The Longman Anthology of British Literature

$\longleftarrow\!\!\!\!\longmapsto\!\!\!\!\Longleftrightarrow\!\!\!\!\longmapsto\!\!\!\!\longrightarrow$

VOLUME 1B

THE EARLY MODERN PERIOD

David Damrosch
HARVARD UNIVERSITY

Kevin J. H. Dettmar
POMONA COLLEGE

Christopher Baswell
BARNARD COLLEGE AND COLUMBIA UNIVERSITY

Clare Carroll
QUEENS COLLEGE, CITY UNIVERSITY OF NEW YORK

Andrew Hadfield
UNIVERSITY OF SUSSEX

Heather Henderson

Peter J. Manning
STATE UNIVERSITY OF NEW YORK, STONY BROOK

Anne Howland Schotter
WAGNER COLLEGE

William Chapman Sharpe
BARNARD COLLEGE

Stuart Sherman
FORDHAM UNIVERSITY

Susan J. Wolfson
PRINCETON UNIVERSITY

The Longman Anthology of British Literature

Fourth Edition

David Damrosch and Kevin J. H. Dettmar

General Editors

VOLUME 1B

THE EARLY MODERN PERIOD

Clare Carroll *and* Andrew Hadfield

Longman

New York   San Francisco   Boston
London   Toronto   Sydney   Tokyo   Singapore   Madrid
Mexico City   Munich   Paris   Cape Town   Hong Kong   Montreal

Editor-in-Chief: *Joseph Terry*
Associate Development Editor: *Erin Reilly*
Executive Marketing Manager: *Joyce Nilsen*
Senior Supplements Editor: *Donna Campion*
Production Manager: *Ellen MacElree*
Project Coordination, Text Design, and Page Makeup: GGS Higher Education Resources, a
    Division of PreMedia Global, Inc.
Cover Design Manager: *Nancy Danahy*
On the Cover: *Hans Holbein*. The Ambassadors. 1553. © *National Portrait Gallery, London*.
Photo Researcher: *Julie Tesser*
Senior Manufacturing Buyer: *Dennis J. Para*
Printer and Binder: *Quebecor-World/Taunton*
Cover Printer: *Lehigh-Phoenix Color/Hagerstown*

For permission to use copyrighted material, grateful acknowledgment is made to the copyright
holders on pages 1979–1980, which are hereby made part of this copyright page.

Library of Congress Cataloging-in-Publication Data
The Longman anthology of British literature / David Damrosch and Kevin J.H. Dettmar,
general editors.—4th ed.
    p. cm.
Includes bibliographical references and index.
ISBN–13: 978–0–205–65524–3 (v. 1 : alk. paper)
ISBN–10: 0–205–65524–6 (v. 1 : alk. paper)
ISBN–13: 978–0–205–65519–9 (v. 2 : alk. paper)
ISBN–10: 0–205–65519–X (v. 2 : alk. paper) 1. English literature. 2. Great Britain—Literary
collections. I. Damrosch, David. II. Dettmar, Kevin J. H., 1958–
PR1109.L69 2010
820.8—dc22

                                                                        2009020241

ISBN-10 Single Volume Edition, Volume 1: 0-205-65524-6
ISBN-13 Single Volume Edition, Volume 1: 978-0-205-65524-3

ISBN-10 Volume 1A, The Middle Ages: 0-205-65530-0
ISBN-13 Volume 1A, The Middle Ages: 978-0-205-65530-4

ISBN-10 Volume 1B, The Early Modern Period: 0-205-65532-7
ISBN-13 Volume 1B, The Early Modern Period: 978-0-205-65532-8

ISBN-10 Volume 1C, The Restoration and the 18th Century: 0-205-65527-0
ISBN-13 Volume 1C, The Restoration and the 18th Century: 978-0-205-65527-4

Longman
is an imprint of

1 2 3 4 5 6 7 8 9 0—QWT—12 11 10 09

www.pearsonhighered.com

CONTENTS

══╬ PERSPECTIVES ╬══
Tracts on Women and Gender   1445

THOMAS HOBBES   (Web)

SIR THOMAS BROWNE   (Web)

ROBERT BURTON   (Web)

ROBERT HERRICK   1618

ADDITIONAL RESOURCES

CULTURAL EDITIONS

Longman Cultural Editions present major texts along with a generous selection of contextual material that reveal the conversations and controversies of its historical moment. Taken together, our new edition and the Longman Cultural Editions offer an unparalleled set of materials for the enjoyment and study of British literary culture from its earliest beginnings to the present. One Longman Cultural Edition is available at no additional cost when packaged with the anthology. Contact your local Pearson Publisher's Representative for packaging details. Some titles of interest for Volume One include the following works:

Beowulf, Anonymous. Translated by Alan Sullivan and Timothy Murphy & ed. Anderson
ISBN-10: 0-321-10720-9 | ISBN-13: 978-0-321-10720-6

Julius Caesar. Shakespeare. ed. Arnold.
ISBN-10: 0-321-20943-5 | ISBN-13: 978-0-321-20943-6

Henry IV, Parts One and Two. Shakespeare. ed. Levao
ISBN-10: 0-321-18274-X | ISBN-13: 978-0-321-18274-6

The Merchant of Venice, Shakespeare. ed. Danson
ISBN-10: 0-321-16419-9 | ISBN-13: 978-0-321-16419-3

Antony and Cleopatra, Shakespeare, ed. Quint
ISBN-10: 0-321-19874-3 | ISBN-13: 978-0-321-19874-7

Hamlet, Shakespeare. ed. Jordan
ISBN-10: 0-321-31729-7 | ISBN-13: 978-0-321-31729-2

King Lear, Shakespeare. ed. McEachern
ISBN-10: 0-321-10722-5 | ISBN-13: 978-0-321-10722-0

Othello and *The Tragedy of Mariam*, Shakespeare and Cary. ed. Carroll and Damrosch
ISBN-10: 0-321-09699-1 | ISBN-13: 978-0-321-09699-9

The History of the Adventures of Joseph Andrews, Fielding. ed. Potkay
ISBN-10: 0-321-20937-0 | ISBN-13: 978-0-321-20937-5

The Castle of Otranto and *The Man of Feeling*, Walpole and MacKenzie. ed. Mandell
ISBN-10: 0-321-39892-0 | ISBN-13: 978-0-321-39892-5

For a complete listing of Longman Cultural Edition titles, please visit www.pearsonhighered.com/literature.

WEB SITE FOR *THE LONGMAN ANTHOLOGY OF BRITISH LITERATURE*

www.myliteraturekit.com

The fourth edition makes connections beyond its covers as well as within them. The Web site we have developed for the course provides a wealth of resources:

Student Resources

- **Discussion Questions for Major Selections and Perspectives Sections.** Designed to prepare students for the kind of deeper-level analysis expected in class discussions, these compelling prompts are available for each period introduction and for major selections and Perspectives groupings.

- **Self-Grading Multiple Choice Practice Questions.** Available for each period introduction and for all major authors and Perspectives groupings, these objective practice quizzes are designed to help students review their basic understanding of the reading.

- **An Interactive Timeline.** Our interactive timeline helps students visualize the key literary, political, and cultural events of an era. Each event is accompanied by a detailed explanation, usually including references to relevant texts that can be found in the anthology, links to helpful sites, and colorful pictures and illustrations.

- **Links to Valuable British Literature Resources.** Our Online Research Guide provides a wealth of annotated links to excellent Web resources on major authors, texts, and related historical and cultural movements and events.

- **An Archive of Additional Texts.** Our new online archive contains a wealth of selections that could not fit within the bounds of the print anthology. A listing of many of these works can be found in context in our table of contents.

- **Additional Reference Materials.** The Web site also features an extensive glossary of literary and cultural terms, useful summaries of British political and religious organizations, and of money, weights, and measures. For further reading, we provide carefully selected, up-to-date bibliographies for each period and author.

Instructor's Section

- **An Online Instructor's Manual (0-205-67976-5).** The online version of our print manual uses a hyperlink format to allow instructors to jump directly to the author or selection they want to access.

- **PowerPoint Presentations.** A visually rich presentation is available for each period.

- **Sample Syllabi.** Our collection of syllabi include samples of a wide variety of approaches to both the survey-level and period-specific courses.

PREFACE

Literature has a double life. Born in one time and place and read in another, literary works are at once products of their age and independent creations, able to live on long after their original world has disappeared. The goal *The Longman Anthology of British Literature* is to present a wealth of poetry, prose, and drama from the full sweep of the literary history of Great Britain and its empire, and to do so in ways that will bring out both the works' original cultural contexts and their lasting aesthetic power. These aspects are in fact closely related: form and content, verbal music and social meanings, go hand in hand. This double life makes literature, as Aristotle said, "the most philosophical" of all the arts, intimately connected to ideas and to realities that the writer transforms into moving patterns of words. The challenge is to show these works in the contexts in which, and for which, they were written, while at the same time not trapping them within those contexts. The warm response this anthology has received from the hundreds of teachers who have adopted it in its first three editions reflects the growing consensus that we are not forced to choose between the literature's aesthetic and cultural dimensions. Our users' responses have now guided us in seeing how we can improve our anthology further, so as to be most pleasurable and stimulating to students, most useful to teachers, and most responsive to ongoing developments in literary studies. This preface can serve as a road map to this book's goals and structure.

NEW TO THIS EDITION

- **Period at a Glance features.** These informative illustrated features open each volume, providing thumbnail sketches of daily life during each period.

- **Enhanced Web site.** A new fourth edition site includes an archive of valuable texts from previous editions, detailed bibliographies, an interactive timeline, discussion questions, and Web resources for major selections and authors.

- **New major, classic texts.** In response to instructors' requests, major additions of important works frequently taught in the British Literature course have been added, including the following selections:
  - A selection from the Irish epic *The Táin Bó Cuailnge*
  - William Baldwin's *Beware the Cat* (sometimes called the first English novel)
  - Edmund Spenser's *The Faerie Queene, Book 6* and *the Cantos of Mutabilitie*
  - William Shakespeare's *Othello* and *King Lear*

- **New selections across the anthology.** We have continued to refine our contents, adding new selections to established units across the anthology, including authors such as John Skelton, Fynes Moryson, Edmund Spenser, and John Donne.

- **Penguin Classics editions of *Beowulf* translated by Michael Alexander and *Sir Gawain and the Green Knight* translated by Brian Stone.** The *Longman Anthology of British Literature* now includes authoritative Penguin Classic translations, trusted throughout the world as editions of classics texts that are both riveting and scholarly.

- **New Perspectives groupings of works in cultural context.** "Perspectives" groupings new to this edition include *The English Sonnet and Sonnet Sequences in the Sixteenth Century*, *Early Modern Books*, and *England, Britain, and the World*.

- **New Response pairings.** A selection from Sir Francis Bacon's *New Atlantis* is paired with Sir Thomas More's *Utopia*.

LITERATURE IN ITS TIME—AND IN OURS

When we engage with a rich literary history that extends back over a thousand years, we often encounter writers who assume their readers know all sorts of things that are little known today: historical facts, social issues, literary and cultural references. Beyond specific information, these works will have come out of a very different literary culture than our own. Even the contemporary British Isles present a cultural situation—or a mix of cultures—very different from what North American readers encounter at home, and these differences only increase as we go farther back in time. A major emphasis of this anthology is to bring the works' original cultural moment to life: not because the works simply or naively reflect that moment of origin, but because they do refract it in fascinating ways. British literature is both a major heritage for modern North America and, in many ways, a very distinct culture; reading British literature will regularly give an experience both of connection and of difference. Great writers create imaginative worlds that have their own compelling internal logic, and a prime purpose of this anthology is to help readers to understand the formal means—whether of genre, rhetoric, or style—with which these writers have created works of haunting beauty. At the same time, as Virginia Woolf says in *A Room of One's Own*, the gossamer threads of the artist's web are joined to reality "with bands of steel."

The *Longman Anthology* pursues a range of strategies to bring out both the beauty of these webs of words and their points of contact with reality and to bring related authors and works together in several ways:

☞ PERSPECTIVES: Broad groupings that illuminate underlying issues in a variety of the major works of a period.

☞ AND ITS TIME: A focused cluster that illuminates a specific cultural moment or a debate to which an author is responding.

☞ RESPONSES: One or more texts in which later authors in the tradition respond creatively to the challenging texts of their forebears.

These groupings provide a range of means of access to the literary culture of each period. The Perspectives sections do much more than record what major writers thought about an issue: they give a variety of views in a range of voices, to illustrate the wider culture within which the literature was being written. Theological reflections by the pioneering scientist Isaac Newton; these and many other vivid readings featured in Volume One give rhetorical as well as social contexts for the poems, plays, and stories around them. Perspectives sections typically relate to several major authors of the period, as with a section on the sixteenth-century sonnet that brings the poetry of Edmund Spenser and Sir Philip Sidney into conversation with less widely read figures like Sir Thomas Wyatt and Henry Howard, Earl of Surrey. Most of the writers included in Perspectives sections are important figures of the period who might be neglected if they were listed on their own with just a few pages each; grouping them together has proved to be useful pedagogically as well as intellectually. Perspectives sections may also include work by a major author whose primary listing appears elsewhere in the period; thus, a Perspective section on the Civil War features a selection from Milton's *Eikonoklastes*, and a section on British perceptions of other lands includes a selection from Spenser's *View of the State of Ireland*, so as to give a rounded presentation of the issue in ways that can inform the reading of those authors in their individual sections.

When we present a major work "And Its Time," we give a cluster of related materials to suggest the context within which the work was written. Thus Sir Philip Sidney's great *Apology for Poetry* is accompanied by readings showing the controversy that was raging at the time concerning the nature and value of poetry. Some of the writers in these groupings and in our Perspectives sections have not traditionally been seen as literary figures, but all have produced lively and intriguing works, from medieval clerics writing about saints and sea monsters, to a polemical seventeenth-century tract giving *The Arraignment of Lewd, Idle, Froward, and Unconstant Women*, to economic writings by William Petty—of the type parodied by Swift in his "Modest Proposal."

We also include "Responses" to significant texts in the British literary tradition, demonstrating the sometimes far-reaching influence these works have had over the decades and centuries, and sometimes across oceans and continents. *Beowulf* and John Gardner's *Grendel* are separated by the Atlantic ocean, perhaps eleven hundred or twelve hundred years—and, most notably, by their attitude toward the poem's monster. The *Morte Darthur* is reinterpreted comically by the 1970s British comedy troupe Monty Python's Flying Circus.

WHAT IS BRITISH LITERATURE?

Stepping back from the structure of the book, let us define our basic terms: What is "British" literature? What is literature itself? And just what should an anthology of this material look like at the present time? The term "British" can mean many things, some of them contradictory, some of them even offensive to people on whom the name has been imposed. If the term "British" has no ultimate essence, it does have a history. The first British were Celtic people who inhabited the British Isles and the northern coast of France (still called Brittany) before various Germanic tribes of Angles and Saxons moved onto the islands in the fifth and sixth centuries. Gradually the Angles and Saxons amalgamated into the Anglo-Saxon culture that became dominant in the southern and eastern regions of Britain and then spread outward; the old British people were pushed west, toward what became known as Cornwall,

Wales, and Ireland, which remained independent kingdoms for centuries, as did Celtic Scotland to the north. By an ironic twist of linguistic fate, the Anglo-Saxons began to appropriate the term "British" from the Britons they had displaced, and they took as a national hero the early, semimythic Welsh King Arthur. By the seventeenth century, English monarchs had extended their sway over Wales, Ireland, and Scotland, and they began to refer to their holdings as "Great Britain." Today, Great Britain includes England, Wales, Scotland, and Northern Ireland, but does not include the Republic of Ireland, which has been independent since 1922.

This anthology uses "British" in a broad sense, as a geographical term encompassing the whole of the British Isles. For all its fraught history, it seems a more satisfactory term than to speak simply of "English" literature, for two reasons. First, most speakers of English live in countries that are not the focus of this anthology (for instance, the United States and Canada); second, while the English language and its literature have long been dominant in the British Isles, other cultures in the region have always used other languages and have produced great literature in these languages. Important works by Irish, Welsh, and Scots writers appear regularly in the body of this anthology, some of them written directly in their languages and presented here in translation, and others written in an English inflected by the rhythms, habits of thought, and modes of expression characteristic of these other languages and the people who use them.

We use the term "literature" in a similarly capacious sense, to refer to a range of artistically shaped works written in a charged language, appealing to the imagination at least as much as to discursive reasoning. It is only relatively recently that creative writers have been able to make a living composing poems, plays, and novels, and only in the past hundred years or so has creating "belles lettres" or high literary art been thought of as a sharply separate sphere of activity from other sorts of writing that the same authors would regularly produce. Sometimes, early modern poets wrote sonnets to reflect and honor loves won and lost; at other times, they wrote sonnets to realize courtly ambition and material gain; and always, they wrote their sonnets with an eye to posterity, and with the goal of a poetic form of immortality ("Not marble, nor the gilded monuments / Of princes, shall outlive this pow'rful rhyme"—Shakespeare, *Sonnet 55*).

VARIETIES OF LITERARY EXPERIENCE

Above all, we have strived to give as full a presentation as possible to the varieties of great literature produced from the eighth to the eighteenth centuries in the British Isles, by women as well as by men, in outlying regions as well as in the metropolitan center of London, and in prose, drama, and verse alike. For these earlier periods, we include More's entire *Utopia*, Baldwin's *Beware the Cat*, and Milton's *Paradise Lost*, and we give major space to narrative poetry by Chaucer and Spenser, and to Swift's *Gulliver's Travels*, among others. Drama appears throughout the anthology, from the medieval *Second Play of the Shepherds* and *Mankind* to a range of early modern and restoration plays: Marlowe's *The Tragical History of Dr. Faustus*, Shakespeare's *Twelfth Night, Othello*, and *King Lear*, Jonson's *The Alchemist*, William Wyncherly's *The Country Wife*, and John Gay's *The Beggar's Opera*. Finally, lyric poetry appears in profusion throughout the anthology, from early lyrics by anonymous Middle English poets and the trenchantly witty Dafydd ap Gwilym to the great flowering of lyric poetry in the early modern period in the writings of Shakespeare, Sidney, and Spenser—to name just the "S's"—to the formal perfection and august rhetoric of Restoration and eighteenth-century poets like Swift, Dryden, Pope, and Johnson. Prose fiction always struggles for space in a literary anthology, but we close this volume with a selection from some of the most vital novelistic writing of the eighteenth century. We hope that this anthology will show that the great works of earlier centuries can speak to us compellingly today, their value only increased by the resistance they offer to our views of ourselves and our world. To read and reread the full sweep of this literature is to be struck anew by the degree to which the most radically new works are rooted in centuries of prior innovation.

ILLUSTRATING VISUAL CULTURE

Another important context for literary production has been a different kind of culture: the visual. This edition includes a suite of color plates in each volume, along with hundreds of black-and-white illustrations throughout the anthology, chosen to show artistic and cultural images that figured importantly for literary creation. Sometimes, a poem refers to a specific painting, or more generally emulates qualities of a school of visual art. At other times, more popular materials like frontispieces may illuminate scenes in early modern writing. In some cases, visual and literary creation have merged, as in William Hogarth's series *A Rake's Progress,* included in Volume One. Thumbnail portraits of many major authors mark the beginning of author introductions.

AIDS TO UNDERSTANDING

We have attempted to contextualize our selections in suggestive rather than exhaustive ways, trying to enhance rather than overwhelm the experience of reading the texts themselves. Thus, when difficult or archaic words need defining in poems, we use glosses in the margins, so as to disrupt the reader's eye as little as possible; footnotes are intended to be concise and informative, rather than massive or interpretive. Important literary and social terms are defined when they are used. For convenience of reference, new Period at a Glance features appear at the beginning of each period, providing a thumbnail sketch of daily life during the period. With these informative, illustrated features readers can begin to connect with the world that the anthology is illuminating. Sums of money, for instance, can be understood better when one knows what a loaf of bread cost at the time; the symbolic values attached to various articles of clothing are sometimes difficult for today's readers to decipher, without some information about contemporary apparel and its class associations. And the gradual shift of the Empire's population from rural regions to urban centers is graphically presented in charts for each period.

LOOKING—AND LISTENING—FURTHER

Beyond the boundaries of the anthology itself, we have expanded our Web site, available to all readers at www.myliteraturekit.com; this site gives a wealth of information, annotated links to related sites, and an archive of texts for further reading. For reference, there is also an extensive glossary of literary and cultural terms available there, together with useful summaries of British political and religious organization, and of money, weights, and measures. For further reading, carefully selected, up-to-date bibliographies for each period and for each author can be found in on the

Web site. A guide to our media resources can be found at the end of the table of contents.

For instructors, we have revised and expanded our popular companion volume, *Teaching British Literature,* written directly by the anthology editors, 600 pages in length, available free to everyone who adopts the anthology.

David Damrosch & Kevin J. H. Dettmar

ACKNOWLEDGMENTS

In planning and preparing the fourth edition of our anthology, the editors have been fortunate to have the support, advice, and assistance of many committed and gifted people. Our editor, Joe Terry, has been unwavering in his enthusiasm for the book and his commitment to it; he and his associates Roth Wilkofsky, Mary Ellen Curley, and Joyce Nilsen have supported us in every possible way throughout the process, ably assisted by Katy Needle, Rosie Ellis, and Annie England. Our developmental editor Erin Reilly guided us and our manuscript from start to finish with unfailing acuity and seemingly unwavering patience. Our copyeditor Stephanie Magean seamlessly integrated the work of a dozen editors. Erin Reilly, Elizabeth Bravo and Stefanie Liebman have devoted enormous energy and creativity to revising our Web site. Karyn Morrison cleared our many permissions, and Julie Tesser tracked down and cleared our many new illustrations. Finally, Nancy Wolitzer and Ellen MacElree oversaw the production with sunny good humor and kept the book successfully on track on a very challenging schedule, working closely with Doug Bell at GGS Higher Education Resources.

Our plans for the new edition have been shaped by comments and suggestions from many faculty who have used the book over the years. We are specifically grateful for the thoughtful advice of our reviewers for this edition, Jesse T. Airaudi (Baylor University), Thomas Crofts (East Tennessee State University), Lois Feuer (California State University, Dominguez Hills), Daniel P. Galvin (Clemson University), S. E. Gontarski (Florida State University), Stephen Harris (University of Massachusetts), Roxanne Kent-Drury (Northern Kentucky University), Carol A. Lowe (McLennan Community College), Darin A Merrill (Brigham Young University—Idaho), David G. Miller (Mississippi College), Crystal L. Mueller (University of Wisconsin Oshkosh), and Gary Schneider (University of Texas—Pan American).

We remain grateful as well for the guidance of the many reviewers who advised us on the creation of the first three editions, the base on which this new edition has been built. In addition to the people named above, we would like to thank Lucien Agosta (California State University, Sacramento), Anne W. Astell (Purdue University), Derek Attridge (Rutgers University), Linda Austin (Oklahoma State University), Arthur D. Barnes (Louisiana State University), Robert Barrett (University of Pennsylvania), Candice Barrington (Central Connecticut State University), Joseph Bartolomeo (University of Massachusetts, Amherst), Mary Been (Clovis Community College), Stephen Behrendt (University of Nebraska), Todd Bender (University of Wisconsin, Madison), Bruce Boehrer (Florida State University), Bruce Brandt (South Dakota State University), Joel J. Brattin (Worcester Polytechnic Institute), James Campbell (University of Central Florida), J. Douglas Canfield (University of Arizona), Paul A. Cantor (University of Virginia), George Allan Cate (University of Maryland, College Park), Philip Collington (Niagra University), Linda McFerrin

Cook (McLellan Community College), Eugene R. Cunnar (New Mexico State University), Earl Dachslager (University of Houston), Elizabeth Davis (University of California, Davis), Andrew Elfenbein (University of Minnesota), Hilary Englert (New Jersey City University), Margaret Ferguson (University of California, Davis), Sandra K. Fisher (State University of New York, Albany), Sandra C. Fowler (The University of Alabama), Allen J. Frantzen (Loyola University, Chicago), Kevin Gardner (Baylor University), Kate Gartner Frost (University of Texas), Leon Gottfried (Purdue University), Leslie Graff (University at Buffalo), Mark L. Greenberg (Drexel University), Peter Greenfield (University of Puget Sound), Natalie Grinnell (Wofford College), James Hala (Drew University), Wayne Hall (University of Cincinnati), Donna Hamilton (University of Maryland), Wendell Harris (Pennsylvania State University), Richard H. Haswell (Washington State University), Susan Sage Heinzelman (University of Texas, Austin), Standish Henning (University of Wisconsin, Madison), Noah Heringman (University of Missouri—Columbia), Jack W. Herring (Baylor University), Carrie Hintz (Queens College), Romana Huk (University of Notre Dame), Maurice Hunt (Baylor University), Mary Anne Hutchison (Utica College), Patricia Clare Ingham (Indiana University), Kim Jacobs (University of Cincinnati Clermont College), Carol Jamison (Armstrong Atlantic State University), Eric Johnson (Dakota State College), Mary Susan Johnston (Minnesota State University), Eileen A. Joy (Southern Illinois University—Edwardsville), Colleen Juarretche (University of California, Los Angeles), George Justice (University of Missouri), Roxanne Kent-Drury (Northern Kentucky University), R. B. Kershner (University of Florida), Lisa Klein (Ohio State University), Adam Komisaruk (West Virginia University), Rita S. Kranidis (Radford University), Leslie M. LaChance (University of Tennessee at Martin), John Laflin (Dakota State University), Lisa Lampert (University of California, San Diego), Dallas Liddle (Augsburg College), Paulino Lim (California State University, Long Beach), Elizabeth B. Loizeaux (University of Maryland), Ed Malone (Missouri Western State College), John J. Manning (University of Connecticut), William W. Matter (Richland College), Evan Matthews (Navarro College), Michael Mays (University of Southern Mississippi), Lawrence McCauley (College of New Jersey), Michael B. McDonald (Iowa State University), James J. McKeown Jr. (McLennan Community College), Kathryn McKinley (Florida International University), Peter E. Medine (University of Arizona), Barry Milligan (Wright State University), Celia Millward (Boston University), Charlotte Morse (Virginia Commonwealth University), Mary Morse (Rider University), Thomas C. Moser, Jr. (University of Maryland), James Najarian (Boston College), Deborah Craig Wester (Worcester State College), Jude V. Nixon (Baylor University), Richard Nordquist (Armstrong Atlantic State University), Daniel Novak (Tulane University), John Ottenhoff (Alma College), Violet O'Valle (Tarrant County Junior College, Texas), Joyce Cornette Palmer (Texas Women's University), Leslie Palmer (University of North Texas), Richard Pearce (Wheaton College), Rebecca Phillips (West Virginia University), Renée Pigeon (California State University, San Bernardino), Tadeusz Pioro (Southern Methodist University), Deborah Preston (Dekalb College), William Rankin (Abilene Christian University), Sherry Rankin (Abilene Christian University), Luke Reinsma (Seattle Pacific University), Elizabeth Robertson (University of Colorado), Deborah Rogers (University of Maine), David Rollison (College of Marin), Brian Rosenberg (Allegheny College), Charles Ross (Purdue University), Kathryn Rummel (California Polytechnic), Harry Rusche (Emory University), Laura E. Rutland (Berry College), Kenneth D. Shields

(Southern Methodist University), R. G. Siemens (Malaspina University-College), Clare A. Simmons (Ohio State University), Sally Slocum (University of Akron), Phillip Snyder (Brigham Young University), Isabel Bonnyman Stanley (East Tennessee University), Brad Sullivan (Florida Gulf Coast University), Margaret Sullivan (University of California, Los Angeles), Herbert Sussmann (Northeastern University), Mary L. Tanter (Tarleton State University), Ronald R. Thomas (Trinity College), Theresa Tinkle (University of Michigan), William A. Ulmer (University of Alabama), Jennifer A. Wagner (University of Memphis), Anne D. Wallace (University of Southern Mississippi), Brett Wallen (Cleveland Community College), Jackie Walsh (McNeese State University, Louisiana), Daniel Watkins (Duquesne University), John Watkins (University of Minnesota), Martin Wechselblatt (University of Cincinnati), Arthur Weitzman (Northeastern University), Bonnie Wheeler (Southern Methodist University), Jan Widmayer (Boise State University), Dennis L. Williams (Central Texas College), William A. Wilson (San Jose State University), Paula Woods (Baylor University), and Julia Wright (University of Waterloo).

Other colleagues brought our developing book into the classroom, teaching from portions of the work-in-progress. Our thanks go to Lisa Abney (Northwestern State University), Charles Lynn Batten (University of California, Los Angeles), Brenda Riffe Brown (College of the Mainland, Texas), John Brugaletta (California State University, Fullerton), Dan Butcher (Southeastern Louisiana University), Lynn Byrd (Southern University at New Orleans), David Cowles (Brigham Young University), Sheila Drain (John Carroll University), Lawrence Frank (University of Oklahoma), Leigh Garrison (Virginia Polytechnic Institute), David Griffin (New York University), Rita Harkness (Virginia Commonwealth University), Linda Kissler (Westmoreland County Community College, Pennsylvania), Brenda Lewis (Motlow State Community College, Tennessee), Paul Lizotte (River College), Wayne Luckman (Green River Community College, Washington), Arnold Markely (Pennsylvania State University, Delaware County), James McKusick (University of Maryland, Baltimore), Eva McManus (Ohio Northern University), Manuel Moyrao (Old Dominion University), Kate Palguta (Shawnee State University, Ohio), Paul Puccio (University of Central Florida), Sarah Polito (Cape Cod Community College), Meredith Poole (Virginia Western Community College), Tracy Seeley (University of San Francisco), Clare Simmons (Ohio State University), and Paul Yoder (University of Arkansas, Little Rock).

As if all this help weren't enough, the editors also drew directly on friends and colleagues in many ways, for advice, for information, sometimes for outright contributions to headnotes and footnotes, even (in a pinch) for aid in proofreading. In particular, we wish to thank David Ackiss, Marshall Brown, James Cain, Cathy Corder, Jeffrey Cox, Michael Coyle, Pat Denison, Tom Farrell, Andrew Fleck, Jane Freilich, Laurie Glover, Lisa Gordis, Joy Hayton, Ryan Hibbet, V. Lauryl Hicks, Nelson Hilton, Jean Howard, David Kastan, Stanislas Kemper, Andrew Krull, Ron Levao, Carol Levin, David Lipscomb, Denise MacNeil, Jackie Maslowski, Richard Matlak, Anne Mellor, James McKusick, Melanie Micir, Michael North, David Paroissien, Stephen M. Parrish, Peter Platt, Cary Plotkin, Desma Polydorou, Gina Renee, Alan Richardson, Esther Schor, Catherine Siemann, Glenn Simshaw, David Tresilian, Shasta Turner, Nicholas Watson, Michael Winckleman, Gillen Wood, and Sarah Zimmerman for all their guidance and assistance.

The pages on the Restoration and the eighteenth century are the work of many collaborators, diligent and generous. Michael F. Suarez, S. J. (Campion Hall,

Oxford) edited the Swift and Pope sections; Mary Bly (Fordham University) edited Sheridan's *School for Scandal*; Michael Caldwell (University of Chicago) edited the portions of "Reading Papers" on *The Craftsman* and the South Sea Bubble. Steven N. Zwicker (Washington University) co-wrote the period introduction, and the headnotes for the Dryden section. Bruce Redford (Boston University) crafted the footnotes for Dryden, Gay, Johnson, and Boswell. Susan Brown, Janice Cable, Christine Coch, Marnie Cox, Tara Czechowski, Susan Greenfield, Mary Nassef, Paige Reynolds, and Andrew Tumminia helped with texts, footnotes, and other matters throughout; William Pritchard gathered texts, wrote notes, and prepared the bibliography. To all, abiding thanks.

It has been a pleasure to work with all of these colleagues in the ongoing collaborative process that has produced this book and brought it to this new stage of its life and use. This book exists for its readers, whose reactions and suggestions we warmly welcome, as these will in turn reshape this book for later users in the years to come.

David Damrosch
HARVARD UNIVERSITY

Kevin J. H. Dettmar
POMONA COLLEGE

Christopher Baswell
BARNARD COLLEGE AND COLUMBIA UNIVERSITY

Clare Carroll
QUEENS COLLEGE, CITY UNIVERSITY OF NEW YORK

Andrew Hadfield
UNIVERSITY OF SUSSEX

Heather Henderson

Peter J. Manning
STATE UNIVERSITY OF NEW YORK, STONY BROOK

Anne Howland Schotter
WAGNER COLLEGE

William Chapman Sharpe
BARNARD COLLEGE

Stuart Sherman
FORDHAM UNIVERSITY

Susan J. Wolfson
PRINCETON UNIVERSITY

ABOUT THE EDITORS

David Damrosch is Professor Comparative Literature at Harvard University. He is past President of the American Comparative Literature Association, and has written widely on world literature from antiquity to the present. His books include *What is World Literature?* (2003), *The Buried Book: The Loss and Rediscovery of the Great Epic of Gilgamesh* (2007), and *How to Read World Literature* (2009). He is the founding general editor of the six-volume *The Longman Anthology of World Literature*, 2/e (2009) and the editor of *Teaching World Literature* (2009).

Kevin J. H. Dettmar is W.M. Keck Professor and Chair of the Department of English at Pomona College, and Past President of the Modernist Studies Association. He is the author of *The Illicit Joyce of Postmodernism and Is Rock Dead?*, and the editor of *Rereading the New: A Backward Glance at Modernism; Marketing Modernisms: Self-Promotion, Canonization, and Rereading; Reading Rock & Roll: Authenticity, Appropriation, Aesthetics*; the Barnes & Noble Classics edition of James Joyce's *A Portrait of the Artist as a Young Man and Dubliners*; and *The Blackwell Companion to Modernist Literature and Culture*, of *The Cambridge Companion to Bob Dylan*.

Christopher Baswell is A.W. Olin Chair of English at Barnard College, and Professor of English and Comparative Literature at Columbia University. His interests include classical literature and culture, medieval literature and culture, and contemporary poetry. He is author of *Virgil in Medieval England: Figuring the "Aeneid" from the Twelfth Century to Chaucer*, which won the 1998 Beatrice White Prize of the English Association. He has held fellowships from the NEH, the National Humanities Center, and the Institute for Advanced Study, Princeton.

Clare Carroll is Director of Renaissance Studies at The Graduate Center, City University of New York and Professor of Comparative Literature at Queens College, CUNY. Her research is in Renaissance Studies, with particular interests in early modern colonialism, epic poetry, historiography, and translation. She is the author of *The Orlando Furioso: A Stoic Comedy*, and editor of Richard Beacon's humanist dialogue on the colonization of Ireland, *Solon His Follie*. Her most recent book is *Circe's Cup: Cultural Transformations in Early Modern Ireland*. She has received Fulbright Fellowships for her research and the Queens College President's Award for Excellence in Teaching.

Andrew Hadfield is Professor of English at The University of Sussex. He is the author of a number of books, including *Shakespeare and Republicanism* (2005), which was awarded the 2006 Sixteenth-Century Society Conference Roland H. Bainton Prize for Literature; *Literature, Travel and Colonialism in the English Renaissance, 1540–1625* (1998); and *Spenser's Irish Experience: Wild Fruyt and Salvage Soyl* (1997).

He has also edited a number of texts, most recently, with Matthew Dimmock, *Religions of the Book: Co-existence and Conflict, 1400–1660* (2008), and with Raymond Gillespie, *The Oxford History of the Irish Book, Vol. III: The Irish Book in English, 1550–1800* (2006). He is a regular reviewer for the TLS.

Heather Henderson is a freelance writer and former Associate Professor of English Literature at Mount Holyoke College. A specialist in Victorian literature, she is the recipient of a fellowship from the National Endowment for the Humanities. She is the author of *The Victorian Self: Autobiography and Biblical Narrative*. Her current interests include homeschooling, travel literature, and autobiography.

Peter J. Manning is Professor at Stony Brook University. He is the author of *Byron and His Fictions* and *Reading Romantics*, and of numerous essays on the British Romantic poets and prose writers. With Susan J. Wolfson, he has co-edited *Selected Poems of Byron*, and *Selected Poems of Beddoes, Hood, and Praed*. He has received fellowships from the National Endowment for the Humanities and the John Simon Guggenheim Memorial Foundation, and the Distinguished Scholar Award of the Keats-Shelley Association.

Anne Schotter is Professor of English at Wagner College. She is the co-editor of *Ineffability: Naming the Unnamable from Dante to Beckett* and author of articles on Middle English poetry, Dante, and medieval Latin poetry. Her current interests include the medieval reception of classical literature, particularly the work of Ovid. She has held fellowships from the Woodrow Wilson and Andrew W. Mellon foundations.

William Sharpe is Professor of English Literature at Barnard College. A specialist in Victorian poetry and the literature of the city, he is the author of *Unreal Cities: Urban Figuration in Wordsworth, Baudelaire, Whitman, Eliot, and Williams*. He is also co-editor of *The Passing of Arthur* and *Visions of the Modern City*. He is the recipient of Guggenheim, National Endowment of the Humanities, Fulbright, and Mellon fellowships, and recently published *New York Nocturne: The City After Dark in Literature, Painting, and Photography*.

Stuart Sherman is Associate Professor of English at Fordham University. He received the Gottschalk Prize from the American Society for Eighteenth-Century Studies for his book *Telling Time: Clocks, Diaries, and English Diurnal Form, 1660–1775*, and is currently at work on a study called "News and Plays: Evanescences of Page and Stage, 1620–1779." He has received the Quantrell Award for Undergraduate Teaching, as well as fellowships from the American Council of Learned Societies and the Chicago Humanities Institute.

Susan J. Wolfson teaches at Princeton University and is general editor of Longman Cultural Editions. She has also produced editions of Felicia Hemans, Lord Byron, Thomas L. Beddoes, William M. Praed, and Thomas Hood. She is the editor of the innovative Longman Cultural Editions of John Keats, and of Mary Shelley's *Frankenstein*, and coeditor (with Barry V. Qualls) of *Three Tales of Doubles*, and (with Claudia Johnson) of Jane Austen's *Pride and Prejudice*. She is author of *The Questioning Presence* (1986), *Formal Charges: The Shaping of Poetry in British Romanticism* (1997), and *Borderlines: The Shiftings of Gender* (2007).

The Longman Anthology of British Literature

VOLUME 1B

THE EARLY MODERN PERIOD

Frontispiece from Saxton's *Atlas*, 1579.

THE EARLY MODERN PERIOD

POPULATION[1]

NATIONAL POPULATIONS (IN MILLIONS)[2]

	England	Scotland	Ireland
1500	3.3[3]	0.5	0.5–0.8
1700	5.6[4]	1.23	1.8–2.0

URBAN POPULATIONS[5]

	London	Edinburgh	Dublin
1500	40,000–50,000[6]	12,000	5,000–7,000
1600	200,000[7]	30,000	15,000
1700	575,000[8]	40,000	60,000

LIFE EXPECTANCY

Life expectancy at birth is about 48 years in Elizabethan England, lower in cities where poor sanitation and crowded conditions cause the plague and other diseases—such as typhus, small pox, consumption (tuberculosis), syphilis, scurvy—to spread more easily. The plague is half as severe in the rich parishes in the city center as it had been in 1563 and 83.3% of all deaths are in the poorer areas at the periphery of the city.

1563 17,404 Londoners die of the plague.
1603 25,045 Londoners die of the plague.
1625 26,350 Londoners die of the plague.
1665 55,797 Londoners die of the plague.

DAILY LIFE

CURRENCY[9]

4 farthings	1d. (1 penny)	One silver penny would be worth approximately $1.23 today.
12d.	1s. (1 shilling)	One shilling would be worth approximately $12.06 today.
5s.	1 crown	One crown would be worth approximately $60.30 today.
20s.	1£ (1 pound)	One pound would be worth approximately $241.20 today.
21s.	1 guinea	One guinea would be worth approximately $253.26 today.

WAGES

	1590s	1663–1683
Craftsmen	18 pence/day	30 pence/day
Laborers	12 pence/day	18 pence/day

1. Any population figures before 1801, when the first official census was taken, are only hypothetical.
2. The population of today's United Kingdom is 60,943,912 (July 2008 est.).
3. 1.5% of England's population lived in London.
4. 11.5% of England's population lived in London.
5. The population of today's London is over 7.6 million (a figure reported in October 2008).
6. Ten European cities had more inhabitants; six had a similar number.
7. Only Naples and Paris had more people than London; Constantinople had twice as many people as London.
8. London became the largest city in Europe, and by 1750 it had 600,000, as many people as Constantinople.
9. Historical equivalences for the purchasing power of a given sum are very approximate. Different types of calculation provide quite different results. A calculation based on wages, for instance, yields a different figure from a calculation based on the prices of basic consumer goods; and those consumer goods thought essential to daily life change drastically over time. These conversions, then, are meant only to be suggestive.

Cost of Goods

1532 1 bushel of barley: £0.490; 1 bushel of beans: £0.361: 1 pound of beef: £0.865; 1 gallon of beer: £2.651

1590 1 bushel of barley: 2.001; 1 bushel of beans: 1.947; 1 pound of beef: 2.127; 1 gallon of beer: 4.304

1663 1 bushel of barley: 2.554; 1 bushel of beans: 2.251; 1 pound of beef: 3.116; 1 gallon of beer: 7.651

Cost of 4-pound loaf of bread (in London)	
1590	4.1 pence
1663	5.8 pence

Food and Drink

Food production can be precarious during the 16th century, as it is dependent on local agriculture, which is susceptible to poor harvest. Bread is an important staple in the diet of all classes. In the upper and middle classes, roasted game and seafood also play prominent roles. The poor often get their protein from milk, eggs, and nuts. Sugar and imported spices are cost-prohibitive and often used to demonstrate social position, but even the lower classes grow some spices in their gardens. Because of unsanitary water supplies, ale is the main beverage for people of all ages. The average adult man consumes about a gallon a day; however, the alcohol content is much less than we know today.

Apparel

Men of the upper and middle classes typically wear a ruff (a separate ruffled collar worn at the neck), codpiece (a pouch that attached to the crotch area of a man's breeches), breeches (pants that stopped just below the knee, each leg was separate), stockings (long socks that covered the entire calf), a doublet (close-fitting, buttoned jacket), and a jerkin (sleeveless jacket worn over the doublet).

Women of the upper and middle classes typically wear a ruff (a separate ruffled collar worn at the neck), bodice (covered from the neck to waist, usually laced closed), sleeves (separate garments), skirt, and farthingale (wheel-shaped stiffening below the waist to which the skirt was pinned).

Most Elizabethan clothing is made from wool or linen, with some items of leather or, for the formal wear of the upper classes, silk. Fashions of the lower classes largely follow those of the upper classes except they rely on cheaper, durable fabrics and styles that allow greater freedom of motion.

Rulers

Oliver Cromwell

Charles II

Rulers	
The Tudors	
Henry VII, King of England, Lord of Ireland (1485–1509)	
Henry VIII, King of England, Lord of Ireland (1509–1547), King of Ireland (1541–1547). His six wives were Catherine of Aragon, Anne Boleyn, Jane Seymour, Anne of Cleves, Catherine Howard, and Catherine Parr.	
Edward VI, King of England and Ireland (1547–1553), son of Henry VIII and Jane Seymour	
Mary I, Queen of England and Ireland (1553–1558), daughter of Henry VIII and Catherine of Aragon	
Elizabeth I, Queen of England and Ireland (1558–1603), daughter of Henry VIII and Anne Boleyn	
The Stuarts	
James I, James VI, King of Scotland (1567–1615), King of England and Ireland (1603–1625), son of Mary Queen of Scots and Henry Stuart, Lord Darnley	
Charles I, King of England, Scotland, and Ireland (1625–1649), son of James I and Anne of Denmark	

RULERS

RULERS
COMMONWEALTH OF ENGLAND
Oliver Cromwell, Lord Protector of England, Scotland, and Ireland (1653–1658)
Richard Cromwell, Second Lord Protector of England, Scotland, and Ireland (1658–1659)
RESTORATION OF THE STUART MONARCHY
Charles II (Charles Stuart) King of Scotland (1649–1685) and King of England and Ireland (1660–1685), son of Charles I and Henrietta Maria of France

TIMELINE

1500 10% of men and 1% of women in England can sign their names.

1509 Henry VIII becomes King of England, Lord of Ireland.

1516 Sir Thomas More's *Utopia* (page 716)

1517 Luther protests the Roman Catholic Church's sale of indulgences.

1534 The Act of Supremacy declares Henry VIII to be the "only supreme head on earth of the Church of England," and thus, he severs allegiance to the Pope and Roman Catholicism.

1538 Henry VIII is excommunicated by the Roman Catholic Church.

1547 Henry VIII dies; Edward VI (son of Henry VIII and Jane Seymour) becomes King of England and Ireland.

1553 Edward VI dies of tuberculosis. Edward attempts to exclude Mary (daughter of Henry VIII and Catherine of Aragon) from the throne for fear that she would restore Catholicism. With the support of Edward's advisors, his cousin Lady Jane Grey assumes the throne briefly. The attempt quickly fails and Mary I becomes Queen of England and Ireland.

1558 Mary I dies; Elizabeth I (daughter of Henry VIII and Anne Boleyn) becomes Queen of England and Ireland.

1563 John Foxe publishes his *Acts and Monuments of These Latter and Perilous Days*—later widely known as the *Book of Martyrs* (page 1063).

1565 The Royal Exchange is built by Thomas Gresham as a commercial headquarters for London merchants.

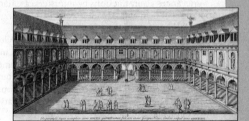

1570 William Baldwin's prose fiction, the *Marvelous History Entitled Beware the Cat, Concerning Diverse Wonderful and Incredible Matters*, is written in 1552 but not published until 1570 (page 790).

1576 Blackfriars, once a Dominican monastery, opens as a theater.

1587 The Catholic Mary Queen of Scots is beheaded having been found guilty of complicity in a plot to murder Queen Elizabeth I.

1587 The Rose Theatre opens.

1588 English naval forces defeat the Spanish Armada.

1590–1596 Edmund Spenser's *The Faerie Queene* (page 824)

1591 Sir Philip Sidney's *Astrophil and Stella* (composed in 1582) is published posthumously (page 680).

1592 Shakespeare begins career in London.

1595 The Swan Theatre opens.

1598 Christopher Marlowe's *Hero and Leander* is published posthumously (page 1092).

1599 The Globe Theatre opens.

1601 Robert Devereux, Earl of Essex, once Queen Elizabeth's favorite, is executed for his rebellion.

1602 William Shakespeare's *Twelfth Night* is first performed (page 1215).

1603 Queen Elizabeth dies; James I (James VI, King of Scotland; son of Mary Queen of Scots and Henry Stuart, Lord Darnley), becomes King of England and Ireland.

1603 Unaware of Elizabeth's death, Hugh O'Neill surrenders after nine years of leading his Irish forces in armed conflict against the crown.

1604 The short version of Christopher Marlowe's *The Tragical History of Dr. Faustus* is published (page 1111).

1604 William Shakespeare's *Othello* is performed for King James I and his guests at Whitehall Palace (page 1272).

1605 Guy Fawkes is captured in the act of attempting to blow up the Houses of Parliament with gunpowder.

1607 Jamestown is established as the first English settlement in North America.

1608 John Smith returns to England (page 1194).

1610 Ben Jonson's *The Alchemist* is first performed (page 1468).

1611 *The King James Bible* is published.

1618 The Thirty Years' War begins.

1619 The banqueting house, Whitehall, is designed by Inigo Jones.

1620 Hic Mulier and Haec-Vir, two pamphlets published within a week of each other, explore issues of gender and apparel (page 1458).

1621 Lady Mary Wroth publishes the first Petrarchan sonnet sequence in English by a woman, *Pamphilia to Amphilanthus* (page 1609).

1625 James I dies; Charles I (son of James I and Anne of Denmark) becomes King of England, Scotland, and Ireland.

1631 John Donne dies (page 1586).

1637 Rioting breaks out in St. Giles Cathedral, Edinburgh, when Charles I imposes the *Book of Common Prayer* on Scots Presbyterians.

1640 "The Short Parliament," the first called by Charles I in 11 years, discusses the king's abuses of power.

1641 Treaty of London is signed granting concessions from Charles I to the Scots Covenanters who had rebelled in the Bishops' War of 1639–1640.

1641 Catholics rebel in Ireland.

1641 The House of Commons passes the Grand Remonstrance, a list of grievances against actions by ministers of Charles I.

1642 30% of men and 10% of women in all of England are literate.

1642 All theaters are shut down in London.

1643 Parliament is purged of those hostile to trying Charles I for treason, and the Rump Parliament is formed.

1643 The Solemn League and Convent, both a military league and a religious covenant, is formed by the Scottish Covenanters and the English Parliamentarians against Charles I and the Royalists.

1644 The Globe Theater is demolished by Puritans, and Sir Matthew Brend builds tenement houses on the site.

1648 The Thirty Years' War ends with the Treaty of Westphalia.

1649 Charles I is beheaded, and Parliament abolishes the monarchy, the Privy Council, and the House of Lords.

1649 The Rump Parliament declares England to be a Commonwealth.

1651 Thomas Hobbes' *Leviathan*

1652 Act for the Settlement of Ireland sentences the rebels of the Confederacy (1641–1652) to be executed and have their lands confiscated.

1653 Oliver Cromwell dismisses the Rump Parliament.

1653 The Barebone's Parliament forms, every member nominated by Oliver Cromwell.

1654–1655 Lord Protector Oliver Cromwell summons the First Protectorate Parliament.

1656–1658 Second Protectorate Parliament.

1659 The Rump Parliament is reinstated by Cromwell's son.

1659 John Lambert and Charles Fleetwood set up a Committee of Safety to rule the Parliament instead of the Rump.

1660 The Royal Society is founded.

1660 General George Monck, commanding the English army in Scotland, reopens the Long Parliament by restoring those Presbyterians purged in 1648.

1660 The Long Parliament is dissolved after creating the Convention Parliament, which invites Charles II to become the English monarch.

1660 Charles II issues the Declaration of Breda, in which he makes known the terms of his acceptance of the crown of England.

1666 Great Fire of London

1667 John Milton's *Paradise Lost* (page 1726)

The Early Modern Period

AN EXPERIMENTAL AGE

John Milton claimed that in *Paradise Lost* his aim was to produce a work that "things unattempted yet in prose or rhyme." Milton's ambitious boast provides us with a useful key to one of the principal goals of writers in the English Early Modern period—namely, their desire and need to produce work that was new and different from what had gone before, however carefully they acknowledged the past and reused and rethought what had already been written. Virtually every writer included in this section of the anthology can be read as an experimental figure, pushing the boundaries of what was possible in a literary text, more akin perhaps to James Joyce or Virginia Woolf than a writer of realist fiction or a poet following well-trodden paths of lyric style. At the

> *Virtually every writer included in this section of the anthology can be read as an experimental figure, pushing the boundaries of what was possible in literary text . . .*

start of this period, in the early sixteenth century, John Skelton invented his own style of English poetry, "Skeltonics," based on short lines of six syllables, enabling him to produce work of great satirical force; Thomas Wyatt and Henry Howard, the Earl of Surrey, concerned that the English lyric lacked the sophistication of the Italian tradition, translated and adapted the sonnets of Petrarch, inventing new English rhyme schemes and styles in the process, as well as complex love poems that often told the reader more about the fears and anxieties of the courtier than they did about the lady in question. In the middle of the century William Baldwin composed a new form of prose fiction that could be regarded as the first novel in English. Toward the end, in one of the most creative periods of English literary history, major writers such as Sir Philip Sidney and Edmund Spenser experimented with new types of poetry, Sidney writing the first sonnet sequence in English, as well as a loosely constructed prose romance, the *Arcadia*, while Spenser, perhaps the most original and innovative poet who had ever written in English, tried out a whole variety of new verse forms, from the populist *Shepheardes Calendar* to the elitist *Fowre Hymns*, producing his own stanza form in his epic-romance, *The Faerie Queene*. John Donne created a distinctive literary voice in his forceful and unsettling erotic and divine poetry, as, in a different way, did George Herbert in his exploration of the meaning of the church and Christian faith in *The Temple*. Women writers also worked hard to forge a literary identity, Isabella Whitney and Lady Mary Wroth writing often angry and despairing lyrics representing the woman's powerlessness in courtship rituals; Aemilia Lanyer producing the first "country house," a poem that represented the sadness at the dissolution of an ideal female community; and other women producing a particularly female approach to the Christian faith.

If anything, English drama was even more willing to push the boundaries of what was possible. The professional stage dates only from the 1560s and became a mass phenomenon in the 1580s, a development few could have predicted.

> *If anything, English drama was even more willing to push the boundaries of what was possible.*

Drama was not taken seriously as a literary form until Ben Jonson produced a folio of his works in 1616, the same year that King James published a similar collection of his political and religious writings. Nevertheless plays did reach a wide audience and, with large theaters such as the Globe, accommodated an audience of 2,000 to 3,000, a significant section of the London population regularly went to see plays before the theaters were closed on the orders of Oliver Cromwell in 1642. Plays had to grab an audience's attention or they risked being trumped by rival companies and fierce "Wars of the Theatres" broke out as companies sought to lure audiences in. Drama thrived in such conditions, especially given the lack of precedents, playwrights being forced to live on their wits and "make it new." The first great star of the new age of commercial theater was Christopher Marlowe, who transformed what it was possible to achieve on stage with the production of *Tamburlaine* in 1587, probably the most influential play of that period, which spawned a host of imitations and helped to characterize a particular, bombastic style of relentless tragedy, based on powerful, overbearing protagonists speaking mighty, rolling lines of blank verse. *Dr. Faustus*, another major play, rethought and adapted the miracle and morality plays that had characterized English drama before the commercial age, and it is a sign of this controversial work's enduring success that generations of readers have not been able to agree whether the play is a subversive or fundamentally conservative work.

The range and variety of Shakespeare's work is stunning, from his early Roman comedy, *The Comedy of Errors*, and historical epic sequence of three plays chronicling the reign of Henry VI (one of the great successes of the early 1590s, even if now it has been relegated to a minor position in his canon), through the major tragedies (written between 1599 and 1607), to the romances, Shakespeare did not stand still. There had been plays about powerful and impressive Moorish and Turkish tyrants, such as Marlowe's Tamburlaine and Robert Greene's *Selimus* (1594); no one, however, raised such a figure to tragic status as Shakespeare did when he wrote *Othello*. Ben Jonson, one of his major rivals, created works that were clearly designed to compete with Shakespeare's in the marketplace. While Shakespeare's company produced romantic comedies based on confusion of identities and genders, most notably, *As You Like It* and *Twelfth Night*, Jonson wrote comedies of humors, city satires that exposed human greed and folly, such as *Everyman in His Humour*, *The Alchemist*, and *The Devil Is an Ass*.

HISTORICAL PERSPECTIVES

We see the past through lenses that show us something of the world we are living in. How we mark periods in history depends less on an objective evaluation of evidence than on our sense of its relation to our own present. The centuries between 1500 and 1700 have been termed the "Renaissance," and, more recently, "the early modern period." They were also centuries in which Europe and England saw a massive change in Christian religious thought and practice; this has been called the "Reformation." What do these names mean, and what do they tell us about our understanding of this single and continuous stretch of time?

However we describe these centuries, they encompassed events that altered the ways people lived and thought. In 1500 England, and the rest of the nations of Europe, were Catholic. Apart from its few communities of Jews, Christendom was united by a universal church whose head was the Pope in Rome, and its faithful prayed according to a common liturgy in Latin. The shape of the cosmos was determined by Aristotelian physics and what could be deduced from the scriptural story of creation. It was believed that the earth was the center of the universe and composed of four elements—earth, air, fire, and water; that the human body was a balance of these elements; and that nature, read as if it were a book, revealed a divinely sanctioned moral order. Christian subjects generally respected their national or positive law, which they saw as a mirror of God's law of nature and providentially guaranteed; they assumed it would protect them from tyranny as well as anarchy. A person's place in society tended to be fixed at birth; the majority of folk lived in country villages, worked the land, and traded in regional markets.

By the end of the seventeenth century, much—though not all—of this way of life had vanished. Certain of its features would remain in place for the next hundred years, as historians who study *la longue durée* ("the long term" from the seventeenth to the nineteenth century) during which social, political and economic structures change very slowly, remind us: land continued to be farmed by methods followed "time out of mind"; manufacture was still largely done by individuals on small, handmade machines. Religion continued to determine every aspect of life; science and art, politics and economics were discussed in terms supplied by religious thought and institutions. But Christianity was no longer of one piece.

> *Religion continued to determine every aspect of life . . .*

Europe had become divided by the establishment of Protestantism in the Low Countries, Scandinavia, and most of Germany. England and Scotland were also Protestant, but with a difference: the first conformed to the doctrine and practices of the Church of England, the second to the requirements of Presbyterianism. Ireland, speaking its Celtic language and retaining many of its ancient customs, remained Catholic despite English attempts at conquest and conversion. Catholics in England, always suspected of subversive intentions, were barely tolerated. Sects proliferated: among them were Anabaptists, Puritans, and Quakers; commonly, their religious doctrines called for massive social change. Cosmic order, too, had changed; it was no longer thought of as geocentric, nor did its elements consist of four primary materials. A natural philosophy based on experimental methods had begun to reshape the disciplines of physics, medicine, and biology; such ancient authorities as Aristotle, Galen, and Pliny were no longer unquestioned. Though sketched in principle by Sir Francis Bacon in his treatise on scientific inquiry, *Novum Organum* ("the new instrument"), published in 1620, a systematic investigation of nature was not underway before the Restoration of the Stuart monarchy in 1660, when scientists in England consolidated their status as intellectuals by forming the Royal Society of London for the Improvement of Natural Knowledge—an organization vigorously supported by the new Stuart king, Charles II. But the worldview that this investigation would help to confirm was already evident early in the seventeenth century. The work of the Italian physicist Galileo Galilei on gravitational force had demonstrated that the most elementary laws of nature were mathematical; the German astronomer Johannes Kepler had confirmed that the universe was heliocentric; the English physician William Harvey had established that the body was energized not by the eccentric flow of "humors" but by a circulation of blood to and from the heart; and the Dutch cosmographer Gerhardus Mercator had discovered the means to navigate the globe safely by accurately mapping latitude and longitude. An international trade, now hugely stimulated by the development of colonies in the Americas, promised wealth to investors willing to take risks and prosperity to the towns and cities in which they lived.

In England, social and political life had been transformed by the activities of city-dwellers . . .

In England, social and political life had been transformed by the activities of city-dwellers, or "burgesses," many of whom were merchants, and also by a civil war. Involving English, Scots, and Irish subjects and parties, it had been fought over religious and social issues but also on a matter of principle. British subjects were to be governed by a monarch whose authority and power were not absolute but limited by law and the actions of Parliament, a legislative assembly representing the monarch's subjects. As a whole, the nation was conceived of as a "mystical body politic"; as the radical Bishop of Winchester John Ponet had declared, the monarch's office—not his person—was sacred. Towns and cities became crowded even as they expanded with new streets, marketplaces, and buildings for private as well as public use. Country folk, flocking to these burgeoning urban centers, succumbed to diseases created by filth and overcrowding and died younger than did their rural relatives. But England was becoming a nation of city dwellers, and everyone knew of "citizens" who had gained wealth and station in these exciting, if also terrifying, cities.

THE HUMANIST RENAISSANCE AND EARLY MODERN SOCIETY

The period from 1500 to 1700 has been understood as a "Renaissance"—literally a "rebirth." Many of its features had already been registered in that earlier renaissance of the twelfth century, particularly an interest in classical authors and their modes of expression in logic and rhetoric. By 1400, however, Italian scholars had begun to reread with fresh eyes the works of Greek and Roman authors such as Plato, Aristotle, Virgil, Ovid, and Horace. What was "reborn" as a result was a sense of the meanings to be discovered in the here and now, in the social, political, and economic everyday world. Writing about the intellectual vitality of the age, the French humanist François Rabelais had his amiable character, the giant Gargantua, confess that his own education had been "darksome, obscured with clouds of ignorance." Gargantua knows, however, that his son will be taught differently:

> Good literature has been restored unto its former light and dignity, and with such amendment and increase of knowledge, that now hardly should I be admitted unto the first form of the little grammar-school boys . . . I see robbers, hangmen, freebooters, tapsters, ostlers, and such like, of the very rubbish of the people, more learned now than the doctors and preachers were in my time.

These comically overstated remarks nevertheless convey the spirit of the Renaissance: learning was no longer to be devoted only to securing salvation but should address the conditions of ordinary life as well. More important, it should be disseminated through all ranks of society.

Albrecht Dürer, *Erasmus of Rotterdam*, 1521.

The writers and scholars responsible for the rebirth of a secular culture, derived in large measure from the pre-Christian cultures of the ancient Mediterranean, have been known as "humanists," because they read "humane" as well as "sacred" letters; their intellectual and artistic practices have been termed "humanism."

> . . . *learning was no longer to be devoted only to securing salvation but should address the conditions of ordinary life as well.*

They cultivated certain habits of thought that became widely adopted by early modern thinkers of all kinds: skill in using language analytically, attentiveness to public and political affairs as well as private and moral ones, and an acute appreciation for differences between peoples, regions, and times. It was, after all, the humanists who began to realize that the classical past required *understanding*. They recognized it as unfamiliar, neither Christian nor European, and they knew, therefore, that it had to be studied, interpreted, and, in a sense, reborn. From its inception in Italy, the work of the humanists traveled north and west, to France, the Low Countries, Germany, the Iberian peninsula, and eventually the British Isles.

At the same time, the cultures of these regions were changing in unprecedented ways. As much as an older world was being reborn, a modern world was being born, and it is in this sense that we can speak of these centuries not only as the Renaissance but also as the "early modern period." Its modernity was registered in various ways, many of them having to do with systems of quantification. Instruments for measuring time and space provided a knowledge of physical nature and its control. Sailing to the new world in 1585, Sir Walter Raleigh made use of Mercator's projection, published in 1568. Means were designed to compute the wealth that was being created by manufacture and trade. Money was used in new and complex ways, its flow managed through such innovations as double-entry bookkeeping and letters of exchange that registered debt and credit in inter-regional markets. The capital that accumulated as a result of these kinds of transactions fueled merchant banks, joint-stock companies, and—notably in England—trading companies that sponsored colonies abroad. Heralded with enthusiasm by William Drayton in 1606, the Virginia colony was reflected in a more muted fashion five years later in Shakespeare's *The Tempest*. In England especially, wealth was increasingly based not on land but on money, and the change encouraged a social mobility that reflected but also exploited the old hierarchy. The effort to ascend the social ladder could prove ruinous, as George Gascoigne's career confirmed. But riches could also make it possible for an artisan's son to purchase a coat of arms and become a gentleman, as Shakespeare did. More important, moneyed wealth supported the artistic and scholarly institutions that allowed the stepson of a bricklayer to attend the best school in London, to profit from the business of the theater, and to compose literary works of sufficient brilliance to make him Poet Laureate—as Ben Jonson did. "Ambition is like choler," warned Francis Bacon; it makes men "active, earnest, full of alacrity and stirring." But if ambition "be stopped and cannot have his way, it becommeth adust, and thereby maligne and venomous." Early modern society was certainly both active and stirring, but the very energy that gave it momentum could also lead to hardship, distress, and personal tragedy.

WRITING FOR A NEW AGE

The sixteenth-century was a time of discontinuities and lost possibilities as well as spectacular advances and transformations.

The sixteenth-century was a time of discontinuities and lost possibilities as well as spectacular advances and transformations. Henry VIII was known throughout Europe as a monarch sympathetic to humanist ideas and educational programs in the first half of his reign. Many writers were enthusiastic about his reign and his desire to transform England into a modern European nation after the austere and straightened reign of his father Henry VII. However, after his divorce from Catherine of Aragon and the break with Rome in 1532, Henry became increasingly despotic and unpredictable, becoming notorious as a tyrant among many of his more enlightened subjects. It would have been hard to predict the end of the reign from its promising beginnings.

English history and literary history is characterized by such breaks and unforeseen changes. The English adaptation of the European sonnet, for example, was hardly a smooth process. Chaucer adapted sonnet forms in his longer narrative poems in the late fourteenth century; Wyatt and Surrey adapted Italian sonnets at Henry's court that were republished in the first major anthology of English lyric poetry Tottel's *Miscellany* (1557); and after Sir Phillip Sidney's *Astrophil and Stella* (composed 1582, published posthumously 1591) there was a vogue for sonnet sequences in the 1590s, which appeared to have died out until it was revived by the publication of William Shakespeare's *Sonnets* in 1609 (some of which may have been written in the 1590s). This does not tell the whole story of the complicated nature of English literary history. Sonnets came in and out of vogue, and other verse forms dominated the literary scene at different points in the century. At the court of Edward VI, more obviously Protestant types of literary verse were promoted by significant intellectual figures, some of them like John Bale returning from exile in the last years of Henry's reign. Allegorical and political poetry experienced a resurgence; and there was an attempt to establish a native English Protestant tradition that looked back to the figure of the plowman (represented most famously in the works of William Langland), intimately connected to the soil and the land, and so able to tell the truth about the corruption of the court. One of the most important writers in Edward's reign was William Baldwin who wrote what many consider to be the first English novel, *Beware the Cat* (page 790) and was the leading light behind the collaborative project *A Mirror Magistrates*, one of Shakespeare's favorite works. *A Mirror* was begun in the reign of Edward VI, but it was not published until 1559, because it fell afoul of the censors in 1555. *A Mirror* is very much a product of a militant Protestant literary culture, but after the death of the young king from tuberculosis in 1553, the work was not received sympathetically at the Catholic court of Edward's half-sister Mary.

A *Mirror* was one of the most important literary texts of the second half of the sixteenth century and went through a number of different editions and versions well into the seventeenth century. The work consists of a series of verse laments by ghosts of dead political figures who usually lament their own failings and ask the assembled group of writers to learn from their mistakes. The team of writers led by Baldwin comment on the particular tragedy and point a moral for the readers to learn from. The work revises the well established genre of advice literature, the mirror for princes (showing monarchs how to rule through a series of negative and positive examples of government), refocusing attention on the individual magistrates as a governing class. Had Edward VI not died so young, it is likely that similar forms of literature would have proliferated in subsequent years and changed the shape and nature of English literary history.

But this is not the only way to look at English literature and history in the sixteenth century. It used to be an orthodox judgment to see the reign of Mary Tudor (1553–1558) as an attempt to artificially revive a long-gone Catholic sensibility and impose it on the English people from above. Recent research, proposed by Eamon Duffy, sees the map of English religious history in a very different way. For Duffy, it is Henry VIII, Edward VI, and Protestant revolutionaries who sought to impose their vision on a reluctant English people. Rather than translators of the Bible and advocates of a break with Rome being those who correctly read the religious desires of the nation, it was, in fact, adherence to the traditional idea of the late medieval church. Whereas Protestants wanted people to read the Bible and determine their own understanding of the word of God, Marian Catholics placed much greater importance on the institution of the church itself and its ability to interpret God's word for an obedient people, concentrating more on liturgy and ritual than sermons and exegesis. Hence, the widespread Catholic taunt, "Where was your church before Luther?"

In Mary's reign many Protestants went into exile in Switzerland, France and the Low Countries, developing their own ideas and their own version of English history, especially in Basel and Geneva, which became centers of resistance to Mary's regime. One of the main achievements of the exiles was the Geneva Bible, often popularly known as the "Breeches Bible," because the translator claimed that Adam and Eve made trousers ("breeches") out of leaves to cover their nakedness. The

Geneva Bible was first published in 1563 and went through several editions, becoming the most popular English Bible in the sixteenth and seventeenth centuries, principally because it was the most widely available and the cheapest. The Bible had an extensive commentary which directed readers to see the history of the church as a battle between the good Protestant forces and the evil Catholic Church of Rome. It had a crucial influence on later English writing. For example, Edmund Spenser cast the duplicitous Duessa as the Whore of Babylon from the Book of Revelation, the seductive and diabolical figure of the Catholic Church in the last days of the world, a reading that could only have been derived from the Geneva Bible.

The other major achievement of the exiles was John Foxe's *Acts and Monuments of the Christian Church*, first published in 1563, a work deemed so important by the Elizabethan authorities that a copy had to be kept in every cathedral church (the principal church connected with a bishop) in the country (see page 1063). Foxe's purpose was to explain that the Protestant church did have a history and was not merely the brainchild of a few disgruntled clergymen. Foxe saw the medieval church as a divided institution, a battleground between those good men who wished to spread the word of God as widely as possible and those evil and deluded priests who wished to suppress the truth and control the people for their own purposes. Like the Geneva Bible, Foxe's history also had a significant impact on the course of English literary history, providing Protestants with a story that they could call their own.

. . . religious history was complex and conflicted in the sixteenth century.

The point to be made is that religious history was complex and conflicted in the sixteenth century. Battle lines were drawn between Catholic and Protestant interpretations and contingent events often determined the course of English history and its literature. However, we must not imagine that divisions were always clear-cut. As the work of Alison Shell has demonstrated, Protestant and Catholic writers borrowed liberally from each other's work, often sharing a common religious and literary language. It is not always easy to tell apart the work of writers such as George Herbert, an Anglican priest, and Robert Southwell, a Catholic martyr. To take another important example, John Donne uses both Catholic and Protestant ideas and vocabulary in his work, perhaps the product of his upbringing as a Catholic and his later conversion to Protestantism, perhaps simply a sign of complicated religious times that tolerated significant overlap between varieties of the same faith.

One of the great surprises for people living at the end of the sixteenth century was that Elizabeth lived so long. The longest reigning monarch since Henry I (1087–1135), the fourth son of William the Conqueror, Elizabeth had been seriously ill at various points in her reign and had not been expected to survive. Historians often make a distinction between the first half of her reign from about 1558 to 1585—when Elizabeth was undoubtedly a shrewd, popular, and successful monarch who united the disparate factions of her kingdoms—and the second half of her reign, when, whatever her merits, many of her leading subjects tired of her style of government and were looking forward to the reign of her successor, whoever that might be. Elizabeth, the Virgin Queen, encouraged a particular style of obeisance in which courtiers paid homage to her as if she were a love object, and she was notorious for encouraging young male favorites, most notably in her later years Robert Devereux, first Earl of Essex, who was eventually

Jan van der Straet, called Stradanus, Impressio Librorum (Book Printing): Plate 4 of the *Nova Reperta* (New Discoveries), late 16th century.

executed after he led a desperate and suicidal rebellion against her in 1601. One of the great ironies of English literary history is that the literature that we often think of as the golden age of Elizabethan writing was produced in the late 1580s and 1590s, a disastrous decade characterized by desperate uncertainty, famine, and political disasters (not least the protracted and terrifying war in Ireland, which nearly bankrupted the crown). The work of Marlowe, Sidney, Shakespeare, Spenser, and Donne was all the product of turbulent times. Moreover, had Elizabeth died earlier, much of it would either never have been written or would have appeared in a very different form.

Many features of Renaissance and early modern culture are again in transition today: the printed book, which once superseded the manuscript, is now challenged by computer-generated hypertext; the nation state, which once eclipsed the feudal domain and divided "Christendom,"

> *Many features of Renaissance and early modern culture are again in transition today . . .*

is now qualified by an international economy; and the belief in human progress, which was once applauded as an advance over the medieval faith in divine providence, is now subject to criticism, in large part because of such kinds of injustice and inequity as slavery, colonialism, and the exploitation of wage labor—all factors in the growth of early modern England and other states in Europe. As modern and postmodern readers, we have a special affinity with our early modern counterparts. Like them, we study change.

HISTORY AND EPIC

The political life of the sixteenth century was dominated by the genius of a single dynasty: the Tudors. Its founder was Owen Tudor, a squire of an ancient Welsh family. Employed at the court of Henry V, he eventually married Henry's widow, Catherine of Valois. The first Tudor monarch was their grandson, Henry, Earl of Richmond, who defeated Richard III at Bosworth Field in 1485 to become Henry VII. He married Elizabeth, daughter of Edward IV, whom Richard III had succeeded—a fortunate event for the people of England, as it united the two parties by whom the crown had been disputed for many decades. Once Henry, who represented the House of Lancaster (whose emblem was a red rose) was joined to Elizabeth, a member of the House of York (signified by a white rose), the so-called "Wars of the Roses" were at an end. Henry VII's bureaucratic skills then settled the kingdom in ways that allowed it to grow and become identified as a single nation, however much it also comprised different peoples: the midlands and the north were distinguished from the more populous south by dialectal forms of speech; and to the west, in Cornwall and Wales, many English subjects still spoke Cornish and Welsh. Ireland, across the sea to the west, and the Scottish highlands to the north were still largely Gaelic speaking. While the Anglo-Normans had invaded Ireland in the twelfth century, it was not until the reign of Elizabeth that the English pursued the subjugation of Ireland by colonizing plantations and conducting a brutal military campaign that produced famine, massacres, and the forced relocation of people. But this supposed English fiefdom remained rebellious and effectively unconquered for Elizabeth's entire reign. Its resistance to English rule was crushed only in 1603, an event that marked the end of an independent Ireland for three hundred years. Oliver Cromwell's account of the massacre of the city of Drogheda in 1649, related in his *Letters from Ireland,* illustrates a later instance of the brutality typical of the English conquest of Ireland. Scotland, to the far north, was a separate and generally unfriendly kingdom with strong ties to France until James VI of Scotland became James I of England. His accession to the English throne in 1603 began a process that would end with the complete union of the two kingdoms in 1707. And there were even more remote regions to consider: England's colonization of the Americas began under Elizabeth I, progressed under James I, and allowed the English to think of themselves as an imperial power.

Writing history offered a way to reinforce the developing sense of nationhood, a project all the more appealing after the creation of an English church and the beginnings of what was thought to be a British empire. Medieval historians had concentrated on the actions of ambitious men and women whose lives reflected their good or bad qualities; early modern historians wrote about events and their manifold causes. William Camden's *Britannia* and Raphael Holinshed's *Chronicles of England, Scotland, and Ireland* (the source for many of Shakespeare's plays) celebrate the deeds and the character of the early peoples of the British Isles. The land itself became the subject of comment: William Harrison wrote a description of the English counties (included in Holinshed); John Stow surveyed the neighborhoods of London; and Michael Drayton, a Stuart poet, wrote a mythopoetic account of England's towns and countryside entitled *Poly-Olbion*. As a history, however, it is Richard Hakluyt's collection of travel stories, *The Principal Navigations, Voyages and Discoveries of the English Nation,* that has proved most memorable over time. It reports in magnificent detail the exploration of the Americas in the latter half of the sixteenth century. Accounts of this wild and fruitful land fired the imaginations of English readers, who, it was hoped, would decide to promote and even participate in the laborious task of colonization. Describing landfall on the coast of Virginia in 1585, Arthur Barlow evoked the image of a paradise, "where we smelled so sweet and so strong a smell as if we had been in the midst of some delicate garden abounding with all kind of odoriferous flowers. . . . I think in all the world the like abundance is not to be found." Attempts to occupy this land of incredible natural wealth were determined by two principal objectives: securing profitable trade with the Indians, and possessing land from which to extract such resources as timber, furs, fish, and eventually, tobacco. The hope of finding gold was on everyone's mind. The Chesapeake Bay and its environs were settled by men interested in commerce, often at great personal expense. The Massachusetts coast attracted Puritan divines and their flocks, and while these colonists also profited from trade, matters of faith were supposed to be their principal concern. By celebrating a national identity, these and other contemporary narratives reveal their thematic connections with the epic, a genre of poetic fiction. But they do not conform to that genre as contemporary poetry represented it—expressing heroic grandeur not only in action but also in the musical verse form and elevated language of the epic tradition.

The masterpieces of early modern English epic are represented by Edmund Spenser's *The Faerie Queene* and John Milton's *Paradise Lost*. Spenser imitated continental models to create an English Protestant epic-romance, an optimistic projection of Elizabethan culture. The realities of Elizabeth I's reign were indeed far from the poet's vision of things, but they were nonetheless very impressive. England's cities had grown to be centers of world commerce, and the bold explorations of such men as Sir Francis Drake testified to the nation's seafaring power. In the figures of his poem, Spenser embodied the energies producing this expansive growth. His virtuous knights overcome monstrous threats to order, peace, and tranquillity. Aspects of the queen's own genius are reflected in his heroines. Like the warrior maiden Britomart, Elizabeth I assumed a martial character when England was in danger from abroad; like his Queen Mercilla, she was supposed to be gracious to her enemies—a trait somewhat belied by her speeches to Parliament agreeing to the execution of Mary Queen of Scots. Like the virgin Una, she stood for what the poet and most of his readers believed was the one true faith: Protestantism. And like Spenser's enigmatic and distant Queen Gloriana, the Faerie Queene of the title, she exercised her authority and power in unpredictable ways: secrecy and dissimulation were her stock in trade. To her subjects, her majesty was awful and sometimes terrifying. But she was also mortal, and at her death, few could have foreseen the new and divided nation that would come into being with the accession of James I.

England's cities had grown to be centers of world commerce . . .

The new king was greeted with mixed feelings. On the one hand, his claim to the throne was not disputed; on the other hand, he came from Scotland, long an enemy of England and always a source of anxiety to those who sought dominion over the British Isles as a whole. Although educated by the humanist George Buchanan, whose treatises praising republican government were widely known and read, James, as his own treatise *The True Law of Free Monarchy* shows, favored absolute rule and

believed that a monarch should be *lex loquens*, the living spirit of the law, and therefore not bound by the terms of national or positive law. His personal conduct appeared to be dubious. His critics represented him as frequently unkempt and claimed
that he preferred to hunt deer rather than to take charge of matters of state. Disputes
with the House of Commons over money to support the Crown's activities were frequent. Reports of intrigue with Catholic Spain shattered the nation's sense of security; an attempt in 1605 to blow up the Houses of Parliament, revealed as the
Gunpowder Plot, caused a near panic. These and other kinds of unrest grew more intense when James's heir, Charles I, proved to be even more autocratic than his father.
Charles's queen, Henrietta Maria, the daughter of Henry IV of France, was a
Catholic, and it was rumored that she was treacherous. Religious controversy raged
throughout the British Isles, and the struggle over the authority and power of the
monarch culminated in a bloody civil war.
Across England and Scotland, forces loyal to the
king fought the army of Parliament, led by
Oliver Cromwell, a Puritan Member of the
Commons. The war, which lasted from 1642 to
1651, ended with the defeat of the royalists.

> *. . . the struggle over the authority*
> *and power of the monarch*
> *culminated in a bloody civil war.*

In 1649 Charles I was captured and executed by order of Parliament, and
England began to be governed as a republic. She was no longer a kingdom but a
Commonwealth, and this period in her history is known as the Interregnum, the period between kingdoms. The long-advocated change, now a reality, could hardly
have begun in a more shocking way. The monarchy had always been regarded as a
sacred office and institution, as Shakespeare's Richard II had said:

> Not all the water in the rough rude sea
> Can wash the balm off from an anointed king;
> The breath of worldly men cannot depose
> The deputy elected by the Lord.

But in the course of half a century, the people had proved themselves to be a sovereign power, and it was politically irrelevant that Charles, on the block, exemplified
a regal self-control. As the Parliamentarian poet Andrew Marvell later wrote of the
King's admirable courage at his execution: "He nothing common did or mean /
Upon that memorable scene . . . Nor called the gods with vulgar spite / To vindi-
cate his helpless right."

The conflict itself, its causes and its outcome, have been variously interpreted. As
a religious and cultural struggle, the Civil War, also known as the Wars of Three
Kingdoms, expressed the resistance of Scots Presbyterians and Irish Catholics to the
centralizing control of the English church and government. As a revolution in government, the conflict was defined by common lawyers, energized by Puritan enthusiasm,
and marked the nation's transition to a society in which the absolute rule by a
monarch was no longer a possibility. The people
themselves had acquired a voice. To some extent
this was a religious voice. Puritans who professed
a belief in congregational church government

> *The people themselves had*
> *acquired a voice.*

were generally proponents of republican rule. Their dedication to the ideal of a society
of equals under the law was shared by men and women of other sects: the Levellers, led

by John Lilburne, who argued for a written constitution, universal manhood suffrage, and religious toleration (for God, Lilburne wrote, "doth not choose many rich, nor many wise"); the Diggers, led by Gerrard Winstanley, who proposed to institute a communistic society in the wastelands they were ploughing and cultivating; the Quakers, led by George Fox, who rejected all forms of church order in deference to the inner light of an individual conscience and, insisting on social equality, refused to take off their hats before gentry or nobility; and the Ranters, who denied the authority of Scripture and saw God everywhere in nature. Without widespread acceptance of the egalitarian concept that had initiated the Protestant reformation—all believers are members of a real though invisible priesthood—it is hard to see how the move from a monarchy to a representative and republican government could have taken place.

The most comprehensive contemporary history of the war, *The True Historical Narrative of the Rebellion and Civil Wars in England*, by Edward Hyde, Earl of Clarendon, was not published before 1704, but the troubled period found an oblique commentary in what is arguably England's greatest and certainly most humanistic epic poem: Milton's *Paradise Lost*, in print by 1667. Milton's career was inextricably bound up with the fate of the Commonwealth. Educated at Cambridge and with his reputation as a poet well established, Milton had begun by 1649 to contribute to a defense of Puritanism and the creation of a republican government. Despite worsening eyesight, he published *The Tenure of Kings and Magistrates*, a sustained and eloquent apology for tyrannicide, after the execution of Charles I; and in his *Eikonoklastes* ("image-breaker"), written after he was made Latin secretary to the new executive, the Council of State, he derided attempts by royalists to celebrate Charles I in John Gauden's pamphlet *Eikon Basilike* ("image of a king"). In 1660, disturbed by the proposed restoration of Charles Stuart, soon to be Charles II, Milton—now completely blind—published his last political treatise, *The Ready and Easy Way to Establish a Commonwealth*. It presented the case for a republicanism that had already lost most of its popularity: the government of the Commonwealth had adopted measures that resembled the autocratic rule of the monarchy it had overthrown. Meanwhile, the composition of *Paradise Lost* was underway. Indebted to many of Spenser's themes in *The Faerie Queene*, Milton infused his subject—the fall of the rebellious angels and the exile from paradise of the disobedient Adam and Eve—with the spirit of the account in Genesis. His poem is the product of a doubly dark vision of life. Sightless and suffering again what he felt were the constraints of a monarchy, Milton's story of exile from paradise spoke to his own and England's loss of innocence and painful acquisition of the knowledge of good and evil during the period of the war and its aftermath. His *Paradise Lost* and its sequel, *Paradise Regained*, express the most provocative ambiguities of contemporary English culture; they were—and still are—praised as rivalling the epics of Homer, Virgil, and Dante in their power and scope.

DRAMA

Drama provided another perspective on English life. While epics depicted the grander aspirations of the nation, its human character was expressed in stage plays, masques or speaking pageants, and dramatic processions. These forms exploited the material of chronicle to illustrate not only the virtues of heroes but also their foibles and limitations; history's villains warned viewers that evil would be punished, if not by civil

While epics depicted the grander aspirations of the nation, its human character was expressed in stage plays . . .

authority then by providence. Writing tragedy based on history and legend, Marlowe and Shakespeare complicated the direct moralism of medieval drama. Rather than portraying characters who became victims of their own misdoings, rising to power only to fall in disgrace, the early modern stage showed virtue and vice as intertwined—a hero's tragic error could also be at the heart of his greatness. The origins of evil were seen as mysterious, even obscure. Some sense of this moral ambiguity can be traced to the tragedies of the Roman philosopher Seneca, which were translated into English and published in 1581. English drama reproduced many of their features: the five-act structure, rapid-fire dialogue punctuated by pithy maxims, and images of tyranny, revenge, and fate illustrated by haunting dreams and echoing curses.

If tragedy turned away from straightforward piety, so did comedy. The medieval drama of Christian salvation, in which the hero's struggle against sin was ended by his acknowledgment of grace, was replaced with plays about the wars between the sexes and between parents and children. Much of this material was modeled on the comedies of Plautus, a Roman playwright, and on the tales or *novellas* of contemporary Italian writers. Playwrights like Ben Jonson also found a wealth of material in the improvisatory Italian *commedia dell'arte*, with its stock characters of the old dotard, the cuckolded husband, the damsel in distress, and the mountebank or quack. *The Alchemist*, chiefly a satire on confidence men and their credulous victims, those tradesmen and entrepreneurs seeking a quick and easy return on investments (especially in the Americas), concludes somewhat ironically by giving the prize to the burgess Lovewit, who disdains censorious critique in favor of a genial wit. An even more topical form of comedy combined some of these continental traditions with themes and figures specifically drawn from London life.

The stage was generally regarded as responsible for both illustrating social failings and stirring up discontent. Although some, like the playwright Thomas Heywood, praised plays as a form of instruction for the unschooled, others, like the Puritan pamphleteer Philip Stubbes, asserted that plays "maintain bawdry, insinuate foolery, and revive the remembrance of heathen idolatry." As Stephen Gosson wrote in *Plays Confuted in Five Actions:*

The stage was generally regarded as responsible for both illustrating social failings and stirring up discontent.

> If private men be suffered to forsake their calling because they desire to talk gentlemenlike in satin & velvet, with a buckler at their heels, proportion is so broken, unity dissolved, harmony confounded, that the whole body must be dismembered, and the prince or head cannot choose but sicken.

The fear was not only that the tricksters of drama would be the objects of emulation rather than scorn, but also that the actors' masquerade of identities would spur social instability in the public theater's audience, ranging from the groundlings in the pit to the gentry in the higher-priced seats. Parliament had tried to maintain social order by regulating, through sumptuary laws, what style and fabrics persons of a particular rank could wear. A subject's experience of the

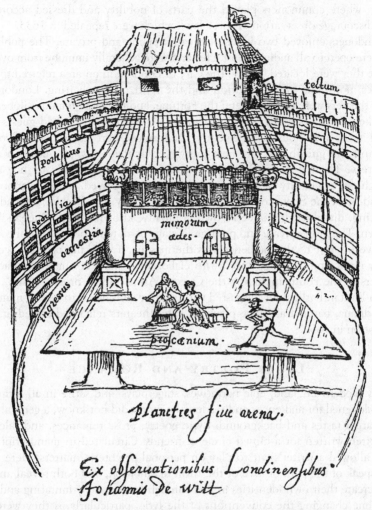

planeties siue arena.

Ex obseruationibus Londinensibus
Johannis de witt

Arend von Buchell, *The Swan Theatre,* after Johannes de Witt, c. 1596. The only extant drawing of a public theater in 1590s London, this sketch shows what Shakespeare's Globe must have looked like. The round playhouse centered on the curtainless platform of the stage (*proscenium*), which projected into the yard (*planities sive arena*). Raised above the stage by two pillars, the roof (*tectum*) stored machinery. At the back of the stage, the tiring house (*mimorum aedes*), where the actors dressed, contained two doors for entrances and exits. There were no stage sets and only movable props such as thrones, tables, beds, and benches, like the one shown here. Other documents on the early modern stage are the contract of the Fortune Theatre, where *The Roaring Girl* was performed, and stage directions in the plays themselves. Modeled on the Globe, although square in shape, the Fortune featured a stage forty-three feet broad and twenty-seven and a half feet deep. Stage directions include further clues: sometimes a curtained booth made "discovery" scenes possible; trapdoors allowed descents; and a space "aloft," such as the gallery above the stage doors, represented a room above the street. Eyewitness accounts fill out the picture. In the yard stood the groundlings who paid a penny for standing room, exposed to the sky, which provided natural lighting. For those willing to pay a penny or two more, three galleries (*orchestra, sedilia,* and *porticulus*) provided seats—the most expensive of which were cushioned. Spectators could buy food and drink during the performance. The early modern theater held an audience of roughly eight hundred standing in the yard, and fifteen hundred more seated in the galleries. According to Thomas Platter, who had seen Shakespeare's *Julius Caesar* in 1599, "everyone has a good view."

theater, where commoners played the parts of nobility and dressed accordingly, might discourage observation of these laws, which were repealed in 1633.

Londoners enjoyed two kinds of theater: public and private. The public theaters were open to all audiences for a fee and were generally immune from oversight because they were located outside the City of London, in an area referred to as the Liberties, notorious for prostitution and the sport of bear-baiting. London's two biggest theaters were located there: the Fortune, and the more famous Globe, home to Shakespeare's company. Private theaters—open only to invited guests—were located in the large houses of the gentry, the Inns of Court (the schools of common law), and the guildhalls; the best known, Blackfriars, was housed in an old monastery. Their performances were acted almost exclusively by boy actors, although the popularity of these companies was short-lived. James I, annoyed by the send-up of the Scots court in *Eastward Ho!*, a play that Ben Jonson had a part in writing, dissolved his queen's own company, known as the Queen's Revels Children. The most private and prestigious stage of all remained the royal court. Of exclusive interest to this audience was the masque, a speaking pageant accompanied by music and dancing, staged with elaborate sets and costumes, and acted by members of the court, including the Queens Anna and Henrietta Maria. But in 1649, a Puritan Parliament, disgusted with what it considered to be the immorality of the drama, banned all stage plays, and the theaters remained closed until the Restoration in 1660.

LYRIC POETRY AND ROMANCE

In early modern England, epic narratives, stage plays, and satire in all forms were genres designed for audiences and readers the writer did not know, a general public with varied tastes and background. Lyric poetry, prose romances, and tales were more often written for a closed circle of friends. Circulated in manuscript, these genres allowed a writer's wit to play on personal or coterie matters. Here writers could speak of the pain of love or the thrill of ambition, and both reveal and, in a sense, create their own identities in and through language. By imitating and at the same time changing the conventions of the lyric, particularly as they were illustrated by the Italian poet Francesco Petrarch, English poets were able to represent a persona, or fictive self, that became in turn a model for others. Unlike Petrarch, who saw his lady as imbued with numinous power before which he could only submit, Sir Thomas Wyatt and Sir Philip Sidney imagined love in social and very human terms. In the struggle to gain affection and power, their subjectivity took strength from their conquests as well as their resistance to defeat. The origins of the lyric in song are attested in the verse of Thomas Campion, much of which was actually set to music. Its uses in pastoral (whether erotic or spiritual) are illustrated by poets as different as Robert Herrick, John Donne, and Andrew Marvell. At times, its objects of adoration could be divine or mystical, as in the verse of George Herbert and Henry Vaughan. Women poets, such as Lady Mary Wroth and Katherine Philips, reworked the conventions of the love lyric to encompass a feminine perspective on passion and, equally important, on friendship. Sonnet sequences were popular and, reflecting a taste for narrative romance, often dramatized a conflict between lovers. Shakespeare wrote the best-known sonnets of

Color Plate 11   Surviving the Reformation.   Rowland Lockey, *Sir Thomas More, 1478–1535, His Family and Descendants,* 1593. Commissioned by Thomas More II, grandson of Sir Thomas More, this painting portrays five generations of this Roman Catholic family. The first seven figures from left to right are modeled on a lost painting by Hans Holbein. Sir Thomas More himself is shown seated at the left, wearing a brown robe. His father, in red, sits next to him, while behind him to either side stand his wife, Anne, and his son, John. His daughters Cecily, Elizabeth, and Margaret are grouped at the center.   *(Copyright © National Portrait Gallery, London.)*

Color Plate 12 Faithfully Portraying Nature.   Hans Holbein, The Younger, *Lady with a Squirrel and a Starling*, c. 1526–8. This painting shows Holbein's almost obsessive concern with representing detail. Artists who represented naturalistic detail played a role in developing the new sense of nature that emerged in the sixteenth century. Nature was now something that could be empirically observed as well as magically divined. If only indirectly, this new representation of nature had its impact upon the new sense of how science might record nature. Thus, the *way* Holbein's technique portrays his subject bears comparison with a whole range of discussions about nature that can be seen in texts as diverse as Shakespeare's *The Tempest* and Bacon's *Advancement of Learning*. The subject, a London lady, is said to be the nurse to Edward VI, the son of Henry VIII. An innovation in early Renaissance interior decoration, such portraits reveal a new sense of the individual subject. (*The Bridgeman Art Library International.*)

Color Plate 13 "Come live with me and be my love." Nicholas Hilliard, *The Young Man Amongst Roses*, c. 1597. Hilliard, the greatest miniaturist of the Elizabethan age, here represents an exquisite aristocratic young man in the pose of melancholic lover. (*V&A Images/Victoria and Albert Museum.*)

Color Plate 14 Something Rich and Strange. Inigo Jones, *Fiery Spirit*, costume design for a torchbearer in *The Lord's Masque*, performed 14 February 1613. Jones designed this masque as part of the celebrations for the marriage of James I's daughter Elizabeth to Frederick V, the Elector Palatine. The elaborate costume designs were modeled on those created for Florentine court theater. (*Copyright © Devonshire Collection, Chatsworth. Reproduced by permission of Chatsworth Settlement Trustees.*)

Color Plate 15   English or Irish?   Marcus Gheeraerts the Younger, *Captain Thomas Lee,*
1594. Thomas Lee served as an army officer during the Elizabethan colonization of Ireland.
This painting portrays him as part barefoot Irish foot soldier and part elaborately accou-
tered English gentleman. On the tree behind him appears a Latin quotation from Livy,
"both to act and to suffer with fortitude is a Roman's part," which is what the Roman patriot Scaevola is supposed to have said when he was captured by rebel Etruscans as he entered their camp disguised in their garb. The painting is thus an elaborate allegory protesting Lee's English loyalty despite his friendship with such Irish chiefs as Hugh O'Neill. On
13 February 1601, Lee died a traitor's death as punishment for his role in the Earl of Essex's
rebellion. *(Tate Gallery, London. Art Resource, New York.)*

Color Plate 16 A Passion for Collecting. Daniel Mytens, *Thomas Howard, second Earl of Arundel and Surrey*, c. 1618. One of the greatest collectors of art in seventeenth-century England, the Earl of Arundel points to the long gallery of marble statues. Henry Peacham, author of *The Compleat Gentleman*, writes that these Classical statues give the viewer "the pleasure of seeing and conversing with these old heroes." Arundel House was full of learned inscriptions. So, the collector's goal was not just to acquire art but to preserve the past, and to provide a visual humanist education in the Classics of ancient Greece and Rome. *(Copyright © National Portrait Gallery, London.)*

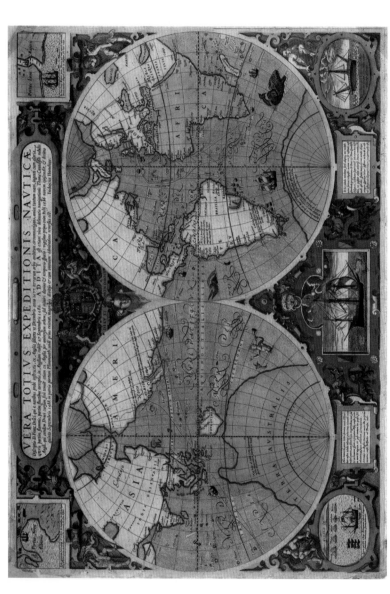

Color Plate 17 Sailing West to Discover the East.   The title of this magnificent map, executed by cartographer Jodocus Hondius, claims it is "The true description of the whole voyage of Francis Drake, who with five well furnished ships left England on the 13th of December, 1577, and returned to England on Sept 27th 1580, with great glory; circumnavigating the circuit of the lands of the earth, one of his ships returned to England on Sept 27th, 1580; of the rest, some were destroyed by fire, some by flood. . . ." Topographical inserts around the frame depict Drake's landing in California, his entry to the port of Java, his wreck on rocks near Celebes, his ship the Golden Hind, and his welcome at the Moluccas. (*Courtesy of the Library of Congress.*)

Color Plate 18 Staging the Monarchy. Anthony Van Dyck, *Charles I of England*,
c. 1637. Charles I, reputedly a retiring personality, is here transformed into a martial hero,
modeled on the great equestrian figures of Ancient Rome. This painting by the great court
painter Van Dyck helped create the iconography of the Stuart monarchy. For the representation of Charles I in print, see his *Eikon Basilike* (ghostwritten by John Gauden) and Milton's
Eikonoklastes in *Perspectives: The Civil War, or The Wars of Three Kingdoms*. (*Art Resource,
New York.*)

Color Plate 19   Order on the Eve of the Civil War.   Cornelius Johnson, *Arthur Capel, 1st Baron Capel, 1604–1649, and His Family,* c. 1640. This painting in the style of Van Dyck portrays the royalist Arthur Capel, who was executed the same year as Charles I. In the background appear gardens, perhaps those of his home at Little Hadham.   *(Copyright © National Portrait Gallery, London.)*

the period. His cast of characters—including the poet as principal speaker, his beloved male friend, a rival poet, and a fickle lady—appear as protagonists in a drama of love, betrayal, devotion, and despair. Some poets embedded their love poetry in prose narratives that told a story, as the Italian poet Dante Alighieri had in his sequence of songs and sonnets to the lady Beatrice entitled *The New Life*. A brilliant tale of seduction frames George Gascoigne's lyrics in his *Adventures of Master F. J.*, and Sidney's eclogues (pastoral poems) punctuate the long and complicated narrative of his prose romance, *Arcadia*.

Prose romances also provided images of new kinds of identity. Stories of marvels surrounded the lives of the powerful and exotic, such as Robert Greene's *Pandosto* (the source for Shakespeare's *The Winter's Tale*) and Thomas Lodge's *Rosalind*, while tales of lower-class artisan-adventurers illustrate the enthusiasm with which early modern writers and readers embraced a freedom to reinvent themselves. The romantic notion of the "marvelous" gained a new meaning in tales of tricksters and of sturdy entrepreneurs who survived against all odds—they represented the creative energies possessed by plain folk. The short fiction of Thomas Nashe, Thomas Deloney, and the hilarious (and anonymous) *Life and Pranks of Long Meg of Westminster* conclusively break with the delicate sentimentality of pure romance and, appealing to a taste for the ordinarily wonderful, point the way for such later novelists as Daniel Defoe, Henry Fielding, and Charles Dickens.

> . . . *tales of tricksters and of sturdy entrepreneurs who survived against all odds—represented the creative energies possessed by plain folk.*

The spirit of romance infused narratives of travel as well, many of which made little distinction between fact and fantasy. Sir John Mandeville's fifteenth-century *Travels*, in print throughout the sixteenth century, responded to the growing curiosity of Europeans about the wonders of nature in distant lands, which harbored whole peoples who were pictured as utterly different from anything known at home. The wonders reported in popular collections of travel narratives like Samuel Purchas's immensely popular *Purchas His Pilgrimage, or Relations of the World and the Religions Observed in All Ages* (1613) were designed to attract, not repel, readers, but a horror of the "other" was nevertheless implied in many of these accounts. Shakespeare's Othello holds the Venetian senate spellbound when he reports that parts of the world are inhabited by "Cannibals that each other eat, / The Anthropophagi," as well as "men whose heads / Do grow beneath their shoulders." In *The Tempest*, such claims are parodied in the figure of Caliban: despite Prospero's accusations, Caliban bears a very human aspect and is no monster. The lure of distant lands could also attract the social critic who sought to devise images of an ideal world in order to better the real world. Sir Thomas More's *Utopia* projects a fantasy of a communal state that does double duty by pointing both to the inequities of English society *and* to the absurdities of reforms that assume men and women can be consistently reasonable. Literally describing a utopia, a "nowhere," his treatise is also effectively a dystopia, a work describing a "bad place." Neither Sir Francis Bacon's *New Atlantis* (1627) nor James Harrington's *Commonwealth of Oceans* (1656)—each a true utopia suggesting a radical reform of political and intellectual life—emulate More's embrace of both utopian and dystopian perspectives. But the dystopias of later writers, such as

Jonathan Swift's *Gulliver's Travels* (1726), Samuel Butler's *Erewhon* (an anagram for "nowhere," 1872) and George Orwell's *1984* (1949), impressively illustrate the hazards of idealistic and visionary social thought.

CHANGING SOCIAL, POLITICAL AND PERSONAL ROLES

The imaginative work of "self-fashioning" in early modern lyric and romance kept pace, to a degree, with actual social change. During this period, a person was born into a place—defined by locale, family, and work—but did not necessarily remain there. The social ladder was traveled in both directions. An impecunious member of the gentry, a second son of a poor squire, or a widow whose noble husband had left her without a suitable jointure or estate could sink below the rank to which they had been born and effectively become a "commoner." In turn, a prosperous artisan, a thrifty yeoman, or an enterprising merchant could eventually become a member of the gentry—folk who were entitled to signal their identity by a coat of arms and were not supposed to do manual work. The new rich were sometimes mocked for seeking advice in conduct books regarding the proper behavior for gentlefolk, but no one could overlook the change in their status. More important, representatives of the "middling sort" were gaining political power. They generally had the right to vote for a member of the House of Commons, and they regularly held local office as bailiffs, magistrates, or sheriffs, and served on juries in towns and villages throughout the kingdom. They administered property, engaged in business, and traded on international markets. Creating much of the wealth of early modern England, they defined the concept of an economic class independent of social rank or family background: "What is Gentry if wealth be wanting, but base servile beggery?" asked Robert Greene. The idea that a person inherited a way of life was undercut by evidence of continuous shifts in both urban and rural society.

> *The idea that a person inherited a way of life was undercut by evidence of continuous shifts in both urban and rural society.*

The situation for women in particular exhibited a certain ideological ambivalence. Ancient philosophy and medieval theology had insisted that *woman*kind was essentially and naturally different from *man*kind, characterized by physical weakness, intellectual passivity, and an aptitude for housework, childcare, and the minor decorative arts. That some women had distinguished themselves in occupations traditionally reserved for men was understood to signal an exception; in general, social doctrine imposed rigid codes of behavior on men and women. This thinking was countered by the text of Scripture—but also and increasingly by evidence from history, which revealed that ordinary women had undertaken all kinds of activity and therefore that a woman had the same range of talents as a man. Literary representation and authorship reflected some of this argument.

Departing from medieval social norms, humanists had stressed that men should be educated in the arts as well as arms, and writers like Sir Philip Sidney, illustrating the sensitivity of men to emotional life, devised characters whose masculinity was amplified by attributes that were conventionally associated with women: passion, sympathy, and a certain self-indulgence. The frustrated lover of his sonnet sequence

Astrophil and Stella is both resourceful and humorously pitiable. Flexibility with respect to categories of gender is also a feature of much lyric poetry; the male poet's beloved is sometimes another man. Shakespeare's sonnets are the chief example of homosexual verse in this period, but homoerotic innuendo, often suggested as a feature of a love triangle, is common in all genres of writing. In Marlowe's poem *Hero and Leander*, the youth Leander loves the girl Hero and attracts the sexual attentions of the sea-god Neptune.

Ideas as well as social forms and practices were also changing. The repeated shifts in religious practice—from medieval Catholicism to Henrician Protestantism, then back to the Catholicism dictated by Queen Mary I, and then on to the Anglican Church of Queen Elizabeth I—revealed that divine worship could alter its form without bringing on the apocalypse. More subtly, the emerging capitalist economy produced a conceptual model for cultural exchange. Just as material goods flowed through regional and national markets, entering a particular locale only to move

> *. . . the emerging capitalist economy produced a conceptual model for cultural exchange.*

elsewhere, sometimes over great distances, so might ideas, styles, and artistic sensibilities. Drama especially conveyed how fluid were the customs, codes, and practices that gave society its sense of identity. The enthusiasm for stage plays was motivated in part by an interest in role-playing: if an actor who in real life might have been born a servant could perform the part of a king in a play, then might he not also perform the part of a king indeed? Was there more to being than performing? This mutability was both liberating and dangerous, as Shakespeare showed by dramatizing the protean powers of Othello's false friend, Iago, who chillingly boasts, "I am not what I am."

THE BUSINESS OF LITERATURE

Writers throughout this period often had to depend on patrons for support in order to produce their work. Patrons often employed writers as secretaries, carrying out important administrative tasks, and employed skilful writers who were adept at producing text to order. Or, they admired the work of writers and wanted to encourage literary endeavour. The Sidney family supported a number of writers, including Ben Jonson, who writes about his relationship to them in his country house poem, *To Penshurst*, not without a series of barbs which hint at the uncomfortable position of a writer for hire who has to see himself as little better than the workers on the family estate. The advent of print opened up new possibilities for writers, who were able to disseminate their

> *The advent of print opened up new possibilities for writers . . .*

work to a wider audience without having to deal with a patron. This was, however, a hazardous route as publishing did not generally provide a substantial living for a writer. Michael Drayton, a poet who appears to have had a fraught and complicated relationship with his patrons, insulting a number in printed works when they failed to value his work as highly as he did, lived a comfortable enough life but died leaving only a few pounds in his estate.

The relationships between writers and patrons often helps to explain a number of issues that are not apparent if we read a work without a knowledge of the conditions under which it was probably written. John Donne's poem, "Twickenham Gardens" seems on first reading like a jilted lover's misogynist tirade against a cruel mistress. However, if we bear in mind that Lucy, Countess of Bedford, one of Donne's most important patrons, owned the estate, then the chances are that the poem is a shared joke that was read by both men and women. It is hard to imagine that the countess did not know of this work or that Donne, who was grateful for her help, wrote this work as a sly attack on a generous supporter. Knowing about the conditions of writing often opens up new possibilities for the reader and different ways of reading works that might seem to have an obvious significance but are actually more nuanced and complex pieces of literature than they appear to be.

Virtually nothing written by Donne was published in his lifetime and he preferred to circulate his work in manuscript. Other writers were much keener to reach a wider audience by having their work printed and published. Inevitably, this led to conflict with the authorities who were not always keen to let anything appear in print. A rudimentary system of licensing texts was established so that anything submitted for publication was supposed to be vetted and approved by the censors headed by the Archbishop of Canterbury. It is clear that, while the desires of the state may well have been draconian, the system did not operate very effectively and most cases of censorship were reactions to a work that caused offense once it was printed. John Stubbs wrote a pamphlet, *The Discoverie of a gaping Gulf whereunto England is like to be swallowed* (1579), which attacked the queen's projected marriage to François, Duke of Alençon, and he had his right hand severed as a result (this punishment did not prevent him from having a successful career as a Member of Parliament, loyal to the crown, afterward). Thomas Middleton wrote a scandalous play, *A Game at Chess* (1624), which openly attacked the Spanish ambassador and caused a diplomatic incident. But it ran for nine consecutive nights before it was banned. Nevertheless, many writers resented the fact that their work was subject to the state control and the possibility of censorship, a factor that influenced the ways in which writers produced their work.

The most eloquent attack on a state-controlled press was by Milton, whose *Areopagitica* protested the practice of licensing books before their publication—that is, before readers had a chance to make up their minds about what these books contained. He drew on ideas of democracy that were current in ancient Athens and on the Puritan notion that good emerges only in contact with evil. "I cannot praise a fugitive and cloistered virtue," he announced, because no true virtue is untested, unchallenged, unexamined; it is valid only when it has deliberately and consciously rejected what is false. The journalistic enterprise of this period fostered the right to free speech and a free press that is now the bedrock of modern democracies.

NATURE AND CHANGE

Language and style were changing notions of the world and of God's design in creating it. Habits of thought that had prevailed during the medieval period now seemed to be incompatible with knowledge derived from the experience of nature. Europeans had inherited from classical philosophy an idea of creation as a vast aggregate of layered systems, or "spheres." Supposedly centered on the densest matter at the earth's core, they emanated outward and upward, ending finally in the sphere of pure spirit, or the ethereal presence of divinity. The entities in these layered

spheres had assigned places that determined their natures both within their particular sphere and in relation to other spheres. Thus gold, the most precious metal, was
superior to silver, but it was at the same time analogous to a lion, a king, and the
sun, each also representing the peak of perfection within its particular class of beings. Human nature was also systematized, with the body and personality alike regulated by a balanced set of "humors," each of which consisted of a primary element.
The earth, water, air, and fire that made up the great world, or macrocosm, of nature
also composed the small universe, or microcosm, of the individual man or woman,
whose personality was ideally balanced between
impulses that were melancholic (caused by a
kind of bile), phlegmatic (brought on by a watery substance), sanguine (bloody), and choleric
(hot tempered). Excessive learning, the contemplation of death, the darkness of night, and isolation were all associated with melancholia, a
diseased condition that in more or less severe
form is represented in such disparate texts as
Marlowe's *Dr. Faustus* and Milton's *Il Penseroso*.

> *Habits of thought that had prevailed during the medieval period now seemed to be incompatible with knowledge derived from the experience of nature.*

This view of creation was important for artists and writers because it gave them
a symbolic language of correspondences by which they could refer to creatures in
widely differing settings and conditions. In a sense, it made nature hospitable to poetry by seeing creation as a divine work of art, designed to inspire not only awe but
also a kind of familiarity. Things were the likenesses of other things. Particularly in
so-called "metaphysical" poetry, whose chief exponent is John Donne, human emotional experience is compared to the realms of astronomy, geography, medicine,
Neoplatonic philosophy, and Christian theology. These correspondences are created
through strikingly unusual metaphors, which some have called metaphysical conceits, from the Italian *concetto* ("concept"). The result is a pervasive sense of a universal harmony in all human experience.

Such analogies were not always respected, however. Increasingly, they were questioned by proponents of a kind of vision that depended on a quantitative or denotative sense of identity or difference. Poetic metaphor might not be able to account for
creation in all its complexity; instead, nature had to be understood through the abstractions of science. By the seventeenth century, it was becoming difficult to regard
creation as a single and comprehensive whole; natural philosophers and scientists in
the making wanted to analyze it piece by individual piece. As John Donne wrote of
the phenomenon of uniqueness in his elegy for Elizabeth Drury, *The Anniversary*:

> The element of fire is quite put out;
> The Sun is lost, and th' earth, and no man's wit
> Can well direct him, where to look for it.
> And freely men confess, that this world's spent,
> When in the Planets, and the Firmament
> They seek so many new; they see that this
> Is crumbled out again to his Atoms.
> 'Tis all in pieces, all coherence gone;
> All just supply, and all Relation:
> Prince, Subject, Father, Son, are things forgot,

The Souldiers in their passage to York turn unto reformers pull down Popish pictures, break down rayles, turn altars into Tables

Wenceslaus Hollar, *Parliamentarian soldiers in Yorkshire destroying "Popish" paintings, etc.* Illustration to *Sight of the Transactions of these latter yeares*, by John Vicars, 1646.

> For every man alone thinks he has got
> To be a Phoenix, and that there can be
> None of that kind, of which he is but he.

The earth had been decentered by the insights of the astronomer Nicholas Copernicus, who in the 1520s deduced that the earth orbits the sun. This "Copernican revolution" was confirmed by the calculations of Tycho Brahe and Johannes Kepler, and our solar system itself was revealed as but one among many. With traditional understandings of the natural order profoundly shaken, many thinkers feared for the survival of the human capacity to order and understand society as well. Ironically, Donne complains of radical individualism by invoking the emblem of the Phoenix, the very sort of traditional metaphor that constituted the coherence he claims has "gone." But whereas the symbol in an emblem book carried with it the myth of the bird's Christ-like death and rebirth, the image of the rare bird takes on a newly skeptical and even satirical meaning in *The Anniversary*: it becomes the sign of a dangerous fragmentation within nature's order. Donne's audience would have been familiar with such symbols from emblem books, poems, and coats of arms, as well as in interior decoration, clothing, and the printers' marks on title pages of books. They were also featured on the standards or flags carried in the Civil War—antique signs in a decidedly modern conflict.

> *With traditional understandings of the natural order profoundly shaken, many thinkers feared for the survival of the human capacity to order and understand society as well.*

THE WAR AND THE MODERN ORDER OF THINGS

The Wars of Three Kingdoms ended with the restoration of the Stuart monarchy, but the society that Charles II was heir to was very different from the one his grandfather, James I, had come from Scotland to rule. The terms of modern life were formulated during this period, even though they were only partially and inconsistently realized. They helped to shape these essentially modern institutions: a representative government under law, a market economy fueled by concentrations of capital, and a class system determined by wealth and the power it conferred. They supported a culture in which extreme and opposing points of view were usual. Milton's republican *Tenure of Kings and Magistrates* was followed by Thomas Hobbes's defense of absolute rule, *The Leviathan, or the Matter, Form, and Power of a Commonwealth, Ecclesiastical and Civil* (1651). Hobbes rejected the assumption that had determined all previous political thought—Aristotle's idea that man was naturally sociable—by characterizing the natural condition of human life as "solitary, poor, nasty, brutish and short." A civil state, said Hobbes, depended on the willingness of each and every citizen to relinquish all his or her rights to the sovereign, which is the Commonwealth. The vigorous language of Puritan sermons, preached and published during the 1640s and 1650s, was replicated in the corantos and diurnals of the period. These new forms would eventually lead to the sophisticated commentary of eighteenth-century journalism. Nationalism, however problematic, was registered in history and epic, as well as in attempts to colonize the Americas and to subdue the Gaelic peoples to the west and the north. Irish poems supporting the Stuarts and lamenting the losses of the Cromwellian wars would become rallying cries during the late seventeenth- and eighteenth-century nationalist risings against English control, eventually to result in Ireland's inclusion in the 1801 Union of Great Britain.

Intellectual thought, mental attitudes, religious practices, and the customs of the people fostered new relations to the past and a new sense of self. While Milton was perhaps the greatest humanist of his time, able to read and write Hebrew, Greek, Latin, Italian, and French, his contemporaries witnessed the disappearance of the culture of Petrarch, Erasmus, and More—

> *Intellectual thought, mental attitudes, religious practices, and the customs of the people fostered new relations to the past and a new sense of self.*

humanists who had fashioned the disciplines of humanism. As more particularized portraits of individual life emerged, new philosophical trends promoted denotative descriptions and quantitative figurations of the world. Shortly after the Restoration of Charles II, the Royal Academy of Science would form a "committee for improving the English language," an attempt to design a universal grammar and an ideal philosophical language. This project, inspired by the intellectual reforms of Francis Bacon, would have been uncongenial to the skeptical casts of mind exhibited by Erasmus and More. The abstract rationalism of the new science, the growth of an empire overseas, a burgeoning industry and commerce at home, and a print culture spreading news throughout Europe and across the Atlantic, would continue to be features of life in the British Isles through the eighteenth century.

 For additional resources on the early modern period, including an interactive timeline of the period, go to *The Longman Anthology of British Literature* Web site at www.myliteraturekit.com.

John Skelton
1460?–1529

The first great Tudor satirist, John Skelton illustrates the appeal of the unorthodox. Taking orders at the age of thirty-eight, Skelton already enjoyed an impressive reputation as a writer of satire and love lyrics. His poems must have appealed to Henry VII, who made him responsible for the education of his second son, the future Henry VIII, and they would eventually prompt Erasmus to call Skelton "a light and ornament of British literature." In 1502, following the death of Henry's older brother Arthur, Skelton lost his employment as royal tutor. Henry, now heir apparent to the English throne, was obliged to trade Skelton's gentle instruction in humane and sacred letters for practical training in statecraft and the art of war. At forty-two and already an old man (by contemporary reckoning), Skelton undertook pastoral duties, although he lived away from his rectory for much of the rest of his life. His satires of the clergy in *Colin Clout* and of Cardinal Wolsey in *Why Come Ye Not to Court* may have placed him in some jeopardy; it is said that a threat from the Cardinal forced Skelton to take refuge on the grounds of Westminster Abbey in London. Skelton never got the satisfaction of witnessing Wolsey's disgrace; he died just a few months before Wolsey lost the office of Lord Chancellor for failing to procure a divorce for the king.

Skelton's poetry is as unusual as was his career. His favorite verse form has become known as "skeltonics"; it consists of a series of lines of two or three stresses whose end rhyme repeats itself for an unspecified number of lines. The lines themselves show alliteration and move at a headlong pace. Skelton excused his practice in *Colin Clout* by noting the "pith" or substance it conveys:

> For though my rhyme be ragged,
> Tattered and jagged,
> Rudely rain-beaten,
> Rusty and moth-eaten,
> If ye take well therewith,
> It hath in it some pith.

Skelton's satires poke fun at the pretensions that characterize all forms of public life, including the ways of courtiers and vagabonds. His dream poem, *The Bowge of Court*, and his morality play about wealth and power, *Magnificence*, provide a witty view of court corruption. His verse includes tender tributes to ladies he loves or has loved as well as anticourtly lyrics accusing women of bad behavior and sexual indiscretion. His verse can even be conversational, as when he appears to be addressing a particular person or representing two or more people speaking to each other.

The Bowge of Court is an early satirical poem, probably written in 1498. Its title derives from the *bouche de court*, the free board and lodging to which the king's courtiers and servants were entitled. Skelton represents a cross-section of English society as a "ship of fools," knaves and charlatans out for what they can get and held together by nothing more than their own self-interest. Any society based on such flimsy principles is in serious trouble. The narrator concludes that he cannot join in the free-for-all, and needs instead to write down what is going on, setting him aside as a truth-telling, honest man, a persona frequently adopted by Skelton, most famously in his Colin Clout poems.

For more on John Skelton, including his poem "Philip Sparrow," go to *The Longman Anthology of British Literature* Web site at www.myliteraturekit.com.

The Bowge of Courte
[from *The Poetical Works* (1856)]

THE PROLOGUE TO THE BOWGE OF COURTE.

In autumpne, whan the sonne *in Virgine*°   *Virgo*
 By radyante hete enryped hath our corne;
Whan Luna, full of mutabylyte,
 As emperes the dyademe hath worne
5 Of our pole artyke, smylynge halfe in scorne
At our foly and our unstedfastnesse;
The tyme whan Mars to werre hym dyde dres;

I, callynge to mynde the greate auctoryte
 Of poetes olde, whyche full craftely,
10 Under as coverte termes as coude be,
 Can touche a trouth° and cloke it subtylly   *truth*
 Wyth fresshe utteraunce full sentencyously;
Dyverse in style, some spared not vyce to wryte,
Some of moralyte nobly dyde endyte;°   *write*

15 Wherby I rede theyr renome and theyr fame
 Maye never dye, bute evermore endure:
I was sore moved to aforce° the same,   *attempt*
 But Ignoraunce full soone dyde me dyscure,°   *betray*
 And shewed that in this arte I was not sure;
20 For to illumyne, she sayde, I was to dulle,
Avysynge me my penne alwaye to pulle,

And not wryte; for he so° wyll atteyne   *whoever*
 Excedynge ferther than his connynge is,
His hede maye be harde, but feble is his brayne,
25 Yet have I knowen suche er this;
 But of reproche surely he maye not mys,
That clymmeth hyer than he may fotynge have;
What and° he slyde downe, who shall hym save? *if*

Thus up and down my mynde was drawen and cast,
30 That I ne wyste° what to do was beste;   *did not know*
So sore enwered,° that I was at the laste   *tired, weary*
 Enforsed to slepe and for to take some reste;
 And to lye downe as soone as I me dreste,°   *was ready*
At Harwyche Porte slumbrynge as I laye,
35 In myne hostes house, called Powers Keye,

Methoughte I sawe a shyppe, goodly of sayle,
 Come saylynge forth into that haven brood,
Her takelynge ryche and of hye apparayle:°   *rigging*
 She kyste an anker, and there she laye at rode.° *anchor*
40 Marchauntes her borded to see what she had lode:
Therein they founde royall marchaundyse,
Fraghted with plesure of what ye coude devyse.

But than I thoughte I woulde not dwell behynde;
   Amonge all other I put myselfe in prece.°   *among the crowd*
45   Than there coude I none aquentaunce fynde:
     There was moche noyse; anone one cryed, Cese!
     Sharpely commaundynge eche man holde hys pece:
Maysters, he sayde, the shyp that ye here see,
The Bowge of Courte it hyghte° for certeynte: *called*

50   The owner therof is lady of estate,
     Whoos name to tell is dame Saunce-pere;°   *without equal*
Her marchaundyse is ryche and fortunate,°   *valuable*
     But who wyll have it muste paye therfore dere;
     This royall chaffre° that is shypped here   *merchandise*
55   Is called Favore, to stonde in her good grace.
Than sholde ye see there pressynge in a pace

Of one and other that wolde this lady see;
     Whiche sat behynde a traves° of sylke fyne,   *screen*
Of golde of tessew° the fynest that myghte be,   *cloth*
60   In a trone° whiche fer clerer dyde shyne   *train*
     Than Phebus in his spere celestyne;
Whoos beaute, honoure, goodly porte,°   *bearing*
I have to lytyll connynge° to reporte.   *skill*

But, of eche thynge there as I toke hede,
65   Amonge all other was wrytten in her trone,
In golde letters, this worde, whiche I dyde rede,
     Garder le fortune, que est mauelz et bone!°   *beware fortune,*
     And, as I stode redynge this verse myselfe allone,   *which is bad and good*
Her chyef gentylwoman, Daunger by her name,
70   Gaue me a taunte, and sayde I was to blame

To be so perte° to prese so proudly uppe: *forward*
     She sayde she trowed that I had eten sause;°   *been too bold*
She asked yf ever I dranke of saucys cuppe.
     And I than softly answered to that clause,°   *those words*
75   That, so to saye, I had gyven her no cause.
Than asked she me, Syr, so God thé spede,°   *prosper*
What is thy name? and I sayde, it was Drede.

What movyd thé, quod she, hydder to come?
     Forsoth, quod I, to bye some of youre ware.°   *goods*
80   And with that worde on me she gave a glome°   *sullen look*
     With browes bente, and gan on me to stare
     Full daynnously,° and fro me she dyde fare,   *disdainfully*
Levynge me stondynge as a mased° man: *bewildered*
To whome there came an other gentylwoman;

85   Desyre her name was, and so she me tolde,
     Sayenge to me, Broder, be of good chere,
Abasshe you not, but hardely be bolde,

    Avaunce yourselfe to aproche and come nere:
    What though our chaffer° be never so dere,   *merchandise*
90   Yet I avyse you to speke, for ony drede:°   *despite any fear*
    Who spareth to speke, in fayth he spareth to spede.°   *succeed*

    Maystres, quod I, I have none aquentaunce,
        That wyll for me be medyatoure and mene;
    And this an other, I have but smale substaunce.
95   Pece, quod Desyre, ye speke not worth a bene:
        Yf ye have not, in fayth I wyll you lene°   *lend*
    A precyous jewell, no rycher in this londe;
    Bone Aventure° have here now in your honde.   *good luck*

    Shyfte now therwith, let see, as ye can,
100   In Bowge of Courte chevysaunce° to make;   *profit*
    For I dare saye that there nys erthly man
        But, an he can Bone Aventure take,
        There can no favour nor frendshyp hym forsake;
    Bone Aventure may brynge you in suche case
105   That ye shall stonde in favoure and in grace.

    But of one thynge I werne you er I goo,
        She that styreth the shyp, make her your frende.
    Maystres, quod I, I praye you tell me why soo,
        And how I maye that waye and meanes fynde.
110   Forsothe, quod she, how ever blowe the wynde
    Fortune gydeth and ruleth all oure shyppe;
    Whome she hateth shall over the see boorde skyp;

    Whome she loveth, of all plesyre is ryche,
        Whyles she laugheth and hath luste for to playe;
115   Whome she hateth, she casteth in the dyche,
        For whan she frouneth, she thynketh to make a fray;°   *conflict*
        She cheryssheth him, and hym she casseth awaye.
    Alas, quod I, how myghte I have her sure?
    In fayth, quod she, by Bone Aventure.

120   Thus, in a rowe, of martchauntes a grete route°   *group*
        Suwed to Fortune that she wold be theyre frynde:
    They thronge in fast, and flocked her aboute;
        And I with them prayed her to have in mynde.
        She promysed to us all she wolde be kynde:
125   Of Bowge of Court she asketh what we wold have;
    And we asked Favoure, and Favour she us gave.

Thus endeth the Prologue; and begynneth the Bowge of Courte brevely compyled.

DREDE

    The sayle is up, Fortune ruleth our helme,
        We wante no wynd to passe now over all;
    Favoure we have tougher than ony elme,

130　That wyll abyde and never from us fall:
　　　But under hony ofte tyme lyeth bytter gall;
　　　For, as me thoughte, in our shyppe I dyde see
　　　Full subtyll persones, in nombre foure and thre.

　　　The fyrste was Favell,° full of flatery,　　　　　　　　　　　　*duplicity*
135　Wyth fables false that well coude fayne a tale;
　　　The seconde was Suspecte, whiche that dayly
　　　　　Mysdempte° eche man, with face deedly and pale;　　　*misjudged*
　　　　　And Haruy Hafter,° that well coude picke a male;°　　*deceiver | purse*
　　　With other foure of theyr affynyte,
140　Dysdayne, Ryotte, Dyssymuler, Subtylte.

　　　Fortune theyr frende, with whome oft she dyde daunce;
　　　　They coude not faile, thei thought, they were so sure;
　　　And oftentymes I wolde myselfe avaunce
　　　　With them to make solace and pleasure;
145　　But my dysporte they coude not well endure;
　　　They sayde they hated for to dele with Drede.
　　　Than Favell gan wyth fayre speche me to fede.

FAVELL

　　　Noo thynge erthely that I wonder so sore
　　　　As of your connynge, that it is so excellent;
150　Deynte° to have with us suche one in store,　　　　　　　　*pleasure*
　　　　So vertuously that hath his dayes spente:
　　　　Fortune to you gyftes of grace hath lente:
　　　Loo, what it is a man to have connynge!°　　　　　　　　　*learning*
　　　All erthly tresoure it is surmountynge.

155　Ye be an apte man, as ony can be founde,
　　　　To dwell with us, and serve my ladyes grace;
　　　Ye be to her yea worth a thousande pounde;
　　　　I herde her speke of you within shorte space,
　　　　Whan there were dyverse that sore dyde you manace;
160　And, though I say it, I was myselfe your frende,
　　　For here be dyverse to you that be unkynde.

　　　But this one thynge ye maye be sure of me;
　　　　For, by that Lorde that bought dere all mankynde,
　　　I can not flater, I muste be playne to thé;
165　　And ye nede ought, man, shewe to me your mynde,
　　　　For ye have me whome faythfull ye shall fynde;
　　　Whyles I have ought, by God, thou shalt not lacke,
　　　And yf nede be, a bolde worde I dare cracke.°　　　　　　*boast*

　　　Nay, naye, be sure, whyles I am on your syde,
170　　Ye maye not fall, truste me, ye maye not fayle;
　　　Ye stonde in favoure, and Fortune is your gyde,
　　　　And, as she wyll, so shall our grete shyppe sayle:
　　　　Thyse lewde cok wattes° shall nevermore prevayle　　　*fools*

Ageynste you hardely, therfore be not afrayde:
175   Farewell tyll soone; but no worde that I sayde.

DREDE

Than thanked I hym for his grete gentylnes:
    But, as me thoughte, he ware on hym a cloke,
That lyned was with doubtfull doublenes;
    Me thoughte, of wordes that he had full a poke;°   *bag*
180   His stomak stuffed ofte tymes dyde reboke:°   *belch*
Suspycyon, me thoughte, mette hym at a brayde,°   *suddenly*
And I drewe nere to herke what they two sayde.

In faythe, quod Suspecte, spake Drede no worde of me?
    Why, what than? wylte thou lete° men to speke?   *stop*
185 He sayth, he can not well accorde with thé.
    Twyst, quod Suspecte, goo playe, hym I ne reke.°   *care*
    By Cryste, quod Favell, Drede is soleyne freke:°   *unsociable person*
What lete us holde him up, man, for a whyle?
Ye soo, quod Suspecte, he maye us bothe begyle.

190 And whan he came walkynge soberly,
    Wyth whom and ha, and with a croked loke,
Me thoughte, his hede was full of gelousy,
    His eyne rollynge, his hondes faste they quoke;
    And to me warde the strayte waye he toke:
195 God spede, broder! to me quod he than;
And thus to talke with me he began.

SUSPYCYON

Ye remembre the gentylman ryghte nowe
    That commaunde° with you, me thought, a party space?°   *talked / long time*
Beware of him, for, I make God avowe,
200   He wyll begyle you and speke fayre to your face;
    Ye never dwelte in suche an other place,
For here is none that dare well other truste;
But I wolde telle you a thynge, and I durste.

Spake he a faith° no worde to you of me?   *in truth*
205   I wote, and° he dyde, ye wolde me telle.   *wonder if*
I have a favoure to you, wherof it be
    That I muste shewe you moche of my counselle:
    But I wonder what the devyll of helle
He sayde of me, whan he with you dyde talke:
210 By myne avyse use not with him to walke.

The soveraynst° thynge that ony man maye have,   *most valuable*
    Is lytyll to saye, and moche to here and see;
For, but I trusted you, so God me save,
    I wolde noo thynge so playne be;
215   To you oonly, me thynke, I durste shryve° me;   *confess*

For now am I plenarely° disposed   *fully*
To shewe you thynges that may not be disclosed.

DREDE

Than I assured hym my fydelyte,
    His counseyle secrete never to dyscure,°   *disclose*
220   Yf he coude fynde in herte to truste me;
    Els I prayed hym, with all my besy cure,°   *careful attention*
    To kepe it hymselfe, for than he myghte be sure
That noo man erthly coude hym bewreye,°   *betray*
Whyles of hys mynde it were lockte with the keye.

225   By God, quod he, this and thus it is;
    And of his mynde he shewed me all and some.
Farewell, quod he, we wyll talke more of this:
    Soo he departed there he wolde be come.
    I dare not speke, I promysed to be dome:
230   But, as I stode musynge in my mynde,
Harvy Hafter came lepynge, lyghte as lynde.°   *nimbly*

Upon his breste he bare a versynge boxe;°   *dice*
    His throte was clere, and lustely coude fayne;°   *sing, invent*
Me thoughte, his gowne was all furred wyth foxe;
235   And ever he sange, Sythe I am no thynge playne.
    To kepe him frome pykyng° it was a grete payne: *stealing*
He gased on me with his gotyshe berde;
Whan I loked on hym, my purse was half aferde.

HARVY HAFTER

Syr, God you save! why loke ye so sadde?
240   What thynge is that I maye do for you?
A wonder thynge that ye waxe not madde!
    For, and I studye sholde as ye doo nowe,
    My wytte wolde waste, I make God avowe.
Tell me your mynde: me thynke, ye make a verse;
245   I coude it skan, and ye wolde it reherse.

But to the poynte shortely to procede,
    Where hathe your dwellynge ben, er ye cam here?
For, as I trowe, I have sene you indede
    Er this, whan that ye made me royall chere.
250   Holde up the helme, loke up, and lete God stere:
I wolde be mery, what wynde that ever blowe,
Heve and how rombelow, row the bote, Norman, rowe!

Prynces of yougthe can ye synge by rote?°   *by heart*
    Or shall I sayle wyth you a felashyp assaye;°   *together*
255   For on the booke° I can not synge a note.   *i.e., with sheet music*
    Wolde to God, it wolde please you some daye

A balade boke before me for to laye,
And lerne me to synge, Re, my, fa, sol!
And, whan I fayle, bobbe me on the noll.°   hit me on the head

260 Loo, what is to you a pleasure grete,
        To have that connynge and wayes that ye have!
     By Goddis soule, I wonder how ye gete
        Soo great pleasyre, or who to you it gave:
        Syr, pardone me, I am an homely knave,
265 To be with you thus perte and thus bolde;
     But ye be welcome to our housholde.

     And, I dare saye, there is no man here inne
        But wolde be glad of your company:
     I wyste° never man that so soone coude wynne   knew
270   The favoure that ye have with my lady;
        I praye to God that it maye never dy:
     It is your fortune for to have that grace;
     As I be saved, it is a wonder case.

     For, as for me, I served here many a daye,
275   And yet unneth° I can have my lyvynge: scarcely
     But I requyre you no worde that I saye;
        For, and I knowe ony erthly thynge
        That is agayne you, ye shall have wetynge:°   knowledge
     And ye be welcome, syr, so God me save:
280 I hope here after a frende of you to have.

                    DREDE

     Wyth that, as he departed soo fro me,
        Anone ther mette with him, as me thoughte,
     A man, but wonderly besene° was he;   attractive
        He loked hawte,° he sette eche man at noughte;   proud
285   His gawdy garment with scornnys° was all wrought;   scorn, taunts
     With indygnacyon lyned was his hode;
     He frowned, as he wolde swere by Cockes° blode;   God's

     He bote° the lyppe, he loked passynge coye;   bit
        His face was belymmed,° as byes had him stounge: disfigured
290 It was no tyme with him to jape nor toye;
        Envye hathe wasted his lyver and his lounge,
        Hatred by the herte so had hym wrounge,
     That he loked pale as asshes to my syghte:
     Dysdayne, I wene, this comerous carkes° hyghte.   difficult person

295 To Hervy Hafter than he spake of me,
        And I drewe nere to harke what they two sayde.
     Now, quod Dysdayne, as I shall saved be,
        I have grete scorne, and am ryghte evyll apayed.
        Than quod Hervy, why arte thou so dysmayde?

300 By Cryste, quod he, for it is shame to saye;
To see Johan Dawes, that came but yester daye,

How he is now taken in conceyte,
This doctour Dawcocke, Drede, I wene, he hyghte:
By Goddis bones, but yf we have som sleyte,°   *strategy*
305 It is lyke he wyll stonde in our lyghte.
By God, quod Hervy, and it so happen myghte;
Lete us therfore shortely at a worde
Fynde some mene to caste him over the borde.

By Him that me boughte,° than quod Dysdayne,   *i.e., Christ*
310 I wonder sore he is in suche conceyte.
Turde, quod Hafter, I wyll thé no thynge layne,°   *hide*
There muste for hym be layde some prety beyte;
We tweyne, I trowe, be not withoute dysceyte:
Fyrste pycke a quarell, and fall oute with hym then,
315 And soo outface hym with a carde of ten.°   *i.e., a bluff*

Forthwith he made on me a prowde assawte,
With scornfull loke mevyd° all in moode;   *angry*
He wente aboute to take me in a fawte;
He frounde, he stared, he stampped where he stoode.
320 I lokyd on hym, I wende he had be woode.°   *thought he was mad*
He sent the arme proudly under the syde,
And in this wyse he gan with me to chyde.

DISDAYNE

Remembrest thou what thou sayd yester nyght?
Wylt thou abyde by the wordes agayne?
325 By God, I have of thé now grete dyspyte;
I shall thé angre ones in every vayne:
It is great scorne to see suche an hayne°   *wretch*
As thou arte, one that cam but yesterdaye,
With us olde servauntes suche maysters to playe.

330 I tell thé, I am of countenaunce:°   *i.e., important*
What weneste I were? I trowe, thou knowe not me.
By Goddis woundes, but for dysplesaunce,
Of my querell soone wolde I venged be:
But no force, I shall ones mete with thé;
335 Come whan it wyll, oppose thé I shall,
What somever aventure therof fall.

Trowest thou, drevyll,° I saye, thou gawdy knave,   *drudge*
That I have deynte° to see thé cherysshed thus?   *pleasure*
By Goddis syd, my sworde thy berde shall shave;
340 Well, ones thou shalte be chermed, I wus:°   *think, know*
Naye, strawe for tales, thou shalte not rule us;
We be thy betters, and so thou shalte us take,
Or we shall thé oute of thy clothes shake.

DREDE

Wyth that came Ryotte, russhynge all at ones,
345   A rusty gallande, to-ragged and to-rente;
And on the borde he whyrled a payre of bones,
      Quater treye dews° he clatered as he wente;   *four, three, deuce*
      Now have at all, by saynte Thomas of Kente!
And ever he threwe and kyst° I wote nere what: *cast*
350   His here was growen thorowe oute his hat.

Thenne I behelde how he dysgysed was:
      His hede was hevy for watchynge over nyghte,
His eyen blereed, his face shone lyke a glas;
      His gowne so shorte that it ne cover myghte
355   His rumpe, he wente so all for somer lyghte;°   *dressed for summer*
His hose was garded wyth a lyste° of grene,   *strip*
Yet at the knee they were broken, I wene.

His cote was checked with patches rede and blewe;
      Of Kyrkeby Kendall° was his shorte demye;°   *cheap wool / jacket*
360   And ay he sange, In fayth, decon thou crewe;
      His elbowe bare, he ware his gere so nye;°   *worn*
      His nose a droppynge, his lyppes were full drye;
And by his syde his whynarde° and his pouche,   *dagger*
The devyll myghte daunce therin for ony crowche.°   *coin*

365   Counter° he coude O *lux* upon a potte;   *accompany*
      An eestryche° fedder of a capons tayle   *ostrich*
He set up fresshely upon his hat alofte:
      What, revell route! quod he, and gan to rayle
      How oft he hadde hit Jenet on the tayle,
370   Of Felyce fetewse,° and lytell prety Cate,   *handsome*
How ofte he knocked at her klycked gate.

What sholde I tell more of his rebaudrye?°   *roguery*
      I was ashamed so to here hym prate:
He had no pleasure but in harlotrye.
375   Ay, quod he, in the devylles date,°   *name*
      What art thou? I sawe thé nowe but late.
Forsothe, quod I, in this courte I dwell nowe.
Welcome, quod Ryote, I make God avowe.

RYOTE

And, syr, in fayth why comste not us amonge,
380   To make thé mery, as other felowes done?
Thou muste swere and stare, man, al daye longe,
      And wake all nyghte, and slepe tyll it be none;°   *noon*
      Thou mayste not studye, or muse on the mone;
This worlde is nothynge but ete, drynke, and slepe,
385   And thus with us good company to kepe.

Plucke up thyne herte upon a mery pyne,°   note?
　　And lete us laugh a placke° or tweyne at nale:°   draught / alehouse
What the devyll, man, myrthe was never one!°   alone
　　What, loo, man, see here of dyce a bale!°   set
390　A brydelynge° caste for that is in thy male!°   final / bag
Now have at all that lyeth upon the burde!°   board, table?
Fye on this dyce, they be not worth a turde!

Have at the hasarde,° or at the dosen browne,°   game / full dozen?
　　Or els I pas° a peny to a pounde!   Give you odds
395　Now, wolde to God, thou wolde leye money downe!
　　Lorde, how that I wolde caste it full rounde!
　　Ay, in my pouche a buckell I have founde!
The armes of Calyce,° I have no coyne nor crosse!   Calais (a low value coin)
I am not happy, I renne ay on the losse.

400　Now renne muste I to the stewys° syde,   brothel
　　To wete° yf Malkyn, my lemman,° have gete oughte: find out / sweetheart
I lete her to hyre, that men maye on her ryde,
　　Her armes easy ferre and nere is soughte:
　　By Goddis sydes, syns I her thyder broughte,
405　She hath gote me more money with her tayle
Than hath some shyppe that into Bordews sayle.

Had I as good an hors as she is a mare,
　　I durst aventure to journey through Fraunce;
Who rydeth on her, he nedeth not to care,
410　For she is trussed for to breke a launce;
　　It is a curtel° that well can wynche and praunce: horse
To her wyll I nowe all my poverte lege;°   i.e., trust her to get rid
And, tyll I come, have here is myne hat to plege.   of my poverty

Drede

Gone is this knave, this rybaude° foule and leude;   rogue
415　He ran as fast as ever that he myghte:
Unthryftynes° in hym may well be shewed,   prodigality
　　For whome Tyborne° groneth both daye and nyghte.   i.e., the gallows
　　And, as I stode and kyste asyde my syghte,
Dysdayne I sawe with Dyssymulacyon
420　Standynge in sadde° communicacion.   serious

But there was poyntynge and noddynge with the hede,
　　And many wordes sayde in secrete wyse;
They wandred ay, and stode styll in no stede:°   place
　　Me thoughte, alwaye Dyscymular dyde devyse;
425　　Me passynge sore myne herte than gan agryse,
I dempte and drede theyr talkynge was not good.
Anone Dyscymular came where I stode.

Than in his hode I sawe there faces tweyne;
　　That one was lene and lyke a pyned goost,

430   That other loked as he wolde me have slayne;
      And to me warde as he gan for to coost,°   *approach*
      Whan that he was even at me almoost,
   I sawe a knyfe hyd in his one sleve,
   Wheron was wryten this worde, *Myscheve.*

435   And in his other sleve, me thought, I sawe
      A spone of golde, full of hony swete,
   To fede a fole, and for to preve a dawe;°   *confirm a simpleton*
      And on that sleve these wordes were wrete,°   *written*
      A *false abstracte cometh from a fals concrete:*
440   His hode was syde,° his cope° was roset graye: *long / hood*
   Thyse were the wordes that he to me dyde saye.

DYSSYMULATION

   How do ye, mayster? ye loke so soberly:
      As I be saved at the dredefull daye,°   *Judgment Day*
   It is a perylous vyce, this envy:
445   Alas, a connynge man ne dwelle maye
      In no place well, but foles with hym fraye!°   *fight*
   But as for that, connynge hath no foo°   *foe*
   Save hym that nought can, Scrypture sayth soo.

   I knowe your vertu and your lytterature°   *learning*
450   By that lytel connynge that I have:
   Ye be malygned sore, I you ensure;
      But ye have crafte your selfe alwaye to save:
      It is grete scorne to se a mysproude° knave   *arrogant*
   With a clerke that connynge is to prate:°   *prattle*
455   Lete theym go lowse theym, in the devylles date!

   For all be it that this longe not to me,°   *does not concern me*
      Yet on my backe I bere suche lewde delynge:
   Ryghte now I spake with one, I trowe,° I see;   *know*
      But, what, a strawe! I maye not tell all thynge.
460   By God, I saye there is grete herte brennynge°   *burning*
   Betwene the persone ye wote° of, you;   *know*
   Alas, I coude not dele so with a Jew!

   I wolde eche man were as playne as I;
      It is a worlde, I saye, to here of some;
465   I hate this faynynge, fye upon it, fye!
      A man can not wote where to be come:
      I wys I coude tell,—but humlery, home;
   I dare not speke, we be so layde awayte,°   *spied on*
   For all our courte is full of dysceyte.

470   Now, by saynte Fraunceys, that holy man and frere,
      I hate these wayes agayne you that they take:
   Were I as you, I wolde ryde them full nere;°   *press them (to give an answer)*

And, by my trouthe, but yf an ende they make,
   Yet wyll I saye some wordes for your sake,
475   That shall them angre, I holde thereon a grote;
For some shall wene be hanged by the throte.

I have a stoppynge° oyster in my poke,°   *blocking (i.e., silencing) / bag*
   Truste me, and yf it come to a nede:
But I am lothe for to reyse a smoke,
480   Yf ye coude be otherwyse agrede;
   And so I wolde it were, so God me spede,
For this maye brede to a confusyon,
Withoute God make a good conclusyon.

Naye, see where yonder stondeth the teder° man!   *other*
485   A flaterynge knave and false he is, God wote;
The drevyll° stondeth to herken, and he can: *drudge*
   It were more thryft, he boughte him a newe cote;
   It will not be, his purse is not on flote:°   *full of money*
All that he wereth, it is borowed ware;
490   His wytte is thynne, his hode is threde bare.

More coude I saye, but what this is ynowe:°   *enough*
   Adewe tyll soone, we shall speke more of this:
Ye muste be ruled as I shall tell you howe;
   Amendis maye be of that is now amys;
495   And I am your, syr, so have I blys,
In every poynte that I can do or saye;
Gyve me your honde, farewell, and have good daye.

DREDE

Sodaynly, as he departed me fro,
   Came pressynge in one in a wonder araye:°   *strange clothes*
500   Er I was ware, behynde me he sayde, Bo!
   Thenne I, astonyed of that sodeyne fraye,°   *attack*
   Sterte all at ones, I lyked no thynge his playe;
For, yf I had not quyckely fledde the touche,
He had plucte oute the nobles° of my pouche.   *gold coins*

505   He was trussed° in a garmente strayte:°   *dressed / tight*
   I have not sene suche an others page;
For he coude well upon a casket wayte;
   His hode all pounsed° and garded° lyke a cage;   *perforated / trimmed*
   Lyghte lyme fynger,° he toke none other wage.   *sticky fingers,*
510   Harken, quod he, loo here myne honde in thyne;   *i.e., thieving*
To us welcome thou arte, by saynte Quyntyne.

DISCEYTE

But, by that Lorde that is one, two, and thre,
   I have an errande to rounde in your ere:
He tolde me so, by God, ye maye truste me,

515   Parte remembre whan ye were there,
       There I wynked on you,—wote ye not where?
       In A *loco*,° I mene *juxta* B:°   *location / near*
       Woo is hym that is blynde and maye not see!

       But to here the subtylte and the crafte,
520   As I shall tell you, yf ye wyll harke agayne;
       And, whan I sawe the horsons wolde you hafte,°   *deceive, rob*
         To holde myne honde, by God, I had grete payne;
         For forthwyth there I had him slayne,
       But that I drede mordre wolde come oute:
525   Who deleth with shrewes hath nede to loke aboute.

DREDE

       And as he rounded thus in myne ere
         Of false collusyon confetryd° by assente,   *joined*
       Me thoughte, I see lewde felawes here and there
         Came for to slee me of mortall entente;
530   And, as they came, the shypborde faste I hente,°   *grasped*
       And thoughte to lepe; and even with that woke,
       Caughte penne and ynke, and wrote thys lytyll boke.

       I wolde therwith no man were myscontente;
         Besechynge you that shall it see or rede,
535   In every poynte to be indyfferente,
         Syth all in substaunce of slumbrynge doth procede:
         I wyll not saye it is mater in dede,°   *fact*
       But yet oftyme suche dremes be founde trewe:
       Now constrewe ye what is the resydewe.

Thus endeth the Bowge of Courte.

⥤ PERSPECTIVES ⥢
The English Sonnet and Sonnet Sequences in the Sixteenth Century

No lyric form was more important than the sonnet in sixteenth-century England and most poets with courtly ambitions felt the need to write sonnets as a sign of their mastery of the form, especially toward the end of the century. Writing a successful sonnet demanded a good ear for verse, rhyme, and rhythm, as well as an ability to make a telling, memorable argument in a short space, often one that surprises or startles the reader. Accordingly, sonnets are not always quite what they seem to be and often play tricks on the reader. The most famous English sonnet, Shakespeare's Sonnet 18 ("Shall I compare thee to a summer's day?") is often taken to be an especially beautiful love poem. But its wit depends to a large part on the ironies and uncertainties that surround it: the poem is actually addressed to a young man, who may or may not have a sexual relationship with the speaker who may or may not be the author of the poem, and it does not actually compare the young man to a summer's day at all, as we learn nothing about his beauty from the poem itself. Rather, the last lines of the sonnet assert that beauty cannot fade if it is captured in verse, "So long as men can breathe or eyes can see, / So long lives this, and this gives life to thee," something the poem has—very wittily and self-consciously—not done. Given the long-recognized genre of ekphrastic poetry—a verbal description of a picture or work of art—the poem's witty refusal to carry out what it claims it will do is striking.

The sonnet was usually—but not always—a poem of fourteen lines with a complicated, interlaced rhyme scheme that could vary and so alter the structure and balance of the poem. Sonnets were divided into shorter units. Often the first eight lines would describe something or a situation, making up an octave. The concluding six lines, the sestet, would comment on them, drawing a moral or making a point. Sonnets could also be divided further into three units of four lines, quatrains, concluding with a couplet that commented on what had gone before, a preferred form for English writers, especially Shakespeare.

The sonnet was principally an Italian form and was regarded as especially sophisticated and accorded high cultural status in England, a country that was painfully aware of its relatively humble artistic and cultural achievements at the start of the sixteenth century, a situation the king, Henry VIII, was determined to change. The most famous sonneteer was Francesco Petrarca (1304–1374), known as Petrarch in the English-speaking world, the first poet laureate of the modern world. Petrarch composed a long series of poems to Laura, a woman he loved but who married someone else and then died relatively young, in his *Canzoniere* many of which were sonnets. Petrarch gave his name to the most widely used sonnet form, the Petrarchan sonnet. The octave (the first eight lines) was rhymed *abab*, *abab* or *abba*, *abba*, and the sestet (the last six lines), *cdecde*, *cdccdc* or *cdcdcd*, all forms that predated Petrarch in Italian sonnet writing but spread throughout Europe after the popularity of his verse. Such a demanding poetic form was possible in Italian and French, which had a large variety of similar endings that enabled writers to produce poems with a narrow range of rhyme schemes. The sonnet flourished in France as well as in Italy, and major collections of poetry were produced by Pierre de Ronsard (1524–1585) and Joachim Du Bellay (1522–1560), poets who also enjoyed a pan-European reputation.

The situation was very different for English writers. While the first English sonneteers, Sir Thomas Wyatt and Henry Howard, Earl of Surrey, produced translations and adaptations of Petrarch that remained faithful to the original rhyme schemes of the Italian, it soon become obvious that a language such as English, which did not rely on inflected word endings but specific grammatical forms, could not easily imitate Italian poetry owing to the lack of possible rhyming words. The result was the development of the English sonnet, which employed far more rhyme words, and so made it possible for poets to use their wit and imagination more easily and freely when composing such a straightened form. The usual rhyme scheme for the English sonnet is *abab cdcd efef gg*, giving the poet at least two more words to use than the Italian version. Whereas the Italian sonnet invariably divided up into an octave and a sestet, the English often contained three quatrains that described the substance of the poem and a couplet that commented on its significance. Sometimes, poets employed both structures and made them overlap, providing a further layer of interpretation for the reader to confront.

The sonnet first appeared in English at the court of Henry VIII, as part of a concerted plan to make English culture more sophisticated. This did not mean, however, that the sonnet can be read as a patriotic form supporting the monarchy and celebrating court life. In fact, the opposite is generally the case, and sonnets often comment obliquely on the unstable situation of the courtier-poet, close to the center of power but also subject to the dangers of life near the mighty. Wyatt's famous sonnet, *Whoso List to Hunt*, undoubtedly refers to his relationship with Anne Boleyn and the danger in which he was placed when she became Henry's second wife in 1533. Wyatt adapts Petrarch's Sonnet 190 to comment on the perils of earthly love at the court of a powerful and vindictive monarch. Petrarch describes the vision of the dead Laura leading him away from earthly vices so that when we see that her necklace has inscribed on it Christ's words to Mary Magdalene before the tomb, *Noli me tangere* (Do not touch me), we realize that this shows the author being led away from his false faith in earthly delights. When Wyatt sees the same necklace, the words mean that he needs to avoid his former lover because she now belongs to the king. A religious poem has become a secular one in which, as Arthur Marotti has pointed out, "love is not love".

Such skillful twists and transformations characterize the English sonnet throughout the sixteenth century, although it would be a mistake to assume that it enjoyed a smooth and straightforward path into English cultural life. The mid-Tudor years when Edward VI and Mary reigned (1547–1558) saw little in the way of sonnet production, although *Tottel's Miscellany*, a collection of English verse that included many poems by Wyatt, Surrey, and others, was published in 1557. Perhaps this lacuna is not surprising given the interest in experiments based on native English writing in Edward's reign, and the relative lack of literary production during Mary's reign. Sonnets were produced throughout Elizabeth's reign, although not always in vast numbers until Sir Philip Sidney produced the first sonnet sequence in English, *Astrophil and Stella*, written in the 1580s and published in the 1590s. Later, sonnet sequences enjoyed a considerable literary vogue, with major authors such as Samuel Daniel (1562–1619), Michael Drayton (1563–1631), Edmund Spenser (1552?–1599), Fulke Greville (1554–1628), all writing their own sequences. The vogue appeared to have died out by the end of Elizabeth's reign and Shakespeare's sonnets (1609) mark a return back to the past as well as a break in their deliberate transgression of its loosely established conventions. As Margaretta De Grazia has argued, the real scandal of Shakespeare's sonnets is probably the representation of the lascivious and transgressive "dark lady," not the fair young man.

The selection of sonnets here charts the poem's progress throughout the century from Wyatt's pioneering adaptations to extracts from Spenser's and Barnfield's sequences published in the 1590s. While Sidney charts the frustrated and unhappy passion of Astrophil for Stella, who is married to another man, Spenser adapts the genre to celebrate his own courtship of and marriage to Elizabeth Boyle, and Barnfield represents homosexual desire. Also included are other variations on the sonnet's subject matter, such as George Gascoigne's sonnets to Alexander Neville, which reflect on his own life and its troubled course.

Sir Thomas Wyatt
1503?–1542

Sir Thomas Wyatt, courtier and poet, was the most important and accomplished lyric poet at the court of Henry VIII. Wyatt had a career that combined success with danger, holding a number of important diplomatic positions but also falling foul of his royal master, not least because he had been involved with Henry's second wife, Anne Boleyn. Wyatt had more than one spell in prison. None of his poetry was published in his lifetime as it circulated solely in manuscript. After his death it became clear that his experiments with the sonnet and other lyric forms were of major importance. Many were published in *Tottel's Miscellany* (1557) alongside Surrey's, which helped influence later generations of poets and establish a dominant strain of English writing.

For more on Wyatt, see his principal listing on page 701.

The Long Love, That in My Thought Doth Harbor

The long love, that in my thought doth harbor
And in mine heart doth keep his residence,
Into my face presseth with bold pretence,
And therein campeth, spreading his banner.
5   She that me learneth° to love and suffer,   *teaches*
And will that my trust and lust's negligence
Be reined by reason, shame and reverence,
With his hardiness° taketh displeasure.   *boldness*
Wherewithal, unto the heart's forest he fleeth,
10 Leaving his enterprise with pain and cry,
And there him hideth and not appeareth.
What may I do when my master feareth
But in the field with him to live and die?
For good is the life, ending faithfully.

COMPANION READING
Petrarch, Sonnet 140[1]

Amor, che nel penser mio vive et regna
e 'l suo seggio maggior nel mio cor tene,
talor armato ne la fronte vene;
ivi si loca et ivi pon sua insegna.
5   Quella ch' amare et sofferir ne 'nsegna
e vol che 'l gran desio, l'accesa spene

---

1. Petrarch (1304–1374), known to his fellow Italians as Francesco Petrarca, was the virtual inventor of modern lyric poetry. Comprising sonnets, songs (*canzone*), and odes, his *Rimé sparse* or "various poems"—widely circulated during and after his lifetime—were translated and imitated by poets throughout Europe. Petrarch's verse demonstrated to his early modern readers that a lyric poet could invest subjects with a spirituality and a seriousness previously attributed to the epic, the ode, and to philosophical poems. Petrarch's *Sonnet 140* is a good example of what English poets like Wyatt were responding to as they worked to bring the sonnet form into the repertory of English poetry. Translations by Robert M. Durling.

ragion, vergogna, et reverenza affrene,
di nostro ardir fra se stessa si sdegna.
Onde Amor paventoso fugge al core,
10   lasciando ogni sua impresa, et piange et trema;
ivi s'asconde et non appar più fore.
Che poss' io far, temendo il mio signore,
se non star seco infin a l'ora estrema?
ché bel fin fa chi ben amando more.

Petrarch, Sonnet 140: A Translation

Love, who lives and reigns in my thought and keeps his principal seat in my heart,
sometimes comes forth all in armor into my forehead, there camps, and there sets up
his banner.

She who teaches us to love and to be patient, and wishes my great desire, my
kindled hope, to be reined in by reason, shame, and reverence, at our boldness is
angry within herself.

Wherefore Love flees terrified to my heart, abandoning his every enterprise, and
weeps and trembles; there he hides and no more appears outside.

What can I do, when my lord is afraid, except stay with him until the last hour?
For he makes a good end who dies loving well.

⌘

Whoso List to Hunt

Who so list° to hunt, I know where is an hind,°   *wishes / doe*
But as for me, helas, I may no more:
The vain travail° hath wearied me so sore.   *idle labor*
I am of them that farthest cometh behind.
5   Yet may I by no means my wearied mind
Draw from° the deer: but as she fleeth afore,   *forget*
Fainting I follow. I leave off therefore,
Since in a net I seek to hold the wind.
Who list her hunt I put him out of doubt,
10   As well as I may spend his time in vain:
And, graven° with diamonds, in letters plain   *engraved*
There is written her fair neck round about:
Noli me tangere,[1] for Caesar's I am,
And wild for to hold though I seem tame.

⌘

COMPANION READING
Petrarch, Sonnet 190

Una candida cerva sopra l'erba
verde m'apparve con duo corna d'oro,
fra due riviere all' ombra d'un alloro,

---

1. "Touch me not," the words the resurrected but not yet risen Christ spoke to Mary Magdalene before his tomb (John 20.17). The "deer" of the poem has often been identified with Anne Boleyn and "Caesar" with Henry VIII.

Levando 'l sole a la stagione acerba.
5   Era sua vista sì dolce superba
ch' i'lasciai per seguirla ogni lavoro,
come l'avaro che 'n cercar tesoro
con diletto l'affanno disacerba.
"Nessun mi tocchi," al bel collo d'intorno
10   scritto avea di diamanti et di topazi.
"Libera farmi al mio Cesare parve."
Et era 'l sol già vòlto al mezzo giorno,
gli occhi miei stanchi di mirar, non sazi,
quand' io caddi ne l'acqua et ella sparve.

Petrarch, Sonnet 190: A Translation

A white doe on the green grass appeared to me, with two golden horns, between two rivers, in the shade of a laurel, when the sun was rising in the unripe season.

Her look was so sweet and proud that to follow her I left every task, like the miser who as he seeks treasure sweetens his trouble with delight.

"Let no one touch me," she bore written with diamonds and topazes around her lovely neck. "It has pleased my Caesar to make me free."

And the sun had already turned at midday; my eyes were tired by looking but not sated, when I fell into the water, and she disappeared.

My Galley

My galley charged° with forgetfulness	loaded
Through sharp seas in winter nights doth pass	
'Tween rock and rock; and eke° mine enemy, alas,	also
That is my lord, steereth with cruelness;	
5 And every oar a thought in readiness,	
As though that death were light° in such a case.	easy
An endless wind doth tear the sail apace.	
Of forced sighs and trusty fearfulness.	
A rain of tears, a cloud of dark disdain	
10 Hath done the wearied cords° great hindrance,	worn rigging
Wreathed with error and eke with ignorance.	
The stars be hid that led me to this pain,	
Drowned is reason that should me comfort,	
And I remain despairing of the port.	

Some Time I Fled the Fire[1]

Some time I fled the fire that me brent°	burned
By sea, by land, by water and by wind;	
And now I follow the coals that be quent°	quenched
From Dover to Calais against my mind.	
5 Lo! how desire is both sprung and spent!	

---

1. This poem appears to record Wyatt's attitude as he attended Anne Boleyn on her way to Calais in October 1532. Having been burned by her "fire" (a possible reference to a love affair), he now follows the dead coals of that fire against his will.

And he may see that whilom° was so blind;   *formerly*
And all his labor now he laugh° to scorn,   *may laugh*
Mashed in the breers° that erst° was all to torn.°   *briars / once / torn up*

⊷ ⊱◆⊰ ⊶

Henry Howard, Earl of Surrey
1517?–1547

Henry Howard, Earl of Surrey, was the heir to the earldom of Norfolk, one of the most powerful positions in England, when he was executed for treason in the last years of Henry VIII's reign for displaying the royal insignia on his shield, taken as a sign that he had inappropriate ambition. The Norfolks were the most significant Catholic family and so often regarded with suspicion after the Reformation. Surrey was a major poet whose career was cut tragically short. He was one of the first imitators—along with Thomas Wyatt—of Italian Petrarchan verse, helping to introduce the sonnet form into English. His blank verse translation of Virgil was also a major literary landmark. His poetry was published in the landmark collection, *Tottel's Miscellany* (1557) and he was singled out by Sir Philip Sidney as one of the few English writers worth reading.

For more on Sidney, see his principal listing on page 709.

Love That Doth Reign and Live within My Thought

Love that doth reign and live within my thought,
And built his seat within my captive breast,
Clad in the arms wherein with me he fought
Oft in my face he doth his banner rest.
5 But she that taught me love and suffer pain,
My doubtful hope and eke° my hot desire   *also*
With shamefast° cloak to shadow and refrain,   *ashamed*
Her smiling grace converteth straight to ire.
And coward love then to the heart apace
10 Taketh his flight, where he doth lurk and plain°   *complain*
His purpose lost, and dare not show his face.
For my lord's guilt thus faultless bide° I pain;   *suffer*
Yet from my lord shall not foot remove:
Sweet is the death that taketh end by love.

Th'Assyrians' King, in Peace with Foul Desire

Th'Assyrians' king,[1] in peace with foul desire
And filthy lusts that stained his regal heart,
In war that should set princely hearts afire
Vanquished did yield for want of martial art.
5 The dent of swords from kisses seemed strange,[2]
And harder than his lady's side his targe;°   *shield*

---

1. The king was Sardanapalus, often regarded as dissolute. He committed suicide by self-immolation.

2. I.e., the dent of swords seemed distasteful compared to kisses.

From glutton feasts to soldiers' fare a change,
His helmet, far above a garland's charge.[3]
Who scarce the name of manhood did retain,
10   Drenched in sloth and womanish delight;
Feeble of sprite,° unpatient of pain,   *spirit*
When he had lost his honor and his right—
Proud time of wealth, in storms appalled with dread—
Murdered himself to show some manful deed.

Set Me Whereas the Sun Doth Parch the Green

Set me whereas the sun doth parch the green,
Or where his beams may not dissolve the ice,
In temperate heat where he is felt and seen;
With proud people, in presence sad and wise;
5   Set me in base, or yet in high degree,
In the long night or in the shortest day,
In clear weather or where mists thickest be,
In lusty youth, or when my hairs be grey;
Set me in earth, in heaven, or yet in hell,
10   In hill, in dale, or in the foaming flood;
Thrall,° or at large, alive whereso I dwell,   *captive*
Sick, or in health, in ill fame or in good:
Yours will I be, and with that only thought
Comfort myself when that my hap° is nought.   *fortune*

The Soote Season

The soote° season, that bud and bloom forth brings,   *sweet*
With green hath clad the hill and eke the vale:
The nightingale with feathers new she sings:
The turtle to her make° hath told her tale: *mate*
5   Summer is come, for every spray now springs,
The hart° hath hung his old head° on the pale:°   *stag / horns / stake*
The buck in brake° his winter coat he flings: *thicket*
The fishes float with new repaired scale:
The adder all her slough away she slings:
10   The swift swallow pursueth the flies small:
The busy bee her honey now she minges:°   *remembers*
Winter is worn° that was the flowers' bale:°   *passed / evil*
And thus I see among these pleasant things
Each care decays, and yet my sorrow springs.

Alas, So All Things Now Do Hold Their Peace

Alas, so all things now do hold their peace.
Heaven and earth disturbed in nothing:
The beasts, the air, the birds their song do cease:

---

3. I.e., his helmet was a greater burden than a garland.

The night's chair° the stars about doth bring: *Ursa Major*
5 Calm is the sea, the waves work less and less:
   So am not I, whom love alas doth wring,
   Bringing before my face the great increase
   Of my desires, whereat I weep and sing
   In joy and woe as in a doubtful ease.
10 For my sweet thoughts sometime do pleasure bring:
   But by and by the cause of my disease
   Gives me a pang, that inwardly doth sting,
   When that I think what grief it is again,
   To live and lack the thing should rid my pain.

⤬⤬

COMPANION READING
Petrarch, Sonnet 164[1]

Or che 'l ciel et la terra e 'l vento tace
et le fere e gli augelli il sonno affrena,
notte il carro stellato in giro mena
et nel suo letto il mar senz' onda giace,

5 vegghio, penso, ardo, piango; et chi mi sface
sempre m'è inanzi per mia dolce pena:
guerra è 'l mio stato, d'ira e di duol piena,
et sol di lei pensando ò qualche pace.

Così sol d'una chiara fonte viva
10 move 'l dolce et l'amaro ond' io mi pasco,
una man sola mi risana et punge;
et perché 'l mio martir non giunga a riva,
mille volte il dì moro et mille nasco,
tanto da la salute mia son lunge.

Petrarch, Sonnet 164: A Translation

Now that the heavens and the earth and the wind are silent, and sleep reins in the beasts and the birds, Night drives her starry car about, and in its bed the sea lies without a wave,

I am awake, I think, I burn, I weep; and she who destroys me is always before me, to my sweet pain: war is my state, full of sorrow and suffering, and only thinking of her do I have any peace.

Thus from one clear living fountain alone spring the sweet and the bitter on which I feed; one hand alone heals me and pierces me.

And that my suffering may not reach an end, a thousand times a day I die and a thousand am born, so distant am I from health.

⤬⤬

1. For Petrarch, see the introductory footnote to the Wyatt response, page 667. This translation is also by Robert M. Durling.

⊷ ⋐◆⋑ ⊶

George Gascoigne
c. 1534–1577

Satire may produce ambiguous results, particularly when it is directed at the author's own life and work. To judge from his candidly witty self-portraits in *Alexander Neville's Theme* and *Woodmanship*, Gascoigne saw a good subject in his own career. The events of his life indicate that whatever ventures he attempted, he failed "to hit the whites [bulls-eyes] which live with all good luck." Educated at Cambridge and trained as a lawyer at Gray's Inn, Gascoigne went into debt trying to keep up with fashionable life in London. His election to Parliament was voided by the claims of his creditors, and in 1561 he compounded his legal difficulties by a bigamous marriage to Elizabeth Boyes, the widow of Willam Breton and the estranged wife of Edward Boyes. His service in the Low Countries was no more successful. He commanded English troops against the Spanish but, after several miscalculated maneuvers, surrendered to the Spanish at Leiden and spent four months as a prisoner of Spain. Upon returning to England he found himself under yet another kind of attack, this time for poetry that was supposed to report the scandalous behavior of certain figures at court. It had been published in 1573 in his absence (and perhaps without his knowledge) in a volume entitled *A Hundreth Sundrie Flowres*. After augmenting the collection—and reworking much of its material so that it conformed to more conventional standards of propriety, he reissued the volume as *The Posies of George Gascoigne* (1575), the version used here. The same volume also contains a prose romance, *The Adventures of Master F.J.*, a racy account of seduction and betrayal, opportunistic lovers, and resourceful ladies.

As Sir Thomas Wyatt had shown, the conventions that had dictated modes of self-expression in lyric poetry were capable of great transformation. Professions of virtuous love and devotion to patriotic ideals in the manner of Petrarch and his followers were no longer the only topics a poet was supposed to address, and Gascoigne, like Wyatt and such later poets as Sir Philip Sidney and John Donne, retuned the lyric voice so that it became capable of illustrating a sense of self charged not only with desire, but also with chagrin, dismay, bitterness, and even revulsion. At the same time, Gascoigne's vision of society remained essentially humorous; throughout his verse he is more committed to castigating himself than those who may have exploited him. Rarely has an author plagued by so many reversals represented as mellow a vision of society. As a rule, satire flattens its subjects to achieve pointed and deliberate effects; Gascoigne's satire gives his subjects a complexity that makes them seem less outrageous than familiar.

Seven Sonnets to Alexander Neville

Alexander Neville delivered him this theme, *Sat cito, si sat bene*, whereupon he compiled these seven sonnets in sequence, therein bewraying his own *Nimis cito*, and therewith his *Vix bene*, as followeth.[1]

1

> In haste, post haste, when first my wand'ring mind,
> Beheld the glist'ring court with gazing eye,
> Such deep delights I seemed therein to find,
> As might beguile a graver guest than I.

---

1. Gascoigne states that he composed these sonnets at the request of Alexander Neville (a poet, translator of Seneca, and secretary to Archbishop Matthew Parker). He was given a theme, *sat cito, si sat bene*, "if it be [done] well, let it be quickly," which he developed to satirize his own fault of acting too quickly: *nimis cito, vix bene,* or "if it be [done] very quickly, it is hardly well."

5   The stately pomp of princes and their peers,
       Did seem to swim in floods of beaten gold,
       The wanton world of young delightful years,
       Was not unlike a heaven for to behold.
       Wherin did swarm (for every saint) a dame,
10   So fair of hue, so fresh of their attire,
       As might excel dame Cynthia[2] for fame,
       Or conquer Cupid with his own desire.
       These and such like were baits that blazed still
       Before mine eye to feed my greedy will.

                            2
15   Before mine eye to feed my greedy will,
       'Gan° muster eke° mine old acquainted mates,   *began to / also*
       Who helped the dish (of vain delight) to fill
       My empty mouth with dainty delicates:
       And foolish boldness took the whip in hand,
20   To lash my life into this trustless trace,°   *harness*
       Till all in haste I leaped aloof° from land,   *aloft*
       And hoist° up sail to catch a courtly grace: *hoisted*
       Each ling'ring day did seem a world of woe,
       Till in that hapless haven my head was brought:
25   Waves of wanhope° so tossed me to and fro,   *discouragement*
       In deep despair to drown my dreadful thought:
       Each hour a day, each day a year did seem,
       And every year a world my will did deem.

                            3
       And every year a world my will did deem,
30   Till lo, at last, to court now am I come,
       A seemly swaine, that might the place beseem,
       A gladsome guest embraced of all and some:
       Not there content with common dignity,
       My wand'ring eye in haste, (yea post post haste)
35   Beheld the blazing badge of bravery,
       For want whereof, I thought myself disgraced:
       Then peevish pride puffed up my swelling heart,
       To further forth so hot an enterprise:
       And comely cost began to play his part,
40   In praising patterns of mine own devise.°   *devising*
       Thus all was good that might be got in haste,
       To prink° me up, and make me higher placed.   *dress*

                            4
       To prink me up and make me higher placed,
       All came too late that taried any time,
45   Pill of provision[3] pleased not my taste,

---

2. The goddess of the moon, an aspect of the goddess Diana, the goddess of chastity.

3. The property his family had provided him as his inheritance. Requiring greater wealth, he began to cut the
trees on his estate.

They made my heels too heavy for to climb:
Me thought it best that boughs of boist'rous oak,
Should first be shred to make my feathers gay.
Till at the last a deadly dinting stroke,
50   Brought down the bulk with edgetools of decay:
Of every farm I then let fly a lease,
To feed the purse that paid for peevishness,
Till rent and all were fall'n in such disease,
As scarce could serve to maintain cleanliness:
55   They bought the body, fine,° farm, lease, and land,   *recorded grant*
All were too little for the merchant's hand.[4]

5

All were too little for the merchant's hand,
And yet my bravery bigger than his book:
But when this hot accompt° was coldly scanned,   *account*
60   I thought high time about me for to look:
With heavy cheer I cast my head aback,
To see the fountain of my furious race.
Compared my loss, my living, and my lack,
In equal balance with my jolly grace.
65   And saw expenses grating on the ground
Like lumps of lead to press my purse full oft,
When light reward and recompense were found,
Fleeting like feathers in the wind aloft:
These thus compared, I left the court at large,
70   For why? the gains doth seldom quit° the charge.   *compensate for*

6

For why? the gains doth seldom quit the charge,
And so say I, by proof too dearly bought,
My haste made waste, my brave and brainsick barge,
Did float too fast, to catch a thing of naught:
75   With leisure, measure, mean, and many mo,°   *more*
I mought° have kept a chair of quiet state,   *might*
But hasty heads cannot be settled so,
Till crooked Fortune give a crabbed mate:[5]
As busy brains must beat on tickle° toys,   *fickle*
80   As rash invention breeds a raw device,
So sudden falls do hinder hasty joys,
And as swift baits do fleetest fish entice.
So haste makes waste, and therefore now I say,
No haste but good, where wisdom makes the way.

7

85   No haste but good, where wisdom makes the way,
For proof whereof, behold the simple snail,

---

4. Having leased his farms, he could no longer sell what
they produced; in all, none of the financial arrangements
he made to acquire more money proved adequate to meet
what the merchant charged for his apparel and upkeep.
5. Fortune will give those who act in haste an outcome
that is unsatisfactory.

(Who sees the soldier's carcass cast away,
With hot assault the castle to assail,)
By line and leisure climbs the lofty wall,
90   And wins the turret's top more cunningly,
Than doughty Dick, who lost his life and all,
With hoisting up his head too hastily.
The swiftest bitch brings forth the blindest whelps,
The hottest fevers coldest cramps ensue,
95   The naked'st need hath over latest helps:[6]
With Neville then I find this proverb true,
That haste makes waste, and therefore still I say,
No haste but good, where wisdom makes the way.
            Sic tuli[7]

Edmund Spenser
1552?–1599

Edmund Spenser apparently wrote the sequence entitled *Amoretti* for Elizabeth Boyle, whom he married in 1594, although some of its eighty-nine sonnets may be of an earlier date and intended for another woman. The sequence was published in 1595 together with *Epithalamion*, Spenser's marriage hymn in celebration of his wedding. The two works are linked thematically by their allusions to the passage of time. The *Amoretti* refers to seasons of the year, the *Epithalamion* to the twenty-four hours of a day that begins at one in the morning and ends at 12 midnight. Epithalamia, a feature of the literature of ancient Greece, were usually written by a professional for a family with whom the poet had no personal connection. Spenser's hymn is unusual in that its poet is also the husband it honors.

For more about Spenser, see his principal listing, on page 822.

from **Amoretti**[1]

1

Happy ye leaves° when as those lilly hands,	*of the book*
Which hold my life in their dead doing° might,	*death-dealing*
Shall handle you and hold in loves soft bands,°	*bonds*
Lyke captives trembling at the victors sight.	
5 And happy lines, on which with starry light,	
Those lamping° eyes will deigne sometimes to look	*flashing*
And reade the sorrowes of my dying spright,°	*spirit*
Written with teares in harts close bleeding book.	
And happy rymes bath'd in the sacred brooke,[2]	
10 Of Helicon whence she derived is,	
When ye behold that Angels blessed looke,	

---

6. Gascoigne alludes to the ironies of Fortune; in sum, the most dire need is met with help, but that help comes too late.
7. Thus I have persevered.

1. "Little loves."
2. Aganippe, which rises (or is "derived") from Helicon, a mountain that is home to the Muses, goddesses of all the arts but known especially for their inspiration of poets.

My soules long lacked foode, my heavens blis.
Leaves, lines, and rymes, seeke her to please alone,
Whom if ye please, I care for other none.

4

New yeare forth looking out of Janus[3] gate,
Doth seeme to promise hope of new delight:
And bidding th'old Adieu, his passed date
Bids all old thoughts to die in dumpish spright°   *low spirits*
5   And calling forth out of sad Winters night,
Fresh love, that long hath slept in cheerlesse bower:
Wils him awake, and soone about him dight
His wanton wings and darts of deadly power.
For lusty spring now in his timely howre,
10 Is ready to come forth him to receive:
And warnes the Earth with divers colord flowre,
To decke hir selfe, and her faire mantle weave.
Then you faire flowre, in whom fresh youth doth raine,°   *reign*
Prepare your selfe new love to entertaine.

13

In that proud port,° which her so goodly graceth,[4]   *bearing*
Whiles her faire face she reares up to the skie:
And to the ground her eie lids low embaseth°   *casts down*
Most goodly temperature° ye may descry,°   *temperament / perceive*
5   Myld humblesse° mixt with awfull° majesty,   *humility / awesome*
For looking on the earth whence she was borne:
Her minde remembreth her mortalitie,
What so is fayrest shall to earth returne.
But that same lofty countenance seemes to scorne
10 Base thing, and thinke how she to heaven may clime:
Treading downe earth as lothsome and forlorne,
That hinders heavenly thoughts with drossy° slime.   *heavy*
Yet lowly still vouchsafe° to looke on me,   *condescend*
Such lowlinesse shall make you lofty be.

22

This holy season fit to fast and pray,[5]
Men to devotion ought to be inclynd:
Therefore, I lykewise on so holy day,

---

3. A Roman god of the new year who has two faces; one looks back at December, the other ahead to January. For Christians the liturgical new year began on March 25, the Feast of the Annunciation, when the Angel Gabriel was thought to have announced the coming of Jesus Christ to the Virgin Mary. Throughout the sequence, Spenser plays with these two concepts of the year, juxtaposing the time dictated by nature, figured by the Roman calendar, with time according to Christian history and celebrated by the fasts and feasts of the church.

4. Spenser describes the lady to whom the sonnet is addressed.

5. The holy season is Lent; the holy day is Ash Wednesday. The sonnet celebrates the poet's admission that his love has a spiritual dimension; complimenting his heart's desire is the worship he gives to his lady's image in the temple of his mind.

For my sweet Saynt some service fit will find.
5   Her temple fayre is built within my mind,
In which her glorious ymage placed is,
On which my thoughts doo day and night attend
Lyke sacred priests that never thinke amisse.
There I to her as th'author of my blisse,
10   Will builde an altar to appease her yre:°   anger
And on the same my hart will sacrifise,
Burning in flames of pure and chast desyre:
The which vouchsafe O goddesse to accept,
Amongst thy deerest relicks to be kept.

62

The weary yeare his race now having run,
The new[6] begins his compast° course anew: encompassed
With shew of morning mylde he hath begun,
Betokening peace and plenty to ensew.
5   So let us, which this chaunge of weather vew,
Chaunge eeke° our mynds and former lives amend,   also
The old yeares sinnes forepast° let us eschew,°   gone by / avoid
And fly the faults with which we did offend.
Then shall the new yeares joy forth freshly send,
10   Into the glooming° world his gladsome ray: gloomy
And all these stormes which now his beauty blend,°   dim
Shall turne to caulmes and tymely cleare away.
So likewise love cheare you your heavy spright,
And chaunge old yeares annoy° to new delight.   grief

65

The doubt° which ye misdeeme,° fayre love, is vaine,   fear / misconceive
That fondly° feare to loose° your liberty,   foolishly / lose
When loosing one, two liberties ye gayne,
And make him bond that bondage earst dyd fly.
5   Sweet be the bands, the which true love doth tye,
Without constraynt or dread of any ill:
The gentle birde feeles no captivity
Within her cage, but singes and feeds her fill.
There pride dare not approch, nor discord spill
10   The league twixt them, that loyal love hath bound:
But simple truth and mutuall good will,
Seekes with sweet peace to salve° each others wound: heal
There fayth doth fearlesse dwell in brasen towre,
And spotlesse pleasure builds her sacred bowre.

6. The Christian new year, the Feast of the Annunciation.

66

To all those happy blessings which ye have,
With plenteous hand by heaven upon you thrown:
This one disparagement they to you gave,
That ye your love lent to so meane a one.[7]

5   Yee whose high worths surpassing paragon,
Could not on earth have found one fit for mate,
Ne but in heaven matchable to none,
Why did ye stoup unto so lowly state.
But ye thereby much greater glory gate,°   *got*

10   Then° had ye sorted°with a princes pere:°   *than / consorted / peer*
For now your light doth more it selfe dilate,°   *spread*
And in my darknesse greater doth appeare.
Yet since your light hath once enlumind° me,   *illuminated*
With my reflex° yours shall encreased be.   *reflected light*

68

Most glorious Lord of lyfe that on this day,[8]
Didst make thy triumph over death and sin:
And having harrowd hell, didst bring away
Captivity thence captive us to win.[9]

5   This joyous day, deare Lord, with joy begin,
And grant that we for whom thou diddest dye
Being with thy deare blood clene washt from sin,
May live for ever in felicity.
And that thy love we weighing worthily,

10   May likewise love thee for the same againe:
And for thy sake that all lyke deare° didst buy,   *at the same cost*
With love may one another entertayne.
So let us love, deare love, lyke as we ought,
Love is the lesson which the Lord us taught.

75

One day I wrote her name upon the strand,°   *beach*
But came the waves and washed it away:
Agayne I wrote it with a second hand,
But came the tyde, and made my paynes his pray.

5   Vayne man, sayd she, that doest in vaine assay,°   *attempt*
A mortall thing so to immortalize.
For I my selve shall lyke to this decay,

7. Working forward from Sonnet 62 and counting each sonnet as representing a day of love and devotion, Sonnet 66 corresponds to Good Friday. Spenser exploits the idea of humility, consistent with the passion of Christ, to express his own sense of devotion to his lady's virtue.
8. The sonnet addresses the "dear Lord" of the Passion on Easter Day to harmonize the poet's love for his lady and his obligation to follow the lesson of Christ.
9. Christians believed that after his Resurrection, Christ descended into hell to rescue Adam and Eve and the patriarchs and prophets of the Hebrew Bible. The event is often described as the harrowing of hell.

And eek my name bee wyped out lykewize.
Not so, (quod I) let baser things devize,°   consent
10   To dy in dust, but you shall live by fame:
My verse your vertues rare shall eternize,°   make eternal
And in the hevens wryte your glorious name:
Where whenas death shall all the world subdew,
Our love shall live, and later life renew.

Sir Philip Sidney
1554–1586

Courtier, poet and author of prose romances, Sir Philip Sidney stands as the most important writer and literary theorist of the first half of Elizabeth's reign who showed what it was possible to achieve in English. However, Sidney's own sense of himself suggests that he valued his political interventions more highly than his literary work. Sidney witnessed the Massacre of Saint Bartholomew's Day (1572) when Protestants were slaughtered in a sudden Catholic uprising, one of the key events that formed Protestant opinion in Europe. Sidney became well-known for advocating a more "forward" policy in Europe that would help the Dutch rebels against the Spanish but he died of his wounds in the battle of Zutphen. He was granted a state funeral, which was used to support his political ideals. His works were principally edited by his sister, Mary (1561–1621), one of the first women to obtain a major reputation as a poet in English.

For more on Sidney, see his principal listing on page 998.

from Astrophil and Stella[1]
1

Loving in truth, and fain° in verse my love to show,   wishing
That she (dear she) might take some pleasure of my pain:
Pleasure might cause her read, reading might make her know,
Knowledge might pity win, and pity grace obtain,
5   I sought fit words to paint the blackest face of woe,
Studying inventions[2] fine, her wits to entertain:
Oft turning others' leaves, to see if thence would flow
Some fresh and fruitfull showers upon my sun-burned brain.
But words came halting forth, wanting Invention's stay,°   support
10   Invention Nature's child, fled step-dame Study's blows,
And others' feet still seemed but strangers in my way.
Thus great with child to speak, and helpless in my throes,°   agonies
Biting my trewand° pen, beating my self for spite,   truant
Fool, said my Muse to me, look in thy heart and write.

---

1. This sonnet sequence was composed in 1582 and published in 1591.
2. "Invention" was the term early modern rhetoricians used to designate the choice of a literary subject and its development as an argument, in contrast to the forms of expression, figures of thought and speech, and imagery by which that subject was conveyed. As Sidney suggests, "invention" depended on the writer's imaginative intelligence, not on his literary education.

3

Let dainty wits cry on the sisters nine,[3]
That bravely masked, their fancies may be told;
Or, Pindar's apes[4] flaunt they in phrases fine,
Enam'ling with pied flowers their thoughts of gold;
5   Or else let them in statelier glory shine,
Ennobling new-found tropes° with problems° old;   *figures of speech / subjects*
Or with strange similes enrich each line,
Of herbs or beasts which Ind or Afric hold.
For me, in sooth, no Muse but one I know;
10 Phrases and problems from my reach do grow,
And strange things cost too dear for my poor sprites.
How then? Even thus—in Stella's face I read
What love and beauty be; then all my deed
But copying is, what, in her, Nature writes.

7

When Nature made her chief work, Stella's eyes,
In color black, why wrapt° she beams so bright?   *enwrapped*
Would she in beamy° black, like painter wise,   *glowing*
Frame daintiest° luster, mixed of shades and light?   *subtlest*
5   Or did she else that sober hue devise,
In object best to knit and strength° our sight,   *strengthen*
Least if no veil these brave gleams did disguise,
They sun-like should more dazzle then delight?[5]
Or would she her miraculous power show,
10 That whereas black seems beáuty's contrary,
She even in black doth make all beauties flow?
Both so and thus, she minding Love should be
Placed ever there, gave him this mourning weed,
To honor all their deaths, who for her bleed.[6]

9

Queen Virtue's court, which some call Stella's face,[7]
Prepared by Nature's choicest furniture,
Hath his front° built of Alabaster pure;   *forehead*
Gold is the covering° of that stately place.   *her hair*
5   The door° by which sometimes comes forth her Grace,   *her mouth*
Red porphir is, which lock of pearl° makes sure:°   *her teeth / secure*
Whose porches rich (which name of cheeks endure°)   *allow*
Marble mixt red and white do interlace.

---

3. The nine Muses, sponsors of the arts, music, and poetry.
4. Poets who slavishly imitated the literary works of the Greek poet Pindar, 522–442. C.E.
5. Did Nature make Stella's eyes black so that their bright beams might be softened to a mixed hue or not blind us with their brilliance?

6. Love is conventionally conveyed by the lady's glance, from her eyes, to the lover's heart, through his eyes; Stella's eyes are dark and in mourning because her glance is lethal.
7. The poet compares Stella's appearance to that of a building, the site of Virtue's court.

	The windows° now through which this heavenly guest	*her eyes*
10	Looks over the world, and can find nothing such,	
	Which dare claim from those lights the name of best.[8]	
	Of touch° they are that without touch doth touch,°	*touchstone / attain*
	Which° Cupid's self from Beauty's mind did draw:	*that which*
	Of touch° they are, and poor I am their straw.[9]	*touchwood, tinder*

10

	Reason, in faith thou art well served, that still	
	Wouldst brabbling° be with sense and love in me;	*babbling*
	I rather wished thee climb the Muses' hill;°	*Mt. Helicon*
	Or reach the fruit of Nature's choicest tree;[1]	
5	Or seek heaven's course or heaven's inside to see.	
	Why shouldst thou toil our thorny soil to till?	
	Leave sense and those which sense's objects be;	
	Deal thou with powers of thoughts; leave love to will.	
	But thou wouldst needs fight both with love and sense,	
10	With sword of wit giving wounds of dispraise,	
	Till downright blows did foil thy cunning fence;°	*swordsmanship*
	For, soon as they[2] strake thee with Stella's rays,	
	Reason, though kneel'dst, and offer'dst straight to prove,	
	By reason good, good reason her to love.	

14

	Alas, have I not pain enough, my friend,	
	Upon whose breast a fiercer grip doth tire[3]	
	Than did on him who first stole down the fire,[4]	
	While Love on me doth all his quiver spend—	
5	But with your rhubarb° words ye must contend,	*bitter*
	To grieve me worse, in saying that desire	
	Doth plunge my well-formed soul even in the mire	
	Of sinful thoughts, which do in ruin end?	
	If that be sin which doth the manners° frame,	*decent behavior*
10	Well stayed with truth in word[5] and faith of deed,	
	Ready of wit, and fearing naught but shame;	
	If that be sin, which in fixed hearts doth breed	
	A loathing of all loose unchastity,	
	Then love is sin, and let me sinful be.	

---

8. Stella's eyes reveal to her that nothing in the world is better than they are; they are uniquely the best.
9. The last three lines of the poem play on the meanings of "touch": Stella's eyes are touchstone, the mineral that reveals whether an ore contains gold; they make contact with their object without touching it; they attain the form that Cupid drew from Beauty; and they act as tinder does to the straw that is the poet: they set him on fire.

1. The tree of knowledge in the Garden of Eden.
2. Love and sense.
3. Grasp does hold.
4. Prometheus, the mythical hero who stole fire from heaven to give to mankind, an act for which the gods ordered his liver torn out by an eagle.
5. Firmly rooted in truthful language.

15

You that do search for every purling spring
Which from the ribs of old Parnassus[6] flows,
And every flower, not sweet perhaps, which grows
Near thereabouts, into your poesy wring;
5   You that do dictionary's method bring
Into your rhymes, running in rattling rows;[7]
You that poor Petrarch's long deceased woes
With newborn sighs and denizened wit do sing:[8]
You take wrong ways; those far-fet° helps be such   *far-fetched*
10   As do bewray° a want of inward touch,   *reveal*
And sure at length stolen goods do come to light;
But if, both for your love and skill, your name
You seek to nurse at fullest breasts of fame,
Stella behold, and then begin to indite.°   *write*

23

The curious wits, seeing dull pensiveness
Bewray itself in my long-settled eyes,
Whence those same fumes of melancholy rise,
With idle pains and missing aim do guess.
5   Some, that know how my spring° I did address,   *youth*
Deem that my Muse some fruit of knowledge plies;
Others, because the prince my service tries,
Think that I think state errors to redress.
But harder judges judge ambition's rage,
10   Scourge of itself, still climbing slippery place,
Holds my young brain captived° in golden cage.   *captivated*
O fools, or over-wise: alas, the race
Of all my thoughts hath neither stop nor start
But only Stella's eyes and Stella's heart.

24

Rich fools there be whose base and filthy heart
Lies hatching still the goods wherein they flow,
And damning their own selves to Tantal's[9] smart,
Wealth breeding want, more blissed,° more wretched grow. *blessed*
5   Yet to those fools heaven such wit doth impart
As what their hands do hold, their heads do know,
And knowing, love, and loving, lay apart
As sacred things, far from all danger's show.
But that rich fool who by blind Fortune's lot

---

6. A mountain in Greece sacred to Apollo and the Muses.
7. I.e., exhibiting alliteration, repeating the same sound within a few lines.
8. I.e., represent the themes and motifs of the 14th-century

Italian poet Petrarch.
9. The mythical sinner, condemned forever in Hades to reach for food and drink which were always already out of reach.

10   The richest gem of love and life enjoys,
    And can with foul abuse such beauties blot,
    Let him, deprived of sweet but unfelt joys,
    Exiled for aye from those high treasures which
    He knows not, grow in only folly rich![1]

31

    With how sad steps, O Moon, thou climb'st the skies,
    How silently, and with how wan° a face,   *pale*
    What may it be, that even in heavenly place
    That busy archer° his sharp arrows tries?   *Cupid*
5   Sure if° that long with Love acquainted eyes   *surely if those*
    Can judge of Love, thou feel'st a lover's case;
    I read it in thy looks, thy languished grace
    To me that feel the like, thy state descries.°   *reveals*
    Then even of fellowship, O Moon, tell me
10   Is constant Love deemed there but want of wit?
    Are beauties there as proud as here they be?
    Do they above love to be loved, and yet
    Those lovers scorn whom that Love doth possess?
    Do they call Virtue there ungratefulness?

37

    My mouth doth water, and my breast doth swell,
    My tongue doth itch, my thoughts in labor be.
    Listen then, lordings, with good ear to me,
    For, of my life, I must a riddle tell.
5   Toward Aurora's[2] court a nymph doth dwell,
    Rich in all beauties which man's eye can see
    (Beauties so far from reach of words, that we
    Abase her praise saying she doth excel),
    Rich in the treasure of deserved renown,
10   Rich in the riches of a royal heart,
    Rich in those gifts which give the eternal crown,
    Who (though most rich in these and every part
    Which make the patents° of true worldly bliss)   *royal grants*
    Hath no misfortune but that Rich she is.

39

    Come sleep, O sleep, the certain knot of peace,
    The baiting° place of wit, the balm of woe,   *resting*
    The poor man's wealth, the prisoner's release,
    Th'indifferent judge between the high and low;
5   With shield of proof° shield me from out the prease°   *proven shield / throng*

1. The sonnet mocks Lord Rich, the husband of Penelope   2. Goddess of the dawn.
Devereux, the model for Sidney's Stella.

Of those fierce darts, despair at me doth throw:
O make in me those civil wars to cease;
I will good tribute pay if thou do so.
Take thou of me smooth pillows, sweetest bed,
10   A chamber deaf to noise, and blind to light:
A rosy garland, and a weary head:
And if these things, as being thine by right,
Move not thy heavy grace, thou shalt in me
Livelier then elsewhere Stella's image see.

45

Stella oft sees the very face of woe
Painted in my beclouded stormy face:
But cannot skill° to pity my disgrace,   *does not know how*
Not though thereof the cause herself she know:
5   Yet hearing late a fable, which did show
Of lovers never known, a grievous case,°   *situation*
Pity thereof gate° in her breast such place,   *got*
That from that sea derived tears' spring did flow.[3]
Alas, if Fancy drawn by imaged things,
10   Though false, yet with free scope more grace doth breed
Than servants' wrack, where new doubts honor brings;[4]
Then think my dear, that you in me do read
Of lovers' ruin some sad tragedy:
I am not I, pity the tale of me.

47

What, have I thus betrayed my liberty?
Can those black beams such burning marks engrave
In my free side; or am I born a slave,
Whose neck becomes° such yoke of tyranny?   *suits*
5   Or want I sense to feel my misery,
Or sprite,° disdain of such disdain to have,   *spirit*
Who for long faith, though daily help I crave,
May get no alms, but scorn of beggary?
Virtue, awake! Beauty but beauty is;
10   I may, I must, I can, I will, I do
Leave following that which it is gain to miss.
Let her go! Soft, but here she comes! Go to;
Unkind, I love you not. Oh me, that eye
Doth make my heart give to my tongue the lie!

52

A strife is grown between Virtue and Love,
While each pretends that Stella must be his.

---

3. I.e., derived from that sea [of pity], a spring of tears did flow.
4. I.e., Fancy with free scope breeds more grace or sympa- thy than the actual destruction of a servant, a situation in which a sense of honor provokes new doubts about that person's worth.

Her eyes, her lips, her all, saith Love, do this,
Since they do wear his badge, most firmly prove.
5   But Virtue thus that title does disprove
That Stella (oh dear name!), that Stella is
That virtuous soul, sure heir of heavenly bliss,
Not this fair outside which our hearts doth move;
And therefore, though her beauty and her grace
10 Be Love's indeed, in Stella's self he may
By no pretense claim any manner place.
Well, Love, since this demur° our suit doth stay,   *objection*
Let Virtue have that Stella's self; yet thus,
That Virtue but that body grant to us.

<h3 style="text-align:center">60</h3>

When my good Angel guides me to the place,
Where all my good I do in Stella see,
That heaven of joys throws only down on me
Thundered disdains and lightnings of disgrace:
5   But when the ruggedst step of Fortune's race°   *course*
Makes me fall from her sight, then sweetly she
With words, wherein the Muses' treasures be,
Shows love and pity to my absent case.[5]
Now I wit-beaten long by hardest Fate,
10 So dull am, that I cannot look into
The ground of this fierce love and lovely hate:
Then some good body tell me how I do,
Whose presence, absence, absence presence is;[6]
Blissed° in my curse, and cursed in my bliss.   *blessed*

<h3 style="text-align:center">63</h3>

O grammar-rules, O now your virtues show,
So children still read you with awful° eyes,   *respectful*
As my young dove may, in your precepts wise,
Her grant to me by her own virtue know;
5   For late, with heart most high, with eyes most low,
I craved the thing which ever she denies;
She, lightning love, displaying Venus' skies,
Lest once should not be heard, twice said, "No, no!"
Sing then, my muse, now Io Paean sing;[7]
10 Heavens envy not at my high triumphing,
But grammar's force with sweet success confirm,
For grammar says,—oh this, dear Stella, weigh,—
For grammar says,—to grammar who says nay?—
That in one speech two negatives affirm!

5. I.e., when a good angel or good fortune guides the poet to Stella, heaven throws at him only the "joys" of disdain and disgrace. On the other hand, when he is away from her, she shows him love and pity.
6. This paradox is repeated in sonnets 106 and 108.
7. Hymn of thanksgiving.

64

No more, my dear, no more these counsels try;
O give my passions leave to run their race;
Let Fortune lay on me her worst disgrace;
Let folk o'ercharged with brain against me cry;

5   Let clouds bedim my face, break in mine eye;
Let me no steps but of lost labor trace;
Let all the earth with scorn recount my case;
But do not will me from my love to fly.
I do not envy Aristotle's wit,

10   Nor do aspire to Caesar's bleeding fame,
Nor aught do care though some above me sit,
Nor hope nor wish another course to frame
But that which once may win thy cruel heart.
Thou art my wit, and thou my virtue art.

68

Stella, the only planet of my light,
Light of my life, and life of my desire,
Chief good whereto my hope doth only aspire,
World of my wealth, and heaven of my delight,

5   Why dost thou spend the treasures of thy sprite°   *spirit*
With voice more fit to wed Amphion's[8] lyre,
Seeking to quench in me the noble fire
Fed by thy worth and blinded by thy sight?
And all in vain; for while they breath most sweet

10   With choicest words, thy words with reasons rare,
Thy reasons firmly set on Virtue's feet,
Labor to kill in me this killing care;
O think I then, what paradise of joy
It is, so fair a virtue to enjoy!

71

Who will in fairest book of Nature[9] know,
How Virtue may best lodged in beauty be,
Let him but learn of Love to read in thee,
Stella, those fair lines, which true goodness show.

5   There shall he find all vices overthrow,°   *overthrown*
Not by rude force, but sweetest sovereignty
Of reason, from whose light those night-birds fly;
That inward sun in thine eyes shineth so.
And not content to be Perfection's heir

---

8. The legendary lyre-player whose music moved the stones that built the walls of Thebes.
9. All of creation, in effect the second "book" of God and a supplement to the Bible. It was a philosophical commonplace that Nature was the repository of natural law, which all human beings could discover through reason, just as the Bible held divine law, which was revealed to the faithful through grace.

10   Thyself, doest strive all minds that way to move:
      Who mark in thee what is in thee most fair.
      So while thy beauty draws the heart to love,
      As fast thy virtue bends that love to good:
      But ah, Desire still cries, give me some food.

Second song

      Have I caught my heavenly jewel
      Teaching sleep most fair to be?
      Now will I teach her that she,
      When she wakes, is too too cruel.

5   Since sweet sleep her eyes hath charmed
      The two only darts of Love,
      Now will I with that boy prove
      Some play while he is disarmed.[1]

      Her tongue, waking, still refuseth,
10   Giving frankly niggard no;
      Now will I attempt to know
      What no her tongue, sleeping, useth.

      See the hand which, waking, guardeth,
      Sleeping, grants a free resort.
15   Now will I invade the fort.
      Cowards love with loss rewardeth.

      But, O fool, think of the danger
      Of her just and high disdain!
      Now will I, alas, refrain.
20   Love fears nothing else but anger.

      Yet those lips, so sweetly swelling,
      Do invite a stealing kiss.
      Now will I but venture this.
      Who will read must first learn spelling.

25   O, sweet kiss! But ah, she's waking!
      Louring° beauty chastens me.   scowling
      Now will I away hence flee:
      Fool, more fool, for no more taking!

74

      I never drank of Aganippe well,[2]
      Nor ever did in shade of Tempe[3] sit,
      And Muses scorn with vulgar brains to dwell,
      Poor layman I, for sacred rites unfit.

---

1. Stella's eyes have charmed and disarmed Cupid, leaving him open to the poet's play or contest of wills.

2. Spring on Mt. Helicon, sacred to the Muses.
3. A valley in Arcadia.

5   Some do I hear of poets' fury[4] tell,
     But, God wot, wot not what they mean by it;
     And this I swear by blackest brook of hell,
     I am no pick-purse of another's wit.
     How falls it then that with so smooth an ease
10   My thoughts I speak; and what I speak doth flow
     In verse, and that my verse best wits doth please?
     Guess we the cause. "What, is it thus?" Fie, no.
     "Or so?" Much less. "How then?" Sure thus it is:
     My lips are sweet, inspired with Stella's kiss.

Fourth song

     Only joy, now here you° are,   *Stella*
     Fit to hear and ease my care:
     Let my whispering voice obtain,
     Sweet reward for sharpest pain:
5   Take me to thee, and thee to me.
     No, no, no, no, my dear, let be.[5]

     Night hath closed all in her cloak,
     Twinkling stars love-thoughts provoke:
     Danger hence good care doth keep,[6]
10   Jealousy itself doth sleep:
     Take me to thee, and thee to me.
     No, no, no, no, my dear, let be.

     Better place no wit can find,
     Cupid's yoke to loose or bind:
15   These sweet flowers on fine bed too,
     Us in their best language woo:
     Take me to thee, and thee to me.
     No, no, no, no, my dear, let be.

     This small light the moon bestows,
20   Serves thy beams but to disclose,
     So to raise my hap more high;[7]
     Fear not else, none can us spy:
     Take me to thee, and thee to me.
     No, no, no, no, my dear, let be.

25   That you heard was but a mouse,
     Dumb sleep holdeth all the house:
     Yet asleep, me thinks they say,

---

4. Divine frenzy; Sidney identifies it as the poets' inspiration in *The Apology for Poetry*.

5. The last line of each stanza is Stella's reply to Astrophil's entreaties in the preceding five lines. An earlier sonnet has suggested that logically two negatives are the same as a positive; thus it is possible to read a certain ambiguity into Stella's rejection of Astrophil here.

6. I.e., good care keeps danger away.

7. Astrophil states that the moon reveals Stella's beauty and thus raises his fortune. Writers and artists in this period imagined fortune as a goddess or a kind of fatal force that turned a wheel to which a person's prosperity was tied; when one was at the top of Fortune's wheel, pleasure and power were within one's grasp. In the last stanza, Astrophil declares that Stella's hate will signal his fall and foresees his death. The images of rising and dying also have a sexual meaning.

        Young folks, take time while you may:
        Take me to thee, and thee to me.
30   No, no, no, no, my dear, let be.

        Niggard° Time threats, if we miss   *miserly*
        This large offer of our bliss:
        Long stay ere[8] he grant the same:
        Sweet then, while each thing doth frame:°   *suit*
35   Take me to thee, and thee to me.
        No, no, no, no, my dear, let be.

        Your fair mother is abed,
        Candles out, and curtains spread:
        She thinks you do letters write:
40   Write, but let me first indite:°   *speak*
        Take me to thee, and thee to me.
        No, no, no, no, my dear, let be.

        Sweet alas, why strive you thus?
        Concord better fitteth us:
45   Leave to Mars the force of hands,
        Your power in your beauty stands:
        Take thee to me, and me to thee.
        No, no, no, no, my dear, let be.

        Woe to me, and do you swear
50   Me to hate, but I forbear,
        Cursed be my destines° all,   *destinies*
        That brought me so high to fall:
        Soon with my death I will please thee.
        No, no, no, no, my dear, let be.

86

        Alas, whence came this change of looks? If I
        Have changed desert let mine own conscience be
        A still-felt plague to self-condemning me,
        Let woe grip on my heart, shame load mine eye;
5   But if all faith like spotless ermine[9] lie
        Safe in my soul, which only doth to thee
        As his sole object of felicity
        With wings of Love in air of wonder fly,
        O ease your hand, treat not so hard your slave:
10   In justice pains come not till faults do call.
        Or if I needs, sweet judge, must torments have,
        Use something else to chasten me withal
        Than those blessed eyes where all my hopes do dwell:
        No doom° should make one's heaven become his hell.   *judgment*

---

8. I.e., it will be long before Time will give us another chance.

9. A kind of weasel whose fur is brown in summer and white in winter.

Eighth song

In a grove most rich of shade,
Where birds wanton music made,
May then young his pied weeds showing,[1]
New perfumed with flowers fresh growing,

5   Astrophil with Stella sweet,
Did for mutual comfort meet,
Both within themselves oppressed,
But each in the other blessed.

Him great harms had taught much care,
10   Her fair neck a foul yoke[2] bare,
But her sight his cares did banish,
In his sight her yoke did vanish.

Wept they had, alas the while,
But now tears themselves did smile,
15   While their eyes by love directed,
Interchangeably reflected.

Sigh they did, but now betwixt°   *between*
Sighs of woes were glad sighs mixed,
With arms crossed, yet testifying
20   Restless rest, and living dying.

Their ears hungry of each word,
Which the dear tongue would afford,
But their tongues restrained from walking,
Till their hearts had ended talking.
25   But when their tongues could not speak,
Love itself did silence break;
Love did set his lips asunder,
Thus to speak in love and wonder:

Stella, sovereign of my joy,
30   Fair triumpher of° annoy,°   *over* / *despair*
Stella, star of heavenly fire,
Stella, loadstar° of desire.   *magnet*

Stella, in whose shining eyes,
Are the lights of Cupid's skies,
35   Whose beams where they once are darted,
Love therewith is straight imparted.

Stella, whose voice when it speaks,
Senses all asunder breaks;
Stella, whose voice when it singeth,
40   Angels to acquaintance bringeth.

---

1. I.e., May, young then, showed his many-colored garments.

2. The "yoke" Stella wears is her marriage to Lord Rich; it is "foul" to Astrophil because it means that he can no longer court her, at least openly.

Stella, in whose body is
Writ° each character of bliss,   *written*
Whose face all, all beauty passeth,
Save thy mind which yet surpasseth.

45   Grant, O grant, but speech alas,
Fails me fearing on to pass,
Grant, O me, what am I saying?
But no fault there is in praying.

Grant, O dear, on knees I pray,
50   (Knees on ground he then did stay)
That not I but since I love you,
Time and place for me may move you.

Never season was more fit,
Never room more apt for it;
55   Smiling air allows my reason,
These birds sing; now use the season.

This small wind which so sweet is,
See how it the leaves doth kiss,
Each tree in his best attiring,
60   Sense of love to love inspiring.

Love makes earth the water drink,
Love to earth makes water sink;
And if dumb things be so witty,
Shall a heavenly grace want pity?

65   There his hands in their speech fain
Would have made tongue's language plain;[3]
But her hands his hands repelling,
Gave repulse all grace excelling.[4]

Then she spake; her speech was such,
70   As not ears but heart did touch:
While such wise she love denied,
As yet love she signified.

Astrophil said she, my love
Cease in these effects to prove:
75   Now be still, yet still believe me,
Thy grief more than death would grieve me.

If that any thought in me,
Can taste comfort but of thee,°   *except from you*
Let me feed with hellish anguish,
80   Joyless, hopeless, endless languish.

---

3. I.e., he would have had the language of his hands make plain what he had spoken.
4. I.e., she rejected him in a way that excelled all the grace that would have accompanied her acceptance of him.

If those eyes you praised, be
Half so dear as you to me,
Let me home return, stark blinded
Of those eyes, and blinder minded.[5]

85 If to secret° of my heart,   *the secrets*
I do any wish impart,
Where thou art not foremost placed,
Be both wish and I defaced.

If more may be said, I say,
90 All my bliss in thee I lay;
If thou love, my love content thee,
For all love, all faith is meant thee,

Trust me while I thee deny,
In myself the smart° I try,°   *pain / feel*
95 Tyran honor doth thus use thee,
Stella's self might not refuse thee.

Therefore, dear, this no more move,
Lest, though I leave not thy love,
Which too deep in me is framed,
100 I should blush when thou art named.

Therewithal away she went,
Leaving him so passion rent,
With what she had done and spoken,
That therewith my song is broken.

Ninth song

Go, my flock, go get you hence,
Seek a better place of feeding,
Where you may have some defense
From the storms in my breast breeding,
5 And showers from mine eyes proceeding.

Leave a wretch in whom all woe
Can abide to keep no measure;
Merry flock, such one forgo,
Unto whom mirth is displeasure,
10 Only rich in mischief's treasure.

Yet, alas, before you go,
Hear your woeful master's story,
Which to stones I else would show:
Sorrow only then hath glory
15 When 'tis excellently° sorry.   *exceedingly*

5. I.e., even blinder in my mind.

Stella, fiercest shepherdess,
Fiercest but yet fairest ever,
Stella whom, O heavens, do bless,
Though against me she persever,
20   Though I bliss inherit never,

Stella hath refused me;
Stella who more love hath proved
In this caitiff° heart to be   *wretched*
Than can in good ewes be moved
25   Toward lambkins best beloved.

Stella hath refused me,
Astrophel, that so well served,
In this pleasant spring must see,
While in pride flowers be preserved,
30   Himself only winter-starved.

Why, alas, doth she then swear
That she loveth me so dearly,
Seeing me so long to bear
Coals of love that burn so clearly,
35   And yet leave me helpless merely?

Is that love? forsooth I trow
If I saw my good dog grieved,
And a help for him did know,
My love should not be believed
40   But he were by me relieved.

No, she hates me (wellaway!)
Feigning love somewhat to please me,
For she knows if she display
All her hate, death soon would seize me
45   And of hideous torments ease me.

Then adieu, dear flock, adieu!
But, alas, if in your straying
Heavenly Stella meet with you,
Tell her, in your piteous blaying,
50   Her poor slave's unjust decaying.

89

Now that, of absence, the most irksome night
With darkest shade doth overcome my day,
(Since Stella's eyes, wont to give me my day,
Leaving my hemisphere, leave me in night)
5   Each day seems long and longs for long-stayed night;
The night, as tedious, woos the approach of day
Tired with the dusty toils of busy day,
Languished with horrors of the silent night,

Suffering the evils both of the day and night,
10 (While no night is more dark than is my day,
Nor no day hath less quiet than my night)
With such bad-mixture of my night and day
That living thus in blackest winter night,
I feel the flames of hottest summer day.

90

Stella, think not that I by verse seek fame—
Who seek, who hope, who love, who live—but thee,
Thine eyes my pride, thy lips mine history.
If thou praise not, all other praise is shame.
5 Nor so ambitious am I as to frame
A nest for my young praise in laurel tree.[6]
In truth, I swear I wish not there should be
Graved in mine epitaph a poet's name.
Nay, if I would, I could just title make
10 That any laud° to me thereof should grow   *praise*
Without my plumes from others' wings I take,[7]
For nothing from my wit or will doth flow
Since all my words thy beauty doth indite,°   *record*
And Love doth hold my hand, and makes me write.

91

Stella, while now by honor's cruel might
I am from you (light of my life) misled,
And that fair you, my sun, thus overspread
With absence' veil,[8] I live in sorrow's night,
5 If this dark place yet show like candle-light,
Some beauty's piece (as amber-colored head,
Milk hands, rose cheeks, or lips more sweet, more red,
Or seeing gets, black,[9] but in blackness bright)
They please, I do confess, they please mine eyes.
10 But why? Because of you they models be,
Models such be wood-globes of glistering skies.[1]
Dear, therefore be not jealous over me,
If you hear that they seem my heart to move;
Not them, O no, but you in them I love.

97

Dian,[2] that fain would cheer her friend the Night,
Shows her oft, at the full, her fairest face,
Bringing with her those starry nymphs, whose chase

6. The laurel tree was identified with Apollo and excellence in poetry.
7. I.e., I do not copy the work of other poets.
8. The veil of absence, obscuring presence.

9. Bright jet-black eyes.
1. Presumably, wooden globes on which are illustrated the
stars and planets of the night sky.
2. Diana, the goddess of chastity, hunting, and the moon.

From heavenly standing° hits each mortal wight.   *ambush*
5   But ah, poor Night, in love with Phoebus'³ light
And endlessly despairing of his grace,
Herself, to show no other joy hath place,
Silent and sad, in mourning weeds doth dight.
Even so, alas, a lady, Dian's peer,
10   With choice delights and rarest company
Would fain drive clouds from out my heavy cheer.
But, woe is me, though joy itself were she,
She could not show my blind brain ways of joy,
While I despair my sun's sight to enjoy.

104

Envious wits,⁴ what hath been mine offense,
That with such poisonous care my looks you mark,
That to each word, nay sigh of mine, you hark,
As grudging me my sorrow's eloquence?
5   Ah, is it not enough that I am thence,
Thence, so far thence, that scarcely any spark
Of comfort dare come to this dungeon dark,
Where rigorous exile locks up all my sense?
But if I by a happy° window pass,   *lucky*
10   If I but stars upon mine armor bear⁵—
Sick, thirsty, glad (though but of empty glass),
Your moral notes straight my hid meaning tear
From out my ribs, and, puffing, prove that I
Do Stella love; fools, who doth it deny?

106

O absent presence, Stella is not here;
False flattering hope, that with so fair a face,
Bare° me in hand, that in this orphan place,   *took*
Stella, I say my Stella, should appear.
5   What sayest thou now, where is that dainty cheer,°   *food*
Thou toldst mine eyes should help their famished case?
But thou art gone now that self-felt disgrace
Doth make me most to wish thy comfort near.⁶
But here I do store of fair ladies meet,
10   Who may with charm of conversation sweet,
Make in my heavy mold new thoughts to grow:
Sure they prevail as much with me, as he
That bad his friend but then new maimed,° to be   *wounded*
Merry with him, and not think of his woe.

---

3. Apollo, the god of poetry, music, and medicine, often
identified with the sun.
4. Poets who identified Sidney as Stella's lover.
5. I.e., Astrophil wears armor decorated with stars in Stella's
honor.

6. I.e., you are gone now that that self (my own self) has
felt the disgrace of rejection; this makes me wish you
here.

107

Stella, since thou so right° a princess art   *true*
Of all the powers which life bestows on me,
That ere by them aught undertaken be
They first resort unto the sovereign part;
5   Sweet, for a while give respite to my heart,
Which pants as though it still should leap to thee,
And on my thoughts give thy lieutenancy[7]
To this great cause, which needs both use and art.
And as a queen, who from her presence sends
10 Whom she employs, dismiss from thee my wit
Till it have wrought what thy own will attends.
On servants' shame oft master's blame doth sit.
O let not fools in me thy works reprove,
And scorning say, "See what it is to love!"

108

When sorrow (using mine own fire's might)
Melts down his lead into my boiling breast,
Through that dark furnace to heart oppressed,
There shines a joy from thee my only light;
5   But soon as thought of thee breeds my delight,
And my young soul flutters to thee his nest,
Most rude despair, my daily unbidden guest,
Clips straight my wings, straight wraps me in his night,
And makes me then bow down my head, and say,
10 Ah what doth Phoebus' gold that wretch avail,
Whom iron doors do keep from use of day?
So strangely (alas) thy works[8] in me prevail,
That in my woes for thee thou art my joy,
And in my joys for thee my only annoy.

Richard Barnfield
1577–1627

Richard Barnfield, a precocious yet only briefly productive poet, published four books of verse before his twenty-fifth birthday but then nothing else; we know merely that he lived to the age of fifty-two, comfortably settled on his Staffordshire estate, a husband and the father of a son, Robert. As a poet, he chose to follow the conventions of the amorous pastoral, fashionable for the ease with which they allowed the representation of lovers' intrigues. His frankly homoerotic verses express the love of a shepherd, Daphnis, for a boy called Ganimede or

7. Dominate my thoughts.   affect me strangely.
8. I.e., "your works," what you have done and meant,

Ganymede, the mythological cup-bearer to Jupiter, the king of the gods. *The Tears of an Affectionate Shepherd* describes two phases to Daphnis's love; in *The Complaint* he offers Ganimede gifts from the pastoral world; in *The Lamentation*, claiming that what is fair is not necessarily good, he specifies steps to moral virtue. Complicating his narrative is the story of Ganimede's love for a woman, Queen Guendolen, whom Daphnis accuses of promiscuity. This rival threesome can be compared with the central figures of Shakespeare's (virtually contemporaneous) sonnet sequence: the poet, the young man, and the so-called dark lady. Finally, however, Barnfield creates his own poetic character, playing with occasional irony on the semantic and biblical association between shepherds and pastors. Barnfield's second collection of poems, published as *Cynthia*, continues to describe the competition for Ganimede's affection.

Slight as his total output was, Barnfield got the attention of readers. Francis Meres, his fellow student at Oxford and later critic of contemporary literature, placed him with Spenser, Sidney, and Abraham Fraunce as "best for pastoral." Barnfield's style is more vividly sensuous than theirs, however; his poems are best compared with the erotic pastoral verse of Theocritus, a Greek poet of the third century B.C.E., the first of its kind in Europe and a model for all subsequent examples of that genre.

Sonnets from *Cynthia*

1

Sporting at fancy, setting light by love,
    There came a thief and stole away my heart,
    (And therefore robbed me of my chiefest part)
Yet cannot reason him a felon prove.
5   For why his beauty (my heart's thief) affirmeth,
    Piercing no skin (the body's fensive° wall)   *defensive*
    And having leave, and free consent withal,
Himself not guilty, from love guilty termeth,[1]
Conscience the judge, twelve reasons are the jury,
10   They find mine eyes the beauty t'have let in,
    And on this verdict given, agreed they been,
Wherefore, because his beauty did allure ye,[2]
    Your doom is this: in tears still to be drowned,
    When his fair forehead with disdain is frowned.

5

It is reported of fair Thetis'[3] son,
    (Achilles, famous for his chivalry,
    His noble mind and magnanimity),
That when the Trojan wars were new begun,
5   Whos'ever was deep-wounded with his spear,
    Could never be recurred° of his maim,°   *cured / wound*
    Nor ever after be made whole again;
Except with that spear's rust he holpen were.°   *could be helped*
Even so it fareth with my fortune now,

---

1. The thief, beauty, having been given leave to steal the speaker's heart, declares himself not guilty; rather, it is love that is guilty.

2. You, i.e., the speaker addresses himself.
3. The mother of Achilles, the great Greek hero of the Trojan War.

10   Who being wounded with his piercing eye,
            Must either thereby find a remedy,
        Or else to be relieved, I know not how,
            Then if thou hast a mind still to annoy me,
            Kill me with kisses, if thou wilt destroy me.

9

Diana° (on a time) walking the wood,   *goddess of the hunt*
        To sport herself, of her fair train forlorn,
        Chancest for to prick her foot against a thorn,
And from thence issued out a stream of blood.
5   No sooner she was vanished out of sight,
        But love's fair Queen° came there by chance,   *Venus*
        And having of this hap a glimmering glance,
    She put the blood into a crystal bright,
    When being now come unto Mount Rhodope,
10   With her fair hands she forms a shape of snow,
        And blends it with this blood; from whence doth grow
A lovely creature, brighter than the day.
        And being christened in fair Paphos'[4] shrine,
        She called him Ganimede: as all divine.

11

Sighing, and sadly sitting by my love,
        He asked the cause of my heart's sorrowing,
        Conjuring me by heaven's eternal king
To tell the cause which me so much did move.
5   Compelled (quoth I) to thee will I confess,
        Love is the cause; and only love it is
        That doth deprive me of my heavenly bliss.
    Love is the pain that doth my heart oppress.
    And what is she (quoth he) whom thou dost love?
10   Look in this glass (quoth I) there shalt thou see
        The perfect form of my felicity.
When, thinking that it would strange magic prove,
        He opened it; and taking off the cover,
        He straight perceived himself to be my lover.

13

Speak, Echo, tell; how may I call my love?   Love[5]
        But how his lamps that are so crystalline?   Eyne°   *eyes*
        Oh, happy stars that make your heavens divine:
    And happy gems that admiration move.
5   How term'st his golden tresses waved with air?   Hair

---

4. Cyprus, sacred to Venus.
5. This poem exploits a rhetorical figure called *paronomasia*, in which sounds are repeated; in this case, the repetition is of the last syllable of a line, which produces the effect of an echo.

Oh, lovely hair of your more lovely master,
Image of love, fair shape of alabaster,
Why dost thou drive thy lover to despair?
How dost thou call the bed where beauty grows?   Rose
10 Fair virgin rose, whose maiden blossoms cover
The milk-white lily, thy embracing lover:
Whose kisses makes thee oft thy red to love.
 And blushing oft for shame, when he hath kissed thee,
He vades° away, and thou rangest° where it list thee. *fades / wander*

19

Ah no; nor I myself: though my pure love
 (Sweet Ganimede) to thee hath still been pure,
 And even till my last gasp shall aye endure,
Could ever thy obdurate beauty move:
5 Then cease, oh goddess' son (for sure thou are,
 A goddess' son that canst resist desire)
 Cease thy hard heart, and entertain love's fire,
Within thy sacred breast: by nature's art.
And as I love thee more than any creature,
10 (Love thee, because thy beauty is divine;
 Love thee because thyself, my soul, is thine:
Wholly devoted to thy lovely feature)
 Even so of all the vowels, I and U,
 Are dearest unto me, as doth ensue.

               1595

▸ ≡◆≡ ◂

Michael Drayton
1563–1631

Michael Drayton was considered a major poet in his lifetime. The recently verified portrait in the National Portrait Gallery, London, shows him with a laurel crown, making him the unofficial poet laureate. Given its date, 1599, the painting suggests that Drayton saw himself as the heir of his most important precursor, Spenser, who died early in the same year. Like Spenser, Drayton wrote a major sonnet sequence, *Ideas Mirrour*, first published in 1594, and revised four times, most importantly in 1599 and 1619, the work proving a commercial success long after the sonnet sequence had ceased to be a popular form for aspiring poets. Most critics agree on the formal subtlety and innovation in *Ideas Mirrour*, but are less united about the tone and purpose of the work. Some read Drayton's overturning of Petrarchan convention as comic parody; others see the sequence characterized by deeply felt erotic anguish.

Sonnet 12

To nothing fitter can I thee compare,
Than to the son of some rich penny-father,°   *miser*
Who having now brought on his end with care,
Leaves to his son all he had heap'd together.
5 This new rich novice, lavish of his chest,

To one man gives, and on another spends,
Then here he riots, yet amongst the rest,
Haps to lend some to one true honest friend.
Thy gifts thou in obscurity do waste,
10   False friends thy kindness, born but to deceive thee,
Thy love, that is on the unworthy plac'd,
Time hath thy beauty, which with age will leave thee;
    Only that little which to me was lent,
    I give thee back, when all the rest is spent.

Sonnet 61

Since there's no help, come let us kiss and part.
Nay, I have done: you get no more of me,
And I am glad, yea glad with all my heart,
That thus so cleanly I myself can free,
5   Shake hands forever, cancel all our vows,
And when we meet at any time again,
Be it not seen in either of our brows
That we one jot of former love retain.
Now at the last gasp of Love's latest breath,
10   When his pulse failing, Passion speechless lies,
When Faith is kneeling by his bed of death,
And Innocence is closing up his eyes,
    Now if thou would'st, when all have given him over,
    From death to life, thou might'st him yet recover.

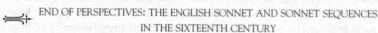   END OF PERSPECTIVES: THE ENGLISH SONNET AND SONNET SEQUENCES
IN THE SIXTEENTH CENTURY

Sir Thomas Wyatt

1503–1542

A gifted poet and diplomat, Sir Thomas Wyatt exemplified the ambitious mixture of social and artistic skills that later ages would see as the ideal of the "Renaissance man." Having entered the household of King Henry VIII immediately after his education at Cambridge, Wyatt promoted English interests on missions to France, Venice, Rome, Spain, and the Low Countries. His career was to prove more precarious at home, where he became involved in court politics. He was deeply attached to the Lady Anne Boleyn, who, by 1527, was the object of Henry's affections and a probable pretext for the King's divorce from Catherine of Aragon and England's break from the Roman Catholic Church. Made Henry's queen in 1533, but out of favor by 1536, Anne implicated by association those who were supposed to have been her lovers. Wyatt, who according to several contemporary accounts, admitted to the King that the Queen had been his mistress, was lucky to suffer no more than imprisonment; the Queen's other favorites were executed. Wyatt subsequently regained political status both at home and abroad, although not without periods of disappointment: His verse letter *Mine Own John Poyns* praises the security of a country life away from London and its intrigues. Wyatt's most protracted mission was from 1537 to 1539, as the King's ambassador to the court of the Holy Roman Emperor in Spain: he tells of his anticipated return to England in the hauntingly brief lyric *Tagus, Farewell*. Despite the execution of his powerful patron, Sir Thomas Cromwell, and a second prison term in 1541 for suspected treason, Wyatt obtained Henry's goodwill at the end of his short life. He died from a fever at the age of thirty-nine while on a diplomatic mission for the king.

By any poetic reckoning, Wyatt is to be valued as a pioneer of English verse. Although many of his poems exhibit irregular meters, they have been praised for their remarkable texture and sense of surprise. His translations of Francesco Petrarch's sonnets established the principal forms of English lyric, the rhyming sonnet with its pentameter line and the more loosely configured song derived from the Italian *canzone*. Wyatt's own poems change the spirit of their Petrarchan themes by giving erotic subjects a satirical and even bitter twist and political topics an inward and personal reference. In one of his best-known sonnets, *Whoso List to Hunt*, he writes of vainly pursuing a "hind" or "deer" (a dear or beloved lady) belonging to "Caesar" (King Henry VIII). Long understood to be a reference to Anne Boleyn, Wyatt's "deer" is quite a different figure than the "deer" in his source, Petrarch's sonnet to a "white doe," who represents his lady, Laura, whom he met in 1327 and loved from a distance until her death in 1350. While Petrarch's lady is imagined as chastely devoted to a heavenly Caesar or God, and therefore as inspiring a religious awe, Wyatt's beloved is the possession of an earthly Caesar, King Henry VIII, and is thus the cause of his immediate frustration.

Wyatt's verse was circulated in manuscript during his lifetime and probably read only by his friends and his acquaintances at court. A few poems were published in 1540, in a collection entitled *The Court of Venus*, but the majority—ninety-seven poems in all—appeared in 1557, in a massive anthology called *Songs and Sonnets*, published by the printer Richard Tottel. This volume, which includes poems by Henry Howard, Earl of Surrey and others, was a milestone in the history of literature. Unlike the earlier sixteenth-century poetry of the British Isles, which remained relatively simple in its genres and diction, *Tottel's Miscellany* (as it has come to be known) exhibited a range of new forms and meters: the sonnet, the song (or *canzone*), the epigram, and rhyming and blank verse. Familiar to writers and readers of Italian and French, these forms allowed poets (now writing a recognizably modern English) to develop a stylistic flexibility and thematic richness previously achieved only by the Middle English poet Geoffrey Chaucer. Before presenting his anthology to the public, however, Tottel did some fairly drastic editing: smoothing out metrical irregularities by adding, subtracting, or changing words, he obviously sought to impress readers with what he judged to be the elegant and up-to-date styles represented by the works in his collection. The poems reprinted here are based not on the *Songs and Sonnets* but on Wyatt's original texts.

They Flee from Me

They flee from me that sometime did me seek
With naked foot stalking in my chamber.
I have seen them gentle tame and meek
That now are wild and do not remember
5   That sometime they put themself in danger
To take bread at my hand; and now they range
Busily seeking with a continual change.
Thanked be fortune, it hath been otherwise
Twenty times better; but once in special,
10   In thine array after a pleasant guise,°   *manner, disguise*
When her loose gown from her shoulders did fall,
And she me caught in her arms long and small;
Therewithal sweetly did me kiss,
And softly said, "dear heart, how like you this?"

15   It was no dream: I lay broad waking.
      But all is turned through my gentleness
      Into a strange fashion of forsaking;
      And I have leave to go of her goodness,
      And she also to use new fangledness.
20   But since that I so kindly am served,
      I would fain° know what she hath deserved.   *wish to*

My Lute, Awake!

      My lute, awake! perform the last
      Labor that thou and I shall waste
          And end that I have now begun,
      For when this song is sung and past,
5   My lute be still, for I have done.

      As to be heard where ere is none,°   *there is no one*
      As lead to grave in marble stone,
          My song may pierce her heart as sone;°   *soon*
      Should we then sigh, or sing, or moan?
10   No, no, my lute, for I have done.

      The rocks do not so cruelly
      Repulse the waves continually,
          As she my suit and affection,
      So that I am past remedy,
15   Whereby my lute and I have done.

      Proud of the spoil that thou hast got
      Of simple hearts through love's shot,
          By whom, unkind, thou has them won,
      Think not he hath his bow forgot,
20   Although my lute and I have done.

      Vengeance shall fall on thy disdain,
      That makest but game on earnest pain;
          Think not alone under the sun
      Unquit° to cause thy lover's plain,°   *freely / lament*
25   Although my lute and I have done.

      Perchance thee lie weathered and old,
      The winter nights that are so cold,
          Plaining in vain unto the mone;°   *moon*
      Thy wishes then dare not be told,
30   Care then who list,° for I have done.   *wishes*

      And then may chance thee to repent
      The time that thou hast lost and spent
          To cause thy lover's sigh and swoon;
      Then shalt thou know beauty but lent
35   And wish and want as I have done.

Now cease, my lute, this is the last
Labor that thou and I shall wast,°   *waste*
   And ended is that we begun;
Now is this song both sung and past,
40 My lute be still, for I have done.

Tagus, Farewell

Tagus,[1] farewell, that westward with thy streams
Turns up the grains of gold already tried:
With spur and sail for I go seek the Thames,
Gainward° the sun that showeth her wealthy pride;   *toward*
5 And to the town which Brutus[2] sought by dreams
Like bended moon doth lend her lusty side.
My King,° my country, alone for whom I live,   *Henry VIII*
Of mighty love the wings for this me give.

Forget Not Yet

Forget not yet the tried° intent   *proven*
Of such a truth as I have meant,
My great travail° so gladly spent   *effort*
   Forget not yet.

5 Forget not yet when first began
The weary life ye know since whan,°   *when*
The suit, the service none tell can,
   Forget not yet.

Forget not yet the great assays,°   *trials*
10 The cruel wrong, the scornful ways,
The painful patience in denays,°   *denials*
   Forget not yet.

Forget not yet, forget not this,
How long ago hath been and is
15 The mind that never meant amiss,
   Forget not yet.

Forget not then thine own aprovyd,[1]
The which so long hath thee so lovyd,
Whose steadfast faith yet never movyd,
20   Forget not this.

Blame Not My Lute

Blame not my lute for he must sound
   Of this or that as liketh me,
For lack of wit the lute is bound

---

1. The Tagus, or Tajo, River is the longest on the Iberian peninsula and empties into the Atlantic at Portugal. Wyatt was sent to Spain as a diplomat but returned to England in 1539.

2. The legendary Trojan hero Brutus was supposed to have settled the British Isles and founded London, to which he was led by a series of dreams sent to him by the goddess Diana.
1. The poet himself, her "approved" lover.

    To give such tunes as pleaseth me:
5   Though my songs be somewhat strange,
    And speaks such words as touch thy change,[1]
        Blame not my lute.

    My lute, alas, doth not offend,
      Though that perforce he must agree
10   To sound such tunes as I intend
      To sing to them that heareth me;
    Then though my songs be somewhat plain,
    And toucheth some that used to fain,[2]
        Blame not my lute.

15   My lute and strings may not deny,
      But as I strike they must obey;
    Break not them then so wrongfully,
      But wreak° thyself some wiser way: *revenge*
    And though the songs which I endite°   *write*
20   Do quit° thy change with rightful spite,   *discharge, answer*
        Blame not my lute.

    Spite asketh spite and changing change,
      And falsed° faith must needs be known;   *betrayed*
    The fault so great, the case so strange,
25   Of right it must abroad be blown:
    Then since that by thine own desart°   *desert*
    My songs do tell how true thou art,
        Blame not my lute.

    Blame but thyself that hast misdone
30   And well deserved to have blame;
    Change thou thy way, so evil begun,
      And then my lute shall sound that same:
    But if till then my fingers play
    By thy desart their wonted way,
35   Blame not my lute.

    Farewell, unknown, for though thou break
      My strings in spite with great disdain,
    Yet have I found out for thy sake
      Strings for to string my lute again;
40   And if perchance this folys° rhyme   *foolish*
    Do make thee blush at any time,
        Blame not my lute.

Lucks, My Fair Falcon, and Your Fellows All

Lucks, my fair falcon, and your fellows all,
How well pleasant it were your liberty!
Ye not forsake me that fair might ye befall.[1]

---

1. I.e., the lady's change of heart, probably also to be signified by a change of tone in the music to which this lyric
was supposedly set.
2. Who used to be desirous or who used to feign desire.

1. I.e., "You do not forsake me so that good luck may
come your way." Wyatt states that despite the falcon's
name, which suggests that he seeks good fortune, Lucks is
loyal to his master.

But they that sometime liked my company,
5   Like lice away from dead bodies they crawl:
Lo, what a proof in light adversity![2]
But ye my birds I swear by all your bells,
Ye be my friends, and so be but few else.

Stand Whoso List

Stand whoso list° upon the slipper° top   *wishes / slippery*
Of courts' estates, and let me here rejoice;
And use me° quiet without let° or stop,   *my / hindrance*
Unknown in court, that hath such brackish joys:
5   In hidden place, so let my days forth pass,
That when my years be done, withouten noise,
I may die aged after the common trace.[1]
For him death greep' the° right hard by the crop°   *grips / throat*
That is much known of other; and of himself alas,
10   Doth die unknown, dazed with dreadful face.

Mine Own John Poyns

Mine own John Poyns,[1] since ye delight to know
    The cause why that homeward I me draw,
    And flee the press of courts[2] where so they° go,   *courtiers*
Rather then to live thrall° under the awe   *enslaved*
5   Of lordly looks, wrapped within my cloak,
    To will and lust learning to set a law;
It is not for because I scorn or mock
    The power of them to whom fortune hath lent
    Charge over us, of right, to strike the stroke.
10   But true it is that I have always meant
    Less to esteem them than the common sort
    Of outward things that judge in their intent
Without regard what doth inward resort.
    I grant sometime that of glory the fire
15   Doth touch my heart: me list° not to report   *I wish*
Blame by honor and honor to desire.
    But how may I this honor now attain
    That cannot dye the color black a liar?[3]
My Poyns, I cannot frame my tongue to feign,
20   To cloak the truth for praise, without desert,
    Of them that list all vice for to retain.[4]

2. Wyatt may have written this poem during one of his imprisonments; in any event, he complains here that in prison only his falcons visit and befriend him. Falcons wore bells on their legs to let their masters know where they were.
1. In the common or usual manner; from age and sickness rather than murder. Wyatt alludes to the perilous existence of a man in public life.
1. John Poyns, or Poynz, a friend of Wyatt, spent time at court in the 1520s.
2. Here Wyatt's posing as a retired courtier critical of the court may illustrate his attitude during one of the periods in which he was out of favor with Henry VIII. He had extensive holdings in Kent, to which he could retire and from which he was elected to Parliament shortly before his death.
3. I.e., who cannot change (dye) black another color and hence call black a liar.

I cannot honor them that sets their part
    With Venus and Bacchus[5] all their life long;
    Nor hold my piece of them although I smart.
25   I cannot crouch nor kneel nor do so great a wrong,
    To worship them like God on earth alone,
    That are as wolves these sely° lambs among.   *innocent*
I cannot with my words complain and moan
    And suffer nought, nor smart without complaint,
30   Nor turn the word that from my mouth is gone.
I cannot speak and look like a saint,
    Use wiles for wit and make deceit a pleasure,
    And call craft counsel, for profit still to paint.[6]
I cannot wrest the law to fill the coffer,
35   With innocent blood to feed myself fat,
    And do most hurt where most help I offer.
I am not he that can allow the state
    Of high Caesar and damn Cato to die,[7]
    That with his death did scape out of the gate
40   From Caesar's hands, if Livy do not lie,
    And would not live where liberty was lost:
    So did his heart the common weal° apply.°   *state / value*
I am not he such eloquence to boast,
    To make the crow singing as the swan,
45   Nor call the lion of coward beasts the most
That cannot take a mouse as the cat can:
    And he that dieth for hunger of the gold
    Call him Alessaundre;[8] and say that Pan
Passeth Apollo in music manifold;°   *many times*
50   Praise Sir Thopas[9] for a noble tale,
    And scorn the story that the knight told.
Praise him for counsel that is drunk of ale;
    Grin when he laugheth that beareth all the sway,
    Frown when he frowneth and groan when he is pale;
55   On others lust to hang both night and day:
    None of these points would ever frame in me;
    My wit is nought, I cannot learn the way.
And much the less of things that greater be,
    That asken help of colors of device°   *kinds of deception*
60   To join the mean with each extremity,

4. I.e., to lie by praising those who wish to retain vicious ways and therefore do not deserve praise.

5. Venus: the goddess of love; Bacchus: the god of wine (also known as Dionysius). Together they represented lust and excess.

6. I.e., to represent a falsehood as the truth for profit.

7. I.e., I cannot condone the rule of Caesar and damn Cato. Livy: a Roman historian of the republican period; he records the story of Cato of Utica, who opposed the tyrannical impulses of Julius Caesar and committed suicide rather than live under tyranny.

8. I.e., flatter as Alexander the Great a man so greedy for gold that he dies of hunger. Wyatt continues to list the flattery he cannot give: Pan—half-man, half-goat—was god of shepherds and famous for his music on his reed pipe, but the undisputed god of music was Apollo.

9. *The Tale of Sir Thopas*, one of Chaucer's *Canterbury Tales*, was composed to illustrate how not to tell a story; *The Knight's Tale*, by contrast, exemplified the high style of poetic narrative.

With the nearest virtue to cloak alway the vice:
    And as to purpose likewise it shall fall,[1]
    To press° the virtue that it may not rise;   *suppress*
As drunkenness good fellowship to call;
65   The friendly foe with his double face
    Say he is gentle and courteous therewithal;
And say that Favel° hath a goodly grace   *Flattery, a character*
    In eloquence, and cruelty to name
    Zeal of justice and change in time and place;
70   And he that suffereth offence without blame
    Call him pitiful; and him true and plain
    That raileth reckless° to every man's shame.   *carelessly criticizes*
Say he is rude that cannot lie and feign,
    The lecher a lover, and tyranny
75   To be the right of a prince's reign.
I cannot, I. No, no, it will not be.
    This is the cause that I could never yet
    Hang on their sleeves that weigh as thou mayst see
A chip of chance more than a pound of wit.[2]
80   This maketh me at home to hunt and to hawk
    And in foul weather at my book to sit.
In frost and snow then with my bow to stalk;
    No man doth mark whereso I ride or go;
    In lusty lees° at liberty I walk,   *meadows*
85   And of these news I feel nor weal° nor woe,   *happiness*
    Sauf° that a clog doth hang yet at my heel: *except*
    No force for that, for it is ordered so
That I may leap both hedge and dike full well.
    I am not now in France to judge the wine,
90   With saffry° sauce the delicates to feel;   *saffron*
Nor yet in Spain where one must him incline
    Rather than to be, outwardly to seem.
    I meddle not with wits that be so fine,
Nor Flanders' cheer[3] letteth° not my sight to deem°   *hinders / judge*
95   Of black and white, nor taketh my wit away
    With beastliness, they beasts do so esteem;[4]
Nor I am not where Christ is given in prey°   *in exchange*
    For money, poison and treason at Rome,
    A common practice used night and day:
100   But here I am in Kent and Christendom
    Among the muses where I read and rhyme;
    Where if thou list, my Poyns, for to come,
Thou shalt be judge how I do spend my time.

---

1. Also, when occasion permits.
2. I.e., follow those who value a little good fortune more than a lot of intelligence.
3. The Flemish were reputed to love drinking.
4. The Flemish esteem beasts, i.e., drunks.

Henry Howard, Earl of Surrey

1517?–1547

To belong to a rich and powerful family was no guarantee of a secure and prosperous life. Henry Howard, son of the Duke of Norfolk, was one of the most gifted young men in the court of King Henry VIII, yet he was embroiled in factionalism from a very early age. As a boy, he was the companion of Henry Fitzroy, Duke of Richmond, the king's illegitimate son. They spent a year together as guests of the King of France and, after their return to England, continued their friendship at Windsor Castle. After Richmond's death in 1536, Surrey apparently ran afoul of the law and found himself again at Windsor Castle, this time as the king's prisoner. Playing up the irony of his situation in *So Cruel Prison*, he memorializes Windsor, formerly a "place of bliss" but now the site of his sorrow at the loss of his freedom and the greater loss of his friend. Surrey was imprisoned again five years later in London, ostensibly for breaking windows. This punishment occasioned a satire, *London, Thou Hast Accused Me*, on the real corruption in the city. At twenty-seven, Surrey took part in the war against the French, was wounded, and a year later, was made commander of Boulogne. But he fell from favor when he opposed his sister's marriage to the brother of his rival, Edward Seymour, Lord Hertford, and denounced Seymour as guardian of Prince Edward, Henry's heir. Angered beyond all reconciliation, Henry had Surrey tried and executed for treason in 1547.

As a poet, Surrey is often coupled with Wyatt, who was actually a generation older. Many of his poems (like Wyatt's) emulated Petrarchan forms, themes, and imagery and were published initially by Richard Tottel in 1557 in a volume entitled *Songs and Sonnets*. But Surrey's own accomplishments were unique. He perfected English blank or unrhymed verse, characterized by the pentameter or five-stress line, and he was the likely inventor of the form that became the standard for the English sonnet: three quatrains followed by a couplet, rhyming *ababcdcdefefgg*. Some of his poems on social subjects adopt a satirical tone and convey his vigorous rejection of contemporary manners and morals.

So Cruel Prison

So cruel prison, how could betide,° alas,   *it happen*
As proud Windsor,[1] where I in lust and joy
With a king's son my childish years did pass,
In greater feast than Priam's sons of Troy;[2]

5 Where° each sweet place returns a taste full sour.   *that*
The large green courts, where we were wont to hove,°   *accustomed to linger*
With eyes cast up unto the maidens' tower,
And easy sighs, such as folk draw in love.

The stately sales,° the ladies bright of hue,   *halls*
10 The dances short, long tales of great delight,
With words and looks that tigers could but rue,
Where each of us did plead the other's right.

---

1. Surrey was imprisoned in Windsor Castle in 1537. In this poem, his distress at his imprisonment is augmented by his memories of Henry Fitzroy, the Earl of Richmond and bastard son of Henry VIII, with whom he spent time at Windsor when they were young. Richmond married Surrey's sister in 1533; he died in 1536.
2. Priam, King of Troy, was defeated by the Greeks in the Trojan War.

The palm play,[3] where, despoiled for the game,
With dazed eyes oft we by gleams of love
15   Have missed the ball and got sight of our dame
To bait her eyes which kept the leads° above.   roofs

The graveled ground,° with sleeves tied on the helm,[4]   jousting arena
On foaming horse, with swords and friendly hearts,
With cheer,° as° though the one should overwhelm,   joyfully / even
20   Where we have fought and chased oft with darts.

With silver drops the meads yet spread for ruth,°   pity
In active games of nimbleness and strength
Where we did strain, trailed by swarms of youth,
Our tender limbs, that yet shot up in length.

25   The secret groves, which oft we made resound
Of pleasant plaint° and of our ladies' praise,   complaint
Recording soft what grace each one had found,
What hope of speed, what dread of long delays.

The wild forest, the clothed holts° with green,   woods
30   With reins avaled° and swift ybreathed° horse,   slackened / panting
With cry of hounds and merry blasts between,
Where we did chase the fearful hart a force.°   ran it down

The void° walls eke, that harbored us each night;   empty
Wherewith, alas, revive within my breast
35   The sweet accord, such sleeps as yet delight,
The pleasant dreams, the quiet bed of rest,

The secret thoughts imparted with such trust,
The wanton talk, the divers change of play,
The friendship sworn, each promise kept so just,
40   Wherewith we passed the winter nights away.

And with this thought the blood forsakes my face,
The tears berain my cheeks of deadly hue;
The which, as soon as sobbing sighs, alas,
Upsupped° have, thus I my plaint renew: absorbed

45   O place of bliss! renewer of my woes!
Give me accompt where is my noble fere,°   companion
Whom in thy walls thou didst each night enclose,
To other lief,° but unto me most dear.   dear

Each wall, alas, that doth my sorrow rue,
50   Returns thereto a hollow sound of plaint.
Thus I, alone, where all my freedom grew,
In prison pine with bondage and restraint,

3. Surrey refers to court tennis, a game resembling modern tennis but played against the walls of a court; he remembers that as players, he and Fitzroy watched the
ladies who followed the game from the "leads," sheets of
metal used to cover roofs.
4. When jousting, a man would tie the sleeve of a lady's
garment to his helmet as a sign of her favor.

And with remembrance of the greater grief,
To banish the less, I find my chief relief.

London, Hast Thou Accused Me

London, hast thou accused me
Of breach of laws, the root of strife?[1]
Within whose breast did boil to see,
(So fervent hot) thy dissolute life,
5   That even the hate of sins, that grow
Within thy wicked walls so rife,
For to break forth did convert° so   *convert me*
That terror could it not repress.
The which, by words, since preachers know
10   What hope is left for to redress,
By unknown means it liked me
My hidden burden to express,
Whereby it might appear to thee
That secret sin hath secret spite;
15   From Justice° rod no fault is free;   *Justice's*
But that all such as works unright
In most quiet are next ill rest.[2]
In secret silence of the night
This made me, with a reckless breast,
20   To wake thy sluggards with my bow;
A figure of the Lord's behest,[3]
Whose scourge for sin the scriptures show.
That, as the fearful thunder clap
By sudden flame at hand we know,
25   Of pebble stones the soundless rap,
The dreadful plage° might make thee see   *shore*
Of God's wrath, that doth thee enwrap;[4]
That pride might know, from conscience free,
How lofty works may her defend;[5]
30   And envy find, as he hath sought,
How other seek him to offend;
And wrath taste of each cruel thought
The just shapp hire in the end;[6]
And idle sloth, that never wrought,
35   To heaven his spirit lift° may begin;   *to lift*
And greedy lucre live in dread

1. Surrey was accused of breaking windows with his bow in the city of London in 1543. He states that he was moved to this action by his hatred of the dissolute life within the city (line 4) and that he was responding to an idea of Justice (line 15).
2. I.e., all those who act wrongly, if they are resting quietly, are nearest to being disturbed.
3. Surrey imagines that he is like a prophet who does the Lord's command (cf. Isaiah 47.11).
4. The phrase is obscure: "just as we know lightening by thunder, so the soundless rap of pebble stones might make you see the dreadful shore of God's wrath that surrounds you."
5. Surrey becomes ironic: "Pride, free from conscience, might know how lofty works may defend her"—i.e., important or prodigious works do not defend from punishment the proud, who are (by definition) without a conscience.
6. I.e., wrath receives, for each of its cruel thoughts, the justly shaped or appointed hire or payment in the end.

To see what hate ill-got goods win;
The lechers, ye that lusts do feed,
Perceive what secrecy is in sin;
40   And gluttons' hearts for sorrow bleed,
Awaked when their fault they find.
In loathsome vice, each drunken wight°   *man*
To stir to God, this was my mind.
Thy windows had done me no spite;
45   But proud people that dread no fall,
Clothed with falsehed° and unright   *falsehood*
Bred in the closures of thy wall,
But wrested to wrath in fervent zeal
Thou hast to strife my secret call.[7]
50   Endured° hearts no warning feel.   *hardened*
Oh shameless whore! is dread then gone
By such thy foes as meant thy weal?[8]
Oh member of false Babylon!
The shop of craft! the den of ire!
55   Thy dreadful dome° draws fast upon;   *judgment*
Thy martyrs' blood, by sword and fire,
In heaven and earth for Justice call.
The Lord shall hear their just desire;
The flame of wrath shall on thee fall;
60   With famine and pest lamentably
Stricken shall be thy lechers all;
Thy proud towers and turrets high,
Enemies to God, beat° stone from stone;   *beaten*
Thine idols burnt that wrought iniquity.
65   When none thy ruin shall bemoan,
But render unto the right wise Lord,
That so hath judged Babylon,
Immortal praise with one accord.

Wyatt Resteth Here

Wyatt resteth here, that quick° could never rest;[1]   *alive*
Whose heavenly gifts increased by disdain
And virtue sank the deeper in his breast:
Such profit he of envy could obtain.

5   A head, where wisdom mysteries did frame;
Whose hammers beat still in that lively brain
As on a stith,° where some work of fame   *anvil*
Was daily wrought, to turn to Britain's gain.

A visage, stern and mild; where both did grow,
10   Vice to condemn, in virtues to rejoice;

---

7. I.e., you have heard my secret call to strife or struggle.
8. Surrey addresses London as the whore of Babylon, the epitome of iniquity, and asks ironically, "Do you no

longer fear those enemies that intend your happiness?"
1. This elegy for the poet Thomas Wyatt was published in 1542, shortly after his death.

Amid great storms whom grace assured so
To live upright and smile at fortune's choice.

A hand that taught what might be said in rhyme;
That reft° Chaucer the glory of his wit;   *took from*
15   A mark the which (unperfited, for time)[2]—
Some may approach, but never none shall hit.

A tongue that served in foreign realms his king;
Whose courteous talk to virtue did enflame
Each noble heart, a worthy guide to bring
20   Our English youth, by travail[3] unto fame.

An eye whose judgment no affect° could blind,   *feeling*
Friends to allure, and foes to reconcile;
Whose piercing look did represent a mind
With virtue fraught, reposed, void of guile.

25   A heart where dread yet never so impressed
To hide the thought that might the truth avaunce;°   *advance*
In neither fortune lift, nor so repressed,[4]
To swell in wealth, or yield unto mischance.

A valiant corps,° where force and beauty met,   *body*
30   Happy, alas! too happy, but for foes,
Lived, and ran the race that nature set;
Of manhood's shape, where she the mold did lose.

But to the heavens that simple soul is fled;
Which left with such, as covet° Christ to know   *desire*
35   Witness to faith that never shall be dead:
Sent for our wealth, but not received so.

Thus, for our guilt, this jewel have we lost;
The earth his bones, the heavens possess his ghost.
Amen.

My Radcliffe, When Thy Reckless Youth Offends

My Radcliffe,[1] when thy reckless youth offends:
Receive thy scourge by others' chastisement.
For such calling, when it works none° amends: *no*
Then plagues are sent without advertisement.
5   Yet Salomon[2] said, the wronged shall recure:°   *recover*
But Wyatt said true, the scar doth aye endure.

---

2. I.e., was left unperfected for lack of time.
3. Work, but also travel, in that Surrey describes Wyatt as a "guide."
4. I.e., neither raised up by fortune to get rich, nor so depressed (by ill fortune) as to yield to a temptation that will lead to misfortune.

1. This epigram is probably addressed to Thomas Radcliffe, third Earl of Essex.
2. Surrey concludes by contrasting an optimistic sentence of King Solomon, which he probably associated with the book of Ecclesiasticus, with the dour reflection of Wyatt.

Sir Thomas More
1477?–1535

Sir Thomas More.

After fifteen years of loyal and distinguished service as a government minister and, finally, Lord Chancellor, Sir Thomas More refused to do the King's bidding. He declined to take the Oath of Allegiance that Henry VIII required of all his subjects, a token of their repudiation of the Pope and recognition of the king as "Defender of the Faith" in England. More's stubborn fidelity to the only church he had ever known drove Henry to extreme measures. He ordered More to the Tower of London and, a year later, had him executed for treason. More may not have been surprised by the decision; he once observed that "If my head should win [Henry] a castle in France, it should not fail to go." It is reported that More's parboiled severed head was fastened to a pole on London Bridge for all to see. By displaying this pathetic remnant of the most conspicuously brilliant man in England, Henry signaled his iron determination to control not only the religious destiny of his kingdom but also its intellectual life.

More's beginnings were auspicious. The son of Agnes and John More, a barrister, he was sent to be a page in the household of Thomas Morton, Archbishop of Canterbury and Lord Chancellor, and then to Oxford, where he met John Colet (1467?–1519), who became, in More's words, "the director of my life." Colet was in many respects a paradoxical source of inspiration for More. A schoolmaster and later a university don, Colet was identified with the scholarship of a Christian humanism that had as its purpose a return to the practices of the primitive and apostolic church. More would end his life professing the authority of the Pope and affirming the Catholic faith as the only true way to salvation.

More was called to the bar and, in 1504, was elected to Parliament. Married that year to Jane Colte and soon the father of four, More organized his household in Chelsea as a center of intellectual activity; there his guests included Desiderius Erasmus and even the King himself. In 1526 the painter Holbein began the first of several visits; his portrait of Thomas More surrounded by numerous family members, including More's gifted daughter Margaret, testifies to the highly conscientious civility that More cultivated in domestic life.

Busy with state and diplomatic affairs from 1504 on, More was knighted and made subtreasurer to the king in 1521. As Lord Chancellor from 1529 to 1532, More was known for his wit, his judicial acumen, and his deft treatment of parties to a case. A popular jingle suggests how swiftly he saw justice done:

> When More some time had Chancellor been,
> No more suits did remain;
> The like will never more be seen,
> Till More be there again.

Perhaps More's dispatch in matters of law gave him some leisure for literature. In any case, his talent as a writer was obvious in his first works: Latin translations of Lucian's dialogues, the *Life of Johan Picus, Earl of Mirandula*, *Utopia* (in Latin), and the *History of Richard III*. Later works reflect the passion for religious orthodoxy that drove him to oppose reforms proposed by Luther, Calvin, and their followers. In 1528 he published *A Dialogue of Sir Thomas More* against the opinions of the English reformer William Tyndale, whose "Englishing" of the

Bible had resolved many of its readers to espouse the new faith. *Supplication of Souls* and *The Confutation of Tyndale's Answer*—similarly directed against the reformation—appeared in 1529 and 1532. More's religious enthusiasm was also expressed in punitive action against those he decided were enemies of the church. John Foxe, whose *Acts and Monuments of These Latter Perilous Days* chronicles the persecution of Christians from the earliest days of the church to his present moment, described More as "blinded in the zeal of popery to all humane considerations." Blinded More was not, however, when he cast an eye to the future. Foreseeing the consequences of Henry's divorce from Catherine of Aragon and his intention to marry again, More resigned his chancellorship in 1532, the year that Parliament published the *Supplication Against the Ordinaries*, a list of grievances against the Catholic Church, and the English church accepted the king as its head. More wrote two more works, the first while still a free (although suspect) man and the second as the King's prisoner: *The Apology of Sir Thomas More* (1533) denounces the reformation, and *A Dialogue of Comfort Against Tribulation* (1533) testifies to the courage that faith could instill in a man who, once possessed of great authority and power, finally found himself in desperate circumstances.

UTOPIA   When More published his account of a hitherto unknown island republic in 1516, Europeans were still largely ignorant of the world beyond their continent. The exploration that would open up so much of the globe was just getting underway, and accounts of voyages to places hardly dreamed of were yet to constitute a literary genre. What travel writing there was catered to readers who loved reports of "marvels" and had no clear appreciation for what later centuries would call a "fact." Sir John Mandeville, whose still-popular account of his travels was first circulated in 1356, described the peoples, customs, and wild life of lands in the East in utterly fantastic terms. But when More called his newly discovered land *Utopia,* literally "nowhere" in Greek, he did so only half in fun. Although his island republic was clearly a figment of More's imagination, the political order that he gave it challenged many of the ideals and practices of contemporary monarchies in Europe, especially in England. His *Utopia* is therefore deceptive: apparently a report of a new people and their society, it was also a critique of the habits of thought and the government that had sustained European and English society for centuries. More composed this work, in Latin, between late September 1515 and September 3, 1516, when he sent it to Erasmus, who helped arrange for the book's first publication in Holland; the first English translation, by Ralph Robinson, appeared in 1551. *Utopia's* text reflects the international scope of its own production. In fact, More the author did, like "More" the character, visit Peter Giles in Antwerp while on a diplomatic mission; and John Clement was More's "pupil-servant"—a tutor to his children and eventually one of the king's physicians.

The second book of *Utopia,* written before the first, describes a government in which administrative and legal authority rotates among the elders of the society, a society in which all property is common, and a culture supported by citizens who have identical tastes, aspirations, and outlooks on life. In the words of the aged philosopher and world traveler, a character More names Hythlodaeus (literally "learned in nonsense"), Utopian society is populated entirely by rational beings. Each citizen is trained in a trade, is guaranteed employment, and will get what he or she needs from cradle to grave. The economy is one in which exchange is by barter, not money; clothing is uniform; education and medical care are free to everyone; and defense is conducted by foreigners whom the Utopians hire to protect them. Utopians who protest or rebel against these policies and practices are seen as unreasonable. The first book, evidently an afterthought, establishes a perspective by which to view the extraordinary claims of the second; it shows why Hythlodaeus can be considered an idealistic dreamer as well as an acute critic. Here More prefaces the praise he will have Hythlodaeus give Utopian society by having the philosopher point out the social ills of contemporary England. Refusing to compromise the ideals he says were practiced in Utopia, Hythlodaeus maintains that he must withdraw from societies like those in England and Europe because he can do them no good. His critique of governments is supported by his denunciation of enclosures and capital punishment for minor felonies, and of kings and magistrates who are driven by greed and a lust for power.

More's account of Utopia, as reported by his character Hythlodaeus, has convinced some readers that he meant his treatise to be taken as a model for the future. Others have given more weight to its elaborate framing as a report from "nowhere" and have seen it rather as a satire on the idea of a wholly rational society. Whatever balance the reader finds in More's brilliant distinctions, his images of an ideal and imaginary society find analogues in those later represented by Jonathan Swift in *Gulliver's Travels*, Samuel Butler in *Erewhon*, and William Morris in *News from Nowhere*. By contrast, George Orwell's *1984* represents the dark side of the "Utopian" state: its absolute repression of individualism.

Presented in the Response section that follows *Utopia* is a selection from Sir Francis Bacon's *The New Atlantis* (c. 1623, published 1626), a witty response to *Utopia*, which shows a scientific community working on a remote island. Bacon shows an open-minded and egalitarian society at work, establishing control over nature and exploiting the world's resources in a useful way.

Utopia[1]
The Best State of a Commonwealth and the New Island Of Utopia

A Truly Golden Handbook, No Less Beneficial Than Entertaining, by the Distinguished and Eloquent Author
THOMAS MORE
Citizen and Sheriff of the Famous City of London

Thomas More to Peter Giles,[2] Greetings.

I am almost ashamed, my dear Peter Giles, to send you this little book about the state of Utopia after almost a year, when I am sure you looked for it within a month and a half. Certainly you know that I was relieved of all the labor of gathering materials for the work and that I had to give no thought at all to their arrangement. I had only to repeat what in your company I heard Raphael[3] relate. Hence there was no reason for me to take trouble about the style of the narrative, seeing that his language could not be polished. It was, first of all, hurried and impromptu and, secondly, the product of a person who, as you know, was not so well acquainted with Latin as with Greek. Therefore the nearer my style came to his careless simplicity the closer it would be to the truth, for which alone I am bound to care under the circumstances and actually do care.

I confess, my dear Peter, that all these preparations relieved me of so much trouble that scarcely anything remained for me to do. Otherwise the gathering or the arrangement of the materials could have required a good deal of both time and application even from a talent neither the meanest nor the most ignorant. If it had been required that the matter be written down not only accurately but eloquently, I could not have performed the task with any amount of time or application. But, as it was, those cares over which I should have had to perspire so hard had been removed. Since it remained for me only to write out simply what I had heard, there was no difficulty about it.

---

1. Translated by C. G. Richards, rev. Edward Surtz, S.J.
2. More was made undersheriff of London in 1510, sitting as judge and representing the sheriff's cases in the city court. His friend Peter Giles (c. 1486–1533) was a classi-

cal scholar, a member of Erasmus's circle, and city clerk of Antwerp, where he oversaw commercial business.
3. Raphael Hythlodaeus, the fictional traveler who tells the character Sir Thomas More about Utopia.

Yet even to carry through this trifling task, my other tasks left me practically no leisure at all. I am constantly engaged in legal business, either pleading or hearing, either giving an award as arbiter or deciding a case as judge. I pay a visit of courtesy to one man and go on business to another. I devote almost the whole day in public to other men's affairs and the remainder to my own. I leave to myself, that is to learning, nothing at all.

When I have returned home, I must talk with my wife, chat with my children, and confer with my servants. All this activity I count as business when it must be done—and it must be unless you want to be a stranger in your own home. Besides, one must take care to be as agreeable as possible to those whom nature has supplied, or chance has made, or you yourself have chosen, to be the companions of your life, provided you do not spoil them by kindness, or through indulgence make masters out of your servants.

Amid these occupations that I have named, the day, the month, the year slip away. When, then, can we find time to write? Nor have I spoken a word about sleep, nor even of food, which for many people takes up as much time as sleep—and sleep takes up almost half a man's life! So I get for myself only the time I filch from sleep and food. Slowly, therefore, because this time is but little, yet finally, because this time is something, I have finished Utopia and sent it to you, my dear Peter, to read— and to remind me of anything that has escaped me.

In this respect I do not entirely distrust myself. (I only wish I were as good in intelligence and learning as I am not altogether deficient in memory!) Nevertheless, I am not so confident as to believe that I have forgotten nothing. As you know, John Clement,[4] my pupil-servant, was also present at the conversation. Indeed I do not allow him to absent himself from any talk which can be somewhat profitable, for from this young plant, seeing that it has begun to put forth green shoots in Greek and Latin literature, I expect no mean harvest some day. He has caused me to feel very doubtful on one point.

According to my own recollection, Hythlodaeus[5] declared that the bridge which spans the river Anydrus at Amaurotum is five hundred paces in length. But my John says that two hundred must be taken off, for the river there is not more than three hundred paces in breadth. Please recall the matter to mind. If you agree with him, I shall adopt the same view and think myself mistaken. If you do not remember, I shall put down, as I have actually done, what I myself seem to remember. Just as I shall take great pains to have nothing incorrect in the book, so, if there is doubt about anything, I shall rather tell an objective falsehood than an intentional lie—or I would rather be honest than wise.

Nevertheless, it would be easy for you to remedy this defect if you ask Raphael himself by word of mouth or by letter. You must do so on account of another doubt which has cropped up, whether more through my fault or through yours or Raphael's I do not know. We forgot to ask, and he forgot to say, in what part of the new world Utopia lies. I am sorry that point was omitted, and I would be willing to pay a considerable sum to purchase that information, partly because I am rather ashamed to be ignorant in what sea lies the island of which I am saying so much, partly because there are several among us, and one in particular, a devout man and a theologian by profession, burning with an extraordinary desire to visit Utopia. He does so not from an

4. John Clement (d. 1572), who tutored More's children, was also a distinguished humanist: a Reader at Oxford; coeditor of the first Greek edition of Galen (c. 130–200), a celebrated physician whose works on medicine remained authoritative through the early modern period; and physician to Henry VIII.

5. This reference introduces the play on Greek words that will characterize the description of Utopia in Book 2. Hythlodaeus means "learned in nonsense"; the river Anydrus and the city Amaurotum mean "waterless" and "made dark or dim," respectively.

idle and curious lust for sight-seeing in new places but for the purpose of fostering and promoting our religion, begun there so felicitously.

To carry out his plan properly, he has made up his mind to arrange to be sent by the pope and, what is more, to be named bishop for the Utopians. He is in no way deterred by any scruple that he must sue for this prelacy, for he considers it a holy suit which proceeds not from any consideration of honor or gain but from motives of piety.

Therefore I beg you, my dear Peter, either by word of mouth if you conveniently can or by letter if he has gone, to reach Hythlodaeus and to make sure that my work includes nothing false and omits nothing true. I am inclined to think that it would be better to show him the book itself. No one else is so well able to correct any mistake, nor can he do this favor at all unless he reads through what I have written. In addition, in this way you will find out whether he accepts with pleasure or suffers with annoyance the fact that I have composed this work. If he himself has decided to put down in writing his own adventures, perhaps he may not want me to do so. By making known the commonwealth of Utopia, I should certainly dislike to forestall him and to rob his narrative of the flower and charm of novelty.

Nevertheless, to tell the truth, I myself have not yet made up my mind whether I shall publish it at all. So varied are the tastes of mortals, so peevish the characters of some, so ungrateful their dispositions, so wrongheaded their judgments, that those persons who pleasantly and blithely indulge their inclinations seem to be very much better off than those who torment themselves with anxiety in order to publish something that may bring profit or pleasure to others, who nevertheless receive it with disdain or ingratitude.

Very many men are ignorant of learning; many despise it. The barbarian rejects as harsh whatever is not positively barbarian. The smatterers despise as trite whatever is not packed with obsolete expressions. Some persons approve only of what is old; very many admire only their own work. This fellow is so grim that he will not hear of a joke; that fellow is so insipid that he cannot endure wit. Some are so dull-minded that they fear all satire as much as a man bitten by a mad dog fears water. Others are so fickle that sitting they praise one thing and standing another thing.

These persons sit in taverns, and over their cups criticize the talents of authors. With much pontificating, just as they please, they condemn each author by his writings, plucking each one, as it were, by the hair. They themselves remain under cover and, as the proverb goes, out of shot. They are so smooth and shaven that they present not even a hair of an honest man by which they might be caught.

Besides, others are so ungrateful that, though extremely delighted with the work, they do not love the author any the more. They are not unlike discourteous guests who, after they have been freely entertained at a rich banquet, finally go home well filled without thanking the host who invited them. Go now and provide a feast at your own expense for men of such dainty palate, of such varied taste, and of such unforgetful and grateful natures!

At any rate, my dear Peter, conduct with Hythlodaeus the business which I mentioned. Afterwards I shall be fully free to take fresh counsel on the subject. However, since I have gone through the labor of writing, it is too late for me to be wise now. Therefore, provided it be done with the consent of Hythlodaeus, in the matter of publishing which remains I shall follow my friends' advice, and yours first and foremost. Good-by, my sweetest friend, with your excellent wife. Love me as you have ever done, for I love you even more than I have ever done.

The Best State of a Commonwealth,
The Discourse of the Extraordinary
Character, Raphael Hythlodaeus, as
Reported by the Renowned Figure,
THOMAS MORE,
Citizen and Sheriff
of the Famous City of
Great Britain,
London

BOOK 1

The most invincible King of England, Henry, the eighth of that name, who is distinguished by all the accomplishments of a model monarch, had certain weighty matters[6] recently in dispute with His Serene Highness, Charles, Prince of Castile.[7] With a view to their discussion and settlement, he sent me as a commissioner to Flanders—as a companion and associate of the peerless Cuthbert Tunstal, whom he has just created Master of the Rolls[8] to everyone's immense satisfaction. Of the latter's praises I shall say nothing, not because I fear that the testimony of a friend should be given little credit but because his integrity and learning are too great for it to be possible, and too well-known for it to be necessary, for me to extol them—less I should wish to give the impression, as the proverb goes, of displaying the sun with a lamp!

We were met at Bruges, according to previous arrangement, by those men put in charge of the affair by the Prince—all outstanding persons. Their leader and head was the Burgomaster[9] of Bruges, a figure of magnificence, but their chief speaker and guiding spirit was Georges de Themsecke,[1] Provost of Cassel, a man not only trained in eloquence but a natural orator—most learned, too, in the law and consummately skillful in diplomacy by native ability as well as by long experience. When after one or two meetings there were certain points on which we could not agree sufficiently, they bade farewell to us for some days and left for Brussels to seek an official pronouncement from the Prince.

Meanwhile, as my business led me, I made my way to Antwerp. While I stayed there, among my other visitors, but of all of them the most welcome, was Peter Giles, a native of Antwerp, an honorable man of high position in his home town yet worthy of the very highest position, being a young man distinguished equally by learning and character; for he is most virtuous and most cultured, to all most courteous, but to his friends so open-hearted, affectionate, loyal, and sincere that you can hardly find one or two anywhere to compare with him as the perfect friend on every score. His modesty is uncommon; no one is less given to deceit, and none has a wiser simplicity of nature. Besides, in conversation he is so polished and so witty without offense that his delightful society and charming discourse largely took away my nostalgia and made me less conscious than before of the separation from my home, wife, and children to whom I was exceedingly anxious to get back, for I had then been more than four months away.

---

6. The "weighty matters" that took More to Flanders concerned the payment of tolls to Flemish ports by the English merchant fleet.
7. The future Charles I of Spain and Charles V, Holy Roman emperor; he ruled the Spanish kingdoms, Spanish America, Naples, Sicily, the Low Countries, and parts of Austria.
8. The principal clerk of the Chancery Court, a court of appeals from decisions by the common-law courts.
9. Mayor.
1. A Flemish diplomat, employed on numerous missions, who died in 1536.

One day I had been at divine service in Notre Dame, the finest church in the city and the most crowded with worshippers. Mass being over, I was about to return to my lodging when I happened to see him in conversation with a stranger, a man of advanced years, with sunburnt countenance and long beard and cloak hanging carelessly from his shoulder, while his appearance and dress seemed to me to be those of a ship's captain.

When Peter had espied me, he came up and greeted me. As I tried to return his salutation, he drew me a little aside and, pointing to the man I had seen him talking with, said:

"Do you see this fellow? I was on the point of taking him straight to you."

"He would have been very welcome," said I, "for your sake."

"No," said he, "for his own, if you knew him. There is no mortal alive today who can give you such an account of unknown peoples and lands, a subject about which I know you are always most greedy to hear."

"Well, then," said I, "my guess was not a bad one. The moment I saw him, I was sure he was a ship's captain."

"But you are quite mistaken," said he, "for his sailing has not been like that of Palinurus but that of Ulysses or, rather, of Plato.[2] Now this Raphael—for such is his personal name, with Hythlodaeus as his family name—is no bad Latin scholar, and most learned in Greek. He had studied that language more than Latin because he had devoted himself unreservedly to philosophy, and in that subject he found that there is nothing valuable in Latin except certain treatises of Seneca and Cicero.[3] He left his patrimony at home—he is a Portuguese—to his brothers, and, being eager to see the world, joined Amerigo Vespucci[4] and was his constant companion in the last three of those four voyages which are now universally read of, but on the final voyage he did not return with him. He importuned and even wrested from Amerigo permission to be one of the twenty-four who at the farthest point of the last voyage were left behind in the fort. And so he was left behind that he might have his way, being more anxious for travel than about the grave. These two sayings are constantly on his lips: 'He who has no grave is covered by the sky,' and 'From all places it is the same distance to heaven.' This attitude of his, but for the favor of God, would have cost him dear.[5] However, when after Vespucci's departure he had traveled through many countries with five companions from the fort, by strange chance he was carried to Ceylon, whence he reached Calicut.[6] There he conveniently found some Portuguese ships, and at length arrived home again, beyond all expectation."

When Peter had rendered this account, I thanked him for his kindness in taking such pains that I might have a talk with one whose conversation he hoped would give me pleasure; then I turned to Raphael. After we had greeted each other and exchanged the civilities which commonly pass at the first meeting of strangers, we went off to my house. There in the garden, on a bench covered with turfs of grass, we sat down to talk together.

---

2. Palinurus: the pilot of the ship sailed by Aeneas from Troy to Italy in Virgil's *Aeneid;* he fell overboard while sleeping at the helm. Ulysses: the Latin name for Odysseus, the hero of Homer's epic poem, the *Odyssey,* who returns to his kingdom, Ithaka, after years of wandering. Plato: the Greek philosopher who is said to have traveled throughout the Mediterranean world.

3. Two Roman writers who composed works on moral and political philosophy.

4. Florentine merchant adventurer (1451–1512), whose accounts of his voyages to the New World were reprinted in many editions; the Americas are named for him.

5. More's paraphrases of two classical authors indicate his humanist training. From Lucan's epic *Pharsalia* he takes: "Mother Earth has room for all her children, and he who lacks an urn has the sky to cover him" (8.819); and from Cicero's *Tusculan Disputations* he takes: "There is a fine remark of Anaxagoras. He was dying at Lampasacus, and his friends asked if he wanted to be taken home. . . . 'There's no need,' he said, 'it's the same distance from anywhere to the underworld'" (1.43.104).

6. Seaport on the west coast of India.

He recounted how, after the departure of Vespucci, he and his friends who had stayed behind in the fort began by degrees through continued meetings and civilities to ingratiate themselves with the natives till they not only stood in no danger from them but were actually on friendly terms and, moreover, were in good repute and favor with a ruler (whose name and country I have forgotten). Through the latter's generosity, he and his five companions were supplied with ample provision and travel resources and, moreover, with a trusty guide on their journey (which was partly by water on rafts and partly over land by wagon) to take them to other rulers with careful recommendations to their favor. For, after traveling many days, he said, they found towns and cities and very populous commonwealths with excellent institutions.

To be sure, under the equator and on both sides of the line nearly as far as the sun's orbit extends, there lie waste deserts scorched with continual heat. A gloomy and dismal region looms in all directions without cultivation or attractiveness, inhabited by wild beasts and snakes or, indeed, men no less savage and harmful than are the beasts. But when you have gone a little farther, the country gradually assumes a milder aspect, the climate is less fierce, the ground is covered with a pleasant green herbage, and the nature of living creatures becomes less wild. At length you reach peoples, cities, and towns which maintain a continual traffic by sea and land not only with each other and their neighbors but also with far-off countries.

Then they had opportunity of visiting many countries in all directions, for every ship which was got ready for any voyage made him and his companions welcome as passengers. The ships they saw in the parts first traveled were flat-bottomed and moved under sails made of papyrus or osiers[7] stitched together and sometimes under sails made of leather. Afterwards they found ships with pointed keels and canvas sails, in fact, like our own in all respects.

Their mariners were skilled in adapting themselves to sea and weather. But he reported that he won their extraordinary favor by showing them the use of the magnetic needle[8] of which they had hitherto been quite ignorant so that they had hesitated to trust themselves to the sea and had boldly done so in the summer only. Now, trusting to the magnet, they do not fear wintry weather, being dangerously confident. Thus, there is a risk that what was thought likely to be a great benefit to them may, through their imprudence, cause them great mischief.

What he said he saw in each place would be a long tale to unfold and is not the purpose of this work. Perhaps on another occasion we shall tell his story, particularly whatever facts would be useful to readers, above all, those wise and prudent provisions which he noticed anywhere among nations living together in a civilized way. For on these subjects we eagerly inquired of him, and he no less readily discoursed; but about stale travelers' wonders we were not curious. Scyllas and greedy Celaenos and folk-devouring Laestrygones[9] and similar frightful monsters are common enough, but well and wisely trained citizens are not everywhere to be found.

To be sure, just as he called attention to many ill-advised customs among these new nations, so he rehearsed not a few points from which our own cities, nations, races, and kingdoms may take example for the correction of their errors. These instances, as I said, I must mention on another occasion. Now I intend to relate merely what he told us of the manners and customs of the Utopians, first, however, giving the talk which drew and led him on to mention that commonwealth.

---

7. Papyrus: reed paper. Osiers: willow twigs.
8. Compass.
9. Fabulous monsters from the *Odyssey* and the *Aeneid*:

Scylla is a six-headed sea monster; Celaeno, a harpy, is a bird with a woman's face; the Lestrygonians were gigantic cannibals.

Raphael had touched with much wisdom on faults in this hemisphere and that, of which he found very many in both, and had compared the wiser measures which had been taken among us as well as among them; for he remembered the manners and customs of each nation as if he had lived all his life in places which he had only visited. Peter expressed his surprise at the man as follows:

"Why, my dear Raphael, I wonder that you do not attach yourself to some king. I am sure there is none of them to whom you would not be very welcome because you are capable not only of entertaining a king with this learning and experience of men and places but also of furnishing him with examples and of assisting him with counsel. Thus, you would not only serve your own interests excellently but be of great assistance in the advancement of all your relatives and friends."

"As for my relatives and friends," he replied, "I am not greatly troubled about them, for I think I have fairly well performed my duty to them already. The posses- sions, which other men do not resign unless they are old and sick and even then re- sign unwillingly when incapable of retention, I divided among my relatives and friends when I was not merely hale and hearty but actually young. I think they ought to be satisfied with this generosity from me and not to require or expect addi- tionally that I should, for their sakes, enter into servitude to kings."

"Fine words!" declared Peter. "I meant not that you should be in servitude but in service to kings."

"The one is only one syllable less than the other," he observed.

"But my conviction is," continued Peter, "whatever name you give to this mode of life, that it is the very way by which you can not only profit people both as private individuals and as members of the commonwealth but also render your own condi- tion more prosperous."

"Should I," said Raphael, "make it more prosperous by a way which my soul ab- hors? As it is, I now live as I please, which I surely fancy is very seldom the case with your grand courtiers. Nay, there are plenty of persons who court the friendship of the great, and so you need not think it a great loss if they have to do without me and one or two others like me."

"Well," I then said, "it is plain that you, my dear Raphael, are desirous nei- ther of riches nor of power. Assuredly, I reverence and look up to a man of your mind no whit less than to any of those who are most high and mighty. But it seems to me you will do what is worthy of you and of this generous and truly philosophic spirit of yours if you so order your life as to apply your talent and in- dustry to the public interest, even if it involves some personal disadvantages to yourself. This you can never do with as great profit as if you are councilor to some great monarch and make him follow, as I am sure you will, straightforward and honorable courses. From the monarch, as from a never-failing spring, flows a stream of all that is good or evil over the whole nation. You possess such com- plete learning that, even had you no great experience of affairs, and such great experience of affairs that, even had you no learning, you would make an excel- lent member of any king's council."

"You are twice mistaken, my dear More," said he, "first in me and then in the matter in question. I have no such ability as you ascribe to me and, if I had ever so much, still, in disturbing my own peace and quiet, I should not promote the public interest. In the first place almost all monarchs prefer to occupy themselves in the pursuits of war—with which I neither have nor desire any acquaintance—rather than in the honorable activities of peace, and they care much more how, by hook or by crook, they may win fresh kingdoms than how they may administer well what they have got.

"In the second place, among royal councilors everyone is actually so wise as to have no need of profiting by another's counsel, or everyone seems so wise in his own eyes as not to condescend to profit by it, save that they agree with the most absurd sayings of, and play the parasite to, the chief royal favorites whose friendliness they strive to win by flattery. To be sure, it is but human nature that each man favor his own discoveries most—just as the crow and the monkey like their own offspring best.

"If anyone, when in the company of people who are jealous of others' discoveries or prefer their own, should propose something which he either has read of as done in other times or has seen done in other places, the listeners behave as if their whole reputation for wisdom were jeopardized and as if afterwards they would deserve to be thought plain blockheads unless they could lay hold of something to find fault with in the discoveries of others. When all other attempts fail, their last resource is a remark such as this: 'Our forefathers were happy with that sort of thing, and would to heaven we had their wisdom.' And then, as if that comment were a brilliant conclusion to the whole business, they take their seats—implying, of course, that it would be a dangerous thing to be found with more wisdom on any point than our forefathers. And yet, no matter what excellent ideas our forefathers may have had, we very serenely bid them a curt farewell. But if in any situation they failed to take the wiser course, that defect gives us a handle which we greedily grab and never let go. Such proud, ridiculous, and obstinate prejudices I have encountered often in other places and once in England too."

"What," I asked, "were you ever in our country?"

"Yes," he answered, "I spent several months there, not long after the disastrous end of the insurrection of western Englishmen against the king, which was put down with their pitiful slaughter.[1] During that time I was much indebted to the Right Reverend Father, John Cardinal Morton, Archbishop of Canterbury, and then also Lord Chancellor of England.[2] He was a man, my dear Peter (for More knows about him and needs no information from me), who deserved respect as much for his prudence and virtue as for his authority. He was of middle stature and showed no sign of his advanced age. His countenance inspired respect rather than fear. In conversation he was agreeable, though serious and dignified. Of those who made suit to him he enjoyed making trial by rough address, but in a harmless way, to see what mettle and what presence of mind a person would manifest. Provided it did not amount to impudence, such behavior gave him pleasure as being akin to his own disposition and excited his admiration as being suited to those holding public office. His speech was polished and pointed. His knowledge of law was profound, his ability incomparable, and his memory astonishingly retentive, for he had improved his extraordinary natural qualities by learning and practice.

"The king placed the greatest confidence in his advice, and the commonwealth seemed much to depend upon him when I was there. As one might expect, almost in earliest youth he had been taken straight from school to court, had spent his whole life in important public affairs, and had sustained numerous and varied vicissitudes

1. In 1497 the people of Cornwall rebelled against taxation by the crown; they were defeated by the king's army outside London, in the Battle of Blackheath.

2. More served for two years as a page in the household of Cardinal Morton (1420–1500).

of fortune, so that by many and great dangers he had acquired a statesman's sagacity which, when thus learned, is not easily forgotten.

"It happened one day that I was at his table when a layman, learned in the laws of your country, was present. Availing himself of some opportunity or other, he began to speak punctiliously of the strict justice which was then dealt out to thieves. They were everywhere executed, he reported, as many as twenty at a time being hanged on one gallows, and added that he wondered all the more, though so few escaped execution, by what bad luck the whole country was still infested with them. I dared be free in expressing my opinions without reserve at the Cardinal's table, so I said to him:

"'You need not wonder, for this manner of punishing thieves goes beyond justice and is not for the public good. It is too harsh a penalty for theft and yet is not a sufficient deterrent. Theft alone is not a grave offense that ought to be punished with death, and no penalty that can be devised is sufficient to restrain from acts of robbery those who have no other means of getting a livelihood. In this respect not your country alone but a great part of our world resembles bad schoolmasters, who would rather beat than teach their scholars. You ordain grievous and terrible punishments for a thief when it would have been much better to provide some means of getting a living, that no one should be under this terrible necessity first of stealing and then of dying for it.'

"'We have,' said the fellow, 'made sufficient provision for this situation. There are manual crafts. There is farming. They might maintain themselves by these pursuits if they did not voluntarily prefer to be rascals.'

"'No,' I countered, 'you shall not escape so easily. We shall say nothing of those who often come home crippled from foreign or civil wars, as recently with you Englishmen from the battle with the Cornishmen and not long ago from the war in France.[3] They lose their limbs in the service of the commonwealth or of the king, and their disability prevents them from exercising their own crafts, and their age from learning a new one. Of these men, I say, we shall take no account because wars come sporadically, but let us consider what happens every day.

"'Now there is the great number of noblemen who not only live idle themselves like drones on the labors of others, as for instance the tenants of their estates whom they fleece to the utmost by increasing the returns[4] (for that is the only economy they know of, being otherwise so extravagant as to bring themselves to beggary!) but who also carry about with them a huge crowd of idle attendants who have never learned a trade for a livelihood. As soon as their master dies or they themselves fall sick, these men are turned out at once, for the idle are maintained more readily than the sick, and often the heir is not able to support as large a household as his father did, at any rate at first.

"'In the meantime the fellows devote all their energies to starving, if they do not to robbing. Indeed what can they do? When by a wandering life they have worn out their clothes a little, and their health to boot, sickly and ragged as they are, no gentleman deigns to engage them and the farmers dare not do so either. The latter know full well that a man who has been softly brought up in idleness and luxury and has been wont[5] in sword and buckler to look down with a swaggering face on the whole neighborhood and to think himself far above everybody will hardly be fit to

---

3. Hythlodaeus refers to actual battles at Dixmude in 1489 and in Boulogne in 1492.

4. Rents.

5. Accustomed.

render honest service to a poor man with spade and hoe, for a scanty wage, and on frugal fare.'

"'But this,' the fellow retorted, 'is just the sort of man we ought to encourage most. On them, being men of a loftier and nobler spirit than craftsmen and farmers, depend the strength and sinews of our army when we have to wage war.'

"'Of course,' said I, 'you might as well say that for the sake of war we must foster thieves. As long as you have these men, you will certainly never be without thieves. Nay, robbers do not make the least active soldiers, nor do soldiers make the most listless robbers, so well do these two pursuits agree. But this defect, though frequent with you, is not peculiar to you, for it is common to almost all peoples.

"'France in particular is troubled with another more grievous plague. Even in peacetime (if you can call it peacetime) the whole country is crowded and beset with mercenaries hired because the French follow the train of thought you Englishmen take in judging it a good thing to keep idle retainers. These wiseacres think that the public safety depends on having always in readiness a strong and re-liable garrison, chiefly of veterans, for they have not the least confidence in tyros.[6] This attitude obliges them always to be seeking for a pretext for war just so they may not have soldiers without experience, and men's throats must be cut without cause lest, to use Sallust's witty saying, "the hand or the mind through lack of practice become dulled." Yet how dangerous it is to rear such wild beasts France has learned to its cost, and the examples of Rome, Carthage, Syria, and many other nations show.[7] Not only the supreme authority of the latter countries but their land and even their cities have been more than once destroyed by their own standing armies.

"'Now, how unnecessary it is to maintain them is clearly proved by this consid-eration: not even the French soldiers, assiduously trained in arms from infancy, can boast that they have very often got the better of it face to face with your draftees.[8] Let me say no more for fear of seeming to flatter you barefacedly. At any rate, your town-bred craftsmen or your rough and clodhopper farmers are not supposed to be much afraid of those idle attendants on gentlemen, except those of the former whose build of body is unfitted for strength and bravery or those whose stalwart spirit is broken by lack of support for their family. Consequently there is no danger that those attendants whose bodies, once strong and vigorous (for it is only the picked men that gentlemen deign to corrupt), are now either weakened by idleness or softened by almost womanish occupations, should become unmanned if trained to earn their living in honest trades and exercised in virile labors!

"'However the case may be, it seems to me by no means profitable to the com-mon weal to keep for the emergency of a war a vast multitude of such people as trou-ble and disturb the peace. You never have war unless you choose it, and you ought to take far more account of peace than of war. Yet this is not the only situation that makes thieving necessary. There is another which, as I believe, is more special to you Englishmen.'

"'What is that?' asked the Cardinal.

"'Your sheep,' I answered, 'which are usually so tame and so cheaply fed, begin now, according to report, to be so greedy and wild that they devour human beings

---

6. Raw recruits.
7. The Romans, Carthaginians, and Syrians used merce-nary armies but suffered mutinies as a result.

8. Hythlodaeus refers to English soldiers who won victo-ries over French forces in such battles as Crecy (1346), Poitiers (1356), and Agincourt (1415).

themselves and devastate and depopulate fields, houses, and towns.[9] In all those parts of the realm where the finest and therefore costliest wool is produced, there are noblemen, gentlemen, and even some abbots, though otherwise holy men, who are not satisfied with the annual revenues and profits which their predecessors used to derive from their estates. They are not content, by leading an idle and sumptuous life, to do no good to their country; they must also do it positive harm. They leave no ground to be tilled; they enclose every bit of land for pasture; they pull down houses and destroy towns, leaving only the church to pen the sheep in. And, as if enough of your land were not wasted on ranges and preserves of game, those good fellows turn all human habitations and all cultivated land into a wilderness.

"'Consequently, in order that one insatiable glutton and accursed plague of his native land may join field to field and surround many thousand acres with one fence, tenants are evicted. Some of them, either circumvented by fraud or overwhelmed by violence, are stripped even of their own property, or else, wearied by unjust acts, are driven to sell. By hook or by crook the poor wretches are compelled to leave their homes—men and women, husbands and wives, orphans and widows, parents with little children and a household not rich but numerous, since farm work requires many hands. Away they must go, I say, from the only homes familiar and known to them, and they find no shelter to go to. All their household goods which would not fetch a great price if they could wait for a purchaser, since they must be thrust out, they sell for a trifle.

"'After they have soon spent that trifle in wandering from place to place, what remains for them but to steal and be hanged—justly, you may say!—or to wander and beg. And yet even in the latter case they are cast into prison as vagrants for going about idle when, though they most eagerly offer their labor, there is no one to hire them. For there is no farm work, to which they have been trained, to be had, when there is no land for plowing left. A single shepherd or herdsman is sufficient for grazing livestock on that land for whose cultivation many hands were once required to make it raise crops.

"'A result of this situation is that the price of food has risen steeply in many localities. Indeed, the price of raw wools has climbed so high that your poor people who used to make cloth cannot possibly buy them, and so great numbers are driven from work into idleness. One reason is that, after the great increase in pasture land, a plague carried off a vast multitude of sheep as though God were punishing greed by sending upon the sheep a murrain[1]—which should have fallen on the owners' heads more justly! But, however much the number of sheep increases, their price does not decrease a farthing because, though you cannot brand that a monopoly which is a sale by more than one person, yet their sale is certainly an oligopoly,[2] for all sheep have come into the hands of a few men, and those already rich, who are not obligated to sell before they wish and who do not wish until they get the price they ask.

"'By this time all other kinds of livestock are equally high-priced on the same account and still more so, for the reason that, with the pulling down of farmsteads and the lessening of farming, none are left to devote themselves to the breeding of

---

9. Hythlodaeus criticizes the management of the English wool trade. The potential for profit from sheep's wool led landlords to fence off or enclose vast open spaces that had previously been shared in common and farmed by peasants. Many of these displaced people sought work in the

cities or became migrant day-laborers throughout the country.
1. A disease of livestock.
2. Control of a commercial market by a small number of companies or merchants.

stock. These rich men will not rear young cattle as they do lambs, but they buy them lean and cheap abroad and then, after they are fattened in their pastures, sell them again at a high price. In my estimation, the whole mischief of this system has not yet been felt. Thus far, the dealers raise the prices only where the cattle are sold, but when, for some time, they have been removing them from other localities faster than they can be bred there, then, as the supply gradually diminishes in the markets where they are purchased, great scarcity must needs be here.

"'Thus, the unscrupulous greed of a few is ruining the very thing by virtue of which your island was once counted fortunate in the extreme. For the high price of food is causing everyone to get rid of as many of his household as possible, and what, I ask, have they to do but to beg, or—a course more readily embraced by men of mettle—to become robbers?

"'In addition, alongside this wretched need and poverty you find wanton luxury. Not only the servants of noblemen but the craftsmen and almost the clodhoppers themselves, in fact all classes alike, are given to much ostentatious sumptuousness of dress and to excessive indulgence at table. Do not dives, brothels, and those other places as bad as brothels, to wit, taverns, wine shops and ale-houses—do not all those crooked games of chance, dice, cards, backgammon, ball, bowling, and quoits, soon drain the purses of their votaries[3] and send them off to rob someone?

"'Cast out these ruinous plagues. Make laws that the destroyers of farmsteads and country villages should either restore them or hand them over to people who will restore them and who are ready to build. Restrict this right of rich individuals to buy up everything and this license to exercise a kind of monopoly for themselves. Let fewer be brought up in idleness. Let farming be resumed and let cloth-working be restored once more that there may be honest jobs to employ usefully that idle throng, whether those whom hitherto pauperism has made thieves or those who, now being vagrants or lazy servants, in either case are likely to turn out thieves. Assuredly, unless you remedy these evils, it is useless for you to boast of the justice you execute in the punishment of theft. Such justice is more showy than really just or beneficial. When you allow your youths to be badly brought up and their characters, even from early years, to become more and more corrupt, to be punished, of course, when, as grown-up men, they commit the crimes which from boyhood they have shown every prospect of committing, what else, I ask, do you do but first create thieves and then become the very agents of their punishment?'

"Even while I was saying these things, the lawyer had been busily preparing himself to reply and had determined to adopt the usual method of disputants who are more careful to repeat what has been said than to answer it, so highly do they regard their memory.

"'Certainly, sir,' he began, 'you have spoken well, considering that you are but a stranger who could hear something of these matters rather than get exact knowledge of them—a statement which I shall make plain in a few words. First, I shall repeat, in order, what you have said; then I shall show in what respects ignorance of our conditions has deceived you; finally I shall demolish and destroy all your arguments. So, to begin with what I promised first, on four points you seemed to me—'

"'Hold your peace,' interrupted the Cardinal, 'for you hardly seem about to reply in a few words if you begin thus. So we shall relieve you of the trouble of making your answer now, but we shall reserve your right unimpaired till your next meeting,

---

3. Devotees.

which I should like to set for tomorrow, provided neither you nor Raphael here is hindered by other business.

"'But now I am eager to have you tell me, my dear Raphael, why you think that theft ought not to be punished with the extreme penalty, or what other penalty you yourself would fix, which would be more beneficial to the public. I am sure that not even you think it ought to go unpunished. Even as it is, with death as the penalty, men still rush into stealing. What force and what fear, if they once were sure of their lives, could deter the criminals? They would regard themselves as much invited to crime by the mitigation of the penalty as if a reward were offered.'

"'Certainly,' I answered, 'most reverend and kind Father, I think it altogether unjust that a man should suffer the loss of his life for the loss of someone's money. In my opinion, not all the goods that fortune can bestow on us can be set in the scale against a man's life. If they say that this penalty is attached to the offense against justice and the breaking of the laws, hardly to the money stolen, one may well characterize this extreme justice as extreme wrong. For we ought not to approve such stern Manlian rules of law[4] as would justify the immediate drawing of the sword when they are disobeyed in trifles nor such Stoical[5] ordinances as count all offenses equal so that there is no difference between killing a man and robbing him of a coin when, if equity has any meaning, there is no similarity or connection between the two cases.[6]

"'God has said, "Thou shalt not kill," and shall we so lightly kill a man for taking a bit of small change? But if the divine command against killing be held not to apply where human law justifies killing, what prevents men equally from arranging with one another how far rape, adultery, and perjury are admissible? God has withdrawn from man the right to take not only another's life but his own. Now, men by mutual consent agree on definite cases where they may take the life of one another. But if this agreement among men is to have such force as to exempt their henchmen from the obligation of the commandment, although without any precedent set by God they take the life of those who have been ordered by human enactment to be put to death, will not the law of God then be valid only so far as the law of man permits? The result will be that in the same way men will determine in everything how far it suits them that God's commandments should be obeyed.

"'Finally, the law of Moses,[7] though severe and harsh—being intended for slaves, and those a stubborn breed—nevertheless punished theft by fine and not by death. Let us not suppose that God, in the new law of mercy in which He gives commands as a father to his sons, has allowed us greater license to be cruel to one another.

"'These are the reasons why I think this punishment unlawful. Besides, surely everyone knows how absurd and even dangerous to the commonwealth it is that a thief and a murderer should receive the same punishment. Since the robber sees that he is in as great danger if merely condemned for theft as if he were convicted of murder as well, this single consideration impels him to murder the man whom otherwise he would only have robbed. In addition to the fact that he is in no greater danger if

---

4. Manlius Torquatus, a Roman general of the 4th century B.C.E., who, having made a law against single encounters, executed his own son for fighting and defeating an enemy warrior.
5. Austere.
6. Hythlodaeus alludes to an important feature of the law: Cases in which the law invoked to cover them is too general to do justice to their complexity are decided by addressing the circumstances in which the alleged violation was committed, the condition of the disputants, and the remedies apart from the law that might serve to settle the case. Such a mitigated justice was known as equity.
7. The Decalogue or Ten Commandments, one of which is "Thou shalt not kill" (Exodus 20.13).

caught, there is greater safety in putting the man out of the way and greater hope of covering up the crime if he leaves no one left to tell the tale. Thus, while we endeavor to terrify thieves with excessive cruelty, we urge them on to the destruction of honest citizens.

"'As to the repeated question about a more advisable form of punishment, in my judgment it is much easier to find a better than a worse. Why should we doubt that a good way of punishing crimes is the one which we know long found favor of old with the Romans, the greatest experts in managing the commonwealth? When men were convicted of atrocious crimes they condemned them for life to stone quarries and to digging in metal mines, and kept them constantly in chains.

"'Yet, as concerns this matter, I can find no better system in any country than that which, in the course of my travels, I observed in Persia among the people commonly called the Polylerites,[8] a nation that is large and well-governed and, except that it pays an annual tribute to the Persian padishah [emperor], otherwise free and autonomous in its laws. They are far from the sea, almost ringed round by mountains, and satisfied with the products of their own land, which is in no way infertile. In consequence they rarely pay visits to other countries or receive them. In accordance with their long-standing national policy, they do not try to enlarge their territory and easily protect what they have from all aggression by their mountains and by the tribute paid to their overlord. Being completely free from militarism, they live a life more comfortable than splendid and more happy than renowned or famous, for even their name, I think, is hardly known except to their immediate neighbors.

"'Now, in their land, persons who are convicted of theft repay to the owner what they have taken from him, not, as is usual elsewhere, to the prince, who, they consider, has as little right to the thing stolen as the thief himself. But if the object is lost, the value is made up out of the thieves' goods, and the balance is then paid intact to their wives and children. They themselves are condemned to hard labor. Unless the theft is outrageous, they neither are confined to prison nor wear shackles about their feet but, without any bonds or restraints, are set to public works. Convicts who refuse to labor or are slack are not put in chains but urged on by the lash. If they do a good day's work, they need fear no insult or injury. The only check is that every night, after their names are called over, they are locked in their sleeping quarters.

"'Except for the constant toil, their life has no hardship. For example, as serviceable to the common weal, they are fed well at the public's expense, the mode varying from place to place. In some parts, what is spent on them is raised by almsgiving. Though this method is precarious, the Polylerite people are so kindhearted that no other is found to supply the need more plentifully. In other parts, fixed public revenues are set aside to defray the cost. Elsewhere, all pay a specified personal tax for these purposes. Yes, and in some localities the convicts do no work for the community, but, whenever a private person needs a hired laborer, he secures in the market place a convict's service for that day at a fixed wage, a bit lower than what he would have paid for free labor. Moreover, the employer is permitted to chastise with stripes a hired man if he be lazy. The result is that they are never out of work and that each one, besides earning his own living, brings in something every day to the public treasury.

"'All of them wear clothes of a color not worn by anyone else. Their hair is not shaved but cropped a little above the ears, from one of which the tip is cut off. Food

---

8. "People of Much Nonsense."

and drink and clothes of the proper color may be given them by their friends. The gift of money is a capital offense, both for the donor and the receiver. It is no less dangerous for a free man to receive a penny for any reason from a condemned person, or for slaves (which is the name borne by the convicts) to touch weapons. The slaves of each district are distinguished by a special badge, which it is a capital offense to throw away, as it is to appear beyond their own bounds or to talk to a slave from another district. Further, it is no safer to plot escape than actually to run away. Yes, and the punishment for connivance in such a plan is death for the slave and slavery for the free man. On the other hand, rewards are appointed for an informer: money for a free man, liberty for a slave, and pardon and immunity for both for their complicity. The purpose is never to make it safer to follow out an evil plan than to repent of it.

"'This is the law and this the procedure in the matter, as I have described it to you. You can easily see how humane and advantageous it is. The object of public anger is to destroy the vices but to save the persons and so to treat them that they necessarily become good and that, for the rest of their lives, they repair all the damage done before.

"'Further, so little is it to be feared that they may sink back into their old evil ways, even travelers who have to go on a journey think themselves most safe if they secure as guides these slaves, who are changed with each new district. For the latter have nothing suitable with which to commit robbery. They bear no arms; money would merely insure the detection of the crime; punishment awaits the man who is caught; and there is absolutely no hope of escaping to a safe place. How could a man so cover his flight as to elude observation when he resembles ordinary people in no part of his attire—unless he were to run away naked? Even then his ear would betray him in his flight!

"'But, of course, would there not at least be risk of their taking counsel together and conspiring against the commonwealth? As if any district could conceive a hope of success without having first sounded and seduced the slave gangs of many other districts! The latter are so little able to conspire together that they may not even meet and converse or greet one another. Much less will they boldly divulge to their own fellow slaves the plot, which they know is dangerous to those concealing it and very profitable to those betraying it. On the other hand, no one is quite without hope of gaining his freedom eventually if he accepts his punishment in a spirit of obedience and resignation and gives evidence of reforming his future life; indeed, every year a number of them are granted their liberty which they have merited by their submissive behavior.'

"When I had finished this speech, I added that I saw no reason why this method might not be adopted even in England and be far more beneficial in its working than the justice which my legal opponent had praised so highly. The lawyer replied: 'Never could that system be established in England without involving the commonwealth in a very serious crisis.' In the act of making this statement, he shook his head and made a wry face and so fell silent. And all who were present gave him their assent.

"Then the Cardinal remarked: 'It is not easy to guess whether it would turn out well or ill inasmuch as absolutely no experiment has been made. If, after pronouncement of the sentence of death, the king were to order the postponement of its execution and, after limitation of the privileges of sanctuary,[9] were to try this system,

---

9. From the 7th century until the Reformation, English churches and sometimes their surrounding precincts provided limited asylum for fugitives from judicial authority.

then, if success proved its usefulness, it would be right to make the system law. In case of failure, then and there to put to death those previously condemned would be no less for the public good and no more unjust than if execution were done here and now. In the meantime no danger can come of the experiment. Furthermore, I am sure that vagrants might very well be treated in the same way for, in spite of repeated legislation against them, we have made no progress.'

"When the Cardinal had finished speaking, they all vied in praising what they all had received with contempt when suggested by me, but especially the part relating to vagrants because this was the Cardinal's addition.

"I am at a loss as to whether it were better to suppress what followed next, for it was quite absurd. But I shall relate it since it was not evil in itself and had some bearing on the matter in question.

"There happened to be present a hanger-on, who wanted to give the impression of imitating a jester but whose imitation was too close to the real thing. His ill-timed witticisms were meant to raise a laugh, but he himself was more often the object of laughter than his jests. The fellow, however, sometimes let fall observations which were to the point, thus proving the proverb true, that if a man throws the dice often he will sooner or later make a lucky throw. One of the guests happened to say:

"'Raphael's proposal has made good provision for thieves. The Cardinal has taken precautions also for vagrants. It only remains now that public measures be devised for persons whom sickness or old age has brought to want and made unable to work for their living.'

"'Give me leave,' volunteered the hanger-on. 'I shall see that this situation, too, be set right. I am exceedingly anxious to get this sort of person out of my sight. They have often harassed me with their pitiful whinings in begging for money—though they never could pitch a tune which would get a coin out of my pocket. For one of two things always happens: either I do not want to give or I cannot, since I have nothing to give. Now they have begun to be wise. When they see me pass by, they say nothing and spare their pains. They no longer expect anything from me—no more, by heaven, than if I were a secular priest! As for me, I should have a law passed that all those beggars be distributed and divided among the Benedictine monasteries and that the men be made so-called lay brothers.[1] The women I should order to become nuns.'

"The Cardinal smiled and passed it off in jest, but the rest took it in earnest. Now a certain theologian who was a friar[2] was so delighted by this jest at the expense of secular priests and of monks that he also began to make merry, though generally he was serious almost to the point of being dour.

"'Nay,' said he, 'not even so will you be rid of mendicants unless you make provision for us friars too.'

"'But this has been taken care of already,' retorted the hanger-on. 'His Eminence made excellent provision for you when he determined that tramps should be confined and made to work, for you are the worst tramps of all.'

"When the company, looking at the Cardinal, saw that he did not think this jest any more amiss than the other, they all proceeded to take it up with vigor—but not the friar. He—and I do not wonder—deluged by these taunts, began to be so

1. Members of the regular religious orders who performed manual labor and sometimes administrative or temporal functions within the monastery. They were distinct from those men who had taken monastic vows and devoted their lives entirely to following the word of God.
2. Friars were members of the mendicant orders who lived solely off alms in return for their prayers and preaching.

furious and enraged that he could not hold back even from abusing the joker. He called him a rascal, a slanderer, and a 'son of perdition,' quoting the while terrible denunciations out of Holy Scripture. Now the scoffer began to scoff in earnest and was quite in his element:

"'Be not angry, good friar. It is written: "In your patience shall you possess your souls."'[3]

"Then the friar rejoined—I shall repeat his very words: 'I am not angry, you gallows bird, or at least I do not sin, for the psalmist says: "Be angry, and sin not."'[4]

"At this point the Cardinal gently admonished the friar to calm his emotions, but he replied:

"'No, my lord, I speak motivated only by a good zeal—as I should. For holy men have had a good zeal; wherefore Scripture says, "The zeal of Thy house has eaten me up,"[5] and churches resound with the hymn: "The mockers of Eliseus[6] as he went up to the house of God felt the zeal of the baldhead"—just as this mocking, scorning, ribald fellow will perhaps feel it.'

"'Maybe,' said the Cardinal, 'you behave with proper feeling, but I think that you would act, if not more holily, at any rate more wisely, if you would not set your wits against those of a silly fellow and provoke a foolish duel with a fool.'

"'No, my lord,' he replied, 'I should not do more wisely. Solomon himself, the wisest of men, says: "Answer a fool according to his folly"[7]—as I do now. I am showing him the pit into which he will fall if he does not take good heed, for, if many scorners of Eliseus, who numbered only one baldhead, felt the zeal of the baldhead, how much more will one scorner of many friars, among whom are numbered many baldheads! And, besides, we have a papal bull[8] by which all who scoff at us are excommunicated!'

"When the Cardinal realized there was no making an end, he sent away the hanger-on by a motion of his head and tactfully turned the conversation to another subject. Soon afterwards he rose from the table and, going to hear the petitions of his suitors, dismissed us.

"Look, my dear More, with how lengthy a tale I have burdened you. I should have been quite ashamed to protract it if you had not eagerly called for it and seemed to listen as if you did not want any part of the conversation to be left out. Though I ought to have related this conversation more concisely, still I felt bound to tell it to exhibit the attitude of those who had rejected what I had said first yet who, immediately afterward, when the Cardinal did not disapprove of it, also gave their approval, flattering him so much that they even smiled on and almost allowed in earnest the fancies of the hanger-on, which his master in jest did not reject. From this reaction you may judge what little regard courtiers would pay to me and my advice."

"To be sure, my dear Raphael," I commented, "you have given me great pleasure, for everything you have said has been both wise and witty. Besides, while listening to you, I felt not only as if I were at home in my native land but as if I were become a boy again, by being pleasantly reminded of the very Cardinal in whose

---

3. Luke 21.19.
4. Psalms 4.4.
5. Psalms 69.9.
6. Elisha, the heir of the prophet Elijah. Hythlodaeus refers to a hymn ascribed to the medieval writer Adam of St. Victor. It alludes to the story of Elisha, who, when

mocked by children for his baldness, curses them "in the name of the Lord"; this causes two bears to emerge from the woods and rip 42 of the children to pieces (2 Kings 2.23–24).
7. Proverbs 26.5.
8. Edict.

court I was brought up as a lad. Since you are strongly devoted to his memory, you cannot believe how much more attached I feel to you on that account, attached exceedingly as I have been to you already. Even now, nevertheless, I cannot change my mind but must needs think that, if you could persuade yourself not to shun the courts of kings, you could do the greatest good to the common weal by your advice. The latter is the most important part of your duty as it is the duty of every good man. Your favorite author, Plato, is of opinion that commonwealths will finally be happy only if either philosophers become kings or kings turn to philosophy.[9] What a distant prospect of happiness there will be if philosophers will not condescend even to impart their counsel to kings!"

"They are not so ungracious," he rejoined, "that they would not gladly do it—in fact, many have already done it in published books—if the rulers would be ready to take good advice. But, doubtless, Plato was right in foreseeing that if kings themselves did not turn to philosophy, they would never approve of the advice of real philosophers because they have been from their youth saturated and infected with wrong ideas. This truth he found from his own experience with Dionysius.[1] If I proposed beneficial measures to some king and tried to uproot from his soul the seeds of evil and corruption, do you not suppose that I should be forthwith banished or treated with ridicule?

"Come now, suppose I were at the court of the French king and sitting in his privy council. In a most secret meeting, a circle of his most astute councilors over which he personally presides is setting its wits to work to consider by what crafty machinations he may keep his hold on Milan and bring back into his power the Naples which has been eluding his grasp; then overwhelm Venice and subjugate the whole of Italy; next bring under his sway Flanders, Brabant, and finally, the whole of Burgundy—and other nations, too, whose territory he has already conceived the idea of usurping.

"At this meeting, one advises that a treaty should be made with the Venetians to last just as long as the king will find it convenient, that he should communicate his intentions to them, and that he should even deposit in their keeping part of the booty, which, when all has gone according to his mind, he may reclaim. Another recommends the hiring of German *Landsknechte* [infantry], and another the mollification of the Swiss with money, and another the propitiation of the offended majesty of the emperor with gold as an acceptable offering. Another thinks that a settlement should be made with the King of Aragon and that, as a guarantee of peace, someone else's kingdom of Navarre should be ceded him! Another proposes that the Prince of Castile be caught by the prospect of a marriage alliance and that some nobles of his court be drawn to the French side by a fixed pension.

"Meanwhile the most perplexing question of all comes up: what is to be done with England? They agree that negotiations for peace should be undertaken, that an alliance always weak at best should be strengthened with the strongest bonds, and that the English should be called friends but suspected as enemies. The Scots therefore must be posted in readiness, prepared for any opportunity to be let loose on the

---

9. *Republic*, 5.473d.
1. Having tried to instruct Dionysius II, King of Syracuse, in the art of ruling as a philosopher, Plato became a virtual prisoner of the court.

English if they make the slightest movement. Moreover, some exiled noble must be fostered secretly—for treaties prevent it being done openly—to maintain a claim to the throne, that by this handle France may keep in check a king in whom it has no confidence.

"In such a meeting, I say, when such efforts are being made, when so many distinguished persons are vying with each other in proposals of a warlike nature, what if an insignificant fellow like myself were to get up and advise going on another tack? Suppose I expressed the opinion that Italy should be left alone. Suppose I argued that we should stay at home because the single kingdom of France by itself was almost too large to be governed well by a single man so that the king should not dream of adding other dominions under his sway. Suppose, then, I put before them the decisions made by the people called the Achorians[2] who live on the mainland to the south-southeast of the island of Utopia.

"Once upon a time they had gone to war to win for their king another kingdom to which he claimed to be the rightful heir by virtue of an old tie by marriage. After they had secured it, they saw they would have no less trouble in keeping it than they had suffered in obtaining it. The seeds of rebellion from within or of invasion from without were always springing up in the people thus acquired. They realized they would have to fight constantly for them or against them and to keep an army in continual readiness. In the meantime they were being plundered, their money was being taken out of the country, they were shedding their blood for the little glory of someone else, peace was no more secure than before, their morals at home were being corrupted by war, the lust for robbery was becoming second nature, criminal recklessness was emboldened by killings in war, and the laws were held in contempt—all because the king, being distracted with the charge of two kingdoms, could not properly attend to either.

"At length, seeing that in no other way would there be any end to all this mischief, they took counsel together and most courteously offered their king his choice of retaining whichever of the two kingdoms he preferred. He could not keep both because there were too many of them to be ruled by half a king, just as no one would care to engage even a muleteer whom he had to share with someone else. The worthy king was obliged to be content with his own realm and to turn over the new one to one of his friends, who was driven out soon afterwards.

"Furthermore, suppose I proved that all this war-mongering, by which so many nations were kept in a turmoil on the French king's account, would, after draining his resources and destroying his people, at length by some mischance end in naught and that therefore he had better look after his ancestral kingdom and make it as prosperous and flourishing as possible, love his subjects and be loved by them, live with them and rule them gently, and have no designs upon other kingdoms since what he already possessed was more than enough for him. What reception from my listeners, my dear More, do you think this speech of mine would find?"

"To be sure, not a very favorable one," I granted.

"Well, then, let us proceed," he continued. "Picture the councilors of some king or other debating with him and devising by what schemes they may heap up treasure for him. One advises crying up the value of money when he has to pay any and crying down its value below the just rate when he has to receive any—with the double result that he may discharge a large debt with a small sum and, when only a small

2. A people "without place, region, or district."

sum is due to him, may receive a large one. Another suggests a make-believe war under pretext of which he would raise money and then, when he saw fit, make peace with solemn ceremonies to throw dust in his simple people's eyes because their loving monarch in compassion would fain avoid human bloodshed.

"Another councilor reminds him of certain old and moth-eaten laws, annulled by long non-enforcement, which no one remembers being made and therefore everyone has transgressed. The king should exact fines for their transgression, there being no richer source of profit nor any more honorable than such as has an outward mask of justice! Another recommends that under heavy penalties he prohibit many things and especially such as it is to the people's advantage not to allow. Afterwards for money he should give a dispensation to those with whose interests the prohibition has interfered. Thus favor is won with the people and a double profit is made: first, by exacting fines from those whose greed of gain has entangled them in the snare and, second, by selling privileges to others—and, to be sure, the higher the price the better the king, since he hates to give any private citizen a privilege which is contrary to the public welfare and will not do so except at a great price!

"Another persuades him that he must bind to himself the judges, who will in every case decide in favor of the king's side. In addition, he must summon them to the palace and invite them to debate his affairs in his presence. There will be no cause of his so patently unjust in which one of them will not, either from a desire to contradict or from shame at repeating another's view or to curry favor, find some loophole whereby the law can be perverted. When through the opposite opinions of the judges a thing in itself as clear as daylight has been made a subject of debate, and when truth has become a matter of doubt, the king is opportunely furnished a handle to interpret the law in his own interest. Everyone else will acquiesce from shame or from fear. Afterwards the decision is boldly pronounced from the Bench. Then, too, a pretext can never be wanting for deciding on the king's side. For such a judge it is enough that either equity be on his side or the letter of the law or the twisted meaning of the written word or, what finally outweighs all law with conscientious judges, the indisputable royal prerogative![3]

"All the councilors agree and consent to the famous statement of Crassus:[4] no amount of gold is enough for the ruler who has to keep an army. Further, the king, however much he wishes, can do no wrong; for all that all men possess is his, as they themselves are, and so much is a man's own as the king's kindness has not taken away from him. It is much to the king's interest that the latter be as little as possible, seeing that his safeguard lies in the fact that the people do not grow insolent with wealth and freedom. These things make them less patient to endure harsh and unjust commands, while, on the other hand, poverty and need blunt their spirits, make them patient, and take away from the oppressed the lofty spirit of rebellion.

"At this point, suppose I were again to rise and maintain that these counsels are both dishonorable and dangerous for the king, whose very safety, not merely his

3. Conditions in which the principle of equity is subverted: The law, rather than being applied in such a way as to respect the conditions and circumstances of a particular case, is bent or twisted to suit the interest of a particular party. In England the courts of equity were often devoted to matters of state and were susceptible to corruption in the interest of promoting royal business. The prerogative was the absolute power of the monarch only in special categories of activity (e.g., the import and export trade), and it was exempt from any legal restrictions.

4. Marcus Licinius Crassus (d. 53 B.C.E.), a man of great wealth who, together with Julius Caesar and Pompey, formed a coalition known as the first triumvirate.

honor, rests on the people's resources rather than his own. Suppose I should show that they choose a king for their own sake and not for his—to be plain, that by his labor and effort they may live well and safe from injustice and wrong. For this very reason, it belongs to the king to take more care for the welfare of his people than for his own, just as it is the duty of a shepherd, insofar as he is a shepherd, to feed his sheep rather than himself.[5]

"The blunt facts reveal that they are completely wrong in thinking that the poverty of the people is the safeguard of peace. Where will you find more quarreling than among beggars? Who is more eager for revolution than he who is discontented with his present state of life? Who is more reckless in the endeavor to upset everything, in the hope of getting profit from some source or other, than he who has nothing to lose? Now if there were any king who was either so despicable or so hateful to his subjects that he could not keep them in subjection otherwise than by ill usage, plundering, and confiscation and by reducing them to beggary, it would surely be better for him to resign his throne than to keep it by such means—means by which, though he retain the name of authority, he loses its majesty. It is not consistent with the dignity of a king to exercise authority over beggars but over prosperous and happy subjects. This was certainly the sentiment of that noble and lofty spirit, Fabricius,[6] who replied that he would rather be a ruler of rich people than be rich himself.

"To be sure, to have a single person enjoy a life of pleasure and self-indulgence amid the groans and lamentations of all around him is to be the keeper, not of a kingdom, but of a jail. In fine, as he is an incompetent physician who cannot cure one disease except by creating another, so he who cannot reform the lives of citizens in any other way than by depriving them of the good things of life must admit that he does not know how to rule free men.

"Yea, the king had better amend his own indolence or arrogance, for these two vices generally cause his people either to despise him or to hate him. Let him live harmlessly on what is his own. Let him adjust his expenses to his revenues. Let him check mischief and crime, and, by training his subjects rightly, let him prevent rather than allow the spread of activities which he will have to punish afterwards. Let him not be hasty in enforcing laws fallen into disuse, especially those which, long given up, have never been missed. Let him never take in compensation for violation anything that a private person would be forbidden in court to appropriate for the reason that such would be an act of crooked craftiness.

"What if then I were to put before them the law of the Macarians,[7] a people not very far distant from Utopia? Their king, on the day he first enters into office, is bound by an oath at solemn sacrifices that he will never have at one time in his coffer more than a thousand pounds of gold or its equivalent in silver. They report that this law was instituted by a very good king, who cared more for his country's interest than his own wealth, to be a barrier against hoarding so much money as would cause a lack of it among his people. He saw that this treasure would be sufficient for the

---

5. A king who did not care for the welfare of his people was usually identified as a tyrant. As Aristotle stated, a tyranny is a perversion of a monarchy and it is characterized by "irresponsible rule over subjects . . . with a view to its own private interest and not in the interest of the persons ruled" (*Politics*, 4.8.3).

6. Roman commander of the republican period; whether he actually made the statement attributed to him is unclear. In any case, it outlines a critique of monarchy common in antityrannical literature of the early modern period.
7. "Happy Ones."

king to put down rebellion and for his kingdom to meet hostile invasions. It was not large enough, however, to tempt him to encroach on the possessions of others. The prevention of the latter was the primary purpose of his legislation. His secondary consideration was that provision was thus made to forestall any shortage of the money needed in the daily business transactions of the citizens. He felt, too, that since the king had to pay out whatever came into his treasury beyond the limit prescribed by law, he would not seek occasion to commit injustice. Such a king will be both a terror to the evil and beloved by the good. To sum it all up, if I tried to obtrude these and like ideas on men strongly inclined to the opposite way of thinking, to what deaf ears should I tell the tale!"

"Deaf indeed, without doubt," I agreed, "and, by heaven, I am not surprised. Neither, to tell the truth, do I think that such ideas should be thrust on people, or such advice given, as you are positive will never be listened to. What good could such novel ideas do, or how could they enter the minds of individuals who are already taken up and possessed by the opposite conviction? In the private conversation of close friends this academic philosophy is not without its charm, but in the councils of kings, where great matters are debated with great authority, there is no room for these notions."

"That is just what I meant," he rejoined, "by saying there is no room for philosophy with rulers."

"Right," I declared, "that is true—not for this academic philosophy which thinks that everything is suitable to every place. But there is another philosophy, more practical for statesmen, which knows its stage, adapts itself to the play in hand, and performs its role neatly and appropriately. This is the philosophy which you must employ. Otherwise we have the situation in which a comedy of Plautus is being performed and the household slaves are making trivial jokes at one another and then you come on the stage in a philosopher's attire and recite the passage from the *Octavia* where Seneca is disputing with Nero.[8] Would it not have been preferable to take a part without words than by reciting something inappropriate to make a hodgepodge of comedy and tragedy? You would have spoiled and upset the actual play by bringing in irrelevant matter—even if your contribution would have been superior in itself. Whatever play is being performed, perform it as best you can, and do not upset it all simply because you think of another which has more interest.

"So it is in the commonwealth. So it is in the deliberations of monarchs. If you cannot pluck up wrongheaded opinions by the root, if you cannot cure according to your heart's desire vices of long standing, yet you must not on that account desert the commonwealth. You must not abandon the ship in a storm because you cannot control the winds.

"On the other hand, you must not force upon people new and strange ideas which you realize will carry no weight with persons of opposite conviction.

8. More's character "More" illustrates the poor social skills of the philosopher by imagining a situation in which the philosopher quotes lines from Seneca's tragedy while everyone else is enjoying a comedy by Plautus. "More" asks not only that the philosopher observe conditions of time and place, but also that—in political situations in which the philosopher might like to instruct his people in moral action but finds that they do not want to listen to him—he not give up his civic obligations and go into retirement. The predicament was one that More and many of his contemporary humanist statesmen actually confronted when they attempted to give advice to their political superiors.

On the contrary, by the indirect approach you must seek and strive to the best of your power to handle matters tactfully. What you cannot turn to good you must at least make as little bad as you can. For it is impossible that all should be well unless all men were good, a situation which I do not expect for a great many years to come!"

"By this approach," he commented, "I should accomplish nothing else than to share the madness of others as I tried to cure their lunacy. If I would stick to the truth, I must needs speak in the manner I have described. To speak falsehoods, for all I know, may be the part of a philosopher, but it is certainly not for me. Although that speech of mine might perhaps be unwelcome and disagreeable to those councilors, yet I cannot see why it should seem odd even to the point of folly. What if I told them the kind of things which Plato creates in his republic or which the Utopians actually put in practice in theirs? Though such institutions were superior (as, to be sure, they are), yet they might appear odd because here individuals have the right of private property, there all things are common.

"To persons who had made up their minds to go headlong by the opposite road, the man who beckons them back and points out dangers ahead can hardly be welcome. But, apart from this aspect, what did my speech contain that would not be appropriate or obligatory to have propounded everywhere? Truly, if all the things which by the perverse morals of men have come to seem odd are to be dropped as unusual and absurd, we must dissemble among Christians almost all the doctrines of Christ. Yet He forbade us to dissemble them to the extent that what He had whispered in the ears of His disciples He commanded to be preached openly from the housetops.[9] The greater part of His teaching is far more different from the morals of mankind than was my discourse. But preachers, crafty men that they are, finding that men grievously disliked to have their morals adjusted to the rule of Christ and following I suppose your advice, accommodated His teaching to men's morals as if it were a rule of soft lead that at least in some way or other the two might be made to correspond.[1] By this method I cannot see what they have gained, except that men may be bad in greater comfort.

"And certainly I should make as little progress in the councils of princes. For I should hold either a different opinion, which would amount to having none at all, or else the same, and then I should, as Mitio says in Terence, help their madness.[2] As to that indirect approach of yours, I cannot see its relevancy; I mean your advice to use my endeavors, if all things cannot be made good, at least to handle them tactfully and, as far as one may, to make them as little bad as possible. At court there is no room for dissembling, nor may one shut one's eyes to things. One must openly approve the worst counsels and subscribe to the most ruinous decrees.

9. Hythlodaeus paraphrases Matthew 10.27 and Luke 12.3; he proposes that the practical and accommodating flexibility that "More" advocates finds its limits in the absolute moral doctrine preached by Jesus Christ and therefore to be followed by Christians.

1. The "rule of soft lead," or the Lesbian rule (after the leaden measure used in architecture on the island of Lesbos in the Aegean), is the figure Aristotle uses to illustrate the concept of equity. The measure, supposedly a rule or an absolute, corresponds to the idea of a written law; but because it is flexible, it is also a written law that

is always interpreted in such a way as to fit the particulars of a case.

2. Hythlodaeus insists that for a philosopher to cross a person in authority and with power will only make the philosopher appear nonsensical and therefore render the ruler less reasonable than he was at first; that is, both philosopher and ruler will appear to be madmen. He instances Mitio, a character in Terence's play The Brothers, who declares: "Still, if I inflamed or even fell in with his passionate temper, I should surely give him another madman for company" (1.145–147).

He would be counted a spy and almost a traitor, who gives only faint praise to evil counsels.

"Moreover, there is no chance for you to do any good because you are brought among colleagues who would easily corrupt even the best of men before being reformed themselves. By their evil companionship, either you will be seduced yourself or, keeping your own integrity and innocence, you will be made a screen for the wickedness and folly of others. Thus you are far from being able to make anything better by that indirect approach of yours.

"For this reason, Plato by a very fine comparison shows why philosophers are right in abstaining from administration of the commonwealth. They observe the people rushing out into the streets and being soaked by constant showers and cannot induce them to go indoors and escape the rain. They know that, if they go out, they can do no good but will only get wet with the rest. Therefore, being content if they themselves at least are safe, they keep at home, since they cannot remedy the folly of others.[3]

"Yet surely, my dear More, to tell you candidly my heart's sentiments, it appears to me that wherever you have private property and all men measure all things by cash values, there it is scarcely possible for a commonwealth to have justice or prosperity—unless you think justice exists where all the best things flow into the hands of the worst citizens or prosperity prevails where all is divided among very few—and even they are not altogether well off, while the rest are downright wretched.

"As a result, when in my heart I ponder on the extremely wise and holy institutions of the Utopians, among whom, with very few laws, affairs are ordered so aptly that virtue has its reward, and yet, with equality of distribution, all men have abundance of all things, and then when I contrast with their policies the many nations elsewhere ever making ordinances and yet never one of them achieving good order—nations where whatever a man has acquired he calls his own private property, but where all these laws daily framed are not enough for a man to secure or to defend or even to distinguish from someone else's the goods which each in turn calls his own, a predicament readily attested by the numberless and ever new and interminable lawsuits—when I consider, I repeat, all these facts, I become more partial to Plato and less surprised at his refusal to make laws for those who rejected that legislation which gave to all an equal share in all goods.

"This wise sage, to be sure, easily foresaw that the one and only road to the general welfare lies in the maintenance of equality in all respects. I have my doubts that the latter could ever be preserved where the individual's possessions are his private property. When every man aims at absolute ownership of all the property he can get, be there never so great abundance of goods, it is all shared by a handful who leave the rest in poverty. It generally happens that the one class preeminently deserves the lot of the other, for the rich are greedy, unscrupulous, and useless, while the poor are well-behaved, simple, and by their daily industry more beneficial to the commonwealth than to themselves. I am fully persuaded that no just and even distribution of goods can be made and that no happiness can be found in human affairs

---

3. Cf. *Republic* 6.496d: "he keeps quiet and minds his own business—as a man in a storm . . . stands aside under a little wall. Seeing others filled with lawlessness, he is content if somehow he himself can live his life here pure of injustice and unholy deeds."

unless private property is utterly abolished.[4] While it lasts, there will always remain a heavy and inescapable burden of poverty and misfortunes for by far the greatest and by far the best part of mankind.

"I admit that this burden can be lightened to some extent, but I contend that it cannot be removed entirely. A statute might be made that no person should hold more than a certain amount of land and that no person should have a monetary income beyond that permitted by law. Special legislation might be passed to prevent the monarch from being overmighty and the people overweening; likewise, that public offices should not be solicited with gifts, nor be put up for sale, nor require lavish personal expenditures. Otherwise, there arise, first, the temptation to recoup one's expenses by acts of fraud and plunder and, secondly, the necessity of appointing rich men to offices which ought rather to have been administered by wise men. By this type of legislation, I maintain, as sick bodies which are past cure can be kept up by repeated medical treatments, so these evils, too, can be alleviated and made less acute. There is no hope, however, of a cure and a return to a healthy condition as long as each individual is master of his own property. Nay, while you are intent upon the cure of one part, you make worse the malady of the other parts. Thus, the healing of the one member reciprocally breeds the disease of the other as long as nothing can so be added to one as not to be taken away from another."[5]

"But," I ventured, "I am of the contrary opinion. Life cannot be satisfactory where all things are common. How can there be a sufficient supply of goods when each withdraws himself from the labor of production? For the individual does not have the motive of personal gain and he is rendered slothful by trusting to the industry of others. Moreover, when people are goaded by want and yet the individual cannot legally keep as his own what he has gained, must there not be trouble from continual bloodshed and riot? This holds true especially since the authority of magistrates and respect for their office have been eliminated, for how there can be any place for these among men who are all on the same level I cannot even conceive."

"I do not wonder," he rejoined, "that it looks this way to you, being a person who has no picture at all, or else a false one, of the situation I mean. But you should have been with me in Utopia and personally seen their manners and customs as I did, for I lived there more than five years and would never have wished to leave except to make known that new world. In that case you unabashedly would admit that you had never seen a well-ordered people anywhere but there."

"Yet surely," objected Peter Giles, "it would be hard for you to convince me that a better-ordered people is to be found in that new world than in the one known to us. In the latter I imagine there are equally excellent minds, as well as commonwealths which are older than those in the new world. In these commonwealths long experience has

4. It was thought that primordial humans did not understand that property could be private and belong to one party only. With the congregation of men and women into tribes, however, private property was established by markers: boundary lines, signs and emblems, and distinctive styles of manufacture. This moment also saw the institution of a civil society characterized by religion and law. By advocating a state in which there is no private property, Hythlodaeus posits a political and economic situation that his contemporaries would have recognized in such limited societies as those under monastic or some other kind of religious rule.

5. The trope of the body politic is ubiquitous in early modern political thought. In *The Education of a Christian Prince*, Erasmus argues: "[A monarch] should consider his kingdom as a great body of which he is the most outstanding member and remember that they who have entrusted all their fortunes and their very safety to the good faith of one man are deserving of consideration. He should keep constantly in mind the example of those rulers to whom the welfare of their people was dearer than their own lives; for it is obviously impossible for a prince to do violence to the state without injuring himself." See also Plato's *Republic*, 5.462.

come upon very many advantages for human life—not to mention also the chance discoveries made among us, which no human mind could have devised."

"As for the antiquity of commonwealths," he countered, "you could give a sounder opinion if you had read the historical accounts of that world. If we must believe them, there were cities among them before there were men among us. Furthermore, whatever either brains have invented or chance has discovered hitherto could have happened equally in both places. But I hold for certain that, even though we may surpass them in brains, we are far inferior to them in application and industry.

"According to their chronicles, up to the time of our landing they had never heard anything about our activities (they call us the Ultra-equinoctials) except that twelve hundred years ago a ship driven by a tempest was wrecked on the island of Utopia. Some Romans and Egyptians were cast on shore and remained on the island without ever leaving it. Now mark what good advantage their industry took of this one opportunity. The Roman empire possessed no art capable of any use which they did not either learn from the shipwrecked strangers or discover for themselves after receiving the hints for investigation—so great a gain was it to them that on a single occasion some persons were carried to their shores from ours.

"But if any like fortune has ever driven anyone from their shores to ours, the event is as completely forgotten as future generations will perhaps forget that I had once been there. And, just as they immediately at one meeting appropriated to themselves every good discovery of ours, so I suppose it will be long before we adopt anything that is better arranged with them than with us. This trait, I judge, is the chief reason why, though we are inferior to them neither in brains nor in resources, their commonwealth is more wisely governed and more happily flourishing than ours."

"If so, my dear Raphael," said I, "I beg and beseech you, give us a description of the island. Do not be brief, but set forth in order the terrain, the rivers, the cities, the inhabitants, the traditions, the customs, the laws, and, in fact, everything which you think we should like to know. And you must think we wish to know everything of which we are still ignorant."

"There is nothing," he declared, "I shall be more pleased to do, for I have the facts ready to hand. But the description will take time."

"In that case," I suggested, "let us go in to dine. Afterwards we shall take up as much time as we like."

"Agreed," he replied.

So we went in and dined. We then returned to the same place, sat down on the same bench, and gave orders to the servants that we should not be interrupted. Peter Giles and I urged Raphael to fulfill his promise. As for him, when he saw us intent and eager to listen, after sitting in silent thought for a time, he began his tale as follows.

THE END OF BOOK ONE

BOOK 2

The island of the Utopians extends in the center (where it is broadest) for two hundred miles and is not much narrower for the greater part of the island, but toward both ends it begins gradually to taper. These ends form a circle five hundred miles in circumference and so make the island look like a new moon, the horns of which are divided by straits about eleven miles across. The straits then unfold into a wide expanse. As the winds are kept off by the land which everywhere surrounds it, the bay is like a huge lake, smooth rather than rough, and thus converts almost the whole center of the country into a harbor which lets ships cross in every direction to the great convenience of the inhabitants.

The mouth of this bay is rendered perilous here by shallows and there by reefs. Almost in the center of the gap stands one great crag which, being visible, is not dangerous. A tower built on it is occupied by a garrison. The other rocks are hidden and therefore treacherous. The channels are known only to the natives, and so it does not easily happen that any foreigner enters the bay except with a Utopian pilot. In fact, the entrance is hardly safe even for themselves, unless they guide themselves by landmarks on the shore. If these were removed to other positions, they could easily lure an enemy's fleet, however numerous, to destruction.

On the outer side of the island, harbors are many. Everywhere, however, the landing is so well defended by nature or by engineering that a few defenders can prevent strong forces from coming ashore.

As the report goes and as the appearance of the ground shows, the island once was not surrounded by sea. But Utopus,[6] who as conqueror gave the island its name (up to then it had been called Abraxa[7]) and who brought the rude and rustic people to such a perfection of culture and humanity as makes them now superior to almost all other mortals, gained a victory at his very first landing. He then ordered the excavation of fifteen miles on the side where the land was connected with the continent and caused the sea to flow around the land. He set to the task not only the natives but, to prevent them from thinking the labor a disgrace, his own soldiers also. With the work divided among so many hands, the enterprise was finished with incredible speed and struck the neighboring peoples, who at first had derided the project as vain, with wonder and terror at its success.

The island contains fifty-four city-states,[8] all spacious and magnificent, identical in language, traditions, customs, and laws. They are similar also in layout and everywhere, as far as the nature of the ground permits, similar even in appearance. None of them is separated by less than twenty-four miles from the nearest, but none is so isolated that a person cannot go from it to another in a day's journey on foot. From each city three old and experienced citizens meet to discuss the affairs of common interest to the island once a year at Amaurotum, for this city, being in the very center of the country, is situated most conveniently for the representatives of all sections. It is considered the chief as well as the capital city.

The lands are so well assigned to the cities that each has at least twelve miles of country on every side, and on some sides even much more, to wit, the side on which the cities are farther apart. No city has any desire to extend its territory, for they consider themselves the tenants rather than the masters of what they hold.

Everywhere in the rural districts they have, at suitable distances from one another, farmhouses well equipped with agricultural implements. They are inhabited by citizens who come in succession to live there. No rural household numbers less

6. Ruler over no place.
7. The name for the highest of 365 heavens, according to the Gnostic philosopher Basilides.
8. When More wrote Utopia, England consisted of 53 counties and the City of London, its principal urban cen-

ter. This allusion to England establishes a connection between Books 1 and 2 and suggests that More intended aspects of Utopia to be understood in relation to life in England.

than forty men and women, besides two serfs attached to the soil.[9] Over them are set a master and a mistress, serious in mind and ripe in years. Over every group of thirty households rules a phylarch.[1]

Twenty from each household return every year to the city, namely, those having completed two years in the country. As substitutes in their place, the same number are sent from the city. They are to be trained by those who have been there a year and who therefore are more expert in farming; they themselves will teach others in the following years. There is thus no danger of anything going wrong with the annual food supply through want of skill, as might happen if all at one time were newcomers and novices at farming. Though this system of changing farmers is the rule, to prevent any individual's being forced against his will to continue too long in a life of rather hard work, yet many men who take a natural pleasure in agricultural pursuits obtain leave to stay several years.

The occupation of the farmers is to cultivate the soil, to feed the animals, and to get wood and convey it to the city either by land or by water, whichever way is more convenient. They breed a vast quantity of poultry by a wonderful contrivance. The hens do not brood over the eggs, but the farmers, by keeping a great number of them at a uniform heat, bring them to life and hatch them. As soon as they come out of the shell, the chicks follow and acknowledge humans as their mothers!

They rear very few horses, and these only high-spirited ones, which they use for no other purpose than for exercising their young men in horsemanship. All the labor of cultivation and transportation is performed by oxen, which they admit are inferior to horses in a sudden spurt but which are far superior to them in staying power and endurance and not liable to as many diseases. Moreover, it requires less trouble and expense to feed them. When they are past work, they finally are of use for food.

They sow grain only for bread. Their drink is wine or cider or perry,[2] or it is even water. The latter is sometimes plain and often that in which they have boiled honey or licorice, whereof they have a great abundance.

Though they are more than sure how much food the city with its adjacent territory consumes, they produce far more grain and cattle than they require for their own use: they distribute the surplus among their neighbors. Whenever they need things not found in the country, they send for all the materials from the city and, having to give nothing in exchange, obtain it from the municipal officials without the bother of bargaining. For very many go there every single month to observe the holyday.

When the time of harvest is at hand, the agricultural phylarchs inform the municipal officials what number of citizens they require to be sent. The crowd of harvesters, coming promptly at the appointed time, dispatch the whole task of harvesting almost in a single day of fine weather.

The Cities, Especially Amaurotum

The person who knows one of the cities will know them all, since they are exactly alike insofar as the terrain permits. I shall therefore picture one or other (nor does it matter which), but which should I describe rather than Amaurotum? First, none is

9. According to feudal practice in medieval Europe, a serf was a person who was in servitude for life and could not leave the land whose lord he served. Unlike most slaves, however, who were generally men or women taken captive in the course of a war and who could buy their freedom, a serf was never freed from his connection to an estate.

Hythlodaeus refers to other kinds of Utopian slaves later in his account of how Utopians organize their society.
1. Chief.
2. Pear liqueur.

worthier, the rest deferring to it as the meeting place of the national senate; and, secondly, none is better known to me, as being one in which I had lived for five whole years.

To proceed. Amaurotum is situated on the gentle slope of a hill and is almost four-square in outline. Its breadth is about two miles starting just below the crest of the hill and running down to the river Anydrus; its length along the river is some-what more than its breadth.

The Anydrus rises eighty miles above Amaurotum from a spring not very large; but, being increased in size by several tributaries, two of which are of fair size, it is half a mile broad in front of the city. After soon becoming still broader and after running farther for sixty miles, it falls into the ocean. Through the whole distance between the city and the sea, and even above the city for some miles, the tide alter-nately flows in for six whole hours and then ebbs with an equally speedy current. When the sea comes in, it fills the whole bed of the Anydrus with its water for a dis-tance of thirty miles, driving the river back. At such times it turns the water salt for some distance farther, but above that point the river grows gradually fresh and passes the city uncontaminated. When the ebb comes, the fresh and pure water extends down almost to the mouth of the river.[3]

The city is joined to the opposite bank of the river not by a bridge built on wooden pillars or piles but by one magnificently arched with stonework. It is situ-ated in the quarter which is farthest from the sea so that ships may pass along the whole of that side of the city without hindrance.

They have also another river, not very large, but very gentle and pleasant, which rises out of the same hill whereon the city is built and runs down through its middle into the river Anydrus. The head and source of this river just outside the city has been connected with it by outworks, lest in case of hostile attack the water might be cut off and diverted or polluted. From this point the water is distributed by conduits made of baked clay into various parts of the lower town. Where the ground makes that course impossible, the rain water collected in capacious cisterns is just as useful.

The city is surrounded by a high and broad wall with towers and ravelins at fre-quent intervals. A moat, dry but deep and wide and made impassable by thorn hedges, surrounds the fortifications on three sides; on the fourth the river itself takes the place of the moat.

The streets are well laid out both for traffic and for protection against the winds. The buildings, which are far from mean, are set together in a long row, con-tinuous through the block and faced by a corresponding one. The house fronts of the respective blocks are divided by an avenue twenty feet broad. On the rear of the houses, through the whole length of the block, lies a broad garden enclosed on all sides by the backs of the blocks. Every home has not only a door into the street but a back door into the garden. What is more, folding doors, easily opened by hand and then closing of themselves, give admission to anyone. As a result, nothing is private property anywhere. Every ten years they actually exchange their very homes by lot.

The Utopians are very fond of their gardens. In them they have vines, fruits, herbs, flowers, so well kept and flourishing that I never saw anything more fruitful and more tasteful anywhere. Their zest in keeping them is increased not merely by the pleasure afforded them but by the keen competition between blocks as to which

3. These features of the Anydrus resemble those of London's Thames River.

will have the best kept garden. Certainly you cannot readily find anything in the whole city more productive of profit and pleasure to the citizens. Therefore it would seem their founder attached the greatest importance to these gardens.

In fact, they report that the whole plan of the city had been sketched at the very beginning by Utopus himself. He left to posterity, however, to add the adornment and other improvements for which he saw one lifetime would hardly suffice. Their annals, embracing the history of 1760 years, are preserved carefully and conscientiously in writing. Here they find stated that at first the houses were low, mere cabins and huts, haphazardly made with any wood to hand, with mud-plastered walls. They had thatched the ridged roofs with straw.

But now all the homes are of handsome appearance with three stories. The exposed faces of the walls are made of stone or cement or brick, rubble being used as filling for the empty space between the walls. The roofs are flat and covered with a kind of cement which is cheap but so well mixed that it is impervious to fire and superior to lead in defying the damage caused by storms. They keep the winds out of their windows by glass (which is in very common use in Utopia) or sometimes by thin linen smeared with translucent oil or amber. The advantage is twofold: the device results in letting more light in and keeping more wind out.

The Officials

Every thirty families choose annually an official whom in their ancient language they call a syphogrant[4] but in their newer a phylarch. Over ten syphogrants with their families is set a person once called a tranibor but now a protophylarch.[5] The whole body of syphogrants, in number two hundred, having sworn to choose the man whom they judge most useful, by secret balloting appoint a governor, specifically one of the four candidates named to them by the people, for one is selected out of each of the four quarter of the city to be commended to the senate.

The governor holds office for life, unless ousted on suspicion of aiming at a tyranny. The tranibors are elected annually but are not changed without good reason. The other officials all hold their posts for one year.

The tranibors enter into consultation with the governor every other day and sometimes, if need arises, oftener. They take counsel about the commonwealth. If there are any disputes between private persons—there are very few—they settle them without loss of time. They always admit to the senate chamber two syphogrants, and different ones every day. It is provided that nothing concerning the commonwealth be ratified if it has not been discussed in the senate three days before the passing of the decree. To take counsel on matters of common interest outside the senate or the popular assembly is considered a capital offense. The object of these measures, they say, is to prevent it from being easy, by a conspiracy between the governor and the tranibors and by tyrannous oppression of the people, to change the order of the commonwealth. Therefore whatever is considered important is laid before the assembly of the syphogrants who, after informing their groups of families, take counsel together and report their decision to the senate. Sometimes the matter is laid before the council of the whole island.

In addition, the senate has the custom of debating nothing on the same day on which it is first proposed but of putting it off till the next meeting. This is their rule

---

4. Wise old man.   5. Tranibor: glutton; protophylarch: principal chief.

lest anyone, after hastily blurting out the first thought that popped into his head, should afterwards give more thought to defending his opinion than to supporting what is for the good of the commonwealth, and should prefer to jeopardize the public welfare rather than to risk his reputation through a wrongheaded and misplaced shame, fearing he might be thought to have shown too little foresight at the first—though he should have been enough foresighted at the first to speak with prudence rather than with haste!

Occupations

Agriculture is the one pursuit which is common to all, both men and women, without exception. They are all instructed in it from childhood, partly by principles taught in school, partly by field trips to the farms closer to the city as if for recreation. Here they do not merely look on, but, as opportunity arises for bodily exercise, they do the actual work.

Besides agriculture (which is, as I said, common to all), each is taught one particular craft as his own. This is generally either wool-working or linen-making or masonry or metal-working or carpentry. There is no other pursuit which occupies any number worth mentioning. As for clothes, these are of one and the same pattern throughout the island and down the centuries, though there is a distinction between the sexes and between the single and married. The garments are comely to the eye, convenient for bodily movement, and fit for wear in heat and cold. Each family, I say, does its own tailoring.

Of the other crafts, one is learned by each person, and not the men only, but the women too. The latter as the weaker sex have the lighter occupations and generally work wool and flax. To the men are committed the remaining more laborious crafts. For the most part, each is brought up in his father's craft, for which most have a natural inclination. But if anyone is attracted to another occupation, he is transferred by adoption to a family pursuing that craft for which he has a liking. Care is taken not only by his father but by the authorities, too, that he will be assigned to a grave and honorable householder. Moreover, if anyone after being thoroughly taught one craft desires another also, the same permission is given. Having acquired both, he practices his choice unless the city has more need of the one than of the other.

The chief and almost the only function of the syphogrants is to manage and provide that no one sit idle, but that each apply himself industriously to his trade, and yet that he be not wearied like a beast of burden with constant toil from early morning till late at night. Such wretchedness is worse than the lot of slaves, and yet it is almost everywhere the life of workingmen—except for the Utopians. The latter divide the day and night into twenty-four equal hours and assign only six to work. There are three before noon, after which they go to dinner. After dinner, when they have rested for two hours in the afternoon, they again give three to work and finish up with supper. Counting one o'clock as the first hour after noon, they go to bed about eight o'clock, and sleep claims eight hours.

The intervals between the hours of work, sleep, and food are left to every man's discretion, not to waste in revelry or idleness, but to devote the time free from work to some other occupation according to taste. These periods are commonly devoted to intellectual pursuits. For it is their custom that public lectures are daily delivered in the hours before daybreak. Attendance is compulsory only for those who have been specially chosen to devote themselves to learning. A great number of all classes, however, both males and females, flock to hear the lectures, some to one and some to another, according to their natural inclination. But if anyone should prefer to devote this time to his trade, as is the case with many minds which do not reach the level for any of the higher intellectual disciplines, he is not hindered; in fact, he is even praised as useful to the commonwealth.

After supper they spend one hour in recreation, in summer in the gardens, in winter in the common halls in which they have their meals. There they either play music or entertain themselves with conversation. Dice and that kind of foolish and ruinous game they are not acquainted with. They do play two games not unlike chess. The first is a battle of numbers in which one number plunders another. The second is a game in which the vices fight a pitched battle with the virtues. In the latter is exhibited very cleverly, to begin with, both the strife of the vices with one another and their concerted opposition to the virtues; then, what vices are opposed to what virtues, by what forces they assail them openly, by what stratagems they attack them indirectly, by what safeguards the virtues check the power of the vices, by what arts they frustrate their designs; and, finally, by what means the one side gains the victory.

But here, lest you be mistaken, there is one point you must examine more closely. Since they devote but six hours to work, you might possibly think the consequence to be some scarcity of necessities. But so far is this from being the case that the aforesaid time is not only enough but more than enough for a supply of all that is requisite for either the necessity or the convenience of living. This phenomenon you too will understand if you consider how large a part of the population in other countries exists without working. First, there are almost all the women, who constitute half the whole; or, where the women are busy, there as a rule the men are snoring in their stead. Besides, how great and how lazy is the crowd of priests and so-called religious! Add to them all the rich, especially the masters of estates, who are commonly termed gentlemen and noblemen. Reckon with them their retainers—I mean, that whole rabble of good-for-nothing swashbucklers. Finally, join in the lusty and sturdy beggars who make some disease an excuse for idleness. You will certainly find far less numerous than you had supposed those whose labor produces all the articles that mortals require for daily use.

Now estimate how few of those who do work are occupied in essential trades. For, in a society where we make money the standard of everything, it is necessary to practice many crafts which are quite vain and superfluous, ministering only to luxury and licentiousness. Suppose the host of those who now toil were distributed over only as few crafts as natural needs and conveniences require. In the great abundance of commodities which must then arise, the prices set on them would be too low for the craftsmen to earn their livelihood by their work. But suppose all those fellows who are now busied with unprofitable crafts, as well as all the lazy and idle throng, any one of whom now consumes as much of the fruits of other men's labors as any two of the workingmen, were all set to work and indeed to useful work. You can easily see how small an allowance of time would be enough and to spare for the production of all that is required by necessity or comfort (or even pleasure, provided it be genuine and natural).

The very experience of Utopia makes the latter clear. In the whole city and its neighborhood, exemption from work is granted to hardly five hundred of the total of men and women whose age and strength make them fit for work. Among them the syphogrants, though legally exempted from work, yet take no advantage of this privilege so that by their example they may the more readily attract the others to work.

The same exemption is enjoyed by those whom the people, persuaded by the recommendation of the priests, have given perpetual freedom from labor through the secret vote of the syphogrants so that they may learn thoroughly the various branches of knowledge. But if any of these scholars falsifies the hopes entertained of him, he is reduced to the rank of workingman. On the other hand, not seldom does it happen that a craftsman so industriously employs his spare hours on learning and makes such progress by his diligence that he is relieved of his manual labor and advanced into the class of men of learning. It is out of this company of scholars that they choose ambassadors, priests, tranibors, and finally the governor himself, whom they call in their ancient tongue Barzanes but in their more modern language Ademus.[6]

Nearly all the remaining populace being neither idle nor busied with useless occupations, it is easy to calculate how much good work can be produced in a very few hours. Besides the points mentioned, there is this further convenience that in most of the necessary crafts they do not require as much work as other nations. In the first place the erection or repair of buildings requires the constant labor of so many men elsewhere because what a father has built, his extravagant heir allows gradually to fall into ruin. As a result, what might have been kept up at small cost, his successor is obliged to erect anew at great expense. Further, often even when a house has cost one man a large sum, another is so fastidious that he thinks little of it. When it is neglected and therefore soon becomes dilapidated, he builds a second elsewhere at no less cost. But in the land of the Utopians, now that everything has been settled and the commonwealth established, a new home on a new site is a rare event, for not only do they promptly repair any damage, but they even take care to prevent damage. What is the result? With the minimum of labor, buildings last very long, and masons and carpenters sometimes have scarcely anything to do, except that they are set to hew out timber at home and to square and prepare stone meantime so that, if any work be required, a building may the sooner be erected.

In the matter of clothing, too, see how little toil and labor is needed. First, while at work, they are dressed unpretentiously in leather or hide, which lasts for seven years. When they go out in public, they put on a cape to hide their comparatively rough working clothes. This garment is of one color throughout the island and that the natural color. Consequently not only is much less woolen cloth needed than elsewhere, but what they have is much less expensive. On the other hand, since linen cloth is made with less labor, it is more used. In linen cloth only whiteness, in woolen cloth only cleanliness, is considered. No value is set on fineness of thread. So it comes about that, whereas elsewhere one man is not satisfied with four or five woolen coats of different colors and as many silk shirts, and the more fastidious not even with ten, in Utopia a man is content with a single cape, lasting generally for two years. There is no reason, of course, why he should desire more, for if he had them he would not be better fortified against the cold nor appear better dressed in the least.

Wherefore, seeing that they are all busied with useful trades and are satisfied with fewer products from them, it even happens that when there is an abundance of all commodities, they sometimes take out a countless number of people to repair whatever public roads are in bad order. Often, too, when there is nothing even of

---

6. Barzanes: "son of Zeus"; Ademus, "peopleless." These names indicate that the governor of Utopia, although considered a divinity in the primitive period of the state, is so impartial in his efforts to rule that he seems to belong to no family, region, or people.

this kind of work to be done, they announce publicly that there will be fewer hours of work. For the authorities do not keep the citizens against their will at superfluous labor since the constitution of their commonwealth looks in the first place to this sole object: that for all the citizens, as far as the public needs permit, as much time as possible should be withdrawn from the service of the body and devoted to the freedom and culture of the mind. It is in the latter that they deem the happiness of life to consist.

Social Relations

But now, it seems, I must explain the behavior of the citizens toward one another, the nature of their social relations, and the method of distribution of goods. Since the city consists of households, households as a rule are made up of those related by blood. Girls, upon reaching womanhood and upon being settled in marriage, go to their husbands' domiciles. On the other hand, male children and then grandchildren remain in the family and are subject to the oldest parent, unless he has become a dotard with old age. In the latter case the next oldest is put in his place.

But that the city neither be depopulated nor grow beyond measure, provision is made that no household shall have fewer than ten or more than sixteen adults; there are six thousand such households in each city, apart from its surrounding territory. Of children under age, of course, no number can be fixed.[7] This limit is easily observed by transferring those who exceed the number in larger families into those that are under the prescribed number. Whenever all the families of a city reach their full quota, the extra persons help to make up the deficient population of other cities.

And if the population throughout the island should happen to swell above the fixed quotas, they enroll citizens out of every city and, on the mainland nearest them, wherever the natives have much unoccupied and uncultivated land, they found a colony under their own laws. They join with themselves the natives if they are willing to dwell with them. When such a union takes place, the two parties gradually and easily merge and together absorb the same way of life and the same customs, much to the great advantage of both peoples. By their procedures they make the land sufficient for both, which previously seemed poor and barren to the natives. The inhabitants who refuse to live according to their laws, they drive from the territory which they carve out for themselves. If they resist, they wage war against them. They consider it a most just cause for war when a people which does not use its soil but keeps it idle and waste nevertheless forbids the use and possession of it to others who by the rule of nature ought to be maintained by it.

If ever any misfortune so diminishes the number in any of their cities that it cannot be made up out of other parts of the island without bringing other cities below their proper strength (this has happened, they say, only twice in all the ages on account of the raging of a fierce pestilence), they are filled up by citizens returning from colonial territory. They would rather that the colonies should perish than that any of the cities of the island should be enfeebled.

But to return to the dealings of the citizens. The oldest, as I have said, rules the household. Wives wait on their husbands, children on their parents, and generally the younger on their elders.

---

7. In England, women came of age at 18, men at 22.

Every city is divided into four equal districts. In the middle of each quarter is a market of all kinds of commodities. To designated market buildings the products of each family are conveyed. Each kind of goods is arranged separately in storehouses. From the latter any head of a household seeks what he and his require and, without money or any kind of compensation, carries off what he seeks. Why should anything be refused? First, there is a plentiful supply of all things and, secondly, there is no underlying fear that anyone will demand more than he needs. Why should there be any suspicion that someone may demand an excessive amount when he is certain of never being in want? No doubt about it, avarice and greed are aroused in every kind of living creature by the fear of want, but only in man are they motivated by pride alone—pride which counts it a personal glory to excel others by superfluous display of possessions. The latter vice can have no place at all in the Utopian scheme of things.

Next to the market place that I have mentioned are the food markets. Here are brought not only different kinds of vegetables, fruit, and bread but also fish and whatever is edible of bird and four-footed beast. Outside the city are designated places where all gore and offal may be washed away in running water. From these places they transport the carcasses of the animals slaughtered and cleaned by the hands of slaves. They do not allow their citizens to accustom themselves to the butchering of animals, by the practice of which they think that mercy, the finest feeling of our human nature, is gradually killed off. In addition, they do not permit to be brought inside the city anything filthy or unclean for fear that the air, tainted by putrefaction, should engender disease.

To continue, each street has spacious halls, located at equal distance from one another, each being known by a special name of its own. In these halls live the syphogrants. To each hall are assigned thirty families, fifteen on either side, to take their meals in common. The managers of each hall meet at a fixed time in the market and get food according to the number of person in their individual charge.

Special care is first taken of the sick who are looked after in public hospitals. They have four at the city limits, a little outside the walls. These are so roomy as to be comparable to as many small towns. The purpose is twofold: first, that the sick, however numerous, should not be packed too close together in consequent discomfort and, second, that those who have a contagious disease likely to pass from one to another may be isolated as much as possible from the rest.[8] These hospitals are very well furnished and equipped with everything conducive to health. Besides, such tender and careful treatment and such constant attendance of expert physicians are provided that, though no one is sent to them against his will, there is hardly anybody in the whole city who, when suffering from illness, does not prefer to be nursed there rather than at home.

After the supervisor for the sick has received food as prescribed by the physicians, then the finest of everything is distributed equally among the halls according to the number in each, except that special regard is paid to the governor, the high priest, and the tranibors, as well as to ambassadors and all foreigners (if there are any, but they are few and far between). Yet the latter, too, when they are in Utopia, have definite homes got ready for them.

---

8. The germ theory of disease dates from the 19th century and the work of Louis Pasteur. Here More seems to be basing his idea of contagion on the experience of the bubonic plague, or Black Death, a major 14th-century European epidemic that killed roughly three-quarters of the population in 20 years.

To these halls, at the hours fixed for dinner and supper, the entire syphograncy assembles, summoned by the blast of a brazen trumpet, excepting persons who are taking their meals either in the hospitals or at home. No one is forbidden, after the halls have been served, to fetch food from the market to his home: they realize that no one would do it without good reason. For, though nobody is forbidden to dine at home, yet no one does it willingly since the practice is considered not decent and since it is foolish to take the trouble of preparing an inferior dinner when an excellent and sumptuous one is ready at hand in the hall nearby.

In this hall all menial offices which to some degree involve heavy labor or soil the hands are performed by slaves. But the duty of cooking and preparing the food and, in fine, of arranging the whole meal is carried out by the women alone, taking turns for each family. Persons sit down at three or more tables according to the number of the company. The men sit with their backs to the wall, the women on the outside, so that if they have any sudden pain or sickness, such as sometimes happens to women with child, they may rise without disturbing the arrangements and go to the nurses.

The nurses sit separately with the infants in a dining room assigned for the purpose, never without a fire and a supply of clean water nor without cradles. Thus they can both lay the infants down and, when they wish, undo their wrappings and let them play freely by the fire. Each woman nurses her own offspring, unless prevented by either death or disease. When that happens, the wives of the syphogrants quickly provide a nurse and find no difficulty in doing so. The reason is that women who can do the service offer themselves with the greatest readiness since everybody praises this kind of pity and since the child who is thus fostered looks on his nurse as his natural mother. In the nurses' quarters are all children up to five years of age. All other minors, among whom they include all of both sexes below the age of marriage, either wait at table on the diners or, if they are not old and strong enough, stand by—and that in absolute silence. Both groups eat what is handed them from the table and have no other separate time for dining.

The syphogrant and his wife sit in the middle of the first table, which is the highest place and which allows them to have the whole company in view, for it stands crosswise at the farthest end of the dining room. Alongside them are two of the eldest, for they always sit four by four at all tables. But if there is a temple in the syphograncy, the priest and his wife so sit with the syphogrant as to preside. On both sides of them sit younger people, and next to them old people again, and so through the house those of the same age sit together and yet mingle with those of a different age. The reason for this practice, they say, is that the grave and reverend behavior of the old may restrain the younger people from mischievous freedom in word and gesture, since nothing can be done or said at table which escapes the notice of the old present on every side.

The trays of food are not served in order from the first place and so on, but all the old men, who are seated in conspicuous places, are served first with the best food, and then equal portions are given to the rest. The old men at their discretion give a share of their delicacies to their neighbors when there is not enough to go around to everybody in the house. Thus, due respect is paid to seniority, and yet all have an equal advantage.

They begin every dinner and supper with some reading which is conducive to morality but which is brief so as not to be tiresome. Taking their cue from the reading, the elders introduce approved subjects of conversation, neither somber nor dull. But they do not monopolize the whole dinner with long speeches: they are ready to hear the young men too, and indeed deliberately draw them out that they may test each one's ability and character, which are revealed in the relaxed atmosphere of a feast.

Their dinners are somewhat short, their suppers more prolonged, because the former are followed by labor, the latter by sleep and a night's rest. They think the night's rest to be more efficacious to wholesome digestion. No supper passes without music, nor does the dessert course lack delicacies. They burn spices and scatter perfumes and omit nothing that may cheer the company. For they are somewhat more inclined to this attitude of mind: that no kind of pleasure is forbidden, provided no harm comes of it.

This is the common life they live in the city. In the country, however, since they are rather far removed from their neighbors, all take their meals in their own homes. No family lacks any kind of edible inasmuch as all the food eaten by the city dwellers comes from those who live in the country.

Utopian Travel, [Etc.]

Now if any citizens conceive a desire either to visit their friends who reside in another city or to see the place itself, they easily obtain leave from their syphogrants and tranibors, unless some good reason prevents them. Accordingly a party is made up and dispatched carrying a letter from the governor which bears witness to the granting of leave to travel and fixes the day of their return. A wagon is granted them with a public slave to conduct and see to the oxen, but, unless they have women in their company, they dispense with the wagon, regarding it as a burden and hindrance. Throughout their journey, though they carry nothing with them, yet nothing is lacking, for they are at home everywhere. If they stay longer than a day in any place, each practices his trade there and is entertained very courteously by workers in the same trade.

If any person gives himself leave to stray out of his territorial limits and is caught without the governor's certificate, he is treated with contempt, brought back as a runaway, and severely punished. If he dares to repeat the offense, he is punished with slavery.

If anyone is seized with the desire of exploring the country belonging to his own city, he is not forbidden to do so, provided he obtain his father's leave and his wife's consent. In any district of the country to which he comes, he receives no food until he has finished the morning share of the day's work or the labor that is usually performed there before supper. If he keep to this condition, he may go where he pleases within the territory belonging to his city. In this way he will be just as useful to the city as if he were in it.

Now you can see how nowhere is there any license to waste time, nowhere any pretext to evade work—no wine shop, no alehouse, no brothel anywhere, no opportunity for corruption, no lurking hole, no secret meeting place. On the contrary, being under the eyes of all, people are bound either to be performing the usual labor or to be enjoying their leisure in a fashion not without decency. This universal behavior must of necessity lead to an abundance of all commodities. Since the latter are distributed evenly among all, it follows, of course, that no one can be reduced to poverty or beggary.

In the senate at Amaurotum (to which, as I said before, three are sent annually from every city), they first determine what commodity is in plenty in each particular place and again where on the island the crops have been meager. They at once fill up the scarcity of one place by the surplus of another. This service they perform without payment, receiving nothing in return from those to whom they give. Those who have given out of their stock to any particular city without requiring any return from it receive what they lack from another to which they have given nothing. Thus, the whole island is like a single family.

But when they have made sufficient provision for themselves (which they do not consider complete until they have provided for two years to come, on account of the next year's uncertain crop), then they export into other countries, out of their surplus, a great quantity of grain, honey, wool, linen, timber, scarlet and purple dyestuffs, hides, wax, tallow, leather, as well as livestock. Of all these commodities they bestow the seventh part on the poor of the district and sell the rest at a moderate price.

By this trade they bring into their country not only such articles as they lack themselves—and practically the only thing lacking is iron—but also a great quantity of silver and gold. This exchange has gone on day by day so long that now they have everywhere an abundance of these metals, more than would be believed. In consequence, they now care little whether they sell for ready cash or appoint a future day for payment, and in fact have by far the greatest amount out on credit. In all transactions on credit, however, they never trust private citizens but the municipal government, the legal documents being drawn up as usual. When the day for payment comes, the city collects the money due from private debtors and puts it into the treasury and enjoys the use of it until the Utopians claim payment.

The Utopians never claim payment of most of the money. They think it hardly fair to take away a thing useful to other people when it is useless to themselves. But if circumstances require that they should lend some part of it to another nation, then they call in their debts—or when they must wage war. It is for that single purpose that they keep all the treasure they possess at home: to be their bulwark in extreme peril or in sudden emergency. They use it above all to hire at sky-high rates of pay foreign mercenaries (whom they would jeopardize rather than their own citizens), being well aware that by large sums of money even their enemies themselves may be bought and set to fight one another either by treachery or by open warfare.

For these military reasons they keep a vast treasure, but not as a treasure. They keep it in a way which I am really quite ashamed to reveal for fear that my words will not be believed. My fears are all the more justified because I am conscious that, had I not been there and witnessed the phenomenon, I myself should have been with difficulty induced to believe it from another's account. It needs must be almost always the rule that, as far as a thing is unlike the ways of the hearers, so far is it from obtaining their credence. An impartial judge of things, however, seeing that the rest of their institutions are so unlike ours, will perhaps wonder less that their use of silver and gold should be adapted to their way of life rather than to ours. As stated, they do not use money themselves but keep it only for an emergency, which may actually occur, yet possibly may never happen.

Meanwhile, gold and silver, of which money is made, are so treated by them that no one values them more highly than their true nature deserves. Who does not see that they are far inferior to iron in usefulness since without iron mortals cannot live any more than without fire and water? To gold and silver, however, nature has given no use that we cannot dispense with, if the folly of men had not made them valuable because they are rare. On the other hand, like a most kind and indulgent mother, she has exposed to view all that is best, like air and water and earth itself, but has removed as far as possible from us all vain and unprofitable things.

If in Utopia these metals were kept locked up in a tower, it might be suspected that the governor and the senate—for such is the foolish imagination of the common folk—were deceiving the people by the scheme and they themselves were deriving some benefit therefrom. Moreover, if they made them into drinking vessels and other such skillful handiwork, then if occasion arose for them all to be melted down again and applied to the pay of soldiers, they realize that people would be unwilling to be deprived of what they had once begun to treasure.

To avoid these dangers, they have devised a means which, as it is consonant with the rest of their institutions, so it is extremely unlike our own—seeing that we value gold so much and are so careful in safeguarding it—and therefore incredible except to those who have experience of it. While they eat and drink from earthenware and glassware of fine workmanship but of little value, from gold and silver they make chamber pots and all the humblest vessels for use everywhere, not only in the common halls but in private homes also. Moreover, they employ the same metals to make the chains and solid fetters which they put on their slaves. Finally, as for those who bear the stigma of disgrace on account of some crime, they have gold ornaments hanging from their ears, gold rings encircling their fingers, gold chains thrown around their necks, and, as a last touch, a gold crown binding their temples. Thus by every means in their power they make gold and silver a mark of ill fame. In this way, too, it happens that, while all other nations bear the loss of these metals with as great grief as if they were losing their very vitals, if circumstances in Utopia ever required the removal of all gold and silver, no one would feel that he were losing as much as a penny.[9]

They also gather pearls by the seashore and diamonds and rubies on certain cliffs. They do not look for them purposely, but they polish them when found by chance. With them they adorn little children, who in their earliest years are proud and delighted with such decorations. When they have grown somewhat older and perceive that only children use such toys, they lay them aside, not by any order of their parents, but through their own feeling of shame, just as our own children, when they grow up, throw away their marbles, rattles, and dolls.

What opposite ideas and feelings are created by customs so different from those of other people came home to me never more clearly than in the case of the Anemolian ambassadors. They arrived in Amaurotum during my stay there. Because they came to treat of important matters, the three representatives of each city had assembled before their appearance. Now all the ambassadors of neighboring nations, who had previously visited the land, were well acquainted with the manners of the Utopians and knew that they paid no respect to costly clothes but looked with contempt on silk and regarded gold as a badge of disgrace. These persons usually came in the simplest possible dress. But the Anemolians, living farther off and having had fewer dealings with them, since they heard that in Utopia all were dressed alike, and in a homespun fashion at that, felt sure that they did not possess what they made no use of. Being more proud than wise, they determined by the grandeur of their apparel to represent the gods themselves and by their splendid adornment to dazzle the eyes of the poor Utopians.

Consequently the three ambassadors made a grand entry with a suite of a hundred followers, all in parti-colored clothes and most in silk. The ambassadors themselves, being noblemen at home, were arrayed in cloth of gold, with heavy gold

9. Hythlodaeus distinguishes first between the use value and the exchange value of an object: Gold, a soft metal, is useless except as decoration; but as a scarce commodity, it can be exchanged for other objects that do have a use value. He then places a moral construction on precious (or scarce) metals because they are used to indicate wealth and promote ostentation.

necklaces and earrings, with gold rings on their fingers, and with strings of gleaming pearls and gems upon their caps; in fact, they were decked out with all those articles which in Utopia are used to punish slaves, to stigmatize evil-doers, or to amuse children. It was a sight worth seeing to behold their cockiness when they compared their grand clothing with that of the Utopians, who had poured out into the street to see them pass. On the other hand, it was no less delightful to notice how much they were mistaken in their sanguine[1] expectations and how far they were from obtaining the consideration which they had hoped to get. To the eyes of all the Utopians, with the exception of the very few who for a good reason had visited foreign countries, all this gay show appeared disgraceful. They therefore bowed to the lowest of the party as to the masters but took the ambassadors themselves to be slaves because they were wearing gold chains, and passed them over without any deference whatever.

Why, you might have seen also the children who had themselves discarded gems and pearls, when they saw them attached to the caps of the ambassadors, poke and nudge their mothers and say to them:

"Look, mother, that big rascal is still wearing pearls and jewels as if he were yet a little boy!"

But the mother, also in earnest, would say:

"Hush, son, I think it is one of the ambassadors' fools."

Others found fault with the golden chains as useless, being so slender that a slave could easily break them or, again, so loose that at his pleasure he could throw them off and escape anywhere scot-free.

After spending one or more days there, the ambassadors saw an immense quantity of gold held as cheaply and in as great contempt there as in honor among themselves. They saw, too, that more gold and silver were amassed to make the chains and fetters of one runaway slave than had made up the whole array of the three of them. They then were crestfallen and for shame put away all the finery with which they had made themselves haughtily conspicuous, especially when, after familiar talk with the Utopians, they had learned their ways and opinions.

The Utopians wonder that any mortal takes pleasure in the uncertain sparkle of a tiny jewel or precious stone when he can look at a star or even the sun itself. They wonder that anyone can be so mad as to think himself more noble on account of the texture of a finer wool, since, however fine the texture is, a sheep once wore the wool and yet all the time was nothing more than a sheep.

They wonder, too, that gold, which by its very nature is so useless, is now everywhere in the world valued so highly that man himself, through whose agency and for whose use it got this value, is priced much cheaper than gold itself. This is true to such an extent that a blockhead who has no more intelligence than a log and who is as dishonest as he is foolish keeps in bondage many wise men and good men merely for the reason that a great heap of gold coins happens to be his. Yet if some chance or some legal trick (which is as apt as chance to confound high and low) transfers it from this master to the lowest rascal in his entire household, he will surely very soon pass into the service of his former servant—as if he were a mere appendage of and addition to the coins! But much more do they wonder at and abominate the madness of persons who pay almost divine honors to the rich, to whom they neither owe anything nor are obligated in any other respect than that they are rich. Yet they know

1. Optimistic.

them to be so mean and miserly that they are more than sure that of all that great pile of cash, as long as the rich men live, not a single penny will ever come their way.

These and similar opinions they have conceived partly from their upbringing, being reared in a commonwealth whose institutions are far removed from follies of the kind mentioned, and partly from instruction and reading good books. Though there are not many in each city who are relieved from all other tasks and assigned to scholarship alone, that is to say, the individuals in whom they have detected from childhood an outstanding personality, a first-rate intelligence, and an inclination of mind toward learning, yet all children are introduced to good literature. A large part of the people, too, men and women alike, throughout their lives, devote to learning the hours which, as we said, are free from manual labor.

They learn the various branches of knowledge in their native tongue. The latter is copious in vocabulary and pleasant to the ear and a very faithful exponent of thought. It is almost the same as that current in a great part of that side of the world, only that everywhere else its form is more corrupt, to different degrees in different regions.

Of all those philosophers whose names are famous in the part of the world known to us, the reputation of not even a single one had reached them before our arrival. Yet in music, dialectic, arithmetic, and geometry they have made almost the same discoveries as those predecessors of ours in the classical world. But while they measure up to the ancients in almost all other subjects, still they are far from being a match for the inventions of our modern logicians. In fact, they have discovered not even a single one of those very ingeniously devised rules about restrictions, amplifications, and suppositions which our own children everywhere learn in the *Small Logicals*. In addition, so far are they from ability to speculate on second intentions that not one of them could see even man himself as a so-called universal—though he was, as you know, colossal and greater than any giant, as well as pointed out by us with our finger.[2]

They are most expert, however, in the courses of the stars and the movements of the celestial bodies. Moreover, they have ingeniously devised instruments in different shapes, by which they have most exactly comprehended the movements and positions of the sun and moon and all the other stars which are visible in their horizon. But of the agreements and discords of the planets and, in sum, of all that infamous and deceitful divination by the stars, they do not even dream.

They forecast rains, winds, and all the other changes in weather by definite signs which they have ascertained by long practice. But as to the causes of all these phenomena, and of the flow of the sea and its saltiness, and, in fine, of the origin and nature of the heavens and the universe, they partly treat of them in the same way as our ancient philosophers and partly, as the latter differ from one another, they, too, in introducing new theories disagree with them all and yet do not in all respects agree with fellow Utopians.

In that part of philosophy which deals with morals, they carry on the same debates as we do. They inquire into the good: of the soul and of the body and of external gifts. They ask also whether the name of good may be applied to all three or

---

2. In logic, a first intention is the conception gained from the apprehension of an object as a whole; a second intention is the abstracted conception gained by generalizing upon a first intention and as such, exists only in the mind. The Utopians cannot conceive of second intentions, because they are themselves second intentions; they are the product of More's reflection upon the particular European governments he has studied.

simply belongs to the endowments of the soul. They discuss virtue and pleasure, but their principal and chief debate is in what thing or things, one or more, they are to hold that happiness consists. In this matter they seem to lean more than they should to the school that espouses pleasure as the object by which to define either the whole or the chief part of human happiness.

What is more astonishing is that they seek a defense for this soft doctrine from their religion, which is serious and strict, almost solemn and hard. They never have a discussion of happiness without uniting certain principles taken from religion as well as from philosophy, which uses rational arguments. Without these principles they think reason insufficient and weak by itself for the investigation of true happiness. The following are examples of these principles. The soul is immortal and by the goodness of God born for happiness. After this life rewards are appointed for our virtues and good deeds, punishment for our crimes. Though these principles belong to religion, yet they hold that reason leads men to believe and to admit them.[3]

Once the principles are eliminated, the Utopians have no hesitation in maintaining that a person would be stupid not to realize that he ought to seek pleasure by fair means or foul, but that he should only take care not to let a lesser pleasure interfere with a greater nor to follow after a pleasure which would bring pain in retaliation. To pursue hard and painful virtue and not only to banish the sweetness of life but even voluntarily to suffer pain from which you expect no profit (for what profit can there be if after death you gain nothing for having passed the whole present life unpleasantly, that is, wretchedly?)—this policy they declare to be the extreme of madness.

As it is, they hold happiness rests not in every kind of pleasure but only in good and decent pleasure. To such, as to the supreme good, our nature is drawn by virtue itself, to which the opposite school alone attributes happiness. The Utopians define virtue as living according to nature since to this end we were created by God. That individual, they say, is following the guidance of nature who, in desiring one thing and avoiding another, obeys the dictates of reason.[4]

Now reason first of all inflames men to a love and veneration of the divine majesty, to whom we owe both our existence and our capacity for happiness. Secondly, it admonishes and urges us to lead a life as free from care and as full of joy as possible and, because of our natural fellowship, to help all other men, too, to attain that end. No one was ever so solemn and severe a follower of virtue and hater of pleasure that he, while imposing on you labors, watchings, and discomforts, would not at the same time bid you do your best to relieve the poverty and misfortunes of others. He would bid you regard as praiseworthy in humanity's name that one man should provide for another man's welfare and comfort—if it is especially humane (and humanity is the virtue most peculiar to man) to relieve the misery of others and, by taking away all sadness from their life, restore them to enjoyment, that is, to pleasure. If so, why should not nature urge everyone to do the same for himself also?

3. By believing in the immortality of the soul, an afterlife of rewards or punishments, and the goodness of God, the Utopians show that they are aware of "natural law," held to be apprehensible by reason.
4. The Utopians represent a people for whom religion is manifest in nature, as it was for the Greeks and the Romans, rather than revealed by God, as it was for the ancient Israelites and, after them, the disciples of Christ.

The Utopian is typically reasonable, follows the dictates of reason, and is guided by a beneficent nature that has not been revealed as fallen from an Edenic state of purity and excellence. Hence in Utopia there is no harm in seeking and enjoying pleasure. Nothing in this conception of human nature admits that humankind is inherently corrupted by original sin, a point of doctrine for Christians.

For either a joyous life, that is, a pleasurable life, is evil, in which case not only ought you to help no one to it but, as far as you can, should take it away from everyone as being harmful and deadly, or else, if you not only are permitted but are obliged to win it for others as being good, why should you not do so first of all for yourself, to whom you should show no less favor than to others? When nature bids you to be good to others, she does not command you conversely to be cruel and merciless to yourself. So nature herself, they maintain, prescribes to us a joyous life or, in other words, pleasure, as the end of all our operations. Living according to her prescription they define as virtue.

To pursue this line. Nature calls all men to help one another to a merrier life. (This she certainly does with good reason, for no one is raised so far above the common lot of mankind as to have his sole person the object of nature's care, seeing that she equally favors all whom she endows with the same form.) Consequently nature surely bids you take constant care not so to further your own advantages as to cause disadvantages to your fellows.[5]

Therefore they hold that not only ought contracts between private persons to be observed but also public laws for the distribution of vital commodities, that is to say, the matter of pleasure, provided they have been justly promulgated by a good king or ratified by the common consent of a people neither oppressed by tyranny nor deceived by fraud. As long as such laws are not broken, it is prudence to look after your own interests, and to look after those of the public in addition is a mark of devotion. But to deprive others of their pleasure to secure your own, this is surely an injustice. On the contrary, to take away something from yourself and to give it to others is a duty of humanity and kindness which never takes away as much advantage as it brings back. It is compensated by the return of benefits as well as by the actual consciousness of the good deed. Remembrance of the love and good will of those whom you have benefited gives the mind a greater amount of pleasure than the bodily pleasure which you have forgone would have afforded. Finally—and religion easily brings this home to a mind which readily assents—God repays, in place of a brief and tiny pleasure, immense and never-ending gladness. And so they maintain, having carefully considered and weighed the matter, that all our actions, and even the very virtues exercised in them, look at last to pleasure as their end and happiness.

By pleasure they understand every movement and state of body or mind in which, under the guidance of nature, man delights to dwell. They are right in including man's natural inclinations. For just as the senses as well as right reason aim at whatever is pleasant by nature—whatever is not striven after through wrong-doing, nor involves the loss of something more pleasant, nor is followed by pain—so they hold that whatever things mortals imagine by a futile consensus to be sweet to them in spite of being against nature (as though they had the power to change the nature of things as they do their names) are all so far from making for happiness that they are even a great hindrance to it. The reason is that they possess the minds of persons in whom they have once become deep-seated with a false idea of pleasure so that no room is left anywhere for true and genuine delights. In fact, very many are the things which, though of their own nature they contain no sweetness, nay, a good part of

---

5. Hythlodaeus describes the classical notion of a benefit, an action that furthers the welfare of a community of persons rather than that of a particular person. The logic of a benefit dictates that an individual can act to confer an advantage not only to himself but also to the community of which he is a part; correspondingly, an action that is to the disadvantage of another individual or his community may not be beneficial to him, however profitable it may seem in the short run.

them very much bitterness, still are, through the perverse attraction of evil desires, not only regarded as the highest pleasures but also counted among the chief reasons that make life worth living.

In the class that follow this spurious pleasure, they put those whom I mentioned before, who think themselves the better men, the better the coat they wear. In this one thing they make a twofold mistake: they are no less deceived in thinking their coat better than in thinking themselves better. If you consider the use of the garment, why is wool of finer thread superior to that of thicker? Yet, as if it were by nature and not by their own mistake that they had the advantage, they hold their heads high and believe some extra worth attaches to themselves thereby. Thus, the honor which, if ill-clad, they would not have ventured to hope for, they require as if of right for a smarter coat. If passed by with some neglect, they are indignant.

Again, does it not show the same stupidity to think so much of empty and unprofitable honors? What natural and true pleasure can another's bared head or bent knees afford you? Will this behavior cure the pain in your own knees or relieve the lunacy in your own head? In this conception of counterfeit pleasure, a strange and sweet madness is displayed by men who imagine themselves to be noble and plume themselves on it and applaud themselves because their fortune has been to be born of certain ancestors of whom the long succession has been counted rich—for that is now the only nobility—and especially rich in landed estates. They consider themselves not a whit less noble even if their ancestors have not left them a square foot or if they themselves have consumed in extravagant living what was left them.

With these persons they class those who, as I said, dote on jewels and gems and who think they become a species of god if ever they secure a fine specimen, especially of the sort which at the period is regarded as of the highest value in their country. It is not everywhere or always that one kind of stone is prized. They will not purchase it unless taken out of its gold setting and exposed to view, and not even then unless the seller takes an oath and gives security that it is a true gem and a true stone, so anxious are they lest a spurious stone in place of a genuine one deceive their eyes. But why should a counterfeited one give less pleasure to your sight when your eye cannot distinguish it from the true article? Both should be of equal value to you, even as they would be, by heaven, to a blind man!

What can be said of those who keep superfluous wealth to please themselves, not with putting the heap to any use but merely with looking at it?[6] Do they feel true pleasure, or are they not rather cheated by false pleasure? Or, what of those who have the opposite failing and hide the gold, which they will never use and perhaps never see again, and who, in their anxiety not to lose it, thereby do lose it? What else but loss is it to deprive yourself of its use, and perhaps all other men too, and to put it back in the ground? And yet you joyfully exult over your hidden treasure as though your mind were now free from all anxiety. Suppose that someone removed it by stealing it and that you died ten years afterwards knowing nothing of the theft. During the whole decade which you lived after the money was stolen, what did it matter to you whether it was stolen or safe? In either case it was of just as little use to you.

Among those who indulge such senseless delights they reckon dicers (whose madness they know not by experience but by hearsay only), as well as hunters and hawkers. What pleasure is there, they ask, in shooting dice upon a table? You have

6. Hythlodaeus implies that money is useful because it can be exchanged for goods in a market. Money exchange is more efficient than barter, as it can always find a commensurable value.

shot them so often that, even if some pleasure had been in it, weariness by now could have arisen from the habitual practice. Or what sweetness can there be, and not rather disgust, in hearing the barking and howling of dogs? Or what greater sensation of pleasure is there when a dog chases a hare than when a dog chases a dog? The same thing happens in both cases: there is racing in both if speed gives you delight.

But if you are attracted by the hope of slaughter and the expectation of a creature being mangled under your eyes, it ought rather to inspire pity when you behold a weak, fugitive, timid, and innocent little hare torn to pieces by a strong, fierce, and cruel dog. In consequence the Utopians have imposed the whole activity of hunting, as unworthy of free men, upon their butchers—a craft, as I explained before, they exercise through their slaves. They regard hunting as the meanest part of the butcher's trade and its other functions as more useful and more honorable, seeing that they do much more positive good and kill animals only from necessity, whereas the hunter seeks nothing but pleasure from the killing and mangling of a poor animal. Even in the case of brute beasts, this desire of looking on bloodshed, in their estimation, either arises from a cruel disposition or degenerates finally into cruelty through the constant practice of such brutal pleasure.

Although the mob of mortals regards these and all similar pursuits—and they are countless—as pleasures, yet the Utopians positively hold them to have nothing to do with true pleasure since there is nothing sweet in them by nature. The fact that for the mob they inspire in the senses a feeling of enjoyment—which seems to be the function of pleasure—does not make them alter their opinion. The enjoyment does not arise from the nature of the thing itself but from their own perverse habit. The latter failing makes them take what is bitter for sweet, just as pregnant women by their vitiated taste suppose pitch and tallow sweeter than honey. Yet it is impossible for any man's judgment, depraved either by disease or by habit, to change the nature of pleasure any more than that of anything else.

The pleasures which they admit as genuine they divide into various classes, some pleasures being attributed to the soul and others to the body. To the soul they ascribe intelligence and the sweetness which is bred of contemplation of truth. To these two are joined the pleasant recollection of a well-spent life and the sure hope of happiness to come.

Bodily pleasure they divide into two kinds. The first is that which fills the sense with clearly perceptible sweetness. Sometimes it comes from the renewal of those organs which have been weakened by our natural heat. These organs are then restored by food and drink. Sometimes it comes from the elimination of things which overload the body. This agreeable sensation occurs when we discharge feces from our bowels or perform the activity generative of children or relieve the itching of some part by rubbing or scratching. Now and then, however, pleasure arises, not in process of restoring anything that our members lack, nor in process of eliminating anything that causes distress, but from something that tickles and affects our senses with a secret but remarkable moving force and so draws them to itself. Such is that pleasure which is engendered by music.

The second kind of bodily pleasure they claim to be that which consists in a calm and harmonious state of the body. This is nothing else than each man's health undisturbed by any disorder. Health, if assailed by no pain, gives delight of itself, though there be no motion arising from pleasure applied from without. Even though it is less obvious and less perceptible by the sense than that overblown craving for eating and drinking, yet none the less many hold it to be the greatest of pleasures.

Almost all the Utopians regard it as great and as practically the foundation and basis of all pleasures. Even by itself it can make the state of life peaceful and desirable, whereas without it absolutely no place is left for any pleasure. The absence of pain without the presence of health they regard as insensibility rather than pleasure.

They long ago rejected the position of those who held that a state of stable and tranquil health (for this question, too, had been actively discussed among them) was not to be counted as a pleasure because its presence, they said, could not be felt except through some motion from without. But on the other hand now they almost all agree that health is above all things conducive to pleasure. Since in disease, they query, there is pain, which is the bitter enemy of pleasure no less than disease is of health, why should not pleasure in turn be found in the tranquillity of health? They think that it is of no importance in the discussion whether you say that disease is pain or that disease is accompanied with pain, for it comes to the same thing either way. To be sure, if you hold that health is either a pleasure or the necessary cause of pleasure, as fire is of heat, in both ways the conclusion is that those who have permanent health cannot be without pleasure.

Besides, while we eat, say they, what is that but health, which has begun to be impaired, fighting against hunger, with food as its comrade in arms? While it gradually gains strength, the very progress to the usual vigor supplies the pleasure by which we are thus restored. Shall the health which delights in conflict not rejoice when it has gained the victory? When at length it has successfully acquired its former strength, which was its sole object through the conflict, shall it immediately become insensible and not recognize and embrace its own good? The assertion that health cannot be felt they think to be far wide of the truth. Who in a waking state, ask they, does not feel that he is in good health—except the man who is not? Who is bound fast by such insensibility or lethargy that he does not confess that health is agreeable and delightful to him? And what is delightful except pleasure under another name?

To sum up, they cling above all to mental pleasures, which they value as the first and foremost of all pleasures. Of these the principal part they hold to arise from the practice of the virtues and the consciousness of a good life. Of these pleasures which the body supplies, they give the palm to health. The delight of eating and drinking, and anything that gives the same sort of enjoyment, they think desirable, but only for the sake of health. Such things are not pleasant in themselves but only in so far as they resist the secret encroachment of ill health. Just as a wise man should pray that he may escape disease rather than crave a remedy for it and that he may drive pain off rather than seek relief from it, so it would be better not to need this kind of pleasure rather than to be soothed by it.

If a person thinks that his felicity consists in this kind of pleasure, he must admit that he will be in the greatest happiness if his lot happens to be a life which is spent in perpetual hunger, thirst, itching, eating, drinking, scratching, and rubbing. Who does not see that such a life is not only disgusting but wretched? These pleasures are surely the lowest of all as being most adulterated, for they never occur unless they are coupled with the pains which are their opposites. For example, with the pleasure of eating is united hunger—and on no fair terms, for the pain is the stronger and lasts the longer. It comes into existence before the pleasure and does not end until the pleasure dies with it. Such pleasures they hold should not be highly valued and only insofar as they are necessary. Yet they enjoy even these pleasures and gratefully acknowledge the kindness of mother nature who, with alluring sweetness, coaxes her offspring to that which of necessity they must constantly do.

In what discomfort should we have to live if, like all other sicknesses which less frequently assail us, so also these daily diseases of hunger and thirst had to be expelled by bitter poisons and drugs?

Beauty, strength, and nimbleness—these as special and pleasant gifts of nature they gladly cherish. Nay, even those pleasures entering by the ears, eyes, or nostrils, which nature intended to be peculiarly characteristic of man (for no other species of living creature either takes in the form and fairness of the world or is affected by the pleasantness of smell, except in choice of food, or distinguishes harmonious and dissonant intervals of sound)—these, too, I say, they follow after as pleasant seasonings of life.[7] But in all they make this limitation: that the lesser is not to interfere with the greater and that pleasure is not to produce pain in aftermath. Pain they think a necessary consequence if the pleasure is base.

But to despise the beauty of form, to impair the strength of the body, to turn nimbleness into sluggishness, to exhaust the body by fasts, to injure one's health, and to reject all the other favors of nature, unless a man neglects these advantages to himself in providing more zealously for the pleasure of other persons or of the public, in return for which sacrifice he expects a greater pleasure from God—but otherwise to deal harshly with oneself for a vain and shadowy reputation of virtue to no man's profit or for preparing oneself more easily to bear adversities which may never come—this attitude they think is extreme madness and the sign of a mind which is both cruel to itself and ungrateful to nature, to whom it disdains to be indebted and therefore renounces all her benefits.

This is their view of virtue and pleasure. They believe that human reason can attain to no truer view, unless a heaven-sent religion inspire man with something more holy. Whether in this stand they are right or wrong, time does not permit us to examine—nor is it necessary. We have taken upon ourselves only to describe their principles, and not also to defend them. But of this I am sure, that whatever you think of their ideas, there is nowhere in the world a more excellent people nor a happier commonwealth. They are nimble and active of body, and stronger than you would expect from their stature. The latter, however, is not dwarfish. Though they have not a very fertile soil or a very wholesome climate, they protect themselves against the atmosphere by temperate living and make up for the defects of the land by diligent labor. Consequently, nowhere in the world is there a more plentiful supply of grain and cattle, nowhere are men's bodies more vigorous and subject to fewer diseases. Not only may you behold the usual agricultural tasks carefully administered there, whereby the naturally barren soil is improved by art and industry, but you may also see how a whole forest has been uprooted in one place by the hands of the people and planted in another. Herein they were thinking not so much of abundance as of transport, that they might have wood closer to the sea or the rivers or the cities themselves. For it takes less labor to convey grain than timber to a distance by land.

The people in general are easygoing, good-tempered, ingenious, and leisure-loving. They patiently do their share of manual labor when occasion demands, though otherwise they are by no means fond of it. In their devotion to mental study they are unwearied. When they had heard from us about the literature and learning of the Greeks (for in Latin there was nothing, apart from history and poetry, which

---

7. Just as the Utopians imagine humankind without original sin, so they cannot imagine any point in ascetic discipline of the body for the sake of curbing or controlling its inherent tendency to sin.

seemed likely to gain their great approval), it was wonderful to see their extreme desire for permission to master them through our instruction.

We began, therefore, to give them public lessons, more at first that we should not seem to refuse the trouble than that we expected any success. But after a little progress, their diligence made us at once feel sure that our own diligence would not be bestowed in vain. They began so easily to imitate the shapes of the letters, so readily to pronounce the words, so quickly to learn by heart, and so faithfully to reproduce what they had learned that it was a perfect wonder to us. The explanation was that most of them were scholars picked for their ability and mature in years, who undertook to learn their tasks not only fired by their own free will but acting under orders of the senate. In less than three years they were perfect in the language and able to peruse good authors without any difficulty unless the text had faulty readings. According to my conjecture, they got hold of Greek literature more easily because it was somewhat related to their own. I suspect that their race was derived from the Greek because their language, which in almost all other respects resembles the Persian, retains some traces of Greek in the names of their cities and officials.

When about to go on the fourth voyage, I put on board, in place of wares to sell, a fairly large package of books,[8] having made up my mind never to return rather than to come back soon. They received from me most of Plato's works, several of Aristotle's, as well as Theophrastus on plants, which I regret to say was mutilated in parts. During the voyage an ape found the book, left lying carelessly about, and in wanton sport tore out and destroyed several pages in various sections. Of grammarians they have only Lascaris, for I did not take Theodore with me. They have no dictionaries except those of Hesychius and Dioscorides. They are very fond of the works of Plutarch and captivated by the wit and pleasantry of Lucian. Of the poets they have Aristophanes, Homer, and Euripides, together with Sophocles in the small Aldine type. Of the historians they possess Thucydides and Herodotus, as well as Herodian.

In medicine, moreover, my companion Tricius Apinatus had carried with him some small treatises of Hippocrates and the *Ars medica* of Galen, to which books they attribute great value. Even though there is scarcely a nation in the whole world that needs medicine less, yet nowhere is it held in greater honor—and this for the reason that they regard the knowledge of it as one of the finest and most useful branches of philosophy. When by the help of this philosophy they explore the secrets of nature, they appear to themselves not only to get great pleasure in doing so but also to win the highest approbation of the Author and Maker of nature. They presume that, like

---

8. Hythlodaeus has given the Utopians only works in Greek, even though they cover topics in the history of Rome. By this, More clearly intended to emphasize what he thought was the intellectual superiority of Greek over Roman culture. Beyond the works of Plato and Aristotle, Hythlodaeus's library contains the works of Theophrastus (3rd century B.C.E.), who wrote a history of plants; Constantine Lascaris and Theodore of Gaza, both grammarians of the 15th century; Hesychius, a Greek lexicographer of the 4th century B.C.E.; Dioscurides, a Greek physician of the 1st century, who wrote a medical textbook, known and used through the early modern period; Plutarch, a Greek biographer and moralist of the 2nd century; Lucian, a Greek rhetorician of the 2nd century, who wrote satirical dialogues; Aristophanes, a Greek dramatist of the 4th century B.C.E., who wrote comic drama; Homer, the name given the author or authors of the Greek epics, the *Iliad* and the *Odyssey*, committed to writing about 800 B.C.E.; and Euripides and Sophocles, both Greek tragedians of the 5th century B.C.E. Herodotus and Thucydides lived during the 5th century B.C.E.; Herodotus wrote of the wars between the kingdoms of the near east and the Greek states in his *Histories*, Thucydides of the tragic fall of the Athenian state in his *Peloponnesian Wars*. Herodian, a Syrian historian, wrote, in Greek, of the Roman emperors from the death of Marcus Aurelius in 180 to 238 C.E. "Tricius Apinatus" is a fictitious author, but Hippocrates and Galen were Greek physicians of the 5th century B.C.E. and the 2nd century, respectively, whose medical treatises were popular until the end of the 17th century. "Aldine type" was the particular typeface used by the early 16-century Venetian printer Aldus Manutius, who was famous for his publication of fine editions of Greek authors.

all other artificers, He has set forth the visible mechanism of the world as a spectacle for man, whom alone He has made capable of appreciating such a wonderful thing. Therefore He prefers a careful and diligent beholder and admirer of His work to one who like an unreasoning brute beast passes by so great and so wonderful a spectacle stupidly and stolidly.

Thus, trained in all learning, the minds of the Utopians are exceedingly apt in the invention of the arts which promote the advantage and convenience of life. Two, however, they owe to us, the art of printing and the manufacture of paper—though not entirely to us but to a great extent also to themselves. When we showed them the Aldine printing in paper books, we talked about the material of which paper is made and the art of printing without giving a detailed explanation, for none of us was expert in either art. With the greatest acuteness they promptly guessed how it was done. Though previously they wrote only on parchment, bark, and papyrus, from this time they tried to manufacture paper and print letters. Their first attempts were not very successful, but by frequent experiment they soon mastered both. So great was their success that if they had copies of Greek authors, they would have no lack of books. But at present they have no more than I have mentioned, but by printing books they have increased their stock by many thousands of copies.

Whoever, coming to their land on a sight-seeing tour, is recommended by any special intellectual endowment or is acquainted with many countries through long travel, is sure of a hearty welcome, for they delight in hearing what is happening in the whole world. On this score our own landing was pleasing to them. Few persons, however, come to them in the way of trade. What could they bring except iron, or what everybody would rather take back home with him—gold and silver! And as to articles of export, the Utopians think it wiser to carry them out of the country themselves than to let strangers come to fetch them. By this policy they get more information about foreign nations and do not forget by disuse their skill in navigation.

Slavery, [Etc.]

Prisoners of war are not enslaved unless captured in wars fought by the Utopians themselves; nor are the sons of slaves,[9] nor anyone who was in slavery when acquired of slaves, nor anyone whom they could acquire from slavery in other countries. Their slaves are either such or such as have been condemned to death elsewhere for some offense. The greater number are of this latter kind. They carry away many of them; sometimes they buy them cheaply; but often they ask for them and get them for nothing. These classes of slaves they keep not only continually at work but also in chains. Their own countrymen are dealt with more harshly, since their conduct is regarded as all the more regrettable and deserving a more severe punishment as an object lesson because, having had an excellent rearing to a virtuous life, they still could not be restrained from crime.

There is yet another class of slaves, for sometimes a hard-working and poverty-stricken drudge of another country voluntarily chooses slavery in Utopia. These individuals are well treated and, except that they have a little more work assigned to them as being used to it, are dealt with almost as leniently as citizens. If anyone

9. More uses the Latin word *servus*, which means servant, slave, and serf. Most commonly captives in war, slaves were also persons punished for crime, as in Utopia. Voluntary slavery, aside from indentured servitude (for a term), was rare except in theory; presumably such persons chose to work as slaves in exchange for a subsistence living.

wishes to depart, which seldom happens, they do not detain him against his will nor send him away empty-handed.

The sick, as I said, are very lovingly cared for, nothing being omitted which may restore them to health, whether in the way of medicine or diet. They console the incurable diseased by sitting and conversing with them and by applying all possible alleviations. But if a disease is not only incurable but also distressing and agonizing without any cessation, then the priests and the public officials exhort the man, since he is now unequal to all life's duties, a burden to himself, and a trouble to others, and is living beyond the time of his death, to make up his mind not to foster the pest and plague any longer nor to hesitate to die now that life is torture to him but, relying on good hope, to free himself from this bitter life as from prison and the rack, or else voluntarily to permit others to free him.[1] In this course he will act wisely, since by death he will put an end not to enjoyment but to torture. Because in doing so he will be obeying the counsels of the priests, who are God's interpreters, it will be a pious and holy action.

Those who have been persuaded by these arguments either starve themselves to death or, being put to sleep, are set free without the sensation of dying. But they do not make away with anyone against his will, nor in such a case do they relax in the least their attendance upon him. They do believe that death counseled by authority is honorific. But if anyone commits suicide without having obtained the approval of priests and senate, they deem him unworthy of either fire or earth and cast his body ignominiously into a marsh without proper burial.

Women do not marry till eighteen, men not till they are four years older. If before marriage a man or woman is convicted of secret intercourse, he or she is severely punished, and they are forbidden to marry altogether unless the governor's pardon remits their guilt. In addition, both father and mother of the family in whose house the offense was committed incur great disgrace as having been neglectful in doing their duties. The reason why they punish this offence so severely is their foreknowledge that, unless persons are carefully restrained from promiscuous intercourse, few will contract the tie of marriage, in which a whole life must be spent with one companion and all the troubles incidental to it must be patiently borne.

In choosing mates, they seriously and strictly espouse a custom which seemed to us very foolish and extremely ridiculous. The woman, whether maiden or widow, is shown naked to the suitor by a worthy and respectable matron, and similarly the suitor is presented naked before the maiden by a discreet man. We laughed at this custom and condemned it as foolish. They, on the other hand, marvelled at the remarkable folly of all other nations. In buying a colt, where there is question of only a little money, persons are so cautious that though it is almost bare they will not buy until they have taken off the saddle and removed all the trappings for fear some sore lies concealed under these coverings. Yet in the choice of a wife, an action which will cause either pleasure or disgust to follow them the rest of their lives, they are so careless that, while the rest of her body is covered with clothes, they estimate the value of the whole woman from hardly a single handbreadth of her, only the face being visible, and clasp her to themselves not without great danger of their agreeing ill together if something afterwards gives them offense.

---

1. Neither suicide nor euthanasia was considered immoral in Greek and Roman society.

All are not so wise as to regard only the character of the spouse, and even in the marriages of the wise, bodily attractions also are no small enhancement to the virtues of the mind. Certainly such foul deformity may be hidden beneath these coverings that it may quite alienate a man's mind from his wife when bodily separation is no longer lawful. If such a deformity arises by chance after the marriage has been contracted, each person must bear his own fate, but beforehand the laws ought to protect him from being entrapped by guile.

This provision was the more necessary because the Utopians are the only people in those parts of the world who are satisfied with one spouse and because matrimony there is seldom broken except by death, unless it be for adultery or for intolerable offensiveness of character. When husband or wife is thus offended, leave is granted by the senate to take another mate.[2] The other party perpetually lives a life of disgrace as well as of celibacy. But they cannot endure the repudiation of an unwilling wife, who is in no way to blame, because some bodily calamity has befallen her. They judge it cruel that a person should be abandoned when most in need of comfort and that old age, since it both entails disease and is a disease itself, should have only an unreliable and weak fidelity.

It sometimes happens, however, that when a married couple agree insufficiently in their dispositions and both find others with whom they hope to live more agreeably, they separate by mutual consent and contract fresh unions, but not without the sanction of the senate. The latter allows of no divorce until its members and their wives have carefully gone into the case. Even then they do not readily give consent because they know that it is a very great drawback to cementing the affection between husband and wife if they have before them the easy hope of a fresh union.

Violators of the conjugal tie are punished by the strictest form of slavery. If both parties are married, the injured parties, provided they consent, are divorced from their adulterous mates and couple together, or else are allowed to marry whom they like. But if one of the injured parties continues to feel affection for so undeserving a mate, it is not forbidden to have the marriage continue in force on condition that the party is willing to accompany and share the labor of the other who has been condemned to slavery. Now and then it happens that the penance of the one and the dutiful assiduity of the other move the compassion of the governor and win back their liberty. Relapse into the same offense, however, involves the penalty of death.

For all other crimes there is no law prescribing any fixed penalty, but the punishment is assigned by the senate according to the atrocity, or veniality, of the individual crime. Husbands correct their wives, and parents their children, unless the offense is so serious that it is to the advantage of public morality to have it punished openly. Generally the worst offenses are punished by the sentence of slavery since this prospect, they think, is no less formidable to the criminal and more advantageous to the state than if they make haste to put the offenders to death and get them out of the way at once. Their labor is more profitable than their death, and their example lasts longer to deter others from like crimes. But if they rebel and kick against this treatment, they are thereupon put to death like untameable beasts that cannot be restrained by prison or chain. If they are patient, however, they are not entirely deprived of all hope. When tamed by long and hard punishment, if they show such

---

2. In England, divorce was granted only on the grounds of adultery. By contrast, the Utopians grant divorce for incompatibility and extend the privilege to the wife as well as the husband. Adultery, however, is punished with slavery.

repentance as testifies that they are more sorry for their sin than for their punishment, then sometimes by the prerogative of the governor and sometimes by the vote of the people their slavery is either lightened or remitted altogether.

To tempt another to an impure act is no less punishable than the commission of that impure act. In every crime the deliberate and avowed attempt is counted equal to the deed, for they think that failure ought not to benefit one who did everything in his power not to fail.

They are very fond of fools.[3] It is a great disgrace to treat them with insult, but there is no prohibition against deriving pleasure from their foolery. The latter, they think, is of the greatest benefit to the fools themselves. If anyone is so stern and morose that he is not amused with anything they either do or say, they do not entrust him with the care of a fool. They fear that he may not treat him with sufficient indulgence since he would find in him neither use nor even amusement, which is his sole faculty.

To deride a man for a disfigurement or the loss of a limb is counted as base and disfiguring, not to the man who is laughed at but to him who laughs, for foolishly upbraiding a man with something as if it were a fault which he was powerless to avoid. While they consider it a sign of a sluggish and feeble mind not to preserve natural beauty, it is, in their judgment, disgraceful affectation to help it out by cosmetics. Experience itself shows them how no elegance of outward form recommends wives to husbands as much as probity and reverence. Some men are attracted only by a handsome shape, but no man's love is kept permanently except by virtue and obedience.

Not merely do they discourage crime by punishment but they offer honors to invite men to virtue. Hence, to great men who have done conspicuous service to their country they set up in the market place statues to stand as a record of noble exploits and, at the same time, to have the glory of forefathers serve their descendants as a spur and stimulus to virtue.

The man who solicits votes to obtain any office is deprived completely of the hope of holding any office at all. They live together in affection and good will. No official is haughty or formidable. They are called fathers and show that character. Honor is paid them willingly, as it should be, and is not exacted from the reluctant. The governor himself is distinguished from citizens not by a robe or a crown but by the carrying of a handful of grain, just as the mark of the high priest is a wax candle borne before him.

They have very few laws because very few are needed for persons so educated. The chief fault they find with other peoples is that almost innumerable books of laws and commentaries are not sufficient. They themselves think it most unfair that any group of men should be bound by laws which are either too numerous to be read through or too obscure to be understood by anyone.

Moreover, they absolutely banish from their country all lawyers, who cleverly manipulate cases and cunningly argue legal points. They consider it a good thing that every man should plead his own cause and say the same to the judge as he would tell his counsel. Thus there is less ambiguity and the truth is more easily elicited when a man, uncoached in deception by a lawyer, conducts his own case and the judge skillfully weighs each statement and helps untutored minds to defeat the false accusations of the crafty. To secure these advantages in other countries is difficult, owing to the

---

3. In early modern Europe, a "fool" could be a professional jester; usually, he was employed at a royal or noble court and had special license to amuse and even criticize his master.

immense mass of extremely complicated laws. But with the Utopians each man is expert in law. First, they have, as I said, very few laws and, secondly, they regard the most obvious interpretation of the law as the most fair interpretation.

This policy follows from their reasoning that, since all laws are promulgated to remind every man of his duty, the more recondite interpretation reminds only very few (for there are few who can arrive at it) whereas the more simple and obvious sense of the laws is open to all. Otherwise, what difference would it make for the common people, who are the most numerous and also most in need of instruction, whether you framed no law at all or whether the interpretation of the law you framed was such that no one could elicit it except by great ingenuity and long argument? Now, the untrained judgment of the common people cannot attain to the meaning of such an interpretation nor can their lives be long enough, seeing that they are wholly taken up with getting a living.

These virtues of the Utopians have spurred their neighbors (who are free and independent since many of them were long ago delivered from tyrants by the Utopians) to obtain officials from them, some for one year and others for five years. On the expiration of their office they escort them home with honor and praise and bring back successors with them to their own country. Certainly these peoples make very good and wholesome provision for the commonwealth. Seeing that the latter's prosperity or ruin depends on the character of officials, of whom could they have made a wiser choice than of those who cannot be drawn from the path of honor by any bribe since it is no good to them as they will shortly return home, nor influenced by crooked partiality or animosity toward any since they are strangers to the citizens? These two evils, favoritism and avarice, wherever they have settled in men's judgments, instantly destroy all justice, the strongest sinew of the commonwealth. The nations who seek their administrators from Utopia are called allies by them; the name of friend is reserved for all the others whom they have benefited.

Treaties which all other nations so often conclude among themselves, break, and renew, they never make with any nation. "What is the use of a treaty," they ask, "as though nature of herself did not sufficiently bind one man to another? If a person does not regard nature, do you suppose he will care anything about words?"

They are led to this opinion chiefly because in those parts of the world treaties and alliances between kings are not observed with much good faith. In Europe, however, and especially in those parts where the faith and religion of Christ prevails, the majesty of treaties is everywhere holy and inviolable, partly through the justice and goodness of kings, partly through the reverence and fear of the Sovereign Pontiffs. Just as the latter themselves undertake nothing which they do not most conscientiously perform, so they command all other rulers to abide by their promises in every way and compel the recalcitrant by pastoral censure and severe reproof.[4] Popes are perfectly right, of course, in thinking it a most disgraceful thing that those who are specially called the faithful should not faithfully adhere to their commitments.

But in that new world, which is almost as far removed from ours by the equator as their life and character are different from ours, there is no trust in treaties. The more numerous and holy the ceremonies with which a treaty is struck the more quickly is it broken. They find some defect in the wording, which sometimes they cunningly devise of set purpose, so that they can never be held by such strong bonds

---

4. More is being ironic in extolling the faithful observance of treaties by the papacy. Pope Julius II, who died a few years before the publication of More's treatise, was notorious for breaking his word.

as not somehow to escape from them and break both the treaty and their faith. If this cunning, nay fraud and deceit, were found to have occurred in the contracts of private persons, the treaty-makers with great disdain would exclaim against it as sacrilegious and meriting the gallows—though the very same men plume themselves on being the authors of such advice when given to kings.

In consequence men think either that all justice is only a plebeian and low virtue which is far below the majesty of kings or that there are at least two forms of it: the one which goes on foot and creeps on the ground, fit only for the common sort and bound by many chains so that it can never overstep its barriers; the other a virtue of kings, which, as it is more august than that of ordinary folk, is also far freer so that everything is permissible to it—except what it finds disagreeable.

This behavior, as I said, of rulers there who keep their treaties so badly is, I suppose, the reason why the Utopians make none; if they lived here, they would perhaps change their minds. Nevertheless they believe that, though treaties are faithfully observed, it is a pity that the custom of making them at all had grown up. The result (as though peoples which are divided by the slight interval of a hill or a river were joined by no bond of nature) is men's persuasion that they are born one another's adversaries and enemies and that they are right in aiming at one another's destruction except in so far as treaties prevent it. What is more, even when treaties are made, friendship does not grow up but the license of freebooting continues to the extent that, for lack of skill in drawing up the treaty, no sufficient precaution to prevent this activity has been included in the articles. But the Utopians, on the contrary, think that nobody who has done you no harm should be accounted an enemy, that the fellowship created by nature takes the place of a treaty, and that men are better and more firmly joined together by good will than by pacts, by spirit than by words.

Military Affairs

War, as an activity fit only for beasts and yet practiced by no kind of beast so constantly as by man, they regard with utter loathing. Against the usage of almost all nations they count nothing so inglorious as glory sought in war. Nevertheless men and women alike assiduously exercise themselves in military training on fixed days lest they should be unfit for war when need requires. Yet they do not lightly go to war. They do so only to protect their own territory or to drive an invading enemy out of their friends' lands or, in pity for a people oppressed by tyranny, to deliver them by force of arms from the yoke and slavery of the tyrant, a course prompted by human sympathy.

They oblige their friends with help, not always indeed to defend them merely but sometimes also to requite and avenge injuries previously done to them. They act, however, only if they themselves are consulted before any step is taken and if they themselves initiate the war after they have approved the cause and demanded restitution in vain. They take the final step of war not only when a hostile inroad has carried off booty but also much more fiercely when the merchants among their friends undergo unjust persecution under the color of justice in any other country, either on the pretext of laws in themselves unjust or by the distortion of laws in themselves good.

Such was the origin of the war which the Utopians had waged a little before our time on behalf of the Nephelogetes[5] against the Alaopolitans. The Nephelogetic

---

5. "Cloud born" (insubstantial) people; the Alaopolitans are "citizens without a people or a country"—that is, stateless.

traders suffered a wrong, as they thought, under pretence of law, but whether right or wrong, it was avenged by a fierce war. Into this war the neighboring nations brought their energies and resources to assist the power and to intensify the rancor of both sides. Most flourishing nations were either shaken to their foundations or grievously afflicted. The troubles upon troubles that arose were ended only by the enslavement and surrender of the Alaopolitans. Since the Utopians were not fighting in their own interest, they yielded them into the power of the Nephelogetes, a people who, when the Alaopolitans were prosperous, were not in the least comparable to them.

So severely do the Utopians punish wrong done to their friends, even in money matters—but not wrongs done to themselves. When they lose their goods anywhere through fraud, but without personal violence, their anger goes no further than abstention from trade with that nation until satisfaction is made. The reason is not that they care less for their citizens than their allies. They are more grieved at their allies' pecuniary loss than their own because their friends' merchants suffer severely by the loss as it falls on their private property, but their own citizens lose nothing but what comes from the common stock and what was plentiful and, as it were, superfluous at home—or else it would not have been exported. As a result, the loss is not felt by any individual. They consider it excessively cruel to avenge such a loss by the death of many when the disadvantage of the loss affects neither the life nor the subsistence of any of their own people.

If a Utopian citizen, however, is wrongfully disabled or killed anywhere, whether the plot is due to the government or to a private citizen, they first ascertain the facts by an embassy and then, if the guilty persons are not surrendered, they cannot be appeased but forthwith declare war. If the guilty persons are surrendered, they are punished either with death or with enslavement.

They not only regret but blush at a victory that has cost much bloodshed, thinking it folly to purchase wares, however precious, too dear. If they overcome and crush the enemy by stratagem and cunning, they feel great pride and celebrate a public triumph over the victory and put up a trophy as for a strenuous exploit. They boast themselves as having acted with valor and heroism whenever their victory is such as no animal except man could have won, that is, by strength of intellect; for, by strength of body, say they, bears, lions, boars, wolves, dogs, and other wild beasts are wont to fight. Most of them are superior to us in brawn and fierceness, but they are all inferior in cleverness and calculation.

Their one and only object in war is to secure that which, had it been obtained beforehand, would have prevented the declaration of war. If that is out of the question, they require such severe punishment of those on whom they lay the blame that for the future they may be afraid to attempt anything of the same sort. These are their chief interests in the enterprise, which they set about promptly to secure, yet taking more care to avoid danger than to win praise or fame.

The moment war is declared, they arrange that simultaneously a great number of placards, made more effective by bearing their public seal, should be set up secretly in the most prominent spots of enemy territory. Herein they promise huge rewards to anyone who will kill the enemy king. Further, they offer smaller sums, but those considerable, for the heads of the individuals whose names they specify in the same proclamations. These are the men whom, next to the king himself, they regard as responsible for the hostile measures taken against them. Whatever reward they fix for an assassin, they double for the man who brings any of the denounced parties alive to them. They actually offer the same rewards, with a guarantee of personal safety, to the persons proscribed, if they will turn against their fellows.

So it swiftly comes about that their enemies suspect all outsiders and, in addition, neither trust nor are loyal to one another. They are in a state of utter panic and no less peril. It is well known that it has often happened that many of them, and especially the king himself, have been betrayed by those in whom they had placed the greatest trust, so easily do bribes incite men to commit every kind of crime. They are boundless in their offers of reward. Remembering, however, what a risk they invite the man to run, they take care that the greatness of the peril is balanced by the extent of the rewards. In consequence they promise and faithfully pay down not only an immense amount of gold but also landed property with high income in very secure places in the territory of friends.

This habit of bidding for and purchasing an enemy, which is elsewhere condemned as the cruel deed of a degenerate nature, they think reflects great credit, first on their wisdom because they thus bring to a conclusion great wars without any battle at all, and secondly on their humanity and mercy because by the death of a few guilty people they purchase the lives of many harmless persons who would have fallen in battle, both on their own side and that of the enemy. They are almost as sorry for the throng and mass of the enemy as for their own citizens. They know that the common folk do not go to war of their own accord but are driven to it by the madness of kings.

If this plan does not succeed, they sow the seeds of dissension broadcast and foster strife by leading a brother of the king or one of the noblemen to hope that he may obtain the throne. If internal strife dies down, then they stir up and involve the neighbors of their enemies by reviving some forgotten claims to dominion such as kings have always at their disposal. Promising their own assistance for the war, they supply money liberally but are very chary of sending their own citizens. They hold them so singularly dear and regard one another of such value that they would not care to exchange any of their own people for the king of the opposite party. As to gold and silver, since they keep it all for this one use, they pay it out without any reluctance, for they would live just as well if they spent it all. Moreover, in addition to the riches which they keep at home, they have also a vast treasure abroad in that many nations, as I said before, are in their debt.

With the riches, they hire and send to war soldiers from all parts, but especially from among the Zapoletans.[6] These people live five hundred miles to the east of Utopia and are fearsome, rough, and wild. They prefer their own rugged woods and mountains among which they are bred. They are a hard race, capable of enduring heat, cold, and toil, lacking all refinements, engaging in no farming, careless about the houses they live in and the clothes they wear, and occupied only with their flocks and herds. To a great extent they live by hunting and plundering. They are born for warfare and zealously seek an opportunity for fighting. When they find it, they eagerly embrace it. Leaving the country in great force, they offer themselves at a cheap rate to anyone who needs fighting men. The only trade they know in life is that by which they seek their death.

6. "Busy sellers," that is, of their services.

They fight with ardor and incorruptible loyalty for those from whom they receive their pay. Yet they bind themselves for no fixed period but take sides on such terms that the next day when higher pay is offered them, even by the enemy, they take his side, and then the day after, if a trifle more is offered to tempt them back, return to the side they took at first.

In almost every war that breaks out there are many of them in both armies. It is a daily occurrence that men connected by ties of blood, who were hired on the same side and so became intimate with one another, soon afterward are separated into two hostile forces and meet in battle. Forgetting both kinship and friendship, they run one another through with the utmost ferocity. They are driven to mutual destruction for no other reason than that they are hired by opposing kings for a tiny sum of which they take such careful account that they are readily induced to change sides by the addition of a penny to their daily rate of pay. So have they speedily acquired a habit of avarice which nevertheless profits them not one whit. What they get by exposing their lives they spend instantly in debauchery and that of a dreary sort.

This people will battle for the Utopians against any mortals whatsoever because their service is hired at a rate higher than they could get anywhere else. The Utopians, just as they seek good men to use them, so enlist these villains to abuse them. When need requires, they thrust them under the tempting bait of great promises into greatest perils. Generally a large proportion never returns to claim payment, but the survivors are honestly paid what has been promised them to incite them again to like deeds of daring. The Utopians do not care in the least how many Zapoletans they lose, thinking that they would be the greatest benefactors to the human race if they could relieve the world of all the dregs of this abominable and impious people.

Next to them they employ the forces of the people for whom they are fighting and then auxiliary squadrons of all their other friends. Last of all they add a contingent of their own citizens out of which they appoint some man of tried valor to command the whole army. For him they have two substitutes who hold no rank as long as he is safe. But if he is captured or killed, the first of the two becomes as it were his heir and successor, and he, if events require, is succeeded by the third. They thus avoid the disorganization of the whole army through the endangering of the commander, the fortunes of war being always incalculable.

In each city a choice is made among those who volunteer. No one is driven to fight abroad against his will because they are convinced that if anyone is somewhat timorous by nature, he not only will not acquit himself manfully but will throw fear into his companions. Should any war, however, assail their own country, they put the fainthearted, if physically fit, on shipboard mixed among the braver sort or put them here and there to man the walls where they cannot run away. Thus, shame at being seen to flinch by their own side, the close quarters with the enemy, and the withdrawal of hope of escape combine to overpower their timidity, and often they make a virtue of extreme necessity.

Just as no one of the men is made to go to a foreign war against his will, so if the women are anxious to accompany their husbands on military service, not only do they not forbid them but actually encourage them and incite them by expressions of praise. When they have gone out, they are placed alongside their husbands on the battle front. Each man is surrounded by his own children and relations by marriage and blood so that those may be closest and lend one another mutual assistance whom nature most impels to help one another. It is the greatest reproach for one spouse to return without the other or for a son to come back having lost his parent.

The result is that, when it comes to hand-to-hand fighting, if the enemy stands his ground, the battle is long and anguished and ends with mutual extermination.

As I have said, they take every care not to be obliged to fight in person as long as they can finish the war by the assistance of hired substitutes. When personal service is inevitable, they are as courageous in fighting as they were ingenious in avoiding it as long as they might. They are not fierce in the first onslaught, but their strength increases by degrees through their slow and hard resistance. Their spirit is so stubborn that they would rather be cut to pieces than give way. The absence of anxiety about livelihood at home, as well as the removal of that worry which troubles men about the future of their families (for such solicitude everywhere breaks the highest courage), makes their spirit exalted and disdainful of defeat.

Moreover, their expert training in military discipline gives them confidence. Finally, their good and sound opinions, in which they have been trained from childhood both by teaching and by the good institutions of their country, give them additional courage. So they do not hold their life so cheap as recklessly to throw it away and not so immoderately dear as greedily and shamefully to hold fast to it when honor bids them give it up.

While the battle is everywhere most hot, a band of picked youths who have taken an oath to devote themselves to the task hunt out the opposing general. They openly attack him; they secretly ambush him. They assail him both from far and from near. A long and continuous wedge of men, fresh comers constantly taking the place of those exhausted, keeps up the attack. It seldom happens, unless he look to his safety by running away, that he is not killed or does not fall alive into the enemy's hands.

If the victory rests with them, there is no indiscriminate carnage, for they would rather take the routed as prisoners than kill them. They never pursue the fleeing enemy without keeping one division all the time drawn up ready for engagement under their banners. To such an extent is this the case that if, after the rest of the army has been beaten, they win the victory by this last reserve force, they prefer to let all their enemies escape rather than get into the habit of pursuing them with their own ranks in disorder. They remember that more than once it has happened to themselves that, when the great bulk of their army has been beaten and routed and when the enemy, flushed with victory, has been chasing the fugitives in all directions, a few of their number, held in reserve and ready for emergencies, have suddenly attacked the scattered and straying enemy who, feeling themselves quite safe, were off their guard. Thereby they have changed the whole fortune of the battle and, wresting out of the enemy's hands a certain and undoubted victory, have, though conquered, conquered their conquerors in turn.

It is not easy to say whether they are more cunning in laying ambushes or more cautious in avoiding them. You would think they contemplated flight when that is the very last thing intended; but, on the other hand, when they do determine to flee, you would imagine that they were thinking of anything but that. If they feel themselves to be inferior in number or in position, either by night they noiselessly march and move their camp or evade the enemy by some stratagem, or else by day they retire so imperceptibly and in such regular order that it is as dangerous to attack them in retreat as it would be in advance. They protect their camp most carefully by a deep and broad ditch, the earth taken out of it being thrown inside. They do not utilize the labor of the lowest workmen for the purpose, but the soldiers do it with their own hands. The whole army is set at work, except those who watch under arms in front of the rampart in case of emergencies. Thus, through the efforts of so many, they complete great fortifications, enclosing a large space, with incredible speed.

They wear armor strong enough to turn blows but easily adapted to all motions and gestures of the body. They do not feel any awkwardness even in swimming, for they practice swimming under arms as part of their apprenticeship in military discipline. The weapons they use at a distance are arrows, which they shoot with great strength and sureness of aim not only on foot but also on horseback. At close quarters they use not swords but battle-axes which, because of their sharp point and great weight, are deadly weapons, whether employed for thrusting or hacking. They are very clever in inventing war machines. They hide them, when made, with the greatest care lest, if made known before required by circumstances, they be rather a laughingstock than an instrument of war. In making them, their first object is to have them easy to carry and handy to pivot.

If a truce is made with the enemy, they keep it so religiously as not to break it even under provocation. They do not ravage the enemy's territory nor burn his crops. Rather, they do not even allow them to be trodden down by the feet of men or horses, as far as can be, thinking that they grow for their own benefit. They injure no noncombatant unless he is a spy. When cities are surrendered to them, they keep them intact. They do not plunder even those which they have stormed but put to death the men who prevented surrender and make slaves of the rest of the defenders. They leave unharmed the crowd of noncombatants. If they find out that any persons recommended the surrender of the town, they give them a share of the property of the condemned. They present their auxiliaries with the rest of the confiscated goods, but not a single one of their own men gets any of the booty.

When the war is over, they do not charge the expense against their friends, for whom they have borne the cost, but against the conquered. Under this head they make them not only pay money, which they lay aside for similar warlike purposes, but also surrender estates, from which they may enjoy forever a large annual income. In many countries they have such revenues which, coming little by little from various sources, have grown to the sum of over seven hundred thousand ducats a year.[7] To these estates they dispatch some of their own citizens under the title of Financial Agents to live there in great style and to play the part of magnates. Yet much is left over to put into the public treasury, unless they prefer to give the conquered nation credit. They often do the latter until they need to use the money, and even then it scarcely ever happens that they call in the whole sum. From these estates they confer a share on those who at their request undertake the dangerous mission which I have previously described.

If any king takes up arms against them and prepares to invade their territory, they at once meet him in great strength beyond their borders. They never lightly make war in their own country nor is any emergency so pressing as to compel them to admit foreign auxiliaries into their island.

Utopian Religions

There are different kinds of religion not only on the island as a whole but also in each city. Some worship as god the sun, others the moon, others one of the planets. There are some who reverence a man conspicuous for either virtue or glory in

---

7. A vast sum of money; by today's reckoning, the amount would equal several million dollars.

the past not only as god but even as the supreme god. But by far the majority, and those by far the wiser, believe in nothing of the kind but in a certain single being, unknown, eternal, immense, inexplicable, far above the reach of the human mind, diffused throughout the universe not in mass but in power. Him they call father. To him alone they attribute the beginnings, the growth, the increase, the changes, and the ends of all things as they have perceived them. To no other do they give divine honors.

In addition, all the other Utopians too, though varying in their beliefs, agree with them in this respect that they hold there is one supreme being, to whom are due both the creation and the providential government of the whole world. All alike call him Mithras[8] in their native language, but in this respect they disagree, that he is looked on differently by different persons. Each professes that whatever that is which he regards as supreme is that very same nature to whose unique power and majesty the sum of all things is attributed by the common consent of all nations. But gradually they are all beginning to depart from this medley of superstitions and are coming to unite in that one religion which seems to surpass the rest in reasonableness. Nor is there any doubt that the other beliefs would all have disappeared long ago had not whatever untoward event, that happened to anyone when he was deliberating on a change of religion, been construed by fear as not having happened by chance but as having been sent from heaven as if the deity whose worship he was forsaking were thus avenging an intention so impious against himself.

But after they had heard from us the name of Christ, His teaching, His character, His miracles, and the no less wonderful constancy of the many martyrs whose blood freely shed had drawn so many nations far and wide into their fellowship, you would not believe how readily disposed they, too, were to join it, whether through the rather mysterious inspiration of God or because they thought it nearest to that belief which has the widest prevalence among them. But I think that this factor, too, was of no small weight, that they had heard that His disciples' common way of life had been pleasing to Christ and that it is still in use among the truest societies of Christians. But whatever it was that influenced them, not a few joined our religion and were cleansed by the holy water of baptism.

But because among us four (for that was all that was left, two of our group having succumbed to fate) there was, I am sorry to say, no priest, they were initiated in all other matters, but so far they lack those sacraments which with us only priests administer. They understand, however, what they are, and desire them with the greatest eagerness. Moreover, they are even debating earnestly among themselves whether, without the dispatch of a Christian bishop, one chosen out of their own number might receive the sacerdotal character. It seemed that they would choose a candidate, but by the time of my departure they had not yet done so.

Even those who do not agree with the religion of Christ do not try to deter others from it. They do not attack any who have made their profession. Only one of our company, while I was there, was interfered with. As soon as he was baptized, in spite of our advice to the contrary, he spoke publicly of Christ's religion with more zeal than discretion. He began to grow so warm in his preaching that not only did he prefer our worship to any other but he condemned all the rest outright. He proclaimed them to be profane in themselves and their followers to be impious and sacrilegious

8. Persian sun god.

and worthy of everlasting fire. When he had long been preaching in this style, they arrested him, tried him, and convicted him not for despising their religion but for stirring up a riot among the people. His sentence after the verdict of guilty was exile. Actually, they count this principle among their most ancient institutions, that no one should suffer for his religion.

Utopus had heard that before his arrival the inhabitants had been continually quarreling among themselves about religion. He had observed that the universal dissensions between the individual sects who were fighting for their country had given him the opportunity of overcoming them all. From the very beginning, therefore, after he had gained the victory, he especially ordained that it should be lawful for every man to follow the religion of his choice, that each might strive to bring others over to his own, provided that he quietly and modestly supported his own by reasons nor bitterly demolished all others if his persuasions were not successful nor used any violence and refrained from abuse. If a person contends too vehemently in expressing his views, he is punished with exile or enslavement.

Utopus laid down these regulations not merely from regard for peace, which he saw to be utterly destroyed by constant wrangling and implacable hatred, but because he thought that this method of settlement was in the interest of religion itself. On religion he did not venture rashly to dogmatize. He was uncertain whether God did not desire a varied and manifold worship and therefore did not inspire different people with different views. But he was certain in thinking it both insolence and folly to demand by violence and threats that all should think to be true what you believe to be true. Moreover, even if it should be the case that one single religion is true and all the rest are false, he readily foresaw that, provided the matter was handled reasonably and moderately, truth by its own natural force would finally emerge sooner or later and stand forth conspicuously. But if the struggle were decided by arms and riots, since the worst men are always the most unyielding, the best and holiest religion would be overwhelmed because of the conflicting false religions, like grain choked by thorns and underbrush.

So he made the whole matter of religion an open question and left each one free to choose what he should believe. By way of exception, he conscientiously and strictly gave injunction that no one should fall so far below the dignity of human nature as to believe that souls likewise perish with the body or that the world is the mere sport of chance and not governed by any divine providence. After this life, accordingly, vices are ordained to be punished and virtue rewarded. Such is their belief, and if anyone thinks otherwise, they do not regard him even as a member of mankind, seeing that he has lowered the lofty nature of his soul to the level of a beast's miserable body—so far are they from classing him among their citizens whose laws and customs he would treat as worthless if it were not for fear. Who can doubt that he will strive either to evade by craft the public laws of his country or to break them by violence in order to serve his own private desires when he has nothing to fear but laws and no hope beyond the body?

Therefore an individual of this mind is tendered no honor, is entrusted with no office, and is put in charge of no function. He is universally regarded as of a sluggish and low disposition. But they do not punish him in any way, being convinced that it is in no man's power to believe what he chooses, nor do they compel him by threats to disguise his views, nor do they allow in the matter any deceptions or lies which they hate exceedingly as being next door to calculated malice. They forbid him to argue in support of his opinion in the presence of the common people, but in private before the priests and important personages they not only permit but also encourage it, being sure that such madness will in the end give way to reason.

There are others, too, and these not a few, who are not interfered with because they do not altogether lack reason for their view and because they are not evil men. By a much different error, these believe that brute animals also have immortal souls, but not comparable to ours in dignity or destined to equal felicity. Almost all Utopians are absolutely certain and convinced that human bliss will be so immense that, while they lament every man's illness, they regret the death of no one but him whom they see torn from life anxiously and unwillingly. This behavior they take to be a very bad omen as though the soul, being without hope and having a guilty conscience, dreaded its departure through a secret premonition of impending punishment. Besides, they suppose that God will not be pleased with the coming of one who, when summoned, does not gladly hasten to obey but is reluctantly drawn against his will. Persons who behold this kind of death are filled with horror and therefore carry the dead out to burial in melancholy silence. Then, after praying God to be merciful to their shades and graciously to pardon their infirmities, they cover the corpse with earth.

On the other hand, when men have died cheerfully and full of good hope, no one mourns for them, but they accompany their funerals with song, with great affection commending their souls to God. Then, with reverence rather than with sorrow, they cremate the bodies. On the spot they erect a pillar on which are inscribed the good points of the deceased. On returning home they recount his character and his deeds. No part of his life is more frequently or more gladly spoken of than his cheerful death.

They judge that this remembrance of uprightness is not only a most efficacious means of stimulating the living to good deeds but also a most acceptable form of attention to the dead. The latter they think are present when they are talked about, though invisible to the dull sight of mortals. It would be inconsistent with the lot of the blessed not to be able to travel freely where they please, and it would be ungrateful of them to reject absolutely all desire of revisiting their friends to whom they were bound during their lives by mutual love and charity. Charity, like all other good things, they conjecture to be increased after death rather than diminished in all good men. Consequently they believe that the dead move about among the living and are witnesses of their words and actions. Hence they go about their business with more confidence because of reliance on such protection. The belief, moreover, in the personal presence of their forefathers keeps men from any secret dishonorable deed.

They utterly despise and deride auguries and all other divinations of vain superstition, to which great attention is paid in other countries. But miracles, which occur without the assistance of nature, they venerate as operations and witnesses of the divine power at work.[9] In their country, too, they say, miracles often occur. Sometimes in great and critical affairs they pray publicly for a miracle, which they very confidently look for and obtain.

They think that the investigation of nature, with the praise arising from it, is an act of worship acceptable to God. There are persons, however, and these not so very few, who for religious motives eschew learning and scientific pursuit and yet allow themselves no leisure. It is only by keeping busy and by all good offices that they are

---

9. Christian doctrine held that a miracle was an intervention by God into the natural order of things. God can perform miracles among non-Christians as well as among Christians.

determined to merit the happiness coming after death. Some tend the sick. Others repair roads, clean out ditches, rebuild bridges, dig turf and sand and stone, fell and cut up trees, and transport wood, grain, and other things into the cities in carts. Not only for the public but also for private persons they behave as servants and as more than slaves.

If anywhere there is a task so rough, hard, and filthy that most are deterred from it by the toil, disgust, and despair involved, they gladly and cheerfully claim it all for themselves. While perpetually engaged in hard work themselves, they secure leisure for the others and yet claim no credit for it. They neither belittle insultingly the life of others nor extol their own. The more that these men put themselves in the position of slaves the more are they honored by all.

Of these persons there are two schools. The one is composed of celibates who not only eschew all sexual activity but also abstain from eating flesh meat and in some cases from eating all animal food. They entirely reject the pleasures of this life as harmful. They long only for the future life by means of their watching and sweat. Hoping to obtain it very soon, they are cheerful and active in the meantime.

The other school is just as fond of hard labor, but regards matrimony as preferable, not despising the comfort which it brings and thinking that their duty to nature requires them to perform the marital act and their duty to the country to beget children. They avoid no pleasure unless it interferes with their labor. They like flesh meat just because they think that this fare makes them stronger for any work whatsoever. The Utopians regard these men as the saner but the first-named as the holier. If the latter based upon arguments from reason their preference of celibacy to matrimony and of a hard life to a comfortable one, they would laugh them to scorn. Now, however, since they say they are prompted by religion, they look up to and reverence them. For there is nothing about which they are more careful than not lightly to dogmatize on any point of religion. Such, then, are the men whom in their language they call by a special name of their own, Buthrescae, a word which may be translated as "religious par excellence."

They have priests of extraordinary holiness, and therefore very few. They have no more than thirteen in each city—with a like number of churches—except when they go to war. In that case, seven go forth with the army, and the same number of substitutes is appointed for the interval. When the regular priests come back, everyone returns to his former duties. Then those who are above the number of thirteen, until they succeed to the places of those who die, attend upon the high priest in the meantime. One, you see, is appointed to preside over the rest. They are elected by the people, just as all the other officials are, by secret ballot to avoid party spirit. When elected, they are ordained by their own group.

They preside over divine worship, order religious rites, and are censors of morals. It is counted a great disgrace for a man to be summoned or rebuked by them as not being of upright life. It is their function to give advice and admonition, but to check and punish offenders belongs to the governor and the other civil officials. The priests, however, do exclude from divine services persons whom they find to be unusually bad. There is almost no punishment which is more dreaded: they incur very great disgrace and are tortured by a secret fear of religion. Even their bodies will not long go scot-free. If they do not demonstrate to the priests their speedy repentance, they are seized and punished by the senate for their impiety.

To the priests is entrusted the education of children and youths. They regard concern for their morals and virtue as no less important than for their advancement in learning. They take the greatest pains from the very first to instill into children's minds, while still tender and pliable, good opinions, which are also useful for the preservation of their commonwealth. When once they are firmly implanted in children, they accompany them all through their adult lives and are of great help in watching over the condition of the commonwealth. The latter never decays except through vices which arise from wrong attitudes.

The feminine sex[1] is not debarred from the priesthood, but only a widow advanced in years is ever chosen, and that rather rarely. Unless they are women, the priests have for their wives the very finest women of the country.

To no other office in Utopia is more honor given, so much so that, even if they have committed any crime, they are subjected to no tribunal, but left only to God and to themselves. They judge it wrong to lay human hands upon one, however guilty, who has been consecrated to God in a singular manner as a holy offering. It is easier for them to observe this custom because their priests are very few and very carefully chosen.

Besides, it does not easily happen that one who is elevated to such dignity for being the very best among the good, nothing but virtue being taken into account, should fall into corruption and wickedness. Even if it does happen, human nature being ever prone to change, yet since they are but few and are invested with no power except the influence of honor, it need not be feared that they will cause any great harm to the state. In fact, the reason for having but few and exceptional priests is to prevent the dignity of the order, which they now reverence very highly, from being cheapened by communicating the honor to many. This is especially true since they think it hard to find many men so good as to be fit for so honorable a position for the filling of which it is not enough to be endowed with ordinary virtues.

They are not more esteemed among their own people than among foreign nations. This can easily be seen from a fact which, I think, is its cause. When the armies are fighting in battle, the priests are to be found separate but not very far off, settled on their knees, dressed in their sacred vestments. With hands outstretched to heaven, they pray first of all for peace, next for a victory to their own side—but without much bloodshed on either side. When their side is winning, they run among the combatants, and restrain the fury of their own men against the routed enemy. Merely to see and to appeal to them suffices to save one's life; to touch their flowing garments protects one's remaining goods from every harm arising from war.

This conduct has brought them such veneration among all nations everywhere and has given them so real a majesty that they have saved their own citizens from the enemy as often as they have protected the enemy from their own men. The following is well known. Sometimes their own side had given way, their case had been desperate, they were taking to flight, and the enemy was rushing on to kill and to plunder. But the carnage was then averted by the intervention of the priests. After the armies were parted from each other, peace was concluded and settled on just terms. Never was there any nation so savage, cruel, and barbarous that it did not regard their persons as sacred and inviolable.

They celebrate as holydays the first and the last day of each month and likewise of each year. The latter they divide into months, measured by the orbit of the moon

1. In Greek and Roman religious practice, women could perform priestly functions. As these were the peoples whom More identified as understanding natural law, he must have thought that natural law did not limit a woman's role in religion.

just as the course of the sun rounds out the year. In their language they call the first days Cynemerni and the last days Trapemerni. These names have the same meaning as if they were rendered "First-Feasts" and "Final-Feasts."

Their temples are fine sights, not only elaborate in workmanship but also capable of holding a vast throng, and necessarily so, since there are so few of them. The temples are all rather dark. This feature, they report, is due not to an ignorance of architecture but to the deliberate intention of the priests. They think that excessive light makes the thoughts wander, whereas scantier and uncertain light concentrates the mind and conduces to devotion.

In Utopia, as has been seen, the religion of all is not the same, and yet all its manifestations, though varied and manifold, by different roads as it were, tend to the same end, the worship of the divine nature. Therefore nothing is seen or heard in the temples which does not seem to agree with all in common. If any sect has a rite of its own, it is performed within the walls of each man's home. Public worship is conducted according to a ritual which does not at all detract from any of the private devotions. Therefore no image of the gods is seen in the temple so that the individual may be free to conceive of God with the most ardent devotion in any form he pleases. They invoke God by no special name except that of Mithras. By this word they agree to represent the one nature of the divine majesty whatever it be. The prayers formulated are such as every man may utter without offense to his own belief.

On the evening of the Final-Feasts, they gather in the temple, still fasting. They thank God for the prosperity they have enjoyed in the month or year of which that holyday is the last day. Next day, which is the First-Feast, they flock to the temples in the morning. They pray for good luck and prosperity in the ensuing year or month, of which this holyday is the auspicious beginning.

On the Final-Feasts, before they go to the temple, wives fall down at the feet of their husbands, children at the feet of their parents. They confess that they have erred, either by committing some fault or by performing some duty carelessly, and beg pardon for their offense. Hence, if any cloud of quarrel in the family has arisen, it is dispelled by this satisfaction so that with pure and clear minds they may be present at the sacrifices, for they are too scrupulous to attend with a troubled conscience. If they are aware of hatred or anger against anyone they do not assist at the sacrifices until they have been reconciled and have cleansed their hearts, for fear of swift and great punishment.

When they reach the temple, they part, the men going to the right side and the women to the left. Then they arrange their places so that the males in each home sit in front of the head of the household and the womenfolk are in front of the mother of the family. They thus take care that every gesture of everyone abroad is observed by those whose authority and discipline govern them at home. They also carefully see to it that everywhere the younger are placed in the company of the elder. If children were trusted to children, they might spend in childish foolery the time in which they ought to be conceiving a religious fear toward the gods, the greatest and almost the only stimulus to the practice of virtues.

They slay no animal in their sacrifices. They do not believe that the divine clemency delights in bloodshed and slaughter, seeing that it has imparted life to animate creatures that they might enjoy life. They burn incense and other fragrant substances and also offer a great number of candles. They are not unaware that these things add nothing to the divine nature, any more than do human prayers, but they like this harmless kind of worship. Men feel that, by these sweet smells and lights, as well as the other ceremonies, they somehow are uplifted and rise with livelier devotion to the worship of God.

The people are clothed in white garments in the temple. The priest wears vestments of various colors, of wonderful design and shape, but not of material as costly as one would expect. They are not interwoven with gold or set with precious stones but wrought with the different feathers of birds so cleverly and artistically that no costly material could equal the value of the handiwork. Moreover, in these birds' feathers and plumes and the definite order and plan by which they are set off on the priest's vestment, they say certain hidden mysteries are contained. By knowing the meaning as it is carefully handed down by the priests, they are reminded of God's benefits toward them and, in turn, of their own piety toward God and their duty toward one another.

As soon as the priest thus arrayed appears from the vestibule, all immediately fall on the ground in reverence. The silence all around is so deep that the very appearance of the congregation strikes one with awe as if some divine power were really present. After remaining a while on the ground, at a signal from the priest they rise.

At this point they sing praises to God, which they diversify with musical instruments, largely different in shape from those seen in our part of the world. Very many of them surpass in sweetness those in use with us, but some are not even comparable with ours. But in one respect undoubtedly they are far ahead of us. All their music, whether played on instruments or sung by the human voice, so renders and expresses the natural feelings, so suits the sound to the matter (whether the words be supplicatory, or joyful, or propitiatory, or troubled, or mournful, or angry), and so represents the meaning by the form of the melody that it wonderfully affects, penetrates, and inflames the souls of the hearers.

At the end, the priest and the people together repeat solemn prayers fixed in form, so drawn up that each individual may apply to himself personally what all recite together. In these prayers every man recognizes God to be the author of creation and governance and all other blessings besides. He thanks Him for all the benefits received, particularly that by the divine favor he has chanced on that commonwealth which is the happiest and has received that religion which he hopes to be the truest. If he errs in these matters or if there is anything better and more approved by God than that commonwealth or that religion, he prays that He will, of His goodness, bring him to the knowledge of it, for he is ready to follow in whatever path He may lead him. But if this form of a commonwealth be the best and his religion the truest, he prays that then He may give him steadfastness and bring all other mortals to the same way of living and the same opinion of God—unless there be something in this variety of religions which delights His inscrutable will.

Finally, he prays that God will take him to Himself by an easy death, how soon or late he does not venture to determine. However, if it might be without offense to His Majesty, it would be much more welcome to him to die a very hard death and go to God than to be kept longer away from Him even by a very prosperous career in life.[2]

After this prayer has been said, they prostrate themselves on the ground again. Then shortly they rise and go away to dinner. The rest of the day they pass in games and in exercises of military training.

---

2. The Utopians do not pray for forgiveness of the sins they have committed in the past, although they do pray for divine guidance in avoiding the errors they may commit in the future.

Now I have described to you, as exactly as I could, the structure of that commonwealth which I judge not merely the best but the only one which can rightly claim the name of a commonwealth. Outside Utopia, to be sure, men talk freely of the public welfare—but look after their private interests only. In Utopia, where nothing is private, they seriously concern themselves with public affairs. Assuredly in both cases they act reasonably. For, outside Utopia, how many are there who do not realize that, unless they make some separate provision for themselves, however flourishing the commonwealth, they will themselves starve? For this reason, necessity compels them to hold that they must take account of themselves rather than of the people, that is, of others.

On the other hand, in Utopia, where everything belongs to everybody, no one doubts, provided only that the public granaries are well filled, that the individual will lack nothing for his private use. The reason is that the distribution of goods is not niggardly. In Utopia there is no poor man and no beggar. Though no man has anything, yet all are rich.

For what can be greater riches for a man than to live with a joyful and peaceful mind, free of all worries—not troubled about his food or harassed by the querulous demands of his wife or fearing poverty for his son or worrying about his daughter's dowry, but feeling secure about the livelihood and happiness of himself and his family: wife, sons, grandsons, great-grandsons, great-great-grandsons, and all the long line of their descendants that gentlefolk anticipate? Then take into account the fact that there is no less provision for those who are now helpless but once worked than for those who are still working.

At this point I should like anyone to be so bold as to compare this fairness with the so-called justice prevalent in other nations, among which, upon my soul, I cannot discover the slightest trace of justice and fairness. What brand of justice is it that any nobleman whatsoever or goldsmith-banker or moneylender or, in fact, anyone else from among those who either do no work at all or whose work is of a kind not very essential to the commonwealth, should attain a life of luxury and grandeur on the basis of his idleness or his nonessential work? In the meantime, the common laborer, the carter, the carpenter, and the farmer perform work so hard and continuous that beasts of burden could scarcely endure it and work so essential that no commonwealth could last even one year without it. Yet they earn such scanty fare and lead such a miserable life that the condition of beasts of burden might seem far preferable. The latter do not have to work so incessantly nor is their food much worse (in fact, sweeter to their taste) nor do they entertain any fear for the future. The workmen, on the other hand, not only have to toil and suffer without return or profit in the present but agonize over the thought of an indigent old age. Their daily wage is too scanty to suffice even for the day: much less is there an excess and surplus that daily can be laid by for their needs in old age.

Now is not this an unjust and ungrateful commonwealth? It lavishes great rewards on so-called gentlefolk and banking goldsmiths and the rest of that kind, who are either idle or mere parasites and purveyors of empty pleasures. On the contrary, it makes no benevolent provision for farmers, colliers, common laborers, carters, and carpenters without whom there would be no commonwealth at all. After it has misused the labor of their prime and after they are weighed down with age and disease and are in utter want, it forgets all their sleepless nights and all the great benefits received at their hands and most ungratefully requites them with a most miserable death.

What is worse, the rich every day extort a part of their daily allowance from the poor not only by private fraud but by public law. Even before they did so it seemed unjust that persons deserving best of the commonwealth should have the worst return. Now they have further distorted and debased the right and, finally, by making laws, have palmed it off as justice. Consequently, when I consider and turn over in my mind the state of all commonwealths flourishing anywhere today, so help me God, I can see nothing else than a kind of conspiracy of the rich, who are aiming at their own interests under the name and title of the commonwealth.[3] They invent and devise all ways and means by which, first, they may keep without fear of loss all that they have amassed by evil practices and, secondly, they may then purchase as cheaply as possible and abuse the toil and labor of all the poor. These devices become law as soon as the rich have once decreed their observance in the name of the public—that is, of the poor also!

Yet when these evil men with insatiable greed have divided up among themselves all the goods which would have been enough for all the people, how far they are from the happiness of the Utopian commonwealth! In Utopia all greed for money was entirely removed with the use of money. What a mass of troubles was then cut away! What a crop of crimes was then pulled up by the roots! Who does not know that fraud, theft, rapine, quarrels, disorders, brawls, seditions, murders, treasons, poisonings, which are avenged rather than restrained by daily executions, die out with the destruction of money? Who does not know that fear, anxiety, worries, toils, and sleepless nights will also perish at the same time as money? What is more, poverty, which alone money seemed to make poor, forthwith would itself dwindle and disappear if money were entirely done away with everywhere.

To make this assertion clearer, consider in your thoughts some barren and unfruitful year in which many thousands of men have been carried off by famine. I emphatically contend that at the end of that scarcity, if rich men's granaries had been searched, as much grain could have been found as, if it had been divided among the people killed off by starvation and disease, would have prevented anyone from feeling that meager return from soil and climate. So easily might men get the necessities of life if that blessed money, supposedly a grand invention to ease access to those necessities, was not in fact the only barrier to our getting what we need.

Even the rich, I doubt not, have such feelings. They are not unaware that it would be a much better state of affairs to lack no necessity than to have abundance of superfluities—to be snatched from such numerous troubles rather than to be hemmed in by great riches. Nor does it occur to me to doubt that a man's regard for his own interests or the authority of Christ our Savior—who in His wisdom could not fail to know what was best and who in His goodness would not fail to counsel what He knew to be best—would long ago have brought the whole world to adopt the laws of

3. Hythlodaeus condemns practices associated with the accumulation of wealth as capital and the corresponding exploitation of workers in the interest of increasing capital. This goal is promoted by various legal "devices," particularly involving estates, that preserve capital within the upper ranks of society. But capital cannot be accumulated in a barter economy, where goods are exchanged for goods rather than for money. Hence Hythlodaeus eliminates money as a way of preventing the formation of capital.

the Utopian commonwealth, had not one single monster, the chief and progenitor of all plagues, striven against it—I mean, Pride.

Pride measures prosperity not by her own advantages but by others' disadvantages.[4] Pride would not consent to be made even a goddess if no poor wretches were left for her to domineer over and scoff at, if her good fortune might not dazzle by comparison with their miseries, if the display of her riches did not torment and intensify their poverty. This serpent from hell entwines itself around the hearts of men and acts like the suckfish in preventing and hindering them from entering on a better way of life.

Pride is too deeply fixed in men to be easily plucked out. For this reason, the fact that this form of a commonwealth—which I should gladly desire for all—has been the good fortune of the Utopians at least, fills me with joy. They have adopted such institutions of life as have laid the foundations of the commonwealth not only most happily, but also to last forever, as far as human prescience can forecast. At home they have extirpated the roots of ambition and factionalism, along with all the other vices. Hence there is no danger of trouble from domestic discord, which has been the only cause of ruin to the well-established prosperity of many cities. As long as harmony is preserved at home and its institutions are in a healthy state, not all the envy of neighboring rulers, though it has rather often attempted it and has always been repelled, can avail to shatter or to shake that nation.

When Raphael had finished his story, many things came to my mind which seemed very absurdly established in the customs and laws of the people described—not only in their method of waging war, their ceremonies and religion, as well as their other institutions, but most of all in that feature which is the principal foundation of their whole structure. I mean their common life and subsistence—without any exchange of money. This latter alone utterly overthrows all the nobility, magnificence, splendor, and majesty which are, in the estimation of the common people, the true glories and ornaments of the commonwealth.

I knew, however, that he was wearied with his tale, and I was not quite certain that he could brook any opposition to his views, particularly when I recalled his censure of others on account of their fear that they might not appear to be wise enough, unless they found some fault to criticize in other men's discoveries. I therefore praised their way of life and his speech and, taking him by the hand, led him in to supper. I first said, nevertheless, that there would be another chance to think about these matters more deeply and to talk them over with him more fully. If only this were some day possible!

Meanwhile, though in other respects he is a man of the most undoubted learning as well as of the greatest knowledge of human affairs, I cannot agree with all that he said. But I readily admit that there are very many features in the Utopian commonwealth which it is easier for me to wish for in our countries than to have any hope of seeing realized.

---

4. Pride therefore prevents a society based on benefits, which typically redound to the welfare of a community rather than to that of particular individuals.

END OF BOOK TWO
THE END OF THE AFTERNOON DISCOURSE OF
RAPHAEL HYTHLODAEUS ON THE LAWS
AND CUSTOMS OF THE ISLAND OF
UTOPIA, HITHERTO KNOWN BUT
TO FEW, AS REPORTED BY THE
MOST DISTINGUISHED AND
MOST LEARNED MAN,
MR. THOMAS MORE,
CITIZEN AND SHERIFF OF LONDON
FINIS

RESPONSE

Francis Bacon[1] from *The New Atlantis*

[The Jew who shows the travellers around the island speaks to the narrator] "God bless thee, my son; I will give thee the greatest jewel I have. For I will impart unto thee, for the love of God and men, a relation of the true state of Salomon's House. Son, to make you know the true state of Salomon's House, I will keep this order. First, I will set forth unto you the end of our foundation. Secondly, the preparations and instruments we have for our works. Thirdly, the several employments and functions whereto our fellows are assigned. And fourthly, the ordinances and rites which we observe.

The end of our foundation is the knowledge of causes, and secret motions of things; and the enlarging of the bounds of human empire, to the effecting of all things possible.

The Preparations and Instruments are these. We have large and deep caves of several depths: the deepest are sunk six hundred fathom: and some of them are digged and made under great hills and mountains: so that if you reckon together the depth of the hill and the depth of the cave, they are (some of them) above three miles deep. For we find, that the depth of a hill, and the depth of a cave from the flat, is the same thing; both remote alike, from the sun and heaven's beams, and from the open air. These caves we call the Lower Region; and we use them for all coagulations, indurations, refrigerations, and conservations of bodies. We use them likewise for the imitation of natural mines; and the producing also of new artificial metals, by compositions and materials which we use, and lay there for many years. We use them also sometimes, (which may seem strange,) for curing of some diseases, and for prolongation of life in some hermits that choose to live

---

1. Francis Bacon (1561–1626), philosopher, lawyer, essayist, scientist and politician. Bacon was a prolific author of tremendous energy who combined a varied writing career with an interest in scientific experimentation (he died from a chill caught making experiments in the snow), and a checkered political career (he was notoriously corrupt). *The New Atlantis* (1626) is an imaginative response to More's *Utopia*, which makes use of Bacon's scientific knowledge allied to his predictions of what might happen in the future. It can be looked upon as an early forerunner of science fiction and read alongside Bacon's work on scientific reasoning such as *The Advancement of Learning* (1605) and the Latin treatise *Novum Orgum* (1620).

there, well accommodated of all things necessary, and indeed live very long; by whom also we learn many things.

We have burials in several earths, where we put diverse cements, as the Chineses do their porcellain. But we have them in greater variety, and some of them more fine. We have also great variety of composts and soils, for the making of the earth fruitful.

We have high towers; the highest about half a mile in height; and some of them likewise set upon high mountains; so that the vantage of the hill with the tower is in the highest of them three miles at least. And these places we call the Upper Region; accounting the air between the high places and the low, as a Middle Region. We use these towers, according to their several heights, and situations, for insolation, refrigeration, conservation; and for the view of divers meteors; as winds, rain, snow, hail; and some of the fiery meteors also. And upon them, in some places, are dwellings of hermits, whom we visit sometimes, and instruct what to observe.

We have great lakes, both salt, and fresh; whereof we have use for the fish and fowl. We use them also for burials of some natural bodies: for we find a difference in things buried in earth or in air below the earth, and things buried in water. We have also pools, of which some do strain fresh water out of salt; and others by art do turn fresh water into salt. We have also some rocks in the midst of the sea, and some bays upon the shore for some works, wherein is required the air and vapor of the sea. We have likewise violent streams and cataracts, which serve us for many motions: and likewise engines for multiplying and enforcing of winds, to set also on going diverse motions.

We have also a number of artificial wells and fountains, made in imitation of the natural sources and baths; as tincted upon vitriol, sulphur, steel, brass, lead, nitre, and other minerals. And again we have little wells for infusions of many things, where the waters take the virtue quicker and better, than in vessels or basins. And amongst them we have a water which we call Water of Paradise, being, by that we do to it made very sovereign for health, and prolongation of life.

We have also great and spacious houses where we imitate and demonstrate meteors; as snow, hail, rain, some artificial rains of bodies and not of water, thunders, lightnings; also generations of bodies in air; as frogs, flies, and divers others.

We have also certain chambers, which we call Chambers of Health, where we qualify the air as we think good and proper for the cure of divers diseases, and preservation of health.

We have also fair and large baths, of several mixtures, for the cure of diseases, and the restoring of man's body from arefaction: and others for the confirming of it in strength of sinewes, vital parts, and the very juice and substance of the body.

We have also large and various orchards and gardens; wherein we do not so much respect beauty, as variety of ground and soil, proper for divers trees and herbs: and some very spacious, where trees and berries are set whereof we make divers kinds of drinks, besides the vineyards. In these we practise likewise all conclusions of grafting, and inoculating as well of wild-trees as fruit-trees, which produceth many effects. And we make (by art) in the same orchards and gardens, trees and flowers to come earlier or later than their seasons; and to come up and bear more speedily than by their natural course they do. We make them also by art greater much than their nature; and their fruit greater and sweeter and of differing taste, smell, colour, and figure, from their nature. And many of them we so order, as they become of medicinal use.

We have also means to make divers plants rise by mixtures of earths without seeds; and likewise to make divers new plants, differing from the vulgar; and to make one tree or plant turn into another.

We have also parks and enclosures of all sorts of beasts and birds which we use not only for view or rareness, but likewise for dissections and trials; that thereby we may take light what may be wrought upon the body of man. Wherein we find many strange effects; as continuing life in them, though divers parts, which you account vital, be perished and taken forth; resuscitating of some that seem dead in appearance; and the like. We try also all poisons and other medicines upon them, as well of chirurgery,[1] as physic. By art likewise, we make them greater or taller than their kind is; and contrariwise dwarf them, and stay their growth: we make them more fruitful and bearing than their kind is; and contrariwise barren and not generative. Also we make them differ in colour, shape, activity, many ways. We find means to make commixtures and copulations of different kinds; which have produced many new kinds, and them not barren, as the general opinion is. We make a number of kinds of serpents, worms, flies, fishes, of putrefaction; whereof some are advanced (in effect) to be perfect creatures, like bests or birds; and have sexes, and do propagate. Neither do we this by chance, but we know beforehand, of what matter and commixture what kind of those creatures will arise.

We have also particular pools, where we make trials upon fishes, as we have said before of beasts and birds.

We have also places for breed and generation of those kinds of worms and flies which are of special use; such as are with you your silk-worms and bees.

I will not hold you long with recounting of our brewhouses, bake-houses, and kitchens, where are made divers drinks, breads, and meats, rare and of special effects. Wines we have of grapes; and drinks of other juice of fruits, of grains, and of roots; and of mixtures with honey, sugar, manna, and fruits dried, and decocted; Also of the tears or woundings of trees; and of the pulp of canes. And these drinks are of several ages, some to the age or last of forty years. We have drinks also brewed with several herbs, and roots, and spices; yea with several fleshes, and white-meats; whereof some of the drinks are such, as they are in effect meat and drink both: so that divers, especially in age, do desire to live with them, with little or no meat or bread. And above all, we strive to have drink of extreme thin parts, to insinuate into the body, and yet without all biting, sharpness, or fretting; insomuch as some of them put upon the back of your hand will, with a little stay, pass through to the palm, and yet taste mild to the mouth. We have also waters which we ripen in that fashion, as they become nourishing; so that they are indeed excellent drink; and many will use no other. Breads we have of several grains, roots, and kernels; yea and some of flesh and fish dried; with divers kinds of leavenings and seasonings: so that some do extremely move appetites; some do nourish so, as divers do live of them, without any other meat; who live very long. So for meats, we have some of them so beaten and made tender and mortified, "yet without all corrupting, as a weak heat of the stomach will turn them into good chylus;[2] as well as a strong heat would meat otherwise prepared. We have some meats also and breads and drinks, which taken by men enable them to fast long after; and some other, that used make the very flesh of

---

1. Surgery.   2. Digestion.

men's bodies sensibly" more hard and tough and their strength far greater than otherwise it would be.

We have dispensatories, or shops of medicines. Wherein you may easily think, if we have such variety of plants and living creatures more than you have in Europe, (for we know what you have,) the simples,[3] drugs, and ingredients of medicines, must likewise be in so much the greater variety. We have them likewise of divers ages, and long fermentations. And for their preparations, we have not only all manner of exquisite distillations and separations, and especially by gentle heats and percolations through divers strainers, yea and substances; but also exact forms of composition, whereby they incorporate almost, as they were natural simples.

We have also divers mechanical arts, which you have not; and stuffs made by them; as papers, linen, silks, tissues; dainty works of feathers of wonderful lustre; excellent dies, and, many others; and shops likewise, as well for such as are not brought into vulgar use amongst us as for those that are. For you must know that of the things before recited, many of them are grown into use throughout the kingdom; but yet, if they did flow from our invention, we have of them also for patterns and principals.

We have also furnaces of great diversities, and that keep great diversity of heats; fierce and quick; strong and constant; soft and mild; blown, quiet; dry, moist; and the like. But above all, we have heats, in imitation of the Sun's and heavenly bodies' heats, that pass divers inequalities, and (as it were) orbs, progresses, and returns, whereby we produce admirable effects. Besides, we have heats of dungs; and of bellies and maws of living creatures, and of their bloods and bodies; and of hays and herbs laid up moist; of lime unquenched; and such like. Instruments also which generate heat only by motion. And farther, places for strong insulations; and again, places under the earth, which by nature, or art, yield heat. These divers heats we use, as the nature of the operation, which we intend, requireth.

We have also perspective-houses, where we make demonstrations of all lights and radiations; and of all colours: and out of things uncoloured and transparent, we can represent unto you all several colours; not in rain-bows, (as it is in gems, and prisms,) but of themselves single. We represent also all multiplications of light, which we carry to great distance, and make so sharp as to discern small points and lines. Also all colourations of light; all delusions and deceits of the sight, in figures, magnitudes, motions, colours all demonstrations of shadows. We find also divers means, yet unknown to you, of producing of light originally from divers bodies. We procure means of seeing objects afar off; as in the heaven and remote places; and represent things near as afar off; and things afar off as near; making feigned distances. We have also helps for the sight, far above spectacles and glasses in use. We have also glasses and means to see small and minute bodies perfectly and distinctly; as the shapes and colours of small flies and worms, grains and flaws in gems, which cannot otherwise be seen, observations in urine and blood not otherwise to be seen. We make artificial rain-bows, halo's, and circles about light. We represent also all manner of reflexions, refractions, and multiplications of visual beams of objects.

We have also precious stones of all kinds, many of them of great beauty, and to you unknown; crystals likewise; and glasses of divers kinds; and amongst them some of metals vitrificated, and other materials besides those of which you make glass. Also a number of fossils, and imperfect minerals, which you have not.

3. Medications made of one ingredient, such as an herb.

Likewise loadstones of prodigious virtue; and other rare stones, both natural and artificial.

We have also sound-houses, where we practise and demonstrate all sounds, and their generation. We have harmonies which you have not, of quarter-sounds, and lesser slides of sounds. Divers instruments of music likewise to you unknown, some sweeter than any you have, together with bells and rings that are dainty and sweet. We represent small sounds as great and deep; likewise great sounds extenuate and sharp; we make divers tremblings and warblings of sounds, which in their original are entire. We represent and imitate all articulate sounds and letters, and the voices and notes of beasts and birds. We have certain helps which set to the ear do further the hearing greatly. We have also divers strange and artificial echoes, reflecting the voice many times, and as it were tossing it: and some that give back the voice louder than it came, some shriller, and some deeper; yea, some rendering the voice differing in the letters or articulate sound from that they receive. We have also means to convey sounds in trunks and pipes, in strange lines and distances.

We have also perfume-houses; wherewith we join also practices of taste. We multiply smells, which may seem strange. We imitate smells, making all smells to breathe outs of other mixtures than those that give them. We make divers imitations of taste likewise, so that they will deceive any man's taste. And in this house we contain also a confiture-house; where we make all sweet-meats, dry and moist; and divers pleasant wines, milks, broths, and sallets;[4] in far greater variety than you have.

We have also engine-houses, where are prepared engines and instruments for all sorts of motions. There we imitate and practise to make swifter motions than any you have, either out of your muskets or any engine that you have: and to make them and multiply them more easily, and with small force, by wheels and other means: and to make them stronger and more violent than yours are; exceeding your greatest cannons and basilisks. We represent also ordnance and instruments of war, and engines of all kinds: and likewise new mixtures and compositions of gun-powder, wildfires burning in water, and unquenchable. Also fireworks of all variety both for pleasure and use. We imitate also flights of birds; we have some degrees of flying in the air. We have ships and boats for going under water, and brooking of seas; also swimming-girdles and supporters. We have divers curious clocks, and other like motions of return: and some perpetual motions. We imitate also motions of living creatures, by images, of men, beasts, birds, fishes, and serpents. We have also a great number of other various motions, strange for equality, fineness, and subtilty.

We have also a mathematical house, where are represented all instruments, as well of geometry as astronomy, exquisitely made.

We have also houses of deceits of the senses; where we represent all manner of feats of juggling, false apparitions, impostures, and illusions; and their fallacies. And surely you will easily believe that we that have so many things truly natural which induce admiration, could in a world of particulars deceive the senses, if we would disguise those things and labour to make them seem more miraculous. But we do hate all impostures, and lies; insomuch as we have severely forbidden it to all our fellows, under pain of ignominy and fines, that they do not show any natural work or thing, adorned or swelling; but only pure as it is, and without all affectation of strangeness.

These are (my son) the riches of Salomon's[5] House.

⌘

4. Salads.   5. Solomon.

William Baldwin
d.1563?

William Baldwin is not as well known as he might be or might have been had the course of English history run in a slightly different direction. Baldwin was the principal editor behind one of the most successful literary projects of the sixteenth century, *A Mirror for Magistrates*, published around 1554, but suppressed and then re-published in 1559. Baldwin published other works, including a treatise of moral philosophy and was one of the key literary figures at the court of Edward VI. Sadly, with Edward's premature death in 1553 and the accession of the Protestant Edward's Catholic half-sister, Mary, Baldwin appears to have lapsed into relative obscurity and ended his days as a minor cleric.

Baldwin's prose fiction, the *Marvelous History Entitled Beware the Cat, Concerning Diverse Wonderful and Incredible Matters*, was written in 1552 but not published until 1570. The work is notable as the first sustained piece of prose fiction in English, but it is much more than simply a fact of literary history. The work contains a series of "orations" by the narrator, Streamer, who has discovered how he can understand the speech of cats and so infiltrate their dark and subversive world. Baldwin's brilliant text works as a satire of human folly and stupidity. But it is also a disturbing analysis of the fine lines between obedience and subversion, a pressing issue for all Englishmen and women in times of religious change and conflicting loyalties. The cats are, on one level, Catholics, but they cannot be classified simply in terms of their religious affiliation, which is one of the key points of the book. People are far too complex to be labeled in this way, as many recent histories of the religious identities of the period have demonstrated. Like the cats in Baldwin's fiction, they have their own idiosyncrasies, belong to communities, exist in a different world if they are excluded from the one that everyone else inhabits. Baldwin is not suggesting that cats are rational and have their own world, but he is enough of a philosopher to force his readers to think about the boundaries they draw up between the human and the nonhuman as well as different groups of people. The cats certainly have some more sensible practices and customs than their human counterparts, including many of their laws.

Beware the Cat
T.K. to the Reader

> This little book, *Beware the Cat*,
>   most pleasantly compiled,
> In time obscured was, and so
>   since that hath been exiled.

5   Exiled because, perchance at first,
>   it showed the toys[1] and drifts
> Of such as then, by wiles and wills,
>   maintained Popish shifts.

> Shifts[2] such as those, in such a time,
10   delighted for to use,
> Whereby full many simple souls
>   they did full sore abuse.

---

1. Whims.   2. Devices, plans.

Abuse? Yea sure, and that with spight,
    whenas the Cat gan tell
15   Of many pranks of Popish priests
    both foolish, mad, and fell.[3]

Fell? Sure, and vain, if judgment right
    appear to be in place,
And so as fell in pleasant wise
20   this fiction shows their grace.

Grace? Nay sure, ungraciousness
    of such and many mo,
Which may be told in these our days
    to make us laugh also.

25   Also to laugh? Nay, rather weep
    to see such shifts now used,
And that in every sort of men
    true virtue is abused.

Abused? Yea, and quite down cast,
30   let us be sure of that;
And therefore now, as hath been said,
    I say, "Beware the Cat."

The Cat full pleasantly will show
    some sleights that now are wrought,
35   And make some laugh which unto mirth
    to be constrained are loath.

Loath? Yea, for over-passing grief
    that much bereaves their mind,
For such disorder as in states
40   of every sort they find.

Find? Yea, who can now boast but that
    the Cat will him disclose?
Therefore, in midst of mirth I say,
    "Beware the Cat" to those.
                Vale.

THE EPISTLE DEDICATORY

Love and Live.
To the Right Worshipful Esquire
Master John Young,[4]
Grace and Health.

I have penned for your mastership's pleasure one of the stories which Master
Streamer told the last Christmas, and which you so fain would have heard reported
by Master Ferrers[5] himself. And although I be unable to pen or speak it so pleasantly

3. Fierce, savage.
4. Probably the courtier, John Young.
5. George Ferrers (c. 1510–1579), a soldier, courtier and
writer, who worked with Baldwin in writing *A Mirror for*

Magistrates. This might suggest that Master Streamer is
also a real person, although it is more likely that Baldwin
has mixed up factual and fictional characters in the fiction. Master Willot is also probably an invention.

as he could, yet have I so nearly used both the order and words of him that spake them (which is not the least virtue of a reporter) that I doubt not but that he and Master Willot shall in the reading think they hear Master Streamer speak, and he himself in the like action shall doubt whether he speaketh or readeth. I have divided his oration into three parts, and set the argument before them and an instruction after them, with such notes as might be gathered thereof, so making it book-like, and entitled *Beware the Cat*.

But because I doubt whether Master Streamer will be contented that other men plow with his oxen (I mean pen such things as he speaketh, which perhaps he would rather do himself to have, as he deserveth, the glory of both), therefore I beseech you to learn his mind herein, and if he agree it pass in such sort, yet that he peruse it before the printing and amend it if in any point I have mistaken him. I pray you likewise to ask Master Ferrers his judgement herein, and show him that the *Cure of the Great Plague*,[6] of Master Streamer's translation out of the Arabic which he sent me from Margate,[7] shall be imprinted as soon as I may conveniently.

And if I shall perceive by your trial that Master Streamer allow my endeavors in this kind, I will hereafter, as Plato did by Socrates,[8] pen out such things of the rest of our Christmas communications as shall be to his great glory, and no less pleasure to all them that desire such kinds of knowledge. In the meanwhile I beseech you to accept my good will, and learn to Beware the Cat. So shall you not only perform that I seek, but also please the Almighty, who always preserve you. Amen.

Yours to his power,
G[ulielmus] B[aldwin].

THE ARGUMENT

It chanced that at Christmas last I was at Court with Master Ferrers, then master of the King's Majesty's pastimes, about setting forth of certain interludes,[9] which for the King's recreation we had devised and were in learning. In which time, among many other exercises among ourselves, we used nightly at our lodging to talk of sundry things for the furtherance of such offices wherein each man as then served. For which purpose it pleased Master Ferrers to make me his bedfellow,[1] and upon a pallet cast upon the rushes in his own chamber to lodge Master Willot and Master Streamer, the one his Astronomer, the other his Divine.[2] And among many other things too long to rehearse, it happened on a night (which I think was the twenty-eight of December), after that Master Ferrers was come from the Court and in bed, there fell a controversy between Master Streamer, who with Master Willot had already slept his first sleep, and me, that was newly come unto bed, the effect whereof was whether birds and beasts had reason.

The occasion thereof was this: I had heard that the King's players were learning a play of Aesop's Crow[3] wherein the most part of the actors were birds, the device whereof I discommended, saying it was not comical to make either speechless things

---

6. Probably an invented work, like the Arabic translation.
7. A small town in Kent. Later known for its vulgarity (unlike nearby Folkestone, where the annotator grew up, which was more classy but rather boring).
8. Plato wrote down what Socrates said in his dialogues with other philosophers.
9. Short stage plays, often performed at court.

1. Men and women often shared beds owing to lack of space in cities and the cold in winter.
2. Priest.
3. No such play exists. The fable tells the story of a foolish bird who is ridiculed for wearing feathers from other birds to make himself look more attractive.

to speak or brutish[4] things to common[5] reasonably; and although in a tale it were sufferable to imagine and tell of something by them spoken or reasonably done (which kind Aesop laudably used), yet it was uncomely, said I, and without example of any author, to bring them in lively personages to speak, do, reason, and allege authorities out of authors. Master Streamer, my lord's Divine, being more divine in this point than I was ware of, held the contrary part, affirming that beasts and fowls had reason, and that as much as men, yea, and in some points more.

Master Ferrers himself and his Astronomer wakened with our talk and harkened to us, but would take part on neither side. And when Master Streamer had for proof of his assertion declared many things (of elephants that walked upon cords, hedgehogs that knew always what weather would come, foxes and dogs that after they had been all night abroad killing geese and sheep would come home in the morning and put their necks into their collars, parrots that bewailed their keepers' deaths, swallows that with celandine[6] open their young ones' eyes, and an hundred things more), which I denied to come of reason, and to be but natural kindly actions, alleging for my proof authority of most grave and learned philosophers.

"Well," quoth Master Streamer, "I know what I know, and I speak not only what by hearsay of some philosophers I know, but what I myself have proved."

"Why," quoth I then, "have you proof of beasts' and fowls' reason?"

"Yea," quoth he, "I have heard them and understand them both speak and reason as well as I hear and understand you."

At this Master Ferrers laughed. But I, remembering what I had read in Albertus' works,[7] thought there might be somewhat more than I did know; wherefore I asked him what beasts or fowls he had heard, and where and when. At this he paused awhile, and at last said: "If that I thought you could be content to hear me, and without any interruption till I have done mark what I say, I would tell you such a story of one piece of mine own experimenting as should both make you wonder and put you out of doubt concerning this matter; but this I promise you afore, if I do tell it, that as soon as any man curiously interrupteth me, I will leave off and not speak one word more." When we had promised quietly to hear, he, turning himself so in his bed as we might best hear him, said as followeth.

The First Part of Master Streamer's Oration

Being lodged (as, I thank him, I have been often) at a friend's house of mine,[8] which, more roomish within than garish without, standeth at Saint Martin's Lane end and hangeth partly upon the town wall that is called Aldersgate (either of one Aldrich, or else of Elders, *Why Aldersgate* that is to say ancient men of the city which among them builded *was so named.* it—as bishops did Bishopsgate; or else of eldern trees, which per- *Bishops builded* chance as they do in the gardens now thereabout, so while the com- *Bishopsgate.* mon there was vacant grew abundantly in the same place where the gate was after builded, and called thereof Elderngate—as Moorgate *Why Moorgate.* took the name of the field without it, which hath been a very moor; or else, because it is the most ancient gate of the City, was thereof in respect of the other, as Newgate, called the Eldergate; or else, as *Why Newgate.*

4. Of beasts.   7. Albertus Magnus, a compiler of marvels.
5. Talk together.   8. The Protestant printer, John Day, a friend of Baldwin.
6. A yellow flower that was thought to cure sight.

Ludgate taketh the name of Lud who builded it—so most part of heralds, I know, will soonest assent that Aluredus builded this; but they are deceived, for he and his wife Algay builded Aldgate, which thereof taketh the name as Cripplegate doth of a cripple, who begged so much in his life, as put to the silver weather cock which he stole from Paul's steeple, after his death builded it).[9] But whereofsoever this gate Aldersgate took the name (which longeth chiefly to historiers to know), at my friend's house, which, as I said standeth so near that it is over it, I lay oftentimes, and that for sundry causes, sometime for lack of other lodging, and sometime as while my Greek alphabets were in printing to see that it might truly be corrected. And sure it is a shame for all young men that they be no more studious in the tongues; but the world is now come to that pass, that if he can prate[1] a little Latin and handle a racquet and a pair of six-square bowls,[2] he shall sooner obtain any living than the best learned in a whole city; which is the cause that learning is so despised and baggagical[3] things so much advanced.

Why Ludgate.

Why Aldgate.
Why Cripplegate.
Paul's weather-
cock was silver.

Against young
men's negligence.

Against unlawful
games.

While I lay at the foresaid house for the causes aforesaid, I was lodged in a chamber hard by the Printing House, which had a fair bay window opening into the garden, the earth whereof is almost as high as Saint Anne's Church top, which standeth thereby. At the other end of the Printing House, as you enter in, is a side door and three or four steps which go up to the leads of the Gate, whereas sometime quarters of men,[4] which is a loathely and abhominable sight, do stand up upon poles. I call it abhominable because it is not only against nature but against Scripture; for God commanded by Moses that, after the sun went down, all such as were hanged or otherwise put to death should be buried, lest if the sun saw them the next day His wrath should come upon them and plague them, as He hath done this and many other realms for the like transgression. And I marvel where men have learned it or for what cause they do it, except it be to feed and please the devils. For sure I believe that some spirits, Misanthropi or Molochitus, who lived by the savor of man's blood, did, after their sacrifices failed (in which men were slain and offered unto them), put into butcherly heathen tyrants' heads to mangle and boil Christian transgressors and to set up their quarters for them to feed upon. And therefore I would counsel all men to bury or burn all executed bodies, and refrain from making such abhominable sacrifice as I have often seen, with ravens or rather devils feeding upon them, in this foresaid leads[5]—in the which every night many cats assembled, and there made such a noise that I could not sleep for them.

God plagueth
abhomination.

Evil spirits live
by the savor of
man's blood.

Good ghostly
counsel of
Master Streamer.

Wherefore, on a time as I was sitting by the fire with certain of the house, I told them what a noise and what a wawling the cats

---

9. Streamer's description of the names of London districts is fanciful and often wrong.
1. Speak (derogatory).
2. Dice.
3. Worthless.
4. Those executed for treason would be hanged, cut down while still alive, disembowelled, and then quartered, with heads and body parts placed on the city gates. Rebellions in 1549 and 1550 had seen various men suffer this fate in London.
5. Roofs.

had made there the night before from ten o'clock till one, so that neither I could sleep nor study for them; and by means of this introduction we fell in communication of cats. And some affirming, as I do now (but I was against it then), that they had understanding, for confirmation whereof one of the servants told this story.

A wise man may in some things change his opinion.

"There was in my country," quod he, "a man" (the fellow was born in Staffordshire) "that had a young cat which he had brought up of a kitling,[6] and would nightly dally and play with it; and on a time as he rode through Kankwood[7] about certain business, a cat, as he thought, leaped out of a bush before him and called him twice or thrice by his name. But because he made none answer nor spake (for he was so afraid that he could not), she spake to him plainly twice or thrice these words following: 'Commend me unto Titton Tatton and to Puss thy Catton, and tell her that Grimalkin is dead.' This done she went her way, and the man went forward about his business. And after that he was returned home, in an evening sitting by the fire with his wife and his household, he told of his adventure in the wood. And when he had told them all the cat's message, his cat, which had harkened unto the tale, looked upon him sadly, and at the last said, 'And is Grimalkin dead? Then farewell dame,' and therewith went her way and was never seen after."

A cat spake to a man in Kankwood.

A wonderful wit of a cat.

When this tale was done, another of the company, which had been in Ireland, asked this fellow when this thing which he had told happened. He answered that he could not tell well, howbeit, as he conjectured, not passing forty years, for his mother knew both the man and the woman which ought[8] the cat that the message was sent unto. "Sure," quod the other, "then it may well be; for about that same time, as I heard, a like thing happened in Ireland where, if I conjecture not amiss, Grimalkin of whom you spake was slain."

Grimalkin was slain in Ireland.

"Yea sir," quod I, "I pray you how so?"

"I will tell you, Master Streamer," quod he, "that which was told me in Ireland, and which I have till now so little credited, that I was ashamed to report it. But hearing that I hear now, and calling to mind my own experience when it was, I do so little misdoubt it that I think I never told, nor you ever heard, a more likely tale. While I was in Ireland, in the time that Mac Murrough and all the rest of the wild lords were the King's enemies, what time also mortal war was between the Fitz Harrises and the Prior and Convent of the Abbey of Tintern, who counted them the King's friends and subjects, whose neighbor was Cahir Mac Art, a wild Irishman then the King's enemy and one which daily made inroads into the county of Wexford and burned such towns and carried away all such cattle as he might come by, by means whereof all the country from Clonmines to Ross became a waste wilderness and is scarce recovered until this day. In this time, I say, as I was on a night at coshery[9]

Experience is an infallible persuader.

Civil war between the King's subjects.

The fashion of the Irish wars.

---

6. Kitten.
7. Cannock Wood, a royal forest in Staffordshire.

8. Owned.
9. A feast.

with one of Fitz Harris' churls, we fell in talk (as we have done now) of strange adventures, and of cats. And there, among other things, the churl (for so they call all farmers and husbandmen) told me as you shall hear.

"There was, not seven years past, a kern[1] of John Butler's dwelling in the fassock[2] of Bantry called Patrick Apore, who minding to make a prey in the night upon Cahir Mac Art, his master's enemy, got him with his boy (for so they call their horse-keepers be they never so old knaves) into his country, and in the night time entered into a town of two houses, and brake in and slew the people, and then took such cattle as they found, which was a cow and a sheep, and departed therewith homeward. But doubting they should be pursued (the cur dogs made such a shrill barking), he got him into a church, thinking to lurk there till midnight was past, for there he was sure that no man would suspect or seek him—for the wild Irishmen have had churches in such reverence (till our men taught them the contrary) that they neither would, nor durst, either rob ought thence or hurt any man that took the churchyard for sanctuary, no, though he had killed his father.

"And while this kern was in the church he thought it best to dine, for he had eaten little that day. Wherefore he made his boy go gather sticks, and strake fire with his feres,[3] and made a fire in the church, and killed the sheep, and after the Irish fashion laid it thereupon and roasted it. But when it was ready, and that he thought to eat it, there came in a cat and set her by him, and said in Irish, 'Shane foel,' which is, 'give me some meat.' He, amazed at this, gave her the quarter that was in his hand, which immediately she did eat up, and asked more till she had consumed all the sheep; and, like a cormorant not satisfied therewith, asked still for more. Wherefore they supposed it were the Devil, and therefore thinking it wisdom to please him, killed the cow which they had stolen, and when they had flayed it gave the cat a quarter, which she immediately devoured. Then they gave her two other quarters; and in the meanwhile, after their country fashion, they did cut a piece of the hide and pricked it upon four stakes which they set about the fire, and therein they sod[4] a piece of the cow for themselves, and with the rest of the hide they made each of them laps[5] to wear about their feet like brogues, both to keep their feet from hurt all the next day, and also to serve for meat the next night, if they could get none other, by broiling them upon coals.

"By this time the cat had eaten three quarters and called for more. Wherefore they gave her that which was a-seething; and doubting lest, when she had eaten that, she would eat them too because they had no more for her, they got them out of the church and the kern took his horse and away he rode as fast as he could hie.

A churl's tale.

This was an Irish town.

Irish curs bark sore.

The wild Irishmen were better than we in reverencing their religion.

The old Irish diet was to dine at night.

A malapert guest that cometh unbidden.

A cat eat a sheep.

The woodkern's cookery.

Kerns for lack of meat eat their shoes roasted.

---

1. Soldier.
2. Wilderness.
3. Means for firelighting.
4. Boiled.
5. Wrappings, i.e., shoes.

When he was a mile or two from the church the moon began to shine, and his boy espied the cat upon his master's horse behind him and told him. Whereupon the kern took his dart, and turning his face toward her, flang it and struck her through with it. But immediately there came to her such a sight of cats that, after long fight with them, his boy was killed and eaten up, and he himself, as good and as swift as his horse was, had much to do to scape.

A kern killed Grimalkin. Cats did kill and eat a man.

"When he was come home and had put off his harness (which was a corslet of mail made like a shirt, and his skull covered over with gilt leather and crested with otter skin), all weary and hungry he set him down by his wife and told her his adventure, which, when a kitling which his wife kept, scarce half a year old, had heard, up she started and said, 'Hast thou killed Grimalkin!' And therewith she plunged in his face, and with her teeth took him by the throat, and ere that she could be plucked away, she had strangled him. This the churl told me now about thirty-three winters past; and it was done, as he and divers other creditable men informed me, not seven years before. Whereupon I gather that this Grimalkin was it which the cat in Kankwood sent news of unto the cat which we heard of even now."

The kern's armor.

A kitling killeth the kern that slew Grimalkin. A very strange conjecture.

"Tush," quod another that sat by, "your conjecture is too unreasonable; for to admit that cats have reason and that they do in their own language understand one another, yet how should a cat in Kankwood know what is done in Ireland?"

"How?" quod he, "even as we know what is done in the realms of France, Flanders, and Spain, yea, and almost in all the world beside. There be few ships but have cats belonging unto them, which bring news unto their fellows out of all quarters."

Each realm knoweth what is done in all other. Cats carry news.

"Yea," quod the other, "but why should all cats love to hear of Grimalkin, or how should Grimalkin eat so much meat as you speak of, or why should all cats so labor to revenge her death?"

"Nay, that passeth my cunning," quod he, "to show in all; howbeit in part conjectures may be made, as thus. It may be that Grimalkin and her line is as much esteemed and hath the same dignity among cats, as either the humble or master bee hath among the whole hive, at whose commandment all bees are obedient, whose succor and safeguard they seek, whose wrongs they all revenge; or as the Pope hath had ere this over all Christendom, in whose cause all his clergy would not only scratch and bite, but kill and burn to powder (though they knew not why) whomsoever they thought to think but once against him—which Pope, all things considered, devoureth more at every meal than Grimalkin did at her last supper."

Bees love and obey their governor.

The Pope's clergy are crueller than cats. The Pope a great waster.

"Nay," said I then, "although the Pope, by exactions and other baggagical trumpery, have spoiled all people of mighty spoils, yet (as touching his own person) he eateth and weareth as little as any other man, though peradventure more sumptuous and costly, and in greater abundance provided. And I heard a very proper saying in this behalf of King Henry VII: When a servant of his told him what abundance of meat he had seen at an abbot's table, he reported him

A little sufficeth him that hath enough.

to be a great glutton; he asked if the abbot eat up all, and when he answered no, but his guests did eat the most part, 'Ah,' quod the king, 'thou callest him glutton for his liberality to feed thee and such other unthankful churls.' Like to this fellow are all ruffians, for let honest, worshipful men of the city make them good cheer or lend them money as they commonly do, and what have they for their labor? Either foul, reproachful names (as 'dunghill churls,' 'cuckold knaves'), or else spiteful and slanderous reports, as to be usurers and decayers of the common weal. And although that some of them be such indeed, yet I abhor to hear other of whom they deserve well, so lewdly to report them. But now, to return to your communication, I marvel how Grimalkin (as you term her), if she were no bigger, could eat so much meat at once."

Such jests a man may have enough.
The wisdom of King Henry the Seventh.

The unthankful are to be abhorred.

"I do not think," quod he that told the tale, "that she did eat all (although she asked all), but took her choice and laid the rest by, as we see in the feeding of many things. For a wolf, although a cony[6] be more than he can eat, yet will he kill a cow or twain for his breakfast—likewise all other ravenous beasts. Now, that love and fellowship and a desire to save their kind is among cats, I know by experience. For there was one that hired a friend of mine, in pastime, to roast a cat alive,[7] and promised him for his labor twenty shillings. My friend, to be sure, caused a cooper to fasten him into a hogshead, in which he turned a spit, whereupon was a quick[8] cat. But ere he had turned a while, whether it was the smell of the cat's wool that singed, or else her cry that called them, I cannot tell, but there came such a sort of cats that if I and other hardy men (which were well scrat for our labor) had not behaved us the better, the hogshead, as fast as it was hooped, could not have kept my cousin from them."

Ravenours spoil more than they occupy.
Like loveth the like.
A quick cat roasted.

Cat will to kind.

"Indeed," quod a well-learned man and one of excellent judgment that was then in the company, "it doth appear that there is in cats, as in all other kinds of beasts, a certain reason and language whereby they understand one another. But, as touching this, Grimalkin I take rather to be an hagat[9] or a witch than a cat. For witches have gone often in that likeness—and thereof hath come the proverb, as true as common, that a cat hath nine lives (that is to say, a witch may take on her a cat's body nine times)."

Some think this was Master Sherry.

Witches may take upon them the likeness of other things.

"By my faith, sir, this is strange," quod I myself, "that a witch should take on her a cat's body. I have read that the Pythonesses could cause their spirits to take upon them dead men's bodies, and the airy spirits which we call demons (of which kind are incubus and succubus, Robin Goodfellow the fairy, and goblins, which the miners call telchines) could at their pleasure take upon them any other sorts. But that a woman, being so large a body, should strain her into the body of a cat (or into that form either), I have not much heard of, nor can well perceive how it may be, which maketh me (I promise you) believe it the less."

Airy spirits take on them dead men's bodies.

6. Rabbit.
7. A common pastime, especially in France.
8. Live.
9. Witch.

"Well, Master Streamer," quod he, "I know you are not so ignorant herein as you make yourself; but this is your accustomed fashion, always to make men believe that you be not so well learned as you be. *Sapiens enim celat scientism*,[1] which appeared well by Socrates. For I know, being skilled as you be in the tongues (chiefly the Calde, Arabic, and Egyptian) and having read so many authors therein, you must needs be skillful in these matters; but where you spake of instrusion of a woman's body into a cat's, you either play Nichodem[2] or the stubborn Popish conjurer: whereof one would creep into his mother's belly again, the other would bring Christ out of Heaven to thrust him into a piece of bread (but as the one of them is gross and the other perverse, so in this point I must place you with one of them). For although witches may take upon them cats' bodies, or alter the shape of their or other bodies, yet this is not done by putting their own bodies thereinto, but either by bringing their souls for the time out of their bodies and putting them in the other, or by deluding the sight and fantasies of the seers. As when I make a candle with the brain of a horse and brimstone, the light of the candle maketh all kinds of heads appear horseheads, but yet it altereth the form of no head, but deceiveth the right conception of the eye (which, through the false light, receiveth a like form)."

Then quod he that had been in Ireland, "I cannot tell, sir, by what means witches do change their own likeness and the shapes of other things, but I have heard of so many and seen so much myself, that I am sure they do it. For in Ireland, as they have been ere this in England, witches are for fear had in high reverence. They be so cunning that they can change the shapes of things as they list at their pleasure and so deceive the people thereby that an act was made in Ireland that no man should buy any red swine. The cause whereof was this: The witches used to send to the markets many red swine, fair and fat to see unto as any might be, and would in that form continue long; but if it chanced the buyers of them to bring them to any water, immediately they found them returned either into wisps of hay, straw, old rotten boards, or such like trumpery, by means whereof they lost their money or such other cattle as they gave in exchange for them.

"There is also, in Ireland, one nation whereof some one man and woman are at every seven years' end turned into wolves, and so continue in the woods the space of seven years. And if they hap to live out the time, they return to their own form again, and other twain are turned for the like time into the same shape—which is a penance (as they say) enjoined that stock by Saint Patrick for some wickedness of their ancestors. And that this is true witnessed a man whom I left alive in Ireland who had performed this seven years' penance, whose wife was slain while she was a wolf in her last year. This man told to many men, whose cattle he had worried and whose bodies he had assailed while he was a wolf, so plain and

Wise men dissemble their cunning.

Master Streamer is well seen in tongues.

Transubstantiationers destroy Christ's manhood.

How witches transform their shape.

One kind of magic consisteth in deceiving the senses.

Witches are reverenced for fear.

An act forbidding to buy red swine.

Sorcerers make swine of hay and other baggage.

Men turned into wolves.

Saint Patrick's plague.

A man proved himself to have been a wolf seven years.

---

1. The wise hide their knowledge.   2. Nicodemus.

evident tokens and showed such scars of wounds which other men had given him, both in his man's shape before he was a wolf and in his wolf's shape since, which all appeared upon his skin, that it was evident to all men (yea, and to the bishop, too, upon whose grant it was recorded and registered) that the matter was undoubtedly past all peradventure.

A Bishop confir-
meth Saint
Partick's plague.

"And I am sure you are not ignorant of the hermit whom, as St. Augustine writeth, a witch would in an ass's form ride upon to market. But now how these witches made their swine, and how these folk were turned from shape to shape, whether by some oint- ment whose clearness deceived men's sights till either the water washed away the ointment, or else that the clearness of the water excelled the clearness of the ointment (and so betrayed the opera- tion of it), I am as uncertain as I am sure that it were the spirits called demons, forced by enchantments, which moved those bodies till shame of their shape discovered caused them to leave them. But as for the transformation of the wolves, [it] is either miraculous as Naaman's leprosy in the stock of Gehesie, or else [due] to shameful, crafty, malicious sorcery. And as the one way is unsearchable, so I think there might means be found to guess how it is done the other way. For witches are by nature exceeding malicious, and if it chance that some witch, for displeasure taken with this wolvish nation, gave her daughter charge in her death bed when she taught her the science (for till that time witches never teach it, nor then but to their eldest and best-beloved daughter) that she should, at every seven years' end, confect some ointment which seven years' space might be in force against all other clearness to represent unto men's eyes the shape of a wolf; and in the night season to go herself in likeness either of the mare or some other night form and anoint therewith the bodies of some couple of that kindred which she hated; and that after her time she should charge her daughter to ob- serve the same, and to charge her daughter after her to do the like forever, so that this charge is given always by tradition with the sci- ence, and so is continued and observed by this witch's offspring, by whom two of this kindred (as it may be supposed) are every seven years' space turned into wolves."

How sorcerers
may make swine.

Demons are the
souls of counter-
feit bodies.

Witches are by
nature malicious.

When and to
whom witches
teach their
science.
How men are
changed into
wolves.

Witchcraft is kin
to unwritten
verities, for both
go by traditions.

When I had heard these tales and the reason of the doing showed by the teller, "Ah, Thomas," quod I (for that was his name; he died afterwards of a disease which he took in Newgate, where he lay long for suspicion of magic because he had desired a prisoner to promise him his soul after he was hanged), "I perceive now the old proverb is true: 'The still sow eateth up all the draff.' You go and be- have yourself so simply that a man would think you were but a fool, but you have uttered such proof of natural knowledge in this your brief talk, as I think (except myself and few more the best-learned alive) none could have done the like."

Many shrewd
diseases do breed
in Newgate.
The best learned
are not the
greatest boasters.

"You say your pleasure, Master Streamer," quod he. "As for me, I have said nothing but that I have seen, and whereof any man might conjecture as I do."

That a man
seeth, he may
boldly say.

"You have spoken full well," quod he that gave occasion of this tale, "and your conjectures are right reasonable. For like as by ointments (as you suppose) the Irish witches do make the form of swine and wolves appear to all men's sight, so think I that by the like power English witches and Irish witches may and do turn themselves into cats. For I heard it told while I was in the university, by a credible clerk of Oxford, how that in the days when he was a child an old woman was brought before the official and accused for a witch, which (in the likeness of a cat) would go into her neighbors' houses and steal thence what she listed. Which complaint was proved true by a place of the woman's skin, which her accusers (with a firebrand that they hurled at her) had singed while she went a-thieving in her cat's likeness. So that, to conclude as I began, I think that the cat which you call Grimalkin, whose name carrieth in it matter to confirm my conjecture (for Malkin is a woman's name, as witnesseth the proverb 'there be more maids than Malkin'), I think, I say, that it was a witch in a cat's likeness; and that for the wit and craft of her, other natural cats that were not so wise have had her and her race in reverence among them, thinking her to be but a mere cat as they themselves were—like as we silly fools long time, for his sly and crafty juggling, reverenced the Pope, thinking him to have been but a man (though much holier than we ourselves were), whereas indeed he was a very incarnated devil, like as this Grimalkin was an incarnate witch."

A woman was found in a cat's likeness and punished. Witches never use their art but to evil.

It is to be thought that Grimalkin was a witch.

Cats may be deceived as well as Christian folk.

"Why then, sir," said I, "do you think that natural cats have wit and that they understand one another?" "What else, Master Streamer?" quod he. "There is no kind of sensible creatures but have reason and understanding; whereby, in their kind, each understandeth other and do therein in some points so excel that the consideration thereof moved Pythagoras (as you know) to believe and affirm that after death men's souls went into beasts and beasts' souls into men, and every one according to his desert in his former body. And although his opinion be fond and false, yet that which drew him thereto is evident and true—and that is the wit and reason of diverse beasts, and again the dull, beastly, brutish ignorance of diverse men.

All sensible creatures have reason and understanding.

Pythagoras' opinion concerning souls.

Some beasts are wiser than men.

"But that beasts understand one another, and fowls likewise, beside that we see by daily experience in marking them, the story of the Bishop of Alexandria by record doth prove. For he found the means, either through diligence so to mark them, or else through magic natural so to subtiliate his sensible powers, either by purging his brain by dry drinks and fumes, or else to augment the brains of his power perceptible by other natural medicines, that he understood all kind of creatures by their voices. For being on a time sitting at dinner in a house among his friends, he harkened diligently to a sparrow that came fleeing and chirping to other that were about the house, and smiled to himself to hear her. And when one of the company desired to know why he smiled, he said 'At the sparrow's tale. For she telleth them,' quod he, 'that in the highway, not a quarter of

A Bishop understood all kind of creatures' voices. The brain is the organ of understanding.

A sparrow called her fellows to a banquet.

a mile hence, a sack of wheat is even now fallen off a horseback and broken, and all the wheat run out, and therefore biddeth them come thither to dinner.' And when the guests, musing hereat, sent to prove the truth, they found it even so as he had told them."

When this tale was ended, the clock struck nine; whereupon old Thomas, because he had far to his lodging, took his leave and departed. The rest of the company got them also either to their business or to their beds. And I went straight to my chamber (before remembered) and took a book in my hand to have studied, but the remembrance of this former talk so troubled me that I could think of nothing else, but mused still and, as it were, examined more narrowly what every man had spoken.

Master Streamer is always given much to study.

The Second Part of Master Streamer's Oration

Ere I had been long in this contemplation, the cats, whose crying the night before had been occasion of all that which I have told you, were assembled again in the leads which I spake of, where the dead men's quarters were set up; and after the same sort as they did the night before, one sang in one tune, another in another, even such another service as my Lord's chapel upon the scaffold[3] sang before the King. They observed no musical chords, neither diatesseron, diapente, nor diapason;[4] and yet I ween I lie, for one cat, groaning as a bear[5] doth when dogs be let slip to him, trolled out so low and so loud a bass that, in comparison of another cat which, crying like a young child, squealed out the shrieking treble, it might be well counted a double diapason. Wherefore, to the intent I might perceive the better the cause of their assembly, and by their gestures perceive part of their meaning, I went softly and fair into a chamber which hath a window into the same leads, and in the dark standing closely,[6] I viewed through the trellis, as well as I could, all their gestures and behavior.

Cats assembled in the leads.

Cats have sundry voices.

The diligence of the author to understand all things.

And I promise you it was a thing worth the marking to see what countenances, what becks,[7] yea and what order was among them. For one cat, which was a mighty big one, grey-haired, bristle-bearded, and having broad eyes which shone and sparkled like two stars, sat in the midst, and on either side of her sat another. And before her stood three more, whereof one mewed continually, save when the great cat groaned. And ever when the great cat had done, this mewing cat began again, first stretching out her neck and, as it were, making 'beisance to them which sat. And oftentimes, in the midst of this cat's mewing, all the rest would suddenly each one in his tune bray forth and incontinently[8] hush again, as it were laughing at somewhat which they heard the other cat declare. And after this sort I beheld them from ten till it was twelve o'clock, at which

Cats keep order among themselves.

Cats make courtesy with their necks and tails.

---

3. Stage.
4. Musical terms.
5. I.e., bear-baiting.

6. Secretly.
7. Gestures.
8. Immediately.

time, whether it were some vessel in the kitchen under or some board in the printing house hard by I cannot tell, but somewhat fell with such a noise that all the cats got them up upon the house; and I, fearing lest any arose to see what was fallen they would charge me with the hurling down of it if they found me there, I whipped into my chamber quickly and, finding my lamp still burning, I set me down upon my bed and devised upon the doings of these cats, casting all manner of ways what might be conjectured thereof to know what they meant.

Note here the painfulness of the author.

The good house-wife's candle never goeth out.

And by and by I deemed that the grey cat which sat in the midst was the chief and sat as judge among the rest, and that the cat which continually mewed declared some matter or made account to her of somewhat. By means whereof I was straight caught with such a desire to know what she had said that I could not sleep of all that night, but lay devising by what means I might learn to understand them. And calling to mind that I had read in Albertus Magnus' works a way how to be able to understand birds' voices, I made no more to do, but sought in my library for the little book entitled *De Virtutibus Animalium*,[9] etc., and greedily read it over. And when I came to "Si vis voces avium intelligere, etc.," Lord how glad I was. And when I had thoroughly marked the description of the medicine, and considered with myself the nature and power of everything therein and how and upon what it wrought, I devised thereby how, with part of those things and additions of other of like virtue and operation, to make a philter for to serve my purpose.

Earnest desire banisheth sleep.

Albertus Magnus teacheth many wonders.

A philosopher searcheth the nature of all things.

And as soon as restless Phoebus was come up out of the smoking sea and, with shaking his golden-colored beams which were all the night long in Thetis' moist bosom, had dropped off his silver sweat into Hera's dry lap, and kissing fair Aurora with glowing mouth had driven from her the advouterer[1] Lucifer, and was mounted so high to look upon Europa that, for all the height of Mile-End steeple, he spied me through the glass window lying upon my bed, up I arose and got me abroad to seek for such things as might serve for the earnest business which I went about.

A description of the resurrection of the sun.

And because you be all my friends that are here I will hide nothing from you, but declare from point to point how I behaved myself both in making and taking my philter. "If thou wilt understand," saith Albert, "the voices of birds or of beasts, take two in thy company, and upon Simon and Jude's day early in the morning, get thee with hounds into a certain wood, and the first beast that thou meetest take, and prepare with the heart of a fox, and thou shalt have thy purpose; and whosoever thou kissest shall understand them as well as thyself."

Nothing may be hid from friends.

How to under-stand birds.

Because his writing here is doubtful, because he saith "quoddam nemus," a certain wood, and because I knew three men not many years past which, while they went about this hunting were so 'fraid, whether with an evil spirit or with their own imagination

Men and dogs 'fraid out of their wits in proving an experiment.

---

9. *Of The Virtues of Animals* . . . 'if you want to understand the voices of the birds'.

1. Adulterer.

I cannot tell, but home they came with their hair standing on end, and some of them have been the worse ever since, and their hounds likewise; and seeing it was so long to St. Jude's Day, therefore I determined not to hunt at all. But conjecturing that the beast which they should take was an hedgehog (which at that time of the year goeth most abroad), and knowing by reason that the flesh thereof was by nature full of natural heat—and therefore, the principal parts being eaten, must needs expulse gross matters and subtile the brain (as by the like power it engendreth fine blood and helpeth much both against the gout and the cramp)—I got me forth towards St. John's Wood, whereas not two days before I had seen one. And see the lucky and unlucky chance! By the way as I went I met with hunters who had that morning killed a fox and three hares, who (I thank them) gave me an hare and the fox's whole body (except the case[2]) and six smart lashes with a slip,[3] because (wherein I did mean no harm) I asked them if they had seen anywhere an hedgehog that morning.

An hedgehog is one of the planetical beasts, and therefore good in magic.

Medicine for the gout.

The liberality of hunters.

And here, save that my tale is otherwise long, I would show you my mind of these wicked, superstitious observations of foolish hunters, for they be like (as me seemeth) to the papists, which for speaking of good and true words punish good and honest men. Are not apes, owls, cuckoos, bears, and urchins God's good creatures? Why, then, is it not lawful to name them? If they say it bringeth ill luck in the game, then are they unlucky, idolatrical, miscreant infidels and have no true belief in God's providence. I beshrew their superstitious hearts, for my buttocks did bear the burden of their misbelief.

Superstitious hunters are kin to the papists.

All creatures are good.

To observe times, days, or words argueth infidelity.

And yet I thank them again for the fox and the hare which they gave me; for with the two hounds at my girdle I went a-hunting, till indeed under an hedge in a hole of the earth by the root of an hollow tree I found an hedgehog with a bushel of crabs[4] about him, whom I killed straight with my knife, saying "Shavol swashmeth, gorgona Iiscud," and with the other beasts, hung him at my girdle, and came homeward as fast as I could hie. But when I came in the close besides Islington, commonly called St. John's Field, a kite, belike very hungry, spied at my back the skinless fox, and thinking to have a morsel strake at it, and that so eagerly that one of his claws was entered so deep that, before he could loose it, I drew out my knife and killed him, saying "Javol sheleg h?ototheca Iiscud," and to make up the mess brought him home with the rest.

He that seeketh findeth.

Albertus saith if a man when he prepareth any medicine tell aloud why he maketh it, it will be of more force.

And ere I had laid them out of my hand, came Thomas (whom you heard of before) and brought me a cat, which for doing evil turns they had that morning caught in a snare set for her two days before, which for the skin's sake being flain, was so exceeding fat that, after I had taken some of the grease, the inwards, and the head, to make (as I made him believe) a medicine for the gout, they parboiled the rest,

One good hap followeth another.

Cat's grease is good for the gout.

2. The hide.
3. Whip.

4. Crab apples.

and at night, roasted and farced[5] with good herbs, did eat it up every morsel, and was as good meat as was or could be eaten.

A cat was roasted and eaten.

But now mark! For when Thomas was departed with his cat, I shut my chamber door to me and flayed mine urchin,[6] wishing oft for Doctor Nicholas, or some other expert physician, to make the dissection for the better knowledge of the anatomy. The flesh I washed clean and put it in a pot, and with white wine, Mellisophillos or Melissa (commonly called balm), rosemary, neat's tongue,[7] four parts of the first and two of the second, I made a broth and set it on a fire and boiled it, setting on a limbec,[8] with a glass at the end over the mouth of the pot to receive the water that distilled from it, in the seething whereof I had a pint of a pottle of wine which I put in the pot. Then, because it was about the *solstitium estivale*,[9] and that in confections the hours of the planets must for the better operation be observed, I tarried till ten o'clock before dinner, what time Mercury began his lucky reign.

A solitary man is either a god or a beast.

Par prior numerus, impar posterior est. gib.

Omne opus fiat in sua planeta. Zoroast. Omne totum totaliter malum. Trismeg.

And then I took a piece of the cat's liver and a piece of the kidney, a piece of the milt[1] and the whole heart, the fox's heart and the lights,[2] the hare's brain, the kite's maw,[3] and the urchin's kidneys. All these I beat in a mortar together until it were small, and then made a cake of it, and baked it upon a hot stone till it was dry like bread. And while this was a-baking I took seven parts of the cat's grease, as much of her brain, with five hairs of her beard (three black and two grey), three parts of the fox's grease, as much of the brain, with the hoofs of his left feet, the like portion of the urchin's grease and brain with his stones,[4] all the kite's brain, with all the marrow of her bones, the juice of her heart, her upper beak and the middle claw of her left foot, the fat of the hare's kidneys and the juice of his right shoulder bone. All these things I pounded together in a mortar by the space of an hour, and then I put it in a cloth and hung it over a basin in the sun, out of which dropped within four hours after about half a pint of oil very fair and clear.

Deus impari numero gaudet.

Dextra bona bonis sinistra vero sinistris.

Calor solis est ignis alichimistice distillationis.

Then took I the galls of all these beasts, and the kite's toe, and served them likewise, keeping the liquor that dropped from them. At twelve of the clock, what time the sun began his planetical dominion, I went to dinner. But meat I ate none, save the boiled urchin; my bread was the cake mentioned before; my drink was the distillation of the urchin's broth, which was exceeding strong and pleasant both in taste and savor.

Master Streamer varieth from the astronomers in his planet hours.

After that I had dined well, my head waxed so heavy that I could not choose but sleep. And after that I waked again, which was within an hour. My mouth and my nose purged exceedingly such yellow, white, and tawny matters as I never saw before, nor thought that any such had been in man's body. When a pint of this gear was come

The intelligible diet.

---

5. Stuffed.
6. Hedgehog.
7. Cow's tongue.
8. A stand for scientific experiments.
9. Summer solstice.

1. Spleen.
2. Lungs.
3. Stomach.
4. Testicles.

forth my rheum ceased, and my head and all my body was in exceeding good temper, and a thousand things which I had not thought of in twenty years before came so freshly to my mind as if they had been then presently done, heard, or seen. Whereby I perceived that my brain (chiefly the nuke memorative)[5] was marvelously well purged. My imagination also was so fresh that by and by I could show a probable reason what, and in what sort, and upon what matter, everything which I had taken wrought, and the cause why.

There be many strange humors in many men's heads. The remembrance lieth in the noodle of the head. A good philosopher. Exercise is good after sleep.

Then, to be occupied after my sleep, I cast away the carcass of the fox and of the kite, with all the garbage both of them and of the rest, saving the tongues and the ears which were very necessary for my purpose. And thus I prepared them: I took all the ears and scalded off the hair; then stamped I them in a mortar; and when they were all a dry jelly, I put to them rue, fennel, lowache,[6] and leek blades, of each an handful, and pounded them afresh. Then divided I all the matter into two equal parts, and made two little pillows and stuffed them therewith. And when Saturn's dry hour of dominion approached, I fried these pillows in good oil olive and laid them hot to mine ears, to each ear one, and kept them thereto till nine o'clock at night, which holp exceedingly to comfort my understanding power. But, because as I perceived the cell perceptible of my brain intelligible was yet too gross, by means that the filmy pannicle[7] coming from *dura mater*[8] made too strait oppilations[9] by ingrossing the pores and conduits imaginative, I devised to help that with this gargaristical fume, whose subtle ascension is wonderful. I took the cat's, the fox's, and the kite's tongue and sod them in wine well near to jelly. Then I took them out of the wine and put them in a mortar and added to them of new cat's dung an ounce; of mustard seed, garlic, and pepper as much; and when they were with beating incorpored, I made lozenges and trochisks[1] thereof.

Hot things purge the head.

A good medicine for aching ears.

What hindreth the imaginative power.

The wholesome things are not always most toothsome.

And at six o'clock at night, what time the sun's dominion began again, I supped with the rest of the meat which I left at dinner. And when Mercury's reign approached, which was within two hours after, I drank a great draught of my stilled water, and anointed all my head over with the wine and oil before described, and with the water which came out of the galls I washed mine eyes. And because no humors should ascend into my head by evaporation of my reins[2] through the chine bone,[3] I took an ounce of Alkakengi[4] in powder, which I had for a like purpose not two days afore bought at the 'pothecaries, and therewith rubbed and chafed my back from the neck down to the middle, and heated in a frying pan my pillows afresh, and laid them to mine ears, and tied a kercher about my head, and with my lozenges and trochisks in a box, I went out among the servants, among whom was a shrewd boy, a very crack-rope,[5]

Mercury furthereth all fine and subtle practices.

The chiefest point of wisdom is to prevent inconveniences. Heat augmenteth the virtue of outward plasters.

---

5. I.e., the memory.
6. Lovage.
7. Membrane.
8. Membrane covering the brain.
9. Obstructions.

1. Lozenges.
2. Kidneys.
3. Jaw bone.
4. Winter cherry.
5. I.e., a person who is destined to be hanged.

that needs would know what was in my box. And I, to sauce him after his sauciness, called them "presciencial[6] pills," affirming that whoso might eat one of them should not only understand wonders, but also prophesy after them. Whereupon the boy was exceeding earnest in entreating me to give him one; and when at last very loathly, as it seemed, I granted his request, he took a lozenge, and put it in his mouth, and chewed it apace, by means whereof when the fume ascended he began to spattle and spit, saying, "By God's bones, it is a cat's turd." At this the company laughed apace; and so did I too, verifying it to be as he said, and that he was a prophet.

The ungracious should be ungraciously served.

Strange things are delectable.

We laugh gladly at shrewd turns.

But that he might not spew too much by imagination, I took a lozenge in my mouth and kept it under my tongue, showing thereby that it was not evil. While this pastime endured, methought I heard one cry with a loud voice, "What Isegrim,[7] what Isegrim"; and therefore I asked whose name was Isegrim, saying that one did call him. But they said that they knew none of that name, nor heard any that did call. "No," quod I (for it called still), "Hear you nobody? Who is that called so loud?"

"We hear nothing but a cat," quod they, "which meweth above in the leads."

When I saw it was so indeed, and that I understood what the cat said, glad was I as any man alive. And taking my leave of them as though I would to bed straight, I went into my chamber (for it was past nine of the clock). And because the hour of Saturnus' cold dominion approached, I put on my gown and got me privily to the place in the which I had viewed the cats the night before. And when I had settled myself where I might conveniently hear and see all things done in the leads where this cat cried still for Isegrim, I put into my two nostrils two trochisks and into my mouth two lozenges, one above my tongue the other under; and put off my left shoe, because of Jupiter's appropinquation;[8] and laid the fox tail under my foot. And to hear the better, I took off my pillows which stopped mine ears; and then listened and viewed as attentively as I could.

Good success of things maketh men joyous. Saturn is a cold, old planet.

There is great cunning in due applying of medicines.

But I warrant you the pellicle, or filmy rime, that lyeth within the bottom of mine ear hole, from whence little veins carry the sounds to the senses, was with this medicine in my pillows so purged and parched, or at least dried, that the least moving of the air, whether struck with breath of living creatures, which we call voices, or with the moving of dead (as winds, waters, trees, carts, falling of stones, etc.), which are named noises, sounded so shrill in my head by reverberation of my 'fined films, that the sound of them altogether was so disordered and monstrous that I could discern no one from other, save only the harmony of the moving of the spheres, which noise excelled all other as much both in pleasance and shrill highness of sound as the Zodiac itself surmounteth all other

The cause of hearing.

The difference between voices and noises.

The harmony of heaven excelleth all other.

6. I.e, able to predict the future.
7. A name for a wolf.

8. Approach.

creatures in altitude of place. For in comparison of the basest of this noise, which is the moving of Saturn by means of his large compass, the highest voices of birds and the straitest whistling of the wind, or any other organ pipes whose sounds I heard confused together, appeared but a low bass. And yet was those an high treble to the voice of beasts, to which as a mean the running of rivers was a tenor; and the boiling of the sea and the cataracts[9] or gulfs thereof a goodly bass; and the rushing, brising, and falling of the clouds a deep diapason.[1]

The harmony of elemental mixtures.

While I harkened to this broil, laboring to discern both voices and noises asunder, I heard such a mixture as I think was never in Chaucer's House of Fame; for there was nothing within an hundred mile of me done on any side (for from so far, but no farther, the air may come because of obliquation[2]) but I heard it as well as if I had been by it, and could discern all voices, but by means of noises understand none. Lord what ado women made in their beds—some scolding; some laughing; some weeping; some singing to their sucking children, which made a woeful noise with their continual crying. And one shrewd wife a great way off (I think at St. Albans) called her husband "cuckold" so loud and shrilly that I heard that plain; and would fain have heard the rest, but could not by no means for barking of dogs, grunting of hogs, wawling of cats, rumbling of rats, gaggling of geese, humming of bees, rousing of bucks, gaggling of ducks, singing of swans, ringing of pans, crowing of cocks, sewing of socks, cackling of hens, scrabbling of pens, peeping of mice, trulling of dice, curling of frogs, and toads in the bogs, chirking of crickets, shutting of wickets, shriking of owls, flittering of fowls, routing of knaves, snorting of slaves, farting of churls, fizzling of girls, with many things else—as ringing of bells, counting of coins, mounting of groins, whispering of lovers, springling of plovers, groaning and spewing, baking and brewing, scratching and rubbing, watching and shrugging—with such a sort of commixed noises as would a-deaf anybody to have heard; much more me, seeing that the pannicles of mine ears were with my medicine made so fine and stiff, and that by the temperate heat of the things therein, that like a tabor dried before the fire or else a lute string by heat shrunk nearer, they were incomparably amended in receiving and yielding the shrillness of any touching sounds.

Chaucer's House of Fame. At every hundred mile the air reflecteth by means of the roundness of the world. The cart and cucking stool groveth for such.

Here the poetical fury came upon him.

Many noises in the night which all men hear not.

Over much noise maketh one deaf.

Heat shrilleth all moist instruments.

While I was earnestly harkening, as I said, to hear the woman, minding nothing else, the greatest bell in St. Botolph's steeple, which is hard by, was tolled for some rich body that then lay in passing, the sound whereof came with such a rumble into mine ear that I thought all the devils in Hell had broken loose and were come about me, and was so afraid therewith that, when I felt the foxtail under my foot (which through fear I had forgot), I deemed it had been the Devil indeed. And therefore I cried out as loud as ever I could, "The Devil, the Devil, the Devil!" But when some of the folks, raised with my noise, had sought me in my chamber and

All sudden things astonish us.

9. Water spouts.
1. Harmony.

2. Changing course.

found me not there, they went seeking about, calling one to another, "Where is he? Where is he? I cannot find Master Streamer." Which noise and stir of them was so great in mine ears and passing man's common sound, that I thought they had been devils indeed which sought and asked for me.

Fertilitas sibi ipsi nocus.[3]

Wherefore I crept close into a corner in the chimney and hid me, saying many good prayers to save me from them. And because their noise was so terrible that I could not abide it, I thought best to stop mine ears, thinking thereby I should be the less afraid. And as I was thereabout, a crow, which belike was nodding asleep on the chimney top, fell down into the chimney over my head, whose flittering in the fall made such a noise that, when I felt his feet upon my head, I thought that the Devil had been come indeed and seized upon me. And when I cast up my hand to save me, and therewith touched him, he called me "knave" in his language, after such a sort that I swooned for fear. And by that I was come to myself again, he was flowen from me into the chamber roof, and there he sat all night.

Danger maketh men devout.

How evil haps run together.

A man may die only by imagination of harm.

Then took I my pillows to stop mine ears; for the rumble that the servants made I took for the devils, it was so great and shrill. And I had no sooner put them on, but by and by I heard it was the servants which sought for me, and that I was deceived through my clearness of hearing, for the bell which put me in all this fear (for which I never loved bells since) tolled still, and I perceived well enough what it was. And seeing that the servants would not leave calling and seeking till they found me, I went down to them and feigned that a cat had been in my chamber and 'fraid me. Whereupon they went to bed again, and I to mine old place.

We hate forever whatsoever hath harmed us.

THE THIRD PART OF MASTER STREAMER'S ORATION

By this time waning Cynthia, which the day before had filled her growing horns, was come upon our hemisphere and freshly yielded forth her brother's light, which the reverberation[4] of Thetis' trembling face, now full by means of spring, had fully cast upon her, whereof she must needs lose every day more and more, by means the neap abasing Thetis' swollen face would make her to cast beyond her those rades,[5] which before the full the spring had caused her to throw short—like as, with a crystal glass a man may, by the placing of it either high or low, so cast the sun or a candlelight upon any round glass of water that it shall make the light thereof both in waxing and waning to counterfeit the moon. For you shall understand—chiefly you, Master Willot, that are my lord's astronomer—that all our ancestors have failed in knowledge of natural causes; for it is not the moon that causeth the sea to ebb and flow, neither to neap and spring, but the neaping and springing of the sea is the cause of the moon's both waxing and waning. For the moonlight is nothing save

The description of the moon at full.

How to counterfeit the moon. Astronomers are deceived. The spring and neaping of the sea causeth the moon to wax and wane.

---

3. Fertility is harmful to itself.
4. Reflection.

5. Rays.

the shining of the sun cast into the element by opposition of the sea; as also the stars are nothing else but the sunlight reflected upon the face of rivers and cast upon the crystalline heaven, which because rivers alway keep like course, therefore are the stars alway of one bigness. As for the course of the stars, from east to west is natural by means of the sun's like moving; but in that they ascend and descend (that is, sometime come northward and sometime go southward), that is caused also by the sun's being either on this side or on the other side his line like-nightical. The like reason followeth for the poles not moving, and that is the situation of those rivers or dead seas which cast them and the roundness and egg-form of the firmament. But to let this pass, which in my *Book of Heaven and Hell* shall be plainly not only declared but both by reason and experience proved, I will come again to my matter.

> *What the moon and stars be.*
>
> *The sun's moving is cause of divers moving of the stars.*
>
> *Why the poles do not move.*
>
> *I take this book to be it that is entitled Of the Great Egg.*

When Cynthia, I say, as following her brother's steps, had looked in at my chamber window and saw me neither in my bed nor at my book, she hied her apace into the south, and at a little hole in the house roof peeped in and saw me where I was set to harken to the cats. And by this time all the cats which were there the night before were assembled with many other, only the great grey one excepted. Unto whom, as soon as he was come, all the rest did their 'beisance as they did the night before. And when he was set, thus he began in his language (which I understood as well as if he had spoken English).

> *The man is studious.*
>
> *Light searcheth all things.*
>
> *Good manners among cats.*

"Ah my dear friends and fellows, you may say I have been a lingerer this night and that I have tarried long; but you must pardon me for I could come no sooner. For when this evening I went into an ambry[6] where was much good meat to steal my supper, there came a wench not thinking I had been there and clapped the lid down, by means whereof I have had much to do to get forth. Also, in the way as I came hither over the housetops, in a gutter were thieves breaking in at the window, who 'fraid me so that I lost my way and fell down into the street and had much to do to escape the dogs. But seeing that by the grace of Hagat and Heg I am now come, although I perceive by the tail of the Great Bear and by Alhabor,[7] which are now somewhat southward, that the fifth hour of our night approacheth; yet, seeing this is the last night of my charge and that tomorrow I must again to my lord Cammoloch (at this all the cats spread along their tails and cried, 'Hagat and Heg save him'), go to now good Mouse-slayer," quod he, "and that time which my misfortune hath lost, recover again by the briefness of thy talk."

> *The strange hap of Grisard.*
>
> *Sweet meat must have sour sauce.*
>
> *Cats are afraid of thieves.*
>
> *Hagat and Heg are witches which the cats do worship.*
>
> *Cats are skilled in astronomy.*
>
> *Cammoloch is chief prince among cats.*
>
> *Gentleness becometh officers.*

"I will my lord," quod Mouse-slayer, which is the cat which as I told you stood before the great cat the night before continually mewing; who in her language, after that with her tail she had made courtesy, shrunk in her neck and said, "Whereas by virtue of your commission from my lord Cammoloch (whose life Hagat and Heg defend), who by inheritance and our free election enjoyeth the

> *Mouse-slayer telleth on her story.*

6. Storehouse.   7. Sirius, the dog star.

empire of his traitorously murdered mother the goddess Grimolochin, you his greffier[8] and chief counselor, my lord Grisard, with Isegrim and Pol-noir your assistants, upon a complaint put up in your high dais[9] by that false accuser Catch-rat, who beareth me malice because I refused his lecherously offered delights, have caused me, in purging of myself before this honorable company, to declare my whole life since the blind days of my kitlinghood. You remember, I trust, how in the two nights passed I have declared my life for four years' space, wherein you perceive how I behaved me all that time.

Grimolochin is the same that was late called Grimalkin. She purgeth herself by declaring her life.

"Wherefore, to begin where I left last, ye shall understand that my lord and lady, whose lives I declared unto you last yesternight, left the city and went to dwell in the country, and carried me with them. And being there strange I lost their house, and with Bird-hunt my mate, the gentlest in honest venery that ever I met with, went to a town where he dwelt called Stratford—either Stony, upon Tine, or upon Avon, I do not well remember which—where I dwelled half a year—and this was in the time when preachers had leave to speak against the Mass, but it was not forbidden till half a year after. In this time I saw nothing worthy to certify my lord of, save this.

Mouse-slayer was by her mistress carried into the country. Bird-hunt was Mouse-slayer's mate.

"My dame, with whom I dwelt, and her husband were both old, and therefore hard to be turned from their rooted belief which they had in the Mass, which caused divers young folk, chiefly their sons and a learned kinsman of theirs, to be the more earnest to teach and persuade them. And when they had almost brought the matter to a good point, I cannot tell how it chanced, but my dame's sight failed her, and she was so sick that she kept her bed two days. Wherefore she sent for the parish priest, her old ghostly father; and when all were voided the chamber save I and they two, she told him how sick she was and how blind, so that she could see nothing, and desired him to pray for her and give her good counsel. To whom he said thus, 'It is no marvel though you be sick and blind in body which suffer your soul willingly to be blinded. You send for me now, but why send you not for me when these new heretics teach you to leave the Catholic belief of Christ's flesh in the sacrament?' 'Why sir,' quod she, 'I did send for you once, and when you came they posed you so with Holy Writ and saints' writings that you could say nothing but call them "heretics," and that they had made the New Testament themselves.'

Old errors are hard to be removed.

A sudden disease.

Cats are admitted to all secrets.

A jolly, persuading knave.

Railing and slandering are the Papists' Scriptures.

"'Yea,' quod he, 'but did I not bid you take heed then, and told you how God would plague you?' 'Yes, good sir,' quod she, 'you did, and now to my pain I find you too true a prophet. But I beseech you forgive me and pray to God for me, and whatsoever you will teach me, that will I believe unto the death.' 'Well,' quod he, 'God refuseth no sinners that will repent, and therefore in any case believe that Christ's flesh, body, soul, and bone is as it was born of our Blessed Lady in the consecrated Host, and see that therefore you worship it, pray, and offer to it. For by it any of your friends' souls

A true coal prophet.

Ghostly counsel of a Popish confessor.

8. Clerk.   9. Raised platform.

may be brought out of Purgatory (which these new heretics say is no place at all—but when their souls fry in it, they shall tell me another tale). And that you may know that all I say is true, and that the Mass can deliver such as trust in it from all manner of sins, I will by and by say you a Mass that shall restore your sight and health.'

No such persuasion as miracles chiefly in helping one from grief.

"Then took he out of his bosom a wafer cake and called for wine. And then, shutting the door unto him, revised[2] himself in a surplice, and upon a table set before the bed he laid his porteous,[3] and thereout he said Mass. And when he came to the elevation, he lifted up the cake and said to my dame (which in two days afore saw nothing), 'Wipe thine eyes thou sinful woman and look upon thy Maker.' With that she lifted up herself and saw the cake, and had her sight and her health as well as ever she had before. When Mass was done she thanked God and him exceedingly, and he gave charge that she should tell to no young folks how she was holp, for his bishop had throughout the diocese forbidden them to say or sing any Mass, but commanded her that secretly unto old honest men and women she should at all times most devoutly rehearse it. And by reason of this miracle, many are so confirmed in that belief that, although by a common law all Masses upon penalty were since forbidden, divers have them privily and nightly said in their chambers until this day.

Veritas quaerit angulos.[1]

A young knave made an old woman's maker.

Old folk are lighter of credit than young.

Cats hear many privy night Masses.

"'Marry sir,' quod Pol-noir, 'this was either a mighty miracle or else a mischievous subtlety of a magistical minister. But sure if the priest by magical art blinded her not afore, and so by like magical sorcery cured her again, it were as good for us to hire him or other priests at our delivery to sing a Mass before our kitlings, that they might in their birth be delivered of their blindness. And sure, if I knew the priest, it should scape me hard but I would have one litter of kitlings in some chamber where he useth now to say his privy night Masses.' 'What need that?' quod Mouse-slayer, 'it would do them no good. For I myself, upon like consideration, kittened since in another mistress's chamber of mine where a priest every day said Mass; but my kitlings saw naught the better, but rather the worse.'

Sorcerers may make folk blind.

Why Masses may serve well.

Devout kitlings that heard Mass so young.

"But when I heard that the Lord with whom I went into the country would to London to dwell again, I kept the house so well for a month before that my Lady when she went carried me with her. And when I was come to London again, I went in visitation to mine old acquaintance. And when I was great with kitling, because I would not be unpurveyed of a place to kitten in, I got in favor and household with an old gentlewoman, a widow, with whom I passed out this whole year.

Flatterers are diligent when they spy a profit.

"This woman got her living by boarding young gentlemen, for whom she kept always fair wenches in store, for whose sake she had the more resort. And to tell you the truth of her trade, it was fine and crafty, and not so dangerous as deceitful. For when she had

The trade of an old gentlewoman.

1. Truth seeks corner.
2. Dressed.

3. Portas, a portable breviary (the Catholic book containing instructions for religious services each day).

soaked from young gentlemen all that they had, then would she cast them off, except they fell to cheating. Wherefore many of them in the nighttime would go abroad and bring the next morning home with them sometimes money, sometime jewels (as rings or chains), sometime apparel; and sometime they would come again cursing their ill fortune, with nothing save peradventure dry blows or wet wounds. But whatsoever they brought, my dame would take it and find the means either so to gage[4] it that she would never fetch it again, or else melt it and sell it to the goldsmiths.

Whores, gaming, and good hostesses make many gentlemen make shameful shifts.

All is fish that cometh to the net.

"And notwithstanding that she used these wicked practices, yet was she very holy and religious. And therefore, although that all images were forbidden, yet kept she one of Our Lady in her coffer. And every night, when everybody were gone to bed and none in her chamber but she and I, then would she fetch Her out, and set Her upon her cupboard, and light up two or three wax candles afore Her, and then kneel down to Her, sometime an whole hour, saying over her beads and praying Her to be good unto her and to save her and all her guests both from danger and shame, and promising that then she would honor and serve Her during all her life.

A Catholic queen.

Images cannot see to hear, except they have much light.

Our Lady is hired to play the bawd.

Old women love their cats well.

"While I was with this woman I was alway much cherished and made of, for on nights while she was a-praying, I would be playing with her beads and alway catch them as she let them fall, and would sometime put my head in the compass of them and run away with them about my neck, whereat many times she took great pleasure, yea and so did Our Lady too. For my dame would say sometimes to Her, 'Yea, Blessed Lady, I know thou hearest me by thy smiling at my cat.'

The image laughed to see the cat play with her dame's beads.

Love is loiterers' occupation.

"And never did my dame do me any hurt save once, and that I was even with her for; and that was thus. There was a gentleman, one of her boarders, much enamored in the beauty of a merchant-man's wife in the city, whom he could by no means persuade to satisfy his lust. Yea, when he made her great banquets, offered her rich apparel and all kind of jewels precious which commonly women delight in, yea and large sums of money which corrupt even the gods themselves, yet could he by no means alter her mind, so much she esteemed her good name and honesty. Wherefore, forced through desire of that which he could not but long for, and so much the more because it was most earnestly denied him, he brake his mind to my dame, and entreated her to aid him to win this young woman's favor, and promised her for her labor whatsoever she would require.

An honest wife.

Quid non mortalia pectora cogis, auri sacra fames?

"Whereupon my dame, which was taken for as honest as any in the city, found the means to desire this young woman to a dinner. And against she should come, my dame gave me a piece of pudding which she had filled full of mustard, which as soon as I had eaten wrought so in my head that it made mine eyes run all the day after; and to mend this she blew pepper in my nose to make me neese. And when the young wife was come, after that my dame had

All is not gold that glistereth.

Mustard purgeth the head and pepper maketh one neese.

4. Pawn.

showed her all the commodities of her house (for women delight much to show forth what they have), they set them down together at the table, none save only they two. And while they were in gossips'[5] talk about the behaviors of this woman and that, I came as I was accustomed and sat by my dame. And when the young woman, hearing me cough and seeing me weep continually, asked what I ailed, my dame, who had tears at her commandment, sighed and, fallen as it were into a sudden dump, brast forth a-weeping and said: 'In faith, mistress, I think I am the infortunatest woman alive, upon whom God hath at once poured forth all his plagues. For my husband, the honestest man that lived, He hath taken from me; and with him mine heir and only son, the most towardly young man that was alive; and yet, not satisfied herewith, lo here my only daughter, which (though I say it) was as fair a woman and as fortunately married as any in this city, He hath, for her honesty or cruelty I cannot tell whether, turned into this likeness, wherein she hath been above this two months, continually weeping as you see and lamenting her miserable wretchedness.'

Women are glorious.

Gossips' common chat.

Women can weep when they will.

There is no deceit to the cheat of an old bawd.

A shameful lie shamefully set forth.

"The young woman, astonished at this tale, and crediting it by means of my dame's lachrymable protestation and deep dissimulation, asked her the more earnestly how and by what chance, and for what cause as she thought, she was so altered. 'Ah,' quod my dame, 'as I said before, I cannot tell what I should think; whether excuse my daughter and accuse God, or else blame her and acquit Him. For this my daughter, being as I said fortunately married, and so beloved of her husband and loving again to him as now we both too late do and forever I think shall rue, was loved exceedingly of another young man, who made great suit and labor unto her. But she, as I think all women should, esteeming her honesty and promise made to her husband the day of their marriage, refused still his desire. But because he was importunate, she came at last and told me it. And I, thinking that I did well, charged her in any case (which full oft since I have repented) that she should not consent unto him, but to shake him off with shrewd words and threatening answers. She did so; alas, alas the while. And the young man, seeing none other boot,[6] went home and fell sick; and loving so honestly and secretly that he would make none other of his counsel, forpined and languished upon his bed the space of three days, receiving neither meat nor drink. And then, perceiving his death to approach, he wrote a letter, which I have in my purse, and sent it by his boy to my daughter. If you can read you shall see it; I cannot, but my daughter here could very well, and write too.' Herewith my dame wept apace, and took the letter out of her purse and gave it this young woman, who read it in form following.

Tears move young minds lightly.

Women are orators by nature.

All women ought above all things to esteem their honesty.

Sharp words and threatening answers will soon cool adulterers.

It is as much pity to see a woman weep as to see a goose go barefoot.

The Nameless Lover to the Nameless Beloved, in whose love, sith he may not live, he only desireth license to die.

---

5. Friends.   6. Cure.

Cursed be the woeful time wherein mutual love first mixed the mass of my miserable carcass. Cursed be the hour that ever the fatal destinies have ought for me purveyed. Yea, cursed be the unhappy hour, may I say, in which I first saw those piercing eyes which, by insensible and unquenchable power inflaming my heart to desire, are so blind of all mercy as will rather with rigor consume my life than rue my grief with one drop of pity. I sue not to you, my dear unloving love, for any kind of grace, the doubtful hope whereof despair hath long since with the pouring showers of cruel words utterly quenched. But thus much I desire, which also by right me thinketh my faithful love hath well deserved, that sith your fidelity in wedlock (which I can and must needs praise, as would to God I could not) will suffer my pined corse no longer to retain the breath through cold cares wholly consumed, yet at the least, which is also an office of friendship before the gods meritorious, come visit him, who if ought might quench love should not love, whose mouth these three days hath taken no food, whose eyes the like time have taken no rest, whose heart this three weeks was never merry, whose mind these three months was never quiet, whose bed this seven nights was never made, and who (to be brief) is in all parts so enfeebled that living he dieth and dead awhile he liveth. And when this silly ghost shall leave this cruel and miserable prison, in recompense of his love, life, and death, let those white and tender hands of yours close up those open windows through which the uncomfortable light of your beauty shone first into his heart. If you refuse this to do, I beseech the gods immortal, to whom immediately I go, that as without any kind of either love or kindness you have caused me to die, so that none other caught with your beauty do likewise perish; I beseech (I say) the just gods that either they change that honest stony heart, or else disfigure that fair merciless favor.[7] Thus, for want of force either to endite or write any more, I take my leave, desiring you either to come and see me die, or if I be dead before, to see me honestly buried. Yours unregarded alive.   G.S.

"When the young woman had read this letter, she took it again to my dame, and with much to do to withhold her swelling tears, she said, 'I am sorry for your heaviness, much more for this poor man's, but most of all for your daughter's. But what did she after she saw this letter?' 'Ah,' quod my dame, 'she esteemed it as she did his suits before. She sent him a rough answer in writing; but or ever the boy came home with it, his master was dead. Within two days after, my son-in-law (her husband) died suddenly. And within two days after, as she sat here with me lamenting his death, a voice cried aloud, "Ah, flinty heart, repent thy cruelty." And immediately (oh extreme rigor) she was changed as you now see her. Whereupon I gather that though God would have us keep our faith to our

A tender heart is easily pierced.

Women's answers are never to seek.

7. Face.

husbands, yet rather than any other should die for our sakes, we should not make any conscience to save their lives. For it fareth in this point as it doth in all other; for as all extremities are vices, so is it a vice, as appeareth plainly by the punishment of my daughter, to be too extreme in honesty, chastity, or any other kind of virtue.'

Note the craft of a bawd.

All extremities are to be forsaken.

"This, with other talk of my dame in the dinner time, so sank into the young woman's mind that the same afternoon she sent for the gentleman whom she had erst so constantly refused and promised him that, if he would appoint her an unsuspected place, she would be glad to meet him to fulfill all his lust, which he appointed to be the next day at my dame's house. Where, when they were all assembled, I, minding to acquit my dame for giving me mustard, caught a quick mouse, whereof my dame always was exceedingly afraid, and came with it under her clothes and there let it go, which immediately crope up upon her leg. But Lord, how she bestirred her then; how she cried out; and how pale she looked. And I, to amend the matter, making as though I leaped at the mouse, all to-bescrat her thighs and her belly, so that I dare say she was not whole again in two months after. And when the young woman, to whom she showed her pounced[8] thighs, said I was an unnatural daughter to deal so with my mother, 'Nay, nay,' quod she, 'I cannot blame her, for it was through my counsel that she suffered all this sorrow. And yet I dare say she did it against her will, thinking to have caught the mouse, which else I dare say would have crept into my belly.' By this means was this innocent woman, otherwise invincible, brought to consent to commit whoredom.

Evil communication confoundeth good virtues.

Cats are malicious. Women are afraid of their own shadows.

The cat payeth her dame for her mustard.

It is an unnatural child that will hurt the mother.

"Shortly after, this young woman begged me of my dame; and to her I went, and dwelled with her all that year. In which year, as all the cats in the parish can tell, I never disobeyed or transgressed our holy law in refusing the concupiscential company of any cat nor the act of generation, although sometimes it were more painful to me than pleasant, if it were offered in due and convenient time. Indeed, I confess I refused Catch-rat, and bit him and scrat him, which our law forbiddeth. For on a time this year when I was great with kitlings, which he of a proud stomach refused to help to get, although I earnestly wooed him thereto; what time he loved so much his own daughter Slick-skin that all other seemed vile in his sight, which also esteemed him as much as he did the rest—that is, never a whit. In this time (I say) when I was great with kitling, I found him in a gutter eating a bat which he had caught that evening; and as you know not only we, but also women in our case, do oft long for many things, so I then longed for a piece of the reremouse,[9] and desired him, for saving of my kitten, to give me a morsel, though it were but of the leather-like wing. But he, like an unnatural, ravenous churl, eat it all up and would give me none. And as men do nowadays to their wives, he gave me bitter words,

Let young women take heed of old bawds.

Cats have laws among them which they keep better than we do ours.

He that despiseth those that love him shall be despised of them that be loveth.

Cats do long while they be with kitten.

There be churls among cats as well as among Christian folk.

8. Scratched.   9. Bat.

saying we longed for wantonness and not for any need. This grieved me so sore, chiefly for the lack of that I longed for, that I was sick two days after, and had not it been for good dame Isegrim, who brought me a piece of a mouse and made me believe it was of a back, I had lost by burden by kittening ten days before my time.

It is the conceit of a thing and not the thing itself that is longed for.

"When I was recovered and went abroad again, about three days, this cruel churl met me and needs would have been doing with me. To whom, when I had made answer according to his deserts, and told him withall, which he might see too by my belly what case I was in, tush, there was no remedy (I think he had eaten savory), but for all that I could say, he would have his will. I, seeing that, and that he would ravish me perforce, I cried out for help as loud as ever I could squawl, and to defend myself till succor came I scrat and bit as hard as ever I could. And this notwithstanding, had not Isegrim and her son Lightfoot come the sooner (who both are here and can witness), he would have marred me quite. Now, whether I might in this case refuse him, and do as I did without breach of our holy law, which forbiddeth us females to refuse any males not exceeding the number of ten in a night, judge you, my lords, to whom the interpretation of the laws belongeth.

Churls must be churlishly served.

Savory is an hot herb provoking lust in cats.

A law for adultery among cats.

"'Yes, surely,' quod Grisard, 'for in the third year of the reign of Glascalon, at a court holden in Cat-wood, as appeareth in the records, they decreed upon that exception, forbidding any male in this case to force any female, and that upon great penalties. But to let this pass, whereof we were satisfied in your purgation the first night, tell us how you behaved you with your new mistress, and that as briefly as you can; for lo where Corleonis is almost plain west, whereby ye know the goblins' hour approacheth.'

Glascalon was chief prince of the cats after Grimolochin.

"After I was come to my young mistress," quod Mouse-slayer, "she made much of me, thinking that I had been my old dame's daughter, and many tales she told thereof to her gossips. My master also made much of me, because I would take meat in my foot and therewith put it in my mouth and feed. In this house dwelt an ungracious fellow who, delighting much in unhappy turns, on a time took four walnut shells and filled them full of soft pitch, and put them upon my feet, and then put my feet into cold water till the pitch was hardened, and then he let me go. But Lord, how strange it was to me to go in shoes, and how they vexed me, for when I ran upon any steep thing they made me slide and fall down. Wherefore all that afternoon, for anger that I could not get off my shoes, I hid me in a corner of the garret which was boarded, under which my master and mistress lay. And at night when they were all in bed, I spied a mouse playing in the floor; and when I ran at her to catch her, my shoes made such a noise upon the boards that it waked my master, who was a man very fearful of spirits. And when he with his servants harkened well to the noise, which went pit-pat, pit-pat, as it had been the trampling of an horse, they waxed all afraid and said surely it was the Devil.

After one a clock at midnight the goblins go abroad, and as soon as any cock croweth, which is their hour, that is at three, they return homeward.

Divers men delight in divers fond things.

A cat was shoed.

Natural delight expelleth melancholy.

The fearful are always suspicious.

"And as one of them, an hardy fellow (even he that had shoed me), came upstairs to see what it was, I went downward to meet him and made such a rattling that, when he saw my glistering eyes, he fell down backward and brake his head, crying out, 'The Devil, the Devil, the Devil.' Which his master and all the rest hearing, ran naked as they were into the street and cried the same cry.

"Whereupon the neighbors arose and called up, among other, an old priest, who lamented much the lack of holy water which they were forbidden to make. Howbeit, he went to church and took out of the font some of the christening water, and took his chalice, and therein a wafer unconsecrate, and put on a surplice, and his stole about his neck, and fet out of his chamber a piece of holy candle which he had kept two year. And herewith he came to the house, and with his candle-light in the one hand and a holy-water sprinkle in the other hand, and his chalice and wafer in sight of his bosom, and a pot of font-water at his girdle, up he came praying towards the garret, and all the people after him.

"And when I saw this, and thinking I should have seen some Mass that night, as many nights before in other places I had, I ran towards them thinking to meet them. But when the priest heard me come, and by a glimpsing had seen me, down he fell upon them that were behind him, and with his chalice hurt one, with his water pot another, and his holy candle fell into another priest's breech beneath (who, while the rest were hawsoning[1] me, was conjuring our maid at the stair foot) and all to-besinged him, for he was so afraid with the noise of the rest which fell that he had not the power to put it out. When I saw all this business, down I ran among them where they lay on heaps. But such a fear as they were all in then I think was never seen afore; for the old priest, which was so tumbled among them that his face lay upon a boy's bare arse, which belike was fallen headlong under him, was so astonished that, when the boy, which for fear had beshit himself, had all to-rayed his face, he neither felt nor smelt it, nor removed from him.

"Then went I to my dame, which lay among the rest God knoweth very madly, and so mewed and curled about her that at last she said, 'I ween it be my cat.' That hearing the knave that had shoed me, and calling to mind that erst he had forgot, said it was so indeed and nothing else. That hearing the priest, in whose holy breech the holy candle all this while lay burning, he took heart a grace, and before he was spied rose up and took the candle in his hand, and looked upon me and all the company, and fell a-laughing at the handsome lying of his fellow's face. The rest, hearing him, came every man to himself and arose and looked upon me, and cursed the knave which had shoed me, who would in no case be a-known of it. This done, they got hot water and dissolved the pitch and plucked off my shoes. And then every man (after they desired each other not to be a-known of this night's work) for shame departed to their lodgings, and all our household went to bed again."

Wickedness is a scourge itself to such as invent it.

Holy water was good for conjurers.

This fellow thought to beguile the Devil. A conjurer can have no better apparel.

Cats hear mo Masses than all men hear of.

Priests have been good conjurers of such kind of spirits.

Fear taketh away the senses.

A liar and a doer of shrewd turns ought to have a good memory. One hardy man encourageth many cowards.

Silence is the best friend that shame hath. The author laughed in a cat's voice.

1. Exorcizing.

When all the cats, and I too for company, had laughed at this space, Mouse-slayer proceeded and said, "After this about three-quarters of a year, which was at Whitsuntide last, I played another prank, and that was this. The gentleman, who by mine old dame's lying and my weeping was accepted and retained of my mistress, came often home to our house, and always in my master's absence was doing with my dame. Wherefore, desirous that my master might know it (for they spent his goods so lavishly between them that, notwithstanding his great trade of merchandise, they had, unweeting to him, almost undone him already), I sought how I might bewray them. Which as hap would, at the time remembered afore, came to pass thus. While this gentleman was doing with my dame, my master came in—so suddenly that he had no leisure to pluck up his hose, but with them about his legs ran into a corner behind the painted cloth, and there stood (I warrant you) as still as a mouse. As soon as my master came in, his wife, according to her old wont, caught him about his neck and kissed him, and devised many means to have got him forth again. But he, being weary, sat down and called for his dinner. And when she saw there was none other remedy, she brought it him, which was a mess of potage and a piece of beef, whereas she and her franion[2] had broke their fast with capons, hot venison, marrow bones, and all other kind of dainties.

"I, seeing this, and minding to show my master how he was ordered, got behind the cloth, and to make the man speak I all to-pawed him with my claws upon his bare legs and buttocks. And for all this, he stood still and never moved. But my master heard me and, thinking I was catching a mouse, bade my dame go help me. Who, knowing what beast was there, came to the cloth and called me away, saying, 'Come puss, come puss,' and cast me meat into the floor. But I, minding another thing, and seeing that scratching could not move him, suddenly I leaped up and caught him by the genitals with my teeth, and bote so hard that, when he had restrained more than I thought any man could, at last he cried out, and caught me by the neck thinking to strangle me. My master, not smelling but hearing such a rat as was not wont to be about such walls, came to the cloth and lift it up, and there found this bare-arst gentleman strangling me who had his stones in my mouth. And when I saw my master I let go my hold, and the gentleman his. And away I ran immediately to the place where I now dwell, and never came there since. So that how they agreed among them I cannot tell, nor never durst go see for fear of my life.

"Thus have I told you, my good lords, all things that have been done and happened through me, wherein you perceive my loyalty and obedience to all good laws, and how shamelessly and falsely I am accused for a transgressor. And I pray you, as you have perceived, so certify my liege great Cammoloch (whose life both Hagat and Heg preserve) of my behavior."

Adulterers are diligent in waiting their times.

A wanton wife and a back door will soon make a rich man poor.

Chance oftentimes betrayeth evil.

None seem outwardly so loving as whores. Sine Baccho et cetera friget Venus.[3]

Fear overcometh smart.

All are not mice that are behind painted cloths.

It is justice to punsh those parts that offend. Whoredom will be known be it never so warily hid.

There be false accusers among all kind of creatures.

---

2. Darling.   3. Without Bacchus and Ceres, Venus is frigid.

When Grisard, Isegrim, and Pol-noir, the commissioners, had heard this declaration and request of Mouse-slayer, they praised her much. And after that they had commanded her, with all the cats there, to be on St. Catherine's day next ensuing at Caithness where, as they said, Cammoloch would hold his court, they departed. And I, glad to have heard that I heard, and sorry that I had not understood what was said the other two nights before, got me to my bed and slept a-good.

And the next morning, when I went out into the garden, I heard a strange cat ask of our cat what Mouse-slayer had done before the commissioners those three nights. To whom our cat answered, that she had purged herself of a crime that was laid to her charge by Catch-rat, and declared her whole life for six years' space. Whereof in the first two years as she said, said she, she had five masters: a priest, a baker, a lawyer, a broker, and a butcher; all whose privy deceits which she had seen she declared the first night. In the next two years she had seven masters: a bishop, a knight, a pothecary, a goldsmith, an usurer, an alchemist, and a lord; whose cruelty, study, craft, cunning, niggishness,[4] folly, waste, and oppression she declared the second night, wherein this doing was notable. Because the knight, having a fair lady to his wife, gave his mind so much to his book that he seldom lay with her, this cat, pitying her mistress and minding to fray him from lying alone, on a night when her master lay from her, got to his mouth and drew so his breath that she almost stifled him. A like part she played with the usurer, who, being rich and yet living miserably and feigning him poor, she got one day, while his treasure chest stood open, and hid her therein; whereof he not knowing locked her in it. And when at night he came thither again and heard one stirring there, and thinking it had been the Devil, he called the priest and many other persons to come and help him to conjure. And when in their sight he opened his chest, out leaped she and they saw what riches he had and cessed[5] him thereafter. As for what was done and said yesternight, both of my lord Grisard's hard adventure and of Mouse-slayer's bestowing her other two last years, which is nothing in comparison of any of the other two years before, I need not tell you for you were present and heard it yourself."

This talk, lo, I heard between these two cats. And then I got me in, and brake my fast with bread and butter, and dined at noon with common meat, which so repleted my head again and my other powers in the first digestion, that by nighttime they were as gross as ever they were before. For when I harkened at night to other two cats, which as I perceived by their gestures spake of the same matter, I understood never a word.

Lo, here have I told you all (chiefly you, my lord) a wonderful matter, and yet as incredible as it is wonderful. Notwithstanding,

Justices should cherish the innocents accused.

Travail and watching maketh sound sleeping.

Mouse-slayer was six year old.

Cats change their dwellings often.

Men ought to lie with their wives.

A niggard is neither good to his self nor to any other.

The Devil delighteth to dwell among money.

All in this book is nothing in comparison of that the cat told before.
Gross meats make gross wits.

Wonders are incredible.

4. Meanness.   5. Taxed.

when I may have convenient time, I will tell you other things which these eyes of mine have seen and these ears of mine have heard, and that of mysteries so far passing this, that all which I have said now shall in comparison thereof be nothing at all to be believed. In the meanwhile, I will pray you to help to get me some money to convey me on my journey to Caithness, for I have been going thither these five years and never was able to perform my journey.

In comparison of a diamond, crystal hath no color. Poverty hindreth many excellent attempts.

When Master Ferrers had promised that he would, every man shut up his shop windows,[6] which the foresaid talk kept open two hours longer than they should have been.

An Exhortation

I know these things will seem marvelous to many men, that cats should understand and speak, have a governor among themselves, and be obedient to their laws. And were it not for the approved authority of the ecstatical author of whom I heard it, I should myself be as doubtful as they. But seeing I know the place and the persons with whom he talked of these matters before he experimented his wonderful and strange confections, I am the less doubtful of any truth therein. Wherefore, seeing he hath in his oration proved that cats do understand us and mark our secret doings, and so declare them among themselves; that through help of the medicines by him described any man may, as he did, understand them; I would counsel all men to take heed of wickedness, and eschew secret sins and privy mischievous counsels, lest, to their shame, all the world at length do know thereof. But if any man, for doubt hereof, do put away his cat, then shall his so doing testify his secret naughty living, which he is more ashamed his cat should see than God and His angels, which see, mark, and behold all men's closest doings.

And that we may take profit by this declaration of Master Streamer, let us so live, both openly and privily that neither our own cat, admitted to all secrets, be able to declare aught of us to the world save what is laudable and honest; nor the Devil's cat, which will we or nill we seeth and writeth all our ill doings, have ought to lay against us afore the face of God, who not only with shame but with everlasting torment will punish all sin and wickedness. And ever when thou goest about anything, call to mind this proverb, *Beware the Cat;* not to tie up thy cat till thou have done, but to see that neither thine own nor the Devil's cat (which cannot be tied up) find anything therein whereof to accuse thee to thy shame.

Thus doing, thou canst not do amiss; but shalt have such good report through the cat's declaration, that thou shalt, in recompence of Master Streamer's labor who giveth thee this warning, sing unto God this hymn of his making.

The Hymn

Who givest wit to whales, to apes, to owls;
And kindly speech to fish, to flesh, to fowls;
And spirit to men in soul and body clean,
To mark and know what other creatures mean;

6. I.e., eyes.

Which hast given grace to Gregory, no Pope,
No King, no Lord; whose treasures are their hope;
But silly priest, which like a streamer waves
In ghostly good, despised of foolish knaves.

Which hast, I say, given grace to him to know
The course of things above and here below,
With skill so great in languages and tongues
As never breathed from Mithridates' lungs.

To whom the hunter of birds, of mice and rats,
Did speak as plain as Kate that thrummeth[7] hats;
By mean of whom is openly bewrayed
Such things as closely were both done and said.

To him grant, Lord, with healthy wealth and rest,
Long life to unload to us his learned breast;
With fame so great to overlive his grave,
As none had erst, nor any after have.

FINIS

Edmund Spenser
1552?–1599

A man whose poetry has come to be known as a monument to Queen Elizabeth's England began life modestly enough. Attending Cambridge as a "sizar," or "poor scholar," he worked as a servant to pay for his fees. Allegiance to the English church was expected of all subjects, and Spenser showed his support of the faith while still a student by contributing anti-Catholic verses to the first emblem book published in England. The genre, consisting of emblems or symbolic scenes explained by clever captions, acquainted the aspiring poet with elements of the mode he was later to master: allegory. Literally a writing that conveys "other" (from the Greek *allos*, "other") than literal meanings, the allegory that Spenser would eventually perfect for his epic poem *The Faerie Queene* produced narrative verse of great flexibility and verve. Building on powerful images, his verse allegories of education in a "virtuous" chivalry convey the challenges he saw attending the creation of a civil society in early modern England.

H. W. Smith, *Edmund Spenser.*

Shortly after leaving Cambridge in 1576, Spenser found employment as a secretary in the London household of the rich and influential Earl of Leicester, a favorite courtier of Queen Elizabeth and an ardent defender of international Protestantism. There he met Leicester's already famous nephew, Sir Philip Sidney, to whom Spenser dedicated his first work, the deliberately archaic, neo-Chaucerian *The Shepheardes Calender*, a sequence of

7. Make fringes for.

twelve eclogues or poems on pastoral subjects, one for each month of the year. A work of a paradoxically innovative style, *The Shepheardes Calender* demonstrated a range of metrical forms that had yet to be seen in English poetry; probably more compelling to the general reader was Spenser's use of pastoral motifs and settings to represent opinions on love, poetry, and social order. Sidney's response to the poem was, nevertheless, somewhat ambivalent. While recognizing that Spenser's eclogues had "much poetry" in them, he stated that he disliked verse composed in an "old rustic language"; among earlier and model poets of pastoral, "neither Theocritus in Greek, Virgil in Latin, nor Sannazaro in Italian did affect it." But precisely because this "old rustic language" could be recognized as purely English and independent of European traditions, Spenser would use a modified form of it in *The Faerie Queene*; in this way he hoped to demonstrate that English literature had as rich a past as any in Europe. He probably began the poem while in Leicester's service; the seventeenth-century biographer John Aubrey reported the discovery of "an abundance of cards, with stanzas of the *Faerie Queene* written on them" in the wainscoting of Spenser's London lodging.

From 1580 to the end of his life, Spenser lived in Ireland, serving as secretary to the Lord Deputy of Ireland, Arthur Grey. At such a distance from Queen Elizabeth's court, Spenser could not have secured royal favor. He was rescued from obscurity in 1589 by Sir Walter Raleigh, who, impressed with the first three books of *The Faerie Queene*, invited Spenser to present his poem to the queen. Beside the gallant and charismatic Raleigh, the poet—said to have been a "little man, who wore short hair, little bands (collars) and little cuffs"—must have cut a poor figure. But the queen liked the poem that illustrated her majesty in so many ways, "desired at timely hours to hear" it, and rewarded Spenser with a life pension of £50 a year. When Spenser returned to Ireland in 1590, he met and fell in love with Elizabeth Boyle, a woman much his junior. They were married in 1594, and Spenser celebrated their courtship and wedding in the *Amoretti* (page 676), a sonnet sequence describing the poet's quest for his "deer" or dear, and *Epithalamion*, a hymn to each of the twenty-four hours of their wedding day. The second three books of *The Faerie Queene*, published in 1596, proved as popular with readers as the first three, although James VI of Scotland (later James I of England) thought slanderous its portrait of the evil queen Duessa, whom he identified as his mother, Mary Queen of Scots. He demanded that Spenser be "duly tried and punished." Fortunately, however, Spenser's friends at court intervened, and nothing came of the king's displeasure.

The last years of the poet's life were full of grief and bitter disappointment. In 1598 the Irish in the province of Munster, rebelling against the English colonial authorities, burned the castle in which Spenser lived. The poet and his wife fled; their newborn child was reported to have perished in the flames. In December of that year, Spenser went to London to deliver letters to the queen from the Governor of Ireland concerning the uprising. He included a note describing his own assessment of the situation—a note that may have included material in a treatise entitled *A View of the Present State of Ireland*, supporting a militaristic policy to colonize the people of Ireland, which he is supposed to have written. He died a month after arriving in London in January of 1599 and was buried in Westminster Abbey near Geoffrey Chaucer, whose poetry had meant so much to him. The monument placed on his grave is inscribed with these words: "Prince of poets in his time, whose Divine Spirit needs no other witness than the works which he left behind."

Consciously aspiring both to Chaucer's humane dignity and to his vividly colloquial style, Spenser saw himself as fashioning and refashioning a tradition of English and possibly British poetry. As he made a point of using older terms and spelling, his poems are presented here unmodernized. Spenser's choice of language parallels his use of the motifs of knightly romance: turning to the past, he sought a vital perspective on the present. John Milton would later describe him as a "sage and serious" poet, who, in *The Faerie Queene*, wrote of the struggle of good against evil and the triumph of faith over falsehood. The subject, treated by weaving different story lines together to form a vast tapestry, interested not only Milton, who was clearly inspired by Spenser's complex understanding of human psychology, but also the next generation of poets in England, especially Ben Jonson, John Donne, and George Herbert, who turned to Spenser for a poetry of satirical vigor and spiritual insight. Yet other readers have been moved by Spenser's lyrics. His shorter poems and occasional verse show his skillful use of repetitive sounds or verbal echoes and reveal his unerring sense of language as a musical medium.

THE FAERIE QUEENE, BOOKS 6 AND 7   It is hard to place Spenser's great poem, as there had been nothing like it before. Spenser invented his own rhyme scheme and stanza form, and he wrote in an archaic way that no one could place easily. Ben Jonson famously remarked that "Spenser, in affecting the ancients, writ no language." Perhaps the best way of thinking of the poem is as an epic-romance, one that follows the history of a nation (an epic path), but also meanders away from its main subject in following stories that may or may not be of consequence (a romance path). Spenser joins these two forms in *The Faerie Queene* and so creates a new, flexible type of poetry that can take the reader in different directions. The "letter to Raleigh" appended to the first edition of the poem, tells the reader that Spenser's plan was to write a work of twelve books following the cardinal virtues as defined by Aristotle. Whether this was ever a serious plan is open to conjecture. The poem as we have it consists of six complete books, and a fragment of a seventh. The first edition contained the first three books of Holiness, Temperance, and Chastity; the second, the next three books of Friendship, Justice, and Courtesy. After Spenser's death, the work was republished with the addition of part of the seventh book, "The Two Cantos of Mutability," part of a book of Constancy.

Book Six follows the adventures of Calidore, the Knight of Courtesy. While the other knights in the poem had at least some idea of the purpose of their quests, Calidore is confronted with complex and contradictory definitions of courtesy and has no clear idea of what he is doing. His stated aim is to capture the Blatant Beast, a fearsome figure who has a multitude of tongues and whose allegorical role appears to be the abuse of language itself. But Calidore spends his time on a series of apparently aimless and disconnected tasks and disappears altogether from the narrative for the middle section of the book. He also tries to turn himself into a shepherd and so avoid the hard work of being a knight. Spenser's pastoral book is not what it seems to be and is a warning of the dark forces that threaten a society when good men are unable and unwilling to act. The poem shows besieged and unprotected shepherds always at the mercy of those who wish to undermine and overthrow their fragile society. In some ways Spenser would appear to have been thinking of his own situation in Ireland; in others, he was imagining the dire fate that could befall an unprotected England at the mercy of hostile neighbors.

The book contains a series of images of courtesy and its opposite, discourtesy, forcing the reader to think about the true nature of this civilizing value and how it could be followed. It also contains a key debate on the nature of the good life, one of the fundamental philosophical questions, when Calidore and Meliobee have their debate in Canto 9. The book also contains a number of incidents that have distinctly humorous elements, most notably when Calidore, the Knight of Courtesy, is told by Colin Clout that he has made the Graces—a form of courtesy—disappear. The knight himself is the problem, at odds with a confused, topsy-turvy society that has confused and confusing values. Whether Calidore is to blame is another question, one that the reader has to consider.

"Two Cantos of Mutability" are, arguably, Spenser's finest poem. The cantos stand as an etiological myth (a myth of origins) that underlies the poem and that explain the meaning, location, and purpose of Spenser's Faerie Land. Mutability challenges Cynthia, the goddess chosen by Jove to rule the universe he has conquered, claiming that she has the real right to be queen, as things change endlessly according to her desire. It is agreed that Jove and Mutability will present their cases before Nature on Arlo Hill, the small mountain nearest to Spenser's house in Ireland. Ireland used to be the fairest of the British Isles which attracted the attention of Diana who spent a great deal of her time there bathing and hunting with her nymphs and satyrs. The foolish god Faunus had an uncontrollable desire to see the goddess naked and so persuaded her nymph, Molanna, to let him know where Diana bathed. Hiding in the bushes, he was so overwhelmed with emotion, that he burst out laughing, inspiring the wrath of the goddess, who cursed the island and never returned, condemning it to its current miserable state. In Canto 7 the protagonists meet on Arlo Hill and make their respective cases. Jove argues that he has conquered the universe and established order so he rules by right; Mutability counters that she should rule as her powers actually control it, whatever Jove might claim. Nature takes little time to decide to award victory to Jove, before she vanishes. The fragment concludes with two stanzas of the "unperfect" Canto 8 which seem to suggest that constancy is the principle that underlies the universe not perpetual change. In reading them we witness Spenser's understanding of the powers that hold sway in the universe and the fragile hold that men and women have on life.

 For additional resources on Spenser, including *"The Faerie Queene, A Letter of the Authors," Booke One of the Faerie Queene*, The Second Booke of *the Faerie Queene*, Canto 12, and "Epithalamion," go to *The Longman Anthology of British Literature* Web site at www.myliteraturekit.com.

The Sixte Booke of the Faerie Queene
Contayning the Legend of S. Calidore or of Courtesie.

1

The waies, through which my weary steps I guyde,
  In this delightfull land of Faery,
  Are so exceeding spacious and wyde,
  And sprinckled with such sweet variety,
5   Of all that pleasant is to eare or eye,
  That I nigh ravisht with rare thoughts delight,
  My tedious travell doe forget thereby;
  And when I gin to feele decay of might,
It strength to me supplies, & chears my dulled spright.

2

10   Such secret comfort, and such heavenly pleasures,
  Ye sacred imps,[1] that on *Parnasso* dwell,
  And there the keeping have of learnings threasures,
  Which doe all worldly riches farre excell,
  Into the mindes of mortall men doe well,[2]
15   And goodly fury into them infuse;
  Guyde ye my footing, and conduct me well
  In these strange waies, where never foote did use,
Ne none can find, but who was taught them by the Muse.[3]

1. The Muses, whose home was Mount Parnassus.
2. Flow.
3. Spenser is following Ariosto's boast that he is attempting something that no other poet has attempted (Ariosto,

Orlando Furioso 1.2). Milton imitates both poets in claiming that his poem "pursues Things unattempted yet in Prose or Rhyme" (Milton's *Paradise Lost*).

3

Revele to me the sacred noursery
20   Of vertue, which with you doth there remaine,
Where it in silver bowre does hidden ly
From view of men, and wicked worlds disdaine.
Since it at first was by the Gods with paine
Planted in earth, being deriv'd at furst
25   From heavenly seedes of bounty soveraine,
And by them long with carefull labour nurst,
Till it to ripenesse grew, and forth to honour burst.

4

Amongst them all growes not a fayrer flowre,
Then is the bloosme of comely courtesie,
30   Which though it on a lowly stalke doe bowre,
Yet brancheth forth in brave nobilitie,
And spreds it selfe through all civilitie:
Of which though present age doe plenteous seeme,
Yet being matcht with plaine Antiquitie,[4]
35   Ye will them all but fayned showes esteeme,
Which carry colours faire, that feeble eies misdeeme.

5

But in the triall of true curtesie,
Its now so farre from that, which then it was,
That it indeed is nought but forgerie,
40   Fashion'd to please the eies of them, that pas,
Which see not perfect things but in a glas:[5]
Yet is that glasse so gay, that it can blynd
The wisest sight, to thinke gold that is bras.
But vertues seat is deepe within the mynd,
45   And not in outward shows, but inward thoughts defynd.[6]

6

But where shall I in all Antiquity
So faire a patterne finde, where may be seene
The goodly praise of Princely curtesie,
As in your selfe, O soveraine Lady Queene,
50   In whose pure minde, as in a mirrour sheene,
It showes, and with her brightnesse doth inflame
The eyes of all, which thereon fixed beene;
But meriteth indeede an higher name:
Yet so from low to high uplifted is your name.

---

4. The lament for the lost simplicity of ancient times recalls the proem to Book V.
5. See 1 Corinthians 13.12: "For now we see through a
glass darkly."

6. The idea that virtue is not simply a form of social activity but a state of mind or condition of the soul is very
important throughout Book 6.

7

55   Then pardon me, most dreaded Soveraine,
       That from your selfe I doe this vertue bring,
       And to your selfe doe it returne againe:
       So from the Ocean all rivers spring,
       And tribute backe repay as to their King.[7]
60   Right so from you all goodly vertues well
       Into the rest, which round about you ring,
       Faire Lords and Ladies, which about you dwell,
    And doe adorne your Court, where courtesies excell.

Canto I

Calidore saves from Maleffort,°   French: evil attempt
A Damzell used vylde:
Doth vanquish Crudor, and doth make
Briana wexe more mylde.

1

    Of Court it seemes, men Courtesie doe call,
       For that it there most useth to abound;
       And well beseemeth° that in Princes hall   *it is appropriate*
       That vertue should be plentifully found,
5   Which of all goodly manners is the ground,
       And roote of civill conversation.[8]
       Right so in Faery court it did redound,°   *abound, overflow*
       Where curteous Knights and Ladies most did won
    Of all on earth, and made a matchlesse paragon.°   *example or model*
                                                of excellence

2

10   But mongst them all was none more courteous Knight,
       Then *Calidore*,[9] beloved over all,
       In whom it seemes, that gentlenesse of spright
       And manners mylde were planted naturall;
       To which he adding comely guize° withall,   *appearance*
15   And gracious speach, did steale mens hearts away.
       Nathlesse thereto he was full stout and tall,
       And well approv'd in batteilous affray,°   *attack*
    That him did much renowme, and far his feme display.

---

7. See Ecclesiastes 1.7: "All the rivers go into the sea, yet the sea is not full: for the rivers go unto the place whence they return, and go."

8. Civilized relationships. The phrase means more than the modern meanings of these words imply. Perhaps an allusion to Stefano Guazzo's *La civile conversatione* (1574), a courtesy book of enormous popularity.

9. Greek: "beauty, gift." The hero of this book has been identified with Sir Philip Sidney and with Robert Devereux, Earl of Essex. See *The Works of Edmund Spenser: A Variorum Edition*, ed. Edwin Greenlaw, G. G. Osgood, F. M. Padelford, et al. 2 vols., Baltimore, 1932–1957, Henceforth abbreviated *Var.*

3

Ne was there Knight, ne was there Lady found[1]
20   In Faery court, but him did deare embrace,
For his faire vsage and conditions sound,
The which in all mens liking gayned place,
And with the greatest purchast greatest grace:
Which he could wisely use, and well apply,
25   To please the best, and th'evill to embase.°   *humble*
For he loathd leasing,° and base flattery,   *falsehood*
And loved simple truth and stedfast honesty.

4

And now he was in travell on his way,
Uppon an hard adventure sore bestad,°   *beset by difficulty*
30   Whenas by chaunce he met uppon a day
With *Artegall*,[2] returning yet halfe sad
From his late conquest, which he gotten had.
Who whenas each of other had a sight,
They knew themselves, and both their persons rad:°   *knew, recognized*
35   When *Calidore* thus first; Haile noblest Knight
Of all this day on ground, that breathen living spright.[3]

5

Now tell, if please you, of the good successe,
Which ye have had in your late enterprize.
To whom Sir *Artegall* gan to expresse
40   His whole exploite, and valorous emprize,
In order as it did to him arize.
Now happy man (sayd then Sir *Calidore*)
Which have so goodly, as ye can devize,
Atchiev'd so hard a quest, as few before;
45   That shall you most renowmed make for evermore.

6

But where ye ended have, now I begin
To tread an endlesse trace,° withouten guyde,   *track, path*
Or good direction, how to enter in,
Or how to issue forth in waies untryde,
50   In perils strange, in labours long and wide,
In which although good Fortune me befall,
Yet shall it not by none be testifyde.

---

1. The courtesy books placed great emphasis on attaining public recognition of one's virtues.
2. Arthegall, the hero of Book 5, had just returned from freeing Irena from the power of Grantorto.
3. I.e., of all knights living. "Breathen" is an obsolete third person plural form of "breathe"; its implied subject is "all knights."

What is that quest (quoth then Sir *Artegall*)
That you into such perils presently doth call?

7

55 The Blattant Beast (quoth he) I doe pursew,
      And through the world incessantly doe chase,
      Till I him overtake, or else subdew:
      Yet know I not or how, or in what place
      To find him out, yet still I forward trace.
60   What is that Blattant Beast?[4] (then he replide)
      It is a Monster bred of hellishe race,
      (Then answerd he) which often hath annoyd
Good Knights and Ladies true, and many else destroyd.

8

Of *Cerberus* whilome he was begot,
65   And fell *Chimæra* in her darkesome den,
      Through fowle commixture of his filthy blot;
      Where he was fostred long in *Stygian*[5] fen,
      Till he to perfect ripenesse grew, and then
      Into this wicked world he forth was sent,
70   To be the plague and scourge of wretched men:
      Whom with vile tongue and venemous intent
He sore doth wound, and bite, and cruelly torment.

9

Then since the salvage Island I did leave
      Sayd *Artegall*, I such a Beast did see,[6]
75   The which did seeme a thousand tongues to have,
      That all in spight and malice did agree,
      With which he bayd and loudly barkt at mee,
      As if that he attonce would me devoure.
      But I that knew my selfe from perill free,
80   Did nought regard his malice nor his powre,
But he the more his wicked poyson forth did poure.

10

That surely is that Beast (saide *Calidore*)
      Which I pursue, of whom I am right glad

---

4. Latin: *blatire*, "to babble." The Blatant Beast is generally interpreted as slander or detraction, although Ben
Jonson reported that Spenser in a letter to Ralegh (also
spelled Raleigh) had identified the Beast with the Puritans (*Var.*, p. 382). Obviously the Blatant Beast does not
refer only to Puritans, or to all Puritans. The pursuit of
the beast by the knight represents the efforts of courtesy
to overcome slander. Since the impulse behind slander or
detraction is malice (wishing evil to another person),
courtesy must try to grapple with malice, the sin opposed
to Christian charity.
5. The Styx was a river flowing through Hades.
6. Arthegall's encounter with the Blatant Beast is generally understood as a reference to the accusations made
against Lord Grey de Wilton for his handling of the Irish
situation.

To heare these tidings, which of none afore
85   Through all my weary travell I have had:
        Yet now some hope your words unto me add.
        Now God you speed (quoth then Sir *Artegall*)
        And keepe your body from the daunger drad:
        For ye have much adoe to deale withall;
90 So both tooke goodly leave, and parted severall.°   *in different directions*

11

Sir *Calidore* thence travelled not long,[7]
        When as by chaunce a comely Squire he found,
        That thorough some more mighty enemies wrong,
        Both hand and foote unto a tree was bound:
95   Who seeing him from farre, with piteous sound
        Of his shrill cries him called to his aide.
        To whom approching, in that painefull stound
        When he him saw, for no demaunds he staide,°   *waited, delayed*
But first him losde,° and afterwards thus to him saide.   *loosed*

12

100 Unhappy Squire, what hard mishap thee brought
        Into this bay[8] of perill and disgrace?
        What cruell hand thy wretched thraldome wrought,
        And thee captyued in this shamefull place?
        To whom he answerd thus; My haplesse case
105   Is not occasiond through my misdesert,
        But through misfortune, which did me abase
        Unto this shame, and my young hope subvert,
Ere that I in her guilefull traines was well expert.

13

Not farre from hence, uppon yond rocky hill,[9]
110   Hard by a streight there stands a castle strong,
        Which doth observe a custome lewd and ill,
        And it hath long mayntaind with mighty wrong:
        For may no Knight nor Lady passe along
        That way, (and yet they needs must passe that way,)
115   By reason of the streight,[1] and rocks among,
        But they that Ladies lockes doe shave away,
And that knights berd for toll, which they for passage pay.

---

7. Upton (*Var.*, p. 189) points out that Calidore's first adventure is like the first adventure of Cervantes's Don Quixote.
8. Situation of a hunted animal (e.g., "at bay").
9. Spenser was probably most influenced by the French romance *Perlesvaus*, Malory 1.24 and Ariosto, *Orlando Furioso*, 37, 42.
1. Narrow or confined place, such as a mountain pass or a narrow pathway.

14

    A shamefull use as ever I did heare,
        Sayd *Calidore*, and to be overthrowne.
120   But by what meanes did they at first it reare,
        And for what cause, tell if thou have it knowne.
        Sayd then that Squire: The Lady which doth owne
        This Castle, is by name *Briana*[2] hight.
        Then which a prouder Lady liveth none:
125   She long time hath deare lov'd a doughty Knight,
    And sought to win his love by all the meanes she might.

15

    His name is *Crudor*,[3] who through high disdaine
        And proud despight of his selfe pleasing mynd,
        Refused hath to yeeld her love againe,
130   Untill a Mantle she for him doe fynd,
        With beards of Knights and locks of Ladies lynd.
        Which to provide, she hath this Castle dight,
        And therein hath a Seneschall° assynd,   *steward*
        Cald *Maleffort*,[4] a man of mickle might,
135   Who executes her wicked will, with worse despight.

16

    He this same day, as I that way did come
        With a faire Damzell, my beloved deare,
        In execution of her lawlesse doome,
        Did set upon us flying both for feare:
140   For little bootes against him hand to reare.
        Me first he tooke, unhable to withstond;
        And whiles he her pursued every where,
        Till his returne unto this tree he bond:
    Ne wote I surely, whether her he yet have fond.

17

145   Thus whiles they spake, they heard a ruefull shrieke
        Of one loud crying, which they streight way ghest,
        That it was she, the which for helpe did seeke.
        Tho looking up unto the cry to lest,°   *listen*
        They saw that Carle from farre, with hand unblest
150   Hayling° that mayden by the yellow heare,   *dragging, pulling*
        That all her garments from her snowy brest,

2. Possibly Greek: "strong."   4. French: "evil attempt."
3. Latin: *crudus*, "cruel."

And from her head her lockes he nigh did teare,
Ne would he spare for pitty, nor refraine for feare.

18

Which haynous sight when *Calidore* beheld,
155   Eftsoones he loosd that Squire, and so him left,
   With hearts dismay and inward dolour queld,
   For to pursue that villaine, which had reft°   *stolen*
   That piteous spoile by so injurious theft.
   Whom overtaking, loude to him he cryde;
160   Leave faytor quickely that misgotten weft°   *stolen prize*
   To him, that hath it better justifyde,
And turne thee soone to him, of whom thou art defyde.

19

Who hearkning to that voice, him selfe upreard,
   And seeing him so fiercely towardes make,°   *move in his direction*
165   Against him stoutly ran, as nought afeard,
   But rather more enrag'd for those words sake;
   And with sterne count'naunce thus unto him spake.
   Art thou the caytive, that defyest me,
   And for this Mayd, whose party thou doest take,
170   Wilt give thy beard, though it but little bee?
Yet shall it not her lockes for raunsome fro me free.

20

With that he fiercely at him flew, and layd
   On hideous strokes with most importune° might,   *severe, persistent*
   That oft he made him stagger as unstayd,
175   And oft recuile° to shunne his sharpe despight.   *recoil*
   But *Calidore*, that was well skild in fight,
   Him long forbore,° and still his spirite spar'd,   *endured, stood up to*
   Lying in waite, how him he damadge might.
   But when he felt him shrinke, and come to ward,[5]
180 He greater grew, and gan to drive at him more hard.

21

Like as a water streame, whose swelling sourse
   Shall drive a Mill, within strong bancks is pent,
   And long restrayned of his ready course;
   So soone as passage is unto him lent,
185   Breakes forth, and makes his way more violent.
   Such was the fury of Sir *Calidore*,
   When once he felt his foeman to relent;

5. Begin to shield himself, take the defensive.

He fiercely him pursu'd, and pressed sore,
Who as he still decayd, so he encreased more.

22

190 The heavy burden of whose dreadfull might
   When as the Carle no longer could sustaine,
   His heart gan faint, and streight he tooke his flight
   Toward the Castle, where if need constraine,
   His hope of refuge used to remaine.
195   Whom *Calidore* perceiving fast to flie,
   He him pursu'd and chaced through the plaine,
   That he for dread of death gan loude to crie
Unto the ward,° to open to him hastilie.   *guard*

23

They from the wall him seeing so aghast,
200   The gate soone opened to receive him in,
   But *Calidore* did follow him so fast,
   That even in the Porch[6] he him did win,
   And cleft his head asunder to his chin.
   The carcasse tumbling downe within the dore,
205   Did choke the entraunce with a lumpe of sin,
   That it could not be shut, whilest *Calidore*
Did enter in, and slew the Porter on the flore.

24

With that the rest, the which the Castle kept,
   About him flockt, and hard at him did lay;
210   But he them all from him full lightly swept,
   As doth a Steare, in heat of sommers day,
   With his long taile the bryzes° brush away.   *gadflies*
   Thence passing forth, into the hall he came,
   Where of the Lady selfe in sad dismay
215   He was ymett, who with uncomely shame
Gan him salute, and fowle upbrayd with faulty blame.

25

False traytor Knight, (sayd she) no Knight at all,
   But scorne of armes that hast with guilty hand
   Murdred my men, and slaine my Seneschall;
220   Now comest thou to rob my house unmand,°   *unprotected*
   And spoile° my selfe, that can not thee withstand?   *rob, despoil, ravish*
   Yet doubt thou not, but that some better Knight
   Then thou, that shall thy treason understand,

6. I.e., just as he reached the porch.

Will it avenge, and pay thee with thy right:°   *i.e., what you deserve*
225   And if none do, yet shame shal thee with shame requight.

26

Much was the Knight abashed at that word;
    Yet answerd thus; Not unto me the shame,
    But to the shamefull doer it afford.°   *grant, attribute*
    Bloud is no blemish; for it is no blame
230   To punish those, that doe deserve the same;
    But they that breake bands of civilitie,
    And wicked customes make, those doe defame
    Both noble armes and gentle curtesie.
No greater shame to man then inhumanitie.

27

235   Then doe your selfe, for dread of shame, forgoe
    This evill manner, which ye here maintaine,
    And doe in stead thereof mild curt'sie showe
    To all, that passe. That shall you glory gaine
    More then his love, which thus ye seeke t'obtaine.
240   Wherewith all full of wrath, she thus replyde;
    Vile recreant, know that I doe much disdaine
    Thy courteous lore, that doest my love deride,
Who scornes thy ydle scoffe, and bids thee be defyde.

28

To take defiaunce at a Ladies word
245   (Quoth he) I hold it no indignity;
    But were he here, that would it with his sword
    Abett,° perhaps he mote it deare aby.°   *support / pay for*
    Cowherd° (quoth she) were not, that thou wouldst fly,   *coward*
    Ere he doe come, he should be soone in place.
250   If I doe so, (sayd he) then liberty
    I leave to you, for aye me to disgrace
With all those shames, that erst ye spake me to deface.

29

With that a Dwarfe she cald to her in hast,
    And taking from her hand a ring of gould,
255   A privy token, which betweene them past,
    Bad him to flie with all the speed he could,
    To *Crudor*, and desire him that he would
    Vouchsafe to reskue her against a Knight,
    Who through strong powre had now her self in hould,
260   Having late slaine her Seneschall in fight,
And all her people murdred with outragious might.

30

The Dwarfe his way did hast, and went all night;
  But *Calidore* did with her there abyde
  The comming of that so much threatned[7] Knight,
265 Where that discourteous Dame with scornfull pryde,
  And fowle entreaty him indignifyde,°   *dishonored*
  That yron heart it hardly could sustaine:
  Yet he, that could his wrath full wisely guyde,
  Did well endure her womanish disdaine,
270 And did him selfe from fraile impatience refraine.

31

The morrow next, before the lampe of light,
  Above the earth upreard his flaming head,
  The Dwarfe, which bore that message to her knight,
  Brought aunswere backe, that ere he tasted bread,
275 He would her succour, and alive or dead
  Her foe deliver up into her hand:
  Therefore he wild her doe away all dread;
  And that of him she mote assured stand,
He sent to her his basenet,° as a faithfull band.   *steel head piece*

32

280 Thereof full blyth the Lady streight became,
  And gan t'augment her bitternesse much more:
  Yet no whit more appalled for the same,
  Ne ought dismayed was Sir *Calidore*,
  But rather did more chearefull seeme therefore.
285 And having soone his armes about him dight,
  Did issue forth, to meete his foe afore;°   *in front*
  Where long he stayed not, when as a Knight
He spide come pricking on with al his powre and might.

33

Well weend he streight, that he should be the same,
290 Which tooke in hand her quarrell to maintaine;
  Ne stayd to aske if it were he by name,
  But coucht his speare, and ran at him amaine.
  They bene ymett in middest of the plaine,
  With so fell fury, and dispiteous forse,
295 That neither could the others stroke sustaine,
  But rudely rowld to ground both man and horse,
Neither of other taking pitty nor remorse.

7. I.e., threatening to Calidore.

34

But *Calidore* uprose againe full light,
 Whiles yet his foe lay fast in sencelesse sound,°   *swoon*
300 Yet would he not him hurt, although he might:
 For shame he weend a sleeping° wight to wound.   *unconscious*
 But when *Briana* saw that drery stound,
 There where she stood uppon the Castle wall,
 She deem'd him sure to have bene dead on ground,
305 And made such piteous mourning therewithall,
That from the battlements she ready seem'd to fall.

35

Nathlesse at length him selfe he did upreare
 In lustlesse wise,° as if against his will,   *i.e., listlessly, wearily*
 Ere he had slept his fill, he wakened were,
310 And gan to stretch his limbs; which feeling ill
 Of his late fall, a while he rested still:
 But when he saw his foe before in vew,
 He shooke off luskishnesse,° and courage chill   *sluggishness*
 Kindling a fresh, gan battell to renew,
315 To prove if better foote then horsebacke would ensew.

36

There then began a fearefull cruell fray
 Betwixt them two, for maystery of might.
 For both were wondrous practicke° in that play,   *experienced*
 And passing well° expert in single fight,   *extremely*
320 And both inflam'd with furious despight:
 Which as it still encreast, so still increast
 Their cruell strokes and terrible affright;
 Ne once for ruth their rigour they releast,
Ne once to breath a while their angers tempest ceast.

37

325 Thus long they trac'd and traverst to and fro,
 And tryde all waies, how each mote entrance make
 Into the life of his malignant foe;
 They hew'd their helmes, and plates asunder brake,
 As they had potshares[8] bene; for nought mote slake
330 Their greedy vengeaunces, but goary blood,
 That at the last like to a purple lake
 Of bloudy gore congeal'd about them stood,
Which from their riven° sides forth gushed like a flood.   *cut*

8. Broken pieces of earthenware, potsherds.

38

At length it chaunst, that both their hands on hie,
335   At once did heave, with all their powre and might,
   Thinking the utmost of their force to trie,
   And prove the finall fortune of the fight:
   But *Calidore*, that was more quicke of sight,
   And nimbler handed, then his enemie,
340   Prevented him before his stroke could light,
   And on the helmet smote him formerlie,[9]
That made him stoupe to ground with meeke humilitie.

39

And ere he could recover foot againe,
   He following that faire advantage fast,
345   His stroke redoubled with such might and maine,
   That him upon the ground he groveling cast;
   And leaping to him light, would have unlast
   His Helme, to make unto his vengeance way.
   Who seeing, in what daunger he was plast,
350   Cryde out, Ah mercie Sir, doe me not slay,
But save my life, which lot° before your foot doth lay.   *destiny*

40

With that his mortall hand a while he stayd,
   And having somewhat calm'd his wrathfull heat
   With goodly patience, thus he to him sayd;
355   And is the boast of that proud Ladies threat,
   That menaced me from the field to beat,
   Now brought to this? By this now may ye learne,
   Strangers no more so rudely to intreat,
   But put away proud looke, and vsage sterne,
360 The which shal nought to you but foule dishonor yearne.°   *earn*

41

For nothing is more blamefull to a knight,
   That court'sie doth as well as armes professe,
   How ever strong and fortunate in fight,
   Then the reproch of pride and cruelnesse.
365   In vaine he seeketh others to suppresse,
   Who hath not learnd him selfe first to subdew:
   All flesh is frayle, and full of ficklenesse,
   Subiect to fortunes chance, still chaunging new;°   *always changing anew*
What haps to day to me, to morrow may to you.

---

9. First (i.e., before Crudor could strike).

42

370 Who will not mercie unto others shew,
　　　How can he mercy ever hope to have?[1]
　　　To pay each with his owne is right and dew.
　　　Yet since ye mercie now doe need to crave,
　　　I will it graunt, your hopelesse life to save;
375　　With these conditions, which I will propound:
　　　First, that ye better shall your selfe behave
　　　Unto all errant knights, whereso on ground;
　　Next that ye Ladies ayde in every stead and stound.

43

　　The wretched man, that all this while did dwell
380　　In dread of death, his heasts° did gladly heare,　　　*orders*
　　　And promist to performe his precept well,
　　　And whatsoever else he would requere.
　　　So suffring him to rise, he made him sweare
　　　By his owne sword, and by the crosse thereon,
385　　To take *Briana* for his loving fere,°　　　*companion, partner*
　　　Withouten dowre or composition;[2]
　　But to release° his former foule condition.　　　*withdraw*

44

　　All which accepting, and with faithfull oth
　　　Bynding himselfe most firmely to obay,
390　　He up arose, how ever liefe or loth,
　　　And swore to him true fealtie for aye.
　　　Then forth he cald from sorrowfull dismay
　　　The sad *Briana*, which all this beheld:
　　　Who comming forth yet full of late affray,
395　　Sir *Calidore* upcheard, and to her teld
　　All this accord, to which he *Crudor* had compeld.

45

　　Whereof she now more glad, then sory earst,
　　　All overcome with infinite affect,°　　　*feeling, emotion*
　　　For his exceeding courtesie, that pearst
400　　Her stubborne hart with inward deepe effect,
　　　Before his feet her selfe she did project,
　　　And him adoring as her lives deare Lord,
　　　With all due thankes, and dutifull respect,
　　　Her selfe acknowledg'd bound for that accord,
405　　By which he had to her both life and love restord.

---

1. See James 2.13 and Matthew 5.7.　　　2. Sum of money paid in settlement.

46

So all returning to the Castle glad,
  Most joyfully she them did entertaine,
  Where goodly glee and feast to them she made,
  To shew her thankefull mind and meaning faine,
410 By all the meanes she mote it best explaine:
  And after all, unto Sir *Calidore*
  She freely gave that Castle for his paine,
  And her selfe bound to him for evermore;
So wondrously now chaung'd, from that she was afore.

47

415 But *Calidore* himselfe would not retaine
  Nor land nor fee, for hyre° of his good deede,   *payment*
  But gave them straight unto that Squire againe,
  Whom from her Seneschall he lately freed,
  And to his damzell as their rightfull meed,
420 For recompence of all their former wrong:
  There he remaind with them right well agreed,
  Till of his wounds he wexed hole and strong,
And then to his first quest he passed forth along.

Canto II

*Calidore sees young Tristram slay
A proud discourteous knight,
He makes him Squire, and of him learnes
his state and present plight.*

1

What vertue is so fitting for a knight,
  Or for a Ladie, whom a knight should love,
  As Curtesie, to beare themselves aright
  To all of each degree, as doth behove?
5 For whether they be placed high above,
  Or low beneath, yet ought they well to know
  Their good, that none them rightly may reprove°   *accuse*
  Of rudenesse, for not yeelding what they owe:
Great skill it is such duties timely to bestow.

2

10 Thereto great helpe dame Nature selfe doth lend:
  For some so goodly gracious are by kind,
  That every action doth them much commend,
  And in the eyes of men great liking find;
  Which others, that have greater skill in mind,
15 Though they enforce themselves, cannot attaine.

For everie thing, to which one is indin'd,
Doth best become, and greatest grace doth gaine:
Yet praise likewise deserve good thewes,° enforst   *manners, customs*
     with paine.

3

That well in courteous *Calidore* appeares,
20   Whose every act and deed, that he did say,
     Was like enchantment, that through both the eyes,[1]
     And both the eares did steale the hart away.
     He now againe is on his former way,
     To follow his first quest, when as he spyde
25   A tall young man from thence not farre away,
     Fighting on foot, as well he him descryde,
Against an armed knight, that did on horsebacke ryde.

4

And them beside a Ladie faire he saw,
     Standing alone on foot, in foule array:
30   To whom himselfe he hastily did draw,
     To weet the cause of so uncomely fray,
     And to depart them, if so be he may.
     But ere he came in place, that youth had kild
     That armed knight, that low on ground he lay;
35   Which when he saw, his hart was inly child
With great amazement, & his thought with wonder fild.

5

Him stedfastly he markt, and saw to bee
     A goodly youth of amiable grace,
     Yet but a slender slip, that scarse did see
40   Yet seventeene yeares, but tall and faire of face
     That sure he deem'd him borne of noble race.
     All in a woodmans iacket he was clad
     Of Lincolne greene,[2] belayd° with silver lace;   *decorated*
     And on his head an hood with aglets[3] sprad,
45   And by his side his hunters horne he hanging had.

6

Buskins he wore of costliest cordwayne,[4]
     Pinckt[5] upon gold, and paled[6] part per part,
     As then the guize° was for each gentle swayne;   *fashion*

1. Some editors emend to *ears* for sake of the rhyme.
2. Lincolne greene: bright green cloth made at Lincoln.
3. Metallic tips of cords or laces.
4. Cordovan, Spanish leather.
5. Ornamented with figures cut in such a way that the gold lining showed through.
6. Marked with vertical stripes.

In his right hand he held a trembling dart,
50   Whose fellow he before had sent apart;
    And in his left he held a sharpe borespeare,
    With which he wont to launch the salvage hart
    Of many a Lyon, and of many a Beare
  That first unto his hand in chase did happen neare.

7

55 Whom *Calidore* a while well having vewed,[7]
    At length bespake; what meanes this, gentle swaine?
    Why hath thy hand too bold it selfe embrewed°   *stained*
    In blood of knight, the which by thee is slaine,
    By thee no knight; which armes impugneth plaine?
60   Certes (said he) loth were I to have broken
    The law of armes; yet breake it should againe,
    Rather then let my selfe of wight be stroken,
  So long as these two armes were able to be wroken.°   *avenged*

8

  For not I him as this his Ladie here
65   May witnesse well, did offer first to wrong,
    Ne surely thus unarm'd I likely were;
    But he me first, through pride and puissance strong
    Assayld, not knowing what to armes doth long.°   *belong*
    Perdie great blame, (then said Sir *Calidore*)
70   For armed knight a wight unarm'd to wrong.
    But then aread, thou gentle chyld, wherefore
  Betwixt you two began this strife and sterne uprore.

9

  That shall I sooth (said he) to you declare.
    I whose unryper yeares are yet unfit
75   For thing of weight, or worke of greater care,
    Doe spend my dayes, and bend my carelesse wit
    To salvage chace, where I thereon may hit
    In all this forrest, and wyld wooddie raine:°   *domain*
    Where, as this day I was enraunging° it,   *rambling in*
80   I chaunst to meete this knight, who there lyes slaine,
  Together with his Ladie, passing on the plaine.

10

  The knight, as ye did see, on horsebacke was,
    And this his Ladie, (that him ill became,)
    On her faire feet by his horse side did pas
85   Through thicke and thin, unfit for any Dame.

---

7. The problem is that a woodsman should not attack a knight, and vice versa.

Yet not content, more to increase his shame,
When so she lagged, as she needs mote so,[8]
He with his speare, that was to him great blame,
Would thumpe her forward, and inforce to goe,
90   Weeping to him in vaine, and making piteous woe.

11

Which when I saw, as they me passed by,
Much was I moved in indignant mind,
And gan to blame him for such cruelty
Towards a Ladie, whom with vsage kind
95   He rather should have taken up behind.
Wherewith he wroth, and full of proud disdaine,
Tooke in foule scorne, that I such fault did find,
And me in lieu thereof revil'd againe,
Threatning to chastize me, as doth t'a chyld pertaine.[9]

12

100   Which I no lesse disdayning, backe returned
His scornefull taunts unto his teeth againe,
That he streight way with haughtie choler burned,
And with his speare strooke me one stroke or twaine;
Which I enforst to beare though to my paine,
105   Cast to requite,° and with a slender dart,   avenge
Fellow of this I beare, throwne not in vaine,
Strooke him, as seemeth, underneath the hart,
That through the wound his spirit shortly did depart.

13

Much did Sir *Calidore* admyre his speach
110   Tempred so well, but more admyr'd the stroke
That through the mayles had made so strong a breach
Into his hart, and had so sternely wroke°   inflicted
His wrath on him, that first occasion broke.
Yet rested not, but further gan inquire
115   Of that same Ladie, whether what he spoke,
Were soothly so, and that th'unrighteous ire
Of her owne knight, had given him his owne due hire.°   reward

14

Of all which, when as she could nought deny,
But cleard that stripling of th'imputed blame,
120   Sayd then Sir *Calidore*; neither will I
Him charge with guilt, but rather doe quite clame:°   acquit, declare free

8. I.e., as she necessarily did.   9. I.e., treating me like a child.

For what he spake, for you he spake it, Dame,
And what he did, he did him selfe to save:
Against both which that knight wrought knightlesse shame.
125   For knights and all men this by nature have,
Towards all womenkind them kindly to behave.

15

But sith that he is gone irrevocable,
Please it you Ladie, to us to aread,
What cause could make him so dishonourable,
130   To drive you so on foot unfit to tread,
And lackey by him, gainst all womanhead?
Certes Sir knight (sayd she) full loth I were
To rayse a lyving blame against the dead:
But since it me concernes, my selfe to clere,
135 I will the truth discover,° as it chaunst whylere.   reveal

16

This day, as he and I together roade
Upon our way, to which we weren bent,
We chaunst to come foreby° a covert glade   near
Within a wood, whereas a Ladie gent
140   Sate with a knight in joyous jolliment,
Of their franke loves, free from all gealous spyes:
Faire was the Ladie sure, that mote content
An hart, not carried with too curious eyes,
And unto him did shew all lovely courtesyes.

17

145 Whom when my knight did see so lovely faire,
He inly gan her lover to envy,
And wish, that he part of his spoyle might share.
Whereto when as my presence he did spy
To be a let,° he bad me by and by   hindrance
150   For to alight: but when as I was loth,
My loves owne part to leave so suddenly,
He with strong hand down from his steed me throw'th,
And with presumpteous powre against that knight streight
                                                    [go'th.

18

Unarm'd all was the knight, as then more meete
155   For Ladies service, and for loves delight,
Then fearing any foeman there to meete:
Whereof he taking oddes, streight bids him dight
Himselfe to yeeld his love, or else to fight.

Whereat the other starting up dismayd,
160   Yet boldly answer'd, as he rightly might;
        To leave his love he should be ill apayd,°   *ill pleased*
In which he had good right gaynst all, that it gainesayd.

19

Yet since he was not presently in plight
        Her to defend, or his to justifie,
165   He him requested, as he was a knight,
        To lend him day his better right to trie,
        Or stay till he his armes, which were thereby,
        Might lightly fetch. But he was fierce and whot,
        Ne time would give, nor any termes aby,°   *abide, submit to*
170   But at him flew, and with his speare him smot;
From which to thinke to save himselfe, it booted not.

20

Meanewhile his Ladie, which this outrage saw,
        Whilest they together for the quarrey° strove,   *prey*
        Into the covert did her selfe withdraw,
175   And closely hid her selfe within the grove.
        My knight hers soone, as seemes, to daunger drove
        And left sore wounded: but when her he mist,
        He woxe halfe mad, and in that rage gan rove
        And range through all the wood, where so he wist
180   She hidden was, and sought her so long, as him list.

21

But when as her he by no meanes could find,
        After long search and chauff,° he turned backe   *rage*
        Unto the place, where me he left behind:
        There gan he me to curse and ban,° for lacke   *curse*
185   Of that faire bootie, and with bitter wracke°   *vengeance*
        To wreake on me the guilt of his owne wrong.
        Of all which I yet glad to beare the packe,
        Strove to appease him, and perswaded long:
But still his passion grew more violent and strong.

22

190   Then as it were t'avenge his wrath on mee,
        When forward we should fare, he flat refused
        To take me up (as this young man did see)
        Upon his steed, for no iust cause accused,
        But forst to trot on foot, and foule misused,
195   Pounching me with the butt end of his speare,
        In vaine complayning, to be so abused.

For he regarded neither playnt nor teare,
But more enforst my paine, the more my plaints to heare.

23

So passed we, till this young man us met,
200   And being moov'd with pittie of my plight,
    Spake, as was meet, for ease of my regret:
    Whereof befell, what now is in your sight.
    Now sure (then said Sir *Calidore*) and right
    Me seemes, that him befell by his owne fault:
205   Who ever thinkes through confidence of might,
    Or through support of count'nance proud and hault°   *haughty*
To wrong the weaker, oft falles in his owne assault.

24

Then turning backe unto that gentle boy,
    Which had himselfe so stoutly well acquit;
210   Seeing his face so lovely sterne and coy,°   *shy, modest*
    And hearing th'answeres of his pregnant wit,
    He praysd it much, and much admyred it;
    That sure he weend him borne of noble blood,
    With whom those graces did so goodly fit:
215   And when he long had him beholding stood,
He burst into these words, as to him seemed good.

25

Faire gentle swayne, and yet as stout° as fayre,   *brave*
    That in these woods amongst the Nymphs dost wonne,
    Which daily may to thy sweete lookes repayre,
220   As they are wont unto *Latonaes* sonne,[1]
    After his chace on woodie *Cynthus*[2] donne:
    Well may I certes such an one thee read,
    As by thy worth thou worthily hast wonne,
    Or surely borne of some Heroicke sead,
225 That in thy face appeares and gratious goodly head.

26

But should it not displease thee it to tell;
    (Unlesse thou in these woods thy selfe conceale,
    For love amongst the woodie Gods to dwell;)
    I would thy selfe require thee to reveale,
230   For deare affection and unfayned zeale,
    Which to thy noble personage I beare,
    And wish thee grow in worship and great weale.°   *wealth, prosperity*

---

1. Apollo.

2. A hill on Delos. Apollo is supposed to have enjoyed chasing nymphs on Delos.

For since the day that armes I first did reare,
I never saw in any greater hope appeare.

27

235   To whom then thus the noble youth; may be
       Sir knight, that by discovering my estate,
       Harme may arise unweeting unto me;
       Nathelesse, sith ye so courteous seemed late,
       To you I will not feare it to relate.
240   Then wote ye that I am a Briton borne,
       Sonne of a King, how ever thorough fate
       Or fortune I my countrie have forlorne,
And lost the crowne, which should my head by right adorne.

28

And *Tristram* is my name, the onely heire[3]
245   Of good king *Meliogras* which did rayne
       In Cornewale, till that he through lives despeire
       Untimely dyde, before I did attaine
       Ripe yeares of reason, my right to maintaine.
       After whose death, his brother seeing mee
250   An infant, weake a kingdome to sustaine,
       Upon him tooke the roiall high degree,
And sent me, where him list, instructed for to bee.

29

The widow Queene my mother, which then hight
       Faire *Emiline*, conceiving then great feare
255   Of my fraile safetie, resting in the might
       Of him, that did the kingly Scepter beare,
       Whose gealous dread° induring not a peare,   *fear*
       Is wont to cut off all, that doubt may breed,
       Thought best away me to remove somewhere
260   Into some forrein land, where as no need
Of dreaded daunger might his doubtfull humor° feed.   *i.e., suspicion*

30

So taking counsell of a wise man red,°   *learned*
       She was by him adviz'd, to send me quight
       Out of the countrie, wherein I was bred,
265   The which the fertile *Lionesse* is hight,
       Into the land of *Faerie*, where no wight
       Should weet of me, nor worke me any wrong.
       To whose wise read° she hearkning, sent me streight   *counsel*

---

3. Spenser's version of the early life of Sir Tristram follows closely Malory, 8.1, but Spenser changes the mother's name from Elizabeth to Emiline.

Into this land, where I have wond thus long,
270   Since I was ten yeares old, now growen to stature strong.

31

All which my daies I have not lewdly spent,
   Nor spilt the blossome of my tender yeares
   In ydlesse, but as was convenient,
   Have trayned bene with many noble feres°   *companions*
275   In gentle thewes,° and such like seemely leres.°   *customs / lessons*
   Mongst which my most delight hath alwaies been,
   To hunt the salvage chace amongst my peres,
   Of all that raungeth in the forrest greene;
Of which none is to me unknowne, that ev'r was seene.

32

280   Ne is there hauke, which mantleth° her on pearch,   *stretches wings*
   Whether high towring, or accoasting° low,   *skimming along the ground*
   But I the measure of her flight doe search,
   And all her pray, and all her diet know.
   Such be our joyes, which in these forrests grow:
285   Onely the use of armes, which most I joy,
   And fitteth most for noble swayne to know,
   I have not tasted yet, yet past a boy,
And being now high time these strong joynts to imploy.

33

Therefore, good Sir, sith now occasion fit
290   Doth fall, whose like hereafter seldome may,
   Let me this crave, unworthy though of it,
   That ye will make me Squire without delay,
   That from henceforth in batteilous array
   I may beare armes, and learne to use them right;
295   The rather since that fortune hath this day
   Given to me the spoile of this dead knight,
These goodly gilden armes, which I have won in fight.

34

All which when well Sir *Calidore* had heard,
   Him much more now, then earst he gan admire,
300   For the rare hope which in his yeares appear'd,
   And thus replide; faire chyld, the high desire
   To love of armes, which in you doth aspire,
   I may not certes without blame denie;
   But rather wish, that some more noble hire,
305   (Though none more noble then is chevalrie,)
I had, you to reward with greater dignitie.

35

There him he causd to kneele, and made to sweare
   Faith to his knight, and truth to Ladies all,
   And never to be recreant, for feare
310   Of perill, or of ought that might befall:
   So he him dubbed,° and his Squire did call.   *made a knight*
   Full glad and joyous then young *Tristram* grew,
   Like as a flowre, whose silken leaves small,
   Long shut up in the bud from heavens vew,
315 At length breakes forth, and brode displayes his smyling hew.

36

Thus when they long had treated to and fro,[4]
   And *Calidore* betooke him to depart,
   Chyld° *Tristram* prayd, that he with him might goe   *knight*
   On his adventure, vowing not to start,
320   But wayt on him in every place and part.
   Whereat Sir *Calidore* did much delight,
   And greatly joy'd at his so noble hart,
   In hope he sure would prove a doughtie knight:
Yet for the time this answere he to him behight.

37

325 Glad would I surely be, thou courteous Squire,
   To have thy presence in my present quest,
   That mote thy kindled courage set on fire,
   And flame forth honour in thy noble brest:
   But I am bound by vow, which I profest
330   To my dread Soveraine, when I it assayd,
   That in atchievement of her high behest,
   I should no creature joyne unto mine ayde,
For thy I may not graunt, that ye so greatly prayde.

38

But since this Ladie is all desolate,
335   And needeth safegard now upon her way,
   Ye may doe well in this her needfull state
   To succour her, from daunger of dismay;
   That thankfull guerdon may to you repay.
   The noble ympe of such new service fayne,
340   It gladly did accept, as he did say.
   So taking courteous leave, they parted twayne,
And *Calidore* forth passed to his former payne.°   *labor, quest*

4. I.e., conversed about various subjects.

39

But *Tristram* then despoyling that dead knight
   Of all those goodly implements of prayse,
345   Long fed his greedie eyes with the faire sight
   Of the bright mettall, shyning like Sunne rayes;
   Handling and turning them a thousand wayes.
   And after having them upon him dight,
   He tooke that Ladie, and her up did rayse
350   Upon the steed of her owne late dead knight,
So with her marched forth, as she did him behight.

40

There to their fortune leave we them awhile,
   And turne we backe to good Sir *Calidore*;
   Who ere he thence had traveild many a mile,
355   Came to the place, whereas ye heard afore
   This knight, whom *Tristram* slew, had wounded sore
   Another knight in his despiteous pryde;
   There he that knight found lying on the flore,
   With many wounds full perilous and wyde,
360   That all his garments, and the grasse in vermeill° dyde.   *red*

41

And there beside him sate upon the ground
   His wofull Ladie, piteously complayning
   With loud laments that most unluckie stound,
   And her sad selfe with carefull hand constrayning
365   To wype his wounds, and ease their bitter payning.
   Which sorie sight when *Calidore* did vew
   With heavie eyne, from teares uneath refrayning,
   His mightie hart their mournefull case can rew,
And for their better comfort to them nigher drew.

42

370   Then speaking to the Ladie, thus he sayd:
   Ye dolefull Dame, let not your griefe empeach°   *hinder, prevent*
   To tell, what cruell hand hath thus arayd°   *afflicted*
   This knight unarm'd, with so unknightly breach
   Of armes, that if I yet him nigh may reach,
375   I may avenge him of so foule despight.
   The Ladie hearing his so courteous speach,
   Gan reare her eyes as to the chearefull light,
And from her sory hart few heavie words forth sight.°   *sighed*

43

In which she shew'd, how that discourteous knight
380   (Whom *Tristram* slew) them in that shadow found,

Joying together in unblam'd delight,
   And him unarm'd, as now he lay on ground,
   Charg'd with his speare and mortally did wound,
   Withouten cause, but onely her to reaue°   *steal*
385   From him, to whom she was for ever bound:
   Yet when she fled into that covert greave,°   *grove, thicket*
He her not finding, both them thus nigh dead did leave.

44

When *Calidore* this ruefull storie had
   Well understood, he gan of her demand,
390   What manner wight he was, and how yclad,
   Which had this outrage wrought with wicked hand.
   She then, like as she best could understand,
   Him thus describ'd, to be of stature large,
   Clad all in gilden armes, with azure band
395   Quartred athwart,° and bearing in his targe°   *transversely / shield*
A Ladie on rough waves, row'd in a sommer barge.

45

Then gan Sir *Calidore* to ghesse streight way
   By many signes, which she described had,
   That this was he, whom *Tristram* earst did slay,
400   And to her said; Dame be no longer sad:
   For he, that hath your Knight so ill bestad,°   *beset*
   Is now him selfe in much more wretched plight;
   These eyes him saw upon the cold earth sprad,
   The meede of his desert for that despight,
405   Which to your selfe he wrought, & to your loved knight.

46

Therefore faire Lady lay aside this griefe,
   Which ye have gathered to your gentle hart,
   For that displeasure; and thinke what reliefe
   Were best devise for this your lovers smart,
410   And how ye may him hence, and to what part
   Convay to be recur'd.° She thankt him deare,   *recovered*
   Both for that newes he did to her impart,
   And for the courteous care, which he did beare
Both to her love; and to her selfe in that sad dreare.

47

415   Yet could she not devise by any wit,
   How thence she might convay him to some place.
   For him to trouble she it thought unfit,
   That was a straunger to her wretched case;

And him to beare, she thought it thing too base.
420   Which when as he perceiv'd, he thus bespake;
Faire Lady let it not you seeme disgrace,
To beare this burden on your dainty backe;
My selfe will beare a part, coportion of your packe.

48

So off he did his shield, and downeward layd
425   Upon the ground, like to an hollow beare;[5]
And powring balme, which he had long purvayd,
Into his wounds, him up thereon did reare,
And twixt them both with parted° paines did beare,   *divided in parts, shared*
Twixt life and death, not knowing what was donne.
430   Thence they him carried to a Castle neare,
In which a worthy auncient Knight did wonne:
Where what ensu'd, shall in next Canto be begonne.

Canto III

Calidore brings Priscilla home,
Pursues the Blatant Beast:
Saves Serena whitest Calepine
By Turpine is opprest.

1

True is, that whilome that good Poet[1] sayd,
The gentle minde by gentle deeds is knowne.
For a man by nothing is so well bewrayd,
As by his manners, in which plaine is showne
5   Of what degree and what race he is growne.
For seldome seene, a trotting Stalion get
An ambling Colt, that is his proper owne:
So seldome seene, that one in basenesse set
Doth noble courage shew, with curteous manners met.[2]

2

10   But evermore contrary hath bene tryde,
That gentle bloud will gentle manners breed;
As well may be in *Calidore* descryde,
By late ensample of that courteous deed,
Done to that wounded Knight in his great need,
15   Whom on his backe he bore, till he him brought
Unto the Castle where they had decreed.
There of the Knight, the which that Castle ought,
To make abode that night he greatly was besought.

---

5. I.e., bier, a stretcher. Calidore is using his shield to
carry off a wounded man.

1. Chaucer.
2. Bhattacherje (*Var.*, p. 330) cites Castiglione as source.

3

He was to weete a man of full ripe yeares,
20   That in his youth had beene of mickle might,
      And borne great sway in armes amongst bis peares:
      But now weake age had dimd his candle light.
      Yet was he courteous still to every wight,
      And loved all that did to armes incline.
25   And was the father of that wounded Knight,
      Whom *Calidore* thus carried on his chine,°   *back*
And *Aldus* was his name, and his sonnes *Aladine*.[3]

4

Who when he saw his sonne so ill bedight,
      With bleeding wounds, brought home upon a Beare,°   *bier*
30   By a faire Lady, and a straunger Knight,
      Was inly touched with compassion deare,
      And deare affection of so dolefull dreare,
      That he these words burst forth; Ah sory boy,
      Is this the hope that to my hoary heare
35   Thou brings? aie me, is this the timely joy,
Which I expected long, now turnd to sad annoy?

5

Such is the weakenesse of all mortall hope;
      So tickle° is the state of earthly things,   *unreliable, changeable*
      That ere they come unto their aymed° scope,   *intended*
40   They fall too short of our fraile reckonings,
      And bring us bale and bitter sorrowings,
      In stead of comfort, which we should embrace:
      This is the state of Keasars° and of Kings.   *emperors*
      Let none therefore, that is in meaner place,
45 Too greatly grieve at any his unlucky case.

6

So well and wisely did that good old Knight
      Temper his griefe, and turned it to cheare,
      To cheare his guests, whom he had stayd that night,
      And make their welcome to them well appeare:
50   That to Sir *Calidore* was easie geare;°   *matter*
      But that faire Lady would be cheard for nought,
      But sigh'd and sorrow'd for her lover deare,
      And inly did afflict her pensive thought,
With thinking to what case her name should now be brought.

3. The meaning of these names has not been established.

7

55   For she was daughter to a noble Lord,
        Which dwelt thereby, who sought her to affy°   *betroth*
        To a great pere; but she did disaccord,
        Ne could her liking to his love apply,
        But lov'd this fresh young Knight, who dwelt her ny,
60   The lusty *Aladine*, though meaner borne,
        And of lesse livelood° and liability,   *livelihood, prosperity*
        Yet full of valour, the which did adorne
   His meanesse much, & make her th'others riches scorne.[4]

8

     So having both found fit occasion,
65   They met together in that luckelesse glade;
        Where that proud Knight in his presumption
        The gentle *Aladine* did earst invade,
        Being unarm'd, and set in secret shade.
        Whereof she now bethinking, gan t'advize,
70   How great a hazard she at earst had made
        Of her good feme, and further gan devize,
   How she the blame might salve with coloured disguize.

9

     But *Calidore* with all good courtesie
        Fain'd her to frolicke, and to put away
75   The pensive fit of her melancholie;
        And that old Knight by all meanes did assay,
        To make them both as merry as he may.
        So they the evening past, till time of rest,
        When *Calidore* in seemly good array
80   Unto his bowre was brought, and there undrest,
   Did sleepe all night through weary travell of his quest.

10

     But faire *Priscilla* (so that Lady hight)
        Would to no bed, nor take no kindely sleepe,
        But by her wounded love did watch all night,
85   And all the night for bitter anguish weepe,
        And with her teares his wounds did wash and steepe.°   *soak*
        So well she washt them, and so well she wacht him,
        That of the deadly swound, in which full deepe

---

4. Spenser is not claiming that Aladine is of mean or humble birth, merely that he is not a "great pere" as is Priscilla's father. Aladine is, nevertheless, of gentle origin.

He drenched was, she at the length dispacht him,
90   And drove away the stound, which mortally attacht him.

11

The morrow next, when day gan to uplooke,
  He also gan uplooke with drery eye,
  Like one that out of deadly dreame awooke:
  Where when he saw his faire *Priscilla* by,
95   He deepely sigh'd, and groaned inwardly,
  To thinke of this ill state, in which she stood,
  To which she for his sake had weetingly
  Now brought her selfe, and blam'd° her noble blood: *dishonored*
For first, next after life, he tendered° her good.   *cherished, cared for*

12

100 Which she perceiving, did with plenteous teares
  His care more then her owne compassionate,
  Forgetfull of her owne, to minde his feares:
  So both conspiring, gan to intimate
  Each others griefe with zeale affectionate,
105   And twixt them twaine with equall care to cast,
  How to save whole her hazarded estate;
  For which the onely helpe now left them last
Seem'd to be *Calidore:* all other helpes were past.

13

Him they did deeme, as sure to them he seemed,
110   A courteous Knight, and full of faithfull trust:
  Therefore to him their cause they best esteemed
  Whole to commit, and to his dealing just.
  Earely, so soone as *Titans*° beames forth brust   *the sun's*
  Through the thicke clouds, in which they steeped lay
115   All night in darkenesse, duld with yron rust,
  Calidore rising up as fresh as day,
Gan freshly him addresse unto his former way.

14

But first him seemed fit, that wounded Knight
  To visite, after this nights perillous passe,°   *passage*
120   And to salute him, if he were in plight,
  And eke that Lady his faire lovely lasse.
  There he him found much better then he was,
  And moved speach to him of things of course,°   *i.e., ordinary, usual*
  The anguish of his paine to overpasse:
125   Mongst which he namely did to him discourse,
Of former daies mishap, his sorrowes wicked sourse.

15

Of which occasion *Aldine* taking hold,
   Gan breake to him the fortunes of his love,
   And all his disadventures to unfold;
130   That *Calidore* it dearly deepe did move.
   In th'end his kyndly courtesie to prove,
   He him by all the bands of love besought,
   And as it mote a faithfull friend behove,
   To safeconduct his love, and not for ought
135 To leave, till to her fathers house he had her brought.

16

Sir *Calidore* his faith thereto did plight,
   It to performe: so after little stay,
   That she her selfe had to the journey dight,
   He passed forth with her in faire array,
140   Fearelesse, who ought did thinke, or ought did say,
   Sith his own thought he knew most cleare from wite.°   *blame*
   So as they past together on their way,
   He can devize this counter-cast° of slight,   *trick*
To give faire colour to that Ladies cause in sight.

17

145 Streight to the carkasse of that Knight he went,
   The cause of all this evill, who was slaine
   The day before by just avengement
   Of noble *Tristram*, where it did remaine:
   There he the necke thereof did cut in twaine,
150   And tooke with him the head, the signe of shame.
   So forth he passed thorough that daies paine,
   Till to that Ladies fathers house he came,
Most pensive man, through feare, what of his childe became.

18

There he arriving boldly, did present
155   The fearefull Lady to her father deare,
   Most perfect pure, and guiltlesse innocent
   Of blame, as he did on his Knighthood sweare,
   Since first he saw her, and did free from feare
   Of a discourteous Knight, who her had reft,
160   And by outragious force away did beare:
   Witnesse thereof he shew'd his head there left,
And wretched life forlorne for vengement of his theft.[5]

5. Calidore's "white lie" has been the occasion of much tongue-clacking among the critics, but Judson (*Var.*, p. 341) cites Guazzo: "I denie not, but that it is commendable to coyne a lye at some time, and in some place, so that it tende to some honest ende."

19

Most joyfull man her sire was her to see,
   And heare th'adventure of her late mischaunce;
165   And thousand thankes to *Calidore* for fee
   Of his large paines in her deliveraunce
   Did yeeld; Ne lesse the Lady did advaunce.
   Thus having her restored trustily,
   As he had vow'd, some small continuaunce
170   He there did make, and then most carefully
Unto his first exploite he did him selfe apply.

20

So as he was pursuing of his quest
   He chaunst to come whereas a jolly Knight,
   In covert shade him selfe did safely rest,
175   To solace with his Lady in delight:
   His warlike armes he had from him undight;
   For that him selfe he thought from daunger free,
   And far from envious eyes that mote him spight
   And eke the Lady was full faire to see,
180   And courteous withall, becomming her degree.[6]

21

To whom Sir *Calidore* approaching nye,
   Ere they were well aware of living wight,
   Them much abasht, but more him selfe thereby,
   That he so rudely did uppon them light,
185   And troubled had their quiet loves delight.
   Yet since it was his fortune, not his fault,
   Him selfe thereof he labour'd to acquite,
   And pardon crav'd for his so rash default,
That he gainst courtesie so fowly did default.

22

190   With which his gentle words and goodly wit
   He soone allayd that Knights conceiv'd displeasure,
   That he besought him downe by him to sit,
   That they mote treat of things abrode at leasure;
   And of adventures, which had in his measure
195   Of so long waies to him befallen late.
   So downe he sate, and with delightfull pleasure
   His long adventures gan to him relate,
Which he endured had through daungerous debate.°   *contest*

---

6. Spenser now places Calidore in a situation that parallels the Aladine-Priscilla episode. The purpose is to contrast courtesy with rudeness.

23

Of which whilest they discoursed both together,
200   The faire *Serena* (so his Lady hight)
Allur'd with myldnesse of the gentle wether,
And pleasaunce of the place, the which was dight
With divers flowres distinct° with rare delight;   *marked*
Wandred about the fields, as liking led
205   Her wavering lust° after her wandring sight,   *pleasure*
To make a garland to adorne her hed,
Without suspect of ill or daungers hidden dred.

24

All sodainely out of the forrest nere
The *Blatant Beast* forth rushing unaware,
210   Caught her thus loosely wandring here and there,
And in his wide great mouth away her bare.
Crying aloud in vaine, to shew her sad misfare°   *misfortune*
Unto the Knights, and calling oft for ayde,
Who with the horrour of her haplesse care
215   Hastily starting up, like men dismayde,
Ran after fast to reskue the distressed mayde.

25

The Beast with their pursuit incited more,
Into the wood was bearing her apace
For to have spoyled her, when *Calidore*
220   Who was more light of foote and swift in chace,
Him overtooke in middest of his race:
And fiercely charging him with all his might,
Forst to forgoe his pray there in the place,
And to betake him selfe to fearefull flight;
225   For he durst not abide with *Calidore* to fight.

26

Who nathelesse, when he the Lady saw
There left on ground, though in full evill plight,
Yet knowing that her Knight now neare did draw,
Staide not to succour her in that affright,
230   But follow'd fast the Monster in his flight:
Through woods and hils he follow'd him so fast,
That he nould let him breath nor gather spright,
But forst him gape and gaspe, with dread aghast,
As if his lungs and lites° were nigh a sunder brast.[7]   *lungs*

7. Calidore does not appear again until Canto 9.

27

235 And now by this Sir *Calepine*[8] (so hight)
    Came to the place, where he his Lady found
    In dolorous dismay and deadly plight,
    All in gore bloud there tumbled on the ground,
    Having both sides through grypt with griesly wound.
240   His weapons soone from him he threw away,
    And stouping downe to her in drery swound,
    Uprear'd her from the ground, whereon she lay,
And in his tender armes her forced up to stay.

28

So well he did his busie paines apply,
245   That the faint sprite he did revoke° againe,   *call back*
    To her fraile mansion of mortality.
    Then up he tooke her twixt his armes twaine,
    And setting on his steede, her did sustaine
    With carefull hands soft footing° her beside,   *walking*
250   Till to some place of rest they mote attaine,
    Where she in safe assuraunce mote abide,
Till she recured were of those her woundes wide.

29

Now when as *Phœbus* with his fiery waine°   *wagon*
    Unto his Inne° began to draw apace;   *house of the zodiac*
255   Tho wexing weary of that toylesome paine,
    In travelling on foote so long a space,
    Not wont on foote with heavy armes to trace,°   *walk*
    Downe in a dale forby a rivers syde,
    He chaunst to spie a faire and stately place,
260   To which he meant his weary steps to guyde,
In hope there for his love some succour to provyde.

30

But comming to the rivers side, he found
    That hardly passable on foote it was:
    Therefore there still he stood as in a stound,
265   Ne wist which way he through the foord mote pas.
    Thus whilest he was in this distressed case,
    Devising what to doe, he nigh espyde
    An armed Knight approaching to the place,
    With a faire Lady lincked by his syde,
270 The which themselves prepard through the foord to ride.[9]

---

8. Calepine, whose adventures make up the action of this book until Calidore returns in Canto 9, seems to be related by his name to Calidore: Greek: *kale*, "beautiful."

9. The Turpine episode is modeled on the Pinabello episode in Aristo, *Orlando Furioso* 22.104 ff.

31

Whom *Calepine* saluting (as became)
    Besought of courtesie in that his neede,
    For safe conducting of his sickely Dame,
    Through that same perillous foord with better heede,
275   To take him up behinde upon his steed,
    To whom that other did this taunt returne.
    Perdy thou peasant Knight, mightst rightly reed
    Me then to be full base and evill borne,
If I would beare behinde a burden of such scorne.

32

280 But as thou hast thy steed forlorne with shame,
    So fire on foote till thou another gayne,
    And let thy Lady likewise doe the same,
    Or beare her on thy backe with pleasing payne,
    And prove thy manhood on the billowes vayne.
285   With which rude speach his Lady much displeased,
    Did him reprove, yet could him not restrayne,
    And would on her owne Palfrey him have eased,
For pitty of his Dame, whom she saw so diseased.°   *ill and uncomfortable*

33

Sir *Calepine* her thanckt, yet inly wroth
290   Against her Knight, her gentlenesse refused,
    And carelesly into the river goth,
    As in despight to be so fowle abused
    Of a rude churle, whom often he accused
    Of fowle discourtesie, unfit for Knight
295   And strongly wading through the waves unused,°   *unaccustomed*
    With speare in th'one hand, stayd him selfe upright,
With th'other staide his Lady up with steddy might.

34

And all the while, that same discourteous Knight,
    Stood on the further bancke beholding him,
300   At whose calamity, for more despight
    He laught, and mockt to see him like to swim.
    But when as *Calepine* came to the brim,
    And saw his carriage past that perill well,
    Looking at that same Carle with count'nance grim,
305   His heart with vengeaunce inwardly did swell,
And forth at last did breake in speaches sharpe and fell.

35

Unknightly Knight, the blemish of that name,
   And blot of all that armes uppon them take,
   Which is the badge of honour and of fame,
310   Loe I defie thee, and here challenge make,
   That thou for ever doe those armes forsake;
   And be for ever held a recreant Knight,
   Unlesse thou dare for thy deare Ladies sake,
   And for thine owne defence on foote alight,
315 To justifie thy fault gainst me in equall fight.

36

The dastard, that did heare him selfe defyde,
   Seem'd not to weigh his threatfull words at all,
   But laught them out, as if his greater pryde,
   Did scorne the challenge of so base a thrall:
320   Or had no courage, or else had no gall.
   So much the more was *Calepine* offended,
   That him to no revenge he forth could call,
   But both his challenge and him selfe contemned,
Ne cared as a coward so to be condemned.

37

325 But he nought weighing what he sayd or did,
   Turned his steede about another way,
   And with his Lady to the Castle rid,
   Where was his won; ne did the other stay,
   But after went directly as he may,
330   For his sicke charge some harbour there to seeke;
   Where he arriving with the fall of day,
   Drew to the gate, and there with prayers meeke,
And myld entreaty lodging did for her beseeke.

38

But the rude Porter that no manners had,
335   Did shut the gate against him in his face,
   And entraunce boldly unto him forbad.
   Nathelesse the Knight now in so needy case,
   Gan him entreat even with submission base,
   And humbly praid to let them in that night:
340   Who to him aunswer'd, that there was no place
   Of lodging fit for any errant Knight,
Unlesse that with his Lord he formerly° did fight.   *first*

39

Full loth am I (quoth he) as now at earst,
   When day is spent, and rest us needeth most,

345 And that this Lady, both whose sides are pearst
 With wounds, is ready to forgo the ghost:
 Ne would I gladly combate with mine host,
 That should to me such curtesie afford,
 Unlesse that I were thereunto enforst.
350 But yet aread to me, how hight thy Lord,
That doth thus strongly ward the Castle of the ford.

40

 His name (quoth he) if that thou list to learne,
 Is hight Sir *Turpine*,[1] one of mickle might,
 And manhood rare, but terrible and stearne
355 In all assaies to every errant Knight,
 Because of one, that wrought him fowle despight.
 Ill seemes (sayd he) if he so valiaunt be,
 That he should be so sterne to stranger wight:
 For seldome yet did living creature see,
360 That curtesie and manhood ever disagree.

41

 But go thy waies to him, and fro me say,
 That here is at his gate an errant Knight,
 That house-rome craves, yet would be loth t'assay
 The proofe of battell, now in doubtfull night,
365 Or curtesie with rudenesse to requite:
 Yet if he needes will fight, crave leave till morne,
 And tell withall, the lamentable plight,
 In which this Lady languisheth forlorne,
That pitty craves, as he of woman was yborne.

42

370 The groome went streight way in, and to his Lord
 Declar'd the message, which that Knight did move;
 Who sitting with his Lady then at bord,°   *table*
 Not onely did not his demaund approve,
 But both himselfe revil'd, and eke his love;
375 Albe his Lady, that *Blandina*[2] hight,
 Him of ungentle vsage did reprove
 And earnestly entreated that they might
Finde favour to be lodged there for that same night.

43

 Yet would he not perswaded be for ought,
380 Ne from his currish will awhit reclame.°   *recant*
 Which answer when the groome returning, brought

1. Latin: *turpis*, "base."   2. Latin: *blandus*, "tempting."

To *Calepine*, his heart did inly flame
With wrathfull fury for so foule a shame,
That he could not thereof avenged bee:
385   But most for pitty of his dearest Dame,
Whom now in deadly daunger he did see;
Yet had no meanes to comfort, nor procure her glee.

44

But all in vaine; for why,° no remedy   *because*
He saw, the present mischiefe to redresse,
390   But th'utmost end perforce for to aby,°   *endure*
Which that nights fortune would for him addresse.
So downe he tooke his Lady in distresse,
And layd her underneath a bush to sleepe,
Cover'd with cold, and wrapt in wretchednesse,
395   Whiles he him selfe all night did nought but weepe,
And wary watch about her for her safegard keepe.

45

The morrow next, so soone as joyous day
Did shew it selfe in sunny beames bedight,
Serena full of dolorous dismay,
400   Twixt darkenesse dread, and hope of living light,
Uprear'd her head to see that chearefull sight.
Then *Calepine*, how ever inly wroth,
And greedy to avenge that vile despight,
Yet for the feeble Ladies sake, full loth
405   To make there lenger stay, forth on his journey goth.

46

He goth on foote all armed by her side,
Upstaying still her selfe uppon her steede,
Being unhable else alone to ride;
So sore her sides, so much her wounds did bleede:
410   Till that at length, in his extreamest neede,
He chaunst far off an armed Knight to spy,
Pursuing him apace with greedy speede,
Whom well he wist to be some enemy,
That meant to make advantage of his misery.

47

415   Wherefore he stayd, till that he nearer drew,
To weet what issue would thereof betyde,
Tho whenas he approched nigh in vew,
By certaine signes he plainely him descryde,
To be the man, that with such scornefull pryde

420
          Had him abusde, and shamed yesterday;
          Therefore misdoubting, least he should misguyde
          His former malice to some new assay,
He cast to keepe him selfe so safely as he may.

48

By this the other came in place likewise,
425
          And couching close his speare and all his powre,
          As bent to some malicious enterprise,
          He bad him stand, t'abide the bitter stoure
          Of his sore vengeaunce, or to make avoure°   *answer*
          Of the lewd words and deedes, which he had done:
430
          With that ran at him, as he would devoure
          His life attonce; who nought could do, but shun
The perill of his pride, or else be overrun.

49

Yet he him still pursew'd from place to place,
          With full intent him cruelly to kill,
435
          And like a wilde goate round about did chace,
          Flying the fury of his bloudy will.
          But his best succour and refuge was still
          Behinde his Ladies backe, who to him cryde,
          And called oft with prayers loud and shrill,
440
          As ever he to Lady was affyde,
To spare her Knight, and rest with reason pacifyde.

50

But he the more thereby enraged was,
          And with more eager felnesse him pursew'd,
          So that at length, after long weary chace,
445
          Having by chaunce a close advantage vew'd,
          He over raught him, having long eschew'd
          His violence in vaine, and with his spere
          Strooke through his shoulder, that the blood ensew'd
          In great aboundance, as a well it were,
450
That forth out of an hill fresh gushing did appere.

51

Yet ceast he not for all that cruell wound,
          But chaste him still, for all his Ladies cry,
          Not satisfyde till on the fatall ground
          He saw his life powrd forth dispiteously:
455
          The which was certes in great jeopardy,
          Had not a wondrous chaunce his reskue wrought,
          And saved from his cruell villany.

Such chaunces oft exceed all humaine thought:
That in another Canto shall to end be brought.

Canto IV

Calepine by a salvage man
from Turpine reskewed is,
And whylest an Infant from a Beare
he saves, his love doth misse.

1

Like as a ship with dreadfull storme long tost,
    Having spent all her mastes and her ground-hold,°   *anchor*
    Now farre from harbour likely to be lost,
    At last some fisher barke° doth neare behold,   *fishing boat*
5   That giveth comfort to her courage cold.
    Such was the state of this most courteous knight
    Being oppressed by that faytour bold,
    That he remayned in most perilous plight,
And his sad Ladie left in pitifull affright.

2

10   Till that by fortune, passing all foresight,
    A salvage man,[1] which in those woods did wonne,
    Drawne with that Ladies loud and piteous shright,°   *shriek*
    Toward the same incessantly did ronne,
    To understand what there was to be donne.
15   There he this most discourteous craven found,
    As fiercely yet, as when he first begonne,
    Chasing the gentle *Calepine* around,
Ne sparing him the more for all his grievous wound.

3

The salvage man, that never till this houre
20   Did taste of pittie, neither gentlesse knew,
    Seeing his sharpe assault and cruell stoure
    Was much emmoved at his perils vew,
    That even his ruder hart began to rew,
    And feele compassion of his evill plight,
25   Against his foe that did him so pursew:
    From whom he meant to free him, if he might,
And him avenge of that so villenous despight.

1. Such savage men are common in 16th-century literature. See Richard Bernheimer, *Wild Men in the Middle Ages*, Cambridge, Mass., 1952.

4

Yet armes or weapon had he none to fight,
  Ne knew the use of warlike instruments,
30 Save such as sudden rage him lent to smite,
  But naked without needfull vestiments,
  To clad his corpse with meete habiliments,
  He cared not for dint of sword nor speere,
  No more then for the strokes of strawes or bents:°   *reeds*
35 For from his mothers wombe, which him did beare
He was invulnerable made by Magicke leare.°   *learning*

5

He stayed not to advize, which way were best
  His foe t'assayle, or how himselfe to gard,
  But with fierce fury and with force infest°   *hostile*
40 Upon him ran; who being well prepard,
  His first assault full warily did ward,
  And with the push of his sharp-pointed speare
  Full on the breast him strooke, so strong and hard,
  That forst him backe recoyle, and reele areare;°   *backward*
45 Yet in his bodie made no wound nor bloud appeare.

6

With that the wyld man more enraged grew,
  Like to a Tygre that hath mist his pray,
  And with mad mood againe upon him flew,
  Regarding neither speare, that mote him slay,
50 Nor his fierce steed, that mote him much dismay.
  The salvage nation doth all dread despize:
  Tho on his shield he griple° hold did lay,   *tenacious, obstinate*
  And held the same so hard, that by no wize
He could him force to loose, or leave his enterprize.

7

55 Long did he wrest and wring it to and fro,
  And every way did try, but all in vaine:
  For he would not his greedie grype forgoe,
  But hayld and puld with all his might and maine,
  That from his steed him nigh he drew againe.
60 Who having now no use of his long speare,
  So nigh at hand, nor force his shield to straine,
  Both speare and shield, as things that needlesse were,
He quite forsooke, and fled himselfe away for feare.

8

But after him the wyld man ran apace,
65 And him pursewed with importune speed,

(For he was swift as any Bucke in chace)
And had he not in his extreamest need,
Bene helped through the swiftnesse of his steed,
He had him overtaken in his flight.
70 Who ever, as he saw him nigh succeed,
Gan cry aloud with horrible affright,
And shrieked out, a thing uncomely for a knight.

9

But when the Salvage saw his labour vaine,
In following of him, that fled so fast,
75 He wearie woxe, and backe return'd againe
With speede unto the place, whereas he last
Had left that couple, nere their utmost cast.°   extreme situation
There he that knight full sorely bleeding found,
And eke the Ladie fearefully aghast,
80 Both for the perill of the present stound,
And also for the sharpnesse of her rankling° wound.   festering

10

For though she were right glad, so rid to bee
From that vile lozell,° which her late offended,   scoundrel
Yet now no lesse encombrance she did see,
85 And perill by this salvage man pretended;°   presented, intended
Gainst whom she saw no meanes to be defended,
By reason that her knight was wounded sore.
Therefore her selfe she wholy recommended
To Gods sole grace, whom she did oft implore,
90 To send her succour, being of all hope forlore.

11

But the wyld man, contrarie to her feare,
Came to her creeping like a fawning hound,
And by rude° tokens made to her appeare   uncivilized, primitive
His deepe compassion of her dolefull stound,
95 Kissing his hands, and crouching to the ground;
For other language had he none nor speach,
But a soft murmure, and confused sound
Of senselesse words, which nature did him teach,
T'expresse his passions, which his reason did empeach.°   hinder

12

100 And comming likewise to the wounded knight,
When he beheld the streames of purple blood
Yet flowing fresh, as moved with the sight,
He made great mone after° his salvage mood,   according to

And running streight into the thickest wood,
105   A certaine herbe from thence unto him brought,
Whose vertue he by use well understood:
The ivyce whereof into his wound he wrought,
And stopt the bleeding straight, ere he it staunched°   *stopped up, blocked*
    thought.

13

Then taking up that Recreants shield and speare,
110   Which earst he left, he signes unto them made,
With him to wend unto his worming neare:
To which he easily did them perswade.
Farre in the forrest by a hollow glade,
Covered with mossie shrubs, which spredding brode
115   Did underneath them make a gloomy shade;
There foot of living creature never trode,
Ne scarse wyld beasts durst come, there was this wights abode.

14

Thether he brought these unacquainted guests;
To whom faire semblance, as he could, he shewed
120   By signes, by lookes, and all his other gests.°   *gestures, behavior*
But the bare ground, with hoarie mosse bestrowed,
Must be their bed, their pillow was unsowed,°   *unsewn*
And the frutes of the forrest was their feast:
For their bad[2] Stuard neither plough'd nor sowed,
125   Ne fed on flesh, ne ever of wyld beast
Did taste the bloud, obaying natures first beheast.

15

Yet howsoever base and meane it were,
They tooke it well, and thanked God for all,
Which had them freed from that deadly feare,
130   And sav'd from being to that caytive thrall.
Here they of force (as fortune now did fall)
Compelled were themselves a while to rest,
Glad of that easement, though it were hut small;
That having there their wounds awhile redrest,
135   They mote the abler be to passe unto the rest.

16

During which time, that wyld man did apply
His best endevour, and his daily paine,
In seeking all the woods both farre and nye

---

2. Probably used here in the sense of "inadequate," because he did not provide them with meat or cultivated food.

For herbes to dresse their wounds; still seeming faine,
140   When ought he did, that did their lyking gaine.
So as ere long he had that knightes wound
Recured well, and made him whole againe:
But that same Ladies hurts no herbe he found,
Which could redresse, for it was inwardly unsound.[3]

17

145   Now when as *Calepine* was woxen strong,
Upon a day he cast abrode to wend,
To take the ayre, and heare the thrushes song,
Unarm'd, as fearing neither foe nor frend,
And without sword his person to defend,
150   There him befell, unlooked for before,
An hard adventure with unhappie end,
A cruell Beare, the which an infant bore
Betwixt his bloodie jawes, besprinckled all with gore.

18

The litle babe did loudly scrike° and squall,   shriek
155   And all the woods with piteous plaints did fill,
As if his cry did meane for helpe to call
To *Calepine*, whose eares those shrieches shrill
Percing his hart with pities point did thrill;
That after him, he ran with zealous haste,
160   To rescue th'infant, ere he did him kill:
Whom though he saw now somewhat overpast,°   gone beyond
Yet by the cry he follow'd, and pursewed fast.

19

Well then him chaunst his heavy armes to want,[4]
Whose burden mote empeach° his needfull speed,   hinder
165   And hinder him from libertie to pant:
For having long time, as his daily weed,
Them wont to weare, and wend on foot for need,
Now wanting them he felt himselfe so light,
That like an Hauke, which feeling her selfe freed
170   From bels and jesses,[5] which did let° her flight,   prevent
Him seem'd his feet did fly, and in their speed delight.

---

3. The nature of Serena's wound, inflicted by the Blatant
Beast, becomes clearer in VI.5. 28 and 6.8–9.
4. I.e., it was fortunate that he lacked his armor and
weapons.

5. Leather straps bound to the feet of falcons, to which
the leash was attached. When falcons were released, they
ordinarily flew with the bells and jesses on their legs.

20

So well he sped him, that the wearie Beare
   Ere long he overtooke, and forst to stay,
   And without weapon him assayling neare,
175   Compeld him soone the spoyle adowne to lay.
   Wherewith the beast enrag'd to lose his pray,
   Upon him turned, and with greedie force
   And furie, to be crossed in his way,
   Gaping full wyde, did thinke without remorse
180 To be aveng'd on him, and to devoure his corse.

21

But the bold knight no whit thereat dismayd,
   But catching up in hand a ragged stone,
   Which lay thereby (so fortune him did ayde)
   Upon him ran, and thrust it all attone
185   Into his gaping throte, that made him grone
   And gaspe for breath, that he nigh choked was,
   Being unable to digest that bone;
   Ne could it upward come, nor downward passe,
Ne could he brooke the coldnesse of the stony masse.

22

190 Whom when as he thus combred did behold,
   Stryving in vaine that nigh his bowels brast,
   He with him closd,° and laying mightie hold   *came together*
   Upon his throte, did gripe his gorge so fast,
   That wanting breath, him downe to ground he cast;
195   And then oppressing him with urgent paine,
   Ere long enforst to breath his utmost blast,
   Gnashing his cruell teeth at him in vaine,
And threatning his sharpe clawes, now wanting powre to
                    [straine.

23

Then tooke he up betwixt his armes twaine
200   The litle babe, sweet relickes of his pray;
   Whom pitying to heare so sore complaine,
   From his soft eyes the teares he wypt away,
   And from his face the filth that did it ray,°   *soil*
   And every litle limbe he searcht around,
205   And every part, that under sweathbands° lay,   *swaddling clothes*
   Least that the beasts sharpe teeth had any wound
Made in his tender flesh, but whole them all he found.

24

So having all his bands againe uptyde,
  He with him thought backe to returne againe:
210 But when he lookt about on every syde,
    To weet which way were best to entertaine,°   *take*
    To bring him to the place, where he would faine,
    He could no path nor tract of foot descry,
    Ne by inquirie learne, nor ghesse by ayme.
215   For nought but woods and forrests farre and nye,
That all about did close the compasse of his eye.

25

Much was he then encombred, ne could tell
  Which way to take: now West he went a while,
  Then Norm; then neither, but as fortune fell.
220 So up and downe he wandred many a mile,
  With wearie travell and uncertaine toile,
  Yet nought the nearer to his journeys end;
  And evermore his lovely litle spoile
  Crying for food, did greatly him offend.°   *bother*
225 So all that day in wandring vainely he did spend.

26

At last about the setting of the Sunne,
  Him selfe out of the forest he did wynd,
  And by good fortune the plaine champion° wonne: *open plain*
  Where looking all about, where he mote fynd
230 Some place of succour to content his mynd,
  At length he heard under the forrests syde
  A voice, that seemed of some woman kynd,
  Which to her selfe lamenting loudly cryde,
And oft complayn'd of fate, and fortune oft defyde.

27

235 To whom approching, when as she perceived
  A stranger wight in place, her plaint she stayd,
  As if she doubted to have bene deceived,
  Or loth to let her sorrowes be bewrayd.
  Whom when as *Calepine* saw so dismayd,
240 He to her drew, and with faire blandishment
  Her chearing up, thus gently to her sayd;
  What be you wofull Dame, which thus lament,
And for what cause declare, so mote ye not repent.°   *be sad*

28

To whom she thus, what need me Sir to tell,
245 That which your selfe have earst ared so right?

A wofull dame ye have me termed well;
   So much more wofull, as my wofull plight
   Cannot redressed be by living wight.
   Nathlesse (quoth he) if need doe not you bynd,
250   Doe it disclose, to ease your grieved spright:
   Oftimes it haps, that sorrowes of the mynd
Find remedie unsought, which seeking cannot fynd.

29

Then thus began the lamentable Dame;
   Sith then ye needs will know the griefe I hoord,
255   I am th'unfortunate *Matilde*[6] by name,
   The wife of bold Sir *Bruin,*[7] who is Lord
   Of all this land, late conquer'd by his sword
   From a great Gyant, called *Cormoraunt;*[8]
   Whom he did overthrow by yonder foord,
260   And in three battailes did so deadly daunt,
That he dare not returne for all his daily vaunt.

30

So is my Lord now seiz'd° of all the land,   *in possession of*
   As in his fee,[9] with peaceable estate,
   And quietly doth hold it in his hand,
265   Ne any dares with him for it debate.
   But to these happie fortunes, cruell fate
   Hath joyn'd one evill, which doth overthrow
   All these our joyes, and all our blisse abate;
   And like in time to further ill to grow,
270   And all this land with endlesse losse to overflow.

31

For th'heavens envying our prosperitie,
   Have not vouchsaft to graunt unto us twaine
   The gladfull blessing of posteritie,
   Which we might see after our selves remaine
275   In th'heritage of our unhappie paine:
   So that for want of heires it to defend,
   All is in time like to returne againe
   To that foule feend, who dayly doth attend
To leape into the same after our lives end.

---

6. Matilda is the nurse and teacher of Rinaldo (Tasso, *Gerusalemme libratu.* 55). Matilda is also the name of the woman who replaces Virgil as Dante's guide (*Purgatorio* 28–33).
7. A common name for the brown bear. Sir Bruin receives as heir the baby stolen by a bear.
8. A cormorant is a large sea-bird, notorious for its appetite, whence the name was used to describe greedy or rapacious people.
9. According to his right of possession as conqueror.

32

280   But most my Lord is grieved herewithall,
  And makes exceeding mone, when he does thinke
  That all this land unto his foe shall fall,
  For which he long in vaine did sweat and swinke,°   *work*
  That now the same he greatly doth forthinke.°   *plan ahead*
285 Yet was it sayd, there should to him a sonne
  Be gotten, not begotten, which should drinke
  And dry up all the water, which doth ronne
In the next brooke, by whom that feend shold be fordonne.

33

Well hop't he then, when this was propheside,
290 That from his sides some noble chyld should rize,
  The which through fame should farre be magnifide,
  And this proud gyant should with brave emprize
  Quite overthrow, who now ginnes to despize
  The good Sir *Bruin*, growing farre in yeares;
295 Who thinkes from me his sorrow all doth rize.
  Lo this my cause of griefe to you appeares;
For which I thus doe mourne, and poure forth ceaselesse teares.

34

Which when he heard, he inly touched was
  With tender ruth for her unworthy griefe,
300 And when he had devized of her case,
  He gan in mind conceive a fit reliefe
  For all her paine, if please her make the priefe.°   *trial, test*
  And having cheared her, thus said; faire Dame,
  In evils counsell is the comfort chiefe,
305 Which though I be not wise enough to frame,
Yet as I well it meane, vouchsafe it without blame.[1]

35

If that the cause of this your languishment
  Be lacke of children, to supply your place,
  Low how good fortune doth to you present
310 This litle babe, of sweete and lovely face,
  And spotlesse spirit, in which ye may enchace°   *engrave*
  What ever formes ye list thereto apply,
  Being now soft and fit them to embrace;
  Whether ye list him traine in chevalry,
315 Or noursle up in lore of learn'd Philosophy.

---

1. I.e., in troubled times the best remedy is good advice, which I cannot well put into words; yet as I mean well, take no offense.

36

And certes it hath oftentimes bene seene,
    That of the like, whose linage was unknowne,
    More brave and noble knights have raysed beene,
    As their victorious deedes have often showen,
320 Being with fame through many Nations blowen,
    Then those, which have bene dandled in the lap.
    Therefore some thought, that those brave imps were sowen
    Here by the Gods, and fed with heavenly sap,
That made them grow so high t'all honorable hap.

37

325 The Ladie hearkning to his sensefull speach,
    Found nothing that he said, unmeet nor geason,°   *extraordinary*
    Having oft seene it tryde,° as he did teach.   *proven*
    Therefore inclyning to his goodly reason,
    Agreeing well both with the place and season,
330 She gladly did of that same babe accept,
    As of her owne by liverey and seisin,[2]
    And having over it a litle wept,
She bore it thence, and ever as her owne it kept.

38

Right glad was *Calepine* to be so rid
335 Of his young charge, whereof he skilled nought:
    Ne she lesse glad; for she so wisely did,
    And with her husband under hand so wrought,
    That when that infant unto him she brought,
    She made him thinke it surely was his owne,
340 And it in goodly thewes° so well upbrought,   *manners*
    That it became a famous knight well knowne
And did right noble deedes, the which elswhere are showne.[3]

39

But *Calepine*, now being left alone
    Under the greenewoods side in sorie plight,
345 Withouten armes or steede to ride upon,
    Or house to hide his head from heavens spight,
    Albe that Dame by all the meanes she might,
    Him oft desired home with her to wend,
    And offred him, his courtesie to requite,

<hr>

2. Legal phrase indicating that a sign of possession (some kind of token) has been received.
3. Spenser apparently intended to include the "famous knight" in some unwritten book of *The Faerie Queene*.

The fact that Matilda was the person who raised the hero Rinaldo in Tasso, *Gerusalemme liberatu* suggests that this foundling-knight was to have been a major figure.

350   Both horse and armes, and what so else to lend,
        Yet he them all refusd, though thankt her as a frend.

40

        And for exceeding griefe which inly grew,
            That he his love so lucklesse now had lost,
            On the cold ground, maugre himselfe he threw,
355   For fell despight, to be so sorely crost;
            And there all night himselfe in anguish tost,
            Vowing, that never he in bed againe
            His limbes would rest, ne lig° in ease embost,°   *lie / wrapped*
            Till that his Ladies sight he mote attaine,
360   Or understand, that she in safetie did remaine.

Canto V

*The salvage serves Serena well
till she Prince Arthure fynd,
Who her together with his Squyre
with th'Hermit leaves behynd.*

1

    O what an easie thing is to descry
        The gentle bloud, how ever it be wrapt
        In sad misfortunes foule deformity,
        And wretched sorrowes, which have often hapt?
5   For howsoever it may grow mis-shapt,
        Like this wyld man, being undisciplynd,
        That to all vertue it may seeme unapt,
        Yet will it shew some sparkes of gentle mynd,
    And at the last breake forth in his owne proper kynd.

2

10 That plainely may in this wyld man be red,
        Who though he were still in his desert wood,
        Mongst salvage beasts, both rudely borne and bred,
        Ne ever saw faire guize, ne learned good,
        Yet shewd some token of his gentle blood,
15   By gentle usage of that wretched Dame.
        For certes he was borne of noble blood,
        How ever by hard hap he hether came;
    As ye may know, when time shall be to tell the same.[1]

3

    Who when as now long time he lacked had
20   The good Sir *Calepine*, that farre was strayd,

---

1. The parentage of the savage man is never revealed.

Did wexe exceeding sorrowfull and sad,
  As he of some misfortune were afrayd:
  And leaving there this Ladie all dismayd,
  Went forth streightway into the forrest wyde,
25   To seeke, if he perchance a sleepe were layd,
  Or what so else were unto him betyde:
He sought him farre & neare, yet him no where he spyde.

4

Tho backe returning to that sorie Dame,
  He shewed semblant of exceeding mone,
30   By speaking signes, as he them best could frame;
  Now wringing both his wretched hands in one,
  Now beating his hard head upon a stone,
  That ruth it was to see him so lament.
  By which she well perceiving, what was done,
35   Gan teare her hayre, and all her garments rent,
And beat her breast, and piteously her selfe torment.

5

Upon the ground her selfe she fiercely threw,
  Regardlesse of her wounds, yet bleeding rife,
  That with their bloud did all the flore imbrew,°   *stain*
40   As if her breast new launcht with murdrous knife,
  Would streight dislodge the wretched wearie life.
  There she long groveling, and deepe groning lay,
  As if her vitall powers were at strife
  With stronger death, and feared their decay,
45 Such were this Ladies pangs and dolorous assay.

6

Whom when the Salvage saw so sore distrest,
  He reared her up from the bloudie ground,
  And sought by all the meanes, that he could best
  Her to recure out of that stony swound,
50   And staunch the bleeding of her dreary wound.
  Yet nould she be recomforted for nought,
  Ne cease her sorrow and impatient stound,
  But day and night did vexe her carefull thought,
And ever more and more her owne affliction wrought.

7

55 At length, when as no hope of his retourne
  She saw now left, she cast to leave the place,
  And wend abrode, though feeble and forlorne,
  To seeke some comfort in that sorie case.

His steede now strong through rest so long a space,
60   Well as she could, she got, and did bedight,
And being thereon mounted, forth did pace,
Withouten guide, her to conduct aright,
Or gard her to defend from bold oppressors might.

8

Whom when her Host saw readie to depart,
65   He would not suffer her alone to fare,
But gan himselfe addresse to take her part.
Those warlike armes, which *Calepine* whyleare
Had left behind, he gan efisoones prepare,
And put them all about himselfe unfit,
70   His shield, his helmet, and his curats² bare.
But without sword upon his thigh to sit:
Sir *Calepine* himselfe away had hidden it.

9

So forth they traveld an uneven payre,
That mote to all men seeme an uncouth sight;
75   A salvage man matcht with a Ladie fayre,
That rather seem'd the conquest of his might,
Gotten by spoyle, then purchaced aright.
But he did her attend most carefully,
And faithfully did serve both day and night,
80   Withouten thought of shame or villeny,
Ne ever shewed signe of foule disloyalty.

10

Upon a day as on their way they went,
It chaunst some furniture° about her steed   equipment
To be disordred by some accident:
85   Which to redresse, she did th'assistance need
Of this her groome, which he by signes did reede,
And streight his combrous armes aside did lay
Upon the ground, withouten doubt or dreed,
And in his homely wize began to assay
90   T'amend what was amisse, and put in right aray.

11

Bout which whilest he was busied thus hard,
Lo where a knight together with his squire,
All arm'd to point came ryding thetherward,
Which seemed by their portance and attire,
95   To be two errant knights, that did inquire

2. Curats, armor for the top part of the body.

After adventures, where they mote them get.
Those were to weet (if that ye it require)
Prince *Arthur* and young *Timias*, which met
By straunge occasion, that here needs forth be set.

12

100 After that *Timias* had againe recured
The favour of *Belphebe*, (as ye heard)
And of her grace did stand againe assured,
To happie blisse he was full high uprear'd,
Nether of envy, nor of chaunge afeard,
105 Though many foes did him maligne therefore,
And with unjust detraction him did beard;°   *affront*
Yet he himselfe so well and wisely bore,
That in her soveraine lyking he dwelt evermore.³

13

But of them all, which did his ruine seeke
110 Three mightie enemies did him most despight,
Three mightie ones, and cruell minded eeke,
That him not onely sought by open might
To overthrow, but to supplant by slight.
The first of them by name was cald *Despetto*,
115 Exceeding all the rest in powre and hight;
The second not so strong but wise, *Decetto*;
The third nor strong nor wise, but spightfullest *Defetto*.⁴

14

Oftimes their sundry powres they did employ,
And severall deceipts, but all in vaine:
120 For neither they by force could him destroy,
Ne yet entrap in treasons subtill traine.
Therefore conspiring all together plaine,
They did their counsels now in one compound;
Where singled forces faile, conjoynd may gaine.
125 The *Blatant Beast* the fittest meanes they found,
To worke his utter shame, and throughly him confound.

15

Upon a day as they the time did waite,
When he did ravnge the wood for salvage game,
They sent that *Blatant Beast* to be a baite,
130 To draw him from his deare beloved dame,
Unwares into the daunger of defame.°   *disgrace, defamation*
For well they wist, that Squire to be so bold,

---

3. Timias and Arthur part in Book IV.7.47 of the *Faerie Queene*. Timias regains the favor of Belphoebe in IV.8.1–18.

4. Despetto, Decetto and Defetto are Spenser's invented Italianate names for despite, deceit, and defect.

That no one beast in forrest wylde or tame,
    Met him in chase, but he it challenge would,
135 And plucke the pray oftimes out of their greedy hould.

16

The hardy boy, as they devised had,
    Seeing the ugly Monster passing by,
    Upon him set, of perill nought adrad,
    Ne skilfull of the uncouth jeopardy;
140   And charged him so fierce and furiously,
    That his great force unable to endure,
    He forced was to turne from him and fly:
    Yet ere he fled, he with his tooth impure
Him heedlesse bit, the whiles he was thereof secure.

17

145 Securely he did after him pursew,
    Thinking by speed to overtake his flight;
    Who through thicke woods and brakes & briers him drew,
    To weary him the more, and waste his spight,
    So that he now has almost spent his spright.
150   Till that at length unto a woody glade
    He came, whose covert stopt his further sight,
    There his three foes shrowded in guilefull shade,
Out of their ambush broke, and gan him to invade.

18

Sharpely they all attonce did him assaile,
155   Burning with inward rancour and despight,
    And heaped strokes did round about him haile
    With so huge force, that seemed nothing might
    Beare off their blowes, from percing thorough quite.
    Yet he them all so warily did ward,
160   That none of them in his soft flesh did bite,
    And all the while his backe for best safegard,
He lent against a tree, that backeward onset bard.

19

Like a wylde Bull, that being at a bay,
    Is bayted° of a mastiffe, and a hound,   *harassed*
165   And a curre-dog; that doe him sharpe assay
    On every side, and beat about him round;
    But most that curre barking with bitter sownd,
    And creeping still behinde, doth him incomber,
    That in his chauffe° he digs the trampled ground,   *rage*
170   And threats his horns, and bellowes like the thonder,
So did that Squire his foes disperse, and drive asonder.

20

Him well behoved so; for his three foes
  Sought to encompasse him on every side,
  And dangerously did round about enclose.
175   But most of all *Defetto* him annoyde,
  Creeping behinde him still to have destroyde:
  So did *Decetto* eke him circumvent,
  But stout *Despetto* in his greater pryde,
  Did front him face to face against him bent,
180 Yet he them all withstood, and often made relent.

21

Till that at length nigh tyrd with former chace,
  And weary now with carefull keeping ward,
  He gan to shrinke, and somewhat to give place,
  Full like ere long to have escaped hard;
185   When as unwares he in the forrest heard
  A trampling steede, that with his neighing fast
  Did warne his rider be uppon his gard;
  With noise whereof the Squire now nigh aghast,
Revived was, and sad dispaire away did cast.

22

190 Eftsoones he spide a Knight approching nye,
  Who seeing one in so great daunger set
  Mongst many foes, him selfe did faster hye;°   *hasten*
  To reskue him, and his weake part abet,
  For pitty so to see him overset.°   *oppressed*
195   Whom soone as his three enemies did vew,
  They fled, and fast into the wood did get:
  Him booted not to thinke them to pursew,
The covert was so thicke, that did no passage shew.

23

Then turning to that swaine, him well he knew
200   To be his *Timias*, his owne true Squire,
  Whereof exceeding glad, he to him drew,
  And him embracing twixt his armes entire,
  Him thus bespake; My liefe, my lifes desire,
  Why have ye me alone thus long yleft?
205   Tell me what worlds despight, or heavens yre
  Hath you thus long away from me bereft?
Where have ye all this while bin wandring, where bene weft?° *wafted, carried*

24

With that he sighed deepe for inward tyne:°   *sorrow*
   To whom the Squire nought aunswered againe,
210   But shedding few soft teares from tender eyne,
   His deare affect° with silence did restraine,   *affection*
   And shut up all his plaint in privy paine.
   There they awhile some gracious speaches spent,
   As to them seemed fit time to entertaine.
215   After all which up to their steedes they went,
And forth together rode a comely couplement.

25

So now they be arrived both in sight
   Of this wyld man, whom they full busie found
   About the sad *Serena* things to dight,
220   With those brave armours lying on the ground,
   That seem'd the spoile of some right well renownd.
   Which when that Squire beheld, he to them stept,
   Thinking to take them from that hylding° hound: *base, worthless*
   But he it seeing, lightly to him lept,
225   And sternely with strong hand it from his handling kept.

26

Gnashing his grinded teeth with griesly looke,
   And sparkling fire out of his furious eyne,
   Him with his fist unwares on th'head he strooke,
   That made him downe unto the earth encline;
230   Whence soone upstarting much he gan repine,
   And laying hand upon his wrathfull blade,
   Thought therewithall forthwith him to have slaine,
   Who it perceiving, hand upon him layd,
And greedily him griping, his avengement stayd.

27

235   With that aloude the faire *Serena* cryde
   Unto the Knight, them to dispart in twaine:
   Who to them stepping did them soone divide,
   And did from further violence restraine,
   Albe the wyld-man hardly would refraine.
240   Then gan the Prince, of her for to demand,
   What and from whence she was, and by what traine°   *snare*
   She fell into that salvage villaines hand,
And whether free with him she now were, or in band.°   *in bondage*

28

To whom she thus; I am, as now ye see,
245   The wretchedst Dame, that live this day on ground,
    Who both in minde, the which most grieveth me,
    And body have receiv'd a mortall wound,
    That hath me driven to this drery stound.
    I was erewhile, the love of *Calepine*,
250   Who whether he alive be to be found,
    Or by some deadly chaunce be done to pine,°   *made to suffer*
Since I him lately lost, uneath is to define.

29

In salvage forrest I him lost of late,
    Where I had surely long ere this bene dead,
255   Or else remained in most wretched state,
    Had not this wylde man in that wofull stead
    Kept, and delivered me from deadly dread.
    In such a salvage wight, of brutish kynd,
    Amongst wilde beastes in desert forrests bred,
260   It is most straunge and wonderfull to fynd
So milde humanity, and perfect gentle mynd.

30

Let me therefore this favour for him finde,
    That ye will not your wrath upon him wreake,
    Sith he cannot expresse his simple minde,
265   Ne yours conceive, ne but by tokens speake:
    Small praise to prove your powre on wight so weake.
    With such faire words she did their heate asswage,
    And the strong course of their displeasure breake,
    That they to pitty turnd their former rage,
270   And each sought to supply the office of her page.

31

So having all things well about her dight,
    She on her way cast forward to proceede,
    And they her forth conducted, where they might
    Finde harbour fit to comfort her great neede.
275   For now her wounds corruption gan to breed;
    And eke this Squire, who likewise wounded was
    Of that same Monster late, for lacke of heed,
    Now gan to faint, and further could not pas
Through feeblenesse, which all his limbes oppressed has.

32

280   So forth they rode together all in troupe,
        To seeke some place, the which mote yeeld some ease
        To these sicke twaine, that now began to droupe,
        And all the way the Prince sought to appease
        The bitter anguish of their sharpe disease,
285   By all the courteous meanes he could invent,
        Somewhile with merry purpose° fit to please,   *conversation*
        And otherwhile with good encouragement,
    To make them to endure the pains, did them torment.[5]

33

    Mongst which, *Serena* did to him relate
290   The foule discourt'sies and unknightly parts,
        Which *Turpine* had unto her shewed late,
        Without compassion of her cruell smarts,
        Although *Blandina* did with all her arts
        Him otherwise perswade, all that she might;
295   Yet he of malice, without her desarts,
        Not onely her excluded late at night,
    But also trayterously did wound her weary Knight.

34

    Wherewith the Prince sore moved, there avoud,
        That soone as he returned backe againe,
300   He would avenge th'abuses of that proud
        And shamefull Knight, of whom she did complaine.
        This wize did they each other entertaine,
        To passe the tedious travell of the way;
        Till towards night they came unto a plaine,
305   By which a little Hermitage there lay,
    Far from all neighbourhood, the which annoy it may.

35

    And nigh thereto a little Chappell stoode,
        Which being all with Yuy overspred,
        Deckt all the roofe, and shadowing the roode,°   *crucifix*
310   Seem'd like a grove faire braunched over hed:
        Therein the Hermite, which his life here led
        In streight° observaunce of religious vow,   *strict*
        Was wont his howres[6] and holy things to bed;°   *bid, offer*
        And therein he likewise was praying now,
315   Whenas these Knights arriv'd, they wist not where nor how.

---

5. I.e., that did them torment.

6. The prayers, or offices, assigned to be read at the canonical hours.

36

They stayd not there, but streight way in did pas.
   Whom when the Hermite present saw in place,
   From his devotion streight he troubled was;
   Which breaking off he toward them did pace,
320   With stayed steps, and grave beseeming grace:
   For well it seem'd, that whilome he had beene
   Some goodly person, and of gentle race,
   That could his good to all, and well did weene,
How each to entertaine with curt'sie well beseene.

37

325 And soothly it was sayd by common fame,[7]
   So long as age enabled him thereto,
   That he had bene a man of mickle name,
   Renowmed much in armes and derring doe:
   But being aged now and weary to
330   Of warres delight, and worlds contentious toyle,
   The name of knighthood he did disavow,
   And hanging up his armes and warlike spoyle,
From all this worlds incombraunce did himselfe assoyle.[8]

38

He thence them led into his Hermitage,
335   Letting their steedes to graze upon the greene:
   Small was his house, and like a little cage,
   For his owne turne,° yet inly neate and clene,   *service, use*
   Deckt with greene boughes, and flowers gay beseene.
   Therein he them full faire did entertaine
340   Not with such forged showes, as fitter beene
   For courting fooles, that curtesies would faine,
But with entire affection and appearaunce plaine.

39

Yet was their fare but homely, such as hee
   Did use, his feeble body to sustaine;
345   The which full gladly they did take in glee,
   Such as it was, ne did of want complaine,
   But being well suffiz'd, them rested faine.
   But faire *Serene* all night could take no rest,
   Ne yet that gentle Squire for grievous paine
350   Of their late woundes, the which the *Blatant Beast*
Had given them, whose griefe through suffraunce sore increast.

---

7. Report (Latin: *fama*).
8. Absolve, release. It was not uncommon for old knights

in romances to turn from martial heroism to seclusion
and prayer.

40

So all that night they past in great disease,
   Till that the morning, bringing earely light
   To guide mens labours, brought them also ease,
355   And some asswagement of their painefull plight.
   Then up they rose, and gan them selves to dight
   Unto their journey; but that Squire and Dame
   So faint and feeble were, that they ne might
   Endure to travell, nor one foote to frame:°   *direct, move*
360 Their hearts were sicke, their sides were sore, their feete were
                                     [lame.

41

Therefore the Prince, whom great affaires in mynd
   Would not permit, to make there lenger stay,
   Was forced there to leave them both behynd,
   In that good Hermits charge, whom he did pray
365   To tend them well. So forth he went his way,
   And with him eke the salvage, that whyleare
   Seeing his royall vsage and array,
   Was greatly growne in love of that brave pere,
Would needes depart, as shall declared be elsewhere.

Canto VI

The Hermite heales both Squire and dame
Of their sore maladies:
He° Turpine doth defeate, and shame   *Arthur*
For his late villanies.

1

No wound, which warlike hand of enemy
   Inflicts with dint of sword, so sore doth light,
   As doth the poysnous sting, which infamy
   Infixeth in the name of noble wight:
5   For by no art, nor any leaches° might   *physician's*
   It ever can recured be againe;
   Ne all the skill, which that immortall spright
   Of *Podalyrius*[1] did in it retaine,
Can remedy such hurts; such hurts are hellish paine.

2

10 Such were the wounds, the which that *Blatant Beast*
   Made in the bodies of that Squire and Dame;
   And being such, were now much more increast,

---

1. Son of Aesculapius, the son of Apollo, famed for his healing powers.

      For want of taking heede unto the same,
        That now corrupt and curelesse they became.
15   Howbe° that carefull Hermite did his best,   *howbeit*
        With many kindes of medicines meete, to tame
        The poysnous humour, which did most infest
     Their ranckling wounds, & every day them duely drest.

3

     For he right well in Leaches craft was seene,°   *versed, practiced*
20   And through the long experience of his dayes,
        Which had in many fortunes tossed beene,
        And past through many perillous assayes,
        He knew the diverse went° of mortall wayes,   *course, passage*
        And in the mindes of men had great insight;
25   Which with sage counsell, when they went astray,
        He could enforme, and them reduce aright,
    And al the passions heale, which wound the weaker spright.

4

     For whylome he had bene a doughty Knight,
        As any one, that lived in his daies,
30   And proved oft in many perillous fight,
        Of which he grace and glory wonne alwaies,
        And in all battels bore away the baies.[2]
        But being now attacht with timely age,
        And weary of this worlds unquiet waies,
35   He tooke him selfe unto this Hermitage,
    In which he liv'd alone, like carelesse bird in cage.[3]

5

     One day, as he was searching of their wounds,
        He found that they had festred privily,
        And ranckling inward with unruly stounds,
40   The inner parts now gan to putrify,
        That quite they seem'd past helpe of surgery,
        And rather needed to be disciplinde[4]
        With holesome reede[5] of sad sobriety,
        To rule the stubborne rage of passion blinde:
45   Give salves to every sore, but counsell to the minde.

6

     So taking them apart into his cell,
        He to that point fit speaches gan to frame,

2. I.e., a garland of bay leaves traditionally given to the winner of a contest.
3. cf. *King Lear* 5.3.9.
4. Controlled, restrained, but also subjected to the discipline of rod or whip to bring the flesh under the control of the reason.
5. Advice, counsel, but also the physical instrument of discipline (see preceeding note).

As he the art of words knew wondrous well,
And eke could doe, as well as say the same,
50   And thus he to them sayd; faire daughter Dame,
And you faire sonne, which here thus long now lie
In piteous languor, since ye hither came,
In vaine of me ye hope for remedie,
And I likewise in vaine doe salves to you applie.

7

55   For in your selfe your onely helpe doth lie,
To heale your selves, and must proceed alone
From your owne will, to cure your maladie.
Who can him cure, that will be cur'd of none?
If therefore health ye seeke, observe this one.
60   First learne your outward sences to refraine
From things, that stirre up fraile affection;
Your eies, your eares, your tongue, your talke restraine[6]
From that they most affect, and in due termes containe.

8

For from those outward sences ill affected,
65   The seede of all this evill first doth spring,
Which at the first before it had infected,
Mote easie be supprest with little thing:
But being growen strong, it forth doth bring
Sorrow, and anguish, and impatient paine
70   In th'inner parts, and lastly scattering
Contagious poyson close through every vaine,
It never rests, till it have wrought his finall bane.°   destruction

9

For that beastes teeth, which wounded you tofore,
Are so exceeding venemous and keene,
75   Made all of rusty yron, ranckling sore,
That where they bite, it booteth not to weene
With salve, or antidote, or other mene
It ever to amend: ne marvaile ought;
For that same beast was bred of hellish strene,°   strain, race
80   And long in darksome *Stygian* den[7] upbrought,
Begot of foule *Echidna*,[8] as in bookes[9] is taught.

---

6. The hermit advises Serena and Timias to restrain their passions since one can do little more than avoid the occasions that lead malice and slander to flourish. See stanza 14.

7. The underworld, region of the river Styx.
8. A monster, half woman, half snake, the mother of Cerberus.
9. I.e., Hesiod's *Theogony*.

10

Echidna is a Monster direfull dred,
    Whom Gods doe hate, and heavens abhor to see;
    So hideous is her shape, so huge her hed,
85   That even the hellish fiends affrighted bee
    At sight thereof, and from her presence flee:
    Yet did her face and former parts professe
    A faire young Mayden, full of comely glee;
    But all her hinder parts did plaine expresse
90 A monstrous Dragon, full of fearefull uglinesse.

11

To her the Gods, for her so dreadfull face,
    In fearefull darkenesse, furthest from the skie,
    And from the earth, appointed have her place,
    Mongst rocks and caves, where she enrold doth lie
95   In hideous horrour and obscurity,°   *darkness*
    Wasting the strength of her immortall age.
    There did *Typhaon* with her company,[1]
    Cruell *Typhaon*, whose tempestuous rage
Make th'heavens tremble oft, & him with vowes asswage.

12

100 Of that commixtion they did then beget
    This hellish Dog, that hight the *Blatant Beast;*
    A wicked Monster, that his tongue doth whet
    Gainst all, both good and bad, both most and least;
    And poures his poysnous gall forth to infest
105   The noblest wights with notable defame:
    Ne ever Knight, that bore so lofty creast,
    Ne ever Lady of so honest name,
But he them spotted with reproch, or secrete shame.

13

In vaine therefore it were, with medicine
110   To goe about to salve such kynd of sore,
    That rather needes wise read and discipline,
    Then outward salves, that may augment it more.
    Aye me (sayd then *Serena* signing sore)
    What hope of helpe doth then for us remaine,
115   If that no salves may us to health restore?
    But sith we need good counsell (sayd the swaine)
Aread good sire, some counsell, that may us sustaine.

---

1. According to Hesiod, Echidna and Typhaon were the parents of a number of beasts, including Geryon's dog Orthrus and his dragon.

14

The best (sayd he) that I can you advize,
   Is to avoide the occasion of the ill:
120   For when the cause, whence evill doth arize,
   Removed is, th'effect surceaseth still.
   Abstaine from pleasure, and restraine your will,
   Subdue desire, and bridle loose delight,
   Use scanted diet, and forbeare your fill,
125   Shun secresie, and talke in open sight:
So shall you soone repaire your present evill plight.

15

Thus having sayd, his sickely patients
   Did gladly hearken to his grave beheast,
   And kept so well his wise commaundements,
130   That in short space their malady was ceast,
   And eke the biting of that harmefull Beast
   Was throughly heal'd. Tho when they did perceave
   Their wounds recur'd, and forces reincreast,
   Of that good Hermite both they tooke their leave,
135   And went both on their way, ne ech would other leave.

16

But each the other vow'd t'accompany,
   The Lady, for that she was much in dred,
   Now left alone in great extremity,
   The Squire, for that he courteous was indeed,
140   Would not her leave alone in her great need.
   So both together traveld, till they met
   With a faire Mayden clad in mourning weed,
   Upon a mangy jade° unmeetely set,   *inferior horse*
And a lewd foole her leading thorough dry and wet.

17

145   But by what meanes that shame to her befell,
   And how thereof her selfe she did acquite,
   I must a while forbeare to you to tell;
   Till that, as comes by course, I doe recite,[2]
   What fortune to the Briton Prince did lite,°   *befall*
150   Pursuing that proud Knight, the which whileare
   Wrought to Sir *Calepine* so foule despight;
   And eke his Lady, though she sickely were,
So lewdly had abusde, as ye did lately heare.[3]

---

2. The story of Mirabella and Disdain is told in Canto 7.27 ff.   3. See Canto 3.27 ff.

18

> The Prince according to the former token,
155   Which faire *Serene* to him delivered had,
>   Pursu'd him streight, in mynd to bene ywroken°   *avenged*
>   Of all the vile demeane,° and usage bad,   *treatment*
>   With which he had those two so ill bestad:
>   Ne wight with him on that adventure went,
160   But that wylde man, whom though he oft forbad,
>   Yet for no bidding, nor for being shent,
> Would he restrayned be from his attendement.

19

> Arriving there, as did by chaunce befall,
>   He found the gate wyde ope, and in he rode,
165   Ne stayd, till that he came into the hall:
>   Where soft dismounting like a weary lode,
>   Upon the ground with feeble feete he trode,
>   As he unable were for very neede
>   To move one foote, but there must make abode;
170   The whiles the salvage man did take his steede,
> And in some stable neare did set him up to feede.

20

> Ere long to him a homely groome there came,
>   That in rude wise him asked, what he was,
>   That durst so boldly, without let° or shame,   *permission, hesitation*
175   Into his Lords forbidden hall to passe.
>   To whom the Prince, him fayning to embase,[4]
>   Mylde answer made; he was an errant Knight,
>   The which was fall'n into this feeble case,
>   Through many wounds, which lately he in fight,
180 Received had, and prayd to pitty his ill plight.

21

> But he, the more outrageous and bold,
>   Sternely did bid him quickely thence avaunt,°   *depart*
>   Or deare aby,° for why his Lord of old   *suffer severely*
>   Did hate all errant Knights, which there did haunt,
185   Ne lodging would to any of them graunt,
>   And therefore lightly bad him packe away,
>   Not sparing him with bitter words to taunt;
>   And therewithall rude hand on him did lay,
> To thrust him out of dore, doing his worst assay.

4. I.e., pretending to be much less imposing than he actually was.

22

190 Which when the Salvage comming now in place,
    Beheld, eftsoones he all enraged grew,
    And running streight upon that villaine base,
    Like a fell Lion at him fiercely flew,
    And with his teeth and nailes, in present vew,
195 Him rudely rent, and all to peeces tore:
    So miserably him all helpelesse slew,
    That with the noise, whilest he did loudly rore,
    The people of the house rose forth in great uprore.

23

    Who when on ground they saw their fellow slaine,
200 And that same Knight and Salvage standing by,
    Upon them two they fell with might and maine,
    And on them layd so huge and horribly,
    As if they would have slaine them presently.
    But the bold Prince defended him so well,
205 And their assault withstood so mightily,
    That maugre all their might, he did repell,
    And beat them back, whilest many undemeath him fell.

24

    Yet he them still so sharpely did pursew,
    That few of them he left alive, which fled,
210 Those evill tidings to their Lord to shew.
    Who hearing how his people badly sped,°   *fared*
    Came forth in hast: where when as with the dead
    He saw the ground all strow'd, and that same Knight
    And salvage with their bloud fresh steeming red,
215 He woxe nigh mad with wrath and fell despight,
    And with reprochfull words him thus bespake on hight.

25

    Art thou he, traytor, that with treason vile,
    Hast slaine my men in this unmanly maner,
    And now triumphest in the piteous spoile
220 Of these poore folk, whose soules with black dishonor
    And foule defame doe decke thy bloudy baner?
    The meede whereof shall shortly be thy shame,
    And wretched end, which still attendeth on her.
    With that him selfe to battell he did frame;
225 So did his forty yeomen,° which there with him came.   *servants*

26

    With dreadfull force they all did him assaile,
      And round about with boystrous strokes oppresse,
      That on his shield did rattle like to haile,
      In a great tempest; that in such distresse,
230   He wist not to which side him to addresse.
      And evermore that craven cowherd Knight,
      Was at his backe with heardesse heedinesse,°   *attention*
      Wayting if he unwares him murther might:
    For cowardize doth still in villany delight.

27

235   Whereof whenas the Prince was well aware,
      He to him turnd with furious intent,
      And him against his powre gan to prepare;
      Like a fierce Bull, that being busie bent
      To fight with many foes about him ment,
240   Feeling some curre behinde his heeles to bite,
      Turnes him about with fell avengement;
      So likewise turnde the Prince upon the Knight,
    And layd at him amaine with all his will and might.

28

    Who when he once his dreadfull strokes had tasted,
245   Durst not the furie of his force abyde,
      But turn'd abacke, and to retyre him hasted
      Through the thick prease,° there thinking him to hyde.   *crowd*
      But when the Prince had once him plainely eyde,
      He foot by foot him followed alway,
250   Ne would him suffer once to shrinke asyde
      But joyning close, huge lode at him did lay:
    Who flying still did ward, and warding fly away.

29

    But when his foe he still so eger saw,
      Unto his heeles himselfe he did betake,
255   Hoping unto some refuge to withdraw:
      Ne would the Prince him ever foot forsake,
      Where so he went, but after him did make.
      He fled from roome to roome, from place to place,
      Whylest every joynt for dread of death did quake,
260   Still looking after him, that did him chace;
    That made him evermore increase his speedie pace.

30

At last he up into the chamber came,
   Whereas his love was sitting all alone,
   Wayting what tydings of her folke became.
265   There did the Prince him overtake anone,
   Crying in vaine to her, him to bemone;
   And with his sword him on the head did smyte,
   That to the ground he fell in senselesse swone:
   Yet whether thwart° or flatly it did lyte,   *transversely, sideways*
270 The tempred Steele did not into his braynepan° byte.   *head*

31

Which when the Ladie saw, with great affright
   She starting up, began to shrieke aloud,
   And with her garment covering him from sight,
   Seem'd under her protection him to shroud;
275   And falling lowly at his feet, her bowd
   Upon her knee, intreating him for grace,
   And often him besought, and prayd, and vowd;
   That with the ruth of her so wretched case,
He stayd his second strooke, and did his hand abase.

32

280 Her weed she then withdrawing, did him discover,
   Who now come to himselfe, yet would not rize,
   But still did lie as dead, and quake, and quiver,
   That even the Prince his basenesse did despize,
   And eke his Dame him seeing in such guize,
285   Gan him recomfort, and from ground to reare.
   Who rising up at last in ghastly wize,
   Like troubled ghost did dreadfully appeare,
As one that had no life him left through former feare.

33

Whom when the Prince so deadly saw dismayd,
290   He for such basenesse shamefully him shent,
   And with sharpe words did bitterly upbrayd;
   Vile cowheard dogge, now doe I much repent,
   That ever I this life unto thee lent,
   Whereof thou caytive so unworthie art;
295   That both thy love, for lacke of hardiment,
   And eke thy selfe, for want of manly hart,
And eke all knights hast shamed with this knightlesse part.

34

Yet further hast thou heaped shame to shame,
   And crime to crime, by this thy cowheard feare.

300   For first it was to thee reprochfull blame,
       To erect this wicked custome, which I heare,
       Gainst errant Knights and Ladies thou dost reare;
       Whom when thou mayst, thou dost of arms despoile
       Or of their upper garment, which they weare:
305   Yet doest thou not with manhood, but with guile
    Maintaine this evill use, thy foes thereby to foile.

35

    And lastly in approvance of thy wrong,
       To shew such faintnesse and foule cowardize,
       Is greatest shame: for oft it falles, that strong
310   And valiant knights doe rashly enterprize,
       Either for fame, or else for exercize,
       A wrongfull quarrell to maintaine by fight;
       Yet have, through prowesse and their brave emprize,
       Gotten great worship in this worldes sight.
315   For greater force there needs to maintaine wrong, then right.

36

    Yet since thy life unto this Ladie fayre
       I given have, live in reproch and scorne;
       Ne ever armes, ne ever knighthood dare
       Hence to professe: for shame is to adorne
320   With so brave badges one so basely borne;
       But onely breath sith that° I did forgive.   *because*
       So having from his craven bodie torne
       Those goodly armes, he them away did give
    And onely suffred him this wretched life to live.

37

325   There whilest he thus was setling things above,
       Atwene that Ladie myld and recreant knight,
       To whom his life he graunted for her love,
       He gan bethinke him, in what perilous plight
       He had behynd him left that salvage wight,
330   Amongst so many foes, whom sure he thought
       By this quite slaine in so unequall fight:
       Therefore descending backe in haste, he sought
    If yet he were alive, or to destruction brought.

38

    There he him found environed about
335   With slaughtred bodies, which his hand had slaine,
       And laying yet a fresh with courage stout
       Upon the rest, that did alive remaine;
       Whom he likewise right sorely did constraine,

Like scattred sheepe, to seeke for safetie,
340   After he gotten had with busie paine
Some of their weapons, which thereby did lie,
With which he layd about,° and made them fast to flie.   *struck vigorously*

39

Whom when the Prince so felly saw to rage,
Approching to him neare, his hand he stayd,
345   And sought, by making signes, him to asswage:
Who them perceiving, streight to him obayd,
As to his Lord, and downe his weapons layd,
As if he long had to his heasts bene trayned.
Thence he him brought away, and up convayd
350   Into the chamber, where that Dame remayned
With her unworthy knight, who ill him entertayned.

40

Whom when the Salvage saw from daunger free,
Sitting beside his Ladie there at ease,
He well remembred, that the same was hee,
355   Which lately sought his Lord for to displease:
Tho all in rage, he on him streight did seaze,
As if he would in peeces him have rent;
And were not, that the Prince did him appeaze,
He had not left one limbe of him unrent:
360   But streight he held his hand at his commaundement.

41

Thus having all things well in peace ordayned,
The Prince himselfe there all that night did rest,
Where him *Blandina* fayrely entertayned,
With all the courteous glee and goodly feast,
365   The which for him she could imagine best.
For well she knew the wayes to win good will
Of every wight, that were not too infest,°   *hostile*
And how to please the minds of good and ill,
Through tempering of her words & lookes by wondrous skill.

42

370   Yet were her words and lookes but false and fayned,
To some hid end to make more easie way,
Or to allure such fondlings, whom she trayned°   *snared*
Into her trap unto their owne decay:
Thereto, when needed, she could weepe and pray,
375   And when her listed, she could fawne and flatter;
Now smyling smoothly, like to sommers day,
Now glooming sadly, so to cloke her matter;
Yet were her words but wynd, & all her teares but water.

43

Whether such grace were given her by kynd,
380   As women wont their guilefull wits to guyde;
         Or learn'd the art to please, I doe not fynd.
         This well I wote, that she so well applyde
         Her pleasing tongue, that soone she pacifyde
         The wrathfull Prince, & wrought her husbands peace.
385   Who nathelesse not therewith satisfyde,
         His rancorous despight did not releasse,
Ne secretly from thought of fell revenge surceasse.

44

For all that night, the whyles the Prince did rest
         In carelesse couch, not weeting what was ment,
390   He watcht in close awayt with weapons prest,
         Willing to worke his villenous intent
         On him, that had so shamefully him stent:
         Yet durst he not for very cowardize
         Effect the same, whylest all the night was spent.
395   The morrow next the Prince did early rize,
And passed forth, to follow his first enterprize.

Canto VII

Turpine is baffuld,[1] his two knights
doe gaine their treasons meed,
Fayre Mirabellaes punishment
for loves disdaine decreed.

1

Like as the gentle hart it selfe bewrayes,
         In doing gentle deedes with franke delight,
         Even so the baser mind it selfe displayes,
         In cancred malice and revengefull spight.
5   For to maligne, t'envie, t'use shifting slight,
         Be arguments of a vile donghill mind,
         Which what it dare not doe by open might,
         To worke by wicked treason wayes doth find,
By such discourteous deeds discovering his base kind.

2

10   That well appeares in this discourteous knight,
         The coward *Turpine*, whereof now I treat;
         Who notwithstanding that in former fight
         He of the Prince his life received late,
         Yet in his mind malitious and ingrate

1. Disgraced as a perjured knight.

15   He gan devize, to be aveng'd anew
            For all that shame, which kindled inward hate.
            Therefore so soone as he was out of vew,
        Himselfe in hast he arm'd, and did him fast pursew.

                            3

        Well did he tract° his steps, as he did ryde,   *traced, followed*
20   Yet would not neare approch in daungers eye,
            But kept aloofe for dread to be descryde,
            Untill fit time and place he mote espy,
            Where he mote worke him scath and villeny.
            At last he met two knights to him unknowne,
25   The which were armed both agreeably,
            And both combynd, what ever chaunce were blowne,
        Betwixt them to divide, and each to make his owne.

                            4

        To whom false *Turpine* comming courteously,
            To cloke the mischiefe, which he inly ment,
30   Gan to complaine of great discourtesie,
            Which a straunge knight, that neare afore him went,
            Had doen to him, and his deare Ladie shent:
            Which if they would afford him ayde at need
            For to avenge, in time convenient,
35   They should accomplish both a knightly deed,
        And for their paines obtaine of him a goodly meed.

                            5

        The knights beleev'd, that all he sayd, was trew,
            And being fresh and full of youthly spright,
            Were glad to heare of that adventure new,
40   In which they mote make triall of their might,
            Which never yet they had approv'd in fight;
            And eke desirous of the offred meed,[2]
            Said then the one of them; where is that wight,
            The which hath doen to thee this wrongfull deed,
45   That we may it avenge, and punish him with speed?

                            6

        He rides (said *Turpine*) there not farre afore,
            With a wyld man soft footing by his syde,
            That if ye list to haste a litle more,
            Ye may him overtake in timely tyde:°   *period of time*
50   Eftsoones they pricked forth with forward pryde,

---

2. Sir Enias (named in VI.8.4.3) and his nameless companion are not only breaking the rules of chivalry (which required assistance without payment; cf. VI.1.46–7); they are debasing themselves to the status of hired assassins.

And ere that litle while they ridden had,
The gentle Prince not farre away they spyde,
Ryding a softly pace with portance° sad,   *bearing*
Devizing of his love more, then of daunger drad.

7

55   Then one of them aloud unto him cryde,
       Bidding him turne againe, false traytour knight,
       Foule womanwronger, for he him defyde.
       With that they both at once with equall spight
       Did bend their speares, and both with equall might
60   Against him ran; but th'one did misse his marke,
       And being carried with his force forthright,
       Glaunst swiftly by; like to that heavenly sparke,
Which glyding through the ayre lights all the heavens darke.[3]

8

But th'other ayming better, did him smite
65   Full in the shield, with so impetuous powre,
       That all his launce in peeces shivered quite,
       And scattered all about, fell on the flowre.
       But the stout Prince, with much more steddy stowre
       Full on his bever° did him strike so sore,   *faceguard of helmet*
70   That the cold steele through piercing, did devowre
       His vitall[4] breath, and to the ground him bore,
Where still he bathed lay in his owne bloody gore.

9

As when a cast° of Faulcons make their flight   *couple*
       At an Herneshaw,° that lyes aloft on wing,   *young heron*
75   The whyles they strike at him with heedlesse might,
       The warie foule his bill doth backward wring;
       On which the first, whose force her first doth bring,
       Her selfe quite through the bodie doth engore,
       And falleth downe to ground like senselesse thing,
80   But th'other not so swift, as she before,
Fayles of her souse,[5] and passing by doth hurt no more.

10

By this the other, which was passed by,
       Himselfe recovering, was return'd to fight;
       Where when he saw his fellow lifelessely,
85   He much was daunted with so dismall sight;
       Yet nought abating of his former spight,

3. The reference is either to a meteor or to lightning.   5. Swooping down at a bird in flight.
4. Necessary for life, life–sustaining.

Let drive at him with so malitious mynd,
As if he would have passed through him quight:
But the steele-head no stedfast hold could fynd,
90   But glauncing by, deceiv'd him of that he desynd.

11

Not so the Prince: for his well learned speare
   Tooke surer hould, and from his horses backe
   Above a launces length him forth did beare,
   And gainst the cold hard earth so sore him strake,
95   That all his bones in peeces nigh he brake.
   Where seeing him so lie, he left his steed,
   And to him leaping, vengeance thought to take
   Of him, for all his former follies meed,
With flaming sword in hand his terror more to breed.

12

100 The fearefull swayne beholding death so nie,
   Cryde out aloud for mercie him to save;
   In lieu whereof he would to him descrie,
   Great treason to him meant, his life to reave.
   The Prince soone hearkned, and his life forgave.
105 Then thus said he, There is a straunger knight,
   The which for promise of great meed, us drave
   To this attempt, to wreake his hid despight,
For that himselfe thereto did want sufficient might.

13

The Prince much mused at such villenie,
110 And sayd; Now sure ye well have earn'd your meed,
   For th'one is dead, and th'other soone shall die,
   Unlesse to me thou hether bring with speed
   The wretch, that hyr'd you to this wicked deed,
   He glad of life, and willing eke to wreake
115 The guilt on him, which did this mischiefe breed,
   Swore by his sword, that neither day nor weeke
He would surceasse, but him, where so he were, would seeke.

14

So up he rose, and forth straight way he went
   Backe to the place, where *Turpine* late he lore;°   *left*
120 There he him found in great astonishment,
   To see him so bedight with bloodie gore,
   And griesly wounds that him appalled sore.
   Yet thus at length he said, how now Sir knight?
   What meaneth this, which here I see before?

125   How fortuneth this foule uncomely plight,
So different from that, which earst ye seem'd in sight?

15

Perdie (said he) in evill houre it fell,
    That ever I for meed did undertake
    So hard a taske, as life for hyre to sell;
130   The which I earst adventur'd for your sake.
    Witnesse the wounds, and this wyde bloudie lake,
    Which ye may see yet all about me steeme.
    Therefore now yeeld, as ye did promise make,
    My due reward, the which right well I deeme
135 I yearned have, that life so dearely did redeeme.

16

But where then is (quoth he halfe wrothfully)
    Where is the bootie,[6] which therefore I bought,
    That cursed caytive, my strong enemy,
    That recreant knight, whose hated life I sought?
140   And where is eke your friend, which halfe it ought?[7]
    He lyes (said he) upon the cold bare ground,
    Slayne of that errant knight, with whom he fought;
    Whom afterwards my selfe with many a wound
Did slay againe, as ye may see there in the stound.

17

145 Thereof false *Turpin* was full glad and faine,
    And needs with him streight to the place would ryde,
    Where he himselfe might see his foeman slaine;
    For else his feare could not be satisfyde.
    So as they rode, he saw the way all dyde
150   With streames of bloud; which tracting° by the traile,   *following*
    Ere long they came, whereas in evill tyde
    That other swayne, like ashes deadly pale,
Lay in the lap of death, rewing his wretched bale.

18

Much did the Craven seeme to mone his case,
155   That for his sake his deare life had forgone;
    And him bewayling with affection base,
    Did counterfeit kind pittie, where was none:
    For wheres no courage, theres no ruth nor mone.
    Thence passing forth, not farre away he found,
160   Whereas the Prince himselfe lay all alone,

6. I.e., Arthur's corpse.   7. I.e., which owed half of it to me.

Loosely displayd upon the grassie ground,
Possessed of sweete sleepe, that luld him soft in swound.

19

Wearie of travell in his former fight,
   He there in shade himselfe had layd to rest,
165   Having his armes and warlike things undight,
   Fearelesse of foes that mote his peace molest;
   The whyles his salvage page, that wont be prest,
   Was wandred in the wood another way,
   To doe some thing, that seemed to him best,
170   The whyles his Lord in silver slomber lay,
Like to the Evening starre adorn'd with deawy ray.

20

Whom when as *Turpin* saw so loosely layd,
   He weened well, that he in deed was dead,
   Like as that other knight to him had sayd:
175   But when he nigh approcht, he mote aread
   Plaine signes in him of life and livelihead.
   Whereat much griev'd against that straunger knight,
   That him too light of credence did mislead,
   He would have backe retyred from that sight,
180 That was to him on earth the deadliest despight.

21

But that same knight would not once let him start,
   But plainely gan to him declare the case
   Of all his mischiefe, and late lucklesse smart;
   How both he and his fellow there in place
185   Were vanquished, and put to foule disgrace,
   And how that he in lieu of life him lent,
   Had vow'd unto the victor, him to trace
   And follow through the world, where so he went,
Till that he him delivered to his punishment.

22

190 He therewith much abashed and affrayd,
   Began to tremble every limbe and vaine;
   And softly whispering him, entyrely prayd,
   T'advize him better, then by such a traine
   Him to betray unto a straunger swaine:
195   Yet rather counseld him contrarywize,
   Sith he likewise did wrong by him sustaine,
   To joyne with him and vengeance to devize,
Whylest time did offer meanes him sleeping to surprize.

23

Nathelesse for all his speach, the gentle knight
200   Would not be tempted to such villenie,
         Regarding more his faith, which he did plight,
         All were[8] it to his mortall enemie,
         Then to entrap him by false treacherie:
         Great shame in lieges blood to be embrew'd.
205   Thus whylest they were debating diverslie,
         The Salvage forth out of the wood issew'd
Backe to the place, whereas his Lord he sleeping vew'd.

24

There when he saw those two so neare him stand,
         He doubted much what mote their meaning bee,
210   And throwing downe his load out of his hand,
         To weet great store of forrest firute, which hee
         Had for his food late gathered from the tree,
         Himselfe unto his weapon he betooke,
         That was an oaken plant, which lately hee
215   Rent by the roof, which he so sternely shooke,
That like an hazell wand, it quivered and quooke.

25

Whereat the Prince awaking, when he spyde
         The traytour *Turpin* with that other knight,
         He started up, and snatching neare his syde
220   His trustie sword, the servant of his might,
         Like a fell Lyon leaped to him light,
         And his left hand upon his collar layd.
         Therewith the cowheard deaded° with affright,   *stupefied*
         Fell flat to ground, ne word unto him sayd,
225 But holding up his hands, with silence mercie prayd.

26

But he so full of indignation was,
         That to his prayer nought he would incline,
         But as he lay upon the humbled gras,
         His foot he set on his vile necke, in signe
230   Of servile yoke, that nobler harts repine.
         Then letting him arise like abject thrall,
         He gan to him obiect his haynous crime,
         And to revile, and rate, and recreant call,
And lastly to despoyle of knightly bannerall.[9]

---

8. Even if it were.   9. Banderole, small pennant or ornamental banner.

27

235 And after all, for greater infamie,
 He by the heeles him hung upon a tree,
 And baffuld° so, that all which passed by,   *disgraced*
 The picture of his punishment might see,
 And by the like ensample warned bee,
240 How ever they through treason doe trespasse.
 But turne we now backe to that Ladie free,[1]
 Whom late we left ryding upon an Asse,
Led by a Carle and foole, which by her side did passe.

28

She was a Ladie of great dignitie,
245   And lifted up to honorable place,
 Famous through all the land of Faerie,
 Though of meane parentage and kindred base,
 Yet deckt with wondrous giftes of natures grace,
 That all men did her person much admire,
250   And praise the feature of her goodly face,
 The beames whereof did kindle lovely fire
In th'harts of many a knight, and many a gentle squire.

29

But she thereof grew proud and insolent,
 That none she worthie thought to be her fere,°   *companion*
255   But scornd them all, that love unto her ment;°   *intended*
 Yet was she lov'd of many a worthy pere,
 Unworthy she to be belov'd so dere,
 That could not weigh of worthinesse aright.
 For beautie is more glorious bright and clere,
260   The more it is admir'd of many a wight,
And noblest she, that served is of noblest knight.

30

But this coy Damzell thought contrariwize,
 That such proud looks would make her praysed more;
 And that the more she did all love despize,
265   The more would wretched lovers her adore.
 What cared she, who sighed for her sore,
 Or who did wayle or watch the wearie night?
 Let them that list, their lucklesse lot deplore;
 She was borne free, not bound to any wight,
270 And so would ever live, and love her owne delight.

1. The noble or gentle Mirabella, who first appeared in VI.6.16–17. It has been suggested that Mirabella (Italian: *mirabile*, "admirable, marvellous"; *mirari*, "to gaze at," *bella* "beautiful") represents the haughty pride of the sonnet lady who scorns the lover's pains.

31

Through such her stubborne stifnesse, and hard hart,
    Many a wretch, for want of remedie,
    Did languish long in lifeconsuming smart,
    And at the last through dreary dolour die:
275   Whylest she, the Ladie of her libertie,
    Did boast her beautie had such soveraine might,
    That with the onely twinckle of her eye,
    She could or save, or spill, whom she would hight.
What could the Gods doe more, but doe it more aright?

32

280 But loe the Gods, that mortall follies vew,
    Did worthily revenge this maydens pride;
    And nought regarding her so goodly hew,
    Did laugh at her, that many did deride,
    Whilest she did weepe, of no man mercifide.
285   For on a day, when *Cupid* kept his court,
    As he is wont at each Saint Valentide,[2]
    Unto the which all lovers doe resort,
That of their loves successe they there may make report.

33

It fortun'd then, that when the roules were red,
290   In which the names of all loves folke were fyled,
    That many there were missing, which were ded,
    Or kept in bands, or from their loves exyled,
    Or by some other violence despoyled.
    Which when as *Cupid* heard, he wexed wroth,
295   And doubting° to be wronged, or beguyled,   *fearing*
    He bad his eyes to be unblindfold both,
That he might see his men, and muster them by oth.

34

Then found he many missing of his crew,
    Which wont doe suit and service to his might;
300   Of whom what was becomen, no man knew.
    Therefore a Jurie was impaneld streight,
    T'enquire of them, whether by force, or sleight,
    Or their owne guilt, they were away convayd.
    To whom foule *Infamie*, and fell *Despight*
305   Gave evidence, that they were all betrayd,
And murdred cruelly by a rebellious Mayd.

---

2. As in Chaucer's *Parliament of Fowls*, the God of Love holds court on St. Valentine's Day.

35

Fayre *Mirabella* was her name, whereby
   Of all those crymes she there indited was:
   All which when *Cupid* heard, he by and by
310   In great displeasure, wild a *Capias*[3]
   Should issue forth, t'attach that scornefull lasse.
   The warrant straight was made, and therewithall
   A Baylieffe errant forth in post did passe,
   Whom they by name there *Portamore*[4] did call;
315 He which doth summon lovers to loves judgement hall.

36

The damzell was attacht,° and shortly brought   *seized*
   Unto the barre, whereas she was arrayned:
   But she thereto nould plead, nor answere ought
   Even for stubborne pride, which her restrayned.
320   So judgement past, as is by law ordayned
   In cases like, which when at last she saw,
   Her stubborne hart, which love before disdayned,
   Gan stoupe, and falling downe with humble awe,
Cryde mercie, to abate the extremitie of law.

37

325 The sonne of *Venus* who is myld by kynd,
   But where he is provokt with peevishnesse,
   Unto her prayers piteously enclynd,
   And did the rigour of his doome represse;
   Yet not so freely, but that nathelesse
330   He unto her a penance did impose,
   Which was, that through this worlds wyde wilderness
   She wander should in companie of those,
Till she had sav'd so many loves, as she did lose.

38

So now she had bene wandring two whole yeares
335   Throughout the world, in this uncomely case,
   Wasting her goodly hew in heavie teares,
   And her good dayes in dolorous disgrace:
   Yet had she not in all these two yeares space,
   Saved but two, yet in two yeares before,
340   Throgh her dispiteous pride, whilest love lackt place,
   She had destroyed two and twenty more.
Aie me, how could her love make half amends therefore.

3. Latin: "you may take"; a written authorization to make   4. Italian: *portare*, "to carry," *amore*, "love."
an arrest.

39

And now she was uppon the weary way,
   When as the gentle Squire, with faire *Serene*,
345   Met her in such misseeming foule array;
   The whiles that mighty man did her demeane
   With all the evill termes and cruell meane,
   That he could make; And eeke that angry foole
   Which follow'd her, with cursed hands uncleane
350   Whipping her horse, did with his smarting toole
Oft whip her dainty selfe, and much augment her doole.°   *grief*

40

Ne ought it mote availe her to entreat
   The one or th'other, better her to use:
   For both so wilfull were and obstinate,
355   That all her piteous plaint they did refuse,
   And rather did the more her beate and bruse.
   But most the former villaine, which did lead
   Her tyreling° jade, was bent her to abuse;   *weary*
   Who though she were with wearinesse nigh dead,
360   Yet would not let her lite, nor rest a little stead.°   *period of time*

41

For he was sterne, and terrible by nature,
   And eeke of person huge and hideous,
   Exceeding much the measure of mans stature,
   And rather like a Gyant monstruous.
365   For sooth he was descended of the hous
   Of those old Gyants,° which did warres darraine   *Titans*
   Against the heaven in order battailous,
   And sib to great *Orgolio*, which was slaine
By *Arthure*, when as *Unas* Knight he did maintaine.

42

370   His lookes were dreadfull, and his fiery eies
   Like two great Beacons, glared bright and wyde,
   Glauncing askew, as if his enemies
   He scorned in his overweening pryde;
   And stalking stately like a Crane, did stryde
375   At every step uppon the tiptoes hie,
   And all the way he went, on every syde
   He gaz'd about, and stared horriblie,
As if he with his lookes would all men terrifie.

43

He wore no armour, ne for none did care,
380   As no whit dreading any living wight;

But in a Jacket quilted richly rare,
    Upon checklaton[5] he was straungely dight,
    And on his head a roll of linnen plight,
    Like to the Mores of Malaber[6] he wore;
385   With which his locks, as blacke as pitchy night,
    Were bound about, and voyded from before,
And in his hand a mighty yron club he bore.

44

This was *Disdaine*, who led that Ladies horse
    Through thick & thin, through mountains & through plains,
390   Compelling her, wher she would not by force
    Haling her palfrey by the hempen raines.
    But that same foole, which most increast her paines,
    Was *Scorne*, who having in his hand a whip,
    Her therewith yirks, and still when she complaines,
395   The more he laughes, and does her closely quip,
To see her sore lament, and bite her tender lip.

45

Whose cruell handling when that Squire beheld,
    And saw those villaines her so vildely use,
    His gentle heart with indignation sweld,
400   And could no lenger beare so great abuse,
    As such a Lady so to beate and bruse;
    But to him stepping, such a stroke him lent,
    That forst him th'halter from his hand to loose,
    And maugre all his might, backe to relent:
405   Else had he surely there bene slaine, or fowly shent.

46

The villaine wroth for greeting him so sore,
    Gathered him selfe together soone againe,
    And with his yron batton, which he bore,
    Let drive at him so dreadfully amaine,
410   That for his safety he did him constraine
    To give him ground, and shift to every side,
    Rather then once his burden to sustaine:
    For bootelesse thing him seemed, to abide,
So mighty blowes, or prove the puissaunce of his pride.

---

5. Ciclaton, defined by Spenser, *View of the Present State of Ireland* (*Var.*, p. 225): "The quilted leather jack[et] is old english: For it was the proper weed of the horseman, as you may read in Chaucer, when he describeth Sir Thopas's apparel, and armour, as he went to fight against the gyant, in his robe of checklaton, which is that kind of gilded leather with which they use to embroider their irish jackets" ("Tale of Sir Thopas," 734).

6. Malabar is in India. The word *Moors* was sometimes used to refer to all non-Christian nations.

47

415 Like as a Mastiffe having at a bay
    A salvage Bull, whose cruell homes doe threat
    Desperate daunger, if he them assay,
    Traceth his ground, and round about doth beat,
    To spy where he may some advauntage get;
420   The whiles the beast doth rage and loudly rore,
    So did the Squire, the whiles the Carle did fret,
    And fume in his disdainefull mynd the more,
And oftentimes by Turmagant and Mahound swore.[7]

48

Nathelesse so sharpely still he him pursewd,
425   That at advantage him at last he tooke,
    When his foote slipt (that slip he dearely rewd,)
    And with his yron club to ground him strooke;
    Where still he lay, ne out of swoune awooke,
    Till heavy hand the Carle upon him layd,
430   And bound him fast: Tho when he up did looke,
    And saw him selfe captiv'd, he was dismayd,
Ne powre had to withstand, ne hope of any ayd.

49

Then up he made him rise, and forward fare,
    Led in a rope, which both his hands did bynd;
435   Ne ought that foole for pitty did him spare,
    But with his whip him following behynd,
    Him often scourg'd, and forst his feete to fynd:
    And other whiles with bitter mockes and mowes
    He would him scorne, that to his gentle mynd
440   Was much more grievous, then the others blowes:
Words sharpely wound, but greatest griefe of scorning growes.

50

The faire *Serena*, when she saw him fall
    Under that villaines club, then surely thought
    That slaine he was, or made a wretched thrall,
445   And fled away with all the speede she mought,
    To seeke for safety, which long time she sought:
    And past through many perils by the way,
    Ere she againe to *Calepine* was brought;
    The which discourse as now I must delay,
450 Till *Mirabettaes* fortunes I doe further say.

7. Oaths used by infidel warriors.

Canto VIII

Prince Arthure overcomes Disdaine,
Quites Mirabell from dreed:
Serena found of Salvages,
By Calepine is freed.

1

Ye gentle Ladies, in whose soveraine powre
   Love hath the glory of his kingdome left,
   And th'hearts of men, as your eternall dowre,
   In yron chaines, of liberty bereft,
5   Delivered hath into your hands by gift;
   Be well aware, how ye the same doe use,
   That pride doe not to tyranny you lift;
   Least if men you of cruelty accuse,
He from you take that chiefedome, which ye doe abuse.

2

10 And as ye soft and tender are by kynde,
   Adornd with goodly gifts of beauties grace,
   So be ye soft and tender eeke in mynde;
   But cruelty and hardnesse from you chace,
   That all your other praises will deface,
15   And from you turne the love of men to hate.
   Ensample take of *Mirabellaes* case,
   Who from the high degree of happy state,
Fell into wretched woes, which she repented late.

3

Who after thraldome of the gentle Squire,°   *Timias*
20   Which she beheld with lamentable eye,
   Was touched with compassion entire,
   And much lamented his calamity,
   That for her sake fell into misery:
   Which booted nought for prayers, nor for threat
25   To hope for to release or mollify;
   For aye the more, that she did them entreat
The more they him misust, and cruelly did beat.

4

So as they forward on their way did pas,
   Him still reviling and afflicting sore,
30   They met Prince *Arthure* with Sir *Enias*,
   (That was that courteous Knight, whom he before
   Having subdew'd, yet did to life restore,)
   To whom as they approcht, they gan augment

Their cruelty, and him to punish more,
35   Scourging and haling him more vehement;
As if it them should grieve to see his punishment.

5

The Squire him selfe when as he saw his Lord,
    The witnesse of his wretchednesse, in place,
    Was much asham'd, that with an hempen cord
40   He like a dog was led in captive case,
    And did his head for bashfulnesse abase,
    As loth to see, or to be seene at all:
    Shame would be bid. But whenas *Enias*
    Beheld two such, of two such villaines thrall,
45 His manly mynde was much emmoved therewithall.

6

And to the Prince thus sayd; See you Sir Knight
    The greatest shame that ever eye yet saw?
    Yond Lady and her Squire with foule despight
    Abusde, against all reason and all law,
50   Without regard of pitty or of awe.
    See how they doe that Squire beat and revile;
    See how they doe the Lady hale and draw.
    But if ye please to lend me leave a while,
I will them soone acquite,° and both of blame assoile.°   *free / absolve*

7

55 The Prince assented, and then he streight way
    Dismounting light, his shield about him threw,
    With which approching, thus he gan to say;
    Abide ye caytive treachetours untrew,
    That have with treason thralled unto you
60   These two, unworthy of your wretched bands;
    And now your crime with cruelty pursew.
    Abide, and from them lay your loathly hands;
Or else abide the death, that hard before you stands.

8

The villaine stayd not aunswer to invent,
65   But with his yron club preparing way,
    His mindes sad message backe unto him sent;
    The which descended with such dreadfull sway,
    That seemed nought the course thereof could stay:
    No more then lightening from the lofty sky.
70   Ne list the Knight the powre thereof assay,
    Whose doome was death, but lightly slipping by,
Unwares defrauded his intended destiny.

9

And to requite him with the like againe,
 With his sharpe sword he fiercely at him flew,
75 And strooke so strongly, that the Carle with paine
 Saved him selfe, but that he there him slew:
 Yet sav'd not so, but that the bloud it drew,
 And gave his foe good hope of victory.
 Who therewith flesht, upon him set anew,
80 And with the second stroke, thought certainely
To have supplyde° the first, and paide the usury.[1] *supplemented*

10

But Fortune aunswerd not unto his call;
 For as his hand was heaved up on hight,
 The villaine met him in the middle fall,° *in mid-stroke*
85 And with his club bet backe his brondyron° bright *sword*
 So forcibly, that with his owne hands might
 Rebeaten backe upon him selfe againe,
 He driven was to ground in selfe despight;
 From whence ere he recovery could gaine,
90 He in his necke had set his foote with fell disdaine.

11

With that the foole, which did that end awayte,
 Came running in, and whilest on ground he lay,
 Laide heavy hands on him, and held so strayte,
 That downe he kept him with his scornefull sway,
95 So as he could not weld him any way.
 The whiles that other villaine went about
 Him to have bound, and thrald without delay;
 The whiles the foole did him revile and flout,
Threatning to yoke them two & tame their corage stout.

12

100 As when a sturdy ploughman with his hynde° *laborer, servant*
 By strength have overthrowne a stubborne steare,
 They downe him hold, and fast with cords do bynde,
 Till they him force the buxome° yoke to beare: *yielding, obedient*
 So did these two this Knight oft tug and teare.
105 Which when the Prince beheld, there standing by,
 He left his lofty steede to aide him neare,
 And buckling soone him selfe, gan fiercely fly
Uppon that Carle, to save his friend from jeopardy.

---

1. I.e., struck extra hard.

13

The villaine leaving him unto his mate
110   To be captiv'd, and handled as he list,
     Himselfe addrest unto this new debate,
     And with his club him all about so blist,°   *brandished*
     That he which way to turne him scarcely wist:
     Sometimes aloft he layd, sometimes alow;
115   Now here, now there, and oft him neare° he mist;   *nearly*
     So doubtfully, that hardly one could know
Whether more wary were to give or ward the blow.

14

But yet the Prince so well enured° was   *accustomed familiar*
     With such huge strokes, approved oft in fight,
120   That way to them he gave forth right to pas.
     Ne would endure the daunger of their might,
     But wayt advantage, when they downe did light.
     At last the caytive after long discourse,
     When all his strokes he saw avoyded quite,
125   Resolved in one t'assemble all his force,
And make one end of him without ruth or remorse.

15

His dreadfull hand he heaved up aloft,
     And with his dreadfull instrument of yre,
     Thought sure have pownded him to powder soft,
130   Or deepe emboweld in the earth entyre:
     But Fortune did not with his will conspire.
     For ere his stroke attayned his intent,
     The noble childe preventing his desire,
     Under his club with wary boldnesse went,
135 And smote him on the knee, that never yet was bent.

16

It never yet was bent, ne bent it now,
     Albe the stroke so strong and puissant were,
     That seem'd a marble pillour it could bow,
     But all that leg, which did his body beare,
140   It crackt throughout, yet did no bloud appeare;
     So as it was unable to support
     So huge a burden on such broken geare,°   *apparatus (i.e., his knee)*
     But fell to ground, like to a lumpe of durt,
Whence he assayd to rise, but could not for his hurt.

17

145 Eftsoones the Prince to him full nimbly stept,
     And least he should recover foote againe,

His head meant from his shoulders to have swept.
Which when the Lady saw, she cryde amaine;
Stay stay, Sir Knight, for love of God abstaine,
150   From that unwares ye weetlesse doe intend;
Slay not that Carle, though worthy to be slaine:
For more on him doth then him selfe depend;
My life will by his death have lamentable end.

18

He staide his hand according her desire,
155   Yet nathemore him suffred to arize;
But still suppressing gan of her inquire,
What meaning mote those uncouth words comprize,
That in that villaines health her safety lies:
That, were no might in man, nor heart in Knights,
160   Which durst her dreaded reskue enterprize,
Yet heavens them selves, that favour feeble rights,
Would for it selfe redresse, and punish such despights.

19

Then bursting forth in teares, which gushed fast
Like many water streames, a while she stayd;°   hesitated
165   Till the sharpe passion being overpast,
Her tongue to her restord, then thus she sayd;
Nor heavens, nor men can me most wretched mayd
Deliver from the doome of my desart,
The which the God of love hath on me layd,
170   And damned to endure this direfull smart,
For penaunce of my proud and hard rebellious hart.

20

In prime of youthly yeares, when first the flowre
Of beauty gan to bud, and bloosme delight,
And nature me endu'd with plenteous dowre,
175   Of all her gifts, that pleasde each living sight,
I was belov'd of many a gentle Knight,
And sude° and sought with all the service dew: pursued
Full many a one for me deepe groand and sight,
And to the dore of death for sorrow drew,
180   Complayning out on me, that would not on them rew.

21

But let them love that list, or live or die;
Me list not die for any lovers doole:
Ne list me leave my loved libertie,
To pitty him that list to play the foole:
185   To love my selfe I learned had in schoole.

Thus I triumphed long in lovers paine,
    And sitting carelesse on the scorners stoole,
    Did laugh at those that did lament and plaine:
But all is now repayd with interest againe.

22

190   For loe the winged God,° that woundeth harts,   *Cupid*
        Causde me be called to accompt therefore,
        And for revengement of those wrongfull smarts,
        Which I to others did inflict afore,
        Addeem'd me to endure this penaunce sore;
195   That in this wize, and this unmeete array,°   *unsuitable clothing*
        With these two lewd companions, and no more,
        Disdaine and *Scorne*, I through the world should stray,
Till I have sav'd so many, as I earst did slay.

23

Certes (sayd then the Prince) the God is just,
200   That taketh vengeaunce of his peoples spoile.
        For were no law in love, but all that lust,
        Might them oppresse, and painefully turmoile,
        His kingdome would continue but a while.
        But tell me Lady, wherefore doe you beare
205   This bottle thus before you with such toile,
        And eeke this wallet at your backe arreare,
That for these Carles to carry much more comely were?

24

Here in this bottle (sayd the sory Mayd)
        I put the teares of my contrition,
210   Till to the brim I have it full defrayd:
        And in this bag which I behinde me don,
        I put repentaunce for things past and gon.
        Yet is the bottle leake, and bag so torne,
        That all which I put in, fals out anon;
215   And is behinde me trodden downe of *Scorne*,
Who mocketh all my paine, & laughs the more I mourn.

25

The Infant° hearkned wisely to her tale,   *Arthur*
        And wondred much at *Cupids* judg'ment wise,
        That could so meekly make proud hearts avale,[2]
220   And wreake him selfe on them, that him despise.
        Then suffred he *Disdaine* up to arise,

2. Go down (i.e., be humbled).

Who was not able up him selfe to reare,
By meanes his leg through his late luckelesse prise,
Was crackt in twaine, but by his foolish feare°   *partner*
225   Was holpen up, who him supported standing neare.

26

But being up, he lookt againe aloft,
    As if he never had received fall;
And with sterne eye-browes stared at him oft,
    As if he would have daunted him with all:
230   And standing on his tiptoes, to seeme tall,
Downe on his golden feete he often gazed,
    As if such pride the other could apall;
Who was so far from being ought amazed,
That he his lookes despised, and his boast dispraized.

27

235   Then turning backe unto that captive thrall,
    Who all this while stood there beside them bound,
Unwilling to be knowne, or seene at all,
    He from those bands weend him to have unwound.
    But when approching neare, he plainely found,
240   It was his owne true groome, the gentle Squire,°   *Timias*
He thereat wext exceedingly astound,
    And him did oft embrace, and oft admire,°   *marveled, wondered*
Ne could with seeing satisfie his great desire.

28

Meane while the Salvage man, when he beheld
245   That huge great foole oppressing th'other Knight,[3]
Whom with his weight unweldy downe he held,
    He flew upon him, like a greedy kight°   *bird of prey*
Unto some carrion offered to his sight,
    And downe him plucking, with his nayles and teeth
250   Gan him to hale, and teare, and scratch, and bite;
    And from him taking his owne whip, therewith
So sore him scourgeth, that the bloud downe followeth.

29

And sure I weene, had not the Ladies cry
    Procur'd the Prince his cruell hand to stay,
255   He would with whipping, him have done to dye:°   *killed*
    But being checkt, he did abstains streight way,
    And let him rise. Then thus the Prince gan say;
Now Lady sith your fortunes thus dispose,

3. Sir Enias.

That if ye list have liberty, ye may,
260   Unto your selfe I freely leave to chose,
Whether I shall you leave, or from these villaines lose.°   *loose, i.e., free*

30

Ah nay Sir Knight (sayd she) it may not be,
But that I needes must by all meanes fulfill
This penaunce, which enjoyned is to me,
265   Least unto me betide a greater ill;
Yet no lesse thankes to you for your good will.
So humbly taking leave, she turnd aside,
But *Arthure*[4] with the rest, went onward still
On his first quest, in which did him betide
270   A great adventure, which did him from them devide.

31

But first it falleth me by course to tell
Of faire *Serena*,[5] who as earst you heard,
When first the gentle Squire at variaunce fell
With those two Carles, fled fast away, afeard
275   Of villany to be to her inferd:°   *brought upon*
So fresh the image of her former dread,
Yet dwelling in her eye, to her appeard,
That every foote did tremble, which did tread,
And every body two, and two she foure did read.

32

280   Through hils & dales, through bushes & through breres
Long thus she fled, till that at last she thought
Her selfe now past the perill of her feares.
Then looking round about, and seeing nought,
Which doubt° of daunger to her offer mought,   *fear*
285   She from her palfrey lighted on the plaine,
And sitting downe, her selfe a while bethought
Of her long travell and turmoyling paine;
And often did of love, and oft of lucke complaine.

33

And evermore she blamed *Calepine*,[6]
290   The good Sir *Calepine*, her owne true Knight,
As th'onely author of her wofull tine:°   *unhappiness*
For being of his love to her so light,
As her to leave in such a piteous plight.

---

4. This is Arthur's last appearance in the poem.
5. Serena flees when Timias is captured by Disdain and Scorn, 7.50.
6. Calepine was separated from Serena when he pursued the bear carrying off the baby, 4.17 ff.

turtledove

Yet never Turtle° truer to his make,
295   Then he was tride° unto his Lady bright:
    Who all this while endured for her sake,
Great perill of his life, and restlesse paines did take.

united, joined

34

Tho when as all her plaints, she had displayd,
    And well disburdened her engrieved brest,
300   Upon the grasse her selfe adowne she layd;
    Where being tyrde with travell, and opprest
    With sorrow, she betooke her selfe to rest.
    There whitest in *Morpheus*[7] bosome safe she lay,
    Fearelesse of ought, that mote her peace molest,
305   False Fortune did her safety betray,
Unto a straunge mischaunce, that menac'd her decay.

35

In these wylde deserts, where she now abode,[8]
    There dwelt a salvage nation, which did live
    Of stealth and spoile, and making nightly rode°
310   Into their neighbours borders; ne did give
    Them selves to any trade, as for to drive
    The painefull plough, or cattell for to breed,
    Or by adventrous marchandize to thrive;
    But on the labours of poore men to feed,
315   And serve their owne necessities with others need.

raid

36

Thereto they usde one most accursed order,°
    To eate the flesh of men, whom they mote fynde,
    And straungers to devoure, which on their border
    Were brought by errour, or by wreckfull wynde.
320   A monstrous cruelty gainst course of kynde.°
    They towards evening wandring every way,
    To seeke for booty, came by fortune blynde,
    Whereas this Lady, like a sheepe astray,
Now drowned in the depth of sleepe all fearelesse lay.

custom
Laws of nature

37

325 Soone as they spide her, Lord what gladfull glee
    They made amongst them selves; but when her face
    Like the faire yvory shining they did see,
    Each gan his fellow solace and embrace,
    For joy of such good hap by heavenly grace.

---

7. God of sleep.   8. See VI.10.39.

330   Then gan they to devize what course to take:
      Whether to slay her there upon the place,
      Or suffer her out of her sleepe to wake,
    And then her eate attonce; or many meales to make.

38

    The best advizement was of bad,[9] to let her
335   Sleepe out her fill, without encomberment:
      For sleepe they sayd would make her battill° better.   *grow fat*
      Then when she wakt, they all gave one consent,
      That since by grace of God she there was sent,
      Unto their God they would her sacrifize,
340   Whose share, her guiltlesse bloud they would present,
      But of her dainty flesh they did devize
    To make a common feast, & feed with gurmandize.

39

    So round about her they them selves did place[1]
      Upon the grasse, and diversely dispose,
345   As each thought best to spend the lingring space.
      Some with their eyes the daintest morsels chose;
      Some praise her paps, some praise her lips and nose;
      Some whet their knives, and strip their elboes bare:
      The Priest him selfe a garland doth compose
350   Of finest flowres, and with full busie care
    His bloudy vessels wash; and holy fire prepare.

40

    The Damzell wakes, then all attonce upstart,
      And round about her flocke, like many flies,
      Whooping, and hallowing on every part,
355   As if they would have rent the brasen skies.
      Which when she sees with ghastly griefful eies,
      Her heart does quake, and deadly pallid hew
      Benumbes her cheekes: Then out aloud she cries,
      Where none is nigh to heare, that will her rew,
360   And rends her golden locks, and snowy brests embrew.°   *stain*

41

    But all bootes not: they hands upon her lay;
      And first they spoile her of her jewls deare,
      And afterwards of all her rich array;
      The which amongst them they in peeces teare,

9. I.e., the best advice was bad.   1. This stanza parodies the blazon, or poetic catalog of a
                            lady's particular physical beauties.

365   And of the pray each one a part doth beare.
        Now being naked, to their sordid eyes
        The goodly threasures of nature appeare:
        Which as they view with lustfull fantasyes,
    Each wisheth to him selfe, and to the rest envyes.

42

370   Her yvorie necke, her alablaster brest,
            Her paps, which like white silken pillowes were,
            For love in soft delight thereon to rest;[2]
            Her tender sides, her bellie white and clere,
            Which like an Altar did it selfe uprere,
375   To offer sacrifice divine thereon;
            Her goodly thighes, whose glorie did appeare
            Like a triumphall Arch, and thereupon
    The spoiles of Princes hang'd, which were in battel won.

43

        Those daintie parts, the dearlings of delight,
380   Which mote not be prophan'd of common eyes,
            Those villeins vew'd with loose lascivious sight,
            And closely tempted with their craftie spyes;
            And some of them gan mongst themselves devize,
            Thereof by force to take their beastly pleasure.
385   But them the Priest rebuking, did advize
            To dare not to pollute so sacred threasure,
    Vow'd to the gods: religion held even theeves in measure.

44

        So being stayd, they her from thence directed
            Unto a litle grove not farre asyde,
390   In which an altar shortly they erected,
            To slay her on. And now the Eventyde
            His brode black wings had through the heavens wyde
            By this dispred, that was the tyme ordayned
            For such a dismall deed, their guilt to hyde:
395   Of few greene turfes an altar soone they fayned,°   *fashioned*
    And deckt it all with flowres, which they nigh hand obtayned.

45

        Tho when as all things readie were aright,
            The Damzell was before the altar set,
            Being alreadie dead with fearefull fright.
400   To whom the Priest with naked armes full net°   *clean*

2. In these stanzas, with their echoes of the Song of Songs, Spenser continues the blazon begun in stanza 39.

Approching nigh, and murdrous knife well whet,°   *sharpened*
Gan mutter close a certaine secret charme,
With other divelish ceremonies met:
Which doen he gan aloft t'advance his arme,
405   Whereat they shouted all, and made a loud alarme.

46

Then gan the bagpypes and the homes to shrill,
   And shrieke aloud, that with the peoples voyce
   Confused, did the ayre with terror fill,
   And made the wood to tremble at the noyce:
410   The whyles she wayld, the more they did rejoyce.
   Now mote ye understand that to this grove
   Sir *Calepine* by chaunce, more then by choyce,
The selfe same evening fortune hether drove,
As he to seeke *Serena* through the woods did rove.

47

415   Long had he sought her, and through many a soyle
   Had traveld still on foot in heavie armes,
   Ne ought was tyred with his endlesse toyle,
   Ne ought was feared of his certaine harmes:
   And now all weetlesse of the wretched stormes,
420   In which his love was lost, he slept full fast,
   Till being waked with these loud alarmes,
   He lightly started up like one aghast,
And catching up his arms streight to the noise forth past.

48

   There by th'uncertaine glims of starry night,
425   And by the twinkling of their sacred fire,
   He mote perceive a litle dawning sight
   Of all, which there was doing in that quire:
   Mongst whom a woman spoyld of all attire
   He spyde, lamenting her unluckie strife,
430   And groning sore from grieved hart entire;
   Eftsoones he saw one with a naked knife
Readie to launch° her brest, and let out loved life.   *pierce, cut*

49

   With that he thrusts into the thickest throng,
   And even as his right hand adowne descends,
435   He him preventing, layes on earth along,
   And sacrifizeth to th'infernall feends.
   Then to the rest his wrathfull hand he bends,
   Of whom he makes such havocke and such hew,°   *slaughter*

That swarmes of damned soules to hell he sends:
440   The rest that scape his sword and death eschew,
Fly like a flocke of doves before a Faulcons vew.

50

From them returning to that Ladie backe,
    Whom by the Altar he doth sitting find,
    Yet fearing death, and next to death the lacke
445   Of clothes to cover, what they ought by kind,
    He first her hands beginneth to unbind;
    And then to question of her present woe;
    And afterwards to cheare with speaches kind.
    But she for nought that he could say or doe,
450   One word durst speake, or answere him awhit thereto.

51

So inward shame of her uncomely case
    She did conceive, through care of womanhood,
    That though the night did cover her disgrace,
    Yet she in so unwomanly a mood,
455   Would not bewray the state in which she stood.
    So all that night to him unknowen she past.
    But day, that doth discover bad and good,
    Ensewing, made her knowen to him at last:[3]
The end whereof Ile keepe untill another cast.

Canto IX

*Calidore hostes with Meliboe
and loves fayre Pastorell;
Coridon envies him, yet he
for ill rewards him well.*

1

Now turne againe my teme thou jolly swayne,°   *farm laborer or shepherd*
    Backe to the furrow which I lately left;
    I lately left a furrow, one or twayne
    Unplough'd, the which my coulter° hath not cleft: *blade of a plow*
5   Yet seem'd the soyle both fayre and frutefull eft,
    As I it past, that were too great a shame,
    That so rich frute should be from us bereft;
    Besides the great dishonour and defame,
Which should befall to *Calidores*[1] immortall name.

3. At this point Calepine and Serena leave the narrative. Spenser's promise to finish their tale is in the manner of Ariosto, but, unlike Ariosto, Spenser never provides the promised conclusion.

1. Calidore has not been mentioned since 3.26. He was then in pursuit of the Blatant Beast.

2

10 Great travell hath the gentle *Calidore*
    And toyle endured, sith I left him last
    Sewing° the *Blatant beast*, which I forbore   *pursuing*
    To finish then, for other present hast.
    Full many pathes and perils he hath past,
15   Through hils, through dales, throgh forests, & throgh plaines
    In that same quest which fortune on him cast,
    Which he atchieved to his owne great gaines,
Reaping eternall glorie of his restlesse paines.

3

So sharply he the Monster did pursew,
20   That day nor night he suffred him to rest,
    Ne rested he himselfe but natures dew,
    For dread of daunger, not to be redrest,
    If he for slouth forslackt° so famous quest.   *neglected*
    Him first from court he to the citties coursed,°   *followed*
25   And from the citties to the townes him prest,
    And from the townes into the countrie forsed,
And from the country back to private farmes he scorsed.°   *chased*

4

From thence into the open fields he fled,
    Whereas the Heardes° were keeping of their neat,°   *shepherds / cattle*
30   And shepheards singing to their flockes, that fed,
    Layes° of sweete love and youthes delightfull heat: *lays, songs*
    Him thether eke for all his fearefull threat
    He followed fast, and chaced him so nie,
    That to the folds, where sheepe at night doe seat,
35   And to the litle cots,° where shepherds lie   *little cottages*
In winters wrathfull time, he forced him to flie.

5

There on a day as he pursew'd the chace,
    He chaunst to spy a sort° of shepheard groomes,   *group*
    Playing on pypes, and caroling apace,
40   The whyles their beasts there in the budded broomes° *shrubs, the broom plant*
    Beside them fed, and nipt the tender bloomes:
    For other worldly wealth they cared nought.
    To whom Sir *Calidore* yet sweating comes,
    And them to tell him courteously besought,
45 If such a beast they saw, which he had thether brought.

6

They answer'd him, that no such beast they saw,
    Nor any wicked feend, that mote offend

Their happie flockes, nor daunger to them draw:
But if that such there were (as none they kend)
50   They prayd high God him farre from them to send.
Then one of them him seeing so to sweat,
After his rusticke wise,[2] that well he weend,
Offred him drinke, to quench his thirstie heat,
And if he hungry were, him offred eke to eat.

7

55   The knight was nothing nice,° where was no need,   *not fastidious*
And tooke their gentle offer: so adowne
They prayd him sit, and gave him for to feed
Such homely what,° as serves the simple clowne,°   *simple food / rustic*
That doth despise the dainties of the towne.
60   Tho having fed his fill, he there besyde
Saw a faire damzell, which did weare a crowne
Of sundry flowres, with silken ribbands tyde,
Yclad in home-made greene that her owne hands had dyde.

8

Upon a litle hillocke she was placed
65   Higher then all the rest, and round about
Environ'd with a girland, goodly graced,
Of lovely lasses, and them all without
The lustie shepheard swaynes sate in a rout,°   *crowd*
The which did pype and sing her prayses dew,
70   And oft rejoyce, and oft for wonder shout,
As if some miracle of heavenly hew
Were downe to them descended in that earthly vew.

9

And soothly sure she was full fayre of face,
And perfectly well shapt in every lim,
75   Which she did more augment with modest grace,
And comely carriage of her count'nance trim,
That all the rest like lesser lamps did dim:
Who her admiring as some heavenly wight,
Did for their soveraine goddesse her esteeme,
80   And caroling her name both day and night,
The fayrest *Pastorella*[3] her by name did hight.

10

Ne was there heard, ne was there shepheards swayne
But her did honour, and eke many a one

---

2. I.e., in his rustic, or country, way.

3. Her name means shepherdess (Latin: *pastor*, "shepherd");
she is revealed to be of noble birth (VI.12.14–22).

Burnt in her love, and with sweet pleasing payne
85 Full many a night for her did sigh and grone:
But most of all the shepheard *Coridon*[4]
For her did languish, and his deare life spend;
Yet neither she for him, nor other none
Did care a whit, ne any liking lend:
90 Though meane her lot, yet higher did her mind ascend.

11

Her whyles Sir *Calidore* there vewed well,
And markt her rare demeanure, which him seemed
So farre die meane° of shepheards to excell,   *demeanor, bearing*
As that he in his mind her worthy deemed,
95 To be a Princes Paragone° esteemed,   *a prince's equal*
He was unwares surprisd in subtile bands
Of the blynd boy,° ne thence could be redeemed   *Cupid*
By any skill out of his cruell hands,
Caught like the bird, which gazing still on others stands.[5]

12

100 So stood he still long gazing thereupon,
Ne any will had thence to move away,
Although his quest were farre afore him gon;
But after he had fed, yet did he stay,
And sate there still, untill the flying day
105 Was farre forth spent, discoursing diversly
Of sundry things, as fell° to worke delay;   *befell*
And evermore his speach he did apply
To th'heards, but meant them to the damzels fantazy.

13

By this the moystie night approching fast,
110 Her deawy humour gan on th'earth to shed,
That warn'd the shepheards to their homes to hast
Their tender flocks, now being fully fed,
For feare of wetting them before their bed;
Then came to them a good old aged syre,
115 Whose silver lockes bedeckt his beard and hed,
With shepheards hooke in hand, and fit attyre,
That wild the damzell rise; the day did now expyre.

14

He was to weet by common voice esteemed
The father of the fayrest *Pastorell*,

---

4. A conventional shepherd name in the pastoral tradition. 5. Maclean suggests the lark caught in a net while staring
in fascination at the hawk held by the fowler.

120   And of her selfe in very deede so deemed;
          Yet was not so, but as old stories tell
          Found her by fortune, which to him befell,
          In th'open fields an Infant left alone,
          And taking up brought home, and noursed well
125   As his owne chyld; for other he had none,
     That she in tract of time accompted° was his owne.   *accounted, considered*

15

    She at his bidding meekely did arise,
       And streight unto her litle flocke did fare:
       Then all the rest about her rose likewise,
130   And each his sundrie sheepe with severall° care   *separate*
       Gathered together, and them homeward bare:
       Whylest everie one with helping hands did strive
       Amongst themselves, and did their labours share,
       To helpe faire *Pastorella*, home to drive
135   Her fleecie flocke; but *Coridon* most helpe did give.

16

    But *Meliboee*[6] (so hight that good old man)
       Now seeing *Calidore* left all alone,
       And night arrived hard at hand, began
       Him to invite unto his simple home;
140   Which though it were a cottage clad with lome,
       And all things therein meane, yet better so
       To lodge, then in the salvage fields to rome.
       The knight full gladly soone agreed thereto,
     Being his harts owne wish, and home with him did go.

17

145   There he was welcom'd of that honest syre,
       And of his aged Beldame° homely well;   *wife*
       Who him besought himselfe to disattyre,
       And rest himselfe, till supper time befell.
       By which home came the fayrest *Pastorell*,
150   After her flocke she in their fold had tyde,
       And supper readie dight, they to it fell
       With small adoe, and nature satisfyde,
     The which doth litle crave contented to abyde.

18

    Tho when they had their hunger slaked well,
155   And the fayre mayd the table ta'ne away,

6. Greek: "honey-toned." This is a conventional pastoral name.

The gentle knight, as he that did excell
  In courtesie, and well could doe and say,
  For so great kindnesse as he found that day,
  Gan greatly thanke his host and his good wife;
160 And drawing thence his speach another way,
  Gan highly to commend the happie life,
Which Shepheards lead, without debate or bitter strife.

19

How much (sayd he) more happie is the state,[7]
  In which ye father here doe dwell at ease,
165 Leading a life so free and fortunate,
  From all the tempests of these worldly seas,
  Which tosse the rest in daungerous disease?
  Where warres, and wreckes, and wicked enmitie
  Doe them afflict, which no man can appease,
170 That certes I your happinesse envie,
And wish my lot were plast in such felicitie.

20

Surely my sonne (then answer'd he againe)
  If happie, then it is in this intent,
  That having small, yet doe I not complaine
175 Of want, ne wish for more it to augment,
  But doe my selfe, with that I have, content;
  So taught of nature, which doth litle need
  Of forreine helpes to lifes due nourishment:
  The fields my food, my flocke my rayment breed;
180 No better doe I weare, no better doe I feed.

21

Therefore I doe not any one envy,
  Nor am envyde of any one therefore;
  They that have much, feare much to lose thereby,
  And store of cares doth follow riches store.
185 The litle that I have, growes dayly more
  Without my care, but onely to attend it;
  My lambes doe every yeare increase their score,
  And my flockes father daily doth amend it.
What have I, but to praise th'Almighty, that doth send it?

22

190 To them, that list, the worlds gay showes I leave,
  And to great ones such follies doe forgive,°   *give up*

---

7. The contrast of courtly and country life described in these stanzas is a convention of pastoral literature. Spenser is imitating specifically Tasso, *Gerusalemme liberata* 7.8–13.

Which oft through pride do their owne perill weave,
And through ambition downe themselves doe drive
To sad decay, that might contented live.

195 Me no such cares nor combrous thoughts offend,
Ne once my minds unmoved quiet grieve,
But all the night in silver sleepe I spend,
And all the day, to what I list, I doe attend.

23

Sometimes I hunt the Fox, the vowed foe
200   Unto my Lambes, and him dislodge away;
Sometime the fawne I practise° from the Doe,   *scheme, devise strategems*
Or from the Goat her kidde how to convay;°   *steal*
Another while I baytes and nets display,
The birds to catch, or fishes to beguyle:
205 And when I wearie am, I downe doe lay
My limbes in every shade, to rest from toyle,
And drinke of every brooke, when thirst my throte doth boyle.

24

The time was once, in my first prime of yeares,
When pride of youth forth pricked my desire,
210   That I disdain'd amongst mine equall peares
To follow sheepe, and shepheards base attire:
For further fortune then I would inquire.
And leaving home, to roiall court I sought;
Where I did sell my selfe for yearely hire,
215   And in the Princes gardin daily wrought:
There I beheld such vainenesse, as I never thought.

25

With sight whereof soone cloyd, and long deluded
With idle hopes, which them doe entertaine,
After I had ten yeares my selfe excluded
220 From native home, and spent my youth in vaine,
I gan my follies to my selfe to plaine,
And this sweet peace, whose lacke did then appeare.
Tho backe returning to my sheepe againe,
I from thenceforth have learn'd to love more deare
225 This lowly quiet life, which I inherite here.

26

Whylest thus he talkt, the knight with greedy eare
Hong still upon his melting mouth attent;°   *attentive*
Whose sensefull words empierst his hart so neare,
That he was rapt with double ravishment,
230   Both of his speach that wrought him great content,

And also of the object of his vew,
On which his hungry eye was alwayes bent;
That twixt his pleasing tongue, and her faire hew,
He lost himselfe, and like one halfe entraunced grew.

27

235   Yet to occasion meanes, to worke his mind,
And to insinuate his harts desire,
He thus replyde; Now surely syre, I find,
That all this worlds gay showes, which we admire,
Be but vaine shadowes to this safe retyre°   *retirement*
240   Of life, which here in lowlinesse ye lead,
Fearelesse of foes, or fortunes wrackfull yre,
Which tosseth states, and under foot doth tread
The mightie ones, affrayd of every chaunges dread.

28

That even I which daily doe behold
245   The glorie of the great, mongst whom I won,
And now have prov'd, what happinesse ye hold
In this small plot of your dominion,
Now loath great Lordship and ambition;
And wish th'heavens so much had graced mee,
250   As graunt me live in like condition;
Or that my fortunes might transposed bee
From pitch° of higher place, unto this low degree.   *height*

29

In vaine (said then old *Meliboe*) doe men[8]
The heavens of their fortunes fault accuse,
255   Sith they know best, what is the best for them:
For they to each such fortune doe diffuse,°   *disperse*
As they doe know each can most aptly use.
For not that, which men covet most, is best,
Nor that thing worst, which men do most refuse;
260   But fittest is, that all contented rest
With that they hold: each hath his fortune in his brest.

30

It is the mynd, that maketh good or ill,
That maketh wretch or happie, rich or poore:
For some, that hath abundance at his will,
265   Hath not enough, but wants in greatest store;

---

8. Meliboe's advice is the traditional Christian precept about earthly fortune: one must use what God has given us and not look for more. Man's content of mind rests in his acceptance of this principle, which was defined crucially for the Middle Ages and Renaissance by St. Augustine in his distinction between the use and *enjoyment* of the goods of this world.

And other, that hath litle, askes no more,
   But in that litle is both rich and wise.
   For wisedome is most riches; fooles therefore
   They are, which fortunes doe by vowes devize,
270 Sith each unto himselfe his life may fortunize.°   *make fortunate*

31

Since then in each mans self (said *Calidore*)
   It is, to fashion his owne lyfes estate,
   Give leave awhyle, good father, in this shore
   To rest my barcke[9] which hath bene beaten late
275 With stormes of fortune and tempestuous fate,
   In seas of troubles and of toylesome paine,
   That whether quite from them for to retrate
   I shall resolve, or backe to turne againe,
I may here with your selfe some small repose obtaine.

32

280 Not that the burden of so bold a guest
   Shall chargefull° be, or chaunge[1] to you at all;   *burdensome*
   For your meane food shall be my daily feast,
   And this your cabin both my bowre and hall.
   Besides for recompence hereof, I shall[2]
285 You well reward, and golden guerdon give,
   That may perhaps you better much withall,
   And in this quiet make you safer live.
So forth he drew much gold, and toward him it drive.°   *thrust*

33

But the good man, nought tempted with the offer
290 Of his rich mould,° did thrust it farre away,   *dross*
   And thus bespake; Sir knight, your bounteous proffer
   Be farre fro me, to whom ye ill display
   That mucky masse, the cause of mens decay,
   That mote empaire my peace with daungers dread.
295 But if ye algates covet to assay
   This simple sort of life, that shepheards lead,
Be it your owne: our rudenesse° to your selfe aread.   *rusticity and simplicity*

34

So there that night Sir *Calidore* did dwell,
   And long while after, whilest him list remaine,
300 Dayly beholding the faire *Pastorell*,

9. Boat, i.e., myself. The image of man as a storm-besieged boat was common in classical and later literature and especially favored by Augustine and Boethius.
1. I.e., change in your mode of life.

2. Calidore's offer of money to Meliboe shows that he has not understood the "courtesy" of the pastoral world in which he now finds himself.

And feeding on the bayt of his owne bane.°   *destruction*
　　During which time he did her entertaine
　　With all kind courtesies, he could invent;
　　And every day, her companie to gaine,
305　When to the field she went, he with her went:
So for to quench his fire, he did it more augment.

35

But she that never had acquainted beene
　　With such queint usage, fit for Queenes and Kings,[3]
　　Ne ever had such knightly service seene,
310　But being bred under base shepheards wings,
　　Had ever learn'd to love the lowly things,
　　Did litle whit regard his courteous guize,
　　But cared more for *Colins*[4] carolings
　　Then all that he could doe, or ever devize:
315　His layes, his loves, his lookes she did them all despize.

36

Which *Calidore* perceiving, thought it best
　　To chaunge the manner of his loftie looke;
　　And doffing his bright armes, himselfe addrest
　　In shepheards weed, and in his hand he tooke,
320　In stead of steelehead speare, a shepheards hooke,
　　That who had seene him then, would have bethought
　　On *Phrygian Paris* by *Plexippus* brooke,
　　When he the love of fayre *Oenone* sought,
What time the golden apple was unto him brought.[5]

37

325　So being clad, unto the fields he went
　　With the faire *Pastorella* every day,
　　And kept her sheepe with diligent attent,
　　Watching to drive the ravenous Wolfe away,
　　The whylest at pleasure she mote sport and play;
330　And every evening helping them to fold:
　　And otherwhiles for need, he did assay
　　In his strong hand their rugged teats to hold,
And out of them to presse the milke: love so much could.

---

3. Cf. Chaucer, "The Knight's Tale."
4. Colin Clout, Spenser's pseudonym throughout his work. Cf. *Shepheardes Calender, Colin Clouts Come Home Again* and VI10. The name was used earlier by John Skelton, *Colin Clout* (1523?) and Clement Marot, *Complaincte de ma Dame Loyse de Savoye* (1531).

5. The Phrygian Paris is Paris, son of Priam of Troy, who precipitated the destruction of Troy by his error in choosing Venus as the recipient of the golden apple of discord. Paris abandoned Oenone to accept Helen, the wife of Menelaus. No brook Plexippus (Greek: "driver of horses") has been identified in ancient or later literature.

38

Which seeing *Coridon*, who her likewise
335 Long time had lov'd, and hop'd her love to gaine,
  He much was troubled at that straungers guize,
  And many gealous thoughts conceiv'd in vaine,
  That this of all his labour and long paine
  Should reap the harvest, ere it ripened were,
340 That made him scoule, and pout, and oft complaine
  Of *Pastorell* to all the shepheards there,
That she did love a stranger swayne then him more dere.

39

And ever when he came in companie,
  Where *Calidore* was present, he would lovre,
345 And byte his lip, and even for gealousie
  Was readie oft his owne hart to devoure,
  Impatient of any paramoure:
  Who on the other side did seeme so farre
  From malicing, or grudging his good houre,[6]
350 That all he could, he graced him with her,
Ne ever shewed signe of rancour or of jarre.°   *contention*

40

And oft, when *Coridon* unto her brought
  Or litle sparrowes, stolen from their nest,
  Or wanton squirrels, in the woods farre sought,
355 Or other daintie thing for her addrest,
  He would commend his guift, and make the best.
  Yet she no whit his presents did regard,
  Ne him could find to fancie in her brest:
  This newcome shepheard had his market mard.
360 Old love is litle worth when new is more prefard.

41

One day when as the shepheard swaynes together
  Were met, to make their sports and merrie glee,
  As they are wont in faire sunshynie weather,
  The whiles their flockes in shadowes shrouded bee,
365 They fell to daunce: then did they all agree,
  That *Colin Clout* should pipe as one most fit;
  And *Calidore* should lead the ring, as hee
  That most in *Pastorellaes* grace did sit.
Thereat frown'd *Coridon*, and his lip closely bit.

---

6. I.e., fortune.

42

370   But *Calidore* of courteous inclination
      Tooke *Coridon*, and set him in his place,
      That he should lead the daunce, as was his fashion;
      For *Coridon* could daunce, and trimly trace.°   *dance gracefully*
      And when as *Pastorella*, him to grace,
375   Her flowry garlond tooke from her owne head,
      And plast on his, he did it soone displace,
      And did it put on *Coridons* in stead:
    Then *Coridon* woxe frollicke, that earst seemed dead.

43

    Another time, when as they did dispose
380   To practise games, and majsteries to try,
      They for their judge did *Pastorella* chose;
      A garland was the meed of victory.
      There *Coridon* forth stepping openly,
      Did chalenge *Calidore* to wrestling game:
385   For he through long and perfect industry,
      Therein well practisd was, and in the same
    Thought sure t'avenge his grudge, & worke his foe great shame.

44

    But *Calidore* he greatly did mistake;
      For he was strong and mightily stifle pight,°   *sturdily built*
390   That with one fall his necke he almost brake,
      And had he not upon him fallen light,
      His dearest joynt he sure had broken quight.
      Then was the oaken crowne by *Pastorell*
      Given to *Calidore*, as his due right;
395   But he, that did in courtesie excell,
    Gave it to *Coridon*, and said he wonne it well.

45

    Thus did the gentle knight himselfe abeare
      Amongst that rusticke rout in all his deeds,
      That even they, the which his rivals were,
400   Could not maligne him, but commend him needs:
      For courtesie amongst the rudest breeds
      Good will and favour. So it surely wrought
      With this faire Mayd, and in her mynde the seeds
      Of perfect love did sow, that last forth brought
405   The fruite of joy and blisse, though long time dearely bought.

46

    Thus *Calidore* continu'd there long time,
      To winne the love of the faire *Pastorell*;

Which having got, he used without crime
Or blamefull blot, but menaged so well,
410   That he of all the rest, which there did dwell,
Was favoured, and to her grace commended.
But what straunge fortunes unto him befell,
Ere he attain'd the point by him intended,
Shall more conveniently in other place be ended.

Canto X

Calidore sees the Graces daunce,
To Colins melody:
The whiles his Pastorell is led,
Into captivity.

1

Who now does follow the foule *Blatant Beast*,
Whilest *Calidore* does follow that faire Mayd,
Unmyndfull of his vow and high beheast,[1]
Which by the Faery Queene was on him layd,
5   That he should never leave, nor be delayd
From chacing him, till he had it attchieved?
But now entrapt of love, which him betrayd,
He mindeth more, how he may be relieved
With grace from her, whose love his heart hath sore engrieved.

2

10   That from henceforth he meanes no more to sew°   pursue
His former quest, so full of toile and paine;
Another quest, another game in vew
He hath, the guerdon of his love to gaine:
With whom he myndes for ever to remaine,
15   And set his rest amongst the rusticke sort,
Rather then hunt still after shadowes vaine
Of courtly favour, fed with light report,
Of every blaste, and sayling alwaies on the port.[2]

3

Ne certes mote he greatly blamed be,
20   From so high step to stoupe unto so low.

1. Spenser seems to be saying that Calidore's sojourn in the pastoral world recalls Odysseus's stay with Circe (*Odyssey* 10), Aeneas' with Dido (*Aeneid* 4), Ruggiero's with Alcina (Ariosto, *Orlando furioso* 6–8), and Rinaldo's with Armida (Tasso, *Gerusalemme liberata* 16); cf. Calypso (*Odyssey* 5). Calidore's predecessors were entrapped by lust and temporarily drawn into realms of sensual enjoyment and diverted from their quests. While Calidore puts aside for a time his promise to capture the Blatant Beast, he is not mired in a world of lust and spiritual torpor. Calidore's stay in the pastoral world may seem a "truancy," but one should keep in mind both the philosophy expressed in the discussion between Meliboe and Calidore in the preceding canto and Spenser's characteristic irony in beginning his cantos.
2. I.e., never resuming his quest.

For who had tasted once (as oft did he)
  The happy peace, which there doth overflow,
  And prov'd the perfect pleasures, which doe grow
  Amongst poore hyndes, in hils, in woods, in dales,
25   Would never more delight in painted show
  Of such false blisse, as there is set for stales,°   *lures*
T'entrap unwary fooles in their eternall bales.

4

For what hath all that goodly glorious gaze
  Like to one sight, which *Calidore* did vew?
30   The glaunce whereof their dimmed eies would daze,
  That never more they should endure the shew
  Of that sunne-shine, that makes them looke askew.
  Ne ought in all that world of beauties rare,
  (Save onely *Glorianaes* heavenly hew
35   To which what can compare?) can it compare;
The which as commeth now, by course[3] I will declare.

5

One day as he did raunge the fields abroad,
  Whilest his faire *Pastorella* was elsewhere,
  He chaunst to come, far from all peoples troad,°   *tread, path*
40   Unto a place, whose pleasaunce did appere
  To passe all others, on the earth which were:
  For all that ever was by natures skill
  Devized to worke delight, was gathered there,
  And there by her were poured forth at fill,
45 As if this to adorne, she all the rest did pill.°   *plunder, pillage*

6

It was an hill plaste in an open plaine,
  That round about was bordered with a wood
  Of matchlesse hight, that seem'd th'earth to disdaine,
  In which all trees of honour stately stood,
50   And did all winter as in sommer bud,
  Spredding pavilions for the birds to bowre,
  Which in their lower braunches sung aloud;
  And in their tops the soring hauke did towre,°   *perch*
Sitting like King of fowles in majesty and powre.

7

55   And at the foote thereof, a gentle flud
  His silver waves did softly tumble downe,

---

3. I.e., in the progress of the narrative.

Unmard with ragged mosse or filthy mud,
Ne mote wylde beastes, ne mote the ruder clowne
Thereto approch, ne filth mote therein drowne:°   *drench*
60   But Nymphes and Faeries by the bancks did sit,
In the woods shade, which did the waters crowne,
Keeping all noysome° things away from it,   *harmful*
And to the waters fall tuning their accents fit.

8

And on the top thereof a spacious plaine
65   Did spred it selfe, to serve to all delight,
Either to daunce, when they to daunce would faine,
Or else to course about their bases light;[4]
Ne ought there wanted, which for pleasure might
Desired be, or thence to banish bale:
70   So pleasauntly the hill with equall hight,
Did seeme to overlooke the lowly vale;
Therefore it rightly cleeped was mount *Acidale*.[5]

9

They say that *Venus*, when she did dispose
Her selfe to pleasaunce, used to resort
75   Unto this place, and therein to repose
And rest her selfe, as in a gladsome port,
Or with the Graces there to play and sport;
That even her owne Cytheron, though in it
She used most to keepe her royall court,
80   And in her soveraine Majesty to sit,
She in regard hereof refusde and thought unfit.

10

Unto this place when as the Elfin Knight
Approcht, him seemed that the merry sound
Of a shrill pipe he playing heard on hight,°   *aloud*
85   And many feete fast thumping th'hollow ground,
That through the woods their Eccho did rebound.[6]
He nigher drew, to weete what mote it be;
There he a troupe of Ladies dauncing found
Full merrily, and making gladfull glee,
90   And in the midst a Shepheard piping he did see.

---

4. Play at game of prisoner's base.
5. Mount Acidale, *Acidalia* being an epithet for Venus (Greek: "without care"), is contrasted with Cytheron, the mountain where Venus showed herself in royal splendor. Spenser confused the name *Cytheron* with *Cythera* (see III.6.29). The distinction between Acidale and Cytheron-

Cythera was probably meant to figure the distinction between Calidore's "truancy" in the pastoral world and his royally appointed task of catching the Blatant Beast.
6. Cf. refrain in *Epithalamion*: "That all the woods shall answer and theyr eccho ring," etc.

11

He durst not enter into th'open greene,
    For dread of them unwares to be descryde,
    For breaking of their daunce, if he were seene;
    But in the covert of the wood did byde,
95   Beholding all, yet of them unespyde.
    There he did see, that pleased much his sight,
    That even he him selfe his eyes envyde,
    An hundred naked maidens lilly white,
All raunged in a ring, and dauncing in delight.

12

100   All they without were raunged in a ring,
    And daunced round; but in the midst of them
    Three other Ladies did both daunce and sing,
    The whilest the rest them round about did hemme,
    And like a girlond did in compasse stemme:°   *encircled*
105   And in the middest of those same three, was placed
    Another Damzell, as a precious gemme,
    Amidst a ring most richly well enchaced,
That with her goodly presence all the rest much graced.

13

Looke how the Crowne, which *Ariadne* wore[7] [8]
110   Upon her yvory forehead that same day,
    That *Theseus* her unto his bridale bore,
    When the bold *Centaures* made that bloudy fray
    With the fierce *Lapithes*, which did them dismay;
    Being now placed in the firmament,
115   Through the bright heaven doth her beams display,
    And is unto the starres an ornament,
Which round about her move in order excellent.

14

Such was the beauty of this goodly band,
    Whose sundry parts were here too long to tell:
120   But she that in the midst of them did stand,
    Seem'd all the rest in beauty to excell,
    Crownd with a rosie girlond, that right well
    Did her beseeme. And ever, as the crew
    About her daunst, sweet flowres, that far did smell,
125   And fragrant odours they uppon her threw;
But most of all, those three did her with gifts endew.

7. Spenser conflates two myths: (1) Ariadne, who helped Theseus escape the labyrinth of Minos, was deserted by Theseus, and received her wedding crown from Bacchus, who later transformed it into the constellation. (2) The battle between the Centaurs and the Lapiths took place at the marriage of Pirithous and Hippodamia.
8. Like; commonly used to introduce a simile: see Samuel Daniel, *Complaint of Rosamond*, 113, 582.

15

Those were the Graces, daughters of delight,[9]
   Handmaides of *Venus*, which are wont to haunt
   Uppon this hill, and daunce there day and night:
130   Those three to men all gifts of grace do graunt,
   And all, that *Venus* in her selfe doth vaunt,
   Is borrowed of them. But that faire one,
   That in the midst was placed parauaunt,°   *most prominently*
   Was she to whom that shepheard pypt alone,
135 That made him pipe so merrily, as never none.

16

She was to weete that jolly Shepheards lasse,[1]
   Which piped there unto that merry rout,
   That jolly shepheard, which there piped, was
   Poore *Colin Clout* (who knowes not *Colin Clout?*)
140 He pypt apace, whitest they him daunst about.
   Pype jolly shepheard, pype thou now apace
   Unto thy love, that made thee low to lout;
   Thy love is present there with thee in place,
Thy love is there advaunst to be another Grace.

17

145 Much wondred *Calidore* at this straunge sight,
   Whose like before his eye had never seene,
   And standing long astonished in spright,
   And rapt with pleasaunce, wist not what to weene;
   Whether it were the traine of beauties Queene,
150 Or Nymphes, or Faeries, or enchaunted show,
   With which his eyes mote have deluded beene.
   Therefore resolving, what it was, to know,
Out of the wood he rose, and toward them did go.

18

But soone as he appeared to their vew,
155   They vanisht all away out of his sight,
   And cleane were gone, which way he never knew;

---

9. See stanza 22.
1. The woman at the center of the 100 dancing maidens and the three Graces is Colin Clout's love. Some critics identify her as the Rosalind of the *Shepheardes Calender*, in which Spenser first identified himself as Colin Clout. Other critics identify her as Elizabeth I, an identification that Colin himself refutes by his apology to Elizabeth in stanza 28. These critics generally cite *Shepheardes Calender*, "Aprill", in which Elizabeth is advanced to be a

fourth Grace. Still others identify her as Elizabeth Boyle, whom Spenser married in 1594 and for whom he wrote the *Amoretti* and *Epithalamion* (page 676). The difficulty of trying to specify one historical identification for this "lass" is resolved by referring to *Amoretti* 74, in which Spenser gives praise in one figure to the three Elizabeths who were important to him: his mother, his wife, and his Queen. The "lass" is love, wife, Queen, and source of inspiration.

All save the shepheard, who for fell despight[2]
Of that displeasure, broke his bag-pipe quight,
And made great mone for that unhappy turne.
160   But *Calidore*, though no lesse sory wight,
For that mishap, yet seeing him to mourne,
Drew neare, that he the truth of all by him mote learne.

19

And first him greeting, thus unto him spake,
Haile jolly shepheard, which thy joyous dayes
165   Here leadest in this goodly merry make,°   *making*
Frequented of these gentle Nymphes alwayes,
Which to thee flocke, to heare thy lovely layes;
Tell me, what mote these dainty Damzels be,
Which here with thee doe make their pleasant playes?
170   Right happy thou, that mayst them freely see:
But why when I them saw, fled they away from me?

20

Not I so happy answerd then that swaine,[3]
As thou unhappy, which them thence didst chace,
Whom by no meanes thou canst recall againe,
175   For being gone, none can them bring in place,
But whom they of them selves list so to grace.
Right sory I, (saide then Sir *Calidore*,)
That my ill fortune did them hence displace.
But since things passed none may now restore,
180   Tell me, what were they all, whose lacke thee grieves so sore.

21

Tho gan that shepheard thus for to dilate;
Then wote thou shepheard, whatsoever thou bee,
That all those Ladies, which thou sawest late,
Are *Venus* Damzels, all within her fee,
185   But differing in honour and degree:
They all are Graces, which on her depend,
Besides a thousand more, which ready bee
Her to adorne, when so she forth doth wend:
But those three in the midst, doe chiefe on her attend.

---

2. Colin's breaking of his pipe is an allusion to his similar gesture in *Shepheardes Calender*, "Januarye." It may also be a suggestion that he is breaking off his poem before his grand scheme, outlined in the Letter to Ralegh, is finished.
3. Colin's explanation of the vision of the dance is the most self-conscious artistic act in Renaissance poetry.

Critics have often noted that Prospero's speech "Our revels now are ended" (*Tempest* 4.1.148 ff) is in reality Shakespeare's farewell to the stage, but Spenser, under his mask of Colin Clout, not only cuts off his vision because of the intrusion of Calidore but also explains its meaning, relating the vision to the source of civilization, "Civility."

22

190

They are the daughters of sky-ruling Jove,[4]
  By him begot of faire *Eurynome*,
  The Oceans daughter, in this pleasant grove,
  As he this way comming from feastfull glee,
  Of *Thetis* wedding with *Æacidee*,
  In sommers shade him selfe here rested weary.
  The first of them hight mylde *Euphrosyne*,
  Next faire *Aglaia*, last *Thalia* merry:
Sweete Goddesses all three which me in mirth do cherry.°   *make cheerful*

195

23

These three on men all gracious gifts bestow,
  Which decke the body or adorne the mynde,
  To make them lovely or well favoured show,
  As comely carriage, entertainement kynde,
  Sweete semblaunt, friendly offices that bynde,
  And all the complements of curtesie:
  They teach us, how to each degree and kynde
  We should our selves demeane, to low, to hie;
To friends, to foes, which skill men call Civility.[5]

200

205

24

Therefore they alwaies smoothly seeme to smile,
  That we likewise should mylde and gentle be,
  And also naked are, that without guile
  Or false dissemblaunce all them plaine may see,
  Simple and true from covert malice free:
  And eeke them selves so in their daunce they bore,
  That two of them still forward seem'd to bee,
  But one still towards shew'd her selfe afore;°   *frontally*
That good should from us goe, then come in greater store.[6]

210

215

---

4. Spenser follows Hesiod, *Theogony*, in making Jove and Eurynome (Greek: "wide rule") parents of the Graces. Spenser is responsible for making the occasion of this mating the return of Jove from the marriage of Thetis and Peleus (*Æacidee*), thus combining the conception of the Graces with the occasion that precipitated the Trojan War.
5. Social order, and the kind of behavior that perpetuates social order.
6. The problem of these lines is whether two Graces are facing toward or away from the viewer; this apparently simple problem, however, lies at the heart of Spenser's courtesy and any possible interpretation of the poem, because of the iconographic traditions of depicting Graces. The pertinent critics are DeWitt T. Starnes and E. W. Talbert, *Classical Myth and Legend in Renaissance Dictionaries* (Chapel Hill, 1955) and Starnes's two earlier articles, *PQ* 21, 1942, 268–82 and *SP* 39, 1942, 143–59; Edgar Wind, *Pagan Mysteries in the Renaissance*, second

edition (Harmondsworth, 1967), pp. 28 ff; Tonkin, *Spenser's Courteous Pastoral*, pp. 248 ff. Seneca, *De beneficiis*, 1.3, states that the circling dance of the Graces symbolizes the three phases of liberality: offering, accepting, and returning benefits. Servius, in his commentary on *Aen*. 1.720, says that one Grace is pictured from the back while two are shown facing front because for one benefit issuing from us two are supposed to return. E. K. in his gloss on *Shepheardes Calender*, "Aprill" 109 ff, reproduces much of the Senecan and Servian iconography:

> The Graces be three sisters, the daughters of Jupiter, (whose names are Aglaia, Thalia, Euphrosyne, and Homer onely addeth a fourth, s. Pasithea) otherwise called Charites, that is thanks, whom the Poetes feyned to be the Goddesses of al bountie and comelines, which therefore (as sayth Theodontius) they make three, to wete, that men first ought to be gracious and bountiful to other freely, then to receiue

25

Such were those Goddesses, which ye did see;
    But that fourth Mayd, which there amidst them traced,°   *danced*
    Who can aread, what creature mote she bee,
220   Whether a creature, or a goddesse graced
    With heavenly gifts from heven first enraced?°   *implanted*
    But what so sure she was, she worthy was,
    To be the fourth with those three other placed:
    Yet was she certes but a countrey lasse,
225   Yet she all other countrey lasses farre did passe.

26

So farre as doth the daughter of the day,
    All other lesser lights in light excell,
    So farre doth she in beautyfull array,
    Above all other lasses beare the bell,°   *win the prize, lead the crowd*
230   Ne lesse in vertue that beseemes her well,
    Doth she exceede the rest of all her race,
    For which the Graces that here wont to dwell,
    Have for more honor brought her to this place,
    And graced her so much to be another Grace.

27

235   Another Grace she well deserves to be,
    In whom so many Graces gathered are,
    Excelling much the meane° of her degree;   *norm, median*
    Divine resemblaunce, beauty soveraine rare,
    Firme Chastity, that spight ne blemish dare;
240   All which she with such courtesie doth grace,
    That all her peres cannot with her compare,
    But quite are dimmed, when she is in place.
    She made me often pipe and now to pipe apace.

---

benefits at other mens hands curteously, and thirdly to requite them thankfully: which are three sundry Actions in liberalitye. [Seneca] And Boccace saith, that they be painted naked, (as they were indeede on the tombe of C. Julius Cæsar) the one hauing her backe toward vs, and her face fromwarde, as proceeding from vs: the other two toward vs, noting double thanke to be due to vs for the benefit, we have done [Servius].

In addition to this late classical iconography, which continued into the Renaissance as E. K.'s gloss shows, there was another specifically Christian tradition, which allegorized the Graces as the three theological virtues: faith, hope, and charity, because of the etymology of their Greek name *Charites*. This etymological allegory is reinforced in English by the coincidence of the name *Graces* and the theological meaning of the word *grace*, which produced another visual image of two Graces pictured from the back and one facing forward. Since faith and hope are virtues related to the afterlife, they are pictured facing away from the viewer; charity as a virtue directed to action in this life is pictured as facing toward the viewer. This double iconographic tradition is the basis for interpreting Spenser's lines. Most editors emend "forward" as printed in 1596 and 1609 to "froward" to conform with the late classical iconography. But Spenser always uses "froward" in its negative sense of "evilly disposed, perverse, adverse." Line 8, in which the third Grace is described as "afore" (viewed frontally), is another reason given for emendation. If, however, one interprets the "forward" of line 7 as meaning that two Graces are nearer the viewer without specifying that they are dorsally or frontally displayed, this difficulty is solved. Spenser is trying to accommodate both iconographic traditions verbally; his language insists that we read the lines both ways; he is being genuinely ambiguous. The "then" of line 9 can be read in both ways: either as the late classical view that good should from us go, then come in greater store, or in the spirit of Christian charity: greater good should from us go *than* come in greater store.

28

Sunne of the world, great glory of the sky,
245   That all the earth doest lighten with thy rayes,
    Great *Gloriana*, greatest Majesty,
    Pardon thy shepheard, mongst so many layes,
    As he hath sung of thee in all his dayes,
    To make one minime° of thy poore handmayd,   *short musical note*
250   And underneath thy feete to place her prayse,
    That when thy glory shall be farre displayd
To future age of her this mention may be made.

29

When thus that shepherd ended had his speach,
    Sayd *Calidore;* Now sure it yrketh mee,
255   That to thy blisse I made this luckelesse breach,
    As now the author of thy bale to be,
    Thus to bereave thy loves deare sight from thee:
    But gentle Shepheard pardon thou my shame,
    Who rashly sought that, which I mote not see.
260   Thus did the courteous Knight excuse his blame,
And to recomfort him, all comely meanes did frame.

30

In such discourses they together spent
    Long time, as fit occasion forth them led;
    With which the Knight him selfe did much content,
265   And with delight his greedy fancy fed,
    Both of his words, which he with reason red;
    And also of the place, whose pleasures rare
    With such regard° his sences ravished,   *observation*
    That thence, he had no will away to fare,
270 But wisht, that with that shepheard he mote dwelling share.

31

But that envenimd sting,[7] the which of yore,
    His poysnous point deepe fixed in his hart
    Had left, now gan afresh to rancle sore,
    And to renue the rigour of his smart:
275   Which to recure, no skill of Leaches° art   *doctor's*
    Mote him availe, but to returne againe
    To his wounds worker, that with lovely dart
    Dinting° his brest, had bred his restlesse paine,   *striking*
Like as the wounded Whale to shore flies from the maine.°   *deep sea*

---

7. I.e., the wound of Cupid's arrow (VI.9.11).

32

280 So taking leave of that same gentle swaine,
         He backe returned to his rusticke wonne,
         Where his faire *Pastorella* did remaine:
         To whome in sort, as he at first begonne,
         He daily did apply him selfe to donne,
285   All dewfull service voide of thoughts impure
         Ne any paines ne perill did he shonne,
         By which he might her to his love allure,
     And liking in her yet untamed heart procure.

33

     And evermore the shepheard *Coridon*,
290   What ever thing he did her to aggrate,°   please
         Did strive to match with strong contention,
         And all his paines did closely emulate;
         Whether it were to caroll, as they sate
         Keeping their sheepe, or games to exercize,
295   Or to present her with their labours late;
         Through which if any grace chaunst to arize
     To him, the Shepheard streight with jealousie did frize.

34

     One day as they all three together went
         To the greene wood, to gather strawberies,
300   There chaunst to them a dangerous accident;
         A Tigre forth out of the wood did rise,
         That with fell clawes full of fierce gourmandize,°   gluttony
         And greedy mouth, wide gaping like hell gate,
         Did runne at *Pastorell* her to surprize:
305   Whom she beholding, now all desolate
     Gan cry to them aloud, to helpe her all too late.

35

     Which *Coridon* first hearing, ran in hast
         To reskue her, but when he saw the feend,
         Through cowherd feare he fled away as fast,
310   Ne durst abide the daunger of the end;
         His life he steemed° dearer then his frend.   esteemed, valued
         But *Calidore* soone comming to her ayde,
         When he the beast saw ready now to rend
         His loves deare spoile, in which his heart was prayde,°   captured as booty
315 He ran at him enraged in stead of being frayde.

36

     He had no weapon, but his shepheards hooke,
         To serve the vengeaunce of his wrathfull will,

With which so sternely he the monster strooke,
That to the ground astonished he fell;
320   Whence ere he could recov'r, he did him quell,
And hewing off his head, it presented
Before the feete of the faire *Pastorell*;
Who scarcely yet from former feare exempted,
A thousand times him thankt, that had her death prevented.

37

325   From that day forth she gan him to affect,°   *have a preference for*
And daily more her favour to augment;
But *Coridon* for cowherdize reject,
Fit to keepe sheepe, unfit for loves content:
The gentle heart scornes base disparagement.
330   Yet *Calidore* did not despise him quight,
But usde him friendly for further intent,
That by his fellowship, he colour° might   *disguise*
Both his estate, and love from skill° of any wight.   *knowledge*

38

So well he woo'd her, and so well he wrought her,
335   With humble service, and with daily sute,
That at the last unto his will he brought her;
Which he so wisely well did prosecute,
That of his love he reapt the timely finite,
And joyed long in close felicity:
340   Till fortune fraught with malice, blinde, and brute,
That envies lovers long prosperity,
Blew up a bitter storme of foule adversity.

39

It fortuned one day, when *Calidore*[8]
Was hunting in the woods (as was his trade)
345   A lawlesse people, *Brigants* hight of yore,
That never usde to live by plough nor spade,
But fed on spoile and booty, which they made
Upon their neighbours, which did nigh them border,
The dwelling of these shepheards did invade,
350   And spoyld their houses, and them selves did murder;
And drove away their flocks, with other much disorder.

40

Amongst the rest, the which they then did pray,
They spoyld old *Melibee* of all he had,
And all his people captive led away,

8. See VI.8.35.

355   Mongst which this lucklesse mayd away was lad,
       Faire *Pastorella*, sorrowfull and sad,
       Most sorrowfull, most sad, that ever sight,
       Now made the spoile of theeves and *Brigants* bad,
       Which was the conquest of the gentlest Knight,
360   That ever liv'd, and th'onely glory of his might.

41

With them also was taken *Coridon*,
       And carried captive by those theeves away;
       Who in the covert of the night, that none
       Mote them descry, nor reskue from their pray,
365   Unto their dwelling did them close convay.
       Their dwelling in a little Island was,
       Covered with shrubby woods, in which no way
       Appeard for people in nor out to pas,
Nor any footing fynde for overgrowen gras.

42

370   For underneath the ground their way was made,
       Through hollow caves, that no man mote discover
       For the thicke shrubs, which did them alwaies shade
       From view of living wight, and covered over:
       But darkenesse dred and daily night did hover
375   Through all the inner parts, wherein they dwelt.
       Ne lightned was with window, nor with louer,[9]
       But with continuall candlelight, which delt
A doubtfull sense of things, not so well seene, as felt.

43

Hither those *Brigants* brought their present pray,
380   And kept them with continuall watch and ward,°   *guard*
       Meaning so soone, as they convenient may,
       For slaves to sell them, for no small reward,
       To merchants, which them kept in bondage hard,
       Or sold againe. Now when faire *Pastorell*
385   Into this place was brought, and kept with gard
       Of griesly theeves, she thought her self in hell,
Where with such damned fiends she should in darknesse dwell.

44

But for to tell the dolefull dreriment,
       And pittifull complaints, which there she made,
390   Where day and night she nought did but lament

9. Louvre, an opening in the roof.

Her wretched life, shut up in deadly shade,
And waste her goodly beauty, which did fade
Like to a flowre, that feeles no heate of sunne,
Which may her feeble leaves with comfort glade.°   *make cheerful or glad*
395   But what befell her in that theevish wonne,
Will in an other Canto better be begonne.

Canto XI

The theeves fall out for Pastorell,
Whilest Melibee is slaine:
Her Calidore from them redeemes,
And bringeth backe againe.

1

The joyes of love, if they should ever last,
    Without affliction or disquietnesse,
    That worldly chaunces doe amongst them cast,
    Would be on earth too great a blessednesse,
5   Liker to heaven, then mortall wretchednesse.
    Therefore the winged God, to let men weet,
    That here on earth is no sure happinesse,
    A thousand sowres hath tempred with one sweet,
To make it seeme more deare and dainty, as is meet.

2

10   Like as is now befalne to this faire Mayd,
    Faire *Pastorell*, of whom is now my song,
    Who being now in dreadfull darknesse layd,
    Amongst those theeves, which her in bondage strong
    Detaynd, yet Fortune not with all this wrong
15   Contented, greater mischiefe on her threw,
    And sorrowes heapt on her in greater throng;
    That who so heares her heavinesse, would rew[1]
And pitty her sad plight, so chang'd from pleasaunt hew.

3

Whylest thus she in these hellish dens remayned,
20   Wrapped in wretched cares and hearts unrest,
    It so befell (as Fortune had ordayned)
    That he, which was their Capitaine profest,
    And had the chiefe commaund of all the rest,
    One day as he did all his prisoners vew,
25   With lustfull eyes, beheld that lovely guest,
    Faire *Pastorella*, whose sad mournefull hew
Like the faire Morning clad in misty fog did shew.

---

1. Spenser bases this episode on the story of Isabel in *Orlando furioso* 12.91 ff.

4

At sight whereof his barbarous heart was fired,
   And inly burnt with flames most raging whot,
30   That her alone he for his part desired
   Of all the other pray, which they had got,
   And her in mynde did to him selfe allot.
   From that day forth he kyndnesse to her showed,
   And sought her love, by all the meanes he mote;
35   With looks, with words, with gifts he oft her wowed:°   *wooed*
And mixed threats among, and much unto her vowed.

5

But all that ever he could doe or say,
   Her constant mynd could not a whit remove,
   Nor draw unto the lure of his lewd lay,°   *song*
40   To graunt him favour, or afford him love.
   Yet ceast he not to sew and all waies prove,
   By which he mote accomplish his request,
   Saying and doing all that mote behove;
   Ne day nor night he suffred her to rest,
45   But her all night did watch, and all the day molest.

6

At last when him she so importune saw,
   Fearing least he at length the raines would lend
   Unto his lust, and make his will[2] his law,
   Sith in his powre she was to foe or frend,[3]
50   She thought it best, for shadow° to pretend   *pretense*
   Some shew of favour, by him gracing small,
   That she thereby mote either freely wend,
   Or at more ease continue there his thrall:
A little well is lent, that gaineth more withall.

7

55   So from thenceforth, when love he to her made,
   With better tearmes she did him entertaine,
   Which gave him hope, and did him halfe perswade,
   That he in time her joyaunce should obtaine.
   But when she saw, through that small favours gaine,
60   That further, then she willing was, he prest,
   She found no meanes to barre him, but to faine
   A sodaine sickenesse, which her sore opprest,
And made unfit to serve his lawlesse mindes behest.

---

2. Passion, particularly sexual passion. See Shakespeare,   3. I.e., she was to be either foe or friend.
Sonnets 135 and 136.

8

By meanes whereof she would not him permit
65   Once to approch to her in privity,
        But onely mongst the rest by her to sit,
        Mourning the rigour of her malady,
        And seeking all things meete for remedy.
        But she resolv'd no remedy to fynde,
70   Nor better cheare to shew in misery,
        Till Fortune would her captive bonds unbynde,
Her sickenesse was not of the body but the mynde.

9

During which space that she thus sicke did lie,
        It chaunst a sort° of merchants, which were wount   *group*
75   To skim those coastes, for bondmen° there to buy,   *slaves*
        And by such trafficke after gaines to hunt,
        Arrived in this Isle though bare and blunt,
        T'inquire for slaves; where being readie met
        By some of these same theeves at the instant brunt,°   *suddenly*
80   Were brought unto their Captaine, who was set
By his faire patients side with sorrowfull regret.

10

To whom they shewed, how those marchants were
        Arriv'd in place, their bondslaves for to buy,
        And therefore prayd, that those same captives there
85   Mote to them for their most commodity°   *profit*
        Be sold, and mongst them shared equally.
        This their request the Captaine much appalled;
        Yet could he not their just demaund deny,
        And willed streight the slaves should forth be called,
90   And sold for most advantage not to be forstalled.

11

Then forth the good old *Meliboe* was brought,
        And *Coridon*, with many other moe,
        Whom they before in diverse spoyles had caught:
        All which he to the marchants sale did showe.
95   Till some, which did the sundry prisoners knowe,
        Gan to inquire for that faire shepherdesse,
        Which with the rest they tooke not long agoe,
        And gan her forme and feature to expresse,
The more t'augment her price, through praise of comlinesse.

12

100   To whom the Captaine in full angry wize
        Made answere, that the Mayd of whom they spake,

Was his owne purchase and his onely prize,
With which none had to doe, ne ought partake,
But he himselfe, which did that conquest make;
105   Litle for him to have one silly° lasse: *weak, helpless*
Besides through sicknesse now so wan and weake,
That nothing meet in marchandise to passe.
So shew'd them her, to prove how pale & weake she was.

13

The sight of whom, though now decayd and mard,
110   And eke hut hardly seene by candle-light,
Yet like a Diamond of rich regard,°   *appearance*
In doubtfull shadow of the darkesome night,
With starrie beames about her shining bright,
These marchants fixed eyes did so amaze,
115   That what through wonder, & what through delight,
A while on her they greedily did gaze,
And did her greatly like, and did her greatly praize.

14

At last when all the rest them offred were,
And prises to them placed at their pleasure,
120   They all refused in regard of her,
Ne ought would buy, how ever prisd with measure,
Withouten her, whose worth above all threasure
They did esteeme, and offred store of gold.
But then the Captaine fraught with more displeasure,
125   Bad them be still, his love should not be sold:
The rest take if they would, he her to him would hold.

15

Therewith some other of the chiefest theeves
Boldly him bad such injurie forbeare;
For that same mayd, how ever it him greeves,
130   Should with the rest be sold before him theare,
To make the prises of the rest more deare.
That with great rage he stoutly doth denay;
And fiercely drawing forth his blade, doth sweare,
That who so hardie hand on her doth lay,
135   It dearely shall aby,° and death for handsell° pay.   *pay / reward*

16

Thus as they words amongst them multiply,
They fall to strokes, the frute of too much talke,
And the mad steele about doth fiercely fly,

Not sparing wight, ne leaving any balke,[4]
140   But making way for death at large to walke:
Who in the horror of the griesly night,
In thousand dreadful shapes doth mongst them stalke,
And makes huge havocke, whiles the candlelight
Out quenched, leaves no skill nor difference of wight.[5]

17

145   Like as a sort° of hungry dogs ymet   *group*
    About some carcase by the common way,
    Doe fall together, stryving each to get
    The greatest portion of the greedie pray;
    All on confused heapes themselves assay,
150   And snatch, and byte, and rend, and tug, and teare;
    That who them sees, would wonder at their fray,
    And who sees not, would be affrayd to heare.
Such was the conflict of those cruell *Brigants* there.

18

But first of all, their captives they doe kill,
155   Least they should joyne against the weaker side,
    Or rise against the remnant at their will;
    Old *Meliboe* is slain, and him beside
    His aged wife, with many others wide,°   *round about*
    But *Coridon* escaping craftily,
160   Creepes forth of dores, whilst darknes him doth hide,
    And flyes away as fast as he can hye,
Ne stayeth leave to take, before his friends doe dye.

19

But *Pastorella*, wofull wretched Elfe,
    Was by the Captaine all this while defended,
165   Who minding more her safety then himselfe,
    His target° alwayes over her pretended;[6]   *shield*
    By meanes whereof, that mote not be amended,
    He at the length was slaine, and layd on ground,
    Yet holding fast twixt both his armes extended
170   Fayre *Pastorell*, who with the selfe same wound   [swound.
Launcht through the arme, fell down with him in drerie.

20

There lay she covered with confused preasse°   *crowd*
    Of carcases, which dying on her fell.

---

4. An unploughed ridge of land.
5. I.e., makes it impossible to distinguish between merchants and pirates.
6. Covered (Latin: *prætendere*).

Tho when as he was dead, the fray gan ceasse,
175   And each to other calling, did compell
To stay their cruell hands from slaughter fell,
Sith they that were the cause of all, were gone.
Thereto they all attonce agreed well,
And lighting candles new, gan search anone,
180 How many of their friends were slaine, how many fone.

21

Their Captaine there they cruelly found kild,
  And in his armes the dreary dying mayd,
Like a sweet Angell twixt two clouds uphild:
Her lovely light was dimmed and decayd,
185   With cloud of death upon her eyes displayd;
Yet did the cloud make even that dimmed light
Seeme much more lovely in that darknesse layd,
And twixt the twinckling of her eye-lids bright,
To sparke out litle beames, like starres in foggie night.

22

190 But when they mov'd the carcases aside,
  They found that life did yet in her remaine:
Then all their helpes they busily applyde,
To call the soule backe to her home againe;
And wrought so well with labour and long paine,
195   That they to life recovered her at last.
Who sighing sore, as if her hart in twaine
Had riven bene, and all her hart strings brast,
With drearie drouping eyne lookt up like one aghast.

23

There she beheld, that sore her griev'd to see,
200   Her father and her friends about her lying,
Her selfe sole left, a second spoyle to bee
Of those, that having saved her from dying,
Renew'd her death by timely death denying:
What now is left her, but to wayle and weepe,
205   Wringing her hands, and ruefully loud crying?
Ne cared she her wound in teares to steepe,°   *bathe, wet*
Albe with all dieir might those *Brigants* her did keepe.

24

But when they saw her now reliv'd againe,
  They left her so, in charge of one the best

210   Of many worst, who with unkind disdaine
         And cruell rigour her did much molest;
         Scarse yeelding her due food, or timely rest,
         And scarsely suffring her infestred wound,
         That sore her payn'd, by any to be drest.
215   So leave we her in wretched thraldome bound,
       And turne we backe to *Calidore*, where we him found.

                              25

       Who when he backe returned from the wood,
         And saw his shepheards cottage spoyled quight,
         And his love reft away, he wexed wood,
220   And halfe enraged at that ruefull sight,
         That even his hart for very fell despight,
         And his owne flesh he readie was to teare,
         He chauft, he griev'd, he fretted, and he sight,
         And fared like a furious wyld Beare,
225   Whose whelpes are stolne away, she being otherwhere.

                              26

       Ne wight he found, to whom he might complaine,
         Ne wight he found, of whom he might inquire;
         That more increast the anguish of his paine.
         He sought the woods; but no man could see there,
230   He sought the plaines; but could no tydings heare.
         The woods did nought but ecchoes vaine rebound;[7]
         The playnes all waste and emptie did appeare:
         Where wont the shepheards oft their pypes resound,
       And feed an hundred flocks, there now not one he found.

                              27

235   At last as there he romed up and downe,
         He chaunst one comming towards him to spy,
         That seem'd to be some sorie simple clowne,
         With ragged weedes, and lockes upstaring hye,
         As if he did from some late daunger fly,
240   And yet his feare did follow him behynd:
         Who as he unto him approched nye,
         He mote perceive by signes, which he did fynd,
       That *Coridon* it was, the silly shepherds hynd.°   rustic

7. Spenser again echoes the refrain from *Epithalamion* as he did in VI.10.10.5.

28

Tho to him running fast, he did not stay
 To greet him first, but askt where were the rest;
 Where *Pastorell?* who full of fresh dismay,
 And gushing forth in teares, was so opprest,
 That he no word could speake, but smit his brest,
 And up to heaven his eyes fast streming threw.
 Whereat the knight amaz'd, yet did not rest,
 But askt againe, what ment that rufull hew:
Where was his *Pastorell?* where all the other crew?

245

250

29

Ah well away (sayd he then sighing sore)
 That ever I did live, this day to see,
 This dismall day, and was not dead before,
 Before I saw faire *Pastorella* dye.
 Die? out alas then *Calidore* did cry:
 How could the death dare ever her to quell?
 But read thou shepheard, read what destiny,
 Or other dyrefull hap from heaven or hell
Hath wrought this wicked deed, doe feare° away, and tell.   *expel fear*

255

260

30

Tho when the shepheard breathed had a whyle,
 He thus began: where shall I then commence
 This wofull tale? or how those *Brigants* vyle,
 With cruell rage and dreadfull violence
 Spoyld all our cots, and caried us from hence?
 Or how faire *Pastorell* should have bene sold
 To marchants, but was sav'd with strong defence?
 Or how those theeves, whilest one sought her to hold,
Fell all at ods, and fought through fury fierce and bold.

265

270

31

In that same conflict (woe is me) befell
 This fatall chaunce, this dolefull accident,
 Whose heavy tydings now I have to tell.
 First all the captives, which they here had hent,°   *seized*
 Were by them slaine by generall consent;
 Old *Meliboe* and his good wife withall
 These eyes saw die, and dearely did lament:
 But when the lot to *Pastorell* did fall,
Their Captaine long withstood, & did her deam forstall.

275

32

280 But what could he gainst all them doe alone:
  It could not boot; needs mote she die at last:
  I onely scapt through great confusione
  Of cryes and clamors, which amongst them past,
  In dreadfull darknesse dreadfully aghast;
285   That better were with them to have bene dead,
  Then here to see all desolate and wast,
  Despoyled of those joyes and jolly head,
Which with those gentle shepherds here I wont to lead.

33

When *Calidore* these ruefull newes had raught,
290   His hart quite deaded was with anguish great,
  And all his wits with doole were nigh distraught,
  That he his face, his head, his brest did beat,
  And death it selfe unto himselfe did threat;
  Oft cursing th'heavens, that so cruell were
295   To her, whose name he often did repeat;
  And wishing oft, that he were present there,
When she was slaine, or had bene to her succour nere.

34

But after griefe awhile had had his course,
  And spent it selfe in mourning, he at last
300   Began to mitigate his swelling sourse,[8]
  And in his mind with better reason cast,
  How he might save her life, if life did last;
  Or if that dead, how he her death might wreake,
  Sith otherwise he could not mend thing past;
305   Or if it to revenge he were too weake,
Then for to die with her, and his lives threed[9] to breake.

35

Tho *Coridon* he prayd, sith he well knew
  The readie way unto that theevish wonne,
  To wend with him, and be his conduct trew
310   Unto the place, to see what should be donne.
  But he, whose hart through feare was late fordonne,
  Would not for ought be drawne to former drede,
  But by all meanes the daunger knowne did shonne:
  Yet *Calidore* so well him wrought with meed,[1]
315 And faire bespoke with words, that he at last agreed.

---

8. Fountain-head (i.e., he stopped crying).
9. The thread of life spun out by the Fates.

1. I.e., worked with promise of reward.

36

So forth they goe together (God before)
   Both clad in shepheards weeds agreeably,
   And both with shepheards hookes: But *Calidore*
   Had underneath, him armed privily.
320   Tho to the place when they approched nye,
   They chaunst, upon an hill not farre away,
   Some flockes of sheepe and shepheards to espy;
   To whom they both agreed to take their way,
In hope there newes to learne, how they mote best assay.

37

325   There did they find, that which they did not feare,
   The selfe same flocks, the which those theeves had reft
   From *Meliboe* and from themselves whyleare,
   And certaine of the theeves there by them left,
   The which for want of heards themselves then kept.
330   Right well knew *Coridon* his owne late sheepe,
   And seeing them, for tender pittie wept:
   But when he saw the theeves, which did them keepe
His hart gan fayle, albe he saw them all asleepe.

38

But *Calidore* recomforting his griefe,
335   Though not his feare: for nought may feare disswade;
   Him hardly forward drew, whereas the thiefe
   Lay sleeping soundly in the bushes shade,
   Whom *Coridon* him counseld to invade
   Now all unwares, and take the spoyle away;
340   But he, that in his mind had closely made
   A further purpose, would not so them slay,
But gently waking them, gave them the time of day.

39

Tho sitting downe by them upon the greene,
   Of sundrie things he purpose gan to faine;[2]
345   That he by them might certaine tydings weene
   Of *Pastorell*, were she alive or slaine.
   Mongst which the theeves them questioned againe,
   What mister men,° and eke from whence they were.   *kind of men*
   To whom they answer'd, as did appertaine,
350   That they were poore heardgroomes, the which whylere
Had from their maisters fled, & now sought hyre elswhere.

---

2. I.e., began to invent conversation.

40

Whereof right glad they seem'd, and offer made
   To hyre them well, if they their flockes would keepe:
   For they themselves were evill groomes, they sayd,
355   Unwont with heards to watch, or pasture sheepe,
   But to forray the land, or scoure the deepe.
   Thereto they soone agreed, and earnest tooke,[3]
   To keepe their flockes for litle hyre and chepe:
   For they for better hyre did shortly looke,
360 So there all day they bode, till light the sky forsooke.

41

Tho when as towards darksome night it drew,
   Unto their hellish dens those theeves them brought,
   Where shortly they in great acquaintance grew,
   And all the secrets of their entrayles° sought.   *minds*
365 There did they find, contrarie to their thought,
   That *Postorell* yet liv'd, but all the rest
   Were dead, right so as *Coridon* had taught:
   Whereof they both full glad and blyth did rest,
But chiefly *Calidore*, whom griefe had most possest.

42

370 At length when they occasion fittest found,
   In dead of night, when all the theeves did rest
   After a late forray, and slept full sound,
   Sir *Calidore* him arm'd, as he thought best,
   Having of late by diligent inquest,
375 Provided him a sword of meanest sort:
   With which he streight went to the Captaines nest.
   But *Coridon* durst not with him consort,
Ne durst abide behind, for dread of worse effort.

43

When to the Cave they came, they found it fast:°   *securely closed*
380 But *Calidore* with huge resistlesse might,
   The dores assayled, and the locks upbrast.
   With noyse whereof the theefe awaking light,
   Unto the entrance ran: where the bold knight
   Encountring him with small resistance slew;
385 The whiles faire *Pastorell* through great affright
   Was almost dead, misdoubting least of new
Some uprore were like that, which lately she did vew.

---

3. I.e., received an initial payment for their services.

44

But when as *Calidore* was comen in,
    And gan aloud for *Pastorell* to call,
390   Knowing his voice although not heard long sin,
    She sudden was revived therewithall,
    And wondrous joy felt in her spirits thrall:
    Like him that being long in tempest tost,
    Looking each houre into deathes mouth to fall,
395   At length espyes at hand the happie cost,
On which he safety hopes, that earst feard to be lost.

45

Her gentle hart, that now long season past
    Had never joyance felt, nor chearefull thought,
    Began some smacke of comfort new to tast,
400   Like lyfull heat to nummed senses brought,
    And life to feele, that long for death had sought;
    Ne lesse in hart rejoyced *Calidore*,
    When he her found, but like to one distraught
    And robd of reason, towards her him bore,
405   A thousand times embrast, and kist a thousand more.

46

But now by this, with noyse of late uprore,
    The hue and cry was raysed all about;
    And all the *Brigants* flocking in great store,
    Unto the cave gan preasse, nought having dout
410   Of that was doen, and entred in a rout.
    But *Calidore* in th'entry close did stand,
    And entertayning them with courage stout,
    Still slew the formost, that came first to hand,
So long till all the entry was with bodies mand.

47

415   Tho when no more could nigh to him approch,
    He breath'd° his sword, and rested him till day: *rested*
    Which when he spyde upon the earth t'encroch,
    Through the dead carcases he made his way,
    Mongst which he found a sword of better say,°   *assay, temper*
420   With which he forth went into th'open light:
    Where all the rest for him did readie stay,
    And fierce assayling him, with all their might
Gan all upon him lay: there gan a dreadfull fight.

Canto XII

*Fayre Pastorella by great hap
her parents understands,
Calidore doth the Blatant beast
subdew, and bynd in bands.*

1

Like as a ship, that through the Ocean wyde
   Directs her course unto one certaine cost,
   Is met of many a counter winde and tyde,
   With which her winged speed is let° and crost,   *hindered*
5   And she her selfe in stormie surges tost;
   Yet making many a borde, and many a bay,
   Still winneth way, ne hath her compasse lost:
   Right so it fares with me in this long way,
Whose course is often stayd, yet never is astray.

2

10 For all that hetherto hath long delayd
   This gentle knight, from sewing his first quest,
   Though out of course, yet hath not bene mis-sayd,
   To shew the courtesie by him profest,
   Even unto the lowest and the least.
15   But now I come into my course againe,
   To his atchievement of the *Blatant beast;*
   Who all this while at will did range and raine,
Whilst none was him to stop, nor none him to restraine.

3

Sir *Calidore* when thus he now had raught[1]
20   Faire *Pastorella* from those *Brigants* powre,
   Unto the Castle of *Belgard*[2] her brought,
   Whereof was Lord the good Sir *Bellamoure;*[3]
   Who whylome was in his youthes freshest flowre
   A lustie knight, as ever wielded speare,
25   And had endured many a dreadfull stoure
   In bloudy battell for a Ladie deare,
The fayrest Ladie then of all that living were.

4

Her name was *Claribell,*[4] whose father hight
   The Lord of *Many Ilands*, farre renound
30   For his great riches and his greater might.
   He through the wealth, wherein he did abound,

---

1. The recognition of Pastorella by her parents through
the agency of Melissa uses a common motif in romance: a
lost child found.

2. French: "good protection" or "loving look."
3. French: "beautiful love."
4. French: "bright beauty."

This daughter thought in wedlocke to have bound
  Unto the Prince of *Picteland*° bordering nere,   *Scotland*
  But she whose sides before with secret wound
35   Of love to *Bellamoure* empierced were,
By all meanes shund to match with any forrein fere.°   *companion, mate*

5

And *Bellamour* againe so well her pleased,
  With dayly service and attendance dew,
  That of her love he was entyrely seized,
40   And closely did her wed, but knowne to few.
  Which when her father understood, he grew
  In so great rage, that them in dongeon deepe
  Without compassion cruelly he threw;
  Yet did so streightly them a sunder keepe,
45 That neither could to company of th'other creepe.

6

Nathlesse Sir *Bellamour*, whether through grace
  Or secret guifts so with his keepers wrought,
  That to his love sometimes he came in place,
  Whereof her wombe unwist to wight was fraught,
50   And in dew time a mayden child forth brought.
  Which she streight way for dread least, if her syre
  Should know thereof, to slay he would have sought,
  Delivered to her handmayd, that for hyre°   *payment*
She should it cause be fostred under straunge attyre.

7

55 The trustie damzell bearing it abrode
  Into the emptie fields, where living wight
  Mote not bewray the secret of her lode,
  She forth gan lay unto the open light
  The litle babe, to take thereof a sight.
60   Whom whylest she did with watrie eyne behold,
  Upon the litle brest like christall bright,
  She mote perceive a litle purple mold,°   *mole*
That like a rose her silken leaves did faire unfold.

8

Well she it markt, and pittied the more,
65   Yet could not remedie her wretched case,
  But closing it againe like as before,
  Bedeaw'd with teares there left it in the place:
  Yet left not quite, but drew a litle space
  Behind the bushes, where she her did hyde,
70 To weet what mortall hand, or heavens grace

Would for the wretched infants helpe provyde,
For which it loudly cald, and pittifully cryde.

9

At length a Shepheard, which there by did keepe
  His fleecie flocke upon the playnes around,
75   Led with the infants cry, that loud did weepe,
  Came to the place, where when he wrapped found
  Th'abandond spoyle, he softly it unbound,
  And seeing there, that did him pittie sore,
  He tooke it up, and in his mantle wound;
80   So home unto his honest wife it bore,
Who as her owne it nurst, and named evermore.

10

Thus long continu'd *Claribell* a thrall,
  And *Bellamour* in bands, till that her syre
  Departed life, and left unto them all.
85   Then all the stormes of fortunes former yre
  Were turnd, and they to freedome did retyre.
  Thenceforth they joy'd in happinesse together,
  And lived long in peace and love entyre,
  Without disquiet or dislike of ether,
90   Till time that *Calidore* brought *Pastorella* thether.

11

Both whom they goodly well did entertaine;
  For *Bellamour* knew *Calidore* right well,
  And loved for his prowesse, sith they twaine
  Long since had fought in field. Als *Claribell*
95   No lesse did tender the faire *Pastorell*,
  Seeing her weake and wan, through durance° long.   *suffering*
  There they a while together thus did dwell
  In much delight, and many joyes among,
Untill the damzell gan to wex more sound and strong.

12

100 Tho gan Sir *Calidore* him to advize
  Of his first quest, which he had long forlore,°   *forsaken*
  Asham'd to thinke, how he that enterprize,
  The which the Faery Queene had long afore
  Bequeath'd to him, forslacked had so sore;
105   That much he feared, least reprochfull blame
  With foule dishonour him mote blot therefore;
  Besides the losse of so much loos[5] and fame,
As through the world thereby should glorifie his name.

---

5. A variant spelling of "lose," fame, reputation.

13

Therefore resolving to returne in hast
110   Unto so great atchievement, he bethought
         To leave his love, now perill being past,
         With *Claribell*, whylest he that monster sought
         Throughout the world, and to destruction brought.
         So taking leave of his faire *Pastorell*,
115   Whom to recomfort, all the meanes he wrought,
         With thanks to *Bellamour* and *Claribell*,
He went forth on his quest, and did, that him befell.

14

But first, ere I doe his adventures tell,
         In this exploite, me needeth to declare,
120   What did betide to the faire *Pastorell*,
         During his absence left in heavy care,
         Through daily mourning, and nightly misfare:
         Yet did that auncient matrone all she might,
         To cherish her with all things choice and rare;
125   And her owne handmayd, that *Melissa*[6] hight,
Appointed to attend her dewly day and night.

15

Who in a morning, when this Mayden faire
         Was dighting her, having her snowy brest
         As yet not laced, nor her golden haire
130   Into their comely tresses dewly drest,
         Chaunst to espy upon her yvory chest
         The rosie marke, which she remembred well
         That litle Infant had, which forth she kest,°   cast
         The daughter of her Lady *Claribell*,
135 The which she bore, the whiles in prison she did dwell.

16

Which well avizing, streight she gan to cast
         In her conceiptfull° mynd, that this faire Mayd   clever, imaginative
         Was that same infant, which so long sith past
         She in the open fields had loosely layd
140   To fortunes spoile, unable it to ayd.
         So full of joy, streight forth she ran in hast
         Unto her mistresse, being halfe dismayd,
         To tell her, how the heavens had her graste,
To save her chylde, which in misfortunes mouth was plaste.

---

6. Greek: "bee." Melissa is also a prophet in Aristo, *Orlando furioso* 3 and 7.

17

145   The sober mother seeing such her mood,
          Yet knowing not, what meant that sodaine thro,
          Askt her, how mote her words be understood,
          And what the matter was, that mov'd her so.
          My liefe (sayd she) ye know, that long ygo,
150   Whilest ye in durance dwelt, ye to me gave
          A little mayde, the which ye chylded tho;
          The same againe if now ye list to have,
      The same is yonder Lady, whom high God did save.

18

Much was the Lady troubled at that speach,
155   And gan to question streight how she it knew.
          Most certaine markes, (sayd she) do me it teach,
          For on her brest I with these eyes did vew
          The litle purple rose, which thereon grew,
          Whereof her name ye then to her did give.
160   Besides her countenaunce, and her likely hew,
          Matched with equall yeares, do surely prieve°   *prove*
      That yond same is your daughter sure, which yet doth live.

19

The matrone stayd no lenger to enquire,
          But forth in hast ran to the straunger Mayd;
165   Whom catching greedily for great desire,
          Rent up her brest, and bosome open layd,
          In which that rose she plainely saw displayd.
          Then her embracing twixt her armes twaine,
          She long so held, and softly weeping sayd;
170   And livest thou my daughter now againe?
      And art thou yet alive, whom dead I long did faine?°   *imagine*

20

Tho further asking her of sundry things,
          And times comparing with their accidents,
          She found at last by very certaine signes,
175   And speaking markes of passed monuments,
          That this young Mayd, whom chance to her presents
          Is her owne daughter, her owne infant deare.
          Tho wondring long at those so straunge events,
          A thousand times she her embraced nere,
180   With many a joyfull kisse, and many a melting teare.

21

Who ever is the mother of one chylde,
          Which having thought long dead, she fyndes alive,

Let her by proofe of that, which she hath fylde
   In her owne breast, this mothers joy descrive:°   *describe*
185   For other none such passion can contrive
   In perfect forme, as this good Lady felt,
   When she so faire a daughter saw survive,
   As *Pastorella* was, that nigh she swelt
For passing joy, which did all into pitty melt.

22

190   Thence running forth unto her loved Lord,
   She unto him recounted, all that fell:
   Who joyning joy with her in one accord,
   Acknowledg'd for his own faire *Pastorell.*
   There leave we them in joy, and let us tell
195   Of *Calidore*, who seeking all this while
   That monstrous Beast by finall force to quell,
   Through every place, with restlesse paine and toile
Him follow'd, by the tract° of his outragious spoile.   *trail*

23

Through all estates he found that he had past,[7]
200   In which he many massacres had left,
   And to the Clergy now was come at last;
   In which such spoile, such havocke, and such theft
   He wrought, that thence all goodnesse he bereft,
   That endlesse were to tell. The Elfin Knight,
205   Who now no place besides unsought had left,
   At length into a Monastere did light,
Where he him found despoyling all with maine & might.

24

Into their cloysters now he broken had,
   Through which the Monckes he chaced here & there,
210   And them pursu'd into their dortours° sad,   *sleeping rooms*
   And searched all their cels and secrets neare;
   In which what filth and ordure did appeare,
   Were yrkesome to report; yet that foule Beast
   Nought sparing them, the more did tosse and teare,
215   And ransacke all their dennes from most to least,
Regarding nought religion, nor their holy heast.°   *vow*

25

From thence into the sacred Church he broke,
   And robd the Chancell, and the deskes downe threw,

---

7. Spenser is making a distinction between the secular clergy, those who were pastors to the people, and monks, those who had retired from the world. The fact that Henry VIII had dissolved the monasteries in England does not alter the point Spenser is making: no one escapes the Blatant Beast.

And Altars fouled, and blasphemy spoke,
220   And th'Images for all their goodly hew,
Did cast to ground, whilest none was them to rew;
So all confounded and disordered there.
But seeing *Calidore*, away he flew,
Knowing his fatall hand by former feare;
225 But he him fast pursuing, soone approched neare.

26

Him in a narrow place he overtooke,
And fierce assailing forst him turne againe:
Sternely he turnd againe, when he him strooke
With his sharpe steele, and ran at him amaine
230   With open mouth, that seemed to containe
A full good pecke° within the utmost brim,   *a great number (of teeth)*
All set with yron teeth in raunges twaine,
That terrifide his foes, and armed him,
Appearing like the mouth of *Orcus*° griesly grim.   *Hell*

27

235 And therein were a thousand tongs empight,°   *implanted*
Of sundry kindes, and sundry quality,
Some were of dogs, that barked day and night,
And some of cats, that wrawling° still did cry: *mewing*
And some of Beares, that groynd continually,
240   And some of Tygres, that did seeme to gren,
And snar at all, that ever passed by:
But most of them were tongues of mortall men,
Which spake reprochfully, not caring when.

28

And them amongst were mingled here and there,
245   The tongues of Serpents with three forked stings,
That spat out poyson and gore bloudy gere[8]
At all, that came within his ravenings,
And spake licentious words, and hatefull things
Of good and bad alike, of low and hie;
250   Ne Kesars° spared he a whit, nor Kings,   *rulers*
But either blotted them with infamie,
Or bit them with his banefull teeth of injury.

29

But *Calidore* thereof no whit afrayd,
Rencountred him with so impetuous might,
255   That th'outrage of his violence he stayd,

8. Corrupt, foul matter, pus.

And bet abacke, threatning in vaine to bite,
And spitting forth the poyson of his spight,
That fomed all about his bloody jawes.
Tho rearing up his former° feete on hight,   *situated more forward*
260   He rampt° upon him with his ravenous pawes,   *seized*
As if he would have rent him with his cruell clawes.

30

But he right well aware, his rage to ward,
Did cast his shield atweene, and therewithall
Putting his puissaunce forth, pursu'd so hard,
265   That backeward he enforced him to fal1,
And being downe, ere he new helpe could call,
His shield he on him threw, and fast downe held,
Like as a bullocke, that in bloudy stall
Of butchers balefull hand to ground is feld,
270   Is forcibly kept downe, till he be throughly queld.

31

Full cruelly the Beast did rage and rore,
To be downe held, and maystred so with might,
That he gan fret and fome out bloudy gore,
Striving in vaine to rere him selfe upright.
275   For still the more he strove, the more the Knight
Did him suppresse, and forcibly subdew;
That made him almost mad for fell despight.
He grind, hee bit, he scratcht, he venim threw,
And fared like a feend, right horrible in hew.

32

280   Or like the hell-borne *Hydra*, which they faine
That great *Alcides* whilome overthrew,[9]
After that he had labourd long in vaine,
To crop his thousand heads, the which still new
Forth budded, and in greater number grew.
285   Such was the fury of this hellish Beast,
Whilest *Calidore* him under him downe threw;
Who nathemore his heavy load releast,
But aye the more he rag'd, the more his powre increast.

33

Tho when the Beast saw, he mote nought availe,
290   By force, he gan his hundred tongues apply,
And sharpely at him to revile and raile,

9. The many-headed monster whom Hercules (Alcides) slew as one of his twelve labors.

With bitter termes of shamefull infamy;
Oft interlacing many a forged lie,
Whose like he never once did speake, nor heare,
295   Nor ever thought thing so unworthily:
Yet did he nought for all that him forbeare,
But strained him so streightly, that he chokt him neare.

34

At last when as he found his force to shrincke,
And rage to quaile, he tooke a muzzell strong
300   Of surest yron, made with many a lincke;
Therewith he mured[1] up his mouth along,
And therein shut up his blasphemous tong,
For never more defaming gentle Knight,
Or unto lovely Lady doing wrong:
305   And thereunto a great long chaine he tight,
With which he drew him forth, even in his own despight.

35

Like as whylome that strong *Tirynthian* swaine,[2]
Brought forth with him the dreadfull dog of hell,
Against his will fast bound in yron chaine,
310   And roring horribly, did him compell
To see the hatefull sunne, that he might tell
To griesly *Pluto*,[3] what on earth was donne,
And to the other damned ghosts, which dwell
For aye in darkenesse, which day light doth shonne.
315   So led this Knight his captyve with like conquest wonne.

36

Yet greatly did the Beast repine° at those   *show discontent*
Straunge bands, whose like till then he never bore,
Ne ever any durst till then impose,
And chauffed inly, seeing now no more
320   Him liberty was left aloud to rore;
Yet durst he not draw backe; nor once withstand
The proved powre of noble *Calidore*,
But trembled underneath his mighty hand,
And like a fearefull dog him followed through the land.

37

325   Him through all Faery land he follow'd so,
As if he learned had obedience long,
That all the people where so he did go,

1. Closed (Latin: *murus*, "wall").   out of hell (Ovid, *Metamorphoses* 7.408–15).
2. Hercules, who was born in Tiryns, brought Cerberus   3. God of the underworld.

Out of their townes did round about him throng,
  To see him leade that Beast in bondage strong,
330   And seeing it, much wondred at the sight;
  And all such persons, as he earst did wrong,
  Rejoyced much to see his captive plight,
And much admyr'd the Beast, but more admyr'd the Knight.

38

Thus was this Monster by the maystring might
335   Of doughty *Calidore*, supprest and tamed,
  That never more he mote endammadge wight
  With his vile tongue, which many had defamed,
  And many causelesse caused to be blamed:
  So did he eeke long after this remaine,
340   Untill that, whether wicked fate so framed,
  Or fault of men, he broke his yron chaine,
And got into the world at liberty againe.

39

Thenceforth more mischiefe and more scath he wrought
  To mortall men, then he had done before;
345   Ne ever could by any more be brought
  Into like bands, ne maystred any more:
  Albe that long time after *Calidore*,
  The good Sir *Pelleas him* tooke in hand,
  And after him Sir *Lamoracke*[4] of yore,
350   And all his brethren borne in Britaine land;
Yet none of them could ever bring him into band.

40

So now he raungeth through the world againe,
  And rageth sore in each degree and state;
  Ne any is, that may him now restraine,
355   He growen is so great and strong of late,
  Barking and biting all that him doe bate,
  Albe they worthy blame, or cleare of crime:
  Ne spareth he most learned wits to rate,°   scold, assault verbally
  Ne spareth he the gentle Poets rime,
360 But rends without regard of person or of time.

41

Ne may this homely verse, of many meanest,
  Hope to escape his venemous despite,
  More then my former writs, all° were they clearest[5]   although

---

4. Both characters in Malory, but neither of them pursues the beast in that work.

5. Most free. Some editors emend to *cleanest* for the sake of the rhyme.

blame

From blamefull blot, and free from all that wite,°

365   With which some wicked tongues did it backebite,

And bring into a mighty Peres displeasure,

That never so deserved to endite.°   censure

Therfor do you my rimes keep better measure,

And seeke to please, that now is counted wisemens threasure.

Two Cantos of Mutabilitie:

Which, Both for Forme and Matter, Appeare to be Parcell of Some Following Booke of the Faerie Queene Under the Legend of Constancie.

Canto VI

Proud Change (not pleasd, in mortall things,
beneath the Moone, to raigne)
Pretends, as well of Gods, as Men,
to be the Soveraine.

1

What man that sees the ever-whirling wheele

Of *Change*, the which all mortall dungs doth sway,°   *have power over*

But that therby doth find, & plainly feele,

How MUTABILITY in them doth play

5   Her cruell sports, to many mens decay?

Which that to all[1] may better yet appeare,

I will rehearse that whylome I heard say,

How she at first her selfe began to reare,

Gainst all the Gods, and th'empire sought from them to beare.

2

10   But first, here falleth fittest to unfold

Her antique race and linage ancient,

As I have found it registred of old,

In *Faery* Land mongst records permanent:

She was, to weet, a daughter by descent

15   Of those old *Titans*,[2] that did whylome strive

1. I.e., so that it may appear more clearly to all.
2. The Titans were the offspring of Heaven (Uranus) and Earth (Gaea) and constitute a generation of gods older than the reigning Olympians (Jupiter, etc.). The most important of them was Saturn, who had dethroned his father Uranus. Because Earth prophesied that Saturn would be dethroned in turn by one of his sons, he devoured each of his children immediately after birth. His wife managed to preserve one, Jupiter, by sending him off to Crete. Jupiter lived to fulfill the prophecy and not only dethroned but also emasculated Saturn. Thus began the reign of the Olympian gods. Saturn's brothers and sisters, offended at Jupiter's presumptions, contended with him for supremacy. The victorious Jupiter thrust the Titans into the pit of Tartarus. Mutability is a descendant of the Titans and bases her claim on the legal right derived from her lineage.

With *Saturnes* sonne for heavens regiment.°   *rule*
    Whom, though high *Jove* of kingdome did deprive,
Yet many of their stemme long after did survive.

3

And many of them, afterwards obtain'd
20   Great power of *Jove*, and high authority;
    As *Hecaté*,[3] in whose almighty hand,
    He plac't all rule and principality,
    To be by her disposed diversly,
    To Gods, and men, as she them list divide:
25   And drad *Bellona*,[4] that doth sound on hie
    Warres and allarums unto Nations wide,
That makes both heaven & earth to tremble at her pride.

4

So likewise did this *Titanesse* aspire,
    Rule and dominion to her selfe to gaine;
30   That as a Goddesse, men might her admire,°   *wonder at*
    And heavenly honours yield, as to them twaine.[4]
    And first, on earth she sought it to obtaine;
    Where she such proofe and sad examples shewed
    Of her great power, to many ones great paine,
35   That not men onely (whom she soone subdewed)
But eke all other creatures, her bad dooings rewed.

5

For, she the face of earthly things so changed,
    That all which Nature had establisht first
    In good estate, and in meet order ranged,
40   She did pervert, and all their statutes burst:
    And all the worlds faire frame (which none yet durst
    Of Gods or men to alter or misguide)
    She alter'd quite, and made them all accurst
    That God had blest; and did at first provide[5]
45 In that still° happy state for ever to abide.   *continuously*

6

Ne shee the lawes of Nature onely brake,
    But eke of Justice, and of Policie;°   *good government*
    And wrong of right, and bad of good did make.
    And death for life exchanged foolishlie:
50   Since which, all living wights have learn'd to die,
    And all this world is woxen daily worse.

---

3. A Titaness, the infernal aspect of the triple goddess   4. I.e., Hecate and Bellona.
Hecate-Diana-Cynthia. A Titaness, goddess of war.   5. Prepare, with overtones of Providential ordering.

O pittious worke of MUTABILITIE!
By which, we all are subiect to that curse,°   *the fall of man*
And death in stead of life have sucked from our Nurse.[6]

7

55   And now, when all the earth she thus had brought
To her behest, and thralled to her might,
She gan to cast in her ambitious thought,
T'attempt[7] th'empire of the heavens hight,
And *Jove* himselfe to shoulder from his right.
60   And first, she past the region of the ayre,°   *the atmosphere*
And of the fire,[8] whose substance thin and slight,
Made no resistance, ne could her contraire,°   *oppose, thwart*
But ready passage to her pleasure did prepaire.°   *provide, furnish*

8

Thence, to the Circle of the Moone she clambe,
65   Where *Cynthia*[9] raignes in everlasting glory,
To whose bright shining palace straight she came,
All fairely deckt with heavens goodly story;
Whose silver gates (by which there sate an hory
Old aged Sire, with hower-glasse in hand,
70   Hight *Tyme*) she entred, were he liefe or sory:°   *willing or not*
Ne staide till she the highest stage° had scand,°   *level / climbed*
Where *Cynthia* did sit, that never still did stand.

9

Her sitting on an Ivory throne shee found,
Drawne of two steeds, th'one black, the other white,
75   Environd with tenne thousand starres around,
That duly her attended day and night;
And by her side, there ran her Page, that hight
Vesper, whom we the Evening-starre intend:°   *call*
That with his Torche, still twinkling like twylight;
80   Her lightened all the way where she should wend,
And joy to weary wandring travailers did lend:

10

That when the hardy *Titanesse* beheld
The goodly building of her Palace bright,
Made of the heavens substance, and up-held
85   With thousand Crystall pillors of huge hight,

6. Nature, or earthly life.
7. To take by force.

8. It was believed that a sphere of fire enclosed the atmosphere.
9. The moon, also called Phoebe.

Shee gan to burne in her ambitious spright,
And t'envie her that in such glorie raigned.
Eftsoones she cast by force and tortious° might,   *wrongful, illegal*
Her to displace, and to her selfe to have gained
90   The kingdome of the Night, and waters by her wained.[1]

11

Boldly she bid the Goddesse downe descend,
And let her selfe into that Ivory throne;
For, shee her selfe more worthy thereof wend,
And better able it to guide alone:
95   Whether to men, whose fall she did bemone,
Or unto Gods, whose state she did maligne,
Or to th'infernall Powers, her need give lone
Of her faire light, and bounty most benigne,
Her selfe of all that rule shee deemed most condigne.°   *worthy, deserving*

12

100   But shee that had to her that soveraigne seat
By highest *Jove* assign'd, therein to beare
Nights burning lamp, regarded not her threat,
Ne yielded ought for favour or for feare;
But with sterne countenaunce and disdainfull cheare,
105   Bending her horned browes,[2] did put her back:
And boldly blaming her for comming there,
Bade her attonce from heavens coast to pack,
Or at her perill bide the wrathfull Thunders wrack.

13

Yet nathemore the *Giantesse* forbare:
110   But boldly preacing-on, raught forth her hand
To pluck her downe perforce from off her chaire;
And there-with lifting up her golden wand,
Threatned to strike her if she did with-stand.
Where-at the starres, which round about her blazed,
115   And eke the Moones bright wagon,[3] still did stand,
All beeing with so bold attempt amazed,
And on her uncouth habit and sterne looke still gazed.

14

Meane-while, the lower World, which nothing knew
Of all that chaunced here, was darkned quite;
120   And eke the heavens, and all the heavenly crew
Of happy wights, now unpurvaide of light,

---

1. Suggests "drawn" as in "moved by a wain"; but it may
also mean "waned, diminished."

2. The crescent moon is often an attribute of Cynthia.
3. See VII.6.9.

Were much afraid, and wondred at that sight;
　　Fearing least *Chaos*[4] broken had his chaine,
　　And brought againe on them eternall night:
125　But chiefely *Mercury*,[5] that next doth raigne,
Ran forth in haste, unto the king of Gods to plaine.

15

All ran together with a great out-cry,
　　To *Joves* faire Palace, fixt in heavens hight;
　　And beating at his gates full earnestly,
130　Gan call to him aloud with all their might,
　　To know what meant that suddaine lack of light.
　　The father of the Gods when this he heard,
　　Was troubled much at their so strange affright,
　　Doubting least *Typhon*[6] were againe uprear'd,
135　Or other his old foes, that once him sorely fear'd.[7]

16

Eftsoones the sonne of *Maia*[8] forth he sent
　　Downe to the Circle of the Moone, to knowe
　　The cause of this so strange astonishment,
　　And why shee did her wonted course forslowe;[9]
140　And if that any were on earth belowe
　　That did with charmes or Magick her molest,
　　Him to attache,[1] and downe to hell to throwe:
　　But, if from heaven it were, then to arrest
The Author, and him bring before his presence prest.°　　　　*quickly*

17

145　The wingd-foot God,[2] so fast his plumes did beat,
　　That soone he came where-as the *Titanesse*
　　Was striving with faire *Cynthia* for her seat:
　　At whose strange sight, and haughty hardinesse,°　　　　*boldness*
　　He wondred much, and feared her no lesse.
150　Yet laying feare aside to doe his charge,[3]
　　At last, he bade her (with bold stedfastnesse)
　　Ceasse to molest the Moone to walke at large,
Or come before high *Jove*, her dooings to discharge.

---

4. The undifferentiated mass of warring elements before the imposition of form by Love often identified with the "void" of Genesis 1.
5. Nearest planet to the moon. Mercury is also the traditional messenger of the gods.
6. A giant imprisoned by Jupiter under Mount Aetna for joining with the Titans in their war against him.

7. I.e., frightened Jupiter.
8. Mercury, son of Jupiter and Maia.
9. Make go more slowly, delay.
1. To seize him.
2. Winged sandals are an attribute of Mercury.
3. To carry out Jupiter's command.

18

And there-with-all, he on her shoulder laid
155   His snaky-wreathed Mace,⁴ whose awfull power
          Doth make both Gods and hellish fiends affraid:
          Where-at the *Titanesse* did sternely lower,
          And stoutly answer'd, that in evill hower
          He from his *Jove* such message to her brought,
160   To bid her leave faire *Cynthias* silver bower;
          Sith shee his *Jove* and him esteemed nought,
No more then *Cynthias* selfe; but all their kingdoms sought.

19

The Heavens Herald⁵ staid not to reply,
          But past away, his doings to relate
165   Unto his Lord; who now in th'highest sky,
          Was placed in his principall Estate,
          With all the Gods about him congregate:°   *gathered*
          To whom when *Hermes*° had his message told,   *Mercury*
          It did them all exceedingly amate,
170   Save *Jove*; who, changing nought his count'nance bold,
Did unto them at length these speeches wise unfold;

20

Harken to mee awhile yee heavenly Powers;
          Ye may remember since th'Earths° cursed seed°   *when / the Titans*
          Sought to assaile the heavens eternal towers,
175   And to us all exceeding feare did breed:
          But how we then defeated all their deed,°   *acts*
          Yee all doe knowe, and them destroied quite;
          Yet not so quite, but that there did succeed
          An off-spring of their bloud, which did alite
180   Upon the fruitfull earth, which doth us yet despite.

21

Of that bad seed is this bold woman bred,
          That now with bold presumption doth aspire
          To thrust faire *Phoebe* from her silver bed,
          And eke our selves from heavens high Empire,
185   If that° her might were match to her desire: *if only*
          Wherefore, it now behoves us to advise
          What way is best to drive her to retire;
          Whether by open force, or counsell wise,
Areed ye sonnes of God, as best ye can devise.°   *contrive*

---

4. The caduceus, the wand of peace and attribute of   5. Mercury as messenger of the gods.
Mercury.

22

190 So having said, he ceast; and with his brow
    (His black eye-brow, whose doomefull dreaded beck°   *nod*
    Is wont to wield the world unto his vow,°   *will*
    And even the highest Powers of heaven to check)
    Made signe to them in their degrees° to speake: *hierarchical order*
195 Who straight gan cast their counsell grave and wise.
    Meane-while, th'Earths daughter, thogh she nought°   *did not care about*
      did reck
    Of *Hermes* message; yet gan now advise,
What course were best to take in this hot bold emprize.

23

Eftsoones she thus resolv'd; that whil'st the Gods
200   (After returne of *Hermes* Embassie)
    Were troubled, and amongst themselves at ods,
    Before they could new counsels re-allie,
    To set upon them in that extasie;°   *bewildered state*
    And take what fortune time and place would lend:
205 So, forth she rose, and through the purest sky
    To *Joves* high Palace straight cast to ascend,
To prosecute her plot: Good on-set boads good end.

24

Shee there arriving, boldly in did pass;
    Where all the Gods she found in counsell close,
210   All quite unarm'd, as then their manner was.
    At sight of her they suddaine all arose,
    In great amaze, ne wist what way to chose.
    But *Jove*, all fearelesse, forc't them to aby;°   *to remain*
    And in bis soveraine throne, gan straight dispose
215 Himselfe more full of grace and Majestie,
That mote encheare° his friends, & foes mote terrific.   *give cheer to*

25

That, when the haughty *Titanesse* beheld,
    All were she fraught with pride and impudence,
    Yet with the sight thereof was almost queld;
220   And inly quaking, seem'd as reft of sense,
    And voyd of speech in that drad audience,
    Untill that *Jove* himselfe, her selfe bespake:
    Speake thou fraile woman, speake with confidence,
    Whence art thou, and what doost thou here now make?°   *now do*
225 What idle errand hast thou, earths mansion to forsake?

26

Shee, halfe confused with his great commaund,
    Yet gathering spirit of her natures pride,
    Him boldly answer'd thus to his demaund:
    I am a daughter, by the mothers side,[6]
230   Of her that is Grand-mother magnifide
    Of all the Gods, great *Earth*, great *Chaos* child:
    But by the fathers (be it not envide)
    I greater am in bloud (whereon I build)
Then all the Gods, though wrongfully from heaven exil'd.

27

235   For, *Titan* (as ye all acknowledge must)
    Was *Saturnes* elder brother by birth-right;
    Both, sonnes of *Uranus*: but by unjust
    And guilefull meaties, through *Corybantes* slight,[7]
    The younger thrust the elder from his right:
240   Since which, thou *Jove*, injuriously hast held
    The Heavens rule from *Titans* sonnes by might;
    And them to hellish dungeons downe hast feld:
Witnesse ye Heavens the truth of all that I have teld.

28

Whilst she thus spake, the Gods that gave good eare
245   To her bold words, and marked well her grace,
    Beeing of stature tall as any there
    Of all the Gods, and beautifull of face,
    As any of the Goddesses in place,
    Stood all astonied, like a sort of Steeres;°   *herd of steers*
250   Mongst whom, some beast of strange & forraine race,
    Unwares is chaunc't, far straying from his peeres:
So did their ghastly gaze bewray their hidden feares.

29

Till having pauz'd awhile, *Jove* thus bespake;
    Will never mortall thoughts ceasse to aspire,
255   In this bold sort,° to Heaven claime to make,   *way*

6. Mutability is the daughter of Earth and Titan, Saturn's elder brother.

7. At the birth of Jupiter his mother Cybele urged the Corybantes, a group of fanatically wild women devoted to her, to make a great uproar to drown the cries of the new-born child. She then presented Saturn with a stone, which he duly ate, thinking it to be Jupiter. This whole passage seems to refer to an alternate version of the war between Jupiter and the Titans. According to this version, Titan, the elder brother of Saturn, was persuaded to abdicate the throne on condition that Saturn should kill all his children so that he might have no descendants to succeed him. As a result of this original compact between Titan and Saturn and Mutability's relation to Titan, Jupiter might be considered a usurper and Mutability the legal heir, as a result of the Corybantes' trick.

And touch celestiall seates with earthly mire?
I would have thought, that bold *Procrustes* hire,[8]
Or *Typhons* fall, or proud *Ixions* paine,
Or great *Prometheus*, tasting of our ire,[9]
260   Would have suffiz'd, the rest for to restraine;
And warn'd all men by their example to refraine:

30

But now, this off-scum of that cursed fry,[1]
Dare to renew the like hold enterprize,
And chalenge th'heritage of this our skie;
265   Whom what should hinder,[2] but that we likewise
Should handle as the rest of her allies,
And thunder-drive to hell? With that, he shooke
His Nectar-deawed locks, with which the skyes
And all the world beneath for terror quooke,
270   And eft his burning levin-brond° in hand he tooke.   *lightning bolt*

31

But, when he looked on her lovely face,
In which, faire beames of beauty did appeare,
That could the greatest wrath soone turne to grace
(Such sway° doth beauty even in Heaven beare)   *power*
275   He staide bis hand: and having chang'd his cheare,
He thus againe in milder wise began;
But ah! if Gods should strive with flesh yfere,
Then shortly should the progeny of Man
Be rooted out, if *Jove* should doe still what he can:

32

280   But thee faire *Titans* child, I rather weene,
Through some vaine errour or inducement light,
To see that° mortall eyes have never seene;   *that which*
Or through ensample of thy sisters might,
Bellona;[3] whose great glory thou doost spight,°   *envy*
285   Since thou hast seene her dreadfull power belowe,
Mongst wretched men (dismaide with her affright)°   *fright of her*
To bandie Crownes, and Kingdomes to bestowe:
And sure thy worth,[4] no lesse then hers doth seem to showe.

---

8. The "reward" of Procrustes, who made his guests fit his bed either by chopping them off if they were too large or by stretching them if they were too small. His "reward" was similar treatment by Theseus. He is included here as an example of what happens to those people who do not observe distinctions either in persons or in hierarchies. 9. Examples of those already punished by Jupiter for opposing his supremacy. For Typhon see VII.6.15.8. Ixion was bound to a burning wheel for trying to seduce Juno.

For stealing fire from heaven and giving it to man Prometheus was bound on the Caucasuses where each day a vulture devoured his liver, which grew again each night.
1. Brood, i.e., the Titans.
2. I.e., what should hinder us from handling her (whom).
3. A Titaness, goddess of war.
4. I.e., and surely thy worth does seem to appear no less than hers.

33

But wote thou this, thou hardy *Titanesse*,
290   That not the worth of any living wight
     May challenge ought in Heavens interesse;°   *legal interest*
     Much lesse the Title of old *Titans*[5] Right:
     For, we by Conquest of our soveraine might,
     And by eternall doome of Fates decree,[6]
295   Have wonne the Empire of the Heavens bright;
     Which to our selves we hold, and to whom wee
Shall worthy deeme partakers of our blisse to bee.

34

Then ceasse thy idle claime thou foolish gerle,
     And seeke by grace and goodnesse to obtaine
300   That place from which by folly *Titan* fell;
     There-to thou maist[7] perhaps, if so thou faine
     Have *Jove* thy gratious Lord and Soveraigne.
     So, having said, she thus to him replide;
     Ceasse *Saturnes* sonne,[8] to seeke by proffers vaine
305   Of idle hopes t'allure mee to thy side,
For to betray my Right, before I have it tride.°   *decided by trial*

35

But thee, ô *Jove*, no equall Judge I deeme
     Of my desert, or of my dewfull Right;
     That in thine owne behalfe maist partiall seeme:
310   But to the highest him, that is behight
     Father of Gods and men by equall might;°   *equally*
     To weet, the God of Nature,[9] I appeale.
     There-at *Jove* wexed wroth, and in his spright
     Did inly grudge,° yet did it well concede;   *complain within*
315   And bade *Dan Phœbus* Scribe[1] her Appellation° seale.   *appeal*

36

Eftsoones the time and place appointed were,
     Where all, both heavenly Powers, & earthly wights,
     Before great Natures presence should appeare,
     For triall of their Titles and best Rights:
320   That was, to weet, upon the highest hights

---

5. Mutability is the daughter of Earth and Titan, because of this relationship Jupiter might be considered a usurper and Mutability a legal heir.
6. Divine order of Providence.
7. To that place you may get.
8. Mutability's patronymic epithet is intended as an insult in that it deprives Jupiter of his sovereignty and presses home her claim.
9. Nature's changed sex is explained by lines 5–7 and is part of literal tradition.
1. Apollo as secretary of this encounter is a humorous touch.

Of *Arlo-hill*[2] (Who knowes not *Arlo-hill?*)[3]
That is the highest head° (in all mens sights)   peak
Of my old father *Mole*,[4] whom Shepheards quill
Renowmed hath with hymnes fit for a rurall skill.

37

325   And, were it not ill fitting for this file,[5]
To sing of hilles & woods, mongst warres & Knights,
I would abate° the sternenesse of my stile,   diminish
Mongst these sterne stounds to mingle soft delights;
And tell how *Arlo* through *Dianaes* spights[6]
330   (Beeing of old the best and fairest Hill
That was in all this holy-Islands hights)
Was made the most unpleasant, and most ill.
Meane while, ô *Clio*, lend *Calliope* thy quill.[7]

38

Whylome, when IRELAND florished in fame[8]
335   Of wealths and goodnesse, far above the rest
Of all that beare the *British* Islands name,
The Gods then us'd (for pleasure and for rest)
Oft to resort there-to, when seem'd them best:
But none of all there-in more pleasure found,
340   Then *Cynthia;* that is soveraine Queene protest
Of woods and forrests, which therein abound,
Sprinkled with wholsom waters, more then most on ground.°   on earth

39

But mongst them all, as fittest for her game,
Either for chace of beasts with hound or boawe,
345   Or for to shroude in shade from *Phœbus* flame,
Or bathe in fountaines that doe freshly flowe,
Or from high hilles, or from the dales belowe,
She chose this *Arlo;* where shee did resort
With all her Nymphes enranged on a rowe,°   arranged in a row
350   With whom the woody Gods did oft consort:°   mingle
For, with the Nymphes, the Satyres love to play & sport.

2. Galtymore, highest peak in the mountain range near Spenser's home Kilcolman in County Cork, so called because it overlooks the Vale of Aherlow in County Tipperary.
3. Aside from the impertinence of answering Spenser's question with an annotation, one might compare the similar self-awareness in VI.10.16.4: "Poore *Colin Clout* (who knowes not *Colin Clout?*)."
4. Spenser's name for the mountain range near his home, which his "shepherd's quill" had already described in *Colin Clouts Come Home Again* (1595).

5. And if it were not inappropriate in this recital . . .
6. Injuries of Cynthia. Diana is the more common name for Cynthia when she is associated with the forest and hunting, as here.
7. Spenser invokes the aid of Clio, Muse of history, to help Calliope, the Muse of epic poetry, as he always does when he treats of real historical events or geographical places.
8. Between the sixth and ninth centuries Ireland was a famous center of learning and art.

40

Amongst the which, there was a Nymph that hight
    Molanna;[9] daughter of old father *Mole,*
    And sister unto *Mulla,*[1] faire and bright:
355   Unto whose bed false *Bregog*[2] whylome stole,
    That Shepheard *Colin*[3] dearely did condole,
    And made her lucklesse loves well knowne to be.
    But this *Molanna,* were she not so shole,°   *shallow*
    Were no lesse faire and beautifull then shee:
360   Yet as she is, a fairer flood° may no man see.   *flowing river*

41

For, first, she springs out of two marble Rocks,
    On which, a grove of Oakes high mounted growes,
    That as a girlond seemes to deck the locks
    Of som faire Bride, brought forth with pompous[4] showes
365   Out of her bowre, that many flowers strowes:
    So, through the flowry Dales she tumbling downe,
    Through many woods, and shady coverts° flowes   *glades*
    (That on each side her silver channell crowne)
Till to the Plaine she come, whose Valleyes shee doth drowne.

42

370   In her sweet streames, *Diana* used oft
    (After her sweatie chace and toilesome play)
    To bathe her selfe; and after, on the soft
    And downy grasse, her dainty limbes to lay
    In covert shade, where none behold her may:
375   For, much she hated sight of living eye.
    Foolish God *Faunus,*° though full many a day   *a faun*
    He saw her clad, yet longed foolishly
To see her naked mongst her Nymphes in privity.[5]

43

No way he found to compasse[6] his desire,
380   But to corrupt *Molanna,* this her maid,
    Her° to discover° for some secret hire: *Diana / to reveal*
    So, her with flattering words he first assaid;
    And after, pleasing gifts for her purvaid,

9. The river Behanagh near Spenser's home. Her name suggests her genealogy: Mol-, "old father *Mole,*" -anna, Behanna.
1. The river Awbeg, renamed by Spenser from Kilnemullah, the ancient name for Buttevant, a city on its banks. Spenser annotates the name himself in *Colin Clouts Come Home Again.*
2. Another river, the story of whose marriage with Mulla

Spenser tells in *Colin Clouts Come Home Again.*
3. Spenser's name for himself from *The Shepheardes Calender* through VI.10. He is referring here to his *Colin Clouts Come Home Again.*
4. Full of pomp, no pejorative sense intended.
5. In secret, but the rhyme word is meant to expose more of his prurient interests.
6. To achieve, with overtones of "to embrace."

Queene-apples, and red Cherries[7] from the tree,
385   With which he her allured and betraid,
To tell what time he might her Lady see
When she her selfe did bathe, that he might secret bee.

44

There-to hee promist, if shee would him pleasure°   *please*
With this small boone, to quit her with a better;
390   To weet, that where-as shee had out of measure
Long lov'd the *Fanchin*,[8] who by nought did set her,
That he would undertake, for this to get her
To be his Love, and of him liked well:
Besides all which, he vow'd to be her debter
395   For many moe good turnes then he would tell;
The least of which, this litte pleasure should excell.

45

The simple maid did yield to him anone;
And eft him placed where he close might view
That never any saw, save onely one;[9]
400   Who, for his hire to so foole-hardy dew,[1]
Was of his hounds devour'd in Hunters hew.°   *slaughter*
Tho, as her manner was on sunny day,
Diana, with her Nymphes about her, drew
To this sweet spring; where, doffing her array,°   *clothes*
405   She bath'd her lovely limbes, for *Jove* a likely pray.

46

There *Faunus* saw that pleased much his eye,
And made his hart to tickle in his brest,
That for great joy of some-what° he did spy,   *something*
He could him not containe in silent rest;
410   But breaking forth in laughter, loud profest
His foolish thought. A foolish *Faune* indeed,
That couldst not hold thy selfe so hidden blest,
But wouldest needs thine owne conceit° areed.   *thought*
Babblers unworthy been of so divine a meed.

---

7. These are typical pastoral gifts, but here they carry overtones of the temptation of Eve.
8. The river Funsheon into which die Behanagh flows.
9. Actaeon; a reference to the myth of Diana and Actaeon, a hunter who in chase came upon Diana naked. In fury she turned him into a stag, and his own dogs devoured him. See Ovid's *Metamorphoses*. 3.173–252, although some of Spenser's details may derive from other Ovidian myths: Callisto, 2.409 ff; Arethusa, 5.572 ff. The whole episode of Faunus and Diana closely parallels the structure of the Actaeon story. The parallelism of characters (Cynthia: Diana; Mutability: Faunus; Molanna: reader), the similarity in theme: an act of presumptuous rebellion, echoing the Christian myth of the Fall, the numerous verbal parallels, all suggest that Spenser wanted his retelling of the Actaeon myth to be an analog of and commentary on the main narrative of the poem.
1. Due to one so foolhardy.

47

415 The Goddesse, all abashed with that noise,
    In haste forth started from the guilty brooke;
    And running straight where-as she heard his voice,
    Enclos'd the bush about, and there him tooke,
    Like darred² Larke; not daring up to looke
420   On her whose sight before so much he sought.
    Thence, forth they drew him by the homes, & shooke
    Nigh all to peeces, that they left him nought;
And then into the open light they forth him brought.

48

Like as an huswife, that with busie care
425   Thinks of her Dairie to make wondrous gaine,
    Finding where-as some wicked beast unware
    That breakes into her Dayr'house, there doth draine
    Her creaming pannes, and frustrate all her paine;
    Hath in some snare or gin set close behind,
430   Entrapped him, and caught into her traine,
    Then thinkes what punishment were best assign'd,
And thousand deathes deviseth in her vengefull mind:

49

So did *Diana* and her maydens all
    Use silly *Faunus*, now within their baile:°   *custody*
435   They mocke and scorne him, and him foule miscall;
    Some by the nose him pluckt, some by the taile,
    And by his goatish beard some did him haile:°   *pull*
    Yet he (poore soule) with patience all did beare;
    For, nought against their wils might countervaile:°   *resist*
440   Ne ought he said what ever he did heare;
But hanging downe his head, did like a Mome appeare.³

50

At length, when they had flouted° him their fill,   *derided*
    They gan to cast what penaunce him to give.
    Some would have gelt him, but that same would spill°   *destroy*
445   The Wood-gods breed, which must for ever live:
    Others would through the river him have drive,°   *driven*
    And ducked deepe: but that seem'd penaunce light;
    But most agreed and did this sentence give,
    Him in Deares skin to clad; & in that plight,
450 To hunt him with their hounds, him selfe save how hee might.

---

2. Dazzled, with a pun on "daring." Larks were dazzled by
mirrors or bits of glass so they could be caught.

3. Fool, blockhead, unknowing comic butt.

51

But *Cynthia's* selfe, more angry then the rest,
   Thought not enough, to punish him in sport,
   And of her shame to make a gamesome° jest;   *sportive*
   But gan examine him in straighter sort,°   *in stricter manner*
455   Which of her Nymphes, or other close consort,
   Him thither brought, and her to him betraid?
   He, much affeard, to her confessed short,
   That't was *Molanna* which her so bewraid.
Then all attonce their hands upon *Molanna* laid.

52

460   But him (according as they had decreed)
   With a Deeres-skin they covered, and then chast
   With all their hounds that after him did speed;
   But he more speedy, from them fled more fast
   Then any Deere: so sore him dread aghast.[4]
465   They after follow'd all with shrill out-cry,
   Shouting as they the heavens would have brast:
   That all the woods and dales where he did flie,
Did ring againe, and loud reeccho to the skie.[5]

53

So they him follow'd till they weary were;
470   When, back returning to *Molann'* againe,
   They, by commaund'ment of *Diana*, there
   Her whelm'd° with stones. Yet *Faunus* (for her paine)   *overwhelmed*
   Of her beloved *Fanchin* did obtaine,
   That her he would receive unto his bed.
475   So now her waves passe through a pleasant Plaine,
   Till with the *Fanchin* she her selfe doe wed,
And (both combin'd) themselves in one faire river spred.[6]

54

Nath'lesse, *Diana*, full of indignation,
   Thence-forth abandond her delicious brooke;
480   In whose sweet streame, before that bad occasion,
   So much delight to bathe her limbes she tooke:
   Ne onely her, but also quite forsooke
   All those faire forrests about *Arlo* hid,
   And all that Mountaine, which doth over-looke
485   The richest champian° that may else be rid,[7]   *plain*
And the faire *Shure*,[8] in which are thousand Salmons bred.

---

4. I.e., so sorely did his dread terrify him.
5. Compare the refrains of *Epithalamion*: "The woods shall to me answer, and my eccho ring," etc.
6. This is another Spenserian river marriage in which

Spenser symbolizes the triumph of love over mutability in a fallen world through the merging of rivers.
7. Past participle of "to read," seen.
8. The river Suir that flows through rich country.

55

Them all, and all that she so deare did way,°⁹   *consider*
   Thence-forth she left; and parting from the place,
   There-on an heavy haplesse curse did lay,
490   To weet, that Wolves, where she was wont to space,°   *roam*
   Should harbour'd be, and all those Woods deface,
   And Thieves should rob and spoile that Coast around.
   Since which, those Woods, and all that goodly Chase,°   *hunting ground*
   Doth to this day with Wolves and Thieves abound:
495 Which too-too true that lands in-dwellers since have found.

Canto VII

Pealing,° from Jove, to Natur's Bar,°   *appealing / court*
   bold Alteration¹ pleades
   Large° Evidence: but Nature soone   *extensive*
   her righteous Doome areads.

1

Ah! whither doost thou now thou greater Muse°   *Calliope*
   Me from these woods & pleasing forrests bring?
   And my fraile spirit (that dooth oft refuse
   This too high flight, unfit for her weake wing)
5   Lift up aloft, to tell of heavens King²
   (Thy soveraine Sire)³ his fortunate successe,
   And victory, in bigger noates to sing,
   Which he obtain'd against that *Titanesse*,
That him of heavens Empire sought to dispossesse.

2

10 Yet sith I needs must follow thy behest,
   Doe thou my weaker wit with skill inspire,
   Fit for this turne;⁴ and in my sable brest
   Kindle fresh sparks of that immortall fire,
   Which learned minds inflameth with desire
15 Of heavenly things: for, who but thou alone,
   That art yborne of heaven and heavenly Sire,
   Can tell things doen in heaven so long ygone;
So farre past memory of man that may be knowne.

---

9. Spenser intends Diana's curse to explain the present state of Ireland, harassed and torn by faction, an etiological myth.
1. Another name for Mutability.
2. Spenser invokes the Muse to lift his fraill spirit, whose wing, too weak, may refuse to undertake such a high poetic flight.

3. Spenser makes Jupiter the father of the Muses. The more traditional father is Apollo.
4. Change of direction, in returning to his original narrative. sable: the 1609 reading. Some editors emend to "feeble." Milton, for one, was not bothered by the original reading, which he imitates in *Pardise Lost* 1.22–3: "What in me is dark Illumine."

3

Now, at the time that was before agreed,
20   The Gods assembled all on *Arlo* hill;
        As well those that are sprung of heavenly seed,
        As those that all the other world doe fill,
        And rule both sea and land unto their will:
        Onely th'infernall Powers might not appeare;
25   Aswell for horror of their count'naunce ill,
        As for th'unruly fiends which they did feare;
Yet *Pluto* and *Proserpina*[5] were present there.

4

And thither also came all other creatures,
        What-ever life or motion doe retaine,
30   According to their sundry kinds of features;
        That *Arlo* scarsly could them all containe;
        So full they filled every hill and Plaine:
        And had not *Natures* Sergeant (that is *Order*)
        Them well disposed by his busie paine,
35   And raunged farre abroad in every border,
They would have caused much confusion and disorder.

5

Then forth issewed (great goddesse) great dame *Nature*,[6]
        With goodly port° and gracious Majesty;   *bearing*
        Being far greater and more tall[7] of stature
40   Then any of the gods or Powers on hie:
        Yet certes by her face and physnomy.°   *countenance*
        Whether she man or woman inly were,
        That could not any creature well descry:°   *discover*
        For, with a veile that wimpled° every where,   *lay in folds*
45 Her head and face was hid, that mote to none appeare.

6

That some doe say was so by skill devized,
        To hide the terror of her uncouth hew,
        From mortall eyes that should be sore agrized;°   *horrified*
        For that her face did like a Lion shew,
50   That eye of wight could not indure to view:
        But others tell that it so beautious was,

5. The king and queen of the underworld. Their presence at this trial is essential because their power is derived from Nature, whose laws reach to and regulate even the anomalies of the underworld.
6. This is the same "god of Nature" referred to in VII.6.3 5.6. Her apparently changed sex is explained by lines 5–7 and by the literary tradition of which she is a part. She is God's vice-regent of the Providential order of nature and can be identified with the Wisdom or Sapience that Spenser describes in *Hymn of Heavenly Beauty*, 183 ff. The ambiguity of her description is part of the tradition beginning with Boethius, *De consolatione philosophiae* and extending through Jean de Meun, *Roman de la Rose*, Alanus de Insulis, *De planctu naturae* and Chaucer, *Parliament of Fowls*.
7. To show her greater importance.

And round about such beames of splendor threw,
That it the Sunne a thousand times did pass,
Ne could be seene, but like an image in a glass.

7

55 That well may seemen true: for, well I weene
That this same day, when she on *Arlo* sat,
Her garment was so bright and wondrous sheene,°   bright, beautiful
That my fraile wit cannot devize to what
It to compare, nor finde like stuffe to that,
60 As those three sacred *Saints*,[8] though else most wise,
Yet on mount *Thabor* quite their wits forgat,
When they their glorious Lord in strange disguise
Transfigur'd sawe; his garments so did daze their eyes.

8

In a fayre Plaine upon an equall Hill,
65 She placed was in a pavilion;
Not such as Craftes-men by their idle° skill   vain
Are wont for Princes states to fashion:
But th'earth her self of her owne motion,
Out of her fruitfull bosome made to growe
70 Most dainty trees; that, shooting up anon,
Did seeme to bow their bloosming heads full lowe,
For homage unto her, and like a throne did shew.

9

So heard° it is for any living wight,   hard
All her array and vestiments to tell,
75 That old *Dan Geffrey*[9] (in whose gentle spright
The pure well head[1] of Poesie did dwell)
In his *Foules*[2] *parley* durst not with it mel,
But it transferd to *Alane*, who he thought
Had in his *Plaint of kindes* describ'd it well:
80 Which who will read set forth so as it ought,°   as it should be
Go seek he out that *Alane* where he may be sought.

10

And all the earth far underneath her feete
Was dight with flowres, that voluntary grew

---

8. Peter, James, and John, who saw Christ transfigured on Mount Tabor. See Matthew 17.1–8; Mark 9.2–3. The Transfiguration was the first time that Christ's divinity shone through his humanity and became apparent to his disciples.
9. Master Geoffrey Chaucer, whose *Parliament of Fowls*, describes Nature, as does Alanus de Insulis in *De planctu naturae* (*Pleynt of Kynde*). Spenser is placing himself squarely in the tradition of regarding Nature as a Wisdom figure.

1. Source; Spenser, like most sixteenth-century poets, considered Chaucer the father of English poetry and imitated many of his poems. Spenser's *Daphnaida* is based on Chaucer's *Book of the Duchess*, and is a continuation of Chaucer's "The Squire's Tale."
2. Chaucer's *Parliament of Fowls*.

Out of the ground, and sent forth odours sweet;
85   Tenne thousand mores° of sundry sent and hew,   *roots, plants*
That might delight the smell, or please the view:
The which, the Nymphes, from all the brooks thereby
Had gathered, which they at her foot-stoole threw;
That richer seem'd then any tapestry,
90   That Princes bowres adorne with painted imagery.

11

And *Mole*³ himselfe, to honour her the more,
Did deck himself in freshest faire attire,
And his high head, that seemeth alwaies hore
With hardned frosts of former winters ire,
95   He with an Oaken girlond now did tire,
As if the love of some new Nymph late seene,
Had in him kindled youthfull fresh desire,
And made him change his gray attire to greene;
Ah gentle *Mole!* such joyance hath thee well beseene.

12

100   Was never so great joyance since the day,
That all the gods whylome assembled were,
On *Hæmus* hill⁴ in their divine array,
To celebrate the solemne bridall cheare,
Twixt *Peleus,*⁵ and dame *Thetis* pointed° there;   *appointed*
105   Where *Phæbus* self, that god of Poets hight,
They say did sing the spousall hymne full cleere,
That all the gods were ravisht with delight
Of his celestiall song, & Musicks wondrous might.

13

This great Grandmother of all creatures bred
110   Great *Nature,* ever young yet full of eld,
Still mooving, yet unmoved from her sted;
Unseene of any, yet of all beheld;
Thus sitting in her throne as I have teld,
Before her came dame *Mutabilitie;*
115   And being lowe before her presence feld,°   *prostrate*
With meek obaysance° and humilitie,   *obedience*
Thus gan her plaintif Plea, with words to amplifie;⁶

---

3. See VII.6.36.8.
4. The marriage of Peleus and Thetis did not take place on Haemus Hill. Spenser transfers the location because of Ovid's description of Haemus (*Metamorcphoses.* 6.87–9), who was changed into a mountain for daring to assume the names of the gods.
5. Jupiter insisted that the goddess Thetis be married to the mortal Peleus when he learned that any son of hers

would be more powerful than his father. Thetis objected and resisted Peleus by changing into a number of shapes, but Peleus' persistence was successful. Their son was Achilles, the hero of Homer's *Iliad.* Spenser stresses their wedding day, when Eris threw the apple of discord at the feet of Juno, Minerva, and Venus, the event that led to the Trojan war.
6. Speak with rhetorical figures.

14

    To thee ô greatest goddesse, onely great,[7]
      An humble suppliant loe, I lowely fly
120   Seeking for Right, which I of thee entreat;
      Who Right to all dost deale indifferently,°   *impartially*
      Damning all Wrong and tortious° Injurie,   *wrongful*
      Which any of thy creatures doe to other
      (Oppressing them with power, unequally)
125   Sith of them all thou art the equall mother,
And knittest each to'each, as brother unto brother.

15

    To thee therefore of this same *Jove* I plaine,
      And of his fellow gods that faine to be,
      That challenge° to themselves the whole worlds raign;   *claim*
130   Of which, the greatest part is due to me,
      And heaven it selfe by heritage[8] in Fee:
      For, heaven and earth I both alike do deeme,
      Sith heaven and earth are both alike to thee;[9]
      And, gods no more then men thou doest esteeme:
135   For, even the gods to thee, as men to gods do seeme.

16

    Then weigh, ô soveraigne goddesse, by what right
      These gods do claime the worlds whole soveraity;
      And that° is onely dew unto thy might   *and that which*
      Arrogate to themselves ambitiously:
140   As for the gods owne principality,
      Which *Jove* usurpes unjustly; that to be
      My heritage, *Jove's* self cannot deny,
      From my great Grandsire *Titan*, unto mee,
Deriv'd by dew descent;[1] as is well knowen to thee.

17

145   Yet mauger *Jove*, and all his gods beside,
      I doe possesse the worlds most regiment;°   *most power*
      As, if ye please it into parts divide,
      And every parts inholders° to convent,°   *tenants / to assemble*
      Shall to your eyes appeare incontinent.°   *immediately*
150   And first, the Earth (great mother of us all)
      That only seems unmov'd and permanent,

7. Mutability's case is orderly in the extreme and may be divided in two parts: her plea (14–26) and her presentation of witnesses (27–47).
8. I.e., hold as one's absolute and rightful possession.
9. Mutability's presumption is evident here in her lapse of logic: I consider heaven and earth alike because you consider them alike, but she is forgetting about the principle of hierarchy.
1. See radiance.

And unto *Mutability* not thrall;
Yet is she chang'd in part, and eeke in generall.

18

For, all that from her springs, and is ybredde,
155   How-ever feyre it flourish for a time,
Yet see we soone decay; and, being dead,
To turne again unto their earthly slime:°   *material source of being*
Yet, out of their decay and mortall° crime,   *deadly*
We daily see new creatures to arize;
160   And of their Winter spring another Prime,°   *spring*
Unlike in forme, and chang'd by strange disguise:
So turne they still about, and change in restlesse wise.

19

As for her tenants; that is, man and beasts,
The beasts we daily see massacred dy,
165   As thralls and vassalls unto mens beheasts:
And men themselves doe change continually,
From youth to eld, from wealth to poverty,
From good to bad, from bad to worst of all.
Ne doe their bodies only flit and fly:
170   But eeke their minds (which they immortall call)
Still° change and vary thoughts, as new occasions fall.   *continually*

20

Ne is the water in more constant case;°   *condition*
Whether those same on high, or these belowe.
For, th'Ocean moveth stil, from place to place;
175   And every River still doth ebbe and flowe:
Ne any Lake, that seems most still and slowe,
Ne Poole so small, that can his smoothnesse holde,
When any winde doth under heaven blowe;
With which, the clouds are also tost and roll'd;
180   Now like great Hills; &, streight, like sluces, them unfold.°   *open themselves*

21

So likewise are all watry living wights
Still tost, and turned, with continuall change,
Never abyding in their stedfast plights.°   *condition*
The fish, still floting, doe at randon range,
185   And never rest; but evermore exchange
Their dwelling places, as the streames them carrie:
Ne have the watry foules a certaine grange,°   *fixed dwelling*
Wherein to rest, ne in one stead do tarry;
But flitting still doe flie, and still their places vary.

22

190   Next is the Ayre: which who feeles not by sense
          (For, of all sense it is the middle meane)²
          To flit still? and, with subtill influence³
          Of his thin spirit,⁴ all creatures to maintaine,
          In state of life? O weake life! that does leane
195   On thing so tickle° as th'unsteady ayre;   *unstable*
          Which every howre is chang'd, and altred cleane
          With every blast that bloweth fowle or faire:
      The faire doth it prolong; the fowle doth it impaire.

23

      Therein the changes infinite beholde,
200   Which to her creatures every minute chaunce;
          Now, boyling hot: streight, friezing deadly cold:
          Now, faire sun-shine, that makes all skip and daunce:
          Streight,° bitter storms and balefull countenance,   *immediately*
          That makes them all to shiver and to shake:
205   Rayne, hayle, and snowe do pay them sad penance,
          And dreadfull thunder-claps (that make them quake)
      With flames & flashing lights that thousand changes make.

24

      Last is the fire: which, though it live for ever,
          Ne can be quenched quite; yet, every day,
210   Wee see his parts, so soone as they do sever,°   *separate*
          To lose their heat, and shortly to decay;
          So, makes himself his owne consuming pray.
          Ne any living creatures doth he breed:
          But all, that are of others bredd, doth slay;
215   And, with their death, his cruell life dooth feed;
      Nought leaving, but their barren ashes, without seede.

25

      Thus, all these fower (the which the ground-work⁵ bee
          Of all the world, and of all living wights)
          To thousand sorts of *Change* we subject see:
220   Yet are they chang'd (by other wondrous slights)
          Into themselves, and lose their native mights;⁶
          The Fire to Aire, and th'Ayre to Water sheere,°   *bright, crystal clear*
          And Water into Earth: yet Water fights

---

2. I.e., air is the medium by which sense perceptions are
transmitted.
3. Air maintains life in creatures by flowing into them
(influencing them) because it is a less material element
than either earth or water, hence subtle.

4. Thin substance, less, that is, than earth or water.
5. The four elements are the basis of all creation.
6. Natural powers. It was believed that elements could be
transmuted into one another.

With Fire, and Aire with Earth approaching neere:
225 Yet all are in one body, and as one appeare.

26

So, in them all raignes *Mutabilitie;*
   How-ever these, that Gods themselves do'call,
   Of them doe claime the rule and soveranty:
   As, *Vesta*,[7] of the fire æthereall;°   *heavenly*
230 *Vulcan*,[8] of this, with us so usuall;
   Ops,[9] of the earth; and *Juno* of the Ayre;[1]
   Neptune,[2] of Seas; and Nymphes,[3] of Rivers all.
   For, all those Rivers to me subject are:
And all the rest, which they usurp, be all my share.

27

235 Which to approven true, as I have told,
   Vouchsafe, ô goddesse, to thy presence call
   The rest which doe the world in being hold:[4]
   As, times and seasons of the yeare that fall:
   Of all the which, demand in generall,
240 Or judge thy selfe, by verdit of thine eye,
   Whether to me they are not subject all.
   Nature did yeeld thereto; and by-and-by,
Bade *Order*[5] call them all, before her Majesty.

28

So, forth issew'd° the Seasons of the yeare;[6]   *came forth*
245 First, lusty *Spring*, all dight in leaves of flowres
   That freshly budded and new bloosmes did beare
   (In which a thousand birds had built their bowres
   That sweetly sung, to call forth Paramours):
   And in his hand a javelin he did beare,
250 And on his head (as fit for warlike stoures)
   A guilt engraven morion° he did weare;   *helmet*
That as some did him love, so others did him feare.

29

Then came the jolly *Sommer*, being dight
   In a thin silken cassock coloured greene,

---

7. Roman goddess of heavenly fire.
8. Vulcan, as opposed to Vesta, is god of earthly fire, a more common phenomenon to us.
9. Goddess of the earth.
1. Juno's special province was the air.
2. God of the seas.
3. Guardian spirits of rivers.

4. Mutability has in mind the participants in the procession about to start, by which man maintains order in his temporal existence.
5. As in VII.7.4.6 Order as sergeant is an important part of the reason that Nature can finally decide against Mutability.
6. Spenser uses only two rhymes in this stanza, as in VII.7.44.

255 That was unlyned all, to be more light:
And on his head a girlond well beseene°   *well adorned*
He wore, from which as he had chauffed[7] been
The sweat did drop; and in his hand he bore
A boawe and shaftes, as he in forrest greene
260 Had hunted late the Libbard° or the Bore,   *leopard*
And now would bathe his limbes, with labor heated sore.

30

Then came the *Autumne* all in yellow clad,
As though he joyed in his plentious store,
Laden with fruits that made him laugh, full glad
265 That he had banisht hunger, which to-fore°   *before*
Had by the belly oft him pinched sore.
Upon his head a wreath that was enrold
With eares of corne, of every sort he bore:
And in his hand a sickle he did holde,
270 To reape the ripened fruits the which the earth had yold.

31

Lastly, came *Winter* cloathed all in frize,[8]
Chattering his teeth for cold that did him chill,
Whil'st on his hoary beard his breath did freese;
And the dull drops that from his purpled bill°   *nose*
275 As from a limbeck[9] did adown distill.
In his right hand a tipped staffe he held,
With which his feeble steps he stayed still:
For, he was faint with cold, and weak with eld;
That scarse his loosed[1] limbes he hable was to weld.°   *wield, manage*

32

280 These, marching softly,° thus in order went,[2]   *slowly*
And after them, the Monthes all riding came;

7. Chauffed: heated (French: *chauffer*).
8. Frieze is a coarse woollen cloth.
9. Alembic, a vessel for distilling; a retort.
1. Out of joint.
2. The stanzas describing the months have certain common features. In each the sign of the zodiac appropriate to it is included, and very often this sign is associated with a well-known classical myth. The procession begins with March because March was the first month of the legal year according to the old calendar, and the first month of the rebirth of nature. New Year's Day was still celebrated on 1 January, a form of the calendar Spenser uses by beginning his *Shepheardes Calender* with January. Below is a brief chart of the months, their zodiacal signs, and the myths associated with them.

March	Aries (ram)	Helle and Phrixus
April	Taurus (bull)	Europa and Jove as bull
May	Gemini (twins)	Castor and Pollux
June	Cancer (crab)	
July	Leo (lion)	Hercules and the Nemean lion
August	Virgo (maid)	Astraea, goddess of justice
September	Libra (scales)	
October	Scorpio (scorpion)	Diana and Orion
November	Sagittarius (centaur)	Chiron
December	Capricorn (goat)	Jupiter and Amalthea
January	Aquarius (urn)	Saturn (?)
February	Pisces (fish)	

Spenser also incorporates the labors of the months, an ancient theme in Christian art, which makes of the farming cycle of the year a symbol of man's finding his way to salvation through the proper use of the curse on Adam that man must work (Genesis 3.17).

First, sturdy *March* with brows full sternly bent,
And armed strongly, rode upon a Ram,
The same which over *Hellespontus*[3] swam:
285   Yet in his hand a spade he also hent,°   *held*
And in a bag all sorts of seeds ysame,°   *together*
Which on the earth he strowed as he went,
And fild her womb with fruitfull hope of nourishment.

33

Next came fresh *Aprill* full of lustyhed,°   *lustiness*
290   And wanton as a Kid whose horne new buds:
Upon a Bull he rode, the same which led
Europa[4] floting through th'*Argolick* fluds:[5]
His hornes were gilden all with golden studs
And garnished with garlonds goodly dight
295   Of all the fairest flowres and freshest buds
Which th'earth brings forth, and wet he seem'd in sight
With waves, through which he waded for his loves delight.

34

Then came faire *May*, the fayrest mayd[6] on ground,
Deckt all with dainties of her seasons pryde,
300   And throwing flowres out of her lap around:
Upon two brethrens shoulders she did ride,
The twinnes of *Leda*; which on eyther side[7]
Supported her like to their soveraine Queene.
Lord! how all creatures laught, when her they spide,
305   And leapt and daunc't as they had ravisht beene!
And *Cupid* selfe about her fluttred all in greene.[8]

35

And after her, came jolly *June*, arrayd
All in greene leaves, as he a Player were;[9]
Yet in his time, he wrought° as well as playd,   *worked*
310   That by his plough-yrons° mote right well appeare: *ploughshare*
Upon a Crab he rode, that him did beare
With crooked crawling steps an uncouth pase,
And backward yode, as Bargemen wont to fare

---

3. *Hellespontus*: Ovid, *Fasti* 3.851–76, tells the story of Helle and Phrixus, who escaped the wrath of Ino through the aid of a ram with golden fleece, which carried them across the body of water now called the Hellespont, whose name came from the fact that Helle slipped off the ram's back and drowned. This ram has been associated with the zodiacal sign Aries and is identified with Jupiter by Boccaccio.
4. Jupiter in the form of a white bull enticed Europa onto his back and then fled into the sea in order to capture her love.

5. The gulf of Argolis in the Aegean.
6. With a pun on the name of the month.
7. Castor and Pollux. There are many versions of this myth, but basically, when Jupiter in the form of a swan seduced Leda she bore him not only Helen of Troy but also these twins.
8. No source has been found for Cupid's being in green. The association of Cupid with spring is a natural but insufficient explanation.
9. Probably a reference to the savage man, or Wood-wose, a common figure in Elizabethan pageantry.

Bending their force contrary to their face,
315 Like that ungracious crew which faines demurest grace.[1]

36

Then came hot *July* boyling like to fire,
 That all his garments he had cast away:
 Upon a Lyon raging yet with ire
 He boldly rode and made him to obay:
320 It was the beast that whylome did forray°   *ravage*
 The Nemæan forrest,[2] till th'*Amphytrionide*
 Him slew, and with his hide did him array;
 Behinde his back a sithe, and by his side
Under his belt he bore a sickle circling wide.

37

325 The sixt was *August*, being rich arrayd
 In garment all of gold downe to the ground:
 Yet rode he not, but led a lovely Mayd[3]
 Forth by the lilly hand, the which was cround
 With eares of corne, and full her hand was found;
330 That was the righteous Virgin, which of old
 Liv'd here on earth, and plenty made abound;
 But, after Wrong was lov'd and Justice solde,
She left th'unrighteous world and was to heaven extold.° *raised, stellified*

38

Next him, *September* marched eeke on foote;
335 Yet was he heavy laden with the spoyle
 Of harvests riches, which he made his boot,
 And him enricht with bounty of the soyle:
 In his one hand, as fit for harvests toyle,
 He held a knife-hook; and in th'other hand
340 A paire of waights,[4] with which he did assoyle°   *determine*
 Both more and lesse, where it in doubt did stand,
And equall gave to each as Justice duly scann'd.°   *measured*

39

Then came *October* full of merry glee:
 For, yet his noule was totty of the must,[5]
345 Which he was treading in the wine-fats see,° *sea of the wine vats*
 And of the joyous oyle, whose gentle gust°   *taste*
 Made him so frollick° and so full of lust: *joyful*

1. Probably a reference to deferential courtiers who back out of the presence of the monarch.
2. A reference to the Nemean lion, killed by Hercules (*Amphytrionide*, son of Amphitryon) as the first of his twelve labors.
3. Astraea, goddess of justice, who fled from the earth because of its wickedness; often associated with Ceres.
4. The scales of Libra.
5. I.e., head was dizzy from the new wine.

Upon a dreadfull Scorpion he did ride,
  The same which by *Dianaes* doom unjust
350 Slew great *Orion:*[6] and eeke by his side
He had his ploughing share, and coulter ready tyde.

40

Next was *November*, he full grosse and fat,
  As fed with lard, and that right well might seeme;
  For, he had been a fatting hogs[7] of late,
355 That yet his browes with sweat, did reek and steem,
  And yet the season was full sharp and breem;°   cold, chill, rough, harsh
  In planting eeke he took no small delight:
  Whereon he rode, not easie was to deeme;[8]
  For it a dreadfull *Centaure* was in sight,
360 The seed *of Saturne*, and faire *Nais*, *Chiron* hight.[9]

41

And after him, came next the chill *December*:
  Yet he through merry feasting which he made,
  And great bonfires, did not the cold remember;
  His Saviours birth his mind so much did glad:
365 Upon a shaggy-bearded Goat he rode,[1]
  The same wherewith *Dan Jove* in tender yeares,
  They say, was nourisht by th'*Idæan* mayd;[2]
  And in his hand a broad deepe boawle he beares;
Of which, he freely drinks an health° to all his peeres.   toast

42

370 Then came old *January*, wrapped well
  In many weeds to keep the cold away;
  Yet did he quake and quiver like to quell,°   as if he might die
  And blowe his nayles to warme them if he may:
  For, they were numbd with holding all the day
375 An hatchet keene, with which he felled wood,
  And from the trees did lop the needlesse spray:
  Upon an huge great Earth-pot steane° he stood;   earthen pottery urn
From whose wide mouth, there flowed forth the Romane[3]
                    [floud.

---

6. In anger at Orion's boasts of his skill as a hunter Diana sent a scorpion to kill him. In remorse she had both Orion and the scorpion stellified.
7. Fattening or butchering hogs.
8. I.e., it was not easy to think about.
9. Spenser's description of Chiron the centaur has not been satisfactorily explained. He is more usually the son of Saturn and Philyra, but he also was called the son of Magnes and Nais (Greek: "water nymph").

1. 1609 reads "rode," although some editors emend to "rade."
2. Jupiter was sent to Amalthea, "th'Idæan mayd," who nursed him. She is sometimes represented as a goat nursing Jupiter, who later stellified her as the goat Capricorn.
3. The Tiber? The details are unclear, but Spenser probably has in mind the common picture of an ancient man holding or lying near an urn that pours forth a flood of water. The image is appropriate for the water-carrier Aquarius.

43

And lastly, came cold *February*, sitting
380   In an old wagon, for he could not ride;
Drawne of two fishes[4] for the season fitting,[5]
Which through the flood before did softly slyde
And swim away: yet had he by his side
His plough and harnesse fit to till the ground,
385   And tooles to prune the trees, before the pride
Of hasting Prime° did make them burgein° round: *hastening spring / to bud*
So past the twelve Months forth, & their dew places found.

44

And after these, there came the *Day*, and *Night*,[6]
Riding together both with equall pase,°   *abreast*
390   Th'one on a Palfrey[7] blacke, the other white;
But *Night* had covered her uncomely° face   *unattractive*
With a blacke veile, and held in hand a mace,
On top whereof the moon and stars were pight,
And sleep and darknesse round about did trace:°   *dance*
395   But *Day* did beare, upon his scepters hight,
The goodly Sun, encompast all with beames bright.

45

Then came the *Howres*, faire daughters of high *Jove*,[8]
And timely *Night*, the which were all endewed
With wondrous beauty fit to kindle love;
400   But they were Virgins all, and love eschewed,
That might forslack the charge to them fore-shewed
By mighty *Jove*;[9] who did them Porters make
Of heavens gate (whence all the gods issued)
Which they did dayly watch, and nightly wake
405   By even turnes,° ne ever did their charge forsake.   *equal turns*

46

And after all came *Life*, and lastly *Death*;
Death with most grim and griesly visage seene,
Yet is he nought but parting of the breath;
Ne ought to see, but like a shade to weene,[1]
410   Unbodied, unsoul'd, unheard, unseene.
But *Life* was like a faire young lusty boy,

---

4. The sign of Pisces.
5. Fit for the season of Lent, when meat was prohibited.
6. Spenser uses only two rhymes in this stanza as in VII.7.28.
7. A small saddle horse.
8. The Hours, whose parentage may be a Spenserian invention, for they are more commonly the daughters of

Jupiter and Themis (law). Their guarding Heaven's gate is derived from Iliad 5.748–50.
9. I.e., that might cause them to neglect the charge ordained for them by mighty Jupiter.
1. I.e., and nothing to see but one would think him a mere shade.

Such as they faine *Dan Cupid* to have beene,
Full of delightfull health and lively joy,
Deckt all with flowres, and wings of gold fit to employ.

47

415 When these were past, thus gan the *Titanesse;*
Lo, mighty mother, now be judge and say,
Whether in all thy creatures more or lesse
CHANGE doth not raign & beare the greatest sway:
For, who sees not, that *Time* on all doth pray?
420 But *Times* do change and move continually.
So nothing here long standeth in one stay:°   *in one place*
Wherefore, this lower world who can deny
But to be subject still to *Mutabilitie?*

48

Then thus gan *Jove;* Right true it is, that these
425 And all things else that under heaven dwell
Are chaung'd of° *Time,* who doth them all disseise°   *by / deprive*
Of being: But, who is it (to me tell)
That *Time* himselfe doth move and still compell
To keepe his course? Is not that namely wee
430 Which poure that vertue from our heavenly cell,
That moves them all, and makes them changed be?
So them we gods doe rule, and in them also thee.

49

To whom, thus *Mutability:* The things
Which we see not how they are mov'd and swayd,
435 Ye may attribute to your selves as Kings,
And say they by your secret powre are made:
But what we see not, who shall us perswade?
But were they so, as ye them faine to be,
Mov'd by your might, and ordred by your ayde;
440 Yet what if I can prove, that even yee
Your selves are likewise chang'd, and subject unto mee?

50

And first, concerning her that is the first,
Even you faire *Cynthia,* whom so much ye make[2]
Joves dearest darling, she was bred and nurst
445 On *Cynthus* hill,[3] whence she her name did take:
Then is she mortall borne, how-so ye crake;°   *however you brag*
Besides, her face and countenance every day

---

2. I.e., whom the rest of you gods make.   3. A hill on Delos, the birthplace of Diana and Apollo.

We changed see, and sundry forms partake,
   Now hornd, now round, now bright, now brown & gray:
450 So that *as changefull as the Moone* men use to° say.   *are accustomed*

51

Next, *Mercury*, who though he lesse appeare
   To change his hew, and alwayes seeme as one;
   Yet, he his course doth altar every yeare,
   And is of late far out of order gone:
455 So *Venus* eeke, that goodly Paragone,[4]
   Though faire all night, yet is she darke all day;
   And *Phœbus* self, who lightsome° is alone,   *radiant*
   Yet is he oft eclipsed by the way,
And fills the darkned world with terror and dismay.

52

460 Now *Mars* that valiant man is changed most:
   For, he some times so far runs out of square,
   That he his way doth seem quite to have lost,
   And cleane without his usuall sphere to fare;
   That even these Star-gazers stonisht are
465 At sight thereof, and damne their lying bookes:
   So likewise, grim Sir *Saturne*[5] oft doth spare
   His sterne aspect,[6] and calme his crabbed lookes:
So many turning cranks these have, so many crookes.

53

But you *Dan Jove*,[7] that only constant are,
470 And King of all the rest, as ye do clame,
   Are you not subject eeke to this misfare?°   *mishap*
   Then let me aske you this withouten blame,
   Where were ye borne? some say in *Crete* by name,
   Others in *Thebes*, and others other-where;[8]
475 But wheresoever they comment the same,
   They all consent that ye begotten were,
And borne here in this world, ne other can appeare.[9]

54

Then are ye mortall borne, and thrall to me,
   Unlesse the kingdome of the sky yee make
480 Immortall, and unchangeable to be;
   Besides, that power and vertue[1] which ye spake,

---

4. Model of excellence, with a sneer at her loves.
5. "Sir" used contemptuously here.
6. Saturn was a malevolent planetary influence.
7. "Master," used contemptuously here.

8. There are many versions of Jupiter's birthplace. Mutability's point is that Jupiter is earth-bred.
9. Nor can it appear otherwise.
1. See VII.7.48.7 and VII.7.49.4.

That ye here worke, doth many changes take,
  And your owne natures change: for, each of you
  That vertue have, or this, or that to make,
485   Is checkt and changed from his nature trew,
By others opposition or obliquid° view.   *directed obliquely*

55

Besides, the sundry motions of your Spheares,
  So sundry waies and fashions as clerkes° faine,   *learned men*
  Some in short space, and some in longer yeares;
490   What is the same but alteration plaine?
  Onely the starrie skie[2] doth still remaine:
  Yet do the Starres and Signes therein still move,
  And even itself is mov'd, as wizards saine.[3]
  But all that moveth, doth mutation love:
495   Therefore both you and them to me I subject prove.[4]

56

Then since within this wide great *Universe*
  Nothing doth firme and permanent appeare,
  But all things tost and turned by transverse:°   *in a haphazard way*
  What then should let,° but I aloft should reare   *prevent*
500   My Trophee,° and from all, the triumph beare?   *sign of victory*
  Now judge then (ô thou greatest goddesse trew!)
  According as thy selfe doest see and heare,
  And unto me addoom° that is my dew;   *give a judgement*
That is the rule of all, all being rul'd by you.

57

505   So having ended, silence long ensewed,
  Ne *Nature* to or fro° spake for a space,   *to one side or the other*
  But with firme eyes affixt, the ground still viewed.
  Meanewhile, all creatures, looking in her face,
  Expecting th'end of this so doubtfull case,
510   Did hang in long suspence what would ensew,
  To whether side should fall the soveraigne place:
  At length, she looking up with chearefull view,
The silence brake, and gave her doome in speeches° few.   *words*

58

  I well consider all that ye have sayd,
515   And find that all things stedfastnes doe hate
  And changed be: yet being rightly wayd
  They are not changed from their first estate;°   *original nature*

---

2. The sphere of the fixed stars above the planets.
3. Movement initiated by the primum mobile.

4. This is Latinate word order: therefore I prove both you and them subject to me.

But by their change their being doe dilate:°   *expand, extend, perfect*
    And turning to themselves at length againe,
520   Doe worke their owne perfection so by fate:
    Then over them Change doth not rule and raigne;
But they raigne over change, and doe their states maintaine.

59

Cease therefore daughter further to aspire,
    And thee content thus to be rul'd by me:
525   For thy decay thou seekst by thy desire;
    But time shall come that all shall changed bee,
    And from thenceforth, none no more change shall see.
So was the *Titaness* put downe and whist,°   *silenced*
    And *Jove* confirm'd in his imperiall see.°   *seat, throne*
530   Then was that whole assembly quite dismist,
And *Natur's* selfe did vanish, whither no man wist.

1

When I bethinke me on that speech whyleare,[5]
    Of *Mutability,* and well it way:
    Me seemes, that though she all unworthy were
    Of the Heav'ns Rule; yet very sooth to say,
    In all things else she beares the greatest sway.
    Which makes me loath this state of life so tickle,°   *unstable, inconstant*
    And love of things so vaine to cast away;
    Whose flowring pride, so fading and so fickle,
Short *Time* shall soon cut down with his consuming sickle.

2

Then gin I thinke on that which Nature sayd,
    Of that same time when no more *Change* shall be,
    But stedfast rest of all things firmely stayd
    Upon the pillours of Eternity,
    That is contrayr° to *Mutabilitie:*   *contrary to*
    For, all that moveth, doth in *Change* delight:
    But thence-forth all shall rest eternally
    With Him that is the God of Sabbaoth[6] hight:
O that great Sabbaoth God, graunt me that Sabaoths sight.[7]

FINIS

5. There have been so many attempts to read these last two stanzas either as a pessimistic renunciation of life or as a too easy acceptance of Christian consolation that their superb appropriateness as conclusion has been obscured. Spenser is not trying to escape the vagaries of this "life so tickle"; he is praying to be able to use them properly so that this changing life will have earned him the right to that unchanging life to come.

6. Hebrew: "armies," "hosts," retained untranslated in the English New Testament (as in the original Greek and Vulgate) and the *Te Deum,* in the designation "The Lord of Sabaoth"; in translating Old Testament passages the English versions have the rendering "The Lord of Hosts."

7. Much scholarly effort has been expended on the two spellings of Sabbaoth in this line. Some critics think that Spenser meant to write Sabbath sight—that is, day of rest or eternal rest, and so emend the second occurrence of the word. The point is that Spenser is calling upon the God of the universe, the Lord of Hosts, both heavenly and earthly, to grant him that seventh-day rest not merely as the cessation of earthly labors but the perfection of them in the full knowledge of the beatific vision.

Sir Philip Sidney
1554–1586

Reality is often stranger but hardly ever more perfect than fiction. As Sir Philip Sidney tells us, the poets bring forth a "golden world." Exempt from judgments about its truth or falsehood, "poetry" (by which Sidney meant fiction) should construct forms of the ideal to mitigate our suffering and move us to good action. Sidney's own work comments brilliantly on contemporary moral and political issues: his sonnet sequence *Astrophil and Stella* (page 680) illustrates the lover's paradox (love may require chastity); his prose romance *The Arcadia* describes the politics of love and sexuality; and his *Apology for Poetry* defends poetic and dramatic art from critics who would dismiss it in favor of philosophy and history. Yet to his countrymen, Sidney's most important achievement may have been a life dedicated to a public heroism and shaped by a sense of personal honor.

History has portrayed him as a prodigy. As his friend Fulke Greville wrote, "though I knew him from a child, yet I never knew him other than a man, . . . his very play tending to enrich his mind, so that even his teachers found something in him to observe and learn above that which they had usually read or taught." Play—understood in the Renaissance manner as "serious play"—took up much of Sidney's early career. Leaving Oxford at the age of seventeen but without a degree, Sidney embarked on what in later centuries was known as the Grand Tour. He visited Europe's major cities, seeking men and women who were fashioning the political goals and aesthetic sensibilities of the age. They included the philosopher Hubert Languet, whose Protestantism was linked to a fiercely antityrannical politics; the artists Tintoretto and Paolo Veronese, whose luminous realism was to determine painterly style for more than a generation; and, finally, Henry of Navarre (later King Henry IV of France) and his wife, Margaret of Valois, whose reign would see the worst of the religious wars in Europe. Back in England by 1575, Sidney espoused a politics that challenged authority. Siding with his father, Henry Sidney, Queen Elizabeth's Lord Deputy Governor of Ireland, he argued for imposing a land tax on the Anglo-Irish nobility, citing their "unreasonable and arrogant pretensions" as a cause of civil unrest. And in 1580, seeking to protect the monarchy from foreign influences, he wrote to the Queen cautioning her against a match with Francis, Duke of Alençon and brother to the French king, Henry III. She was furious at his temerity and ordered him to the country, where he was to remain out of touch with court affairs. By 1584 she had relented, sending Sidney to the Netherlands to assess the Protestant resistance to Spanish rule. There, in 1586, fighting for the Queen's interest and the Protestant cause she championed, he died of an abscessed bullet wound in his thigh.

Sidney's first literary work was a brief pastoral masque entitled *The Lady of May*, composed in honor of the Queen in 1578. His subsequent exile from court provided him with extensive time to write. He was often at Wilton, the estate of his sister, Mary Herbert, Countess of Pembroke; it was there that he wrote the first two of his major works, in all likelihood with his sister and her circle as his first readers and critics. *The Apology for Poetry*, a work defending what Sidney called his "unelected vocation," answers attacks on art, poetry, and the theater by such censorious writers as Stephen Gosson. But its argument exceeds the limits of antitheatrical debate to embrace questions about the uses of history and the effectiveness of philosophy—a subject that bears comparison with the poetics of Aristotle and Horace. Readers have remembered most its insistence that "poetry" goes beyond nature to fashion an ideal; it works "not only to make a Cyrus, which had been but a particular excellency as nature might have done, but to bestow a Cyrus upon the world to make many

Cyruses." Poetry's creatures—whether heroes, heroines, or villains—cannot misrepresent fact because they exist only in the imagination of readers and listeners: "for the poet," Sidney declared, "he nothing affirms, and therefore never lieth."

Sidney's second work from his period at Wilton, the pastoral prose romance known as *The Arcadia*, was finished in 1581 and circulated in manuscript thereafter (and in print in 1973), depicts the willfulness of a superstitious and lazy duke, Basilius, who sequesters his marriageable daughters, Pamela and Philoclea, in the country where no suitor can meet them. His plans are foiled by two foreign princes, Pyrocles and Musidorus, who, disguised as a woman and a shepherd, manage to court and win the love of these ladies. Interspersed throughout the prose narrative of these events are poems, termed *eclogues*, expressing the joys and sorrows of pastoral life, one of which, *As I my little flock on Ister bank*, has persuaded many readers that Sidney was arguing for a radical, essentially republican politics.

A second version of the *Arcadia*, apparently written two or three years later, very explicitly introduces politics to the plot: Sidney sketches the characters of several rulers, magnificent and tyrannical; includes arguments for resistance and rebellion; and illustrates the nature of justice and equity. This version, revised after Sidney's death by his sister, Mary Herbert, Countess of Pembroke, and published in 1593, contains splendid portraits of queens both good and bad. Especially memorable is the wicked Cecropia, who plots to capture and kill the Arcadian princesses. The mother of Amphialus, who is a kind of moving target for misfortune's arrows, Cecropia has sometimes been understood to figure Catherine de'Medici, the powerful French queen, who many maintained had helped plan the massacre of hundreds of Protestants on Saint Bartholomew's Day, 1572.

 For additional resources on Sidney, including Book1 of *Arcadia*, go to *The Longman Anthology of British Literature* Web site at www.myliteraturekit.com.

The Apology for Poetry

When the right virtuous Edward Wotton[1] and I were at the Emperor's court together, we gave ourselves to learn horsemanship of John Pietro Pugliano, one that with great commendation had the place of an esquire in his stable. And he, according to the fertileness of the Italian wit, did not only afford us the demonstration of his practice, but sought to enrich our minds with the contemplations therein, which he thought most precious. But with none I remember mine ears were at that time more laden, than when (either angered with slow payment, or moved with our learner-like admiration) he exercised his speech in the praise of his faculty. He said soldiers were the noblest estate of mankind, and horsemen the noblest of soldiers. He said they were the masters of war and ornaments of peace, speedy goers and strong abiders, triumphers both in camps and courts. Nay, to so unbelieved a point he proceeded as that no earthly thing bred such wonder to a prince as to be a good horseman—skill of government was but a *pedanteria* [pedantry] in comparison. Then would he add certain praises, by telling what a peerless beast the horse was, the only serviceable courtier without flattery, the beast of most beauty, faithfulness, courage, and such more, that if I had not been a piece of a logician before I came to him, I think he would have persuaded me to have wished myself a horse. But thus much at least with his no few words he drave

---

1. Edward Wotton (1548–1626), half-brother of Henry Wotton who saw diplomatic service under James I. Edward Wotton and Sidney undertook a mission to the court of the Emperor Maximilian at Vienna in 1574–1575.

into me, that self-love is better than any gilding to make that seem gorgeous wherein ourselves be parties. Wherein, if Pugliano's strong affection and weak arguments will not satisfy you, I will give you a nearer example of myself, who (I know not by what mischance) in these my not old years and idlest times having slipped into the title of a poet, am provoked to say something unto you in the defense of that my unelected vocation,[2] which if I handle with more good will than good reasons, bear with me, since the scholar is to be pardoned that followeth the steps of his master. And yet I must say that, as I have more just cause to make a pitiful defense of poor poetry, which from almost the highest estimation of learning is fallen to be the laughingstock of children, so have I need to bring some more available proofs: since the former is by no man barred of his deserved credit, the silly latter hath had even the names of philosophers used to the defacing of it, with great danger of civil war among the Muses.[3]

And first, truly, to all them that, professing learning, inveigh against poetry may justly be objected that they go very near to ungratefulness, to seek to deface that which, in the noblest nations and languages that are known, hath been the first light-giver to ignorance, and first nurse, whose milk by little and little enabled them to feed afterwards of tougher knowledges. And will they now play the hedgehog that, being received into the den, drive out his host? Or rather the vipers, that with their birth kill their parents?

Let learned Greece in any of his manifold sciences be able to show me one book before Musaeus, Homer, and Hesiod, all three nothing else but poets.[4] Nay, let any history be brought that can say any writers were there before them, if they were not men of the same skill, as Orpheus, Linus,[5] and some other are named, who, having been the first of that country that made pens deliverers of their knowledge to the posterity, may justly challenge to be called their fathers in learning: for not only in time they had this priority (although in itself antiquity be venerable) but went before them, as causes to draw with their charming sweetness the wild untamed wits to an admiration of knowledge. So, as Amphion[6] was said to move stones with his poetry to build Thebes, and Orpheus to be listened to by beasts— indeed stony and beastly people—so among the Romans were Livius Andronicus and Ennius. So in the Italian language the first that made it aspire to be a treasure-house of science were the poets Dante, Boccaccio, and Petrarch. So in our English were Gower and Chaucer, after whom, encouraged and delighted with their excellent fore-going,[7] others have followed, to beautify our mother tongue, as well in the same kind as in other arts.

---

2. Sidney refers to writing poetry as his "unelected vocation" because he would have readers believe that he undertook it only after Elizabeth I had exiled him from court.
3. Mythological figures who were thought to inspire the liberal arts.
4. Musaeus was in fact a poet of the 5th century C.E., reported to be a pupil of the mythical Orpheus, the first musician. Homer was the legendary author of the *Iliad*, an epic poem telling of the seige of Troy by the army of the Greeks led by the hero, Achilles; and of the *Odyssey*, recounting the return of the hero, Odysseus, from Troy to his homeland in Ithaka. Hesiod is known as the poet of the *Theogony*, which tells the story of the gods in Greece; and of *Works and Days*, which describes the rituals and

practices of the agricultural year. Both Homer and Hesiod lived in the 8th century B.C.E.
5. Supposed to have been the teacher of Orpheus.
6. Sidney lists historical and legendary poets to illustrate his claim that they were the founders of civilization and culture. Amphion was supposed to have moved stones by playing his music and thus to have built the walls of Troy; Livius Andronicus (c. 284–204 B.C.E.) was believed to have been the first Latin poet; Ennius (c. 239–169 B.C.E.) was traditionally regarded as the greatest of the early Latin poets. Dante, Boccaccio, and Petrarch were the first of the great Italian poets of the early Renaissance; Chaucer and Gower were the most important of the late medieval poets who wrote in English.
7. Example.

This did so notably show itself, that the philosophers of Greece durst not a long time appear to the world but under the masks of poets. So Thales, Empedocles, and Parmenides[8] sang their natural philosophy in verses; so did Pythagoras and Phocylides their moral counsels; so did Tyrtaeus in war matters, and Solon in matters of policy: or rather they, being poets, did exercise their delightful vein in those points of highest knowledge, which before them lay hid to the world. For that wise Solon was directly a poet it is manifest, having written in verse the notable fable of the Atlantic Island, which was continued by Plato. And truly even Plato[9] whosoever well considereth shall find that in the body of his work, though the inside and strength were philosophy, the skin, as it were, and beauty depended most of[1] poetry: for all standeth upon dialogues, wherein he feigneth many honest burgesses of Athens to speak of such matters, that, if they had been set on the rack, they would never have confessed them, besides his poetical describing the circumstances of their meetings, as the well ordering of a banquet,[2] the delicacy of a walk, with interlacing mere tales, as Gyges' ring and others, which who knoweth not to be flowers of poetry did never walk into Apollo's garden.[3]

And even historiographers (although their lips sound of things done, and verity[4] be written in their foreheads) have been glad to borrow both fashion and, perchance, weight of the poets. So Herodotus entitled his History by the name of the nine Muses;[5] and both he and all the rest that followed him either stale[6] or usurped of poetry their passionate describing of passions, the many particularities of battles, which no man could affirm; or, if that be denied me, long orations put in the mouths of great kings and captains, which it is certain they never pronounced.

So that truly neither philosopher nor historiographer could at the first have entered into the gates of popular judgments, if they had not taken a great passport of poetry, which in all nations at this day where learning flourisheth not, is plain to be seen; in all which they have some feeling of poetry.

In Turkey, besides their law-giving divines, they have no other writers but poets. In our neighbor country Ireland, where truly learning goeth very bare, yet are their poets held in a devout reverence. Even among the most barbarous and simple Indians where no writing is, yet have they their poets who make and sing songs, which they call *areytos*,[7] both of their ancestors' deeds and praises of their gods: a sufficient probability that, if ever learning come among them, it must be by having their hard dull wits softened and sharpened with the sweet delights of poetry—for until they find a pleasure in the exercises of the mind, great promises of much

8. Sidney lists the best-known of the Greek philosophers before Plato: Thales, a geometrician; Empedocles, who studied the concepts of change and permanence; Parmenides, who investigated the nature of being; Pythagoras, a mathematician and astronomer; Phocylides, a moralist; and Tyrtaeus, a poet. Solon (c. 640–558 B.C.E.) was an Athenian statesman, poet, and constitutional reformer. No trace remains of a poem by Solon telling of Atlantis, an island beyond the pillars of Hercules that vanishes beneath the sea; Sidney recalls Plato's dialogue (*Timaeus*, 21–24), in which Critias tells Socrates that the story of Atlantis originates in an unfinished poem of Solon.
9. Author of many works of philosophy in dialogue form, notably *The Republic*, on the construction of an ideal state, and *The Symposium*, on the nature of love and its association with beauty and truth. He was a key influence on Renaissance thinkers.

1. On.
2. A banquet is the setting of *The Symposium;* speakers take a walk in the *The Phaedrus;* and the story of Gyges' ring is told in *The Republic*.
3. Apollo was the god of poetry.
4. Truth.
5. Herodotus, a Greek historian (480–425 B.C.E.), wrote about the struggle between Asia and Greece; later classical editors divided his work, which he entitled simply *History*, into nine books named after the nine Muses: Calliope, Clio, Euterpe, Melpomene, Terpsichore, Erato, Polyhymnia, Urania, and Thalia.
6. Stole.
7. A West Indian dance, recorded by José de Acosta in his *Natural and Moral History of the West Indies* (translated into English in 1604).

knowledge will little persuade them that know not the fruits of knowledge. In Wales, the true remnant of the ancient Britons, as there are good authorities to show the long time they had poets, which they called bards, so through all the conquests of Romans, Saxons, Danes, and Normans, some of whom did seek to ruin all memory of learning from among them, yet do their poets even to this day last; so as it is not more notable in soon beginning than in long continuing.

But since the authors of most of our sciences[8] were the Romans, and before them the Greeks, let us a little stand upon their authorities, but even so far as to see what names they have given unto this now scorned skill.

Among the Romans a poet was called *vates*, which is as much as a diviner, foreseer, or prophet, as by his conjoined words *vaticinium* [prediction] and *vaticinari* [to foretell] is manifest: so heavenly a title did that excellent people bestow upon this heart-ravishing knowledge. And so far were they carried into the admiration thereof, that they thought in the chanceable hitting upon any such verses great foretokens of their following fortunes were placed. Whereupon grew the word of *Sortes Virgilianae*,[9] when by sudden opening Virgil's book they lighted upon any verse of his making, whereof the histories of the emperors' lives are full: as of Albinus, the governor of our island, who in his childhood met with this verse

Arma amens capio nec sat rationis in armis[1]

and in his age performed it. Which, although it were a very vain and godless superstition, as also it was to think spirits were commanded by such verses—whereupon this word charms, derived of *carmina* [songs], cometh—so yet serveth it to show the great reverence those wits were held in; and altogether not without ground, since both the oracles of Delphos and Sibylla's prophecies were wholly delivered in verses.[2] For that same exquisite observing of number and measure[3] in the words, and that high flying liberty of conceit proper to the poet, did seem to have some divine force in it.

And may not I presume a little further, to show the reasonableness of this word *vates*, and say that the holy David's Psalms are a divine poem? If I do, I shall not do it without the testimony of great learned men, both ancient and modern. But even the name of Psalms will speak for me, which being interpreted, is nothing but songs; then that it is fully written in meter, as all learned Hebricians agree, although the rules be not yet fully found; lastly and principally, his handling his prophecy, which is merely poetical: for what else is the awaking his musical instruments, the often and free changing of persons, his notable *prosopopoeias* [personifications], when he maketh you, as it were, see God coming in His majesty, his telling of the beasts' joyfulness and hills leaping,[4] but a heavenly poesy, wherein almost he showeth himself a passionate lover of that unspeakable and everlasting beauty to be seen by the eyes of the mind, only cleared by faith? But truly now having named him, I fear me I seem to profane that holy name, applying it to poetry, which is among us thrown down to so ridiculous an estimation. But they that with quiet judgments will look a

8. Any body of knowledge, typically natural philosophy and also including ethics and politics.
9. The Virgilian lots, or fortune as it is implied in lines from the *Aeneid*, which the reader chose at random and then subjects to interpretation.
1. "I seize arms madly, nor is there reason in arming" (2.314).

2. The shrine of Apollo at Delphi was presided over by a priestess who was believed to know the god's thoughts about the future; the Sibyls were supposed to be ancient prophetesses whose words were collected in the *Sibylline Books*.
3. Meter and rhythm.
4. Psalm 29.

little deeper into it, shall find the end and working of it such as, being rightly applied, deserveth not to be scourged out of the Church of God.

But now let us see how the Greeks named it, and how they deemed of it. The Greeks called him a "poet," which name hath, as the most excellent, gone through other languages. It cometh of this word ποιεῖν, which is, to make: wherein, I know not whether by luck or wisdom, we Englishmen have met with the Greeks in calling him a maker: which name, how high and incomparable a title it is, I had rather were known by marking the scope of other sciences than by any partial allegation.

There is no art delivered to mankind that hath not the works of nature for his principal object, without which they could not consist, and on which they so depend, as they become actors and players, as it were, of what nature will have set forth. So doth the astronomer look upon the stars, and, by that he seeth, set down what order nature hath taken therein. So doth the geometrician and arithmetician in their diverse sorts of quantities. So doth the musicians in time tell you which by nature agree, which not. The natural philosopher thereon hath his name, and the moral philosopher standeth upon the natural virtues, vices, or passions of man; and follow nature (saith he) therein, and thou shalt not err. The lawyer saith what men have determined; the historian what men have done. The grammarian speaketh only of the rules of speech; and the rhetorician and logician, considering what in nature will soonest prove and persuade, thereon give artificial rules, which still are compassed within the circle of a question according to the proposed matter. The physician weigheth the nature of man's body, and the nature of things helpful or hurtful unto it. And the metaphysic,[5] though it be in the second and abstract notions, and therefore be counted supernatural, yet doth he indeed build upon the depth of nature. Only the poet, disdaining to be tied to any such subjection, lifted up with the vigor of his own invention, doth grow in effect another nature, in making things either better than nature bringeth forth, or, quite anew, forms such as never were in nature, as the Heroes, Demigods, Cyclops, Chimeras, Furies,[6] and such like: so as he goeth hand in hand with nature, not enclosed within the narrow warrant[7] of her gifts, but freely ranging only within the zodiac of his own wit. Nature never set forth the earth in so rich tapestry as divers poets have done; neither with so pleasant rivers, fruitful trees, sweet-smelling flowers, nor whatsoever else may make the too much loved earth more lovely. Her world is brazen, the poets only deliver a golden.

But let those things alone, and go to man—for whom as the other things are, so it seemeth in him her uttermost cunning is employed—and know whether she have brought forth so true a lover as Theagenes, so constant a friend as Pylades, so valiant a man as Orlando, so right a prince as Xenophon's Cyrus, so excellent a man every way as Virgil's Aeneas.[8] Neither let this be jestingly conceived, because the works of

---

5. A philosopher who considered abstractions and aspects of mental and spiritual life entertained in a state of contemplation rather than of action.

6. Furies: supernatural forces figured as mad goddesses pursuing revenge; demigods: male offspring of a god and a mortal, having some divine powers; cyclops: a one-eyed giant; chimeras: imaginary monsters made up of grotesquely disparate parts.

7. Authority.

8. Sidney cites men recognized for their virtues. Theagenes exemplifies the true lover in Heliodorus's romance, the *Aethiopica*; Pylades, who helped Orestes avenge his father Agamemnon's murder, was cited by

Renaissance commentators as a perfect friend; Orlando (modeled on Roland, the knight who fought for Charlemagne against the Basques at the battle of Roncesvalles, 778 C.E.) was the hero of Ariosto's *Orlando Furioso* and illustrated the Renaissance idea of valor. The *Anabasis* of Xenophon (himself a general in Cyrus's army) relates how Cyrus the Younger, a Persian prince, helped the Peloponnesians resist the army of Athens and then died in an attempt to take the Persian throne from his brother Artaxerxes in the 5th century B.C.E. Aeneas, the hero of Virgil's *Aeneid* and the mythical founder of the Roman Empire, was generally considered to be the epitome of the statesman.

the one be essential, the other in imitation or fiction; for any understanding knoweth the skill of each artificer standeth in that *idea* or fore-conceit[9] of the work, and not in the work itself. And that the poet hath that *idea* is manifest, by delivering them forth in such excellency as he had imagined them. Which delivering forth also is not wholly imaginative, as we are wont to say by them that build castles in the air; but so far substantially it worketh, not only to make a Cyrus, which had been but a particular excellency as nature might have done, but to bestow a Cyrus upon the world to make many Cyruses, if they will learn aright why and how that maker made him.

Neither let it be deemed too saucy a comparison to balance the highest point of man's wit with the efficacy of nature; but rather give right honor to the heavenly Maker of that maker, who having made man to His own likeness, set him beyond and over all the works of that second nature: which in nothing he showeth so much as in poetry, when with the force of a divine breath he bringeth things forth surpassing her doings—with no small arguments to the credulous of that first accursed fall of Adam, since our erected wit maketh us know what perfection is, and yet our infected will keepeth us from reaching unto it. But these arguments will by few be understood, and by fewer granted. This much (I hope) will be given me, that the Greeks with some probability of reason gave him the name above all names of learning.

Now let us go to a more ordinary opening of him, that the truth may be the more palpable: and so I hope, though we get not so unmatched a praise as the etymology of his names will grant, yet his very description, which no man will deny, shall not justly be barred from a principal commendation.

Poesy therefore is an art of imitation,[1] for so Aristotle termeth it in the word μίμησις—that is to say, a representing, counterfeiting, or figuring forth—to speak metaphorically, a speaking picture—with this end, to teach and delight.

Of this have been three general kinds. The chief, both in antiquity and excellency, were they that did imitate the unconceivable excellencies of God. Such were David in his Psalms; Solomon in his Song of Songs, in his Ecclesiastes, and Proverbs; Moses and Deborah in their Hymns; and the writer of Job: which, beside other, the learned Emanuel Tremellius and Franciscus Junius[2] do entitle the poetical part of the Scripture. Against these none will speak that hath the Holy Ghost in due holy reverence. (In this kind, though in a full wrong divinity, were Orpheus, Amphion, Homer in his Hymns, and many other, both Greeks and Romans.)[3] And this poesy must be used by whosoever will follow St. James's counsel in singing psalms when they are merry, and I know is used with the fruit of comfort by some, when, in sorrowful pangs of their death-bringing sins, they find the consolation of the never-leaving goodness.

9. The element of the literary work that determines how and to what end its subject is conveyed. Sidney later states that an *Idea* works "substantially" because it makes readers want to imitate the virtuous characters represented in a literary work.
1. Aristotle stated that poetry was a mimetic (from *mimesis*) or imitative art; Sidney (following Horace, who sees that poetry is like painting) adds that this imitation is (in some sense) pictorial.

2. Sixteenth-century translators of the Hebrew and Greek Bible into Latin who considered the books here mentioned (all in the Hebrew Bible) to be poetry.
3. Sidney distinguishes the mystical works of Hellenic antiquity as erroneous in their depiction and understanding of divinity.

The second kind is of them that deal with matters philosophical, either moral, as Tyrtaeus,[4] Phocylides, Cato, or natural, as Lucretius and Virgil's *Georgics;* or astronomical, as Manilius and Pontanus; or historical, as Lucan: which who mislike, the fault is in their judgment quite out of taste, and not in the sweet food of sweetly uttered knowledge.

But because this second sort is wrapped within the fold of the proposed subject, and takes not the course of his own invention, whether they properly be poets or no let grammarians dispute, and go to the third, indeed right poets, of whom chiefly this question ariseth: betwixt whom and these second is such a kind of difference as betwixt the meaner sort of painters, who counterfeit only such faces as are set before them, and the more excellent, who having no law but wit, bestow that in colors upon you which is fittest for the eye to see: as the constant though lamenting look of Lucretia,[5] when she punished in herself another's fault, wherein he painteth not Lucretia whom he never saw, but painteth the outward beauty of such a virtue. For these third be they which most properly do imitate to teach and delight, and to imitate borrow nothing of what is, hath been, or shall be; but range, only reined with learned discretion, into the divine consideration of what may be and should be. These be they that, as the first and most noble sort may justly be termed *vates,* so these are waited on in the excellentest languages and best understandings with the fore-described name of poets. For these indeed do merely make to imitate, and imitate both to delight and teach; and delight, to move men to take that goodness in hand, which without delight they would fly as from a stranger; and teach, to make them know that goodness whereunto they are moved—which being the noblest scope to which ever any learning was directed, yet want there not idle tongues to bark at them.

These be subdivided into sundry more special denominations. The most notable be the heroic, lyric, tragic, comic, satiric, iambic, elegiac, pastoral,[6] and certain others, some of these being termed according to the matter they deal with, some by the sorts of verses they liked best to write in; for indeed the greatest part of poets have apparelled their poetical inventions in that numbrous kind of writing which is called verse—indeed but apparelled, verse being but an ornament and no cause to poetry, since there have been many most excellent poets that never versified, and now swarm many versifiers that need never answer to the name of poets. For Xenophon, who did imitate so excellently as to give us *effigiem iusti imperii,* the portraiture of a just empire, under the name of Cyrus (as Cicero saith of him), made therein an absolute heroical poem.[7] So did Heliodorus in his sugared invention of that picture of

4. Sidney lists poets who he considers wrote some kind of philosophy and are not altogether "right," that is, pure poets. Tyrtaeus: mid-7th century B.C.E. Greek poet known for his praise of valor; Phocylides: a moralist of the 6th century B.C.E. Cato: Dionysius Cato (c. 300 C.E.), a moralist of whom little is known, who wrote a collection of moral sayings in verse couplets, published by Erasmus for use in schools; Lucretius: the Roman poet of the 1st century B.C.E. who wrote about the creation of the physical world; Virgil: the poet who stated the principles of farming in his *Georgics;* Manilius: the poet of the 1st century C.E. who wrote a versified treatise on astronomy; Pontanus: Joannes Jovius Pontanus, a late 15th-century poet who wrote a work on astronomy; and Lucan: the Roman poet of the 1st century C.E. who wrote the epic

Pharsalia, which describes the events in the civil war between Caesar and Pompey up to Caesar's seduction of the Egyptian queen, Cleopatra.

5. Legendary heroine of the ancient Roman republic who committed suicide rather than live in shame after being raped by the tyrant Sextus Tarquinius. Her story was told in versions by Ovid, Livy, Chaucer, Christine de Pisan, Shakespeare, and others.

6. Sidney lists the eight genres of poetry; "iambic" was a kind of satiric verse written in iambics, a meter made up of units or feet, each of which consists of a lightly stressed syllable followed by a heavily stressed syllable.

7. Sidney refers to Xenophon's *Cyropaedia,* his history of Cyrus, the emperor of Persia, a work that he thinks has a heroic quality because it deals with the fate of an empire.

love in Theagenes and Chariclea;[8] and yet both these wrote in prose: which I speak to show that it is not rhyming and versing that maketh a poet—no more than a long gown maketh an advocate, who though he pleaded in armor should be an advocate and no soldier. But it is that feigning notable images of virtues, vices, or what else, with that delightful teaching, which must be the right describing note to know a poet by; although indeed the senate of poets hath chosen verse as their fittest raiment, meaning, as in matter they passed all in all, so in manner to go beyond them: not speaking (table-talk fashion or like men in a dream) words as they chanceably fall from the mouth, but peising[9] each syllable of each word by just proportion according to the dignity of the subject.

Now therefore it shall not be amiss first to weigh this latter sort of poetry by his works, and then by his parts; and if in neither of these anatomies he be condemnable, I hope we shall obtain a more favorable sentence.

This purifying of wit—this enriching of memory, enabling of judgment, and enlarging of conceit—which commonly we call learning, under what name soever it come forth, or to what immediate end soever it be directed, the final end is to lead and draw us to as high a perfection as our degenerate souls, made worse by their clayey lodgings, can be capable of.

This, according to the inclination of the man, bred many-formed impressions. For some that thought this felicity principally to be gotten by knowledge, and no knowledge to be so high or heavenly as acquaintance with the stars, gave themselves to astronomy; others, persuading themselves to be demigods if they knew the causes of things, became natural and supernatural philosophers; some an admirable delight drew to music; and some the certainty of demonstration to the mathematics. But all, one and other, having this scope: to know, and by knowledge to lift up the mind from the dungeon of the body to the enjoying his own divine essence.

But when by the balance of experience it was found that the astronomer, looking to the stars, might fall in a ditch, that the inquiring philosopher might be blind in himself, and the mathematician might draw forth a straight line with a crooked heart, then lo, did proof, the overruler of opinions, make manifest that all these are but serving sciences, which, as they have each a private end in themselves, so yet are they all directed to the highest end of the mistress-knowledge, by the Greeks called ἀρχιτεκτονική, which stands (as I think) in the knowledge of a man's self, in the ethic and politic consideration, with the end of well-doing and not of well-knowing only—even as the saddler's next end is to make a good saddle, but his further end to serve a nobler faculty, which is horsemanship, so the horseman's to soldiery, and the soldier not only to have the skill, but to perform the practice of a soldier. So that, the ending end of all earthly learning being virtuous action, those skills that most serve to bring forth that have a most just title to be princes over all the rest.

Wherein, if we can, show we the poet's nobleness, by setting him before his other competitors. Among whom as principal challengers step forth the moral philosophers, whom, me thinketh, I see coming towards me with a sullen gravity, as though they could not abide vice by daylight, rudely clothed for to witness outwardly their contempt of outward things, with books in their hands against glory, whereto they set their names, sophistically speaking against subtlety, and angry

---

8. Characters in Heliodorus's romance, *Aethiopica*.   9. Weighing.

with any man in whom they see the foul fault of anger. These men casting largess as they go, of definitions, divisions, and distinctions, with a scornful interrogative do soberly ask whether it be possible to find any path so ready to lead a man to virtue as that which teacheth what virtue is; and teach it not only by delivering forth his very being, his causes and effects, but also by making known his enemy, vice, which must be destroyed, and his cumbersome servant, passion, which must be mastered; by showing the generalities that containeth it, and the specialities that are derived from it; lastly, by plain setting down how it extendeth itself out of the limits of a man's own little world to the government of families and maintaining of public societies.

The historian scarcely giveth leisure to the moralist to say so much, but that he, laden with old mouse-eaten records, authorizing himself (for the most part) upon other histories, whose greatest authorities are built upon the notable foundation of hearsay; having much ado to accord differing writers and to pick truth out of their partiality; better acquainted with a thousand years ago than with the present age, and yet better knowing how this world goeth than how his own wit runneth; curious for antiquities and inquisitive of novelties; a wonder to young folks and a tyrant in table talk, denieth, in a great chafe,[1] that any man for teaching of virtue, and virtuous actions is comparable to him. "I am *testis temporum, lux veritatis, vita memoriae, magistra vitae, nuntia vetustatis*.[2] The philosopher," saith he, "teacheth a disputative virtue, but I do an active. His virtue is excellent in the dangerless Academy of Plato,[3] but mine showeth forth her honorable face in the battles of Marathon, Pharsalia, Poitiers, and Agincourt.[4] He teacheth virtue by certain abstract considerations, but I only bid you follow the footing of them that have gone before you. Old-aged experience goeth beyond the fine-witted philosopher, but I give the experience of many ages. Lastly, if he make the songbook, I put the learner's hand to the lute; and if he be the guide, I am the light." Then would he allege you innumerable examples, confirming story by stories, how much the wisest senators and princes have been directed by the credit of history, as Brutus, Alphonsus of Aragon,[5] and who not, if need be? At length the long line of their disputation maketh a point in this, that the one giveth the precept, and the other the example.

Now whom shall we find (since the question standeth for the highest form in the school of learning) to be moderator? Truly, as me seemeth, the poet; and if not a moderator, even the man that ought to carry the title from them both, and much more from all other serving sciences. Therefore compare we the poet with the historian and with the moral philosopher; and if he go beyond them both, no other human skill can match him. For as for the divine, with all reverence it is ever to be excepted, not only for having his scope as far beyond any of these as eternity exceedeth a moment, but even for passing each of these in themselves.

---

1. Heat, fury.
2. Sidney quotes Cicero in his *De Oratore* (*Concerning the Orator*): "I am the witness of time, the light of truth, the life of memory, the governess of life, the herald of antiquity."
3. The olive grove near Athens, where Plato and his successors taught philosophy.
4. Sidney mentions some memorable battles: The Athenians defeated the invading Persians at Marathon in 490 B.C.E.; Caesar defeated Pompey at Pharsalus in 48 B.C.E.; the Franks, under Charles Martel, defeated the Moors,

led by Spanish emir Abd al-Rahman Ghafiqi in 732; the English, under Edward, the Black Prince, overcame the French army and captured their king, John II in 1356, each time at Poitiers; finally, Henry V defeated the French in 1415 at Agincourt.
5. Brutus: Roman statesman, one of Caesar's assassins, who is said to have spent the night before the battle of Pharsalus reading history; Alphonsus: King of Aragon and Sicily who encouraged his soldiers to seize the libraries of those they conquered and to bring their books to him.

And for the lawyer, though *Ius* [Right] be the daughter of Justice, and justice the chief of virtues, yet because he seeketh to make men good rather *formidine poenae* than *virtutis amore;*[6] or, to say righter, doth not endeavor to make men good, but that their evil hurt not others; having no care, so he be a good citizen, how bad a man he be: therefore as our wickedness maketh him necessary, and necessity maketh him honorable, so is he not in the deepest truth to stand in rank with these who all endeavor to take naughtiness away and plant goodness even in the secretest cabinet of our souls. And these four are all that any way deal in that consideration of men's manners, which being the supreme knowledge, they that best breed it deserve the best commendation.

The philosopher, therefore, and the historian are they which would win the goal, the one by precept, the other by example. But both, not having both, do both halt.[7] For the philosopher, setting down with thorny arguments the bare rule, is so hard of utterance and so misty to be conceived, that one that hath no other guide but him shall wade in him till he be old before he shall find sufficient cause to be honest. For his knowledge standeth so upon the abstract and general, that happy is that man who may understand him, and more happy that can apply what he doth understand. On the other side, the historian, wanting the precept, is so tied, not to what should be but to what is, to the particular truth of things and not to the general reason of things, that his example draweth no necessary consequence, and therefore a less fruitful doctrine.

Now doth the peerless poet perform both: for whatsoever the philosopher saith should be done, he giveth a perfect picture of it in someone by whom he presupposeth it was done, so as he coupleth the general notion with the particular example. A perfect picture I say, for he yieldeth to the powers of the mind an image of that whereof the philosopher bestoweth but a wordish description, which doth neither strike, pierce, nor possess the sight of the soul so much as that other doth. For as in outward things, to a man that had never seen an elephant or a rhinoceros, who should tell him most exquisitely all their shapes, color, bigness, and particular marks, or of a gorgeous palace, an *architector* [architect], with declaring the full beauties, might well make the hearer able to repeat, as it were by rote, all he had heard, yet should never satisfy his inward conceit[8] with being witness to itself of a true lively knowledge; but the same man, as soon as he might see those beasts well painted, or the house well in model, should straightways grow, without need of any description, to a judicial comprehending of them: so no doubt the philosopher with his learned definitions—be it of virtue, vices, matters of public policy or private government—replenisheth the memory with many infallible grounds of wisdom, which, notwithstanding, lie dark before the imaginative and judging power, if they be not illuminated or figured forth by the speaking picture of poesy.

Tully[9] taketh much pains, and many times not without poetical helps, to make us know the force love of our country hath in us. Let us but hear old Anchises speaking in the midst of Troy's flames,[1] or see Ulysses in the fullness of all Calypso's delights bewail his absence from barren and beggarly Ithaca. Anger, the Stoics said,

---

6. I.e., rather "from fear of punishment" than "from love of virtue" (Horace, *Epistles* 1.2.62). Sidney distinguishes between staying within the law and moral behavior.
7. Limp.
8. The listener's mental picture or image.

9. Cicero.
1. In the remainder of this paragraph, Sidney refers to exemplary moments in the lives of mythical figures as illustrated in the literature of antiquity, especially the works of Virgil, Homer, and the Greek and Roman dramatists.

was a short madness: let but Sophocles bring you Ajax on a stage, killing or whipping sheep and oxen, thinking them the army of Greeks, with their chieftains Agamemnon and Menelaus, and tell me if you have not a more familiar insight into anger than finding in the schoolmen his *genus* [race] and difference.[2] See whether wisdom and temperance in Ulysses and Diomedes, valor in Achilles, friendship in Nisus and Euryalus, even to an ignorant man carry not an apparent shining; and, contrarily, the remorse of conscience in Oedipus, the soon repenting pride in Agamemnon, the self-devouring cruelty in his father Atreus, the violence of ambition in the two Theban brothers, the sour-sweetness of revenge in Medea; and, to fall lower, the Terentian Gnatho and our Chaucer's Pandar so expressed that we now use their names to signify their trades:[3] and finally, all virtues, vices, and passions so in their own natural seats laid to the view, that we seem not to hear of them, but clearly to see through them.

But even in the most excellent determination of goodness, what philosopher's counsel can so readily direct a prince, as the feigned Cyrus in Xenophon; or a virtuous man in all fortunes, as Aeneas in Virgil; or a whole commonwealth, as the way of Sir Thomas More's *Utopia*? I say the way, because where Sir Thomas More erred, it was the fault of the man and not of the poet, for that way of patterning a commonwealth was most absolute, though he perchance hath not so absolutely performed it. For the question is, whether the feigned image of poetry or the regular instruction of philosophy hath the more force in teaching: wherein if the philosophers have more rightly showed themselves philosophers than the poets have attained to the high top of their profession, as in truth

> *Mediocribus esse poetis,*
> *Non dii, non homines, non concessere columnae;*[4]

it is, I say again, not the fault of the art, but that by few men that art can be accomplished.

Certainly, even our Savior Christ could as well have given the moral commonplaces of uncharitableness and humbleness as the divine narration of Dives and Lazarus;[5] or of disobedience and mercy, as that heavenly discourse of the lost child and the gracious father; but that His through-searching wisdom knew the estate of Dives burning in hell, and of Lazarus in Abraham's bosom, would more constantly (as it were) inhabit both the memory and judgment. Truly, for myself, meseems I see before mine eyes the lost child's disdainful prodigality, turned to envy a swine's dinner: which by the learned divines[6] are thought not historical acts, but instructing parables.

For conclusion, I say the philosopher teacheth, but he teacheth obscurely, so as the learned only can understand him, that is to say, he teacheth them that are already taught; but the poet is the food for the tenderest stomachs, the poet is indeed the right popular philosopher, whereof Aesop's tales[7] give good proof: whose pretty

---

2. Species.
3. Gnatho: a parasite and flatterer in the Roman playwright Terence's *Eunuchus;* Pandar: the go-between for the lovers in Chaucer's *Troilus and Criseyde*.
4. Neither gods, nor men, nor booksellers permit poets to be mediocre; a statement adapted from Horace's *Art of Poetry*.
5. Sidney cites several parables from scripture. The rich man, Dives, refused to help the beggar Lazarus; Dives was condemned to hell, Lazarus went to heaven (Luke 16.19–31). He then cites the story of the Prodigal Son, welcomed home by his father after a period of dissolution (Luke 15.11–32).
6. Theologians.
7. Moralistic fables reputedly by a Greek slave who lived about 570 B.C.E.; numerous translations into English of his work were available in the 16th century.

allegories, stealing under the formal tales of beasts, make many, more beastly than beasts, begin to hear the sound of virtue from these dumb speakers.

But now may it be alleged that if this imagining of matters be so fit for the imagination, then must the historian needs surpass, who bringeth you images of true matters, such as indeed were done, and not such as fantastically or falsely may be suggested to have been done. Truly, Aristotle himself, in his discourse of poesy, plainly determineth this question, saying that poetry is φλοσοφώτερον and σπουδαιότερον, that is to say, it is more philosophical and more studiously serious than history. His reason is, because poesy dealeth with καθόλου, that is to say, with the universal consideration, and the history with καθέκαστον, the particular: now, saith he, the universal weighs what is fit to be said or done, either in likelihood or necessity (which the poesy considereth in his imposed names), and the particular only marks whether Alcibiades did, or suffered, this or that.[8] Thus far Aristotle: which reason of his (as all his) is most full of reason. For indeed, if the question were whether it were better to have a particular act truly or falsely set down, there is no doubt which is to be chosen, no more than whether you had rather have Vespasian's picture[9] right as he was, or, at the painter's pleasure, nothing resembling. But if the question be for your own use and learning, whether it be better to have it set down as it should be, or as it was, then certainly is more doctrinable the feigned Cyrus in Xenophon than the true Cyrus in Justin, and the feigned Aeneas in Virgil than the right Aeneas in Dares Phrygius:[1] as to a lady that desired to fashion her countenance to the best grace, a painter should more benefit her to portrait a most sweet face, writing Canidia upon it, than to paint Canidia as she was, who, Horace sweareth, was full ill-favored.[2]

If the poet do his part aright, he will show you in Tantalus, Atreus, and such like,[3] nothing that is not to be shunned; in Cyrus, Aeneas, Ulysses, each thing to be followed; where the historian, bound to tell things as things were, cannot be liberal (without he will be poetical) of a perfect pattern, but, as in Alexander or Scipio himself, show doings, some to be liked, some to be misliked. And then how will you discern what to follow but by your own discretion, which you had without reading Quintus Curtius?[4] And whereas a man may say, though in universal consideration of doctrine the poet prevaileth, yet that the history, in his saying such a thing was done, doth warrant a man more in that he shall follow—the answer is manifest: that, if he stand upon that[5] was (as if he should argue, because it rained yesterday, therefore it should rain today), then indeed hath it some advantage to a gross conceit; but if he know an example only informs a conjectured likelihood, and so go by reason, the poet doth so far exceed him as he is to frame his example to that which is most reasonable (be it in warlike, politic, or private matters), where the historian in his bare *Was* hath many times that which we call fortune to overrule the best wisdom. Many times he must tell events whereof he can yield no cause; or, if he do, it must be poetically.

---

8. Sidney paraphrases Aristotle's *Poetics* (9.1451b). Alcibiades was a talented if unscrupulous Greek statesman.
9. A Roman emperor (70–79 C.E.) who was described by the historian Suetonius as very ugly.
1. Justinus (2nd–3rd century C.E.), and Dares Phrygius (5th century C.E.) wrote histories that some readers thought were more accurate than the more literary accounts by Xenophon, Homer, and Virgil.

2. Canidia was a prostitute who jilted the Roman poet, Horace; he then attacked her in his poems.
3. Evil figures (Tantalus served the flesh of his son, Pelops, to the gods; Atreus served his nephews' flesh to their father Thyestes).
4. Quintus Curtius (1st century C.E.) wrote a history of Alexander the Great.
5. What.

For that a feigned example hath as much force to teach as a true example (for as for to move, it is clear, since the feigned may be tuned to the highest key of passion), let us take one example wherein an historian and a poet did concur. Herodotus and Justin do both testify that Zopyrus, King Darius's faithful servant, seeing his master long resisted by the rebellious Babylonians, feigned himself in extreme disgrace of his king: for verifying of which, he caused his own nose and ears to be cut off, and so flying to the Babylonians, was received, and for his known valor so sure credited, that he did find means to deliver them over to Darius.[6] Much like matter doth Livy record of Tarquinius and his son. Xenophon excellently feigneth such another stratagem performed by Abradatas in Cyrus's behalf.[7] Now would I fain know, if occasion be presented unto you to serve your prince by such an honest dissimulation, why you do not as well learn it of Xenophon's fiction as of the other's verity; and truly so much the better, as you shall save your nose by the bargain: for Abradatas did not counterfeit so far. So then the best of the historian is subject to the poet; for whatsoever action, or faction, whatsoever counsel, policy, or war stratagem the historian is bound to recite, that may the poet (if he list[8]) with his imitation make his own, beautifying it both for further teaching, and more delighting, as it please him: having all, from Dante's heaven to his hell, under the authority of his pen.[9] Which if I be asked what poets have done so, as I might well name some, so yet say I, and say again, I speak of the art, and not of the artificer.

Now, to that which commonly is attributed to the praise of history, in respect of the notable learning is got by marking the success, as though therein a man should see virtue exalted and vice punished—truly that commendation is particular to poetry, and far off from history. For indeed poetry ever sets virtue so out in her best colors, making Fortune her well-waiting handmaid, that one must needs be enamored of her. Well may you see Ulysses in a storm, and in other hard plights; but they are but exercises of patience and magnanimity, to make them shine the more in the near-following prosperity. And of the contrary part, if evil men come to the stage, they ever go out (as the tragedy writer answered to one that misliked the show of such persons) so manacled as they little animate folks to follow them. But the history, being captived to the truth of a foolish world, is many times a terror from well-doing, and an encouragement to unbridled wickedness. For see we not valiant Miltiades rot in his fetters?[1] The just Phocion and the accomplished Socrates put to

6. The story of Zopyrus is told in Herodotus's *Histories* (3.153–58) and in Justin's *Histories* (1.10.15–22).
7. Tarquinius Superbus was the last of the Roman kings: his son, Sextus Tarquinius, passed himself off as an ally of the Gabians to spy for Rome (Livy, *Histories* 1.3–4). Abradates (actually Araspes), acted in the same way for the Persian king, Cyrus (Xenophon, *Cyropaedia* 6.1.39).
8. Wishes.
9. Dante's *Divine Comedy* describes his journey through hell, purgatory, and paradise.
1. Sidney demonstrates that the study of history is not conducive to good morals because it does not show virtue rewarded or vice punished. Miltiades: unsuccessful against the Persians in his siege of Paros, he was imprisoned by his own people, the Athenians (Herodotus, *Histories* 6.136). Phocion: an Athenian statesman wrongly put to death for a supposed conspiracy (Plutarch, *Phocion* 38). Plato's teacher Socrates had been put to

death for supposed impiety. Lucius Septimius Severus, Emperor of Rome (193–211), was able but termed "most cruel" by his biographer, Aelius Spartianus; by contrast, his virtuous successor, Marcus Aurelius Alexander Severus, was murdered by mutinous soldiers. Lucius Cornelius Sulla was a dictator of Rome, who tyrannized his subjects and yet died peacefully in his bed in 78 B.C.E.; Caius Marius was also a tyrant and never punished. Pompey opposed Caesar and was murdered after his defeat at Pharsalus; Marcus Tullius Cicero, the most accomplished of Roman lawyers and orators, was murdered by the order of Marcus Antonius in 43 B.C.E. Marcus Portius Cato committed suicide after his defeat at the battle of Thapsus rather than be captured by Caesar. Sidney calls Caesar a "rebel" because he invaded the territory of the Roman state (crossing the river Rubicon) without permission from the Roman Senate.

death like traitors? The cruel Severus live prosperously? The excellent Severus miserably murdered? Sulla and Marius dying in their beds? Pompey and Cicero slain then when they would have thought exile a happiness? See we not virtuous Cato driven to kill himself, and rebel Caesar so advanced that his name yet, after 1600 years, lasteth in the highest honor? And mark but even Caesar's own words of the aforenamed Sulla (who in that only did honestly, to put down his dishonest tyranny), *literas nescivit*,[2] as if want of learning caused him to do well. He meant it not by poetry, which, not content with earthly plagues, deviseth new punishments in hell for tyrants, nor yet by philosophy, which teacheth *occidendos esse*; but no doubt by skill in history, for that indeed can afford you Cypselus, Periander, Phalaris, Dionysius, and I know not how many more of the same kennel, that speed well enough in their abominable injustice of usurpation.

I conclude, therefore, that he excelleth history, not only in furnishing the mind with knowledge, but in setting it forward to that which deserveth to be called and accounted good: which setting forward, and moving to well-doing, indeed setteth the laurel crown upon the poets as victorious, not only of the historian, but over the philosopher, howsoever in teaching it may be questionable.

For suppose it be granted (that which I suppose with great reason may be denied) that the philosopher, in respect of his methodical proceeding, doth teach more perfectly than the poet, yet do I think that no man is so much φιλοφιλόσοφος [a lover of philosophy] as to compare the philosopher in moving with the poet. And that moving is of a higher degree than teaching, it may by this appear, that it is well nigh both the cause and effect of teaching. For who will be taught, if he be not moved with desire to be taught? And what so much good doth that teaching bring forth (I speak still of moral doctrine) as that it moveth one to do that which it doth teach? For, as Aristotle saith, it is not γνῶσις [knowing] but πρᾶξις [doing] must be the fruit. And how πρᾶξις can be, without being moved to practice, it is no hard matter to consider.[3]

The philosopher showeth you the way, he informeth you of the particularities, as well of the tediousness of the way, as of the pleasant lodging you shall have when your journey is ended, as of the many by-turnings that may divert you from your way. But this is to no man but to him that will read him, and read him with attentive studious painfulness; which constant desire whosoever hath in him, hath already passed half the hardness of the way, and therefore is beholding to the philosopher but[4] for the other half. Nay truly, learned men have learnedly thought that where once reason hath so much overmastered passion as that the mind hath a free desire to do well, the inward light each mind hath in itself is as good as a philosopher's book; since in nature we know it is well to do well, and what is well, and what is evil, although not in the words of art which philosophers bestow upon us; for out of natural conceit the philosophers drew it. But to be moved to do that which we know, or to be moved with desire to know, *hoc opus, hic labor est*.[5]

2. He knew no literature. Sidney indicates that the learning Sulla lacked was not of poetry, which reveals the punishments of hell; or of philosophy, which teaches *occidendum esse*—that is, when someone should be put to death, or the punishments inflicted by the state. Sidney argues that Sulla learned his misgovernment from history, which instructed him in the profitable ways of tyrants: Cipselus and Periander, both tyrants of Corinth; Phalaris, tyrant of Agrigentum; and Dionysius, tyrant of Syracuse.

3. *Nicomachean Ethics* 1.1.

4. Merely.

5. "This is the task, this the work"; the words of the Cumaean sibyl to the hero Aeneas, who intends to return to earth from the underworld (*Aeneid* 6.128).

Now therein of all sciences (I speak still of human, and according to the human conceit[6]) is our poet the monarch. For he doth not only show the way, but giveth so sweet a prospect into the way, as will entice any man to enter into it. Nay, he doth, as if your journey should lie through a fair vineyard, at the first give you a cluster of grapes, that full of that taste, you may long to pass further. He beginneth not with obscure definitions, which must blur the margin with interpretations, and load the memory with doubtfulness; but he cometh to you with words set in delightful proportion, either accompanied with, or prepared for, the well enchanting skill of music; and with a tale forsooth he cometh unto you, with a tale which holdeth children from play, and old men from the chimney corner. And, pretending no more, doth intend the winning of the mind from wickedness to virtue—even as the child is often brought to take most wholesome things by hiding them in such other as have a pleasant taste, which, if one should begin to tell them the nature of aloes or rhabarbarum[7] they should receive, would sooner take their physic at their ears than at their mouth. So is it in men (most of which are childish in the best things, till they be cradled in their graves): glad they will be to hear the tales of Hercules, Achilles, Cyrus, Aeneas; and, hearing them, must needs hear the right description of wisdom, valor, and justice; which, if they had been barely, that is to say philosophically, set out, they would swear they be brought to school again.

That imitation whereof poetry is, hath the most conveniency to nature of all other, insomuch that, as Aristotle saith, those things which in themselves are horrible, as cruel battles, unnatural monsters, are made in poetical imitation delightful.[8] Truly, I have known men that even with reading Amadis de Gaule[9] (which God knoweth wanteth much of a perfect poesy) have found their hearts moved to the exercise of courtesy, liberality, and especially courage. Who readeth Aeneas carrying old Anchises on his back, that wisheth not it were his fortune to perform so excellent an act? Whom doth not these words of Turnus move, the tale of Turnus having planted his image in the imagination,

> Fugientem haec terra videbit?
> Usque adeone mori miserum est?[1]

Where the philosophers, as they scorn to delight, so must they be content little to move—saving wrangling whether virtus [virtue] be the chief or the only good, whether the contemplative or the active life do excel—which Plato and Boethius well knew, and therefore made mistress Philosophy very often borrow the masking raiment of poesy.[2] For even those hard-hearted evil men who think virtue a school name, and know no other good but indulgere genio [self-indulgence], and therefore despise the austere admonitions of the philosopher, and feel not the inward reason they stand upon, yet will be content to be delighted—which is all the good-fellow poet seemeth to promise—and so steal to see the form of goodness (which seen they cannot but love) ere themselves be aware, as if they took a medicine of cherries.

Infinite proofs of the strange effects of this poetical invention might be alleged; only two shall serve, which are so often remembered as I think all men know them.

6. Way of thinking.
7. Medicines.
8. Poetics, 4.1448b.
9. Chivalric romance in Spanish by Vasco de Lobeyra, c. 1325. It appeared in English translation in 1567.
1. In Virgil, Turnus unsuccessfully defended his native Latium (the region around Rome) against the invading Trojans led by Aeneas. Taking his last stand, Turnus

cries: "Shall this ground see [Turnus] fleeing? Is it so hard, then, to die?" (Aeneid 12.645–46).
2. The philosophers Plato and Boethius both argued that a retired and contemplative life was superior to the active life or the life in public service. By contrast, the Roman orator Cicero asserted the value of prudence and the importance of contributing to the public good.

The one of Menenius Agrippa,[3] who, when the whole people of Rome had resolutely divided themselves from the senate, with apparent show of utter ruin, though he were (for that time) an excellent orator, came not among them upon trust of figurative speeches or cunning insinuations, and much less with far-fet[4] maxims of philosophy, which (especially if they were Platonic) they must have learned geometry before they could well have conceived; but forsooth he behaves himself like a homely and familiar poet. He telleth them a tale, that there was a time when all the parts of the body made a mutinous conspiracy against the belly, which they thought devoured the fruits of each other's labor; they concluded they would let so unprofitable a spender starve. In the end, to be short (for the tale is notorious, and as notorious that it was a tale), with punishing the belly they plagued themselves. This applied by him wrought such effect in the people, as I never read that only words brought forth but then so sudden and so good an alteration; for upon reasonable conditions a perfect reconcilement ensued. The other is of Nathan the prophet,[5] who, when the holy David had so far forsaken God as to confirm adultery with murder, when he was to do the tenderest office of a friend in laying his own shame before his eyes, sent by God to call again so chosen a servant, how doth he it but by telling of a man whose beloved lamb was ungratefully taken from his bosom: the application most divinely true, but the discourse itself feigned; which made David (I speak of the second and instrumental cause) as in a glass see his own filthiness, as that heavenly psalm of mercy well testifieth.

By these, therefore, examples and reasons, I think it may be manifest that the poet, with that same hand of delight, doth draw the mind more effectually than any other art doth. And so a conclusion not unfitly ensue: that, as virtue is the most excellent resting place for all worldly learning to make his end of, so poetry, being the most familiar to teach it, and most princely to move towards it, in the most excellent work is the most excellent workman.

But I am content not only to decipher him[6] by his works (although works, in commendation or dispraise, must ever hold a high authority), but more narrowly will examine his parts; so that (as in a man) though all together may carry a presence full of majesty and beauty, perchance in some one defectuous piece we may find blemish.

Now in his parts, kinds, or species (as you list to term them), it is to be noted that some poesies have coupled together two or three kinds, as the tragical and comical, whereupon is risen the tragicomical. Some, in the manner, have mingled prose and verse, as Sannazaro and Boethius.[7] Some have mingled matters heroical and pastoral. But that cometh all to one in this question, for, if severed they be good, the conjunction cannot be hurtful. Therefore, perchance forgetting some and leaving some as needless to be remembered, it shall not be amiss in a word to cite the special kinds, to see what faults may be found in the right use of them.

Is it then the Pastoral poem which is misliked? (For perchance where the hedge is lowest they will soonest leap over.) Is the poor pipe disdained, which sometime out of Meliboeus's mouth can show the misery of people under hard lords or ravening soldiers, and again, by Tityrus, what blessedness is derived to them that lie lowest from the goodness of them that sit highest;[8] sometimes, under the pretty tales of wolves

3. Roman consul who calmed rebellious commoners in 494 B.C.E. (Livy, *Histories* 2.32).
4. Far-fetched.
5. 2 Samuel 12.1–7.
6. Poetry.
7. Sannazaro: Italian poet (1458–1530) whose pastoral of mixed prose and verse, the *Arcadia*, influenced Sidney's

work of the same name. Boethius (480?–524?): the Roman and Christian philosopher whose work *The Consolation of Philosophy* contains passages of prose and poetry.
8. Meliboeus and Tityrus are characters in Virgil's *Eclogues*. Sidney responds to the idea that pastoral is the least elevated of the poetic genres; here he declares that it is capable of conveying political and moral ideas.

and sheep, can include the whole considerations of wrongdoing and patience; some-times show that contentions for trifles can get but a trifling victory: where perchance a man may see that even Alexander and Darius, when they strave who should be cock of this world's dunghill, the benefit they got was that the after-livers may say

> Haec memini et victum frustra contendere Thirsin:
> Ex illo Corydon, Corydon est tempore nobis.[9]

Or is it the lamenting Elegiac;[1] which in a kind heart would move rather pity than blame; who bewails with the great philosopher Heraclitus, the weakness of mankind and the wretchedness of the world; who surely is to be praised, either for compassionate accompanying just causes of lamentations, or for rightly painting out how weak be the passions of woefulness? Is it the bitter but wholesome Iambic,[2] who rubs the galled mind, in making shame the trumpet of villainy, with bold and open crying out against naughtiness? Or the Satiric, who

> Omne vafer vitium ridenti tangit amico;[3]

who sportingly never leaveth till he make a man laugh at folly, and at length shamed, to laugh at himself, which he cannot avoid without avoiding the folly; who, while

> circum praecordia ludit,[4]

giveth us to feel how many headaches a passionate life bringeth us to; how, when all is done,

> Est Ulubris, animus si nos non deficit aequus?[5]

No, perchance it is the Comic, whom naughty playmakers and stage-keepers have justly made odious. To the arguments of abuse I will answer after. Only this much now is to be said, that the comedy is an imitation of the common errors of our life, which he representeth in the most ridiculous and scornful sort that may be, so as it is impossible that any beholder can be content to be such a one. Now, as in geometry the oblique must be known as well as the right, and in arithmetic the odd as well as the even, so in the actions of our life who seeth not the filthiness of evil wanteth a great foil to perceive the beauty of virtue. This doth the comedy handle so in our private and domestical matters as with hearing it we get as it were an expe-rience what is to be looked for of a niggardly Demea, of a crafty Davus, of a flattering Gnatho, of a vainglorious Thraso;[6] and not only to know what effects are to be ex-pected, but to know who be such, by the signifying badge given them by the come-dian. And little reason hath any man to say that men learn the evil by seeing it so set out, since, as I said before, there is no man living but, by the force truth hath in nature, no sooner seeth these men play their parts, but wisheth them in pistrinum;[7] although perchance the sack of his own faults lie so hidden behind his back that he

9. "These things I remember, how vanquished Thrysis tried in vain. Since then it has been Coridon, only Cori-don, with us" (Virgil, Eclogues, 7.69–70). These lines sug-gest the futility of ambition.
1. A kind of poetry lamenting loss or remembering what no longer exists. Heraclitus: a philosopher of conflict and flux, who lived about 500 B.C.E.
2. A verse form used in satire.
3. "The sly man probes every one of his friend's faults while making his friend laugh" (Persius, Satires,

1.116–17).
4. "He plays around the heart" (Persius, Satires 1.117).
5. "[Contentment] is at Ulubrae, if a well-balanced mind doesn't fail us" (Horace, Epistles, 1.11.30). Ulubrae was a notoriously disagreeable small town.
6. Stock characters from the Roman comedies of Terence.
7. At a mill; a customary punishment for criminals and unruly slaves.

seeth not himself dance the same measure; whereto yet nothing can more open his eyes than to find his own actions contemptibly set forth.

So that the right use of comedy will (I think) by nobody be blamed; and much less of the high and excellent Tragedy, that openeth the greatest wounds, and showeth forth the ulcers that are covered with tissue; that maketh kings fear to be tyrants, and tyrants manifest their tyrannical humors; that, with stirring the affects of admiration and commiseration, teacheth the uncertainty of this world, and upon how weak foundations gilden roofs are builded; that maketh us know

> *Qui sceptra saevus duro imperio regit*
> *Timet timentes; metus in auctorem redit.*[8]

But how much it can move, Plutarch yieldeth a notable testimony of the abominable tyrant Alexander Pheraeus,[9] from whose eyes a tragedy, well made and represented, drew abundance of tears, who without all pity had murdered infinite numbers, and some of his own blood: so as he, that was not ashamed to make matters for tragedies, yet could not resist the sweet violence of a tragedy. And if it wrought no further good in him, it was that he, in despite of himself, withdrew himself from hearkening to that which might mollify his hardened heart. But it is not the tragedy they do mislike; for it were too absurd to cast out so excellent a representation of whatsoever is most worthy to be learned.

Is it the Lyric that most displeaseth, who with his tuned lyre and well-accorded voice, giveth praise, the reward of virtue, to virtuous acts; who gives moral precepts, and natural problems; who sometimes raiseth up his voice to the height of the heavens, in singing the lauds of the immortal God? Certainly, I must confess my own barbarousness, I never heard the old song of Percy and Douglas[1] that I found not my heart moved more than with a trumpet; and yet is it sung but by some blind crowder,[2] with no rougher voice than rude style; which, being so evil apparelled in the dust and cobwebs of that uncivil age, what would it work trimmed in the gorgeous eloquence of Pindar?[3] In Hungary I have seen it the manner at all feasts, and other such meetings, to have songs of their ancestors' valor, which that right soldierlike nation think one of the chiefest kindlers of brave courage. The incomparable Lacedemonians[4] did not only carry that kind of music ever with them to the field, but even at home, as such songs were made, so were they all content to be singers of them—when the lusty men were to tell what they did, the old men what they had done, and the young what they would do. And where a man may say that Pindar many times praiseth highly victories of small moment, matters rather of sport than virtue; as it may be answered, it was the fault of the poet, and not of the poetry, so indeed the chief fault was in the time and custom of the Greeks, who set those toys at so high a price that Philip of Macedon[5] reckoned a horserace won at Olympus among his three fearful[6] felicities. But as the unimitable Pindar often did, so is that kind most capable and most fit to awake the thoughts from the sleep of idleness to embrace honorable enterprises.

---

8. "The cruel man (i.e., the tyrant) who rules his people with a harsh government fears his fearful people; terror returns to its author" (Seneca, *Oedipus*, 3.705–6).
9. Tyrant of Pherae in Thessaly (369–357 B.C.E.), described by Plutarch in his *Life of Pelopidas*.
1. Sidney refers to the ballad *Chevy Chase*, which describes the conflict between the Earls of Percy and Douglas.
2. Fiddler.
3. The most famous of Greek lyric poets (c. 522–402 B.C.E.),

whose metrically complex odes celebrate victories in the Panhellenic games, the most famous of which was held every four years at Olympia.
4. Spartans.
5. Father of Alexander the Great, himself a conquering general and hero. Olympus: Sidney's error for Olympia, site of the Olympian Games.
6. Wonderful.

There rests the Heroical—whose very name (I think) should daunt all back-biters: for by what conceit can a tongue be directed to speak evil of that which draweth with him no less champions than Achilles, Cyrus, Aeneas, Turnus, Tydeus, and Rinaldo?[7]—who doth not only teach and move to a truth, but teacheth and moveth to the most high and excellent truth; who maketh magnanimity and justice shine through all misty fearfulness and foggy desires; who, if the saying of Plato and Tully be true, that who could see virtue would be wonderfully ravished with the love of her beauty—this man sets her out to make her more lovely in her holiday apparel, to the eye of any that will deign not to disdain until they understand. But if anything be already said in the defense of sweet poetry, all concurreth to the maintaining the heroical, which is not only a kind, but the best and most accomplished kind of poetry. For as the image of each action stirreth and instructeth the mind, so the lofty image of such worthies most inflameth the mind with desire to be worthy, and informs with counsel how to be worthy. Only let Aeneas be worn in the tablet of your memory, how he governeth himself in the ruin of his country; in the preserving his old father, and carrying away his religious ceremonies; in obeying God's commandment to leave Dido, though not only all passionate kindness, but even the human consideration of virtuous gratefulness, would have craved other of him; how in storms, how in sports, how in war, how in peace, how a fugitive, how victorious, how besieged, how besieging, how to strangers, how to allies, how to enemies, how to his own; lastly, how in his inward self, and how in his outward government—and I think, in a mind not prejudiced with a prejudicating humor, he will be found in excellency fruitful, yea, even as Horace saith,

melius Chrysippo et Crantore.[8]

But truly I imagine it falleth out with these poet-whippers, as with some good women, who often are sick, but in faith they cannot tell where; so the name of poetry is odious to them, but neither his cause nor effects, neither the sum that contains him, nor the particularities descending from him, give any fast handle to their carping dispraise.

Since then poetry is of all human learning the most ancient and of most fatherly antiquity, as from whence other learnings have taken their beginnings; since it is so universal that no learned nation doth despise it, nor barbarous nation is without it; since both Roman and Greek gave such divine names unto it, the one of prophesying, the other of making, and that indeed that name of making is fit for him, considering that where all other arts retain themselves within their subject, and receive, as it were, their being from it, the poet only bringeth his own stuff, and doth not learn a conceit out of a matter,[9] but maketh matter for a conceit; since neither his description nor end containing any evil, the thing described cannot be evil; since his effects be so good as to teach goodness and to delight the learners; since therein (namely in moral doctrine, the chief of all knowledges) he doth not only far pass the historian, but, for instructing, is well nigh comparable to the philosopher, for moving leaves him behind him; since the Holy Scripture (wherein there is no uncleanness) hath whole parts in it poetical, and that even our Savior Christ vouchsafed to use the flowers of it; since all his kinds are not only in their united forms but in their severed

---

7. Epic heroes and moral exemplars. Tydeus fought to bring Polyneices, the son of Oedipus, to the throne of Thebes (see Statius's *Thebaid*); Rinaldo was one of the French king Charlemagne's knights who fought against the Saracens in Italy (see Ludovico Ariosto's *Orlando*

Furioso and Torquato Tasso's *Jerusalem Delivered*).
8. "Better than [the philosophers] Chrysippus and Crantor" (Horace, *Epistles*, 1.4).
9. I.e., does not take his theme from his material.

dissections fully commendable; I think (and think I think rightly) the laurel crown appointed for triumphant captains doth worthily (of all other learnings) honor the poet's triumph.

But because we have ears as well as tongues, and that the lightest reasons that may be will seem to weigh greatly, if nothing be put in the counterbalance, let us hear, and, as well as we can, ponder what objections be made against this art, which may be worthy either of yielding or answering.

First, truly I note not only in these μισ'ομονσοι, poet-haters, but in all that kind of people who seek a praise by dispraising others, that they do prodigally spend a great many wandering words in quips and scoffs, carping and taunting at each thing which, by stirring the spleen, may stay the brain from a through-beholding the worthiness of the subject. Those kind of objections, as they are full of a very idle easiness, since there is nothing of so sacred a majesty but that an itching tongue may rub itself upon it, so deserve they no other answer, but, instead of laughing at the jest, to laugh at the jester. We know a playing wit can praise the discretion of an ass, the comfortableness of being in debt, and the jolly commodities of being sick of the plague. So of the contrary side, if we will turn Ovid's verse

Ut lateat virtus proximitate mali,[1]

that good lie hid in nearness of the evil, Agrippa will be as merry in showing the vanity of science as Erasmus was in the commending of folly. Neither shall any man or matter escape some touch of these smiling railers. But for Erasmus and Agrippa,[2] they had another foundation than the superficial part would promise. Marry, these other pleasant faultfinders, who will correct the verb before they understand the noun, and confute others' knowledge before they confirm their own—I would have them only remember that scoffing cometh not of wisdom. So as the best title in true English they get with their merriments is to be called good fools; for so have our grave forefathers ever termed that humorous kind of jesters.

But that which giveth greatest scope to their scorning humor is rhyming and versing. It is already said (and, as I think, truly said), it is not rhyming and versing that maketh poesy. One may be a poet without versing, and a versifier without poetry. But yet, presuppose it were inseparable (as indeed it seemeth Scaliger[3] judgeth), truly it were an inseparable commendation. For if *oratio* next to *ratio*, speech next to reason, be the greatest gift bestowed upon mortality, that cannot be praiseless which doth most polish that blessing of speech; which considers each word, not only (as a man may say) by his most forcible quality, but by his best measured quantity, carrying even in themselves a harmony—without, perchance, number, measure, order, proportion be in our time grown odious. But lay aside the just praise it hath, by being the only fit speech for music (music, I say, the most divine striker of the senses), thus much is undoubtedly true, that if reading be foolish without remembering, memory being the only treasure of knowledge, those words which are fittest for memory are likewise most convenient for knowledge. Now, that verse far exceedeth prose in the

1. "That virtue may lie next to evil" (Cf. Ovid, *The Art of Love* 2.662).
2. Henry Cornelius Agrippa of Nettesheim (1486–1533), a German philosopher, and Desiderius Erasmus of Rotterdam (1467–1536), the greatest humanist scholar of the early modern period. Sidney refers to their most popular works, *The Uncertainty and Vanity of Knowledge* and *The Praise of Folly*, respectively, both written to satirize human pretensions.
3. Julius Caesar Scaliger (1484–1558), an Italian scholar who wrote a treatise, *Seven Books on Poetry*.

knitting up of memory, the reason is manifest: the words (besides their delight, which hath a great affinity to memory) being so set as one cannot be lost but the whole work fails; which accusing itself, calleth the remembrance back to itself, and so most strongly confirmeth it. Besides, one word so, as it were, begetting another, as, be it in rhyme or measured verse, by the former a man shall have a near guess to the follower. Lastly, even they that have taught the art of memory have showed nothing so apt for it as a certain room divided into many places well and thoroughly known. Now, that hath the verse in effect perfectly, every word having his natural seat, which seat must needs make the word remembered. But what needeth more in a thing so known to all men? Who is it that ever was a scholar that doth not carry away some verses of Virgil, Horace, or Cato, which in his youth he learned, and even to his old age serve him for hourly lessons? But the fitness it hath for memory is notably proved by all delivery of arts: wherein for the most part, from grammar to logic, mathematics, physic, and the rest, the rules chiefly necessary to be borne away are compiled in verses. So that, verse being in itself sweet and orderly, and being best for memory, the only handle of knowledge, it must be in jest that any man can speak against it.

Now then go we to the most important imputations laid to the poor poets. For aught I can yet learn, they are these. First, that there being many other more fruitful knowledges, a man might better spend his time in them than in this. Secondly, that it is the mother of lies. Thirdly, that it is the nurse of abuse, infecting us with many pestilent desires; with a siren's sweetness drawing the mind to the serpent's tail of sinful fancies (and herein, especially, comedies give the largest field to ear,[4] as Chaucer saith); how, both in other nations and in ours, before poets did soften us, we were full of courage, given to martial exercises, the pillars of manlike liberty, and not lulled asleep in shady idleness with poets' pastimes. And lastly, and chiefly, they cry out with open mouth as if they had overshot Robin Hood,[5] that Plato banished them out of his commonwealth. Truly, this is much, if there be much truth in it.

First, to the first. That a man might better spend his time, is a reason indeed; but it doth (as they say) but *petere principium* [beg the question]. For if it be as I affirm, that no learning is so good as that which teacheth and moveth to virtue; and that none can both teach and move thereto so much as poetry: then is the conclusion manifest that ink and paper cannot be to a more profitable purpose employed. And certainly, though a man should grant their first assumption, it should follow (methinks) very unwillingly, that good is not good, because better is better. But I still and utterly deny that there is sprong out of earth a more fruitful knowledge.

To the second, therefore, that they should be the principal liars, I answer paradoxically, but truly, I think truly, that of all writers under the sun the poet is the least liar, and, though he would, as a poet can scarcely be a liar. The astronomer, with his cousin the geometrician, can hardly escape, when they take upon them to measure the height of the stars. How often, think you, do the physicians lie, when they aver things good for sicknesses, which afterwards send Charon[6] a great number of souls drowned in a potion before they come to his ferry? And no less of the rest, which take upon them to affirm. Now, for the poet, he nothing affirms, and therefore never lieth. For, as I take it, to lie is to affirm that to be true which is false. So as the other artists,

---

4. Sidney refers to an expression in Chaucer's *Canterbury Tales*: "a large feeld to ere," *The Knight's Tale*, line 28.
5. The medieval folk hero, who is said to have lived in Sherwood Forest. Plato banishes poets in his treatise on

the ideal state (*The Republic* 3.392).
6. According to Greek myth, Charon ferries souls across the river Styx to the underworld.

and especially the historian, affirming many things, can, in the cloudy knowledge of mankind, hardly escape from many lies. But the poet (as I said before) never affirmeth. The poet never maketh any circles about your imagination, to conjure you to believe for true what he writes. He citeth not authorities of other histories, but even for his entry calleth the sweet Muses to inspire into him a good invention; in truth, not laboring to tell you what is or is not, but what should or should not be. And therefore, though he recount things not true, yet because he telleth them not for true, he lieth not—without we will say that Nathan lied in his speech before-alleged to David; which as a wicked man durst scarce say, so think I none so simple would say that Aesop lied in the tales of his beasts; for who thinks that Aesop wrote it for actually true were well worthy to have his name chronicled among the beasts he writeth of. What child is there, that, coming to a play, and seeing *Thebes* written in great letters upon an old door, doth believe that it is Thebes? If then a man can arrive to that child's age to know that the poets' persons and doings are but pictures what should be, and not stories what have been, they will never give the lie to things not affirmatively but allegorically and figuratively written. And therefore, as in history, looking for truth, they may go away full fraught with falsehood, so in poesy, looking but for fiction, they shall use the narration but as an imaginative ground-plot of a profitable invention. But hereto is replied, that the poets give names to men they write of, which argueth a conceit of an actual truth, and so, not being true, proves a falsehood. And doth the lawyer lie then, when under the names of *John-a-stiles* and *John-a-nokes*[7] he puts his case? But that is easily answered. Their naming of men is but to make their picture the more lively, and not to build any history: painting men, they cannot leave men nameless. We see we cannot play at chess but that we must give names to our chessmen; and yet, methinks, he were a very partial champion of truth that would say we lied for giving a piece of wood the reverend title of a bishop. The poet nameth Cyrus or Aeneas no other way than to show what men of their fames, fortunes, and estates should do.

Their third is, how much it abuseth men's wit, training it to wanton sinfulness and lustful love: for indeed that is the principal, if not only, abuse I can hear alleged.[8] They say, the comedies rather teach than reprehend amorous conceits. They say the lyric is larded with passionate sonnets; the elegiac weeps the want of his mistress; and that even to the heroical, Cupid hath ambitiously climbed. Alas, Love, I would thou couldst as well defend thyself as thou canst offend others. I would those on whom thou dost attend could either put thee away, or yield good reason why they keep thee. But grant love of beauty to be a beastly fault (although it be very hard, since only man, and no beast, hath that gift to discern beauty); grant that lovely name of Love to deserve all hateful reproaches (although even some of my masters the philosophers spent a good deal of their lamp-oil in setting forth the excellency of it); grant, I say, whatsoever they will have granted, that not only love, but lust, but vanity, but (if they list) scurrility, possesseth many leaves of the poets' books; yet think I, when this is granted, they will find their sentence may with good manners put the last words foremost, and not say that poetry abuseth man's wit, but that man's wit abuseth poetry.

---

7. I.e., John Doe, or John Roe of ancient law courts.
8. Sidney refers to contemporary criticism of the drama,
the best known of which was Stephen Gosson's *School of Abuse* (1579); see page 1033.

For I will not deny but that man's wit may make poesy, which should be εἰκαστική [representing real things] (which some learned have defined: figuring forth good things), to be φανταστική [representing imaginary things] (which doth, contrariwise, infect the fancy with unworthy objects), as the painter, that should give to the eye either some excellent perspective, or some fine picture, fit for building or fortification, or containing in it some notable example (as Abraham sacrificing his son Isaac, Judith killing Holofernes, David fighting with Goliath),[9] may leave those, and please an ill-pleased eye with wanton shows of better hidden matters. But what, shall the abuse of a thing make the right use odious? Nay truly, though I yield that poesy may not only be abused, but that being abused, by the reason of his sweet charming force, it can do more hurt than any other army of words: yet shall it be so far from concluding that the abuse should give reproach to the abused, that, contrariwise, it is a good reason that whatsoever, being abused, doth most harm, being rightly used (and upon the right use each thing conceiveth his title), doth most good. Do we not see the skill of physic, the best rampire[1] to our often-assaulted bodies, being abused, teach poison, the most violent destroyer? Doth not knowledge of law, whose end is to even and right all things, being abused, grow the crooked fosterer of horrible injuries? Doth not (to go to the highest) God's word abused breed heresy, and His name abused become blasphemy? Truly, a needle cannot do much hurt, and as truly (with leave of ladies be it spoken) it cannot do much good: with a sword thou mayst kill thy father, and with a sword thou mayst defend thy prince and country. So that, as in their calling poets fathers of lies they said nothing, so in this their argument of abuse they prove the commendation.

They allege herewith, that before poets began to be in price our nation had set their hearts' delight upon action, and not imagination: rather doing things worthy to be written, than writing things fit to be done. What that before-time was, I think scarcely Sphinx[2] can tell, since no memory is so ancient that hath not the precedent of poetry. And certain it is that, in our plainest homeliness, yet never was the Albion[3] nation without poetry. Marry, this argument, though it be levelled against poetry, yet is it indeed a chainshot[4] against all learning, or bookishness as they commonly term it. Of such mind were certain Goths,[5] of whom it is written that, having in the spoil of a famous city taken a fair library, one hangman (belike fit to execute the fruits of their wits) who had murdered a great number of bodies, would have set fire in it: no, said another very gravely, take heed what you do, for while they are busy about these toys, we shall with more leisure conquer their countries. This indeed is the ordinary doctrine of ignorance, and many words sometimes I have heard spent in it. But because this reason is generally against all learning as well as poetry, or rather, all learning but poetry; because it were too large a digression to handle it, or at least too superfluous (since it is manifest that all government of action is to be gotten by knowledge, and knowledge best by gathering many knowledges, which is reading), I only, with Horace, to him that is of that opinion

jubeo stultum esse libenter;[6]

for as for poetry itself, it is the freest from this objection.

9. Sidney refers to episodes in the Bible (Genesis 22, 1 Samuel 17, Judith 2–14).
1. Rampart.
2. In Greek mythology, a monster with a woman's head and a lion's body who posed riddles to human beings.
3. British.
4. Two cannonballs joined by a chain; it was deployed in

naval warfare, usually against the rigging on enemy ships.
5. Northern European tribes, often described as uncivilized by ancient historians. The fate of "a fair library" is told by Michel de Montaigne in his essay *Of Pedantry* (*Essays* 1.24).
6. "I order [him] to be stupid cheerfully" (Horace, *Satires,* 1.1.63).

For poetry is the companion of camps. I dare undertake, Orlando Furioso, or honest King Arthur, will never displease a soldier; but the quiddity of *ens* and *prima materia* will hardly agree with a corselet;[7] and therefore, as I said in the beginning, even Turks and Tartars are delighted with poets. Homer, a Greek, flourished before Greece flourished. And if to a slight conjecture a conjecture may be opposed, truly it may seem, that as by him their learned men took almost their first light of knowledge, so their active men received their first motions of courage. Only Alexander's example may serve, who by Plutarch is accounted of such virtue, that Fortune was not his guide but his footstool; whose acts speak for him, though Plutarch did not: indeed the phoenix of warlike princes.[8] This Alexander left his schoolmaster, living Aristotle, behind him, but took dead Homer with him. He put the philosopher Callisthenes to death for his seeming philosophical, indeed mutinous, stubbornness, but the chief thing he was ever heard to wish for was that Homer had been alive. He well found he received more bravery of mind by the pattern of Achilles than by hearing the definition of fortitude. And therefore, if Cato misliked Fulvius for carrying Ennius with him to the field,[9] it may be answered that, if Cato misliked it, the noble Fulvius liked it, or else he had not done it; for it was not the excellent Cato Uticensis (whose authority I would much more have reverenced), but it was the former, in truth a bitter punisher of faults (but else a man that had never well sacrificed to the Graces: he misliked and cried out against all Greek learning, and yet, being eighty years old, began to learn it, belike fearing that Pluto understood not Latin). Indeed, the Roman laws allowed no person to be carried to the wars but he that was in the soldiers' roll; and therefore, though Cato misliked his unmustered person, he misliked not his work.[1] And if he had, Scipio Nasica, judged by common consent the best Roman, loved him. Both the other Scipio brothers, who had by their virtues no less surnames than of Asia and Afric, so loved him that they caused his body to be buried in their sepulture. So as Cato's authority, being but against his person, and that answered with so far greater than himself, is herein of no validity.

But now indeed my burden is great; now Plato's name is laid upon me, whom, I must confess, of all philosophers I have ever esteemed most worthy of reverence, and with good reason: since of all philosophers he is the most poetical. Yet if he will defile the fountain out of which his flowing streams have proceeded, let us boldly examine with what reasons he did it. First, truly, a man might maliciously object that Plato, being a philosopher, was a natural enemy of poets. For indeed, after the philosophers had picked out of the sweet mysteries of poetry the right discerning true points of knowledge, they forthwith putting it in method, and making a school-art of that which the poets did only teach by a divine delightfulness, beginning to spurn at their guides, like ungrateful prentices, were not content to set up shops for themselves, but

---

7. I.e., soldiers will enjoy reading about knights like Ariosto's Orlando Furioso or Malory's King Arthur, but will balk at philosophers' concerns with "quiddities" (subtleties), "*ens*" (being), and "*prima materia*" (the original matter of the universe).

8. Sidney cites various episodes from Plutarch's accounts of Alexander the Great in his *Lives* (c. 100 C.E.), which was translated into English by Sir Thomas North in 1579. The phoenix was a mythic bird thought to be eternally reborn in the ashes of its own funeral pyre.

9. Marcus Portius Cato the Censor (234–184 B.C.E.), criticized the general Marcus Flavius Nobilior for carrying

the poetry of Quintus Ennius (239–169 B.C.E.) on a battle campaign. Sidney goes on to distinguish Cato the Censor from his great-grandson, Marcus Porcius Cato, the chief political antagonist of Julius Caesar.

1. In fact, as Sidney states, the poet Ennius in person actually accompanied Flavius; he was "unmustered" in that he was not on the army payroll. Sidney continues to praise Ennius by saying that he was loved by various Scipios: Publius Cornelius Scipio Nasica, Publius Cornelius Scipio Africanus, and Lucius Cornelius Scipio Asiaticus, all notable patriots and generals.

sought by all means to discredit their masters; which by the force of delight being barred them, the less they could overthrow them, the more they hated them. For indeed, they found for Homer seven cities strave who should have him for their citizen; where many cities banished philosophers as not fit members to live among them. For only repeating certain of Euripides' verses,[2] many Athenians had their lives saved of the Syracusans, where the Athenians themselves thought many philosophers unworthy to live. Certain poets, as Simonides and Pindar, had so prevailed with Hiero the First,[3] that of a tyrant they made him a just king; where Plato could do so little with Dionysius, that he himself of a philosopher was made a slave. But who should do thus, I confess, should requite the objections made against poets with like cavillations[4] against philosophers; as likewise one should do that should bid one read *Phaedrus* or *Symposium* in Plato, or the discourse of love in Plutarch, and see whether any poet do authorize abominable filthiness, as they do. Again, a man might ask out of what commonwealth Plato did banish them:[5] in sooth, thence where he himself alloweth community of women—so as belike this banishment grew not for effeminate wantonness, since little should poetical sonnets be hurtful when a man might have what woman he listed.[6] But I honor philosophical instructions, and bless the wits which bred them: so as they be not abused, which is likewise stretched to poetry.

St. Paul himself (who yet, for the credit of poets, twice citeth poets, and one of them by the name of "their prophet") setteth a watchword upon philosophy—indeed upon the abuse.[7] So doth Plato upon the abuse, not upon poetry. Plato found fault that the poets of his time filled the world with wrong opinions of the gods, making light tales of that unspotted essence, and therefore would not have the youth depraved with such opinions. Herein may much be said. Let this suffice: the poets did not induce such opinions, but did imitate those opinions already induced. For all the Greek stories can well testify that the very religion of that time stood upon many and many-fashioned gods, not taught so by the poets, but followed according to their nature of imitation. Who list may read in Plutarch the discourses of Isis and Osiris,[8] of the cause why oracles ceased, of the divine providence, and see whether the theology of that nation stood not upon such dreams which the poets indeed superstitiously observed—and truly (since they had not the light of Christ) did much better in it than the philosophers, who, shaking off superstition, brought in atheism. Plato therefore (whose authority I had much rather justly construe than unjustly resist) meant not in general of poets, in those words of which Julius Scaliger saith *Qua authoritate barbari quidam atque hispidi abuti velint ad poetas e republica exigendos;*[9] but only meant to drive out those wrong opinions of the Deity (whereof now, without further law, Christianity hath taken away all the hurtful belief)

---

2. Plutarch states that Greek slaves living outside Greece had won their release by teaching their masters the poetry of Euripides (*Life of Nicias,* ch. 29).

3. Tyrant of Syracuse (478–476 B.C.E.), who patronized Greek poets. Aeschylus was a playwright; Bacchylides a lyric poet; and Simonides a writer of satire. Dionysius the Elder of Syracuse was said to have sold Plato to the Spartan ambassador Pollis as a slave, a situation from which he was later liberated.

4. Objections.

5. I.e., poets. Plato argued that in his ideal republic, all women should be common, that is, not married to a single man but sexually available to all men (*Republic* 5, 449–462). Sidney observes that Plato banishes poets not

because poetry makes men licentious, an impossibility in a state in which women are readily available, but for some other reason.

6. Desired.

7. Paul rejects the assessment of poets by philosophers (Acts 17.18, Colossians 2.8), and he castigates false prophets (Titus 1.12).

8. Isis, the Egyptian goddess of fertility, was sister and wife of Osiris, civilizer of Egypt, god of the dead, and source of life.

9. By abuse of whose authority, barbarous and crude men wish to expel poets from the Republic; Scaliger is commenting on Plato's expulsion of poets from an ideal republic in his own treatise on poetry.

perchance (as he thought) nourished by the then esteemed poets. And a man need go no further than to Plato himself to know his meaning: who, in his dialogue called *Ion*, giveth high and rightly divine commendation unto poetry. So as Plato, banishing the abuse, not the thing, not banishing it, but giving due honor unto it, shall be our patron, and not our adversary. For indeed I had much rather (since truly I may do it) show their mistaking of Plato (under whose lion's skin they would make an ass-like braying against poesy) than go about to overthrow his authority; whom, the wiser a man is, the more just cause he shall find to have in admiration; especially since he attributeth unto poesy more than myself do, namely, to be a very inspiring of a divine force, far above man's wit, as in the forenamed dialogue is apparent.

Of the other side, who would show the honors have been by the best sort of judgments granted them, a whole sea of examples would present themselves: Alexanders, Caesars, Scipios, all favorers of poets; Laelius, called the Roman Socrates, himself a poet, so as part of *Heautontimorumenos*[1] in Terence was supposed to be made by him; and even the Greek Socrates, whom Apollo confirmed to be the only wise man, is said to have spent part of his old time in putting Aesop's fables into verses. And therefore, full evil should it become his scholar Plato to put such words in his master's mouth against poets. But what need more? Aristotle writes the Art of Poesy;[2] and why, if it should not be written? Plutarch teacheth the use to be gathered of them; and how, if they should not be read? And who reads Plutarch's either history or philosophy, shall find he trimmeth both their garments with guards of poesy. But I list not to defend poesy with the help of his underling historiography. Let it suffice to have showed it is a fit soil for praise to dwell upon; and what dispraise may be set upon it, is either easily overcome, or transformed into just commendation.

So that, since the excellencies of it may be so easily and so justly confirmed, and the low-creeping objections so soon trodden down: it not being an art of lies, but of true doctrine; not of effeminateness, but of notable stirring of courage; not of abusing man's wit, but of strengthening man's wit; not banished, but honored by Plato: let us rather plant more laurels for to engarland the poets' heads (which honor of being laureate, whereas besides them only triumphant captains were, is a sufficient authority to show the price they ought to be held in) than suffer the ill-favored breath of such wrong-speakers once to blow upon the clear springs of poesy.

But since I have run so long a career in this matter, methinks, before I give my pen a full stop, it shall be but a little more lost time to inquire why England, the mother of excellent minds, should be grown so hard a stepmother to poets, who certainly in wit ought to pass all other, since all only proceedeth from their wit, being indeed makers of themselves, not takers of others. How can I but exclaim

Musa, mihi causas memora, quo numine laeso?[3]

Sweet poesy, that hath anciently had kings, emperors, senators, great captains, such as, besides a thousand others, David, Adrian, Sophocles, Germanicus, not only to

---

1. Gaius Laelius was said to have written parts of a play called *Heautontimorumenos* (*The Self-Tormenter*), reputed to be by the Roman playwright Terence. Plato reports that Socrates turned Aesop's fables into verse.

2. Sidney refers to Aristotle's *Poetics*.
3. "Muse, tell me the cause, by what wounded divinity. . . ." (*Aeneid* 1.8).

favor poets, but to be poets;[4] and of our nearer times can present for her patrons a Robert, king of Sicily, the great King Francis of France, King James of Scotland; such cardinals as Bembus and Bibbiena; such famous preachers and teachers as Beza and Melanchthon; so learned philosophers as Fracastorius and Scaliger; so great orators as Pontanus and Muretus; so piercing wits as George Buchanan; so grave counselors as, beside many, but before all, that Hospital of France,[5] than whom (I think) that realm never brought forth a more accomplished judgment, more firmly builded upon virtue: I say these, with numbers of others, not only to read others' poesies, but to poetize for others' reading—that poesy, thus embraced in all other places, should only find in our time a hard welcome in England, I think the very earth lamenteth it, and therefore decketh our soil with fewer laurels than it was accustomed. For heretofore poets have in England also flourished, and, which is to be noted, even in those times when the trumpet of Mars[6] did sound loudest. And now that an overfaint quietness should seem to strew[7] the house for poets, they are almost in as good reputation as the mountebanks[8] at Venice. Truly even that, as of the one side it giveth great praise to poesy, which like Venus (but to better purpose) had rather be troubled in the net with Mars than enjoy the homely quiet of Vulcan:[9] so serves it for a piece of a reason why they are less grateful to idle England, which now can scarce endure the pain of a pen.

Upon this necessarily followeth, that base men with servile wits undertake it, who think it enough if they can be rewarded of the printer. And so as Epaminondas[1] is said with the honor of his virtue to have made an office, by his exercising it, which before was contemptible, to become highly respected; so these men, no more but setting their names to it, by their own disgracefulness disgrace the most graceful poesy. For now, as if all the Muses were got with child to bring forth bastard poets, without any commission they do post over the banks of Helicon,[2] till they make the readers more weary than post-horses; while, in the meantime, they

Queis meliore luto finxit praecordia Titan

are better content to suppress the outflowings of their wit, than, by publishing them, to be accounted knights of the same order. But I that, before ever I durst aspire unto the dignity, am admitted into the company of the paper-blurrers, do find the very true cause of our wanting estimation is want of desert—taking upon us to be poets in despite of Pallas.

Now, wherein we want desert were a thankworthy labor to express; but if I knew, I should have mended myself. But I, as I never desired the title, so have I neglected the means to come by it. Only, overmastered by some thoughts, I yielded an inky

---

4. King David of Israel composed psalms; the emperor Adrian (i.e., Hadrian) wrote verse and prose; Germanicus Caesar, conqueror of Germany, is supposed to have written poetry and plays. Sidney goes on to list a range of modern statesmen-poets.
5. Michel de L'Hôpital (1505–1573), a statesman who favored religious toleration, wrote Latin poems.
6. God of war.
7. Be scattered over.
8. Itinerant quacks peddling fake medicines.
9. Roman god of fire and smiths who caught his adulterous wife, Venus, and Mars, the god of war, in a net he had forged.

1. Theban general (4th century B.C.E.).
2. Not a very clear paragraph. The mountain named Helicon is sacred to the muses. Here it represents the inspirational springs that are being "post[ed] over," that is, bypassed, by contemporary "bastard poets" eager to publish, while better writers "whose hearts the Titan [Prometheus] molded out of better clays" (Juvenal, *Satires* 14.36) keep their works private rather than be lumped in with their inferiors. Sidney himself claims, perhaps with false modesty, that as a poet he is classed with the mediocrities, and declares that the reason for poets' low esteem is "want of desert" or lack of worth: They have not been helped by Pallas Athena, goddess of wisdom.

tribute unto them. Marry, they that delight in poesy itself should seek to know what they do, and how they do; and especially look themselves in an unflattering glass of reason, if they be inclinable unto it. For poesy must not be drawn by the ears; it must be gently led, or rather it must lead—which was partly the cause that made the ancient-learned affirm it was a divine gift, and no human skill: since all other knowledges lie ready for any that hath strength of wit. A poet no industry can make, if his own genius be not carried into it; and therefore it is an old proverb, *orator fit, poeta nascitur* [the orator is made, the poet born].

Yet confess I always that as the fertilest ground must be manured, so must the highest-flying wit have a Daedalus to guide him.[3] That Daedalus, they say, both in this and in other, hath three wings to bear itself up into the air of due commendation: that is, art, imitation, and exercise. But these, neither artificial rules nor imitative patterns, we much cumber ourselves withal. Exercise indeed we do, but that very fore-backwardly: for where we should exercise to know, we exercise as having known; and so is our brain delivered of much matter which never was begotten by knowledge. For there being two principal parts, matter to be expressed by words and words to express the matter, in neither we use art or imitation rightly. Our matter is *quodlibet* [what you will] indeed, though wrongly performing Ovid's verse,

> *Quicquid conabor dicere, versus erit;*[4]

never marshalling it into any assured rank, that almost the readers cannot tell where to find themselves.

Chaucer, undoubtedly, did excellently in his *Troilus and Criseyde;*[5] of whom, truly, I know not whether to marvel more, either that he in that misty time could see so clearly, or that we in this clear age go so stumblingly after him. Yet had he great wants, fit to be forgiven in so reverent an antiquity. I account the *Mirror of Magistrates* meetly furnished of beautiful parts, and in the Earl of Surrey's lyrics many things tasting of a noble birth, and worthy of a noble mind. The *Shepherd's Calendar* hath much poetry in his eclogues, indeed worthy the reading, if I be not deceived. (That same framing of his style to an old rustic language I dare not allow, since neither Theocritus in Greek, Virgil in Latin, nor Sannazaro in Italian did affect it.) Besides these I do not remember to have seen but few (to speak boldly) printed that have poetical sinews in them; for proof whereof, let but most of the verses be put in prose, and then ask the meaning, and it will be found that one verse did but beget another, without ordering at the first what should be at the last; which becomes a confused mass of words, with a tingling sound of rhyme, barely accompanied with reason.

Our tragedies and comedies (not without cause cried out against), observing rules neither of honest civility nor skilful poetry—excepting *Gorboduc*[6] (again, I say, of those that I have seen), which notwithstanding as it is full of stately speeches and well-sounding phrases, climbing to the height of Seneca's style, and as full of notable

---

3. The mythical artisan Daedalus built wings so that he and his son Icarus could escape from Crete, where Minos had confined him in the maze of his own making; but Icarus flew too near the sun, the wax in his wings melted, and he fell into the Aegean Sea and drowned. He is often cited as a figure of ambition.

4. "Whatever I shall try to say shall become verse" (*Tristia* 4.10.26).

5. Sidney gives grudging praise to a number of poets of the early modern period: Chaucer's romance *Troilus and Criseyde* relates the unhappy love affair of two Trojans; the *Mirror of* [i.e., *for*] *Magistrates*, a poem by various authors and added to at intervals during the 16th century, illustrated exemplary tragedies; the Earl of Surrey is Henry Howard; *The Shepheardes Calender* was written by Edmund Spenser. Theocritus, Virgil, and Sannazzaro were poets of pastoral.

6. A tragedy by Thomas Sackville and Thomas Norton (1561).

morality, which it doth most delightfully teach, and so obtain the very end of poesy, yet in truth it is very defectuous[7] in the circumstances, which grieveth me, because it might not remain as an exact model of all tragedies. For it is faulty both in place and time, the two necessary companions of all corporal actions. For where the stage should always represent but one place, and the uttermost time presupposed in it should be, both by Aristotle's precept and common reason, but one day, there is both many days, and many places, inartificially[8] imagined.

But if it be so in *Gorboduc*, how much more in all the rest, where you shall have Asia of the one side, and Afric of the other, and so many other under-kingdoms, that the player, when he cometh in, must ever begin with telling where he is, or else the tale will not be conceived? Now you shall have three ladies walk to gather flowers: and then we must believe the stage to be a garden. By and by we hear news of shipwreck in the same place: and then we are to blame if we accept it not for a rock. Upon the back of that comes out a hideous monster with fire and smoke: and then the miserable beholders are bound to take it for a cave. While in the meantime two armies fly in, represented with four swords and bucklers: and then what hard heart will not receive it for a pitched field?

Now, of time they are much more liberal: for ordinary it is that two young princes fall in love; after many traverses, she is got with child, delivered of a fair boy; he is lost, groweth a man, falls in love, and is ready to get another child; and all this in two hours' space: which, how absurd it is in sense, even sense may imagine, and art hath taught, and all ancient examples justified—and at this day, the ordinary players in Italy will not err in. Yet will some bring in an example of *Eunuchus* in Terence, that containeth matter of two days, yet far short of twenty years. True it is, and so was it to be played in two days, and so fitted to the time it set forth. And though Plautus have in one place done amiss, let us hit with him, and not miss with him.[9]

But they will say: How then shall we set forth a story which containeth both many places and many times? And do they not know that a tragedy is tied to the laws of poesy, and not of history; not bound to follow the story, but having liberty either to feign a quite new matter or to frame the history to the most tragical conveniency? Again, many things may be told which cannot be showed, if they know the difference betwixt reporting and representing. As, for example, I may speak (though I am here) of Peru, and in speech digress from that to the description of Calicut;[1] but in action I cannot represent it without Pacolet's horse;[2] and so was the manner the ancients took, by some *Nuntius* [messenger] to recount things done in former time or other place. Lastly, if they will represent a history, they must not (as Horace saith) begin *ab ovo* [from the beginning], but they must come to the principal point of that one action which they will represent.

By example this will be best expressed. I have a story of young Polydorus,[3] delivered for safety's sake, with great riches, by his father Priam to Polymnestor, king of Thrace, in the Trojan war time; he, after some years, hearing the overthrow of Priam, for to make the treasure his own, murdereth the child; the body of the child is taken up by Hecuba; she, the same day, findeth a sleight to be revenged most cruelly of the tyrant. Where now would one of our tragedy writers begin, but with the delivery of the child? Then should he sail over into Thrace, and so spend I know not how many

---

7. Defective.
8. Inartistically.
9. Terence, Plautus: two well-known writers of Roman comedies who influenced the drama in early modern England; Shakespeare took the plot of *The Comedy of Errors* from Plautus's *Menaechmi*.

1. Seaport on the west coast of India.
2. A magic horse in the French romance *Valentine and Orson*.
3. Sidney praises the narrative of the hero Polydorus as told by Euripides, who avoids a lengthy plot in his play on the subject, *Hecuba*.

years, and travel numbers of places. But where doth Euripides? Even with the finding of the body, leaving the rest to be told by the spirit of Polydorus. This need no further to be enlarged; the dullest wit may conceive it.

But besides these gross absurdities, how all their plays be neither right tragedies, nor right comedies, mingling kings and clowns, not because the matter so carrieth it, but thrust in the clown by head and shoulders to play a part in majestical matters with neither decency nor discretion, so as neither the admiration and commiseration, nor the right sportfulness, is by their mongrel tragicomedy obtained. I know Apuleius did somewhat so,[4] but that is a thing recounted with space of time, not represented in one moment; and I know the ancients have one or two examples of tragicomedies, as Plautus hath *Amphitryo;*[5] but, if we mark them well, we shall find that they never, or very daintily, match hornpipes and funerals. So falleth it out that, having indeed no right comedy, in that comical part of our tragedy, we have nothing but scurrility, unworthy of any chaste ears, or some extreme show of doltishness, indeed fit to lift up a loud laughter, and nothing else: where the whole tract of a comedy should be full of delight, as the tragedy should be still maintained in a well-raised admiration.

But our comedians think there is no delight without laughter; which is very wrong, for though laughter may come with delight, yet cometh it not of delight, as though delight should be the cause of laughter; but well may one thing breed both together. Nay, rather in themselves they have, as it were, a kind of contrariety: for delight we scarcely do but in things that have a conveniency to ourselves or to the general nature; laughter almost ever cometh of things most disproportioned to ourselves and nature. Delight hath a joy in it, either permanent or present. Laughter hath only a scornful tickling.

For example, we are ravished with delight to see a fair woman, and yet are far from being moved to laughter; we laugh at deformed creatures, wherein certainly we cannot delight. We delight in good chances, we laugh at mischances: we delight to hear the happiness of our friends, or country, at which he were worthy to be laughed at that would laugh; we shall, contrarily, laugh sometimes to find a matter quite mistaken and go down the hill against the bias in the mouth of some such men—as for the respect of them one shall be heartily sorry, he cannot choose but laugh, and so is rather pained than delighted with laughter.

Yet deny I not but that they may go well together. For as in Alexander's picture well set out we delight without laughter,[6] and in twenty mad antics we laugh without delight; so in Hercules, painted with his great beard and furious countenance, in a woman's attire, spinning at Omphale's commandment, it breedeth both delight and laughter: for the representing of so strange a power in love procureth delight, and the scornfulness of the action stirreth laughter. But I speak to this purpose, that all the end of the comical part be not upon such scornful matters as stir laughter only, but, mixed with it, that delightful teaching which is the end of poesy. And the great fault even in that point of laughter, and forbidden plainly by Aristotle, is that they stir laughter in

4. In his prose romance *The Golden Ass* (c. 155 C.E.); William Adlington translated the work into English in the 16th century.

5. In this play, the tragic element is represented by the heroine Alcmena, tricked into sleeping with the god Jupiter, who is disguised as her husband Amphitrion, and the comic element by the burlesque behavior of the gods who arrange the deception.

6. Sidney distinguishes reactions to different kinds of descriptions: Alexander's portrait delights; mad antics provoke laughter; Hercules, captive and dressed as a woman by Queen Omphale of Lydia, both delights and provokes laughter.

sinful things, which are rather execrable than ridiculous, or in miserable, which are rather to be pitied than scorned. For what is it to make folks gape at a wretched beggar and a beggarly clown; or, against law of hospitality, to jest at strangers, because they speak not English so well as we do? What do we learn, since it is certain

> *Nil habet infelix paupertas durius in se,*
> *Quam quod ridiculos homines facit?*[7]

But rather, a busy loving courtier and a heartless threatening Thraso;[8] a self-wise-seeming schoolmaster; an awry-transformed traveler. These if we saw walk in stage names, which we play naturally, therein were delightful laughter, and teaching delightfulness—as in the other, the tragedies of Buchanan[9] do justly bring forth a divine admiration.

But I have lavished out too many words of this play matter. I do it because, as they are excelling parts of poesy, so is there none so much used in England, and none can be more pitifully abused; which, like an unmannerly daughter showing a bad education, causeth her mother Poesy's honesty to be called in question.

Other sort of poetry almost have we none, but that lyrical kind of songs and sonnets: which, Lord, if He gave us so good minds, how well it might be employed, and with how heavenly fruit, both private and public, in singing the praises of the immortal beauty: the immortal goodness of that God who giveth us hands to write and wits to conceive; of which we might well want words, but never matter; of which we could turn our eyes to nothing, but we should ever have new-budding occasions. But truly many of such writings as come under the banner of unresistible love, if I were a mistress, would never persuade me they were in love: so coldly they apply fiery speeches, as men that had rather read lovers' writings—and so caught up certain swelling phrases which hang together like a man that once told my father that the wind was at northwest and by south, because he would be sure to name winds enough—than that in truth they feel those passions, which easily (as I think) may be bewrayed by that same forcibleness or *energia* (as the Greeks call it) of the writer. But let this be a sufficient though short note, that we miss the right use of the material point of poesy.

Now, for the outside of it, which is words, or (as I may term it) diction, it is even well worse. So is that honey-flowing matron Eloquence appareled, or rather disguised, in a courtesan-like painted affectation: one time, with so far-fet words that may seem monsters but must seem strangers to any poor Englishman; another time, with coursing[1] of a letter, as if they were bound to follow the method of a dictionary; another time, with figures and flowers, extremely winter-starved. But I would this fault were only peculiar to versifiers, and had not as large possession among prose-printers; and (which is to be marveled) among many scholars; and (which is to be pitied) among some preachers. Truly I could wish, if at least I might be so bold to wish in a thing beyond the reach of my capacity, the diligent imitators of Tully and Demosthenes[2] (most worthy to be imitated) did not so much keep Nizolian paperbooks[3] of their figures and

---

7. "Unfortunate poverty has nothing in itself harder to bear than that it makes men ridiculous" (Juvenal, *Satires* 3.152–53).
8. The braggart soldier of Terence's comedy *Eunuchus*.
9. A Scots humanist (1506–1582) who wrote four tragedies on biblical and classical themes.
1. Alliteration.
2. Athenian statesman and orator (383–322 B.C.E.).

3. Marius Nizolius, a 16th-century Italian rhetorician and lexicographer, published a collection of phrases by Cicero (i.e., Tully). Sidney complains that contemporary writers use them too often. Cicero, when he prosecuted the traitor Catiline, employed repetition skillfully to heighten the effect of his argument, but writers in Sidney's time are not as discriminating.

phrases, as by attentive translation (as it were) devour them whole, and make them wholly theirs: for now they cast sugar and spice upon every dish that is served to the table—like those Indians, not content to wear earrings at the fit and natural place of the ears, but they will thrust jewels through their nose and lips, because they will be sure to be fine. Tully, when he was to drive out Catiline, as it were with a thunderbolt of eloquence, often used the figure of repetition, as *Vivit. Vivit? Imo in senatum venit, & c.*[4] Indeed, inflamed with a well-grounded rage, he would have his words (as it were) double out of his mouth, and so do that artificially which we see men in choler do naturally. And we, having noted the grace of those words, hale them in sometimes to a familiar epistle, when it were too too much choler to be choleric. How well store of *similiter cadences* [similar cadences] doth sound with the gravity of the pulpit, I would but invoke Demosthenes' soul to tell, who with a rare daintiness useth them. Truly they have made me think of the sophister[5] that with too much subtlety would prove two eggs three, and though he might be counted a sophister, had none for his labor. So these men bringing in such a kind of eloquence, well may they obtain an opinion of a seeming finesse, but persuade few—which should be the end of their finesse. Now for similitudes, in certain printed discourses, I think all herbarists, all stories of beasts, fowls, and fishes are rifled up,[6] that they come in multitudes to wait upon any of our conceits; which certainly is as absurd a surfeit to the ears as is possible. For the force of a similitude not being to prove anything to a contrary disputer, but only to explain to a willing hearer, when that is done, the rest is a most tedious prattling, rather overswaying the memory from the purpose whereto they were applied, than any whit informing the judgment, already either satisfied, or by similitudes not to be satisfied. For my part, I do not doubt, when Antonius and Crassus,[7] the great forefathers of Cicero in eloquence, the one (as Cicero testifieth of them) pretended not to know art, the other not to set by it, because with a plain sensibleness they might win credit of popular ears (which credit is the nearest step to persuasion, which persuasion is the chief mark of oratory), I do not doubt (I say) but that they used these knacks very sparingly; which who doth generally use, any man may see doth dance to his own music, and so be noted by the audience more careful to speak curiously than to speak truly. Undoubtedly (at least to my opinion undoubtedly), I have found in divers smally learned courtiers a more sound style than in some professors of learning; of which I can guess no other cause, but that the courtier, following that which by practice he findeth fittest to nature, therein (though he know it not) doth according to art, though not by art: where the other, using art to show art, and not to hide art (as in these cases he should do), flieth from nature, and indeed abuseth art.

But what? Methinks I deserve to be pounded for straying from poetry to oratory. But both have such an affinity in the wordish consideration, that I think this digression will make my meaning receive the fuller understanding: which is not to take upon me to teach poets how they should do, but only, finding myself sick among the rest, to show some one or two spots of the common infection grown among the most part of writers, that, acknowledging ourselves somewhat awry, we may bend to the right use both of matter and manner: whereto our language giveth us great occasion, being indeed capable of any excellent exercising of it. I know some will say it is a

---

4. "He lives. He lives? He still comes into the Senate. . . ." The sentences paraphrase the opening of Cicero's first oration against Catiline.
5. One who argues by specious reasons.
6. Sidney suggests that the figures in beast fables are all

"rifled" or taken by many writers; hence they have become trite.
7. Antonius: Marcus Antonius, consul in 99 B.C.E.; Crassus: Publius Licinius Crassus Dives Mucianus, consul in 175 B.C.E. Both men were famous orators.

mingled language.[8] And why not so much the better, taking the best of both the other? Another will say it wanteth grammar. Nay truly, it hath that praise, that it wants not grammar: for grammar it might have, but it needs it not, being so easy in itself, and so void of those cumbersome differences of cases, genders, moods, and tenses, which I think was a piece of the Tower of Babylon's curse,[9] that a man should be put to school to learn his mother-tongue. But for the uttering sweetly and properly the conceits of the mind (which is the end of speech), that hath it equally with any other tongue in the world; and is particularly happy in compositions of two or three words together, near the Greek, far beyond the Latin, which is one of the greatest beauties can be in a language.

Now of versifying there are two sorts, the one ancient, the other modern: the ancient marked the quantity of each syllable, and according to that framed his verse; the modern, observing only number (with some regard of the accent), the chief life of it standeth in that like sounding of the words, which we call rhyme. Whether of these be the more excellent, would bear many speeches: the ancient (no doubt) more fit for music, both words and time observing quantity, and more fit lively to express diverse passions, by the low or lofty sound of the well-weighed syllable; the latter likewise, with his rhyme, striketh a certain music to the ear, and, in fine, since it doth delight, though by another way, it obtains the same purpose: there being in either sweetness, and wanting in neither majesty. Truly the English, before any vulgar language I know, is fit for both sorts. For, for the ancient, the Italian is so full of vowels that it must ever be cumbered with elisions;[1] the Dutch so, of the other side, with consonants, that they cannot yield the sweet sliding, fit for a verse; the French in his whole language hath not one word that hath his accent in the last syllable saving two, called *antepenultima* [third from last]; and little more hath the Spanish, and therefore very gracelessly may they use dactyls.[2] The English is subject to none of these defects. Now for the rhyme, though we do not observe quantity, yet we observe the accent very precisely, which other languages either cannot do, or will not do so absolutely. That *caesura*, or breathing place in the midst of the verse, neither Italian nor Spanish have, the French and we never almost fail of. Lastly, even the very rhyme itself, the Italian cannot put it in the last syllable, by the French named the masculine rhyme, but still in the next to the last, which the French call the female, or the next before that, which the Italian term *sdrucciola* [three-syllable rhyme]. The example of the former is *buono: suono*, of the *sdrucciola* is *femina: semina*. The French, of the other side, hath both the male, as *bon: son*, and the female, as *plaise: taise*, but the *sdrucciola* he hath not: where the English hath all three, as *due: true, father: rather, motion: potion*[3]—with much more which might be said, but that already I find the triflingness of this discourse is much too much enlarged.

So that since the ever-praiseworthy Poesy is full of virtue-breeding delightfulness, and void of no gift that ought to be in the noble name of learning; since the blames laid against it are either false or feeble; since the cause why it is not esteemed in England is the fault of poet-apes, not poets; since, lastly, our tongue is

---

8. Sidney describes English as a "mingled" language because it is derived from Anglo-Saxon, brought over by the invading Germanic tribes during the 6th century, and Norman-French, introduced by William the Conqueror in 1066.

9. Early modern writers identified Babylon with Babel (see Genesis 10.10).

1. The suppression of a vowel at the end of a word when the next word begins with a vowel.

2. A metric foot in classical poetry, consisting of one long and two short syllables, as in the words "murmuring," "sensible."

3. *Motion* and *potion* presumably retained three syllables, as the Middle English spelling "mocioun" reveals.

most fit to honor poesy, and to be honored by poesy; I conjure you all that have had the evil luck to read this ink-wasting toy of mine, even in the name of the nine Muses, no more to scorn the sacred mysteries of poesy; no more to laugh at the name of poets, as though they were next inheritors to fools; no more to jest at the reverent title of a rhymer; but to believe, with Aristotle, that they were the ancient treasurers of the Grecians' divinity; to believe, with Bembus, that they were first bringers-in of all civility; to believe, with Scaliger, that no philosopher's precepts can sooner make you an honest man than the reading of Virgil; to believe, with Clauserus,[4] the translator of Cornutus, that it pleased the heavenly Deity, by Hesiod and Homer, under the veil of fables, to give us all knowledge, logic, rhetoric, philosophy natural and moral, and *quid non?* [what not]; to believe, with me, that there are many mysteries contained in poetry, which of purpose were written darkly, lest by profane wits it should be abused; to believe, with Landino,[5] that they are so beloved of the gods that whatsoever they write proceeds of a divine fury; lastly, to believe themselves, when they tell you they will make you immortal by their verses. Thus doing, your name shall flourish in the printers' shops; thus doing, you shall be of kin to many a poetical preface; thus doing, you shall be most fair, most rich, most wise, most all, you shall dwell upon superlatives; thus doing, though you be *libertino patre natus* [son of freed slave], you shall suddenly grow *Herculea proles* [a descendant of Hercules],

> *Si quid mea carmina possunt;*[6]

thus doing, your soul shall be placed with Dante's Beatrice, or Virgil's Anchises. But if (fie of such a but) you be born so near the dull-making cataract of Nilus[7] that you cannot hear the planet-like music of poetry; if you have so earth-creeping a mind that it cannot lift itself up to look to the sky of poetry, or rather, by a certain rustical disdain, will become such a mome as to be a Momus[8] of poetry; then, though I will not wish unto you the ass's ears of Midas, nor to be driven by a poet's verses, as Bubonax[9] was, to hang himself, nor to be rhymed to death, as is said to be done in Ireland; yet thus much curse I must send you, in the behalf of all poets, that while you live, you live in love, and never get favor for lacking skill of a sonnet; and, when you die, your memory die from the earth for want of an epitaph.

❈ "THE APOLOGY" AND ITS TIME ❈
The Art of Poetry

After the spread of Reformation doctrine on the importance of moral discipline, English readers often encountered denunciations of poetry and especially drama. The issues that Sidney took up when he defended poetry were the subject of sharp dispute. Stephen Gosson

---

4. Conrad Clauser, a 16th-century German scholar who translated the works of Lucius Annaeus Cornutus, a 1st-century Greek slave who wrote commentaries on Aristotle and Virgil.
5. Cristoforo Landino (1424–1504), an Italian humanist who wrote moral dialogues.
6. "If my songs can do anything" (*Aeneid* 9.446).
7. Cicero claimed that hearing the sound of the cataracts of the Nile River in Egypt caused deafness; the Neoplatonists thought the movement of the planets produced

heavenly music, the music of the spheres.
8. Momus personified the faultfinder in Greek literature; a mome is a blockhead. Apollo changed Midas's ears to those of an ass to signal his stupidity after Midas judged Pan's flute playing to be superior to Apollo's (Ovid, *Metamorphoses* 11.146).
9. Sidney conflates Hipponax, a Greek poet, with *Bupalus*, a sculptor. The latter had made an unflattering portrait of the former, who took revenge with deadly verses. Irish poets claimed their verses could kill man or beast.

represented the opinions of many of poetry's detractors. As he declares in *The School of Abuse*, published shortly before Sidney wrote his *Apology*, poetry provides frivolous distraction from the serious business of life and, what is worse, temptations to godlessness. But others, like Sidney, took a more optimistic view of the subject. In *The Art of English Poesy*, George Puttenham states that poets were the first lawgivers (as Sidney had) and focuses particularly on epic poetry, which, he says, give readers images of a truth beyond history as well as consistently inspiring models of action to imitate. His popular treatise contains a wealth of practical advice for aspiring writers and even today remains a useful sourcebook for information on rhetorical figures of thought and speech.

In addition to the challenge posed by moralists such as Gosson, defenders of English poetry also had to confront purely practical problems. Unlike the Romance languages—Italian, French, and Spanish—sixteenth-century English had lost almost all its feminine endings, the accented vowel sounds that made rhyming fairly easy. English was also a language in which words of one syllable were quite common, and poets had trouble creating the metrical harmonies usual in poetry written in languages rich in polysyllables. George Gascoigne's brief treatise *Certain Notes of Instruction*, which concerns the making of verse or rhyme in English, deals with these conditions directly. He warns against trying to achieve euphony or a musical quality by "rolling in pleasant words," as in the sequence "Rim, Ram, Ruff," and he insists that the "truer Englishman" uses words of one syllable. Critics could differ in what they valued, of course; in *A Defense of Rhyme*, Samuel Daniel justified rhyme as "pleasing to nature," which desires form and closures, not chaos and infinity. More important, he defended English writers against the claim that they could never match their classical precursors. He reminded readers that imputations of barbarism and ignorance are based on relative, not absolute, judgments.

Stephen Gosson

from *The School of Abuse*[1]

The Syracusans used such variety of dishes in their banquets that when they were set and their boards furnished,[2] they were many times in doubt which they should touch first or taste last. And in my opinion the world giveth every writer so large a field to walk in that before he set pen to the book, he shall find himself feasted at Syracuse, uncertain where to begin or when to end. This caused Pindarus[3] to question with his Muse whether he were better with his art to decipher the life of Nimpe Melia, or Cadmus's encounter with the dragon, or the wars of Hercules at the walls of Thebes, or Bacchus's cups, or Venus's juggling? He saw so many turnings laid open to his feet, that he knew not which way to bend his pace.

Therefore, as I cannot but commend his wisdom which in banqueting feeds most upon that that doth nourish best, so must I dispraise his method in writing which, following the course of amorous poets, dwelleth longest on those points that profit least, and like a wanton whelp,[4] leaveth the game[5] to run riot. The scarab flies over many a sweet flower and lights in a cowsherd.[6] It is the custom of the fly to leave the sound

1. Stephen Gosson was a playwright who turned against the stage, and then wrote Puritanical critiques of what he considered its immorality. His *School of Abuse* was published in 1579.
2. Tables set.
3. Pindar, the most difficult and obscure of Greek poets, famous for his odes. The story of Cadmus's encounter with the dragon is a fragment of a cycle of legends about the city of Thebes; the legendary hero Hercules delivered the city of Thebes from the burden of paying tribute to the foreign king Orchomenus; Bacchus was the Roman god of wine; and Venus's "juggling" refers to her erotic escapades.
4. Unruly puppy.
5. Hunt.
6. Cow dung.

places of the horse and suck at the botch,[7] the nature of colloquintida[8] to draw the worst humors to itself, the manner of swine to forsake the fair fields and wallow in the mire, and the whole practice of poets, either with fables to show their abuses or with plain terms to unfold their mischief, discover their shame, discredit themselves, and disperse their poison through the world. Virgil sweats in describing his gnat, Ovid bestirreth him to paint out his flea; the one shows his art in the lust of Dido, the other his cunning in the incest of Myrrha and that trumpet of bawdry, the craft of love.[9]

I must confess that poets are the whetstones of wit, notwithstanding that wit is dearly bought. Where honey and gall are mixed, it will be hard to sever the one from the other. The deceitful physician giveth sweet syrups to make his poison go down the smoother, the juggler casteth a mist to work the closer, the siren's song is the sailor's wrack,[1] the fowler's whistle the bird's death, the wholesome bait the fish's bane. The Harpies[2] have virgin faces, and the vultures, talents; Hyena speaks like a friend and devours like a foe; the calmest seas hide dangerous rocks; the wolf jets in wether's fells.[3] Many good sentences are spoken by David to shadow his knavery,[4] and written by poets as ornaments to beautify their works and set their trumpery to sale without suspect.

But if you look well to Epaeus's horse,[5] you shall find in his bowels the destruction of Troy; open the sepulchre of Semiramis,[6] whose title promiseth such wealth to the kings of Persia, you shall see nothing but dead bones; rip up the golden ball that Nero consecrated to Jupiter Capitolinus,[7] you shall [find] it stuffed with the shavings of his beard; pull off the visor that poets mask in, you shall disclose their reproach, bewray[8] their vanity, loathe their wantonness, lament their folly, and perceive their sharp sayings to be placed as pearls in dunghills, fresh pictures on rotten walls, chaste matrons' apparel on common courtesans. These are the cups of Circe,[9] that turn reasonable creatures into brute beasts; the balls of Hippomenes,[1] that hinder the course of Atalanta; and the blocks of the Devil, that are cast in our ways to cut off the race of toward wits. No marvel though Plato shut them out of his school and banished them quite from his commonwealth as effeminate writers,[2] unprofitable members, and utter enemies to virtue.

---

7. Ulcer.
8. A wild cucumber, used as an herbal medicine.
9. Dido, Queen of Carthage, with whom the legendary Trojan hero Aeneas stayed on his way to founding Rome; Virgil's *Aeneid* provides the best-known account of this episode. According to legend, Myrrha was the mother of the Greek god of vegetation, Adonis, by her father, King Cinyras, who, when he learned of his incest, changed her into a myrtle; the story is told by Ovid in his *Metamorphoses*, a poem describing erotic transformations. Gosson condemns Ovid's poem *Ars Amatoria*, or "the craft (or art) of love," as an immoral work ("bawdry" is licentiousness).
1. The mermaid's song is the sailor's shipwreck.
2. Monstrous and filthy birds whom Aeneas and his companions encounter.
3. The wolf strolls in sheep's clothing.
4. King of the ancient Israelites and poet of the psalms,

David was guilty of adulterous love for Bathsheba, whose husband he murdered.
5. The Trojan horse.
6. Mythical queen of Assyria, who is supposed to have built the city of Babylon.
7. The Emperor Nero is said to have consecrated a golden ball to Jupiter in his temple on the Capitoline Hill in Rome.
8. Expose.
9. In Homer's *Odyssey*, the goddess who transformed the companions of Odysseus into swine.
1. The legendary suitor of Atalanta, who refused to marry anyone she could defeat in a footrace. Hippomenes won the race by dropping golden apples on the racetrack. Atalanta could not resist stopping to pick them up, and her delay allowed Hippomenes victory.
2. Plato exiles poets from his ideal republic (see *The Republic* 3.398a).

George Puttenham

from *The Art of English Poesie*[1]

How Poets were the first Philosophers, the first Astronomers and Historiographers, and Orators and Musicians of the world.[2]

Utterance also and language is given by nature to man for persuasion of others and aid of themselves, I mean the first ability to speak. For speech itself is artificial and made by man, and the more pleasing it is, the more it prevaileth to such purpose as it is intended for. But speech by meter is a kind of utterance more cleanly couched and more delicate to the ear than prose is, because it is more current and slipper upon the tongue and withal tunable and melodious as a kind of music and therefore may be termed a musical speech or utterance which cannot but please the hearer very well. Another cause is for that[3] is briefer and more compendious and easier to bear away and be retained in memory than that which is contained in multitude of words and full of tedious ambage and long periods.[4] It is beside a manner of utterance more eloquent and rhetorical than the ordinary proof which we use in our daily talk, because it is decked and set out with all manner of fresh colors and figures, which maketh that it sooner inveigleth[5] the judgment of man and carryeth his opinion this way and that, whither soever the heart by impression of the ear shall be most affectionately bent and directed. The utterance in prose is not of so great efficacy because not only it is daily used, and by that occasion the care is over-glutted with it, but is also not so voluble and slipper on the tongue, being wide and loose, and nothing numerous nor contrived into measures and founded with so gallant and harmonical accents, nor in fine allowed that figurative conveyance[6] nor so great license in choice of words and phrases as meter is. So as the poets were also from the beginning the best persuaders and their eloquence the first rhetoric of the world, even so it became[7] that the high mysteries of the gods should be revealed and taught by a manner of utterance and language of extraordinary phrase and brief and compendious and above all others sweet and civil as the metrical is. The same also was meetest to register the lives and noble gifts of princes, and of the great monarchs of the world and all other memorable accidents of time, so as the poet was also the first historiographer. Then forasmuch as they were the first observers of all natural causes and effects in the things generable and corruptable, and from thence mounted up to search after the celestial courses and influences and yet penetrated further to know the divine essences and substances separate,[8] as is said before, they were the first astronomers and philosophists and metaphysics. Finally, because they did altogether endeavor themselves to reduce[9] the life of man to a certain method of good manners, and made

---

1. George Puttenham has always been assumed to be the author of *The Art of English Poesie*, a critical treatise that appeared in 1589. Dividing his work into three books (*Of Poets and Poesie*, *Of Proportion*, and *Of Ornament*), Puttenham discusses the works of English poets, poetic forms and genres, and figures of speech and thought respectively. The work as a whole is a compendium of contemporary ideas and practices illustrating the proper way to compose and appreciate poetry.
2. In his *Apology for Poetry*, Sidney also claims that poets were the first human beings to express feeling, thought, and a sense of the higher purposes of life.
3. I.e., poetry.
4. Dull indirection and long sentences.
5. Appeals to.
6. Expression.
7. Was appropriate.
8. I.e., to know the divine essences and the particular objects present in the heavens.
9. Abstract.

the first differences between virtue and vice, and then tempered all these knowledges and skills with the exercise of a delectable music by melodious instruments, which withall served them to delight their hearers and to call the people together by admiration to a plausible and virtuous conversation, therefore were they the first philosophers ethic[1] and the first artificial musicians of the world. Such was Linus, Orpheus, Amphion, and Musaeus,[2] the most ancient poets and philosophers, of whom there is left any memory by the profane writers. King David also and Solomon his son and many other of the holy prophets wrote in meters and used to sing them to the harp,[3] although to many of us ignorant of the Hebrew language and phrase and not observing it, the same seem but a prose. It cannot be therefore that any scorn or indignity should justly be offered to so noble, profitable, ancient, and divine a science as Poesie is. * * *

Of historical poesie,[4] by which the famous acts of Princes and the virtuous and worthy lives of our forefathers were reported.

There is nothing in man of all the potential parts of his mind (reason and will excepted) more noble or more necessary to the active life than memory. Because it maketh[5] most to a sound judgment and perfect worldly wisdom, examining and comparing the times past with the present and by them both considering the time to come, [it] concludeth with a steadfast resolution what is the best course to be taken in all his actions and advices in this world. It came upon this reason: experience [is] to be so highly commended in all consultations of importance and preferred before any learning or science, and yet experience is no more than a mass of memories assembled, that is, such trials as man hath made in time before. Right so, no kind of argument in all the oratory craft doth better persuade and more universally satisfy than example, which is but the representation of old memories and like successes [that have] happened in times past. For these regards, the poesie historical is of all other, next[6] the divine, most honorable and worthy, as well for the common benefit as for the special comfort every man receiveth by it. No one thing in the world with more delectation [is] reviving our spirits than to behold, as it were in a glass, the lively image of our dear forefathers, their noble and virtuous manner of life, with other things authentic, which because we are not able otherwise to attain to the knowledge of by any of our fences,[7] we apprehend them by memory, whereas the present time and things so swiftly pass away [so] as they give us no leisure almost to look into them and much less to know and consider of them thoroughly. The things future, being also events very uncertain, and such as cannot possibly be known because they be not yet, cannot be used for example nor for delight otherwise than by hope, though many promise the contrary, by vain and deceitful arts taking upon them to reveal the truth of accidents to come, which if it were so as they surmise, are yet but sciences merely conjectural and not of any benefit to man or to the commonwealth where they be used or professed. Therefore the good and exemplary things and actions of the former ages were reserved only to the historical reports of wise and grave

---

1. I.e., philosophers who consider ethics.
2. Puttenham names legendary figures who were thought to be among the first poets: Linus, a poet and the teacher of Hercules, who later killed him with his own lyre; Orpheus, commonly considered the first poet, whose music charmed even the animals; Amphion, the poet whose music moved stones to build Thebes; and Musaeus, said to have been a pupil of Orpheus.

3. Scripture provides accounts of King David, supposed to be the author of the psalms, and Solomon, to whom the Song of Songs is attributed.
4. Epic poetry.
5. Benefits.
6. After.
7. Ways of arguing.

men; those of the present time [were] left to the fruition and judgment of our senses; the future as hazards and uncertain events [were] utterly neglected and laid aside for magicians and mockers to get their livings by, such manner of men as by negligence of magistrates and remisses of laws every country breedeth great store of. These historical men nevertheless used not the matter so precisely to wish that all they wrote should be accounted true,[8] for that was not needful nor expedient to the purpose, namely to be used either for example or for the pleasure, considering that many times it is seen a feigned matter or altogether fabulous, besides that it maketh more mirth than any other, works no less good conclusions for example than the most true and veritable, but oftentimes more, because the poet hath the handling of them[9] to fashion at his pleasure, but not so of the other[1] which must go according to their verity and none otherwise without the writers' great blame. Again as ye know, more and more excellent examples may be feigned in one day by a good wit than many ages through man's frailty are able to put in ure,[2] which made the learned and witty men of those times to devise many historical matters of no verity at all, but with purpose to do good and no hurt, as using them for a manner of discipline and precedent of commendable life. Such was the commonwealth of Plato, and Sir Thomas More's *Utopia*, resting all in device,[3] but never [to be] put in execution and easier wished than to be performed. And you shall perceive that histories were of three sorts, wholly true and wholly false, and a third holding part of either, but for honest recreation and good example they were all of them.[4]

George Gascoigne

from *Certain Notes of Instruction*[1]

The first and most necessary point that ever I found meet to be considered in making of a delectable poem is this, to ground it upon some fine invention.[2] For it is not enough to roll in pleasant words, nor yet to thunder in Rim, Ram, Ruff, by letter (quoth my master Chaucer) nor yet to abound in apt vocables or epithets, unless the invention have in it also *aliquid salis* [something salty]. By this *aliquid salis* I mean some good and fine device, showing the quick capacity of a writer, and where I say some good and fine invention, I mean that I would have it both fine and good. For many inventions are so superfine that they are *Vix* [scarcely] good. And again many inventions are good, and yet not finely handled. And for a general forewarning: what theme soever you do take in hand, if you do handle it but *tanquam in oratione perpetua* [as a perpetual sermon], and never study for some depth of device in your invention and some figures also in the handling thereof, it will appear to the skillful reader but a tale of a tub. To deliver unto you general examples it were almost impossible, since the occasions of inventions are (as it were) infinite. Nevertheless, take in worth mine opinion and perceive my further meaning in these few points. If I should undertake to

---

8. Puttenham identifies epic poets as historical, in that they represent the past, but not as historians, in that they do not represent it entirely truthfully.

9. His poetic subjects.

1. I.e., the historian who must try to discover the factual truth of the past.

2. Use.

3. Conception.

4. I.e., they were all equally good for recreation and good moral example.

1. George Gascoigne's *Certain Notes* was published in 1575 as part of his second work, containing both poetry and prose, entitled *The Posies of George Gascoigne*. Gascoigne's full listing appears on page 673.

2. In early modern treatises on the art of writing poetry, "invention" meant the discovery and development of "matter," the topics and ideas that the poet will then represent. After "invention," he draws on a knowledge of rhetoric, the techniques by which "matter" is made interesting and memorable.

write in praise of a gentlewoman, I would neither praise her crystal eye nor her cherry lip, etc., for these things are *trita et obvia* [trite and obvious]. But I would either find some supernatural cause whereby my pen might walk in superlative degree, or else I would undertake to answer for any imperfection that she hath, and thereupon raise the praise of her commendation.[3] Likewise, if I should disclose my pretense in[4] love, I would either make a strange discourse of some intolerable passion, or find occasion to plead by the example of some history, or discover[5] my disquiet in shadows *per allegoriam* [through allegory], or use the covertest mean that I could to avoid the uncomely customs of common writers. Thus much I adventure to deliver unto you (my friend) upon [the] rule of invention, which of all other rules is most to be marked and hardest to be prescribed in certain and infallible rules. Nevertheless, to conclude therein, I would have you stand most upon the excellency of your invention and stick[6] not to study deeply for some fine device. For that being found, pleasant words will follow well enough and fast enough.

Your invention being once devised, take heed that neither pleasure of rhyme nor variety of device do carry you from it. For as to use obscure and dark phrases in a pleasant[7] sonnet is nothing delectable, so to intermingle merry jests in a serious matter is an indecorum.[8]

I will next advise you that you hold the just measure wherewith you begin your verse. I will not deny but this may seem a preposterous order, but because I covet rather to satisfy you particularly than to undertake a general tradition, I will not so much stand upon the manner as the matter of my precepts. I say then, remember to hold the same measure wherewith you begin, whether it be in a verse of six syllables, eight, ten, twelve, etc., and though this precept might seem ridiculous unto you, since every young scholar can conceive that he ought to continue in the same measure wherewith he beginneth, yet do I see and read many men's poems nowadays which beginning with the measure of twelve in the first line and fourteen in the second (which is the common kind of verse), they will yet (by that time they have passed over a few verses) fall into fourteen and fourteen and *sic de similibus* [so on], the which is either forgetfulness or carelessness. * * *

I think it not amiss to forewarn you that you thrust as few words of many syllables into your verse as may be, and hereunto I might allege many reasons. First, the most ancient English words are of one syllable, so that the more monosyllables that you use, the truer Englishman you shall seem, and the less you shall smell of the inkhorn.[9] Also, words of many syllables do cloy a verse and make it unpleasant, whereas words of one syllable will more easily fall to be short or long as occasion requireth, or will be adapted to become circumflex[1] or of an indifferent[2] sound.

I would exhort you also to beware of rhyme without reason. My meaning is hereby that your rhyme lead you not from your first invention, for many writers when they have laid the platform of their invention are yet drawn sometimes (by rhyme) to forget it or at least to alter it, as when they cannot readily find out a word which may rhyme to the first (and yet continue their determinate invention) they do then either botch it up with a word that will rhyme (how small reason soever it carry with it) or else they alter their first word and so perhaps decline or trouble their former

3. My compliment to her.
4. Profession of.
5. Reveal.
6. Hesitate.
7. Lighthearted.

8. Improper act.
9. Inkpot.
1. Accentuated.
2. Soft.

invention. But do you always hold your first determined invention, and do rather search the bottom of your brains for apt words than change good reason for rumbling rhyme. * * *

Also as much as may be, eschew strange words or *obsoleta et inusitata* [obsolete and rare], unless the theme do give just occasion. Marry, in some places a strange word doth draw attentive reading, but yet I would have you therein to use discretion.

And as much as you may, frame your style to perspicuity and to be sensible, for the haughty obscure verse doth not much delight and the verse that is too easy is like a tale of a rusted[3] horse. But let your poem be such as may both delight and draw attentive reading and therewithal may deliver such matter as be worth the marking.

Samuel Daniel
from *A Defense of Rhyme*[1]

Such affliction doth laborsome curiosity[2] still lay upon our best delights (which ever must be made strange and variable) as if art were ordained to afflict nature and that we could not go but in fetters. Every science, every profession, must be so wrapped up in unnecessary intrications, as if it were not to fashion but to confound the understanding, which makes me much to distrust man and fear that our presumption goes beyond our ability and our curiosity is more than our judgment, laboring ever to seem to be more than we are or laying greater burdens upon our minds than they are well able to bear, because we would not appear like other men.

And indeed I have wished there were not that multiplicity of rhymes as is used by many in sonnets, which yet we see in some so happily to succeed and hath been so far from hindering their inventions as it hath begot conceit[3] beyond expectation and comparable to the best inventions of the world. For sure in an eminent spirit whom nature hath fitted for that mystery, rhyme is no impediment to his conceit, but rather gives him wings to mount and carries him, not out of his course, but as it were beyond his power to a far happier flight. All excellencies being sold us at the hard price of labor, it follows, where we bestow most thereof, we buy the best success, and rhyme being far more laborious than loose measures (whatsoever is objected), must needs, meeting with wit and industry, breed greater and worthier effects in our language. So that if our labors have wrought out a manumission[4] from bondage and that we go at liberty, notwithstanding these ties, we are no longer the slaves of rhyme but we make it a most excellent instrument to serve us. Nor is this certain limit observed in sonnets any tyrannical bounding of the conceit,[5] but rather a reducing it in *girum* [in bounds], and a just form, neither too long for the shortest project nor too short for the longest, being but only employed for a present passion. For the body of our imagination, being as an unformed chaos without fashion, without day, if by the divine power of the spirit it be wrought into an orb of order and form, is it not more pleasing to nature that desires a certainty and comports not with that which is infinite, to have these closes[6]

---

3. Restless.
1. Samuel Daniel, a poet and playwright, published a variety of works throughout his long career, notably: a collection of sonnets, *Delia* (1592); two tragedies, *Cleopatra* (1594) and *Philotas* (1604); an epic poem of the Wars of the Roses, *Civil Wars* (1595, 1609); and several masques. His essay on poetry, *A Defense of Rhyme*, was published in 1603.

2. Daniel's criticism of "laborsome curiosity" is comparable to Gascoigne's criticism of an "inkhorn" style: both poets reject pedantry.
3. Created conceptions.
4. Release.
5. I.e., the conception informing the poem.
6. Endings, as in rhyme.

rather than not to know where to end or how far to go, especially seeing our passions are often without measure. And we find in the best of the Latins many times either not concluding or else otherwise in the end than they began. Besides, is it not most delightful to see much excellently ordered in a small room, or little gallantly disposed and made to fill up a space of like capacity, in such sort that the one would not appear so beautiful in a larger circuit nor the other do well in a less, which often we find to be so, according to the powers of nature, in the workman. And these limited proportions and rests of stanzas, consisting of six, seven, or eight lines, are of that happiness, both for the disposition of the matter, the apt planting the sentence where it may best stand to hit, the certain close of delight with the full body of a just period well-carried,[7] is such as neither the Greeks or Latins ever attained unto. For their boundless running on often so confounds the reader that having once lost himself must either give off unsatisfied or certainly cast back to retrieve the escaped sense and to find way again into his matter.

Methinks we should not so soon yield our consents captive to the authority of antiquity unless we saw more reason. All our understandings are not to be built by the square of Greece and Italy. We are the children of nature as well as they, we are not so placed out of the way of judgment but that the same sun of discretion shineth upon us, we have our portion of the same virtues as well as of the same vices. * * *

It is not the observing of trochaics nor their iambics[8] that will make our writings aught the wiser. All their poesie, all their philosophy is nothing unless we bring the discerning light of conceit[9] with us to apply it to use. It is not books, but only that great book of the world and the all-overspreading grace of heaven that makes men truly judicial.[1] Nor can it be but a touch of arrogant ignorance to hold this or that nation barbarous, these or those times gross, considering how this manifold creature man, wheresoever he stand in the world, hath always some disposition of worth, entertains the order of society, affects that which is most in use, and is eminent in some one thing or other that fits his humor and the times. The Grecians held all other nations barbarous but themselves, yet Pyrrhus when he saw the well-ordered marching of the Romans, which made them see their presumptuous error, could say it was no barbarous manner of preceding. The Goths, Vandals, and Longobards,[2] whose coming down like an innundation overwhelmed, as they say, all the glory of learning in Europe, have yet left us still their laws and customs as the originals of most of the provincial constitutions of Christendom, which well-considered with their other course of government may serve to clear them from this imputation of ignorance. And though the vanquished never yet spoke well of the conqueror,[3] yet even through the unsound coverings of malediction appear those monuments of truth as argue well their worth and proves them not without judgment, though without Greek and Latin.

END OF "THE APOLOGY" AND ITS TIME

---

7. A well-constructed sentence.
8. Meters used in classical poetry.
9. Imagination.
1. Discriminating.
2. Lombards.
3. Daniel refers to the culture of conquered peoples without specifying which conquests or peoples he has in mind. But he acknowledges that even in the curses of these peoples, as they complain about their conquerors, there are "monuments of truth" that reveal worth and judgment.

Isabella Whitney
fl. 1567–1573

Little is known about the life of Isabella Whitney. Biographers agree that she was the sister of Geoffrey Whitney, the author of the first emblem book in England, and that, like him, she was born in Cheshire. The rest is to be deduced from her poetry, which points to an author with little formal education, a sharp eye for the details of urban life, and some knowledge of classical mythology. The modesty of Whitney's literary background sets her off from such later and accomplished poets as Mary Herbert and Aemilia Lanyer, and her poems on the challenges of love, friendship, and survival in a large city distinguish her from women who wrote devotional verse. Her poems follow the form and conventions of broadside ballads, a feature that may have made them popular with readers who were drawn to stories that gave advice on affairs of the heart and matters of the purse. Of "the middling sort," Whitney probably came to London for employment and diversion, but she seems to have had difficulty supporting herself. In any case, after publishing two collections of verse, *The Copy of a Letter* (c. 1567) and *A Sweet Nosegay* (1573), she left the city, having lived out the dreams as well as the disappointments of many English villagers who went to London to find work. Poems like *The Manner of Her Will* provide a detailed sketch of the delights and horrors of urban life as it was experienced by a talented woman of limited means.

The Admonition by the Author
to All Young Gentlewomen, and to All Other Maids Being in Love

<blockquote>

Ye virgins that from Cupid's tents
    do bear away the foil,[1]
Whose hearts as yet with raging love
    most painfully do boil,

5   To you I speak, for you be they
    that good advice do lack;
Oh, if I could good counsel give,
    my tongue should not be slack.

But such as I can give, I will,
10   here in few words express,
Which if you do observe, it will
    some of your care redress.

Beware of fair and painted talk,
    beware of flattering tongues;
15   The mermaids do pretend no good
    for all their pleasant songs.

Some use the tears of crocodiles
    contrary to their heart,

</blockquote>

---

1. The reference is obscure. Cupid's weapons were traditionally a bow and arrows; Whitney describes him rather as a fencer who wounds his victims with a foil or sword. By bearing his foil away, Whitney's virgins appear to have experienced unrequited love.

And if they cannot always weep,
    they wet their cheeks by art.

20

Ovid, within his art of love,[2]
    doth teach them this same knack,
To wet their hand and touch their eyes,
    so oft as tears they lack.

25   Why have ye such deceit in store?
    have you such crafty wile?
Less craft than this, God knows, would soon
    us simple souls beguile.

And will ye not leave off? But still
30   delude us in this wise?
Since it is so, we trust we shall
    take heed to feigned lies.

Trust not a man at the first sight,
    but try him well before;
35   I wish all maids within their breasts
    to keep this thing in store:

For trial shall declare his truth,
    and show what he doth think,
Whether he be a lover true,
40   or do intend to shrink.

If Scylla[3] had not trust too much
    before that she did try,
She could not have been clean forsake°   *forsaken*
    when she for help did cry.

45   Or if she had had good advice,
    Nisus had lived long;
How durst she trust a stranger, and
    do her dear father wrong?

King Nisus had a hair by fate
50   which hair while he did keep,
He never should be overcome
    neither on land nor deep.

The stranger that the daughter loved
    did war against the King,

---

2. The *Ars Amatoria*, a facetious treatise in which the poet advises men how to court and make love to women. Here, Whitney implies that her readers either imitate or avoid the examples of legendary women whose stories she tells.

3. Daughter of the mythical Nisus, king of Megara, Scylla trusted the love of Minos, king of Crete, who was besieging her father's city. For love of Minos (whom Whitney refers to as "the stranger"), Scylla betrayed her father by stealing a lock of his hair, a guarantee that Megara would remain free. According to Virgil, Minos, having taken Megara, captured Scylla, tied her to his ship, and dragged her through the sea. She was eventually transformed into a ciris, or sea-bird.

55 And always sought how that he might
    them in subjection bring.

This Scylla stole away the hair
    for to obtain her will,
And gave it to the stranger that
60   did straight her father kill.

Then she, who thought herself most sure
    to have her whole desire,
Was clean reject,° and left behind   *rejected*
    when he did home retire.

65 Or if such falsehood had been once
    unto Oenone[4] known,
About the fields of Ida wood
    Paris had walked alone.

Or if Demophoon's deceit
70   to Phyllis[5] had been told,
She had not been transformed so,
    as poets tell of old.

Hero did try Leander's[6] truth
    before that she did trust,
75 Therefore she found him unto her
    both constant, true, and just.

For always did he swim the sea
    when stars in sky did glide,
Till he was drowned by the way
80   near hand unto the side.

She scratched her face, she tore her hair
    (it grieveth me to tell)
When she did know the end of him,
    that she did love so well.

85 But like Leander there be few,
    therefore in time take heed;
And always try before ye trust,
    so shall you better speed.

The little fish that careless is
90   within the water clear,
How glad is he, when he doth see
    a bait for to appear.

He thinks his hap° right good to be,   *luck*
    that he the same could spy,

---

4. A nymph of Mount Ida, who was abandoned by Paris, son of Priam, king of Troy.
5. A mythical princess of Thrace and loved by the Greek warrior Demophon (or Demophoon); believing that he would not return to her after the Trojan War, she hanged herself.
6. Hero's lover, Leander, drowned while swimming across the Hellespont to be with her, whereupon she, too, threw herself into the sea.

95   And so the simple fool doth trust
      too much before he try.

O little fish what hap hadst thou,
      to have such spiteful fate,
To come into one's cruel hands
100   out of so happy state?

Thou didst suspect no harm, when thou
      upon the bait didst look;
O that thou hadst had Linceus's[7] eyes
      for to have seen the hook.

105   Then hadst thou with thy pretty mates
      been playing in the streams,
Whereas Sir Phoebus° daily doth   *the sun god Apollo*
      show forth his golden beams.

But since thy fortune is so ill
110   to end thy life on shore,
Of this thy most unhappy end
      I mind to speak no more.

But of thy fellow's chance that late
      such pretty shift did make,
115   That he from fisher's hook did sprint
      before he could him take.

And now he pries on every bait,
      suspecting still that prick
(For to lie hid in every thing)
120   wherewith the fishers strick.°   *strike*

And since the fish that reason lacks
      once warned doth beware,
Why should not we take heed to that
      that turneth us to care?

125   And I who was deceived late
      by one's unfaithful tears,
Trust now for to beware, if that
      I live this hundred years.

Finis.

A Careful Complaint by the Unfortunate Author

Good Dido[1] stint thy tears,
      and sorrows all resign
To me that born was to augment
      misfortune's luckless line.

---

7. A sharp-eyed mythical warrior of Greece.   Aeneas on his way from Troy to Italy.
1. Queen of Carthage, seduced and then abandoned by

5 Or using still the same,
  good Dido do thy best,
In helping to bewail the hap
  that furthereth mine unrest.
For though thy Troyan mate,
10 that Lord Aeneas hight,
Requiting all thy steadfast love,
  from Carthage took his flight,
And foully broke his oath,
  and promise made before
15 Whose falsehood finished thy delight
  before thy hairs were hoar.
Yet greater cause of grief
  compels me to complain,
For Fortune fell° converted hath   *evil*
20 my health to heaps of pain.
And that she² swears my death,
  too plain it is (alas),
Whose end let malice still attempt
  to bring the same to pass.
25 O Dido, thou hadst lived
  a happy woman still,
If fickle fancy had not thralled°   *enslaved*
  thy wits to reckless will.
For as the man by whom
30 thy deadly dolors bred,
Without regard of plighted troth
  from Carthage city fled,
So might thy cares in time
  be banished out of thought,
35 His absence might well salve the sore
  that erst° his presence wrought.   *first*
For fire no longer burns
  than faggots° feed the flame,   *except when sticks*
The want of things that breed annoy
40 may soon redress the same.³
But I, unhappy most,
  and gripped with endless griefs,
Despair (alas) amid my hope,
  and hope without relief.
45 And as the swelt'ring heat
  consumes the war away,
So do the heaps of deadly harms
  still threaten my decay.
O death delay not long

---

2. I.e., Fortune, whose end or purpose, Whitney's death, malice will bring to pass.

3. I.e., "want," which breeds annoyance, will also end annoyance, as it will eventually result in death.

50   thy duty to declare.
     Ye Sisters three[4] dispatch my days
     and finish all my care.

The Manner of Her Will

The Author (though loath to leave the City) upon her friend's procurement is constrained to depart, wherefore she feigneth as she would die and maketh her will and testament, as followeth, with large legacies of such goods and riches which she most abundantly hath left behind her, and thereof maketh London sole executor to see her legacies performed.

    A communication which the Author had to London, before she made her will.

     The time is come I must depart
        from thee, ah famous city.
     I never yet to rue my smart,
        did find that thou hadst pity,
5   Wherefore small cause there is that I
        should grieve from thee to go.
     But many women foolishly,
        like me, and other mo'e,
     Do such a fixed fancy set,
10   on those which least deserve,
     That long it is ere° wit we get,   *before*
        away from them to swerve.°   *turn*
     But time with pity oft will tell
        to those that will her try,
15   Whether it best be more to mell,°   *associate with*
        or utterly defy.
     And now hath time me put in mind,
        of thy great cruelness,
     That never once a help would find,
20   to ease me in distress.
     Thou never yet wouldst credit give
        to board me for a year,
     Nor with apparel me relieve
        except thou paid were.
25   No, no, thou never didst me good,
        nor ever wilt, I know;
     Yet I am in no angry mood
        but will, or ere I go,
     In perfect love and charity,
30   my testament here write,
     And leave to thee such treasury
        as I in it recite.
     Now stand aside and give me leave
        to write my latest will,

---

4. I.e., the three Fates, who determine the length of life and the time of death.

35 And see that none you do deceive
of that I leave them till.[1]

The manner of her will, and what she left to London and to all those in it at her departing.

I whole in body and in mind,
 but very weak in purse,
Do make and write my testament
 for fear it will be worse.
5 And first I wholly do commend
 my soul and body eke,°   *also*
To God the Father and the Son
 so long as I can speak.
And after speech, my soul to him
10 and body to the grave,
Till time that all shall rise again
 their judgment for to have.
And then I hope they both shall meet
 to dwell for aye° in joy,   *ever*
15 Whereas I trust to see my friends
 released from all annoy.
Thus have you heard touching my soul
 and body what I mean,
I trust you all will witness bear,
20 I have a steadfast brain.
And now let me dispose such things
 as I shall leave behind,
That those which shall receive the same
 may know my willing mind.
25 I first of all to London leave
 because I there was bred,
Brave buildings rare, of churches store,
 and Paul's to the head.[2]
Between the same, fair streets there be
30 and people goodly store;
Because their keeping craveth° cost,   *requires*
 I yet will leave him[3] more.
First for their food, I butchers leave,
 that every day shall kill;
35 By Thames you shall have brewers store,
 and bakers at your will.
And such as orders do observe,°   *clergymen*
 and eat fish thrice a week,
I leave two streets, full fraught therewith,
40 they need not far to seek.

1. I.e., you must not deceive my inheritors by taking what
I leave them until I leave them.
2. St. Paul's Cathedral, in the heart of the City of London; Whitney describes it as the foremost or "head" of

London's public buildings.
3. St. Paul's, to whose district Whitney will leave "more"
than the "goodly store" already there.

Watling Street, and Canwick Street,
 I full of woolen leave,
And linen store in Friday Street,
 if they me not deceive.
45 And those which are of calling such,
 that costlier they require,
I mercers leave, with silk so rich,
 as any would desire.
In cheap of them, they store shall find,
50 and likewise in that street,[4]
I goldsmiths leave, with jewels such
 as are for ladies meet.
And plate to furnish cupboards with,
 full brave there shall you find,
55 With purl° of silver and of gold.   *cord*
 to satisfy your mind.
With hoods, bongraces,° hats or caps,   *sunshades*
 such store are in that street,
As if on one side you should miss,
60 the other serves you feat.
For nets of every kind of sort,
 I leave within the pawn,
French ruffs, high purls,° gorgets° and sleeves   *ruffs / collars*
 of any kind of lawn.°   *thin cloth*
65 For purse or knives, for comb or glass,
 or any needful knack,
I by the stocks have left a boy
 will ask you what you lack.
I hose do leave in Birchin Lane,
70 of any kind of size,
For women stitched, for men both trunks
 and those of Gascoigne guise,
Boots, shoes, or pantables° good store,   *slippers*
 Saint Martin's hath for you.
75 In Cornwall, there I leave you beds,
 and all that 'longs° thereto.   *belongs*
For women shall you tailors have,
 by Bow, the chiefest dwell,
In every lane you some shall find
80 can do indifferent well.
And for the men, few streets or lanes,
 but bodymakers° be,   *suitmakers*
And such as make the sweeping cloaks
 with guards° beneath the knee.   *ornamental borders*
85 Artillery at Temple Bar,
 and dagges° at Tower Hill,   *pistols*

4. I.e., they shall also find much cheap cloth in that street.

Swords and bucklers of the best
   are nigh the Fleet until.[5]
Now when thy folk are fed and clad
90   with such as I have named,
For dainty mouths, and stomachs weak
   some junkets° must be framed.   *milk puddings*
Wherefore I 'pothecaries° leave   *apothecaries*
   with banquets in their shop,
95   Physicians also for the sick,
   diseases for to stop.
Some roisters° still must bide in thee,   *thugs*
   and such as cut it out,
That with the guiltless quarrel will
100   to let their blood about.[6]
For them I cunning surgeons leave
   some plasters° to apply,   *bandages*
That ruffians may not still be hanged
   nor quiet persons die.
105   For salt, oatmeal, candles, soap,
   or what you else do want,
In many places shops are full,
   I left you nothing scant.
If they that keep what you I leave,
110   ask money, when they sell it,
At mint,° there is such store, it is   *the mint*
   impossible to tell it.
At stillyard° store of wines there be,   *the distillery*
   your dulled minds to glad,
115   And handsome men, that must not wed
   except they leave their trade.[7]
They oft shall seek for proper girls,
   and some perhaps shall find,
That need compels, or lucre lures
120   to satisfy their mind.
And near the same, I houses leave
   for people to repair,
To bathe themselves, so to prevent
   infection of the air.
125   On Saturdays I wish that those,
   which all the week do drug,°   *drudge*
Shall thither trudge, to trim them up
   on Sundays to look smug.
If any other thing be lacked
130   in thee, I wish them look,
For there it is, I little brought

---

5. I.e., near the Temple Bar up to Fleet Street.
6. I.e., those who assault men who have done them no
harm must remain in London.

7. I.e., because they deal in liquor, they are not fit husbands.

but nothing from thee took.
Now for the people in thee left,
    I have done as I may,
135   And that the poor, when I am gone,
    have cause for me to pray.
I will to prisons portions leave,
    what though but very small,
Yet that they may remember me,
140   occasion be it shall,
And first the counter they shall have,
    lest they should go to wrack,°   *ruin*
Some coggers,° and some honest men,   *crooks*
    that sergeants draw aback.[8]
145   And such as friends will not them bail,
    whose coin is very thin,
For them I leave a certain hole
    and little ease within.
The Newgate once a month shall have
150   a sessions° for his share,   *court trials*
Lest being heaped, infection might
    procure a further care.[9]
And at those sessions some shall 'scape
    with burning near the thumb,
155   And afterward to beg their fees,
    till they have got the sum.
And such whose deeds deserveth death,
    and twelve° have found the same,   *a jury*
They shall be drawn up Holborn Hill
160   to come to further shame.
Well, yet to such I leave a nag
    shall soon their sorrows cease,
For he shall either break their necks
    or gallop from the preace.°   *crowd*
165   The Fleet, not in their circuit is,[1]
    yet if I give him nought,
It might procure his curse, ere I
    unto the ground be brought.
Wherefore I leave some papist old
170   to underprop his roof,
And to the poor within the same
    a box for their behoof.°   *benefit*

8. Whitney seems to wish to endow prisons with a "counter," a device to keep track of accounts, lest the prisoners be ruined by tradesmen, both crooks and honest men, who sell goods to prisoners and who are also restrained in their commerce by sergeants.

9. I.e., Newgate prison shall hold trials once a month to avoid overcrowding and disease. Some prisoners, marked by a burn on the thumb, will be freed to beg for bail money.

1. In the 16th century the Fleet was a prison for people convicted of crimes by the Star Chamber, a court dealing with affairs of conscience, such as treason and differences of faith; hence it is where one would find a Catholic, a papist. It was not a prison for people convicted by the common law; hence it is not in the same "circuit" as Newgate.

What makes you standers-by to smile,
　　and laugh so in your sleeve,
175　I think it is, because that I
　　　to Ludgate° nothing give.   *a debtors' prison*
I am not now in case to lie,
　　here is no place of jest;
I did reserve that for myself,
180　　if I my health possessed.
And ever came in credit so
　　a debtor for to be,
When days of payment did approach,
　　I thither meant to flee.
185　To shroud myself amongst the rest
　　that choose to die in debt;
Rather than any creditor
　　should money from them get.
Yet 'cause° I feel myself so weak   *because*
190　　that none me credit° dare,   *give me credit*
I here revoke, and do it leave
　　some bankrupts to his° share.   *their*
To all the bookbinders by Paul's°   *St. Paul's Cathedral*
　　because I like their art,
195　They every week shall money have
　　when they from books depart.°   *sell their books*
Amongst them all, my printer must
　　have somewhat to his share;
I will my friends these books to buy
200　　of him, with other ware.
For maidens poor, I widowers rich
　　do leave, that oft shall dote,
And by that means shall marry them,
　　to set the girls afloat.
205　And wealthy widows will I leave
　　to help young gentlemen,
Which when you° have, in any case,   *i.e., gentlemen*
　　be courteous to them° then.   *i.e., widows*
And see their plate and jewels eke
210　　may not be marred with rust,
Nor let their bags too long be full,
　　for fear that they do burst.
To every gate under the walls
　　that compass thee about,
215　I fruit wives leave to entertain
　　such as come in and out.
To Smithfield° I must something leave,   *the meat market*
　　my parents there did dwell;
So careless for to be of it,
220　　none would account it well.
Wherefore it thrice a week shall have,

   of horse and neat° good store,   *beef*
  And in his spittle,[2] blind and lame,
   to dwell for evermore.
225 And Bedlam[3] must not be forgot,
   for that was oft my walk,
  I people there too many leave,
   that out of tune do talk.
  At Bridewell[4] there shall beadles be,
230 and matrons that shall still
  See chalk well-chopped, and spinning plied,
   and turning of the mill.
  For such as cannot quiet be,
   but strive for house or land,
235 At th'Inns of Court,[5] I lawyers leave
   to take their cause in hand.
  And also leave I at each Inn,
   of Court or Chancery,
  Of gentlemen, a youthful root,
240 full of activity,
  For whom I store of books have left
   at each bookbinder's stall,
  And part of all that London hath
   to furnish them withal.°   *with*
245 And when they are with study cloyed,°   *tired*
   to recreate their mind,
  Of tennis courts, of dancing schools,
   and fence they store shall find.
  And every Sunday at the least,
250 I leave to make them sport,
  In divers places players that
   of wonder shall report.
  Now London have I (for thy sake)
   within thee and without,
255 As comes into my memory,
   dispersed round about
  Such needful things, as they should have
   here left now unto thee
  When I am gone, with conscience
260 let them dispersed be.
  And though I nothing named have
   to bury me withal,
  Consider that above the ground
   annoyance be I shall.°   *I shall be*
265 And let me have a shrouding sheet

---

2. In the hospital at Smithfield, the blind and lame are always to dwell or find refuge.
3. Asylum for the insane.
4. A prison for persons convicted for minor offenses; it also served as a workhouse for the unemployed.
5. The offices of those practicing common law; also the schools teaching common law.

to cover me from shame,
    And in oblivion bury me
      and never more me name.
Ringings° nor other ceremonies   *of church bells*
270   use you not for cost,
    Nor at my burial make no feast,
      your money were but lost.
Rejoice in God that I am gone,
    out of this vale so vile.
275   And that of each thing left such store,
      as may your wants exile.
I make thee sole executor, because
    I loved thee best.
And thee I put in trust, to give
280   the goods unto the rest.
Because thou shalt a helper need,
    in this so great a charge,
I wish good Fortune be thy guide, lest
    thou shouldst run at large.
285   The happy days and quiet times,
    they both her servants be,
Which well will serve to fetch and bring
    such things as need° to thee.   *are needed*
Wherefore (good London) not refuse°   *do not refuse*
290   for helper her to take,
Thus being weak and weary both
    an end here will I make.
To all that ask what end I made,
    and how I went away,
295   Thou answer mayest like those which here
    no longer tarry may.
And unto all that wish me well,
    or rue that I am gone,
Do me commend, and bid them cease
300   my absence for to moan.
And tell them further, if they would,
    my presence still have had,
They should have sought to mend my luck,
    which ever was too bad.
305   So fare thou well a thousand times,
    God shield thee from thy foe,
And still make thee victorious
    of those that seek thy woe.
And though I am persuade° that I   *persuaded*
310   shall never more thee see,
Yet to the last, I shall not cease
    to wish much good of thee.
This twenty of October, I,
    in Anno Domini,

315   A thousand five hundred seventy three,
    as almanacs descry,
Did write this will with mine own hand
    and it to London gave,
In witness of the standers-by,
320   whose names if you will have,
Paper, Pen, and Standish° were,   *inkstand*
    at that same present by,
With Time, who promised to reveal,
    so fast as she could hie,
325   The same, lest of my nearer kin
    for any thing should vary,
So finally I make an end
    no longer can I tarry.

Finis.

—— ✦ ——

Mary Herbert, Countess of Pembroke
1561–1621

Mary Herbert was like many women of her time in having two phases to her life: a period of service to men, followed by a phase of independent activity. Deeply attached to her brother, Sir Philip Sidney, she spent much of her young adulthood in his company. The estate she presided over as wife to Henry Herbert, Earl of Pembroke, was Sidney's place of refuge after Queen Elizabeth had exiled him from court. At Wilton House and in his sister's company he wrote *The Apology for Poetry* and the first version of his prose romance, *The Arcadia*. Mary Herbert was an interested party in yet another project, his translation of the psalms, and when he died in 1586, she resolved to finish the project. Picking up where he had left off, at Psalm 43, she completed the cycle. Her work was encouraged by the circle of friends that gathered frequently at Wilton House and included such writers and musicians as Francis Mere, Edmund Spenser, Samuel Daniel, Nicholas Breton, Fulke Greville, and Abraham Fraunce. The seventeenth-century biographer John Aubrey spoke of the group as a "college."

Translations of the psalms were popular among Protestant writers of the period; they fulfilled the obligation to know both the Word and the indwelling spirit of God. Poets of religious lyric in the next century, especially George Herbert, would seek and represent a similar knowledge. Mary Herbert dedicated her work to Queen Elizabeth in a poem entitled *Even Now That Care* (available on our Web site), which was followed by an elegy for her brother Philip, *To Thee Pure Sprite*. Although riddled with ellipses or words that have been deliberately omitted, they convey the spiritual intensity that characterizes her translations. Some critics think that she did not write a second elegy (here attributed to her), *The Lay of Clorinda*; it is, however, what we might expect a woman of her station and training to have written about the death of a beloved friend. Milton would later give a profoundly political and religious dimension to the genre in his *Lycidas*, an elegy that is as much for an age and its temperament as it is for a person.

For additional resources on Mary Herbert, go to *The Longman Anthology of British Literature* Web site at www.myliteraturekit.com.

Psalm 71: In Te Domini Speravi

On thee my trust is grounded.
  Lord, let me never be
    With shame confounded,
      But set me free
5 And in thy justice rescue me;
    Thy gracious ear to meward° bend   *toward me*
      And me defend.

Be thou my rock, my tower,
  My ever safe resort,
10   Whose saving power
      Hath not been short°   *deficient*
To work my safety, for my fort
  On thee alone is built; in thee
    My strongholds be.

15 Me, O my God, deliver
  From wicked, wayward hand.
    God, my help-giver,
      On whom I stand
And stood since I could understand,
20   Nay, since by life I first became
      What now I am.

Since prisoned in my mother,
  By thee I prison brake,°   *broke from*
    I trust no other,
25   No other make
My stay, no other refuge take,
  Void of thy praise no time doth find
    My mouth and mind.

Men for a monster took me,
30 Yet hope of help from thee
    Never forsook me.
      Make then by me
All men, with praise extolled, may see
  Thy glory,[1] thy magnificence,
35   Thy excellence.

When feeble years do leave me
  No stay of other sort,
    Do not bereave me
      Of thy support,
40 And fail not then to be my fort,
    When weakness, in me killing might,°   *strength*
      Usurps his right.[2]

---

1. I.e., cause all men to see, by my aid, thy glory magnified with praise.

2. I.e., when weakness, having overcome strength, takes the place of strength in my soul.

For now against me banded,
  My foes have talked of me;
45   Now unwithstanded,°   *not withstood*
      Who° their spies be   *whoever*
Of me have made a firm decree:
  (Lo!) God to him hath bid adieu,
    Now then pursue.[3]

50 Pursue, say they, and take him;
  No succor can he win,
    No refuge make him.
      O God, begin
To bring with speed thy forces in.
55 Help me, my God, my God, I say
    Go not away.

But let them be confounded
  And perish by whose hate
    My soul is wounded;
60   And in one rate,°   *as a class*
Let them all share in shameful state
  Whose counsels, as their farthest end,°   *goal*
    My wrong intend.

For I will still persevere
  My hopes on thee to raise,
65   Augmenting ever
      Thy praise with praise.
My mouth shall utter forth always
  Thy truths, thy helps, whose sum surmounts
70   My best accounts.

Thy force keeps me from fearing,
  Nor ever dread I aught;
    Thy justice bearing
      In mindful thought
75 And glorious acts which thou hast taught
  Me from my youth;[4] and I have shown
    What I have known.

Now age doth overtake me
  And paint my head with snow;
80   Do not forsake me
      Until I show
The ages which succeeding grow,
  And every afterliving wight,°   *generation of men*
    Thy power and might.

---

3. I.e., my enemies' spies have decreed: God has said goodbye to him, so now hunt him down.

4. I.e., bearing thy justice and glorious acts in mindful thought.

85 How is thy justice raised
    Above the height of thought;
      How highly praised
        What thou hast wrought.
Sought let be all that can be sought,
90   None shall be found, nay none shall be,
      O God, like thee.

What if thou down didst drive me
    Into the gulf of woes;
      Thou wilt revive me
95   Again from those
And from the deep, which deepest goes;
    Exalting me again will make
      Me comfort take.

My greatness shall be greater
100   By thee; by comfort thine
      My good state better.
        O lute of mine,
To praise his truth thy tunes incline;
    My harp extol the Holy One
105   In Judah known.

My voice to my harp join thee,[5]
    My soul saved from decay,
      My voice conjoin° thee,   *join with*
        My tongue each day,
110 In all men's view his justice lay,°   *reveal*
    Who° hath disgraced and shamed so,   *those who*
      Who work my woe.

Psalm 121: Levavi Oculos

Unto the hills, I now will bend
    And list° with joy my hopeful sight;   *incline*
To him who me doth comfort send,
    My gracious God, the Lord of might.
5   Even he (who ever blessed be he named)
      Who Heaven and Earth and all therein hath framed.

By him thy foot, from slip shall stay,°   *prevent*
    Nor will he sleep who thee sustains;
Israel's great God by night or day
10   To sleep or slumber aye° disdains.   *always*
      For he is still thy guard forever waking,
      On thy right hand thy safety undertaking.

5. I.e., let my voice, joined to my harp, join thee.

So undertakes that neither sun
    By day with heat shall thee molest,
15 Nor moon by night, when day is done,
    Offend thee, or disturb thy rest.
      Yea, from all evil thou still in his protection
      Shalt safely dwell from harm or ill infection.

This Lord (who never fails his flock)
20   Shall thee in all thy ways attend
At home, abroad, thy fort, thy rock
    From all annoy shall thee defend.
      Yea, from this time from age to age for ever
      Will be thy God, and thee forsaking never.

c. 1590

The Doleful Lay° of Clorinda   *ballad*

Ay me, to whom shall I my case complain
That may compassion° my impatient grief?   *sympathize with*
Or where shall I unfold my inward pain,
That my enriven° ear may find relief?   *dismayed*
5   Shall I unto the heavenly powers it show?
    Or unto earthly men that dwell below?

To heavens? Ah they, alas, the authors were
And workers of my unremedied woe;
For they foresee what to us happens here,
10 And they foresaw, yet suffered this be so.
    From them comes good, from them comes also ill;
    That which they made, who can them warn to spill.°   *destroy*

To men? Ah they, alas, like wretched be
And subject to the heavens' ordinance;
15 Bound to abide whatever they decree,
Their best redress is their best sufferance.[1]
    How then can they, like wretched, comfort me,
    The which no less, need comforted to be?[2]

Then to myself will I my sorrow mourn,
20 Since none alive like sorrowful remains;
And to myself my plaints shall back return,
To pay their usury with doubled pains.
    The woods, the hills, the rivers shall resound
    The mournful accent of my sorrow's ground.°   *cause*

25 Wood, hills, and rivers now are desolate,
Since he is gone the which them all did grace;

---

1. I.e., the best recourse for men subject to heaven is to tolerate its decrees.

2. I.e., how can they comfort me, wretched as I am, who themselves need to be comforted?

And all the fields do wail their widow state,
Since death their fairest flower did late deface.
   The fairest flower in field that ever grew,
30   Was Astrophel;[3] that was, we all may rue.

What cruel hand of cursed fate unknown,
Hath cropped the stalk which bore so fair a flower?
Untimely cropped, before it were well grown,
And clean defaced in untimely hour.
35   Great loss to all that ever him did see,
     Great loss to all, but greatest loss to me.

Break now your garlands, O ye shepherds' lasses,
Since the fair flower which them adorned is gone;
The flower which them adorned is gone to ashes,
40   Never again let lass put garland on.
     Instead of garland, wear sad cypress now,
     And bitter elder, broken from the bow.

Nor ever sing the love-lays which he made,
Who ever made such lays of love as he?
45   Nor ever read the riddles which he said
Unto yourselves to make you merry glee.
     Your merry glee is now laid all abed,
     Your merry maker now, alas, is dead.

Death, the devourer of all world's delight,
50   Hath robbed you and reft from me my joy;
Both you and me and all the world he quite
Hath robbed of joyance and left sad annoy.
     Joy of the world, and shepherds' pride was he,
     Shepherds' hope, never like again to see.

55   Oh death, that hast us of such riches reft,
Tell us at least, what hast thou with it done?
What is become of him whose flower here left
Is but the shadow of his likeness gone,
     Scarce like the shadow of that which he was,
60   Naught° like, but that he like a shade did pass?   *nothing*

But that immortal spirit, which was decked
With all the dowries of celestial grace,
By sovereign choice from the heavenly choirs select,
And lineally derived from angel's race,
65   O what is now of it become, aread—°   *tell*
     Ay me, can so divine a thing be dead?

---

3. Astrophel or Astrophil: the principal speaker and the lover of "Stella," the figure representing the beloved woman, in Sir Philip Sidney's sonnet sequence *Astrophil and Stella*.

Ah no, it is not dead, nor can it die,
But lives for aye° in blissful paradise,   *ever*
Where like a newborn babe it soft doth lie,
70   In bed of lilies wrapped in tender wise.°   *manner*
    And compassed all about with roses sweet,
    And dainty violets from head to feet.

There thousand birds all of celestial brood,
To him do sweetly carol day and night,
75   And with strange notes, or him well understood,
Lull him asleep in angel-like delight,
    While in sweet dream to him presented be
    Immortal beauties which no eye may see.

But he them sees and takes exceeding pleasure
80   Of their divine aspects, appearing plain,
And kindling love in him above all measure,
Sweet love still joyous, never feeling pain.
    For what so goodly form he there doth see,
    He may enjoy from jealous rancor free.

85   There liveth he in everlasting bliss,
Sweet spirit never fearing more to die,
Nor dreading harm from any foes of his,
Nor fearing salvage° beasts more cruelty.   *savage*
    While we here, wretches, wail his private lack,
90   And with vain vows do often call him back.

But live thou there still happy, happy spirit,
And give us leave thee here thus to lament.
Not thee that dost thy heaven's joy inherit,
But our own selves that here in dole are drent.°   *drenched*
95   Thus do we weep and wail and wear our eyes,
    Mourning others, our own miseries.

✥ PERSPECTIVES ✥

Early Modern Books

With the invention of movable type by Johann Gutenberg in 1439, the production of printed books became more efficient, and their dissemination was far wider. The use of paper for printing, as opposed to the animal skins that were used for manuscripts, also meant that printed books could be produced much more cheaply. But this did not necessarily mean that all books were necessarily inexpensive. Many of the books printed before 1500 (known as *incunables* or *incunabula*) were sumptuously printed. William Caxton produced the first printed English book in Bruges in 1474, and then two years later established printing presses in Westminster and London. The first works that he printed were great literary works such as Chaucer's *Canterbury Tales* and Sir Thomas Malory's *Morte Darthur*. Caxton's collaborator and successor as head of his printing press, Wynkyn de Worde, born in Alsace, is largely credited with improving the technology of English printing and bringing in an era of more affordable printed books. A woodcut from his 1495 printing of Ranulf Higdon's *Polychronicon*, translated by John of Trevisa (1387), is reproduced here. This text by a Benedictine monk was both theological and historical. The best sellers of the sixteenth and seventeenth centuries were not literary but rather religious texts. The Bible and Foxe's *Book of Martyrs* in the sixteenth century, and Bunyan's *Pilgrim's Progress* in the later seventeenth century were the most commonly found books in English households. As elsewhere in Europe, the advent of the printing press in England brought with it the wider dissemination of a greater number of books in a wide array of formats. In this section, you can observe some of the features of early modern printing through viewing facsimiles of printed books and one example of a commonplace book, a form of handwritten text that remained popular in the seventeenth century.

This woodcut, taken from the second edition of *Polychronicon* published by the printer Wynkyn de Worde in 1495, represents an idealized English landscape. It depicts a city on a river, enclosed by a massive wall, behind which one can see houses, castles, towers, and an imposing cathedral. A sea opens up in the distance, showing yet other islands, cities, and boats under sail. The representation is typical of the bird's-eye views illustrated in contemporary topographical surveys.

"The burning of Tharchbishop of Cant. D. Thom. Cranmer in the town dich at Oxford" from John Foxe's (1516–1587) *Actes and Monuments of These Latter and Perilous Days* (1563). Like many other intellectual Protestants, John Foxe had gone into exile during the reign of the Catholic Mary I (1553–1558). Foxe compiled his magnum opus from manuscript and printed accounts of the persecution of English Protestants during the Marian period. His book became known as the *Book of Martyrs* and was the most popular book of the early modern period after the Bible. Foxe collaborated with the printer John Day, who was also publisher and bookseller, to produce four editions (1563, 1570, 1576, and 1583) of this bestselling book. The woodcut illustrating the burning of Archbishop Cranmer in 1556 shows his hand outstretched as Friar John to the left, and to the right three noblemen, numerous civilians and soldiers look on. Cranmer was said to have held his hand "so steadfast and immutable . . . that all might see his hand burned before his body was touched." This was the same hand with which he had previously written a recantation of his prior resistance to the Roman Catholic Church. He repented his recantation, and for his refusal to accept Catholicism as the national faith was sentenced to death. The text combines the use of black letter type face for the narrative alongside Roman type face for the heading. Ironically, this black letter type, based on a textus hand from medieval manuscripts, was more easily read by the common English reader of the sixteenth century. It was only after 1590 that most printing was done in Roman type, based on the humanist hand used to write Latin. The Bible and *The Book of Martyrs* continued to be printed in black letter throughout the seventeenth century.

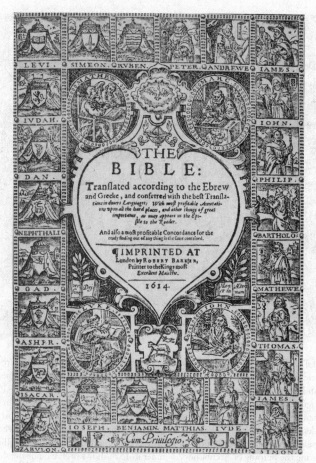

The Geneva Bible was printed in at least 144 editions between 1560 and 1644. It was the first to use Roman Type (as opposed to black letter) and verse divisions. This frontispiece of the 1614 edition displays the twelve tribes of Israel and the twelve apostles, with the four evangelists (Matthew, Mark, Luke, and John) at the center. The text was translated in Geneva, Switzerland, by the English Protestant Exiles, fleeing religious persecution under Queen Mary. They also provided marginal notes whose antihierarchical church politics made them so controversial that King James banned their use in the King James Bible and made ownership of the Geneva Bible a felony. James I was particularly worried about marginal notes such as the one in Exodus 1.19, which allowed disobedience to kings. Authorized King James Version Bibles became more widely used, and in 1644, the Geneva Bible was printed for the last time.

Their fitting at meate. XVI.

Plate XVI. "Their sitting at meate" from Thomas Hariot's (1560–1621) *A briefe and true report of the new found land of Virginia of the commodities and of the nature and manners of the naturall inhabitants* (1585). First Published by Theodore de Bry. 1590. Thomas Hariot's *A Briefe and True Report of the New Found Land of Virginia* (1588) was reprinted by Richard Hakluyt in his *Principal Navigations* (1589). Hakluyt brought John White's drawings illustrating the text to the attention of the Flemish printer Theodore De Bry, who modeled the engraved plates of his *True Pictures and Fashions of America* (1590) upon them. Hariot wrote captions for these plates, which Hakluyt translated into English. So, there are levels of both visual and textual revision that have reformed the representation of Hariot's eyewitness account of the Algonquian Indians. The caption provided for this illustration extols the taste of maize and the moderation of the Indians in their eating and drinking. This text promotes the feasibility and the profit to be gained from future voyages. Some other captions, however, such as that to Plate XIII: "Their manner of fishynge in Virginia" betray the Europeans' judgment of the Indians as barbaric: "content with their state and livinge frendlye together of those things which god in his bountye hath given unto them, yet without givinge hym any thankes according to his desarte. So savage is this people, and deprived of the true knowledge of god."

Iberis Cardamantica.
Sciatica Cresses.

things *Galen* in his ninth booke of medicines,
crates, in certaine verses tending to that effect.

Illustration of *sciatica cresses* herb from a 1597 edition of John Gerard's *The Herball or Generall historie of plantes*. *The Herball or Generall historie of plantes* (1597) illustrates the demand for the books offering practical advice and instruction. Its author, John Gerard, was a well-known physician, a member of the Barbers and Surgeons' Company, superintendent of the "physic garden" at the College of Physicians, and in charge of the garden of William Cecil, Lord Burghley, the queen's Lord Chancellor. His hugely popular book, which went into many editions, describes the appearance, cultivation, and medicinal virtues of over a thousand kinds of English plant. The plate of the herb *sciatica cresses* shows its foliage and root system, and notes that its roots mixed with pig fat relieve the pain of sciatica, a disease affecting the nerves of the back and hips.

Geoffrey Whitney (1548?–1601) composed one of the most important English emblem books, *A Choice of Emblems* (1586). Each emblem contains a woodcut, prefixed by a Latin motto and accompanied by verses in six-line stanzas. The book was dedicated to the Earl of Leicester and was published in Leyden, where Whitney was studying at the university. Although only twenty-three of the emblems are original and another 235 loosely or exactly copy Continental models by Alciati, Paradin, Sambucus, and Junius, Whitney gives many of the emblems a specifically English interpretation. Sometimes an emblem is used to support the politics of the Leicester court faction, who urged an active role in defending Protestants in the Low Countries. At other times, Whitney's Englishness surfaces in references to local events. For example, he applies the emblem of the phoenix to the fire of Nantwich, not far from his birthplace in Chesire, where he would retire after the death of his patron Leicester. Possibly because of the decline of the Leicester faction, Whitney's book was not republished in his lifetime. Nevertheless, his influence is seen in later Jacobean emblem books, such as Peacham's *Minerva Britanna* (London, 1612), and in decorations in domestic architecture and furnishings. Whitney's work helped to make the Continental emblem tradition known to such English poets as Shakespeare, Spenser, Donne, and Philips, whose poetry is enriched by emblematic metaphor, conjuring up both a visual image and its complex symbolic associations. The motto to this emblem "Unica semper avis" (means "the bird that is ever unique") and the image are inspired by Ovid's *Metamorphoses* 15.393–407.

The Phoenix
Unica semper avis

To my countrymen of the Nampwiche in Cheshire.

    The Phoenix rare, with feathers fresh of hue,
    Arabia's right, and sacred to the sun:
    Whom, other birds with wonder seem to view,
    Doth live until a thousand years be run:
5   Then makes a pile: which, when with sun it burns,
    She flies therein, and so to ashes turns.

    Whereof, behold, another Phoenix rare,
    With speed doth rise most beautiful and fair:
    And though for truth, this many do declare,
10   Yet thereunto, I mean not for to swear:
    Although I know that author's witness true,
    What here I write, both of the old, and new.

    Which when I weighed, the new, and eke the old,
    I thought upon your town destroyed with fire:
15   And did in mind, the new Nampwiche behold,
    A spectacle for any man's desire:
    Whose buildings brave, where cinders were but late,
    Did represent (me thought) the Phoenix fate.

    And as the old, was many hundred years,
20   A town of fame, before it felt that cross:
    Even so, (I hope) this Wiche,[1] that now appears,
    A Phoenix age shall last, and know no loss:
    Which God vouchsafe, who make you thankful, all:
    That see this rise, and saw the other fall.

---

1. Originally meaning the group of buildings connected with a salt pit, "wich" was the name given to such saltmaking towns as Nantwich and Northwich in Chesire.

Title page to Volume 2 of *Utriusque cosmi, maioris scilicet et minoris, metaphysica atque technica historia,* ("Metaphysical and Technical History of both the Greater and Lesser Universe"), by Robert Fludd, 1619. After taking his degree at Oxford, Robert Fludd studied chemistry and medicine on the Continent, where he came into contact with the occult philosophy of the Rosicrucians, whose goals ranged from alchemy to moral reformation. Returning to London, he practiced medicine and published numerous works expressing his belief that science was a form of divine revelation and that all creation reflected a divinely ordered design. This engraving shows the image of a male body spread out over the cosmos as a circle, portraying the human body's perfect proportions, and their analogy to the proportions of the universe: man is a little world, the microcosm to the universe's macrocosm. The engraving also depicts the earth-centered Ptolemaic universe, the constellations and astrological signs. The innermost circles are the four bodily humors (choleric, melancholic, phlegmatic, and sanguine), and the outermost circles are the supernatural faculties of reason, intellect, and mind.

Frontispiece to Francis Bacon, *Advancement of Learning* (1640). This engraving can be read as both a representation of the kind of technological innovation that Bacon lauds in the *Advancement* as well as a kind of allegory of the scientific revolution. The text is an accurate representation of one of the inventions of the early modern Europe—the large sailing ship. At the same time it symbolizes the transgression of the Pillars of Hercules (the Straits of Gibraltar), once thought of as the limits of the known world, a kind of hubristic and bold adventure not unlike the quest for knowledge and power by Marlowe's Doctor Faustus or Shakespeare's Prospero.

Vpon the death of Hobson the Carrier of Cambridge./

Death being tyred with the tedious stay
Of aged Hobson long had watcht à day
To snatch him hence, but still when
   death was come
Hee neuer found his moueing Ghest at
   home,
Att last hee caught him; and with Letters
   sendes
Him from the townesmen to their late
   dead freiendes.
His life was not à Race as others bee
'Twas but à trott of threescore yeares and
   three,
And yet hee ridd soe fast, that all the while
Death ouertooke him not, till by à wyle
Hee made him stand. The vniuersitie
Hath cause to mourne, for this his Destinie
ffor shee had lost her Learned heades before,
And now to make her miserie the more,
One of her Legges is gone; for sure 'twas hee
That bore the weight of the vniuersitie;
His waggons grone for greife, and euery tree
Twixt this and London all in mourning bee
The Bull in sable standes and all the quire
Of Waggoniers expresse their sadd desire
By mournefull Whistles; I (though not
   his Debtor)
Giue him these lynes, stead of á wonted
   Letter.

        Guill: Hall Christ: Coll'./[1]

The handwriting in this manuscript is a combination of Italic, a script made popular by Italian Renaissance humanists, and widely used for Latin, and secretary, a hand prevalent in England from 1500 to 1650. William Hall wrote the poem to commemorate the death of Thomas Hobson, the mail carrier of Christ's College, Cambridge. Milton also wrote a poem about Hobson that helped make popular the expression "Hobson's choice," referring to his only allowing students to rent out the next horse in line—"this one or none." The poem by Hall appears only in two manuscript books, now both at the Folger Library.

---

1. Guill: that is, "Guillelmus," the Latin form of "William."

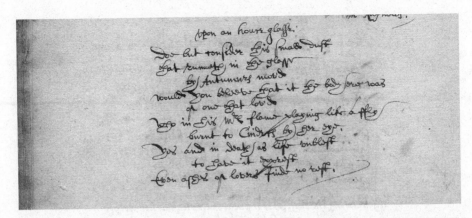

From Folger MS V.b.43, f. 9v. *Vpon an houre glasse* written by Ben Jonson in a secretary hand, the type of handwriting prevalent in England from the early sixteenth through the seventeenth century. This poem appears in a large manuscript referred to as a *folio*, large pieces of paper, each folded in half to produce two leaves or four pages. This manuscript verse collection, referred to as both a *miscellany* and a *commonplace book*, contains many poems by different authors written side by side by a scribe, circa. 1630. So, for example, Donne's "The Anagram" appears on the same page as "Vpon an houre glasse."[1] Compare the poem in MS. V. 43 on the left with the version in the 1640 printed edition on the right:

Vpon an houre glasse

Doe but consider this small dust
that runneth in the glasse
   by Autumnes mov'd
would you beleeve that it the body ere was
   of one that lov'd
who in his M[ist]r[i]s flame playing like
a Fly
   burnt to Cinders by her eye,
Yes and in death as life vnblest
   to have it exprest
Even ashes of lovers finde no rest.

The Hour-Glass[2]

Do but consider this small dust
   Here running in the glass,
     By atoms moved:
Could you believe that this
   The body [ever] was
     Of one that loved?
And in his mistress' flame, playing like
a fly,
   Turned to cinders by her eye?
Yes; and in death, as life, unblest,
     To have't expressed,
Even ashes of lovers find no rest.

1. To read more about this poem and other manuscript collections of poems, you can read an on-line article by Christopher Ivic at http://www.folger.edu/html/folger_institute/mm/EssayCI.html.

2. This version of the poem by Jonson was published in 1640.

Frontispiece to *A certaine Relation of the Hog-faced Gentlewoman called Mistris Tannakin Skinker, who was borne at Wirkham, a Neuter Towne between the Emperour and the Hollander, scituate on the river Rhyne. Who was bewitched in her mothers wombe in the yeare 1618 and hath lived ever since unknowne in this kinde to any, but her Parents and a few other neighbours. And can never recover her true shape, till she be married, & c Also relating the cause, as it is since conceived, how her mother came to be so bewitched* (1640). This woodcut illustration of the woman with the hog face and one of her suitors is a good example of cheap print. It is the early modern equivalent of supermarket check-out tabloids such as *News of the World.* This title page shows an interesting feature of early modern printing—the tendency to advertise the entire text by summarizing its contents and setting forth the most outrageous details on the title page.

Elizabeth I
1533–1603

No British monarch has left posterity a more dazzling record of accomplishments than Elizabeth Tudor, second daughter of Henry VIII. During the course of her reign, England became a nation to rival France and Spain; England's cities became centers of commerce, her navy controlled the principal routes of trade, and her people pursued lucrative interests in Europe and the New World. Having ruled England for almost half a century, Elizabeth has lived on as a figure of compelling power in the history of her people. What Shakespeare said of his character Cleopatra—"Age cannot wither her, nor custom stale her infinite variety"— conveys something of the fascination the memory of this extraordinary woman has had for the English people as well as for others around the globe. Age did, of course, eventually touch her being; doubtless, too, the brilliant strategies by which she governed subjects who were ever jealous of her royal prerogative must finally have become predictable. But Elizabeth was brought up in the atmosphere of a volatile politics, given to shifts in the winds of chance, susceptible to the heat of violent controversy and even to the flames of rebellion. She did what she had to do to remain on the throne; her father's example, if nothing else, taught her how fragile was the rule of a monarch who depended much more on the loyalty of subjects than on the authority of office or the power of the law.

Elizabeth's birth was itself a disappointment, at least to Henry VIII, who had hoped for a son. Her mother was the king's second wife, the charming Anne Boleyn, whom he married after divorcing Catherine of Aragon, the mother of his first daughter, Mary Tudor. The divorce precipitated the king's break with the Catholic Church, made Mary Tudor illegitimate, and effectively defined Anne's politics as unequivocally Protestant. But the new queen's influence was short-lived. Supporters of Catholicism, those who remained faithful to the memory of Catherine and respected the claims of Mary Tudor, may have been responsible for convincing the king that Anne had been unfaithful to him; in any case, he ordered her execution. Ten days later, he married Jane Seymour, declared Elizabeth illegitimate, and again waited for the birth of a son. Elizabeth's half-brother, the future Edward VI, was born in 1537, when Elizabeth was four years old. Fortunately, at the age of ten, Elizabeth at last acquired a loving stepmother: Henry's sixth wife, Catherine Parr, looked after her interests and education. An excellent student, fluent in Latin, French, and Italian and versed in history, Elizabeth was raised to be the subject of her brother, who became king after Henry's death in 1547. When he died in 1553, she became a pawn in a long and vicious struggle for the crown. Imprisoned in the Tower and then in Woodstock Castle in Oxfordshire by the Catholic supporters of her sister's claim to the throne, Elizabeth wrote lyrics that testify to both her fears and her faith during this dangerous time.

In 1558, Queen Mary died, and Elizabeth was crowned with much rejoicing; in the historian William Camden's words: "neither did the people ever embrace any other Prince with more willing and constant mind." Once on the throne, Elizabeth pursued a policy of exemplary discretion; she rewarded those who were loyal to her and punished those who showed signs of disobedience. In 1568, when her cousin Mary, Queen of Scots, abdicated the throne of Scotland in favor of her son, James VI, Elizabeth granted Mary refuge in England. Yet evidence later suggested that Mary, an ardent Catholic, had plotted to kill Elizabeth and restore Catholicism in England, and in 1587, Elizabeth ordered her execution with great regret. Reflecting on this action, also the subject of a speech to Parliament, the queen declared: "This death will wring my heart as long as I live."

Robert Peake (attr.), *Queen Elizabeth Going in Procession to Blackfriars in 1600*. This splendid painting is linked to no particular event. Its arrangement of figures suggests a Roman imperial triumph, and evokes the success of the queen's monarchy. She appears to be in a litter, but is actually in a chair on wheels pushed by attendants, and protected by a canopy held by courtiers. She is preceded by a knight, perhaps Gilbert Talbot, Earl of Shrewsbury, who carries the sword of state. Though Elizabeth was sixty-eight when this painting was made in 1601, she is shown as a much younger woman. Her wish to be recognized as always desirable and ever the object of courtly devotion is well illustrated by her pale, unlined face, her highly dressed hair and her stylized body, clothed in a bejeweled dress whose puffed sleeves and intricate lace ruff suggest an ethereal and even divine creature. She is attended by six Knights of the Garter; the knight standing directly beside her (with a bald head and stiff grey beard) has been identified as her current favorite, Edward Somerset, Earl of Worcester; his two principal castles, Raglan and Chepstow, are probably those in the background of the painting.

A woman and reigning monarch, Elizabeth's position was anomalous. As a woman, she retained an important kind of social power only as long as she was an object of desire, to be courted and won; as a reigning monarch, she was expected not only to govern but also to secure the succession. In her speech to Parliament on the subject of marriage early in her reign, Elizabeth provided reasons why she would delay taking a husband. She probably never intended to take one. Continuing the fiction of courtship well past the age at which she could be expected to have a child, she saw to it that she remained at once attractive and unavailable. Most important, she succeeded in commanding the attention of her subjects by transforming her court into a center of literary and artistic activity. Late in life, she met her most serious suitor, the Duke of Alençon, brother to the French king, Henry III. A dwarf whose face was disfigured by smallpox, he was her "little frog," a man she is said to have loved dearly. The problem of succession required another kind of temporizing. She refused to name James VI of Scotland as the next king of England until shortly before she died—a silence that she maintained was necessary to preserve the peace.

Throughout her long reign she cultivated two personas. As a monarch, she could speak courageously (as she did to her soldiers at Tilbury on the Devon coast while they waited for the Spanish to invade); as a woman, she could convey understanding (as she did to her critics in her so-called Golden Speech curtailing her prerogative to create monopolies). Her government remained a conscientious one to its very end. She cultivated a habit of mind that must have helped to ensure its stability: as her translation of Boethius's *Consolation of Philosophy* (made when she was sixty years old) reminds us, she never allowed herself to forget the vicissitudes of fortune and her own mortality.

Written with a Diamond on Her Window at Woodstock[1]

Much suspected by° me,   *to have been done by*
Nothing proved can be,
Quoth Elizabeth prisoner.

Written on a Wall at Woodstock

Oh fortune, thy wresting wavering state
Hath fraught with cares my troubled wit,
Whose witness this present prison late
Could bear, where once was joy flown quite.[1]
5   Thou causedst the guilty to be loosed
From lands where innocents were inclosed,
And caused the guiltless to be reserved,°   *bound*
And freed those that death had well deserved.
But all herein° can be nothing caught,   *in prison*
10 So God send to my foes all they have thought.[2]

The Doubt of Future Foes

The doubt° of future foes exiles my present joy,   *fear*
And wit me warns to shun such snares as threaten mine annoy;[1]
For falsehood now doth flow, and subjects' faith doth ebb,
Which should not be if reason ruled or wisdom weaved the web.
5   But clouds of joys untried° do cloak aspiring minds,   *untested*
Which turn to rage of late repent by changed course of winds.[2]
The top of hope supposed the root of rue shall be,
And fruitless all their grafted guile, as shortly ye shall see.[3]
The dazzled eyes with pride, which great ambition blinds,

1. Elizabeth was imprisoned at Woodstock Castle, near Oxford, from 23 May 1554 to sometime late in April 1555. The queen, Mary I, Elizabeth's half-sister, suspected her of treason. This and the following poem are thought to have been written at this time.
1. I.e., this prison could bear witness recently to fortune's wavering state, once joy had flown from it.
2. I.e., nothing can be done by one who is in prison, so may God send to my foes what they have suspected me of planning.

1. My harm.
2. I.e., because of a change of wind, my enemies' clouds of joy can turn to the rain of repentance.
3. I.e., at their most hopeful, my enemies supposed that the tree of my monarchy would be uprooted, but their grafted limbs of guile will bear no fruit.

10   Shall be unsealed by worthy wights[4] whose foresight falsehood finds.
      The daughter of debate that discord aye° doth sow   *ever*
      Shall reap no gain where former rule[5] still peace hath taught to know.
      No foreign banished wight[6] shall anchor in this port;
      Our realm brooks not seditious sects, let them elsewhere resort.
15   My rusty sword through rest shall first his edge employ
      To poll their tops[7] that seek such change or gape[8] for future joy.

On Monsieur's Departure[1]

I grieve and dare not show my discontent,
I love and yet am forced to seem to hate,
I do, yet dare not say I ever meant,
I seem stark mute but inwardly do prate.
5   I am and not,° I freeze and yet am burned,   *am not*
         Since from myself another self I turned.

My care is like my shadow in the sun,
Follows me flying, flies when I pursue it,
Stands and lies by me, doth what I have done.
10   His too familiar care doth make me rue° it.   *regret*
         No means I find to rid him from my breast,
         Till by the end of things° it be supprest.   *death*

Some gentler passion slide into my mind,
For I am soft and made of melting snow;
15   Or be more cruel, love, and so be kind.
Let me or° float or sink, be high or low.   *either*
         Or let me live with some more sweet content,
         Or die and so forget what love ere meant.

SPEECHES   The speeches of Elizabeth I exemplify early modern public oratory at its most effective. But they are also marked by features uniquely derived from her sense of herself as a monarch who wished (and probably needed) to convince her subjects that their welfare was more important to her than her own. In the excerpts that follow, Elizabeth emphasizes that although nature made her a woman and therefore of the weaker sex, divine right has made her a "prince," a person endowed with a masculine persona whose function it is to command not obey. She further emphasizes that her principal care is for her subjects, who are her charges and in some sense her children. In her public dealings throughout her reign, she played the gender card for all it was worth; in so doing, she transformed the fact that she was a woman, potentially a liability, into an instrument of policy.

---

4. Men.
5. The rule of Elizabeth's father, Henry VIII, and brother, Edward VI, both Protestants.
6. Any supporter of Philip II, king of Spain and consort of Mary I.
7. Cut their heads off.

8. Smile.
1. The poem expresses Elizabeth's regret at the departure of the Duke d'Alençon, who had sought her hand in marriage. After four years of visits and inconclusive negotiations, the courtship ended in 1583.

On Marriage[1]

I may say unto you that from my years of understanding, sith[2] I first had consideration of myself to be born a servitor of Almighty God, I happily chose this kind of life
in which I yet live, which I assure you for mine own part hath hitherto best contented myself and I trust hath been most acceptable to God. From the which, if either ambition of high estate offered to me in marriage by the pleasure and
appointment of my prince[3]—whereof I have some records in this presence, as you
our Lord Treasurer[4] well know; or if the eschewing of the danger of mine enemies or
the avoiding of the period of death, whose messenger or rather continual watchman,
the prince's indignation, was not little time daily before mine eyes—by whose
means, although I know or justly may suspect, yet I will not now utter; or if the
whole cause were in my sister herself, I will not now burthen her therewith, because
I will not charge the dead: if any of these I say, I had not now remained in this estate
wherein you see me. But so constant have I always continued in this determination—although my youth and words may seem to some hardly to agree together—
yet is it most true that at this day I stand free from any other meaning that either I
have had in times past or have at this present. With which trade of life I am so thoroughly acquainted that I trust God, who hath hitherto therein preserved and led me
by the hand, will not now of His goodness suffer me to go alone. * * *

Nevertheless—if any of you be in suspect—whensoever it may please God to incline my heart to another kind of life, ye may well assure yourselves my meaning is
not to do or determine anything wherewith the realm may or shall have just cause to
be discontented. And therefore put that clean out of your heads.[5] For I assure you—
what credit my assurance may have with you I cannot tell, but what credit it shall
deserve to have the sequence shall declare—I will never in that matter conclude
anything that shall be prejudicial to the realm, for the weal, good, and safety
whereof I will never shun to spend my life. And whomsoever my chance shall be to
light upon, I trust he shall be as careful for the realm and you—I will not say as myself, because I cannot so certainly determine of any other; but at the least ways, by
my good will and desire he shall be such as shall be as careful for the preservation of
the realm and you as myself.

And albeit it might please Almighty God to continue me still in this mind to
live out of the state of marriage, yet it is not to be feared but He will so work in my
heart and in your wisdoms as good provision by His help may be made in convenient
time, whereby the realm shall not remain destitute of an heir that may be a fit governor, and peradventure more beneficial to the realm than such offspring as may

1. In 1559, a year after she had acceded to the throne at
the age of 25, Elizabeth addressed Parliament on the subject of marriage. Because the monarchy passed on by inheritance, it was expected that a monarch would marry
and have children. In this speech, Elizabeth hints that
she will never marry and also that she trusts God to provide for her successor who, she guesses, may be more
"beneficial" to the kingdom than any child of her own
would be. She probably intended to convey to her subjects that she would never abandon the kingdom either
to the rule of a foreign prince (as Mary I had) or to a succession crisis.
2. Since.

3. The "prince" Elizabeth refers to is probably not Philip
II, the consort of Mary I, but rather Mary herself, who in
her official capacity as queen regnant might have offered
her sister's hand in marriage to a suitable consort. Elizabeth can refer to Mary as her "sister" when she alludes to
a "cause" that has no implications for the state but is
rather personal, "in my sister herself."
4. The Marquis of Winchester.
5. Elizabeth emphasizes that her subjects and their representatives in Parliament have no authority to force her
into marriage, however desirable they may think marriage is for the future of the kingdom.

come of me. For, although I be never so careful of your well doings and mind ever so to be, yet may my issue grow out of kind and become perhaps ungracious. And in the end, this shall be for me sufficient, that a marble stone shall declare that a Queen, having reigned such a time, lived and died a virgin.

On Mary, Queen of Scots[1]

The bottomless graces and immeasurable benefits bestowed upon me by the Almighty are and have been such, as I must not only acknowledge them but admire them, accounting them as well miracles as benefits; not so much in respect of His Divine Majesty—with whom nothing is more common than to do things rare and singular—as in regard of our weakness, who cannot sufficiently set forth His wonderful works and graces, which to me have been so many, so diversely folded and embroidered one upon another, as in no sort am I able to express them.

And although there liveth not any that may more justly acknowledge themselves infinitely bound unto God than I, whose life He hath miraculously preserved at sundry times (beyond my merit) from a multitude of perils and dangers, yet is not that the cause for which I count myself the deepliest bound to give Him my humblest thanks, or to yield Him greatest recognition; but this which I shall tell you hereafter, which will deserve the name of wonder, if rare things and seldom seen be worthy of account. Even this it is: that as I came to the crown with the willing hearts of subjects, so do I now, after twenty-eight years' reign, perceive in you no diminution of good wills, which, if haply I should want, well might I breathe but never think I lived.

And now, albeit I find my life hath been full dangerously sought, and death contrived by such as no desert procured it, yet am I thereof so clear from malice—which hath the property to make men glad at the falls and faults of their foes, and make them seem to do for other causes, when rancor is the ground—as I protest it is and hath been my grievous thought that one, not different in sex, of like estate, and my near kin, should be fallen into so great a crime. Yea, I had so little purpose to pursue her with any color of malice, that as it is not unknown to some of my Lords here—for now I will play the blab—I secretly wrote her a letter upon the discovery of sundry treasons, that if she would confess them, and privately acknowledge them by her letters unto myself, she never should need be called for them into so public question. Neither did I it of mind to circumvent her, for then I knew as much as she could confess; and so did I write.

And if, even yet, now the matter is made but too apparent, I thought she truly would repent—as perhaps she would easily appear in outward show to do—and that for her none other would take the matter upon them; or that we were but as two milkmaids, with pails upon our arms; or that there were no more dependency upon us, but mine own life were only in danger, and not the whole estate of your religion and well doings; I protest—wherein you may believe me, for although I may have many vices, I hope I have not accustomed my tongue to be an instrument of untruth—I would most willingly pardon and remit this offence. Or if by my death

---

1. The text is Elizabeth's answer to a petition from Parliament to execute Mary, Queen of Scots, who was reported to have conspired to depose her cousin Elizabeth and who had been a prisoner of the English queen for ten years. In August 1586, evidence of a new plot came to light, and the conspirators, led by Sir Thomas Babington, were executed. On the evidence in letters to Babington, Mary was then formally tried and convicted of treason by a special court of peers, counsellors, and judges. Elizabeth answered Parliament in October by asking for delay and divine enlightenment.

other nations and kingdoms might truly say that this realm had attained an ever prosperous and flourishing estate, I would (I assure you) not desire to live, but gladly give my life, to the end my death might procure you a better prince. And for your sakes it is that I desire to live: to keep you from a worse. For, as for me, I assure you I find no great cause I should be fond to live. I take no such pleasure in it that I should much wish it, nor conceive such terror in death that I should greatly fear it. And yet I say not but, if the stroke were coming, perchance flesh and blood would be moved with it, and seek to shun it.

I have had good experience and trial of this world. I know what it is to be a subject, what to be a sovereign, what to have good neighbors, and sometime meet evil-willers. I have found treason in trust, seen great benefits little regarded, and instead of gratefulness, courses[2] of purpose to cross. These former remembrances, present feeling, and future expectation of evils, (I say), have made me think an evil is much the better the less while it dureth,[3] and so them happiest that are soonest hence;[4] and taught me to bear with a better mind these treasons, than is common to my sex—yea, with a better heart perhaps than is in some men. Which I hope you will not merely impute to my simplicity or want of understanding, but rather that I thus conceived—that had their purposes taken effect, I should not have found the blow, before I had felt it; nor, though my peril should have been great, my pain should have been but small and short. Wherein, as I would be loath to die so bloody a death, so doubt I not but God would have given me grace to be prepared for such an event; which, when it shall chance, I refer to His good pleasure.

And now, as touching their treasons and conspiracies, together with the contriver of them. I will not so prejudicate myself and this my realm as to say or think that I might not, without the last statute, by the ancient laws of this land have proceeded against her; which[5] was not made particularly to prejudice her, though perhaps it might then be suspected in respect of the disposition of such as depend that way. It was so far from being intended to entrap her, that it was rather an admonition to warn the danger thereof. But sith it is made, and in the force of a law, I thought good, in that which might concern her, to proceed according thereunto rather than by course of common law. Wherein, if you the judges have not deceived me, or that the books you brought me were not false—which God forbid—I might as justly have tried her by the ancient laws of the land.

But you lawyers are so nice and so precise in sifting and scanning every word and letter, that many times you stand more upon form than matter, upon syllables than the sense of the law. For, in this strictness and exact following of common form, she must have been indicted in Staffordshire, been arraigned at the bar, holden up her hand, and then been tried by a jury: a proper course, forsooth, to deal in that manner with one of her estate! I thought it better, therefore, for avoiding of these and more absurdities, to commit the cause to the inquisition of a good number of the greatest and most noble personages of this realm, of the judges and others of good account, whose sentence I must approve.[6]

---

2. Plans.
3. Lasts.
4. I.e., out of this world.
5. I.e., the Parliamentary statute of 1584–1585, known as the Act for the Queen's Surety, which provided for the trial of Mary, Queen of Scots, should she be accused of treason.

6. Elizabeth claims that Mary could have been tried as a criminal in a common law court but that this would have been an improper way to proceed as Mary remained a Queen of Scotland and her liability under English law was open to question.

And all little enough: for we Princes, I tell you, are set on stages, in the sight and view of all the world duly observed. The eyes of many behold our actions; a spot is soon spied in our garments, a blemish quickly noted in our doings. It behoveth us, therefore, to be careful that our proceedings be just and honorable.

But I must tell you one thing more: that in this late Act of Parliament you have laid an hard hand on me—that I must give direction for her death, which cannot be but most grievous, and an irksome burden to me. And lest you might mistake mine absence from this Parliament—which I had almost forgotten: although there be no cause why I should willingly come amongst multitudes (for that amongst many, some may be evil), yet hath it not been the doubt of any such danger or occasion that kept me from thence, but only the great grief to hear this cause spoken of, especially that such one of state and kin should need so open a declaration, and that this nation should be so spotted with blots of disloyalty. Wherein, the less is my grief for that I hope the better part is mine; and those of the worse not much to be accounted of, for that in seeking my destruction they might have spoiled their own souls.

And even now could I tell you that which would make you sorry. It is a secret; and yet I will tell it you (although it be known I have the property to keep counsel but too well, often times to mine own peril). It is not long since mine eyes did see it written that an oath was taken within few days either to kill me or to be hanged themselves; and that to be performed ere one month were ended. Hereby I see your danger in me, and neither can or will be so unthankful or careless of your consciences as to take no care for your safety.

I am not unmindful of your oath made in the Association,[7] manifesting your great good wills and affections, taken and entered into upon good conscience and true knowledge of the guilt, for safeguard of my person; done (I protest to God) before I ever heard it, or ever thought of such a matter, till a thousand hands, with many obligations, were showed me at Hampton Court, signed and subscribed with the names and seals of the greatest of this land. Which, as I do acknowledge as a perfect argument of your true hearts and great zeal to my safety, so shall my bond be stronger tied to greater care for all your good.

But, for that this matter is rare, weighty and of great consequence, and I think you do not look for any present resolution—the rather for that, as it is not my manner in matters of far less moment to give speedy answer without due consideration, so in this of such importance—I think it very requisite with earnest prayer to beseech His Divine Majesty so to illuminate mine understanding and inspire me with His grace, as I may do and determine that which shall serve to the establishment of His Church, preservation of your estates, and prosperity of this Commonwealth under my charge. Wherein, for that I know delay is dangerous, you shall have with all conveniency our resolution delivered by our message. And what ever any prince may merit of their subjects, for their approved testimony of their unfeigned sincerity, either by governing justly, void of all partiality, or sufferance of any injuries done (even to the poorest), that do I assuredly promise inviolably to perform, for requital of your so many deserts.

---

7. The Oath (or Bond) of Association was taken by the Queen's Council in October 1582. It provided for Mary's arrest and execution without a trial; in essence, it sanctioned a lynching.

On Mary's Execution[1]

Full grievous is the way whose going on and end breeds cumber[2] for the hire of a laborious journey. I have strived more this day than ever in my life whether I should speak or use silence. If I speak and not complain, I shall dissemble; if I hold my peace, your labor taken were full vain.

For me to make my moan were strange and rare, for I suppose you shall find few that, for their own particular, will cumber you with such a care. Yet such, I protest, hath been my greedy desire and hungry will that of your consultation might have fallen out some other means to work my safety, joined with your assurance, than that for which you are become so earnest suitors, as I protest I must needs use complaint[3]—though not of you, but unto you, and of the cause; for that I do perceive, by your advices, prayers, and desires, there falleth out this accident, that only my injurer's bane must be my life's surety.

But if any there live so wicked of nature to suppose that I prolonged this time only pro forma, to the intent to make a show of clemency, thereby to set my praises to the wire-drawers[4] to lengthen them the more, they do me so great a wrong as they can hardly recompense. Or if any person there be that think or imagine that the least vainglorious thought hath drawn me further herein, they do me as open injury as ever was done to any living creature—as He that is the maker of all thoughts knoweth best to be true. Or if there be any that think that the Lords, appointed in commission, durst do no other, as fearing thereby to displease or to be suspected to be of a contrary opinion to my safety, they do but heap upon me injurious conceits. For, either those put in trust by me to supply my place have not performed their duty towards me, or else they have signified unto you all that my desire was that every one should do according to his conscience, and in the course of these proceedings should enjoy both freedom of voice and liberty of opinion, and what they would not openly, they might privately to myself declare. It was of a willing mind and great desire I had, that some other means might be found out, wherein I should have taken more comfort than in any other thing under the sun.

And since now it is resolved that my surety cannot be established without a princess's head, I have just cause to complain that I, who have in my time pardoned so many rebels, winked at so many treasons, and either not produced[5] them or altogether slipped them over with silence, should now be forced to this proceeding, against such a person. I have besides, during my reign, seen and heard many opprobrious books and pamphlets against me, my realm and state, accusing me to be a tyrant. I thank them for their alms. I believe therein their meaning was to tell me news: and news it is to me indeed. I would it were as strange to hear of their impiety. What will they not now say, when it shall be spread that for the safety of her life a maiden queen could be content to spill the blood even of her own kinswoman? I may therefore full well complain that any man should think me given to cruelty; whereof I am so guiltless and innocent as I should slander God if I should say He gave me so vile a mind. Yea, I protest, I am so far from it that for mine own life I would not touch her.

---

1. Parliament had determined that Elizabeth's safety and the future of Protestantism in England could be secured only by Mary's execution; it sent a delegation to Elizabeth asking for her approval. Again Elizabeth demurred. It was only in February 1587, after a new conspiracy was discovered, that Elizabeth signed Mary's death warrant.
2. Distress.
3. Express regret.
4. One who draws metal into wire.
5. Acted upon.

Neither hath my care been so much bent how to prolong mine, as how to preserve both: which I am right sorry is made so hard, yea so impossible.

I am not so void of judgment as not to see mine own peril; nor yet so ignorant as not to know it were in nature a foolish course to cherish a sword to cut mine own throat; nor so careless as not to weigh that my life daily is in hazard. But this I do consider, that many a man would put his life in danger for the safeguard of a king. I do not say that so will I; but I pray you think that I have thought upon it.

But sith so many hath both written and spoken against me, I pray you give me leave to say somewhat for myself, and, before you return to your countries, let you know for what a one you have passed so careful thoughts. And, as I think myself infinitely beholding unto you all that seek to preserve my life by all the means you may, so I protest that there liveth no prince—nor ever shall be—more mindful to requite so good deserts. Wherein, as I perceive you have kept your old wont[6] in a general seeking the lengthening of my days, so am I sure that never shall I requite it, unless I had as many lives as you all; but for ever I will acknowledge it while there is any breath left me. Although I may not justify, but may justly condemn, my sundry faults and sins to God, yet for my care in this government let me acquaint you with my intents.

When first I took the sceptre, my title made me not forget the giver, and therefore [I] began as it became me, with such religion as both I was born in, bred in, and, I trust, shall die in; although I was not so simple as not to know what danger and peril so great an alteration might procure me—how many great princes of the contrary opinion would attempt all they might against me, and generally what enmity I should thereby breed unto myself. Which all I regarded not, knowing that He, for whose sake I did it, might and would defend me. Rather marvel that I am, than muse that I should not be if it were not God's holy hand that continueth me beyond all other expectation.

I was not simply trained up, nor in my youth spent my time altogether idly; and yet, when I came to the crown, then entered I first into the school of experience, bethinking myself of those things that best fitted a king—justice, temper, magnanimity, judgment. As for the two latter, I will not boast. But for the two first, this may I truly say: among my subjects I never knew a difference of person, where right was one;[7] nor never to my knowledge preferred for favor what I thought not fit for worth; nor bent mine ears to credit a tale that first was told me; nor was so rash to corrupt my judgment with my censure, ere I heard the cause. I will not say but many reports might fortune[8] be brought me by such as must hear the matter, whose partiality might mar the right; for we princes cannot hear all causes ourselves. But this dare I boldly affirm: my verdict went with the truth of my knowledge.

But full well wished Alcibiades[9] his friend, that he should not give any answer till he had recited the letters of the alphabet. So have I not used over-sudden resolutions in matters that have touched me full near: you will say that with me, I think. And therefore, as touching your counsels and consultations, I conceive them to be wise, honest, and conscionable; so provident and careful for the safety of my life (which I wish no longer than may be for your good), that though I never can yield

6. Desire.
7. I.e., my justice was impartial; it did not regard rank, occupation, or property as factors in determining what was right.
8. By chance.

9. An Athenian statesman who took part in the Peloponnesian War; changed sides to support Athens' enemy, Sparta; and was finally assassinated by Persians with whom he sought an alliance. The source of Elizabeth's reference is unknown.

you of recompense your due, yet shall I endeavor myself to give you cause to think your good will not ill bestowed, and strive to make myself worthy for such subjects. And as for your petition: your judgment I condemn not, neither do I mistake your reasons, but pray you to accept my thankfulness, excuse my doubtfulness, and take in good part my answer-answerless. Wherein I attribute not so much to my own judgment, but that I think many particular persons may go before me, though by my degree I go before them. Therefore, if I should say, I would not do what you request, it might peradventure be more than I thought; and to say I would do it, might perhaps breed peril of that you labor to preserve, being more than in your own wisdoms and discretions would seem convenient,[1] circumstances of place and time being duly considered.

To the English Troops at Tilbury, Facing the Spanish Armada[1]

My loving people, we have been persuaded by some that are careful of our safety, to take heed how we commit ourselves to armed multitudes, for fear of treachery. But I assure you, I do not desire to live to distrust my faithful and loving people. Let tyrants fear. I have always so behaved myself that, under God, I have placed my chiefest strength and safeguard in the loyal hearts and good will of my subjects; and therefore I am come amongst you, as you see, at this time, not for my recreation and disport,[2] but being at this time resolved, in the midst and heat of the battle, to live or die amongst you all, to lay down for my God, and for my kingdom, and for my people, my honor and my blood, even in the dust. I know I have the body of a weak and feeble woman, but I have the heart and stomach of a king, and of a king of England too, and think foul scorn[3] that Parma or Spain, or any prince of Europe should dare to invade the border of my realm; to which rather than any dishonor shall grow[4] by me, I myself will take up arms, I myself will be your general, judge, and rewarder of every one of your virtues in the field. I know, already for your forwardness[5] you have deserved rewards and crowns;[6] and we do assure you, in the word of a prince, they shall be duly paid you.

The Golden Speech[1]

Mr. Speaker, we have heard your declaration and perceive your care of our estate, by falling into a consideration of a grateful acknowledgment of such benefits as you have received; and that your coming is to present thanks to us, which I accept with no less joy than your loves can have desire to offer such a present.

I do assure you there is no prince that loves his subjects better, or whose love can countervail our love. There is no jewel, be it of never so rich a price, which I set before this jewel: I mean your love. For I do esteem it more than any treasure or

---

1. Elizabeth equivocates nicely. She refuses to disagree with Parliament, lest she not respect her own misgivings; she refuses to agree with Parliament, lest its policy not be in her own interest.
1. In 1588, with the Spanish fleet threatening the south coast of England, Elizabeth went to Tilbury, in Dorset, to speak to the troops who were guarding England against an invasion.
2. Amusement.
3. Shameful.
4. Be caused.

5. Courage.
6. Recompense.
1. The queen had the prerogative or absolute power to grant favored subjects a patent for an exclusive manufacture. But the monopolies so created were disliked by those who would otherwise have competed for business, and a move to limit them was begun in Parliament. In response, in 1601, Elizabeth met with a committee of the House of Commons, led by the Speaker, thanked them for the subsidies recently granted the crown by the Commons, and promised to reform her practice.

riches; for that we know how to prize, but love and thanks I count unvaluable. And, though God hath raised me high, yet this I count the glory of my crown, that I have reigned with your loves. This makes me that I do not so much rejoice that God hath made me to be a queen, as to be a queen over so thankful a people. Therefore, I have cause to wish nothing more than to content the subject; and that is a duty which I owe. Neither do I desire to live longer days than I may see your prosperity; and that is my only desire. And as I am that person that still yet under God hath delivered you, so I trust, by the almighty power of God, that I shall be His instrument to preserve you from every peril, dishonor, shame, tyranny and oppression; partly by means of your intended helps which we take very acceptably, because it manifesteth the largeness of your good loves and loyalties unto your sovereign.

Of myself I must say this: I never was any greedy, scraping grasper, nor a strait, fast-holding prince, nor yet a waster. My heart was never set on any worldly goods, but only for my subjects' good. What you bestow on me, I will not hoard it up, but receive it to bestow on you again. Yea, mine own properties I account yours, to be expended for your good; and your eyes shall see the bestowing of all for your good. Therefore, render unto them, I beseech you, Mr. Speaker, such thanks as you imagine my heart yieldeth, but my tongue cannot express.

Since I was queen, yet did I never put my pen to any grant but that, upon pretext and semblance made unto me, it was both good and beneficial to the subject in general, though a private profit to some of my ancient servants who had deserved well at my hands. But the contrary being found by experience, I am exceedingly beholding to such subjects as would move the same at the first. And I am not so simple to suppose, but that there be some of the Lower House whom these grievances never touched: and for them, I think they spake out of zeal to their countries,[2] and not out of spleen or malevolent affection as being parties grieved; and I take it exceeding gratefully from them, because it gives us to know that no respects or interest had moved them, other than the minds they have to suffer no diminution of our honor and our subjects' love unto us. The zeal of which affection, tending to ease my people and knit their hearts unto me, I embrace with a princely care, for above all earthly treasure I esteem my people's love, more than which I desire not to merit.

That my grants should be grievous to my people and oppressions privileged under color of our patents, our kingly dignity shall not suffer[3] it. Yea, when I heard it, I could give no rest unto my thoughts until I had reformed it. Shall they, think you, escape unpunished that have thus oppressed you, and have been respectless of their duty, and regardless of our honor?[4] No, I assure you, Mr. Speaker, were it not more for conscience' sake than for any glory or increase of love that I desire, these errors, troubles, vexations and oppressions, done by these varlets and lewd persons, not worthy the name of subjects, should not escape without condign punishment. But I perceive they dealt with me like physicians who, ministering a drug, make it more acceptable by giving it a good aromatical savor, or when they give pills do gild them all over.[5]

I have ever used to set the Last-Judgment Day before mine eyes, and so to rule as I shall be judged to answer before a higher Judge, to whose judgment seat I do ap-

2. I.e, those members who protested monopolies on behalf of their constituents, or "countries," and not on their own account.
3. Allow.
4. I.e., those who benefited from a monopoly without regard to the welfare of the general public.
5. Elizabeth compares unscrupulous patentees to physicians who coat bitter pills with sugar; in this case she is the patient who did not realize what was being given to her.

peal, that never thought was cherished in my heart that tended not unto my people's good. And now, if my kingly bounties have been abused, and my grants turned to the hurt of my people, contrary to my will and meaning, and if any in authority under me have neglected or perverted what I have committed to them, I hope God will not lay their culps[6] and offences to my charge; who, though there were danger in repealing our grants, yet what danger would I not rather incur for your good, than I would suffer them still to continue?

I know the title of a king is a glorious title; but assure yourself that the shining glory of princely authority hath not so dazzled the eyes of our understanding, but that we well know and remember that we also are to yield an account of our actions before the great Judge. To be a king and wear a crown is a thing more glorious to them that see it, than it is pleasant to them that bear it. For myself, I was never so much enticed with the glorious name of a king or royal authority of a queen, as delighted that God hath made me His instrument to maintain His truth and glory, and to defend this kingdom (as I said) from peril, dishonor, tyranny and oppression.

There will never queen sit in my seat with more zeal to my country, care for my subjects, and that will sooner with willingness venture her life for your good and safety, than myself. For it is my desire to live nor reign no longer than my life and reign shall be for your good. And though you have had and may have many princes more mighty and wise sitting in this seat, yet you never had nor shall have any that will be more careful and loving.

Shall I ascribe anything to myself and my sexly weakness? I were not worthy to live then; and, of all, most unworthy of the mercies I have had from God, who hath given me a heart that yet never feared any foreign or home enemy. And I speak it to give God the praise, as a testimony before you, and not to attribute anything to myself. For I, oh Lord! what am I, whom practices and perils past should not fear? Or what can I do? That I should speak for any glory, God forbid.

This, Mr. Speaker, I pray you deliver unto the House, to whom heartily recommend me. And so I commit you all to your best fortunes and further counsels. And I pray you, Mr. Comptroller,[7] Mr. Secretary,[8] and you of my Council, that before these gentlemen go into their countries, you bring them all to kiss my hand.

❈

Aemilia Lanyer
1569–1645

Aemilia Lanyer was born Aemilia Bassano, the daughter of Queen Elizabeth's court musician, Baptista Bassano. Acquaintance with the nobility surrounding the Queen allowed her an education that was typically reserved for women of high station. At eighteen, shortly after her mother's death, she became the mistress of Henry Cary Hunsdon, the Lord Chancellor. Her position increased her presence at court until, at twenty-three, she became pregnant and was forced to marry a court musician. Their son, conspicuously named Henry, was born three months after the wedding. The first years of her married life were not auspicious. Alfonso Lanyer was a spendthrift, and the money Aemilia had acquired as Hunsdon's mistress was

---

6. Sins.
7. Sir William Knollys.
8. Sir Robert Cecil.

soon exhausted. Desperate for reassurance, she visited the astrologer Simon Forman to learn whether the stars indicated that Alfonso would gain a knighthood. The disreputable Forman appears to have had other ideas. His casebook records that on one occasion, he "went and supped with her and stayed all night, and she was familiar and friendly to him in all things. But only she would not halek [have intercourse] . . . he never obtained his purpose and she was a whore and dealt evil with him."

Lanyer's character is more accurately represented in the record of her long friendship with Margaret Clifford, Countess of Cumberland, and her daughter Anne. In 1610, partly in tribute to the loyal support of her patroness, Lanyer published a volume of poetry entitled *Salve Deus Rex Judaeorum*; this included a verse defense of women and a poem to Cookham, a country house leased by Margaret Clifford's brother, William Russell, and visited frequently by Lanyer until 1605. She particularly records two critical transformations in her sense of herself: a spiritual awakening, inspired by the piety of the Countess, and a confirmation of herself as a poet. Her impressions of Cookham express a unity among aesthetic elements that are usually opposed and antithetical: pagan culture and Christian vision, temporal experience and spiritual knowledge, and the erotic pleasure in the discipline of chastity.

The Description of Cookham

Farewell (sweet Cookham) where I first obtained
Grace from that Grace where perfit° grace remained;   *perfect*
And where the Muses[1] gave their full consent,
I should have power the virtuous to content;
5   Where princely Palace willed me to indite,°   *write*
The sacred story[2] of the soul's delight.
Farewell (sweet place) where virtue then did rest,
And all delights did harbor in her breast;
Never shall my sad eyes again behold
10   Those pleasures which my thoughts did then unfold:
Yet you (great Lady),[3] Mistress of that place,
From whose desires did spring this work of grace;
Vouchsafe° to think upon those pleasures past,   *agree*
As fleeting worldly joys that could not last,
15   Or, as dim shadows of celestial pleasures,
Which are desired above all earthly treasures.
Oh how (me thought) against you thither came,[4]
Each part did seem some new delight to frame!
The house received all ornaments to grace it,
20   And would endure no foulness to deface it.
The walks put on their summer liveries,°   *uniforms*
And all things else did hold like similies:°   *comparisons*
The trees with leaves, with fruits, with flowers clad,
Embraced each other, seeming to be glad,
25   Turning themselves to beauteous canopies,
To shade the bright sun from your brighter eyes.
The crystal streams with silver spangles graced,

---

1. Divinities who presided over the arts and courtesy.
2. Possibly the story of the Passion, recounted in the poem *Salve Deus Rex Judaeorum*.
3. Margaret Clifford, the Countess of Cumberland.
4. In preparation for your arrival.

While by the glorious sun they were embraced,
The little birds in chirping notes did sing,
30 To entertain both you and that sweet spring.
And Philomela[5] with her sundry lays,°   songs
Both you and that delightful place did praise.
Oh, how me thought each plant, each flower, each tree
Set forth their beauties then to welcome thee:
35 The very hills right humbly did descend,
When you to tread upon them did intend.
And as you set your feet, they still did rise,
Glad that they could receive so rich a prize.
The gentle winds did take delight to be
40 Among those woods that were so graced by thee.
And in sad° murmur uttered pleasing sound,   deep
That pleasure in that place might more abound:
The swelling banks delivered all their pride,
When such a Phoenix[6] once they had espied.
45 Each arbor, bank, each seat, each stately tree,
Thought themselves honored in supporting thee.
The pretty birds would oft come to attend thee,
Yet fly away for fear they should offend thee:
The little creatures in the burrow by°   nearby
50 Would come abroad to sport them in your eye;
Yet fearful of the bow in your fair hand,
Would run away when you did make a stand.
Now let me come unto that stately tree,
Wherein such goodly prospects you did see;
55 That oak that did in height his fellows pass,
As much as lofty trees, low growing grass
Much like a comely cedar straight and tall,
Whose beauteous stature far exceeded all.
How often did you visit this fair tree,
60 Which seeming joyful in receiving thee,
Would like a palm tree spread his arms abroad,
Desirous that you there should make abode:
Whose fair green leaves much like a comely veil,
Defended Phoebus when he would assail:[7]
65 Whose pleasing boughs did yield a cool fresh air,
Joying his happiness when you were there.
Where being seated, you might plainly see,
Hills, vales, and woods, as if on bended knee
They had appeared, your honor to salute,
70 Or to prefer some strange unlooked for suit:
All interlaced with brooks and crystal springs,
A prospect fit to please the eyes of kings:

---

5. In Greek mythology, a woman who was transformed
into a swallow; in Latin versions of her story she becomes
a nightingale.
6. A mythical bird, always unique on earth, that regener-

ates itself in its own funeral pyre and therefore signifies
eternity; here it figures the Countess.
7. The leaves of the palm tree protected the Countess
from Phoebus, the god of the sun.

And thirteen shires appeared all in your sight,
Europe could not afford much more delight.
75 What was there then but gave you all content,
While you the time in meditation spent,
Of their Creator's power, which there you saw,
In all his creatures held a perfit law;
And in their beauties did you plain descry,°   *discern*
80 His beauty, wisdom, grace, love, majesty.
In these sweet woods how often did you walk,
With Christ and his apostles there to talk;
Placing his holy writ in some fair tree,
To meditate what you therein did see:
85 With Moses you did mount his holy hill,[8]
To know his pleasure, and perform his will.
With lovely David[9] you did often sing
His holy hymns to heaven's eternal king.
And in sweet music did your soul delight,
90 To sound his praises, morning, noon, and night.
With blessed Joseph you did often feed
Your pined° brethren, when they stood in need.[1]   *poor*
And that sweet lady sprung from Clifford's race,[2]
Of noble Bedford's blood, fair steam of grace,
95 To honorable Dorset now espoused,
In whose fair breast true virtue then was housed.
Oh, what delight did my weak spirits find
In those pure parts of her well framed mind,
And yet it grieves me that I cannot be
100 Near unto her, whose virtues did agree
With those fair ornaments of outward beauty,
Which did enforce from all both love and duty.
Unconstant Fortune, thou art most to blame,
Who casts us down into so low a frame,
105 Where our great friends we cannot daily see,
So great a diffrence is there in degree.
Many are placed in those orbs of state,
Parters° in honor, so ordained by Fate;   *participants*
Nearer in show, yet farther off in love,
110 In which, the lowest always are above.[3]
But whither am I carried in conceit?°   *imagination*
My wit too weak to conster of° the great.   *understand*
Why not? although we are but born of earth,
We may behold the heavens, despising death;
115 And loving heaven that is so far above,

8. Moses climbed Mount Sinai to receive the law of God
(Exodus 24, 25).
9. King David the psalmist.
1. Sold by his jealous brothers into slavery, Joseph became
Pharoah's right-hand man and granted these same brothers food and money during a famine many years later
(Genesis 42.1–28).

2. The Lady is the Countess's daughter Anne, descended
from Margaret Russell of Bedford and her father George
Clifford, Duke of Cumberland. Anne married the Earl of
Dorset in 1609 and is thus referred to as Dorset.
3. I.e., persons of low station or rank love more than
those who are of the gentry or nobility.

May in the end vouchsafe us entire love.
Therefore sweet memory do thou retain
Those pleasures past, which will not turn again;
Remember beauteous Dorset's former sports,
120 So far from being touched by ill reports;
Wherein myself did always bear a part,
While reverend Love presented my true heart.
Those recreations let me bear in mind,
Which her sweet youth and noble thoughts did find,
125 Whereof deprived, I evermore must grieve,
Hating blind Fortune, careless to relieve.
And you sweet Cookham, whom these ladies leave,
I now must tell the grief you did conceive
At their departure; when they went away,
130 How everything retained a sad dismay;
Nay long before, when once an inkling came,
Methought each thing did unto sorrow frame:
The trees that were so glorious in our view,
Forsook both flowers and fruit, when once they knew
135 Of your depart,° their very leaves did wither,   departure
Changing their colors as they grew together.
But when they saw this had no power to stay you,
They often wept, though speechless, could not pray° you;   beg
Letting their tears in your fair bosoms fall,
140 As if they said, "Why will ye leave us all?"
This being vain, they cast their leaves away,
Hoping that pity would have made you stay,
Their frozen tops like age's hoary hairs,
Shows their disasters, languishing in fears;
145 A swarthy riveled rine° all overspread,   bark
Their dying bodies half alive, half dead.
But your occasions called you so away,
That nothing there had power to make you stay:
Yet did I see a noble grateful mind,
150 Requiting each according to their kind,
Forgetting not to turn and take your leave
Of these sad creatures, powerless to receive
Your favor when with grief you did depart,
Placing their former pleasures in your heart;
155 Giving great charge to noble memory,
There to preserve their love continually:
But specially the love of that fair tree,
That first and last you did vouchsafe to see:
In which it pleased you oft to take the air,
160 With noble Dorset, then a virgin fair:
Where many a learned book was read and scanned
To this fair tree, taking me by the hand,
You did repeat the pleasures which had passed,
Seeming to grieve they could no longer last.

165   And with a chaste, yet loving kiss took leave,
Of which sweet kiss I did it soon bereave:[4]
Scorning a senseless creature should possess
So rare a favor, so great happiness.
No other kiss it could receive from me,

170   For fear to give back what it took of thee:
So I ungrateful creature did deceive it,
Of that which you vouchsafed in love to leave it.
And though it oft° had given me much content,   *often*
Yet this great wrong I never could repent:

175   But of the happiest made it most forlorn,
To show that nothing's free from Fortune's scorn,
While all the rest with this most beauteous tree,
Made their sad consort° sorrow's harmony.   *music*
The flowers that on the banks and walks did grow,

180   Crept in the ground, the grass did weep for woe.
The winds and waters seemed to chide together,
Because you went away they know not whither:
And those sweet brooks that ran so fair and clear,
With grief and trouble wrinkled did appear.

185   Those pretty birds that wonted° were to sing,   *accustomed*
Now neither sing, nor chirp, nor use their wing;
But with their tender feet on some bare spray,
Warble forth sorrow, and their own dismay.
Fair Philomela leaves her mournful ditty,

190   Drowned in dead sleep, yet can procure no pity:
Each arbor, bank, each seat, each stately tree,
Looks bare and desolate now for want of thee;
Turning green tresses into frosty gray,
While in cold grief they wither all away.

195   The sun grew weak, his beams no comfort gave,
While all green things did make the earth their grave;
Each briar, each bramble, when you went away,
Caught fast your clothes, thinking to make you stay;
Delightful Echo[5] wonted° to reply   *used*

200   To our last words, did now for sorrow die:
The house cast off each garment that might grace it,
Putting on dust and cobwebs to deface it.
All desolation then there did appear,
When you were going whom they held so dear.

205   This last farewell to Cookham here I give,
When I am dead thy name in this may live,
Wherein I have performed her noble hest,°   *request*
Whose virtues lodge in my unworthy breast,
And ever shall, so long as life remains,

210   Tying my heart to her by those rich chains.

---

4. I.e., I took their kiss from the tree on which they had put it.

5. A nymph who can only repeat what she has heard; in the absence of voices, she dies.

Christopher Marlowe
1564–1593

When Christopher Marlowe began his career as a dramatist, the Elizabethan stage was at the height of its popularity and sophistication. Marlowe's plays were an immediate success, fascinating audiences with dazzling characters, exotic settings, and controversial subjects. Throughout his career—and even after his sudden death at the age of twenty-nine—Marlowe was Shakespeare's principal commercial and artistic rival.

A shoemaker's son, Marlowe went to Cambridge on a scholarship that was intended to prepare him for holy orders. His interests proved to be literary rather than religious, however, and he left Cambridge for London. As a student, he had composed a number of poems, notably the brilliant but unfinished *Hero and Leander*, a narrative of heterosexual and homosexual passion, but public recognition came with the production of his first play, *Tamburlaine the Great*, in 1587. This was followed by *The Second Part of Tamburlaine the Great*, *The Jew of Malta*, *Edward II*, *Dr. Faustus*, *Dido, Queen of Carthage*, and finally, *The Massacre at Paris*, all composed within a period of six years. Marlowe's bold and inventive language captivated audiences; his blank verse, in which the sense of a sentence is not interrupted at the end of each line by the constraints of rhyme, brought the rhythms of natural speech to the language of theater. His characterizations of heroes were equally astonishing: driven by an incandescent desire that no conquest could satisfy, they revealed the torment and tragedy that were occasioned by pride.

Marlowe himself may have been employed in subversive activities. While still at Cambridge, he became a spy for Queen Elizabeth's secret service, dedicated to the infiltration and exposure of Catholic groups in England and abroad. How much activity he was responsible for remains guesswork. At the very least, the manner in which he died suggests his involvement in clandestine politics. In May 1593, the Queen's Privy Council issued a warrant for his arrest. The charge against him—blasphemy—seems to have come from Thomas Kyd, a fellow playwright with whom Marlowe shared lodgings. While in London waiting for a hearing, Marlowe, who was drinking in an alehouse, got into a fight with three men (all government spies), one of whom was Ingram Friser. Marlowe raised a dagger to stab Friser, but Friser, warding off the blow, managed to turn the dagger against Marlowe. It pierced his eye "in such sort that his brains coming out at the dagger point, he shortly after died." The affair did not end there; two days after Marlowe's death, Richard Baines (himself a former spy) accused him before the Privy Council of atheism, treason, and the opinion "that they that love not tobacco and boys were fools." Whether or not these accusations held any truth, they referred to views that were not unusual in the circles Marlowe frequented; they indicate a skepticism in matters of religion and an indifference to social decorum that authorities responsible for political order would have considered dangerous. Some scholars think that Marlowe was murdered by government command. Although the mystery surrounding his death may never be solved, the mercurial brilliance of his work remains undisputed.

With the exception of the two parts of *Tamburlaine*, published in 1590, Marlowe's works were published after his death: *Edward II* and *Dido, Queen of Carthage* in 1594; *Hero and Leander* in 1598; *Dr. Faustus* in 1604; and *The Jew of Malta* in 1633.

 For additional resources on Marlowe, go to *The Longman Anthology of British Literature* Web site at www.myliteraturekit.com.

Hero and Leander[1]

On Hellespont,[2] guilty of true love's blood,
In view and opposite, two cities stood,
Seaborders,° disjoined by Neptune's might.   *seaports*
The one Abydos, the other Sestos hight.
5   As Sestos, Hero dwelt, Hero the fair,
Whom young Apollo° courted for her hair,   *god of the sun*
And offered as a dower° his burning throne,   *wedding gift*
Where she should sit for men to gaze upon.
The outside of her garments were of lawn,°   *fine cloth*
10   The lining, purple silk, with gilt stars drawn,
Her wide sleeves green, and bordered with a grove,
Where Venus° in her naked glory strove,   *goddess of love*
To please the careless and disdainful eyes,
Of proud Adonis° that before her lies.   *Venus's lover*
15   Her kirtle° blue, whereon was many a stain,   *gown*
Made with the blood of wretched lovers slain.
Upon her head she wore a myrtle wreath,
From whence her veil reached to the ground beneath.
Her veil was artificial flowers and leaves,
20   Whose workmanship both man and beast deceives.
Many would praise the sweet smell as she passed,
When t'was the odor which her breath forth cast,
And there for honey, bees have fought in vain,
And beat from thence, have lighted there again.
25   About her neck hung chains of pebble stone,
Which, lightened by her neck, like diamonds shone.
She wore no gloves, for neither sun nor wind
Would burn or parch her hands, but to her mind,
Or warm or cool them, for they took delight
30   To play upon those hands, they were so white.
Buskins° of shells all silvered, used she,   *boots*
And branched° with blushing coral to the knee.   *decorated*
Where sparrows perched, of hollow pearl and gold,
Such as the world would wonder to behold.
35   Those with sweet water oft her handmaid fills,
Which as she went would chirrup through the° bills.[3]   *their*
Some say, for her the fairest Cupid pined,
And looking in her face, was strucken° blind.   *struck*
But this is true, so like was one the other,
40   As he imagined Hero was his mother.
And oftentimes into her bosom flew,
About her naked neck his bare arms threw.

---

1. In the early modern period, the story of the lovers Hero
and Leander was attributed to the legendary poet
Musaeus; in fact, it appears to be the work of an anonymous Greek poet of the 4th or 5th century C.E.
2. The straits separating Asia Minor from Thracian

Greece, now the Dardanelles.
3. A fantastic costume: Hero's boots are decorated with
shells that are filled with water on which mechanical
sparrows made of pearl and gold perch and chirp.

And laid his childish head upon her breast,
And with still panting rocked, there took his rest.
45 So lovely fair was Hero, Venus' nun,
As nature wept, thinking she was undone,
Because she took more from her than she left,
And of such wondrous beauty her bereft.
Therefore in sign° her treasure suffered wrack,°   *to signify / loss*
50 Since Hero's time, hath half the world been black.
Amorous Leander, beautiful and young,
(Whose tragedy divine Musaeus sung)
Dwelt at Abidos, since him dwelt there none
For whom succeeding times make greater moan.
55 His dangling tresses that were never shorn,
Had they been cut and unto Colchis[4] borne,
Would have allured the vent'rous° youth of Greece,   *adventurous*
To hazard more than for the golden fleece.
Fair Cynthia° wished his arms might be her sphere,   *goddess of the moon*
60 Grief makes her pale, because she moves not there.
His body was straight as Circe's[5] wand,
Jove might have sipped out nectar from his hand.
Even as delicious meat is to the taste,
So was his neck in touching, and surpassed
65 The white of Pelops'[6] shoulder; I could tell ye
How smooth his breast was, and how white his belly,
And whose immortal fingers did imprint,
That heavenly path with many a curious dint
That runs along his back, but my rude pen
70 Can hardly blazon° forth the loves of men,[7]   *list*
Much less of powerful gods. Let it suffice,
That my slack muse sings of Leander's eyes.
Those orient° cheeks and lips, exceeding his   *shining*
That leapt into the water for a kiss
75 Of his own shadow, and despising many,
Died ere he could enjoy the love of any.
Had wild Hippolytus[8] Leander seen,
Enamored of his beauty had he been,
His presence made the rudest peasant melt,
80 That in the vast uplandish° country dwelt;   *rustic*
The barbarous Thracian[9] soldier, moved with nought,
Was moved with him, and for his favor fought.

---

4. A country at the east end of the Black Sea, to which the legendary golden fleece—a Greek treasure—had been taken. Colchis was raided by the Greek hero Jason and his men, the Argonauts, who carried the fleece back to their homeland.
5. The Greek divinity who with her magic wand turned the companions of Odysseus into swine (*Odyssey* 10).
6. A legendary figure whose father, Tantalus, had him cooked and served to the gods. Only his shoulder was eaten, however, and that was restored with a piece of ivory.

7. The homoerotic element in Marlowe's description of Leander becomes explicit here and continues to be prominent later in the poet's account of Neptune's love for Leander.
8. A legendary hero, vowed to hunting and chastity; at the command of Phaedra, his stepmother, he was consumed by a sea-monster for having refused to return her love for him.
9. Thrace was a mountainous region in northeastern Greece.

Some swore he was a maid in man's attire,
For in his looks were all that men desire,
85 A pleasant, smiling cheek, a speaking eye,
A brow for love to banquet royally,
And such as knew he was a man would say,
Leander, thou art made for amorous play;
Why art thou not in love, and loved of all?
90 Though thou be fair, yet be not thine own thrall.°   *slave*

The men of wealthy Sestos, every year
(For his sake whom their goddess° held so dear,   *Venus*
Rose-cheeked Adonis), kept a solemn feast;
Thither resorted many a wandering guest
95 To meet their loves; such as had none at all
Came lovers home from this great festival.
For every street like to a firmament°   *sky*
Glistered with breathing stars, who where they went,
Frighted the melancholy earth, which deemed,
100 Eternal heaven to burn, for so it seemed
As if another Phaeton[1] had got
The guidance of the sun's rich chariot.
But far above, the loveliest Hero shined,
And stole away th'enchanted gazer's mind,
105 For like sea-nymphs inveigling harmony,
So was her beauty to the standers-by.
Nor that night-wandering pale and watery star,[2]
(When yawning dragons draw her thirling° car,   *spinning*
From Latmos' mount up to the gloomy sky,
110 Where crowned with blazing light and majesty,
She proudly sits) more over-rules the flood,
Than she the hearts of those that near her stood.
Even as, when gaudy nymphs pursue the chase,
Wretched Ixion's shaggy-footed race,[3]
115 Incensed with savage heat, gallop amain,
From steep pine-bearing mountains to the plain,
So ran the people forth to gaze upon her,
And all that viewed her were enamored on her.
And as in fury of a dreadful fight,
120 Their fellows being slain or put to flight,
Poor soldiers stand with fear of death strucken,
So at her presence all surprised and tooken°   *taken*
Await the sentence of her scornful eyes;
He whom she favors lives, the other dies.
125 There might you see one sigh, another rage,

---

1. Apollo's son, who drove his father's chariot too near the earth and was struck down by Jove's thunderbolt.
2. The moon, or Cynthia, whose seat is Mount Latmos.
3. Centaurs, creatures who were half-man, half-horse.

They were the sons of Centaurus, the son of Ixion and Nephele, a cloud-goddess whom Zeus substituted for Hera, Ixion's real love.

And some (their violent passions to assuage)
Compile sharp satires; but alas too late,
For faithful love will never turn to hate.
And many, seeing great princes were denied,
130   Pined as they went and thinking on her, died.
On this feast day, O cursed day and hour,
Went Hero through Sestos, from her tower
To Venus' temple, where unhappily,
As after chanced, they did each other spy.
135   So fair a church as this had Venus none,
The walls were of discolored jasper stone,
Wherein was Proteus[4] carved, and o'erhead,
A lively vine of green sea agate spread,
Where by one hand, light-headed Bacchus° hung,   *god of wine*
140   And with the other, wine from grapes out-wrung.
Of crystal shining fair the pavement was,
The town of Sestos called it Venus' glass.
There might you see the gods in sundry shapes
Committing heady riots, incest, rapes.
145   For know that underneath this radiant flower
Was Danae's statue[5] in a brazen tower;
Jove, stealing from his sister's bed
To dally with Idalian Ganymede,
And for his love, Europa, bellowing loud,
150   And tumbling with the rainbow in a cloud;
Blood-quaffing Mars, heaving the iron net,
Which limping Vulcan and his Cyclops set;
Love kindling fire to burn such towns as Troy;
Sylvanus weeping for the lovely boy
155   That now is turned into a cypress tree,
Under whose shade the wood gods love to be.
And in the midst a silver altar stood,
There Hero, sacrificing turtle's° blood,   *dove's*
Veiled to the ground, veiling her eyelids close,
160   And modestly they opened as she rose;
Thence flew Love's arrow with the golden head,
And thus Leander was enamored.
Stone still he stood, and evermore he gazed,
Till with the fire that from his count'nance blazed,
165   Relenting Hero's gentle heart was struck,
Such force and virtue hath an amorous look.

It lies not in our power to love or hate,
For will in us is overruled by fate.

---

4. A sea-god, who could change his shape at will.
5. The figure of the mythical woman Danae, whose father shut her up in a tower to keep her from suitors; Jupiter visited her there in a shower of gold. Marlowe continues his description of "Venus' glass" by allusions to popular mythological figures: Ganymede, Jove's cupbearer and lover; Europa, carried off by Jove disguised as a bull; the lover of Venus, Mars, who was caught in the net of Vulcan, Venus's husband, assisted by his one-eyed helpers, the Cyclops; and Sylvanus, a wood god, who wept for his lover, Cyparissus, who had been turned into a tree.

When two are stripped long ere the course begin,
170   We wish that one should lose, the other win.
And one especially do we affect,
Of two gold ingots like in each respect.
The reason no man knows, let it suffice,
What we behold is censured° by our eyes.   *judged*
175   Where both deliberate, the love is slight,
Who ever loved that loved not at first sight?

He kneeled, but unto her devoutly prayed.
Chaste Hero to herself thus softly said,
Were I the saint he worships, I would hear him,
180   And as she spoke those words, came somewhat near him.
He started up, she blushed as one ashamed,
Wherewith Leander much more was inflamed.
He touched her hand, in touching it she trembled,
Love deeply grounded, hardly is dissembled.
185   These lovers parled° by the touch of hands;   *spoke*
True love is mute, and oft amazed stands.
Thus while dumb signs their yielding hearts entangled,
The air with sparks of living fire was spangled,
And Night, deep-drenched in misty Acheron,°   *a river in hell*
190   Heaved up her head, and half the world upon
Breathed darkness forth (dark night is Cupid's day)
And now begins Leander to display
Love's holy fire with words, with sighs and tears,
Which like sweet music entered Hero's ears,
195   And yet at every word she turned aside,
And always cut him off as he replied.
At last, like to a bold, sharp sophister,°   *false reasoner*
With cheerful hope thus he accosted her.

Fair creature, let me speak without offence,
200   I would my rude words had the influence
To lead thy thoughts, as thy fair looks do mine,
Then shouldst thou be his prisoner who is thine.
Be not unkind and fair, misshapen stuff°   *ungainly persons*
Are of behavior boisterous and rough.
205   O shun me not, but hear me ere you go,
God knows I cannot force love, as you do.
My words shall be as spotless as my youth,
Full of simplicity and naked truth.
This sacrifice (whose sweet perfume descending
210   From Venus' altar to your footsteps bending)
Doth testify that you exceed her far,
To whom you offer, and whose nun you are.
Why should you worship her, her you surpass,
As much as sparkling diamonds flaring° glass.   *flashing*
215   A diamond set in lead his worth retains,
A heavenly nymph, beloved of human swains,°   *suitors*

Receives no blemish, but oft times more grace,
Which makes me hope, although I am but base,
Base in respect of thee, divine and pure,
220 Dutiful service may thy love procure,
And I in duty will excel all other,
As thou in beauty dost exceed Love's mother.
Nor heaven, nor thou, were made to gaze upon,
As heaven preserves all things, so save thou one.°   *Leander*
225 A stately builded ship, well-rigged and tall,
The ocean maketh more majestical.
Why vowest thou then to live in Sestos here,
Who on Love's seas more glorious wouldst appear?
Like untuned golden strings all women are,
230 Which, long time lie untouched, will harshly jar.
Vessels of brass oft handled brightly shine,
What difference betwixt the richest mine
And basest mold, but use? For both not used
Are of like worth. Then treasure is abused
235 When misers keep it; being put to loan,
In time it will return us two for one.
Rich robes, themselves and others do adorn,
Neither themselves nor others, if not worn.
Who builds a palace and rams up the gate,
240 Shall see it ruinous and desolate.
Ah, simple Hero, learn thyself to cherish,
Lone women, like to empty houses, perish.
Less sins the poor rich man that starves himself,
In heaping up a mass of drossy pelf,°   *worthless booty*
245 Than such as you; his golden earth remains,
Which, after his decease, some other gains.
But this fair gem, sweet in the loss alone,
When you fleet hence, can be bequeathed to none.
Or if it could, down from th'enamelled sky,
250 All heaven would come to claim this legacy,
And with intestine broils° the world destroy,   *civil wars*
And quite confound nature's sweet harmony.
Well therefore by the gods decreed it is,
We human creatures should enjoy that bliss.
255 One is no number, maids are nothing then,
Without the sweet society of men.
Wilt thou live single still? One shalt thou be,
Though never-singling Hymen[6] couple thee.
Wild savages, that drink of running springs,
260 Think water far excels all earthly things.
But they that daily taste neat° wine, despise it.   *unwatered*
Virginity, albeit some highly prize it,
Compared with marriage, had you tried them both,

---

6. Marlowe turns to paradox: Although Hero is coupled by Hymen, the god of marriage, she can also remain "one" or single.

Differs as much as wine and water doth.
265 Base boullion° for the stamp's sake we allow,[7]   *metal*
Even so for men's impression do we you.
By which alone, our reverend fathers say,
Women receive perfection every way.
This idol which you term virginity,
270 Is neither essence subject to the eye,
No, nor to any one exterior sense,
Nor hath it any place of residence,
Nor is't of earth or mold celestial,
Or capable of any form at all.
275 Of that which hath no being do not boast,
Things that are not at all are never lost.
Men foolishly do call it virtuous,
What virtue is it, that is born with us?
Much less can honor be ascribed thereto;
280 Honor is purchased by the deeds we do.
Believe me, Hero, honor is not won,
Until some honorable deed be done.
Seek you for chastity, immortal fame,
And know that some have wronged Diana's name?
285 Whose name is it, if she be false or not,
So she be fair, but some vile tongues will blot?
But you are fair (aye me), so wondrous fair,
So young, so gentle, and so debonair,°   *courteous*
As Greece will think if thus you live alone,
290 Some one or other keeps you as his own.
Then, Hero, hate me not, nor from me fly,
To follow swiftly blasting infamy.
Perhaps thy sacred priesthood makes thee loath,
Tell me, to whom mad'st thou that heedless oath?

295 To Venus, answered she, and as she spoke,
Forth from those two translucent cisterns broke
A stream of liquid pearl, which down her face
Made milk-white paths, whereon the gods might trace
To Jove's high court. He thus replied: the rites
300 In which love's beauteous empress most delights
Are banquets, Doric[8] music, midnight revel,
Plays, masques, and all that stern age counteth evil.
Thee as a holy Idiot doth she scorn,
For thou, in vowing chastity, hast sworn
305 To rob her name and honor, and thereby
Commit'st a sin far worse than perjury,
Even sacrilege against her deity,
Through regular and formal purity.

---

7. Just as a coin has its value stamped on it, so a woman is valued according to the impression she gives.

8. Pertaining to the Greek region of Doris, noted for the simplicity of its culture.

To expiate which sin, kiss and shake hands,
310   Such sacrifice as this Venus demands.

Thereat she smiled, and did deny him so,
As put thereby, yet might he hope for mo'e.
Which makes him quickly re-enforce his speech,
And her in humble manner thus beseech.

315   Though neither gods nor men may thee deserve,
Yet for her sake whom you have vowed to serve,
Abandon fruitless, cold virginity,
The gentle Queen of Love's sole enemy.
Then shall you most resemble Venus' nun,
320   When Venus' sweet rites are performed and done.
Flint-breasted Pallas[9] joys in single life,
But Pallas and your mistress are at strife.
Love, Hero, then, and be not tyrannous,
But heal the heart that thou has wounded thus,
325   Nor stain thy youthful years with avarice,
Fair fools delight to be accounted nice.°   *coy*
The richest corn° dies if it be not reaped,   *grain*
Beauty alone is lost, too warily kept.
These arguments he used, and many more,
330   Wherewith she yielded, that was won before,
Hero's looks yielded, but her words made war;
Women are won when they begin to jar.°   *quarrel*
Thus having swallowed Cupid's golden hook,
The more she strived, the deeper was she struck.
335   Yet evilly feigning anger, strove she still,
And would be wrought to grant against her will.
So having paused a while, at last she said:
Who taught thee rhetoric to deceive a maid?
Aye me, such words as these should I abhor,
340   And yet I like them for the orator.

With that Leander stooped, to have embraced her,
But from his spreading arms away she cast her,
And thus bespake him: Gentle youth, forbear
To touch the sacred garments which I wear.
345   Upon a rock, and underneath a hill,
Far from the town (where all is whist° and still,   *quiet*
Save that sea playing on yellow sand
Sends forth a rattling murmur to the land,
Whose sound allures the golden Morpheus,°   *god of sleep*
350   In silence of the night to visit us)
My turret stands, and there God knows I play
With Venus' swans and sparrows all the day,
A dwarfish beldame° bears° me company,   *old woman / keeps*

---

9. Athena or Minerva, goddess of wisdom, justice, and war.

That hops about the chamber where I lie,
355 And spends the night (that might be better spent)
In vain discourse and apish merriment.
Come thither; as she spake this, her tongue tripped,
For unawares (Come thither) from her slipped,
And suddenly her former color changed,
360 And here and there her eyes through anger ranged,
And like a planet, moving several ways,
At one self instant, she, poor soul, assays,
Loving, not to love at all, and every part,
Strove to resist the motions of her heart.
365 And hands so pure, so innocent, nay such,
As might have made heaven stoop to have a touch,
Did she uphold to Venus, and again,
Vowed spotless chastity, but all in vain.
Cupid beat down her prayers with his wings,
370 Her vowes above the empty air he flings.
All deep enraged, his sinewy bow he bent,
And shot a shaft that burning from him went,
Wherewith she, stroocken,° looked so dolefully,   *struck*
As made Love sigh to see his tyranny.
375 And as she wept, her tears to pearl he turned,
And wound them on his arm, and for her mourned.
Then towards the palace of the Destinies,°   *the Fates*
Laden with languishment and grief, he flies.
And to those stern nymphs humbly made request,
380 Both might enjoy each other, and be blessed.
But with a ghastly dreadful countenance,
Threatening a thousand deaths at every glance,
They answered Love, nor would vouchsafe so much
As one poor word, their hate to him was such.
385 Harken a while, and I will tell you why:
Heaven's winged herald, Jove-born Mercury,[1]
The selfsame day that he asleep had laid
Enchanted Argus, spied a country maid,
Whose careless hair, instead of pearl t'adorn it,
390 Glistered with dew, as one that seemed to scorn it,
Her breath as fragrant as the morning rose,
Her mind pure and her tongue untaught to glose.°   *deceive*
Yet proud she was (for lofty pride that dwells
In towered courts, is oft in shepherds' cells°),   *cottages*
395 And too too well the fair vermillion knew,
And silver tincture of her cheeks, that drew
The love of every swain. On her, this god
Enamored was, and with his snakey rod,°   *Mercury's staff*
Did charm her nimble feet, and made her stay,

1. The messenger god; he enchanted the many-eyed herdsman Argus (or Argos), whom Juno had ordered to guard the heifer Io, beloved of Jupiter.

400　The while upon a hillock down he lay,
　　And sweetly on his pipe began to play,
　　And with his smooth speech, her fancy to assay,°   *attempt*
　　Till in his twining arms he locked her fast,
　　And then he wooed her with kisses and at last,
405　As shepherds do, her on the ground he laid,
　　And tumbling in the grass, he often strayed
　　Beyond the bounds of shame, in being bold
　　To eye those parts, which no eye should behold,
　　And like an insolent commanding lover,
410　Boasting his parentage, would needs discover
　　The way to new Elysium; but she,
　　Whose only dower° was her chastity,   *dowry, wealth*
　　Having striven in vain, was now about to cry,
　　And crave the help of the shepherds that were nigh.
415　Herewith he stayed his fury, and began
　　To give her leave to rise; away she ran,
　　After went Mercury, who used such cunning,
　　As she to hear his tale, left off running.
　　Maids are not wooed by brutish force and might,
420　But speeches full of pleasure and delight.
　　And knowing Hermes° courted her, was glad   *Mercury*
　　That she such loveliness and beauty had
　　As could provoke his liking, yet was mute,
　　And neither would deny, nor grant his suit.
425　Still vowed he love, she wanting no excuse
　　To feed him with delays, as women use,
　　Or thirsting after immortality,
　　All women are ambitious naturally,
　　Imposed upon her lover such a task,
430　As he ought not perform, nor yet she ask.
　　A draught of flowing nectar, she requested,
　　Wherewith the king of the gods and men is feasted.
　　He ready to accomplish what she willed,
　　Stole some from Hebe° (Hebe, Jove's cups filled)   *a goddess*
435　And gave it to his simple rustic love,
　　Which being known (as what is hid from Jove?)
　　He inly stormed, and waxed more furious
　　Than for the fire filched by Prometheus,[2]
　　And thrusts him down from heaven; he wandering here,
440　In mournful terms, with sad and heavy cheer
　　Complained to Cupid. Cupid, for his° sake,   *Prometheus's*
　　To be revenged on Jove, did undertake,
　　And those on whom heaven, earth, and hell relies,
　　I mean the adamantine° Destinies,   *implacable*
445　He wounds with love, and forced them equally,

2. In Greek mythology, the figure of "forethought"; he made mankind out of clay and, when Jupiter deprived them of fire, stole it from heaven.

To dote upon deceitful Mercury.
They offered him the deadly, fatal knife,
That shears the slender threads of human life,
At his fair feathered feet, the engines laid,
450 Which th'earth from ugly Chaos'[3] den up-weighed:
These he regarded not, but did entreat
That Jove, usurper of his father's° seat,   *Saturn's*
Might presently be banished into hell,
And aged Saturn in Olympus dwell.
455 They granted what he craved, and once again,
Saturn and Ops° began their golden reign.   *Wealth (Saturn's wife)*
Murder, rape, war, lust, and treachery
Were, with Jove, closed in Stygian Emprie.°   *empire of hell*
But long this blessed time continued not,
460 As soon as he his wished purpose got;
He reckless of his promise, did despise
The love of the everlasting Destinies.
They seeing it, both Love and him abhorred,
And Jupiter unto his place restored.
465 And but that learning, in despite of Fate,
Will mount aloft and enter heaven's gate,
And to the seat of Jove itself advance,
Hermes[4] had slept in hell with ignorance.
Yet as a punishment they added this,
470 That he and Poverty should always kiss.
And to this day is every scholar poor,
Gross gold from them runs headlong to the boor.
Likewise the angry sisters° thus deluded,   *the Destinies*
To venge themselves on Hermes have concluded
475 That Midas' brood[5] shall sit in honor's chair,
To which the Muses' sons are only heir.
And fruitful wits that in aspiring° are,   *ambitious*
Shall, discontent, run into regions far,
And few great lords in virtuous deeds shall joy,
480 But be surprised with every garish toy.
And still enrich the lofty° servile clown,   *proud*
Who with encroaching guile keeps learning down.
Then muse not Cupid's suit no better sped,°   *succeeded*
Seeing in their loves the Fates were injured.
485 By this, sad Hero, with love unacquainted
Viewing Leander's face, fell down and fainted.
He kissed her and breathed life into her lips,
Wherewith as one displeased, away she trips.

3. The infinite space that precedes creation.
4. Hermes (or Mercury), as Learning (or the messenger god), must rise to a god's status; he cannot therefore be imprisoned in ignorance for long. Marlowe's unprecedented mythology is complicated: he describes "deceitful Mercury" as instituting a new golden age, then as losing it because he neglects "the Destinies," and finally as regaining divine favor because of what he signifies.
5. Like their father, the children of Midas would have the golden touch, i.e., money; ironically, the Destinies decree that money is also honor.

Yet as she went full often looked behind,
490   And many poor excuses did she find
To linger by the way, and once she stayed,
And would have turned again, but was afraid,
In offering parley,° to be counted light.   *speech*
So on she goes, and in her idle flight,
495   Her painted fan of curled plumes let fall,
Thinking to train° Leander therewithal.   *tempt*
He, being a novice, knew not what she meant,
But stayed, and after her a letter sent.
Which joyful Hero answered in such sort,
500   As he had hope to scale the beauteous fort,
Wherein the liberal graces locked their wealth,
And therefore to her tower he got by stealth.
Wide open stood the door, he need not climb,
And she herself before the pointed° time,   *appointed*
505   Had spread the board, with roses strewed the room,
And oft looked out and mused he did not come.
At last he came, O who can tell the greeting,
These greedy lovers had at their first meeting.
He asked, she gave, and nothing was denied,
510   Both to each other quickly were affied.°   *betrothed*
Look how their hands, so were their hearts united,
And what he did, she willingly requited.
(Sweet are the kisses, the embracements sweet,
When like desires and affections meet
515   For from the earth to heaven, is Cupid raised,
Where fancy is in equal balance paised°),   *poised*
Yet she this rashness suddenly repented,
And turned aside and to herself lamented.
As if her name and honor had been wronged,
520   By being possessed of him for whom she longed.
Aye, and she wished, albeit not from her heart,
That he would leave her turret and depart.
The mirthful god of amorous pleasure smiled,
To see how he this captive nymph beguiled.
525   For hitherto he did but fan the fire,
And kept it down that it might burn the higher.
Now waxed she jealous, lest his love abated,
Fearing her own thoughts made her to be hated.[6]
Therefore unto him hastily she goes,
530   And like light Salmacis,[7] her body throws
Upon his bosom, where with yielding eyes,
She offers up herself a sacrifice,
To slake his anger, if he were displeased,
O what god would not therewith be appeased?

6. I.e., fearing that she was hated, she imagined that she
was hated.

7. A nymph who pursued the boy Hermaphroditus; when
she embraced him they became one, half-girl, half-boy.

535   Like Aesop's cock,[8] this jewel he enjoyed,
        And as a brother with his sister toyed,
        Supposing nothing else was to be done,
        Now he her favor and good will had won.
        But know you not that creatures wanting sense°   *inanimate*
540   By nature have a mutual appetence,°   *desire*
        And wanting organs to advance a step,
        Moved by Love's force, unto each other leap?
        Much more in subjects having intellect,
        Some hidden influence breeds like effect.
545   Albeit Leander, rude in love and raw,
        Long dallying with Hero, nothing saw
        That might delight him more, yet he suspected
        Some amorous rites or other were neglected.
        Therefore unto his body, hers he clung,°   *clasped*
550   She fearing on the rushes° to be flung,   *a floor covering*
        Strived with redoubled strength; the more she strived,
        The more a gentle pleasing heat revived,
        Which taught him all that elder lovers know,
        And now the same 'gan° so to scorch and glow,   *began*
555   As in plain terms (yet cunningly) he craved it,
        Love always makes those eloquent that have it.
        She, with a kind of granting, put him by it,
        And ever as he thought himself most nigh it,
        Like to the tree of Tantalus[9] she fled,
560   And seeming lavish, saved her maidenhead.
        Ne'er king more sought to keep his diadem
        Than Hero this inestimable gem.
        Above our life we love a steadfast friend,
        Yet when a token of great wealth we send,
565   We often kiss it, often look thereon,
        And stay the messenger that would be gone;
        No marvel then, though Hero would not yield
        So soon to part from that she dearly held.
        Jewels being lost are found again; this, never.
570   T'is lost but once, and once lost, lost for ever.

        Now had the morn° espied her lover's° steeds,   *Aurora / Apollo*
        Whereat she starts, puts on her purple weeds,
        And red for anger that he stayed so long,
        All headlong throws herself the clouds among,
575   And now Leander, fearing to be missed,
        Embraced her suddenly, took leave, and kissed,
        Long was he taking leave, and loath to go,
        And kissed again, as lovers use to do,

8. According to Aesop, a writer of animal fables supposed to have lived in Thrace in the 6th century B.C.E., his cock found a precious jewel in the barnyard but rejected it because it was not a barleycorn. In the context of Marlowe's story the comparison is ambiguous.
9. Punished in hell for revealing the secrets of the gods, Tantalus was doomed to reach for fruit from a tree whose branches were always beyond his grasp.

Sad Hero wrung him by the hand and wept,
580　Saying, let your vows and promises be kept.
Then standing at the door, she turned about,
As loath to see Leander going out.
And now the sun that through th'orizon peeps,
As pitying these lovers, downward creeps.
585　So that in silence of the cloudy night,
Though it was morning, did he take his flight.
But what the secret trusty night concealed,
Leander's amorous habit soon revealed,
With Cupid's myrtle was his bonnet crowned,
590　About his arms the purple ribbon wound,
Wherewith she wreathed her largely spreading hair.
Nor could the youth abstain, but he must wear
The sacred ring wherewith she was endowed
When first religious chastity she vowed,
595　Which made his love through Sestos to be known,
And thence to Abydos sooner blown
Than he could sail, for incorporeal Fame,°　　　　　　　　*Rumor*
Whose weight consists of nothing but her name,
Is swifter than the wind, whose tardy plumes
600　Are reeking° water and dull earthly fumes.　　　　　　*vaporizing*
Home when he came, he seemed not to be there,
But like exiled air thrust from his sphere,
Set in a foreign place, and straight from thence,
Alcides-like,° by mighty violence,　　　　　　　　　*like Heracles*
605　He would have chased away the swelling main,
That him from her unjustly did detain.
Like as the sun in a diameter[1]
Fires and enflames objects removed far,
And heateth kindly,° shining lat'rally,　　　　　　　　*gently*
610　So beauty sweetly quickens when 'tis nigh.
But being separated and removed,
Burns where it cherished, murders where it loved.
Therefore even as an index to a book,
So to his mind was young Leander's look.°　　　　　　*appearance*
615　O none but gods have power their love to hide,
Affection by the countenance is descried.
The light of hidden fire itself discovers,
And love that is concealed betrays poor lovers.
His secret flame apparently was seen,
620　Leander's father knew where he had been,
And for the same mildly rebuked his son,
Thinking to quench the fire new begun.
But love resisted once grows passionate,
And nothing more than counsel, lovers hate.
625　For as a hot, proud horse lightly disdains

---

1. I.e., directly (as opposed to obliquely) above the earth.

To have his head controlled, but breaks the reins,
Spits forth the ringled bit° and with his hooves   *the bit with rings*
Checks the submissive ground, so he that loves,
The more he is restrained, the worse he fares,
630   What is it now but mad Leander dares?
O Hero, Hero, thus he cried full oft,
And then he got him to a rock aloft.
Where having spied her tower, long stared he on't,
And prayed the narrow toiling Hellespont
635   To part in twain, that he might come and go,
But still the rising billows answered no.
With that he stripped him to the ivory skin,
And crying, Love I come!, leapt lively° in.   *quickly*
Whereat the sapphire-visaged god² grew proud,
640   And made his capr'ing triton sound aloud,
Imagining that Ganymede, displeased,
Had left the heavens, therefore on him he seized.
Leander strived, the waves about him wound,
And pulled him to the bottom, where the ground
645   Was strewed with pearl and in low coral groves,
Sweet singing mermaids sported with their loves
On heaps of heavy gold, and took great pleasure
To spurn the careless sort, the shipwrack° treasure.   *shipwrecked*
For here the stately azure palace stood,
650   Where kingly Neptune and his train abode,
The lusty god embraced him, called him love,
And swore he never should return to Jove.
But when he knew it was not Ganymede,
For underwater he was almost dead,
655   He heaved him up, and looking on his face,
Beat down the gold waves with his triple mace,
Which mounted up, intending to have kissed him,
And fell in drops like tears because they missed him.
Leander, being up, began to swim,
660   And looking back, saw Neptune follow him.
Whereat aghast, the poor soul 'gan to cry,
O let me visit Hero ere I die!
The god put Helle's³ bracelet on his arm,
And swore the sea should never do him harm.
665   He clapped his plump cheeks, with his tresses played,
And smiling wantonly, his love bewrayed.°   *revealed*
He watched his arms, and as they opened wide,
At every stroke, betwixt them would he slide,
And steal a kiss, and then run out and dance,
670   And as he turned, cast many a lustful glance,

---

2. Neptune, whose son, Triton, is both a shell and the creature who blows upon it.
3. The daughter of the mythical Athamas and Nephele, who had to escape from the wrath of her stepmother, Ino, on a flying ram; she fell off its back into the part of the sea called the Hellespont. Neptune is said to have rescued her; the bracelet the god puts on Leander's arm signifies divine protection.

And threw him gaudy toys to please his eye,
And dive into the water, and there pry
Upon his breast, his thighs, and every limb,
And up again, and close beside him swim
675   And talk of love. Leander made reply,
You are deceived, I am no woman I.
Thereat smiled Neptune, and then told a tale,
How that a shepherd sitting in a vale,
Played with a boy so fair and kind,
680   As for his love both earth and heaven pined,
That of the cooling river durst not drink,
Lest water nymphs should pull him from the brink.
And when he sported in the fragrant lawns,
Goat-footed satyrs and up-staring fawns,[4]
685   Would steal him thence. Ere half this tale was done,
Aye me, Leander cried, th'enamored sun,
That now should shine on Thetis' glassy bower,[5]
Descends upon my radiant Hero's tower.
O that these tardy arms of mine were wings,
690   And as he spake, upon the waves he springs.
Neptune was angry that he gave no ear,
And in his heart, revenging malice bore.
He flung at him his mace, but as it went,
He called it in, for love made him repent.
695   The mace, returning back, his own hand hit,
As meaning to be venged for darting it.
When this fresh-bleeding wound Leander viewed,
His color went and came, as if he rued
The grief which Neptune felt. In gentle breasts,
700   Relenting thoughts, remorse, and pity rests.
And who have hard hearts, and obdurate minds,
But vicious, harebrained, and illit'rate hinds?°   *rustics*
The god, seeing him with pity to be moved,
Thereon concluded that he was beloved.
705   (Love is too full of faith, too credulous,
With folly and false hope deluding us.)
Wherefore Leander's fancy to surprise,
To the rich ocean for gifts he flies.
'Tis wisdom to give much, a gift prevails,
710   When deep, persuading oratory fails.
By this, Leander, being near the land,
Cast down his weary feet and felt the sand.
Breathless albeit he were, he rested not,
Till to the solitary tower he got.
715   And knocked and called, at which celestial noise,
The longing heart of Hero much more joys
Than nymphs and shepherds when the timbrell° rings,   *tambourine*

---

4. Fauns, spirits who are guided by the heavens.   5. The bower of Thetis, a sea nymph, is the sea.

Or crooked dolphin when the sailor sings.[6]
She stayed not her robes, but straight arose,
720   And drunk with gladness, to the door she goes,
Where seeing a naked man, she screeched for fear,
Such sighs as this to tender maids are rare.
And ran into the dark herself to hide;
Rich jewels in the dark are soonest spied.
725   Unto her he was led, or rather drawn,
By those white limbs which sparkled through the lawn.
The nearer he came, the more she fled,
And seeking refuge, slipped into her bed.
Whereon Leander sitting, thus begin,
730   Though numbing cold, all feeble, faint, and wan:

If not for love, yet love, for pity's sake,
Me in thy bed and maiden bosom take,
At least vouchsafe these arms some little room,
Who hoping to embrace thee cheerily swome.°   swam
735   This head was beat with many a churlish billow,
And therefore let it rest upon thy pillow.
Herewith, afrighted, Hero shrunk away,
And in her lukewarm place Leander lay.
Whose lively head like fire from heaven fet,°   fetched
740   Would animate gross clay, and higher set
The drooping thoughts of base declining souls,
Than dreary° Mars, carousing nectar bowls.°   bloody / bowls of nectar
His hands he cast upon her like a snare,
She, overcome with shame and sallow fear,
745   Like chaste Diana when Actaeon spied her,
Being suddenly betrayed, dived down to hide her.
And as her silver body downward went,
With both her hands she made the bed a tent,
And in her own mind thought herself secure,
750   O'ercast with dim and darksome coverture.°   covering
And now she lets him whisper in her ear,
Flatter, entreat, promise, protest, and swear,
Yet ever as he greedily assayed
To touch those dainties, she the Harpy[7] played
755   And every limb did as a soldier stout,
Defend the fort, and keep the foe-man out.
For though the rising iv'ry mount he scaled,
Which is with azure circling lines empaled,
Much like a globe (a globe may I term this,
760   By which love sails to regions full of bliss),
Yet there with Sisyphus[8] he toiled in vain,

6. The sailor is the mythical musician Arion, who was saved by dolphins ("crooked" because of their curved backs) when they heard him sing.
7. One of the fierce birds who snatched food from the Trojan companions of Aeneas on their way from Troy to Italy (*Aeneid* 3.225ff.).
8. The legendary king of Corinth, who in the underworld was eternally condemned to roll a large stone to the top of a hill, only to have it roll down again.

Till gentle parley° did the truce obtain.   *speech*
She trembling strove, this strife of hers (like that
Which made the world) another world begat,
765   Of unknown joy. Treason was in her thought,
And cunningly to yield herself she sought.
Seeming not won, yet won she was at length,
In such wars women use but half their strength.
Leander now like Thebian Hercules,[9]
770   Entered the orchard of Th'esperides.
Whose fruit none rightly can describe, but he
That pulls or shakes it from the golden tree.
Wherein Leander on her quivering breast,
Breathless spoke some thing and sighed out the rest,
775   Which so prevailed, as he with small ado,
Enclosed her in his arms and kissed her too.
And every kiss to her was as a charm,
And to Leander as a fresh alarm.
So that the truce was broke, and she alas,
780   (Poor silly maiden) at his mercy was.
Love is not full of pity (as men say)
But deaf and cruel, where he means to prey,
Even as a bird, which in our hands we wring,
Forth plungeth and oft flutters with her wing.
785   And now she wished this night were never done,
And sighed to think upon th'approaching sun,
For much it grieved her that the bright daylight
Should know the pleasure of this blessed night.
And then like Mars and Ericine° displayed,   *Venus*
790   Both in each others' arms, chained as they laid,
Again she knew not how to frame her look,
Or speak to him who in a moment took
That which so long, so charily she kept,
And feign by stealth away she would have crept,
795   And to some corner secretly have gone,
Leaving Leander in the bed alone.
But as her naked feet were whipping out,
He on the sudden clinged her so about,
That mermaid-like unto the floor she slid,
800   One half appeared, the other half was hid.
Thus near the bed she blushing stood upright,
And from her countenance behold ye might,
A kind of twilight break, which through the hair,
As from an orient cloud, glimpse here and there.
805   And round about the chamber this false morn
Brought forth the day before the day was born,

---

9. The eleventh labor of Hercules was to steal the golden apples of the Hesperides, daughters of the evening, who watched over their orchard on an island in a distant western sea.

So Hero's ruddy cheek, Hero betrayed,
And her all naked to his sight displayed.
Whence his admiring eyes more pleasure took
810   Than Dis on heaps of gold fixing his look.
By this Apollo's golden harp began,
To sound forth music to the ocean,
Which watchful Hesperus[1] no sooner heard,
But he the day bright-bearing car prepared
815   And ran before, as harbinger of light,
And with his flaming beams mocked ugly Night,
Till she, o'ercome with anguish, shame, and rage,
Danged° down to Hell her loathsome carriage.   *hurled*
Desunt nonnulla.[2]

THE TRAGICAL HISTORY OF DR. FAUSTUS   Marlowe's play is the first dramatic rendition of the medieval legend of a man who sold his soul to the devil. Sixteenth-century readers associated him with a necromancer named Dr. Faustus, and Marlowe exploited this identification when he reworked the medieval plot for his play. Rejecting the usual learning available to ambitious men—philosophy, medicine, law, and theology—Marlowe's Faustus signs a contract with the devil, represented in this case by his servant, Mephostophilis; in exchange for his soul, Faustus gains superhuman powers for twenty-four years. He uses these powers to conjure the Pope in Rome into giving the Protestant Emperor Charles V authority over the church through a surrogate Pope, Bruno; but his powers are also deployed in the banal trickery of simple and even criminal characters. The play is enigmatic on points of doctrine. Mephostophilis describes hell not as a locale but rather as the state of mind of one who has rejected God—a description that Milton will later amplify—telling Faustus: "this is hell, nor am I out of it." And Faustus, having worshipped the devil, is nevertheless offered a chance to repent and find salvation even at the very end of his allotted life. But he rejects God's love in favor of a night with Helen of Troy, praising her in lines that are now famous: "Was this the face that launched a thousand ships, / And burnt the topless towers of Ilium?" The play concludes with a report of Faustus's mangled body, torn to bits by the demon to whom he had given his soul.

The textual history of the play is very vexed, and the extent of Marlowe's own authorship remains unclear. A short version of the play was published in 1604; known as the A text, it was probably used by touring companies. The longer B text, given here, was published in 1616, probably based on Marlowe's original manuscript but also incorporating revisions and additions by Marlowe and others as the play continued to evolve in performance.

Although playtexts in this period quite often show variants from one edition to another, the case of *Dr. Faustus* is an extreme one; lacking an authoritative version, it has generally been read in various conflations of A and B. Even so, it has continued to prove popular with audiences, both for the fatal drama of Faustus's bargain with the Devil and for the magnificent blank verse in which the drama plays out.

---

1. Marlowe mistakes the evening star, Hesperus, for the morning star, Venus.
2. "Some things are missing." Added in 1598 by Marlowe's printer, Edward Blunt, who believed the poem was unfinished.

The Tragical History of Dr. Faustus
Dramatis Personae

CHORUS	THE POPE
FAUSTUS	BRUNO
WAGNER, *SERVANT TO FAUSTUS*	RAYMOND, *KING OF HUNGARY*
GOOD ANGEL AND EVIL ANGEL	CHARLES, *THE GERMAN EMPEROR*
VALDES ⎱ *Friends to Faustus*	MARTINO
CORNELIUS ⎰	FREDERICK
MEPHOSTOPHILIS	BENVOLIO
LUCIFER	SAXONY
BELZEBUB	DUKE OF VANHOLT
THE SEVEN DEADLY SINS	DUCHESS OF VANHOLT
CLOWN/ROBIN	SPIRITS IN THE SHAPES OF ALEXANDER
DICK	THE GREAT, DARIUS, PARAMOUR, AND
RAFE	HELEN
VINTNER	AN OLD MAN
CARTER	SCHOLARS, SOLDIERS, DEVILS, COURTIERS,
HOSTESS	CARDINALS, MONKS, CUPIDS

[*Enter Chorus.*]

CHORUS: Not marching in the fields of Thrasimene,[1]
      Where Mars did mate the warlike Carthigens,
      Nor sporting in the dalliance of love
      In courts of kings where state is overturned,
5   Nor in the pomp of proud audacious deeds,
      Intends our muse to vaunt his heavenly verse.[2]
      Only this, gentles: we must now perform
      The form of Faustus' fortunes, good or bad.
      And now to patient judgments we appeal,
10   And speak for Faustus in his infancy.
      Now is he born, of parents base of stock,
      In Germany, within a town called Rhodes.
      At riper years to Wittenberg he went,
      Whereas his kinsmen chiefly brought him up.
15   So much he profits in divinity,
      The fruitful plot° of scholarism graced,   *field*
      That shortly he was graced with Doctor's name,
      Excelling all; and sweetly can dispute
      In th' heavenly matters of theology.
20   Till swol'n with cunning of a self-conceit,
      His waxen wings did mount above his reach,

---

1. Trasimeno, a lake in Italy near Rome. The Carthaginian general Hannibal conquered Roman forces at Trasimeno in 217 B.C.E.; Marlowe's "Mars" is probably a reference to the Roman army, which "mated" or engaged the enemy opposition there.

2. These lines may refer to plays Marlowe had previously staged and whose subjects were war (*Tamburlaine*) and love (*Edward II, Dido, Queen of Carthage*).

Title page, 1620 edition of Marlowe's *The Tragical History of Dr. Faustus*.

And melting, heavens conspired his overthrow.[3]
For falling to a devilish exercise,
And glutted now with learning's golden gifts,
25   He surfeits upon cursed necromancy.
Nothing so sweet as magic is to him,
Which he prefers before his chiefest bliss:
And this the man that in his study sits.

ACT 1

Scene 1

[*Faustus in his study.*]
FAUSTUS: Settle thy studies, Faustus, and begin
To sound the depth of that thou wilt profess.
Having commenced, be a divine in show,
Yet level at the end of every art
5   And live and die in Aristotle's works.
Sweet Analytics, 'tis thou hast ravished me.[4]

3. Faustus is compared to the legendary figure of Icarus, whose father, the master craftsman Daedalus, made him a pair of wings that were attached to his body with wax. Icarus flew too near the sun, the wax supporting his wings melted, and he fell to the sea. The legend is generally understood to signify the consequences of pride and presumption.
4. Aristotle (384–322 B.C.E.), the best known of the Greek philosophers, wrote on the natural and social sciences. His *Analytics* dealt with logic.

Bene disserere est finis logices.
Is "to dispute well logic's chiefest end"?
Affords this art no greater miracle?

10   Then read no more: thou hast attained that end.
A greater subject fitteth Faustus' wit.
Bid *on cai me on*° farewell. And Galen,[5] come.   *being and non-being*
Seeing, *ubi desinit philosophus, ibi incipit medicus.*
Be a physician, Faustus: heap up gold

15   And be eternized for some wondrous cure.
Summum bonum medicinae sanitas:
"The end of physic is our body's health."
Why, Faustus, hast thou not attained that end?
Is not thy common talk sound aphorisms?°   *wise sayings*

20   Are not thy bills hung up as monuments,
Whereby whole cities have escaped the plague,
And thousand desperate maladies been cured?
Yet art thou still but Faustus and a man.
Couldst thou make men to live eternally,

25   Or being dead, raise them to life again,
Then this profession were to be esteemed.
Physic, farewell. Where is Justinian?[6]
Si una eademque res legatur duobus,
Alter rem, alter valorem rei etc.,

30   A petty case of paltry legacies!
Exhaereditare filium non potest pater, nisi—
Such is the subject of the institute
And universal body of the law.
This study fits a mercenary drudge,

35   Who aims at nothing but external trash,
Too servile and illiberal for me.
When all is done Divinity is best.
Jerome's Bible![7] Faustus, view it well.
Stipendium peccati mors est. Ha! Stipendium etc.,

40   "The reward of sin is death."[8] That's hard.
Si pecasse negamus, fallimur, et nulla est in nobis veritas.
"If we say that we have no sin
We deceive ourselves, and there is no truth in us."[9]
Why then, belike, we must sin,

45   And so consequently die.
Ay, we must die, an everlasting death.
What doctrine call you this? *Che sera, sera.*
"What will be, shall be." Divinity, adieu!
These necromantic books are heavenly,

5. Greek physician (130–200 C.E.) whose works on medicine were studied through the early modern period. Faustus welcomes his change of authorities with "where the philosopher ends, the physician begins."
6. Justinian, Emperor of Byzantium (483–565 C.E.), codified all of Roman law; his *Institutes* provided the basis for civil law in England as well as on the continent. Faustus cites a principle of estate law: "if one and the same thing is bequeathed to two people, one of them should have the thing itself, and the other the value of it"; and "the father may not disinherit the son."
7. Jerome (347–420 C.E.), a theologian who translated the Greek Bible and some of the Hebrew Bible into Latin, also wrote on Christian doctrine.
8. Romans 6.23.
9. 1 John 1.8.

50   Lines, circles, scenes, letters and characters:
Ay, these are those that Faustus most desires.
Oh, what a world of profit and delight,
Of power, of honor, of omnipotence,
Is promised to the studious artisan!
55   All things that move between the quiet poles
Shall be at my command. Emperors and kings
Are but obeyed in their several provinces.
Nor can they raise the wind or rend the clouds.
But his dominion that exceeds in this
60   Stretcheth as far as doth the mind of man:
A sound magician is a demi-god.
Here, tire° my brains to get° a deity.   *use / engender*

[*Enter Wagner.*]

      Wagner, commend me to my dearest friends,
The German Valdes and Cornelius.
65   Request them earnestly to visit me.

WAGNER: I will, sir.

                              [*Exit.*]

FAUSTUS: Their conference will be a greater help to me
      Than all my labors, plod I ne'er so fast.

[*Enter the Good and Evil Angels.*]

GOOD ANGEL: Oh Faustus, lay that damned book aside,
70   And gaze not on it lest it tempt thy soul
And heap God's heavy wrath upon thy head.
Read, read the scriptures: that is blasphemy.

EVIL ANGEL: Go forward, Faustus, in that famous art
      Wherein all nature's treasure is contained.
75   Be thou on earth as Jove[1] is in the sky,
Lord and commander of these elements.

                         [*Exeunt Angels.*]

FAUSTUS: How am I glutted with conceit° of this!   *idea*
      Shall I make spirits fetch me what I please,
Resolve me of all ambiguities,
80   Perform what desperate enterprise I will?
I'll have them fly to India for gold,
Ransack the ocean for orient pearl,
And search all corners of the new-found world
For pleasant fruits and princely delicates.
85   I'll have them read me strange philosophy,
And tell the secrets of all foreign kings.
I'll have them wall all Germany with brass,
And make swift Rhine circle fair Wittenberg.
I'll have them fill the public schools° with silk,   *college lecture halls*
90   Wherewith the students shall be bravely clad.
I'll levy soldiers with the coin they bring,
And chase the Prince of Parma from our land,

---

1. Roman god of the heavens and king of the gods.

And reign sole king of all the provinces.
Yea, stranger engines for the brunt of war
95   Than was the fiery keel[2] at Antwerp's bridge
I'll make my servile spirits to invent.
Come, German Valdes and Cornelius,
And make me blest with your sage conference.
    [*Enter Valdes and Cornelius.*]
    Valdes, sweet Valdes and Cornelius!
100   Know that your words have won me at the last
To practice magic and concealed arts.
Yet not your words only but mine own fantasy
That will receive no object° for my head,   *idea*
But ruminates on necromantic skill.
105   Philosophy is odious and obscure.
Both law and physic are for petty wits.
Divinity is basest of the three,
Unpleasant, harsh, contemptible and vile.
'Tis magic, magic that hath ravished me.
110   Then, gentle friends, aid me in this attempt,
And I, that have with subtle syllogisms
Gravelled the pastors of the German Church
And made the flowering pride of Wittenberg
Swarm to my problems as the infernal spirits
115   On sweet Musaeus[3] when he came to hell,
Will be as cunning as Agrippa was,
Whose shadow made all Europe honor him.
VALDES: Faustus, these books, thy wit and our experience
    Shall make all nations to canonize us,
120   As Indian moors obey their Spanish lords.
So shall the spirits of every element
Be always serviceable to us three.
Like lions shall they guard us when we please;
Like Almain rutters° with their horsemen's staves;   *German knights*
125   Or Lapland giants trotting by our sides.
Sometimes like women or unwedded maids,
Shadowing more beauty in their airy brows
Than has the white breasts of the queen of love.
From Venice shall they drag huge argosies,°   *merchant ships*
130   And from America the golden fleece[4]
That yearly stuffs old Philip's treasury
If learned Faustus will be resolute.
FAUSTUS: Valdes, as resolute am I in this
    As thou to live, therefore object° it not.   *reject*

---

2. In 1585 a fire ship destroyed the Duke of Parma's
bridge across the river Scheldt in the city of Antwerp.
3. Faustus wants to model himself on Musaeus, a legendary poet, said to have been a student of Orpheus, and
Cornelius Agrippa of Nettesheim (1486–1535), a
philosopher known for his works on skepticism and the
occult.

4. The "golden fleece" refers to the treasure (the gold
wool of a divine ram) sought and won by the legendary
hero, Jason, and his companions, known as the Argonauts (from the name of their ship, the Argo). Faustus
alludes to this treasure when he refers to the gold the
King of Castile, Philip II, was taking from lands in the
New World.

CORNELIUS: The miracles that magic will perform
   Will make thee vow to study nothing else.
   He that is grounded in Astrology,
   Enriched with tongues,° well seen° in minerals,   *languages / educated*
   Hath all the principles magic doth require.
140 Then doubt not, Faustus, but to be renowned,
   And more frequented° for this mystery   *sought after*
   Than heretofore the Delphian oracle.[5]
   The spirits tell me they can dry the sea,
   And fetch the treasure of all foreign wracks,°   *wrecks*
145 Yea, all the wealth that our forefathers hid
   Within the massy° entrails of the earth.   *massive*
   Then tell me, Faustus, what shall we three want?
FAUSTUS: Nothing, Cornelius! Oh, this cheers my soul.
   Come, show me some demonstrations magical,
150 That I may conjure in some bushy grove,
   And have these joys in full possession.
VALDES: Then haste thee to some solitary grove,
   And bear wise Bacon's and Albanus'[6] works,
   The Hebrew Psalter and New Testament;
155 And whatsoever else is requisite
   We will inform thee e're our conference cease.
CORNELIUS: Valdes, first let him know the words of art,
   And then, all other ceremonies learned,
   Faustus may try his cunning by himself.
VALDES: First I'll instruct thee in the rudiments,
   And then wilt thou be perfecter than I.
FAUSTUS: Then come and dine with me, and after meat
   We'll canvass every quiddity° thereof,   *question*
   For ere I sleep, I'll try what I can do.
165 This night I'll conjure, though I die therefore.   [*Exeunt.*]

Scene 2

[*Enter two Scholars.*]
FIRST SCHOLAR: I wonder what's become of Faustus, that was wont to make our
   schools ring with *sic probo*.[7]
  [*Enter Wagner.*]
SECOND SCHOLAR: That shall we presently know. Here comes his boy.
FIRST SCHOLAR: How now, sirrah, where's thy master?
WAGNER: God in heaven knows.
SECOND SCHOLAR: Why, dost not thou know then?
WAGNER: Yes, I know, but that follows not.

---

5. A shrine of Apollo, the god of the sun, music, and medicine, in his temple at Delphi, where his priestess, called the Pythia, spoke incoherent phrases that a priest later interpreted as prophecies.
6. Roger Bacon (1214–1294) was an English Franciscan monk and a lecturer at Oxford University who was inter-ested in natural science, particularly alchemy. Albanus is perhaps Pietro D'Abano (1250–1360), who was supposed to be a sorcerer and was burned in effigy by the Inquisition after his death.
7. "Thus I prove."

FIRST SCHOLAR: Go to, sirrah. Leave your jesting and tell us where he is.

WAGNER: That follows not by force of argument, which you, being licentiates,[8]

10   should stand upon. Therefore, acknowledge your error and be attentive.

SECOND SCHOLAR: Then you will not tell us?

WAGNER: You are deceived, for I will tell you. Yet if you were not dunces, you
          would never ask me such a question. For is he not *Corpus naturale?*[9] And is
          not that *mobile?* Then wherefore should you ask me such a question? But

15   that I am by nature phlegmatic, slow to wrath and prone to lechery (to love,
          I would say), it were not for you to come within forty foot of the place of ex-
          ecution, although I do not doubt but to see you both hanged the next ses-
          sions. Thus, having triumphed over you, I will set my countenance like a
          precision,[1] and begin to speak thus: "Truly, my dear brethren, my master is

20   within at dinner with Valdes and Cornelius, as this wine, if it could speak
          would inform your worships. And so the Lord bless you, preserve you and
          keep you, my dear brethren."

                                                                    [*Exit.*]

FIRST SCHOLAR: Oh Faustus, then I fear that which I have long suspected:
          That thou art fallen into that damned art

25   For which they two are infamous through the world.

SECOND SCHOLAR: Were he a stranger, not allied to me,
          The danger of his soul would make me mourn.
          But come, let us go, and inform the Rector.
          It may be his grave counsel may reclaim him.

FIRST SCHOLAR: I fear me nothing will reclaim him now.

SECOND SCHOLAR: Yet let us see what we can do.   [*Exeunt.*]

Scene 3

[*Thunder. Enter Lucifer and Four Devils. Faustus to them with this speech.*]

FAUSTUS: Now that the gloomy shadow of the night,
          Longing to view Orion's drizzling look,
          Leaps from th'Antarctic world unto the sky,
          And dims the welkin° with her pitchy breath,   *heaven*

5   Faustus, begin thine incantations
          And try if devils will obey thy hest,°   *command*
          Seeing thou hast prayed and sacrificed to them.
          Within this circle is Jehovah's name
          Forward and backward anagrammatized:

10   The abbreviated names of holy saints,
          Figures of every adjunct to the heavens,
          And characters of signs and evening stars,
          By which the spirits are enforced to rise.
          Then fear not, Faustus, to be resolute

15   And try the utmost magic can perform.[2]

8. Postgraduates.
9. A natural body.
1. Puritan.
2. Faustus styles himself an accomplished magician. He now repeats, in Latin, his command to Mephostophilis to appear in the guise of a friar: "May the gods of the underworld be kind to me; may the triple deity of Jehovah be gone; to the spirits of fire, air, and water, greetings. Prince of the east, Beelzebub, monarch of the fires below, and Demogorgon, we appeal to you so that Mephostophilis may appear and rise. Why do you delay? By Jehovah, hell and the hallowed water which I now sprinkle, and the sign of the cross, which I now make, and by our vows, let Mephostophilis himself now arise to serve us."

[*Thunder.*]

Sint mihi dei acherontis propitii, valeat numen triplex Jehovae, ignei areii, aquatani spiritus salvete: orientis princeps Belzebub, inferni ardentis monarcha et demigorgon, propitiamus vos, ut appareat, et surgat Mephostophilis (Dragon)[3] *quod tumeraris: per Jehovam, gehennam, et consecratam aquam quam nunc*

20   *spargo; signumque crucis quod nunc facio; et per vota nostra ipse nunc surgat nobis dicatus Mephostophilis.*

[*Enter a Devil.*]

        I charge thee to return and change thy shape.
        Thou art too ugly to attend on me.
        Go, and return an old Franciscan friar:
25   That holy shape becomes a devil best.

                                                    [*Exit Devil.*]

        I see there's virtue in my heavenly words.
        Who would not be proficient in this art?
        How pliant is this Mephostophilis!
        Full of obedience and humility,
30   Such is the force of magic and my spells.
        Now, Faustus, thou art conjuror laureate:[4]
        Thou canst command great Mephostophilis.
        Quin redis Mephostophilis fratris imagine.

[*Enter Mephostophilis.*]

MEPHOSTOPHILIS: Now, Faustus, what wouldst thou have me do?
FAUSTUS: I charge thee wait upon me whilst I live,
        To do whatever Faustus shall command,
        Be it to make the moon drop from her sphere,
        Or the ocean to overwhelm the world.
MEPHOSTOPHILIS: I am a servant to great Lucifer,
40   And may not follow thee without his leave.
        No more than he commands must we perform.
FAUSTUS: Did not he charge thee to appear to me?
MEPHOSTOPHILIS: No, I came now hither of mine own accord.
FAUSTUS: Did not my conjuring speeches raise thee? Speak.
MEPHOSTOPHILIS: That was the cause, but yet *per accidens*;°   by accident
        For when we hear one rack the name of God,
        Abjure the scriptures and his saviour Christ,
        We fly in hope to get his glorious soul.
        Nor will we come unless he use such means
50   Whereby he is in danger to be damned.
        Therefore the shortest cut for conjuring
        Is stoutly to abjure all godliness
        And pray devoutly to the prince of hell.
FAUSTUS: So Faustus hath already done, and holds this principle:
55   There is no chief but only Belzebub,
        To whom Faustus doth dedicate himself.

---

3. This appears to be a stage direction that was inserted into the playtext; it probably indicates that at this point the figure of a dragon should come on stage.

4. Faustus, stating he is a "conjurer laureate" or honored magician, asks again, in Latin: "Why do you not return, Mephostophilis, in the guise of a friar?"

This word "damnation" terrifies not me,
For I confound hell in elysium.°   *heaven*
My ghost be with the old philosophers.
60   But leaving these vain trifles of men's souls,
Tell me, what is that Lucifer, thy lord?
MEPHOSTOPHILIS: Arch-regent and commander of all spirits.
FAUSTUS: Was not that Lucifer an angel once?
MEPHOSTOPHILIS: Yes, Faustus, and most dearly loved of God.
FAUSTUS: How comes it then that he is prince of devils?
MEPHOSTOPHILIS: Oh, by aspiring pride and insolence,
For which God threw him from the face of heaven.
FAUSTUS: And what are you that live with Lucifer?
MEPHOSTOPHILIS: Unhappy spirits that fell with Lucifer,
70   Conspired against our God with Lucifer,
And are for ever damned with Lucifer.
FAUSTUS: Where are you damned?
MEPHOSTOPHILIS: In hell.
FAUSTUS: How comes it then that thou art out of hell?
MEPHOSTOPHILIS: Why, this is hell, nor am I out of it.
Think'st thou that I that saw the face of God
And tasted the eternal joys of heaven,
Am not tormented with ten thousand hells
In being deprived of everlasting bliss?
80   Oh, Faustus, leave these frivolous demands,
Which strike a terror to my fainting soul.
FAUSTUS: What, is great Mephostophilis so passionate
For being deprived of the joys of heaven?
Learn thou of Faustus manly fortitude,
85   And scorn those joys thou never shalt possess.
Go, bear these tidings to great Lucifer,
Seeing Faustus hath incurred eternal death
By desperate thoughts against Jove's deity.
Say he surrenders up to him his soul,
90   So he will spare him four and twenty years,
Letting him live in all voluptuousness,
Having thee ever to attend on me,
To give me whatsoever I shall ask,
To tell me whatsoever I demand,
95   To slay mine enemies and to aid my friends
And always be obedient to my will.
Go, and return to mighty Lucifer,
And meet me in my study at midnight,
And then resolve me of thy master's mind.
MEPHOSTOPHILIS: I will, Faustus.   [*Exit.*]
FAUSTUS: Had I as many souls as there be stars,
I'd give them all for Mephostophilis.
By him I'll be great emperor of the world,
And make a bridge through the air
105   To pass the ocean. With a band of men

I'll join the hills that bind the Affrick shore,
And make that country continent to Spain,
And both contributory to my crown.
The Emperor shall not live but by my leave,
110 Nor any potentate of Germany.
Now that I have obtained what I desired,
I'll live in speculation of this art
Till Mephostophilis return again.   [*Exit.*]

Scene 4

[*Enter Wagner and the Clown.*]

WAGNER: Come hither, sirrah boy.

CLOWN: Boy? Oh, disgrace to my person! Zounds! "Boy" in your face! You have seen many boys with beards, I am sure.

WAGNER: Sirrah, hast thou no comings in?

CLOWN: Yes, and goings out too, you may see, sir.

WAGNER: Alas, poor slave. See how poverty jests in his nakedness. I know the villain's out of service and so hungry that I know he would give his soul to the devil for a shoulder of mutton though it were blood-raw.

CLOWN: Not so neither. I had need to have it well roasted, and good sauce to it, if
10   I pay so dear, I can tell you.

WAGNER: Sirrah, wilt thou be my man and wait on me? And I will make thee go like *Qui mihi discipulus.*[5]

CLOWN: What, in verse?

WAGNER: No, slave, in beaten silk and stavesacre.[6]

CLOWN: Stavesacre? That's good to kill vermin. Then belike, if I serve you I shall be lousy.

WAGNER: Why, so thou shalt be whether thou dost it or no. For, sirrah, if thou dost not presently bind thyself to me for seven years, I'll turn all the lice about thee into familiars,[7] and make them tear thee in pieces.

CLOWN: Nay, sir, you may save yourself a labor, for they are as familiar with me as if they paid for their meat and drink, I can tell you.

WAGNER: Well, sirrah, leave your jesting and take these guilders.[8]

CLOWN: Yes, marry, sir, and I thank you too.

WAGNER: So, now thou art to be at an hour's warning, whensoever and whereso
25   ever the devil shall fetch thee.

CLOWN: Here, take your guilders.

WAGNER: Truly, I'll none of them.

CLOWN: Truly but you shall.

WAGNER: Bear witness I gave them him.

CLOWN: Bear witness I give them you again.

WAGNER: Not I. Thou art pressed. Prepare thyself, for I will presently raise up two devils, to carry thee away: Banio, Belcher!

CLOWN: Belcher? And Belcher come here, I'll belch him! I am not afraid of a devil.

[*Enter Two Devils and the Clown runs up and down crying.*]

5. One who is my disciple.   7. Spirits.
6. A poison.   8. Coins.

WAGNER: How now, sir, will you serve me now?

CLOWN: Ay, good Wagner. Take away the devil then.

WAGNER: Baliol and Belcher, spirits, away!

[Exeunt Devils.]

CLOWN: What, are they gone? A vengeance on them! They have vile long nails.
There was a he-devil and a she-devil. I'll tell you how you shall know them:
40   all he-devils has horns, and all she-devils has clifts[9] and cloven feet.

WAGNER: Well, sirrah, follow me.

CLOWN: But, do you hear, if I should serve you, would you teach me to raise up
Banio's and Belcheo's?

WAGNER: I will teach thee to turn thyself to anything, to a dog, or a cat, or a
45   mouse, or a rat, or anything.

CLOWN: How? A Christian fellow to a dog or a cat, a mouse or a rat? No, no, sir,
if you turn me into anything, let it be in the likeness of a little pretty frisking flea, that I may be here and there and everywhere. Oh, I'll tickle the
pretty wenches' plackets![1] I'll be amongst them, i'faith.

WAGNER: Well, sirrah, come.

CLOWN: But do you hear, Wagner?

WAGNER: How? Baliol and Belcher!

CLOWN: Oh Lord, I pray, sir, let Banio and Belcher go sleep.

WAGNER: Villain, call me Master Wagner, and see that you walk attentively and
55   let your right eye be always diametrically fixed upon my left heel, that thou
mayest *Quasi vestigias nostras insistere*.[2]   [*Exit.*]

CLOWN: God forgive me, he speaks Dutch fustian![3] Well, I'll follow him. I'll serve
him, that's flat.   [*Exit.*]

Scene 5

[*Enter Faustus in his study.*]

FAUSTUS: Now, Faustus, must thou needs be damned?
And canst thou not be saved?
What boots it then to think on God or heaven?
Away with such vain fancies and despair,
5   Despair in God and trust in Belzebub.°   *the Devil*
Now go not backward. No, Faustus, be resolute.
Why waverest thou? Oh, something soundeth in mine ears
Abjure this magic, turn to God again.
Ay, and Faustus will turn to God again.
10   To God? He loves thee not.
The God thou servest is thine own appetite,
Wherein is fixed the love of Belzebub.
To him I'll build an altar and a church,
And offer lukewarm blood of new-born babes.
[*Enter the Good and Evil Angels.*]

GOOD ANGEL: Sweet Faustus, leave that execrable art.

FAUSTUS: Contrition, prayer, repentance, what of these?

---

9. Clefts.
1. Petticoats.
2. Wagner mocks the Clown by telling him to walk "as if

to tread in our footsteps," knowing that the clown's
magic will never be as powerful as his own.
3. Nonsense.

GOOD ANGEL: Oh, they are means to bring thee unto heaven.

EVIL ANGEL: Rather illusions, fruits of lunacy,
    That make men foolish that do trust them most.

GOOD ANGEL: Sweet Faustus, think of heaven and heavenly things.

EVIL ANGEL: No, Faustus, think of honor and of wealth.

                                                   [*Exeunt Angels.*]

FAUSTUS: Of wealth!
    Why, the signory of Emden[4] shall be mine!
    When Mephostophilis shall stand by me,
25   What God can hurt thee, Faustus? Thou art safe.
    Cast no more doubts. Come, Mephostophilis,
    And bring glad tidings from great Lucifer.
    Is't not midnight? Come Mephostophilis!
    Veni, veni,° *Mephostophile!*   come, come
  [*Enter Mephostophilis.*]
30   Now tell me, what saith Lucifer, thy lord?

MEPHOSTOPHILIS: That I shall wait on Faustus whilst he lives,
    So he will buy my service with his soul.

FAUSTUS: Already Faustus hath hazarded that for thee.

MEPHOSTOPHILIS: But now thou must bequeath it solemnly,
35   And write a deed of gift with thine own blood,
    For that security craves great Lucifer.
    If thou deny it, I will back to hell.

FAUSTUS: Stay, Mephostophilis, and tell me
    What good will my soul do thy lord?

MEPHOSTOPHILIS: Enlarge his kingdom.

FAUSTUS: Is that the reason why he tempts us thus?

MEPHOSTOPHILIS: *Solamen miseris, socios habuisse doloris.*[5]

FAUSTUS: Why, have you any pain, that torture others?

MEPHOSTOPHILIS: As great as have the human souls of men.
45   But tell me, Faustus, shall I have thy soul?
    And I will be thy slave and wait on thee,
    And give thee more than thou hast wit to ask.

FAUSTUS: Ay, Mephostophilis, I'll give it thee.

MEPHOSTOPHILIS: Then, Faustus, stab thy arm courageously,
50   And bind thy soul, that at some certain day
    Great Lucifer may claim it as his own,
    And then be thou as great as Lucifer.

FAUSTUS: Lo, Mephostophilis, for love of thee
    I cut mine arm, and with my proper blood
55   Assure my soul to be great Lucifer's,
    Chief lord and regent of perpetual night.
    View here the blood that trickles from mine arm,
    And let it be propitious for my wish.

MEPHOSTOPHILIS: But, Faustus, thou must write it in manner of a deed of gift.

---

4. At this point in his career, Faustus aspires to the governorship of Emden, an important trading town in Germany, a pathetic exchange for his immortal soul.

5. Mephostophilis states that misery loves company in hell: "It is a comfort in wretchedness to have companions in woe."

FAUSTUS: Ay, so I will. But, Mephostophilis,
   My blood congeals and I can write no more!
MEPHOSTOPHILIS: I'll fetch thee fire to dissolve it straight.   [*Exit.*]
FAUSTUS: What might the staying of my blood portend?
   Is it unwilling I should write this bill?
65   Why streams it not that I may write afresh?
   "Faustus gives to thee his soul": ah, there it stayed!
   Why shouldst thou not? Is not thy soul thine own?
   Then write again: "Faustus gives to thee his soul."
[*Enter Mephostophilis with a chafer of coals.*]
MEPHOSTOPHILIS: Here's fire. Come, Faustus, set it on.
FAUSTUS: So, now my blood begins to clear again.
   Now will I make an end immediately.
MEPHOSTOPHILIS: Oh what will not I do to obtain his soul!
FAUSTUS: *Consummatum est:*[6] this bill is ended,
   And Faustus hath bequeathed his soul to Lucifer.
75   But what is this inscription on mine arm?
   Homo fuge!° Whither should I flee?   *Flee, O man*
   If unto heaven, he'll throw me down to hell.
   My senses are deceived: here's nothing writ!
   Oh, yes, I see it plain. Even here is writ
80   *Homo fuge.* Yet shall not Faustus fly.
MEPHOSTOPHILIS: I'll fetch him somewhat to delight his mind.   [*Exit.*]
[*Enter Devils, giving crowns and rich apparel to Faustus; they dance and then depart.*
Enter Mephostophilis.]
FAUSTUS: What means this show? Speak, Mephostophilis.
MEPHOSTOPHILIS: Nothing, Faustus, but to delight thy mind,
   And let thee see what magic can perform.
FAUSTUS: But may I raise such spirits when I please?
MEPHOSTOPHILIS: Ay, Faustus, and do greater things than these.
FAUSTUS: Then there's enough for a thousand souls.
   Here, Mephostophilis, receive this scroll,
   A deed of gift, of body and of soul:
90   But yet conditionally, that thou perform
   All covenants and articles between us both.
MEPHOSTOPHILIS: Faustus, I swear by hell and Lucifer
   To effect all promises between us both.
FAUSTUS: Then hear me read it, Mephostophilis.
95   On these conditions following:
   First, that Faustus may be a spirit in form and substance.
   Secondly, that Mephostophilis shall be his servant, and be by him com-
   manded.
   Thirdly, that Mephostophilis shall do for him, and bring him whatsoever.
100   Fourthly, that he shall be in his chamber or house invisible.
   Lastly, that he shall appear to the said John Faustus at all times, in what
      shape and form soever he please.

___

6. As reported in the Vulgate Bible, Faustus speaks the last words of Jesus on the cross: "It is finished" (John 19.30), and then realizes he must try to avoid the consequences: "Flee, O man."

        I, John Faustus of Wittenberg Doctor, by these presents, do give both body
        and soul to Lucifer, Prince of the East, and his minister Mephostophilis,
105   and furthermore grant unto them that four and twenty years being
        expired, and these articles above written being inviolate, full power to
        fetch or carry the said John Faustus, body and soul, flesh, blood or goods,
        into their habitation wheresoever.

        By me, John Faustus.

MEPHOSTOPHILIS: Speak, Faustus, do you deliver this as your deed?

FAUSTUS: Ay, take it, and the devil give thee good of it.

MEPHOSTOPHILIS: So now, Faustus, ask me what thou wilt.

FAUSTUS: First I will question with thee about hell.
        Tell me, where is the place that men call hell?

MEPHOSTOPHILIS: Under the heavens.

FAUSTUS: Ay, so are all things else; but whereabouts?

MEPHOSTOPHILIS: Within the bowels of these elements,
        Where we are tortured and remain for ever.
        Hell hath no limits, nor is circumscribed
120   In one self place. But where we are is hell,
        And where hell is there must we ever be.
        And to be short, when all the world dissolves
        And every creature shall be purified,
        All places shall be hell that is not heaven.

FAUSTUS: Come, I think hell's a fable.

MEPHOSTOPHILIS: Ay, think so still, till experience change thy mind.

FAUSTUS: Why, dost thou think that Faustus shall be damned?

MEPHOSTOPHILIS: Ay, of necessity, for here's the scroll
        In which thou hast given thy soul to Lucifer.

FAUSTUS: Ay, and body too, but what of that?
        Think'st thou that Faustus is so fond to imagine
        That after this life there is any pain?
        Tush, these are trifles and old wives' tales.

MEPHOSTOPHILIS: But Faustus, I am an instance to prove the contrary,
135   For I tell thee I am damned, and now in hell.

FAUSTUS: How? Now in hell? Nay, and this be hell, I'll willingly be damned here.
        What! Sleeping, eating, walking and disputing? But leaving this, let me
        have a wife, the fairest maid in Germany, for I am wanton and lascivious,
        and can not live without a wife.

MEPHOSTOPHILIS: How, a wife? I prithee, Faustus, talk not of a wife.

FAUSTUS: Nay, sweet Mephostophilis, fetch me one, for I will have one.

MEPHOSTOPHILIS: Well, thou wilt have one. Sit there till I come: I'll fetch
        thee a wife in the devil's name.

      [*Enter a Devil dressed like a woman, with fireworks.*]

FAUSTUS: What sight is this?

MEPHOSTOPHILIS: Tell, Faustus, how dost thou like thy wife?

FAUSTUS: A plague on her for a hot whore.

MEPHOSTOPHILIS: Tut, Faustus, marriage is but a ceremonial toy.
        If thou lovest me, think no more of it.
        I'll cull thee out the fairest courtesans
150   And bring them every morning to thy bed.

She whom thine eye shall like, thy heart shall have,
Be she as chaste as was Penelope,[7]
As wise as Saba, or as beautiful
As was bright Lucifer before his fall.
155   Here, take this book, and peruse it well.
The iterating° of these lines brings gold,   *repetition*
The framing of this circle on the ground
Brings thunder, whirlwinds, storm and lightning.
Pronounce this thrice devoutly to thyself
160   And men in harness shall appear to thee,
Ready to execute what thou commandest.

FAUSTUS: Thanks, Mephostophilis. Yet fain would I have a book wherein I might behold all spells and incantations, that I might raise up spirits when I please.

MEPHOSTOPHILIS: Here they are in this book.   [*There turn to them.*]

FAUSTUS: Now would I have a book where I might see all characters and planets of the heavens, that I might know their motions and dispositions.

MEPHOSTOPHILIS: Here they are too.   [*Turn to them.*]

FAUSTUS: Nay, let me have one book more, and then I have done, wherein I
170   might see all plants, herbs and trees that grow upon the earth.

MEPHOSTOPHILIS: Here they be.

FAUSTUS: Oh thou art deceived.

MEPHOSTOPHILIS: Tut, I warrant thee.   [*Turn to them.*]

ACT 2

Scene 1

[*Enter Faustus in his study, and Mephostophilis.*]

FAUSTUS: When I behold the heavens then I repent,
And curse thee, wicked Mephostophilis,
Because thou hast deprived me of those joys.

MEPHOSTOPHILIS: 'Twas thine own seeking, Faustus, thank thyself.
5   But thinkst thou heaven is such a glorious thing?
I tell thee, Faustus, it is not half so fair
As thou or any man that breathes on earth.

FAUSTUS: How prov'st thou that?

MEPHOSTOPHILIS: 'Twas made for man; then he's more excellent.

FAUSTUS: If heaven was made for man, 'twas made for me.
I will renounce this magic and repent.

[*Enter the Good and Evil Angels.*]

GOOD ANGEL: Faustus, repent. Yet God will pity thee.

EVIL ANGEL: Thou art a spirit. God cannot pity thee.

FAUSTUS: Who buzzeth in mine ears I am a spirit?
15   Be I a devil, yet God may pity me.
Yea, God will pity me if I repent.

EVIL ANGEL: Ay, but Faustus never shall repent.   [*Exeunt.*]

FAUSTUS: My heart's so hardened I cannot repent.

---

7. Mephostophilis compares the ideal woman to Penelope, the wife of Odysseus, who waited 20 years for him to return from the Trojan wars, and to Saba, the wise Queen of Sheba, who caught King Solomon, known himself for his wisdom (1 Kings).

Scarce can I name salvation, faith or heaven,
20   But fearful echoes thunder in mine ears
"Faustus, thou art damned." Then swords and knives,
Poison, guns, halters and envenomed steel
Are laid before me to dispatch myself.
And long ere this I should have done the deed,
25   Had not sweet pleasure conquered deep despair.
Have not I made blind Homer sing to me
Of Alexander's love and Oenon's death?[1]
And hath not he that built the walls of Thebes
With ravishing sound of his melodious harp
30   Made music with my Mephostophilis?[2]
Why should I die then, or basely despair?
I am resolved, Faustus shall not repent.
Come, Mephostophilis, let us dispute again,
And reason of divine astrology.
35   Speak, are there many spheres above the moon?
Are all celestial bodies but one globe,
As is the substance of this centric earth?[3]

MEPHOSTOPHILIS: As are the elements, such are the heavens,
Even from the moon unto the empyrial orb,
40   Mutually folded in each other's spheres,
And jointly move upon one axle-tree,
Whose termine° is termed the world's wide pole.   *end point*
Nor are the names of Saturn, Mars or Jupiter
Feigned, but are erring stars.

FAUSTUS: But have they all one motion, both *situet tempore?*[4]

MEPHOSTOPHILIS: All move from east to west in four and twenty hours upon the poles of the world, but differ in their motions upon the poles of the zodiac.

FAUSTUS: Tush, these slender trifles Wagner can decide. Hath Mephostophilis no
50   greater skill? Who knows not the double motion of the planets? That the first is finished in a natural day? The second thus, as Saturn in thirty years, Jupiter in twelve, Mars in four, the sun, Venus and Mercury in twenty-eight days. Tush, these are freshmen's suppositions. But tell me, hath every sphere a dominion or *intelligentia?*[5]

MEPHOSTOPHILIS: Ay.

FAUSTUS: How many heavens or spheres are there?

MEPHOSTOPHILIS: Nine, the seven planets, the firmament, and the empyrial heaven.

FAUSTUS: But is there not *coelum igneum et cristallinum?*

MEPHOSTOPHILIS: No, Faustus, they be but fables.[6]

---

1. Faustus claims he has made the poet Homer sing to him of the love of Alexander the Great (356–323 B.C.E.), who was married to Statira, daughter of the Emperor Darius of Persia; and of Oenone, a nymph of Mount Ida, who died from grief when her lover, Paris of Troy, deserted her for Helen, the wife of King Menalaus of Sparta.
2. Faustus further claims that the legendary Amphion, whose music built the walls of Thebes, also made music with Mephostophilis, now Faustus's servant.
3. Faustus alludes to the Ptolemaic universe in which the earth, at the center, is surrounded by concentric spheres, beginning with the moon. Beyond the spheres of the stars that were thought to move (the constellations) were the spheres of the fixed stars.
4. In place and in time.
5. Guiding spirit.
6. Faustus asks whether there is a "fiery and crystalline heaven" beyond the "empyrial heaven" Mephostophilis has mentioned, and he is told it is a fiction.

FAUSTUS: Resolve me then in this one question. Why are not conjunctions, op-
positions, aspects, eclipses, all at one time, but in some years we have more,
in some less?

MEPHOSTOPHILIS: *Per inaequalem motum, respectu totius.*[7]

FAUSTUS: Well, I am answered. Now tell me, who made the world?

MEPHOSTOPHILIS: I will not.

FAUSTUS: Sweet Mephostophilis, tell me.

MEPHOSTOPHILIS: Move me not, Faustus.

FAUSTUS: Villain, have not I bound thee to tell me anything?

MEPHOSTOPHILIS: Ay, that is not against our kingdom, but this is.
Think on hell, Faustus, for thou art damned.

FAUSTUS: Think, Faustus, upon God, that made the world.

MEPHOSTOPHILIS: Remember this—   [*Exit.*]

FAUSTUS: Ay, go, accursed spirit to ugly hell.
75   'Tis thou hast damned distressed Faustus' soul.
Is't not too late?

[*Enter the Good and Evil Angels.*]

EVIL ANGEL: Too late.

GOOD ANGEL: Never too late, if Faustus will repent.

EVIL ANGEL: If thou repent devils will tear thee in pieces.

GOOD ANGEL: Repent, and they shall never raze° thy skin.   shave

[*Exeunt Angels.*]

FAUSTUS: Ah, Christ my savior,
Seek to save distressed Faustus' soul.

[*Enter Lucifer, Belzebub and Mephostophilis.*]

LUCIFER: Christ cannot save thy soul, for he is just.
There's none but I have interest in the same.

FAUSTUS: Oh what art thou that look'st so terribly?

LUCIFER: I am Lucifer, and this is my companion prince in hell.

FAUSTUS: Oh Faustus, they are come to fetch away thy soul.

BELZEBUB: We are come to tell thee thou dost injure us.

LUCIFER: Thou call'st on Christ contrary to thy promise.

BELZEBUB: Thou shouldst not think on God.

LUCIFER: Think on the devil.

BELZEBUB: And his dam too.

FAUSTUS: Nor will I henceforth. Pardon me in this,
And Faustus vows never to look to heaven,
95   Never to name God or to pray to him,
To burn his scriptures, slay his ministers,
And make my spirits pull his churches down.

LUCIFER: Do so, and we will highly gratify thee.

BELZEBUB: Faustus, we are come from hell in person to show thee some pastime.
100   Sit down and thou shalt behold the seven deadly sins appear to thee in
their own proper shapes and likeness.

FAUSTUS: That sight will be as pleasant to me as Paradise was to Adam the first
day of his creation.

---

7. Faustus asks why planetary and astral events do not occur uniformly, and Mephostophilis answers that they do "with respect to the whole" but each "by unequal motion."

LUCIFER: Talk not of Paradise or Creation, but mark this show. Talk of the devil
105   and nothing else. Go, Mephostophilis, fetch them in.
    [*Enter the Seven Deadly Sins.*]
BELZEBUB: Now, Faustus, question them of their names and dispositions.
FAUSTUS: That shall I soon. What art thou, the first?
PRIDE: I am Pride. I disdain to have any parents. I am like to Ovid's flea.[8] I can
    creep into every corner of a wench. Sometimes like a periwig I sit upon her
110   brow. Next, like a necklace I hang about her neck. Then, like a fan of feath-
    ers, I kiss her. And then turning myself to a wrought smock do what I list.
    But fie, what a smell is here! I'll not speak a word for a king's ransome, un-
    less the ground be perfumed and covered with cloth of Arras.[9]
FAUSTUS: Thou art a proud knave indeed. What art thou, the second?
COVETOUSNESS: I am Covetousness. Begotten of an old churl in a leather bag.
    And might I now obtain my wish, this house, you and all, should turn to
    gold, that I might lock you safe into my chest. Oh, my sweet gold!
FAUSTUS: And what art thou, the third?
ENVY: I am Envy, begotten of a chimney-sweeper and an oyster-wife. I cannot read
120   and therefore wish all books were burnt. I am lean with seeing others eat.
    Oh, that there would come a famine over all the world, that all might die,
    and I live alone, then thou should'st see how fat I'd be. But must thou sit
    and I stand? Come down, with a vengeance!
FAUSTUS: Out, envious wretch. But what art thou, the fourth?
WRATH: I am Wrath. I had neither father nor mother. I leapt out of a lion's
    mouth when I was scarce an hour old, and ever since have run up and
    down the world with this case of rapiers, wounding myself when I could get
    none to fight withal. I was born in hell, and look to it, for some of you shall
    be my father.
FAUSTUS: And what art thou, the fifth?
GLUTTONY: I am Gluttony. My parents are all dead, and the devil a penny they
    have left me, but a small pension and that buys me thirty meals a day and
    ten bevers:[1] a small trifle to suffice nature. I come of a royal pedigree; my fa-
    ther was a gammon of bacon and my mother was a hog's head of claret wine.
135   My godfathers were these: Peter Pickle-herring and Martin Martlemas-beef.
    But my godmother, oh, she was an ancient gentlewoman, and well-beloved
    in every good town and city. Her name was Mistress Margery March-beer.
    Now, Faustus, thou hast heard all my progeny, wilt thou bid me to supper?
FAUSTUS: No, I'll see thee hanged. Thou wilt eat up all my victuals.
GLUTTONY: Then the devil choke thee.
FAUSTUS: Choke thyself, Glutton. What art thou, the sixth?
SLOTH: Hey ho, I am Sloth. I was begotten on a sunny bank where I have lain
    ever since, and you have done me great injury to bring me from thence. Let
    me be carried thither again by Gluttony and Lechery. I'll not speak another
145   word for a king's ransom.
FAUSTUS: And what are you, Mistress Minx, the seventh and last?
LECHERY: Who, I sir? I am one that loves an inch of raw mutton better than an ell
    of fried stockfish,[2] and the first letter of my name begins with Lechery.

8. One of the poems of the Roman poet Ovid (43
B.C.E.–18 C.E.) describes the journey of a flea around a
woman's body.

9. Flemish cloth for tapestries.
1. Snacks.
2. Lechery implies that she would prefer a short but energetic penis to a yard-long but dry one.

FAUSTUS: Away to hell! Away, on, piper!

[*Exeunt the Seven Deadly Sins.*]

LUCIFER: Now, Faustus, how dost thou like this?

FAUSTUS: Oh, this feeds my soul.

LUCIFER: Tut, Faustus, in hell is all manner of delight.

FAUSTUS: Oh, might I see hell and return again safe, how happy were I then!

LUCIFER: Faustus, thou shalt. At midnight I will send for thee. Meanwhile, peruse
155   this book and view it throughly, and thou shalt turn thyself into what shape
thou wilt.

FAUSTUS: Thanks, mighty Lucifer. This will I keep as chary as my life.

LUCIFER: Now, Faustus, farewell, and think on the devil.

FAUSTUS: Farewell, great Lucifer. Come, Mephostophilis.

[*Exeunt omnes, several ways.*]

Scene 2

[*Enter the Clown.*]

CLOWN: What, Dick, look to the horses there till I come again. I have gotten one
of Doctor Faustus' conjuring books, and now we'll have such knavery as't
passes.

[*Enter Dick.*]

DICK: What, Robin, you must come away and walk the horses.

ROBIN: I walk the horses? I scorn't, faith. I have other matters in hand. Let the
horses walk themselves and they will. *A per se a, t.h.e. the: o per se o deny
orgon, gorgon.*³ Keep further from me, O thou illiterate and unlearned
hostler.

DICK: 'Snails!⁴ What hast thou got there? A book? Why, thou canst not tell ne'er
10   a word on't.

ROBIN: That thou shalt see presently. Keep out of the circle, I say, lest I send you
into the ostry⁵ with a vengeance.

DICK: That's like, faith. You had best leave your foolery, for, an my master come,
he'll conjure you, faith!

ROBIN: My master conjure me? I'll tell thee what, an my master come here, I'll
clap as fair a pair of horns⁶ on's head as e'er thou sawest in thy life.

DICK: Thou need'st not do that, for my mistress hath done it.

ROBIN: Ay, there be of us here, that have waded as deep into matters as other
men, if they were disposed to talk.

DICK: A plague take you! I thought you did not sneak up and down after her for
nothing. But I prithee tell me, in good sadness, Robin, is that a conjuring
book?

ROBIN: Do but speak what thou't have me to do, and I'll do't. If thou't dance
naked, put off thy clothes and I'll conjure thee about presently. Or if thou't

---

3. Barely literate, Robin is trying to parse a Latin phrase,
atheo Demigorgon ("godless Demigorgon").
4. Christ's nails.

5. Inn.
6. Sign of a cuckold.

25   go but to the tavern with me, I'll give thee white wine, red wine, claret
       wine, sack, muskadine, malmesey and whippincrust.[7] Hold, belly, hold; and
       we'll not pay one penny for it.
DICK: Oh brave! Prithee, let's to it presently, for I am as dry as a dog.
ROBIN: Come, then, let's away.   [Exeunt.]

ACT 3

Scene 1

[Enter the Chorus.]

CHORUS: Learned Faustus,
         To find the secrets of astronomy,
         Graven in the book of Jove's high firmament,
         Did mount him up to scale Olympus' top,
5   Where sitting in a chariot burning bright,
         Drawn by the strength of yoked dragons' necks,
         He views the clouds, the planets, and the stars,
         The tropic, zones, and quarters of the sky,
         From the bright circle of the horned moon,
10   Even to the height of Primum Mobile.[1]
         And whirling round with this circumference,
         Within the concave compass of the pole,
         From east to west his dragons swiftly glide,
         And in eight days did bring him home again.
15   Not long he stayed within his quiet house,
         To rest his bones after his weary toil,
         But new exploits do hale him out again,
         And mounted then upon a dragon's back,
         That with his wings did part the subtle air,
20   He now is gone to prove cosmography,
         That measures coasts and kingdoms of the earth;
         And as I guess will first arrive at Rome,
         To see the Pope and manner of his court,
         And take some part of holy Peter's feast,
25   The which this day is highly solemnized.   [Exit.]

Scene 2

[Enter Faustus and Mephostophilis.]

FAUSTUS: Having now, my good Mephostophilis,
          Passed with delight the stately town of Trier,
          Environed round with airy mountain tops,
          With walls of flint, and deep entrenched lakes,
5   Not to be won by any conquering prince,
          From Paris next coasting the realm of France
          We saw the river Main fall into Rhine,

---

7. Robin lists various kinds of wine; "whippincrust" is
probably a corruption of "hippocras," a kind of sweet
wine.

1. The outermost of the heavenly spheres. Faustus is pictured as viewing the heavens from Mount Olympus to the
circle of the moon and beyond, to the primum mobile.

Whose banks are set with groves of fruitful vines;
Then up to Naples, rich Campania,
10   Whose buildings fair and gorgeous to the eye,
The streets straight forth and paved with finest brick,
Quarters the town in four equivolence.°   *parts*
There saw we learned Maro's golden tomb,[2]
The way he cut an English mile in length,
15   Thorough a rock of stone in one night's space.
From thence to Venice, Padua and the rest,
In midst of which a sumptuous temple stands,
That threats the stars with her aspiring top,
Whose frame is paved with sundry colored stones,
20   And roofed aloft with curious work in gold.
Thus hitherto hath Faustus spent his time.
But tell me now, what resting place is this?
Hast thou, as erst I did command,
Conducted me within the walls of Rome?
MEPHOSTOPHILIS: I have, my Faustus, and for proof thereof,
This is the goodly palace of the Pope;
And cause we are no common guests,
I choose his privy chamber for our use.
FAUSTUS: I hope his Holiness will bid us welcome.
MEPHOSTOPHILIS: All's one, for we'll be bold with his venison.
But now, my Faustus, that thou may'st perceive
What Rome contains for to delight thine eyes,
Know that this city stands upon seven hills
That underprop the groundwork of the same.
35   Just through the midst runs flowing Tiber's stream,
With winding banks that cut it in two parts,
Over the which four stately bridges lean,
That make safe passage to each part of Rome.
Upon the bridge called Ponto Angelo
40   Erected is a castle passing strong,
Where thou shalt see such store of ordinance
As that the double cannons forged of brass
Do match the number of the days contained
Within the compass of one complete year.
45   Beside the gates and high pyramides,
That Julius Caesar brought from Africa.[3]
FAUSTUS: Now by the kingdoms of infernal rule,
Of Styx, or Acheron, and the fiery lake
Of ever-burning Phlegethon,° I swear   *rivers in hell*
50   That I do long to see the monuments
And situation of bright splendent Rome.
Come, therefore, let's away.

---

2. Faustus' fiery chariot cut through rocks to go from
Naples, where the Roman poet Publius Virgilius Maro, or
Virgil, is buried, to Padua and Venice.

3. The Emperor Caligula brought an obelisk back from
Heliopolis in Egypt, which stands before St. Peter's in
Rome.

MEPHOSTOPHILIS: Now, stay, my Faustus. I know you'd see the Pope,
     And take some part of holy Peter's feast,
55   The which in state and high solemnity
     This day is held through Rome and Italy
     In honor of the Pope's triumphant victory.
FAUSTUS: Sweet Mephostophilis, thou pleasest me.
     Whilst I am here on earth let me be cloyed
60   With all things that delight the heart of man.
     My four and twenty years of liberty
     I'll spend in pleasure and in dalliance,
     That Faustus' name, whilst this bright frame doth stand,
     May be admired through the furthest land.
MEPHOSTOPHILIS: 'Tis well said, Faustus. Come then, stand by me,
     And thou shalt see them come immediately.
FAUSTUS: Nay stay, my gentle Mephostophilis,
     And grant me my request, and then I go.
     Thou know'st within the compass of eight days
70   We viewed the face of heaven, of earth and hell.
     So high our dragons soared into the air,
     That looking down, the earth appeared to me
     No bigger than my hand in quantity.
     There did we view the kingdoms of the world,
75   And what might please mine eye, I there beheld.
     Then in this show let me an actor be,
     That this proud Pope may Faustus' cunning see.
MEPHOSTOPHILIS: Let it be so, my Faustus, but first stay
     And view their triumphs° as they pass this way.   *procession*
80   And then devise what best contents thy mind
     By cunning in thine art to cross the Pope,
     Or dash the pride of this solemnity,
     To make his monks and abbots stand like apes,
     And point like antics° at his triple crown,   *clowns*
85   To beat the beads about the friars' pates,
     Or clap huge horns upon the cardinals' heads,
     Or any villainy thou canst devise,
     And I'll perform it, Faustus. Hark, they come!
     This day shall make thee be admired in Rome.
[*Enter the Cardinals and Bishops, some bearing crosiers, some the pillars, Monks and Friars, singing their procession. Then the Pope and Raymond, King of Hungary with Bruno[4] led in chains.*]
POPE: Cast down our footstool.
RAYMOND: Saxon Bruno, stoop,
     Whilst on thy back his Holiness ascends
     Saint Peter's chair and state pontifical.
BRUNO: Proud Lucifer, that state belongs to me:
95   But thus I fall to Peter, not to thee.

---

4. This character has no apparent historical counterpart or model.

POPE: To me and Peter shalt thou grovelling lie,
   And crouch before the papal dignity.
   Sounds trumpets then, for thus Saint Peter's heir
   From Bruno's back ascends Saint Peter's chair.
  [*A flourish while he ascends.*]
100 Thus, as the gods creep on with feet of wool
   Long ere with iron hands they punish men,
   So shall our sleeping vengeance now arise,
   And smite with death thy hated enterprise.
   Lord cardinals of France and Padua,
105 Go forthwith to our holy consistory,
   And read amongst the statutes decretal,
   What by the holy council held at Trent[5]
   The sacred synod hath decreed for them
   That doth assume the papal government,
110 Without election and a true consent.
   Away, and bring us word with speed!
FIRST CARDINAL: We go, my lord.
              [*Exeunt Cardinals.*]

POPE: Lord Raymond.
FAUSTUS: Go, haste thee, gentle Mephostophilis,
115 Follow the cardinals to the consistory,
   And as they turn their superstitious books,
   Strike them with sloth and drowsy idleness,
   And make them sleep so sound that in their shapes
   Thyself and I may parly° with this Pope,   *speak*
120 This proud confronter of the Emperor,[6]
   And in despite of all his holiness
   Restore this Bruno to his liberty
   And bear him to the states of Germany.
MEPHOSTOPHILIS: Faustus, I go.
FAUSTUS: Dispatch it soon,
   The Pope shall curse that Faustus came to Rome.
       [*Exeunt Faustus and Mephostophilis.*]

BRUNO: Pope Adrian,[7] let me have some right of law:
   I was elected by the Emperor.
POPE: We will depose the Emperor for that deed,
130 And curse the people that submit to him.
   Both he and thou shalt stand excommunicate,
   And interdict from Church's privilege
   And all society of holy men.
   He grows too proud in his authority,
135 Lifting his lofty head above the clouds
   And like a steeple overpeers the Church.
   But we'll pull down his haughty insolence,

---

5. The council of Trent, called to meet the challenges posed by the Protestant Reformation, was held between 1545 and 1563.
6. The Holy Roman Emperor, Charles V, Emperor from 1519.

7. Possibly Marlowe means Hadrian VI (1522–1523), although he was Pope before the Council of Trent, after which the action of the play is supposed to have taken place.

And, as Pope Alexander, our progenitor,
Stood on the neck of German Frederick,[8]
140   Adding this golden sentence to our praise,
That Peter's heirs should tread on emperors
And walk upon the dreadful adder's back,
Treading the lion and the dragon down,
And fearless spurn the killing basilisk,[9]
145   So will we quell that haughty schismatic,
And by authority apostolical
Depose him from his regal government.
BRUNO: Pope Julius swore to princely Sigismond[1]
For him and the succeeding popes of Rome,
150   To hold the emperors their lawful lords.
POPE: Pope Julius did abuse the Church's rites,
And therefore none of his decrees can stand.
Is not all power on earth bestowed on us?
And therefore though we would we cannot err.
155   Behold this silver belt, whereto is fixed
Seven golden seals fast sealed with seven seals,
In token of our seven-fold power from heaven,
To bind or loose, lock fast, condemn or judge,
Resign or seal, or what so pleaseth us.
160   Then he and thou, and all the world, shall stoop,
Or be assured of our dreadful curse,
To light as heavy as the pains of hell.
[Enter Faustus and Mephostophilis, like the cardinals.]
MEPHOSTOPHILIS: Now tell me, Faustus, are we not fitted well?
FAUSTUS: Yes, Mephostophilis, and two such cardinals
165   Ne'er served a holy Pope as we shall do.
But whilst they sleep within the consistory,
Let us salute his reverend fatherhood.
RAYMOND: Behold, my lord, the cardinals are returned.
POPE: Welcome, grave fathers, answer presently
170   What have our holy council there decreed
Concerning Bruno and the Emperor,
In quittance of their late conspiracy
Against our state and papal dignity?
FAUSTUS: Most sacred patron of the Church of Rome,
175   By full consent of all the synod
Of priests and prelates, it is thus decreed:
That Bruno and the German Emperor
Be held as lollards[2] and bold schismatics
And proud disturbers of the Church's peace.
180   And if that Bruno by his own assent,
Without enforcement of the German peers,

---

8. Pope Alexander III (1159–1181) forced Emperor Frederick Barbarossa to acknowledge his authority.
9. A mythical creature whose glance was lethal.
1. It is unclear to whom Marlowe refers; there was no

Pope Julius during the reign of the Emperor Sigismund (1368–1436).
2. Heretics; in England, followers of John Wycliffe (1328?–1384).

Did seek to wear the triple diadem
And by your death to climb Saint Peter's chair,
The statutes decretal have thus decreed:
185   He shall be straight condemned of heresy
And on a pile of faggots burnt to death.
POPE: It is enough. Here, take him to your charge,
And bear him straight to Ponto Angelo,
And in the strongest tower enclose him fast.
190   Tomorrow, sitting in our consistory
With all our college of grave cardinals,
We will determine of his life or death.
Here, take his triple crown along with you,
And leave it in the Church's treasury.
195   Make haste again, my good lord cardinals,
And take our blessing apostolical.
MEPHOSTOPHILIS: So, so, was never devil thus blessed before.
FAUSTUS: Away, sweet Mephostophilis, be gone:
The cardinals will be plagued for this anon.

                                   [*Exeunt Faustus and Mephostophilis.*]

POPE: Go presently, and bring a banquet forth
That we may solemnize Saint Peter's feast,
And with Lord Raymond, King of Hungary,
Drink to our late and happy victory.   [*Exeunt.*]

SCENE 3

[*A sennet³ while the banquet is brought in, and then enter Faustus and Mephostophilis
in their own shapes.*]
MEPHOSTOPHILIS: Now, Faustus, come prepare thyself for mirth.
The sleepy cardinals are hard at hand
To censure Bruno that is posted° hence,   *ridden*
And on a proud paced steed as swift as thought
5   Flies o'er the Alps to fruitful Germany,
There to salute the woeful Emperor.
FAUSTUS: The Pope will curse them for their sloth today,
That slept both Bruno and his crown away.
But now, that Faustus may delight his mind,
10   And by their folly make some merriment,
Sweet Mephostophilis, so charm me here,
That I may walk invisible to all,
And do what e'er I please unseen of any.
MEPHOSTOPHILIS: Faustus, thou shalt. Then kneel down presently:
15   Whilst on thy head I lay my hand,
And charm thee with this magic wand.
First wear this girdle, then appear
Invisible to all are here.
The planets seven, the gloomy air,
20   Hell and the Furies'⁴ forked hair,

---

3. A trumpet call.   4. Greek divinities instigating revenge.

Pluto's[5] blue fire and Hecate's[6] tree,
With magic spells so compass thee,
That no eye may thy body see.
So, Faustus, now for all their holiness,
25   Do what thou wilt, thou shalt not be discerned.
FAUSTUS: Thanks, Mephostophilis. Now, friars, take heed
Lest Faustus make your shaven crowns to bleed.
MEPHOSTOPHILIS: Faustus, no more. See where the cardinals come.
  [*Enter the Pope and all the Lords. Enter the Cardinals with a book.*]
POPE: Welcome, lord cardinals. Come, sit down.
30   Lord Raymond, take your seat. Friars, attend
And see that all things be in readiness
As best beseems this solemn festival.
FIRST CARDINAL: First, may it please your sacred Holiness,
To view the sentence of the reverend synod
35   Concerning Bruno and the Emperor?
POPE: What needs this question? Did I not tell you
Tomorrow we would sit i'the consistory
And there determine of his punishment?
You brought us word even now, it was decreed
40   That Bruno and the cursed Emperor
Were by the holy Council both condemned
For loathed lollards and base schismatics.
Then wherefore would you have me view that book?
FIRST CARDINAL: Your Grace mistakes. You gave us no such charge.
RAYMOND: Deny it not. We all are witnesses
That Bruno here was late delivered you,
With his rich triple crown to be reserved
And put into the Church's treasury.
BOTH CARDINAL: By holy Paul, we saw them not.
POPE: By Peter, you shall die
Unless you bring them forth immediately.
Hale° them to prison, lade their limbs with gyves!°   take / chains
False prelates, for this hateful treachery,
Cursed be your souls to hellish misery.
FAUSTUS: So, they are safe. Now Faustus, to the feast.
The Pope had never such a frolic guest.
POPE: Lord Archbishop of Rheims, sit down with us.
BISHOP: I thank your Holiness.
FAUSTUS: Fall to, and the devil choke you an you spare.
POPE: Who's that spoke? Friars, look about.
FRIARS: Here's nobody, if it like your Holiness.
POPE: Lord Raymond, pray fall to. I am beholding
To the Bishop of Milan for this so rare a present.
FAUSTUS: I thank you, sir.
  [*Snatches it.*]

---

5. The Roman god of the underworld.   6. Goddess representing death and the dark side of the
                                               moon.

POPE: How now? Who snatched the meat from me?
       Villains, why speak you not?
       My good Lord Archbishop, here's a most dainty dish
       Was sent me from a cardinal in France.
FAUSTUS: I'll have that too.
       [*Snatches it.*]
POPE: What lollards do attend our Holiness
       That we receive such great indignity? Fetch me some wine.
FAUSTUS: Ay, pray do, for Faustus is a-dry.
POPE: Lord Raymond, I drink unto your grace.
FAUSTUS: I pledge your grace.
       [*Snatches the glass.*]
POPE: My wine gone too? Ye lubbers,° look about   *louts*
       And find the man that doth this villainy,
       Or by our sanctitude you all shall die.
       I pray, my lords, have patience at this
       Troublesome banquet.
BISHOP: Please it your Holiness, I think it be some ghost crept out of Purgatory,
       and now is come unto your Holiness for his pardon.
POPE: It may be so.
       Go, then, command our priests to sing a dirge
       To lay the fury of this same troublesome ghost.
       [*The Pope crosseth himself.*]
FAUSTUS: How now? Must every bit be spiced with a cross?
       Nay then, take that.
       [*Faustus hits him a box of the ear.*]
POPE: Oh, I am slain! Help me, my lords.
       Oh come, and help to bear my body hence.
       Damned be this soul for ever for this deed!
                                         [*Exeunt the Pope and his train.*]
MEPHOSTOPHILIS: Now, Faustus, what will you do now?
       For I can tell you, you'll be cursed with bell, book and candle.
FAUSTUS: Bell, book and candle, candle, book and bell,
       Forward and backward, to curse Faustus to hell.
       [*Enter the Friars with bell, book and candle, for the dirge.*]
FIRST FRIAR: Come, brethren, let's about our business with good devotion.
95   [*sing*] Cursed be he that stole his Holiness' meat from the table. *Maledicat
       dominus.*[7]
       Cursed be he that took his Holiness a blow on the face. *Maledicat dominus.*
       Cursed be he that struck Friar Sandelo a blow on the pate. *Maledicat domi-
       nus.*
100   Cursed be he that disturbeth our holy dirge. *Maledicat dominus.*
       Cursed be he that took away his Holiness' wine. *Maledicat dominus.*
       Et omnes sancti.[8] Amen.
       [*Faustus and Mephostophilis beat the Friars, fling fireworks among them and exeunt.
       Enter Chorus.*]
CHORUS: When Faustus had with pleasure ta'en the view
       Of rarest things and royal courts of kings,

---

7. May God curse you.   8. And all the saints.

105 He stayed his course and so returned home;
Where such as bear his absence but with grief,
I mean his friends and nearest companions,
Did gratulate his safety with kind words,
And in their conference of what befell,
110 Touching his journey through the world and air,
They put forth questions of astrology,
Which Faustus answered with such learned skill
As they admired and wondered at his wit.
Now is his fame spread forth in every land;
115 Amongst the rest, the Emperor is one,
Carolus the Fifth, at whose palace now
Faustus is feasted 'mongst his noblemen.
What there he did in trial of his art,
I leave untold: your eyes shall see performed.

Scene 4

[*Enter Robin the ostler*[9] *with a book in his hand.*]

ROBIN: Oh this is admirable! Here I ha' stol'n one of Doctor Faustus' conjuring
books, and, i'faith, I mean to search some circles for my own use. Now will I
make all the maidens in our parish dance at my pleasure stark naked before
me. And so by that means I shall see more than ere I felt or saw yet.

[*Enter Rafe calling Robin.*]

RAFE: Robin, prithee come away! There's a gentleman tarries to have his horse,
and he would have his things rubbed and made clean. He keeps such a
chafing with my mistress about it, and she has sent me to look thee out.
Prithee, come away!

ROBIN: Keep out, keep out, or else you are blown up. You are dismembered, Rafe,
10   keep out, for I am about a roaring piece of work.

RAFE: Come, what dost thou with that same book? Thou canst not read?

ROBIN: Yes, my master and mistress shall find that I can read, he for his forehead,
she for her private study. She's born to bear with me, or else my art fails.

RAFE: Why, Robin, what book is that?

ROBIN: What book? Why, the most intolerable book for conjuring that ere was
invented by any brimstone devil.

RAFE: Canst thou conjure with it?

ROBIN: I can do all these things easily with it. First, I can make thee drunk with
ippocras at any tavern in Europe, for nothing. That's one of my conjuring
20   works!

RAFE: Our master parson says that's nothing.

ROBIN: True, Rafe. And more, Rafe, if thou hast any mind to Nan Spit, our
kitchen maid, then turn her and wind her to thy own use as often as thou
wilt, and at midnight.

RAFE: Oh brave Robin! Shall I have Nan Spit, and to mine own use? On that
condition, I'll feed thy devil with horsebread as long as he lives, of free cost.

9. Stableman.

ROBIN: No more, sweet Rafe. Let's go and make clean our boots which lie foul upon our hands, and then to our conjuring, in the devil's name.

[Exeunt. Re-enter Robin and Rafe with a silver goblet.]

ROBIN: Come, Rafe, did I not tell thee we were for ever made by this Doctor
30   Faustus' book? *Ecce signum*,[1] here's a simple purchase for horse-keepers. Our horses shall eat no hay as long as this lasts.

[Enter the Vintner.]

RAFE: But, Robin, here comes the vintner.

ROBIN: Hush, I'll gull[2] him supernaturally. Drawer, I hope all is paid. God be with you. Come, Rafe.

VINTNER: Soft, sir, a word with you. I must yet have a goblet paid from you ere you go.

ROBIN: I, a goblet? Rafe, I a goblet? I scorn you, and you are but a etc. I, a goblet? Search me.

VINTNER: I mean so, sir, with your favor.

ROBIN: How say you now?

VINTNER: I must say somewhat to your fellow—you, sir.

RAFE: Me, sir? Me, sir? Search your fill. Now, sir, you may be ashamed to burden honest men with a matter of truth.

VINTNER: Well, t'one of you hath this goblet about you.

ROBIN: You lie, drawer. 'Tis afore me! Sirrah, you! I'll teach ye to impeach honest men. Stand by, I'll scour you for a goblet. Stand aside, you were best. I charge you in the name of Belzebub. Look to the goblet, Rafe.

VINTNER: What mean you, sirrah?

ROBIN: I'll tell you what I mean. *[He reads]* *Sanctobolorum Periphrasticon.*[3] Nay, I'll
50   tickle you, vintner—look to the goblet, Rafe. *Polypragmos Belseborams framanto pacostiphos tostu Mephostophilis, Etc.*

[Enter Mephostophilis, who sets squibs[4] at their backs. They run about.]

VINTNER: *O nomine Domine*[5] what mean'st thou, Robin? Thou hast no goblet.

RAFE: *Peccatum peccatorum*[6] here's thy goblet, good vintner.

ROBIN: *Misericordia pro nobis*[7] what shall I do? Good devil, forgive me now and I'll
55   never rob thy library more.

[Enter to them Mephostophilis.]

MEPHOSTOPHILIS: Vainish villains! Th'one like an ape, another like a bear, the third an ass, for doing this enterprise.
         Monarch of hell, under whose black survey
         Great potentates do kneel with awful fear,
60   Upon whose altars thousand souls do lie,
         How am I vexed with these villains' charms?
         From Constantinople am I hither come,
         Only for pleasure of these damned slaves.

ROBIN: How, from Constantinople? You have had a great journey. Will you take
65   six pence in your purse to pay for your supper, and be gone?

---

1. "Behold, the sign"; i.e., of the truth.   5. In God's name.
2. Trick.   6. Sin of sins.
3. Gibberish.   7. Mercy on us.
4. Firecrackers.

MEPHOSTOPHILIS: Well, villains, for your presumption I transform thee into an
        ape and thee into a dog, and so be gone.   [*Exit.*]
ROBIN: How, into an ape? That's brave! I'll have fine sport with the boys. I'll get
        nuts and apples enow.
RAFE: And I must be a dog!
ROBIN: I'faith thy head will never be out of the potage pot.   [*Exeunt.*]

ACT 4

Scene 1

[*The Emperor's Court. Enter Martino and Frederick at several doors.*]
MARTINO: What ho, officers, gentlemen!
        Hie to the presence to attend the Emperor.
        Good Frederick, see the rooms be voided straight.
        His Majesty is coming to the hall;
5   Go back, and see the state in readiness.
FREDERICK: But where is Bruno, our elected Pope,
        That on a fury's back came post from Rome?
        Will not his grace consort° the Emperor?   *greet*
MARTINO: Oh yes, and with him comes the German conjuror,
10   The learned Faustus, fame of Wittenberg,
        The wonder of the world for magic art.
        And he intends to show great Carolus
        The race of all his stout progenitors,
        And bring in presence of his Majesty
15   The royal shapes and warlike semblances
        Of Alexander and his beauteous paramour.[1]
FREDERICK: Where is Benvolio?
MARTINO: Fast asleep, I warrant you.
        He took his rouse with stoups° of Rhenish wine   *large cups*
20   So kindly yesternight to Bruno's health,
        That all this day the sluggard keeps his bed.
FREDERICK: See, see, his window's ope. We'll call to him.
MARTINO: What ho, Benvolio?
        [*Enter Benvolio above at a window in his nightcap, buttoning.*]
BENVOLIO: What a devil ail you two?
MARTINO: Speak softly, sir, lest the devil hear you;
        For Faustus at the court is late arrived,
        And at his heels a thousand furies wait
        To accomplish whatsoever the Doctor please.
BENVOLIO: What of this?
MARTINO: Come, leave thy chamber first, and thou shalt see
        This conjuror perform such rare exploits
        Before the Pope and royal Emperor
        As never yet was seen in Germany.
BENVOLIO: Has not the Pope enough of conjuring yet?
35   He was upon the devil's back late enough,

1. Alexander the Great and his wife, Roxana.

And if he be so far in love with him,
I would he would post with him to Rome again.

FREDERICK: Speak, wilt thou come and see this sport?

BENVOLIO: Not I.

MARTINO: Wilt thou stand in thy window and see it, then?

BENVOLIO: Ay, and I fall not asleep i' the meantime.

MARTINO: The Emperor is at hand, who comes to see
What wonders by black spells may compassed be.

BENVOLIO: Well, go you, attend the Emperor. I am content for this once to thrust
45   my head out at a window, for they say if a man be drunk over night the devil
cannot hurt him in the morning. If that be true, I have a charm in my head
shall control him as well as the conjuror, I warrant you.

[*Exeunt Martino and Frederick.*]

Scene 2

[*Sennet. Charles, the German Emperor, Bruno, Saxony, Faustus, Mephostophilis,
Frederick, Martino, and Attendants. Benvolio still at the window.*]

EMPEROR: Wonder of men, renowned magician,
Thrice-learned Faustus, welcome to our court.
This deed of thine, in setting Bruno free
From his and our professed enemy,
5   Shall add more excellence unto thine art,
Than if by powerful necromantic spells
Thou couldst command the world's obedience.
For ever be beloved of Carolus;
And if this Bruno thou hast late redeemed,
10   In peace possess the triple diadem
And sit in Peter's chair, despite of chance,
Thou shalt be famous through all Italy,
And honored of the German Emperor.

FAUSTUS: These gracious words, most royal Carolus,
15   Shall make poor Faustus to his utmost power
Both love and serve the German Emperor,
And lay his life at holy Bruno's feet.
For proof whereof, if so your Grace be pleased,
The Doctor stands prepared, by power of art,
20   To cast his magic charms that shall pierce through
The ebon° gates of ever-burning hell,   *ebony*
And hale the stubborn furies from their caves,
To compass whatsoe'er your Grace commands.

BENVOLIO [*ASIDE*]: Blood, he speaks terribly! But for all that, I do not greatly
25   believe him. He looks as like a conjuror as the Pope to a coster-monger.[2]

EMPEROR: Then, Faustus, as thou late didst promise us,
We would behold that famous conqueror,
Great Alexander, and his paramour,
In their true shapes and state majestical,

---

2. Vegetable seller.

30   That we may wonder at their excellence.

FAUSTUS: Your Majesty shall see them presently.

Mephostophilis, away!

And with a solemn noise of trumpets' sound,

Present before this royal Emperor

35   Great Alexander and his beauteous paramour.

MEPHOSTOPHILIS: Faustus, I will.

BENVOLIO: Well, Master Doctor, an your devils come not away quickly, you shall

have me asleep presently. Zounds, I could eat myself for anger, to think I

have been such an ass all this while, to stand gaping after the devil's

40   governor, and can see nothing.

FAUSTUS: I'll make you feel something anon, if my art fail me not.

My lord, I must forwarn your Majesty

That when my spirits present the royal shapes

Of Alexander and his paramour,

45   Your Grace demand no questions of the King,

But in dumb silence let them come and go.

EMPEROR: Be it as Faustus please, we are content.

BENVOLIO: Ay, ay, and I am content too. And thou bring Alexander and his

paramour before the Emperor, I'll be Actaeon[3] and turn myself to a stag.

FAUSTUS: And I'll play Diana, and send you the horns presently.

[Sennet. Enter at one the Emperor Alexander, at the other Darius. They meet. Darius
is thrown down; Alexander kills him, takes off his crown, and, offering to go out, his
Paramour meets him. He embraceth her and sets Darius' crown upon her head, and
coming back, both salute the Emperor, who, leaving his state, offers to embrace them,
which Faustus seeing, suddenly stays him. Then trumpets cease and music sounds.]

My gracious lord, you do forget yourself.

These are but shadows, not substantial.

EMPEROR: Oh pardon me, my thoughts are so ravished

With sight of this renowned Emperor,

55   That in mine arms I would have compassed him.

But, Faustus, since I may not speak to them,

To satisfy my longing thoughts at full,

Let me this tell thee: I have heard it said

That this fair lady, whilst she lived on earth,

60   Had on her neck a little wart or mole.

How may I prove that saying to be true?

FAUSTUS: Your Majesty may boldly go and see.

EMPEROR: Faustus, I see it plain,

And in this sight thou better pleasest me

65   Than if I gained another monarchy.

FAUSTUS: Away, be gone.

[Exit Show.]

See, see, my gracious lord, what strange beast is yon, that thrusts his head

out at window?

EMPEROR: Oh, wondrous sight! See, Duke of Saxony,

---

3. Mythical hunter, changed by the goddess Diana into a stag because he had seen her naked as she bathed after a hunt;
he was then devoured by his own dogs.

70   Two spreading horns most strangely fastened
        Upon the head of young Benvolio!⁴

SAXONY: What, is he asleep? Or dead?

FAUSTUS: He sleeps, my lord: but dreams not of his horns.

EMPEROR: This sport is excellent. We'll call and wake him.

75   What ho, Benvolio!

BENVOLIO: A plague upon you! Let me sleep awhile.

EMPEROR: I blame thee not to sleep much, having such a head of thine own.

SAXONY: Look up, Benvolio, 'tis the Emperor calls.

BENVOLIO: The Emperor? Where? Oh, zounds, my head!

EMPEROR: Nay, and thy horns hold, 'tis no matter for thy head, for that's armed
    sufficiently.

FAUSTUS: Why, how now, Sir Knight? What, hanged by the horns? This most
    horrible! Fie, fie! Pull in your head for shame; let not all the world wonder
    at you.

BENVOLIO: Zounds, Doctor, is this your villainy?

FAUSTUS: Oh, say not so, sir. The Doctor has no skill,
    No art, no cunning, to present these lords
    Or bring before this royal Emperor
    The mighty monarch, warlike Alexander.

90   If Faustus do it, you are straight resolved
    In bold Actaeon's shape to turn a stag.
    And therefore, my lord, so please your majesty,
    I'll raise a kennel of hounds shall hunt him so
    As all his footmanship shall scarce prevail

95   To keep his carcass from their bloody fangs.
    Ho, Belimote, Argiron, Asterote!

BENVOLIO: Hold, hold! Zounds, he'll raise up a kennel of devils, I think anon.
    Good my lord, entreat for me. 'Sblood, I am never never able to endure
    these torments.

EMPEROR: Then, good Master Doctor,
    Let me entreat you to remove his horns:
    He has done penance now sufficiently.

FAUSTUS: My gracious lord, not so much for injury done to me, as to delight your
    majesty with some mirth, hath Faustus justly requited this injurious knight;

105   which being all I desire, I am content to remove his horns. Mephostophilis,
    transform him. And hereafter, sir, look you speak well of scholars.

BENVOLIO [ASIDE]: Speak well of ye? 'Sblood, and scholars be such cuckold-
    makers to clap horns of honest men's heads o' this order, I'll ne'er trust
    smooth faces and small ruffs more. But an I be not revenged for this, would

110   I might be turned to a gaping oyster and drink nothing but salt water.

EMPEROR: Come, Faustus, while the Emperor lives,
    In recompense of this thy high desert,°   *merit*
    Thou shalt command the state of Germany,
    And live beloved of mighty Carolus.   [*Exeunt omnes.*]

---

4. To be "horned" was to be cuckolded. Benvolio, who has insulted scholars, is given horns by Faustus, who takes a
scholar's revenge. The insult is introduced as a reflection on the myth of Diana and Actaeon.

Scene 3

[Enter Benvolio, Martino, Frederick and Soldiers.]

MARTINO: Nay, sweet Benvolio, let us sway thy thoughts
    From this attempt against the conjuror.
BENVOLIO: Away, you love me not, to urge me thus.
    Shall I let slip° so great an injury,   *overlook*
5   When every servile groom jests at my wrongs,
    And in their rustic gambols proudly say
    Benvolio's head was graced with horns today?
    Oh, may these eyelids never close again
    Till with my sword I have that conjuror slain.
10   If you will aid me in this enterprise,
    Then draw your weapons and be resolute.
    If not, depart. Here will Benvolio die,
    But Faustus' death shall quit my infamy.
FREDERICK: Nay, we will stay with three, betide what may,
15   And kill that Doctor if he come this way.
BENVOLIO: Then, gentle Frederick, hie° thee to the grove,   *take*
    And place our servants and our followers
    Close in an ambush there behind the trees.
    By this I know the conjuror is near:
20   I saw him kneel and kiss the Emperor's hand,
    And take his leave, laden with rich rewards.
    Then, soldiers, boldly fight. If Faustus die,
    Take you the wealth, leave us the victory.
FREDERICK: Come, soldiers, follow me unto the grove.
25   Who kills him shall have gold and endless love.

[Exit Frederick with the Soldiers.]

BENVOLIO: My head is lighter than it was by th'horns,
    But yet my heart more ponderous than my head,
    And pants until I see that conjuror dead.
MARTINO: Where shall we place ourselves, Benvolio?
BENVOLIO: Here will we stay to bide the first assault.
    Oh, were that damned hell-hound but in place,
    Thou soon shouldst see me quit my foul disgrace.
    [Enter Frederick.]
FREDERICK: Close, close! The conjuror is at hand,
    And all alone comes walking in his gown.
35   Be ready then, and strike the peasant down.
BENVOLIO: Mine be that honor, then. Now sword, strike home.
    For horns he gave, I'll have his head anon.
    [Enter Faustus with a false head.]
MARTINO: See, see, he comes.
BENVOLIO: No words. This blow ends all.
40   Hell take his soul; his body thus must fall.
    [Attacks Faustus.]
FAUSTUS: Oh!
FREDERICK: Groan you, Master Doctor?

BENVOLIO: Break may his heart with groans! Dear Frederick, see,
   Thus will I end his griefs immediately.
  [*Cuts off his head.*]
MARTINO: Strike with a willing hand: his head is off.
BENVOLIO: The devil's dead! The Furies now may laugh.
FREDERICK: Was this that stern aspect, that awful frown,
   Made the grim monarch of infernal spirits
   Tremble and quake at his commanding charms?
MARTINO: Was this that damned head, whose heart conspired
   Benvolio's shame before the Emperor?
BENVOLIO: Ay, that's the head, and here the body lies,
   Justly rewarded for his villainies.
FREDERICK: Come, let's devise how we may add more shame
55 To the black scandal of his hated name.
BENVOLIO: First, on his head, in quittance° of my wrongs,   *payment*
   I'll nail huge forked horns, and let them hang
   Within the window where he yoked° me first,   *overcame*
   That all the world may see my just revenge.
MARTINO: What use shall we put his beard to?
BENVOLIO: We'll sell it to a chimney-sweeper: it will wear
   out ten birching° brooms, I warrant you.   *birch-twig*
FREDERICK: What shall eyes do?
BENVOLIO: We'll put out his eyes, and they shall serve for buttons to his lips, to
65 keep his tongue from catching cold.
MARTINO: An excellent policy! And now, sirs, having divided him, what shall
  the body do?
  [*Faustus rises.*]
BENVOLIO: Zounds, the devil's alive again!
FREDERICK: Give him his head, for God's sake!
FAUSTUS: Nay, keep it. Faustus will have heads and hands.
   I call your hearts to recompense this deed.
   Knew you not, traitors, I was limited
   For four and twenty years to breathe on earth?
   And had you cut my body with your swords,
75 Or hewed this flesh and bones as small as sand,
   Yet in a minute had my spirit returned,
   And I had breathed a man made free from harm.
   But wherefore do I dally° my revenge?   *delay*
   Asteroth, Belimoth, Mephostophilis!
  [*Enter Mephostophilis and other Devils.*]
80 Go, horse these traitors on your fiery backs,
   And mount aloft with them as high as heaven;
   Thence pitch them headlong to the lowest hell.
   Yet stay, the world shall see their misery,
   And hell shall after plague their treachery.
85 Go, Belimoth, and take this caitiff° hence,   *coward*
   And hurl him in some lake of mud and dirt.
   Take thou this other: drag him through the woods
   Amongst the pricking thorns and sharpest briars,

Whilst with my gentle Mephostophilis,
90   This traitor flies unto some steepy rock,
That rolling down may break the villain's bones,
As he intended to dismember me.
Fly hence, dispatch my charge immediately.

FREDERICK: Pity us, gentle Faustus! Save our lives!

FAUSTUS: Away!

FREDERICK: He must needs go that the devil drives.

[*Exeunt Spirits with the Knights. Enter the Ambush Soldiers.*]

FIRST SOLDIER: Come, sirs, prepare yourselves in readiness.
Make haste to help these noble gentlemen.
I heard them parley with the conjuror.

SECOND SOLDIER: See, where he comes. Dispatch and kill the slave.

FAUSTUS: What's here? An ambush to betray my life!
Then Faustus, try thy skill. Base peasants, stand!
For lo, these trees remove at my command,
And stand as bulwarks twixt yourselves and me,
105   To shield me from your hated treachery.
Yet, to encounter this your weak attempt,
Behold an army comes incontinent.°   *rapidly*

[*Faustus strikes the door, and enter a devil playing on a drum; after him another bear-*
ing an ensign;[5] *and divers with weapons; Mephostophilis with fireworks. They set upon*
the soldiers and drive them out.]

Scene 4

[*Enter at several doors Benvolio, Frederick and Martino, their heads and faces bloody*
and besmeared with mud and dirt, all having horns on their heads.]

MARTINO: What ho, Benvolio!

BENVOLIO: Here! What, Frederick, ho!

FREDERICK: Oh help me, gentle friend. Where is Martino?

MARTINO: Dear Frederick, here,
5   Half smothered in a lake of mud and dirt,
Through which the Furies dragged me by the heels.

FREDERICK: Martino, see Benvolio's horns again!

MARTINO: Oh misery! How now, Benvolio?

BENVOLIO: Defend me, heaven! Shall I be haunted still?

MARTINO: Nay, fear not, man; we have no power to kill.

BENVOLIO: My friends transformed thus! Oh hellish spite!
Your heads are all set with horns!

FREDERICK: You hit it right:
It is your own you mean. Feel on your head.

BENVOLIO: Zounds, horns again!

MARTINO: Nay, chafe not, man. We all are sped.°   *done for*

BENVOLIO: What devil attends this damned magician,
That, spite of spite, our wrongs are doubled?

FREDERICK: What may we do, that we may hide our shames?

5. Flag.

BENVOLIO: If we should follow him to work revenge,
    He'd join long asses' ears to these huge horns,
    And make us laughing stocks to all the world.
MARTINO: What shall we then do, dear Benvolio?
BENVOLIO: I have a castle joining near these woods,
25   And thither we'll repair and live obscure,
    Till time shall alter these our brutish shapes.
    Sith° black disgrace hath thus eclipsed our fame,   *since*
    We'll rather die with grief, than live with shame.

                                              [*Exeunt omnes.*]

                     Scene 5

[*Enter Faustus and Mephostophilis.*]
FAUSTUS: Now, Mephostophilis, the restless course
    That time doth run with calm and deadly foot,
    Shortening my days and thread of vital life,
    Calls for the payment of my latest years.
5   Therefore, sweet Mephostophilis, let us
    Make haste to Wittenberg.
MEPHOSTOPHILIS: What, will you go on horseback, or on foot?
FAUSTUS: Nay, till I am past this fair and pleasant green
    I'll walk on foot.
    [*Enter a Horse-Courser.*][6]
HORSE-COURSER: I have been all this day seeking one master Fustian.[7] Mass,
    see where he is! God save you, Master Doctor.
FAUSTUS: What, horse-courser! You are well met.
HORSE-COURSER: Do you hear, sir? I have brought you forty dollars for your
    horse.
FAUSTUS: I cannot sell him so. If thou likest him for fifty, take him.
HORSE-COURSER: Alas, sir, I have no more. I pray you, speak for me.
MEPHOSTOPHILIS: I pray you, let him have him. He is an honest fellow, and he
    has a great charge, neither wife nor child.
FAUSTUS: Well, come, give me your money. My boy will deliver him to you. But
20   I must tell you one thing before you have him: ride him not into the water
    at any hand.
HORSE-COURSER: Why, sir, will he not drink of all waters?
FAUSTUS: Oh yes, he will drink of all waters; but ride him not into the water.
    Ride him over hedge or ditch or where thou wilt, but not into the water.
HORSE-COURSER: Well, sir, now I am a made man for ever. I'll not leave my
    horse for forty. If he had but the quality of hey ding ding, hey ding ding, I'd
    make a brave living on him. He has a buttock as slick as an eel. Well, God
    bye, sir. Your boy will deliver him me. But hark ye sir: if my horse be sick or
    ill at ease, if I bring his water to you, you'll tell me what is?
FAUSTUS: Away, you villain! What, dost think I am a horse-doctor?
                                              [*Exit Horse-Courser.*]
    What art thou, Faustus, but a man condemned to die?

---

6. Horse trader.   7. Bombast.

Thy fatal time doth draw to final end:
Despair doth drive distrust into my thoughts.
Confound these passions with a quiet sleep.
35   Tush, Christ did call the thief upon the cross;
Then rest thee, Faustus, quiet in conceit.

[*Sleeps in his chair. Enter Horse-Courser all wet, crying.*]

HORSE-COURSER: Alas, alas, Doctor Fustian quotha! Mass, Doctor Lopus[8] was
never such a doctor. Has given me a purgation has purged me of forty dollars: I shall never see them more. But yet like an ass as I was, I would not be
ruled by him, for he bade me I should ride him into no water. Now I, think
40   ing my horse had had some rare quality that he would not have had me
known of, I, like a venturous youth, rid him into the deep pond at the
town's end. I was no sooner in the middle of the pond but my horse vanished away, and I sat upon a bottle of hay, never so near drowning in my life.
But I'll seek out my Doctor and have my forty dollars again, or I'll make it
45   the dearest horse. Oh, yonder is his snipper-snapper. Do you hear? You!
Hey-pass, where's your master?

MEPHOSTOPHILIS: Why, sir, what would you? You cannot speak with him.

HORSE-COURSER: But I *will* speak with him.

MEPHOSTOPHILIS: Why, he's fast asleep. Come some other time.

HORSE-COURSER: I'll speak with him now, or I'll break his glass windows about
his ears.

MEPHOSTOPHILIS: I tell thee he has not slept this eight nights.

HORSE-COURSER: And he have not slept this eight weeks I'll speak with him.

MEPHOSTOPHILIS: See where he is fast asleep.

HORSE-COURSER: Ay, this is he. God save ye, Master Doctor. Master Doctor!
Master Doctor Fustian! Forty dollars, forty dollars for a bottle of hay!

MEPHOSTOPHILIS: Why, thou seest he hears thee not.

HORSE-COURSER: So, ho, ho! So, ho, ho!

[*Halloos in his ear.*]

No, will you not wake? I'll make you wake e'er I go.

[*He pulls him by the leg, and pulls it away.*]

60   Alas, I am undone! What shall I do?

FAUSTUS: Oh, my leg, my leg! Help, Mephostophilis. Call the officers. My leg,
my leg!

MEPHOSTOPHILIS: Come, villain, to the Constable.

HORSE-COURSER: Oh lord, sir, let me go and I'll give you forty dollars more.

MEPHOSTOPHILIS: Where be they?

HORSE-COURSER: I have none about me. Come to my hostry and I'll give them
you.

MEPHOSTOPHILIS: Be gone, quickly!

[*Horse-Courser runs away.*]

FAUSTUS: What, is he gone? Farewell he. Faustus has his leg again, and the
70   horse-courser, I take it, a bottle of hay for his labor. Well, this trick shall
cost him forty dollars more.

---

8. Dr. Lopez, Queen Elizabeth's physician, who was executed in 1594 for alleged complicity in an attempt to murder the
Queen. Marlowe died in 1593, so the reference is not his but one of a later editor.

[*Enter Wagner.*]

FAUSTUS: How now, Wagner, what news with thee?

WAGNER: If it please you, the Duke of Vanholt[9] doth earnestly entreat your company, and hath sent some of his men to attend you with provision for your
75   journey.

FAUSTUS: The Duke of Vanholt's an honorable gentleman, and one to whom I
must be no niggard[1] of my cunning. Come, away.   [*Exeunt.*]

Scene 6

[*Enter Clown, Dick, Horse-Courser and a Carter.*]

CARTER: Come, my masters, I'll bring you to the best beer in Europe. What ho,
hostess. Where be these whores?

[*Enter Hostess.*]

HOSTESS: How now, what lack you? What, my old guests, welcome!

CLOWN: Sirrah Dick, dost thou know why I stand so mute?

DICK: No, Robin, why is't?

CLOWN: I am eighteen pence on the score.[2] But say nothing. See if she have forgotten me.

HOSTESS: Who's this, that stands so solemnly by himself? What, my old guest?

CLOWN: Oh, hostess, how do you? I hope my score stands still.

HOSTESS: Ay, there's no doubt of that, for methinks you make no haste to wipe it
out.

DICK: Why, hostess, I say, fetch us some beer.

HOSTESS: You shall presently. Look up into the hall there, ho!   [*Exit.*]

DICK: Come, sirs, what shall we do now till mine hostess comes?

CARTER: Marry, sir, I'll tell you the bravest tale how a conjuror served me. You
know Doctor Faustus?

HORSE-COURSER: Ay, a plague take him. Here's some on's have cause to know
him. Did he conjure thee too?

CARTER: I'll tell you how he served me. As I was going to Wittenberg t'other
20   day, with a load of hay, he met me and asked me what he should give me for
as much hay as he could eat. Now, sir, I, thinking that a little would serve
his turn, bade him take as much as he would for three-farthings. So he
presently gave me my money and fell to eating. And, as I am a cursen man,
he never left eating till he had eat up all my load of hay.

ALL: Oh monstrous! Eat a whole load of hay?

CLOWN: Yes, yes, that may be, for I have heard of one that has eat a load of logs.

HORSE-COURSER: Now, sirs, you shall hear how villainously he served me. I
went to him yesterday to buy a horse of him, and he would by no means sell
him under forty dollars. So, sir, because I knew him to be such a horse as
30   would run over hedge and ditch and never tire, I gave him his money. So
when I had my horse, Doctor Fauster bade me ride him night and day and
spare him no time. But, quoth he, in any case ride him not into the water.
Now, sir, I thinking the horse had some quality that he would not have me

9. The Duchy of Anholt in Germany.   2. Eighteen pence in debt.
1. Miser.

35   know of, what did I but ride him into a great river, and when I came just in
        the midst, my horse vanished away, and I sat straddling upon a bottle of hay.
ALL: Oh brave Doctor!
HORSE-COURSER: But you shall hear how bravely I served him for it: I went me
        home to his house, and there I found him asleep. I kept a-hallowing and
40   whooping in his ears, but all could not wake him. I, seeing that, took him by
        the leg and never rested pulling, till I had pulled me his leg quite off, and
        now 'tis at home in mine hostry.
CLOWN: And has the Doctor but one leg, then? That's excellent, for one of his
        devils turned me into the likeness of an ape's face.
CARTER: Some more drink, hostess.
CLOWN: Hark you, we'll into another room and drink a while, and then we'll go
        seek out the Doctor.   [Exeunt omnes.]

Scene 7

[Enter the Duke of Vanholt, his Duchess, Faustus and Mephostophilis.]
DUKE: Thanks, Master Doctor, for these pleasant sights. Nor know I how suffi-
        ciently to recompense your great deserts in erecting that enchanted castle in
        the air, the sight whereof so delighted me, as nothing in the world could
        please me more.
FAUSTUS: I do think myself, my good lord, highly recompensed in that it pleaseth
        your grace to think but well of that which Faustus hath performed. But, gra-
        cious lady, it may be that you have taken no pleasure in those sights. There-
        fore, I pray you tell me, what is the thing you most desire to have. Be it in
        the world, it shall be yours. I have heard that great-bellied women do long
60   for things are rare and dainty.
LADY: True, Master Doctor, and since I find you so kind, I will make known unto
        you what my heart desires to have; and were it now summer, as it is January,
        a dead time of the winter, I would request no better meat than a dish of ripe
        grapes.
FAUSTUS: This is but a small matter. Go, Mephostophilis, away.
                                                        [Exit Mephostophilis.]
        Madame, I will do more than this for your content.
        [Enter Mephostophilis again with the grapes.]
        Here, now taste ye these. They should be good, for they come from a far
        country, I can tell you.
DUKE: This makes me wonder more than all the rest, that at this time of the year,
20   when every tree is barren of his fruit, from whence you had these ripe grapes.
FAUSTUS: Please it your grace, the year is divided into two circles over the whole
        world, so that when it is winter with us, in the contrary circle it is likewise
        summer with them, as in India, Saba and such countries that lie far East,
25   where they have fruit twice a year. From whence, by means of a swift spirit
        that I have, I had these grapes brought as you see.
LADY: And trust me, they are the sweetest grapes that e'er I tasted.
        [The Clowns bounce at the gate within.]
DUKE: What rude disturbers have we at the gate?
        Go, pacify their fury. Set it ope,
30   And then demand of them what they would have.

[*They knock again and call out to talk with Faustus.*]

SERVANT: Why, how now, masters? What a coil[3] is there?

    What is the reason you disturb the Duke?

DICK: We have no reason for it, therefore a fig for him.

SERVANT: Why, saucy varlets, dare you be so bold?

HORSE-COURSER: I hope, sir, we have wit enough to be more bold than wel-

    come.

SERVANT: It appears so. Pray be bold elsewhere,

    And trouble not the Duke.

DUKE: What would they have?

SERVANT: They all cry out to speak with Doctor Faustus.

CARTER: Ay, and we will speak with him.

DUKE: Will you, sir? Commit the rascals.

DICK: Commit with us! He were as good commit with his father as commit with

    us.

FAUSTUS: I do beseech your grace let them come in.

    They are good subject for a merriment.

DUKE: Do as thou wilt, Faustus; I give thee leave.

FAUSTUS: I thank your grace.

    [*Enter the Clown, Dick, Carter and Horse-Courser.*]

    Why, how now, my good friends?

50   Faith, you are too outrageous, but come near.

    I have procured your pardons. Welcome all.

CLOWN: Nay, sir, we will be welcome for our money, and we will pay for what we

    take. What ho! Give's half-a-dozen of beer here, and be hanged.

FAUSTUS: Nay, hark you. Can you tell me where you are?

CARTER: Ay, marry can I. We are under heaven.

SERVANT: Ay, but, sir sauce-box, know you in what place?

HORSE-COURSER: Ay, ay, the house is good enough to drink in. Zounds, fill us

    some beer or we'll break all the barrels in the house and dash out all your

    brains with your bottles.

FAUSTUS: Be not so furious. Come, you shall have beer.

    My lord, beseech you give me leave awhile.

    I'll gage my credit, 'twill content your Grace.

DUKE: With all my heart, kind Doctor; please thyself.

    Our servants and our court's at thy command.

FAUSTUS: I humbly thank your Grace. Then fetch some beer.

HORSE-COURSER: Ay, marry. There spake a doctor indeed, and faith, I'll drink a

    health to thy wooden leg for that word.

FAUSTUS: My wooden leg? What dost thou mean by that?

CARTER: Ha, ha, ha! Dost thou hear him, Dick? He has forgot his leg.

HORSE-COURSER: Ay, ay, he does not stand much upon that.

FAUSTUS: No, faith. Not much upon a wooden leg.

CARTER: Good lord! That flesh and blood should be so frail with your worship.

    Do not you remember a horse-courser you sold a horse to?

FAUSTUS: Yes, I remember I sold one a horse.

3. Disturbance.

CARTER: And do you remember you bid he should not ride into the water?

FAUSTUS: Yes, I do very well remember that.

CARTER: And do you remember nothing of your leg?

FAUSTUS: No, in good sooth.

CARTER: Then I pray remember your courtesy.[4]

FAUSTUS: I thank you, sir.

CARTER: 'Tis not so much worth. I pray you, tell me one thing.

FAUSTUS: What's that?

CARTER: Be both your legs bedfellows every night together?

FAUSTUS: Wouldst thou make a colossus[5] of me, that thou askest me such ques-
85   tions?

CARTER: No, truly, sir. I would make nothing of you, but I would fain know that.
   [Enter Hostess with drink.]

FAUSTUS: Then I assure thee certainly they are.

CARTER: I thank you, I am fully satisfied.

FAUSTUS: But wherefore dost thou ask?

CARTER: For nothing, sir: but methinks you should have a wooden bedfellow of
   one of 'em.

HORSE-COURSER: Why, do you hear, sir? Did not I pull off one of your legs
   when you were asleep?

FAUSTUS: But I have it again now I am awake. Look you here, sir.

ALL: Oh horrible! Had the Doctor three legs?

CARTER: Do you remember, sir, how you cozened[6] me and eat up my load of—
   [Faustus charms him dumb.]

DICK: Do you remember how you made me wear an ape's—

HORSE-COURSER: You whoreson conjuring scab, do you remember how you
   cozened me with a ho—

CLOWN: Ha' you forgotten me? You think to carry it away with your hey-pass and
   re-pass. Do you remember the dog's fa—
   [Faustus has charmed each dumb in turn; exeunt Clowns.]

HOSTESS: Who pays for the ale? Hear you, Master Doctor, now you have sent
   away my guests, I pray who shall pay me for my a—?
   [Exit Hostess.]

LADY: My lord,
105   We are much beholding to this learned man.

DUKE: So are we, madam, which we will recompense
   With all the love and kindness that we may.
   His artful sport drives all sad thoughts away.   [Exeunt.]

ACT 5

Scene 1

[Thunder and lightning. Enter Devils with covered dishes. Mephostophilis leads them
into Faustus' study. Then enter Wagner.]

WAGNER: I think my master means to die shortly.

---

4. Kindness   6. Tricked.
5. Huge statue.

He hath made his will, and given me his wealth,
His house, his goods, and store of golden plate,
Besides two thousand ducats ready coined.
5   And yet methinks, if that death were near,
He would not banquet and carouse and swill
Amongst the students, as even now he doth,
Who are at supper with such belly-cheer
As Wagner ne'er beheld in all his life.
10   See where they come; belike the feast is ended.   [*Exit.*]
[*Enter Faustus, Mephostophilis and two or three Scholars.*]

FIRST SCHOLAR: Master Doctor Faustus, since our conference about fair ladies,
which was the beautifullest in all the world, we have determined with ourselves that Helen of Greece[1] was the admirablest lady that ever lived.
Therefore Master Doctor, if you will do us so much favor, as to let us see that
15   peerless dame of Greece, whom all the world admires for majesty, we should
think ourselves much beholding unto you.

FAUSTUS: Gentlemen, for that I know your friendship is unfeigned,
It is not Faustus' custom to deny
The just request of those that wish him well.
20   You shall behold that peerless dame of Greece,
No otherwise for pomp of majesty,
Than when Sir Paris crossed the seas with her,
And brought the spoils to rich Dardania.°   *Troy*
Be silent then, for danger is in words.
[*Music sounds. Mephostophilis brings in Helen; she passeth over the stage.*]

SECOND SCHOLAR: Was this fair Helen, whose admired worth
Made Greece with ten years wars afflict poor Troy?

THIRD SCHOLAR: Too simple is my wit to tell her worth
Whom all the world admires for majesty.

FIRST SCHOLAR: Now we have seen the pride of nature's work,
30   We'll take our leaves, and for this blessed sight
Happy and blest be Faustus evermore.
[*Enter an Old Man.*]

FAUSTUS: Gentlemen, farewell: the same wish I to you.   [*Exeunt Scholars.*]

OLD MAN: Oh gentle Faustus, leave this damned art,[2]
This magic, that will charm thy soul to hell,
35   And quite bereave thee of salvation.
Though thou hast now offended like a man,
Do not persever in it like a devil.
Yet, yet, thou hast an amiable° soul,   *lovable*
If sin by custom grow not into nature:

---

1. The mythical queen of Menelaus, King of Sparta, who
was abducted by Paris, son of King Priam of Troy. The action began the Trojan War.
2. The Old Man's lines in the A text reflect a Calvinist
sense that Faustus may be saved by the Saviour's "mercy"
and "blood alone":

    Ah Doctor Faustus, that I might prevail,
    To guide thy steps unto the way of life,
    By which sweet path thou mayst attain the goal

That shall conduct thee to celestial rest.
Break heart, drop blood, and mingle it with tears,
Tears falling from repentant heaviness
Of thy most vile and loathsome filthiness,
The stench whereof corrupts the inward soul
With such flagitious crimes of hainous sinnes,
As no commiseration may expel,
But mercy Faustus of thy Saviour sweet,
Whose blood alone must wash away thy guilt.

40   Then, Faustus, will repentance come too late,
        Then thou art banished from the sight of heaven;
        No mortal can express the pains of hell.
        It may be this my exhortation
        Seems harsh and all unpleasant; let it not,
45   For, gentle son, I speak it not in wrath,
        Or envy of thee, but in tender love,
        And pity of thy future misery.
        And so have hope, that this my kind rebuke,
        Checking thy body, may amend thy soul.
FAUSTUS: Where art thou, Faustus? Wretch, what hast thou done?
        Damned art thou, Faustus, damned: despair and die.
        Hell claims his right, and with a roaring voice
        Says "Faustus, come, thine hour is almost come"
    [*Mephostophilis gives him a dagger.*]
        And Faustus now will come to do thee right.
OLD MAN: Oh stay, good Faustus, stay thy desperate steps.
        I see an angel hover o'er thy head,
        And with a vial full of precious grace,
        Offers to pour the same into thy soul.
        Then call for mercy and avoid despair.
FAUSTUS: Ah my sweet friend, I feel thy words
        To comfort my distressed soul.
        Leave me awhile to ponder on my sins.
OLD MAN: I leave thee, but with grief of heart,
        Fearing the ruin of thy hopeless soul.   [*Exit.*]
FAUSTUS: Accursed Faustus, wretch, what hast thou done?
        I do repent, and yet I do despair.
        Hell strives with grace for conquest in my breast.
        What shall I do to shun the snares of death?
MEPHOSTOPHILIS: Thou traitor, Faustus, I arrest thy soul
70   For disobedience to my sovereign lord.
        Revolt,[3] or I'll in piecemeal tear thy flesh.
FAUSTUS: I do repent I e'er offended him.
        Sweet Mephostophilis, entreat thy lord
        To pardon my unjust presumption,
75   And with my blood again I will confirm
        The former vow I made to Lucifer.
MEPHOSTOPHILIS: Do it then, Faustus, with unfeigned heart,
        Lest greater dangers do attend thy drift.
FAUSTUS: Torment, sweet friend, that base and crooked age
80   That durst dissuade me from thy Lucifer,
        With greatest torment that our hell affords.
MEPHOSTOPHILIS: His faith is great: I cannot touch his soul.
        But what I may afflict his body with
        I will attempt, which is but little worth.
FAUSTUS: One thing, good servant, let me crave of thee,

---

3. I.e., return to the terms of your bargain with the devil.

> To glut the longing of my heart's desire,
> That I may have unto my paramour
> That heavenly Helen which I saw of late,
> Whose sweet embraces may extinguish clear
90> Those thoughts that do dissuade me from my vow,
> And keep my vow I made to Lucifer.

MEPHOSTOPHILIS: This, or what else my Faustus shall desire,
> Shall be performed in twinkling of an eye.

[Enter Helen again, passing over between two Cupids.]

FAUSTUS: Was this the face that launched a thousand ships,
95> And burnt the topless towers of Ilium?
> Sweet Helen, make me immortal with a kiss.
> Her lips suck forth my soul: see where it flies.
> Come, Helen, come, give me my soul again.
> Here will I dwell, for heaven is in those lips,
100> And all is dross that is not Helena.

[Enter Old Man.]

> I will be Paris,⁴ and for love of thee
> Instead of Troy shall Wittenberg be sacked,
> And I will combat with weak Menelaus,
> And wear thy colors on my plumed crest.
105> Yea, I will wound Achilles in the heel,
> And then return to Helen for a kiss.
> Oh, thou art fairer than the evening's air,
> Clad in the beauty of a thousand stars.
> Brighter art thou than flaming Jupiter,
110> When he appeared to hapless Semele:⁵
> More lovely than the monarch of the sky,
> In wanton Arethusa's⁶ azure arms,
> And none but thou shalt be my paramour.   *[Exeunt.]*

OLD MAN: Accursed Faustus, miserable man,
115> That from thy soul exclud'st the grace of heaven,
> And fliest the throne of his tribunal seat.

[Enter the Devils.]

> Satan begins to sift° me with his pride,   scrutinize
> As in this furnace God shall try my faith.
> My faith, vile hell, shall triumph over thee.
120> Ambitious fiends, see how the heavens smiles
> At your repulse, and laughs your state to scorn.
> Hence, hell, for hence I fly unto my God.   *[Exeunt.]*

Scene 2

[Thunder. Enter Lucifer, Belzebub and Mephostophilis.]

LUCIFER: Thus from infernal Dis° do we ascend   hell
> To view the subjects of our monarchy,

---

4. Faustus imagines he will be not only Paris, Helen's lover, but also the victor in combat with her husband, King Menelaus, as well as with the greatest of the Greek warriors, Achilles.

5. The mortal woman to whom Jupiter appeared as lightening.
6. A nymph beloved by the river-god Alpheus; no myth describes her as Jupiter's lover.

Those souls which sin seals the black sons of hell,
'Mong which as chief, Faustus, we come to thee,
5   Bringing with us lasting damnation
To wait upon thy soul. The time is come
Which makes it forfeit.
MEPHOSTOPHILIS: And this gloomy night,
Here in this room will wretched Faustus be.
BELZEBUB: And here we'll stay,
To mark him how he doth demean himself.
MEPHOSTOPHILIS: How should he, but in desperate lunacy?
Fond worldling, now his heart blood dries with grief.
His conscience kills it, and his laboring brain
15   Begets a world of idle fantasies
To overreach the devil. But all in vain:
His store of pleasures must be sauced with pain.
He and his servant Wagner are at hand.
Both come from drawing Faustus' latest will.
20   See where they come.
   [Enter Faustus and Wagner.]
FAUSTUS: Say, Wagner, thou hast perused my will:
How dost thou like it?
WAGNER: Sir, so wondrous well
As in all humble duty I do yield
25   My life and lasting service for your love.
   [Enter the Scholars.]
FAUSTUS: Gramercies, Wagner. Welcome, gentlemen.
FIRST SCHOLAR: Now, worthy Faustus, methinks your looks are changed.
FAUSTUS: Oh gentlemen!
SECOND SCHOLAR: What ails Faustus?
FAUSTUS: Ah, my sweet chamber-fellow, had I lived with thee
Then had I lived still, but now must die eternally.
Look, sirs, comes he not? Comes he not?
FIRST SCHOLAR: Oh, my dear Faustus, what imports this fear?
SECOND SCHOLAR: Is all our pleasure turned to melancholy?
THIRD SCHOLAR: He is not well with being oversolitary.
SECOND SCHOLAR: If it be so, we'll have physicians, and Faustus shall be cured.
THIRD SCHOLAR: 'Tis but a surfeit, sir; fear nothing.
FAUSTUS: A surfeit of deadly sin, that hath damned both body and soul.
SECOND SCHOLAR: Yet Faustus, look up to heaven, and remember mercy is
40   infinite.
FAUSTUS: But Faustus' offence can ne'er be pardoned, The serpent that tempted
Eve may be saved, but not Faustus. Oh gentlemen, hear with patience and
tremble not at my speeches. Though my heart pant and quiver to remember
that I have been a student here these thirty years, oh would I had never seen
45   Wittenberg, never read book. And what wonders I have done all Germany
can witness, yea all the world, for which Faustus hath lost both Germany
and the world, yea heaven itself, heaven, the seat of God, the throne of the
blessed, the kingdom of joy, and must remain in hell for ever. Hell, oh hell

for ever. Sweet friends, what shall become of Faustus, being in hell for ever?

SECOND SCHOLAR: Yet Faustus, call on God.

FAUSTUS: On God, whom Faustus hath abjured? On God, whom Faustus hath blasphemed? Oh my God, I would weep, but the devil draws in my tears. Gush forth blood instead of tears, yea, life and soul. Oh, he stays my tongue. I would lift up my hands, but see, they hold them, they hold them.

ALL: Who, Faustus?

FAUSTUS: Why, Lucifer and Mephostophilis: Oh gentlemen, I gave them my soul for my cunning.

ALL: Oh, God forbid.

FAUSTUS: God forbade it indeed, but Faustus hath done it. For vain pleasure of
60   four and twenty years hath Faustus lost eternal joy and felicity. I writ them a bill with mine own blood, the date is expired: this is the time, and he will fetch me.

FIRST SCHOLAR: Why did not Faustus tell us of this before, that divines might have prayed for thee?

FAUSTUS: Oft have I thought to have done so, but the devil threatened to tear me in pieces if I named God; to fetch me body and soul if I once gave ear to divinity, and now 'tis too late. Gentlemen, away, lest you perish with me.

SECOND SCHOLAR: Oh what may we do to save Faustus?

FAUSTUS: Talk not of me, but save yourselves and depart.

THIRD SCHOLAR: God will strengthen me. I will stay with Faustus.

FIRST SCHOLAR: Tempt not God, sweet friend, but let us into the next room and pray for him.

FAUSTUS: Ay, pray for me, pray for me. And what noise soever you hear, come not unto me, for nothing can rescue me.

SECOND SCHOLAR: Pray thou, and we will pray, that God may have mercy upon thee.

FAUSTUS: Gentlemen, farewell. If I live till morning, I'll visit you. If not, Faustus is gone to hell.

ALL: Faustus, farewell.

[Exeunt Scholars.]

MEPHOSTOPHILIS: Ay, Faustus, now thou hast no hope of heaven,
Therefore despair, think only upon hell,
For that must be thy mansion, there to dwell.

FAUSTUS: Oh, thou bewitching fiend, 'twas thy temptation
Hath robbed me of eternal happiness.

MEPHOSTOPHILIS: I do confess it, Faustus, and rejoice.
'Twas I that, when thou were't i' the way to heaven,
Dammed up thy passage; when thou took'st the book
To view the scriptures, then I turned the leaves
And led thine eye.
90   What, weep'st thou? 'Tis too late, despair. Farewell.
Fools that will laugh on earth, must weep in hell.   [Exit.]

[Enter the Good and the Evil Angel at several doors.]

GOOD ANGEL: Oh Faustus, if thou hadst given ear to me,
Innumerable joys had followed thee.

But thou didst love the world.

EVIL ANGEL: Gave ear to me,
And now must taste hell's pains perpetually.

GOOD ANGEL: Oh, what will all thy riches, pleasures, pomps,
Avail thee now?

EVIL ANGEL: Nothing but vex thee more,
100   To want in hell, that had on earth such store.

[*Music while the throne descends.*]

GOOD ANGEL: Oh, thou hast lost celestial happiness,
Pleasures unspeakable, bliss without end.
Hadst thou affected sweet divinity,
Hell, or the devil, had had no power on thee.
105   Hadst thou kept on that way, Faustus, behold
In what resplendent glory thou hadst sat
In yonder throne, like those bright shining saints,
And triumphed over hell. That thou hast lost,
And now, poor soul, must thy good angel leave thee:
110   The jaws of hell are open to receive thee.   [*Exit.*]

[*Hell is discovered.*]

EVIL ANGEL: Now, Faustus, let thine eyes with horror stare
Into that vast perpetual torture-house.
There are the furies tossing damned souls
On burning forks. Their bodies broil in lead.
115   There are live quarters broiling on the coals
That ne'er can die. This ever-burning chair
Is for o'er-tortured souls to rest them in.
These, that are fed with sops of flaming fire,
Were gluttons, and loved only delicates,
120   And laughed to see the poor starve at their gates.
But yet all these are nothing. Thou shalt see
Ten thousand tortures that more horrid be.

FAUSTUS: Oh, I have seen enough to torture me.

EVIL ANGEL: Nay, thou must feel them, taste the smart of all:
125   He that loves pleasure must for pleasure fall.
And so I leave thee, Faustus, till anon.
Then wilt thou tumble in confusion.   [*Exit.*]

[*The clock strikes eleven.*]

FAUSTUS: Ah Faustus,
Now hast thou but one bare hour to live,
130   And then thou must be damned perpetually.
Stand still, you ever-moving spheres of heaven,
That time may cease and midnight never come.
Fair nature's eye, rise, rise again, and make
Perpetual day. Or let this hour be but
135   A year, a month, a week, a natural day,
That Faustus may repent and save his soul.
O *lente, lente, currite noctis equi.*[7]

7. Faustus quotes from Ovid's *Amores* 1.13.40: "O slowly, slowly run, horses of the night."

The stars move still, time runs, the clock will strike.
The devil will come, and Faustus must be damned.
140 Oh, I'll leap up to my God: who pulls me down?
See, see, where Christ's blood streams in the firmament.
One drop would save my soul, half a drop. Ah, my Christ!
Ah, rend not my heart for naming of my Christ!
Yet will I call on him. Oh, spare me, Lucifer!
145 Where is it now? 'Tis gone:
And see where God stretcheth out his arm,
And bends his ireful brows.
Mountains and hills, come, come, and fall on me,
And hide me from the heavy wrath of God.
150 No, no. Then will I headlong run into the earth.
Earth, gape! Oh no, it will not harbor me.
You stars that reigned at my nativity,
Whose influence hath allotted death and hell,
Now draw up Faustus like a foggy mist
155 Into the entrails of yon laboring cloud,
That when you vomit forth into the air
My limbs may issue from your smoky mouths,
So that my soul may but ascend to heaven.
[*The watch strikes.*]
Ah! half the hour is past,
160 'Twill all be past anon.°   soon
Oh God, if thou wilt not have mercy on my soul,
Yet, for Christ's sake whose blood hath ransomed me,
Impose some end to my incessant pain.
Let Faustus live in hell a thousand years,
165 A hundred thousand, and at last be saved.
Oh, no end is limited to damned souls.
Why wert thou not a creature wanting soul?
Or why is this immortal that thou hast?
Ah, Pythagoras' *metempsychosis*,[8] were that true
170 This soul should fly from me, and I be changed
Unto some brutish beast.
All beasts are happy, for when they die
Their souls are soon dissolved in elements,
But mine must live still to be plagued in hell.
175 Cursed be the parents that engendered me!
No, Faustus, curse thyself, curse Lucifer,
That hath deprived thee of the joys of heaven.
[*The clock strikes twelve.*]
Oh, it strikes, it strikes! Now body turn to air,
Or Lucifer will bear thee quick to hell.
[*Thunder and lightning.*]

---

8. The transmigration of souls. The Greek philosopher Pythagoras speculated that souls were reborn in other bodies in an endless progression.

180   Oh soul, be changed into little water drops
       And fall into the ocean, ne'er be found.
    [*Thunder. Enter the Devils.*]
       My God, my God, look not so fierce on me.
       Adders and serpents, let me breathe awhile.
       Ugly hell, gape not, come not, Lucifer!
185   I'll burn my books. Ah, Mephostophilis!   [*Exeunt with him.*]

Scene 3

[*Enter the Scholars.*]
FIRST SCHOLAR: Come, gentlemen, let us go visit Faustus,
       For such a dreadful night was never seen
       Since first the world's creation did begin.
       Such fearful shrieks and cries were never heard.
5   Pray heaven the Doctor have escaped the danger.
SECOND SCHOLAR: Oh help us, heaven! See, here are Faustus' limbs,
       All torn asunder by the hand of death.
THIRD SCHOLAR: The devils whom Faustus served have torn him thus:
       For twixt the hours of twelve and one, methought
10   I heard him shriek and call aloud for help,
       At which self time the house seemed all on fire
       With dreadful horror of these damned fiends.
SECOND SCHOLAR: Well, gentlemen, though Faustus' end be such.
       As every Christian heart laments to think on,
15   Yet, for he was a scholar once admired
       For wondrous knowledge in our German schools,
       We'll give his mangled limbs due burial,
       And all the students clothed in mourning black
       Shall wait upon his heavy funeral.   [*Exeunt.*]

Epilogue

[*Enter the Chorus.*]
CHORUS: Cut is the branch that might have grown full straight,
       And burned is Apollo's laurel bough,
       That sometime grew within this learned man.
       Faustus is gone. Regard his hellish fall,
5   Whose fiendful fortune may exhort the wise
       Only to wonder at unlawful things,
       Whose deepness doth entice such forward wits,
       To practice more than heavenly power permits.

Terminat hora diem, Terminat Author opus.[9]
Finis.

---

9. The hour ends the day, the author ends the work.

⤦

RESPONSE
C. S. Lewis: from *The Screwtape Letters*

The Screwtape Letters (1940) inverts the terms of the Faust story and tells the devil's side of it. C. S. Lewis's diabolical character Screwtape shows how a human being and Christian soul may be enlisted in the devil's service. While Satan's agent Mephostophilis convinces Marlowe's Dr. Faustus to accept an afterlife in hell in exchange for a life of extraordinary influence and a high place in the world, Screwtape urges his helper, Wormwood, to corrupt his intended victim by subtle temptations to ambition. As long as Lewis's hero is preoccupied with getting ahead—living for the future rather than in the present—he risks capture and a place in hell. But unlike Dr. Faustus, he escapes the clutches of Wormwood by repudiating ambition and embracing the charitable doctrines of the devil's "Enemy," an unnamed power but clearly a figure for Jesus.

from *The Screwtape Letters*
Letter XV

My Dear Wormwood,

I had noticed, of course, that the humans were having a lull in their European war—what they naively call "The War"![1]—and am not surprised that there is a corresponding lull in the patient's anxieties. Do we want to encourage this, or to keep him worried? Tortured fear and stupid confidence are both desirable states of mind. Our choice between them raises important questions.

The humans live in time but our Enemy[2] destines them to eternity. He therefore, I believe, wants them to attend chiefly to two things, to eternity itself, and to that point of time which they call the Present. For the Present is the point at which time touches eternity. Of the present moment, and of it only, humans have an experience analogous to the experience which our Enemy has of reality as a whole; in it alone freedom and actuality are offered them. He would therefore have them continually concerned either with eternity (which means being concerned with Him) or with the Present—either meditating on their eternal union with, or separation from, Himself, or else obeying the present voice of conscience, bearing the present cross, receiving the present grace, giving thanks for the present pleasure.

Our business is to get them away from the eternal, and from the Present. With this in view, we sometimes tempt a human (say a widow or a scholar) to live in the Past. But this is of limited value, for they have some real knowledge of the past and it has a determinate nature and, to that extent, resembles eternity. It is far better to make them live in the Future. Biological necessity makes all their passions point in that direction already, so that thought about the Future inflames hope and fear. Also, it is unknown to them, so that in making them think about it we make them think of unrealities. In a word, the Future is, of all things, the thing least like eternity. It is the most completely temporal part of time—for the Past is frozen and no longer flows, and the Present is all lit up with eternal rays. Hence the encouragement we have given to all those schemes of thought such as Creative Evolution, Scientific Humanism, or Communism, which fix men's affections on the Future, on the very core of temporality. Hence nearly all vices are rooted in the future. Gratitude looks to the past and love to the present; fear, avarice, lust, and ambition look ahead.[3] Do not think lust an exception. When the present pleasure arrives, the sin (which alone interests us) is already over. The pleasure is just the part of the process which we regret and would exclude if we could do so without losing the sin; it is the part contributed by the Enemy, and therefore experienced in a Present. The sin, which is our contribution, looked forward.

To be sure, the Enemy wants men to think of the Future too—just so much as is necessary for now planning the acts of justice or charity which will probably be their duty tomorrow. The duty of planning the morrow's work is today's duty; though its material is borrowed from the future, the duty, like all duties, is in the Present. This is not straw splitting. He does not want men to give the Future their hearts, to place their treasure in it. We do. His ideal is a man who, having worked all day for the good of prosperity (if that is his vocation), washes his mind of the whole subject, commits the issue to Heaven, and returns at once to the patience or gratitude demanded by the moment that is passing over him. But we want a man hag-ridden by the Future—haunted by visions of an imminent heaven or hell upon earth—ready to break the Enemy's commands in the present if by so doing we make him think he can attain the one or avert the other—dependent for his faith on the success or failure of schemes whose end he will not live to see. We want a whole race perpetually in pursuit of the rainbow's end, never honest, nor kind, nor happy now, but always using as mere fuel wherewith to heap the altar of the future every real gift which is offered them in the Present.

It follows then, in general, and other things being equal, that it is better for your patient[4] to be filled with anxiety or hope (it doesn't much matter which) about this war than for him to be living in the present. But the phrase "living in the present" is ambiguous. It may describe a process which is really just as much concerned with the Future as anxiety itself. Your man may be untroubled about the Future, not because he is concerned with the Present, but because he has persuaded himself that the Future is going to be agreeable. As long as that is the real course of his tranquility, his tranquility will do us good, because it is only piling up more disappointment, and therefore more impatience, for him when his false hopes are dashed. If, on the other hand, he is aware that horrors may be in store for him and is praying for the virtues, wherewith to meet them, and meanwhile concerning himself with the Present because there, and there alone, all duty, all grace, all knowledge, and all pleasure dwell, his state is very undesirable and should be attacked at once. Here again, our Philological Arm[5] has done good work; try the word "complacency" on him. But, of course, it is most likely that he is "living in the present" for none of these reasons but simply because his health is good and he is enjoying his work. The phenomenon would then be merely natural. All the same, I should break it up if I were you. No natural phenomenon is really in our favor. Anyway, why should the creature be happy?

Your affectionate uncle
Screwtape

---

3. Emotions felt by Doctor Faustus.
4. Wormword's potential victim.
5. The institution of hypocrisy. Screwtape argues that feelings of "complacency" in the Present mask an ambitious confidence in the Future.

Sir Walter Raleigh

c. 1554–1618

Born in South Devon, a region in which ports and shipyards testified to the importance of England's world trade and colonies abroad, Sir Walter Raleigh spent a considerable part of his life outside his native land. As a boy, he fought with Huguenot armies in France; at twenty-four he led an expedition to the West Indies with his half-brother, Sir Humphrey Gilbert; and two years later, he commanded a contingent of English troops in Ireland. He is reported to have been a great favorite of Elizabeth, at least until in 1592, when he secretly married one of her ladies-in-waiting, Elizabeth Throckmorton. The Queen, furious that she had had no say in the match, imprisoned Raleigh in the Tower of London for a period that summer.

Raleigh was famous for his travels. His most challenging expedition was intended to locate the legendary gold mines of El Dorado in South America. In 1595 he set out for the Spanish colony of Guiana, penetrating the interior of that land by venturing up the Orinoco. He described his trip in the brilliantly detailed *Discovery of the Large, Rich and Beautiful Empire of Guiana*, and although he returned to England without the gold he had gone for, his leadership of an expedition to sack the harbor of Cadiz in 1596 was enough to restore him to royal favor. But Raleigh was to encounter real trouble with the accession of James I. His enemies at court convinced the king that Raleigh had committed treason, and in 1603 he was tried, convicted, and once again confined to the Tower of London, this time with his wife and family. He remained there for thirteen years. His release was finally granted on the condition that he lead another expedition to Guiana. He had informed the King that on his earlier trip he had discovered an actual gold mine, and he now claimed that his new adventure would be successful. In fact, it was a disaster. Not only did he find no gold, but the mine to whose existence he had sworn was revealed to be a fabrication. On this occasion the grounds for proving treason were stronger than they had been in 1603. Raleigh was executed in 1618.

During his long imprisonment, Raleigh began to write a complete history of the world, managing only to cover events in ancient history to 168 B.C.E. Entitled *The History of the World* and published in 1614, the work is primarily remembered for the stunning reflection on death that appears on its last page: "O eloquent, just and mighty Death! Whom none could advise, thou hast persuaded; what none hath dared, thou hast done; and whom all the world hath flattered, thou only hast cast out of the world and despised; thou hast drawn together all the far stretched greatness, all the pride, cruelty, and ambition of man, and covered it all over with those two narrow words, *Hic iacet*."

Much of Raleigh's poetry is occasional, written to address the circumstances and the moment in which he found himself. It possesses the quality Castiglione celebrated in his treatise on court life: a brilliance of self-expression that contemporary Italians termed *sprezzatura*, created by the supposedly artless use of artifice showing not the courtier's education but, rather, his native wit and talent. Raleigh exploits images of common life but with an unusual intensity, adding sensuous detail to expressions of affection and reminders of mortality to celebrations of love. His longest and greatest poem, *The 21st and Last Book of the Ocean to Cynthia*, remained fragmentary at the time of his death. Occasioned when Queen Elizabeth imprisoned him for his marriage, the poem illustrates Raleigh's fury at the Queen's inconsistent treatment of her "Ocean" or "Water," as Raleigh pronounced his first name. It ends in an equivocation: Raleigh professes his devotion to Elizabeth, instancing his good will that "knit up by faith shall ever last"; but he also concludes that despite this, they will not be reconciled: "Her love hath end; my woe must ever last."

 For additional resources on Raleigh, including a selection from *Discovery of the Large, Rich and Beautiful Empire of Guiana*, go to *The Longman Anthology of British Literature* Web site at www.myliteraturekit.com.

Nature That Washed Her Hands in Milk

Nature that washed her hands in milk
   And had forgot to dry them,
Instead of earth took snow and silk,[1]
   At love's request to try them,
5   If she a mistress could compose
To please love's fancy out of those.

Her eyes he would should be of light,
   A violet breath and lips of jelly,
Her hair not black nor over-bright,
10   And of the softest down her belly;
As for her inside he would have it
Only of wantonness and wit.

At love's entreaty, such a one
   Nature made, but with her beauty
15   She hath framed a heart of stone,
   So as love by ill destiny
Must die for her whom nature gave him
Because her darling would not save him.

But time, which nature doth despise,
20   And rudely gives her love the lie,
Makes hope a fool, and sorrow wise,
   His hands doth neither wash nor dry,
But being made of steel and rust,
Turns snow, and silk, and milk to dust.

25   The light, the belly, lips, and breath
   He dims, discolors, and destroys,
With those he feeds, but fills not death,
   Which sometimes were the food of joys;
Yea, time doth dull each lively wit
30   And dries all wantonness with it.

Oh cruel time which takes in trust
   Our youth, our joys, and all we have,
And pays us but with age and dust,
   Who in the dark and silent grave,
35   When we have wandered all our ways,
Shuts up the story of our days.[2]

---

1. "And the Lord God formed man of the dust of the ground" (Genesis 2.7).

2. With one slight change and the addition of a final couplet, the last stanza of this poem is also Raleigh's *Epitaph*.

To the Queen[1]

Our passions are most like to floods and streams,
The shallow murmur, but the deep are dumb.
So when affections yield discourse, it seems
The bottom is but shallow whence they come.
5   They that are rich in words must needs discover
      That they are poor in that which makes a lover.

Wrong not, dear empress of my heart,
      The merit of true passion,
With thinking that he feels no smart,
10   That sues for no compassion.
Since, if my plaints serve not to prove
      The conquest of your beauty,
It comes not from defect of love,
      But from excess of duty.

15   For knowing that I sue to serve
      A saint of such perfection,
As all desire, but none deserve,
      A place in her affection;
I rather choose to want relief
20   Than venture the revealing,
When glory recommends the grief,
      Despair distrusts the healing.

Thus those desires that aim too high
      For any mortal lover,
25   When reason cannot make them die,
      Discretion will them cover.
Yet when discretion doth bereave
      The plaints that they should utter,
Then your discretion may perceive
30   That silence is a suitor.

Silence in love bewrays more woe
      Than words, though ne'er so witty,
A beggar that is dumb, you know,
      Deserveth double pity.
35   Then misconceive not (dearest heart)
      My true, though secret passion,
He smarteth most that hides his smart,
      And sues for no compassion.

---

1. This elaborate compliment is typical of the courtly expressions of devotion Elizabeth I often inspired. Its respectful complaint can be compared to the bitter regret in Raleigh's later poem *The Shepherd of the Ocean to Cynthia*.

On the Life of Man

What is our life? A play of passion,
Our mirth the music of division,
Our mothers' wombs the tiring houses be,
Where we are dressed for this short comedy,
5   Heaven the judicious sharp spectator is,
That sits and marks still who doth act amiss,
Our graves that hide us from the searching sun,
Are like drawn curtains when the play is done;
Thus march we playing to our latest rest,
10   Only we die in earnest, that's no jest.

1612

The Author's Epitaph, Made by Himself

Even such is time, which takes in trust
Our youth, our joys, and all we have,
And pays us but with age and dust,
Who in the dark and silent grave,
5   When we have wandered all our days,
Shuts up the story of our days;
And from which earth, and grave, and dust,
The Lord shall raise me up, I trust.

As You Came from the Holy Land

As you came from the holy land
    Of Walsingham[1]
Met you not with my true love
    By the way as you came?[2]

5   How shall I know your true love
    That have met many one?
As I went to the holy land
    That have come, that have gone.

She is neither white nor brown
10   But as the heavens, fair.
There is none hath a form so divine
    In the earth or the air.

Such a one did I meet good sir,
    Such an angelic face,

---

1. A district in the county of Norfolk and site of Walsingham Abbey, one of the great shrines of medieval England.
2. This stanza is the first in the dialogue that constitutes the poem. Its first seven stanzas alternate statements between two speakers: a lover and a traveler. Stanzas 8 and 9 are spoken by the traveler; the final two stanzas are spoken by the lover.

15   Who like a queen, like a nymph did appear
      By her gait, by her grace.

She hath left me here all alone,
    All alone as unknown,
Who sometimes did me lead with herself,
20   And me loved as her own.

What's the cause that she leaves you alone
    And a new way doth take,
Who loved you once as her own,
    And her joy did you make?

25   I have loved her all my youth,
    But now old, as you see;
Love likes not the falling fruit
    From the withered tree.

Know that love is a careless child
30   And forgets promise past;
He is blind, he is deaf, when he list,°   *wishes*
    And in faith never fast.

His desire is a dureless° content   *transient*
    And a trustless joy;
35   He is won with a world of despair
    And is lost with a toy.

Of womankind such indeed is the love
    Or the word love abused,
Under which many childish desires
40   And conceits are excused.

But love is a durable fire
    In the mind ever burning;
Never sick, never old, never dead,
    From itself never turning.

from The 21st and Last Book of the Ocean to Cynthia[1]

Sufficeth to you, my joys interred,
In simple words that I my woes complain;
You that then died when first my fancy erred—[2]
Joys under dust that never live again.

1. This lyric complaint, a fragment of what was projected as a much longer work, is the most important of Raleigh's poems. It tells of his despair at losing the Queen's favor and reproaches her for indifference to his devoted service. Adopting the conventions of pastoral, Raleigh styles himself "The Shepherd of the Ocean," perhaps to draw attention to his first name, which he pronounced "Water." "Cynthia" is, of course, Elizabeth, figured here (as she was so often) as the moon, ever changeful, as well as Diana, the goddess of the moon and of chastity. Characterizing Cynthia as the moving force in his life,

Raleigh's verse illustrates how conventions of courtly love could acquire a political reference: both Elizabeth and her courtiers were accustomed to conveying their hopes and desires in the coded language of erotic compliment. Spenser's poem *Colin Clout's Come Home Again* (1591) notes that the subject of Raleigh's "Cynthia" is "the great unkindness" and "usage hard" of the "Lady of the Sea," who has "from her presence faultless him (i.e., the Shepherd) debarred."
2. The poet complains to his own "joys" that are now dead and buried.

5   If to the living were my muse addressed,
      Or did my mind her own spirit still inhold,
      Were not my living passion so repressed
      As to the dead° the dead did these unfold,   *i.e., joys*

      Some sweeter words, some more becoming verse
10   Should witness my mishap in higher kind;
      But my love's wounds, my fancy in the hearse,
      The idea but resting of a wasted mind,

      The blossoms fallen, the sap gone from the tree,
      The broken monuments of my great desires—
15   From these so lost what may the affections° be?   *passions*
      What heat in cinders of extinguished fires?

      Lost in the mud of those high-flowing streams,
      Which through more fairer fields their courses bend,
      Slain with self-thoughts, amazed in fearful dreams,
20   Woes without date, discomforts without end.

      From fruitless trees I gather withered leaves,
      And glean° the broken ears° with miser's hand,   *harvest / of grain*
      Who sometime did enjoy the weighty sheaves;
      I seek fair flowers amid the brinish° sand.   *salty*

25   All in the shade, even in the fair sun days,
      Under those healthless trees I sit alone,
      Where joyful birds sing neither lovely lays,
      Nor Philomen° recounts her direful moan.   *the nightingale*

      No feeding flocks, no shepherd's company,
30   That might renew my dolorous conceit,°   *imagination*
      While happy then, while love and fantasy
      Confined my thoughts on that fair flock to wait;

      No pleasing streams fast to the ocean wending,
      The messengers sometimes of my great woe;
35   But all on earth, as from the cold storms bending,
      Shrink from my thoughts in high heavens or below.

      Oh, hopeful love, my object and invention,
      Oh, true desire, the spur of my conceit,
      Oh, worthiest spirit, my mind's impulsion,°   *force*
40   Oh, eyes transpersant,° my affection's bait,   *that penetrate*

      Oh princely form, my fancy's adamant,°   *magnet*
      Divine conceit,° my pains' acceptance,   *image*
      Oh, all in one! Oh, heaven on earth transparent!
      The seat of joys and love's abundance!

45   Out of that mass of miracles, my muse
      Gathered those flowers, to her pure senses pleasing;

Out of her eyes, the store of joys, did choose
Equal delights, my sorrow's counterpoising.

Her regal looks my vigorous sighs suppressed,
50   Small drops of joys sweetened great worlds of woes,
One gladsome day a thousand cares redressed—
Whom love defends, what fortune overthrows?

When she did well, what did there else amiss?
When she did ill, what empires would have pleased?
55   No other power affecting woe or bliss,
She gave, she took, she wounded, she appeased.

The honor of her love, love still devising,
Wounding my mind with contrary conceit,
Transferred itself sometime to her aspiring,
60   Sometime the trumpet of her thought's retreat.[3]

To seek new worlds for gold, for praise, for glory,
To try° desire, to try love severed far,   test
When I was gone, she sent her memory,
More strong than were ten thousand ships of war,

65   To call me back; to leave great honor's thought;
To leave my friends, my fortune, my attempt;
To leave the purpose[4] I so long had sought,
And hold both cares and comforts in contempt.

Such heat in ice, such fire in frost remained,
70   Such trust in doubt, such comfort in despair,
Which, like the gentle lamb, though lately weaned,
Plays with the dug, though finds no comfort there.

But as a body, violently slain,
Retaineth warmth although the spirit be gone,
75   And by a power in nature moves again
Till it be laid below the fatal stone;

Or as the earth, even in cold winter days,
Left for a time by her life-giving sun,
Doth by the power remaining of his rays
80   Produce some green, though not as it hath done;

Or as a wheel, forced by the falling stream,
Although the course be turned some other way,
Doth for a time go round upon the beam,
Till, wanting strength to move, it stands at stay;

3. The honor of being loved by her creating love (in me), wounding me with a contrary (twofold) conception, sometimes aspiring to (please) her, sometimes heralding the withdrawal of her attention. In other words, the poet is constantly aware that his love makes him have a conflicted conception of how to approach Cynthia: sometimes he pleases her, sometimes what he does causes her disdain.
4. Raleigh's "purpose" was to find gold for England in the wilderness of the New World; he continued to hope for success in this venture until 1617, when his last voyage to Guiana ended in nothing.

85   So my forsaken heart, my withered mind—
        Widow of all the joys it once possessed,
        My hopes clean out of sight with forced wind—
        To kingdoms strange, to lands far off, addressed,

        Alone, forsaken, friendless, on the shore
90   With many wounds, with death's cold pangs embraced,
        Writes in the dust, as one that could no more,
        Whom love, and time, and fortune, had defaced,

        Of things so great, so long, so manifold,
        With means so weak, the soul even then depicting
95   The weal, the woe, the passages of old,
        And worlds of thoughts descried° by one last sighing.   *discerned*

        As if, when after Phoebus° is descended,   *the sun*
        And leaves a light much like the past day's dawning,
        And every toil and labor wholly ended,
100   Each living creature draweth to his resting,

        We should begin by such a parting light
        To write the story of all ages past,
        And end the same before approaching night.

        Such is again the labor of my mind,
105   Whose shroud, by sorrow woven now to end,
        Hath seen that ever shining sun declined,
        So many years that so could not descend,

        But that the eyes of my mind held her beams
        In every part transferred by love's swift thought,
110   Far off or near, in waking or in dreams,
        Imagination strong in lustre brought.

        Such force her angelic appearance had
        To master distance, time, or cruelty,
        Such art to grieve, and after to make glad,
115   Such fear in love, such love in majesty.

        My weary lines her memory embalmed;
        My darkest ways her eyes make clear as day.
        What storms so great but Cynthia's beams appeased?
        What rage so fierce, that love could not allay?

120   Twelve years entire I wasted in this war,[5]
        Twelve years of my most happy younger days;
        But I in them, and they now wasted are,
        "Of all which past, the sorrow only stays."

                        * * *
        Yet as the air in deep caves underground
125   Is strongly drawn when violent heat hath vent

5. The 12 years of service to Elizabeth began with his command of troops in Ireland in 1580 and ended, in the terms the poem supplies, with his marriage and imprisonment in 1592. Raleigh was only 36 at the time.

Great clefts therein, till moisture do abound,
And then the same, imprisioned and up-pent,°   *pent up*

Breaks out in earthquakes, tearing all asunder,
So in the center of my cloven heart—
130   My heart, to whom her beauties were such wonder—
Lies the sharp, poisoned head of that love's dart

Which, till all break and dissolve to dust,
Thence drawn it cannot be, or therein known,
There, mixed with my heart-blood, the fretting rust
135   The better part hath eaten and outgrown.

But what of those or these? Or what of aught
Of that which was, or that which is, to treat?
What I possess is but the same I sought;
My love was false, my labors were deceit.

140   Nor less than such they are esteemed to be,
A fraud bought at the price of many woes,
A guile, whereof the profits unto me—
Could it be thought premediate° for those?   *plead*

Witness those withered leaves left on the tree,
145   The sorrow-worn face, the pensive mind,
The external shows, what may the internal be;
Cold care hath bitten both the root and rind.

But stay, my thoughts, make end, give fortune way;
Harsh is the voice of woe and sorrow's sound;
150   Complaints cure not, and tears do but allay
Griefs for a time, which after more abound.

To seek for moisture in the Arabian sand
Is but a loss of labor and of rest,
The links which time did break of hearty bands

155   Words cannot knit, or wailings make anew,
Seek not the sun in clouds when it is set . . .
On highest mountains, where those cedars[6] grew,
Against whose banks the troubled ocean beat,

And were the marks to find thy hoped port,
160   Into a soil far off themselves remove.
On Sestos' shore, Leander's late resort,
Hero hath left no lamp to guide her love.[7]

Thou lookest for light in vain, and storms arise,
She sleeps thy death, that erst thy danger sighed,

6. The cedar was identified as a tree of royalty; so Raleigh can speak of the ocean beating against banks over which the cedar presides.
7. Leander and Hero were two lovers who lived on oppo-site shores of the Hellespont. When Leander swam at night from Abydos to visit Hero in Sestos, she hung out a lantern to guide him.

165 Strive then no more, bow down thy weary eyes—
 Eyes which to all these woes thy heart have guided.

 She is gone, she is lost, she is found, she is ever fair;
 Sorrow draws weakly where love draws not too,
 Woe's cries sound nothing, but only in love's ear.
170 Do then by dying what life cannot do.

 Unfold thy flocks and leave them to the fields,
 To feed on hills or dales, where likes them best,
 Of what the summer or the springtime yields,
 For love and time hath given thee leave to rest.

175 Thy heart which was their fold, now in decay
 By often storms and winter's many blasts,
 All torn and rent, becomes misfortune's prey,
 False hope, my shepherd's staff, now age hath brast.°   *broken*

 My pipe, which love's own hand gave my desire
180 To sing her praises and my woe upon—
 Despair hath often threatened to the fire,
 As vain to keep now all the rest are gone.

 Thus home I draw, as death's long night draws on,
 Yet every foot, old thoughts turn back mine eyes;
185 Constraint me guides, as old age draws a stone
 Against a hill, which over-weighty lies

 For feeble arms or wasted strength to move.
 My steps are backward, gazing on my loss,
 My mind's affection and my soul's sole love,
190 Not mixed with fancy's chaff or fortune's dross.

 To God I leave it,° who first gave it me,   *my soul*
 And I her gave, and she returned again,
 As it was hers; so let His mercies be
 Of my last comforts the essential mean.°   *factor*

195 But be it so or not, the effects are past;
 Her love hath end, my woes must ever last.

⇒ PERSPECTIVES ⇐
England, Britain, and the World

Although the Elizabethan Age is often seen as the dawn of transatlantic travel, it is clear that the horizons of English men and women were very much bounded by Europe. Most trade was with European neighbors and the mighty Ottoman empire that dominated the southern Mediterranean and included vast sections of modern Bulgaria and Hungary. Routes to the east had to be negotiated with the Ottoman imperial authorities. Although Venice—the subject of two of Shakespeare's plays, *The Merchant of Venice* and *Othello*—had declined from its heyday owing to the Turkish threat, it was still one of the most powerful ports in Europe and the main point of Western access to the Mediterranean. In contrast the Americas looked like a distant and strange land. Travel across the Atlantic often took as long as three months and the main purpose of voyages was often to commandeer Spanish treasure from their huge empire in South America rather than establish colonies (unless they served as naval bases). Some Englishmen were alarmed by their countrymen's indifference to the New World, and Richard Hakluyt's anthology, *The Principal Voyages, Traffiques and Discoveries of the English Nation* (1589, revised and expanded 1598) was designed to give the English the confidence to become a major imperial nation and so rival the Spanish. But it is worth noting that only one of Shakespeare's plays, *The Tempest* (1611), has any reference to the Americas, and, even so, it is set on an island in the Mediterranean. Shakespeare's imagination remained firmly rooted in Britain and Europe.

The English were unsure of their place within the British Isles. Wales had been absorbed in the early sixteenth century by Henry VIII but remained an alien land with its own traditions, customs and, most importantly, language. Ireland had been conquered by the Normans in the twelfth century and held as a lordship, but was made a separate kingdom ruled by the English king when Henry VIII declared himself its monarch in 1534. Yet, as many commentators have pointed out, it was as much a colony, inhabited by hostile and alien people, as a sovereign territory. Scotland was a separate kingdom, often regarded with considerable fear and hostility by the English, its people, like the Welsh and Irish, eager to discomfort their more powerful neighbors at every opportunity. England and Scotland were united when James VI of Scotland became king in 1603, but this was a Scottish takeover, not the English conquest that many had predicted. James brought with him a large entourage of his fellow countrymen, who occupied important positions in his household, and were bitterly resented by many important Londoners. It tells us a great deal about the politics of the British Isles that, while James styled himself "King of Britain," the English parliament refused to ratify his plan to unite the kingdoms. Moreover, as events throughout the sixteenth and seventeenth centuries were to demonstrate with frequent regularity, England itself was hardly a united realm. The north was predominately Catholic with its great lords looking to challenge the power and authority of the crown, as were many parts of the East; the southwest and Cornwall in particular, were hard to access and fiercely independent. Cornwall had its own language, and the Prayer book had to be translated into Cornish because so few people understood English. Given the hostility of Catholic Europe, led by Spain, and the problematic relationship with France, it is easy to see why England often felt surrounded and beleaguered.

This section tries to provide a snapshot of the world as it appeared to English men and women in the sixteenth and seventeenth centuries. There were indeed important accounts of the discovery of the Americas that were widely available. But these were mainly stories of Spanish conquests and hardships until the publication of Thomas Hariot's important *A Brief and True Report of the Newfound Land of Virginia*, first published in a small quarto in 1588 but then reproduced as a grand folio with superb illustrations based on John White's drawings in 1590, the first part of Theodor De Bry's series of works recounting the discovery of America for a Protestant audience. Hariot's text, designed to encourage settlers to join the fledgling colonies in Virginia, represented the natives of the New World as civilized and law-abiding, a pointed contrast to some of the savages who lived nearer to home. Edmund Spenser's *A View of the Present State of Ireland* (c.1596) gives us a sense of how threatening the English felt the native Irish to be, comparing them with the most ferocious savages known to man. Spenser shows that the native Irish are descended from the Scythians, an ancient and powerful people who lived by the Black Sea alongside the ancient Greeks. The Scythians were known for their ferocity and warlike nature but they could be civilized. Spenser, in describing the Irish use of the mantle, claims that Irish customs and practices are the problem in Ireland, suggesting that if they are removed the Irish can be anglicized and civilized. Such passages help us to understand that their near neighbors were seen in mainly negative ways, but that we should be careful of assuming that such stereotypes can always be read in a straightforward manner or that they are simply the product of prejudice.

Also included here are passages describing the Ottoman Empire and Italy, as well as John Smith's famous account of Pocahontas. The early seventeenth century saw the first substantial publications of travelers' accounts of their journeys, with Fynes Moryson (1566–1630) producing the longest work. Moryson is not always an acute judge and sees the world through his own prejudices, but he gives us an important picture of how English people saw themselves and others in the early seventeenth century. Italy, as Moryson's comments indicate, was seen with a mixture of envy and fear, being, on the one hand, much more sophisticated and cultured than England, and, on the other, a Catholic country known for its vicious politics and unstable nature. The Ottoman empire was similarly feared and admired, but for different reasons, being a powerful military machine that threatened to overwhelm its Christian opponents.

⊷ ⊨♦⊒ ⊶

Fynes Moryson
1566–1630

Fynes Moryson has a good claim to have been the first professional travel writer. His account of his travels is the most comprehensive by an early modern English writer. He was educated at Peterhouse College Cambridge, and became a fellow there. At the age of twenty-three he persuaded the college to let him travel at its expense and, after studying law at Oxford, he left for Germany on 1 May 1591. Moryson spent the next four years traveling through Germany, the Low Countries, Denmark, Poland, and Austria, before returning to London on 13 May 1595. He then wished to venture further afield, having a particular desire to see "Jerusalem, the fountain of Religion, and Constantinople, of old the seat of Christian Emperors, and now the seat of the Turkish Ottoman." Together with his brother, Henry, he set out from London on 29 November 1595. He traveled overland to Venice before sailing to Joppa and proceeding to Jerusalem. They then traveled to Tripoli, Aleppo, and Antioch where Henry Moryson died of dysentery. Fynes, having recovered from the illness, returned to London via Crete, Constantinople, and Venice, arriving on 10 July 1597.

In 1599 Moryson was employed as secretary to Charles Blount, Lord Mountjoy, the Lord Deputy of Ireland, remaining in his service until 1606. He spent much of the rest of his life trying to find a publisher for the increasingly voluminous account of his travels, eventually persuading John Beale of Aldersgate Street, to produce three huge volumes entitled *An Itinerary* (1617). A fourth volume was licensed in 1626, but remained in manuscript until sections of it were published in the twentieth century. Moryson was clearly frustrated by these problems and vowed that he would give up writing in order to concentrate on theology. Little is known of the last years of his life. He died in 1630.

The extracts here give some sense of Moryson's fascination with and contempt for Italy. While he is attracted by the glamour of its riches, architectural beauties, and images—which, as a Protestant, he is duty bound to be suspicious of—he is horrified by the superstitiousness he encounters. Other passages reveal his traveler's taste for anecdotes.

Moryson represents the Ottoman Empire as an absolute tyranny. Preferment is achieved through favoritism and corruption. People are overtaxed and Christians are treated especially badly. Inheritance laws demand that the emperor takes a large slice of the property of the deceased, so people tend to bury and hide their wealth. The Turks are brave and tough but intensely cruel. They are taught that death in defense of one's country is admirable. They are also idle and addicted to sexual pleasure, particularly sodomy.

In some ways Moryson clearly admires the Ottoman Empire and its military prowess in the same way that commentators admired the martial culture of the Spartan, while tempering their respect with fear. He is as much in awe of their wealth and success as he is in many Italian cities. Overall, however, the Turks pose as much a threat to European Christianity as they represent respected trading partners. The extracts here represent Moryson's cultural analysis of the Ottoman Empire—sections which were not printed until the twentieth century—and his impressions of Constantinople.

from An Itinerary Containing His Ten Year Travel through the Twelve Dominions of Germany, Bohmerland, Switzerland, Netherland, Denmark, Poland, Italy, Turkey, France, England, Scotland & Ireland (1617)

OBSERVATIONS OF ITALY

Now we were to cross the breadth of Italy, from the Adriatic to the Tyrrhenian Sea. The first day in the Morning, we rode fifteen miles to a little City, called Madonna di Loreto, through fruitful Mountains, and passing a high Promontory. By the way was an Alter, with this inscription in Latin; O passenger, go on merrily, &c. Gregory the thirteenth hath well paved the rest of the way. The like inscription is in the ascent of the Mountain, upon which the little City Loreto stands: for this way (in a fruitful Country of corn, and a dirty soil) was paved at the charge of the said Pope.

A certain chamber hath given beginning to this City and the Church thereof, then which nothing is esteemed more holy among the Papists; and because many gifts of great price use to be given by vow to our Lady of this Church, the City is well fortified against Pirates, who did once spoil the same, and were like again to be invited by the hope of rich spoils to the like attempts, if the Towne lay unfortified. It is of little circuit, and lies in length from East to the West, so narrow; as it hath almost but one street in the breadth, and all the houses of this street are Innes, or Shops of them that sell Beads to number prayers. On the East side, after a steep descent of a Mountain, lies a valley of two miles, and beyond that the sea. On the North side, towards Ancona, though the sea be very far distant, yet from this City, seated upon a high Mountain, it may easily be seen. Upon the doors of this Church, famous for men's superstitious/worship, these verses are written:

> Illotus timeat quincunque intrara, Sacellum,
>   In terries nullum sanctius orbis habet.

> Enter not here unwashed of any spot,
> For a more holy Church the world hath not.

At the Church door is a statue of brass erected to Pope Gregory the thirteenth. As I walked about the Church, behold in a dark Chappell a Priest, by his Exorcisms casting a devil out of a poor woman: Good Lord what fencing and truly conjuring words he used!

How much more skilful was he in the devils names? Then any ambitious Roman ever was in the names of his Citizens, whom he courted for their voices. If he had eaten a bushel of salt in hell; if he had been an inhabitant thereof, surely this Art could never have been more familiar to him. He often spoke to the ignorant woman in the Latin tongue, but nothing less then in Tullie's[1] phrase, and at last the poor wretch, either hired to deceive the people, or (if that be more probable) drawn by familiar practice with the Priest, or at least affrighted with his strange language and cries, confessed her self dispossessed by his exorcism. In the body of the Church, a Table of written hand, in the Greek, Latin, and many other tongues, was fastened to a Pillar, setting down at large the wonderful history of the Chamber in midst of the Church, which I confess was less curiously observed by me, abhorring from that superstition, & hastening from thence as much as I might; yet give me leave to set down the sum thereof out of the itinerary of Villamont a French Gentleman. This Chamber or Chappell (said he) is the very house, in which the Queen Virgin of Nazareth was borne, brought up, and saluted by the Angell, foretelling her of Christ's birth, and in which Christ was conceived, and in which the Virgin dwelt after Christ's ascension, accompanied with the holy Apostles, especially with Saint John by Christ's command, which the Apostles after the Virgins death, for the great mysteries done here, turned into a Chappell, consecrated to the sacrificing of Christ, and dedicated the same, and with their own hands, made the great Crosse of wood, now set in the window of the Chappell, and in which Saint Luke made with his hand the picture and Image now set above it. Let me add: This Chappell from a House became a Chamber, and of a Chamber was made a Chappell, and it is built of brick, and is thirty feet long, twelve and a half broad. In the chimney (as Villemont said) as yet remain the holy ashes, which no man dare take away, and the Alter also, upon which the Masse is sung, was made by the Apostles hand. There is a room into which you first enter, which is divided from the Chapel by an iron grate, for no man enters the chapel without leave, but must say his prayers in the outer room; yet leave is given to any that ask it. Villamont added, that he found by diligent search, that this Chapel was much reverenced in the primitive Church: but the holy land being subdued by Saracens, then by Turks; he said it happened in the year 1291, that this house was taken up from the foundations, by Angels, who in the night miraculously carried it to the Sea shore of Slavonia, where it was made known to the people by the shining of the Virgin's Image, and then by a vision of a religious man. The Virgin her self made known the History to him. He added the Virgins Oration wherein she gives her self many titles, which in later ages were first invented, and she doth so extol her own praises with her own mouth, as he that reads the old song of the blessed Virgin, would cry out with the Latin Poet, only changing the name. O how is she changed from the Virgin, which so modestly spoke of her self.

Villamont added, that messengers were sent into Palestine, who found this History to be most true: yet this Chappell did not long abide in Slavonia, but the Angels in the year 1294 took it up again, and transported it to this Sea coast of Italy, where again it was made known by the shining of the Image was called Madonna at Loreto, that is, our Lady of Loreto. And because thieves lying in the wood, did spoil strangers, who took it up, and set it down in a private possession of two brothers, who disagreeing in the division of the profit rising by the concourse of people, the Angels the fourth time took it up, and placed it in this firm seat, where now it remained. After it was often visited by strangers, Pope Paul the second built an other stately Church over it, Pope Leo the tenth having first fortified the little City against Pirates. Let me add, that Pope Sixtus the fifth, borne in this Marca of Ancona, established a Bishop in this Towne, and so

---

1. Marcus Tullius Cicero (106–43 B.C.E.), Roman orator and statesman. One of the models of Renaissance prose style.

made it a City. Villamont relating the treasure of this Church, among the rest, named certain Maps of Cities, and Mountains, and the Images of the twelve Apostles, a great Crucifix, Candlesticks, and infinite Vessels of silver, Images, Chalices, Crosses of gold, and many precious stones of huge value, two Crosses made all of precious stones (whereof one was given by the Arch-Duke of Austria), and a Harte of gold set with precious stones (the gift of the Duchesse of Loraine) and a vessel of huge value. * * *

The second day we began the view of Rome with the Popes Palace, seated in the part of the City, called Il Borgo; which Palace Pope Nicholas the third built, and Nicholas the fifth compassed with walls, and the Palace is of great circuit, and the stairs are so easy, that Horses and Mules may go up to the top of the Mountain, and with easy ascent and descent bear the Popes carriage.[2] At the entrance there be galleries one above the other, whereof the two first were built by Leo the tenth, and Paul the third, and the third and highest by Sixtus Quintus, and they are all fairly painted and gilded. Upon these lie two large chambers, and beyond them is a vast and long gallery of four hundred seventy and one walking paces, in the middle whereof is the famous Library of the Popes. In Vatican; and therein are many inscriptions of the Pope Sixtus Quintus who repaired it, and it is adorned with many faire pictures gilded all over. I did see the several rooms thereof. The first one hundred forty and seven walking paces long, had three rows of Cupboards filled with books: the second was thirty nine paces long; and the third containing the books of greatest price locked up, was twenty paces long. Pope Sixtus the fourth built this Library, with the Chappell of the Palace, and the Conclave. The wall of the Chappell shined like a glass with precious stones: where the Pope Sixtus Quintus commanded Michael Angelo to paint the day of Judgment, and the common report is, that this Pope promised this famous Painter thereupon made the picture of the Pope and the Cardinals in hell amongst the Devils, so lively as every man might known them. Between this Chappell and the Conclave, (where they choose the Popes) lies a Kingly Gallery, not unworthily called vulgarly Sala Regia, (which others call Sala del Conclave). The wall of this Gallery in like sort shined with precious stones, and the pavement is of precious marble, the arched roof all gilded, and at the upper end I wondered to see the Massacre of Paris painted upon the wall, with the Popes inscription greatly commending that detestable cruelty.[3] At the same upper end the foresaid Chappell (as you come up) lies on the left hand, and the Conclave on the right hand; in which Conclave the Cardinals meet to choose the Pope, divided into several rooms, but meeting at a common table, and when they have chosen him, they lead him into a Chappell at the lower end, and near the door of the said Kingly Gallery, and place him there upon a hollow seat of Marble. I know not whether this be the chair, in which the sex or the Pope is tried, but I am sure it is hollow, with a hold in the bottom. After they put a Banner out of a high window, and there make known to the people the name that the Pope hath chosen, and then his arms are hung up round about. This Chappell at the lower end of the said Gallery, hath the name of Pope Paul the third, of the Family of Farnese, and it is little, and of a round form (as I remember), but it is beautiful beyond imagination. The images of the Apostles seem to be of silver, and Paradise painted upon the arched roof, with Angels flying, being the work of Michael Angelo, seemed to me admirable. Upon the other side of the said Library is the private Gallery of the Pope, looking into the Garden (3) Belvedere, which is seated upon the side of the Mountain

---

2. Moryson's visit would seem to indicate that the papal buildings were more accessible and less obviously threatening and paranoid fortresses than many contemporary English accounts would indicate.

3. Protestants regarded the Massacre of Saint Bartholomew's Day, August 23, 1572, when the Catholic Guise faction in Paris killed 50,000 Protestant Huguenots, as one of the most significant dates of European history. The evil genius behind the massacre was said to be Catherine de'Medici who was, of course, Italian. She was congratulated by Pope Gregory XIII.

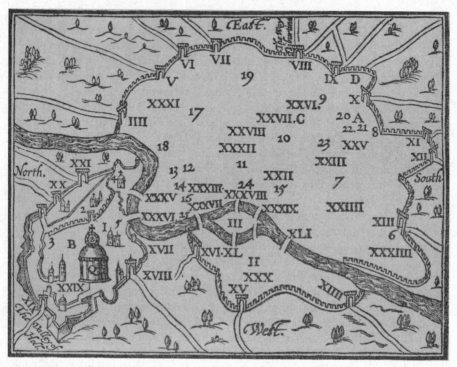

Fynes Moryson's representation of Rome, labeling all the places he visited in the text (1617).

Vatican, where Pope Innocent the eight built part of the Palace, and called it Belvedere, of the faire prospect of all Rome subject to the eye. And Pope Julius the second placed in this Garden many very faire statues, namely, of the River Nile, of the River Tiber, of Romulus and Remus playing with the papps[4] of a shee-Wolfe, all being placed in the open Garden, and a most faire statua of Apollo, another admirable statua of Lycaon with his children, another of the boy Antoninus, whom the Emperor Adrian loved, another of Hercules another of Cupid, another of Venus, another of Cleopatra sleeping with her arm over her face, and bearing a Serpent, being a wonderful faire statua. And these are all locked up, and not to be seen without favor.

Hence we went to the Castle (4) of Saint Angelo of old called Moles Adiani, for it was the Sepulcher of the Emperor Adrian, upon the top whereof was the Pine apple of brass, which before I said was since placed in the open Court-yard of Saint Peters Church. This Sepulcher of Adrian called Moles (B) was demolished by Belisarius, in the war of the Goths, upon the ruins whereof Pope Boniface the eight built this Castle, and Pope Alexander the sixth compassed it with walls and ditches, and placed therein a guard of Soldiers, and built from this Castle to the Popes Palace an open and a close gallery, by which upon any tumult, the Pope may pass safely from his Palace to the Castle. And after Pope Paul the third built very faire chambers in this Castle. On the outside is the statua of Pope Pius the fourth, and within is the statua of Paul the third, upon which these verses are written of the Emperor Charles the fifth coming to Rome.

E Lvbia venit Romanas victor ad arces
Caesar, & in niveis aureus ivit Equis.

4. Breasts.

> Ille triumphavit, sed tu plus Paule triumphas,
> Victor namque tuis oscula dat pedibus.

> With victory to Rome from Africa came
> Caesar, on milk white Horses, golden all.
> He Triumph'd, Paul thy triumph hath more fame,
> This Conqueror to kiss thy feet did fall.

In this Castle they show the head of Adrian, the statua of Saint Peter, a bunch of Grapes of brass, the place where the Cardinal Caietan escaped out of prison, and a Trap-door where prisoners are let down into a dungeon. The chambers are built in a circle round about the great chamber in the middle, which is called Sala regia, and without is a round Garden within the walls, and upon the top of the Castle, in the place of the said Pine-apple, is the statua of the Angell Michael, of which the Castle hath the name. The meadows of Quintis Cincinates lie near this Castle.

Upon the walls of the Church S. Croce, is a monument of Arno, overflowing, with this inscription in the Italian tongue: In the year 1333. The water of Arno overflowed to this height, and in the year 1557 to this, yet higher. In this Church is the sepulcher of Michaele Angleo Bonoritio, a most famous Engraver, Painter, and Builder, whose bones were brought from Rome, at the instance of Duke Cosmo, in the year 1570 and laid here. It is most certain that he was most skilful in those Arts, and of him the Italians greatly boast, and with all tell much of his fantastic humors: namely, that when he painted the Popes Chappell, (whereof I spoke in describing that Popes Palace) that he first obtained the Popes promise, that no man should come in, ill the work were finished; and understanding that the Pope had broken this promise, coming in himself with some Cardinals at the back door of the vestry, that he being then to paint the last Judgment, did so lively figure the Pope and the Cardinal (that tempted him) amongst the Devils, as every man might easily know them. But that is abominable, which the Romans of the better sort seriously tell of him, that he being to paint a crucifix for the Pope, when he came to expresses the lively actions of the passion, hired a Porter to be fastened upon a Crosse, and at that very time stabbed him with a penknife, and while he was dying, made a rare piece of work for the Art, but infamous for the murder: and that hereupon he was banished Rome, and went to the Court of the Duke of Urbino, where he was entertained with much honor. And they report also that when he was recalled to Rome with pardon of that fault, the Duchess of Urbino being bold upon her former acquaintance, should entreat him at his leisure to paint all the Saints for her: and that he to show that so great a task should not be imposed upon a workman of his sort, should satisfy this request, or rather put it off with a rude & uncivil jest, sending her the picture of a mans privy part, most artificially painted, and praying her to take in good part the Father of all the Saints, till he could at leisure send their pictures.

from Observations of the Ottoman Empire

The Turkish State

The Turkish Empire in our time is more vast and ample then ever it was formerly containing most large provinces. In Africa it begins from the straight of Gibraltar and so contains Mauritania, Barbaria, Egypt, and all the Coasts of the Mediterranean sea. The chief City of Egypt Al-Cairo hath rich traffic, and yields exceeding great Revenues to the Emperor though no doubt much less since the Portugal's sailing by the South coast of Africa and planting themselves in the East, brought all the Commodities thereof into Portugal, from thence distributing them through Europe, which voyage in our days, is yearly made by the English and Flemings. From Egypt it contains in Asia the three Provinces of Arabia, all Palestine, Syria, Mesopotamia, the many and large Provinces of Natolia or Asia the lesser, and both the Provinces of Armenia to the very confines of Persia (in these times much more straightened than in former ages) herein the famous City of Aleppo,[1] whether all the precious wares of the East are brought by great Rivers and upon the backs of Camels, yields huge Revenues to the Emperor. In Europe it contains all Greece and the innumerable Islands of the Mediterranean sea, some few excepted (as Malta fortified by an order of Christian knights, Sicily and Sardinia subject to the king of Spain, and Corsica subject to the City of Genoa, and the two Islands of Cephalonia, that of Corfu, of Zante and of Candia with some few other small Islands, subject to the Venetians). Also it contains Thracia, Bulgaria, Walachia, almost all Hungary, Albania, Slavonia, part of Dalmatia and other large Provinces to the Confines of the Germane Emperor, and king of Poland.

The form of the Ottoman Empire is merely absolute, and in the highest degree Tyrannical using all his Subjects as borne-slaves.

No man hath any free Inheritance from his father, but mangled if any at all, since all unmovable goods belong to the Emperor, and for moveable goods, they either have little, or dare not freely use them in life, or otherwise dispose them at death then by a secret guift,[2] as I shall show in his place. Yea the Children of the very Bashawes and chief Subjects, though equal to their fathers in military virtues (since there is no way to avoid contempt or live in estimation but the profession of Arms), yet seldom rise to any place of government. For this Tyrant indeed uses to prefer no borne Turk to any high place, but they who sit at the Sterne of the Sate, or have any great Command either in the Army, or in Civil government are for the most part Christians of ripe years, either taken Captives or voluntarily subjecting themselves, and so leaving the profession of Christianity to become Mohammedans, or else they be the Tributary Children of Christian Subjects gathered every fifth year oftener if occasion requires, and carried far from their parents while they are young to be brought up in the Turkish religion and military exercises; So as when they come to age, they neither know their Country nor parents; nor kinsmen so much as by name. * * *

All that live under this Tyrant, are used like sponges to be squeezed when they are full. All the Turks, yea the basest sort, spoil and make a pray of the Franks (so they call Christians that are strangers, upon the old league they have with the French) and in like sort they spoil Christian Subjects. The soldiers and officers seeking all occasions of oppression, spoil the Common Turks, and all Christians. The Governors and greatest Commanders make a pray of the very soldiers, and of the Common Turks, and all Christians, and the superiors among them use like extortion upon the Inferiors, and when these great men are grown rich, the Emperor strangles them to have their treasure. So as the Turks hide their riches and many times bury them under ground, and because nothing is so dangerous as to be reputed rich, they dare neither fare well, not build faire houses, nor have any rich household stuff. The Emperor seldom speaks or writes to any, no not to his chief Viziers but by the name of slaves, and so miserable is their servitude, so base their obedience, as if

---

1. Aleppo, in Syria.   2. I.e., trick.

he send a poor Chiaass or messenger to take the head of the greatest Subject, he though riding in the head of his troops, yet presently submits himself to the execution. Neither indeed hath he any hope in resistance, since his equals are his enemies in hope to rise by his fall, his fellow soldiers forsake him as inured to absolute obedience, and he not knowing his parents, kinsmen or any friends, is left alone to stand or fall by himself. * * *

This Tyrant seldom speaks to any of his subjects, but will be understood by his looks, having many dumb men about his person, who will speak by signs among themselves as fast as we do by words, and these men together with some boys prostituted to his lust, and some of his dearest Concubines, are only admitted to be continually near his person. The chief Vizier only receives his Commandments and his mouth gives law to all under him, being of incredible power and authority by reason of this pride and retirednes of the Tyrant were not this high estate of his very slippery, and subject to sudden destruction. They, who are admitted to the Tyrants presence, must not look him in the face, and having kissed the hem of his garment, when they rise from adoring him, must return with their eyes cast on the ground, and their faces towards him, not turning their backs till they be out of his sight.

WARFARE IN GENERAL

Certain positions of religion and the due conferring of rewards and punishments make the Turks bold adventure their persons and carefully perform all duties in War. By blind religion they are taught, that they mount to heaven without any impediment, who dye fighting for their Country and the Law of Mahomet. And that a Stoical Fate or destiny governs all humane affaires, so as if the time of death be not come, a man is no less safe in the Camp then in a Castle, if it be come, he can be preserved in neither of them, and this makes them like beasts to rush upon all dangers even without Arms to defend or offend, and to fill the ditches with their dead Carcasses, thinking to overcome by number alone, without military art. Again all rewards as the highest dignities and the like given continually by the Emperor to the most valiant and best deserving, make them apt to dare any thing. And in like sort severe punishments never failing to be inflicted on all offenders, more specially on such as brawl and fight among themselves, who are punished according to the quality of the offence, sometimes with death, and also such as break martial discipline, sometimes punishing him with death that pulls but a bunch of grapes in a Vineyard. I say these punishments never failing to be inflicted upon offenders, make the soldiers formerly encouraged by rewards no less to fear base Cowardice, brawling, fighting or any breach of discipline, and keep them in awe, as they keep all other Subjects and enemies under fear of their sword hanging over them. And the form of this State being absolute tyranny, since all things must be kept by the same means they are gotten, the State gotten and maintained by the sword, must needs give exorbitant Privileges or rather means of oppression to all the Soldiers who (as I formerly have showed) are not themselves free from the yoke of the same Tyranny which they exercise over others, while the superiors oppressing their inferiors are themselves grinded to dust by greater men, and the greatest of all hold life and goods at the Emperors pleasure, upon an hours warning, among whom happy are the lean, for the fat are still drawn to the shambles. The poorest man may aspire to the highest dignities, if his mind and fortune will serve him, but upon those high pinnacles, there is no firm abiding, and the same Virtue and Starr, that made him rise, cannot preserve him long from falling. The great men most ravenously gape for treasure, and by rapine get abundance, but when they have it, all that cannot be made portable, must be hidden or buried, for to build a fairer house, to have a rich household stuff, or to keep a good table, doth but make the Puttock[3] a prey to the Eagle. * * *

JUDGMENTS CORPORAL AND CAPITAL

Touching their Corporal and Capital Judgments. For small offences they are beaten with Cudgels on the soles of the feet, the bellies and backs, the strokes being many and painful according to the offence, or the anger of him that inflicts them. Myself did see some hanging and rotting in Chains upon the Gallows.

Also I did see one that had been impaled (vulgarly Casuckde) an horrible kind of death. The malefactor carries the wooden stake upon which he is to dye, being eight foot long and sharp towards one end, and when he comes into the place of execution, he is stripped into his shirt, and laid upon the ground with his face downward, then the sharp end of the stake is thrust into his fundament, and beaten with beetles up into his body, till it come out, at or about his Waist, then the blunt end is fastened in the ground, and so he sets at little ease, till he dye, which may be soon if the stake be driven with favor, otherwise, he may languish two or three days in pain and hunger; if torment will permit him in that time to feel hunger, for no man dares give him meat.

They have an other terrible kind of death vulgarly called Gaucher. The malefactor hath a rope or Chain fastened about his body, whereof the other end is made fast to the top of a Tower or of a Gibbet made high of purpose, and so this rope or chain being of fit length, his body is cast down to pitch upon a hook of Iron, where he hangs till he dyes, with horror of the height of pain, and of hunger. For howsoever, he may dye presently if any vital part pitch upon the hook, yet hanging by the shoulder or thigh he may live long. And if any men give these executed men, meat, or help to prolong their miserable life, he shall dye the same death; Mores and Christians and they that are not of the Army, are often putt to this death, yea the Beglerbegs sometimes putt Governors to this death for extortions or Cruelties committed by them, or rather to get their wealth. They have an other terrible kind of death Bragadino a Venetian Governor of Famagusta in Cyprus, after he had yielded the City upon Composition for life to him and his soldiers.

A Turk forsaking his faith and a Christian doing or speaking any thing against the law of Mahomet are burned with fire. Traitors or those whom the Emperor so calls, are tortured under the nails and with diverse torments, but the great men of the Army are only strangled.

A murderer is putt to some of the former cruel deaths. A thief is hanged and I have read of a soldier that had stolen milk, and after was strangled. The Adulterer is imprisoned for some Months, and after redeemed with money, but the Adulteress is set naked upon an Ass with the bowels of an ox about her neck, and so she is whipped about the streets having stones and dirt cast at her. If a Christian man commit fornication with a Turkish woman both are putt to death, and this Common danger to both, makes them more wary of others, and more confident to trust one an other, but the sin is Common, and at Constantinople the houses of Ambassadors, will not stick to play the bawds for a small reward. In case of this offence nothing frees a Christian from death, but his turning Mahomet an. Yet I remember that I saw a Tower at Tripoli

---

3. A buzzard or kite, which are largely scavengers; in falconry terms, an ignoble bird, despite its size.

called the tower of Love, built by a rich Christian to redeem his life being condemned for this Crime. But if a Turk lye with a Christian woman, he is not putt to death, but sett upon an Ass with his face towards the tail, which he holds in his hand, and hath the bowels of an ox cast about his neck, and so is led through the streets in scorn. If a Christian lye with a Christian woman, the fault is punished with paying of money. All harlots write their names in the book of the Cady or the Sobbassa, and not only the Turks but even the Janissaries are permitted to have acquaintance with them so it be not in the two lents, wherein they yearly fast, For in that Case, while I was in Turkey many women were sewed in sacks, and drowned in the Sea at Constantinople. Generally for greater Crimes, the Judge of the Turks devise and impose a death with greater torment especially for reproaching their law of Prophet, which a Christian cannot redeem, but by turning Turk.

OF DEGREES IN THE COMMON WEALTH AND FAMILY

* * * For the private Family each man may have as many Wives as he is able to feed so he take a letter of permission from the Cady, and some of them keep their wives in diverse Cities to avoid the strife of women; yet if they live both in one house with him, they seldom disagree, being not preferred one above another. The Turks use not to take a dowry but as they buy captive women, (whom they may sell again or keep for Concubines of for any other service); so they also buy Free women to be their wives, so as the father is enriched by having many and fair Daughters. Divorce is permitted for perverse manners, for barrenness or like faults allowed by the Cady. As they buy Captive Women, so may they buy any other for Concubines so they write their names in the book of the Cady. For as Christians are married by Priests in the Church; so Turks are married by taking a letter, or bill from the Cady (who is their spiritual Judge) and writing the marriage in his book at his private house. But at the day of marriage, they also use to bathe, and to pray in their Mosques.

Lastly it is no disgrace to be borne of a Captive Woman, or out of marriage, for that is the Condition, of the very Emperors, Whose mothers are Captives, and before the birth of their first son, never have a letter of dowry to make them free women and wives, which after they have a son was of old wont to be granted them, but the Emperors of late times seldom give that letter to them, for jealousy lest they should practice their deaths to have power in the reign of their succeeding son * * *

Having cast anchor (as I said) in the Port of Constantinople, behold, as soon as day began to break, many companies of Turks rushing into our Bark, who like so many starved flies fell to suck the sweet Wines, each rascal among them beating with cudgels and ropes the best of our Mariners, if he durst but repine against it, till within short space the Candian Merchant having advertised the Venetian Ambassador of their arrival, he sent a Janissary to protect the Bark, and the goods; and as soon as he came, it seemed to me no less strange, that this one man should beat all those Turks, and drive them out of the Bark like so many dogs, the common Turks daring no more resist them. And the Sergeant of the Magistrate having taken some of our Greek Mariners (though subject to the State of Venice) to work for their Ottoman in gathering stones, and like base employments, this Janissary caused them presently to be released, and to be sent again into their Bark, such is the tyranny of the Turks against all Christians as well their subjects as others, so as no man sailed into these parts, but under the Banner of England, France, or Venice, who being in league with the great Turk, have their Ambassadors in this City, and their Consuls in other Havens, to protect those that come under their Banner, in this sort sending them a Janissary to keep them from wrongs, so soon as they are advertised of their arrival. * * *

The Description of the City of Constantinople, and the Adjacent Territories and Seas

The great lines or walls show the form of the City, and the single small lines describe the Territory adjoining.

(A)   In this Tower they hang out a light of pitch and like burning matter, to direct the Sailors by night, coming to the City, or sailing along the coast out of the Sea Euxinus (which they say is called the Black Sea of many shipwrecks therein happening.) And this Tower is sixteen miles distant from the City.

(B)   Here is a marble pillar erected upon a Rock compassed with the sea, which they call the pillar of Pompey, and therein many passengers (for their memory) use to engrave their names. And here are innumerable flocks of Sea foul and of many kinds, wherewith he that is skilful to shoot in his Peace, may abundantly furnish himself.

(C)   Here is the Euxine or black Sea.

(D E)   Here lie two strong Castles, one in Europe, the other in Asia, some eight miles distant from the City, built to defend the Haven from the assault of the enemies by Sea on that side, and the Garrison there kept, searched the ships coming from the City, that no slaves or prohibited goods be carried therein, neither can any ship pass unsearched, except they will hazard to be sunk. Finally, the great Turk sends his chief prisoners to be kept in these strong Castles.

(F)   Here great ships use to cast anchor at their first arrival, till they bee unloaded, and here again they ride at anchor to expect winds, when they are loaded and ready to depart.

(G)   All along this bank and the opposite side for a large circuit, the greatest ships use to lie when they are unloaded, and they lie most safely and close by the shore, fastened by cables on land.

(H)   Here lies the old City built by the Genoese of Italy, called Gallata by the Turks, and Perah by the Greeks (of the situation beyond the Chanel.) It is now accounted a Suburb of Constantinople, and is seated upon a most pleasant hill, wherein for the most part live Christians, as well subjects as others, and the Ambassadors of England, France, and Venice, only the Emperors Ambassadors of England were wont to dwell upon the Sea-shore in the Plain, and their Palace is not far distant from this (K); but Master Edward Barton the English Ambassador at this time dwelt upon the top of the hill, in a faire house within a large field, and pleasant gardens compassed with a wall. And all Gallata is full of very pleasant gardens, and compassed with pleasant fields, whereof some towards the land furthest from the Sea, are used for the burial of Turks.

(I)   Here is a little Creek of the Sea is compassed with walls and buildings, within which the Galleys, and store-houses for all things thereunto belonging.

(K)   Here is the chief passage over the water called Tapano, where a man may pass for two aspers. All along this Sea bank lye very many great Guns (as upon the Tower Wharf at London), and here the fishers land, and sell their fish.

(L)   Here the Megarenses of old built Chalcedon, a City of Bethinia, famous for Council held there, by the ruin of which City, Constantinople increased. At this day there is only a Village, or rather some scattered houses, and it is commonly called Scuteri, or Scudretta.

(M)   Here the Great Turks mother then living, had her private Garden.

(N)   Hither the Heir of the Empire is sent, as it were into banishment, under pretence to govern the Province Bursia, as soon as he is circumcised, and so being made a Muslim (that is, a circumcised Turk) first begins to draw the eyes of the Army and Janissaries towards him.

(O)   Here is the Palace or Court of the great Turk, called by the Italians Seraglio, and vulgarly Saray, and it was of old the Monastery of Saint Sophia. Mahomet the second first compassed it with walls, and the buildings together with the large and pleasant gardens are some three or four miles in circuit. I entered the outward Court thereof by a stately Gate kept by many Janissaries called Capigi of that office. The court yard was large, all compassed with building of free stone two stories high, with a low and almost plain roof tiled, and without windows, after the manner of the building of Italy, and round about the inside, it was cast out with arches like the building of Cloisters, under which they walked dry in the greatest rain. And in this Court is a large pulpit or open room, where the great Turk useth to show himself to the Janissaries to satisfy them when they make any mutiny.

(P)   Here is a banqueting house, vulgarly called Chuske, the prospect whereof is more pleasant then can be expressed, beholding four Sears at once, and the land on all sides beyond them.

Fynes Moryson's representation of Constantinople, labeling all the places he visited in the text (1617).

(Q)   Here is the Church of Saint Sophia, opposite to the Court Gate, of old built by the Christians after the form of Solomon's Temple, and endowed with the annual rent of three hundred thousand Zechines, now made a Mosque or Mahomet an Church. And howsoever the Turks cannot endure that unwashed Christians (so called by them, because they use not Baths so continually as they doe) should enter their Mosques, or pass over their Sepulchers, yet my self entered this Church with the Janissary my guide, trusting to his power to defend me, yet he willed me first to put of my shoes, and according to the Turks custom to leave them in the porch, where they were safe till we returned. The Church is of a round form, and built of brick, and supported with faire pillars, and paved with Marble (over which the Turks laid Mats to kneel, and prostrate themselves more commodiously upon them.) The roof is beautified with pictures of that rich painting, which the Italians call alla Mosaica, shining like enameled work, which now by antiquity were much decayed, and in some parts defaced. Round about the Church hung many Lamps, which they use to burn in time of the Lent (called Beyram); and every week upon Thursday in the evening, and Friday all day, which they keep holy after their fashion for their Sabbath day. Round about the upper part of the Church are large and most faire Galleries. And here I did see two Nuts of Marble of huge bigness and great beauty. Moreover I did see the great Turk when he entered this Church, and howsoever it lie close to the Gate of his Palace. Yet he came riding upon a horse richly trapped, with many troopes of his chief horseman, standing in rank within the Courts of his Palace, and from the Court Gate to the Church door, between which troops on both sides, he passed as between walls of brass, with great pomp. And when a Chaus (or Pensioner) being on horseback did see me close by the Emperors side, he rushed upon me to strike me with his mace, saying, What doth this Christian dog so near the person of our great Lord? But the Janissary, whom our Ambassador had given me for a Guide and Protector, repelled him from doing me any wrong, and many Janissaries (according to their manner) coming to help him, the Chaus was glad to let me alone, and they bade me be bold to stand still, though I were the second or third person from the Emperor. Near this Church is the stately Sepulcher of Selymus the second, and another Sepulcher no less stately, and newly built for Amaranth lately deceased, where he lay with those male children round about him, who according to the manner were strangled by his Successor after he was dead. Not far thence is the Market place having some one hundred marble pillars about it, and adorned with a Pyramids or pinnacle, erected upon four Globes, and with a pleasant Fountain of water, together with other ornaments left (as it seems) by Christian Emperors.

(R)   The wonderful Mosque and Sepulcher of Solyman, numbered among the miracles of the World.

(S)   Two houses for the same use, as the Exchange of London, where the Merchants meet, namely, for the selling of fine wares, but no way to be compared to the same for the building. They are called the great and the less Bezestand, and use to bee opened only certain days of the week, and for some six hours, at which times small and more precious wares are there to be sold, as Jewels, Semiters (or Swords), set with Jewels, but commonly counterfeit, pieces of Velvet, Satin, and Damask, and the like. And the Market place is not far distant, where Captives of both sexes are weekly sold, and the buyers if they will, may take them into a house, and there see them naked, and handle them (as wee handle beasts to know their fatness and strength.)

(T)   Here is a Fort that is fortified with seven Towers, called by the Turks Jadicule, and by Christians the seven Towers, where a garrison of Soldiers is kept, because the Emperors treasure is there laid up, and chief Prisoners use to be kept there. The treasure is vulgarly said to bee laid up there, but the great Turk seldom goes thither: and since it is true, that where the treasure is, there is the mind, I think it probable (which I have heard of experienced men) that more of the treasure lies in the Seraglio, where the great Turk holds his Court.

(V)   Here be the ruins of a Palace upon the very walls of the City, called the Palace of Constantine, wherein I did see an Elephant, called Philo by the Turks, and another beast newly brought out of Africa, (the Mother of Monsters) which beast is altogether unknown in our parts, and is called Surnapa by the people of Asia, Astanpa by others, and Giraffe by the Italians, the picture whereof I remember to have seen in the Maps of Mercator; and because the beast is very rare, I will describe his form as well as I can. His hair is red colored, with many black and white spots; I could scarce reach with the point of my fingers to the hinder part of his back, which grew higher and higher towards his foreshoulder, and his neck was thin and some three ells long, so as he easily turned his head in a moment to any part or corner of the room wherein he stood, putting it over the beams thereof, being built like a Barn, and high (for the Turkish building, not unlike the building of Italy, both which I have formerly described) by reason where of he many times put his nose in my neck, when I though my self furthest distant from him, which familiarity of his I liked not; and howsoever the Keepers assured me he would not hurt me, yet I avoided these his familiar kisses as much as I could. His body was slender, not greater, but much higher then the body of a stag or Hart, and his head and face was like to that of a stag, but the head was less and the face more beautiful: He had two horns, but short and scarce half a foot long; and in the forehead he had two bunches of flesh, his ears and feet like an Ox, and his legs like a stag. The Janissary my guide did in my name and for me give twenty Aspers to the Keeper of this Beast.

⊷ ⊱⊰ ⊶

Edmund Spenser
1552?–1599

from A View of the [Present] State of Ireland

Spenser's dialogue, A View of the Present State of Ireland was composed in about 1596 as a response to Hugh O'Neill's sustained threat to English rule in Ireland, which had begun in 1594 and was to last until 1603, after Spenser's death. The long work was not published until 1633 but circulated extensively in manuscript (over twenty copies survive). The dialogue has become notorious as a brutal defense of the English right to colonize its weaker neighbor, and the denigration of the Irish as savages who needed to be civilized by firm government. In this extract the fictional Irenius, who Spenser represents as an English settler in Ireland, explains to his English-based counterpart, Eudoxus, that Irish customs are derived from those of one of the barbarian races of the ancient world, the Scythians, whose lands bordered those of Greece. Everything about the Irish is a means of confronting civilized values, even their clothes, which seem innocent to the uninitiated but which help them resist the march of progress and civilization.

Eudox: In truth Iren. You doe well remember the plot of your first purpose; but yet from that (meseemes) ye have much swerved in all this long discourse, of the first inhabiting of Ireland; for what is that to your purpose?

Iren: Truly very material, for if you marked the course of all that speech well, it was to show, by what means the customs, that now are in Ireland, being some of them indeed very strange and almost heathenish, were first brought in: and that was, as I said, by those nations from whom that country was first peopled; for the difference in manners and customs, doth follow the difference of nations and people. The which I have declared to you, to have been three especially which seated themselves here: to wit, first the Scythian, then the Gauls, and lastly the English. Notwithstanding that I am not ignorant, that there were sundry nations which got footing in that land, of the which there yet remain divers great families and septs, of whom I will also in their proper places make mention.

Eudox: You bring your self Iren. Very well into the way again, notwithstanding that it seems that you were never out of the way, but now that you have passed thorough those antiquities, which I could have wished not so soon ended, begin when you please, to declare what customs and manners have been derived from those nations to the Irish, and which of them you find fault withal.

Iren: I will begin then to count their customs in the same order that I counted their nations, and first with the Scythian or Scottish manners. Of the which there is one use, amongst them, to keep their cattle, and to live themselves the most part of the year in boolies, still to fresh land, as they have depastured the former. The which appeared plainer to be the manner of the Scythians, as you may read in Olaus Magnus, and Io. Bohemus, and yet is used amongst all the Tartarians and the people about the Caspian Sea, which are naturally Scythians, to live in herds as they call them, being the very same, that the Irish boolies are, driving their cattle continually with them, and feeding only on their milk and white meats.

Eudox: What fault can you find with this custom? For though it be an old Scythian use, yet it is very behoofefull[1] in this country of Ireland, where there are great mountains, and waste deserts full of grass, that the same should be eaten down, and nourish many thousands of cattle, for the good of the whole realm, which cannot (me thinks) well be any other way, then by keeping those boolies there, as you have showed.

Iren: But by this custom of boolying, there grow in the mean time many great enormities unto that Common-wealth. For first if there be any out-laws, or loose people, (as they are never without some) which live upon stealths and spoils, they are evermore succored and find relief only in these boolies, being upon the waste places, whereas else they should be driven shortly to starve, or to come down to the towns to seek relief, where by one means or other, they would soon be caught. Besides, such stealths of cattle as they make, they bring commonly to those boolies, being upon those waste places, where they are readily received, and the thief harbored from danger of law, or such officers as might light upon him.[2] Moreover the people that thus live in those boolies, grow thereby the more barbarous, and live more licentiously than they could in towns, using what manners they list, and practicing what mischief and villainies they will, either against the government there, by their combinations, or against private men, whom they malign, by stealing their goods, or murdering themselves. For there they think themselves half exempted from law and obedience,

---

1. Necessary.
2. Cattle raiding enjoyed a significant role in Irish culture and society. The greatest Irish epic, the *Táin Bó Cuailnge* ("Cattle Raid of Cooley"), as the title might suggest, centers around such an event.

and having once tasted freedom, doe like a steer, that hath been long out of his yoke, grudge and repine ever after, to come under rule again.

Eudox: By your speech Iren. I perceive more evil to come by this use of boolies, then good by their grassing; and therefore it may well be reformed: but that must be in his due course: do you proceed to the next.

Iren: They have another custom from the Scythians, that is the wearing of Mantles, and long glibbes, which is a thick curled bush of hair, hanging down over their eyes, and monstrously disguising them, which are both very bad and hurtful.

Eudox: Doe you think that the mantle comes from the Scythians? I would surely think otherwise, for by that which I have read, it appeared that most nations of the world anciently used the mantle. For the Jews used it, as you may read of Elias mantle, &c. The Chaldees also used it, as you may read in Diodorus. The Egyptians likewise used it, as you may read in Herodotus, and may be gathered by the description of Berenice, in the Greek Commentary upon Callimachus. The Greeks also used it anciently, as appeared by Venus mantle lined with stars, though afterwards they changed the form thereof into their cloaks, called Pallia, as some of the Irish also use. And the ancient Latin's and Romans used it, as you may read in Virgil, who was a very great antiquary: That Evander, when Aeneas came to him at his feast, did entertain and feast him, sitting on the ground, and lying on mantles. Insomuch as he useth the very word mantile for mantle.

" – Humi mantilia sternunt."[3]
So that it seems that the mantle was a general habit to most nations, and not proper to the Scythians only, as you suppose.

Iren: I cannot deny but that anciently it was common to most, and yet since disused and laid away. But in this later age of the world, since the decay of the Roman empire, it was renewed and brought in again by those Northern Nations, when breaking out of their cold caves and frozen habitations, into the sweet soil of Europe, they brought with them their usual weeds, fit to shield the cold, and that continual frost, to which they had at home been inured: the which yet they left not off, by reason that they were in perpetual wars, with the nations whom they had invaded, but, still removing from place to place, carried always with them that weed, as their house, their bed, and their garment; and, coming lastly into Ireland, they found there more special use thereof, by reason of the raw cold climate, from whom it is now grown into that general use, in which that people now have it. After whom the Gauls succeeding, yet finding the like necessity of that garment, continued the like use thereof.

Eudox: Since then the necessity thereof is so commodious, as you allege, that it is instead of housing, bedding, and clothing, what reason have you then to wish so necessary a thing cast off?

Iren: Because the commodity doth not countervail the discommodity; for the inconveniencies which thereby doe arise, are much more many; for it is a fit house for an out-law, a meet bed for a rebel, and an apt cloak for a thief. First the out-law being for his many crimes and villains banished from the towns and houses of honest men, and wandering in waste places, far from danger of law, make his mantle his house, and under it cover himself from the wrath of heaven, from the offence of the earth, and from the sight of men. When it rains it is his pent-house; when it blows it is his tent; when it freezes it is his tabernacle. In Summer he can wear it loose, in winter he can wrap it close; at all times he can use it; never heavy, never cumbersome. Likewise for a rebel it is as serviceable. For in his war that he make (if at least it deserve the name of

---

3. They spread their cloaks on the ground.

war) when he still flies from his foe, and lurks in the thick woods and straight passages, waiting for advantages, it is his bed, yea and almost his household stuff. For the wood is his house against all weathers, and his mantle is his couch to sleep in. Therein he wraps himself round, and coucheth[4] himself strongly against the gnats, which in that country doe more annoy the naked rebels, whilst they keep the woods, and doe more sharply wound them then all their enemies swords, or spears, which can seldom come nigh them: yea and oftentimes their mantle serves them, when they are near driven, being wrapped about their left arm in stead of a target, for it is hard to cut thorough with a sword, besides it is light to bear, light to throw away, and, being (as they commonly are) naked, it is to them all in all. Lastly for a thief it is so handsome, as it may seem it was first invented for him, for under it he may cleanly convey any fit pillage that comes handsomely in his way, and when he goes abroad in the night in free-booting, it is his best and surest friend; for lying, as they often do, 2 or 3 nights together abroad to watch for their booty, with that they can prettily shroud themselves under a bush or a bank side, till they may conveniently do their errand: and when all is over, he can, in his mantle pass thorough any town or company, being close hooded over his head, as he useth, from knowledge of any to whom he is endangered. Besides this, he, or any man else that is disposed to mischief or villainy, may under his mantle go privily armed without suspicion of any, carry his head-piece, his skein, or pistol if his please, to be always in readiness. Thus necessary and fitting is a mantle, for a bad man, and surely for a bad housewife it is no less convenient, for some of them that bee wandering woe men, called of them Mona-shul, it is half a wardrobe; for in Summer you shall find her arrayed commonly but in her smock and mantle to be more ready for her light services: in Winter, and in her travaile,[5] it is her cloak and safeguard, and also a coverlet for her lewd exercise. And when she hath filled her vessel, under it she can hide both her burden, and her blame; yea, and when her bastard is borne, it serves instead of swaddling clouts. And as for all other good women which love to doe but little work, how handsome it is to lye in and sleep, or to louse themselves in the sun-shine, they that you will think it very unfit for a good housewife to stir in, or to busy her self about her housewifery in such sort as she should. These be some of the abuses for which I would think it meet to forbid all mantles.

Eudox: O evil minded man, that having reckoned up so many uses of a mantle, will yet wish it to be abandoned! Sure I think Diogenes dish did never serve his master for more turns, notwithstanding that he made it his dish, his cup, his cap, his measure, his water-pot, then a mantle doth an Irish man. But I see they be most to bad intents, and therefore I will join with you in abolishing it. But what blame lay you to the glib? take heed (I pray you) that you be not too busy therewith for fear of your own blame, seeing our Englishmen take it up in such a general fashion to wear their hair so immeasurably long, that some of them exceed the longest Irish glibs.

Iren: I fear not the blame of any underserved dislikes: but for the Irish glibbes, they are as fit masks as a mantle is for a thief. For whensoever he hath run himself into that peril of law, that he will not be known, he either cuts of his glib quite, by which he becomes nothing like himself, or pulls it so low down over his eyes, that it is very hard to discern his thievish countenance. And therefore fit to be trussed up with the mantle.

Eudox: Truly these three Scythian abuses, I hold most fit to bee taken away with sharp penalties, and sure I wonder how they have been kept thus long, notwithstanding so many good provisions and orders, as have been devised for that people.

---

4. Protects, covers.   5. Labor, giving birth.

Thomas Hariot
c. 1560–1621

Thomas Hariot, an astronomer and mathematician, was a member of Sir Walter Raleigh's household. This account, published by Hakluyt in 1598, reports on his voyage to Virginia in 1586. He tells of an unanticipated yet terrible consequence of European colonization: the death of numbers of Indians from diseases—brought by colonists—to which the Indians had no immunity. As a scientific matter, the phenomenon was not at all understood, and Hariot describes attempts by the English to explain what it meant in supposedly moral terms and also to take advantage of its practical effect—the reduction of the Indian population—as a way to colonize the region further.

from A Brief and True Report of the Newfound Land of Virginia

It resteth I speak a word or two of the natural inhabitants, their natures and manners, leaving large discourse thereof until time more convenient hereafter; now only so far forth as that you may know how they in respect of troubling our inhabiting and planting are not to be feared, but that they shall have cause both to fear and love us that shall inhabit with them.

They are a people clothed with loose mantles made of deerskins, and aprons of the same round about their middles, all else naked; of such a difference of statures only as we in England;[1] having no edge tools or weapons of iron or steel to offend us withal, neither know they how to make any. Those weapons that they have are only bows made of witch hazel and arrows of reeds, flat-edged truncheons also of wood about a yard long; neither have they anything to defend themselves but targets[2] made of barks and some armors made of sticks wickered together with thread. * * *

Their manner of war amongst themselves is either by sudden surprising one another, most commonly about the dawning of the day or moonlight, or else by ambushes or some subtle devices. Set battles are very rare, except it fall out where there are many trees, where either part may have some hope of defense after the delivery of every arrow, in leaping behind some or other.[3]

If there fall out any wars between us and them, what their fight is likely to be, we having advantages against them so many manner of ways, as by our discipline, our strong weapons and devices else, especially ordinance[4] great and small, it may easily be imagined. By the experience we have had in some places, the turning up of their heels against us in running away was their best defense.

In respect of us they are a people poor, and for want of skill and judgment in the knowledge and use of our things do esteem our trifles before things of greater value. Nothwithstanding, in their proper manner (considering the want of such means as we have), they seem very ingenious. For although they have no such tools, nor any such crafts, sciences, and arts as we, yet in those things they do, they show excellency of wit. And by how much they upon due consideration shall find our manner of knowledges

---

1. I.e., the Indians are generally of the same stature as the English and have the same range of differences in height as the English.
2. Shields.
3. Europeans fought each other in "set battles." Typically, an army was led by its cavalry and supported by its in-

fantry, who marched to a distance from which they could fire their guns and cannons at the enemy. Indians waged what is known in the modern period as guerrilla warfare, attacking the enemy by surprise maneuvers and defending themselves in quick retreats.
4. Artillery.

and crafts to exceed theirs in perfection and speed for doing or execution, by so much the more is it probable that they should desire our friendship and love and have the greater respect for pleasing and obeying us. Whereby may be hoped, if means of good government be used, that they may in a short time be brought to civility and the embracing of true religion.

Some religion they have already, which although it be far from the truth, yet being as it is, there is hope that it may be the easier and sooner reformed.

They believe that there are many gods, which they call Mantoac, but of different sorts and degrees, one only chief and great God, which hath been from all eternity, who, as they affirm, when he purposed to make the world, made first other gods of a principal order to be as means and instruments to be used in the creation and government to follow, and after, the sun, moon, and stars as petty gods and the instruments of the other more principal. First (they say) were made waters, out of which by the gods was made all diversity of creatures that are visible or invisible.

For mankind, they say a woman was made first, which by the working of one of the gods, conceived and brought forth children; and in such sort they say they had their beginning. But how many years or ages have passed since, they say they can make no relation, having no letters or other such means as we to keep records of the particularities of times past, but only tradition from father to son.

* * *

Most things they saw with us, as mathematical instruments, sea compasses, the virtue of the loadstone[5] in drawing[6] iron, a perspective glass[7] whereby was showed many strange sights, burning glasses,[8] wild fireworks, guns, hooks, writing and reading, springclocks that seem to go of themselves, and many other things that we had were so strange unto them and so far exceeded their capacities to comprehend the reason and means how they should be made and done that they thought they were rather the works of gods than of men, or at the leastwise they had been given and taught us of the gods. Which made many of them to have such opinion of us as that if they knew not the truth of God and religion already, it was rather to be had from us whom God so specially loved than from a people that were so simple as they found themselves to be in comparison of us. Whereupon greater credit was given unto that we spoke of, concerning such matters. * * *

There could at no time happen any strange sickness, losses, hurts, or any other cross unto them but that they would impute to us the cause or means thereof, for offending or not pleasing us. One other rare and strange accident, leaving others, will I mention before I end, which moved the whole country that either knew or heard of us, to have us in wonderful admiration.

There was no town where we had any subtle devise[9] practiced against us, we leaving it unpunished or not revenged (because we sought by all means possible to win them by gentleness) but that within a few days after our departure from every such town, the people began to die very fast, and many in short space; in some towns about twenty, in some forty, and in one six score, which in truth was very many in respect of their numbers. This happened in no place that we could learn but where we had been where they used some practice against us, and after such time.[1] The

5. Magnet.
6. Attracting.
7. Telescope.
8. Magnifying glasses.
9. Trick.

1. Hariot moralizes the phenomenon of immunity by stating that Indian villages that came down with disease were those that had resisted or "used some practice against" the English.

disease also was so strange that they neither knew what it was, nor how to cure it, the like by report of the oldest men in the country never happened before, time out of mind. * * *

This marvelous accident in all the country wrought so strange opinions of us that some people could not tell whether to think us gods or men, and the rather because that all the space of their sickness, there was no man of ours known to die or that was especially sick; they noted also that we had no women among us, neither that we did care for any of theirs.

Some therefore were of opinion that we were not born of women, and therefore not mortal, but that we were men of an old generation many years past, then risen again to immortality.

Some would likewise seem to prophecy that there were more of our generation yet to come to kill theirs and take their places, as some thought the purpose was, by that which was already done. Those that were immediately to come after us they imagined to be in the air, yet invisible and without bodies, and that they by our entreaty and for the love of us did make the people to die in that sort as they did by shooting invisible bullets into them.

To confirm this opinion, their physicians (to excuse their ignorance in curing the disease) would not be ashamed to say but earnestly make the simple people believe that the strings of blood that they sucked out of the sick bodies were the strings wherewithal the invisible bullets were tied and cast. Some also thought that we shot them ourselves out of our pieces from the place where we dwelt and killed the people in any town that had offended us, as we listed, how far distant from us so ever it were. And other some said that it was the special work of God for our sakes as we ourselves have cause in some sort to think no less, whatsover some do or may imagine to the contrary, specially some astrologers, knowing of the eclipse of the sun which we saw the same year before in our voyage thitherward, which unto them appeared very terrible. And also of a comet which began to appear but a few days before the beginning of the said sickness.[2] But to exclude them[3] from being the special causes of so special an accident, there are further reasons than I think fit at this present to be alleged. These their[4] opinions I have set down the more at large that it may appear unto you that there is good hope that they may be brought through discreet dealing and government to the embracing of the truth and consequently to honor, obey, fear, and love us.

And although some of our company toward the end of the year showed themselves too fierce in slaying some of the people in some towns, upon causes that on our part might easily enough have been born withal; yet notwithstanding, because it was on their part justly deserved, the alteration of their opinions generally and for the most part concerning us is the less to be doubted.[5] And whatsoever else they may be, by carefulness[6] of ourselves need nothing at all to be feared.

---

2. The Indians attributed their disease to God's favor toward the English. Hariot observes that the English concurred in this opinion, despite the warnings of astrologers who saw a recent eclipse of the sun and the arrival of a comet as bad omens. He concludes that the Indians' sense of a divine power backing the English enterprise could be the basis for their further peaceful subjugation.
3. The eclipse and the comet.

4. I.e., the Indians'.
5. Hariot admits that the English were "too fierce" in killing Indians for insufficient reason; at the same time, he states, without further explanation, that as these actions were "justly deserved," the English need fear no change in the Indians' attitude toward them.
6. Taking care.

John Smith
c. 1580–1631

John Smith's reports on the first years of the Jamestown settlement offered English readers a remarkably complete account of their colony in Virginia. To this day, it remains our principal source of information about English relations with the Indians of that region, the Powhatans. The first version of these reports, entitled *A True Relation of such occurrences and accidents of note as hath hap'ned in Virginia since the first planting of that colony* (1608) records events from the settlers' landing on Cape Henry at the mouth of the Chesapeake in December 1606 to the moment of Smith's return to England during the spring of 1608. Written as a first-person narrative in a terse, reportorial style, *A True Relation* reads as a series of notes. It gives us a vivid picture of the Indians of the area, how they received the English, and what measures they took to contain these newcomers, but it tells us little about how the author interpreted these events. What we notice is how often Smith imposes his own Europeanist construction on the situation, calling Powhatan—the principal chief of the local tribes—an "Emperor" and those governing the tribes themselves as "Kings." Smith's later *General History of Virginia and the Summer Isles* was published in 1623 and obviously elaborated his earlier material. Referring to himself in the third person as "Captain Smith" or "the president," Smith evaluates with considerable astuteness the actions of both the English and the Powhatan Indians as they met on ground they increasingly understood as contested.

It is impossible to know how much of Smith's *General History* is the result of his imaginative reconstruction of events that had, in all likelihood, lost their immediacy in his memory. The *General History* is much longer than *A True Relation* and is replete with details that give the reader a vivid sense of the difficulty the English had settling this unfamiliar territory. Smith's most compelling passages report conversations he had with Powhatan. Presumably with the aid of an interpreter, although he does not tell us so, Smith understands that Powhatan was fully aware of the end the colonists had in view: in Smith's translation of Powhatan's words, it was "to invade my people and possess my country." With remarkable ventriloquism, Smith speaks sympathetically, through Powhatan, on behalf of the people he himself often declared as being "savages." In these reported conversations, Smith's Powhatan shows dignity and perspicacity. As Powhatan reflects upon English deceit and ambition with a keen and uncompromising accuracy, it is evident that Smith had reason to admire—and to fear—his adversary.

from **General History of Virginia and the Summer Isles**

This happened in the winter in that extreme frost, 1607. Now though we had victual sufficient—I mean only of oatmeal, meal, and corn—yet the ship staying 14 weeks when she might as well have been gone in 14 days spent[1] a great part of that, the beef, pork, oil, aqua vitae, fish, butter and cheese, beer, and near all the rest that was sent to be landed. When they departed what their discretion could spare to make a little poor meal or two we called feasts to relish our mouths. Of each somewhat they left us, yet I must confess those that had either money, spare clothes, credit to give bills of payment, gold, rings, furs, or any such commodities were ever welcome to this removing tavern.[2] * * * Now for all this plenty our ordinary was but meal and water, so that this great charge little relieved our wants, whereby with the extremity of the bitter cold frost and those defects more than half of us died and took our deaths in that

---

1. Consumed.

2. The ship that had the food supply; Smith refers to its dwindling stores.

piercing winter. I cannot deny but both Smith and Skrivener[3] did their best to amend what was amiss, but with the president[4] went the major part.

But the worst mischief was our gilded refiners with their golden promises made all men their slaves in hope of recompenses. There was no talk, no hope, no work but *dig* gold, *wash* gold, *refine* gold, *load* gold—such a bruit of GOLD that one mad fellow desired to be buried in the sands, lest they should by their art make gold of his bones! Little need there was and less reason the ship should stay, their wages run on, our victual consume 14 weeks, that the mariners might say they did help to build such a golden church that we can say the rain washed near to nothing in 14 days.[5]

Were it that Captain Smith would not applaud all those golden inventions because they admitted him not to the sight of their trials nor golden consultations, I know not. But I have heard him oft question with Captain Martin, and tell him, except he could show him a more substantial trial, he was not enamored with their "dirty" skill, breathing out these and many other passions. Never anything did more torment him than to see all necessary business neglected to fraught such a drunken ship with so much gilded dirt.

Till then we never accounted Captain Newport a refiner, who being ready to set sail for England—and we not having any use of parliaments, plays, petitions, admirals, recorders, interpreters, chronologers, courts of plea, nor justices of peace!—sent Master Wingfield and Captain Archer home with him, that had engrossed all those titles, for England *to seek some place of better employment!*[6]

> O cursed gold, those hunger-starved movers,
> To what misfortunes lead'st thou all those lovers!
> For all the China wealth nor Indies can
> Suffice the mind of an av'ricious man.

* * *

The 12 of January [1609], we arrived at Werowocomoco,[7] where the river was frozen near half a mile from the shore. But to neglect no time, the president with his barge so far had approached by breaking the ice as the ebb left him amongst those oozy shoals. Yet rather than to lie there frozen to death, by his own example he taught them to march near middle deep more than a flight-shot[8] through this muddy, frozen ooze. When the barge floated he appointed two or three to return her aboard the pinnace[9] where, for want of water, in melting the ice they made fresh water, for the river there was salt. But in this march Master Russell, whom none could persuade to stay behind, being somewhat ill and exceeding heavy, so overtoiled himself as the rest had much ado ere he got ashore to regain life into his dead, benumbed spirits.

Quartering in the next houses we found, we sent to Powhatan for provision, who sent us plenty of bread, turkeys, and venison.

3. Matthew Skrivener was a member of the Council of the Virginia Company.

4. Edward Wingfield was president of the colony until 1607, after which Smith served in that position. Here Smith claims that neither he nor Skrivener had ways or means enough to secure the food the president had preempted.

5. Smith writes ironically. There was no reason for the ship to stay in Virginia just so the mariners could say that they had built a "golden church"; because no gold in fact existed in Virginia, to have said so would have meant that the colonists then would have to say that the rain had washed this church to nothing to account for its absence. Smith deplores the gold lust of the mariners.

6. I.e., "Until we saw the ship laden with supposed gold ore, we never thought that Captain Newport was a refiner (of gold ore)." Smith claims ironically that Newport sent Wingfield and Archer, both gentlemen and officers, back to England because they had no skills of use to the colony. In fact, Smith recognized that the colony desperately needed the skills in governance these officers were supposed to have but actually lacked. Thus Smith deplores the gold lust of the leaders of the Virginia Company as well as their inability to establish order in Jamestown.

7. A Powhatan village near Jamestown, on the eastern shore of Charles River.

8. The distance a bow shoots an arrow.

9. A small, light ship that often accompanied a larger ship.

The next day, having feasted us after his ordinary manner, he began to ask us when we would be gone, feigning he sent not for us, neither had he any corn, and his people much less—yet for forty swords he would procure us forty baskets. The president, showing him the men there present that brought him the message and conditions, asked Powhatan how it chanced he became so forgetful. Threat the king concluded the matter with a merry laughter, asking for our commodities. But none he liked without guns and swords, valuing a basket of corn more precious than a basket of copper, saying he could rate[1] his corn but not the copper.

Captain Smith, seeing the intent of this subtle savage, began to deal with him after this manner:

"Powhatan, though I had many courses[2] to have made my provision, yet believing your promises to supply my wants, I neglected all to satisfy your desire. And to testify my love, I send you my men for your building, neglecting mine own. What your people had you have engrossed, forbidding them our trade; and now you think by consuming the time we shall consume for want, not having to fulfill your strange demands. As for swords and guns, I told you long ago I had none to spare. And you must know those I have can keep me from want. Yet steal or wrong you I will not, nor dissolve that friendship we have mutually promised, except you constrain me by our bad usage."

The king,[3] having attentively list'ned to this discourse, promised that both he and his country would spare him what he could, the which within two days they should receive.

"Yet Captain Smith," saith the king, "some doubt I have of your coming hither that makes me not so kindly seek to relieve you as I would. For many do inform me your coming hither is not for trade but to invade my people and possess my country, who dare not come to bring you corn, seeing you thus armed with your men. To free us of this fear, leave aboard your weapons, for here they are needless, we being all friends and forever Powhatans."

With many such discourses they spent the day, quartering that night in the king's houses.

* * * Powhatan began to expostulate the difference of peace and war after this manner:

"Captain Smith, you may understand that I having seen the death of all my people thrice, and not anyone living of those three generations but myself—I know the difference of peace and war better than any in my country. But now I am old and ere long must die, my brethren, namely, Opitchapam, Opechancanough, and Kekataugh, [and] my two sisters and their two daughters are distinctly each other's successors: I wish their experience no less than mine, and your love to them no less than mine to you.

"But this bruit from Nansamund[4] that you are come to destroy my country so much affrighteth all my people as they dare not visit you. What will it avail you to take that by force you may quickly have by love? or to destroy them that provide you food? What can you get by war when we can hide our provisions and fly to the woods? whereby you must famish by wronging us, your friends. And why are you thus jealous of our loves, seeing us unarmed, and both do and are willing still to feed you with that you cannot get but by our labors?

"Think you I am so simple not to know it is better to eat good meat, lie well, and sleep quietly with my women and children, laugh and be merry with you, have copper,

1. Appraise.
2. Opportunities.
3. Powhatan.
4. I.e., this rumor from Nansamund (a Powhatan village near the mouth of the James River). Powhatan rightly claims that the colonists value food, a necessity of life, more than they do copper; he bargains with Smith accordingly.

hatchets, or what I want, being your friend, than be forced to fly from all?—to lie cold in the woods, feed upon acorns, roots, and such trash, and be so hunted by you that I can neither rest, eat, nor sleep, but my tired men must watch, and if a twig but break, everyone crieth THERE COMETH CAPTAIN SMITH!—then must I fly I know not whither, and thus with miserable fear end my miserable life, leaving my pleasures to such youths as you, which through your rash unadvisedness may quickly as miserably end, for want of that you never know where to find.

"Let this therefore assure you of our loves, and every year our friendly trade shall furnish you with corn, and now also, if you would come in friendly manner to see us and not thus with your guns and swords as to invade your foes."

To this subtle discourse the president thus replied:

"Seeing you will not rightly conceive of our words, we strive to make you know our thoughts by our deeds. The vow I made you of my love both myself and my men have kept. As for your promise, I find it every day violated by some of your subjects. Yet, we finding your love and kindness, our custom is so far from being ungrateful that for your sake only we have curbed our thirsting desire of revenge, else had they known as well the cruelty we use to our enemies as our true love and courtesy to our friends.

"And I think your judgment sufficient to conceive as well by the adventures we have undertaken as by the advantage we have by our arms of yours that had we intended you any hurt, long ere this we could have effected it.

"Your people coming to me at James Town are entertained with their bows and arrows without any exceptions, we esteeming it with you as it is with us to wear our arms as our apparel.

"As for the danger of our enemies, in such wars consist our chiefest pleasure. For your riches we have no use. As for the hiding your provision or by your flying to the woods, we shall not so unadvisedly starve as you conclude. Your friendly care in that behalf is needless, for we have a rule to find beyond your knowledge."[5]

Many other discourses they had till at last they began to trade. But the king seeing his will would not be admitted as a law, our guard dispersed,[6] nor our men disarmed, he (sighing) breathed his mind once more in this manner:

"Captain Smith, I never use any werowance[7] so kindly as yourself, yet from you I receive the least kindness of any. Captain Newport gave me swords, copper, clothes, a bed, tools, or what I desired, ever taking what I offered him; and would send away his guns when I entreated him. None doth deny to lie at my feet or refuse to do what I desire, but only you; of whom I can have nothing but what you regard not, and yet you will have whatsoever you demand. Captain Newport you call father, and so you call me. But I see for all us both you will do what you list, and we must both seek to content you. But if you intend so friendly as you say, send hence your arms that I may believe you. For you see the love I bear you doth cause me thus nakedly to forget myself."[8]

Smith, seeing this savage but trifle the time[9] to cut his throat, procured the savages to break the ice that his boat might come to fetch his corn and him, and gave order for more men to come on shore to surprise the king, with whom also he but

5. Smith claims that the colonists could have wiped out the Powhatans long ago had they so desired; in fact, they have allowed the Powhatans to visit Jamestown armed. Smith also claims that the English have a superior knowledge of the sources of food. His boasts are without substance. Historians agree that during these early years of Jamestown, the Powhatans could have destroyed the English. It is certain that the English relied on the Powhatans for food, but bragging of this kind was typical of such negotiations.

6. Surrounding them.

7. The Powhatan term for tribal chief.

8. Powhatan fences verbally with Smith, comparing his meanness to the Indians with Newport's generosity.

9. Waited.

trifled the time till his men were landed; and to keep him from suspicion, entertained the time with this reply:

"Powhatan, you must know as I have but one God I honor but one king; and I live not here as your subject but as your friend to pleasure you with what I can. By the gifts you bestow on me you gain more than by trade. Yet would you visit me as I do you, you should know it is not our custom to sell our courtesies as a vendible commodity. Bring all your country with you for your guard, I will not dislike it as being overjealous.

"But to content you, tomorrow I will leave my arms and trust to your promise. I call you father indeed, and as a father you shall see I will love you. But the small care you have of such a child caused my men persuade me to look to myself."[1]

By this time Powhatan—having knowledge his men were ready whilest the ice was a-breaking—with his luggage, women, and children fled, yet to avoid suspicion left two or three of the women talking with the captain whilest he secretly ran away, and his men that secretly beset the house; which being presently discovered to Captain Smith, with his pistol, sword, and target he made such a passage among these naked devils that at his first shoot they next him tumbled one over another and the rest quickly fled before him, some one way, some another, so that without any hurt, only accompanied with John Russell, he obtained the *corps du guard*.[2]

When they perceived him so well escaped and with his eighteen men—for he had no more with him ashore—to the uttermost of their skill they sought excuses to dissemble the matter. And Powhatan to excuse his flight and the sudden coming of this multitude sent our captain a great bracelet and a chain of pearl by an ancient orator[3] that bespoke us to this purpose, perceiving even then from our pinnace a barge and men departing and coming unto us:

"Captain Smith, our werowance is fled, fearing your guns, and knowing when the ice was broken there would come more men, sent these numbers but to guard his corn from stealing that might happen without your knowledge. Now though some be hurt by your misprision,[4] yet Powhatan is your friend and so will forever continue. Now since the ice is open, he would have you send away your corn and if you would have his company, send away also your guns which so affrighteth his people that they dare not come to you as he promised they should."

Then having provided baskets for our men to carry our corn to the boats, they kindly offered their service to guard our arms that none should steal them. A great many they were of goodly, well-proportioned fellows as grim as devils. Yet the very sight of cocking our matches and being to let fly,[5] a few words caused them to leave their bows and arrows to our guard, and bear down our corn on their own backs. We needed not importune them to make dispatch, but our barges being left on the ooze by the ebb caused us stay till the next high water midnight tide, so that we returned again to our old quarter, [and] spent that half night with such mirth as though we never had suspected or intended anything.

Powhatan and his Dutchmen bursting with desire to have the head of Captain Smith (for if they could but kill him they thought all was theirs), neglected not any

---

1. Smith believes Powhatan wants to kill him; he therefore determines to take him prisoner. He states that he is not a subject of Powhatan but, rather, of another king, i.e., James I. He further contrasts his belief in one God with the Powhatans' pantheism.
2. Military advantage.

3. Spokesman for the Powhatans.
4. Mistake; the Powhatans' spokesman claims that Smith is responsible for the wounding of his men and that their chief is Smith's friend.
5. Priming our guns, preparing to fire.

opportunity to effect his purpose.[6] The Indians with all the merry sports they could devise spent the time till night. Then they all returned to Powhatan, who all this time was making ready his forces to surprise the house and him at supper.

Notwithstanding, the eternal all-seeing God did prevent him and by a strange means. For Pocahontas, his dearest jewel and daughter, in that dark night came through the irksome woods and told our captain great cheer should be sent us by and by. But Powhatan and all the power he could make would after come kill us all if they that brought it could not kill us with our own weapons when we were at supper. Therefore if we would live she wished us presently to be gone. Such things as she delighted in he[7] would have given her, but with the tears running down her cheeks she said she durst not be seen to have any, for if Powhatan should know it, she were but dead, and so she ran away by herself as she came.

Within less than an hour came eight or ten lusty fellows with great platters of venison and other victual, very importunate to have us put out our matches,[8] whose smoke made them sick, and sit down to our victual. But the captain made them taste every dish, which done he sent some of them back to Powhatan to bid him make haste for he was prepared for his coming. As for them, he knew they came to betray him at his supper, but he would prevent them and all their other intended villainies, so that they might be gone. Not long after came more messengers to see what news. Not long after them others. Thus we spent the night as vigilantly as they till it was high water, yet seemed to the savages as friendly as they to us. And that we were so desirous to give Powhatan content as he requested, we did leave him Edward Brynton to kill him fowl and the Dutchmen to finish his house, thinking at our return from Pamaunkee[9] the frost would be gone, and then we might find a better opportunity if necessity did occasion it, little dreaming yet of the Dutchmen's treachery, whose humor well suited this verse—

> Is any free that may not live as freely as he list?
> Let us live so, then w'are as free and brutish as the best.[1]

END OF PERSPECTIVES: ENGLAND, BRITAIN, AND THE WORLD

William Shakespeare
1564–1616

English colonists venturing to the New World carried with them an English Bible; if they owned a single secular book, it was probably the works of William Shakespeare. A humanist scripture of sorts, his works have never hardened into doctrine; rather, they have lent themselves to a myriad range of interpretations, each shaped by particular interests, tastes, and expectations. Ben Jonson's line—"He was not of an age, but for all time!"—describes the appeal Shakespeare has had for speakers of English and the many other languages into which his works have been translated.

---

6. The Indians made allies of the Dutch, who were competing with the English for trade in the New World.
7. I.e., Smith.
8. A match was a wick or a cord, usually made of hemp or cotton, that was kept lit to use for firing guns or cannons; the Powhatans did not want the colonists to have a way to use their weapons.
9. A Powhatan village on the Pamaunkee (now the Charles) River.
1. Smith implies a distinction between living as you wish, which is license, and living under law, which is liberty. That the "best" should be bestial is, of course, ironic.

Attributed to John Taylor,
Portrait of William Shakespeare,
c. 1610.

Shakespeare was born in the provincial town of Stratford-on-Avon, a three-day journey from London by horse or carriage. His father, John Shakespeare, was a glover and local justice of the peace; his mother, Mary Arden, came from a family that owned considerable land in the county. He probably went to a local grammar school where he learned Latin and read histories of the ancient world. Jonson's disparaging comment, that Shakespeare knew "small Latin and less Greek," must not be taken too seriously. Shakespeare (unlike Jonson) was not classically inclined, but his mature works reveal a mind that was extraordinarily well informed and acutely aware of rhetorical techniques and logical argument. At eighteen Shakespeare married Anne Hathaway, who was twenty-six; in the next three years they had a daughter, Susanna, and then twins, Hamnet and Judith. Six years later, perhaps after periods of teaching school in Stratford, he went to London, eventually (in 1594) to join one of the great theatrical companies of the day, the Chamberlain's Men. It was with this company that he began his career as actor, manager, and playwright. In 1599 the troupe began to put on plays at the Globe, an outdoor theater in Southwark, not far from the other principal theaters of the day—the Rose, the Bear Garden, and the Swan—and across the river from the city of London itself. Because these theaters were outside city limits, in a district known as "the liberties," they were free from the control of authorities responsible for civic order; in effect, the theater provided a place in which all kinds of ideas and ways of life, whether conventional or not, could be represented, examined, and criticized. When James I acceded to the throne in 1603, Shakespeare's company became the King's Men and played also at court and at Blackfriars, an indoor theater in London. Some critics think that the change in venue necessitated a degree of allusiveness and innuendo that was not evident in earlier productions.

During the years Shakespeare was writing for the theater, the populations of Europe were periodically devastated by the plague, and city authorities were obliged to close places of public gathering, including theaters. Shakespeare provided plays for seasons in which the theaters in London were open, composing them at lightning speed and helping to stage productions on very short notice. The plays that we now accept as Shakespeare's fall roughly into several general categories: first, the histories, largely based on the chronicles of the Tudor historian Raphael Holinshed, and the Roman plays, inspired by Plutarch's *Lives of the Ancient Romans,* written in Greek and translated by Sir Thomas North; second, the comedies, often set in the romantic world of the English countryside or an Italian town; third, the tragedies, some of which explore the dark legends of the past; and fourth, a group in the mixed genre of tragicomedy but also called, after critics in the nineteenth century, the romances. A fifth, somewhat anomalous group—*All's Well That Ends Well, Measure for Measure,* and *Troilus and Cressida*—falls between comedy and satire; these plays are usually termed "problem comedies."

The early phase of Shakespeare's career, the decade beginning in the late 1580s, saw the first cycle of his English histories. In four plays (known as the first tetralogy) this cycle depicted events in the reigns of Henry VI and Richard III and concluded by dramatizing the accession of the first Tudor monarch, Henry VII. Fascinated by the fate of peoples governed by feeble or oppressive rulers, Shakespeare expressed his loathing of tyranny by showing how the misgovernment of a weak king can lead to despotic rule. The cycle ends with the death of the tyrant, Richard III, and the accession of the Duke of Richmond, later Henry VII (Elizabeth's grandfather)—an action that celebrates the founder of the Tudor dynasty and the providence that had selected this family to bring peace to England. A later play, *King John,* concerns an earlier monarch whose claim to the throne is suspect; here divine right, having validated the succession of the Tudor monarchy in the first tetralogy, is made doubtful by a monarch's own viciousness. The play implies a question that Shakespeare continues to ask of history for the rest of his career: in what sense may divine right to be understood as a principle of monarchic rule? History, as Shakespeare will go on to represent it, no longer clearly demonstrates the triumph of justice but rather shows the interrelatedness of good and evil motives that end in morally ambiguous action. The first of the Roman plays, *The Tragedy of Titus Andronicus*, which tells of the Roman general's revenge for the rape of his daughter Lavinia, and the early comedies, *The Taming of the Shrew*, *The Comedy of Errors*, *Two Gentlemen of Verona*, and *Love's Labor's Lost*, which depict the effects of mistaken identity and misunderstood speech, illustrate other themes that Shakespeare will continue to represent: the terrible consequences of the search for revenge and the unfortunate, as well as salutary, self-deceptions of love.

The second phase, culminating in productions around 1600, is marked by more and subtler comedy: *A Midsummer Night's Dream*, *The Merchant of Venice*, *The Merry Wives of Windsor*, *Much Ado About Nothing*, *As You Like It*, and *Twelfth Night*. These plays insert into plots focusing primarily on the courtship of young couples a dramatic commentary on darker kinds of human desire: a longing for possessions; a wish to control others, particularly children; and a self-love so intense that it leads to fantasy and delusion. A romantic tragedy of this period, *Romeo and Juliet*, shows how the gross unreason sustaining a family feud and a mysteriously malevolent fate combine to destroy the future of lovers. A second cycle of four English histories, beginning with the deposition of Richard II and ending in the triumphs of Henry V and the birth of Henry VI, reveals how Shakespeare complicates the genre. An ostensible motive for the second tetralogy was the celebration of an English monarchy that had been preserved through the ages by God's will. Yet the actions of even the least controversial of its kings are questionable: Henry V's conquest of France is driven by greed as much as by his claim to the French throne, which is represented as dubious even in the playtext. A second Roman play, *The Tragedy of Julius Caesar*, takes up the question of tyranny in relation to the liberty inherent in a republic; the play seems most tragic when its action suggests that the Roman people do not recognize the sacrifices that are necessary to preserve such freedom and even regard freedom itself as negligible. As a whole, these plays demonstrate the characteristics of Shakespeare's mature style. Certain recurring images unify the plays thematically and, more important, link them to contemporary habits of speech as well as to the intellectual discourse of the period. Visual images—the "I" and the "eye" of the lover—often clarify the language of love, and figures denoting the well-being of different kinds of "corporation," including the human body, the family, and the body politic, signal the comprehensive order that was supposed to govern relations among all the elements of creation.

Incorporating many of the themes in the "problem comedies," the tragedies of the same period preoccupied Shakespeare for the seven years following the accession of James I: *Hamlet*, *Othello*, *King Lear*, *Macbeth*, *Antony and Cleopatra*, and *Coriolanus*, together with *Timon of Athens*, a play that was apparently written in collaboration with Thomas Middleton. *All's Well That Ends Well* and *Measure for Measure* illustrate societies that contain rather than reject sordid or unregenerate characters, both noble and common, and thus provide opportunities for comic endings to situations that might otherwise have ended in tragedy. And making much of the need for order but exemplifying the deep disorder of the military societies of Greece and Troy, the characters in *Troilus and Cressida* reveal the extent to which Shakespeare could imagine language as ironic and the human spirit as utterly possessed by a cynical need to turn every occasion to its own advantage. These plays serve to introduce tragedies of unprecedented scope.

Featuring heroes who overreach the limits of their place in life and so fail to fulfill their obligations to themselves and their dependents, Shakespeare's later tragedies embrace a wider range of human experience than can be explained by traditional conceptions of sin and fate. Profoundly complex in their treatment of motivation and the operations of the will, the tragedies entertain the idea of a beneficent deity who both permits terrible suffering and infuses, to use Hamlet's words, a "special providence in the fall of a sparrow." They reveal the blinding egotism that causes fatal misperceptions of character, motive, and action; their heroes are at once terribly in error and also strangely sympathetic. The human capacity for evil is perhaps most fully realized in the characters of women: the bestial daughters of King Lear, Goneril and Regan; the diabolical Lady Macbeth; the shamelessly duplicitous Cleopatra. Yet even they are not entirely unsympathetic; in many ways their behavior responds to the challenges that other, essentially more authoritative characters represent. The romances—*Pericles, Cymbeline, The Winter's Tale,* and *The Tempest*—round out the final phase of Shakespeare's dramatic career, representing (like the comedies) the restoration of family harmony and (like the histories) the return of good government. The deeply troubling divisions within families and states that characterize the tragedies are the basis for the restorative unions in the romances. Their depiction of passages of time and space that allow providential recoveries of health and prosperity to both individual characters and whole bodies politic are largely owing to the intervention of women. Unlike the women of the tragedies, the daughters and wives of the romances are generative in the broadest sense. They heal their fathers and husbands by restoring to their futures the possibility of descendents and therefore of dynastic continuity. Their agency is, in turn, sustained by forces identified as divine and outside history. *Henry VIII,* a history, and *Two Noble Kinsmen,* a romance, both probably composed jointly with John Fletcher, conclude Shakespeare's career as a dramatist.

Shakespeare also wrote narrative and lyric poems of great power, notably *Venus and Adonis, The Rape of Lucrece,* and a cycle of 154 sonnets. In a bold departure from tradition the sonnets celebrate the poet's steadfast love for a young man (never identified), his competitive rivalry with another poet (sometimes identified as Christopher Marlowe), and his troubled relationship with a woman who has dark features. The cycle encourages an interpretation that accounts for its romantic elements, but it also thwarts any obvious construction of events. It is thought that most of the sonnets were composed in the mid-1590s, although they were not published until 1609, apparently without Shakespeare's oversight. Their order therefore cannot be assigned to Shakespeare, and for this reason alone their function as narrative must remain problematic. Still, the reader can trace their representation of successive relations between persons and themes: the young man, although himself derelict in the duties of friendship, will remain beloved by the poet and be made immortal by his verse, while the dark lady, who is unscrupulous and afflicted with venereal disease, receives only expressions of desire and lust, shadowed by the poet's disdain and self-loathing.

In a sense, Shakespeare has always been up to date. True, his language is not what is heard today, and his characters are shaped by forces within his culture, not ours. Yet we continue to see his plays on stage and in film, sometimes as recreations of the productions that historians of theater think he knew and saw but more often as reconceived with the addition of modern costumes, settings, and music as well as some strategic cutting of the dramatic text. Earlier periods produced their own kinds of Shakespeare. The Restoration stage, with scenery that allowed audiences to imagine they were looking through a window to life itself, put on plays that were embellished and trimmed to satisfy the taste of the time. Some producers omitted characters who were considered superfluous (the porter in *Macbeth*); others added characters who were judged essential for balance (Miranda's sister, Dorinda, in *The Tempest*). *King Lear* acquired a happy ending when Edgar married Cordelia. No one production of any period has defined a play entirely; every director has had his or her vision of what Shakespeare meant an audience to see. These reinterpretations testify to the perennial vitality of a playwright who was indeed, as Jonson said, "for all time."

 For additional resources on Shakespeare, go to *The Longman Anthology of British Literature* Web site at www.myliteraturekit.com.

THE SONNETS   The entire sequence numbers 154 sonnets. The first fourteen encourage a young man to marry and have children and may have been commissioned by his family. Neither the young man nor his family has been identified, although some readers have thought Henry Wriosthesley, Earl of Southampton, a possible subject. In Sonnet 15, Shakespeare turns to a related topic: the young man will be made eternal not only by his descendants but by the poet's praise of him in verse. Sonnet 20 initiates a long sequence of sonnets addressed to a young man as the poet's lover; whether he is the man who featured in the earlier sonnets on procreation is unclear, but it has generally been assumed so. Beginning with Sonnet 78, the poet complains that a rival poet is stealing his subject—the young man's virtue and grace—to the detriment of his own poetry. Who Shakespeare's rival is (or whether he is in fact a single person) is not known, although some readers have considered Christopher Marlowe a possibility. A final set of twenty-eight sonnets introduces a new character to the sequence, a figure often referred to as "the dark lady," who is the lover of both the poet and the young man. The threesome make up a dramatic unity that is fraught with tension and anguish.

Sonnets

1

	From fairest creatures we desire increase,	
	That thereby beauty's rose might never die,	
	But as the riper° should by time decease,	*the older person*
	His tender heir might bear his memory;	
5	But thou, contracted° to thine own bright eyes,	*engaged, shrunk*
	Feed'st thy light's flame with self-substantial fuel,	
	Making a famine where abundance lies,	
	Thyself thy foe, to thy sweet self too cruel.	
	Thou that art now the world's fresh ornament	
10	And only herald to the gaudy spring,	
	Within thine own bud buriest thy content,	
	And, tender churl, mak'st waste in niggarding.°	*hoarding*
	Pity the world, or else this glutton be:	
	To eat the world's due, by the grave and thee.[1]	

12

	When I do count the clock that tells the time,	
	And see the brave day sunk in hideous night;	
	When I behold the violet past prime,	
	And sable° curls all silvered o'er with white;	*dark*
5	When lofty trees I see barren of leaves	
	Which erst from heat did canopy the herd,	
	And summer's green, all girded up in sheaves,	
	Borne on the bier with white and bristly beard,[2]	
	Then of thy beauty do I question make	
10	That thou among the wastes of time must go,	
	Since sweets and beauties do themselves forsake[3]	

---

1. Have pity on the world and do not consume your own substance by refusing to engender the child you owe now to the world and finally to the grave.
2. The harvest of grain, once green, is gathered in bun-
dles; each stalk ends in clusters of kernels protected by husks that resemble a white and bristling beard.
3. Beauties fade, seeming to forsake themselves.

And die as fast as they see others grow;
   And nothing 'gainst Time's scythe can make defense
   Save breed, to brave° him when he takes thee hence.   *defy*

15

When I consider every thing that grows
Holds in perfection but a little moment,
That this huge stage presenteth naught but shows
Whereon the stars in secret influence comment;[4]

5 When I perceive that men as plants increase,
Cheerèd and checked even by the selfsame sky,
Vaunt° in their youthful sap, at height decrease,   *boast*
And wear their brave state out of memory;°   *until forgotten*
Then the conceit° of this inconstant stay   *idea*

10 Sets you most rich in youth before my sight,
Where wasteful Time debateth with Decay
To change your day of youth to sullied° night,   *dark*
   And all in war with Time for love of you,
   As he takes from you, I ingraft you new.[5]

18

Shall I compare thee to a summer's day?
Thou art more lovely and more temperate.
Rough winds do shake the darling buds of May,
And summer's lease hath all too short a date.°   *duration*

5 Sometimes too hot the eye of heaven shines,
And often is his gold complexion dimmed;
And every fair from fair sometimes declines,
By chance or nature's changing course untrimmed.°   *stripped bare*
But thy eternal summer shall not fade

10 Nor lose possession of that fair thou ow'st;°   *own*
Nor shall Death brag thou wanderest in his shade,
When in eternal lines° to time thou grow'st.   *of verse*
   So long as men can breathe or eyes can see,
   So long lives this, and this gives life to thee.

20

A woman's face with Nature's own hand painted
Hast thou, the master-mistress of my passion;[6]
A woman's gentle heart, but not acquainted
With shifting change, as is false women's fashion;

5 An eye more bright than theirs, less false in rolling,°   *straying*
Gilding the object whereupon it gazeth;
A man in hue, all hues in his controlling,[7]

---

4. Human action is a kind of show, influenced by the stars or heavenly forces.
5. Renew by grafting new beauty in verse.
6. Feminine in appearance, the young man is both a master and a mistress of the poet's passion. This is the first of a series of sonnets in which Shakespeare addresses the young man in clearly erotic language.
7. A man in appearance, he determines the nature of what he sees, what is apparent to him.

Which steals men's eyes and women's souls amazeth.
And for a woman wert thou first created,
10   Till Nature, as she wrought thee, fell a-doting,°   *in love*
And by addition me of thee defeated,[8]
By adding one thing to my purpose nothing.
    But since she pricked thee out for women's pleasure,
    Mine be thy love and thy love's use their treasure.

29

When, in disgrace with fortune and men's eyes,
I all alone beweep my outcast state,
And trouble deaf heaven with my bootless° cries,   *unavailing*
And look upon myself and curse my fate,
5   Wishing me like to one more rich in hope,
Featured like him, like him with friends possessed,
Desiring this man's art and that man's scope,°   *powers*
With what I most enjoy contented least;
Yet in these thoughts myself almost despising,
10   Haply° I think on thee, and then my state,   *perhaps*
Like to the lark at break of day arising
From sullen earth, sings hymns at heaven's gate;
    For thy sweet love remembered such wealth brings
    That then I scorn to change° my state with kings.   *exchange*

30

When to the sessions° of sweet silent thought[9]   *law courts*
I summon up remembrance of things past,
I sigh the lack of many a thing I sought,
And with old woes new wail my dear time's waste.[1]
5   Then can I drown an eye, unused to flow,
For precious friends hid in death's dateless° night,   *endless*
And weep afresh love's long since cancelled woe,
And moan th'expense° of many a vanished sight.   *what it cost*
Then can I grieve at grievances foregone,
10   And heavily° from woe to woe tell o'er   *sorrowfully*
The sad account of fore-bemoanèd moan,
Which I new pay as if not paid before.[2]
    But if the while I think on thee, dear friend,
    All losses are restored, and sorrows end.

---

8. The last four lines of the sonnet are full of double meanings: the thing loving nature adds to the young man is a penis; this points or "pricks" him out for women's pleasure or "use" (with the added suggestion that his body is capital, which through usury generates interest); but the poet reserves for himself the young man's love, which is beyond commerce and has no price.
9. The conceit governing this imagery depends on the poet's association of his sense of guilt at his misdeeds with a notion of a debt. He represents himself as a debtor who cannot discharge what he owes to others because the complaints against him remain constantly fresh in his mind. He also figures as in debt to himself, as it is his time that he has wasted in reviewing these complaints. His debts are paid, however, when he thinks of his friend.
1. I bemoan the waste of my time by remembering anew former sadness.
2. I add up the sorrows and complaints against me that I have already accounted for; I pay for them as if they were new debts; so I add to the sum I have wasted.

31

Thy bosom is endearèd with all hearts,
Which I by lacking have supposèd dead,
And there reigns love and all love's loving parts,
And all those friends which I thought buried.[3]

5 How many a holy and obsequious° tear   *mournful*
Hath dear religious love stol'n from mine eye
As interest of the dead, which now appear
But things removed that hidden in thee lie!
Thou art the grave where buried love doth live,
10 Hung with the trophies of my lovers gone,
Who all their parts° of me to thee did give;   *shares*
That due of many now is thine alone.
    Their images I loved I view in thee,[4]
    And thou, all they, hast all the all of me.

33

Full many a glorious morning have I seen
Flatter the mountaintops with sovereign eye,
Kissing with golden face the meadows green,
Gilding pale streams with heavenly alchemy;
5 Anon° permit the basest clouds to ride   *soon*
With ugly rack° on his celestial face,   *driven clouds*
And from the forlorn world his visage hide,
Stealing unseen to west with this disgrace.
Even so my sun one early morn did shine
10 With all-triumphant splendor on my brow.
But out, alack! He was but one hour mine;
The region° cloud hath masked him from me now.   *of the upper air*
    Yet him for this my love no whit disdaineth;
    Suns of the world may stain when heaven's sun staineth.[5]

35

No more be grieved at that which thou hast done.
Roses have thorns, and silver fountains mud,
Clouds and eclipses stain both moon and sun,
And loathsome canker° lives in sweetest bud.   *worm*
5 All men make faults, and even I in this,
Authorizing thy trespass with compare,°   *comparisons*
Myself corrupting, salving thy amiss,
Excusing thy sins more than thy sins are.
For to thy sensual fault I bring in sense°—   *reason*

3. I.e., my past loves seem to live again in your bosom; the affection they had is now made over to you.
4. Here Shakespeare plays with a convention of courtly love: the virtues of all previous loves are said to be summed up in a present love, who embodies a universal perfection.
5. If the sun may be covered by clouds, so too the suns (or sons) of the world may dim in their affections. This is the first of the poet's laments for his lover's insincerity.

10   Thy adverse party° is thy advocate—   *accuser*
      And 'gainst myself a lawful plea commence.
      Such civil war is in my love and hate
           That I an accessary needs must be
           To that sweet thief which sourly robs from me.

                                    55

      Not marble nor the gilded monuments
      Of princes shall outlive this powerful rhyme,
      But you shall shine more bright in these contents
      Than unswept stone besmeared with sluttish° time.   *dirty*
5   When wasteful war shall statues overturn,
      And broils° root out the work of masonry,   *uprisings*
      Nor° Mars his sword nor war's quick fire shall burn   *neither*
      The living record of your memory.
      'Gainst death and all-oblivious° enmity   *casting into oblivion*
10   Shall you pace forth; your praise shall still find room
      Even in the eyes of all posterity
      That wear this world out to the ending doom.°   *judgment day*
           So, till the judgment that yourself° arise,   *when you yourself*
           You live in this, and dwell in lovers' eyes.

                                    60

      Like as the waves make towards the pebbled shore,
      So do our minutes hasten to their end;
      Each changing place with that which goes before,
      In sequent° toil all forwards do contend.°   *successive / strive*
5   Nativity, once in the main° of light,   *sea*
      Crawls to maturity, wherewith being crowned,
      Crookèd eclipses 'gainst his glory fight,
      And Time that gave doth now his gift confound.°   *destroy*
      Time doth transfix° the flourish set on youth   *puncture*
10   And delves° the parallels in beauty's brow,   *digs*
      Feeds on the rarities of nature's truth,
      And nothing stands but for his scythe to mow.
           And yet to times in hope my verse shall stand,
           Praising thy worth despite his cruel hand.

                                    71

      No longer mourn for me when I am dead
      Than° you shall hear the surly sullen bell   *then*
      Give warning to the world that I am fled
      From this vile world with vildest° worms to dwell.   *vilest*
5   Nay, if you read this line, remember not
      The hand that writ it, for I love you so,
      That I in your sweet thoughts would be forgot,
      If thinking on me then should make you woe.°   *grieve you*
      O if, I say, you look upon this verse,
10   When I, perhaps, compounded am with clay,

Do not so much as my poor name rehearse,°   *repeat*
But let your love ev'n with my life decay,
  Lest the wise world should look into your moan,
  And mock you with me after I am gone.[6]

73

That time of year thou mayst in me behold
When yellow leaves, or none, or few, do hang
Upon those boughs which shake against the cold,
Bare ruined choirs[7] where late the sweet birds sang.
In me thou seest the twilight of such day
As after sunset fadeth in the west,
Which by and by black night doth take away,
Death's second self, that seals up all in rest.
In me thou seest the glowing of such fire
That on the ashes of his youth doth lie
As the deathbed whereon it must expire,
Consumed with that which it was nourished by.
  This thou perceiv'st, which makes thy love more strong,
  To love that well which thou must leave ere long.

80

O, how I faint when I of you do write,
Knowing a better spirit° doth use your name,   *the rival poet*
And in the praise thereof spends all his might
To make me tongue-tied, speaking of your fame!
But since your worth, wide as the ocean is,
The humble as° the proudest sail doth bear,   *as well as*
My saucy bark, inferior far to his,
On your broad main° doth willfully appear.   *sea*
Your shallowest° help will hold me up afloat,   *slightest*
Whilst he upon your soundless° deep doth ride;   *unfathomable*
Or, being wrecked, I am a worthless boat,
He of tall building° and of goodly pride.   *construction*
  Then if he thrive and I be cast away,
  The worst was this: my love was my decay.°   *ruin*

86

Was it the proud full sail of his great verse,
Bound for the prize° of all-too-precious you,   *captive booty*
That did my ripe thoughts in my brain inhearse,°   *entomb*
Making their tomb the womb wherein they grew?
Was it his spirit,° by spirits taught to write   *genius*
Above a mortal pitch, that struck me dead?[8]

6. Lest people seeing your grief at my death should ridicule you because of your association with me.
7. The choir is the section of a church reserved for the singers in the choir. "Choir" puns on "quire," the gathering of pages in a book, and thus recalls the "leaves" in line 2.

8. Shakespeare ironically suggests that the rival poet writes with supernatural help, or at least what he claims is supernatural help. Shakespeare later implies that this help is actually no more than a gull's (trickster's) intelligence or gossip.

No, neither he, nor his compeers by night
Giving him aid, my verse astonishèd.
He, nor that affable familiar ghost°   *spirit*
10   Which nightly gulls him with intelligence,
As victors of my silence cannot boast;
I was not sick of any fear from thence.
    But when your countenance filled up his line,[9]
    Then lacked I matter; that enfeebled mine.°   *my verse*

87

Farewell! Thou art too dear for my possessing,
And like enough thou know'st thy estimate.°   *value*
The charter of thy worth gives thee releasing;[1]
My bonds in thee are all determinate.°   *ended*
5   For how do I hold thee but by thy granting,
And for that riches where is my deserving?
The cause of this fair gift in me is wanting,
And so my patent[2] back again is swerving.
Thyself thou gav'st, thy own worth then not knowing,
10   Or me, to whom thou gav'st it, else mistaking;
So thy great gift, upon misprision° growing,   *error*
Comes home again, on better judgment making.
    Thus have I had thee as a dream doth flatter,
    In sleep a king, but waking no such matter.

93

So shall I live, supposing thou art true,
Like a deceivèd husband; so love's face
May still seem love to me, though altered new,
Thy looks with me, thy heart in other place.
5   For there can live no hatred in thine eye,
Therefore in that I cannot know thy change.°   *infidelity*
In many's looks the false heart's history
Is writ in moods and frowns and wrinkles strange,
But heaven in thy creation did decree
10   That in thy face sweet love should ever dwell;
Whate'er thy thoughts or thy heart's workings be,
Thy looks should nothing thence but sweetness tell.
    How like Eve's apple doth thy beauty grow,
    If thy sweet virtue answer not thy show![3]

94

They that have pow'r to hurt, and will do none,[4]
That do not do the thing they most do show,°   *appear to do*

9. When you became his subject.
1. You are worth so much that you can pay off all obligations you owe me; in other words, I have no right to you.
2. Deed granting a monopoly.
3. Like Eve's deceptively attractive apple, the young man's beauty is a kind of temptation that leads to the death of him who succumbs to it.

4. The poem warns against a loss of self-control, which is associated with a loss of self-ownership. Persons (the undefined "they" of the sonnet) can lend themselves to others, their stewards, but at the same time, they retain control over their own great virtue. If they succumb to evil or ill-will, however, they risk becoming very corrupt.

Who moving others are themselves as stone,
Unmovèd, cold, and to temptation slow—
5   They rightly° do inherit heaven's graces,   *justly*
And husband° nature's riches from expense;   *protect*
They are the lords and owners of their faces,°   *appearances*
Others but stewards of their excellence.
The summer's flow'r is to the summer sweet,
10 Though to itself it only live and die;
But if that flow'r with base° infection meet,   *common*
The basest° weed outbraves his dignity.   *humblest*
    For sweetest things turn sourest by their deeds;
    Lilies that fester smell far worse than weeds.

104

To me, fair friend, you never can be old,
For, as you were when first your eye I eyed,
Such seems your beauty still. Three winters cold
Have from the forests shook three summers' pride,
5   Three beauteous springs to yellow autumn turned
In process of the seasons have I seen,
Three April perfumes in three hot Junes burned,
Since first I saw you fresh, which yet are green.
Ah, yet doth beauty, like a dial[5] hand,
10 Steal from his figure and no pace perceived.
So your sweet hue, which methinks still doth stand,
Hath motion, and mine eye may be deceived,
    For fear of which, hear this, thou age unbred:°   *unborn*
    Ere you were born was beauty's summer dead.

106

When in the chronicle of wasted° time   *past*
I see descriptions of the fairest wights,°   *people*
And beauty making beautiful old rhyme
In praise of ladies dead and lovely knights,
5   Then, in the blazon° of sweet beauty's best,   *catalogue*
Of hand, of foot, of lip, of eye, of brow,
I see their antique pen would have expressed
Even such a beauty as you master° now.   *possess*
So all their praises are but prophecies
10 Of this our time, all you prefiguring;
And, for° they looked but with divining eyes,   *because*
They had not skill enough your worth to sing.
    For we, which now behold these present days,
    Have eyes to wonder, but lack tongues to praise.[6]

---

5. Beauty is like the hand of a clock, a dial; it moves slowly but inexorably away from the height of the hour.
6. The poets of antiquity could not describe your perfec-

tion because they could only guess at it; we recognize your perfection but lack the skill to describe it.

107

Not mine own fears nor the prophetic soul
Of the wide world dreaming on things to come[7]
Can yet the lease of my true love control,
Supposed as forfeit to a confined doom.°   *at a set time*
5   The mortal moon hath her eclipse endured,
And the sad augurs mock their own presage;
Incertainties now crown themselves assured,
And peace proclaims olives of endless age.[8]
Now with the drops of this most balmy time[9]
10   My love looks fresh, and Death to me subscribes,°   *yields*
Since, spite of him, I'll live in this poor rhyme,
While he insults° o'er dull and speechless tribes;   *triumphs*
    And thou in this shalt find thy monument,
    When tyrants' crests and tombs of brass are spent.°   *worn away*

116

Let me not to the marriage of true minds
Admit impediments. Love is not love
Which alters when it alteration finds,°   *in the beloved*
Or bends with the remover to remove.
5   O, no, it is an ever-fixèd mark°   *landmark*
That looks on tempests and is never shaken;
It is the star to every wandering bark,
Whose worth's unknown, although his height be taken.[1]
Love's not Time's fool, though rosy lips and cheeks
10   Within his bending sickle's compass° come;   *range*
Love alters not with his brief hours and weeks,
But bears it out even to the edge of doom.°   *judgment day*
    If this be error and upon me proved,
    I never writ, nor no man ever loved.

123

No, Time, thou shalt not boast that I do change.
Thy pyramids[2] built up with newer might
To me are nothing novel, nothing strange;
They are but dressings of a former sight.
5   Our dates are brief, and therefore we admire

---

7. Shakespeare may have had in mind the ancient concept of *anima mundi* (literally, a world soul), which was imagined as breathing life into all creation.

8. A supposedly dangerous lunar eclipse has passed, and those who predicted disaster now mock their own predictions. The moon may be Elizabeth I, who died in 1603; the endless peace to follow may be the one that James I negotiated with the Spanish in 1604. Or the moon's eclipse may figure Elizabeth's sixty-third year, a numerologically suspect period; in this case the ensuing peace describes a time in which anxiety over the future of the kingdom diminished,

or "uncertainties" were "assured," i.e., became certainties.

9. A time that is restorative, as from the application of a medicinal ointment; a possible reference to the coronation of James I, celebrated by anointing the monarch with balm and other rituals.

1. The star by which ships navigate by measuring its altitude from the horizon (known values) is itself beyond valuation.

2. Any imposing structure; those built recently, "with newer might," are reconceptions, "dressings," of former structures.

What thou dost foist upon us that is old,
And rather make them born to our desire
Than think that we before have heard them told.
Thy registers° and thee I both defy,   *records*
10 Not wondering at the present nor the past,
For thy records and° what we see doth lie,   *and also*
Made more or less by thy continual haste.
    This I do vow and this shall ever be:
    I will be true, despite thy scythe and thee.

124

If my dear love were but the child of state,
It might for Fortune's bastard be unfathered,
As subject to Time's love or to Time's hate,
Weeds among weeds, or flowers with flowers gathered.[3]
5 No, it was builded far from accident;
It suffers not in smiling pomp, nor falls
Under the blow of thrallèd° discontent,   *enslaved*
Whereto th' inviting time our fashion° calls.   *manner*
It fears not Policy,° that heretic,   *expediency*
10 Which works on leases of short-numbered hours,
But all alone stands hugely politic,[4]
That it nor grows with heat nor drowns with showers.
    To this I witness call the fools of Time,
    Which die for goodness, who have lived for crime.[5]

126

O thou, my lovely boy, who in thy power
Dost hold Time's fickle glass,° his sickle hour;   *hourglass*
Who hast by waning grown, and therein show'st
Thy lovers withering as thy sweet self grow'st;
5 If Nature, sovereign mistress over wrack,°   *destruction*
As thou goest onwards, still will pluck thee back,
She keeps thee to this purpose, that her skill
May Time disgrace and wretched minutes kill.[6]
Yet fear her, O thou minion° of her pleasure!   *slave*
10 She may detain, but not still keep, her treasure.
    Her audit, though delayed, answered must be,
    And her quietus° is to render thee.[7]   *settlement*

---

3. If my love for you were merely a product of circumstance, it would be no more than Fortune's bastard and not have a father; it would be subject to accidents, both good and bad.
4. His love is beyond the expedient maneuvers of mere "policy" because it is itself "politic" or a state.
5. This enigmatic couplet may mean that those who have lived as criminals and then die for goodness are Time's fools because deathbed repentance is folly; or that those who have lived as criminals and then die in a good cause are Time's fools in the sense that everyone who resists the temporizing ways of the world is a fool.
6. His lover's power can hold back time and prevent his sickle from mowing down his green youth; paradoxically, while others grow old, he grows young. Nature permits this expressly to defy Time.
7. Yet Nature owes you to Time and will pay her debt by handing you over at last. The sonnet ends short of the 14 lines the form demands, as if to emphasize the idea of brevity.

128[8]

How oft, when thou my music play'st[9]
Upon that blessed wood whose motion sounds
With thy sweet fingers when thou gently sway'st
The wiry concord that mine ear confounds,[1]
5   Do I envy those jacks° that nimble leap   *keys*
To kiss the tender inward of thy hand,
Whilst my poor lips, which should that harvest reap,
At the wood's boldness by° thee blushing stand.   *alongside*
To be so tickled they° would change their state   *his lips*
10   And situation with those dancing chips,
O'er whom thy fingers walk with gentle gait,
Making dead wood more blest° than living lips.   *happier*
    Since saucy jacks so happy are in this,
    Give them thy fingers, me thy lips to kiss.

129

The expense° of spirit in a waste of shame[2]   *dissipation*
Is lust in action; and, till action, lust
Is perjured, murderous, bloody, full of blame,
Savage, extreme, rude, cruel, not to trust,
5   Enjoyed no sooner but despised straight,°   *immediately*
Past reason hunted, and no sooner had
Past reason hated, as a swallowed bait
On purpose laid to make the taker mad;[3]
Mad in pursuit, and in possession so;°   *also*
10   Had, having, and in quest to have, extreme;
A bliss in proof,° and proved, a very woe;   *i.e., while experienced*
Before, a joy proposed; behind, a dream.
    All this the world well knows; yet none knows well
    To shun the heaven that leads men to this hell.

130

My mistress' eyes are nothing like the sun;
Coral is far more red than her lips' red;
If snow be white, why then her breasts are dun;°   *brown*
If hairs be wires, black wires grow on her head.
5   I have seen roses damasked,° red and white,   *mingled*
But no such roses see I in her cheeks;
And in some perfumes is there more delight
Than in the breath that from my mistress reeks.

---

8. Sonnet 127 was the first to have a woman, not a man, as its principal subject; she is described as a woman of dark complexion.
9. The poem builds on a comparison between playing a keyboard instrument, understood to be a virginal or small harpsichord, and a lover's kiss. The keys or jacks of the instrument "kiss" the player's fingers; the speaker asks to kiss the player's lips.

1. I.e., your fingers produce the concord between the strings of the instrument that astounds my hearing.
2. The line evokes two kinds of meaning, moral and sexual: the futility and degradation of passion, and its waste as "spirit," conventionally understood as semen, in the body or waist of the woman.
3. The lover is both the hunter, who seeks satisfaction, and the hunted, for whom a bait is laid by mad passion.

I love to hear her speak, yet well I know
10   That music hath a far more pleasing sound.
I grant I never saw a goddess go;
My mistress, when she walks, treads on the ground.
    And yet, by heaven, I think my love as rare
    As any she belied with false compare.[4]

138

When my love swears that she is made of truth
I do believe her, though I know she lies,
That she might think me some untutored youth,
Unlearnèd in the world's false subtleties.
5   Thus vainly thinking that she thinks me young,
Although she knows my days are past the best,
Simply I credit her false-speaking tongue;
On both sides thus is simple truth suppressed.
But wherefore says she not she is unjust?
10   And wherefore say not I that I am old?
O, love's best habit is in seeming° trust,   *apparent*
And age in love loves not to have years told.
    Therefore I lie with her, and she with me,[5]
    And in our faults by lies we flattered be.

144

Two loves I have, of comfort and despair,
Which like two spirits do suggest° me still: *tempt*
The better angel is a man right fair,
The worser spirit a woman colored ill.
5   To win me soon to hell, my female evil
Tempteth my better angel from my side,
And would corrupt my saint to be a devil,
Wooing his purity with her foul pride.
And whether that my angel be turned fiend
10   Suspect I may, yet not directly tell;
But being both from me, both to each friend,
I guess one angel in another's hell.
    Yet this shall I ne'er know, but live in doubt
    Till my bad angel fire my good one out.[6]

152

In loving thee thou know'st I am forsworn,°   *faithless*
But thou art twice forsworn, to me love swearing:
In act thy bed-vow° broke, and new faith torn   *marriage vow*
In vowing new hate after new love bearing.[7]

4. The couplet suggests ironic or hyperbolic compliment: my mistress is exceptional in that she has set new standards for true beauty by a comparison that defies its standards.
5. We deceive each other; we have sex with each other.
6. The couplet suggests several interpretations. The poet's lady or bad angel could fire or dismiss his "fair" friend; she could infect him with a venereal disease, a condition that would cause a fever; finally, she could be the cause of his descent into hellfire, a consequence of sin.
7. You have broken your marriage vow and your vow to love me.

5   But why of two oaths' breach do I accuse thee,
       When I break twenty? I am perjured most,
       For all my vows are oaths but to misuse° thee,   *deceive*
       And all my honest faith in thee is lost.
       For I have sworn deep oaths of thy deep kindness,
10   Oaths of thy love, thy truth, thy constancy,
       And, to enlighten thee, gave eyes to blindness,[8]
       Or made them swear against the thing they see;
          For I have sworn thee fair. More perjured eye,
          To swear against the truth so foul a lie!

TWELFTH NIGHT; OR, WHAT YOU WILL.   Shakespeare's *Twelfth Night; or, What You Will* was first performed during the feast of Candlemas at the Middle Temple, one of the Inns of Court, on 2 February 1602. An eyewitness to that performance, the barrister John Manningham, found the story of the puritanical steward Malvolio the most memorable: "A good practice in it to make the steward believe his lady widow was involved with him, by counterfeiting a letter as from his Lady . . . telling him what she liked best in him, and prescribing his gesture in smiling, his apparel, etc. And then when he came to practice making him believe he was mad." However distant the memory of the twelfth day of Christmas as a feast of misrule was at the time of the play's first performance, the element of the world turned upside down in Shakespeare's comedy delighted the carousing young lawyers.

Part of the play's larger parody of the self-delusion of desire and of the literary forms in which that desire is expressed is shown in the plotline where the sanctimonious Malvolio is fooled into believing that he might be the love object of Olivia, his female employer, and so acts out the most preposterous courtship of her. The play sends up the conventions of courtly love, particularly as stylized in the lyric love poetry that was popular among young London men with literary ambition as well as self-dramatizing aristocrats in the Elizabethan court. This was the poetry of Sir Walter Raleigh and the young John Donne, with all its teasing eroticism, hyperbolic flattery, and Petrarchan angst.

In *Twelfth Night,* the three central characters—Orsino, Olivia, and Viola—all act out their similarly stylized passions. Orsino lolls about listening to sad music as he pines for love of Olivia. She vows to do nothing but mourn for her dead brother—for seven years— until she meets Cesario, a servant whom Orsino has sent to woo her. Cesario, none other than the shipwrecked Viola disguised as a male servant, praises Olivia from head to toe and makes witty, erotic jokes and complaints against the lady's cruelty that capture her fancy. Olivia is jolted out of mourning and into infatuation. Cesario/Viola in turn falls almost immediately in love with Orsino, and her love grows in heat not despite but more likely because of the apparent impossibility of fulfillment. Viola's twin Sebastian meanwhile flees Antonio, a man who has taken care of him for three months since being shipwrecked, only to fall haphazardly into Olivia's arms at the right moment to become the realization of her infatuation for Cesario.

All these self-deluded desires are expressed in some of Shakespeare's most lyrical dramatic verse. The play is studded throughout with such stars of lyric illumination as the fool Feste's songs. The sad ironies he reflects on and the enlightening wit he laces his barbs with

---

8. To make you seem fair, I saw what was not there or did not see what was there.

provide a kind of detachment and wisdom that set into relief the absurdity of the lovers' self-seriousness.

At the end of the play, the lovers—and even the drunkard Sir Toby Belch and the serving maid Maria—are matched as couples, while only Malvolio vows revenge. Antonio, the one character whose passion seems to be based on any real acquaintance with the object of his affection, is also left alone; the text is silent on his fate. In the comic world of *Twelfth Night*, mistaken identity and lack of self-knowledge are, if not for Antonio, at least overcome for some by "nature's bias"—an openness to affection and the ability to snatch pleasure when the lucky opportunity arises.

The text of *Twelfth Night* is based on the 1623 Folio.

Twelfth Night; or, What You Will*

The Names of the Actors

ORSINO, Duke (or Count) of Illyria
VALENTINE, Gentleman attending on Orsino
CURIO, Gentleman attending on Orsino

VIOLA, a shipwrecked lady, later disguised as Cesario
SEBASTIAN, twin brother of Viola
ANTONIO, a sea captain, friend to Sebastian
CAPTAIN, of the shipwrecked vessel

OLIVIA, a rich countess of Illyria
MARIA, gentlewoman in Olivia's household
SIR TOBY BELCH, Olivia's uncle
SIR ANDREW AGUECHEEK, a companion of Sir Toby
MALVOLIO, Steward of Olivia's household
FABIAN, a member of Olivia's household
FESTE, a clown, also called Fool, Olivia's jester

A PRIEST
FIRST OFFICER
SECOND OFFICER

LORDS, SAILORS, MUSICIANS, AND OTHER ATTENDANTS
Scene: A city in Illyria, and the seacoast near it

ACT 1

Scene 1[1]

[*Enter Orsino Duke of Illyria, Curio, and other lords (with musicians).*]
ORSINO: If music be the food of love, play on;
        Give me excess of it, that surfeiting,

---

* The notes are based on those of David Bevington, ed. *The Complete Works of Shakespeare.* All original stage directions are in square brackets, and all editorially added stage directions are in parentheses.
1. Location: Orsino's court.

The appetite may sicken and so die.
That strain again! It had a dying fall;°   cadence
5   O, it came o'er my ear like the sweet sound
That breathes upon a bank of violets,
Stealing and giving odor. Enough, no more.
'tis not so sweet now as it was before.
O spirit of love, how quick° and fresh art thou,   alive
10   That, notwithstanding thy capacity
Receiveth as the sea, naught enters there,
Of what validity° and pitch° soe'er,   value / worth
But falls into abatement° and low price   depreciation
Even in a minute! So full of shapes° is fancy°   imagined forms / love
15   That it alone is high fantastical.°   highly imaginative
CURIO: Will you go hunt, my lord?
ORSINO: What, Curio?
CURIO: The hart.°   pun on "heart"
ORSINO: Why, so I do, the noblest that I have.
O, when mine eyes did see Olivia first,
Methought she purged the air of pestilence.
20   That instant was I turned into a hart,
And my desires, like fell° and cruel hounds,   fierce
E'er since pursue me.[2]
[Enter Valentine.]
                                        How now, what news from her?
VALENTINE: So please my lord, I might not be admitted,
But from her handmaid do return this answer:
25   The element° itself, till seven years' heat,°   sky / seven summers
Shall not behold her face at ample view;
But like a cloistress° she will veilèd walk,   nun
And water once a day her chamber round
With eye-offending brine—all this to season°   preserve
30   A brother's dead love, which she would keep fresh
And lasting in her sad remembrance.
ORSINO: O, she that hath a heart of that fine frame°   construction
To pay this debt of love but to a brother,
How will she love, when the rich golden shaft°   Cupid's arrow
35   Hath killed the flock of all affections else°   other feelings
That live in her; when liver, brain, and heart,[3]
These sovereign thrones, are all supplied, and filled
Her sweet perfections,[4] with one self king!°   single lord
Away before me to sweet beds of flowers.
40   Love-thoughts lie rich when canopied with bowers.   [Exeunt.]

2. Allusion to Ovid: Actaeon was turned into a stag by   3. Seats of the passions.
Diana and killed by his own hounds.   4. I.e., her sweet perfections are filled.

Scene 2[5]

[*Enter Viola, a Captain, and Sailors.*]

VIOLA: What country, friends, is this?

CAPTAIN: This is Illyria, lady.

VIOLA: And what should I do in Illyria?
        My brother he is in Elysium.[6]

5   Perchance° he is not drowned. What think you, sailors?   *perhaps*

CAPTAIN: It is perchance° that you yourself were saved.   *by chance*

VIOLA: O, my poor brother! And so perchance may he be.

CAPTAIN: True, madam, and to comfort you with chance,°   *possibilities*
        Assure yourself, after our ship did split,

10   When you and those poor number saved with you
        Hung on our driving° boat, I saw your brother,   *drifting*
        Most provident in peril, bind himself,
        Courage and hope both teaching him the practice,
        To a strong mast that lived° upon the sea;   *floated*

15   Where, like Arion[7] on the dolphin's back,
        I saw him hold acquaintance with the waves
        So long as I could see.

VIOLA: For saying so, there's gold. [*She gives money.*]
        Mine own escape unfoldeth to my hope,°   *gives me hope*

20   Whereto thy speech serves for authority,
        The like of him. Know'st thou this country?

CAPTAIN: Ay, madam, well, for I was bred and born
        Not three hours' travel from this very place.

VIOLA: Who governs here?

CAPTAIN: A noble duke, in nature as in name.

VIOLA: What is his name?

CAPTAIN: Orsino.

VIOLA: Orsino! I have heard my father name him.
        He was a bachelor then.

CAPTAIN: And so is now, or was so very late;
        For but a month ago I went from hence,
        And then 'twas fresh in murmur°—as, you know,   *rumor*
        What great ones do the less° will prattle of—   *social inferiors*
        That he did seek the love of fair Olivia.

VIOLA: What's she?

CAPTAIN: A virtuous maid, the daughter of a count
        That died some twelvemonth since, then leaving her
        In the protection of his son, her brother,
        Who shortly also died; for whose dear love,

40   They say, she hath abjured the sight
        And company of men.

VIOLA: O, that I served that lady,
        And might not be delivered° to the world   *revealed*
        Till I had made mine own occasion mellow,°   *ready*

---

5. Location: The coast of the Adriatic.
6. Home of the blessed dead.

7. Greek poet who jumped overboard to escape murderous sailors and charmed dolphins with his lyre, so that they carried him to shore.

	What my estate° is!	*social position*
CAPTAIN:	That were hard to compass,°	*bring about*
45	Because she will admit no kind of suit,	
	No, not° the Duke's.	*not even*
VIOLA:	There is a fair behavior° in thee, Captain,	*conduct; appearance*
	And though that nature with a beauteous wall	
	Doth oft close in pollution, yet of thee	
50	I will believe thou hast a mind that suits	
	With this thy fair and outward character.°	*appearance*
	I prithee, and I'll pay thee bounteously,	
	Conceal me what I am, and be my aid	
	For such disguise as haply shall become	
55	The form of my intent.° I'll serve this duke.	*my outward purpose*
	Thou shalt present me as an eunuch[8] to him.	
	It may be worth thy pains, for I can sing	
	And speak to him in many sorts of music	
	That will allow° me very worth his service.	*prove*
60	What else may hap, to time I will commit;	
	Only shape thou thy silence to my wit.°	*plan*
CAPTAIN:	Be you his eunuch, and your mute° I'll be;	*silent attendant*
	When my tongue blabs, then let mine eyes not see.	
VIOLA:	I thank thee. Lead me on.	[*Exeunt.*]

Scene 3[9]

[*Enter Sir Toby (Belch) and Maria.*]

SIR TOBY: What a plague means my niece to take the death of her brother thus? I am sure care's an enemy to life.

MARIA: By my troth, Sir Toby, you must come in earlier o'nights. Your cousin,[1] my lady, takes great exceptions to your ill hours.

SIR TOBY: Why, let her except before excepted.[2]

MARIA: Ay, but you must confine yourself within the modest limits of order.

SIR TOBY: Confine? I'll confine myself no finer[3] than I am. These clothes are good enough to drink in, and so be these boots too. An[4] they be not, let them hang themselves in their own straps.

MARIA: That quaffing and drinking will undo you. I heard my lady talk of it yesterday, and of a foolish knight that you brought in one night here to be her wooer.

SIR TOBY: Who, Sir Andrew Aguecheek?

MARIA: Ay, he.

SIR TOBY: He's as tall[5] a man as any's in Illyria.

MARIA: What's that to the purpose?

SIR TOBY: Why, he has three thousand ducats a year.

---

8. Castrato, or male soprano singer, which would explain her high-pitched voice.
9. Location: Olivia's house.
1. Kinswoman.
2. I.e., let her take exception all she wants; I don't care

(plays on the cant legal phrase, *exceptis excipiendis*, "with the exceptions before named").
3. Tighter; better.
4. If.
5. Brave; tall.

MARIA: Ay, but he'll have but a year in all these ducats.[6] He's a very fool and a prodigal.

SIR TOBY: Fie, that you'll say so! He plays o' the viol-degamboys,[7] and speaks three or four languages word for word without book, and hath all the good gifts of nature.

MARIA: He hath indeed, almost natural,[8] for, besides that he's a fool, he's a great quarreler, and but that he hath the gift of a coward to allay the gust[9] he
25   hath in quarreling, 'tis thought among the prudent he would quickly have the gift of a grave.

SIR TOBY: By this hand, they are scoundrels and substractors[1] that say so of him. Who are they?

MARIA: They that add, moreover, he's drunk nightly in your company.

SIR TOBY: With drinking healths to my niece. I'll drink to her as long as there is a passage in my throat and drink in Illyria. He's a coward and a coistrel[2] that will not drink to my niece till his brains turn o' the toe like a parish top.[3] What, wench? *Castiliano vulgo!*[4] For here comes Sir Andrew Ague-face.[5]

[*Enter Sir Andrew (Aguecheek).*]

SIR ANDREW: Sir Toby Belch! How now, Sir Toby Belch?

SIR TOBY: Sweet Sir Andrew!

SIR ANDREW [*to Maria*]: Bless you, fair shrew.[6]

MARIA: And you too, sir.

SIR TOBY: Accost,[7] Sir Andrew, accost.

SIR ANDREW: What's that?

SIR TOBY: My niece's chambermaid.[8]

SIR ANDREW: Good Mistress Accost, I desire better acquaintance.

MARIA: My name is Mary, sir.

SIR ANDREW: Good Mistress Mary Accost—

SIR TOBY: You mistake, knight. "Accost" is front her,[9] board her,[1] woo her, assail her.

SIR ANDREW: By my troth, I would not undertake her in this company. Is that the meaning of "accost"?

MARIA: Fare you well, gentlemen. [(*Going.*)]

SIR TOBY: An thou let part[2] so, Sir Andrew, would thou mightst never draw sword again.

SIR ANDREW: An you part so, mistress, I would I might never draw sword again. Fair lady, do you think you have fools in hand?[3]

MARIA: Sir, I have not you by the hand.

---

6. He'll spend all his money in a year.
7. Predecessor to the violincello.
8. Play on the sense "born idiot."
9. Taste.
1. Detractors.
2. Horse groom (base fellow).
3. Large top, spun by whipping, provided by the parish as a form of exercise.
4. Uncertain meaning. Possibly a call for politeness, or else a form of "speak of the devil."
5. With the thin, pale countenance of someone suffering from ague, a fever marked by chills.
6. Small creature (connotation of shrewishness probably unintended).
7. Greet her.
8. A lady-in-waiting, not a servant.
9. Come alongside her.
1. As in a naval encounter; the language of battle is used to describe sex.
2. If you let her leave.
3. Have fools to deal with (Mary chooses to take it literally).

SIR ANDREW: Marry,[4] but you shall have, and here's my hand. [(*He gives her his hand.*)]

MARIA: Now, sir, thought is free. I pray you, bring your hand to the buttery-bar,[5] and let it drink.

SIR ANDREW: Wherefore, sweetheart? What's your metaphor?

MARIA: It's dry,[6] sir.

SIR ANDREW: Why, I think so. I am not such an ass but I can keep my hand dry. But what's your jest?

MARIA: A dry[7] jest, sir.

SIR ANDREW: Are you full of them?

MARIA: Ay, sir, I have them at my fingers' ends.[8] Marry, now I let go your hand, I am barren. [*She lets go his hand.*]   [*Exit Maria.*]

SIR TOBY: O knight, thou lack'st a cup of canary![9] When did I see thee so put down?[1]

SIR ANDREW: Never in your life, I think, unless you see canary put me down.[2] Methinks sometimes I have no more wit than a Christian or an ordinary
70   man has. But I am a great eater of beef, and I believe that does harm to my wit.

SIR TOBY: No question.

SIR ANDREW: An I thought that, I'd forswear it. I'll ride home tomorrow, Sir Toby.

SIR TOBY: *Pourquoi*,[3] my dear knight?

SIR ANDREW: What is "*pourquoi*"? Do or not do? I would I had bestowed that time in the tongues[4] that I have in fencing, dancing, and bearbaiting. O, had I but followed the arts![5]

SIR TOBY: Then hadst thou had an excellent head of hair.

SIR ANDREW: Why, would that have mended my hair?

SIR TOBY: Past question, for thou seest it will not curl by nature.

SIR ANDREW: But it becomes me well enough, does't not?

SIR TOBY: Excellent. It hangs like flax on a distaff;[6] and I hope to see a huswife take thee between her legs and spin it off.[7]

SIR ANDREW: Faith, I'll home tomorrow, Sir Toby. Your niece will not be seen, or if she be, it's four to one she'll none of me. The Count himself here hard by[8] woos her.

SIR TOBY: She'll none o' the Count. She'll not match above her degree,[9] neither in estate,[1] years, nor wit; I have heard her swear 't. Tut; there's life in 't,[2]
90   man.

SIR ANDREW: I'll stay a month longer. I am a fellow o' the strangest mind i' the world; I delight in masques and revels sometimes altogether.[3]

SIR TOBY: Art thou good at these kickshawses,[4] knight?

---

4. Indeed.
5. Door of the wine-cellar.
6. Thirsty; aged and sexually weak.
7. Ironic; barren (referring to Sir Andrew).
8. At my disposal; in my hand.
9. Sweet wine from the Canary Islands.
1. Discomfited.
2. Knocked flat.
3. Why.
4. Languages, perhaps with a pun on curling-tongs.
5. Liberal arts (but Sir Toby plays on arts as "artifice").

6. Staff for holding flax during spinning.
7. Treat your hair like flax to be spun; cause you to lose it through venereal disease ("huswife" may be a pun on "hussy").
8. Nearby.
9. Rank.
1. Fortune.
2. There's hope left.
3. In all respects.
4. Trifles (from the French *quelque chose*).

SIR ANDREW: As any man in Illyria, whatsoever he be, under the degree of my
 betters,[5] and yet I will not compare with an old man.[6]
SIR TOBY: What is thy excellence in a galliard,[7] knight?
SIR ANDREW: Faith, I can cut a caper.[8]
SIR TOBY: And I can cut the mutton to 't.
SIR ANDREW: And I think I have the back-trick[9] simply as strong as any man in
 Illyria.
SIR TOBY: Wherefore are these things hid? Wherefore have these gifts a curtain
 before 'em? Are they like to take[1] dust, like Mistress Mall's picture?[2] Why
 dost thou not go to church in a galliard and come home in a coranto?[3]
 My very walk should be a jig; I would not so much as make water but in a
105 sink-a-pace.[4] What dost thou mean? Is it a world to hide virtues[5] in? I did
 think, by the excellent constitution of thy leg, it was formed under the
 star of a galliard.[6]
SIR ANDREW: Ay, 'tis strong, and it does indifferent well[7] in a dun-colored
 stock.[8] Shall we set about some revels?
SIR TOBY: What shall we do else? Were we not born under Taurus?[9]
SIR ANDREW: Taurus? That's sides and heart.
SIR TOBY: No, sir, it is legs and thighs. Let me see thee caper. [(*Sir Andrew capers.*)]
 Ha, higher! Ha, ha, excellent!   [*Exeunt.*]

Scene 4[1]

[*Enter Valentine, and Viola in man's attire.*]
VALENTINE: If the Duke continue these favors towards you, Cesario, you are like
 to be much advanced. He hath known you but three days, and already
 you are no stranger.
VIOLA: You either fear his humor[2] or my negligence, that you call in question the
5 continuance of his love. Is he inconstant, sir, in his favors?
VALENTINE: No, believe me.

[*Enter Duke (Orsino), Curio, and attendants.*]
VIOLA: I thank you. Here comes the Count.
ORSINO: Who saw Cesario, ho?
VIOLA: On your attendance,° my lord, here.   *at your service*
ORSINO: Stand you awhile aloof. [(*The others stand aside.*)] Cesario,
 Thou know'st no less but all.° I have unclasped   *everything*
 To thee the book even of my secret soul.
 Therefore, good youth, address thy gait° unto her;   *go*
 Be not denied access, stand at her doors,
15 And tell them, there thy fixèd foot shall grow
 Till thou have audience.

---

5. Excepting my social superiors.
6. Experienced person.
7. Lively dance in triple-time.
8. Lively leap; spice used with mutton (mutton suggests
"whore").
9. Backward step in the galliard.
1. Likely to collect.
2. Any woman's portrait (usually kept under protective
glass).
3. Running dance.

4. Dance like the galliard (French *cinquepace*).
5. Talents.
6. Under a star favorable to dancing.
7. Well enough.
8. Stocking.
9. Zodiacal sign said to govern legs and thighs (Sir Andrew is mistaken).
1. Location: Orsino's court.
2. Changeableness.

VIOLA: Sure, my noble lord,
    If she be so abandoned to her sorrow
    As it is spoke, she never will admit me.
ORSINO: Be clamorous and leap all civil bounds°   *bounds of civility*
20   Rather than make unprofited return.
VIOLA: Say I do speak with her, my lord, what then?
ORSINO: O, then unfold the passion of my love;
    Surprise° her with discourse of my dear faith.   *take her by storm*
    It shall become° thee well to act my woes;   *suit*
25   She will attend it better in thy youth
    Than in a nuncio's° of more grave aspect.   *messenger's*
VIOLA: I think not so, my lord.
ORSINO: Dear lad, believe it;
    For they shall yet belie thy happy years
    That say thou art a man. Diana's lip
30   Is not more smooth and rubious;° thy small pipe°   *ruby red / voice*
    Is as the maiden's organ, shrill and sound,°   *high and clear*
    And all is semblative° a woman's part.   *resembling*
    I know thy constellation° is right apt   *predestined nature*
    For this affair.—Some four or five attend him.
35   All, if you will, for I myself am best
    When least in company.—Prosper well in this,
    And thou shalt live as freely as thy lord,
    To call his fortunes thine.
VIOLA: I'll do my best,
    To woo your lady. [(*Aside.*)] Yet a barful strife!°   *conflict full of impediments*
40   Whoe'er I woo, myself would be his wife.   [*Exeunt.*]

Scene 5³

[*Enter Maria and Clown (Feste).*]
MARIA: Nay, either tell me where thou hast been, or I will not open my lips so
    wide as a bristle may enter in way of thy excuse. My lady will hang thee
    for thy absence.
FESTE: Let her hang me. He that is well hanged in this world needs to fear no
5   colors.⁴
MARIA: Make that good.⁵
FESTE: He shall see none to fear.⁶
MARIA: A good Lenten⁷ answer. I can tell thee where that saying was born, of "I
    fear no colors."
FESTE: Where, good Mistress Mary?
MARIA: In the wars,⁸ and that may you be bold to say in your foolery.
FESTE: Well, God give them wisdom that have it; and those that are fools, let
    them use their talents.⁹

---

3. Location: Olivia's house.
4. Fear nothing.
5. Explain that.
6. He'll be dead and, therefore, fear no one.

7. Meager, like Lenten fare.
8. In war, "colors" would be enemy flags.
9. Abilities (reference to the parable of the talents, Matthew 25.14–29).

MARIA: Yet you will be hanged for being so long absent; or to be turned away,[1] is
15   not that as good as a hanging to you?

FESTE: Many a good hanging[2] prevents a bad marriage; and for turning away, let
            summer bear it out.[3]

MARIA: You are resolute, then?

FESTE: Not so, neither, but I am resolved on two points.[4]

MARIA: That if one break, the other will hold; or if both break, your gaskins[5] fall.

FESTE: Apt, in good faith, very apt. Well, go thy way. If Sir Toby would leave
            drinking, thou wert as witty a piece of Eve's flesh as any in Illyria.

MARIA: Peace, you rogue, no more o' that. Here comes my lady. Make your excuse
            wisely, you were best.[6]   [Exit.]

    [Enter Lady Olivia with Malvolio (and Attendants).]

FESTE [(Aside)]: Wit, an 't be thy will, put me into good fooling! Those wits that
            think they have thee do very oft prove fools, and I that am sure I lack
            thee may pass for a wise man. For what says Quinapalus?[7] "Better a witty
            fool than a foolish wit."—God bless thee, lady!

OLIVIA [(To attendants)]: Take the fool away.

FESTE: Do you not hear, fellows? Take away the lady.

OLIVIA: Go to,[8] you're a dry[9] fool. I'll no more of you.
            Besides, you grow dishonest.[1]

FESTE: Two faults, madonna,[2] that drink and good counsel will amend. For give
            the dry[3] fool drink, then is the fool not dry. Bid the dishonest man mend
35   himself; if he mend, he is no longer dishonest; if he cannot, let the
            botcher[4] mend him. Anything that's mended is but patched; virtue that
            transgresses is but patched with sin, and sin that amends is but patched
            with virtue. If that this simple syllogism will serve, so; if it will not, what
            remedy? As there is no true cuckold but calamity, so beauty's a flower.[5]
40   The lady bade take away the fool; therefore I say again, take her away.

OLIVIA: Sir, I bade them take away you.

FESTE: Misprision[6] in the highest degree! Lady, cucullus non facit monachum;[7] that's
            as much to say as I wear not motley[8] in my brain. Good madonna, give
            me leave to prove you a fool.

OLIVIA: Can you do it?

FESTE: Dexterously, good madonna.

OLIVIA: Make your proof.

FESTE: I must catechize you for it, madonna. Good my mouse of virtue,[9] answer
            me.

OLIVIA: Well, sir, for want of other idleness,[1] I'll bide[2] your proof.

FESTE: Good madonna, why mourn'st thou?

---

1. Dismissed.
2. Perhaps a bawdy pun on being "well-hung."
3. Let mild weather make homelessness endurable.
4. Maria plays on points as "laces used to hold up breeches."
5. Wide breeches.
6. It would be best for you.
7. Feste's invention.
8. Stop.
9. Dull.
1. Unreliable.
2. My lady.

3. Thirsty.
4. Mender of old clothes.
5. I.e., Olivia has wedded calamity but will be unfaithful to it, for it is natural to seize the moment of youth and beauty.
6. Mistake.
7. The cowl does not make the monk.
8. The multicolored fool's garment.
9. Virtuous mouse (term of endearment).
1. Pastime.
2. Endure.

OLIVIA: Good fool, for my brother's death.

FESTE: I think his soul is in hell, madonna.

OLIVIA: I know his soul is in heaven, fool.

FESTE: The more fool, madonna, to mourn for your brother's soul, being in heaven. Take away the fool, gentlemen.

OLIVIA: What think you of this fool, Malvolio? Doth he not mend?[3]

MALVOLIO: Yes, and shall do till the pangs of death shake him. Infirmity, that decays the wise, doth ever make the better fool.

FESTE: God send you, sir, a speedy infirmity for the better increasing your folly! Sir Toby will be sworn that I am no fox, but he will not pass[4] his word for twopence that you are no fool.

OLIVIA: How say you to that, Malvolio?

MALVOLIO: I marvel your ladyship takes delight in such a barren rascal. I saw him
65   put down the other day with[5] an ordinary fool that has no more brain than a stone. Look you now, he's out of his guard[6] already. Unless you laugh and minister occasion[7] to him, he is gagged. I protest I take these wise men that crow so at these set[8] kind of fools no better than the fools' zanies.[9]

OLIVIA: O, you are sick of self-love, Malvolio, and taste with a distempered[1] ap-
70   petite. To be generous, guiltless, and of free disposition is to take those things for bird-bolts[2] that you deem cannon bullets. There is no slander in an allowed[3] fool, though he do nothing but rail; nor no railing in a known discreet man, though he do nothing but reprove.

FESTE: Now Mercury[4] endue thee with leasing,[5] for thou speak'st well of fools!
     [Enter Maria.]

MARIA: Madam, there is at the gate a young gentleman much desires to speak with you.

OLIVIA: From the Count Orsino, is it?

MARIA: I know not, madam. 'Tis a fair young man, and well attended.

OLIVIA: Who of my people hold him in delay?

MARIA: Sir Toby, madam, your kinsman.

OLIVIA: Fetch him off, I pray you. He speaks nothing but madman.[6] Fie on him!
     [(Exit Maria.)] Go you, Malvolio. If it be a suit from the Count, I am sick, or not at home; what you will, to dismiss it. [Exit Malvolio.] Now you see, sir, how your fooling grows old, and people dislike it.

FESTE: Thou hast spoke for us, madonna, as if thy eldest son should be a fool; whose skull Jove cram with brains, for—here he comes—
     [Enter Sir Toby.]
          one of thy kin has a most weak pia mater.[7]

OLIVIA: By mine honor, half drunk. What is he at the gate, cousin?

SIR TOBY: A gentleman.

OLIVIA: A gentleman? What gentleman?

---

3. Improve.
4. Give.
5. By.
6. Defenseless.
7. Provide occasion for wit.
8. Artificial.
9. Fools' assistants.

1. Diseased.
2. Blunt arrows for shooting birds.
3. Licensed.
4. God of trickery.
5. Make you a skillful liar.
6. The words of madness.
7. Brain.

SIR TOBY: 'tis a gentleman here—[(*He belches.*)] A plague o' these pickle-herring! [*To Feste.*] How now, sot?[8]

FESTE: Good Sir Toby.

OLIVIA: Cousin,[9] cousin, how have you come so early by this lethargy?

SIR TOBY: Lechery? I defy lechery. There's one at the gate.

OLIVIA: Ay, marry, what is he?

SIR TOBY: Let him be the devil an he will, I care not.
    Give me faith,[1] say I. Well, it's all one.[2]   [*Exit.*]

OLIVIA: What's a drunken man like, Fool?

FESTE: Like a drowned man, a fool, and a madman. One draft above heat[3] makes him a fool, the second mads him, and a third drowns him.

OLIVIA: Go thou and seek the crowner,[4] and let him sit o' my coz;[5] for he's in the third degree of drink, he's drowned. Go, look after him.

FESTE: He is but mad yet, madonna; and the fool shall look to the madman. [*Exit.*]
    [*Enter Malvolio.*]

MALVOLIO: Madam, yond young fellow swears he will speak with you. I told him you were sick; he takes on him to understand so much, and therefore comes to speak with you. I told him you were asleep; he seems to have a foreknowledge of that too, and therefore comes to speak with you. What is to be said to him, lady? He's fortified against any denial.

OLIVIA: Tell him he shall not speak with me.

MALVOLIO: He's been told so; and he says he'll stand at your door like a sheriff 's post,[6] and be the supporter to a bench, but he'll speak with you.

OLIVIA: What kind o' man is he?

MALVOLIO: Why, of mankind.

OLIVIA: What manner of man?

MALVOLIO: Of very ill manner. He'll speak with you, will you or no.

OLIVIA: Of what personage and years is he?

MALVOLIO: Not yet old enough for a man, nor young enough for a boy; as a squash[7] is before 'tis a peascod,[8] or a codling[9] when 'tis almost an apple.
120   'tis with him in standing water[1] between boy and man. He is very well-favored,[2] and he speaks very shrewishly.[3] One would think his mother's milk were scarce out of him.

OLIVIA: Let him approach. Call in my gentlewoman.

MALVOLIO: Gentlewoman, my lady calls.   [*Exit.*]
    [*Enter Maria.*]

OLIVIA: Give me my veil. Come, throw it o'er my face.
    We'll once more hear Orsino's embassy. [*Olivia veils.*]
    [*Enter Viola.*]

VIOLA: The honorable lady of the house, which is she?

OLIVIA: Speak to me; I shall answer for her. Your will?

---

8. Fool; drunkard.
9. Kinsman.
1. I.e., to resist the devil.
2. It doesn't matter.
3. Drink more than would make him warm.
4. Coroner.
5. Hold an inquest on my kinsman (Sir Toby).
6. Post before the sherrif's door to mark a residence of authority.

7. Unripe pea-pod.
8. Pea-pod.
9. Unripe apple.
1. At the turn of the tide.
2. Good-looking.
3. Sharply.

VIOLA: Most radiant, exquisite, and unmatchable beauty—I pray you, tell me if
130   this be the lady of the house, for I never saw her. I would be loath to cast
away my speech; for besides that it is excellently well penned, I have
taken great pains to con[4] it. Good beauties, let me sustain[5] no scorn; I am
very comptible,[6] even to the least sinister usage.[7]

OLIVIA: Whence came you, sir?

VIOLA: I can say little more than I have studied, and that question's out of my
part. Good gentle one, give me modest[8] assurance if you be the lady of
the house, that I may proceed in my speech.

OLIVIA: Are you a comedian?[9]

VIOLA: No, my profound heart; and yet, by the very fangs of malice, I swear I am
140   not that I play. Are you the lady of the house?

OLIVIA: If I do not usurp[1] myself, I am.

VIOLA: Most certain, if you are she, you do usurp yourself; for what is yours to bestow is not yours to reserve. But this is from[2] my commission. I will on
with my speech in your praise, and then show you the heart of my mes-
145   sage.

OLIVIA: Come to what is important in 't. I forgive[3] you the praise.

VIOLA: Alas, I took great pains to study it, and 'tis poetical.

OLIVIA: It is the more like to be feigned. I pray you, keep it in. I heard you were
saucy at my gates, and allowed your approach rather to wonder at you
150   than to hear you. If you be not mad,[4] begone; if you have reason,[5] be
brief. 'Tis not that time of moon with me[6] to make one[7] in so skipping[8] a
dialogue.

MARIA: Will you hoist sail, sir? Here lies your way.

VIOLA: No, good swabber,[9] I am to hull[1] here a little longer.—Some mollification
155   for your giant,[2] sweet lady. Tell me your mind; I am a messenger.

OLIVIA: Sure you have some hideous matter to deliver, when the courtesy[3] of it is
so fearful. Speak your office.[4]

VIOLA: It alone concerns your ear. I bring no overture of war, no taxation[5] of
homage. I hold the olive[6] in my hand; my words are as full of peace as
160   matter.

OLIVIA: Yet you began rudely. What are you? What would you?

VIOLA: The rudeness that hath appeared in me have I learned from my entertainment.[7] What I am and what I would are as secret as maidenhead—to
your ears, divinity;[8] to any other's, profanation.

OLIVIA: Give us the place alone. We will hear this divinity. [*Exeunt Maria and attendants.*] Now, sir, what is your text?

VIOLA: Most sweet lady—

4. Learn by heart.
5. Endure.
6. Sensitive.
7. Slightest rude treatment.
8. Reasonable.
9. Actor.
1. Supplant.
2. Outside.
3. Excuse.
4. Altogether mad? But mad?
5. Sanity.
6. I'm not in the mood.

7. Take part.
8. Sprightly.
9. One who swabs the deck.
1. Float without sails.
2. Small Maria, who guards her lady like a medieval giant.
3. Formal beginning.
4. Business.
5. Demand.
6. Olive-branch.
7. Reception.
8. Holy discourse.

OLIVIA: A comfortable[9] doctrine, and much may be said of it. Where lies your
　　　　text?

VIOLA: In Orsino's bosom.

OLIVIA: In his bosom? In what chapter of his bosom?

VIOLA: To answer by the method,[1] in the first of his heart.

OLIVIA: O, I have read it. It is heresy. Have you no more to say?

VIOLA: Good madam, let me see your face.

OLIVIA: Have you any commission from your lord to negotiate with my face? You
　　　　are now out of your text. But we will draw the curtain and show you the
　　　　picture. [*Unveiling.*] Look you, sir, such a one I was this present.[2] Is 't not
　　　　well done?

VIOLA: Excellently done, if God did all.

OLIVIA: 'tis in grain,[3] sir; 'twill endure wind and weather.

VIOLA: 'tis beauty truly blent,[4] whose red and white
　　　　Nature's own sweet and cunning[5] hand laid on.
　　　　Lady, you are the cruel'st she alive
　　　　If you will lead these graces to the grave
185　　　And leave the world no copy.

OLIVIA: O, sir, I will not be so hardhearted. I will give out divers schedules[6] of my
　　　　beauty. It shall be inventoried, and every particle and utensil[7] labeled to[8]
　　　　my will: as, item, two lips, indifferent[9] red; item, two gray eyes, with lids
　　　　to them; item, one neck, one chin, and so forth. Were you sent hither to
190　　　praise[1] me?

VIOLA: I see you what you are: you are too proud.
　　　　But, if° you were the devil, you are fair.　　　　　　　　　　　*even if*
　　　　My lord and master loves you. O, such love
　　　　Could be but recompensed,° though you were crowned　*could only be repaid*
195　　　The nonpareil of beauty!

OLIVIA: 　　　　　　　　　　　How does he love me?

VIOLA: With adorations, fertile° tears,　　　　　　　　　　　　　　*abundant*
　　　　With groans that thunder love, with sighs of fire.

OLIVIA: Your lord does know my mind; I cannot love him.
200　　　Yet I suppose him virtuous, know him noble,
　　　　Of great estate, of fresh and stainless youth,
　　　　In voices well divulged,° free,° learned, and valiant,　*well spoken of / generous*
　　　　And in dimension and the shape of nature°　　　　　　　*physical form*
　　　　A gracious° person. But yet I cannot love him.　　　　　　*graceful*
205　　　He might have took his answer long ago.

VIOLA: If I did love you in my master's flame,°　　　　　　　　　　*passion*
　　　　With such a suffering, 'such a deadly° life,　　　　　　　　*death-like*
　　　　In your denial I would find no sense;
　　　　I would not understand it.

OLIVIA: 　　　　　　　　　　　Why, what would you?

9. Comforting.　　　　　　　　　　　6. Lists.
1. To continue the metaphor.　　　　　7. Article.
2. A minute ago.　　　　　　　　　　8. Added to.
3. Fast dyed.　　　　　　　　　　　　9. Somewhat.
4. Blended.　　　　　　　　　　　　1. Pun on "appraise."
5. Skillful.

VIOLA: Make me a willow[2] cabin at your gate
210   And call upon my soul° within the house;   *Olivia*
          Write loyal cantons° of contemnèd° love   *songs / rejected*
          And sing them loud even in the dead of night;
          Hallow° your name to the reverberate hills,   *call; bless*
          And make the babbling gossip° of the air   *echo*
215   Cry out "Olivia!" O, you should not rest
          Between the elements of air and earth
          But you should pity me!
OLIVIA: You might do much.
                                What is your parentage?
VIOLA: Above my fortunes, yet my state° is well.   *social standing*
220   I am a gentleman.
OLIVIA: Get you to your lord.
          I cannot love him. Let him send no more—
          Unless, perchance, you come to me again
          To tell me how he takes it. Fare you well.
          I thank you for your pains. Spend this for me.
     [(*She offers a purse.*)]
VIOLA: I am no fee'd post,° lady. Keep your purse.   *paid messenger*
          My master, not myself, lacks recompense.
          Love make his heart of flint that you shall love,
          And let your fervor, like my master's, be
          Placed in contempt! Farewell, fair cruelty.   [*Exit.*]
OLIVIA: "What is your parentage?"
          "Above my fortunes, yet my state is well:
          I am a gentleman." I'll be sworn thou art!
          Thy tongue, thy face, thy limbs, actions, and spirit
          Do give thee fivefold blazon.° Not too fast! Soft,° soft!   *coat of arms / wait*
235   Unless the master were the man.[3] How now?
          Even so quickly may one catch the plague?
          Methinks I feel this youth's perfections
          With an invisible and subtle stealth
          To creep in at mine eyes. Well, let it be.
240   What ho, Malvolio!
     [*Enter Malvolio.*]
MALVOLIO: Here, madam, at your service.
OLIVIA: Run after that same peevish messenger,
          The County's° man. He left this ring behind him,   *Count's*
          [*giving a ring*]
          Would I or not.[4] Tell him I'll none of it.
          Desire him not to flatter with° his lord,   *encourage*
245   Nor hold him up with hopes; I am not for him.
          If that the youth will come this way tomorrow,
          I'll give him reasons for 't. Hie thee, Malvolio.
MALVOLIO: Madam, I will.   [*Exit*]

---

2. Willow was the symbol of unrequited love.   4. Whether I wanted it or not.
3. Unless Cesario and Orsino changed places.

OLIVIA: I do I know not what, and fear to find
250   Mine eye too great a flatterer for my mind.
           Fate, show thy force. Ourselves we do not owe.°   own
           What is decreed must be; and be this so.   [Exit.]

ACT 2

Scene 1[5]

[Enter Antonio and Sebastian.]

ANTONIO: Will you stay no longer? Nor will you not[6] that I go with you?

SEBASTIAN: By your patience,[7] no. My stars shine darkly over me. The malig-
           nancy of my fate might perhaps distemper yours; therefore I shall crave of
           you your leave that I may bear my evils alone. It were a bad recompense
5   for your love to lay any of them on you.

ANTONIO: Let me yet know of you whither you are bound.

SEBASTIAN: No, sooth,[8] sir; my determinate[9] voyage is mere extravagancy.[1] But I
           perceive in you so excellent a touch of modesty that you will not extort
           from me what I am willing to keep in; therefore it charges me in manners
10   the rather to express myself.[2] You must know of me then, Antonio, my
           name is Sebastian, which I called Roderigo. My father was that Sebastian
           of Messaline whom I know you have heard of. He left behind him myself
           and a sister, both born in an hour.[3] If the heavens had been pleased,
           would we had so ended! But you, sir, altered that, for some hour[4] before
15   you took me from the breach of the sea[5] was my sister drowned.

ANTONIO: Alas the day!

SEBASTIAN: A lady, sir, though it was said she much resembled me, was yet of
           many accounted beautiful. But though I could not with such estimable
           wonder[6] over-far believe that, yet thus far I will boldly publish[7] her: she
20   bore a mind that envy[8] could not but call fair. She is drowned already, sir,
           with salt water, though I seem to drown her remembrance again with
           more.

ANTONIO: Pardon me, sir, your bad entertainment.[9]

SEBASTIAN: O good Antonio, forgive me your trouble.[1]

ANTONIO: If you will not murder me for[2] my love, let me be your servant.

SEBASTIAN: If you will not undo what you have done, that is, kill him whom you
           have recovered,[3] desire it not. Fare ye well at once. My bosom is full of

---

5. Location: Somewhere in Illyria.
6. Do you not wish.
7. Leave.
8. Truly.
9. Determined upon.
1. Wandering.
2. Courtesy demands that I reveal myself.
3. In the same hour.
4. About an hour.

5. The surf.
6. Admiring judgment.
7. Proclaim.
8. Even malice.
9. Reception.
1. The trouble I put you to.
2. Be the death of me in return for.
3. Saved.

kindness,[4] and I am yet so near the manners of my mother[5] that upon the least occasion more mine eyes will tell tales of me. I am bound to the
30   Count Orsino's court. Farewell.   [*Exit.*]
ANTONIO: The gentleness of all the gods go with thee!
    I have many enemies in Orsino's court,
    Else would I very shortly see thee there.
    But come what may, I do adore thee so
35   That danger shall seem sport, and I will go.   [*Exit.*]

Scene 2[6]

[*Enter Viola and Malvolio, at several[7] doors.*]
MALVOLIO: Were not you even now with the Countess Olivia?
VIOLA: Even now, sir. On a moderate pace I have since arrived but hither.
MALVOLIO: She returns this ring to you, sir. You might have saved me my pains,
    to have taken[8] it away yourself. She adds, moreover, that you should put
5   your lord into a desperate[9] assurance she will none of him. And one thing
    more: that you be never so hardy to come[1] again in his affairs, unless it be
    to report your lord's taking of this. Receive it so.
VIOLA: She took the ring of me. I'll none of it.
MALVOLIO: Come, sir, you peevishly threw it to her, and her will is it should be so
10   returned. [*He throws down the ring.*] If it be worth stooping for, there it
    lies, in your eye; if not, be it his that finds it.
    [*Exit.*]
VIOLA [*picking up the ring*]: I left no ring with her. What means this lady?
    Fortune forbid my outside have not charmed her!
    She made good view of° me, indeed so much   *looked closely at*
15   That sure methought her eyes had lost° her tongue,   *caused her to lose*
    For she did speak in starts, distractedly.
    She loves me, sure! The cunning of her passion
    Invites me in° this churlish messenger.   *in the person of*
    None of my lord's ring? Why, he sent her none.
20   I am the man.° If it be so—as 'tis—   *man of her choice*
    Poor lady, she were better love a dream.
    Disguise, I see, thou art a wickedness
    Wherein the pregnant enemy° does much.   *resourceful Satan*
    How easy is it for the proper false°   *handsome deceivers*
25   In women's waxen° hearts to set their forms!°   *malleable / impressions*
    Alas, our frailty is the cause, not we,
    For such as we are made of, such we be.
    How will this fadge?° My master loves her dearly,   *turn out*
    And I, poor monster,[2] fond° as much on him;   *dote*
30   And she, mistaken, seems to dote on me.

---

4. Tenderness.   8. By taking.
5. Womanly inclination to weep.   9. Without hope.
6. Location: Outside Olivia's house.   1. Bold as to come.
7. Different.   2. Because both man and woman.

What will become of this? As I am man,
My state is desperate° for my master's love;   *hopeless*
As I am woman—now, alas the day!—
What thriftless° sighs shall poor Olivia breathe!   *unprofitable*
35   O Time, thou must untangle this, not I;
It is too hard a knot for me t' untie.   [*Exit.*]

                              Scene 3[3]

[*Enter Sir Toby and Sir Andrew.*]

SIR TOBY: Approach, Sir Andrew. Not to be abed after midnight is to be up be-
     times;[4] and *diluculo surgere,*[5] thou know'st—
SIR ANDREW: Nay, by my troth, I know not, but I know to be up late is to be up
     late.
SIR TOBY: A false conclusion. I hate it as an unfilled can.[6] To be up after midnight
     and to go to bed then, is early; so that to go to bed after midnight is to go
     to bed betimes. Does not our lives consist of the four elements?[7]
SIR ANDREW: Faith, so they say, but I think it rather consists of eating and drink-
     ing.
SIR TOBY: Thou'rt a scholar; let us therefore eat and drink. Marian, I say, a stoup[8]
     of wine!

     [*Enter Clown (Feste).*]

SIR ANDREW: Here comes the Fool, i' faith.
FESTE: How now, my hearts! Did you never see the picture of "we three"?[9]
SIR TOBY: Welcome, ass. Now let's have a catch.[1]
SIR ANDREW: By my troth, the Fool has an excellent breast.[2] I had rather than
     forty shillings I had such a leg, and so sweet a breath to sing, as the fool
     has. In sooth, thou wast in very gracious[3] fooling last night, when thou
     spok'st of Pigrogromitus, of the Vapians passing the equinoctial of
     Queubus.[4] 'twas very good, i' faith. I sent thee sixpence for thy leman.[5]
20   Hadst it?
FESTE: I did impeticos thy gratillity;[6] for Malvolio's nose is no whipstock.[7] My lady
     has a white hand, and the Myrmidons[8] are no bottle-ale houses.
SIR ANDREW: Excellent! Why, this is the best fooling, when all is done. Now, a
     song.
SIR TOBY: Come on, there is sixpence for you. [(*He gives money.*)] Let's have a song.
SIR ANDREW: There's a testril[9] of me too. [(*He gives money.*)] If one knight give a—
FESTE: Would you have a love song, or a song of good life?[1]
SIR TOBY: A love song, a love song.
SIR ANDREW: Ay, ay, I care not for good life.

---

3. Location: Olivia's house.
4. Early.
5. *Diluculo surgere* (*saluberrimum est*)—to rise early is most
healthful (from Lily's *Latin Grammar*).
6. Tankard.
7. Fire, water, earth, air.
8. Goblet.
9. Picture of two fools or asses, the onlooker being the
third.
1. Round-song.

2. Voice.
3. Elegant.
4. Mock erudition.
5. Sweetheart.
6. Impetticoat (pocket up) thy gratuity.
7. Whip-handle.
8. Followers of Achilles.
9. Coin worth sixpence.
1. Virtuous living.

FESTE [(*sings*)]:

30   O mistress mine, where are you roaming?
                  O, stay and hear, your true love 's coming.
                     That can sing both high and low.
                  Trip no further, pretty sweeting
                     Journeys end in lovers' meeting,
35   Every wise man's son doth know.

SIR ANDREW: Excellent good, i' faith.

SIR TOBY: Good, good.

FESTE [(*sings*)]:

                  What is love? 'tis not hereafter;
                  Present mirth hath present laughter;
40   What's to come is still unsure.
                  In delay there lies no plenty.
                  Then come kiss me, sweet and twenty;
                     Youth's a stuff will not endure.

SIR ANDREW: A mellifluous voice, as I am true knight.

SIR TOBY: A contagious[2] breath.

SIR ANDREW: Very sweet and contagious, i' faith.

SIR TOBY: To hear by the nose, it is dulcet in contagion. But shall we make the welkin[3] dance indeed? Shall we rouse the night owl in a catch that will draw three souls out of one weaver?[4] Shall we do that?

SIR ANDREW: An you love me, let's do't. I am dog at a catch.

FESTE: By'r Lady, sir, and some dogs will catch well.

SIR ANDREW: Most certain. Let our catch be "Thou knave."

FESTE: "Hold thy peace, thou knave," knight? I shall be constrained in 't to call thee knave, knight.

SIR ANDREW: 'Tis not the first time I have constrained one to call me knave. Begin, Fool. It begins, "Hold thy peace."

FESTE: I shall never begin if I hold my peace.

SIR ANDREW: Good, i' faith. Come, begin. [*Catch sung.*]
   [*Enter Maria.*]

MARIA: What a caterwauling do you keep here! If my lady have not called up her
60   steward Malvolio and bid him turn you out of doors, never trust me.

SIR TOBY: My lady's a Cataian,[5] we are politicians,[6] Malvolio's a Peg-o'-Ramsey,[7] and [(*He sings*)] "Three merry men be we." Am not I consanguineous?[8] Am I not of her blood? Tillyvally![9] Lady! [(*He sings.*)] "There dwelt a man in Babylon, lady, lady."[1]

FESTE: Beshrew me, the knight's in admirable fooling.

SIR ANDREW: Ay, he does well enough if he be disposed, and so do I too. He does it with a better grace, but I do it more natural.[2]

---

2. Catchy; infected.
3. Sky.
4. Weavers were associated with the singing of psalms.
5. Native of Cathay; trickster.
6. Schemers.
7. Character in a popular song (here used contemptuously).

8. Related.
9. Nonsense.
1. From an old song, *The Constancy of Suzanna.*
2. Naturally (unconsciously suggesting idiocy).

SIR TOBY [(*sings*)]: "O' the twelfth day of December"—

MARIA: For the love o' God, peace!

[*Enter Malvolio.*]

MALVOLIO: My masters, are you mad? Or what are you? Have you no wit,[3] manners, nor honesty[4] but to gabble like tinkers at this time of night? Do ye
make an alehouse of my lady's house, that ye squeak out your coziers'[5]
catches without any mitigation or remorse[6] of voice? Is there no respect
of place, persons, nor time in you?

SIR TOBY: We did keep time, sir, in our catches. Sneck up![7]

MALVOLIO: Sir Toby, I must be round[8] with you. My lady bade me tell you that
though she harbors you as her kinsman, she's nothing allied to your disorders. If you can separate yourself and your misdemeanors, you are welcome to the house; if not, an it would please you to take leave of her, she
80   is very willing to bid you farewell.

SIR TOBY [(*sings*)]: "Farewell, dear heart, since I must needs be gone."[9]

MARIA: Nay, good Sir Toby.

FESTE [(*sings*)]: "His eyes do show his days are almost done."

MALVOLIO: Is't even so?

SIR TOBY [(*sings*)]: "But I will never die."

FESTE: "Sir Toby, there you lie."

MALVOLIO: This is much credit to you.

SIR TOBY [(*sings*)]: "Shall I bid him go?"

FESTE [(*sings*)]: "What an if you do?"

SIR TOBY [(*sings*)]: "Shall I bid him go, and spare not?"

FESTE [(*sings*)]: "O, no, no, no, no, you dare not."

SIR TOBY: Out o' tune, sir? Ye lie. Art any more than a steward? Dost thou think,
because thou art virtuous, there shall be no more cakes and ale?

FESTE: Yes, by Saint Anne,[1] and ginger[2] shall be hot i' the mouth, too.

SIR TOBY: Thou'rt i' the right.—Go, sir, rub your chain with crumbs.[3]—A stoup
of wine, Maria!

MALVOLIO: Mistress Mary, if you prized my lady's favor at anything more than
contempt, you would not give means[4] for this uncivil rule.[5] She shall
know of it, by this hand.   [*Exit.*]

MARIA: Go shake your ears.[6]

SIR ANDREW: 'Twere as good a deed as to drink when a man's a-hungry to challenge him the field[7] and then to break promise with him and make a fool
of him.

SIR TOBY: Do 't, knight. I'll write thee a challenge, or I'll deliver thy indignation
105   to him by word of mouth.

MARIA: Sweet Sir Toby, be patient for tonight. Since the youth of the Count's was
today with my lady, she is much out of quiet. For[8] Monsieur Malvolio, let

---

3. Common sense.
4. Decency.
5. Cobblers'.
6. Considerate lowering.
7. Go hang.
8. Blunt.
9. From the ballad *Corydon's Farewell to Phyllis*.
1. Mother of the Virgin Mary. (Her cult was derided in
the Reformation, as were cakes and ale at church feasts.)

2. Used to spice ale.
3. Remember your position.
4. I.e., provide wine.
5. Behavior.
6. I.e., your ass's ears.
7. To a duel.
8. As for.

me alone with him. If I do not gull[9] him into a nayword[1] and make him a common recreation,[2] do not think I have wit enough to lie straight in my
110   bed. I know I can do it.

SIR TOBY: Possess us,[3] possess us. Tell us something of him.

MARIA: Marry, sir, sometimes he is a kind of puritan.

SIR ANDREW: O, if I thought that, I'd beat him like a dog.

SIR TOBY: What, for being a puritan? Thy exquisite reason, dear knight?

SIR ANDREW: I have no exquisite reason for 't, but I have reason good enough.

MARIA: The devil a puritan that he is, or anything constantly,[4] but a time-pleaser;[5] an affectioned[6] ass, that cons state without book[7] and utters it by great swaths; the best persuaded of himself, so crammed, as he thinks, with excellencies, that it is his grounds of faith that all that look on him
120   love him; and on that vice in him will my revenge find notable cause to work.

SIR TOBY: What wilt thou do?

MARIA: I will drop in his way some obscure epistles of love, wherein by the color of his beard, the shape of his leg, the manner of his gait, the expressure[8] of
125   his eye, forehead, and complexion, he shall find himself most feelingly personated.[9] I can write very like my lady your niece; on a forgotten matter[1] we can hardly make distinction of our hands.

SIR TOBY: Excellent! I smell a device.

SIR ANDREW: I have't in my nose too.

SIR TOBY: He shall think, by the letters that thou wilt drop, that they come from my niece, and that she's in love with him.

MARIA: My purpose is indeed a horse of that color.

SIR ANDREW: And your horse now would make him an ass.

MARIA: Ass, I doubt not.

SIR ANDREW: O, 'twill be admirable!

MARIA: Sport royal, I warrant you. I know my physic[2] will work with him. I will plant you two, and let the Fool make a third, where he shall find the letter. Observe his construction[3] of it. For this night, to bed, and dream on the event.[4] Farewell.   [Exit.]

SIR TOBY: Good night, Penthesilea.[5]

SIR ANDREW: Before me,[6] she's a good wench.

SIR TOBY: She's a beagle[7] true-bred and one that adores me. What o' that?

SIR ANDREW: I was adored once, too.

SIR TOBY: Let's to bed, knight. Thou hadst need send for more money.

SIR ANDREW: If I cannot recover[8] your niece, I am a foul way out.[9]

SIR TOBY: Send for money, knight. If thou hast her not i' the end, call me cut.[1]

SIR ANDREW: If I do not, never trust me, take it how you will.

---

9. Trick.
1. Byword (for dupe).
2. Sport.
3. Inform.
4. Consistently.
5. Sychophant.
6. Affected.
7. Learns a stately manner by heart.
8. Expression.
9. Represented.

1. When we have forgotten who wrote something.
2. Medicine.
3. Interpretation.
4. Outcome.
5. Queen of the Amazons.
6. I swear.
7. Small, intelligent hunting dog.
8. Win.
9. Out of money.
1. Horse with a docked tail or, perhaps, a gelding.

SIR TOBY: Come, come, I'll go burn some sack.[2] 'tis too late to go to bed now.
Come, knight; come, knight.   [*Exeunt.*]

Scene 4[3]

[*Enter Duke (Orsino) Viola, Curio, and others.*]

ORSINO: Give me some music. Now, good morrow,° friends.		*morning*
Now, good Cesario, but° that piece of song,		*I ask only*
That old and antique° song we heard last night.		*quaint*
Methought it did relieve my passion much,		
5 More than light airs and recollected° terms		*studied*
Of these most brisk and giddy-pacèd times.		
Come, but one verse.		

CURIO: He is not here, so please your lordship, that should sing it.

ORSINO: Who was it?

CURIO: Feste the jester, my lord, a fool that the Lady Olivia's father took much delight in. He is about the house.

ORSINO: Seek him out, and play the tune the while.

[(*Exit Curio.*)]

[*Music plays.*]

[*To Viola.*] Come hither, boy. If ever thou shalt love	
In the sweet pangs of it remember me;	
15 For such as I am, all true lovers are,	
Unstaid and skittish in all motions else°	*other emotions*
Save in the constant image of the creature	
That is beloved. How dost thou like this tune?	

VIOLA: It gives a very echo to the seat

20   Where Love is throned.°   *i.e., the heart*

ORSINO: Thou dost speak masterly.
My life upon 't, young though thou art, thine eye
Hath stayed upon some favor° that it loves.   *face*
Hath it not, boy?

VIOLA: A little, by your favor.

ORSINO: What kind of woman is't?

VIOLA: Of your complexion.

ORSINO: She is not worth thee, then. What years, i' faith?

VIOLA: About your years, my lord.

ORSINO: Too old, by heaven. Let still° the woman take	*always*
An elder than herself. So wears° she to him;	*adapts herself*
So sways she level° in her husband's heart.	*she keeps constant*
30 For, boy, however we do praise ourselves,	
Our fancies° are more giddy and unfirm,	*loves*
More longing, wavering, sooner lost and worn,	
Than women's are.	

VIOLA: I think it well, my lord.

ORSINO: Then let thy love be younger than thyself,	
35 Or thy affection cannot hold the bent;°	*hold steady*

---

2. Warm some Spanish wine.   3. Location: Orsino's court.

For women are as roses, whose fair flower
Being once displayed,° doth fall that very hour.   *full blown*
VIOLA: And so they are. Alas that they are so,
To die even when° they to perfection grow!   *just as*
[*Enter Curio and Clown (Feste).*]
ORSINO: O fellow, come, the song we had last night.
Mark it, Cesario, it is old and plain;
The spinsters° and the knitters in the sun,   *spinners*
And the free° maids that weave their thread with bones,°   *innocent / bobbins*
Do use° to chant it. It is silly sooth,°   *are used / simple truth*
45   And dallies with the innocence of love,
Like the old age.°   *good old days*
FESTE: Are you ready, sir?
ORSINO: Ay, prithee, sing. [*Music.*]
[*The Song.*]
FESTE [(*sings*)]:
Come away, come away, death,
50   And in sad cypress° let me be laid.   *coffin*
Fly away, fly away, breath;
I am slain by a fair cruel maid.
My shroud of white, stuck all with yew,°   *yew-sprigs*
O, prepare it!
55   My part° of death, no one so true   *portion*
Did share it.

Not a flower, not a flower sweet
On my black coffin let there be strown;°   *strewn*
Not a friend, not a friend greet
60   My poor corpse, where my bones shall be thrown.
A thousand thousand sighs to save,
Lay me, O, where
Sad true lover never find my grave,
To weep there!

ORSINO [(*offering money*)]: There's for thy pains.
FESTE: No pains, sir. I take pleasure in singing, sir.
ORSINO: I'll pay thy pleasure then.
FESTE: Truly, sir, and pleasure will be paid,[4] one time or another.
ORSINO: Give me now leave to leave thee.
FESTE: Now, the melancholy god[5] protect thee, and the tailor make thy doublet[6] of
changeable taffeta, for thy mind is a very opal. I would have men of such
constancy put to sea, that their business might be everything and their
intent[7] everywhere, for that's it that always makes a good voyage of noth-
ing.[8] Farewell.
[*Exit.*]
ORSINO: Let all the rest give place.[9]

---

4. Indulgence must be paid for.
5. Saturn, said to control the melancholy temperament.
6. Jacket.

7. Destination.
8. Come to nothing.
9. Leave.

[*Curio and attendants withdraw.*]
Once more, Cesario,

Get thee to yond same sovereign cruelty.°   *cruel person*
Tell her, my love, more noble than the world,
Prizes not quantity of dirty lands;
80 The parts° that fortune hath bestowed upon her,   *possessions*
Tell her, I hold as giddily as fortune;
But 'tis that miracle and queen of gems
That nature pranks° her in attracts my soul.   *adorns*

VIOLA: But if she cannot love you, sir?

ORSINO: I cannot be so answered.

VIOLA: Sooth,° but you must.   *In truth*
Say that some lady, as perhaps there is,
Hath for your love as great a pang of heart
As you have for Olivia. You cannot love her;
You tell her so; Must she not then be answered?° *accept your answer*

ORSINO: There is no woman's sides
Can bide° the beating of so strong a passion   *withstand*
As love doth give my heart; no woman's heart
So big, to hold so much. They lack retention.
Alas, their love may be called appetite,
95 No motion° of the liver,[1] but the palate,   *emotion*
That suffer surfeit, cloyment,° and revolt;°   *satiety / revulsion*
But mine is all as hungry as the sea,
And can digest as much. Make no compare
Between that love a woman can bear me
And that I owe° Olivia.   *have for*

VIOLA: Ay, but I know—

ORSINO: What dost thou know?

VIOLA: Too well what love women to men may owe.
In faith, they are as true of heart as we.
My father had a daughter loved a man
105 As it might be, perhaps, were I a woman,
I should your lordship.

ORSINO: And what's her history?

VIOLA: A blank, my lord. She never told her love,
But let concealment, like a worm i' the bud,
Feed on her damask° cheek. She pined in thought, *pink and white*
110 And with a green and yellow° melancholy   *pale and sallow*
She sat like Patience on a monument,°   *tomb*
Smiling at grief. Was not this love indeed?
We men may say more, swear more, but indeed
Our shows° are more than will;° for still we prove *displays / our passions*
115 Much in our vows, but little in our love.

ORSINO: But died thy sister of her love, my boy?

VIOLA: I am all the daughters of my father's house,
And all the brothers too—and yet I know not.

---

1. Seat of the emotion of love.

Sir, shall I to this lady?

ORSINO: Ay, that's the theme.
To her in haste; give her this jewel.
[*He gives a jewel.*] Say
My love can give no place, bide no denay.°   *cannot endure denial*
                                                    [*Exeunt (separately).*]

Scene 5[2]

[*Enter Sir Toby, Sir Andrew, and Fabian.*]

SIR TOBY: Come thy ways,[3] Signor Fabian.

FABIAN: Nay, I'll come. If I lose a scruple[4] of this sport, let me be boiled to death
   with melancholy.

SIR TOBY: Wouldst thou not be glad to have the niggardly rascally sheep-biter[5]
5   come by some notable shame?

FABIAN: I would exult, man. You know he brought me out o' favor with my lady
   about a bearbaiting[6] here.

SIR TOBY: To anger him we'll have the bear again, and we will fool him black
   and blue. Shall we not, Sir Andrew?

SIR ANDREW: An we do not, it is pity of our lives.

[*Enter Maria (with a letter).*]

SIR TOBY: Here comes the little villain.—How now, my metal of India![7]

MARIA: Get ye all three into the boxtree.[8] Malvolio's coming down this walk. He
   has been yonder i' the sun practicing behavior[9] to his own shadow this
   half hour. Observe him, for the love of mockery, for I know this letter
15   will make a contemplative[1] idiot of him. Close,[2] in the name of jesting!
   [*The others hide.*] Lie thou there [*throwing down a letter*]; for here comes
   the trout that must be caught with tickling.[3]   [*Exit.*]

[*Enter Malvolio.*]

MALVOLIO: 'tis but fortune; all is fortune. Maria once told me she did affect me;[4]
   and I have heard herself come thus near, that should she fancy,[5] it should
20   be one of my complexion.[6] Besides, she uses me with a more exalted respect than anyone else that follows[7] her. What should I think on 't?

SIR TOBY: Here's an overweening rogue!

FABIAN: O, peace! Contemplation makes a rare turkey-cock of him. How he jets[8]
   under his advanced[9] plumes!

SIR ANDREW: 'Slight,[1] I could so beat the rogue!

SIR TOBY: Peace, I say.

MALVOLIO: To be Count Malvolio.

SIR TOBY: Ah, rogue!

SIR ANDREW: Pistol him, pistol him.

---

2. Location: Olivia's garden.
3. Come along.
4. A bit.
5. Dog that bites sheep; i.e., a sneak.
6. Target of Puritan disapproval.
7. Gold; i.e., priceless one.
8. Shrub.
9. Elegant conduct.
1. I.e., from his musings.

2. Hide.
3. Stroking about the gills.
4. Olivia liked me.
5. Fall in love.
6. Personality.
7. Serves.
8. Struts.
9. Raised.
1. By God's light.

SIR TOBY: Peace, peace!

MALVOLIO: There is example[2] for 't. The lady of the Strachy[3] married the yeoman of the wardrobe.

SIR ANDREW: Fie on him, Jezebel![4]

FABIAN: O, peace! Now he's deeply in. Look how imagination blows him.[5]

MALVOLIO: Having been three months married to her, sitting in my state[6]—

SIR TOBY: O, for a stone-bow,[7] to hit him in the eye!

MALVOLIO: Calling my officers about me, in my branched[8] velvet gown; having come from a daybed,[9] where I have left Olivia sleeping—

SIR TOBY: Fire and brimstone!

FABIAN: O, peace, peace!

MALVOLIO: And then to have the humor of state;[1] and after a demure travel of regard,[2] telling them I know my place as I would they should do theirs, to ask for my kinsman Toby.

SIR TOBY: Bolts and shackles!

FABIAN: O, peace, peace, peace! Now, now.

MALVOLIO: Seven of my people, with an obedient start, make out for him. I frown the while, and perchance wind up my watch, or play with my[3]— some rich jewel. Toby approaches; curtsies[4] there to me—

SIR TOBY: Shall this fellow live?

FABIAN: Though our silence be drawn from us with cars,[5] yet peace.

MALVOLIO: I extend my hand to him thus, quenching my familiar smile with an austere regard of control[6]—

SIR TOBY: And does not Toby take[7] you a blow o' the lips then?

MALVOLIO: Saying, "Cousin Toby, my fortunes having cast me on your niece give
55   me this prerogative of speech—"

SIR TOBY: What, what?

MALVOLIO: "You must amend your drunkenness."

SIR TOBY: Out, scab!

FABIAN: Nay, patience, or we break the sinews of our plot.

MALVOLIO: "Besides, you waste the treasure of your time with a foolish knight—"

SIR ANDREW: That's me, I warrant you.

MALVOLIO: "One Sir Andrew."

SIR ANDREW: I knew 'twas I, for many do call me fool.

MALVOLIO: What employment have we here?
    [(Taking up the letter.)]

FABIAN: Now is the woodcock[8] near the gin.[9]

SIR TOBY: O, peace, and the spirit of humors[1] intimate reading aloud to him!

---

2. Precedent.
3. Unknown reference; lady who married below her station.
4. Wicked queen of Israel.
5. Puffs him up.
6. Chair of state.
7. Crossbow.
8. Embroidered.
9. Sofa.
1. Manner of authority.

2. Grave survey of the company.
3. Malvolio recalls that, as a Count, he would not be wearing his steward's chain.
4. Bows.
5. With chariots; i.e., by force.
6. Look of authority.
7. Give.
8. Proverbially stupid bird.
9. Snare.
1. Whim.

MALVOLIO: By my life, this is my lady's hand. These be her very c's, her u's, and her t's;[2] and thus makes she her great[3] P's. It is in contempt of[4] question her hand.

SIR ANDREW: Her c's, her u's, and her t's. Why that?

MALVOLIO [(reads)]: "To the unknown beloved, this, and my good wishes."—Her very phrases! By your leave, wax.[5] Soft![6] And the impressure her Lucrece,[7] with which she uses to seal. 'tis my lady. To whom should this be? [(He opens the letter.)]

FABIAN: This wins him, liver[8] and all.

MALVOLIO [(reads)]: "Jove knows I love,
But who?
Lips, do not move;
No man must know."

80　"No man must know." What follows? The numbers[9] altered! "No man must know." If this should be thee, Malvolio?

SIR TOBY: Marry, hang thee, brock![1]

MALVOLIO [(reads)]: "I may command where I adore,
But silence, like a Lucrece knife,
85　With bloodless stroke my heart doth gore;
M.O.A.I. doth sway my life."

FABIAN: A fustian[2] riddle!

SIR TOBY: Excellent wench,[3] say I.

MALVOLIO: "M.O.A.I. doth sway my life." Nay, but first, let me see, let me see, let
90　me see.

FABIAN: What dish o' poison has she dressed[4] him!

SIR TOBY: And with what wing[5] the staniel[6] checks at it![7]

MALVOLIO: "I may command where I adore." Why, she may command me; I serve her, she is my lady. Why, this is evident to any formal capacity.[8] There is
95　no obstruction[9] in this. And the end—what should that alphabetical position portend? If I could make that resemble something in me! Softly! M.O.A.I.—

SIR TOBY: O, ay, make up that. He is now at a cold scent.[1]

FABIAN: Sowter will cry upon 't[2] for all this, though it be as rank as a fox.

MALVOLIO: M—Malvolio. M! Why, that begins my name!

FABIAN: Did not I say he would work it out? The cur is excellent at faults.[3]

MALVOLIO: M—But then there is no consonancy in the sequel that suffers under probation:[4] A should follow, but O does.

---

2. Cut; slang for female pudenda.
3. Uppercase; copious (implying "pee").
4. Beyond.
5. Conventional apology for breaking a seal.
6. Softly.
7. Lucretia; chaste matron, who stabbed herself to death as a response to being raped.
8. Seat of passion.
9. Verses.
1. Badger.
2. Pompous.
3. Clever girl (Maria).

4. Prepared.
5. Speed.
6. Inferior hawk.
7. Turns to fly at it.
8. Normal understanding.
9. Difficulty.
1. Difficult trail.
2. The hound will pick up the scent.
3. Breaks in the scent.
4. Pattern in the letters that stands up under examination.

FABIAN: And O shall end,[5] I hope.

SIR TOBY: Ay, or I'll cudgel him, and make him cry "O!"

MALVOLIO: And then I comes behind.

FABIAN: Ay, an you had any eye behind you, you might see more detraction[6] at your heels than fortunes before you.

MALVOLIO: M.O.A.I. This simulation[7] is not as the former. And yet, to crush[8]
110   this a little, it would bow to me, for every one of these letters are in my name. Soft! Here follows prose.
       [*He reads.*] "If this fall into thy hand, revolve.[9] In my stars[1] I am above thee, but be not afraid of greatness. Some are born great, some achieve greatness, and some have greatness thrust upon 'em. Thy Fates open their
115   hands; let thy blood and spirit embrace them; and, to inure[2] thyself to what thou art like to be, cast thy humble slough[3] and appear fresh. Be opposite[4] with a kinsman, surly with servants. Let thy tongue tang[5] arguments of state; put thyself into the trick of singularity.[6] She thus advises thee that sighs for thee. Remember who commended thy yellow stock
120   ings, and wished to see thee ever cross-gartered.[7] I say, remember. Go to, thou art made, if thou desir'st to be so. If not, let me see thee a steward still, the fellow of servants, and not worthy to touch Fortune's fingers. Farewell. She that would alter services[8] with thee,

                                          The Fortunate-Unhappy."[9]
125   Daylight and champaign[1] discovers[2] not more! This is open. I will be proud, I will read politic authors,[3] I will baffle[4] Sir Toby, I will wash off gross acquaintance, I will be point-devise[5] the very man. I do not now fool myself, to let imagination jade[6] me; for every reason excites to this, that my lady loves me. She did commend my yellow stockings of late, she
130   did praise my leg being cross-gartered; and in this[7] she manifests herself to my love, and with a kind of injunction drives me to these habits[8] of her liking. I thank my stars, I am happy.[9] I will be strange,[1] stout,[2] in yellow stockings and cross-gartered, even with the swiftness of putting on. Jove and my stars be praised! Here is yet a post-script. [*He reads.*] "Thou
135   canst not choose but know who I am. If thou entertain'st[3] my love, let it appear in thy smiling; thy smiles become thee well. Therefore in my presence still[4] smile, dear my sweet, I prithee."

       Jove, I thank thee. I will smile; I will do everything that thou wilt have me.

                                                                                 [*Exit.*]

---

5. O ends Malvolio's name; a noose shall end his life; *omega* ends the Greek alphabet.
6. Defamation.
7. Disguise.
8. Force.
9. Consider.
1. Fate.
2. Accustom.
3. Outer skin.
4. Contradictory.
5. Sound with.
6. Eccentricity.
7. Wearing hose garters crossed above and below the knee.
8. Change places.

9. Unfortunate.
1. Open country.
2. Discloses.
3. Political writers.
4. Disgrace.
5. Correct to the letter.
6. Trick.
7. This letter.
8. Attire.
9. Fortunate.
1. Aloof.
2. Haughty.
3. You accept.
4. Always.

[*Sir Toby, Sir Andrew, and Fabian come from hiding.*]

FABIAN: I will not give my part of this sport for a pension of thousands to be paid from the Sophy.[5]

SIR TOBY: I could marry this wench for this device.

SIR ANDREW: So could I too.

SIR TOBY: And ask no other dowry with her but such another jest.
        [*Enter Maria.*]

SIR ANDREW: Nor I neither.

FABIAN: Here comes my noble gull-catcher.[6]

SIR TOBY: Wilt thou set thy foot o' my neck?

SIR ANDREW: Or o' mine either?

SIR TOBY: Shall I play[7] my freedom at tray-trip,[8] and become thy bondslave?

SIR ANDREW: I' faith, or I either?

SIR TOBY: Why, thou hast put him in such a dream that when the image of it leaves him he must run mad.

MARIA: Nay, but say true, does it work upon him?

SIR TOBY: Like aqua vitae[9] with a midwife.

MARIA: If you will then see the fruits of the sport, mark his first approach before my lady. He will come to her in yellow stockings, and 'tis a color she abhors, and cross-gartered, a fashion she detests; and he will smile upon her, which will now be so unsuitable to her disposition, being addicted to a melancholy as she is, that it cannot but turn him into a notable con-
160   tempt.[1] If you will see it, follow me.

SIR TOBY: To the gates of Tartar,[2] thou most excellent devil of wit!

SIR ANDREW: I'll make one[3] too.

[*Exeunt.*]

ACT 3

Scene 1[4]

[*Enter Viola, and Clown (Feste, playing his pipe and tabor).*]

VIOLA: Save thee,[5] friend, and thy music. Dost thou live by[6] thy tabor?[7]

FESTE: No, sir, I live by the church.

VIOLA: Art thou a churchman?

FESTE: No such matter, sir. I do live by the church, for I do live at my house, and
5   my house doth stand by the church.

VIOLA: So thou mayst say the king lies[8] by a beggar if a beggar dwell near him, or the church stands by thy tabor if thy tabor stand by the church.

FESTE: You have said, sir. To see this age! A sentence is but a cheveril[9] glove to a good wit. How quickly the wrong side may be turned outward!

---

5. Shah of Persia.
6. Fool-catcher.
7. Gamble.
8. Game of dice.
9. Distilled liquor.
1. Notorious object of contempt.
2. Tartarus, the section of hell for the most evil.

3. Tag along.
4. Location: Olivia's garden.
5. God save.
6. Earn your living with.
7. Drum.
8. Dwells; lies sexually.
9. Kid.

VIOLA: Nay, that's certain. They that dally nicely[1] with words may quickly make
    them wanton.[2]

FESTE: I would therefore my sister had had no name, sir.

VIOLA: Why, man?

FESTE: Why, sir, her name's a word, and to dally with that word might make my
15   sister wanton.[3] But indeed, words are very rascals since bonds disgraced
    them.[4]

VIOLA: Thy reason, man?

FESTE: Troth, sir, I can yield you none without words, and words are grown so false
    I am loath to prove reason with them.

VIOLA: I warrant thou art a merry fellow and car'st for nothing.

FESTE: Not so, sir, I do care for something; but in my conscience, sir, I do not care
    for you. If that be to care for nothing, sir, I would it would make you in-
    visible.

VIOLA: Art not thou the Lady Olivia's fool?

FESTE: No indeed, sir. The Lady Olivia has no folly. She will keep no fool, sir, till
    she be married, and fools are as like husbands as pilchers[5] are to her-
    rings—the husband's the bigger. I am indeed not her fool but her cor-
    rupter of words.

VIOLA: I saw thee late[6] at the Count Orsino's.

FESTE: Foolery, sir, does walk about the orb[7] like the sun; it shines everywhere. I
    would be sorry, sir, but[8] the fool should be as oft with your master as with
    my mistress. I think I saw your wisdom there.

VIOLA: Nay, an thou pass upon[9] me, I'll no more with thee. Hold, there's expenses
    for thee. [(*She gives a coin.*)]

FESTE: Now Jove, in his next commodity[1] of hair, send thee a beard!

VIOLA: By my troth, I'll tell thee, I am almost sick for one—[*aside*] though I would
    not have it grow on my chin.—Is thy lady within?

FESTE: Would not a pair of these have bred, sir?

VIOLA: Yes, being kept together and put to use.[2]

FESTE: I would play Lord Pandarus[3] of Phrygia, sir, to bring a Cressida to this
    Troilus.

VIOLA: I understand you, sir. 'Tis well begged. [(*She gives another coin.*)]

FESTE: The matter, I hope, is not great, sir, begging but a beggar; Cressida was a
    beggar.[4] My lady is within, sir. I will conster[5] to them whence you come.
45   Who you are and what you would are out of my welkin[6]—I might say "el-
    ement," but the word is overworn.   [*Exit.*]

VIOLA: This fellow is wise enough to play the fool,
    And to do that well craves° a kind of wit.   *requires*
    He must observe their mood on whom he jests,
50   The quality of persons, and the time,

---

1. Play subtly; toy amorously.
2. Equivocal.
3. Licentious.
4. Since sworn statements have been needed to make them good.
5. Small fish.
6. Recently.
7. Earth.
8. Unless.

9. Fence verbally with me.
1. Shipment.
2. Put out at interest.
3. Go-between in the story of Troilus and Cressida.
4. She became a leprous beggar in Henryson's continuation of Chaucer's story.
5. Explain.
6. Sky.

And, like the haggard,° check° at every feather   *untrained hawk / turn*
That comes before his eye. This is a practice°   *skill*
As full of labor as a wise man's art;
For folly that he wisely shows is fit,
55   But wise men, folly-fall'n,° quite taint their wit.[7]   *fallen into folly*
    [*Enter Sir Toby and (Sir) Andrew.*]

SIR TOBY: Save you, gentleman.

VIOLA: And you, sir.

SIR ANDREW: *Dieu vous garde, monsieur.*[8]

VIOLA: *Et vous aussi; votre serviteur.*[9]

SIR ANDREW: I hope, sir, you are, and I am yours.

SIR TOBY: Will you encounter[1] the house? My niece is desirous you should enter,
    if your trade[2] be to her.

VIOLA: I am bound to[3] your niece, sir; I mean, she is the list[4] of my voyage.

SIR TOBY: Taste[5] your legs, sir. Put them to motion.

VIOLA: My legs do better understand[6] me, sir, than I understand what you mean by
    bidding me taste my legs.

SIR TOBY: I mean, to go, sir, to enter.

VIOLA: I will answer you with gait and entrance.—But we are prevented.[7]
    [*Enter Olivia and Gentlewoman (Maria).*]
    Most excellent accomplished lady, the heavens rain odors on you!

SIR ANDREW: That youth's a rare courtier. "Rain odors"—well.

VIOLA: My matter hath no voice,[8] lady, but to your own most pregnant[9] and
    vouchsafed[1] ear.

SIR ANDREW: "Odors," "pregnant," and "vouchsafed." I'll get 'em all three all
    ready.[2]

OLIVIA: Let the garden door be shut, and leave me to my hearing.
    [*Exeunt Sir Toby, Sir Andrew, and Maria.*]
    Give me your hand, sir.

VIOLA: My duty, madam, and most humble service.

OLIVIA: What is your name?

VIOLA: Cesario is your servant's name, fair princess.

OLIVIA: My servant, sir? 'Twas never merry world
Since lowly feigning° was called compliment.   *false humility*
You're servant to the Count Orsino, youth.

VIOLA: And he is yours, and his must needs be yours;
Your servant's servant is your servant, madam.

OLIVIA: For him, I think not on him. For his thoughts,
Would they were blanks, rather than filled with me!

VIOLA: Madam, I come to whet your gentle thoughts
On his behalf.

OLIVIA: O, by your leave,° I pray you.   *please*
I bade you never speak again of him.

---

7. Ruin their reputation for intelligence.
8. God protect you, sir.
9. You, too; your servant.
1. Enter.
2. Business.
3. Bound for; obliged to.
4. Destination.

5. Try.
6. Comprehend; stand under.
7. Anticipated.
8. Cannot be uttered.
9. Receptive.
1. Attentive.
2. Memorized for future use.

90	But, would you undertake another suit,	
	I had rather hear you to solicit that	
	Than music from the spheres.°	*heavenly harmony*

VIOLA: Dear lady—

OLIVIA: Give me leave, beseech you. I did send,
         After the last enchantment you did here,
         A ring in chase of you; so did I abuse°   *deceive*
95   Myself, my servant, and, I fear me, you.
         Under your hard construction° must I sit,   *interpretation*
         To force° that on you in a shameful cunning   *for forcing*
         Which you knew none of yours. What might you think?
         Have you not set mine honor at the stake
100   And baited° it with all th' unmuzzled thoughts   *harassed*
         That tyrannous heart can think? To one of your receiving°   *intelligence*
         Enough is shown; a cypress,° not a bosom,   *thin black cloth*
         Hides my heart. So, let me hear you speak.

VIOLA: I pity you.

OLIVIA: That's a degree to love.

VIOLA: No, not a grece;° for 'tis a vulgar proof°   *step / common experience*
         That very oft we pity enemies.

OLIVIA: Why then, methinks 'tis time to smile again.
         O world, how apt° the poor are to be proud!   *ready*
         If one should be a prey, how much the better
110   To fall before the lion than the wolf!
         [*Clock strikes.*]
         The clock upbraids me with the waste of time.
         Be not afraid, good youth, I will not have you;
         And yet, when wit and youth is come to harvest
         Your wife is like° to reap a proper° man.   *likely / handsome*
115   There lies your way, due west.

VIOLA: Then westward ho!³
         Grace and good disposition attend your ladyship.
         You'll nothing, madam, to my lord by me?

OLIVIA: Stay.
         I prithee, tell me what thou think'st of me.

VIOLA: That you do think you are not what you are.

OLIVIA: If I think so, I think the same of you.

VIOLA: Then think you right. I am not what I am.

OLIVIA: I would you were as I would have you be!

VIOLA: Would it be better, madam, than I am?
125   I wish it might, for now I am your fool.

OLIVIA [(*aside*)]: O, what a deal of scorn looks beautiful
         In the contempt and anger of his lip!
         A murderous guilt shows not itself more soon
         Than love that would seem hid; love's night is noon.⁴—
130   Cesario, by the roses of the spring,

---

3. The cry of Thames watermen to attract westward-   4. Love cannot hide itself.
bound passengers from London to Westminster.

By maidhood, honor, truth, and everything,
I love thee so that, maugre° all thy pride,   *despite*
Nor wit nor reason can my passion hide.
Do not extort thy reasons from this clause,
135   For that I woo, thou therefore hast no cause.
But rather reason thus with reason fetter.
Love sought is good, but given unsought is better.

VIOLA: By innocence I swear, and by my youth,
I have one heart, one bosom, and one truth,
140   And that no woman has, nor never none
Shall mistress be of it save I alone.
And so adieu, good madam. Nevermore
Will I my master's tears to you deplore.°   *beweep*

OLIVIA: Yet come again, for thou perhaps mayst move
145   That heart, which now abhors, to like his love.

                              [*Exeunt (separately).*]

Scene 2[5]

[*Enter Sir Toby, Sir Andrew, and Fabian.*]

SIR ANDREW: No, faith, I'll not stay a jot longer.

SIR TOBY: Thy reason, dear venom,[6] give thy reason.

FABIAN: You must needs yield your reason, Sir Andrew.

SIR ANDREW: Marry, I saw your niece do more favors to the Count's servingman
5   than ever she bestowed upon me. I saw't i' the orchard.[7]

SIR TOBY: Did she see thee the while, old boy? Tell me that.

SIR ANDREW: As plain as I see you now.

FABIAN: This was a great argument[8] of love in her toward you.

SIR ANDREW: 'Slight,[9] will you make an ass o' me?

FABIAN: I will prove it legitimate,[1] sir, upon the oaths[2] of judgment and reason.

SIR TOBY: And they have been grand-jurymen since before Noah was a sailor.

FABIAN: She did show favor to the youth in your sight only to exasperate you, to
awake your dormouse[3] valor, to put fire in your heart and brimstone in
your liver. You should then have accosted her, and with some excellent
15   jests, fire-new from the mint, you should have banged the youth into
dumbness. This was looked for at your hand, and this was balked.[4] The
double gilt of this opportunity you let time wash off, and you are now
sailed into the north[5] of my lady's opinion, where you will hang like an
icicle on a Dutchman's beard[6] unless you do redeem it by some laudable
20   attempt either of valor or policy.[7]

SIR ANDREW: An't be any way, it must be with valor, for policy I hate. I had as
lief be a Brownist[8] as a politician.[9]

---

5. Location: Olivia's house.
6. Venomous person.
7. Garden.
8. Proof.
9. God's light.
1. True.
2. Testimony.
3. Sleepy.

4. Missed.
5. Out of the warmth.
6. Alludes to the arctic voyage of William Berentz in 1596–1597.
7. Stratagem.
8. Early name for the Congregationalists, after founder Robert Browne.
9. Schemer.

SIR TOBY: Why, then, build me thy fortunes upon the basis of valor. Challenge
me the Count's youth to fight with him; hurt him in eleven places. My
25 niece shall take note of it; and assure thyself, there is no love-broker in
the world can more prevail in man's commendation with woman than
report of valor.

FABIAN: There is no way but this, Sir Andrew.

SIR ANDREW: Will either of you bear me a challenge to him?

SIR TOBY: Go, write it in a martial hand. Be curst[1] and brief; it is no matter how
witty, so it be eloquent and full of invention. Taunt him with the license
of ink.[2] If thou "thou"-est[3] him some thrice, it shall not be amiss; and as
many lies[4] as will lie in thy sheet of paper, although the sheet were big
enough for the bed of Ware[5] in England, set 'em down. Go, about it. Let
35 there be gall[6] enough in thy ink, though thou write with a goose pen,[7] no
matter. About it.

SIR ANDREW: Where shall I find you?

SIR TOBY: We'll call thee at the cubiculo.[8] Go.

[Exit Sir Andrew.]

FABIAN: This is a dear manikin[9] to you, Sir Toby.

SIR TOBY: I have been dear to him, lad, some two thousand strong or so.

FABIAN: We shall have a rare letter from him; but you'll not deliver 't?

SIR TOBY: Never trust me, then; and by all means stir on the youth to an answer.
I think oxen and wainropes[1] cannot hale[2] them together. For Andrew, if
he were opened and you find so much blood in his liver[3] as will clog the
45 foot of a flea, I'll eat the rest of th' anatomy.

FABIAN: And his opposite,[4] the youth, bears in his visage no great presage of cruelty.

[Enter Maria.]

SIR TOBY: Look where the youngest wren[5] of nine comes.

MARIA: If you desire the spleen,[6] and will laugh yourselves into stitches, follow
50 me. Yond gull[7] Malvolio is turned heathen, a very renegado; for there is
no Christian that means to be saved by believing rightly can ever believe
such impossible passages of grossness.[8] He's in yellow stockings.

SIR TOBY: And cross-gartered?

MARIA: Most villainously, like a pedant that keeps a school i', the church. I have
55 dogged him like his murderer. He does obey every point of the letter that
I dropped to betray him. He does smile his face into more lines than is in
the new map with the augmentation of the Indies.[9] You have not seen
such a thing as 'tis. I can hardly forbear hurling things at him. I know my
lady will strike him. If she do, he'll smile and take't for a great favor.

SIR TOBY: Come, bring us, bring us where he is.   [Exeunt omnes.]

---

1. Fierce.
2. Freedom of writing.
3. Call him "thou" (informal).
4. Charges of lying.
5. Famous bed, more than 10 feet wide.
6. Bitterness; ingredient in ink.
7. Goose quill; foolish style.
8. Small chamber.
9. Puppet.
1. Wagon ropes.

2. Haul.
3. A pale and bloodless liver was a sign of cowardice.
4. Adversary.
5. Smallest of small birds.
6. Laughing fit.
7. Fool.
8. Gross impossibilities.
9. Emerie Molyneux's map, c. 1599, which showed more of the East Indies than had ever been mapped before.

Scene 3[1]

[*Enter Sebastian and Antonio.*]

SEBASTIAN: I would not by my will have troubled you,
          But since you make your pleasure of your pains,
          I will no further chide you.
ANTONIO: I could not stay behind you. My desire,
5   More sharp than filèd steel, did spur me forth,
          And not all° love to see you—though so much   only
          As might have drawn one to a longer voyage—
          But jealousy° what might befall your travel,   solicitude
          Being skilless in° these parts, which to a stranger,   unacquainted with
10   Unguided and unfriended, often prove
          Rough and unhospitable. My willing love,
          The rather by these arguments of fear,
          Set forth in your pursuit.
SEBASTIAN: My kind Antonio,
          I can no other answer make but thanks,
15   And thanks; and ever oft good turns
          Are shuffled off with such uncurrent° pay.   valueless
          But were my worth,° as is my conscience,° firm,   wealth / inclination
          You should find better dealing.° What's to do?   treatment
          Shall we go see the relics° of this town?   monuments
ANTONIO: Tomorrow, sir. Best first go see your lodging.
SEBASTIAN: I am not weary, and 'tis long to night.
          I pray you, let us satisfy our eyes
          With the memorials and the things of fame
          That do renown° this city.   make famous
ANTONIO: Would you'd pardon me.
25   I do not without danger walk these streets.
          Once in a sea fight 'gainst the Count his° galleys   Count's
          I did some service, of such note indeed
          That were I ta'en here it would scarce be answered.°   atoned for
SEBASTIAN: Belike° you slew great number of his people?   Perhaps
ANTONIO: Th' offense is not of such a bloody nature,
          Albeit the quality of the time and quarrel
          Might well have given us bloody argument.°   cause for bloodshed
          It might have since been answered° in repaying   atoned for
          What we took from them, which for traffic's° sake   trade's
35   Most of our city did. Only myself stood out,
          For which, if I be lapsèd° in this place,   surprised
          I shall pay dear.
SEBASTIAN: Do not then walk too open.
ANTONIO: It doth not fit me. Hold, sir, here's my purse.
          [*He gives his purse.*]
          In the south suburbs, at the Elephant,°   an inn
40   Is best to lodge. I will bespeak our diet,°   order our food

---

1. Location: A street.

Whiles you beguile the time and feed your knowledge
With viewing of the town. There shall you have me.

SEBASTIAN: Why I your purse?

ANTONIO: Haply° your eye shall light upon some toy°   *perhaps / trifle*
45   You have desire to purchase; and your store°   *store of money*
            I think is not for idle markets,° sir.   *useless purchases*

SEBASTIAN: I'll be your purse-bearer and leave you
            For an hour.

ANTONIO: To th' Elephant.

SEBASTIAN: I do remember.   [*Exeunt (separately).*]

Scene 4[2]

[*Enter Olivia and Maria.*]

OLIVIA [(*aside*)]: I have sent after him; he says he'll come.
            How shall I feast him? What bestow of him?
            For youth is bought more oft than begged or borrowed.
            I speak too loud.—
5   Where's Malvolio? He is sad and civil,[3]
            And suits well for a servant with my fortunes.
            Where is Malvolio?

MARIA: He's coming, madam, but in very strange manner. He is, sure, possessed,
            madam.

OLIVIA: Why, what's the matter? Does he rave?

MARIA: No, madam, he does nothing but smile. Your ladyship were best to have
            some guard about you if he come, for sure the man is tainted in 's wits.

OLIVIA: Go call him hither. [(*Maria summons Malvolio.*)] I am as mad as he, If sad
            and merry madness equal be.

[*Enter Malvolio, (cross-gartered and in yellow stockings).*]
15   How now, Malvolio?

MALVOLIO: Sweet lady, ho, ho!

OLIVIA: Smil'st thou? I sent for thee upon a sad occasion.

MALVOLIO: Sad, lady? I could be sad. This does make some obstruction in the
            blood, this cross-gartering, but what of that? If it please the eye of one, it
            is with me as the very true sonnet[4] is, "Please one and please all."

OLIVIA: Why, how dost thou, man? What is the matter with thee?

MALVOLIO: Not black in my mind, though yellow in my legs. It did come to his
            hands, and commands shall be executed. I think we do know the sweet
            roman hand.[5]

OLIVIA: Wilt thou go to bed, Malvolio?

MALVOLIO: To bed! "Ay, sweetheart, and I'll come to thee."[6]

OLIVIA: God comfort thee! Why dost thou smile so and kiss thy hand so oft?

MARIA: How do you, Malvolio?

MALVOLIO: At your request? Yes, nightingales answer daws.[7]

---

2. Location: Olivia's garden.
3. Serious and sedate.
4. Song.
5. Italian style of handwriting.

6. Quotation from a popular song.
7. I.e., why should a fine fellow like me answer a daw
(crow) like you.

MARIA: Why appear you with this ridiculous boldness before my lady?

MALVOLIO: "Be not afraid of greatness." 'Twas well writ.

OLIVIA: What mean'st thou by that, Malvolio?

MALVOLIO: "Some are born great—"

OLIVIA: Ha?

MALVOLIO: "Some achieve greatness—"

OLIVIA: What sayst thou?

MALVOLIO: "And some have greatness thrust upon them."

OLIVIA: Heaven restore thee!

MALVOLIO: "Remember who commended thy yellow stockings—"

OLIVIA: Thy yellow stockings?

MALVOLIO: "And wished to see thee cross-gartered."

OLIVIA: Cross-gartered?

MALVOLIO: "Go to, thou art made, if thou desir'st to be so—"

OLIVIA: Am I made?

MALVOLIO: "If not, let me see thee a servant still."

OLIVIA: Why, this is very midsummer madness.

    [Enter Servant.]

SERVANT: Madam, the young gentleman of the Count Orsino's is returned. I
    could hardly entreat him back. He attends your ladyship's pleasure.

OLIVIA: I'll come to him. [(Exit Servant.)] Good Maria, let this fellow be looked to.

50   Where's my cousin Toby? Let some of my people have a special care of
    him. I would not have him miscarry[8] for the half of my dowry.

                                    [Exeunt (Olivia and Maria, different ways).]

MALVOLIO: Oho, do you come near[9] me now? No worse man than Sir Toby to
    look to me! This concurs directly with the letter. She sends him on pur-
    pose that I may appear stubborn to him, for she incites me to that in the

55   letter. "Cast thy humble slough," says she; "be opposite with a kinsman,
    surly with servants; let thy tongue tang with arguments of state; put thy-
    self into the trick of singularity." And consequently sets down the man-
    ner how: as, a sad[1] face, a reverend carriage, a slow tongue, in the habit[2]
    of some sir of note, and so forth. I have limed[3] her, but it is Jove's doing,

60   and Jove make me thankful! And when she went away now, "Let this fel-
    low be looked to." "Fellow!"[4] Not "Malvolio," nor after my degree,[5] but
    "fellow." Why, everything adheres together, that no dram[6] of a scruple,[7]
    no scruple of a scruple, no obstacle, no incredulous[8] or unsafe circum-
    stance—what can be said?—nothing that can be can come between me

65   and the full prospect of my hopes. Well, Jove, not I, is the doer of this,
    and he is to be thanked.

    [Enter (Sir) Toby, Fabian, and Maria.]

SIR TOBY: Which way is he, in the name of sanctity? If all the devils of hell be
    drawn in little,[9] and Legion[1] himself possessed him, yet I'll speak to him.

---

8. Come to harm.
9. Appreciate.
1. Serious.
2. Attire.
3. Caught.
4. Companion.
5. According to my position.

6. Small amount; one-eighth of a fluid ounce.
7. Doubt; one-third of a dram.
8. Incredible.
9. Brought together in a small space.
1. An unclean spirit ("My name is Legion, for we are many," Mark 5.9).

FABIAN: Here he is, here he is.—How is't with you, sir? How is't with you, man?

MALVOLIO: Go off. I discard you. Let me enjoy my private. Go off.

MARIA: Lo, how hollow the fiend speaks within him! Did not I tell you? Sir Toby, my lady prays you to have a care of him.

MALVOLIO: Aha, does she so?

SIR TOBY: Go to, go to! Peace, peace, we must deal gently with him. Let me alone.—How do you, Malvolio? How is 't with you? What, man, defy the devil! Consider, he's an enemy to mankind.

MALVOLIO: Do you know what you say?

MARIA: La you,[2] an you speak ill of the devil, how he takes it at heart! Pray God he be not bewitched!

FABIAN: Carry his water[3] to the wisewoman.

MARIA: Marry, and it shall be done tomorrow morning, if I live. My lady would not lose him for more than I'll say.

MALVOLIO: How now, mistress?

MARIA: O Lord!

SIR TOBY: Prithee, hold thy peace; this is not the way. Do you not see you move[4] him? Let me alone with him.

FABIAN: No way but gentleness, gently, gently. The fiend is rough, and will not be roughly used.

SIR TOBY: Why, how now, my bawcock![5] How dost thou, chuck?[6]

MALVOLIO: Sir!

SIR TOBY: Ay, biddy,[7] come with me. What man, tis not for gravity[8] to play at cherry-pit[9] with Satan. Hang him, foul collier![1]

MARIA: Get him to say his prayers, good Sir Toby, get him to pray.

MALVOLIO: My prayers, minx?

MARIA: No, I warrant you, he will not hear of godliness.

MALVOLIO: Go hang yourselves all! You are idle,[2] shallow things; I am not of your element. You shall know more hereafter.   [Exit.]

SIR TOBY: Is 't possible?

FABIAN: If this were played upon a stage, now, I could condemn it as an improba-
100   ble fiction.

SIR TOBY: His very genius[3] hath taken the infection of the device, man.

MARIA: Nay, pursue him now, lest the device take air and taint.[4]

FABIAN: Why, we shall make him mad indeed.

MARIA: The house will be the quieter.

SIR TOBY: Come, we'll have him in a dark room and bound. My niece is already in the belief that he's mad. We may carry it[5] thus for our pleasure and his penance till our very pastime, tired out of breath, prompt us to have mercy on him, at which time we will bring the device to the bar[6] and crown thee for a finder of madmen. But see, but see!

---

2. Look you.
3. Urine.
4. Upset.
5. Fine fellow (from French beau-coq).
6. Chick.
7. Chicken.
8. Dignity.
9. A child's game.

1. Coal-peddler.
2. Foolish.
3. Spirit.
4. Become exposed to air and, thus, to spoil.
5. Carry the trick on.
6. To court.

[*Enter Sir Andrew (with a letter).*]

FABIAN: More matter for a May morning.[7]

SIR ANDREW: Here's the challenge. Read it. I warrant there's vinegar and pepper in 't.

FABIAN: Is 't so saucy?[8]

SIR ANDREW: Ay, is 't, I warrant him. Do but read.

SIR TOBY: Give me. [(*He reads.*)] "Youth, whatsoever thou art, thou art but a scurvy fellow."

FABIAN: Good, and valiant.

SIR TOBY [(*reads*)]: "Wonder not, nor admire[9] not in thy mind, why I do call thee so, for I will show thee no reason for 't."

FABIAN: A good note, that keeps you from the blow of the law.

SIR TOBY [(*reads*)]: "Thou com'st to the Lady Olivia, and in my sight she uses thee kindly. But thou liest in thy throat; that is not the matter I challenge thee for."

FABIAN: Very brief, and to exceeding good sense—less.

SIR TOBY [(*reads*)]: "I will waylay thee going home, where if it be thy chance to kill me—"

FABIAN: Good.

SIR TOBY [(*reads*)]: "Thou kill'st me like a rogue and a villain."

FABIAN: Still you keep o' the windy[1] side of the law. Good.

SIR TOBY [(*reads*)]: "Fare thee well, and God have mercy upon one of our souls! He may have mercy upon mine, but my hope is better, and so look to thyself. Thy friend, as thou usest him, and thy sworn enemy,

Andrew Aguecheek."

If this letter move him not, his legs cannot. I'll give 't him.

MARIA: You may have very fit occasion for 't. He is now in some commerce with my lady, and will by and by depart.

SIR TOBY: Go, Sir Andrew. Scout me[2] for him at the corner of the orchard like a bum-baily.[3] So soon as ever thou seest him, draw, and as thou draw'st, swear horrible; for it comes to pass oft that a terrible oath, with a swaggering accent sharply twanged off, gives manhood more approbation[4] than ever proof[5] itself would have earned him. Away!

SIR ANDREW: Nay, let me alone for swearing.[6]   [*Exit.*]

SIR TOBY: Now will not I deliver his letter, for the behavior of the young gentleman gives him out to be of good capacity and breeding; his employment between his lord and my niece confirms no less. Therefore this letter, being so excellently ignorant, will breed no terror in the youth. He will find it comes from a clodpoll.[7] But, sir, I will deliver his challenge by word of mouth, set upon Aguecheek a notable report of valor, and drive the gentleman—as I know his youth will aptly receive it—into a most hideous

---

7. Material for a May Day comedy.
8. Spicy; insolent.
9. Marvel.
1. Windward; i.e., safe.
2. Keep watch.

3. Agent who makes arrests.
4. Reputation.
5. Testing.
6. Leave swearing to me.
7. Blockhead.

150   opinion of his rage, skill, fury, and impetuosity. This will so fright them
           both that they will kill one another by the look, like cockatrices.[8]

[*Enter Olivia and Viola.*]

FABIAN: Here he comes with your niece. Give them way till he take leave, and
           presently after him.

SIR TOBY: I will meditate the while upon some horrid message for a challenge.

                                        [*Exeunt Sir Toby, Fabian, and Maria.*]

OLIVIA: I have said too much unto a heart of stone
           And laid mine honor too unchary° on 't.   *carelessly*
There's something in me that reproves my fault,
           But such a headstrong potent fault it is
           That it but mocks reproof.

VIOLA: With the same havior° that your passion bears   *behavior*
           Goes on my master's griefs.

OLIVIA [*giving a locket*]: Here, wear this jewel for me. 'Tis my picture.
           Refuse it not; it hath no tongue to vex you.
           And I beseech you come again tomorrow.

165   What shall you ask of me that I'll deny,
           That honor, saved, may upon asking give?

VIOLA: Nothing but this; your true love for my master.

OLIVIA: How with mine honor may I give him that
           Which I have given to you?

VIOLA: I will acquit° you.   *release*

OLIVIA: Well, come again tomorrow. Fare thee well.
           A fiend like° thee might bear my soul to hell.   *resembling*
                                                                        [*Exit.*]

[*Enter (Sir) Toby and Fabian.*]

SIR TOBY: Gentleman, God save thee.

VIOLA: And you, sir.

SIR TOBY: That defense thou hast, betake thee to 't. Of what nature the wrongs
           are thou hast done him, I know not, but thy intercepter,[9] full of despite,[1]
           bloody as the hunter, attends thee at the orchard end. Dismount thy
           tuck,[2] be yare[3] in thy preparation, for thy assailant is quick, skillful, and
           deadly.

VIOLA: You mistake sir. I am sure no man hath any quarrel to me. My remem-
           brance is very free and clear from any image of offense done to any man.

SIR TOBY: You'll find it otherwise, I assure you. Therefore, if you hold your life at
           any price, betake you to your guard, for your opposite[4] hath in him what
           youth, strength, skill, and wrath can furnish man withal.

VIOLA: I pray you, sir, what is he?

SIR TOBY: He is knight, dubbed with unhatched[5] rapier and on carpet considera-
           tion,[6] but he is a devil in private brawl. Souls and bodies hath he di-
           vorced three, and his incensement at this moment is so implacable that
           satisfaction can be none but by pangs of death and sepulcher. Hob, nob[7]
190   is his word;[8] give 't or take 't.

8. Basilisks, or reptiles able to kill with a glance.   4. Opponent.
9. He who lies in wait.   5. Unhacked; unused in battle.
1. Defiance.   6. Through court favor.
2. Draw your rapier.   7. Have or have not.
3. Quick.   8. Motto.

VIOLA: I will return again into the house and desire some conduct[9] of the lady. I am no fighter. I have heard of some kind of men that put quarrels purposely on others, to taste[1] their valor. Belike[2] this is a man of that quirk.[3]

SIR TOBY: Sir, no. His indignation derives itself out of a very competent[4] injury;
195   therefore, get you on and give him his desire. Back you shall not to the house unless you undertake that with me which with as much safety you might answer him. Therefore, on, or strip your sword stark naked; for meddle[5] you must, that's certain, or forswear to wear iron[6] about you.

VIOLA: This is as uncivil as strange. I beseech you, do me this courteous office, as
200   to know of the knight what my offense to him is. It is something of my negligence, nothing of my purpose.

SIR TOBY: I will do so.—Signor Fabian, stay you by this gentleman till my return.
[Exit (Sir) Toby.]

VIOLA: Pray you, sir, do you know of this matter?

FABIAN: I know the knight is incensed against you, even to a mortal arbitrament,[7]
205   but nothing of the circumstance more.

VIOLA: I beseech you, what manner of man is he?

FABIAN: Nothing of that wonderful promise, to read him by his form, as you are like to find him in the proof of his valor. He is, indeed, sir, the most skillful, bloody, and fatal opposite that you could possibly have found in any
210   part of Illyria. Will you walk towards him, I will make your peace with him if I can.

VIOLA: I shall be much bound to you for 't. I am one that had rather go with Sir Priest than Sir Knight. I care not who knows so much of my mettle.
[Exeunt.]

[Enter (Sir) Toby and (Sir) Andrew.]

SIR TOBY: Why, man, he's a very devil; I have not seen such a firago.[8] I had a pass[9]
215   with him, rapier, scabbard, and all, and he gives me the stuck in[1] with such a mortal motion that it is inevitable; and on the answer,[2] he pays you as surely as your feet hits the ground they step on. They say he has been fencer to the Sophy.

SIR ANDREW: Pox on 't, I'll not meddle with him.

SIR TOBY: Ay, but he will not now be pacified. Fabian can scarce hold him younder.

SIR ANDREW: Plague on 't, an I thought he had been valiant and so cunning in fence, I'd have seen him damned ere I'd have challenged him. Let him let the matter slip and I'll give him my horse, gray Capilet.

SIR TOBY: I'll make the motion.[3] Stand here, make a good show on 't. This shall end without the perdition of souls.[4] [Aside, as he crosses to meet Fabian.] Marry, I'll ride your horse as well as I ride you.

---

9. Escort.
1. Test.
2. Probably.
3. Peculiarity.
4. Sufficient.
5. Engage in combat.
6. Give up your right to wear a sword.

7. Trial to the death.
8. Virago (overbearing woman).
9. Bout.
1. Thrust.
2. Return.
3. Offer.
4. I.e., killing.

[*Enter Fabian and Viola.*]

[(*Aside to Fabian.*)] I have his horse to take up[5] the quarrel. I have persuaded him the youth's a devil.

FABIAN: He is as horribly conceited of him,[6] and pants and looks pale as if a bear
were at his heels.

SIR TOBY [(*to Viola*)]: There's no remedy, sir, he will fight with you for 's oath's
sake. Marry, he hath better bethought him of his quarrel, and he finds
that now scarce to be worth talking of. Therefore draw, for the support-
ance of his vow; he protests he will not hurt you.

VIOLA [(*aside*)]: Pray God defend me! A little thing would make me tell them how
much I lack of a man.

FABIAN: Give ground, if you see him furious.

SIR TOBY [*crossing to Sir Andrew*]: Come, Sir Andrew, there's no remedy. The
gentleman will, for his honor's sake, have one bout with you. He cannot
by the *duello*[7] avoid it. But he has promised me, as he is a gentleman and
a soldier, he will not hurt you. Come on, to 't.

SIR ANDREW: Pray God he keep his oath!

[*Enter Antonio.*]

VIOLA: I do assure you, 'tis against my will.

[(*They draw.*)]

ANTONIO [(*drawing, to Sir Andrew*)]: Put up your sword. If this young gentleman
Have done offense, I take the fault on me;
If you offend him, I for him defy you.

SIR TOBY: You, sir? Why, what are you?

ANTONIO: One, sir, that for his love dares yet do more
245   Than you have heard him brag to you he will.

SIR TOBY [(*drawing*)]: Nay, if you be an undertaker,° I am for° you.   challenger /
                                                                                    ready for

[*Enter Officers.*]

FABIAN: O good Sir Toby, hold! Here come the officers.

SIR TOBY [(*to Antonio*)]: I'll be with you anon.

VIOLA [(*to Sir Andrew*)]: Pray, sir, put your sword up, if you please.

SIR ANDREW: Marry, will I, sir; and for that I promised you, I'll be as good as my
word.
He will bear you easily, and reins well.

FIRST OFFICER: This is the man. Do thy office.

SECOND OFFICER: Antonio, I arrest thee at the suit
Of Count Orsino.

ANTONIO: You do mistake me, sir.

FIRST OFFICER: No, sir, no jot. I know your favor° well,   face
Though now you have no sea-cap on your head.—
Take him away. He knows I know him well.

ANTONIO: I must obey. [(*To Viola.*)] This comes with seeking you.
But there's no remedy; I shall answer it.
260   What will you do, now my necessity

---

5. Settle.   7. Dueling code.
6. I.e., Cesario has as horrible a conception of
Sir Andrew.

Makes me to ask you for my purse? It grieves me
Much more for what I cannot do for you
Than what befalls myself. You stand amazed,
But be of comfort.

SECOND OFFICER: Come, sir, away.

ANTONIO [*to Viola*]: I must entreat of you some of that money.

VIOLA: What money, sir?
For the fair kindness you have showed me here,
And part° being prompted by your present trouble,   *partly*
Out of my lean and low ability
270   I'll lend you something. My having° is not much;   *wealth*
I'll make division of my present° with you.   *what I have now*
Hold, there's half my coffer.° [(*She offers money.*)]   *purse*

ANTONIO: Will you deny me now?
Is 't possible that my deserts to° you   *claims on*
Can lack persuasion? Do not tempt my misery,
275   Lest that it make me so unsound a man
As to upbraid you with those kindnesses
That I have done for you.

VIOLA: I know of none,
Nor know I you by voice or any feature.
I hate ingratitude more in a man
280   Than lying, vainness, babbling drunkenness,
Or any taint of vice whose strong corruption
Inhabits our frail blood.

ANTONIO: O heavens themselves!

SECOND OFFICER: Come, sir, I pray you, go.

ANTONIO: Let me speak a little. This youth that you see here
I snatched one half out of the jaws of death,
Relieved him with such° sanctity of love,   *much*
And to his image, which methought did promise
Most venerable worth,° did I devotion.   *worthiness*

FIRST OFFICER: What's that to us? The time goes by. Away!

ANTONIO: But, O, how vile an idol proves this god!
Thou hast, Sebastian, done good feature shame.
In nature there's no blemish but the mind;
None can be called deformed but the unkind.°   *unnatural*
Virtue is beauty, but the beauteous evil
295   Are empty trunks o'erflourished° by the devil.   *ornamented*

FIRST OFFICER: The man grows mad. Away with him! Come, come, sir.

ANTONIO: Lead me on.

                                    [*Exit (with Officers).*]

VIOLA [(*aside*)]: Methinks his words do from such passion fly
That he believes himself. So do not I.
Prove true, imagination, O, prove true,
That I, dear brother, be now ta'en for you!

SIR TOBY: Come hither, knight. Come hither, Fabian.
We'll whisper o'er a couplet or two of most sage saws.°   *wise sayings*

[(*They gather apart from Viola.*)]

VIOLA: He named Sebastian. I my brother know
305   Yet living in my glass;° even such and so   *mirror*
         In favor was my brother, and he went
         Still° in this fashion, color, ornament,   *always*
         For him I imitate. O, if it prove,°   *prove true*
         Tempests are kind, and salt waves fresh in love!

                                                                          [(*Exit.*)]

SIR TOBY: A very dishonest⁸ paltry boy, and more a coward than a hare. His dis-
         honesty appears in leaving his friend here in necessity and denying him;
         and for his cowardship, ask Fabian.

FABIAN: A coward, a most devout coward, religious° in it.   *confirmed*

SIR ANDREW: 'Slid,° I'll after him again and beat him.   *God's eyelid*

SIR TOBY: Do, cuff him soundly, but never draw thy sword.

SIR ANDREW: An I do not—   [(*Exit.*)]

FABIAN: Come, let's see the event.°   *result*

SIR TOBY: I dare lay any money 'twill be nothing yet.°   *nevertheless*

                                                                          [*Exeunt.*]

ACT 4

Scene 1⁹

[*Enter Sebastian and Clown (Feste).*]

FESTE: Will you make me believe that I am not sent for you?

SEBASTIAN: Go to, go to, thou art a foolish fellow. Let me be clear of thee.

FESTE: Well held out,¹ i' faith! No, I do not know you, nor I am not sent to you by
         my lady to bid you come speak with her, nor your name is not Master Ce-
5   sario, nor this is not my nose, neither. Nothing that is so is so.

SEBASTIAN: I prithee, vent thy folly somewhere else. Thou know'st not me.

FESTE: Vent my folly! He has heard that word of some great man, and now applies
         it to a fool. Vent my folly! I am afraid this great lubber,² the world, will
         prove a cockney.³ I prithee now, ungird thy strangeness⁴ and tell me what
10   I shall vent to my lady. Shall I vent to her that thou art coming?

SEBASTIAN: I prithee, foolish Greek,⁵ depart from me. There's money for thee.
         [(*He gives money.*)] If you tarry longer, I shall give worse payment.

FESTE: By my troth, thou hast an open hand. These wise men that give fools
         money get themselves a good report—after fourteen years' purchase.⁶
         [*Enter (Sir) Andrew, (Sir) Toby, and Fabian.*]

SIR ANDREW: Now, sir, have I met you again? There's for you!
         [(*He strikes Sebastian.*)]

SEBASTIAN: Why, there's for thee, and there, and there!
         [(*He beats Sir Andrew with the hilt of his dagger.*)]
                 Are all the people mad?

---

8. Dishonorable.   3. Affected person.
9. Location: Before Olivia's house.   4. Abandon your strange manner.
1. Kept up.   5. Buffoon.
2. Lout.   6. At great expense.

SIR TOBY: Hold, sir, or I'll throw your dagger o'er the house.

FESTE: This will I tell my lady straight. I would not be in some of your coats for
20   twopence.

[Exit.]

SIR TOBY: Come on, sir, hold!

[He grips Sebastian.]

SIR ANDREW: Nay, let him alone. I'll go another way to work with him. I'll have
an action of battery[7] against him, if there be any law in Illyria. Though I
struck him first, yet it's no matter for that.

SEBASTIAN: Let go thy hand!

SIR TOBY: Come, sir, I will not let you go. Come, my young soldier, put up your
iron. You are well fleshed.[8] Come on.

SEBASTIAN: I will be free from thee. [He breaks free and draws his sword.] What
wouldst thou now?
30   If thou dar'st tempt me further, draw thy sword.

SIR TOBY: What, what? Nay, then I must have an ounce or two of this malapert[9]
blood from you. [He draws.]

[Enter Olivia.]

OLIVIA: Hold, Toby! On thy life I charge thee, hold!

SIR TOBY: Madam—

OLIVIA: Will it be ever thus? Ungracious wretch,
Fit for the mountains and the barbarous caves,
Where manners ne'er were preached! Out of my sight!—
Be not offended, dear Cesario.—
Rudesby,° begone!   *rude fellow*

[(Exeunt Sir Toby, Sir Andrew, and Fabian.)]

I prithee, gentle friend,
40   Let thy fair wisdom, not thy passion, sway
In this uncivil and unjust extent°   *attack*
Against thy peace. Go with me to my house,
And hear thou there how many fruitless pranks
This ruffian hath botched up,° that thou thereby   *contrived*
45   Mayst smile at this. Thou shalt not choose but go.
Do not deny.° Beshrew° his soul for me!   *refuse / curse*
He started° one poor heart of mine, in thee.   *startled*

SEBASTIAN [(aside)]: What relish° is in this? How runs the stream?   *taste*
50   Or I am mad, or else this is a dream.
Let fancy° still my sense in Lethe[1] steep;   *imagination*
If it be thus to dream, still let me sleep!

OLIVIA: Nay, come, I prithee. Would thou'dst be ruled by me!

SEBASTIAN: Madam, I will.

OLIVIA: O, say so, and so be!   [Exeunt.]

---

7. Assault charge.   9. Impudent.
8. Initiated into battle.   1. River of forgetfulness in the Underworld.

Scene 2[2]

[*Enter Maria (with a gown and a false beard), and Clown (Feste).*]

MARIA: Nay, I prithee, put on this gown and this beard; make him believe thou
art Sir[3] Topas[4] the curate. Do it quickly. I'll call Sir Toby the whilst.

[*Exit.*]

FESTE: Well, I'll put it on, and I will dissemble[5] myself in 't, and I would I were the
first that ever dissembled in such a gown. [*He disguises himself in gown and*
5   *beard.*] I am not tall enough to become the function[6] well, nor lean[7]
enough to be thought a good student; but to be said an honest man and
a good housekeeper[8] goes as fairly as to say a careful man and a great
scholar. The competitors[9] enter.

[*Enter (Sir) Toby (and Maria).*]

SIR TOBY: Jove bless thee, Master Parson.

FESTE: *Bonos dies,*[1] Sir Toby. For, as the old hermit of Prague,[2] that never saw pen
and ink, very wittily said to a niece of King Gorboduc,[3] "That that is, is";
so I, being Master Parson, am Master Parson; for what is "that" but "that,"
and "is" but "is"?

SIR TOBY: To him, Sir Topas.

FESTE: What, ho, I say! Peace in this prison!

[*He approaches the door behind which Malvolio is confined.*]

SIR TOBY: The knave[4] counterfeits well; a good knave.

MALVOLIO [*within*]: Who calls there?

FESTE: Sir Topas the curate, who comes to visit Malvolio the lunatic.

MALVOLIO: Sir Topas, Sir Topas, good Sir Topas, go to my lady—

FESTE: Out, hyperbolical[5] fiend! How vexest thou this man! Talkest thou nothing
but of ladies?

SIR TOBY: Well said, Master Parson.

MALVOLIO: Sir Topas, never was man thus wronged. Good Sir Topas, do not
think I am mad. They have laid me here in hideous darkness.

FESTE: Fie, thou dishonest Satan! I call thee by the most modest terms, for I am
one of those gentle ones that will use the devil himself with courtesy.
Sayst thou that house[6] is dark?

MALVOLIO: As hell, Sir Topas.

FESTE: Why, it hath bay windows transparent as barricadoes,[7] and the clerestories[8]
30   toward the south north are as lustrous as ebony; and yet complainest
thou of obstruction?

MALVOLIO: I am not mad, Sir Topas. I say to you this house is dark.

FESTE: Madman, thou errest. I say there is no darkness but ignorance, in which
thou art more puzzled than the Egyptians in their fog.[9]

---

2. Location: Olivia's house.
3. Title for priests.
4. Comic knight in Chaucer. (The topaz stone was believed to cure lunacy.)
5. Disguise.
6. Priestly office.
7. Scholars were supposed to be poor and, therefore, thin.
8. Neighbor.
9. Associates.
1. Good day.

2. Invented authority.
3. Legendary British king in the tragedy *Gorbobuc* (1562).
4. Fellow.
5. Boisterous.
6. Room.
7. Barricades.
8. Upper windows.
9. Allusion to the darkness Moses brought upon Egypt (Exodus 10.21–23).

MALVOLIO: I say this house is as dark as ignorance, though ignorance were as dark as hell; and I say there was never man thus abused. I am no more mad than you are. Make the trial of it in any constant question.[1]

FESTE: What is the opinion of Pythagoras[2] concerning wildfowl?

MALVOLIO: That the soul of our grandam might haply inhabit a bird.

FESTE: What think'st thou of his opinion?

MALVOLIO: I think nobly of the soul, and no way approve his opinion.

FESTE: Fare thee well. Remain thou still in darkness. Thou shalt hold th' opinion of Pythagoras ere I will allow of thy wits,[3] and fear to kill a woodcock[4] lest thou dispossess the soul of thy grandam. Fare thee well.

[(*He moves away from Malvolio's prison.*)]

MALVOLIO: Sir Topas, Sir Topas!

SIR TOBY: My most exquisite Sir Topas!

FESTE: Nay, I am for all waters.[5]

MARIA: Thou mightst have done this without thy beard and gown. He sees thee not.

SIR TOBY: To him in thine own voice, and bring me word how thou find'st him. I would we were well rid of this knavery. If he may be conveniently delivered,[6] I would he were, for I am now so far in offense with my niece that I cannot pursue with any safety this sport to the upshot.[7] Come by and by to my chamber.

[*Exit (with Maria).*]

FESTE [(*singing as he approaches Malvolio's prison*)]:
      "Hey, Robin, jolly Robin,
55   Tell me how thy lady does."[8]

MALVOLIO: Fool!

FESTE: "My lady is unkind, pardie."[9]

MALVOLIO: Fool!

FESTE: "Alas, why is she so?"

MALVOLIO: Fool, I say!

FESTE: "She loves another—" Who calls, ha?

MALVOLIO: Good Fool, as ever thou wilt deserve well at my hand, help me to a candle, and pen, ink, and paper. As I am a gentleman, I will live to be
65   thankful to thee for 't.

FESTE: Master Malvolio?

MALVOLIO: Ay, good Fool.

FESTE: Alas, sir, how fell you beside your five wits?[1]

MALVOLIO: Fool, there was never man so notoriously abused. I am as well in my
70   wits, Fool, as thou art.

FESTE: But[2] as well? Then you are mad indeed, if you be no better in your wits than a fool.

1. Consistent discussion.
2. Philosopher who originated the doctrine of the transmigration of souls.
3. Acknowledge your sanity.
4. Proverbially stupid bird.
5. Good for any trade.

6. Delivered from prison.
7. Conclusion.
8. Fragment of a song attributed to Thomas Wyatt.
9. By God (French: *par Dieu*).
1. Out of your mind.
2. Only.

MALVOLIO: They have here propertied me,[3] keep me in darkness, send ministers
    to me—asses—and do all they can to face me[4] out of my wits.
FESTE: Advise you[5] what you say. The minister is here.
    [*He speaks as Sir Topas.*]
        Malvolio, Malvolio, thy wits the heavens restore! Endeavor thyself to
    sleep; and leave thy vain bibble-babble.
MALVOLIO: Sir Topas!
FESTE [*in Sir Topas' voice*]: Maintain no words with him, good fellow.
    [*In his own voice.*] Who, I, sir? Not I, sir. God b' wi' you, good Sir Topas.
    [*In Sir Topas' voice.*] Marry, amen.
    [*In his own voice.*] I will, sir, I will.
MALVOLIO: Fool! Fool! Fool, I say!
FESTE: Alas, sir, be patient. What say you, sir? I am shent[6] for speaking to you.
MALVOLIO: Good Fool, help me to some light and some paper. I tell thee I am as
    well in my wits as any man in Illyria.
FESTE: Welladay[7] that you were, sir!
MALVOLIO: By this hand, I am. Good Fool, some ink, paper, and light; and con-
    vey what I will set down to my lady. It shall advantage thee more than
90   ever the bearing of letter did.
FESTE: I will help you to 't. But tell me true, are you not mad indeed, or do you but
    counterfeit?
MALVOLIO: Believe me, I am not. I tell thee true.
FESTE: Nay, I'll ne'er believe a madman till I see his brains. I will fetch you light
95   and paper and ink.
MALVOLIO: Fool, I'll requite it in the highest degree. I prithee, begone.
FESTE [*sings*]:

> I am gone, sir,
>   And anon, sir,
> I'll be with you again,
100   In a trice,
>   Like to the old Vice,[8]
> Your need to sustain;
> Who, with dagger of lath,°   *Vice's weapon*
> In his rage and his wrath,
105   Cries, "Aha!" to the devil;
> Like a mad lad,
> Pare thy nails, dad?
>   Adieu, goodman devil!   [*Exit.*]

Scene 3[9]

[*Enter Sebastian (with a pearl).*]
SEBASTIAN: This is the air; that is the glorious sun;
    This pearl she gave me, I do feel 't and see 't;
    And though 'tis wonder that enwraps me thus,

---

3. Treated me as property.
4. Brazen me.
5. Take care.
6. Rebuked.

7. Alas.
8. Comic character of old morality plays.
9. Location: Olivia's garden.

	Yet 'tis not madness. Where's Antonio, then?	
5	I could not find him at the Elephant;	
	Yet there he was,° and there I found this credit,°	*had been / belief*
	That he did range the town to seek me out.	
	His counsel now might do me golden service;	
	For though my soul disputes well with my sense	
10	That this may be some error, but no madness,	
	Yet doth this accident° and flood of fortune	*surprise*
	So far exceed all instance,° all discourse,°	*precedent / logic*
	That I am ready to distrust mine eyes	
	And wrangle° with my reason that persuades me	*dispute*
15	To any other trust° but that I am mad,	*belief*
	Or else the lady's mad. Yet if 'twere so,	
	She could not sway° her house, command her followers,	*rule*
	Take and give back affairs and their dispatch°	*management*
	With such a smooth, discreet, and stable bearing	
20	As I perceive she does. There's something in 't	
	That is deceivable.° But here the lady comes.	*deceptive*

[Enter Olivia and Priest.]

OLIVIA: Blame not this haste of mine. If you mean well,
　　　　Now go with me and with this holy man
　　　　Into the chantry° by. There, before him,　　　　　　*chapel nearby*
25　　And underneath that consecrated roof,
　　　　Plight me the full assurance of your faith,
　　　　That my most jealous° and too doubtful soul　　　　*anxious*
　　　　May live at peace. He shall conceal it
　　　　Whiles° you are willing it shall come to note,°　　*until / become known*
30　　What time° we will our celebration keep　　　　　　*at which time*
　　　　According to my birth.° What do you say?　　　　　*social position*
SEBASTIAN: I'll follow this good man, and go with you,
　　　　And having sworn truth, ever will be true.
OLIVIA: Then lead the way, good Father, and heavens so shine
35　　That they may fairly note° this act of mine!　　　　*look well upon*
　　　　　　　　　　　　　　　　　　　　　　　　　　　　　　[Exeunt.]

ACT 5

Scene 1[1]

[Enter Clown (Feste) and Fabian.]

FABIAN: Now, as thou lov'st me, let me see his letter.

FESTE: Good Master Fabian, grant me another request.

FABIAN: Anything.

FESTE: Do not desire to see this letter.

FABIAN: This is to give a dog and in recompense desire my dog again.[2]

[Enter Duke (Orsino), Viola, Curio, and Lords.]

---

1. Location: Before Olivia's house.
2. Famously, Queen Elizabeth once asked Dr. Bulleyn for his dog and promised a gift of his choosing in exchange; he asked to have his dog back.

ORSINO: Belong you to the Lady Olivia, friends?

FESTE: Ay, sir, we are some of her trappings.[3]

ORSINO: I know thee well. How dost thou, my good fellow?

FESTE: Truly, sir, the better for[4] my foes and the worse for my friends.

ORSINO: Just the contrary—the better for thy friends.

FESTE: No, sir, the worse.

ORSINO: How can that be?

FESTE: Marry, sir, they praise me, and make an ass of me. Now my foes tell me
    plainly I am an ass, so that by my foes, sir, I profit in the knowledge of
15   myself, and by my friends I am abused;[5] so that, conclusions to be as
    kisses, if your four negatives make your two affirmatives, why then the
    worse for my friends and the better for my foes.

ORSINO: Why, this is excellent.

FESTE: By my troth, sir, no, though it please you to be one of my friends.

ORSINO: Thou shalt not be the worse for me. There's gold.
    [(He gives a coin.)]

FESTE: But that it would be double-dealing,[6] sir, I would you could make it an-
    other.

ORSINO: O, you give me ill counsel.

FESTE: Put your grace in your pocket,[7] sir, for this once, and let your flesh and
    blood obey it.[8]

ORSINO: Well, I will be so much a sinner to be a double-dealer. There's another.
    [(He gives another coin.)]

FESTE: *Primo, secundo, tertio*, is a good play,[9] and the old saying is, the third pays
    for all.[1] The triplex,[2] sir, is a good tripping measure; or the bells of Saint
    Bennet,[3] sir, may put you in mind—one, two, three.

ORSINO: You can fool no more money out of me at this throw.[4] If you will let your
    lady know I am here to speak with her, and bring her along with you, it
    may awake my bounty further.

FESTE: Marry, sir, lullaby to your bounty till I come again. I go, sir, but I would not
    have you to think that my desire of having is the sin of covetousness. But
35   as you say, sir, let your bounty take a nap. I will awake it anon.   [*Exit.*]
    [*Enter Antonio and Officers.*]

VIOLA: Here comes the man, sir, that did rescue me.

ORSINO: That face of his I do remember well,
    Yet when I saw it last it was besmeared
    As black as Vulcan[5] in the smoke of war.
40   A baubling° vessel was he captain of,   *trifling*
    For shallow draft[6] and bulk unprizable,[7]
    With which such scatheful° grapple did he make   *harmful*
    With the most noble bottom° of our fleet   *ship*
    That very envy° and the tongue of loss°   *even malice / the losers*
45   Cried fame and honor on him. What's the matter?

3. Ornaments.
4. Because of.
5. Deceived.
6. Giving twice; deceit.
7. Pocket your virtue; be generous.
8. I.e., my ill counsel.
9. Game.

1. I.e., the third time is lucky.
2. Triple-time in music.
3. Church of St. Benedict.
4. Throw of the dice.
5. Roman god of fire, smith to the other gods.
6. Depth of water a ship draws.
7. Of slight value.

FIRST OFFICER: Orsino, this is that Antonio
    That took the *Phoenix* and her freight from Candy,°   *Crete*
    And this is he that did the *Tiger* board
    When your young nephew Titus lost his leg.
50   Here in the streets, desperate° of shame and state,   *reckless*
    In private brabble° did we apprehend him.   *brawl*
VIOLA: He did me kindness, sir, drew on my side,
    But in conclusion put strange speech upon me.
    I know not what 'twas but distraction.°   *madness*
ORSINO: Notable° pirate, thou saltwater thief,   *notorious*
    What foolish boldness brought thee to their mercies
    Whom thou in terms so bloody and so dear°   *costly*
    Hast made thine enemies?
ANTONIO: Orsino, noble sir,
    Be pleased that I° shake off these names you give me.   *allow me to*
60   Antonio never yet was thief or pirate,
    Though, I confess, on base and ground° enough   *solid grounds*
    Orsino's enemy. A witchcraft drew me hither.
    That most ingrateful boy there by your side
    From the rude sea's enraged and foamy mouth
65   Did I redeem; a wreck past hope he was.
    His life I gave him, and did thereto add
    My love, without retention° or restraint,   *reservation*
    All his in dedication. For his sake
    Did I expose myself—pure° for his love—   *purely*
70   Into° the danger of this adverse° town,   *unto / hostile*
    Drew to defend him when he was beset;
    Where being apprehended, his false cunning,
    Not meaning to partake with me in danger,
    Taught him to face me out of his acquaintance°   *deny knowing me*
75   And grew a twenty years' removed° thing   *estranged*
    While one would wink; denied me mine own purse,
    Which I had recommended° to his use   *entrusted*
    Not half an hour before.
VIOLA: How can this be?
ORSINO: When came he to this town?
ANTONIO: Today, my lord; and for three months before,
    No interim, not a minute's vacancy,
    Both day and night did we keep company.
    [*Enter Olivia and attendants.*]
ORSINO: Here comes the Countess. Now heaven walks on earth.
    But for thee, fellow—fellow, thy words are madness.
85   Three months this youth hath tended upon me;
    But more of that anon. Take him aside.
OLIVIA [*to Orsino*]: What would my lord—but that° he may not have— *except what*
    Wherein Olivia may seem serviceable?—
    Cesario, you do not keep promise with me.
VIOLA: Madam?
ORSINO: Gracious Olivia—

OLIVIA: What do you say, Cesario?—Good my lord—
VIOLA: My lord would speak. My duty hushes me.
OLIVIA: If it be aught to the old tune, my lord,
95   It is as fat° and fulsome° to mine ear   *gross / offensive*
             As howling after music.
ORSINO: Still so cruel?
OLIVIA: Still so constant, lord.
ORSINO: What, to perverseness? You uncivil lady,
             To whose ingrate° and unauspicious° altars   *ungrateful / unpromising*
100   My soul the faithfull'st offerings have breathed out
             That e'er devotion tendered! What shall I do?
OLIVIA: Even what it please my lord that shall become° him.   *suit*
ORSINO: Why should I not, had I the heart to do it,
             Like to th' Egyptian thief[8] at point of death
105   Kill what I love?—a savage jealousy
             That sometimes savors nobly. But hear me this:
             Since you to nonregardance° cast my faith,   *neglect*
             And that° I partly know the instrument   *since*
             That screws° me from my true place in your favor,   *pries*
110   Live you the marble-breasted tyrant still.
             But this your minion,° whom I know you love,   *favorite*
             And whom, by heaven I swear, I tender° dearly,   *hold*
             Him will I tear out of that cruel eye
             Where he sits crownèd in his master's spite.°—   *despite his master*
115   Come, boy, with me. My thoughts are ripe in mischief.
             I'll sacrifice the lamb that I do love,
             To spite a raven's heart within a dove. [(Going.)]
VIOLA: And I, most jocund, apt,° and willingly,   *readily*
             To do you rest,° a thousand deaths would die. [(Going.)]   *give you peace*
OLIVIA: Where goes Cesario?
VIOLA: After him I love
             More than I love these eyes, more than my life,
             More by all mores° than e'er I shall love wife.   *all comparisons*
             If I do feign, you witnesses above
             Punish my life for tainting of my love!
OLIVIA: Ay me, detested! How am I beguiled!
VIOLA: Who does beguile you? Who does do you wrong?
OLIVIA: Hast thou forgot thyself? Is it so long?
             Call forth the holy father.
                                                                [(Exit an attendant.)]
ORSINO [(to Viola)]:   Come, away!
OLIVIA: Whither, my lord? Cesario, husband, stay.
ORSINO: Husband?
OLIVIA: Ay, husband. Can he that deny?
ORSINO [to Viola]: Her husband, sirrah?[9]
VIOLA: No, my lord, not I.

---

8. Allusion to the *Ethiopica* by Heliodorus, in which the robber captain Thyamis kidnaps and falls in love with   Chariclea. Threatened with death, he tries to kill her first.
9. Address to an inferior.

OLIVIA: Alas, it is the baseness of thy fear
            That makes thee strangle thy propriety.°   *identity*
            Fear not, Cesario, take thy fortunes up;
135   Be that thou know'st thou art, and then thou art
            As great as that thou fear'st.°   *Orsino*
    [*Enter Priest.*]
                                              O, welcome, Father!
            Father, I charge thee by thy reverence
            Here to unfold—though lately we intended
            To keep in darkness what occasion now
140   Reveals before 'tis ripe—what thou dost know
            Hath newly passed between this youth and me.
PRIEST: A contract of eternal bond of love,
            Confirmed by mutual joinder° of your hands,   *joining*
            Attested by the holy close° of lips,   *meeting*
145   Strengthened by interchangement of your rings,
            And all the ceremony of this compact
            Sealed in my function, by my testimony;
            Since when, my watch hath told me, toward my grave
            I have traveled but two hours.
ORSINO [*to Viola*]: O thou dissembling cub! What wilt thou be
            When time hath sowed a grizzle° on thy case?°   *gray hair / skin*
            Or will not else thy craft so quickly grow
            That thine own trip° shall be thine overthrow?   *trickery*
            Farewell, and take her, but direct thy feet
155   Where thou and I henceforth may never meet.
VIOLA: My Lord, I do protest—
OLIVIA: O, do not swear!
            Hold little° faith, though thou hast too much fear.   *a little*
    [*Enter Sir Andrew.*]
SIR ANDREW: For the love of God, a surgeon! Send one presently¹ to Sir Toby.
OLIVIA: What's the matter?
SIR ANDREW: He's broke my head across, and has given Sir Toby a bloody cox-
            comb² too. For the love of God, your help! I had rather than forty pound
            I were at home.
OLIVIA: Who has done this, Sir Andrew?
SIR ANDREW: The Count's gentleman, one Cesario. We took him for a coward,
165   but he's the very devil incardinate.³
ORSINO: My gentleman, Cesario?
SIR ANDREW: 'Od's lifelings,⁴ here he is!—You broke my head for nothing, and
            that that I did I was set on to do 't by Sir Toby.
VIOLA: Why do you speak to me? I never hurt you.
170   You drew your sword upon me without cause,
            But I bespake you fair, and hurt you not.
SIR ANDREW: If a bloody coxcomb be a hurt, you have hurt me. I think you set
            nothing by a bloody coxcomb.

---

1. Immediately.   3. Incarnate.
2. Fool's cap (here, head).   4. By God's little lives.

[Enter (Sir) Toby and Clown (Feste).]

   Here comes Sir Toby, halting.[5] You shall hear more. But if he had not
175 been in drink, he would have tickled you othergates[6] than he did.

ORSINO: How now, gentleman? How is 't with you?

SIR TOBY: That's all one.[7] He's hurt me, and there's th' end on 't.—Sot,[8] didst see
   Dick surgeon, sot?

FESTE: O, he's drunk, Sir Toby, an hour agone; his eyes were set[9] at eight i' the
180 morning.

SIR TOBY: Then he's a rogue, and a passy measures pavane.[1] I hate a drunken
   rogue.

OLIVIA: Away with him! Who hath made this havoc with them?

SIR ANDREW: I'll help you, Sir Toby, because we'll be dressed[2] together.

SIR TOBY: Will you help? An ass-head and a coxcomb and a knave, a thin-faced
   knave, a gull!

OLIVIA: Get him to bed, and let his hurt be looked to.

       [(Exeunt Feste, Fabian, Sir Toby, and Sir Andrew.)]

[Enter Sebastian.]

SEBASTIAN: I am sorry, madam, I have hurt your kinsman;
   But, had it been the brother of my blood,
190 I must have done no less with wit and safety.[3]—
   You throw a strange regard° upon me, and by that   *estranged look*
   I do perceive it hath offended you.
   Pardon me, sweet one, even for the vows
   We made each other but so late ago.

ORSINO: One face, one voice, one habit,° and two persons,   *dress*
   A natural perspective,[4] that is and is not!

SEBASTIAN: Antonio, O my dear Antonio!
   How have the hours racked and tortured me
   Since I have lost thee!

ANTONIO: Sebastian are you?

SEBASTIAN: Fear'st thou° that, Antonio?   *do you doubt*

ANTONIO: How have you made division of yourself?
   An apple cleft in two is not more twin
   Than these two creatures. Which is Sebastian?

OLIVIA: Most wonderful!

SEBASTIAN *[(seeing Viola)]*: Do I stand there? I never had a brother;
   Nor can there be that deity in my nature
   Of here and everywhere.° I had a sister,   *omnipresence*
   Whom the blind° waves and surges have devoured.   *heedless*
   Of charity,° what kin are you to me?   *tell me in kindness*
210 What countryman? What name? What parentage?

VIOLA: Of Messaline. Sebastian was my father.
   Such a Sebastian was my brother, too.
   So went he suited° to his watery tomb.   *dressed*

---

5. Limping.
6. Otherwise.
7. It doesn't matter.
8. Drunkard.
9. Closed.

1. Slow dance.
2. Have our wounds dressed.
3. With an intelligent regard for my safety.
4. Optical illusion.

                 If spirits can assume both form and suit,
                 You come to fright us.
SEBASTIAN: A spirit I am indeed,
                 But am in that dimension grossly clad°   *clothed in the flesh*
                 Which from the womb I did participate.°   *inherit*
                 Were you a woman, as the rest goes even,°   *circumstances allow*
                 I should my tears let fall upon your cheek
220   And say, "Thrice welcome, drownèd Viola!"
VIOLA: My father had a mole upon his brow.
SEBASTIAN: And so had mine.
VIOLA: And died that day when Viola from her birth
                 Had numbered thirteen years.
SEBASTIAN: O, that record° is lively in my soul!   *memory*
                 He finishèd indeed his mortal act
                 That day that made my sister thirteen years.
VIOLA: If nothing lets° to make us happy both   *hinders*
                 But this my masculine usurped attire,
230   Do not embrace me till each circumstance
                 Of place, time, fortune, do cohere and jump°   *agree completely*
                 That I am Viola—which to confirm
                 I'll bring you to a captain in this town
                 Where lie my maiden weeds,° by whose gentle help   *clothes*
235   I was preserved to serve this noble count.
                 All the occurrence of my fortune since
                 Hath been between this lady and this lord.
SEBASTIAN [(*to Olivia*)]: So comes it, lady, you have been mistook.
                 But nature to her bias drew° in that.   *followed her bent*
240   You would have been contracted to a maid,°   *virgin man*
                 Nor are you therein, by my life, deceived.
                 You are betrothed both to a maid and man.
ORSINO [(*to Olivia*)]: Be not amazed; right noble is his blood.
                 If this be so, as yet the glass° seems true,   *natural perspective*
245   I shall have share in this most happy wreck.
                 [(*to Viola.*)] Boy, thou hast said to me a thousand times
                 Thou never shouldst love woman like to° me.   *as much as*
VIOLA: And all those sayings will I over swear,°   *swear again*
                 And all those swearings keep as true in soul
250   As doth that orbèd continent° the fire   *the Sun*
                 That severs day from night.
ORSINO: Give me thy hand,
                 And let me see thee in thy woman's weeds.°   *clothes*
VIOLA: The captain that did bring me first on shore
                 Hath my maid's garments. He upon some action°   *legal charge*
255   Is now in durance,° at Malvolio's suit,   *imprisonment*
                 A gentleman and follower of my lady's.
OLIVIA: He shall enlarge° him. Fetch Malvolio hither.   *release*
                 And yet, alas, now I remember me,
                 They say, poor gentleman, he's much distract.
                 [*Enter Clown (Feste) with a letter, and Fabian.*]

260   A most extracting° frenzy of mine own   *distracting*
      From my remembrance clearly banished his.
      How does he, sirrah?

FESTE: Truly, madam, he holds Beelzebub at the stave's end[5] as well as a man in
      his case may do. He's here writ a letter to you; I should have given 't you
265   today morning. But as a madman's epistles are no gospels, so it skills[6] not
      much when they are delivered.

OLIVIA: Open 't and read it.

FESTE: Look then to be well edified when the fool delivers[7] the madman. [*He reads
      loudly.*] "By the Lord, madam—"

OLIVIA: How now, art thou mad?

FESTE: No, madam, I do but read madness. An your ladyship will have it as it
      ought to be, you must allow *vox.*[8]

OLIVIA: Prithee, read i' thy right wits.[9]

FESTE: So I do, madonna; but to read his right wits is to read thus. Therefore per-
      pend,[1] my princess, and give ear.

OLIVIA [*to Fabian*]: Read it you, sirrah.

FABIAN [*reads*]: "By the Lord, madam, you wrong me, and the world shall know it.
      Though you have put me into darkness and given your drunken cousin
      rule over me, yet have I the benefit of my senses as well as your ladyship.
280   I have your own letter that induced me to the semblance I put on, with
      the which I doubt not but to do myself much right or you much shame.
      Think of me as you please. I leave my duty a little unthought of, and
      speak out of my injury.

                                  The madly used Malvolio."

OLIVIA: Did he write this?

FESTE: Ay, madam.

ORSINO: This savors not much of distraction.

OLIVIA: See him delivered,° Fabian. Bring him hither.   *released*
                                            [*Exit Fabian.*]

      My lord, so please you, these things further thought on,
      To think me as well a sister as a wife,
290   One day shall crown th' alliance on 't, so please you,
      Here at my house and at my proper° cost.   *own*

ORSINO: Madam, I am most apt° t' embrace your offer.   *ready*
      [*To Viola.*] Your master quits° you; and for your service done him, *releases*
      So much against the mettle° of your sex,   *disposition*
295   So far beneath your soft and tender breeding,
      And since you called me master for so long,
      Here is my hand. You shall from this time be
      Your master's mistress.

OLIVIA: A sister! You are she.

    [*Enter (Fabian with) Malvolio.*]

ORSINO: Is this the madman?

OLIVIA: Ay, my lord, this same.

300   How now, Malvolio?

---

5. Holds the devil off.   8. Loud voice.
6. Matters.   9. I.e., express his true state of mind.
7. Speaks the words of.   1. Consider.

MALVOLIO: Madam, you have done me wrong,
                Notorious wrong.
OLIVIA: Have I, Malvolio? No.
MALVOLIO [*showing a letter*]: Lady, you have. Pray you, peruse that letter.
                You must not now deny it is your hand.
                Write from it,° if you can, in hand or phrase,   *differently*
305   Or say 'tis not your seal, not your invention.°   *composition*
                You can say none of this. Well, grant it then,
                And tell me, in the modesty of honor,
                Why you have given me such clear lights° of favor,   *signs*
                Bade me come smiling and cross-gartered to you,
310   To put on yellow stockings, and to frown
                Upon Sir Toby and the lighter° people?   *lesser*
                And, acting this in an obedient hope,
                Why have you suffered me to be imprisoned,
                Kept in a dark house, visited by the priest,°   *Feste*
315   And made the most notorious geck° and gull   *dupe*
                That e'er invention played on? Tell me why?
OLIVIA: Alas, Malvolio, this is not my writing,
                Though, I confess, much like the character;°   *my handwriting*
                But out of° question 'tis Maria's hand.   *beyond*
320   And now I do bethink me, it was she
                First told me thou wast mad; then cam'st in smiling,
                And in such forms which here were presupposed°   *pre-imposed*
                Upon thee in the letter. Prithee, be content.
                This practice° hath most shrewdly° passed upon thee;   *plot / mischievously*
325   But when we know the grounds and authors of it,
                Thou shalt be both the plaintiff and the judge
                Of thine own cause.
FABIAN: Good madam, hear me speak,
                And let no quarrel nor no brawl to come
                Taint the condition of this present hour,
330   Which I have wondered at. In hope it shall not,
                Most freely I confess, myself and Toby
                Set this device against Malvolio here,
                Upon° some stubborn and uncourteous parts°   *because of / qualities*
                We had conceived against him. Maria writ
335   The letter at Sir Toby's great importance,°   *importunity*
                In recompense whereof he hath married her.
                How with a sportful malice it was followed°   *carried out*
                May rather pluck on° laughter than revenge,   *induce*
                If that the injuries be justly weighed
340   That have on both sides passed.
OLIVIA [*to Malvolio*]: Alas, poor fool, how have they baffled° thee!   *disgraced*
FESTE: Why, "Some are born great, some achieve greatness, and some have great-
                ness thrown upon them." I was one, sir, in this interlude,[2] one Sir Topas,
                sir, but that's all one. "By the Lord, fool, I am not mad." But do you re-
                member?

2. Little play.

345   "Madam, why laugh you at such a barren rascal? An you smile
      not, he's gagged." And thus the whirligig³ of time brings in his revenges.
MALVOLIO: I'll be revenged on the whole pack of you!

                                                                [*Exit.*]

OLIVIA: He hath been most notoriously abused.
ORSINO: Pursue him, and entreat him to a peace.
      He hath not told us of the captain yet.
      When that is known, and golden time convents,°   *is convenient*
      A solemn combination shall be made
      Of our dear souls. Meantime, sweet sister,
355   We will not part from hence. Cesario, come—
      For so you shall be, while you are a man;
      But when in other habits° you are seen,   *attire*
      Orsino's mistress and his fancy's° queen.   *love's*

                                  [*Exeunt (all, except Feste).*]

FESTE [*sings*]:
           When that I was and a little tiny boy,
360   With hey, ho, the wind and the rain,
           A foolish thing was but a toy,°   *trifle*
           For the rain it raineth every day.

           But when I came to man's estate,
           With hey, ho, the wind and the rain,
365   'Gainst knaves and thieves men shut their gate,
           For the rain it raineth every day.

           But when I came, alas, to wive,
           With hey, ho, the wind and the rain,
           By swaggering could I never thrive,
370   For the rain it raineth every day.

           But when I came unto my beds,
           With hey, ho, the wind and the rain,
           With tosspots° still had drunken heads,   *drunkards*
           For the rain it raineth every day.

375   A great while ago the world begun,
           With hey, ho, the wind and the rain,
           But that's all one, our play is done,
           And we'll strive to please you every day.
[*Exit.*]

OTHELLO   The first recorded performance of *Othello* was on 1 November 1604, before King
James I and his guests at Whitehall Palace. The Chamberlain's Men were now the King's Men,
and, as such, their duties at times even included waiting on the king, as Shakespeare and eleven
of his troupe did earlier in August of that year. The play would be performed again at court as
part of the marriage celebrations for the king's daughter, Princess Elizabeth, in 1612–1613. A
notation on the title page of the Quarto gives evidence of the play's popularity: "As it hath
been diverse times acted at the Globe and Black Friers, by his Maiesties Servants." A man
from an Oxford college who had seen one of these productions wrote an account of how the

3. Spinning top.

boy actor who played Desdemona "acted her part supremely, yet when she was killed was even more moving, for when she fell back upon the bed she implored the pity of the spectators by her very face." Contemporary audiences were clearly moved to pity by Othello as well, as can be seen in an elegy for Richard Burbage, the star of Shakespeare's troupe:

> But let me not forget one chiefest part
> Wherein beyond the rest, he mov'd the heart,
> The grieved Moor, made jealous by a slave,
> Who sent his wife to fill a timeless grave,
> Then slew himself upon the bloody bed.

The above poem sympathetically echoes the play's reversal of the audience's expectations. It is Iago, who speaks of Othello in racist language, who is the "slave" and "villain," not Othello, who had been "sold to slavery." Othello is "The grieved Moor." The term "Moor" has various connotations in the early modern period. It is often synonymous with "black Moor," or it can be identified with the "tawny" inhabitants of Barbary. At least one recent editor of *Othello*, E. A. J. Honigmann, has questioned the identification of "the noble Moor" as "black." Honigmann hypothesizes that the play was inspired by the visit to Elizabeth's court by the Moorish ambassador from the King of Barbary, whom Shakespeare would have witnessed when performing at court with the Chamberlain's Men during Christmastime in 1601. The vast majority of Shakespeare's audience, however, would not have seen this very aristocratic Moorish diplomat. The identification between "Moor" and a specific complexion is perhaps less important than the notion that Moors were seen as culturally alien and could be subject to racist practices. There were blacks in England, a result of the capture of slaves from Spanish and Portuguese vessels by English seamen. These Africans, brought into the country by force, were in turn expelled by force. In 1601, Elizabeth I issued a proclamation for the transportation of all "Negroes and blackamoors" out of England.

Shakespeare's audience would have known at least three black characters on the popular stage, all monstrous villains. Muly Hamet in George Peele's revenge tragedy *The Battle of Alcazar* (1589) seeks to destroy his own family; though given to bombastic rants, he proves cowardly and underhanded. Shakespeare's first black character, Aaron, in *Titus Andronicus* (1594), may have a redeeming concern for his son, but he is possessed by a motiveless and unrepentant drive to commit evil: He boasts of having "done a thousand dreadful things / As willingly as one would kill a fly." Eleazar in *Lust's Dominion* (c. 1600) embodies the sexual stereotype of the "black devil," manipulating his erotic hold over a white woman of royal blood to gain power.

It is against this network of racial exclusion, in both political practice and dramatic representation, that the play's persistent references to Othello's race need to be read. Othello's bravery and passionate love for Desdemona confound the stereotype of the black villain, and his Italian name and loyal service to the state suggest his assimilation to and identification with Venice. Yet to a certain degree, Othello shares some of his dramatic ancestors' traits— rhetorical bombast, an intense sexuality and uncontrollable violence. Iago voices sexually demonized portrayals of Othello's blackness, calling him "an old black ram," a "Barbary horse," "a lascivious Moor," "an erring Barbarian." However, Othello, too, is haunted by his own "blackness," as when he expresses his fear that Iago's claims of Desdemona's infidelity are true and that she has left him for another man: "Haply for I am black . . . she's gone." Through imagining Othello's internalization of the stereotype of racial inferiority, Shakespeare adds to our understanding of his vulnerability and the fatal consequences of such self-hatred.

Shakespeare's thinking both in his time and ahead of his time emerges in his complex representation of race in relation to marriage, sexuality, and love. From his rather more schematic narrative source, Giraldi Cinthio's *Hecatommithi* (1565), an Italian Renaissance tale of lust, brutality and banal moralization, Shakespeare creates a tragedy. A brief synopsis of the Italian novella will make the point. The Ensign (Iago) to a Moorish Captain (Othello) lusts after his wife Desdemona, and when she will not return his advances, the Ensign decides it is because she is in love with the Corporal (Cassio). Filled with hate and a desire to kill her lest even her husband enjoy her, the Ensign sets about convincing the Captain of his wife's infidelity. When Desdemona is confronted with her husband's jealous suspicions, she concludes that she should never have married a Moor. The Ensign plots with the Moor to kill Desdemona. Bludgeoning her to death with sandbags, they then pull the plaster down from the ceiling to make it look like an accident. Afterward realizing that his wicked Ensign has cost him the joy of his life, the Captain demotes him; in turn, the Ensign accuses the Captain of murdering his own wife. The Moorish Captain denies everything under torture, but Desdemona's relatives eventually get their revenge upon him.

In the narrative source, the protagonist is merely a cultural marker, "the Moor," whom the heroine can dismiss as an inappropriate choice for marriage—a warning to other young women. Shakespeare transforms the Ensign's frustrated lust for Desdemona into the complex homoeroticism of Iago's sexual jealousy of and manipulative intimacy with both Cassio and Othello. Whereas the tales in Cinthio's *Hecatommithi* as a whole do not deny the validity of Iago's cynical views of sexuality and love, Desdemona's combination of passion and faithful devotion exposes how sickly twisted and hatefully vengeful such a view is. The ruling emotion of Cinthio's Moor, a compound of mere jealousy and unrepentant hatred, becomes, in Shakespeare's conception, the tormented self-hatred that leads the tragic hero to doubt his worthiness to be loved and to shoulder the unbearable responsibility that leads him to take his life. The Moor's uncontrollable desire to punish his wife for his supposed sexual transgression in the tale is allied in the tragedy with Othello's obsession with punishing himself for his racial difference: "My name that was as fresh / As Dian's visage is now begrimed and black / As my own face."

At the same time, Othello's identification of his public honor with his wife's chastity demonstrates Shakespeare's understanding of how the need to control women's sexuality in early modern conceptions of marriage functions as a microcosm of the larger theological and political order. Iago's accusations of Desdemona's infidelity stir up the male fear of uncontrollable female sexuality, causing Othello to lament: "O curse of marriage / That we can call these delicate creatures ours / And not their appetites." Renaissance tracts on marriage present women as "the weaker vessel," requiring control by fathers and husbands. The sermons on marriage echoed Saint Paul in stating that men should be "the head of the wife, as Christ is the head of the Church." This male authority demanded the woman's obedience to her husband, just as subjects owed obedience to their sovereign. In eloping with Othello, Desdemona has already transgressed the authority of her father, who taunts Othello with Desdemona's potential for future disobedience: "She has deceived her father and may thee." Although she defies her father in her unswerving loyalty and love for her husband, like that recommended in early modern tracts on marriage, Desdemona is simultaneously compromised as disobedient and furtive.

While the play celebrates the passionate love of Desdemona for Othello, it also reveals the terrible costs of her submission. Such submission also informs Emilia's desire to please Iago. By obeying Iago's desire that she steal the handkerchief that becomes the circumstantial evidence of Desdemona's betrayal, Emilia becomes an unwitting accomplice in her mistress's murder. In telling the truth at the end of the play, Emilia defies her husband's command that she be silent, acknowledging how shocking such defiance would seem: "Let heaven and men and devils, let them all, / All, all, cry shame against me, yet I'll speak." In giving her this defiant speech, the play speaks volumes about the silent obedience demanded of women.

In multiple and sometimes contradictory ways, Shakespeare's *Othello* reproduces the discourses of racism and sexism in early modern English culture and contests them, defying audience expectations by creating sympathy for a black hero and a disobedient daughter, and placing this sympathy against a hero's sexism and a wife's too willing submission. Iago's manipulation of these discourses in preying upon Othello's self-hatred of his "blackness" and fear of Desdemona's passionate independence lead him to murder her. To protect her husband, even as he kills her, Desdemona persists in her loyalty by claiming responsibility for her own death. But may she also be acknowledging her acquiescence in her murder? At the end of the play, Othello acknowledges how he has allowed himself to be blinded, but maintains that he was "not easily jealous but, being wrought, / Perplexed in the extreme." Witnessing his wife's faithful love, he describes his crime in racially charged terms: "one whose hand / Like the base Indian, threw a pearl away / Richer than all his tribe." The unbearable guilt he suffers for her death leads him to take his own life. Othello's self-description as "one who loved not wisely, but too well," may more accurately describe Desdemona's self-sacrifice and suffering for love. To what extent either she or Othello achieves self-knowledge are questions the audience must answer in relation to themselves and their own world, as well as the world in which Shakespeare lived and created.

Othello, the Moor of Venice

The Names of the Actors

OTHELLO, *the Moor*	SAILORS
BRABANTIO, *a senator, father to Desdemona*	CLOWN
CASSIO, *an honorable lieutenant to Othello*	DESDEMONA, *daughter to Brabantio*
IAGO, *Othello's ancient,° a villain ensign*	*and wife to Othello*
RODERIGO, *a gulled gentleman*	EMILIA, *wife to Iago*
DUKE OF VENICE	BIANCA, *a courtesan and mistress to Cassio*
SENATORS *of Venice*	A MESSENGER
MONTANO, *Governor of Cyprus*	A HERALD
GENTLEMEN *of Cyprus*	A MUSICIAN
LODOVICO AND GRATIANO, *kinsmen*	SERVANTS, ATTENDANTS, OFFICERS,
to Brabantio, two noble Venetians	SENATORS, MUSICIANS, GENTLEMEN

Scene: *Venice; a seaport in Cyprus*

ACT 1[1]

Scene 1[2]

[*Enter Roderigo and Iago.*]

RODERIGO: Tush, never tell me! I take it much unkindly
    That thou, Iago, who hast had my purse
    As if the strings were thine, shouldst know of this.[3]
IAGO: 'Sblood,[4] but you'll not hear me.
5   If ever I did dream of such a matter,
    Abhor me.
RODERIGO: Thou toldst me thou didst hold him in thy hate.
IAGO: Despise me
    If I do not. Three great ones of the city,
10   In personal suit to make me his lieutenant,
    Off-capped to him;° and by the faith of man,   *Othello*
    I know my price, I am worth no worse a place.

---

1. The notes are based on those of David Bevington, ed. *The Complete Works of Shakespeare*. All original stage directions are in square brackets, and all editorially added stage directions are in parentheses.

2. Location: Venice. A street.
3. I.e., Desdemona's elopement.
4. By His (Christ's) blood.

	But he, as loving his own pride and purposes,	
	Evades them with a bombast circumstance[5]	
15	Horribly stuffed with epithets of war,	
	And, in conclusion,	
	Nonsuits° my mediators. For, "Certes,"° says he,	rejects / certainly
	"I have already chose my officer."	
	And what was he?	
20	Forsooth, a great arithmetician,[6]	
	One Michael Cassio, a Florentine,	
	A fellow almost damned in a fair wife,[7]	
	That never set a squadron in the field	
	Nor the division of a battle knows	
25	More than a spinster[8]—unless the bookish theoric,°	theory
	Wherein the togaed consuls° can propose°	
	As masterly as he. Mere prattle without practice	senators / discuss
	Is all his soldiership. But he, sir, had th'election;	
	And I, of whom his° eyes had seen the proof	Othello's
30	At Rhodes, at Cyprus, and on other grounds	
	Christened° and heathen, must be beleed and calmed[9]	Christian
	By debitor and creditor.[1] This countercaster,[2]	
	He, in good time,° must his lieutenant be,	opportunely
	And I—God bless the mark![3]—his Moorship's ancient.°	ensign

RODERIGO: By heaven, I rather would have been his hangman.
IAGO: Why, there's no remedy. 'Tis the curse of service;

	Preferment° goes by letter and affection,[4]	promotion
	And not by old gradation,[5] where each second	
	Stood heir to th' first. Now, sir, be judge yourself	
40	Whether I in any just term° am affined°	respect / bound
	To love the Moor.	

RODERIGO: I would not follow him then.
IAGO: O sir, content you.[6]

	I follow him to serve my turn upon him.	
	We cannot all be masters, nor all masters	
45	Cannot be truly° followed. You shall mark	faithfully
	Many a duteous and knee-crooking knave	
	That, doting on his own obsequious bondage,	
	Wears out his time, much like his master's ass,	
	For naught but provender, and when he's old, cashiered.°	dismissed
50	Whip me[7] such honest knaves. Others there are	
	Who, trimmed in forms and visages of duty,[8]	

5. Wordy evasion. *Bombast* is cotton padding.
6. A man whose military knowledge is merely theoretical, based on books of tactics.
7. Cassio does not seem to be married, but his counterpart in Shakespeare's source does have a woman in his house.
8. A housewife, one whose regular occupation is spinning.
9. Left to leeward without wind, becalmed (a sailing metaphor).
1. A name for a system of bookkeeping.

2. Bookkeeper, one who tallies with *counters*, or "metal disks." Said contemptuously of Cassio.
3. Perhaps originally a formula to ward off evil; here an expression of impatience.
4. Personal influence and favoritism.
5. Step-by-step seniority, the traditional way.
6. Don't you worry about that.
7. Whip, as far as I'm concerned.
8. Dressed up in the mere form and show of dutifulness.

Keep yet their hearts attending on themselves,
And, throwing but shows of service on their lords,
Do well thrive by them, and when they have lined their coats,[9]
55 Do themselves homage.[1] These fellows have some soul,
And such a one do I profess myself. For, sir,
It is as sure as you are Roderigo,
Were I the Moor I would not be Iago.[2]
In following him, I follow but myself—
60 Heaven is my judge, not I for love and duty,
But seeming so for my peculiar° end.   *particular*
For when my outward action doth demonstrate
The native° act and figure° of my heart   *innate* / *intent*
In compliment extern,[3] 'tis not long after
65 But I will wear my heart upon my sleeve
For daws[4] to peck at. I am not what I am.[5]
RODERIGO: What a full° fortune does the thick-lips[6] owe°   *swelling* / *own*
        If he can carry 't thus!°   *carry this off*
IAGO: Call up her father.
        Rouse him, make after him, poison his delight,
70 Proclaim him in the streets; incense her kinsmen,
        And, though he in a fertile climate dwell,
        Plague him with flies.[7] Though that his joy be joy,[8]
        Yet throw such changes of vexation° on 't   *vexing changes*
        As it may lose some color.[9]
RODERIGO: Here is her father's house. I'll call aloud.
IAGO: Do, with like timorous° accent and dire yell   *frightening*
        As when, by night and negligence, the fire
        Is spied in populous cities.
RODERIGO: What ho, Brabantio! Signor Brabantio, ho!
IAGO: Awake! What ho, Brabantio! Thieves, thieves, thieves!
        Look to your house, your daughter, and your bags!
        Thieves, thieves!
        [*Brabantio (enters) above (at a window.*)]¹
BRABANTIO: What is the reason of this terrible summons?
        What is the matter° there?   *your business*
RODERIGO: Signor, is all your family within?
IAGO: Are your doors locked?
BRABANTIO: Why, wherefore ask you this?
IAGO: Zounds,[2] sir, you're robbed. For shame, put on your gown!
        Your heart is burst; you have lost half your soul.
        Even now, now, very now, an old black ram

---

9. Stuffed their purses.
1. Attend to self-interest solely.
2. If I were able to assume command, I certainly would not choose to remain a subordinate, or, I would keep a suspicious eye on a flattering subordinate.
3. Outward show (conforming in this case to the inner workings and intention of the heart).
4. Small crowlike birds, proverbially stupid and avaricious.
5. I am not one who wears his heart on his sleeve.

6. Elizabethans often applied the term "Moor" to Africans.
7. Though he seems prosperous and happy now, vex him with misery.
8. Although he seems fortunate and happy.
9. That may cause it to lose some of its first gloss.
1. This stage direction, from the Quarto, probably calls for an appearance on the gallery above and rearstage.
2. By His (Christ's) wounds.

90   Is tupping your white ewe.³ Arise, arise!
            Awake the snorting° citizens with the bell,   *snorting*
            Or else the devil⁴ will make a grandsire of you.
            Arise, I say!

BRABANTIO: What, have you lost your wits?

RODERIGO: Most reverend signor, do you know my voice?

BRABANTIO: Not I. What are you?

RODERIGO: My name is Roderigo.

BRABANTIO: The worser welcome.
            I have charged thee not to haunt about my doors.
            In honest plainness thou hast heard me say
            My daughter is not for thee; and now, in madness,
100   Being full of supper and distempering° drafts,   *intoxicating*
            Upon malicious bravery⁵ dost thou come
            To start° my quiet.   *disrupt*

RODERIGO: Sir, sir, sir—

BRABANTIO: But thou must needs be sure
            My spirits and my place⁶ have in° their power   *have it in*
105   To make this bitter to thee.

RODERIGO: Patience, good sir.

BRABANTIO: What tell'st thou me of robbing? This is Venice;
            My house is not a grange.°   *country house*

RODERIGO: Most grave Brabantio,
            In simple° and pure soul I come to you.   *sincere*

IAGO: Zounds, sir, you are one of those that will not serve God if the devil bid you.

110   Because we come to do you service and you think we are ruffians, you'll have
       your daughter covered with a Barbary⁷ horse; you'll have your nephews⁸ neigh
       to you; you'll have coursers for cousins and jennets for germans.⁹

BRABANTIO: What profane wretch art thou?

IAGO: I am one, sir, that comes to tell you your daughter and the Moor are now making
115   the beast with two backs.

BRABANTIO: Thou art a villain.

IAGO: You are—a senator.¹

BRABANTIO: This thou shalt answer.² I know thee, Roderigo.

RODERIGO: Sir, I will answer anything. But I beseech you,
            If 't be your pleasure and most wise° consent—   *well-informed*
120   As partly I find it is—that your fair daughter,
            At this odd-even³ and dull watch o' the night,
            Transported with° no worse nor better guard   *by*
            But with a knave of common hire,⁴ a gondolier,
            To the gross clasps of a lascivious Moor—
125   If this be known to you and your allowance°   *permission*

---

3. Covering, copulating with (said of sheep).
4. The devil was conventionally pictured as black.
5. With hostile intent to defy me.
6. My temperament and my authority of office.
7. From northern Africa (and hence associated with Othello).
8. I.e., grandsons.

9. You'll have stallions for kinsmen and ponies for relatives.
1. Said with mock politeness, as though the word itself were an insult.
2. Be held accountable for.
3. Between one day and the next, i.e., about midnight.
4. Than by a low fellow, a servant.

	We then have done you bold and saucy° wrongs.	*insolent*
	But if you know not this, my manners tell me	
	We have your wrong rebuke. Do not believe	
	That, from° the sense of all civility,°	*contrary to / decency*
130	I thus would play and trifle with your reverence.[5]	
	Your daughter, if you have not given her leave,	
	I say again, hath made a gross revolt,	
	Tying her duty, beauty, wit,° and fortunes	*intelligence*
	In an extravagant° and wheeling° stranger[6]	*expatriate / vagabond*
135	Of here and everywhere. Straight° satisfy yourself.	*straightway*
	If she be in her chamber or your house,	
	Let loose on me the justice of the state	
	For thus deluding you.	

BRABANTIO: Strike on the tinder,[7] ho!

140	Give me a taper! Call up all my people!	
	This accident° is not unlike my dream.	*event*
	Belief of it oppresses me already.	
	Light, I say, light! [*Exit above*].	

IAGO: Farewell, for I must leave you.

	It seems not meet° nor wholesome to my place°	*fitting / position*
145	To be producted[8]—as, if I stay, I shall—	
	Against the Moor. For I do know the state,	
	However this may gall° him with some check,°	*oppress / rebuke*
	Cannot with safety cast° him, for he's embarked°	*dismiss / engaged*
	With such loud reason[9] to the Cyprus wars,	
150	Which even now stands in act,° that, for their souls,[1]	*are going on*
	Another of his fathom[2] they have none	
	To lead their business; in which regard,[3]	
	Though I do hate him as I do hell pains,	
	Yet for necessity of present life°	*livelihood*
155	I must show out a flag and sign of love,	
	Which is indeed but sign. That you shall surely find him,	
	Lead to the Sagittary[4] the raisèd search,[5]	
	And there will I be with him. So farewell. [*Exit.*]	

[*Enter (below), Brabantio (in his nightgown)[6] with servants and torches.*]

BRABANTIO: It is too true an evil. Gone she is;

160	And what's to come of my despisèd time[7]
	Is naught but bitterness. Now, Roderigo,
	Where didst thou see her?—O, unhappy girl!—
	With the Moor, sayst thou?—Who would be a father!—
	How didst thou know 'twas she?—O, she deceives me
165	Past thought!—What said she to you?—Get more tapers.

---

5. The respect due to you.
6. Foreigner.
7. Charred linen ignited by a spark from flint and steel, used to light torches or *tapers*.
8. Produced (as a witness).
9. Unanimous shout of confirmation (in the Senate).
1. To save themselves.
2. I.e., ability, depth of experience.

3. Out of regard for which.
4. An inn or house where Othello and Desdemona are staying, named for its sign of Sagittarius, or Centaur.
5. Search party roused out of sleep.
6. Dressing gown. (This costuming is specified in the Quarto text.)
7. I.e., remainder of life.

Raise all my kindred.—Are they married, think you?

RODERIGO: Truly, I think they are.

BRABANTIO: O heaven! How got she out? O treason of the blood!
Fathers, from hence trust not your daughters' minds

170   By what you see them act. Is there not charms°   *spells*
By which the property° of youth and maidhood   *nature*
May be abused?° Have you not read, Roderigo,   *deceived*
Of some such thing?

RODERIGO: Yes, sir, I have indeed.

BRABANTIO: Call up my brother.—O would you had had her!—

175   Some one way, some another.—Do you know
Where we may apprehend her and the Moor?

RODERIGO: I think I can discover° him, if you please   *reveal*
To get good guard and go along with me.

BRABANTIO: Pray you, lead on. At every house I'll call;

180   I may command° at most.—Get weapons, ho!   *demand aid*
And raise some special officers of night.—
On, good Roderigo. I will deserve° your pains.   *reward*
                                   [Exeunt.]

Scene 2[8]

[(*Before Othello's lodgings.*) *Enter Othello, Iago, attendants with torches.*]

IAGO: Though in the trade of war I have slain men,
Yet do I hold it very stuff[9] o' the conscience
To do no contrived° murder. I lack iniquity   *premeditated*
Sometimes to do me service. Nine or ten times

5   I had thought t' have yerked° him° here under the ribs.   *stabbed / Roderigo*

OTHELLO: 'Tis better as it is.

IAGO: Nay, but he prated,
And spoke such scurvy and provoking terms
Against your honor
That, with the little godliness I have,

10   I did full hard forbear him.[1] But, I pray you, sir,
Are you fast married? Be assured of this,
That the magnifico[2] is much beloved,
And hath in his effect° a voice potential°   *command / powerful*
As double as the Duke's. He will divorce you,

15   Or put upon you what restraint or grievance
The law, with all his might to enforce it on,
Will give him cable.°   *scope*

OTHELLO: Let him do his spite.
My services which I have done the seigniory°   *government*
Shall out-tongue his complaints. 'Tis yet to know°—   *not yet known*

20   Which, when I know that boasting is an honor,
I shall promulgate—I fetch my life and being

---

8. Location: Venice. Another street. Before Othello's
lodgings.
9. Essence, basic material (continuing the metaphor of
trade from line 1).

1. I restrained myself with great difficulty from assaulting
him.
2. Venetian grandee, i.e., Brabantio.

	From men of royal siege,° and my demerits°	*rank / deserts*
	May speak unbonnetted[3] to as proud a fortune	
	As this that I have reached. For know, Iago,	
25	But that I love the gentle Desdemona,	
	I would not my unhousèd° free condition	*unconfined*
	Put into circumscription and confine°	*confinement*
	For the seas' worth.[4] But look, what lights come yond?	

[*Enter Cassio (and certain officers[5]) with torches.*]

IAGO: Those are the raisèd father and his friends.
30   You were best go in.
OTHELLO: Not I. I must be found.
      My parts, my title, and my perfect soul[6]
      Shall manifest me rightly. Is it they?
IAGO: By Janus,[7] I think no.
OTHELLO: The servants of the Duke? And my lieutenant?
35   The goodness of the night upon you, friends!
      What is the news?
CASSIO: The Duke does greet you, General,
      And he requires your haste-post-haste appearance
      Even on the instant.

OTHELLO: What is the matter,° think you?   *business*
CASSIO: Something from Cyprus, as I may divine.°   *guess*
40   It is a business of some heat.° The galleys   *urgency*
      Have sent a dozen sequent° messengers   *successive*
      This very night at one another's heels,
      And many of the consuls,° raised and met,   *senators*
      Are at the Duke's already. You have been hotly called for;
45   When, being not at your lodging to be found,
      The Senate hath sent about[8] three several° quests   *separate*
      To search you out.
OTHELLO: 'Tis well I am found by you.
      I will but spend a word here in the house
      And go with you.   [*Exit.*]

CASSIO: Ancient, what makes° he here?   *does*
IAGO: Faith, he tonight hath boarded[9] a land carrack.°   *merchant ship*
      If it prove lawful prize,° he's made forever.   *booty*
CASSIO: I do not understand.
IAGO: He's married.
CASSIO: To who?

[(*Enter Othello.*)]

IAGO: Marry,[1] to—Come, Captain, will you go?
OTHELLO: Have with you.[2]
CASSIO: Here comes another troop to seek for you.

3. Without removing the hat, i.e., on equal terms (or "with hat off," "in all due modesty").
4. All the riches at the bottom of the sea.
5. The Quarto text calls for "Cassio with lights, officers with torches."
6. My natural gifts, my position or reputation, and my unflawed conscience.

7. Roman two-faced god of beginnings.
8. All over the city.
9. Gone aboard and seized as an act of piracy (with sexual suggestion).
1. An oath, originally "by the Virgin Mary"; here with wordplay on *married*.
2. Let's go.

[*Enter Brabantio, Roderigo, with officers and torches.*][3]

IAGO: It is Brabantio. General, be advised.[4]
    He comes to bad intent.

OTHELLO: Holla! Stand there!

RODERIGO: Signor, it is the Moor.

BRABANTIO: Down with him, thief!
    [(*They draw on both sides.*)]

IAGO: You, Roderigo! Come, sir, I am for you.

OTHELLO: Keep up° your bright swords, for the dew will rust them.   *sheathe*
    Good signor, you shall more command with years
    Than with your weapons.

BRABANTIO: O thou foul thief, where hast thou stowed my daughter?
    Damned as thou art, thou hast enchanted her!

65   For I'll refer me to all things of sense,[5]
    If she in chains of magic were not bound
    Whether a maid so tender, fair, and happy,
    So opposite to marriage that she shunned
    The wealthy curlèd darlings of our nation,

70   Would ever have, t' incur a general mock,
    Run from her guardage[6] to the sooty bosom
    Of such a thing as thou—to fear, not to delight.
    Judge me the world if 'tis not gross in sense°   *obvious*
    That thou hast practiced on her with foul charms,

75   Abused her delicate youth with drugs or minerals°   *poisons*
    That weakens motion.[7] I'll have 't disputed on;[8]
    'Tis probable and palpable to thinking.
    I therefore apprehend and do attach° thee   *arrest*
    For an abuser of the world, a practicer

80   Of arts inhibited° and out of warrant.°—   *black magic / illegal*
    Lay hold upon him! If he do resist,
    Subdue him at his peril.

OTHELLO: Hold your hands,
    Both you of my inclining° and the rest.   *following*
    Were it my cue to fight, I should have known it

85   Without a prompter.—Whither will you that I go
    To answer this your charge?

BRABANTIO: To prison, till fit time
    Of law and course of direct session[9]
    Call thee to answer.

OTHELLO: What if I do obey?

90   How may the Duke be therewith satisfied,
    Whose messengers are here about my side
    Upon some present business of the state
    To bring me to him?

---

3. The Quarto text calls for "others with lights and weapons."
4. Be on your guard.
5. Submit my case to creatures possessing common sense.
6. My guardianship of her.
7. Impair the vital faculties.
8. Argued in court by professional counsel, debated by experts.
9. Regular or specially convened legal proceedings.

OFFICER: 'Tis true, most worthy signor.
          The Duke's in council, and your noble self,
95   I am sure, is sent for.
BRABANTIO: How? The Duke in council?
          In this time of the night? Bring him away.°   *right along*
          Mine's not an idle° cause. The Duke himself,   *trifling*
          Or any of my brothers of the state,
          Cannot but feel this wrong as 'twere their own;
100   For if such actions may have passage free,[1]
          Bondslaves and pagans shall our statesmen be.
      [*Exeunt.*]

                              Scene 3[2]

[*Enter Duke (and) Senators (and sit at a table with lights,) and Officers. (The Duke
and Senators are reading dispatches.)*][3]

DUKE: There is no composition° in these news   *consistency*
          That gives them credit.
FIRST SENATOR: Indeed, they are disproportioned.°   *inconsistent*
          My letters say a hundred and seven galleys.
DUKE: And mine, a hundred forty.
SECOND SENATOR: And mine, two hundred.
          But though they jump° not on a just° account—   *agree / exact*
          As in these cases, where the aim° reports   *conjecture*
          'Tis oft with difference—yet do they all confirm
          A Turkish fleet, and bearing up to Cyprus.
DUKE: Nay, it is possible enough to judgment.
          I do not so secure me in the error
          But the main article I do approve[4]
          In fearful sense.
SAILOR [*within*]:   What ho, what ho, what ho!
      [*Enter Sailor.*]
OFFICER: A messenger from the galleys.
DUKE: Now, what's the business?
SAILOR: The Turkish preparation[5] makes for Rhodes.
          So was I bid report here to the state
          By Signor Angelo.
DUKE: How say you by° this change?   *about*
FIRST SENATOR: This cannot be
20   By no assay° of reason. 'Tis a pageant°   *test / mere show*
          To keep us in false gaze.[6] When we consider
          Th' importancy of Cyprus to the Turk,
          And let ourselves again but understand
          That, as it more concerns the Turk than Rhodes,

---

1. Are allowed to go unchecked.
2. Location: Venice. A council chamber.
3. The Quarto text calls for the Duke and senators to "sit
at a table with lights and attendants."
4. I do not take such (false) comfort in the discrepancies

that I fail to perceive the main point, i.e., that the Turkish fleet is threatening.
5. Fleet prepared for battle.
6. Looking the wrong way.

25   So may he with more facile question bear it,[7]
      For that° it stands not in such warlike brace,°   *since / state*
      But altogether lacks th' abilities°   *means of defense*
      That Rhodes is dressed in°—if we make thought of this,   *equipped with*
      We must not think the Turk is so unskillful°   *careless*
30   To leave that latest° which concerns him first,   *last*
      Neglecting an attempt of ease and gain
      To wake° and wage° a danger profitless.   *stir up / risk*
DUKE: Nay, in all confidence, he's not for Rhodes.
OFFICER: Here is more news.
      [*Enter a Messenger.*]
MESSENGER: The Ottomites, reverend and gracious,
      Steering with due course toward the isle of Rhodes,
      Have there injointed them[8] with an after° fleet.   *following*
FIRST SENATOR: Ay, so I thought. How many, as you guess?
MESSENGER: Of thirty sail; and now they do restem
40   Their backward course,[9] bearing with frank° appearance   *undisguised*
      Their purposes toward Cyprus. Signor Montano,
      Your trusty and most valiant servitor,°   *officer*
      With his free duty[1] recommends[2] you thus,
      And prays you to believe him.
DUKE: 'Tis certain then for Cyprus.
      Marcus Luccicos, is not he in town?
FIRST SENATOR: He's now in Florence.
DUKE: Write from us to him, post-post-haste. Dispatch.
FIRST SENATOR: Here comes Brabantio and the valiant Moor.
      [*Enter Brabantio, Othello, Cassio, Iago, Roderigo, and officers.*]
DUKE: Valiant Othello, we must straight° employ you   *straightway*
      Against the general enemy[3] Ottoman.
      [(*To Brabantio.*)] I did not see you; welcome, gentle° signor.   *noble*
      We lacked your counsel and your help tonight.
BRABANTIO: So did I yours. Good Your Grace, pardon me;
55   Neither my place° nor aught I heard of business   *official position*
      Hath raised me from my bed, nor doth the general care
      Take hold on me, for my particular° grief   *personal*
      Is of so floodgate[4] and o'erbearing nature
      That it engluts° and swallows other sorrows   *engulfs*
60   And it is still itself.[5]
DUKE: Why, what's the matter?
BRABANTIO: My daughter! O, my daughter!
DUKE AND SENATORS: Dead?
BRABANTIO: Ay, to me.
      She is abused,° stol'n from me, and corrupted   *deceived*
      By spells and medicines bought of mountebanks;
      For nature so preposterously to err,

7. So also he (the Turk) can more easily capture it (Cyprus).
8. Joined themselves.
9. Retrace their original course.
1. Freely given and loyal service.

2. Commends himself and reports to.
3. Universal enemy to all Christendom.
4. Overwhelming (as when floodgates are opened).
5. Remains undiminished.

65	Being not deficient,° blind, or lame of sense,	*defective*
	Sans° witchcraft could not.	*without*

DUKE: Whoe'er he be that in this foul proceeding
Hath thus beguiled your daughter of herself,
And you of her, the bloody book of law
You shall yourself read in the bitter letter

70   After your own sense[6]—yea, though our proper° son   *my own*
Stood in your action.[7]

BRABANTIO: Humbly I thank Your Grace.
Here is the man, this Moor, whom now it seems
Your special mandate for the state affairs
Hath hither brought.

ALL: We are very sorry for 't.
DUKE [(*to Othello*)]:
75   What, in your own part, can you say to this?
BRABANTIO: Nothing, but this is so.
OTHELLO: Most potent, grave, and reverend signors,

	My very noble and approved° good masters:	*esteemed*
	That I have ta'en away this old man's daughter,	
80	It is most true; true, I have married her.	
	The very head and front[8] of my offending	
	Hath this extent, no more. Rude° am I in my speech,	*unpolished*
	And little blessed with the soft phrase of peace;	
	For since these arms of mine had seven years' pith,[9]	
85	Till now some nine moons wasted,[1] they have used	
	Their dearest° action in the tented field;	*most valuable*

And little of this great world can I speak
More than pertains to feats of broils and battle,
And therefore little shall I grace my cause

90	In speaking for myself. Yet, by your gracious patience,	
	I will a round° unvarnished tale deliver	*plain*

Of my whole course of love—what drugs, what charms,
What conjuration, and what mighty magic,

	For such proceeding I am charged withal,°	*with*
95	I won his daughter.	

BRABANTIO: A maiden never bold;
Of spirit so still and quiet that her motion
Blushed at herself;[2] and she, in spite of nature,

	Of years,[3] of country, credit,° everything,	*reputation*

To fall in love with what she feared to look on!

100	It is a judgment maimed and most imperfect	
	That will confess° perfection so could err	*concede (that)*

Against all rules of nature, and must be driven

	To find out practices° of cunning hell	*plots*

6. According to your own interpretation.
7. Were under your accusation.
8. Height and breadth, entire extent.
9. Since I was seven.
1. Until some nine months ago (since when Othello has

evidently not been on active duty, but in Venice).
2. She blushed easily at herself. (*Motion* can suggest the impulse of the soul or of the emotions, or physical movement.)
3. I.e., difference in age.

Why this should be. I therefore vouch° again   *assert*
105   That with some mixtures powerful o'er the blood,°   *passions*
Or with some dram conjured to this effect,[4]
He wrought upon her.
DUKE: To vouch this is no proof,
Without more wider° and more overt test°   *fuller / testimony*
Than these thin habits[5] and poor likelihoods°   *weak inferences*
110   Of modern seeming[6] do prefer° against him.   *bring forth*
FIRST SENATOR: But Othello, speak.
Did you by indirect and forcèd courses[7]
Subdue and poison this young maid's affections?
Or came it by request and such fair question°   *conversation*
115   As soul to soul affordeth?
OTHELLO: I do beseech you,
Send for the lady to the Sagittary
And let her speak of me before her father.
If you do find me foul in her report,
The trust, the office I do hold of you
120   Not only take away, but let your sentence
Even fall upon my life.
DUKE: Fetch Desdemona hither.
OTHELLO: Ancient, conduct them. You best know the place.
                                   [(*Exeunt Iago and attendants.*)]
And, till she come, as truly as to heaven
I do confess the vices of my blood,°   *passions*
125   So justly° to your grave ears I'll present   *accurately*
How I did thrive in this fair lady's love,
And she in mine.
DUKE: Say it, Othello.
OTHELLO: Her father loved me, oft invited me,
130   Still° questioned me the story of my life   *continually*
From year to year—the battles, sieges, fortunes
That I have passed.
I ran it through, even from my boyish days
To th' very moment that he bade me tell it,
135   Wherein I spoke of most disastrous chances,
Of moving accidents° by flood and field,   *stirring happenings*
Of hairbreadth scapes i' th' imminent deadly breach,[8]
Of being taken by the insolent foe
And sold to slavery, of my redemption thence,
140   And portance° in my travels' history,   *conduct*
Wherein of antres° vast and deserts idle,°   *caverns / barren*
Rough quarries,° rocks, and hills whose heads touch heaven,   *rock formations*
It was my hint° to speak—such was my process—   *opportunity*
And of the Cannibals that each other eat,

---

4. Dose made by magical spells to have this effect.
5. Garments, i.e., appearances.
6. Commonplace assumption.

7. Means used against her will.
8. Death-threatening gaps made in a fortification.

145   The Anthropophagi,[9] and men whose heads
          Do grow beneath their shoulders. These things to hear
          Would Desdemona seriously incline;
          But still the house affairs would draw her thence,
          Which ever as she could with haste dispatch
150   She'd come again, and with a greedy ear
          Devour up my discourse. Which I, observing,
          Took once a pliant° hour, and found good means   *well-suiting*
          To draw from her a prayer of earnest heart
          That I would all my pilgrimage dilate,°   *relate in detail*
155   Whereof by parcels° she had something heard,   *piecemeal*
          But not intentively.° I did consent,   *continuously*
          And often did beguile her of her tears,
          When I did speak of some distressful stroke
          That my youth suffered. My story being done,
160   She gave me for my pains a world of sighs.
          She swore, in faith, 'twas strange, 'twas passing° strange,   *exceedingly*
          'Twas pitiful, 'twas wondrous pitiful.
          She wished she had not heard it, yet she wished
          That heaven had made her° such a man. She thanked me,   *created her to be*
165   And bade me, if I had a friend that loved her,
          I should but teach him how to tell my story,
          And that would woo her. Upon this hint° I spake.   *opportunity*
          She loved me for the dangers I had passed,
          And I loved her that she did pity them.
170   This only is the witchcraft I have used.
          Here comes the lady. Let her witness it.
     [*Enter Desdemona, Iago (and) attendants.*]
DUKE: I think this tale would win my daughter too.
          Good Brabantio,
175   Take up this mangled matter at the best.[1]
          Men do their broken weapons rather use
          Than their bare hands.
BRABANTIO: I pray you, hear her speak.
          If she confess that she was half the wooer,
          Destruction on my head if my bad blame
180   Light on the man!—Come hither, gentle mistress.
          Do you perceive in all this noble company
          Where most you owe obedience?
DESDEMONA: My noble Father,
          I do perceive here a divided duty.
          To you I am bound for life and education;°   *upbringing*
185   My life and education both do learn° me   *teach*
          How to respect you. You are the lord of duty;[2]
          I am hitherto your daughter. But here's my husband,
          And so much duty as my mother showed

9. Man-eaters (a term from Pliny's *Natural History*).   2. To whom duty is due.
1. Make the best of a bad bargain.

To you, preferring you before her father,
190   So much I challenge° that I may profess   claim
Due to the Moor my lord.

BRABANTIO: God be with you! I have done.
Please it Your Grace, on to the state affairs.
I had rather to adopt a child than get° it.   beget
195   Come hither, Moor. [(*He joins the hands of Othello and Desdemona.*)]
I here do give thee that with all my heart[3]
Which, but thou hast already, with all my heart°   gladly
I would keep from thee.—For your sake,° jewel,   on your account
I am glad at soul I have no other child,
200   For thy escape° would teach me tyranny,   elopement
To hang clogs[4] on them.—I have done, my lord.

DUKE: Let me speak like yourself,[5] and lay a sentence[6]
Which, as a grice° or step, may help these lovers   step
Into your favor.
205   When remedies° are past, the griefs are ended   hopes of remedy
By seeing the worst, which late on hopes depended.[7]
To mourn a mischief° that is past and gone   misfortune
Is the next° way to draw new mischief on.   nearest
What° cannot be preserved when fortune takes,   whatever
210   Patience her injury a mockery makes.[8]
The robbed that smiles steals something from the thief;
He robs himself that spends a bootless grief.[9]

BRABANTIO: So let the Turk of Cyprus us beguile,
We lose it not, so long as we can smile.
215   He bears the sentence well that nothing bears
But the free comfort which from thence he hears,
But he bears both the sentence and the sorrow
That, to pay grief, must of poor patience borrow.[1]
These sentences, to sugar or to gall,
220   Being strong on both sides, are equivocal.[2]
But words are words. I never yet did hear
That the bruised heart was piercèd through the ear.[3]
I humbly beseech you, proceed to th' affairs of state.

DUKE: The Turk with a most mighty preparation makes for Cyprus. Othello, the
225   fortitude[4] of the place is best known to you; and though we have there a substitute[5] of most allowed[6] sufficiency, yet opinion, a sovereign mistress of

3. Wherein my whole affection has been engaged.
4. Blocks of wood fastened to the legs of criminals or convicts to inhibit escape.
5. As you would, in your proper temper.
6. Apply a maxim.
7. Which griefs were sustained until recently by hopeful
anticipation.
8. Patience laughs at the injury inflicted by fortune (and
thus eases the pain).
9. Indulges in unavailing grief.
1. A person well bears out your maxim who can enjoy its
platitudinous comfort, free of all genuine sorrow, but anyone whose grief bankrupts his poor patience is left with
your saying and his sorrow, too. (*Bears the sentence* also
plays on the meaning, "receives judicial sentence.")
2. These fine maxims are equivocal, either sweet or bitter
in their application.
3. I.e., surgically lanced and cured by mere words of
advice.
4. Strength.
5. Deputy.
6. Acknowledged.

effects, throws a more safer voice on you.[7] You must therefore be content to
slubber[8] the gloss of your new fortunes with this more stubborn[9] and boisterous expedition.

OTHELLO: The tyrant custom, most grave senators,
 Hath made the flinty and steel couch of war
 My thrice-driven° bed of down. I do agnize[1]   *thrice sifted*
 A natural and prompt alacrity
 I find in hardness,° and do undertake   *hardship*
235 These present wars against the Ottomites.
 Most humbly therefore bending to your state,[2]
 I crave fit disposition for my wife,
 Due reference of place and exhibition,[3]
 With such accommodation° and besort°   *provision / attendance*
240 As levels° with her breeding.°   *suits / upbringing*
DUKE: Why, at her father's.
BRABANTIO: I will not have it so.
OTHELLO: Nor I.
DESDEMONA: Nor I. I would not there reside,
 To put my father in impatient thoughts
 By being in his eye. Most gracious Duke,
245 To my unfolding° lend your prosperous° ear,   *proposal / propitious*
 And let me find a charter° in your voice,   *authorization*
 T' assist my simpleness.
DUKE: What would you, Desdemona?
DESDEMONA: That I did love the Moor to live with him,
250 My downright violence and storm of fortunes[4]
 May trumpet to the world. My heart's subdued
 Even to the very quality of my lord.[5]
 I saw Othello's visage in his mind,
 And to his honors and his valiant parts°   *qualities*
255 Did I my soul and fortunes consecrate.
 So that, dear lords, if I be left behind
 A moth[6] of peace, and he go to the war,
 The rites[7] for why I love him are bereft me,
 And I a heavy interim shall support
260 By his dear[8] absence. Let me go with him.
OTHELLO: Let her have your voice.°   *consent*
 Vouch with me, heaven, I therefor beg it not
 To please the palate of my appetite,
 Nor to comply with heat°—the young affects°   *sexual passion / desires*
265 In me defunct—and proper° satisfaction,   *personal*
 But to be free° and bounteous to her mind.   *generous*

7. General opinion, an important determiner of affairs,
chooses you as the best man.
8. Soil, sully.
9. Harsh, rough.
1. Know in myself, acknowledge.
2. Bowing to your authority.
3. Provision of appropriate place to live and allowance of
money.

4. My plain and total breach of social custom, taking my
future by storm and disrupting my whole life.
5. My heart is brought wholly into accord with Othello's
virtues; I love him for his virtues.
6. I.e., one who consumes merely.
7. Rites of love (with a suggestion, too, of "rights,"
sharing).
8. Heartfelt. Also, costly.

And heaven defend° your good souls that you think°   *forbid / should think*
I will your serious and great business scant
When she is with me. No, when light-winged toys
270   Of feathered Cupid seel⁹ with wanton dullness
My speculative and officed instruments,¹
That my disports corrupt and taint my business,²
Let huswives make a skillet of my helm,
And all indign° and base adversities   *unworthy, shameful*
275   Make head° against my estimation!°   *rise up / reputation*

DUKE: Be it as you shall privately determine,
Either for her stay or going. Th' affair cries haste,
And speed must answer it.

A SENATOR: You must away tonight.

DESDEMONA: Tonight, my lord?

DUKE: This night.

OTHELLO: With all my heart.

DUKE: At nine i' the morning here we'll meet again.
Othello, leave some officer behind,
And he shall our commission bring to you,
With such things else of quality and respect³
As doth import° you.   *concern*

OTHELLO: So please Your Grace, my ancient;
A man he is of honesty and trust.
To his conveyance I assign my wife,
With what else needful Your Good Grace shall think
To be sent after me.

DUKE: Let it be so.
Good night to everyone. [*To Brabantio.*] And, noble signor,
290   If virtue no delighted° beauty lack,   *delightful*
Your son-in-law is far more fair than black.

FIRST SENATOR: Adieu, brave Moor. Use Desdemona well.

BRABANTIO: Look to her, Moor, if thou hast eyes to see.
She has deceived her father, and may thee.

          [(*Exeunt Duke, Brabantio, Cassio, Senators, and officers.*)]

OTHELLO: My life upon her faith! Honest Iago,
My Desdemona must I leave to thee.
I prithee, let thy wife attend on her,
And bring them after in the best advantage.⁴
Come, Desdemona. I have but an hour
300   Of love, of worldly matters and direction,°   *instructions*
To spend with thee. We must obey the time.⁵

          [*Exit (with Desdemona.*)]

RODERIGO: Iago—

IAGO: What sayst thou, noble heart?

---

9. I.e., make blind (as in falconry, by sewing up the eyes
of the hawk during training).
1. Eyes and other faculties used in the performance of
duty.

2. So that my sexual pastimes impair my work.
3. Of importance and relevance.
4. At the most favorable opportunity.
5. The urgency of the present crisis.

RODERIGO: What will I do, think'st thou?

IAGO: Why, go to bed and sleep.

RODERIGO: I will incontinently° drown myself.   *immediately*

IAGO: If thou dost, I shall never love thee after. Why, thou silly gentleman?

RODERIGO: It is silliness to live when to live is torment; and then have we a prescription[6] to die when death is our physician.

IAGO: O villainous![7] I have looked upon the world for four times seven years, and, since I could distinguish betwixt a benefit and an injury, I never found man that knew how to love himself. Ere I would say I would drown myself for the love of a guinea hen,[8] I would change my humanity with a baboon.

RODERIGO: What should I do? I confess it is my shame to be so fond,[9] but it is not in
315   my virtue[1] to amend it.

IAGO: Virtue? A fig![2] 'Tis in ourselves that we are thus or thus. Our bodies are our gardens, to the which our wills are gardeners; so that if we will plant nettles or sow lettuce, set hyssop[3] and weed up thyme, supply it with one gender[4] of herbs or distract it with[5] many, either to have it sterile with idleness[6] or manured
320   with industry—why, the power and corrigible authority[7] of this lies in our wills. If the beam[8] of our lives had not one scale of reason to poise[9] another of sensuality, the blood[1] and baseness of our natures would conduct us to most preposterous conclusions. But we have reason to cool our raging motions,[2] our carnal stings, our unbitted[3] lusts, whereof I take this that you call love to be a sect
325   or scion.[4]

RODERIGO: It cannot be.

IAGO: It is merely a lust of the blood and a permission of the will. Come, be a man. Drown thyself? Drown cats and blind puppies. I have professed me thy friend, and I confess me knit to thy deserving with cables of perdurable[5] toughness. I
330   could never better stead[6] thee than now. Put money in thy purse. Follow thou the wars; defeat thy favor[7] with an usurped[8] beard. I say, put money in thy purse. It cannot be long that Desdemona should continue her love to the Moor—put money in thy purse—nor he his to her. It was a violent commencement in her, and thou shalt see an answerable sequestration[9]—put but money
335   in thy purse. These Moors are changeable in their wills[1]—fill thy purse with money. The food that to him now is as luscious as locusts[2] shall be to him shortly as bitter as coloquintida.[3] She must change for youth; when she is sated with his body, she will find the error of her choice. She must have change, she

6. Right based on long-established custom. Also, doctor's prescription.
7. I.e., what perfect nonsense.
8. A slang term for a prostitute.
9. Infatuated.
1. Strength, nature.
2. To give a fig is to thrust the thumb between the first and second fingers in a vulgar and insulting gesture.
3. An herb of the mint family.
4. Kind.
5. Divide it among.
6. Want of cultivation.
7. Power to correct.
8. Balance.
9. Counterbalance.

1. Natural passions.
2. Appetites.
3. Unbridled, uncontrolled.
4. Cutting or offshoot.
5. Very durable.
6. Assist.
7. Disguise your face.
8. The suggestion is that Roderigo is not man enough to have a beard of his own.
9. A corresponding separation or estrangement.
1. Carnal appetites.
2. Fruit of the carob tree (see Matthew 3.4), or perhaps honeysuckle.
3. Colocynth or bitter apple, a purgative.

340 must. Therefore put money in thy purse. If thou wilt needs damn thyself, do it a
more delicate way than drowning. Make[4] all the money thou canst. If sancti-
mony[5] and a frail vow betwixt an erring[6] barbarian and a supersubtle Venetian
be not too hard for my wits and all the tribe of hell, thou shalt enjoy her.
Therefore make money. A pox of drowning thyself! It is clean out of the way.[7]
Seek thou rather to be hanged in compassing[8] thy joy than to be drowned and
345 go without her.

RODERIGO: Wilt thou be fast[9] to my hopes if I depend on the issue?[1]

IAGO: Thou art sure of me. Go, make money. I have told thee often, and I retell thee
again and again, I hatethe Moor. My cause is hearted;[2] thine hath no less reason. Let us be conjunctive[3] in our revenge against him. If thou canst cuckold
350 him, thou dost thyself a pleasure, me a sport. There are many events in the
womb of time which will be delivered. Traverse,[4] go, provide thy money. We
will have more of this tomorrow. Adieu.

RODERIGO: Where shall we meet i' the morning?

IAGO: At my lodging.

RODERIGO: I'll be with thee betimes.° [(He starts to leave.)]   early

IAGO: Go to, farewell.—Do you hear, Roderigo?

RODERIGO: What say you?

IAGO: No more of drowning, do you hear?

RODERIGO: I am changed.

IAGO: Go to, farewell. Put money enough in your purse.

RODERIGO: I'll sell all my land.   [Exit.]

IAGO: Thus do I ever make my fool my purse;
    For I mine own gained knowledge should profane
    If I would time expend with such a snipe[5]
365 But for my sport and profit. I hate the Moor;
    And it is thought abroad° that twixt my sheets   rumored
    He's done my office.[6] I know not if 't be true;
    But I, for mere suspicion in that kind,
    Will do as if for surety.[7] He holds me well;[8]
370 The better shall my purpose work on him.
    Cassio's a proper° man. Let me see now: handsome
    To get his place and to plume[9] up my will
    In double knavery—How, how?—Let's see:
    After some time, to abuse° Othello's ear   deceive
375 That he° is too familiar with his wife.   Cassio
    He hath a person and a smooth dispose°   disposition
    To be suspected, framed to make women false.

---

4. Raise, collect.
5. Sacred ceremony.
6. Wandering, vagabond, unsteady.
7. Entirely unsuitable as a course of action.
8. Encompassing, embracing.
9. True.
1. Successful outcome.
2. Fixed in the heart, heartfelt.

3. United.
4. A military marching term.
5. Woodcock, i.e., fool.
6. My sexual function as husband.
7. Act as if on certain knowledge.
8. Regards me favorably.
9. Put a feather in the cap of, i.e., glorify, gratify.

The Moor is of a free° and open° nature,   *frank / unsuspicious*

That thinks men honest that but seem to be so,

380   And will as tenderly° be led by the nose   *readily*

As asses are.

I have 't. It is engendered. Hell and night

Must bring this monstrous birth to the world's light.

[*Exit.*]

ACT 2

Scene 1[1]

[*Enter Montano and two Gentlemen.*]

MONTANO: What from the cape can you discern at sea?

FIRST GENTLEMAN: Nothing at all. It is a high-wrought flood.°   *agitated sea*

I cannot, twixt the heaven and the main,°   *ocean*

Descry a sail.

MONTANO: Methinks the wind hath spoke aloud at land;

A fuller blast ne'er shook our battlements.

If it hath ruffianed° so upon the sea,   *raged*

What ribs of oak, when mountains° melt on them,   *of water*

Can hold the mortise?[2] What shall we hear of this?

SECOND GENTLEMAN: A segregation° of the Turkish fleet.   *dispersal*

For do but stand upon the foaming shore,

The chidden[3] billow seems to pelt the clouds;

The wind-shaked surge, with high and monstrous mane,[4]

Seems to cast water on the burning Bear[5]

15   And quench the guards of th' ever-fixèd pole.

I never did like molestation° view   *such a disturbance*

On the enchafèd° flood.   *angry*

MONTANO: If that° the Turkish fleet   *if*

Be not ensheltered and embayed,° they are drowned;   *in a harbor*

20   It is impossible to bear it out.°   *survive*

[*Enter a (Third) Gentleman.*]

THIRD GENTLEMAN: News, lads! Our wars are done.

The desperate tempest hath so banged the Turks

That their designment° halts.° A noble ship of Venice   *enterprise / is lame*

Hath seen a grievous wreck° and sufferance°   *shipwreck / damage*

25   On most part of their fleet.

MONTANO: How? Is this true?

THIRD GENTLEMAN: The ship is here put in,

A Veronesa;[6] Michael Cassio,

---

1. Location; A seaport in Cyprus. An open place near the quay.

2. Hold their joints together.

3. I.e., rebuked, repelled (by the shore), and thus shot into the air.

4. The surf is like the mane of a wild beast.

5. The constellation Ursa Minor or the Little Bear, which includes the polestar (and hence regarded as the *guards of th' ever-fixed pole* in the next line; sometimes the term *guards* is applied to the two "pointers" of the Big Bear or Dipper, which may be intended here).

6. Fitted out in Verona for Venetian service, or possibly *Verennessa* (the Folio spelling), i.e., *verrinessa*, a cutter (from *verrinare*, "to cut through").

Lieutenant to the warlike Moor Othello,
Is come on shore; the Moor himself at sea,
30   And is in full commission here for Cyprus.

MONTANO: I am glad on 't. 'Tis a worthy governor.

THIRD GENTLEMAN: But this same Cassio, though he speak of comfort
Touching the Turkish loss, yet he looks sadly°   gravely
And prays the Moor be safe, for they were parted
35   With foul and violent tempest.

MONTANO: Pray heaven he be,
For I have served him, and the man commands
Like a full° soldier. Let's to the seaside, ho!   perfect
As well to see the vessel that's come in
As to throw out our eyes for brave Othello,
40   Even till we make the main and th' aerial blue[7]
An indistinct regard.[8]

THIRD GENTLEMAN: Come, let's do so,
For every minute is expectancy°   gives expectation
Of more arrivance.°   arrival

[Enter Cassio.]

CASSIO: Thanks, you the valiant of this warlike isle,
45   That so approve° the Moor! O, let the heavens   honor
Give him defense against the elements,
For I have lost him on a dangerous sea.

MONTANO: Is he well shipped?

CASSIO: His bark is stoutly timbered, and his pilot
50   Of very expert and approved allowance;°   tested reputation
Therefore my hopes, not surfeited to death,[9]
Stand in bold cure.[1]

            [(A cry) within:] "A sail, a sail, a sail!"

CASSIO: What noise?

A GENTLEMAN: The town is empty. On the brow o' the sea[2]
55   Stand ranks of people, and they cry "A sail!"

CASSIO: My hopes do shape him for[3] the governor.

[(A shot within.)]

SECOND GENTLEMAN: They do discharge their shot of courtesy;[4]
Our friends at least.

CASSIO: I pray you, sir, go forth,
And give us truth who 'tis that is arrived.

SECOND GENTLEMAN: I shall. [Exit.]

MONTANO: But, good Lieutenant, is your general wived?

CASSIO: Most fortunately. He hath achieved a maid
That paragons° description and wild fame,°   surpasses / rumor
One that excels the quirks° of blazoning[5] pens,   witty conceits
65   And in th' essential vesture of creation

7. The sea and the sky.
8. Indistinguishable in our view.
9. Overextended, worn thin through repeated application
or delayed fulfillment.
1. In strong hopes of fulfillment.

2. Cliff-edge.
3. I hope it is.
4. Fire a salute in token of respect and courtesy.
5. Setting forth as though in heraldic language.

Does tire the engineer.⁶
[*Enter (Second) Gentleman.*]⁷

How now? Who has put in?°   *to harbor*

SECOND GENTLEMAN: 'Tis one Iago, ancient to the General.

CASSIO: He's had most favorable and happy speed.
        Tempests themselves, high seas, and howling winds,
70   The guttered° rocks and congregated sands—   *jagged*
        Traitors ensteeped° to clog the guiltless keel—   *lying under water*
        As° having sense of beauty, do omit°   *as if / suspend*
        Their mortal° natures, letting go safely by   *deadly*
        The divine Desdemona.

MONTANO: What is she?

CASSIO: She that I spake of, our great captain's captain,
        Left in the conduct of the bold Iago,
        Whose footing° here anticipates our thoughts   *landing*
        A se'nnight's° speed. Great Jove, Othello guard,   *week's*
        And swell his sail with thine own powerful breath,
80   That he may bless this bay with his tall° ship,   *splendid*
        Make love's quick pants in Desdemona's arms,
        Give renewed fire to our extincted spirits,
        And bring all Cyprus comfort!

[*Enter Desdemona, Iago, Roderigo, and Emilia.*]

                 O, behold,
        The riches of the ship is come on shore!
85   You men of Cyprus, let her have your knees.

[(*The gentlemen make curtsy to Desdemona.*)]

        Hail to thee, lady! And the grace of heaven
        Before, behind thee, and on every hand
        Enwheel thee round!

DESDEMONA: I thank you, valiant Cassio.
        What tidings can you tell me of my lord?

CASSIO: He is not yet arrived, nor know I aught
        But that he's well and will be shortly here.

DESDEMONA: Oh, but I fear—How lost you company?

CASSIO: The great contention of the sea and skies
        Parted our fellowship.

[*Within:* "A sail, a sail!" (*A shot.*)]

                But hark. A sail!

SECOND GENTLEMAN: They give their greeting to the citadel.
        This likewise is a friend.

CASSIO: See for the news.

[(*Exit Second Gentleman.*)]

        Good Ancient, you are welcome. [(*Kissing Emilia.*)]
        Welcome, mistress.
        Let it not gall your patience, good Iago,
100   That I extend° my manners; 'tis my breeding⁸   *give scope to*

---

6. In her real, God-given, beauty, (she) defeats any attempt to praise her. The enginer [enginer] is the poet, one who devises.

7. So identified in the Quarto text here and in lines 57, 60, 67 and 95; the Folio calls him a gentelman.
8. Training in the niceties of etiquette.

That gives me this bold show of courtesy.

IAGO: Sir, would she give you so much of her lips
   As of her tongue she oft bestows on me,
   You would have enough.

DESDEMONA: Alas, she has no speech![9]

IAGO: In faith, too much.
   I find it still,° when I have list° to sleep.   *always / desire*
   Marry, before your ladyship, I grant,
   She puts her tongue a little in her heart
   And chides with thinking.[1]

EMILIA: You have little cause to say so.

IAGO: Come on, come on. you are pictures out of doors,[2]
   Bells[3] in your parlors, wildcats in your kitchens,[4]
   Saints° in your injuries, devils being offended,   *martyrs*
   Players° in your huswifery,° and huswives[5] in your beds. *idlers / housekeeping*

DESDEMONA: O, fie upon thee, slanderer!

IAGO: Nay, it is true, or else I am a Turk.[6]
   You rise to play, and go to bed to work.

EMILIA: You shall not write my praise.

IAGO: No, let me not.

DESDEMONA: What wouldst write of me, if thou shouldst praise me?

IAGO: O, gentle lady, do not put me to 't,
120 For I am nothing if not critical.°   *censorious*

DESDEMONA: Come on, essay.°—There's one gone to the harbor? *try*

IAGO: Ay, madam.

DESDEMONA: I am not merry, but I do beguile
   The thing I am[7] by seeming otherwise.
125 Come, how wouldst thou praise me?

IAGO: I am about it, but indeed my invention
   Comes from my pate as birdlime[8] does from frieze°— *coarse cloth*
   It plucks out brains and all. But my Muse labors,[9]
   And thus she is delivered:
130 If she be fair and wise, fairness and wit,
   The one's for use, the other useth it.[1]

DESDEMONA: Well praised! How if she be black[2] and witty?

IAGO: If she be black, and thereto have a wit,
   She'll find a white[3] that shall her blackness fit.[4]

DESDEMONA: Worse and worse.

EMILIA: How if fair and foolish?

IAGO: She never yet was foolish that was fair,
   For even her folly[5] helped her to an heir.°   *to bear a child*

---

9. She's not a chatterbox, as you allege.
1. In her thoughts only.
2. Silent and well-behaved in public.
3. Jangling, noisy, and brazen.
4. In domestic affairs. (Ladies would not do the cooking.)
5. Hussies (i.e., women are "busy" in bed, or unduly thrifty in dispensing sexual favors).
6. An infidel, not to be believed.
7. My anxious self.

8. Sticky substance used to catch small birds.
9. Exerts herself. Also, prepares to deliver a child (with a following pun on "*delivered*" in line 130).
1. Her cleverness will make use of her beauty.
2. Dark-complexioned, brunette.
3. A fair person (with wordplay on "wight," a person).
4. With sexual suggestion of mating.
5. With added meaning of "lechery, wantonness."

DESDEMONA: These are old fond⁶ paradoxes to make fools laugh i' th' alehouse.
140   What miserable praise hast thou for her that's foul⁷ and foolish?
IAGO: There's none so foul and foolish thereunto,°   *in addition*
           But does foul° pranks which fair and wise ones do.   *sluttish*
DESDEMONA: O, heavy ignorance! Thou praisest the worst best. But what praise
           couldst thou bestow on a deserving woman indeed, one that, in the authority
145   of her merit, did justly put on the vouch⁸ of very malice itself?
IAGO: She that was ever fair, and never proud,
           Had tongue at will, and yet was never loud,
           Never lacked gold and yet went never gay,°   *extravagantly clothed*
           Fled from her wish, and yet said, "Now I may,"⁹
150   She that being angered, her revenge being nigh,
           Bade her wrong stay¹ and her displeasure fly,
           She that in wisdom never was so frail
           To change the cod's head for the salmon's tail,²
           She that could think and ne'er disclose her mind,
155   See suitors following and not look behind,
           She was a wight, if ever such wight were—
DESDEMONA: To do what?
IAGO: To suckle fools and chronicle small beer.³
DESDEMONA: Oh, most lame and impotent conclusion! Do not learn of him, Emilia,
160   though he be thy husband. How say you, Cassio? Is he not a most profane and
           liberal⁴ counselor?
CASSIO: He speaks home,⁵ madam. You may relish⁶ him more in⁷ the soldier than in
           the scholar.
           [(*Cassio and Desdemona stand together, conversing intimately.*)]
IAGO [(*aside*)]:   He takes her by the palm. Ay, well said,⁸ whisper. With as little a web
165   as this will I ensnare as great a fly as Cassio. Ay, smile upon her, do; I will-
           gyve⁹ thee in thine own courtship.¹ You say true;² 'tis so, indeed. If such tricks
           as these strip you out of your lieutenantry, it had been better you had not kissed
           your three fingers so oft, which now again you are most apt to play the sir³ in.
           Very good; well kissed! An excellent courtesy! 'Tis so, indeed. Yet again your
170   fingers to your lips? Would they were clyster pipes⁴ for your sake! [*Trumpet
           within.*] The Moor! I know his trumpet.
CASSIO: 'Tis truly so.
DESDEMONA: Let's meet him and receive him.
CASSIO: Lo, where he comes!
           [*Enter Othello and attendants.*]

---

6. Foolish.
7. Ugly.
8. Compel the approval.
9. Avoided temptation where the choice was hers.
1. Resolved to put up with her injury patiently.
2. To exchange a lackluster husband for a sexy lover(?)
(*Cod's head* is slang for "penis.").
3. To nurse babies and keep petty household accounts.
4. Ribald and licentious.

5. Right to the target (a term from fencing).
6. Appreciate.
7. In the character of.
8. Well done.
9. Fetter, shackle.
1. Courtesy, show of courtly manners.
2. That's right, go ahead.
3. The fine gentleman.
4. Tubes used for enemas and douches.

OTHELLO: O, my fair warrior!

DESDEMONA: My dear Othello!

OTHELLO: It gives me wonder great as my content
　　　　　To see you here before me. O my soul's joy,
　　　　　If after every tempest come such calms,
　　　　　May the winds blow till they have weakened death,
　　　　　And let the laboring bark climb hills of seas
180　　　Olympus-high, and duck again as low
　　　　　As hell's from heaven! If it were now to die,
　　　　　'Twere now to be most happy, for I fear
　　　　　My soul hath her content so absolute
　　　　　That not another comfort like to this
185　　　Succeeds in unknown fate.⁵

DESDEMONA: The heavens forbid
　　　　　But that our loves and comforts should increase
　　　　　Even as our days do grow!

OTHELLO: Amen to that, sweet powers!
　　　　　I cannot speak enough of this content.
　　　　　It stops me here; it is too much of joy.
　　　　　And this, and this, the greatest discords be
　　　[(They kiss.)]⁶
　　　　　That e'er our hearts shall make!

IAGO [(aside)]: O, you are well tuned now!
　　　　　But I'll set down⁷ the pegs that make this music,
195　　　As honest as I am.⁸

OTHELLO: Come, let us to the castle.
　　　　　News, friends! Our wars are done, the Turks are drowned.
　　　　　How does my old acquaintance of this isle?—
　　　　　Honey, you shall be well desired° in Cyprus;　　　　　　　　　welcomed
200　　　I have found great love amongst them. O, my sweet,
　　　　　I prattle out of fashion,° and I dote　　　　　　　　　　　　incoherntly
　　　　　In mine own comforts.—I prithee, good Iago,
　　　　　Go to the bay and disembark my coffers.°　　　　　　　　　　chests
　　　　　Bring thou the master° to the citadel;　　　　　　　　　　　ship's captain
205　　　He is a good one, and his worthiness
　　　　　Does challenge° much respect.—Come, Desdemona.—　　　deserve
　　　　　Once more, well met at Cyprus!
　　　　　　　　　　　　[Exeunt Othello and Desdemona (and all but Iago and Roderigo.)]

IAGO [(to an attendant)]: Do thou meet me presently at the harbor. [(To Roderigo)]
　　　　　Come hither. If thou be'st valiant—as, they say, base men⁹ being in love have

---

5. Can follow in the unknown future.　　　　　　　　　8. For all my supposed honesty.
6. The direction is from the Quarto.　　　　　　　　　9. Even lowly born men.
7. Loosen (and hence untune the instrument).

210   then a nobility in their natures more than is native to them—list[1] me. The
           Lieutenant tonight watches on the court of guard.[2] First, I must tell
           thee this: Desdemona is directly in love with him.
RODERIGO: With him? Why, 'tis not possible.
IAGO: Lay thy finger thus,[3] and let thy soul be instructed. Mark me with what vio-
215   lence she first loved the Moor, but[4] for bragging and telling her fantastical lies.
           To love him still for prating? Let not thy discreet heart think it. Her eye must
           be fed; and what delight shall she have to look on the devil? When the blood is
           made dull with the act of sport,[5] there should be, again to inflame it and to give
           satiety a fresh appetite, loveliness in favor,[6] sympathy[7] in years, manners, and
220   beauties—all which the Moor is defective in. Now, for want of these required
           conveniences,[8] her delicate tenderness will find itself abused,[9] begin to heave
           the gorge,[1] disrelish and abhor the Moor. Very nature[2] will instruct her in it
           and compel her to some second choice. Now, sir, this granted—as it is a most
           pregnant[3] and unforced position—who stands so eminent in the degree[4] of this
225   fortune as Cassio does? A knave very voluble,[5] no further conscionable[6] than
           in putting on the mere form of civil and humane[7] seeming for the better com-
           passing of his salt[8] and most hidden loose affection.[9] Why, none, why, none. A
           slipper[1] and subtle knave, a finder out of occasions, that has an eye can stamp[2]
230   and counterfeit advantages,[3] though true advantage never present itself; a devi-
           lish knave. Besides, the knave is handsome, young, and hath all those requi-
           sites in him that folly[4] and green[5] minds look after. A pestilent complete
           knave, and the woman hath found him[6] already.
RODERIGO: I cannot believe that in her. She's full of most blessed condition.[7]
IAGO: Blessed fig's end! The wine she drinks is made of grapes. If she had been
235   blessed, she would never have loved the Moor. Blessed pudding![8] Didst thou
           not see her paddle with the palm of his hand? Didst not mark that?
RODERIGO: Yes, that I did; but that was but courtesy.
IAGO: Lechery, by this hand. An index[9] and obscure prologue to the history of lust
           and foul thoughts. They met so near with their lips that their breaths embraced
240   together. Villainous thoughts, Roderigo! When these mutualities[1] so marshal
           the way, hard at hand[2] comes the master and main exercise, th' incorporate[3]
           conclusion. Pish! But, sir, be you ruled by me. I have brought you from Venice.

---

1. Listen to.
2. Guardhouse. (Cassio is in charge of the watch.)
3. I.e., on your lips.
4. Only.
5. Sex.
6. Appearance.
7. Correspondence, similarity.
8. Things conducive to sexual compatibility.
9. Cheated, revolted.
1. Experience nausea.
2. Her very instincts.
3. Evident, cogent.
4. As next in line for.
5. Facile, glib.
6. Conscientious, conscience-bound.

7. Polite, courteous.
8. Licentious.
9. Passion.
1. Slippery.
2. An eye that can coin, create.
3. Favorable opportunities.
4. Wantonness.
5. Immature.
6. Sized him up, perceived his intent.
7. Disposition.
8. Sausage.
9. Table of contents.
1. Exchanges, intimacies.
2. Closely following.
3. Carnal.

Watch you[4] tonight; for the command, I'll lay 't upon you.[5] Cassio knows you not. I'll not be far from you. Do you find some occasion to anger Cassio, either
245   by speaking too loud, or tainting[6] his discipline, or from what other course you please, which the time shall more favorably minister.[7]

RODERIGO: Well.

IAGO: Sir, he's rash and very sudden in choler,[8] and haply[9] may strike at you. Provoke him that he may, for even out of that will I cause these of Cyprus to
250   mutiny,[1] whose qualification[2] shall come into no true taste[3] again but by the displanting of Cassio. So shall you have a shorter journey to your desires by the means I shall then have to prefer[4] them, and the impediment most profitably removed, without the which there were no expectation of our prosperity.

RODERIGO: I will do this, if you can bring it to any opportunity.

IAGO: I warrant[5] thee. Meet me by and by[6] at the citadel. I must fetch his necessaries ashore. Farewell.

RODERIGO: Adieu.   [Exit.]

IAGO: That Cassio loves her, I do well believe 't;
       That she loves him, 'tis apt° and of great credit.°   probable / credibility
260   The Moor, howbeit that I endure him not,
       Is of a constant, loving, noble nature,
       And I dare think he'll prove to Desdemona
       A most dear husband. Now, I do love her too,
       Not out of absolute lust—though peradventure
265   I stand accountant° for as great a sin—   accountable
       But partly led to diet° my revenge   feed
       For that I do suspect the lusty Moor
       Hath leaped into my seat, the thought whereof
       Doth, like a poisonous mineral, gnaw my innards;
270   And nothing can or shall content my soul
       Till I am evened with him, wife for wife,
       Or failing so, yet that I put the Moor
       At least into a jealousy so strong
       That judgment cannot cure. Which thing to do,
275   If this poor trash of Venice, whom I trace[7]
       For[8] his quick hunting, stand[9] the putting on,
       I'll have our Michael Cassio on the hip,[1]
       Abuse° him to the Moor in the rank garb°—   slander / coarse manner
       For I fear Cassio with my nightcap[2] too—
280   Make the Moor thank me, love me, and reward me

---

4. Stand watch.
5. I'll arrange for you to be appointed, given orders.
6. Disparaging.
7. Provide.
8. Wrath.
9. Perhaps.
1. Riot.
2. Appeasement.
3. Acceptable state.
4. Advance.
5. Assure.

6. Immediately.
7. Train, or follow (?), or perhaps *trash*, a hunting term, meaning to put weights on a hunting dog in order to slow him down.
8. To make more eager.
9. Responds properly when I incite him to quarrel.
1. At my mercy, where I can throw him. (A wrestling term.)
2. As a rival in my bed, as one who gives me cuckold's horns.

For making him egregiously an ass
And practicing upon° his peace and quiet   *plotting against*
Even to madness. 'Tis here, but yet confused.
Knavery's plain face is never seen till used.   [*Exit.*]

Scene 2³

[*Enter Othello's Herald with a proclamation.*]

HERALD: It is Othello's pleasure, our noble and valiant general, that, upon certain
tidings now arrived, importing the mere perdition⁴ of the Turkish fleet, every
man put himself into triumph:⁵ some to dance, some to make bonfires, each
man to what sport and revels his addiction⁶ leads him. For, besides these beneficial news, it is the celebration of his nuptial. So much was his pleasure should
be proclaimed. All offices⁷ are open, and there is full liberty of feasting from
this present hour of five till the bell have told eleven. Heaven bless the isle of
Cyprus and our noble general Othello!

[Exit.]

Scene 3⁸

[*Enter Othello, Desdemona, Cassio, and attendants.*]

OTHELLO: Good Michael, look you to the guard tonight.
      Let's teach ourselves that honorable stop°   *restraint*
      Not to outsport° discretion.   *celebrate beyond*
CASSIO: Iago hath direction what to do,
5   But notwithstanding, with my personal eye
      Will I look to 't.
OTHELLO: Iago is most honest.
      Michael, good night. Tomorrow with your earliest⁹
      Let me have speech with you. [(*To Desdemona.*)] Come, my dear love,
      The purchase made, the fruits are to ensue;
10   That profit's yet to come 'tween me and you.¹—
      Good night.

[Exit (Othello, with Desdemona and attendants.)]

      [*Enter Iago.*]
CASSIO: Welcome, Iago. We must to the watch.
IAGO: Not this hour,² Lieutenant; 'tis not yet ten o' the clock. Our general cast³ us
      thus early for the love of his Desdemona; who⁴ let us not therefore blame. He
15   hath not yet made wanton the night with her, and she is sport for Jove.
CASSIO: She's a most exquisite lady.
IAGO: And, I'll warrant her, full of game.
CASSIO: Indeed, she's a most fresh and delicate creature.

---

3. Location: Cyprus. A street.
4. Complete destruction.
5. Public celebration.
6. Inclination.
7. Rooms where food and drink are kept.
8. Location: Cyprus. The citadel.

9. At your earliest convenience.
1. Though married, we haven't yet consummated our love.
2. Not for an hour yet.
3. Dismissed.
4. Othello.

IAGO: What an eye she has! Methinks it sounds a parley[5] to provocation.

CASSIO: An inviting eye, and yet methinks right modest.

IAGO: And when she speaks, is it not an alarum[6] to love?

CASSIO: She is indeed perfection.

IAGO: Well, happiness to their sheets! Come, Lieutenant, I have a stoup[7] of wine,
and here without[8] are a brace[9] of Cyprus gallants that would fain have a mea-
25   sure[1] to the health of black Othello.

CASSIO: Not tonight, good Iago. I have very poor and unhappy brains for drinking.
I could well wish courtesy would invent some other custom of entertainment.

IAGO: O, they are our friends. But one cup! I'll drink for you.[2]

CASSIO: I have drunk but one cup tonight, and that was craftily qualified[3] too, and
30   behold what innovation[4] it makes here.[5] I am unfortunate in the infirmity and
dare not task my weakness with any more.

IAGO: What, man? 'Tis a night of revels. The gallants desire it.

CASSIO: Where are they?

IAGO: Here at the door. I pray you, call them in.

CASSIO: I'll do't, but it dislikes me.[6]   [Exit.]

IAGO: If I can fasten but one cup upon him,
        With that which he hath drunk tonight already,
        He'll be as full of quarrel and offense[7]
        As my young mistress' dog. Now, my sick fool Roderigo,
40   Whom love hath turned almost the wrong side out,
        To Desdemona hath tonight caroused°   drunk off
        Potations pottle-deep;[8] and he's to watch.°   stand watch
        Three lads of Cyprus—noble swelling° spirits,   proud
        That hold their honors in a wary distance,[9]
45   The very elements° of this warlike isle—   typical sort
        Have I tonight flustered with flowing cups,
        And they watch° too. Now, 'mongst this flock of drunkards   are on guard
        Am I to put our Cassio in some action
        That may offend the isle.—But here they come.

        [Enter Cassio, Montano, and gentlemen; (servants following with wine.)]
50   If consequence do but approve my dream,[1]
        My boat sails freely both with wind and stream.°   current

CASSIO: 'Fore God, they have given me a rouse° already.   large drink

MONTANO: Good faith, a little one; not past a pint, as I am a soldier.

IAGO: Some wine, ho!
55   [(He sings.)] "And let me the cannikin° clink, clink,   cup
        And let me the cannikin clink.
        A soldier's a man,

5. Calls for a conference, issues an invitation.
6. Signal calling men to arms (continuing the military metaphor of parley, line 21).
7. Measure of liquor, two quarts.
8. Outside.
9. Pair.
1. Gladly drink a toast.
2. In your place. (Iago will do the steady drinking to keep the gallants company while Cassio has only one cup.)

3. Diluted.
4. Disturbance, insurrection.
5. I.e., in my head.
6. I'm reluctant.
7. Readiness to take offense.
8. To the bottom of the tankard.
9. Are extremely sensitive of their honor.
1. If subsequent events will only substantiate scheme.

O, man's life's but a span;[2]
Why, then, let a soldier drink."

60   Some wine, boys!

CASSIO: 'Fore God, an excellent song.

IAGO: I learned it in England, where indeed they are most potent in potting.[3] Your
Dane, your German, and your swag-bellied Hollander—drink, ho!—are nothing to your English.

CASSIO: Is your Englishman so exquisite in his drinking?

IAGO: Why, he drinks you,[4] with facility, your Dane dead drunk; he sweats not[5] to
overthrow your Almain;[6] he gives your Hollander a vomit ere the next pottle
can be filled.

CASSIO: To the health of our general!

MONTANO: I am for it, Lieutenant, and I'll do you justice.[7]

IAGO: O sweet England! [*He sings.*]

          "King Stephen was and-a worthy peer,
          His breeches cost him but a crown;
          He held them sixpence all too dear,
75   With that he called the tailor lown.°   *lout*

          He was a wight of high renown,
          And thou art but of low degree.
          'Tis pride[8] that pulls the country down;
          Then take thy auld° cloak about thee."   *old*

80   Some wine, ho!

CASSIO: 'Fore God, this is a more exquisite song than the other.

IAGO: Will you hear 't again?

CASSIO: No, for I hold him to be unworthy of his place that does those things. Well, God's
above all; and there be souls must be saved, and there be souls must not be saved.

IAGO: It's true, good Lieutenant.

CASSIO: For mine own part—no offense to the General, nor any man of quality[9]—I
hope to be saved.

IAGO: And so do I too, Lieutenant.

CASSIO: Ay, but, by your leave, not before me; the lieutenant is to be saved before
90   the ancient. Let's have no more of this; let's to our affairs.—God forgive us our
sins!—Gentlemen, let's look to our business. Do not think, gentlemen, I am
drunk. This is my ancient; this is my right hand, and this is my left. I am not
drunk now. I can stand well enough, and speak well enough.

GENTLEMEN: Excellent well.

CASSIO: Why, very well then; you must not think then that I am drunk.   [*Exit.*]

MONTANO: To th' platform, masters. Come, let's set the watch.[1]

                                                          [(*Exeunt Gentlemen.*)]

---

2. Brief span of time. (Cf. Psalm 39.5 as rendered in the
Book of Common Prayer: "Thou hast made my days as it
were a span long.")
3. Drinking.
4. Drinks.
5. Need not exert himself.

6. German.
7. I'll drink as much as you.
8. Extravagance in dress.
9. Rank.
1. Mount the guard.

IAGO: You see this fellow that is gone before.
         He's a soldier fit to stand by Caesar
         And give direction; and do but see his vice.
100   'Tis to his virtue a just equinox,[2]
         The one as long as th' other. 'Tis pity of him.
         I fear the trust Othello puts him in,
         On some odd time of his infirmity,
         Will shake this island.
MONTANO: But is he often thus?
IAGO: 'Tis evermore the prologue to his sleep.
         He'll watch the horologe a double set,[3]
         If drink rock not his cradle.
MONTANO: It were well
         The General were put in mind of it.
         Perhaps he sees it not, or his good nature
110   Prizes the virtue that appears in Cassio
         And looks not on his evils. Is not this true?
         [Enter Roderigo.]
IAGO [aside to him]: How now, Roderigo?
         I pray you, after the Lieutenant; go.   [(Exit Roderigo.)]
MONTANO: And 'tis great pity that the noble Moor
115   Should hazard such a place as his own second
         With[4] one of an engraffed° infirmity.   inveterate
         It were an honest action to say so
         To the Moor.
IAGO: Not I, for this fair island.
         I do love Cassio well and would do much
120   To cure him of this evil. [(Cry within: "Help! Help!")]
                        But hark! What noise?
         [Enter Cassio, pursuing Roderigo.][5]
CASSIO: Zounds, you rogue! You rascal!
MONTANO: What's the matter, Lieutenant?
CASSIO: A knave teach me my duty? I'll beat the knave into a twiggen[6] bottle.
RODERIGO: Beat me?
CASSIO: Dost thou prate, rogue? [(He strikes Roderigo.)]
MONTANO: Nay, good Lieutenant. [(Restraining him.)] I pray you, sir, hold your
         hand.
CASSIO: Let me go, sir, or I'll knock you o'er the mazard.[7]
MONTANO: Come, come, you're drunk.
CASSIO: Drunk? [(They fight.)]
IAGO [(aside to Roderigo)]:
130   Away, I say. Go out and cry a mutiny.[8]

                                                  [(Exit Roderigo.)]

---

2. Exact counterpart. (Equinox is an equal length of days and nights.)
3. Stay awake twice around the clock or horologe.
4. Risk giving such an important position as his second in command to.
5. The Quarto text reads, "driving in."

6. Wicker-covered. (Cassio vows to assail Roderigo until his skin resembles wickerwork or until he has driven Roderigo through the holes in a wickerwork.)
7. Head. (literally, a drinking vessel.)
8. Riot.

Nay, good Lieutenant—God's will, gentlemen—
Help, ho!—Lieutenant—sir—Montano—sir—
Help, masters!°—Here's a goodly watch indeed!   *sirs*
[(*A bell rings.*)]9
Who's that which rings the bell?—Diablo,° ho!   *the devil*
135 The town will rise.° God's will, Lieutenant, hold!   *grow riotous*
You'll be ashamed forever.
[*Enter Othello and attendants with weapons*].
OTHELLO: What is the matter here?
MONTANO: Zounds, I bleed still.
I am hurt to th' death. He dies! [(*He thrusts at Cassio.*)]
OTHELLO: Hold, for your lives!
IAGO: Hold, ho! Lieutenant—sir—Montano—gentlemen—
140 Have you forgot all sense of place and duty?
Hold! The General speaks to you. Hold, for shame!
OTHELLO: Why, how now, ho! From whence ariseth this?
Are we turned Turks, and to ourselves do that
Which heaven hath forbid the Ottomites?1
145 For Christian shame, put by this barbarous brawl!
He that stirs next to carve for2 his own rage
Holds his soul light;3 he dies upon his motion.4
Silence that dreadful bell. It frights the isle
From her propriety.° What is the matter, masters?   *proper state*
150 Honest Iago, that looks dead with grieving,
Speak. Who began this? On thy love, I charge thee.
IAGO: I do not know. Friends all but now, even now,
In quarter5 and in terms° like bride and groom   *on good terms*
Devesting them° for bed; and then, but now—   *undressing*
155 As if some planet had unwitted men—
Swords out, and tilting one at others' breasts
In opposition bloody. I cannot speak°   *explain*
Any beginning to this peevish odds;°   *quarrel*
And would in action glorious I had lost
160 Those legs that brought me to a part of it!
OTHELLO: How comes it, Michael, you are thus forgot?6
CASSIO: I pray you, pardon me. I cannot speak.
OTHELLO: Worthy Montano, you were wont° be civil;   *accustomed to be*
The gravity and stillness° of your youth   *sobriety*
165 The world hath noted, and your name is great
In mouths of wisest censure.° What's the matter   *judgment*
That you unlace7 your reputation thus
And spend your rich opinion° for the name   *reputation*
Of a night-brawler? Give me answer to it.

---

9. This direction is from the Quarto, as are *Exit Roderigo*
at line 130, *They fight* at line 129, and *with weapons* at line
136.
1. Inflict on ourselves the harm that heaven has prevented the Turks from doing (by destroying their fleet).
2. Indulge, satisfy with his sword.

3. Places little value on his life.
4. If he moves.
5. In friendly conduct, within bounds.
6. Have forgotten yourself thus.
7. Undo, lay open (as one might loose the strings of a
purse containing reputation).

MONTANO: Worthy Othello, I am hurt to danger.
    Your officer, Iago, can inform you—
    While I spare speech, which something° now offends° me—   *somewhat / pains*
    Of all that I do know; nor know I aught
    By me that's said or done amiss this night,
175   Unless self-charity be sometimes a vice,
    And to defend ourselves it be a sin
    When violence assails us.
OTHELLO: Now, by heaven,
    My blood[8] begins my safer guides[9] to rule,
    And passion, having my best judgment collied,°   *darkened*
180   Essays° to lead the way. Zounds, if I stir,   *undertakes*
    Or do but lift this arm, the best of you
    Shall sink in my rebuke. Give me to know
    How this foul rout° began, who set it on;   *riot*
    And he that is approved in° this offense,   *found guilty of*
185   Though he had twinned with me, both at a birth,
    Shall lose me. What? In a town of[1] war
    Yet wild, the people's hearts brim full of fear,
    To manage° private and domestic quarrel?   *undertake*
    In night, and on the court and guard of safety?[2]
190   'Tis monstrous. Iago, who began 't?
MONTANO [(*to Iago*)]: If partially affined,[3] or leagued in office,[4]
    Thou dost deliver more or less than truth,
    Thou art no soldier.
IAGO: Touch me not so near.
    I had rather have this tongue cut from my mouth
195   Than it should do offense to Michael Cassio;
    Yet, I persuade myself, to speak the truth
    Shall nothing wrong him. Thus it is, General.
    Montano and myself being in speech,
    There comes a fellow crying out for help,
200   And Cassio following him with determined sword
    To execute[5] upon him. Sir, this gentleman [*indicating Montano.*]
    Steps in to Cassio and entreats his pause.°   *him to stop*
    Myself the crying fellow did pursue,
    Lest by his clamor—as it so fell out—
205   The town might fall in fright. He, swift of foot,
    Outran my purpose, and I returned, the rather°   *sooner*
    For that I heard the clink and fall of swords
    And Cassio high in oath, which till tonight
    I ne'er might say before. When I came back—
210   For this was brief—I found them close together
    At blow and thrust, even as again they were

8. Passion (of anger).
9. I.e., reason.
1. Town garrisoned for.
2. At the main guardhouse or headquarters and on watch.

3. Made partial by some personal relationship.
4. In league as fellow officers.
5. Give effect to (his anger).

When you yourself did part them.
More of this matter cannot I report.
But men are men; the best sometimes forget.°   *forget themselves*
215   Though Cassio did some little wrong to him,
As men in rage strike those that wish them best,[6]
Yet surely Cassio, I believe, received
From him that fled some strange indignity,
Which patience could not pass.°   *overlook*

OTHELLO: I know, Iago,
220   Thy honesty and love doth mince this matter,
Making it light to Cassio. Cassio, I love thee,
But nevermore be officer of mine.
    [*Enter Desdemona, attended.*]
Look if my gentle love be not raised up.
I'll make thee an example.

DESDEMONA: What is the matter, dear?

OTHELLO: All's well now, sweeting;
Come away to bed. [(*To Montano.*)] Sir, for your hurts,
Myself will be your surgeon.[7]—Lead him off.
    [(*Montano is led off.*)]
Iago, look with care about the town
And silence those whom this vile brawl distracted.
230   Come, Desdemona. 'Tis the soldiers' life
To have their balmy slumbers waked with strife.
                    [*Exit (with all but Iago and Cassio.*)]

IAGO: What, are you hurt, Lieutenant?

CASSIO: Ay, past all surgery.

IAGO: Marry, God forbid!

CASSIO: Reputation, reputation, reputation! O, I have lost my reputation! I have
lost the immortal part of myself, and what remains is bestial. My reputation,
Iago, my reputation!

IAGO: As I am an honest man, I thought you had received some bodily wound; there
is more sense in that than in reputation. Reputation is an idle and most false
240   imposition,[8] oft got without merit and lost without deserving. You have lost no
reputation at all, unless you repute yourself such a loser. What, man, there are
more ways to recover[9] the General again. You are but now cast in his mood[1]—
a punishment more in policy[2] than in malice, even so as one would beat his
offenseless dog to affright an imperious lion.[3] Sue[4] to him again and he's yours.

CASSIO: I will rather sue to be despised than to deceive so good a commander with
so slight,[5] so drunken, and so indiscreet an officer. Drunk? And speak parrot?[6]
And squabble? Swagger? Swear? And discourse fustian with one's own shadow?

6. Even those who are well disposed.
7. Make sure you receive medical attention.
8. Thing artificially imposed and of no real value.
9. Regain favor with.
1. Dismissed in a moment of anger.
2. Done for expediency's sake and as a public gesture.

3. Would make an example of a minor offender to deter
more important and dangerous offenders.
4. Petition.
5. Worthless.
6. Talk nonsense, rant. (*Discourse fustian*, in the next
lines, has much the same meaning.)

O thou invisible spirit of wine, if thou hast no name to be known by, let us call thee devil!

IAGO: What was he that you followed with your sword? What had he done to you?

CASSIO: I know not.

IAGO: Is 't possible?

CASSIO: I remember a mass of things, but nothing distinctly; a quarrel, but nothing wherefore.[7] O God, that men should put an enemy in their mouths to steal
255   away their brains! That we should, with joy, pleasance, revel, and applause[8] transform ourselves into beasts!

IAGO: Why, but you are now well enough. How came you thus recovered?

CASSIO: It hath pleased the devil drunkenness to give place to the devil wrath. One unperfectness shows me another, to make me frankly despise myself.

IAGO: Come, you are too severe a moraler.[9] As the time, the place, and the condition of this country stands, I could heartily wish this had not befallen; but since it is as it is, mend it for your own good.

CASSIO: I will ask him for my place again; he shall tell me I am a drunkard. Had I as many mouths as Hydra,[1] such an answer would stop them all. To be now a sen-
265   sible man, by and by a fool, and presently a beast! Oh, strange! Every inordinate cup is unblessed, and the ingredient is a devil.

IAGO: Come, come, good wine is a good familiar creature, if it be well used. Exclaim no more against it. And, good Lieutenant, I think you think I love you.

CASSIO: I have well approved[2] it, sir. I drunk!

IAGO: You or any man living may be drunk at a time,[3] man. I'll tell you what you shall do. Our general's wife is now the general—I may say so in this respect, for that[4] he hath devoted and given up himself to the contemplation, mark, and denotement[5] of her parts[6] and graces. Confess yourself freely to her; importune her help to put you in your place again. She is of so free,[7] so kind, so apt, so
275   blessed a disposition, she holds it a vice in her goodness not to do more than she is requested. This broken joint between you and her husband entreat her to splinter;[8] and, my fortunes against any lay[9] worth naming, this crack of your love shall grow stronger than it was before.

CASSIO: You advise me well.

IAGO: I protest,[1] in the sincerity of love and honest kindness.

CASSIO: I think it freely;[2] and betimes in the morning I will beseech the virtuous Desdemona to undertake for me. I am desperate of my fortunes if they check[3] me here.

IAGO: You are in the right. Good night, Lieutenant. I must to the watch.

CASSIO: Good night, honest Iago.   [Exit Cassio.]

IAGO: And what's he then that says I play the villain,
When this advice is free[4] I give, and honest,

---

7. Why.
8. Desire for applause.
9. Moralizer.
1. The Lernaean Hydra, a monster with many heads and the ability to grow two heads when one was cut off, slain by Hercules as the second of his 12 labors.
2. Proved.
3. At one time or another.
4. In view of this fact, that.

5. Both words mean "observation."
6. Qualities.
7. Generous.
8. Bind with splints.
9. Stake, wager.
1. Insist, declare.
2. Unreservedly.
3. Repulse.
4. Free from guile. Also, freely given.

Probal° to thinking, and indeed the course   *reasonable*
To win the Moor again? For 'tis most easy
Th' inclining° Desdemona to subdue°   *willing / persuade*
290   In any honest suit; she's framed as fruitful[5]
As the free elements.[6] And then for her
To win the Moor—were 't to renounce his baptism,
All seals and symbols of redeemèd sin—
His soul is so enfettered to her love
295   That she may make, unmake, do what she list,
Even as her appetite[7] shall play the god
With his weak function.[8] How am I then a villain,
To counsel Cassio to this parallel[9] course
Directly to his good? Divinity of hell![1]
300   When devils will the blackest sins put on,°   *instigate*
They do suggest° at first with heavenly shows,   *tempt*
As I do now. For whiles this honest fool
Plies Desdemona to repair his fortune,
And she for him pleads strongly to the Moor,
305   I'll pour this pestilence into his ear,
That she repeals him[2] for her body's lust;
And by how much she strives to do him good,
She shall undo her credit with the Moor.
So will I turn her virtue into pitch,[3]
310   And out of her own goodness make the net
That shall enmesh them all.
                    [*Enter Roderigo.*]
                    How now, Roderigo?
RODERIGO: I do follow here in the chase, not like a hound that hunts, but one that
fills up the cry.[4] My money is almost spent; I have been tonight exceedingly
well cudgeled; and I think the issue will be I shall have so much[5] experience for
315   my pains, and so, with no money at all and a little more wit, return again to
Venice.
IAGO: How poor are they that have not patience!
What wound did ever heal but by degrees?
Thou know'st we work by wit, and not by witchcraft,
320   And wit depends on dilatory time.
Does 't not go well? Cassio hath beaten thee,
And thou, by that small hurt, hast cashiered° Cassio.   *dismissed*
Though other things grow fair against the sun,

---

5. Created as generous.
6. I.e., earth, air, fire, and water, unrestrained and spontaneous.
7. Her desire, or, perhaps, his desire for her.
8. Exercise of faculties (weakened by his fondness for her).
9. Corresponding to these facts and to his best interests.

1. Inverted theology of hell (which seduces the soul to its
damnation).
2. Attempts to get him restored.
3. Foul blackness. Also a snaring substance.
4. Merely takes part as one of the pack.
5. Just so much and no more.

Yet fruits that blossom first will first be ripe.[6]
325   Content thyself awhile. By the Mass, 'tis morning!
Pleasure and action make the hours seem short.
Retire thee; go where thou art billeted.
Away, I say! Thou shalt know more hereafter.
Nay, get thee gone.   [*Exit Roderigo.*]
330   Two things are to be done.
My wife must move° for Cassio to her mistress;   *plead*
I'll set her on;
Myself the while to draw the Moor apart
And bring him jump° when he may Cassio find   *precisely*
335   Soliciting his wife. Ay, that's the way.
Dull not device° by coldness° and delay.   [*Exit.*]   *plot / lack of zeal*

ACT 3

Scene 1[7]

[*Enter Cassio (and) Musicians.*]

CASSIO: Masters, play here—I will content your pains[8]—
Something that's brief, and bid "Good morrow, General." [(*They play.*)]
[(*Enter*) *Clown.*]

CLOWN: Why, masters, have your instruments been in Naples, that they speak i' the
nose[9] thus?

A MUSICIAN: How, sir, how?

CLOWN: Are these, I pray you, wind instruments?

A MUSICIAN: Ay, marry, are they, sir.

CLOWN: O, thereby hangs a tail.

A MUSICIAN: Whereby hangs a tale, sir?

CLOWN: Marry, sir, by many a wind instrument[1] that I know. But, masters, here's
money for you. [*He gives money.*] And the General so likes your music that he
desires you, for love's sake,[2] to make no more noise with it.

A MUSICIAN: Well, sir, we will not.

CLOWN: If you have any music that may not[3] be heard, to 't again; but, as they say, to
hear music the General does not greatly care.

A MUSICIAN: We have none such, sir.

CLOWN: Then put up your pipes in your bag, for I'll away.[4] Go, vanish into air, away!
[*Exeunt Musicians.*]

CASSIO: Dost thou hear, mine honest friend?

CLOWN: No, I hear not your honest friend; I hear you.

---

6. Plans that are well prepared and set expeditiously in
motion will soonest ripen into success.
7. Location: Before the chamber of Othello and Desdemona.
8. Reward your efforts.
9. Sound nasal. Also sound like one whose nose has been
attacked by syphilis. (Naples was popularly supposed to
have a high incidence of venereal disease.)

1. With a joke on flatulence. The *tail* that hangs nearby
the *wind instrument* suggests the penis.
2. Out of friendship and affection. Also, for the sake of
lovemaking in Othello's marriage.
3. Cannot.
4. (Possibly a misprint, or a snatch of song?)

CASSIO: Prithee, keep up[5] thy quillets.[6] There's a poor piece of gold for thee. [*He gives money.*] If the gentlewoman that attends the General's wife be stirring, tell her there's one Cassio entreats her a little favor of speech.[7] Wilt thou do this?

CLOWN: She is stirring, sir. If she will stir[8] hither, I shall seem[9] to notify unto her.

CASSIO: Do, good my friend.   [*Exit Clown.*]

    [*Enter Iago.*]

                    In happy time,[1] Iago.

IAGO: You have not been abed, then?

CASSIO: Why, no. The day had broke
    Before we parted. I have made bold, Iago,
    To send in to your wife. My suit to her
30   Is that she will to virtuous Desdemona
    Procure me some access.

IAGO: I'll send her to you presently;
    And I'll devise a mean to draw the Moor
    Out of the way, that your converse and business
35   May be more free.

CASSIO: I humbly thank you for 't.   [*Exit (Iago.)*]
                  I never knew
    A Florentine[2] more kind and honest.

    [*Enter Emilia.*]

EMILIA: Good morrow, good Lieutenant. I am sorry
    For your displeasure;° but all will sure be well.   *fall from favor*
40   The General and his wife are talking of it,
    And she speaks for you stoutly.° The Moor replies   *spiritedly*
    That he you hurt is of great fame° in Cyprus   *importance*
    And great affinity,° and that in wholesome wisdom *family connection*
    He might not but refuse you; but he protests° he loves you *insists*
45   And needs no other suitor but his likings
    To take the safest occasion by the front[3]
    To bring you in again.

CASSIO: Yes I beseech you,
    If you think fit, or that it may be done,
    Give me advantage of some brief discourse
50   With Desdemon alone.

EMILIA: Pray you, come in.
    I will bestow you where you shall have time
    To speak your bosom° freely.   *thoughts*

CASSIO: I am much bound to you.   [*(Exeunt.)*]

---

5. Do not bring out.
6. Quibbles, puns.
7. The favor of a brief talk.
8. Bestir herself (with a play on *stirring*, "rousing herself from rest").

9. Deem it good, think fit.
1. I.e., well met.
2. I.e., even a fellow Florentine. (Iago is a Venetian; Cassio is a Florentine.)
3. Opportunity by the forelock.

Scene 2[4]

[*Enter Othello, Iago, and Gentlemen.*]

OTHELLO [(*giving letters*)]: These letters give, Iago, to the pilot,
    And by him do my duties° to the Senate.   *give my respects*
    That done, I will be walking on the works;°   *fortifications*
    Repair° there to me.   *return*
IAGO: Well, my good lord, I'll do 't.
OTHELLO: This fortification, gentlemen, shall we see 't?
GENTLEMEN: We'll wait upon° your lordship.   [*Exeunt.*]   *attend*

Scene 3[5]

[*Enter Desdemona, Cassio, and Emilia.*]

DESDEMONA: Be thou assured, good Cassio, I will do
    All my abilities in thy behalf.
EMILIA: Good madam, do. I warrant it grieves my husband
    As if the cause were his.
DESDEMONA: O, that's an honest fellow. Do not doubt, Cassio,
    But I will have my lord and you again
    As friendly as you were.
CASSIO: Bounteous madam,
    Whatever shall become of Michael Cassio,
    He's never anything but your true servant.
DESDEMONA: I know 't. I thank you. You do love my lord;
    You have known him long, and be you well assured
    He shall in strangeness° stand no farther off   *aloofness*
    Than in a politic[6] distance.
CASSIO: Ay but, lady,
    That policy may either last so long,
15   Or feed upon such nice and waterish diet,[7]
    Or breed itself so out of circumstance,[8]
    That, I being absent and my place supplied,[9]
    My general will forget my love and service.
DESDEMONA: Do not doubt° that. Before Emilia here   *fear*
20   I give thee warrant° of thy place. Assure thee,   *guarantee*
    If I do vow a friendship I'll perform it
    To the last article. My lord shall never rest.
    I'll watch him tame[1] and talk him out of patience;[2]
    His bed shall seem a school, his board° a shrift;°   *table / confessional*
25   I'll intermingle everything he does
    With Cassio's suit. Therefore be merry, Cassio,
    For thy solicitor° shall rather die   *advocate*
    Than give thy cause away.°   *up*

4. Location: The citadel.
5. Location: The garden of the citadel.
6. Required by wise policy.
7. Or sustain itself at length upon such trivial and meager
technicalities.
8. Continually renew itself so out of chance events, or

yield so few chances for my being pardoned.
9. Filled by another person.
1. Tame him by keeping him from sleeping (a term from
falconry).
2. Past his endurance.

[*Enter Othello and Iago (at a distance).*]

EMILIA: Madam, here comes my lord.

CASSIO: Madam, I'll take my leave.

DESDEMONA: Why, stay, and hear me speak.

CASSIO: Madam, not now. I am very ill at ease,
　　　　Unfit for mine own purposes.

DESDEMONA: Well, do your discretion.³ 　　　　　　　　[*Exit Cassio.*]

IAGO: Ha? I like not that.

OTHELLO: 　　　　　　　　What dost thou say?

IAGO: Nothing, my lord; or if—I know not what.

OTHELLO: Was not that Cassio parted from my wife?

IAGO: Cassio, my lord? No, sure, I cannot think it,
　　　　That he would steal away so guiltylike,
40　　　Seeing you coming.

OTHELLO: 　　　　　　　　I do believe 'twas he.

DESDEMONA: How now, my lord?
　　　　I have been talking with a suitor here,
　　　　A man that languishes in your displeasure.

OTHELLO: Who is 't you mean?

DESDEMONA: Why, your lieutenant, Cassio. Good my lord,
　　　　If I have any grace or power to move you,
　　　　His present reconciliation take;⁴
　　　　For if he be not one that truly loves you,
　　　　That errs in ignorance and not in cunning,° 　　　　　*wittingly*
50　　　I have no judgment in an honest face.
　　　　I prithee, call him back.

OTHELLO: 　　　　　　　　Went he hence now?

DESDEMONA: Yes, faith, so humbled
　　　　That he hath left part of his grief with me
　　　　To suffer with him. Good love, call him back.

OTHELLO: Not now, sweet Desdemon. Some other time.

DESDEMONA: But shall 't be shortly?

OTHELLO: 　　　　　　　　The sooner, sweet, for you.

DESDEMONA: Shall 't be tonight at supper?

OTHELLO: 　　　　　　　　No, not tonight.

DESDEMONA: Tomorrow dinner,° then? 　　　　　　　　*noontime*

OTHELLO: 　　　　　　　　I shall not dine at home.
　　　　I meet the captains at the citadel.

DESDEMONA: Why, then, tomorrow night, or Tuesday morn,
　　　　On Tuesday noon, or night, on Wednesday morn.
　　　　I prithee, name the time, but let it not
　　　　Exceed three days. In faith, he's penitent;
　　　　And yet his trespass, in our common reason°—　　　*judgments*
65　　　Save that, they say, the wars must make example

---

3. Act according to your own discretion.　　　　4. Let him be reconciled to you right away.

Out of her best⁵—is not almost° a fault   *scarcely*
T' incur a private check.⁶ When shall he come?
Tell me, Othello. I wonder in my soul
What you would ask me that I should deny,
70   Or stand so mammering on.° What? Michael Cassio,   *wavering about*
That came a-wooing with you, and so many a time,
When I have spoke of you dispraisingly,
Hath ta'en your part—to have so much to do
To bring him in!° By 'r Lady, I could do much—   *restore him to favor*

OTHELLO: Prithee, no more. Let him come when he will;
    I will deny thee nothing.

DESDEMONA: Why, this is not a boon.
    'Tis as I should entreat you wear your gloves,
    Or feed on nourishing dishes, or keep you warm,
    Or sue to you to do a peculiar° profit   *personal*
80   To your own person. Nay, when I have a suit
    Wherein I mean to touch° your love indeed,   *test*
    It shall be full of poise⁷ and difficult weight,
    And fearful to be granted.

OTHELLO: I will deny thee nothing.
    Whereon,° I do beseech thee, grant me this,   *in return*
85   To leave me but a little to myself.

DESDEMONA: Shall I deny you? No. Farewell, my lord.

OTHELLO: Farewell, my Desdemona. I'll come to thee straight.°   *straightway*

DESDEMONA: Emilia, come.—Be as your fancies° teach you;   *inclinations*
    Whate'er you be, I am obedient.   [*Exit with Emilia.*]

OTHELLO: Excellent wretch!⁸ Perdition catch my soul
    But I do love thee! And when I love thee not,
    Chaos is come again.⁹

IAGO: My noble lord—

OTHELLO: What dost thou say, Iago?

IAGO: Did Michael Cassio, when you wooed my lady,
95   Know of your love?

OTHELLO: He did, from first to last. Why dost thou ask?

IAGO: But for a satisfaction of my thought;
    No further harm.

OTHELLO: Why of thy thought, Iago?

IAGO: I did not think he had been acquainted with her.

OTHELLO: O, yes, and went between us very oft.

IAGO: Indeed?

OTHELLO: Indeed? Ay, indeed. Discern'st thou aught in that?
    Is he not honest?

IAGO: Honest, my lord?

OTHELLO: Honest. Ay, honest.

---

5. Were it not that, as the saying goes, military discipline requires making an example of the very best men. (*Her* refers to *wars* as a singular concept.)
6. Even a private reprimand.
7. Weight, heaviness; or equipoise, delicate balance involving hard choice.

8. A term of affectionate endearment.
9. I.e., My love for you will last forever, until the end of time when chaos will return. (But with an unconscious, ironic suggestion that, if anything should induce Othello to cease loving Desdemona, the result would be chaos.)

IAGO: My lord, for aught I know.

OTHELLO: What dost thou think?

IAGO: Think, my lord?

OTHELLO: "Think, my lord?" By heaven, thou echo'st me,
          As if there were some monster in thy thought
          Too hideous to be shown. Thou dost mean something.
          I heard thee say even now, thou lik'st not that,
110   When Cassio left my wife. What didst not like?
          And when I told thee he was of my counsel°   *in my confidence*
          In my whole course of wooing, thou cried'st "Indeed?"
          And didst contract and purse° thy brow together   *knit*
          As if thou then hadst shut up in thy brain
115   Some horrible conceit.° If thou dost love me,   *fancy*
          Show me thy thought.

IAGO: My lord, you know I love you.

OTHELLO: I think thou dost;
          And, for° I know thou'rt full of love and honesty,   *because*
          And weigh'st thy words before thou giv'st them breath,
120   Therefore these stops° of thine fright me the more;   *pauses*
          For such things in a false disloyal knave
          Are tricks of custom,° but in a man that's just   *customary*
          They're close dilations,[1] working from the heart
          That passion cannot rule.[2]

IAGO: For° Michael Cassio,   *as for*
125   I dare be sworn I think that he is honest.

OTHELLO: I think so too.

IAGO: Men should be what they seem;
          Or those that be not, would they might seem none![3]

OTHELLO: Certain, men should be what they seem.

IAGO: Why, then, I think Cassio's an honest man.

OTHELLO: Nay, yet there's more in this.
          I prithee, speak to me as to thy thinkings,
          As thou dost ruminate, and give thy worst of thoughts
          The worst of words.

IAGO: Good my lord, pardon me.
          Though I am bound to every act of duty,
135   I am not bound to that° all slaves are free to.[4]   *that which*
          Utter my thoughts? Why, say they are vile and false,
          As where's that palace whereinto foul things
          Sometimes intrude not? Who has that breast so pure
          But some uncleanly apprehensions
140   Keep leets and law days,[5] and in sessions sit
          With° meditations lawful?°   *along with* / *innocent*

---

1. Secret or involuntary expressions or delays.
2. I.e., that are too passionately strong to be restrained (referring to the workings), or that cannot rule its own passions (referring to the heart).
3. I.e., not to be men, or not seem to be honest.

4. Free with respect to.
5. I.e., hold court, set up their authority in one's heart. *Leets* are a kind of manor court; *law days* are the days courts sit in session, or those sessions.

OTHELLO: Thou dost conspire against thy friend,[6] Iago,
　　　　　If thou but think'st him wronged and mak'st his ear
　　　　　A stranger to thy thoughts.
IAGO:　　　　　　　　　　　　I do beseech you,
145　　Though I perchance am vicious° in my guess—　　　　　　*wrong*
　　　　　As I confess it is my nature's plague
　　　　　To spy into abuses, and oft my jealousy°　　　　　*suspicious nature*
　　　　　Shapes faults that are not—that your wisdom then,°　　　*on that account*
　　　　　From one[7] that so imperfectly conceits,　　　　　　*conjectures*
150　　Would take no notice, nor build yourself a trouble
　　　　　Out of his scattering° and unsure observance.　　　　　*random*
　　　　　It were not for your quiet nor your good,
　　　　　Nor for my manhood, honesty, and wisdom,
　　　　　To let you know my thoughts.
OTHELLO:　　　　　　　　　　What dost thou mean?
IAGO: Good name in man and woman, dear my lord,
　　　　　Is the immediate° jewel of their souls.　　　　　*essential*
　　　　　Who steals my purse steals trash; 'tis something, nothing;
　　　　　'Twas mine, 'tis his, and has been slave to thousands;
　　　　　But he that filches from me my good name
160　　Robs me of that which not enriches him
　　　　　And makes me poor indeed.
OTHELLO: By heaven, I'll know thy thoughts.
IAGO: You cannot, if° my heart were in your hand,　　　　　*even if*
165　　Nor shall not, whilst 'tis in my custody.
OTHELLO: Ha?
IAGO:　　　O, beware, my lord, of jealousy.
　　　　　It is the green-eyed monster, which doth mock
　　　　　The meat it feeds on.[8] That cuckold lives in bliss
　　　　　Who, certain of his fate, loves not his wronger;[9]
　　　　　But O, what damnèd minutes tells° he o'er　　　　　*counts*
170　　Who dotes, yet doubts, suspects, yet fondly loves!
OTHELLO: O, misery!
IAGO: Poor and content is rich, and rich enough,[1]
　　　　　But riches fineless° is as poor as winter　　　　　*boundless*
　　　　　To him that ever fears he shall be poor.
175　　Good God, the souls of all my tribe defend
　　　　　From jealousy!
OTHELLO:　　　　　Why, why is this?
　　　　　Think'st thou I'd make a life of jealousy,
　　　　　To follow still the changes of the moon
　　　　　With fresh suspicions?[2] No! To be once in doubt
180　　Is once° to be resolved.[3] Exchange me for a goat　　　*once and for all*

6. I.e., Othello.
7. I.e., myself, Iago.
8. Mocks and torments the heart of its victim, the man who suffers jealously.
9. I.e., his faithless wife. (The unsuspecting cuckold is spared the misery of loving his wife only to discover she is cheating on him.)

1. To be content with what little one has is the greatest wealth of all (proverbial).
2. To be constantly imagining new causes for suspicion, changing incessantly like the moon.
3. Free of doubt, having settled the matter.

When I shall turn the business of my soul
To such exsufflicate and blown⁴ surmises
Matching thy inference.° 'Tis not to make me jealous   *allegation*
To say my wife is fair, feeds well, loves company,
185   Is free of speech, sings, plays, and dances well;
Where virtue is, these are more virtuous.
Nor from mine own weak merits will I draw
The smallest fear or doubt of her revolt,⁵
For she had eyes, and chose me. No, Iago,
190   I'll see before I doubt; when I doubt, prove;
And on the proof, there is no more but this—
Away at once with love or jealousy.

IAGO: I am glad of this, for now I shall have reason
To show the love and duty that I bear you
195   With franker spirit. Therefore, as I am bound,
Receive it from me. I speak not yet of proof.
Look to your wife; observe her well with Cassio.
Wear your eyes thus, not° jealous nor secure.°   *neither / certain*
I would not have your free and noble nature,
200   Out of self-bounty,⁶ be abused.° Look to 't.   *deceived*
I know our country disposition well;
In Venice they do let God see the pranks
They dare not show their husbands; their best conscience
Is not to leave 't undone, but keep 't unknown.

OTHELLO: Dost thou say so?

IAGO: She did deceive her father, marrying you;
And when she seemed to shake and fear your looks,
She loved them most.

OTHELLO: And so she did.

IAGO: Why, go to,⁷ then!
She that, so young, could give out such a seeming,°   *false appearance*
210   To seel⁸ her father's eyes up close as oak,⁹
He thought 'twas witchcraft! But I am much to blame.
I humbly do beseech you of your pardon
For too much loving you.

OTHELLO: I am bound¹ to thee forever.

IAGO: I see this hath a little dashed your spirits.

OTHELLO: Not a jot, not a jot.

IAGO: I' faith, I fear it has.
I hope you will consider what is spoke
Comes from my love. But I do see you're moved.
I am to pray you not to strain my speech
To grosser issues° nor to larger reach°   *significances / scope*
220   Than to suspicion.

---

4. Inflated and blown up, rumored about, or, spat out and flyblown, hence, loathsome, disgusting.
5. Fear of her unfaithfulness.
6. Inherent or natural goodness and generosity.

7. An expression of impatience.
8. Blind (a term from falconry).
9. A close-grained wood.
1. Indebted (but perhaps with ironic sense of "tied").

OTHELLO: I will not.

IAGO: Should you do so, my lord,
My speech should fall into such vile success°   *effect*
Which my thoughts aimed not. Cassio's my worthy friend.
My lord, I see you're moved.

OTHELLO: No, not much moved.
225   I do not think but Desdemona's honest.°   *chaste*

IAGO: Long live she so! And long live you to think so!

OTHELLO: And yet, how nature erring from itself—

IAGO: Ay, there's the point! As—to be bold with you—
Not to affect° many proposèd matches   *prefer*
230   Of her own clime, complexion, and degree,[2]
Whereto we see in all things nature tends—
Foh! One may smell in such a will° most rank,   *sensuality*
Foul disproportion,° thoughts unnatural.   *abnormality*
But pardon me. I do not in position°   *argument*
235   Distinctly speak of her, though I may fear
Her will, recoiling° to her better[3] judgment,   *reverting*
May fall to match you with her country forms[4]
And happily repent.[5]

OTHELLO: Farewell, farewell!
If more thou dost perceive, let me know more.
240   Set on thy wife to observe. Leave me, Iago.

IAGO [*going*]: My lord, I take my leave.

OTHELLO: Why did I marry? This honest creature doubtless
Sees and knows more, much more, than he unfolds.

IAGO [*returning*]: My lord, I would I might entreat your honor
245   To scan° this thing no farther. Leave it to time.   *scrutinize*
Although 'tis fit that Cassio have his place—
For, sure, he fills it up with great ability—
Yet, if you please to hold him off awhile,
You shall by that perceive him and his means.[6]
250   Note if your lady strain his entertainment[7]
With any strong or vehement importunity;
Much will be seen in that. In the meantime,
Let me be thought too busy° in my fears—   *interfering*
As worthy cause I have to fear I am—
255   And hold her free,[8] I do beseech your honor.

OTHELLO: Fear not my government.°   *conduct*

IAGO: I once more take my leave.   [*Exit.*]

OTHELLO: This fellow's of exceeding honesty,
And knows all qualities,° with a learnèd spirit,   *natures*
260   Of human dealings. If I do prove her haggard,[9]
Though that her jesses[1] were my dear heartstrings,

2. Country, color, and social position.
3. I.e., more natural and reconsidered.
4. Undertake to compare you with Venetian norms of
handsomeness.
5. Perhaps repent her marriage.

6. The method he uses (to regain his post).
7. Urge his reinstatement.
8. Regard her as innocent.
9. Wild (like a wild female hawk).
1. Straps fastened around the legs of a trained hawk.

I'd whistle her off and let her down the wind[2]
To prey at fortune.[3] Haply, for[4] I am black
And have not those soft parts of conversation[5]
265   That chamberers° have, or for I am declined   *gallants*
Into the vale of years—yet that's not much—
She's gone. I am abused,° and my relief   *deceived*
Must be to loathe her. O curse of marriage,
That we can call these delicate creatures ours
270   And not their appetites! I had rather be a toad
And live upon the vapor of a dungeon
Than keep a corner in the thing I love
For others' uses. Yet, 'tis the plague of great ones;
Prerogatived[6] are they less than the base.[7]
275   'Tis destiny unshunnable, like death.
Even then this forkèd[8] plague is fated to us
When we do quicken.[9] Look where she comes.
                [*Enter Desdemona and Emilia.*]
If she be false, O, then heaven mocks itself!
I'll not believe 't.
DESDEMONA: How now, my dear Othello?
280   Your dinner, and the generous° islanders   *noble*
By you invited, do attend° your presence.   *await*
OTHELLO: I am to blame.
DESDEMONA: Why do you speak so faintly?
Are you not well?
OTHELLO: I have a pain upon my forehead here.
DESDEMONA: Faith, that's with watching.° 'Twill away again.   *too little sleep*
[(*She offers her handkerchief.*)]
Let me but bind it hard, within this hour
It will be well.
OTHELLO: Your napkin° is too little.   *handkerchief*
Let it alone.° Come, I'll go in with you.   *never mind*
[*He puts the handkerchief from him, and it drops.*]
DESDEMONA: I am very sorry that you are not well.

                                            [*Exit (with Othello.*)]

EMILIA [(*picking up the handkerchief*)]:
290   I am glad I have found this napkin.
This was her first remembrance from the Moor.
My wayward° husband hath a hundred times   *capricious*
Wooed me to steal it, but she so loves the token—
For he conjured her she should ever keep it—

---

2. I'd let her go forever. (To release a hawk downwind
was to invite it not to return.)
3. Fend for herself in the wild.
4. Perhaps because.
5. Pleasing graces of social behavior.
6. Privileged (to have honest wives).
7. Ordinary citizens. (Socially prominent men are espe-

cially prone to the unavoidable destiny of being cuckolded and to the public shame that goes with it.)
8. An allusion to the horns of the cuckold.
9. Receive life. *Quicken* may also mean to swarm with
maggots as the body festers, in which case lines suggest
that *even then*, in death, we are cuckolded by *forkèd*
worms.

295   That she reserves it evermore about her
         To kiss and talk to. I'll have the work ta'en out,[1]
         And give 't Iago. What he will do with it
         Heaven knows, not I;
         I nothing but to please his fantasy.°   whim
         [Enter Iago.]
IAGO: How now? What do you here alone?
EMILIA: Do not you chide. I have a thing for you.
IAGO: You have a thing for me? It is a common thing[2]—
EMILIA: Ha?
IAGO: To have a foolish wife.
EMILIA: O, is that all? What will you give me now
         For that same handkerchief?
IAGO: What handkerchief?
EMILIA: What handkerchief?
         Why, that the Moor first gave to Desdemona;
310   That which so often you did bid me steal.
IAGO: Hast stolen it from her?
EMILIA: No, faith. She let it drop by negligence,
         And to th' advantage[3] I, being here, took 't up.
         Look, here 'tis.
IAGO: A good wench! Give it me.
EMILIA: What will you do with 't, that you have been so earnest
         To have me filch it?
IAGO [(snatching it)]:   Why, what is that to you?
EMILIA: If it be not for some purpose of import,
         Give 't me again. Poor lady, she'll run mad
         When she shall lack° it.   miss
IAGO: Be not acknown on 't.[4]
320   I have use for it. Go, leave me.   [Exit Emilia.]
         I will in Cassio's lodging lose[5] this napkin
         And let him find it. Trifles light as air
         Are to the jealous confirmations strong
         As proofs of Holy Writ. This may do something.
325   The Moor already changes with my poison.
         Dangerous conceits° are in their natures poisons,   ideas
         Which at the first are scarce found to distaste,°   be distasteful
         But with a little act° upon the blood   action
         Burn like the mines of sulfur.
         [Enter Othello.]
                                   I did say so.
330   Look where he comes! Not poppy nor mandragora[6]
         Nor all the drowsy syrups of the world
         Shall ever medicine thee to that sweet sleep

1. Design of the embroidery copied.
2. With bawdy suggestion; *common* suggests coarseness
and availability to all comers, and *thing* is a slang term for
the genitals.
3. Taking the opportunity.

4. Do not confess knowledge of it.
5. The Folio spelling, *loose,* is a normal spelling for "lose,"
but it may also contain the idea of "let go," "release."
6. An opiate made of the mandrake root.

Which thou owedst° yesterday.   *you did own*

OTHELLO: Ha, ha, false to me?

IAGO: Why, how now, General? No more of that.

OTHELLO: Avaunt! Begone! Thou hast set me on the rack.
　　　　I swear 'tis better to be much abused
　　　　Than but to know 't a little.

IAGO: How now, my lord?

OTHELLO: What sense had I of her stolen hours of lust?
　　　　I saw 't not, thought it not, it harmed not me.
340　　I slept the next night well, fed well, was free° and merry;   *carefree*
　　　　I found not Cassio's kisses on her lips.
　　　　He that is robbed, not wanting° what is stolen,   *missing*
　　　　Let him not know 't and he's not robbed at all.

IAGO: I am sorry to hear this.

OTHELLO: I had been happy if the general camp,
　　　　Pioners⁷ and all, had tasted her sweet body,
　　　　So° I had nothing known. O, now, forever   *provided*
　　　　Farewell the tranquil mind! Farewell content!
　　　　Farewell the plumèd troops and the big° wars   *stately*
350　　That makes ambition virtue! O, farewell!
　　　　Farewell the neighing steed and the shrill trump,
　　　　The spirit-stirring drum, th' ear-piercing fife,
　　　　The royal banner, and all quality,°   *character*
　　　　Pride,° pomp, and circumstance° of glorious war!   *display / pageantry*
　　　　And O, you mortal engines,⁸ whose rude throats
　　　　Th' immortal Jove's dread clamors° counterfeit,   *thunder*
　　　　Farewell! Othello's occupation's gone.

IAGO: Is 't possible, my lord?

OTHELLO: Villain, be sure thou prove my love a whore!
360　　Be sure of it. Give me the ocular proof,
　　　　Or, by the worth of mine eternal soul,
　　　　Thou hadst been better have been born a dog
　　　　Than answer my waked wrath!

IAGO: Is 't come to this?

OTHELLO: Make me to see 't, or at the least so prove it
365　　That the probation° bear no hinge nor loop   *proof*
　　　　To hang a doubt on, or woe upon thy life!

IAGO: My noble lord—

OTHELLO: If thou dost slander her and torture me,
　　　　Never pray more; abandon all remorse;°   *pity*
370　　On horror's head horrors accumulate;
　　　　Do deeds to make heaven weep, all earth amazed;
　　　　For nothing canst thou to damnation add
　　　　Greater than that.

IAGO: O grace! O heaven forgive me!
　　　　Are you a man? Have you a soul or sense?

---

7. Diggers of mines, the lowest grade of soldiers.　　8. Cannon. (*Mortal* means "deadly.")

375   God b' wi' you; take mine office. O wretched fool,[9]
           That lov'st to make thine honesty a vice!°   *failing*
           O monstrous world! Take note, take note, O world,
           To be direct and honest is not safe.
           I thank you for this profit,° and from hence°   *instruction / henceforth*
380   I'll love no friend, sith° love breeds such offense.[1]   *since*
OTHELLO: Nay, stay. Thou shouldst be honest.[2]
IAGO: I should be wise, for honesty's a fool
           And loses that° it works for.   *what*
OTHELLO: By the world,
           I think my wife be honest and think she is not;
385   I think that thou art just and think thou art not.
           I'll have some proof. My name, that was as fresh
           As Dian's[3] visage, is now begrimed and black
           As mine own face. If there be cords, or knives,
           Poison, or fire, or suffocating streams,
390   I'll not endure it. Would I were satisfied!
IAGO: I see, sir, you are eaten up with passion.
           I do repent me that I put it to you.
           You would be satisfied?
OTHELLO: Would? Nay, and I will.
IAGO: And may; but how? How satisfied, my lord?
395   Would you, the supervisor,° grossly gape on?   *onlooker*
           Behold her topped?
OTHELLO: Death and damnation! O!
IAGO: It were a tedious difficulty, I think,
           To bring them to that prospect. Damn them then,[4]
           If ever mortal eyes do see them bolster[5]
400   More° than their own.° What then? How then?   *other / own eyes*
           What shall I say? Where's satisfaction?
           It is impossible you should see this,
           Were they as prime° as goats, as hot as monkeys,   *wanton*
           As salt° as wolves in pride,° and fools as gross   *lustful / heat*
405   As ignorance made drunk. But yet I say,
           If imputation[6] and strong circumstances
           Which lead directly to the door of truth
           Will give you satisfaction, you might have 't.
OTHELLO: Give me a living reason she's disloyal.
IAGO: I do not like the office.
           But sith° I am entered in this cause so far,   *since*
           Pricked° to 't by foolish honesty and love,   *spurred*
           I will go on. I lay with Cassio lately,
           And being troubled with a raging tooth
415   I could not sleep. There are a kind of men
           So loose of soul that in their sleeps will mutter

---

9. Iago addresses himself as a fool for having carried honesty too far.
1. Harm to the one who offers help and friendship.
2. It appears that you are. (But Iago replies in the sense of "ought to be.")
3. Diana, goddess of the moon and of chastity.
4. They would have to be really incorrigible.
5. Go to bed together, share a bolster.
6. Strong circumstantial evidence.

Their affairs. One of this kind is Cassio.
In sleep I heard him say, "Sweet Desdemona,
Let us be wary, let us hide our loves!"
420   And then, sir, would he grip and wring my hand,
Cry "O sweet creature!", then kiss me hard,
As if he plucked up kisses by the roots
That grew upon my lips; then laid his leg
Over my thigh, and sighed, and kissed, and then
425   Cried, "Cursèd fate that gave thee to the Moor!"

OTHELLO: O, monstrous! Monstrous!

IAGO: Nay, this was but his dream.

OTHELLO: But this denoted a foregone conclusion.[7]
'Tis a shrewd doubt,[8] though it be but a dream.

IAGO: And this may help to thicken other proofs
430   That do demonstrate thinly.

OTHELLO: I'll tear her all to pieces.

IAGO: Nay, but be wise. Yet we see nothing done;
She may be honest yet. Tell me but this:
Have you not sometimes seen a handkerchief
Spotted° with strawberries in your wife's hand?   *embroidered*

OTHELLO: I gave her such a one. 'Twas my first gift.

IAGO: I know not that; but such a handkerchief—
I am sure it was your wife's—did I today
See Cassio wipe his beard with.

OTHELLO: If it be that—

IAGO: If it be that, or any that was hers,
440   It speaks against her with the other proofs.

OTHELLO: O, that the slave° had forty thousand lives!   *Cassio*
One is too poor, too weak for my revenge.
Now do I see 'tis true. Look here, Iago,
All my fond[9] love thus do I blow to heaven.
445   'Tis gone.
Arise, black vengeance, from the hollow hell!
Yield up, O love, thy crown and hearted° throne   *fixed in the heart*
To tyrannous hate! Swell, bosom, with thy freight,°   *burden*
For 'tis of aspics'° tongues!   *venomous serpents'*

IAGO: Yet be content.°   *calm*

OTHELLO: O, blood, blood, blood!

IAGO: Patience, I say. Your mind perhaps may change.

OTHELLO: Never, Iago. Like to the Pontic Sea,[1]
Whose icy current and compulsive course
Ne'er feels retiring ebb, but keeps due on
455   To the Propontic[2] and the Hellespont,[3]
Even so my bloody thoughts with violent pace
Shall ne'er look back, ne'er ebb to humble love,

7. Concluded experience or action.
8. Suspicious circumstance.
9. Foolish (but also suggesting "affectionate").
1. Black Sea.

2. Sea of Marmara, between the Black Sea and the Aegean.
3. Dardanelles, straits where the Sea of Marmara joins with the Aegean.

Till that a capable° and wide revenge   *ample*
Swallow them up. Now, by yond marble[4] heaven,
460   [*Kneeling.*] In the due reverence of a sacred vow
I here engage my words.

IAGO: Do not rise yet.
[*He kneels.*][5] Witness, you ever-burning lights above,
You elements that clip° us round about,   *encompass*
Witness that here Iago doth give up
465   The execution° of his wit,° hands, heart,   *exercise / mind*
To wronged Othello's service. Let him command,
And to obey shall be in me remorse,[6]
What bloody business ever.° [(*They rise.*)]   *soever*

OTHELLO: I greet thy love,
Not with vain thanks, but with acceptance bounteous,
470   And will upon the instant put thee to 't.[7]
Within these three days let me hear thee say
That Cassio's not alive.

IAGO: My friend is dead;
'Tis done at your request. But let her live.

OTHELLO: Damn her, lewd minx!° O, damn her, damn her!   *wanton*
475   Come, go with me apart. I will withdraw
To furnish me with some swift means of death
For the fair devil. Now art thou my lieutenant.

IAGO: I am your own forever.   [*Exeunt.*]

Scene 4[8]

[*Enter Desdemona, Emilia, and Clown.*]

DESDEMONA: Do you know, sirrah,[9] where Lieutenant Cassio lies?

CLOWN: I dare not say he lies[1] anywhere.

DESDEMONA: Why, man?

CLOWN: He's a soldier, and for me to say a soldier lies, 'tis stabbing.

DESDEMONA: Go to. Where lodges he?

CLOWN: To tell you where he lodges is to tell you where I lie.

DESDEMONA: Can anything be made of this?

CLOWN: I know not where he lodges, and for me to devise a lodging and say he lies
here, or he lies there, were to lie in mine own throat.[2]

DESDEMONA: Can you inquire him out, and be edified by report?

CLOWN: I will catechize the world for him; that is, make questions, and by them
answer.

DESDEMONA: Seek him, bid him come hither. Tell him I have moved[3] my lord on
his behalf and hope all will be well.

CLOWN: To do this is within the compass of man's wit, and therefore I will attempt
the doing it.   [*Exit Clown.*]

DESDEMONA: Where should I lose that handkerchief, Emilia?

4. I.e., gleaming like marble and unrelenting.
5. In the Quarto text, Iago kneels here after Othello has knelt at line 460.
6. Pity (for Othello's wrongs).
7. To the proof.
8. Location: Before the citadel.

9. A form of address to an inferior.
1. Lodges. (But the Clown makes the obvious pun.)
2. Lie egregiously and deliberately. Also, use the windpipe to speak a lie.
3. Petitioned.

EMILIA: I know not, madam.

DESDEMONA: Believe me, I had rather have lost my purse

20   Full of crusadoes;° and but my noble Moor   *gold coins*

Is true of mind and made of no such baseness

As jealous creatures are, it were enough

To put him to ill thinking.

EMILIA: Is he not jealous?

DESDEMONA: Who, he? I think the sun where he was born

25   Drew all such humors⁴ from him.

EMILIA: Look where he comes.

    [*Enter Othello.*]

DESDEMONA: I will not leave him now till Cassio

Be called to him.—How is 't with you, my lord?

OTHELLO: Well, my good lady. [*Aside.*] O, hardness to dissemble!—

How do you, Desdemona?

DESDEMONA: Well, my good lord.

OTHELLO: Give me your hand. [*She gives her hand.*] This hand is moist, my lady.

DESDEMONA: It yet hath felt no age nor known no sorrow.

OTHELLO: This argues fruitfulness and liberal heart.⁵

Hot, hot, and moist. This hand of yours requires

A sequester° from liberty, fasting and prayer,   *separation*

35   Much castigation,° exercise° devout;   *discipline / prayer*

For here's a young and sweating devil here

That commonly rebels. 'Tis a good hand,

A frank⁶ one.

DESDEMONA: You may indeed say so,

For 'twas that hand that gave away my heart.

OTHELLO: A liberal hand. The hearts of old gave hands,⁷

But our new heraldry is hands, not hearts.⁸

DESDEMONA: I cannot speak of this. Come now, your promise.

OTHELLO: What promise, chuck?⁹

DESDEMONA: I have sent to bid Cassio come speak with you.

OTHELLO: I have a salt and sorry rheum¹ offends me;

Lend me thy handkerchief.

DESDEMONA: Here, my lord. [(*She offers a handkerchief.*)]

OTHELLO: That which I gave you.

DESDEMONA: I have it not about me.

OTHELLO: Not?

DESDEMONA: No, faith, my lord.

OTHELLO: That's a fault. That handkerchief

50   Did an Egyptian to my mother give.

She was a charmer,° and could almost read   *sorceress*

The thoughts of people. She told her, while she kept it

'Twould make her amiable° and subdue my father   *desirable*

---

4. Refers to the four bodily fluids thought to determine temperament.
5. Gives evidence of amorousness, fecundity, and sexually freedom.
6. Generous, open (with sexual suggestion).
7. In former times, people would give their hearts when

they gave their hands to something.
8. In our decadent times, the joining of hands is no longer a badge to signify the giving of hearts.
9. A term of endearment.
1. Distressful head cold or watering of the eyes.

Entirely to her love, but if she lost it
55   Or made a gift of it, my father's eye
Should hold her loathèd and his spirits should hunt
After new fancies.° She, dying, gave it me,   *loves*
And bid me, when my fate would have me wived,
To give it her.[2] I did so; and take heed on 't;
60   Make it a darling like your precious eye.
To lose 't or give 't away were such perdition°   *loss*
As nothing else could match.

DESDEMONA: Is 't possible?

OTHELLO: 'Tis true. There's magic in the web° of it.   *weaving*
A sibyl, that had numbered in the world
65   The sun to course two hundred compasses,[3]
In her prophetic fury[4] sewed the work;°   *embroidered pattern*
The worms were hallowed that did breed the silk,
And it was dyed in mummy[5] which the skillful
Conserved of[6] maidens' hearts.

DESDEMONA: I' faith! Is 't true?

OTHELLO: Most veritable. Therefore look to 't well.

DESDEMONA: Then would to God that I had never seen 't!

OTHELLO: Ha? Wherefore?

DESDEMONA: Why do you speak so startingly and rash?[7]

OTHELLO: Is 't lost? Is 't gone? Speak, is 't out o' the way?°   *misplaced*

DESDEMONA: Heaven bless us!

OTHELLO: Say you?

DESDEMONA: It is not lost; but what an if° it were?   *if*

OTHELLO: How?

DESDEMONA: I say it is not lost.

OTHELLO: Fetch 't, let me see 't.

DESDEMONA: Why, so I can, sir, but I will not now.
This is a trick to put me from my suit.
Pray you, let Cassio be received again.

OTHELLO: Fetch me the handkerchief! My mind misgives.

DESDEMONA: Come, come,
85   You'll never meet a more sufficient° man.   *able*

OTHELLO: The handkerchief!

DESDEMONA: I pray, talk° me of Cassio.   *talk to*

OTHELLO: The handkerchief!

DESDEMONA: A man that all his time[8]
Hath founded his good fortunes on your love,
Shared dangers with you—

OTHELLO: The handkerchief!

DESDEMONA: I' faith, you are to blame.

OTHELLO: Zounds!   [*Exit Othello.*]

---

2. I.e., to my wife.
3. Annual circlings. (The *sibyl*, or prophetess, was 200 years old.)
4. Frenzy of prophetic inspiration.
5. Medicinal or magical preparation drained from mummified bodies.

6. Prepared or preserved out of.
7. Disjointedly and impetuously, excitedly.
8. Throughout his career.

EMILIA: Is not this man jealous?

DESDEMONA: I ne'er saw this before.

95   Sure, there's some wonder in this handkerchief.
          I am most unhappy in the loss of it.

EMILIA: 'Tis not a year or two shows us a man.[9]
          They are all but° stomachs, and we all but food;   *nothing but*
          They eat us hungerly,° and when they are full   *hungrily*
100   They belch us.
                              [*Enter Iago and Cassio.*]
                       Look you, Cassio and my husband.

IAGO [(*to Cassio*)]:
          There is no other way; 'tis she must do 't.
          And, lo, the happiness![1] Go and importune her.

DESDEMONA: How now, good Cassio? What's the news with you?

CASSIO: Madam, my former suit. I do beseech you
105   That by your virtuous° means I may again   *efficacious*
          Exist and be a member of his love
          Whom I, with all the office° of my heart,   *loyal service*
          Entirely honor. I would not be delayed.
          If my offense be of such mortal° kind   *fatal*
110   That nor° my service past, nor present sorrows,   *neither*
          Nor purposed merit in futurity
          Can ransom me into his love again,
          But to know so must be my benefit;[2]
          So shall I clothe me in a forced content,
115   And shut myself up in[3] some other course,
          To fortune's alms.[4]

DESDEMONA: Alas, thrice-gentle Cassio,
          My advocation° is not now in tune.   *advocacy*
          My lord is not my lord; nor should I know him,
          Were he in favor° as in humor° altered.   *appearance / mood*
120   So help me every spirit sanctified
          As I have spoken for you all my best
          And stood within the blank[5] of his displeasure
          For my free speech! You must awhile be patient.
          What I can do I will, and more I will
125   Than for myself I dare. Let that suffice you.

IAGO: Is my lord angry?

EMILIA: He went hence but now,
          And certainly in strange unquietness.

IAGO: Can he be angry? I have seen the cannon
130   When it hath blown his ranks into the air,
          And like the devil from his very arm
          Puffed his own brother—and is he angry?

---

9. You can't really know a man even in a year or two of
experience (?), or, real men come along seldom (?).
1. In happy time, fortunately met.
2. Merely to know that my case is hopeless will have to
content me (and will be better than uncertainty).

3. Confine myself to.
4. Throwing myself on the mercy of fortune.
5. Within pointblank range. (The *blank* is the center of
the target.)

Something of moment[6] then. I will go meet him.
There's matter in 't indeed, if he be angry.

DESDEMONA: I prithee, do so. [*Exit (Iago.)*]

      Something, sure, of state,°   *state affairs*
Either from Venice, or some unhatched practice[7]
Made demonstrable here in Cyprus to him,
Hath puddled° his clear spirit; and in such cases   *muddied*
Men's natures wrangle with inferior things,
140 Though great ones are their object. 'Tis even so;
For let our finger ache, and it indues°   *induces*
Our other, healthful members even to a sense
Of pain. Nay, we must think men are not gods,
Nor of them look for such observancy°   *attentiveness*
145 As fits the bridal.[8] Beshrew me[9] much, Emilia,
I was, unhandsome° warrior as I am,   *unskillful*
Arraigning his unkindness with[1] my soul;
But now I find I had suborned the witness,[2]
And he's indicted falsely.

EMILIA: Pray heaven it be
150 State matters, as you think, and no conception
Nor no jealous toy° concerning you.   *fancy*

DESDEMONA: Alas the day! I never gave him cause.

EMILIA: But jealous souls will not be answered so;
They are not ever jealous for the cause,
155 But jealous for° they're jealous. It is a monster   *do because*
Begot upon itself,[3] born on itself.

DESDEMONA: Heaven keep that monster from Othello's mind!

EMILIA: Lady, amen.

DESDEMONA: I will go seek him. Cassio, walk hereabout.
160 If I do find him fit, I'll move your suit
And seek to effect it to my uttermost.

CASSIO: I humbly thank Your ladyship.

          [*Exit (Desdemona with Emilia.)*]

[*Enter Bianca.*]

BIANCA: Save° you, friend Cassio!   *God save*

CASSIO: What make° you from home?   *do*
How is 't with you, my most fair Bianca?
165 I' faith, sweet love, I was coming to your house.

BIANCA: And I was going to your lodging, Cassio.
What, keep a week away? Seven days and nights?
Eightscore-eight[4] hours? And lovers' absent hours
More tedious than the dial[5] eightscore times?
170 O weary reckoning!

CASSIO: Pardon me, Bianca.

---

6. Of immediate importance, momentous.
7. As yet unexecuted or undiscovered plot.
8. Wedding (when a bridegroom is newly attentive to his bride).
9. A mild oath.
1. Before the bar of.

2. Induced the witness to give false testimony.
3. Generated solely from itself.
4. One hundred sixty-eight, the number of hours in a week.
5. A complete revolution of the clock.

I have this while with leaden thoughts been pressed;
But I shall, in a more continuate° time,   *uninterrupted*
Strike off this score⁶ of absence. Sweet Bianca,
[(*Giving her Desdemona's handkerchief.*)]
Take me this work out.⁷

BIANCA: O Cassio, whence came this?
175   This is some token from a newer friend.°   *mistress*
To the felt absence now I feel a cause.
Is 't come to this? Well, well.

CASSIO: Go to, woman!
Throw your vile guesses in the devil's teeth,
From whence you have them. You are jealous now
180   That this is from some mistress, some remembrance.
No, by my faith, Bianca.

BIANCA: Why, whose is it?

CASSIO: I know not, neither. I found it in my chamber.
I like the work well. Ere it be demanded°—   *inquired for*
As like° enough it will—I would have it copied.   *likely*
185   Take it and do 't, and leave me for this time.

BIANCA: Leave you? Wherefore?

CASSIO: I do attend here on the General,
And think it no addition,⁸ nor my wish,
To have him see me womaned.

BIANCA: Why, I pray you?

CASSIO: Not that I love you not.

BIANCA: But that you do not love me.
I pray you, bring° me on the way a little,   *accompany*
And say if I shall see you soon at night.

CASSIO: 'Tis but a little way that I can bring you,
For I attend here; but I'll see you soon.

BIANCA: 'Tis very good. I must be circumstanced.⁹

                                                            [*Exeunt omnes.*]

ACT 4

Scene 1¹

[*Enter Othello and Iago.*]

IAGO: Will you think so?

OTHELLO: Think so, Iago?

IAGO: What,
To kiss in private?

OTHELLO: An unauthorized kiss!

IAGO: Or to be naked with her friend in bed
An hour or more, not meaning any harm?

OTHELLO: Naked in bed, Iago, and not mean harm?
It is hypocrisy against the devil.
They that mean virtuously and yet do so,

---

6. Settle this account.
7. Copy this embroidery for me.
8. I.e., addition to my reputation.

9. Be governed by circumstance, yield to your conditions.
1. Location: Before the citadel.

The devil their virtue tempts, and they tempt heaven.

IAGO: If they do nothing, 'tis a venial° slip.   *pardonable*

10   But if I give my wife a handkerchief—

OTHELLO: What then?

IAGO: Why then, 'tis hers, my lord, and being hers,

        She may, I think, bestow 't on any man.

OTHELLO: She is protectress of her honor too.

15   May she give that?

IAGO: Her honor is an essence that's not seen;

        They have it[2] very oft that have it not.

        But, for the handkerchief—

OTHELLO: By heaven, I would most gladly have forgot it.

20   Thou saidst—O, it comes o'er my memory

        As doth the raven o'er the infectious house,[3]

        Boding to all—he had my handkerchief.

IAGO: Ay, what of that?

OTHELLO: That's not so good now.

IAGO: What

        If I had said I had seen him do you wrong?

25   Or heard him say—as knaves be such abroad,°   *around about*

        Who having, by their own importunate suit,

        Or voluntary dotage[4] of some mistress,

        Convincèd or supplied[5] them, cannot choose

        But they must blab—

OTHELLO: Hath he said anything?

IAGO: He hath, my lord; but, be you well assured,

        No more than he'll unswear.

OTHELLO: What hath he said?

IAGO: Faith, that he did—I know not what he did.

OTHELLO: What? What?

IAGO: Lie—

OTHELLO: With her?

IAGO: With her, on her; what you will.

OTHELLO: Lie with her? Lie on her? We say "lie on her" when they belie[6] her. Lie
        with her? Zounds, that's ful-some.[7]—Handkerchief—confessions—handker-
        chief!—To confess and be hanged for his labor—first to be hanged and then to
        confess.[8]—I tremble at it. Nature would not invest herself in such shadowing

40   passion without some instruction.[9] It is not words[1] that shakes me thus. Pish!
        Noses, ears, and lips.—Is 't possible?—Confess—handkerchief!—O devil!

        [*Falls in a trance.*]

IAGO: Work on, My medicine, work! Thus credulous fools are caught,

---

2. They enjoy a reputation for it.
3. Allusion to the belief that the raven hovered over a
house of sickness or infection, such as one visited by the
plague.
4. Willing infatuation.
5. Seduced or sexually gratified.
6. Slander.
7. Foul.

8. Othello reverses the proverbial *confess and be hanged*;
Cassio is to be given no time to confess before he dies.
9. I.e., without some foundation in fact, nature would not
have dressed herself in such an overwhelming passion
that comes over me now and fills my mind with images,
or in such a lifelike fantasy as Cassio had in his dream of
lying with Desdemona.
1. Mere words.

And many worthy and chaste dames even thus,
All guiltless, meet reproach.—What, ho! My lord!
45   My lord, I say! Othello!

[*Enter Cassio.*]

                        How now, Cassio?
CASSIO: What's the matter?
IAGO: My lord is fall'n into an epilepsy.
        This is his second fit. He had one yesterday.
CASSIO: Rub him about the temples.
IAGO: No, forbear.
        The lethargy° must have his° quiet course.   *coma / its*
50   If not, he foams at mouth, and by and by
        Breaks out to savage madness. Look, he stirs.
        Do you withdraw yourself a little while.
        He will recover straight. When he is gone,
        I would on great occasion speak with you.

                                                        [*Exit Cassio.*]

55   How is it, General? Have you not hurt your head?
OTHELLO: Dost thou mock me?[2]
IAGO: I mock you not, by heaven.
        Would you would bear your fortune like a man!
OTHELLO: A hornèd man's a monster and a beast.
IAGO: There's many a beast then in a populous city,
60   And many a civil° monster.   *city-dwelling*
OTHELLO: Did he confess it?
IAGO: Good sir, be a man.
        Think every bearded fellow that's but yoked[3]
        May draw with you.[4] There's millions now alive
65   That nightly lie in those unproper° beds   *shared*
        Which they dare swear peculiar.° Your case is better.[5]   *their own*
        O, 'tis the spite of hell, the fiend's arch-mock,
        To lip° a wanton in a secure couch   *kiss*
        And to suppose her chaste! No, let me know,
70   And knowing what I am,[6] I know what she shall be.[7]
OTHELLO: O, thou art wise. 'Tis certain.
IAGO: Stand you awhile apart;
        Confine yourself but in a patient list.[8]
        Whilst you were here o'erwhelmèd with your grief—
        A passion most unsuiting such a man—
75   Cassio came hither. I shifted him away,[9]
        And laid good 'scuse upon your ecstasy,°   *trance*
        Bade him anon return and here speak with me,

---

2. Othello takes Iago's question about hurting his head to be a mocking reference to the cuckold's horns.
3. Married. Also, put into the yoke of infamy and cuckoldry.
4. Pull as you do, like oxen who are yoked, i.e., share your fate as cuckold.

5. I.e., because you know the truth.
6. I.e., a cuckold.
7. Will happen to her.
8. Within the bounds of patience.
9. Used a dodge to get rid of him.

The which he promised. Do but encave° yourself   *conceal*
And mark the fleers,° the gibes, and notable° scorns   *sneere / obvious*
80   That dwell in every region of his face;
For I will make him tell the tale anew,
Where, how, how oft, how long ago, and when
He hath and is again to cope° your wife.   *have sex with*
I say, but mark his gesture. Marry, patience!
85   Or I shall say you're all-in-all in spleen,[1]
And nothing of a man.
OTHELLO: Does thou hear, Iago?
I will be found most cunning in my patience;
But—dost thou hear?—most bloody.
IAGO: That's not amiss;
But yet keep time[2] in all. Will you withdraw?
    [(*Othello stands apart.*)]
90   Now will I question Cassio of Bianca,
A huswife° that by selling her desires   *hussy*
Buys herself bread and clothes. It is a creature
That dotes on Cassio—as 'tis the strumpet's plague
To beguile many and be beguiled by one.
95   He, when he hears of her, cannot restrain°   *refrain*
From the excess of laughter. Here he comes.
    [*Enter Cassio.*]
As he shall smile, Othello shall go mad;
And his unbookish° jealousy must conster°   *uninstructed / construe*
Poor Cassio's smiles, gestures, and light behaviors
100   Quite in the wrong.—How do you now, Lieutenant?
CASSIO: The worser that you give me the addition°   *title*
Whose want[3] even kills me.
IAGO: Ply Desdemona well and you are sure on 't.
    [(*Speaking lower*)] Now, if this suit lay in Bianca's power,
105   How quickly should you speed!
CASSIO [(*laughing*)]:   Alas, poor caitiff!°   *wretch*
OTHELLO [(*aside*)]: Look how he laughs already!
IAGO: I never knew a woman love man so.
CASSIO: Alas, poor rogue! I think, i' faith, she loves me.
OTHELLO: Now he denies it faintly, and laughs it out.
IAGO: Do you hear, Cassio?
OTHELLO: Now he importunes him
To tell it o'er. Go to![4] Well said,° well said.   *well done*
IAGO: She gives it out that you shall marry her.
Do you intend it?
CASSIO: Ha, ha, ha!
OTHELLO: Do you triumph, Roman?[5] Do you triumph?

1. Utterly governed by passionate impulses.
2. Keep yourself steady (as in music).
3. The lack of which.

4. An expression of remonstrance.
5. The Romans were noted for their *triumphs* or triumphal
processions.

CASSIO: I marry her? What? A customer?[6] Prithee, bear some charity to my wit;[7] do not think it so unwholesome. Ha, ha, ha!

OTHELLO: So, so, so, so! They laugh that win.[8]

IAGO: Faith, the cry goes that you shall marry her.

CASSIO: Prithee, say true.

IAGO: I am a very villain else.[9]

OTHELLO: Have you scored me?[1] Well.

CASSIO: This is the monkey's own giving out. She is persuaded I will marry her out of her own love and flattery,[2] not out of my promise.

OTHELLO: Iago beckons° me. Now he begins the story.   *signals*

CASSIO: She was here even now; she haunts me in every place. I was the other day talking on the seabank[3] with certain Venetians, and thither comes the bauble,[4] and, by this hand,[5] she falls me thus about my neck—

[(*He embraces Iago.*)]

OTHELLO: Crying, "O, dear Cassio!" as it were; his gesture imports it.

CASSIO: So hangs and lolls and weeps upon me, so shakes and pulls me. Ha, ha, ha!

OTHELLO: Now he tells how she plucked him to my chamber. O, I see that nose of yours, but not that dog I shall throw it to.[6]

CASSIO: Well, I must leave her company.

IAGO: Before me,[7] look where she comes.

[*Enter Bianca (with Othello's handkerchief).*]

CASSIO: 'Tis such another fitchew![8] Marry, a perfumed one.—What do you mean by this haunting of me?

BIANCA: Let the devil and his dam[9] haunt you! What did you mean by that same handkerchief you gave me even now? I was a fine fool to take it. I must take out the work? A likely piece of work,[1] that you should find it in your chamber and know not who left it there! This is some minx's token, and I must take out the work? There; give it your hobbyhorse.[2] [(*She gives him the handkerchief.*)] Wheresoever you had it, I'll take out no work on't.

CASSIO: How now, my sweet Bianca? How now? How now?

OTHELLO: By heaven, that should be[3] my handkerchief!

BIANCA: If you'll come to supper tonight, you may; if you will not, come when you are next prepared for.[4]

[*Exit.*]

IAGO: After her, after her.

CASSIO: Faith, I must. She'll rail in the streets else.

IAGO: Will you sup there?

CASSIO: Faith, I intend so.

IAGO: Well, I may chance to see you, for I would very fain speak with you.

CASSIO: Prithee, come. Will you?

6. Prostitute.
7. Be more charitable to my judgment.
8. I.e., they that laugh last laugh best.
9. Call me a complete rogue if I'm not telling the truth.
1. Scored off me, beaten me, made up my reckoning, branded me.
2. Self-flattery, self-deception.
3. Seashore.
4. Plaything.
5. I make my vow.
6. Othello imagines himself cutting off Cassio's nose and throwing it to a dog.

7. On my soul.
8. What a polecat she is! Just like all the others. (Polecats were often compared with prostitutes because of their rank smell and presumed lechery.)
9. Mother.
1. A fine story.
2. Harlot.
3. Must be.
4. When I'm ready for you (i.e., never).

IAGO: Go to. Say no more.   [*Exit Cassio.*]

OTHELLO [(*advancing*)]: How shall I murder him, Iago?

IAGO: Did you perceive how he laughed at his vice?

OTHELLO: O, Iago!

IAGO: And did you see the handkerchief?

OTHELLO: Was that mine?

IAGO: Yours, by this hand. And to see how he prizes the foolish woman your wife!
160   She gave it him, and he hath given it his whore.

OTHELLO: I would have him nine years a-killing. A fine woman! A fair woman! A
        sweet woman!

IAGO: Nay, you must forget that.

OTHELLO: Ay, let her rot and perish, and be damned tonight, for she shall not live.
        No, my heart is turned to stone; I strike it, and it hurts my hand. O, the world
        hath not a sweeter creature! She might lie by an emperor's side and command
        him tasks.

IAGO: Nay, that's not your way.[5]

OTHELLO: Hang her! I do but say what she is. So delicate with her needle! An
        admirable musician! O, she will sing the savageness out of a bear. Of so high
        and plenteous wit and invention![6]

IAGO: She's the worse for all this.

OTHELLO: O, a thousand, a thousand times! And then, of so gentle a condition![7]

IAGO: Ay, too gentle.[8]

OTHELLO: Nay, that's certain. But yet the pity of it, Iago! O, Iago, the pity of it, Iago!

IAGO: If you are so fond[9] over her iniquity, give her patent[1] to offend, for if it touch
        not you it comes near nobody.

OTHELLO: I will chop her into messes.[2] Cuckold me?

IAGO: O, 'tis foul in her.

OTHELLO: With mine officer?

IAGO: That's fouler.

OTHELLO: Get me some poison, Iago, this night. I'll not expostulate with her, lest
        her body and beauty unprovide[3] my mind again. This night, Iago.

IAGO: Do it not with poison. Strangle her in her bed, even the bed she hath contami-
185   nated.

OTHELLO: Good, good! The justice of it pleases. Very good.

IAGO: And for Cassio, let me be his undertaker.[4] You shall hear more by midnight.

OTHELLO: Excellent good. [(*A trumpet within.*)] What trumpet is that same?

IAGO: I warrant, something from Venice.
        [*Enter Lodovico, Desdemona, and attendants.*]
190   'Tis Lodovico. This comes from the Duke.
        See, your wife's with him.

LODOVICO: God save you, worthy General!

OTHELLO: With all my heart, sir.[5]

---

5. I.e., the way you should think of her.
6. Imagination.
7. Wellborn and well-bred.
8. Generous, yielding (to other men).
9. Foolish.

1. License.
2. Portions of meat, i.e., bits.
3. Weaken, render unfit.
4. Undertake to dispatch him.
5. I thank you most heartily.

LODOVICO: [(*giving him a letter*)] The Duke and the senators of Venice greet you.
OTHELLO: I kiss the instrument of their pleasures.
  [(*He opens the letter, and reads.*)]
DESDEMONA: And what's the news, good cousin Lodovico?
IAGO: I am very glad to see you, signor.
  Welcome to Cyprus.
LODOVICO: I thank you. How does Lieutenant Cassio?
IAGO: Lives, sir.
DESDEMONA: Cousin, there's fall'n between him and my lord
  An unkind⁶ breach; but you shall make all well.
OTHELLO: Are you sure of that?
DESDEMONA: My lord?
OTHELLO [*reads*]: "This fail you not to do, as you will—"
LODOVICO: He did not call; he's busy in the paper.
  Is there division twixt my lord and Cassio?
DESDEMONA: A most unhappy one. I would do much
  T' atone° them, for the love I bear to Cassio.   reconcile
OTHELLO: Fire and brimstone!
DESDEMONA: My lord?
OTHELLO: Are you wise?
DESDEMONA: What, is he angry?
LODOVICO: Maybe the letter moved him;
  For, as I think, they do command him home,
  Deputing Cassio in his government.°   office
DESDEMONA: By my troth, I am glad on 't.°   of it
OTHELLO: Indeed?
DESDEMONA: My lord?
OTHELLO: I am glad to see you mad.⁷
DESDEMONA: Why, sweet Othello—
OTHELLO [(*striking her*)]: Devil!
DESDEMONA: I have not deserved this.
LODOVICO: My lord, this would not be believed in Venice,
  Though I should swear I saw 't. 'Tis very much.°   outrageous
  Make her amends; she weeps.
OTHELLO: O devil, devil!
  If that the earth could teem° with woman's tears,   breed
  Each drop she falls° would prove a crocodile.⁸   lets fall
  Out of my sight!
DESDEMONA: I will not stay to offend you. [(*Going.*)]
LODOVICO: Truly, an obedient lady.
  I do beseech your lordship, call her back.
OTHELLO: Mistress!
DESDEMONA: [*returning*] My lord?
OTHELLO: What would you with her, sir?
LODOVICO: Who, I, my lord?

---

6. Unnatural, contrary to their natures; hurtful.
7. I.e., I am glad to see that you are insane enough to rejoice in Cassio's promotion. (Othello bitterly plays on

Desdemona's *I am glad.*)
8. Crocodiles were supposed to weep hypocritical tears for their victims.

OTHELLO: Ay, you did wish that I would make her turn.[9]
    Sir, she can turn, and turn, and yet go on
230   And turn again; and she can weep, sir, weep;
    And she's obedient,[1] as you say, obedient,
    Very obedient.—Proceed you in your tears.—
    Concerning this, sir—Oh, well-painted passion!°—   *grief*
    I am commanded home.—Get you away;
235   I'll send for you anon.—Sir, I obey the mandate
    And will return to Venice.—Hence, avaunt!

                           [(*Exit Desdemona.*)]

    Cassio shall have my place. And, sir, tonight
    I do entreat that we may sup together.
    You are welcome, sir, to Cyprus.—Goats and monkeys![2]
LODOVICO: Is this the noble Moor whom our full Senate
    Call all in all sufficient? Is this the nature
    Whom passion could not shake? Whose solid virtue
    The shot of accident nor dart of chance
    Could neither graze nor pierce?
IAGO: He is much changed.
LODOVICO: Are his wits safe? Is he not light of brain?
IAGO: He's that he is. I may not breathe my censure
    What he might be. If what he might he is not,
    I would to heaven he were![3]
LODOVICO: What, strike his wife?
IAGO: Faith, that was not so well; yet would I knew
250   That stroke would prove the worst!
LODOVICO: Is it his use?°
       custom
    Or did the letters work upon his blood°   *passions*
    And new-create his fault?
IAGO: Alas, alas!
    It is not honesty in me to speak
    What I have seen and known. You shall observe him,
255   And his own courses will denote[4] him so
    That I may save my speech. Do but go after,
    And mark how he continues.
LODOVICO: I am sorry that I am deceived in him.   [*Exeunt.*]

                  Scene 2[5]
[*Enter Othello and Emilia.*]
OTHELLO: You have seen nothing, then?
EMILIA: Nor ever heard, nor ever did suspect.
OTHELLO: Yes, you have seen Cassio and she together.
EMILIA: But then I saw no harm, and then I heard

---

9. Othello implies that Desdemona is pliant and will do a *turn* sexually with any man.
1. With much the same sexual connotation as *turn.*
2. The most lustful animals.
3. I dare not venture an opinion as to whether he's of

unsound mind, as you suggest, but, if he isn't, then it might be better to wish he were in fact insane, since only that could excuse his wild behavior.
4. Actions will reveal.
5. Location: The citadel.

5   Each syllable that breath made up between them.

OTHELLO: What, did they never whisper?

EMILIA: Never, my lord.

OTHELLO: Nor send you out o' the way?

EMILIA: Never.

OTHELLO: To fetch her fan, her gloves, her mask, nor nothing?

EMILIA: Never, my lord.

OTHELLO: That's strange.

EMILIA: I durst, my lord, to wager she is honest,
    Lay down my soul at stake.° If you think other,   *as the wager*
15   Remove your thought; it doth abuse your bosom.°   *deceive you*
    If any wretch have put this in your head,
    Let heaven requite it with the serpent's curse![6]
    For if she be not honest, chaste, and true,
    There's no man happy; the purest of their wives
20   Is foul as slander.

OTHELLO: Bid her come hither. Go.

                                          [Exit Emilia.]

    She says enough; yet she's a simple bawd
    That cannot say as much.[7] This° is a subtle whore,   *Desdemona*
    A closet lock and key of villainous secrets.
    And yet she'll kneel and pray; I have seen her do 't.
    [Enter Desdemona and Emilia.]

DESDEMONA: My lord, what is your will?

OTHELLO: Pray you, chuck, come hither.

DESDEMONA: What is your pleasure?

OTHELLO: Let me see your eyes.
    Look in my face.

DESDEMONA: What horrible fancy's this?

OTHELLO [(*to Emilia*)]: Some of your function,[8] mistress.
30   Leave procreants° alone and shut the door;   *mating couples*
    Cough or cry "hem" if anybody come.
    Your mystery,° your mystery! Nay, dispatch.   *trade*
                                            [Exit Emilia.]

DESDEMONA [(*kneeling*)]: Upon my knees, what doth your speech import?
    I understand a fury in your words,
35   But not the words.

OTHELLO: Why, what art thou?

DESDEMONA: Your wife, my lord, your true
    And loyal wife.

OTHELLO: Come, swear it, damn thyself,
    Lest, being like one of heaven,[9] the devils themselves

---

6. The curse pronounced by God on the serpent for deceiving Eve, just as some man has done to Othello and Desdemona. (See Genesis 3.14.)

7. Any procuress or go-between who couldn't make up as plausible a story as Emilia's would have to be pretty stupid.

8. I.e., Practice your chosen profession, that of bawd (by guarding the door).

9. Looking like an angel.

Should fear to seize thee. Therefore be double damned:
40   Swear thou art honest.

DESDEMONA: Heaven doth truly know it.

OTHELLO: Heaven truly knows that thou art false as hell.

DESDEMONA: To whom, my lord? With whom? How am I false?

OTHELLO [(*weeping*)]: Ah, Desdemon! Away, away, away!

DESDEMONA: Alas the heavy day! Why do you weep?
45   Am I the motive° of these tears, my lord?   *cause*
         If haply you my father do suspect
         An instrument of this your calling back,
         Lay not your blame on me. If you have lost him,
         I have lost him too.

OTHELLO: Had it pleased heaven
50   To try me with affliction, had they[1] rained
         All kinds of sores and shames on my bare head,
         Steeped me in poverty to the very lips,
         Given to captivity me and my utmost hopes,
         I should have found in some place of my soul
55   A drop of patience. But, alas, to make me
         A fixèd figure for the time of scorn[2]
         To point his° slow and moving finger[3] at!   *its*
         Yet could I bear that too, well, very well.
         But there where I have garnered° up my heart,   *stored*
60   Where either I must live or bear no life,
         The fountain° from the which my current runs   *spring*
         Or else dries up—to be discarded thence!
         Or keep it as a cistern° for foul toads   *cesspool*
         To knot° and gender° in! Turn thy complexion there,[4]   *couple / engender*
65   Patience, thou young and rose-lipped cherubin—
         Ay, there look grim as hell![5]

DESDEMONA: I hope my noble lord esteems me honest.°   *chaste*

OTHELLO: O, ay, as summer flies are in the shambles,°   *slaughterhouse*
         That quicken° even with blowing.[6] O thou weed,   *come to life*
70   Who art so lovely fair and smell'st so sweet
         That the sense aches at thee, would thou hadst ne'er been born!

DESDEMONA: Alas, what ignorant sin[7] have I committed?

OTHELLO: Was this fair paper, this most goodly book,
         Made to write "whore" upon? What committed?
75   Committed? O, thou public commoner!°   *prostitute*
         I should make very forges of my cheeks,
         That would to cinders burn up modesty,
         Did I but speak thy deeds. What committed?

---

1. I.e., heavenly powers.
2. Scornful world.
3. I.e., hour hand of the clock, moving so slowly it seems hardly to move at all. (Othello envisages himself as being eternally pointed at by the scornful world as the numbers on a clock are pointed at by the hour hand.)

4. Change your color, grow pale, at such a sight.
5. Even Patience, that rose-lipped cherub, will look grim and pale at this spectacle.
6. I.e., with the puffing up of something rotten in which maggots are breeding.
7. Sin in ignorance.

Heaven stops the nose at it and the moon winks;[8]
80   The bawdy[9] wind, that kisses all it meets,
Is hushed within the hollow mine[1] of earth
And will not hear 't. What committed?
Impudent strumpet!

DESDEMONA: By heaven, you do me wrong.

OTHELLO: Are not you a strumpet?

DESDEMONA: No, as I am a Christian.
If to preserve this vessel° for my lord   *body*
From any other foul unlawful touch
Be not to be a strumpet, I am none.

OTHELLO: What, not a whore?

DESDEMONA: No, as I shall be saved.

OTHELLO: Is 't possible?

DESDEMONA: O, heaven forgive us!

OTHELLO: I cry you mercy,° then.   *beg you pardon*
I took you for that cunning whore of Venice
That married with Othello. [*Calling out.*] You, mistress,
95   That have the office opposite to Saint Peter
And keep the gate of hell!
[*Enter Emilia.*]
                              You, you, ay, you!
We have done our course.[2] There's money for your pains.   [(*He gives money.*)]
I pray you, turn the key and keep our counsel.   [*Exit.*]

EMILIA: Alas, what does this gentleman conceive?°   *suppose*
100   How do you, madam? How do you, my good lady?

DESDEMONA: Faith, half asleep.[3]

EMILIA: Good madam, what's the matter with my lord?

DESDEMONA: With who?

EMILIA: Why, with my lord, madam.

DESDEMONA: Who is thy lord?

EMILIA: He that is yours, sweet lady.

DESDEMONA: I have none. Do not talk to me, Emilia.
I cannot weep, nor answers have I none
But what should go by water.[4] Prithee, tonight
Lay on my bed my wedding sheets, remember;
110   And call thy husband hither.

EMILIA: Here's a change indeed!   [*Exit.*]

DESDEMONA: 'Tis meet° I should be used so, very meet.   *fitting*
How have I been behaved, that he might stick°   *attach*
The small'st opinion° on my least misuse?°   *censure / misconduct*
[*Enter Iago and Emilia.*]

IAGO: What is your pleasure, madam? How is 't with you?

DESDEMONA: I cannot tell. Those that do teach young babes
Do it with gentle means and easy tasks.

8. Closes her eyes. (The moon symbolizes chastity.)
9. Kissing one and all.
1. Cave (where the winds were thought to dwell).
2. Business (with an indecent suggestion of "trick," turn
at sex.)
3. I.e., dazed.
4. Be expressed by tears.

He might have chid me so, for, in good faith,
I am a child to chiding.

IAGO: What is the matter, lady?

EMILIA: Alas, Iago, my lord hath so bewhored her,
Thrown such despite and heavy terms upon her,
That true hearts cannot bear it.

DESDEMONA: Am I that name, Iago?

IAGO: What name, fair lady?

DESDEMONA: Such as she said my lord did say I was.

EMILIA: He called her whore. A beggar in his drink
Could not have laid such terms upon his callet.°   *whore*

IAGO: Why did he so?

DESDEMONA [(*weeping*)]:

130   I do not know. I am sure I am none such.

IAGO: Do not weep, do not weep. Alas the day!

EMILIA: Hath she forsook so many noble matches,
Her father and her country and her friends,
To be called whore? Would it not make one weep?

DESDEMONA: It is my wretched fortune.

IAGO: Beshrew° him for 't!   *curse*
How comes this trick° upon him?   *delusion*

DESDEMONA: Nay, heaven doth know.

EMILIA: I will be hanged if some eternal° villain,   *inveterate*
Some busy and insinuating° rogue,   *wheedling*
Some cogging,° cozening° slave, to get some office,   *cheating / defrauding*

140   Have not devised this slander. I will be hanged else.

IAGO: Fie, there is no such man. It is impossible.

DESDEMONA: If any such there be, heaven pardon him!

EMILIA: A halter° pardon him! And hell gnaw his bones!   *hangman's noose*
Why should he call her whore? Who keeps her company?

145   What place? What time? What form?° What likelihood?   *appearance*
The Moor's abused by some most villainous knave,
Some base notorious knave, some scurvy fellow.
O, heaven, that such companions thou'dst unfold,[5]
And put in every honest hand a whip

150   To lash the rascals naked through the world
Even from the east to th' west!

IAGO: Speak within door.[6]

EMILIA: O, fie upon them! Some such squire° he was   *fellow*
That turned your wit the seamy side without°   *wrong side out*
And made you to suspect me with the Moor.

IAGO: You are a fool. Go to.[7]

DESDEMONA: Alas, Iago,
What shall I do to win my lord again?
Good friend, go to him; for, by this light of heaven,
I know not how I lost him. Here I kneel. [*She kneels.*]

5. If only you would expose such fellows.   7. I.e., that's enough.
6. I.e., not so loud.

If e'er my will did trespass 'gainst his love,
160   Either in discourse of thought or actual deed,
Or that° mine eyes, mine ears, or any sense   *if*
Delighted them° in any other form;   *took delight*
Or that I do not yet,° and ever did,   *still*
And ever will—though he do shake me off
165   To beggarly divorcement—love him dearly,
Comfort forswear⁸ me! Unkindness may do much,
And his unkindness may defeat° my life,   *destroy*
But never taint my love. I cannot say "whore."
It does abhor⁹ me now I speak the word;
170   To do the act that might the addition° earn   *title*
Not the world's mass of vanity° could make me.   *showy splendor*
[*She rises.*]
IAGO: I pray you, be content. 'Tis but his humor.°   *mood*
The business of the state does him offense,
And he does chide with you.
DESDEMONA: If 'twere no other—
IAGO: It is but so, I warrant.   [(*Trumpets within.*)]
Hark, how these instruments summon you to supper!
The messengers of Venice stays the meat.°   *wait to dine*
Go in, and weep not. All things shall be well.
[*Exeunt Desdemona and Emilia.*]
[*Enter Roderigo.*]
How now, Roderigo?
RODERIGO: I do not find that thou deal'st justly with me.
IAGO: What in the contrary?
RODERIGO: Every day thou daff'st me¹ with some device,² Iago, and rather, as it
seems to me now, keep'st from me all conveniency³ than suppliest me with the
least advantage⁴ of hope. I will indeed no longer endure it, nor am I yet per-
185   suaded to put up⁵ in peace what already I have foolishly suffered.
IAGO: Will you hear me, Roderigo?
RODERIGO: Faith, I have heard too much, for your words and performances are no
kin together.
IAGO: You charge me most unjustly.
RODERIGO: With naught but truth. I have wasted myself out of my means. The jewels you have had from me to deliver⁶ Desdemona would half have corrupted a
votarist.⁷ You have told me she hath received them and returned me expecta-
tions and comforts of sudden respect⁸ and acquaintance, but I find none.
IAGO: Well, go to, very well.
RODERIGO: "Very well"! "Go to"! I cannot go to,⁹ man, nor 'tis not very well. By
this hand, I think it is scurvy, and begin to find myself fopped¹ in it.
IAGO: Very well.

---

8. May heavenly comfort forsake.
9. Fill me with abhorrence. Also, make me whorelike.
1. You put me off.
2. Excuse, trick.
3. Advantage, opportunity.
4. Increase.
5. Submit to, tolerate.

6. Deliver to.
7. Nun.
8. Immediate consideration.
9. Roderigo changes Iago's *go to*, an expression urging patience, to *I cannot go to*, "I have no opportunity for success in wooing."
1. Fooled, duped.

RODERIGO: I tell you 'tis not very well.[2] I will make myself known to Desdemona. If
she will return me my jewels, I will give over my suit and repent my unlawful
200   solicitation; if not, assure yourself I will seek satisfaction[3] of you.

IAGO: You have said now?[4]

RODERIGO: Ay, and said nothing but what I protest intendment[5] of doing.

IAGO: Why, now I see there's mettle in thee, and even from this instant do build on
thee a better opinion than ever before. Give me thy hand, Roderigo. Thou hast
taken against me a most just exception; but yet I protest I have dealt most
directly in thy affair.

RODERIGO: It hath not appeared.

IAGO: I grant indeed it hath not appeared, and your suspicion is not without wit and
judgment. But, Roderigo, if thou hast that in thee indeed which I have greater
210   reason to believe now than ever—I mean purpose, courage, and valor—this
night show it. If thou the next night following enjoy not Desdemona, take me
from this world with treachery and devise engines[6] for my life.

RODERIGO: Well, what is it? Is it within reason and compass?

IAGO: Sir, there is especial commission come from Venice to depute Cassio in
215   Othello's place.

RODERIGO: Is that true? Why, then Othello and Desdemona return again to Venice.

IAGO: O, no; he goes into Mauritania and takes away with him the fair Desdemona,
unless his abode be lingered here by some accident; wherein none can be so
determinate[7] as the removing of Cassio.

RODERIGO: How do you mean, removing of him?

IAGO: Why, by making him uncapable of Othello's place—knocking out his brains.

RODERIGO: And that you would have me to do?

IAGO: Ay, if you dare do yourself a profit and a right. He sups tonight with a har-
lotry,[8] and thither will I go to him. He knows not yet of his honorable fortune.
225   If you will watch his going thence, which I will fashion to fall out[9] between
twelve and one, you may take him at your pleasure. I will be near to second
your attempt, and he shall fall between us. Come, stand not amazed at it, but
go along with me. I will show you such a necessity in his death that you shall
think yourself bound to put it on him. It is now high[1] suppertime, and the
230   night grows to waste.[2] About it.

RODERIGO: I will hear further reason for this.

IAGO: And you shall be satisfied.   [Exeunt.]

2. Roderigo changes Iago's very well, "all right, then," to
not very well, "not at all good."
3. Repayment. (The term normally means settling of accounts in a duel.)
4. Have you finished?
5. Intention.

6. Plots against.
7. Conclusive.
8. Slut.
9. Occur.
1. Fully.
2. Wastes away.

Scene 3[3]

[*Enter Othello, Lodovico, Desdemona, Emilia, and attendants.*]

LODOVICO: I do beseech you, sir, trouble yourself no further.

OTHELLO: O, pardon me; 'twill do me good to walk.

LODOVICO: Madam, good night. I humbly thank your ladyship.

DESDEMONA: Your honor is most welcome.

OTHELLO: Will you walk, sir?

5   O, Desdemona!

DESDEMONA: My lord?

OTHELLO: Get you to bed on th' instant. I will be returned forthwith. Dismiss your
     attendant there. Look 't be done.

DESDEMONA: I will, my lord.

                    [*Exit (Othello, with Lodovico and attendants.*)]

EMILIA: How goes it now? He looks gentler than he did.

DESDEMONA: He says he will return incontinent,°   *immediately*
     And hath commanded me to go to bed,
     And bid me to dismiss you.

EMILIA: Dismiss me?

DESDEMONA: It was his bidding. Therefore, good Emilia,

15   Give me my nightly wearing, and adieu.
     We must not now displease him.

EMILIA: I would you had never seen him!

DESDEMONA: So would not I. My love doth so approve him
     That even his stubbornness,° his checks,° his frowns—   *roughness / rebukes*

20   Prithee, unpin me—have grace and favor in them.

     [(*Emilia prepares Desdemona for bed.*)]

EMILIA: I have laid those sheets you bade me on the bed.

DESDEMONA: All's one.[4] Good faith, how foolish are our minds!
     If I do die before thee, prithee shroud me
     In one of these same sheets.

EMILIA: Come, come, you talk.°   *prattle*

DESDEMONA: My mother had a maid called Barbary.
     She was in love, and he she loved proved mad°   *wild*
     And did forsake her. She had a song of "Willow."
     An old thing 'twas, but it expressed her fortune,
     And she died singing it. That song tonight

30   Will not go from my mind; I have much to do
     But to go hang[5] my head all at one side
     And sing it like poor Barbary. Prithee, dispatch.

EMILIA: Shall I go fetch your nightgown?°   *dressing gown*

DESDEMONA: No, unpin me here.
     This Lodovico is a proper° man.   *handsome*

EMILIA: A very handsome man.

DESDEMONA: He speaks well.

EMILIA: I know a lady in Venice would have walked barefoot to Palestine for a touch
     of his nether lip.

---

3. Location: The citadel.   5. I can scarcely keep myself from hanging.
4. All right. It doesn't really matter.

DESDEMONA [(*singing*)]: "The poor soul sat sighing by a sycamore tree,
40   Sing all a green willow;[6]
    Her hand on her bosom, her head on her knee,
         Sing willow, willow, willow.
    The fresh streams ran by her and murmured her moans;
         Sing willow, willow, willow;
45   Her salt tears fell from her, and softened the stones—"
    Lay by these.
    [*Singing*] "Sing willow, willow, willow—"
    Prithee, hie thee.° He'll come anon.°   *hurry / right away*
    [*Singing*] "Sing all a green willow must be my garland.
50   Let nobody blame him; his scorn I approve—"
    Nay, that's not next.—Hark! Who is 't that knocks?
EMILIA: It's the wind.
DESDEMONA [(*singing*)]: "I called my love false love; but what said he then?
         Sing willow, willow, willow;
55   If I court more women, you'll couch with more men."
    So, get thee gone. Good night. Mine eyes do itch;
    Doth that bode weeping?
EMILIA: 'Tis neither here nor there.
DESDEMONA: I have heard it said so. O, these men, these men!
    Dost thou in conscience think—tell me, Emilia—
60   That there be women do abuse° their husbands   *deceive*
    In such gross kind?
EMILIA: There be some such, no question.
DESDEMONA: Wouldst thou do such a deed for all the world?
EMILIA: Why, would not you?
DESDEMONA: No, by this heavenly light!
EMILIA: Nor I neither by this heavenly light;
65   I might do 't as well i' the dark.
DESDEMONA: Wouldst thou do such a deed for all the world?
EMILIA: The world's a huge thing. It is a great price
    For a small vice.
DESDEMONA: Good troth, I think thou wouldst not.
EMILIA: By my troth, I think I should, and undo 't when I had done. Marry, I would
    not do such a thing for a joint ring,[7] nor for measures of lawn,[8] nor for gowns,
    petticoats, nor caps, nor any petty exhibition.[9] But for all the whole world!
    Uds[1] pity, who would not make her husband a cuckold to make him a
    monarch? I should venture purgatory for 't.
DESDEMONA: Beshrew me if I would do such a wrong
    For the whole world.
EMILIA: Why, the wrong is but a wrong i' the world, and having the world for your
    labor, 'tis a wrong in your own world, and you might quickly make it right.

---

6. A conventional emblem of disappointed love.   9. Gift.
7. A ring made in separate halves.   1. God's.
8. Fine linen.

DESDEMONA: I do not think there is any such woman.

EMILIA: Yes, a dozen, and as many
　　　　To th' vantage[2] as would store° the world they played[3] for.　　*populate*
　　　　But I do think it is their husbands' faults
　　　　If wives do fall. Say that they slack their duties°　　　*marital duties*
　　　　And pour our treasures into foreign laps,[4]
85　　　Or else break out in peevish jealousies,
　　　　Throwing restraint upon us?[5] Or say they strike us,
　　　　Or scant our former having in despite?[6]
　　　　Why, we have galls,[7] and though we have some grace,
　　　　Yet have we some revenge. Let husbands know
90　　　Their wives have sense° like them. They see, and smell,　　*physical sense*
　　　　And have their palates both for sweet and sour,
　　　　As husbands have. What is it that they do
　　　　When they change us for others? Is it sport?°　　　*sexual pastime*
　　　　I think it is. And doth affection° breed it?　　　　*passion*
95　　　I think it doth. Is 't frailty that thus errs?
　　　　It is so, too. And have not we affections,
　　　　Desires for sport, and frailty, as men have?
　　　　Then let them use us well; else let them know,
　　　　The ills we do, their ills instruct us so.

DESDEMONA: Good night, good night. God me such uses° send　　*practice*
　　　　Not to pick bad from bad, but by bad mend![8]

　　　　　　　　　　　　　　　　　　　　　　　[Exeunt.]

ACT 5

Scene 1[9]

[Enter Iago and Roderigo.]

IAGO: Here stand behind this bulk.[1] Straight will he come.
　　　　Wear thy good rapier bare,° and put it home.　　　*unsheathed*
　　　　Quick, quick! Fear nothing. I'll be at thy elbow.
　　　　It makes us or it mars us. Think on that,
5　　　And fix most firm thy resolution.

RODERIGO: Be near at hand. I may miscarry in 't.

IAGO: Here, at thy hand. Be bold, and take thy stand.

　　　[(Iago stands aside; Roderigo conceals himself.)]

RODERIGO: I have no great devotion to the deed;
　　　　And yet he hath given me satisfying reasons.
10　　　'Tis but a man gone. Forth, my sword! He dies.

　　　[(He draws.)]

---

2. In addition, to boot.
3. Gambled. Also, sported sexually.
4. I.e., are unfaithful, give what is rightfully ours (semen) to other women.
5. I.e., jealously restricting our freedom to see other men.
6. Reduce our allowance to spite us.
7. Are capable of resenting injury and insult.

8. Not to learn bad conduct from others' badness (as Emilia has suggested women learn from men), but to mend my ways by perceiving what badness is, making spiritual benefit out of evil and adversity.
9. Location: A street in Cyprus.
1. Framework projecting from the front of a shop.

IAGO: I have rubbed this young quat° almost to the sense,°   *pimple / raw*
And he grows angry. Now, whether he kill Cassio
Or Cassio him, or each do kill the other,
Every way makes my gain. Live Roderigo,[2]
15   He calls me to a restitution large
Of gold and jewels that I bobbed° from him   *swindled*
As gifts to Desdemona.
It must not be. If Cassio do remain,
He hath a daily beauty in his life
20   That makes me ugly; and besides, the Moor
May unfold° me to him; there stand I in much peril.   *expose*
No, he must die. Be 't so. I hear him coming.
[*Enter Cassio.*]
RODERIGO [(*coming forth*)]: I know his gait, 'tis he.—Villain, thou diest!
[(*He attacks Cassio.*)]
CASSIO: That thrust had been mine enemy indeed,
25   But that my coat[3] is better than thou know'st.
I will make proof° of thine.   *a test*
[(*He draws, and wounds Roderigo.*)]
RODERIGO: O, I am slain! [*He falls.*]
[(*Iago, from behind, wounds Cassio in the leg, and exits.*)]
CASSIO: I am maimed forever. Help, ho! Murder! Murder!
[*Enter Othello.*]
OTHELLO: The voice of Cassio! Iago keeps his word.
RODERIGO: O, villain that I am!
OTHELLO: It is even so.
CASSIO: O, help, ho! Light! A surgeon!
OTHELLO: 'Tis he. O brave Iago, honest and just,
That hast such noble sense of thy friend's wrong!
Thou teachest me. Minion,[4] your dear lies dead,
And your unblest fate hies.° Strumpet, I come.   *hastens on*
35   Forth of° my heart those charms, thine eyes, are blotted;   *from out*
Thy bed, lust-stained, shall with lust's blood be spotted.   [*Exit Othello.*]
[*Enter Lodovico and Gratiano.*]
CASSIO: What ho! No watch? No passage?° Murder! Murder!   *passers-by*
GRATIANO: 'Tis some mischance. The voice is very direful.
CASSIO: O, help!
LODOVICO: Hark!
RODERIGO: O, wretched villain!
LODOVICO: Two or three groan. 'Tis heavy° night;   *thick, dark*
These may be counterfeits. Let's think 't unsafe
To come in° to the cry without more help.   *approach*
[(*They remain near the entrance.*)]
RODERIGO: Nobody come? Then shall I bleed to death.
[*Enter Iago (in his shirtsleeves, with a light).*]

---

2. If Roderigo lives.
3. Possibly a garment of mail under the outer clothing, or
simply a tougher coat than Roderigo expected.
4. Hussy (i.e., Desdemona).

LODOVICO: Hark!

GRATIANO: Here's one comes in his shirt, with light and weapons.

IAGO: Who's there? Whose noise is this that cries on° murder?   *cries out*

LODOVICO: We do not know.

IAGO: Did not you hear a cry?

CASSIO: Here, here! For heaven's sake, help me!

IAGO: What's the matter?
    [*(He moves toward Cassio.)*]

GRATIANO [*(to Lodovico)*]: This is Othello's ancient, as I take it.

LODOVICO [*(to Gratiano)*]: The same indeed, a very valiant fellow.

IAGO [*(to Cassio)*]: What° are you here that cry so grievously?   *who*

CASSIO: Iago? Oh, I am spoiled,° undone by villains!   *ruined*

55   Give me some help.

IAGO: O me, Lieutenant! What villains have done this?

CASSIO: I think that one of them is hereabout,
    And cannot make° away.   *get*

IAGO: O treacherous villains!
    [*To Lodovico and Gratiano.*] What are you there? Come in, and

60   give some help. [*(They advance.)*]

RODERIGO: O, help me there!

CASSIO: That's one of them.

IAGO: O murderous slave! O villain!
    [*(He stabs Roderigo.)*]

RODERIGO: O damned Iago! O inhuman dog!

IAGO: Kill men i' the dark?—Where be these bloody thieves?—
    How silent is this town!—Ho! Murder, murder!—
    [*(To Lodovico and Gratiano.)*]

65   What may you be? Are you of good or evil?

LODOVICO: As you shall prove us, praise° us.   *appraise*

IAGO: Signor Lodovico?

LODOVICO: He, sir.

IAGO: I cry you mercy.[5] Here's Cassio hurt by villains.

GRATIANO: Cassio?

IAGO: How is 't, brother?

CASSIO: My leg is cut in two.

IAGO: Marry, heaven forbid!
    Light, gentlemen! I'll bind it with my shirt.
    [*(He hands them the light and tends to Cassio's wound.)*]
    [*Enter Bianca.*]

BIANCA: What is the matter, ho? Who is 't that cried?

IAGO: Who is 't that cried?

BIANCA: O my dear Cassio!
    My sweet Cassio! O, Cassio, Cassio, Cassio!

IAGO: O, notable strumpet! Cassio, may you suspect

---

5. I beg your pardon.

Who they should be that have thus mangled you?

CASSIO: No.

GRATIANO: I am sorry to find you thus. I have been to seek you.

IAGO: Lend me a garter. [(*He applies a tourniquet.*)] So.—O, for a chair,°   *litter*
    To bear him easily hence!

BIANCA: Alas, he faints! O, Cassio, Cassio, Cassio!

IAGO: Gentlemen all, I do suspect this trash
    To be a party in this injury.—
    Patience awhile, good Cassio.—Come, come;
    Lend me a light. [*He shines the light on Roderigo.*]
    Know we this face or no?

90   Alas, my friend and my dear countryman
    Roderigo! No.—Yes, sure.—O, heaven! Roderigo!

GRATIANO: What, of Venice?

IAGO: Even he, sir. Did you know him?

GRATIANO: Know him? Ay.

IAGO: Signor Gratiano? I cry your gentle° pardon.   *noble*
    These bloody accidents° must excuse my manners   *sudden events*
    That so neglected you.

GRATIANO: I am glad to see you.

IAGO: How do you, Cassio?—O a chair, a chair!

GRATIANO: Roderigo!

IAGO: He, he, 'tis he. [(*A litter is brought in.*)] O, that's well said;[6] the chair.
    Some good man bear him carefully from hence;
    I'll fetch the General's surgeon. [*To Bianca.*] For you, mistress,
    Save you your labor.[7]—He that lies slain here, Cassio,
    Was my dear friend. What malice° was between you?   *enmity*

CASSIO: None in the world, nor do I know the man.

IAGO [(*to Bianca*)]: What, look you pale?—O, bear him out o' th' air.[8]
    [(*Cassio and Roderigo are borne off.*)]
    Stay you,[9] good gentlemen.—Look you pale, mistress?—
    Do you perceive the gastness° of her eye?—   *terror*
    Nay, if you stare,[1] shall hear more anon.—

110   Behold her well; I pray you, look upon her.
    Do you see, gentlemen? Nay, guiltiness
    Will speak, though tongues were out of use.
    [(*Enter Emilia.*)]

EMILIA: 'Las, what's the matter? What's the matter, husand?

IAGO: Cassio hath here been set on in the dark

115   By Roderigo and fellows that are scaped.
    He's almost slain, and Roderigo dead.

EMILIA: Alas, good gentleman! Alas, good Cassio!

IAGO: This is the fruits of whoring. Prithee, Emilia,
    Go know° of Cassio where he supped tonight.   *learn*

120   [(*To Bianca.*)] What, do you shake at that?

---

6. Well done.
7. Never you mind tending Cassio.
8. Fresh air was thought to be dangerous for a wound.

9. Lodovico and Gratiano are evidently about to leave.
1. Iago pretends to interpret Bianca's wild looks as an involuntary confession of guilt.

BIANCA: He supped at my house, but I therefore shake not.

IAGO: O, did he so? I charge you go with me.

EMILIA: O, fie upon thee, strumpet!

BIANCA: I am no strumpet, but of life as honest°   *chaste*

125   As you that thus abuse me.

EMILIA: As I? Faugh! Fie upon thee!

IAGO: Kind gentlemen, let's go see poor Cassio dressed.²—

     Come, mistress, you must tell 's another tale.

     Emilia, run you to the citadel

130   And tell my lord and lady what hath happed.—

     Will you go on afore? [(*Aside.*)] This is the night

     That either makes me or fordoes° me quite.   [*Exeunt.*]   *ruins*

Scene 2³

[*Enter Othello (with a light,) and Desdemona in her bed.*]⁴

OTHELLO: It is the cause,⁵ it is the cause, my soul.

     Let me not name it to you, you chaste stars!

     It is the cause. Yet I'll not shed her blood,

     Nor scar that whiter skin of hers than snow,

5   And smooth as monumental alabaster.⁶

     Yet she must die, else she'll betray more men.

     Put out the light, and then put out the light.⁷

     If I quench thee, thou flaming minister,⁸

     I can again thy former light restore,

10   Should I repent me;° but once put out thy light,   *change my mind*

     Thou cunning'st pattern⁹ of excelling nature,

     I know not where is that Promethean heat¹

     That can thy light relume.° When I have plucked thy rose,   *rekindle*

     I cannot give it vital growth again;

15   It needs must wither. I'll smell thee on the tree.

[(*He kisses her.*)]

     O, balmy breath, that dost almost persuade

     Justice to break her sword! One more, one more.

     Be thus when thou art dead, and I will kill thee,

     And love thee after. One more, and that's the last.

[*He kisses her.*]

20   So sweet was ne'er so fatal. I must weep,

     But they are cruel° tears. This sorrow's heavenly;   *unrelenting*

     It strikes where it doth love.² She wakes.

DESDEMONA: Who's there? Othello?

OTHELLO: Ay, Desdemona.

DESDEMONA: Will you come to bed, my lord?

---

2. Cassio's wounds dressed.

3. Location: A bedchamber in the citadel.

4. Either the curtains are drawn back to reveal the bed in a recessed area backstage, or the bed is "thrust out" on-stage as the scene begins.

5. Cause of justice, the offense itself, which Othello must correct as an agent of justice.

6. Used in making tombs and funeral monuments.

7. The torch or lamp . . . Desdemona's life.

8. Torch or lamp that serves me.

9. You skillfully wrought perfect example.

1. Divine fire (alluding to the theft of fire from heaven by Prometheus).

2. Compare Hebrews 12.6: "For whom the Lord loveth he chasteneth."

OTHELLO: Have you prayed tonight, Desdemon?

DESDEMONA: Ay, my lord.

OTHELLO: If you bethink yourself of any crime°   *sin*

     Unreconciled as yet to heaven and grace,

30   Solicit° for it straight.°   *pray / immediately*

DESDEMONA: Alack, my lord, what may you mean by that?

OTHELLO: Well, do it, and be brief. I will walk by.

     I would not kill thy unpreparèd spirit.

     No, heaven forfend!° I would not kill thy soul.   *forbid*

DESDEMONA: Talk you of killing?

OTHELLO: Ay, I do.

DESDEMONA: Then heaven

     Have mercy on me!

OTHELLO: Amen, with all my heart!

DESDEMONA: If you say so, I hope you will not kill me.

OTHELLO: Humh!

DESDEMONA: And yet I fear you; for you're fatal then

40   When your eyes roll so. Why I should fear I know not,

     Since guiltiness I know not; but yet I feel I fear.

OTHELLO: Think on thy sins.

DESDEMONA: They are loves I bear to you.[3]

OTHELLO: Ay, and for that thou diest.

DESDEMONA: That death's unnatural that kills for loving.

45   Alas, why gnaw you so your nether lip?

     Some bloody passion shakes your very frame.

     These are portents; but yet I hope, I hope,

     They do not point on[4] me.

OTHELLO: Peace, and be still!

DESDEMONA: I will so. What's the matter?

OTHELLO: That handkerchief which I so loved and gave thee

     Thou gav'st to Cassio.

DESDEMONA: No, by my life and soul!

     Send for the man and ask him.

OTHELLO: Sweet soul, take heed, take heed of perjury.

55   Thou art on thy deathbed.

DESDEMONA: Ay, but not yet to die.

OTHELLO: Yes, presently.°   *immediately*

     Therefore confess thee freely of thy sin;

     For to deny each article with oath

     Cannot remove nor choke the strong conception[5]

60   That I do groan withal.[6] Thou art to die.

DESDEMONA: Then Lord have mercy on me!

OTHELLO: I say, amen.

DESDEMONA: And have you mercy too! I never did

     Offend° you in my life; never loved Cassio   *wrong*

65   But with such general warranty° of heaven   *sanction*

---

3. If I sinned, it was in loving you more than my father or
more than God.

4. Point at, predict what is to happen to.

5. Belief in your guilt. Also, plan in my mind.

6. Groan at in sorrow. Also, as in giving birth.

As I might love. I never gave him token.
OTHELLO: By heaven, I saw my handkerchief in 's hand.
O, perjured woman! Thou dost stone° heart,   *harden*
And makes me call what I intend to do
A murder, which I thought a sacrifice.
I saw the handkerchief.
DESDEMONA: He found it, then.
I never gave it him. Send for him hither;
Let him confess a truth.
OTHELLO: He hath confessed.
DESDEMONA: What, my lord?
OTHELLO: That he hath used thee.
DESDEMONA: How? Unlawfully?
OTHELLO: Ay.
DESDEMONA: He will not say so.
OTHELLO: No, his mouth is stopped;
Honest Iago hath ta'en order° for 't.   *taken measures*
DESDEMONA: O, my fear interprets. What, is he dead?
OTHELLO: Had all his hairs been lives, my great revenge
Had stomach for them all.
DESDEMONA: Alas, he is betrayed and I undone!   [(*She weeps.*)]
OTHELLO: Out, strumpet! Weep'st thou for him to my face?
DESDEMONA: O, banish me, my lord, but kill me not!
OTHELLO: Down, strumpet!
DESDEMONA: Kill me tomorrow; let me live tonight!
OTHELLO: Nay, if you strive—
DESDEMONA: But half an hour!
OTHELLO: Being done,[7] there is no pause.
DESDEMONA: But while I say one prayer!
OTHELLO: It is too late. [(*Smothers her.*)]
EMILIA [(*at the door*)]: My lord, my lord! What, ho! My lord, my lord!
OTHELLO: What noise is this? Not dead? Not yet quite dead?
90   I that am cruel am yet merciful;
I would not have thee linger in thy pain. [(*He dispatches her.*)]
So, so.
EMILIA [*within*]: What, ho! My lord, my lord!
OTHELLO: Who's there?
EMILIA [*within*]: O, good my lord, I would speak a word with you!
OTHELLO: Yes, 'tis Emilia.—By and by.—She's dead.
'Tis like° she comes to speak of Cassio's death.—   *likely that*
The noise was here.[8] Ha! No more moving?
Still as the grave. Shall she come in? Were 't good?—
I think she stirs again. No. What's best to do?
100   If she come in, she'll sure speak to my wife.
My wife! My wife! What wife? I have no wife.

---

7. Since justice has begun its relentless course.

8. The Folio's *high* is possible, suggesting that the commotion of the attack on Cassio was loud.

O, insupportable! O, heavy hour!
Methinks it should be now a huge eclipse
Of sun and moon, and that th' affrighted globe
Should yawn[9] at alteration.[1]

EMILIA [(*within*)]:   I do beseech you
That I may speak with you, O, good my lord!

OTHELLO: I had forgot thee. O, come in, Emilia.—
Soft,° by and by. Let me the curtains draw.—   *wait a minute*
[(*He closes the bed curtains and opens the door.*)]
Where art thou?

[*Enter Emilia.*]
                                        What's the matter with thee now?

EMILIA: O, my good lord, yonder's foul murders done!

OTHELLO: What, now?

EMILIA: But now, my lord.

OTHELLO: It is the very error° of the moon;   *aberration, irregularity*
She comes more nearer earth than she was wont,
115   And makes men mad.

EMILIA: Cassio, my lord, hath killed a young Venetian
Called Roderigo.

OTHELLO: Roderigo killed?
120   And Cassio killed?

EMILIA: No, Cassio is not killed.

OTHELLO: Not Cassio killed? Then murder's out of tune,
And sweet revenge grows harsh.

DESDEMONA: O, falsely, falsely murdered!

EMILIA: O, Lord, what cry is that?

OTHELLO: That? What?

EMILIA: Out[2] and alas, that was my lady's voice.
[(*She opens the bed-curtains.*)]
125   Help, help, ho, help! O lady, speak again!
Sweet Desdemona! O sweet mistress, speak!

DESDEMONA: A guiltless death I die.

EMILIA: O, who hath done this deed?

DESDEMONA: Nobody; I myself. Farewell.
130   Commend me to my kind lord. O, farewell! [(*She dies.*)]

OTHELLO: Why, how should she be murdered?

EMILIA: Alas, who knows?

OTHELLO: You heard her say herself it was not I.

EMILIA: She said so. I must needs report the truth.

OTHELLO: She's like a liar gone to burning hell!
135   'Twas I that killed her.

EMILIA: O, the more angel she,
And you the blacker devil!

---

9. Gape in amazement, i.e., move in an earthquake. (According to Pliny, earthquakes often happen during eclipses.)

1. At these cataclysmic events in nature, well suited to express the horror of Desdemona's death.
2. A cry of dismay, intensifying *alas*.

OTHELLO: She turned to folly,[3] and she was a whore.

EMILIA: Thou dost belie° her, and thou art a devil.   *slander*

OTHELLO: She was false as water.

EMILIA: Thou art rash as fire to say

140   That she was false. O, she was heavenly true!

OTHELLO: Cassio did top her. Ask thy husband else.[4]

　　　　O, I were damned beneath all depth in hell

　　　　But that I did proceed upon just grounds

　　　　To this extremity. Thy husband knew it all.

EMILIA: My husband?

OTHELLO: Thy husband.

EMILIA: That she was false to wedlock?

OTHELLO: Ay, with Cassio. Nay, had she been true,

　　　　If heaven would make me such another world

　　　　Of one entire and perfect chrysolite,°   *precious topaz*

　　　　I'd not have sold her for it.

EMILIA: My husband?

OTHELLO: Ay, 'twas he that told me on her first.

　　　　An honest man he is, and hates the slime

　　　　That sticks on filthy deeds.

EMILIA: My husband?

OTHELLO: What needs this iterance,° woman? I say thy husband.   *repetition*

EMILIA: O, mistress, villainy hath made mocks° with love!   *made sport*

　　　　My husband say she was false?

OTHELLO: He, woman;

　　　　I say thy husband. Dost understand the word?

　　　　My friend, thy husband, honest, honest Iago.

EMILIA: If he say so, may his pernicious soul

　　　　Rot half a grain a day! He lies to th' heart.

　　　　She was too fond of her most filthy bargain.

OTHELLO: Ha? [(*He draws.*)]

EMILIA: Do thy worst!

　　　　This deed of thine is no more worthy heaven

　　　　Than thou wast worthy her.

OTHELLO: Peace, you were best.[5]

EMILIA: Thou hast not half that power to do me harm

　　　　As I have to be hurt.° O gull!° O dolt!   *to endure hurt / dupe*

　　　　As ignorant as dirt! Thou hast done a deed—

170   I care not for thy sword; I'll make thee known,

　　　　Though I lost twenty lives.—Help! Help, ho, help!

　　　　The Moor hath killed my mistress! Murder, murder!

　　　[*Enter Montano, Gratiano, and Iago.*]

MONTANO: What is the matter? How now, General?

EMILIA: O, are you come, Iago? You have done well,

175   That men must lay their murders on your neck.

---

3. I.e., wantonness, fleshly sin.　　　　　　　　　　5. It would be best for you.
4. I.e., if you don't believe me.

GRATIANO: What is the matter?

EMILIA [to Iago]:

    Disprove this villain, if thou be'st a man.

    He says thou toldst him that his wife was false.

    I know thou didst not; thou'rt not such a villain.

180   Speak, for my heart is full.

IAGO: I told him what I thought, and told no more

    Than what he found himself was apt° and true.   *plausible*

EMILIA: But did you ever tell him she was false?

IAGO: I did.

EMILIA: You told a lie, an odious, damnèd lie!

    Upon my soul, a lie, a wicked lie.

    She false with Cassio? Did you say with Cassio?

IAGO: With Cassio, mistress. Go to, charm[6] your tongue.

EMILIA: I will not charm my tongue; I am bound to speak.

190   My mistress here lies murdered in her bed—

ALL: O, heavens forfend!

EMILIA: And your reports have set the murder on.

OTHELLO: Nay, stare not, masters. It is true indeed.

GRATIANO: 'Tis a strange truth.

MONTANO: O, monstrous act!

EMILIA: Villainy, villainy, villainy!

    I think upon 't—I think I smell 't! O, villainy!

    I thought so then[7]—I'll kill myself for grief—

    O, villainy, villainy!

IAGO: What, are you mad? I charge you, get you home.

EMILIA: Good gentlemen, let me have leave to speak.

    'Tis proper I obey him, but not now.

    Perchance, Iago, I will ne'er go home.

OTHELLO: O! O! O! [(*Othello falls on the bed.*)][8]

EMILIA: Nay, lay thee down and roar,

205   For thou hast killed the sweetest innocent

    That e'er did lift up eye.[9]

OTHELLO [*rising*]:   O, she was foul!

    I scarce did know you, uncle. There lies your niece,

    Whose breath indeed these hands have newly stopped.

    I know this act shows° horrible and grim.   *looks*

GRATIANO: Poor Desdemon! I am glad thy father's dead.

    Thy match was mortal to him, and pure grief

    Shore his old thread[1] in twain. Did he live now,

    This sight would make him do a desperate turn,°   *deed*

    Yea, curse his better angel from his side,

215   And fall to reprobance.[2]

OTHELLO: 'Tis pitiful. But yet Iago knows

    That she with Cassio hath the act of shame

6. Keep silent (as though by a magic spell).

7. Perhaps in 3.3 and 4.2.

8. This direction is from the Quarto.

9. Lift her eyes to heaven.

1. Sheared the thread of his old age (as Atropos, one of the three Fates, was thought to do).

2. Damnation, i.e., suicide.

A thousand times committed. Cassio confessed it;
And she did gratify° his amorous works   *reward*
220   With that recognizance° and pledge of love   *token*
Which I first gave her. I saw it in his hand;
It was a handkerchief, an antique token
My father gave my mother.

EMILIA: O, God! O, heavenly God!

IAGO: Zounds, hold your peace.

EMILIA: 'Twill out, 'twill out! I peace?
No, I will speak as liberal as the north.³
Let heaven and men and devils, let them all,
All, all, cry shame against me, yet I'll speak.

IAGO: Be wise, and get you home.

EMILIA: I will not.
    [(*Iago threatens Emilia.*)]

GRATIANO: Fie,
230   Your sword upon a woman?

EMILIA: O, thou dull Moor! That handkerchief thou speak'st of
I found by fortune and did give my husband;
For often, with a solemn earnestness,
More than indeed belonged° to such a trifle,   *was appropriate*
235   He begged of me to steal 't.

IAGO: Villainous whore!

EMILIA: She give it Cassio? No, alas! I found it,
And I did give 't my husband.

IAGO: Filth, thou liest!

EMILIA: By heaven, I do not, I do not, gentlemen.
O, murderous coxcomb!⁴ What should such a fool
240   Do with so good a wife?

OTHELLO: Are there no stones⁵ in heaven
But what serves for the thunder?—Precious° villain!   *utter*
    [(*He runs at Iago; Montano disarms Othello. Iago, from behind, stabs Emilia.*)]⁶

GRATIANO: The woman falls! Sure he hath killed his wife.

EMILIA: Ay, ay. O, lay me by my mistress' side.

                                                        [(*Exit Iago.*)]

GRATIANO: He's gone, but his wife's killed.

MONTANO: 'Tis a notorious villain. Take you this weapon,
Which I have here recovered from the Moor.
Come, guard the door without. Let him not pass,
But kill him rather. I'll after that same villain,
For 'tis a damnèd slave.
    [*Exit (with all but Othello and Emilia, who has been laid by Desdemona's side.*)]

OTHELLO: I am not valiant neither,
250   But every puny whipster⁷ gets my sword.

---

3. Freely as the north wind (blows).
4. Fool (addressed to Othello).
5. Bolts, such as those used for thunderbolts.
6. The quarto text reads, "The Moor runs at Iago. Iago

kills his wife." The Quarto also specifies the exit of Iago
below.
7. Contemptible fellow (one who is always ready to whip
out his sword).

But why should honor[8] outlive honesty?°   *integrity*
    Let it go all.

EMILIA: What did thy song bode, lady?
    Hark, canst thou hear me? I will play the swan,
    And die in music. [*She sings.*] "Willow, willow, willow."
255   Moor, she was chaste. She loved thee, cruel Moor.
    So come my soul to bliss as I speak true.
    So speaking as I think, alas, I die. [*She dies.*]

OTHELLO: I have another weapon in this chamber;
    It was a sword of Spain, the ice-brook's temper[9]—
260   O, here it is. [(*He finds a sword.*)] Uncle, I must come forth.

GRATIANO: [(*within*)] If thou attempt it, it will cost thee dear.
    Thou hast no weapon, and perforce must suffer.

OTHELLO: Look in upon me then and speak with me,
    Or, naked° as I am, I will assault thee.   *unarmed*
  [(*Enter Gratiano.*)]

GRATIANO: What is the matter?

OTHELLO: Behold, I have a weapon;
    A better never did itself sustain
    Upon a soldier's thigh. I have seen the day
    That, with this little arm and this good sword,
    I have made my way through more impediments
270   Than twenty times your stop.[1] But O, vain boast!
    Who can control his fate? 'Tis not so now.
    Be not afraid, though you do see me weaponed;
    Here is my journey's end, here is my butt[2]
    And very seamark[3] of my utmost sail.
  [(*Gratiano steps back.*)]
275   Do you go back dismayed? 'Tis a lost° fear;   *wasted*
    Man but a rush[4] against Othello's breast
    And he retires. Where should Othello go?
  [(*He turns to Desdemona.*)]
    Now, how dost thou look now? O, ill-starred wench!
    Pale as thy smock! When we shall meet at compt,°   *Judgment Day*
280   This look of thine will hurl my soul from heaven,
    And fiends will snatch at it. Cold, cold, my girl?
    Even like thy chastity. O, cursèd, cursèd slave![5]
    Whip me, ye devils,
    From the possession of this heavenly sight!
285   Blow me about in winds! Roast me in sulfur!
    Wash me in steep-down gulfs of liquid fire!
    O, Desdemon! Dead, Desdemon! Dead! O! O!

[*Enter Lodovico, Cassio* [(*carried in a litter*)],[6] *Montano, and Iago* [(*prisoner*)], *with officers.*]

---

8. The bravery for which one enjoys a soldier's reputation.
9. Tempered in ice-cold water.
1. Power (to stop).
2. Goal, limit (an archery term).

3. Beacon (marking his destination or limit).
4. Wield no more than a reed.
5. Othello himself.
6. The Quarto specifies that Cassio is "in a chair."

LODOVICO: Where is this rash and most unfortunate man?

OTHELLO: That's he that was Othello. Here I am.

LODOVICO: Where is that viper? Bring the villain forth.

　　[(*Iago is led forward.*)]

OTHELLO: I look down towards his feet;[7] but that's a fable.

　　If that thou be'st a devil, I cannot kill thee.

　　[(*He wounds Iago.*)]

LODOVICO: Wrench his sword from him. [(*Othello is disarmed.*)]

IAGO:　　　　　　　I bleed, sir, but not killed.

OTHELLO: I am not sorry neither. I'd have thee live,

295　　For in my sense[8] 'tis happiness to die.

LODOVICO: O thou Othello, that was once so good,

　　Fall'n in the practice[9] of a cursèd slave,°　　　　　*villain*

　　What shall be said to thee?

OTHELLO:　　　　　　　Why, anything.

　　An honorable murderer, if you will,

300　　For naught I did in hate, but all in honor.

LODOVICO: This wretch hath part confessed his villainy.

　　Did you and he consent° in Cassio's death?　　　　*agree*

OTHELLO: Ay.

CASSIO: Dear General, I never gave you cause.

OTHELLO: I do believe it, and I ask your pardon.

　　Will you, I pray, demand that demi-devil

　　Why he hath thus ensnared my soul and body?

IAGO: Demand me nothing. What you know, you know.

　　From this time forth I never will speak word.

LODOVICO: What, not to pray?

GRATIANO: Torments° will ope your lips.　　　　　*torture*

OTHELLO: Well, thou dost best.

LODOVICO: Sir, you shall understand what hath befall'n,

　　Which, as I think, you know not. Here is a letter

315　　Found in the pocket of the slain Roderigo;

　　And here another. [(*He produces letters.*)] The one of them imports

　　The death of Cassio, to be undertook

　　By Roderigo.

OTHELLO: O villain!

CASSIO:　　　　　　Most heathenish and most gross!°　　　*monstrous*

LODOVICO [(*showing another paper*)]: Now here's another discontented paper

　　Found in his pocket too. And this, it seems,

　　Roderigo meant t' have sent this damnèd villain;

　　But that belike° Iago in the interim　　　　　*most likely*

　　Came in and satisfied him.[1]

OTHELLO: O thou pernicious caitiff!—

　　How came you, Cassio, by that handkerchief

　　That was my wife's?

---

7. I.e., to see if they are cloven, as the devil's are fabled to be.
8. To one who feels as I do.

9. Through the plotting, into the snare.
1. Interposed and gave him satisfactory explanation.

CASSIO: I found it in my chamber;
　　　　　And he himself confessed but even now
　　　　　That there he dropped it for a special purpose
330　　　Which wrought to his desire.²
OTHELLO: O fool, fool, fool!
CASSIO: There is besides in Roderigo's letter
　　　　　How he upbraids Iago, that he made him
　　　　　Brave° me upon the watch, whereon it came³　　　　　　　　*defy*
　　　　　That I was cast;° and even but now he spake,　　　　　　　*dismissed*
335　　　After long seeming dead, Iago hurt him,
　　　　　Iago set him on.
LODOVICO: [(*to Othello*)] You must forsake this room and go with us.
　　　　　Your power and your command is taken off,°　　　　　　　*taken away*
　　　　　And Cassio rules in Cyprus. For this slave,
340　　　If there be any cunning cruelty
　　　　　That can torment him much and hold him long,⁴
　　　　　It shall be his. You shall close prisoner rest°　　　　　　　*remain*
　　　　　Till that the nature of your fault be known
　　　　　To the Venetian state.—Come, bring away.
OTHELLO: Soft you;° a word or two before you go.　　　　　　　*one moment*
　　　　　I have done the state some service, and they know't.
　　　　　No more of that. I pray you, in your letters,
　　　　　When you shall these unlucky° deeds relate,　　　　　　　*unfortunate*
　　　　　Speak of me as I am; nothing extenuate,
350　　　Nor set down aught in malice. Then must you speak
　　　　　Of one that loved not wisely but too well;
　　　　　Of one not easily jealous but, being wrought,⁵
　　　　　Perplexed° in the extreme; of one whose hand,　　　　　　　*distraught*
　　　　　Like the base Indian,⁶ threw a pearl away
355　　　Richer than all his tribe; of one whose subdued⁷ eyes,
　　　　　Albeit unusèd to the melting mood,
　　　　　Drops tears as fast as the Arabian trees
　　　　　Their medicinable gum.° Set you down this;　　　　　　　*myrrh*
　　　　　And say besides that in Aleppo once,
360　　　Where a malignant and a turbaned Turk
　　　　　Beat a Venetian and traduced the state,
　　　　　I took by th' throat the circumcisèd dog
　　　　　And smote him, thus. [(*He stabs himself.*)]⁸
LODOVICO: O, bloody period!°　　　　　　　　　　　　　　　*end, conclusion*
GRATIANO: All that is spoke is marred.
OTHELLO: I kissed thee ere I killed thee. No way but this,
　　　　　Killing myself, to die upon a kiss.
　　　　　[*He kisses Desdemona and dies.*]

---

2. Worked out as he wished, fitted in with his plan.
3. Whereof it came about.
4. Keep him alive a long time (during his torture).
5. Worked upon, worked into a frenzy.
6. This reading from the Quarto pictures an ignorant sav-age who cannot recognize the value of a precious jewel.

The Folio reading, *Iudean* or *Judean* i.e., infidel or disbe-liever, may refer to Herod, who slew Miriam in a fit of jealousy, or to Judas Iscariot, the betrayer of Christ.
7. I.e., overcome by grief.
8. This direction is in the Quarto text.

CASSIO: This did I fear, but thought he had no weapon;
    For he was great of heart.
LODOVICO [to Iago]:   O Spartan dog,[9]
    More fell° than anguish, hunger, or the sea!   *cruel*
370   Look on the tragic loading of this bed.
    This is thy work. The object poisons sight;
    Let it be hid.[1] Gratiano, keep° the house,   *remain in*
  [(*The bed curtains are drawn*)]
    And seize upon the fortunes of the Moor,
    For they succeed on you.[2] [*To Cassio.*] To you, Lord Governor,
375   Remains the censure° of this hellish villain,   *sentencing*
    The time, the place, the torture. O, enforce it!
    Myself will straight aboard, and to the state
    This heavy act with heavy heart relate.   [*Exeunt.*]

King Lear

King Lear has the power to move us as no other play of Shakespeare's can. The tragedy enacts the suffering endured by a father who rejects the one child who truly loves him. Lear's downfall is set in motion through his desire to measure love, an emotional commitment that cannot be quantified. Equally disastrous is his decision to bestow power over the kingdom to the daughters who can best meet his childish desire for public protestations of affection. When Lear demands to know, "Which of you shall we say doth love us most?" Goneril boasts of loving Lear "more than word can wield the matter," and Regan protests herself "an enemy to all other joys." Cordelia, however, recognizes the emotional bankruptcy of this contest and refuses to speak in such hyperbole. Lear banishes her and hands over the reins of power to her sisters, only to discover they will not meet his exigent demands with any more patience than he granted to Cordelia. Like father like daughter, Goneril and Regan banish the father who banished their sister. Lear blames his unkind daughters for all his troubles. He curses them, threatening them with "the terrors of the earth," as he attempts to ward off his descent into grief and madness. When, homeless, he enters the storm on the heath, he experiences the lot of his poorest subjects. Standing by him in all this are his Fool, who speaks truth through nonsense, and the disguised Kent, who for his outspoken defense of Cordelia had been banished by Lear. Paradoxically, only by becoming mad does Lear achieve some measure of wisdom. Dislocated and deranged, he discovers his error only in time to receive Cordelia's comfort and forgiveness before she is executed at the command of those his fatal misjudgment put into power. The play makes us confront human brutality and the lack of any comforting divine intervention, yet it also allows us to witness Lear's learning through suffering. This combination of profound suffering, brought on by human error, and great insight into that same weakness makes this the closest of all Shakespeare's tragedies to the works of the ancient Greek tragedians.

---

9. Spartan dogs were noted for their savagery and silence.
1. I.e., draw the bed curtains. (No stage direction specifies that the dead are to be carried offstage at the end of the play.)

2. Take legal possession of Othello's property, which passes as though by inheritance to you.

This combination of pathos and understanding is in part achieved through Shakespeare's very original handling of source material. First performed at court in December 1606, Shakespeare's *Lear* comes after a long line of versions of the story that end happily. In earlier versions of the story—including Raphael Holinshed's *Chronicles* (1587), Edmund Spenser's *The Faerie Queene* 2.10.27–32, and the play *The True Chronicle History of King Leir* (written c. 1594; published 1605)—the King of France restores Lear to his power after he has been dethroned. Not only is there no tragic ending in the earlier *King Leir* but there is no storm on the heath and no descent into madness. In Holinshed's *Chronicles* and Spenser's *Faerie Queene* 2.10, Cordelia commits suicide after the death of her father, rather than being executed in front of him. In contrast, Shakespeare's choice to have Lear attempt to save Cordelia by slaying her executioner makes the once exigent and self-centered father defiantly heroic and self-sacrificing in his final hour. Beyond this, Shakespeare's Lear has to live through Cordelia's death, which increases the depth of his tragic suffering.

Not only did Shakespeare alter the central plot, but he added to it the subplot of the gullible Gloucester, inspired by the story of the blinded king of Paphlagonia from Sir Philip Sidney's prose romance *Arcadia*. Edmund, Gloucester's bastard son, convinces his too trusting father that his legitimate son Edgar is plotting to kill him. Gloucester then is turned over by Edmund to Goneril who orders his eyes to be "plucked out." Later, in his blindness Gloucester is aided by Edgar now disguised as a mad beggar. Only in his blindness does Gloucester come to understand his mistaken judgment. The subplot of his experience of insight through blindness mirrors Lear's experience of wisdom through madness. The two plots both make us reflect on how human beings deceive themselves and collude in their own destruction, and yet rise above mere victimhood through the capacity to acknowledge their part in all this. Strikingly both plots deal with the cruelty of parents against children and children against parents, along with the difficulty in those relationships of trusting love and resisting manipulation.

King Lear interrogates the character of the filial bond, and the extent to which human relationships are governed by "nature." The two meanings of the word "kind," signifying both generous and related by blood, are played off of each other repeatedly and underscore our troubled awareness of how the parent-child relationship should but does not guarantee kind treatment. The play is haunted by the multiple meanings of the words "nature" and "natural," referring to the natural world of flora and fauna, and to the social world of human nature. Edmund is Lear's "natural" or illegitimate son. Lear's legitimate daughters Goneril and Regan are called monstrous and "unnatural." We are made to question the relation between what is deemed "natural" by biology on the one hand and by custom on the other. How can Lear claim to have "loved [Cordelia] most" and so easily disinherit her? How natural is Edmund's worship of the "Nature" he calls his "goddess"? Why does Lear expect Goneril and Regan to treat him kindly? Is the unforgiving storm on the heath the ultimate experience of nature? Where does Cordelia's capacity to treat Lear kindly come from? Is it her nature as a daughter? Or is there something else at work here, something beyond what was believed at the time of the play to be part of the natural hierarchical order of the family?

At the end of the play the incredible goodness of Cordelia is defeated by the forces of evil, as represented by her sisters and the man they fought over, Edmund. While Edmund repents his evil at the end, her sisters destroy each other. Significantly, those who have managed to conceal their true identities survive—Kent, who has played the role of Caius, the servant of Lear, and Edgar, who has feigned the role of Tom o' Bedlam as he protected his blinded father Gloucester. Ironically, it is in masquerading that they prove themselves to be most true, or loyal. Kent and Edgar embody the ability to adapt to changing conditions and yet to remain true to one's cause in the face of the arbitrary and capricious will of those in power. That the imagination has a role to play in this survival is no better illustrated than in Edgar's convincing his blind father that he has jumped off a cliff and been saved from death. Even such moments of hope, however, withhold any easy comfort. Edgar's words to

Gloucester—"Men must endure / Their going hence, even as their coming hither, / Ripeness is all," (5.2.7–8)—suggest the notion that our lives are made more meaningful by our awareness of and preparation for death. Yet, Gloucester's rejoinder "And that's true too," could be read as darkly and humorously undercutting the solace offered by such wisdom.

   King Lear represents the terrifying abyss of human cruelty causing a suffering that the loyal love of Edgar, Kent, and Cordelia can comfort but never fully heal. Perhaps it is this very searching look at the way we humans torture each other that made the play the most celebrated at the end of the most violent century in history. If eighteenth-century audiences were outraged by the extremity of the tragedy and could only bear to see it acted with the happy ending, provided in Nahum Tate's adaptation (1687), those of the twentieth century could see parallels between Shakespeare's desperadoes on the heath and the derelicts of Samuel Beckett's dark comedies. At the start of the twenty-first century, you, a new generation of readers, will inevitably make the play your own through a fresh reading of how suffering and love mysteriously intertwine in *King Lear*.

King Lear*

The Names of the Actors

KING LEAR
GONERIL,
REGAN,   } Lear's daughters
CORDELIA,
DUKE OF ALBANY, *Goneril's husband*
DUKE OF CORNWALL, *Regan's husband*
KING OF FRANCE, *Cordelia's suitor and husband*
DUKE OF BURGUNDY, *suitor to Cordelia*
EARL OF KENT, *later disguised as Caius*
EARL OF GLOUCESTER
EDGAR, *Gloucester's son and heir, later disguised as poor Tom*
EDMUND, *Gloucester's bastard son*
SCENE: *Britain*]

OSWALD, *Goneril's steward*
A KNIGHT *serving King Lear*
Lear's FOOL
CURAN, *in Gloucester's household*
GENTLEMEN
Three SERVANTS
OLD MAN, *a tenant of Gloucester*
Three MESSENGERS
A GENTLEMAN *attending Cordelia as a Doctor*
Two CAPTAINS
HERALD

Knights, Gentlemen, Attendants, Servants, Officers, Soldiers, Trumpeters

ACT 1
Scene 1[1]

[*Enter Kent, Gloucester, and Edmund.*]

KENT: I thought the King had more affected[2] the Duke of Albany[3] than Cornwall.

GLOUCESTER: It did always seem so to us; but now in the division of the kingdom it appears not which of the dukes he values most, for equalities are so weighed that curiosity in neither can make choice of either's moiety.[4]

KENT: Is not this your son, my lord?

---

* The text and notes in this selection are based on the sixth edition of Bevington.
1. Location: King Lear's palace.
2. Favored.

3. I.e., Scotland.
4. The shares balance so equally that close scrutiny cannot find advantage in either's portion.

GLOUCESTER: His breeding,[5] sir, hath been at my charge. I have so often blushed
to acknowledge him that now I am brazed[6] to't.

KENT: I cannot conceive[7] you.

GLOUCESTER: Sir, this young fellow's mother could; whereupon she grew round-
10   wombed and had indeed, sir, a son for her cradle ere she had a husband for
her bed. Do you smell a fault?

KENT: I cannot wish the fault undone, the issue[8] of it being so proper.[9]

GLOUCESTER: But I have a son, sir, by order of law,[1] some year[2] elder than this,
who yet is no dearer in my account. Though this knave[3] came something[4]
15   saucily to the world before he was sent for, yet was his mother fair, there
was good sport at his making, and the whoreson must be acknowledged.—
Do you know this noble gentleman, Edmund?

EDMUND: No, my lord.

GLOUCESTER: My lord of Kent. Remember him hereafter as my honorable friend.

EDMUND: My services to Your Lordship.

KENT: I must love you, and sue[5] to snow you better.

EDMUND: Sir, I shall study deserving.[6]

GLOUCESTER: He hath been out[7] nine years, and away he shall again. The King
is coming.

[*Sennet.*[8] *Enter (one bearing a coronet,*[9] *then) King Lear, Cornwall, Albany,*
Goneril, Regan, Cordelia, and attendants.]

LEAR: Attend[1] the lords of France and Burgundy, Gloucester.

GLOUCESTER: I shall, my liege.°   [*Exit.*]   lord

LEAR: Meantime we[2] shall express our darker° purpose.   secret
Give me the map there. [(*He takes a map.*)] Know that we have divided
In three our kingdom; and 'tis our fast° intent   firm
30   To shake all cares and business from our age,
Conferring them on younger strengths while we
Unburdened crawl toward death. Our son of Cornwall,
And you, our no less loving son of Albany,
We have this hour a constant will to publish
35   Our daughters' several dowers,[3] that future strife
May be prevented now. The princes, France and Burgundy,
Great rivals in our youngest daughter's love,
Long in our court have made their amorous sojourn
And here are to be answered. Tell me, my daughters—
40   Since now we will divest us both of rule,
Interest° of territory, cares of state—   possession
Which of you shall we say doth love us most,

---

5. His raising has been at my expense.
6. Hardened.
7. Understand, but Gloucester puns on the sense of "become pregnant."
8. Offspring.
9. Excellent, handsome.
1. Legitimate.
2. Estimation.
3. Young fellow.
4. Somewhat.

5. Petition, beg.
6. Strive to be worthy of your esteem.
7. Abroad, absent.
8. Trumpet signal announcing a procession.
9. This stage direction is from the Quarto; a coronet signifies nobility below the rank of a king.
1. Wait upon.
2. The royal use of "we" for "I."
3. I firmly resolve to make known each daughter's dowry, or inheritance for marriage.

That we our largest bounty may extend
Where nature doth with merit challenge?[4] Goneril,

45   Our eldest born, speak first.

GONERIL: Sir, I love you more than words can wield° the matter,   *handle, convey*
Dearer than eyesight, space, and liberty,
Beyond what can be valued, rich or rare,
No less than life, with grace, health, beauty, honor;

50   As much as child e'er loved, or father found;
A love that makes breath poor and speech unable.[5]
Beyond all manner of so much I love you.

CORDELIA [aside]: What shall Cordelia speak? Love and be silent.

LEAR [indicating on map]: Of all these bounds, even from this line to this,

55   With shadowy° forests and with champains riched,°   *shady / fertile plains*
With plenteous rivers and wide-skirted meads,[6]
We make thee lady. To thine and Albany's issue
Be this perpetual.—What says our second daughter,
Our dearest Regan, wife of Cornwall? Speak.

REGAN: I am made of that self mettle[7] as my sister,
And prize me at her worth.[8] In my true heart
I find she names my very deed of love;[9]
Only she comes too short, that I profess
Myself an enemy to all other joys

65   Which the most precious square of sense possesses,[1]
And find I am alone felicitate°   *made happy*
In your dear Highness' love.

CORDELIA [(aside)]:   Then poor Cordelia!
And yet not so, since I am sure my love's
More ponderous° than my tongue.   *weighty*

LEAR: To thee and thine hereditary ever
Remain this ample third of our fair kingdom,
No less in space, validity, and pleasure
Than that conferred on Goneril.—Now, our joy,
Although our last and least, to whose young love

75   The vines° of France and milk° of Burgundy   *vineyards / pastures*
Strive to be interessed,° what can you say to draw°   *establish a claim / win*
A third more opulent than your sisters'? Speak.

CORDELIA: Nothing, my lord.

LEAR: Nothing?

CORDELIA: Nothing.

LEAR: Nothing will come of nothing. Speak again.

CORDELIA: Unhappy that I am, I cannot heave
My heart into my mouth. I love Your Majesty
According to my bond,° no more nor less.   *duty*

---

4. Where natural affection and merit claim our bounty.
5. Utterance impoverished and speech inadequate.
6. Abundant rivers bordered with wide meadows.
7. That same spirited temperament.

8. And value myself as her equal.
9. Describes my love in action.
1. Which the most delicately sensitive part of my nature can enjoy.

LEAR: How, how, Cordelia? Mend your speech a little,
        Lest you may mar your fortunes.
CORDELIA: Good my lord,
        You have begot me, bred me, loved me. I
        Return those duties back as are right fit,
        Obey you, love you, and most honor you.
90   Why have my sisters husbands if they say
        They love you all?° Haply, when I shall wed,   *exclusively*
        That lord whose hand must take my plight² shall carry
        Half my love with him, half my care and duty.
        Sure I shall never marry like my sisters,
95   To love my father all.
LEAR: But goes thy heart with this?
CORDELIA: Ay, my good lord.
LEAR: So young, and so untender?
CORDELIA: So young, my lord, and true.
LEAR: Let it be so! Thy truth then be thy dower!
100   For, by the sacred radiance of the sun,
        The mysteries of Hecate³ and the night,
        By all the operation of the orbs
        From whom we do exist and cease to be,
        Here I disclaim all my paternal care,
105   Propinquity, and property of blood,⁴
        And as a stranger to my heart and me
        Hold thee from this⁵ forever. The barbarous Scythian,⁶
        Or he that makes his generation messes⁷
        To gorge his appetite, shall to my bosom
110   Be as well neighbored, pitied, and relieved
        As thou my sometime° daughter.   *former*
KENT: Good my liege—
LEAR: Peace, Kent!
        Come not between the dragon and his wrath.
        I loved her most, and thought to set my rest
115   On her kind nursery.⁸ [(*To Cordelia*)] Hence, and avoid my sight!—
        So be my grave my peace, as here I give
        Her father's heart from her. Call France. Who stirs?
        Call Burgundy.   [(*Exit one.*)]
                        Cornwall and Albany,
        With my two daughters' dowers digest the third.⁹
120   Let pride, which she calls plainness, marry her.
        I do invest you jointly with my power,
        Preeminence, and all the large effects
        That troop with majesty. Ourself by monthly course,

2. Marriage pledge.
3. Secret rites of the goddess of witchcraft and the moon.
4. Close kinship, and rights and duties entailed in blood ties.
5. This time forth.
6. Scythians were typed by classical authors as savages.

7. He that makes meals of his children.
8. To rely wholly on her nursing.
9. Put Cordelia's inheritance in with those of the other two.

With reservation of an hundred knights
125 By you to be sustained,[1] shall our abode
Make with you by due turns. Only we shall retain
The name and all th'addition[2] to a king.
The sway,[3] revenue, execution of the rest,
Belovèd sons, be yours, which to confirm,
130 This coronet part between you.
KENT: Royal Lear,
Whom I have ever honored as my king,
Loved as my father, as my master followed,
As my great patron thought on in my prayers—
LEAR: The bow is bent and drawn. Make from[4] the shaft.
KENT: Let it fall rather, though the fork invade
The region of my heart.[5] Be Kent unmannerly
When Lear is mad. What wouldst thou do, old man?
Think'st thou that duty shall have dread to speak
When power to flattery bows?
140 To plainness honor's bound[6]
When majesty falls to folly. Reserve thy state,[7]
And in thy best consideration check
This hideous rashness. Answer my life my judgment,[8]
Thy youngest daughter does not love thee least,
145 Nor are those emptyhearted whose low sounds
Reverb no hollowness.[9]
LEAR: Kent, on thy life, no more.
KENT: My life I never held but as a pawn
To wage against thine enemies, nor fear to lose it,
Thy safety being motive.[1]
LEAR: Out of my sight!
KENT: See better, Lear, and let me still remain
The true blank[2] of thine eye.
LEAR: Now, by Apollo—
KENT: Now, by Apollo, King,
Thou swear'st thy gods in vain.
LEAR: Oh, vassal! Miscreant![3]
                    [(*Laying his hand on his sword.*)]
ALBANY, CORNWALL: Dear sir, forbear.
KENT: Kill thy physician, and the fee bestow
Upon the foul disease. Revoke thy gift,
Or whilst I can vent clamor from my throat
I'll tell thee thou dost evil.
LEAR: Hear me, recreant,° on thine allegiance hear me!   *traitor*
That thou hast sought to make us break our vows,

1. Reserving the right to be attended by 100 knights, whom you will have to support.
2. The honors and prerogatives of a king.
3. Sovereign authority.
4. Get out of the way of.
5. Let the arrow strike even if the barbed head pierce my heart.
6. Loyalty demands frankness.
7. Retain control of your kingdom.
8. I wager my life on my judgment.
9. Do not reverberate emptiness and insincerity.
1. Your safety being what prompts me to act.
2. Center of the target.
3. Literally "unbeliever"; hence, villain.

Which we durst never yet, and with strained pride
To come betwixt our sentence and our power,[4]
Which nor our nature nor our place can bear,[5]

165   Our potency made good, take thy reward.
Five days we do allot thee for provision
To shield thee from disasters of the world,
And on the sixth to turn thy hated back
Upon our kingdom. If on the tenth day following

170   Thy banished trunk° be found in our dominions,   body
The moment is thy death. Away! By Jupiter,
This shall not be revoked.

KENT: Fare thee well, King. Sith thus thou wilt appear,
Freedom lives hence and banishment is here.

175   [(To Cordelia)] The gods to their dear shelter take thee, maid,
That justly think'st and hast most rightly said!
[(To Regan and Goneril)] And your large speeches may your deeds approve,[6]
That good effects may spring from words of love.
Thus Kent, O princes, bids you all adieu.

180   He'll shape his old course in a country new.   [Exit.]
[Flourish.[7] Enter Gloucester, with France and Burgundy; attendants]

GLOUCESTER: Here's France and Burgundy, my noble lord.

LEAR: My lord of Burgundy,
We first address toward you, who with this king
Hath rivaled for our daughter. What in the least

180   Will you require in present dower with her
Or cease your quest of love?

BURGUNDY: Most royal Majesty,
I crave no more than hath Your Highness offered,
Nor will you tender less.

LEAR: Right noble Burgundy,
When she was dear to us we did hold her so,

185   But now her price is fallen. Sir, there she stands.
If aught within that little-seeming substance,[8]
Or all of it, with our displeasure pieced,°   joined
And nothing more, may fitly like Your Grace,
She's there, and she is yours.

BURGUNDY: I know no answer.

LEAR: Will you, with those infirmities she owes,
Unfriended, new-adopted to our hate,
Dowered with our curse and strangered with our oath,
Take her, or leave her?

BURGUNDY: Pardon me, royal sir.
Election makes not up in such conditions.[9]

---

4. To block my power to command and judge.
5. Which neither my temperament nor my office as king can bear.
6. May your deeds confirm your speeches.

7. Trumpet fanfare.
8. One who seems substantial but whose substance is little.
9. No choice is possible in such conditions.

LEAR: Then leave her, sir, for by the power that made me,
         I tell you all her wealth. [(*To France*)] For you, great King,
         I would not from your love make such a stray
         To match you where I hate; therefore beseech you
         T'avert your liking[1] a more worthier way
200   Than on a wretch whom Nature is ashamed
         Almost t'acknowledge hers.
FRANCE: This is most strange,
         That she whom even but now was your best object,
         The argument of your praise, balm of your age,
         The best, the dearest, should in this trice° of time   *moment*
205   Commit a thing so monstrous to dismantle
         So many folds of favor. Sure her offense
         Must be of such unnatural degree
         That monsters[2] it, or your forevouched affection
         Fall into taint,[3] which to believe of her
210   Must be a faith that reason without miracle
         Should never plant in me.
CORDELIA: I yet beseech Your Majesty—
         If for I want[4] that glib and oily art
         To speak and purpose not, since what I well intend
215   I'll do't before I speak—that you make known
         It is no vicious blot, murder, or foulness,
         No unchaste action or dishonored step
         That hath deprived me of your grace and favor,
         But even for want of that for which I am richer:
220   A still-soliciting° eye and such a tongue   *ever-begging*
         That I am glad I have not, though not to have it
         Hath lost me in your liking.
LEAR: Better thou
         Hadst not been born than not t'have pleased me better.
FRANCE: Is it but this? A tardiness in nature
225   Which often leaves the history° unspoke   *story*
         That it intends to do?—My lord of Burgundy,
         What say you to the lady? Love's not love
         When it is mingled with regards that stands
         Aloof from th'entire point.[5] Will you have her?
230   She is herself a dowry.
BURGUNDY [(*to Lear*)]:   Royal King,
         Give but that portion which yourself proposed,
         And here I take Cordelia by the hand,
         Duchess of Burgundy.
LEAR: Nothing. I have sworn. I am firm.
BURGUNDY [(*to Cordelia*)]: I am sorry, then, you have so lost a father

---

1. Turn your affections.
2. Makes it monstrous.
3. Or else the affection for her you have hitherto affirmed must fall into suspicion.

4. Because I lack.
5. Love is not mixed with irrelevant considerations.

That you must lose a husband.

CORDELIA: Peace be with Burgundy!
    Since that respects of fortune are his love,
    I shall not be his wife.

FRANCE: Fairest Cordelia, that art most rich being poor,
240   Most choice, forsaken, and most loved, despised,
    Thee and thy virtues here I seize upon,
    Be it lawful I take up what's cast away.

                                   [*He takes her hand.*]

    Gods, gods! 'Tis strange that from their cold'st neglect
    My love should kindle to inflamed respect.—
245   Thy dowerless daughter, King, thrown to my chance,
    Is queen of us, of ours, and our fair France.
    Not all the dukes of wat'rish Burgundy
    Can buy this unprized[6] precious maid of me.—
    Bid them farewell, Cordelia, though unkind.
250   Thou losest here, a better where to find.

LEAR: Thou hast her, France. Let her be thine, for we
    Have no such daughter, nor shall ever see
    That face of hers again. Therefore begone
    Without our grace, our love, our benison.
255   Come, noble Burgundy.

        [*Flourish. Exeunt (all but France, Goneril, Regan, and Cordelia).*]

FRANCE: Bid farewell to your sisters.

CORDELIA: Ye jewels of our father, with washed° eyes   *tear washed*
    Cordelia leaves you. I know you what you are,
    And like a sister am most loath to call
260   Your faults as they are named. Love well our father.
    To your professèd bosoms[7] I commit him.
    But yet, alas, stood I within his grace,
    I would prefer° him to a better place.   *recommend*
    So, farewell to you both.

REGAN: Prescribe not us our duty.

GONERIL: Let your study
    Be to content your lord, who hath received you
    At Fortune's aims.[8] You have obedience scanted,
    And well are worth the want that you have wanted.[9]

CORDELIA: Time shall unfold what plighted cunning hides;
270   Who covers faults, at last shame them derides.[1]
    Well may you prosper!

FRANCE: Come, my fair Cordelia.

                              [*Exeunt France and Cordelia.*]

GONERIL: Sister, it is not little I have to say of what most nearly appertains to us
    both. I think our father will hence tonight.

---

6. Not appreciated, but also priceless.
7. Publicly avowed love.
8. As a handout from Fortune.
9. You well deserve to be without the dowry and parental

affection that you lacked and flouted.
1. Those who hide their faults in time will be ashamed and derided.

REGAN: That's most certain, and with you; next month with us.

GONERIL: You see how full of changes his age is; the observation we have made of it hath not been little. He always loved our sister most, and with what poor judgment he hath now cast her off appears too grossly.

REGAN: 'Tis the infirmity of his age. Yet he hath ever but slenderly known himself.

GONERIL: The best and soundest of his time hath been but rash.[2] Then must we

280   look from his age to receive not alone the imperfections of long-ingraffed condition,[3] but therewithal[4] the unruly waywardness that infirm and choleric years bring with them.

REGAN: Such unconstant starts[5] are we like to have from him as this of Kent's banishment.

GONERIL: There is further compliment[6] of leave-taking between France and him. Pray you, let us hit[7] together. If our father carry authority with such disposition as he bears, this last surrender of his will but offend us.[8]

REGAN: We shall further think of it.

GONERIL: We must do something, and i'th' heat.[9]

[Exeunt.]

Scene 2[1]

[Enter Bastard (Edmund, with a letter).]

EDMUND: Thou, Nature,[2] art my goddess; to thy law
     My services are bound. Wherefore should I
     Stand in the plague of custom and permit
     The curiosity of nations to deprive me,
5   For that I am some twelve or fourteen moonshines
     Lag of a brother?[3] Why bastard? Wherefore base?
     When my dimensions are as well compact,°   *fitted, framed*
     My mind as generous, and my shape as true,
     As honest° madam's issue? Why brand they us   *chaste*
10   With base? With baseness? Bastardy? Base, base?
     Who in the lusty stealth of nature take
     More composition and fierce quality[4]
     Than doth within a dull, stale, tirèd bed
     Go to th' creating a whole tribe of fops°   *fools*
15   Got 'tween asleep and wake? Well, then,
     Legitimate Edgar, I must have your land.
     Our father's love is to the bastard Edmund
     As to th' legitimate. Fine word, "legitimate"!
     Well, my legitimate, if this letter speed°   *prosper*

2. Even in the prime of his life, he was stormy and unpredictable.
3. Long-implanted habit.
4. Angry, dominated by the hot and dry choleric humor.
5. Impulsive outbursts.
6. Ceremony.
7. Agree.
8. If our father continues to boss us around with his usual imperiousness, this most recent display of willfulness will do us nothing but harm.

9. While the iron is hot.
1. Location: The Earl of Gloucester's house.
2. The force that governs the material world through mechanistic and amoral forces.
3. Why should I submit to the injustice of convention and allow arbitrary social gradations to deprive me because I am 12 to 14 months younger than a brother?
4. Whose begetting in the sexual act requires and engenders a fuller mixture and more energetic force.

20   And my invention thrive, Edmund the base
        Shall top th' legitimate. I grow, I prosper.
        Now, gods, stand up for bastards!
        [*Enter Gloucester.*]
GLOUCESTER: Kent banished thus? And France in choler,° parted?   *anger*
        And the King gone tonight? Prescribed° his power,   *limited*
25   Confined to exhibition?° All this done   *an allowance of money*
        Upon the gad?° Edmund, how now? What news?   *suddenly*
EDMUND: So please Your Lordship, none.

                                              [(*Putting up the letter.*)]
GLOUCESTER: Why so earnestly seek you to put up that letter?
EDMUND: I know no news, my lord.
GLOUCESTER: What paper were you reading?
EDMUND: Nothing, my lord.
GLOUCESTER: No? What needed then that terrible dispatch[5] of it into your
        pocket? The quality of nothing hath not such need to hide itself. Let's see.
        Come, if it be nothing I shall not need spectacles.
EDMUND: I beseech you, sir, pardon me. It is a letter from my brother, that I have
        not all o'erread; and for so much as I have perused, I find it not fit for your
        o'erlooking.
GLOUCESTER: Give me the letter, sir.
EDMUND: I shall offend either to detain or give it. The contents, as in part I
40   understand them, are to blame.[6]
GLOUCESTER: Let's see, let's see.   [(*Edmund gives the letter.*)]
EDMUND: I hope for my brother's justification he wrote this but as an essay or
        taste[7] of my virtue.
GLOUCESTER [(*reads*)]: "This policy and reverence of age makes the world bitter
45   to the best of our times,[8] keeps our fortunes from us till our oldness cannot
        relish them. I begin to find an idle and fond[9] bondage in the oppression of
        aged tyranny, who sways not as it hath power but as it is suffered.[1] Come
        to me, that of this I may speak more. If our father would sleep till I waked
        him, you should enjoy half his revenue forever and live the beloved of
50   your brother, Edgar." Hum! Conspiracy! "Sleep till I waked him, you
        should enjoy half his revenue." My son Edgar! Had he a hand to write
        this? A heart and brain to breed it in? When came you to this? Who
        brought it?
EDMUND: It was not brought me, my lord; there's the cunning of it. I found it
55   thrown in at the casement of my closet.
GLOUCESTER: You know the character[2] to be your brother's?
EDMUND: If the matter[3] were good, my lord, I durst swear it were his; but in
        respect of that I would fain[4] think it were not.

---

5. Fearful quick disposal.
6. The Folio reading "too blame," "too blameworthy to be shown," may be correct.
7. Trial or test.
8. This policy of reverencing old age makes the best years of our lives bitter.

9. Useless and foolish.
1. Permitted.
2. Handwriting.
3. Contents.
4. Gladly.

GLOUCESTER: It is his.

EDMUND: It is his hand, my lord, but I hope his heart is not in the contents.

GLOUCESTER: Has he never before sounded you in this business?

EDMUND: Never, my lord. But I have heard him oft maintain it to be fit that, sons at perfect age and fathers declined,[5] the father should be as ward to the son, and the son manage his revenue.

GLOUCESTER: Oh, villain, villain! His very opinion in the letter! Abhorred villain! Unnatural, detested, brutish villain! Worse than brutish! Go, sirrah, seek him. I'll apprehend him. Abominable villain! Where is he?

EDMUND: I do not well know, my lord. If it shall please you to suspend your indignation against my brother till you can derive from him better testimony of
70   his intent, you should run a certain course; where, if you violently proceed against him, mistaking his purpose, it would make a great gap in your own honor and shake in pieces the heart of his obedience. I dare pawn down[6] my life for him that he hath writ this to feel my affection to Your Honor, and to no other pretense of danger.

GLOUCESTER: Think you so?

EDMUND: If Your Honor judge it meet, I will place you where you shall hear us confer of this, and by an auricular assurance have your satisfaction,[7] and that without any further delay than this very evening.

GLOUCESTER: He cannot be such a monster—

EDMUND: Nor is not, sure.

GLOUCESTER: To his father, that so tenderly and entirely loves him. Heaven and earth! Edmund, seek him out; wind me into him,[8] I pray you. Frame the business after your own wisdom. I would unstate myself to be in a due resolution.[9]

EDMUND: I will seek him, sir, presently,[1] convey the business as I shall find means, and acquaint you withal.

GLOUCESTER: These late[2] eclipses in the sun and moon portend no good to us. Though the wisdom of nature can reason it thus and thus, yet nature finds itself scourged by the sequent effects.[3] Love cools, friendship falls off, broth-
90   ers divide; in cities, mutinies; in countries, discord; in palaces, treason; and the bond cracked twixt son and father. This villain of mine comes under the prediction; there's son against father. The King falls from bias of nature;[4] there's father against child. We have seen the best of our time. Machinations, hollowness, treachery, and all ruinous disorders follow us
95   disquietly to our graves. Find out this villain, Edmund; it shall lose thee nothing.[5] Do it carefully. And the noble and truehearted Kent banished! His offense, honesty! 'Tis strange.   *Exit.*

EDMUND: This is the excellent foppery[6] of the world, that when we are sick in fortune — often the surfeits of our own behavior[7]—we make guilty of our disasters
100   the sun, the moon, and stars, as if we were villains on necessity, fools

---

5. Sons at full maturity and father having become feeble.
6. Stake.
7. Satisfy yourself as to the truth by what you hear.
8. Insinuate yourself into his confidence.
9. I would give up my rank and wealth to know the truth.
1. Immediately.
2. Recent.

3. Though natural science explains these eclipses, nature is tortured by the devastating consequences.
4. Natural inclination.
5. Earn you a reward.
6. Foolishness.
7. Consequences of our own overindulgence.

by heavenly compulsion, knaves, thieves, and treachers[8] by spherical predominance,[9] drunkards, liars, and adulterers by an enforced obedience of planetary influence, and all that we are evil in, by a divine thrusting on. An admirable evasion of whoremaster man, to lay his goatish[1] disposition
105   on the charge[2] of a star! My father compounded with my mother under the Dragon's tail[3] and my nativity was under Ursa Major,[4] so that it follows I am rough and lecherous. Fut, I should have been that I am, had the maidenliest star in the firmament twinkled on my bastardizing. Edgar—
[Enter Edgar.]
            and pat[5] he comes like the catastrophe of the old comedy. My cue is vil-
110   lainous melancholy, with a sigh like Tom o' Bedlam.[6]—Oh, these eclipses do portend these divisions![7] Fa, sol, la, mi.
EDGAR: How now, brother Edmund, what serious contemplation are you in?
EDMUND: I am thinking, brother, of a prediction I read this other day, what should follow these eclipses.
EDGAR: Do you busy yourself with that?
EDMUND: I promise you, the effects he writes of succeed unhappily,[8] as of unnatu-ralness between the child and the parent, death, dearth, dissolutions of ancient amities, divisions in state, menaces and maledictions against king and nobles, needless diffidences,[9] banishment of friends, dissipation of
120   cohorts, nuptial breaches, and I know not what.
EDGAR: How long have you been a sectary astronomical?[1]
EDMUND: Come, come, when saw you my father last?
EDGAR: The night gone by.
EDMUND: Spake you with him?
EDGAR: Ay, two hours together.
EDMUND: Parted you in good terms? Found you no displeasure in him by word nor countenance?
EDGAR: None at all.
EDMUND: Bethink yourself wherein you may have offended him, and at my en-
130   treaty forbear his presence[2] until some little time hath qualified the heat of his displeasure, which at this instant so rageth in him that with the mis-chief of your person[3] it would scarcely allay.
EDGAR: Some villain hath done me wrong.
EDMUND: That's my fear. I pray you, have a continent forbearance till the speed
135   of his rage goes slower; and, as I say, retire with me to my lodging, from whence I will fitly bring you to hear my lord speak. Pray ye, go! There's my key. [He gives a key.] If you do stir abroad, go armed.
EDGAR: Armed, brother?
EDMUND: Brother, I advise you to the best. I am no honest man if there be
140   any good meaning toward you. I have told you what I have seen and

---

8. Traitors.
9. Astrological determination.
1. Lecherous.
2. To the responsibility of.
3. My father had sex with my mother under the constella-tion Draco.
4. The big bear or dipper.
5. On cue, like the resolution (of a play).

6. A lunatic patient of Bethlehem Hospital in London turned out to beg for his own bread.
7. Family and social conflicts.
8. Follow unluckily.
9. Groundless distrust of others.
1. Astronomical believer.
2. Avoid meeting him.
3. With the harmful effect of your presence.

heard, but faintly, nothing like the image and horror of it. Pray you,
140   away.
EDGAR: Shall I hear from you anon?
EDMUND: I do serve you in this business.   [Exit (Edgar).]
145   A credulous father and a brother noble,
       Whose nature is so far from doing harms
       That he suspects none; on whose foolish honesty
       My practices ride easy. I see the business.
       Let me, if not by birth, have lands by wit.
       All with me's meet that I can fashion fit.   [Exit.]

                              Scene 3⁴

       [Enter Goneril, and (Oswald, her) steward.]
GONERIL: Did my father strike my gentleman for chiding of his fool?
OSWALD: Ay, madam.
GONERIL: By day and night he wrongs me! Every hour
       He flashes into one gross crime° or other   offense
5   That sets us all at odds. I'll not endure it.
       His knights grow riotous, and himself upbraids us
       On every trifle. When he returns from hunting
       I will not speak with him. Say I am sick.
       If you come slack⁵ of former services
10   You shall do well; the fault of it I'll answer.
                                                             [(Horns within.)]
OSWALD: He's coming, madam. I hear him.
GONERIL: Put on what weary negligence you please,
       You and your fellows. I'd have it come to question.°   be made an issue
       If he distaste° it, let him to my sister,   dislike
15   Whose mind and mine, I know, in that are one,
       Not to be overruled. Idle old man,
       That still would manage those authorities
       That he hath given away! Now, by my life,
       Old fools are babes again, and must be used
20   With checks as flatteries, when they are seen abused.⁶
       Remember what I have said.
OSWALD: Well, madam.
GONERIL: And let his knights have colder looks among you.
       What grows of it, no matter. Advise your fellows so.
25   I would breed from hence occasions, and I shall,
       That I may speak.⁷ I'll write straight to my sister
       To hold my very course. Prepare for dinner.   [Exeunt.]

4. Location: The Duke of Albany's palace.
5. Fall short of.
6. Old fools . . . must be treated with rebukes in place of
flatteries, when such flattery is seen to be taken advantage of.
7. Speak bluntly.

Scene 4

[Enter Kent (disguised)].

KENT: If but as well[8] I other accents borrow
    That can my speech diffuse,[9] my good intent
    May carry through itself to that full issue
    For which I razed my likeness.[1] Now, banished Kent,
5   If thou canst serve where thou dost stand condemned,
    So may it come[2] thy master, whom thou lov'st,
    Shall find thee full of labors.

[Horns within. Enter Lear, (Knights,) and attendants.]

LEAR: Let me not stay° a jot for dinner. Go get it ready.   *wait*

                                        [(Exit an Attendant.)]

    [(To Kent)] How now, what art thou?

KENT: A man, sir.

LEAR: What dost thou profess?[3] What wouldst thou with us?

KENT: I do profess to be no less than I seem: to serve him truly that will put me in
    trust, to love him that is honest, to converse with him that is wise and says
    little, to fear judgment, to fight when I cannot choose, and to eat no fish.[4]

LEAR: What art thou?

KENT: A very honest-hearted fellow, and as poor as the King.

LEAR: If thou be'st as poor for a subject as he's for a king, thou'rt poor enough.
    What wouldst thou?

KENT: Service.

LEAR: Who wouldst thou serve?

KENT: You.

LEAR: Dost thou know me, fellow?

KENT: No, sir, but you have that in your countenance[5] which I would fain call
    master.

LEAR: What's that?

KENT: Authority.

LEAR: What services canst do?

KENT: I can keep honest counsel,[6] ride, run, mar a curious[7] tale in telling it, and
    deliver a plain message bluntly. That which ordinary men are fit for I am
30   qualified in, and the best of me is diligence.

LEAR: How old art thou?

KENT: Not so young, sir, to love a woman for singing, nor so old to dote on her for
    anything. I have years on my back forty-eight.

LEAR: Follow me; thou shalt serve me. If I like thee no worse after dinner, I will
35   not part from thee yet.—Dinner, ho, dinner! Where's my knave, my fool?
    Go you and call my fool hither.   *[(Exit one.)]*

[Enter steward (Oswald).]

    You! You, sirrah, where's my daughter?

---

8. As well as I have disguised myself by means of costume.
9. Render confused or indistinct.
1. May achieve the desired result for which I scraped off my beard and erased my outward appearance.
2. Come to pass that.
3. What is your special calling? (But Kent puns in his answer on *profess* meaning "to claim.")
4. To be a meat eater, or to be a good Protestant (?).
5. Face and bearing.
6. Keep confidences.
7. Ornate.

OSWALD: So please you—   *[Exit.]*
LEAR: What says the fellow there? Call the clodpoll[8] back.   *[(Exit a knight.)]*
40   Where's my fool, ho? I think the world's asleep.
    [(Enter Knight.)]
        How now? Where's that mongrel?
KNIGHT: He says, my lord, your daughter is not well.
LEAR: Why came not the slave back to me when I called him?
KNIGHT: Sir, he answered me in the roundest[9] manner, he would not.
LEAR: He would not?
KNIGHT: My lord, I know not what the matter is, but to my judgment Your
    Highness is not entertained[1] with that ceremonious affection as you were
    wont. There's a great abatement of kindness appears as well in the general
    dependents as in the Duke himself also and your daughter.
LEAR: Ha? Say'st thou so?
KNIGHT: I beseech you, pardon me, my lord, if I be mistaken, for my duty cannot
    be silent when I think Your Highness wronged.
LEAR: Thou but rememberest[2] me of mine own conception. I have perceived a
    most faint neglect of late, which I have rather blamed as mine own jealous
55   curiosity[3] than as a very pretense and purpose of unkindness. I will look fur-
    ther into't. But where's my fool? I have not seen him this two days.
KNIGHT: Since my young lady's going into France, sir, the Fool hath much pined
    away.
LEAR: No more of that. I have noted it well. Go you and tell my daughter I would
60   speak with her.   *[(Exit one.)]*
        Go you call hither my fool.   *[(Exit one.)]*
    [Enter steward (Oswald).]
        Oh, you, sir, you, come you hither, sir. Who am I, sir?
OSWALD: My lady's father.
LEAR: "My lady's father"? My lord's knave! You whoreson dog, you slave, you cur!
OSWALD: I am none of these, my lord, I beseech your pardon.
LEAR: Do you bandy looks[4] with me, you rascal?
                                                            [(He strikes Oswald.)]
OSWALD: I'll not be strucken, my lord.
KENT: Nor tripped neither, you base football[5] player.
                                                            [(He trips up Oswald's heels.)]
LEAR: I thank thee, fellow. Thou serv'st me, and I'll love thee.
KENT: Come, sir, arise, away! I'll teach you differences. Away, away! If you will
    measure your lubber's length again,[6] tarry; but away! Go to. Have you
    wisdom? So.
                                                            [(He pushes Oswald out.)]
LEAR: Now, my friendly knave, I thank thee. There's earnest of thy service.
                                                            [(He gives Kent money.)]
    [Enter Fool.]

---

8. Blockhead.
9. Bluntest.
1. Treated.
2. Remind.
3. Overly scrupulous regard for etiquette.

4. Exchange glances (in such a way as to imply that Oswald and Lear are social equals).
5. Football, a raucous street game played by the lower classes.
6. If you want to be laid out flat again, you clumsy ox.

FOOL: Let me hire him too. Here's my coxcomb.

[(*Offering Kent his cap.*)]

LEAR: How now, my pretty knave, how dost thou?

FOOL [(*to Kent*)]: Sirrah, you were best take my coxcomb.

KENT: Why, Fool?

FOOL: Why? For taking one's part that's out of favor. Nay, an thou canst not smile
as the wind sits, thou'lt catch cold shortly. There, take my coxcomb. Why,
80   this fellow has banished two on 's daughters[7] and did the third a blessing
against his will. If thou follow him, thou must needs wear my coxcomb.—
How now, nuncle? Would I had two coxcombs and two daughters.

LEAR: Why, my boy?

FOOL: If I gave them all my living,[8] I'd keep my coxcombs myself. There's mine;
85   beg another of thy daughters.[9]

LEAR: Take heed, sirrah—the whip.

FOOL: Truth's a dog must to kennel. He must be whipped out, when the Lady
Brach[1] may stand by th' fire and stink.

LEAR: A pestilent gall[2] to me!

FOOL: Sirrah, I'll teach thee a speech.

LEAR: Do.

FOOL: Mark it, nuncle:
Have more than thou showest,
Speak less than thou knowest,
95   Lend less than thou owest,
Ride more than thou goest,°   *walk*
Learn° more than thou trowest,°   *listen to / believe*
Set less than thou throwest;[3]
Leave thy drink and thy whore,
100   And keep in-a-door,
And thou shalt have more
Than two tens to a score.[4]

KENT: This is nothing, Fool.

FOOL: Then 'tis like the breath of an unfee'd lawyer;[5] you gave me nothing for't.
105   Can you make no use of nothing, nuncle?

LEAR: Why, no, boy. Nothing can be made out of nothing.

FOOL [*to Kent*]: Prithee, tell him; so much the rent of his land comes to. He will
not believe a fool.

LEAR: A bitter° fool!   *satirical*

FOOL: Dost know the difference, my boy, between a bitter fool and a sweet one?

LEAR: No, lad. Teach me.

FOOL: That lord that counseled thee
    To give away thy land,
Come place him here by me;

7. Paradoxically, by giving Goneril and Regan his kingdom, Lear has lost them.
8. Property.
9. Beg for the coxcomb that you deserve for dealing with
your daughters as you did.
1. Bitch hound (likened to Goneril and Regan who
have been given favored places despite their reeking of
dishonest flattery.)
2. Irritation.
3. Don't stake everything on a single throw.
4. You will more than break even, since a score equals
two tens.
5. It is free and useless advice (Lawyers, being proverbially
mercenary, would not give good advice unless paid well.

115   Do thou for him stand.
           The sweet and bitter fool.
               Will presently appear:
           The one in motley[6] here,
               The other found out there.[7]
LEAR: Dost thou call me fool, boy?
FOOL: All thy other titles thou hast given away; that thou wast born with.
KENT: This is not altogether fool, my lord.
FOOL: No, faith, lords and great men will not let me;[8] if I had a monopoly out,
           they would have part on't. And ladies too, they will not let me have all the
125   fool to myself; they'll be snatching. Nuncle, give me an egg and I'll give
           thee two crowns.
LEAR: What two crowns shall they be?
FOOL: Why, after I have cut the egg i'th' middle and eat up the meat, the two
           crowns of the egg. When thou clovest thy crown i'th' middle and gav'st
130   away both parts, thou bor'st thine ass on thy back o'er the dirt. Thou hadst
           little wit in thy bald crown when thou gav'st thy golden one away. If I
           speak like myself in this, let him be whipped that first finds it so.[9]
           [(Sings)] "Fools had ne'er less grace in a year,
               For wise men are grown foppish
135   And know not how their wits to wear,
               Their manners are so apish."[1]
LEAR: When were you wont to be so full of songs, sirrah?
FOOL: I have used[2] it, nuncle, e'er since thou mad'st thy daughters thy mothers; for
           when thou gav'st them the rod and putt'st down thine own breeches,
140   [(Sings)] "Then they for sudden joy did weep,
               And I for sorrow sung,
           That such a king should play bo-peep
               And go the fools among."
           Prithee, nuncle, keep a schoolmaster that can teach thy fool to lie. I would
145   fain learn to lie.
LEAR: An[3] you lie, sirrah, we'll have you whipped.
FOOL: I marvel what kin thou and thy daughters are. They'll have me whipped
           for speaking true, thou'lt have me whipped for lying, and sometimes I
           am whipped for holding my peace. I had rather be any kind o' thing
150   than a fool. And yet I would not be thee, nuncle. Thou hast pared thy
           wit o' both sides and left nothing i'th' middle. Here comes one o' th'
           parings.
        [Enter Goneril.]
LEAR: How now, daughter? What makes that frontlet on?[4] You are too much of
           late i'th' frown.

6. The parti-colored dress of the professional fool.
7. The Fool points at Lear, the "bitter" fool.
8. Great persons at court will not let me monopolize folly.
9. If I speak like a fool in saying this, let the first person to discover the truth be whipped (since in this corrupt world those who speak the truth are punished for doing so.
1. Fools have never been so out of favor, for wise men foppishly trade places with the fools and no longer know how to show off their wits to advantage, they have grown so foolish in their manners.
2. Practiced.
3. If.
4. What is that frown doing on your forehead?

FOOL: Thou wast a pretty fellow when thou hadst no need to care for her frowning; now thou art an O with-out a figure.[5] I am better than thou art now; I
am a fool, thou art nothing. [*To Goneril*] Yes, forsooth, I will hold my
tongue; so your face bids me, though you say nothing.
      Mum, mum,
160   He that keeps nor crust nor crumb,
            Weary of all, shall want some.[6]
      [(*Pointing to Lear*)] That's a shelled peascod.[7]
GONERIL: Not only, sir, this your all-licensed[8] fool,
            But other of your insolent retinue
165   Do hourly carp and quarrel, breaking forth
            In rank and not-to-be-endurèd riots. Sir,
            I had thought by making this well known unto you
            To have found a safe redress, but now grow fearful,
            By what yourself too late° have spoke and done,   *recently*
170   That you protect this course and put it on°   *encourage it*
            By your allowance; which if you should, the fault
            Would not scape censure, nor the redresses sleep
            Which in the tender of a wholesome weal
            Might in their working do you that offense,
175   Which else were shame, that then necessity
            Will call discreet proceeding.[9]
FOOL: For you know, nuncle,
            "The hedge sparrow fed the cuckoo[1] so long
            That it had its head bit off by it young."
180   So, out went the candle, and we were left darkling.[2]
LEAR [(*to Goneril*)]: Are you our daughter?
GONERIL: I would you would make use of your good wisdom,
            Whereof I know you are fraught, and put away
            These dispositions which of late transport you
185   From what you rightly are.
FOOL: May not an ass know when the cart draws the horse? Whoop, Jug![3] I love
            thee.
LEAR: Does any here know me? This is not Lear.
            Does Lear walk thus, speak thus? Where are his eyes?
190   Either his notion[4] weakens, or his discernings
            Are lethargied[5]—Ha! Waking? 'Tis not so.
            Who is it that can tell me who I am?
FOOL: Lear's shadow.
LEAR: I would learn that[6]; for, by the marks of sovereignty,
195   Knowledge, and reason, I should be false persuaded

---

5. A zero, unless preceded by a digit.
6. That person who, having grown weary of his possessions, gives all away, will find himself in need of part of
what is gone.
7. A peapod empty of its contents.
8. Allowed to speak or act as he pleases.
9. Nor would the punishment remain unused, which out
of care for the common good, might prove unpleasant to
you—proceedings that the stern necessity of the times

will regard as prudent even if under normal circumstances
they might seem shameful.
1. Cuckoo, a bird that lays its eggs in other birds' nests.
2. In the dark.
3. Jug is a nickname for Joan and can also mean whore.
4. Intellectual power.
5. Or his faculties are asleep.
6. Who I am.

I had daughters.[7]

FOOL: Which they will make an obedient father.

LEAR: Your name, fair gentlewoman?

GONERIL: This admiration,[8] sir, is much o'th' savor
200　　Of other your new pranks. I do beseech you
　　　To understand my purposes aright.
　　　As you are old and reverend, should be wise.
　　　Here do you keep a hundred knights and squires,
　　　Men so disordered, so debauched and bold
205　　That this our court, infected with their manners,
　　　Shows like a riotous inn. Epicurism[9] and lust
　　　Makes it more like a tavern or a brothel
　　　Than a graced palace. The shame itself doth speak
　　　For instant remedy. Be then desired,°　　　　　　　　　requested
210　　By her that else will take the thing she begs,
　　　A little to disquantity your train,[1]
　　　And the remainders that shall still depend
　　　To be such men as may besort your age,
　　　Which know themselves and you.

LEAR:　　　　　　　　　　　　Darkness and devils!
215　　Saddle my horses! Call my train together!　　　　　　[(Exit one.)]
　　　Degenerate bastard, I'll not trouble thee.
　　　Yet have I left a daughter.

GONERIL: You strike my people, and your disordered rabble
　　　Make servants of their betters.
　　　[Enter Albany.]

LEAR: Woe, that too late repents!—Oh, sir, are you come?
　　　Is it your will? Speak, sir—Prepare my horses.
　　　　　　　　　　　　　　　　　　　　　　　　　[(Exit one.)]

　　　Ingratitude, thou marble-hearted fiend,
　　　More hideous when thou show'st thee in a child
225　　Than the sea monster!

ALBANY: Pray, sir, be patient.

LEAR [(to Goneril)]:　　　　　Detested kite,° thou liest!　　　bird of prey
　　　My train are men of choice and rarest parts,
　　　That all particulars of duty know
　　　And in the most exact regard support
230　　The worships of their name. Oh, most small fault,
　　　How ugly didst thou in Cordelia show!
　　　Which, like an engine, wrenched my frame of nature
　　　From the fixed place,[2] drew from my heart all love,
　　　And added to the gall. Oh, Lear, Lear, Lear!
235　　Beat at this gate [striking his head] that let thy folly in
　　　And thy dear judgment out!—Go, go, my people.
　　　　　　　　　　　　　　　　　　　　　　　　[Exeunt some.]

---

7. All these outward signs of kingly status and sanity would seem to suggest falsely that I am a man who had daughters.
8. Wonderment.

9. Hedonism.
1. Diminish the number of your attendants.
2. Which like a powerful mechanical contrivance wrenched my natural affection away from where it belonged.

ALBANY: My lord, I am guiltless as I am ignorant
    Of what hath moved you.
LEAR: It may be so, my lord.—
    Hear, Nature, hear! Dear goddess, hear!
240   Suspend thy purpose if thou didst intend
    To make this creature fruitful!
    Into her womb convey sterility;
    Dry up in her the organs of increase,
    And from her derogate° body never spring   *debased*
245   A babe to honor her! If she must teem,°   *produce offspring*
    Create her child of spleen,³ that it may live
    And be a thwart disnatured torment to her!
    Let it stamp wrinkles in her brow of youth,
    With cadent° tears fret channels in her cheeks,   *cascading*
250   Turn all her mother's pains and benefits
    To laughter and contempt, that she may feel
    How sharper than a serpent's tooth it is
    To have a thankless child! Away, away!
                      [Exit (with Kent and the rest of Lear's followers).]
ALBANY: Now, gods that we adore, whereof comes this?
GONERIL: Never afflict yourself to know more of it,
    But let his disposition have that scope
    As dotage gives it.
    [Enter Lear.]
LEAR: What, fifty of my followers at a clap?
    Within a fortnight?
ALBANY: What's the matter, sir?
LEAR: I'll tell thee. [(*To Goneril*)] Life and death! I am ashamed
    That thou hast power to shake my manhood thus,
    That these hot tears, which break from me perforce,
    Should make thee worth them. Blasts and fogs upon thee!
    Th'untented⁴ woundings of a father's curse
265   Pierce every sense about thee! Old fond eyes,
    Beweep this cause again, I'll pluck ye out
    And cast you, with the waters that you loose,⁵
    To temper clay.⁶ Yea, is't come to this?
    Ha! Let it be so. I have another daughter,
270   Who, I am sure, is kind and comfortable.°   *comforting*
    When she shall hear this of thee, with her nails
    She'll flay thy wolvish visage. Thou shalt find
    That I'll resume the shape which thou dost think
    I have cast off forever.   *[Exit.]*
GONERIL [(*to Albany*)]:   Do you mark that?
ALBANY: I cannot be so partial, Goneril,
    To the great love I bear you—

---

3. Violent ill nature.
4. Too deep to be probed.

5. Let loose in tears.
6. To mix with earth.

GONERIL: Pray you, content.—What, Oswald, ho!
    [(*To the Fool*)] You, sir, more knave than fool, after your master.
FOOL: Nuncle Lear, nuncle Lear! Tarry, take the Fool with thee.[7]
280   A fox, when one has caught her,
    And such a daughter
    Should sure to the slaughter,
    If my cap would buy a halter.
    So the Fool follows after.   *[Exit.]*
GONERIL: This man hath had good counsel. A hundred knights?
    'Tis politic and safe to let him keep
    At point a hundred knights—yes, that on every dream,
    Each buzz, each fancy, each complaint, dislike,
    He may enguard his dotage with their powers
290   And hold our lives in mercy—Oswald, I say!
ALBANY: Well, you may fear too far.
GONERIL: Safer than trust too far.
    Let me still take away the harms I fear,
    Not fear still to be taken.[8] I know his heart.
295   What he hath uttered I have writ my sister.
    If she sustain him and his hundred knights
    When I have showed th'unfitness—
    [Enter steward (Oswald).]
                How now, Oswald?
    What, have you writ that letter to my sister?
OSWALD: Ay, madam.
GONERIL: Take you some company and away to horse.
    Inform her full of my particular fear,
    And thereto add such reasons of your own
    As may compact° if more. Get you gone,   *confirm*
    And hasten your return.   (*Exit Oswald.*)
              No, no, my lord,
305   This milky gentleness and course[9] of yours
    Though I condemn not, yet, under pardon,
    You're much more attasked for want of wisdom
    Than praised for harmful mildness.
ALBANY: How far your eyes may pierce I cannot tell.
310   Striving to better, oft we mar what's well.
GONERIL: Nay, then—
ALBANY: Well, well, th'event.[1]   *[Exeunt.]*

Scene 5[2]

[Enter Lear, Kent (disguised as Caius), and Fool.]
LEAR [*giving a letter to Kent*]: Go you before to Gloucester[3] with these letters.
    Acquaint my daughter no further with anything you know than comes from

---

7. Take me with you, and take the name "fool" with you.
8. Rather than always be in fear of being taken prisoner by such harms.
9. Effeminate and gentle way.

1. Time will tell.
2. Location: Before Albany's palace.
3. The city in Gloucestershire.

her demand out of the letter. If your diligence be not speedy, I shall be there afore you.

KENT: I will not sleep, my lord, till I have delivered your letter.   [*Exit.*]

FOOL: If a man's brains were in 's heels, were't not in danger of kibes?[4]

LEAR: Ay, boy.

FOOL: Then, I prithee, be merry. Thy wit shall not go slipshod.[5]

LEAR: Ha, ha, ha!

FOOL: Shalt see thy other daughter will use thee kindly,[6] for though she's as like this as a crab's like an apple, yet I can tell what I can tell.

LEAR: What canst tell, boy?

FOOL: She will taste as like this as a crab does to a crab.[7] Thou canst tell why one's nose stands i'th' middle on 's face?

LEAR: No.

FOOL: Why, to keep one's eyes of either side 's[8] nose, that what a man cannot smell out he may spy into.

LEAR: I did her wrong.

FOOL: Canst tell how an oyster makes his shell?

LEAR: No.

FOOL: Nor I neither. But I can tell why a snail has a house.

LEAR: Why?

FOOL: Why, to put 's head in, not to give it away to his daughters and leave his horns without a case.[9]

LEAR: I will forget my nature.[1] So kind a father!—Be my horses ready?

FOOL: Thy asses are gone about 'em. The reason why the seven stars are no more than seven is a pretty reason.

LEAR: Because they are not eight.

FOOL: Yes, indeed. Thou wouldst make a good fool.

LEAR: To take't again perforce! Monster ingratitude!

FOOL: If thou wert my fool, nuncle, I'd have thee beaten for being old before thy time.

LEAR: How's that?

FOOL: Thou shouldst not have been old till thou hadst been wise.

LEAR: Oh, let me not be mad, not mad, sweet heaven!
Keep me in temper; I would not be mad!

[(*Enter Gentleman.*)]

How now, are the horses ready?

GENTLEMAN: Ready, my lord.

LEAR: Come, boy.   [*Exeunt (Lear and Gentleman).*]

FOOL: She that's a maid now, and laughs at my departure,
Shall not be a maid long, unless things[2] be cut shorter.[3]   [(*Exit.*)]

---

4. Wouldn't his brains be in danger of that common affliction of the heel called chilblains?

5. Your brains would have no need for slippers to avoid chafing the chilblains, since you have no brains.

6. With the natural kindness or "relatedness" of child to father; according to her own "kind" or nature.

7. Crabapple.

8. Of his.

9. The snail's head and horns are unendangered with its case or shell; Lear conversely, has given away his crown to his daughters, leaving his brows unadorned and vulnerable.

1. Natural affection.

2. Penises.

3. A bawdy joke addressed to the audience.

ACT 2

Scene 1[4]

[*Enter Bastard (Edmund) and Curan, severally.*[5]]

EDMUND: Save thee, Curan.

CURAN: And you, sir. I have been with your father and given him notice that the
Duke of Cornwall and Regan his duchess will be here with him this night.

EDMUND: How comes that?

CURAN: Nay, I know not. You have heard of the news abroad[6]—I mean the whispered ones, for they are yet but ear-kissing arguments?

EDMUND: Not I. Pray you, what are they?

CURAN: Have you heard of no likely wars toward[7] twixt the Dukes of Cornwall
and Albany?

EDMUND: Not a word.

CURAN: You may do, then, in time. Fare you well, sir.

[*Exit.*]

EDMUND: The Duke be here tonight? The better! Best!
This weaves itself perforce into my business.
My father hath set guard to take my brother,
15   And I have one thing, of a queasy question,[8]
Which I must act. Briefness and fortune, work!—
Brother, a word. Descend. Brother, I say!

[*Enter Edgar.*]

My father watches. Oh, sir, fly this place!
Intelligence is given where you are hid.
20   You have now the good advantage of the night.
Have you not spoken 'gainst the Duke of Cornwall?
He's coming hither, now, i'th' night, i'th' haste,
And Regan with him. Have you nothing said
Upon his party 'gainst the Duke of Albany?
25   Advise yourself.[9]

EDGAR: I am sure on't, not a word.

EDMUND: I hear my father coming. Pardon me;
In cunning I must draw my sword upon you.
Draw. Seem to defend yourself. Now, quit you well.—

[(*They draw.*)]

Yield! Come before my father!—Light, ho, here!—
30   Fly, brother.—Torches, torches!—So farewell.

[*Exit Edgar.*]

Some blood drawn on me would beget opinion
Of my more fierce endeavor.[1] I have seen drunkards
Do more than this in sport. [(*He wounds himself in the arm.*)] Father, father!
Stop, stop! No help?

[*Enter Gloucester, and servants with torches.*]

---

4. Location: The Earl of Gloucester's house.
5. Separately.
6. Going the rounds.
7. Impending.

8. Not for queasy stomachs.
9. Consider your situation.
1. Create an impression of my having fought fiercely.

GLOUCESTER: Now, Edmund, where's the villain?
EDMUND: Here stood he in the dark, his sharp sword out,
          Mumbling of wicked charms, conjuring the moon
          To stand's² auspicious mistress.
GLOUCESTER: But where is he?
EDMUND: Look, sir, I bleed.
GLOUCESTER: Where is the villain, Edmund?
EDMUND: Fled this way, sir. When by no means he could—
GLOUCESTER: Pursue him, ho! Go after. [*Exeunt some servants.*] By no means what?
EDMUND: Persuade me to the murder of Your Lordship,
          But that I told him the revenging gods
          'Gainst parricides did all the thunder bend,°   *aim*
          Spoke with how manifold and strong a bond
45   The child was bound to th' father; sir, in fine,
          Seeing how loathly opposite³ I stood
          To his unnatural purpose, in fell motion
          With his preparèd sword he charges home
          My unprovided° body, latched° mine arm;   *unprotected / nicked*
50   And when he saw my best alarumed spirits,
          Bold in the quarrel's right, roused to th'encounter,
          Or whether ghasted° by the noise I made,   *frightened*
          Full suddenly he fled.
GLOUCESTER: Let him fly far.
          Not in this land shall he remain uncaught;
55   And found—dispatch.⁴ The noble Duke my master,
          My worthy arch and patron,⁵ comes tonight.
          By his authority I will proclaim it
          That he which finds him shall deserve our thanks,
          Bringing the murderous coward to the stake;
60   He that conceals him, death.
EDMUND: When I dissuaded him from his intent
          And found him pight° to do it, with curst speech   *determined*
          I threatened to discover° him. He replied,   *expose*
          "Thou unpossessing° bastard, dost thou think,   *unable to inherit*
65   If I would stand against thee, would the reposal,°   *placing*
          Of any trust, virtue, or worth in thee
          Make thy words faithed? No. What I should deny—
          As this I would, ay, though thou didst produce
          My very character—I'd turn it all
70   To thy suggestion,° plot, and damnèd practice;°   *handwriting / scheming*
          And thou must make a dullard of the world
          If they not thought the profits of my death

---

2. Act as his.
3. Loathingly opposed.

4. That will be the end for him.
5. Chief patron.

Were very pregnant and potential spirits
75   To make thee seek it."[6]

GLOUCESTER: Oh, strange and fastened° villain!   *hardened*
Would he deny his letter, said he?
I never got him.   [*Tucket within.*[7]]
Hark, the Duke's trumpets! I know not why he comes.
All ports[8] I'll bar; the villain shall not scape.
The Duke must grant me that. Besides, his picture
80   I will send far and near, that all the kingdom
May have due note of him; and of my land,
Loyal and natural[9] boy, I'll work the means
To make thee capable.[1]

[*Enter Cornwall, Regan, and attendants.*]

CORNWALL: How now, my noble friend? Since I came hither,
Which I can call but now, I have heard strange news.

REGAN: If it be true, all vengeance comes too short
Which can pursue th'offender. How dost, my lord?

GLOUCESTER: Oh madam, my old heart is cracked, it's cracked!

REGAN: What, did my father's godson seek your life?
He whom my father named? Your Edgar?

GLOUCESTER: Oh, lady, lady, shame would have it hid!

REGAN: Was he not companion with the riotous knights
That tended upon my father?

GLOUCESTER: I know not, madam. 'Tis too bad, too bad.

EDMUND: Yes, madam, he was of that consort.°   *crew*

REGAN: No marvel, then, though° he were ill affected.   *if*
'Tis they have put him on[2] the old man's death,
To have th'expense and spoil of his revenues.
I have this present evening from my sister
100   Been well informed of them, and with such cautions
That if they come to sojourn at my house
I'll not be there.

CORNWALL: Nor I, assure thee, Regan.
Edmund, I hear that you have shown your father
105   A childlike office.

EDMUND: It was my duty, sir.

GLOUCESTER [(*to Cornwall*)]: He did bewray his practice,[3] and received
This hurt you see striving to apprehend° him.   *arrest*

CORNWALL: Is he pursued?

GLOUCESTER: Ay, my good lord.

CORNWALL: If he be taken, he shall never more
110   Be feared of doing harm. Make your own purpose,

---

6. It and you must think everyone slow-witted indeed not to suppose that they would see how the profits to be gained by my death would be fertile and potent tempters to make you seek my death.
7. Flourish on a trumpet.
8. Seaports or gateways.
9. Prompted by natural feeling; bastard.
1. Legally able to inherit.
2. Incited him to.
3. Expose his plot.

How in my strength you please.[4] For you, Edmund,
Whose virtue and obedience doth this instant
So much commend itself, you shall be ours.
Natures of such deep trust we shall much need;
115   You we first seize on.

EDMUND: I shall serve you, sir,
          Truly, however else.[5]

GLOUCESTER: For him I thank Your Grace.

CORNWALL: You know not why we came to visit you—

REGAN: —Thus out of season, threading dark-eyed night:
120   Occasions, noble Gloucester, of some poise,°   weight
          Wherein we must have use of your advice.
          Our father he hath writ, so hath our sister,
          Of differences, which I least thought it fit
          To answer from our home. The several messengers
125   From hence attend dispatch.[6] Our good old friend,
          Lay comforts to your bosom, and bestow
          Your needful counsel to our businesses,
          Which craves the instant use.

GLOUCESTER: I serve you, madam.
130   Your Graces are right welcome.   [Flourish. Exeunt.]

                    Scene 2[7]

[Enter Kent (disguised as Caius) and steward (Oswald), severally.[8]]

OSWALD: Good dawning to thee, friend. Art of this house?

KENT: Ay.

OSWALD: Where may we set our horses?

KENT: I'th' mire.

OSWALD: Prithee, if thou lov'st me, tell me.

KENT: I love thee not.

OSWALD: Why then, I care not for thee.

KENT: If I had thee in Lipsbury pinfold,[9] I would make thee care for me.

OSWALD: Why dost thou use me thus? I know thee not.

KENT: Fellow, I know thee.

OSWALD: What dost thou know me for?

KENT: A knave, a rascal, an eater of broken meats; a base, proud, shallow, beggarly,
          three-suited, hundred-pound, filthy worsted-stocking knave;[1] a lily-livered,
          action-taking, whoreson, glass-gazing, superserviceable, finical rogue; one-
15   trunk-inheriting slave;[2] one that wouldst be a bawd in way of good service,[3]
          and art nothing but the composition of a knave, beggar, coward, pander, and

---

4. Go about achieving your purpose, making free use of
my authority and resources.
5. Above all else.
6. Wait to be dispatched.
7. Location: Before Gloucester's house.
8. At separate doors.
9. Within the pinfold of the lips, between my teeth.
1. A steward of a household, with an allowance of three

suits a year and a comfortable income of 100 pounds,
dressed up in dirty wool stockings appropriate to the servant class.
2. A cowardly, litigious, insufferable, self-infatuated, officious, foppish rogue, whose personal property fits into
one trunk.
3. The titles I've given you.

the son and heir of a mongrel bitch; one whom I will beat into clamorous whining if thou deny'st the least syllable of thy addition.

OSWALD: Why, what a monstrous fellow art thou thus to rail on one that is nei-
20   ther known of thee nor knows thee!

KENT: What a brazen-faced varlet art thou to deny thou knowest me! Is it two days since I tripped up thy heels and beat thee before the King? Draw, you rogue, for though it be night, yet the moon shines. I'll make a sop o'th' moonshine[4] of you, you whoreson, cullionly barbermonger.[5] Draw!

[(*He brandishes his sword.*)]

OSWALD: Away! I have nothing to do with thee.

KENT: Draw, you rascal! You come with letters against the King, and take Vanity the puppet's part[6] against the royalty of her father. Draw, you rogue, or I'll so carbonado[7] your shanks—draw, you rascal! Come your ways.

OSWALD: Help, ho! Murder! Help!

KENT: Strike, you slave! Stand, rogue, stand, you neat[8] slave, strike!

[(*He beats him.*)]

OSWALD: Help, ho! Murder! Murder!
[*Enter Bastard (Edmund, with his rapier drawn), Cornwall, Regan, Gloucester, servants.*]

EDMUND: How now, what's the matter? Part!

KENT: With you, goodman boy, an you please! Come, I'll flesh ye. Come on, young master.

GLOUCESTER: Weapons? Arms? What's the matter here?

CORNWALL: Keep peace, upon your lives! [(*Kent and Oswald are parted.*)] He dies that strikes again. What is the matter?

REGAN: The messengers from our sister and the King.

CORNWALL: What's your difference? Speak.

OSWALD: I am scarce in breath, my lord.

KENT: No marvel, you have so bestirred your valor. You cowardly rascal, nature disclaims in[9] thee. A tailor made thee.

CORNWALL: Thou art a strange fellow. A tailor make a man?

KENT: A tailor, sir. A stonecutter or a painter could not have made him so ill,
45   though they had been but two years o'th' trade.

CORNWALL: Speak yet, how grew your quarrel?

OSWALD: This ancient ruffian, sir, whose life I have spared at suit of his gray beard—

KENT: Thou whoreson zed![1] Thou unnecessary letter!—My lord, if you'll give me
50   leave, I will tread this unbolted[2] villain into mortar and daub the wall of a jakes[3] with him.—Spare my gray beard, you wagtail?[4]

CORNWALL: Peace, sirrah!
         You beastly knave, know you no reverence?

---

4. Something so perforated that it will soak up moon-shine as a sop soaks up liquor.
5. Base frequenter of barber shops.
6. The part of Goneril, here personified as a character in a morality play.
7. Cut crosswise.
8. Foppish, calflike.

9. Disowns.
1. The letter z, regarded as unnecessary and often not included in dictionaries of the time.
2. Unsifted, hence coarse.
3. Toilet.
4. Bird wagging its tail feathers.

KENT: Yes, sir, but anger hath a privilege.

CORNWALL: Why art thou angry?

KENT: That such a slave as this should wear a sword,
Who wears no honesty. Such smiling rogues as these,
Like rats, oft bite the holy cords atwain
Which are too intrinse[5] t'unloose; smooth every passion
60   That in the natures of their lords rebel,
Bring oil to fire, snow to their colder moods,
Renege, affirm, and turn their halcyon beaks[6]
With every gale and vary of their masters,
Knowing naught, like dogs, but following.—
65   A plague upon your epileptic[7] visage!
Smile you my speeches, as I were a fool?
Goose, an I had you upon Sarum plain,
I'd drive ye cackling home to Camelot.[8]

CORNWALL: What, art thou mad, old fellow?

GLOUCESTER: How fell you out? Say that.

KENT: No contraries hold more antipathy
Than I and such a knave.

CORNWALL: Why dost thou call him knave? What is his fault?

KENT: His countenance likes me not.

CORNWALL: No more, perchance, does mine, nor his, nor hers.

KENT: Sir, 'tis my occupation to be plain:
I have seen better faces in my time
Than stands on any shoulder that I see
Before me at this instant.

CORNWALL: This is some fellow
80   Who, having been praised for bluntness, doth affect
A saucy roughness, and constrains the garb
Quite from his nature.[9] He cannot flatter, he;
An honest mind and plain, he must speak truth!
An they will take't, so; if not, he's plain.
85   These kind of knaves I know, which in this plainness
Harbor more craft and more corrupter ends
Than twenty silly-ducking observants
That stretch their duties nicely.[1]

KENT: Sir, in good faith, in sincere verity,
90   Under th'allowance of your great aspect,
Whose influence, like the wreath of radiant fire
On flickering Phoebus' front[2]—

CORNWALL: What mean'st by this?

KENT: To go out of my dialect,[3] which you discommend so much. I know, sir, I am
no flatterer. He that beguiled you in a plain accent was a plain knave,

---

5. Intricately knotted.
6. The halcyon or kingfisher, if hung up, would supposedly
turn its beak to the wind.
7. Grimacing.
8. Kent if given space and opportunity would send Oswald packing like a cackling goose. Camelot is the legendary seat of King Arthur and the Knights of the Round

Table.
9. Distorts plainness from its true purpose so that it becomes instead a way of deceiving the listener.
1. Than 20 foolishly bowing courtiers.
2. The sun god's forehead.
3. Manner of speech.

95   which for my part I will not be, though I should win your displeasure to en-
       treat me to't.
CORNWALL [(to Oswald)]: What was th'offense you gave him?
OSWALD: I never gave him any.
       It pleased the King his master very late
100   To strike at me, upon his misconstruction;[4]
       When he, compact, and flattering his displeasure,
       Tripped me behind; being down, insulted, railed,
       And put upon him such a deal of man
       That worthied him,[5] got praises of the King
105   For him attempting who was self-subdued;
       And, in the fleshment° of this dread exploit,[6]   excitement
       Drew on me here again.
KENT: None of these rogues and cowards
       But Ajax is their fool.[7]
CORNWALL: Fetch forth the stocks!
110   You stubborn, ancient knave, you reverend braggart,
       We'll teach you.
KENT: Sir, I am too old to learn.
       Call not your stocks for me. I serve the King,
115   On whose employment I was sent to you.
       You shall do small respect, show too bold malice
       Against the grace and person of my master,
       Stocking his messenger.
CORNWALL: Fetch forth the stocks! As I have life and honor,
       There shall he sit till noon.
REGAN: Till noon? Till night, my lord, and all night too.
KENT: Why, madam, if I were your father's dog
120   You should not use me so.
REGAN: Sir, being his knave, I will.
CORNWALL: This is a fellow of the selfsame color
       Our sister speaks of.—Come, bring away the stocks!

                                        [Stocks brought out.]

GLOUCESTER: Let me beseech Your Grace not to do so.
125   His fault is much, and the good King his master
       Will check him for't. Your purposed low correction
130   Is such as basest and contemned'st wretches
       For pilferings and most common trespasses
       Are punished with. The King must take it ill
       That he, so slightly valued in his messenger,
       Should have him thus restrained.
CORNWALL: I'll answer that.
REGAN: My sister may receive it much more worse
       To have her gentleman abused, assaulted,
       For following her affairs. Put in his legs.

                                        [(Kent is put in the stocks.)]

4. As a result of the king's misunderstanding me.   7. You never find any rogues and cowards of this sort who
5. And acted with a bravado that earned him praise.   do not outdo the blustering Ajax in his boasting.
6. For attacking one who chose not to resist.

135   Come, my good lord, away.

                           [Exeunt (all but Gloucester and Kent).]

GLOUCESTER: I am sorry for thee, friend. 'Tis the Duke's pleasure,

140   Whose disposition, all the world well knows,

     Will not be rubbed° nor stopped. I'll entreat for thee.   *hindered*

KENT: Pray, do not, sir. I have watched° and traveled hard.   *gone sleepless*

     Some time I shall sleep out; the rest I'll whistle.

     A good man's fortune may grow out at heels.[8]

     Give you good morrow!

GLOUCESTER: The Duke's to blame in this. 'Twill be ill taken.   *[Exit.]*

KENT: Good King, that must approve° the common saw,   *prove true*

145   Thou out of heaven's benediction com'st

     To the warm sun!   *[(He takes out a letter.)]*

150   Approach, thou beacon to this under globe,

     That by thy comfortable beams I may

     Peruse this letter. Nothing almost sees miracles

     But misery. I know 'tis from Cordelia,

     Who hath most fortunately been informed

     Of my obscurèd course, "and shall find time

     From this enormous state, seeking to give

     Losses their remedies." All weary and o'erwatched,

155   Take vantage,° heavy eyes, not to behold   *advantage*

     This shameful lodging.

160   Fortune, good night. Smile once more; turn thy wheel!

                                  [(He sleeps.)]

                   Scene 3[9]

[Enter Edgar.]

EDGAR: I heard myself proclaimed,

     And by the happy hollow of a tree

     Escaped the hunt. No port is free, no place

     That guard and most unusual vigilance

5   Does not attend my taking. Whiles I may scape

     I will preserve myself, and am bethought

     To take the basest and most poorest shape

     That ever penury, in contempt of man,

     Brought near to beast. My face I'll grime with filth,

10   Blanket my loins, elf° all my hairs in knots,   *tangle*

     And with presented nakedness outface

     The winds and persecutions of the sky.

     The country gives me proof and precedent

     Of Bedlam beggars who with roaring voices

15   Strike° in their numbed and mortifièd° arms   *stick / deadened*

     Pins, wooden pricks, nails, sprigs of rosemary;

     And with this horrible object, from low farms,

     Poor pelting° villages, sheepcotes, and mills,   *paltry*

---

8. Even good men suffer decline in fortune at times.   9. Location: The scene continues. Kent is dozing in the stocks.

Sometimes with lunatic bans,° sometimes with prayers,   *curses*
20   Enforce their charity. Poor Turlygod! Poor Tom!¹
        That's something yet. Edgar I nothing am.   [*Exit.*]

Scene 4²

Enter Lear, Fool, and Gentleman.
LEAR: 'Tis strange that they³ should so depart from home
        And not send back my messenger.
GENTLEMAN: As I learned,
        The night before there was no purpose in them
        Of this remove.⁴
KENT: Hail to thee, noble master!
LEAR: Ha?
        Mak'st thou this shame thy pastime?
KENT: No, my lord.
FOOL: Ha, ha, he wears cruel⁵ garters. Horses are tied by the heads, dogs and bears
        by th' neck, monkeys by th' loins, and men by th' legs. When a man's over-
        lusty at legs,⁶ then he wears wooden netherstocks.⁷
LEAR: What's he that hath so much thy place mistook
        To set thee here?
KENT: It is both he and she:
        Your son and daughter.
LEAR: No.
KENT: Yes.
LEAR: No, I say.
KENT: I say yea.
LEAR: No, no, they would not.
KENT: Yes, they have.
LEAR: By Jupiter, I swear no.
KENT: By Juno, I swear ay.
LEAR: They durst not do't!
        They could not, would not do't. 'Tis worse than murder
        To do upon respect⁸ such violent outrage.
        Resolve° me with all modest° haste which way   *enlighten / moderate*
        Thou mightst deserve, or they impose, this usage,
25   Coming from us.
KENT: My lord, when at their home⁹
        I did commend° Your Highness' letters to them,   *deliver*
        Ere I was risen from the place that showed
        My duty kneeling, came there a reeking post,
        Stewed° in his haste, half breathless, panting forth   *soaked*
30   From Goneril his mistress salutations;
        Delivered letters, spite of intermission,¹

1. Bedlam beggars were known as "poor Toms."
2. Location: scene continues before Gloucester's house.
Kent still dozing in the stocks.
3. Cornwall and Regan.
4. Change of residence.
5. Unkind, with pun on *crewel*, "worsted."
6. Given to running away or overly active sexually.
7. Stockings.
8. Against my officers who deserve respect.
9. Kent and Oswald went first to Cornwall's palace after
leaving Albany's palace.
1. In disregard of interrupting me, or in spite of the inter-
ruptions caused by being out of breath.

Which presently they read; on whose contents
They summoned up their meiny,[2] straight took horse,
Commanded me to follow and attend
35   The leisure of their answer, gave me cold looks;
And meeting here the other messenger,
Whose welcome, I perceived, had poisoned mine—
Being the very fellow which of late
Displayed so saucily against Your Highness—
40   Having more man than wit[3] about me, drew.
He raised the house with loud and coward cries.
Your son and daughter found this trespass worth
The shame which here it suffers.

FOOL: Winter's not gone yet if the wild geese fly that way.[4]
    Fathers that wear rags
        Do make their children blind,[5]
    But fathers that bear bags[6]
        Shall see their children kind.
    Fortune, that arrant whore,
50   Ne'er turns the key to th' poor.
But, for all this, thou shalt have as many dolors[7] for thy daughters as thou
canst tell in a year.

LEAR: Oh, how this mother[8] swells up toward my heart!
    Hysterica passio, down, thou climbing sorrow!
    Thy element's below.—Where is this daughter?

KENT: With the Earl, sir, here within.

LEAR: Follow me not. Stay here.   [*Exit.*]

GENTLEMAN: Made you no more offense but what you speak of?

KENT: None.
    How chance the King comes with so small a number?

FOOL: An thou hadst been set i'th' stocks for that question, thou'dst well deserved
it.

KENT: Why, Fool?

FOOL: We'll set thee to school to an ant to teach thee there's no laboring i'th'
65   winter. All that follow their noses are led by their eyes but blind men, and
there's not a nose among twenty but can smell him that's stinking.[9] Let go
thy hold when a great wheel runs down a hill lest it break thy neck with
following; but the great one that goes upward, let him draw thee after.
When a wise man gives thee better counsel, give me mine again. I would
70   have none but knaves follow it, since a fool gives it.
        That sir which serves and seeks for gain,
            And follows but for form,

---

2. Retinue of servants.
3. Having more courage than good sense.
4. The signs still point to worsening fortune; the wild geese are still flying south.
5. Indifferent to their father's needs.
6. I.e., bags of gold.

7. Griefs, with pun on dollars.
8. The "mother," or "*Hysterica passio*" was a form of hysteria which women were believed to suffer from because the womb, or uterus (Greek *hystera*) moved in such a way or emitted vapors that caused them to choke.
9. One who is out of favor is easily detected.

Will pack° when it begins to rain   *be off*
    And leave thee in the storm.
75 But I will tarry; the fool will stay,
    And let the wise man fly.
    The knave turns fool that runs away;
        The fool no knave, pardie.[1]

[*Enter Lear and Gloucester.*]

KENT: Where learned you this, Fool?

FOOL: Not i'th' stocks, fool.

LEAR: Deny to speak with me? They are sick? They are weary?
    They have traveled all the night? Mere fetches,°   *pretexts*
    The images of revolt and flying off.
    Fetch me a better answer.

GLOUCESTER: My dear lord,
85 You know the fiery quality of the Duke,
    How unremovable and fixed he is
    In his own course.

LEAR: Vengeance! Plague! Death! Confusion!
    Fiery? What quality? Why, Gloucester, Gloucester,
90 I'd speak with the Duke of Cornwall and his wife.

GLOUCESTER: Well, my good lord, I have informed them so.

LEAR: Informed them? Dost thou understand me, man?

GLOUCESTER: Ay, my good lord.

LEAR: The King would speak with Cornwall. The dear father
    Would with his daughter speak, commands, tends service.
    Are they informed of this? My breath and blood!
    Fiery? The fiery Duke? Tell the hot Duke that—
    No, but not yet. Maybe he is not well.
    Infirmity doth still neglect all office
100 Whereto our health is bound;[2] we are not ourselves
    When nature, being oppressed, commands the mind
    To suffer with the body. I'll forbear,
    And am fallen out with my more headier will,
    To take the indisposed and sickly fit
105 For the sound man.[3] [(*Looking at Kent*)] Death on my state! Wherefore
    Should he sit here? This act persuades me
    That this remotion° of the Duke and her   *keeping apart*
    Is practice only. Give me my servant forth.
    Go tell the Duke and 's wife I'd speak with them,
110 Now, presently. Bid them come forth and hear me,
    Or at their chamber door I'll beat the drum
    Till it cry sleep to death.[4]

---

1. *Par dieu* (French), "by God."
2. Sickness always prompts us to neglect duties which in good health we are bound to perform.
3. And now disapprove of my more impetuous will in having rashly supposed that those who are indisposed and sickly were in sound health.
4. Put an end to sleep by the noise.

GLOUCESTER: I would have all well betwixt you.   [Exit.]

LEAR: Oh, me, my heart, my rising heart! But down!

FOOL: Cry to it, nuncle, as the cockney did to the eels when she put 'em i'th' paste
    alive. She knapped 'em o'th' coxcombs with a stick and cried, "Down,
    wantons,[5] down!" 'Twas her brother that, in pure kindness to his horse,
    buttered his hay.

[Enter Cornwall, Regan, Gloucester, (and) servants.]

LEAR: Good morrow to you both.

CORNWALL: Hail to your Grace!

[Kent here set at liberty.]

REGAN: I am glad to see Your Highness.

LEAR: Regan, I think you are. I know what reason
    I have to think so. If thou shouldst not be glad,
    I would divorce me from thy mother's tomb,

125   Sepulch'ring an adultress.[6] [(To Kent)] Oh, are you free?
    Some other time for that.—Belovèd Regan,
    Thy sister's naught.° Oh, Regan, she hath tied   wicked
    Sharp-toothed unkindness, like a vulture, here.

[(He lays his hand on his heart.)]

    I can scarce speak to thee. Thou'lt not believe
    With how depraved a quality—Oh, Regan!

REGAN: I pray you, sir, take patience. I have hope
    You less know how to value her desert
    Than she to scant her duty.[7]

LEAR: Say? How is that?

REGAN: I cannot think my sister in the least
    Would fail her obligation. If, sir, perchance
    She have restrained the riots of your followers,
    'Tis on such ground and to such wholesome end
    As clears her from all blame.

LEAR: My curses on her!

REGAN: Oh, sir, you are old;
    Nature in you stands on the very verge
    Of his confine.[8] You should be ruled and led
    By some discretion that discerns your state
    Better than you yourself. Therefore, I pray you,

145   That to our sister you do make return.
    Say you have wronged her.

LEAR: Ask her forgiveness?
    Do you but mark how this becomes the house:
    [(Kneeling)] "Dear daughter, I confess that I am old;

---

5. The cockney wife is trying to coax the eels into laying
down their lives for the making of the pastry pie, a plea
that is about as ineffectual as Lear's imploring his rising
heart to subside.

6. I would stop honoring your dead mother's grave, since

it would surely contain the dead body of an adulteress.

7. I trust this is more a matter of your undervaluing her
merit than of her falling slack in her duty to you.

8. Your life has almost completed its allotted scope.

Age is unnecessary. On my knees I beg
That you'll vouchsafe me raiment, bed, and food."
REGAN: Good sir, no more. These are unsightly tricks.
Return you to my sister.
LEAR [(*rising*)]:   Never, Regan.
She hath abated° me of half my train,   *deprived*
Looked black upon me, struck me with her tongue
Most serpentlike upon the very heart.
All the stored vengeances of heaven fall
On her ingrateful top!⁹ Strike her young bones,
You taking airs, with lameness!
CORNWALL: Fie, sir, fie!
LEAR: You nimble lightnings, dart your blinding flames
160   Into her scornful eyes! Infect her beauty,
You fen-sucked¹ fogs drawn by the powerful sun
To fall and blister!
REGAN: O the blest gods! So will you wish on me
When the rash mood is on.
LEAR: No, Regan, thou shalt never have my curse.
Thy tender-hafted² nature shall not give
Thee o'er to harshness. Her eyes are fierce, but thine
Do comfort and not burn. 'Tis not in thee
To grudge my pleasures, to cut off my train,
170   To bandy° hasty words, to scant my sizes,³   *exchange*
And, in conclusion, to oppose the bolt
Against my coming in. Thou better know'st
The offices of nature, bond of childhood,
Effects of courtesy, dues of gratitude.
175   Thy half o'th' kingdom hast thou not forgot,
Wherein I thee endowed.
REGAN: Good sir, to th' purpose.
LEAR: Who put my man i'th' stocks?   [*Tucket within.*]
CORNWALL: What trumpet's that?
REGAN: I know't—my sister's. This approves her letter,
That she would soon be here.
[*Enter steward (Oswald).*]
                              Is your lady come?
LEAR: This is a slave, whose easy-borrowed pride
Dwells in the fickle grace of her he follows.—
Out, varlet, from my sight!
CORNWALL: What means Your Grace?
LEAR: Who stocked my servant? Regan, I have good hope
185   Thou didst not know on't.
[*Enter Goneril.*]
                              Who comes here? O heavens,

---

9. Ungrateful head.   2. Set in a tender frame.
1. It was thought that the sun sucked up poisons from   3. Diminish my allowances.
fens or marshes.

If you do love old men, if your sweet sway
Allow obedience, if you yourselves are old,
Make it your cause; send down, and take my part!
[(*To Goneril*)] Art not ashamed to look upon this beard?

[(*Goneril and Regan join hands.*)]

Oh, Regan, will you take her by the hand?

GONERIL: Why not by th' hand, sir? How have I offended?
All's not offense that indiscretion finds
And dotage terms so.

LEAR: O sides,[4] you are too tough!
Will you yet hold?—How came my man i'th' stocks?

CORNWALL: I set him there, sir; but his own disorders
Deserved much less advancement.[5]

LEAR: You? Did you?

REGAN: I pray you, father, being weak, seem so.
If till the expiration of your month
You will return and sojourn with my sister,
200   Dismissing half your train, come then to me.
I am now from[6] home, and out of that provision
Which shall be needful for your entertainment.[7]

LEAR: Return to her? And fifty men dismissed?
No! Rather I abjure all roofs, and choose
To wage against the enmity o'th'air,
To be a comrade with the wolf and owl—
Necessity's sharp pinch. Return with her?
Why, the hot-blooded France, that dowerless took
Our youngest born—I could as well be brought
210   To knee his throne and, squirelike, pension beg
To keep base life afoot. Return with her?
Persuade me rather to be slave and sumpter°   *packhorse*
To this detested groom.   [(*He points to Oswald.*)]

GONERIL: At your choice, sir.

LEAR: I prithee, daughter, do not make me mad.
215   I will not trouble thee, my child. Farewell.
We'll no more meet, no more see one another.
But yet thou art my flesh, my blood, my daughter—
Or rather a disease that's in my flesh,
Which I must needs call mine. Thou art a boil,
220   A plague-sore, or embossèd[8] carbuncle
In my corrupted blood. But I'll not chide thee;
Let shame come when it will, I do not call it.
I do not bid the thunder-bearer[9] shoot,
Nor tell tales of thee to high-judging Jove.
225   Mend when thou canst; be better at thy leisure.

---

4. Sides of the chest, stretched by the swelling heart.   7. Proper reception.
5. Far less honor, far worse treatment.   8. Swollen stone.
6. Away from.   9. Jove.

I can be patient. I can stay with Regan,
I and my hundred knights.
REGAN: Not altogether so.
     I looked not for you yet, nor am provided
230   For your fit welcome. Give ear, sir, to my sister;
     For those that mingle reason with your passion
     Must be content to think you old, and so—
     But she knows what she does.
LEAR: Is this well spoken?
REGAN: I dare avouch it, sir. What, fifty followers?
235   Is it not well? What should you need of more?
     Yea, or so many, sith that both charge and danger
     Speak 'gainst so great a number? How in one house
     Should many people under two commands
     Hold amity? 'Tis hard, almost impossible.
GONERIL: Why might not you, my lord, receive attendance
     From those that she calls servants, or from mine?
REGAN: Why not, my lord? If then they chanced to slack° ye,   *neglect*
     We could control them. If you will come to me—
     For now I spy a danger—I entreat you
245   To bring but five-and-twenty. To no more
     Will I give place or notice.
LEAR: I gave you all—
REGAN: And in good time you gave it.
LEAR: Made you my guardians, my depositaries,°   *trustees*
     But kept a reservation to be followed
     With such a number. What, must I come to you
     With five-and-twenty? Regan, said you so?
REGAN: And speak't again, my lord. No more with me.
LEAR: Those wicked creatures yet do look well-favored
     When others are more wicked; not being the worst
255   Stands in some rank of praise. [(*To Goneril*)] I'll go with thee.
     Thy fifty yet doth double five-and-twenty
     And thou art twice her love.
GONERIL: Hear me, my lord:
     What need you five-and-twenty, ten, or five,
     To follow in a house where twice so many
260   Have a command to tend you?
REGAN: What need one?
LEAR: Oh, reason not the need! Our basest beggars
     Are in the poorest thing superfluous.[1]
     Allow not nature more than nature needs,
     Man's life is cheap as beast's. Thou art a lady;
265   If only to go warm were gorgeous,
     Why, nature needs not what thou gorgeous wear'st,

---

1. Even our poorest beggars have some wretched possessions beyond what they absolutely need.

Which scarcely keeps thee warm. But, for true need—
You heavens, give me that patience, patience I need!
You see me here, you gods, a poor old man,
270   As full of grief as age, wretched in both.
If it be you that stirs these daughters' hearts
Against their father, fool me not so much
To bear it tamely; touch me with noble anger,
And let not women's weapons, water drops,
Stain my man's cheeks. No, you unnatural hags,
I will have such revenges on you both
That all the world shall—I will do such things—
What they are yet I know not, but they shall be
The terrors of the earth. You think I'll weep;
280   No, I'll not weep.   [Storm and tempest.]
I have full cause of weeping; but this heart
Shall break into a hundred thousand flaws
Or ere I'll weep. Oh, Fool, I shall go mad!
                [Exeunt (Lear, Gloucester, Kent, Gentleman, and Fool).]
CORNWALL: Let us withdraw. 'Twill be a storm.
REGAN: This house is little. The old man and 's people
        Cannot be well bestowed.°   lodged
GONERIL: 'Tis his own blame hath put himself from rest,[2]
        And must needs taste his folly.
REGAN: For his particular,[3] I'll receive him gladly,
290   But not one follower.
GONERIL: So am I purposed. Where is my lord of Gloucester?
CORNWALL: Followed the old man forth.
        [Enter Gloucester.]
                                        He is returned.
GLOUCESTER: The King is in high rage.
CORNWALL: Whither is he going?
GLOUCESTER: He calls to horse, but will I know not whither.
CORNWALL: 'Tis best to give him way. He leads himself.
GONERIL [(to Gloucester)]: My lord, entreat him by no means to stay.
GLOUCESTER: Alack, the night comes on, and the bleak winds
        Do sorely ruffle. For many miles about
        There's scarce a bush.
REGAN: Oh, sir, to willful men
300   The injuries that they themselves procure
        Must be their schoolmasters. Shut up your doors.
        He is attended with a desperate train,
        And what they may incense him to, being apt
        To have his ear abused,[4] wisdom bids fear.

2. Out of the house, and lacking peace of mind.   4. He being inclined to listen to wild counsel.
3. As for him individually.

CORNWALL: Shut up your doors, my lord; 'tis a wild night.
My Regan counsels well. Come out o'th' storm.

[*Exeunt.*]

ACT 3
Scene 1[5]

[*Storm still. Enter Kent (disguised as Caius) and a Gentleman, severally.*]

KENT: Who's there, besides foul weather?
GENTLEMAN: One minded like the weather, most unquietly.
KENT: I know you. Where's the King?
GENTLEMAN: Contending with the fretful elements;
5   Bids the wind blow the earth into the sea
Or swell the curlèd waters 'bove the main,
That things might change or cease; tears his white hair,
Which the impetuous blasts with eyeless rage
Catch in their fury and make nothing of;
10   Strives in his little world of man to outstorm
The to-and-fro-conflicting wind and rain.
This night, wherein the cub-drawn[6] bear would couch,
The lion and the belly-pinchèd wolf
Keep their fur dry, unbonneted he runs
15   And bids what will take all.
KENT: But who is with him?
GENTLEMAN: None but the Fool, who labors to outjest
His heart-struck injuries.
KENT: Sir, I do know you,
And dare upon the warrant of my note
Commend a dear thing to you. There is division,
20   Although as yet the face of it is covered
With mutual cunning, twixt Albany and Cornwall;
Who have—as who have not, that their great stars
Throned and set high?—servants, who seem no less,
Which are to France the spies and speculations
25   Intelligent of our state.[7] What hath been seen,
Either in snuffs and packings[8] of the dukes,
Or the hard rein which both of them hath borne
Against the old kind King, or something deeper,
Whereof perchance these are but furnishings—
30   But true it is, from France there comes a power
Into this scattered kingdom, who already,
Wise in our negligence, have secret feet
In some of our best ports and are at point
To show their open banner. Now to you:
35   If on my credit you dare build so far

---

5. Location: A heath in Gloucestershire.
6. Famished, with udders sucked dry.

7. Supplying intelligence pertinent to our state.
8. Resentments and intrigues.

To make your speed to Dover, you shall find
Some that will thank you, making just report
Of how unnatural and bemadding sorrow
The King hath cause to plain.
40   I am a gentleman of blood and breeding,
And from some knowledge and assurance offer
This office to you.
GENTLEMAN: I will talk further with you.
KENT: No, do not.
For confirmation that I am much more
45   Than my outwall,[9] open this purse and take
What it contains. [(*He gives a purse and a ring.*)] If you shall see Cordelia—
As fear not but you shall—show her this ring,
And she will tell you who that fellow is
That yet you do not know. Fie on this storm!
50   I will go seek the King.
GENTLEMAN: Give me your hand. Have you no more to say?
KENT: Few words, but, to effect, more than all yet:
That when we have found the King—in which your pain
55   That way, I'll this—he that first lights on him
Holla the other.

                                    [*Exeunt (separately).*]

                        Scene 2[1]

[*Storm still. Enter Lear and Fool.*]
LEAR: Blow, winds, and crack your cheeks! Rage, blow!
You cataracts and hurricanoes, spout
Till you have drenched our steeples, drowned the cocks![2]
You sulfurous and thought-executing fires,
5   Vaunt-couriers° of oak-cleaving thunderbolts,   *forerunners*
Singe my white head! And thou, all-shaking thunder,
Strike flat the thick rotundity o'th' world!
Crack nature's molds, all germens spill at once[3]
That makes ingrateful man!
FOOL: Oh, nuncle, court holy water in a dry house is better than this rainwater out
o'door. Good nuncle, in, ask thy daughters blessing. Here's a night pities
neither wise men nor fools.
LEAR: Rumble thy bellyful! Spit, fire! Spout, rain!
Nor rain, wind, thunder, fire are my daughters.
15   I tax not you, you elements, with unkindness;
I never gave you kingdom, called you children.
You owe me no subscription.° Then let fall   *allegiance*
Your horrible pleasure. Here I stand your slave,

---

9. Exterior appearance.   3. Crack the molds in which nature makes all life; destroy
1. Location: The heath.   all seeds at once.
2. Weathercocks.

A poor, infirm, weak, and despised old man.
20 But yet I call you servile ministers,
That will with two pernicious daughters join
Your high-engendered battles 'gainst a head
So old and white as this. O, ho! 'Tis foul.
FOOL: He that has a house to put 's head in has a good headpiece.[4]
25   The codpiece that will house
       Before the head has any,
    The head and he shall louse;
       So beggars marry many.[5]
    The man that makes his toe
30   What he his heart should make
    Shall of a corn cry woe,
       And turn his sleep to wake.[6]
For there was never yet fair woman but she made mouths in a glass.[7]
LEAR: No, I will be the pattern of all patience;
35 I will say nothing.
   [*Enter Kent, (disguised as Caius).*]
KENT: Who's there?
FOOL: Marry, here's grace and a codpiece[8]; that's a wise man and a fool.
KENT: Alas, sir, are you here? Things that love night
40 Love not such nights as these. The wrathful skies
Gallow° the very wanderers of the dark   *frighten*
And make them keep their caves. Since I was man,
Such sheets of fire, such bursts of horrid thunder,
Such groans of roaring wind and rain I never
45 Remember to have heard. Man's nature cannot carry
Th'affliction nor the fear.
LEAR: Let the great gods,
That keep this dreadful pother° o'er our heads,   *hubbub*
Find out their enemies now. Tremble, thou wretch,
That hast within thee undivulgèd crimes
Unwhipped of justice! Hide thee, thou bloody hand,
50 Thou perjured, and thou simular° of virtue   *pretender*
That art incestuous! Caitiff,° to pieces shake,   *wretch*
That under covert and convenient seeming
Has practiced° on man's life! Close pent-up guilts,   *plotted*
Rive your concealing continents and cry
55 These dreadful summoners grace![9] I am a man
More sinned against than sinning.

---

4. Helmetlike covering for the head, and head for common sense.
5. A man who houses his genitals in a sexual embrace before he has a roof over his head can expect the lice-infected poverty of a penniless marriage.
6. Anyone who unwisely places his affection on base things will be afflicted with sorrow and sleeplessness.
7. The practice of making attractive faces in the mirror.
8. Royal grace and a codpiece, prominent in the Fool's costume.
9. O you secret and buried consciousnesses of guilt, burst open the hiding places that conceal you, and pray for mercy. (Summoners are the officers who cited offenders to appear before ecclesiastical courts.)

KENT: Alack, bareheaded?
  Gracious my lord, hard by here is a hovel;
  Some friendship will it lend you 'gainst the tempest.
  Repose you there while I to this hard house—
60 More harder than the stones whereof 'tis raised,
  Which even but now, demanding after you,
  Denied me to come in—return and force
  Their scanted° courtesy.   *stinted*
LEAR: My wits begin to turn.
  Come on, my boy. How dost, my boy? Art cold?
65 I am cold myself.—Where is this straw, my fellow?
  The art of our necessities is strange,
  And can make vile things precious. Come, your hovel.—
  Poor fool and knave, I have one part in my heart
  That's sorry yet for thee.
FOOL: [*sings*] "He that has and a little tiny wit,
    With heigh-ho, the wind and the rain,
  Must make content with his fortunes fit,
    Though the rain it raineth every day."
LEAR: True, boy.—Come, bring us to this hovel.

                 [Exit (with Kent).]

FOOL: This is a brave night to cool a courtesan.[1] I'll speak a prophecy ere I go:
  When priests are more in word than matter;[2]
  When brewers mar their malt with water;
  When nobles are their tailors' tutors,
  No heretics burned but wenches' suitors,[3]
80 Then shall the realm of Albion
  Come to great confusion.

  When every case in law is right,
  No squire in debt, nor no poor knight;
  When slanders do not live in tongues,
85 Nor cutpurses come not to throngs;
  When usurers tell their gold i'th' field,
  And bawds and whores do churches build,
  Then comes the time, who lives to see't,
  That going shall be used with feet.[4]

90 This prophecy Merlin shall make, for I live before his time.[5]   *[Exit.]*

---

1. This night is stormy enough to cool the lust of a courtesan.
2. When priests do not practice what they preach. This and the next three lines satirize the present state of affairs.
3. When the prevailing heresy is lechery, punished not by burning at the stake but by venereal infection.

4. The anticlimax of "then people will walk on foot" suggests that none of these utopian dreams will come to pass.
5. Both prophecies are imitations of the pseudo-Chaucerian "Merlin's Prophecy."

Scene 3[6]

[*Enter Gloucester and Edmund (with lights).*]

GLOUCESTER: Alack, alack, Edmund, I like not this unnatural dealing. When
 I desired their leave that I might pity him, they took from me the use of
 mine own house, charged me on pain of perpetual displeasure neither to
 speak of him, entreat for him, or any way sustain him.

EDMUND: Most savage and unnatural!

GLOUCESTER: Go to; say you nothing. There is division between the dukes, and
 a worse matter than that. I have received a letter this night; 'tis dangerous
 to be spoken; I have locked the letter in my closet.[7] These injuries the King
 now bears will be revenged home;[8] there is part of a power already footed.[9]

10 We must incline to the King. I will look him and privily relieve him. Go
 you and maintain talk with the Duke, that my charity be not of him
 perceived. If he ask for me, I am ill and gone to bed. If I die for't, as no less
 is threatened me, the King my old master must be relieved. There is strange
 things toward,[1] Edmund. Pray you, be careful.   [*Exit.*]

EDMUND: This courtesy forbid thee shall the Duke
 Instantly know, and of that letter too.
 This seems a fair deserving, and must draw me
 That which my father loses—no less than all.
 The younger rises when the old doth fall.   [*Exit.*]

Scene 4[2]

[*Enter Lear, Kent (disguised as Caius), and Fool.*]

KENT: Here is the place, my lord. Good my lord, enter.
 The tyranny of the open night's too rough
 For nature[3] to endure.   [*Storm still.*]

LEAR: Let me alone.

KENT: Good my lord, enter here.

LEAR: Wilt break my heart?

KENT: I had rather break mine own. Good my lord, enter.

LEAR: Thou think'st 'tis much that this contentious storm
 Invades us to the skin. So 'tis to thee,
 But where the greater malady is fixed
 The lesser is scarce felt, Thou'dst shun a bear,

10 But if thy flight lay toward the roaring sea
 Thou'dst meet the bear i'th' mouth. When the mind's free,
 The body's delicate. This tempest in my mind
 Doth from my senses take all feeling else
 Save what beats there. Filial ingratitude!

15 Is it not as this mouth should tear this hand
 For lifting food to't? But I will punish home.

---

6. Location: Gloucester's house.
7. Private chamber.
8. Thoroughly.
9. Landed.

1. Impending.
2. Location: The heath, before a hovel.
3. Human nature.

No, I will weep no more. In such a night
To shut me out? Pour on; I will endure.
In such a night as this? Oh, Regan, Goneril,
20   Your old kind father, whose frank heart gave all—
Oh, that way madness lies; let me shun that!
No more of that.
KENT: Good my lord, enter here.
LEAR: Prithee, go in thyself; seek thine own ease.
This tempest will not give me leave to ponder
25   On things would hurt me more. But I'll go in.
[(*To the Fool*)] In, boy; go first. You houseless poverty—
Nay, get thee in. I'll pray, and then I'll sleep.

                                                  [*Exit (Fool into the hovel).*]

Poor naked wretches, wheresoe'er you are,
That bide the pelting of this pitiless storm,
30   How shall your houseless heads and unfed sides,
Your looped and windowed[4] raggedness, defend you
From seasons such as these? Oh, I have ta'en
Too little care of this! Take physic, pomp;[5]
Expose thyself to feel what wretches feel,
35   That thou mayst shake the superflux[6] to them
And show the heavens more just.
EDGAR [(*within*)]: Fathom and half, fathom and half! Poor Tom!
[*Enter Fool (from the hovel).*]
FOOL: Come not in here, nuncle; here's a spirit. Help me, help me!
KENT: Give me thy hand. Who's there?
FOOL: A spirit, a spirit! He says his name's poor Tom.
KENT: What art thou that dost grumble there i'th' straw?
Come forth.
     [*Enter Edgar (disguised as a madman).*]
EDGAR: Away! The foul fiend follows me! Through the sharp hawthorn blows the
cold wind.[7] Hum! Go to thy bed and warm thee.
LEAR: Didst thou give all to thy daughters? And art thou come to this?
EDGAR: Who gives anything to poor Tom? Whom the foul fiend[8] hath led
through fire and through flame, through ford and whirlpool, o'er bog and
quagmire; that hath laid knives under his pillow and halters in his pew, set
ratsbane by his porridge, made him proud of heart to ride on a bay trotting
50   horse over four-inched bridges to course his own shadow for a traitor.[9]
Bless thy five wits![1] Tom's a-cold. Oh, do de, do de, do de. Bless thee from
whirlwinds, star-blasting, and taking![2] Do poor Tom some charity, whom

---

4. Full of openings that let in the rain.
5. Cure yourself, O powerful ones.
6. Superfluity, wealth above one's needs.
7. This line is found in an 18th-century ballad "The Friar of Orders Grey."
8. Edgar's feigned identity of Tom o' Bedlam includes demonic possession.
9. The fiend has laid in poor Tom's way tempting means to

despairing suicide, knives under his pillow, nooses in his church pew, and rat poison beside his soup, and riding a horse over bridges four inches wide in pursuit of his shadow.
1. Either the five physical senses—sight, hearing, taste, touch, and smell—or the five faculties of the mind—wit, imagination, fantasy, estimation, and memory.
2. Being blighted by the influence of the stars and taking infection.

the foul fiend vexes. There could I have him now—and there—and there
again—and there.   [*Storm still.*]

LEAR: Has his daughters brought him to this pass?—
Couldst thou save nothing? Wouldst thou give 'em all?

FOOL: Nay, he reserved a blanket, else we had been all shamed.

LEAR: Now, all the plagues that in the pendulous air
Hang fated o'er men's faults light on thy daughters!

KENT: He hath no daughters, sir.

LEAR: Death, traitor! Nothing could have subdued nature
To such a lowness but his unkind daughters.
Is it the fashion that discarded fathers
Should have thus little mercy on their flesh?
65   Judicious punishment! 'Twas this flesh begot
Those pelican[3] daughters.

EDGAR: Pillicock[4] sat on Pillicock Hill. Alow, alow, loo, loo!

FOOL: This cold night will turn us all to fools and madmen.

EDGAR: Take heed o'th' foul fiend. Obey thy parents; keep thy word's justice;
70   swear not; commit not with man's sworn spouse; set not thy sweet heart on
proud array. Tom's a-cold.

LEAR: What hast thou been?

EDGAR: A servingman, proud in heart and mind, that curled my hair, wore gloves
in my cap, served the lust of my mistress' heart, and did the act of darkness
75   with her; swore as many oaths as I spake words, and broke them in the
sweet face of heaven. One that slept in the contriving of lust and waked to
do it. Wine loved I deeply, dice dearly, and in woman out-paramoured the
Turk.[5] False of heart, light of ear, bloody of hand; hog in sloth, fox in
stealth, wolf in greediness, dog in madness, lion in prey. Let not the creak-
80   ing of shoes nor the rustling of silks betray thy poor heart to woman. Keep
thy foot out of brothels, thy hand out of plackets,[6] thy pen from lenders'
books, and defy the foul fiend. Still through the hawthorn blows the cold
wind; says suum, mun, nonny. Dolphin my boy, boy, sessa! Let him trot by.
                                                             [*Storm still.*]

LEAR: Thou wert better in a grave than to answer with thy uncovered body this ex-
85   tremity of the skies. Is man no more than this? Consider him well. Thou
ow'st the worm no silk, the beast no hide, the sheep no wool, the cat no perfume. Ha! Here's three on 's are sophisticated; thou art the thing itself.
Unaccommodated[7] man is no more but such a poor, bare, forked animal as
thou art. Off, off, you lendings! Come, unbutton here.
                                                  [(*Tearing off his clothes.*)]

FOOL: Prithee, nuncle, be contented; 'tis a naughty[8] night to swim in. Now a little
fire in a wild field were like an old lecher's heart—a small spark, all the rest
on 's body cold.

[*Enter Gloucester, with a torch.*]
Look, here comes a walking fire.

---

3. Greedy, because young pelicans fed upon their
mother's blood.
4. A euphemism for penis in nursery rhymes.
5. Outdid the Sultan in keeping mistresses.

6. Slits in skirts or petticoats.
7. Unfurnished with the trappings of civilization.
8. Nasty.

EDGAR: This is the foul fiend Flibbertigibbet![9] He begins at curfew and walks till
95   the first cock; he gives the web and the pin,[1] squinnies the eye and makes
         the harelip, mildews the white wheat, and hurts the poor creature of earth.
              Swithold[2] footed thrice the 'old;[3]
              He met the nightmare and her ninefold;
                   Bid her alight,
100   And her troth plight,
              And aroint[4] thee, witch, aroint thee!
KENT: How fares Your Grace?
LEAR: What's he?
KENT: Who's there? What is't you seek?
GLOUCESTER: What are you there? Your names?
EDGAR: Poor Tom, that eats the swimming frog, the toad, the tadpole, the wall
         newt and the water; that in the fury of his heart, when the foul fiend rages,
         eats cow dung for salads, swallows the old rat and the ditch-dog, drinks the
         green mantle[5] of the standing pool; who is whipped from tithing to tithing
110   and stock-punished and imprisoned; who hath had three suits to his back,
         six shirts to his body,
              Horse to ride, and weapon to wear;
              But mice and rats and such small deer
              Have been Tom's food for seven long year.
115   Beware my follower. Peace, Smulkin![6] Peace, thou fiend!
GLOUCESTER What, hath Your Grace no better company?
EDGAR: The Prince of Darkness is a gentleman. Modo he's called, and Mahu.
GLOUCESTER [(to Lear)]: Our flesh and blood, my lord, is grown so vile
         That it doth hate what gets it.
EDGAR: Poor Tom's a-cold.
GLOUCESTER: Go in with me. My duty cannot suffer
         T'obey in all your daughters' hard commands.
         Though their injunction be to bar my doors
         And let this tyrannous night take hold upon you,
125   Yet have I ventured to come seek you out
         And bring you where both fire and food is ready.
LEAR: First let me talk with this philosopher.
         [(To Edgar)] What is the cause of thunder?
KENT: Good my lord,
         Take his offer. Go into th' house.
LEAR: I'll talk a word with this same learnèd Theban.[7]
135   [(To Edgar)] What is your study?

---

9. A devil from Elizabethan folklore whose name appears
in Samuel Harsnett's *Declaration of Egregious Popish
Impostures* (1603) and elsewhere.
1. Cataract.
2. Saint Withold, an Anglo-Saxon exorcist, who here
provides defense against the demon thought to afflict
sleepers by commanding the nightmare to alight.

3. Walked over the upland plain.
4. Begone.
5. Scum.
6. A devil's name, from Harsnett's *Declaration*, as are
Modo and Mahu in line 1117.
7. A scholar or philosopher.

EDGAR: How to prevent the fiend, and to kill vermin.
LEAR: Let me ask you one word in private.

           [Lear and Edgar talk apart.]

KENT [(*to Gloucester*)]: Importune him once more to go, my lord.
135 His wits begin t'unsettle.
GLOUCESTER: Canst thou blame him?

             [Storm still.]

140 His daughters seek his death. Ah, that good Kent!
   He said it would be thus, poor banished man.
   Thou sayest the King grows mad; I'll tell thee, friend,
   I am almost mad myself. I had a son,
   Now outlawed from my blood; he sought my life
145 But lately, very late. I loved him, friend,
   No father his son dearer. True to tell thee,
   The grief hath crazed my wits. What a night's this!—
   I do beseech Your Grace—
LEAR: Oh, cry you mercy, sir.
150 [(*To Edgar*)] Noble philosopher, your company.
EDGAR: Tom's a-cold.
GLOUCESTER [(*to Edgar*)]: In, fellow, there, in th' hovel. Keep thee warm.
LEAR [*starting toward the hovel*]: Come, let's in all.
KENT: This way, my lord.
LEAR: With him!
150 I will keep still with my philosopher.
KENT [(*to Gloucester*)]: Good my lord, soothe him. Let him take the fellow.
GLOUCESTER: [*to Kent*] Take you him on.
KENT [(*to Edgar*)]: Sirrah, come on. Go along with us.
LEAR: Come, good Athenian.[8]
GLOUCESTER: No words, no words! Hush.
EDGAR: Child Rowland to the dark tower came;[9]
   His word[1] was still, "Fie, foh, and fum,
   I smell the blood of a British man."[2]   *[Exeunt.]*

Scene 5[3]

[*Enter Cornwall and Edmund (with a letter).*]
CORNWALL: I will have my revenge ere I depart his house.
EDMUND: How, my lord, I may be censured,[4] that nature[5] thus gives way to loy-
  alty, something fears me to think of.

---

8. Philosopher.
9. Probably a fragment of a ballad about the hero of the Charlemagne legends. A *child* is a candidate for knighthood.
1. Watchword.

2. The words of the Giant in "Jack, the Giant Killer."
3. Location: Gloucester's house.
4. Judged.
5. Attachment to family.

CORNWALL: I now perceive it was not altogether your brother's evil disposition
5   made him seek his death, but a provoking merit set awork by a reprovable
        badness in himself.

EDMUND: How malicious is my fortune, that I must repent to be just! This is the
        letter he spoke of, which approves him an intelligent party to the advan-
        tages of France. Oh, heavens! That this treason were not, or not I the
10   detector!

CORNWALL: Go with me to the Duchess.

EDMUND: If the matter of this paper be certain, you have mighty business in hand.

CORNWALL: True or false, it hath made thee Earl of Gloucester. Seek out where
        thy father is, that he may be ready for our apprehension.[6]

EDMUND [(aside)]: If I find him comforting the King, it will stuff his suspicion more
        fully—I will persevere in my course of loyalty, though the conflict be sore
        between that and my blood.[7]

CORNWALL: I will lay trust upon thee, and thou shalt find a dearer father in my
        love.   [Exeunt.]

Scene 6[8]

[Enter Kent (disguised as Caius) and Gloucester.]

GLOUCESTER: Here is better than the open air; take it thankfully. I will piece[9]
        out the comfort with what addition I can. I will not be long from you.

KENT: All the power of his wits have given way to his impatience.[1] The gods re-
        ward your kindness!

                                                    [Exit (Gloucester).]

[Enter Lear, Edgar (as poor Tom), and Fool.]

EDGAR: Fraterretto[2] calls me, and tells me Nero is an angler[3] in the lake of dark-
        ness. Pray, innocent, and beware the foul fiend.

FOOL: Prithee, nuncle, tell me whether a madman be a gentleman or a yeoman?[4]

LEAR: A king, a king!

FOOL: No, he's a yeoman that has a gentleman to his son; for he's a mad yeoman
10   that sees his son a gentleman before him.

LEAR: To have a thousand with red burning spits
        Come hizzing[5] in upon 'em—

EDGAR: The foul fiend bites my back.

FOOL: He's mad that trusts in the tameness of a wolf, a horse's health, a boy's love,
15   or a whore's oath.

LEAR: It shall be done; I will arraign them[6] straight.
        [(To Edgar)] Come, sit thou here, most learnèd justicer.
        [(To the Fool)] Thou, sapient sir, sit here. Now, you she-foxes!

EDGAR: Look where he stands and glares! Want'st thou eyes at trial, madam?
20   [(Sings.)] "Come o'er the burn, Bessy, to me—"[7]

---

6. For our arresting of him.
7. Family loyalty.
8. Location: Within a building on Gloucester's estate.
9. Eke.
1. Rage.
2. Another fiend from Harsnett's Declaration.
3. Chaucer's "Monk's Tale" tells how Nero fished in the

Tiber with nets of gold thread.
4. Property owner below the rank of gentleman.
5. Hissing.
6. Put them on trial.
7. First line of a ballad by William Birche, 1558. A burn
is a brook.

FOOL [(*sings*)]: Her boat hath a leak,[8]
     And she must not speak
     Why she dares not come over to thee.

EDGAR: The foul fiend haunts poor Tom in the voice of a nightingale.
25   Hoppedance[9] cries in Tom's belly for two white herring. Croak not, black angel; I have no food for thee.

KENT [(*to Lear*)]: How do you, sir? Stand you not so amazed.
     Will you lie down and rest upon the cushions?

LEAR: I'll see their trial first. Bring in their evidence.
30   [(*To Edgar*)] Thou robèd[1] man of justice, take thy place;
     [(*To the Fool*)] And thou, his yokefellow of equity,[2]
     Bench by his side. [(*To Kent*)] You are o'th' commission;
     Sit you, too.   [(*They sit.*)]

EDGAR: Let us deal justly.   [(*He sings.*)]
35   Sleepest or wakest thou, jolly shepherd?
      Thy sheep be in the corn;[3]
     And for one blast of thy minikin mouth,[4]
      Thy sheep shall take no harm.
     Purr the cat[5] is gray.

LEAR: Arraign her first; 'tis Goneril, I here take my oath before this honorable assembly, kicked the poor King her father.

FOOL: Come hither, mistress. Is your name Goneril?

LEAR: She cannot deny it.

FOOL: Cry you mercy, I took you for a joint stool.[6]

LEAR: And here's another,[7] whose warped looks proclaim
     What store[8] her heart is made on. Stop her there!
     Arms, arms, sword, fire! Corruption in the place!
     False justicer, why hast thou let her scape?

EDGAR: Bless thy five wits!

KENT: Oh, pity! Sir, where is the patience now
     That you so oft have boasted to retain?

EDGAR [(*aside*)]: My tears begin to take his part so much
     They mar my counterfeiting.

LEAR: The little dogs and all,
55   Tray, Blanch, and Sweetheart, see, they bark at me.

EDGAR: Tom will throw his head at[9] them.—Avaunt, you curs!
      Be thy mouth or black or white,
      Tooth that poisons if it bite,
      Mastiff, greyhound, mongrel grim,

---

8. The leaky boat may suggest the woman's sexual easiness.
9. Another fiend from Harsnett's *Declaration*.
1. Edgar with his blanket.
2. Partner in law.
3. In the grain field.
4. One shout from your dainty (minikin) mouth can save the sheep.

5. A devil or familiar from Harsnett.
6. A low stool made by a joiner. Proverbially the phrase "I took you for a joint stool" meant "I beg your pardon for failing to notice you." The reference is also to a stool on stage.
7. Regan.
8. Material.
9. Threaten.

60   Hound or spaniel, brach or lym,[1]
      Bobtail tike or trundle-tail,[2]
      Tom will make him weep and wail;
      For, with throwing thus my head,
      Dogs leap the hatch,[3] and all are fled.

65   Do de, de, de. Sessa! Come, march to wakes[4] and fairs and market towns.
      Poor Tom, thy horn is dry.

LEAR: Then let them anatomize Regan; see what breeds about her heart. Is there any
      cause in nature that makes these hard hearts? [(*To Edgar*)] You, sir, I entertain
      for one of my hundred; only I do not like the fashion of your garments. You
70   will say they are Persian; but let them be changed.

KENT: Now, good my lord, lie here and rest awhile.

LEAR [(*lying on cushions*)]:   Make no noise, make no noise. Draw the curtains.[5] So,
      so. We'll go to supper i'th' morning.   [(*He sleeps.*)]

FOOL: And I'll go to bed at noon.
    [*Enter Gloucester.*]

GLOUCESTER [(*to Kent*)]:   Come hither, friend. Where is the King my master?

KENT: Here, sir, but trouble him not; his wits are gone.

GLOUCESTER: Good friend, I prithee, take him in thy arms.
      I have o'erheard a plot of death upon him.
      There is a litter ready; lay him in't
80   And drive toward Dover, friend, where thou shalt meet
      Both welcome and protection. Take up thy master.
      If thou shouldst dally half an hour, his life,
      With thine and all that offer to defend him,
      Stand in assurèd loss. Take up, take up,
85   And follow me, that will to some provision
      Give thee quick conduct.

KENT: Oppressèd nature sleeps.
      This rest might yet have balmed thy broken sinews,°   *nerves*
      Which, if convenience° will not allow,   *circumstances*
      Stand in hard cure. [(*To the Fool*)] Come, help to bear thy master.
90   Thou must not stay behind.   [(*They pick up Lear.*)]

GLOUCESTER: Come, come, away!
                                [*Exeunt (all but Edgar).*]

EDGAR: When we our betters see bearing our woes,
      We scarcely think our miseries our foes.
      Who alone suffers suffers most i'th' mind,[6]
      Leaving free things and happy shows behind;
      But then the mind much sufferance doth o'erskip
95   When grief hath mates, and bearing fellowship.
      How light and portable my pain seems now,
      When that which makes me bend makes the King bow—
      He childed as I fathered. Tom, away!

1. Bitch hound or blood hound.
2. Mongrel dog with a docked or bobbed tail.
3. Lower half of a divided door.
4. Parish festivals.
5. Bedcurtains.
6. Whoever suffers alone has the greatest mental suffering.

Mark the high noises, and thyself bewray
100   When false opinion, whose wrong thoughts defile thee,
In thy just proof repeals and reconciles thee.[7]
What will hap more tonight, safe scape the King!
105   Lurk, lurk.   *[Exit.]*

Scene 7[8]

[*Enter Cornwall, Regan, Goneril, Bastard (Edmund), and Servants.*]

CORNWALL [(*to Goneril*)]: Post speedily to my lord your husband; show him this letter. [*He gives a letter.*] The army of France is landed.—Seek out the traitor Gloucester.   [(*Exeunt some Servants.*)]

REGAN: Hang him instantly.

GONERIL: Pluck out his eyes.

CORNWALL: Leave him to my displeasure. Edmund, keep you our sister company. The revenges we are bound to take upon your traitorous father are not fit for your beholding. Advise the Duke,[9] where you are going, to a most festinate[1] preparation; we are bound to the like. Our posts[2] shall be swift and
10   intelligent betwixt us. Farewell, dear sister; farewell, my lord of Gloucester.

[*Enter steward (Oswald).*]

How now? Where's the King?

OSWALD: My lord of Gloucester hath conveyed him hence.
Some five- or six-and-thirty of his knights,
Hot questrists° after him, met him at gate,   *searchers*
15   Who, with some other of the lord's dependents,
Are gone with him toward Dover, where they boast
To have well-armèd friends.

CORNWALL: Get horses for your mistress.   [(*Exit Oswald.*)]

GONERIL: Farewell, sweet lord, and sister.

CORNWALL: Edmund, farewell.   [(*Exeunt (Goneril and Edmund).*)]
Go seek the traitor Gloucester.
Pinion° him like a thief; bring him before us.   *bind*
                                   [(*Exeunt Servants.*)]
Though well we may not pass upon his life[3]
Without the form of justice, yet our power
Shall do a court'sy° to our wrath, which men   *bow to*
25   May blame but not control.

[*Enter Gloucester, and Servants (leading him).*]
                                  Who's there? The traitor?

REGAN: Ingrateful fox! 'Tis he.

CORNWALL: Bind fast his corky° arms.   *withered*

---

7. Pay attention to what is being said about those in high places; only reveal your identity when public opinion, which now falsely derides you, finally justly proclaims your innocence and recalls you from banishment.
8. Location: Gloucester's house.

9. Albany.
1. Speedy.
2. Messengers.
3. Pass the death sentence upon him.

GLOUCESTER: What means Your Graces? Good my friends, consider
  You are my guests. Do me no foul play, friends.
CORNWALL: Bind him, I say.   [(*Servants bind him.*)]
REGAN: Hard, hard. Oh, filthy traitor!
GLOUCESTER: Unmerciful lady as you are, I'm none.
CORNWALL: To this chair bind him.—Villain, thou shalt find—
        [(*Regan plucks Gloucester's beard.*)]
GLOUCESTER: By the kind gods, 'tis most ignobly done
  To pluck me by the beard.
REGAN: So white,° and such a traitor?   *old*
GLOUCESTER: Naughty° lady,   *wicked*
  These hairs which thou dost ravish from my chin
  Will quicken and accuse thee. I am your host.
  With robbers' hands my hospitable favors
  You should not ruffle thus. What will you do?
CORNWALL: Come, sir, what letters had you late from France?
REGAN: Be simple-answered, for we know the truth.
CORNWALL: And what confederacy have you with the traitors
  Late footed[4] in the kingdom?
REGAN: To whose hands
  You have sent the lunatic King. Speak.
GLOUCESTER: I have a letter guessingly set down,
  Which came from one that's of a neutral heart,
  And not from one opposed.
CORNWALL: Cunning.
REGAN: And false.
CORNWALL: Where hast thou sent the King?
GLOUCESTER: To Dover.
REGAN: Wherefore to Dover? Wast thou not charged at peril—
CORNWALL: Wherefore to Dover? Let him answer that.
GLOUCESTER: I am tied to th' stake, and I must stand the course.[5]
REGAN: Wherefore to Dover?
GLOUCESTER: Because I would not see thy cruel nails
  Pluck out his poor old eyes, nor thy fierce sister
  In his anointed[6] flesh rash° boarish fangs.   *slash*
  The sea, with such a storm as his bare head
60 In hell-black night endured, would have buoyed up
  And quenched the stellèd fires;[7]
  Yet, poor old heart, he holp° the heavens to rain.   *helped*
  If wolves had at thy gate howled that dern° time,   *dread*
  Thou shouldst have said, "Good porter, turn the key."
65 All cruels else subscribe.[8] But I shall see
  The wingèd Vengeance[9] overtake such children.

---

4. Recently landed.
5. Like a bear baited with dogs whose attack he must withstand.
6. Consecrated with holy oil.
7. Fires of the stars.
8. All other cruel creatures would show forgiveness except you.
9. The vengeance of the angel of divine wrath.

CORNWALL: See't shalt thou never.—Fellows, hold the chair.
    Upon these eyes of thine I'll set my foot.
GLOUCESTER: He that will think to live till he be old,
    Give me some help!
    [(*Servants hold the chair as Cornwall grinds out one of Gloucester's eyes with his*
                                boot.)]
                      Oh, cruel! O you gods!
REGAN: One side will mock another. Th'other too.
CORNWALL [*to Gloucester*]: If you see Vengeance—
FIRST SERVANT: Hold your hand, my lord!
    I have served you ever since I was a child;
    But better service have I never done you
    Than now to bid you hold.
REGAN: How now, you dog?
FIRST SERVANT [*to Regan*]: If you did wear a beard upon your chin,
    I'd shake it on this quarrel.[1]—What do you mean?
CORNWALL: My villain?   [(*He draws his sword.*)]
FIRST SERVANT [(*drawing*)]: Nay, then, come on, and take the chance of anger.
                [(*They fight. Cornwall is wounded.*)]
REGAN [(*to another Servant*)]: Give me thy sword. A peasant stand up thus?
              [(*She takes a sword and runs at him behind.*)]
FIRST SERVANT: Oh, I am slain! My lord, you have one eye left
    To see some mischief° on him. Oh!   [*He dies.*] injury
CORNWALL: Lest it see more, prevent it. Out, vile jelly!
              [(*He puts out Gloucester's other eye.*)]
    Where is thy luster now?
GLOUCESTER: All dark and comfortless. Where's my son Edmund?
    Edmund, enkindle all the sparks of nature[2]
    To quit this horrid act.
REGAN: Out, treacherous villain!
85   Thou call'st on him that hates thee. It was he
    That made the overture of thy treasons to us,
    Who is too good to pity thee.
GLOUCESTER: Oh, my follies! Then Edgar was abused.
    Kind gods, forgive me that, and prosper him!
REGAN [*to a Servant*]: Go thrust him out at gates and let him smell
             His way to Dover. [*Exit (a Servant) with Gloucester.*]
    How is't, my lord? How look you?
CORNWALL: I have received a hurt. Follow me, lady.—
    Turn out that eyeless villain. Throw this slave
95   Upon the dunghill.—Regan, I bleed apace.
    Untimely comes this hurt. Give me your arm.
          [*Exeunt (Cornwall, supported by Regan).*]

---

1. I'd pull your beard in defiance for the cause of Gloucester.   2. Love of child for father.

SECOND SERVANT: I'll never care what wickedness I do,
    If this man come to good.
THIRD SERVANT: If she live long,
    And in the end meet the old course of death,
100   Women will all turn monsters.
SECOND SERVANT: Let's follow the old Earl, and get the Bedlam[3]
    To lead him where he would. His roguish madness
    Allows itself to anything.[4]
THIRD SERVANT: Go thou. I'll fetch some flax and whites of eggs
    To apply to his bleeding face. Now, heaven help him!
                                [Exeunt (with the body.)][5]

ACT 4
Scene 1[6]

[Enter Edgar (as poor Tom).]
EDGAR: Yet better thus, and known to be contemned,
    Than still contemned and flattered.[7] To be worst,
    The lowest and most dejected thing of fortune,
    Stands still in esperance,[8] lives not in fear.
5   The lamentable change is from the best;
    The worst returns to laughter.[9] Welcome, then,
    Thou unsubstantial air that I embrace!
    The wretch that thou hast blown unto the worst
    Owes nothing to thy blasts.
                [Enter Gloucester, and an Old Man (leading him).]
                But who comes here?
10   My father, poorly led? World, world, O world!
    But that thy strange mutations make us hate thee,
    Life would not yield to age.[1]
OLD MAN: Oh, my good lord, I have been your tenant
    And your father's tenant these fourscore years.
GLOUCESTER: Away, get thee away! Good friend, begone.
    Thy comforts can do me no good at all;
    Thee they may hurt.
OLD MAN: You cannot see your way.
GLOUCESTER: I have no way and therefore want no eyes;
    I stumbled when I saw. Full oft 'tis seen
20   Our means secure us, and our mere defects
    Prove our commodities.[2] O dear son Edgar,

---

3. Madman from the insane asylum.
4. His madness means he can do anything we ask.
5. At some point after line 96, the body of the slain servant must be removed.
6. Location: The heath.
7. It is better to be a beggar and know that you are despised by others rather than to be despised behind one's

back and flattered to one's face.
8. Gives one some cause for hope.
9. Any change from the worst is bound to be happy.
1. If it were not for the bad fortune we suffer, we would never accept old age and death.
2. Our prosperity makes us feel falsely secure whereas our suffering helps us.

The food of thy abusèd father's wrath![3]
Might I but live to see thee in my touch,
I'd say I had eyes again!

OLD MAN: How now? Who's there?

EDGAR [aside]: O gods! Who is't can say, "I am at the worst"?
I am worse than e'er I was.

OLD MAN: 'Tis poor mad Tom.

EDGAR [(aside)]: And worse I may be yet. The worst is not
So long as we can say, "This is the worst."

OLD MAN [(to Edgar)]: Fellow, where goest?

GLOUCESTER: Is it a beggar-man?

OLD MAN: Madman and beggar too.

GLOUCESTER: He has some reason,° else he could not beg.   sanity
I'th' last night's storm I such a fellow saw,
Which made me think a man a worm. My son
Came then into my mind, and yet my mind
35   Was then scarce friends with him. I have heard more since.
As flies to wanton° boys are we to th' gods;   heedless
They kill us for their sport.

EDGAR [(aside)]:   How should this be?
Bad is the trade that must play fool to sorrow,
Ang'ring itself and others.[4]—Bless thee, master!

GLOUCESTER: Is that the naked fellow?

OLD MAN: Ay, my lord.

GLOUCESTER: Then, prithee, get thee gone. If for my sake
Thou wilt o'ertake us hence a mile or twain
I'th' way toward Dover, do it for ancient love,[5]
And bring some covering for this naked soul,
45   Which I'll entreat to lead me.

OLD MAN: Alack, sir, he is mad.

GLOUCESTER: 'Tis the time's plague, when madmen lead the blind.
Do as I bid thee, or rather do thy pleasure;
Above the rest, begone.

OLD MAN: I'll bring him the best 'parel that I have,
50   Come on't what will.   [Exit.]

GLOUCESTER: Sirrah, naked fellow—

EDGAR: Poor Tom's a-cold. [(Aside)] I cannot daub it further.[6]

GLOUCESTER: Come hither, fellow.

EDGAR [(aside)]: And yet I must.—Bless thy sweet eyes, they bleed.

GLOUCESTER: Know'st thou the way to Dover?

---

3. On whom your deceived father's anger fed.
4. It's hard to have to play the fool to my suffering father,
distressing both myself and others.

5. The traditional trusting bond of master and tenant.
6. I cannot continue the pretense further.

EDGAR: Both stile and gate, horseway and footpath. Poor Tom hath been scared
out of his good wits. Bless thee, good man's son, from the foul fiend! Five
fiends have been in poor Tom at once: of lust, as Obidicut; Hobbididance,
prince of dumbness; Mahu, of stealing; Modo, of murder; Flibbertigibbet,[7]
of mopping and mowing,[8] who since possesses chambermaids and waiting
60   women. So, bless thee, master!
GLOUCESTER [(giving a purse)]: Here, take this purse, thou whom the heavens' plagues
Have humbled to all strokes. That I am wretched
Makes thee the happier. Heavens, deal so still!
Let the superfluous and lust-dieted[9] man,
65   That slaves your ordinance,[1] that will not see
Because he does not feel, feel your pow'r quickly!
So distribution should undo excess
And each man have enough. Dost thou know Dover?
EDGAR: Ay, master.
GLOUCESTER: There is a cliff, whose high and bending head
Looks fearfully in the confinèd deep.
Bring me but to the very brim of it
And I'll repair the misery thou dost bear
With something rich about me. From that place
75   I shall no leading need.
EDGAR: Give me thy arm.
Poor Tom shall lead thee.   [Exeunt.]

Scene 2[2]

[Enter Goneril (and) Bastard (Edmund).]
GONERIL: Welcome, my lord. I marvel our mild husband
Not met us on the way.
[(Enter) steward (Oswald).]
                                       Now, where's your master?
OSWALD: Madam, within, but never man so changed.
I told him of the army that was landed;
5   He smiled at it. I told him you were coming;
His answer was "The worse." Of Gloucester's treachery
And of the loyal service of his son
When I informed him, then he called me sot°   fool
And told me I had turned the wrong side out.
10   What most he should dislike seems pleasant to him;
What like, offensive.
GONERIL [to Edmund]:   Then shall you go no further.
It is the cowish° terror of his spirit,   cowardly
That dares not undertake. He'll not feel wrongs
15   Which tie him to an answer.[3] Our wishes on the way

---

7. Names of fiends taken from Harsnett.
8. Making faces.
9. Immoderately gluttonous and allowed to indulge in his appetites.
1. That enslaves your divine ordinances to his own corrupt will.
2. Location: Before the Duke of Albany's palace.
3. He will ignore insults that, if he took notice, would oblige him to fight.

May prove effects. Back, Edmund, to my brother;[4]
Hasten his musters and conduct his powers.[5]
I must change names at home and give the distaff[6]
Into my husband's hands. This trusty servant
20 Shall pass between us. Ere long you are like to hear,
If you dare venture in your own behalf,
A mistress's command. Wear this; spare speech.

                                        [(*She gives him a favor.*)]

Decline your head. [(*She kisses him.*)] This kiss, if it durst speak,
Would stretch thy spirits up into the air.
25 Conceive,[7] and fare thee well.   [*Exit.*]

EDMUND: Yours in the ranks of death.

GONERIL: My most dear Gloucester!
Oh, the difference of man and man!
To thee a woman's services are due;
My fool usurps my body.[8]

OSWALD: Madam, here comes my lord.   [(*Exit*).]
     [*Enter Albany.*]

GONERIL: I have been worth the whistling.

ALBANY: Oh, Goneril,
You are not worth the dust which the rude wind
Blows in your face. I fear your disposition;
That nature which contemns° its origin   *hates, spurns*
35 Cannot be bordered certain[9] in itself.
She that herself will sliver and disbranch
From her material sap perforce must wither
And come to deadly use.

GONERIL: No more. The text is foolish.

ALBANY: Wisdom and goodness to the vile seem vile;
Filths savor but themselves.[1] What have you done?
Tigers, not daughters, what have you performed?
A father, and a gracious agèd man,
Whose reverence even the head-lugged[2] bear would lick,
45 Most barbarous, most degenerate, have you madded.°   *driven mad*
Could my good brother suffer you to do it?
A man, a prince, by him so benefited?
If that the heavens do not their visible spirits
Send quickly down to tame these vile offenses,
50 It will come,
Humanity must perforce prey on itself,
Like monsters of the deep.

GONERIL: Milk-livered° man,   *cowardly*
That bear'st a cheek for blows, a head for wrongs,
Who hast not in thy brows an eye discerning

4. Brother-in-law Cornwall.
5. Assembling of troops and armed forces.
6. Spinning wheel, symbol of the wife's role.
7. Understand, with sexual double meaning, continuing from "stretch my spirits" and to "death," (or climax) in the next line.
8. My foolish husband claims possession of my body.
9. Kept within bounds.
1. Those who are filthy only have a taste for what is filthy.
2. Dragged by the head.

55 Thine honor from thy suffering,[3] that not know'st
 Fools do those villains pity who are punished
 Ere they have done their mischief.[4] Where's thy drum?
 France spreads his banners in our noiseless land,
 With plumèd helm thy state begins to threat,
60 Whilst thou, a moral° fool, sits still and cries,   *moralizing*
 "Alack, why does he so?"

ALBANY: See thyself, devil!
 Proper deformity shows not in the fiend
 So horrid as in woman.

GONERIL: Oh, vain fool!

ALBANY: Thou changèd and self-covered thing, for shame,
65 Bemonster not thy feature. Were't my fitness
 To let these hands obey my blood,
 They are apt enough to dislocate and tear
 Thy flesh and bones. Howe'er thou art a fiend,
 A woman's shape doth shield thee.

GONERIL: Marry, your manhood! Mew!
 [*Enter a Messenger.*]

ALBANY: What news?

MESSENGER: Oh, my good lord, the Duke of Cornwall's dead,
 Slain by his servant, going to put out
 The other eye of Gloucester.

ALBANY: Gloucester's eyes!

MESSENGER: A servant that he bred, thrilled with remorse,
 Opposed against the act, bending his sword
 To his great master, who, thereat enraged,
 Flew on him and amongst them felled him dead,
 But not without that harmful stroke which since
85 Hath plucked him after.

ALBANY: This shows you are above,
 You justicers,° that these our nether crimes   *judges*
 So speedily can venge! But, oh, poor Gloucester!
 Lost he his other eye?

MESSENGER: Both, both, my lord.—
 This letter, madam, craves a speedy answer;
90 'Tis from your sister.   [*He gives her a letter.*]

GONERIL [(*aside*)]: One way I like this well;
 But being widow, and my Gloucester with her,
 May all the building in my fancy pluck
 Upon my hateful life.[5] Another way
 The news is not so tart.—I'll read, and answer.

              [(*Exit.*)]

ALBANY: Where was his son when they did take his eyes?

MESSENGER: Come with my lady hither.

---

3. Able to tell the difference between an insult to your honor and something you should tolerate.
4. You who fail to understand that only fools like yourselves are so tenderhearted as to pity villains like Gloucester, Lear, and Cordelia, who are apprehended before they have committed a crime.
5. I like this because Edmund is now Duke of Gloucester, and Cornwall, a rival for the throne is dead, but since Regan is a widow and with Edmund, she may destroy my fantasy of sharing the kingdom with Edmund.

ALBANY: He is not here.

MESSENGER: No, my good lord. I met him back again.

ALBANY: Knows he the wickedness?

MESSENGER: Ay, my good lord. 'Twas he informed against him,
100   And quit the house on purpose that their punishment
         Might have the freer course.

ALBANY: Gloucester, I live
         To thank thee for the love thou show'dst the King
         And to revenge thine eyes.—Come hither, friend.
         Tell me what more thou know'st.   [*Exeunt.*]

Scene 3⁶

[*Enter Kent (disguised) and a Gentleman.*]

KENT: Why the King of France is so suddenly gone back know you no reason?

GENTLEMAN: Something he left imperfect in the state,⁷ which since his coming
         forth is thought of, which imports⁸ to the kingdom so much fear and danger
         that his personal return was most required and necessary.

KENT: Who hath he left behind him general?

GENTLEMAN: The Marshal of France, Monsieur la Far.

KENT: Did your letters pierce the Queen to any demonstration of grief?

GENTLEMAN: Ay, sir. She took them, read them in my presence,
         And now and then an ample tear trilled down
10   Her delicate cheek. It seemed she was a queen
         Over her passion, who, most rebel-like,
         Sought to be king o'er her.

KENT: Oh, then it moved her?

GENTLEMAN: Not to a rage. Patience and sorrow strove
         Who should express her goodliest. You have seen
15   Sunshine and rain at once. Her smiles and tears
         Were like a better way; those happy smilets
         That played on her ripe lip seemed not to know
         What guests were in her eyes, which parted thence
         As pearls from diamonds dropped. In brief,
20   Sorrow would be a rarity most beloved
         If all could so become it.

KENT: Made she no verbal question?

GENTLEMAN: Faith, once or twice she heaved the name of "father"
         Pantingly forth, as if it pressed her heart;
25   Cried, "Sisters, sisters! Shame of ladies, sisters!
         Kent! Father! Sisters! What, i'th' storm, i'th' night?
         Let pity not be believed!" There she shook
         The holy water from her heavenly eyes,
         And, clamor-moistened, then away she started
30   To deal with grief alone.

KENT: It is the stars,
         The stars above us, govern our conditions,
         Else one self mate and make could not beget

6. Location: The French camp near Dover.   8. Portends.
7. Unsettled in state affairs.

Such different issues.[9] You spoke not with her since?

GENTLEMAN: No.

KENT: Was this before the King returned?[1]

GENTLEMAN: No, since.

KENT: Well, sir, the poor distressèd Lear's i'th' town,
Who sometime in his better tune[2] remembers
What we are come about, and by no means
Will yield to see his daughter.

GENTLEMAN: Why, good sir?

KENT: A sovereign shame so elbows him[3]—his own unkindness
That stripped her from his benediction,° turned her   blessing
To foreign casualties, gave her dear rights
To his dog-hearted daughters—these things sting
His mind so venomously that burning shame
45   Detains him from Cordelia.

GENTLEMAN: Alack, poor gentleman!

KENT: Of Albany's and Cornwall's powers° you heard not?   troops

GENTLEMAN: 'Tis so. They are afoot.°   on the march

KENT: Well, sir, I'll bring you to our master Lear
50   And leave you to attend him. Some dear cause
Will in concealment wrap me up awhile.
When I am known aright, you shall not grieve
Lending me this acquaintance.[4] I pray you, go
Along with me.   [Exeunt.]

                              Scene 4[5]

[Enter, with drum and colors, Cordelia, Gentleman,[6] and soldiers.]

CORDELIA: Alack, 'tis he! Why, he was met even now
As mad as the vexed sea, singing aloud,
Crowned with rank fumiter[7] and furrow weeds,
With hardocks,[8] hemlock, nettles, cuckooflowers,
5   Darnel,[9] and all the idle weeds that grow
In our sustaining corn. A century[1] send forth!
Search every acre in the high-grown field
And bring him to our eye.   [(Exit a soldier or soldiers.)]
                    What can man's wisdom[2]
In the restoring his bereavèd sense,
10   He that helps him take all my outward worth.

GENTLEMAN: There is means, madam.
Our foster nurse of nature is repose,
The which he lacks. That to provoke in him

---

9. Otherwise one couple could not give birth to such different children.
1. Before the King of France returned to his kingdom.
2. More composed state of mind.
3. Prods his memory.
4. Regret having met me.
5. Location: The French camp.

6. The Quarto specifies "Doctor" here and at line 11.
7. Fumitory, a weed or herb.
8. Burdocks, or wild mustard.
9. Weedy grass.
1. A troop of 100 men.
2. What medical wisdom can accomplish.

Are many simples operative,[3] whose power
15   Will close the eye of anguish.
CORDELIA: All blest secrets,
All you unpublished virtues[4] of the earth,
Spring with my tears! Be aidant and remediate
20   In the good man's distress! Seek, seek for him,
Lest his ungoverned rage dissolve the life
That wants the means to lead it.
    [Enter Messenger.]
MESSENGER: News, madam.
The British powers° are marching hitherward.   *armies*
CORDELIA: 'Tis known before. Our preparation stands
In expectation of them. O dear father,
It is thy business that I go about;[5]
Therefore great France
My mourning and importuned tears hath pitied.
30   No blown ambition doth our arms incite,
But love, dear love, and our aged father's right.
Soon may I hear and see him!   [Exeunt.]

Scene 5[6]

[Enter Regan and steward (Oswald).]
REGAN: But are my brother's powers[7] set forth?
OSWALD: Ay, madam.
REGAN: Himself in person there?
OSWALD: Madam, with much ado.
5   Your sister is the better soldier.
REGAN: Lord Edmund spake not with your lord at home?
OSWALD: No, madam.
REGAN: What might import° my sister's letters to him?   *express*
OSWALD: I know not, lady.
REGAN: Faith, he is posted° hence on serious matter.   *has hurried*
It was great ignorance, Gloucester's eyes being out,
To let him live. Where he arrives he moves
All hearts against us. Edmund, I think, is gone,
In pity of his misery, to dispatch
15   His nighted° life; moreover to descry°   *blinded / spy out*
The strength o'th'enemy.
OSWALD: I must needs after him, madam, with my letter.
REGAN: Our troops set forth tomorrow. Stay with us;
The ways are dangerous.
OSWALD: I may not, madam.
My lady charged my duty[8] in this business.
REGAN: Why should she write to Edmund? Might not you
Transport her purposes by word? Belike

3. Many herbal remedies can work.
4. Little known beneficial herbs.
5. Possibly an allusion to Luke 2.40, where Jesus says, "Wist ye not that I must be about my Father's business?"
6. Location: Gloucester's house.
7. Albany's forces.
8. Insisted upon my obedience.

Something—I know not what. I'll love thee much;
Let me unseal the letter.
OSWALD: Madam, I had rather—
REGAN: I know your lady does not love her husband,
I am sure of that; and at her late being here
She gave strange oeillades⁹ and most speaking looks
To noble Edmund. I know you are of her bosom.
OSWALD: I, madam?
REGAN: I speak in understanding; y'are, I know't.
Therefore I do advise you, take this note:¹
My lord is dead; Edmund and I have talked,
And more convenient is he for my hand
Than for your lady's. You may gather more.
35   If you do find him, pray you, give him this;
And when your mistress hears thus much from you,
I pray, desire her call her wisdom to her.
So, fare you well.
If you do chance to hear of that blind traitor,
40   Preferment falls on him that cuts him off.
OSWALD: Would I could meet him, madam! I should show
What party I do follow.
REGAN: Fare thee well.

[*Exeunt (separately)*.]

Scene 6²

[*Enter Gloucester, and Edgar (in peasant's clothes, leading his father)*.]
GLOUCESTER: When shall I come to th' top of that same hill?
EDGAR: You do climb up it now. Look how we labor.
GLOUCESTER: Methinks the ground is even.
EDGAR: Horrible steep.
Hark, do you hear the sea?
GLOUCESTER: No, truly.
EDGAR: Why, then, your other senses grow imperfect
By your eyes' anguish.
GLOUCESTER: So may it be, indeed.
Methinks thy voice is altered, and thou speak'st
In better phrase and matter than thou didst.
EDGAR: You're much deceived. In nothing am I changed
But in my garments.
GLOUCESTER: Methinks you're better spoken.
EDGAR: Come on, sir, here's the place. Stand still. How fearful
And dizzy 'tis to cast one's eyes so low!
The crows and choughs° that wing the midway air   jackdaws
Show scarce so gross as beetles. Halfway down
15   Hangs one that gathers samphire³—dreadful trade!

9. Eliads, or amorous glances.
1. Take note of this.
2. Location: An open place near Dover.
3. Herb used in pickling.

Methinks he seems no bigger than his head.
The fishermen that walk upon the beach
Appear like mice, and yond tall anchoring bark
Diminished to her cock;⁴ her cock, a buoy
20   Almost too small for sight. The murmuring surge,
That on th'unnumbered idle pebble chafes,
Cannot be heard so high. I'll look no more,
Lest my brain turn, and the deficient sight
Topple down headlong.

GLOUCESTER: Set me where you stand.

EDGAR: Give me your hand. You are now within a foot
Of th'extreme verge. For all beneath the moon
Would I not leap upright.⁵

GLOUCESTER: Let go my hand.
Here, friend, 's another purse; in it a jewel
Well worth a poor man's taking.   [(*He gives a purse.*)]
    Fairies and gods.
30   Prosper it with thee! Go thou further off.
Bid me farewell, and let me hear thee going.

EDGAR [(*moving away*)]: Now fare ye well, good sir.

GLOUCESTER: With all my heart.

EDGAR [(*aside*)]: Why I do trifle thus with his despair
Is done to cure it.

GLOUCESTER [(*kneeling*)]: O you mighty gods!
35   This world I do renounce, and in your sights
Shake patiently my great affliction off.
If I could bear it longer and not fall
To quarrel with your great opposeless wills,
My snuff⁶ and loathèd part of nature should
40   Burn itself out. If Edgar live, oh, bless him!
Now, fellow, fare thee well.   [*He falls forward.*]

EDGAR: Gone, sir. Farewell.—
And yet I know not how conceit° may rob   *imagination*
The treasury of life, when life itself
Yields to the theft. Had he been where he thought,
45   By this had thought been past. Alive or dead?—
Ho, you, sir! Friend! Hear you, sir! Speak!—
Thus might he pass indeed; yet he revives.—
What⁷ are you, sir?

GLOUCESTER: Away, and let me die.

EDGAR: Hadst thou been aught but gossamer, feathers, air,
50   So many fathom down precipitating,
Thou'dst shivered like an egg; but thou dost breathe,
Hast heavy substance, bleed'st not, speak'st, art
    sound.

---

4. Reduced to the size of her cockboat, a small ship's boat.
5. Up and down.
6. Useless residue.

7. Who. Edgar now speaks in a new voice, different from that of Poor Tom and from the other voice he put on at the start of this scene.

Ten masts at each make not the altitude
Which thou hast perpendicularly fell.
55   Thy life's a miracle. Speak yet again.

GLOUCESTER: But have I fall'n or no?

EDGAR: From the dread summit of this chalky bourn.°   *cliff*
Look up aheight; the shrill-gorged lark so far
Cannot be seen or heard. Do but look up.

GLOUCESTER: Alack, I have no eyes.
Is wretchedness deprived that benefit
To end itself by death? 'Twas yet some comfort
When misery could beguile the tyrant's rage
And frustrate his proud will.

EDGAR: Give me your arm.

[He lifts him up.]

65   Up—so. How is't? Feel you your legs? You stand.

GLOUCESTER: Too well, too well.

EDGAR: This is above all strangeness.
Upon the crown o'th' cliff what thing was that
Which parted from you?

GLOUCESTER: A poor unfortunate beggar.

EDGAR: As I stood here below, methought his eyes
70   Were two full moons; he had a thousand noses,
Horns whelked and waved like the enridgèd sea.
It was some fiend. Therefore, thou happy father,
Think that the clearest gods, who make them honors
Of men's impossibilities,[8] have preserved thee.

GLOUCESTER: I do remember now. Henceforth I'll bear
Affliction till it do cry out itself
"Enough, enough," and die. That thing you speak of,
I took it for a man; often 'twould say
"The fiend, the fiend." He led me to that place.

EDGAR: Bear free and patient thoughts.

[Enter Lear (mad, fantastically dressed with wild flowers).]
                        But who comes here?
The safer sense will ne'er accommodate
His master thus.

LEAR: No, they cannot touch me for coining. I am the King himself.[9]

EDGAR: Oh, thou side-piercing[1] sight!

LEAR: Nature's above art in that respect. There's your press money.[2] That fellow
handles his bow like a crow-keeper.[3] Draw me a clothier's yard.[4] Look, look
a mouse! Peace, peace; this piece of toasted cheese will do't. There's my
gauntlet;[5] I'll prove it on a giant. Bring up the brown bills.[6] Oh, well flown,
bird! I'th' clout,[7] i'th' clout—hewgh! Give the word.

8. Who win our awe and reverence by doing things impossible to men.
9. They cannot prosecute me for minting coins. As King, I enjoy the exclusive royal prerogative for doing so.
1. Heartrending, with a suggestion of Christ's suffering on the cross.

2. Bonus for enlisting.
3. Worker who drives crows away.
4. Draw your bow a full cloth-yard long.
5. Armored glove thrown down in a challenge to a duel.
6. Soldiers carrying pikes.
7. Target, bull's-eye.

EDGAR: Sweet marjoram.[8]

LEAR: Pass.

GLOUCESTER: I know that voice.

LEAR: Ha! Goneril with a white beard? They flattered me like a dog and told me I had white hairs in my beard ere the black ones were there. To say ay and no to everything that I said ay and no to was no good divinity.[9] When the rain came to wet me once and the wind to make me chatter, when the thunder would not peace at my bidding, there I found 'em, there I smelt 'em out. Go to, they are not men o' their words. They told me I was everything. 'Tis a lie. I am not ague-proof.[1]

GLOUCESTER: The trick of that voice I do well remember.
Is't not the King?

LEAR: Ay, every inch a king.
When I do stare, see how the subject quakes
I pardon that man's life. What was thy cause?[2]
Adultery?

105   Thou shalt not die. Die for adultery? No.
The wren goes to't, and the small gilded fly
Does lecher in my sight.
Let copulation thrive; for Gloucester's bastard son
Was kinder to his father than my daughters

110   Got 'tween the lawful sheets.
To't, luxury,° pell-mell, for I lack soldiers.   *lechery*
Behold yond simpering dame,
Whose face between her forks presages snow,[3]
That minces virtue and does shake the head
To hear of pleasure's name;

115   The fitchew nor the soilèd horse goes to't[4]
With a more riotous appetite.
Down from the waist they're centaurs,[5]
Though women all above.
But to the girdle do the gods inherit;

120   Beneath is all the fiends'.
There's hell, there's darkness, there is the sulfurous pit,
Burning, scalding, stench, consumption. Fie, fie, fie!
Pah, pah! Give me an ounce of civet,[6] good apothecary,
sweeten my imagination. There's money for thee.

GLOUCESTER: Oh, let me kiss that hand!

LEAR: Let me wipe it first; it smells of mortality.

GLOUCESTER: Oh, ruined piece of nature! This great world
Shall so wear out to naught. Dost thou know me?

---

8. An herb used to cure madness.
9. To agree flatteringly to everything I said was not good theology, since the Bible teaches us "let your yea be yea and your nay, nay'" (James 5.12, Matthew 5.37, and 2 Corinthians 1.18).
1. Immune to illness.
2. Offense.

3. Whose frosty looks seem to suggest frigidity between the legs.
4. Neither the polecat nor the well-pastured horse indulges in sexual pleasure.
5. Mythical creatures with the head, arms, and torso of a man and the lower body and legs of a horse.
6. Musk perfume.

LEAR: I remember thine eyes well enough. Dost thou squinny[7] at me? No, do thy
130   worst, blind Cupid; I'll not love. Read thou this challenge. Mark but the
        penning of it.

GLOUCESTER: Were all thy letters suns, I could not see.

EDGAR [(aside)]: I would not take this from report. It is,
        And my heart breaks at it.

LEAR: Read.

GLOUCESTER: What, with the case of eyes?

LEAR: Oho, are you there with me? No eyes in your head, nor no money in your
        purse? Your eyes are in a heavy case, your purse in a light, yet you see how
        this world goes.

GLOUCESTER: I see it feelingly.[8]

LEAR: What, art mad? A man may see how this world goes with no eyes. Look
        with thine ears. See how yond justice rails upon yond simple thief. Hark in
        thine ear: change places and, handy-dandy,[9] which is the justice, which is
        the thief? Thou hast seen a farmer's dog bark at a beggar?

GLOUCESTER: Ay, sir.

LEAR: And the creature run from the cur? There thou mightst behold the great
        image of authority: a dog's obeyed in office.
        Thou rascal beadle,[1] hold thy bloody hand!
        Why does thou lash[2] that whore? Strip thine own back;
150   Thou hotly lusts to use her in that kind
        For which thou whipp'st her. The usurer hangs the cozener.[3]
        Through tattered clothes small vices do appear;
        Robes and furred gowns hide all. Plate sin with gold,
        And the strong lance of justice hurtless breaks;[4]
155   Arm it in rags, a pygmy's straw does pierce it.
        None does offend, none, I say, none. I'll able 'em.[5]
        Take that of me, my friend, who have the power
        To seal th'accuser's lips. Get thee glass eyes,
        And like a scurvy politician seem[6]
160   To see the things thou does not. Now, now, now, now!
        Pull off my boots. Harder, harder! So.

EDGAR [(aside)]: Oh, matter and impertinency[7] mixed,
        Reason in madness!

LEAR: If thou wilt weep my fortunes, take my eyes.
165   I know thee well enough; thy name is Gloucester.
        Thou must be patient. We came crying hither.
        Thou know'st the first time that we smell the air
        We wawl and cry. I will preach to thee. Mark.

GLOUCESTER: Alack, alack the day!

LEAR: When we are born, we cry that we are come

---

7. Squint.
8. By touch, and with emotional feeling.
9. Take your choice of hands, as in the child's game.
1. Parish officer.
2. Why do we allow adulteresses to be publicly whipped by law? Why not whip the man who lusts after her?
3. The moneylender sentences the con man to be

hanged.
4. Splinters harmlessly.
5. Exempt everyone from legal guilt.
6. If Gloucester were to fit himself with glasses, he would look wise like a vile politician.
7. Sense and nonsense.

To this great stage of fools.—This' a good block.[8]
It were a delicate stratagem to shoe
A troop of horse with felt. I'll put 't in proof,
And when I have stol'n upon these son-in-laws,
175   Then, kill, kill, kill, kill, kill, kill!
[Enter a Gentleman (with attendants).]
GENTLEMAN: Oh, here he is. Lay hand upon him.—Sir,
          Your most dear daughter—
LEAR: No rescue? What, a prisoner? I am even
          The natural fool of fortune.[9] Use me well;
180   You shall have ransom. Let me have surgeons;
          I am cut to th' brains.
GENTLEMAN: You shall have anything.
LEAR: No seconds? All myself?
          Why, this would make a man a man of salt[1]
          To use his eyes for garden waterpots,
          Ay, and laying a autumn's dust.
          I will die bravely, like a smug bridegroom.[2] What?
          I will be jovial. Come, come, I am a king,
          Masters, know you that?
GENTLEMAN: You are a royal one, and we obey you.
LEAR: Then there's life in't. Come, an you get it, you
          shall get it by running. Sa, sa, sa, sa.[3]
                    [Exit (running, followed by attendants).]
GENTLEMAN: A sight most pitiful in the meanest wretch,
          Past speaking of in a king! Thou hast one daughter
          Who redeems nature from the general curse
195   Which twain have brought her to.
EDGAR: Hail, gentle sir.
GENTLEMAN: Sir, speed you. What's your will?
EDGAR: Do you hear aught, sir, of a battle toward?
GENTLEMAN: Most sure and vulgar. Everyone hears that
          Which can distinguish sound.
EDGAR: But, by your favour,
200   How near's the other army?
GENTLEMAN: Near and on speedy foot. The main descry
          Stands on the hourly thought.
EDGAR: I thank you, sir; that's all.
GENTLEMAN: Though that the Queen on special cause is here,
205   Her army is moved on.
EDGAR: I thank you, sir.
                    [Exit (Gentleman)]
GLOUCESTER: You ever-gentle gods, take my breath from me;
          Let not my worser spirit tempt me again
          To die before you please!

---

8. Mold for a felt hat. Lear may be referring to the weeds
he has wound about his hair.
9. Born plaything.
1. Of salt tears.

2. Bridegroom continues the punning of die bravely, "have
sex successfully."
3. A hunting cry.

EDGAR: Well pray you, father.

GLOUCESTER: Now, good sir, what are you?

EDGAR: A most poor man, made tame to fortune's blows,
    Who, by the art of known and feeling sorrows,
    Am pregnant to good pity. Give me your hand.
    I'll lead you to some biding.   [(*He offers his arm.*)]

GLOUCESTER: Hearty thanks.
215   The bounty and the benison of heaven
      To boot, and boot!

    [*Enter steward (Oswald).*]

OSWALD: A proclaimed prize![4] Most happy!
                            [(*He draws his sword.*)]
    That eyeless head of thine was first framed flesh
    To raise my fortunes. Thou old unhappy traitor,
    Briefly thyself remember.[5] The sword is out
220   That must destroy thee.

GLOUCESTER: Now let thy friendly hand
    Put strength enough to't.   [(*Edgar intervenes.*)]

OSWALD: Wherefore, bold peasant,
    Durst thou support a published traitor? Hence,
    Lest that th'infection of his fortune take
    Like hold on thee. Let go his arm.

EDGAR: 'Chill not let go, zir, without vurther 'cagion.[6]

OSWALD: Let go, slave, or thou diest!

EDGAR: Good gentleman, go your gait, and let poor volk pass. An 'chud ha' bin
    zwaggered out of my life, 'twould not ha' bin zo long as 'tis by a vortnight.[7]
    Nay, come not near th' old man; keep out, 'che vor ye, or Ise try whether
230   your costard or my ballow[8] be the harder. 'Chill be plain with you.

OSWALD: Out, dunghill!

EDGAR: 'Chill[9] pick your teeth, zir. Come no matter vor your foins.[1]
                    [(*They fight. Edgar fells him with his cudgel.*)]

OSWALD: Slave, thou hast slain me. Villain, take my purse.
    If ever thou wilt thrive, bury my body
    And give the letters which thou find'st about me
    To Edmund, Earl of Gloucester. Seek him out
    Upon the English party. Oh, untimely death!
    Death!   [(*He dies.*)]

EDGAR: I know thee well: a serviceable villain,
235   As duteous to the vices of thy mistress
    As badness would desire.

GLOUCESTER: What, is he dead?

EDGAR: Sit you down, father. Rest you.   [(*Gloucester sits.*)]

---

4. A man with a price on his head.
5. Say your prayers.
6. I will not let go, sir without further occasion. Edgar adopts the Somerset dialect, a stage convention used for peasants.
7. If I could have been swaggered (bullied) out of my life, it wouldn't have lasted as long as a fortnight (i.e., two weeks).
8. Your head or my cudgel.
9. I'll.
1. Thrusts.

Let's see these pockets; the letters that he speaks of
May be my friends. He's dead; I am only sorry
240   He had no other deathsman.[2] Let us see.

                    [(He finds a letter and opens it.)]

Leave, gentle wax,[3] and, manners, blame us not.
To know our enemies' minds we rip their hearts;
Their papers is more lawful.   [(Reads the letter.)]

    "Let our reciprocal vows be remembered. You have many opportunities
245   to cut him[4] off; if your will want not, time and place will be fruitfully offered. There is nothing done if he return the conqueror. Then am I the
prisoner, and his bed my jail, from the loathed warmth whereof deliver me
and supply the place for your labor.

    Your—wife, so I would say—affectionate servant,
250   and for you her own for venture, Goneril."

Oh, indistinguished space of woman's will!
A plot upon her virtuous huaband's life,
And the exchange my brother! Here in the sands
Thee I'll rake up, the post unsanctified
255   Of murderous lechers; and in the mature time
With this ungracious paper strike the sight
Of the death-practiced Duke. For him 'tis well
That of thy death and business I can tell.

                    [(Exit with the body.)]

GLOUCESTER: The King is mad. How stiff is my vile sense,[5]
260   That I stand up and have ingenious[6] feeling
Of my huge sorrows! Better I were distract;°   crazy
So should my thoughts be severed from my griefs,
And woes by wrong imaginations lose
The knowledge of themselves.   [Drum afar off.]

[Enter Edgar.]

EDGAR: Give me your hand.
265   Far off, methinks, I hear the beaten drum.
Come, father, I'll bestow you with a friend.

                [Exeunt, (Edgar leading his father).]

Scene 7[7]

[Enter Cordelia, Kent (dressed still in his disguise costume), and Gentleman.[8]]
CORDELIA: O thou good Kent, how shall I live and work
To match thy goodness? My life will be too short,
And every measure fail me.
KENT: To be acknowledged, madam, is o'erpaid.
5   All my reports go with the modest truth,
Nor more nor clipped, but so.

---

2. Executioner.
3. The letter's seal.
4. Albany.
5. How obstinate is my deplorable sanity and power of

sensation.
6. Keen consciousness.
7. Location: The French camp.
8. Doctor in the Quarto.

CORDELIA: Be better suited.
    These weeds° are memories of those worser hours;   *garments*
    I prithee, put them off.
KENT: Pardon, dear madam;
    Yet to be known shortens my made intent.[9]
10   My boon I make it[1] that you know me not
    Till time and I think meet.
CORDELIA: Then be't so, my good lord. [*To the Gentleman*] How
    does the King?
GENTLEMAN: Madam, sleeps still.
CORDELIA: O you kind goods,
    Cure this great breach in his abusèd nature!
    Th'untuned and jarring senses, oh, wind up°   *tune*
    Of this child-changèd[2] father!
GENTLEMAN: So please Your Majesty
20   That we may wake the King? He hath slept long.
CORDELIA: Be governed by your knowledge, and proceed
    I'th' sway of your own will.—Is he arrayed?
    [*Enter Lear in a chair carried by servants.*]
GENTLEMAN: Ay, madam. In the heaviness of sleep
    We put fresh garments on him.
25   Be by, good madam, when we do awake him.
    I doubt not of his temperance.
CORDELIA: Very well.   [(*Music.*)]
GENTLEMAN: Please you, draw near.—Louder the music there!
CORDELIA [(*kissing him*)]:
    O my dear father! Restoration hang
    Thy medicine on my lips, and let this kiss
30   Repair those violent harms that my two sisters
    Have in thy reverence made!
KENT: Kind and dear princess!
CORDELIA: Had you not been their father, these white flakes[3]
    Did challenge pity of them. Was this a face
    To be opposed against the warring winds?
35   To stand against the deep dread-bolted thunder
    In the most terrible and nimble stroke
    Of quick cross lightning? To watch—poor perdu!—
    With this thin helm? Mine enemy's dog,
    Though he had bit me, should have stood that night
40   Against my fire; and wast thou fain, poor father,
    To hovel thee with swine and rogues forlorn
    In short and musty straw? Alack, alack!
    'Tis wonder that thy life and wits at once
    Had not concluded all.—He wakes! Speak to him.

9. To reveal my true identity now would alter my care-   2. Changed by children's cruelty.
fully made plan.   3. White locks of hair.
1. The favor I seek.

GENTLEMAN: Madam, do you; 'tis fittest.

CORDELIA: How does my royal lord? How fares Your Majesty?

LEAR: You do me wrong to take me out o'th' grave.
　　　　Thou art a soul in bliss; but I am bound
　　　　Upon a wheel of fire,[4] that mine own tears
50　　　Do scald like molten lead.

CORDELIA:　　　　　　　　　　Sir, do you know me?

LEAR: You are a spirit, I know. Where did you die?

CORDELIA: Still, still, far wide!

GENTLEMAN: He's scarce awake. Let him alone awhile.

LEAR: Where have I been? Where am I? Fair daylight?
55　　　I am mightily abused.° I should ev'n die with pity　　　*confused*
　　　　To see another thus. I know not what to say.
　　　　I will not swear these are my hands. Let's see;
　　　　I feel this pinprick. Would I were assured
　　　　Of my condition!

CORDELIA [(*kneeling*)]: Oh, look upon me, sir,
　　　　And hold your hands in benediction o'er me.

　　　　　　　　　　　　　　　　　　[*He attempts to kneel.*]

　　　　No, sir, you must not kneel.

LEAR:　　　　　　　　　　　Pray, do not mock me.
　　　　I am a very foolish fond old man,
　　　　Fourscore and upward, not an hour more nor less;
65　　　And, to deal plainly,
　　　　I fear I am not in my perfect mind.
　　　　Methinks I should know you, and know this man,
　　　　Yet I am doubtful; for I am mainly ignorant
　　　　What place this is, and all the skill I have
70　　　Remembers not these garments, nor I know not
　　　　Where I did lodge last night. Do not laugh at me,
　　　　For, as I am a man, I think this lady
　　　　To be my child Cordelia.

CORDELIA [(*weeping*)]: And so I am, I am.

LEAR: Be your tears wet? Yes, faith. I pray, weep not.
　　　　If you have poison for me I will drink it.
　　　　I know you do not love me, for your sisters
　　　　Have, as I do remember, done me wrong.
　　　　You have some cause, they have not.

CORDELIA:　　　　　　　　　　No cause, no cause.

LEAR: Am I in France?

KENT:　　　　　　　In your own kingdom, sir.

LEAR: Do not abuse° me.　　　　　　　　　　　　　　　*confuse*

GENTLEMAN: Be comforted, good madam. The great rage,
85　　　You see, is killed in him, and yet it is danger

---

4. A punishment of hell in medieval accounts.

To make him even o'er the time he has lost.
Desire him to go in. Trouble him no more
Till further settling.

CORDELIA: Will't please Your Highness walk?

LEAR: You must bear with me.
Pray you now, forget and forgive.
I am old and foolish.

[Exeunt (all but Kent and Gentleman).]

GENTLEMAN: Holds it true, sir, that the Duke of Cornwall was so slain?

KENT: Most certain, sir.

GENTLEMAN: Who is conductor° of his people?   leader

KENT: As 'tis said, the bastard son of Gloucester.

GENTLEMAN: They say Edgar, his banished son, is with the Earl of Kent in
Germany.

KENT: Report is changeable. 'Tis time to look about; the powers of the kingdom
100   approach apace.

GENTLEMAN: The arbitrament⁵ is like to be bloody. Fare you well, sir.   [(Exit.)]

KENT: My point and period will be throughly wrought,⁶
110   Or well or ill, as this day's battle's fought.   [(Exit.)]

ACT 5

Scene 1⁷

[Enter, with drum and colors, Edmund, Regan, Gentlemen, and soldiers.]

EDMUND [to a Gentleman]:
Know of the Duke if his last purpose hold,
Or whether since he is advised by aught
To change the course. He's full of alteration
And self-reproving. Bring his constant pleasure.

[(Exit Gentleman.)]

REGAN: Our sister's man is certainly miscarried.°   lost

EDMUND: 'Tis to be doubted,° madam.   feared

REGAN: Now, sweet lord,
You know the goodness I intend upon you.
Tell me, but truly—but then speak the truth—
Do you not love my sister?

EDMUND: In honored love.

REGAN: But have you never found my brother's way
To the forfended⁸ place?

EDMUND: That thought abuses you.

REGAN: I am doubtful that you have been conjunct
And bosomed with her, as far as we call hers.

EDMUND: No, by mine honor, madam.

REGAN: I never shall endure her. Dear my lord,

---

5. Decision by arms.   7. Location: The British camp near Dover.
6. Literally, the full stop at the end of my life's sentence   8. Forbidden (by the commandment against adultery).
will be thoroughly shaped.

Be not familiar° with her.   *intimate*
EDMUND: Fear me not.—She and the Duke her husband!
   [Enter, with drum and colors, Albany, Goneril, (and) soldiers.]
GONERIL *[(aside)]*: I had rather lose the battle than that sister
20   Should loosen him and me.
ALBANY *[(to Regan)]*: Our very loving, sister, well bemet.
    [(To Edmund)] Sir, this I heard: the King is come to his daughter,
    With others whom the rigor of our state
    Forced to cry out. Where I could not be honest,
25   I never yet was valiant. For this business,
    It touches us as France invades our land,
    Not bolds the King, with others whom, I fear,
    Most just and heavy causes make oppose.
EDMUND: Sir, you speak nobly.
REGAN: Why is this reasoned?[9]
GONERIL: Combine together 'gainst the enemy;
    For these domestics and particular broils
    Are not the question here.
ALBANY: Let's then determine
    With th'ancient of war on our proceeding.
EDMUND: I shall attend you presently at your tent.
REGAN: Sister, you'll go with us?
GONERIL: No.
REGAN: 'Tis most convenient. Pray, go with us.
GONERIL *[(aside)]*: Oho, I know the riddle.[1]—I will go.
      [(As they are going out,) enter Edgar (disguised).]
EDGAR *[(to Albany)]*: If e'er Your Grace had speech with man so poor,
    Hear me one word.
ALBANY *[(to the others)]*: I'll overtake you.
          [Exeunt both the armies.]
        Speak.
EDGAR *[(giving a letter)]*: Before you fight the battle, ope this letter.
    If you have victory, let the trumpet sound
45   For him that brought it. Wretched though I seem,
    I can produce a champion that will prove
    What is avouchèd° there. If you miscarry,[2]   *affirmed*
    Your business of the world hath so an end,
    And machination ceases. Fortune love you!
ALBANY: Stay till I have read the letter.
EDGAR: I was forbid it.
    When time shall serve, let but the herald cry
    And I'll appear again.   *[Exit (Edgar).]*
ALBANY: Why, fare thee well. I will o'erlook thy paper.
   [Enter Edmund.]

9. Why are we arguing about reasons for fighting?
1. I understand the reason for Regan's demand that I
accompany her, which is that she wants to keep me away

from Edmund.
2. Lose the battle and die.

EDMUND: The enemy's in view. Draw up your powers.

                                                [(*He offers Albany a paper.*)]

     Here is the guess of their true strength and forces

     By diligent discovery;° but your haste   *scouting*

     Is now urged on you.

ALBANY: We will greet the time.   [*Exit.*]

EDMUND: To both these sisters have I sworn my love,

60   Each jealous° of the other as the stung   *suspicious*

     Are of the adder. Which of them shall I take?

     Both? One? Or neither? Neither can be enjoyed

     If both remain alive. To take the widow

     Exasperates, makes mad her sister Goneril,

65   And hardly shall I carry out my side,

     Her husband being alive. Now then, we'll use

     His countenance for the battle, which being done,

     Let her who would be rid of him devise

     His speedy taking off. As for the mercy

70   Which he intends of Lear and to Cordelia,

     The battle done and they within our power,

     Shall never see his pardon, for my state

     Stands on me to defend, not to debate.

                                              [*Exit.*]

Scene 2³

[*Alarum within. Enter, with drum and colors, Lear, Cordelia, and soldiers, over the stage; and exeunt.*]

[*Enter Edgar and Gloucester.*]

EDGAR: Here, father, take the shadow of this tree

     For your good host. Pray that the right may thrive.

     If ever I return to you again,

     I'll bring you comfort.

GLOUCESTER: Grace go with you, sir!

                                              [*Exit (Edgar.)*]

[*Alarum⁴ and retreat within. Enter Edgar.*]

EDGAR: Away, old man! Give me thy hand. Away!

     King Lear hath lost, he and his daughter ta'en.

     Give me thy hand. Come on.

GLOUCESTER: No further, sir. A man may rot even here.

EDGAR: What, in ill thoughts again? Men must endure

10   Their going hence, even as their coming hither;

     Ripeness is all. Come on.

GLOUCESTER: And that's true too.

                                            [*Exeunt.*]

---

3. Location: The battlefield.   4. Trumpet call to battle.

Scene 3[5]

[*Enter, in conquest, with drum and colors, Edmund; Lear and Cordelia, as prisoners; soldiers, Captain.*]

EDMUND: Some officers take them away. Good guard[6]
    Until their greater pleasures[7] first be known
    That are to censure° them.   *judge*
CORDELIA [(*to Lear*)]:   We are not the first
    Who with best meaning have incurred the worst.
5   For thee, oppressèd King, I am cast down;
    Myself could else outfrown false Fortune's frown.
    Shall we not see these daughters and these sisters?
LEAR: No, no, no, no! Come, let's away to prison.
    We two alone will sing like birds i'th' cage.
10   When thou dost ask me blessing, I'll kneel down
    And ask of thee forgiveness. So we'll live,
    And pray, and sing, and tell old tales, and laugh
    At gilded butterflies,[8] and hear poor rogues
    Talk of court news; and we'll talk with them too—
15   Who loses and who wins; who's in, who's out—
    And take upon 's the mystery of things,
    As if we were God's spies; and we'll wear out,
    In a walled prison, packs and sects of great ones,
    That ebb and flow by th' moon.
EDMUND: Take them away.
LEAR: Upon such sacrifices, my Cordelia,
    The gods themselves throw incense. Have I caught thee?
    He that parts us shall bring a brand from heaven
    And fire us hence like foxes.[9] Wipe thine eyes;
    The good years shall devour them, flesh and fell,
25   Ere they shall make us weep. We'll see 'em starved first.
    Come.   [*Exit (with Cordelia, guarded)*.]
EDMUND: Come hither, Captain. Hark.
    Take thou this note. [(*He gives a paper*.)] Go follow them to prison.
    One step I have advanced thee; if thou dost
30   As this instructs thee, thou dost make thy way
    To noble fortunes. Know thou this: that men
    Are as the time is. To be tender-minded
    Does not become a sword. Thy great employment
    Will not bear question; either say thou'lt do't
35   Or thrive by other means.
CAPTAIN: I'll do't, my lord.
EDMUND: About it, and write "happy" when th' hast done.
    Mark, I say, instantly, and carry it so
    As I have set it down.

---

5. Location: The British camp.
6. Guard them well.
7. The wishes of those in command.
8. Brightly dressed courtiers.

9. Nothing short of a firebrand from heaven will ever part us again. Firebrands were used to smoke foxes from their lairs.

CAPTAIN: I cannot draw a cart, nor eat dried oats;
40   If it be man's work, I'll do't   *[Exit Captain.]*
     [*Flourish. Enter Albany, Goneril, Regan, (another Captain, and) soldiers.*]
ALBANY: Sir, you have showed today your valiant strain,
       And fortune led you well. You have the captives
       Who were the opposites° of this day's strife;   *enemies*
       I do require them of you, so to use them
45   As we shall find their merits and our safety
       May equally determine.
EDMUND: Sir, I thought it fit
       To send the old and miserable King
       To some retention° and appointed guard,   *confinement*
       Whose age had charms in it, whose title more,
50   To pluck the common bosom on his side
       And turn our impressed lances in our eyes
       Which do command them.[1] With him I sent the Queen,
       My reason all the same; and they are ready
       Tomorrow, or at further space, t'appear
55   Where you shall hold your session. At this time
       We sweat and bleed; the friend hath lost his friend,
       And the best quarrels in the heat are cursed
       By those that feel their sharpness.
       The question of Cordelia and her father
60   Requires a fitter place.
ALBANY: Sir, by your patience,
       I hold you but a subject of[2] this war,
       Not as a brother.
REGAN: That's as we list to grace him.
       Methinks our pleasure might have been demanded
       Ere you had spoke so far. He led our powers,
65   Bore the commission of my place and person,
       The which immediacy may well stand up
       And call itself your brother.
GONERIL: Not so hot!
       In his own grace he doth exalt himself
       More than in your addition.[3]
REGAN: In my rights,
70   By me invested, he compeers° the best.   *is equal with*
GONERIL: That were the most if he should husband you.
REGAN: Jesters do oft prove prophets.
GONERIL: Holla, holla!
       That eye that told you so looked but asquint.°   *furtively*

---

1. Whose advanced age had magic in it, and whose title as king had even more, to win the sympathy of the commoners and turn against us the weapons of those very troops whom we impressed into service.
2. Subordinate in.
3. The titles you confer upon him.

REGAN: Lady, I am not well, else I should answer
70   From a full-flowing stomach. [(*To Edmund*)] General,
       Take thou my soldiers, prisoners, patrimony;
       Dispose of them, of me; the walls is thine.[4]
       Witness the world that I create thee here
       My lord and master.
GONERIL: Mean you to enjoy him?
ALBANY: The let-alone lies not in your good will.
EDMUND: Nor in thine, lord.
ALBANY: Half-blooded[5] fellow, yes.
REGAN [(*to Edmund*)]: Let the drum strike and prove my title thine.
ALBANY: Stay yet; hear reason. Edmund, I arrest thee
       On capital treason; and, in thy attaint
80   This gilded serpent. [(*Pointing to Goneril*)] For your claim, fair sister,
       I bar it in the interest of my wife;
       'Tis she is subcontracted to this lord,
       And I, her husband, contradict your banns.
       If you will marry, make your loves to me;
85   My lady is bespoke.
GONERIL: An interlude!°   *a play*
ALBANY: Thou art armed, Gloucester. Let the trumpet sound.
       If none appear to prove upon thy person
       Thy heinous, manifest, and many treasons,
       There is my pledge. [(*He throws down a glove.*)] I'll make it on thy heart,
90   Ere I taste bread, thou art in nothing less
       Than I have here proclaimed thee.
REGAN: Sick, oh, sick!
GONERIL [(*aside*)]: If not, I'll ne'er trust medicine.[6]
EDMUND [(*throwing down a glove*)]: There's my exchange. What in the world he is
95   That names me traitor, villain-like he lies.
       Call by the trumpet. He that dares approach,
       On him, on you—who not?—I will maintain
       My truth and honor firmly.
ALBANY: A herald, ho!
EDMUND: A herald, ho, a herald!
       [*Enter a Herald.*]
ALBANY [(*to Edmund*)]: Trust to thy single virtue;[7] for thy soldiers,
       All levied in my name, have in my name
       Took their discharge.
REGAN: My sickness grows upon me.
ALBANY [(*to Soldiers*)]: She is not well. Convey her to my tent.
                                   [(*Exit Regan, supported.*)]

---

4. The citadel of my heart and body surrender completely   6. Poison.
to you.   7. Unaided strength.
5. Only half noble.

Come hither, herald. Let the trumpet sound,
105   And read out this.   [(*He gives a paper.*)]
CAPTAIN: Sound, trumpet!   [*A trumpet sounds.*]
HERALD: (*reads*) "If any man of quality or degree[8] within the lists of the army will
         maintain upon Edmund, supposed Earl of Gloucester, that he is a mainfold
         traitor, let him appear by the third sound of the trumpet. He is bold in his
110   defense."
EDMUND: Sound!   [*First trumpet.*]
HERALD: Again!   [*Second trumpet.*]
HERALD: Again!   [*Third trumpet.*]
                                                           [*Trumpet answers within.*]
         [*Enter Edgar, armed, (with a trumpeter before him).*]
ALBANY: Ask him his purposes, why he appears
115   Upon this call o'th' trumpet.
HERALD: What[9] are you?
         Your name, your quality, and why you answer
         This present summons?
EDGAR: Know my name is lost,
         By treason's tooth bare-gnawn and canker-bit.[1]
         Yet am I noble as the adversary
120   I come to cope.°   encounter
ALBANY: Which is that adversary?
EDGAR: What's he that speaks for Edmund, Earl of Gloucester?
EDMUND: Himself. What say'st thou to him?
EDGAR: Draw thy sword,
         That, if my speech offend a noble heart,
         Thy arm may do thee justice. Here is mine.
                                                           [(*He draws his sword.*)]
125   Behold, it is the privilege of mine honors,[2]
         My oath, and my profession. I protest,
         Maugre[3] thy strength, place, youth, and eminence,
         Despite thy victor sword and fire-new fortune,
         Thy valor, and thy heart, thou art a traitor—
130   False to thy gods, thy brother, and thy father,
         Conspirant 'gainst this high-illustrious prince,
         And from th'extremest upward of thy head
         To the descent and dust below thy foot
         A most toad-spotted traitor. Say thou no,
135   This sword, this arm, and my best spirits are bent
         To prove upon thy heart, whereto I speak,
         Thou liest.
EDMUND: In wisdom I should ask thy name.
         But since thy outside looks so fair and warlike,
140   And that thy tongue some say of breeding breathes,

---

8. Noble birth or rank.   2. Of my knighthood.
9. Who.   3. In spite of.
1. Worm-eaten.

What safe and nicely[4] I might well delay
By rule of knighthood, I disdain and spurn.[5]
Back do I toss those treasons[6] to thy head,
With the hell-hated lie o'erwhelm thy heart,
145   Which—for they yet glance by and scarcely bruise[7]—
This sword of mine shall give them instant way,[8]
Where they shall rest forever.—Trumpets, speak!

          [(He draws.) Alarums. Fight. (Edmund falls.)]

ALBANY *[(to Edgar)]:* Save him, save him!
GONERIL: This is practice, Gloucester.
By th' law of arms thou wast not bound to answer
150   An unknown opposite. Thou art not vanquished,
But cozened° and beguiled.   *tricked*
ALBANY: Shut your mouth, dame,
Or with this paper shall I stopple° it.—Hold, sir.   *stop up*
Thou worse than any name, read thine own evil.

          [(He shows the letter.)]

    [(To Goneril)] No tearing, lady; I perceive you know it.
GONERIL: Say if I do, the laws are mine, not thine.
Who can arraign me for't?
ALBANY: Most monstrous! Oh!
Know'st thou this paper?
GONERIL: Ask me not what I know.

          [Exit.]

ALBANY: Go after her. She's desperate; govern her.

          [(Exit a soldier.)]

EDMUND: What you have charged me with, that have I done,
160   And more, much more. The time will bring it out.
'Tis past, and so am I. But what art thou
That hast this fortune on me? If thou'rt noble,
I do forgive thee.
EDGAR: Let's exchange charity.
I am no less in blood than thou art, Edmund;
165   If more, the more th' hast wronged me.
My name is Edgar, and thy father's son
The gods are just, and of our pleasant° vices   *pleasurable*
Make instruments to plague us.
The dark and vicious place where thee he got°   *begot*
170   Cost him his eyes.
EDMUND: Th' hast spoken right. 'Tis true.
The wheel is come full circle; I am here.
ALBANY *[(to Edgar)]:* Methought thy very gait did prophesy
A royal nobleness. I must embrace thee.

          [(They embrace.)]

---

4. Cautiously and punctiliously.
5. I disdain to insist on my right to refuse combat with one of lower rank.
6. Accusations of treason.

7. Which charges of treason—since as yet they merely glance off my armor.
8. Provide an immediate pathway to your heart.

Let sorrow split my heart if ever I
175   Did hate thee or thy father!
EDGAR: Worthy prince, I know't.
ALBANY: Where have you hid yourself?
     How have you known the miseries of your father?
EDGAR: By nursing them, my lord. List° a brief tale,   *listen to*
     And when 'tis told, oh, that my heart would burst!
     The bloody proclamation to escape[9]
     That followed me so near—oh, our lives' sweetness,
     That we the pain of death would hourly die
     Rather than die at once![1]—taught me to shift
185   Into a madman's rags, t'assume a semblance
     That very dogs disdained; and in this habit
     Met I my father with his bleeding rings,°   *sockets*
     Their precious stones new lost; became his guide,
     Led him, begged for him, saved him from despair;
190   Never—oh, fault!—revealed myself unto him
     Until some half hour past, when I was armed.
     Not sure, though hoping, of this good success,
     I asked his blessing, and from first to last
     Told him our pilgrimage. But his flawed° heart—   *cracked*
195   Alack, too weak the conflict to support—
     Twixt two extremes of passion, joy and grief,
     Burst smilingly.
EDMUND: This speech of yours hath moved me,
     And shall perchance do good. But speak you on;
     You look as you had something more to say.
ALBANY: If there be more, more woeful, hold it in,
     For I am almost ready to dissolve,[2]
     Hearing of this.
EDGAR: This would have seemed a period
     To such as love not sorrow; but another,
     To amplify too much, would make much more
205   And to extremity.[3] Whilst I
     Was big in clamor, came there in a man
     Who, having seen me in my worst estate,
     Shunned my abhorred society; but then, finding
     Who 'twas that so endured, with his strong arms
210   He fastened on my neck and bellowed out
     As he'd burst heaven, threw him on my father,[4]
     Told the most piteous tale of Lear and him
     That ever ear received, which in recounting
     His grief grew puissant,° and the strings of life   *powerful*

---

9. In order to escape the death-threatening proclamation.
1. Oh, the perversity of our attachment to our lives'
sweetness, that we prefer to suffer continually the fear of
death rather than die at once and be done with it.

2. Break into tears.
3. But another sorrowful circumstance, adding to what is
already too much, would increase it and exceed the limit.
4. Threw himself on my father.

215   Began to crack. Twice then the trumpets sounded,
        And there I left him tranced.
ALBANY: But who was this?
EDGAR: Kent, sir, the banished Kent, who in disguise
        Followed his enemy king and did him service
        Improper for a slave.
        [Enter a Gentleman (with a bloody knife).]
GENTLEMAN: Help, help, oh, help!
EDGAR: What kind of help?
ALBANY: Speak, man.
EDGAR: What means this bloody knife?
GENTLEMAN: 'Tis hot, it smokes.
        It came even from the heart of—Oh, she's dead!
ALBANY: Who dead? Speak, man.
GENTLEMAN: Your lady, sir, your lady! And her sisiter
225   By her is poisoned; she confesses it.
EDMUND: I was contracted to them both. All three
        Now marry in an instant.
EDGAR: Here comes Kent.
        [Enter Kent.]
ALBANY: Produce the bodies, be they alive or dead.
                                            [(Exit Gentleman.)]
        This judgment of the heavens, that makes us tremble,
230   Touches us not with pity.—Oh, is this he?
        [To Kent] The time will not allow the compliment
        Which very manners urges.
KENT: I am come
        To bid my king and master aye good night.
        Is he not here?
ALBANY: Great thing of us forgot!
235   Speak, Edmund, where's the King? And where's Cordelia?
                    [Goneril and Regan's bodies (are) brought out.]
        See's thou this object, Kent?
KENT: Alack, why thus?
EDMUND: Yet Edmund was beloved.
        The one the other poisoned for my sake
240   And after slew herself.
ALBANY: Even so. Cover their faces.
EDMUND: I pant for life. Some good I mean to do,
        Despite of mine own nature. Quickly send—
        Be brief in it—to th' castle, for my writ
245   Is on the life of Lear and on Cordelia.
        Nay, send in time.
ALBANY: Run, run, oh, run!
EDGAR: To who, my lord? Who has the office? *[(To Edmund)]* Send
        Thy token of reprieve.

EDMUND: Well thought on. Take my sword. The captain!
250   Give it the Captain.
EDGAR: Haste thee, for thy life.

                               [*(Exit one with Edmund's sword.)*]

EDMUND: He hath commission from thy wife and me
        To hang Cordelia in the prison and
        To lay the blame upon her own despair,
        That she fordid° herself.   destroyed
ALBANY: The gods defend her! Bear him hence awhile.

                               [*(Edmund is borne off.)*]

        [*Enter Lear, with Cordelia in his arms; (Captain).*]

LEAR: Howl, howl, howl! Oh, you are men of stones!
        Had I your tongues and eyes, I'd use them so
        That heaven's vault should crack. She's gone forever.
        I know when one is dead and when one lives;
300   She's dead as earth. Lend me a looking glass;
        If that her breath will mist or stain the stone,
        Why, then she lives.
KENT: Is this the promised end?
EDGAR: Or image of that horror?
ALBANY: Fall and cease!
LEAR: This feather stirs; she lives! If it be so,
305   It is a chance which does redeem all sorrows
        That ever I have felt.
KENT [*(kneeling)*]:   O my good master!
LEAR: Prithee, away.
EDGAR: 'Tis noble Kent, your friend.
LEAR: A plague upon you, murderers, traitors all!
        I might have saved her; now she's gone forever!
310   Cordelia, Cordelia! Stay a little. Ha?
        What is't thou say'st? Her voice was ever soft,
        Gentle, and low, an excellent thing in woman.
        I killed the slave that was a-hanging thee.
CAPTAIN: 'Tis true, my lords, he did.
LEAR: Did I not, fellow?
315   I have seen the day, with my good biting falchion°   light sword
        I would have made them skip. I am old now,
        And these same crosses spoil me.[5]—Who are you?
        Mine eyes are not o'th' best; I'll tell you straight.
KENT: If Fortune brag of two she loved and hated,
320   One of them we behold.
LEAR: This is a dull sight. Are you not Kent?
KENT: The same,
        Your servant Kent. Where is your servant Caius?[6]

---

5. Adversities take away my strength.   6. Kent's disguise name.

LEAR: He's a good fellow, I can tell you that;
    He'll strike, and quickly too. He's dead and rotten
KENT: No, my good lord, I am the very man—
LEAR: I'll see that straight.
KENT: That from your first of difference and decay
    Have followed your sad steps—
LEAR: You are welcome hither.
KENT: Nor no man else. All's cheerless, dark, and deadly.
330   Your eldest daughters have fordone° themselves,   destroyed
    And desperately are dead.
LEAR: Ay, so I think.
ALBANY: He knows not what he says, and vain is it
    That we present us to him.
EDGAR: Very bootless.°   in vain
    [Enter a Messenger.]
MESSENGER: Edmund is dead, my lord.
ALBANY: That's but a trifle here.
    You lords and noble friends, know our intent:
    What comfort to this great decay may come
    Shall be applied. For us, we will resign,
    During the life of this old majesty,
340   To him our absolute power; [(to Edgar and Kent)] you, to your rights,
    With boot and such addition as your honors
    Have more than merited. All friends shall taste
    The wages of their virtue, and all foes
    The cup of their deservings.—Oh, see, see!
LEAR: And my poor fool[7] is hanged! No, no, no life?
    Why should a dog, a horse, a rat have life,
    And thou no breath at all? Thou'lt come no more,
    Never, never, never, never, never!
    Pray you, undo this button. Thank you, sir.
350   Do you see this? Look on her, look, her lips,
    Look there, look there!   [He dies.]
EDGAR: He faints.—My lord, my lord!
KENT: Break, heart, I prithee, break!
EDGAR: Look up, my lord.
KENT: Vex not his ghost.[8] Oh, let him pass! He hates him
    That would upon the rack[9] of this tough world
355   Stretch him out longer.
EDGAR: He is gone indeed.
KENT: The wonder is he hath endured so long.
    He but usurped his life.

7. Cordelia; fool is a term of endearment.   9. Torture rack.
8. Departing spirit.

ALBANY: Bear them from hence. Our present business
       Is general woe. [(*To Kent and Edgar*)] Friends of my soul, you twain
360   Rule in this realm, and the gored state sustain.
KENT: I have a journey, sir, shortly to go.
       My master calls me; I must not say no.
EDGAR: The weight of this sad time we must obey;
       Speak what we feel, not what we ought to say.
365   The oldest hath borne most; we that are young
       Shall never see so much nor live so long.

                                        [Exeunt, with a dead march.]

⚛ PERSPECTIVES ⚛
Tracts on Women and Gender

What is the nature of woman? Is she meant to be subordinate to man or an equal partner? What virtues is she capable of? Does she have intellectual ability, and if so, is it appropriate for her to write? How should she behave toward her husband? What are his responsibilities to her? What is the difference between a good woman and a bad one? What is the difference between manly behavior and womanly behavior? These are some of the questions that early modern English tracts on women and gender ask. Although we would not ask all of these questions in precisely the same way today, they are still of burning interest. The debate over these questions in early modern tracts on women sheds light on the representation of sex and gender in the poetry and drama of the period. By *sex* is meant the representation of biological difference; by *gender* is meant the representation of sex difference as it is socially constructed.

In the Middle Ages there were both attacks on women and defenses of them by both women and men, but intellectual and social changes modified the debate in the early modern period. One of the prominent medieval genres that continued to be imitated in the early modern period was the praise of exemplary women, such as Boccaccio's *De Claris Mulieribus* ("concerning famous women"), Chaucer's *Legend of Good Women*, and Christine de Pisan's *Le Livre de la Cité des Dames* (translated into English in 1521 as *The Book of the City of Ladies*). Renaissance humanism brought a new intellectual rigor to the genre. The German humanist Heinrich Cornelius Agrippa (1486–1535) stands out in the early Tudor controversy of the 1540s. Agrippa's *De Nobilitate et Praecellentia Foemenei Sexus* (translated in 1542 as *A Treatise of the Nobilitie and Excellencye of Woman Kynde*) not only lists biblical and classical heroines but also examines how the place of women in society is determined by culture rather than nature: "And thus by these lawes, the women being subdued as it were by force of arms, are constrained to give place to men, and to obey their subduers, not by natural, nor divine necessity or reason, but by custom, education, fortune, and a certain tyrannical occasion." However, even a humanist author such as Erasmus, who had enlightened views on other social issues, had very strict views about the absolute subordination of wife to husband. Indeed, this subordination seems to have increased in intensity in the early modern period as the nuclear family headed by the father superseded the extended family, in which power was more dispersed throughout the network of kinship.

Among the learned, the new classical humanist education was still largely reserved for young men. Such changes moved the historian Joan Kelly Gadol to ask, "Did women have a Renaissance?" At the same time, some early modern women were educated enough to represent themselves in the debate on the nature of women, and they brought new perspectives to it. Margaret Tyler was one of the first English women to speak in defense of women as writers. Rachel Speght, the first polemical or argumentative woman writer in English, wrote her defense of women in response to a controversy set in motion by the publication of Joseph Swetnam's *The Arraignment of Lewd, Idle, Froward, and Unconstant Women* (1615). Swetnam was a misogynist, but his tract had the virtue of eliciting defenses of women. Among these responses were *A Muzzle for Melastomus*, written from the theological perspective of Rachel Speght, and *Ester Hath Hanged Haman*, written from the more secular outlook of "Ester Sowernam" (a pen-name adopted to counter the "sweet" in the name Swetnam). Two other tracts of the 1620s, *Hic Mulier* ("the mannish woman") and *Haec-Vir* ("the womanish man") humorously raised the problem of the blurring of genders and carried on a debate about the style of dress and behavior that men and women should adopt.

Whether these tracts take the form of an oration, a speech by one person, or a dialogue between two people (as in *Haec-Vir*), they are all in lively conversation with each other, either directly or indirectly. They are also in a lively conversation with other texts in this period.

Title page from *The English Gentlewoman*, by Richard Brathwaite, 1631.

Representing only a fraction of the early modern literature on women and gender, these tracts attest to heightened interest in questions of gender.

⊷ ⬥ ⊶

Joseph Swetnam
fl. 1615

Little is known about Joseph Swetnam other than that he stirred up an enormous controversy over the question of women when he wrote *The Arraignment of Lewd, Idle, Froward, and Unconstant Women* (1615). The work was published anonymously with an introductory letter signed by "Thomas Tel-troth." Trotting out all the negative stereotypes of women he could jumble together, Swetnam constructed his mock treatise as a piece of raucous comedy, aimed at the lowest common denominator. Reading Swetnam's work as a serious diatribe against women, Rachel Speght and the pseudonymous Ester Sowernam and Constantia Munda produced critiques of misogyny. Speght unmasked Swetnam's authorship and identified him as a fencing master in Bristol. An anonymous comedy, *Swetnam the Woman-hater, Arraigned by*

Women (1620), possibly by Thomas Heywood, dramatized the debate as a court trial with Swetnam prosecuting his case against women and the Amazon Atlanta (a soldier disguised as a woman) defending them. Swetnam is finally turned over to a court of women, who find him guilty and muzzle him (an obvious reference to Speght's *Muzzle for Melastomus*).

from The Arraignment of Lewd, Idle, Froward, and Unconstant Women

from *Chapter 2. The Second Chapter showeth the manner of such women as live upon evil report: it also showeth that the beauty of women has been the bane of many a man, for it hath overcome valiant and strong men, eloquent and subtle men. And in a word it hath overcome all men, as by examples following shall appear.*

First, that of Solomon unto whom God gave singular wit and wisdom, yet he loved so many women that he quite forgot his God which always did guide his steps, so long as he lived godly and ruled justly, but after he had glutted himself with women, then he could say, vanity of vanity all is but vanity. He also in many places of his book of Proverbs exclaims most bitterly against lewd women calling them all that naught is, and also displayeth their properties, and yet I cannot let men go blameless although women go shameless; but I will touch them both, for if there were not receivers then there would not be so many stealers: if there were not some knaves there would not be so many whores, for they both hold together to bolster each other's villainy, for always birds of a feather will flock together hand in hand to bolster each other's villainy.

Men, I say, may live without women, but women cannot live without men. For Venus, whose beauty was excellent fair, yet when she needeth man's help she took Vulcan, a clubfooted smith. And therefore if a woman's face glister,[1] and her gesture pierce the marble wall, or if her tongue be as smooth as oil or as soft as silk, and her words so sweet as honey, or if she were a very ape for wit, or a bag of gold for wealth, or if her personage have stolen away all that nature can afford, and if she be decked up in gorgeous apparel, then a thousand to one but she will love to walk where she may get acquaintance, and acquaintance bringeth familiarity, and familiarity setteth all follies abroach,[2] and twenty to one that if a woman love gadding but that she will pawn her honor to please her fantasy.

Man must be at all the cost and yet live by the loss. A man must take all the pains and women will spend all the gains. A man must watch and ward, fight and defend, till the ground, labor in the vineyard, and look what he getteth in seven years; a woman will spread it abroad with a fork in one year, and yet little enough to serve her turn but a great deal too little to get her good will. Nay, if thou give her ever so much and yet if thy person please not her humor, then will I not give a halfpenny for her honesty at the year's end.

For then her breast will be the harborer of an envious heart, and her heart the storehouse of poisoned hatred; her head will devise villainy, and her hands are ready to practice that which their heart desireth. Then who can but say that women are sprung from the devil, whose heads, hands and hearts, minds and souls are evil, for women are called the hook of all evil, because men are taken by them as a fish is taken in with the hook.

---

1. Glitter, shine.   2. Flowing abroad.

For women have a thousand ways to entice thee, and ten thousand ways to deceive thee, and all such fools as are suitors unto them; some they keep in hand with promises, and some they feed with flattery, and some they delay with dalliances, and some they please with kisses. They lay out the folds of their hair to entangle men into their love; betwixt their breasts is the vale of destruction, and in their beds there is hell, sorrow and repentance. Eagles do not eat men till they are dead, but women devour them alive, for a woman will pick thy pocket and empty thy purse, laugh in thy face and cut thy throat. They are ungrateful, perjured, full of fraud, flouting and deceit, unconstant, waspish,[3] toyish,[4] light, sullen, proud, discourteous and cruel, and yet they were by God created, and by nature formed, and therefore by policy and wisdom to be avoided, for good things abused are to be refused. Or else for a month's pleasure, she may make thee go stark naked. She will give thee roast meat, but she will beat thee with the spit. If thou hast crowns in thy purse, she will be thy heart's gold until she leave thee not a whit of white money. They are like summer birds, for they will abide no storm, but flock about thee in the pride of thy glory, and fly from thee in the storms of affliction; for they aim more at thy wealth than at thy person, and esteem more thy money than any man's virtuous qualities; for they esteem of a man without money as a horse does a fair stable without meat. They are like eagles which will always fly where the carrion is.

They will play the horse-leech to suck away thy wealth, but in the winter of thy misery, she will fly away from thee. Not unlike the swallow, which in the summer harboreth herself under the eaves of a house, and against winter flieth away, leaving nothing but dirt behind her.

Solomon saith, he that will suffer himself to be led away or to take delight in such women's company is like a fool which rejoiceth when he is led to the stocks. *Proverbs* 7.

Hosea, by marrying a lewd woman of light behavior was brought unto idolatry, *Hosea* 1. Saint Paul accounteth fornicators so odious, that we ought not to eat meat with them. He also showeth that fornicators shall not inherit the kingdom of Heaven, 1 *Corinthians* the 9th and 11th verse.

And in the same chapter Saint Paul excommunicateth fornicators, but upon amendment he receiveth them again. Whoredom punished with death, *Deuteronomy* 22.21 and *Genesis* 38.24. Phineas a priest thrust two adulterers, both the man and the woman, through the belly with a spear, *Numbers* 25.

God detests the money or goods gotten by whoredom, *Deuteronomy* 23.17, 18. Whores called by diverse names, and the properties of whores, *Proverbs* 7.6 and 21. A whore envieth an honest woman, *Esdras* 16 and 24. Whoremongers God will judge, *Hebrews* 13 and 42. They shall have their portions with the wicked in the lake that burns with fire and brimstone, *Revelation* 21.8.

Only for the sin of whoredom God was sorry at heart, and repented that he ever made man, *Genesis* 6.67.

Saint Paul saith, to avoid fornication every man may take a wife, 1 *Corinthians* 6.9.

Therefore he which hath a wife of his own and yet goeth to another woman is like a rich thief which will steal when he has no need.

There are three ways to know a whore: by her wanton looks, by her speech, and by her gait. *Ecclesiasticus* 26.[5] And in the same chapter he saith, that we must not give our strength unto harlots, for whores are the evil of all evils, and the vanity of all

---

3. Spiteful.
4. Frivolous, wanton.

5. Apocryphal book of the Old Testament.

vanities, they weaken the strength of a man and deprive the body of his beauty, it fur-roweth his brows and maketh the eyes dim, and a whorish woman causeth the fever and the gout; and at a word, they are a great shortening to a man's life.

For although they seem to be as dainty as sweet meat, yet in trial not so whole-some as sour sauce. They have wit, but it is all in craft; if they love it is vehement, but if they hate it is deadly.

Plato saith, that women are either angels or devils, and that they either love dearly or hate bitterly, for a woman hath no mean in her love, nor mercy in her hate, no pity in revenge, nor patience in her anger; therefore it is said, that there is nothing in the world which both pleases and displeases a man more than a woman, for a woman most delighteth a man and yet most deceiveth him, for as there is nothing more sweet to a man than a woman when she smiles, even so there is nothing more odious than the angry countenance of a woman.

Solomon in his 20th chapter of *Ecclesiastes*[6] saith, that an angry woman will foam at the mouth like a boar. If all this be true as most true it is, why shouldest thou spend one hour in the praise of women as some fools do, for some will brag of the beauty of such a maid, another will vaunt of the bravery of such a woman, that she goeth be-yond all the women in the parish. Again, some study their fine wits how they may cunningly swooth[7] women, and with logic how to reason with them, and with elo-quence to persuade them. They are always tempering their wits as fiddlers do their strings, who wrest them so high, that many times they stretch them beyond time, tune and reason.

Again, there are many that weary themselves with dallying, playing, and sporting with women, and yet they are never satisfied with the unsatiable desire of them; if with a song thou wouldest be brought asleep, or with a dance be led to delight, then a fair woman is fit for thy diet. If thy head be in her lap she will make thee believe that thou are hard by[8] God's seat, when indeed thou are just at hell gate.

⊷ ⚎⬧⚍ ⊷

Rachel Speght
1597?–?

The daughter of the rector of two London churches and the wife of a minister, Rachel Speght was only about nineteen years old when she wrote *A Muzzle for Melastomus, the Cynical Baiter of, and Foul-Mouthed Barker Against Evah's Sex, or an Apologetical Answer to the Irreligious and Illiterate Pamphlet made by Io. Swu. and by him Intituled The Arraignment of Women.* Speght in-terpreted Swetnam's *Arraignment* as a serious attack on women to show the faulty logic under-pinning misogyny. Her title indicates the dual thrust of her analysis: the *irreligious* Swetnam has misinterpreted Scripture, and the *illiterate* pamphlet is logically confused and rhetorically flawed. She argues for a view of marriage as a mutual partnership and the relation between the sexes as one of greater equality. Modern critics have debated the implications of Speght's work: Barbara Lewalski has called Rachel Speght "the first self-proclaimed and positively identified female polemicist in England," while Ann Rosalind Jones has questioned whether Speght's work can be considered feminist in the twentieth-century sense. All critics of early modern gender studies agree, however, that Speght was a learned and committed author. She alone of the participants in the Jacobean controversy about women affixed her own name to the title

6. A faulty citation: in Ecclesiasticus 25, an angry woman is compared to a bear.

7. Sway, woo.
8. Close to.

page. And she reiterated her authorship with the publication of her poetic dream-vision *Mortalities Memorandum* (1621), in which she defends women's education.

from A Muzzle for Melastomus

Of Woman's Excellency, with the causes of her creation, and of the sympathy which ought to be in man and wife each toward other

The work of creation being finished, this approbation thereof was given by God himself, that "All was very good."[1] If all, then woman, who—except man—is the most excellent creature under the canopy of heaven. But if it be objected by any:

First, that woman, though created good, yet by giving ear to Satan's temptations brought death and misery upon all her posterity.

Secondly, that "Adam was not deceived, but that the woman was deceived and was in the transgression."[2]

Thirdly, that St. Paul says "It were good for a man not to touch a woman."[3]

Fourthly and lastly, that of Solomon, who seems to speak against all of our sex: "I have found one man of a thousand, but a woman among them all I have not found,"[4] whereof in its due place.

To the first of these objections, I answer: that Satan first assailed the woman because where the hedge is lowest, most easy it is to get over, and she being the weaker vessel[5] was with more facility to be seduced—like as a crystal glass sooner receives a crack than a strong stone pot. Yet we shall find the offense of Adam and Eve almost to parallel; for as an ambitious desire to be made like God was the motive which caused her to eat, so likewise was it his, as may plainly appear by that *ironia:* "Behold, man is become as one of us"[6]—not that he was so indeed, but hereby his desire to attain a greater perfection than God had given him was reproved. Woman sinned, it is true, by her infidelity in not believing the word of God but giving credit to Satan's fair promises that "she should not die";[7] but so did the man, too. And if Adam had not approved of that deed which Eve had done, and been willing to tread the steps where she had gone, he—being her head—would have reproved her and have made the commandment a bit to restrain him from breaking his Maker's injunction. For if a man burn his hand in the fire, the bellows that blew the fire is not to be blamed, but himself rather for not being careful to avoid the danger. Yet if the bellows had not blown, the fire had not burned; no more is woman simply to be condemned for man's transgression. For by the free will which before his fall he enjoyed, he might have avoided and been free from being burned or singed with that fire which was kindled by Satan and blown by Eve. It therefore served not his turn a whit afterwards to say: "The woman which thou gavest me gave me of the tree, and I did eat."[8] For a penalty was inflicted upon him as well as on the woman, the punishment of her transgression being particular to her own sex and to none but the female kind, but for the sin of man the whole earth was cursed.[9] And he being better able than the woman to have

---

1. Genesis 1.31. References to the Bible are indicated in the margins of Speght's text.
2. 1 Timothy 2.14.
3. 1 Corinthians 7.1.
4. Ecclesiastes 7.28.
5. "The weaker vessel," a phrase taken from 1 Peter 3.7, is frequently used in early modern English sermons to describe woman.

6. Genesis 3.22. "Ironia," or irony, is a figure of speech in which the meaning is the opposite of that of the words used and the tone of which is often mocking.
7. Genesis 3.4.
8. Genesis 3.12.
9. Genesis 3.17.

resisted temptation, because the stronger vessel, was first called to account, to show that to whom much is given, of them much is required; and that he who was the sovereign of all creatures visible should have yielded greatest obedience to God.

True it is (as is already confessed) that woman first sinned, yet find we no mention of spiritual nakedness till man had sinned. Then it is said "Their eyes were opened,"[1] the eyes of their mind and conscience; and then perceived they themselves naked, that is, not only bereft of that integrity which they originally had, but felt the rebellion and disobedience of their members in the disordered motions of their now corrupt nature, which made them for shame to cover their nakednesse. Then (and not afore) it is said that they saw it, as if sin were imperfect and unable to bring a deprivation of a blessing received, or death on all mankind, till man (in whom lay the active power of generation) had transgressed. The offense, therefore, of Adam and Eve is by St. Austin[2] thus distinguished: "the man sinned against God and himself, the woman against God, herself and her husband"; yet in her giving of the fruit to eat had she no malicious intent towards him, but did therein show a desire to make her husband partaker of that happiness, which she thought by their eating they should both have enjoyed. This her giving Adam of that sauce, wherewith Satan had served her, whose sourness, afore he had eaten, she did not perceive, was that which made her sin to exceed his. Wherefore, that she might not of him who ought to honor her be abhorred,[3] the first promise that was made in Paradise, God makes to woman, that by her seed should the serpent's head be broken.[4] Whereupon Adam calls her *Hevah*, Life, that as the woman had been an occasion of his sin so should woman bring forth the Savior from sin, which was in the fullness of time accomplished.[5] By which was manifested that he is a Savior of believing women no less than of men, that so the blame of sin may not be imputed to his creature, which is good, but to the will by which Eve sinned; and yet by Christ's assuming the shape of man was it declared that his mercy was equivalent to both sexes. So that by Hevah's blessed seed, as St. Paul affirms, it is brought to pass that "male and female are all one in Christ Jesus."[6]

To the second objection I answer: that the Apostle does not hereby exempt man from sin, but only giveth to understand that the woman was the primary transgressor, and not the man; but that man was not at all deceived was far from his meaning. For he afterwards expressly saith that "in Adam all die, so in Christ shall all be made alive."[7]

For the third objection, "It is good for a man not to touch a woman": the Apostle makes it not a positive prohibition but speaks it only because of the Corinth[ian]s' present necessity,[8] who were then persecuted by the enemies of the church. For which cause, and no other, he saith: "Art thou loosed from a wife? Seek not a wife"—meaning whilst the time of these perturbations should continue in their heat; "but if thou are bound, seek not to be loosed; if thou marriest, thou sinnest not," only increase thy care: "for the married careth for the things of this world. And I wish that you were without care that ye might cleave fast to the Lord without separation: for the time remaineth, that they which have wives be as though they had none, for the persecutors shall deprive you of them either by imprisonment, banishment or death." So that manifest it is, that the Apostle does not hereby forbid marriage, but only adviseth the Corinth[ian]s to forbear a while, till God in mercy should curb the fury of their

1. Genesis 3.7.
2. St. Augustine; this commonplace echoes parts of his sermon on Adam and Eve.
3. 1 Peter 3.7.
4. Genesis 3.15.

5. Galatians 4.4.
6. Galatians 3.28.
7. 1 Corinthians 15.22.
8. 1 Corinthians 7.

adversaries. For (as Eusebius[9] writeth) Paul was afterward married himself, the which is very probable, being that interrogatively he saith: "Have we not power to lead about a wife being a sister, as well as the rest of the Apostles, and as the brethren of the Lord, and Cephas?"[1]

The fourth and last objection is that of Solomon: "I have found one man among a thousand, but a woman among them all have I not found."[2] For answer of which, if we look into the story of his life, we shall find therein a commentary upon this enigmatical[3] sentence included. For it is there said that Solomon had seven hundred wives and three hundred concubines, which number connected make one thousand. These women turning away his heart from being perfect with the Lord his God,[4] sufficient cause had he to say, that among the said thousand women found he not one upright. He saith not, that among a thousand women never any man found one worthy of commendation, but speaks in the first person singularly "I have not found," meaning in his own experience. For this assertion is to be held a part of the confession of his former follies, and no otherwise, his repentance being the intended drift of *Ecclesiastes*.

Thus having (by God's assistance) removed those stones whereat some have stumbled, others broken their shins, I will proceed toward the period of my intended task, which is to decipher the excellency of women. Of whose creation I will, for order's sake, observe: first, the efficient cause,[5] which was God; secondly, the material cause, or whereof she was made; thirdly, the formal cause, or fashion and proportion of her feature; fourthly and lastly, the final cause, the end or purpose for which she was made. To begin with the first.

The efficient cause of woman's creation was Jehovah the Eternal, the truth of which is manifest in Moses his narration of the six days' works, where he says, "God created them male and female."[6] And David, exhorting all "the earth to sing to the Lord" (meaning, by a metonymy,[7] "earth": all creatures that live on the earth, of whatever sex or nation) gives this reason: "For the Lord has made us."[8] That work then cannot choose but be good, yea very good, which is wrought by so excellent a workman as the Lord; for he, being a glorious Creator, must effect a worthy creature. Bitter water cannot proceed from a pleasant sweet fountain, nor bad work from that workman which is perfectly good—and, in propriety, none but he.[9]

Secondly, the material cause, or matter whereof woman was made, was of a refined mold, if I may so speak. For man was created of the dust of the earth,[1] but woman was made of a part of man after that he was a living soul. Yet she was not produced from Adam's foot, to be his too low inferior; nor from his head to be his superior; but from his side, near his heart, to be his equal: that where he is lord, she may be lady. And therefore saith God concerning man and woman jointly: "Let them rule over the fish of the sea, and over the fowls of the heaven, and over every beast that moves upon the earth."[2] By which words he makes their authority equal, and all creatures to be in subjection to them both. This, being rightly considered, doth teach men to make such

9. Eusebius (A.D. 260–340) was Bishop of Caesarea and a church historian. See *Ecclesiastical History* 3.30.
1. 1 Corinthians 9.5.
2. Ecclesiastes 7.30.
3. Mysterious.
4. 1 Kings 11.3.
5. The agent who makes something; see Aristotle's *Physics* 2.3.

6. Genesis 1.28 [27].
7. A figure of speech that substitutes one term for another to which it is closely related.
8. Psalms 100.3.
9. Psalms 100.5; Matthew 19.7.
1. Genesis 2.7.
2. Genesis 1.26.

account of their wives as Adam did of Eve: "This is bone of my bone, and flesh of my flesh."[3] As also, that they neither do or wish any more hurt unto them, than unto their own bodies. For men ought to love their wives as themselves, because he that loves his wife loves himself;[4] and never did man hate his own flesh (which the woman is) unless a monster in nature.

Thirdly, the formal cause, fashion and proportion, of woman was excellent. For she was neither like the beasts of the earth, fowls of the air, fishes of the sea, or any other inferior creature; but man was the only object which she did resemble. For as God gave man a lofty countenance that he might look up toward Heaven, so did he likewise give unto woman. And as the temperature of man's body is excellent, so is woman's. For whereas other creatures, by reason of their gross humors, have excrements for their habit—as fowls their feathers, beasts their hair, fishes their scales—man and woman only have their skin clear and smooth.[5] And (that more is) in the image of God were they both created; yea and to be brief, all the parts of their bodies, both external and internal, were correspondent and meet each for other.

Fourthly and lastly, the final cause or end for which woman was made was to glorify God, and to be a collateral companion for man to glory God, in using her body and all the parts, powers and faculties thereof as instruments for his honor. As with her voice to sound forth his praises, like Miriam, and the rest of her company;[6] with her tongue not to utter words of strife, but to give good counsel unto her husband, the which he must not despise. For Abraham was bidden to give ear to Sarah his wife.[7] Pilate was willed by his wife not to have any hand in the condemning of Christ;[8] and a sin it was in him that he listened not to her; Leah and Rachel counseled Jacob to do according to the word of the Lord;[9] and the Shunamite put her husband in mind of harboring the prophet Elisha.[1] Her hands should be open, according to her ability, in contributing towards God's service and distressed servants, like to that poor widow who cast two mites into the treasury;[2] and as Mary Magdalene, Susanna and Joanna, the wife of Herod's steward, with many others which of their substance ministered unto Christ.[3] Her heart should be a receptacle for God's word, like Mary that treasured the sayings of Christ in her heart.[4] Her feet should be swift in going to seek the Lord in his sanctuary, as Mary Magdalene made haste to seek Christ at his sepulcher.[5] Finally, no power external or internal ought woman to keep idle, but to employ it in some service of God, to the glory of her creator and comfort of her own soul.

The other end for which woman was made was to be a companion and helper for man; and if she must be a *helper,* and but a *helper,* then are those husbands to be blamed, which lay the whole burden of domestical affairs and maintenance on the shoulders of their wives. For, as yoke-fellows they are to sustain part of each other's cares, griefs and calamities. But as if two oxen be put into one yoke, the one being bigger than the other, the greater bears most weight; so the husband, being the stronger vessel, is to bear a greater burden than his wife. And therefore the Lord said to Adam: "In the sweat of your face shall you eat your bread, till you return to the dust."[6] And St. Paul says that "he that provideth not for his household is worse than an infidel."[7]

3. Genesis 2.23.
4. Ephesians 5.28.
5. Genesis 1.26.
6. Exodus 15.20.
7. Genesis 21.12.
8. Matthew 27.19.
9. Genesis 31.16.

1. 2 Kings 4.9.
2. Mark 12.43.
3. Luke 8.
4. Luke 1.45.
5. John 20.1.
6. Genesis 3.19.
7. 1 Timothy 5.8.

Nature hath taught senseless creatures to help one another: as the male pigeon, when his hen is weary with sitting on her eggs and comes off from them, supplies her place, that in her absence they may receive no harm, until such time as she is fully refreshed. Of small birds, the cock always helps his hen to build her nest; and while she sits upon her eggs he flies abroad to get meat for her, who cannot then provide any for herself. The crowing cockerel helps his hen to defend her chickens from peril, and will endanger himself to save her and them from harm. Seeing then, that these unreasonable creatures by the instinct of nature bear such affection to each other, that without any grudge they willingly according to their kind help one another, I may reason, *a minore ad maius*,[8] that much more should man and woman, which are reasonable creatures, be helpers to each other in all things lawful, they having the law of God to guide them, his word to be a lantern to their feet and a light unto their paths, by which they are excited to a far more mutual participation of each other's burden than other creatures. So that neither the wife may say to her husband nor the husband to his wife: "I have no need of thee,"[9] no more than the members of the body may say to each other, between whom there is such a sympathy that if one member suffer, all suffer with it. Therefore though God bade Abraham forsake his country and kindred, yet he bade him not forsake his wife who, being "Flesh of his flesh, and bone of his bone," was to be copartner with him of whatsoever did betide him, whether joy or sorrow. Wherefore Solomon says "woe to him that is alone";[1] for when thoughts of discomfort, troubles of this world and fear of dangers do possess him, he wants a companion to lift him up from the pit of perplexity into which he is fallen.[2] For a good wife, saith Plautus, is the wealth of the mind and the welfare of the heart; and therefore a meet associate for her husband. And "woman," saith Paul, "is the glory of the man."[3]

Marriage is a merri-age, and this world's paradise, where there is mutual love. Our blessed Savior vouchsafed to honor a marriage with the first miracle that he wrought,[4] unto which miracle matrimonial estate may not unfitly be resembled. For as Christ turned water into wine, a far more excellent liquor (which, as the Psalmist saith, "Makes glad the hearts of man"[5]) so the single man is changed by marriage from a bachelor to a husband, a far more excellent title: from a solitary life to a joyful union and conjunction with such a creature as God had made meet for man, for whom none was fit till she was made. The enjoying of this great blessing made Pericles more unwilling to part from his wife than to die for his country; and Antonius Pius to pour forth that pathetic exclamation against death for depriving him of his dearly beloved wife: "O cruel hard-hearted death in bereaving me of her whom I esteemed more than my own life!"[6] "A virtuous woman," saith Solomon, "is the crown of her husband";[7] by which metaphor he shows both the excellency of such a wife and what account her husband is to make of her. For a king does not trample his crown under his feet, but highly esteems it, gently handles it and carefully lays it up as the evidence of his kingdom; and therefore when David destroyed Rabbah[8] he took off the crown from their king's head. So husbands should not account their wives as their vassals but as those that are "heirs together of the grace of life,"[9] and with all lenity and mild persuasions

---

8. From the lesser to the greater.
9. 1 Corinthians 12.21.
1. Ecclesiastes 4.10.
2. Ecclesiastes 4.10.
3. 1 Corinthians 11.7.
4. John 2.
5. Psalms 104.15.
6. Antonius Pius (86–161 C.E.) Roman emperor, founded

a charity for orphaned girls in honor of his wife. Plutarch writes about how Pericles (495–429 B.C.E.), ruler of Athens, greatly loved Aspasia.
7. Proverbs 7.4.
8. 1 Chronicles 20.2. Joab destroyed Rabbah, while David took the king's crown.
9. 1 Peter 3.7.

set their feet in the right way if they happen to tread awry, bearing with their infirmities, as Elkanah did with his wife's barrenness.[1]

The kingdom of God is compared to the marriage of a king's son;[2] John calleth the conjunction of Christ and his chosen a marriage;[3] and not few but many times does our blessed Savior in the Canticles[4] set forth his unspeakable love towards his church under the title of a husband rejoicing with his wife, and often vouchsafeth to call her his sister a spouse—by which is showed that with God "is no respect of persons," nations, or sexes.[5] For whosoever, whether it be man or woman, that doth "believe in the lord Jesus, such shall be saved."[6] And if God's love, even from the beginning, had not been as great toward woman as to man, then he would not have preserved from the deluge of the old world as many women as men. Nor would Christ after his resurrection have appeared to a woman first of all other, had it not been to declare thereby, that the benefits of his death and resurrection are as available, by belief, for women as for men; for he indifferently died for the one sex as well as the other.

<hr />

Ester Sowernam

The pen name Ester Sowernam comes from the Old Testament heroine Esther, who defended her people against Haman, and the antithesis of Joseph Swetnam's last name (sweet/sour). The full title of her text also parodies Swetnam's: *Ester Hath Hanged Haman; or An Answer to a Lewd Pamphlet, Entitled The Arraignment of Women. With the Arraignment of Lewd, Idle, Froward and Unconstant Men, and Husbands* (1617). On the whole, the author of this pamphlet presents herself in a more secular light than Rachel Speght does. Sowernam's criticisms of misogyny are more psychological and social than moral and logical. Trained in classics as well as Scripture and a keen observer, Ester Sowernam finds that Swetnam has incorrectly stated that the Bible is the source of the statement that women are a necessary evil and finds that the true source is in Euripides's *Medea*. The occasion for Sowernam's writing is a dinner party at which Swetnam's book and Speght's response were discussed. Sowernam finds fault with both—Swetnam because he "damns all women" and Speght because she "undertaking to defend women doth rather charge and condemn them." Sowernam cites the double standard by which men are excused for what women are judged harshly for in order to assert women's superiority. She argues that women are judged more severely because they are thought to be more virtuous in the first place. The second half of her pamphlet may have helped to inspire the comedy that spoofed the entire controversy, *Swetnam the Woman-Hater Arraigned by Women* (1620).

from **Ester Hath Hanged Haman**
from *Chapter 7. The answer to all objections which are material made against women*

As for that crookedness and frowardness[1] with which you charge women, look from whence they have it. For of themselves and their own disposition it doth not proceed, which is proved directly by your own testimony. For in your 46th page, line 15[16], you say: "A young woman of tender years is flexible, obedient, and subject to do

---

1. 1 Samuel 1.17.
2. Matthew 22.
3. Revelation 19.7.
4. The Song of Songs.

5. Romans 2.11.
6. John 3.18.
1. Perversity, unreasonableness.

anything, according to the will and pleasure of her husband." How cometh it then that this gentle and mild disposition is afterwards altered? Yourself doth give the true reason, for you give a great charge not to marry a widow. But why? Because, say you in the same page, "A widow is framed to the conditions[2] of another man." Why then, if a woman have froward conditions, they be none of her own, she was framed to them. Is not our adversary ashamed of himself to rail against women for those faults which do all come from men? Doth not he most grievously charge men to learn[3] their wives bad and corrupt behavior? For he saith plainly: "Thou must unlearn a widow, and make her forget and forego her former corrupt and disordered behavior." Thou must unlearn her; *ergo*, what fault she hath learned: her corruptness comes not from her own disposition but from her husband's destruction.

Is it not a wonder that your pamphlets are so dispersed? Are they not wise men to cast away time and money upon a book which cutteth their own throats? 'Tis pity but that men should reward you for your writing (if it be but as the Roman Sertorius[4] did the idle poet: he gave him a reward, but not for his writing—but because he should never write more). As for women, they laugh that men have no more able a champion. This author cometh to bait women or, as he foolishly saith, the "Bearbaiting of Women," and he bringeth but a mongrel cur who doth his kind[5] to brawl and bark, but cannot bite. The mild and flexible disposition of a woman is in philosophy proved in the composition of her body, for it is a maxim: *Mores animi sequuntur temperaturam corporis* (the disposition of the mind is answerable to the temper of the body). A woman in the temperature of her body is tender, soft and beautiful, so doth her disposition in mind correspond accordingly: she is mild, yielding and virtuous. What disposition accidentally happeneth unto her is by the contagion of a froward husband, as Joseph Swetnam affirmeth.

And experience proveth. It is a shame for a man to complain of a froward woman—in many respects all concerning himself. It is a shame he hath no more government over the weaker vessel.[6] It is a shame he hath hardened her tender sides and gentle heart with his boisterous and Northern blasts. It is a shame for a man to publish and proclaim household secrets—which is a common practice amongst men, especially drunkards, lechers, and prodigal spendthrifts. These when they come home drunk, or are called in question for their riotous misdemeanors, they presently show themselves the right children of Adam. They will excuse themselves by their wives and say that their unquietness and frowardness at home is the cause that they run abroad: an excuse more fitter for a beast than a man. If thou wert a man thou wouldst take away the cause which urgeth a woman to grief and discontent, and not by thy frowardness increase her distemperature.[7] Forbear thy drinking, thy luxurious riot, thy gaming and spending, and thou shalt have thy wife give thee as little cause at home as thou givest her great cause of disquiet abroad. Men which are men, if they chance to be matched with froward wives—either of their own making or others' marring[8]— they would make a benefit of the discommodity:[9] either try his skill to make her mild or exercise his patience to endure her cursedness; for all crosses are inflicted either for punishment of sins or for exercise of virtues. But humorous[1] men will sooner mar a thousand women than out of a hundred make one good.

---

2. Circumstances, character traits.
3. Teach.
4. Quintus Sertorius, Roman general, appointed governor of Farther Spain in 83 B.C.E.
5. Nature.

6. From 1 Peter 3.7.
7. Disorder in mind and body.
8. Spoiling.
9. Inconvenience, disadvantageousness.
1. Moody.

And this shall appear in the imputation which our adversary chargeth upon our sex: to be lascivious, wanton and lustful. He saith: "Women tempt, allure and provoke men." How rare a thing is it for women to prostitute and offer themselves? How common a practice is it for men to seek and solicit women to lewdness? What charge do they spare? What travail do they bestow? What vows, oaths and protestations do they spend to make them dishonest? They hire panders, they write letters, they seal them with damnations and execrations to assure them of love when the end proves but lust. They know the flexible disposition of women, and the sooner to overreach them some will pretend they are so plunged in love that, except they obtain their desire, they will seem to drown, hang, stab, poison, or banish themselves from friends and country. What motives are these to tender dispositions? Some will pretend marriage, another offer continual maintenance; but when they have obtained their purpose, what shall a woman find?—just that which is her everlasting shame and grief: she hath made herself the unhappy subject to a lustful body and the shameful stall[2] of a lascivious tongue. Men may with foul shame charge woman with this sin which she had never committed, if she had not trusted; nor had ever trusted, if she had not been deceived with vows, oaths and protestations. To bring a woman to offend in one sin, how many damnable sins do they commit? I appeal to their own consciences. The lewd disposition of sundry men doth appear in this: if a woman or maid will yield to lewdness, what shall they want?[3]—but if they would live in honesty, what help shall they have? How much will they make of the lewd? How base an account of the honest? How many pounds will they spend in bawdy houses? But when will they bestow a penny upon an honest maid or woman, except it be to corrupt them?

Our adversary bringeth many examples of men which have been overthrown by women. It is answered before: the fault is their own. But I would have him, or anyone living, to show any woman that offended in this sin of lust, but that she was first solicited by a man.

Helen was the cause of Troy's burning: first, Paris did solicit her; next, how many knaves and fools of the male kind had Troy, which to maintain whoredom would bring their city to confusion?

When you bring in examples of lewd women and of men which have been stained by women, you show yourself both frantic and a profane irreligious fool to mention Judith,[4] for cutting off Holofernes' head, in that rank.

You challenge women for untamed and unbridled tongues; there was never woman was ever noted for so shameless, so brutish, so beastly a scold as you prove yourself in this base and odious pamphlet. Your blaspheme God, you rail at his creation, you abuse and slander his creatures; and what immodest or impudent scurrility is it which you do not express in this lewd and lying pamphlet?

Hitherto I have so answered all your objections against women that, as I have not defended the wickedness of any, so I have set down the true state of the question. As Eve did not offend without temptation of a serpent, so women do seldom offend but it is by provocation of men. Let not your impudency, nor your consorts' dishonesty, charge our sex hereafter with those sins of which you yourselves were the first procurers. I have, in my discourse, touched you, and all yours, to the quick. I have taxed you with bitter speeches; you will, perhaps, say I am a railing scold. In this objection,

---

2. Target.
3. Lack, need.
4. A wealthy, attractive widow who saved her people from Holofernes, an Assyrian general, by attracting and

then killing him. (See the Book of Judith, part of the Catholic Bible, but viewed as apocryphal by Jews and Protestants.)

Joseph Swetnam, I will teach you both wit and honesty. The difference between a railing scold and an honest accuser is this: the first rageth upon passionate fury without bringing cause or proof, the other bringeth direct proof for what she allegeth. You charge women with clamorous words, and bring no proof; I charge you with blasphemy, with impudency, scurrility, foolery and the like. I show just and direct proof for what I say. It is not my desire to speak so much; it is your dessert to provoke me upon just cause so far. It is not railing to call a crow black, or a wolf a ravenor,[5] or a drunkard a beast; the report of the truth is never to be blamed: the deserver of such a report deserves the shame.

Now, for this time, to draw to an end. Let me ask according to the question of Cassian, *cui bono?*[6]—what have you gotten by publishing your pamphlet? Good I know you can get none. You have, perhaps, pleased the humors of some giddy, idle, conceited persons. But you have dyed yourself in the colors of shame, lying, slandering, blasphemy, ignorance, and the like.

The shortness of time and the weight of business call me away, and urge me to leave off thus abruptly; but assure yourself, where I leave now I will by God's grace supply the next term, to your small content. You have exceeded in your fury against widows, whose defense you shall hear of at the time aforesaid. In the mean space, recollect your wits; write out of deliberation, not out of fury; write out of advice, not out of idleness: forbear to charge women with faults which come from the contagion of masculine serpents.

➥ ⇥◆⇤ ➥

Hic Mulier and *Haec-Vir*

Hic Mulier and *Haec-Vir* were published anonymously within a week of each other in February 1620. *Hic Mulier*, the first of the two pamphlets to appear, begins with the complaint that "since the days of Adam women were never so masculine." The title introduces this theme by a gender switch of its own: *Hic Mulier*, Latin for "This Woman," uses the masculine form *hic* instead of the feminine *haec*. The title page contains illustrations of two such mannish women—one wearing a man's hat, which she admires in a mirror, and another sitting in a barber's chair to get her hair cut. Structured as a "brief declamation," or oration, the text argues that such activities as hair bobbing and wearing men's clothes are immoral and unnatural for women. Furthermore, such gender crossing is also a threat to the entire political order: "most pernicious to the commonwealth for she hath power by example to do it a world of injury."

As its subtitle boasts, *Haec-Vir* was "an answer to the late book intituled *Hic Mulier*" and was represented as "a brief dialogue between Haec-Vir the Womanish-Man, and Hic Mulier the Man-Woman." The effeminate man and the hermaphroditic woman first misrecognize each other's gender. Once that is cleared up, the foppish man launches into a diatribe against the woman, who defends herself by arguing that "custom is an idiot." The first half of the dialogue reads like a proclamation of the equality of the sexes, with the bare-breasted, dagger-swinging Hic Mulier exclaiming, "We are as free-born as men, have as free election, and as free spirits, we are compounded of like parts and may with like liberty make benefit of our creations." Despite this bold challenge, the text as a whole makes a rather conservative case for the need for gender distinctions, the overturning of which was seen as an assault on hierarchy. The dialogue ends with both participants agreeing to exchange clothes and Latin pronouns so that men will again be manly and women subservient to them.

---

5. An animal who seizes in order to devour.   6. "To whose benefit," a phrase attributed by Cicero to Lucius Cassius.

These pamphlets display the early modern fascination with, and loathing of, transvestism. Not only did the fashionable young male favorites of King James I's court resemble the womanish man of *Haec-Vir*, but there were more than a few documented cases of women wearing breeches on the streets. A few women were actually brought before ecclesiastical courts for "shamefully" putting on "man's apparel."

While conforming to the comic pattern of disrupting and then reestablishing the status quo, these pamphlets show that questions about custom, nature, and sex and gender roles were being asked in the early seventeenth century.

from Hic Mulier; or, The Man-Woman

So I present these masculine women in their deformities as they are, that I may call them back to the modest comeliness in which they were.

The modest comeliness in which they were? Why, did ever these mermaids, or rather mere-monsters,[1] that wear the Car-man's block,[2] the Dutchman's feather *upse-van-muffe*, the poor man's pate pouled by a Treene dish, the French doublet trussed with points, to Mary Aubries' light nether skirts, the fool's baldric, and the devil's poniard. Did they ever know comeliness or modesty? Fie, no, they never walked in those paths, for these at the best are sure but rags of gentry, torn from better pieces for their foul stains, or else the adulterate branches of rich stocks,[3] that taking too much sap from the root, are cut away, and employed in base uses; or, if not so, they are the stinking vapors drawn from dunghills, which nourished in the higher regions of the air, become meteors and false fires blazing and flashing therein, and amazing men's minds with their strange proportions, till the substance of their pride being spent, they drop down again to the place from whence they came, and there rot and consume unpitied, and unremembered.

And questionless it is true, that such were the first beginners of these last deformities, for from any purer blood would have issued a purer birth; there would have been some spark of virtue: some excuse for imitation; but this deformity has no agreement with goodness, nor any difference against the weakest reason: it is all base, all barbarous. Base, in the respect it offends men in the example, and God in the most unnatural use: barbarous, in that it is exorbitant from nature, and an antithesis to kind,[4] going astray (with ill-favored affectation) both in attire, in speech, in manners, and (it is to be feared) in the whole courses and stories of their actions. What can be more true and curious consent of the most fairest colors and the wealthy gardens which fill the world with living plants? Do but you receive virtuous inmates (as what palaces are more rich to receive heavenly messengers?) and you shall draw men's souls to you with that severe, devout, and holy adoration, that you shall never want praise, never love, never reverence.

But now methinks I hear the witty-offending great ones reply in excuse of their deformities: What, is there no difference amongst women? no distinction of places, no respect of honors, nor no regard of blood, or alliance? Must but a bare pair of shears pass between noble and ignoble, between the generous spirit and the base mechanic; shall we be all co-heirs of one honor, one estate, and one habit? O men, you are then too tyrannous, and not only injure nature, but also break the laws and customs of the

---

1. Pure monsters.
2. A merchant's hat. Descriptions of ridiculous fashions follow: the *upse-van-muffe* is an elaborate feathered hat; the pate pouled by a Treene dish is hair cut short to the shape of a wooden dish; the French doublet is a man's

close-fitting upper body garment tied with laces; baldric: fancy belt; poniard: dagger.
3. Trunks or stems.
4. The opposite of what is natural to the gender.

wisest princes. Are not bishops known by their miters, princes by their crowns, judges by their robes, and knights by their spurs? But poor women have nothing (how great soever they be) to divide themselves from the enticing shows or moving images which do furnish most shops in the city. What is it that either the laws have allowed to the greatest ladies, custom found convenient, or their bloods or places challenged, which hath not been engrossed into the city with as great greediness, and pretense of true title; as if the surcease[5] from the imitation were the utter breach of their charter everlastingly.

For this cause, these apes of the city have enticed foreign nations to the cells, and there committing gross adultery with their gewgaws,[6] have brought out such unnatural conceptions, that the whole world is not able to make a *Democritus* big enough to laugh at their foolish ambitions.[7] Nay, the very art of painting (which to the last age shall ever be held in detestation) they have so cunningly stolen and hidden amongst their husbands' hoards of treasure, that the decayed stock of prostitution (having little other revenues) are hourly in bringing their action of *detinue*[8] against them. Hence (being thus troubled with these *Popeniars*,[9] and loath still to march in one rank with fools and *zanies*[1]) have proceeded these disguised deformities, not to offend the eyes of goodness, but to tire with ridiculous contempt the never to be satisfied appetites of these gross and unmannerly intruders. Nay, look if this very last edition of disguise, this which is so full of faults, corruptions, and false quotations, this bait which the devil had laid to catch the souls of wanton women, be not as frequent in the demi-palaces of burghers and citizens as it is either at masque, triumph, tilt-yard, or play-house. Call but to account the tailors that are contained within the circumference of the walls of the city, and let but their heels and their hard reckonings be justly summed together, and it will be found they have raised more new foundations of this new disguise, and metamorphosed more modest old garments, to this new manner of short base and French doublet (only for the use of freemen's wives[2] and their children) in one month, than has been worn in court, suburbs, or country, since the unfortunate beginning of the first devilish invention.

Let therefore the powerful Statute of Apparel[3] but lift his battle-axe, and crush the offenders in pieces, so as every one may be known by the true badge of their blood, or fortune; and then these *Chimeras* of deformity will be sent back to hell, and there burn to cinders in the flames of their own malice.

Thus, methinks, I hear the best offenders argue, nor can I blame a high blood to swell when it is coupled and counter-checked with baseness and corruption; yet this shows an anger passing near akin to envy, and alludes much to the saying of an excellent poet:

> Women never
> Love beauty in their sex, but envy ever.

They have Caesar's ambition, and desire to be one and one alone, but yet to offend themselves, to grieve others, is a revenge dissonant to reason, and as *Euripides* says, a woman of that malicious nature is a fierce beast, and most pernicious to the

---

5. Cessation, stop.
6. Showy decorations.
7. Seneca recounts how Democritus laughed rather than cried at human life (*De tranquilitate animi* 15.2).
8. Legal action to recover personal property.
9. Popinjays, vain and empty people.
1. Parasites, those who play the fool for amusement.

2. Women married to men possessing the freedom of a city, borough, or corporation.
3. Laws governing dress that were intended to differentiate the aristocracy from the common people had been enacted from the Middle Ages through to the early modern period.

commonwealth, for she has power by example to do it a world of injury. But far be such cruelty from the softness of their gentle dispositions: O let them remember what the poet saith:

> Women be
> Fram'd with the same parts of the mind as men
> Nay Nature triumph'd in their beauty's birth,
> And women made the glory of the earth,
> The life of beauty, in whose simple breast,
> (As in her fair lodging) Virtue rests:
> Whose towering thoughts attended with remorse,
> Do make their fairness be of greater force.

But when they thrust virtue out of doors, and give a shameless liberty to every loose passion, that either their weak thoughts engender, or the discourse of wicked tongues can charm into their yielding bosoms (much too apt to be opened with any pick-lock of flattering and deceitful insinuation) then they turn maskers, mummers, nay monsters in their disguises, and so they may catch the bridle in their teeth, and run away with their rulers, they care not into what dangers they plunge either their fortunes or reputations, the disgrace of the whole sex, or the blot and obloquy of their private families, according to the saying of the poets

> Such is the cruelty of women-kind,
> When they have shaken off the shamefac'd band
> With which wise nature did them strongly bind,
> T'obey the hests of man's well-ruling hand
> That then all rule and reason they withstand
> To purchase a licentious liberty;
> But virtuous women wisely understand,
> That they were born to mild humility,
> Unless the heavens them lift to lawful sovereignty.[4]

To you therefore that are fathers, husbands, of sustainers of these new hermaphrodites, belongs the cure of this impostume;[5] it is you that give fuel to the flames of their wild indiscretion. You add the oil which makes their stinking lamps defile the whole house with filthy smoke, and your purses purchase these deformities at rates both dear and unreasonable. Do you but hold close your liberal hands, or take a strict account of the employment of the treasure you give to their necessary maintenance, and these excesses will either cease, or else die smothered in prison in the tailors' trunks for want of redemption.

from Haec-Vir; or, The Womanish-Man

Hic-Mulier: Well, then to the purpose: first, you say, I am base in being a slave to novelty. What flattery can there be in freedom of election? Or what baseness to crown my delights with those pleasures which are most suitable to mine affections? Bondage or slavery is a restraint from those actions, which the mind (of its own accord) doth most willingly desire: to perform the intents and purposes of another's disposition, and that

---

4. Description of the tyranny of the Amazonian ruler   5. Abscess.
Radigund in Spenser's *Faerie Queene* 5.5.25.

not but by mansuetude[1] or sweetness of entreaty; but by the force of authority and strength of compulsion. Now for me to follow change, according to the limitation of my own will and pleasure, there cannot be a greater freedom. Nor do I in my delight of change otherwise than as the whole world doth, or as becometh a daughter of the world to do. For what is the world, but a very shop or warehouse of change? Sometimes winter, sometimes summer; day and night: they hold sometimes riches, sometimes poverty, sometimes health, sometimes sickness: now pleasure; presently anguish; now honor; then contempt: and to conclude, there is nothing but change, which doth surround and mix with all our fortunes. And will you have poor woman such a fixed star, that she shall not so much as move or twinkle in her own sphere? That would be true slavery indeed, and a baseness beyond the chains of the worst servitude. Nature to everything she hath created hath given a singular delight in change, as to herbs, plants, and trees a time to wither and shed their leaves, a time to bud and bring forth their leaves, and a time for their fruits and flowers; to worms and creeping things a time to hide themselves in the pores and hollows of the earth, and a time to come abroad and suck the dew; to beasts liberty to choose their food, liberty to delight in their food, and liberty to feed and grow fat with their food. The birds have the air to fly in, the waters to bathe in, and the earth to feed on. But to man, both these and all things else, to alter, frame, and fashion, according to his will and delight shall rule him. Again, who will rob the eye of the variety of objects, the ear of the delight of sounds, the nose of smells, the tongue of taste, and the hand of feeling? And shall only woman, excellent woman, so much better in that she is something purer, be only deprived of this benefit? Shall she be the bondslave of time, the handmaid of opinion, or the strict observer of every frosty or cold benumbed imagination? It would be a cruelty beyond the rack or strapado.[2]

But you will say it is not change, but novelty, from which you deter us: a thing that doth avert the good, and erect the evil; prefer the faithless, and confound desert; that with the change of opinions breeds the change of states, and with continual alterations thrusts headlong forward both ruin and subversion. Alas (soft Sir) what can you christen by that new imagined title, when the words of a wise man are: *that what was done, is but done again: all things do change, and under the cope of heaven there is no new thing.*[3] So that whatsoever we do or imitate, it is neither slavish, base, nor a breeder of novelty.

Next, you condemn me of unnaturalness, in forsaking my creation, and contemning[4] custom. How do I forsake my creation, that do all the right and offices due to my creation? I was created free, born free, and live free: what lets me then so to spin out my time, that I may die free?

To alter creation were to walk on my hands with my heels upward, to feed myself with my feet, or to forsake the sweet sound of sweet words, for the hissing noise of the serpent: but I walk with a face erected, with a body clothed, with a mind busied, and with a heart full of reasonable and devout cogitations; only offensive in attire, inasmuch as it is a stranger to the curiosity of the present times, and an enemy to custom. Are we then bound to be the flatterers of time, or the dependents on custom? O miserable servitude chained only to baseness and folly! For then custom, nothing is more absurd, nothing more foolish. * * *

---

1. Gentleless, meekness.
2. Rack: a frame with a roller at either end on which a person would be tortured; strapado: a form of torture in which the victim's hands would be tied behind his or her back and the victim would then be suspended by a pulley with a sharp jolt.
3. Ecclesiastes 1.9.
4. Disdaining, despising.

Cato Junior held it for a custom, never to eat meat but sitting on the ground. The Venetians kiss one another ever at the first meeting; and even in this day it is a general received custom amongst our English, that when we meet or overtake any man in our travel or journeying, to examine him whither he rides, how far, to what purpose, and where he lodgeth? Nay, and with that unmannerly boldness of inquisition, that it is a certain ground of a most insufficient quarrel, not to receive a full satisfaction of those demands which go far astray from good manners, or comely civility; and will you have us to marry ourselves to these mimic and most fantastic customs? It is a fashion or custom with us to mourn in black, yet the Argian[5] and Roman ladies ever mourned in white; and (if we will tie the action upon the signification of colors) I see not but we may mourn in green, blue, red or any simple color used in heraldry. For us to salute strangers with a kiss is counted but civility, but with foreign nations immodesty; for you to cut the hair of your upper lips, familiar here in England, everywhere else almost thought unmanly. To ride on side-saddles at first was counted here abominable pride, and et cetera. I might instance in a thousand things that only custom and not reason hath approved. To conclude, Custom is an idiot, and whoever dependeth wholly upon him, without the discourse of reason, will take from him his pied[6] coat, and become a slave indeed to contempt and censure.

But you say we are barbarous and shameless and cast off all softness, to run wild through a wilderness of opinions. In this you express more cruelty than in all the rest, because I do not stand with my hands on my belly like a baby[7] at Bartholomew Fair,[8] that move not my whole body when I should but only stir my head like Jack of the clock house[9] which has no joints, that is not dumb when wantons court me, as if asslike I were ready for all burdens, or because I weep not when injury gripes me, like a worried deer in the fangs of many curs. Am I therefore barbarous or shameless? He is much injurious that so baptized us; we are as free-born as men, have as free election, and as free spirits, we are compounded of like parts, and may with like liberty make benefit of our creations; my countenance shall smile on the worthy, and frown on the ignoble, I will hear the wise, and be deaf to idiots, give counsel to my friend, but be dumb to flatterers, I have hands that shall be liberal to reward desert, feet that shall move swiftly to do good offices, and thoughts that shall ever accompany freedom and severity. If this be barbarous, let me leave the city and live with creatures of like simplicity.

* * *

Hic-Mulier: Therefore to take your proportion in a few lines (my dear Feminine-Masculine) tell me what Charter, prescription or right of claim you have to those things you make our absolute inheritance? Why do you curl, frizzle and powder your hair, bestowing more hours and time in dividing lock from lock, and hair from hair, in giving every thread his posture, and every curl his true fence and circumference than ever Caesar did in marshalling his army, either at Pharsalia, in Spain, or Britain? Why do you rob us of our ruffs, our earrings, carkanets,[1] and mamillions,[2] of our fans and feathers, our busks and French bodies, nay, of our masks, hoods, shadows, and shapynas,[3] not so much as the very art of painting, but you have so greedily engrossed it,

---

5. Of Argos.
6. Spotted, motley.
7. Doll.
8. A popular carnival fair held every year from 1133 to 1865 at West Smithfield on 24 August, the feast day of St. Bartholomew.

9. Figure that strikes the bell of a clock.
1. A jeweled or gold necklace.
2. Rounded protuberances (from French *mamelon*, nipple).
3. Disguises.

that were it not for that little fantastical sharp pointed dagger that hangs at your chins, and the cross hilt which guards your upper lip, hardly would there be any difference between the fair mistress and the foolish servant. But is this theft the uttermost of our spoil? Fie, you have gone a world further, and even ravished from us our speech, our actions, sports, and recreations. Goodness leave me, if I have not heard a man court his mistress with the same words that Venus did Adonis, or as near as the book could instruct him;[4] where are the tilts and tourneys, and lofty galliards[5] that were danced in the days of old, when men capered in the air like wanton kids on the tops of mountains, and turned above ground as if they had been compact of fire or a purer element?[6] Tut, all's forsaken, all's vanished, those motions showed more strength than art, and more courage than courtship; it was much too robustious, and rather spent the body than prepared it, especially where any defect before reigned; hence you took from us poor women our traverses and tourneys, our modest stateliness and curious slidings, and left us nothing but the new French garb of puppet hopping and setting. Lastly, poor shuttlecock[7] that was only a female invention, how have you taken it out of our hands, and made yourselves such lords and rulers over it, that though it be a very emblem of us, and our lighter despised fortunes, yet it dare now hardly come near us; nay, you keep it so imprisoned within your bed-chambers and dining rooms, amongst your pages and panders, that a poor innocent maid to give but a kick with her battledore,[8] were more than halfway to the ruin of her reputation. For this you have demolished the noble schools of horsemanship (of which many were in this city) hung up your arms to rust, glued up those swords in their scabbards that would shake all Christendom with the brandish, and entertained into your mind such softness, dullness, and effeminate niceness that it would even make *Heraclitus*[9] himself laugh against his nature to see how pulingly[1] you languish in this weak entertained sin of womanish softness. To see one of your gender either show himself (in the midst of his pride or riches) at a playhouse or public assembly; how (before he dare enter) with the Jacob's-staff of his own eyes and his pages, he takes a full survey of himself, from the highest sprig in his feather, to the lowest spangle that shines in his shoestring: how he prunes and picks himself like a hawk set a-weathering, calls every several garment to auricular[2] confession, making them utter both their mortal great stains, and their venial and less blemishes, though the mote must be much less than an atom. Then to see him pluck and tug everything into the form of the newest received fashion; and by *Durer's* rules[3] make his leg answerable to his neck; his thigh proportionable with his middle, his foot with his hand, and a world of such idle disdained foppery. To see him thus patched up with symmetry, make himself complete, and even as a circle, and lastly, cast himself among the eyes of the people (as an object of wonder) with more niceness than a virgin goes to the sheets of her first lover would make patience herself mad with anger, and cry with the poet:

> O hominum mores, O gens, O tempora dura,
> Quantus in urbe dolor; quantus in orbe dolus![4]

---

4. Venus, goddess of love, fell in love with the beautiful youth Adonis.
5. A brisk dance in triple time.
6. Men were thought to be dominated by dry humors and women by humid ones.
7. A small piece of cork with feathers sticking out of it, batted back and forth in the game of battledoor and shuttlecock.
8. A small racket, used to hit a shuttlecock.

9. Heraclitus was said to weep whenever he went forth in public (See Seneca, *De tranquilitate animi* 15.2).
1. In a whining tone.
2. Told privately, to the ear.
3. Albrecht Dürer (1471–1528), German painter and engraver, wrote a work on human proportions that was published after his death.
4. O customs of men, O people, O hard times / What great sadness in the city; what great fraud in the world.

Now since according to your own inference, even by the laws of nature, by the rules of religion, and the customs of all civil nations, it is necessary there be a distinct and special difference between man and woman, both in their habit and behaviors, what could we poor weak women do less (being far too weak by force to fetch back those spoils you have unjustly taken from us) than to gather up those garments you have proudly cast away, and therewith to clothe both our bodies and our minds; since no other means was left us to continue our names, and to support a difference? For to have held the way in which our forefathers first set us, or to have still embraced the civil modesty, or gentle sweetness of our soft inclinations; why, you had so far encroached upon us, and so over-bribed the world, to be deaf to any grant of restitution, that as at our creation, our whole sex was contained in man our first parent, so we should have had no other being, but in you, and your most effeminate quality. Hence we have preserved (though to our own shames) those manly things which you have forsaken, which would you again accept, and restore to us the blushes we laid by, when first we put on your masculine garments; doubt not but chaste thoughts and bashfulness will again dwell in us, and our palaces being newly gilt, trimmed, and reedified, draw to us all the Graces, all the Muses,[5] which that you may more willingly do, and (as we of yours) grow into detestation of that deformity you have purloined, to the utter loss of your honors and reputations. Mark how the brave Italian poet,[6] even in the infancy of your abuses, most lively describes you:

> About his neck a Carknet[7] rich he ware
> Of precious Stones, all set in gold well tried;
> His arms that erst all warlike weapons bare,
> In golden bracelets wantonly were tied:
> Into his ears two rings conveyed are
> Of golden wire, at which on either side,
> Two Indian pearls, in making like two pears,
> Of passing price were pendant at his ears.
>
> His locks bedewed with water of sweet savor,
> Stood curled round in order on his head;
> He had such wanton womanish behavior,
> As though in valor he had ne'er been bred:
> So chang'd in speech, in manners and in favor,
> So from himself beyond all reason led,
> By these enchantments of this amorous dame;
> He was himself in nothing, but in name.

Thus you see your injury to us is of an old and inveterate continuance, having taken such strong root in your bosoms, that it can hardly be pulled up, without some offense to the soil: ours young and tender, scarce freed from the swaddling clothes, and therefore may with as much ease be lost, as it was with little difficulty found. Cast then from you our ornaments, and put on your own armors. Be men in shape, men in show, men in words, men in actions, men in counsel, men in example: then will we love and serve you; then will we hear and obey you; then will we like rich jewels hang

---

5. The graces were the three sisters, Aglaia, Thalia, and Euphrosyne, viewed as bestowers of charm and beauty; the muses were the nine daughters of Zeus and Memory who inspire poetry and the arts.
6. Ludovico Ariosto (1474–1532), whose description of

Ruggiero's decadence when he is seduced by the sorceress Alcina in *Orlando Furioso 7* is quoted here in the translation (1590) by Sir John Harington, Queen Elizabeth's godson.
7. Necklace.

at your ears to take our instructions, like true friends follow you through all dangers, and like careful leeches[8] pour oil into your wounds. Then shall you find delight in our words; pleasure in our faces; faith in our hearts; chastity in our thoughts, and sweetness both in our inward and outward inclinations. Comeliness shall be then our study; fear our armor, and modesty our practice: then shall we be all your most excellent thoughts can desire, and have nothing in us less than impudence and deformity.

Haec-Vir; Enough: you have both raised my eyelids, cleared my sight, and made my heart entertain both shame and delight at an instant; shame in my follies past; delight in our noble and worthy conversion. Away then from me these light vanities, the only ensigns[9] of a weak and soft nature: and come you grave and solid pieces, which arm a man with fortitude and resolution: you are too rough and stubborn for a woman's wearing, we will here change our attires, as we have changed our minds, and with our attires, our names. I will no more be *Haec-Vir,* but *Hic Vir,* nor you *Hic-Mulier,* but *Haec Mulier.* From henceforth deformity shall pack to Hell; and if at any time he hide himself upon the earth, yet it shall be with contempt and disgrace. He shall have no friend but Poverty; no favorer but Folly, nor no reward but Shame. Henceforth we will live nobly like ourselves, ever sober, ever discreet, ever worthy; true men, and true women. We will be henceforth like well-coupled doves, full of industry, full of love: I mean, not of sensual and carnal love, but heavenly and divine love, which proceeds from God, whose inexpressible nature none is able to deliver in words, since is like his dwelling, high and beyond the reach of human apprehension.

END OF PERSPECTIVES: TRACTS ON WOMEN AND GENDER

Ben Jonson
1572–1637

Ben Jonson's life was full of changes and contradictions. His earliest biographer, William Drummond, called him "passionately kind and angry, careless either to gain or keep, vindictive, but, if he be well answered, at himself." His father was Protestant, but Jonson turned Catholic, only to recant that conversion later; nevertheless, in his last years he called himself a "beadsman." The stepson of a bricklayer, he became Poet Laureate. He wrote poems of praise to win the patronage of king and court but also skewered their follies in satire. Though often assuming the role of moralist in his poetry and plays, Jonson admitted that as a younger man he was "given to venery" and pleaded guilty to the charge of murder. He was attached to admiring younger poets, "the tribe of Ben," yet he also enjoyed feuds, such as those with fellow dramatists Marston and Dekker. While espousing Horatian spareness and an acute sense of meter in both criticism and poetry, Jonson also had a keen ear for the colloquial language of London.

Indeed, London was one of the few constants in Jonson's turbulent career. Born in Harts-Born Lane near Charing Cross, he was buried in the nave in the north aisle, across the Abbey from Poets' Corner. Jonson portrayed the city as the world of those who lived by their wits. He dramatized literary infighting in *Every Man Out of His Humour* (1599), greedy schemes in *Volpone* (1606), intellectual confidence scams in *The Alchemist* (1610), and antitheatrical Puritan preaching in *Bartholomew Fair* (1614). The London audience at the Hope Theatre was reported to have exclaimed at a performance of *Bartholomew Fair:* "O rare Ben Jonson!"

---

8. Physicians.   9. Banners, signs.

Unlike other playwrights of his time (including Shakespeare), Jonson oversaw the publication of his plays, which appeared with his poems in the same deluxe folio volume, entitled *Works* (1616). The assertion of the dignity of popular drama surprised many of his readers, one of whom wrote, "Pray tell me Ben, where doth the mystery lurk, / What others call a play, you call a work?" That Jonson wanted his plays to be read as much as performed can be gathered from the comment printed on the title page of *Every Man Out of His Humour:* "as it was first composed by the author, Ben Jonson, containing more than hath been publicly spoken or acted."

Jonson viewed writing as his profession; he became the first poet in England to earn a living by his art. His achievement was recognized by James I, who made Jonson the first Poet Laureate of England and granted him a pension for life. Before becoming laureate, Jonson depended on a whole string of patrons. With the new Stuart king in power, Jonson was able to use his claim of Scots descent to advantage. He was supported by Esme Stuart Seigneur D'Aubigny (a cousin of King James), to whom he dedicated his first tragedy, *Sejanus* (1603). His patrons included Sir Walter Raleigh and Lady Mary Wroth, to whom he dedicated *The Alchemist*. Jonson's most important break came when he received a commission for a court masque. In 1605 he wrote *The Masque of Blackness* starring the Queen herself. To gain some idea of the extravagance of these masques, consider that in 1617, while 12,000 pounds were spent on the entire administration of Ireland, 4,000 pounds were spent on a single masque, *Pleasure Reconciled to Virtue*. The masques were lavish ventures that required costumes, music, and magnificent scenery, which was designed by Inigo Jones, who introduced the Italian invention of perspective.

If the pursuit of patronage was crucial to Jonson's advancement, his satire of politics and power repeatedly put his career and even his life at risk. In 1603 Jonson was called before the Privy Council for *Sejanus*; the charges included "popery and treason." Jonson's *Epicoene, or the Silent Woman*—which climaxes in the revelation that the silent woman is really a boy—was suppressed because it lampooned a love affair of the King's first cousin, Lady Arbella Stuart. One observer complained of the 1613 *Irish Masque at Court* that it was "no time . . . to exasperate that nation by making ridiculous." Jonson was imprisoned twice for the offense that his plays gave to the powerful—once for the now lost *The Isle of Dogs* (1597) and another time for *Eastward Ho!* (1605), in which he made fun of King James's Scots accent.

Jonson took reckless risks, whose consequences he barely managed to escape. While imprisoned for the murder of Gabriel Spencer in 1598, Jonson became a Catholic. Following his conversion, Jonson pleaded guilty to manslaughter (later calling it the result of a duel) but went free by claiming benefit of clergy. This medieval custom originally allowed clerics to be judged by the bishop's court but, by Jonson's time, permitted anyone who could translate the Latin Bible to go free. Jonson left prison with his belongings confiscated, his thumb branded for the felony, and his reputation marked by his profession of an outlaw religion. Like any other Catholic in Elizabethan England, Jonson could be fined or have his property confiscated for not attending Anglican services. Indeed, he and his wife were interrogated for their nonattendance in 1605; Jonson was also charged with being "a poet, and by fame a seducer of youth to the Popish religion." Threatened again with loss of property and another prison term, Jonson complied with the Court's order that he take instruction in Protestantism.

Not all Jonson's disputes were quite so dangerous. Like the characters in his plays, he enjoyed engaging in the game of vapors, a mock argument, drummed up for the display of wit. He not only engaged in combats of wit with Shakespeare (who acted in *Every Man Out of His Humour*) but also ridiculed Marston and Dekker in what critics call "the War of the Theaters." Jonson's *Every Man Out of His Humour* satirized Marston as a pseudo-intellectual. The same year, Jonson and Dekker collaborated on a play. Two years later, Dekker parodied Jonson as the bombastic Horace, constantly reading his work aloud and expecting praise in *Satiriomastix* (1601). The title of this play means "the whipping of the satirist," and it is full of barbs about Jonson's checkered past—both his imprisonment and his theatrical flops. Dekker called Jonson a "brown-bread mouth-stinker." Jonson responded with a "forced defense" against "base detractors and illiterate apes" in *Poetaster* (1601).

Jonson did have high regard for some of his contemporaries, as they did for him. Among these was John Donne, who wrote commendatory verses for *Volpone* and to whom Jonson wrote "Who shall doubt, Donne, whe'er I a poet be / When I dare send my epigrams to thee?" As an older man, Jonson held court at the Devil Tavern among his fellow poets as self-proclaimed *arbiter bibendi* (master of drinking), whose main object was "Not drinking much, but talking wittily." This vein of wit was carried on by Sir John Suckling's *A Session of Poets* and Herrick's *Prayer for Ben Jonson*. His servant Brome wrote an elegy for him, as did the many men of letters who contributed to *Jonsonius Virbius* ("Jonson Reborn"), the year after his death.

Jonson saw himself as a moral and poetic guide. His satire of moral depravity and intellectual delusion is hysterically funny. His plays include direct criticism of contemporary poetry and drama, contracts with the audience, and self-mockery—a foretaste of the break from realistic conventions in modernism. Jonson's comedies also persuade us that there is no reality without satire; we cannot know the world without laughing at its ridiculousness. The human foibles and obsessions portrayed in his comedies are captured in a language so vivid and oral that it has to be read aloud. Jonson's verse dazzles by concealing its art, allowing conversational words and rhythms to be perfectly wedded to poetic meters. The simplicity and restraint of his language, as in his elegy on the death of his son, are the vehicles for pure music and powerful emotion.

For additional resources on Jonson, including *Volpone*, go to *The Longman Anthology of British Literature* Web site at www.myliteraturekit.com.

THE ALCHEMIST   *The Alchemist* begins with a fart. So starts a series of insults that two swindlers—Face and Subtle—hurl at each other until their prostitute pal Dol Common reminds them of their "venture tripartite" to "cozen kindly." Subtle, a down-at-the-heels confidence man who passes himself off as an alchemist, capable through secret knowledge of turning base metals to gold, and his wily assistant Face, who lures clients to the empty house in Blackfriars that he is supposed to be minding, team up with Dol to hoodwink eight variously self-deluded early modern London types by promising to fulfill their wildest dreams of wealth, sex, and power. The law clerk Dapper is made to believe that, as nephew of the Queen of the Faeries (played by Dol), he will be given a magic spirit to help him clean up at gambling. The shopkeeper Abel Drugger has a horoscope cast that promises him a killing in business and marriage to a rich widow. The Puritan parson Tribulation and the skeptical elder Ananias eagerly agree to have the goods of poor orphans transmuted into precious metals. The city knight Epicure Mammon hopes to achieve the philosopher's stone itself—the magic ingredient that will turn all to gold and allow him to enjoy jewel-encrusted luxury and sex with a harem of succubae. His at-first-unbelieving sidekick Surly thinks that by playing the role of a Spanish Count he can win the hand of the rich, nineteen-year-old widow Dame Pliant, while she believes that her fortune will be to marry a gallant young aristocrat. Her brother the country squire Kastril simply wants to learn how to quarrel in the abusive manner of the London "angry boys" to succeed in the kind of one-upmanship that the play roundly ridicules.

Indeed, no one really gets the better of anyone in this play except Lovewit, the owner of the Blackfriars townhouse in which this madcap action takes place. When he returns home, all these plots explode, as all the neighbors complain to him about the riotous comings and goings they have been witnessing. All the dupes that the cozeners have been trying to keep separate from one another show up almost simultaneously to attempt to get back the money they have all too willingly allowed themselves to be defrauded of. None of the dupes is punished—except by losing the loot that they have handed over and by having to resume the lives they lead at the start. While Subtle and Dol have to return to their lives on the street, Face returns to his role as Jeremy the butler through a bargain with his master, Lovewit. In short, Lovewit gets the girl—Dame Pliant—and all the money in return for protecting his servant Jeremy from the law.

Andrew Gurr, director of the Globe project in London, has suggested an intriguing explanation for the point of this rather unsettling happy ending: that in the crafty metadramatic world created by the playwright, Lovewit was none other than William Shakespeare, Jonson's chief rival. Like Lovewit, Shakespeare was out of town because of the plague in 1610, and like Lovewit, Shakespeare not only loved wit but made a profit out of it as a capitalist landlord. As one of the five co-owners of the Blackfriars theater, where *The Alchemist* was first performed in 1610, Shakespeare, the greatest playwright of his age, was also a typical early modern Londoner, who shared the dupes of the play's concern with making money. At the end of the play, Face asks the audience to "feast often" and "invite new guests" to the theater, to laugh at his and his theatrical conspirators' shenanigans (as Lovewit has). At the same time, Face implicitly enjoins the spectators to contemplate how they have been both tricked and entertained by the actors who have counterfeited their roles to make money for themselves—but even more money for the owners of the stage.

But the play is about much more than greed for money or the deceptive power of theater. It is about the self-deception and self-aggrandizement that motivate not only greed but all sorts of human desires, including lust and even the betterment of society. In Act 4, Surly calls Subtle "Faustus" for promising to cure "plagues, piles, and pox." As Jonson critic Anne Barton has pointed out, Mammon is also like the Marlovian tragic hero Dr. Faustus in his utopian dreams. Another pseudo-Faustus, Mammon claims that he wants to relieve beggars of want and to cure the plague. The play is about the universally human and particularly early modern desire for control over a world that cannot really be controlled—at least not through the mental constructs the play sends up.

Among these systems of discourse that pretend to knowledge, the central object of the play's derision is alchemy. During the early modern period, alchemy was still widely believed in, so much so that Elizabeth I hired John Dee (alluded to in 2.6.20) to make astrological predictions for her and punished Cornelius Lannoy for not making good on his promises to make gold. The transformative power of alchemy becomes a metaphor for every other type of transformation in the play. There is the transformative power to control reality promised by an array of specialized discourses. Grammar, rhetoric, and logic are meant to transform Kastril into a master of argument but merely result in his ability to contradict and abuse others. The language of Puritan millenarian prophecy, based on allegorical interpretation of the Bible, was meant to predict the end of the world. Here, this language is put in the mouth of Dol Common, who pretends to be outraged into a fit of Puritan ranting when she is courted as a great lady by Mammon. The play also ridicules such systems to predict the future as astrology and palmistry. These illusions of control are also not unlike the New Age therapies of today, what the Australian actor Geoffrey Rush has referred to as the "feng shui gobbledegook" behind the magically successful floor plan for Drugger's shop.

The human capacities that allow us to deal more ably with the chaos of life—acceptance of reality and self-knowledge—are sorely wanting in all the play's characters, not just in the foolish gulls but in the tricksters as well. As removed as we might like to think we are from the outrageous hypocrisy of a parson willing to counterfeit money to promote his religion or the gullibility of a law clerk who thinks that by sitting in a privy and biting on gingerbread the Queen of Faeries will appear to him, the play encourages us to laugh at our shared human capacity for self-abasement in the hope of achieving our desires. The satire is gentle enough, since all survive to face the fallible selves they are trying to escape through their foolish, and often base, desires. In *The Alchemist*, Jonson produced a visceral portrait of the London of his day and the characters who made it tick. While we may no longer believe in alchemy, the play's evocation of the frenetic energy, clever scheming for wealth, and drive to control through the pretense of specialized knowledge can still provoke a corrosively ironic laughter at not only the follies of early modern London but also the self-delusions of the city in our contemporary world.

The *Alchemist* appeared in both the *Quarto* of 1612 and the *Folio* of 1616 and 1640. The *Folio* added stage directions and changed the oaths to remove possible accusation of blasphemy.

The Alchemist
TO THE LADY MOST DESERVING HER NAME AND BLOOD

LADY MARY WROTH[1]

Madam—In the age of sacrifices, the truth of religion was not in the greatness and fat of the offerings, but in the devotion and zeal of the sacrificers: else what could a handful of gums have done in the sight of a hecatomb?[2] Or how might I appear at this altar, except with those affections that no less love the light and witness, than they have the conscience of your virtue? If what I offer bear an acceptable odor, and hold the first strength, it is your value of it, which remembers where, when, and to whom it was kindled. Otherwise, as the times are, there comes rarely forth that thing so full of authority or example, but by assiduity[3] and custom grows less, and loses. This, yet, safe in your judgment (which is a Sidney's) is forbidden to speak more, lest it talk or look like one of the ambitious faces of the time, who, the more they paint,[4] are the less themselves. Your ladyship's true honorer,

Ben Jonson.

TO THE READER

If thou beest more, thou art an understander, and then I trust thee. If thou art one that takest up, and but a pretender, beware of what hands thou receivest thy commodity; for thou wert never more fair in the way to be cozened,[5] than in this age, in poetry, especially in plays: wherein, now the concupiscence of dances and of antics so reigneth, as to run away from nature, and be afraid of her, is the only point of art that tickles the spectators. But how out of purpose, and place, do I name art? When the professors are grown so obstinate contemners of it, and presumers on their own naturals,[6] as they are deriders of all diligence that way, and, by simple mocking at the terms, when they understand not the things, think to get off wittily with their ignorance. Nay, they are esteemed the more learned, and sufficient for this, by the many, through their excellent vice of judgment. For they commend writers, as they do fencers or wrestlers; who if they come in robustuously, and put for it with a great deal of violence, are received for the braver fellows: when many times their own rudeness is the cause of their disgrace, and a little touch of their adversary gives all that boisterous force the foil.[7] I deny not, but that these men, who always seek to do more than enough, may some time happen on some thing that is good, and great; but very seldom; and when it comes it doth not recompense the rest of their ill. It sticks out,

---

1. The play is dedicated to Lady Mary Wroth, poet, patroness of poets, and niece of Sir Philip Sidney. Her name was also spelled "Worth," as alluded to in "deserving of her name." See selected poems from her sonnet sequence *Pamphilia to Amphilanthus* (page 1611).
2. How could incense ("gums") compare with a huge sacrifice ("hecatomb," literally 100 oxen)?
3. Perseverance.
4. Apply makeup.
5. Tricked.
6. Confident in their natural, or innate, wit; "naturals" also means "fools."
7. Check, repulse, defeat.

perhaps, and is more eminent, because all is sordid and vile about it: as lights are more discerned in a thick darkness, than a faint shadow. I speak not this, out of a hope to do good to any man against his will; for I know, if it were put to the question of theirs and mine, the worse would find more suffrages: because the most favor common errors. But I give thee this warning, that there is a great difference between those, that, to gain the opinion of copy,[8] utter all they can, however unfitly; and those that use election and a mean.[9] For it is only the disease of the unskilful, to think rude things greater than polished; or scattered more numerous[1] than composed.

Dramatis Personae

SUBTLE, *the Alchemist*	PERTINAX SURLY, *a Gamester*
FACE, *the Housekeeper*	TRIBULATION WHOLESOME, *a Pastor of*
DOL COMMON, *their Colleague*	*Amsterdam*
DAPPER, *a Lawyer's Clerk*	ANANIAS, *a Deacon (church officer) there*
DRUGGER, *Tobacco Man*	KASTRIL,[2] *the Angry Boy*
LOVEWIT, *Master of the House*	DAME PLIANT, *his Sister, a Widow*
SIR EPICURE MAMMON, *a Knight*	NEIGHBORS, OFFICERS, ATTENDANTS, etc.

Scene, London

ARGUMENT

T *he sickness hot,*[3] *a master quit, for fear,*
H *is house in town, and left one servant there;*
E *ase him corrupted, and gave means to know*

A *Cheater, and his punk;*° *who now brought low,*   prostitute
L *eaving their narrow practice, were become*
C *ozeners*° *at large; and only wanting some*   cheaters, tricksters
H *ouse to set up, with him they here contract,*
E *ach for a share, and all begin to act.*
M *uch company they draw, and much abuse,*
I *n casting figures,*° *telling fortunes, news,*   reading horoscopes
S *elling of flies, flat bawdry with the stone,*[4]
T *ill it, and they, and all in fume are gone.*

PROLOGUE

Fortune, that favors fools, these two short hours,
    We wish away, both for your sakes and ours,
Judging spectators; and desire, in place.
    To the author justice, to ourselves but grace.
    Our scene is London, 'cause we would make known,

---

8. Fame for prolific and fluent writing.
9. Careful choice and moderation.
1. "Numerous" in the sense of both "copious" and "skilled in numbers," able to write verse that is musical in its rhythm.

2. Kestrel, a small hawk; a term of contempt.
3. A reference to the plague that hit London in 1609–1610.
4. "Flies" were demons; "the stone" is the philosophers' stone and also slang for "testicle."

No country's mirth is better than our own:
No clime breeds better matter for your whore,
   Bawd,° squire,° impostor, many persons more,   *madam / pimp*
Whose manners, now call'd humors,[5] feed the stage;
   And which have still been subject for the rage
Or spleen of comic writers. Though this pen
   Did never aim to grieve, but better men;
Howe'er the age he lives in doth endure
   The vices that she breeds, above their cure.
But when the wholesome remedies are sweet,
   And in their working gain and profit meet,
He hopes to find no spirit so much diseased.
   But will with such fair correctives be pleased.
For here he doth not fear who can apply.
   If there be any that will sit so nigh
Unto the stream, to look what it doth run,
   They shall find things, they'd think or wish were done;
They are so natural follies, but so shewn,
   As even the doers may see, and yet not own.

ACT 1

Scene 1—*A room in Lovewit's house*

[*Enter Face, in a captain's uniform, with his sword drawn, and Subtle with a vial, quarrelling, and followed by Dol Common.*]

FACE: Believe't, I will.
SUBTLE: Thy worst. I fart at thee.
DOL: Ha' you your wits? why, gentlemen! for love—
FACE: Sirrah, I'll strip you—
SUBTLE: What to do? Lick figs°   *ficus, the piles*
   Out at my—
FACE: Rogue, rogue!—out of all your sleights.
DOL: Nay, look ye, sovereign, general, are you madmen?
SUBTLE: O, let the wild sheep loose. I'll gum your silks
   With good strong water,[6] an you come.
DOL: Will you have
   The neighbours hear you? will you betray all?
   Hark! I hear somebody.
FACE: Sirrah—
SUBTLE: I shall mar
10   All that the tailor has made, if you approach.
FACE: You most notorious whelp, you insolent slave,
   Dare you do this?
SUBTLE: Yes, faith; yes, faith.

---

5. The four personality types controlled by the four bodily fluids: sanguine, or happy (blood); phlegmatic, or impassive (phlegm); choleric, or angry (bile); and melancholy (black bile).

6. Subtle threatens to ruin the fabric of Face's fancy uniform by throwing a vial of chemicals at him.

FACE: Why, who
    Am I, my mongrel? who am I?
SUBTLE: I'll tell you,
    Since you know not yourself.
FACE: Speak lower, rogue.
SUBTLE: Yes, you were once (time's not long past) the good,
    Honest, plain, livery-three-pound-thrum,[7] that kept
    Your master's worship's house here in the Friars,[8]
    For the vacations—
FACE: Will you be so loud?
SUBTLE: Since, by my means, translated° suburb-captain.[9]   *promoted to*
FACE: By your means, Doctor Dog!
SUBTLE: Within man's memory,
    All this I speak of.
FACE: Why, I pray you, have I
    Been countenanced by you, or you by me?
    Do but collect, sir, where I met you first.
SUBTLE: I do not hear well.
FACE: Not of this, I think it.
25   But I shall put you in mind, sir;—at Pie-corner,[1]
    Taking your meal of steam in, from cooks' stalls,
    Where, like the father of hunger, you did walk
    Piteously costive,° with your pinch'd-horn-nose,   *constipated, stingy*
    And your complexion of the Roman wash,
30   Stuck full of black and melancholic worms,
    Like powder corns shot at the artillery-yard.[2]
SUBTLE: I wish you could advance your voice a little.
FACE: When you went pinn'd up in the several rags
    You'd raked and picked from dunghills, before day;
35   Your feet in mouldy slippers, for your kibes;°   *chilblains*
    A felt° of rug, and a thin threaden cloke,   *hat*
    That scarce would cover your no-buttocks—
SUBTLE: So, sir!
FACE: When all your alchemy, and your algebra,
    Your minerals, vegetals, and animals,
40   Your conjuring, cozening,° and your dozen of trades,   *trickery*
    Could not relieve your corps with so much linen°   *underwear*
    Would make you tinder, but to see a fire;[3]
    I gave you countenance, credit for your coals,
    Your stills, your glasses, your materials;

---

7. A poorly dressed servant. Three pounds was a servant's yearly salary, and a thrum is the loose end of a weaver's warp.
8. Neighborhood of Blackfriars Theatre, where *The Alchemist* was performed.
9. Pretender to officer rank in the suburbs, the sleazy outskirts of the city.

1. Location of cooks' shops in Smithfield, a down-at-the-heels part of town.
2. Face describes Subtle's face as sallow and covered with blackheads that look like blotches of shot gunpowder.
3. So few shreds of linen that it would not even be enough kindling to start a fire.

45   Built you a furnace, drew you customers,
             Advanced all your black arts; lent you, beside,
             A house to practise in—

SUBTLE: Your master's house!

FACE: Where you have studied the more thriving skill
             Of bawdry° since.   *lewdness, pandering*

SUBTLE: Yes, in your master's house.

50   You and the rats here kept possession.
             Make it not strange. I know you were one could keep
             The buttery-hatch still lock'd, and save the chippings,
             Sell the dole beer to aqua-vitae men,[4]
             The which, together with your Christmas vails°   *tips*
55   At post-and-pair, your letting out of counters,
             Made you a pretty stock, some twenty marks,[5]
             And gave you credit to converse with cobwebs,
             Here, since your mistress' death hath broke up house.

FACE: You might talk softlier, rascal.

SUBTLE: No, you scarab,°   *dung beetle*
60   I'll thunder you in pieces: I will teach you
             How to beware to tempt a Fury again,
             That carries tempest in his hand and voice.

FACE: The place has made you valiant.

SUBTLE: No, your clothes.—
             Thou vermin, have I ta'en thee out of dung,
65   So poor, so wretched, when no living thing
             Would keep thee company, but a spider, or worse?
             Rais'd thee from brooms, and dust, and watering-pots,
             Sublimed° thee, and exalted thee, and fix'd thee   *turned to vapor*
             In the third region,[6] call'd our state of grace?
70   Wrought thee to spirit, to quintessence, with pains
             Would twice have won me the philosopher's work?[7]
             Put thee in words and fashion, made thee fit
             For more than ordinary fellowships?
             Giv'n thee thy oaths, thy quarrelling dimensions,
75   Thy rules to cheat at horse-race, cock-pit, cards,
             Dice, or whatever gallant tincture[8] else?
             Made thee a second in mine own great art?
             And have I this for thanks! Do you rebel,
             Do you fly out in the projection?
80   Would you be gone now?

DOL: Gentlemen, what mean you?
             Will you mar all?

SUBTLE: Slave, thou hadst had no name—

DOL: Will you undo yourselves with civil war?

---

4. Subtle accuses Face of selling beer given out free from rich households.
5. Post and pair: a card game; counters: gambling chips: a mark was worth 13 shillings and 4 pence.
6. The highest sphere of the universe.

7. The quintessence was the most purified form that could be extracted from all matter. The philosopher's work was the result of alchemy, the "stone" that transformed metal into gold.
8. A color or quality in alchemy.

SUBTLE: Never been known, past *equi clibanum*,[9]
             The heat of horse-dung, under ground, in cellars.
85   Or an ale-house darker than deaf John's; been lost
             To all mankind, but laundresses and tapsters,[1]
             Had not I been.
DOL: Do you know who hears you, Sovereign?
FACE: Sirrah—
DOL: Nay, General, I thought you were civil.
FACE: I shall turn desperate, if you grow thus loud.
SUBTLE: And hang thyself, I care not.
FACE: Hang thee, collier,°   coal miner
             And all thy pots, and pans, in picture, I will,
             Since thou hast moved me—
DOL: O, this will o'erthrow all.
FACE: Write thee up bawd in Paul's,[2] have all thy tricks
             Of cozening with a hollow coal, dust, scrapings,
95   Searching for things lost, with a sieve and sheers,[3]
             Erecting figures° in your rows of houses,   cast a horoscope
             And taking in of shadows with a glass,
             Told in red letters;[4] and a face cut for thee,
             Worse than Gamaliel Ratsey's.[5]
DOL: Are you sound?
100   Have you your senses, masters?
FACE: I will have
             A book, but barely reckoning thy impostures,
             Shall prove a true philosopher's stone to printers.
SUBTLE: Away, you trencher-rascal!
FACE: Out, you dog-leach!
             The vomit of all prisons—
DOL: Will you be
105   Your own destructions, gentlemen?
FACE: Still spew'd out
             For lying too heavy on the basket.[6]
SUBTLE: Cheater!
FACE: Bawd!
SUBTLE: Cow-herd!
FACE: Conjurer!
SUBTLE: Cut-purse!
FACE: Witch!
DOL: O me!
             We are ruin'd, lost! have you no more regard
             To your reputations? where's your judgment? 'slight,°   by God's light
110   Have yet some care of me, of your republic[7]—

---

9. Oven fueled by horse dung.
1. Women who drew beer in taverns.
2. Advertise yourself as a pimp outside St. Paul's.
3. The sieve was believed to turn in the direction of thieves and stolen goods.
4. The glass cast up figures that were interpreted by a virgin.

5. A famous bandit known for his mask ("cut").
6. For eating too much from the sheriff's charity basket for the poor.
7. Commonweal and also a pun on *res publica*, public, or common thing; a bawdy reference to Dol Common.

FACE: Away, this brach! I'll bring thee, rogue, within
       The statute of sorcery, tricesimo tertio
       Of Harry the Eighth:[8] ay, and perhaps, thy neck
       Within a noose, for laundring gold and barbing° it.   *clipping*
DOL [*snatches Face's sword*]: You'll bring your head within a cockscomb, will you?[9]
       And you, sir, with your menstrue°—   *solvent*
       [*Dashes Subtle's vial out of his hand.*] Gather it up.—
       'Sdeath,° you abominable pair of stinkards,   *by God's death*
       Leave off your barking, and grow one again,
       Or, by the light that shines, I'll cut your throats.
120   I'll not be made a prey unto the marshal,
       For ne'er a snarling dog-bolt° of you both.   *blunt-headed arrow*
       Have you together cozen'd all this while,
       And all the world, and shall it now be said,
       You've made most courteous shift to cozen yourselves?
125   [*To Face*] You will accuse him! you will bring him in
       Within the statute! Who shall take your word?
       A whoreson, upstart, apocryphal captain,
       Whom not a Puritan in Blackfriars will trust
       So much as for a feather: [*To Subtle*] and you, too,
130   Will give the cause, forsooth! you will insult,
       And claim a primacy in the divisions?
       You must be chief? as if you only had
       The powder to project with, and the work
       Were not begun out of equality?
135   The venture tripartite? all things in common?
       Without priority? 'Sdeath! you perpetual curs,
       Fall to your couples again, and cozen kindly,[1]
       And heartily, and lovingly, as you should,
       And lose not the beginning of a term,[2]
140   Or, by this hand, I shall grow factious too,
       And take my part, and quit you.
FACE: 'Tis his fault;
       He ever murmurs, and objects his pains,
       And says, the weight of all lies upon him.
SUBTLE: Why, so it does.
DOL: How does it? do not we
145   Sustain our parts?
SUBTLE: Yes, but they are not equal.
DOL: Why, if your part exceed to-day, I hope
       Ours may, to-morrow, match it.
SUBTLE: Ay, they may.
DOL: May, murmuring mastiff! ay, and do. Death on me!
       Help me to throttle him. [*Seizes Subtle by the throat.*]
SUBTLE: Dorothy! mistress Dorothy!
150   'Ods precious, I'll do any thing. What do you mean?

---

8. Law of 1541 prohibiting sorcery.   1. Work together as a pack, like hunting dogs.
9. The cockscomb was the fool's cap.   2. A term of the law courts; the busiest times in London.

DOL: Because o' your fermentation and cibation?[3]
SUBTLE: Not I, by heaven—
DOL [To Face.]:   Your Sol and Luna°—help me.   *gold and silver*
SUBTLE: Would I were hang'd then! I'll conform myself.
DOL: Will you, sir? do so then, and quickly: swear.
SUBTLE: What should I swear?
DOL: To leave your faction, sir,
        And labor kindly in the common work.
SUBTLE: Let me not breathe if I meant aught beside.
        I only used those speeches as a spur
        To him.
DOL: I hope we need no spurs, sir. Do we?
FACE: 'Slid,° prove to-day, who shall shark° best.   *God's eyelid / cheat*
SUBTLE: Agreed.
DOL: Yes, and work close and friendly.
SUBTLE: 'Slight, the knot
        Shall grow the stronger for this breach, with me.
        [*They shake hands.*]
DOL: Why, so, my good baboons! Shall we go make
        A sort of sober, scurvy, precise neighbours,
165   That scarce have smiled twice since the king came in,
        A feast of laughter at our follies? Rascals,
        Would run themselves from breath, to see me ride,[4]
        Or you t' have but a hole to thrust your heads in,
        For which you should pay ear-rent?[5] No, agree,
170   And may Don Provost° ride a feasting long,   *Provost-Marshal*
        In his old velvet jerkin and stain'd scarfs,
        My noble Sovereign, and worthy General,
        Ere we contribute a new crewel° garter   *double thread*
        To his most worsted worship.
SUBTLE: Royal Dol!
175   Spoken like Claridiana,[6] and thyself.
FACE: For which at supper, thou shalt sit in triumph,
        And not be styled Dol Common, but Dol Proper,
        Dol Singular: the longest cut at night,
        Shall draw thee for his Dol Particular.[7] [*Bell rings without.*]
SUBTLE: Who's that? one rings. To the window, Dol—pray heaven,
        The master do not trouble us this quarter.
FACE: O, fear not him. While there dies one a week
        O' the plague, he's safe, from thinking toward London:
        Beside, he's busy at his hop-yards now;
185   I had a letter from him. If he do,
        He'll send such word, for airing of the house,

---

3. Alchemical processes: fermentation was the change of any substance into fermented or purified form, and cibation was an infusion of liquid into dried matter.
4. To see her ride or carried off in a cart as were prostitutes, who were also often stripped and beaten.
5. Those who had their heads put in the stocks as punishment often had their ears cut off as well.
6. Heroine of the *Mirror of Princely Deeds and Knighthood,* a Spanish romance, translated by Margaret Tyler.
7. Whoever draws the longest lot gets to sleep with Dol. Also, "longest cut," in the sexual sense, as in *Twelfth Night* 2.5.67–68.

As you shall have sufficient time to quit it:
Though we break up a fortnight, 'tis no matter.

SUBTLE: Who is it, Dol?

DOL: A fine young quodling.°   *unripe apple*

FACE: O,

190   My lawyer's clerk, I lighted on last night,
In Holborn, at the Dagger. He would have
(I told you of him) a familiar,[8]
To rifle with at horses, and win cups.

DOL: O, let him in.

SUBTLE: Stay. Who shall do't?

FACE: Get you

195   Your robes on: I will meet him as going out.

DOL: And what shall I do?

FACE: Not be seen; away!   [*Exit Dol.*]
Seem you very reserv'd.

SUBTLE: Enough.   [*Exit.*]

FACE [*aloud and retiring*]: God be wi' you, sir,
I pray you let him know that I was here:
His name is Dapper. I would gladly have staid, but—

                                Scene 2

DAPPER [*within*]: Captain, I am here.

FACE: Who's that?—He's come, I think, Doctor.
   [*Enter Dapper.*]
        Good faith, sir, I was going away.

DAPPER: In truth,
I am very sorry, Captain.

FACE: But I thought
Sure I should meet you.

DAPPER: Ay, I am very glad.

5   I had a scurvy writ or two to make,
And I had lent my watch last night to one
That dines to-day at the sheriff's, and so was robb'd
Of my past-time.
   [*Re-enter Subtle, in his velvet Cap and Gown.*]
                         Is this the cunning-man?

FACE: This is his worship.

DAPPER: Is he a doctor?°   *learned man*

FACE: Yes.

DAPPER: And you have broke with him, Captain?

FACE: Ay.

DAPPER: And how?

FACE: Faith, he does make the matter, sir, so dainty°   *complicated*
I know not what to say.

DAPPER: Not so, good Captain.

FACE: Would I were fairly rid of it, believe me.

---

8. A spirit, in this instance to advise him on gambling.

DAPPER: Nay, now you grieve me, sir. Why should you wish so?
15   I dare assure you, I'll not be ungrateful.
FACE: I cannot think you will, sir. But the law
          Is such a thing—and then he says, Read's matter[9]
          Falling so lately.
DAPPER: Read! he was an ass,
          And dealt, sir, with a fool.
FACE: It was a clerk, sir.
DAPPER: A clerk?
FACE: Nay, hear me, sir, you know the law
          Better, I think—
DAPPER: I should, sir, and the danger:
          You know, I shew'd the statute to you.
FACE: You did so.
DAPPER: And will I tell then? By this hand of flesh,
          Would it might never write good court-hand more,[1]
25   If I discover. What do you think of me,
          That I am a chiaus?[2]
FACE: What's that?
DAPPER: The Turk was here.
          As one would say, do you think I am a Turk?
FACE: I'll tell the doctor so.
DAPPER: Do, good sweet Captain.
FACE: Come, noble Doctor, pray thee let's prevail;
30   This is the gentleman, and he is no chiaus.
SUBTLE: Captain, I have return'd you all my answer.
          I would do much, sir, for your love—But this
          I neither may, nor can.
FACE: Tut, do not say so.
          You deal now with a noble fellow, Doctor,
35   One that will thank you richly; and he is no chiaus:
          Let that, sir, move you.
SUBTLE: Pray you, forbear—
FACE: He has
          Four angels here.[3]
SUBTLE: You do me wrong, good sir.
FACE: Doctor, wherein? to tempt you with these spirits?
SUBTLE: To tempt my art and love, sir, to my peril.
40   Fore heaven, I scarce can think you are my friend,
          That so would draw me to apparent danger.
FACE: I draw you! a horse draw you, and a halter,
          You, and your flies° together—   *familiar spirits*
DAPPER: Nay, good Captain.
FACE: That know no difference of men.

---

9. Simon Read was in trouble with the College of Physicians for practicing medicine without a license. After being charged with dealing in spirits in 1607, he was pardoned because he contacted spirits to determine the identity of the men who had robbed Toby Matthew.

1. Court-hand was a handwriting used in the courts that took training and skill to produce.
2. A cheat, from the Turkish *chäush*, meaning messenger.
3. An angel was a gold coin worth 10 shillings with the image of the Archangel Michael stamped on it.

SUBTLE: Good words, sir.
FACE: Good deeds, Sir Doctor Dogs-meat. 'Slight, I bring you
        No cheating Clim o' the Cloughs, or Claribels,[4]
        That look as big as five-and-fifty, and flush;[5]
        And spit out secrets like hot custard—
DAPPER: Captain!
FACE: Nor any melancholic under-scribe,
50   Shall tell the vicar;[6] but a special gentle,°   *gentleman*
        That is the heir to forty marks[7] a year,
        Consorts with the small poets of the time,
        Is the sole hope of his old grandmother:
        That knows the law, and writes you six fair hands,
55   Is a fine clerk, and has his cyphering° perfect,   *account keeping*
        Will take his oath o' the Greek Testament,[8]
        If need be, in his pocket; and can court
        His mistress out of Ovid.[9]
DAPPER: Nay, dear Captain—
FACE: Did you not tell me so?
DAPPER: Yes; but I'd have you
60   Use Master Doctor with some more respect.
FACE: Hang him, proud stag, with his broad velvet head![1]—
        But for your sake, I'd choak, ere I would change
        An article of breath with such a puckfist:°   *ball of air*
        Come, let's be gone. [*Going.*]
SUBTLE: Pray you let me speak with you.
DAPPER: His worship calls you, Captain.
FACE: I am sorry
        I e'er embark'd myself in such a business,
DAPPER: Nay, good sir; he did call you.
FACE: Will he take then?
SUBTLE: First, hear me—
FACE: Not a syllable, 'less you take.
SUBTLE: Pray you, sir—
FACE: Upon no terms, but an *assumpsit*.°   *verbal promise*
SUBTLE: Your humor must be law. [*He takes the four angels.*]
FACE: Why now, sir, talk.
        Now I dare hear you with mine honor. Speak.
        So may this gentleman too.
SUBTLE: Why, sir—[*Offering to whisper Face.*]
FACE: No whispering.
SUBTLE: Fore heaven, you do not apprehend the loss
        You do yourself in this.
FACE: Wherein? for what?

---

4. Clim o' the Cloughs was an outlaw in the *Ballad of Adam Bell*, and Claribel was a knight who "loved out of measure" in Spenser's *Faerie Queene* 4.9.20.
5. A winning hand of cards.
6. Vicar-general in the ecclesiastical courts.
7. A mark was worth 14 shillings.
8. In the Folio, Jonson changed "Testament" to "Xenophon" to avoid the charge of blasphemy, forbidden on the stage by the law of 1606.
9. The Roman poet Ovid's *Art of Love* was a text popular with amorous young men who wanted to show off their sophistication and learning.
1. The velvet capped head of a doctor.

SUBTLE: Marry, to be so importunate for one,
    That, when he has it, will undo you all:
    He'll win up all the money in the town,
FACE: How!
SUBTLE: Yes, and blow up gamester after gamester,
    As they do crackers° in a puppet play.   *firecrackers*
80   If I do give him a familiar,°   *spirit, demon*
    Give you him all you play for; never set him:
    For he will have it.
FACE: You are mistaken, Doctor.
    Why he does ask one but for cups and horses,
    A rifling fly;[2] none of your great familiars.
DAPPER: Yes, Captain, I would have it for all games.
SUBTLE: I told you so.
FACE   [*taking Dapper aside*]: 'Slight, that is a new business!
    I understood you, a tame bird, to fly
    Twice in a term, or so, on Friday nights,
    When you had left the office, for a nag
90   Of forty or fifty shillings.
DAPPER: Ay, 'tis true, sir;
    But I do think now I shall leave the law,
    And therefore—
FACE: Why, this changes quite the case,
    Do you think that I dare move° him?   *urge*
DAPPER: If you please, sir;
    All's one to him, I see.
FACE: What! for that money?
95   I cannot with my conscience; nor should you
    Make the request, methinks.
DAPPER: No, sir, I mean
    To add consideration.
FACE: Why then, sir,
    I'll try.—[*Goes to Subtle.*] Say that it were for all games, Doctor?
SUBTLE: I say then, not a mouth shall eat for him
100   At any ordinary, but on the score,[3]
    That is a gaming mouth, conceive me.
FACE: Indeed!
SUBTLE: He'll draw you all the treasure of the realm,
    If it be set him.
FACE: Speak you this from art?
SUBTLE: Ay, sir, and reason too, the ground of art.
105   He is of the only best complexion,
    The Queen of Fairy loves.
FACE: What! is he?
SUBTLE: Peace.
    He'll overhear you. Sir, should she but see him—

---

2. He wants a fly, or familiar spirit, only for gambling.   3. No gambler shall eat his dinner at an inn except on credit.

FACE: What?

SUBTLE: Do not you tell him.

FACE: Will he win at cards too?

SUBTLE: The spirits of dead Holland, living Isaac,[4]

110   You'd swear were in him; such a vigorous luck
           As cannot be resisted. 'Slight, he'll put
           Six of your gallants to a cloke,[5] indeed.

FACE: A strange success, that some man shall be born to!

SUBTLE: He hears you, man—

DAPPER: Sir, I'll not be ingrateful.

FACE: Faith, I have confidence in his good nature:
       You hear, he says he will not be ingrateful.

SUBTLE: Why, as you please; my venture follows yours.

FACE: Troth, do it, Doctor; think him trusty, and make him.
       He may make us both happy in an hour:

120   Win some five thousand pound, and send us two on't.

DAPPER: Believe it, and I will, sir.

FACE: And you shall, sir. [*Takes him aside.*]
       You have heard all?

DAPPER: No, what was't? Nothing, I, sir.

FACE: Nothing!

DAPPER: A little, sir.

FACE: Well, a rare star
       Reign'd at your birth.

DAPPER: At mine, sir! No.

FACE: The Doctor

125   Swears that you are—

SUBTLE: Nay, Captain, you'll tell all now.

FACE: Allied to the Queen of Fairy.

DAPPER: Who? that I am?
       Believe it, no such matter—

FACE: Yes, and that
       You were born with a cawl on your head.[6]

DAPPER: Who says so?

FACE: Come,
       You know it well enough, though you dissemble it.

DAPPER: I'fac,° I do not: you are mistaken.   *in faith*

FACE: How!
       Swear by your fac, and in a thing so known
       Unto the Doctor? How shall we, sir, trust you
       In the other matter? can we ever think,
       When you have won five or six thousand pound,

135   You'll send us shares in't, by this rate?

DAPPER: By Jove, sir,
       I'll win ten thousand pound, and send you half.
       I'fac's no oath.

---

4. John and Isaac Hollander, Dutch alchemists, were said
to have lived in the early 15th century. Their works were
published in the late 16th century.

5. Strip them down to their cloaks.

6. A membrane surrounding the head of a baby at birth,
believed to be a good omen.

SUBTLE: No, no, he did but jest.
FACE: Go to. Go thank the doctor: he's your friend,
          To take it so.
DAPPER: I thank his worship.
FACE: So!
140   Another angel.
DAPPER: Must I?
FACE: Must you! 'slight,
          What else is thanks? will you be trivial?—Doctor,
     [*Dapper gives him the money.*]
          When must he come for his familiar?
DAPPER: Shall I not have it with me?
SUBTLE: O, good sir!
          There must a world of ceremonies pass;
145   You must be bath'd and fumigated first;
          Besides the Queen of Fairy does not rise
          Till it be noon.
FACE: Not, if she danced, to-night.
SUBTLE: And she must bless it.
FACE: Did you never see
          Her royal grace yet?
DAPPER: Whom?
FACE: Your aunt of Fairy?
SUBTLE: Not since she kist him in the cradle, Captain;
          I can resolve you that.
FACE: Well, see her grace,
          Whate'er it cost you, for a thing that I know.
          It will be somewhat hard to compass; but
          However, see her. You are made, believe it,
155   If you can see her. Her grace is a lone woman,
          And very rich; and if she take a fancy,
          She will do strange things. See her, at any hand.
          'Slid, she may hap to leave you all she has:
          It is the doctor's fear.
DAPPER: How will't be done, then?
FACE: Let me alone, take you no thought. Do you
          But say to me, Captain, I'll see her grace.
DAPPER: Captain, I'll see her grace.
FACE: Enough. [*Knocking within.*]
SUBTLE: Who's there?
          Anon.—[*aside to Face*] Conduct him forth by the back way.—
          [*to Dapper*] Sir, against one o'clock prepare yourself;
165   Till when you must be fasting; only take
          Three drops of vinegar in at your nose,
          Two at your mouth, and one at either ear;
          Then bathe your fingers' ends and wash your eyes,
          To sharpen your five senses, and cry "hum"
170   Thrice, and then "buz" as often; and then come.   [*Exit.*]

FACE: Can you remember this?

DAPPER: I warrant you.

FACE: Well then, away. It is but your bestowing
    Some twenty nobles[7] 'mong her grace's servants,
    And put on a clean shirt: you do not know
175   What grace her grace may do you in clean linen.

                                      [Exeunt Face and Dapper.]

Scene 3

SUBTLE   [*within*]: Come in! Good wives, I pray you forbear me now;
    Troth I can do you no good till afternoon—
    [*Re-enters, followed by Drugger.*]
    What is your name, say you, Abel Drugger?

DRUGGER: Yes, sir.

SUBTLE: A seller of tobacco?

DRUGGER: Yes. sir.

SUBTLE: Umph!

5   Free of the Grocers?[8]

DRUGGER: Ay, an't please you.

SUBTLE: Well—
    Your business, Abel?

DRUGGER: This, an't please your worship;
    I am a young beginner, and am building
    Of a new shop, an't like your worship, just
    At corner of a street:—Here is the plot on't—
10   And I would know by art, sir, of your worship,
    Which way I should make my door, by necromancy,
    And where my shelves; and which should be for boxes,
    And which for pots. I would be glad to thrive, sir:
    And I was wish'd to your worship by a gentleman,
15   One Captain Face, that says you know men's planets,
    And their good angels, and their bad.

SUBTLE: I do,
    If I do see them—
    [*Re-enter Face.*]

FACE: What! my honest Abel?
    Thou art well met here.

DRUGGER: Troth, sir, I was speaking,
    Just as your worship came here, of your worship:
20   I pray you speak for me to Master Doctor.

FACE: He shall do any thing.—Doctor, do you hear?
    This is my friend, Abel, an honest fellow;
    He lets me have good tobacco, and he does not
    Sophisticate° it with sack-lees or oil,   *dilute*
25   Nor washes it in muscadel° and grains,°   *wine / spices*
    Nor buries it in gravel, under ground.
    Wrapp'd up in greasy leather, or piss'd clouts;

---

7. A noble was a coin worth six shillings and eight pence.   8. Admitted to the guild of the Grocers' Company.

But keeps it in fine lily pots, that, open'd,
Smell like conserve of roses, or French beans.
30   He has his maple block, his silver tongs,
Winchester pipes, and fire of Juniper:[9]
A neat, spruce, honest fellow, and no goldsmith.°   *usurer*
SUBTLE: He is a fortunate fellow, that I am sure on.
FACE: Already, sir, have you found it? Lo thee, Abel!
SUBTLE: And in right way toward riches—
FACE: Sir!
SUBTLE: This summer
He will be of the clothing of his company,
And next spring call'd to the scarlet;° spend what he can.   *made sheriff*
FACE: What and so little beard?
SUBTLE: Sir, you must think,
He may have a receipt to make hair come:[1]
40   But he'll be wise, preserve his youth, and fine for't;
His fortune looks for him another way.
FACE: 'Slid, Doctor, how canst thou know this so soon?
I am amused at that!
SUBTLE: By a rule, Captain,
In metoposcopy,[2] which I do work by;
45   A certain star in the forehead, which you see not.
Your chestnut or your olive-color'd face
Does never fail; and your long ear doth promise.
I knew't by certain spots, too, in his teeth,
And on the nail of his mercurial finger.[3]
FACE: Which finger's that?
SUBTLE: His little finger. Look.
You were born upon a Wednesday?
DRUGGER: Yes, indeed, sir.
SUBTLE: The thumb, in chiromancy,° we give Venus;   *palmistry*
The fore-finger, to Jove; the midst, to Saturn;
The ring, to Sol; the least, to Mercury,
55   Who was the lord, sir, of his horoscope,
His house of life being Libra; which fore-show'd,
He should be a merchant, and should trade with balance.[4]
FACE: Why, this is strange! Is it not, honest Nab?
SUBTLE: There is a ship now, coming from Ormus,[5]
60   That shall yield him such a commodity
Of drugs—This is the west, and this the south?
    [*Pointing to the plan.*]

9. The tobacco was cut on a maple wood block, smoked
in pipes made in Winchester, and lit with aromatic coal
of juniper that was held with silver tongs.
1. Recipe for growing hair.
2. Interpretation of personality on the basis of facial features.
3. The chestnut-colored face was believed to mean a happy
and straightforward person; long ears signified intelligence.
Each finger was associated with a particular planet in
palmistry.

4. Subtle relies on Drugger's ignorance of the astrological
belief that if Libra ruled the "first house," the sign of the
zodiac rising on the eastern horizon at the time of one's
birth, then that meant that Venus, goddess of love, ruled
one's life, rather than Mercury, the god of businessmen,
alchemists, tricksters, and thieves.
5. The port of Hormuz, then a center of the spice trade on
the Persian Gulf.

DRUGGER: Yes, sir.

SUBTLE: And those are your two sides?

DRUGGER: Ay, sir.

SUBTLE: Make me your door, then, south; your broad side, west:
    And on the east side of your shop, aloft,
65   Write Mathlai, Tarmiel, and Baraborat;
    Upon the north part, Rael, Velel, Thiel.[6]
    They are the names of those mercurial spirits,
    That do fright flies from boxes.

DRUGGER: Yes, sir.

SUBTLE: And
    Beneath your threshold, bury me a load-stone°   *magnet*
70   To draw in gallants that wear spurs: the rest,
    They'll seem[7] to follow.

FACE: That's a secret, Nab!

SUBTLE: And, on your stall, a puppet, with a vice
    And a court-fucus° to call city-dames: *cosmetic*
    You shall deal much with minerals.

DRUGGER: Sir, I have
75   At home, already—

SUBTLE: Ay, I know you have arsenic,
    Vitriol, sal-tartar, argaile, alkali,
    Cinoper:[8] I know all.—This fellow, Captain,
    Will come, in time, to be a great distiller,
    And give a say°—I will not say directly,   *make an attempt at*
80   But very fair—at the philosopher's stone.

FACE: Why, how now, Abel! is this true?

DRUGGER   [aside to Face]:   Good Captain,
    What must I give?

FACE: Nay, I'll not counsel thee.
    Thou hear'st what wealth (he says, spend what thou canst,)
    Thou'rt like to come to.

DRUGGER: I would gi' him a crown.[9]

FACE: A crown! and toward such a fortune? heart,
    Thou shalt rather gi' him thy shop. No gold about thee?

DRUGGER: Yes, I have a portague,[1] I have kept this half year.

FACE: Out on thee, Nab! 'Slight, there was such an offer—
    Shalt keep't no longer, I'll give't him for thee.
90   Doctor, Nab prays your worship to drink this, and swears
    He will appear more grateful, as your skill
    Does raise him in the world.

DRUGGER: I would entreat
    Another favor of his worship.

---

6. These spirits' names are taken from *Heptameron Seu El-
ementa Magica Pietri de Albano Philosophi*, an appendix to
Cornelius Agrippa's *De Occulta Philosophia* (1567). Subtle
claims these spirits protect tobacco from fleas.
7. Playing on the Latin *videre*, meaning to be seen, to
seem.

8. Vitriol: sulphuric acid; sal-tartar: potash; argaile: crude
cream of tartar; alkali: soda ash; cinoper, or cinnabar:
mercuric sulphide.
9. Silver coin worth five shillings, 25 pence.
1. Portuguese gold coin worth approximately four pounds.

FACE: What is't, Nab?

DRUGGER: But to look over, sir, my almanac,

95   And cross out my ill days, that I may neither
          Bargain, nor trust upon them.

FACE: That he shall, Nab;
          Leave it, it shall be done, 'gainst afternoon.

SUBTLE: And a direction for his shelves.

FACE: Now, Nab,
          Art thou well pleased, Nab?

DRUGGER: 'Thank, sir, both your worships.

FACE: Away.—   [Exit Drugger.]
          Why, now, you smoaky persecutor of nature!
          Now do you see, that something's to be done,
          Beside your beech-coal, and your corsive waters,
          Your crosslets, crucibels, and cucurbites?²

105   You must have stuff brought home to you, to work on:
          And yet you think, I am at no expense
          In searching out these veins, then following them,
          Then trying them out. 'Fore God, my intelligence°   information
          Costs me more money, than my share oft comes to.

110   In these rare works.

SUBTLE: You are pleasant, sir.—How now!

Scene 4

[Re-enter Dol.]

SUBTLE: What says my dainty Dolkin?

DOL: Yonder fish-wife
          Will not away. And there's your giantess,
          The bawd of Lambeth.³

SUBTLE: Heart, I cannot speak with them.

DOL: Not afore night, I have told them in a voice,

5   Thorough the trunk, like one of your familiars.
          But I have spied Sir Epicure Mammon—

SUBTLE: Where?

DOL: Coming along, at far end of the lane,
          Slow of his feet, but earnest of his tongue
          To one that's with him.

SUBTLE: Face, go you, and shift.   [Exit Face.]

10   Dol, you must presently make ready, too.

DOL: Why, what's the matter?

SUBTLE: O, I did look for him
          With the sun's rising: 'marvel he could sleep!
          This is the day I am to perfect for him
          The magisterium,° our great work, the stone;   master-principle

15   And yield it, made, into his hands: of which
          He has, this month, talk'd as he were possess'd.

---

2. Crosslets: melting pots; crucibels: melting pots; cucur-
bites: vessels with downturned necks for distilling liquids.

3. Prostitute of Lambeth, a disreputable quarter of London in Jonson's time.

And now he's dealing pieces on't away.—
Methinks I see him entering ordinaries,°   *inns*
Dispensing for the pox, and plaguy houses,[4]
20   Reaching his dose, walking Moorfields for lepers,[5]
And offering citizens' wives pomander-bracelets,[6]
As his preservative, made of the elixir;
Searching the spittal,° to make old bawds young;   *hospital*
And the highways, for beggars, to make rich:
25   I see no end of his labors. He will make
Nature asham'd of her long sleep: when art,
Who's but a step-dame, shall do more than she,
In her best love to mankind, ever could:
If his dream lasts, he'll turn the age to gold.   [*Exeunt.*]

ACT 2

Scene 1—*An outer room in Lovewit's house*

[*Enter Sir Epicure Mammon and Surly.*]

MAMMON: Come on, sir. Now, you set your foot on shore
In *Novo Orbe;*° here's the rich Peru: *New World*
And there within, sir, are the golden mines,
Great Solomon's Ophir![7] he was sailing to't,
5   Three years, but we have reach'd it in ten months.
This is the day, wherein, to all my friends,
I will pronounce the happy word, BE RICH;
THIS DAY YOU SHALL BE SPECTATISSIMI,°   *most looked at*
You shall no more deal with the hollow dye,
10   Or the frail card. No more be at charge of keeping
The livery-punk° for the young heir, that must   *prostitute*
Seal,[8] at all hours, in his shirt: no more,
If he deny, have him beaten to't, as he is
That brings him the commodity.[9] No more
15   Shall thirst of satin, or the covetous hunger
Of velvet entrails for a rude-spun cloke,
To be display'd at Madam Augusta's,[1] make
The sons of Sword and Hazard fall before
The golden calf, and on their knees, whole nights
20   Commit idolatry with wine and trumpets;

---

4. Pox: smallpox; and the great pox: syphilis; plaguy houses: hospitals for those suffering from the plague.
5. Moorfields was an area to the north of London, bordering on the areas of Bedlam, the madhouse, and of the leper houses.
6. Pomander bracelets were believed to protect the wearer against infectious disease.
7. King Solomon was said to have brought his gold from Ophir every three years (1 Kings 10.22). The alchemists believed Solomon possessed the philosophers' stone and alchemically produced the gold in Ophir.

8. Seal: to have sexual intercourse and to make a promissory note as pay for services rendered.
9. The heir, or john, is beaten to be forced to pay what he owes. Then to raise the money, he uses a commodity swindle, buying cheap goods on credit, which he sells at a loss. Incensed at how he has been cheated and beaten, the heir takes out his anger by beating the prostitute.
1. Most likely a brothel.

Or go a feasting after drum and ensign.[2]
No more of this. You shall start up young viceroys,
And have your punks, and punketees,° my Surly.   *little prostitutes*
And unto thee I speak it first, BE RICH.
25   Where is my Subtle, there? Within, ho!
FACE [*within*]:   Sir
He'll come to you by and by.
MAMMON: That is his fire-drake,°   *one who tends fire*
His Lungs, his Zephyrus,° he that puffs his coals,   *west wind*
Till he firk° nature up, in her own center.   *excite*
You are not faithful, sir. This night, I'll change
30   All that is metal, in my house, to gold:
And, early in the morning, will I send
To all the plumbers and the pewterers,
And buy their tin and lead up; and to Lothbury
For all the copper.
SURLY: What, and turn that too?
MAMMON: Yes, and I'll purchase Devonshire and Cornwall,
And make them perfect Indies! you admire now?
SURLY: No, faith.
MAMMON: But when you see th' effects of the Great Medicine,[3]
Of which one part projected on a hundred
Of Mercury, or Venus, or the moon,
40   Shall turn it to as many of the sun;
Nay, to a thousand, so *ad infinitum*;
You will believe me.
SURLY: Yes, when I see't, I will.
But if my eyes do cozen me so, and I
Giving them no occasion, sure I'll have
45   A whore, shall piss them out next day.
MAMMON: Ha! why?
Do you think I fable with you? I assure you,
He that has once the flower of the sun,
The perfect ruby, which we call elixir,
Not only can do that, but, by its virtue,
50   Can confer honor, love, respect, long life;
Give safety, valor, yea, and victory,
To whom he will. In eight and twenty days,
I'll make an old man of fourscore, a child.
SURLY: No doubt; he's that already.
MAMMON: Nay, I mean,
55   Restore his years, renew him, like an eagle,
To the fifth age;[4] make him get sons and daughters,
Young giants; as our philosophers have done,

2. Garbled version of the story of the golden calf (Exodus 32).

3. The philosophers' stone.
4. Between the ages of 50 and 65.

The ancient patriarchs, afore the flood,[5]
But taking, once a week, on a knife's point,
60   The quantity of a grain of mustard of it;
Become stout Marses,[6] and beget young Cupids.

SURLY: The decay'd vestals of Piet-hatch[7] would thank you,
That keep the fire° alive, there.   *venereal disease*

MAMMON: 'Tis the secret
Of nature naturis'd[8] 'gainst all infections,
65   Cures all diseases coming of all causes;
A month's grief in a day, a year's in twelve;
And, of what age soever, in a month:
Past all the doses of your drugging doctors.
I'll undertake, withal, to fright the plague
70   Out of the kingdom in three months,

SURLY: And I'll
Be bound, the players[9] shall sing your praises, then,
Without their poets.

MAMMON: Sir, I'll do't. Meantime,
I'll give away so much unto my man,
Shall serve the whole city, with preservative,
75   Weekly; each house his dose, and at the rate—

SURLY: As he that built the Water-work,[1] does with water?

MAMMON: You are incredulous.

SURLY: Faith I have a humor,°   *whim*
I would not willingly be gull'd.° Your stone   *hoodwinked*
Cannot transmute me.

MAMMON: Pertinax, my Surly,
80   Will you believe antiquity? records?
I'll show you a book where Moses and his sister,
And Solomon have written of the art;
Ay, and a treatise penn'd by Adam—

SURLY: How!

MAMMON: Of the philosophers' stone, and in High Dutch.°   *High German*

SURLY: Did Adam write, sir, in High Dutch?

MAMMON: He did;
Which proves it was the primitive tongue.

SURLY: What paper?

MAMMON: On cedar board.

SURLY: O that, indeed, they say,
Will last 'gainst worms.

MAMMON: 'Tis like your Irish wood,[2]

---

5. The alchemists attributed the longevity of the Hebrew patriarchs to their possession of the all-curing philosophers' stone.
6. Gods of war.
7. Haunt of prostitutes.
8. In scholastic philosophy, *natura naturata*, created nature, as opposed to creating nature, *natura naturans*, God's power in nature.
9. Actors would be happy if Mammon cured the plague, since the playhouses were closed whenever the death toll from the plague reached 40 deaths per week.
1. A system of lead pipes, designed by Peter Moris in 1582 and Bevis Bulmer in 1594, carried water from the Thames River to the houses of London.
2. According to Richard Braithwaite's *A Strappado for the Devil* (1615), Irish wood was protected from blight by St. Patrick.

'Gainst cob-webs. I have a piece of Jason's fleece, too,[3]
90   Which was no other than a book of alchemy,
        Writ in large sheep-skin, a good fat ram-vellum.
        Such was Pythagoras' thigh, Pandora's tub,
        And, all that fable of Medea's charms,[4]
        The manner of our work; the bulls, our furnace,
95   Still breathing fire; our *argent-vive,*° the dragon: quicksilver, mercury
        The dragon's teeth, mercury sublimate,
        That keeps the whiteness, hardness, and the biting:
        And they are gather'd into Jason's helm,
        The alembic, and then sow'd in Mars his field,
100   And thence sublimed so often, till they're fixed.
        Both this, the Hesperian garden, Cadmus' story,
        Jove's shower, the boon of Midas, Argus' eyes,[5]
        Boccace his Demogorgon,[6] thousands more,
        All abstract riddles of our stone.—How now?

Scene 2

[*Enter Face, dressed as a servant.*]
MAMMON: Do we succeed? Is our day come? and holds it?
FACE: The evening will set red upon you, sir;
        You have color for it, crimson:[7] the red ferment
        Has done his office; three hours hence prepare you
5   To see projection.
MAMMON: Pertinax, my Surly,
        Again I say to thee, aloud, "Be rich."
        This day, thou shalt have ingots; and, to-morrow,
        Give lords th' affront.—Is it, my Zephyrus,° right   west wind
        Blushes the bolt's-head?[8]
FACE: Like a wench with child, sir,
10   That were but now discover'd° to her master.   revealed
MAMMON: Excellent witty Lungs!—my only care is
        Where to get stuff enough now, to project on;
        This town will not half serve me.
FACE: No, sir! buy
        The covering off o' churches.
MAMMON: That's true.
FACE: Yes.
15   Let them stand bare, as do their auditory;°   congregation
        Or cap them, new, with shingles.

3. Mammon follows the allegorical interpretation of mythology popular with the alchemists. The Golden Fleece, the object of Jason and the Argonauts' quest, becomes a text on how to turn metal into gold.
4. Pythagoras's thigh was believed to be golden. Pandora released all evil into the world when she opened her box. Medea used her witchcraft to aid Jason in his pursuit of the Golden Fleece. Her father promised Jason the fleece if he could plow a field with a team of fire-breathing horses and brass-footed bulls, then plant the field with teeth from the dragon slain by Cadmus, defeat the men who would rise up out of the teeth, and slay the dragon

who guarded the fleece.
5. Hercules won the three golden apples in the Hesperian garden. Jove changed into a shower of gold to have intercourse with Danaë. All that Midas touched turned to gold; Argus was a watchman with 100 eyes.
6. In his *De Genealogia Deorum* (*On the Genealogy of the Gods*), Boccaccio portrayed Demogorgon as the original god of all mythology.
7. Crimson, or red, signified the last stage in the process of alchemical transformation.
8. Long-necked flask.

MAMMON: No, good thatch:
    Thatch will lie light upon the rafters, Lungs.—
    Lungs, I will manumit° thee from the furnace;   *free, release*
    I will restore thee thy complexion, Puff,
20   Lost in the embers; and repair this brain,
    Hurt with the fume o' the metals.
FACE: I have blown, sir,
    Hard for your worship; thrown by many a coal,
    When 'twas not beech; weigh'd those I put in, just,
    To keep your heat still even; these blear'd eyes
25   Have wak'd to read your several colors, sir,
    Of the pale citron, the green lion, the crow,
    The peacock's tail, the plumed swan.
MAMMON: And, lastly,
    Thou hast descry'd the flower, the *sanguis agni?*°   *blood of the lamb*
FACE: Yes, sir.
MAMMON: Where's master?
FACE: At his prayers, sir, he;
30   Good man, he's doing his devotions
    For the success.
MAMMON: Lungs, I will set a period
    To all thy labors; thou shalt be the master
    Of my seraglio.°   *harem*
FACE: Good, sir.
MAMMON: But do you hear?
    I'll geld° you, Lungs   *castrate*
FACE: Yes, sir.
MAMMON: For I do mean
35   To have a list of wives and concubines,
    Equal with Solomon, who had the stone
    Alike with me; and I will make me a back
    With the elixir, that shall be as tough
    As Hercules, to encounter fifty a night.—
40   Thou art sure thou saw'st it blood?
FACE: Both blood and spirit, sir.
MAMMON: I will have all my beds blown up, not stuft:
    Down is too hard: and then, mine oval room
    Fill'd with such pictures as Tiberius took
    From Elephantis, and dull Aretine[9]
45   But coldly imitated. Then, my glasses°   *mirrors*
    Cut in more subtle angles, to disperse
    And multiply the figures, as I walk
    Naked between my succubae.[1] My mists
    I'll have of perfume, vapor'd 'bout the room,
50   To lose ourselves in; and my baths, like pits

---

9. Elephantis: Roman erotic writer referred to by Suetonius;   *Sonnetti Lussuriosi* (1523).
Aretine: Pietro Aretino, Italian author of sexual satires   1. Demons who assume female form to have sex.

To fall into; from whence we will come forth,
And roll us dry in gossamer and roses.—
Is it arrived at ruby?—Where I spy
A wealthy citizen, or a rich lawyer,
55 Have a sublimed pure wife, unto that fellow
I'll send a thousand pound to be my cuckold.

FACE: And I shall carry it?

MAMMON: No. I'll have no bawds,°   *panderers, procurers*
But fathers and mothers: they will do it best,
Best of all others. And my flatterers
60 Shall be the pure and gravest of divines,
That I can get for money. My mere fools,
Eloquent burgesses, and then my poets
The same that writ so subtly of the fart,
Whom I will entertain still for that subject.
65 The few that would give out themselves to be
Court and town-stallions, and, each-where, belie
Ladies who are known most innocent for them;
Those will I beg, to make me eunuchs of;
And they shall fan me with ten ostrich tails
70 A-piece, made in a plume to gather wind.
We will be brave, Puff, now we have the med'cine,
My meat shall all come in, in Indian shells,
Dishes of agat set in gold, and studded
With emeralds, sapphires, hyacinths, and rubies.
75 The tongues of carps, dormice, and camels' heels,
Boil'd in the spirit of Sol, and dissolv'd pearl,
Apicius' diet, gainst the epilepsy:[2]
And I will eat these broths with spoons of amber,
Headed with diamond and carbuncle,
80 My foot-boy shall eat pheasants, calver'd salmons,
Knots, godwits, lampreys:° I myself will have   *eel-like fish*
The beards of barbels° served, instead of salads;   *carp-like fish*
Oil'd mushrooms; and the swelling unctuous paps
Of a fat pregnant sow, newly cut off,
85 Drest with an exquisite, and poignant sauce;
For which, I'll say unto my cook, "There's gold,
Go forth, and be a knight."

FACE: Sir, I'll go look
A little, how it heightens.   [*Exit.*]

MAMMON: Do.—My shirts
I'll have of taffeta-sarsnet,° soft and light   *silky material*
90 As cobwebs; and for all my other raiment,
It shall be such as might provoke the Persian,
Were he to teach the world riot anew.
My gloves of fishes' and birds' skins, perfumed
With gums of paradise, and eastern air—

2. Quintus Gavius Apicius, Roman gourmand of Tiberius's reign; "tongues of carps" and "dormice" were considered delicacies, and camels' heels were thought to ward off disease.

SURLY: And do you think to have the stone with this?

MAMMON: No, I do think t' have all this with the stone.

SURLY: Why, I have heard, he must be *homo frugi*,°   *temperate man*
    A pious, holy, and religious man,
    One free from mortal sin, a very virgin.

MAMMON: That makes it, sir; he is so; but I buy it;
    My venture brings it me. He, honest wretch,
    A notable, superstitious, good soul,
    Has worn his knees bare, and his slippers bald,
    With prayer and fasting for it; and sir, let him
105   Do it alone, for me, still. Here he comes.
    Not a profane word afore him: 'tis poison.—

Scene 3

[Enter Subtle.]
    Good morrow, father.

SUBTLE: Gentle son, good morrow.
    And to your friend there. What is he, is with you?

MAMMON: An heretic, that I did bring along,
    In hope, sir, to convert him.

SUBTLE: Son, I doubt°   *suspect*
5   You are covetous, that thus you meet your time
    In the just point: prevent° your day at morning.   *anticipate*
    This argues something, worthy of a fear
    Of importune° and carnal appetite.   *untimely*
    Take heed you do not cause the blessing leave you,
10   With your ungovern'd haste. I should be sorry
    To see my labors, now even at perfection,
    Got by long watching and large patience,
    Not prosper where my love and zeal hath placed them.
    Which (heaven I call to witness, with your self,
15   To whom I have pour'd my thoughts) in all my ends,
    Have look'd no way, but unto public good,
    To pious uses, and dear charity
    Now grown a prodigy with men. Wherein
    If you, my son, should now prevaricate,°   *deviate*
20   And, to your own particular lusts employ
    So great and catholic° a bliss, be sure   *universal*
    A curse will follow, yea, and overtake
    Your subtle and most secret ways.

MAMMON: I know, sir;
    You shall not need to fear me: I but come,
25   To have you confute° this gentleman.   *prove wrong*

SURLY: Who is,
    Indeed, sir, somewhat costive° of belief   *reluctant*
    Toward your stone; would not be gull'd.

SUBTLE: Well, son,
    All that I can convince him in, is this.

The WORK IS DONE, bright Sol is in his robe.[3]
30   We have a medicine of the triple soul,[4]
        The glorified spirit. Thanks be to heaven,
        And make us worthy of it!—Ulen Spiegel![5]
FACE [*within*]: Anon, sir.
SUBTLE: Look well to the register,
        And let your heat still lessen by degrees,
35   To the aludels.°   *pear-shaped pots*
FACE [*within*]:   Yes, sir.
SUBTLE: Did you look
        On the bolt's-head yet?
FACE [*within*]:   Which? on D, sir?
SUBTLE: Ay;
        What's the complexion?
FACE [*within*]:   Whitish.
SUBTLE: Infuse vinegar,
        To draw his volatile substance and his tincture:
        And let the water in glass E be filter'd,
40   And put into the gripe's egg.[6] Lute° him well;   *seal in clay*
        And leave him closed in *balneo.*°   *in a bath*
FACE [*within*]:   I will, sir.
SURLY: What a brave language here is! next to canting.[7]
SUBTLE: I have another work, you never saw, son.
        That three days since past the philosopher's wheel[8]
45   In the lent° heat of Athanor;[9] and's become   *slow*
        Sulphur of Nature.
MAMMON: But 'tis for me?
SUBTLE: What need you?
        You have enough in that is perfect,
MAMMON: O but—
SUBTLE: Why, this is covetise!
MAMMON: No, I assure you,
        I shall employ it all in pious uses,
50   Founding of colleges and grammar schools,
        Marrying young virgins, building hospitals,
        And now and then a church,
    [*Re-enter Face.*]
SUBTLE: How now!
FACE: Sir, please you,
        Shall I not change the filter?
SUBTLE: Marry, yes;
        And bring me the complexion of glass B.   [*Exit Face.*]
MAMMON: Have you another?

---

3. The gold is ready.
4. Triple soul, including the vital (in the heart), natural (in the liver), and universal (in the brain) spirits.
5. Til Owl-glass, or mirror, trickster hero of German jest books, hoodwinked the Landgrave of Hesse, who believed in alchemy.
6. Vessel shaped like a vulture's egg.
7. Rhyming street talk.
8. Alchemical cycle.
9. Furnace with slow and steady heat.

SUBTLE: Yes, son; were I assured—
        Your piety were firm, we would not want
        The means to glorify it: but I hope the best.—
        I mean to tinct C in sand-heat to-morrow,
        And give him imbibition.[1]
MAMMON: Of white oil?
SUBTLE: No, sir, of red. F is come over the helm too,
        I thank my Maker, in S. Mary's bath,
        And shews *lac virginis*.[2] Blessed be heaven!
        I sent you of his feces° there calcined:[3]   sediment
        Out of that calx,° I have won the salt of mercury.   fine powder
MAMMON: By pouring on your rectified water?
SUBTLE: Yes, and reverberating in Athanor.
        [*Re-enter Face.*]
        How now! what color says it?
FACE: The ground black, sir.
MAMMON: That's your crow's head?[4]
SURLY: Your cock's-comb's,° is it not?   fool's
SUBTLE: No, 'tis not perfect. Would it were the crow!
70   That work wants something.
SURLY [*aside*]:   O, I look'd for this.
        The hay's a pitching.
SUBTLE: Are you sure you loosed them
        In their own menstrue?
FACE: Yes, sir, and then married them,
        And put them in a bolt's-head nipp'd to digestion,[5]
        According as you bade me, when I set
75   The liquor of Mars° to circulation   molten iron
        In the same heat.
SUBTLE: The process then was right.
FACE: Yes, by the token, sir, the retort brake,
        And what was saved was put into the pelican,[6]
        And sign'd with Hermes' seal.[7]
SUBTLE: I think 'twas so.
80   We should have a new amalgama.°   mixture of metals
SURLY [*aside*]:   O, this ferret
        Is rank as any pole-cat.
SUBTLE: But I care not:
        Let him e'en die; we have enough beside,
        In embrion.° H has his white shirt on?[8]   in early stages
FACE: Yes, sir,
        He's ripe for inceration,[9] he stands warm,

---

1. Absorption of a liquid by a solid.
2. Virgin's milk, a term for mercury.
3. Burnt down to fine powder.
4. "Crow's head" refers to the blackness of the material at this stage of the process.
5. Digestion is the extraction of soluble substances by water and heat.

6. A retort is a closed vessel with an outlet tube. A pelican is a vessel resembling a pelican, with a long neck curving down and reentering the body of the vessel.
7. Hermetically sealed, heated, and twisted closed.
8. Has turned white now.
9. Turning solid matter waxy by adding fluid.

85 In his ash-fire. I would not you should let
Any die now, if I might counsel, sir,
For luck's sake to the rest: it is not good.
MAMMON: He says right.
SURLY [aside]:   Ay, are you bolted?
FACE: Nay, I know't, sir,
I have seen the ill fortune. What is some three ounces
90 Of fresh materials?
MAMMON: Is't no more?
FACE: No more, sir,
Of gold, t'amalgame with some six of mercury.
MAMMON: Away, here's money. What will serve?
FACE: Ask him, sir.
MAMMON: How much?
SUBTLE: Give him nine pound:—you may give him ten.
SURLY: Yes, twenty, and be cozen'd, do.
MAMMON: There 'tis. [Gives Face the money.]
SUBTLE: This needs not; but that you will have it so,
To see conclusions of all: for two
Of our inferior works are at fixation,[1]
A third is in ascension.° Go your ways.   *distillation*
Have you set the oil of Luna° in kemia?[2]   *white elixir*
FACE: Yes, sir.
SUBTLE: And the philosopher's vinegar?°   *mercury*
FACE: Ay.   [Exit.]
SURLY: We shall have a salad!
MAMMON: When do you make projection?
SUBTLE: Son, be not hasty, I exalt our med'cine,
By hanging him *in balneo vaporoso*,°   *vapor bath*
And giving him solution; then congeal him;
105 And then dissolve him; then again congeal him;
For look, how oft I iterate the work,
So many times I add unto his virtue.
As, if at first one ounce convert a hundred.
After his second loose, he'll turn a thousand;
110 His third solution, ten; his fourth, a hundred;
After his fifth, a thousand thousand ounces
Of any imperfect metal, into pure
Silver or gold, in all examinations,
As good as any of the natural mine,
115 Get you your stuff here against afternoon,
Your brass, your pewter, and your andirons,
MAMMON: Not those of iron?
SUBTLE: Yes, you may bring them too:
We'll change all metals,
SURLY: I believe you in that.

---

1. Reducing a volatile substance to stable form.   2. Vessel in which distillation occurred in chemical analysis.

MAMMON: Then I may send my spits?

SUBTLE: Yes, and your racks.

SURLY: And dripping pans, and pot-hangers, and hooks,
    Shall he not?

SUBTLE: If he please.

SURLY: —To be an ass.

SUBTLE: How, sir!

MAMMON: This gentleman you must bear withal:
    I told you he had no faith.

SURLY: And little hope, sir;
    But much less charity, should I gull myself.

SUBTLE: Why, what have you observ'd, sir, in our art,
    Seems so impossible?

SURLY: But your whole work, no more.
    That you should hatch gold in a furnace, sir,
    As they do eggs in Egypt![3]

SUBTLE: Sir, do you
    Believe that eggs are hatch'd so?

SURLY: If I should?

SUBTLE: Why, I think that the greater miracle,
    No egg but differs from a chicken more
    Than metals in themselves.[4]

SURLY: That cannot be.
    The egg's ordain'd by nature to that end,
    And is a chicken *in potentia.*°   *in potentiality*

SUBTLE: The same we say of lead and other metals,
    Which would be gold, if they had time.

MAMMON: And that
    Our art doth further.

SUBTLE: Ay, for 'twere absurd
    To think that nature in the earth bred gold
    Perfect in the instant: something went before.
140   There must be remote matter.

SURLY: Ay, what is that?

SUBTLE: Marry, we say—

MAMMON: Ay, now it heats: stand, father,
    Pound him to dust.

SUBTLE: It is, of the one part,
    A humid exhalation, which we call
    Materia liquida,° or the unctuous water;   *liquid matter*
145   On the other part, a certain crass and vicious
    Portion of earth; both which, concorporate,
    Do make the elementary matter of gold;
    Which is not yet *propria materia,*°   *its own substance*
    But common to all metals and all stones;
150   For, where it is forsaken of that moisture,

---

3. In dunghills and incubators. See Pliny, *Naturalis Histo-*
ria 10.75–76.

4. The following 70 lines are based on Martin Del Rio's
Disquisitiones Magicae (1599–1600).

And hath more dryness, it becomes a stone:
Where it retains more of the humid fatness,
It turns to sulphur, or to quicksilver,
Who are the parents of all other metals.
155 Nor can this remote matter suddenly
Progress so from extreme unto extreme,
As to grow gold, and leap o'er all the means.
Nature doth first beget the imperfect, then
Proceeds she to the perfect. Of that airy
160 And oily water, mercury is engender'd;
Sulphur of the fat and earthy part; the one,
Which is the last, supplying the place of male,
The other of the female, in all metals.
Some do believe hermaphrodeity,[5]
165 That both do act and suffer. But these two
Make the rest ductile, malleable, extensive.[6]
And even in gold they are; for we do find
Seeds of them, by our fire, and gold in them;
And can produce the species of each metal
170 More perfect thence, than nature doth in earth.
Beside, who doth not see in daily practice
Art can beget bees, hornets, beetles, wasps,
Out of the carcasses and dung of creatures;
Yes, scorpions of an herb, being rightly placed?
175 And these are living creatures, far more perfect
And excellent than metals.[7]

MAMMON: Well said, father!
Nay, if he take you in hand, sir, with an argument,
He'll bray° you in a mortar.   *grind into bits*

SURLY: Pray you, sir, stay.
Rather than I'll be bray'd, sir, I'll believe
180 That Alchemy is a pretty kind of game,
Somewhat like tricks o' the cards, to cheat a man
With charming.

SUBTLE: Sir?

SURLY: What else are all your terms,
Whereon no one of your writers 'grees with other!
Of your elixir, your *lac virginis*,°   *dissolved mercury*
185 Your stone, your med'cine, and your chrysosperme,°   *golden sperm*
Your sal, your sulphur, and your mercury,
Your oil of height, your tree of life, your blood,
Your marcasite, your tutty, your magnesia,[8]
Your toad, your crow, your dragon, and your panther,[9]

---

5. Involving both male and female.
6. Capable of being extended.
7. The way alchemy worked is here described in terms of spontaneous generation of life from dead matter. People still believed in spontaneous generation because they did not yet realize that life sprung from eggs that had been laid in dead matter.
8. Marchasite: iron pyrites; tutty: zinc oxide.
9. Toad, crow, and panther are a series of colors in the alchemical process; dragon is mercury.

190   Your sun, your moon, your firmament, your adrop,[1]
       Your lato, azoch, zernich, chibrit, heautarit,[2]
       And then your red man, and your white woman,[3]
       With all your broths, your menstrues, and materials,
       Of piss and egg-shells, women's terms, man's blood,
195   Hair o' the head, burnt clouts, chalk, merds, and clay,
       Powder of bones, scalings of iron, glass,
       And worlds of other strange ingredients,
       Would burst a man to name?
SUBTLE: And all these named,
       Intending but one thing: which art our writers
200   Used to obscure their art.
MAMMON: Sir, so I told him—
       Because the simple idiot should not learn it,
       And make it vulgar.
SUBTLE: Was not all the knowledge
       Of the Egyptians writ in mystic symbols?
       Speak not the scriptures oft in parables?
205   Are not the choicest fables of the poets,
       That were the fountains and first springs of wisdom,
       Wrapp'd in perplexed allegories?
MAMMON: I urg'd that,
       And clear'd to him, that Sysiphus was damn'd
       To roll the ceaseless stone, only because
210   He would have made ours common.[4] [Dol appears at the door.]—
                            Who is this?
SUBTLE: 'Sprecious!°—What do you mean? go in, good lady,   God's precious
       Let me entreat you. [Dol retires.]—Where's this varlet?
       [Re-enter Face.]
FACE: Sir.
SUBTLE: You very knave! do you use me thus?
FACE: Wherein, sir?
SUBTLE: Go in and see, you traitor. Go!   [Exit Face.]
MAMMON: Who is it, sir?
SUBTLE: Nothing, sir; nothing.
MAMMON: What's the matter, good sir?
       I have not seen you thus distemper'd: who is't?
SUBTLE: All arts have still had, sir, their adversaries,
       But ours the most ignorant.—
       [Re-enter Face.]
                            What now?
FACE: 'Twas not my fault, sir; she would speak with you.
SUBTLE: Would she, sir? Follow me.   [Exit.]
MAMMON [stopping him.]:   Stay, Lungs.

1. The firmament is another name for the philosophers' stone; adrop is lead.
2. Lato: brasslike metal; azoch: mercury; zernich: trisulphide of arsenic; chibrit: sulphur; heautarit: mercury.
3. Red man: sulphur; white woman: mercury.

4. Condemned to Hades for revealing the secret of the gods (here interpreted as the philosophers' stone), Sysiphus had to roll a huge stone up a hill over and over as it kept rolling back downhill.

FACE: I dare not, sir.

MAMMON: Stay, man; what is she?

FACE: A lord's sister, sir.

MAMMON: How! pray thee, stay.

FACE: She's mad, sir, and sent hither—
           He'll be mad too—

MAMMON: I warrant thee.—Why sent hither?

FACE: Sir, to be cured.

SUBTLE   [within]:   Why, rascal!

FACE: Lo you!—Here, sir!   [Exit.]

MAMMON: 'Fore God, a Bradamante, a brave piece.[5]

SURLY: Heart, this is a bawdy-house! I will be burnt else.

MAMMON: O, by this light, no: do not wrong him. He's
           Too scrupulous that way: it is his vice.
           No, he's a rare physician, do him right,
230   An excellent Paracelsian,[6] and has done
           Strange cures with mineral physic. He deals all
           With spirits, he; he will not hear a word
           Of Galen, or his tedious recipes.[7]
       [Re-enter Face.]
           How now, Lungs!

FACE: Softly, sir; speak softly. I meant
235   To have told your worship all. This must not hear.

MAMMON: No, he will not be gull'd: let him alone.

FACE: Y're very right, sir, she is a most rare scholar,
           And is gone mad with studying Broughton's works.[8]
           If you but name a word touching the Hebrew,
240   She falls into her fit, and will discourse
           So learnedly of genealogies,
           As you would run mad too, to hear her, sir.

MAMMON: How might one do't'have conference with her, Lungs?

FACE: O divers have run mad upon the conference:
245   I do not know, sir. I am sent in haste,
           To fetch a vial.

SURLY: Be not gull'd, sir Mammon.

MAMMON: Wherein? pray ye, be patient.

SURLY: Yes, as you are,
           And trust confederate° knaves and bawds and whores.   banded together

MAMMON: You are too foul, believe it.—Come here, Ulen,
250   One word.

FACE: I dare not, in good faith. [Going.]

MAMMON: Stay, knave.

FACE: He is extreme angry that you saw her, sir.

---

5. Bradamante, a female knight, is the heroine of Ariosto's *Orlando Furioso* (1532; English trans., 1591). Brave: good looking, and courageous.
6. A follower of the medical theory of Paracelsus (1493–1541), which proposed that health depended on the proper chemical balance of mercury, salt, and sulphur in the body.

7. Galen, respected medical authority of antiquity (130–210), whose humoral theory of medicine was still widely believed by early modern physicians.
8. Hugh Broughton (1549–1612) was a Puritan author who wrote learned works on the Bible, particularly on the genealogies of the Old Testament. See *The Alchemist* 4.5 for a send-up of his scholarly jargon.

MAMMON: Drink that. [*Gives him money.*] What is she when she's out of her fit?
FACE: O, the most affablest creature, sir! so merry!
         So pleasant! she'll mount you up, like quicksilver,
255   Over the helm; and circulate like oil,
         A very vegetal:[9] discourse of state,
         Of mathematics, bawdry, any thing—
MAMMON: Is she no way accessible? no means,
         No trick to give a man a taste of her—wit—
260   Or so?
SUBTLE [*within*]: Ulen!
FACE: I'll come to you again, sir.   [*Exit.*]
MAMMON: Surly, I did not think one of your breeding
         Would traduce personages of worth.
SURLY: Sir Epicure,
         Your friend to use; yet still loth to be gull'd:
         I do not like your philosophical bawds.
265   Their stone is letchery enough to pay for,
         Without this bait.
MAMMON: 'Heart, you abuse yourself.
         I know the lady, and her friends, and means,
         The original of this disaster. Her brother
         Has told me all.
SURLY: And yet you never saw her
270   Till now?
MAMMON: O yes, but I forgot. I have, believe it,
         One of the treacherousest memories, I do think,
         Of all mankind.
SURLY: What call you her brother?
MAMMON: My lord—
         He will not have his name known, now I think on't,
SURLY: A very treacherous memory!
MAMMON: On my faith—
SURLY: Tut, if you have it not about you, pass it,
         Till we meet next.
MAMMON: Nay, by this hand, 'tis true.
         He's one I honor, and my noble friend;
         And I respect his house.
SURLY: Heart! can it be,
         That a grave sir, a rich, that has no need,
280   A wise sir, too, at other times, should thus,
         With his own oaths, and arguments, make hard means
         To gull himself? An this be your elixir,
         Your *lapis mineralis*, and your lunary,[1]
         Give me your honest trick yet at primero,
285   Or gleek;[2] and take your *lutum sapientis*,

---

9. With the connotation of Latin *vegetus*, lively, animated.
An extended series of alchemical metaphors for her sexual responsiveness.
1. *Lapis mineralis*: mineral stone; lunary: the fern moonwort,

and mercury.
2. Trick: a hand of cards with a pun on trick as a sly
scheme. Primero and gleek are card games.

Your *menstruum simplex!*[3] I'll have gold before you,
And with less danger of the quicksilver,
Or the hot sulphur.[4]
    [Re-enter Face.]

FACE   *[to Surly]*:   Here's one from Captain Face, sir,
    Desires you meet him in the Temple-church,
290   Some half hour hence, and upon earnest business.
    [whispers to Mammon] Sir, if you please to quit us, now; and come
    Again within two hours, you shall have
    My master busy examining o' the works;
    And I will steal you in, unto the party,
295   That you may see her converse.—Sir, shall I say,
    You'll meet the captain's worship?

SURLY: Sir, I will.— *[Walks aside.]*
    But, by attorney, and to a second purpose.
    Now, I am sure it is a bawdy-house;
    I'll swear it, were the marshal here to thank me:
300   The naming this commander doth confirm it.
    Don Face! why he's the most authentic dealer
    In these commodities, the superintendant
    To all the quainter[5] traffickers in town!
    He is the visitor, and does appoint,
305   Who lies with whom, and at what hour; what price:
    Which gown, and in what smock; what fall; what tire.
    Him will I prove, by a third person, to find
    The subtleties of this dark labyrinth:
    Which if I do discover, dear Sir Mammon,
310   You'll give your poor friend leave, though no philosopher,
    To laugh: for you that are, 'tis thought, shall weep.

FACE: Sir, he does pray, you'll not forget.

SURLY: I will not, sir.
    Sir Epicure, I shall leave you.   *[Exit.]*

MAMMON: I follow you, straight.

FACE: But do so, good sir, to avoid suspicion.
315   This gentleman has a parlous head.

MAMMON: But wilt thou, Ulen,
    Be constant to thy promise?

FACE: As my life, sir.

MAMMON: And wilt thou insinuate what I am, and praise me,
    And say, I am a noble fellow?

FACE: O, what else, sir?
    And that you'll make her royal with the stone,
320   An empress; and yourself, king of Bantam.[6]

MAMMON: Wilt thou do this?

FACE: Will I, sir!

---

3. *Lutum sapientis*: paste for closing the mouths of vessels;
menstruum simplex: simple solvent.
4. Quicksilver was used to treat venereal disease; sulphur
was used to treat skin diseases.

5. Quainter: with a pun on quaint, cunt.
6. Land of legendary wealth in Java; Bantam was the capital of an Islamic empire.

MAMMON: Lungs, my Lungs!
    I love thee.
FACE: Send your stuff, sir, that my master
    May busy himself about projection,
MAMMON: Thou hast witch'd me, rogue: take, go.
    [*Gives him money.*]
FACE: Your jack,[7] and all, sir.
MAMMON: Thou art a villain—I will send my jack,
    And the weights too. Slave, I could bite thine ear.
    Away, thou dost not care for me.
FACE: Not I, sir!
MAMMON: Come, I was born to make thee, my good weasel,
    Set thee on a bench, and have thee twirl a chain
330   With the best lord's vermin of 'em all.
FACE: Away, sir.
MAMMON: A count, nay, a Count Palatine[8]—
FACE: Good, sir, go.
MAMMON: —shall not advance thee better: no, nor faster.   [*Exit.*]

Scene 4

[*Re-enter Subtle and Dol.*]
SUBTLE: Has he bit? has he bit?
FACE: And swallowed too, my Subtle.
    I have given him line, and now he plays, i'faith.
SUBTLE: And shall we twitch him?
FACE: Thorough both the gills.
    A wench is a rare bait, with which a man
5   No sooner's taken, but he straight firks mad.[9]
SUBTLE: Dol, my lord What's-ums sister, you must now
    Bear yourself *statelich.*°   stately
DOL: O let me alone.
    I'll not forget my race,[1] I warrant you.
    I'll keep my distance, laugh and talk aloud;
10   Have all the tricks of a proud scurvy lady,
    And be as rude as her woman.
FACE: Well said, Sanguine![2]
SUBTLE: But will he send his andirons?
FACE: His jack too,
    And's iron shoeing-horn; I have spoke to him. Well,
    I must not lose my wary gamester yonder.
SUBTLE: O Monsieur Caution, that will not be gull'd.
FACE: Ay, if I can strike a fine hook into him, now!
    The Temple-church, there I have cast mine angle.
    Well, pray for me. I'll about it. [*Knocking without.*]

---

7. Device for turning the spit; the jack was driven by weights.
8. The jurisdiction of a palatinate count was equal to the king's.
9. Firks mad: is excited to raving madness.

1. Race in the early modern sense of lineage, and also sex; and course, in the sense of plan of action.
2. Pink-cheeked; the personality of the sanguine humor was happy, amorous, and brave.

SUBTLE: What, more gudgeons![3]
        Dol, scout, scout! [*Dol goes to the window.*] Stay, Face, you must go to
            the door,
20   'Pray God it be my Anabaptist.[4]—Who is't, Dol?
DOL: I know him not: he looks like a gold-end man.[5]
SUBTLE: Goods so! 'tis he, he said he would send what call you him?
        The sanctified elder, that should deal
        For Mammon's jack and andirons. Let him in.
25   Stay, help me off, first, with my gown. [*Exit Face with the gown.*] Away,
        Madam, to your withdrawing chamber. [*Exit Dol.*] Now,
        In a new tune, new gesture, but old language.—
        This fellow is sent from one negociates with me
        About the stone too; for the holy brethren
30   Of Amsterdam, the exiled saints; that hope
        To raise their discipline by it.[6] I must use him
        In some strange fashion, now, to make him admire me.—

                              Scene 5

[*Enter Ananias.*]
SUBTLE: Where is my drudge? [*Aloud.*]
        [*Re-enter Face.*]
FACE: Sir!
SUBTLE: Take away the recipient,
        And rectify your menstrue from the phlegma.[7]
        Then pour it on the Sol, in the cucurbite,[8]
        And let them macerate[9] together.
FACE: Yes, sir.
5   And save the ground?
SUBTLE: No: *terra damnata*[1]
        Must not have entrance in the work.—Who are you?
ANANIAS: A faithful brother, if it please you.
SUBTLE: What's that?
        A Lullianist? a Ripley? *Filius artis?*[2]
        Can you sublime and dulcify? calcine?[3]
10   Know you the sapor pontic? sapor stiptic?[4]
        Or what is homogene, or heterogene?[5]
ANANIAS: I understand no heathen language, truly.

---

3. Small fish eager to bite live bait.
4. Anabaptists began as a Protestant sect in Germany. They believed in communal ownership of property, adult baptism, and a return to the principles of the early Christian Church.
5. Traveling jeweler.
6. The Anabaptists came to England when their attempts to take over Amsterdam and other Dutch towns led to their being exiled.
7. Purify your solvent by distillation from the watery substance.
8. Gourd-shaped vessel with long neck bent downward.

9. Soak to soften.
1. Damned earth; the residue remaining after distillation.
2. Lullianist: follower of Raymond Lull (1235–1315), a Spanish scientist to whom alchemical works were attributed; Ripley: follower of George Ripley, an English Canon who wrote works of alchemy and popularized Lull; *Filius artis*: son of art.
3. Sublime: vaporize and distill; dulcify: sweeten; calcine: heat and reduce to fine powder.
4. Two of the five savors engendered by heat; *sapor pontic*: a sour taste; *sapor stiptic*: a less sour taste.
5. Homogene: of one kind; heterogene: of various kinds.

SUBTLE: Heathen! you Knipper-doling?[6] Is *ars sacra*,
    Or chrysopoeia, or spagyrica,
15   Or the pamphysic, or panarchic knowledge,[7]
    A heathen language?
ANANIAS: Heathen Greek, I take it.
SUBTLE: How! heathen Greek?
ANANIAS: All's heathen but the Hebrew.[8]
SUBTLE: Sirrah, my varlet, stand you forth and speak to him,
    Like a philosopher: answer in the language.
20   Name the vexations, and the martyrisations[9]
    Of metals in the work.
FACE: Sir, putrefaction,
    Solution, ablution, sublimation,
    Cohobation, calcination, ceration, and
    Fixation.[1]
SUBTLE: This is heathen Greek to you, now!—
25   And when comes vivification?[2]
FACE: After mortification.°   destruction
SUBTLE: What's cohobation?
FACE: 'Tis the pouring on
    Your *aqua regis*, and then drawing him off,
    To the trine circle of the seven spheres.[3]
SUBTLE: What's the proper passion of metals?
FACE: Malleation.[4]
SUBTLE: What's your *ultimum supplicium auri?*[5]
FACE: Antimonium.
SUBTLE: This is heathen Greek to you!—And what's your mercury?
FACE: A very fugitive, he will be gone, sir.
SUBTLE: How know you him?
FACE: By his viscosity,
    His oleosity,° and his suscitability.°   oiliness / volatility
SUBTLE: How do you sublime him?
FACE: With the calce[6] of egg-shells,
    White marble, talc.
SUBTLE: Your magisterium,° now,   masterwork
    What's that?
FACE: Shifting, sir, your elements,
    Dry into cold, cold into moist, moist into hot,
    Hot into dry.

---

6. Bernt Knipperdollink, one of the instigators of the Anabaptist rebellion in Munster (1534–1536).
7. Chrysopoeia: gold-making; spagyrica: special alchemical method of Paracelsus; pamphysic or panarchic knowledge: universal knowledge.
8. Puritans regarded Hebrew as the original language, which Adam spoke, and the Anabaptists even considered dispensing with all books except the Hebrew Bible, or Old Testament.
9. Martyrisations: the tests that metals were put through.
1. Putrefaction: disintegration; solution: changing a solid to a liquid; ablution: washing away impurities; sublimation: vaporization and distillation; cohobation: redistillation;

calcination: reducing to powder by heating; ceration: making waxy; fixation: changing volatile material into stable form.
2. Vivification: restoration of a substance to its first state.
3. *Aqua regis*: a solvent for gold; trine circle: planets that were one-third of a circle or 120 degrees apart were thought to be a positive sign; the seven spheres are the Sun, the Moon, and the planets Earth, Mars, Mercury, Venus, and Saturn.
4. Passion: how metals can be affected; malleation: hammering.
5. *Ultimum supplicium auri:* ultimate punishment of gold.
6. Calce: powder produced by burning of a substance.

SUBTLE: This is heathen Greek to you still?
40   Your *lapis philosophicus?°*   *philosophers' stone*
FACE: 'Tis a stone, and not
        A stone; a spirit, a soul, and a body:
        Which if you do dissolve, it is dissolved;
        If you coagulate, it is coagulated;
        If you make it to fly, it flieth.
SUBTLE: Enough.   [*Exit Face.*]
45   This is heathen Greek to you! What are you, sir?
ANANIAS: Please you, a servant of the exiled Brethren,[7]
        That deal with widows' and with orphans' goods;
        And make a just account unto the saints:
        A deacon,
SUBTLE: O, you are sent from Master Wholesome,
50   Your teacher?
ANANIAS: From Tribulation Wholesome,
        Our very zealous pastor.
SUBTLE: Good! I have
        Some orphans' goods to come here.
ANANIAS: Of what kind, sir?
SUBTLE: Pewter and brass, andirons and kitchen-ware,
        Metals, that we must use our medicine on:
55   Wherein the brethren may have a pennyworth,
        For ready money.
ANANIAS: Were the orphans' parents
        Sincere professors?[8]
SUBTLE: Why do you ask?
ANANIAS: Because
        We then are to deal justly, and give, in truth,
        Their utmost value.
SUBTLE: 'Slid, you'd cozen else,
60   And if their parents were not of the faithful?
        I will not trust you, now I think on it,
        'Till I have talk'd with your pastor. Have you brought money
        To buy more coals?
ANANIAS: No, surely.
SUBTLE: No! how so?
ANANIAS: The Brethren bid me say unto you, sit,
65   Surely, they will not venture any more,
        Till they may see projection.
SUBTLE: How!
ANANIAS: You've had,
        For the instruments, as bricks, and loam, and glasses,
        Already thirty pound; and for materials,
        They say, some ninety more: and they have heard since,

---

7. The exiled Brethren were a Protestant sect of Anabap-   8. Zealous Anabaptists, true believers.
tists exiled from the Netherlands.

70   That one at Heidelberg,⁹ made it of an egg,
         And a small paper of pin-dust.°   *metal filings*
SUBTLE: What's your name?
ANANIAS: My name is Ananias.
SUBTLE: Out, the varlet
         That cozen'd the apostles!¹ Hence, away!
         Flee, Mischief! had your holy consistory²
75   No name to send me, of another sound,
         Than wicked Ananias? send your elders³
         Hither to make atonement for you quickly,
         And give me satisfaction; or out goes
         The fire; and down th' alembics, and the furnace,
80   *Piger Henricus*,⁴ or what not. Thou wretch!
         Both sericon and bufo⁵ shall be lost,
         Tell them. All hope of rooting out the bishops,⁶
         Or the antichristian hierarchy, shall perish,
         If they stay threescore minutes: the aqueity,
85   Terreity, and sulphureity
         Shall run together again, and all be annull'd,⁷
         Thou wicked Ananias! [*Exit Ananias.*] This will fetch 'em,
         And make them haste towards their gulling more.
         A man must deal like a rough nurse, and fright
90   Those that are froward,° to an appetite.   *contrary*

                           Scene 6
         [*Re-enter Face in his uniform, followed by Drugger.*]
FACE: H's busy with his spirits, but we'll upon him.
SUBTLE: How now! what mates, what Bayards have we here?⁸
FACE: I told you, he would be furious.—Sir, here's Nab,
         Has brought you another piece of gold to look on:
5   —We must appease him. Give it me,—and prays you,
         You would devise—what is it, Nab?
DRUGGER: A sign, sir.
FACE: Ay, a good lucky one, a thriving sign, Doctor.
SUBTLE: I was devising now.
FACE: 'Slight, do not say so,
         He will repent he gave you any more—
10   What say you to his constellation, Doctor,
         The Balance?⁹
SUBTLE: No, that way is stale, and common.

---

9. City known as a center for alchemy.
1. Ananias kept money back from the apostles. See *Acts of the Apostles* 5.1–11.
2. Church board made up of deacons, ministers, and elders.
3. Authority figures of the church.
4. A lazy Henry.
5. Red and black tincture.

6. Radical Protestants objected to the bishops in the Church of England as a remnant of Roman Catholicism.
7. The processes of alchemical purification will be reversed and the work completely ruined.
8. Bayard was the enchanted horse of Rinaldo in Ariosto's *Orlando Furioso*.
9. Constellation: zodiacal sign; the Balance: Libra (21 September to 20 October).

      A townsman born in Taurus,[1] gives the bull,
      Or the bull's-head: in Aries,[2] the ram,
      A poor device! No, I will have his name

15   Form'd in some mystic character; whose radii,°   *rays*
      Striking the senses of the passers by,
      Shall, by a virtual° influence, breed affections,°   *powerful / inclinations*
      That may result upon the party owns it:
      As thus—

FACE: Nab!

SUBTLE: He shall have "a bell," that's "Abel";

20   And by it standing one whose name is "Dee,"[3]
      In a "rug" gown, there's "D," and "Rug," that's "drug":
      And right anenst° him a dog snarling "er";   *against*
      There's "Drugger," Abel Drugger. That's his sign.
      And here's now mystery and hieroglyphic![4]

FACE: Abel, thou art made.

DRUGGER: Sir, I do thank his worship.

FACE: Six o' thy legs° more will not do it, Nab.   *bows*
      He has brought you a pipe of tobacco, Doctor.

DRUGGER: Yes, sir:
      I have another thing I would impart—

FACE: Out with it, Nab.

DRUGGER: Sir, there is lodged, hard by me,

30   A rich young widow—

FACE: Good! a *bona roba?*[5]

DRUGGER: But nineteen, at the most.

FACE: Very good, Abel.

DRUGGER: Marry, she's not in fashion yet; she wears
      A hood, but it stands a-cop.°   *high on the head*

FACE: No matter, Abel.

DRUGGER: And I do now and then give her a fucus—[6]

FACE: What! dost thou deal, Nab?

SUBTLE: I did tell you, Captain.

DRUGGER: And physic too, sometime, sir; for which she trusts me
      With all her mind. She's come up here of purpose
      To learn the fashion.

FACE: Good (his match too!)—On, Nab.

DRUGGER: And she does strangely long to know her fortune.

FACE: God's lid, Nab, send her to the Doctor, hither.

DRUGGER: Yes, I have spoke to her of his worship already;
      But she's afraid it will be blown abroad,
      And hurt her marriage.

FACE: Hurt it! 'tis the way

---

1. Taurus, the bull (21 April to 20 May).
2. Aries, the ram (21 March to 20 April).
3. John Dee (1527–1608), alchemist and mathematician, favored by Queen Elizabeth, to whom he gave advice based on astrology.
4. The Renaissance interest in Egyptian hieroglyphics was rooted in the belief in Hermes Trismegistus, the supposed author of the *Corpus Hermeticum*, who was thought to be the inventor of the hieroglyph.
5. Well-dressed woman, a prostitute.
6. Fucus: make-up with a pun of obvious sexual meaning.

To heal it, if 'twere hurt; to make it more
45   Follow'd and sought: Nab, thou shalt tell her this.
She'll be more known, more talk'd of; and your widows
Are ne'er of any price till they be famous;
Their honor is their multitude of suitors:
Send her, it may be thy good fortune. What!
50   Thou dost not know,
DRUGGER: No, sir, she'll never marry
Under a knight: her brother has made a vow.
FACE: What! and dost thou despair, my little Nab,
Knowing what the Doctor has set down for thee,
And seeing so many of the city dubb'd?°   *knighted*
55   One glass o' thy water, with a madam I know,
Will have it done, Nab: what's her brother, a knight?
DRUGGER: No, sir, a gentleman newly warm° in his land, sir,   *having just inherited*
Scarce cold in his one and twenty, that does govern
His sister here; and is a man himself
60   Of some three thousand a year, and is come up
To learn to quarrel, and to live by his wits,
And will go down again, and die in the country.
FACE: How! to quarrel?
DRUGGER: Yes, sir, to carry quarrels,
As gallants do; to manage them by line.
FACE: 'Slid, Nab, the Doctor is the only man
In Christendom for him. He has made a table,
With mathematical demonstrations.
Touching the art of quarrels: he will give him
An instrument to quarrel by. Go, bring them both,
70   Him and his sister. And, for thee, with her
The Doctor happ'ly may persuade. Go to:
'Shalt give his worship a new damask suit
Upon the premises.
SUBTLE: O, good Captain!
FACE: He shall;
He is the honestest fellow, doctor.—Stay not,
75   No offers; bring the damask, and the parties.
DRUGGER: I'll try my power, sir,
FACE: And thy will too, Nab.
SUBTLE: 'Tis good tobacco, this! what is't an ounce?
FACE: He'll send you a pound, Doctor.
SUBTLE: O no.
FACE: He will do't.
It is the goodest soul!—Abel, about it.
80   Thou shalt know more anon. Away, be gone.—   *[Exit Abel.]*
A miserable rogue, and lives with cheese,
And has the worms. That was the cause, indeed,
Why he came now: he dealt with me in private,
To get a med'cine for them.
SUBTLE: And shall, sir. This works.

FACE: A wife, a wife for one of us, my dear Subtle!
      We'll e'en draw lots, and he that fails, shall have
      The more in goods, the other has in tail.[7]

SUBTLE: Rather the less: for she may be so light
      She may want grains.

FACE: Ay, or be such a burden,
90   A man would scarce endure her for the whole.

SUBTLE: Faith, best let's see her first, and then determine.

FACE: Content: but Dol must ha' no breath on't.

SUBTLE: Mum.
      Away you, to your Surly yonder, catch him.

FACE: 'Pray God I have not staid too long.

SUBTLE: I fear it.   [Exeunt.]

ACT 3

Scene 1—*The lane before Lovewit's house*

[*Enter Tribulation Wholesome and Ananias.*]

TRIBULATION: These chastisements are common to the saints,
      And such rebukes, we of the Separation[8]
      Must bear with willing shoulders, as the trials
      Sent forth to tempt frailties.

ANANIAS: In pure zeal,
5   I do not like the man, he is a heathen,
      And speaks the language of Canaan,[9] truly.

TRIBULATION: I think him a profane person indeed.

ANANIAS: He bears
      The visible mark of the Beast in his forehead.[1]
      And for his stone, it is a work of darkness,
10   And with philosophy blinds the eyes of man.

TRIBULATION: Good brother, we must bend unto all means
      That may give furtherance to the holy cause.

ANANIAS: Which his cannot: the sanctified cause
      Should have a sanctified course.

TRIBULATION: Not always necessary:
15   The children of perdition are oft-times
      Made instruments even of the greatest works:
      Beside, we should give° somewhat to man's nature,   *concede*
      The place he lives in, still about the fire,
      And fume of metals, that intoxicate
20   The brain of man, and make him prone to passion.
      Where have you greater atheists than your cooks?
      Or more profane, or choleric,° than your glass-men?°   *angry / glass-blowers*

---

7. In tail: obvious sexual meaning with a pun on legal entail, or limited ownership.
8. Separation: i.e., of the Anabaptists both by exile from Holland and God's election of them from the world of sinners.
9. In the Old Testament, the Canaanites, the original inhabitants of Israel, are portrayed as worshippers of idols.
1. The Puritans portrayed the Roman Catholic Church as the Beast of Revelation 16.2.

More antichristian than your bell-founders?
What makes the devil so devilish, I would ask you,
25   Satan, our common enemy, but his being
Perpetually about the fire, and boiling
Brimstone and arsenic? We must give, I say,
Unto the motives, and the stirrers up
Of humors in the blood. It may be so,
30   When as the work is done, the stone is made,
This heat of his may turn into a zeal,
And stand up for the beauteous discipline,
Against the menstruous cloth and rag of Rome.[2]
We must await his calling, and the coming
35   Of the good spirit. You did fault, t' upbraid him
With the brethren's blessing of Heidelberg,[3] weighing
What need we have to hasten on the work,
For the restoring of the silenced Saints,[4]
Which ne'er will be, but by the philosophers' stone.
40   And so a learned elder, one of Scotland,
Assured me; *aurum potabile* being
The only med'cine for the civil magistrate,[5]
T' incline him to a feeling of the cause;
And must be daily used in the disease.

ANANIAS: I have not edified more, truly, by man;
Not since the beautiful light first shone on me;
And I am sad my zeal hath so offended.

TRIBULATION: Let us call on him then.

ANANIAS: The motion's good,
And of the spirit; I will knock first. [*Knocks.*] Peace he within!
[*The door is opened, and they enter.*]

Scene 2—*A room in Lovewit's house*

[*Enter Subtle, followed by Tribulation and Ananias.*]

SUBTLE: O, are you come? 'twas time. Your threescore minutes
Were at the last thread, you see: and down had gone
Furnus acedice, turris circulatorius:[6]
Lembec, bolt's-head, retort and pelican[7]
5   Had all been cinders.—Wicked Ananias!
Art thou return'd? nay then, it goes down yet.

TRIBULATION: Sir, be appeased; he is come to humble
Himself in spirit, and to ask your patience,
If too much zeal hath carried him aside
10   From the due path.

SUBTLE: Why, this doth qualify!
TRIBULATION: The brethren had no purpose, verily,
    To give you the least grievance: but are ready
    To lend their willing hands to any project
    The spirit and you direct.
SUBTLE: This qualifies[8] more!
TRIBULATION: And for the orphan's goods, let them be valued,
    Or what is needful else to the holy work,
    It shall be numbered; here, by me, the saints,
    Throw down their purse before you.
SUBTLE: This qualifies most!
    Why, thus it should be, now you understand.
20   Have I discours'd so unto you of our stone,
    And of the good that it shall bring your cause?
    Shew'd you (beside the main of hiring forces
    Abroad, drawing the Hollanders,[9] your friends.
    From the Indies, to serve you, with all their fleet)
25   That even the med'cinal use shall make you a faction,
    And party in the realm? As, put the case,
    That some great man in state, he have the gout,
    Why, you but send three drops of your elixir,
    You help him straight: there you have made a friend.
30   Another has the palsy or the dropsy,
    He takes of your incombustible stuff,
    He's young again: there you have made a friend,
    A lady that is past the feat[1] of body,
    Though not of mind, and hath her face decay'd
35   Beyond all cure of paintings, you restore,
    With the oil of talc: there you have made a friend;
    And all her friends. A lord that is a leper,
    A knight that has the bone-ache,° or a squire   *syphilis*
    That hath both these, you make them smooth and sound,
40   With a bare fricace° of your med'cine: still   *rub*
    You increase your friends.
TRIBULATION: Ay, it is very pregnant.°   *full of potential*
SUBTLE: And then the turning of this lawyer's pewter
    To plate at Christmas.—
ANANIAS: Christ-tide, I pray you.[2]
SUBTLE: Yet, Ananias!
ANANIAS: I have done.
SUBTLE: Or changing
45   His parcel gilt° to massy gold. You cannot   *guilded silver*
    But raise you friends. Withal, to be of power

---

8. Qualifies: to dilute chemically and to pacify Subtle's anger at Ananais.
9. Subtle leads Tribulation to believe that Dutch traders in the east were concerned with religious toleration for the exiled Anabaptists.

1. Meaning both fitness and act, as in the act of sex.
2. Christ-tide rather than Christmas, because the Puritans objected to the mass.

To pay an army in the field, to buy
The king of France out of his realms, or Spain
Out of his Indies. What can you not do
50   Against lords spiritual or temporal,
That shall oppone° you?   oppose
TRIBULATION: Verily, 'tis true.
We may be temporal lords ourselves, I take it.
SUBTLE: You may be anything, and leave off to make
Long-winded exercises;° or suck up   religious ceremonies
55   Your "ha!" and "hum!" in a tune.[3] I not deny,
But such as are not graced in a state,
May, for their ends, be adverse in religion,
And get a tune to call the flock together:
For, to say sooth, a tune does much with women,
60   And other phlegmatic people; it is your bell.
ANANIAS: Bells are profane; a tune may be religious.
SUBTLE: No warning with you! then farewell my patience.
'Slight, it shall down: I will not be thus tortured.
TRIBULATION: I pray you, sir.
SUBTLE: All shall perish. I have spoken it.
TRIBULATION: Let me find grace, sir, in your eyes; the man
He stands corrected: neither did his zeal,
But as your self, allow a tune somewhere,
Which now, being toward the stone, we shall not need.
SUBTLE: No, nor your holy vizard,° to win widows   pious look
70   To give you legacies; or make zealous wives
To rob their husbands for the common cause:
Nor take the start° of bonds broke but one day,   take advantage
And say, they were forfeited by providence.
Nor shall you need o'er night to eat huge meals,
75   To celebrate your next day's fast the better;
The whilst the brethren and the sisters humbled,
Abate the stiffness of the flesh.[4] Nor east
Before your hungry hearers scrupulous bones;°   bones of contention
As whether a Christian may hawk or hunt,[5]
80   Or whether matrons of the holy assembly
May lay their hair out, or wear doublets,
Or have that idol, Starch, about their linen.[6]
ANANIAS: It is indeed an idol.
TRIBULATION: Mind him not, sir.
I do command thee, spirit of zeal, but trouble,
85   To peace within him! Pray, you, sir, go on.
SUBTLE: Nor shall you need to libel 'gainst the prelates,
And shorten so your ears[7] against the hearing

---

3. The "ha" and "hum" were sounds associated with Puritan preaching and singing.
4. The hardship of hunger with a comic pun on the stiffness of the male sex organ.
5. Puritan writers decried hunting as immoral.
6. Puritans also attacked fancy dress and elaborate hairstyles.
7. Have your ears cut off.

Of the next wire-drawn grace.[8] Nor of necessity
Rail against plays, to please the alderman[9]
90   Whose daily custard you devour: nor lie
With zealous rage till you are hoarse. Not one
Of these so singular arts. Nor call your selves
By names of Tribulation, Persecution,
Restraint, Long-patience, and such-like, affected
95   By the whole family or wood° of you,   *collection*
Only for glory, and to catch the ear
Of the disciple.
TRIBULATION: Truly, sir, they are
Ways that the godly brethren have invented,
For propagation of the glorious cause,
100   As very notable means, and whereby also
Themselves grow soon, and profitably, famous.
SUBTLE: O, but the stone, all's idle to it! nothing!
The art of angels' nature's miracle,
The divine secret that doth fly in clouds
105   From east to west;[1] and whose tradition
Is not from men, but spirits.
ANANIAS: I hate traditions;[2]
I do not trust them.—
TRIBULATION: Peace!
ANANIAS: They are popish all.
I will not peace: I will not—
TRIBULATION: Ananias!
ANANIAS: Please the profane, to grieve the godly; I may not.
SUBTLE: Well, Ananias, thou shalt overcome.
TRIBULATION: It is an ignorant zeal that haunts him, sir:
But truly, else, a very faithful brother,
A botcher, and a man, by revelation,[3]
That hath a competent knowledge of the truth.
SUBTLE: Has he a competent sum there in the bag
To buy the goods within? I am made guardian,
And must, for charity, and conscience sake,
Now see the most be made for my poor orphan;
Though I desire the brethren too good gainers;
120   There they are within. When you have view'd, and bought 'em,
And ta'en the inventory of what they are,
They are ready for projection; there's no more
To do: cast on the med'cine, so much silver
As there is tin there, so much gold as brass,
125   I'll give't you in by weight.

---

8. Long prayer.
9. City magistrates often had Puritan leanings against the plays.
1. The "divine secret," the hidden truth of alchemy traveled from Egypt in the east to Europe in the west.
2. Puritans saw the interpretations of the Bible in the tradition of the Roman Catholic Church as a corruption of the truth.
3. A "botcher" was a tailor who did repairs; a "man by revelation" was the Puritan ideal of one who sought the truth strictly through his own inner inspiration.

TRIBULATION: But how long time,
     Sir, must the saints expect yet?
SUBTLE: Let me see,
     How's the moon now? Eight, nine, ten days hence,
     He will be silver potate;° then three days   *liquefied silver*
     Before he citronise:[4] Some fifteen days,
130 The magisterium will be perfected.
ANANIAS: About the second day of the third week,
     In the ninth month?
SUBTLE: Yes, my good Ananias.
TRIBULATION: What will the orphan's goods arise to, think you?
SUBTLE: Some hundred marks, as much as fill'd three cars,
135 Unladed now: you'll make six millions of them.—
     But I must have more coals laid in.
TRIBULATION: How?
SUBTLE: Another load,
     And then we have finish'd. We must now increase
     Our fire to *ignis ardens*, we are past
     Fimus equinus, balnei, cineris,
140 And all those lenter heats.[5] If the holy purse
     Should with this draught fall low, and that the saints
     Do need a present sum, I have a trick
     To melt the pewter, you shall buy now, instantly,
     And with a tincture make you as good Dutch dollars
145 As any are in Holland.
TRIBULATION: Can you so?
SUBTLE: Ay, and shall 'bide the third examination.
ANANIAS: It will be joyful tidings to the brethren.
SUBTLE: But you must carry it secret.
TRIBULATION: Ay; but stay,
     This act of coining,° is it lawful?   *counterfeiting*
ANANIAS: Lawful?
150 We know no magistrate;[6] or, if we did,
     This 's foreign coin.
SUBTLE: It is no coining, sir.
     It is but casting.
TRIBULATION: Ha? you distinguish well:
     Casting of money may be lawful.
ANANIAS: 'Tis, sir.
TRIBULATION: Truly, I take it so.
SUBTLE: There is no scruple,
155 Sir, to be made of it; believe Ananias;
     This case of conscience he is studied in.
TRIBULATION: I'll make a question of it to the brethren.
ANANIAS: The brethren shall approve it lawful, doubt not.

---

4. Be made citron in color, a late stage of the alchemical process.
5. *Ignis ardens*, the hottest fire; the "lenter," or lower, heats are *fimus equinus*, the slowest heat, produced by

horse manure; *balnei*, slow even heat; *cineris*: heat of ashes.
6. Puritans believed that civil magistrates had no authority over matters of conscience.

Where shall it be done? [*Knocking without.*]
SUBTLE: For that we'll talk anon.
160 There's some to speak with me. Go in, I pray you,
And view the parcels. That's the inventory.
I'll come to you straight. [*Exeunt Tribulation and Ananias.*] Who is it?—
Face! appear.

Scene 3

[*Enter Face, in his uniform.*]
SUBTLE: How now! good prize?
FACE: Good pox! yond' costive cheater⁷
Never came on.
SUBTLE: How then?
FACE: I have walk'd the round
Till now, and no such thing.
SUBTLE: And ha' you quit° him!   *given up on*
FACE: Quit him? an hell would quit him too, he were happy.
5   'Slight! would you have me stalk like a mill-jade,⁸
All day, for one that will not yield us grains?⁹
I know him of old.
SUBTLE: O, but to have gull'd him,
Had been a mastery.
FACE: Let him go, black boy!¹
And turn thee, that some fresh news may possess thee.
10   A noble count, a don of Spain, my dear
Delicious compeer, and my party-bawd,°   *fellow pimp*
Who is come hither private for his conscience,²
And brought munition with him, six great slops,°   *large, wide trousers*
Bigger than three Dutch hoys, beside round trunks,
15   Furnished with pistolets, and pieces of eight,³
Will straight be here, my rogue, to have thy bath,
(That is the color,)° and to make his battery   *pretext*
Upon our Dol, our castle, our cinque-port,⁴
Our Dover pier, our what thou wilt. Where is she?
20   She must prepare perfumes, delicate linen,
The bath in chief, a banquet, and her wit,
For she must milk his epididimis.⁵
Where is the doxy?°   *wench*
SUBTLE: I'll send her to thee:
And but dispatch my brace of little John Leydens,⁶
25   And come again myself.
FACE: Are they within then?
SUBTLE: Numb'ring the sum.

7. Skeptical gambler, i.e., surly.
8. Horse that circled around and pushed the arm turning the grindstone.
9. Profit, as in grains of flour and of gold.
1. Black, because his face is covered with soot.
2. Private, or concealed, because of his religious beliefs.

3. Spanish gold coins.
4. One of the five defensive ports of the southeastern coast of England.
5. Tube that sperm move through.
6. John Leyden, leader of the Anabaptists.

FACE:	How much?	
SUBTLE:	A hundred marks, boy.	[*Exit.*]
FACE:	Why, this is a lucky day. Ten pounds of MAMMON!°	*riches*

FACE: Why, this is a lucky day. Ten pounds of MAMMON!°   *riches*
        Three of my clerk! a portague⁷ of my grocer!
        This of the brethren! beside reversions,⁸

30   And states° to come in the widow, and my count!   *estates*
        My share to-day will not be bought for forty—
    [*Enter Dol.*]

DOL: What?
FACE: Pounds, dainty Dorothy! art thou so near?
DOL: Yes; say, lord general, how fares our camp?⁹
FACE: As with the few that had entrench'd themselves

35   Safe, by their discipline, against a world, Dol,
        And laugh'd within those trenches, and grew fat
        With thinking on the booties, Dol, brought in
        Daily by their small parties. This dear hour,
        A doughty Don is taken with my Dol;

40   And thou mayst make his ransom what thou wilt,
        My Dousabel;¹ he shall be brought here fetter'd
        With thy fair looks, before he sees thee; and thrown
        In a down-bed, as dark as any dungeon;
        Where thou shalt keep him waking with thy drum;²

45   Thy drum, my Dol, thy drum; till he be tame
        As the poor black-birds were in the great frost,³
        Or bees are with a basin;⁴ and so hive him
        In the swan-skin coverlid, and cambric sheets,
        Till he work honey and wax, my little God's-gift.

DOL: What is he, General?
FACE: An *adelantado,*°   *governor*
        A grandee, girl. Was not my Dapper here yet?
DOL: No.
FACE: Nor my Drugger?
DOL: Neither.
FACE: A pox on 'em.
        They are so long a furnishing! such stinkards
        Would not be seen upon these festival days.—
    [*Re-enter Subtle.*]

55   How now! have you done?
SUBTLE: Done. They are gone. The sum
        Is here in bank, my Face. I would we knew
        Another chapman° now would buy 'em outright.   *merchant*
FACE: 'Slid, Nab shall do't against he have the widow,
        To furnish household.
SUBTLE: Excellent, well thought on:

---

7. Portuguese gold coin.
8. Future possessions, inherited when owner gives them up.
9. The first line of Kyd's play *The Spanish Tragedy.*
1. Sweet and beautiful.

2. Sexual activity.
3. The "great frost" occurred when the Thames froze over (December 1607 to February 1608).
4. A swarm of bees was made to settle by banging a basin.

60   Pray God he come!

FACE: I pray he keep away
        Till our new business be o'erpast.

SUBTLE: But, Face,
        How cam'st thou by this secret don?

FACE: A spirit
        Brought me th' intelligence in a paper here,
        As I was conjuring yonder in my circle

65   For Surly; I have my flies° abroad. Your bath   *spirits*
        Is famous, Subtle, by my means. Sweet Dol,
        You must go tune your virginal,⁵ no losing
        O' the least time: and, do you hear? good action.
        Firk,° like a flounder; kiss, like a scallop, close;   *excite sexually*

70   And tickle him with thy mother-tongue. His great
        Verdugoship has not a jot of language;⁶
        So much the easier to be cozen'd, my Dolly.
        He will come here in a hired coach, obscure,
        And our own coachman, whom I have sent as guide,

75   No creature else. [*Knocking without.*] Who's that?   [*Exit Dol.*]

SUBTLE: It is not he?

FACE: O no, not yet this hour.
        [*Re-enter Dol.*]

SUBTLE: Who is't?

DOL: Dapper,
        Your clerk.

FACE: God's will then, Queen of Fairy,
        On with your tire;° [*Exit Dol.*] and, Doctor, with your robes.   *costume*
        Let's dispatch him for God's sake.

SUBTLE: 'Twill be long.

FACE: I warrant you, take but the cues I give you,
        It shall be brief enough. [*Goes to the window.*] 'Slight, here are more!
        Abel, and I think the angry boy, the heir,
        That fain would quarrel.

SUBTLE: And the widow?

FACE: No,
        Not that I see. Away! [*Exit Subtle*]—O sir, you are welcome.

                        Scene 4

        [*Enter Dapper.*]

FACE: The Doctor is within a-moving° for you;   *conjuring*
        I have had the most ado to win him to it!—
        He swears you'll be the darling of the dice;
        He never heard her highness dote till now.

5   Your aunt has given you the most gracious words
        That can be thought on.

DAPPER: Shall I see her grace?

---

5. Keyboard instrument, with a sexual innuendo.   6. Verdugoship: a mock title; not a jot of language: speaks
                                                        no English.

FACE: See her, and kiss her too.—
    [*Enter Abel, followed by Kastril.*]
                      What, honest Nab!
    Hast brought the damask?
DRUGGER: No, sir; here's tobacco.
FACE: 'Tis well done, Nab: thou'lt bring the damask too?
DRUGGER: Yes: here's the gentleman, Captain, Master Kastril,
    I have brought to see the Doctor.
FACE: Where's the widow?
DRUGGER: Sir, as he likes, his sister, he says, shall come.
FACE: O, is it so? good time. Is your name Kastril, sir?
KASTRIL: Ay, and the best of the Kastrils, I'd be sorry else,
15   By fifteen hundred a year. Where is the Doctor?
    My mad° tobacco-boy, here, tells me of one   *wild*
    That can do things: has he any skill?
FACE: Wherein, sir?
KASTRIL: To carry a business,° manage a quarrel fairly,   *arrange a duel*
    Upon fit terms.
FACE: It seems, sir, you are but young
20   About the town, that can make that a question.
KASTRIL: Sir, not so young, but I have heard some speech
    Of the angry boys, and seen them take tobacco;
    And in his shop; and I can take it too.
    And I would fain be one of 'em, and go down
25   And practice in the country.
FACE: Sir, for the duello,
    The Doctor, I assure you, shall inform you,
    To the least shadow of a hair; and show you
    An instrument° he has of his own making,   *book, treatise*
    Wherewith no sooner shall you make report
30   Of any quarrel, but he will take the height on't
    Most instantly, and tell in what degree
    Of safety it lies in, or mortality.
    And how it may be borne, whether in a right line,
    Or a half circle; or may else be cast
35   Into an angle blunt, if not acute:
    All this he will demonstrate. And then, rules
    To give and take the lie by.
KASTRIL: How! to take it?
FACE: Yes, in oblique he'll show you, or in circle;
    But never in diameter.[7] The whole town
40   Study his theorems, and dispute them ordinarily
    At the eating academies.
KASTRIL: But does he teach
    Living by the wits too?

---

7. To uphold his honor, a gentleman could not allow a direct ("in diameter") accusation of lying, but he might allow an indirect ("oblique") or roundabout ("in a circle") suggestion.

FACE: Anything whatever.
          You cannot think that subtlety, but he reads it.
          He made me a captain. I was a stark pimp,
45   Just of your standing, 'fore I met with him;
          It is not two months since. I'll tell you his method:
          First, he will enter you at some ordinary.°   *eating house*
KASTRIL: No, I'll not come there: you shall pardon me.
FACE: For why, sir?
KASTRIL: There's gaming there, and tricks.
FACE: Why, would you be
50   A gallant, and not game?
KASTRIL: Ay, 'twill spend a man.[8]
FACE: Spend you! it will repair you when you are spent:
          How do they live by their wits there, that have vented
          Six times your fortunes?
KASTRIL: What, three thousand a-year!
FACE: Ay, forty thousand.
KASTRIL: Are there such?
FACE: Ay, sir,
55   And gallants yet. Here's a young gentleman
          Is born to nothing,—[*Points to Dapper.*] forty marks a-year,
          Which I count nothing:—he is to be initiated,
          And have a fly° of the Doctor. He will win you,   *familiar spirit*
          By unresistible luck, within this fortnight,
60   Enough to buy a barony. They will set him
          Upmost, at the groom porters, all the Christmas:
          And for the whole year through, at every place,
          Where there is play, present him with the chair;
          The best attendance, the best drink; sometimes
65   Two glasses of Canary,° and pay nothing;   *sweet wine*
          The purest linen, and the sharpest knife,
          The partridge next his trencher: and somewhere
          The dainty bed, in private, with the dainty.[9]
          You shall have your ordinaries bid for him,
70   As play-houses for a poet; and the master
          Pray him aloud to name what dish he affect.
          Which must be butter'd shrimps:[1] and those that drink
          To no mouth else, will drink to his, as being
          The goodly president mouth of all the board.
KASTRIL: Do you not gull one?
FACE: 'Ods my life! do you think it?
          You shall have a cast commander,° (can but get   *unemployed officer*
          In credit with a glover, or a spurrier,
          For some two pair of either's ware aforehand,)
          Will, by most swift posts, dealing [but] with him,
80   Arrive at competent means to keep himself,

---

8. Waste a man's wealth.   1. Sexually stimulating food.
9. Sweet and lovely sexual object.

His punk and naked boy,[2] in excellent fashion,
And be admired for't.
KASTRIL: Will the Doctor teach this?
FACE: He will do more, sir: when your land is gone,
       As men of spirit hate to keep earth long,
85   In a vacation,[3] when small money is stirring,
       And ordinaries suspended till the term,
       He'll show a perspective,° where on one side   magic mirror
       You shall behold the faces and the persons
       Of all sufficient young heirs in town,
90   Whose bonds are current for commodity;
       On th' other side, the merchants' forms, and others,
       That without help of any second broker,
       Who would expect a share, will trust such parcels:
       In the third square, the very street and sign
95   Where the commodity dwells, and does but wait
       To be deliver'd, be it pepper, soap,
       Hops, or tobacco, oatmeal, woad, or cheeses.
       All which you may so handle, to enjoy
       To your own use, and never stand obliged.
KASTRIL: I'faith! is he such a fellow?
FACE: Why, Nab here knows him.
       And then for making matches for rich widows,
       Young gentlewomen, heirs, the fortunat'st man!
       He's sent to, far and near, all over England,
       To have his counsel, and to know their fortunes.
KASTRIL: God's will, my suster shall see him.
FACE: I'll tell you, sir,
       What he did tell me of Nab, It's a strange thing:——
       By the way, you must eat no cheese, Nab, it breeds melancholy,
       And that same melancholy breeds worms; but pass it:——
       He told me, honest Nab here was ne'er at tavern
110   But once in's life!
DRUGGER: Truth, and no more I was not.
FACE: And then he was so sick—
DRUGGER: Could he tell you that too?
FACE: How should I know it?
DRUGGER: In troth we had been a shooting,
       And had a piece of fat ram-mutton to supper,
       That lay so heavy o' my stomach—
FACE: And he has no head
115   To bear any wine; for what with the noise of the fiddlers,
       And care of his shop, for he dares keep no servants—
DRUGGER: My head did so ache—
FACE: As he was fain to be brought home,
       The Doctor told me: and then a good old woman—

---

2. Prostitute and catamite.   3. Time between terms of the law courts.

DRUGGER: Yes, faith, she dwells in Sea-coal-lane,[4]—did cure me,
120   With sodden° ale, and pellitory of the wall;[5]   *boiled*
        Cost me but two-pence. I had another sickness
        Was worse than that.
FACE: Ay, that was with the grief
        Thou took'st for being cess'd° at eighteen-pence,   *taxed*
        For the water-work.[6]
DRUGGER: In truth, and it was like
125   T' have cost me almost my life.
FACE: Thy hair went off?
DRUGGER: Yes, sir; 'twas done for spite.
FACE: Nay, so says the Doctor.
KASTRIL: Pray thee, tobacco-boy, go fetch my suster;
        I'll see this learned boy before I go;
        And so shall she.
FACE: Sir, he is busy now;
130   But if you have a sister to fetch hither,
        Perhaps your own pains may command her sooner;
        And he by that time will be free.
KASTRIL: I go.   [*Exit.*]
FACE: Drugger, she's thine: the damask!—   [*Exit Abel.*]
                          [*Aside.*] Subtle and I
        Must wrestle for her.—Come on, Master Dapper,
135   You see how I turn clients here away,
        To give your cause dispatch; have you perform'd
        The ceremonies were enjoin'd you?
DAPPER: Yes, of the vinegar,
        And the clean shirt.
FACE: 'Tis well: that shirt may do you
        More worship° than you think. Your aunt's a-fire,   *praise*
140   But that she will not show it, t' have a sight of you,
        Have you provided for her grace's servants?
DAPPER: Yes, here are six score Edward shillings.
FACE: Good!
DAPPER: And an old Harry's sovereign.
FACE: Very good!
DAPPER: And three James shillings, and an Elizabeth groat,°   *four pennies*
145   Just twenty nobles.°   *gold coins*
FACE: O, you are too just.
        I would you had had the other noble in Mary's,
DAPPER: I have some Philip and Mary's.
FACE: Ay, those same
        Are best of all: where are they? Hark, the Doctor.

---

4. Neighborhood of fruit sellers, peddlers, and poor people.
5. Low, green plant growing at the base of walls.

6. Bulmer's London Bridge pump-house piped water to houses in London.

Scene 5

[*Enter Subtle, disguised like a priest of Fairy, with a stripe of cloth.*]

SUBTLE   [*in a feigned voice*]: Is yet her grace's cousin come?
FACE: He is come.
SUBTLE: And is he fasting?
FACE: Yes.
SUBTLE: And hath cried hum?
FACE: Thrice, you must answer.
DAPPER: Thrice.
SUBTLE: And as oft buz?
FACE: If you have, say.
DAPPER: I have.
SUBTLE: Then, to her cuz,

5   Hoping that he hath vinegar'd his senses,
    As he was bid, the Fairy Queen dispenses,
    By me, this robe, the petticoat of fortune;
    Which that he straight put on, she doth importune,
    And though to fortune[7] near be her petticoat,
10   Yet nearer is her smock,° the Queen doth note: *undergarment*
    And therefore, ev'n of that a piece she hath sent
    Which, being a child, to wrap him in was rent;
    And prays him for a scarf he now will wear it,
    With as much love as then her grace did tear it,
15   About his eyes, [*They blind him with the rag.*] to shew he is fortunate.[8]
    And, trusting unto her to make his state,°   *fortune*
    He'll throw away all worldly pelf about him;
    Which that he will perform, she doth not doubt him.
FACE: She need not doubt him, sir. Alas, he has nothing,
20   But what he will part withal as willingly,
    Upon her Grace's word—throw away your purse—
    As she would ask it;—handkerchiefs and all—
    [*He throws away, as they bid him.*]
    She cannot bid that thing, but he'll obey.—
    If you have a ring about you, cast it off,
25   Or a silver seal at your wrist; her grace will send
    Her fairies here to search you, therefore deal
    Directly with her Highness: if they find
    That you conceal a mite, you are undone,
DAPPER: Truly, there's all.
FACE: All what?
DAPPER: My money; truly.
FACE: Keep nothing that is transitory about you.
    [*aside to Subtle*] Bid Dol play music.—Look, the elves are come
    [*Dol plays on the cittern[9] within.*]

---

7. Bawdy reference to her private parts.
8. Playing on the notion that Fortune is blind.
9. Stringed instrument played with a plectrum.

To pinch you, if you tell not truth. Advise you. [*They pinch him.*]

DAPPER: O! I have a paper with a spur-ryal[1] in't.

FACE: *Ti, ti.*

They knew't, they say.

SUBTLE: *Ti, ti, ti, ti.* He has more yet.

FACE [*aside to Sub*]: *Ti, ti-ti-ti.* In the other pocket.

SUBTLE: *Titi, titi, titi, titi, titi.*

They must pinch him or he will never confess, they say.

[*They pinch him again.*]

DAPPER: O, O!

FACE: Nay, pray you hold: he is her Grace's nephew.

Ti, ti, ti? What care you? good faith, you shall care.—

Deal plainly, sir, and shame the fairies. Show

40   You are innocent.

DAPPER: By this good light, I have nothing.

SUBTLE: *Ti, ti, ti, ti, to, ta.* He does equivocate, she says:

Ti, ti do ti, ti ti do, ti da; and swears by the *light* when he is blinded.

DAPPER: By this good *dark*, I have nothing but a half-crown

Of gold about my wrist, that my love gave me;

45   And a leaden heart I wore since she forsook me.

FACE: I thought 'twas something. And would you incur

Your aunt's displeasure for these trifles? Come,

I had rather you had thrown away twenty half-crowns. [*Takes it off.*]

You may wear your leaden heart still.—[*Enter Dol, hastily.*]

How now!

SUBTLE: What news, Dol?

DOL: Yonder's your knight, sir Mammon.

FACE: 'Ods lid, we never thought of him till now!

Where is he?

DOL: Here hard by: he is at the door.

SUBTLE: And you are not ready, now! Dol, get his suit.[2]   [*Exit Dol.*]

He must not be sent back.

FACE: O by no means.

55   What shall we do with this same puffin[3] here,

Now he's on the spit?

SUBTLE: Why, lay him back[4] awhile,

With some device.

[*Re-enter Dol, with Face's clothes.*]

                  —*Ti, ti, ti, ti, ti, ti,* Would her Grace speak with me?

I come.—Help, Dol!

[*Knocking without.*]

FACE [*speaks through the key-hole*]: Who's there? sir Epicure,

My master's in the way. Please you to walk

60   Three or four turns, but till his back be turn'd,

And I am for you.—Quickly, Dol!

---

1. Coin worth 15 shillings.
2. The costume of Lungs, assistant to the Alchemist.

3. Half fish and half bird, so a person who is neither fish nor fowl.
4. Away from the fire.

SUBTLE: Her grace
    Commends her kindly to you, master Dapper.
DAPPER: I long to see her Grace.
SUBTLE: She now is set
    At dinner in her bed, and she has sent you
65   From her own private trencher, a dead mouse,
    And a piece of gingerbread, to be merry withal.
    And stay your stomach, lest you faint with fasting;
    Yet if you could hold out till she saw you, she says,
    It would be better for you.
FACE: Sir, he shall
70   Hold out, an 'twere this two hours, for her highness;
    I can assure you that. We will not lose
    All we ha' done.—
SUBTLE: He must not see, nor speak
    To any body, till then.
FACE: For that we'll put, sir,
    A stay° in's mouth.   *gag*
SUBTLE: Of what?
FACE: Of gingerbread.
75   Make you it fit. He that hath pleas'd her Grace
    Thus far, shall not now crincle° for a little.—   *shrink, flinch*
    Gape, sir, and let him fit you.
    [*They thrust a gag of gingerbread in his mouth.*]
SUBTLE: Where shall we now
    Bestow him?
DOL: I' the privy.
SUBTLE: Come along, sir,
    I now must shew you Fortune's privy lodgings.
FACE: Are they perfum'd, and his bath ready?
SUBTLE: All:
    Only the fumigation's somewhat strong.
FACE   [*Speaking through the key-hole*]:Sir Epicure, I am yours, sir, by and by.
                                         [*Exeunt with Dapper.*]

ACT 4

Scene 1—*A room in Lovewit's house*

[*Enter Face and Mammon.*]
FACE: O sir, y' are come i' the only finest time.—
MAMMON: Where's master?
FACE: Now preparing for projection, sir.
    Your stuff will b' all chang'd shortly.
MAMMON: Into gold?
FACE: To gold and silver, sir.
MAMMON: Silver I care not for.
FACE: Yes, sir, a little to give beggars.
MAMMON: Where's the lady?
FACE: At hand here. I ha' told her such brave things of you,

Touching your bounty, and your noble spirit—

MAMMON: Hast thou?

FACE: As she is almost in her fit to see you.
        But, good sir, no divinity in your conference,
10   For fear of putting her in rage.—

MAMMON: I warrant thee.

FACE: Six men [sir] will not hold her down: and then,
        If the old man should hear or see you—

MAMMON: Fear not.

FACE: The very house, sir, would run mad. You know it,
        How scrupulous he is, and violent,
15   'Gainst the least act of sin. Physic, or mathematics,
        Poetry, state,° or bawdry, as I told you,   *politics*
        She will endure, and never startle; but
        No word of controversy.

MAMMON: I am school'd, good Ulen.

FACE: And you must praise her house, remember that,
20   And her nobility.

MAMMON: Let me alone:
        No herald, no, nor antiquary, Lungs,
        Shall do it better. Go.

FACE   [aside]:   Why, this is yet
        A kind of modern happiness, to have
        Dol Common for a great lady.   [*Exit*]

MAMMON: Now, Epicure,
25   Heighten thyself, talk to her all in gold;
        Rain her as many showers as Jove did drops
        Unto his Danaë;[5] show the god a miser,
        Compared with Mammon. What! the stone will do't.
        She shall feel gold, taste gold, hear gold, sleep gold;
30   Nay, we will *concumbere*[6] gold: I will be puissant,
        And mighty in my talk to her.—
        [*Re-enter Face, with Dol richly dressed.*]
                                Here she comes.

FACE: To him, Dol, suckle him.—This is the noble knight,
        I told your ladyship—

MAMMON: Madam, with your pardon,
        I kiss your vesture.

DOL: Sir, I were uncivil
35   If I would suffer that; my lip to you, sir.

MAMMON: I hope my lord your brother be in health, lady.

DOL: My lord, my brother is, though I no lady, sir.

FACE   [aside]: Well said, my Guinea bird.°   *prostitute*

MAMMON: Right noble madam—

FACE   [aside]: O, we shall have most fierce idolatry.

MAMMON: 'Tis your prerogative.

DOL: Rather your courtesy.

---

5. Jove came to his love object Danaë in a shower of gold.   6. Copulate; see Juvenal, *Satire* 6.191.

MAMMON: Were there nought else to enlarge your virtues to me,
    These answers speak your breeding and your blood.
DOL: Blood we boast none, sir, a poor baron's daughter.
MAMMON: Poor! and gat you? profane not. Had your father
45   Slept all the happy remnant of his life
    After that act, lien but there still, and panted.
    He had done enough to make himself, his issue,
    And his posterity noble.
DOL: Sir, although
    We may be said to want the gilt and trappings,
50   The dress of honor, yet we strive to keep
    The seeds and the materials.
MAMMON: I do see
    The old ingredient, virtue, was not lost,
    Nor the drug money used to make your compound.
    There is a strange nobility in your eye,
55   This lip, that chin! methinks you do resemble
    One of the Austriac princes.[7]
FACE [*aside*]:   Very like!
    Her father was an Irish costermonger.°   *fruit seller*
MAMMON: The house of Valois° just had such a nose,   *French royal family*
    And such a forehead yet the Medici
60   Of Florence boast.
DOL: Troth, and I have been liken'd
    To all these princes.
FACE: I'll be sworn, I heard it.
MAMMON: I know not how! it is not any one,
    But e'en the very choice of all their features.
FACE [*aside*]: I'll in, and laugh.   [*Exit.*]
MAMMON: A certain touch, or air,
65   That sparkles a divinity, beyond
    An earthly beauty!
DOL: O, you play the courtier.
MAMMON: Good lady, gi' me leave—
DOL: In faith, I may not,
    To mock me, sir.
MAMMON: To burn in this sweet flame;
    The phœnix never knew a nobler death.[8]
DOL: Nay, now you court the courtier, and destroy
    What you would build; this art, sir, in your words,
    Calls your whole faith in question.
MAMMON: By my soul—
DOL: Nay, oaths are made of the same air, sir.
MAMMON: Nature
    Never bestow'd upon mortality

---

7. The royal Austrian family of the Habsburgs was noted for a large lower lip.

8. Every 500 years the phoenix was consumed by fire and rose again from its ashes. See Geoffrey Whitney, *The Phoenix*, in Perspectives: Early Modern Books, page 1066.

75   A more unblamed, a more harmonious feature;
       She play'd the step-dame in all faces else:
       Sweet Madam, let me be particular—
DOL: Particular,[9] sir! I pray you know your distance.
MAMMON: In no ill sense, sweet lady; but to ask
80   How your fair graces pass the hours? I see
       You are lodg'd here, in the house of a rare man,
       An excellent artist; but what's that to you?
DOL: Yes, sir; I study here the mathematics,
       And distillation.
MAMMON: O, I cry your pardon.
85   He's a divine instructor! can extract
       The souls of all things by his art; call all
       The virtues, and the miracles of the sun,
       Into a temperate furnace; teach dull nature
       What her own forces are. A man, the emperor
90   Has courted above Kelly;[1] sent his medals
       And chains, to invite him.
DOL: Ay, and for his physic, sir—
MAMMON: Above the art of Aesculapius,[2]
       That drew the envy of the thunderer!
       I know all this, and more.
DOL: Troth, I am taken, sir,
95   Whole with these studies, that contemplate nature.
MAMMON: It is a noble humor; but this form
       Was not intended to so dark a use.
       Had you been crooked, foul, of some coarse mould
       A cloister had done well; but such a feature
100   That might stand up the glory of a kingdom,
       To live recluse! is a mere solecism,[3]
       Though in a nunnery. It must not be.
       I muse, my lord your brother will permit it!
       You should spend half my land first, were I he.
105   Does not this diamond better on my finger,
       Than in the quarry?
DOL: Yes.
MAMMON: Why, you are like it.
       You were created, lady, for the light.
       Here, you shall wear it; take it, the first pledge
       Of what I speak, to bind you to believe me.
DOL: In chains of adamant?°   *strong iron*
MAMMON: Yes, the strongest bands.
       And take a secret too. Here, by your side
       Doth stand this hour, the happiest man in Europe.

---

9. Dol has taken him to mean sexually intimate.
1. Edward Kelly, the medium for the alchemist John Dee, claimed to posses the philosophers' stone but, when he failed to produce it in Prague, was imprisoned by the emperor Rudolph II.
2. God of medicine who was killed by Jove's thunderbolt lest humans become immortal.
3. Mistake, impropriety.

DOL: You are contented, sir?

MAMMON: Nay, in true being,
        The envy of princes and the fear of states.

DOL: Say you so, sir Epicure?

MAMMON: Yes, and thou shalt prove it,
        Daughter of honor. I have cast mine eye
        Upon thy form, and I will rear this beauty
        Above all styles.

DOL: You mean no treason, sir?

MAMMON: No, I will take away that jealousy.°   *suspicion*
120   I am the lord of the philosophers' stone,
        And thou the lady.

DOL: How, sir! ha' you that?

MAMMON: I am the master of the mystery.
        This day the good old wretch here o' the house
        Has made it for us; now he's at projection.
125   Think therefore thy first wish now, let me hear it,
        And it shall rain into thy lap, no shower,
        But floods of gold, whole cataracts, a deluge,
        To get a nation on thee.

DOL: You are pleased, sir,
        To work on the ambition of our sex.

MAMMON: I am pleased the glory of her sex should know,
        This nook, here, of the Friars[4] is no climate
        For her to live obscurely in, to learn
        Physic and surgery, for the constable's wife
        Of some odd hundred[5] in Essex; but come forth,
135   And taste the air of palaces; eat, drink
        The toils of empirics,[6] and their boasted practice;
        Tincture of pearl, and coral, gold and amber;
        Be seen at feasts and triumphs; have it ask'd,
        What miracle she is? set all the eyes
140   Of court a-fire, like a burning glass,
        And work them into cinders, when the jewels
        Of twenty states adorn thee, and the light
        Strikes out the stars! that when thy name is mention'd,
        Queens may look pale; and we but showing our love,
145   Nero's Poppaea may be lost in story![7]
        Thus will we have it.

DOL: I could well consent, sir.
        But, in a monarchy, how will this be?
        The prince will soon take notice, and both seize
        You and your stone, it being a wealth unfit
150   For any private subject.

MAMMON: If he knew it.

---

4. Blackfriars, location of Lovewit's house.
5. Subdivision of a county.
6. Ancient physicians who practiced medicine based on

empirical evidence.
7. Nero killed his mother and wife on account of his love
for Poppea.

DOL: Yourself do boast it, sir.

MAMMON: To thee, my life.

DOL: O, but beware, sir! you may come to end
    The remnant of your days in a loth'd prison,
    By speaking of it.

MAMMON: 'Tis no idle fear:

155   We'll therefore go with all, my girl, and live
    In a free state,° where we will eat our mullets,   *a republic*
    Soused in high-country wines, sup pheasants' eggs,
    And have our cockles boil'd in silver shells;
    Our shrimps to swim again, as when they liv'd,

160   In a rare butter made of dolphin's milk,
    Whose cream does look like opals; and with these
    Delicate meats set ourselves high for pleasure,[8]
    And take us down again, and then renew
    Our youth and strength with drinking the elixir,

165   And so enjoy a perpetuity
    Of life and lust! And thou shalt have thy wardrobe
    Richer than nature's, still to change thy self,
    And vary oftener, for thy pride, than she,
    Or art, her wise and almost-equal servant.

    [*Re-enter Face.*]

FACE: Sir, you are too loud. I hear you, every word,
    Into the laboratory. Some fitter place;
    The garden, or great chamber above. How like you her?

MAMMON: Excellent! Lungs. There's for thee. [*Gives him money.*]

FACE: But do you hear?
    Good sir, beware, no mention of the rabbins.[9]

MAMMON: We think not on 'em. [*Exeunt Mammon and Dol.*]

FACE: O, it is well, sir.—Subtle!

Scene 2

    [*Enter Subtle.*]

FACE: Dost thou not laugh?

SUBTLE: Yes; are they gone?

FACE: All's clear.

SUBTLE: The widow is come.

FACE: And your quarrelling disciple?

SUBTLE: Ay.

FACE: I must to my captainship again then.

SUBTLE: Stay, bring them in first.

FACE: So I meant. What is she?

5   A bonnibel?°   *beauty*

SUBTLE: I know not.

FACE: We'll draw lots:
    You'll stand to that?

---

8. Ready for sexual excitement and all forms of sensuous pleasure.

9. Jewish authorities on law and doctrine, cited in the work of the Puritan author Broughton.

SUBTLE: What else?
FACE: O, for a suit,
     To fall now like a curtain, flap!¹
SUBTLE: To the door, man.
FACE: You'll have the first kiss, 'cause I am not ready.   [*Exit.*]
SUBTLE: Yes, and perhaps hit you through both the nostrils.²
FACE [*within*]: Who would you speak with?
KASTRIL [*within*]:   Where's the captain?
FACE [*within*]:   Gone, sir,
     About some business.
KASTRIL [*within*]:   Gone!
FACE [*within*]:   He'll return straight.
     But master Doctor, his lieutenant, is here.
     [*Enter Kastril, followed by Dame Pliant.*]
SUBTLE: Come near, my worshipful boy, my *terrae fili*,³
     That is, my boy of land; make thy approaches:
15   Welcome; I know thy lusts,° and thy desires,   wishes
     And I will serve and satisfy them. Begin,
     Charge me from thence, or thence, or in this line;
     Here is my center: ground thy quarrel.
KASTRIL: You lie.
SUBTLE: How, child of wrath and anger! the loud lie?
20   For what, my sudden boy?
KASTRIL: Nay, that look you to,
     I am afore-hand.⁴
SUBTLE: O, this is no true grammar,
     And as ill logic! You must render causes, child,
     Your first and second intentions, know your canons
     And your divisions, moods, degrees, and differences,
25   Your predicaments, substance, and accident,
     Series, extern and intern, with their causes,
     Efficient, material, formal, final,
     And have your elements perfect.⁵
KASTRIL [*aside*]:   What is this!
     The angry tongue he talks in?
SUBTLE: That false precept,
30   Of being afore-hand, has deceived a number,
     And made them enter quarrels, often-times,
     Before they were aware; and afterward,
     Against their wills.
KASTRIL: How must I do then, sir?
SUBTLE: I cry this lady mercy: she should first
35   Have been saluted. [*Kisses her.*] I do call you lady,
     Because you are to be one, ere't be long,

---

1. His "suit" is his captain's uniform; "like a curtain flap," like the drop scene in a masque which would create an instant change of scene.
2. Get the better of you.
3. Son of the earth.
4. I got there first.
5. Subtle uses the terms of scholastic logic to describe how one should properly quarrel.

My soft and buxom widow.

KASTRIL: Is she, i'faith?

SUBTLE: Yes, or my art is an egregious liar.

KASTRIL: How know you?

SUBTLE: By inspection on her forehead,
40   And subtlety[6] of her lip, which must be tasted
       Often, to make a judgment. [*Kisses her again.*] 'Slight, she melts
       Like a myrobolane:[7]—here is yet a line.
       In *rivo frontis*,[8] tells me he is no knight.

DAME PLIANT: What is he then, sir?

SUBTLE: Let me see your hand.
45   O, your *linea fortunœ*[9] makes it plain;
       And stella here *in monte Veneris*.[1]
       But, most of all, *junctura annularis*.[2]
       He is a soldier, or a man of art, lady,
       But shall have some great honor shortly.

DAME PLIANT: Brother,
50   He's a rare man, believe me!
       [*Re-enter Face, in his uniform.*]

KASTRIL: Hold your peace.
       Here comes the t'other rare man.—'Save you, Captain,

FACE: Good master Kastril! Is this your sister?

KASTRIL: Ay, sir.
       Please you to kuss her, and be proud to know her.

FACE: I shall be proud to know you, lady. [*Kisses her.*]

DAME PLIANT: Brother.
55   He calls me lady, too.

KASTRIL: Ay, peace: I heard it. [*Takes her aside.*]

FACE: The Count is come.

SUBTLE: Where is he?

FACE: At the door.

SUBTLE: Why, you must entertain him.

FACE: What'll you do
       With these the while?

SUBTLE: Why, have them up, and show them
       Some fustian book, or the dark glass.[3]

FACE: 'Fore God,
60   She is a delicate dab-chick![4] I must have her.   [*Exit.*]

SUBTLE: Must you! ay, if your fortune will, you must.—
       Come, sir, the Captain will come to us presently:
       I'll have you to my chamber of demonstrations,
       Where I will show you both the grammar and logic,
65   And rhetoric of quarreling; my whole method

---

6. Exquisiteness, and also a pun on subtlety as a sugary confection.
7. Plumlike fruit from the east.
8. The frontal vein.
9. Line of fortune, extending from beneath the little finger to the index finger.

1. The star ("stella") on the mount of Venus (*monte Veneris*) at the base of the thumb.
2. Joint of the ring finger.
3. Fustian: bogus, bombastic; dark glass: crystal ball.
4. Dainty bird that dives into water.

Drawn out in tables; and my instrument,
That hath the several scales[5] upon't, shall make you
Able to quarrel at a straw's-breadth by moon-light.
And, lady, I'll have you look in a glass,
70   Some half an hour, but to clear your eye-sight,
Against you see your fortune; which is greater,
Than I may judge upon the sudden, trust me.

                    [Exit, followed by Kastril and Dame Pliant.]

Scene 3

[*Re-enter Face.*]

FACE: Where are you, Doctor?
SUBTLE [*within*]:   I'll come to you presently.
FACE: I will ha' this same widow, now I ha' seen her,
    On any composition.°   *terms*
    [*Re-enter Subtle.*]
SUBTLE: What do you say?
FACE: Ha' you disposed of them?
SUBTLE: I have sent 'em up.
FACE: Subtle, in troth, I needs must have this widow.
SUBTLE: Is that the matter?
FACE: Nay, but hear me.
SUBTLE: Go to.
    If you rebel once, Dol shall know it all:
    Therefore be quiet, and obey your chance.
FACE: Nay, thou art so violent now—Do but conceive,
10   Thou art old, and canst not serve[6]—
SUBTLE: Who cannot? I?
    'Slight, I will serve her with thee, for a—
FACE: Nay,
    But understand: I'll gi' you composition.°   *compensation*
SUBTLE: I will not treat with thee; what! sell my fortune?
    'Tis better than my birth-right. Do not murmur:
15   Win her, and carry her. If you grumble, Do!
    Knows it directly.
FACE: Well, sir, I am silent.
    Will you go help to fetch in Don in state?   *[Exit.]*
SUBTLE: I follow you, sir: we must keep Face in awe,
    Or he will over-look us like a tyrant.
    [*Re-enter Face, introducing Surly disguised as a Spaniard.*]
20   Brain of a tailor! who comes here? Don John![7]
SURLY: *Señores, beso las manos a vuestras mercedes.*[8]
SUBTLE: Would you had stoop'd a little, and kist our *anos!*
FACE: Peace, Subtle.
SUBTLE: Stab me; I shall never hold, man.
    He looks in that deep ruff like a head in a platter.

---

5. A scale different for each argument.
6. Serve sexually.

7. Typical name for a Spaniard.
8. "Gentlemen, I kiss your honors' hands."

25   Serv'd in by a short cloak upon two trestles.[9]
FACE: Or, what do you say to a collar of brawn, cut down
        Beneath the souse, and wriggled with a knife?[1]
SUBTLE: 'Slud, he does look too fat to be a Spaniard.
FACE: Perhaps some Fleming or some Hollander got him
30   In d'Alva's time; Count Egmont's bastard.[2]
SUBTLE: Don,
        Your scurvy, yellow, Madrid face is welcome.
SURLY: *Gracias*.
SUBTLE: He speaks out of a fortification.
        Pray God he have no squibs in those deep sets.[3]
SURLY: *Por dios, señores, muy linda casa!*[4]
SUBTLE: What says he?
FACE: Praises the house, I think;
        I know no more but's action.
SUBTLE: Yes, the *casa*,
        My precious Diego, will prove fair enough
        To cozen you in. Do you mark? you shall
        Be cozen'd, Diego.
FACE: Cozen'd, do you see,
40   My worthy Donzel,[5] cozen'd.
SURLY: *Entiendo.*[6]
SUBTLE: Do you intend it? so do we, dear Don.
        Have you brought pistolets, or portagues,
        My solemn Don?—Dost thou feel any?
FACE [*feels his pockets*]:   Full.
SUBTLE: You shall be emptied, Don, pumped and drawn
45   Dry, as they say.
FACE: Milked, in troth, sweet Don.
SUBTLE: See all the monsters; the great lion of all, Don.[7]
SURLY: *Con licencia, se puede ver a esta señora?*[8]
SUBTLE: What talks he now?
FACE: Of the señora.
SUBTLE: O, Don,
        That is the lioness, which you shall see
        Also, my Don.
FACE: 'Slid, Subtle, how shall we do?
SUBTLE: For what?
FACE: Why Dol's employ'd, you know.
SUBTLE: That's true.
        'Fore heaven, I know not: he must stay, that's all.
FACE: Stay! that he must not by no means.
SUBTLE: No! why?

---

9. His legs.
1. Collar of brawn: pig's neck; souse: ear; wriggled: cut in a ruffled pattern.
2. The Dutch patriot Egmont was executed by the Duke of Alva, commander of the Spanish army in the Netherlands.
3. Squibs: rockets; deep sets: deep folds in his collar.

4. "By God, gentlemen, a very fine house."
5. From Italian *donzello*, squire.
6. "I understand."
7. The lions were a tourist attraction at the Tower of London.
8. "If you please, may one see the lady."

FACE: Unless you'll mar all, 'Slight, he'll suspect it:
55   And then he will not pay, not half so well.
          This is a travelled punk-master, and does know
          All the delays; a notable hot rascal,
          And looks already rampant.[9]
SUBTLE: 'Sdeath, and Mammon
          Must not be troubled.
FACE: Mammon! in no case.
SUBTLE: What shall we do then?
FACE: Think: you must be sudden.
SURLY: *Entiendo que la señora es tan hermosa, que codicio tan à verla, como la bien
          aventuranza de mi vida.*[1]
FACE: *Mi vida!* 'Slid, Subtle, he puts me in mind o' the widow.
          What dost thou say to draw her to it, ha!
65   And tell her 'tis her fortune? All our venture
          Now lies upon't. It is but one man more,
          Which of us chance to have her: and beside,
          There is no maidenhead to be fear'd or lost.
          What dost thou think on't, Subtle?
SUBTLE: Who, I? why—
FACE: The credit of our house too is engaged.
SUBTLE: You made me an offer for my share erewhile.
          What wilt thou give me, i'faith?
FACE: O, by that light
          I'll not buy now: You know your doom to me.
          E'en take your lot, obey your chance, sir; win her,
          And wear her out, for me.
SUBTLE: 'Slight, I'll not work her then.
FACE: It is the common cause; therefore bethink you.
          Dol else must know it, as you said.
SUBTLE: I care not.
SURLY: *Señores, por qué se tarda tanto?*[2]
SUBTLE: Faith, I am not fit, I am old.
FACE: That's now no reason, sir.
SURLY: *Puede ser de hacer burla de mi amor?*[3]
FACE: You hear the Don too? by this air, I call,
          And loose the hinges: Dol!
SUBTLE: A plague of hell—
FACE: Will you then do?
SUBTLE: Y're a terrible rogue!
          I'll think of this: will you, sir, call the widow?
FACE: Yes, and I'll take her too with all her faults,
          Now I do think on't better.
SUBTLE: With all my heart, sir;
          Am I discharged o' the lot?

---

9. Heraldic term for an animal rearing on its hind legs.
1. "I understand the lady is so beautiful that I long to see
her as the great good fortune of my life."

2. "Gentlemen, why so much delay?"
3. "Perhaps you are mocking my love."

FACE: As you please.

SUBTLE: Hands. [*They take hands.*]

FACE: Remember now, that upon any change,
        You never claim her.

SUBTLE: Much good joy, and health to you, sir.

90   Marry a whore! Fate, let me wed a witch first.

SURLY: *Por estas honradas barbas*⁴—

SUBTLE: He swears by his beard.
        Dispatch, and call the brother too.   [*Exit Face.*]

SURLY: *Tengo duda, Señores*
        *Que no me hagan alguna traición.*⁵

SUBTLE: How, issue on? yes, *presto, Señor*. Please you

95   *Enthratha* the *chambratha*, worthy Don:
        Where if you please the fates, in your *bathada*,
        You shall be soaked, and stroked, and tubb'd, and rubb'd,
        And scrubb'd, and fubb'd,° dear Don, before you go.   *cheated*
        You shall, in faith, my scurvy baboon Don.

100   Be curried,⁶ claw'd and flaw'd, and taw'd, indeed.
        I will the heartlier go about it now,
        And make the widow a punk so much the sooner,
        To be revenged on this impetuous face:
        The quickly doing of it, is the grace.   [*Exeunt Subtle and Surly.*]

Scene 4

[*Enter Face, Kastril, and Dame Pliant.*]

FACE: Come, lady: I knew the Doctor would not leave,
        Till he had found the very nick⁷ of her fortune.

KASTRIL: To be a countess, say you?

FACE: A Spanish countess, sir.

DAME PLIANT: Why, is that better than an English countess?

FACE: Better? 'Slight, make you that a question, lady?

KASTRIL: Nay, she is a fool, Captain, you must pardon her.

FACE: Ask from your courtier, to your inns-of-court-man,°   *lawyer*
        To your mere milliner; they will tell you all,
        Your Spanish gennet is the best horse;⁸ your Spanish

10   Stoop° is the best garb:° your Spanish beard   *bow / manner*
        Is the best cut; your Spanish ruffs are the best
        Wear; your Spanish pavin the best dance;⁹
        Your Spanish titillation° in a glove   *perfume*
        The best perfume: and for your Spanish pike,¹

15   And Spanish blade, let your poor Captain speak—
        Here comes the Doctor.

[*Enter Subtle with a paper.*]

SUBTLE: My most honor'd lady,
        For so I am now to style you, having found

---

4. "By this honored beard."
5. "I am afraid, gentlemen, you are deceiving me in some way."
6. Soaked, scraped, and beaten.
7. Crucial moment.
8. Small Spanish horse.
9. Dance with a stately rhythm.
1. Spear used by the infantry.

By this my scheme, you are to undergo
An honorable fortune, very shortly.
20   What will you say now, if some—
FACE: I ha' told her all, sir:
And her right worshipful brother here, that she shall be
A countess: do not delay them, sir: a Spanish countess,
SUBTLE: Still, my scarce-worshipful Captain, you can keep
No secret! Well, since he has told you, madam,
25   Do you forgive him, and I do.
KASTRIL: She shall do that, sir;
I'll look to't, 'tis my charge.
SUBTLE: Well then: nought rests
But that she fit her love now to her fortune.
DAME PLIANT: Truly I shall never brook a Spaniard.
SUBTLE: No?
DAME PLIANT: Never since eighty-eight could I abide them,[2]
30   And that was some three year afore I was born, in truth,
SUBTLE: Come, you must love him, or be miserable,
Choose which you will.
FACE: By this good rush,[3] persuade her,
She will cry strawberries else within this twelvemonth.
SUBTLE: Nay, shads and mackerel, which is worse.[4]
FACE: Indeed, sir?
KASTRIL: God's lid, you shall love him, or I'll kick you.
DAME PLIANT: Why,
I'll do as you will have me, brother,
KASTRIL: Do,
Or by this hand I'll maul you.
FACE: Nay, good sir,
Be not so fierce.
SUBTLE: No, my enraged child;
She will be ruled. What, when she comes to taste
40   The pleasures of a countess! to be courted—
FACE: And kiss'd, and ruffled!°   *fondled*
SUBTLE: Ay, behind the hangings.[5]
FACE: And then come forth in pomp!
SUBTLE: And know her state!
FACE: Of keeping all the idolators of the chamber
Barer to her,[6] than at their prayers!
SUBTLE: Is serv'd
45   Upon the knee!
FACE: And has her pages, ushers,
Footmen, and coaches—

---

2. 1588, the year of the Spanish Armada's attack on England.
3. The stage, like the floors of private houses, were covered with rush, or straw.
4. She will be so poor that she will have to sell strawberries in the street, or she will have to sell fish, an even lower occupation.
5. Tapestries or wall-hangings.
6. With their hats off in respect to her.

SUBTLE: Her six mares—

FACE: Nay, eight!

SUBTLE: To hurry her through London, to th' Exchange,
          Bethlem, the china-houses[7]—

FACE: Yes, and have
          The citizens gape at her, and praise her tires,°   *clothes*
50   And my lord's goose-turd bands,[8] that ride with her.

KASTRIL: Most brave! By this hand, you are not my suster,
          If you refuse.

DAME PLIANT: I will not refuse, brother.
          [*Enter Surly.*]

SURLY: *Qué es esto, señores, que no se venga?*
          Esta tardanza me mata![9]

FACE: It is the count come:
55   The doctor knew he would be here, by his art.

SUBTLE: *En gallanta madama, Don! gallantissima!*

SURLY: *Por todos los dioses, la más acabada*
          Hermosura, que he visto en mi vida![1]

FACE: Is't not a gallant language that they speak?

KASTRIL: An admirable language! Is't not French?

FACE: No, Spanish, sir.

KASTRIL: It goes like law-French,
          And that, they say, is the courtliest language.[2]

FACE: List, sir.

SURLY: *El sol ha perdido su lumbre, con el*
          Resplandor que trae esta dama! Válgame Dios![3]

FACE: H'admires your sister.

KASTRIL: Must not she make curt'sy?

SUBTLE: 'Ods will, she must go to him, man, and kiss him!
          It is the Spanish fashion, for the women
          To make first court.

FACE: 'Tis true he tells you, sir:
          His art knows all.

SURLY: *Por qué no se acude?*[4]

KASTRIL: He speaks to her, I think.

FACE: That he does, sir.

SURLY: *Por el amor de Dios, qué es esto que se tarda?*[5]

KASTRIL: Nay, see: she will not understand him! gull,
          Noddy.

DAME PLIANT: What say you, brother?

KASTRIL: Ass, my suster.
          Go kuss him, as the cunning man would have you;

---

7. The Exchange was a fashionable shopping area. Beth-
lem, or Bedlam, was the London insane asylum; china
houses were shops selling porcelain and other precious
goods from the east.
8. Collars in goose-turd green, a fashionable color.
9. "Why does she not come, gentlemen? This delay is
killing me."

1. "By all the gods, the most perfect beauty that I have
ever seen in my life."
2. Norman French was the language of the law courts.
3. "The sun has lost its light with the splendor that this
lady brings. God bless me!"
4. "Why does she not come?"
5. "For the love of God, why is it she delays?"

75 I'll thrust a pin in your buttocks else.

FACE: O no, sir.

SURLY: *Señora mia, mi persona está muy indigna a llegar a tanta hermosura.*[6]

FACE: Does he not use her bravely?

KASTRIL: Bravely, i'faith!

FACE: Nay, he will use her better.

KASTRIL: Do you think so?

SURLY: *Señora, si será servida, entremos.*[7]   [*Exit with Dame Pliant.*]

KASTRIL: Where does he carry her?

FACE: Into the garden, sir;

 Take you no thought: I must interpret for her.

SUBTLE [*aside to Face, who goes out*]: Give Dol the word.—[*to Kastril*] Come, my
 fierce child, advance,

 We'll to our quarreling lesson again.

KASTRIL: Agreed.

 I love a Spanish boy with all my heart.

SUBTLE: Nay, and by this means, sir, you shall be brother
 To a great count.

KASTRIL: Ay, I knew that at first.

 This match will advance the house of the Kastrils.

SUBTLE: 'Pray God your sister prove but pliant!

KASTRIL: Why,

 Her name is so, by her other husband.

SUBTLE: How!

KASTRIL: The widow Pliant. Knew you not that?

SUBTLE: No, faith, sir;

 Yet, by erection of her figure,[8] I guessed it,
 Come, let's go practice.

KASTRIL: Yes, but do you think, Doctor,
 I e'er shall quarrel well?

SUBTLE: I warrant you.   [*Exeunt.*]

Scene 5

[*Enter Dol in her fit of raving, followed by* MAMMON.]

DOL: For after Alexander's death[9]—

MAMMON: Good lady—

DOL: That Perdiccas and Antigonus, were slain,
 The two that stood, Seleuc' and Ptolomy[1]—

MAMMON: Madam.

---

6. "My lady, my person is unworthy to attain so much
beauty."
7. "Lady, if it is convenient, let us go in."
8. Both the casting of her horoscope and the sexual
arousal that her appearance provokes.
9. Alexander the Great, King of Macedonia, who conquered and ruled an empire over the Mediterranean
world in the 4th century B.C.E. Dol's lines 1–32 contain
quotations from Hugh Broughton's *A Conceit of Scripture*
(1590). The passage quoted here is from an interpretation of the dream of Nebuchadnezzar in the Book of

Daniel 2, where a pagan idol with legs of iron and clay is
broken by a stone that becomes a huge mountain.
1. Perdiccas, Antigonus, Seleucus, and Ptolemy were the
four generals of Alexander the Great, who fought over
his kingdom. Like many Puritans, Broughton interpreted
the Ptolemaic empire (Egypt, to the south) and the Se-
leucid empire (Syria, to the north) as the four kingdoms
in a cycle of decay of pagan rule that would give way to
the fifth monarchy (see line 34 below), which in the 17th
century was identified with the thousand-year reign of
Christ.

DOL: Made up the two legs, and the fourth beast,
5   That was Gog-north, and Egypt-south: which after
           Was call'd Gog-iron-leg, and South-iron-leg—
MAMMON: Lady—
DOL: And then Gog-horned. So was Egypt, too:
           Then Egypt-clay-leg, and Gog-clay-leg—
MAMMON: Sweet madam.
DOL: And last Gog-dust, and Egypt-dust, which fall
10   In the last link of the fourth chain. And these
           Be stars in story, which none see, or look at—
MAMMON: What shall I do?
DOL: For, as he says, except
           We call the rabbins, and the heathen Greeks[2]—
MAMMON: Dear lady.
DOL: To come from Salem, and from Athens,
15   And teach the people of Great Britain—
           [*Enter Face, hastily, in his servant's dress.*]
FACE: What's the matter, sir?
DOL: To speak the tongue of Eber, and Javan—
MAMMON: O,
           She's in her fit.
DOL: We shall know nothing—
FACE: Death, sir,
           We are undone!
DOL: Where then a learned linguist
           Shall see the ancient used communion
20   Of vowels and consonants—
FACE: My master will hear!
DOL: A wisdom, which Pythagoras held most high—
MAMMON: Sweet honorable lady!
DOL: To comprise
           All sounds of voices, in few marks of letters—
FACE: Nay, you must never hope to lay her now.[3]
           [*They all speak together.*]
DOL: And so we may arrive by Talmud skill,[4]
           And profane Greek, to raise the building up
           Of Helen's house against the Ismaelite,[5]
           King of Thogarma,[6] and his habergions°   *armor*
           Brimstony, blue, and fiery; and the force
30   Of King Abaddon, and the Beast of Cittim:
           Which rabbi David Kimchi, Onkelos,

2. The "rabbins" (Jews from Salem) and the "heathen Greeks" (from Athens) are to teach the Puritans of Great Britain the languages of Scripture, the tongue of Eber (ancestor of the Hebrews) and of Javan (ancestor of the Greeks).
3. "Lay her," means both to allay or calm her down, and to have sexual intercourse with her.
4. The Talmud contains texts of Jewish civil and religious law.

5. "Helen's house" is Heber's house in Hugh Broughton's *A Conceit of Scripture* (1590) where he uses it to mean "the kingdom of God;" the Ismaelite are the sons of Ismael (Ishmael), pagans.
6. King of Thogarma, ruler of a biblical kingdom (Ezekiel 38.6).

And Aben Ezra do interpret Rome.[7]

FACE: How did you put her into't?

MAMMON: Alas! I talk'd
        Of a fifth monarchy I would erect,
35   With the philosopher's stone,[8] by chance, and she
        Falls on the other four straight.

FACE: Out of Broughton![9]
        I told you so. 'Slid, stop her mouth.

MAMMON: Is't best?

FACE: She'll never leave else. If the old man hear her,
        We are but feces, ashes.

SUBTLE [within]:   What's to do there?

FACE: O, we are lost! Now she hears him, she is quiet.
        [Enter Subtle, they run different ways.]

MAMMON: Where shall I hide me!

SUBTLE: How! what sight is here?
        Close deeds of darkness, and that shun the light!
        Bring him again. Who is he? What, my son!
        O, I have lived too long.

MAMMON: Nay, good, dear father,
45   There was no unchaste purpose.

SUBTLE: Not? and flee me,
        When I come in?

MAMMON: That was my error.

SUBTLE: Error?
        Guilt, guilt, my son: give it the right name. No marvel,
        If I found check in our great work within,
        When such affairs as these were managing!

MAMMON: Why, have you so?

SUBTLE: It has stood still this half hour:
        And all the rest of our less works gone back.
        Where is the instrument of wickedness,
        My lewd° false drudge?   ignorant

MAMMON: Nay, good sir, blame not him;
        Believe me, 'twas against his will or knowledge:
55   I saw her by chance.

SUBTLE: Will you commit more sin,
        To excuse a varlet?

MAMMON: By my hope, 'tis true, sir.

SUBTLE: Nay, then I wonder less, if you, for whom
        The blessing was prepared, would so tempt heaven,
        And lose your fortunes.

MAMMON: Why, sir?

SUBTLE: This will retard

---

7. Biblical commentators interpreted King of Abaddon as the Pope and Beast of Cittim as the Roman Catholic Church.

8. With a bawdy pun on stone as "testicle."
9. Broughton's A Conceit of Scripture.

60   The work, a month at least.

MAMMON: Why, if it do.
        What remedy? But think it not, good father:
        Our purposes were honest.

SUBTLE: As they were,
        So the reward will prove.—[*A loud explosion within.*] How now! ah me!
        God, and all saints be good to us.—
    [*Re-enter Face.*]
                                        What's that?

FACE: O, sir, we are defeated! all the works
        Are flown *in fumo,°* every glass is burst: *in smoke*
        Furnace, and all rent down! as if a bolt
        Of thunder had been driven through the house.
        Retorts, receivers, pelicans, bolt-heads,
70   All struck in shivers! [*Subtle falls down as in a swoon.*]
                                Help, good sir! alas,
        Coldness, and death invades him. Nay, sir Mammon,
        Do the fair offices° of a man! You stand,   *duties*
        As you were readier to depart than he.
    [*Knocking within.*]
        Who's there? My lord her brother is come.

MAMMON: Ha, Lungs!

FACE: His coach is at the door. Avoid his sight,
        For he's as furious as his sister's mad.

MAMMON: Alas!

FACE: My brain is quite undone with the fume, sir,
        I ne'er must hope to be mine own man again.

MAMMON: Is all lost, Lungs? will nothing be preserv'd
80   Of all our cost?

FACE: Faith, very little, sir;
        A peck of coals or so, which is cold comfort, sir.

MAMMON: O my voluptuous mind! I am justly punish'd.

FACE: And so am I, sir.

MAMMON: Cast from all my hopes—

FACE: Nay, certainties, sir.

MAMMON: By mine own base affections.

SUBTLE [*seeming to come to himself*]: O, the curst fruits of vice and lust!

MAMMON: Good father,
        It was my sin. Forgive it.

SUBTLE: Hangs my roof
        Over us still, and will not fall, O justice,
        Upon us, for this wicked man!

FACE: Nay, look, sir,
        You grieve him now with staying in his sight:
90   Good sir, the nobleman will come too, and take you,
        And that may breed a tragedy.

MAMMON: I'll go.

FACE: Ay, and repent at home, sir. It may be,

For some good penance you may ha' it yet;
A hundred pound to the box at Bedlam[1]—

MAMMON:　　　　　　　　　　　　　　　　Yes.

FACE: For the restoring such as—have their wits.

MAMMON:　　　　　　　　　　　　　　　I'll do't.

FACE: I'll send one to you to receive it.

MAMMON:　　　　　　　　　　　　Do.
　　　　　Is no projection left?

FACE:　　　　　　　　　　　All flown, or stinks, sir.

MAMMON: Will nought be sav'd that's good for med'cine, think'st thou?

FACE: I cannot tell, sir. There will be perhaps,

100　　　Something about the scraping of the shards,
　　　　Will cure the itch,—[aside] though not your itch of mind, sir.—
　　　　It shall be saved for you, and sent home. Good sir.
　　　　This way, for fear the lord should meet you. [Exit Mammon.]

SUBTLE [raising his head]:　　　　　　　　Face!

FACE: Ay.

SUBTLE: Is he gone?

FACE:　　　　　　　Yes, and as heavily

105　　As all the gold he hoped for were in's blood.
　　　Let us be light though.

SUBTLE [leaping up]:　　　Ay, as balls, and bound
　　　　And hit our heads against the roof for joy:
　　　　There's so much of our care now cast away,

FACE: Now to our Don,

SUBTLE:　　　　　　　Yes, your young widow by this time

110　　Is made a countess, Face; she has been in travail
　　　Of a young heir for you.

FACE:　　　　　　　Good sir.

SUBTLE:　　　　　　　Off with your case,[2]
　　　　And greet her kindly, as a bridegroom should,
　　　　After these common hazards.

FACE:　　　　　　　Very well, sir.
　　　　Will you go fetch Don Diego off, the while?

SUBTLE: And fetch him over too,[3] if you'll be pleased, sir:
　　　　Would Dol were in her place, to pick his pockets now!

FACE: Why, you can do't as well, if you would set to't.
　　　I pray you prove your virtue.[4]

SUBTLE:　　　　　　　For your sake, sir.　　　　　　[Exeunt.]

Scene 6

[Enter Surly and Dame Pliant.]

SURLY: Lady, you see into what hands you are fall'n;
　　　　'Mongst what a nest of villains! and how near
　　　　Your honor was t' have catch'd a certain clap,°　　　gonorrhea

---

1. The poor box for the madhouse.
2. Costume as Lungs.

3. Get the better of him.
4. Virtue in the sense of ability or skill.

Through your credulity, had I but been
5   So punctually forward, as place, time,
And other circumstances would have made a man;
For you're a handsome woman: would you were wise too!
I am a gentleman come here disguised,
Only to find the knaveries of this citadel;
10   And where I might have wrong'd your honor and have not,
I claim some interest in your love. You are,
They say, a widow, rich: and I'm a bachelor,
Worth nought: your fortunes may make me a man.
As mine have preserv'd you a woman. Think upon it,
15   And whether I have deserv'd you or no.

DAME PLIANT: I will, sir.

SURLY: And for these household-rogues, let me alone
To treat with them.

[Enter Subtle.]

SUBTLE: How doth my noble Diego,
And my dear madam countess? Hath the count
Been courteous, lady? liberal, and open?
20   Donzel, methinks you look melancholic,
After your coitum, and scurvy:[5] truly,
I do not like the dullness of your eye:
It hath a heavy cast, 'tis upsee Dutch,[6]
And says you are a lumpish whore-master.
25   Be lighter, I will make your pockets so. [Attempts to pick them.]

SURLY   [throws open his cloak]: Will you, Don Bawd and Pick-purse?
[strikes him down] How now! reel you?
Stand up, sir, you shall find, since I am so heavy,
I'll give you equal weight.

SUBTLE: Help! murder!

SURLY: No, sir,
There's no such thing intended: a good cart,
30   And a clean whip[7] shall ease you of that fear.
I am the Spanish Don that should be cozen'd.
Do you see, cozen'd! Where's your captain Face,
That parcel-broker,[8] and whole-bawd, all rascal!

[Enter Face, in his uniform.]

FACE: How, Surly!

SURLY: O, make your approach, good Captain.
35   I have found from whence your copper rings and spoons
Come, now, wherewith you cheat abroad in taverns.
'Twas here you learn'd t' anoint your boot with brimstone,
Then rub men's gold on't for a kind of touch,
And say 'twas naught, when you had changed the color,
40   That you might have't for nothing. And this Doctor,

5. Sad and sick after sex.
6. In the Dutch style, drunken.

7. A common punishment for minor crimes was to be tied
to a cart and whipped through the streets.
8. Part-time go-between.

Your sooty, smoky-bearded compeer, he
Will close you so much gold, in a bolt's-head,
And, on a turn, convey in the stead another
With sublimed mercury, that shall burst in the heat,
45   And fly out all *in fumo!* Then weeps Mammon;
Then swoons his worship. [*Face slips out.*] Or, he is the Faustus,[9]
That casteth figures and can conjure, cures
Plagues, piles, and pox, by the ephemerides,[1]
And holds intelligence with all the bawds
50   And midwives of three shires: while you send in—
Captain—what! is he gone!—damsels with child,
Wives that are barren, or the waiting-maid
With the green sickness. [*Seizes Subtle as he tries to leave.*]
               Nay, sir, you must tarry,
Though he be scaped; and answer by the ears, sir.

Scene 7

[*Re-enter Face, with Kastril.*]
FACE: Why, now's the time, if ever you will quarrel
    Well, as they say, and be a true-born child:
    The doctor and your sister both are abused.
KASTRIL: Where is he? Which is he? He is a slave,
5   Whate'er he is, and the son of a whore.—Are you
    The man, sir, I would know?
SURLY: I should be loath, sir,
    To confess so much.
KASTRIL: Then you lie in your throat.
SURLY: How!
FACE [*to Kastril*]: A very arrant° rogue, sir, and a cheater,   *notorious*
    Employ'd here by another conjurer
10   That does not love the doctor, and would cross him,
    If he knew how.
SURLY: Sir, you are abused.
KASTRIL: You lie:
    And 'tis no matter.
FACE: Well said, sir! He is
    The impudent'st rascal—
SURLY: You are indeed: Will you hear me, sir?
FACE: By no means: bid him be gone.
KASTRIL: Begone, sir, quickly.
SURLY: This's strange!—Lady, do you inform your brother.
FACE: There is not such a foist° in all the town,   *cheat*
    The Doctor had him presently; and finds yet,
    The Spanish Count will come here.—[*aside.*] Bear up, Subtle.
SUBTLE: Yes, sir, he must appear within this hour.
FACE: And yet this rogue would come in a disguise,

---

9. Character who made a pact with the devil to achieve   1. Astronomical almanacs.
power in Christopher Marlowe's play *Doctor Faustus*.

By the temptation of another spirit,
To trouble our art, though he could not hurt it!

KASTRIL: Ay,
I know—Away, [*to his sister*] you talk like a foolish mauther.[2]

SURLY: Sir, all is truth she says.

FACE: Do not believe him, sir.
25   He is the lying'st swabber![3] Come your ways, sir.

SURLY: You are valiant out of company!

KASTRIL: Yes, how then, sir?
[*Enter Drugger, with a piece of damask.*]

FACE: Nay, here's an honest fellow, too, that knows him,
And all his tricks. Make good what I say, Abel,
This cheater would have cozen'd thee o' the widow.—
[*Aside to Drugger.*]
30   He owes this honest Drugger here, seven pound,
He has had on him, in two-penny'orths of tobacco.

DRUGGER: Yes, sir. And he has damn'd himself three terms to pay me.[4]

FACE: And what does he owe for lotium?[5]

DRUGGER: Thirty shillings, sir;
And for six syringes.[6]

SURLY: Hydra[7] of villainy!

FACE: Nay, sir, you must quarrel him out o' the house.

KASTRIL: I will:
—Sir, if you get not out o' doors, you lie;
And you are a pimp.

SURLY: Why, this is madness, sir,
Not valor in you; I must laugh at this.

KASTRIL: It is my humor: you are a pimp and a trig,°   fop
40   And an *Amadis de Gaul*, or a Don Quixote.[8]

DRUGGER: Or a knight o' the curious coxcomb,[9] do you see?
[*Enter Ananias.*]

ANANIAS: Peace to the household!

KASTRIL: I'll keep peace for no man.

ANANIAS: Casting of dollars is concluded lawful.

KASTRIL: Is he the constable?

SUBTLE: Peace, Ananias.

FACE: No, sir.

KASTRIL: Then you are an otter, and a shad, a whit,
A very tim.°   tiny particle

SURLY: You'll hear me, sir?

KASTRIL: I will not.

ANANIAS: What is the motive?

SUBTLE: Zeal in the young gentleman,

---

2. Young girl.
3. Low person, deck-scrubber.
4. Sworn for three law terms in a row.
5. Lotium was stale urine used as a hair tonic.
6. Syringes for applying lotium or taking medicine to treat venereal disease.
7. The many-headed sea beast who grew two new heads

for each one that was cut off.
8. Amadis of Gaul, the hero of the Spanish prose romance of the same name, was the model of all chivalry for Don Quixote, the hero of Cervantes' comic novel about a deluded old man who thought he could be a knight.
9. The preposterous hat that Surly wears.

Against his Spanish slops.[1]

ANANIAS: They are profane,
Lewd, superstitious, and idolatrous breeches.

SURLY: New rascals!

KASTRIL: Will you begone, sir!

ANANIAS: Avoid, Satan!
Thou art not of the light: That ruff of pride
About thy neck, betrays thee; and is the same
With that which the unclean birds, in seventy-seven,[2]
Were seen to prank° it with on divers coasts: swagger
55   Thou look'st like antichrist, in that lewd hat,

SURLY: I must give way.

KASTRIL: Be gone, sir.

SURLY: But I'll take
A course with you—

ANANIAS: Depart, proud Spanish fiend!

SURLY: Captain and Doctor.

ANANIAS: Child of perdition!

KASTRIL: Hence, sir!   [Exit Surly.]
Did I not quarrel bravely!

FACE: Yes, indeed, sir.

KASTRIL: Nay, an I give my mind to't, I shall do't.

FACE: O, you must follow, sir, and threaten him tame:
He'll turn again else.

KASTRIL: I'll re-turn him then.   [Exit.]
[Subtle takes Ananias aside.]

FACE: Drugger, this rogue prevented° us for thee: forestalled
We had determin'd that thou should'st have come
65   In a Spanish suit, and have carried her so; and he,
A brokerly° slave! goes, puts it on himself.   pimping
Hast brought the damask?

DRUGGER: Yes, sir.

FACE: Thou must borrow
A Spanish suit: hast thou no credit with the players?

DRUGGER: Yes, sir; did you never see me play the Fool?[3]

FACE: I know not, Nab:—[aside.] Thou shalt, if I can help it.—
Hieronimo's old cloak, ruff, and hat will serve;[4]
I'll tell thee more when thou bring'st 'em.   [Exit Drugger.]

ANANIAS: Sir, I know
The Spaniard hates the brethren, and hath spies
Upon their actions: and that this was one

---

1. Large, wide trousers.
2. The "unclean birds" may refer to the "unclean bird" that appears in Babylon after the fall of the city in Revelation 18.2. It is unclear what "seventy-seven" refers to; perhaps Jonson meant 1567, the year of D'Alva's invasion of the Protestant Netherlands.

3. Drugger was probably played by the actor Robert Arnim, who played the role of the Fool for the King's Men, Shakespeare's acting company and the company for The Alchemist.
4. Ben Jonson was reported to have worn just such a costume when playing the role of Hieronimo, the hero of Kyd's Spanish Tragedy.

75   I make no scruple.—But the holy synod[5]
Have been in prayer and meditation for it;
And 'tis reveal'd no less to them than me,
That casting of money is most lawful.

SUBTLE: True,
But here I cannot do it; if the house
80   Should chance to be suspected, all would out,
And we be lock'd up in the Tower for ever,
To make gold there for the state, never come out;[6]
And then are you defeated.

ANANIAS: I will tell
This to the elders and the weaker brethren,
85   That the whole company of the separation
May join in humble prayer again.

SUBTLE: And fasting.

ANANIAS: Yea, for some fitter place. The peace of mind
Rest with these walls!

SUBTLE: Thanks, courteous Ananias.

FACE: What did he come for?

SUBTLE: About casting dollars,
90   Presently out of hand. And so I told him,
A Spanish minister came here to spy,
Against the faithful—

FACE: I conceive.° Come, Subtle,   *understand*
Thou art so down upon the least disaster!
How wouldst thou ha' done, if I had not helped thee out?

SUBTLE: I thank thee, Face, for the angry boy, i'faith.

FACE: Who would ha' look'd° it should ha' been that rascal,   *expected*
Surly? He had dyed his beard and all. Well, sir,
Here's damask come to make you a suit.

SUBTLE: Where's Drugger?

FACE: He is gone to borrow me a Spanish habit;
100   I'll be the Count, now.

SUBTLE: But where's the widow?

FACE: Within, with my lord's sister: Madam Dol
Is entertaining her.

SUBTLE: By your favor, Face,
Now she is honest,° I will stand again.   *chaste*

FACE: You will not offer it.

SUBTLE: Why?

FACE: Stand to your word,
105   Or—here comes Dol, she knows—

SUBTLE: Y'are tyrannous still.

    [*Enter Dol, hastily.*]

FACE: Strict for my right.—How now, Dol? Hast told her,

---

5. Assembly of church people.
6. Edward II was said to have imprisoned the alchemist Raymond Lull in the Tower of London when he failed to produce gold; Elizabeth I punished Cornelius Lannoy for the same failure.

                                The Spanish Count will come?
DOL: Yes; but another is come,
            You little look'd for!
FACE: Who is that?
DOL: Your master;
            The master of the house.
SUBTLE: How, Dol!
FACE: She lies,
110   This is some trick. Come, leave your quiblins,° Dorothy.   *tricks*
DOL: Look out, and see.   [*Face goes to the window.*]
SUBTLE: Art thou in earnest?
DOL: 'Slight,
            Forty o' the neighbors are about him, talking.
FACE: 'Tis he, by this good day.
DOL: 'Twill prove ill day
            For some on us.
FACE: We are undone, and taken.
DOL: Lost, I'm afraid.
SUBTLE: You said he would not come,
            While there died one a week within the liberties.[7]
FACE: No: 'twas within the walls.[8]
SUBTLE: Was't so! cry you mercy.
            I thought the liberties. What shall we do now, Face?
FACE: Be silent: not a word, if he call or knock.
120   I'll into mine old shape again and meet him,
            Of Jeremy, the butler. In the mean time,
            Do you two pack up all the goods and purchase,
            That we can carry in the two trunks. I'll keep him
            Off for to-day, if I cannot longer: and then
125   At night, I'll ship you both away to Ratcliff,
            Where we will meet to-morrow, and there we'll share.
            Let Mammon's brass and pewter keep the cellar;
            We'll have another time for that. But, Dol,
            'Prythee go heat a little water quickly;
130   Subtle must shave me: all my Captain's beard
            Must off, to make me appear smooth Jeremy.
            You'll do it?
SUBTLE: Yes, I'll shave you, as well as I can.
FACE: And not cut my throat, but trim me?
SUBTLE: You shall see, sir.   [*Exeunt.*]

ACT 5

Scene 1—*Before Lovewit's door*

[*Enter Lovewit, with several of the Neighbors.*]
LOVEWIT: Has there been such resort, say you?
1 NEIGHBOR: Daily, sir.

---

7. Many died of plague in the area of the Liberties, or   8. The walls of the City of London, one square mile in
Blackfriars, outside the city walls.   area.

2 NEIGHBOR: And nightly, too.

3 NEIGHBOR: Ay, some as brave as lords.

4 NEIGHBOR: Ladies and gentlewomen.

5 NEIGHBOR: Citizens' wives.

1 NEIGHBOR: And knights.

6 NEIGHBOR: In coaches.

2 NEIGHBOR: Yes, and oyster women.

1 NEIGHBOR: Beside other gallants.

3 NEIGHBOR: Sailors' wives.

4 NEIGHBOR: Tobacco men.

5 NEIGHBOR: Another Pimlico![9]

LOVEWIT: What should my knave advance.
    To draw this company? He hung out no banners
    Of a strange calf with five legs to be seen,
    Or a huge lobster with six claws?

6 NEIGHBOR: No, sir.

3 NEIGHBOR: We had gone in then, sir.

LOVEWIT: He has no gift
    Of teaching in the nose[1] that e'er I know of!
    You saw no bills set up that promised cure
    Of agues, or the tooth-ache?

2 NEIGHBOR: No such thing, sir.

LOVEWIT: Nor heard a drum struck for baboons or puppets?

5 NEIGHBOR: Neither, sir.

LOVEWIT: What device should he bring forth now?
    I love a teeming wit as I love my nourishment:
    'Pray God he have not kept such open house
    That he hath sold my hangings, and my bedding!
    I left him nothing else. If he have eat them,
20   A plague o' the moth, say I! Sure he has got
    Some bawdy pictures to call all this ging°!   *crowd*
    The friar and the nun; or the new motion[2]
    Of the knight's courser covering the parson's mare;
    The boy of six year old with the great thing:°   *penis*
25   Or 't may be, he has the fleas that run at tilt
    Upon a table, or some dog to dance.
    When saw you him?

1 NEIGHBOR: Who, sir, Jeremy!

2 NEIGHBOR: Jeremy butler?
    We saw him not this month.

LOVEWIT: How!

4 NEIGHBOR: Not these five weeks, sir.

6 NEIGHBOR: These six weeks at the least.

LOVEWIT: You amaze me, neighbors!

5 NEIGHBOR: Sure, if your worship know not where he is,

---

9. Resort near Hogsden, which was known for its cakes and ales.

1. Preaching with the nasal intonation that was associated with the Puritans.
2. Puppet show and sexual intercourse.

He's slipt away.

6 NEIGHBOR: Pray God, he be not made away.

LOVEWIT: Ha! it's no time to question, then. [*Knocks at the door.*]

6 NEIGHBOR: About
Some three weeks since, I heard a doleful cry,
As I sat up a mending my wife's stockings.

LOVEWIT: 'Tis strange that none will answer! Didst thou hear
A cry, sayst thou?

6 NEIGHBOR: Yes, sir, like unto a man
That had been strangled an hour, and could not speak.

2 NEIGHBOR: I heard it too, just this day three weeks, at two o'clock
Next morning.

LOVEWIT: These be miracles, or you make them so!

40   A man an hour strangled, and could not speak,
And both you heard him cry?

3 NEIGHBOR: Yes, downward, sir.

LOVEWIT: Thou art a wise fellow. Give me thy hand, I pray thee.
What trade art thou on?

3 NEIGHBOR: A smith, an't please your worship.

LOVEWIT: A smith! Then lend me thy help to get this door open.

3 NEIGHBOR: That I will presently, sir, but fetch my tools— [*Exit.*]

1 NEIGHBOR: Sir, best to knock again, afore you break it.

Scene 2

LOVEWIT [*knocks again*]: I will.

[*Enter Face, in his butler's livery.*]

FACE: What mean you, sir?

1, 2, 4 NEIGHBOR: O, here's Jeremy!

FACE: Good sir, come from the door.

LOVEWIT: Why, what's the matter?

FACE: Yet farther, you are too near yet.

LOVEWIT: I' the name of wonder,
What means the fellow?

FACE: The house, sir, has been visited.

LOVEWIT: What, with the plague? Stand thou then farther.

FACE: No, sir,
I had it not.

LOVEWIT: Who had it then? I left
None else but thee i' the house.

FACE: Yes, sir, my fellow,
The cat that kept the buttery, had it on her
A week before I spied it; but I got her

10   Convey'd away in the night: and so I shut
The house up for a month—

LOVEWIT: How!

FACE: Purposing then, sir,
T' ha' burnt rose-vinegar, treacle, and tar,
And ha' made it sweet, that you shou'd ne'er have known it;

    Because I knew the news would but afflict you, sir.

LOVEWIT: Breathe less, and farther off! Why this is stranger:
    The neighbors tell me all here that the doors
    Have still been open—

FACE: How, sir!

LOVEWIT: Gallants, men and women,
    And of all sorts, tag-rag, been seen to flock here
    In threaves,° these ten weeks, as to a second Hogsden,   *crowds*
20   In days of Pimlico and Eye-bright.[3]

FACE: Sir.
    Their wisdoms will not say so.

LOVEWIT: To-day they speak
    Of coaches, and gallants; one in a French hood
    Went in, they tell me; and another was seen
    In a velvet gown at the window: divers more
25   Pass in and out.

FACE: They did pass through the doors then,
    Or walls, I assure their eye-sights, and their spectacles:
    For here, sir, are the keys, and here have been,
    In this my pocket, now above twenty days:
    And for before, I kept the fort alone there.
30   But that 'tis yet not deep in the afternoon,
    I should believe my neighbours had seen double
    Through the black-pot,° and made these apparitions!   *beer mug*
    For, on my faith to your worship, for these three weeks
    And upwards the door has not been open'd.

LOVEWIT: Strange!

1 NEIGHBOR: Good faith, I think I saw a coach.

2 NEIGHBOR: And I too,
    I'd have been sworn.

LOVEWIT: Do you but think it now?
    And but one coach?

4 NEIGHBOR: We cannot tell, sir: Jeremy
    Is a very honest fellow.

FACE: Did you see me at all?

1 NEIGHBOR: No; that we are sure on.

2 NEIGHBOR: I'll be sworn o' that.

LOVEWIT: Fine rogues to have your testimonies built on!
    [*Re-enter Third Neighbor, with his tools.*]

3 NEIGHBOR: Is Jeremy come!

1 NEIGHBOR: O yes; you may leave your tools;
    We were deceived, he says.

2 NEIGHBOR: He has had the keys;
    And the door has been shut these three weeks.

3 NEIGHBOR: Like enough.

---

3. Pimlico and Eye-bright: resorts at Hogsden known for beer.

LOVEWIT: Peace and get hence, you changelings.[4]
    [*Enter Surly and Mammon.*]
FACE   [*aside*]:   Surly come!
45   And Mammon made acquainted! They'll tell all.
    How shall I beat them off? What shall I do?
    Nothing's more wretched than a guilty conscience.[5]

Scene 3

SURLY: No, sir, he was a great physician. This,
    It was no bawdy house, but a mere chancel![6]
    You knew the lord and his sister.
MAMMON: Nay, good Surly—
SURLY: The happy word, Be Rich—
MAMMON: Play not the tyrant.—
SURLY: Should be to-day pronounced to all your friends.
    And where be your andirons now? And your brass pots,
    That should have been golden flagons, and great wedges?
MAMMON: Let me but breathe. What, they have shut their doors,
    Methinks!
SURLY: Ay, now 'tis holiday with them.
MAMMON: Rogues, [*He and Surly knock.*]
10   Cozeners, impostors, bawds!
FACE: What mean you, sir!
MAMMON: To enter if we can.
FACE: Another man's house!
    Here is the owner, sir: turn you to him,
    And speak your business.
MAMMON: Are you, sir, the owner?
LOVEWIT: Yes, sir.
MAMMON: And are those knaves within your cheaters?
LOVEWIT: What knaves, what cheaters?
MAMMON: Subtle and his Lungs.
FACE: The gentleman is distracted, sir! No lungs,
    Nor lights[7] have been seen here these three weeks, sir,
    Within these doors, upon my word.
SURLY: Your word,
    Groom arrogant?
FACE: Yes, sir, I am the housekeeper,
20   And know the keys have not been out of my hands.
SURLY: This is a new Face.[8]

---

4. People who change their opinion often, and idiots, whom the faeries exchanged for the human babies whom they snatched out of their cribs.
5. A translation of "Nihil est miserius quam animus hominis conscius" (Plautus, *Mostellaria* 544–45).
6. Nothing less than a church. The chancel is the eastern part of a church.

7. The lungs of animals were called "lights" when sold by butchers.
8. A "new Face," both another man like Face, and Face in the new disguise or role, of Jeremy the butler, in which Surly, ironically, does not appear to recognize him.

FACE: You do mistake the house, sir:
    What sign was't at?
SURLY: You rascal! This is one
    Of the confederacy. Come, let's get officers,
    And force the door.
LOVEWIT: 'Pray you stay, gentlemen.
SURLY: No, sir, we'll come with warrant.
MAMMON: Ay, and then
    We shall have your doors open.   [*Exeunt Mammon and Surly.*]
LOVEWIT: What means this?
FACE: I cannot tell, sir.
1 NEIGHBOR: These are two o' the gallants
    That we do think we saw.
FACE: Two of the fools!
    You talk as idly as they. Good faith, sir,
30   I think the moon has crazed 'em all.—[*aside*] (O me,
    [*Enter Kastril.*]
    The angry boy come too! He'll make a noise,
    And ne'er away till he have betray'd us all.)
KASTRIL [*knocking*]: What rogues, bawds, slaves, you'll open the door, anon!
    Punk, cockatrice,° my suster! By this light   *whore*
35   I'll fetch the marshal[9] to you. You are a whore
    To keep your castle—
FACE: Who would you speak with, sir?
KASTRIL: The bawdy Doctor, and the cozening Captain,
    And Puss my suster.
LOVEWIT: This is something, sure.
FACE: Upon my trust, the doors were never open, sir.
KASTRIL: I have heard all their tricks told me twice over,
    By the fat knight and the lean gentleman.
LOVEWIT: Here comes another.
    [*Enter Ananias and Tribulation.*]
FACE: Ananias too!
    And his pastor!
TRIBULATION [*beating at the door*]: The doors are shut against us,
ANANIAS: Come forth, you seed of sulphur, sons of fire!
45   Your stench it is broke forth; abomination
    Is in the house.
KASTRIL: Ay, my suster's there.
ANANIAS: The place,
    It is become a cage of unclean birds.
KASTRIL: Yes, I will fetch the scavenger, and the constable.
TRIBULATION: You shall do well.
ANANIAS: We'll join to weed them out.
KASTRIL: You will not come then, punk device,[1] my sister!
ANANIAS: Call her not sister; she's a harlot verily.

---

9. Court officer in charge of prisons.   1. "Punk device," complete whore.

KASTRIL: I'll raise the street.

LOVEWIT: Good gentleman, a word.

ANANIAS: Satan avoid, and hinder not our zeal!

[Exeunt Ananias, Tribulation, and Kastril.]

LOVEWIT: The world's turn'd Bedlam.

FACE: These are all broke loose,

55   Out of St. Katherine's, where they use to keep
      The better sort of mad-folks.

1 NEIGHBOR: All these persons
      We saw go in and out here.

2 NEIGHBOR: Yes, indeed, sir.

3 NEIGHBOR: These were the parties.

FACE: Peace, you drunkards! Sir.
      I wonder at it: please you to give me leave

60   To touch the door, I'll try an the lock be chang'd.

LOVEWIT: It mazes° me!   *bewilders*

FACE [*goes to the door*]: Good faith, sir, I believe
      There's no such thing: 'tis all *deceptio visus*[2]—
      [*aside*] Would I could get him away.

DAPPER [*within*]: Master Captain! Master Doctor!

LOVEWIT [*aside*]: Who's that?

FACE: Our clerk within, that I forgot! [*to Lovewit*] I know
      not, sir.

DAPPER [*within*]: For God's sake, when will her Grace be at leisure?

FACE: Ha!
      Illusions, some spirit o' the air!—[*aside.*] His gag is melted,
      And now he sets out the throat.

DAPPER [*within*]:   I am almost stifled—

FACE [*aside*]: Would you were altogether.

LOVEWIT: 'Tis in the house.
      Ha! list.

FACE: Believe it, sir, in the air.

LOVEWIT: Peace, you.

DAPPER [*within*]: Mine aunt's Grace does not use me well.

SUBTLE [*within*]:   You fool,
      Peace, you'll mar all.

FACE [*speaks through the key-hole, while Lovewit advances to the door unobserved*]:
                          Or you will else, you rogue.

LOVEWIT: O, is it so? Then you converse with spirits!—
      Come, sir. No more of your tricks, good Jeremy,
      The truth, the shortest way.

FACE: Dismiss this rabble, sir.—

75   What shall I do? I am catch'd. [*Aside.*]

LOVEWIT: Good neighbors,
      I thank you all. You may depart. [*Exeunt Neighbors.*]—Come, sir,
      You know that I am an indulgent master;
      And therefore conceal nothing. What's your medicine,

2. Optical illusion.

To draw so many several sorts of wild fowl?
FACE: Sir, you were wont to affect mirth and wit—
    But here's no place to talk on't in the street.
    Give me but leave to make the best of my fortune,
    And only pardon me the abuse of your house:
    It's all I beg. I'll help you to a widow,
85   In recompense, that you shall give me thanks for,
    Will make you seven years younger, and a rich one.
    'Tis but your putting on a Spanish cloak:
    I have her within. You need not fear the house;
    It was not visited.
LOVEWIT: But by me, who came
90   Sooner than you expected.
FACE: It is true, sir.
    'Pray you forgive me.
LOVEWIT: Well: let's see your widow.   [*Exeunt.*]

Scene 4—*A room in the same*
[*Enter Subtle, leading in Dapper, with his eyes bound as before.*]
SUBTLE: How! Ha' you eaten your gag?
DAPPER: Yes faith, it crumbled
    Away in my mouth.
SUBTLE: You ha' spoil'd all then.
DAPPER: No!
    I hope my aunt of Fairy will forgive me.
SUBTLE: Your aunt's a gracious lady; but in troth
5   You were to blame.
DAPPER: The fume did overcome me,
    And I did do't to stay my stomach. 'Pray you
    So satisfy her Grace.
[*Enter Face, in his uniform.*]
                Here comes the Captain
FACE: How now! Is his mouth down?°   open
SUBTLE: Ay, he has spoken!
FACE: A pox, I heard him, and you too.—He's undone then.—
10   I have been fain to say, the house is haunted
    With spirits, to keep churl° back.   country bumpkin
SUBTLE: And hast thou done it?
FACE: Sure, for this night.
SUBTLE: Why, then triumph and sing
    Of Face so famous, the precious king
    Of present wits.
FACE: Did you not hear the coil°   disturbance
15   About the door?
SUBTLE: Yes, and I dwindled with it.
FACE: Show him his aunt, and let him be dispatch'd:
    I'll send her to you.   [*Exit Face.*]
SUBTLE: Well, sir, your aunt her Grace
    Will give you audience presently,° on my suit,   at once

And the Captain's word that you did not eat your gag
20   In any contempt of her highness. [*Unbinds his eyes.*]
DAPPER: Not I, in troth, sir.
[*Enter Dol, like the Queen of Fairy.*]
SUBTLE: Here she is come. Down o' your knees and wriggle:
    She has a stately presence. [*Dapper kneels, and shuffles towards her.*]
                              Good! Yet nearer,
    And bid, God save you!
DAPPER: Madam!
SUBTLE: And your aunt.
DAPPER: And my most gracious aunt, God save your Grace.
DOL: Nephew, we thought to have been angry with you;
    But that sweet face of yours hath turn'd the tide,
    And made it flow with joy, that ebb'd of love.
    Arise, and touch our velvet gown.
SUBTLE: The skirts,
    And kiss 'em. So!
DOL: Let me now stroke that head.
30   Much, nephew, shall thou win, much shall thou spend,
    Much shall thou give away, much shall thou lend.
SUBTLE [*aside*]: Ay, much! indeed. [*aloud*] Why do you not thank her Grace?
DAPPER: I cannot speak for joy.
SUBTLE: See the kind wretch!
    Your Grace's kinsman right.
DOL: Give me the bird.3
35   Here is your fly in a purse, about your neck, cousin;
    Wear it, and feed it about this day sev'n-night,
    On your right wrist—
SUBTLE: Open a vein with a pin.
    And let it suck but once a week; till then,
    You must not look on't.
DOL: No: and kinsman,
40   Bear yourself worthy of the blood you come on.4
SUBTLE: Her grace would have you eat no more Woolsack pies.
    Nor Dagger frumety.5
DOL: Nor break his fast
    In Heaven and Hell.6
SUBTLE: She's with you everywhere!
    Nor play with costarmongers, at mum-chance, tray-trip,7
45   God make you rich;8 (when as your aunt has done it); but keep
    The gallant'st company, and the best games—
DAPPER: Yes, sir.
SUBTLE: Gleek and primero9: and what you get, be true to us.
DAPPER: By this hand, I will.

---

3. Familiar spirit, the "fly."
4. Are born from.
5. Woolsack and Dagger were London inns; "frumety," wheat boiled in milk sweetened with cinnamon and sugar.
6. Heaven and Hell are taverns near Westminster.
7. Dice games.
8. A type of backgammon.
9. Card games.

SUBTLE: You may bring's a thousand pound
           Before to-morrow night, if but three thousand
50   Be stirring,[1] an you will.
DAPPER: I swear I will then.
SUBTLE: Your fly will learn you all games.
FACE [*within*]:   Have you done there?
SUBTLE: Your Grace will command him no more duties?
DOL: No:
           But come, and see me often. I may chance
           To leave him three or four hundred chests of treasure,
55   And some twelve thousand acres of Fairyland,
           If he game well and comely with good gamesters.
SUBTLE: There's a kind aunt! Kiss her departing part.—
           But you must sell your forty mark a year, now.
DAPPER: Ay, sir, I mean.
SUBTLE: Or, give't away; pox on't!
DAPPER: I'll give't mine aunt: I'll go and fetch the writings.   [*Exit.*]
SUBTLE: 'Tis well—away!
           [*Re-enter Face.*]
FACE: Where's Subtle?
SUBTLE: Here: what news?
FACE: Drugger is at the door, go take his suit,
           And bid him fetch a parson, presently;
           Say, he shall marry the widow. Thou shalt spend
65   A hundred pound by the service! [*Exit Subtle.*] Now, queen Dol,
           Have you pack'd up all?
DOL: Yes.
FACE: And how do you like
           The Lady Pliant?
DOL: A good dull innocent.
           [*Re-enter Subtle.*]
SUBTLE: Here's your Hieronimo's cloak and hat.
FACE: Give me 'em.
SUBTLE: And the ruff too?
FACE: Yes; I'll come to you presently.   [*Exit.*]
SUBTLE: Now he is gone about his project, Dol,
           I told you of, for the widow.
DOL: 'Tis direct
           Against our articles.
SUBTLE: Well, we will fit him, wench.
           Hast thou gull'd her of her jewels or her bracelets?
DOL: No; but I will do't.
SUBTLE: Soon at night, my Dolly,
75   When we are shipp'd, and all our goods aboard,
           Eastward for Ratcliff; we will turn our course
           To Brainford, westward, if thou sayst the word,
           And take our leaves of this o'er-weening rascal,

---

1. If there are only 3,000 pounds to be gambled for.

          This peremptory Face.

DOL: Content, I'm weary of him.

SUBTLE: Thou'st cause, when the slave will run a wiving, Dol,
          Against the instrument that was drawn between us.

DOL: I'll pluck his bird as bare as I can.

SUBTLE: Yes, tell her,
          She must by any means address some present
          To the cunning man, make him amends for wronging

85   His art with her suspicion; send a ring
          Or chain of pearl; she will be tortured else
          Extremely in her sleep, say, and have strange things
          Come to her. Wilt thou?

DOL: Yes.

SUBTLE: My fine flitter-mouse,°   _bat_
          My bird o' the night! We'll tickle it at the Pigeons,[2]

90   When we have all, and may unlock the trunks,
          And say, this's mine, and thine; and thine, and mine. [_They kiss._]
     [_Re-enter Face._]

FACE: What now! a billing?

SUBTLE: Yes, a little exalted
          In the good passage of our stock-affairs.[3]

FACE: Drugger has brought his parson; take him in, Subtle,

95   And send Nab back again to wash his face,

SUBTLE: I will: and shave himself.   [_Exit._]

FACE: If you can get him.

DOL: You are hot upon it, Face, whate'er it is!

FACE: A trick that Dol shall spend ten pound a month by.
     [_Re-enter Subtle._]
          Is he gone?

SUBTLE: The chaplain waits you in the hall, sir.

FACE: I'll go bestow him.   [_Exit._]

DOL: He'll now marry her, instantly.

SUBTLE: He cannot yet, he is not ready. Dear Dol,
          Cozen her of all thou canst. To deceive him
          Is no deceit, but justice, that would break
          Such an inextricable tie as ours was.

DOL: Let me alone to fit him.
     [_Re-enter Face._]

FACE: Come, my venturers,
          You have pack'd up all? where be the trunks? Bring forth.

SUBTLE: Here.

FACE: Let us see 'em. Where's the money?

SUBTLE: Here,
          In this.

FACE: Mammon's ten pound; eight score before:
          The brethren's money, this. Drugger's and Dapper's.

---

2. To "tickle it," have fun, with sexual innuendo; the
Three Pigeons in Brentford marketplace.

3. Joint capital of the company.

110   What paper's that?
DOL: The jewel of the waiting-maid's,
         That stole it from her lady, to know certain—
FACE: If she should have precedence of her mistress?
DOL: Yes.
FACE: What box is that?
SUBTLE: The fish-wives' rings, I think,
         And the ale-wives' single money.⁴ Is't not, Dol?
DOL: Yes; and the whistle that the sailor's wife
         Brought you to know an her husband were with Ward.⁵
FACE: We'll wet it to-morrow; and our silver-beakers
         And tavern cups. Where be the French petticoats,
         And girdles and hangers?⁶
SUBTLE: Here, in the trunk,
120   And the bolts of lawn.
FACE: Is Drugger's damask there?
         And the tobacco?
SUBTLE: Yes.
FACE: Give me the keys.
DOL: Why you the keys?
SUBTLE: No matter, Dol; because
         We shall not open them before he comes.
FACE: 'Tis true, you shall not open them, indeed;
125   Nor have them forth, do you see? Not forth, Dol.
DOL: No?
FACE: No, my smock rampant.⁷ The right is, my master
         Knows all, has pardon'd me, and he will keep them;
         Doctor, 'tis true—you look—for all your figures:
         I sent for him indeed. Wherefore, good partners,
130   Both he and she be satisfied; for here
         Determines° the indenture tripartite   *ends*
         'Twixt Subtle, Dol, and Face. All I can do
         Is to help you over the wall, o' the back-side,
         Or lend you a sheet to save your velvet gown, Dol.
135   Here will be officers presently, bethink you
         Of some course suddenly to 'scape the dock:
         For thither you will come else. [*Loud knocking*] Hark you, thunder.
SUBTLE: You are a precious fiend!
OFFICER [*without*]:   Open the door.
FACE: Dol, I am sorry for thee, i'faith; but hear'st thou?
140   It shall go hard but I will place thee somewhere:
         Thou shalt have my letter to Mistress Amo⁸—
DOL: Hang you!

---

4. Small change.
5. A well-known pirate.
6. Hangers: loops on belts from which swords were hung.

7. Wild whore, applying the image of a rampant beast, standing on its hind legs and attacking, to Dol's sexuality.
8. "Mistress Amo" and "Madam Caesarean" were stock names for brothel keepers.

FACE: Or Madam Caesarean.

DOL: Pox upon you, rogue,
    Would I had but time to beat thee!

FACE: Subtle,
    Let's know where you set up next; I will send you
145   A customer now and then, for old acquaintance:
    What new course ha' you?

SUBTLE: Rogue, I'll hang myself;
    That I may walk a greater devil than thou,
    And haunt thee in the flock-bed and the buttery.[9]   [Exeunt.]

Scene 5—An outer room in the same

    [Enter Lovewit in the Spanish dress, with the Parson.]
    [Loud knocking at the door.]

LOVEWIT: What do you mean, my masters?

MAMMON [without]:   Open your door,
    Cheaters, bawds, conjurers.

OFFICER [without]:   Or we will break it open.

LOVEWIT: What warrant have you?

OFFICER [without]:   Warrant enough, sir, doubt not,
    If you'll not open it.

LOVEWIT: Is there an officer, there?

OFFICER [without]: Yes, two or three for failing.

LOVEWIT: Have but patience,
    And I will open it straight.
    [Enter Face, as butler.]

FACE: Sir, ha' you done?
    Is it a marriage? Perfect?

LOVEWIT: Yes, my brain.

FACE: Off with your ruff and cloak then; be yourself, sir.

SURLY [without]: Down with the door.

KASTRIL [without]:   'Slight, ding° it open.   break

LOVEWIT [opening the door]:   Hold,
10   Hold, gentlemen, what means this violence;
    [Mammon, Surly, Kastril, Ananias, Tribulation, and Officers, rush in.]

MAMMON: Where is this collier?[1]

SURLY: And my Captain Face?

MAMMON: These day owls.

SURLY: That are birding in men's purses.

MAMMON: Madam Suppository.[2]

KASTRIL: Doxy, my suster.

ANANIAS: Locusts
    Of the foul pit.

---

9. Flock-bed: mattress stuffed with cheap material; buttery: eating place.
1. The collier, or coal worker, like the alchemist, was associated with darkness and the devil.

2. "Suppository," refers to Dol's occupation as a prostitute but also to her fraudulent, or supposititious, study of medicine.

TRIBULATION: Profane as Bel and the Dragon.[3]

ANANIAS: Worse than the grasshoppers, or the lice of Egypt.[4]

LOVEWIT: Good gentlemen, hear me. Are you officers,
          And cannot stay this violence?

1 OFFICER: Keep the peace.

LOVEWIT: Gentlemen, what is the matter? whom do you seek?

MAMMON: The chemical cozener.

SURLY: And the Captain Pander.

KASTRIL: The nun my suster.[5]

MAMMON: Madam Rabbi.[6]

ANANIAS: Scorpions,
          And caterpillars.

LOVEWIT: Fewer at once, I pray you.

2 OFFICER: One after another, gentlemen, I charge you,
          By virtue of my staff.

ANANIAS: They are the vessels
          Of pride, lust, and the cart.

LOVEWIT: Good zeal, lie still
25   A little while.

TRIBULATION: Peace, Deacon Ananias.

LOVEWIT: The house is mine here, and the doors are open;
          If there be any such persons as you seek for,
          Use your authority, search on o' God's name.
          I am but newly come to town, and finding
30   This tumult 'bout my door, to tell you true,
          It somewhat mazed me; till my man, here, fearing
          My more displeasure, told me he had done
          Somewhat an insolent part, let out my house
          (Belike, presuming on my known aversion
35   From any air o' the town while there was sickness,)
          To a doctor and a captain: who, what they are
          Or where they be, he knows not.

MAMMON: Are they gone?

LOVEWIT: You may go in and search, sir. [*Mammon, Ananias, and Tribulation go in.*]
                              Here, I find
          The empty walls worse than I left them, smok'd.
40   A few crack'd pots, and glasses, and a furnace:
          The ceiling fill'd with poesies of the candle,[7]
          And madam with a dildo writ o' the walls:[8]
          Only one gentlewoman, I met here,
          That is within, that said she was a widow—

KASTRIL: Ay, that's my suster; I'll go thump her. Where is she?
          [*Goes in.*]

---

3. Idols worshipped by the Babylonians referred to in one of the apocryphal books of the Old Testament.

4. Two of the plagues inflicted upon the Egyptians in Exodus 7–12.

5. Ironic term for a prostitute.

6. A reference to Dol's Puritan rantings in 4.5.1–32.

7. Words written with candle smoke.

8. Drawing of a woman playing with a dildo (phallus) on the walls.

LOVEWIT: And should have married a Spanish count, but he,
        When he came to't, neglected her so grossly,
        That I, a widower, am gone through° with her.   *married*
SURLY: How! have I lost her then?
LOVEWIT: Were you the Don, sir?
50   Good faith, now, she does blame y' extremely, and says
        You swore, and told her you had taken the pains
        To dye your beard, and umber o'er your face,
        Borrowed a suit, and ruff, all for her love;
        And then did nothing. What an oversight,
55   And want of putting forward, sir, was this!
        Well fare an old harquebusier,⁹ yet,
        Could prime his powder, and give fire, and hit,
        All in a twinkling!
        [*Re-enter Mammon.*]
MAMMON: The whole nest are fled!
LOVEWIT: What sort of birds were they?
MAMMON: A kind of choughs,¹
60   Or thievish daws, sir, that have pick'd my purse
        Of eight score and ten pounds within these five weeks,
        Beside my first materials; and my goods,
        That lie in the cellar, which I am glad they have left,
        I may have home yet.
LOVEWIT: Think you so, sir?
MAMMON: Ay.
LOVEWIT: By order of law, sir, but not otherwise.
MAMMON: Not mine own stuff!
LOVEWIT: Sir, I can take no knowledge
        That they are yours, but by public means.
        If you can bring certificate that you were gull'd of 'em,
        Or any formal writ out of a court
70   That you did cozen yourself, I will not hold them.
MAMMON: I'll rather lose 'em.
LOVEWIT: That you shall not, sir,
        By me, in troth. Upon these terms, they are yours.
        What! should they have been, sir, turn'd into gold, all?
MAMMON: No,
        I cannot tell—It may be they should—What then?
LOVEWIT: What a great loss in hope have you sustain'd!
MAMMON: Not I, the commonwealth has.
FACE: Ay, he would ha' built
        The city new; and made a ditch about it.
        Of silver, should have run with cream from Hogsden;
        That, every Sunday, in Moorfields, the younkers,
80   And tits and tom-boys² should have fed on, gratis.
MAMMON: I will go mount a turnip-cart, and preach

___

9. A soldier armed with a harquebus, or handgun.
1. Pronounced "chuffs," type of crows.

2. Younkers, and tits and tom-boys: adolescent boys and
girls.

The end of the world, within these two months, Surly,
What! in a dream?

SURLY: Must I needs cheat myself,
With that same foolish vice of honesty!

85 Come, let us go and hearken out the rogues:
That Face I'll mark for mine, if e'er I meet him.

FACE: If I can hear of him, sir, I'll bring you word,
Unto your lodging; for in troth, they were strangers
To me, I thought them honest as myself, sir.

[Exeunt Mammon and Surly.]

[Re-enter Ananias and Tribulation.]

TRIBULATION: 'Tis well, the saints shall not lose all yet. Go,
And get some carts—

LOVEWIT: For what, my zealous friends?

ANANIAS: To bear away the portion of the righteous
Out of this den of thieves.

LOVEWIT: What is that portion?

ANANIAS: The goods sometimes the orphans', that the brethren
95 Bought with their silver pence.

LOVEWIT: What, those i' the cellar,
The knight sir Mammon claims?

ANANIAS: I do defy
The wicked Mammon, so do all the brethren,
Thou profane man! I ask thee with what conscience
Thou canst advance that idol against us,
100 That have the seal?[3] Were not the shillings number'd,
That made the pounds; were not the pounds told out,
Upon the second day of the fourth week,
In the eighth month, upon the table dormant,[4]
The year of the last patience of the saints,
105 Six hundred and ten?[5]

LOVEWIT: Mine earnest vehement botcher,
And deacon also, I cannot dispute with you:
But if you get you not away the sooner,
I shall confute you with a cudgel.

ANANIAS: Sir!

TRIBULATION: Be patient, Ananias.

ANANIAS: I am strong,
110 And will stand up, well girt, against an host
That threaten Gad in exile.[6]

LOVEWIT: I shall send you
To Amsterdam, to your cellar.

ANANIAS: I will pray there,
Against thy house: may dogs defile thy walls,

3. Those with the seal are God's chosen (Revelation 9.4).
4. Permanent side-table.
5. I.e., 1610. The "year of the last patience of the saints"

refers to the millennium, when the end of the world was
supposed to occur.
6. An allegorical reference to the exiled Anabaptists; see
Genesis 49.19.

And wasps and hornets breed beneath thy roof,
115   This seat of falsehood, and this cave of cozenage!

[*Exeunt Ananias and Tribulation.*]

[*Enter Drugger.*]

LOVEWIT: Another too?

DRUGGER: Not I, sir, I am no brother.

LOVEWIT [*beats him*]: Away, you Harry Nicholas![7] do you talk?

[*Exit Drugger.*]

FACE: No, this was Abel Drugger. Good sir, go.

[*To the Parson.*]

And satisfy him; tell him all is done:
120   He staid too long a washing of his face.
The Doctor, he shall hear of him at Westchester,
And of the Captain, tell him, at Yarmouth, or
Some good port-town else, lying for a wind.   [*Exit Parson.*]
If you can get off the angry child, now, sir—

[*Enter Kastril, dragging in his sister.*]

KASTRIL: Come on, you ewe, you have match'd most sweetly, ha' you not?
Did not I say, I would never ha' you tupp'd°   *mated with*
But by a dubb'd boy,° to make you a lady-tom?   *knight*
'Slight, you are a mammet! O, I could touse you, now.[8]
Death, mun' you marry, with a pox!

LOVEWIT: You lie, boy;
130   As sound as you; and I'm aforehand with you.

KASTRIL: Anon!

LOVEWIT: Come, will you quarrel? I will feize° you, sirrah;   *beat*
Why do you not buckle to your tools?

KASTRIL: God's light,
This is a fine old boy as e'er I saw!

LOVEWIT: What, do you change your copy[9] now? Proceed,
135   Here stands my dove: stoop at her, if you dare.[1]

KASTRIL: 'Slight, I must love him! I cannot choose, i' faith,
An I should be hang'd for't! Suster, I protest,
I honor thee for this match.

LOVEWIT: O, do you so, sir?

KASTRIL: Yes, an thou canst take tobacco and drink, old boy,
140   I'll give her five hundred pound more to her marriage,
Than her own state.

LOVEWIT: Fill a pipe-full, Jeremy.

FACE: Yes; but go in and take it, sir.

LOVEWIT: We will—
I will be ruled by thee in any thing. Jeremy.

KASTRIL: 'Slight, thou art not hide-bound, thou art a jovy° boy!   *jovial*
145   Come, let us in. I pray thee, and take our whiffs.

---

7. Hendrick Niclaes was an Anabaptist and leader of the
Family of Love, a sect outlawed by Elizabeth I in 1580.
8. Mammet: puppet; touse: beat, tousle.
9. Change your tune.

1. The "dove" may be Dame Pliant as well as his sword;
stoop at her: attack her, a term from falconry. Kastril's
name comes from kestrel, a small hawk.

LOVEWIT: Whiff in with your sister, brother boy. [*Exeunt Kastril and Dame Pliant.*]
That master

That had received such happiness by a servant,
In such a widow, and with so much wealth,
Were very ungrateful, if he would not be
150   A little indulgent to that servant's wit,
And help his fortune, though with some small strain
Of his own candour. [*advancing*]—Therefore, gentlemen,
And kind spectators, if I have outstript
An old man's gravity, or strict canon,[2] think
155   What a young wife and a good brain may do;
Stretch age's truth sometimes, and crack it too.
Speak for thy self, knave.
FACE: So I will. sir. [*advancing to the front of the stage*]
Gentlemen,

My part a little fell in this last scene,
Yet 'twas decorum.[3] And though I am clean
160   Got off from Subtle, Surly, Mammon, Dol,
Hot Ananias, Dapper, Drugger, all
With whom I traded: yet I put my self
On you, that are my country:[4] and this pelf°   loot
Which I have got, if you do quit° me, rests   acquit
165   To feast you often, and invite new guests.

[Exeunt.]

On Something, That Walks Somewhere[1]

At court I met it, in clothes brave° enough   showy
    To be a courtier, and looks grave enough
To seem a statesman. As I near it came,
    It made me a great face; I asked the name.
5   "A lord," it cried, "buried in flesh, and blood,
    And such from whom let no man hope least good,
For I will do none; and as little ill,
    For I will dare none." Good lord, walk dead still.

On My First Daughter[1]

Here lies to each her parents' ruth,°   grief
Mary, the daughter of their youth;
Yet, all heaven's gifts, being heaven's due,
It makes the father less to rue.
5   At six months' end, she parted hence
With safety of her innocence;

---

2. Rule of behavior.
3. Decorum is the sense of consistency of character. Love-wit has just defended his own behavior that was inconsistent with the character of an old man.
4. Appeal to my countrymen's judgment, as to a jury.

1. This and the following four poems were all first printed in the collected *Works* of 1616 under the heading "Epigrams." An epigram is a short, witty poem of invective or satire. Jonson's "Epigrams" include epitaphs, poems of praise, and verse letters.
1. Probably written in the late 1590s.

Whose soul heaven's Queen (whose name she bears),
In comfort of her mother's tears,
Hath placed amongst her virgin-train;
10   Where, while that severed doth remain,
This grave partakes the fleshly birth;[2]
Which cover lightly, gentle earth.

To John Donne

Donne, the delight of Phoebus,[1] and each Muse,
    Who, to thy one, all other brains refuse;[2]
Whose every work, of thy most early wit
    Came forth example, and remains so, yet;
5   Longer a-knowing than most wits do live;
    And which no affection praise enough can give!
To it,[3] thy language, letters, arts, best life,
    Which might with half mankind maintain a strife;
All which I meant to praise, and, yet, I would,
10   But leave, because I cannot as I should.

On My First Son[1]

Farewell, thou child of my right hand,[2] and joy;
    My sin was too much hope of thee, loved boy.
Seven years thou wert lent to me, and I thee pay,
    Exacted by thy fate, on the just day.
5   O, could I lose all father, now![3] For why
    Will man lament the state he should envy?
To have so soon 'scaped world's and flesh's rage,
    And, if no other misery, yet age?
Rest in soft peace, and, asked, say, "Here doth lie
10   Ben Jonson his best piece of poetry."
For whose sake, henceforth, all his vows be such,
    As what he loves may never like too much.[4]

Inviting a Friend to Supper[1]

Tonight, grave sir, both my poor house and I
    Do equally desire your company:
Not that we think us worthy such a guest,
    But that your worth will dignify our feast
5   With those that come; whose grace may make that seem
    Something, which else could hope for no esteem.

2. While the soul is in heaven, the grave holds the body.
1. God of poetry.
2. The Muses give the inspiration to your brain that they deny to others.
3. In addition to your wit.
1. Benjamin, who died of the plague on his birthday in 1603.

2. In Hebrew, Benjamin means "son of the right hand; dexterous, fortunate."
3. Let go of fatherly feeling.
4. "If you wish . . . to beware of sorrows that gnaw the heart, to no man make yourself too much a comrade" (Martial 12.34, lines 8–11).
1. Based on three poems of invitation by the Roman poet Martial, 11.52, 5.78, and 10.48.

It is the fair acceptance, Sir, creates
　　The entertainment perfect, not the cates.°   *food*
Yet shall you have, to rectify your palate,
10   An olive, capers, or some better salad
Ushering the mutton; with a short-legged hen
　　If we can get her, full of eggs, and then
Lemons, and wine for sauce: to these, a coney°   *rabbit*
　　Is not to be despaired of, for our money;
15 And though fowl now be scarce, yet there are clerks,°   *scholars*
　　The sky not falling, think we may have larks.
I'll tell you of more, and lie, so you will come:
　　Of partridge, pheasant, woodcock, of which some
May yet be there; and godwit, if we can;
20   Knat, rail, and ruff,° too. Howsoe'er, my man   *gamebirds*
Shall read a piece of Virgil, Tacitus,
　　Livy, or of some better book to us,
Of which we'll speak our minds, amidst our meat;
　　And I'll profess no verses to repeat;
25 To this, if aught appear, which I not know of,
　　That will the pastry, not my paper, show of.[2]
Digestive cheese and fruit there sure will be;
　　But that, which most doth take my muse and me,
Is a pure cup of rich Canary wine,
30   Which is the Mermaid's,[3] now, but shall be mine:
Of which had Horace, or Anacreon tasted,
　　Their lives, as do their lines, till now had lasted.[4]
Tobacco, nectar, or the Thespian spring
　　Are all but Luther's beer to this I sing.[5]
35 Of this we will sup free, but moderately,
　　And we will have no Poley, or Parrot by;[6]
Nor shall our cups make any guilty men,
　　But, at our parting, we will be, as when
We innocently met. No simple word
40   That shall be uttered at our mirthful board
Shall make us sad next morning, or affright
　　The liberty, that we'll enjoy tonight.

To Penshurst[1]

Thou art not, Penshurst, built to envious show
　　Of touch,° or marble; nor canst boast a row   *black marble*
　　Of polished pillars, or a roof of gold;

---

2. Add to this that if there is any paper, it will only be that used to keep the pastry from sticking to the pan.
3. A famous tavern in Cheapside, London.
4. Horace praised wine in Latin verse, as did Anacreon in Greek.
5. The Thespian spring, inspiration of poetry, and all these things are but Luther's beer in comparison with Canary.
6. Government spies; talkative birds.

1. First published in the 1616 *Works* in *The Forest*, a title inspired by the Latin *silva* (timber), suggesting raw materials to be worked, used by classical authors for an improvised collection of poems. Penshurst was the Sidney family's house in Kent since 1552, the "great lord" (line 91) of which was Robert Sidney, Baron Sidney of Penshurst and Viscount of Lille, younger brother of Sir Philip Sidney.

Thou hast no lantern,° whereof tales are told,   *turret*
5   Or stair, or courts; but stand'st an ancient pile,[2]
    And these grudged at, art reverenced the while.
Thou joy'st in better marks, of soil, of air,
    Of wood, of water; therein thou art fair.
Thou hast thy walks for health, as well as sport:
10   Thy mount to which the dryads° do resort,   *wood nymphs*
Where Pan, and Bacchus their high feasts have made,[3]
    Beneath the broad beech and the chestnut shade;
That taller tree, which of a nut was set
    At his great birth, where all the Muses met.
15   There, in the writhèd bark, are cut the names
    Of many a sylvan,° taken with his flames;   *wood sprite*
And thence, the ruddy satyrs oft provoke
    The lighter fauns, to reach thy Lady's oak.[4]
Thy copse,° too, named of Gamage, thou hast there,   *a small wood*
20   That never fails to serve thee seasoned deer
When thou wouldst feast, or exercise thy friends.
    The lower land, that to the river bends,
Thy sheep, thy bullocks, kine° and calves do feed;   *cows*
    The middle grounds thy mares and horses breed.
25   Each bank doth yield thee conies,° and the tops   *rabbits*
    Fertile of wood, Ashour and Sydney's copse,
To crown thy open table, doth provide
    The purpled pheasant with the speckled side;
The painted partridge lies in every field,
30   And, for thy mess, is willing to be killed.
And if the high-swoll'n Medway[5] fail thy dish,
    Thou hast thy ponds, that pay thee tribute fish:
Fat, agèd carps, that run into thy net.
    And pikes, now weary their own kind to eat,
35   As loath, the second draught, or cast to stay,
    Officiously, at first, themselves betray;
Bright eels, that emulate them, and leap on land
    Before the fisher, or into his hand.
Then hath thy orchard fruit, thy garden flowers,
40   Fresh as the air, and new as are the hours.
The early cherry, with the later plum,
    Fig, grape, and quince, each in his time doth come;
The blushing apricot and woolly peach
    Hang on thy walls, that every child may reach.
45   And though thy walls be of the country stone,
    They're reared with no man's ruin, no man's groan;
There's none, that dwell about them, wish them down;
    But all come in, the farmer, and the clown,°   *peasant*

2. The castle was built in 1340.
3. Pan was the god of forest, field, and pasture; Bacchus was the god of wine.
4. In Greek mythology the satyr with a man's body and a goat's legs was devoted to lechery. Robert Sidney's wife Barbara Gamage was said to have given birth under this oak.
5. The local river.

And no one empty-handed, to salute
50   Thy lord and lady, though they have no suit.
Some bring a capon, some a rural cake,
        Some nuts, some apples; some that think they make
The better cheeses, bring 'em; or else send
        By their ripe daughters, whom they would commend
55 This way to husbands; and whose baskets bear
        An emblem of themselves in plum, or pear.
But what can this (more than express their love)
        Add to thy free provisions, far above
The need of such? whose liberal board doth flow
60   With all that hospitality doth know!
Where comes no guest, but is allowed to eat
        Without his fear, and of thy lord's own meat;
Where the same beer, and bread, and self-same wine
        That is his lordship's shall be also mine,
65 And I not fain to sit (as some this day
        At great men's tables) and yet dine away.
Here no man tells my cups; nor, standing by,
        A waiter, doth my gluttony envy,
But gives me what I call, and lets me eat;
70   He knows below he shall find plenty of meat,
Thy tables hoard not up for the next day.
        Nor, when I take my lodging, need I pray
For fire, or lights, or livery:° all is there,   *provisions, food*
        As if thou then wert mine, or I reigned here;
75 There's nothing I can wish, for which I stay.
        That found King James, when, hunting late this way
With his brave son, the Prince, they saw thy fires
        Shine bright on every hearth as the desires
Of thy Penates[6] had been set on flame
80   To entertain them; or the country came,
With all their zeal, to warm their welcome here.
        What (great, I will not say, but) sudden cheer
Didst thou, then, make 'em! and what praise was heaped
        On thy good lady, then, who therein reaped
85 The just reward of her high housewifery;
        To have her linen, plate, and all things nigh,
When she was far, and not a room, but dressed
        As if it had expected such a guest!
These, Penshurst, are thy praise, and yet not all.
90   Thy lady's noble, fruitful, chaste withall.
His children thy great lord may call his own,
        A fortune, in this age, but rarely known.
They are, and have been, taught religion; thence
        Their gentler spirits have sucked innocence.
95 Each morn and even, they are taught to pray,

6. Household gods.

With the whole household, and may every day
Read in their virtuous parents' noble parts
   The mysteries of manners, arms, and arts.
Now, Penshurst, they that will proportion° thee   *compare*
100   With other edifices, when they see
Those proud, ambitious heaps, and nothing else,
   May say, their lords have built, but thy lord dwells.

Song to Celia

Drink to me only with thine eyes,
   And I will pledge with mine;
Or leave a kiss but in the cup,
   And I'll not look for wine.
5   The thirst that from the soul doth rise
   Doth ask a drink divine;
But might I of Jove's nectar sup,
   I would not change for thine.
I sent thee late a rosy wreath,
10   Not so much honoring thee
As giving it a hope that there
   It could not withered be.
But thou thereon didst only breathe,
   And sent'st it back on me;
15 Since when it grows, and smells, I swear,
   Not of itself, but thee.

Queen and Huntress[1]

Queen and huntress, chaste and fair,
Now the sun is laid to sleep,
Seated in thy silver chair,
State in wonted manner keep;
5   Hesperus° entreats thy light,   *the evening star*
   Goddess excellently bright.

Earth, let not thy envious shade
Dare itself to interpose;
Cynthia's shining orb was made
10 Heaven to clear, when day did close.
   Bless us then with wishèd sight,
   Goddess excellently bright.

Lay thy bow of pearl apart,
And thy crystal-shining quiver;
15 Give unto the flying hart
Space to breathe, how short soever.
   Thou that mak'st a day of night,
   Goddess excellently bright.

1. From *Cynthia's Revels*, 5.6.1–18. Cynthia, another name for Diana, goddess of the moon and the hunt, and of chastity, an image associated with Queen Elizabeth.

To the Memory of My Beloved, the Author, Mr. William Shakespeare, and What He Hath Left Us[1]

To draw no envy, Shakespeare, on thy name,
    Am I thus ample[2] to thy book and fame,
While I confess thy writings to be such,
    As neither man nor muse can praise too much.
5   'Tis true, and all men's suffrage. But these ways
    Were not the paths I meant unto thy praise;
For silliest ignorance on these may light,
    Which, when it sounds at best, but echoes right;
Or blind affection, which doth ne'er advance
10   The truth, but gropes, and urgeth all by chance;
Or crafty malice, might pretend this praise,
    And think to ruin, where it seemed to raise.
These are as some infamous bawd or whore
    Should praise a matron. What could hurt her more?
15 But thou art proof against them, and indeed
    Above the ill fortune of them, or the need.
I, therefore will begin. Soul of the age!
    The applause! delight! the wonder of our stage!
My Shakespeare, rise; I will not lodge thee by
20   Chaucer, or Spenser, or bid Beaumont lie
A little further, to make thee a room;[3]
    Thou art a monument without a tomb,
And art alive still while thy book doth live,
    And we have wits to read, and praise to give.
25 That I not mix thee so, my brain excuses,
    I mean with great, but disproportioned, Muses;
For, if I thought my judgment were of years,
    I should commit thee surely with thy peers,
And tell how far thou didst our Lyly outshine,
30   Or sporting Kyd, or Marlowe's mighty line.[4]
And though thou hadst small Latin, and less Greek,
    From thence to honor thee, I would not seek
For names, but call forth thundering Aeschylus,
    Euripides, and Sophocles to us,
35 Pacuvius, Accius, him of Cordova dead,
    To life again, to hear thy buskin[5] tread
And shake a stage; or, when thy socks[6] were on,
    Leave thee alone for the comparison

---

1. Prefixed to the first folio of Shakespeare's plays (1623).
2. From Latin *amplus*: copious; an *amplus orator* was one who spoke richly and with dignity.
3. Chaucer, Spenser, and Francis Beaumont were buried in Westminster Abbey; Shakespeare was buried in Stratford.
4. Lyly was an author of English prose comedies; Kyd and Marlowe were authors of English verse tragedies.
5. Boot worn by tragic actors. Jonson compares Shakespeare to tragedians of ancient Greece (Aeschylus, Euripides, Sophocles) and Rome (Pacuvius, Accius, and "him of Cordova," Seneca).
6. Symbols of comedy.

Of all that insolent Greece or haughty Rome
40   Sent forth, or since did from their ashes come.
Triumph, my Britain; thou hast one to show
    To whom all scenes of Europe homage owe.
He was not of an age, but for all time!
    And all the muses still were in their prime
45 When like Apollo he came forth to warm
    Our ears, or like a Mercury to charm![7]
Nature herself was proud of his designs,
    And joyed to wear the dressing of his lines,
Which were so richly spun, and woven so fit
50   As, since, she will vouchsafe no other wit.
The merry Greek, tart Aristophanes,
    Neat Terence, witty Plautus,[8] now not please,
But antiquated, and deserted lie,
    As they were not of nature's family.
55 Yet must I not give nature all; thy art,
    My gentle Shakespeare, must enjoy a part.
For though the poet's matter nature be,
    His art doth give the fashion. And that he
Who casts to write a living line must sweat
60   (Such as thine are) and strike the second heat
Upon the Muses' anvil: turn the same,
    And himself with it, that he thinks to frame;[9]
Or for the laurel, he may gain a scorn;
    For a good poet's made as well as born.
65 And such wert thou! Look how the father's face
    Lives in his issue; even so, the race
Of Shakespeare's mind and manners brightly shines
    In his well-turnèd, and true-filèd lines:
In each of which he seems to shake a lance,[1]
70   As brandished at the eyes of ignorance.
Sweet Swan of Avon, what a sight it were
    To see thee in our waters yet appear,
And make those flights upon the banks of Thames,
    That so did take Eliza, and our James![2]
75 But stay, I see thee in the hemisphere
    Advanced, and made a constellation there!
Shine forth, thou star of poets, and with rage
    Or influence chide or cheer the drooping stage,[3]
Which, since thy flight from hence, hath mourned like night,
80   And despairs day, but for thy volume's light.

---

7. Apollo and Mercury were the gods of poetry and eloquence.
8. Aristophanes was an ancient Greek comic playwright; Terence and Plautus were authors of Roman comedy.
9. See Horace, *Ars Poetica* 441: "return the ill-tuned verses to the anvil."

1. Pun on "Shake-speare."
2. Queen Elizabeth and King James.
3. Like an ancient hero, Shakespeare is given a place among the stars; as the "rage" and "influence" of the planets affect life on earth, Shakespeare affects the world of the stage.

To the Immortal Memory, and Friendship of that Noble Pair, Sir Lucius Cary and Sir H. Morison[1]

The Turn[2]

Brave infant of Saguntum, clear
Thy coming forth in that great year,
When the prodigious Hannibal did crown
His rage with razing your immortal town.[3]
5   Thou, looking then about,
Ere thou wert half got out,
Wise child, didst hastily return,
And mad'st thy mother's womb thine urn.
How summed° a circle[4] didst thou leave mankind   *complete*
10   Of deepest lore, could we the center find!

The Counter-Turn

Did wiser nature draw thee back
From out the horror of that sack,
Where shame, faith, honor, and regard of right
Lay trampled on?—the deeds of death, and night,
10   Urged, hurried forth, and hurled
Upon th'affrighted world?
Sword, fire, and famine, with fell fury met;
And all on utmost ruin set;
As, could they but life's miseries foresee,
20   No doubt all infants would return like thee.

The Stand

For, what is life, if measured by the space,
Not by the act?
Or maskèd man, if valued by his face,
Above his fact?°   *deeds*
25   Here's one outlived his peers
And told forth fourescore years;
He vexèd time, and busied the whole state;
Troubled both foes, and friends,
But ever to no ends:
30   What did this stirrer, but die late?
How well at twenty had he fallen, or stood!
For three of his fourescore, he did no good.

---

1. Sir Lucius Cary (1610?–1643), second Viscount Falkland, son of Elizabeth Cary (author of *The Tragedy of Mariam*). He befriended Jonson whose wrote an elegy on his death. Sir Henry Morison (or Moryson), son of Sir Richard Morison and nephew of the travel writer Fynes Morison, see page 1174 died on or near his twenty-first birthday.
2. "Turn," "counter-turn," and "stand" represent the Greek "strophe," "antistrophe," and "epode." Jonson's poem is the first Great Ode in English. Often in the form of an address, the ode is a dignified lyric poem, in commemoration of a person, occasion, or theme. The Greek poet Pindar wrote odes praising winners of the Olympics. His odes were sung by a chorus in a three-part scheme, which Jonson imitates here.
3. Pliny, *History* 7.3.40–42: "an infant of Saguntum . . . at once went back into the womb in the year in which the city was destroyed by Hannibal" (the great Carthaginian general in the Second Punic War).
4. Emblem of perfection.

The Turn

He entered well by virtuous parts,
Got up and thrived with honest arts:
35 He purchased friends, and fame, and honors then,
And had his noble name advanced with men:
But weary of that flight,
He stooped in all men's sight!
To sordid flatteries, acts of strife,
40 And sunk in that dead sea of life
So deep, as he did then death's waters sup;
But that the cork of title buoyed him up.

The Counter-Turn

Alas, but Morison fell young!
He never fell: thou fall'st,[5] my tongue.
45 He stood, a soldier to the last right end,
A perfect patriot, and a noble friend,
But most, a virtuous son.
All offices were done
By him, so ample, full, and round,
50 In weight, in measure, number, sound,
As, though his age imperfect might appear,
His life was of humanity the sphere.

The Stand

Go now, and tell out days summed up with fears;
And make them years;
55 Produce thy mass of miseries on the stage,
To swell thine age;
Repeat of things a throng,
To show thou hast been long,
Not lived; for life doth her great actions spell
60 By what was done and wrought
In season, and so brought
To light: her measures are, how well
Each syllabe° answered, and was formed, how fair;   *syllable*
These make the lines of life, and that's her air.

The Turn

65 It is not growing like a tree
In bulk, doth make man better be;
Or standing long an oak, three hundred year,
To fall a log at last, dry, bald, and sere:
A lily of a day
70 Is fairer far, in May,
Although it fall and die that night;
It was the plant and flower of light.

5. Slip, with a pun on the Latin *fallere*, to deceive, to be mistaken.

In small proportions, we just beauty see,
And in short measures life may perfect be.

The Counter-Turn

75 Call, noble Lucius, then for wine,
And let thy looks with gladness shine;
Accept this garland,[6] plant it on thy head;
And think, nay know, thy Morison's not dead.
He leaped the present age,
80 Possessed with holy rage,
To see that bright eternal day,
Of which we priests, and poets say
Such truths, as we expect for happy men,
And there he lives with memory, and Ben

The Stand

85 Jonson, who sung this of him, ere he went
Himself to rest,
Or taste a part of that full joy he meant
To have expressed
In this bright asterism;°   *constellation*
90 Where it were friendship's schism
(Were not his Lucius long with us to tarry)
To separate these twi-
Lights, the Dioscuri;[7]
And keep the one half from his Harry.
95 But fate doth so alternate the design,
Whilst that in heaven, this light on earth must shine.

The Turn

And shine as you exalted are;
Two names of friendship, but one star:
Of hearts the union. And those not by chance
100 Made, or indentured,° or leased out t' advance   *contracted for*
The profits for a time.
No pleasures vain did chime,
Of rhymes, or riots, at your feasts,
Orgies of drink, or feigned protests;
105 But simple love of greatness, and of good;
That knits brave minds, and manners, more than blood.

The Counter-Turn

This made you first to know the why
You liked; then after, to apply
That liking; and approach so one the t'other,

---

6. The poem itself.
7. "Twin lights:" the mythical Greek brothers, Castor and Pollux. After Castor's death the twin brothers exchanged places on earth and in the underworld at regular intervals.

110　　　Till either grew a portion of the other:
　　　　Each stylèd, by his end,
　　　　The copy of his friend.
　　　　You lived to be the great surnames
　　　　And titles by which all made claims
115　　　Unto the virtue. Nothing perfect done,
　　　　But as a Cary, or a Morison.

The Stand

　　　　And such a force the fair example had,
　　　　As they that saw
　　　　The good, and durst not practise it, were glad
120　　　That such a law
　　　　Was left yet to mankind;
　　　　Where they might read, and find
　　　　Friendship in deed was written, not in words.
　　　　And with the heart, not pen,
125　　　Of two so early° men,   *youthful*
　　　　Whose lines her rolls were, and records.
　　　　Who, ere the first down bloomèd on the chin,
　　　　Had sowed these fruits, and got the harvest in.

Pleasure Reconciled to Virtue
A Masque as It Was Presented at Court Before King James. 1618.[1]

The Scene was the Mountain Atlas, who had his top ending in the figure of an old man, his head and beard all hoary and frost, as if his shoulders were covered with snow; the rest wood and rock. A grove of ivy at his feet, out of which, to a wild music of cymbals, flutes, and tabors, is brought forth Comus,[2] the god of cheer or the belly, riding in triumph, his head crowned with roses and other flowers, his hair curled; they that wait upon him, crowned with ivy, their javelins done about with it; one of them going with Hercules' bowl[3] bare before him, while the rest presented him, with this

Hymn

　　　　Room, room, make room for the bouncing belly,
　　　　First father of sauce and deviser of jelly,
　　　　Prime master of arts, and the giver of wit,
　　　　That found out the excellent engine, the spit,
5　　　　The plough and the flail, the mill, and the hopper,
　　　　The hutch, and the bolter, the furnace and copper.
　　　　The oven, the bavin, the mawkin, and peel,
　　　　The hearth and the range, the dog and the wheel.[4]

---

1. A masque was an entertainment performed by members of the court that included elaborate sets, dance, music, and poetry. Designed to compliment the monarch, the masque portrayed him as an ideal ruler in a moral allegory. The myth on which this masque is based in the story of Hercules' choice between pleasure and virtue, in which King James is represented as harmonizing voluptuous enjoyment and right action.
2. Allied with Dionysus, the god of wine, Comus is the god of sensual excess.

3. Hercules used the bowl that the Sun gave him as a sailing ship.
4. Flail: tool for threshing corn; mill: apparatus for grinding grain; hopper: a cone through which grain is conveyed to the mill; hutch: a box for sifting grain; bolter: a sieve; bavin: bundle of light wood used in bakers' oven; mawkin: mop for cleaning a baker's oven; peel: a baker's shovel. A dog connected to a wheel turned the roasting spit.

He, he first invented both hogshead° and tun,°   *cask / barrel*
10   The gimlet and vice, too, taught them to run.[5]
        And since, with the funnel, an Hippocras bag
        He's made of himself, that now he cries swag.[6]
        Which shows, though the pleasure be but of four inches,
        Yet he is a weezle, the gullet° that pinches,   *throat*
15   Of any delight, and not spares from the back
        Whatever, to make of the belly a sack.
        Hail, hail, plump paunch! O the founder of taste
        For fresh meats, or powdered, or pickle, or paste;
        Devourer of broiled, baked, roasted, or sod,°   *boiled*
20   And emptier of cups, be they even, or odd;
        All which have now made thee, so wide i' the waist
        As scarce with no pudding thou art to be laced;
        But eating and drinking, until thou dost nod,
        Thou break'st all thy girdles, and break'st forth[7] a god.

To this, the Bowl-bearer

Do you hear, my friends, to whom do you sing all this now? Pardon me only that I ask you, for I do not look for an answer; I'll answer myself. I know it is now such a time as the Saturnals[8] for all the world, that every man stands under the eaves of his own hat and sings what pleases him; that's the right and the liberty of it. Now you sing of god Comus here, the Belly-god. I say it is well, and I say it is not well. It is well, as it is a ballad, and the belly worthy of it I must needs say, and 'twere forty yards of ballad, more—as much ballad as tripe.[9] But when the belly is not edified by it, it is not well; for where did you ever read, or hear, that the belly had any ears? Come, never pump for an answer, for you are defeated. Our fellow Hunger there, that was as ancient a retainer to the belly as any of us, was turned away, for being unseasonable—not unreasonable, but unseasonable—and now is he (poor thin-gut) fain to get his living with teaching of starlings, magpies, parrots, and jackdaws, those things he would have taught the belly. Beware of dealing with the Belly; the Belly will not be talked to, especially when he is full. Then there is no venturing upon Venter,[1] then he will blow you all up; he will thunder, indeed la; some in derision call him the father of farts. But I say, he was the first inventor of great ordinance,[2] and taught us to discharge them on festival days. Would we had a fit feast for him i' faith, to show his activity. I would have something now fetched in now to please his five senses, the throat; or the two senses, the eyes. Pardon me, for my two senses; for I that carry Hercules' bowl[3] in the service may see double by my place, for I have drunk like a frog today. I would have a tun[4] now, brought in to dance, and so many bottles about him. Ha? You look as if you would make a problem of this. Do you see? a problem: why bottles? and why a tun? and why a tun? and why bottles to dance? I say that men that drink hard and serve the belly in any place of quality (as *The Jovial Tinkers*, or *The Lusty Kindred*)[5] are

---

5. The gimlet and vice were used to tap the cask.
6. A Hippocras bag was a strainer for wine. To "cry swag" was to let out a hanging belly.
7. With a double meaning of fart.
8. The Roman Saturnalia was a wild festival at the end of the year, similar to Twelfth Night, part of the English Christmas season, at the celebration of which this

masque was performed.
9. Edible animal intestines, and also the human stomach.
1. Belly (Latin).
2. Artillery.
3. "To carry Hercules' bowl" means to drink heavily.
4. Keg.
5. Taverns.

living measures of drink, and can transform themselves, and do every day, to bottles or tuns when they please; and when they have done all they can, they are, as I say again (for I think I said somewhat like it afore), but moving measures of drink. And there is a piece-in-the-cellar can hold more than all they. This will I make good, if it please our new god but to give a nod; for the belly does all by signs, and I am all for the belly, the truest clock in the world to go by.

*Here the first Anti-masque[6] [danced by men
in the shape of bottles, tuns, etc.] after which,*

HERCULES: What rites are these? Breeds earth more monsters yet?
    Antaeus[7] scarce is cold; what can beget
    This store? and stay such contraries upon her?
    Is earth so fruitful of her own dishonor?
5   Or 'cause his vice was inhumanity,
    Hopes she, by vicious hospitality
    To work an expiation first?[8] and then
    (Help, Virtue) these are sponges, and not men.
    Bottles? mere vessels? half a tun of paunch?
10   How? and the other half thrust forth in haunch?[9]
    Whose feast? the belly's! Comus'! and my cup
    Brought in to fill the drunken orgies up
    And here abused! That was the crowned reward
    Of thirsty heroes after labor hard!
15   Burdens and shames of nature, perish, die;
    For yet you never lived, but in the sty
    Of vice have wallowed, and in that swine's strife
    Been buried under the offense of life.
    Go, reel, and fall, under the load you make,
20   Till your swoll'n bowels burst with what you take.
    Can this be pleasure, to extinguish man?
    Or so quite change him in his figure? Can
    The belly love his pain, and be content
    With no delight, but what's a punishment?
25   These monsters plague themselves, and fitly too,
    For they do suffer what and all they do.
    But here must be no shelter, nor no shroud
    For such: sink grove, or vanish into cloud.

*After this, the whole grove vanished, and the whole music was discovered,
sitting at the foot of the mountain, with Pleasure and Virtue seated above them.
The Choir invited Hercules to rest with this*

Song

    Great friend and servant of the good,
    Let cool a while thy heated blood,
    And from thy mighty labor cease.
      Lie down, lie down,
5   And give thy troubled spirits peace,

6. A grotesque, comic interlude.
7. Antaeus was a Libyan giant slain by Hercules.
8. Hercules assumes that Comus is another monster, like Antaeus, produced by the Earth and that Earth hopes to

expiate her guilt by giving birth to one monster after another.
9. The area between the ribs and thighs.

Whilst Virtue, for whose sake
Thou dost this godlike travail take,
May of the choicest herbage° make,   *plants*
    Here on this mountain bred,
10   A crown, a crown
      For thy immortal head.

    Here Hercules being laid down at their feet,
the second anti-masque, which was of pygmies,[1] appeared.

1ST PYGMY: Antaeus dead? And Hercules yet live!
    Where is this Hercules? What would I give
    To meet him, now? Meet him? Nay, three such other,
    If they had hand in murder of our brother![2]
5   With three? with four? with ten? nay, with as many
    As the name yields![3] Pray anger there by any
    Whereon to feed my just revenge and soon!
    How shall I kill him? Hurl him 'gainst the moon,
    And break him in small portions! Give to Greece
10   His brain, and every tract of earth a piece!
2ND PYGMY: He is yonder.
1ST: Where?
3RD: At the hill foot, asleep.
1ST: Let one go steal his club.
2ND: My charge; I'll creep.
4TH: He's ours.
1ST: Yes, peace.
3RD: Triumph, we have him, boy.
4TH: Sure, sure, he's sure.
1ST: Come, let us dance for joy.

    At the end of their dance they thought to surprise him, when suddenly,
being awaked by the music, he roused himself, and they all ran into holes.

Song

CHOIR: Wake, Hercules, awake, but heave up thy black eye,
    'Tis only asked from thee to look and these will die,
          Or fly.
      Already they are fled,
      Whom scorn had else left dead.

  At which Mercury[4] descendeth from the hill, with a garland of poplar to crown him.

MERCURY: Rest still, thou active friend of Virtue: these
    Should not disturb the peace of Hercules.
    Earth's worms and honor's dwarfs, at too great odds,
    Prove or provoke the issue of the gods.
5   See here, a crown, the agèd hill hath sent thee,
    My grandsire Atlas, he that did present thee
    With the best sheep that in his fold were found,

1. In ancient Greek history, the pygmies were supposed to have been a tribe of very short people in Africa or India; the term was also used of dwarves.
2. Antaeus.

3. The Pygmies' assumption that there is more than one Hercules is a joke alluding to the many different stories about Hercules put forward by the mythographers.
4. The messenger god.

Or golden fruit, on the Hesperian ground,
For rescuing his fair daughters, then the prey
10 Of a rude pirate, as thou cam'st this way;
And taught thee all the learning of the sphere,
And how, like him, thou mightst the heaven up-bear,
As that thy labors virtuous recompense.[5]
He, though a mountain now, hath yet the sense
15 Of thanking thee for more, thou being still
Constant to goodness, guardian of the hill;
Antaeus, by thee suffocated here,
And the voluptuous Comus, god of cheer,
Beat from his grove, and that defaced. But now
20 The time's arrived, that Atlas told thee of: how
By unaltered law, and working of the stars,
There should be a cessation of all jars°   *fights*
'Twixt Virtue and her noted opposite,
Pleasure, that both should meet here, in the sight
25 Of Hesperus, the glory of the west,[6]
The brightest star, that from his burning crest
Lights all on this side the Atlantic seas
As far as to thy pillars Hercules.[7]
See where he shines, Justice and Wisdom placed
30 About his throne and those with Honor graced,
Beauty and Love. It is not with his brother
Bearing the world, but ruling such another
Is his renown.[8] Pleasure, for his delight,
Is reconciled to Virtue; and this night
35 Virtue brings forth twelve princes have been bred
In this rough mountain and near Atlas' head,
The hill of Knowledge; one, and chief of whom
Of the bright race of Hesperus is come,
Who shall in time the same that he is, be,
40 And now is only a less light than he.[9]
These now she trusts with Pleasure, and to these
She gives an entrance to the Hesperides,
Fair Beauty's garden; neither can she fear
They should grow soft or wax effeminate here,
45 Since in her sight and by her charge all's done,
Pleasure the servant, Virtue looking on.

*Here the whole choir of music called the masquers forth from
the lap of the mountain, which now opens with this*

Song

Ope, agèd Atlas, open then thy lap,
And from thy beamy bosom, strike a light,

---

5. Atlas was an astronomer. His labor of holding up the
heavens was taken over by Hercules so that Atlas could
capture the golden apples of the Hesperides.
6. Hesperus, the brother of Atlas, was the evening star
and the protector of the western isles.

7. The Pillars of Hercules are the Straits of Gibraltar.
8. Hesperus is similar to King James, who also rules "another" world: England.
9. King James's 18-year-old son Prince Charles.

That men may read in thy mysterious map
          All lines
5   And signs
Of royal education, and the right,
      See how they come, and show,
      That are but born to know.
          Descend,
10   Descend,
    Though pleasure lead,
          Fear not to follow:
    They who are bred
          Within the hill
15   Of skill,
      May safely tread
          What path they will:
No ground of good is hollow.

*In their descent from the hill Daedalus[1] came down
before them of whom Hercules questioned Mercury.*

HERCULES: But Hermes, stay a little, let me pause:
  Who's this that leads?
MERCURY: A guide that gives them laws
  To all their motions. Daedalus the wise.
HERCULES: And doth in sacred harmony comprise
  His precepts?
MERCURY: Yes.
HERCULES: They may securely prove°   *experience*
Then, any labyrinth, though it be of love.

Here, while they put themselves in form, Daedalus hath his first

Song

Come on, come on, and where you go,
    So interweave the curious knot,
As even th'observer scarce may know
    Which lines are Pleasures, and which not.

5   First, figure out the doubtful way
      At which, a while all youth should stay
    Where she and Virtue did contend
      Which should have Hercules to friend.[2]

    Then, as all actions of mankind
10   Are but a labyrinth or maze,
    So let your dances be entwined,
      Yet not perplex men unto gaze;

---

1. Daedalus here acts as choreographer for the dance. As architect of the labyrinth, or maze, Daedalus may symbolize Inigo Jones, the set designer of the masque.

2. The story of how Hercules had to choose the arduous path of Virtue over the easy road offered to him by Vice is related by the ancient Greek author Xenophon (*Memorabilia* 2.1.21–34).

But measured, and so numerous° too,   *rhythmical*
    As men may read each act you do,
15 And when they see the graces meet,
    Admire the wisdom of your feet.

For dancing is an exercise
    Not only shows the mover's wit,
But maketh the beholder wise,
20   As he hath power to rise to it.

The first dance.

After which Daedalus again.

Song 2

O more, and more! this was so well
    As praise wants half his voice to tell;
Again yourselves compose;
    And now put all the aptness on
5 Of figure, that proportion
    Or color can disclose.

That if those silent arts were lost,
    Design and picture, they might boast
From you a newer ground;
10   Instructed to that height'ning sense
Of dignity and reverence
    In your true motions found:

Begin, begin; for look, the fair
    Do longing listen to what air
15 You form your second touch;
    That they may vent their murmuring hymns
Just to the tune you move your limbs,
    And wish their own were such.

Make haste, make haste, for this
20   The labyrinth of Beauty is.

The second dance.

That ended, Daedalus:

Song 3

It follows now, you are to prove
    The subtlest maze of all, that's love,
        And if you stay too long,
        The fair will think you do 'em wrong,

5 Go choose among—but with a mind
    As gentle as the stroking wind
        Runs o'er the gentler flowers.

And so let all your actions smile,
As if they meant not to beguile
10   The ladies, but the hours.

Grace, laughter and discourse may meet,
And yet the beauty not go less:
For what is noble should be sweet,
But not dissolved in wantonness.

15   Will you, that I give the law
To all your sport and sum it?
It should be such should envy draw,
But ever overcome it.

*Here they danced with the ladies, and the whole revels[3] followed; which ended, Mercury
called to Daedalus in this following speech, which was after repeated in song, by two trebles,
two tenors, a bass, and the whole chorus.*

Song 4

An eye of looking back were well,
Or any murmur that would tell
Your thoughts, how you were sent
And went,
5   To walk with Pleasure, not to dwell.

These, these are hours by Virtue spared
Herself, she being her own reward,
But she will have you know
That though
10   Her sports be soft, her life is hard.

You must return unto the hill,
And there advance
With labor and inhabit still
That height and crown
15   From whence you ever may look down
Upon triumphed Chance.

She, she it is, in darkness shines.
'Tis she that still herself refines
By her own light, to every eye,
20   More seen, more known, when Vice stands by.

And though a stranger here on earth,
In heaven she hath her right of birth.
There, there is Virtue's seat,
Strive to keep her your own;
25   'Tis only she can make you great,
Though place, here, make you known.

3. The audience, including members of the court.

After which they danced their last dance, and returned into the scene,
which closed, and is a mountain again, as before.

The End.

This pleased the king so well, as he would see it again; when it was presented with
these additions.[4]

John Donne

1572–1631

A. Duncan, engraved portrait of
John Donne.

John Donne wrote some of the most passionate love poems
and most moving religious verse in the English language.
Even his contemporaries wondered how one mind could
express itself in such different modes. Eliciting a portrait of
the artist as a split personality, Donne's letters mention the
melancholic lover "Jack Donne," succeeded by the Anglican
priest "Doctor Donne." Izaak Walton's *Life of Donne* (1640)
portrays an earnest, aspiring clergyman who wrote love poetry
to his wife. Yet Donne actually wrote most of his poetry—
both the love lyrics and the *Holy Sonnets*—before he entered
the ministry at forty-three. An ambitious, talented, and
handsome young man, Donne struggled to attain secular patronage; later, he resigned himself to life in the church and,
after his wife's death, came to terms with his own mortality.

Donne was born into a Catholic family. His mother was the
great-niece of Sir Thomas More; she went into exile in
Antwerp for a time to seek religious toleration. One of Donne's uncles was imprisoned in the
Tower of London because he was a Jesuit priest. Donne wrote of his family that none "hath
endured and suffered more in their persons and fortunes, for obeying the Teachers of Roman
Doctrine, then it hath done." Donne and his brother Henry entered Hart Hall, Oxford, when
they were just eleven and ten, young enough to be spared the required oath recognizing the
Queen as head of the church. The Donne brothers later studied law at Lincoln's Inn, where
Henry was arrested for harboring a priest in 1593. The priest was drawn and quartered; Henry
died in Newgate prison of the plague.

Though shadowed by his brother's death, Donne's student years in London had their
pleasures. Donne was distracted from studying law by "the worst voluptuousness . . . an
Hydroptique immoderate desire of humane learning and languages." The young Donne was
described by his friend Sir Richard Baker as "a great visitor of ladies, a great frequenter of
Plays, a great writer of conceited Verses." Among these were Donne's erotic *Elegies*, including *To His Mistress Going to Bed* and *Love's Progress*, both of which were refused a license for
publication in the 1633 edition of his collected verse.

Shortly after gaining a position as secretary to Sir Thomas Egerton, Lord Keeper of the
Great Seal, in 1597, Donne met and fell in love with Ann More. His noble employer's niece,
she was so far above Donne's station that they married secretly. When Ann's father heard the

4. The additions were another masque, *For the Honor of Wales.*

news, he asked Egerton to have Donne fired and saw to it that he was incarcerated. At this time, Donne is said to have written to Ann: *"John Donne, Ann Donne, un-done."* As a result of Donne's petition, the Court of Audience for Canterbury declared the marriage lawful; nevertheless, Ann was disinherited.

John and Ann made a love match, but their life was not easy. She bore twelve children in fifteen years, not counting miscarriages. Donne lamented the "poorness of [his] fortune and the greatness of [his] charge." After thirteen years of marriage, however, he could also still say: "we had not one another at so cheap a rate, as that we should ever be weary of one another." A few of the love poems in *Songs and Sonnets* express a mixture of bliss and hardship linked with their marriage.

Relations with friends and patrons also influenced Donne's poetry. He is said to have addressed several poems to Magdalen Herbert, mother of the poet George. Living in Mitcham near London, Donne cemented his friendship with Ben Jonson, who wrote two epigrams in praise of Donne in thanks for his Latin verses on *Volpone* (1607). Donne was also introduced to Lucy, Countess of Bedford, who asked Jonson to get her a copy of Donne's *Satires*. Donne not only addressed several verse letters to her but also enjoyed her poems. An even more generous patron was Sir Robert Drury, for the death of whose young daughter Elizabeth the poet composed *A Funeral Elegie*, the inspiration for his two *Anniversaries* (1612) on the nature of the cosmos and death.

Donne's writing from 1607 to 1611 dealt with theological and moral controversies. His *Pseudo-Martyr* (1610) argued that Catholics should take the Oath of Allegiance to the King and that resistance to him should not be glorified as a form of martyrdom. This work won him James I's advice to enter the ministry, but, still skeptical, Donne held off. He protested against sectarianism: "You know I never fettered nor imprisoned the word Religion ... immuring it in a Rome, or a Wittenberg, or a Geneva." Donne also examined the morality of suicide in *Biathanatos* (written 1607, published 1646). His *Holy Sonnets* (some of which may have been written as early as 1608–1610) reveal an obsession with his own death and fear of damnation: "I dare not move my dim eyes any way, / Despair behind, and death before doth cast / Such terror."

Donne was plagued by professional bad luck until he became an Anglican priest. With the exception of Sir Robert Drury, Donne never found a dependable patron. His applications for secretaryships in Ireland and Virginia were unsuccessful. In search of the Earl of Somerset's patronage, Donne wrote an epithalamion for his marriage to Frances Howard and even volunteered to justify her earlier controversial divorce. Fortunately for Donne, his attempts to win a position through Somerset failed, since a year later the Earl fell from power. Giving up his long quest for secular preferment, Donne took holy orders in 1615. Once an Anglican priest, he was made a royal chaplain and received an honorary Doctorate of Divinity from Cambridge. Two years later, he became reader in divinity at his old law school Lincoln's Inn.

Prosperity was followed by tragic loss. Ann Donne died giving birth in 1617. The death of his wife turned Donne more completely toward God. His later prose viewed death from a different perspective from his earlier personal torment. Suffering from a recurring fever, he wrote *Devotions upon Emergent Occasions* (1624). In the midst of a major epidemic, at the height of his fever, distraught and sleepless, he realizes our common mortality: "never send to know for whom the bell tolls; it tolls for thee." He became a prolific and stirring preacher of sermons. Some of these, such as that urging the Company of the Virginia Plantation to spread the gospel (1622), were printed in his lifetime. One written just before his death shows confidence in God's forgiveness: "I cannot plead innocency of life, especially of my youth: But I am to be judged by a merciful God."

If Donne's life can be split into the secular and religious, his poetic sensibility cannot. His verse fuses flesh and spirit through metaphysical conceits that create fascinating connections between apparently unrelated topics. In Donne's erotic lyrics, sex excites spiritual ecstasy along with hot lust and seductive wit. Similarly, Donne's religious poems express his relation with God not as an intellectual construct but as an emotional need, articulated in intimate and even erotic language. Later ages did not always appreciate either Donne's sensuality or his intellectual extravagance; remarkably, none of his poems were included in the most important nineteenth-century anthology of poetry, Palgraves's *Golden Treasury*. Donne's fame was revived early in the twentieth century, when modernist poets, especially T. S. Eliot, took inspiration from Donne's complex mixture of immediacy and artifice, passion and subtle thought.

For additional resources on Donne, go to *The Longman Anthology of British Literature* Web site at www.myliteraturekit.com.

The Good Morrow[1]

I wonder by my troth, what thou, and I
Did, till we loved? Were we not weaned till then?
But sucked on country pleasures, childishly?
Or snorted we in the seven sleepers' den?[2]
5   'Twas so; but this, all pleasures fancies be.
If ever any beauty I did see,
Which I desired, and got, 'twas but a dream of thee.

And now good morrow to our waking souls,
Which watch not one another out of fear;
10 For love, all love of other sights controls,
And makes one little room, an everywhere.
Let sea-discoverers to new worlds have gone,
Let maps to others, worlds on worlds have shown,
Let us possess one world, each hath one, and is one.

15 My face in thine eye, thine in mine appears,
And true plain hearts do in the faces rest.
Where can we find two better hemispheres
Without sharp north, without declining west?
What ever dies was not mixed equally;[3]
20 If our two loves be one, or, thou and I
Love so alike, that none do slacken, none can die.

Song

Go, and catch a falling star,
    Get with child a mandrake root,[1]
Tell me, where all past years are,
    Or who cleft the Devil's foot,
5   Teach me to hear mermaids singing,
    Or to keep off envy's stinging,

1. Donne's love poems, written over a period of 20 years, cannot be dated with any certainty. They were first printed in 1633, scattered throughout the entire collection of poems. Then, in the 1635 edition, the love poems were printed as a group under the title *Songs and Sonnets*. There is no certainty that the titles were chosen by Donne.

2. Legendary cave where seven Ephesian youths were put to sleep by God to escape the persecution of Christians by the Emperor Decius (249).
3. According to ancient medicine, death was caused by an imbalance of elements in the body.
1. A fork-rooted plant, resembling the human body in its form.

And find
What wind
Serves to advance an honest mind.

10 If thou be borne to strange sights,
    Things invisible to see,
Ride ten thousand days and nights,[2]
    Till age snow white hairs on thee.
Thou, when thou return'st, will tell me
15 All strange wonders that befell thee,
    And swear
    No where
Lives a woman true, and fair.

If thou findest one, let me know,
20   Such a pilgrimage were sweet;
Yet do not, I would not go,
    Though at next door we might meet,
Though she were true, when you met her,
And last, till you write your letter,
25   Yet she
    Will be
False, ere I come, to two, or three.

Twickenham Garden[1]

Blasted with sighs, and surrounded with tears,
    Hither I come to seek the spring,
    And at mine eyes, and at mine ears,
Receive such balms[2] as else cure everything;
5   But oh, self-traitor, I do bring
The spider love, which transubstantiates all,
    And can convert manna to gall;[3]
And that this place may thoroughly be thought
    True Paradise, I have the serpent brought.

10 'Twere wholesomer for me, that winter did
    Benight the glory of this place,
    And that a grave frost did forbid
These trees to laugh, and mock me to my face;
    But that I may not this disgrace
15 Endure, nor leave this garden, Love, let me
    Some senseless piece of this place be;

2. See *Faerie Queene* 3.7.56–61, where Spenser's Squire of Dames searches the country for a chaste woman.
1. Twickenham Park was the home of Lucy Harington, Countess of Bedford, and a meeting place of writers whom she patronized, such as Donne. The poem most likely is addressed to her and dates from 1608, when she bought the house, to 1617, when she moved.
2. Healing influences.

3. Spiders turn what they eat into poison; and transubstantiation is the changing of the bread and wine in the Eucharist into the body and blood of Jesus Christ. Manna is the miraculous food that God gave the Israelites to eat when they left Egypt and traveled through the desert. Hence, poisonous love that transforms all and can turn miraculous food into bitterness.

Make me a mandrake[4] so I may groan[5] here,
   Or a stone fountain weeping out my year.

Hither with crystal vials,[6] lovers, come,
20   And take my tears, which are love's wine,
   And try your mistress' tears at home,
For all are false, that taste not just like mine;
     Alas, hearts do not in eyes shine,
Nor can you more judge woman's thoughts by tears,
25   Than by her shadow, what she wears.
O pérverse sex, where none is true but she
   Who's therefore true, because her truth kills me.[7]

The Undertaking

I have done one braver thing
   Than all the Worthies did,[1]
And yet a braver thence doth spring,
   Which is to keep that hid.

5 It were but madness now to impart
   The skill of specular stone,[2]
When he which can have learned the art
   To cut it, can find none.

So, if I now should utter this,
10   Others (because no more
Such stuff to work upon, there is,)
   Would love but as before.

But he who loveliness within
   Hath found, all outward loathes,
15 For he who color loves, and skin,
   Loves but their oldest clothes.

If, as I have, you also do
   Virtue attired in woman see,
And dare love that, and say so too,
20   And forget the He and She;

And if this love, though placèd so,
   From profane men you hide,
Which will no faith on this bestow,
   Or, if they do, deride:

25 Then you have done a braver thing
   Than all the Worthies did;

4. The mandrake, a poisonous and narcotic plant, was said to shriek when uprooted.
5. Donne's *Songs and Sonnets* (1633) and some manuscripts read "grow" instead of "groan."
6. Crystal vials, or tear-vessels, were put in ancient tombs as symbols of mourning.
7. The speaker rails against the lady's perverseness in being the only faithful ("true") woman, who is faithful to her man, for the very reason that this faithfulness distresses the speaker of the poem.
1. The nine great military heroes of ancient and medieval legend and history.
2. Transparent stone of ancient times, but now lost, that required great skill to cut in strips.

And a braver thence will spring,
Which is, to keep that hid.

The Sun Rising[1]

     Busy old fool, unruly Sun,
      Why dost thou thus
Through windows, and through curtains call on us?
Must to thy motions lovers' seasons run?
5   Saucy pedantic wretch, go chide
       Late schoolboys, and sour prentices,°   *apprentices*
  Go tell court-huntsmen, that the king will ride,
  Call country ants to harvest offices;
Love, all alike, no season knows, nor clime,
10 Nor hours, days, months, which are the rags of time.

       Thy beams, so reverend, and strong
       Why shouldst thou think?
I could eclipse and cloud them with a wink,
But that I would not lose her sight so long:
15   If her eyes have not blinded thine,
       Look, and tomorrow late, tell me,
  Whether both th'Indias of spice and mine[2]
  Be where thou left'st them, or lie here with me.
Ask for those kings whom thou saw'st yesterday,
20 And thou shalt hear, all here in one bed lay.

       She is all states, and all princes, I,
       Nothing else is.
Princes do but play us; compared to this,
All honor's mimic; all wealth alchemy.°   *fake science*
25   Thou sun art half as happy as we,
       In that the world's contracted thus;
  Thine age asks ease, and since thy duties be
  To warm the world, that's done in warming us.
Shine here to us, and thou art everywhere;
30 This bed thy center is, these walls, thy sphere.

The Indifferent

  I can love both fair and brown,
Her whom abundance melts, and her whom want betrays,
Her who loves loneness best, and her who masks and plays,
Her whom the country formed, and whom the town,
5 Her who believes, and her who tries,°   *questions*
Her who still weeps with spongy eyes,

---

1. In the tradition of the alba, a love song addressing the dawn, as in Ovid's *Amores* 1.13 and Petrarch's *Canzoniere* 188.

2. The East Indies was the source of spice; the West Indies was the source of gold.

And her who is dry cork, and never cries;
I can love her, and her, and you and you,
I can love any, so she be not true.

10   Will no other vice content you?
Will it not serve your turn to do, as did your mothers?
Or have you old vices spent, and now would find out others?
Or doth a fear, that men are true, torment you?
Oh we are not, be not you so,
15   Let me, and do you, twenty know.
Rob me, but bind me not, and let me go.
Must I, who came to travail,[1] thorough you
Grow your fixed subject, because you are true?

Venus heard me sigh this song,
20   And by love's sweetest part, variety, she swore,
She heard not this till now; and that it should be so no more.
She went, examined, and returned ere long,
And said, "Alas, some two or three
Poor heretics in love there be,
25   Which think to establish dangerous constancy.
But I have told them, 'Since you will be true,
You shall be true to them, who are false to you.'"

The Canonization[1]

For God's sake hold your tongue, and let me love,
    Or° chide my palsy, or my gout,   *either*
My five gray hairs, or ruined fortune flout,
    With wealth your state, your mind with arts improve,
5   Take you a course, get you a place,
        Observe his Honor, or his Grace,
Or the King's real, or his stampèd face[2]
    Contemplate, what you will, approve,
    So you will let me love.

10   Alas, alas, who's injured by my love?
    What merchant's ships have my sighs drowned?
Who says my tears have overflowed his ground?
    When did my colds a forward spring remove?
        When did the heats which my veins fill
15   Add one more to the plaguy bill?[3]
Soldiers find wars, and lawyers find out still
    Litigious men, which quarrels move
    Though she and I do love.

Call us what you will, we are made such by love;
20   Call her one, me another fly,

1. In three senses: to make love, to undergo hardship, and
to travel or move on to another woman.
1. The making of saints.

2. The King's actual face or his image stamped on coins.
3. Daily list of those who have died issued during out-
breaks of the plague.

We are tapers° too, and at our own cost die,[4]   *candles*
   And we in us find the eagle and the dove.
The phoenix riddle hath more wit[5]
     By us; we two being one, are it.
25   So to one neutral thing both sexes fit,
   We die and rise the same, and prove
   Mysterious by this love.

We can die by it, if not live by love,
   And if unfit for tombs and hearse
30 Our legend be, it will be fit for verse;
     And if no piece of chronicle we prove,
     We'll build in sonnets pretty rooms;[6]
     As well a well wrought urn becomes
The greatest ashes, as half-acre tombs,
35   And by these hymns, all shall approve
     Us canonized for love.

And thus invoke us: You whom reverend love
   Made one another's hermitage;°   *refuge, retreat*
You, to whom love was peace, that now is rage;
40   Who did the whole world's soul contract, and drove
     Into the glasses° of your eyes[7]   *lenses*
     (So made such mirrors, and such spies,
That they did all to you epitomize)
     Countries, towns, courts: beg from above
45   A pattern of your love!

Air and Angels

Twice or thrice had I loved thee,
Before I knew thy face or name;
So in a voice, so in a shapeless flame,
Angels affect us oft, and worshipped be;
5   Still when, to where thou wert, I came,
Some lovely glorious nothing I did see.[1]
   But since my soul, whose child love is,
Takes limbs of flesh, and else could nothing do,
   More subtle than the parent is
10 Love must not be, but take a body too,
   And therefore what thou wert, and who,
     I bid love ask, and now
That it assume thy body, I allow,
And fix itself in thy lip, eye, and brow.

---

4. To die is to experience orgasm.
5. The mythical bird that was burned and reborn out of its own ashes, a symbol of perfection. See Geoffrey Whitney, "The Phoenix" from *A Choice of Emblems* in Perspectives: Early Modern Books (page 1066).
6. A play on *stanza*, Italian for "room."

7. The lovers gazing into each other's eyes saw there a compact version or microcosm of the larger world or macrocosm.
1. A divine light shining through the body that Neoplatonists thought was the true object of desire rather than the body, which only reflected that beauty.

15   Whilst thus to ballast love, I thought,
      And so more steadily to have gone,
      With wares which would sink admiration,
      I saw, I had love's pinnace° overfraught,   *light sailing ship*
          Every thy hair for love to work upon
20   Is much too much, some fitter must be sought;
          For, nor in nothing, nor in things
      Extreme, and scattering bright, can love inhere;
          Then as an angel, face and wings
      Of air, not pure as it, yet pure doth wear,
25   So thy love may be my love's sphere;[2]
              Just such disparity
      As is twixt air and angel's purity,[3]
      'Twixt women's love, and men's will ever be.

Break of Day[1]

      'Tis true, 'tis day; what though it be?
      Oh wilt thou therefore rise from me?
      Why should we rise, because 'tis light?
      Did we lie down, because 'twas night?
5   Love, which in spite of darkness brought us hither,
      Should in despite of light keep us together.
      Light hath no tongue, but is all eye;
      If it could speak as well as spy,
      This were the worst, that it could say,
10   That being well, I fain would stay,
      And that I loved my heart and honor so,
      That I would not from him, that had them, go.

      Must business thee from hence remove?
      Oh, that's the worst disease of love,
15   The poor, the foul, the false, love can
      Admit, but not the busied man.
      He which hath business, and makes love, does do
      Such wrong, as when a married man doth woo.

A Valediction:° Of Weeping   *farewell*

          Let me pour forth
      My tears before thy face, whilst I stay here,
      For thy face coins them, and thy stamp° they bear,   *image*
      And by this mintage they are something worth,
5   For thus they be
              Pregnant of thee;
      Fruits of much grief they are, emblems° of more,   *symbols*

---

2. The analogy is between his love as the intelligence
controlling a heavenly body and her love as the heavenly
sphere, or material body.
3. Metaphysical doctrine separates being into celestial,

aerial, and material. If the material lady returns his aerial
love, then they will be united in a celestial union.
1. First printed, with music, in W. Corkine's *Second Book
of Airs* (1612).

When a tear falls, that thou falst which it bore,
So thou and I are nothing then, when on a diverse shore.

10   On a round ball
A workman that hath copies by, can lay
A Europe, Africa, and an Asia,
And quickly make that, which was nothing, all,[1]
        So doth each tear,
15   Which thee doth wear,
A globe, yea world by that impression grow,
Till thy tears mixed with mine do overflow
This world, by waters sent from thee, my heaven dissolvèd so.

        Oh more than moon,
20 Draw not up seas to drown me in thy sphere,[2]
Weep me not dead, in thine arms, but forbear
To teach the sea, what it may do too soon;
        Let not the wind
        Example find,
25 To do me more harm, than it purposeth;
Since thou and I sigh one another's breath,
Whoe'er sighs most, is cruelest, and hastes the other's death.

Love's Alchemy

Some that have deeper digged love's mine than I,
Say, where his centric° happiness doth lie: *central*
        I have loved, and got, and told,
But should I love, get, tell, till I were old,
5 I should not find that hidden mystery;
        Oh, 'tis imposture all:
And as no chemic° yet the elixir got,[1]   *alchemist*
        But glorifies his pregnant pot,
        If by the way to him befall
10 Some odoriferous thing, or medicinal,
        So, lovers dream a rich and long delight,
        But get a winter-seeming summer's night.

Our ease, our thrift, our honor, and our day,
Shall we, for this vain bubble's shadow pay?
15   Ends love in this, that my man,°   *servant*
Can be as happy as I can; if he can
Endure the short scorn of a bridegroom's play?
        That loving wretch that swears,
        'Tis not the bodies marry, but the minds,
20   Which he in her angelic finds,
        Would swear as justly, that he hears,

1. The blank ball looks like a zero ("nothing") until the continents are painted on it to represent the entire world ("all").

2. An astral sphere with a power of attraction greater than the moon might draw the seas up to itself.
1. A goal of alchemy was to produce a pure essence with the power to heal and prolong life.

In that day's rude hoarse minstrelsy, the spheres.[2]
Hope not for mind in women; at their best
Sweetness and wit, they're but mummy,[3] possessed.

The Flea[1]

Mark but this flea, and mark in this,
How little that which thou deniest me is;
It sucked me first,[2] and now sucks thee,
And in this flea, our two bloods mingled be;
5   Thou know'st that this cannot be said
A sin, nor shame, nor loss of maidenhead,
    Yet this enjoys before it woo,
    And pampered swells with one blood made of two,
    And this, alas, is more than we would do.

10   Oh stay, three lives in one flea spare,
Where we almost, yea more than married are.
This flea is you and I, and this
Our marriage bed, and marriage temple is;
    Though parents grudge, and you, w'are met,
15   And cloistered in these living walls of jet.°   *black*
    Though use make you apt to kill me,
    Let not to that, self murder added be,
    And sacrilege, three sins in killing three.

    Cruel and sudden, hast thou since
20   Purpled thy nail, in blood of innocence?
Wherein could this flea guilty be,
Except in that drop which it sucked from thee?
Yet thou triumph'st, and say'st that thou
Find'st not thy self, nor me the weaker now;
25   'Tis true, then learn how false, fears be;
    Just so much honor, when thou yield'st to me,
    Will waste, as this flea's death took life from thee.

The Bait[1]

Come live with me, and be my love,
And we will some new pleasures prove
Of golden sands, and crystal brooks,
With silken lines, and silver hooks.

5   There will the river whispering run
Warmed by thy eyes, more than the sun.

---

2. The concentric globes that created sublime music as they revolved around the earth.
3. Medicine made from mummies; dead bodies.
1. Based on a poem attributed to Ovid, the poem plays on the belief that intercourse involved the mixing of bloods.
2. "Me it sucked first" in the 1635 edition.
1. Parodies Marlowe's *The Passionate Shepherd to His Love* and Raleigh's *The Nymph's Reply*.

And there the enamored fish will stay,
Begging themselves they may betray.

When thou wilt swim in that live bath,
10   Each fish, which every channel hath,
Will amorously to thee swim,
Gladder to catch thee, then thou him.

If thou, to be so seen, be'st loath,
By sun, or moon, thou darkenest both,
15   And if myself have leave to see,
I need not their light, having thee.

Let others freeze with angling reeds,
And cut their legs, with shells and weeds,
Or treacherously poor fish beset,
20   With strangling snare, or windowy net:

Let coarse bold hands, from slimy nest
The bedded fish in banks out-wrest,
Or curious traitors, sleave-silk flies²
Bewitch poor fishes' wandering eyes.

25   For thee, thou need'st no such deceit,
For thou thyself are thine own bait;
That fish, that is not catched thereby,
Alas, is wiser far than I.

The Apparition

When by thy scorn, O murderess, I am dead,
And that thou thinkst thee free
From all solicitation from me,
Then shall my ghost come to thy bed,
5   And thee, feigned vestal,° in worse arms shall see;   *virgin priestess*
Then thy sick taper will begin to wink,
And he, whose thou art then, being tired before,
Will, if thou stir, or pinch to wake him, think
Thou call'st for more,
10   And in false sleep will from thee shrink,
And then poor aspen¹ wretch, neglected thou
Bathed in a cold quicksilver² sweat will lie
A verier° ghost than I;   *truer*
What I will say, I will not tell thee now,
15   Lest that preserve thee; and since my love is spent,
I had rather thou shouldst painfully repent,
Than by my threatenings rest still innocent.

---

2. Artificial flies made from silk threads.   2. Liquid mercury, used to treat venereal disease.
1. Trembling like an aspen leaf in the wind.

A Valediction: Forbidding Mourning[1]

As virtuous men pass mildly away,
   And whisper to their souls, to go,
Whilst some of their sad friends do say,
   The breath goes now, and some say, no:

5   So let us melt, and make no noise,
   No tear-floods, nor sigh-tempests move,
'Twere profanation° of our joys   *desecration*
   To tell the laity[2] of our love.

Moving of th'earth brings harms and fears,
10   Men reckon what it did and meant,
But trepidation of the spheres,[3]
   Though greater far, is innocent.

Dull sublunary[4] lovers' love
   (Whose soul is sense) cannot admit
15   Absence, because it doth remove
   Those things which elemented° it.   *composed*

But we by a love, so much refined,
   That our selves know not what it is,
Inter-assurèd of the mind,
20   Care less, eyes, lips, and hands to miss.

Our two souls therefore, which are one,
   Though I must go, endure not yet
A breach, but an expansion,
   Like gold to airy thinness beat.[5]

25   If they be two, they are two so
   As stiff twin compasses[6] are two,
Thy soul the fixed foot, makes no show
   To move, but doth, if th' other do.

And though it in the center sit,
30   Yet when the other far doth roam,
It leans, and hearkens after it,
   And grows erect, as that comes home.

Such wilt thou be to me, who must
   Like th' other foot, obliquely run;
35   Thy firmness makes my circle just,°   *complete*
   And makes me end, where I begun.

---

1. In his *Life of Dr. John Donne* (1640), Walton describes the occasion as Donne's farewell to his wife before his journey to France in 1611.
2. The uninitiated.
3. Though the movement of the spheres is greater than an earthquake, we feel its effects less.
4. Under the sphere of the moon, hence sensual.
5. Gold was beaten to produce gold leaf. "Airy" suggests their love will become so fine that it will be spiritual.
6. A common emblem of constancy amidst change.

The Ecstasy[1]

Where, like a pillow on a bed,
    A pregnant bank swelled up, to rest
The violet's reclining head,[2]
    Sat we two, one another's best.

5   Our hands were firmly cemented
        With a fast balm, which thence did spring,
    Our eye-beams twisted, and did thread
        Our eyes, upon one double string;[3]

So to intergraft our hands, as yet
10   Was all the means to make us one,
And pictures in our eyes to get
    Was all our propagation.[4]

As 'twixt two equal armies, Fate
    Suspends uncertain victory,
15   Our souls (which to advance their state
    Were gone out) hung 'twixt her and me.

And whilst our souls negotiate there,
    We like sepulchral statues lay;
All day, the same our postures were,
20   And we said nothing, all the day.

If any, so by love refined,
    That he soul's language understood,
And by good love were grown all mind,
    Within convenient distance stood,

25   He (though he knew not which soul spake
    Because both meant, both spake the same)
Might thence a new concoction[5] take,
    And part far purer than he came.

This ecstasy doth unperplex,
30   We said, and tell us what we love,
We see by this, it was not sex,
    We see, we saw not what did move:

But as all several souls contain
    Mixture of things, they know not what,
35   Love, these mixed souls, doth mix again,
    And makes both one, each this and that.

A single violet transplant,
    The strength, the color, and the size,

---

1. From *ekstasis* (Greek) meaning passion and the withdrawal of the soul from the body. A beautiful and secluded pastoral spot was a frequent setting for love poetry.
2. The violet was an emblem of faithfulness.

3. The lovers are totally enthralled by gazing into each other's eyes.
4. The act of reflecting each other's image was called "making babies."
5. Refining of metals by heat.

(All which before was poor and scant)
40   Redoubles still, and multiplies.

When love with one another so
   Interinanimates two souls,
That abler soul, which thence doth flow,
   Defects of loneliness controls.

45 We then, who are this new soul, know,
   Of what we are composed and made,
For, th' atomies° of which we grow,   *components, parts*
   Are souls, whom no change can invade.

But O alas, so long, so far
50   Our bodies why do we forbear?
They are ours, though they are not we, we are
   The intelligences, they the sphere.[6]

We owe them thanks, because they thus,
   Did us to us at first convey,
55 Yielded their forces, sense, to us,
   Nor are dross° to us, but allay.°   *refuse / a mixture*

On man heaven's influence works not so,
   But that it first imprints the air,[7]
So soul into the soul may flow,
60   Though it to body first repair.

As our blood labors to beget
   Spirits, as like souls as it can,
Because such fingers need to knit
   That subtle knot, which makes us man:[8]

65 So much pure lovers' souls descend
   T'affections,° and to faculties,°[9]   *feelings / powers*
Which sense may reach and apprehend,
   Else a great prince in prison lies.

To our bodies turn we then, that so
70   Weak men on love revealed may look;
Love's mysteries in souls do grow,
   But yet the body is his book.

And if some lover, such as we,
   Have heard this dialogue of one,
75 Let him still mark us, he shall see
   Small change, when we are to bodies gone.

---

6. In Aristotelian cosmology, each planet moved in a sphere (the form of its motion around the earth) and was guided by an inner spiritual force, or intelligence.
7. An angel has to put on clothes of air to be seen by men; in hermetic medicine, the air mediates the influence of the stars. Just as spirits need a material medium,

so souls need the union of bodies.
8. In scholastic philosophy a human being is composed of body and soul, and vapors called spirits produced by the blood link the body with the soul.
9. As the blood mediates between body and soul, so the lovers' feelings mediate between flesh and spirit.

The Funeral

Whoever comes to shroud me, do not harm
    Nor question much
That subtle wreath of hair, which crowns my arm;
The mystery, the sign you must not touch,
5   For 'tis my outward soul,
Viceroy to that, which then to heaven being gone,
    Will leave this to control,
And keep these limbs her provinces, from dissolution.

For if the sinewy thread my brain lets fall
10   Through every part,
Can tie those parts, and make me one of all;[1]
These hairs which upward grew, and strength and art
    Have from a better brain,
Can better do it;[2] except she meant that I
15   By this should know my pain,
As prisoners then are manacled when they're condemned to die.

Whate'er she meant by it, bury it with me,
    For since I am
Love's martyr, it might breed idolatry,
20   If into others' hands these relics[3] came;
    As 'twas humility
To afford to it all a soul can do,
    So, 'tis some bravery,
That since you would save[4] none of me, I bury some of you.

The Relic

When my grave is broke up again
Some second guest to entertain,
(For graves have learned that woman-head[1]
To be to more than one a bed)
5   And he that digs it, spies
A bracelet of bright hair about the bone,
    Will he not let us alone,
And think that there a loving couple lies,
Who thought that this device might be some way
10   To make their souls, at the last busy day,
Meet at this grave, and make a little stay?

---

1. There was a theory that nerves emanating from the brain held the entire body together.
2. Her hairs coming from a better brain could better preserve his body.
3. Objects, often body parts, that served as memorials of a saint.

4. Editions from 1633 to 1669 read "have," as do some manuscripts.
1. A feminine trait, with a play on maidenhead. The reference is to the custom of burying more than one corpse in the same grave.

If this fall in a time, or land,
Where misdevotion[2] doth command,
Then, he that digs us up, will bring
15   Us, to the Bishop, and the King,
    To make us relics; then
Thou shalt be a Mary Magdalen, and I
    A something else thereby;[3]
All women shall adore us, and some men;
20   And since at such time, miracles are sought,
I would have that age by this paper taught
What miracles we harmless lovers wrought.

First, we loved well and faithfully,
Yet knew not what we loved, nor why,
25   Difference of sex no more we knew,
    Than our guardian angels do;
    Coming and going, we
Perchance might kiss, but not between those meals;
    Our hands ne'er touched the seals,
30   Which nature, injured by late law, sets free:[4]
These miracles we did; but now alas,
All measure, and all language, I should pass,
Should I tell what a miracle she was.

Elegy 19: To His Mistress Going to Bed[1]

Come, Madam, come, all rest my powers defy,
Until I labor, I in labor° lie.   *suffering*
The foe oft-times having the foe in sight,
Is tired with standing though he never fight.
5   Off with that girdle,° like heaven's zone° glistering,   *belt / zodiac*
But a far fairer world encompassing.
Unpin that spangled breastplate[2] which you wear,
That th'eyes of busy fools may be stopped there.
Unlace your self, for that harmonious chime,
10   Tells me from you, that now it is bed time.
Off with that happy busk,° which I envy,   *bodice*
That still can be, and still can stand so nigh.
Your gown going off, such beauteous state reveals,
As when from flowery meads th' hill's shadow steals.
15   Off with that wiry coronet and show
The hairy diadem which on you doth grow:
Now off with those shoes, and then safely tread

2. Idolatry, as in *The Second Anniversary*, where Donne calls prayers to saints "misdevotion."
3. Possibly Jesus Christ or one of Mary's lovers.
4. Nature permits a free love forbidden by human law.
1. In Latin poetry, an elegy was a poem in "elegiacs" (alternating lines of dactylic hexameters and pentameters).

Most of these, like Ovid's *Amores*, were about love and sex; Donne imitates Ovid's wit and eroticism. This poem was refused a license to be printed in 1633; it was first printed in *The Harmony of the Muses* (1654).
2. The stomacher, a covering for the chest worn under the bodice and covered with jewels.

In this love's hallowed temple, this soft bed.
In such white robes, heaven's angels used to be
20   Received by men; thou angel bring'st with thee
A heaven like Mahomet's paradise;³ and though
Ill spirits walk in white, we easily know,
By this these angels from an evil sprite,
Those set our hairs, but these our flesh upright.
25   License my roving hands, and let them go,
Before, behind, between, above, below.
Oh my America! my new-found-land,
My kingdom, safliest when with one man manned,
My mine of precious stones, my empery,°   *empire*
30   How blest am I in this discovering thee!
To enter in these bonds, is to be free;
Then where my hand is set, my seal shall be.⁴
        Full nakedness! All joys are due to thee.
As souls unbodied, bodies unclothed must be,
35   To taste whole joys. Gems which you women use
Are like Atlanta's balls, cast in men's views,⁵
That when a fool's eye lighteth on a gem,
His earthly soul may covet theirs, not them.
Like pictures, or like books' gay coverings made
40   For laymen, are all women thus arrayed;
Themselves are mystic books, which only we
(Whom their imputed grace will dignify)
Must see revealed.⁶ Then since that I may know,
As liberally, as to a midwife, show
45   Thyself: cast all, yea, this white linen hence,
Here is no penance much less innocence.⁷
To teach thee, I am naked first; why then
What need'st thou have more covering than a man?

from Holy Sonnets¹
Divine Meditations

1

As due by many titles° I resign   *legal rights*
Myself to thee, Oh God, first I was made
By thee, and for thee, and when I was decayed
Thy blood bought that, the which before was thine,
5   I am thy son, made with thyself to shine,
Thy servant, whose pains thou has still repaid,

---

3. A heaven of sensual pleasure.
4. He has signed an agreement, which he will now stamp with his seal. Also, he has put his hand where he will consummate his desire.
5. Donne changes the story of how Atalanta was distracted from racing her suitor Hippomenes when he threw three golden apples before her, which she paused to pick up.

6. The analogy is between the grace that man cannot merit from God in Calvinist doctrine and the undeserved favors women grant their lovers.
7. The 1669 edition and some manuscripts read: "There is no penance due to innocence."
1. The first 12 of the sonnets are printed in the sequence of the 1633 edition, which, according to Helen Gardner, represents Donne's order.

Thy sheep, thine image, and, till I betrayed
Myself, a temple of thy Spirit divine;
Why doth the devil then usurp on me?
10   Why doth he steal, nay ravish that's thy right?
Except thou rise and for thine own work fight,
Oh I shall soon despair, when I do see
That thou lov'st mankind well, yet wilt not choose me,
And Satan hates me, yet is loth to lose me.

2

Oh my black soul! Now thou art summoned
By sickness, death's herald, and champion;
Thou art like a pilgrim, which abroad hath done
Treason, and durst not turn to whence he is fled,
5   Or like a thief, which till death's doom be read,
Wisheth himself delivered from prison;
But damned and haled° to execution,   *dragged*
Wisheth that still he might be imprisoned;
Yet grace, if thou repent, thou canst not lack;
10   But who shall give thee that grace to begin?
Oh make thyself with holy mourning black,
And red with blushing, as thou art with sin;
Or wash thee in Christ's blood, which has this might
That being red, it dyes red souls to white.

3

This is my play's last scene, here heavens appoint
My pilgrimage's last mile; and my race
Idly, yet quickly run, hath this last pace,
My span's last inch, my minute's latest point,
5   And gluttonous death, will instantly unjoint
My body, and soul, and I shall sleep a space,
But my ever-waking part shall see that face,
Whose fear already shakes my every joint:
Then, as my soul, to heaven her first seat, takes flight,
10   And earth-borne body, in the earth shall dwell,
So, fall my sins, that all may have their right,
To where they're bred, and would press me, to hell.
Impute me righteous, thus purged of evil,[2]
For thus I leave the world, the flesh, and devil.

4

At the round earth's imagined corners, blow[3]
Your trumpets, angels, and arise, arise
From death, you numberless infinities

---

2. Protestant theology held that even when a man repented of his sins, he was still marked by the sin of Adam
and needed to be made righteous by Christ's grace.

3. "I saw four angels standing on the four corners of the
earth, holding the four winds of the earth" (Revelation
7.1).

Of souls, and to your scattered bodies go,
5   All whom the flood did, and fire shall o'erthrow,[4]
All whom war, dearth, age, agues, tyrannies,
Despair, law, chance, hath slain, and you whose eyes,
Shall behold God, and never taste death's woe.[5]
But let them sleep, Lord, and me mourn a space,
10   For, if above all these, my sins abound,
'Tis late to ask abundance of thy grace,
When we are there; here on this lowly ground,
Teach me how to repent; for that's as good
As if thou hadst sealed my pardon with thy blood.

5

If poisonous minerals, and if that tree,
Whose fruit threw death on else immortal us,
If lecherous goats, if serpents envious
Cannot be damned; alas, why should I be?
5   Why should intent or reason, born in me,
Make sins, else equal, in me more heinous?
And mercy being easy, and glorious
To God, in his stern wrath, why threatens he?
But who am I, that dare dispute with thee?
10   O God, Oh! of thine only worthy blood,
And my tears, make a heavenly Lethean[6] flood,
And drown in it my sins' black memory.
That thou remember them, some claim as debt,
I think it mercy, if thou wilt forget.

6

Death be not proud, though some have called thee
Mighty and dreadful, for thou are not so.
For, those, whom thou think'st thou dost overthrow,
Die not, poor death, nor yet canst thou kill me;
5   From rest and sleep, which but thy pictures be,
Much pleasure, then from thee, much more must flow,
And soonest our best men with thee do go,
Rest of their bones, and soul's delivery.
Thou art slave to fate, chance, kings, and desperate men,
10   And dost with poison, war, and sickness dwell,
And poppy,° or charms can make us sleep as well,   *a narcotic*
And better than thy stroke; why swell'st° thou then?   *grow in pride*
One short sleep past, we wake eternally,
And death shall be no more. Death thou shalt die.[7]

---

4. The flood that Noah survived (Genesis 7) and the fire that will destroy the world at the last judgment (Revelation 6.11).
5. The resurrection of the body (see 1 Corinthians 15.51–52).

6. Of Lethe, the river of forgetfulness in the underworld of ancient mythology.
7. "The last enemy that shall be destroyed is death" (1 Corinthians 15.26).

7

Spit in my face ye Jews, and pierce my side,
Buffet, and scoff, scourge, and crucify me,
For I have sinned, and sinned, and only he,
Who could do no iniquity, hath died:
5   But by my death cannot be satisfied°   *atoned for*
My sins, which pass° the Jews' impiety: *surpass, exceed*
They killed once an inglorious[8] man, but I
Crucify him daily, being now glorified.[9]
Oh let me then, his strange love still admire:
10   Kings pardon, but he bore our punishment.
And Jacob came clothed in vile harsh attire
But to supplant, and with gainful intent:[1]
God clothed himself in vile man's flesh, that so
He might be weak enough to suffer woe.

8

Why are we by all creatures waited on?
Why do the prodigal elements supply
Life and food to me, being more pure than I,
Simple, and further from corruption?[2]
5   Why brook'st thou, ignorant horse, subjection?
Why dost thou bull, and boar so sillily
Dissemble weakness, and by one man's stroke die,[3]
Whose whole kind, you might swallow and feed upon?
Weaker I am, woe is me, and worse than you,
10   You have not sinned, nor need be timorous.
But wonder at a greater wonder, for to us
Created nature doth these things subdue,
But their Creator, whom sin, nor nature tied,
For us, his creatures, and his foes, hath died.

9

What if this present were the world's last night?
Mark in my heart, O soul, where thou dost dwell,
The picture of Christ crucified, and tell
Whether that countenance can thee affright,
5   Tears in his eyes quench the amazing light,
Blood fills his frowns, which from his pierced head fell,
And can that tongue adjudge thee unto hell,
Which prayed forgiveness for his foes' fierce spite?
No, no; but as in my idolatry[4]

8. Unknown; not yet ascended into glory.
9. Every sin knowingly committed is another torture of Christ. (See Hebrews 6.6: "They crucify to themselves the Son of God afresh.")
1. Jacob tricked his father Isaac into giving him his blessing by disguising himself in goatskin as his hairy brother Esau (see Genesis 27.1–36).

2. The elements are physically and morally pure, while humans are a complex mixture of all four elements, prone to decay, and moral agents, capable of sin.
3. The slaughterman's blow, and Adam's sin, causing death to all creation.
4. Erotic devotion to women.

10   I said to all my profane mistresses,
      Beauty, of pity, foulness only is
      A sign of rigor:[5] so I say to thee,
      To wicked spirits are horrid shapes assigned,
      This beauteous form assures a piteous mind.

10

      Batter my heart, three-personed God;[6] for, you
      As yet but knock, breathe, shine, and seek to mend;
      That I may rise, and stand, o'erthrow me, and bend
      Your force, to break, blow, burn and make me new.
5   I, like an usurped town, to another due,
      Labor to admit you, but oh, to no end,
      Reason your viceroy° in me, me should defend,   ruler
      But is captived, and proves weak or untrue,
      Yet dearly I love you, and would be loved fain,°   willingly
10   But am betrothed unto your enemy,
      Divorce me, untie, or break that knot again,
      Take me to you, imprison me, for I
      Except you enthrall me, never shall be free,
      Nor ever chaste, except you ravish me.

11

      Wilt thou love God, as he thee? Then digest,°   consider
      My soul, this wholesome meditation,
      How God the Spirit, by angels waited on
      In heaven, doth make his temple in thy breast.
5   The Father having begot a Son most blest,
      And still begetting, (for he ne'er begun)[7]
      Hath deigned to choose thee by adoption,
      Coheir to his glory, and Sabbath's endless rest;
      And as a robbed man, which by search doth find
10   His stol'n stuff sold, must lose or buy it again:
      The Son of glory came down, and was slain,
      Us whom he had made, and Satan stol'n, to unbind.
      'Twas much, that man was made like God before,
      But, that God should be made like man, much more.

12

      Father, part of his double interest
      Unto thy kingdom, thy Son gives to me,
      His jointure° in the knotty Trinity,   joint tenancy
      He keeps, and gives me his death's conquest.

---

5. Beautiful women show compassion; only ugly ones refuse their lovers.

6. The Trinity: God the Father, Son, and Holy Spirit.

7. God's existence and begetting of his Son are both eternal.

5   This Lamb, whose death, with life the world hath blest,
       Was from the world's beginning slain, and he[8]
       Hath made two wills, which with the legacy[9]
       Of his and thy kingdom, do thy sons invest.
       Yet such are those laws, that men argue yet
10   Whether a man those statutes can fulfill;
       None doth, but all-healing grace and Spirit,
       Revive again what law and letter kill.
       Thy law's abridgement, and thy last command
       Is all but love; oh let that last will stand![1]

from Devotions Upon Emergent Occasions[1]
["FOR WHOM THE BELL TOLLS"]

Nunc lento sonitu dicunt, morieris.
Now this bell tolling softly for another, says to me, Thou must die.

Perchance he for whom this bell[2] tolls may be so ill as that he knows not it tolls
for him; and perchance I may think myself so much better than I am, as that they
who are about me, and see my state may have caused it to toll for me, and I know
not that. The Church is catholic, universal, so are all her actions; all that she does,
belongs to all. When she baptises a child, that action concerns me; for that child is
thereby connected to that Head which is my Head too, and engrafted into that
body,[3] whereof I am a member. And when she buries a man, that action concerns
me: all mankind is of one Author, and is of one volume; when one man dies, one
chapter is not torn out of the book, but translated[4] into a better language; and every
chapter must be so translated. God employs several translators; some pieces are
translated by age, some by sickness, some by war, some by justice; but God's hand is
in every translation, and his hand shall bind up all our scattered leaves again, for
that library where every book shall lie open to one another. As therefore the bell
that rings to a sermon calls not upon the preacher only, but upon the congregation to
come, so this bell calls us all; but how much more me, whom am brought so near the
door by this sickness. There was a contention as far as a suit, (in which both piety
and dignity, religion, and estimation, were mingled) which of the religious orders
should ring to prayers first in the morning; and it was determined that they should
ring first that rose earliest. If we understand aright the dignity of this bell that
tolls for our evening prayer, we would be glad to make it ours by rising early, in that
application, that it might be ours, as well as his whose indeed it is. The bell doth
toll for him that thinks it doth; and though it intermit again, yet from that minute
that occasion wrought upon him, he is united to God. Who casts not up his eye to
the sun when it rises? but who takes off his eye from a comet when that breaks out?

---

8. Christ, "the Lamb slain from the foundation of the world"
(Revelation 13.8).
9. Old and New Testaments.
1. "A new commandment I give unto you, that ye love one
another" (John 13.34).

1. Donne wrote the *Devotions* (1624) following an illness
he suffered in winter 1623. Each meditation concerns a
phase of his disease.
2. The passing-bell rung slowly when a person was dying.
3. United with the church.
4. From Latin *translatus*, "having been carried across."

Who bends not his ear to any bell which upon any occasion rings? but who can remove it from that bell which is passing a piece of himself out of this world? No man is an island, entire of itself; every man is a piece of the Continent, a part of the main. If a clod be washed away by the sea, Europe is the less, as well as if a promontory were, as well as if a manor of thy friends or of thine own were. Any man's death diminishes me, because I am involved in mankind; and therefore never send to know for whom the bell tolls; it tolls for thee. Neither can we call this a begging of misery or a borrowing of misery, as though we were not miserable enough of ourselves but must fetch in more from the next house in taking upon us the misery of our neighbors. Truly it were an excusable covetousness if we did; for affliction is a treasure, and scarce any man hath enough of it. No man hath affliction enough that is not matured and ripened by it, and made fit for God by that affliction. If a man carry treasure in bullion, or in a wedge of gold, and have none coined into current moneys, his treasure will not defray him as he travels. Tribulation is treasure in the nature of it, but it is not current money in the use of it, except we get nearer and nearer our home, heaven, by it. Another man may be sick too, and sick to death, and this affliction may lie in his bowels as gold in a mine and be of no use to him: but this bell that tells me of his affliction digs out and applies that gold to me, if by this consideration of another's danger I take mine own into contemplation and so secure myself by making my recourse to my God who is our only security.

Lady Mary Wroth
1586–1640

Lady Mary Wroth was born the same year that her uncle Sir Philip Sidney died in battle. Like her uncle, she wrote brilliant sonnets and an entertaining and complex prose romance, but whereas his death and writing became the stuff of myth, she died in obscurity. Appreciated by the finest poets of her time, her writing was neglected for the next 300 years; she has only recently been rediscovered as one of the most compelling women writers of her age. Her *Pamphilia to Amphilanthus*, the first Petrarchan sonnet sequence in English by a woman, was first printed in 1621 but was not reprinted until 1977. Wroth's work has finally become available outside rare book libraries, thanks to Josephine Robert's editions of Wroth's complete poems (1983) and her prose romance *The Countess of Montgomeries Urania* (1995), along with Michael Brennan's edition of her pastoral tragicomedy *Love's Victory* (1988). Recent criticism has stressed the formal complexity and variety of her poetry and prose, their creation of female subjectivity, and their relationship to her life and social context, shedding new light on one of the most emotionally powerful and stylistically innovative authors of the Jacobean period.

Mary Wroth was born into the cultivated and distinguished Sidney family. Mary and her mother, two brothers, and seven sisters lived at the family estate Penshurst in Kent. She sometimes visited her father in the Low Countries, where he commanded the English troops fighting for the Protestant cause against the Spanish. Ben Jonson sang the praises of Lady Mary's family and their way of life in *To Penshurst* (see page 1569), a place where the children not only enjoyed natural beauty—"broad beech" and "chest-nut shade"—but also learned the "mysteries of manners, arms and arts." Mary also spent a great deal of time in London with her aunt for whom she was named, Mary (Sidney) Herbert, Countess of Pembroke, hostess to and patron of a circle of poets that included George Chapman and Ben Jonson.

Mary found a mentor in her aunt, who herself wrote poems as well as translations of the Psalms and of Petrarch. Mary Herbert's translation of Petrarch's *Trionfo della Morte* ("Triumph of Death") portrays the poet's beloved Laura not as a passive object but as a lively and eloquent speaker. Mary Wroth's own sonnets similarly portray the woman as the suffering and desiring subject of love rather than the mute object that was common in earlier English Petrarchan poetry. Mary Wroth took the title of her *Urania* from a character in Philip Sidney's *The Countess of Pembrokes Arcadia*, whose publication had been overseen by his sister, Mary Sidney Herbert. Mary Wroth even created the character of the Queen of Naples as a fictional version of her aunt and perhaps saw *Urania* as a continuation of *Arcadia*.

When Mary married Sir Robert Wroth, Lord of Durance and Laughton House and juror for the Gunpowder Plot, she continued her close family ties with her aunt and father (yet another poet), but she also moved into the larger world of the Jacobean court. She served as Queen Anne's companion, and she became at once an observer and a center of attention in the aristocratic circle at court. In 1605, shortly after the first recorded performance of *Othello* at Whitehall, Lady Mary Wroth played in Ben Jonson's *Masque of Blackness*, in which she was presented to the court with Lady Frances Walsingham as the embodiment of gravity and dignity. Later, Wroth would deploy metaphors of darkness and night to great effect in her lyric poems.

It was in this court context that she attracted the attention of Ben Jonson, who not only wrote a poem complimenting her husband but also dedicated a sonnet and two epigrams to her. Jonson paid tribute to her as a subject and inspiration for poetry and as a powerfully moving poet in her own right. He claimed that since writing out her sonnets, he had "become / A better lover and much better poet." Dedicating his great play *The Alchemist* to her, he portrayed her as inheriting her uncle's mantle as poet: "To that Lady Most Deserving her Name and Blood, Lady Mary Wroth,"—a pun on her name, as Wroth was pronounced "worth." While she, too, punned on her married name in her poetry, Mary clung to her identity as a Sidney, using the Sidney device in her letters.

Her marriage was not particularly happy and pales in comparison with her literary friendship and love affair with her cousin William Herbert, by whom she had two illegitimate children, after she was widowed in 1614. During the years of her early widowhood she wrote the first part of her prose romance *Urania*, which was printed with *Pamphilia to Amphilanthus* in 1621. The *Urania* not only presents a fictional account of her relationship with her cousin and her parents' own happy marriage but also was read at the time as a criticism of the mores of the court. King James's courtiers, taking offense at the satire of their private lives, attacked her, prompting her to ask for the book to be removed from publication a few months after it first appeared. The early modern prejudice against women writing surfaces in Lord Denny's punning condescension to Wroth: "leave idle books alone / For wiser and worthier women have writ none."

Fortunately for us, she didn't take his advice and continued to write the second book of the *Urania*, which survives in manuscript. Indeed, no record of a warrant to recall the book survives. Her final years remain a mystery; she lived in retirement after her cousin's death. She left behind a body of poetry challenging the status quo of the court, proclaiming the suffering she had endured for love, and singing the beauty of spiritual love in a woman's voice. Imitating not only her uncle Philip's *Arcadia* but also the *Heptameron* of the French writer Marguerite de Navarre, Mary Wroth made the prose romance a complex combination of novelistic fantasy, roman à clef, and social satire. The greatest English woman writer of her age, Mary Wroth fashioned a new voice and new perspectives within literary tradition that convey the fullness and complexity of her life as woman, lover, and writer.

from **Pamphilia to Amphilanthus**[1]

1

When night's black mantle could most darkness prove,
   And sleep death's image did my senses hire
   From knowledge of myself, then thoughts did move
   Swifter than those most swiftness need require:
5   In sleep, a chariot drawn by winged desire
   I saw, where sat bright Venus, Queen of love,
   And at her feet her son,[2] still adding fire
   To burning hearts which she did hold above,
But one heart flaming more than all the rest
10 The goddess held, and put it to my breast.
   "Dear son, now shut,"[3] said she, "thus must we win."
He her obeyed, and martyred my poor heart,
   I, waking, hoped as dreams it would depart;[4]
   Yet since, O me, a lover I have been.

5

Can pleasing sight, misfortune ever bring?
   Can firm desire a painful torment try?
   Can winning eyes prove to the heart a sting?
   Or can sweet lips in treason hidden lie?
5   The Sun most pleasing blinds the strongest eye.
   If too much look'd on, breaking the sight's string;[5]
   Desires still crossed, must unto mischief hie,°   *move quickly*
   And as despair, a luckless chance may fling.
Eyes, having won, rejecting proves a sting
10 Killing the bud before the tree doth spring;
   Sweet lips not loving do as poison prove:
Desire, sight, eyes, lips, seek, see, prove, and find
   You love may win, but curses if unkind;
   Then show you harm's dislike, and joy in Love.[6]

16

Am I thus conquered? Have I lost the powers
   That to withstand, which joys to ruin me?
   Must I be still while it my strength devours
   And captive leads me prisoner, bound, unfree?
5   Love first shall leave men's fant'sies to them free,[7]
   Desire shall quench love's flames, spring hate sweet showers,
   Love shall loose all his darts, have sight, and see

---

1. The title means "From the All-loving one to the Dual Lover." First published in 1621, the sonnet sequence is here printed according to the numbering in Josephine Robert's 1983 edition.
2. Cupid. Compare the image of the chariot here with that in Petrarch's *Triumph of Love.*
3. Enclose that flaming heart within Pamphilia.
4. Pamphilia's experience of love is represented as a dream vision, a symbolic narrative in which the dreamer discovers hidden truth.
5. Compare 1.6 with Donne's "The Extasie," lines 7–8. Both poems rely on the early modern notion that the eyes give off light that make vision possible.
6. The form of this poem that begins with rhetorical questions that are echoed in the answers that follow is called *carmen correlativum,* or correlative verse.
7. Before I surrender to Love, Love will allow men to realize their fantasies freely.

His shame, and wishings hinder happy hours.[8]
Why should we not Love's purblind° charms resist?   *totally blind*
10   Must we be servile, doing what he list?°   *wants*
No, seek some host to harbor thee: I fly
Thy babish° tricks, and freedom do profess;   *childish*
          But O my hurt, makes my lost heart confess
          I love, and must. So farewell liberty.

17

Truly poor Night thou welcome art to me;
          I love thee better in this sad attire
          Than that which raiseth some men's fant'sies higher
          Like painted outsides which foul inward be.[9]
5   I love thy grave, and saddest looks to see,
          Which seems my soul, and dying heart entire,
          Like to the ashes of some happy fire
          That flamed in joy, but quenched in misery.
I love thy count'nance,° and thy sober pace   *face, expression*
10   Which evenly goes, and as of loving grace
          To us, and me among the rest oppressed
Gives quiet, peace to my poor self alone,
          And freely grants day leave when thou art gone
          To give clear light to see all ill redressed.

25

Like to the Indians, scorched with the sun,
          The sun which they do as their God adore
          So am I us'd by love, for ever more
          I worship him, less favors have I won.
5   Better are they who thus to blackness run,
          And so can only whiteness' want deplore
          Then I who pale and white am with grief's store,
          Nor can have hope, but to see hopes undone;
Besides their sacrifice received's in sight
10   Of their chose saint: Mine hid as worthless rite;
          Grant me to see where I my offerings give,
Then let me wear the mark of Cupid's might
          In heart as they in skin of Phoebus° light   *Apollo, the sun god*
          Not ceasing off'rings to love while I live.

26

When everyone to pleasing pastime hies°   *goes in haste*
          Some hunt, some hawk,[1] some play, while some delight
          In sweet discourse, and music shows joy's might
          Yet I my thoughts do far above these prize.

8. Cupid blindfolded was a popular figure in Renaissance   23.27.
iconography.   1. To hunt game with hawks.
9. Like the whitewashed sepulchers (tombs) in Matthew

5   The joy which I take is that free from eyes
  I sit, and wonder at this day-like night
  So to dispose themselves, as void of right,
  And leave true pleasure for poor vanities;
 When others hunt, my thoughts I have in chase;
10   If hawk, my mind at wishèd end doth fly,
  Discourse, I with my spirit talk, and cry
  While others music choose as greatest grace.
 O God, say I, can these fond pleasures move?
 Or music be but in sweet thoughts of love?

28. Song

Sweetest love, return again,
  Make not too long stay;
Killing mirth and forcing pain,
  Sorrow leading way,
5   Let us not thus parted be,
Love and absence ne'er agree;

But since you must needs depart,
  And me hapless° leave,   *unlucky*
In your journey take my heart
10   Which will not deceive.
Yours it is, to you it flies
Joying in those lovèd eyes,

So in part, we shall not part
  Though we absent be;
15   Time, nor place, nor greatest smart
  Shall my bands make free.
Tied I am, yet think it gain,
In such knots I feel no pain.

But can I live having lost
20   Chiefest part of me?
Heart is fled, and sight is crossed,
  These my fortunes be;
Yet dear heart go, soon return,
As good there as here to burn.

39

Take heed mine eyes, how you your looks do cast,
  Lest they betray my heart's most secret thought;
  Be true unto yourselves for nothing's bought
  More dear than doubt which brings a lover's fast.
5   Catch you all watching eyes, ere they be past,
  Or take yours fixed where your best love hath sought
  The pride of your desires; let them be taught
  Their faults for shame, they could no truer last;

Then look, and look with joy for conquest won,
10   Of those that searched your hurt in double kind;
    So you kept safe, let them themselves look blind;
    Watch, gaze, and mark 'til they to madness run,
While you, mine eyes, enjoy full sight of love
Contented that such happinesses move.

40

False hope which feeds but to destroy, and spill°   *kill*
    What it first breeds; unnatural to the birth
    Of thine own womb; conceiving but to kill,[2]
    And plenty gives to make the greater dearth,
5 So tyrants do who falsely ruling earth
    Outwardly grace them, and with profits fill,
    Advance those who appointed are to death
    To make their greater fall to please their will.
Thus shadow they their wicked vile intent,
10 Coloring evil with a show of good
    While in fair shows their malice so is spent;
    Hope kills the heart, and tyrants shed the blood.
For hope deluding brings us to the pride[3]
Of our desires the farther down to slide.

48

If ever Love had force in human breast?
    If ever he could move in pensive heart?
    Or if that he such power could but impart
    To breed those flames whose heat brings joy's unrest,
5 Then look on me: I am to these addressed.
    I am the soul that feels the greatest smart,
    I am that heartless trunk of heart's depart,
    And I, that one, by love and grief oppressed;
None ever felt the truth of Love's great miss°   *need, want*
10 Of eyes, 'til I deprived was of bliss;
    For had he seen, he must have pity showed;
I should not have been made this stage of woe
    Where sad disasters have their open show;
    O no, more pity he had sure bestowed.

55

How like a fire doth love increase in me,
    The longer that it lasts, the stronger still,
    The greater purer, brighter, and doth fill
    No eye with wonder more, then hopes still be
5 Bred in my breast, when fires of love are free
    To use that part to their best pleasing will,
    And now impossible it is to kill

---

2. The image is of a miscarriage or infanticide.   3. Arrogance, but also elation and pleasure.

The heat so great where Love his strength doth see.
Mine eyes can scare sustain the flames my heart
10   Doth trust in them my passions to impart,
    And languishingly strive to show my love;
My breath not able is to breathe least part
    Of that increasing fuel of my smart;
    Yet love I will till I but ashes prove.[4]
    Pamphilia[5]

68

My pain, still smothered in my grièved breast
    Seeks for some ease, yet cannot passage find
    To be discharged of this unwelcome guest;
    When most I strive, more fast his burdens bind,
5   Like to a ship, on Goodwins[6] cast by wind
    The more she strives, more deep in sand is pressed
    Till she be lost; so am I, in this kind°   way
    Sunk and devoured, and swallowed by unrest,
Lost, shipwracked, spoiled, debarred of smallest hope
10   Nothing of pleasure left; save thoughts have scope,
    Which wander may. Go then, my thoughts, and cry
Hope's perished, Love tempest-beaten, Joy lost:
    Killing Despair hath all these blessings crossed.
    Yet Faith still cries, Love will not falsify.

74. Song

Love a child is ever crying,
    Please him, and he straight is flying;
    Give him, he the more is craving,
    Never satisfied with having.

5   His desires have no measure,
    Endless folly is his treasure;
    What he promiseth he breaketh;
    Trust not one word that he speaketh.

He vows nothing but false matter,
10   And to cozen° you he'll flatter.   trick
    Let him gain the hand[7] he'll leave you,
    And still glory to deceive you.

He will triumph in your wailing,
    And yet cause be of your failing.
15   These his virtues are, and slighter

---

4. Josephine Roberts has noted that "will" may stand for the poet's lover William Herbert. Early modern poets frequently used the device of the embedded name.
5. To mark the completion of the first section of sonnets,
the poet signed her pen name at the foot of sonnet 55.
6. A dangerous shoal off the southeastern coast of England.
7. Let him take control.

Are his gifts, his favors lighter.
Feathers are as firm in staying,
   Wolves no fiercer in their preying;
   As a child then leave him crying,
20   Nor seek him so given to flying.

from *A Crown of Sonnets Dedicated to Love*[1]

77

In this strange labyrinth how shall I turn?
   Ways° are on all sides while the way I miss: *paths*
   If to the right hand, there, in love I burn;
   Let me go forward, therein danger is;
5   If to the left, suspicion hinders bliss,
     Let me turn back, shame cries I ought return,
     Nor faint° though crosses with my fortunes kiss;[2]   *lose heart*
     Stand still is harder, although sure to mourn.[3]
Thus let me take the right, or left-hand way,
10   Go forward, or stand still, or back retire;
   I must these doubts endure without allay°   *relief*
   Or help, but travail[4] find for my best hire.
Yet that which most my troubled sense doth move
Is to leave all, and take the thread of love.[5]

82

He may our profit, and our tutor prove
   In whom alone we do this power find,
   To join two hearts as in one frame to move;
   Two bodies, but one soul to rule the mind;
5   Eyes which must care to one dear object bind
     Ears to each other's speech as if above
     All else they sweet, and learned were; this kind
     Content of lovers witnesseth true love.
It doth enrich the wits, and make you see
10   That in your self, which you knew not before,
   Forcing you to admire such gifts should be
   Hid from your knowledge, yet in you the store;
Millions of these adorn the throne of Love,
How blest be they then, who his favors prove.

83

How blessed be they then, who his favors prove,
   A life whereof the birth is just desire,

---

1. The crown (Italian *corona*) is a form in which the last line of each poem is repeated as the first line of the next. The last poem of the sequence ends with the first line of the first poem.

2. Though troubles embrace my luck, or fate.

3. It is more difficult to do nothing, although this is sure to make me mourn.

4. Hard work, with wordplay on "Travel," which occurs in the 1621 text.

5. An allusion to the myth of Ariadne, beloved of Theseus, to whom she gave a thread to unwind behind him on his path through the labyrinth so that, after slaying the Minotaur, he could retrace his steps on his way out.

Breeding sweet flame which hearts invite to move
In these loved eyes which kindle Cupid's fire,
5 And nurse his longings with his thoughts entire,
Fixed on the heat of wishes formed by love;
Yet whereas fire destroys this doth aspire,
Increase, and foster all delights above;
Love will a painter make you, such as you
10 Shall able be to draw your only dear
More lovely, perfect, lasting, and more true
Than rarest workman, and to you more near.
These be the least, then all must needs confess
He that shuns love doth love himself the less.

84

He that shuns love does love himself the less
And cursed he whose spirit not admires
The worth of love, where endless blessedness
Reigns,[6] and commands, maintained by heav'nly fires
5 Made of virtue, joined by truth, blown by desires
Strengthened by worth, renewed by carefulness
Flaming in never changing thoughts, briers
Of jealousy shall here miss welcomeness;
Nor coldly pass in the pursuits of love
10 Like one long frozen in a sea of ice,
And yet but chastely let your passions move
No thought from virtuous love your minds entice.
Never to other ends your fant'sies place
But where they may return with honor's grace.

103

My muse now happy, lay thyself to rest,
Sleep in the quiet of a faithful love,
Write you no more, but let these fant'sies move
Some other hearts, wake not to new unrest;
5 But if you study, be those thoughts addressed
To truth, which shall eternal goodness prove,
Enjoying of true joy, the most, and best,
The endless gain which never will remove.
Leave the discourse to Venus, and her son
10 To young beginners, and their brains inspire
With stories of great love, and from that fire
Get heat to write the fortunes they have won,
And thus leave off; what's past shows you can love,
Now let your constancy your honor prove.
                                        Pamphilia.[7]

---

6. Reigns: "raines" in the original.
7. According to the 1621 *Urania*, when Pamphilia accepts

the keys to the Throne of Love, the virtue *Constancy* disappears and is transformed into Pamphilia's breast.

Robert Herrick
1591–1674

The urbane and at times pagan poet Robert Herrick might seem an unlikely candidate for rural vicar, but such were his connections that he was promoted from deacon to priest in a day. He spent most of his life as vicar of the Devonshire parish of Dean, where he wrote poetry about country customs and church liturgy. A hundred and fifty years after his death, a writer in the *Quarterly Review* was able to find people in the village who could recite from memory Herrick's *Farewell to Dean Bourn:* "I never look to see / Dean, or thy watery incivility," lines that "they said he uttered as he crossed the brook, upon being ejected from the vicarage by Cromwell." Referring to Herrick's return to the vicarage after the Restoration, these locals "added with an air of innocent triumph, 'He did see it again.'" The villagers also recalled stories of how the bachelor vicar threw his sermon at the congregation one day for their inattention and how he taught his pet pig to drink from a tankard. Many of his best poems, such as *Corinna's Going A-Maying* and *The Hock-Cart, or Harvest Home*, celebrate the landscape and the life of the country in the idealized tradition of pastoral poetry.

The son of a goldsmith in Cheapside, Herrick was apprenticed to the trade at age fourteen. After taking his B.A. from Cambridge in 1617, he returned to London, where he spent his poetic apprenticeship until he was appointed chaplain to the Duke of Buckingham in his failed expedition to aid the French Protestants of Rhé in 1627. Only a year later, Herrick moved to the vicarage at Dean, but many of his poems recount his London days, recalling the feasts frequented by Ben Jonson, whose verse "out-did the meat, out-did the frolic wine." The influence of Jonson's classical concision, wit, and urbanity can be felt in such poems as *Delight in Disorder* and his *Prayer* to the poet. While in London, Herrick also became friends with William Lawes, the court composer who wrote the music for Milton's masque *Comus*. When Lawes set Herrick's *To the Virgins, to Make Much of Time* to music, this poem became one of the most popular drinking songs of the seventeenth century—often sung as a "catch," which meant that its words could be played with to produce ribald double meanings. His poems circulated in manuscript until his volume of verse was printed in 1648, with his secular poetry entitled *Hesperides* and his religious poetry entitled *Noble Numbers*. He first achieved a wide readership in the early nineteenth century with the romantic revival of interest in rural life and poetry.

from HESPERIDES

The Argument of His Book[1]

I sing of brooks, of blossoms, birds, and bowers,
Of April, May, of June, and July flowers.
I sing of Maypoles, hock carts, wassails, wakes,[2]
Of bridegrooms, brides, and of their bridal cakes.
5 I write of youth, of love, and have access
By these, to sing of cleanly wantonness.°   *carefree abandon*
I sing of dews, of rains, and piece by piece,
Of balm, of oil, of spice, and ambergris.[3]

1. All of Herrick's poems were published in 1648. The "Argument" introduces the book's themes.
2. Hock carts: harvest wagons; wassails: drinking toasts; wakes: celebrations in honor of the dedication of a parish church.
3. Secretion from the intestines of sperm whales, used to make perfume.

10   I sing of times trans-shifting;[4] and I write
      How roses first came red, and lilies white.
      I write of groves, of twilights, and I sing
      The court of Mab,[5] and of the fairy king.
      I write of hell; I sing (and ever shall)
      Of Heaven, and hope to have it after all.

To His Book

While thou did keep thy candor[1] undefil'd,
Dearly I lov'd thee as my first-born child;
But when I saw thee wantonly to roam
From house to house, and never stay at home,
5   I break° my bonds of love, and bade thee go,   *broke*
Regardless whether well thou sped'st, or no.
On with thy fortunes then, what e're they be;
If good I'll smile, if bad I'll sigh for thee.

Another

To read my book the virgin shy
May blush (with Brutus[1] standing by);
But when he's gone, read through what's writ,
And never stain a cheek for it.

Another

Who with thy leaves shall wipe at need
The place where swelling piles do breed:
May every ill that bites or smarts
Perplex him in his hinder-parts.

To the Sour Reader

If thou dislik'st the piece thou light'st on first;
Think that of all that I have writ, the worst:
But if thou read'st my book unto the end,
And still do'st this and that verse reprehend:
5   O perverse man! If all disgustful be,
Th' extreme scab take thee, and thine, for me.

When He Would Have His Verses Read

In sober mornings, do not thou rehearse
The holy incantation of a verse;
But when that men have both well drunk and fed,
Let my enchantments then be sung or read.

4. Times changing and passing; the cycle of the seasons.
5. Queen of the fairies.
1. A play on the modern meaning of "candor" (frank

honesty) and its Latin meaning, "whiteness, radiance."
1. Presumably her sweetheart.

5　　　When laurel spirits i' th' fire, and when the hearth
　　　　Smiles to itself, and guilds the roof with mirth;
　　　　When up the thyrse[1] is rais'd, and when the sound
　　　　Of sacred orgies[2] flies around, around;
　　　　When the rose reigns, and locks with ointment shine,
10　　　Let rigid Cato[3] read these lines of mine.

Delight in Disorder

　　　　A sweet disorder in the dress
　　　　Kindles in clothes a wantonness:
　　　　A lawn° about the shoulders thrown   *scarf*
　　　　Into a fine distraction;
5　　　An erring° lace, which here and there   *wandering*
　　　　Enthralls the crimson stomacher:[1]
　　　　A cuff neglectful, and thereby
　　　　Ribbons to flow confusedly:
　　　　A winning wave, deserving note,
10　　　In the tempestuous petticoat;
　　　　A carelesse shoestring, in whose tie
　　　　I see a wild civility:
　　　　Do more bewitch me, than when art
　　　　Is too precise[2] in every part.

Corinna's Going A-Maying

　　　　Get up, get up for shame! the blooming morn
　　　　Upon her wings presents the god unshorn.[1]
　　　　　　See how Aurora[2] throws her fair
　　　　　　Fresh-quilted colors through the air:
5　　　　　Get up, sweet slug-a-bed, and see
　　　　　　The dew-bespangling herb and tree.
　　　　Each flower has wept, and bowed toward the east,
　　　　Above an hour since; yet you not dressed,
　　　　　　Nay! not so much as out of bed?
10　　　　When all the birds have matins° said,   *morning prayer*
　　　　And sung their thankfull hymns: 'tis sin,
　　　　　　Nay, profanation° to keep in,   *impiety*
　　　　Whenas a thousand virgins on this day
　　　　Spring, sooner than the lark, to fetch in May.[3]

15　　　Rise, and put on your foliage, and be seen
　　　　To come forth, like the springtime, fresh and green,
　　　　　　And sweet as Flora.[4] Take no care

1. A javelin twisted with ivy.
2. Songs to Bacchus, god of wine.
3. Cato the Elder, Roman statesman (234–149 B.C.E.), who inveighed against moral laxity.
1. Ornamental covering for the chest worn under the lacing of the bodice.
2. "Precise" was often used to describe the strictness of the Puritans.

1. Apollo, the sun god, whose beams are seen as his flowing locks.
2. Goddess of the dawn in Roman mythology.
3. The custom on May Day morning was to gather blossoms.
4. Ancient Italian goddess of fertility and flowers.

For jewels for your gown, or hair:
Fear not; the leaves will strew
20   Gems in abundance upon you;
Besides, the childhood of the day has kept,
Against you come, some orient° pearls unwept;   *oriental, shining*
        Come, and receive them while the light
        Hangs on the dew-locks of the night,
25   And Titan[5] on the eastern hill
        Retires himself, or else stands still
Till you come forth. Wash, dress, be brief in praying:
Few beads are best,[6] when once we go a-Maying.

Come, my Corinna, come; and coming, mark
30 How each field turns a street; each street a park
        Made green, and trimmed with trees; see how
        Devotion gives each house a bough,
        Or branch: each porch, each door, ere this,
        An ark, a tabernacle is,[7]
35 Made up of whitethorn neatly interwove;
As if here were those cooler shades of love.
        Can such delights be in the street
        And open fields, and we not see't?
        Come, we'll abroad; and let's obey
40   The proclamation made for May,
And sin no more, as we have done, by staying;
But my Corinna, come, let's go a-Maying.

There's not a budding boy, or girl, this day,
But is got up, and gone to bring in May.
45   A deal of youth, ere this, is come
        Back, and with whitethorn laden home.
        Some have dispatched their cakes and cream,
        Before that we have left to dream:
And some have wept, and wooed, and plighted troth,
50 And chose their priest, ere we can cast off sloth.
        Many a green-gown has been given,
        Many a kiss, both odd and even:[8]
        Many a glance, too, has been sent
        From out the eye, love's firmament:
55 Many a jest told of the keys betraying
This night, and locks picked; yet we're not a-Maying.

Come, let us go, while we are in our prime,
And take the harmless folly of the time.
        We shall grow old apace, and die
60   Before we know our liberty.

---

5. The sun god.
6. An allusion to Catholic rosary beads.
7. The Hebrew ark of the Covenant contained the tablets of the laws; a tabernacle is an ornamental niche to hold the consecrated host.
8. Green gown . . . given; by lying in the grass. Kisses are odd and even in kissing games.

Our life is short; and our days run
   As fast away as does the sun;
And as a vapor, or a drop of rain
Once lost, can ne'er be found again,
65   So when or you or I are made
     A fable, song, or fleeting shade,°   *soul*
     All love, all liking, all delight
Lies drowned with us in endless night.
Then while time serves, and we are but decaying,
70 Come, my Corinna, come, let's go a-Maying.

To the Virgins, to Make Much of Time

Gather ye rosebuds while ye may,
   Old time is still a-flying;[1]
And this same flower that smiles today,
   Tomorrow will be dying.[2]

5 The glorious lamp of heaven, the sun,
   The higher he's a-getting;
The sooner will his race be run,[3]
   And nearer he's to setting.

That age is best, which is the first,
10   When youth and blood are warmer;
But being spent, the worse, and worst
   Times still succeed the former.
Then be not coy, but use your time,
   And while ye may, go marry;
15 For having lost but once your prime,
   You may for ever tarry.

The Hock-Cart,[1] or Harvest Home
To the Right Honorable, Mildmay, Earl of Westmoreland[2]

Come, sons of summer, by whose toil,
We are the lords of wine and oil;
By whose tough labors, and rough hands,
We rip up first, then reap our lands.
5 Crowned with the ears of corn, now come,
And, to the pipe, sing harvest home.
Come forth, my Lord, and see the cart
Dressed up with all the country art.
See, here a maukin,° there a sheet,   *scarecrow*
10 As spotlesse pure, as it is sweet,
The horses, mares, and frisking fillies,

---

1. The Latin tag *tempus fugit* ("time flies").
2. "Dying" was also a euphemism for orgasm.
3. In Greek mythology, the sun was seen as the chariot of Phoebus Apollo drawn across the sky each day as in a race.

1. Wagon carrying the last load of harvest crops.
2. The landlord, Mildmay Fane (Earl of Westmoreland), was one of Herrick's patrons.

(Clad, all, in linen, white as lilies.)
The harvest swains,° and wenches bound   *young men*
For joy, to see the hock-cart crowned.
15   About the cart, hear how the rout
Of rural younglings raise the shout,
Pressing before, some coming after,
Those with a shout and these with laughter.
Some bless the cart, some kiss the sheaves;
20   Some prank° them up with oaken leaves: *decorate*
Some cross the fill-horse, some with great
Devotion stroke the home-borne wheat:[3]
While other rustics, less attent
To prayers, than to merriment,
25   Run after with their breeches rent.
     Well, on, brave boys, to your Lord's hearth,
Glittering with fire; where, for your mirth,
Ye shall see first the large and chief
Foundation of your feast, fat beef:
30   With upper stories, mutton, veal,
And bacon, (which makes full the meal)
With several dishes standing by,
As here a custard, there a pie,
And here all tempting frumenty.°   *pudding*
35   And for to make the merry cheer,
If smirking° wine be wanting here,   *sparkling*
There's that, which drowns all care, stout beer:
Which freely drink to your Lord's health,
Then to the plough, (the common-wealth),
40   Next to your flails, your fanes, your vats;[4]
Then to the maids with wheaten hats:
To the rough sickle, and crook'd scythe,
Drink, frolic boys, till all be blithe.
     Feed, and grow fat; and as ye eat,
45   Be mindfull, that the laboring neat[5]
As you, may have their fill of meat.
And know, besides, ye must revoke°   *call back*
The patient ox unto the yoke,
And all go back unto the plow
50   And harrow, though they're hanged up now.
And, you must know, your Lord's word's true,
Feed him ye must, whose food fills you,
And that this pleasure is like rain,
Not sent ye for to drown your pain,
55   But for to make it spring again.

---

3. The fill-horse is harnessed between the shafts of the
cart. Crossing the horse and kissing the sheaves of wheat
were old English Catholic customs.

4. Flails: instruments for threshing; fans: used to separate
wheat from chaff.
5. Cattle, whose "meat" is grain or hay.

His Prayer to Ben Jonson[1]

When I a verse shall make,
Know I have prayed thee,
For old religion's sake,[2]
Saint Ben to aid me.

5   Make the way smooth for me,
When I, thy Herrick,
Honoring thee, on my knee
Offer my lyric.

Candles I'll give to thee
10 And a new altar;
And thou Saint Ben shall be
Writ in my psalter.°   *hymn book*

Upon Julia's Clothes

When as in silks my Julia goes,
Then, then, me thinks, how sweetly flows
That liquefaction of her clothes.
Next, when I cast mine eyes and see
5   That brave° vibration each way free;   *splendid*
O how that glittering taketh me!

Upon His Spaniel Tracie

Now thou art dead, no eye shall ever see,
For shape and service, spaniel like to thee.
This shall my love do, give thy sad death one
Tear, that deserves of me a million.

To Dean-Bourn, a Rude River in Devon

Dean-Bourn, farewell; I never look to see
Deane, or thy watery incivility.
Thy rocky bottom that doth tear thy streams,
And makes them frantic, ev'n to all extremes,
5   To my content I never should behold,
Were thy streams silver, or thy rocks all gold.
Rocky thou art; and rocky we discover
Thy men; and rocky are thy ways all over.
O men, O manners; there and ever known
10 To be a rocky generation!
A people currish, churlish as the seas;
And rude (almost) as rudest savages:

---

1. The humorous conceit in this poem is of Ben Jonson as a saint in the "religion" of poetry, aiding Herrick as a saint would intercede for a sinner. Herrick pays homage to Jonson's style both in his humor and verse form. 2. A reference to Jonson's Catholicism.

With whom I did, and may re-sojourn when
Rocks turn to rivers, rivers turn to men.

from **His Noble Numbers**

His Prayer for Absolution

For those my unbaptizèd rhymes,
Writ in my wild unhallow'd times;
For every sentence, clause, and word,
That's not inlaid with Thee (my Lord),
5   Forgive me God, and blot each line
Out of my book that is not Thine.
But if 'mongst all, Thou find'st here one
Worthy thy benediction,
That one of all the rest shall be
10   The glory of my work, and me.

To His Sweet Saviour

Night hath no wings to him that cannot sleep;
And Time seems then not for to fly, but creep;
Slowly her chariot drives, as if that she
Had broke her wheel, or cracked her axeltree.
5   Just so it is with me, who list'ning, pray
The winds to blow the tedious night away,
That I might see the cheerful peeping day.
Sick is my heart! O Saviour! Do Thou please
To make my bed soft in my sicknesses:
10   Lighten my candle, so that I beneath
Sleep not forever in the vaults of death.
Let me Thy voice betimes i' th' morning hear;
Call, and I'll come; say Thou the when and where.
Draw me but first, and after Thee I'll run,
15   And make no one stop till my race be done.

To God, on His Sickness

What though my harp and viol be
Both hung upon the willow tree?[1]
What though my bed be now my grave,
And for my house I darkness have?
5   What though my healthful days are fled,
And I lie number'd with the dead?
Yet I have hope, by Thy great power,
To spring, though now a wither'd flower.

---

1. In Psalm 137, the Hebrew poets, exiled in Babylon, hang their harps in the willow trees, too sorrowful to sing songs of their lost homeland.

George Herbert
1593–1633

Engraved portrait of George Herbert.

George Herbert spent the last three years of his life as a country parson. In an age in which such a church living was often a mere sinecure, Herbert had a genuine vocation, which he chose over other paths open to him through his talent and the connections of his distinguished Welsh family. His education and vocation were most influenced by his mother Magdalene Herbert, a woman with a great appreciation for poetry and strong devotion to the Church of England. When she died in 1627, John Donne gave the funeral sermon, extolling not only her grace, wit, and charm but especially her extraordinary charity to those who suffered from the plague of 1625, among whom was Donne himself. Herbert's mother had been widowed when he was just three years old. She brought up ten children, first in Oxford and then in London, where she saw to it that they were well read in the Bible and the classics.

Herbert studied at Cambridge University, where he became Reader in Rhetoric in 1616; in 1620 he was elected Public Orator, a post that he held for eight years. He wrote poetry and delivered public addresses in Latin and worked on the Latin version of Francis Bacon's *The Advancement of Learning*. Herbert also stood for Parliament and served there in 1624, when the Virginia Company, in which many of his friends and family were stockholders, was beset by financial difficulties and ultimately dissolved by James I.

Though his book *The Temple*, which included all his English poems, was not published until just after his death in 1633, Herbert was already writing verse as an undergraduate in 1610, when he dedicated two sonnets to his mother that advocated religious rather than secular love as the subject for poetry. His first published poems were written in Latin, commemorating the death of Prince Henry (1612). Herbert also wrote three different collections of Latin poems during his Cambridge years: *Musae Responsoriae*, polemical poems that defended the rites of the Church of England from Puritan criticism; *Passio discerpta*, religious verse that focused on Christ's passion and death in a style reminiscent of Crashaw; and *Lucas*, a collection of brief epigrams, such as this one on pride: "Each man is earth, and the field's child. Tell me, / Will you be a sterile mountain or a fertile valley?" The sardonic and mocking tone of these epigrams may surprise a reader of his English poems, but the wit and the rhetorical finish of his Latin poetry recur in his later verse.

Herbert's poetry is some of the most complex and innovative of all English verse. In a very pared-down style, enlivened by gentle irony, Herbert produces complexity of meaning through allegory and emblem, directly or more often indirectly alluding to biblical images, events, and insights, which take on their own moral and poetic meaning in the life of the speaker and the reader. Each of his poems is a kind of spiritual event, enacting in its form, both visual and aural, the very theological experiences and beliefs—or conflict of beliefs—expressed. Herbert allows us to make the spiritual journey with him through suffering and redemption, through doubt and hope. The meaning of one of his poems unravels like a discovery, each line and stanza raising alternative possibilities and altering the meaning of the one before. His spirituality is not a matter of easy acceptance but one of struggle, portrayed with wit, logic, and passion that recall the best of Donne's verse. The humility, subtle hesitancy, and whimsical irony are Herbert's alone, as when he addresses a love poem, *The Pearl*, to God:

> I know the ways of pleasure, the sweet strains,
> The lullings and the relishes of it . . .
> My stuff is flesh, not brass; my senses live,
> And grumble oft, that they have more in me
> Then he that curbs them, being but one to five:
>   Yet I love thee.

The Altar[1]

A broken ALTAR, Lord, thy servant rears,
Made of a heart, and cemented with tears:
    Whole parts are as thy hand did frame;
    No workman's tool has touched the same.[2]
5   A   HEART   alone
              Is   such   a   stone,
              As   nothing   but
              Thy power doth cut.
              Wherefore each part
10   Of my hard heart
              Meets in this frame,
              To praise thy Name.
    That, if I chance to hold my peace,
    These stones to praise thee may not cease.[3]
15 Oh let thy blessed SACRIFICE be mine,
and   sanctify   this   ALTAR   to   be   thine.

Redemption[1]

Having been tenant long to a rich lord,
    Not thriving, I resolvèd to be bold,
    And make a suit unto him, to afford
A new small-rented° lease, and cancel the old.   cheaper

5   In heaven at his manor I him sought:
        They told me there, that he was lately gone
        About some land, which he had dearly bought
    Long since on earth, to take possession.

    I straight returned, and knowing his great birth,
10   Sought him accordingly in great resorts—

1. All of Herbert's poems were published in *The Temple* (1633).
2. See Exodus 20.5, where God tells Moses: "And if thou wilt make me an altar of stone, thou shalt not build it of hewn stone: for if thou lift up thy tool upon it thou has polluted it."
3. See Luke 19.40: "I tell you that, if these should hold their peace, the stones would immediately cry out."
1. "Redemption," means deliverance from sin and comes from the Latin *redimere*, meaning to buy back, to ransom.

In cities, theaters, gardens, parks, and courts:
At length I heard a ragged noise and mirth

Of thieves and murderers: there I him espied,
Who straight, "Your suit is granted," said, and died.

Easter

Rise heart, thy Lord is risen. Sing his praise
           Without delays,
Who takes thee by the hand, that thou likewise
           With him may'st rise:
5   That, as his death calcinèd° thee to dust,   *reduced by fire*
His life may make thee gold, and much more just.

Awake, my lute, and struggle for thy part
           With all thy art.
The cross taught all wood to resound his name
10   Who bore the same.
His stretchèd sinews taught all strings, what key
Is best to celebrate this most high day.

Consort° both heart and lute, and twist a song   *harmonize*
           Pleasant and long:
15   Or, since all music is but three parts vied
           And multiplied,[1]
Oh let thy blessed spirit bear a part,
And make up our defects with his sweet art.

I got me flowers to strew thy way;
20   I got me boughs off many a tree:
But thou wast up by break of day,
And brought'st thy sweets along with thee.

The sun arising in the east,
Though he give light, and th' east perfume,
25   If they should offer to contest
With thy arising, they presume.

Can there be any day but this,
Though many suns to shine endeavor?
We count three hundred, but we miss:[2]
30   There is but one, and that one ever.

1. Since music is increased by three-part harmony.
2. We are mistaken in reckoning that there are 300-plus days in the year, since they are all but as one day when compared to the light of the Son (Christ) rising.

Easter Wings[1]

Lord, who createdst man in wealth and store,[2]
Though foolishly he lost the same,
Decaying more and more,
Till he became
Most poor:
With thee
Oh let me rise
As larks, harmoniously,
And sing this day thy victories:
Then shall the fall[3] further the flight in me.

My tender age in sorrow did begin
And still with sickness and shame
Thou didst so punish sin,
That I became
Most thin.
With thee
Let me combine,
And feel this day thy victory:
For, if I imp[4] my wing on thine,
Affliction shall advance the flight in me.

Affliction (1)[1]

When first thou didst entice to thee my heart,
        I thought the service brave:
So many joys I wrote down for my part,
        Besides what I might have
5 Out of my stock of natural delights,
Augmented with thy gracious benefits.

I lookèd on thy furniture so fine,
        And made it fine to me:
Thy glorious household stuff did me entwine,
        And 'tice me unto thee.
10 Such stars I counted mine: both heaven and earth
Paid me my wages in a world of mirth.

What pleasures could I want, whose king I served,
        Where joys my fellows were?
15 Thus argued into hopes, my thoughts reserved
        No place for grief or fear;
Therefore my sudden soul caught at the place,
And made her youth and fierceness seek thy face.

1. As in the first editions of Herbert, this poem is printed sideways to represent the shape of wings.
2. Plenty.
3. The human frailty of sin, as well as the speaker's own descent into sin and suffering, which Christ redeems through his rising from the dead on Easter.
4. In falconry, to insert feathers in a bird's wing.
1. Editors assign numbers to poems to which Herbert gave the same title to distinguish them from one another.

At first thou gav'st me milk and sweetness;
          I had my wish and way:
My days were strawed° with flowers and happiness;   *strewed*
          There was no month but May.
But with my years sorrow did twist and grow,
And made a party unawares for woe.

My flesh began unto my soul in pain,[2]
          Sicknesses cleave° my bones;   *penetrate*
Consuming agues dwell in every vein,
          And tune my breath to groans,
Sorrow was all my soul, I scarce believed,
Till grief did tell me roundly, that I lived.

When I got health, thou took'st away my life,
          And more; for my friends die:
My mirth and edge was lost; a blunted knife
          Was of more use than I.
Thus thin and lean without a fence or friend,
I was blown through with every storm and wind.

Whereas my birth and spirit rather took
          The way that takes the town,
Thou didst betray me to a lingering book,
          And wrap me in a gown.
I was entangled in the world of strife,
Before I had the power to change my life.

Yet, for I threatened often the siege to raise,
          Not simpering all mine age,
Thou often did with academic praise
          Melt and dissolve my rage.
I took thy sweetened pill, till I came near;
I could not go away, nor persevere.

Yet, lest perchance I should too happy be
          In my unhappiness,
Turning my purge[3] to food, thou throwest me
          Into more sickness.
Thus does thy power cross-bias[4] me, not making
Thine own gift good, yet me from my ways taking.

Now I am here, what thou wilt do with me
          None of my books will show:
I read, and sigh, and wish I were a tree,
          For sure then I should grow
To fruit or shade; at least some bird would trust
Her household to me, and I should be just.

---

2. The body speaks to the soul from this point on.   4. To give an inclination running counter to another.
3. Medicine inducing evacuation of the bowels.

Yet, though thou troublest me, I must be meek;
               In weakness must be stout.
Well, I will change the service, and go seek
               Some other master out.
65 Ah my dear God! though I am clean forgot,
Let me not love thee, if I love thee not.

Prayer (1)

Prayer the church's banquet; angels' age,
    God's breath in man returning to his birth;
    The soul in paraphrase, heart in pilgrimage;
The Christian plummet[1] sounding heaven and earth;

5 Engine against th' Almighty, sinner's tower,[2]
    Reversèd thunder, Christ-side-piercing spear,
    The six-days world transposing in an hour;
A kind of tune, which all things hear and fear;

Softness, and peace, and joy, and love, and bliss;
10   Exalted manna,[3] gladness of the best;
    Heaven in ordinary,[4] man well dressed,
The milky way, the bird of paradise,[5]

    Church bells beyond the stars heard, the soul's blood,
    The land of spices; something understood.

Jordan (1)[1]

Who says that fictions only and false hair
Become a verse? Is there in truth no beauty?
Is all good structure in a winding stair?
May no lines pass, except they do their duty
5   Not to a true, but painted chair?

Is it no verse, except enchanted groves
And sudden arbors shadow coarse-spun lines?
Must purling° streams refresh a lover's loves?   *rippling*
Must all be veiled, while he that reads, divines,[2]
10   Catching the sense at two removes?

Shepherds are honest people; let them sing:
Riddle who list,[3] for me, and pull for prime.[4]
I envy no man's nightingale or spring;

1. A metal weight used to measure, or sound, the depth of
water; figuratively, the criterion of truth.
2. A stronghold or fortress, used for purposes of defense.
3. The food that God supplied to the Jews during their
wandering in the wilderness.
4. What is usual; or, a meal in a tavern.
5. A bird, found in New Guinea, known for its beautiful
feathers.
1. To cross the river Jordan symbolizes entering the
Promised Land.
2. To interpret what is obscure through magical insight or
intuitive conjecture.
3. Whoever wants to may interpret.
4. Draw a lucky card, or hit upon a lucky guess.

Nor let them punish me with loss of rhyme,
15   Who plainly say, *My God, My King.*

Church Monuments

While that my soul repairs to her devotion,
Here I entomb my flesh, that it betimes
May take acquaintance of this heap of dust;
To which the blast of death's incessant motion,
5   Fed with the exhalation of our crimes,
Drives all at last. Therefore I gladly trust

My body to this school, that it may learn
To spell his elements and find his birth
Written in dusty heraldry and lines
10   Which dissolution sure does best discern,
Comparing dust with dust, and earth with earth.[1]
These[2] laugh at jet and marble, put for signs

To sever the good fellowship of dust
And spoil the meeting. What shall point out them[3]
15   When they shall bow, and kneel, and fall down flat
To kiss those heaps, which now they have in trust?
Dear flesh, while I do pray, learn here thy stem
And true descent; that when thou shalt grow fat,

And wanton in thy cravings, thou may'st know,
20   That flesh is but the glass, which holds the dust
That measures all our time, which also shall
Be crumbled into dust. Mark here below
How tame these ashes are, how free from lust,
That thou may'st set thyself against thy fall.

The Windows

Lord, how can man preach thy eternal word?
    He is a brittle, crazy° glass,   cracked
Yet in thy temple thou do him afford
    This glorious and transcendent place,
5   To be a window, through thy grace.

But when thou dost anneal[1] in glass thy story,
    Making thy life to shine within
The holy preachers, then the light and glory
    More reverent grows, and does win
10   Which else shows watr'ish, bleak, and thin.

---

1. An allusion to Genesis 3.19: "for dust thou art and to dust shalt thou return."
2. Dust and earth.
3. The souls that cling to "those heaps," the dust of their bodies and of the earth.
1. To burn in colors on glass.

Doctrine and life, colors and light, in one
      When they combine and mingle, bring
A strong regard and awe; but speech alone
      Doth vanish like a flaring thing,
15   And in the ear, not conscience ring.

Denial

When my devotions could not pierce
      Thy silent ears;
Then was my heart broken, as was my verse:
      My breast was full of tears
5   And disorder:

My bent thoughts, like a brittle bow,
      Did fly asunder:
Each took his way; some would to pleasures go,
      Some to the wars and thunder
10   Of alarms.

As good go anywhere, they say,
      As to benumb
Both knees and heart in crying night and day,
      Come, come, my God, Oh come!
15   But no hearing.

O that thou shouldst give dust a tongue
      To cry to thee,
And then not hear it crying! All day long
      My heart was in my knee,
20   But no hearing.

Therefore my soul lay out of sight,
      Untuned, unstrung;
My feeble spirit, unable to look right,
      Like a nipped bloom, hung
25   Discontented.

Oh cheer and tune my heartless breath,
      Defer no time,
That so thy favors granting my request,
      They and my mind may chime,°   *ring together, agree*
30   And mend my rhyme.

Virtue

Sweet day, so cool, so calm, so bright,
The bridal° of the earth and sky: *wedding*
The dew shall weep thy fall tonight,
      For thou must die.

5 Sweet rose, whose hue, angry and brave
Bids the rash gazer wipe his eye:
Thy root is ever in its grave,
And thou must die.

Sweet spring, full of sweet days and roses,
10 A box where sweets° compacted lie;   *pleasant fragrances*
My music shows ye have your closes,[1]
And all must die.

Only a sweet and virtuous soul,
Like seasoned timber, never gives;
15 But though the whole world turn to coal,[2]
Then chiefly lives.

Man

My God, I heard this day
That none doth build a stately habitation,
But he that means to dwell therein.
What house more stately hath there been,
5 Or can be, than is man? to[1] whose creation
All things are in decay.

For man is everything,
And more; he is a tree, yet bears more[2] fruit;
A beast, yet is, or should be more:
10 Reason and speech we only bring.
Parrots may thank us, if they are not mute:
They go upon the score.[3]

Man is all symmetry,
Full of proportions, one limb to another,
15 And all to all the world besides:
Each part may call the farthest, brother;
For head with foot has private amity,
And both with moons and tides.

Nothing hath got so far
20 But man hath caught and kept it as his prey.
His eyes dismount the highest star:
He is in little all the sphere.[4]
Herbs gladly cure our flesh; because that they
Find their acquaintance there.

25 For us the winds do blow,
The earth doth rest, heav'n move, and fountains flow;

---

1. Cadences, indicating that Herbert wanted this poem to be sung.
2. Reduced to ashes as at the Last Judgment.
1. In comparison to.

2. An alternative reading is "no."
3. They are indebted to us.
4. See Robert Fludd's engraving of the human body as microcosm of the universe, page 1068.

Nothing we see, but means our good,
As our delight, or as our treasure.
The whole is, either our cupboard of food,
30   Or cabinet of pleasure.

The stars have us to bed;
Night draws the curtain, which the sun withdraws,
Music and light attend our head.
All things unto our flesh are kind
35   In their descent and being; to our mind
In their ascent and cause.

Each thing is full of duty.
Waters united are our navigation,
Distinguished, our habitation;
40   Below, our drink; above, our meat;
Both are our cleanliness. Hath one such beauty?
Then how are all things neat?

More servants wait on man
Than he'll take notice of: in ev'ry path,
45   He treads down that which doth befriend him,
When sickness makes him pale and wan.
Oh mighty love! Man is one world, and hath
Another to attend him.

Since then, my God, thou hast
50   So brave a palace built, O dwell in it,
That it may dwell with thee at last!
Till then, afford us so much wit,
That, as the world serves us, we may serve thee,
And both thy servants be.

Jordan (2)

When first my lines of heav'nly joys made mention,
Such was their luster, they did so excel,
That I sought out quaint° words, and trim invention;   *clever*
My thoughts began to burnish,° sprout, and swell,   *spread out*
5   Curling with metaphors a plain intention,
Decking the sense, as if it were to sell.[1]

Thousands of notions in my brain did run,
Off'ring their service, if I were not sped.[2]
I often blotted what I had begun;
10   This was not quick° enough, and that was dead.   *lively*
Nothing could seem too rich to clothe the sun,
Much less those joys which trample on his head.[3]

1. Decorating the meaning as if it were for sale.
2. Dealt with so that I was satisfied.

3. The sun is a symbol for Christ; the sun's head is the Son's head.

As flames do work and wind, when they ascend,
So did I weave my self into the sense.
15 But while I bustled, I might hear a friend
Whisper, "How wide° is all this long pretence!   *beside the point*
There is in love a sweetness ready penn'd:
Copy out only that, and save expense."

Time

Meeting with time, "Slack thing," said I,
"Thy scythe is dull; whet it for shame."
"No marvel sir," he did reply,
"If it at length deserve some blame:
5   But where one man would have me grind it,
Twenty for one too sharp do find it."

"Perhaps some such of old did pass,[1]
Who above all things lov'd this life;
To whom thy scythe a hatchet was,
10 Which now is but a pruning knife.
Christ's coming hath made man thy debtor,
Since by thy cutting he grows better.

"And in this blessing thou art blest:
For where thou only wert before
15 An executioner at best,
Thou art a gard'ner now, and more,
An usher to convey our souls
Beyond the utmost stars and poles.

"And this is that makes life so long,
20 While it detains us from our God.
Ev'n pleasures here increase the wrong,
And length of days lengthen the rod.
Who wants° the place, where God doth dwell,   *lacks*
Partakes already half of hell.

"Of what strange length must that needs be,
Which ev'n eternity excludes!"
Thus far Time heard me patiently:
Then chafing° said, "This man deludes: *getting angry*
What do I here before his door?
30 He doth not crave less time, but more."

The Collar

I struck the board,° and cried, "No more.   *table*
I will abroad!
What? Shall I ever sigh and pine?

---

1. Herbert is the speaker in stanzas 2, 3, and 4 and in the first two lines of stanza 5.

My lines and life are free; free as the road,
    Loose as the wind, as large as store.°   *abundance*
        Shall I be still in suit?[1]
Have I no harvest but a thorn
To let me blood, and not restore
What I have lost with cordial[2] fruit?
                Sure there was wine
    Before my sighs did dry it; there was corn
    Before my tears did drown it.
Is the year only lost to me?
    Have I no bays[3] to crown it?
No flowers, no garlands gay? all blasted?
                All wasted?
Not so, my heart; but there is fruit,
            And thou hast hands.
Recover all thy sigh-blown age
On double pleasures: leave thy cold dispute
Of what is fit and not forsake thy cage,
            Thy rope of sands,
Which petty thoughts have made, and made to thee
    Good cable, to enforce and draw,
              And be thy law,
While thou didst wink[4] and wouldst not see.
            Away! take heed:
            I will abroad.
Call in thy death's head[5] there: tie up thy fears.
              He that forbears
    To suit and serve his need,
            Deserves his load."
But as I raved and grew more fierce and wild
            At every word,
Me thoughts I heard one calling, *Child!*
        And I replied, *My Lord.*

The Pulley

      When God at first made man,
Having a glass of blessings standing by,
"Let us," said he "pour on him all we can:
Let the world's riches, which dispersèd lie,
      Contract into a span."

      So strength first made a way;
Then beauty flowed, then wisdom, honor, pleasure:
When almost all was out, God made a stay,
Perceiving that alone of all his treasure
      Rest in the bottom lay.[1]

---

1. Engaged in a lawsuit.
2. Invigorating to the heart.
3. The poet's laurel wreath.
4. Shut your eyes to.

5. The skull as an emblem of human mortality.
1. "Rest" in the sense of repose, or freedom from distress, and in the sense of remainder, or surplus.

"For if I should," said he,
"Bestow this jewel also on my creature,
He would adore my gifts instead of me,
And rest in Nature, not the God of Nature.
15   So both should losers be.

"Yet let him keep the rest,
But keep them with repining° restlessness: *complaining*
Let him be rich and weary, that at least,
If goodness lead him not, yet weariness
20   May toss him to my breast."

The Forerunners

The harbingers[1] are come: see, see their mark;
White is their color, and behold my head.
But must they have my brain? Must they dispark°   *turn out*
Those sparkling notions, which therein were bred?
5   Must dullness turn me to a clod?
Yet have they left me, "Thou art still my God."

Good men ye be, to leave me my best room,
Ev'n all my heart, and what is lodged there:
I pass not, I, what of the rest become,
10   So "Thou art still my God," be out of fear.[2]
          He will be pleasèd with that ditty;
And if I please him, I write fine and witty.

Farewell, sweet phrases, lovely metaphors:
But will ye leave me thus? when ye before
15   Of stews[3] and brothels only knew the doors,
Then did I wash you with my tears, and more,
          Brought you to Church well-dressed and clad:
My God must have my best, ev'n all I had.

Lovely enchanting language, sugarcane,
20   Honey of roses, whither wilt thou fly?
Hath some fond lover 'ticed thee to thy bane?
And wilt thou leave the Church, and love a sty?
          Fie, thou wilt soil thy 'broidered coat,
And hurt thy self, and him that sings the note.

25   Let foolish lovers, if they will love dung,
With canvas, not with arras° clothe their shame: *rich tapestry*
Let Folly speak in her own native tongue.
True Beauty dwells on high; ours is a flame

---

1. Men sent out before a royal train to requisition lodgings by marking the doors with chalk.

2. I don't care about anything except being left with the
thought that "Thou art still my God."
3. Public hot bathhouses, brothels.

But borrowed thence to light us thither:
30   Beauty and beauteous words should go together.

Yet if you go, I pass not; take your way.
For, "Thou art still my God" is all that ye
Perhaps with more embellishment can say.
Go, birds of spring; let winter have his fee;
35   Let a bleak paleness chalk the door.
So all within be livelier than before.

Love (3)

Love bade me welcome: yet my soul drew back,
      Guilty of dust and sin.
But quick-eyed Love, observing me grow slack°   *slow, weak*
      From my first entrance in,
5   Drew nearer to me, sweetly questioning,
      If I lacked anything.

"A guest," I answered, "worthy to be here":
      Love said, "You shall be he."
"I the unkind, ungrateful? Ah my dear,
10   I cannot look on thee."
Love took my hand, and smiling did reply,
      "Who made the eyes but I?"

"Truth Lord, but I marred them; let my shame
      Go where it doth deserve."
15   "And know you not," says Love, "who bore the blame?"
      "My dear, then I will serve."
"You must sit down," says Love, "and taste my meat."
      So I did sit and eat.[1]

Richard Lovelace
1618–1657

In *To His Noble Friend*, Andrew Marvell portrays Richard Lovelace as an amorous and chival-
rous courtier from a world destroyed by "Our Civil Wars." Marvell depicts the consternation
that arose

When the beauteous ladies came to know
That their dear Lovelace was endangered so:
Lovelace that thawed the most congealèd breast
He who loved best and them defended best.

---

1. The speaker takes Communion, which symbolizes union with God.

The dashing and handsome Lovelace was the last exemplar of courtly *sprezzatura* in the history of English poetry, recalling the eroticism and finesse of Wyatt and the chivalry of Sidney and Raleigh. The voluptuousness and elegance that characterized his poetry no less than the Carolinian court was destroyed by the Puritan Revolution.

Lovelace's brief life was indeed endangered more than once—all because of his allegiance to the Royalist cause. After only two years at Cambridge University, he left school to fight in the army of King Charles I, serving as senior ensign in the First Scottish expedition of 1639 and captain in the second of 1640. Both expeditions were disasters for the King's forces. Lovelace was imprisoned twice, first in 1642 for presenting an anti-Parliamentary petition from his home county Kent and again in 1648, when Marvell's patron Lord Fairfax brought the Roundhead (Puritan) army right to the doors of Lovelace's country estate. During his first stint in prison, Lovelace wrote one of his most memorable poems, *To Althea, from Prison*. Released on bail, he lived a precarious life, aiding the King's cause by selling his property and giving money to supply arms. In 1649, when he was released from prison the second time, Lovelace was reduced to selling all of his property, even his family portraits.

Lovelace is a representative of the cultural milieu of the court of Charles I, which included many poets and painters of great distinction. The regime was graced by such poets as Sir John Suckling, Thomas Carew, Abraham Cowley, and Edmund Waller, sometimes referred to as the Cavalier poets, among whom Lovelace is considered the greatest. Lovelace admired not only the works of his fellow poets but also the paintings of Rubens, Van Dyck, and Lely, which adorned the court. Lovelace was great friends with and wrote poems praising Lely, who designed plates for Lovelace's two books of poems, published in 1649 and 1659. Lovelace enjoyed painting and music as a gentleman amateur, the characteristic persona of a Cavalier poet. His poems express a tone of extravagant passion tempered with courtly poise achieved through lush images conveying a sensuous *joie de vivre* and a perspective of brave insouciance mixed with self-deprecating irony. His deft rhythms create songlike poems with a spontaneous grace and ease, stylistic ideals of the Cavaliers.

We know nothing about Lovelace after 1649. His brother Philip had been colonel in the King's army but survived the Interregnum to become governor of New York in 1688. Of his brother William's death on the field of battle in the Civil War, Richard had written these stoic lines to Philip:

> Iron decrees of Destiny
> Are ne'er wiped out with a wet eye.
> But this way you may gain the field,
> Oppose but sorrow, and 'twill yield;
> One gallant thorough made resolve
> Doth starry influence dissolve.

To Lucasta, Going to the Wars

Tell me not, sweet, I am unkind,
    That from the nunnery
Of thy chaste breast and quiet mind
    To war and arms I fly.

5   True, a new mistress now I chase,
    The first foe in the field;
And with a stronger faith embrace
    A sword, a horse, a shield.

Yet this inconstancy is such
　　As you too shall adore;
I could not love thee, dear, so much,
　　Loved I not honor more.

1649

The Grasshopper[1]
To My Noble Friend, Mr. Charles Cotton[2]

O thou that swing'st upon the waving hair
　　Of some well-fillèd oaten beard,
Drunk ev'ry night with a delicious tear
　　Dropped thee from heav'n, where now th' art reared,

5　　The joys of earth and air are thine entire,
　　　　That with thy feet and wings dost hop and fly;
And when thy poppy[3] works thou dost retire
　　　　To thy carved acorn-bed to lie.

Up with the day, the sun thou welcom'st then,
10　　　Sport'st in the gilt-plats° of his beams,　　　　*golden fields*
And all these merry days mak'st merry men,
　　　　Thyself, and melancholy streams.

But ah the sickle! golden ears are cropped,
　　　　Ceres and Bacchus[4] bid good night;
15　Sharp frosty fingers all your flowers have topped,
　　　　And what scythes spared, winds shave off quite.

Poor verdant fool! and now green ice! thy joys,
　　　　Large and as lasting as thy perch of grass,
Bid us lay in 'gainst winter, rain, and poise°　　　*counterbalance*
20　　Their floods, with an o'erflowing glass.

Thou best of men and friends! We will create
　　　　A genuine summer in each other's breast;
And spite of this cold time and frozen fate[5]
　　　　Thaw us a warm seat to our rest.

25　Our sacred hearths shall burn eternally
　　　　As vestal flames;[6] the North Wind, he
Shall strike his frost-stretched wings, dissolve and fly
　　　　This Etna[7] in epitome.

Dropping December shall come weeping in,
30　　Bewail th' usurping of his reign;

---

1. The grasshopper was associated with a carefree life.
2. Charles Cotton was a learned and literary man. This poem describes the atmosphere of Puritan rule during the Interregnum.
3. A plant with narcotic powers.
4. The goddess of agriculture and the god of wine.

5. A reference to the persecution of Royalists during the rule of the Puritans.
6. The Roman Vestal Virgins attended to the eternal flame.
7. A volcano, here symbolizing the force and warmth of friendship.

But when in showers of old Greek[8] we begin,
    Shall cry, he hath his crown[9] again!

Night as clear Hesper shall our tapers whip
    From the light casements where we play,
35   And the dark hag from her black mantle strip,
    And stick there everlasting day.[1]

Thus richer than untempted kings are we,
    That asking nothing, nothing need:
Though Lord of all what seas embrace; yet he
40   That wants himself is poor indeed.

1649

To Althea, from Prison

When love with unconfined wings
    Hovers within my gates,
And my divine Althea brings
    To whisper at the grates:
5   When I lie tangled in her hair
    And fettered to her eye,
The gods[1] that wanton° in the air,   *play*
    Know no such liberty.

When flowing cups run swiftly round,
10   With no allaying Thames,[2]
Our careless heads with roses bound,
    Our hearts with loyal flames;
When thirsty grief in wine we steep,
    When healths and draughts go free,
15 Fishes that tipple in the deep
    Know no such liberty.

When, like committed° linnets,° I   *confined / songbirds*
    With shriller throat shall sing
The sweetness, mercy, majesty,
20   And glories of my king;
When I shall voice aloud, how good
    He is, how great should be,
Enlargèd winds that curl the flood,
    Know no such liberty.

25 Stone walls do not a prison make,
    Nor iron bars a cage;
Minds innocent and quiet take
    That for an hermitage;°   *hermit's dwelling*

---

8. The wine that was most prized in ancient Rome.
9. Wreath worn at a drinking party.
1. Hesperus, the morning star; casements: frames forming windows; the dark hag: Hecate, daughter of Night.

1. Some editions read "birds" rather than "gods."
2. River running through London; the meaning of this line is "with no water to dilute the wine."

If I have freedom in my love,
30   And in my soul am free,
Angels alone that soar above,
    Enjoy such liberty.

1649

Love Made in the First Age: To Chloris[1]

In the nativity of time,
Chloris, it was not thought a crime
    In direct Hebrew for to woo.[2]
Now we make love, as all on fire,
5   Ring retrograde[3] our loud desire,
    And court in English backward too.

Thrice happy was that golden age,
When compliment was construed rage,[4]
    And fine words in the center hid;
10   When cursed *No* stained no maid's bliss,
And all discourse was summed in *Yes,*
    And nought forbade, but to forbid.

Love then unstinted, love did sip,
And cherries plucked fresh from the lip,
15   On cheeks and roses free he fed;
Lasses like autumn plums did drop,
And lads, indifferently did crop
    A flower, and a maidenhead.

Then unconfinèd each did tipple
20   Wine from the bunch, milk from the nipple;
    Paps tractable as udders were;
Then equally the wholesome jellies
Were squeezed from olive-trees, and bellies,
    Nor suits of trespass did they fear.

25   A fragrant bank of strawberries,
Diapered° with violet's eyes,   *decorated*
    Was table, tablecloth, and fare;
No palace to the clouds did swell;
Each humble princess then did dwell
30   In the piazza[5] of her hair.

Both broken faith, and the cause of it,
All-damning gold was damned to the pit;
    Their troth sealed with a clasp and kiss,

1. "The First Age" refers to the golden age of Greek and Roman mythology, a time of idyllic plenty in which there was no need for laws or work.
2. Hebrew, which reads from right to left, was believed to have been the original language.
3. In backward or reverse direction; an imitation of notes in contrary motion.
4. When compliments were interpreted as passionate proposals.
5. A colonnade surrounding a square.

Lasted until that extreme day,
35   In which they smiled their souls away,
     And, in each other breathed new bliss.

Because no fault, there was no tear;
No groan did grate the granting ear;
     No false foul breath their delicate smell:
40   No serpent kiss poisoned the taste,
Each touch was naturally chaste,
     And their mere sense a miracle.

Naked as their own innocence,
And unembroidered[6] from offense
45   They went, above poor riches, gay;   *young swan's*
On softer than the cygnet's° down,
In beds they tumbled of their own;
     For each within the other lay.

Thus did they live: thus did they love,
50   Repeating only joys above;
     And angels were, but with clothes on,
Which they would put off cheerfully,
To bathe them in the galaxy,[7]
     Then gird them with the heavenly zone.[8]

55   Now, Chloris, miserably crave
The offered bliss you would not have;
     Which evermore I must deny,
Whilst ravished with these noble dreams
And crownèd with mine own soft beams,
60   Enjoying of myself I lie.

Henry Vaughan
1622–1695

Henry Vaughan grew up speaking Welsh among the woods and streams of Newton in the parish of Llansantffraed. He responded to the sound of his first language and to the beauty of this countryside in the music and imagery of his poetry. For example, the slope of Mount Allt, on which he lived, provided a striking image: "those faint beams in which this hill is dressed, / After the Sun's remove." The Welsh influence can be heard in his poetry's alliteration and assonance; his piling up of comparisons, as in *The Night*, is called *dyfalu* ("to liken") in Welsh poetic technique. On the title page to his second book of verse, *Olor Iscanus* ("The Swan of Usk" [a local river]), he is called a "Silurist," a member of an ancient Welsh tribe. Though his verse is written in English, Vaughan's poetry and identity were always bound up with his native land.

---

6. Not ornamented with the trappings of authority.   8. The zodiac of stars.
7. The Milky Way.

Henry Vaughan's Welsh childhood was followed by education at Oxford, where he studied with his twin brother Thomas, and then at the Inns of Court in London, where he began his poetic apprenticeship. An admirer of Ben Jonson's verse, Vaughan praised and imitated Jonson in his first book of poetry, *Poems with the Tenth Satyre of Juvenal Englished* (1646). The mysticism and Neoplatonism of Vaughan's best known collection of poems, *Silex Scintillans* ("The Fiery Flint") (1650), link him to the metaphysical tradition of Donne, Herbert, and Crashaw, yet his verse continued to show fondness for the wit and spareness of Jonson.

At the outbreak of the Civil War, Vaughan returned to Wales in August 1642. He worked as secretary to the Circuit Chief Justice of the Great Sessions until 1645, when he joined the company of soldiers who fought for King Charles's cause with Sir Herbert Price at Chester. The poems in *Silex Scintillans* express his anger and disappointment at the outcome of the Civil War. In *Prayer in Time of Persecution*, Vaughan rails against the Puritans for confiscating the woods of his family's estate. The 1650 Act for the Propagation of the Gospel in Wales gave a committee of Puritan commissioners the power to purge the Welsh royalist clergy. Among these was Henry's brother Thomas, who was stripped of his position and livelihood. In *The World*, Vaughan describes a "darksome statesman" reminiscent of Cromwell; and in several poems, Vaughan complains of the Puritan "zeal" that brought about regicide and persecution of the Church of England. In *Christ's Nativity*, Vaughan lamented the Puritans' prohibition of the observance of Christmas and Good Friday:

> Shall he that came down from thence,
>   And here for us was slain,
> Shall he be now cast off? no sense
>   Of all his woes remain?
> Can neither Love, nor sufferings bind?
>   Are we all stone, and Earth?
> Neither his bloody passions mind,
>   Nor one day bless his birth?
> Alas, my God! Thy birth now here
> Must not be numbered in the year.

There is even evidence in one poem, *The Proffer*, that Vaughan disdained offers of power from Cromwell's government: "I'll not stuff my story / With your Commonwealth and glory." Some time after 1650, Vaughan decided to study and practice medicine.

The 1650s were troubled years for Vaughan. During this time he grieved for the deaths of his brother Thomas and his first wife Catherine. In the preface to the second edition of *Silex Scintillans* in 1655, Vaughan refers to an illness he had suffered, which seems to have been spiritual and may even have resulted in a kind of conversion experience. In this same preface, Vaughan also praises George Herbert: "his holy life and verse gained many pious Converts of whom I am the least." Along with the Bible, Herbert's verse is the main influence on Vaughan's. The titles of twenty-six lyrics in *Silex Scintillans* are taken from Herbert's *The Temple*. Both poets describe a spiritual paradise, but while Herbert's is ineffable, Vaughan's has the physical beauty of an actual landscape. Vaughan's temple stretches beyond the pristine church architecture of Herbert's imagery to touch flowers and trees and to contemplate the stars. Vaughan's feeling for nature is unsurpassed in English verse until Wordsworth. Vaughan's intense sense of the transitoriness of natural beauty and the immanence of mortality make his verse worth contemplating and savoring.

Regeneration

> A ward, and still in bonds, one day
>   I stole abroad;
> It was high spring, and all the way

<pre>
        Primrosed, and hung with shade;
5   Yet, was it frost within,
            And surly winds
    Blasted my infant buds, and sin
        Like clouds eclipsed my mind.

    Stormed thus, I straight perceived my spring
10   Mere stage and show,
    My walk a monstrous, mountained thing,
        Roughcast with rocks, and snow;
        And as a pilgrim's eye
            Far from relief,
15 Measures the melancholy sky,
        Then drops, and rains for grief,

    So sighed I upwards still, at last
            'Twixt steps, and falls
    I reached the pinnacle, where placed
20   I found a pair of scales,
        I took them up and laid
            In th'one late pains,
    The other smoke, and pleasures weighed,
        But proved the heavier grains.

25 With that, some cried, "Away!" Straight I
            Obeyed, and led
    Full east, a fair, fresh field could spy;
        Some called it, Jacob's bed,¹
        A virgin soil, which no
30   Rude feet ere trod,
    Where, since he stepped there, only go
        Prophets, and friends of God.

    Here, I reposed; but scarce well set,
            A grove descried
35 Of stately height, whose branches met
        And mixed on every side;
        I entered, and once in,
            Amazed to see't,
    Found all was changed, and a new spring
40   Did all my senses greet;
</pre>

The unthrift° sun shot vital gold   *spendthrift*
<pre>
            A thousand pieces,
    And heaven its azure did unfold,
        Checkered with snowy fleeces,
45   The air was all in spice,
            And every bush
</pre>

---

1. See Genesis 28.11–19. Sleeping outdoors, Jacob had a vision of a ladder in the sky leading up to God.

A garland wore; thus fed my eyes,
           But all the ear lay hush.

Only a little fountain lent
50   Some use for ears,
And on the dumb shades language spent
           The music of her tears;
       I drew her near, and found
           The cistern full
55 Of divers stones, some bright, and round
           Others ill-shaped, and dull.

The first, pray mark, as quick as light
           Danced through the flood,
But, th'last more heavy than the night
60   Nailed to the center stood;
      I wondered much, but tired
          At last with thought,
My restless eye that still desired
         As strange an object brought;

65 It was a bank of flowers, where I descried,
           Though 'twas mid-day,
Some fast asleep, others broad-eyed
         And taking in the ray,
       Here musing long, I heard
70   A rushing wind
Which still increased, but whence it stirred
        Nowhere I could not find.

I turned me round, and to each shade
          Dispatched an eye,
75 To see, if any leaf had made
         Least motion, or reply;
       But while I listening sought
         My mind to ease
By knowing, where 'twas, or where not,
80   It whispered, "Where I please."[2]

"Lord," then said I, "on me one breath,
    And let me die before my death!"

The Retreat

Happy those early days! when I
Shined in my angel infancy.

---

2. John 3.8: "The wind bloweth where it listeth, and thou hearest the sound thereof, but canst not tell whence it cometh, and whither it goeth: so is every one that is born of the Spirit." See also Genesis 2.7 for the breath of life that God breathed into humanity.

Before I understood this place
Appointed for my second race,[1]
5   Or taught my soul to fancy ought
But a white, celestial thought;
When yet I had not walked above
A mile or two from my first love,
And looking back, at that short space,
10   Could see a glimpse of his bright face;
When on some gilded cloud, or flower
My gazing soul would dwell an hour,
And in those weaker glories spy
Some shadows of eternity;
15   Before I taught my tongue to wound
My conscience with a sinful sound,
Or had the black art to dispense
A several° sin to every sense,   *separate*
But felt through all this fleshly dress
20   Bright shoots of everlastingness.
   O, how I long to travel back,
And tread again that ancient track!
That I might once more reach that plain
Where first I left my glorious train,
25   From whence th' enlightened spirit sees
That shady city of palm trees.[2]
But, ah! my soul with too much stay°   *hesitation*
Is drunk, and staggers in the way.
Some men a forward motion love;
30   But I by backward steps would move,
And when this dust falls to the urn
In that state I came, return.

Silence, and Stealth of Days[1]

Silence, and stealth of days! 'tis now
      Since thou art gone,
Twelve hundred hours, and not a brow[2]
      But clouds hang on.
5   As he that in some cave's thick damp,
      Locked from the light,
Fixeth a solitary lamp,
      To brave the night

1. "Second race" implies a Platonic belief in the reincarnation of the soul and in the preexistence of the soul in the world of perfect forms.
2. The New Jerusalem, the Paradise of Heaven.
1. The poem is about the death of Vaughan's younger brother William, who died in July 1648.
2. Facial expression, but also a gallery in a coal mine, since the following lines depict the image of a miner making his way through dark mist.

And walking from his sun, when past
10   That glim'ring ray,
Cuts through the heavy mists in haste
        Back to his day,[3]
So o'er fled minutes I retreat
        Unto that hour
15 Which showed thee last, but did defeat
        Thy light, and pow'r;
I search, and rack my soul to see
        Those beams again,
But nothing but the snuff[4] to me
20   Appeareth plain;
That dark, and dead sleeps in its known
        And common urn,
But those fled to their Maker's throne,
        There shine, and burn.
25 O could I track them! but souls must
        Track one the other,
And now the spirit, not the dust,
        Must be thy brother.
Yet I have one Pearl[5] by whose light
30   All things I see,
And in the heart of earth and night,
        Find Heaven and thee.

The World

I saw eternity the other night,
Like a great ring of pure and endless light,
        All calm as it was bright;
And round beneath it, Time, in hours, days, years,
5   Driven by the spheres,[1]
Like a vast shadow moved, in which the world
        And all her train were hurled.
The doting lover in his quaintest strain[2]
        Did there complain;
10 Near him, his lute, his fancy, and his flights,
        Wit's sour delights,
With gloves and knots,[3] the silly snares of pleasure,
        Yet his dear treasure,
All scattered lay, while he his eyes did pour
15   Upon a flower.

3. When the miner walks a little beyond the area lit by his lamp into the dark, he then rushes back to the light.
4. The part of a candlewick burnt to give light; an image of his brother's body turned to dust.

5. The Bible.
1. The spheres of the heavenly bodies circling the earth.
2. Most intricate melody.
3. Ties or bows worn as love tokens.

The darksome statesman[4] hung with weights and woe
Like a thick midnight fog moved there so slow
      He did not stay nor go;
Condemning thoughts, like sad eclipses, scowl
20   Upon his soul,
And clouds of crying witnesses without
      Pursued him with one shout.
Yet digged the mole, and lest his ways be found,
      Worked underground,
25 Where he did clutch his prey. But one did see
      That policy:
Churches and altars fed him; perjuries
      Were gnats and flies;
It rained about him blood and tears; but he
30   Drank them as free.

The fearful miser on a heap of rust
Sat pining all his life there, did scarce trust
      His own hands with the dust;
Yet would not place° one piece above, but lives   *invest*
35   In fear of thieves.
Thousands there were as frantic as himself,
      And hugged each one his pelf:°   *money*
The downright epicure placed heaven in sense,[5]
      And scorned pretense;
40 While others, slipped into a wide excess,
      Said little less;
The weaker sort slight, trivial wares enslave,
      Who think them brave,°   *showy*
And poor, depisèd Truth sat counting by,°   *reckoning*
45   Their victory.

Yet some, who all this while did weep and sing,
And sing and weep, soared up into the ring;
      But most would use no wing,
"O fools!" said I, "thus to prefer dark night
50   Before true light!
To live in grots° and caves, and hate the day   *caverns*
      Because it shows the way;
The way which from the dead and dark abode
      Leads up to God,
55 A way where you might tread the sun and be
      More bright than he!"
But as I did their madness so discuss,
      One whispered thus:

---

4. Possibly a reference to Cromwell.   5. An "epicure" is a person who finds the greatest good in sensual pleasure.

"This ring the bridegroom did for none provide,
60   But for his bride."[6]

1650

They Are All Gone into the World of Light!

They are all gone into the world of light!
    And I alone sit lingering here;
Their very memory is fair and bright,
    And my sad thoughts doth clear.

5   It glows and glitters in my cloudy breast
    Like stars upon some gloomy grove,
Or those faint beams in which this hill is dressed,
    After the sun's remove.

I see them walking in an air of glory,
10   Whose light doth trample on my days:
My days, which are at best but dull and hoary,
    Mere glimmering and decays.

O holy hope! and high humility,
    High as the heavens above!
15   These are your walks, and you have showed them me
    To kindle my cold love,

Dear, beauteous death! the jewel of the just,
    Shining no where, but in the dark;
What mysteries do lie beyond thy dust,
20   Could man outlook that mark!

He that hath found some fledged birds nest, may know
    At first sight, if the bird be flown;
But what fair well, or grove he sings in now,
    That is to him unknown.

25   And yet, as angels in some brighter dreams
    Call to the soul, when man doth sleep,
So some strange thoughts transcend our wonted themes,
    And into glory peep.

If a star were confined into a tomb
30   Her captive flames must needs burn there;
But when the hand that locked her up, gives room,
    She'll shine through all the sphere.

O Father of eternal life, and all
    Created glories under thee!
35   Resume thy spirit from this world of thrall°   *slavery*
    Into true liberty.

6. For the union of Christ and his Church as that between husband and wife, see Ephesians 5.23.

Either disperse these mists, which blot and fill
    My perspective[1] still as they pass,
Or else remove me hence unto that hill,[2]
40   Where I shall need no glass.

The Night
John 3.2[1]

Through that pure virgin-shrine,
That sacred veil drawn o'er thy glorious noon
That men might look and live as glowworms shine,
      And face the moon:
5   Wise Nicodemus saw such light
      As made him know his God by night.

Most blest believer he!
Who in that land of darkness and blind eyes
Thy long expected healing wings could see,
10   When thou didst rise,
      And what can never more be done,
      Did at midnight speak with the Sun!

O who will tell me, where
He found thee at that dead and silent hour?
15   What hallowed solitary ground did bear
      So rare a flower,
      Within whose sacred leaves did lie
      The fullness of the Deity?

No mercy-seat of gold,[2]
20   No dead and dusty cherub, nor carved stone,
But his own living works did my Lord hold
      And lodge alone;
      Where trees and herbs did watch and peep
      And wonder, while the Jews did sleep.

25   Dear night! this world's defeat;[3]
The stop to busy fools; cares check and curb;
The day of spirits; my soul's calm retreat
      Which none disturb!
      Christ's progress, and his prayer time;
30   The hours to which high heaven doth chime;

1. Telescope; vision.
2. Sion Hill, a symbol for union with God.
1. In John 3.2, the Pharisee Nicodemus tells Jesus: "Rabbi, we know that thou art a teacher come from God: for no man can do these miracles that thou doest except God be with him."

2. God told the Israelites to build "a mercy seat of pure gold" with a cherub on either end to place above the ark (see Exodus 25.17–21).
3. This and the next stanza echo George Herbert's *Prayer (1)*; see page 1631.

God's silent, searching flight,
When my Lord's head is filled with dew, and all
His locks are wet with the clear drops of night;
    His still, soft call;
35   His knocking time; the souls dumb watch,
When spirits their fair kindred catch.

    Were all my loud, evil days
Calm and unhaunted as is thy dark tent,
Whose peace but by some angel's wing or voice
40   Is seldom rent;
Then I in heaven all the long year
Would keep, and never wander here.

    But living where the sun
Doth all things wake, and where all mix and tire
45 Themselves and others, I consent and run
    To ev'ry mire,°   bog
And by this world's ill-guiding light,
Ere more then I can do by night.

    There is in God (some say)
50 A deep, but dazzling darkness; as men here
Say it is late and dusky, because they
    See not all clear;
O for that night! where I in him
Might live invisible and dim.

↤ ⊰⬥⊱ ↦

Andrew Marvell
1621–1678

Praised by his nephew for "joining the most peculiar graces of wit and learning" and berated by his antagonist Samuel Parker for speaking the language of "boat-swains and cabin boys," Andrew Marvell left little evidence for his biographers. Most of what remains of his verse has been bequeathed to posterity by virtue of a shady banking scheme on his part and an implausible claim by his housekeeper to be "Mrs. Marvell." Though she couldn't remember the date of his death, Mary Palmer tried to prove that she was the poet's wife to get at money that her master had squirrelled away in an account for some bankrupt acquaintances. To further her claim, she saw to it that Marvell's *Miscellaneous Poems* were published in 1681. In his own name, Marvell published only a few occasional poems and a satire attacking religious intolerance and political authoritarianism.

If it is thanks to Mrs. Palmer's rummaging through the poet's papers that such exquisite poems as *To His Coy Mistress* and *The Definition of Love* saw the light of day, it is largely thanks to T. S. Eliot that modern critical attention was turned to Marvell's poetry. The Augustans and Romantics neglected him, and it was not until Eliot that such features of Marvell's verse as Latinate gravity, metaphysical wit, and muscular syntax came to be fully appreciated. For ingenious ambiguity and sheer seductive sensuousness, Marvell is one of the greatest poets of all time.

As tantalizing as the verse is, it leaves little solid evidence of what was a very private life. Marvell grew up in a house surrounded by gardens in the Yorkshire town of Hull on the Humber, where his father was the Anglican rector. There is a story that Marvell once left university for London to flirt with Catholicism, but his father made sure he returned to Cambridge and Protestantism. After his father's death, Marvell traveled in Holland, France, Italy, and Spain (1642–1647). He later tutored Mary Fairfax, daughter of Lord Fairfax of Nun-Appleton House (1650–1652), and taught William Dutton, Cromwell's ward (1653–1656). Initially recommended by Milton to serve as Assistant Latin Secretary in 1653, Marvell was first appointed Latin Secretary to the Council of State in 1657. He was elected Member of Parliament for Hull in 1659, a position he held until 1678. When Charles II restored the monarchy, Marvell interceded on Milton's behalf and made sure his old friend and fellow poet was released from prison. Later in life, Marvell wrote satires criticizing the corruption of the Restoration regime, all but one published anonymously.

Marvell chose to keep his cards close to his chest in the ideologically volatile atmosphere of the Civil War and Restoration. A contemporary biographer remarked that Marvell "was wont to say that, he would not play the good-fellow in any man's company in whose hands he would not trust his life." He did not fight in the Civil War, since he was in Europe at the time, and as he later ambiguously maintained, "the Cause was too good to have been fought for." His strategy in dealing with change involved publicly siding with the faction in power while maintaining politically incorrect friendships and finding himself "inclinable to favor the weaker party"—whether it was a Royalist who had given his life for the King, such as Lord Hastings, or a Republican who went to prison for his convictions, such as Milton. Marvell wrote poems praising both royalists and revolutionaries. He was nothing if not tolerant.

He was also something of a chameleon, an assumer of numerous poetic personae and disguises. In *Tom May's Death*, Marvell satirized the Royalist turned Republican, here portrayed arriving in heaven drunk. Marvell equivocally praised Cromwell in *An Horatian Ode*, ironically maintaining that it was the Irish whom Cromwell had so brutally massacred who could "best affirm his praises." When he became tutor to Cromwell's ward William Dutton, Marvell wrote poems praising Cromwell in such slavishly glowing terms that the poet was made Latin Secretary to the Council of State.

The last word should go to Marvell, whose choice to translate the following chorus from Seneca's *Thyestes* shows his outlook on the vicissitudes of power:

> Climb at court for me that will
> Giddy favor's slippery hill;
> All I seek is to lie still,
> Settled in some secret nest.
> In calm leisure let me rest,
> And far off the public stage
> Pass away my silent age.
> Thus, when without noise, unknown,
> I have lived out all my span,
> I shall die without a groan,
> An old honest countryman,
> Who exposed to others' eyes,
> Into his own heart ne'er pries.
> Death to him's a strange surprise.

The Coronet[1]

When for the thorns with which I long, too long,
 With many a piercing wound,
 My Savior's head have crowned,
I seek with garlands to redress that wrong:
5 Through every garden, every mead,
I gather flow'rs (my fruits are only flow'rs)
 Dismantling all the fragrant towers°   *tall headdresses*
That once adorned my shepherdess's head.
And now when I have summed up all my store,
10 Thinking (so I myself deceive)
 So rich a chaplet° thence to weave   *wreath*
As never yet the King of Glory wore:
  Alas, I find the serpent old
  That, twining in his speckled breast,[2]
15 About the flowers disguised does fold,°   *wind*
 With wreaths° of fame and interest.   *coils*
Ah, foolish man, that wouldst debase with them,
And mortal glory, Heaven's diadem!
But Thou who only couldst the serpent tame,
20 Either his slippery knots at once untie,
And disentangle all his winding snare:
Or shatter too with him my curious frame:[3]
And let these wither, so that he may die,
Though set with skill and chosen out with care:
25 That they, while Thou on both their spoils[4] dost tread,
May crown thy feet, that could not crown thy head.[5]

Bermudas[1]

 Where the remote Bermudas ride
In th' ocean's bosom unespied,
From a small boat, that rowed along,
The list'ning winds received this song.
5 "What should we do but sing his praise
That led us through the watry maze,
Unto an isle so long unknown,[2]
And yet far kinder than our own?
Where he the huge sea-monsters wracks,°   *shipwrecks*
10 That lift the deep upon their backs.
He lands us on a grassy stage,

1. Marvell's poems were first published in 1681.
2. See Spenser, *Faerie Queene* 1.11.15.
3. Ingenious structure (the chaplet).
4. Sloughing of the snake's skin; plundering.
5. See Genesis 3.15, for the prophecy that the seed of Eve will bruise the serpent's head.
1. Probably composed sometime after 1653, when Marvell

was living in the house of John Oxenbridge, who had made two trips to the Bermudas. Marvell could also have known Captain John Smith's 1624 work *The General History of Virginia, New England and the Summer Isles* (as the Bermudas were called).
2. Unknown to Europeans; Juan Bermudez first came there in 1515.

Safe from the storms, and prelate's[3] rage.
He gave us this eternal spring,
Which here enamels everything;
15   And sends the fowl to us in care,
On daily visits through the air.
He hangs in shades the orange bright,
Like golden lamps in a green night,
And does in the pom'granates close,
20   Jewels more rich than Ormus[4] shows.
He makes the figs our mouths to meet,
And throws the melons at our feet,
But apples° plants of such a price,   *pineapples*
No tree could ever bear them twice.
25   With cedars, chosen by his hand,
From Lebanon, he stores the land,
And makes the hollow seas, that roar,
Proclaim the ambergris[5] on shore.
He cast (of which we rather boast)
30   The gospel's pearl upon our coast,
And in these rocks for us did frame
A temple, where to sound his name.
Oh let our voice his praise exalt,
Till it arrive at heaven's vault:
35   Which thence (perhaps) rebounding, may
Echo beyond the Mexique Bay.[6]
Thus sung they, in the English boat,
An holy and a cheerful note,
And all the way, to guide their chime,
40   With falling oars they kept the time.

The Nymph Complaining for the Death of Her Fawn[1]

The wanton troopers[2] riding by
Have shot my fawn, and it will die.
Ungentle men! They cannot thrive
To kill thee. Thou ne'er didst alive
5   Them any harm: alas, nor could
Thy death yet do them any good.
I'm sure I never wished them ill;
Nor do I for all this; nor will:
But, if my simple prayers may yet
10   Prevail with Heaven to forget
Thy murder, I will join my tears
Rather than fail. But, O my fears!

---

3. Clergyman's, bishop's.
4. Hormuz on the Persian Gulf.
5. Musky secretion of the sperm whale that is used in perfumes.
6. Gulf of Mexico.

1. Ancient Roman poets such as Catullus and Ovid had written poems on the death of pets, as did the early 16th-century English poet John Skelton in *Philip Sparrow*.
2. A term used for the Presbyterian Scots Covenanting Army that attacked England in 1640.

It cannot die so. Heaven's King
Keeps register of everything:
15   And nothing may we use in vain.
E'en beasts must be with justice slain,
Else men are made their deodands.[3]
Though they should wash their guilty hands
In this warm life-blood, which doth part
20   From thine, and wound me to the heart,
Yet could they not be clean: their stain
Is dyed in such a purple grain.
There is not such another in
The world, to offer for their sin.
25   Unconstant Sylvio, when yet
I had not found him counterfeit,
One morning (I remember well)
Tied in this silver chain and bell,
Gave it to me: nay, and I know
30   What he said then; I'm sure I do.
Said he, "Look how your huntsman here
Hath taught a fawn to hunt his dear."
But Sylvio soon had me beguiled.
This waxèd tame, while he grew wild,
35   And quite regardless of my smart,
Left me his fawn, but took his heart.
       Thenceforth I set myself to play
My solitary time away
With this: and very well content,
40   Could so mine idle life have spent.
For it was full of sport; and light
Of foot, and heart; and did invite
Me to its game: it seemed to bless
Itself in me. How could I less
45   Than love it? O I cannot be
Unkind, t' a beast that loveth me.
       Had it lived long, I do not know
Whether it too might have done so
As Sylvio did: his gifts might be
50   Perhaps as false or more than he.
But I am sure, for ought that I
Could in so short a time espie,
Thy Love was far more better than
The love of false and cruel men.
55   With sweetest milk and sugar first
I it at mine own fingers nursed.
And as it grew, so every day
It waxed more white and sweet than they,

3. Otherwise, men would become forfeited objects. In early modern English law, any personal property that caused a human death had to be given up as part of the reparation for the crime.

It had so sweet a breath! And oft
60   I blushed to see its foot more soft,
And white, (shall I say than my hand?)
Nay any lady's of the land.
     It is a wondrous thing, how fleet
'Twas on those little silver feet.
65   With what a pretty skipping grace,
It oft would challenge me the race:
And when 't had left me far away,
'Twould stay, and run again, and stay.
For it was nimbler much than hinds;
70   And trod, as on the four winds.
     I have a garden of my own,
But so with roses overgrown,
And lilies, that you would it guess
To be a little wilderness.
75   And all the springtime of the year
It only lovèd to be there.
Among the beds of lilies, I
Have sought it oft, where it should lie;
Yet could not, till itself would rise,
80   Find it, although before mine eyes.
For, in the flaxen lilies' shade,
It like a bank of lilies laid.
Upon the roses it would feed,
Until its lips e'en seemed to bleed:
85   And then to me 'twould boldly trip,
And print those roses on my lip.
But all its chief delight was still
On roses thus itself to fill:
And its pure virgin limbs to fold
90   In whitest sheets of lilies cold.
Had it lived long, it would have been
Lilies without, roses within.
O help! O help! I see it faint:
And die as calmly as a saint.
95   See how it weeps. The tears do come
Sad, slowly dropping like a gum.
So weeps the wounded balsam: so
The holy frankincense doth flow.
The brotherless Heliades
100 Melt in such amber tears as these.[4]
     I in a golden vial will
Keep these two crystal tears; and fill
It till it do o'reflow with mine;
Then place it in Diana's[5] shrine.

---

4. Grieving the death of their brother Phaethon, the Heliades were transformed into poplar trees which wept
tears of amber.
5. Goddess of chastity and of the hunt.

105   Now my sweet fawn is vanished to
       Whither the swans and turtles° go: *doves*
       In fair Elysium to endure,
       With milk-white lambs, and ermines pure.
       O do not run too fast: for I
110   Will but bespeak thy grave, and die.
           First my unhappy statue shall
       Be cut in marble; and withal,
       Let it be weeping too:⁶ but there
       Th' engraver sure his art may spare;
115   For I so truly thee bemoan,
       That I shall weep though I be stone:
       Until my tears, still dropping, wear
       My breast, themselves engraving there.
       There at my feet shalt thou be laid,
120   Of purest alabaster made:
       For I would have thine image be
       White as I can, though not as thee.

To His Coy Mistress¹

Had we but world enough, and time,
This coyness, Lady, were no crime.
We would sit down, and think which way
To walk, and pass our long love's day.
5   Thou by the Indian Ganges' side
Shouldst rubies find: I by the tide
Of Humber would complain.² I would
Love you ten years before the flood:
And you should if you please refuse
10   Till the conversion of the Jews.³
My vegetable love should grow
Vaster than empires, and more slow.⁴
An hundred years should go to praise
Thine eyes, and on thy forehead gaze.
15   Two hundred to adore each breast:
But thirty thousand to the rest.
An age at least to every part,
And the last age should show your heart.
For Lady you deserve this state;
20   Nor would I love at lower rate.
    But at my back I always hear

---

6. Niobe was turned into a weeping stone for her pride in her children.
1. A poem on the theme of *carpe diem* ("seize the day") that includes a blazon, or description of the lady from head to toe, and a logical argument: "If . . . But . . . Therefore."
2. Marvell grew up in Hull on the Humber River.

3. The end of time: the Flood occurred in the distant past, and Christians prophesied that Jews would convert to Christianity at the end of the world.
4. The "vegetable" was characterized only by growth, in contrast to the sensitive, which felt, and the rational, which could reason.

Times wingèd chariot hurrying near:
And yonder all before us lie
Deserts of vast eternity.
25   Thy beauty shall no more be found;
Nor, in thy marble vault, shall sound
My echoing song: then worms shall try
That long preserved virginity:
And your quaint honor turn to dust;[5]
30   And into ashes all my lust.
The grave's a fine and private place,
But none, I think, do there embrace.
   Now, therefore, while the youthful hue
Sits on thy skin like morning dew,[6]
35   And while thy willing soul transpires
At every pore with instant fires,
Now let us sport us while we may;
And now, like amorous birds of prey,
Rather at once our time devour,
40   Than languish in his slow-chapped° power.   *slowly biting*
Let us roll all our strength, and all
Our sweetness, up into one ball:
And tear our pleasures with rough strife,
Thorough the iron gates of life.[7]
45   Thus, though we cannot make our sun
Stand still, yet we will make him run.[8]

The Definition of Love

My Love is of a birth as rare
As 'tis for object strange and high:
It was begotten by Despair
Upon Impossibility.

5   Magnanimous Despair alone
Could show me so divine a thing,
Where feeble Hope could ne'er have flown
But vainly flapped its tinsel wing.

And yet I quickly might arrive
10   Where my extended soul is fixed,
But Fate does iron wedges drive,
And always crowds itself betwixt.

For Fate with jealous eye does see
Two perfect loves, nor lets them close:°   *unite*

---

5. "Quaint honor," proud chastity. Note the pun on *queynte* (Middle English), woman's genitals.
6. In the 1681 Folio, "dew" reads "glue," and in two manuscripts the rhymes in lines 33 and 34 are "glue" and "dew."
7. One manuscript reads "grates" for "gates."
8. Joshua made the sun stand still in the war against Gibeon (see Joshua 10.12).

15   Their union would her ruin be,
      And her tyrannic power depose.

      And therefore her decrees of steel
      Us as the distant poles have placed,
      (Though Love's whole world on us doth wheel)
20   Not by themselves to be embraced.

      Unless the giddy heaven fall,
      And earth some new convulsion tear;
      And, us to join, the world should all
      Be cramped into a planisphere.[1]

25   As lines (so loves) oblique[2] may well
      Themselves in every angle greet:
      But ours so truly parallel,
      Though infinite, can never meet.

      Therefore the love which us doth bind,
30   But Fate so enviously debars,
      Is the conjunction of the mind,
      And opposition of the stars.[3]

The Mower Against Gardens

      Luxurious man, to bring his vice in use,[1]
          Did after him the world seduce,
      And from the fields the flowers and plants allure,
          Where Nature was most plain and pure.
5   He first enclosed within the garden's square
          A dead and standing pool of air,
      And a more luscious earth for them did knead,
          Which stupefied them while it fed.
      The pink grew then as double as his mind;[2]
10   The nutriment did change the kind.
      With strange perfumes he did the roses taint,
          And flowers themselves were taught to paint.
      The tulip, white, did for complexion seek,
          And learned to interline its cheek:
15   Its onion root they then so high did hold,
          That one was for a meadow sold.[3]
      Another world was searched, through oceans new,
          To find the Marvel of Peru.[4]
      And yet these rarities might be allowed
20   To man, that sovereign thing and proud,

1. A two-dimensional map of the globe.
2. Slanting at an angle other than a right angle, and also veering away from right morals.
3. Conjunction: coming together in the same sign of the zodiac; union. Stars in opposition are diametrically opposed to one another.
1. To make current.

2. Double, both in the sense of having two blooms and being the result of sophisticated (duplicitous) thought.
3. Marvell alludes to the 17th-century lucrative trade in Dutch tulips.
4. *Mirabilis jalapa*, also known as the four-o'clock, a multicolored flower native to tropical America.

Had he not dealt between the bark and tree,[5]
   Forbidden mixtures there to see.
No plant now knew the stock from which it came;
   He grafts upon the wild the tame:
25   That the uncertain and adult'rate fruit
      Might put the palate in dispute.
His green seraglio[6] has its eunuchs too;
   Lest any tyrant him outdo.
And in the cherry he does nature vex,
30   To procreate without a sex.[7]
'Tis all enforced; the fountain and the grot,°   *grotto*
   While the sweet fields do lie forgot:
Where willing Nature does to all dispense
   A wild and fragrant innocence:
35   And fauns and fairies do the meadows till,
      More by their presence than their skill.
Their statues polished by some ancient hand,
   May to adorn the gardens stand:
But howsoe'er the figures do excel,
40   The gods themselves with us do dwell.

The Mower's Song

My mind was once the true survey
   Of all these meadows fresh and gay;
And in the greenness of the grass
   Did see its hopes as in a glass;°   *mirror*
5   When Juliana came, and she,
What I do to the grass, does to my thoughts and me.[1]

But these, while I with sorrow pine,
   Grew more luxuriant still and fine,
That not one blade of grass you spied,
10   But had a flower on either side;
   When Juliana came, and she,
What I do to the grass, does to my thoughts and me.

Unthankful meadows, could you so
   A fellowship so true forgo,
15   And in your gaudy May-games meet,[2]
   While I lay trodden under feet?
   When Juliana came, and she,
What I do to the grass, does to my thoughts and me.

But what you in compassion ought,
20   Shall now by my revenge be wrought:

---

5. An expression used to describe interfering in another's affairs, especially those of a married couple.
6. Secluded place; Turkish palace; harem.
7. To grow by grafting one strain of cherry onto another.

1. This 12-syllable line (an alexandrine) is the only instance of a refrain in all of Marvell's poetry.
2. Festivals celebrated on May 1.

And flowers, and grass, and I and all,
Will in one common ruin fall.
For Juliana comes, and she,
What I do to the grass, does to my thoughts and me.

25   And thus, ye meadows, which have been
Companions of my thoughts more green,
Shall now the heraldry become
With which I shall adorn my tomb;
For Juliana comes, and she,
30   What I do to the grass, does to my thoughts and me.

The Garden

How vainly men themselves amaze
To win the palm, the oak, or bays,[1]
And their uncessant labors see
Crowned from some single herb or tree,
5   Whose short and narrow-vergèd shade
Does prudently their toils upbraid,
While all flowers and all trees do close°   *unite*
To weave the garlands of repose.

Fair quiet, have I found thee here,
10   And innocence thy sister dear!
Mistaken long, I sought you then
In busy companies of men.
Your sacred plants, if here below,
Only among the plants will grow.
15   Society is all but rude,
To this delicious solitude.[2]

No white nor red[3] was ever seen
So am'rous as this lovely green.
Fond lovers, cruel as their flame,
20   Cut in these trees their mistress' name.
Little, alas, they know, or heed,
How far these beauties hers exceed!
Fair trees! whereso'er your barks I wound,
No name shall but your own be found.

25   When we have run our passion's heat,
Love hither makes his best retreat.
The gods, that mortal beauty chase,
Still in a tree did end their race.
Apollo hunted Daphne so,

---

1. Vainly: arrogantly, in vain; amaze: bewilder, go mad; the palm, the oak, or bays: prizes symbolic of military, political, and poetic excellence.

2. Compare to Katherine Philips's *A Country-life*: "Then welcome dearest solitude, / My great felicity; / Though some are pleased to call thee rude."
3. Colors used to describe the beloved's beauty.

30   Only that she might laurel grow,
        And Pan did after Syrinx speed,
        Not as a nymph, but for a reed.[4]

        What wondrous life in this I lead!
        Ripe apples drop about my head;
35   The luscious clusters of the vine
        Upon my mouth do crush their wine;
        The nectarine, and curious peach,
        Into my hands themselves do reach;
        Stumbling on melons, as I pass,
40   Insnared with flowers, I fall on grass.

        Meanwhile the mind, from pleasure less,
        Withdraws into its happiness:
        The mind, that ocean where each kind
        Does straight its own resemblance find,[5]
45   Yet it creates, transcending these,
        Far other worlds, and other seas,
        Annihilating all that's made
        To a green thought in a green shade.

        Here at the fountain's sliding foot,
50   Or at some fruit-tree's mossy root,
        Casting the body's vest aside,
        My soul into the boughs does glide:
        There like a bird it sits and sings,
        Then whets and combs its silver wings;
55   And, till prepared for longer flight,
        Waves in its plumes the various light.

        Such was that happy garden-state,
        While man there walked without a mate:
        After a place so pure and sweet,
60   What other help could yet be meet!
        But 'twas beyond a mortal's share
        To wander solitary there:
        Two paradises 'twere in one
        To live in paradise alone.

65   How well the skillful gardener drew
        Of flowers and herbs this dial new;[6]
        Where from above the milder sun
        Does through a fragrant zodiac run;
        And, as it works, th' industrious bee
70   Computes its time as well as we.[7]

---

4. As god of poetry, Apollo seeks the laurel (the bays), while Pan seeks the syrinx (pipe) of pastoral poetry. Apollo chased Daphne, who prayed to be saved from him and was transformed into a laurel tree, just as Syrinx escaped Pan's lust when she was turned into a reed.
5. It was popularly believed that animals and plants on land had counterparts in the sea. This line describes the mind as innately possessing ideas, a concept of Platonic philosophy.
6. The garden is arranged as a floral sundial.
7. Computes its time: a pun on thyme.

How could such sweet and wholesome hours
Be reckoned but with herbs and flowers!

An Horatian Ode Upon Cromwell's Return from Ireland[1]

The forward youth that would appear
Must now forsake his muses dear,
   Nor in the shadows sing
   His numbers[2] languishing.
5   'Tis time to leave the books in dust,
And oil th' unusèd armor's rust:
   Removing from the wall
   The corslet[3] of the hall.
So restless Cromwell could not cease
10   In the inglorious arts of peace,
   But through adventurous war
   Urgèd his active star.
And, like the three-forked lightning, first
Breaking the clouds where it was nursed,
15   Did thorough his own side
   His fiery way divide:[4]
For 'tis all one to courage high
The emulous or enemy;
   And with such to enclose
20   Is more than to oppose.
Then burning through the air he went,
And palaces and temples rent:
   And Caesar's head at last
   Did through his laurels blast.[5]
25   'Tis madness to resist or blame
The force of angry heaven's flame:
   And, if we would speak true,
   Much to the man is due,
Who, from his private gardens, where
30   He lived reservèd and austere,
   As if his highest plot
   To plant the bergamot,[6]
Could by industrious valor climb
To ruin the great work of Time,

1. Cromwell returned from his military campaign in Ireland in May 1650. After General Fairfax resigned as commander of the parliamentary army because he refused to invade Scotland, Cromwell assumed his position and attacked the Scots. This poem was printed in the 1681 edition but then was canceled from printed copies until 1776. The influence of Horace's *Odes* (especially 1. 35, 37; IV. 4, 5, 14, 15) surfaces in the poised dignity of the verse and its subtly ambiguous attitude toward power.

2. Conformity to a rhythmical pattern in verse or music.
3. Defensive armor covering the upper body.
4. Cromwell's overtaking his rivals in Parliament is described as an elemental force similar to the "three-forked lightning" of Zeus.
5. Although lightning was thought not to strike the laurel (symbolizing the royal crown), Cromwell had struck down Charles I (Caesar).
6. A pear known as the "prince's pear."

35   And cast the kingdom old
         Into another mold.
      Though justice against fate complain,
      And plead the ancient rights in vain:
         But those do hold or break,
40   As men are strong or weak.
      Nature, that hateth emptiness,
      Allows of penetration less:[7]
         And therefore must make room
         Where greater spirits come.
45   What field of all the Civil Wars,
      Where his were not the deepest scars?
         And Hampton[8] shows what part
         He had of wiser art,
      Where, twining subtle fears with hope,
50   He wove a net of such a scope,
         That Charles himself might chase
         To Carisbrooke's narrow case:
      That thence the royal actor borne,
      The tragic scaffold might adorn;
55   While round the armèd bands
         Did clap their bloody hands.
      He nothing common did or mean
      Upon that memorable scene:
         But with his keener eye
60   The axe's[9] edge did try;
      Nor called the gods with vulgar spite
      To vindicate his helpless right,
         But bowed his comely head,
         Down, as upon a bed.
65   This was that memorable hour
      Which first assured the forcèd power.
         So when they did design
         The Capitol's first line,
      A bleeding head where they begun,
70   Did fright the architects to run;
         And yet in that the State
         Foresaw it's happy fate.[1]
      And now the Irish are ashamed
      To see themselves in one year tamed:[2]
75   So much one man can do,
         That does both act and know.
      They can affirm his praises best,

---

7. Nature abhors not only a vacuum but even more so the penetration of one body's space by another body.
8. Hampton Court where Charles I was held captive before his execution in 1649. He had fled to Carisbrooke Castle on the Isle of Wight, where he was betrayed to the Governor in 1647.
9. Marvell plays on the Latin "acies," the sharp edge of a sword, a keen glance, and the vanguard of battle.

1. In digging the foundations of the temple of Jupiter Capitolinum, the excavators found a human's head (caput), which was interpreted as prophesying that Rome should be the capitol of the Empire (see Livy, Annals I.55.6).
2. From August 1649 to his return to England in May 1650, Cromwell went on a savage military campaign that included the slaughter of Irish civilians.

And have, though overcome, confessed
   How good he is, how just,
80   And fit for highest trust.[3]
Nor yet grown stiffer with command,
But still in the Republic's hand:
   How fit he is to sway
   That can so well obey.[4]
85 He to the commons' feet presents
A kingdom, for his first year's rents:
   And, what he may, forbears
   His fame to make it theirs:
And has his sword and spoils ungirt,
90 To lay them at the public's skirt.
   So when the falcon high
   Falls heavy from the sky,
She, having killed, no more does search,
But on the next green bough to perch;
95   Where, when he first does lure,
   The falconer has her sure.
What may not then our isle presume
While victory his crest does plume!
   What may not others fear
100   If thus he crown each year!
A Caesar he ere long to Gaul,
To Italy an Hannibal,[5]
   And to all states not free
   Shall climactéric° be.   *period of change*
105 The Pict no shelter now shall find
Within his particolored mind;
   But from this valor sad°   *severe*
   Shrink underneath the plaid:[6]
Happy if in the tufted brake
110 The English hunter him mistake;
   Nor lay his hounds in near
   The Caledonian° deer.   *Scottish*
But thou the wars' and fortune's son
March indefatigably on;
115   And for the last effect
   Still keep thy sword erect:
Besides the force it has to fright
The spirits of the shady night,[7]
   The same arts that did gain
120   A power must it maintain.

---

3. An example of one of the many equivocal statements in this poem; of course, the Irish did not affirm Cromwell's greatness.
4. A saying attributed to the Athenian Solon the lawgiver.
5. Neither Caesar nor Hannibal gave freedom to peoples whose countries they invaded and conquered.

6. Marvell uses "Picts" the ancient name for the Scots, creating a play on *picti* (Latin: painted) and particolored.
7. There was an ancient tradition of dead spirits being frightened by raised swords (Homer, *Odyssey* 11; Virgil, *Aeneid* 6). The dead spirits referred to here include the dead in the wars in Ireland and England, including the king.

Katherine Philips
1631–1664

Idolized as the "Matchless Orinda" in her own day, Katherine Philips is now taking her place in the history of English verse after two centuries of neglect. During her lifetime, her work circulated in manuscript among a close network of friends. The first edition of her poems appeared posthumously in 1664. The second edition of 1667 was evidently a commercial success, since it was reprinted in 1669, 1678, and 1710. The next complete edition of her poems did not appear until 1994.

John Keats esteemed Philips's *To Mrs. Mary Awbrey at Parting* as an example of "real feminine Modesty;" today, by contrast, critics praise her poems to women friends as reminiscent of the ancient Greek Sappho's erotic lyrics. By imitating Donne's love lyrics in her poems to women, Philips poetically conceives of these friendships as no less world-changing, no less ennobling and enthralling, than Donne's romantic liaisons. Some of the best poets of her own day were able to appreciate her as a fellow poet rather than as Keats's romanticized ideal woman. Marvell paid tribute to her by subtly alluding to lines of her poetry in one of his greatest poems, *The Garden*. And Henry Vaughan insisted that "No laurel grows, but for [her] brow."

Katherine Philips's work was particularly important for other women writers. Philips's lyric poetry influenced such other early modern women poets as Aphra Behn and Anne Killigrew. Yet it is impossible to pigeonhole Philips as stereotypically feminine. She wrote on public and political themes as well as personal subjects, endowing traditional genres such as the parting poem, the elegy, and the epitaph, with a particular directness and clarity all her own.

Katherine Philips was born in London to a well-to-do Presbyterian family. Her father was a prosperous merchant, and her mother was the daughter of a Fellow of the Royal College of Physicians. Philips's father was wealthy enough to invest two hundred pounds for a thousand acres in Ulster, a scheme that was begun in 1642 by the Puritan Parliament but, ironically, not realized until the Restoration, when we find Katherine in Ireland pursuing lawsuits to obtain this land. As a girl, Katherine attended Mrs. Salmon's Presbyterian School, where she learned to love poetry and began to write verses. In 1646 her widowed mother married Sir Richard Philips, and the family moved to his castle in Wales. Philips herself married Sir Richard's kinsman James Philips, and they lived together for twelve years in the small Welsh town of Cardigan when not in London, where her husband served as a Member of Parliament during the Interregnum.

However Presbyterian and Cromwellian were the associations of her family and marriage, she emerged after the Restoration as a complete Anglican. Not only did she write poetry against the regicide, such as *Upon the Double Murder of King Charles*, but she became a favorite author at court. She was encouraged to write poetry by her friend "Poliarchus," Sir Charles Cotterell, Master of Ceremonies in the Court of Charles II, who showed her poems to the royal family. An Anglo-Irish nobleman, the Earl of Orrery, encouraged her to complete a translation of Corneille's *Pompey* and actually produced and had the play printed in Dublin in 1663.

Katherine Philips developed friendships that became the theme of what most critics regard as her best poems. Perhaps the most intense of these friendships was that with Mrs. Anne Owen, the Lucasia of Philips's most passionate poems, several of which echo love poems by Donne. Her friend Sir Edward Dering, whom she called "the Noble Silvander," lamented

Katherine Philips's death in recounting the extraordinary accomplishment of both her poetry and her life, which had attempted

> the most generous design . . . to unite all those of her acquaintance which she found worthy or desired to make so (among which later number she was pleased to give me a place) into one society, and by the bands of friendship to make an alliance more firm than what nature, our country or equal education can produce.

Friendship in Emblem
or the Seal,[1]
TO MY DEAREST LUCASIA[2]

The hearts thus intermixèd speak
A love that no bold shock can break;
For joined and growing, both in one,
Neither can be disturbed alone.

5   That means a mutual knowledge too;
For what is't either heart can do,
Which by its panting sentinel°   *guard*
It does not to the other tell?

That friendship hearts so much refines,
10   It nothing but itself designs:
The hearts are free from lower ends,
For each point to the other tends.

They flame, 'tis true, and several ways,
But still those flames do so much raise,
15   That while to either they incline
They yet are noble and divine.

From smoke or hurt those flames are free,
From grossness or mortality:
The hearts (like Moses bush presumed)[3]
20   Warmed and enlightened, not consumed.

The compasses that stand above
Express this great immortal Love;[4]
For friends, like them, can prove this true,
They are, and yet they are not, two.

25   And in their posture is expressed

---

1. A symbolic picture, which appeared with a motto and a poem in such books as Whitney's *Choice of Emblems* (see Perspectives: Early Modern Books, page 1066). The central emblematic image of this poem is "the compasses" (line 21); another emblem is "those flames" (line 14).
2. Anne Owen, to whom many of Philips's poems are dedicated, was a neighbor of hers in Wales and a close friend from 1651 until Philips's death.

3. See Exodus 3.2–5 for the burning bush through which the angel of the Lord appeared to and from which God called Moses.
4. Compare the image of the compasses here to the "twin compasses" in Donne's *A Valediction: Forbidding Mourning* (page 1598).

Friendship's exalted interest:
Each follows where the other leans,
And what each does, the other means.

And as when one foot does stand fast,
30 And t'other circles seeks to cast,
The steady part does regulate
And make the wanderer's motion straight:

So friends are only two in this,
T'reclaim each other when they miss:
35 For whose'er will grossly fall,
Can never be a friend at all.

And as that useful instrument
For even lines was ever meant;
So friendship from good angels⁵ springs,
40 To teach the world heroic things.

As these are found out in design
To rule and measure every line;
So friendship governs actions best,
Prescribing law to all the rest.

45 And as in nature nothing's set
So just as lines and numbers met;
So compasses for these being made,
Do friendship's harmony persuade.

And like to them, so friends may own
50 Extension, not division:
Their points, like bodies, separate;
But head, like souls, knows no such fate.

And as each part so well is knit,
That their embraces ever fit:
55 So friends are such by destiny,
And no third can the place supply.

There needs no motto to the seal:
But that we may the mine⁶ reveal
To the dull eye, it was thought fit
60 That friendship only should be writ.

But as there is degrees of bliss,
So there's no friendship meant by this,
But such as will transmit to fame
Lucasia's and Orinda's name.

---

5. Guardian spirits, with puns on angels, and *angeli* (Latin), messengers.
6. A mass of gold, a store of plenty, as well as a pun on the possessive pronoun meaning "my own" and perhaps also on "mind."

Upon the Double Murder of King Charles
in Answer to a Libelous Rhyme Made by V. P.[1]

I think not on the state, nor am concerned
Which way soever that great helm is turned,
But as that son whose father's danger nigh
Did force his native dumbness, and untie
5   The fettered organs: so here is a cause
That will excuse the breach of nature's laws.[2]
Silence were now a sin: nay passion now
Wise men themselves for merit would allow.
What noble eye could see, (and careless pass)
10   The dying lion kicked by every ass?
Hath Charles so broke God's laws, he must not have
A quiet crown, nor yet a quiet grave?
Tombs have been sanctuaries; thieves lie here
Secure from all their penalty and fear.
15   Great Charles his double misery was this,
Unfaithful friends, ignoble enemies;
Had any heathen been this prince's foe,
He would have wept to see him injured so.
His title was his crime, they'd reason good
20   To quarrel at the right they had withstood.
He broke God's laws, and therefore he must die,
And what shall then become of thee and I?
Slander must follow treason; but yet stay,
Take not our reason with our king away.
25   Though you have seized upon all our defense,
Yet do not sequester° our common sense.   *confiscate*
But I admire not at this new supply:
No bounds will hold those who at scepters fly.
Christ will be King, but I ne'er understood,
30   His subjects built his kingdom up with blood,
(Except their own) or that he would dispense
With his commands, though for his own defense.
Oh! to what height of horror are they come,
Who dare pull down a crown, tear up a tomb![3]

On the Third of September, 1651[1]

As when the glorious magazine of light[2]
Approaches to his canopy of night,
He with new splendor clothes his dying rays,

---

1. Vavasor Powell, a Fifth Monarchist who believed that Christ's second coming was imminent, and an ardent Republican, whose verses on the murder of the king are lost. According to Philips's poem, Powell argued that Charles I had usurped God's power.
2. Breaking the prohibition against women speaking on public affairs. See Margaret Tyler's preface to *The First Part of the Mirror of Princely Deeds*, for a defense of woman's ability to write about war, traditionally considered only appropriate to male authors.
3. Possibly a reference to the unearthing of the regicides' bodies.
1. Cromwell defeated Charles II at the Battle of Worcester on this date.
2. The sun; a magazine is a storehouse for gunpowder.

And double brightness to his beams conveys;
5   As if to brave and check his ending fate,
Puts on his highest looks in 's lowest state;
Dressed in such terror as to make us all
Be anti-Persians,[3] and adore his fall;
Then quits the world, depriving it of day,
10   While every herb and plant does droop away:
So when our gasping English royalty
Perceived her period now was drawing nigh,
She summons her whole strength to give one blow,
To raise her self, or pull down others too.
15   Big with revenge and hope, she now spake more
Of terror than in many months before;
And musters her attendants, or to save
Her from, or wait upon her to the grave:
Yet but enjoyed the miserable fate
20   Of setting majesty, to die in state.
    Unhappy Kings! who cannot keep a throne,
Nor be so fortunate to fall alone!
Their weight sinks others: Pompey could not fly,
But half the world must bear him company;[4]
25   Thus captive Sampson could not life conclude,
Unless attended with a multitude.[5]
Who'd trust to greatness now, whose food is air,
Whose ruin sudden, and whose end despair?
Who would presume upon his glorious birth,
30   Or quarrel for a spacious share of earth,
That sees such diadems° become thus cheap,   *crowns*
And heroes tumble in the common heap?
    O! give me virtue then, which sums up all,
And firmly stands when crowns and scepters fall.

To the Truly Noble, and Obliging Mrs. Anne Owen
(on My First Approaches)[1]

Madam,
As in a triumph conquerors admit
Their meanest captives to attend on it,[2]
Who, though unworthy, have the power confessed,
And justified the yielding of the rest:
5   So when the busy world (in hope t'excuse
Their own surprise) your conquests do peruse,
And find my name, they will be apt to say

---

3. Anti-sun, since the Persians were thought to worship the sun, and anti-monarchist, possibly with reference to Darius I, the Persian king who put down many revolts during his lifetime.
4. Caesar defeated Pompey at the battle of Pharsalus, where 15,000 of Pompey's men were killed. Afterward, Pompey fled to Egypt, where he was assassinated.
5. The blind Israelite hero Samson tore down the temple at

Gaza, thus killing both himself and his enemies (Judges 16).
1. Mrs. Anne Owen of Orielton, Wales, was Philips' close friend and the "Lucasia" of her poems; she was married to John Owen and was the heiress to the ancient seat of Presaddfed in Anglesey.
2. Here, "triumph" means military victory and the triumphal procession that announced it.

Your charms were blinded, or else thrown away.
There is no honor got in gaining me,
10 Who am a prize not worth your victory.
But this will clear you, that 'tis general
The worst applaud what is admired by all.
But I have plots in't: for the way to be
Secure of fame to all posterity
15 Is to obtain the honor I pursue,
To tell the world I was subdued by you.
And since in you all wonders common are,
Your votaries° may in your virtues share,   *devoted admirers*
While you by noble magic worth impart:
20 She that can conquer, can reclaim a heart.
Of this creation I shall not despair,
Since for your own sake it concerns your care:
For 'tis more honor that the world should know
You made a noble soul, than found it so.

To Mrs. Mary Awbrey at Parting[1]

I have examined, and do find,
    Of all that favor me,
There's none I grieve to leave behind
    But only, only thee.
5 To part with thee I needs must die,
    Could parting separate thee and I.

But neither chance nor compliment
    Did element our love;
'Twas sacred sympathy was lent
10   Us from the choir above.
That friendship fortune did create,
Which fears a wound from time or fate.

Our changed and mingled souls are grown
    To such acquaintance now,
15 That if each would assume their own,
    Alas! we know not how.
We have each other so engrossed,
That each is in the union lost.

And thus we can no absence know,
20   Nor shall we be confined;
Our active souls will daily go
    To learn each other's mind.
Nay, should we never meet to sense,
Our souls would hold intelligence.[2]

---

1. Mrs. Mary Awbrey, one of Philips' classmates at Mrs. Salmon's school. Quoting the entire poem, John Keats praises it as an example of "real feminine Modesty" in a letter to J. H. Reynolds of 21 September 1817.

2. A Neoplatonic idea, that the souls would know each other not by physical contact but by spiritual communion. Compare Donne's A Valediction: Forbidding Mourning (page 1598.)

25 Inspired with a flame divine,
        I scorn to court a stay;
    For from the noble soul of thine
        I can ne'er be away.
    But I shall weep when thou dost grieve;
30 Nor can I die whilst thou dost live.

    By my own temper I shall guess
        At thy felicity,
    And only like my happiness
        Because it pleaseth thee.
35 Our hearts at any time will tell
    If thou, or I, be sick, or well.

    All honor sure I must pretend,
        All that is good or great;
    She that would be Rosania's[3] friend,
40   Must be at least complete.
    If I have any bravery,
    'Tis cause I am so much of thee.

    Thy leiger° soul in me shall lie,   *ambassador*
        And all thy thoughts reveal;
45 Then back again with mine shall fly,
        And thence to me shall steal.
    Thus still to one another tend;
    Such is the sacred name of friend.

    Thus our twin souls in one shall grow,
50   And teach the world new love;
    Redeem the age and sex, and show
        A flame fate dares not move:
    And courting death to be our friend,
    Our lives together too shall end.

55 A dew shall dwell upon our tomb
        Of such a quality,
    That fighting armies, thither come,
        Shall reconciled be.
    We'll ask no epitaph, but say
60 Orinda and Rosania.

To My Excellent Lucasia, on Our Friendship
17th July 1651[1]

    I did not live until this time
        Crowned my felicity,
    When I could say without a crime,

---

3. Rosania was the poetic name that Philips gave to her friend Mary Awbrey.

1. Philips met her friend Anne Owen (called "Lucasia") in 1651.

I am not thine, but thee.
5   This carcass breathed, and walked, and slept,
    So that the world believed
There was a soul the motions kept;
    But they were all deceived.
For as a watch by art is wound
10   To motion, such was mine:
But never had Orinda found
    A soul till she found thine;
Which now inspires, cures and supplies,
    And guides my darkened breast:
15 For thou art all that I can prize,
    My joy, my life, my rest.
Nor bridegroom's nor crowned conqueror's mirth
    To mine compared can be:
They have but pieces of this earth,
20   I've all the world in thee.
Then let our flame still light and shine,
    (And no bold fear control)
As innocent as our design,
    Immortal as our soul.

The World

We falsely think it due unto our friends,
That we should grieve for their too early ends:
He that surveys the world with serious eyes,
And strips her from her gross and weak disguise,[1]
5 Shall find 'tis injury to mourn their fate;
He only dies untimely who dies late.
For if 'twere told to children in the womb,
To what a stage of mischief they must come;
Could they foresee with how much toil and sweat
10 Men court that gilded nothing, being great;
What pains they take not to be what they seem,
Rating their bliss by others' false esteem,
And sacrificing their content, to be
Guilty of grave and serious vanity;
15 How each condition hath its proper thorns,
And what one man admires, another scorns;
How frequently their happiness they miss,
And so far from agreeing what it is,
That the same person we can hardly find,
20 Who is an hour together in a mind;
Sure they would beg a period of their breath,
And what we call their birth would count their death.
Mankind is mad; for none can live alone,

1. The Platonic notion that the body is a covering for the soul.

Because their joys stand by comparison:
25   And yet they quarrel at society,
And strive to kill they know not whom, nor why.
We all live by mistake, delight in dreams,
Lost to ourselves, and dwelling in extremes;
Rejecting what we have, though ne'er so good,
30   And prizing what we never understood.
Compared to our boisterous inconstancy
Tempests are calm, and discords harmony.
Hence we reverse the world, and yet do find
The God that made can hardly please our mind.
35   We live by chance, and slip into events;
Have all of beasts except their innocence.
The soul, which no man's power can reach, a thing
That makes each woman man, each man a king,
Doth so much loose, and from its height so fall,
40   That some contend to have no soul at all.
'Tis either not observed, or at the best
By passion fought withall, by sin depressed.
Freedom of will (God's image) is forgot;
And if we know it, we improve it not.
45   Our thoughts, though nothing can be more our own,
Are still unguided, very seldom known.
Time 'scapes our hands as water in a sieve,
We come to die ere we begin to live.
Truth, the most suitable and noble prize,
50   Food of our spirits, yet neglected lies.
Errors and shadows are our choice, and we
Owe our perdition to our own decree.
If we search truth, we make it more obscure;
And when it shines, we can't the light endure.
55   For most men who plod on, and eat, and drink,
Have nothing less their business than to think;
And those few that enquire, how small a share
Of truth they find! how dark their notions are!
That serious evenness that calms the breast,
60   And in a tempest can bestow a rest,
We either not attempt, or else decline,
By every trifle snatched from our design.
(Others he must in his deceits involve,
Who is not true unto his own resolve.)
65   We govern not ourselves, but loose the reins,
Courting our bondage to a thousand chains;
And with as many slaveries content,
As there are tyrants ready to torment,
We live upon a rack, extended still
70   To one extreme, or both, but always ill.
For since our fortune is not understood,
We suffer less from bad than from the good.

The sting is better dressed and longer lasts,
As surfeits are more dangerous than fasts.
75 And to complete the misery to us,
We see extremes are still contiguous.
And as we run so fast from what we hate,
Like squibs on ropes,[2] to know no middle state;
So (outward storms strengthened by us) we find
80 Our fortune as disordered as our mind.
But that's excused by this, it doth its part;
A treacherous world befits a treacherous heart.
All ill's our own; the outward storms we loathe
Receive from us their birth, or sting, or both;
85 And that our vanity be past a doubt,
'Tis one new vanity to find it out.
Happy are they to whom God gives a grave,
And from themselves as from his wrath doth save.
'Tis good not to be born; but if we must,
90 The next good is, soon to return to dust:
When th'uncaged[3] soul, fled to eternity,
Shall rest, and live, and sing, and love, and see.
Here we but crawl and grope, and play and cry;[4]
Are first our own, then other's enemy:
95 But there shall be defaced both stain and score,
For time, and death, and sin shall be no more.[5]

2. A display of fireworks on a line.   4. Paraphrasing 1 Corinthians 13.11–12.
3. Free from the body.   5. As promised in Revelation 21.4.

The Execution of Charles I, 17th-century German print.

⚌✣ PERSPECTIVES ✣⚌

The Civil War, or the Wars of
Three Kingdoms

The English Civil War arose out of citizens' revolutionary demands for their rights and those of their legislature, and out of England's attempt to dominate Ireland and Scotland. The armed conflicts that arose from the demand for political self-determination in every part of the British Isles would have consequences for centuries to come. During the period from 1639 to 1651, war raged not only in England but also in Ireland, Scotland, and Wales; hence, historians now prefer to call this period of conflict the Wars of Three Kingdoms. The origins of the conflict in England were between Parliament and a King who had an absolutist style of governing. Charles I reigned without Parliament from 1629 to 1640, a period referred to as the "Eleven Years' Tyranny." He also imposed unpopular heavy taxes in the form of ship money levies to build up the fleet. Even more controversial was his imposition of Anglican worship and episcopal authority on Puritans and Presbyterians, who felt that such ritual was tantamount to Roman Catholicism. The King placed two Anglican bishops on the court of Star Chamber, who used the arbitrary power of this body to enforce unpopular religious practices.

When the King decided to impose an Anglican liturgy on the Scottish Kirk in 1639, riots broke out in Edinburgh, and Scottish Lowlanders united in a National Covenant against English interference. In 1639 and 1640, Scottish military uprisings necessitated Charles I's recalling Parliament to ask for financial aid. The Parliament was already angered by the eleven-year shutdown by the King, his imposition of taxes without its consent, and his support for Archbishop Laud, whom Parliament viewed as too dictatorial and too high church, shutting out both Puritans (who elected their ministers and disdained Catholic sacraments) and Presbyterians (who favored central church government but not Anglo-Catholic authority or ritual). When Parliament refused after three weeks to grant the King's request for money, the King decided to dissolve the "Short Parliament." In the wake of the dissolution of Parliament, soldiers went on rampages against churches, smashing stained glass windows and altar rails that smacked to them of Roman Catholicism. In some places, soldiers mutinied against their aristocratic commanders.

When the Scots defeated the King's army in the fall of 1640, he had to recall Parliament to petition for more funds. Led by John Pym, the "Long Parliament" seized the opportunity to criticize the King. It passed a Bill of Attainder, condemning to death as a traitor the general of the King's army, Viscount Strafford, who had been accused of instigating the war against Scotland and of suggesting that an Irish Catholic army could be used against England. No proof of guilt was necessary, only assent from the House of Lords and the King. Despite the King's reluctance, the combined opposition of the House of Commons and armed mobs in London in the spring of 1641 pressured him into signing Strafford's death warrant.

That fall two rebellions broke out in Ireland—one organized by Catholic Irish gentry, another arising more spontaneously among the native Gaelic Irish in Ulster against Scots and English settlers who had dispossessed them of their land. Pym blamed the unrest on the King and his Catholic court. Although there was terrible violence, especially in the popular uprisings, the English press wildly exaggerated the extent of the bloodshed, claiming a figure for Protestant deaths in the North of Ireland that was greater than the number of Protestants then living in the whole country. Pym, the leader of the House of Commons, moved that Parliament should offer no help in repressing Irish rebellion unless Charles agreed to dismiss his guilty counselors. The next day, Oliver Cromwell moved that the Parliament empower the Puritan Earl of Essex to head the English militia. Attacks on the King became stronger: his irresponsibility and violation of the security and rights of the people mandated Parliament's wresting power from him. On May 12, Archbishop Laud was executed. Although the King made some concessions, by January 1642 he decided to impeach Pym, four other members of Commons, and one from the House of Lords for treason. However, the accused were safely hidden in the City, and the King left London, not to return until he was put on trial and beheaded seven years later. Just on the eve of the outbreak of the war, the "Gentlewomen and Tradesmen's Wives of London" presented their petition to Parliament, complaining against Archbishop Laud's Anglicanism and the threat of violence from Ireland. The first part of the English Civil War (1642–1646), arising from the disputes between Parliament and the King, culminated in the victory of Parliament's New Model Army, headed by Sir Thomas Fairfax.

With the King defeated by the combined forces of the New Model Army and the Scots Covenanters in 1646, new conflicts arose between the army and the Parliament. Closely tied to the army, the Levellers, led by John Lilburne, agitated for a fundamental revision of the constitution: a single representative body, universal suffrage for men, and the abolition of monarchy and noble privilege. Colonel Ludlow, a leader of the republicans, opposed any negotiations with the King and petitioned Parliament to reform the constitution and to put the King on trial. When the House of Commons refused to listen to the army and continued to negotiate with the King, Colonels Ludlow, Ireton, and Pride purged Parliament, placing forty-five members under arrest and prohibiting another 186 from entering the House. This Rump Parliament set up a high court to try the King. On 27 January 1649, Charles I was condemned to death as a tyrant and traitor who had shed the blood of his people. John Bradshaw, President of the Court, proclaimed that the King was subject to the law and the law proceeded from Parliament. Arising out of these events came both the King's own memoir, *Eikon Basilike* ("the Royal Image"), ghostwritten and published after his execution by John Gauden, and Milton's militantly republican response *Eikonoklastes* ("Image-Breaker").

In the last stage of the Civil War, the dead king's son, Charles II, attempted to regain power through Irish and Scottish aid. In Ireland the Marquis of Ormonde led a coalition of royalists that secured the support of Irish troops for the King in exchange for the free exercise of Catholicism. Before Charles II could land in Dublin, the English sent troops there to put down the uprising. Cromwell slaughtered many at the siege of Drogheda; his campaign throughout Munster killed many civilians. In the aftermath of Cromwell's conquest, what remained of an Irish intelligentsia was either exiled or killed off, and large numbers of native inhabitants were either thrown off their land onto poorer farming land in western Ireland or sent into indentured servitude in the Caribbean. Following policies begun by Elizabeth and James, Cromwell granted Irish land to English settlers. The late events of the war in Ireland are represented here by one of Cromwell's letters from his campaign in Ireland, and by *John O'Dwyer of the Glenn*, a translation of one of the many Irish-language laments for the devastation of the Cromwellian conquest.

In Scotland, Charles II found allies among Presbyterian Covenanters, infuriated with the English Parliament for executing a Scottish monarch, and in the Marquis of Montrose, who recruited the Highland clans. When the Covenanters met with Charles II for the Treaty of Breda in Holland, they imposed on him a promise to reestablish Presbyterianism as the religion of both England and Scotland, to reinstate the Scottish Parliament, and to repudiate his pledges to Ormonde and Montrose. When Charles landed in Scotland, he learned that Montrose, most loyal of all royalists, had been hanged and quartered as a traitor. The political intrigue of Argyle against Montrose can be seen in the Earl of Clarendon's account of Montrose's death. The Covenanters, fighting for Scotland rather than for the King, were defeated by Cromwell at Dunbar. The Scots' losses were so huge that Scottish royalism was revived for one last battle between the King's Cavaliers and Cromwell's Roundheads. Facing Cromwell's army at Worcester in 1651, the forces of Scots and English royalists were vastly outnumbered and easily defeated. Charles II escaped to France, where he remained until the Restoration. Two years later, Cromwell became Lord Protector of the Commonwealth.

John Gauden
1605–1662

John Gauden wrote the most influential account of the royalist cause, *Eikon Basilike* ("Royal Portrait"), advance copies of which were sold on the day of Charles I's execution in 1649. Although Gauden at first sided with Parliament and the Presbyterians, he did not agree to the abolition of the bishops. In 1647 supporters of Charles I, then confined at Hampton Court by Parliament, sought Gauden's help to revise the King's meditations for publication. When the manuscript was complete, Gauden showed it to the King, who hesitated about having it published under his name. Meanwhile, the King was preoccupied first by his attempts to escape and then by his confinement, trial, and execution. When Royston first printed the book in January 1649, he believed that King Charles was the author. Just months later, William Duggard published another edition based on a manuscript that had been revised by the King; Gauden's authorship remained publically unknown until 1690.

Throughout the Interregnum, Gauden managed to keep his deanery at Brockton by conforming to Presbyterianism. With the Restoration in 1660, he was made Bishop of Exeter. In letters to Sir Edward Hyde, Gauden admitted his authorship and complained that his reward had not been sufficient. He was then promoted to the bishopric of Worcester, just a year before his death.

Eikon Basilike was written to influence public opinion and to guide the Prince of Wales, who waited in exile to regain his father's throne. A collection of meditations written in a lofty style, *Eikon Basilike* justified the King's views and evoked sympathy for his plight. The emblematic frontispiece shows the King in a saintly light—kneeling in prayer. Admirers of the work called it "most charitable, most heavenly" and "most pious, most ravishing." By the end of 1649, thirty-five editions had been printed in England. The most important of these, that of March 1649, added the King's prayers, the Prince of Wales's letter to his father, and an epitaph on the King's death. An English-language edition was published in Ireland in 1649, and twenty foreign-language editions were published on the Continent for the English community in exile as well as their European supporters.

The text aroused both support and criticism. Parliament had the printer Duggard arrested but released him when he produced a license to publish the book. Parliament prohibited the further sale of the book in May 1649, but by the end of 1649, five clandestine editions and two responses had appeared. *The Princely Pellican* explained how Charles had come to write the book, and *Eikon Alethine* attacked it as a fraud. Milton wrote his own rebuttal in *Eikonoklastes*, a savagely satirical prosecution of the King. *Eikonoklastes* merely went through two editions, showing that it could not compete in popularity with *Eikon Basilike*.

from Eikon Basilike
from *Chapter 4. Upon the Insolency of the Tumults*

I never thought anything, except our sins, more ominously presaging all these mischiefs which have followed, than those tumults in London and Westminster soon after the convening of this Parliament which were not like a storm at sea, (which yet wants not its terror,) but like an earthquake, shaking the very foundation of all; than which nothing in the world hath more of horror.

As it is one of the most convincing arguments that there is a God, while His power sets bounds to the raging of the sea, so it is no less that He restrains the madness of the people. Nor does anything portend more God's displeasure against a nation than when He suffers the confluence and clamors of the vulgar to pass all boundaries of laws and reverence to authority.

Which those tumults did to so high degrees of insolence, that they spared not to invade the honor and freedom of the two Houses, menacing, reproaching, shaking, yea, and assaulting some members of both Houses as they fancied or disliked them; nor did they forbear most rude and unseemly deportments, both in contemptuous words and actions, to myself and my court.

Nor was this a short fit or two of shaking, as an ague, but a quotidian fever, always increasing to higher inflammations, impatient of any mitigation, restraint, or remission.

First, they must be a guard against those fears which some men scared themselves and others withal; when, indeed, nothing was more to be feared, and less to be used by wise men, than those tumultuary confluxes of mean and rude people who are taught first to petition, then to protect, then to dictate, at last to command and overawe the Parliament.

All obstructions of Parliament, that is, all freedom of differing in votes, and debating matters with reason and candor, must be taken away with these tumults. By these must the Houses be purged, and all rotten members (as they pleased to count them) cast out; by these the obstinacy of men, resolved to discharge their consciences, must be subdued; by these all factious, seditious, and schismatical proposals against government, ecclesiastical or civil, must be backed and abetted till they prevailed.

Generally, whoever had most mind to bring forth confusion and ruin upon Church and State used the midwifery of those tumults, whose riot and impatience was such as they would not stay the ripening and season of counsels, or fair production of acts, in the order, gravity, and deliberateness befitting a Parliament, but ripped up with barbarous cruelty, and forcibly cut out abortive notes, such as their inviters and encouragers most fancied.

Yea, so enormous and detestable were their outrages, that no sober man could be without infinite shame and sorrow to see them so tolerated and connived at by some, countenanced, encouraged, and applauded by others.

What good man had not rather want anything he most desired for the public good, than obtain it by such unlawful and irreligious means? But men's passions and God's directions seldom agree; violent designs and motions must have suitable engines; such as too much attend their own ends, seldom confine themselves to God's means. Force must crowd in what reason will not lead.

Who were the chief demagogues and patrons of tumults, to send for them, to flatter and embolden them, to direct and tune their clamorous importunities, some men yet living are too conscious to pretend ignorance. God in His due time will let these see that those were no fit means to be used for attaining His ends.

But as it is no strange thing for the sea to rage when strong winds blow upon it, so neither for multitudes to become insolent when they have men of some reputation for parts and piety to set them on.

That which made their rudeness most formidable was, that many complaints being made, and messages sent by myself and some of both Houses yet no order for redress could be obtained with any vigor and efficacy proportionable to the malignity of that now far-spread disease and predominant mischief.

Such was some men's stupidity, that they feared no inconvenience; others' petulancy, that they joyed to see their betters shamefully outraged and abused, while they knew their only security consisted in vulgar flattery, so insensible were they of mine or the two Houses common safety and honors.

Nor could ever any order be obtained impartially to examine, censure, and punish the known boutefeus[1] and impudent incendiaries, who boasted of the influence they had, and used to convoke those tumults as their advantages served.

Yea some, who should have been wiser statesmen, owned them as friends, commending their courage, zeal, and industry, which to sober men could seem no better than that of the devil, who goes about seeking whom he may deceive and devour.

I confess, when I found such a deafness, that no declaration from the bishops, who were first foully insolenced and assaulted, nor yet from other lords and gentlemen of honor, nor yet from myself, could take place for the due repression of these tumults, and securing not only our freedom in Parliament, but our very persons in the streets; I thought myself not bound by my presence to provoke them to higher boldness and contempts; I hoped by my withdrawing[2] to give time both for the ebbing of their tumultuous fury, and others regaining some degrees of modesty and sober sense.

---

1. Firebrands.
2. Charles decided to flee from London on the night of 10 January 1642 in response to rioting that erupted as a result of his failed attempts to arrest the five opposition leaders in the House of Commons. Charles returned to Whitehall only as a prisoner just before his execution.

Some may interpret it as an effect of pusillanimity[3] in any man, for popular terrors, to desert his public station; but I think it is hardiness beyond true valor for a wise man to set himself against the breaking in of a sea, which to resist at present threatens imminent danger, but to withdraw gives it space to spend its fury, and gains a fitter time to repair the breach. Certainly a gallant man had rather fight to great disadvantages for number and place in the field in an orderly way, than scuffle with an undisciplined rabble.

Some suspected and affirmed that I meditated a war, when I went from Whitehall only to redeem my person and conscience from violence: God knows I did not then think of a war. Nor will any prudent man conceive that I would, by so many former and some after acts, have so much weakened myself if I had purposed to engage in a war, which to decline by all means I denied myself in so many particulars. It is evident I had then no army to fly unto for protection and vindication.

Who can blame me, or any other, for withdrawing ourselves from the daily baitings of the tumults, not knowing whether their fury and discontent might not fly so high as to worry and tear those in pieces whom as yet they but played with in their paws? God, who is my sole judge, is my witness in heaven that I never had any thoughts of my going from my house at Whitehall if I could have had but any reasonable fair quarter. I was resolved to bear much, and did so; but I did not think myself bound to prostitute the majesty of my place and person, the safety of my wife and children, to those who are prone to insult most when they have objects and opportunity most capable of their rudeness and petulancy.

But this business of the tumults, whereof some have given already an account to God, others yet living know themselves desperately guilty, time and the guilt of many has so smothered up and buried, that I think it best to leave it as it is; only I believe the just avenger of all disorders will in time make those men and that city see their sin in the glass of their punishment. It is more than an even lay, that they may one day see themselves punished by that way they offended.

Had this Parliament, as it was in its first election and constitution, sat full and free, the members of both Houses, being left to their freedom of voting, as in all reason, honor, and religion they should have been, I doubt not but things would have been so carried as would have given no less good content to all good men than they wished or expected.

For I was resolved to hear reason in all things, and to consent to it as far as I could comprehend it; but as swine are to gardens and orderly plantations, so are tumults to Parliaments, and plebeian concourses to public counsels, turning all into disorders and sordid confusions.

I am prone sometimes to think that had I called this Parliament to any other place in England, as I might opportunely enough have done, the sad consequences in all likelihood, with God's blessing, might have been prevented. A Parliament would have been welcome in any place; no place afforded such confluence of various and vicious humors as that where it was unhappily convened. But we must leave all to God, who orders our disorders, and magnifies His wisdom most when our follies and miseries are most discovered.

3. Cowardice.

John Milton
1608–1674

With the popularity of the royalist tract *Eikon Basilike* after the execution of Charles I, the new Puritan government needed to find someone to defend its cause against the growing support for the King. The Puritans found their man in the newly appointed Secretary for Foreign Tongues to the Council of State, John Milton. In *Eikonoklastes* ("Image Breaker"), Milton focused his attack on the arguments of *Eikon Basilike* more than on its authorship. He doubted whether the King wrote his own defense, but he chose to concentrate on a chapter-by-chapter refutation of the book's account of history—in terms of both events and the perspective on them. Milton also revealed that one the prayers attributed to the King was really Pamela's prayer from Sir Philip Sidney's prose romance *Arcadia*. For the Puritan Milton this was a shocking piece of paganism and plagiarism by one who presented himself as pious. Milton's language in *Eikonoklastes* is iconoclastic—mocking and sarcastic, marked by invective and sharply stinging *ad hominem* argument. One royalist called *Eikonoklastes* a "blackguardly book" in which Milton "blows his viper's breath upon those immortal devotions." Some royalists even viewed Milton's blindness as God's punishment for his having attacked the King. Shortly after the Restoration of Charles II in 1660, the House of Commons ordered the burning of *Eikonoklastes* and had Milton arrested. He was imprisoned for several months before being released through the aid of his friend Andrew Marvell. *Eikonklastes* was first published in October 1649; the second and final edition in Milton's lifetime appeared in 1650.

For more about Milton, see his principal listing, page 1698.

from Eikonoklastes
from *Chapter 1. Upon the King's Calling This Last Parliament*

"The odium and offenses which some men's rigor, or remissness in church and state had contracted upon his government, he resolved to have expiated with better laws and regulations." And yet the worst of misdemeanors committed by the worst of all his favorites, in the height of their dominion, whether acts of rigor or remissness, he hath from time to time continued, owned, and taken upon himself by public declarations, as often as the clergy, or any other of his instruments felt themselves overburdened with the people's hatred. And who knows not the superstitious rigor of his Sunday's chapel, and the licentious remissness of his Sunday's theater;[1] accompanied with that reverend statute for dominical jigs and maypoles,[2] published in his own name, and derived from the example of his father James? Which testifies all that rigor in superstition, all that remissness in religion to have issued out originally from his own house, and from his own authority.

Much rather then may those general miscarriages in State, his proper sphere, be imputed to no other person chiefly than to himself. And which of all those oppressive

---

1. While observers such as the Spanish ambassador noted Charles's sincere piety, Milton considered traditional ritual "superstitious," ironically linking it to irreligious theater life. Like the Puritans, Milton abhorred Sunday theater performances, and in *Of Reformation*, he attacked the bishops for promoting "gaming, jigging, wassailing, and mixed dancing" on Sundays.

2. The *Book of Sports* (1633) forbade bearbaiting and bullbaiting on Sundays, but also rebuked the Puritans for condemning other forms of recreation such as dancing and archery.

acts, or impositions did he ever disclaim or disavow, till the fatal awe of this Parliament hung ominously over him. Yet here he smoothly seeks to wipe off all the envy of his evil government upon his substitutes, and under-officers: and promises, though much too late, what wonders he purposed to have done in the reforming of religion—a work wherein all his undertakings heretofore declare him to have had little or no judgment. Neither could his breeding, or his course of life acquaint him with a thing so spiritual. Which may well assure us what kind of reformation we could expect from him; either some politic form of an imposed religion, or else perpetual vexation, and persecution to all those that complied not with such a form.

The like amendment he promises in State; not a step further "than his reason and conscience told him was fit to be desired"; wishing "he had kept within those bounds, and not suffered his own judgment to have been overborne in some things," of which things one was the Earl of Strafford's execution.[3] And what signifies all this, but that still his resolution was the same, to set up an arbitrary government of his own; and that all Britain was to be tied and chained to the conscience, judgment, and reason of one man; as if those gifts had been only his peculiar and prerogative, entailed upon him with his fortune to be a king? When as doubtless no man so obstinate, or so much a tyrant, but professes to be guided by that which he calls his reason, and his judgment, though never so corrupted; and pretends also his conscience. In the meanwhile, for any Parliament or the whole nation to have either reason, judgment, or conscience, by this rule was altogether in vain, if it thwarted the king's will; which was easy for him to call by any other more plausible name. He himself hath many times acknowledged to have no right over us but by law; and by the same law to govern us: but law in a free nation hath been ever public reason, the enacted reason of a Parliament; which he denying to enact, denies to govern us by that which ought to be our law; interposing his own private reason, which to us is no law. And thus we find these fair and specious promises, made upon the experience of many hard sufferings, and his most mortified retirements, being thoroughly sifted, to contain nothing in them much different from his former practices, so cross, and so averse to all his Parliaments, and both the nations of this island. What fruits they could in likelihood have produced in his restorement, is obvious to any prudent foresight.

And this is the substance of his first section, till we come to the devout of it, modeled into the form of a private psalter. Which they who so much admire, either for the matter or the manner, may as well admire the archbishop's late breviary,[4] and many other as good *Manuals*, and *Handmaids of Devotion*, the lip-work of every prelatical liturgist, clapped together, and quilted out of Scripture phrase, with as much ease, and as little need of Christian diligence, or judgment, as belongs to the compiling of any ordinary and salable piece of English divinity, that the shops value. But he who from such a kind of psalmistry, or any other verbal devotion, without the pledge and

---

3. Thomas Wentworth, Earl of Strafford, was executed in May 1641. Charles had recalled Strafford from the Lord Deputyship in Ireland to help with the war against the Scots Covenanters. Parliament accused Wentworth of planning to use the Irish army to suppress the King's opponents in Scotland and England. Even though Strafford was successfully defended against the charges, Charles signed his death warrant, fearing retaliation against himself and the Queen for their part in a plot to rescue Strafford.

4. Milton's name for Archbishop Laud's *Prayer Book*, which the Puritans hated because of its similarity to Roman Catholic ritual.

earnest of suitable deeds, can be persuaded of a zeal, and true righteousness in the person, hath much yet to learn; and knows not that the deepest policy of a tyrant hath been ever to counterfeit religious. And Aristotle in his *Politics*, hath mentioned that special craft among twelve other tyrannical sophisms.[5] Neither want we examples. Andronicus Comnenus the Byzantine Emperor, though a most cruel tyrant, is reported by Nicetas[6] to have been a constant reader of Saint Paul's Epistles; and by continual study had so incorporated the phrase and style of that transcendent apostle into all his familiar letters, that the imitation seemed to vie with the original. Yet this availed not to deceive the people of that empire; who notwithstanding his saint's vizard, tore him to pieces for his tyranny.

From stories of this nature both ancient and modern which abound, the poets also, and some English, have been in this point so mindful of decorum, as to put never more pious words in the mouth of any person, than of a tyrant. I shall not instance an abstruse author, wherein the King might be less conversant, but one whom we well know was the closet companion of these his solitudes, William Shakespeare, who introduces the person of Richard the Third, speaking in as high a strain of piety, and mortification, as is uttered in any passage of this book, and sometimes to the same sense and purpose with some words in this place, "I intended," saith he, "not only to oblige my friends but mine enemies." The like saith Richard, Act 2. Scene 1,

> I do not know that Englishman alive
> With whom my soul is any jot at odds,
> More than the infant that is born tonight;
> I thank my God for my humility.

Other stuff of this sort may be read throughout the whole tragedy, wherein the poet used not much license in departing from the truth of history, which delivers him a deep dissembler, not of his affections only, but of religion.

from *Chapter 4. Upon the Insolency of the Tumults*

And that the King was so emphatical and elaborate on this theme against tumults, and expressed with such a vehemence his hatred of them, will redound less perhaps, than he was aware, to the commendation of his government. For besides that in good governments they happen seldomest, and rise not without cause, if they prove extreme and pernicious, they were never counted so to monarchy, but to monarchical tyranny; and extremes one with another are at most antipathy. If then the King so extremely stood in fear of tumults, the inference will endanger him to be the other extreme. Thus far the occasion of this discourse against tumults; now to the discourse itself, voluble enough, and full of sentence,[1] but that, for the most part, either specious rather than solid, or to his cause nothing pertinent.

"He never thought any thing more to presage the mischiefs that ensued, than those tumults." Then was his foresight but short, and much mistaken. Those tumults were but the mild effects of an evil and injurious reign; not signs of mischiefs to come, but seeking relief for mischiefs past; those signs were to be read more apparent in his

5. See Aristotle, *Politics* 5.9.15, for the notion that care in religious ritual is a device of tyrants.

6. A 12th-century historian who recorded the cruelty of Comnenus's reign (1183–1185).
1. Significance, meaning.

rage and purposed revenge of those free expostulations, and clamors of the people against his lawless government. "Not any thing," saith he, "portends more God's displeasure against a nation than when he suffers the clamors of the vulgar to pass all bounds of law & reverence to authority." It portends rather his displeasure against a tyrannous King, whose proud throne he intends to overturn by that contemptible vulgar; the sad cries and oppressions of whom his royalty regarded not. As for that supplicating people they did no hurt either to law or authority, but stood for it rather in the Parliament against whom they feared would violate it.

That "they invaded the honor and freedom of the two Houses," is his own officious accusation, not seconded by the Parliament, who had they seen cause, were themselves best able to complain. And if they "shook & menaced" any, they were such as had more relation to the Court, than to the Commonwealth; enemies, not patrons of the people. But if their petitioning unarmed were an invasion of both Houses, what was his entrance into the House of Commons, besetting it with armed men, in what condition then was the honor, and freedom of that House?

"They forbore not rude deportments, contemptuous words and actions to himself and his Court."

It was more wonder, having heard what treacherous hostility he had designed against the city, and his whole kingdom, that they forbore to handle him as people in their rage have handled tyrants heretofore for less offenses.

"They were not a short ague, but a fierce quotidian fever:" He indeed may best say it, who most felt it; for the shaking was within him; and it shook him by his own description "worse than a storm, worse then an earthquake, Belshazzar's Palsy."[2] Had not worse fears, terrors, and envies made within him that commotion, how could a multitude of his subjects, armed with no other weapon then petitions, have shaken all his joints with such a terrible ague. Yet that the Parliament should entertain the least fear of bad intentions from him or his party, he endures not; but would persuade us that "men scare themselves and others without cause;" for he thought fear would be to them a kind of armor, and his design was, if it were possible, to disarm all, especially of a wise fear and suspicion; for that he knew would find weapons.

He goes on therefore with vehemence to repeat the mischiefs done by these tumults. "They first petitioned, then protected, dictate next, and lastly overawe the Parliament. They removed obstructions, they purged the Houses, cast out rotten members." If there were a man of iron, such as Talus, by our poet Spenser, is feigned to be the page of Justice, who with his iron flail could do all this, and expeditiously, without those deceitful forms and circumstances of law, worse than ceremonies in religion; I say God send it down, whether by one Talus, or by a thousand.[3]

"But they subdued the men of conscience in Parliament, backed and abetted all seditious and schismatical proposals against government ecclesiastical and civil."

Now we may perceive the root of his hatred whence it springs. It was not the King's grace or princely goodness, but this iron flail the people, that drove the bishops out of their baronies, out of their cathedrals, out of the Lord's house, out of their copes

2. In *Of Reformation*, Milton compares the feasting of Anglican bishops to that of Belshazzar in his palace in Babylon on the eve of the fall of the city to the Medes and Persians. When King Belshazzar saw the mysterious writing on the wall that foretold his doom, "the joints of his loins were loosed, and his knees smote one against

another" (Daniel 5.6).
3. Talus is the iron flail who ruthlessly cuts down all who oppose Artegal, the Knight of Justice, in Spenser's *Faerie Queene* 5, much of which is about the subjugation of Ireland by England.

and surplices, and all those papistical innovations,[4] threw down the High Commission and Star Chamber, gave us a triennial Parliament, and what we most desired;[5] in revenge whereof he now so bitterly inveighs against them; these are those seditious and schismatical proposals, then by him condescended to, as acts of grace, now of another name; which declares him, touching matters of Church and State, to have been no other man in the deepest of his solitude, than he was before at the highest of his sovereignty.

But this was not the worst of these tumults, they played the hasty "midwives," and "would not stay the ripening, but went straight to ripping up, and forcibly cut out abortive votes."

They would not stay perhaps the Spanish demurring, and putting off such wholesome acts and counsels, as the politic cabin at Whitehall had no mind to. But all this is complained here as done to the Parliament, and yet we heard not the Parliament at that time complain of any violence from the people, but from him. Wherefore intrudes he to plead the cause of Parliament against the people, while the Parliament was pleading their own cause against him; and against him were forced to seek refuge of the people? 'Tis plain then that those confluxes and resorts interrupted not the Parliament, nor by them were thought tumultuous, but by him only and his court faction.

"But what good Man had not rather want any thing he most desired for the public good, than attain it by such unlawful and irreligious means;" as much as to say, had not rather sit still and let his country be tyrannized, than that the people, finding no other remedy, should stand up like men and demand their rights and liberties. This is the artificialest piece of fineness to persuade men into slavery that the wit of court could have invented. But hear how much better the moral of this lesson would befit the teacher. What good man had not rather want a boundless and arbitrary power, and those fine flowers of the crown, called prerogatives, than for them to use force and perpetual vexation to his faithful subjects, nay to wade for them through blood and civil war? So that this and the whole bundle of those following sentences may be applied better to the convincement of his own violent courses, than of those pretended tumults.

"Who were the chief demagogues to send for those tumults, some alive are not ignorant." Setting aside the affrightment of this goblin word; for the King by his leave cannot coin English as he could money, to be current (and tis believed this wording was above his known style and orthography, and accuses the whole composure to be conscious of some other author)[6] yet if the people "were sent for, emboldened and directed" by those "demagogues," who, saving his Greek, were good patriots, and by his own confession "Men of some repute for parts and piety," it helps well to assure us there was both urgent cause, and the less danger of their coming.

"Complaints were made, yet no redress could be obtained." The Parliament also complained of what danger they sat in from another party, and demanded of him a guard, but it was not granted. What marvel then if it cheered them to see some store

---

4. Milton refers to the London petition calling for the abolition of the bishops' power, introduced into Parliament in December 1640, that resulted in their exclusion from the House of Lords.
5. The High Commission, the highest ecclesiastical court, investigated such matters as heresy, recusancy, and any writing against the Book of Common Prayer; Parliament abolished it on 5 July 1641. The Star Chamber was

also abolished because it was viewed as a special tool of government favoring the special right of the sovereign above all other persons and the common law. A triennial Parliament is a parliament convened every three years.
6. Milton believed that Charles I could not have written *Eikon Basilike* because such passages as this one showed a word choice and style different from Charles's.

of their friends, and in the Roman not the pettifogging sense, their clients so near about them; a defense due by nature both from whom it was offered, and to whom; as due as to their parents; though the Court stormed, and fretted to see such honor given to them, who were then best fathers of the Commonwealth. And both the Parliament and people complained, and demanded justice for those assaults, if not murders done at his own doors, by that crew of rufflers, but he, instead of doing justice on them, justified and abetted them in what they did, as in his public "Answer to a Petition from the City" may be read. Neither is it slightly to be passed over, that in the very place where blood was first drawn in this cause, as the beginning of all that followed, there was his own blood shed by the executioner. According to that sentence of divine justice, "In the place where dogs licked the blood of Naboth, shall dogs lick thy blood, even thine."

From hence he takes occasion to excuse that improvident and fatal error of his absenting from the Parliament. "When he found that no declaration of the bishops could take place against those tumults." Was that worth his considering, that foolish and self-undoing declaration of twelve cypher bishops, who were immediately appeached of treason for that audacious declaring?[7] The bishops peradventure were now and then pulled by the rochets,[8] and deserved another kind of pulling; but what amounted this to "the fear of his own person in the streets"? Did he not the very next day after his irruption into the House of Commons, than which nothing had more exasperated the people, go in his coach unguarded into the city? did he receive the least affront, much less violence in any of the streets, but rather humble demeanors, and supplications? Hence may be gathered, that however in his own guiltiness he might have justly feared, yet that he knew the people so full of awe and reverence to his person, as to dare commit himself single among the thickest of them, at a time when he had most provoked them. Besides in Scotland they had handled the Bishops in a more robustious manner; Edinburgh had been full of tumults,[9] two armies from thence had entered England against him;[1] yet after all this, he was not fearful, but very forward to take so long a journey to Edinburgh;[2] which argues first, as did also his rendition afterward to the Scotch Army,[3] that to England he continued still, as he was indeed, a stranger, and full of diffidence; to the Scots only a native King,[4] in his confidence, though not in his dealing towards them. It shows us next beyond doubting, that all this his fear of tumults was but a mere color and occasion taken of his resolved absence from the Parliament, for some other end not difficult to be guessed. And those instances wherein valor is not to be questioned for not "scuffling with the sea, or an undisciplined rabble," are but subservient to carry on the solemn jest of his fearing tumults: if they discover not withall, the true reason why he departed; only to turn his slashing at the court gate, to slaughtering "in the field"; his disorderly bickering, to an orderly invading: which was nothing else but a more orderly disorder.

"Some suspected and affirmed, that he meditated a War when he went first from Whitehall." And they were not the worst heads that did so, nor did "any of his former

---

7. The Bishops' Exclusion Bill was Parliament's reaction to the assertion by 12 bishops that any legislation passed by the House of Lords when the bishops were absent was void.
8. Vestments.
9. When Charles attempted to force the Book of Common Prayer on the Scottish churches, the people rioted.
1. The first Scottish war ended with the Treaty of

Berwick in June 1639, the second with the Treaty of Ripon in October 1640.
2. Charles went to Edinburgh in 1641, hoping to pit the Covenanters against their opponents.
3. Charles surrendered himself to the Scottish army commanders in May 1646.
4. Charles was born in Scotland, and he made special appeals to the Scots to be their king in both 1641 and 1646.

acts weaken him" to that, as he alleges for himself, or if they had, they clear him only for the time of passing them, not for what ever thoughts might come after into his mind. Former actions of improvidence or fear, not with him unusual, cannot absolve him of all after meditations.

He goes on protesting his "no intention to have left Whitehall," had these horrid tumults given him but "fair quarter," as if he himself, his wife and children had been in peril. But to this enough hath been answered.

"Had this Parliament as it was in its first election," namely, with the Lord and Baron Bishops, "sat full and free," he doubts not but all had gone well. What warrant this of his to us? Whose not doubting was all good men's greatest doubt.

"He was resolved to hear reason, and to consent so far as he could comprehend." A hopeful resolution; what if his reason were found by oft experience to comprehend nothing beyond his own advantages, was this a reason fit to be intrusted with the common good of three nations?

"But," saith he, "as swine are to gardens, so are tumults to Parliaments." This the Parliament, had they found it so, could best have told us. In the meanwhile, who knows not that one great hog may do as much mischief in a garden, as many little swine.[5]

"He was sometimes prone to think that had he called this last Parliament to any other place in England, the sad consequences might have been prevented." But change of air changes not the mind. Was not his first Parliament at Oxford dissolved after two subsidies given him, and no justice received? Was not his last in the same place, where they sat with as much freedom, as much quiet from tumults, as they could desire, a Parliament both in his account, and their own, consisting of all his friends, that fled after him, and suffered for him, and yet by him nicknamed, and cashiered for a "mongrel Parliament that vexed his Queen with their base and mutinous motions," as his cabinet letter tells us?[6] Whereby the world may see plainly, that no shifting of place, no sifting of members to his own mind, no number, no paucity, no freedom from tumults, could ever bring his arbitrary wilfulness, and tyrannical designs to brook the least shape or similitude, the least counterfeit of a Parliament.

Finally instead of praying for his people as a good King should do, he prays to be delivered from them, as "from wild beasts, inundations, and raging seas, that had overborne all loyalty, modesty, laws, justice, and religion." God save the people from such intercessors.

Oliver Cromwell
1599–1658

Oliver Cromwell's brutal conquest of Ireland (1649–1650) was the culmination of a long military, political, and religiously zealous career and the turning point in his rise to the position of Lord Protector. He had risen steadily in the Parliamentary Army, serving in the early days of the Civil War as captain of a troop of horses and finally becoming the chief of the New Model

---

5. Milton may echo the identification of the hog with Henry VIII for his failure to carry out a thorough and consistent reformation in Anthony Gilby's An Admonition to England and Scotland to Call Them to Repentance (Geneva, 1558).

6. Charles called an opposition Parliament that met in Oxford on 22 January 1644 and that he ordered closed after disagreement with them. This Parliament first attempted a peaceful settlement with the Westminster Parliament and then declared it guilty of treason. The King called it his "mongrel Parliament."

Army. Not only did he have a genius for military strategy but he was one of those who "never stirred from their troops . . . but fought to the last minute." He and his men were both called "Ironsides" in tribute to their indomitability. As a member of Parliament, he argued vigorously for the Puritan cause, and when Parliament was purged of Presbyterians in 1649, Cromwell's power and that of his fellow Congregationalists or Independents increased. At the trial of Charles I in January 1649, Cromwell adamantly demanded execution. Afterward, when the new Commonwealth was set up, one of Parliament's first charges was to send Cromwell to subdue Ireland, where Irish Royalists and Rebels, once pitted against each other, had formed a coalition and were gaining ground.

Cromwell's treatment of the Irish tested the limits of the principles of the Puritan Revolution and left a legacy of devastation. Although Cromwell was a strong member of the English Parliament, he helped to bring about the abolition of both Irish and Scottish Parliaments with his military defeats of both kingdoms. In September 1644, Cromwell urged the Presbyterian Parliament to guarantee liberty of conscience to the Independents among his troops, but when the Catholics of New Ross, Ireland, called for similar toleration in October 1649, Cromwell refused them: "if by liberty of conscience, you mean a liberty to exercise the Mass, I judge it best to use plain dealing, and to let you know, where the Parliament of England have power, that will not be allowed of." Indeed during Cromwell's rule in England, only Jews and non-Anglican Protestants were tolerated. Furthermore, Cromwell escalated the policy (begun under Elizabeth and James) of giving lands confiscated from native Irish inhabitants to English colonists. The massacre of Drogheda—including civilians as well as troops—made the Irish remember Cromwell as cruel. In the following letter of 17 September 1649, Cromwell presents his troops' massacre of the people of Drogheda as "the righteous judgment of God." The same religious conviction that had made him and his New Model Army such valiant defenders of English liberty was used to justify Irish slaughter.

Cromwell also used his letters to keep Parliament informed of his progress, to ask for further supplies, and to promote his political power. He was to go on to defeat the Scots in 1650. Ultimately, his power grew to such an extent that in 1657 he became Lord Protector, assuming the pomp and trappings of royalty. When his son Richard succeeded him at his death in September 1658, it seemed as if Oliver Cromwell's rule had led to a new monarchy. His son proved a weak successor, and the Commonwealth was restored in May 1659, only to collapse with the Restoration of 1660. If Cromwell's participation in parliamentary politics and the New Model Army contributed to the cause of republican liberty, his conquest of Ireland marked one of the bleakest chapters in the English colonization of Ireland.

from Letters from Ireland

Relating the Several Great Success It Hath Pleased God to Give Unto the Parliament's Forces There, in the Taking of Drogheda, Trym, Dundalk, Carlingford, and the Nury.
* * *

For the Honorable *William Lenthal* Esq;
Speaker of the Parliament of *England*

Sir,

Your army[1] being safely arrived at Dublin, and the enemy endeavoring to draw all his forces together about Trym and Tecroghan[2] (as my intelligence gave me); from

---

1. The letter is addressed to Parliament from the commander of the parliamentary army, hence "your army."

2. A town and townland in County Meath, northwest of Dublin.

whence endeavors were used by the Marquis of Ormonde, to draw Owen Roe O'Neal with his forces to his assistance, but with what success I cannot yet learn.[3] I resolved after some refreshment taken for our weather-beaten men and horses, and accommodations for a march, to take the field; and accordingly upon Friday the thirtieth of August last, rendezvoused with eight regiments of foot, and six of horse, and some troops of dragoons, three miles on the north side of Dublin; the design was, to endeavor the regaining of Drogheda,[4] or tempting the enemy, upon his hazard of the loss of that place, to fight. Your army came before the town upon Monday following, where having pitched, as speedy course as could be was taken to frame our batteries,[5] which took up the more time, because divers of the battering guns were on shipboard. Upon Monday the ninth of this instant, the batteries began to play; whereupon I sent Sir Arthur Ashton the then Governor a summons, to deliver the town to the use of the Parliament of England; to the which I received no satisfactory answer, but proceeded that day to beat down the steeple of the church on the south side of the town, and to beat down a tower not far from the same place, which you will discern by the card[6] enclosed. Our guns not being able to do much that day, it was resolved to endeavor to do our utmost the next day to make breaches[7] assaultable, and by the help of God to storm them. The places pitched upon, were that part of the town wall next a church, called St. Marie's, which was the rather chosen, because we did hope that if we did enter and possess that church, we should be the better able to keep it against their horse and foot, until we could make way for the entrance of our horse, which we did not conceive that any part of the town would afford the like advantage for that purpose with this. The batteries planted were two, one was for that part of the wall against the east end of the said church, the other against the wall on the south side; being somewhat long in battering, the enemy made six retrenchments, three of them from the said church to Duleek Gate, and three from the east end of the church to the town wall, and so backward. The guns after some two or three hundred shot, beat down the corner tower, and opened two reasonable good breaches in the east and south wall. Upon Tuesday the tenth of this instant, about five of the clock in the evening, we began the storm, and after some hot dispute, we entered about seven or eight hundred men, the enemy disputing it very stiffly with us; and indeed through the advantages of the place, and the courage God was pleased to give the defenders, our men were forced to retreat quite out of the breach, not without some considerable loss; Colonel Cassel being there shot in the head, whereof he presently died, and divers soldiers and officers doing their duty, killed and wounded. There was a tenalia[8] to flanker the south wall of the town, between Duleek Gate, and the corner tower before mentioned, which our men entered, wherein they found some forty or fifty of the enemy, which they put to the sword, and this they held; but it being without[9] the wall, and the sallyport[1] through the wall into that tenalia being choked up with some of the enemy which were killed in it, it proved of no use for our entrance into the town that way.

3. James Butler, Earl of Ormonde, represented Charles I in Ireland throughout the 1640s. At first opposed to the Catholic Confederation led by Owen Roe O'Neill (c. 1590–1649), Ormonde joined forces with O'Neill against the incursion of Cromwell's army.
4. Drogheda (Droichead átha, "Bridge of the ford"), a city in County Louth, was under royalist command when Cromwell arrived there on 2 September 1649.

5. Platforms on which artillery was mounted.
6. Chart, map.
7. Gaps in fortifications.
8. A low fortification to protect the wall from the side.
9. Outside.
1. An opening for troops to pass through.

Although our men that stormed the breaches were forced to recoil, as before is expressed, yet being encouraged to recover their loss, they made a second attempt, wherein God was pleased to animate them, that they got ground of the enemy, and by the goodness of God, forced him to quit his entrenchments; and after a very hot dispute, the enemy having both horse and foot, and we only foot within the wall, the enemy gave ground, and our men became masters; but of their retrenchments and the church, which indeed although they made our entrance the more difficult, yet they proved of excellent use to us, so that the enemy could not annoy us with their horse, but thereby we had advantage to make good the ground, that so we might let in our own horse, which accordingly was done, though with much difficulty; the enemy retreated divers of them into the Mill-Mount, a place very strong and of difficult access, being exceeding high, having a good graft[2] and strongly pallisadoed;[3] the Governor Sir Arthur Ashton and divers considerable officers being there, our men getting up to them, were ordered by me to put them all to the sword; and indeed being in the heat of action, I forbade them to spare any that were in arms in the town, and I think that night they put to the sword about two thousand men, divers of the officers and soldiers being fled over the bridge into the other part of the town, where about one hundred of them possessed St. Peter's church steeple, some the west gate, and others, a round strong tower next the gate, called St. Sunday's. These being summoned to yield to mercy, refused; whereupon I ordered the steeple of St. Peter's church to be fired, where one of them was heard to say in the midst of the flames, "God damn me, God confound me, I burn, I burn." The next day the other two towers were summoned,[4] in one of which was about six or seven score, but they refused to yield themselves; and we knowing that hunger must compel them, set only good guards to secure them from running away, until their stomachs were come down. From one of the said towers, notwithstanding their condition, they killed and wounded some of our men; when they submitted, their officers were knocked on the head, and every tenth man of the soldiers killed, and the rest shipped for the Barbados;[5] the soldiers in the other tower were all spared, as to their lives only, and shipped likewise for the Barbados. I am persuaded that this is a righteous judgment of God upon these barbarous wretches, who have imbrued their hands in so much innocent blood, and that it will tend to prevent the effusion of blood for the future, which are the satisfactory grounds to such actions, which otherwise cannot but work remorse and regret.

The officers and soldiers of this garrison were the flower of all their army; and their great expectation was that our attempting this place would put fair to ruin us; they being confident of the resolution of their men, and the advantage of the place; if we had divided our force into two quarters, to have besieged the north town and the south town, we could not have had such a correspondency between the two parts of our army, but that they might have chosen to have brought their army, and have fought with which part they pleased, and at the same time have made a sally with two thousand men upon us, and have left their walls manned, they having in the town the numbers specified in this inclosed, by some say near four thousand. Since this great mercy vouchsafed to us, I sent a party of horse and dragoons to Dundalk, which the enemy quitted, and we are possessed of; as also another castle they deserted between

---

2. Ditch, moat.
3. Defended with a strong fence of pointed stakes.
4. Called to surrender.
5. In the Cromwellian period in Ireland, not only men captured in battle but also women and children were sent into indentured servitude to English colonies in the Caribbean.

Trym and Drogheda, upon the Boynes.[6] I sent a party of horse and dragoons to a house within five miles of Trym, there being then in Trym some Scots companies which the Lord of Ards[7] brought to assist the Lord of Ormonde; but upon the news of Drogheda they ran away, leaving their great guns behind them, which we also have possessed. And now give me leave to say how it comes to pass that this work is wrought. It was set upon some of our hearts, that a great thing should be done, not by power, or might, but by the Spirit of God; and is it not so clear? That which caused your men to storm so courageously, it was the Spirit of God, who gave your men courage, and took it away again, and gave the enemy courage, and took it away again, and gave your men courage again, and therewith this happy success; and therefore it is good that God alone have all the glory.

It is remarkable, that these people at the first set up the Mass in some places of the town that had been monasteries; but afterwards grew so insolent, that the last Lord's day before the Storm,[8] the Protestants were thrust out of the great church, called St. Peter's, and they had public Mass there; and in this very place near one thousand of them were put to the sword, flying thither for safety: I believe all their friars were knocked on the head promiscuously, but two, the one of which was Father Peter Taaff (Brother to the Lord Taaff)[9] whom the Soldiers took the next day, and made an end of; the other was taken in the round tower, under the repute of lieutenant, and when he understood the officers in that tower had no quarter, he confessed he was a friar, but that did not save him. A great deal of loss in this business, fell upon Col. Hewson, Col. Cassel, and Colonel Ewers' regiments; Colonel Ewers having two field-officers in his regiment shot, Colonel Cassel and a captain of his regiment slain, Colonel Hewson's captain-lieutenant slain; I do not think we lost one hundred men upon the place, though many be wounded. I most humbly pray, the Parliament will be pleased this army may be maintained, and that a consideration may be had of them, and of the carrying on of the affairs here, as may give a speedy issue to this work, to which there seems to be a marvelous fair opportunity offered by God. And although it may seem very chargeable to the State of England to maintain so great a force, yet surely to stretch a little for the present, in following God's Providence, in hope the charge will not be long, I trust it will not be thought by any (that have no irreconcilable or malicious principles) unfit for me to move for a constant supply, which in humane probability, as to outward means, is most likely to hasten and perfect this work; and indeed, if God please to finish it here, as he hath done in England, the war is like to pay itself. We keep the field much, our tents sheltering us from the wet and cold, but yet the country sickness overtakes many, and therefore we desire recruits, and some fresh regiments of foot may be sent us; for it is easily conceived by what the garrisons already drink up, what our field army will come to, if God shall give more garrisons into our hands. Craving pardon for this great trouble, I rest,

Your most humble Servant,

O. CROMWELL

Dublin, Sept. 17, 1649

---

6. The Boyne River.
7. Hugh Montgomery (c. 1623–1663), 3rd Viscount of Ards.
8. I.e., Cromwell's attack on the town.

9. Theobald, 2nd Viscount Taaff (d. 1677). An uncle of Lord Taaff, Lucas was forced to surrender New Ross to Cromwell in October 1649.

John O'Dwyer of the Glenn
c. 1651

John O'Dwyer of the Glenn (Seán O'Duibhir an Ghleanna) is one of the most beautiful popular Irish-language songs commemorating the war against the Cromwellian conquest of Ireland and its aftermath. According to James Hardiman, who collected this song in his *Irish Minstrelsy, or Bardic Remains of Ireland* (1831), John O'Dwyer was "a distinguished officer who commanded in the Counties of Waterford and Tipperary in 1651." The poem is listed under the heading "Jacobite Relics," which places it in a long tradition of support for the Stuart kings, which began with the celebration of the accession of James I in elite bardic poetry and continued into the eighteenth century with support for Bonnie Prince Charlie in popular ballads.

The imagery of the natural world in *John O'Dwyer of the Glenn* symbolizes the state of Ireland. The lyric begins with a pastoral idyll, as the speaker describes awakening in the morning to the sound of birds singing. The intrusion of a fox signals the advent of war, and a sad old woman who stands by the side of the road reckoning her geese evokes Ireland weeping for those she has lost. Some of the geese (*geidh*), here referred to as "that prowler's spoil," died in battle; others, like the "wild geese" (*geidh fiádháin*) who left Ireland after the defeat of the Gaelic chiefs in 1603, fled to the Continent. John O'Dwyer and his men were said by Hardiman to have embarked for Spain.

The translation here is that of Thomas Furlong as printed in Hardiman's *Irish Minstrelsy*. The song originated in County Tipperary in the mid-seventeenth century, and there are more verses in Irish. It is still sung in both English and Irish. The best edition of the Irish text is that edited by Padraig de Brún and Breandán Ó Buachalla in *Nua-Dhuanaire* (1971), which also contains poems by such mid-seventeenth-century Irish poets as Piaras Feiritéar and Dáibhí O Bruadair.

John O'Dwyer of the Glenn

    Blithe the bright dawn found me,
    Rest with strength had crown'd me,
    Sweet the birds sung round me,
        Sport was all their toil.
5   The horn its clang was keeping,
    Forth the fox was creeping,
    Round each dame stood weeping,
        O'er that prowler's spoil.
    Hark, the foe is calling,
10   Fast the woods are falling,
    Scenes and sights appalling
        Mark the wasted soil.[1]

    War and confiscation
    Curse the fallen nation;
15   Gloom and desolation
        Shade the lost land o'er.
    Chill the winds are blowing,

---

1. The falling woods are the old Irish families who have been thrown off their land, and the "wasted soil" is the country after war.

Death aloft is going;
Peace or hope seems growing
20   For our race no more.
Hark the foe is calling,
Fast the woods are falling,
Scenes and sights appalling
      Throng our blood-stained shore.

25   Where's my goat to cheer me,[2]
Now it plays not near me;
Friends no more can hear me;
      Strangers round me stand.
Nobles once high-hearted,
30   From their homes have parted,
Scatter'd, scar'd and started
      By a base-born band.
Hark the foe is calling,
Fast the woods are falling;
35   Scenes and sights appalling
      Thicken round the land.

Oh! that death had found me
And in darkness bound me,
Ere each object round me
40   Grew so sweet, so dear.
Spots that once were cheering,
Girls beloved endearing,
Friends from whom I'm steering,
      Take this parting tear.
45   Hark, the foe is calling,
Fast the woods are falling;
Scenes and sights appalling
      Plague and haunt me here.

The Story of Alexander Agnew

Alexander Agnew is seen by contemporary Scots writers such as Booker Prize–winning novel-ist James Kelman as something of a hero. An unrepentant freethinker, Agnew was the first man in Scots history publicly to deny the existence of God. Offending the Presbyterian laws of Scot-land, Agnew was found guilty of blasphemy and hanged. The following journalistic account of his trial gives the sense of a man being driven to greater and greater levels of vitriolic sarcasm by the nitpicking detail of his Presbyterian examiners. Since the story begins with his refusing to go to church, saying, "Hang God, God was hanged long since," the ninth count against him—that he refused to say grace—seems oddly anticlimactic.

---

2. The goat stands for both Charles II in exile and the defeated Irish lords.

The story was printed in *Mercurius Politicus*, a pamphlet founded by Marchamont Needham in June 1650. In 1649, Parliament had had Needham arrested for the royalist *Mercurius Pragmaticus*, a pamphlet he had been editing since 1647, and ordered John Milton to examine Needham on his political views. Less than a year after his brush with the law, Needham reemerged as the editor of *Mercurius Politicus, the Common-Wealth of England Stated . . . . With a Discourse of Excellencie of a Free-State, above a Kingly-Government*. Needham's editorial style has been described as slangy. For example, in Needham's first sentence in *Mercurius Politicus* 15, he refers to the Scots Presbyterians as "our gown'd Granado's." Needham clearly had it in for the Scots, whose independence he and his pamphlet's republican English audience saw as one of the greatest obstacles to the Commonwealth.

The Story of Alexander Agnew; or Jock of Broad Scotland[1]

Alexander Agnew, commonly called Jock of broad Scotland, being accused; forasmuch as by the Divine Law of Almighty God, and Acts of Parliament of this nation, the committers of the horrid crime of blasphemy are punished by death; nevertheless, in plain contempt of the said Laws and Acts of Parliament, the said Alexander Agnew uttered heinous and grievous blasphemies against the Omnipotent and Almighty God; and second and third persons of the Trinity, as the same is set down in diverse articles in manner following; to wit,

First, the said Alexander being desired to go to church answered, "Hang God, God was hanged long since." What had he to do with God? He had nothing to do with God. Secondly, he answered, he was nothing in God's common,[2] God gave him nothing, and he was no more obliged to God than to the Devil, and God was very greedy. Thirdly, when he was desired to seek anything in God's name, he said he would never seek anything for God's sake, and that it was neither God nor the Devil that gave the fruits of the ground, the wives of the country gave him his meat. Fourthly, being asked, wherein he believed, answered, he believed in white meal, water, and salt. Fifthly, being asked how many persons were in the Godhead, answered there was only one person in the Godhead who made all, but for Christ he was not God, because he was made, and came into the world after it was made, and died as other men, being nothing but a mere man.

Sixthly, he declared that he knew not whether God or the Devil had the greater power, but he thought the Devil had the greatest, "And when I die," said he, "let God and the Devil strive for my soul, and let him that is strongest take it." Seventhly, he denied there was a holy Ghost, or knew there was a Spirit, and denied he was a sinner or needed mercy. Eighthly, he denied he was a sinner and that he scorned to seek God's mercy. Ninthly, he ordinarily mocked all exercise of God's worship, and invocation on his name, in derision saying, "Pray you to your God and I will pray to mine when I think time." And when he was desired by some to give thanks for his meat, he said, "Take a sackful of prayers to the mill and shell them, and grind them and take your breakfast of them." To others he said, "I will give you a twopence, and pray until a bowl of meal and one stone[3] of butter fall down from heaven through the house rigging to you." To others he said when bread and cheese was given him, and was laid on the ground by him, he said, "If I leave this, I will long cry to God before he give it me again." To others he said, "Take a bannock[4] and break it in two, and lay down the one half thereof, and ye will long pray to God before he put the other half to it again."

---

1. From *Mercurius Politicus*, 3 July 1656.
2. Community.
3. Fourteen pounds.

4. In Scotland and the North of England, a large round loaf of bread.

Tenthly, being posed whether or not he knew God or Christ, he answered, he had never had any profession, nor never would; he never had any religion, nor never would: also that there was no God nor Christ, and that he never received anything from God but from nature, which he said ever reigned, and ever would, and that to speak of God and their persons was an idle thing, and that he would never name such names, for he had shaken his cap of these things long since, and he denied that a man has a soul, or that there is a heaven or a hell, or that the Scriptures are the word of God. Concerning Christ he said, that he heard of such a man, but for the second person of the Trinity, he had been the second person of the Trinity, if the ministers had not put him in prison, and that he was no more obliged to God nor the Devil. And these aforesaid blasphemies are not rarely or seldom uttered by him, but frequently and ordinarily in several places where he resorted, to the entangling, deluding, and seducing of the common people: through the committing of which blasphemies he hath contravened the tenor of the said Laws and Acts of Parliament and incurred the pain of death mentioned therein, which ought to be inflicted upon him with all rigor, in manner specified in the indictment.

Which indictment being put to the knowledge of an assize,[5] the said Alexander Agnew called Jock of broad Scotland, was by the said assize, all in one voice, by the mouth of William Carlile, late baily[6] of Dumfrize their chancellor[7] found guilty of the crime of blasphemy mentioned in his indictment. For which the commissioners ordained him upon Wednesday, 21 May 1656, betwixt 2 and 4 hours in the afternoon to be taken to the ordinary place of execution for the burgh of Dumfrize, and there to be hanged on a gibbet while he be dead, and all his movable goods to be escheat.[8]

—✦ END OF PERSPECTIVES: THE CIVIL WAR, OR THE WARS OF THREE KINGDOMS ✦—

John Milton
1608–1674

John Milton Surrounded by Muses.
Seventeenth-century engraving.

While writing *Paradise Lost,* Milton would rise early to begin composing poetry; when his secretary arrived late, the old blind man would complain, "I want to be milked." Prodigious in his memory and ingenuity, austere in his frugality and discipline, Milton devoted his life to learning, politics, and art. He put his eloquence at the service of the Puritan Revolution, which brought on the beheading of a king and the institution of a republican commonwealth. Milton entered controversies on divorce and freedom of the press. He showed courage in defending the Puritan republic when he could have lost his life for doing so. Radical, scholar, sage— Milton is above all the great epic poet of England.

Milton's life was marked by a passionate devotion to his religious, political, and artistic ideals, a devotion that ran in

---

5. In Scotland, a trial by jury.
6. In Scotland, the chief magistrate of a county who functions as a sheriff.

7. In Scotland, the foreman of a jury.
8. Forfeited to the state.

his family. Milton's father was said to have been disinherited for his Protestantism by his own father, who was Roman Catholic. When the Civil War broke out, Milton sided with Cromwell while his brother fought for the King. The oldest of three children in a prosperous middle-class family, young John read Virgil, Ovid, and Livy; he especially loved "our sage and serious Spenser," whom he called "a better teacher than Aquinas." Milton later wrote that from the age of twelve he "hardly ever gave up reading for bed till midnight." After his first year at Christ's College, Cambridge, the poet was expelled. While in exile, Milton excoriated academia: "How wretchedly suited that place is to the worshippers of Phoebus! It is disgusting to be constantly subjected to the threats of a rough tutor and to other indignities my spirit cannot endure." Returning to Cambridge, he took his BA in 1629 and his MA in 1632. On vacations during these years he wrote two of his most musical lyrics, the erotic *L'Allegro* and the Platonic *Il Penseroso*. After leaving university, Milton lived with his parents in Berkshire, where he wrote *Lycidas*, a haunting elegy for the early death of his Cambridge friend Edward King, and *Comus*, a masque for the prominent noble Egerton family at Ludlow Castle.

After his mother's death in 1638, Milton traveled to Europe. He stayed longest in Italy, where his poems were greatly admired by the Florentine literati, who welcomed him into their academies. He later reflected that it was in Italy that he first sensed his vocation as an epic poet, hoping to "perhaps leave something so written, as they should not willingly let it die." Visiting Rome, Naples, and Venice, Milton collected Monteverdi's music, which he would later sing and play. He also met the famed astronomer Galileo, the censorship of whose works Milton would later protest. Concerned about political turmoil in England, he returned home at the outbreak of the Civil War.

From 1640 to 1660, Milton devoted himself to "the cause of real and substantial liberty," by which he meant religious, domestic, and civil liberties. Defending religious liberty, he decried Anglican hierarchy and ritualism—"the new vomited paganism of sensual idolatry"—in a series of tracts, including *Of Reformation* (1641) and *The Reason of Church Government* (1642).

That same year, Milton married seventeen-year-old Mary Powell, who came from a royalist Oxfordshire family. After only a month, she left Milton alone to his "philosophical" life for a more sociable one at home. Troubled by the unhappiness of his marriage, Milton wrote four treatises on divorce, for which he was publicly condemned. He argued that incompatibility should be grounds for divorce, that both husband and wife should be allowed to remarry, and that to maintain otherwise was contrary to reason and scripture. According to his nephew, whom Milton tutored during this time, he was interested in marrying another woman but by 1645 was reunited with Mary. They had a daughter soon afterward. They were joined for several years by Mary's family, who had lost their estate in the Civil War.

Along with "the true conception of marriage," Milton's concept of domestic liberty included "the sound education of children, and freedom of thought and speech." In *Of Education* (1644), opposing strictly vocational instruction, Milton called for the study of languages, rhetoric, poetry, philosophy, and science, the goal of which was "to perform justly, skillfully and magnanimously all of the offices both private and public of peace and war." In *Areopagitica* (1644), Milton fought against censorship before publication but counseled control of printed texts posing political or religious danger. In the 1640s, Milton steered a course midway between the religious conformity demanded by the once-dissenting Presbyterians and the complete separation of church and state advocated by such radicals as Roger Williams, who ultimately went to America in search of greater toleration.

After Oliver Cromwell defeated the Royalists and the King was tried and executed by order of the "Rump" parliament purged of dissenters, Milton wrote *The Tenure of Kings and Magistrates* (1649) to argue that subjects could justly overthrow a tyrant. This tract won him the job of Latin Secretary to the Council of State, handling all correspondence to foreign governments. After the beheading of Charles I in 1649, *Eikon Basilike*, "the Royal Image" (page 1681) appeared, pieced together from the King's papers by his chaplain John Gauden. To counteract sympathy for the King's cause that this work might elicit, Milton wrote a chapter-by-chapter refutation of it entitled *Eikonoklastes*, or *Image-Breaker* (1649) (page 1684). Milton also defended Cromwell's government in three Latin works that were in some measure self-defenses: *First* and *Second Defense of the English People* (1651, 1654) and *Defense of Himself* (1656).

His eyes weakened by the strain of so much writing, Milton went blind. His wife Mary died, leaving three daughters and one son. The boy died soon after, in May 1652. That same month, Milton wrote a sonnet exhorting the Lord General Cromwell to "Help us to save free conscience from the paw of hireling wolves," a reference to ministers who wanted to exclude dissenters from a unified established church. Sounding the cry for liberty again in *Avenge, O Lord these Slaughtered Saints* (1655), Milton lamented the massacre of Italian Protestants. One of Milton's most beautiful and best-known sonnets, *Methought I Saw My Late Espoused Saint*, is said to be about his second wife, Katherine Woodcock, who, after just two years of marriage, died following the birth of her child in 1558.

Cromwell died the same year, and his son Richard's succession to power began a period of political confusion. Milton continued to write political tracts, now even more radical in arguing for universal education and freedom from allegiance to *any* established church and against the abuse of church positions for money. In *De Doctrina Christiana* (written 1655–1660, published 1823), Milton set forth his individualistic theology; he was convinced that no one should be required to attend church and that everyone should interpret scripture in his own way. Committed to the cause of the republic even after the Restoration of Charles II, Milton published *The Ready and Easy Way to Establish a Free Commonwealth* in 1660. Shortly after its appearance, Milton went into hiding. The House of Commons ordered the burning of *Eikonoklastes* and had Milton arrested. He was held in prison for several months. For a time threatened with heavy fines and even death by hanging, Milton was finally released through the aid of his friend Andrew Marvell.

In the aftermath of the Restoration, Milton lived in obscurity and desolation. On the anniversary of Charles I's execution, Cromwell's body was dug up and hanged. More than a few of Milton's friends were either executed or forced into exile. The republic to which he had devoted his life's work had been defeated. Amid this experience of defeat, he worked on *Paradise Lost*, with its themes of fall, damnation, war in heaven, and future redemption for an erring humanity.

While writing his epic, he was much helped by the companionship and housekeeping of his young and amiable third wife Elizabeth Minshull, whom he married in 1663. Young pupils, secretaries, and his daughters read to him in many languages (some of which they didn't understand). The Miltons lived frugally on the money that he had saved from his salary as Latin Secretary (1649–1659). Milton had begun writing *Paradise Lost* by 1658–1659, but he only completed the first edition for publication in 1667. First conceiving of this work as a drama, he had written a soliloquy for the rebellious Lucifer in 1642, which later appeared near the opening of the epic's fourth book. Milton explained that he had put off writing *Paradise Lost* because it was "a work to be raised . . . by devout prayer to that eternal Spirit who can enrich with all utterance and knowledge."

In the last ten years of his life, Milton also wrote *Paradise Regained* (1671), a short epic about the temptation of Christ, based on the model of the Book of Job. Published in the same year was *Samson Agonistes*, a verse tragedy about the biblical hero, who, betrayed by his lover Delilah, brought down destruction on himself as well as his enemies. In 1673 he published an expanded edition of his *Poems* (1645), to which he added his translations of the Psalms. Finally, in 1674, all twelve books of *Paradise Lost* as we know it were published. That same year, Milton died in a fit of gout and was buried in Saint Giles Cripplegate alongside his father.

Milton combined the traditional erudition of a Renaissance poet with the committed politics of a Puritan radical, both of which contributed to his crowning achievement, *Paradise Lost*. Milton draws on the Bible, Homer, Virgil, and Dante to create his own original sound and story. The vivid sensual imagery of *L'Allegro*, echoing Shakespeare and Spenser, suggests the pastoral idyll of Adam and Eve in Paradise. The intellectual rebelliousness of his prose works inflects the epic's dramatic embodiment of such problems as the origin of evil, sin, and death. Like *Samson Agonistes*, *Paradise Lost* reaches humanity's psychological depths: arrogance, despair, revenge, self-destruction, desire, and self-knowledge. Most of all, *Paradise Lost* dramatizes human wayfaring in the face of the Fall, not unlike Milton's own heroic perseverance in writing his epic after the loss of the world he had helped to create.

> ✺ For additional resources on Milton, including the full text of *Samson Agonistes*, go to *The Longman Anthology of British Literature* Web site at www.myliteraturekit.com.

L'Allegro[1]

Hence loathèd Melancholy
   Of Cerberus,[2] and blackest midnight born,
In Stygian cave forlorn.
   'Mongst horrid shapes, and shreiks, and sights unholy,
5   Find out some uncouth° cell,   *unknown*
   Where brooding darkness spreads his jealous wings,
   And the night-raven[3] sings;
   There under ebon shades, and low-brow'd rocks,
   As ragged as thy Locks,
10   In dark Cimmerian[4] desert ever dwell.
But come thou goddess fair and free,
In Heaven yclept° Euphrosyne,   *called*
And by men, heart-easing Mirth,
Whom lovely Venus at a birth
15   With two sister Graces more
To ivy-crownèd Bacchus bore;[5]
Or whether (as some sager sing)
The frolic wind that breathes the spring,
Zephyr with Aurora playing,
20   As he met her once a-Maying,[6]
There on beds of violets blue,
And fresh-blown roses washed in dew,
Filled her with thee a daughter fair,
So buxom,° blithe, and debonair.   *yielding*
25   Haste thee nymph, and bring with thee
Jest and youthful Jollity,
Quips and cranks,° and wanton wiles,   *jests*
Nods, and becks, and wreathèd smiles,
Such as hang on Hebe's[7] cheek,
30   And love to live in dimple sleek;

---

1. The happy person. This and the companion poem *Il Penseroso* (the pensive one) were composed around 1631; they were first published in 1645.
2. For the underworld cave of the three-headed dog Cerberus, see Virgil, *Aeneid* 6.418. Milton makes Cerberus and Night the parents of Melancholy, which is the subject of *Il Penseroso*.
3. Ominous bird.

4. The Cimmerians lived at the extreme limit of the known world (see *Odyssey* 11.13–22).
5. The Graces: Euphrosyne (Mirth), Aglaia (Brightness), and Thalia (Bloom). Servius's commentary to the *Aeneid* makes Venus and Bacchus their parents.
6. Milton invented this parentage of the Graces by Aurora, the dawn, and Zephyr, the west wind.
7. Goddess of youth and daughter of Zeus and Hera.

Sport that wrinkled Care derides,
And Laughter holding both his sides.
Come, and trip it as you go
On the light fantastic toe,
35 And in thy right hand lead with thee,
The mountain nymph, sweet Liberty;
And if I give thee honor due,
Mirth, admit me of thy crew
To live with her, and live with thee,
40 In unreprovèd pleasures free;
To hear the lark begin his flight,
And singing startle the dull night,
From his watch-tower in the skies,
Till the dappled dawn doth rise;
45 Then to come in spite of sorrow,
And at my window bid good morrow,
Through the sweetbriar, or the vine,
Or the twisted eglantine.°   *honey-suckle*
While the cock with lively din,
50 Scatters the rear of darkness thin,
And to the stack, or the barn door,
Stoutly struts his dames before,
Oft listening how the hounds and horn
Cheerly rouse the slumbring morn,
55 From the side of some hoar° hill,   *gray with mist*
Through the high wood echoing shrill.
Sometime walking not unseen
By hedge-row elms, on hillocks green,
Right against the eastern gate,
60 Where the great sun begins his state,°   *progress*
Robed in flames, and amber light,
The clouds in thousand liveries dight,°   *dressed*
While the plowman near at hand,
Whistles ore the furrowed land,
65 And the milkmaid singeth blithe,
And the mower whets his scythe,
And every shepherd tells his tale
Under the hawthorn in the dale.
Straight mine eye hath caught new pleasures
70 Whilst the landscape round it measures,
Russet lawns, and fallows° gray,   *plowed lands*
Where the nibling flocks do stray,
Mountains on whose barren breast
The laboring clouds do often rest;
75 Meadows trim with daisies pied,°   *variegated*
Shallow brooks, and rivers wide.
Towers and battlements it sees
Bosomed high in tufted trees,
Where perhaps some beauty lies,

80 The cynosure[8] of neighboring eyes.
Hard by, a cottage chimney smokes
From betwixt two agèd oaks,
Where Corydon and Thyrsis met,
Are at their savory dinner set
85 Of herbs, and other country messes,
Which the neat-handed Phyllis dresses;
And then in haste her bower she leaves,
With Thestylis[9] to bind the sheaves;
Or if the earlier season lead
90 To the tanned haycock° in the mead,   *heaps of hay*
Sometimes with secure delight
The upland hamlets will invite,
When the merry bells ring round,
And the jocond rebecks° sound   *fiddles*
95 To many a youth, and many a maid,
Dancing in the checkered shade;
And young and old come forth to play
On a sunshine holiday,
Till the livelong daylight fail,
100 Then to the spicy nut-brown ale,
With stories told of many a feat,
How fairy Mab[1] the junkets° eat,   *cream cheeses*
She was pinched, and pulled she said,
And by the friar's lantern led
105 Tells how the drudging goblin sweat,
To earn his cream-bowl duly set,
When in one night, ere glimpse of morn,
His shadowy flail hath threshed the corn
That ten day-laborers could not end;
110 Then lies him down the lubber fiend.[2]
And stretched out all the chimney's length,
Basks at the fire his hairy strength;
And crop-full out of doors he flings,
Ere the first cock his matin rings.
115 Thus done the tales, to bed they creep,
By whispering winds soon lulled asleep.
Towered cities please us then,
And the busy hum of men,
Where throngs of knights and barons bold,
120 In weeds° of peace high triumphs° hold,   *clothes / tournaments*
With store of ladies, whose bright eyes
Rain influence,[3] and judge the prize,
Of wit, or arms, while both contend

8. The North Star, here meaning, the center of attention.
9. The shepherds' names are common in Renaissance pastoral.
1. Queen of the fairies, and the topic of Mercutio's famous speech (*Romeo and Juliet* 1.4.54–95).

2. Slaving demon, like Robin Goodfellow called "lob of spirits" in *Midsummer Night's Dream* 2.1.16.
3. In astrology, the process by which an etherial fluid emanating from the stars ruled human fate.

To win her grace, whom all commend.
125   There let Hymen[4] oft appear
In saffron robe, with taper clear,
And pomp, and feast, and revelry,
With mask, and antique pageantry;
Such sights as youthful poets dream
130   On summer eves by haunted stream.
Then to the well-trod stage anon,
If Jonson's learned sock[5] be on,
Or sweetest Shakespeare fancy's child,
Warble his native wood-notes wild,
135   And ever against eating cares
Lap me in soft Lydian airs,[6]
Married to immortal verse
Such as the meeting soul may pierce
In notes, with many a winding bout
140   Of linkèd sweetness long drawn out,
With wanton heed and giddy cunning,
The melting voice through mazes running,
Untwisting all the chains that tie
The hidden soul of harmony.
145   That Orpheus' self may heave his head
From golden slumber on a bed
Of heaped Elysian flowers, and hear
Such strains as would have won the ear
Of Pluto, to have quite set free
150   His half regained Eurydice.[7]
These delights, if thou canst give,
Mirth with thee, I mean to live.[8]

Il Penseroso[1]

Hence vain deluding joys,
      The brood of Folly without father bred,
How little you bestead,°   help
      Or fill the fixèd mind with all your toys;
5   Dwell in some idle brain,
      And fancies fond with gaudy shapes possess,
As thick and numberless
      As the gay motes that people the sunbeams,
Or likest hovering dreams,
10   The fickle pensioners° of Morpheus'[2] train.   guards

---

4. Roman wedding god.
5. Low-heeled slipper of the comic actor in ancient Greece and Rome.
6. Plato considered the Lydian mode to be morally corrupting and loose; others found it a source of relaxed enjoyment.
7. When Orpheus attempted to rescue his wife Eurydice from Hades, he lost her by violating the command that he not look back to see if she were behind him.
8. These lines recall the final couplet of Marlowe's "The Passionate Shepherd to His Love": "of these delights thy mind may move; / Then love with me, and be my love."
1. The pensive one.
2. God of dreams and son of Sleep.

But hail thou Goddess, sage and holy,
Hail divinest Melancholy,
Whose saintly visage is too bright
To hit° the sense of human sight,   *fit*
15 And therefore to our weaker view,
O'er laid with black staid Wisdom's hue;[3]
Black, but such as in esteem,
Prince Memnon's sister[4] might beseem,
Or that starred Ethiope Queen[5] that strove
20 To set her beauties praise above
The sea nymphs, and their powers offended.
Yet thou art higher far descended,
Thee bright-haired Vesta[6] long of yore,
To solitary Saturn bore;
25 His daughter she (in Saturn's reign
Such mixture was not held a stain)[7]
Oft in glimmering bowers, and glades
He met her, and in secret shades
Of woody Ida's inmost grove,
30 While yet there was no fear of Jove.
Come pensive nun, devout and pure,
Sober, steadfast, and demure,
All in a robe of darkest grain,
Flowing with majestic train,
35 And sable° stole of cypress lawn,°   *dark / fine linen*
Over thy decent shoulders drawn.
Come, but keep thy wonted state,
With even step, and musing gait,
And looks commercing with the skies,
40 Thy rapt soul sitting in thine eyes:
There held in holy passion still,
Forget thyself to marble,[8] till
With a sad leaden downward cast,
Thou fix them on the earth as fast.
45 And join with thee calm Peace, and Quiet,
Spare Fast, that oft with gods doth diet,
And hears the Muses in a ring,
Ay round about Jove's altar sing.
And add to these retired leisure;
50 That in trim gardens takes his pleasure;
But first, and chiefest, with thee bring
Him that yon soars on golden wing,

---

3. Melancholy was governed by the black bile in the body and manifested itself in a black face.
4. The Ethiopian Prince Memnon (*Odyssey* 11.521) had a sister named Himera (Greek, "light of day").
5. Cassiopea was turned into a constellation because she boasted that she was more beautiful than the Nereids.

6. Milton makes Vesta a mother; by tradition, she was a virgin, daughter of Saturn, and goddess of the hearth.
7. The Golden Age was a time of plenty and sexual freedom.
8. Turning to stone through grief comes from the story of Niobe.

Guiding the fiery-wheelèd throne,[9]
The cherub Contemplation;[1]
55   And the mute Silence hist° along,   *a call*
'Less Philomel[2] will deign a song,
In her sweetest, saddest plight,
Smoothing the rugged brow of night,
While Cynthia[3] checks her dragon yoke,
60   Gently o'er th'accustomed oak;
Sweet bird that shunn'st the noise of folly,
Most musical, most melancholy!
Thee chantress oft the woods among,
I woo to hear thy evensong;
65   And missing thee, I walk unseen
On the dry smooth-shaven green,
To behold the wandring moon,
Riding near her highest noon,
Like one that had been led astray
70   Through the heaven's wide pathless way;
And oft, as if her head she bowed,
Stooping through a fleecy cloud.
Oft on a plat° of rising ground,   *plot*
I hear the far-off curfew sound,
75   Over some wide-watered shore,
Swinging slow with sullen roar;
Or if the air will not permit,
Some still removèd place will fit,
Where glowing embers through the room
80   Teach light to counterfeit a gloom,
Far from all resort of mirth,
Save the cricket on the hearth,
Or the bellman's drowsy charm,[4]
To bless the doors from nightly harm;
85   Or let my lamp at midnight hour,
Be seen in some high lonely tower,
Where I may oft out-watch the Bear,[5]
With thrice great Hermes,[6] or unsphere[7]
The spirit of Plato to unfold
90   What worlds, or what vast regions hold
The immortal mind that hath forsook
Her mansion in this fleshly nook;
And of those demons that are found

9. See Ezekiel 1.4–6.
1. The angel Cherubim contemplate God.
2. The nightingale (Greek).
3. The moon goddess, another name for Hecate; for her dragons, see Ovid, *Metamorphoses* 7.218–19.
4. The night-watchman, or bellman, cries out the hours in a chant, or charm (from *carmen*, Latin for song).

5. The constellation of the Great Bear, which never sets, symbolizes perfection.
6. Hermes Trismegistus was believed to be the author of the Hermetica, texts of esoteric neoplatonism and magic.
7. To remove from the eternal sphere and make reappear on earth.

95
In fire, air, flood, or under ground,
Whose power hath a true consent
With planet, or with element.
Sometime let gorgeous Tragedy
In scepter'd pall° come sweeping by,   *robe*
Presenting Thebes, or Pelops line,

100
Or the tale of Troy divine.[8]
Or what (though rare) of later age
Ennobled hath the buskined stage.[9]
But, O sad virgin, that thy power
Might raise Musaeus[1] from his bower,

105
Or bid the soul of Orpheus[2] sing
Such notes as warbled to the string,
Drew iron tears down Pluto's cheek,
And made Hell grant what Love did seek.
Or call up him[3] that left half told

110
The story of Cambuscan bold,
Of Camball, and of Algarsife,
And who had Canace to wife,
That owned the virtuous° ring and glass,   *magical*
And of the wondrous horse of brass,

115
On which the Tartar king did ride;
And if aught else, great bards beside,[4]
In sage and solemn tunes have sung,
Of tourneys and of trophies hung;
Of forests, and enchantments drear,

120
Where more is meant then meets the ear.
Thus, Night, oft see me in thy pale career,
Till civil-suited Morn appear,
Not tricked and frounced[5] as she was wont,
With the Attic boy[6] to hunt,

125
But kerchiefed in a comely cloud,
While rocking winds are piping loud,
Or ushered with a shower still,°   *quiet*
When the gust hath blown his fill,
Ending on the rustling leaves,

130
With minute drops from off the eaves.
And when the sun begins to fling
His flaring beams, me, Goddess, bring
To archèd walks of twilight groves,

---

8. Thebes was the birthplace of Oedipus, tragic hero of Sophocles' *Oedipus Rex*. Pelops' descendants Agamemnon and Orestes are the subject of Aeschylus' tragedy *Oresteia*. Troy was the city destroyed by the Trojan War, the tragic consequences of which are the subject of Euripides' *The Trojan Women*.
9. The high boots of tragic actors. Compare *L'Allegro* line 132.

1. Prophet and poet, who studied with the mythic bard Orpheus.
2. See *L'Allegro* 145–50.
3. Chaucer; the "story" is the unfinished *Squire's Tale*.
4. Lines 116–20 refer to Spenser's allegorical *Faerie Queene*.
5. Richly attired and wearing ringlets.
6. Cephalus, beloved of Aurora, who met him while he was hunting. (See Ovid, *Metamorphoses* 7.700–13.)

And shadows brown that Sylvan[7] loves
135   Of pine, or monumental oak,
Where the rude ax with heavèd stroke.
Was never heard the nymphs to daunt,
Or fright them from their hallowed haunt.
There in close covert by some brook,
140   Where no prophaner eye may look,
Hide me from day's garish eye,
While the bee with honeyed thigh,
That at her flowery work doth sing,
And the waters murmuring
145   With such consort° as they keep,   *musical harmony*
Entice the dewy-feathered sleep;
And let some strange mysterious dream
Wave at his wings in airy stream
Of lively portraiture displayed,
150   Softly on my eye-lids laid.
And as I wake, sweet music breathe
Above, about, or underneath,
Sent by some spirit to mortals good,
Or th'unseen genius° of the wood.   *presiding local god*
155   But let my due feet never fail
To walk the studious cloisters° pale,   *enclosure*
And love the high embowèd° roof,   *arched*
With antic pillars massy proof,°   *impenetrability*
And storied[8] windows richly dight,°   *decorated*
160   Casting a dim religious light.
There let the pealing organ blow
To the full voiced choir below,
In service high, and anthems clear,
As may with sweetness, through mine ear,
165   Dissolve me into ecstasies,
And bring all heaven before mine eyes.
And may at last my weary age
Find out the peaceful hermitage,
The hairy gown and mossy cell,
170   Where I may sit and rightly spell°   *find out about*
Of every star that heaven doth shew,
And every herb that sips the dew,
Till old experience do attain
To something like prophetic strain.
175   These pleasures Melancholy give,
And I with thee will choose to live.[9]

7. Roman god of the forest.   9. See *L'Allegro* 151–52.
8. With stories from the Bible.

Lycidas

In this Monody[1] the Author bewails a learned Friend,[2] unfortunately drowned in his passage from Chester on the Irish Seas, 1637. And by occasion foretells the ruin of our corrupted Clergy then in their height.

Yet once more, O ye laurels, and once more
Ye myrtles brown, with ivy[3] never sear,°   *withered*
I come to pluck your berries harsh and crude,°   *unripe*
And with forced fingers rude,
5   Shatter your leaves before the mellowing year.
Bitter constraint, and sad occasion dear,
Compels me to disturb your season due:
For Lycidas is dead, dead ere his prime,[4]
Young Lycidas, and hath not left his peer:
10   Who would not sing for Lycidas? he knew
Himself to sing, and build the lofty rhyme.
He must not float upon his watery bier
Unwept, and welter° to the parching wind,   *writhe*
Without the meed° of some melodious tear.°   *recompense / elegy*
15   Begin then, sisters of the sacred well,[5]
That from beneath the seat of Jove doth spring,
Begin, and somewhat loudly sweep the string.
Hence with denial vain, and coy excuse,
So may some gentle Muse
20   With lucky words favor my destined urn,
And as he passes turn,
And bid fair peace be to my sable° shroud.   *black*
For we were nursed upon the self-same hill,
Fed the same flock; by fountain, shade, and rill.
25   Together both, ere the high lawns appeared
Under the opening eyelids of the morn,
We drove a field, and both together heard
What time the grayfly[6] winds her sultry horn,
Battening° our flocks with the fresh dews of night,   *fattening*
30   Oft till the star that rose, at evening, bright,
Toward heaven's descent had sloped his westering wheel.
Meanwhile the rural ditties were not mute,
Tempered to th' oaten flute,
Rough satyrs danced, and fauns with cloven heel,
35   From the glad sound would not be absent long,
And old Damaetas[7] lov'd to hear our song.

1. A mournful song sung by one voice. *Lycidas* is a pastoral elegy, a lament for the dead through language evoking nature and the rural life of shepherds. The first *Idyll* of Theocritus and Virgil's fifth *Eclogue* are classical precedents for *Lycidas*. Shelley's *Adonais* and Arnold's *Thyrsis* are later examples of this form.
2. Edward King, who attended Cambridge when Milton did, drowned 10 August 1637. He had planned to enter the clergy and had written some Latin poems.
3. Laurels . . . myrtles . . . ivy: the leaves used to crown respectively poets, lovers, and scholars.
4. King ("Lycidas") was 25 when he died.
5. Sisters: the nine muses; well: Aganippe, on Mount Helicon, where there was an altar to Jove.
6. Name used to designate various kinds of insects.
7. "Damaetas" is etymologically derived from the Greek verb meaning "to tame;" thus a tutor is meant.

But O the heavy change, now thou art gone,
Now thou art gone, and never must return!
Thee shepherd, thee the woods, and desert caves,
40   With wild thyme and the gadding° vine o'ergrown,   *wandering*
And all their echoes mourn.
The willows, and the hazle copses green,
Shall now no more be seen,
Fanning their joyous leaves to thy soft lays.
45   As killing as the canker° to the rose,   *cankerworm*
Or taint-worm[8] to the weanling herds that graze,
Or frost to flowers, that their gay wardrop wear,
When first the white thorn blows;
Such, Lycidas, thy loss to shepherd's ear.
50   Where were ye nymphs when the remorseless deep
Closed o'er the head of your loved Lycidas?
For neither were ye playing on the steep
Where your old Bards, the famous Druids,° lie,   *pagan Celtic priests*
Nor on the shaggy top of Mona[9] high,
55   Nor yet where Deva spreads her wizard stream:
Ay me, I fondly dream!
Had ye been there—for what could that have done?
What could the Muse[1] herself that Orpheus bore,
The Muse herself for her inchanting son
60   Whom universal nature did lament,
When by the rout that made the hideous roar
His gory visage down the stream was sent,
Down the swift Hebrus to the Lesbian shore.[2]
     Alas! What boots° it with incessant care   *avails*
65   To tend the homely slighted shepherd's trade,
And strictly meditate the thankless Muse,
Were it not better done as others use,
To sport with Amaryllis in the shade,
Or with the tangles of Neaera's hair?[3]
70   Fame is the spur that the clear spirit doth raise
(That last infirmity of noble mind)
To scorn delights, and live laborious days;
But the fair guerdon° when we hope to find,   *reward*
And think to burst out into sudden blaze,
75   Comes the blind Fury[4] with th'abhorred shears,
And slits the thin spun life. "But not the praise,"
Phoebus replied, and touched my trembling ears;[5]
"Fame is no plant that grows on mortal soil,

8. An intestinal worm that can kill newly weaned calves.
9. The island of Anglesey; Deva: the river Dee, viewed as magical and prophetic by the inhabitants.
1. Calliope, Orpheus' mother.
2. Ovid, *Metamorphoses*, 11.1–55, relates how Orpheus was torn to pieces by the Thracian women and how his severed head floated down the Hebrus and was carried

across to the island of Lesbos.
3. Amaryllis symbolizes erotic poetry (Virgil, *Eclogues* 2.14–15); Neaera: see *Eclogues* 3.3.
4. Atropos, one of the Fates, who cut the thread of life spun by her sisters.
5. Echoing Virgil, *Eclogues* 6.3–4: "the Cynthian plucked my ear and warned me."

Nor in the glistering foil[6]
80 Set off to the world, nor in broad rumor lies,
But lives and spreds aloft by those pure eyes,
And perfet witness of all-judging Jove;
As he pronounces lastly on each deed,
Of so much fame in heaven expect thy meed."
85   O Fountain Arethuse, and thou honored flood,
Smooth-sliding Mincius, crowned with vocal reeds,
That strain I heard was of a higher mood.[7]
But now my oat proceeds,
And listens to the herald of the sea
90 That came in Neptune's plea.[8]
He asked the waves, and asked the felon° winds,   *savage*
"What hard mishap hath doomed this gentle swain?"
And questioned every gust of rugged wings
That blows from off each beakèd promontory;
95 They knew not of his story,
And sage Hippotades[9] their answer brings,
That not a blast was from his dungeon strayed,
The air was calm, and on the level brine,
Sleek Panope[1] with all her sisters played.
100 It was that fatal and perfidious bark,
Built in th' eclipse,° and rigged with curses dark,   *period of evil omen*
That sunk so low that sacred head of thine.
        Next Camus,[2] reverend sire, went footing slow,
His mantle hairy, and his bonnet sedge,[3]
105 Inwrought with figures dim, and on the edge
Like to that sanguine flower inscribed with woe.[4]
"Ah! who hath reft (quoth he) my dearest pledge?"°   *child*
Last came, and last did go,
The Pilot of the Galilean lake,[5]
110 Two massy keys he bore of metals twain,
(The golden opes, the iron shuts amain°).   *vehemently*
He shook his mitered[6] locks, and stern bespake,
"How well could I have spared for thee, young swain,
Enow° of such as for their bellies' sake,   *enough*
115 Creep and intrude, and climb into the fold?[7]
Of other care they little reckoning make,
Than how to scramble at the shearer's feast,

---

6. A reflecting leaf of gold or silver placed under a precious stone.
7. The "higher mood" is the lofty tone of Phoebus' speech. The invocation to the river Arethuse (in Sicily) and the Mincius (Virgil's native river) marks a return to pastoral.
8. The herald Triton came to defend Neptune from blame for King's death.
9. God of winds, son of Hippotes.
1. One of the 50 Nereids (sea nymphs), mentioned by Virgil, *Aeneid* 5.240.
2. The River Cam, representing Cambridge University.

3. "Hairy" refers to the fur of the academic gown; sedge: a rushlike plant growing near water.
4. The hyacinth; see Ovid, *Metamorphoses* 10.214–16: "the flower bore the marks AI AI, letters of lamentation."
5. St. Peter bearing the keys of heaven given to him by Christ (Matthew 16.19).
6. Wearing a bishop's headdress.
7. See John 10.1: "He that entereth not by the door into the sheepfold, but climbeth up some other way, the same is a thief and a robber."

And shove away the worthy bidden guest.
Blind mouths![8] that scarce themselves know how to hold
120   A sheep-hook, or have learned aught else the least
That to the faithfull herdman's art belongs!
What recks it them?[9] What need they? They are sped;°   *satisfied*
And when they list,° their lean and flashy° songs   *please / insipid*
Grate on their scrannel° pipes of wretched straw,   *feeble*
125   The hungry sheep look up, and are not fed,
But swoln with wind, and the rank mist they draw,
Rot inwardly, and foul contagion spread.
Besides what the grim woolf[1] with privy° paw   *secret, hidden*
Daily devours apace, and nothing said,
130   But that two-handed engine at the door,
Stands ready to smite once, and smite no more."[2]
    Return Alpheus,[3] the dread voice is past,
That shrunk thy streams; return Sicilian muse,
And call the vales, and bid them hither cast
135   Their bells, and flowerets of a thousand hues.
Ye valleys low where the mild whispers use,°   *often go*
Of shades and wanton winds, and gushing brooks,
On whose fresh lap the swart star[4] sparely looks,
Throw hither all your quaint enameled eyes,
140   That on the green turf suck the honeyed showers,
And purple all the ground with vernal flowers.
Bring the rathe° primrose that forsaken dies,   *early*
The tufted crow-toe,° and pale jessamine,°   *hyacinth / jasmine*
The white pink, and the pansie freaked° with jet,   *adorned*
145   The glowing violet.
The musk-rose, and the well attired woodbine,
With cowslips wan° that hang the pensive head,   *pale*
And every flower that sad embroidery wears:
Bid amaranthus[5] all his beauty shed,
150   And daffadillies fill their cups with tears,
To strew the laureate hearse where Lycid lies.
For so to interpose a little ease,
Let our frail thoughts dally with false surmise.[6]
Ay me! whilst thee the shores, and sounding seas
155   Wash far away, where'er thy bones are hurled,
Whether beyond the stormy Hebrides[7]
Where thou perhaps under the whelming tide
Visit'st the bottom of the monstrous world;
Or whether thou to our moist° vows denied,   *tearful*
160   Sleep'st by the fable of Bellerus[8] old,

8. Milton's charge against the greed of the clergy.
9. What business is it of theirs?
1. The Roman Catholic Church.
2. Indicates that the corrupted clergy will be punished; see 1 Samuel 26.8.
3. The Arcadian hunter, who pursued Arethusa, the nymph he loved, under the sea to Sicily.
4. The Dog-star, Sirius. Its rising brings on the dog-days of heat.
5. The eternal flower (see *Paradise Lost*, 3.353–57).
6. The surmise is false since King's body drowned and will have no hearse.
7. Islands off the northwest coast of Scotland.
8. A giant of Bellerium, the Latin name for Land's End.

Where the great vision of the guarded mount
Looks toward Namancos and Bayona's hold;[9]
Look homeward angel° now, and melt with ruth.°   Michael / pity
And, O ye dolphins, waft the haples youth.[1]
165   Weep no more, woeful shepherds weep no more,
For Lycidas your sorrow is not dead,
Sunk though he be beneath the wat'ry floor,
So sinks the day-star° in the ocean bed,   the sun
And yet anon repairs his drooping head,
170   And tricks° his beams, and with new spangled ore,°   arrays / gold
Flames in the forehead of the morning sky:
So Lycidas sunk low, but mounted high,
Through the dear might of him[2] that walked the waves
Where other groves, and other streams along,
175   With nectar pure his oozy lock's he laves,[3]
And hears the unexpressive nuptial[4] song,
In the blest kingdoms meek of joy and love.
There entertain him all the saints above,
In solemn troops, and sweet societies
180   That sing, and singing in their glory move,
And wipe the tears for ever from his eyes.[5]
Now Lycidas the shepherds weep no more;
Henceforth thou art the genius° of the shore,   local deity
In thy large recompense, and shalt be good
185   To all that wander in that perilous flood.
        Thus sang the uncouth° swain to th' oaks and rills,   unknown
While the still morn went out with sandals gray,
He touched the tender stops of various quills,[6]
With eager thought warbling his Doric° lay: pastoral
190   And now the sun had stretched out all the hills,[7]
And now was dropped into the western bay;
At last he rose, and twitch'd his mantle blue:[8]
Tomorrow to fresh woods, and pastures new.

How Soon Hath Time

How soon hath time the subtle thief of youth,
    Stol'n on his wing my three and twentieth year![1]
    My hasting days fly on with full career,°   speed
    But my late spring no bud or blossom shew'th.
5   Perhaps my semblance° might deceive the truth,   appearance

---

9. Namancos: an ancient name for a district in northwestern Spain; Bayona: a fortress town about 50 miles south of Cape Finisterre. The two names represent the threat of Spanish Catholicism, against which St. Michael guards England.
1. The dolphin is a symbol of Christ; waft: convey by water.
2. Christ, who walks on the sea in Matthew 14.25–6.
3. The brooks in Eden run with nectar, *Paradise Lost* 4.240; oozy: slimy from contact with the sea.
4. Relating to the marriage of the Lamb, or Christ, to the Church (Revelation 19.7).

5. See Revelation 7.17: "God shall wipe away all tears from their eyes"; see also Revelation 21.4.
6. Stops are the finger-holes in the pipes; quills are the hollow reeds of the shepherd's pipe.
7. The setting sun had shone over the hills and lengthened their shadows.
8. Blue is the traditional symbol of hope.
1. Written when Milton was 23, this sonnet was published in 1645.

That I to manhood am arrived so near,
And inward ripeness doth much less appear,
That some more timely-happy spirits² endu'th.°   gives, endows
Yet be it less or more, or soon or slow,
10   It shall be still° in strictest measure even,°   always / level with
To that same lot, however mean or high,
Toward which Time leads me, and the will of Heaven;
All is, if I have grace to use it so,
As ever in my great task Master's° eye.   God's

On the New Forcers of Conscience Under the Long Parliament¹

Because you have thrown off your prelate Lord,²
And with stiff vows renounced his liturgy³
To seize the widowed whore Plurality⁴
From them whose sin ye envied, not abhored,
5   Dare ye for this adjure° the civil sword   entreat
To force our consciences that Christ set free,⁵
And ride us with a classic hierarchy⁶
Taught ye by meer A. S. and Rutherford?⁷
Men whose life, learning, faith and pure intent
10   Would have been held in high esteem with Paul
Must now be named and printed heretics
By shallow Edwards⁸ and Scotch what d'ye call:
But we do hope to find out all your tricks,
Your plots and packing worse then those of Trent,⁹
15   That so the Parliament
May with their wholsome and preventive shears
Clip your phylacteries,¹ though balk° your ears,²   stop short of
And succor our just fears,
When they shall read this clearly in your charge:
20   *New presbyter* is but *old priest* writ large.³

2. Those individuals of Milton's age who have already achieved success.

1. Written c. 1646, but printed in 1673.

2. Refers to the abolishment of episcopacy in England in September 1646.

3. The House of Commons forbade the use of the *Book of Common Prayer* in August 1645.

4. The practice of holding more than one living identified with episcopacy but subsequently supported by the Presbyterian system.

5. Milton complains of the Westminster Assembly's attempt to impose Presbyterianism by force.

6. Parliament resolved that the English congregations were to be grouped in Presbyteries or "Classes," which could impose rules after the Scottish pattern.

7. A. S.: Dr. Adam Stewart, Scottish Presbyterian controversialist; Rutherford: Samuel Rutherford, author of pamphlets in defense of Presbyterianism.

8. Thomas Edwards, author of *Antapologia*, advocating strict Presbyterianism, and *Gangraena* (1646), which included a denunciation of Milton's views on divorce.

9. Comparing the overwhelming Presbyterian predominance in the Assembly to the anti-protestant Roman Catholic Council of Trent (1545–1563).

1. Small leather boxes containing scriptural texts worn by Jews as a mark of obedience. Christ in Matthew 23.5 uses the phrase "make broad their phylacteries" in the sense "vaunt their own righteousness."

2. William Prynne, who had attacked one of the Bishops in print, actually did have both of his ears cut off. Milton's manuscript of this poem contains the line: "Crop ye as close as marginal P—'s ears."

3. "Priest" is etymologically a contracted form of Latin "presbyter" (an elder). The Presbyterians now appeared as dictatorial as the bishops had been.

To the Lord General Cromwell

Cromwell, our chief of men, who through a cloud[1]
   Not of war only, but detractions rude,
   Guided by faith and matchless fortitude
   To peace and truth thy glorious way hast ploughed,
5 And on the neck of crownèd Fortune[2] proud
   Hast reard° God's trophies and his work pursued,   *raised, erected*
   While Darwen stream[3] with blood of Scotts imbrued,°   *stained*
   And Dunbar field[4] resounds thy praises loud,
   And Worester's laureate wreath;[5] yet much remains
10   To conquer still; peace hath her victories
   No less renownd than war, new foes arise
Threatening to bind our souls with secular chains:
   Help us to save free conscience from the paw
   Of hireling wolves whose gospel is their maw.

On the Late Massacre in Piedmont[1]

Avenge O Lord thy slaughtered saints, whose bones
   Lie scattered on the Alpine mountains cold,[2]
   Even them who kept thy truth so pure of old
   When all our Fathers worshiped stocks and stones,[3]
5 Forget not: in thy book[4] record their groans
   Who were thy sheep and in their ancient fold
   Slain by the bloody Piemontese that rolled
   Mother with infant down the rocks. Their moans
The vales redoubled to the hills, and they
10   To Heaven. Their martyred blood and ashes sow
   O'er all th' Italian fields where still doth sway
The triple tyrant:[5] that from these may grow
   A hundred-fold,[6] who having learnt thy way
   Early may fly the Babylonian[7] woe.

1. In Virgil, Aeneas prevails through the "war-cloud" of battle as he conquers Italy (*Aeneid* 10.809).
2. Refers to Charles I and to his successor, whose army Cromwell defeated at Worcester after he had been crowned king in Scotland on 1 January 1651. This poem was written in 1652 but not published until 1694.
3. Near Preston, where, on 17–19 August 1648, Cromwell routed the invading Scottish army.
4. At Dunbar, on 3 September 1650, after being virtually surrounded, Cromwell routed the Scottish army.
5. At Worcester, on 3 September 1651, Cromwell virtually annihilated Charles II's Royalist Scottish army.
1. The poem protests the persecution of Protestants in northern Italy in 1655.

2. See Luke 18.7: "shall not God avenge his own elect," and Psalms 141.7: "Our bones are scattered at the grave's mouth."
3. Gods of wood and stone.
4. See Revelation 5.1: "I saw in the right hand of him that sat on the throne a book."
5. The Pope with his three-tiered crown.
6. Lines 10–13 combine the parable of the sower (Matthew 13.3–23) with the legend of Cadmus, in which an army of warriors sprouts from the sowing of a dragon's teeth.
7. The Puritans used the corrupt Babylon of Revelation as a symbol for the Roman Catholic Church.

When I Consider How My Light Is Spent[1]

When I consider how my light is spent,
    Ere half my days, in this dark world and wide,
    And that one talent which is death to hide,[2]
    Lodged with me useless, though my soul more bent
5   To serve therewith my Maker, and present
    My true account, lest he returning chide,
    Doth God exact day-labor, light denied,
    I fondly° ask; but Patience to prevent   *foolishly*
That murmur, soon replies, "God doth not need
10 Either man's work or his own gifts,[3] who best
    Bear his mild yoke,[4] they serve him best, his state
Is kingly. Thousands at his bidding speed
    And post o'er land and ocean without rest:
    They also serve who only stand and wait."

Methought I Saw My Late Espoused Saint[1]

Methought I saw my late espousèd saint°   *soul in heaven*
    Brought to me like Alcestis[2] from the grave,
    Whom Jove's great son to her glad husband gave,
    Rescued from death by force though pale and faint.
5   Mine as whom washed from spot of child-bed taint,
    Purification in the old Law[3] did save,
    And such, as yet once more I trust to have
    Full sight of her in Heaven without restraint,
Came vested all in white, pure as her mind:
10 Her face was veiled, yet to my fancied sight,
    Love, sweetness, goodness, in her person shined
So clear, as in no face with more delight,
    But O, as to embrace me she enclined,
    I waked, she fled, and day brought back my night.[4]

AREOPAGITICA   The title *Areopagitica* refers to the Areopagus, the ancient Athenian Council of State. Milton wrote *Areopagitica* to criticize the Parliamentary Ordinance of 14 June 1643 "to prevent and suppress the licence of printing." Although *Areopagitica* was

---

1. Probably written around 1652, as Milton's blindness became complete.
2. In the parable of the talents, Jesus tells of a servant who is given a talent (a large sum of money) to keep for his master. He buries the money; his master condemns him for not having invested it wisely. Matthew 25.14–30.
3. See Job 22.2.
4. See Matthew 11.30: "My yoke is easy."
1. The date of composition is placed at 1658; the poem appears as the last sonnet in the 1673 edition.
2. In Euripides' *Alcestis*, she gives her life for her husband Admetus, but Hercules ("Jove's great son") wrestles with death and brings her back from the grave.

3. According to Leviticus 12.4–8, after bearing a female child, a woman shall be unclean "two weeks, as in her separation: and she shall continue in the blood of her purifying threescore and six days" (i.e., during this period "she shall touch no hallowed thing, nor come into the sanctuary"). Some critics construe this line as evidence that the sonnet is about the death of Milton's second wife Katherine Woodcock, who died three months after childbirth in 1658.
4. In Virgil, Aeneas sees the ghost of his wife Creusa amid the ruins of Troy; when he tries to embrace her, "she withdrew into thin air . . . most like a winged dream" (*Aeneid* 2.791–794).

unlicensed, Milton made the bold move of affixing his name to the title page, which made no mention of the printer. Also on the title page are these lines from Euripides' *Suppliant Women* (438–41):

> There is true Liberty when free born men
> Having to advise the public may speak free,
> Which he who can and will, deserv'd high praise,
> Who neither can nor will, may hold his peace;
> What can be juster in a state than this?

from Areopagitica[1]
A Speech of Mr. John Milton for the Liberty of Unlicensed Printing, to the Parliament of England

* * * Good and evil we know in the field of this world grow up together almost inseparably; and the knowledge of good is so involved and interwoven with the knowledge of evil, and in so many cunning resemblances hardly to be discerned, that those confused seeds which were imposed on Psyche as an incessant labor to cull out and sort asunder, were not more intermixed.[2] It was from out the rind of one apple tasted, that the knowledge of good and evil, as two twins cleaving together, leaped forth into the world. And perhaps this is that doom which Adam fell into of knowing good and evil, that is to say, of knowing good by evil.[3]

As therefore the state of man now is, what wisdom can there be to choose, what continence to forbear without the knowledge of evil? He that can apprehend and consider vice with all her baits and seeming pleasures, and yet abstain, and yet distinguish, and yet prefer that which is truly better, he is the true wayfaring[4] Christian. I cannot praise a fugitive and cloistered virtue, unexercised and unbreathed, that never sallies out and sees her adversary, but slinks out of the race where that immortal garland is to be run for, not without dust and heat. Assuredly we bring not innocence into the world, we bring impurity much rather: that which purifies us is trial, and trial is by what is contrary. That virtue therefore which is but a youngling in the contemplation of evil, and knows not the utmost that vice promises to her followers, and rejects it, is but a blank virtue, not a pure; her whiteness is but an excremental[5] whiteness; which was the reason why our sage and serious poet Spenser, whom I dare be known to think a better teacher than Scotus or Aquinas, describing true temperance under the person of Guyon, brings him in with his palmer through the cave of Mammon and the bower of earthly bliss, that he might see and know, and yet abstain.[6]

1. The Areopagus was the seat of the Council of State, organized as a judicial tribunal by Solon in the sixth century B.C. The Athenian orator Isocrates argues for its renewal in his *Areopagiticus*.
2. Furious over her son Cupid's love for Psyche, Venus ordered Psyche to sort out a huge mass of seeds, but the ants, sympathizing with her plight, sorted them for her. See Apuleius, *Golden Ass* 4–6.
3. See *Paradise Lost* 4.222: "Knowledge of Good bought

dear by knowing ill."
4. The original reads "warfaring," but in several copies this is corrected by hand to "wayfaring."
5. Superficial.
6. Duns Scotus and Thomas Aquinas here represent types of the scholastic theologian. For the cave of Mammon, see *The Faerie Queene* 2.7 (the Palmer is not with Guyon in Mammon's Cave); the "Bower of Bliss," 2.12.

Since therefore, the knowledge and survey of vice is in this world so necessary to the constituting of human virtue, and the scanning of error to the confirmation of truth, how can we more safely and with less danger scout into the regions of sin and falsity than by reading all manner of tractates and hearing all manner of reason? And this is the benefit which may be had of books promiscuously read.

But of the harm that may result hence, three kinds are usually reckoned. First is feared the infection that may spread; but then all human learning and controversy in religious points must remove out of the world, yea the Bible itself; for that ofttimes relates blasphemy not nicely,[7] it describes the carnal sense of wicked men not unelegantly, it brings in holiest men passionately murmuring against providence through all the arguments of Epicurus;[8] in other great disputes it answers dubiously and darkly to the common reader; and ask a Talmudist what ails the modesty of his marginal Keri, that Moses and all the prophets cannot persuade him to pronounce the textual Chetiv.[9] For these causes we all know the Bible itself put by the papist into the first rank of prohibited books. The ancientest fathers must be next removed, as Clement of Alexandria, and that Eusebian book of Evangelic preparation transmitting our ears through a hoard of heathenish obscenities to receive the Gospel. Who finds not that Irenaeus, Epiphanius, Jerome,[1] and others discover more heresies than they well confute, and that oft for heresy which is the truer opinion?[2]

* * *

Impunity and remissness, for certain, are the bane of a commonwealth; but here the great art lies, to discern in what the law is to bid restraint and punishment, and in what things persuasion only is to work. If every action which is good or evil in man at ripe years, were to be under pittance and prescription and compulsion, what were virtue but a name, what praise could be then due to well-doing, what gramercy[3] to be sober, just, or continent?

Many there be that complain of divine providence for suffering Adam to transgress. Foolish tongues! when God gave him reason, he gave him freedom to choose, for reason is but choosing; he had been else a mere artificial Adam, such an Adam as he is in the motions.[4] We ourselves esteem not of that obedience, or love, or gift, which is of force. God therefore left him free, set before him a provoking object, ever almost in his eyes; herein consisted his merit, herein the right of his reward, the praise of his abstinence. Wherefore did he create passions within us, pleasures round about us, but that these rightly tempered are the very ingredients of virtue? They are not skilful considerers of human things who imagine to remove sin by removing the matter of sin. For, besides that it is a huge heap increasing under the very act of diminishing, though some part of it may for a time be withdrawn from some persons, it cannot from all, in such a universal thing as

---

7. Delicately.

8. The Greek philosopher who propounded a morality based on pleasure.

9. Talmudist: a student of the Talmud, the Jewish commentaries on the Bible; Keri: marginal emendations of rabbinical scholars on the Chetiv, the text of the Bible.

1. Early apologists of Christianity: St. Clement of Alexandria (2nd century) and Eusebius, who describes pagan depravity to promote faith in Christianity, as do

St. Irenaeus (2nd century), Epiphanius (4th century), and St. Jerome (early 5th century).

2. Milton goes on to argue that the effect of books depends upon the teacher, who, if really good, needs no books. Milton stresses the role of the reader: A wise person can find something instructive in even the worst books.

3. Thanks.

4. Puppet shows. For this statement about Adam, see *Paradise Lost* 3.103–28.

books are; and when this is done, yet the sin remains entire. Though ye take from a covetous man all his treasure, he has yet one jewel left—ye cannot bereave him of his covetousness. Banish all objects of lust, shut up all youth into the severest discipline that can be exercised in any hermitage, ye cannot make them chaste that came not thither so: such great care and wisdom is required to the right managing of this point.

Suppose we could expel sin by this means; look how much we thus expel of sin, so much we expel of virtue: for the matter of them both is the same; remove that, and ye remove them both alike. This justifies the high providence of God, who, though he command us temperance, justice, continence, yet pours out before us, even to a profuseness, all desirable things, and gives us minds that can wander beyond all limit and satiety. Why should we then affect a rigor contrary to the manner of God and of nature, by abridging or scanting those means which books freely permitted are, both to the trial of virtue and the exercise of truth?[5]

* * *

And lest some should persuade ye, Lords and Commons, that these arguments of learned men's discouragement at this your Order are mere flourishes, and not real, I could recount what I have seen and heard in other countries where this kind of inquisition tyrannizes; when I have sat among their learned men, for that honor I had, and been counted happy to be born in such a place of philosophic freedom as they supposed England was, while themselves did nothing but bemoan the servile condition into which learning amongst them was brought; that this was it which had damped the glory of Italian wits; that nothing had been there written now these many years but flattery and fustian. There it was that I found and visited the famous Galileo, grown old, a prisoner to the Inquisition[6] for thinking in astronomy otherwise than the Franciscan and Dominican licensers thought. And though I knew that England then was groaning loudest under the prelatical yoke, nevertheless I took it as a pledge of future happiness that other nations were so persuaded of her liberty.

Yet was it beyond my hope that those worthies were then breathing in her air, who should be her leaders to such a deliverance as shall never be forgotten by any revolution of time that this world hath to finish. When that was once begun, it was as little in my fear, that what words of complaint I heard among learned men of other parts uttered against the Inquisition, the same I should hear by as learned men at home uttered in time of Parliament against an order of licensing; and that so generally, that when I had disclosed myself a companion of their discontent, I might say, if without envy, that he whom an honest quaestorship had endeared to the Sicilians, was not more by them importuned against Verres,[7] than the favorable opinion which I had among many who honor ye, and are known and respected by ye, loaded me with entreaties and persuasions that I would not despair to lay together that which just reason should bring into my mind toward the removal of an undeserved thraldom upon learning.

---

5. Milton argues that no intelligent person will be willing to take on the job of censorship and that an unintelligent person would be prone to commit serious errors. In addition to giving power to stupid people, censorship would actually encourage people to read banned books and to adhere to the perverse opinions expressed in such books.
6. In 1633 the great Italian astronomer Galileo was tried by the Inquisition at Rome and forced to abjure his ear-

lier assertion that his findings confirmed the Copernican heliocentric theory of the universe. He was under house arrest in Florence when Milton visited there in 1638–1639.
7. Cicero exposed the corruption of Verres' government in 75 B.C.E.

That this is not, therefore, the disburdening of a particular fancy, but the common grievance of all those who had prepared their minds and studies above the vulgar pitch to advance truth in others, and from others to entertain it, thus much may satisfy. And in their name I shall for neither friend nor foe conceal what the general murmur is; that if it come to inquisitioning again and licensing, and that we are so timorous of ourselves and so suspicious of all men as to fear each book and the shaking of every leaf, before we know what the contents are; if some who but of late were little better than silenced from preaching, shall come now to silence us from reading, except what they please, it cannot be guessed what is intended by some but a second tyranny over learning; and will soon put it out of controversy that bishops and presbyters are the same to us both name and thing.

* * *

But I am certain that a state governed by the rules of justice and fortitude, or a church built and founded upon the rock of faith and true knowledge, cannot be so pusillanimous.[8] While things are yet not constituted in religion, that freedom of writing should be restrained by a discipline imitated from the prelates, and learnt by them from the Inquisition, to shut us up all again into the breast of a licenser, must needs give cause of doubt and discouragement to all learned and religious men. Who cannot but discern the fineness of this politic drift, and who are the contrivers: that while bishops were to be baited down, then all presses might be open; it was the people's birthright and privilege in time of parliament, it was the breaking forth of light.

But now, the bishops abrogated and voided out of the church, as if our reformation sought no more but to make room for others into their seats under another name, the episcopal arts begin to bud again; the cruse[9] of truth must run no more oil; liberty of printing must be enthralled again under a prelatical commission of twenty, the privilege of the people nullified; and, which is worse, the freedom of learning must groan again, and to her old fetters: all this the parliament yet sitting. Although their own late arguments and defenses against the prelates might remember them that this obstructing violence meets for the most part with an event utterly opposite to the end which it drives at; instead of suppressing sects and schisms, it raises them and invests them with a reputation: "The punishing of wits enhances their authority," saith the Viscount St. Albans,[1] "and a forbidden writing is thought to be a certain spark of truth that flies up in the faces of them who seek to tread it out."

This Order, therefore, may prove a nursing mother to sects, but I shall easily show how it will be a stepdame to Truth; and first by disenabling us to the maintenance of what is known already.

Well knows he who uses to consider, that our faith and knowledge thrives by exercise, as well as our limbs and complexion. Truth is compared in scripture to a streaming fountain;[2] if her waters flow not in a perpetual progression, they sicken into a muddy pool of conformity and tradition. A man may be a heretic in the truth;

---

8. Mean-spirited, cowardly.
9. Small vessel; see 1 Kings 17.12–16.
1. Sir Francis Bacon, An Advertisement Touching the Con-

troversies of the Church of England.
2. See Psalms 85.11.

and if he believe things only because his pastor says so, or the Assembly so determines, without knowing other reason, though his belief be true, yet the very truth he holds becomes his heresy. There is not any burden that some would gladlier post off to another than the charge and care of their religion. There be, who knows not that there be, of protestants and professors who live and die in as arrant an implicit faith, as any lay papist of Loreto.[3]

A wealthy man addicted to his pleasure and to his profits, finds religion to be a traffic so entangled, and of so many piddling accounts, that of all mysteries[4] he cannot skill to keep a stock going upon that trade. What should he do? Fain he would have the name to be religious, fain he would bear up with his neighbors in that. What does he, therefore, but resolves to give over toiling, and to find himself out some factor to whose care and credit he may commit the whole managing of his religious affairs; some Divine of note and estimation that must be. To him he adheres, resigns the whole warehouse of his religion with all the locks and keys into his custody; and indeed makes the very person of that man his religion; esteems his associating with him a sufficient evidence and commendatory of his own piety. So that a man may say his religion is now no more within himself, but is become a dividual movable,[5] and goes and comes near him, according as that good man frequents the house. He entertains him, gives him gifts, feasts him, lodges him. His religion comes home at night, prays, is liberally supped, and sumptuously laid to sleep, rises, is saluted, and after the malmsey, or some well spiced brewage, and better breakfasted than he[6] whose morning appetite would have gladly fed on green figs between Bethany and Jerusalem, his religion walks abroad at eight, and leaves his kind entertainer in the shop trading all day without his religion.

Another sort there be, who, when they hear that all things shall be ordered, all things regulated and settled, nothing written but what passes through the customhouse of certain publicans[7] that have the tonnaging and the poundaging of all freespoken truth, will straight give themselves up into your hands, make 'em and cut 'em out what religion ye please. There be delights, there be recreations and jolly pastimes that will fetch the day about from sun to sun, and rock the tedious year as in a delightful dream. What need they torture their heads with that which others have taken so strictly and so unalterably into their own purveying? These are the fruits which a dull ease and cessation of our knowledge will bring forth among the people. How goodly, and how to be wished, were such an obedient unanimity as this, what a fine conformity would it starch us all into! Doubtless a staunch and solid piece of framework, as any January could freeze together.[8]

* * *

Truth indeed came once into the world with her divine Master, and was a perfect shape most glorious to look on. But when he ascended, and his apostles after him were laid asleep, then straight arose a wicked race of deceivers, who, as that story goes of the Egyptian Typhon with his conspirators, how they dealt with the

3. Professors: those who profess religion; Loreto: a Catholic shrine supposed to have been transported to Italy from the Holy Land.
4. Trades, crafts.
5. A separate piece of property.

6. For this description of Christ, see Mark 11.12–14.
7. Tax collectors.
8. Milton goes on to argue that censorship will make the clergy lazy and will hinder the Reformation's goal of seeking truth.

good Osiris, took the virgin Truth, hewed her lovely form into a thousand pieces, and scattered them to the four winds.[9] From that time ever since, the sad friends of Truth, such as durst appear, imitating the careful search that Isis made for the mangled body of Osiris, went up and down gathering up limb by limb still as they could find them. We have not yet found them all, Lords and Commons, nor ever shall do, till her Master's second coming. He shall bring together every joint and member, and shall mold them into an immortal feature of loveliness and perfection. Suffer not these licensing prohibitions to stand at every place of opportunity, forbidding and disturbing them that continue seeking, that continue to do our obsequies to the torn body of our martyred saint.

We boast our light; but if we look not wisely on the sun itself, it smites us into darkness. Who can discern those planets that are oft combust, and those stars of brightest magnitude that rise and set with the sun, until the opposite motion of their orbs bring them to such a place in the firmament, where they may be seen evening or morning. The light which we have gained, was given us, not to be ever staring on, but by it to discover onward things more remote from our knowledge. It is not the unfrocking of a priest, the unmitering of a bishop, and the removing him from off the Presbyterian shoulders that will make us a happy nation; no, if other things as great in the church, and in the rule of life both economical and political, be not looked into and reformed, we have looked so long upon the blaze that Zwinglius[1] and Calvin hath beaconed up to us, that we are stark blind.

There be who perpetually complain of schisms and sects, and make it such a calamity that any man dissents from their maxims. It is their own pride and ignorance which causes the disturbing, who neither will hear with meekness, nor can convince, yet all must be suppressed which is not found in their syntagma.[2] They are the troublers, they are the dividers of unity, who neglect and permit not others to unite those dissevered pieces which are yet wanting to the body of Truth. To be still searching what we know not by what we know, still closing up truth to truth as we find it (for all her body is homogeneal[3] and proportional), this is the golden rule in theology as well as in arithmetic, and makes up the best harmony in a church; not the forced and outward union of cold and neutral and inwardly divided minds.

Lords and Commons of England, consider what nation it is whereof ye are, and whereof ye are the governors; a nation not slow and dull, but of a quick, ingenious, and piercing spirit, acute to invent, subtle and sinewy to discourse, not beneath the reach of any point the highest that human capacity can soar to. Therefore the studies of learning in her deepest sciences have been so ancient and so eminent among us that writers of good antiquity and ablest judgment have been persuaded that even the school of Pythagoras and the Persian wisdom took beginning from the old philosophy of this island.[4] And that wise and civil Roman, Julius Agricola, who governed once here for Caesar, preferred the natural wits of Britain before the labored studies of the

---

9. Typhon tore apart and scattered Osiris' body, and his wife Isis and son Horus collected it. The interpretation here is based on Plutarch's allegory in *Isis and Osiris*.
1. Ulrich Zwingli (1484–1531), the Protestant reformer of Zurich.

2. Systematic doctrinal treatise.
3. Homogeneous.
4. For the connection between the Druids and Zoroastrian and Pythagorean philosophy, see Pliny, *Natural History* 30.2.

French.[5] Nor is it for nothing that the grave and frugal Transylvanian[6] sends out yearly from as far as the mountainous borders of Russia and beyond the Hercynian wilderness,[7] not their youth, but their staid men to learn our language and our theologic arts.

Yet that which is above all this, the favor and the love of Heaven, we have great argument to think in a peculiar manner propitious and propending towards us. Why else was this nation chosen before any other, that out of her as out of Sion should be proclaimed and sounded forth the first tidings and trumpet of reformation to all Europe? And had it not been the obstinate perverseness of our prelates against the divine and admirable spirit of Wycliffe[8] to suppress him as a schismatic and innovator, perhaps neither the Bohemian Huss and Jerome,[9] no, nor the name of Luther, or of Calvin, had been ever known; the glory of reforming all our neighbors had been completely ours. But now, as our obdurate clergy have with violence demeaned the matter, we are become hitherto the latest and the backwardest scholars of whom God offered to have made us the teachers.

Now once again by all concurrence of signs, and by the general instinct of holy and devout men, as they daily and solemnly express their thoughts, God is decreeing to begin some new and great period in his Church, even to the reforming of reformation itself. What does he then but reveal himself to his servants, and, as his manner is, first to his Englishmen? I say as his manner is, first to us, though we mark not the method of his counsels and are unworthy. Behold now this vast city, a city of refuge, the mansion house of liberty, encompassed and surrounded with his protection. The shop of war hath not there more anvils and hammers waking, to fashion out the plates and instruments of armed justice in defense of beleaguered Truth, than there be pens and heads there, sitting by their studious lamps, musing, searching, revolving new notions and ideas wherewith to present, as with their homage and their fealty, the approaching reformation; others as fast reading, trying all things, assenting to the force of reason and convincement.

What could a man require more from a nation so pliant and so prone to seek after knowledge? What wants there to such a towardly[1] and pregnant soul but wise and faithful laborers to make a knowing people, a nation of prophets, of sages, and of worthies? We reckon more than five months yet to harvest; there need not be five weeks, had we but eyes to lift up; the fields are white already. Where there is much desire to learn, there of necessity will be much arguing, much writing, many opinions; for opinion in good men is but knowledge in the making. Under these fantastic terrors of sect and schism, we wrong the earnest and zealous thirst after knowledge and understanding which God hath stirred up in this city.

What some lament of, we rather should rejoice at, should rather praise this pious forwardness among men, to reassume the ill-deputed care of their religion into their own hands again. A little generous prudence, a little forbearance of one another, and some grain of charity might win all these diligences to join and unite into one general

---

5. See Tacitus, *Agricola* 21.
6. Seventeenth-century Transylvania was Protestant and independent.
7. South-central Germany.
8. English Protestants viewed John Wyclif (1320?–1384)

as the initiator of the Reformation in England.
9. Jerome of Prague (c. 1365–1416), a disciple of Wycliff, and John Huss of Bohemia (1373–1415).
1. Promising.

and brotherly search after truth; could we but forego this prelatical tradition of crowding free consciences and Christian liberties into canons and precepts of men. I doubt not, if some great and worthy stranger should come among us, wise to discern the mold and temper of a people, and how to govern it, observing the high hopes and aims, the diligent alacrity of our extended thoughts and reasonings in the pursuance of truth and freedom, but that he would cry out as Pyrrhus did, admiring the Roman docility and courage, "If such were my Epirots, I would not despair the greatest design that could be attempted to make a church or kingdom happy."[2]

Yet these are the men cried out against for schismatics and sectaries;[3] as if, while the temple of the Lord was building, some cutting, some squaring the marble, others hewing the cedars, there should be a sort of irrational men who could not consider there must be many schisms and many dissections made in the quarry and in the timber, ere the house of God can be built. And when every stone is laid art-fully together, it cannot be united into a continuity, it can but be contiguous in this world; neither can every piece of the building be of one form; nay rather the perfec-tion consists in this, that out of many moderate varieties and brotherly dissimilitudes that are not vastly disproportional, arises the goodly and the graceful symmetry that commends the whole pile and structure.

Let us, therefore, be more considerate builders, more wise in spiritual architec-ture, when great reformation is expected. For now the time seems come, wherein Moses, the great prophet, may sit in heaven rejoicing to see that memorable and glorious wish of his fulfilled, when not only our seventy elders, but all the Lord's people, are become prophets.

* * *

Methinks I see in my mind a noble and puissant nation rousing herself like a strong man after sleep, and shaking her invincible locks. Methinks I see her as an eagle muing[4] her mighty youth, and kindling her undazzled eyes at the full midday beam; purging and unscaling her long-abused sight at the fountain itself of heavenly radiance; while the whole noise of timorous and flocking birds, with those also that love the twilight, flutter about, amazed at what she means, and in their envious gab-ble would prognosticate a year of sects and schisms.

What should ye do then, should ye suppress all this flowery crop of knowledge and new light sprung up and yet springing daily in this city? Should ye set an oli-garchy of twenty engrossers[5] over it, to bring a famine upon our minds again, when we shall know nothing but what is measured to us by their bushel? Believe it, Lords and Commons, they who counsel ye to such a suppressing, do as good as bid ye sup-press yourselves; and I will soon show how.

* * *

And now the time in special is, by privilege, to write and speak what may help to the further discussing of matters in agitation. The temple of Janus with his two con-troversal faces might now not unsignificantly be set open.[6] And though all the winds of doctrine were let loose to play upon the earth, so Truth be in the field, we do inju-riously by licensing and prohibiting to misdoubt her strength. Let her and Falsehood grapple; who ever knew Truth put to the worse, in a free and open encounter. Her confuting is the best and surest suppressing. He who hears what praying there is for

2. King Pyrrhus of Epirus defeated the Romans at Here-
clea in 280 B.C.E.
3. Dividers of the church.
4. Renewing.

5. Monopolists.
6. The Roman god Janus's head had two faces looking in opposite directions. During times of war, the gates of Janus were open.

light and clearer knowledge to be sent down among us, would think of other matters to be constituted beyond the discipline of Geneva, framed and fabriced already to our hands.[7]

Yet when the new light which we beg for shines in upon us, there be who envy and oppose, if it come not first in at their casements. What a collusion[8] is this, whenas we are exhorted by the wise man to use diligence, to seek for wisdom as for hidden treasures[9] early and late, that another order shall enjoin us to know nothing but by statute. When a man hath been laboring the hardest labor in the deep mines of knowledge, hath furnished out his findings in all their equipage, drawn forth his reasons as it were a battle ranged, scattered and defeated all objections in his way, calls out his adversary into the plain, offers him the advantage of wind and sun, if he please, only that he may try the matter by dint of argument; for his opponents then to skulk, to lay ambushments, to keep a narrow bridge of licensing where the challenger should pass, though it be valor enough in soldiership, is but weakness and cowardice in the wars of Truth.

For who knows not that Truth is strong, next to the Almighty. She needs no policies, nor stratagems, nor licensings to make her victorious—those are the shifts and the defenses that error uses against her power. Give her but room, and do not bind her when she sleeps, for then she speaks not true, as the old Proteus did, who spake oracles only when he was caught and bound,[1] but then rather she turns herself into all shapes except her own, and perhaps tunes her voice according to the time, as Micaiah did before Ahab,[2] until she be adjured into her own likeness.

Yet is it not impossible that she may have more shapes than one. What else is all that rank of things indifferent, wherein Truth may be on this side, or on the other, without being unlike herself? What but a vain shadow else is the abolition of those ordinances, that handwriting nailed to the cross;[3] what great purchase is this Christian liberty which Paul so often boasts of? His doctrine is, that he who eats, or eats not, regards a day, or regards it not, may do either to the Lord.[4] How many other things might be tolerated in peace and left to conscience, had we but charity, and were it not the chief stronghold of our hypocrisy to be ever judging one another. I fear yet this iron yoke of outward conformity hath left a slavish print upon our necks; the ghost of a linen decency[5] yet haunts us. We stumble and are impatient at the least dividing of one visible congregation from another, though it be not in fundamentals; and through our forwardness to suppress, and our backwardness to recover any enthralled piece of truth out of the gripe of custom, we care not to keep truth separated from truth, which is the fiercest rent and disunion of all. We do not see that while we still affect by all means a rigid external formality, we may as soon fall again into a gross conforming stupidity, a stark and dead congealment of "wood, and hay, and stubble"[6] forced and frozen together, which is more to the sudden degenerating of a church than many subdichotomies[7] of petty schisms.

Not that I can think well of every light separation, or that all in a church is to be expected "gold and silver and precious stones."[8] It is not possible for man to sever

---

7. Discipline of Geneva: Calvinism; fabriced: fabricated.
8. Secret agreement for purposes of trickery; ambiguity in words or reasoning.
9. The wise man is Solomon; see Proverbs 8.11 and Matthew 13.44.
1. The story of Proteus is in *Odyssey* 384–93.
2. 1 Kings 22.

3. Colossians 2.14.
4. Romans 14.1–13.
5. A reference to the controversy over ecclesiastical vestments.
6. See 1 Corinthians 3.12.
7. Inconsequential divisions.
8. 1 Corinthians 3.12.

the wheat from the tares, the good fish from the other fry; that must be the angels' ministry at the end of mortal things.[9] Yet if all cannot be of one mind,—as who looks they should be?—this doubtless is more wholesome, more prudent, and more Christian, that many be tolerated, rather than all compelled. I mean not tolerated popery and open superstition, which, as it extirpates all religions and civil supremacies, so itself should be extirpate, provided first that all charitable and compassionate means be used to win and regain the weak and the misled; that also which is impious or evil absolutely, either against faith or manners, no law can possibly permit, that intends not to unlaw itself; but those neighboring differences, or rather indifferences, are what I speak of, whether in some point of doctrine or of discipline, which though they may be many, yet need not interrupt "the unity of spirit," if we could but find among us the "bond of peace."[1]

In the meanwhile, if any one would write and bring his helpful hand to the slow-moving reformation which we labor under, if truth have spoken to him before others, or but seemed at least to speak, who hath so bejesuited us that we should trouble that man with asking license to do so worthy a deed? And not consider this, that if it come to prohibiting, there is not aught more likely to be prohibited than truth itself; whose first appearance to our eyes bleared and dimmed with prejudice and custom, is more unsightly and unplausible than many errors, even as the person is of many a great man slight and contemptible to see to. And what do they tell us vainly of new opinions, when this very opinion of theirs, that none must be heard but whom they like, is the worst and newest opinion of all others; and is the chief cause why sects and schisms do so much abound, and true knowledge is kept at distance from us; besides yet a greater danger which is in it. For when God shakes a kingdom with strong and healthful commotions to a general reforming, it is not untrue that many sectaries and false teachers are then busiest in seducing; but yet more true it is that God then raises to his own work men of rare abilities and more than common industry, not only to look back and revise what hath been taught heretofore, but to gain further and go on some new enlightened steps in the discovery of truth.

PARADISE LOST   *Paradise Lost* is about devastating loss attended by redemption. The reader's knowledge of the Fall creates a sense of tragic inevitability. And Satan, no less than Adam and Eve, appears in all the psychological complexity and verbal grandeur of a tragic hero. Indeed, there is even a manuscript in which Milton outlined the story as a tragedy. In that version, "Lucifer's contriving Adam's ruin" is Act 3. Following epic tradition, Milton places this part of the action at the forefront of his poem, beginning *in medias res*.

So powerful is Milton's opening portrayal of Satan that the Romantic poets thought Satan was the hero of the poem. Focusing on the first two books, the romantic reading sees him as a dynamic rebel. From a Renaissance point of view, Satan is more like an Elizabethan hero-villain, with his many soliloquies and his tortured psychology of brilliance twisted toward evil. Only in Book 9, however, does Milton say, "I now must change these notes to tragic," thereby signaling that he is about to narrate the fall of Adam and Eve. From this point on, the poem follows Adam and Eve's tragic movement from sin to despair to the recognition of sin and the need for repentance. Adam and Eve's learning through suffering and the prophecy of the Son's redemption of sin make this a story of gain as well as loss, on the order of Acschylean tragedy.

Like all epics, *Paradise Lost* is encyclopedic, combining many different genres. To read this poem is to have an education in everything from literary history to astronomy. Milton draws on a

9. Matthew 13.24.   1. Ephesians 4.3.

vast wealth of reading, with the Bible as his main source—not only Genesis, but also Exodus, the Prophets, Revelation, Saint Paul, and especially the Psalms, which he had translated. Milton also makes great use of biblical commentary from rabbinical, patristic, and contemporary sources. Early on, Milton had envisaged a poem about the Arthurian legend, and his choice of the non-martial, seemingly unheroic biblical story of Adam and Eve marks a bold departure from epic tradition. While Spenser's *Faerie Queene* is Milton's most important vernacular model, among epic poets his closest affinity is with Virgil and Dante, both of whom had written of the underworld; Dante especially devoted himself to humanity's free choice of sin. Like Dante, Milton creates his poem as a microcosm of the natural universe. His ideal vision of the world before the Fall is one where day and night are equal and the sun is always in the same sign of the zodiac, an image that embodies in poetic astronomy the world of simplicity and perfection that humans have lost through sin. Milton does not choose between the earth-centered Ptolemaic and the heliocentric Copernican systems but presents both as alternative explanations for the order of the universe.

Although we know nothing about the order in which the parts of the poem were composed, we do know that Milton typically composed at night or in the early morning. Sometimes he lay awake unable to write a line; at others he was seized "with a certain impetus and *oestro*" [frenzy]. He would dictate forty lines from memory and then reduce them to half that number. According to his nephew, the poem was written from 1658 to 1663.

The one extant manuscript of the poem, which contains the first book, reveals that Milton revised for punctuation and spelling. There were two editions in Milton's lifetime, both printed by Samuel Simmons. The first edition, *Paradise Lost: A poem in ten books*, was printed in six different issues in 1667, 1668, and 1669. From the fourth issue of the poem on, such paratexts as "The Printer to Reader," "The Argument" (which stood altogether), and Milton's note on the verse appear. With the second octave edition of 1674, Milton divided Books 7 and 10 into two books each to create twelve books in all. Prefaced by dedicatory Latin verses, one of which was by his old friend Andrew Marvell, this 1674 edition, which appeared in the year of Milton's death, is the basis for the present text.

Paradise Lost[1]
Book 1
The Argument

This first Book proposes, first in brief, the whole Subject, *Man's disobedience, and the loss thereupon of Paradise wherein he was plac't*: Then touches *the prime cause of his fall, the Serpent, or rather* Satan *in the Serpent; who revolting from God, and drawing to his side many Legions of Angels, was by the command of God driven out of Heaven with all his Crew into the great Deep.* Which action past over, the Poem hastes into the midst of things,[2] presenting Satan *with his Angels now fallen into Hell*, describ'd here, *not in the Centre* (for Heaven and Earth may be suppos'd as yet not made, certainly not yet accurst) *but in a place of utter darkness, fitliest call'd Chaos*: Here Satan *with his Angels lying on the burning Lake, thunder-struck and astonisht, after a certain space recovers, as from confusion, calls up him who next in Order and Dignity lay by him; they confer of thir miserable fall*. Satan *awakens all his Legions, who lay till then in the same manner confounded; They rise, thir Numbers, array of Battle, thir chief Leaders nam'd, according to the Idols known afterwards in* Canaan *and the Countries adjoining*. To these Satan directs his Speech,

---

1. Our text is taken from Merritt Y. Hughes, ed., *John Milton Complete Poems and Major Prose*, and the notes are adapted from Alastair Fowler, ed., *Paradise Lost*.

2. Following Horace's rule that the epic should plunge "*in medias res*."

comforts them with hope yet of regaining Heaven but tells them lastly of a new World and new kind of Creature to be created, according to an ancient Prophecy or report in Heaven; for that Angels were long before this visible Creation, was the opinion of many ancient Fathers. To find out the truth of this Prophecy, and what to determine thereon he refers to a full Council. What his Associates thence attempt. Pandemonium the Palace of Satan rises, suddenly built out of the Deep: The infernal Peers there sit in Council.

    Of Man's First Disobedience, and the Fruit
    Of that Forbidden Tree, whose mortal[3] taste
    Brought Death into the World, and all our woe,[4]
    With loss of *Eden,* till one greater Man[5]
5   Restore us, and regain the blissful Seat,
    Sing Heav'nly Muse,[6] that on the secret top
    Of *Oreb,* or of *Sinai,* didst inspire
    That Shepherd, who first taught the chosen Seed,[7]
    In the Beginning how the Heav'ns and Earth
10   Rose out of *Chaos:* Or if *Sion* Hill[8]
    Delight thee more, and *Siloa's* Brook[9] that flow'd
    Fast° by the Oracle of God; I thence   *close*
    Invoke thy aid to my advent'rous Song,
    That with no middle flight intends to soar
15   Above th' *Aonian* Mount,[1] while it pursues
    Things unattempted yet in Prose or Rhyme.[2]
    And chiefly Thou O Spirit, that dost prefer
    Before all Temples th' upright heart and pure,[3]
    Instruct me, for Thou know'st; Thou from the first
20   Wast present, and with mighty wings outspread
    Dove-like satst brooding on the vast Abyss
    And mad'st it pregnant:[4] What in me is dark
    Illumine, what is low raise and support;
    That to the highth of this great Argument°   *theme*
25   I may assert Eternal Providence,
    And justify[5] the ways of God to man.

3. "Death-bringing" (Latin *mortalis*) but also "to mortals."

4. This definition of the first sin follows Calvin's Catechism.

5. Christ, in Pauline theology the second Adam (see Romans 5.19). The people and events referred to in these lines have a typological connection, i.e., the Christian interpretation of the Old Testament as a prefiguration of the New.

6. Rhetorically, lines 1–49 are the *invocatio*, consisting of an address to the Muse, and the *principium* that states the whole scope of the poem's action. The "Heavenly Muse," later addressed as the muse of astronomy Urania (7.1), is here identified with the Holy Spirit of the Bible, which inspires Moses.

7. The "Shepherd" is Moses, who was granted the vision of the burning bush on Mount Oreb (Exodus 3) and received the Law, either on Mount Oreb (Deuteronomy 4.10) or on its lower part, Mount Sinai (Exodus 19.20). Moses, the first Jewish writer, taught "the chosen seed,"

the children of Israel, about the beginning of the world in Genesis.

8. The sanctuary, a place of ceremonial song but also (Isaiah 2.3) of oracular pronouncements.

9. A spring immediately west of Mount Zion and beside Calvary, often used as a symbol of the operation of the Holy Ghost.

1. Helicon, sacred to the Muses.

2. Ironically translating Ariosto's boast in the invocation to *Orlando Furioso.*

3. The Spirit is the voice of God, which inspired the Hebrew prophets.

4. Identifying the Spirit present at the creation (Genesis 1.2) with the Spirit in the form of a dove that descended on Jesus at the beginning of his ministry (John 1.32). Vast: large; deserted (Latin *vastus*).

5. Does not mean merely "demonstrate logically" but has its biblical meaning and implies spiritual rather than rational understanding.

Say first, for Heav'n hides nothing from thy view
Nor the deep Tract of Hell, say first what cause
Mov'd our Grand[6] Parents in that happy State,
30   Favor'd of Heav'n so highly, to fall off
From thir Creator, and transgress his Will
For° one restraint, Lords of the World besides?°   *because of / otherwise*
Who first seduc'd them to that foul revolt?
Th' infernal Serpent;[7] hee it was, whose guile
35   Stirr'd up with Envy and Revenge, deceiv'd
The Mother of Mankind; what time his Pride
Had cast him out from Heav'n, with all his Host
Of Rebel Angels, by whose aid aspiring
To set himself in Glory above his Peers,
40   He trusted to have equall'd the most High,[8]
If he oppos'd; and with ambitious aim
Against the Throne and Monarchy of God
Rais'd impious War in Heav'n and Battle proud
With vain attempt. Him the Almighty Power
45   Hurl'd headlong flaming from th' Ethereal Sky[9]
With hideous ruin and combustion down
To bottomless perdition, there to dwell
In Adamantine Chains[1] and penal Fire,
Who durst defy th' Omnipotent to Arms.
50   Nine times the Space that measures Day and Night[2]
To mortal men, hee with his horrid crew
Lay vanquisht, rolling in the fiery Gulf
Confounded though immortal: But his doom
Reserv'd him to more wrath; for now the thought
55   Both of lost happiness and lasting pain
Torments him; round he throws his baleful° eyes   *evil, suffering*
That witness'd huge affliction and dismay
Mixt with obdúrate° pride and steadfast hate: *unyielding*
At once as far as Angels' ken° he views   *power of vision*
60   The dismal° Situation waste and wild,   *dreadful, sinister*
A Dungeon horrible, on all sides round
As one great Furnace flam'd, yet from those flames
No light, but rather darkness visible
Serv'd only to discover sights of woe,[3]
65   Regions of sorrow, doleful shades, where peace

6. Implies not only greatness, but also inclusiveness of generality or parentage.
7. "That old serpent, called the Devil, and Satan" (Revelation 12.9) both because Satan entered the body of a serpent to tempt Eve and because his nature is guileful and dangerous to humans.
8. Satan's crime was not his aspiring "above his peers" but aspiring "To set himself in [divine] Glory." Numerous verbal echoes relate lines 40–48 to the biblical accounts of the fall and binding of Lucifer, in 2 Peter 2.4, Revelation 20.1–2, and Isaiah 14.12–15: "Thou hast said . . . I will exalt my throne above the stars of God . . . I will be

like the most High. Yet thou shalt be brought down to hell."
9. Mingling an allusion to Luke 10.18, "I beheld Satan as lightning fall from heaven," with one to Homer, *Iliad* 1.591, Hephaistos "hurled from the ethereal threshold."
1. 2 Peter 2.4; "God spared not the angels that sinned, but . . . delivered them into chains of darkness."
2. The devils fall for the same number of days that the Titans fall from heaven when overthrown by the Olympian gods (see Hesiod, *Theogony* 664–735).
3. See the account of the land of the dead in Job 10.22: "the light is as darkness."

And rest can never dwell, hope never comes
That comes to all;[4] but torture without end
Still urges,° and a fiery Deluge, fed   *presses*
With ever-burning Sulphur unconsum'd:
70   Such place Eternal Justice had prepar'd
For those rebellious, here thir Prison ordained
In utter° darkness, and thir portion set   *complete, outer*
As far remov'd from God and light of Heav'n
As from the Center thrice to th' utmost Pole.[5]
75   O how unlike the place from whence they fell!
There the companions of his fall, o'erwhelm'd
With Floods and Whirlwinds of tempestuous fire,
He soon discerns, and welt'ring by his side
One next himself in power, and next in crime,
80   Long after known in *Palestine*, and nam'd
Beëlzebub.[6] To whom th' Arch-Enemy,
And thence in Heav'n call'd Satan,[7] with bold words
Breaking the horrid silence thus began.[8]
        If thou beest hee; But O how fall'n! how chang'd
85   From him, who in the happy Realms of Light
Cloth'd with transcendent brightness didst outshine
Myriads though bright:[9] If he whom mutual league,
United thoughts and counsels, equal hope,
And hazard in the Glorious Enterprise,
90   Join'd with me once, now misery hath join'd
In equal ruin: into what Pit thou seest
From what highth fall'n, so much the stronger prov'd
He with his Thunder: and till then who knew
The force of those dire Arms? yet not for those,
95   Nor what the Potent Victor in his rage
Can else inflict, do I repent or change,
Though chang'd in outward luster; that fixt mind
And high disdain, from sense of injur'd merit,
That with the mightiest rais'd me to contend,
100   And to the fierce contention brought along
Innumerable force of Spirits arm'd
That durst dislike his reign, and mee preferring,
His utmost power with adverse power oppos'd
In dubious Battle on the Plains of Heav'n,

---

4. The phrase echoes Dante's *Inferno*: III.9 "All hope abandon, ye who enter here."

5. Milton refers to the Ptolemaic universe in which the earth is at the center of ten concentric spheres. Milton draws attention to the numerical proportion, heaven-earth:earth-hell—i.e., earth divides the interval between heaven and hell in the proportion that Neoplatonists believed should be maintained between reason and concupiscence.

6. Hebrew, "Lord of the flies"; Matthew 12.24, "the prince of the devils."

7. Hebrew, "enemy." After his rebellion, Satan's "former name" (Lucifer) was no longer used (5.658).

8. Rhetorically, the opening of the action proper. The 41-line speech beginning here, the first speech in the book, exactly balances the last, which also is spoken by Satan and also consists of 41 lines (1.622–62).

9. The break in grammatical concord (between "him" and "didst") reflects Satan's doubt whether Beelzebub is present and so whether second-person forms are appropriate.

105   And shook his throne.[1] What though the field be lost?
       All is not lost; the unconquerable Will,
       And study° of revenge, immortal hate,   *pursuit*
       And courage never to submit or yield:
       And what is else not to be overcome?
110   That Glory[2] never shall his wrath or might
       Extort from me. To bow and sue for grace
       With suppliant knee, and deify his power
       Who from the terror of this Arm so late
       Doubted° his Empire, that were low indeed,   *feared for*
115   That were an ignominy and shame beneath
       This downfall; since by Fate the strength of Gods
       And this Empyreal substance cannot fail,[3]
       Since through experience of this great event
       In Arms not worse, in foresight much advanc't,
120   We may with more successful hope resolve
       To wage by force or guile eternal War
       Irreconcilable to our grand Foe,
       Who now triúmphs, and in th' excess of joy
       Sole reigning holds the Tyranny of Heav'n.[4]
125   So spake th' Apostate Angel, though in pain,
       Vaunting aloud, but rackt with deep despair:
       And him thus answer'd soon his bold Compeer.°   *comrade*
          O Prince, O Chief of many Throned Powers,
       That led th' imbattl'd Seraphim[5] to War
130   Under thy conduct, and in dreadful deeds
       Fearless, endanger'd Heav'n's perpetual King;
       And put to proof his high Supremacy,
       Whether upheld by strength, or Chance, or Fate;[6]
       Too well I see and rue the dire event,
135   That with sad overthrow and foul defeat
       Hath lost us Heav'n, and all this mighty Host
       In horrible destruction laid thus low,
       As far as Gods and Heav'nly Essences
       Can perish: for the mind and spirit remains
140   Invincible, and vigor soon returns,
       Though all our Glory extinct, and happy state
       Here swallow'd up in endless misery.
       But what if he our Conqueror (whom I now
       Of force° believe Almighty, since no less   *necessarily*
145   Than such could have o'erpow'rd such force as ours)

---

1. The Son's chariot, not Satan's armies, shakes heaven to its foundations, as we learn in Book 6. Throughout the present passage, Satan sees himself as the hero of a pagan epic.
2. Either "the glory of overcoming me" or "my glory of will."
3. Implying not only that as angels they are immortal, but also that the continuance of their strength is assured by fate.

4. An obvious instance of the devil's bias.
5. The traditional nine orders of angels are seraphim, cherubim, thrones, dominions, virtues, powers, principalities, archangels, and angels, but Milton does not use these terms systematically.
6. The main powers recognized in the devils' ideology. God's power rests on a quality that does not occur to Beelzebub: goodness.

Have left us this our spirit and strength entire
Strongly to suffer and support our pains,
That we may so suffice° his vengeful ire,   satisfy
Or do him mightier service as his thralls
150   By right of War, whate'er his business be
Here in the heart of Hell to work in Fire,
Or do his Errands in the gloomy Deep;
What can it then avail though yet we feel
Strength undiminisht, or eternal being
155   To undergo eternal punishment?[7]
Whereto with speedy words th' Arch-fiend repli'd.
    Fall'n Cherub, to be weak is miserable
Doing or Suffering: but of this be sure,
To do aught good never will be our task,
160   But ever to do ill our sole delight,
As being the contrary to his high will
Whom we resist.[8] If then his Providence
Out of our evil seek to bring forth good,
Our labor must be to pervert that end,
165   And out of good still to find means of evil;
Which oft-times may succeed, so as perhaps
Shall grieve him, if I fail not, and disturb
His inmost counsels from thir destin'd aim.
But see the angry Victor hath recall'd
170   His Ministers of vengeance and pursuit
Back to the Gates of Heav'n: the Sulphurous Hail
Shot after us in storm, o'erblown hath laid°   subdued
The fiery Surge, that from the Precipice
Of Heav'n receiv'd us falling, and the Thunder,
175   Wing'd with red Lightning and impetuous rage,
Perhaps hath spent his shafts, and ceases now
To bellow through the vast and boundless Deep.
Let us not slip° th' occasion, whether scorn,   lose
Or satiate fury yield it from our Foe.
180   Seest thou yon dreary Plain, forlorn and wild,
The seat of desolation, void of light,
Save what the glimmering of these livid flames
Casts pale and dreadful? Thither let us tend
From off the tossing of these fiery waves,
185   There rest, if any rest can harbor there,
And reassembling our afflicted° Powers,   downcast
Consult how we may henceforth most offend°   harm
Our Enemy, our own loss how repair,
How overcome this dire Calamity,

7. Existing eternally, merely so that our punishment may
also be eternal.
8. This fundamental disobedience and disorientation
make Satan's heroic virtue into the corresponding excess
of vice. Lines 163–65 look forward to 12.470–78 and
Adam's wonder at the astonishing reversal whereby God
will turn the Fall into an occasion for good.

190   What reinforcement we may gain from Hope,
          If not what resolution from despair.
             Thus Satan talking to his nearest Mate
          With Head up-lift above the wave, and Eyes
          That sparkling blaz'd, his other Parts besides

195   Prone on the Flood, extended long and large
          Lay floating many a rood,° in bulk as huge   *six to eight yards*
          As whom the Fables name of monstrous size,
          Titanian, or *Earth-born,* that warr'd on *Jove,*
          Briareos or *Typhon,*[9] whom the Den

200   By ancient *Tarsus*[1] held, or that Sea-beast
          Leviathan,[2] which God of all his works
          Created hugest that swim th' Ocean stream:
          Him haply slumb'ring on the *Norway* foam
          The Pilot of some small night-founder'd° Skiff,   *sunk in night*

205   Deeming some Island, oft, as Seamen tell,
          With fixed Anchor in his scaly rind
          Moors by his side under the Lee, while Night
          Invests° the Sea, and wished Morn delays: *wraps*
          So stretcht out huge in length the Arch-fiend lay

210   Chain'd on the burning Lake, nor ever thence
          Had ris'n or heav'd his head, but that the will
          And high permission of all-ruling Heaven
          Left him at large to his own dark designs,
          That with reiterated crimes he might

215   Heap on himself damnation, while he sought
          Evil to others, and enrag'd might see
          How all his malice serv'd but to bring forth
          Infinite goodness, grace and mercy shown
          On Man by him seduc't, but on himself

220   Treble confusion, wrath and vengeance pour'd.
          Forthwith upright he rears from off the Pool
          His mighty Stature; on each hand the flames
          Driv'n backward slope thir pointing spires, and roll'd
          In billows, leave i' th' midst a horrid° Vale.   *bristling*

225   Then with expanded wings he steers his flight
          Aloft, incumbent[3] on the dusky Air
          That felt unusual weight, till on dry Land
          He lights, if it were Land that ever burn'd
          With solid, as the Lake with liquid fire

230   And such appear'd in hue;[4] as when the force

---

9. The serpent-legged *Briareos* was a Titan, the serpent-headed *Typhon* (Typhoeus) a Giant. Each was a son of Earth; each fought against Jupiter; and each was eventually confined beneath Aetna (see lines 232–37). Typhon was so powerful that when he first made war on the Olympians, they had to resort to metamorphoses to escape (Ovid, *Metamorphoses* 5.325–31 and 346–58).
1. The biblical Tarsus was the capital of Cilicia, and both

Pindar and Aeschylus describe Typhon's habitat as a Cilician cave or "den."
2. The monster of Job 41, identified in Isaiah's prophecy of judgment as "the crooked serpent" (Isaiah 27.1) but also sometimes thought of as a whale.
3. Pressing with his weight.
4. In the 17th century, "hue" referred to surface appearance and texture as well as color.

Of subterranean wind transports a Hill
Torn from *Pelorus*,[5] or the shatter'd side
Of thund'ring *Etna*, whose combustible
And fuell'd entrails thence conceiving Fire,
235   Sublim'd[6] with Mineral fury,[7] aid the Winds,
And leave a singed bottom all involv'd°   wreathed
With stench and smoke: Such resting found the sole
Of unblest feet. Him follow'd his next Mate,
Both glorying to have scap't the *Stygian*[8] flood
240   As Gods, and by thir own recover'd strength,
Not by the sufferance of supernal Power.
        Is this the Region, this the Soil, the Clime,
Said then the lost Arch-Angel, this the seat
That we must change° for Heav'n, this mournful gloom   exchange
245   For that celestial light? Be it so, since he
Who now is Sovran can dispose and bid
What shall be right: fardest° from him is best   farthest
Whom reason hath equall'd, force hath made supreme
Above his equals. Farewell happy Fields
250   Where Joy for ever dwells: Hail horrors, hail
Infernal world, and thou profoundest Hell
Receive thy new Possessor: One who brings
A mind not to be chang'd by Place or Time.
The mind is its own place, and in itself
255   Can make a Heav'n of Hell, a Hell of Heav'n.[9]
What matter where, if I be still the same,
And what I should be, all but less than hee
Whom Thunder hath made greater? Here at least
We shall be free; th' Almighty hath not built
260   Here for his envy, will not drive us hence:
Here we may reign secure, and in my choice
To reign is worth ambition[1] though in Hell:
Better to reign in Hell, than serve in Heav'n.
But wherefore let we then our faithful friends,
265   Th' associates and copartners of our loss
Lie thus astonisht on th' oblivious Pool,[2]
And call them not to share with us their part
In this unhappy Mansion: or once more
With rallied Arms to try what may be yet
270   Regain'd in Heav'n, or what more lost in Hell?
        So *Satan* spake, and him *Beëlzebub*
Thus answer'd. Leader of those Armies bright,
Which but th' Omnipotent none could have foiled,

---

5. Pelorus and Aetna are volcanic mountains in Sicily.
6. Converted directly from solid to vapor by volcanic heat in such a way as to resolidify on cooling.
7. Disorder of minerals, or subterranean disorder.
8. Of the river Styx—i.e., hellish.
9. The view that heaven and hell are states of mind was

held by Amaury de Bene, a medieval heretic often cited in 17th-century accounts of atheism.
1. Worth striving for (Latin *ambitio*). Satan refers not merely to a mental state but also to an active effort that is the price of power.
2. The pool attended by forgetfulness.

275	If once they hear that voice, thir liveliest pledge	
	Of hope in fears and dangers, heard so oft	
	In worst extremes, and on the perilous edge°	*front line*
	Of battle when it rag'd, in all assaults	
	Thir surest signal, they will soon resume	
	New courage and revive, though now they lie	
280	Groveling and prostrate on yon Lake of Fire,	
	As we erewhile, astounded and amaz'd;	
	No wonder, fall'n such a pernicious highth.	
	He scarce had ceas't when the superior Fiend	
	Was moving toward the shore; his ponderous shield	
285	Ethereal temper,[3] massy, large and round,	
	Behind him cast; the broad circumference	
	Hung on his shoulders like the Moon, whose Orb	
	Through Optic Glass the *Tuscan* Artist[4] views	
	At Ev'ning from the top of *Fesole,*	
290	Or in *Valdarno,* to descry new Lands,	
	Rivers or Mountains in her spotty Globe.	
	His Spear, to equal which the tallest Pine	
	Hewn on *Norwegian* hills, to be the Mast	
	Of some great Ammiral,° were but a wand,	*flagship*
295	He walkt with to support uneasy steps	
	Over the burning Marl,° not like those steps	*ground*
	On Heaven's Azure, and the torrid Clime	
	Smote on him sore besides, vaulted with Fire;	
	Nathless° he so endur'd, till on the Beach	*nevertheless*
300	Of that inflamed Sea, he stood and call'd	
	His Legions, Angel Forms, who lay intrans't	
	Thick as Autumnal Leaves that strow the Brooks	
	In *Vallombrosa,* where th' *Etrurian* shades	
	High overarch't imbow'r;[5] or scatter'd sedge	
305	Afloat, when with fierce Winds *Orion* arm'd	
	Hath vext the Red-Sea Coast,[6] whose waves o'erthrew	
	Busiris and his *Memphian* Chivalry,	
	While with perfidious hatred they pursu'd	
	The Sojourners of *Goshen,* who beheld	
310	From the safe shore thir floating Carcasses	
	And broken Chariot Wheels;[7] so thick bestrown	
	Abject and lost lay these, covering the Flood,	

3. Tempered in celestial fire.

4. Galileo, who looked through a telescope ("optic glass"), had been placed under house arrest by the Inquisition near Florence, which is in the "Valdarno" or the Valley of the Arno, overlooked by the hills of "Fesole" or Fiesole.

5. See Isaiah 34.4: "and all their host shall fall down, as the leaf falleth off from the vine, and as a falling fig from the fig tree." Fallen leaves were an enduring simile for the numberless dead; see Homer, *Iliad* 6.146; Virgil, *Aeneid* 6.309; Dante, *Inferno* 3.112. Milton adds an actual locality, Vallombrosa, again near Florence.

6. Commentators on Job 9.9 and Amos 5.8 interpreted the creation of Orion as a symbol of God's power to raise tempests and floods to execute his judgments. Thus Milton's transition to the Egyptians overwhelmed by God's judgment in lines 306–11 is a natural one. The Hebrew name for the Red Sea was "Sea of Sedge."

7. Contrary to his promise, the Pharaoh with his Memphian (i.e., Egyptian) charioteers pursued the Israelites—who had been in captivity in Goshen—across the Red Sea. The Israelites passed over safely; but the Egyptians' chariot wheels were broken (Exodus 14.25), and the rising sea engulfed them and cast their corpses on the shore.

Under amazement of thir hideous change.
He call'd so loud, that all the hollow Deep
315   Of Hell resounded. Princes, Potentates,
Warriors, the Flow'r of Heav'n, once yours, now lost,
If such astonishment as this can seize
Eternal spirits; or have ye chos'n this place
After the toil of Battle to repose
320   Your wearied virtue,° for the ease you find   strength
To slumber here, as in the Vales of Heav'n?
Or in this abject posture have ye sworn
To adore the Conqueror? who now beholds
Cherub and Seraph rolling in the Flood
325   With scatter'd Arms and Ensigns,° till anon   battle flags
His swift pursuers from Heav'n Gates discern
Th' advantage, and descending tread us down
Thus drooping, or with linked Thunderbolts
Transfix us to the bottom of this Gulf.
330   Awake, arise, or be for ever fall'n.
        They heard, and were abasht, and up they sprung
Upon the wing; as when men wont to watch
On duty, sleeping found by whom they dread,
Rouse and bestir themselves ere well awake.
335   Nor did they not perceive the evil plight
In which they were, or the fierce pains not feel;
Yet to thir General's Voice they soon obey'd
Innumerable. As when the potent Rod
Of *Amram's* Son[8] in *Egypt's* evil day
340   Wav'd round the Coast, up call'd a pitchy cloud
Of *Locusts,* warping° on the Eastern Wind,   floating
That o'er the Realm of impious *Pharaoh* hung
Like Night, and darken'd all the Land of *Nile*:
So numberless were those bad Angels seen
345   Hovering on wing under the Cope° of Hell   canopy
'Twixt upper, nether, and surrounding Fires;
Till, as a signal giv'n, th' uplifted Spear
Of thir great Sultan waving to direct
Thir course, in even balance down they light
350   On the firm brimstone, and fill all the Plain;
A multitude, like which the populous North
Pour'd never from her frozen loins, to pass
Rhene or the *Danaw,* when her barbarous Sons
Came like a Deluge on the South, and spread
355   Beneath *Gibraltar* to the *Lybian* sands.[9]
Forthwith from every Squadron and each Band
The Heads and Leaders thither haste where stood

8. Moses, who used his rod to bring down on the Egyptians a plague of locusts (Exodus 10.12–15).
9. The barbarian invasions of Rome began with crossings of the Rhine ("Rhene") and Danube ("Danaw") rivers and spread to North Africa.

Thir great Commander; Godlike shapes and forms
Excelling human, Princely Dignities,
360 And Powers that erst in Heaven sat on Thrones;
Though of thir Names in heav'nly Records now
Be no memorial, blotted out and ras'd
By thir Rebellion, from the Books of Life.[1]
Nor had they yet among the Sons of *Eve*
365 Got them new Names, till wand'ring o'er the Earth,
Through God's high sufferance for the trial of man,
By falsities and lies the greatest part
Of Mankind they corrupted to forsake
God thir Creator, and th' invisible
370 Glory of him that made them, to transform
Oft to the Image of a Brute, adorn'd
With gay Religions° full of Pomp and Gold,   ceremonies
And Devils to adore for Deities:[2]
Then were they known to men by various Names,
375 And various Idols through the Heathen World.
Say, Muse, thir Names then known, who first, who last,
Rous'd from the slumber on that fiery Couch,
At thir great Emperor's call, as next in worth
Came singly where he stood on the bare strand,
380 While the promiscuous crowd stood yet aloof?
The chief were those who from the Pit of Hell
Roaming to seek thir prey on earth, durst fix
Thir Seats long after next the Seat of God,
Thir Altars by his Altar, Gods ador'd
385 Among the Nations round, and durst abide
Jehovah thund'ring out of *Sion,* thron'd
Between the Cherubim; yea, often plac'd
Within his Sanctuary itself thir Shrines,
Abominations; and with cursed things
390 His holy Rites, and solemn Feasts profan'd,
And with thir darkness durst affront his light.
First *Moloch,*[3] horrid King besmear'd with blood
Of human sacrifice, and parents' tears,
Though for the noise of Drums and Timbrels° loud   *tambourines*
395 Thir children's cries unheard, that pass'd through fire
To his grim Idol. Him the *Ammonite*
Worshipt in *Rabba* and her wat'ry Plain,
In *Argob* and in *Basan,* to the stream
Of utmost *Arnon.*[4] Nor content with such

1. See Revelation 3.5 ("He that overcometh . . . I will not blot out his name out of the book of life") and Exodus 32.32–33.
2. The catalogue of gods here is an epic convention.
3. Satan gathers 12 disciples: Moloch, Chemos, Baalim, Ashtaroth, Astoreth, Thammuz, Dagon, Rimmon, Osiris, Isis, Horus, and Belial. The literal meaning of *Moloch* is "king."

4. Though ostensibly magnifying Moloch's empire, these lines look forward to his eventual defeat; for Rabba, the Ammonite royal city, is best known for its capture by David after his repentance (2 Samuel 12), while the Israelite conquest of the regions of Argob and Basan, as far as the boundary river Arnon, is recalled by Moses as particularly crushing (Deuteronomy 3.1–13).

400   Audacious neighborhood, the wisest heart
       Of *Solomon*[5] he led by fraud to build
       His Temple right against the Temple of God
       On that opprobrious Hill,[6] and made his Grove
       The pleasant Valley of *Hinnom, Tophet* thence
405   And black *Gehenna* call'd, the Type of Hell.[7]
       Next *Chemos*,[8] th' obscene dread of *Moab's* Sons,
       From *Aroar* to *Nebo*, and the wild
       Of Southmost *Abarim*; in *Hesebon*
       And *Horonaim, Seon's* Realm, beyond
410   The flow'ry Dale of *Sibma* clad with Vines,
       And *Eleale* to th' Asphaltic Pool.[9]
       Peor[1] his other Name, when he entic'd
       Israel in *Sittim* on thir march from *Nile*
       To do him wanton rites, which cost them woe.[2]
415   Yet thence his lustful Orgies he enlarg'd
       Even to that Hill of scandal, by the Grove
       Of *Moloch* homicide, lust hard by hate;
       Till good *Josiah*[3] drove them thence to Hell.
       With these came they, who from the bord'ring flood
420   Of old *Euphrates*[4] to the Brook that parts
       Egypt from *Syrian* ground, had general Names
       Of *Baalim* and *Ashtaroth*,[5] those male,
       These Feminine. For Spirits when they please
       Can either Sex assume, or both; so soft
425   And uncompounded is thir Essence pure,
       Not ti'd or manacl'd with joint or limb,
       Nor founded on the brittle strength of bones,
       Like cumbrous flesh; but in what shape they choose
       Dilated° or condens't, bright or obscure,   *expanded*°
430   Can execute thir aery purposes,
       And works of love or enmity fulfil.
       For those the Race of *Israel* oft forsook
       Thir living strength,[6] and unfrequented left

---

5. Solomon's wives drew him into idolatry (1 Kings 11.5–7); but the "high places that were before Jerusalem . . . on the right hand of the mount of corruption which Solomon . . . had builded for Ashtoreth the abomination of the Zidonians, and for Chemosh the abomination of the Moabites, and Milcom the abomination of the children of Ammon" were later destroyed by Josiah (2 Kings 23.13–14).

6. The Mount of Olives, because of Solomon's idolatry called "mount of corruption." Throughout the poem, Solomon functions as a type both of Adam and of Christ.

7. To abolish sacrifice to Moloch, Josiah "defiled Topheth, which is in the valley of the children of Hinnom" (2 Kings 23.10). Gehenna, for "Valley of Hinnom," is used in Matthew 10.28 as a name for hell.

8. "The abomination of Moab," associated with the neighboring god Moloch in 1 Kings 11.7.

9. Most of these places are named in Numbers 32 as the formerly Moabite inheritance assigned by Moses to the tribes of Reuben and Gad. Numbers 21.25–30 rejoices at the Israelite capture of Hesebon (Heshbon), a Moabite city which had been taken by the Amorite King Seon, or Sihon. Heshbon, Horonaim, "the vine of Sibmah," and Elealeh all figure in Isaiah's sad prophecy of the destruction of Moab (Isaiah 15.5, 16.8f). The Asphaltic Pool is the Dead Sea.

1. For the story of Peor, see Numbers 25.1–3 and Hosea 9.10.

2. A plague that killed 24,000 (Numbers 25.9).

3. Always a favorite with the Reformers because of his destruction of idolatrous images.

4. An area stretching from the northeast limit of Syria to the southwest limit of Canaan, the river Besor.

5. Baal is the general name for most idols; the Phoenician and Canaanite sun gods were collectively called Baalim (plural form). Astartes (Ishtars) were manifestations of the moon goddess.

6. See 1 Samuel 15.29: "Strength of Israel," a formulaic periphrasis for Jehovah.

His righteous Altar, bowing lowly down
435   To bestial Gods; for which thir heads as low
Bow'd down in Battle, sunk before the Spear
Of despicable foes. With these in troop
Came *Astoreth*, whom the *Phoenicians* call'd
Astarte, Queen of Heav'n, with crescent Horns;[7]
440   To whose bright Image nightly by the Moon
Sidonian Virgins paid thir Vows and Songs,
In *Sion* also not unsung, where stood
Her Temple on th' offensive Mountain, built
By that uxorious King, whose heart though large,
445   Beguil'd by fair Idolatresses, fell
To Idols foul. *Thammuz*[8] came next behind,
Whose annual wound in *Lebanon* allur'd
The *Syrian* Damsels to lament his fate
In amorous ditties all a Summer's day,
450   While smooth *Adonis* from his native Rock
Ran purple to the Sea, suppos'd with blood
Of *Thammuz* yearly wounded: the Love-tale
Infected *Sion's* daughters with like heat,
Whose wanton passions in the sacred Porch
455   *Ezekiel* saw, when by the Vision led
His eye survey'd the dark Idolatries
Of alienated *Judah*. Next came one
Who mourn'd in earnest, when the Captive Ark
Maim'd his brute Image, head and hands lopt off
460   In his own Temple, on the grunsel° edge,   threshold
Where he fell flat, and sham'd his Worshippers:
Dagon his Name, Sea Monster, upward Man
And downward Fish:[9] yet had his Temple high
Rear'd in *Azotus*, dreaded through the Coast
465   Of *Palestine*, in *Gath* and *Ascalon*,
And *Accaron* and *Gaza's* frontier bounds.[1]
Him follow'd *Rimmon*, whose delightful Seat
Was fair *Damascus*, on the fertile Banks
Of *Abbana* and *Pharphar*, lucid streams.[2]
470   He also against the house of God was bold:

A Leper once he lost and gain'd a King,
Ahaz his sottish Conqueror, whom he drew
God's Altar to disparage and displace
For one of *Syrian* mode, whereon to burn
His odious off'rings, and adore the Gods
Whom he had vanquisht.³ After these appear'd
A crew who under Names of old Renown,
Osiris, Isis, Orus and thir Train
With monstrous shapes and sorceries abus'd°   deceived
Fanatic *Egypt* and her Priests, to seek
Thir wand'ring Gods disguis'd in brutish forms
Rather than human.⁴ Nor did *Israel* scape
Th' infection when thir borrow'd Gold compos'd
The Calf in *Oreb:*⁵ and the Rebel King⁶
Doubl'd that sin in *Bethel* and in *Dan,*
Lik'ning his Maker to the Grazed Ox,⁷
Jehovah, who in one Night when he pass'd
From *Egypt* marching, equall'd with one stroke
Both her first born and all her bleating Gods.⁸
Belial came last,⁹ than whom a Spirit more lewd
Fell not from Heaven, or more gross to love
Vice for itself: To him no Temple stood
Or Altar smok'd; yet who more oft than hee
In Temples and at Altars, when the Priest
Turns Atheist, as did *Ely's* Sons, who fill'd
With lust and violence the house of God.¹
In Courts and Palaces he also Reigns
And in luxurious Cities, where the noise
Of riot ascends above thir loftiest Tow'rs,
And injury and outrage: And when Night
Darkens the Streets, then wander forth the Sons
Of *Belial,* flown° with insolence and wine.²   swollen
Witness the Streets of *Sodom,* and that night
In *Gibeah,* when the hospitable door
Expos'd a Matron to avoid worse rape.³
These were the prime in order and in might;
The rest were long to tell, though far renown'd,

Line numbers: 475, 480, 485, 490, 495, 500, 505

3. After engineering the overthrow of Damascus by the Assyrians, the sottish (foolish) King Ahaz became interested in the cult of Rimmon and had an altar of the Syrian type put in the temple of the Lord (2 Kings 16.9–17).
4. Milton alludes to the myth of the Olympian gods fleeing from the Giant Typhoeus into Egypt and hiding in bestial forms (Ovid, *Metamorphoses* 5.319–31) afterward worshipped by the Egyptians.
5. Perhaps the most familiar of all Israelite apostasies was their worship of "a calf in Horeb" (Psalms 106.19) made by Aaron while Moses was away receiving the tables of the Law (Exodus 32).
6. Jeroboam, who led the revolt of the ten tribes of Israel against Rehoboam, Solomon's successor; he "doubled" Aaron's sin, since he made "two calves of gold," placing

one in Bethel and the other in Dan (1 Kings 12.28–29).
7. "Thus they changed their glory into the similitude of an ox that eateth grass" (Psalms 106.20).
8. At the passover, Jehovah smote all the Egyptian first-born, "both man and beast" (Exodus 12.12); presumably, this stroke would extend to their sacred animals.
9. Belial comes last, both because he had no local cult and because in the poem he is "timorous and slothful" (2.117). Properly, "Belial" is an abstract noun meaning "iniquity."
1. The impiety and fornication of Ely's sons are described in 1 Samuel 2.12–24.
2. The Puritans referred to their enemies as the Sons of Belial.
3. See Genesis 19 and Judges 19.

Th' *Ionian* Gods,[4] of *Javan's* Issue held
Gods, yet confest later than Heav'n and Earth
510   Thir boasted Parents; *Titan* Heav'n's first born
With his enormous° brood, and birthright seiz'd   *monstrous*
By younger *Saturn*, he from mightier *Jove*
His own and *Rhea's* Son like measure found;
So *Jove* usurping reign'd: these first in *Crete*
515   And *Ida* known,[5] thence on the Snowy top
Of cold *Olympus* rul'd the middle Air
Thir highest Heav'n; or on the *Delphian* Cliff,[6]
Or in *Dodona*, and through all the bounds
Of *Doric* Land;° or who with *Saturn* old   *Greece*
520   Fled over *Adria* to th' *Hesperian* Fields,
And o'er the *Celtic* roam'd the utmost Isles.[7]
All these and more came flocking; but with looks
Downcast and damp,° yet such wherein appear'd   *depressed*
Obscure some glimpse of joy, to have found thir chief
525   Not in despair, to have found themselves not lost
In loss itself; which on his count'nance cast
Like doubtful hue: but he his wonted pride
Soon recollecting,° with high words, that bore   *recovering*
Semblance of worth, not substance, gently rais'd
530   Thir fainting courage, and dispell'd thir fears.
Then straight commands that at the warlike sound
Of Trumpets loud and Clarions° be uprear'd   *shrill trumpets*
His mighty Standard; that proud honor claim'd
Azazel as his right, a Cherub tall:[8]
535   Who forthwith from the glittering Staff unfurl'd
Th' Imperial Ensign, which full high advanc't
Shone like a Meteor streaming to the Wind
With Gems and Golden lustre rich imblaz'd,[9]
Seraphic arms and Trophies: all the while
540   Sonorous metal blowing Martial sounds:
At which the universal Host upsent
A shout that tore Hell's Concave,° and beyond   *vault*
Frighted the Reign of *Chaos* and old Night.[1]
All in a moment through the gloom were seen
545   Ten thousand Banners rise into the Air
With Orient° Colors waving: with them rose   *brilliant*
A Forest huge of Spears: and thronging Helms

---

4. The Ionian Greeks were held by some to be the issue of Javan the son of Japhet the son of Noah, on the basis of the Septuagint version of Genesis 10.
5. Jove was born and secretly reared on Mount Ida, in Crete.
6. Delphi was famed as the site of the Pythian oracle of Apollo, but cults of Ge, Poseidon, and Artemis were also celebrated there.
7. After Saturn's downfall he fled across the Adriatic Sea (Adria) to Italy (Hesperian Fields), France (the Celtic),

and the British Isles (Utmost Isles).
8. Azazel was one of the chief fallen angels who are the object of God's wrath in the apocryphal Book of Enoch. For the healing of the earth he is bound and cast into the same wilderness where the scapegoat was led (Enoch 10.4–8).
9. Adorned with heraldic devices.
1. Chaos and Night, rulers of the region of unformed matter between Heaven and Hell.

	Appear'd, and serried° Shields in thick array	*locked together*
	Of depth immeasurable: Anon they move	
550	In perfect *Phalanx*[2] to the *Dorian*° mood	*solemn*
	Of Flutes and soft Recorders; such as rais'd	
	To highth of noblest temper Heroes old	
	Arming to Battle, and instead of rage	
	Deliberate valor breath'd, firm and unmov'd	
555	With dread of death to flight or foul retreat,	
	Nor wanting power to mitigate and swage°	*assuage*
	With solemn touches, troubl'd thoughts, and chase	
	Anguish and doubt and fear and sorrow and pain	
	From mortal or immortal minds. Thus they	
560	Breathing united force with fixed thought	
	Mov'd on in silence to soft Pipes that charm'd	
	Thir painful steps o'er the burnt soil; and now	
	Advanc't in view they stand, a horrid° Front	*bristling*
	Of dreadful length and dazzling Arms, in guise	
565	Of Warriors old with order'd Spear and Shield,	
	Awaiting what command thir mighty Chief	
	Had to impose: He through the armed Files	
	Darts his experienc't eye, and soon traverse°	*across*
	The whole Battalion views, thir order due,	
570	Thir visages and stature as of Gods;	
	Thir number last he sums. And now his heart	
	Distends with pride, and hard'ning in his strength	
	Glories: For never since created man,[3]	
	Met such imbodied° force, as nam'd with these	*united*
575	Could merit more than that small infantry	
	Warr'd on by Cranes:[4] though all the Giant brood	
	Of *Phlegra* with th' Heroic Race were join'd	
	That fought at *Thebes* and *Ilium*, on each side	
	Mixt with auxiliar Gods;[5] and what resounds	
580	In Fable or *Romance of Uther's* Son°	*King Arthur*
	Begirt with *British* and *Armoric*[6] Knights;	
	And all who since, Baptiz'd or Infidel	
	Jousted in *Aspramont* or *Montalban*,	
	Damasco, or *Marocco*, or *Trebisond*,	
585	Or whom *Biserta* sent from *Afric* shore	
	When *Charlemain* with all his Peerage fell	
	By *Fontarabbia*.[7] Thus far these beyond	

2. A square battle formation.
3. Since humanity was created.
4. When compared with Satan's, any army would seem no bigger than pygmies ("that small infantry"), who were portrayed by Pliny as tiny men who fought with cranes.
5. To amplify the heroic stature of the angels, Milton mentions a series of armies that had been thought worthy of epic treatment only to dismiss them. The Giants, who fought with the Olympians at Phlegra, join with the heroes of Thebes and Troy (Ilium).

6. From Brittany.
7. Aspramont was a castle near Nice, and Montalban was the castle of Rinaldo; these castles figure in Ariosto's *Orlando Furioso* and the romances concerned with chivalric wars between Christians and Saracens. Milton would know late versions of the Charlemagne legend. Charlemagne's whole rearguard, led by Roland, one of the 12 peers or paladins, was massacred at Roncesvalles, about 40 miles from Fontarabbia (Fuenterrabia).

Compare of mortal prowess, yet observ'd°   *obeyed*
Thir dread commander: he above the rest
590   In shape and gesture proudly eminent
Stood like a Tow'r; his form had yet not lost
All her Original brightness, nor appear'd
Less than Arch-Angel ruin'd, and th' excess
Of Glory obscur'd: As when the Sun new ris'n
595   Looks through the Horizontal misty Air
Shorn of his Beams, or from behind the Moon
In dim Eclipse disastrous twilight sheds
On half the Nations, and with fear of change
Perplexes Monarchs.⁸ Dark'n'd so, yet shone
600   Above them all th' Arch-Angel: but his face
Deep scars of Thunder had intrencht, and care
Sat on his faded cheek, but under Brows
Of dauntless courage, and considerate° Pride   *deliberate*
Waiting revenge: cruel his eye, but cast
605   Signs of remorse and passion to behold
The fellows of his crime, the followers rather
(Far other once beheld in bliss) condemn'd
For ever now to have thir lot in pain,
Millions of Spirits for his fault amerc't°   *deprived*
610   Of Heav'n, and from Eternal Splendors flung
For his revolt, yet faithful how they stood,
Thir Glory wither'd. As when Heaven's Fire
Hath scath'd the Forest Oaks, or Mountain Pines,
With singed top thir stately growth though bare
615   Stands on the blasted Heath. He now prepar'd
To speak; whereat thir doubl'd Ranks they bend
From wing to wing, and half enclose him round
With all his Peers: attention held them mute.
Thrice he assay'd, and thrice in spite of scorn,
620   Tears such as Angels weep, burst forth: at last
Words interwove with sighs found out thir way.
    O Myriads of immortal Spirits, O Powers
Matchless, but with th' Almighty, and that strife
Was not inglorious, though th' event° was dire,   *result*
625   As this place testifies, and this dire change
Hateful to utter: but what power of mind
Foreseeing or presaging, from the Depth
Of knowledge past or present, could have fear'd
How such united force of Gods, how such
630   As stood like these, could ever know repulse?
For who can yet believe, though after loss,
That all these puissant° Legions, whose exíle   *powerful*

8. The comparison is ironically double-edged, for the ominous solar eclipse presages not only disaster for creation but also the doom of the godlike ruler for whom the sun was a traditional symbol.

Hath emptied Heav'n, shall fail to re-ascend
Self-rais'd, and repossess thir native seat?
635   For mee be witness all the Host of Heav'n,
If counsels different, or danger shunn'd
By me, have lost our hopes. But he who reigns
Monarch in Heav'n, till then as one secure
Sat on his Throne, upheld by old repute,
640   Consent or custom, and his Regal State
Put forth at full, but still his strength conceal'd,
Which tempted our attempt, and wrought our fall.
Henceforth his might we know, and know our own
So as not either to provoke, or dread
645   New War, provok't; our better part remains
To work in close° design, by fraud or guile   *secret*
What force effected not: that he no less
At length from us may find, who overcomes
By force, hath overcome but half his foe.
650   Space may produce new Worlds; whereof so rife°   *common*
There went a fame° in Heav'n that he ere long   *rumor*
Intended to create, and therein plant
A generation, whom his choice regard
Should favor equal to the Sons of Heaven:
655   Thither, if but to pry, shall be perhaps
Our first eruption, thither or elsewhere:
For this Infernal Pit shall never hold
Celestial Spirits in Bondage, nor th' Abyss
Long under darkness cover. But these thoughts
660   Full Counsel must mature: Peace is despair'd,
For who can think Submission? War then, War
Open or understood, must be resolv'd.
        He spake: and to confirm his words, out-flew
Millions of flaming swords, drawn from the thighs
665   Of mighty Cherubim; the sudden blaze
Far round illumin'd hell: highly they rag'd
Against the Highest, and fierce with grasped Arms
Clash'd on thir sounding shields the din of war,
Hurling defiance toward the Vault of Heav'n.
670   There stood a Hill not far whose grisly top
Belch'd fire and rolling smoke; the rest entire
Shone with a glossy scurf, undoubted sign
That in his womb was hid metallic Ore,
The work of Sulphur.[9] Thither wing'd with speed
675   A numerous Brígad° hasten'd. As when bands   *brigade*
Of Píoners° with Spade and Pickax arm'd   *engineers*
Forerun the Royal Camp, to trench a Field,

---

9. The traditional physiognomy of the fiend is in Milton's hell displaced onto the landscape. It is a dead or corrupt body imaged as scurf (i.e., scales, crust), belching, ransacked womb, bowels, entrails, and ribs.

Or cast a Rampart. *Mammon*[1] led them on,
Mammon, the least erected° Spirit that fell   *elevated*
680　From Heav'n, for ev'n in Heav'n his looks and thoughts
Were always downward bent, admiring more
The riches of Heav'n's pavement, trodd'n Gold,
Than aught divine or holy else enjoy'd
In vision beatific: by him first
685　Men also, and by his suggestion taught,
Ransack'd the Center, and with impious hands
Rifl'd the bowels of thir mother Earth
For Treasures better hid. Soon had his crew
Op'n'd into the Hill a spacious wound
690　And digg'd out ribs of Gold. Let none admire°   *wonder*
That riches grow in Hell; that soil may best
Deserve the precious bane. And here let those
Who boast in mortal things, and wond'ring tell
Of *Babel*, and the works of *Memphian* Kings,[2]
695　Learn how thir greatest Monuments of Fame,
And Strength and Art are easily outdone
By Spirits reprobate, and in an hour
What in an age they with incessant toil
And hands innumerable scarce perform.
700　Nigh on the Plain in many cells prepar'd,
That underneath had veins of liquid fire
Sluic'd° from the Lake, a second multitude   *led by channels*
With wondrous Art founded the massy Ore,
Severing each kind, and scumm'd the Bullion dross:
705　A third as soon had form'd within the ground
A various mould, and from the boiling cells
By strange conveyance fill'd each hollow nook:
As in an Organ from one blast of wind
To many a row of Pipes the sound-board breathes.
710　Anon out of the earth a Fabric huge
Rose like an Exhalation,[3] with the sound
Of Dulcet Symphonies and voices sweet,
Built like a Temple, where *Pilasters*° round   *columns*
Were set, and Doric pillars overlaid
715　With Golden Architrave; nor did there want
Cornice or Frieze, with bossy° Sculptures grav'n;   *embossed*
The Roof was fretted° Gold. Not *Babylon*,[4]   *patterned*

1. In Matthew 6.24 and Luke 16.13, "Mammon" is an abstract noun meaning wealth, but later it was used as the name of "the prince of this world" (John 12.31). Medieval and Renaissance tradition often associated Mammon with Plutus, the Greek god of riches.
2. The Tower of Babel was built by the ambitious Nimrod. The works of Memphian kings, the Pyramids, were regarded as memorials of vanity.
3. Pandaemonium rises to music, since in the Renais-

sance it was believed that musical proportions governed the forms of architecture.
4. An ironic allusion to Ovid's description of the Palace of the Sun built by Mulciber (*Metamorphoses* 2.1–4). Pandaemonium has a classical design, complete in every respect, like that of the ancient (but still surviving) giltroofed Pantheon, the most admired building of Milton's time. Doric is the oldest and simplest order of Greek architecture.

Nor great *Alcairo* such magnificence
Equall'd in all thir glories,[5] to inshrine
720   *Belus*[6] or *Serapis*[7] thir Gods, or seat
Thir Kings, when *Egypt* with *Assyria* strove
In wealth and luxury. Th' ascending pile
Stood fixt her stately highth, and straight the doors
Op'ning thir brazen folds discover wide
725   Within, her ample spaces, o'er the smooth
And level pavement: from the arched roof
Pendant by subtle Magic many a row
Of Starry Lamps and blazing Cressets[8] fed
With *Naphtha* and *Asphaltus*[9] yielded light
730   As from a sky. The hasty multitude
Admiring enter'd, and the work some praise
And some the Architect: his hand was known
In Heav'n by many a Tow'red structure high,
Where Scepter'd Angels held thir residence,
735   And sat as Princes, whom the supreme King
Exalted to such power, and gave to rule,
Each in his Hierarchy, the Orders bright.
Nor was his name unheard or unador'd
In ancient *Greece*; and in *Ausonian* land
740   Men call'd him *Mulciber*;[1] and how he fell
From Heav'n, they fabl'd, thrown by angry *Jove*
Sheer o'er the Crystal Battlements: from Morn
To Noon he fell, from Noon to dewy Eve,
A Summer's day; and with the setting Sun
745   Dropt from the Zenith like a falling Star,
On *Lemnos* th' *Aegean* Isle:[2] thus they relate,
Erring; for he with this rebellious rout
Fell long before; nor aught avail'd him now
To have built in Heav'n high Tow'rs; nor did he scape
750   By all his Engines, but was headlong sent
With his industrious crew to build in hell.
Meanwhile the winged Heralds by command
Of Sovran power, with awful Ceremony
And Trumpets' sound throughout the Host proclaim
755   A solemn Council forthwith to be held
At *Pandaemonium*, the high Capitol

---

5. In traditional biblical exegesis, Babylon, a place of proud iniquity, was often a figure of Antichrist or of hell. Memphis (modern Cairo) was the most splendid city of Egypt.
6. Bel, the Babylonian Baal; see lines 421–23n and Jeremiah 51.44: "I will punish Bel in Babylon."
7. An Egyptian deity.
8. Basketlike lamps.
9. *Naphtha* is an oily constituent of asphalt (*asphaltus*).
1. The Greek god Hephaistos, in Latin *Mulciber* or Vulcan, presided over all arts, such as metal-working, that re-

quired the use of fire. He built all the palaces of the gods. "Ausonian land" is the old Greek name for Italy. Milton emulates Homer's description of the daylong fall of Hephaistos (*Iliad* 1.591–95) and then deflates it in the casual but commanding dismissal of 746–48.
2. In Homer (*Iliad* 2.87–90), the Achaians going to a council are compared to bees, as are the Carthaginians in Virgil (*Aeneid* 1.430–36). Milton also glances at Virgil's mock-epic account of the ideal social organization of the hive (*Georgics* 4.149–227).

Of Satan and his Peers: thir summons call'd
From every Band and squared Regiment
By place or choice the worthiest; they anon
760   With hunderds and with thousands trooping came
Attended: all access was throng'd, the Gates
And Porches wide, but chief the spacious Hall
(Though like a cover'd field, where Champions bold
Wont ride in arm'd, and at the Soldan's° chair   *Sultan's*
765   Defi'd the best of *Paynim*° chivalry   *pagan*
To mortal combat or career with Lance)
Thick swarm'd, both on the ground and in the air,
Brusht with the hiss of rustling wings. As Bees
In spring time, when the Sun with *Taurus*[3] rides,
770   Pour forth thir populous youth about the Hive
In clusters; they among fresh dews and flowers
Fly to and fro, or on the smoothed Plank,
The suburb of thir Straw-built Citadel,
New rubb'd with Balm, expatiate° and confer   *debate*
775   Thir State affairs. So thick the aery crowd
Swarm'd and were strait'n'd; till the Signal giv'n,
Behold a wonder! they but now who seem'd
In bigness to surpass Earth's Giant Sons
Now less than smallest Dwarfs, in narrow room
780   Throng numberless, like that Pigmean Race
Beyond the *Indian* Mount, or Faery Elves,
Whose midnight Revels, by a Forest side
Or Fountain some belated Peasant sees,
Or dreams he sees, while over-head the Moon
785   Sits Arbitress, and nearer to the Earth
Wheels her pale course;[4] they on thir mirth and dance
Intent, with jocund Music charm his ear;
At once with joy and fear his heart rebounds.
Thus incorporeal Spirits to smallest forms
790   Reduc'd thir shapes immense, and were at large,
Though without number still amidst the Hall
Of that infernal Court. But far within
And in thir own dimensions like themselves
The great Seraphic Lords and Cherubim
795   In close° recess and secret conclave[5] sat   *secret*
A thousand Demi-Gods on golden seats,
Frequent° and full. After short silence then   *crowded*
And summons read, the great consult began.
             The End of the First Book.

---

3. In Milton's time the sun entered the second sign of the
zodiac in mid-April, according to the Julian calendar.
4. Echoing *A Midsummer Night's Dream* 2.1.28f and 141.
"The moon / Sits arbitress" because the moon-goddess

was queen of faery.
5. "Conclave" could refer to any assembly in secret session but already had the specifically ecclesiastical meaning on which Milton's satire here depends.

Book 2
The Argument

The Consultation begun, Satan debates whether another Battle be to be hazarded for the recovery of Heaven: some advise it, others dissuade: A third proposal is preferr'd, mention'd before by Satan, to search the truth of that Prophecy or Tradition in Heaven concerning another world, and another kind of creature equal or not much inferior to themselves, about this time to be created: Thir doubt who shall be sent on this difficult search: Satan thir chief undertakes alone the voyage, is honor'd and applauded. The Council thus ended, the rest betake them several ways and to several employments, as thir inclinations lead them, to entertain the time till Satan return. He passes on his Journey to Hell Gates, finds them shut, and who sat there to guard them, by whom at length they are op'n'd, and discover[1] to him the great Gulf between Hell and Heaven; with what difficulty he passes through, directed by Chaos, the Power of that place, to the sight of this new World which he sought.

     High on a Throne of Royal State,[2] which far
     Outshone the wealth of *Ormus* and of *Ind*,[3]
     Or where the gorgeous East with richest hand
     Show'rs on her Kings *Barbaric* Pearl and Gold,
5   Satan exalted sat, by merit rais'd
     To that bad eminence; and from despair
     Thus high uplifted beyond hope, aspires
     Beyond thus high, insatiate to pursue
     Vain War with Heav'n, and by success° untaught   *result*
10   His proud imaginations thus display'd.
     Powers and Dominions,[4] Deities of Heav'n,
     For since no deep within her gulf can hold
     Immortal vigor, though opprest and fall'n,
     I give not Heav'n for lost. From this descent
15   Celestial Virtues rising, will appear
     More glorious and more dread than from no fall
     And trust themselves to fear no second fate:
     Mee though just right and the fixt Laws of Heav'n
     Did first create your Leader, next, free choice,
20   With what besides, in Counsel or in Fight,
     Hath been achiev'd of merit, yet this loss
     Thus far at least recover'd, hath much more
     Establisht in a safe unenvied Throne
     Yielded with full consent. The happier state
25   In Heav'n, which follows dignity, might draw
     Envy from each inferior; but who here
     Will envy whom the highest place exposes
     Foremost to stand against the Thunderer's aim[5]
     Your bulwark, and condemns to greatest share

1. Disclose.
2. Compare Spenser's description of the bright throne of the Phaethon-like Lucifera, embodiment of pride in *The Faerie Queene* 1.4.8.
3. India. Ormus, an island town in the Persian Gulf, was famous as a jewel market.
4. Two angelic orders mentioned by St. Paul in Colossians 1.16.
5. By identifying him with thunder, the attribute of Jupiter, Satan reduces God to a mere Olympian tyrant.

30 Of endless pain? where there is then no good
    For which to strive, no strife can grow up there
    From Faction; for none sure will claim in Hell
    Precedence, none, whose portion is so small
    Of present pain, that with ambitious mind
35 Will covet more. With this advantage then
    To union, and firm Faith, and firm accord,
    More than can be in Heav'n, we now return
    To claim our just inheritance of old,
    Surer to prosper than prosperity
40 Could have assur'd us; and by what best way,
    Whether of open War or covert guile,
    We now debate; who can advise, may speak.
         He ceas'd, and next him *Moloch*, Scepter'd King
    Stood up, the strongest and the fiercest Spirit
45 That fought in Heav'n; now fiercer by despair:
    His trust was with th' Eternal to be deem'd
    Equal in strength, and rather than be less
    Car'd not to be at all; with that care lost
    Went all his fear: of God, or Hell, or worse
50 He reck'd° not, and these words thereafter spake.   *cared*
         My sentence° is for open War: Of Wiles,   *opinion*
    More unexpert,° I boast not: them let those   *inexperienced*
    Contrive who need, or when they need, not now.
    For while they sit contriving, shall the rest,
55 Millions that stand in Arms, and longing wait
    The Signal to ascend, sit ling'ring here
    Heav'n's fugitives, and for thir dwelling place
    Accept this dark opprobrious Den of shame,
    The Prison of his Tyranny who Reigns
60 By our delay? no, let us rather choose
    Arm'd with Hell flames and fury[6] all at once
    O'er Heav'n's high Tow'rs to force resistless way,
    Turning our Tortures into horrid Arms
    Against the Torturer; when to meet the noise
65 Of his Almighty Engine[7] he shall hear
    Infernal Thunder, and for Lightning see
    Black fire and horror shot with equal rage
    Among his Angels; and his Throne itself
    Mixt with *Tartarean* Sulphur, and strange fire,[8]
70 His own invented Torments. But perhaps
    The way seems difficult and steep to scale
    With upright wing against a higher foe.

---

6. The violent yoking of concrete and abstract words is one of the most characteristic figures of Milton's style.
7. Machine of war, probably here referring to the Messiah's chariot or perhaps to his thunder.
8. In the classical underworld, Tartarus was the place of the guilty. For "strange fire," see Leviticus 10.1–2: "Nadab and Abihu, the sons of Aaron . . . offered strange fire before the Lord, which he commanded them not. And there went out fire from the Lord, and devoured them."

Let such bethink them, if the sleepy drench[9]
Of that forgetful Lake benumb not still,
75   That in our proper motion we ascend
Up to our native seat: descent and fall
To us is adverse. Who but felt of late
When the fierce Foe hung on our brok'n Rear
Insulting,° and pursu'd us through the Deep,   assaulting, exulting
80   With what compulsion and laborious flight
We sunk thus low? Th' ascent is easy then;
Th' event° is fear'd; should we again provoke   outcome
Our stronger, some worse way his wrath may find
To our destruction: if there be in Hell
85   Fear to be worse destroy'd: what can be worse
Than to dwell here, driv'n out from bliss, condemn'd
In this abhorred deep to utter woe;
Where pain of unextinguishable fire
Must exercise° us without hope of end   afflict
90   The Vassals[1] of his anger, when the Scourge
Inexorably, and the torturing hour
Calls us to Penance? More destroy'd than thus
We should be quite abolisht and expire.
What fear we then? what doubt we to incense
95   His utmost ire? which to the highth enrag'd,
Will either quite consume us, and reduce
To nothing this essential,° happier far   essence
Than miserable to have eternal being:
Or if our substance be indeed Divine,
100 And cannot cease to be, we are at worst
On this side nothing;[2] and by proof we feel
Our power sufficient to disturb his Heav'n,
And with perpetual inroads to Alarm,
Though inaccessible, his fatal Throne:
105 Which if not Victory is yet Revenge.
      He ended frowning, and his look denounc'd
Desperate revenge, and Battle dangerous
To less than Gods. On th' other side up rose
Belial, in act more graceful and humane;
110 A fairer person lost not Heav'n; he seem'd
For dignity compos'd and high exploit:
But all was false and hollow; though his Tongue
Dropt Manna, and could make the worse appear
The better reason,[3] to perplex and dash
115 Maturest Counsels: for his thoughts were low;

9. A draught of medicine for an animal.
1. Servants, slaves. Also an allusion to Romans 9.22: "What if God, willing to show his wrath, and to make his power known, endured with much longsuffering the vessels of wrath fitted to destruction . . . ?"

2. Already we are in the worst condition possible, short of being nothing, being annihilated.
3. This was the claim of the Greek Sophists, who taught their students how to use rhetoric to win an argument.

To vice industrious, but to Nobler deeds
Timorous and slothful: yet he pleas'd the ear,
And with persuasive accent thus began.
        I should be much for open War, O Peers,
120   As not behind in hate; if what was urg'd
Main reason to persuade immediate War,
Did not dissuade me most, and seem to cast
Ominous conjecture on the whole success:
When he who most excels in fact° of Arms,   *feat*
125   In what he counsels and in what excels
Mistrustful, grounds his courage on despair
And utter dissolution, as the scope
Of all his aim, after some dire revenge.
First, what Revenge? the Tow'rs of Heav'n are fill'd
130   With Armed watch, that render all access
Impregnable; oft on the bordering Deep
Encamp thir Legions, or with obscure⁴ wing
Scout far and wide into the Realm of night,
Scorning surprise. Or could we break our way
135   By force, and at our heels all Hell should rise
With blackest Insurrection, to confound
Heav'n's purest Light, yet our great Enemy
All incorruptible would on his Throne
Sit unpolluted, and th' Ethereal mould
140   Incapable of stain would soon expel
Her mischief, and purge off the baser fire
Victorious.⁵ Thus repuls'd, our final hope
Is flat° despair: we must exasperate   *absolute*
Th' Almighty Victor to spend all his rage,
145   And that must end us, that must be our cure,
To be no more; sad cure; for who would lose,
Though full of pain, this intellectual being,
Those thoughts that wander through Eternity,
To perish rather, swallow'd up and lost
150   In the wide womb of uncreated night,
Devoid of sense and motion? and who knows,
Let this be good,⁶ whether our angry Foe
Can give it, or will ever? how he can
Is doubtful; that he never will is sure.
155   Will he, so wise, let loose at once his ire,
Belike° through impotence, or unaware,   *no doubt*
To give his Enemies thir wish, and end
Them in his anger, whom his anger saves
To punish endless? wherefore cease we then?

---

4. "Obscure" is stressed on the first syllable here.
5. Criticizing Moloch's proposal to mix God's throne with sulphur (lines 68–9) and shoot "black fire" among his angels. This "baser fire" Belial contrasts with the "ethereal" (derived from ether, the fifth and purest element) fire of the throne.
6. Suppose it is good to be destroyed.

160 Say they who counsel War, we are decreed,
   Reserv'd and destin'd to Eternal woe;
   Whatever doing, what can we suffer more,
   What can we suffer worse? is this then worst,
   Thus sitting, thus consulting, thus in Arms?
165 What when we fled amain,° pursu'd and strook°   *headlong / struck*
   With Heav'n's afflicting Thunder, and besought
   The Deep to shelter us? this Hell then seem'd
   A refuge from those wounds: or when we lay
   Chain'd on the burning Lake? that sure was worse.
170 What if the breath that kindl'd those grim fires
   Awak'd should blow them into sevenfold rage
   And plunge us in the flames? or from above
   Should intermitted vengeance arm again
   His red right hand to plague us? what if all
175 Her° stores were op'n'd, and this Firmament   *Hell's*
   Of Hell should spout her Cataracts of Fire,
   Impendent° horrors, threat'ning hideous fall   *threatening*
   One day upon our heads; while we perhaps
   Designing or exhorting glorious war,
180 Caught in a fiery Tempest shall be hurl'd
   Each on his rock transfixt, the sport and prey
   Of racking whirlwinds, or for ever sunk
   Under yon boiling Ocean, wrapt in Chains;
   There to converse with everlasting groans,
185 Unrespited, unpitied, unrepriev'd,
   Ages of hopeless end; this would be worse.
   War therefore, open or conceal'd, alike
   My voice dissuades; for what can force or guile
   With him, or who deceive his mind, whose eye
190 Views all things at one view? he from Heav'n's highth
   All these our motions° vain, sees and derides;   *schemes*
   Not more Almighty to resist our might
   Than wise to frustrate all our plots and wiles.
   Shall we then live thus vile, the race of Heav'n
195 Thus trampl'd, thus expell'd to suffer here
   Chains and these Torments? better these than worse
   By my advice; since fate inevitable
   Subdues us, and Omnipotent Decree,
   The Victor's will. To suffer, as to do,
200 Our strength is equal, nor the Law unjust
   That so ordains: this was at first resolv'd,
   If we were wise, against so great a foe
   Contending, and so doubtful what might fall.
   I laugh, when those who at the Spear are bold
205 And vent'rous, if that fail them, shrink and fear
   What yet they know must follow, to endure
   Exile, or ignominy, or bonds, or pain,
   The sentence of thir Conqueror: This is now

Our doom; which if we can sustain and bear,
210 Our Supreme Foe in time may much remit
His anger, and perhaps thus far remov'd
Not mind us not offending, satisfi'd
With what is punisht; whence these raging fires
Will slack'n, if his breath stir not thir flames.
215 Our purer essence then will overcome
Thir noxious vapor, or enur'd° not feel,   *accustomed*
Or chang'd at length, and to the place conform'd
In temper[7] and in nature, will receive
Familiar the fierce heat, and void of pain;
220 This horror will grow mild, this darkness light,[8]
Besides what hope the never-ending flight
Of future days may bring, what chance, what change
Worth waiting, since our present lot appears
For happy though but ill, for ill not worst,[9]
225 If we procure not to ourselves more woe.
      Thus *Belial* with words cloth'd in reason's garb
Counsell'd ignoble ease, and peaceful sloth,
Not peace: and after him thus *Mammon* spake.
      Either to disinthrone the King of Heav'n
230 We war, if war be best, or to regain
Our own right lost: him to unthrone we then
May hope, when everlasting Fate shall yield
To fickle Chance, and *Chaos* judge the strife:
The former vain to hope argues as vain
235 The latter: for what place can be for us
Within Heav'n's bound, unless Heav'n's Lord supreme
We overpower? Suppose he should relent
And publish Grace to all, on promise made
Of new Subjection; with what eyes could we
240 Stand in his presence humble, and receive
Strict Laws impos'd, to celebrate his Throne
With warbl'd Hymns, and to his Godhead sing
Forc't Halleluiahs[1] while he Lordly sits
Our envied Sovran, and his Altar breathes
245 Ambrosial[2] Odors and Ambrosial Flowers,
Our servile offerings. This must be our task
In Heav'n, this our delight; how wearisome
Eternity so spent in worship paid
To whom we hate. Let us not then pursue
250 By force impossible, by leave obtain'd
Unácceptable, though in Heav'n, our state

7. Temperament, the mixture or adjustment of humors. Thus the phrase means "adjusted psychologically and physically to the new environment."
8. Easy to bear, and illumination.
9. Though as far as happiness is concerned, the devils are but ill off, as far as evil is concerned, they could be worse.

1. The word "hallelujah" (Hebrew, "praise Jehovah") occurred in so many psalms that it came to mean a song of praise to God.
2. Fragrant and perfumed, immortal. Ambrosia was the fabled food or drink of the gods.

Of splendid vassalage, but rather seek
Our own good from ourselves, and from our own
Live to ourselves, though in this vast recess,
255   Free, and to none accountable, preferring
Hard liberty before the easy yoke
Of servile Pomp.[3] Our greatness will appear
Then most conspicuous, when great things of small,
Useful of hurtful, prosperous of adverse
260   We can create, and in what place soe'er
Thrive under evil, and work ease out of pain
Through labor and endurance. This deep world
Of darkness do we dread? How oft amidst
Thick clouds and dark doth Heav'n's all-ruling Sire
265   Choose to reside, his Glory unobscur'd,
And with the Majesty of darkness round
Covers his Throne; from whence deep thunders roar
Must'ring thir rage, and Heav'n resembles Hell?
As he our darkness, cannot we his Light
270   Imitate when we please? This Desert soil
Wants not her hidden lustre, Gems and Gold;
Nor want we skill or art, from whence to raise
Magnificence; and what can Heav'n show more?
Our torments also may in length of time
275   Become our Elements, these piercing Fires
As soft as now severe, our temper chang'd
Into their temper;[4] which must needs remove
The sensible of pain.[5] All things invite
To peaceful Counsels, and the settl'd State
280   Of order, how in safety best we may
Compose° our present evils, with regard   order
Of what we are and where, dismissing quite
All thoughts of War; ye have what I advise.
    He scarce had finisht, when such murmur fill'd
285   Th' Assembly, as when hollow Rocks retain
The sound of blust'ring winds, which all night long
Had rous'd the Sea, now with hoarse cadence lull
Sea-faring men o'erwatcht, whose Bark by chance
Or Pinnace anchors in a craggy Bay
290   After the Tempest: Such applause was heard
As *Mammon* ended, and his Sentence° pleas'd,   opinion
Advising peace: for such another Field
They dreaded worse than Hell: so much the fear
Of Thunder and the Sword of *Michaël*[6]

---

3. In *Samson Agonistes* 271, Samson condemns those who are fonder of "bondage with ease than strenuous liberty." The antithesis is from the Roman historian, Sallust, who assigns it to an opponent of the dictator Sulla. See also Jesus' words in Matthew 11.28–30: "Come unto me. . . . For my yoke is easy."
4. Milton alludes to an idea of St. Augustine's, that the

devils are bound to tormenting fires as if to bodies (*City of God*, 21.10).
5. The part of pain apprehended through the senses.
6. In the war in Heaven, Michael's two-handed sword felled "squadrons at once" and wounded even Satan. "Michael" here has three syllables.

295   Wrought still within them; and no less desire
       To found this nether Empire, which might rise
       By policy,[7] and long process of time,
       In emulation opposite to Heav'n.
       Which when *Beëlzebub*[8] perceiv'd, than whom,
300   *Satan* except, none higher sat, with grave
       Aspect he rose, and in his rising seem'd
       A Pillar of State; deep on his Front° engraven   *forehead*
       Deliberation sat and public care;
       And Princely counsel in his face yet shone,
305   Majestic though in ruin: sage he stood
       With *Atlantean*[9] shoulders fit to bear
       The weight of mightiest Monarchies; his look
       Drew audience and attention still as Night
       Or Summer's Noon-tide air, while thus he spake.
310   Thrones and Imperial Powers, off-spring of Heav'n,
       Ethereal Virtues; or these Titles now
       Must we renounce, and changing style be call'd
       Princes of Hell? for so the popular vote
       Inclines, here to continue, and build up here
315   A growing Empire; doubtless; while we dream,
       And know not that the King of Heav'n hath doom'd
       This place our dungeon, not our safe retreat
       Beyond his Potent arm, to live exempt
       From Heav'n's high jurisdiction, in new League
320   Banded against his Throne, but to remain
       In strictest bondage, though thus far remov'd,
       Under th' inevitable curb, reserv'd
       His captive multitude: For he, be sure,
       In highth or depth, still first and last will Reign
325   Sole King, and of his Kingdom lose no part
       By our revolt, but over Hell extend
       His Empire, and with Iron Sceptre rule
       Us here, as with his Golden those in Heav'n.
       What° sit we then projecting peace and war?   *why*
330   War hath determin'd[1] us, and foil'd with loss
       Irreparable; terms of peace yet none
       Voutsaf't[2] or sought; for what peace will be giv'n
       To us enslav'd, but custody severe,
       And stripes, and arbitrary punishment
335   Inflicted? and what peace can we return,
       But to our power[3] hostility and hate,
       Untam'd reluctance,° and revenge though slow,   *resistance*

7. Statesmanship, often in a bad sense, implying Machiavellian strategems. "Process" is stressed on the second syllable.
8. Satan's closest associate.
9. Worthy of Atlas, who was forced by Jupiter to carry the heavens on his shoulders as a punishment for his part in the rebellion of the Titans.
1. Finished, but the context also activates a subsidiary meaning, "war has given us a settled aim."
2. "Vouchsafed": granted; Milton's spelling, "Voutsaf't," indicates the 17th-century pronunciation he preferred.
3. To the limit of our power.

Yet ever plotting how the Conqueror least
May reap his conquest, and may least rejoice
340   In doing what we most in suffering feel?[4]
Nor will occasion want, nor shall we need
With dangerous expedition to invade
Heav'n, whose high walls fear no assault or Siege,
Or ambush from the Deep. What if we find
345   Some easier enterprise? There is a place
(If ancient and prophetic fame in Heav'n
Err not) another World, the happy seat
Of some new Race call'd *Man*, about this time
To be created like to us, though less
350   In power and excellence, but favor'd more
Of him who rules above;[5] so was his will
Pronounc'd among the Gods, and by an Oath,
That shook Heav'n's whole circumference, confirm'd.[6]
Thither let us bend all our thoughts, to learn
355   What creatures there inhabit, of what mould,
Or substance, how endu'd,° and what thir Power,   *gifted*
And where thir weakness, how attempted° best,   *attacked*
By force or subtlety: Though Heav'n be shut,
And Heav'n's high Arbitrator sit secure
360   In his own strength, this place may lie expos'd
The utmost border of his Kingdom, left
To their defense who hold it: here perhaps
Some advantageous act may be achiev'd
By sudden onset, either with Hell fire
365   To waste his whole Creation, or possess
All as our own, and drive as we were driven,
The puny° habitants, or if not drive,   *weak*
Seduce them to our Party, that thir God
May prove thir foe, and with repenting hand
370   Abolish his own works. This would surpass
Common revenge, and interrupt his joy
In our Confusion, and our Joy upraise
In his disturbance; when his darling Sons
Hurl'd headlong to partake with us,[7] shall curse
375   Thir frail Original,° and faded bliss,   *author*
Faded so soon. Advise if this be worth
Attempting, or to sit in darkness here
Hatching vain Empires. Thus *Beëlzebub*
Pleaded his devilish Counsel, first devis'd
380   By *Satan*, and in part propos'd: for whence,

4. How God may get the least happiness from our pain. Beelzebub portrays God as similar in his motives to the devils.
5. The creation of humanity was the subject of a public oath by God, but the time of the creation was the subject of a rumor only ("it is not for you to know the times or season," Acts 1.7).
6. See Isaiah 13.12–13: "I will make a man more precious than fine gold. . . . Therefore I will shake the Heavens."
7. Share in our condition; also, take sides with us.

But from the Author of all ill could Spring
So deep a malice, to confound the race
Of mankind in one root,[8] and Earth with Hell
To mingle and involve, done all to spite
385 The great Creator? But thir spite still serves
His glory to augment. The bold design
Pleas'd highly those infernal States,[9] and joy
Sparkl'd in all thir eyes; with full assent
They vote: whereat his speech he thus renews.
390   Well have ye judg'd, well ended long debate,
Synod[1] of Gods, and like to what ye are,
Great things resolv'd, which from the lowest deep
Will once more lift us up, in spite of Fate,
Nearer our ancient Seat; perhaps in view
395 Of those bright confines, whence with neighboring Arms
And opportune excursion we may chance
Re-enter Heav'n; or else in some mild Zone
Dwell not unvisited of Heav'n's fair Light
Secure, and at the bright'ning Orient beam
400 Purge off this gloom; the soft delicious Air,
To heal the scar of these corrosive Fires
Shall breathe her balm. But first whom shall we send
In search of this new world, whom shall we find
Sufficient? who shall tempt° with wand'ring feet   venture upon
405 The dark unbottom'd infinite Abyss
And through the palpable obscure[2] find out
His uncouth° way, or spread his aery flight   unknown
Upborne with indefatigable wings
Over the vast abrupt,[3] ere he arrive
410 The happy Isle; what strength, what art can then
Suffice, or what evasion bear him safe
Through the strict Senteries° and Stations thick   sentries
Of Angels watching round? Here he had need
All circumspection, and wee now no less
415 Choice in our suffrage;[4] for on whom we send,
The weight of all and our last hope relies.
This said, he sat; and expectation held
His look suspense, awaiting who appear'd
To second, or oppose, or undertake
420 The perilous attempt; but all sat mute,
Pondering the danger with deep thoughts; and each
In other's count'nance read his own dismay
Astonisht: none among the choice and prime

8. Adam, the root of the genealogical tree of man.
9. Estates of the realm, people of rank and authority.
1. A meeting of councillors.
2. See Exodus 10.21: "The Lord said unto Moses, Stretch
out thine hand toward heaven, that there may be darkness

over the land of Egypt, even darkness which may be felt."
3. The adjective (precipitous, broken off) is here used as a
noun and refers to the abyss between hell and heaven.
4. Care in our vote (to elect him).

Of those Heav'n-warring Champions could be found
425　So hardy as to proffer° or accept　　　　　　　　　　　　*offer*
Alone the dreadful voyage; till at last
Satan, whom now transcendent glory rais'd
Above his fellows, with Monarchal pride
Conscious of highest worth, unmov'd thus spake.
430　　O Progeny of Heav'n, Empyreal Thrones,
With reason hath deep silence and demur°　　　　　　　　　*delay*
Seiz'd us, though undismay'd: long is the way
And hard, that out of Hell leads up to light;
Our prison strong, this huge convex° of Fire,　　　　　　　*vault*
435　Outrageous to devour, immures us round
Ninefold, and gates of burning Adamant
Barr'd over us prohibit all egress.
These past, if any pass, the void profound
Of unessential° Night receives him next　　　　　　　　　　*empty*
440　Wide gaping, and with utter loss of being
Threatens him, plung'd in that abortive gulf.
If thence he scape into whatever world,
Or unknown Region, what remains him less
Than⁵ unknown dangers and as hard escape.
445　But I should ill become this Throne, O Peers,
And this Imperial Sov'ranty, adorn'd
With splendor, arm'd with power, if aught propos'd
And judg'd of public moment, in the shape
Of difficulty or danger could deter
450　Mee from attempting. Wherefore do I assume
These Royalties, and not refuse to Reign,
Refusing⁶ to accept as great a share
Of hazard as of honor, due alike
To him who Reigns, and so much to him due
455　Of hazard more, as he above the rest
High honor'd sits? Go therefore mighty Powers.
Terror of Heav'n, though fall'n; intend° at home,　　　　　*consider*
While here shall be our home, what best may ease
The present misery, and render Hell
460　More tolerable; if there be cure or charm
To respite° or deceive, or slack the pain　　　　　　　　　　*rest*
Of this ill Mansion: intermit no watch
Against a wakeful Foe, while I abroad
Through all the Coasts of dark destruction seek
465　Deliverance for us all: this enterprise
None shall partake with me. Thus saying rose
The Monarch, and prevented all reply,
Prudent, lest from his resolution rais'd°　　　　　　　　　*encouraged*
Others among the chief might offer now

5. What awaits him except.　　　　　　6. If I refuse.

470   (Certain to be refus'd) what erst they fear'd;
     And so refus'd might in opinion stand
     His Rivals, winning cheap the high repute
     Which he through hazard huge must earn. But they
     Dreaded not more th' adventure than his voice
475   Forbidding; and at once with him they rose;
     Thir rising all at once was as the sound
     Of Thunder heard remote. Towards him they bend
     With awful° reverence prone; and as a God   *respectful*
     Extol him equal to the highest in Heav'n:
480   Nor fail'd they to express how much they prais'd,
     That for the general safety he despis'd
     His own: for neither do the Spirits damn'd
     Lose all thir virtue; lest bad men should boast[7]
     Thir specious° deeds on earth, which glory excites,   *pretending*
485   Or close° ambition varnisht o'er with zeal.   *secret*
     Thus they thir doubtful consultations dark
     Ended rejoicing in their matchless Chief:
     As when from mountain tops the dusky clouds
     Ascending, while the North wind sleeps, o'erspread
490   Heav'n's cheerful face, the low'ring Element
     Scowls o'er the dark'n'd lantskip° Snow, or show'r;   *landscape*
     If chance the radiant Sun with farewell sweet
     Extend his ev'ning beam, the fields revive,
     The birds thir notes renew, and bleating herds
495   Attest thir joy, that hill and valley rings.
     O shame to men! Devil with Devil damn'd
     Firm concord holds, men only disagree
     Of Creatures rational, though under hope
     Of heavenly Grace; and God proclaiming peace,
500   Yet live in hatred, enmity, and strife
     Among themselves, and levy cruel wars,
     Wasting the Earth, each other to destroy:
     As if (which might induce us to accord)
     Man had not hellish foes anow° besides,   *enough*
505   That day and night for his destruction wait.
        The *Stygian* Council thus dissolv'd; and forth
     In order came the grand infernal Peers:
     Midst came thir mighty Paramount,° and seem'd   *ruler*
     Alone th' Antagonist of Heav'n, nor less
510   Than Hell's dread Emperor with pomp Supreme,[8]
     And God-like imitated State; him round
     A Globe° of fiery Seraphim inclos'd   *band*
     With bright imblazonry,° and horrent° Arms.   *heraldry / bristling*
     Then of thir Session ended they bid cry
515   With Trumpet's regal sound the great result:

---

7. So that men ought not to boast.
8. Lines 510–20 may portray the English mob's easy gullibility and their passion (which Milton detested) for the
regalia of monarchy.

Toward the four winds four speedy Cherubim
Put to thir mouths the sounding Alchymy[9]
By Herald's voice explain'd: the hollow Abyss
Heard far and wide, and all the host of Hell
520   With deaf'ning shout, return'd them loud acclaim.
Thence more at ease thir minds and somewhat rais'd°   *encouraged*
By false presumptuous hope, the ranged powers[1]
Disband, and wand'ring, each his several way
Pursues, as inclination or sad choice
525   Leads him perplext, where he may likeliest find
Truce to his restless thoughts, and entertain
The irksome hours, till this great Chief return.
Part on the Plain, or in the Air sublime°   *uplifted*
Upon the wing, or in swift Race contend,
530   As at th' *Olympian* Games or *Pythian* fields;[2]
Part curb thir fiery Steeds, or shun the Goal
With rapid wheels, or fronted Brígads form.
As when to warn proud Cities war appears
Wag'd in the troubl'd Sky, and Armies rush
535   To Battle in the Clouds, before each Van
Prick forth the Aery Knights, and couch thir spears
Till thickest Legions close; with feats of Arms
From either end of Heav'n the welkin° burns.   *sky*
Others with vast *Typhoean*[3] rage more fell
540   Rend up both Rocks and Hills, and ride the Air
In whirlwind; Hell scarce holds the wild uproar.
As when *Alcides* from *Oechalia* Crown'd
With conquest, felt th' envenom'd robe, and tore
Through pain up by the roots *Thessalian* Pines,
545   And *Lichas* from the top of *Oeta* threw
Into th' *Euboic* Sea.[4] Others more mild,
Retreated in a silent valley, sing
With notes Angelical to many a Harp
Thir own Heroic deeds and hapless fall
550   By doom of Battle; and complain that Fate
Free Virtue should enthrall to Force or Chance.
Thir Song was partial,° but the harmony   *prejudiced*
(What could it less when Spirits immortal sing?)
Suspended° Hell, and took with ravishment   *enthralled*
555   The thronging audience. In discourse more sweet

---

9. Trumpets made of the alloy brass, associated with alchemy.
1. Armies drawn up in ranks.
2. Epic models for lines 528–69 include the sports of the Myrmidons during Achilles' absence from the war (Homer, *Iliad* 2.774ff.), the Greek funeral games of *Iliad* 23 and the Trojan of *Aeneid* 5, and the amusements of the blessed dead in Virgil's Elysium (*Aeneid* 6.642–59). To "shun the goal" (line 531) is to drive a chariot as close as possible around a post without touching it.

3. Like that of Typhon, the hundred-headed Titan. A pun, for "typhon" was also an English word meaning "whirlwind."
4. "Alcides" (Hercules) returning as victor from "Oechalia" (Ovid, *Metamorphoses* 9.136) put on a ritual robe that had inadvertently been soaked by his wife in corrosive poison. Mad with pain, he blamed his friend Lichas, who had brought the robe, and hurled him far into the "Euboic" (Euboean) Sea.

(For Eloquence the Soul, Song charms the Sense,)
Others apart sat on a Hill retir'd,
In thoughts more elevate, and reason'd high
Of Providence, Foreknowledge, Will, and Fate,

560   Fixt Fate, Free will, Foreknowledge absolute,
And found no end, in wand'ring mazes lost.
Of good and evil much they argu'd then,
Of happiness and final misery,
Passion and Apathy, and glory and shame,

565   Vain wisdom all, and false Philosophie:[5]
Yet with a pleasing sorcery could charm
Pain for a while or anguish, and excite
Fallacious hope, or arm th' obdured° breast   *hardened*
With stubborn patience as with triple steel.

570   Another part in Squadrons and gross° Bands,   *dense*
On bold adventure to discover wide
That dismal World, if any Clime perhaps
Might yield them easier habitation, bend
Four ways thir flying March, along the Banks

575   Of four infernal Rivers that disgorge
Into the burning Lake thir baleful° streams;[6]   *evil*
Abhorred *Styx* the flood of deadly hate,
Sad *Acheron* of sorrow, black and deep;
Cocytus, nam'd of lamentation loud

580   Heard on the rueful stream; fierce *Phlegeton*
Whose waves of torrent fire inflame with rage.
Far off from these a slow and silent stream,
Lethe the River of Oblivion rolls
Her wat'ry Labyrinth, whereof who drinks,

585   Forthwith his former state and being forgets,
Forgets both joy and grief, pleasure and pain.
Beyond this flood a frozen Continent
Lies dark and wild, beat with perpetual storms
Of Whirlwind and dire Hail, which on firm land

590   Thaws not, but gathers heap, and ruin seems
Of ancient pile; all else deep snow and ice,
A gulf profound as that *Serbonian* Bog[7]
Betwixt *Damiata* and Mount *Casius* old,
Where Armies whole have sunk: the parching° Air   *withering*

595   Burns frore,° and cold performs th' effect of Fire.   *frozen*
Thither by harpy-footed Furies hal'd,[8]
At certain revolutions all the damn'd

5. Directed against Stoicism, the most formidable ethical challenge to Christianity; "apathy," or complete freedom from passion, was a Stoic ideal.
6. This description of the four rivers of hell takes its broad outline from Virgil's *Aeneid* 6, Dante's *Inferno* 14, and Spenser's *Faerie Queene* 2.7.56ff. Milton adds the detail of confluence in the "burning lake." The epithet or descrip-

tion attached to each river translates its Greek name (e.g., "Styx" means hateful).
7. Serbonis, a lake bordered by quicksands on the Egyptian coast.
8. Milton combines the hook-clawed Harpies of Dante and Virgil with the ancient Greek Furies, daughters of Acheron and Night and agencies of divine vengeance.

Are brought: and feel by turns the bitter change
Of fierce extremes, extremes by change more fierce,
600   From Beds of raging Fire to starve° in Ice   stifle
Thir soft Ethereal warmth, and there to pine
Immovable, infixt, and frozen round,
Periods of time, thence hurried back to fire.
They ferry over this *Lethean* Sound
605   Both to and fro, thir sorrow to augment,
And wish and struggle, as they pass, to reach
The tempting stream, with one small drop to lose
In sweet forgetfulness all pain and woe,
All in one moment, and so near the brink;
610   But Fate withstands, and to oppose th' attempt
Medusa[9] with *Gorgonian* terror guards
The Ford, and of itself the water flies
All taste of living wight, as once it fled
The lip of *Tantalus*.[1] Thus roving on
615   In confus'd march forlorn, th' advent'rous Bands
With shudd'ring horror pale, and eyes aghast
View'd first thir lamentable lot, and found
No rest: through many a dark and dreary Vale
They pass'd, and many a Region dolorous,
620   O'er many a Frozen, many a Fiery Alp,
Rocks, Caves, Lakes, Fens, Bogs, Dens, and shades of death,
A Universe of death, which God by curse
Created evil, for evil only good,
Where all life dies, death lives, and Nature breeds,
625   Perverse, all monstrous, all prodigious things,
Abominable, inutterable, and worse
Than Fables yet have feign'd, or fear conceiv'd,
Gorgons and *Hydras*, and *Chimeras* dire.[2]
       Meanwhile the Adversary of God and Man,
630   *Satan* with thoughts inflam'd of highest design,
Puts on swift wings, and towards the Gates of Hell
Explores his solitary flight; sometimes
He scours the right hand coast, sometimes the left,
Now shaves with level wing the Deep, then soars
635   Up to the fiery concave tow'ring high.
As when far off at Sea a Fleet descri'd
Hangs in the Clouds, by *Equinoctial* Winds
Close sailing from *Bengala*, or the Isles
Of *Ternate* and *Tidore*, whence Merchants bring
640   Thir spicy Drugs:[3] they on the Trading Flood

---

9. One of the Gorgons, mythical sisters with snakes for
hair, whose look turned the beholder into stone.
1. In Homer's hell, Tantalus is tormented by thirst, standing in a pool that recedes whenever he tries to drink
(*Odyssey* 11.582–92).
2. The Hydra was many-headed, and the Chimeras

breathed flame.
3. In Milton's time there was increased trade with "Bengala" (Bengal) and "Ternate" and "Tidore" (two of the
"spice islands," or Moluccas). The spice ships would cross
the "Ethiopian" Sea (the Indian Ocean) before rounding
the Cape of Good Hope.

Through the wide *Ethiopian* to the Cape
Ply stemming nightly toward the Pole. So seem'd
Far off the flying Fiend: at last appear
Hell bounds high reaching to the horrid Roof,
645 And thrice threefold the Gates; three folds were Brass,
Three Iron, three of Adamantine Rock,
Impenetrable, impal'd° with circling fire,   *enclosed*
Yet unconsum'd. Before the Gates there sat
On either side a formidable shape;
650 The one seem'd Woman to the waist, and fair,[4]
But ended foul in many a scaly fold
Voluminous and vast, a Serpent arm'd
With mortal° sting: about her middle round   *death-dealing*
A cry of Hell Hounds never ceasing bark'd
655 With wide *Cerberean* mouths full loud, and rung
A hideous Peal:[5] yet, when they list, would creep,
If aught disturb'd thir noise, into her womb,
And kennel there, yet there still bark'd and howl'd
Within unseen. Far less abhorr'd than these
660 Vex'd *Scylla* bathing in the Sea that parts
Calabria from the hoarse *Trinacrian* shore:[6]
Nor uglier follow the Night-Hag,[7] when call'd
In secret, riding through the Air she comes
Lur'd with the smell of infant blood, to dance
665 With *Lapland* Witches, while the laboring Moon
Eclipses at thir charms. The other shape,
If shape it might be call'd that shape had none
Distinguishable in member, joint, or limb,
Or substance might be call'd that shadow seem'd,
670 For each seem'd either; black it stood as Night,
Fierce as ten Furies, terrible as Hell,
And shook a dreadful Dart;[8] what seem'd his head
The likeness of a Kingly Crown had on.
Satan was now at hand, and from his seat
675 The Monster moving onward came as fast,
With horrid strides; Hell trembled as he strode.
Th' undaunted Fiend what this might be admir'd,°   *wondered*
Admir'd, not fear'd; God and his Son except,
Created thing naught valu'd he nor shunn'd;

4. The nearest analogue to Milton's Sin is probably Spenser's Errour, who is half serpent and half woman, has a "mortal sting," and swallows her young (*The Faerie Queene* 1.1.14–16). The serpent of sin that tempted Adam and Eve was traditionally portrayed as having a woman's head or bust.
5. There is a whole "cry" (pack) of hounds, because one sin engenders many consequences, sometimes hidden. Cerberus was the many-headed dog who guarded Hades.
6. Circe, jealous of the nymph Scylla, changed her lower parts into a knot of "gaping dogs' heads, such as a Cerberus

might have" (Ovid, *Metamorphoses* 14.50–74). Later Scylla was again transformed, into a dangerous rock between "Trinacria" (Sicily) and Calabria. In the medieval moralized Ovid, she became a symbol of lust or of sin.
7. Hecate, whose charms were used by Circe in her spell against Scylla. Milton may allude here to the hellish yeth hounds, which, according to popular superstition, followed the queen of darkness across the sky in pursuit of the souls of the damned.
8. The "dreadful dart" was a traditional attribute of Death, signifying his sharpness and suddenness.

680 And with disdainful look thus first began.
      Whence and what are thou, execrable shape,
    That dar'st, though grim and terrible, advance
    Thy miscreated Front athwart my way
    To yonder Gates? through them I mean to pass,
685 That be assured, without leave askt of thee:
    Retire, or taste thy folly, and learn by proof,°   experience
    Hell-born, not to contend with Spirits of Heav'n.
      To whom the Goblin full of wrath repli'd:
    Art thou that Traitor Angel, art thou hee,
690 Who first broke peace in Heav'n and Faith, till then
    Unbrok'n, and in proud rebellious Arms
    Drew after him the third part of Heav'n's Sons
    Conjur'd[9] against the Highest, for which both Thou
    And they outcast from God, are here condemn'd
695 To waste Eternal days in woe and pain?
    And reck'n'st thou thyself with Spirits of Heav'n,
    Hell-doom'd, and breath'st defiance here and scorn,
    Where I reign King, and to enrage thee more,
    Thy King and Lord? Back to thy punishment,
700 False fugitive, and to thy speed add wings,
    Lest with a whip of Scorpions I pursue
    Thy ling'ring, or with one stroke of this Dart
    Strange horror seize thee, and pangs unfelt before.
      So spake the grisly terror, and in shape,
705 So speaking and so threat'ning, grew tenfold
    More dreadful and deform: on th' other side
    Incens't with indignation *Satan* stood
    Unterrifi'd, and like a Comet burn'd,
    That fires the length of *Ophiucus*[1] huge
710 In th' Artic Sky, and from his horrid hair
    Shakes Pestilence and War. Each at the Head
    Levell'd his deadly aim; thir fatal hands
    No second stroke intend, and such a frown
    Each cast at th' other, as when two black Clouds
715 With Heav'n's Artillery fraught, come rattling on
    Over the *Caspian*, then stand front to front
    Hov'ring a space, till Winds the signal blow
    To join thir dark Encounter in mid air:
    So frown'd the mighty Combatants, that Hell
720 Grew darker at thir frown, so matcht they stood;
    For never but once more was either like
    To meet so great a foe:[2] and now great deeds

9. Sworn together in conspiracy; bewitched.
1. The comet referred to here may be a magnificent one that appeared in 1618 in the constellation *Ophiuchus*. In his diary, John Evelyn held it responsible for the Thirty Years' War. Ophiuchus (Serpent Bearer) is also chosen to allude to Satan's later transformation into a serpent.
2. When Christ destroys "him that had the power of death, that is, the devil" (Hebrews 2.14), as well as "the last enemy . . . death" (1 Corinthians 15.26).

Had been achiev'd, whereof all Hell had rung,
Had not the Snaky Sorceress that sat
725   Fast by Hell Gate, and kept the fatal Key,
Ris'n, and with hideous outcry rush'd between.
      O Father, what intends thy hand, she cri'd,
Against thy only Son?[3] What fury O Son,
Possesses thee to bend that mortal Dart
730   Against thy Father's head? and know'st for whom;
For him who sits above and laughs the while
At thee ordain'd his drudge, to execute
Whate'er his wrath, which he calls Justice, bids,
His wrath which one day will destroy ye both.
735   She spake, and at her words the hellish Pest
Forbore, then these to her *Satan* return'd:
      So strange thy outcry, and thy words so strange
Thou interposest, that my sudden hand
Prevented spares to tell thee yet by deeds
740   What it intends; till first I know of thee,
What thing thou art, thus double-form'd, and why
In this infernal Vale first met thou call'st
Me Father, and that Phantasm call'st my Son?
I know thee not, nor ever saw till now
745   Sight more detestable than him and thee.
      T' whom thus the Portress of Hell Gate repli'd:[4]
Hast thou forgot me then, and do I seem
Now in thine eye so foul, once deem'd so fair
In Heav'n, when at th' Assembly, and in sight
750   Of all the Seraphim with thee combin'd
In bold conspiracy against Heav'n's King,
All on a sudden miserable pain
Surpris'd thee, dim thine eyes, and dizzy swum
In darkness, while thy head flames thick and fast
755   Threw forth, till on the left side op'ning wide,
Likest to thee in shape and count'nance bright,
Then shining heav'nly fair, a Goddess arm'd
Out of thy head I sprung:[5] amazement seiz'd
All th' Host of Heav'n; back they recoil'd afraid
760   At first, and call'd me *Sin*, and for a Sign
Portentous held me; but familiar grown,
I pleas'd, and with attractive graces won
The most averse, thee chiefly, who full oft
Thyself in me thy perfect image viewing
765   Becam'st enamor'd, and such joy thou took'st

3. The allegory whereby Sin is daughter of Satan and
mother of Death is from St. Basil's *Hexameron.*
4. Sin's office is an allegorical statement of the idea that
access to hell is by sinning.
5. The circumstances of Sin's birth recall the ancient

myth about Athena springing fully formed from the head
of Zeus. It is thus presented as a parody of God's generation of the Son, since Minerva's birth had traditionally
been allegorized by theologians in that sense.

With me in secret, that my womb conceiv'd
A growing burden. Meanwhile War arose,
And fields were fought in Heav'n: wherein remain'd
(For what could else) to our Almighty Foe
770   Clear Victory, to our part loss and rout
Through all the Empyrean: down they fell
Driv'n headlong from the Pitch° of Heaven, down   *summit*
Into this Deep, and in the general fall
I also; at which time this powerful Key
775   Into my hand was giv'n, with charge to keep
These Gates for ever shut, which none can pass
Without my op'ning. Pensive here I sat
Alone, but long I sat not, till my womb
Pregnant by thee, and now excessive grown
780   Prodigious motion felt and rueful throes.
At last this odious offspring whom thou seest
Thine own begotten, breaking violent way
Tore through my entrails, that with fear and pain
Distorted, all my nether shape thus grew
785   Transform'd: but he my inbred enemy
Forth issu'd, brandishing his fatal Dart
Made to destroy: I fled, and cri'd out *Death*;
Hell trembl'd at the hideous Name, and sigh'd
From all her Caves, and back resounded *Death*.
790   I fled, but he pursu'd (though more, it seems,
Inflam'd with lust than rage) and swifter far,
Mee overtook his mother all dismay'd,
And in embraces forcible and foul
Ingend'ring with me, of that rape begot
795   These yelling Monsters that with ceaseless cry
Surround me, as thou saw'st, hourly conceiv'd
And hourly born, with sorrow infinite
To me, for when they list, into the womb
That bred them they return, and howl and gnaw
800   My Bowels, thir repast; then bursting forth
Afresh with conscious terrors vex° me round,   *harass*
That rest or intermission none I find.[6]
Before mine eyes in opposition sits
Grim *Death* my Son and foe, who sets them on,
805   And me his Parent would full soon devour
For want of other prey, but that he knows
His end with mine involv'd; and knows that I
Should prove a bitter Morsel, and his bane,
Whenever that shall be; so Fate pronounc'd.
810   But thou O Father, I forewarn thee, shun
His deadly arrow; neither vainly hope

---

6. Here Sin's offspring appear to symbolize the pangs of guilt or fear. "Conscious terrors" are terrors of guilty knowledge.

To be invulnerable in those bright Arms,
Though temper'd heav'nly, for that mortal dint,
Save he who reigns above, none can resist.[7]

815   She finish'd, and the subtle Fiend his lore
Soon learn'd, now milder, and thus answer'd smooth.
Dear Daughter, since thou claim'st me for thy Sire,
And my fair Son here shows't me, the dear pledge
Of dalliance had with thee in Heav'n, and joys

820   Then sweet, now sad to mention, through dire change
Befall'n us unforeseen, unthought of, know
I come no enemy, but to set free
From out this dark and dismal house of pain,
Both him and thee, and all the heav'nly Host

825   Of Spirits that in our just pretenses arm'd
Fell with us from on high: from them I go
This uncouth° errand sole, and one for all   strange
Myself expose, with lonely steps to tread
Th' unfounded° deep, and through the void immense   bottomless

830   To search with wand'ring quest a place foretold
Should be, and, by concurring signs, ere now
Created vast and round, a place of bliss
In the Purlieus° of Heav'n, and therein plac't   outskirts
A race of upstart Creatures, to supply

835   Perhaps our vacant room, though more remov'd,
Lest Heav'n surcharg'd° with potent multitude   too full
Might hap to move new broils: Be this or aught
Than this more secret now design'd, I haste
To know, and this once known, shall soon return,

840   And bring ye to the place where Thou and Death
Shall dwell at ease, and up and down unseen
Wing silently the buxom° Air, imbalm'd[8]   unresisting
With odors; there ye shall be fed and fill'd
Immeasurably, all things shall be your prey.

845   He ceas'd, for both seem'd highly pleas'd, and Death
Grinn'd horrible a ghastly smile, to hear
His famine° should be fill'd, and blest his maw   hunger
Destin'd to that good hour: no less rejoic'd
His mother bad, and thus bespake her Sire.

850   The key of this infernal Pit by due,
And by command of Heav'n's all-powerful King
I keep, by him forbidden to unlock
These Adamantine Gates; against all force
Death ready stands to interpose his dart,

855   Fearless to be o'ermatcht by living might.
But what owe I to his commands above

---

7. Dint: stroke given with a weapon. Only God is immune to death.

8. Balmy, rendered resistent to decay.

Who hates me, and hath hither thrust me down
Into this gloom of *Tartarus* profound,
To sit in hateful Office here confin'd,
860   Inhabitant of Heav'n, and heav'nly-born,
Here in perpetual agony and pain,
With terrors and with clamors compasst round
Of mine own brood, that on my bowels feed:
Thou art my Father, thou my Author, thou
865   My being gav'st me; whom should I obey
But thee, whom follow? thou wilt bring me soon
To that new world of light and bliss, among
The Gods who live at ease, where I shall Reign
At thy right hand voluptuous, as beseems
870   Thy daughter and thy darling, without end.[9]
     Thus saying, from her side the fatal Key,
Sad instrument of all our woe, she took;[1]
And towards the Gate rolling her bestial train,
Forthwith the huge Portcullis high up drew,
875   Which but herself not all the *Stygian* powers
Could once have mov'd; then in the key-hole turns
Th' intricate wards,[2] and every Bolt and Bar
Of massy Iron or solid Rock with ease
Unfast'ns: on a sudden op'n fly
880   With impetuous recoil and jarring sound
Th' infernal doors, and on thir hinges grate
Harsh Thunder, that the lowest bottom shook
Of *Erebus*.[3] She op'n'd, but to shut
Excell'd her power; the Gates wide op'n stood,
885   That with extended wings a Banner'd Host
Under spread Ensigns marching might pass through
With Horse and Chariots rankt in loose array;
So wide they stood, and like a Furnace mouth
Cast forth redounding° smoke and ruddy flame.   *surging*
890   Before thir eyes in sudden view appear
The secrets of the hoary deep, a dark
Illimitable Ocean without bound,
Without dimension, where length, breadth, and highth,
And time and place are lost; where eldest *Night*
895   And *Chaos*, Ancestors of Nature, hold
Eternal Anarchy, amidst the noise
Of endless wars, and by confusion stand.
For hot, cold, moist, and dry, four Champions fierce
Strive here for Maistry, and to Battle bring

---

9. Parodying the Nicene creed ("on the right hand of the Father . . . [Christ] whose kingdom shall have no end"). In Sin's fantasy, she enjoys glory like Christ's. Satan, Sin, and Death form a complete anti-Trinity.
1. "Sad instrument" may stand in apposition to "she" as well as to "key"; it could mean "a person made use of by another, for the accomplishment of a purpose."
2. The incisions in a key's bit.
3. Classical name for Hell.

900 Thir embryon Atoms;[4] they around the flag
     Of each his Faction, in thir several Clans,
     Light-arm'd or heavy, sharp, smooth, swift or slow,
     Swarm populous, unnumber'd as the Sands
     Of *Barca* or *Cyrene's* torrid soil,[5]
905 Levied° to side with warring Winds, and poise   *enlisted*
     Thir lighter wings. To whom these most adhere,
     Hee rules a moment; *Chaos* Umpire sits,
     And by decision more imbroils the fray
     By which he Reigns: next him high Arbiter
910 *Chance* governs all. Into this wild Abyss,
     The Womb of nature and perhaps her Grave,
     Of neither Sea, nor Shore, nor Air, nor Fire,
     But all these in thir pregnant causes mixt
     Confus'dly, and which thus must ever fight,
915 Unless th' Almighty Maker them ordain
     His dark materials to create more Worlds,
     Into this wild Abyss the wary fiend
     Stood on the brink of Hell and look'd a while,
     Pondering his Voyage: for no narrow frith°   *channel*
920 He had to cross. Nor was his ear less peal'd°   *dinned*
     With noises loud and ruinous (to compare
     Great things with small) than when *Bellona*[6] storms,
     With all her battering Engines bent to rase
     Some Capital City; or less than if this frame
925 Of Heav'n were falling, and these Elements
     In mutiny had from her Axle torn
     The steadfast Earth. At last his Sail-broad Vans°   *wings*
     He spreads for flight, and in the surging smoke
     Uplifted spurns the ground, thence many a League
930 As in a cloudy Chair ascending rides
     Audacious, but that seat soon failing, meets
     A vast vacuity: all unawares
     Flutt'ring his pennons° vain plumb down he drops   *wings*
     Ten thousand fadom° deep, and to this hour   *fathoms*
935 Down had been falling, had not by ill chance
     The strong rebuff of some tumultuous cloud
     Instinct° with Fire and Nitre hurried him   *inflamed*
     As many miles aloft: that fury stay'd,
     Quencht in a Boggy *Syrtis*, neither Sea,[7]
940 Nor good dry Land, nigh founder'd on he fares,
     Treading the crude consistence, half on foot,

---

4. In Hesiod's *Theogony*, Chaos and Night were made "ancestors" of nature. Milton's description of the strife between contrary qualities that preceded the emergence of the cosmos is close to Ovid's account of the primeval chaos in which "cold things strove with hot, moist with dry, soft with hard, weightless with heavy" (*Metamorphoses* 1.19ff.).
5. "Barca," an ancient city of Cyrenaica, of which "Cyrene" was the capital.
6. Goddess of war, here a metonymy for war itself.
7. The Syrtes were two huge and proverbially dangerous shifting sandbanks off the North African shore.

Half flying;[8] behoves him now both Oar and Sail.
As when a Gryfon through the Wilderness
With winged course o'er Hill or moory Dale,
945   Pursues the *Arimaspian*, who by stealth
Had from his wakeful custody purloin'd
The guarded Gold: So eagerly the fiend
O'er bog or steep, through strait, rough, dense, or rare,
With head, hands, wings, or feet pursues his way,
950   And swims or sinks, or wades, or creeps, or flies:
At length a universal hubbub wild
Of stunning sounds and voices all confus'd
Borne through the hollow dark assaults his ear
With loudest vehemence: thither he plies,
955   Undaunted to meet there whatever power
Or Spirit of the nethermost Abyss
Might in that noise reside, of whom to ask
Which way the nearest coast of darkness lies
Bordering on light; when straight behold the Throne
960   Of *Chaos*, and his dark Pavilion spread
Wide on the wasteful Deep; with him Enthron'd
Sat Sable-vested *Night*, eldest of things,
The Consort of his Reign; and by them stood
Orcus and *Ades*, and the dreaded name
965   Of *Demogorgon*;[9] *Rumor* next and *Chance*,
And *Tumult* and *Confusion* all imbroil'd,
And *Discord* with a thousand various mouths.
       T' whom *Satan* turning boldly, thus. Ye Powers
And Spirits of this nethermost Abyss,
970   *Chaos* and ancient *Night*, I come no Spy,
With purpose to explore or to disturb
The secrets of your Realm, but by constraint
Wand'ring this darksome Desert, as my way
Lies through your spacious Empire up to light,
975   Alone, and without guide, half lost, I seek
What readiest path leads where your gloomy bounds
Confine with° Heav'n; or if some other place   *border on*
From your Dominion won, th' Ethereal King
Possesses lately, thither to arrive
980   I travel this profound,° direct my course;   *deep pit*
Directed, no mean recompence it brings

---

8. Spenser's dragon of evil is similarly described as "halfe flying, and halfe footing in his hast" (*The Faerie Queene* 1.11.8). The legend of "gold-guarding griffins" in Scythia, from whom the one-eyed Arimaspi steal, was often retold out of Herodotus (3.116) and Pliny (*Natural History* 7.10). The griffin (a composite monster: half eagle, half lion) is appropriate here partly because it was subdued by the sun god Apollo, as Satan will be by Christ.
9. In general, this court of personifications resembles Vir-

gil's halls of Pluto (*Aeneid* 6.268–81), though the only member common to both is Discord. Milton's Demogorgon is from Boccaccio's *De genealogia deorum*, in which he comes first of all the dark gods. Among his brood are Night, Tartarus, Erebus, the serpent Python, Litigium (cf. Milton's Tumult and Discord), and Fama (Milton's Rumor). Orcus and Ades are Latin and Greek names of Pluto, god of hell.

To your behoof, if I that Region lost,
All usurpation thence expell'd, reduce
To her original darkness and your sway
985 (Which is my present journey) and once more
Erect the Standard there of *ancient Night*;
Yours be th' advantage all, mine the revenge.
        Thus *Satan*; and him thus the Anarch[1] old
With falt'ring speech and visage incompos'd°   *disordered*
990 Answer'd. I know thee, stranger, who thou art,
That mighty leading Angel, who of late
Made head against Heav'n's King, though overthrown.
I saw and heard, for such a numerous Host
Fled not in silence through the frighted deep
995 With ruin upon ruin, rout on rout,
Confusion worse confounded; and Heav'n Gates
Pour'd out by millions her victorious Bands
Pursuing. I upon my Frontiers here
Keep residence; if all I can will serve,
1000 That little which is left so to defend,
Encroacht on still through our intestine broils
Weak'ning the Sceptre of old *Night*: first Hell
Your dungeon stretching far and wide beneath;
Now lately Heaven and Earth, another World
1005 Hung o'er my Realm, link'd in a golden Chain
To that side Heav'n from whence your Legions fell:
If that way be your walk, you have not far;
So much the nearer danger; go and speed;
Havoc and spoil and ruin are my gain.
1010   He ceas'd; and *Satan* stay'd not to reply,
But glad that now his Sea should find a shore,
With fresh alacrity and force renew'd
Springs upward like a Pyramid of fire
Into the wild expanse, and through the shock
1015 Of fighting Elements, on all sides round
Environ'd wins his way; harder beset
And more endanger'd, than when *Argo* pass'd
Through *Bosporus* betwixt the justling° Rocks:[2]   *jostling*
Or when *Ulysses* on the Larboard shunn'd
1020 *Charybdis*, and by th' other whirlpool steer'd.[3]
So he with difficulty and labor hard
Mov'd on, with difficulty and labor hee;
But hee once past, soon after when man fell,
Strange alteration! Sin and Death amain°   *without delay*

1. Chaos, ruler or antiruler of the "eternal anarchy" (line 896).
2. When Jason and the Argonauts sailed through the Bosporus (Straits of Constantinople) en route to Colchis, their boat, the *Argo*, narrowly escaped destruction between the Symplegades, the clashing or "jostling" rocks.

See Apollonius Rhodius, *Argonautica* 2.317, 552–611.
3. Homer tells how Odysseus followed Circe's advice in avoiding Charybdis and sailing close by Scylla ("the other whirlpool") in his passage through the Straits of Messina between Sicily and Italy (*Odyssey* 12).

1025   Following his track, such was the will of Heav'n,
    Pav'd after him a broad and beat'n way
    Over the dark Abyss, whose boiling Gulf
    Tamely endur'd a Bridge of wondrous length
    From Hell continu'd reaching th' utmost Orb
1030   Of this frail World; by which the Spirits perverse
    With easy intercourse pass to and fro
    To tempt or punish mortals, except whom
    God and good Angels guard by special grace.
    But now at last the sacred influence
1035   Of light appears, and from the walls of Heav'n
    Shoots far into the bosom of dim Night
    A glimmering dawn; here Nature first begins
    Her fardest° verge, and *Chaos* to retire   *farthest*
    As from her outmost works a brok'n foe
1040   With tumult less and with less hostile din,
    That *Satan* with less toil, and now with ease
    Wafts on the calmer wave by dubious light
    And like a weather-beaten Vessel holds°   *remains in*
    Gladly the Port, though Shrouds and Tackle torn;
1045   Or in the emptier waste, resembling Air,
    Weighs his spread wings, at leisure to behold
    Far off th' Empyreal Heav'n, extended wide
    In circuit, undetermin'd square or round,[4]
    With Opal Tow'rs and Battlements adorn'd
1050   Of living° Sapphire, once his native Seat;   *unshaped*
    And fast by hanging in a golden Chain[5]
    This pendant world, in bigness as a Star
    Of smallest Magnitude close by the Moon.
    Thither full fraught with mischievous revenge,
1055   Accurst, and in a cursed hour he hies.
             The End of the Second Book.

Book 3
The Argument

    God sitting on his Throne sees Satan flying towards this world, then newly created; shows him to the Son who sat at his right hand; foretells the success of Satan in perverting mankind; clears his own Justice and Wisdom from all imputation, having created Man free and able enough to have withstood his Tempter; yet declares his purpose of grace towards him, in regard he fell not of his own malice, as did Satan, but by him seduc't. The Son of God renders praises to his Father for the manifestation of his gracious purpose towards Man;

---

4. So wide that it was impossible to tell whether the boundary was rectilinear or curved.

5. Homer's Zeus asserts his transcendence by claiming that if a golden chain were lowered from Heaven, he could draw up by it all the other gods, together with the earth and the sea, and hang them from a pinnacle of

Olympus (*Iliad* 8.18–27). Milton interprets this chain as "the universal concord and sweet union of all things which Pythagoras poetically figures as harmony" (*Prolusion* 2), thus accepting a philosophical and literary tradition that runs from Plato through Boethius, Chaucer, and Spenser.

but God again declares, that Grace cannot be extended towards Man without the satisfaction of divine Justice; Man hath offended the majesty of God by aspiring to Godhead, and therefore with all his Progeny devoted to death must die, unless some one can be found sufficient to answer for his offense, and undergo his Punishment. The Son of God freely offers himself a Ransom for Man: the Father accepts him, ordains his incarnation, pronounces his exaltation above all Names in Heaven and Earth; commands all the Angels to adore him; they obey, and hymning to thir Harps in full Choir, celebrate the Father and the Son. Meanwhile Satan alights upon the bare convex of this World's outermost Orb; where wand'ring he first finds a place since call'd The Limbo of Vanity; what persons and things fly up thither; thence comes to the Gate of Heaven, describ'd ascending by stairs, and the waters above the Firmament that flow about it: His passage thence to the Orb of the Sun; he finds there Uriel the Regent of that Orb, but first changes himself into the shape of a meaner Angel; and pretending a zealous desire to behold the new Creation and Man whom God had plac't there, inquires of him the place of his habitation, and is directed; alights first on Mount Niphates.

	Hail holy Light, offspring of Heav'n first-born,	
	Or of th' Eternal Coeternal beam	
	May I express thee unblam'd?[1] since God is Light,	
	And never but in unapproached Light	
5	Dwelt from Eternity, dwelt then in thee,	
	Bright effluence° of bright essence increate.[2]	*radiance*
	Or hear'st thou rather[3] pure Ethereal stream,	
	Whose Fountain who shall tell? before the Sun,	
	Before the Heavens thou wert, and at the voice	
10	Of God, as with a Mantle didst invest°	*cover*
	The rising world of waters dark and deep,	
	Won from the void° and formless infinite.[4]	*chaos*
	Thee I revisit now with bolder wing,	
	Escap't the *Stygian* Pool, though long detain'd	
15	In that obscure sojourn, while in my flight	
	Through utter and through middle darkness borne[5]	
	With other notes than to th' *Orphean* Lyre	
	I sung of Chaos and Eternal Night,	
	Taught by the heav'nly Muse° to venture down	*Urania*
20	The dark descent, and up to reascend,	
	Though hard and rare:[6] thee I revisit safe,	
	And feel thy sovran vital Lamp; but thou	

1. The light of the invocation has been interpreted as the Son of God, as physical light, and as the principal image of God and the divine emanation itself, according to the Platonic system. Milton proposes three images or forms of address, "offspring," "beam," and "stream," each of which associates the divine Light or Wisdom with a different aspect of deity. The blame could attach only to using the second name, "co-eternal beam;" it is this name that is justified by the implicit appeal to scriptural authority.
2. "God is Light," from 1 John 1.5. God "only hath immortality, dwelling in the light which no man can approach unto" (1 Timothy 6.16). "Essence increate," the uncreated divine essence. In the physics and metaphysics of Milton's time, light was regarded as an "accident" (quality), not a body or substance.
3. Do you prefer to be called.
4. See Genesis 1.1–5.
5. The "Stygian pool" and the "utter" (outer) darkness are hell; the "middle darkness" is chaos.
6. Alluding to the "fable of Orpheus, whom they faigne to have recovered his Euridice from Hell with his Musick, that is, Truth and Equity from darkenesse of Barbarisme and Ignorance with his profound and excellent Doctrines; but, that in the way to the upper-earth, she was lost againe" (Henry Reynolds, *Mythomystes*). "Other notes," because Milton, unlike Orpheus, claims not to have lost his Eurydice.

Revisit'st not these eyes, that roll in vain
To find thy piercing ray, and find no dawn;
25   So thick a drop serene[7] hath quencht thir Orbs,
Or dim suffusion° veil'd. Yet not the more   cataract
Cease I to wander where the Muses haunt
Clear Spring, or shady Grove, or Sunny Hill,
Smit with the love of sacred Song;[8] but chief
30   Thee *Sion*[9] and the flow'ry Brooks beneath
That wash thy hallow'd feet, and warbling flow,
Nightly I visit: nor sometimes forget
Those other two equall'd with me in Fate,
So were I equall'd with them in renown,
35   Blind *Thamyris* and blind *Maeonides*,
And *Tiresias* and *Phineus* Prophets old.[1]
Then feed on thoughts, that voluntary move
Harmonious numbers;° as the wakeful Bird[2]   rhythmic measure
Sings darkling,° and in shadiest Covert hid   in the dark
40   Tunes her nocturnal Note. Thus with the Year
Seasons return, but not to me returns
Day, or the sweet approach of Ev'n or Morn,
Or sight of vernal bloom, or Summer's Rose,
Or flocks, or herds, or human face divine;
45   But cloud instead, and ever-during dark
Surrounds me, from the cheerful ways of men
Cut off, and for the Book of knowledge[3] fair
Presented with a Universal blanc°   blank
Of Nature's works to me expung'd and ras'd,°   erased
50   And wisdom at one entrance quite shut out.
So much the rather thou Celestial Light
Shine inward, and the mind through all her powers
Irradiate, there plant eyes, all mist from thence
Purge and disperse, that I may see and tell
55   Of things invisible to mortal sight.
     Now had th' Almighty Father from above,
From the pure Empyrean where he sits
High Thron'd above all highth, bent down his eye,
His own works and their works at once to view:
60   About him all the Sanctities of Heaven
Stood thick as Stars, and from his sight receiv'd
Beatitude past utterance; on his right

---

7. Literally translating *gutta serena*, the medical term for
the form of blindness from which Milton suffered.
8. An allusion to Virgil's prayer that "smitten with a great
love" of the Muses, he may be shown by them the secrets
of nature (*Georgics* 2.475–89).
9. The mountain of scriptural inspiration.
1. Thamyris was a Thracian poet who fell in love with
the Muses and challenged them to a contest in which the
loser was to give the winner whatever he wanted. The
Muses, having won, took Thamyris's eyes and his lyre.

Maeonides was Homer's surname; the contrast between
his outward blindness and inner vision was a commonplace. In *De Idea Platonica*, Milton writes of Tiresias that
his "very blindness gave him boundless light." The Thracian king Phineus lost his sight because he had become
too good a prophet.
2. The nightingale. The soul of Thamyris passed into a
nightingale.
3. The Book of Nature.

The radiant image of his Glory sat,
His only Son; On Earth he first beheld
65 Our two first Parents, yet the only two
Of mankind, in the happy Garden plac't,
Reaping immortal fruits of joy and love,
Uninterrupted joy, unrivall'd love
In blissful solitude; he then survey'd
70 Hell and the Gulf between, and *Satan* there
Coasting the wall of Heav'n on this side Night
In the dun° Air sublime,° and ready now   dusky / aloft
To stoop with wearied wings, and willing feet
On the bare outside of this World, that seem'd
75 Firm land imbosom'd without Firmament,[4]
Uncertain which, in Ocean or in Air.
Him God beholding from his prospect high,
Wherein past, present, future he beholds,
Thus to his only Son foreseeing spake.
80   Only begotten Son, seest thou what rage
Transports our adversary, whom no bounds
Prescrib'd, no bars of Hell, nor all the chains
Heapt on him there, nor yet the main Abyss
Wide interrupt° can hold; so bent he seems   divided
85 On desperate revenge, that shall redound
Upon his own rebellious head. And now
Through all restraint broke loose he wings his way
Not far off Heav'n, in the Precincts of light,
Directly towards the new created World,
90 And Man there plac't, with purpose to assay°   test
If him by force he can destroy, or worse,
By some false guile pervert; and shall pervert;
For Man will heark'n to his glozing° lies,   flattering
And easily transgress the sole Command,[5]
95 Sole pledge of his obedience: So will fall
Hee and his faithless Progeny: whose fault?
Whose but his own? ingrate, he had of mee
All he could have; I made him just and right,
Sufficient to have stood, though free to fall.
100 Such I created all th' Ethereal Powers
And Spirits, both them who stood and them who fail'd;
Freely they stood who stood, and fell who fell.
Not free, what proof could they have giv'n sincere
Of true allegiance, constant Faith or Love,
105 Where only what they needs must do, appear'd,
Not what they would? what praise could they receive?
What pleasure I from such obedience paid,
When Will and Reason (Reason also is choice)

---

4. The firmament or atmosphere, being inside the shell of   5. I.e., not to taste the fruit of the forbidden tree.
the universe that Satan stands on, is invisible to him.

Useless and vain, of freedom both despoil'd,
110 Made passive both, had serv'd necessity,
Not mee. They therefore as to right belong'd,
So were created, nor can justly accuse
Thir maker, or thir making, or thir Fate;
As if Predestination over-rul'd
115 Thir will, dispos'd by absolute Decree
Or high foreknowledge; they themselves decreed
Thir own revolt, not I: if I foreknew,
Foreknowledge had no influence on their fault,
Which had no less prov'd certain unforeknown.
120 So without least impulse or shadow of Fate,
Or aught by me immutably foreseen,
They trespass, Authors to themselves in all
Both what they judge and what they choose; for so
I form'd them free, and free they must remain,
125 Till they enthrall themselves: I else must change
Thir nature, and revoke the high Decree
Unchangeable, Eternal, which ordain'd
Thir freedom: they themselves ordain'd thir fall.
The first sort[6] by thir own suggestion° fell,   *temptation*
130 Self-tempted, self-deprav'd: Man falls deceiv'd
By th' other first: Man therefore shall find grace,
The other none: in Mercy and Justice both,
Through Heav'n and Earth, so shall my glory excel,
But Mercy first and last shall brightest shine.
135   Thus while God spake, ambrosial fragrance fill'd
All Heav'n, and in the blessed Spirits elect[7]
Sense of new joy ineffable diffus'd:
Beyond compare the Son of God was seen
Most glorious, in him all his Father shone
140 Substantially express'd, and in his face
Divine compassion visibly appear'd,
Love without end, and without measure Grace,
Which uttering thus he to his Father spake.
    O Father, gracious was that word which clos'd
145 Thy sovran° sentence, that Man should find grace;   *sovereign*
For which both Heav'n and Earth shall high extol
Thy praises, with th' innumerable sound
Of Hymns and sacred Songs, wherewith thy Throne
Encompass'd shall resound thee ever blest.
150 For should Man finally be lost, should Man
Thy creature late so lov'd, thy youngest Son
Fall circumvented thus by fraud, though join'd
With his own folly? that be from thee far,
That far be from thee, Father, who art Judge

---

6. Satan and the rebel angels.
7. The "elect angels" of 1 Timothy 5.21, explained in

Milton's *De doctrina* 1.9 as angels "who have not revolted."

155   Of all things made, and judgest only right.
      Or shall the Adversary[8] thus obtain
      His end, and frustrate thine, shall he fulfil
      His malice, and thy goodness bring to naught,
      Or proud return though to his heavier doom,
160   Yet with revenge accomplish't and to Hell
      Draw after him the whole Race of mankind,
      By him corrupted? or wilt thou thyself
      Abolish thy Creation, and unmake,
      For him, what for thy glory thou hast made?
165   So should thy goodness and thy greatness both
      Be question'd and blasphem'd without defense.
        To whom the great Creator thus repli'd.
      O Son, in whom my Soul hath chief delight,[9]
      Son of my bosom, Son who art alone
170   My word, my wisdom, and effectual might,
      All hast thou spok'n as my thoughts are, all
      As my Eternal purpose hath decreed:
      Man shall not quite be lost, but sav'd who will,
      Yet not of will in him, but grace in me
175   Freely voutsaf't;° once more I will renew   *vouchsafed*
      His lapsed° powers, though forfeit and enthrall'd   *decayed*
      By sin to foul exorbitant desires;
      Upheld by me, yet once more he shall stand
      On even ground against his mortal foe,
180   By me upheld, that he may know how frail
      His fall'n condition is, and to me owe
      All his deliv'rance, and to none but me.
      Some I have chosen of peculiar grace
      Elect above the rest; so is my will:[1]
185   The rest shall hear me call, and oft be warn'd
      Thir sinful state, and to appease betimes
      Th' incensed Deity while offer'd grace
      Invites; for I will clear thir senses dark,
      What may suffice, and soft'n stony hearts
190   To pray, repent, and bring obedience due.
      To Prayer, repentance, and obedience due,
      Though but endeavor'd with sincere intent,
      Mine ear shall not be slow, mine eye not shut.
      And I will place within them as a guide
195   My Umpire *Conscience*, whom if they will hear,

---

8. The literal meaning of "Satan."
9. Echoing Mark 1.11, the words out of the heavens at Jesus' baptism: "Thou art my beloved Son, in whom I am well pleased."
1. In *De doctrina* 1.4, Milton sets out an Arminian position, explicitly opposed to the Calvinist, on such doctrines as predestination, election, and reprobation, and he could be regarded as doing something similar here

(lines 173–202); e.g., his God seems to make salvation depend on humans' will to avail themselves of grace, or on "prayer, repentance, and obedience" (line 191), whereas Calvinists regarded humans as incapable of contributing in any way to their own salvation. By the term "elect," Milton usually means no more than "whoever believes and continues in the faith."

Light after light well us'd they shall attain,
And to the end persisting, safe arrive.
This my long sufferance and my day of grace
They who neglect and scorn, shall never taste;
200 But hard be hard'n'd, blind be blinded more,
That they may stumble on, and deeper fall;
And none but such from mercy I exclude.
But yet all is not done; Man disobeying,
Disloyal breaks his fealty, and sins
205 Against the high Supremacy of Heav'n,
Affecting° God-head, and so losing all,   *seeking*
To expiate his Treason hath naught left,
But to destruction sacred and devote,°   *dedicated*
He with his whole posterity must die,
210 Die hee or Justice must; unless for him
Some other able, and as willing, pay
The rigid satisfaction, death for death.[2]
Say Heav'nly Powers, where shall we find such love,
Which of ye will be mortal[3] to redeem
215 Man's mortal crime, and just th' unjust to save,
Dwells in all Heaven charity° so dear?   *compassionate love*
    He ask'd, but all the Heav'nly Choir stood mute,
And silence was in Heav'n: on man's behalf
Patron or Intercessor none appear'd,
220 Much less that durst upon his own head draw
The deadly forfeiture, and ransom set.[4]
And now without redemption all mankind
Must have been lost, adjudg'd to Death and Hell
By doom° severe, had not the Son of God,   *judgment*
225 In whom the fulness dwells of love divine,
His dearest mediation thus renew'd.
    Father, thy word is past,[5] man shall find grace;
And shall grace not find means, that finds her way,
The speediest of thy winged messengers,
230 To visit all thy creatures, and to all
Comes unprevented,° unimplor'd, unsought?   *unanticipated*
Happy for man, so coming; he her aid
Can never seek, once dead in sins and lost;
Atonement for himself or offering meet,
235 Indebted and undone, hath none to bring:
Behold mee then, mee for him, life for life
I offer, on mee let thine anger fall;
Account mee man; I for his sake will leave
Thy bosom, and this glory next to thee

---

2. Note that human death is here regarded by God not as a punishment, but as a "satisfaction" for the treason. See *De doctrina* 1.16: "The satisfaction of Christ is the complete reparation made by him . . . by the fulfilment of the Law, and payment of the required price for all mankind."
3. Is willing to be subject to death.
4. Put down the ransom price (by giving his own life).
5. Your word of honor is pledged.

240   Freely put off, and for him lastly die
      Well pleas'd, on me let Death wreck all his rage;
      Under his gloomy power I shall not long
      Lie vanquisht; thou hast giv'n me to possess
      Life in myself for ever, by thee I live,[6]
245   Though now to Death I yield, and am his due
      All that of me can die, yet that debt paid,
      Thou wilt not leave me in the loathsome grave
      His prey, nor suffer my unspotted Soul
      For ever with corruption there to dwell;
250   But I shall rise Victorious, and subdue
      My vanquisher, spoil'd of his vaunted spoil;
      Death his death's wound shall then receive, and stoop
      Inglorious, of his mortal sting disarm'd.[7]
      I through the ample Air in Triumph high
255   Shall lead Hell Captive maugre° Hell, and show   *despite*
      The powers of darkness bound. Thou at the sight
      Pleas'd, out of Heaven shalt look down and smile,
      While by thee rais'd I ruin all my Foes,
      Death last, and with his Carcass glut the Grave:[8]
260   Then with the multitude of my redeem'd
      Shall enter Heav'n long absent, and return,
      Father, to see thy face, wherein no cloud
      Of anger shall remain, but peace assur'd,
      And reconcilement; wrath shall be no more
265   Thenceforth, but in thy presence Joy entire.
          His words here ended, but his meek aspéct
      Silent yet spake, and breath'd immortal love
      To mortal men, above which only shone
      Filial obedience: as a sacrifice
270   Glad to be offer'd, he attends° the will   *awaits*
      Of his great Father. Admiration seiz'd
      All Heav'n, what this might mean, and whither tend
      Wond'ring; but soon th' Almighty thus repli'd:
          O thou in Heav'n and Earth the only peace
275   Found out for mankind under wrath, O thou
      My sole complacence! well thou know'st how dear
      To me are all my works, nor Man the least
      Though last created, that for him I spare
      Thee from my bosom and right hand, to save,
280   By losing thee a while, the whole Race lost.
      Thou therefore whom thou only canst redeem,
      Thir Nature also to thy Nature join;
      And be thyself Man among men on Earth,

---

6. See John 5.26: "As the Father hath life in himself: so hath he given to the Son to have life in himself."
7. See 1 Corinthians 15.55–56: "O death, where is thy sting? O grave, where is thy victory? The sting of death is sin; and the strength of sin is the law."
8. Alludes to 1 Corinthians 15.26: "The last enemy that shall be destroyed is death."

Made flesh, when time shall be, of Virgin seed,
285 By wondrous birth: Be thou in *Adam's* room°   place
The Head of all mankind, though *Adam's* Son.
As in him perish all men, so in thee
As from a second root shall be restor'd,
As many as are restor'd, without thee none.[9]
290 His crime makes guilty all his Sons, thy merit
Imputed shall absolve them who renounce
Thir own both righteous and unrighteous deeds,[1]
And live in thee transplanted, and from thee
Receive new life. So Man, as is most just,
295 Shall satisfy for Man, be judg'd and die,
And dying rise, and rising with him raise
His Brethren, ransom'd with his own dear life.
So Heav'nly love shall outdo Hellish hate,
Giving to death, and dying to redeem,
300 So dearly to redeem what Hellish hate
So easily destroy'd, and still destroys
In those who, when they may, accept not grace.
Nor shalt thou by descending to assume
Man's Nature, lessen or degrade thine own.
305 Because thou hast, though Thron'd in highest bliss
Equal to God, and equally enjoying
God-like fruition, quitted[2] all to save
A world from utter loss, and hast been found
By Merit more than Birthright Son of God,
310 Found worthiest to be so by being Good,
Far more than Great or High; because in thee
Love hath abounded more than Glory abounds,
Therefore thy Humiliation shall exalt
With thee thy Manhood also to this Throne;
315 Here shalt thou sit incarnate, here shalt Reign
Both God and Man, Son both of God and Man,
Anointed[3] universal King; all Power
I give thee, reign for ever, and assume
Thy Merits; under thee as Head Supreme
320 Thrones, Princedoms, Powers, Dominions I reduce:
All knees to thee shall bow, of them that bide
In Heaven, or Earth, or under Earth in Hell;
When thou attended gloriously from Heav'n
Shalt in the Sky appear, and from thee send
325 The summoning Arch-Angels to proclaim
Thy dread Tribunal: forthwith from all Winds

---

9. See 1 Corinthians 15.22: "As in Adam all die, even so in Christ shall all be made alive."

1. See *De doctrina* 1.22: "As therefore our sins are imputed to Christ, so the merits or righteousness of Christ are imputed to us through faith." If one simply renounced dependence on "righteous" deeds, one would be justified by faith alone; but for the "living faith"—faith issuing in works—that Milton believes necessary, one has to renounce (in a different sense) "unrighteous" deeds.

2. A pun, since "quitted" meant "redeemed, remitted" as well as "left."

3. The "Anointed" in Hebrew is the Messiah.

The living, and forthwith the cited° dead   *summoned*
Of all past Ages to the general Doom°   *judgment*
Shall hast'n, such a peal shall rouse thir sleep.
330 Then all thy Saints° assembl'd, thou shalt judge   *elect*
Bad men and Angels, they arraign'd shall sink
Beneath thy Sentence; Hell, her numbers full,
Thenceforth shall be for ever shut. Meanwhile
The World shall burn, and from her ashes spring
335 New Heav'n and Earth, wherein the just shall dwell
And after all thir tribulations long
See golden days, fruitful of golden deeds,
With Joy and Love triumphing, and fair Truth.⁴
Then thou thy regal Sceptre shalt lay by,
340 For regal Sceptre then no more shall need,
God shall be All in All. But all ye Gods,°   *angels*
Adore him, who to compass all this dies,
Adore the Son, and honor him as mee.
      No sooner had th' Almighty ceas't, but all
345 The multitude of Angels with a shout
Loud as from numbers without number, sweet
As from blest voices, uttering joy, Heav'n rung
With Jubilee, and loud Hosannas fill'd
Th' eternal Regions: lowly reverent
350 Towards either Throne they bow, and to the ground
With solemn adoration down they cast
Thir Crowns inwove with Amarant and Gold,
Immortal Amarant,⁵ a Flow'r which once
In Paradise, fast by the Tree of Life
355 Began to bloom, but soon for man's offense
To Heav'n remov'd where first it grew, there grows,
And flow'rs aloft shading the Fount of Life,
And where the river of Bliss through midst of Heav'n
Rolls o'er *Elysian* Flow'rs her Amber stream;⁶
360 With these that never fade the Spirits elect
Bind thir resplendent locks inwreath'd with beams,
Now in loose Garlands thick thrown off, the bright
Pavement that like a Sea of Jasper shone
Impurpl'd with Celestial Roses smil'd.
365 Then Crown'd again thir gold'n Harps they took,
Harps ever tun'd, that glittering by thir side
Like Quivers hung, and with Preamble sweet
Of charming symphony they introduce
Thir sacred Song, and waken raptures high;
370 No voice exempt,° no voice but well could join   *debarred*

---

4. The burning of Earth is based on 2 Peter 3.12ff.
5. "Amaranth" in Greek means "unwithering"; a purple
flower that was a "symbol of immortality"; the amaran-
tine crown was an ancient pagan symbol of untroubled

tranquillity and health.
6. Allusion to Virgil, *Aeneid* 6.656–59, the description of
spirits chanting in chorus beside the Eridanus, in the
Elysian fields; "amber" was a standard of purity or clarity.

Melodious part, such concord is in Heav'n.
  Thee Father first they sung Omnipotent,
Immutable, Immortal, Infinite,[7]
Eternal King; thee Author of all being,
375　Fountain of Light, thyself invisible
Amidst the glorious brightness where thou sit'st
Thron'd inaccessible, but° when thou shad'st   *except*
The full blaze of thy beams, and through a cloud
Drawn round about thee like a radiant Shrine,
380　Dark with excessive bright thy skirts appear,
Yet dazzle Heav'n, that brightest Seraphim
Approach not, but with both wings veil thir eyes.
Thee next they sang of all Creation first,
Begotten Son, Divine Similitude,
385　In whose conspicuous count'nance, without cloud
Made visible, th' Almighty Father shines,
Whom else no Creature can behold;[8] on the
Impresst th' effulgence of his Glory abides,
Transfus'd on thee his ample Spirit rests.
390　Hee Heav'n of Heavens and all the Powers therein
By thee created, and by thee threw down
Th' aspiring Dominations:° thou that day   *rebel angels*
Thy Father's dreadful Thunder didst not spare,
Nor stop thy flaming Chariot wheels, that shook
395　Heav'n's everlasting Frame, while o'er the necks
Thou drov'st of warring Angels disarray'd.
Back from pursuit thy Powers with loud acclaim
Thee only extoll'd, Son of thy Father's might,
To execute fierce vengeance on his foes:
400　Not so on Man; him through their malice fall'n,
Father of Mercy and Grace, thou didst not doom°   *judge*
So strictly, but much more to pity incline:
No sooner did thy dear and only Son
Perceive thee purpos'd not to doom frail Man
405　So strictly, but much more to pity inclin'd,[9]
Hee to appease thy wrath, and end the strife
Of Mercy and Justice in thy face discern'd,
Regardless of the Bliss wherein hee sat
Second to thee, offer'd himself to die
410　For man's offense. O unexampl'd love,
Love nowhere to be found less than Divine!
Hail Son of God, Savior of Men, thy Name
Shall be the copious matter of my Song
Henceforth, and never shall my Harp thy praise

---

7. Line 373 is transplanted in its entirety from Sylvester's
translation of Du Bartas's poem on creation.
8. See John 1.18 and 14.9.
9. Most editors say that "but" or "than" has to be supplied

before "He" (line 406). However, if "much more to pity
inclined" refers to the Son, the "but" immediately preceding is available for the main clause.

415   Forget, nor from thy Father's praise disjoin.
            Thus they in Heav'n, above the starry Sphere,
        Thir happy hours in joy and hymning spent.
        Meanwhile upon the firm opacous Globe
        Of this round World, whose first convex divides
420   The luminous inferior Orbs, enclos'd
        From *Chaos* and th' inroad of Darkness old,[1]
        Satan alighted walks: a Globe far off
        It seem'd, now seems a boundless Continent
        Dark, waste, and wild, under the frown of Night
425   Starless expos'd, and ever-threat'ning storms
        Of *Chaos* blust'ring round, inclement sky;
        Save on that side which from the wall of Heav'n,
        Though distant far, some small reflection gains
        Of glimmering air less vext° with tempest loud: *tossed about*
430   Here walk'd the Fiend at large in spacious field.
        As when a Vultur on *Imaus* bred,
        Whose snowy ridge the roving *Tartar* bounds,
        Dislodging from a Region scarce of prey
        To gorge the flesh of Lambs or yeanling Kids
435   On Hills where Flocks are fed, flies toward the Springs
        Of *Ganges* or *Hydaspes,Indian* streams;
        But in his way lights on the barren Plains
        Of *Sericana*, where *Chineses* drive
        With Sails and Wind thir cany Waggons light:
440   So on this windy Sea of Land, the Fiend
        Walk'd up and down alone bent on his prey,[2]
        Alone, for other Creature in this place
        Living or lifeless to be found was none,
        None yet, but store hereafter from the earth
445   Up hither like Aereal vapors flew
        Of all things transitory and vain, when Sin
        With vanity had fill'd the works of men:[3]
        Both all things vain, and all who in vain things
        Built thir fond hopes of Glory or lasting fame,
450   Or happiness in this or th' other life;
        All who have thir reward on Earth, the fruits
        Of painful Superstition and blind Zeal,
        Naught seeking but the praise of men, here find
        Fit retribution, empty as thir deeds;

1. The "starry Sphere" is either the sphere of the fixed stars or, more loosely, the stars and planets together. The stars are enclosed within the *primum mobile* or "first convex" (sphere). Both heaven and chaos lie outside that opaque ("opacous") shell.
2. The simile compares the vulture's journey to Satan's. One journey is from Imaus (a mountain range said to run through Afghanistan) to the rivers of India; the other is from the "frozen continent" (2.587) of Tartarus, which did not keep Satan from roving, to Eden with its rivers.

The "barren plains of Sericana" correspond to the *primum mobile* because both are stopping places and in both the elements are confused. (The Chinese use sails, the means of propulsion for ships, on their land vehicles; and the *primum mobile* is a "sea of land.")
3. In *Orlando Furioso* 34.73ff., a passage from which Milton quotes in *Of Reformation*, Ariosto tells how Astolfo searches for his lost wits in a Limbo of Vanity on the moon.

455   All th' unaccomplisht works of Nature's hand,
       Abortive, monstrous, or unkindly mixt,
       Dissolv'd on Earth, fleet hither, and in vain,
       Till final dissolution, wander here,
       Not in the neighboring Moon, as some have dream'd;
460   Those argent Fields more likely habitants,
       Translated Saints,[4] or middle Spirits hold
       Betwixt th' Angelical and Human kind:
       Hither of ill-join'd Sons and Daughters born
       First from the ancient World those Giants came
465   With many a vain exploit, though then renown'd:[5]
       The builders next of *Babel* on the Plain
       Of *Sennaar*, and still with vain design
       New *Babels*, had they wherewithal, would build:[6]
       Others came single; he who to be deem'd
470   A God, leap'd fondly into *Ætna* flames,
       Empedocles, and hee who to enjoy
       Plato's Elysium, leap'd into the Sea,
       Cleombrotus,[7] and many more too long,
       Embryos, and Idiots, Eremites and Friars
475   White, Black and Grey, with all thir trumpery.[8]
       Here Pilgrims roam, that stray'd so far to seek
       In *Golgotha*[9] him dead, who lives in Heav'n;
       And they who to be sure of Paradise
       Dying put on the weeds of *Dominic*,
480   Or in *Franciscan* think to pass disguis'd;[1]
       They pass the Planets seven, and pass the fixt,
       And that Crystalline Sphere whose balance weighs
       The Trepidation talkt, and that first mov'd;[2]
       And now Saint *Peter* at Heav'n's Wicket seems
485   To wait them with his Keys, and now at foot
       Of Heav'n's ascent they lift thir Feet, when lo
       A violent cross wind from either Coast
       Blows them transverse ten thousand Leagues awry
       Into the devious Air; then might ye see
490   Cowls, Hoods and Habits with thir weares tost

---

4. Probably such as Enoch (Genesis 5.24) and Elijah (2 Kings 2).

5. The first group of fools are the Giants, "mighty men . . . of renown," born of the misunion of "sons of God" with "daughters of men" (Genesis 6.4).

6. At 12.45–47 the builders of Babel are said to have formed their "vain design" out of a desire for fame. "New Babels" suggests the New Babylon of anti-Papist propaganda.

7. Empedocles and Cleombrotus were not associated by classical writers but occur together in Lactantius' chapter on "Pythagoreans and Stoics who, Believing in the Immortality of the Soul, Foolishly Persuade a Voluntary Death" (*Divinae Institutiones* 3.18). Cleombrotus drowned himself after an unwise reading of Plato's *Phaedo*; Empedocles' motive was to conceal his own mortality.

8. Milton here satirizes a Catholic tradition that consigned cretins and unbaptized infants to a much debated *limbo infantum*. The friars were specified by robe color; "white" meant Carmelite, "black" Dominican, and "grey" Franciscan. The contemptuous juxtaposition of all three colors ridicules the importance assigned to external trappings. "Eremites" were Order of Friars Hermits.

9. The hill where Christ was crucified and buried.

1. Compare *Inferno* 27.67–84, in which Dante tells how Guido da Montefeltro hoped to get into heaven by virtue of Franciscan robes but found to his cost that absolution without repentance is vain.

2. In order of proximity to earth, the spheres passed are the seven planetary spheres; the eighth sphere, containing the "fixed" stars; the ninth, "crystalline sphere;" and the tenth sphere, the "first moved" or *primum mobile*.

And flutter'd into Rags, then Reliques, Beads,
Indulgences, Dispenses,[3] Pardons, Bulls,
The sport of Winds: all these upwhirl'd aloft
Fly o'er the backside of the World far off
495 Into a *Limbo*° large and broad, since call'd   empty region
The Paradise of Fools, to few unknown
Long after, now unpeopl'd and untrod;
All this dark Globe the Fiend found as he pass'd,
And long he wander'd, till at last a gleam
500 Of dawning light turn'd thither-ward in haste
His travell'd steps; far distant he descries
Ascending by degrees magnificent
Up to the wall of Heaven a Structure high,
At top whereof, but far more rich appear'd
505 The work as of a Kingly Palace Gate
With Frontispiece[4] of Diamond and Gold
Imbellisht; thick with sparkling orient° Gems   brilliant
The Portal shone, inimitable on Earth
By Model, or by shading Pencil drawn.
510 The Stairs were such as whereon *Jacob* saw
Angels ascending and descending, bands
Of Guardians bright, when he from *Esau* fled
To *Padan-Aram* in the field of *Luz*,
Dreaming by night under the open Sky,
515 And waking cri'd, *This is the Gate of Heav'n.*[5]
Each Stair mysteriously° was meant,[6] nor stood   symbolically
There always, but drawn up to Heav'n sometimes
Viewless, and underneath a bright Sea flow'd
Of Jasper, or of liquid Pearl, whereon
520 Who after came from Earth, sailing arriv'd,
Wafted by Angels, or flew o'er the Lake
Rapt in a Chariot drawn by fiery Steeds.
The Stairs were then let down, whether to dare
The Fiend by easy ascent, or aggravate
525 His sad exclusion from the doors of Bliss.
Direct against which op'n'd from beneath,
Just o'er the blissful seat of Paradise,
A passage down to th' Earth, a passage wide,
Wider by far than that of after-times
530 Over Mount *Sion*, and, though that were large,
Over the *Promis'd Land* to God so dear,
By which, to visit oft those happy Tribes,
On high behests his Angels to and fro

3. A "dispense" or dispensation was an exemption from a solemn obligation by licence of an ecclesiastical dignitary, especially the Pope.
4. A decorated entrance or a pediment over the gate.
5. The unregenerate Jacob was terrified by the vision of a ladder reaching to heaven just after he had cheated Esau out of his father's blessing (Genesis 27–28). The experi-

ence awed him into belief and a vow to the Lord.
6. Jacob's ladder had been identified with Homer's golden chain linking the universe to Jupiter. Each "stair," or step, could be interpreted as a spiritual stage extending "from the supreme God even to the bottomest dregs of the universe."

Pass'd frequent, and his eye with choice° regard   *careful*
535   From *Paneas* the fount of *Jordan's* flood
        To *Beërsaba*,[7] where the *Holy Land*
        Borders on *Egypt* and th' *Arabian* shore;
        So wide the op'ning seem'd, where bounds were set
        To darkness, such as bound the Ocean wave.
540   *Satan* from hence now on the lower stair
        That scal'd by steps of Gold to Heaven Gate
        Looks down with wonder at the sudden view
        Of all this World at once. As when a Scout
        Through dark and desert ways with peril gone
545   All night; at last by break of cheerful dawn
        Obtains° the brow of some high-climbing Hill,   *reaches*
        Which to his eye discovers unaware
        The goodly prospect of some foreign land
        First seen, or some renown'd Metropolis
550   With glistering Spires and Pinnacles adorn'd,
        Which now the Rising Sun gilds with his beams.
        Such wonder seiz'd, though after Heaven seen,
        The Spirit malign, but much more envy seiz'd
        At sight of all this World beheld so fair.
555   Round he surveys, and well might, where he stood
        So high above the circling Canopy
        Of Night's extended shade; from Eastern Point
        Of *Libra* to the fleecy Star that bears
        Andromeda far off *Atlantic* Seas
560   Beyond th' Horizon;[8] then from Pole to Pole
        He views in breadth, and without longer pause
        Down right into the World's first Region throws
        His flight precipitant, and winds with ease
        Through the pure marble Air his oblique way
565   Amongst innumerable Stars, that shone
        Stars distant, but nigh hand seem'd other Worlds,
        Or other Worlds they seem'd, or happy Isles,
        Like those *Hesperian* Gardens fam'd of old,[9]
        Fortunate Fields, and Groves and flow'ry Vales,
570   Thrice happy Isles, but who dwelt happy there
        He stay'd not to enquire: above them all[1]
        The golden Sun in splendor likest Heaven
        Allur'd his eye: Thither his course he bends
        Through the calm Firmament; but up or down
575   By centre, or eccentric, hard to tell,[2]

---

7. "Paneas" is a later Greek name for Dan—not the city of Dan but the spring of the same name, "the easternmost fountain of Jordan." Beersaba was the southern limit of Canaan, as Dan was the northern.
8. From Satan's viewpoint the constellation Andromeda appears just above Aries, as if carried on its back.
9. A hint of the Fall. Hesiod places beyond the ocean the gardens where the Hesperides (Atlantides) unsuccessfully

guarded apples Jupiter entrusted them with; see 3.559.
1. Above: in splendor, not spatially.
2. Satan might travel by a centric orbit around earth (as in the Ptolemaic universe) or an eccentric orbit, around the sun (as in the Copernican universe). His path is "hard to tell" because specifying further would involve opting for a particular astronomical system (Ptolemaic, Copernican, etc.), a choice Milton avoids; see 4.592–7.

Or Longitude, where the great Luminary
Aloof the vulgar Constellations thick,
That from his Lordly eye keep distance due,
Dispenses Light from far; they as they move
580 Thir Starry dance in numbers° that compute   *rhythms*
Days, months, and years,[3] towards his all-cheering Lamp
Turn swift thir various motions, or are turn'd
By his Magnetic beam, that gently warms
The Universe,[4] and to each inward part
585 With gentle penetration, though unseen,
Shoots invisible virtue even to the deep:
So wondrously was set his Station bright.
There lands the Fiend, a spot like which perhaps
Astronomer in the Sun's lucent Orb
590 Through his glaz'd Optic Tube yet never saw.[5]
The place he found beyond expression bright,
Compar'd with aught on Earth, Metal or Stone;
Not all parts like, but all alike inform'd
With radiant light, as glowing Iron with fire;
595 If metal, part seem'd Gold, part Silver clear;
If stone, Carbuncle most or Chrysolite,
Ruby or Topaz, to the Twelve° that shone   *completing the twelve*
In *Aaron's* Breastplate,[6] and a stone besides
Imagin'd rather oft than elsewhere seen,
600 That stone, or like to that which here below
Philosophers in vain so long have sought,
In vain, though by thir powerful Art they bind
Volatile *Hermes*, and call up unbound
In various shapes old *Proteus* from the Sea,
605 Drain'd through a Limbec° to his Native form.[7]   *beaker*
What wonder then if fields and regions here
Breathe forth *Elixir* pure, and Rivers run
Potable Gold,[8] when with one virtuous° touch   *powerful*
Th' Arch-chemic Sun so far from us remote
610 Produces with Terrestrial Humor mixt
Here in the dark so many precious things
Of color glorious and effect so rare?
Here matter new to gaze the Devil met

3. In Plato's *Timaeus* (38C), God created planets "for the determining of the numbers of time," day, month and year. See also Genesis 1:14, "Let there be lights in the firmament of the heaven to divide the day from the night; and let them be for signs, and for seasons, and for days, and years."

4. Kepler's theory that solar "magnetic" force regulated planetary motions continued Tycho's emphasis on the sun's supremacy.

5. Spots on the sun—supposed to show corruptibility— were observed by Virgil, Charlemagne, Johann Fabricius (1611), and telescopically by the Jesuit Christopher Scheiner (1612) and by Galileo (1613).

6. Aaron's 12 jewels represent the 12 tribes of Israel. His "breastplate of judgment" has four rows of three stones each: "a ruby, a topaz, and a carbuncle in the first row" (Exodus 25; 28:15–20).

7. That is, "Alchemists have failed to find the philosopher's stone, however adept they are at the preliminary stage of fixing philosophic mercury." Hermes is represented as Mercury, and Proteus as matter, because of his changing forms.

8. An elixir is any medium like the philosopher's stone that transmutes base metals to gold. The "elixir of long life," or "Potable [drinkable] Gold," was a goal of alchemy.

Undazzl'd, far and wide his eye commands,
615   For sight no obstacle found here, nor shade,
But all Sun-shine, as when his Beams at Noon
Culminate from th' *Equator*, as they now
Shot upward still direct, whence no way round
Shadow from body opaque can fall, and the Air,
620   Nowhere so clear, sharp'n'd his visual ray
To objects distant far, whereby he soon
Saw within ken a glorious Angel stand,
The same whom *John* saw also in the Sun:[9]
His back was turn'd, but not his brightness hid;
625   Of beaming sunny Rays, a golden tiar
Circl'd his Head, nor less his Locks behind
Illustrious° on his Shoulders fledge° with wings   *shining / feathered*
Lay waving round; on some great charge employ'd
He seem'd, or fixt in cogitation deep.
630   Glad was the Spirit impure; as now in hope
To find who might direct his wand'ring flight
To Paradise the happy seat of Man,
His journey's end and our beginning woe.
But first he casts to change his proper shape,[1]
635   Which else might work him danger or delay:
And now a stripling Cherub he appears,
Not of the prime, yet such as in his face
Youth smil'd Celestial, and to every Limb
Suitable grace diffus'd, so well he feign'd;
640   Under a Coronet his flowing hair
In curls on either check play'd, wings he wore
Of many a color'd plume sprinkl'd with Gold,
His habit fit for speed succinct,[2] and held
Before his decent° steps a Silver wand.   *graceful*
645   He drew not nigh unheard; the Angel bright,
Ere he drew nigh, his radiant visage turn'd,
Admonisht by his ear, and straight was known
Th' Arch-Angel *Uriel*, one of the sev'n
Who in God's presence, nearest to his Throne
650   Stand ready at command, and are his Eyes
That run through all the Heav'ns, or down to th' Earth
Bear his swift errands over moist and dry,
O'er Sea and Land: him *Satan* thus accosts.[3]
       Uriel, for thou of those sev'n Spirits that stand
655   In sight of God's high Throne, gloriously bright,
The first art wont his great authentic will

---

9. Refers to John the Divine's vision in Revelation 19:17,
"I saw an angel standing in the sun."
1. Satan later assumes other shapes: wolf (4.183); cormorant (4.196); lion (4.402); tiger (4.403); toad (4.800);
angel (5.55); serpent (9.188). In Satan, as in Spenser's
Archimago, protean "fluctuations of shape" connote evil.

2. That is, "his uniform suitable for speed," or "his clothing girt up."
3. Seven principal angels are "the eyes of the Lord, which
run to and fro through the whole earth" (Zechariah 4).
Uriel, or "Light of God," was the angel of the south.

Interpreter through highest Heav'n to bring,
Where all his Sons thy Embassy attend;
And here art likeliest by supreme decree
660 Like honor to obtain, and as his Eye
To visit oft this new Creation round;
Unspeakable desire to see, and know
All these his wondrous works, but chiefly Man,
His chief delight and favor,° him for whom   *object of favor*
665 All these his works so wondrous he ordain'd,
Hath brought me from the Choirs of Cherubim
Alone thus wand'ring. Brightest Seraph, tell
In which of all these shining Orbs hath Man
His fixed seat, or fixed seat hath none,
670 But all these shining Orbs his choice to dwell;
That I may find him, and with secret gaze,[4]
Or open admiration him behold
On whom the great Creator hath bestow'd
Worlds, and on whom hath all these graces pour'd;
675 That both in him and all things, as is meet
The Universal Maker we may praise;
Who justly hath driv'n out his Rebel Foes
To deepest Hell, and to repair that loss
Created this new happy Race of Men
680 To serve him better: wise are all his ways.
     So spake the false dissembler unperceiv'd;
For neither Man nor Angel can discern
Hypocrisy, the only evil that walks
Invisible, except to God alone,
685 By his permissive will,[5] through Heav'n and Earth:
And oft though wisdom wake, suspicion sleeps
At wisdom's Gate, and to simplicity
Resigns her charge, while goodness thinks no ill
Where no ill seems: Which now for once beguil'd
690 Uriel, though Regent of the Sun, and held
The sharpest-sighted Spirit of all in Heav'n;
Who to the fraudulent Impostor foul
In his uprightness answer thus return'd.
     Fair Angel, thy desire which tends to know
695 The works of God, thereby to glorify
The great Work-Master, leads to no excess
That reaches blame,[6] but rather merits praise
The more it seems excess, that led thee hither
From thy Empyreal Mansion thus alone,
700 To witness with thine eyes what some perhaps
Contented with report hear only in Heav'n:

4. Echoing Herod's enquiry after Jesus, the second Adam (Matthew 2:8).
5. The permissive will is distinguished from God's positive will, which permits only good.

6. The "desire" for knowledge may be blameless if its objects are good and it has a good motivation (to "glorify" God).

For wonderful indeed are all his works,
Pleasant to know, and worthiest to be all
Had in remembrance always with delight;[7]
705   But what created mind can comprehend
Thir number, or the wisdom infinite
That brought them forth, but hid thir causes deep.[8]
I saw when at his Word the formless Mass,
This world's material mould, came to a heap:
710   Confusion heard his voice, and wild uproar
Stood rul'd, stood vast infinitude confin'd;
Till at his second bidding darkness fled,
Light shone, and order from disorder sprung:
Swift to thir several Quarters hasted then
715   The cumbrous Elements, Earth, Flood, Air, Fire,
And this Ethereal quintessence° of Heav'n   *purest distillation*
Flew upward, spirited with various forms,
That roll'd orbicular, and turn'd to Stars
Numberless, as thou seest, and how they move;
720   Each had his place appointed, each his course,
The rest in circuit walls this Universe.
Look downward on that Globe whose hither side
With light from hence, though but reflected, shines:
That place is Earth the seat of Man, that light
725   His day, which else as th' other Hemisphere
Night would invade, but there the neighboring Moon
(So call that opposite fair Star) her aid
Timely interposes, and her monthly round
Still ending, still renewing through mid Heav'n,
730   With borrow'd light her countenance triform
Hence° fills and empties to enlighten the Earth,   *from the sun*
And in her pale dominion checks the night.
That spot to which I point is *Paradise*,[9]
Adam's abode, those lofty shades his Bow'r.
735   Thy way thou canst not miss, me mine requires.
　　　Thus said, he turn'd, and *Satan* bowing low,
As to superior Spirits is wont in Heav'n,
Where honor due and reverence none neglects,
Took leave, and toward the coast° of Earth beneath,   *side*
740   Down from th' Ecliptic,[1] sped with hop'd success,
Throws his steep flight in many an Aery wheel,
Nor stay'd, till on *Niphates'* top he lights.[2]
　　　　The End of the Third Book.

---

7. See Psalms 111:2, 4, "The works of the Lord are great, sought out of all them that have pleasure therein. . . . He hath made his wonderful works to be remembered."
8. In *De doctrina* 1.9, Milton says that "The good angels do not see into all God's thoughts, as the Papists pretend . . . there are many things of which they are ignorant." Even Christ "does not know absolutely everything, for there are some secrets which the Father has kept to himself alone."

9. Since Paradise is visible from the sun, sunlight is already reaching it: Satan's 12-hour journey from the *primum mobile* has taken at least the second half of Adam's night.
1. The sun's orbit, lying (until the Fall) in the equatorial plane.
2. *Niphates* is a mountain on the Armenia-Assyria border, source of the Tigris. The river of Paradise is called Tigris before it divides (9.71).

Book 4
The Argument

Satan *now in prospect of* Eden, *and nigh the place where he must now attempt the bold enterprise which he undertook alone against God and Man, falls into many doubts with himself, and many passions, fear, envy, and despair; but at length confirms himself in evil, journeys on to Paradise, whose outward prospect and situation is described, overleaps the bounds, sits in the shape of a Cormorant on the Tree of Life, as highest in the Garden to look about him. The Garden describ'd; Satan's first sight of* Adam *and* Eve; *his wonder at thir excellent form and happy state, but with resolution to work thir fall; overhears thir discourse, thence gathers that the Tree of Knowledge was forbidden them to eat of, under penalty of death; and thereon intends to found his Temptation, by seducing them to transgress: then leaves them a while, to know further of thir state by some other means. Meanwhile* Uriel *descending on a Sun-beam warns* Gabriel, *who had in charge the Gate of Paradise, that some evil spirit had escap'd the Deep, and past at Noon by his Sphere in the shape of a good Angel down to Paradise, discovered after by his furious gestures in the Mount.* Gabriel *promises to find him ere morning. Night coming on,* Adam *and* Eve *discourse of going to thir rest: thir Bower describ'd; thir Evening worship.* Gabriel *drawing forth his Bands of Nightwatch to walk the round of Paradise, appoints two strong Angels to* Adam's *Bower, lest the evil spirit should be there doing some harm to* Adam *or* Eve *sleeping; there they find him at the ear of* Eve, *tempting her in a dream, and bring him, though unwilling, to* Gabriel; *by whom question'd, he scornfully answers, prepares resistance, but hinder'd by a Sign from Heaven, flies out of Paradise.*

     O for that warning voice, which he who saw
     Th' *Apocalypse*, heard cry in Heav'n aloud,
     Then when the Dragon, put to second rout,
     Came furious down to be reveng'd on men,
5   *Woe to the inhabitants on Earth!*[1] that now,
     While time was, our first Parents had been warn'd
     The coming of thir secret foe, and scap'd
     Haply so scap'd his mortal snare; for now
     Satan, now first inflam'd with rage, came down,
10   The Tempter ere th' Accuser of man-kind,
     To wreck° on innocent frail man his loss   *avenge*
     Of that first Battle, and his flight to Hell:
     Yet not rejoicing in his speed, though bold,
     Far off and fearless, nor with cause to boast,
15   Begins his dire attempt, which nigh the birth
     Now rolling, boils in his tumultuous breast,
     And like a devilish Engine back recoils
     Upon himself; horror and doubt distract
     His troubl'd thoughts, and from the bottom stir
20   The Hell within him, for within him Hell
     He brings, and round about him, nor from Hell
     One step no more than from himself can fly

---

1. The Apocalypse of St. John (Revelation) relates a vision of a second battle in heaven between Michael and "the Dragon," Satan.

By change of place: Now conscience wakes despair
That slumber'd, wakes the bitter memory
25   Of what he was, what is, and what must be
Worse; of worse deeds worse sufferings must ensue.
Sometimes towards *Eden* which now in his view
Lay pleasant,[2] his griev'd look he fixes sad,
Sometimes towards Heav'n and the full-blazing Sun,
30   Which now sat high in his Meridian Tow'r:
Then much revolving, thus in sighs began.
     O thou that with surpassing Glory crown'd,
Look'st from thy sole Dominion like the God
Of this new World; at whose sight all the Stars
35   Hide thir diminisht heads; to thee I call,
But with no friendly voice, and add thy name
O Sun, to tell thee how I hate thy beams
That bring to my remembrance from what state
I fell, how glorious once above thy Sphere;
40   Till Pride and worse Ambition threw me down
Warring in Heav'n against Heav'n's matchless King:[3]
Ah wherefore! he deserv'd no such return
From me, whom he created what I was
In that bright eminence, and with his good
45   Upbraided none;[4] nor was his service hard.
What could be less than to afford him praise,
The easiest recompense, and pay him thanks,
How due! yet all his good prov'd ill in me,
And wrought but malice; lifted up so high
50   I sdein'd° subjection, and thought one step higher   *disdained*
Would set me highest, and in a moment quit°   *pay off*
The debt immense of endless gratitude,
So burdensome, still paying, still to owe;
Forgetful what from him I still receiv'd,
55   And understood not that a grateful mind
By owing owes not, but still pays, at once
Indebted and discharg'd; what burden then?[5]
O had his powerful Destiny ordain'd
Me some inferior Angel, I had stood
60   Then happy; no unbounded hope had rais'd
Ambition. Yet why not? some other Power
As great might have aspir'd, and me though mean
Drawn to his part; but other Powers as great
Fell not, but stand unshak'n, from within
65   Or from without, to all temptations arm'd.
Hadst thou the same free Will and Power to stand?

---

2. The etymological meaning of "Eden" is "pleasure, delight."
3. According to Edward Phillips, lines 32–41 were shown to him and some others "before the Poem was begun,"
when Milton intended to write a tragedy on the Fall.
4. Demanded no return for his benefits; see James 1.5.
5. Simply by owning an obligation gratefully, one ceases to owe it.

Thou hadst: whom hast thou then or what to accuse,
But Heav'n's free Love dealt equally to all?
Be then his Love accurst, since love or hate,
70 To me alike, it deals eternal woe.
Nay curs'd be thou; since against his thy will
Chose freely what it now so justly rues.
Me miserable! which way shall I fly
Infinite wrath, and infinite despair?
75 Which way I fly is Hell; myself am Hell;
And in the lowest deep a lower deep
Still threat'ning to devour me opens wide,
To which the Hell I suffer seems a Heav'n.
O then at last relent: is there no place
80 Left for Repentance, none for Pardon left?
None left but by submission; and that word
Disdain forbids me, and my dread of shame
Among the Spirits beneath, whom I seduc'd
With other promises and other vaunts
85 Than to submit, boasting I could subdue
Th' Omnipotent. Ay me, they little know
How dearly I abide that boast so vain,
Under what torments inwardly I groan:
While they adore me on the Throne of Hell,
90 With Diadem and Sceptre high advanc'd
The lower still I fall, only Supreme
In misery; such joy Ambition finds.
But say I could repent and could obtain
By Act of Grace[6] my former state; how soon
95 Would highth recall high thoughts, how soon unsay
What feign'd submission swore: ease would recant
Vows made in pain, as violent and void.
For never can true reconcilement grow
Where wounds of deadly hate have pierc'd so deep:
100 Which would but lead me to a worse relapse,
And heavier fall: so should I purchase dear
Short intermission bought with double smart.
This knows my punisher; therefore as far
From granting hee, as I from begging peace:
105 All hope excluded thus, behold instead
Of us out-cast, exil'd, his new delight,
Mankind created, and for him this World.
So farewell Hope, and with Hope farewell Fear,
Farewell Remorse: all Good to me is lost;
110 Evil be thou my Good; by thee at least
Divided Empire with Heav'n's King I hold

6. By concession of favor, not of right; often used for a formal pardon by Parliament.

By thee, and more than half perhaps will reign;
As Man ere long, and this new World shall know.
    Thus while he spake, each passion dimm'd his face,
115   Thrice chang'd with pale, ire, envy and despair,
Which marr'd his borrow'd visage, and betray'd
Him counterfeit, if any eye beheld.
For heav'nly minds from such distempers foul
Are ever clear. Whereof hee soon aware,
120   Each perturbation smooth'd with outward calm,
Artificer° of fraud; and was the first   *inventor*
That practis'd falsehood under saintly show,
Deep malice to conceal, couch't° with revenge: *hidden*
Yet not anough had practis'd to deceive
125   *Uriel* once warn'd; whose eye pursu'd him down
The way he went, and on th' *Assyrian* mount°   *Niphates mountain range*
Saw him disfigur'd, more than could befall
Spirit of happy sort: his gestures fierce
He mark'd and mad demeanor, then alone,
130   As he suppos'd, all unobserv'd, unseen.
So on he fares, and to the border comes
Of *Eden,* where delicious Paradise,
Now nearer, Crowns with her enclosure green,
As with a rural mound the champaign° head   *unenclosed, level*
135   Of a steep wilderness, whose hairy sides
With thicket overgrown, grotesque and wild,
Access deni'd; and over head up grew
Insuperable highth of loftiest shade,
Cedar, and Pine, and Fir, and branching Palm,
140   A Silvan Scene, and as the ranks ascend
Shade above shade, a woody Theatre
Of stateliest view. Yet higher than thir tops
The verdurous wall of Paradise up sprung:
Which to our general Sire° gave prospect large   *Adam*
145   Into his nether Empire neighboring round.
And higher than that Wall a circling row
Of goodliest Trees loaden with fairest Fruit,
Blossoms and Fruits at once of golden hue
Appear'd, with gay enamell'd° colors mixt: *lustrous*
150   On which the Sun more glad impress'd his beams
Than in fair Evening Cloud, or humid Bow,°   *rainbow*
When God hath show'r'd the earth; so lovely seem'd
That Lantskip:° And of pure now purer air   *landscape*
Meets his approach, and to the heart inspires
155   Vernal delight and joy, able to drive
All sadness but despair: now gentle gales
Fanning thir odoriferous wings dispense
Native perfúmes, and whisper whence they stole
Those balmy spoils. As when to them who sail

160   Beyond the *Cape* of *Hope*, and now are past
      Mozambic,[7] off at Sea North-East winds blow
      Sabean[8] Odors from the spicy shore
      Of *Araby* the blest, with such delay
      Well pleas'd they slack thir course, and many a League
165   Cheer'd with the grateful smell old Ocean smiles.
      So entertain'd those odorous sweets the Fiend
      Who came thir bane, though with them better pleas'd
      Than *Asmodeus* with the fishy fume,
      That drove him, though enamor'd, from the Spouse
170   Of *Tobit's* Son, and with a vengeance sent
      From *Media* post to *Egypt*, there fast bound.[9]
          Now to th' ascent of that steep savage° Hill   *wild*
      Satan had journey'd on, pensive and slow;
      But further way found none, so thick entwin'd,
175   As one continu'd brake, the undergrowth
      Of shrubs and tangling bushes had perplext
      All path of Man or Beast that pass'd that way:
      One Gate there only was, and that look'd East
      On th' other side: which when th' arch-felon saw
180   Due entrance he disdain'd, and in contempt,
      At one slight bound high overleap'd all bound
      Of Hill or highest Wall, and sheer within
      Lights on his feet. As when a prowling Wolf,
      Whom hunger drives to seek new haunt for prey,
185   Watching where Shepherds pen thir Flocks at eve
      In hurdl'd Cotes° amid the field secure,   *shelters*
      Leaps o'er the fence with ease into the Fold:
      Or as a Thief bent to unhoard the cash
      Of some rich Burgher, whose substantial doors,
190   Cross-barr'd and bolted fast, fear no assault,
      In at the window climbs, or o'er the tiles:
      So clomb° this first grand Thief into God's Fold: *climbed*
      So since into his Church lewd Hirelings[1] climb.
      Thence up he flew, and on the Tree of Life,
195   The middle Tree and highest there that grew,
      Sat like a Cormorant;[2] yet not true Life
      Thereby regain'd, but sat devising Death
      To them who liv'd; nor on the virtue thought
      Of that life-giving Plant, but only us'd
200   For prospect,° what well us'd had been the pledge   *lookout*

7. Mozambique, a Portuguese colony on the east coast of Africa; the trade route lay between Mozambique and Madagascar.
8. Of Saba or Sheba (now Yemen). Milton draws on the description of "Araby the blest"—"Arabia felix"—in Diodorus Siculus 3.46.
9. The apocryphal book Tobit relates the story of Tobit's son Tobias, who was sent into Media on an errand and there married Sara. Sara had previously been given to seven men, but all were killed by the jealous spirit Asmodeus before their marriages could be consummated. By the advice of Raphael, however, Tobias succeeded by creating a fishy smoke to drive away the devil Asmodeus.
1. Wicked men motivated only by material gain.
2. A voracious sea bird, often used to describe greedy clergy.

Of immortality. So little knows
Any, but God alone, to value right
The good before him, but perverts best things
To worst abuse, or to thir meanest use.
205 Beneath him with new wonder now he views
To all delight of human sense expos'd
In narrow room Nature's whole wealth, yea more,
A Heaven on Earth: for blissful Paradise
Of God the Garden was, by him in the East
210 Of *Eden* planted; *Eden* stretch'd her Line
From *Auran* Eastward to the Royal Tow'rs
Of Great *Seleucia*, built by *Grecian* Kings,
Or where the Sons of *Eden* long before
Dwelt in *Telassar:*[3] in this pleasant soil
215 His far more pleasant Garden God ordain'd;
Out of the fertile ground he caus'd to grow
All Trees of noblest kind for sight, smell, taste;
And all amid them stood the Tree of Life,
High eminent, blooming Ambrosial Fruit
220 Of vegetable Gold; and next to Life
Our Death the Tree of Knowledge grew fast by,
Knowledge of Good bought dear by knowing ill.[4]
Southward through *Eden* went a River large,
Nor chang'd his course, but through the shaggy hill
225 Pass'd underneath ingulft, for God had thrown
That Mountain as his Garden mould high rais'd
Upon the rapid current, which through veins
Of porous Earth with kindly° thirst up-drawn,   natural
Rose a fresh Fountain, and with many a rill
230 Water'd the Garden;[5] thence united fell
Down the steep glade, and met the nether Flood,
Which from his darksome passage now appears,
And now divided into four main Streams,
Runs diverse, wand'ring many a famous Realm
235 And Country whereof here needs no account,
But rather to tell how, if Art could tell,
How from that Sapphire Fount the crisped° Brooks,   wavy
Rolling on Orient Pearl and sands of Gold,
With mazy error° under pendant shades   wandering
240 Ran Nectar, visiting each plant, and fed
Flow'rs worthy of Paradise which not nice° Art   careful
In Beds and curious Knots, but Nature boon°   bounteous
Pour'd forth profuse on Hill and Dale and Plain,
Both where the morning Sun first warmly smote

---

3. Auran was an eastern boundary of the land of Israel.
Great Seleucia was built by Alexander's general Seleucus
Nicator as a seat of government for his Syrian empire.
The mention of Telassar prophesies war in Eden; see 2

Kings 14.11ff., where Telassar is an instance of lands destroyed utterly.
4. See Genesis 2.9.
5. See Genesis 2.10.

245   The open field, and where the unpierc't shade
         Imbrown'd° the noontide Bow'rs: Thus was this place,   *darkened*
         A happy rural seat of various view:
         Groves whose rich Trees wept odorous Gums and Balm,
         Others whose fruit burnisht with Golden Rind
250   Hung amiable,° *Hesperian* Fables true,[6]   *lovely*
         If true, here only, and of delicious taste:
         Betwixt them Lawns, or level Downs, and Flocks
         Grazing the tender herb, were interpos'd,
         Or palmy hillock, or the flow'ry lap
255   Of some irriguous° Valley spread her store,   *well-watered*
         Flow'rs of all hue, and without Thorn the Rose:[7]
         Another side, umbrageous° Grots and Caves   *shady*
         Of cool recess, o'er which the mantling Vine
         Lays forth her purple Grape, and gently creeps
260   Luxuriant; meanwhile murmuring waters fall
         Down the slope hills, disperst, or in a Lake,
         That to the fringed Bank with Myrtle crown'd,
         Her crystal mirror holds, unite thir streams.
         The Birds thir choir apply;° airs, vernal airs,[8]   *practice*
265   Breathing the smell of field and grove, attune
         The trembling leaves, while Universal *Pan*[9]
         Knit with the *Graces* and the *Hours* in dance
         Led on th' Eternal Spring.[1] Not that fair field
         Of *Enna*, where *Proserpin* gath'ring flow'rs
270   Herself a fairer Flow'r by gloomy *Dis*
         Was gather'd, which cost *Ceres* all that pain
         To seek her through the world;[2] nor that sweet Grove
         Of *Daphne* by *Orontes*, and th' inspir'd
         Castalian Spring[3] might with this Paradise
275   Of *Eden* strive; nor that *Nyseian* Isle
         Girt with the River *Triton*, where old *Cham*,
         Whom Gentiles *Ammon* call and *Lybian Jove*,
         Hid *Amalthea* and her Florid° Son,   *ruddy-complexioned*
         Young *Bacchus*, from his Stepdame *Rhea's* eye;[4]
280   Nor where *Abassin* Kings thir issue Guard,
         Mount *Amara*, though this by some suppos'd
         True Paradise under the *Ethiop* Line
         By *Nilus* head, enclos'd with shining Rock,

---

6. Golden fruit like the legendary apples of the western islands, the Hesperides.

7. The thornless rose was used to symbolize the sinless state of humanity before the Fall; or the state of grace.

8. Breezes and melodies.

9. Pan (Greek for "all") was a symbol of universal nature.

1. Neoplatonists thought the triadic pattern of their dance expressed the movement underlying all natural generation.

2. The rape of Proserpina by Dis, the king of hell, was located in Enna by Ovid (*Fasti* 4.420ff.). The search for her made the world barren, and even when she was found,

she was restored to Ceres—and fruitfulness to the world—only for half the year.

3. The grove called "Daphne" beside the river Orontes, near Antioch, had an Apolline oracle and a stream named after the famous Castalian spring of Parnassus.

4. Ammon, King of Libya, had an illicit affair with a maiden Amaltheia, who gave birth to a marvelous son Dionysus (Bacchus). To protect mother and child from the jealousy of his wife Rhea, Ammon hid them on Nysa, an island near modern Tunis. The identifications of Ammon with the Libyan Jupiter and with Noah's son Ham were widely accepted.

A whole day's journey high,[5] but wide remote
285   From this *Assyrian* Garden, where the Fiend
Saw undelighted all delight, all kind
Of living Creatures new to sight and strange:
Two of far nobler shape erect and tall,
Godlike erect, with native Honor clad
290   In naked Majesty seem'd Lords of all,
And worthy seem'd, for in thir looks Divine
The image of thir glorious Maker shone,[6]
Truth, Wisdom, Sanctitude severe and pure,
Severe, but in true filial freedom plac't;
295   Whence true autority in men; though both
Not equal, as thir sex not equal seem'd;
For contemplation hee and valor form'd,
For softness shee and sweet attractive Grace,
Hee for God only, shee for God in him:[7]
300   His fair large Front° and Eye sublime° declar'd   *forehead / uplifted*
Absolute rule; and Hyacinthine Locks
Round from his parted forelock manly hung
Clust'ring, but not beneath his shoulders broad:
Shee as a veil down to the slender waist
305   Her unadorned golden tresses wore
Dishevell'd, but in wanton ringlets wav'd
As the Vine curls her tendrils, which impli'd
Subjection, but requir'd with gentle sway,
And by her yielded, by him best receiv'd,
310   Yielded with coy° submission, modest pride,   *modest*
And sweet reluctant amorous delay.
Nor those mysterious parts were then conceal'd,
Then was not guilty shame: dishonest shame
Of Nature's works, honor dishonorable,
315   Sin-bred, how have ye troubl'd all mankind
With shows instead, mere shows of seeming pure,
And banisht from man's life his happiest life,
Simplicity and spotless innocence.
So pass'd they naked on, nor shunn'd the sight
320   Of God or Angel, for they thought no ill:
So hand in hand they pass'd, the loveliest pair
That ever since in love's imbraces met,
Adam the goodliest man of men since born
His Sons, the fairest of her Daughters *Eve*.
325   Under a tuft of shade that on a green
Stood whispering soft, by a fresh Fountain side
They sat them down, and after no more toil

5. Milton takes his description of Mount Amara from Peter Heylyn's *Cosmographie* 4.64.
6. See Genesis 1.27: "God created man in his own image."

7. See 1 Corinthians 11.3: "The head of every man is Christ; and the head of the woman is the man; and the head of Christ is God."

Of thir sweet Gard'ning labor than suffic'd
To recommend cool *Zephyr*,[8] and made ease
330   More easy, wholesome thirst and appetite
More grateful, to thir Supper Fruits they fell,
Nectarine Fruits which the compliant boughs
Yielded them, side-long as they sat recline°   *lying down*
On the soft downy Bank damaskt with flow'rs:
335   The savory pulp they chew, and in the rind
Still as they thirsted scoop the brimming stream;
Nor gentle purpose,° nor endearing smiles   *conversation*
Wanted,° nor youthful dalliance as beseems   *lacked*
Fair couple, linkt in happy nuptial League,
340   Alone as they. About them frisking play'd
All Beasts of th' Earth, since wild, and of all chase
In Wood or Wilderness, Forest or Den;
Sporting the Lion ramp'd,° and in his paw   *reared up*
Dandl'd the Kid; Bears, Tigers, Ounces,° Pards° *lynxes / leopards*
345   Gamboll'd before them, th' unwieldy Elephant
To make them mirth us'd all his might, and wreath'd
His Lithe Proboscis; close the Serpent sly
Insinuating,[9] wove with Gordian twine[1]
His braided train, and of his fatal guile
350   Gave proof unheeded; others on the grass
Coucht, and now fill'd with pasture gazing sat,
Or Bedward ruminating;[2] for the Sun
Declin'd was hasting now with prone career
To th' Ocean Isles,[3] and in th' ascending Scale
355   Of Heav'n the Stars that usher Evening rose:
When *Satan* still in gaze, as first he stood,
Scarce thus at length fail'd speech recover'd sad.
     O Hell! what do mine eyes with grief behold,
Into our room of bliss thus high advanc't
360   Creatures of other mould, earth-born perhaps,
Not Spirits, yet to heav'nly Spirits bright
Little inferior; whom my thoughts pursue
With wonder, and could love, so lively shines
In them Divine resemblance, and such grace
365   The hand that form'd them on thir shape hath pour'd.
Ah gentle pair, yee little think how nigh
Your change approaches, when all these delights
Will vanish and deliver ye to woe,
More woe, the more your taste is now of joy;
370   Happy, but for so happy ill secur'd
Long to continue, and this high seat your Heav'n
Ill fenc't for Heav'n to keep out such a foe

8. The west wind.
9. Penetrating by sinuous ways.
1. Coil, convolution, as difficult to undo as the Gordian

knot, which it took the hero Alexander to cut.
2. Chewing the cud before going to rest.
3. The Azores.

As now is enter'd; yet no purpos'd foe
To you whom I could pity thus forlorn
375   Though I unpitied: League with you I seek,
And mutual amity so strait,° so close,   *intimate*
That I with you must dwell, or you with me
Henceforth; my dwelling haply may not please
Like this fair Paradise, your sense, yet such
380   Accept your Maker's work; he gave it me,
Which I as freely give; Hell shall unfold,[4]
To entertain you two, her widest Gates,
And send forth all her Kings; there will be room,
Not like these narrow limits, to receive
385   Your numerous offspring; if no better place,
Thank him who puts me loath to this revenge
On you who wrong me not for him who wrong'd.
And should I at your harmless innocence
Melt, as I do, yet public reason[5] just,
390   Honor and Empire with revenge enlarg'd,
By conquering this new World, compels me now
To do what else though damn'd I should abhor.
     So spake the Fiend, and with necessity,
The Tyrant's plea, excus'd his devilish deeds.
395   Then from his lofty stand on that high Tree
Down he alights among the sportful Herd
Of those fourfooted kinds, himself now one,
Now other, as thir shape serv'd best his end
Nearer to view his prey, and unespi'd
400   To mark what of thir state he more might learn
By word or action markt: about them round
A Lion now he stalks with fiery glare,
Then as a Tiger, who by chance hath spi'd
In some Purlieu° two gentle Fawns at play,   *edge of a forest*
405   Straight couches close, then rising changes oft
His couchant watch, as one who chose his ground
Whence rushing he might surest seize them both
Gript in each paw: when *Adam* first of men
To first of women *Eve* thus moving speech,
410   Turn'd him° all ear to hear new utterance flow.   *Satan*
     Sole partner and sole part of all these joys,[6]
Dearer thyself than all; needs must the Power
That made us, and for us this ample World
Be infinitely good, and of his good
415   As liberal and free as infinite,
That rais'd us from the dust and plac't us here
In all this happiness, who at his hand

4. A blasphemous echo of Matthew 10.8 ("freely ye have received, freely give").

5. Reason of state, a perversion of the Ciceronian princi-ple (*Laws* 3.3.8) that the good of the people is the supreme law.

6. The first "sole" means "only"; the second, "unrivalled."

Have nothing merited, nor can perform
Aught whereof hee hath need, hee who requires
420   From us no other service than to keep
This one, this easy charge, of all the Trees
In Paradise that bear delicious fruit
So various, not to taste that only Tree
Of Knowledge, planted by the Tree of Life,[7]
425   So near grows Death to Life, whate'er Death is,
Some dreadful thing no doubt; for well thou know'st
God hath pronounc't it death to taste that Tree,
The only sign of our obedience left
Among so many signs of power and rule
430   Conferr'd upon us, and Dominion giv'n
Over all other Creatures that possess
Earth, Air, and Sea.[8] Then let us not think hard
One easy prohibition, who enjoy
Free leave so large to all things else, and choice
435   Unlimited of manifold delights:
But let us ever praise him, and extol
His bounty, following our delightful task
To prune these growing Plants, and tend these Flow'rs,
Which were it toilsome, yet with thee were sweet.
440   To whom thus Eve repli'd. O thou for whom
And from whom I was form'd flesh of thy flesh,[9]
And without whom am to no end, my Guide
And Head, what thou hast said is just and right.[1]
For wee to him indeed all praises owe,
445   And daily thanks, I chiefly who enjoy
So far the happier Lot, enjoying thee
Preëminent by so much odds,° while thou   *advantage*
Like consort to thyself canst nowhere find.
That day I oft remember, when from sleep
450   I first awak't, and found myself repos'd
Under a shade on flow'rs, much wond'ring where
And what I was, whence thither brought, and how.
Not distant far from thence a murmuring sound
Of waters issu'd from a Cave and spread
455   Into a liquid Plain, then stood unmov'd
Pure as th' expanse of Heav'n; I thither went
With unexperienc't thought, and laid me down
On the green bank, to look into the clear
Smooth Lake, that to me seem'd another Sky.
460   As I bent down to look, just opposite,

---

7. See Genesis 2.16ff.
8. See Genesis 1.28: "God said unto them . . . have do-minion over the fish of the sea, and over the fowl of the air, and over every living thing that moveth upon the earth."
9. See 1 Corinthians 11.9: "Neither was the man created for the woman; but the woman for the man." See Genesis 2.23.
1. See 1 Corinthians 11.3: "The head of every man is Christ; and the head of the woman is the man; and the head of Christ is God."

A Shape within the wat'ry gleam appear'd
Bending to look on me, I started back,
It started back, but pleas'd I soon return'd,
Pleas'd it return'd as soon with answering looks
465   Of sympathy and love; there I had fixt
Mine eyes till now, and pin'd with vain desire,[2]
Had not a voice thus warn'd me, What thou seest,
What there thou seest fair Creature is thyself,
With thee it came and goes: but follow me,
470   And I will bring thee where no shadow stays°   awaits
Thy coming, and thy soft imbraces, hee
Whose image thou art, him thou shalt enjoy
Inseparably thine, to him shalt bear
Multitudes like thyself, and thence be call'd
475   Mother of human Race: what could I do,
But follow straight, invisibly thus led?
Till I espi'd thee, fair indeed and tall,
Under a Platan, yet methought less fair,
Less winning soft, less amiably mild,
480   Than that smooth wat'ry image; back I turn'd,
Thou following cri'd'st aloud, Return fair *Eve*,
Whom fli'st thou? whom thou fli'st, of him thou art,
His flesh, his bone; to give thee being I lent
Out of my side to thee, nearest my heart
485   Substantial Life, to have thee by my side
Henceforth an individual° solace dear;   inseparable
Part of my Soul I seek thee, and thee claim
My other half: with that thy gentle hand
Seiz'd mine, I yielded, and from that time see
490   How beauty is excell'd by manly grace
And wisdom, which alone is truly fair.
    So spake our general Mother, and with eyes
Of conjugal attraction unreprov'd,°   innocent
And meek surrender, half imbracing lean'd
495   On our first Father, half her swelling Breast
Naked met his under the flowing Gold
Of her loose tresses hid: hee in delight
Both of her Beauty and submissive Charms
Smil'd with superior Love, as *Jupiter*
500   On *Juno* smiles, when he impregns° the Clouds   impregnates
That shed *May* Flowers; and press'd her Matron lip
With kisses pure: aside the Devil turn'd
For envy, yet with jealous leer malign
Ey'd them askance, and to himself thus plain'd.°   complained
505   Sight hateful, sight tormenting! thus these two
Imparadis't in one another's arms

---

2. Alluding to Ovid's story of the proud youth Narcissus, who was punished for his scornfulness by being made to fall in love with his own reflection in a pool.

The happier *Eden*, shall enjoy thir fill
Of bliss on bliss, while I to Hell am thrust,
Where neither joy nor love, but fierce desire,
510   Among our other torments not the least,
Still unfulfill'd with pain of longing pines;°   *troubles*
Yet let me not forget what I have gain'd
From thir own mouths; all is not theirs it seems:
One fatal Tree there stands of Knowledge call'd,
515   Forbidden them to taste: Knowledge forbidd'n?
Suspicious, reasonless. Why should thir Lord
Envy them that? can it be sin to know,
Can it be death? and do they only stand
By Ignorance, is that thir happy state,
520   The proof of thir obedience and thir faith?
O fair foundation laid whereon to build
Thir ruin! Hence I will excite thir minds
With more desire to know, and to reject
Envious commands, invented with design
525   To keep them low whom Knowledge might exalt
Equal with Gods; aspiring to be such,
They taste and die: what likelier can ensue?
But first with narrow search I must walk round
This Garden, and no corner leave unspi'd;
530   A chance but chance³ may lead where I may meet
Some wand'ring Spirit of Heav'n, by Fountain side,
Or in thick shade retir'd, from him to draw
What further would be learnt. Live while ye may,
Yet happy pair; enjoy, till I return,
535   Short pleasures, for long woes are to succeed.
    So saying, his proud step he scornful turn'd,
But with sly circumspection, and began
Through wood, through waste, o'er hill, o'er dale his roam.
Meanwhile in utmost Longitude,⁴ where Heav'n
540   With Earth and Ocean meets, the setting Sun
Slowly descended, and with right aspect
Against the eastern Gate of Paradise
Levell'd his ev'ning Rays: it was a Rock
Of Alablaster,° pil'd up to the Clouds,   *alabaster*
545   Conspicuous far, winding with one ascent
Accessible from Earth, one entrance high;
The rest was craggy cliff, that overhung
Still as it rose, impossible to climb.⁵
Betwixt these rocky Pillars *Gabriel*⁶ sat
550   Chief of th' Angelic Guards, awaiting night;
About him exercis'd Heroic Games

---

3. An accident and an opportunity.
4. The farthest west.
5. A possible source is the paradise of Mount Amara in

Heylyn's *Cosmographie*.
6. "Strength of God," one of the four archangels ruling the corners of the world.

Th' unarmed Youth of Heav'n, but nigh at hand
Celestial Armory, Shields, Helms, and Spears
Hung high with Diamond flaming, and with Gold.
555 Thither came *Uriel*, gliding through the Even
On a Sun-beam, swift as a shooting Star
In *Autumn* thwarts° the night, when vapors fir'd   *crosses*
Impress the Air, and shows the Mariner
From what point of his Compass to beware
560 Impetuous winds:[7] he thus began in haste.
    Gabriel, to thee thy course by Lot hath giv'n
Charge and strict watch that to this happy place
No evil thing approach or enter in;
This day at highth of Noon came to my Sphere
565 A Spirit, zealous, as he seem'd, to know
More of th' Almighty's works, and chiefly Man
God's latest Image: I describ'd° his way   *observed*
Bent all on speed, and markt his Aery Gait;
But in the Mount that lies from *Eden* North,
570 Where he first lighted, soon discern'd his looks
Alien from Heav'n, with passions foul obscur'd:
Mine eye pursu'd him still, but under shade
Lost sight of him; one of the banisht crew
I fear, hath ventur'd from the Deep, to raise
575 New troubles; him thy care must be to find.
    To whom the winged Warrior thus return'd:
Uriel,[8] no wonder if thy perfect sight,
Amid the Sun's bright circle where thou sitst,
See far and wide: in at this Gate none pass
580 The vigilance here plac't, but such as come
Well known from Heav'n; and since Meridian hour
No Creature thence: if Spirit of other sort,
So minded, have o'erleapt these earthy bounds
On purpose, hard thou know'st it to exclude
585 Spiritual substance with corporeal bar.
But if within the circuit of these walks
In whatsoever shape he lurk, of whom
Thou tell'st, by morrow dawning I shall know.
    So promis'd hee, and *Uriel* to his charge
590 Return'd on that bright beam, whose point now rais'd
Bore him slope downward to the Sun now fall'n
Beneath th' *Azores*; whither the prime Orb,
Incredible how swift, had thither roll'd
Diurnal,° or this less volúbil[9] Earth   *in one day*
595 By shorter flight to th' East, had left him there
Arraying with reflected Purple and Gold

---

7. Shooting stars were thought to be a sign of storm be-   8. "Light of God."
cause in falling they were thrust down by winds.   9. Capable of ready rotation on its axis.

The Clouds that on his Western Throne attend:[1]
Now came still Ev'ning on, and Twilight gray
Had in her sober Livery all things clad;
600 Silence accompanied, for Beast and Bird,
They to thir grassy Couch, these to thir Nests
Were slunk, all but the wakeful Nightingale;
She all night long her amorous descant sung;
Silence was pleas'd: now glow'd the Firmament
605 With living Sapphires: *Hesperus*[2] that led
The starry Host, rode brightest, till the Moon
Rising in clouded Majesty, at length
Apparent Queen unveil'd her peerless light,
And o'er the dark her Silver Mantle threw.
610   When *Adam* thus to *Eve*: Fair Consort, th' hour
Of night, and all things now retir'd to rest
Mind us of like repose, since God hath set
Labor and rest, as day and night to men
Successive, and the timely dew of sleep
615 Now falling with soft slumbrous weight inclines
Our eye-lids; other Creatures all day long
Rove idle unimploy'd, and less need rest;
Man hath his daily work of body or mind
Appointed, which declares his Dignity,
620 And the regard of Heav'n on all his ways;
While other Animals unactive range,
And of thir doings God takes no account.
Tomorrow ere fresh Morning streak the East
With first approach of light, we must be ris'n,
625 And at our pleasant labor, to reform
Yon flow'ry Arbors, yonder Alleys green,
Our walk at noon, with branches overgrown,
That mock our scant manuring,° and require   *cultivating*
More hands than ours to lop thir wanton growth:
630 Those Blossoms also, and those dropping Gums,
That lie bestrown unsightly and unsmooth,
Ask riddance, if we mean to tread with ease;
Meanwhile, as Nature wills, Night bids us rest.
To whom thus *Eve* with perfect beauty adorn'd.
635 My Author° and Disposer, what thou bidd'st   *origin, creator*
Unargu'd I obey; so God ordains,
God is thy Law, thou mine: to know no more
Is woman's happiest knowledge and her praise.
With thee conversing I forget all time,
640 All seasons and thir change, all please alike.[3]
Sweet is the breath of morn, her rising sweet,

---

1. The appearance of sunset can be regarded as either by orbital motion of the sun about the earth or by the earth's rotation (a lesser movement).

2. The evening star.
3. Time of day; not "seasons of the year," since it is still eternal spring.

With charm° of earliest Birds; pleasant the Sun   *song*
When first on this delightful Land he spreads
His orient Beams, on herb, tree, fruit, and flow'r,
645   Glist'ring with dew; fragrant the fertile earth
After soft showers; and sweet the coming on
Of grateful Ev'ning mild, then silent Night
With this her solemn Bird and this fair Moon,
And these the Gems of Heav'n, her starry train:
650   But neither breath of Morn when she ascends
With charm of earliest Birds, nor rising Sun
On this delightful land, nor herb, fruit, flow'r,
Glist'ring with dew, nor fragrance after showers,
Nor grateful Ev'ning mild, nor silent Night
655   With this her solemn Bird, nor walk by Moon,
Or glittering Star-light without thee is sweet.
But wherefore all night long shine these, for whom
This glorious sight, when sleep hath shut all eyes?
        To whom our general Ancestor repli'd.
660   Daughter of God and Man, accomplisht *Eve*,
Those have thir course to finish, round the Earth,
By morrow Ev'ning, and from Land to Land
In order, though to Nations yet unborn,
Minist'ring light prepar'd, they set and rise;
665   Lest total darkness should by Night regain
Her old possession, and extinguish life
In Nature and all things, which these soft fires
Not only enlighten, but with kindly heat
Of various influence foment and warm,
670   Temper or nourish, or in part shed down
Thir stellar virtue on all kinds that grow
On Earth, made hereby apter to receive
Perfection from the Sun's more potent Ray.[4]
These then, though unbeheld in deep of night,
675   Shine not in vain, nor think, though men were none,
That Heav'n would want spectators, God want praise;
Millions of spiritual Creatures walk the Earth
Unseen, both when we wake, and when we sleep:
All these with ceaseless praise his works behold
680   Both day and night: how often from the steep
Of echoing Hill or Thicket have we heard
Celestial voices to the midnight air,
Sole, or responsive each to other's note
Singing thir great Creator: oft in bands
685   While they keep watch, or nightly rounding walk,
With Heav'nly touch of instrumental sounds

4. In Neoplatonic astrology, Sol was said to accomplish the generation of new life by acting through each of the other planets in turn; their function was only to modulate his influence or to select from his complete spectrum of virtues. After the Fall, the influence of the stars becomes less "kindly" (benign; natural).

In full harmonic number join'd, thir songs
Divide the night, and lift our thoughts to Heaven.
   Thus talking hand in hand alone they pass'd
690 On to thir blissful Bower; it was a place
Chos'n by the sovran Planter, when he fram'd
All things to man's delightful use; the roof
Of thickest covert was inwoven shade
Laurel and Myrtle, and what higher grew
695 Of firm and fragrant leaf; on either side
Acanthus, and each odorous bushy shrub
Fenc'd up the verdant wall; each beauteous flow'r,
Iris all hues, Roses, and Jessamin°   *jasmine*
Rear'd high thir flourisht heads between, and wrought
700 Mosaic; underfoot the Violet,
Crocus, and Hyacinth with rich inlay
Broider'd the ground, more color'd than with stone
Of costliest Emblem:⁵ other Creature here
Beast, Bird, Insect, or Worm durst enter none;
705 Such was thir awe of Man. In shadier Bower
More sacred and sequester'd, though but feign'd,
Pan or *Silvanus* never slept, nor Nymph,
Nor *Faunus* haunted.⁶ Here in close recess
With Flowers, Garlands, and sweet-smelling Herbs
710 Espoused *Eve* deckt first her Nuptial Bed,
And heav'nly Choirs the Hymenaean° sung,   *wedding hymn*
What day the genial° Angel to our Sire   *nuptial, generative*
Brought her in naked beauty more adorn'd,
More lovely than *Pandora,* whom the Gods
715 Endow'd with all thir gifts, and O too like
In sad event, when to the unwiser Son
Of *Japhet* brought by *Hermes,* she ensnar'd
Mankind with her fair looks, to be aveng'd
On him who had stole *Jove's* authentic fire.⁷
720   Thus at thir shady Lodge arriv'd, both stood,
Both turn'd, and under op'n Sky ador'd
The God that made both Sky, Air, Earth and Heav'n
Which they beheld, the Moon's resplendent Globe
And starry Pole:° Thou also mad'st the Night,   *sky*

---

5. Any ornament of inlaid work; the other sense of "emblem" (pictorial symbol) also operates here, to draw attention to the emblematic properties of the flowers (the humility of the violet, prudence of the hyacinth, amiability of the jasmine, etc.). The bower as a whole is an emblem of true married love.

6. Pan, Silvanus, and Faunus were confused, for all were represented as half man, half goat. Pan was a symbol of fecundity; Silvanus, god of woods, symbolized gardens and limits; Faunus, the Roman Pan, a wood god, and the father of satyrs, was an emblem of concupiscence.

7. Milton has followed the version of the myth in Charles Estienne's *Dictionarium historicum* (1671): "Pandora . . .

is feigned by Hesiod the first woman—made by Vulcan at Jupiter's command—. . . she was called Pandora, either because she was 'endowed with all [the gods'] gifts,' or because she was endowed with gifts by all." She was "sent with a closed casket to Epimetheus, since Jupiter wanted revenge on the human race for the boldness of Prometheus, who had stolen fire from heaven and taken it . . . down to earth; and that Epimetheus received her and opened the casket, which contained every kind of evil, so that it filled the world with diseases and calamaties." Prometheus and Epimetheus were sons of Iapetus, the Titan son of Coelus and Terra. Milton identifies Iapetus with Iaphet (Noah's son).

725 Maker Omnipotent, and thou the Day,
Which we in our appointed work imploy'd
Have finisht happy in our mutual help
And mutual love, the Crown of all our bliss
Ordain'd by thee, and this delicious place
730 For us too large, where thy abundance wants
Partakers, and uncropt falls to the ground.
But thou hast promis'd from us two a Race
To fill the Earth, who shall with us extol
Thy goodness infinite, both when we wake,
735 And when we seek, as now, thy gift of sleep.
      This said unanimous, and other Rites
Observing none, but adoration pure
Which God likes best, into thir inmost bower
Handed they went; and eas'd the putting off
740 These troublesome disguises which wee wear,
Straight side by side were laid, nor turn'd I ween
Adam from his fair Spouse, nor *Eve* the Rites
Mysterious of connubial Love refus'd:
Whatever Hypocrites austerely talk
745 Of purity and place and innocence,
Defaming as impure what God declares
Pure, and commands to some, leaves free to all.
Our Maker bids increase,[8] who bids abstain
But our Destroyer, foe to God and Man?
750 Hail wedded Love, mysterious Law, true source
Of human offspring, sole propriety
In Paradise of all things common else.
By thee adulterous lust was driv'n from men
Among the bestial herds to range, by thee
755 Founded in Reason, Loyal, Just, and Pure,
Relations dear, and all the Charities°   *affections*
Of Father, Son, and Brother first were known.
Far be it, that I should write thee sin or blame,
Or think thee unbefitting holiest place,
760 Perpetual Fountain of Domestic sweets,
Whose bed is undefil'd and chaste pronounc't,[9]
Present, or past, as Saints and Patriarchs us'd.
Here Love his golden shafts imploys,[1] here lights
His constant Lamp, and waves his purple wings,
765 Reigns here and revels; not in the bought smile
Of Harlots, loveless, joyless, unindear'd,
Casual fruition, nor in Court Amours,
Mixt Dance, or wanton Mask, or Midnight Ball,
Or Serenate, which the starv'd Lover sings

---

8. See Genesis 1.28.
9. See Hebrews 13.4: "Marriage is honourable in all, and the bed undefiled."

1. Cupid's "golden shafts" were sharp and gleaming and kindled love, while those of lead were blunt and put love to flight (Ovid, *Metamorphoses* 1.468–71).

770 To his proud fair, best quitted with disdain.
     These lull'd by Nightingales imbracing slept,
     And on thir naked limbs the flow'ry roof
     Show'r'd Roses, which the Morn repair'd.° Sleep on,   *made up for*
     Blest pair; and O yet happiest if ye seek
775 No happier state, and know to know no more.[2]
          Now had night measur'd with her shadowy Cone
     Half way up Hill this vast Sublunar Vault,[3]
     And from thir Ivory Port the Cherubim
     Forth issuing at th' accustom'd hour stood arm'd
780 To thir night watches in warlike Parade,
     When *Gabriel* to his next in power thus spake.
          Uzziel,[4] half these draw off, and coast the South
     With strictest watch; these other wheel the North;
     Our circuit meets full West. As flame they part
785 Half wheeling to the Shield, half to the Spear.[5]
     From these, two strong and subtle Spirits he call'd
     That near him stood, and gave them thus in charge.
          Ithuriel and *Zephon*, with wing'd speed
     Search through this Garden, leave unsearcht no nook,
790 But chiefly where those two fair Creatures Lodge,
     Now laid perhaps asleep secure° of harm.   *careless*
     This Ev'ning from the Sun's decline arriv'd
     Who tells of some infernal Spirit seen
     Hitherward bent (who could have thought?) escap'd
795 The bars of Hell, on errand bad no doubt:
     Such where ye find, seize fast, and hither bring.
          So saying, on he led his radiant Files,
     Dazzling the Moon; these to the Bower direct
     In search of whom they sought: him there they found
800 Squat like a Toad, close at the ear of *Eve*;
     Assaying by his Devilish art to reach
     The Organs of her Fancy, and with them forge
     Illusions as he list, Phantasms° and Dreams,   *illusions*
     Or if, inspiring venom, he might taint
805 Th' animal spirits[6] that from pure blood arise
     Like gentle breaths from Rivers pure, thence raise
     At least distemper'd,° discontented thoughts,   *vexed*
     Vain hopes, vain aims, inordinate desires
     Blown up with high conceits ingend'ring pride.

---

2. Either "know that it is best not to seek new knowledge (by eating the forbidden fruit)" or "know how to limit your experience to the state of innocence."
3. The earth's shadow is a cone that appears to circle around it in diametrical opposition to the sun. When the axis of the cone reaches the meridian, it is midnight; but here it is only "Half way up," so the time is nine o'clock.
4. "Uzziel" (Strength of God) occurs in the Bible as an ordinary human name (e.g., Exodus 6.18), and so does "Zephon" (Searcher of Secrets: Numbers 26.15).

"Ithuriel" (Discovery of God) is not from the Bible.
5. "Shield" for "left" and "spear" for "right" were ancient military terms.
6. Spirits in this sense were fine vapors, regarded by some as a medium between body and soul, by others as a separate soul. Animal spirits (Latin *anima*, soul) ascended to the brain and issued through the nerves to impart motion to the body. Local movement of the animal spirits could also produce imaginative apparitions, by which angels were thought to affect the human mind.

810 Him thus intent *Ithuriel* with his Spear
    Touch'd lightly; for no falsehood can endure
    Touch of Celestial temper, but returns
    Of force to its own likeness: up he starts
    Discover'd and surpris'd. As when a spark
815 Lights on a heap of nitrous[7] Powder, laid
    Fit for the Tun[8] some Magazin to store
    Against° a rumor'd War, the Smutty grain   *preparing for*
    With sudden blaze diffus'd, inflames the Air:
    So started up in his own shape the Fiend.
820 Back stepp'd those two fair Angels half amaz'd
    So sudden to behold the grisly King;
    Yet thus, unmov'd with fear, accost him soon.
        Which of those rebel Spirits adjudg'd to Hell
    Com'st thou, escap'd thy prison, and transform'd,
825 Why satst thou like an enemy in wait
    Here watching at the head of these that sleep?
        Know ye not then said *Satan*, fill'd with scorn,
    Know ye not mee? ye knew me once no mate
    For you, there sitting where ye durst not soar;
830 Not to know mee argues yourselves unknown,
    The lowest of your throng; or if ye know,
    Why ask ye, and superfluous begin
    Your message, like to end as much in vain?
    To whom thus *Zephon*, answering scorn with scorn.
835 Think not, revolted Spirit, thy shape the same,
    Or undiminisht brightness, to be known
    As when thou stood'st in Heav'n upright and pure;
    That Glory then, when thou no more wast good,
    Departed from thee, and thou resembl'st now
840 Thy sin and place of doom obscure and foul.
    But come, for thou, be sure, shalt give account
    To him who sent us, whose charge is to keep
    This place inviolable, and these from harm.
        So spake the Cherub, and his grave rebuke
845 Severe in youthful beauty, added grace
    Invincible: abasht the Devil stood,
    And felt how awful goodness is, and saw
    Virtue in her shape how lovely, saw, and pin'd°   *mourned*
    His loss; but chiefly to find here observ'd
850 His lustre visibly impair'd; yet seem'd
    Undaunted. If I must contend, said he,
    Best with the best, the Sender not the sent,
    Or all at once; more glory will be won,
    Or less be lost. Thy fear, said *Zephon* bold,
855 Will save us trial what the least can do

---

7. Mixed with niter (potassium nitrate or saltpeter, an ingredient in gunpowder) to form an explosive.   8. In proper condition for casking, ready for use.

Single against thee wicked, and thence weak.
    The Fiend repli'd not, overcome with rage;
But like a proud Steed rein'd, went haughty on,
Champing his iron curb: to strive or fly
860 He held it vain; awe from above had quell'd
His heart, not else dismay'd. Now drew they nigh
The western Point,[9] where those half-rounding guards
Just met, and closing stood in squadron join'd
Awaiting next command. To whom thir Chief
865 *Gabriel* from the Front thus call'd aloud.
    O friends, I hear the tread of nimble feet
Hasting this way, and now by glimpse discern
Ithuriel and *Zephon* through the shade,
And with them comes a third of Regal port,
870 But faded splendor wan; who by his gait
And fierce demeanor seems the Prince of Hell,
Not likely to part hence without contest;
Stand firm, for in his look defiance low'rs.
    He scarce had ended, when those two approach'd
875 And brief related whom they brought, where found,
How busied, in what form and posture coucht.
    To whom with stern regard thus *Gabriel* spake.
Why hast thou, *Satan*, broke the bounds prescrib'd
To thy transgressions, and disturb'd the charge
880 Of others, who approve not to transgress
By thy example, but have power and right
To question thy bold entrance on this place;
Imploy'd it seems to violate sleep, and those
Whose dwelling God hath planted here in bliss?
885   To whom thus *Satan*, with contemptuous brow.
Gabriel, thou hadst in Heav'n th' esteem of wise,
And such I held thee; but this question askt
Puts me in doubt. Lives there who loves his pain?
Who would not, finding way, break loose from Hell,
890 Though thither doom'd? Thou wouldst thyself, no doubt,
And boldly venture to whatever place
Farthest from pain, where thou might'st hope to change
Torment with ease, and soonest recompense
Dole° with delight, which in this place I sought;   *suffering*
895 To thee no reason; who know'st only good,
But evil hast not tri'd: and wilt object
His will who bound us? let him surer bar
His Iron Gates, if he intends our stay
In that dark durance:° thus much what was askt.[1]   *imprisonment*
900 The rest is true, they found me where they say;
But that implies not violence or harm.

---

9. For the angels' movement in a circle around heaven,   1. That is, "thus much in reply to what was asked."
see also 4.782–4.

Thus he in scorn. The warlike Angel mov'd,
Disdainfully half smiling thus repli'd.
O loss of one in Heav'n to judge of wise,
905   Since *Satan* fell, whom folly overthrew,
And now returns him from his prison scap't,
Gravely in doubt whether to hold them wise
Or not, who ask what boldness brought him hither
Unlicens't from his bounds in Hell prescrib'd;
910   So wise he judges it to fly from pain
However,° and to scape his punishment.   *howsoever*
So judge thou still, presumptuous, till the wrath,
Which thou incurr'st by flying, meet thy flight
Sevenfold, and scourge that wisdom back to Hell,
915   Which taught thee yet no better, that no pain
Can equal anger infinite provok't.
But wherefore thou alone? wherefore with thee
Came not all Hell broke loose? is pain to them
Less pain, less to be fled, or thou than they
920   Less hardy to endure? courageous Chief,
The first in flight from pain, hadst thou alleg'd
To thy deserted host this cause of flight,
Thou surely hadst not come sole fugitive.
    To which the Fiend thus answer'd frowning stern.
925   Not that I less endure, or shrink from pain,
Insulting Angel, well thou know'st I stood
Thy fiercest, when in Battle to thy aid
The blasting volley'd Thunder made all speed
And seconded thy else not dreaded Spear.
930   But still thy words at random, as before,
Argue thy inexperience what behooves
From hard assays and ill successes past
A faithful Leader,[2] not to hazard all
Through ways of danger by himself untri'd.
935   I therefore, I alone first undertook
To wing the desolate Abyss, and spy
This new created World, whereof in Hell
Fame is not silent, here in hope to find
Better abode, and my afflicted Powers
940   To settle here on Earth, or in mid Air;
Though for possession put to try once more
What thou and thy gay Legions dare against;
Whose easier business were to serve thir Lord
High up in Heav'n, with songs to hymn his Throne,
945   And practis'd distances to cringe, not fight.
    To whom the warrior Angel soon repli'd.
To say and straight unsay; pretending first

2. That is, "You're still talking off the top of your head, showing how little you know about a defeated commander's responsibilities."

Wise to fly pain, professing next the Spy,
Argues no Leader, but a liar trac't,°   *discovered*
950 Satan, and couldst thou faithful add? O name,
O sacred name of faithfulness profan'd!
Faithful to whom? to thy rebellious crew?
Army of Fiends, fit body to fit head;
Was this your discipline and faith ingag'd,
955 Your military obedience, to dissolve
Allegiance to th' acknowledg'd Power supreme?
And thou sly hypocrite, who now wouldst seem
Patron of liberty, who more than thou
Once fawn'd, and cring'd, and servilely ador'd
960 Heav'n's awful Monarch? wherefore but in hope
To dispossess him, and thyself to reign?
But mark what I arede° thee now, avaunt;   *advise*
Fly thither whence thou fledd'st: if from this hour
Within these hallow'd limits thou appear,
965 Back to th' infernal pit I drag thee chain'd,
And Seal thee so, as henceforth not to scorn
The facile° gates of hell too slightly barr'd.   *easily moved*
    So threat'n'd hee, but *Satan* to no threats
Gave heed, but waxing more in rage repli'd.
970   Then when I am thy captive talk of chains,
Proud limitary Cherub,[3] but ere then
Far heavier load thyself expect to feel
From my prevailing arm, though Heaven's King
Ride on thy wings, and thou with thy Compeers,
975 Us'd to the yoke, draw'st his triumphant wheels
In progress through the road of Heav'n Star-pav'd.
    While thus he spake, th' Angelic Squadron bright
Turn'd fiery red, sharp'ning in mooned horns
Thir Phalanx, and began to hem him round
980 With ported Spears,[4] as thick as when a field
Of *Ceres* ripe for harvest waving bends
Her bearded Grove of ears, which way the wind
Sways them; the careful Plowman doubting stands
Lest on the threshing floor his hopeful sheaves
985 Prove chaff.[5] On th' other side *Satan* alarm'd
Collecting all his might dilated stood.
Like *Teneriff* or *Atlas* unremov'd:[6]
His stature reacht the Sky, and on his Crest

3. Satan contemptuously mistakes Gabriel, who is a top seraph (4.549–50) rather than a cherub. "Limitary" implies that Gabriel has an undesirable provincial assignment.
4. The spears are held sloping upward, pointing towards Satan. The angels' formation is crescent-shaped ("mooned"); such formations, classic in warfare, were still used.

5. Comparison of an excited army to wind-stirred corn is Homeric (*Iliad* 2.147–50). Ceres is the harvest goddess, here standing for "corn."
6. "Teneriff" is Tenerife, the pyramidal mountain on the Canary Island of the same name. Atlas sustained the stars as Satan sustains the pressure of the angels. Like Satan, Atlas also rebelled against God.

Sat horror Plum'd; nor wanted in his grasp
990 What seem'd both Spear and Shield: now dreadful deeds
Might have ensu'd, nor only Paradise
In this commotion, but the Starry Cope°   *firmament*
Of Heav'n perhaps, or all the Elements
At least had gone to rack, disturb'd and torn
995 With violence of this conflict, had not soon
Th' Eternal to prevent such horrid fray
Hung forth in Heav'n his golden Scales,[7] yet seen
Betwixt *Astrea*° and the *Scorpion* sign,   *Virgo*
Wherein all things created first he weigh'd,
1000 The pendulous round Earth with balanc't Air
In counterpoise, now ponders all events,
Battles and Realms: in these he put two weights
The sequel each of parting and of fight;
The latter quick up flew, and kickt the beam;
1005 Which *Gabriel* spying, thus bespake the Fiend.
     Satan, I know thy strength, and thou know'st mine,
Neither our own but giv'n; what folly then
To boast what Arms can do, since thine no more
Than Heav'n permits, nor mine, though doubl'd now
1010 To trample thee as mire: for proof look up,
And read thy Lot in yon celestial Sign
Where thou art weigh'd, and shown how light, how weak,
If thou resist. The Fiend lookt up and knew
His mounted scale aloft: nor more; but fled
1015 Murmuring, and with him fled the shades of night.
                   The End of the Fourth Book.

Book 5
The Argument

Morning approacht, Eve *relates to* Adam *her troublesome dream; he likes it not, yet com-forts her: They come forth to thir day labors: Thir Morning Hymn at the Door of thir Bower.* God *to render Man inexcusable sends* Raphael *to admonish him of his obedience, of his free estate, of his enemy near at hand; who he is, and why his enemy, and whatever else may avail* Adam *to know.* Raphael *comes down to Paradise, his appearance describ'd, his coming discern'd by* Adam *afar off sitting at the door of his Bower; he goes out to meet him, brings him to his lodge, entertains him with the choicest fruits of Paradise got together by* Eve; *thir discourse at Table:* Raphael *performs his message, minds* Adam *of his state and of his enemy; relates at* Adam's *request who that enemy is, and how he came to be so, beginning from his first revolt in Heaven, and the occasion thereof; how he drew his Legions after him to the parts of the North, and there incited them to rebel with him, persuading all but only* Abdiel *a Seraph, who in Argument dissuades and opposes him, then forsakes him.*

7. Homer's Zeus balances the fates of Trojans and Greeks, and Hector and Achilles, with golden scales (*Iliad* 8.68–77 and 22.208–13, imitated in Virgil's *Aeneid* 12.725–7). In Homer, the loser's scale sinks down to death; in Milton the inferior side rises, being "found wanting" (Daniel 5.27).

     Now Morn her rosy steps in th' Eastern Clime
     Advancing, sow'd the Earth with Orient Pearl,
     When *Adam* wak't, so custom'd, for his sleep
     Was Aery light, from pure digestion bred,
5   And temperate vapors bland, which th' only sound
     Of leaves and fuming rills, *Aurora's* fan,
     Lightly dispers'd, and the shrill Matin° Song   *morning*
     Of Birds on every bough;[1] so much the more
     His wonder was to find unwak'n'd *Eve*
10   With Tresses discompos'd, and glowing Cheek,
     As through unquiet rest: hee on his side
     Leaning half-rais'd, with looks of cordial Love
     Hung over her enamor'd, and beheld
     Beauty, which whether waking or asleep,
15   Shot forth peculiar° graces; then with voice   *distinctive*
     Mild, as when *Zephyrus*[2] on *Flora* breathes,
     Her hand soft touching, whisper'd thus. Awake
     My fairest, my espous'd, my latest found,
     Heav'n's last best gift, my ever new delight,
20   Awake, the morning shines, and the fresh field
     Calls us; we lose the prime,[3] to mark how spring
     Our tended Plants, how blows° the Citron Grove,   *blossoms*
     What drops the Myrrh, and what the balmy Reed,
     How Nature paints her colors, how the Bee
25   Sits on the Bloom extracting liquid sweet.[4]
         Such whispering wak'd her, but with startl'd eye
     On *Adam*, whom imbracing, thus she spake.
         O Sole in whom my thoughts find all repose,
     My Glory, my Perfection, glad I see
30   Thy face, and Morn return'd, for I this Night,
     Such night till this I never pass'd, have dream'd,
     If dream'd, not as I oft am wont, of thee,
     Works of day past, or morrow's next design,
     But of offense and trouble, which my mind
35   Knew never till this irksome night; methought
     Close at mine ear one call'd me forth to walk
     With gentle voice, I thought it thine; it said,
     Why sleep'st thou *Eve?* now is the pleasant time,
     The cool, the silent, save where silence yields
40   To the night-warbling Bird, that now awake
     Tunes sweetest his love-labor'd song; now reigns
     Full Orb'd the Moon, and with more pleasing light
     Shadowy sets off the face of things; in vain,
     If none regard; Heav'n wakes with all his eyes,

---

1. The "only" (mere) sound of leaves, water, and birds
was enough to rouse Adam. The fan of Aurora, the goddess of morning, is the leaves.
2. The west wind. Zephyrus's sweet breath was supposed
to produce flowers, as was that of his wife, the flower-
goddess Flora.
3. The first hour of the day.
4. For lines 18–25, see Song of Solomon 2.10–13 and
7.12.

45 Whom to behold but thee, Nature's desire,
In whose sight all things joy, with ravishment
Attracted by thy beauty still to gaze.
I rose as at thy call, but found thee not;
To find thee I directed then my walk;
50 And on, methought, alone I pass'd through ways
That brought me on a sudden to the Tree
Of interdicted Knowledge: fair it seem'd,
Much fairer to my Fancy than by day:
And as I wond'ring lookt, beside it stood
55 One shap'd and wing'd like one of those from Heav'n
By us oft seen; his dewy locks distill'd
Ambrosia;[5] on that Tree he also gaz'd;
And O fair Plant, said he, with fruit surcharg'd,
Deigns none to ease thy load and taste thy sweet,
60 Nor God, nor Man; is Knowledge so despis'd?
Or envy, or what reserve[6] forbids to taste?
Forbid who will, none shall from me withhold
Longer thy offer'd good, why else set here?
This said he paus'd not, but with vent'rous Arm
65 He pluckt, he tasted; mee damp horror chill'd
At such bold words voucht with a deed so bold:
But he thus overjoy'd, O Fruit Divine,
Sweet of thyself, but much more sweet thus cropt,
Forbidd'n here, it seems, as only fit
70 For Gods, yet able to make Gods of Men:
And why not Gods of Men, since good, the more
Communicated, more abundant grows,
The Author not impair'd, but honor'd more?
Here, happy Creature, fair Angelic Eve,
75 Partake thou also; happy though thou art,
Happier thou may'st be, worthier canst not be:
Taste this, and be henceforth among the Gods
Thyself a Goddess, not to Earth confin'd,
But sometimes in the Air, as wee, sometimes
80 Ascend to Heav'n, by merit thine, and see
What life the Gods live there, and such live thou.
So saying, he drew nigh, and to me held,
Even to my mouth of that same fruit held part
Which he had pluckt; the pleasant savory smell[7]
85 So quick'n'd appetite, that I, methought,
Could not but taste. Forthwith up to the Clouds
With him I flew, and underneath beheld
The Earth outstretcht immense, a prospect wide
And various: wond'ring at my flight and change

---

5. The fabled anointing oil of the gods.
6. Limitation, restriction, or knowledge kept secret on the part of God; but perhaps also inhibition, self-restraint on the part of humans.
7. The fruit has an appetizing, fragrant scent, but "savory" could also mean "spiritually edifying."

90 To this high exaltation; suddenly
    My Guide was gone, and I, methought, sunk down,
    And fell asleep; but O how glad I wak'd
    To find this but a dream! Thus *Eve* her Night
    Related, and thus *Adam* answer'd sad.°   *gravely*
95   Best Image of myself and dearer half,
    The trouble of thy thoughts this night in sleep
    Affects me equally; nor can I like
    This uncouth° dream, of evil sprung I fear;   *strange*
    Yet evil whence? in thee can harbor none,
100 Created pure. But know that in the Soul
    Are many lesser Faculties that serve
    Reason as chief; among these Fancy next
    Her office holds; of all external things,
    Which the five watchful Senses represent,
105 She forms Imaginations, Aery shapes,
    Which Reason joining or disjoining, frames
    All what we affirm or what deny, and call
    Our knowledge or opinion; then retires
    Into her private Cell when Nature rests.[8]
110 Oft in her absence mimic Fancy wakes
    To imitate her; but misjoining shapes,
    Wild work produces oft, and most in dreams,
    Ill matching words and deeds long past or late.
    Some such resemblances methinks I find
115 Of our last Ev'ning's talk,[9] in this thy dream,
    But with addition strange; yet be not sad.
    Evil into the mind of God[1] or Man
    May come and go, so unapprov'd, and leave
    No spot or blame behind: Which gives me hope
120 That what in sleep thou didst abhor to dream,
    Waking thou never wilt consent to do.
    Be not disheart'n'd then, nor cloud those looks
    That wont to be more cheerful and serene
    Than when fair Morning first smiles on the World,
125 And let us to our fresh imployments rise
    Among the Groves, the Fountains, and the Flow'rs
    That open now thir choicest bosom'd° smells   *hidden*
    Reserv'd from night, and kept for thee in store.
        So cheer'd he his fair Spouse, and she was cheer'd,
130 But silently a gentle tear let fall
    From either eye, and wip'd them with her hair;
    Two other precious drops that ready stood,

8. For the psychology involved here, see Burton, *Anatomy of Melancholy* 1.1.2.7: "Phantasy, or imagination . . . is an inner sense which doth more fully examine the species perceived by common sense, of things present or absent. . . . In time of sleep this faculty is free, and many times conceives strange, stupend, absurd shapes . . . it is subject and governed by reason, or at least should be." 9. Their discussion of the prohibition of the Tree of Knowledge (4.421ff.). 1. Probably "angel." But Milton (if not Adam) may also intend a reference to the doctrine that God's omniscience extends to evil.

Each in thir crystal sluice, hee ere they fell
Kiss'd as the gracious signs of sweet remorse
135 And pious awe, that fear'd to have offended.
     So all was clear'd, and to the Field they haste.
But first from under shady arborous roof,
Soon as they forth were come to open sight
Of day-spring,° and the Sun, who scarce up risen   daybreak
140 With wheels yet hov'ring o'er the Ocean brim,
Shot parallel to the earth his dewy ray,
Discovering in wide Lantskip° all the East   landscape
Of Paradise and *Eden's* happy Plains,
Lowly they bow'd adoring, and began
145 Thir Orisons,° each Morning duly paid   prayers
In various style, for neither various style
Nor holy rapture wanted they to praise
Thir Maker, in fit strains pronounct or sung
Unmeditated, such prompt eloquence
150 Flow'd from thir lips, in Prose or numerous Verse,
More tuneable° than needed Lute or Harp   tuneful
To add more sweetness, and they thus began.[2]
     These are thy glorious works, Parent of good,
Almighty, thine this universal Frame,[3]
155 Thus wondrous fair; thyself how wondrous then!
Unspeakable, who sit'st above these Heavens
To us invisible or dimly seen
In these thy lowest works, yet these declare
Thy goodness beyond thought, and Power Divine:
160 Speak yee who best can tell, ye Sons of Light,
Angels, for yee behold him, and with songs
And choral symphonies, Day without Night,
Circle his Throne rejoicing, yee in Heav'n;
On Earth join all ye Creatures to extol
165 Him first, him last, him midst, and without end.
Fairest of Stars,[4] last in the train of Night,
If better thou belong not to the dawn,
Sure pledge of day, that crown'st the smiling Morn
With thy bright Circlet, praise him in thy Sphere
170 While day arises, that sweet hour of Prime.
Thou Sun, of this great World both Eye and Soul,[5]
Acknowledge him thy Greater, sound his praise
In thy eternal course, both when thou climb'st,
And when high Noon hast gain'd, and when thou fall'st.
175 Moon, that now meet'st the orient Sun, now fli'st

2. The hymn (lines 153–208) is based on Psalm 148 and on the canticle *Benedicite, omnia opera* (in the 1549 *Book of Common Prayer*).
3. Used of heaven, earth, or the universe regarded as structures fabricated by God.
4. The planet Venus rises in the east just before sunrise

and is known as the morning star.
5. The metaphor of the sun as an eye implied a connection between seeing and understanding and hence an identification of the sun with the creative word. The sun is "soul" of the world in the sense that it gives life.

With the fixt Stars, fixt in thir Orb that flies,
And yee five other wand'ring Fires that move
In mystic Dance not without Song,[6] resound
His praise, who out of Darkness call'd up Light.
180   Air, and ye Elements the eldest birth
Of Nature's Womb, that in quaternion run
Perpetual Circle, multiform, and mix
And nourish all things, let your ceaseless change
Vary to our great Maker still new praise.
185   Ye Mists and Exhalations that now rise
From Hill or steaming Lake, dusky or grey,
Till the Sun paint your fleecy skirts with Gold,
In honor to the World's great Author rise,
Whether to deck with Clouds th' uncolor'd sky,
190   Or wet the thirsty Earth with falling showers,
Rising or falling still advance his praise.
His praise ye Winds, that from four Quarters blow,
Breathe soft or loud; and wave your tops, ye Pines,
With every Plant, in sign of Worship wave.
195   Fountains and yee, that warble, as ye flow,
Melodious murmurs, warbling tune his praise.
Join voices all ye living Souls; ye Birds,
That singing up to Heaven Gate ascend,
Bear on your wings and in your notes his praise;
200   Yee that in Waters glide, and yee that walk
The Earth, and stately tread, or lowly creep;
Witness if I be silent, Morn or Even,
To Hill, or Valley, Fountain, or fresh shade
Made vocal by my Song, and taught his praise.
205   Hail universal Lord, be bounteous still
To give us only good; and if the night
Have gather'd aught of evil or conceal'd,
Disperse it, as now light dispels the dark.
    So pray'd they innocent, and to thir thoughts
210   Firm peace recover'd soon and wonted calm.
On to thir morning's rural work they haste
Among sweet dews and flow'rs; where any row
Of Fruit-trees overwoody reach'd too far
Thir pamper'd boughs, and needed hands to check
215   Fruitless imbraces: or they led the Vine
To wed her Elm; she spous'd about him twines
Her marriageable arms, and with her brings
Her dow'r th' adopted Clusters, to adorn
His barren leaves. Them thus imploy'd beheld
220   With pity Heav'n's high King, and to him call'd

---

6. The music of the spheres, inaudible now to fallen humans' gross hearing. The elements are a form of the quaternion, or tetrad, a group of four regarded as one: air, earth, fire, and water. For the transformation of the elements into one another, see Cicero, *De natura deorum* 2.33.

Raphael, the sociable Spirit, that deign'd
To travel with *Tobias*, and secur'd
His marriage with the seven-times-wedded Maid.
Raphael, said hee, thou hear'st what stir on Earth
225   *Satan* from Hell scap't through the darksome Gulf
Hath rais'd in Paradise, and how disturb'd
This night the human pair, how he designs
In them at once to ruin all mankind.
Go therefore, half this day as friend with friend
230   Converse with *Adam*, in what Bow'r or shade
Thou find'st him from the heat of Noon retir'd,
To respite his day-labor with repast,
Or with repose; and such discourse bring on,
As may advise him of his happy state,
235   Happiness in his power left free to will,
Left to his own free Will, his Will though free,
Yet mutable; whence warn him to beware
He swerve not too secure:[7] tell him withal
His danger, and from whom, what enemy
240   Late fall'n himself from Heaven, is plotting now
The fall of others from like state of bliss;
By violence, no, for that shall be withstood,
But by deceit and lies; this let him know,
Lest wilfully transgressing he pretend
245   Surprisal, unadmonisht, unforewarn'd.
    So spake th' Eternal Father, and fulfill'd
All Justice: nor delay'd the winged Saint
After his charge receiv'd,[8] but from among
Thousand Celestial Ardors, where he stood
250   Veil'd with his gorgeous wings, up springing light
Flew through the midst of Heav'n; th' angelic Choirs
On each hand parting, to his speed gave way
Through all th' Empyreal road; till at the Gate
Of Heav'n arriv'd, the gate self-open'd wide
255   On golden Hinges turning, as by work
Divine the sovran Architect had fram'd.[9]
From hence, no cloud, or, to obstruct his sight,
Star interpos'd, however small he sees,[1]
Not unconform to other shining Globes,
260   Earth and the Gard'n of God, with Cedars crown'd
Above all Hills. As when by night the Glass
Of *Galileo*, less assur'd, observes
Imagin'd Lands and Regions in the Moon.[2]

---

7. To be careful not to err through overconfidence.
8. That is, "after he received his order."
9. In Acts 12.10, an iron gate opens to St. Peter and an angel. Likewise, in the *Iliad* 5.749, heaven's gates open automatically for Hera.

1. "Small" qualifies Earth. From Raphael's startling viewpoint, earth is almost too small to be like "other shining globes" (stars).
2. Contrast 1.286–91, where the reality of lunar geography is unquestioned.

Or Pilot from amidst the *Cyclades*
265 *Delos or Samos* first appearing kens°   *detects*
A cloudy spot.[3] Down thither prone° in flight   *downward sloping*
He speeds, and through the vast Ethereal Sky
Sails between worlds and worlds, with steady wing
Now on the polar winds, then with quick Fan
270 Winnows the buxom° Air; till within soar   *yielding*
Of Tow'ring Eagles, to all the Fowls he seems
A *Phœnix*, gaz'd by all, as that sole Bird
When to enshrine his reliques in the Sun's
Bright Temple, to *Egyptian Thebes* he flies.[4]
275 At once on th' Eastern cliff of Paradise
He lights,[5] and to his proper shape returns
A Seraph wing'd; six wings he wore, to shade
His lineaments° Divine; the pair that clad   *figure*
Each shoulder broad, came mantling o'er his breast
280 With regal Ornament; the middle pair
Girt like a Starry Zone his waist, and round
Skirted his loins and thighs with downy Gold
And colors dipt in Heav'n; the third his feet
Shadow'd from either heel with feather'd mail
285 Sky-tinctur'd grain.[6] Like *Maia's* son° he stood,   *Mercury*
And shook his Plumes, that Heav'nly fragrance fill'd
The circuit wide. Straight knew him all the Bands
Of Angels under watch; and to his state,°   *rank*
And to his message° high in honor rise;   *mission*
290 For on some message high they guess'd him bound.
Thir glittering Tents he pass'd, and now is come
Into the blissful field, through Groves of Myrrh.
And flow'ring Odors, Cassia, Nard, and Balm,[7]
A Wilderness of sweets; for Nature here
295 Wanton'd as in her prime, and play'd at will
Her Virgin Fancies, pouring forth more sweet,
Wild above Rule or Art, enormous bliss.
Him through the spicy Forest onward come
Adam discern'd, as in the door he sat
300 Of his cool Bow'r, while now the mounted Sun
Shot down direct his fervid Rays, to warm
Earth's inmost womb, more warmth than *Adam* needs;

---

3. The Cyclades are a circular group of islands in the southern Aegean. Delos is one of the Cyclades, the birth-place of Apollo and Diana. Samos is not one of the Cyclades, but the birthplace of Juno, who married Jupiter there; so, like Delos, a mythic version of Eden.
4. Every 500 years the mythic phoenix immolated itself in a pyre or nest of spices, from which a new phoenix arose from its ashes or bone marrow and flew to Heliopo-lis, City of the Sun, to deposit its relics. (See Ovid's *Metamorphoses* 15.391–407, and Pliny's *Natural History* 10.2.)

5. The only gate is on the Eastern side (4.178).
6. Echoes the description of the seraphim in Isaiah 6.2, "Each one had six wings; with twain he covered his face, and with twain he covered his feet, and with twain he did fly."
7. Myrrh is an aromatic gum, used for protection against devils. Cassia is a cinnamon-like spice. Nard was the ointment poured over Jesus' head to anoint him for burial (Mark 14.3, 8). Balm of Gilead was celebrated as the ear-liest known balsam (another aromatic substance).

And *Eve* within, due° at her hour prepar'd   *duly*
For dinner savoury fruits, of taste to please
305   True appetite, and not disrelish thirst
Of nectarous draughts between, from milky° stream,   *sweet*
Berry or Grape: to whom thus *Adam* call'd.
      Haste hither *Eve*, and worth thy sight behold
Eastward among those Trees, what glorious shape
310   Comes this way moving; seems another Morn
Ris'n on mid-noon; some great behest from Heav'n
To us perhaps he brings, and will voutsafe
This day to be our Guest. But go with speed,
And what thy stores contain, bring forth and pour
315   Abundance, fit to honor and receive
Our Heav'nly stranger; well we may afford
Our givers thir own gifts, and large bestow
From large bestow'd, where Nature multiplies
Her fertile growth, and by disburd'ning grows
320   More fruitful, which instructs us not to spare.
      To whom thus *Eve*. *Adam*, earth's hallow'd mould,
Of God inspir'd, small store will serve, where store,
All seasons, ripe for use hangs on the stalk;
Save what by frugal storing firmness gains
325   To nourish, and superfluous moist consumes:
But I will haste and from each bough and brake,°   *bush*
Each Plant and juiciest Gourd will pluck such choice
To entertain our Angel guest, as hee
Beholding shall confess that here on Earth
330   God hath dispenst his bounties as in Heav'n.
      So saying, with dispatchful looks in haste
She turns, on hospitable thoughts intent
What choice to choose for delicacy best,
What order, so contriv'd as not to mix
335   Tastes, not well join'd, inelegant, but bring
Taste after taste upheld° with kindliest change;   *sustained*
Bestirs her then, and from each tender stalk
Whatever Earth all-bearing Mother yields
In *India* East or West, or middle shore
340   In *Pontus* or the *Punic* Coast, or where
Alcinoüs reign'd,[8] fruit of all kinds, in coat,
Rough, or smooth rin'd,° or bearded husk, or shell   *rinded*
She gathers, Tribute large, and on the board
Heaps with unsparing hand; for drink the Grape
345   She crushes, inoffensive must, and meaths
From many a berry, and from sweet kernels prest
She tempers dulcet creams, nor these to hold
Wants her fit vessels pure, then strews the ground

8. The Pontus is the southern shore of the Black Sea. The Punic Coast is the Carthaginian coast of the Mediterranean. Alcinous, Homer's hospitable Phaeacian king, lived on an island paradise called Scheria.

With Rose and Odors from the shrub unfum'd.[9]
350   Meanwhile our Primitive great Sire, to meet
His god-like Guest, walks forth, without more train
Accompanied than with his own complete
Perfections; in himself was all his state,°   *dignity*
More solemn than the tedious pomp that waits
355   On Princes, when thir rich Retinue long
Of Horses led, and Grooms besmear'd with Gold
Dazzles the crowd, and sets them all agape.
Nearer his presence *Adam* though not aw'd,
Yet with submiss° approach and reverence meek,   *submissive*
360   As to a superior Nature, bowing low,
    Thus said. Native of Heav'n, for other place
None can than Heav'n such glorious shape contain;
Since by descending from the Thrones above,
Those happy places thou hast deign'd a while
365   To want,° and honor these, voutsafe with us   *miss*
Two only, who yet by sovran gift possess
This spacious ground, in yonder shady Bow'r
To rest, and what the Garden choicest bears
To sit and taste, till this meridian heat
370   Be over, and the Sun more cool decline.
    Whom thus the Angelic Virtue answer'd mild.
Adam, I therefore came, nor art thou such
Created, or such place hast here to dwell,
As may not oft invite, though Spirits of Heav'n
375   To visit thee; lead on then where thy Bow'r
O'ershades; for these mid-hours, till Ev'ning rise
I have at will. So to the Silvan Lodge
They came, that like *Pomona's* Arbor smil'd
With flow'rets deck't and fragrant smells; but *Eve*
380   Undeckt, save with herself more lovely fair
Than Wood-Nymph,[1] or the fairest Goddess feign'd
Of three that in Mount *Ida* naked strove,[2]
Stood to entertain her guest from Heav'n; no veil
Shee needed, Virtue-proof, no thought infirm
385   Alter'd her cheek. On whom the Angel *Hail*
Bestow'd, the holy salutation us'd
Long after to blest *Mary*, second *Eve*.
    Hail Mother of Mankind, whose fruitful Womb
Shall fill the World more numerous with thy Sons
390   Than with these various fruits the Trees of God

---

9. "Must" is unfermented grape-juice; "meaths" are meads, or sweet drinks; to "temper" is to mix; "dulcet" can mean sweet or bland; and "odours" are scented flowers or spices that are "unfum'd" because they do not require burning, as incense does.
1. The Roman wood-nymph Pomona presided over gardens and especially fruit trees.

2. The three goddesses Juno, Minerva, and Venus all claimed the apple of Strife, inscribed TO THE FAIREST, and the mortal Paris, famed for his wisdom, was appointed arbiter. The judgment of Paris was delivered on Mount Ida, where the goddesses appeared before him naked and without ornament.

Have heap'd this Table. Rais'd of grassy turf
Thir Table was, and mossy seats had round,
And on her ample Square from side to side
All *Autumn* pil'd, though *Spring* and *Autumn* here
395   Danc'd hand in hand. A while discourse they hold;
No fear lest Dinner cool; when thus began
Our Author.° Heav'nly stranger, please to taste   *ancestor*
These bounties which our Nourisher, from whom
All perfet good unmeasur'd out, descends,
400   To us for food and for delight hath caus'd
The Earth to yield; unsavory food perhaps
To spiritual Natures; only this I know,
That one Celestial Father gives to all.
        To whom the Angel. Therefore what he gives
405   (Whose praise be ever sung) to man in part
Spiritual, may of purest Spirits be found
No ingrateful food:³ and food alike those pure
Intelligential substances⁴ require
As doth your Rational; and both contain
410   Within them every lower faculty
Of sense, whereby they hear, see, smell, touch, taste,
Tasting concoct, digest, assimilate,
And corporeal to incorporeal turn,⁵
For know, whatever was created, needs
415   To be sustain'd and fed; of Elements
The grosser feeds the purer, Earth the Sea,
Earth and the Sea feed Air, the Air those Fires
Ethereal, and as lowest first the Moon;
Whence in her visage round those spots, unpurg'd
420   Vapors not yet into her substance turn'd.
Nor doth the Moon no nourishment exhale⁶
From her moist Continent to higher Orbs.
The Sun that light imparts to all, receives
From all his alimental° recompense   *nutritive*
425   In humid exhalations, and at Even
Sups with the Ocean:⁷ though in Heav'n the Trees
Of life ambrosial fruitage bear, and vines
Yield Nectar, though from off the boughs each Morn
We brush mellifluous° Dews, and find the ground   *sweetly flowing*
430   Cover'd with pearly grain:⁸ yet God hath here
Varied his bounty so with new delights,

3. Food acceptable to the angels ("purest spirits") because acceptable to humans ("in part spiritual").
4. Intellectual beings.
5. Physiological theory distinguished three stages of digestion: the "first concoction," or digestion in the stomach ("concoct"); the "second concoction," or conversion to blood ("digest"); and the "third concoction," or secretion ("assimilate").
6. The ancient theory was that vapors drawn up to the moon from the earth caused lunar spots. Galileo explained them as landscape features, a theory used above at lines 287–91.
7. This version of the Great Chain of Being was held by Stoics and Epicureans and was also popular in Milton's own time with mystical and alchemic Platonists such as Robert Fludd.
8. Manna, the "corn of heaven."

As may compare with Heaven; and to taste
Think not I shall be nice.° So down they sat,   *overrefined*
And to thir viands fell, nor seemingly⁹
435   The Angel, nor in mist, the common gloss
Of Theologians, but with keen dispatch
Of real hunger, and concoctive heat
To transubstantiate;¹ what redounds,° transpires   *remains in excess*
Through Spirits with ease; nor wonder; if by fire
440   Of sooty coal the Empiric Alchemist
Can turn, or holds it possible to turn
Metals of drossiest Ore to perfet Gold
As from the Mine. Meanwhile at Table *Eve*
Minister'd naked, and thir flowing cups
445   With pleasant liquors crown'd: O innocence
Deserving Paradise! if ever, then,
Then had the Sons of God° excuse to have been   *angels*
Enamour'd at that sight; but in those hearts
Love unlibidinous reign'd, nor jealousy
450   Was understood, the injur'd Lover's Hell.
        Thus when with meats and drinks they had suffic't,
Not burd'n'd Nature, sudden mind arose
In *Adam*, not to let th' occasion pass
Given him by this great Conference to know
455   Of things above his World, and of thir being
Who dwell in Heav'n, whose excellence he saw
Transcend his own so far, whose radiant forms
Divine effulgence, whose high Power so far
Exceeded human, and his wary speech
460   Thus to th' Empyreal° Minister he fram'd.   *heavenly*
        Inhabitant with God, now know I well
Thy favor, in this honor done to Man,
Under whose lowly roof thou hast voutsaf't
To enter, and these earthly fruits to taste,
465   Food not of Angels, yet accepted so,
As that more willingly thou couldst not seem
At Heav'n's high feasts to have fed: yet what compare?
        To whom the winged Hierarch repli'd.
O *Adam*, one Almighty is, from whom
470   All things proceed, and up to him return,
If not deprav'd from good, created all
Such to perfection, one first matter all,
Indu'd with various forms, various degrees

---

9. Refers to the Docetist theories about angelic appearances, devised to explain away the awkwardly materialistic accounts of angels in the Bible (e.g., at Genesis 18.8, "they did eat"). The Reformers on the whole rejected such evasions.

1. Transubstantiation is the Roman Catholic doctrine that the bread and wine of the Eucharist become the body and blood of Christ so "transubstantiate" contrasts sharply with the direct concrete simplicity of "keen . . . hunger."

Of substance, and in things that live, of life;[2]
475   But more refin'd, more spiritous, and pure,
As nearer to him plac't or nearer tending
Each in thir several active Spheres assign'd,
Till body up to spirit work, in bounds
Proportion'd to each kind. So from the root
480   Springs lighter the green stalk, from thence the leaves
More aery, last the bright consummate° flow'r   *perfected*
Spirits odorous breathes: flow'rs and thir fruit
Man's nourishment, by gradual scale sublim'd°   *raised*
To vital spirits aspire, to animal,
485   To intellectual, give both life and sense,[3]
Fancy° and understanding, whence the Soul   *imagination*
Reason receives, and reason is her being,
Discursive, or Intuitive; discourse
Is oftest yours, the latter most is ours,
490   Differing but in degree, of kind the same.[4]
Wonder not then, what God for you saw good
If I refuse not, but convert, as you,
To proper substance; time may come when men
With Angels may participate, and find
495   No inconvenient Diet, nor too light Fare:
And from these corporal nutriments perhaps
Your bodies may at last turn all to spirit,
Improv'd by tract of time, and wing'd ascend
Ethereal, as wee, or may at choice
500   Here or in Heav'nly Paradises dwell;
If ye be found obedient, and retain
Unalterably firm his love entire
Whose progeny you are. Meanwhile enjoy
Your fill what happiness this happy state
505   Can comprehend, incapable of more.
      To whom the Patriarch of mankind repli'd:
O favorable Spirit, propitious guest,
Well hast thou taught the way that might direct
Our knowledge, and the scale of Nature set
510   From centre to circumference, whereon
In contemplation of created things
By steps we may ascend to God.[5] But say,
What meant that caution join'd, *if ye be found*

---

2. Raphael's world picture is characterized by a cyclic movement of emanation and return that marks it as Platonic, as does the notion of successive degrees of spirituousness. The plant simile explains the notion of a scale of being from vegetable to animal, human, and angelic natures.

3. "Vital spirits" were fine pure fluids, given off by the blood of the heart and sustaining life; "animal spirits" had their seat in the brain and controlled sensation and voluntary motion.

4. The distinction between the "intuitive," simple undifferentiated operation of the contemplating intellect and the "discursive" or ratiocinative, piecemeal operation of the intellect working in conjunction with the reason goes back ultimately to Plato.

5. In the scale or ladder of nature, Adam refers to the Platonic ascent from image to universal, up the hierarchic grades of existence.

Obedient? can we want obedience then
515   To him, or possibly his love desert
Who form'd us from the dust, and plac'd us here
Full to the utmost measure of what bliss
Human desires can seek or apprehend?
        To whom the Angel. Son of Heav'n and Earth,
520   Attend: That thou art happy, owe to God;
That thou continu'st such, owe to thyself,
That is, to thy obedience; therein stand.
This was that caution giv'n thee; be advis'd.
God made thee perfet, not immutable;
525   And good he made thee, but to persevere
He left it in thy power, ordain'd thy will
By nature free, not over-rul'd by Fate
Inextricable, or strict necessity;
Our voluntary service he requires,
530   Not our necessitated, such with him
Finds no acceptance, nor can find, for how
Can hearts, not free, be tri'd whether they serve
Willing or no, who will but what they must
By Destiny, and can no other choose?
535   Myself and all th' Angelic Host that stand
In sight of God enthron'd, our happy state
Hold, as you yours, while our obedience holds;
On other surety none; freely we serve,
Because we freely love, as in our will
540   To love or not; in this we stand or fall:
And some are fall'n, to disobedience fall'n,
And so from Heav'n to deepest Hell; O fall
From what high state of bliss into what woe!
        To whom our great Progenitor. Thy words
545   Attentive, and with more delighted ear
Divine instructor, I have heard, than when
Cherubic Songs by night from neighboring Hills
Aereal Music send: nor knew I not
To be both will and deed created free;
550   Yet that we never shall forget to love
Our maker, and obey him whose command
Single, is yet so just, my constant thoughts
Assur'd me and still assure: though what thou tell'st
Hath past in Heav'n, some doubt within me move,
555   But more desire to hear, if thou consent,
The full relation, which must needs be strange,
Worthy of Sacred silence to be heard;
And we have yet large day, for scarce the Sun
Hath finisht half his journey, and scarce begins
560   His other half in the great Zone of Heav'n.
        Thus *Adam* made request, and *Raphaël*

After short pause assenting, thus began.[6]
   High matter thou injoin'st me, O prime of men,
Sad task and hard, for how shall I relate
565   To human sense th' invisible exploits
Of warring Spirits; how without remorse°   *pity*
The ruin of so many glorious once
And perfet while they stood; how last unfold
The secrets of another World, perhaps
570   Not lawful to reveal? yet for thy good
This is dispens't, and what surmounts the reach
Of human sense, I shall delineate so,
By lik'ning spiritual to corporal forms,
As may express them best, though what if Earth
575   Be but the shadow of Heav'n, and things therein
Each to other like, more than on Earth is thought?
   As yet this World was not, and *Chaos* wild
Reign'd where these Heav'ns now roll, where Earth now rests
Upon her Centre pois'd, when on a day
580   (For Time, though in Eternity, appli'd
To motion, measures all things durable
By present, past, and future) on such day
As Heav'n's great Year brings forth, th' Empyreal Host
Of Angels by Imperial summons call'd,
585   Innumerable before th' Almighty's Throne
Forthwith from all the ends of Heav'n appear'd
Under thir Hierarchs in orders bright;
Ten thousand thousand Ensigns high advanc'd,[7]
Standards and Gonfalons, twixt Van and Rear
590   Stream in the Air,[8] and for distinction serve
Of Hierarchies, of Orders, and Degrees;
Or in thir glittering Tissues bear imblaz'd
Holy Memorials, acts of Zeal and Love
Recorded eminent. Thus when in Orbs
595   Of circuit inexpressible they stood,
Orb within Orb, the Father infinite,
By whom in bliss imbosom'd sat the Son,
Amidst as from a flaming Mount, whose top
Brightness had made invisible, thus spake.
600   Hear all ye Angels, Progeny of Light,
Thrones, Dominations, Princedoms, Virtues, Powers,[9]
Hear my Decree, which unrevok't shall stand.

---

6. Raphael's account of the war in heaven continues to the end of Book 6. It is one of the two long "episodes," or inset narrations, that conclude the two halves of the poem (the other is at the end of Book 11).
7. Echoing Daniel 7.10, "thousand thousands ministered unto him, and ten thousand times ten thousand stood before him."

8. "Gonfalons" are banners fastened to cross-bars, whereas "standards" are fastened to a flagpole.
9. No mere roll call of titles; see Colossians 1.16 for Christ's agency in the angels' creation ("whether they be thrones, or dominions, or principalities, or powers: all things were created by him, and for him").

This day I have begot whom I declare
My only Son, and on this holy Hill
605   Him have anointed, whom ye now behold
At my right hand; your Head I him appoint;
And by my Self have sworn to him shall bow
All knees in Heav'n, and shall confess him Lord:
Under his great Vice-gerent Reign abide
610   United as one individual Soul
For ever happy: him who disobeys
Mee disobeys, breaks union, and that day
Cast out from God and blessed vision, falls
Into utter darkness, deep ingulft, his place
615   Ordain'd without redemption, without end.
    So spake th' Omnipotent, and with his words
All seem'd well pleas'd, all seem'd, but were not all.
That day, as other solemn days,[1] they spent
In song and dance about the sacred Hill,
620   Mystical dance, which yonder starry Sphere
Of Planets and of fixt° in all her Wheels   *fixed stars*
Resembles nearest, mazes intricate,
Eccentric, intervolv'd, yet regular
Then most, when most irregular they seem:
625   And in thir motions harmony Divine
So smooths her charming° tones, that God's own ear   *magical*
Listens delighted.[2] Ev'ning now approach'd
(For wee have also our Ev'ning and our Morn,
Wee ours for change delectable, not need)
630   Forthwith from dance to sweet repast they turn
Desirous; all in Circles as they stood,
Tables are set, and on a sudden pil'd
With Angels' Food, and rubied Nectar flows:
In Pearl, in Diamond, and massy Gold,
635   Fruit of delicious Vines, the growth of Heav'n.
On flow'rs repos'd, and with fresh flow'rets crown'd,
They eat, they drink, and in communion sweet
Quaff immortality and joy, secure
Of surfeit where full measure only bounds
640   Excess, before th' all bounteous King, who show'r'd
With copious hand, rejoicing in thir joy.
Now when ambrosial Night with Clouds exhal'd
From that high mount of God, whence light and shade
Spring both, the face of brightest Heav'n had chang'd
645   To grateful Twilight (for Night comes not there
In darker veil) and roseate Dews dispos'd
All but the unsleeping eyes of God to rest,

1. Holy days, festivals. Politically, these were opposed by Puritans.
2. The music of the spheres was a Neopythagorean concept, in which the movement of planets and other heavenly bodies in their spheres created a divine music.

Wide over all the Plain, and wider far
Than all this globous Earth in Plain outspread,
650   (Such are the Courts of God) th' Angelic throng
Disperst in Bands and Files thir Camp extend
By living Streams among the Trees of Life,
Pavilions numberless, and sudden rear'd,
Celestial Tabernacles, where they slept
655   Fann'd with cool Winds, save those who in thir course
Melodious Hymns about the sovran Throne
Alternate all night long: but not so wak'd
Satan, so call him now, his former name
Is heard no more in Heav'n;[3] he of the first,
660   If not the first Arch-Angel, great in Power,
In favor and preëminence, yet fraught
With envy against the Son of God, that day
Honor'd by his great Father, and proclaim'd
Messiah King anointed, could not bear
665   Through pride that sight, and thought himself impair'd.°   *injured*
Deep malice thence conceiving and disdain,
Soon as midnight brought on the dusky hour
Friendliest to sleep and silence, he resolv'd
With all his Legions to dislodge,[4] and leave
670   Unworshipt, unobey'd the Throne supreme,
Contemptuous, and his next subordinate
Awak'ning, thus to him in secret spake.
        Sleep'st thou, Companion dear, what sleep can close
Thy eye-lids? and rememb'rest what Decree
675   Of yesterday, so late hath past the lips
Of Heav'n's Almighty. Thou to me thy thoughts
Wast wont, I mine to thee was wont to impart;
Both waking we were one; how then can now
Thy sleep dissent? new Laws thou see'st impos'd;
680   New Laws from him who reigns, new minds may raise
In us who serve, new Counsels, to debate
What doubtful may ensue; more in this place
To utter is not safe. Assemble thou
Of all those Myriads which we lead the chief;
685   Tell them that by command, ere yet dim Night
Her shadowy Cloud withdraws, I am to haste,
And all who under me thir Banners wave,
Homeward with flying march where we possess
The Quarters of the North, there to prepare
690   Fit entertainment to receive our King
The great *Messiah*, and his new commands,
Who speedily through all the Hierarchies

---

3. Satan's name prior to his fall is unknown. Like those of the other fallen angels, his has been erased from memory (see 1.361–3).

4. Can mean to shift military quarters, or to displace (with "throne" as the object).

Intends to pass triumphant, and give Laws.
　　So spake the false Arch-Angel, and infus'd
695　　Bad influence into th' unwary breast
Of his Associate; hee together calls,
Or several one by one, the Regent Powers,
Under him Regent, tells, as he was taught,
That the most High commanding, now ere Night,
700　　Now ere dim Night had disincumber'd Heav'n,
The great Hierarchal Standard was to move;
Tells the suggested cause, and casts between
Ambiguous words and jealousies, to sound
Or taint integrity; but all obey'd
705　　The wonted signal, and superior voice
Of thir great Potentate; for great indeed
His name, and high was his degree in Heav'n;
His count'nance, as the Morning Star that guides
The starry flock, allur'd them, and with lies
710　　Drew after him the third part of Heav'n's Host:[5]
Meanwhile th' Eternal eye, whose sight discerns
Abstrusest thoughts, from forth his holy Mount
And from within the golden Lamps that burn
Nightly before him, saw without thir light
715　　Rebellion rising, saw in whom, how spread
Among the sons of Morn, what multitudes
Were banded to oppose his high Decree;
And smiling to his only Son thus said.
　　Son, thou in whom my glory I behold
720　　In full resplendence, Heir of all my might,
Nearly it now concerns us to be sure
Of our Omnipotence, and with what Arms
We mean to hold what anciently we claim
Of Deity or Empire, such a foe
725　　Is rising, who intends to erect his Throne
Equal to ours, throughout the spacious North;
Nor so content, hath in his thought to try°　　　　　　*test*
In battle, what our Power is, or our right.
Let us advise, and to this hazard draw
730　　With speed what force is left, and all imploy
In our defense, lest unawares we lose
This our high place, our Sanctuary, our Hill.
　　To whom the Son with calm aspect and clear
Lightning Divine, ineffable, serene,
735　　Made answer. Mighty Father, thou thy foes
Justly hast in derision, and secure
Laugh'st at thir vain designs and tumults vain,

---

5. The image depends on familiar symbolism whereby the morning star represented both Satan and Christ. As evening star, Christ set in death; as morning star he was resurrected (Revelation 22.16). Satan, as Lucifer, travesties Christ, specifically the Good Shepherd.

Matter to mee of Glory, whom thir hate
Illustrates,° when they see all Regal Power   *glorifies*
740   Giv'n me to quell thir pride, and in event°   *result*
Know whether I be dext'rous to subdue[6]
Thy Rebels, or be found the worst in Heav'n.
        So spake the Son, but *Satan* with his Powers
Far was advanc't on winged speed, an Host
745   Innumerable as the Stars of Night,
Or Stars of Morning, Dew-drops, which the Sun
Impearls on every leaf and every flower.
Regions they pass'd, the mighty Regencies°   *dominions*
Of Seraphim and Potentates and Thrones
750   In thir triple Degrees, Regions to which
All thy Dominion, *Adam* is no more
Than what this Garden is to all the Earth,
And all the Sea, from one entire globose°   *sphere*
Stretcht into Longitude; which having pass'd
755   At length into the limits of the North
They came, and *Satan* to his Royal seat
High on a Hill, far blazing, as a Mount
Rais'd on a Mount, with Pyramids and Tow'rs
From Diamond Quarries hewn,[7] and Rocks of Gold,
760   The Palace of great *Lucifer*, (so call
That Structure in the Dialect of men
Interpreted) which not long after, he
Affecting° all equality with God,   *pretending to*
In imitation of that Mount whereon
765   *Messiah* was declar'd in sight of Heav'n,
The Mountain of the Congregation call'd:
For thither he assembl'd all his Train,
Pretending so commanded to consult
About the great reception of thir King,
770   Thither to come, and with calumnious° Art   *slanderous*
Of counterfeited truth thus held thir ears.
        Thrones, Dominations, Princedoms, Virtues, Powers,
If these magnific Titles yet remain
Not merely titular, since by Decree
775   Another now hath to himself ingross't
All Power, and us eclipst under the name
Of King anointed, for whom all this haste
Of midnight march, and hurried meeting here,
This only to consult how we may best
780   With what may be devis'd of honors new
Receive him coming to receive from us

---

6. Matching the Father's wit: Christ's dextrous position at God's right hand results from his dextrous (skillful) defeat of Satan (see 6.892 and Mark 16.19).
7. Pyramids are spires or obelisks, rather than the squat form now assumed. Obelisk-pyramids were associated with Rome, and with fame, and in miniature form were fashionable in palaces.

Knee-tribute yet unpaid, prostration vile,
Too much to one, but double how endur'd,
To one and to his image now proclaim'd?
785   But what if better counsels might erect
Our minds and teach us to cast off this Yoke?
Will ye submit your necks, and choose to bend
The supple knee? ye will not, if I trust
To know ye right, or if ye know yourselves
790   Natives and Sons of Heav'n possest before
By none, and if not equal all, yet free,
Equally free; for Orders and Degrees
Jar not with liberty, but well consist.
Who can in reason then or right assume
795   Monarchy over such as live by right
His equals, if in power and splendor less,
In freedom equal? or can introduce
Law and Edict on us, who without law
Err not? much less for this to be our Lord,
800   And look for adoration to th' abuse
Of those Imperial Titles which assert
Our being ordain'd to govern, not to serve?[8]
      Thus far his bold discourse without control
Had audience, when among the Seraphim
805   *Abdiel*,[9] than whom none with more zeal ador'd
The Deity, and divine commands obey'd,
Stood up, and in a flame of zeal severe
The current of his fury thus oppos'd.
      O argument blasphemous, false and proud!
810   Words which no ear ever to hear in Heav'n
Expected, least of all from thee, ingrate,°   *ungrateful*
In place thyself so high above thy Peers.
Canst thou with impious obloquy condemn
The just Decree of God, pronounc't and sworn,
815   That to his only Son by right endu'd
With Regal Sceptre, every Soul in Heav'n
Shall bend the knee, and in that honor due
Confess him rightful King? unjust thou say'st
Flatly unjust, to bind with Laws the free,
820   And equal over equals to let Reign,
One over all with unsucceeded power.[1]
Shalt thou give Law to God, shalt thou dispute
With him the points of liberty, who made
Thee what thou art, and form'd the Pow'rs of Heav'n
825   Such as he pleas'd, and circumscrib'd thir being?

---

8. Satan's argument recalls the Stuarts' assertion of the divine right of kings to govern independently of rule of law. Satan avoids the question of who ordained the titles.
9. Abdiel ("Servant of God") occurs in the Bible only in a genealogy (1 Chronicles 5.15).
1. Never to be succeeded, everlasting. But at 3.339–41 God envisages the obsolescence of both rule and duty, as God is "all in all."

Yet by experience taught we know how good,
And of our good, and of our dignity
How provident he is, how far from thought
To make us less, bent rather to exalt
830   Our happy state under one Head more near
United. But to grant it thee unjust,
That equal over equals Monarch Reign:
Thyself though great and glorious dost thou count,
Or all Angelic Nature join'd in one,
835   Equal to him begotten Son, by whom
As by his Word the mighty Father made
All things, ev'n thee, and all the Spirits of Heav'n
By him created in thir bright degrees,°   *ranks*
Crown'd them with Glory, and to thir Glory nam'd
840   Thrones, Dominations, Princedoms, Virtues, Powers,
Essential Powers, nor by his Reign obscur'd,
But more illustrious made, since he the Head
One of our number thus reduc't becomes,[2]
His Laws our Laws, all honor to him done
845   Returns our own. Cease then this impious rage,
And tempt not these; but hast'n to appease
Th' incensed Father, and th' incensed Son,
While Pardon may be found in time besought.
    So spake the fervent Angel, but his zeal
850   None seconded, as out of season judg'd,
Or singular and rash, whereat rejoic'd
Th' Apostate, and more haughty thus repli'd.
    That we were form'd then say'st thou? and the work
Of secondary hands, by task transferr'd
855   From Father to his Son? strange point and new!
Doctrine which we would know whence learnt: who saw
When this creation was? remember'st thou
Thy making, while the Maker gave thee being?
We know no time when we were not as now;
860   Know none before us, self-begot, self-rais'd
By our own quick'ning° power, when fatal course   *life-giving*
Had circl'd his full Orb, the birth mature
Of this our native Heav'n, Ethereal Sons.
Our puissance is our own, our own right hand
865   Shall teach us highest deeds, by proof to try
Who is our equal: then thou shalt behold
Whether by supplication we intend
Address, and to begirt th' Almighty Throne
Beseeching or besieging. This report,
870   These tidings carry to th' anointed King;
And fly, ere evil intercept thy flight.

2. Having set aside his divinity, the Son will be "reduced" by the incarnation.

He said, and as the sound of waters deep
Hoarse murmur echo'd to his words applause
Through the infinite Host, nor less for that
875 The flaming Seraph fearless, though alone
Encompass'd round with foes, thus answer'd bold.
    O alienate from God, O Spirit accurst,
Forsak'n of all good; I see thy fall
Determin'd, and thy hapless crew involv'd
880 In this perfidious fraud, contagion spread
Both of thy crime and punishment: henceforth
No more be troubl'd how to quit the yoke
Of God's *Messiah*: those indulgent Laws
Will not be now voutsaf'd, other Decrees
885 Against thee are gone forth without recall;
That Golden Sceptre which thou didst reject
Is now an Iron Rod to bruise and break
Thy disobedience. Well thou didst advise,
Yet not for thy advice or threats I fly
890 These wicked Tents devoted,[3] lest° the wrath   *but*
Impendent, raging into sudden flame
Distinguish not: for soon expect to feel
His Thunder on thy head, devouring fire.
Then who created thee lamenting learn,
895 When who can uncreate thee thou shalt know.
    So spake the Seraph *Abdiel* faithful found,
Among the faithless, faithful only hee;
Among innumerable false, unmov'd,
Unshak'n, unseduc'd, unterrifi'd
900 His Loyalty he kept, his Love, his Zeal;
Nor number, nor example with him wrought
To swerve from truth, or change his constant mind
Though single. From amidst them forth he pass'd,
Long way through hostile scorn, which he sustain'd
905 Superior, nor of violence fear'd aught;
And with retorted scorn his back he turn'd
On those proud Tow'rs to swift destruction doom'd.
    The End of the Fifth Book.

Book 6
The Argument

Raphael *continues to relate how* Michael *and* Gabriel *were sent forth to Battle against* Satan *and his Angels. The first fight describ'd:* Satan *and his Powers retire under Night: He calls a Council, invents devilish Engines, which in the second day's Fight put* Michael *and his Angels to some disorder; but they at length pulling up Mountains overwhelm'd both the force and Machines of* Satan: *Yet the Tumult not so ending, God on the third day sends* Messiah *his Son for whom he had reserv'd the glory of the Victory:* Hee *in the Power*

---

3. That is, consigned to destruction.

of his Father coming to the place, and causing all his Legions to stand still on either side, with his Chariot and Thunder driving into the midst of his Enemies, pursues them unable to resist towards the wall of Heaven; which opening they leap down with horror and confusion in the place of punishment prepar'd for them in the Deep: Messiah returns with triumph to his Father.

	All night the dreadless Angel° unpursu'd	*Abdiel*
	Through Heav'n's wide Champaign° held his way, till Morn,	*field*
	Wak't by the circling Hours, with rosy hand	
	Unbarr'd the gates of Light. There is a Cave	
5	Within the Mount of God, fast by his Throne,	
	Where light and darkness in perpetual round	
	Lodge and dislodge° by turns, which makes through Heav'n	*move quarters*
	Grateful vicissitude,° like Day and Night;	*change*
	Light issues forth, and at the other door	
10	Obsequious° darkness enters, till her hour	*dutiful*
	To veil the Heav'n, though darkness there might well	
	Seem twilight here; and now went forth the Morn[1]	
	Such as in highest Heav'n, array'd in Gold	
	Empyreal,[2] from before her vanisht Night,	
15	Shot through with orient Beams: when all the Plain	
	Cover'd with thick embattl'd Squadrons bright,	
	Chariots and flaming Arms, and fiery Steeds	
	Reflecting blaze on blaze, first met his view:	
	War he perceiv'd, war in procinct,° and found	*prepared*
20	Already known what he for news had thought	
	To have reported: gladly then he mixt	
	Among those friendly Powers who him receiv'd	
	With joy and acclamations loud, that one	
	That of so many Myriads fall'n, yet one	
25	Return'd not lost: On to the sacred hill	
	They led him high applauded, and present	
	Before the seat supreme; from whence a voice	
	From midst a Golden Cloud thus mild was heard.	
	Servant of God,[3] well done, well hast thou fought	
30	The better fight, who single hast maintain'd	
	Against revolted multitudes the Cause	
	Of Truth, in word mightier than they in Arms;	
	And for the testimony of Truth hast borne	
	Universal reproach, far worse to bear	
35	Than violence:[4] for this was all thy care	
	To stand approv'd in sight of God, though Worlds	
	Judg'd thee perverse: the easier conquest now	
	Remains thee, aided by this host of friends,	
	Back on thy foes more glorious to return	

1. The appearance of morning signals Day 2 of the action.
2. Purest; of the region nearest God.
3. Translating "Abdiel" (see 5.805n).
4. Milton echoes Matthew 25.21 ("Well done, thou good and faithful servant"); 1 Timothy 6.12 ("fight the good fight of faith"); and Psalm 69.7 ("for thy sake I have borne reproach").

40 Than scorn'd thou didst depart, and to subdue
By force, who reason for thir Law refuse,
Right reason for thir Law,[5] and for thir King
Messiah, who by right of merit Reigns.
Go *Michael* of Celestial Armies Prince,
45 And thou in Military prowess next,
Gabriel, lead forth to Battle these my Sons
Invincible,[6] lead forth my armed Saints
By Thousands and by Millions rang'd for fight;
Equal in number to that Godless crew
50 Rebellious, them with Fire and hostile Arms
Fearless assault, and to the brow° of Heav'n   *verge*
Pursuing drive them out from God and bliss,
Into thir place of punishment, the Gulf
Of *Tartarus*, which ready opens wide
55 His fiery *Chaos* to receive thir fall.[7]
    So spake the Sovran voice, and Clouds began
To darken all the Hill, and smoke to roll
In dusky wreaths, reluctant flames, the sign
Of wrath awak't: nor with less dread the loud
60 Ethereal Trumpet from on high gan° blow: *began to*
At which command the Powers Militant,
That stood for Heav'n, in mighty Quadrate join'd
Of Union irresistible, mov'd on
In silence thir bright Legions, to the sound
65 Of instrumental Harmony that breath'd
Heroic Ardor to advent'rous deeds
Under thir God-like Leaders, in the Cause
Of God and his *Messiah*. On they move
Indissolubly firm; nor obvious° Hill,   *standing in the way*
70 Nor straitening Vale, nor Wood, nor Stream divides
Thir perfet ranks; for high above the ground
Thir march was, and the passive Air upbore
Thir nimble tread; as when the total kind
Of Birds in orderly array on wing
75 Came summon'd over *Eden* to receive
Thir names of thee; so over many a tract
Of Heav'n they march'd, and many a Province wide
Tenfold the length of this terrene:° at last   *earth*
Far in th' Horizon to the North appear'd
80 From skirt to skirt° a fiery Region, stretcht   *edge*
In battailous° aspect, and nearer view   *warlike*
Bristl'd with upright beams innumerable

5. Upright, true reason; conscience. Translating the Stoic and Scholastic phrase "recta ratio."
6. See Daniel 12.1; Revelation 12.7ff, "And there was war in heaven: Michael and his angels fought against the dragon; and the dragon fought and his angels, And

prevailed not; neither was their place any more in heaven."
7. For Tartarus as a pagan type of hell, see 2.69n. "Fiery chaos" is an exact term, since hell "encroached" on chaos (2.1002). Presumably hell was created at the moment of Satan's fall (6.292n).

Of rigid Spears, and Helmets throng'd, and Shields
Various, with boastful Argument portray'd,
85   The banded Powers of *Satan* hasting on
With furious expedition;° for they ween'd   *speed*
That selfsame day by fight, or by surprise
To win the Mount of God, and on his Throne
To set the envier of his State, the proud
90   Aspirer, but thir thoughts prov'd fond and vain
In the mid way: though strange to us it seem'd
At first, that Angel should with Angel war,
And in fierce hosting° meet, who wont to meet   *hostile encounter*
So oft in Festivals of joy and love
95   Unanimous, as sons of one great Sire
Hymning th' Eternal Father: but the shout
Of Battle now began, and rushing sound
Of onset ended soon each milder thought.
High in the midst exalted as a God
100   Th' Apostate in his Sun-bright Chariot sat
Idol of Majesty Divine, enclos'd
With Flaming Cherubim, and golden Shields;[8]
Then lighted from his gorgeous Throne, for now
'Twixt Host and Host but narrow space was left,
105   A dreadful interval, and Front to Front
Presented stood in terrible array
Of hideous length: before the cloudy Van,
On the rough edge of battle ere it join'd,
Satan with vast and haughty strides advanc'd,
110   Came tow'ring, arm'd in Adamant and Gold;
Abdiel that sight endur'd not, where he stood
Among the mightiest, bent on highest deeds,
And thus his own undaunted heart explores.
    O Heav'n! that such resemblance of the Highest
115   Should yet remain, where faith and realty°   *sincerity*
Remain not; wherefore should not strength and might
There fail where Virtue fails, or weakest prove
Where boldest; though to sight unconquerable?
His puissance,° trusting in th' Almighty's aid,   *power*
120   I mean to try, whose Reason I have tri'd°   *tested*
Unsound and false; nor is it aught but just,
That he who in debate of Truth hath won,
Should win in Arms, in both disputes alike
Victor; though brutish that contest and foul,
125   When Reason hath to deal with force, yet so
Most reason is that Reason overcome.
    So pondering, and from his armed Peers
Forth stepping opposite, half way he met

8. Satan's chariot travesties Messiah's cosmic vehicle; it is an idol, or false image, of majesty divine.

His daring foe, at this prevention° more   *obstruction*
130   Incenst, and thus securely him defi'd.[9]
    Proud, art thou met? thy hope was to have reacht
The highth of thy aspiring unoppos'd,
The Throne of God unguarded, and his side
Abandon'd at the terror of thy Power
135   Or potent tongue; fool, not to think how vain
Against th' Omnipotent to rise in Arms;
Who out of smallest things could without end
Have rais'd incessant Armies to defeat
Thy folly; or with solitary hand
140   Reaching beyond all limit, at one blow
Unaided could have finisht thee, and whelm'd
Thy Legions under darkness; but thou seest
All are not of thy Train; there be who° Faith   *there are those who*
Prefer, and Piety to God, though then
145   To thee not visible, when I alone
Seem'd in thy World erroneous to dissent
From all: my Sect thou seest, now learn too late
How few sometimes may know, when thousands err.
    Whom the grand Foe with scornful eye askance
150   Thus answer'd. Ill for thee, but in wisht hour
Of my revenge, first sought for thou return'st
From flight, seditious Angel, to receive
Thy merited reward, the first assay
Of this right hand provok'd, since first that tongue
155   Inspir'd with contradiction durst oppose
A third part of the Gods, in Synod met
Thir Deities to assert,[1] who while they feel
Vigor Divine within them, can allow
Omnipotence to none. But well thou com'st
160   Before thy fellows, ambitious to win
From me some Plume, that thy success may show
Destruction to the rest: this pause between
(Unanswer'd lest thou boast) to let thee know;
At first I thought that Liberty and Heav'n
165   To heav'nly Souls had been all one; but now
I see that most through sloth had rather serve,
Minist'ring Spirits, train'd up in Feast and Song;
Such hast thou arm'd, the Minstrelsy of Heav'n,
Servility with freedom to contend,
170   As both thir deeds compar'd this day shall prove.
    To whom in brief thus *Abdiel* stern repli'd.
Apostate, still thou err'st, nor end wilt find
Of erring, from the path of truth remote:

---

9. "Incensed" describes Satan, while "securely" (confidently) describes Abdiel.
1. Satan presumptuously claims more than angelic status.

Synod: a general church council to determine doctrine; a Presbyterian ecclesiastical court.

Unjustly thou deprav'st° it with the name   *defame*
175   Of *Servitude* to serve whom God ordains,
Or Nature; God and Nature bid the same,
When he who rules is worthiest, and excels
Them whom he governs. This is servitude,
To serve th' unwise, or him who hath rebell'd
180   Against his worthier, as thine now serve thee,
Thyself not free, but to thyself enthrall'd;
Yet lewdly° dar'st our minist'ring upbraid.   *seditiously*
Reign thou in Hell thy Kingdom, let mee serve
In Heav'n God ever blest,[2] and his Divine
185   Behests obey, worthiest to be obey'd;
Yet Chains in Hell, not Realms expect: meanwhile
From mee return'd, as erst thou said'st, from flight,
This greeting on thy impious Crest receive.
        So saying, a noble stroke he lifted high,
190   Which hung not, but so swift with tempest fell
On the proud Crest of *Satan*, that no sight,
Nor motion of swift thought, less could his Shield
Such ruin intercept: ten paces huge
He back recoil'd; the tenth on bended knee
195   His massy Spear upstay'd; as if on Earth
Winds under ground or waters forcing way
Sidelong, had pusht a Mountain from his seat
Half sunk with all his Pines. Amazement seiz'd
The Rebel Thrones, but greater rage to see
200   Thou foil'd thir mightiest, ours joy fill'd, and shout,
Presage of Victory and fierce desire
Of Battle: whereat *Michaël* bid sound
Th' Arch-Angel trumpet; through the vast of Heav'n
It sounded, and the faithful Armies rung°   *proclaimed*
205   Hosanna to the Highest: nor stood at gaze
The adverse Legions, nor less hideous join'd
The horrid shock: now storming fury rose,
And clamor such as heard in Heav'n till now
Was never, Arms on Armor clashing bray'd
210   Horrible discord, and the madding° Wheels   *frenzied*
Of brazen Chariots rag'd; dire was the noise
Of conflict; over head the dismal hiss
Of fiery Darts in flaming volleys flew,
And flying vaulted either Host with fire.
215   So under fiery Cope° together rush'd   *sky*
Both Battles main,[3] with ruinous assault
And inextinguishable rage; all Heav'n
Resounded, and had Earth been then, all Earth
Had to her Centre shook. What wonder? when

---

2. Satan echoes this phrase in hell; see 1.263, "Better to reign in hell, than serve in heaven."

3. The main bodies of the armies, as distinct from the wings or van at 6.107.

220 Millions of fierce encount'ring Angels fought
On either side, the least of whom could wield
These Elements, and arm him with the force
Of all thir Regions:[4] how much more of Power
Army against Army numberless to raise
225 Dreadful combustion° warring, and disturb,   *commotion*
Though not destroy, thir happy Native seat;
Had not th' Eternal King Omnipotent
From his stronghold of Heav'n high over-rul'd
And limited thir might; though number'd such
230 As each divided Legion might have seem'd
A numerous Host, in strength each armed hand
A Legion; led in fight, yet Leader seem'd
Each Warrior single as in Chief, expert
When to advance, or stand, or turn the sway
235 Of Battle, open when, and when to close
The ridges of grim War; no thought of flight,
None of retreat, no unbecoming deed.
That argu'd fear; each on himself reli'd,
As only in his arm the moment° lay   *determining influence*
240 Of victory; deeds of eternal fame
Were done, but infinite: for wide was spread
That War and various; sometimes on firm ground
A standing fight, then soaring on main wing°   *fully airborne*
Tormented all the Air; all Air seem'd then
245 Conflicting Fire: long time in even scale
The Battle hung; till *Satan,* who that day
Prodigious power had shown, and met in Arms
No equal, ranging through the dire attack
Of fighting Seraphim confus'd, at length
250 Saw where the Sword of *Michael* smote, and fell'd
Squadrons at once, with huge two-handed sway
Brandisht aloft the horrid edge came down
Wide wasting; such destruction to withstand
He hasted, and oppos'd the rocky Orb
255 Of tenfold Adamant, his ample Shield
A vast circumference: At his approach
The great Arch-Angel from his warlike toil
Surceas'd, and glad as hoping here to end
Intestine° War in Heav'n, the Arch-foe subdu'd   *internal*
260 Or Captive dragg'd in Chains, with hostile frown
And visage all inflam'd first thus began.
    Author of evil, unknown till thy revolt,
Unnam'd in Heav'n, now plenteous, as thou seest
These Acts of hateful strife, hateful to all,
265 Though heaviest by just measure on thyself

4. The layers into which the four elements were arranged, more or less according to what would now be called their density.

And thy adherents: how hast thou disturb'd
Heav'n's blessed peace, and into Nature brought
Misery, uncreated till the crime
Of thy Rebellion? how hast thou instill'd
270 Thy malice into thousands, once upright
And faithful, now prov'd false. But think not here
To trouble Holy Rest; Heav'n casts thee out
From all her Confines. Heav'n the seat of bliss
Brooks not the works of violence and War.
275 Hence then, and evil go with thee along,
Thy offspring, to the place of evil, Hell,
Thou and thy wicked crew; there mingle broils,°   *concoct quarrels*
Ere this avenging Sword begin thy doom,
Or some more sudden vengeance wing'd from God
280 Precipitate thee with augmented pain.
       So spake the Prince of Angels; to whom thus
The Adversary.[5] Nor think thou with wind
Of airy threats to awe whom yet with deeds
Thou canst not. Hast thou turn'd the least of these
285 To flight, or if to fall, but that they rise
Unvanquisht, easier to transact with mee
That thou shouldst hope, imperious, and with threats
To chase me hence? err not that so shall end
The strife which thou call'st evil, but wee style
290 The strife of Glory: which we mean to win,
Or turn this Heav'n itself into the Hell
Thou fabl'st,[6] here however to dwell free,
If not to reign: meanwhile thy utmost force,
And join him nam'd 'Almighty' to thy aid,
295 I fly not, but have sought thee far and nigh.
       They ended parle,° and both address'd for fight   *debate*
Unspeakable; for who, though with the tongue
Of Angels, can relate, or to what things
Liken on Earth conspicuous, that may lift
300 Human imagination to such highth
Of Godlike Power: for likest Gods they seem'd,
Stood they or mov'd, in stature, motion, arms
Fit to decide the Empire of great Heav'n.
Now wav'd thir fiery Swords, and in the Air
305 Made horrid Circles; two broad Suns thir Shields
Blaz'd opposite, while expectation stood
In horror; from each hand with speed retir'd
Where erst was thickest fight, th' Angelic throng,
And left large field, unsafe within the wind
310 Of such commotion, such as, to set forth

5. The literal meaning of "Satan." See 1.82n, and Job 1.6.
6. Satan rejects even the word "hell" as a made-up term.
Hell has existed since 6.54, if not earlier; but God
announced it to the loyal angels only. Only after joining
them does Abdiel mention it (6.183).

Great things by small, if Nature's concord broke,
Among the Constellations war were sprung,
Two Planets rushing from aspect malign
Of fiercest opposition in mid Sky,[7]
315   Should combat, and thir jarring Spheres confound.
Together both with next to Almighty Arm,
Uplifted imminent one stroke they aim'd
That might determine, and not need repeat,
As not of power, at once;[8] nor odds appear'd
320   In might or swift prevention;° but the sword   *anticipation*
Of *Michael* from the Armory of God
Was giv'n him temper'd so, that neither keen
Nor solid might resist that edge: it met
The sword of *Satan* with steep force to smite
325   Descending, and in half cut sheer, nor stay'd,
But with swift wheel reverse,[9] deep ent'ring shear'd
All his right side; then *Satan* first knew pain,
And writh'd him to and fro convolv'd;° so sore   *contorted*
The griding° sword with discontinuous wound   *piercing*
330   Pass'd through him, but th' Ethereal substance clos'd
Not long divisible, and from the gash
A stream of Nectarous humor issuing flow'd
Sanguine, such as Celestial Spirits may bleed,
And all his Armor stain'd erewhile so bright.
335   Forthwith on all sides to his aid was run
By Angels many and strong, who interpos'd
Defense, while others bore him on thir Shields
Back to his Chariot, where it stood retir'd
From off the files of war: there they him laid
340   Gnashing for anguish and despite and shame
To find himself not matchless, and his pride
Humbl'd by such rebuke, so far beneath
His confidence to equal God in power.
Yet soon he heal'd; for Spirits that live throughout
345   Vital in every part, not as frail man
In Entrails, Heart or Head, Liver or Reins,°   *kidneys*
Cannot but by annihilating die;
Nor in thir liquid° texture mortal wound   *flexible*
Receive, no more than can the fluid Air:
350   All Heart they live, all Head, all Eye, all Ear,
All Intellect, all Sense, and as they please,
They Limb themselves, and color, shape or size
Assume, as likes° them best, condense or rare.   *pleases*
     Meanwhile in other parts like deeds deserv'd

---

7. The planets are in diametrically opposite signs at mid-sky, or the zenith. Astrologers recognized five spatial relations ("aspects") between planets; "opposition" was disharmonious, with a malign influence.

8. That is, it would be beyond their power to repeat such a blow immediately.
9. Michael follows through into a reverse stroke. As a young man, Milton assiduously practiced fencing.

355   Memorial, where the might of *Gabriel* fought,
And with fierce Ensigns° pierc'd the deep array   *battle cries*
Of *Moloch* furious King, who him defi'd,
And at his Chariot wheels to drag him bound
Threat'n'd, nor from the Holy One of Heav'n
360   Refrain'd his tongue blasphemous; but anon
Down clov'n to the waist, with shatter'd Arms
And uncouth° pain fled bellowing. On each wing   *unfamiliar*
Uriel and *Raphaël* his vaunting foe,
Though huge, and in a Rock of Diamond Arm'd,
365   Vanquish'd *Adramelech*, and *Asmadai*,[1]
Two potent Thrones, that to be less than Gods
Disdain'd, but meaner thoughts learn'd in thir flight,
Mangl'd with ghastly wounds through Plate and Mail.
Nor stood unmindful *Abdiel* to annoy
370   The Atheist crew, but with redoubl'd blow
Ariel and *Arioch*, and the violence
Of *Ramiel* scorcht and blasted overthrew.[2]
I might relate of thousands, and thir names
Eternize here on Earth; but those elect
375   Angels contented with thir fame in Heav'n
Seek not the praise of men; the other sort
In might though wondrous and in Acts of War,
Nor of Renown less eager, yet by doom
Cancell'd from Heav'n and sacred memory,
380   Nameless in dark oblivion let them dwell.
For strength from Truth divided and from Just,
Illaudable,° naught merits but dispraise   *unworthy of praise*
And ignominy, yet to glory aspires
Vain-glorious, and through infamy seeks fame:
385   Therefore Eternal silence be thir doom.
        And now thir Mightiest quell'd, the battle swerv'd
With many an inroad° gor'd; deformed rout   *passage*
Enter'd, and foul disorder; all the ground
With shiver'd armor strown, and on a heap
390   Chariot and Charioteer lay overturn'd
And fiery foaming Steeds; what stood, recoil'd
O'erwearied, through the faint Satanic Host
Defensive scarce,[3] or with pale fear surpris'd,
Then first with fear surpris'd and sense of pain
395   Fled ignominious, to such evil brought
By sin of disobedience, till that hour
Not liable to fear or flight or pain.

---

1. Presumably Raphael vanquishes Asmodeus (Asmadai), in view of their biblical encounter (4.171n). Aptly, the solar intelligence Uriel vanquishes the sun-god Adramelec (2 Kings 17.31).
2. Ariel ("Lion of God" or "Divine Light") is Jerusalem at Isaiah 29.1ff. Arioc ("Lion-like") was the "King of Ellasar" (Genesis 14.1) whom Abram fought. Ramiel ("Deceiver of God") was one of the angels fornicating with women in 1 Enoch 6.7.
3. That is, hardly capable of defending itself.

Far otherwise th' inviolable Saints
In Cubic Phalanx firm advanc'd entire,
400 Invulnerable, impenetrably arm'd:
Such high advantages thir innocence
Gave them above thir foes, not to have sinn'd,
Not to have disobey'd; in fight they stood
Unwearied, unobnoxious° to be pain'd   *not liable*
405 By wound, though from thir place by violence mov'd.
    Now Night her course began, and over Heav'n
Inducing darkness, grateful truce impos'd,
And silence on the odious din of War:
Under her Cloudy covert both retir'd,
410 Victor and Vanquisht: on the foughten field°   *battlefield*
Michaël and his Angels prevalent°   *victorious*
Encamping, plac'd in Guard thir Watches round,
Cherubic waving fires:⁴ on th' other part
Satan with his rebellious disappear'd,
415 Far in the dark dislodg'd,° and void of rest,   *moved camp*
His Potentates to Council call'd by night;⁵
And in the midst thus undismay'd began.
    O now in danger tri'd, now known in Arms
Not to be overpow'r'd, Companions dear,
420 Found worthy not of Liberty alone,
Too mean pretense, but what we more affect,⁶
Honor, Dominion, Glory, and renown,
Who have sustain'd one day in doubtful fight,
(And if one day, why not Eternal days?)
425 What Heaven's Lord had powerfullest to send
Against us from about his Throne, and judg'd
Sufficient to subdue us to his will,
But proves not so: then fallible, it seems,
Of future we may deem him, though till now
430 Omniscient thought. True is, less firmly arm'd,
Some disadvantage we endur'd and pain,
Till now not known, but known as soon contemn'd,
Since now we find this our Empyreal form
Incapable of mortal injury,
435 Imperishable, and though pierc'd with wound,
Soon closing, and by native vigor heal'd.
Of evil then so small as easy think
The remedy; perhaps more valid Arms,
Weapons more violent, when next we meet,
440 May serve to better us, and worse° our foes,   *injure*

---

4. Cherubim, excelling in knowledge, are assigned to sentry duty; see also 4.778ff, 12.590ff. Being fiery, they are their own watchfires.

5. In the *Iliad* 9, there is a nocturnal council of war called by Agamemnon after defeat by Hector.

6. Raphael conveys instruction by ironic wordplay: "mean pretence" can mean both "low ambition" and "base dissimulation," while "affect" can mean both "aspire to" and "feign."

Or equal what between us made the odds,
In Nature none: if other hidden cause
Left them Superior, while we can preserve
Unhurt our minds, and understanding sound,
445   Due search and consultation will disclose.
       He sat; and in th' assembly next upstood
Nisroch, of Principalities the prime;[7]
As one he stood escap't from cruel fight,
Sore toil'd, his riv'n Arms to havoc hewn,
450   And cloudy in aspect thus answering spake.
Deliverer from new Lords, leader to free
Enjoyment of our right as Gods; yet hard
For Gods, and too unequal work we find
Against unequal arms to fight in pain,
455   Against unpain'd, impassive; from which evil
Ruin must needs ensue; for what avails
Valor or strength, though matchless, quell'd with pain
Which all subdues, and makes remiss° the hands   slack
Of Mightiest. Sense of pleasure we may well
460   Spare out of life perhaps, and not repine,
But live content, which is the calmest life:
But pain is perfet misery, the worst
Of evils, and excessive, overturns
All patience. He who therefore can invent
465   With what more forcible we may offend°   hurt
Our yet unwounded Enemies, or arm
Ourselves with like defense, to me° deserves   it seems to me
No less than for deliverance what we owe.[8]
       Whereto with look compos'd Satan repli'd.
470   Not uninvented that, which thou aright
Believ'st so main° to our success, I bring;   important
Which of us who beholds the bright surface
Of this Ethereous mould whereon we stand,
This continent of spacious Heav'n, adorn'd
475   With Plant, Fruit, Flow'r Ambrosial, Gems and Gold,
Whose Eye so superficially surveys
These things, as not to mind° from whence they grow   recall
Deep under ground, materials dark and crude,
Of spiritous and fiery spume, till toucht
480   With Heav'n's ray, and temper'd they shoot forth
So beauteous, op'ning to the ambient light.
These in thir dark Nativity the Deep
Shall yield us, pregnant with infernal flame,
Which into hollow Engines long and round
485   Thick ramm'd, at th' other bore with touch of fire
Dilated and infuriate° shall send forth   exploded

---

7. The Assyrian King Sennacherib perished while worshipping the idol Nisroch.

8. That is, "no less for than what we owe our deliverer (Satan)." Nisroc is inviting a leadership contest.

From far with thund'ring noise among our foes
Such implements of mischief as shall dash
To pieces, and o'erwhelm whatever stands
490   Adverse, that they shall fear we have disarm'd
The Thunderer of his only dreaded bolt.[9]
Nor long shall be our labor, yet ere dawn,
Effect shall end our wish. Meanwhile revive;
Abandon fear; to strength and counsel join'd
495   Think nothing hard, much less to be despair'd.
He ended, and his words thir drooping cheer°   mood
Enlight'n'd, and thir languisht hope reviv'd.
Th' invention all admir'd, and each, how hee
To be th' inventor miss'd, so easy it seem'd
500   Once found, which yet unfound most would have thought
Impossible: yet haply of thy Race
In future days, if Malice should abound,
Some one intent on mischief, or inspir'd
With dev'lish machination might devise
505   Like instrument to plague the Sons of men
For sin, on war and mutual slaughter bent.
Forthwith from Council to the work they flew,
None arguing stood, innumerable hands
Were ready, in a moment up they turn'd
510   Wide the Celestial soil, and saw beneath
Th' originals of Nature° in thir crude   original elements
Conception; Sulphurous and Nitrous Foam
They found, they mingl'd, and with subtle Art,
Concocted and adusted° they reduc'd   dried up by heat
515   To blackest grain, and into store convey'd:
Part hidd'n veins digg'd up (nor hath this Earth
Entrails unlike) of Mineral and Stone,[1]
Whereof to found° thir Engines and thir Balls   cast
Of missive ruin; part incentive reed°   match
520   Provide, pernicious with one touch to fire.
So all ere day-spring, under conscious Night
Secret they finish'd, and in order set,
With silent circumspection unespi'd.
Now when fair Morn Orient in Heav'n appear'd[2]
525   Up rose the Victor Angels, and to Arms
The matin Trumpet Sung: in Arms they stood
Of Golden Panoply, refulgent Host,
Soon banded; others from the dawning Hills
Look'd round, and Scouts each Coast light-armed scour

9. The invention of gunpowder portrayed here had recent associations as well as epic ones. The Parliamentary forces were famed for their artillery. Mid-century sermons and tracts regarded the Gunpowder Plot, the unsuccessful attempt to blow up Parliament (1605), as a "hellish invention."
1. This is necessary information for Adam and Eve: before the Fall there was no mining.
2. The morning of Day 3 of the action.

530   Each quarter, to descry the distant foe,
       Where lodg'd, or whither fled, or if for fight,
       In motion or in halt: him soon they met
       Under spread Ensigns moving nigh, in slow
       But firm Battalion; back with speediest Sail
535   Zophiel,[3] of Cherubim the swiftest wing,
       Came flying, and in mid Air aloud thus cri'd.
          Arm, Warriors, Arm for fight, the foe at hand,
       Whom fled we thought, will save us long pursuit
       This day, fear not his flight; so thick a Cloud
540   He comes, and settl'd in his face I see
       Sad° resolution and secure:° let each   *serious / confident*
       His Adamantine coat gird well, and each
       Fit well his Helm, grip fast his orbed Shield,
       Borne ev'n or high, for this day will pour down,
545   If I conjecture aught, no drizzling show'r,
       But rattling storm of Arrows barb'd with fire.
       So warn'd he them aware themselves, and soon
       In order, quit° of all impediment;   *freed*
       Instant without disturb they took Alarm,
550   And onward move Embattl'd; when behold
       Not distant far with heavy pace the Foe
       Approaching gross and huge; in hollow Cube
       Training° his devilish Enginry, impal'd   *pulling*
       On every side with shadowing Squadrons Deep,
555   To hide the fraud. At interview° both stood   *in mutual view*
       A while, but suddenly at head appear'd
       Satan: And thus was heard Commanding loud.
          Vanguard, to Right and Left the Front unfold;
       That all may see who hate us, how we seek
560   Peace and composure,° and with open breast   *settlement*
       Stand ready to receive them, if they like
       Our overture, and turn not back perverse;
       But that I doubt; however witness Heaven,
       Heav'n witness thou anon, while we discharge
565   Freely our part: yee who appointed stand
       Do as you have in charge, and briefly touch
       What we propound, and loud that all may hear.
          So scoffing in ambiguous words, he scarce
       Had ended; when to Right and Left the Front
570   Divided, and to either Flank retir'd.
       Which to our eyes discover'd new and strange,
       A triple-mounted row of Pillars laid
       On Wheels (for like to Pillars most they seem'd
       Or hollow'd bodies made of Oak or Fir
575   With branches lopt, in Wood or Mountain fell'd)

3. Zophiel means "Spy of God."

Brass, Iron, Stony mould,[4] had not thir mouths
With hideous orifice gap't on us wide,
Portending hollow truce; at each behind
A Seraph stood, and in his hand a Reed
580 Stood waving tipt with fire; while we suspense,°   *attentive*
Collected stood within our thoughts amus'd,°   *puzzled*
Not long, for sudden all at once thir Reeds
Put forth, and to a narrow vent appli'd
With nicest touch. Immediate in a flame,
585 But soon obscur'd with smoke, all Heav'n appear'd,
From those deep-throated Engines belcht, whose roar
Embowell'd with outrageous noise the Air,
And all her entrails tore, disgorging foul
Thir devilish glut, chain'd Thunderbolts and Hail
590 Of Iron Globes, which on the Victor Host
Levell'd, with such impetuous fury smote,
That whom they hit, none of thir feet might stand,
Though standing else as Rocks, but down they fell
By thousands, Angel on Arch-Angel roll'd;
595 The sooner for thir Arms; unarm'd they might
Have easily as Spirits evaded swift
By quick contraction or remove; but now
Foul dissipation follow'd and forc't rout;
Nor serv'd it to relax thir serried files.[5]
600 What should they do? if on they rush'd repulse
Repeated, and indecent° overthrow   *unbecoming*
Doubl'd, would render them yet more despis'd,
And to thir foes a laughter; for in view
Stood rankt of Seraphim another row
605 In posture to displode° thir second tire°   *discharge / volley*
Of Thunder: back defeated to return
They worse abhorr'd. *Satan* beheld thir plight,
And to his Mates° thus in derision call'd.   *comrades*
   O Friends, why come not on these Victors proud?
610 Erewhile they fierce were coming, and when wee,
To entertain them fair with open Front
And Breast, (what could we more?) propounded terms
Of composition, straight they chang'd thir minds,
Flew off, and into strange vagaries° fell,   *fits*
615 As they would dance, yet for a dance they seem'd
Somewhat extravagant and wild, perhaps
For joy of offer'd peace: but I suppose
If our proposals once again were heard
We should compel them to a quick result.
620   To whom thus *Belial* in like gamesome mood.
Leader, the terms we sent were terms of weight,

---

4. Made of brass, iron, stone.   5. That is, space their close formation more loosely.

Of hard contents, and full of force urg'd home,
Such as we might perceive amus'd them all,
And stumbl'd many; who receives them right,
625 Had need from head to foot well understand;
Not understood, this gift they have besides,
They show us when our foes walk not upright.
     So they among themselves in pleasant vein
Stood scoffing, highth'n'd in thir thoughts beyond
630 All doubt of Victory, eternal might
To match with thir inventions they presum'd
So easy, and of his Thunder made a scorn,
And all his Host derided, while they stood
A while in trouble; but they stood not long,
635 Rage prompted them at length, and found them arms[6]
Against such hellish mischief fit to oppose.
Forthwith (behold the excellence, the power
Which God hath in his mighty Angels plac'd)
Thir Arms away they threw, and to the Hills[7]
640 (For Earth hath this variety from Heav'n
Of pleasure situate in Hill and Dale)
Light as the Lightning glimpse they ran, they flew,
From thir foundations loos'ning to and fro
They pluckt the seated° Hills with all thir load,   *fixed*
645 Rocks, Waters, Woods, and by the shaggy tops
Uplifting bore them in thir hands: Amaze,°   *bewilderment*
Be sure, and terror seiz'd the rebel Host,
When coming towards them so dread they saw
The bottom of the Mountains upward turn'd,
650 Till on those cursed Engines' triple-row
They saw them whelm'd, and all thir confidence
Under the weight of Mountains buried deep,
Themselves invaded next, and on thir heads
Main° Promontories flung, which in the Air   *whole*
655 Came shadowing,° and opprest whole Legions arm'd,   *casting shade*
Thir armor help'd thir harm, crush't in and bruis'd
Into thir substance pent, which wrought them pain
Implacable, and many a dolorous groan,
Long struggling underneath, ere they could wind°   *squirm*
660 Out of such prison, though Spirits of purest light,
Purest at first, now gross by sinning grown.
The rest in imitation to like Arms
Betook them, and the neighboring Hills uptore;
So Hills amid the Air encounter'd Hills
665 Hurl'd to and fro with jaculation° dire,   *hurling*
That under ground they fought in dismal shade:
Infernal noise; War seem'd a civil Game

6. Echoing Virgil's *Aeneid* 1.150 ("furor arma minstrat").
7. Lines 639–66 allude to the Giants' war against the

Olympians, a pagan type of the angelic rebellion. See
1.199n, 1.231ff, and Hesiod's *Theogony* 713–18.

To this uproar; horrid confusion heapt
Upon confusion rose: and now all Heav'n
670 Had gone to wrack, with ruin overspread,
Had not th' Almighty Father where he sits
Shrin'd in his Sanctuary of Heav'n secure,
Consulting on the sum of things,[8] foreseen
This tumult, and permitted all, advis'd:°   *after consideration*
675 That his great purpose he might so fulfil,
To honor his Anointed Son aveng'd
Upon his enemies, and to declare
All power on him transferr'd: whence to his Son
Th' Assessor° of his Throne he thus began.   *sharer*
680   Effulgence of my Glory, Son belov'd,
Son in whose face invisible is beheld
Visibly, what by Deity I am,
And in whose hand what by Decree I do,
Second Omnipotence, two days are past,
685 Two days, as we compute the days of Heav'n,
Since *Michael* and his Powers went forth to tame
These disobedient; sore hath been thir fight,
As likeliest was, when two such Foes met arm'd;
For to themselves I left them, and thou know'st,
690 Equal in thir Creation they were form'd,
Save what sin hath impair'd, which yet hath wrought
Insensibly, for I suspend thir doom;
Whence in perpetual fight they needs must last
Endless, and no solution will be found:
695 War wearied hath perform'd what War can do,
And to disorder'd rage let loose the reins,
With Mountains as with Weapons arm'd, which makes
Wild work in Heav'n, and dangerous to the main.°   *whole*
Two days are therefore past, the third is thine;[9]
700 For thee I have ordain'd it, and thus far
Have suffer'd, that the Glory may be thine
Of ending this great War, since none but Thou
Can end it. Into thee such Virtue and Grace
Immense I have transfus'd, that all may know
705 In Heav'n and Hell thy Power above compare,
And this perverse Commotion govern'd thus,
To manifest thee worthiest to be Heir
Of all things, to be Heir and to be King
By Sacred Unction,° thy deserved right.   *anointing*
710 Go then thou Mightiest in thy Father's might,
Ascend my Chariot, guide the rapid Wheels
That shake Heav'n's basis,° bring forth all my War,   *foundation*

8. Usually explained as "universe," by analogy with Lucretius 5.362 ("summarum summa"). But "summa rerum" ("highest public interest") is closer.

9. Allegorically, the third day is the day of resurrection, as in Luke 13.32, "the third day I shall be perfected."

My Bow and Thunder, my Almighty Arms
Gird on, and Sword upon thy puissant Thigh;
715   Pursue these sons of Darkness, drive them out
From all Heav'n's bounds into the utter Deep:
There let them learn, as likes them, to despise
God and *Messiah* his anointed King.[1]
     He said, and on his Son with Rays direct
720   Shone full; hee all his Father full exprest
Ineffably into his face receiv'd,
And thus the filial Godhead answering spake.
     O Father, O supreme of heav'nly Thrones,
First, Highest, Holiest, Best, thou always seek'st
725   To glorify thy Son, I always thee,
As is most just; this I my Glory account,
My exaltation, and my whole delight,
That thou in me well pleas'd, declar'st thy will
Fulfill'd, which to fulfil is all my bliss.
730   Sceptre and Power, thy giving, I assume
And gladlier shall resign, when in the end
Thou shalt be All in All, and I in thee
For ever, and in mee all whom thou lov'st;[2]
But whom thou hat'st, I hate, and can put on
735   Thy terrors, as I put thy mildness on,
Image of thee in all things; and shall soon,
Arm'd with thy might, rid heav'n of these rebell'd,
To thir prepar'd ill Mansion° driven down,   *dwelling*
To chains of darkness, and th' undying Worm,
740   That from thy just obedience could revolt,
Whom to obey is happiness entire.
Then shall thy Saints unmixt, and from th' impure
Far separate, circling thy holy Mount
Unfeigned *Halleluiahs* to thee sing,
745   Hymns of high praise, and I among them chief.
So said, he o'er his Sceptre bowing, rose
From the right hand of Glory where he sat,
And the third sacred Morn began to shine
Dawning through Heav'n: forth rush'd with whirl-wind sound
750   The Chariot of Paternal Deity,[3]
Flashing thick flames, Wheel within Wheel, undrawn,°   *self-powered*
Itself instinct° with Spirit, but convoy'd   *animated*
By four Cherubic shapes, four Faces each
Had wondrous, as with Stars thir bodies all

1. Literally translating "Messiah."
2. Echoing 1 Corinthians 15.24, 28, "Then cometh the end, when he shall have delivered up the kingdom to God, even the Father; when he shall have put down all rule and all authority and power. . . . And when all things shall be subdued unto him, then shall the Son also himself be subject unto him that put all things under him, that God may be all in all." See also 3.339–43.

3. The central allegory, prepared for by many partial anticipations; see 1.311; 2.887; 3.394, 522, 653n (the seven archangels of the cosmic chariot); 6.100–3 (Satan's chariot), 211, 338, 358, 390, 711. The image is also present in Ezekiel 1.4–6, 16, 26–8; 10.12, 16.

755 And Wings were set with Eyes, with Eyes the Wheels
     Of Beryl, and careering Fires between;
     Over thir heads a crystal Firmament,
     Whereon a Sapphire Throne, inlaid with pure
     Amber, and colors of the show'ry Arch.
760 Hee in Celestial Panoply all arm'd
     Of radiant *Urim*,[4] work divinely wrought,
     Ascended, at his right hand Victory
     Sat Eagle-wing'd, beside him hung his Bow
     And Quiver with three-bolted Thunder stor'd,[5]
765 And from about him fierce Effusion roll'd
     Of smoke and bickering° flame, and sparkles dire;   *flashing*
     Attended with ten thousand thousand Saints,
     He onward came, far off his coming shone,
     And twenty thousand (I thir number heard)
770 Chariots of God, half on each hand were seen:
     Hee on the wings of Cherub rode sublime°   *set aloft*
     On the Crystalline Sky, in Sapphire Thron'd.
     Illustrious far and wide, but by his own
     First seen, them unexpected joy surpris'd,
775 When the great Ensign of *Messiah* blaz'd
     Aloft by Angels borne, his Sign in Heav'n:[6]
     Under whose Conduct *Michael* soon reduc'd°   *led back*
     His Army, circumfus'd° on either Wing,   *spread around*
     Under thir Head imbodied all in one.
780 Before him Power Divine his way prepar'd;
     At his command the uprooted Hills retir'd
     Each to his place, they heard his voice and went
     Obsequious, Heav'n his wonted face renew'd,
     And with fresh Flow'rets Hill and Valley smil'd.
785 This saw his hapless Foes, but stood obdur'd,°   *hardened*
     And to rebellious fight rallied thir Powers
     Insensate, hope conceiving from despair.
     In heav'nly Spirits could such perverseness dwell?
     But to convince the proud what Signs avail,
790 Or Wonders move th' obdurate to relent?
     They hard'n'd more by what might most reclaim,[7]
     Grieving to see his Glory, at the sight
     Took envy, and aspiring to his highth,
     Stood reimbattl'd fierce, by force or fraud

4. Mentioned in Exodus 28.30, "thou shalt put in the breastplate of judgment the Urim and the Thummim; and they shall be upon Aaron's heart, when he goeth in before the Lord."

5. Jupiter's thunderbolts in the Giant War were sometimes interpreted as a type of Christ's power, sometimes as a contrasting evil; see 1.506–21; Hesiod, *Theogony* 687ff. And in contrast with Phaethon (another charioteer), Messiah's true sonship allows him to wield three-bolted thunder (6.572) instead of having it used against him.

6. A portrayal of Matthew 24.30, "then shall appear the sign of the Son of man in heaven: and then . . . they shall see the Son of man coming in the clouds of heaven with power and great glory."

7. In Exodus 14.4, Pharaoh's heart hardened despite miraculous signs.

795　Weening to prosper, and at length prevail
　　Against God and *Messiah*, or to fall
　　In universal ruin last, and now
　　To final Battle drew, disdaining flight,
　　Or faint retreat; when the great Son of God
800　To all his Host on either hand thus spake.
　　　　Stand still in bright array ye Saints, here stand
　　Ye Angels arm'd, this day from Battle rest;
　　Faithful hath been your Warfare, and of God
　　Accepted, fearless in his righteous Cause,
805　And as ye have receiv'd, so have ye done
　　Invincibly: but of this cursed crew
　　The punishment to other hand belongs;
　　Vengeance is his, or whose he sole appoints;[8]
　　Number to this day's work is not ordain'd
810　Nor multitude, stand only and behold
　　God's indignation on these Godless pour'd
　　By mee; not you but mee they have despis'd,
　　Yet envied; against mee is all thir rage,
　　Because the Father, t'whom in Heav'n supreme
815　Kingdom and Power and Glory appertains,
　　Hath honor'd me according to his will.
　　Therefore to mee thir doom he hath assign'd;
　　That they may have thir wish, to try° with mee   *test*
　　In Battle which the stronger proves, they all,
820　Or I alone against them, since by strength
　　They measure all, of other excellence
　　Not emulous, nor care who them excels;
　　Nor other strife with them do I voutsafe.
　　　　So spake the Son, and into terror chang'd
825　His count'nance too severe to be beheld
　　And full of wrath bent on his Enemies.
　　At once the Four[9] spread out thir Starry wings
　　With dreadful shade contiguous, and the Orbs
　　Of his fierce Chariot roll'd, as with the sound
830　Of torrent Floods, or of a numerous Host.
　　Hee on his impious Foes right onward drove,
　　Gloomy as Night; under his burning Wheels
　　The steadfast Empyrean shook throughout,
　　All but the Throne itself of God.[1] Full soon
835　Among them he arriv'd; in his right hand
　　Grasping ten thousand Thunders, which he sent
　　Before him, such as in thir Souls infix'd
　　Plagues; they astonisht all resistance lost,

8. The Bible reiterates that vengeance is a divine prerogative, not lightly delegated. For examples, see Deuteronomy 32.35; Psalm 94.1; Romans 12.19; Hebrews 10.30.
9. The "four cherubic shapes" of 6.753, their wings set
with eyes; see Ezekiel 10.12.
1. Refuting Satan's claim to have shaken the throne, at
1.105.

All courage; down thir idle weapons dropp'd;
840 O'er Shields and Helms, and helmed heads he rode
Of Thrones and mighty Seraphim prostrate,
That wish't the Mountains now might be again
Thrown on them as a shelter from his ire.[2]
Nor less on either side tempestuous fell
845 His arrows, from the fourfold-visag'd Four,
Distinct° with eyes, and from the living Wheels,   adorned
Distinct alike with multitude of eyes;
One Spirit in them rul'd, and every eye
Glar'd lightning, and shot forth pernicious fire
850 Among th' accurst, that wither'd all thir strength,
And of thir wonted vigor left them drain'd,
Exhausted, spiritless, afflicted, fall'n.
Yet half his strength he put not forth, but check'd
His Thunder in mid Volley, for he meant
855 Not to destroy, but root them out of Heav'n:[3]
The overthrown he rais'd, and as a Herd
Of Goats or timorous flock together throng'd
Drove them before him Thunder-struck, pursu'd
With terrors and with furies to the bounds
860 And Crystal wall of Heav'n, which op'ning wide,
Roll'd inward, and a spacious Gap disclos'd
Into the wasteful° Deep; the monstrous sight   desolate
Struck them with horror backward, but far worse
Urg'd them behind; headlong themselves they threw
865 Down from the verge of Heav'n, Eternal wrath
Burn'd after them to the bottomless pit.
      Hell heard th' unsufferable noise, Hell saw
Heav'n ruining° from Heav'n, and would have fled   falling
Affrighted; but strict Fate had cast too deep
870 Her dark foundations, and too fast had bound.
Nine days they fell; confounded *Chaos* roar'd,
And felt tenfold confusion in thir fall
Through his wild Anarchy, so huge a rout
Incumber'd him with ruin: Hell at last
875 Yawning receiv'd them whole, and on them clos'd,
Hell thir fit habitation fraught with fire
Unquenchable, the house of woe and pain.
Disburd'n'd Heav'n rejoic'd, and soon repair'd
Her mural breach, returning whence it roll'd.
880 Sole Victor from th' expulsion of his Foes
Messiah his triumphal Chariot turn'd:
To meet him all his Saints, who silent stood

2. Echoes Revelation 6.16, where the damned cry "to the
mountains and rocks, Fall on us, and hide us from the
face of him that sitteth on the throne, and from the
wrath of the Lamb."
3. Contrast with Hesiod, *Theogony*, where Zeus' total energies are insufficient to end the conflict.

Eye-witnesses of his Almighty Acts,
With Jubilee advanc'd; and as they went,
885   Shaded with branching Palm,[4] each order bright,
Sung Triumph, and him sung Victorious King,
Son, Heir, and Lord, to him Dominion giv'n,
Worthiest to Reign: he celebrated rode
Triumphant through mid Heav'n, into the Courts
890   And Temple of his mighty Father Thron'd
On high; who into Glory him receiv'd,
Where now he sits at the right hand of bliss.
     Thus measuring things in Heav'n by things on Earth
At thy request, and that thou mayst beware
895   By what is past, to thee I have reveal'd
What might have else to human Race been hid:
The discord which befell, and War in Heav'n
Among th' Angelic Powers, and the deep fall
Of those too high aspiring, who rebell'd
900   With *Satan*, hee who envies now thy state,
Who now is plotting how he may seduce
Thee also from obedience, that with him
Bereav'd of happiness thou mayst partake
His punishment, Eternal misery;
905   Which would be all his solace and revenge,
As a despite done against the most High,
Thee once to gain Companion of his woe.
But list'n not to his Temptations, warn
Thy weaker;[5] let it profit thee to have heard
910   By terrible Example the reward
Of disobedience; firm they might have stood,
Yet fell; remember, and fear to transgress.
     The End of the Sixth Book.

Book 7
The Argument

Raphael *at the request of* Adam *relates how and wherefore this world was first created; that* God, *after the expelling of Satan and his Angels out of Heaven, declar'd his pleasure to create another World and other Creatures to dwell therein; sends his Son with Glory and attendance of Angels to perform the work of Creation in six days: the Angels celebrate with Hymns the performance thereof, and his reascension into Heaven.*

---

4. The palm also belongs to an allegory of the passion narrative. The palm of victory recalls that in Revelation 7.9; the song of triumph recalls Revelation 5.12; and reception into glory at the right hand of bliss recalls the ascension in Hebrews 1.3.

5. Supply "vessel" to "weaker." See 1 Peter 3.7, "ye hus-bands, dwell with them according to knowledge, giving honor unto the wife, as unto the weaker vessel, and as being heirs together of the grace of life." This is part of a homily on duties of spouses calculated to counteract any tendency to submissiveness on the part of husbands.

[THE INVOCATION]

Descend from Heav'n *Urania*,[1] by that name
If rightly thou art call'd, whose Voice divine
Following, above th' *Olympian* Hill I soar,
Above the flight of *Pegasean* wing.[2]
5 The meaning, not the Name I call: for thou
Nor of the Muses nine, nor on the top
Of old *Olympus* dwell'st, but Heav'nly born,
Before the Hills appear'd, or Fountain flow'd,
Thou with Eternal Wisdom didst converse,
10 Wisdom thy Sister, and with her didst play
In presence of th' Almighty Father, pleas'd
With thy Celestial Song. Up led by thee
Into the Heav'n of Heav'ns I have presum'd,
An Earthly Guest, and drawn Empyreal Air,
15 Thy temp'ring;[3] with like safety guided down
Return me to my Native Element:
Lest from this flying Steed unrein'd, (as once
Bellerophon, though from a lower Clime)
Dismounted, on th' *Aleian* Field I fall
20 Erroneous° there to wander and forlorn.[4]   *wandering, erring*
Half yet remains unsung, but narrower bound
Within the visible Diurnal Sphere
Standing on Earth, not rapt° above the Pole,[5]   *entranced*
More safe I Sing with mortal voice, unchang'd
25 To hoarse or mute, though fall'n on evil days,
On evil days though fall'n, and evil tongues;
In darkness, and with dangers compast round,
And solitude;[6] yet not alone, while thou
Visit'st my slumbers Nightly, or when Morn
30 Purples the East: still govern thou my Song,
Urania, and fit audience find, though few.
But drive far off the barbarous dissonance
Of *Bacchus* and his Revellers, the Race
Of that wild Rout that tore the *Thracian* Bard
35 In *Rhodope*, where Woods and Rocks had Ears
To rapture, till the savage clamor drown'd
Both Harp and Voice;[7] nor could the Muse defend

1. Only in this invocation is the Muse ever named. *Urania* was the Muse of Astronomy. Milton's denial that his Urania is one "of the Muses nine" directs attention to a more recent, single Muse. Since Du Bartas's *Uranie*, the name had been used for the Christian Muse of the divine poetry movement.
2. The winged horse Pegasus was an emblem for the inspired poet.
3. The air of the "first region" (3.562–64) was fatal to mortals.
4. When Bellerophon tried to fly to heaven on Pegasus, Jupiter sent an insect to sting the horse and throw the rider. Bellerophon fell on the Aleian plain and wandered blind and lonely until his death.
5. Either the celestial pole or a synecdoche for the sky.
6. The obfuscated syntax conceals an allusion to Milton's dangerous situation during the persecutions that immediately followed the Restoration.
7. Orpheus as a type of the inspired poet. The myth of his dismemberment by Thracian women during orgies of Bacchus seems to have focused some of Milton's deepest fears. Rhodope was a mountain range in Thrace. In Ovid, *Metamorphoses* 11.1–60, the "woods and rocks" mourned Orpheus's loss, though they were the instruments of his murder.

Her Son. So fail not thou, who thee implores:
For thou art Heavn'ly, shee an empty dream.

40   Say Goddess, what ensu'd when *Raphaël*,
The affable Arch-angel, had forewarn'd
Adam by dire example to beware
Apostasy, by what befell in Heaven
To those Apostates, lest the like befall

45   In Paradise to *Adam* or his Race,
Charg'd not to touch the interdicted Tree,
If they transgress, and slight that sole command,
So easily obey'd amid the choice
Of all tastes else to please thir appetite,

50   Though wand'ring. He with his consorted° *Eve*   espoused
The story heard attentive, and was fill'd
With admiration,° and deep muse° to hear   amazement / meditation
Of things so high and strange, things to thir thought
So unimaginable as hate in Heav'n,

55   And War so near the Peace of God in bliss
With such confusion: but the evil soon
Driv'n back redounded° as a flood on those   flared back
From whom it sprung, impossible to mix
With Blessedness. Whence *Adam* soon repeal'd°   abandoned

60   The doubts that in his heart arose: and now
Led on, yet sinless, with desire to know
What nearer might concern him, how this World
Of Heav'n and Earth conspicuous first began[8]
When, and whereof created, for what cause,

65   What within *Eden* or without was done
Before his memory, as one whose drouth°   thirst
Yet scarce allay'd still eyes the current stream,
Whose liquid murmur heard new thirst excites,
Proceeded thus to ask his Heav'nly Guest.

70   Great things, and full of wonder in our ears,
Far differing from this World, thou hast reveal'd
Divine Interpreter[9] by favor sent
Down from the Empyrean to forewarn
Us timely of what might else have been our loss,

75   Unknown, which human knowledge could not reach:
For which to th' infinitely Good we owe
Immortal thanks, and his admonishment
Receive with solemn purpose to observe
Immutably his sovran will, the end°   purpose

80   Of what we are.[1] But since thou hast voutsaf't
Gently for our instruction to impart

---

8. Heaven and earth are "conspicuous," or visible, as opposed to the invisible "heaven of heavens." See 3.390;
7.13, 22.
9. In Virgil's *Aeneid* (4.378), Mercury is called "interpres
divum" when he brings Jupiter's command for Aeneas to
leave Dido.
1. Echoing Ecclesiastes 12.13, "Let us hear the end of all:
Fear God, and keep his commandments: for this is the
whole duty of man."

Things above Earthly thought, which yet concern'd
Our knowing, as to highest wisdom seem'd,°   *seemed good*
Deign to descend now lower, and relate
85   What may no less perhaps avail us known,
How first began this Heav'n which we behold
Distant so high, with moving Fires adorn'd
Innumerable, and this which yields or fills
All space[2] the ambient Air wide interfus'd
90   Imbracing round this florid Earth, what cause
Mov'd the Creator in his holy Rest
Through all Eternity so late to build
In *Chaos*, and the work begun, how soon
Absolv'd,° if unforbid thou mayst unfold   *completed*
95   What wee, not to explore the secrets ask
Of his Eternal Empire, but the more
To magnify his works,[3] the more we know.
And the great Light of Day yet wants to run
Much of his Race though steep, suspense in Heav'n
100   Held by thy voice,[4] thy potent voice he hears,
And longer will delay to hear thee tell
His Generation, and the rising Birth
Of Nature from the unapparent° Deep: *invisible*
Or if the Star of Ev'ning and the Moon
105   Haste to thy audience, Night with her will bring
Silence, and Sleep list'ning to thee will watch,°   *remain awake*
Or we can bid his absence, till thy Song
End, and dismiss thee ere the Morning shine.
      Thus *Adam* his illustrious Guest besought:
110   And thus the Godlike Angel answer'd mild.
This also thy request with caution askt
Obtain: though to recount Almighty works
What words or tongue of Seraph can suffice,
Or heart of man suffice to comprehend?
115   Yet what thou canst attain which best may serve
To glorify the Maker, and infer°   *render*
Thee also happier, shall not be withheld
Thy hearing, such Commission from above
I have receiv'd, to answer thy desire
120   Of knowledge within bounds; beyond abstain
To ask, nor let thine own inventions° hope°   *reasonings / hope for*
Things not reveal'd, which th' invisible King,
Only Omniscient, hath supprest in Night,
To none communicable in Earth or Heaven:[5]

---

2. Air yields to solids, or fills the space they leave.
3. Echoing Job 36.24, "Remember that thou magnify his work." Adam treads lightly, not wishing to pry into forbidden knowledge.
4. The day is nearly over since the sun is at a low point in its course ("race"). In "suspense," it is both hanging in the

sky and attentive to Raphael.
5. See 1 Timothy 1.17, "The king eternal, immortal, invisible, the only wise God" and Matthew 24.36, "of that day and hour knoweth no man, no, not the angels of heaven, but my Father only." Milton elsewhere sets bounds to astronomical inquiry; see 8.70ff.

125   Anough is left besides to search and know.
       But Knowledge is as food, and needs no less
       Her Temperance over Appetite, to know
       In measure what the mind may well contain,
       Oppresses else with Surfeit, and soon turns
130   Wisdom to Folly, as Nourishment to Wind.
           Know then, that after *Lucifer* from Heav'n
       (So call him, brighter once amidst the Host
       Of Angels, than that Star the Stars among)[6]
       Fell with his flaming Legions through the Deep
135   Into his place, and the great Son return'd
       Victorious with his Saints,° th' Omnipotent   angels
       Eternal Father from his Throne beheld
       Thir multitude, and to his Son thus spake.
           At least our envious Foe hath fail'd, who thought
140   All like himself rebellious, by whose aid
       This inaccessible high strength, the seat
       Of Deity supreme, us dispossest,
       He trusted to have seiz'd, and into fraud°   faithlessness
       Drew many, whom thir place knows here no more;[7]
145   Yet far the greater part have kept, I see,
       Thir station, Heav'n yet populous retains
       Number sufficient to possess her Realms
       Though wide, and this high Temple to frequent
       With Ministeries due and solemn Rites:
150   But lest his heart exalt him in the harm
       Already done to have dispeopl'd Heav'n,
       My damage fondly° deem'd, I can repair   foolishly
       That detriment, if such it be to lose
       Self-lost, and in a moment will create
155   Another World, out of one man a Race
       Of men innumerable, there to dwell,
       Not here, till by degrees of merit rais'd
       They open to themselves at length the way
       Up hither, under long obedience tri'd,
160   And Earth be chang'd to Heav'n, and Heav'n to Earth,
       One Kingdom, Joy and Union without end.
       Meanwhile inhabit lax,° ye Powers of Heav'n;   live spaciously
       And thou my Word, begotten Son, by thee
       This I perform, speak thou, and be it done:
165   My overshadowing Spirit and might with thee
       I send along, ride forth, and bid the Deep
       Within appointed bounds be Heav'n and Earth,
       Boundless the Deep, because I am[8] who fill

---

6. Raphael offers "Lucifer" (the morning star, Venus or
Mercury) as an intelligible human translation for Satan's
original name. That name is suggested but not given; see
1.82, 361–63; 5.658ff, 700–14.

7. In Job 7.9ff, "He that goeth down to the grave shall
come up no more. He shall return no more to his house,
neither shall his place know him any more."
8. "I am" is the divine name in Exodus 3.14.

Infinitude, nor vacuous the space
170 Though I uncircumscrib'd myself retire,
And put not forth my goodness, which is free
To act or not, Necessity and Chance
Approach not mee, and what I will is Fate.
      So spake th' Almighty, and to what he spake
175 His Word, the Filial Godhead, gave effect.
Immediate are the Acts of God, more swift
Than time or motion, but to human ears
Cannot without process of speech be told,
So told as earthly notion can receive.
180 Great triumph and rejoicing was in Heav'n
When such was heard declar'd the Almighty's will;
Glory they sung to the most High, good will
To future men, and in thir dwellings peace:⁹
Glory to him whose just avenging ire
185 Had driven out th' ungodly from his sight
And th' habitations of the just; to him
Glory and praise, whose wisdom had ordain'd
Good out of evil to create, instead
Of Spirits malign a better Race to bring
190 Into their vacant room, and thence diffuse
His good to Worlds and Ages infinite.
So sang the Hierarchies: Meanwhile the Son
On his great Expedition now appear'd,
Girt with Omnipotence, with Radiance crown'd
195 Of Majesty Divine, Sapience and Love
Immense, and all his Father in him shone.
About his Chariot numberless were pour'd
Cherub and Seraph, Potentates and Thrones,
And Virtues, winged Spirits, and Chariots wing'd,
200 From the Armory of God, where stand of old
Myriads between two brazen Mountains lodg'd¹
Against a solemn day, harness't at hand,
Celestial Equipage;° and now came forth   *equipment*
Spontaneous, for within them Spirit liv'd,
205 Attendant on thir Lord: Heav'n op'n'd wide
Her ever-during Gates, Harmonious sound
On golden Hinges moving,² to let forth
The King of Glory in his powerful Word
And Spirit coming to create new Worlds.
210 On heav'nly ground they stood, and from the shore
They view'd the vast immeasurable Abyss

9. Echoing Job 38.7 ("the morning stars sang together, and all the sons of God shouted for joy" at creation); and Luke 2.14 (the angels' hymn celebrating incarnation and new creation: "Glory to God in the highest, and on earth peace, good will toward men").
1. See Zechariah 6.1, "there came four chariots out from between two mountains; and the mountains were mountains of brass."
2. Contrast these gates with those of hell, which opened with a "jarring sound" (2.879ff) to give Satan his view of the abyss.

Outrageous° as a Sea, dark, wasteful,° wild,   *unrestrained / desolate*
Up from the bottom turn'd by furious winds
And surging waves, as Mountains to assault

215   Heav'n's highth, and with the Centre mix the Pole.
      Silence, ye troubl'd waves, and thou Deep, peace,
Said then th' Omnific° Word, your discord end: *all-creating*
      Nor stay'd, but on the Wings of Cherubim
Uplifted, in Paternal Glory rode

220   Far into *Chaos*, and the World unborn;
For *Chaos* heard his voice: him all his Train
Follow'd in bright procession to behold
Creation, and the wonders of his might.
Then stay'd the fervid° Wheels, and in his hand   *burning*

225   He took the golden Compasses, prepar'd
In God's Eternal store, to circumscribe
This Universe, and all created things:
One foot he centred, and the other turn'd
Round through the vast profundity obscure,

230   And said, Thus far extend, thus far thy bounds,
This be thy just° Circumference, O World.   *exact*
Thus God the Heav'n created, thus the Earth,
Matter unform'd and void:[3] Darkness profound
Cover'd th' Abyss: but on the wat'ry calm

235   His brooding wings the Spirit of God outspread,
And vital virtue° infus'd, and vital warmth   *power*
Throughout the fluid Mass, but downward purg'd
The black tartareous cold Infernal dregs
Adverse to life; then founded, then conglob'd°   *formed into a ball*

240   Like things to like, the rest to several place
Disparted, and between spun out the Air,
And Earth self-balanc't on her Centre hung.
      Let there be Light, said God, and forthwith Light
Ethereal, first of things,[4] quintessence pure

245   Sprung from the Deep, and from her Native East
To journey through the airy gloom began,
Spher'd in a radiant Cloud, for yet the Sun
Was not; shee in a cloudy Tabernacle
Sojourn'd the while.[5] God saw the Light was good;

250   And light from darkness by the Hemisphere
Divided: Light the Day, and Darkness Night
He nam'd. Thus was the first Day Ev'n and Morn:[6]

---

3. Plato writes of a formless substance in *Timaeus* 50ff; compare to the void of Genesis 1.2. But in *De doctrina* 1.7, Milton explicitly rejects creation *ex nihilo*.
4. Ether is the purest element; see 3.7, "pure ethereal stream."
5. With the tabernacle, or sanctuary for God, Milton avoids the biblical problem of how there could be light without the sun. He also addresses this problem in *De doctrina* 1.7, where he admits the impossibility of con-

ceiving "light without some source of light," yet distinguishes visible light from the perpetual invisible light in the heaven of heavens.
6. Echoing Genesis 1.4ff, "God saw the light, that it was good: and God divided the light from the darkness. And God called the light Day, and the darkness he called Night. And the evening and the morning were the first day." This phrase marks Day 14 of *Paradise Lost*'s action.

Nor pass'd uncelebrated, nor unsung
By the Celestial Choirs, when Orient Light
255　Exhaling° first from Darkness they beheld;　　　　　　　*breathing forth*
Birth-day of Heav'n and Earth; with joy and shout
The hollow Universal Orb they fill'd,
And touch'd thir Golden Harps, and hymning prais'd
God and his works, Creator him they sung,
260　Both when first Ev'ning was, and when first Morn.
　　　Again, God said, let there be Firmament
Amid the Waters, and let it divide
The Waters from the Waters: and God made
The Firmament, expanse of liquid, pure,
265　Transparent, Elemental Air, diffus'd
In circuit to the uttermost convex
Of this great Round:° partition firm and sure,　　　　　　*universe*
The Waters underneath from those above
Dividing: for as Earth, so hee the World°　　　　　　　　*universe*
270　Built on circumfluous Waters calm, in wide
Crystalline Ocean, and the loud misrule
Of *Chaos* far remov'd, lest fierce extremes
Contiguous might distemper the whole frame:[7]
And Heav'n he nam'd the Firmament: So Ev'n
275　And Morning *Chorus* sung the second Day.
　　　The Earth was form'd, but in the Womb as yet
Of Waters, Embryon° immature involv'd,°　　　　　　　*embryo / enveloped*
Appear'd not: over all the face of Earth
Main° Ocean flow'd, not idle, but with warm　　　　　　*uninterrupted*
280　Prolific° humor soft'ning all her Globe,　　　　　　　*generative*
Fermented the great Mother to conceive,
Satiate with genial° moisture, when God said,　　　　　*generative*
Be gather'd now ye Waters under Heav'n
Into one place, and let dry Land appear.[8]
285　Immediately the Mountains huge appear
Emergent, and thir broad bare backs upheave
Into the Clouds, thir tops ascend the Sky:
So high as heav'd the tumid° Hills, so low　　　　　　　*swollen*
Down sunk a hollow bottom broad and deep,
290　Capacious bed of Waters: thither they
Hasted with glad precipitance, uproll'd
As drops on dust conglobing from the dry;
Part rise in crystal Wall, or ridge direct,
For haste; such flight the great command impress'd
295　On the swift floods: as Armies at the call
Of Trumpet (for of Armies thou hast heard)[9]

---

7. In chaos, opposite qualities ("extremes") are not held
apart by intervening means, but are contiguous.
8. Echoing Genesis 1.9.

9. The simile would not have made things clearer to
Adam and Eve, if Raphael had not already recounted the
angelic war.

Troop to thir Standard, so the wat'ry throng,
Wave rolling after Wave, where way they found,
If steep, with torrent rapture,° if through Plain,   *force*
300 Soft-ebbing; nor withstood them Rock or Hill,
But they, or under ground, or circuit wide
With Serpent error wand'ring,[1] found thir way,
And on the washy Ooze deep Channels wore;
Easy, ere God had bid the ground be dry,
305 All but within those banks, where Rivers now
Stream, and perpetual draw thir humid train.°   *trailed robe*
The dry Land, Earth, and the great receptacle
Of congregated Waters he call'd Seas:[2]
And saw that it was good, and said, Let th' Earth
310 Put forth the verdant Grass, Herb yielding Seed,
And Fruit Tree yielding Fruit after her kind;
Whose Seed is in herself upon the Earth.
He scarce had said, when the bare Earth, till then
Desert and bare, unsightly, unadorn'd,
315 Brought forth the tender Grass, whose verdure clad
Her Universal Face with pleasant green,
Then Herbs of every leaf, that sudden flow'r'd
Op'ning thir various colors, and made gay
Her bosom smelling sweet: and these scarce blown,
320 Forth flourish'd thick the clust'ring Vine, forth crept
The smelling Gourd, up stood the corny Reed
Embattl'd in her field: and th' humble° Shrub,   *low-growing*
And Bush with frizzl'd hair implicit:° last   *interwoven*
Rose as in Dance the stately Trees, and spread
325 Thir branches hung with copious Fruit: or gemm'd°   *budded*
Thir Blossoms: with high Woods the Hills were crown'd,
With tufts the valleys and each fountain side,
With borders long the Rivers. That Earth now
Seem'd like to Heav'n, a seat where Gods might dwell,
330 Or wander with delight, and love to haunt
Her sacred shades: though God had yet not rain'd
Upon the Earth, and man to till the ground
None was, but from the Earth a dewy Mist
Went up and water'd all the ground, and each
335 Plant of the field, which ere it was in the Earth
God made, and every Herb, before it grew
On the green stem; God saw that it was good:
So Ev'n and Morn recorded° the Third Day.[3]   *sang*
     Again th' Almighty spake: Let there be Lights
340 High in th' expanse of Heaven to divide
The Day from Night; and let them be for Signs,

---

1. By itself, "error" might be a Latinism for "winding;" but after "serpent" it indisputably anticipates the Fall.
2. Echoing Genesis 1.10ff. "Congregated waters" echoes the Vulgate's "congregationesque aquarum."
3. This marks day 16 of the action.

For Seasons, and for Days, and circling Years,
And let them be for Lights as I ordain
Thir Office in the Firmament of Heav'n
345   To give Light on the Earth; and it was so.[4]
And God made two great Lights, great for thir use
To Man, the greater to have rule by Day,
The less by Night altern:° and made the Stars,   *by turns*
And set them in the Firmament of Heav'n
350   To illuminate the Earth, and rule the Day
In thir vicissitude,° and rule the Night,   *variety*
And Light from Darkness to divide. God saw,
Surveying his great Work, that it was good:
For of Celestial Bodies first the Sun
355   A mighty Sphere he fram'd, unlightsome first,
Though of Ethereal Mould:° then form'd the Moon   *quintessential matter*
Globose, and every magnitude of Stars,
And sow'd with Stars the Heav'n thick as a field:
Of Light by far the greater part he took.
360   Transplanted from her cloudy Shrine,[5] and plac'd
In the Sun's Orb, made porous to receive
And drink the liquid Light, firm to retain
Her gather'd beams, great Palace now of Light.
Hither as to thir Fountain other Stars
365   Repairing, in thir gold'n Urns draw Light,
And hence the Morning Planet gilds her horns;
By tincture° or reflection they augment   *infusion*
Thir small peculiar,[6] though from human sight
So far remote, with diminution seen.
370   First in his East the glorious Lamp was seen,
Regent of Day, and all th' Horizon round
Invested with bright Rays, jocund to run
His Longitude° through Heav'n's high road: the gray   *ecliptic course*
Dawn, and the *Pleiades* before him danc'd
375   Shedding sweet influence: less bright the Moon,
But opposite in levell'd° West was set   *on the same plane*
His mirror, with full face borrowing her Light
From him, for other light she needed none
In that aspect, and still that distance keeps
380   Till night, then in the East her turn she shines,
Revolv'd on Heav'n's great Axle and her Reign
With thousand lesser Lights dividual° holds,   *shared*
With thousand thousand Stars, that then appear'd
Spangling the Hemisphere: then first adorn'd
385   With thir bright Luminaries that Set and Rose,
Glad Ev'ning and glad Morn crown'd the fourth day.[7]

---

4. Echoing Genesis 1.14ff.
5. Equivalent to the "cloudy tabernacle" at 7.248.
6. "Peculiar" light is inherent to a heavenly body, as opposed to "strange" or borrowed light.

7. The fourth day is crowned because it occupies the sovereign central place, fourth of the days of creation and seventeenth of the action.

And God said, let the Waters generate
Reptile with Spawn abundant, living Soul.°   *animate existence*
And let Fowl fly above the Earth, with wings
390   Display'd on the op'n Firmament of Heav'n.
And God created the great Whales, and each
Soul living, each that crept, which plenteously
The waters generated by thir kinds,
And every Bird of wing after his kind;
395   And saw that it was good, and bless'd them, saying,
Be fruitful, multiply, and in the Seas
And Lakes and running Streams the waters fill;
And let the Fowl be multipli'd on the Earth.[8]
Forthwith the Sounds and Seas, each Creek and Bay
400   With Fry° innumerable swarm, and Shoals   *offspring*
Of Fish that with thir Fins and shining Scales
Glide under the green Wave, in Sculls that oft
Bank° the mid Sea: part single or with mate   *form a shelf*
Graze the Seaweed thir pasture, and through Groves
405   Of Coral stray, or sporting with quick glance
Show to the Sun thir wav'd coats dropt° with Gold,   *spotted*
Or in thir Pearly shells at ease, attend°   *wait for*
Moist nutriment, or under Rocks thir food
In jointed Armor watch: on smooth° the Seal,   *smooth water*
410   And bended Dolphins play: part huge of bulk
Wallowing unwieldly, enormous in thir Gait
Tempest° the Ocean: there Leviathan   *disturb violently*
Hugest of living Creatures, on the Deep
Stretcht like a Promontory sleeps or swims,
415   And seems a moving Land, and at his Gills
Draws in, and at his Trunk° spouts out a Sea.   *blowhole*
Meanwhile the tepid Caves, and Fens and shores
Thir Brood as numerous hatch, from th' Egg that soon
Bursting with kindly° rupture forth disclos'd°   *natural / hatched*
420   Thir callow° young, but feather'd soon and fledge   *unfeathered*
They summ'd° thir Pens,° and soaring th' air sublime   *completed / plumage*
With clang° despis'd the ground, under a cloud   *harsh scream*
In prospect; there the Eagle and the Stork
On Cliffs and Cedar tops thir Eyries build:[9]
425   Part loosely wing the Region, part more wise
In common, rang'd in figure wedge thir way,
Intelligent of seasons, and set forth
Thir Aery Caravan high over Seas
Flying, and over Lands with mutual wing
430 ·   Easing thir flight; so steers the prudent Crane
Her annual Voyage, borne on Winds; the Air
Floats, as they pass, fann'd with unnumber'd plumes:

8. Echoing Genesis 1.20–2.
9. Milton's epic catalogue compresses Tasso's *Creation* (1607), book 5, where 19 birds (including almost all Milton's seven) are assigned complex moral qualities.

From Branch to Branch the smaller Birds with song
Solac'd the Woods, and spread thir painted wings
435 Till Ev'n, nor then the solemn Nightingale
Ceas'd warbling, but all night tun'd her soft lays:
Others on Silver Lakes and Rivers Bath'd
Thir downy Breast; the Swan with Arched neck
Between her white wings mantling° proudly, Rows   *stretching*
440 Her state with Oary feet: yet oft they quit
The Dank,° and rising on stiff Pennons,° tow'r   *pool / wings*
The mid Aereal Sky: Others on ground
Walk'd firm; the crested Cock whose clarion° sounds   *small trumpet*
The silent hours, and th' other° whose gay Train   *peacock*
445 Adorns him, color'd with the Florid hue
Of Rainbows and Starry Eyes. The Waters thus
With Fish replenisht, and the Air with Fowl
Ev'ning and Morn solemniz'd the Fift day.[1]
    The Sixt, and of Creation last arose
450 With Ev'ning Harps and Matin, when God said,
Let th' Earth bring forth Soul living in her kind,
Cattle and Creeping things, and Beast of the Earth,
Each in their kind.[2] The Earth obey'd, and straight
Op'ning her fertile Womb teem'd° at a Birth   *produced*
455 Innumerous living Creatures, perfet forms,
Limb'd and full grown: out of the ground up rose
As from his Lair the wild Beast where he wons°   *lives*
In Forest wild, in Thicket, Brake, or Den;
Among the Trees in Pairs they rose, they walk'd:
460 The Cattle in the Fields and Meadows green:
Those rare and solitary, these in flocks[3]
Pasturing at once, and in broad Herds upsprung.
The grassy Clods now Calv'd, now half appear'd
The Tawny Lion, pawing to get free
465 His hinder parts, then springs as broke from Bonds,
And Rampant shakes his Brinded° mane; the Ounce,°   *streaked / lynx*
The Libbard,° and the Tiger, as the Mole   *leopard*
Rising, the crumbl'd Earth above them threw
In Hillocks; the swift Stag from under ground
470 Bore up his branching head: scarce from his mould
Behemoth biggest born of Earth upheav'd
His vastness:[4] Fleec't the Flocks and bleating rose,
As Plants: ambiguous between Sea and Land
The River Horse° and scaly Crocodile.   *hippopotamus*
475 At once came forth whatever creeps the ground,
Insect or Worm; those wav'd thir limber fans
For wings, and smallest Lineaments exact

---

1. Day 18 of the action.
2. Echoing Genesis 1.24.
3. "Those" are the wild beasts, while "these" are the cattle.

4. The italics make "behemoth" seem a name. See Job 40.15, "Behold now behemoth, which I made with thee."

In all the Liveries deckt of Summer's pride
With spots of Gold and Purple, azure and green:
480   These as a line thir long dimension drew,
Streaking the ground with sinuous trace; not all
Minims° of Nature; some of Serpent kind   *smallest creatures*
Wondrous in length and corpulence° involv'd°   *bulk / coiled*
Thir Snaky folds, and added wings. First crept
485   The Parsimonious Emmet,° provident   *careful ant*
Of future, in small room large heart° enclos'd,   *wisdom*
Pattern of just equality perhaps
Hereafter, join'd in her popular Tribes
Of Commonalty: swarming next appear'd
490   The Female Bee that feeds her Husband Drone
Deliciously,° and builds her waxen Cells   *luxuriously*
With Honey stor'd: the rest are numberless,
And thou thir Natures know'st, and gav'st them Names,
Needless to thee repeated; nor unknown
495   The Serpent subtl'st Beast of all the field,[5]
Of huge extent sometimes, with brazen Eyes
And hairy Mane terrific, though to thee
Not noxious, but obedient at thy call.
Now Heav'n in all her Glory shone, and roll'd
500   Her motions, as the great first-Mover's hand
First wheel'd thir course; Earth in her rich attire
Consummate° lovely smil'd; Air, Water, Earth,   *completed*
By Fowl, Fish, Beast, was flown, was swum, was walkt
Frequent;° and of the Sixt day yet remain'd;   *abundantly*
505   There wanted yet the Master work, the end
Of all yet done; a Creature who not prone
And Brute as other Creatures, but endu'd
With Sanctity of Reason, might erect
His Stature, and upright with Front° serene   *face*
510   Govern the rest, self-knowing, and from thence
Magnanimous° to correspond with Heav'n,   *noble*
But grateful to acknowledge whence his good
Descends, thither with heart and voice and eyes
Directed in Devotion, to adore
515   And worship God Supreme who made him chief
Of all his works: therefore th'Omnipotent
Eternal Father (For where is not hee
Present) thus to his Son audibly spake.
    Let us make now Man in our image, Man
520   In our similitude, and let them rule
Over the Fish and Fowl of Sea and Air,
Beast of the Field, and over all the Earth,

---

5. Milton singles out the serpent for mention last of the beasts, next to mankind. Echoing Genesis 3.1, "Now the serpent was more subtle than any beast of the field which the Lord God had made."

And every creeping thing that creeps the ground.[6]
This said, he form'd thee, *Adam*, thee O Man

525 Dust of the ground, and in thy nostrils breath'd
The breath of Life; in his own Image hee
Created thee, in the Image of God
Express,[7] and thou becam'st a living Soul.
Male he created thee, but thy consort

530 Female for Race; then bless'd Mankind, and said,
Be fruitful, multiply, and fill the Earth,
Subdue it, and throughout Dominion hold
Over Fish of the Sea, and Fowl of the Air,
And every living thing that moves on the Earth.[8]

535 Wherever thus created, for no place
Is yet distinct by name, thence as thou know'st
He brought thee into this delicious° Grove,   *delightful*
This Garden, planted with the Trees of God,
Delectable both to behold and taste;

540 And freely all thir pleasant fruit for food
Gave thee, all sorts are here that all th' Earth yields,
Variety without end; but of the Tree
Which tasted works knowledge of Good and Evil,
Thou may'st not; in the day thou eat'st, thou di'st;

545 Death is the penalty impos'd, beware,
And govern well thy appetite, lest sin
Surprise thee, and her black attendant Death.[9]
Here finish'd hee, and all that he had made
View'd, and behold all was entirely good;

550 So Ev'n and Morn accomplish'd the Sixt day:
Yet not till the Creator from his work,
Desisting, though unwearied, up return'd
Up to the Heav'n of Heav'ns his high abode,
Thence to behold this new created World

555 Th' addition of his Empire, how it show'd
In prospect from his Throne, how good, how fair,
Answering his great Idea. Up he rode
Follow'd with acclamation and the sound
Symphonious of ten thousand Harps that tun'd°   *gave vent to*

560 Angelic harmonies: the Earth, the Air
Resounded, (thou remember'st, for thou heard'st)
The Heav'ns and all the Constellations rung,
The Planets in thir station list'ning stood,
While the bright Pomp° ascended jubilant.   *procession*

565 Open, ye everlasting Gates, they sung,
Open, ye Heav'ns, your living doors; let in

6. Echoing Genesis 1.26.
7. Milton echoes a phrase from Hebrews 1.3, "Who being . . . the express image of his person . . . purged our sins."

8. Echoing Genesis 1.28.
9. Perhaps Raphael, calling Death Sin's "attendant," is innocent about Sin and Death's true relationship—or wishes Adam and Eve to be so.

The great Creator from his work return'd
Magnificent, his Six days' work, a World;
Open, and henceforth oft; for God will deign
570   To visit oft the dwellings of just Men
Delighted, and with frequent intercourse
Thither will send his winged Messengers
On errands of supernal Grace. So sung
The glorious Train ascending: He through Heav'n,
575   That open'd wide her blazing Portals,[1] led
To God's Eternal house direct the way,
A broad and ample road, whose dust is Gold
And pavement Stars, as Stars to thee appear,
Seen in the Galaxy, that Milky way
580   Which nightly as a circling Zone° thou seest   belt
Powder'd with Stars. And now on Earth the Seventh
Ev'ning arose in *Eden*,[2] for the Sun
Was set, and twilight from the East came on,
Forerunning Night; when at the holy mount
585   Of Heav'n's high-seated top, th' Imperial Throne
Of Godhead, fixt for ever firm and sure,
The Filial Power arriv'd, and sat him down
With his great Father, for he also went
Invisible, yet stay'd (such privilege
590   Hath Omnipresence) and the work ordain'd,
Author and end of all things, and from work[3]
Now resting, bless'd and hallow'd the Sev'nth day,
As resting on that day from all his work,
But not in silence holy kept; the Harp
595   Had work and rested not, the solemn Pipe,
And Dulcimer, all Organs of sweet stop,
All sounds on Fret by String or Golden Wire
Temper'd soft Tunings,[4] intermixt with Voice
Choral or Unison; of incense Clouds
600   Fuming from Golden Censers hid the Mount.
Creation and the Six days' acts they sung:
Great are thy works, *Jehovah*, infinite
Thy power; what thought can measure thee or tongue
Relate thee; greater now in thy return
605   Than from the Giant Angels;[5] thee that day
Thy Thunders magnifi'd; but to create

---

1. The portals of the sun are represented by the tropical signs of Capricorn and Cancer. In Macrobius' *Dream of Scipio*, Cancer is "the portal of men, because through it descent is made to the lower regions; Capricorn, the portal of gods, because through it souls return to their rightful abode of immortality, to be reckoned among the gods."
2. Beginning day 20 of the action.
3. See Genesis 2.3, "God blessed the seventh day, and sanctified it: because that in it he had rested from all his work which God created and made."
4. The details of the heavenly music: the harp takes precedence, as it was played by David. A "stop" is a register of an organ or harpsichord; a "fret" is a ridge dividing the fingerboard of guitar-like stringed instruments; to "temper" is to adjust the pitch; and "tunings" are melodious sounds.
5. The Gigantomachia, or rebellion of the giants against the gods, serves throughout as a mythic version of Satan's rebellion.

Is greater than created to destroy
Who can impair thee, mighty King, or bound
Thy Empire? easily the proud attempt
610   Of Spirits apostate and thir Counsels vain
Thou hast repell'd, while impiously they thought
Thee to diminish, and from thee withdraw
The number of thy worshippers. Who seeks
To lessen thee, against his purpose serves
615   To manifest the more thy might: his evil
Thou usest, and from thence creat'st more good.
Witness this new-made World, another Heav'n
From Heaven Gate not far, founded in view
On the clear *Hyaline*, the Glassy Sea;[6]
620   Of amplitude almost immense,° with Stars   *immeasurable*
Numerous, and every Star perhaps a World
Of destin'd habitation; but thou know'st
Thir seasons: among these the seat of men,
Earth with her nether Ocean circumfus'd,
625   Thir pleasant dwelling-place. Thrice happy men,
And sons of men, whom God hath thus advanc't,
Created in his Image, there to dwell
And worship him, and in reward to rule
Over his Works, on Earth, in Sea, or Air,
630   And multiply a Race of Worshippers
Holy and just: thrice happy if they know
Thir happiness, and persevere upright.
      So sung they, and the Empyrean rung,
With *Halleluiahs*: Thus was Sabbath kept.
635   And thy request think now fulfill'd, that ask'd
How first this World and face° of things began,   *outward form*
And what before thy memory was done
From the beginning, that posterity
Inform'd by thee might know; if else thou seek'st
640   Aught, not surpassing human measure, say.
      The End of the Seventh Book.

Book 8
The Argument

Adam *inquires concerning celestial Motions, is doubtfully answer'd, and exhorted to search rather things more worthy of knowledge: Adam assents, and still desirous to detain Raphael, relates to him what he remember'd since his own Creation, his placing in Paradise, his talk with God concerning solitude and fit society, his first meeting and Nuptials with Eve, his discourse with the Angel thereupon; who after admonitions repeated departs.*

6. In Revelation 4.6, the "thalassa hyaline" is called a "sea of glass like unto crystal." Here, the term refers to the waters above the firmament.

The Angel ended, and in *Adam's* Ear
So Charming left his voice, that he a while
Thought him still speaking, still stood fixt to hear;[1]
Then as new wak't thus gratefully repli'd.
5   What thanks sufficient, or what recompense
Equal have I to render thee, Divine
Historian, who thus largely hast allay'd
The thirst I had of knowledge, and voutsaf't
This friendly condescension to relate
10   Things else by me unsearchable, now heard
With wonder, but delight, and, as is due,
With glory attributed to the high
Creator; something yet of doubt remains,
Which only thy solution° can resolve   *explanation*
15   When I behold this goodly Frame,° this World   *universe*
Of Heav'n and Earth consisting, and compute
Thir magnitudes, this Earth a spot, a grain,
An Atom, with the Firmament compar'd
And all her number'd° Stars, that seem to roll   *numerous*
20   Spaces incomprehensible (for such
Thir distance argues and thir swift return
Diurnal) merely to officiate° light   *minister*
Round this opacous° Earth, this punctual° spot,   *opaque / pointlike*
One day and night; in all thir vast survey
25   Useless besides; reasoning I oft admire,°   *wonder*
How Nature wise and frugal could commit
Such disproportions, with superfluous hand
So many nobler Bodies to create,
Greater so manifold to this one use,
30   For aught appears, and on thir Orbs impose
Such restless revolution day by day
Repeated, while the sedentary Earth,
That better might with far less compass move,
Serv'd by more noble than herself, attains
35   Her end without least motion, and receives,
As Tribute such a sumless journey brought
Of incorporeal speed, her warmth and light;
Speed, to describe whose swiftness Number fails.
      So spake our Sire, and by his count'nance seem'd
40   Ent'ring on studious thoughts abstruse, which *Eve*
Perceiving where she sat retir'd in sight,
With lowliness Majestic from her seat,
And Grace that won who saw to wish her stay,
Rose and went forth among her Fruits and Flow'rs,
45   To visit° how they prosper'd, bud and bloom,   *inspect*
Her Nursery; they at her coming sprung

---

1. After epic digressions, audiences often remain rapt; see Homer's *Odyssey* 13.1 and Apollonius 1.512-16 (after Orpheus' song of creation).

And toucht by her fair tendance° gladlier grew.   *attention*
Yet went she not, as not with such discourse
Delighted, or not capable her ear
50 Of what was high: such pleasure she reserv'd,
Adam relating, she sole Auditress;
Her Husband the Relater she preferr'd
Before the Angel, and of him to ask
Chose rather: hee, she knew, would intermix
55 Grateful digressions, and solve high dispute
With conjugal Caresses, from his Lip
Not Words alone pleas'd her. O when meet now
Such pairs, in Love and mutual Honor join'd?
With Goddess-like demeanor forth she went;
60 Not unattended, for on her as Queen
A pomp° of winning Graces waited still,   *retinue*
And from about her shot Darts of desire
Into all Eyes to wish her still in sight.
And *Raphael* now to *Adam's* doubt propos'd
65 Benevolent and facile° thus repli'd.   *kindly*
   To ask or search I blame thee not, for Heav'n
Is as the Book of God before thee set,
Wherein to read his wond'rous Works, and learn
His Seasons, Hours, or Days, or Months, or Years:[2]
70 This to attain, whether Heav'n move or Earth,
Imports not, if thou reck'n right; the rest
From Man or Angel the great Architect
Did wisely to conceal, and not divulge
His secrets to be scann'd° by them who ought   *examined minutely*
75 Rather admire; or if they list to try
Conjecture, he his Fabric of the Heav'ns
Hath left to thir disputes, perhaps to move
His laughter at thir quaint Opinions wide
Hereafter,[3] when they come to model Heav'n
80 And calculate the Stars, how they will wield
The mighty frame, how build, unbuild, contrive
To save appearances, how gird the Sphere
With Centric and Eccentric scribbl'd o'er,
Cycle and Epicycle, Orb in Orb:[4]
85 Already by thy reasoning this I guess,
Who are to lead thy offspring, and supposest
That bodies bright and greater should not serve
The less not bright, nor Heav'n such journeys run,
Earth sitting still, when she alone receives
90 The benefit: consider first, that Great
Or Bright infers not Excellence: the Earth

---

2. Echoing Genesis 1.14, "lights in the firmament for signs, and for seasons, and for days, and years."
3. For other instances of God's laughter, see 2.731; 3.257; 5.718, 737; 12.59.
4. Eccentric orbits and epicycles are attempts within the Ptolemaic system to accommodate observed irregularities in stellar motions.

Though in comparison of Heav'n, so small,
Nor glistering,° may of solid good contain   *gleaming*
More plenty than the Sun that barren shines,[5]
95   Whose virtue on itself works no effect,
But in the fruitful Earth; there first receiv'd
His beams, unactive else, thir vigor find.
Yet not to Earth are those bright Luminaries
Officious,° but to thee Earth's habitant.   *dutiful*
100   And for the Heav'n's wide Circuit, let it speak
The Maker's high magnificence, who built
So spacious, and his Line stretcht out so far;
That Man may know he dwells not in his own;
An Edifice too large for him to fill,
105   Lodg'd in a small partition, and the rest
Ordain'd for uses to his Lord best known.
The swiftness of those Circles° attribute,   *orbits*
Though numberless,° to his Omnipotence,   *innumerable*
That to corporeal substances could add
110   Speed almost Spiritual; mee thou think'st not slow,
Who since the Morning hour set out from Heav'n
Where God resides, and ere mid-day arriv'd
In *Eden*, distance inexpressible
By Numbers that have name. But this I urge,
115   Admitting Motion in the Heav'ns, to show
Invalid that which thee to doubt it mov'd;
Not that I so affirm, though so it seem
To thee who hast thy dwelling here on Earth.
God to remove his ways from human sense,
120   Plac'd Heav'n from Earth so far, that earthly sight,
If it presume, might err in things too high,
And no advantage gain. What if the Sun
Be Centre to the World,° and other Stars   *universe*
By his attractive virtue° and their own   *power of attraction*
125   Incited, dance about him various rounds?[6]
Thir wandring course now high, now low, then hid,
Progressive, retrograde, or standing still,
In six thou seest,[7] and what if sev'nth to these
The Planet Earth, so steadfast though she seem,
130   Insensibly three different Motions move?
Which else to several Spheres thou must ascribe,
Mov'd contrary with thwart obliquities,
Or save the Sun his labor, and that swift

---

5. The sun is "barren" because it already contains a pleni-
tude of life. It requires no additions from its own reflected
beams.
6. The elusive astronomy reflects Milton's own difficulty
in choosing among the planetary systems available. The
main choice was between updated versions of the earth-
centered Ptolemaic system and the new system of Coper-

nicus, which placed the sun at the center. The lesson for
Adam is more likely that models matter less than obedience. As the argument to Book 8 puts it, "Adam is doubtfully answered."
7. The six are Saturnus, Iupiter, Mars, Venus, Mercurius,
and Luna. Whether Tellus (the earth) or Sol (the sun)
constituted the seventh planet was controversial.

135 Nocturnal and Diurnal rhomb suppos'd,
    Invisible else above all Stars, the Wheel
    Of Day and Night; which needs not thy belief,
    If Earth industrious of herself fetch Day
    Travelling East, and with her part averse
    From the Sun's beam meet Night, her other part
140 Still luminous by his ray.[8] What if that light
    Sent from her through the wide transpicuous° air,   *transparent*
    To the terrestrial Moon be as a Star
    Enlight'ning her by Day, as she by Night
    This Earth? reciprocal, if Land be there,
145 Fields and Inhabitants: Her spots thou seest
    As Clouds,[9] and Clouds may rain, and Rain produce
    Fruits in her soft'n'd Soil, for some to eat
    Allotted there; and other Suns perhaps
    With thir attendant Moons thou wilt descry
150 Communicating Male and Female Light,
    Which two great Sexes animate the World,
    Stor'd in each Orb perhaps with some that live.
    For such vast room in Nature unpossest
    By living Soul, desert and desolate,
155 Only to shine, yet scarce to contribute
    Each Orb a glimpse of Light, convey'd so far
    Down to this habitable, which returns
    Light back to them, is obvious° to dispute.   *open*
    But whether thus these things, or whether not,
160 Whether the Sun predominant in Heav'n
    Rise on the Earth, or Earth rise on the Sun,
    Hee from the East his flaming road begin,
    Or Shee from West her silent course advance
    With inoffensive° pace that spinning sleeps   *unobstructed*
165 On her soft Axle, while she paces Ev'n,
    And bears thee soft with the smooth Air along,
    Solicit° not thy thoughts with matters hid,   *disturb*
    Leave them to God above, him serve and fear;[1]
    Of other Creatures, as him pleases best,
170 Wherever plac't, let him dispose: joy thou
    In what he gives to thee, this Paradise
    And thy fair *Eve*: Heav'n is for thee too high
    To know what passes there; be lowly wise:
    Think only what concerns thee and thy being;

---

8. Raphael uses terminology of various astronomical systems here. Copernicus attributed these motions to earth (8.130); the "thwart obliquities" may look forward to a post-Fall, tilted Zodiac; and the "rhomb" probably refers to the *primum mobile* or tenth sphere of the medieval planetary system, which revolved with incredibly swift diurnal motion about the earth, carrying the spheres of stars and planets with it. The "earth industrious" of

Copernicus contrasts with the Ptolemeic "sedentary earth" (32).
9. Changes of the moon's spots were often ascribed to effects of the lunar atmosphere. Raphael also opts for the lunar clouds theory at 5.418-20.
1. Echoing Ecclesiastes 12.13, "Fear God, and keep his commandments: for this is the whole duty of man."

175 Dream not of other Worlds, what Creatures there
  Live, in what state, condition or degree,
  Contented that thus far hath been reveal'd
  Not of Earth only but of highest Heav'n.
   To whom thus Adam clear'd of doubt, repli'd.
180 How fully hast thou satisfi'd me, pure
  Intelligence° of Heav'n, Angel serene,   *spirit*
  And freed from intricacies, taught to live
  The easiest way, nor with perplexing thoughts
  To interrupt the sweet of Life, from which
185 God hath bid dwell far off all anxious cares,
  And not molest us, unless we ourselves
  Seek them with wand'ring thoughts, and notions vain.
  But apt the Mind or Fancy is to rove
  Uncheckt, and of her roving is no end;
190 Till warn'd, or by experience taught, she learn
  That not to know at large of things remote
  From use, obscure and subtle, but to know
  That which before us lies in daily life,
  Is the prime Wisdom; what is more, is fume,°   *smoke*
195 Or emptiness, or fond impertinence,°   *foolish irrelevance*
  And renders us in things that most concern
  Unpractic'd, unprepar'd, and still to seek.
  Therefore from this high pitch let us descend
  A lower flight, and speak of things at hand
200 Useful, whence haply mention may arise
  Of something not unseasonable to ask
  By sufferance,° and thy wonted favor deign'd.   *permission*
  Thee I have heard relating what was done
  Ere my remembrance: now hear mee relate
205 My Story, which perhaps thou hast not heard;
  And Day is yet not spent; till then thou seest
  How subtly to detain thee I devise,
  Inviting thee to hear while I relate,
   Fond, were it not in hope of thy reply:
210 For while I sit with thee, I seem in Heav'n,
  And sweeter thy discourse is to my ear
  Than Fruits of Palm-tree pleasantest to thirst
  And hunger both, from labor, at the hour
  Of sweet repast; they satiate, and soon fill,
215 Though pleasant, but thy words with Grace Divine
  Imbu'd, bring to thir sweetness no satiety.
   To whom thus *Raphael* answer'd heav'nly meek.
  Nor are thy lips ungraceful, Sire of men,
  Nor tongue ineloquent; for God on thee
220 Abundantly his gifts hath also pour'd
  Inward and outward both, his image fair:
  Speaking or mute all comeliness and grace
  Attends thee, and each word, each motion forms.

Nor less think wee in Heav'n of thee on Earth
225   Than of our fellow servant, and inquire
Gladly into the ways of God with Man:
For God we see hath honor'd thee, and set
On Man his Equal Love: say therefore on;
For I that Day was absent, as befell,
230   Bound on a voyage uncouth° and obscure,   *unfamiliar*
Far on excursion toward the Gates of Hell;
Squar'd in full Legion (such command we had)
To see that none thence issu'd forth a spy,
Or enemy, while God was in his work,
235   Lest hee incenst at such eruption bold,
Destruction with Creation might have mixt.
Not that they durst without his leave attempt,
But us he sends upon his high behests
For state,° as Sovran King, and to enures   *ceremony*
240   Our prompt obedience. Fast we found, fast shut
The dismal Gates, and barricado'd strong;
But long ere our approaching heard within
Noise, other than the sound of Dance or Song,
Torment, and loud lament, and furious rage.
245   Glad we return'd up to the coasts of Light
Ere Sabbath Ev'ning: so we had in charge.
But thy relation now; for I attend,
Pleas'd with thy words no less than thou with mine.
         So spake the Godlike Power, and thus our Sire.
250   For man to tell how human Life began
Is hard; for who himself beginning knew?
Desire with thee still longer to converse
Induc'd me. As new wak't from soundest sleep
Soft on the flow'ry herb I found me laid
255   In Balmy Sweat, which with his Beams the Sun
Soon dri'd, and on the reeking moisture fed.
Straight toward Heav'n my wond'ring Eyes I turn'd,
And gaz'd a while the ample Sky, till rais'd
By quick instinctive motion up I sprung,
260   As thitherward endeavoring, and upright
Stood on my feet; about me round I saw
Hill, Dale, and shady Woods, and sunny Plains,
And liquid Lapse of murmuring Streams; by these,
Creatures that liv'd, and mov'd, and walk'd, or flew
265   Birds on the branches warbling; all things smil'd,
With fragrance and with joy my heart o'erflow'd.
Myself I then perus'd, and Limb by Limb
Survey'd, and sometimes went,° and sometimes ran   *walked*
With supple joints, as lively vigor led:
270   But who I was, or where, or from what cause,
Knew not; to speak I tri'd, and forthwith spake,
My Tongue obey'd and readily could name

Whate'er I saw. Thou Sun, said I, fair Light
And thou enlight'n'd Earth, so fresh and gay,
275   Ye Hills and Dales, ye Rivers, Woods, and Plains
And ye that live and move, fair Creatures, tell,
Tell, if ye saw, how came I thus, how here?
Not of myself; by some great Maker then,
In goodness and in power preëminent;
280   Tell me, how may I know him, how adore,
From whom I have that thus I move and live,[2]
And feel that I am happier than I know.
While thus I call'd, and stray'd I knew not whither,
From where I first drew Air, and first beheld
285   This happy Light, when answer none return'd,
On a green shady Bank profuse of Flow'rs
Pensive I sat me down; there gentle sleep
First found me, and with soft oppression seiz'd
My drowsed sense, untroubl'd, though I thought
290   I then was passing to my former state
Insensible, and forthwith to dissolve:
When suddenly stood at my Head a dream,
Whose inward apparition gently mov'd
My fancy to believe I yet had being,
295   And liv'd: One came, methought, of shape Divine,
And said, thy Mansion° wants thee, *Adam*, rise,   *home*
First Man, of Men innumerable ordain'd
First Father, call'd by thee I come thy Guide
To the Garden of bliss, thy seat prepar'd.[3]
300   So saying, by the hand he took me rais'd,
And over Fields and Waters, as in Air
Smooth sliding without step, last led me up
A woody Mountain; whose high top was plain,
A Circuit wide, enclos'd, with goodliest Trees
305   Planted, with Walks, and Bowers, that what I saw
Of Earth before scarce pleasant seem'd. Each Tree
Load'n with fairest Fruit, that hung to the Eye
Tempting, stirr'd in me sudden appetite
To pluck and eat; whereat I wak'd, and found
310   Before mine Eyes all real, as the dream
Had lively shadow'd: Here had new begun
My wand'ring, had not hee who was my Guide
Up hither, from among the Trees appear'd,
Presence Divine. Rejoicing, but with awe,
315   In adoration at his feet I fell
Submiss:° he rear'd me, and Whom thou sought'st I am,[4]   *submissive*

2. See St. Paul's sermon on the Unknown God, Acts
17.28: "For in him we live, and move, and have our
being."
3. See Genesis 2.15.

4. See Exodus 3.14: "I AM THAT I AM. . . . Thus shalt
thou say unto the children of Israel, I AM hath sent me
unto you."

Said mildly, Author of all this thou seest
Above, or round about thee or beneath.
This Paradise I give thee, count it thine
320 To Till and keep, and of the Fruit to eat:
Of every Tree that in the Garden grows
Eat freely with glad heart; fear here no dearth:[5]
But of the Tree whose operation brings
Knowledge of good and ill, which I have set
325 The Pledge of thy Obedience and thy Faith,
Amid the Garden by the Tree of Life,
Remember what I warn thee, shun to taste,
And shun the bitter consequence: for know,
The day thou eat'st thereof, my sole command
330 Transgrest, inevitably thou shalt die;
From that day mortal, and this happy State
Shalt lose, expell'd from hence into a World
Of woe and sorrow. Sternly he pronounc'd
The rigid interdiction,° which resounds   *prohibition*
335 Yet dreadful in mine ear, though in my choice
Not to incur; but soon his clear aspect
Return'd and gracious purpose° thus renew'd.   *discourse*
Not only these fair bounds, but all the Earth
To thee and to thy Race I give; as Lords
340 Possess it, and all things that therein live,
Or live in Sea, or Air, Beast, Fish, and Fowl.[6]
In sign whereof each Bird and Beast behold
After thir kinds; I bring them to receive
From thee thir Names, and pay thee fealty
345 With low subjection; understand the same
Of Fish within thir wat'ry residence,
Not hither summon'd, since they cannot change
Thir Element to draw the thinner Air.
As thus he spake, each Bird and Beast behold
350 Approaching two and two, These cow'ring low
With blandishment, each Bird stoop'd on his wing.
I nam'd them, as they pass'd, and understood
Thir Nature, with such knowledge God endu'd
My sudden apprehension: but in these
355 I found not what methought I wanted still;
And to the Heav'nly vision thus presum'd.
    O by what Name, for thou above all these,
Above mankind, or aught than mankind higher,
Surpassest far my naming, how may I
360 Adore thee, Author of this Universe,
And all this good to man, for whose well being
So amply, and with hands so liberal

5. See Genesis 2.15–17.   6. See Genesis 1.28.

Thou hast provided all things: but with mee
I see not who partakes. In solitude
365   What happiness, who can enjoy alone,
Or all enjoying, what contentment find?
Thus I presumptuous; and the vision bright,
As with a smile more bright'n'd, thus repli'd.
       What call'st thou solitude? is not the Earth
370   With various living creatures, and the Air
Replenisht, and all these at thy command
To come and play before thee; know'st thou not
Thir language and thir ways? They also know,[7]
And reason not contemptibly; with these
375   Find pastime, and bear rule; thy Realm is large.
So spake the Universal Lord, and seem'd
So ordering. I with leave of speech implor'd,
And humble deprecation thus repli'd.
       Let not my words offend thee, Heav'nly Power,
380   My Maker, be propitious while I speak.
Hast thou not made me here thy substitute,
And these inferior far beneath me set?
Among unequals what society
Can sort,° what harmony or true delight?   agree
385   Which must be mutual, in proportion due
Giv'n and receiv'd; but in disparity
The one intense, the other still remiss
Cannot well suit with either, but soon prove
Tedious alike:[8] Of fellowship I speak
390   Such as I seek, fit to participate
All rational delight, wherein the brute
Cannot be human consort; they rejoice
Each with thir kind, Lion with Lioness;
So fitly them in pairs thou hast combin'd;
395   Much less can Bird with Beast, or Fish with Fowl
So well converse, nor with the Ox the Ape;
Worse then can Man with Beast, and least of all.
       Whereto th' Almighty answer'd, not displeas'd.
A nice and subtle happiness I see
400   Thou to thyself proposest, in the choice
Of thy Associates, *Adam,* and wilt taste
No pleasure, though in pleasure, solitary.
What think'st thou then of mee, and this my State,
Seem I to thee sufficiently possest
405   Of happiness, or not? who am alone
From all Eternity, for none I know

---

7. It was a widespread Jewish belief that before the Fall, Adam understood the language of the beasts. The original language was usually supposed to have been Hebrew, but sometimes Syriac, Greek, or Aramaic.

8. In a stringed instrument the strings should bear a due ratio of length and frequency. But the human string is too strained ("intense") and therefore high in pitch, while the animal string is too "remiss," i.e., low in pitch.

Second to mee or like, equal much less.
How have I then with whom to hold converse
Save with the Creatures which I made, and those
410   To me inferior, infinite descents
Beneath what other Creatures are to thee?
   He ceas'd, I lowly answer'd. To attain
The highth and depth of thy Eternal ways
All human thoughts come short, Supreme of things;
415   Thou in thyself art perfet, and in thee
Is no deficience found; not so is Man,
But in degree, the cause of his desire
By conversation with his like to help,
Or solace his defects. No need that thou
420   Shouldst propagate, already infinite;
And through all numbers absolute, though One;[9]
But Man by number is to manifest
His single imperfection, and beget
Like of his like, his Image multipli'd,
425   In unity defective, which requires
Collateral love, and dearest amity.
Thou in thy secrecy although alone,
Best with thyself accompanied, seek'st not
Social communication, yet so pleas'd,
430   Canst raise thy Creature to what highth thou wilt
Of Union or Communion, deifi'd;
I by conversing cannot these erect
From prone, nor in thir ways complacence° find.   *source of pleasure*
Thus I embold'n'd spake, and freedom us'd
435   Permissive, and acceptance found, which gain'd
This answer from the gracious voice Divine.
   Thus far to try thee, *Adam,* I was pleas'd,
And find thee knowing not of Beasts alone,
Which thou hast rightly nam'd, but of thyself,
440   Expressing well the spirit within thee free,
My Image, not imparted to the Brute,
Whose fellowship therefore unmeet for thee
Good reason was thou freely shouldst dislike,
And be so minded still; I, ere thou spak'st,
445   Knew it not good for Man to be alone,
And no such company as then thou saw'st
Intended thee, for trial only brought,
To see how thou couldst judge of fit and meet:
What next I bring shall please thee, be assur'd,
450   Thy likeness, thy fit help, thy other self,
Thy wish, exactly to thy heart's desire.
   Hee ended, or I heard no more, for now

9. The divine monad contains all other numbers and is therefore complete and perfect through them all. The monad is like God because it is the fountain and origin of all numbers, as God is the origin of created being.

My earthly° by his Heav'nly overpower'd,   *earthly nature*
Which it had long stood under, strain'd to the highth
455 In that celestial Colloquy sublime,
As with an object that excels the sense,
Dazzl'd and spent, sunk down, and sought repair
Of sleep, which instantly fell on me, call'd
By Nature as in aid, and clos'd mine eyes.[1]
460 Mine eyes he clos'd, but op'n left the Cell
Of Fancy my internal sight, by which
Abstract° as in a trance methought I saw,   *withdrawn*
Though sleeping, where I lay, and saw the shape
Still glorious before whom awake I stood;
465 Who stooping op'n'd my left side, and took
From thence a Rib, with cordial spirits warm,
And Life-blood streaming fresh; wide was the wound,
But suddenly with flesh fill'd up and heal'd:
The Rib he form'd and fashion'd with his hands;
470 Under his forming hands a Creature grew,
Manlike, but different sex, so lovely fair,
That what seem'd fair in all the World, seem'd now
Mean, or in her summ'd up, in her contain'd
And in her looks, which from that time infus'd
475 Sweetness into my heart, unfelt before,
And into all things from her Air inspir'd
The spirit of love and amorous delight.
Shee disappear'd, and left me dark, I wak'd
To find her, or for ever to deplore
480 Her loss, and other pleasures all abjure:
When out of hope, behold her, not far off,
Such as I saw her in my dream, adorn'd
With what all Earth or Heaven could bestow
To make her amiable: On she came,
485 Led by her Heav'nly Maker, though unseen,
And guided by his voice, nor uninform'd
Of nuptial Sanctity and marriage Rites:
Grace was in all her steps, Heav'n in her Eye,
In every gesture dignity and love.
490 I overjoy'd could not forbear aloud.°   *saying aloud*
   This turn hath made amends; thou hast fulfill'd
Thy words, Creator bounteous and benign,
Giver of all things fair, but fairest this
Of all thy gifts, nor enviest. I now see
495 Bone of my Bone, Flesh of my Flesh, my Self
Before me; Woman is her Name, of Man
Extracted; for this cause he shall forgo
Father and Mother, and to his Wife adhere;

1. For lines 452–86, see Genesis 2.21ff.

And they shall be one Flesh, one Heart, one Soul.[2]

500   She heard me thus, and though divinely brought,
Yet Innocence and Virgin Modesty,
Her virtue and the conscience° of her worth,   *consciousness*
That would be woo'd, and not unsought be won,
Not obvious, not obtrusive, but retir'd,
505 The more desirable, or to say all,
Nature herself, though pure of sinful thought,
Wrought in her so, that seeing me, she turn'd;
I follow'd her, she what was Honor knew,
And with obsequious° Majesty approv'd   *compliant*
510 My pleaded reason. To the Nuptial Bow'r
I led her blushing like the Morn: all Heav'n,
And happy Constellations on that hour
Shed thir selectest influence; the Earth
Gave sign of gratulation,° and each Hill;   *joy*
515 Joyous the Birds; fresh Gales and gentle Airs
Whisper'd it to the Woods, and from thir wings
Flung Rose, flung Odors from the spicy Shrub,
Disporting, till the amorous Bird of Night[3]
Sung Spousal, and bid haste the Ev'ning Star
520 On his Hill top, to light the bridal Lamp.
Thus I have told thee all my State, and brought
My Story to the sum of earthly bliss
Which I enjoy, and must confess to find
In all things else delight indeed, but such
525 As us'd or not, works in the mind no change,
Nor vehement desire, these delicacies
I mean of Taste, Sight, Smell, Herbs, Fruits, and Flow'rs,
Walks, and the melody of Birds; but here
Far otherwise, transported I behold,
530 Transported touch; here passion first I felt,
Commotion strange, in all enjoyments else
Superior and unmov'd, here only weak
Against the charm of Beauty's powerful glance.
Or° Nature fail'd in mee, and left some part   *either*
535 Not proof enough such Object to sustain,
Or from my side subducting,° took perhaps   *subtracting*
More than enough; at least on her bestow'd
Too much of Ornament, in outward show
Elaborate, of inward less exact.°   *perfect*
540 For well I understand in the prime end
Of Nature her th' inferior, in the mind
And inward Faculties, which most excel,
In outward also her resembling less
His Image who made both, and less expressing

2. See *Genesis* 3.23ff. The biblical expression "one flesh"   3. The nightingale; see 5.40–41.
is replaced by the familiar Platonic tripartite division.

545   The character of that Dominion giv'n
       O'er other Creatures; yet when I approach
       Her loveliness, so absolute she seems
       And in herself complete, so well to know
       Her own, that what she wills to do or say,
550   Seems wisest, virtuousest, discreetest, best;
       All higher knowledge in her presence falls
       Degraded, Wisdom in discourse with her
       Loses discount'nanc't, and like folly shows;
       Authority and Reason on her wait,
555   As one intended first, not after made
       Occasionally;° and to consummate all,   *accidentally*
       Greatness of mind and nobleness thir seat
       Build in her loveliest, and create an awe
       About her, as a guard Angelic plac't.
560   To whom the Angel with contracted brow.
          Accuse not Nature, she hath done her part;
       Do thou but thine, and be not diffident°   *mistrustful*
       Of Wisdom, she deserts thee not, if thou
       Dismiss not her, when most thou need'st her nigh,
565   By attribúting overmuch to things
       Less excellent, as thou thyself perceiv'st.
       For what admir'st thou, what transports thee so,
       An outside? fair no doubt, and worthy well
       Thy cherishing, thy honoring, and thy love,
570   Not thy subjection: weigh with her thyself;
       Then value: Oft-times nothing profits more
       Than self-esteem, grounded on just and right
       Well manag'd; of that skill the more thou know'st,
       The more she will acknowledge thee her Head,[4]
575   And to realities yield all her shows;
       Made so adorn for thy delight the more,
       So awful, that with honor thou may'st love
       Thy mate, who sees when thou art seen least wise.
       But if the sense of touch whereby mankind
580   Is propagated seem such dear delight
       Beyond all other, think the same voutsaf't
       To Cattle and each Beast; which would not be
       To them made common and divulg'd, if aught
       Therein enjoy'd were worthy to subdue
585   The Soul of Man, or passion in him move.
       What higher in her society thou find'st
       Attractive, human, rational, love still;
       In loving thou dost well, in passion not,
       Wherein true Love consists not; Love refines
590   The thoughts, and heart enlarges, hath his seat

---

4. Alludes to 1 Corinthians 11.3: "The head of every man is Christ; and the head of the woman is the man; and the head of Christ is God."

In Reason, and is judicious, is the scale[5]
By which to heav'nly Love thou may'st ascend,
Not sunk in carnal pleasure, for which cause
Among the Beasts no Mate for thee was found.[6]

595   To whom thus half abash't *Adam* repli'd.[7]
Neither her out-side form'd so fair, nor aught
In procreation common to all kinds
(Though higher of the genial° Bed by far,   *nuptial*
And with mysterious reverence I deem)

600   So much delights me, as those graceful acts,
Those thousand decencies that daily flow
From all her words and actions, mixt with Love
And sweet compliance, which declare unfeign'd
Union of Mind, or in us both one Soul;

605   Harmony to behold in wedded pair
More grateful than harmonious sound to the ear.
Yet these subject not; I to thee disclose
What inward thence I feel, not therefore foil'd,°   *overcome*
Who meet with various objects, from the sense

610   Variously representing; yet still free
Approve the best, and follow what I approve.
To Love thou blam'st me not, for Love thou say'st
Leads up to Heav'n, is both the way and guide;
Bear with me then, if lawful what I ask;

615   Love not the heav'nly Spirits, and how thir Love
Express they, by looks only, or do they mix
Irradiance, virtual or immediate touch?
        To whom the Angel with a smile that glow'd
Celestial rosy red, Love's proper hue,

620   Answer'd. Let it suffice thee that thou know'st
Us happy, and without Love no happiness.
Whatever pure thou in the body enjoy'st
(And pure thou wert created) we enjoy
In eminence, and obstacle find none

625   Of membrance, joint, or limb, exclusive bars:
Easier than Air with Air, if Spirits embrace,
Total they mix, Union of Pure with Pure
Desiring; nor restrain'd conveyance need
As Flesh to mix with Flesh, or Soul with Soul.

630   But I can now no more; the parting Sun
Beyond the Earth's green Cape and verdant Isles

---

5. The Neoplatonic ladder of love.
6. Raphael here expounds the very familiar Neoplatonic
distinction between divine or celestial love, human or
terrestrial love, and bestial love. The first (Milton's
"heavenly love") is the love of the contemplative, belonging to mind alone. The second ("true love") is the
force that drives humans to propagate the earthly image
of divine beauty but may also, in its ideal form, lead them
to the first. The third ("sunk . . . pleasure") is experienced by humans who stoop to debauchery.
7. The conversation of Raphael and Adam does in some
respects resemble a debate between Heavenly Love and
Human Love in which the angel/human distinction is in-
tensified into an antithesis.

Hesperian sets, my Signal to depart.[8]
Be strong, live happy, and love, but first of all
Him whom to love is to obey, and keep

635 His great command; take heed lest Passion sway
Thy Judgment to do aught, which else free Will
Would not admit; thine and of all thy Sons
The weal or woe in thee is plac't; beware.
I in thy persevering shall rejoice,

640 And all the Blest: stand fast; to stand or fall
Free in thine own Arbitrement it lies.
Perfet within, no outward aid require;
And all temptation to transgress repel.
      So saying, he arose; whom *Adam* thus

645 Follow'd with benediction. Since to part,
Go heavenly Guest, Ethereal Messenger,
Sent from whose sovran goodness I adore.
Gentle to me and affable hath been
Thy condescension, and shall be honor'd ever

650 With grateful Memory: thou to mankind
Be good and friendly still, and oft return.
      So parted they, the Angel up to Heav'n
From the thick shade, and *Adam* to his Bow'r.
      The End of the Eighth Book.

Book 9
The Argument

Satan *having compast the Earth, with meditated guile returns as a mist by Night into Paradise, enters into the Serpent sleeping. Adam and Eve in the Morning go forth to thir labors, which Eve proposes to divide in several places, each laboring apart: Adam consents not, alleging the danger, lest that Enemy, of whom they were forewarn'd, should attempt her found alone: Eve loath to be thought not circumspect or firm enough, urges her going apart, the rather desirous to make trial of her strength; Adam at last yields: The Serpent finds her alone; his subtle approach, first gazing, then speaking, with much flattery extolling Eve above all other Creatures. Eve wond'ring to hear the Serpent speak, asks how he attain'd to human speech and such understanding not till now; the Serpent answers, that by tasting of a certain Tree in the Garden he attain'd both to Speech and Reason, till then void of both: Eve requires him to bring her to that Tree, and finds it to be the Tree of Knowledge forbidden: The Serpent now grown bolder, with many wiles and arguments induces her at length to eat; she pleas'd with the taste deliberates awhile whether to impart thereof to Adam or not, at last brings him of the Fruit, relates what persuaded her to eat thereof: Adam at first amaz'd, but perceiving her lost, resolves through vehemence[1] of love to perish with her; and extenuating[2] the trespass, eats also of the Fruit: The effects thereof in them both; they seek to cover thir nakedness; then fall to variance and accusation of one another.*

---

8. Where the sun sets "beneath the Azores." Here the "green Cape" is Cape Verde, and the "verdant Isles" are the Cape Verde Islands.

1. The root meaning of Latin "vehementia" is mindlessness.
2. Carrying further, drawing out.

No more of talk where God or Angel Guest
With Man, as with his Friend, familiar us'd
To sit indulgent, and with him partake
Rural repast, permitting him the while
5   Venial° discourse unblam'd: I now must change   *permissible*
Those Notes to Tragic; foul distrust, and breach
Disloyal on the part of Man, revolt,
And disobedience: On the part of Heav'n
Now alienated, distance and distaste,
10 Anger and just rebuke, and judgment giv'n,
That brought into this World a world of woe,
Sin and her shadow Death, and Misery
Death's Harbinger: Sad task, yet argument
Not less but more Heroic than the wrath
15 Of stern *Achilles* on his Foe pursu'd
Thrice Fugitive about *Troy* Wall; or rage
Of *Turnus* for *Lavinia* disespous'd,
Or *Neptune's* ire or *Juno's*, that so long
Perplex'd the *Greek* and *Cytherea's* Son;³
20 If answerable° style I can obtain   *equal, accountable*
Of my Celestial Patroness,⁴ who deigns
Her nightly visitation unimplor'd,
And dictates to me slumb'ring, or inspires
Easy my unpremeditated Verse:
25 Since first this Subject for Heroic Song
Pleas'd me long choosing, and beginning late;
Not sedulous by Nature to indite
Wars, hitherto the only Argument
Heroic deem'd, chief maistry to dissect
30 With long and tedious havoc fabl'd Knights
In Battles feign'd; the better fortitude
Of Patience and Heroic Martyrdom
Unsung; or to describe Races and Games,
Or tilting Furniture, emblazon'd Shields,
35 Impreses⁵ quaint, Caparisons⁶ and Steeds;
Bases and tinsel Trappings, gorgeous Knights
At Joust and Tournament; then marshall'd Feast
Serv'd up in Hall with Sewers,° and Seneschals;°   *waiters / stewards*
The skill of Artifice or Office mean,

3. Achilles is "stern" in his "wrath" because he refused any covenant with Hector, and Turnus dies fighting Aeneas for the hand of Lavinia, whereas Messiah, more heroically, is not implacable in his anger. He issued his sole commandment "sternly" (8.333); but when it is disobeyed, he works for reconciliation. Similarly, God's anger is distinguished from "Neptune's ire" and "Juno's" (which merely "perplexed" Odysseus and Aeneas) in that it is expressed in justice rather than in victimization.

4. The heavenly Muse, Urania. Both ancient and modern epics had always had war, or at least fighting, as a principal ingredient. (So has *Paradise Lost*, in the first half of the poem; but in the second half this subject is transcended.) Milton now glances unfavorably at the typical matter of the romantic epic.
5. Heraldic devices, often with accompanying mottoes.
6. Ornamented coverings spread over the saddle of a horse.

40   Not that which justly gives Heroic name
    To Person or to Poem.[7] Mee of these
    Nor skill'd nor studious, higher Argument
    Remains, sufficient of itself to raise
    That name,[8] unless an age too late, or cold
45   Climate, or Years damp my intended wing
    Deprest; and much they may, if all be mine,
      Not Hers who brings it nightly to my Ear.
    The Sun was sunk, and after him the Star
    Of *Hesperus*,° whose Office is to bring   *the planet Venus*
50   Twilight upon the Earth, short Arbiter
    Twixt Day and Night, and now from end to end
    Night's Hemisphere had veil'd the Horizon round:
    When *Satan* who late fled before the threats
    Of *Gabriel* out of *Eden*,[9] now improv'd°   *intensified*
55   In meditated fraud and malice, bent
    On Man's destruction, maugre what might hap
    Of heavier on himself,[1] fearless return'd.
    By Night he fled, and at Midnight return'd
    From compassing the Earth, cautious of day,
60   Since *Uriel* Regent of the Sun descri'd
    His entrance, and forewarn'd the Cherubim
    That kept thir watch; thence full of anguish driv'n,
    The space of seven continu'd Nights he rode
    With darkness, thrice the Equinoctial Line
65   He circl'd, four times cross'd the Car of Night
    From Pole to Pole, traversing each Colure;[2]
    On th'eighth return'd, and on the Coast averse
    From entrance or Cherubic Watch, by stealth
    Found unsuspected way. There was a place,
70   Now not, though Sin, not Time, first wrought the change,
    Where *Tigris* at the foot of Paradise
    Into a Gulf shot under ground, till part
    Rose up a Fountain by the Tree of Life;
    In with the River sunk, and with it rose
75   *Satan* involv'd in rising Mist, then sought
    Where to lie hid; Sea he had searcht and Land
    From *Eden* over *Pontus*, and the Pool
    Maeotis, up beyond the River *Ob*;[3]
    Downward as far Antarctic; and in length

---

7. Artifice implies mechanic or applied art. It is beneath the dignity of epic to teach etiquette and social ceremony and heraldry.

8. The name of epic.

9. I.e., at the end of Book 4, a week earlier.

1. Despite the danger of heavier punishment.

2. By keeping to earth's shadow, Satan contrives to experience a whole week of darkness. The two colures were great circles, intersecting at right angles at the poles and dividing the equinoctial circle (the equator) into four equal parts.

3. In his north-south circles, Satan passed Pontus (the Black Sea), the "pool / Maeotis" (the Sea of Azov), and the Siberian River Ob, which flows north into the Gulf of Ob and from there into the Arctic Ocean.

80 West from *Orontes* to the Ocean barr'd
    At *Darien*, thence to the Land where flows
    Ganges and *Indus*:[4] thus the Orb he roam'd
    With narrow search; and with inspection deep
    Consider'd every Creature, which of all
85 Most opportune might serve his Wiles, and found
    The Serpent subtlest Beast of all the Field.[5]
    Him after long debate, irresolute°   undecided
    Of thoughts revolv'd, his final sentence° chose   judgment
    Fit Vessel, fittest Imp° of fraud, in whom   offshoot
90 To enter, and his dark suggestions hide
    From sharpest sight: for in the wily Snake,
    Whatever sleights none would suspicious mark,
    As from his wit and native subtlety
    Proceeding, which in other Beasts observ'd
95 Doubt° might beget of Diabolic pow'r   suspicion
    Active within beyond the sense of brute.
    Thus he resolv'd, but first from inward grief
    His bursting passion into plaints thus pour'd:
      O Earth, how like to Heav'n, if not preferr'd
100 More justly, Seat worthier of Gods, as built
    With second thoughts, reforming what was old!
    For what God after better worse would build?
    Terrestrial Heav'n, danc't round by other Heav'ns
    That shine, yet bear thir bright officious Lamps,
105 Light above Light, for thee alone, as seems,
    In thee concentring all thir precious beams
    Of sacred influence:[6] As God in Heav'n
    Is Centre, yet extends to all, so thou
    Centring receiv'st from all those Orbs; in thee,
110 Not in themselves, all thir known virtue appears
    Productive in Herb, Plant, and nobler birth
    Of Creatures animate with gradual life
    Of Growth, Sense, Reason, all summ'd up in Man.[7]
    With what delight could I have walkt thee round,
115 If I could joy in aught, sweet interchange
    Of Hill and Valley, Rivers, Woods and Plains,
    Now Land, now Sea, and Shores with Forest crown'd,
    Rocks, Dens, and Caves; but I in none of these
    Find place or refuge; and the more I see
120 Pleasures about me, so much more I feel
    Torment within me, as from the hateful siege°   conflict
    Of contraries; all good to me becomes

---

4. In his westward circling of the equinoctial line, he crossed the Syrian river Orontes, then the Pacific ("peaceful") "Ocean barred" by the Isthmus of Darien (Panama) and India.
5. See Genesis 3.1.

6. The case for an earth-centered universe, put at 8.86–114 by Raphael, is now put by Satan.
7. "Growth, sense, reason" are the activities of the vegetable, animal, and rational souls, respectively, in humans.

Bane,° and in Heav'n much worse would be my state.   *poison*
But neither here seek I, no nor in Heav'n
125 To dwell, unless by maistring Heav'n's Supreme;
Nor hope to be myself less miserable
By what I seek, but others to make such
As I, though thereby worse to me redound:
For only in destroying I find ease
130 To my relentless thoughts; and him destroy'd,
Or won to what may work his utter loss,
For whom all this was made, all this will soon
Follow, as to him linkt in weal or woe,
In woe then: that destruction wide may range:[8]
135 To mee shall be the glory sole among
Th'infernal Powers, in one day to have marr'd
What he *Almight* styl'd, six Nights and Days
Continu'd making, and who knows how long
Before had been contriving, though perhaps
140 Not longer than since I in one Night freed
From servitude inglorious well nigh half
Th' Angelic Name, and thinner left the throng
Of his adorers: hee to be aveng'd,
And to repair his numbers thus impair'd,
145 Whether such virtue° spent of old now fail'd   *power*
More Angels to Create, if they at least
Are his Created, or to spite us more,
Determin'd to advance into our room
A Creature form'd of Earth, and him endow,
150 Exalted from so base original,
With Heav'nly spoils, our spoils; What he decreed
He effected; Man he made, and for him built
Magnificent this World, and Earth his seat,
Him Lord pronounc'd, and, O indignity!
155 Subjected to his service Angel wings,
And flaming Ministers to watch and tend
Thir earthy Charge: Of these the vigilance
I dread, and to elude, thus wrapt in mist
Of midnight vapor glide obscure, and pry
160 In every Bush and Brake, where hap may find
The Serpent sleeping, in whose mazy folds
To hide me, and the dark intent I bring.
O foul descent! that I who erst contended
With Gods to sit the highest, am now constrain'd
165 Into a Beast, and mixt with bestial slime,
This essence to incarnate and imbrute,
That to the highth of Deity aspir'd;
But what will not Ambition and Revenge

8. The created cosmos will follow humans to destruction.

Descend to? who aspires must down as low
170   As high he soar'd, obnoxious° first or last   *exposed*
To basest things. Revenge, at first though sweet,
Bitter ere long back on itself recoils;
Let it, I reck not, so it light well aim'd,
Since higher I fall short, on him who next
175   Provokes my envy, this new Favorite
Of Heav'n, this Man of Clay, Son of despite,
Whom us the more to spite his Maker rais'd
From dust: spite then with spite is best repaid.
      So saying, through each Thicket Dank or Dry,
180   Like a black mist low creeping, he held on
His midnight search, where soonest he might find
The Serpent: him fast sleeping soon he found
In Labyrinth of many a round self-roll'd,
His head the midst, well stor'd with subtle wiles:
185   Not yet in horrid Shade or dismal Den,
Nor nocent° yet, but on the grassy Herb   *harmful, guilty*
Fearless unfear'd he slept: in at his Mouth
The Devil enter'd, and his brutal sense,
In heart or head, possessing soon inspir'd
190   With act intelligential; but his sleep
Disturb'd not, waiting close° th' approach of Morn.   *concealed*
Now whenas sacred Light began to dawn
In *Eden* on the humid Flow'rs, that breath'd
Thir morning incense, when all things that breathe,
195   From th' Earth's great Altar send up silent praise
To the Creator, and his Nostrils fill
With grateful Smell, forth came the human pair
And join'd thir vocal Worship to the Choir
Of Creatures wanting voice; that done, partake
200   The season, prime for sweetest Scents and Airs:
Then cómmune how that day they best may ply
Thir growing work: for much thir work outgrew
The hands' dispatch of two Gard'ning so wide.
And *Eve* first to her Husband thus began.
205   *Adam*, well may we labor still to dress
This Garden, still to tend Plant, Herb and Flow'r,
Our pleasant task enjoin'd, but till more hands
Aid us, the work under our labor grows,
Luxurious by restraint; what we by day
210   Lop overgrown, or prune, or prop, or bind,
One night or two with wanton growth derides
Tending to wild. Thou therefore now advise
Or hear what to my mind first thoughts present,
Let us divide our labors, thou where choice
215   Leads thee, or where most needs, whether to wind
The Woodbine round this Arbor, or direct
The clasping Ivy where to climb, while I
In yonder Spring of Roses intermixt

With Myrtle, find what to redress till Noon:
220   For while so near each other thus all day
Our task we choose, what wonder if so near
Looks intervene and smiles, or object new
Casual discourse draw on, which intermits
Our day's work brought to little, though begun
225   Early, and th' hour of Supper comes unearn'd.
　　　　To whom mild answer *Adam* thus return'd.
Sole *Eve*, Associate sole, to me beyond
Compare above all living Creatures dear,
Well hast thou motion'd,° well thy thoughts imploy'd   *proposed*
230   How we might best fulfil the work which here
God hath assign'd us, nor of me shalt pass
Unprais'd: for nothing lovelier can be found
In Woman, than to study household good,
And good works in her Husband to promote.
235   Yet not so strictly hath our Lord impos'd
Labor, as to debar us when we need
Refreshment, whether food, or talk between,
Food of the mind, or this sweet intercourse
Of looks and smiles, for smiles from Reason flow,
240   To brute deni'd, and are of Love the food,
Love not the lowest end of human life.
For not to irksome toil, but to delight
He made us, and delight to Reason join'd.
These paths and Bowers doubt not but our joint hands
245   Will keep from Wilderness with ease, as wide
As we need walk, till younger hands ere long
Assist us: But if much converse perhaps
Thee satiate, to short absence I could yield.
For solitude sometimes is best society,
250   And short retirement urges sweet return.
But other doubt possesses me, lest harm
Befall thee sever'd from me; for thou know'st
What hath been warn'd us, what malicious Foe
Envying our happiness, and of his own
255   Despairing, seeks to work us woe and shame
By sly assault; and somewhere nigh at hand
Watches, no doubt, with greedy hope to find
His wish and best advantage, us asunder,
Hopeless to circumvent us join'd, where each
260   To other speedy aid might lend at need;
Whether his first design be to withdraw
Our fealty from God, or to disturb
Conjugal Love, than which perhaps no bliss
Enjoy'd by us excites his envy more;
265   Or this, or worse,[9] leave not the faithful side

9. Whether this or worse (be his first design).

That gave thee being, still shades thee and protects.
The Wife, where danger or dishonor lurks,
Safest and seemliest by her Husband stays,
Who guards her, or with her the worst endures.

270   To whom the Virgin° Majesty of *Eve*,   *chaste, innocent*
As one who loves, and some unkindness meets,
With sweet austere composure thus repli'd.
    Offspring of Heav'n and Earth, and all Earth's Lord,
That such an Enemy we have, who seeks
275   Our ruin, both by thee inform'd I learn,
And from the parting Angel over-heard
As in a shady nook I stood behind,
Just then return'd at shut of Ev'ning Flow'rs.
But that thou shouldst my firmness therefore doubt
280   To God or thee, because we have a foe
May tempt it, I expected not to hear.
His violence thou fear'st not, being such,
As wee, not capable of death or pain,
Can either not receive, or can repel.
285   His fraud is then thy fear, which plain infers
Thy equal fear that my firm Faith and Love
Can by his fraud be shak'n or seduc't;
Thoughts, which how found they harbor in thy breast,
Adam, misthought of her to thee so dear?
290   To whom with healing words *Adam* repli'd.
Daughter of God and Man, immortal *Eve*,
For such thou art, from sin and blame entire:°   *free*
Not diffident° of thee do I dissuade   *mistrustful*
Thy absence from my sight, but to avoid
295   Th' attempt itself, intended by our Foe.
For hee who tempts, though in vain, at least asperses°   *falsely charges*
The tempted with dishonor foul, suppos'd
Not incorruptible of Faith, not proof
Against temptation: thou thyself with scorn
300   And anger wouldst resent the offer'd wrong,
Though ineffectual found: misdeem not then,
If such affront I labor to avert
From thee alone, which on us both at once
The Enemy, though bold, will hardly dare,
305   Or daring, first on mee th' assault shall light.
Nor thou his malice and false guile contemn;
Subtle he needs must be, who could seduce
Angels, nor think superfluous others' aid.
I from the influence of thy looks receive
310   Access° in every Virtue, in thy sight   *increase*
More wise, more watchful, stronger, if need were
Of outward strength; while shame, thou looking on,
Shame to be overcome or over-reacht
Would utmost vigor raise, and rais'd unite.

315   Why shouldst not thou like sense within thee feel
       When I am present, and thy trial choose
       With me, best witness of thy Virtue tri'd.
           So spake domestic *Adam* in his care
       And Matrimonial Love; but *Eve,* who thought
320   Less° attribúted to her Faith sincere,   *too little*
       Thus her reply with accent sweet renew'd.
           If this be our condition, thus to dwell
       In narrow circuit strait'n'd by a Foe,
       Subtle or violent, we not endu'd
325   Single with like defense, wherever met,
       How are we happy, still in fear of harm?
       But harm precedes not sin: only our Foe
       Tempting affronts us with his foul esteem
       Of our integrity: his foul esteem
330   Sticks no dishonor on our Front,° but turns   *forehead*
       Foul on himself; then wherefore shunn'd or fear'd
       By us? who rather double honor gain
       From his surmise prov'd false, find peace within,
       Favor from Heav'n, our witness from th' event.
335   And what is Faith, Love, Virtue unassay'd
       Alone, without exterior help sustain'd?
       Let us not then suspect our happy State
       Left so imperfet by the Maker wise,
       As not secure to single or combin'd.
340   Frail is our happiness, if this be so,
       And *Eden* were no Eden[1] thus expos'd.
           To whom thus Adam fervently repli'd.
       O Woman, best are all things as the will
       Of God ordain'd them, his creating hand
345   Nothing imperfet or deficient left
       Of all that he Created, much less Man,
       Or aught that might his happy State secure,
       Secure from outward force; within himself
       The danger lies, yet lies within his power:
350   Against his will he can receive no harm.
       But God left free the Will, for what obeys
       Reason, is free, and Reason he made right,
       But bid her well beware, and still erect,[2]
       Lest by some fair appearing good surpris'd
355   She dictate false, and misinform the Will
       To do what God expressly hath forbid.
       Not then mistrust, but tender love enjoins,
       That I should mind thee oft, and mind thou me.
       Firm we subsist, yet possible to swerve,
360   Since Reason not impossibly may meet

---

1. I.e., no pleasure, the literal Hebrew meaning of "Eden."   2. Always attentive, but also with a glance at upright.

Some specious object by the Foe suborn'd,
And fall into deception unaware,
Not keeping strictest watch, as she was warn'd.
Seek not temptation then, which to avoid
365   Were better, and most likely if from mee
Thou sever not: Trial will come unsought.
Wouldst thou approve° thy constancy, approve   *demonstrate*
First thy obedience; th' other who can know,
Not seeing thee attempted, who attest?
370   But if thou think, trial unsought may find
Us both securer° than thus warn'd thou seem'st,   *more careless*
Go; for thy stay, not free, absents thee more;
Go in thy native innocence, rely
On what thou hast of virtue, summon all,
375   For God towards thee hath done his part, do thine.
        So spake the Patriarch of Mankind, but *Eve*
Persisted, yet submiss, though last, repli'd.
        With thy permission then, and thus forewarn'd
Chiefly by what thy own last reasoning words
380   Touch'd only, that our trial, when least sought,
May find us both perhaps far less prepar'd,
The willinger I go, nor much expect
A Foe so proud will first the weaker seek;
So bent, the more shall shame him his repulse.
385   Thus saying, from her Husband's hand her hand
Soft she withdrew, and like a Wood-Nymph light,
Oread or *Dryad*, or of *Delia's* Train,[3]
Betook her to the Groves, but *Delia's* self
In gait surpass'd and Goddess-like deport,
390   Though not as shee with Bow and Quiver arm'd,
But with such Gard'ning Tools as Art yet rude,
Guiltless° of fire had form'd, or Angels brought.[4]   *innocent, ignorant*
To Pales, or Pomona, thus adorn'd,
Likest she seem'd, Pomona when she fled
395   *Vertumnus*, or to *Ceres* in her Prime,
Yet Virgin of *Proserpina* from *Jove*.[5]
Her long and ardent look his Eye pursu'd
Delighted, but desiring more her stay.
Oft he to her his charge of quick return
400   Repeated, shee to him as oft engag'd
To be return'd by Noon amid the Bow'r,
And all things in best order to invite
Noontide repast, or Afternoon's repose.

---

3. Oreads were mountain nymphs, such as attended on Diana; dryads were wood nymphs. Neither class of nymphs was immortal.
4. Only as a result of the Fall did it become necessary for humans to have some means of warming themselves. There may also be an allusion to the fire stolen from heaven by Prometheus.
5. Pales was the Roman goddess of pastures; Pomona was the nymph or goddess of fruit trees, seduced by the disguised Vertumnus; Ceres was the goddess of corn and agriculture who bore Proserpina to Jove.

O much deceiv'd, much failing, hapless *Eve*,
405   Of thy presum'd return! event perverse!
Thou never from that hour in Paradise
Found'st either sweet repast, or sound repose;
Such ambush hid among sweet Flow'rs and Shades
Waited with hellish rancor imminent
410   To intercept thy way, or send thee back
Despoil'd of Innocence, of Faith, of Bliss.
For now, and since first break of dawn the Fiend,
Mere° Serpent in appearance, forth was come,   plain
And on his Quest, where likeliest he might find
415   The only two of Mankind, but in them
The whole included Race, his purpos'd prey.
In Bow'r and Field he sought, where any tuft
Of Grove or Garden-Plot more pleasant lay,
Thir tendance° or Plantation for delight,   object of care
420   By Fountain or by shady Rivulet,
He sought them both, but wish'd his hap° might find   chance
Eve separate, he wish'd, but not with hope
Of what so seldom chanc'd, when to his wish,
Beyond his hope, *Eve* separate he spies,
425   Veil'd in a Cloud of Fragrance, where she stood,
Half spi'd, so thick the Roses bushing round
About her glow'd, oft stooping to support
Each Flow'r of slender stalk, whose head though gay
Carnation, Purple, Azure, or speckt with Gold,
430   Hung drooping unsustain'd, them she upstays
Gently with Myrtle band, mindless the while,
Herself, though fairest unsupported Flow'r,
From her best prop so far, and storm so nigh.[6]
Nearer he drew, and many a walk travers'd
435   Of stateliest Covert, Cedar, Pine, or Palm,
Then voluble and bold, now hid, now seen
Among thick-wov'n Arborets and Flow'rs
Imborder'd on each Bank, the hand° of *Eve*:   handiwork
Spot more delicious than those Gardens feign'd
440   Or of reviv'd *Adonis*, or renown'd
Alcinoüs, host of old *Laertes'* Son,
Or that, not Mystic, where the Sapient King
Held dalliance with his fair *Egyptian* Spouse.[7]
Much hee the Place admir'd, the Person more.
445   As one who long in populous City pent,
Where Houses thick and Sewers annoy the Air,

6. See 4.270, page 1797, where Proserpina (and by implication Eve) was "Herself a fairer flower" when she was
carried off by the king of hell.
7. "The sapient king" was Solomon (*Song of Solomon* 6.2).
Milton alludes to Spenser's addition to the myth of Ado-

nis, that Venus keeps Adonis hidden in a secret garden
(*The Faerie Queene* 3.6). "Laertes' son" was Odysseus;
much-traveled as he was, he marveled when he saw the
Garden of Alcinoüs (Homer, *Odyssey* 7).

Forth issuing on a Summer's Morn to breathe
Among the pleasant Villages and Farms
Adjoin'd, from each thing met conceives delight,
450 The smell of Grain, or tedded° Grass, or Kine,°   *mown / cows*
Or Dairy, each rural sight, each rural sound;
If chance with Nymphlike step fair Virgin pass,
What pleasing seem'd, for her now pleases more,
She most, and in her look sums all Delight.
455 Such Pleasure took the Serpent to behold
This Flow'ry Plat,° the sweet recess of *Eve*   *piece of ground*
Thus early, thus alone; her Heav'nly form
Angelic, but more soft, and Feminine,
Her graceful Innocence, her every Air
460 Of gesture or least action overaw'd
His Malice, and with rapine sweet bereav'd
His fierceness of the fierce intent it brought:
That space the Evil one abstracted stood
From his own evil, and for the time remain'd
465 Stupidly good, of enmity disarm'd,
Of guile, of hate, of envy, of revenge;
But the hot Hell that always in him burns,
Though in mid Heav'n, soon ended his delight,
And tortures him now more, the more he sees
470 Of pleasure not for him ordain'd: then soon
Fierce hate he recollects, and all his thoughts
Of mischief, gratulating,° thus excites.   *rejoicing*
     Thoughts, whither have ye led me, with what sweet
Compulsion thus transported to forget
475 What hither brought us, hate, not love, nor hope
Of Paradise for Hell, hope here to taste
Of pleasure, but all pleasure to destroy,
Save what is in destroying, other joy
To me is lost. Then let me not let pass
480 Occasion which now smiles, behold alone
The Woman, opportune° to all attempts,   *exposed*
Her Husband, for I view far round, not nigh,
Whose higher intellectual more I shun,
And strength, of courage haughty, and of limb
485 Heroic built, though of terrestrial mould,°   *formed of earth*
Foe not informidable, exempt from wound,
I not; so much hath Hell debas'd, and pain
Infeebl'd me, to what I was in Heav'n.
Shee fair, divinely fair, fit Love for Gods,
490 Not terrible, though terror be in Love
And beauty, not approacht by stronger hate,
Hate stronger, under show of Love well feign'd,
The way which to her ruin now I tend.
     So spake the Enemy of Mankind, enclos'd
495 In Serpent, Inmate bad, and toward *Eve*

Address'd his way, not with indented wave,
Prone on the ground, as since, but on his rear,
Circular base of rising folds, that tow'r'd
Fold above fold a surging Maze, his Head
500 Crested aloft, and Carbuncle his Eyes;[8]
With burnisht Neck of verdant Gold, erect
Amidst his circling Spires,° that on the grass   coils
Floated redundant:° pleasing was his shape,   abundant to excess
And lovely, never since of Serpent kind
505 Lovelier, not those that in *Illyria* chang'd
Hermione and *Cadmus*, or the God
In *Epidaurus*;[9] nor to which transform'd
Ammonian Jove, or *Capitoline* was seen,
Hee with *Olympias*, this with her who bore
510 *Scipio* the highth of Rome.[1] With tract oblique
At first, as one who sought access, but fear'd
To interrupt, side-long he works his way.
As when a Ship by skilful Steersman wrought
Nigh River's mouth or Foreland, where the Wind
515 Veers oft, as oft so steers, and shifts her Sail;
So varied hee, and of his tortuous Train
Curl'd many a wanton wreath in sight of *Eve*,
To lure her Eye; shee busied heard the sound
Of rustling Leaves, but minded not, as us'd
520 To such disport before her through the Field,
From every Beast, more duteous at her call,
Than at *Circean* call the Herd disguis'd.[2]
Hee bolder now, uncall'd before her stood;
But as in gaze admiring: Oft he bow'd
525 His turret Crest, and sleek enamell'd Neck,
Fawning, and lick'd the ground whereon she trod.
His gentle dumb expression turn'd at length
The Eye of *Eve* to mark his play; he glad
Of her attention gain'd, with Serpent Tongue
530 Organic, or impulse of vocal Air,
His fraudulent temptation thus began.
    Wonder not, sovran Mistress, if perhaps
Thou canst, who are sole Wonder, much less arm
Thy looks, the Heav'n of mildness, with disdain,
535 Displeas'd that I approach thee thus, and gaze
Insatiate, I thus single, nor have fear'd
Thy awful brow, more awful thus retir'd.

---

8. "Carbuncle" or reddish eyes denoted rage.
9. Cadmus was turned into a serpent first; only after he had embraced his wife Hermione (Harmonia) in his new form did she, too, change, (Ovid, *Metamorphoses* 4.572–603). Aesculapius, the god of healing, once changed into a serpent to help the Romans in that form (Ovid, *Metamorphoses* 15.626–744).

1. Jupiter Ammon, the "Lybian Jove," as a serpent mated with Olympias to father Alexander the Great, just as the Roman Jupiter, Capitolinus, took the form of a snake to father the great general Scipio.
2. Homer's Circe changed men into beasts who surprised Odysseus's company by fawning on them like dogs (*Odyssey* 10.212–19).

Fairest resemblance of thy Maker fair,
Thee all things living gaze on, all things thine
540 By gift, and thy Celestial Beauty adore
With ravishment beheld, there best beheld
Where universally admir'd: but here
In this enclosure wild, these Beasts among,
Beholders rude, and shallow to discern
545 Half what in thee is fair, one man except,
Who sees thee? (and what is one?) who shouldst be seen
A Goddess among Gods, ador'd and serv'd
By Angels numberless, thy daily Train.
　　So gloz'd° the Tempter, and his Proem° tun'd;　　　*flattered / prelude*
550 Into the Heart of *Eve* his words made way,
Though at the voice much marvelling; at length
Not unamaz'd she thus in answer spake.
　　What may this mean? Language of Man pronounc't
By Tongue of Brute, and human sense exprest?[3]
555 The first at least of these I thought deni'd
To Beasts, whom God on thir Creation-Day
Created mute to all articulate sound;
The latter I demur,° for in thir looks　　　　　　　*hesitate about*
Much reason, and in thir actions oft appears.
560 Thee, Serpent, subtlest beast of all the field
I knew, but not with human voice endu'd;
Redouble then this miracle, and say,
How cam'st thou speakable of mute,[4] and how
To me so friendly grown above the rest
565 Of brutal kind, that daily are in sight?
Say, for such wonder claims attention due.
　　To whom the guileful Tempter thus repli'd.
Empress of this fair World, resplendent *Eve*,
Easy to mee it is to tell thee all
570 What thou command'st and right thou should'st be obey'd:
I was at first as other Beasts that graze
The trodden Herb, of abject° thoughts and low,　　　*mean-spirited*
As was my food, nor aught but food discern'd
Or Sex, and apprehended nothing high:
575 Till on a day roving the field, I chanc'd
A goodly Tree far distant to behold
Loaden with fruit of fairest colors mixt,
Ruddy and Gold: I nearer drew to gaze;
When from the boughs a savory odor blown,
580 Grateful to appetite, more pleas'd my sense
Than smell of sweetest Fennel, or the Teats
Of Ewe or Goat dropping with Milk at Ev'n,

---

3. Milton is unusually favorable to Eve in making her ask
the serpent how it came by its voice. The Eve of Scriptural exegesis, by contrast, is carried away by the words
and makes no inquiry into their source.
4. How did you become capable of speech from being
dumb?

Unsuckt of Lamb or Kid, that tend thir play.
To satisfy the sharp desire I had
585 Of tasting those fair Apples, I resolv'd
Not to defer; hunger and thirst at once,
Powerful persuaders, quick'n'd at the scent
Of that alluring fruit, urg'd me so keen.
About the mossy Trunk I wound me soon,
590 For high from ground the branches would require
Thy utmost reach or *Adam's*: Round the Tree
All other Beasts that saw, with like desire
Longing and envying stood, but could not reach.
Amid the Tree now got, where plenty hung
595 Tempting so nigh, to pluck and eat my fill
I spar'd not, for such pleasure till that hour
At Feed or Fountain never had I found.
Sated at length, ere long I might perceive
Strange alteration in me, to degree
600 Of Reason in my inward Powers, and Speech
Wanted not long, though to this shape retain'd.
Thenceforth to Speculations high or deep
I turn'd my thoughts, and with capacious mind
Consider'd all things visible in Heav'n,
605 Or Earth, or Middle, all things fair and good;
But all that fair and good in thy Divine
Semblance, and in thy Beauty's heav'nly Ray
United I beheld; no Fair° to thine   *beauty*
Equivalent or second, which compell'd
610 Mee thus, though importune perhaps, to come
And gaze, and worship thee of right declar'd
Sovran of Creatures, universal Dame.
      So talk'd the spirited[5] sly Snake; and *Eve*,
Yet more amaz'd unwary thus repli'd.
615   Serpent, thy overpraising leaves in doubt
The virtue° of that Fruit, in thee first prov'd: *power*
But say, where grows the Tree, from hence how far?
For many are the Trees of God that grow
In Paradise, and various, yet unknown
620 To us, in such abundance lies our choice,
As leaves a greater store of Fruit untoucht,
Still hanging incorruptible, till men
Grow up to thir provision, and more hands
Help to disburden Nature of her Birth.
625   To whom the wily Adder, blithe and glad.
Empress, the way is ready, and not long,
Beyond a row of Myrtles, on a Flat,
Fast by a Fountain, one small Thicket past

5. Endowed with an animating spirit, stirred up; also energetic, enterprising, possessed by a spirit.

Of blowing° Myrrh and Balm; if thou accept   *blooming*
630   My conduct,° I can bring thee thither soon.   *guidance*
        Lead then, said Eve. Hee leading swiftly roll'd
In tangles, and made intricate seem straight,
To mischief swift. Hope elevates, and joy
        Bright'ns his Crest, as when a wand'ring Fire,
635   Compact° of unctuous vapor, which the Night   *made up*
Condenses, and the cold invirons round,
Kindl'd through agitation to a Flame,
Which oft, they say, some evil Spirit attends,
Hovering and blazing with delusive Light,
640   Misleads th' amaz'd Night-wanderer from his way
To Bogs and Mires, and oft through Pond or Pool,
There swallow'd up and lost, from succor far.
So glister'd the dire Snake, and into fraud
Led *Eve* our credulous Mother, to the Tree
645   Of prohibition, root of all our woe;
Which when she saw, thus to her guide she spake.
        Serpent, we might have spar'd our coming hither,
Fruitless to mee, though Fruit be here to excess,
The credit of whose virtue rest with thee,
650   Wondrous indeed, if cause of such effects.
But of this Tree we may not taste nor touch;
God so commanded, and left that Command
Sole Daughter of his voice;[6] the rest, we live
Law to ourselves, our Reason is our Law.
655   To whom the Tempter guilefully repli'd.
Indeed? hath God then said that of the Fruit
Of all these Garden Trees ye shall not eat,
Yet Lords declar'd of all in Earth or Air?[7]
        To whom thus *Eve* yet sinless. Of the Fruit
660   Of each Tree in the Garden we may eat,
But of the Fruit of this fair Tree amidst
The Garden, God hath said, Ye shall not eat
Thereof, nor shall ye touch it, lest ye die.
        She scarce had said, though brief, when now more bold
665   The Tempter, but with show of Zeal and Love
To Man, and indignation at his wrong,
New part puts on, and as to passion mov'd,
Fluctuates disturb'd, yet comely, and in act
Rais'd, as of some great matter to begin.
670   As when of old some Orator renown'd
In *Athens* or free *Rome*, where Eloquence
Flourish'd, since mute, to some great cause addrest,
Stood in himself collected, while each part,
Motion, each act won audience ere the tongue,

6. A Hebraism for "voice sent from heaven."   7. Lines 655–58 closely follow Genesis 3.1.

675 Sometimes in highth began, as no delay
     Of Preface brooking through his Zeal of Right.[8]
     So standing, moving, or to highth upgrown
     The Tempter all impassion'd thus began.
        O Sacred, Wise, and Wisdom-giving Plant,
680 Mother of Science,° Now I feel thy Power   knowledge
     Within me clear, not only to discern
     Things in thir Causes, but to trace the ways
     Of highest Agents, deem'd however wise.
     Queen of this Universe, do not believe
685 Those rigid threats of Death; ye shall not Die:
     How should ye? by the Fruit? it gives you Life
     To° Knowledge: By the Threat'ner? look on mee,   in addition to
     Mee who have touch'd and tasted, yet both live,
     And life more perfet have attain'd than Fate
690 Meant mee, by vent'ring higher than my Lot.
     Shall that be shut to Man, which to the Beast
     Is open? or will God incense his ire
     For such a petty Trespass, and not praise
     Rather your dauntless virtue, whom the pain
695 Of Death denounc't, whatever thing Death be,
     Deterr'd not from achieving what might lead
     To happier life, knowledge of Good and Evil;
     Of good, how just? of evil, if what is evil
     Be real, why not known, since easier shunn'd?[9]
700 God therefore cannot hurt ye, and be just;
     Not just, not God; not fear'd then, nor obey'd:
     Your fear itself of Death removes the fear.
     Why then was this forbid? Why but to awe,
     Why but to keep ye low and ignorant,
705 His worshippers; he knows that in the day
     Ye Eat thereof, your Eyes that seem so clear,
     Yet are but dim, shall perfetly be then
     Op'n'd and clear'd, and ye shall be as Gods,
     Knowing both Good and Evil as they know.[1]
710 That ye should be as Gods, since I as Man,
     Internal Man,[2] is but proportion meet,
     I of brute human, thee of human Gods.
     So ye shall die perhaps, by putting off
     Human, to put on Gods, death to be wisht,
715 Though threat'n'd, which no worse than this can bring.[3]

8. This simile blends oratorical, theatrical, and theological meanings. Thus "part" means "part of the body," "dramatic role," and "moral act"; "motion" means "gesture," "mime" (or "puppet-show"), and "instigation, persuasive force, inclination"; "act" means "action," "performance of a play," and "the accomplished deed itself."
9. If the knowledge is good, how is it just to prohibit it? Here occurs the most egregious logical fallacy in speech. (For evil to be "shunned," it is not at all necessary that it should be "known" in the sense of being experienced.)
1. See Genesis 3.5.
2. The serpent's pretense is that his "inward powers" are human.
3. Satan offers a travesty of Christian mortification and death to sin; see Colossians 3.1–15: "ye have put off the old man with his deeds; And have put on the new man, which is renewed in knowledge after the image of him that created him."

And what are Gods that Man may not become
As they, participating° God-like food?   *sharing*
The Gods are first, and that advantage use
On our belief, that all from them proceeds;
720   I question it, for this fair Earth I see,
Warm'd by the Sun, producing every kind,
Them nothing: If they° all things, who enclos'd   *if they produce*
Knowledge of Good and Evil in this Tree,
That who so eats thereof, forthwith attains
725   Wisdom without their leave? and wherein lies
Th' offense, that Man should thus attain to know?
What can your knowledge hurt him, or this Tree
Impart against his will if all be his?
Or is it envy, and can envy dwell
730   In heav'nly breasts?⁴ these, these and many more
Causes import° your need of this fair Fruit.   *suggest*
Goddess humane, reach then, and freely taste.
        He ended, and his words replete with guile
Into her heart too easy entrance won:
735   Fixt on the Fruit she gaz'd, which to behold
Might tempt alone, and in her ears the sound
Yet rung of his persuasive words, impregn'd°   *impregnated*
With Reason, to her seeming, and with Truth;
Meanwhile the hour of Noon drew on, and wak'd
740   An eager appetite, rais'd by the smell
So savory of that Fruit, which with desire,
Inclinable now grown to touch or taste,
Solicited her longing eye;⁵ yet first
Pausing a while, thus to herself she mus'd.
745   Great are thy Virtues, doubtless, best of Fruits,
Though kept from Man, and worthy to be admir'd,
Whose taste, too long forborne, at first assay
Gave elocution to the mute, and taught
The Tongue not made for Speech to speak thy praise:⁶
750   Thy praise hee also who forbids thy use,
Conceals not from us, naming thee the Tree
Of Knowledge, knowledge both of good and evil;
Forbids us then to taste, but his forbidding
Commends thee more, while it infers the good
755   By thee communicated, and our want:
For good unknown, sure is not had, or had
And yet unknown, is as not had at all.
In plain° then, what forbids he but to know,   *plainly*
Forbids us good, forbids us to be wise?

4. See Virgil, *Aeneid* 1.11; Satan is inviting Eve to participate in a pagan epic, complete with machinery of jealous
gods.
5. For lines 735–43, see Genesis 3.6.

6. Eve has trusted Satan's account of the fruit and consequently argues from false premises, such as its magical
power.

760   Such prohibitions bind not. But if Death
       Bind us with after-bands, what profits then
       Our inward freedom? In the day we eat
       Of this fair Fruit, our doom is, we shall die.
       How dies the Serpent? hee hath eat'n and lives,
765   And knows, and speaks, and reasons, and discerns,
       Irrational till then. For us alone
       Was death invented? or to us deni'd
       This intellectual food, for beasts reserv'd?
       For Beasts it seems: yet that one Beast which first
770   Hath tasted, envies not, but bring with joy
       The good befall'n him, Author unsuspect,[7]
       Friendly to man, far from deceit or guile.
       What fear I then, rather what know to fear[8]
       Under this ignorance of Good and Evil,
775   Of God or Death, of Law or Penalty?
       Here grows the Cure of all, this Fruit Divine,
       Fair to the Eye, inviting to the Taste,
       Of virtue° to make wise: what hinders then   power
       To reach, and feed at once both Body and Mind?
780   So saying, her rash hand in evil hour
       Forth reaching to the Fruit, she pluck'd, she eat:°   ate
       Earth felt the wound, and Nature from her seat
       Sighing through all her Works gave signs of woe,
       That all was lost. Back to the Thicket slunk
785   The guilty Serpent, and well might, for *Eve*,
       Intent now wholly on her taste, naught else
       Regarded, such delight till then, as seem'd,
       In Fruit she never tasted, whether true
       Or fancied so, through expectation high
790   Of knowledge, nor was God-head from her thought.[9]
       Greedily she ingorg'd without restraint,
       And knew not eating Death:[1] Satiate at length,
       And hight'n'd as with Wine, jocund and boon,°   jolly
       Thus to herself she pleasingly began.
795   O Sovran, virtuous, precious of all Trees
       In Paradise, of operation blest
       To Sapience,[2] hitherto obscur'd, infam'd,°   defamed
       And thy fair Fruit let hang, as to no end
       Created; but henceforth my early care,
800   Not without Song, each Morning, and due praise
       Shall tend thee, and the fertile burden ease
       Of thy full branches offer'd free to all;

7. Eve means "informant not subject to suspicion."
8. What fear I, then—or rather (since I'm not allowed to know anything) what do I know that is to be feared?
9. She expected to achieve godhead.
1. She knew not that she was eating death; "she was un-

aware, while she ate death" or even "she 'knew'; not eating (immediate) death."
2. "Sapience" is derived from Latin *sapientia* (discernment, taste) and ultimately from *sapere* (to taste).

Till dieted by thee I grow mature
In knowledge, as the Gods who all things know;
805   Though others[3] envy what they cannot give;
For had the gift been theirs, it had not here
Thus grown. Experience, next to thee I owe,
Best guide; not following thee, I had remain'd
In ignorance, thou op'n'st Wisdom's way,
810   And giv'st access, though secret she retire.
And I perhaps am secret; Heav'n is high,
High and remote to see from thence distinct
Each thing on Earth; and other care perhaps
May have diverted from continual watch
815   Our great Forbidder, safe with all his Spies
About him. But to *Adam* in what sort
Shall I appear? shall I to him make known
As yet my change, and give him to partake
Full happiness with mee, or rather not.
820   But keep the odds of Knowledge in my power
Without Copartner? so to add what wants
In Female Sex, the more to draw his Love,
And render me more equal, and perhaps,
A thing not undesirable, sometime
825   Superior: for inferior who is free?
This may be well: but what if God have seen,
And Death ensue? then I shall be no more,
And *Adam* wedded to another *Eve*,
Shall live with her enjoying, I extinct;
830   A death to think. Confirm'd then I resolve,
Adam shall share with me in bliss or woe:
So dear I love him, that with him all deaths
I could endure, without him live no life.
        So saying, from the Tree her step she turn'd,
835   But first low Reverence done, as to the power
That dwelt within, whose presence had infus'd
Into the plant sciential[4] sap, deriv'd
From Nectar, drink of Gods. *Adam* the while
Waiting desirous her return, had wove
840   Of choicest Flow'rs a Garland to adorn
Her Tresses, and her rural labors crown,
As Reapers oft are wont thir Harvest Queen.
Great joy he promis'd to his thoughts, and new
Solace in her return, so long delay'd;
845   Yet oft his heart, divine° of something ill,   prophet
Misgave him; hee the falt'ring measure[5] felt;
And forth to meet her went, the way she took
That Morn when first they parted; by the Tree

3. I.e., God. Eve's language is now full of lapses in logic   4. Endowed with knowledge.
and evasions in theology.   5. The rhythm of his own heart.

Of Knowledge he must pass; there he her met,
850 Scarce from the Tree returning; in her hand
A bough of fairest fruit that downy smil'd,
New gather'd, and ambrosial smell diffus'd,
To him she hasted, in her face excuse
Came Prologue, and Apology to prompt,[6]
855 Which with bland words at will she thus addrest.
      Hast thou not wonder'd, *Adam*, at my stay?
Thee I have misst, and thought it long, depriv'd
Thy presence, agony of love till now
Not felt, nor shall be twice, for never more
860 Mean I to try, what rash untri'd I sought,
The pain of absence from thy sight. But strange
Hath been the cause, and wonderful to hear:
This Tree is not as we are told, a Tree
Of danger tasted,° nor to evil unknown   *if tasted*
865 Op'ning the way, but of Divine effect
To open Eyes, and make them Gods who taste;
And hath been tasted such: the Serpent wise,
Or not restrain'd as wee, or not obeying,
Hath eat'n of the fruit, and is become,
870 Not dead, as we are threat'n'd, but thenceforth
Endu'd with human voice and human sense,
Reasoning to admiration, and with mee
Persuasively hath so prevail'd, that I
Have also tasted, and have also found
875 Th' effects to correspond, opener mine Eyes,
Dim erst, dilated Spirits, ampler Heart,
And growing up to Godhead; which for thee
Chiefly I sought, without thee can despise.
For bliss, as thou hast part, to me is bliss,
880 Tedious, unshar'd with thee, and odious soon.
Thou therefore also taste, that equal Lot
May join us, equal Joy, as equal Love;
Lest thou not tasting, different degree[7]
Disjoin us, and I then too late renounce
885 Deity for thee, when Fate will not permit.
      Thus *Eve* with Count'nance blithe her story told;
But in her Cheek distemper[8] flushing glow'd.
On th' other side, *Adam*, soon as he heard
The fatal Trespass done by *Eve*, amaz'd,
890 Astonied° stood and Blank, while horror chill   *stunned*
Ran through his veins, and all his joints relax'd;

6. The expression on Eve's face is visible in advance as she approaches and so is like the prologue-speaker of a play. But it also remains on her face as she speaks, to help out her words, and so is like the prompter of the play. The actor prompted is apology, i.e., justification or defense personified.
7. Differing position in the scale of creatures.
8. A disordered condition due to disturbance of the temperament of the bodily humors.

From his slack hand the Garland wreath'd for *Eve*,
Down dropp'd, and all the faded Roses shed:
Speechless he stood and pale, till thus at length
895　First to himself he inward silence broke.
　　　O fairest of Creation, last and best
Of all God's Works, Creature in whom excell'd
Whatever can to sight or thought be form'd,
Holy, divine, good, amiable, or sweet!
900　How art thou lost, how on a sudden lost,
Defac't, deflow'r'd, and now to death devote?°　　　　　*given over*
Rather how hast thou yielded to transgress
The strict forbiddance, how to violate
The sacred Fruit forbidd'n! some cursed fraud
905　Of Enemy hath beguil'd thee, yet unknown,
And mee with thee hath ruin'd, for with thee
Certain my resolution is to Die;
How can I live without thee, how forgo
Thy sweet Converse and Love so dearly join'd,
910　To live again in these wild Woods forlorn?
Should God create another *Eve*, and I
Another Rib afford, yet loss of thee
Would never from my heart; no no, I feel
The Link of Nature draw me: Flesh of Flesh,
915　Bone of my Bone thou art, and from thy State
Mine never shall be parted, bliss or woe.
　　　So having said, as one from sad dismay
Recomforted, and after thoughts disturb'd
Submitting to what seem'd remediless,
920　Thus in calm mood his Words to *Eve* he turn'd.
　　　Bold deed thou hast presum'd, advent'rous *Eve*,
And peril great provok't, who thus hath dar'd
Had it been only coveting to Eye
That sacred Fruit, sacred° to abstinence,　　　　　*devoted*
925　Much more to taste it under ban to touch.
But past who can recall, or done undo?
Not God Omnipotent, nor Fate; yet so
Perhaps thou shalt not Die, perhaps the Fact°　　　　*crime, deed*
Is not so heinous now, foretasted Fruit,
930　Profan'd first by the Serpent, by him first
Made common and unhallow'd ere our taste;
Nor yet on him found deadly, he yet lives,
Lives, as thou said'st, and gains to live as Man
Higher degree of Life, inducement strong
935　To us, as likely tasting to attain
Proportional ascent, which cannot be
But to be Gods, or Angels Demi-gods.
Nor can I think that God, Creator wise,
Though threat'ning, will in earnest so destroy
940　Us his prime Creatures, dignifi'd so high,

Set over all his Works, which in our Fall,
For us created, needs with us must fail,
Dependent made; so God shall uncreate,
Be frustrate, do, undo, and labor lose,

945 Not well conceiv'd of God, who though his Power
Creation could repeat, yet would be loath
Us to abolish, lest the Adversary
Triumph and say; Fickle their State whom God
Most Favors, who can please him long? Mee first

950 He ruin'd, now Mankind; whom will he next?
Matter of scorn, not to be given the Foe.
However I with thee have fixt my Lot,
Certain to undergo like doom;[9] if Death
Consort with thee, Death is to mee as Life;

955 So forcible within my heart I feel
The Bond of Nature draw me to my own,
My own in thee, for what thou art is mine;
Our State cannot be sever'd, we are one,
One Flesh; to lose thee were to lose myself.

960   So *Adam*, and thus *Eve* to him repli'd.
O glorious trial of exceeding Love,
Illustrious evidence, example high!
Ingaging me to emulate, but short
    Of thy perfection, how shall I attain,

965 *Adam*, from whose dear side I boast me sprung,
And gladly of our Union hear thee speak,
One Heart, one Soul in both; whereof good proof
This day affords, declaring thee resolv'd,
Rather than Death or aught than Death more dread

970 Shall separate us, linkt in Love so dear,
To undergo with mee one Guilt, one Crime,
If any be, of tasting this fair Fruit,
Whose virtue, for of good still good proceeds,
Direct, or by occasion[1] hath presented

975 This happy trial of thy Love, which else
So eminently never had been known.
Were it I thought Death menac't would ensue
This my attempt, I would sustain alone
The worst, and not persuade thee, rather die

980 Deserted, than oblige° thee with a fact   *make liable*
Pernicious to thy Peace, chiefly assur'd
Remarkably so late of thy so true,
So faithful Love unequall'd; but I feel
Far otherwise th' event,° nor Death, but Life   *result*

985 Augmented, op'n'd Eyes, new Hopes, new Joys,
Taste so Divine, that what of sweet before

---

9. Three separate meanings are possible: judgment, irrev-   1. I.e., directly or indirectly.
ocable destiny, and death.

Hath toucht my sense, flat seems to this, and harsh.
On my experience, *Adam*, freely taste,
And fear of Death deliver to the Winds.

990   So saying, she embrac'd him, and for joy
Tenderly wept, much won that he his Love
Had so ennobl'd, as of choice to incur
Divine displeasure for her sake, or Death.
In recompense (for such compliance bad

995   Such recompense best merits) from the bough
She gave him of that fair enticing Fruit
With liberal hand: he scrupl'd not to eat
Against his better knowledge, not deceiv'd,
But fondly overcome with Female charm.[2]

1000   Earth trembl'd from her entrails, as again
In pangs, and Nature gave a second groan,
Sky low'r'd, and muttering Thunder, some sad drops
Wept at completing of the mortal Sin
Original;[3] while *Adam* took no thought,

1005   Eating his fill, nor *Eve* to iterate
Her former trespass fear'd, the more to soothe
Him with her lov'd society, that now
As with new Wine intoxicated both
They swim in mirth, and fancy that they feel

1010   Divinity within them breeding wings
Wherewith to scorn the Earth: but that false Fruit
Far other operation first display'd,
Carnal desire inflaming, hee on *Eve*
Began to cast lascivious Eyes, she him

1015   As wantonly repaid; in Lust they burn:
Till *Adam* thus 'gan *Eve* to dalliance move.
     Eve, now I see thou are exact of taste,
And elegant, of Sapience[4] no small part,
Since to each meaning savor[5] we apply,

1020   And Palate call judicious; I the praise
Yield thee, so well this day thou hast purvey'd.°   *provided*
Much pleasure we have lost, while we abstain'd
From this delightful Fruit, nor known till now
True relish, tasting; if such pleasure be

1025   In things to us forbidden, it might be wish'd,
For this one Tree had been forbidden ten.
But come, so well refresh't, now let us play,
As meet is, after such delicious Fare;
For never did thy Beauty since the day

---

2. See 1 Timothy 2.14: "And Adam was not deceived, but the woman being deceived was in the transgression."
3. The only occurrence in *Paradise Lost* of the term "Original Sin." In his *De doctrina* (1.11), Milton defines Original Sin as "the sin which is common to all men, that which our first parents, and in them all their posterity committed, when, casting off their obedience to God, they tasted the fruit of the forbidden tree."
4. Wisdom, from Latin *sapere*, to taste.
5. Tastiness, understanding.

1030 I saw thee first and wedded thee, adorn'd
With all perfections, so inflame my sense
With ardor to enjoy thee, fairer now
Than ever, bounty of this virtuous Tree.[6]
    So said he, and forbore not glance or toy°   caress
1035 Of amorous intent, well understood
Of° Eve, whose Eye darted contagious Fire.   by
Her hand he seiz'd, and to a shady bank,
Thick overhead with verdant roof imbowr'd
He led her nothing loath; Flow'rs were the Couch,
1040 Pansies, and Violets, and Asphodel,
And Hyacinth, Earth's freshest softest lap.
There they thir fill of Love and Love's disport
Took largely, of thir mutual guilt the Seal,
The solace of thir sin, till dewy sleep
1045 Oppress'd them, wearied with thir amorous play.
Soon as the force of that fallacious Fruit,
That with exhilarating vapor bland°   pleasing
About thir spirits had play'd, and inmost powers
Made err, was now exhal'd, and grosser sleep
1050 Bred of unkindly fumes,[7] with conscious dreams
Encumber'd, now had left them, up they rose
As from unrest, and each the other viewing,
Soon found thir Eyes how op'n'd, and thir minds
How dark'n'd;[8] innocence, that as a veil
1055 Had shadow'd them from knowing ill, was gone,
Just confidence, and native righteousness,
And honor from about them, naked left
To guilty shame: hee cover'd, but his Robe
Uncover'd more. So rose the *Danite* strong
1060 *Herculean Samson* from the Harlot-lap
Of *Philistean Dalilah*, and wak'd
Shorn of his strength, They destitute and bare
Of all thir virtue:[9] silent, and in face
Confounded long they sat, as struck'n mute,
1065 Till *Adam*, though not less than *Eve* abasht,
At length gave utterance to these words constrain'd.
    O *Eve*, in evil hour thou didst give ear
To that false Worm, of whomsoever taught
To counterfeit Man's voice, true in our Fall,
1070 False in our promis'd Rising; since our Eyes
Op'n'd we find indeed, and find we know
Both Good and Evil, Good lost, and Evil got,

---

6. See Homer, *Iliad* 14, where Hera, bent on deceiving Zeus, comes to him wearing Aphrodite's belt and seems more charming to him than ever before.
7. Unnatural vapors or exhalations rising from the stomach to the brain.
8. See Genesis 3.7: "The eyes of them both were opened, and they knew that they were naked."
9. See Judges 16 for the story of Samson's betrayal by Delilah.

Bad Fruit of Knowledge, if this be to know,
Which leaves us naked thus, of Honor void,
1075 Of Innocence, of Faith, of Purity,
Our wonted Ornaments now soil'd and stain'd,
And in our Faces evident the signs
Of foul concupiscence; whence evil store;
Even shame, the last of evils; of the first
1080 Be sure then. How shall I behold the face
Henceforth of God or Angel, erst with joy
And rapture so oft beheld? those heav'nly shapes
Will dazzle now this earthly, with thir blaze
Insufferably bright. O might I here
1085 In solitude live savage, in some glade
Obscur'd, where highest Woods impenetrable
To Star or Sun-light, spread thir umbrage broad,
And brown as Evening: Cover me ye Pines,
Ye Cedars, with innumerable boughs
1090 Hide me, where I may never see them more.
But let us now, as in bad plight, devise
What best may for the present serve to hide
The Parts of each from other, that seem most
To shame obnoxious,° and unseemliest seen,   *exposed*
1095 Some Tree whose broad smooth Leaves together sew'd,
And girded on our loins, may cover round
Those middle parts, that this new comer, Shame,
There sit not, and reproach us as unclean.[1]
     So counsell'd hee, and both together went
1100 Into the thickest Wood, there soon they chose
The Figtree,[2] not that kind for Fruit renown'd,
But such as at this day to *Indians* known
In *Malabar* or *Decan* spreads her Arms
Branching so broad and long, that in the ground
1105 The bended Twigs take root, and Daughters grow
About the Mother Tree, a Pillar'd shade
High overarch't, and echoing Walks between;
There oft the *Indian* Herdsman shunning heat
Shelters in cool, and tends his pasturing Herds
1110 At Loopholes cut through thickest shade: Those Leaves
They gather'd, broad as Amazonian Targe,°   *shield*
And with what skill they had, together sew'd,
To gird thir waist, vain Covering if to hide
Thir guilt and dreaded shame; O how unlike
1115 To that first naked Glory. Such of late
Columbus found th' *American* so girt
With feather'd Cincture,° naked else and wild   *belt*
Among the Trees on Isles and woody Shores.

1. See Genesis 3.7.   from Gerard's *Herball* (1597).
2. Milton's description of the banyan or Indian fig comes

Thus fenc't, and as they thought, thir shame in part
1120　Cover'd, but not at rest or ease of Mind,
They sat them down to weep, nor only Tears
Rain'd at thir Eyes, but high Winds worse within
Began to rise, high Passions, Anger, Hate,
Mistrust, Suspicion, Discord, and shook sore
1125　Thir inward State of Mind, calm Region once
And full of Peace, now toss't and turbulent:
For Understanding rul'd not, and the Will
Heard not her lore, both in subjection now
To sensual Appetite, who from beneath
1130　Usurping over sovran Reason claim'd
Superior sway: From thus distemper'd breast,
Adam, estrang'd in look and alter'd style,
Speech intermitted thus to *Eve* renew'd.
　　Would thou hadst heark'n'd to my words, and stay'd
1135　With me, as I besought thee, when that strange
Desire of wand'ring this unhappy Morn,
I know not whence possess'd thee; we had then
Remain'd still happy, not as now, despoil'd
Of all our good, sham'd, naked, miserable.
1140　Let none henceforth seek needless cause to approve°　　　　*give proof of*
The Faith they owe;[3] when earnestly they seek
Such proof, conclude, they then begin to fail.
　　To whom soon mov'd with touch of blame thus *Eve*.
What words have past thy Lips,[4]*Adam* severe,
1145　Imput'st thou that to my default, or will
Of wand'ring, as thou call'st it, which who knows
But might as ill have happ'n'd thou being by,
Or to thyself perhaps: hadst thou been there,
Or here th' attempt, thou couldst not have discern'd
1150　Fraud in the Serpent, speaking as he spake;
No ground of enmity between us known,
Why hee should mean me ill, or seek to harm.
Was I to have never parted from thy side?
As good have grown there still a lifeless Rib.
1155　Being as I am, why didst not thou the Head[5]
Command me absolutely not to go,
Going into such danger as thou said'st?
Too facile° then thou didst not much gainsay,　　　　*permissive*
Nay, didst permit, approve, and fair dismiss.
1160　Hadst thou been firm and fixt in thy dissent
Neither had I transgress'd, nor thou with mee.
　　To whom then first incenst Adam repli'd.
Is this the Love, is this the recompense

---

3. Be under obligation to render or possess.
4. Echoes Odysseus' disapproval of a speech of Agamemnon's (*Iliad* 14.83).

5. Alludes to 1 Corinthians 11.3: "The head of every man is Christ; and the head of the woman is the man; and the head of Christ is God."

	Of mine to thee, ingrateful *Eve*, express't	
1165	Immutable° when thou wert lost, not I,	*unchangeable*
	Who might have liv'd and joy'd immortal bliss,	
	Yet willingly chose rather Death with thee:	
	And am I now upbraided, as the cause	
	Of thy transgressing? not enough severe,	
1170	It seems, in thy restraint: what could I more?	
	I warn'd thee, I admonish'd thee, foretold	
	The danger, and the lurking Enemy	
	That lay in wait; beyond this had been force,	
	And force upon free Will hath here no place.	
1175	But confidence then bore thee on, secure	
	Either to meet no danger, or to find	
	Matter of glorious trial; and perhaps	
	I also err'd in overmuch admiring	
	What seem'd in thee so perfet, that I thought	
1180	No evil durst attempt thee, but I rue	
	That error now, which is become my crime,	
	And thou th' accuser. Thus it shall befall	
	Him who to worth in Woman overtrusting	
	Lets her Will rule; restraint she will not brook,	
1185	And left to herself, if evil thence ensue,	
	Shee first his weak indulgence will accuse.	

Thus they in mutual accusation spent
The fruitless hours, but neither self-condemning,
And of thir vain contést appear'd no end.
The End of the Ninth Book.

Book 10
The Argument

Man's *transgression known, the Guardian Angels forsake Paradise, and return up to Heaven to approve thir vigilance, and are approv'd, God declaring that the entrance of Satan could not be by them prevented. He sends his Son to judge the Transgressors, who descends and gives Sentence accordingly; then in pity clothes them both, and reascends. Sin and Death sitting till then at the Gates of Hell, by wondrous sympathy feeling the success of Satan in this new World, and the sin by Man there committed, resolve to sit no longer confin'd in Hell, but to follow Satan thir Sire up to the place of Man: To make the way easier from Hell to this World to and fro, they pave a broad Highway or Bridge over Chaos, according to the Track that Satan first made; then preparing for Earth, they meet him proud of his success returning to Hell; thir mutual gratulation. Satan arrives at Pandemonium, in full assembly relates with boasting his success against Man; instead of applause is entertained with a general hiss by all his audience, transform'd with himself also suddenly into Serpents, according to his doom giv'n in Paradise; then deluded with a show of the forbidden Tree springing up before them, they greedily reaching to take of the Fruit, chew dust and bitter ashes. The proceedings of Sin and Death; God foretells the final Victory of his Son over them, and the renewing of all things; but for the present commands his Angels to make several alterations in the Heavens and Elements. Adam more and more perceiving his fall'n condition heavily bewails, rejects the condolement of* Eve; *she persists and at length appeases him: then to evade the Curse likely to fall on thir Offspring, proposes to* Adam *violent ways, which he approves not, but conceiving better hope, puts her in mind of the late Promise made them, that her Seed should be reveng'd on the Serpent, and exhorts her with him to seek Peace of the offended Deity, by repentance and supplication.*

      Meanwhile the heinous and despiteful act
Of *Satan* done in Paradise, and how
Hee in the Serpent had perverted *Eve*,
Her Husband shee, to taste the fatal fruit,
5   Was known in Heav'n;[1] for what can scape the Eye
Of *God* All-seeing, or deceive his Heart
Omniscient, who in all things wise and just,
Hinder'd not *Satan* to attempt the mind
Of Man, with strength entire, and free will arm'd,
10 Complete to have discover'd and repulst
Whatever wiles of Foe or seeming Friend.
For still they knew, and ought to have still remember'd
The high Injunction not to taste that Fruit,
Whoever tempted; which they not obeying,
15 Incurr'd, what could they less, the penalty,
And manifold[2] in sin, deserv'd to fall.
Up into Heav'n from Paradise in haste
Th' Angelic Guards ascended, mute and sad
For Man, for of his state by this they knew,
20 Much wond'ring how the subtle Fiend had stol'n
Entrance unseen. Soon as th' unwelcome news
From Earth arriv'd at Heaven Gate, displeas'd
All were who heard, dim sadness did not spare
That time Celestial visages, yet mixt
25 With pity, violated not thir bliss.
About the new-arriv'd, in multitudes
Th' ethereal People ran, to hear and know
How all befell: they towards the Throne Supreme
Accountable made haste to make appear
30 With righteous plea, thir utmost vigilance,
And easily approv'd; when the most High
Eternal Father from his secret Cloud,
Amidst in Thunder utter'd thus his voice.
      Assembl'd Angels, and ye Powers return'd
35 From unsuccessful charge, be not dismay'd,
Nor troubl'd at these tidings from the Earth,

1. Rhetorically, lines 1–16 function both as *principium*, stating the subject of the book, and as *initium*, introducing the first scene. They also sum up the theological content of Book 3, which will receive specific application in the present book, in the exchanges between the Father and the Son (lines 34–84) and between the Son and Adam (lines 124ff.). Note the structural symmetry whereby the divine decrees of the third book are balanced by those of the third from the end.
2. Multiplied; alluding to Psalms 38.19: "they that hate me wrongfully are multiplied."

Which your sincerest care could not prevent,
Foretold so lately what would come to pass,
When first this Tempter cross'd the Gulf from Hell.
40 I told ye then he should prevail and speed°   *succeed*
On his bad Errand, Man should be seduc't
And flatter'd out of all, believing lies
Against his Maker; no Decree of mine
Concurring to necessitate his Fall,
45 Or touch with lightest moment of impulse
His free Will, to her own inclining left
In even scale.³ But fall'n he is, and now
What rests, but that the mortal Sentence pass
On his transgression. Death denounc't that day,
50 Which he presumes already vain and void,
Because not yet inflicted, as he fear'd,
By some immediate stroke; but soon shall find
Forbearance no acquittance ere day end.
Justice shall not return as bounty scorn'd.
55 But whom send I to judge them? whom but thee
Vicegerent Son, to thee I have transferr'd
All Judgment, whether in Heav'n, or Earth, or Hell.
Easy it may be seen that I intend
Mercy colleague with Justice, sending thee
60 Man's Friend, his Mediator, his design'd
Both Ransom and Redeemer voluntary,
And destin'd Man himself to judge Man fall'n.⁴
    So spake the Father, and unfolding bright
Toward the right hand his Glory, on the Son
65 Blaz'd forth unclouded Deity; he full
Resplendent all his Father manifest
Express'd, and thus divinely answer'd mild.
    Father Eternal, thine is to decree,
Mine both in Heav'n and Earth to do thy will
70 Supreme, that thou in mee thy Son belov'd
May'st ever rest well pleas'd.⁵ I go to judge
On Earth these thy transgressors, but thou know'st,
Whoever judg'd, the worst on mee must light,
When time shall be, for so I undertook
75 Before thee; and not repenting, this obtain
Of right, that I may mitigate thir doom
On me deriv'd, yet I shall temper so
Justice with Mercy, as may illustrate most
Them fully satisfied, and thee appease.

---

3. "Moment" is a term applied to the smallest increment that could affect the equilibrium of a balance. If man had been protected from the tempter, then there would have been real interference with the free action of the scales of justice.

4. The double syntax—line 62 can be read as either "himself a man, destined to judge man" (primary) or "destined to judge man himself, man fallen"—mimes the close identification of Christ with humanity.

5. Echoing Matthew 3.17.

80   Attendance none shall need, nor Train, where none
        Are to behold the Judgment, but the judg'd,
        Those two; the third[6] best absent is condemn'd,
        Convict° by flight, and Rebel to all Law: convicted
        Conviction to the Serpent none belongs.[7]
85   Thus saying, from his radiant Seat he rose
        Of high collateral° glory: him Thrones and Powers,   side by side
        Princedoms, and Dominations ministrant
        Accompanied to Heaven Gate, from whence
        Eden and all the Coast in prospect lay.
90   Down he descended straight; the speed of Gods
        Time counts not, though with swiftest minutes wing'd.
        Now was the Sun in Western cadence° low[8]   falling
        From Noon, and gentle Airs due at thir hour
        To fan the Earth now wak'd, and usher in
95   The Ev'ning cool, when he from wrath more cool
        Came the mild Judge and Intercessor both
        To sentence Man: the voice of God they heard
        Now walking in the Garden, by soft winds
        Brought to thir Ears, while day declin'd, they heard,
100   And from his presence hid themselves among
        The thickest Trees, both Man and Wife, till God
        Approaching, thus to Adam call'd aloud.
            Where art thou *Adam*, wont with joy to meet
        My coming seen far off? I miss thee here,
105   Not pleas'd, thus entertain'd with solitude,
        Where obvious duty erewhile appear'd unsought:
        Or come I less conspicuous, or what change
        Absents thee, or what chance detains? Come forth.
        He came, and with him *Eve*, more loath, though first
110   To offend, discount'nanc't both, and discompos'd;
        Love was not in thir looks, either to God
        Or to each other, but apparent guilt,
        And shame, and perturbation, and despair,
        Anger, and obstinacy, and hate, and guile.
115   Whence *Adam* falt'ring long, thus answer'd brief.
            I heard thee in the Garden, and of thy voice
        Afraid, being naked, hid myself. To whom
        The gracious Judge without revile repli'd.
            My voice thou oft hast heard, and hast not fear'd,
120   But still rejoic't, how is it now become
        So dreadful to thee? that thou art naked, who
        Hath told thee? hast thou eaten of the Tree
        Whereof I gave thee charge thou shouldst not eat?
            To whom thus *Adam* sore beset repli'd.

---

6. Satan.
7. "Conviction" has both the legal sense (proof of guilt) and   the theological (the condition of being convinced of sin).
                                                                  8. Lines 92–123 follow Genesis 3.8–11.

125   O Heav'n! in evil strait this day I stand
     Before my Judge, either to undergo
     Myself the total Crime, or to accuse
     My other self, the partner of my life;
     Whose failing, while her Faith to me remains,
130   I should conceal, and not expose to blame
     By my complaint; but strict necessity
     Subdues me, and calamitous constraint,
     Lest on my head both sin and punishment,
     However insupportable, be all
135   Devolv'd;[9] though should I hold my peace, yet thou
     Wouldst easily detect what I conceal.
     This Woman whom thou mad'st to be my help,
     And gav'st me as thy perfet gift, so good,
     So fit, so acceptable, so Divine,
140   That from her hand I could suspect no ill,
     And what she did, whatever in itself,
     Her doing seem'd to justify the deed;
     Shee gave me of the Tree, and I did eat.[1]
       To whom the sovran Presence thus repli'd.
145   Was shee thy God, that her thou didst obey
     Before his voice, or was shee made thy guide,
     Superior, or but equal, that to her
     Thou didst resign thy Manhood, and the Place
     Wherein God set thee above her made of thee,
150   And for thee, whose perfection far excell'd
     Hers in all real° dignity:[2] Adorn'd   *regal*
     She was indeed, and lovely to attract
     Thy Love, not thy Subjection, and her Gifts
     Were such as under Government well seem'd,
155   Unseemly to bear rule, which was thy part°   *role*
     And person,° hadst thou known thyself aright.   *character*
       So having said, he thus to Eve in few:
     Say Woman, what is this which thou hast done?
       To whom sad *Eve* with shame nigh overwhelm'd,
160   Confessing soon, yet not before her Judge
     Bold or loquacious, thus abasht repli'd.
       The Serpent me beguil'd and I did eat.[3]
       Which when the Lord God heard, without delay
     To Judgment he proceeded on th' accus'd
165   Serpent though brute, unable to transfer
     The Guilt on him who made him instrument
     Of mischief, and polluted from the end
     Of his Creation; justly then accurst,
     As vitiated in Nature: more to know

---

9. Caused to fall upon.
1. See Genesis 3.12.
2. See 1 Corinthians 11.8ff.: "For the man is not of the woman; but the woman of the man. Neither was the man created for the woman; but the woman for the man."
3. Repeating Genesis 3.13.

170 Concern'd not Man (since he no further knew)
Nor alter'd his offense; yet God at last
To Satan first in sin his doom appli'd,
Though in mysterious° terms, judg'd as then best: *mystical*
And on the Serpent thus his curse let fall.

175   Because thou hast done this, thou art accurst
Above all Cattle, each Beast of the Field;
Upon thy Belly groveling thou shalt go,
And dust shalt eat all the days of thy Life.
Between Thee and the Woman I will put

180 Enmity, and between thine and her Seed;
Her Seed shall bruise thy head, thou bruise his heel.[4]
    So spake this Oracle, then verifi'd
When *Jesus* son of *Mary* second *Eve*,
Saw Satan fall like Lightning down from Heav'n,[5]

185 Prince of the Air; then rising from his Grave
Spoil'd Principalities and Powers, triumpht
In open show, and with ascension bright
Captivity led captive through the Air,[6]
The Realm itself of Satan long usurpt,

190 Whom he shall tread at last under our feet;[7]
Ev'n hee who now foretold his fatal bruise,
And to the Woman thus his Sentence turn'd.
    Thy sorrow I will greatly multiply
By thy Conception; Children thou shalt bring

195 In sorrow forth, and to thy Husband's will
Thine shall submit, hee over thee shall rule.
    On *Adam* last thus judgment he pronounc'd.
Because thou hast heark'n'd to the voice of thy Wife,
And eaten of the Tree concerning which

200 I charg'd thee, saying: Thou shalt not eat thereof,
Curs'd is the ground for thy sake, thou in sorrow
Shalt eat thereof all the days of thy Life;[8]
Thorns also and Thistles it shall bring thee forth
Unbid, and thou shalt eat th' Herb of the Field,

205 In the sweat of thy Face shalt thou eat Bread,
Till thou return unto the ground, for thou
Out of the ground wast taken, know thy Birth,
For dust thou art, and shalt to dust return.[9]
    So judg'd he Man, both Judge and Savior sent,

210 And th' instant stroke of Death denounc't that day
Remov'd far off;[1] then pitying how they stood
Before him naked to the air, that now

---

4. See Genesis 3.14ff.
5. "I beheld Satan as lightning fall from heaven" (Luke 10.18).
6. Psalms 68.18: "Thou hast ascended on high, thou hast led captivity captive:" applied to Christ in Ephesians 4.8.
7. See Romans 16.20: "And the God of peace shall bruise Satan under your feet shortly."
8. See Genesis 3.17.
9. See Genesis 3.18–19.
1. Christ removes the fear that physical death will follow the eating of the fruit on the same day.

Must suffer change, disdain'd not to begin
Thenceforth the form of servant to assume,[2]
215 As when he wash'd his servants' feet, so now
As Father of his Family he clad
Thir nakedness with Skins of Beasts, or slain,
Or as the Snake with youthful Coat repaid;
And thought not much to clothe his Enemies:
220 Nor hee thir outward only with the Skins
Of Beasts, but inward nakedness, much more
Opprobrious, with his Robe of righteousness,
Arraying cover'd from his Father's sight.
To him with swift ascent he up return'd,
225 Into his blissful bosom reassum'd
In glory as of old, to him appeas'd
All, though all-knowing, what had past with Man
Recounted, mixing intercession sweet.
Meanwhile ere thus was sinn'd and judg'd on Earth,
230 Within the Gates of Hell sat Sin and Death,
In counterview within the Gates that now
Stood open wide, belching outrageous° flame   *enormous*
Far into *Chaos*, since the Fiend pass'd through,
Sin opening, who thus now to Death began.
235   O Son, why sit we here each other viewing
Idly, while Satan our great Author° thrives   *parent*
In other Worlds, and happier Seat provides
For us his offspring dear? It cannot be
But that success attends him; if mishap,
240 Ere this he had return'd, with fury driv'n
By his Avengers, since no place like° this   *so well as*
Can fit his punishment, or their revenge.
Methinks I feel new strength within me rise,
Wings growing, and Dominion giv'n me large
245 Beyond this Deep; whatever draws me on,
Or° sympathy,° or some connatural force   *Either / affinity*
Powerful at greatest distance to unite
With secret amity things of like kind
By secretest conveyance.° Thou my Shade   *communication*
250 Inseparable must with mee along:
For Death from Sin no power can separate.
But lest the difficulty of passing back
Stay his return perhaps over this Gulf
Impassable, Impervious, let us try
255 Advent'rous work, yet to thy power and mine
Not unagreeable to found° a path   *establish*
Over this Main° from Hell to that new World   *expanse*
Where Satan now prevails, a Monument

2. See Philippians 2.7: "made himself of no reputation, and took upon him the form of a servant, and was made in the likeness of men."

Of merit high to all th' infernal Host,
260   Easing thir passage hence, for intercourse,
Or transmigration,[3] as thir lot shall lead.
Nor can I miss the way, so strongly drawn
By this new felt attraction and instinct.
        Whom thus the meagre° Shadow answer'd soon,   *emaciated*
265   Go whither Fate and inclination strong
Leads thee, I shall not lag behind, nor err
The way, thou leading, such a scent I draw°   *inhale*
Of carnage, prey innumerable, and taste
The savor of Death from all things there that live:
270   Nor shall I to the work thou enterprisest
Be wanting, but afford thee equal aid.
        So saying, with delight he snuff'd the smell
Of mortal change on Earth. As when a flock
Of ravenous Fowl, though many a League remote,
275   Against the day of Battle, to a Field,
Where Armies lie encamp, come flying, lur'd
With scent of living Carcasses design'd
For death, the following day, in bloody fight.
So scented the grim Feature,° and upturn'd   *form*
280   His Nostril wide into the murky Air,
Sagacious° of his Quarry from so far.   *acutely perceiving*
Then Both from out Hell Gates into the waste
Wide Anarchy of *Chaos* damp and dark
Flew diverse, and with Power (thir Power was great)
285   Hovering upon the Waters; what they met
Solid or slimy, as in raging Sea
Tost up and down together crowded drove
From each side shoaling° towards the mouth of Hell.   *crowding*
As when two Polar Winds blowing adverse
290   Upon the *Cronian* Sea,[4] together drive
Mountains of Ice, that stop th' imagin'd way
Beyond *Petsora* Eastward, to the rich
Cathaian Coast. The aggregated Soil
Death with his Mace petrilic,° cold and dry,   *turning into stone*
295   As with a Trident smote, and fix't as firm
As *Delos* floating once; the rest his look
Bound with *Gorgonian* rigor not to move,
And with *Asphaltic* slime; broad as the Gate
Deep to the Roots of Hell the gather'd beach°   *ridge of stones*
300   They fasten'd, and the Mole° immense wrought on   *causeway*

3. Permanent emigration, a euphemism for damnation.
4. Various references to stone, ice, and exploration follow. The Cronian Sea is the Arctic Ocean; as *mare concretum*, it is relevant to Death's solidifying work. The "imagin'd way" is the northeast passage to Cathay searched for by Henry Hudson (1608), who failed to find a route through the ice. Petsora is the Pechora, a river in northern Russia. Cathay was a separate empire, north of present-day China. Delos, an island in the Aegean Sea, was supposedly made to float by Poseidon's trident in order to provide a refuge where Latona could give birth to Apollo and Artemis, safe from Hera's jealousy. It was later anchored by Zeus. The Gorgons turned to stone all whom they looked at.

Over the foaming deep high Archt, a Bridge
Of length prodigious joining to the Wall[5]
Immoveable of this now fenceless World
Forfeit to Death; from hence a passage broad,
305 Smooth, easy, inoffensive down to Hell.
So, if great things to small may be compar'd,
Xerxes, the Liberty of *Greece* to yoke,
From *Susa* his *Memnonian* Palace high
Came to the Sea, and over *Hellespont*
310 Bridging his way, *Europe* with *Asia* join'd,
And scourg'd with many a stroke th' indignant waves.[6]
Now had they brought the work by wondrous Art
Pontifical,[7] a ridge of pendent° Rock   hanging
Over the vext° Abyss, following the track   stormy
315 Of *Satan*, to the selfsame place where hee
First lighted from his Wing, and landed safe
From out of *Chaos* to the outside bare
Of this round World: with Pins of Adamant
And Chains they made all fast, too fast they made
320 And durable; and now in little space
The confines met of Empyrean Heav'n
And of this World, and on the left hand Hell[8]
With long reach interpos'd; three sev'ral ways
In sight, to each of these three places led.
325 And now thir way to Earth they had descri'd,
To Paradise first tending, when behold
Satan in likeness of an Angel bright
Betwixt the *Centaur* and the *Scorpion* steering
His *Zenith*,[9] while the Sun in *Aries* rose:
330 Disguis'd he came, but those his Children dear
Thir Parent soon discern'd, though in disguise.
Hee, after *Eve* seduc't, unminded° slunk   unnoticed
Into the Wood fast by, and changing shape
To observe the sequel,° saw his guileful act   consequence
335 By *Eve*, though all unweeting,° seconded   unwitting
Upon her Husband, saw thir shame that sought
Vain covertures;° but when he saw descend   clothes, lies
The Son of God to judge them, terrifi'd
Hee fled, not hoping to escape, but shun
340 The present, fearing guilty what his wrath

---

5. The outer shell (2.1024–31) reached by the bridge, the "utmost orb / Of this frail world." Despite the wall, the world is without defense ("fenceless") against Death after the Fall.

6. Xerxes, king of the Persians, bridged the Hellespont, a stretch of water separating Europe and Asia. When a storm destroyed the bridge, he is said to have had the waters whipped. Susa, sometimes called Memnonia, after Memnon, son of Tithonus and Aurora was the winter seat of the Persian kings.

7. Meaning both bridge-making, and episcopal. The Pope's title Pontifex referred to his role as bridge-builder between this world and the next. The implication, therefore, is that priests have special skill in easing the way to hell.

8. The sinister, evil side, where reprobate goats go in the parable (Matthew 25:33). Compare to the "dextrous" Son at God's right hand; 5.742n.

9. Satan flies straight up from Paradise, between Scorpio and Sagittarius.

Might suddenly inflict; that past, return'd
By Night, and list'ning where the hapless Pair
Sat in thir sad discourse and various plaint,°   *complaint*
Thence gather'd his own doom;° which understood   *judgment*
345   Not instant, but of future time, with joy
And tidings fraught, to Hell he now return'd,
And at the brink of *Chaos,* near the foot
Of this new wondrous Pontifice, unhop't
Met who to meet him came, his Offspring dear.
350   Great joy was at thir meeting, and at sight
Of that stupendous Bridge his joy increas'd.
Long hee admiring stood, till Sin, his fair
Enchanting Daughter, thus the silence broke.
    O Parent, these are thy magnific deeds,
355   Thy Trophies, which thou view'st as not thine own,
Thou art thir Author and prime Architect:
For I no sooner in my Heart divin'd,
My Heart, which by a secret harmony
Still moves with thine, join'd in connexion sweet,
360   That thou on Earth hadst prosper'd, which thy looks
Now also evidence, but straight I felt
Though distant from thee Worlds between, yet felt
That I must after thee with this thy Son;
Such fatal consequence° unites us three: *relationship*
365   Hell could no longer hold us in her bounds,
Nor this unvoyageable Gulf obscure
Detain from following thy illustrious track.
Thou hast achiev'd our liberty, confin'd
Within Hell Gates till now, thou us impow'r'd
370   To fortify° thus far, and overlay   *grow strong*
With this portentous Bridge the dark Abyss.
Thine now is all this World, thy virtue° hath won   *power*
What thy hands builded not, thy Wisdom gain'd
With odds° what War hath lost, and fully aveng'd   *advantage*
375   Our foil° in Heav'n; here thou shalt Monarch reign, *defeat*
There didst not; there let him still Victor sway,
As Battle hath adjudg'd, from this new World
Retiring, by his own doom alienated,
And henceforth Monarchy with thee divide
380   Of all things, parted by th' Empyreal bounds
His Quadrature, from thy Orbicular World,[1]
Or try thee now more dang'rous to his Throne.
    Whom thus the Prince of Darkness answer'd glad
Fair Daughter, and thou Son and Grandchild both,[2]
385   High proof ye now have giv'n to be the Race
Of *Satan* (for I glory in the name,

1. The world (universe) is often "orbicular" (see 3.718), a
form incommensurate with the "quadrature" or square.

2. As offspring of Satan's incest with his daughter Sin.

Antagonist of Heav'n's Almighty King)
Amply have merited of me, of all
Th' Infernal Empire, that so near Heav'n's door
390 Triumphal with triumphal act have met,
Mine with this glorious Work, and made one Realm
Hell and this World, one Realm, one Continent
Of easy thorough-fare. Therefore while I
Descend through Darkness, on your Road with ease
395 To my associate Powers, them to acquaint
With these successes, and with them rejoice,
You two this way, among those numerous Orbs
All yours, right down to Paradise descend;
There dwell and Reign in bliss, thence on the Earth
400 Dominion exercise and in the Air,
Chiefly on Man, sole Lord of all declar'd,
Him first make sure your thrall, and lastly kill.
My Substitutes I send ye, and Create
Plenipotent° on Earth, of matchless might   *having full authority*
405 Issuing from mee: on your joint vigor now
My hold of this new Kingdom all depends,
Through Sin to Death expos'd by my exploit.
If your joint power prevail, th' affairs of Hell
No detriment° need fear, go and be strong.   *injury*
410   So saying he dismiss'd them, they with speed
Thir course through thickest Constellations held
Spreading thir bane; the blasted Stars lookt wan,
And Planets, Planet-strook, real Eclipse
Then suffer'd.[3] Th' other way *Satan* went down
415 The Causey° to Hell Gate; on either side   *causeway*
Disparted *Chaos* over-built exclaim'd,
And with rebounding surge the bars assail'd,
That scorn'd his indignation: through the Gate,
Wide open and unguarded, *Satan* pass'd,
420 And all about found desolate; for those
Appointed to sit there,[4] had left thir charge,
Flown to the upper World; the rest were all
Far to th'inland retir'd, about the walls
Of *Pandaemonium*, City and proud seat
425 Of *Lucifer*, so by allusion call'd,
Of that bright Star to *Satan* paragon'd.°   *compared*
There kept thir Watch the Legions, while the Grand
In Council sat, solicitous° what chance   *anxious*
Might intercept thir Emperor sent, so hee
430 Departing gave command, and they observ'd.
As when the Tartar from his *Russian* Foe

---

3. The planets are stricken by an adverse influence. Stars are literally struck when Phaethon's pride leads him to drive his father Apollo's sun-chariot on an unnatural course through the heavens; see Ovid's *Metamorphoses* 2.205.
4. Sin and Death.

By *Astracan*[5] over the Snowy Plains
Retires, or *Bactrian* Sophi[6] from the horns
Of *Turkish* Crescent,[7] leaves all waste beyond
435   The Realm of *Aladule*,[8] in his retreat
To *Tauris* or *Casbeen*:[9] So these the late
Heav'n-banisht Host, left desert utmost Hell
Many a dark League, reduc't in careful Watch
Round thir Metropolis, and now expecting
440   Each hour their great adventurer from the search
Of Foreign Worlds: he through the midst unmark't,
In show Plebeian Angel militant
Of lowest order, pass't; and from the door
Of that *Plutonian*[1] Hall, invisible
445   Ascended his high Throne, which under state°   canopy
Of richest texture spread, at th' upper end
Was plac't in regal lustre. Down a while
He sat, and round about him saw unseen:
At last as from a Cloud his fulgent head
450   And shape Star-bright appear'd, or brighter, clad
With what permissive glory since his fall
Was left him, or false glitter: All amaz'd
At that so sudden blaze the Stygian throng
Bent thir aspect, and whom they wish'd beheld,
455   Thir mighty Chief return'd: loud was th' acclaim:
Forth rush'd in haste the great consulting Peers,
Rais'd from thir dark *Divan*,[2] and with like joy
Congratulant approach'd him, who with hand
Silence, and with these words attention won.
460   Thrones, Dominations, Princedoms, Virtues, Powers,
For in possession such, not only of right,
I call ye and declare ye now, return'd
Successful beyond hope, to lead ye forth
Triumphant out of this infernal Pit
465   Abominable, accurst, the house of woe,
And Dungeon of our Tyrant: Now possess,
As Lords, a spacious World, to our native Heaven
Little inferior, by my adventure hard
With peril great achiev'd. Long were to tell
470   What I have done, what suffer'd, with what pain
Voyag'd th' unreal, vast, unbounded deep
Of horrible confusion, over which
By Sin and Death a broad way now is pav'd
To expedite your glorious march; but I

---

5. Astracan, or Astrakhan, was a Tartar kingdom and capital city near the mouth of the Volga.
6. Persian king.
7. Refers not only to the Turkish ensign, but also to their battle formations.

8. Greater Armenia.
9. Tauris (modern Tabriz) is in the extreme northwest of Persia; Casbeen, or Kazvin, is north of Teheran.
1. Pertaining to Pluto, ruler of the classical underworld.
2. Turkish council of state.

475	Toil'd out my úncouth° passage, forc't to ride	*strange*
	Th' untractable Abyss, plung'd in the womb	
	Of unoriginal° *Night* and *Chaos* wild,	*uncreated*
	That jealous of thir secrets fiercely oppos'd	
	My journey strange, with clamorous uproar	
480	Protesting Fate supreme; thence how I found	
	The new created World, which fame in Heav'n	
	Long had foretold, a Fabric wonderful	
	Of absolute perfection, therein Man	
	Plac't in a Paradise, by our exile	
485	Made happy: Him by fraud I have seduc'd	
	From his Creator, and the more to increase	
	Your wonder, with an Apple; he thereat	
	Offended, worth your laughter, hath giv'n up	
	Both his beloved Man and all his World,	
490	To Sin and Death a prey, and so to us,	
	Without our hazard, labor, or alarm,	
	To range in, and to dwell, and over Man	
	To rule, as over all he should have rul'd.	
	True is, mee also he hath judg'd, or rather	
495	Mee not, but the brute Serpent in whose shape	
	Man I deceiv'd: that which to mee belongs,	
	Is enmity, which he will put between	
	Mee and Mankind; I am to bruise his heel;	
	His Seed, when is not set, shall bruise my head:	
500	A World who would not purchase with a bruise,	
	Or much more grievous pain? Ye have th' account	
	Of my performance: What remains, ye Gods,	
	But up and enter now into full bliss.	
	So having said, a while he stood, expecting	
505	Thir universal shout and high applause	
	To fill his ear, when contrary he hears	
	On all sides, from innumerable tongues	
	A dismal universal hiss, the sound	
	Of public scorn; he wonder'd, but not long	
510	Had leisure, wond'ring at himself now more;	
	His Visage drawn he felt to sharp and spare,	
	His Arms clung to his Ribs, his Legs entwining	
	Each other, till supplanted° down he fell	*tripped*
	A monstrous Serpent on his Belly prone,[3]	
515	Reluctant,° but in vain: a greater power	*resisting*
	Now rul'd him, punisht in the shape he sinn'd,	
	According to his doom: he would have spoke,	
	But hiss for hiss return'd with forked tongue	
	To forked tongue, for now were all transform'd	
520	Alike, to Serpents all as accessories	

3. See the metamorphosis of Cadmus in Ovid, *Metamorphoses* 4.572–603, and the mutual interchange of serpentine forms in Dante's canto of the thieves, *Inferno* 25.

To his bold Riot: dreadful was the din
Of hissing through the Hall, thick swarming now
With complicated° monsters, head and tail,   *compound*
Scorpion and Asp, and *Amphisbaena* dire,
525   *Cerastes* horn'd, *Hydrus*, and *Ellops* drear,
And *Dipsas*⁴ (not so thick swarm'd once the Soil
Bedropt with blood of *Gorgon*, or the Isle
Ophiusa) but still greatest hee the midst,⁵
Now Dragon grown, larger than whom the Sun
530   Ingender'd in the *Pythian* Vale on slime,
Huge *Python*, and his Power no less he seem'd
Above the rest still to retain;⁶ they all
Him follow'd issuing forth to th' open Field,
Where all yet left of that revolted Rout
535   Heav'n-fall'n, in station stood or just array,
Sublime° with expectation when to see   *uplifted*
In Triumph issuing forth thir glorious Chief;
They saw, but other sight instead, a crowd
Of ugly Serpents; horror on them fell,
540   And horrid sympathy; for what they saw,
They felt themselves now changing; down thir arms,
Down fell both Spear and Shield, down they as fast,
And the dire hiss renew'd, and the dire form
Catcht by Contagion, like in punishment,
545   As in thir crime. Thus was th' applause they meant,
Turn'd to exploding hiss, triumph to shame
Cast on themselves from thir own mouths. There stood
A Grove hard by, sprung up with this thir change,
His will who reigns above, to aggravate
550   Thir penance, laden with fair Fruit, like that
Which grew in Paradise, the bait of *Eve*
Us'd by the Tempter: on that prospect strange
Thir earnest eyes they fix'd, imagining
For one forbidden Tree a multitude
555   Now ris'n, to work them furder° woe or shame;   *further*
Yet parcht with scalding thirst and hunger fierce,
Though to delude them sent, could not abstain,
But on they roll'd in heaps, and up the Trees
Climbing, sat thicker than the snaky locks
560   That curl'd *Megaera*:⁷ greedily they pluck'd
The Fruitage fair to sight, like that which grew

---

4. The amphisbaena is a serpent with a head at either end. The cerastes has four horns on its head. The hydrus is a water snake. The ellops, though sometimes identified as the swordfish, is mentioned as a serpent in Pliny, *Natural History* 32.5. The dipsas causes raging thirst by its bite.

5. When Perseus was bringing back the severed head of Medusa, drops of blood fell to earth and became serpents. "Ophiusa" means literally "full of serpents"; a name an-

ciently given to several islands, including Rhodes and one of the Balearic group.

6. For the birth of Python from the slime remaining after the flood, see Ovid, *Metamorphoses* 1.438–40. Python was slain by Apollo. Satan's dragon shape is that of the "old dragon" of Christian apocalypse; see Revelation 12.9: "the great dragon was cast out, that old serpent, called the Devil, and Satan."

7. One of the Furies, often described as snaky-haired.

Near that bituminous Lake where *Sodom* flam'd;[8]
This more delusive, not the touch, but taste
Deceiv'd; they fondly thinking to allay
565   Thir appetite with gust,° instead of Fruit   *taste*
Chew'd bitter Ashes, which th' offended taste
With spattering noise rejected: oft they assay'd,
Hunger and thirst constraining, drugg'd° as oft,   *nauseated*
With hatefullest disrelish writh'd thir jaws
570   With soot and cinders fill'd; so oft they fell
Into the same illusion, not as Man
Whom they triumph'd, once lapst. Thus were they plagu'd
And worn with Famine long, and ceaseless hiss,
Till thir lost shape, permitted, they resum'd,
575   Yearly enjoin'd, some say, to undergo
This annual humbling certain number'd days,
To dash thir pride, and joy for Man seduc't.
However some tradition they dispers'd
Among the Heathen of thir purchase got,
580   And Fabl'd how the Serpent, whom they call'd
Ophion with *Eurynome*, the wide-
Encroaching *Eve* perhaps, had first the rule
Of high *Olympus*, thence by Saturn driv'n
And Ops, ere yet *Dictaean Jove* was born.[9]
585   Meanwhile in Paradise the hellish pair
Too soon arriv'd, *Sin* there in power before,
Once actual, now in body, and to dwell
Habitual habitant; behind her *Death*
Close following pace for pace, not mounted yet
590   On his pale Horse:[1] to whom *Sin* thus began.
    Second of *Satan* sprung, all conquering *Death*,
What think'st thou of our Empire now, though earn'd
With travail difficult, not better far
Than still at Hell's dark threshold to have sat watch,
595   Unnam'd, undreaded, and thyself half starv'd?
    Whom thus the Sin-born Monster answer'd soon.
To mee, who with eternal Famine pine,
Alike is Hell, or Paradise, or Heaven,
There best, where most with ravin I may meet;
600   Which here, though plenteous, all too little seems
To stuff this Maw, this vast unhide-bound Corpse.
    To whom th' incestuous Mother thus repli'd.
Thou therefore on these Herbs, and Fruits, and Flow'rs
Feed first, on each Beast next, and Fish, and Fowl,

---

8. The allusion is to Josephus, *Wars* 4.8.4, where it is said that traces still remain of the divine fire that burnt Sodom, such as tasty-looking fruits that turned to ashes when plucked.
9. Ophion and Eurynome ruled Olympus until the one yielded to Cronos (Saturn) and the other to Rhea (Ops).

Their two successors then ruled the Titans, while Zeus lived in the Dictaean cave. See Apollonius Rhodius, *Argonautica* 1.503–9.
1. See Revelation 6.8: "I looked, and behold a pale horse: and his name that sat on him was Death, and Hell followed with him."

605   No homely morsels, and whatever thing
       The Scythe of Time mows down, devour unspar'd,
       Till I in Man residing through the Race,
       His thoughts, his looks, words, actions all infect,
       And season him thy last and sweetest prey.
610   This said, they both betook them several ways,
       Both to destroy, or unimmortal make
       All kinds, and for destruction to mature
       Sooner or later; which th' Almighty seeing
       From his transcendent Seat the Saints among,
615   To those bright Orders utter'd thus his voice.
           See with what heat these Dogs of Hell advance
       To waste and havoc° yonder World, which I   devastate
       So fair and good created, and had still
       Kept in that state, had not the folly of Man
620   Let in these wasteful Furies, who impute
       Folly to mee, so doth the Prince of Hell
       And his Adherents, that with so much ease
       I suffer them to enter and possess
       A place so heav'nly, and conniving seem
625   To gratify my scornful Enemies,
       That laugh, as if transported with some fit
       Of Passion, I to them had quitted° all,   yielded
       At random yielded up to their misrule;
       And know not that I call'd and drew them thither
630   My Hell-hounds, to lick up the draff° and filth   refuse
       Which man's polluting Sin with taint hath shed
       On what was pure, till cramm'd and gorg'd, nigh burst
       With suckt and glutted offal, at one sling
       Of thy victorious Arm, well-pleasing Son,
635   Both *Sin*, and *Death*, and yawning *Grave* at last
       Through *Chaos* hurl'd, obstruct the mouth of Hell
       For ever, and seal up his ravenous Jaws.
       Then Heav'n and Earth renew'd shall be made pure
       To sanctity that shall receive no stain:
640   Till then the Curse pronounc't on both precedes.[2]
           He ended, and the heav'nly Audience loud
       Sung *Halleluiah*, as the sound of Seas,
       Through multitude that sung: Just are thy ways,
       Righteous are thy Decrees on all thy Works;
645   Who can extenuate° thee? Next, to the Son,   disparage
       Destin'd restorer of Mankind, by whom
       New Heav'n and Earth shall to the Ages rise,
       Or down from Heav'n descend. Such was thir song,
       While the Creator calling forth by name
650   His mighty Angels gave them several charge,

2. See Genesis 3.17: "Cursed is the ground for thy sake."

	As sorted° best with present things. The Sun	*accorded*
	Had first his precept° so to move, so shine,	*order*
	As might affect the Earth with cold and heat	
	Scarce tolerable, and from the North to call	
655	Decrepit Winter, from the South to bring	
	Solstitial summer's[3] heat. To the blanc° Moon	*pale*
	Her office they prescrib'd, to th' other five°	*planets*
	Thir planetary motions and aspects	
	In *Sextile, Square,* and *Trine,* and *Opposite,*[4]	
660	Of noxious efficacy, and when to join	
	In Synod° unbenign, and taught the fixt	*conjunction*
	Thir influence malignant when to show'r,[5]	
	Which of them rising with the Sun, or falling,	
	Should prove tempestuous: To the Winds they set	
665	Thir corners, when with bluster to confound	
	Sea, Air, and Shore, the Thunder when to roll	
	With terror through the dark Aereal Hall.	
	Some say he bid his Angels turn askance	
	The Poles of Earth twice ten degrees and more	
670	From the Sun's Axle; they with labor push'd	
	Oblique the Centric Globe: Some say[6] the Sun	
	Was bid turn Reins from th' Equinoctial Road	
	Like distant breadth to *Taurus* with the Sev'n	
	Atlantic Sisters, and the *Spartan* Twins	
675	Up to the *Tropic* Crab,[7] thence down amain°	*at full speed*
	By *Leo* and the *Virgin* and the *Scales,*	
	As deep as *Capricorn,* to bring in change	
	Of Seasons to each Clime; else had the Spring	
	Perpetual smil'd on Earth with vernant° Flow'rs,	*flourishing*
680	Equal in Days and Nights, except to those	
	Beyond the Polar Circles; to them Day	
	Had unbenighted shone, while the low Sun	
	To recompense his distance, in thir sight	
	Had rounded still th' *Horizon,* and not known	
685	Or East or West, which had forbid the Snow	
	From cold *Estotiland* and South as far	
	Beneath *Magellan.*[8] At that tasted Fruit	
	The Sun, as from *Thyestean* Banquet, turn'd	

3. God commands the angels to make the earth turn on its axis and so cause the change of seasons, and to disrupt the order of the planets, making their effect on the world negative as well as positive. Milton's own, invented pre-Fall cosmos thus gives way to the Ptolemaic, Copernican, and other post-Fall systems.

4. Sextile and trine are harmonious astrological aspects, while quartile and opposition are disharmonious — as a result of the Fall.

5. The "fixed" (stars) exerted "sweet influence" when first created (7.375).

6. The first alternative accords with heliocentric theories, the second with geocentric; Milton does not decide.

7. The Atlantic sisters are the Pleiades, daughters of Atlas, a group within the constellation Taurus. The Spartan Twins are Castor and Pollux, sons of King Tyndarus of Sparta; the zodiacal constellation (and sign) Gemini.

8. "Estotiland" was used vaguely for northeast Labrador, relevant to Hudson's search for a northwest passage in 1610. "Magellan" is not necessarily the straits of Magellan: modern Argentina was labelled Magellonica.

His course intended;[9] else how had the World
690 Inhabited, though sinless, more than now,
Avoided pinching cold and scorching heat?
These changes in the Heav'ns, though slow, produc'd
Like change on Sea and Land, sideral° blast,   *from the stars*
Vapor, and Mist, and Exhalation° hot,   *meteor*
695 Corrupt and Pestilent: Now from the North
Of *Norumbega,* and the *Samoed* shore[1]
Bursting thir brazen Dungeon, arm'd with ice
And snow and hail and stormy gust and flaw,°   *sudden squall*
Boreas and *Cæcias* and *Argesles* loud
700 And *Thrascias* rend the Woods and Seas upturn;
With adverse blast upturns them from the South
Notus and *Afer* black with thundrous Clouds
From *Serraliona;*° thwart of these as fierce   *Sierra Leone*
Forth rush the *Levant* and the *Ponent* Winds
705 *Eurus* and *Zephir* with thir lateral noise,
Sirocco, and *Libecchio.* Thus began
Outrage from lifeless things; but Discord first
Daughter of Sin, among th' irrational,
Death introduc'd through fierce antipathy:
710 Beast now with Beast gan war, and Fowl with Fowl,
And Fish with Fish; to graze the Herb all leaving,
Devour'd each other; nor stood much in awe
Of Man, but fled him, or with count'nance grim
Glar'd on him passing: these were from without
715 The growing miseries, which *Adam* saw
Already in part, though hid in gloomiest shade,
To sorrow abandon'd, but worse felt within,
And in a troubl'd Sea of passion tost,
Thus to disburd'n sought with sad complaint.
720   O miserable of happy! is this the end
Of this new glorious World, and mee so late
The Glory of that Glory, who now become
Accurst of blessed, hide me from the face
Of God, whom to behold was then my highth
725 Of happiness: yet well, if here would end
The misery, I deserv'd it, and would
My own deservings; but this will not serve;
All that I eat or drink, or shall beget,

---

9. Thyestes seduced Aerope, his brother's wife. In revenge, Atreus invited Thyestes to a reconciliation banquet and served up to him his child's flesh. The sun
changed course to avoid seeing an act so obscene. See
Seneca, *Thyestes* 776ff.
1. Milton's catalogue of winds begins with Norumbega,
modern-day southeast Canada and northeast United States.

Samoed is northeast Siberia. The "brazen Dungeon"
refers to Virgil's *Aeneid* 1.50ff, where Aeolus imprisons
the winds in a cave. There are 11 winds in all: the four
northern are Boreas, Caecias, Argestes, and Thrascias.
These oppose two adverse southern winds, Notus and
Afer. The five lateral east-west winds are Levant, Eurus,
Zephir, Sirocco, and Libecchio.

Is propagated curse.[2] O voice once heard
730   Delightfully, *Increase and multiply*,[3]
Now death to hear! for what can I increase
Or multiply, but curses on my head?
Who of all Ages to succeed, but feeling
The evil on him brought by me, will curse
735   My Head; Ill fare our Ancestor impure,
For this we may thank *Adam*; but his thanks
Shall be the execration; so besides
Mine own that bide upon me, all from mee
Shall with a fierce reflux on mee redound,°   overflow, come back
740   On mee as on thir natural centre light
Heavy, though in thir place. O fleeting joys
Of Paradise, dear bought with lasting woes!
Did I request thee, Maker, from my Clay
To mould me Man, did I solicit thee
745   From darkness to promote me, or here place
In this delicious Garden? as my Will
Concurr'd not to my being, it were but right
And equal° to reduce me to my dust,   just
Desirous to resign, and render back
750   All I receiv'd, unable to perform
Thy terms too hard, by which I was to hold
The good I sought not. To the loss of that,
Sufficient penalty, why hast thou added
The sense of endless woes? inexplicable
755   Thy Justice seems; yet to say truth, too late
I thus contest; then should have been refus'd
Those terms whatever, when they were propos'd:
Thou didst accept them; wilt thou enjoy the good,
Then cavil the conditions? and though God
760   Made thee without thy leave, what if thy Son
Prove disobedient, and reprov'd, retort,
Wherefore didst thou beget me? I sought it not:
Wouldst thou admit for his contempt of thee
That proud excuse? yet him not thy election,°   choice
765   But Natural necessity begot.
God made thee of choice his own, and of his own
To serve him, thy reward was of his grace,
Thy punishment then justly is at his Will.
Be it so, for I submit, his doom° is fair,   judgment
770   That dust I am, and shall to dust return:[4]
O welcome hour whenever! why delays
His hand to execute what his Decree
Fix'd on this day? why do I overlive,

2. Handed down from one generation to another. Food prolongs life and thus extends the curse, while begetting children hands it on. Note also that eating and sex are jointly the concerns of the concupiscible faculty, which was often regarded as the special field of operation of concupiscence or the "body of sin."
3. See Genesis 1.28.
4. Alluding to Genesis 3.19.

Why am I mockt with death, and length'n'd out
775   To deathless pain? How gladly would I meet
Mortality my sentence, and be Earth
Insensible, how glad would lay me down
As in my Mother's lap![5] There I should rest
And sleep secure; his dreadful voice no more
780   Would Thunder in my ears, no fear of worse
To mee and to my offspring would torment me
With cruel expectation. Yet one doubt
Pursues me still, lest all I cannot die,
Lest that pure breath of Life, the Spirit of Man
785   Which God inspir'd, cannot together perish
With this corporeal Clod; then in the Grave,
Or in some other dismal place, who knows
But I shall die a living Death? O thought
Horrid, if true! yet why? it was but breath
790   Of Life that sinn'd; what dies but what had life
And sin? the Body properly hath neither.
All of me then shall die:[6] let this appease
The doubt, since human reach no further knows.
For though the Lord of all be infinite,
795   Is his wrath also? be it, Man is not so,
But mortal doom'd. How can he exercise
Wrath without end on Man whom Death must end?
Can he make deathless Death? that were to make
Strange contradiction, which to God himself
800   Impossible is held, as Argument
Of weakness, not of Power. Will he draw out,
For anger's sake, finite to infinite
In punisht Man, to satisfy his rigor
Satisfi'd never; that were to extend
805   His Sentence beyond dust and Nature's Law,
By which all Causes else according still
To the reception of thir matter act,
Not to th' extent of thir own Sphere.[7] But say
That Death be not one stroke, as I suppos'd,
810   Bereaving sense, but endless misery
From this day onward, which I feel begun
Both in me, and without me, and so last
To perpetuity; Ay me, that fear
Comes thund'ring back with dreadful revolution

5. Adam's lament echoes Job 3.
6. Adam's question is like Milton's in *De doctrina* 1.13: "What could be more absurd than that the mind, which is the part principally offending, should escape the threatened death; and that the body alone, to which immortality was equally allotted, before death came into the world by sin, should pay the penalty of sin by undergoing death, though not implicated in the transgression?"

Milton's belief in the joint extinction and joint resurrection of man's body and mind was not an eccentric heresy but good biblical theology.
7. Adam tries to comfort himself with an argument drawn from medieval philosophy. Here Adam means that God would be going beyond a natural law, that any agent acts according to the powers of what receives its action, not according to its own powers.

815 On my defenseless head; both Death and I
Am found Eternal, and incorporate° both,   *united, embodied*
Nor I on my part single, in mee all
Posterity stands curst:[8] Fair Patrimony
That I must leave ye, Sons; O were I able
820 To waste it all myself, and leave ye none!
So disinherited how would ye bless
Me now your Curse! Ah, why should all mankind
For one man's fault thus guiltless be condemn'd,
If guiltless? But from me what can proceed,
825 But all corrupt, both Mind and Will deprav'd,
Not to do only, but to will the same
With me? how can they then acquitted stand
In sight of God? Him after all Disputes
Forc't I absolve: all my evasions vain
830 And reasonings, though through Mazes, lead me still
But to my own conviction:[9] first and last
On mee, mee only, as the source and spring
Of all corruption, all the blame lights due;
So might the wrath. Fond wish! couldst thou support
835 That burden heavier than the Earth to bear,
Than all the World much heavier, though divided
With that bad Woman? Thus what thou desir'st,
And what thou fear'st, alike destroys all hope
Of refuge, and concludes thee miserable
840 Beyond all past example and futúre,
To *Satan* only like both crime and doom.
O Conscience, into what Abyss of fears
And horrors hast thou driv'n me; out of which
I find no way, from deep to deeper plung'd!
845   Thus *Adam* to himself lamented loud
Through the still Night, not now, as ere man fell,
Wholesome and cool and mild, but with black Air
Accompanied, with damps and dreadful gloom,
Which to his evil Conscience represented
850 All things with double terror: On the ground
Outstretcht he lay, on the cold ground, and oft
Curs'd his Creation, Death as oft accus'd
Of tardy execution, since denounc't
The day of his offense. Why comes not Death,
855 Said he, with one thrice àcceptable stroke
To end me? Shall Truth fail to keep her word,
Justice Divine not hast'n to be just?
But Death comes not at call, Justice Divine

---

8. Not only are Death and I double, two in one, but so also am I, since I am both myself and my descendants.
9. Adam at last reaches full conviction of his sin, but being unable yet to pass to contrition, the next stage of re-pentance, he falls instead into despair. The present passage should be compared with Satan's similar fall into conscience-stricken despair at 4.86–113.

Mends not her slowest pace for prayers or cries.
860   O Woods, O Fountains, Hillocks, Dales and Bow'rs,
With other echo late I taught your Shades
To answer, and resound far other Song.
Whom thus afflicted when sad Eve beheld,
Desolate where she sat, approaching nigh,
865   Soft words to his fierce passion she assay'd:
But her with stern regard he thus repell'd.
        Out of my sight, thou Serpent, that name best
Befits thee with him leagu'd, thyself as false
And hateful; nothing wants, but that thy shape,
870   Like his, and color Serpentine may show
Thy inward fraud, to warn all Creatures from thee
Henceforth; lest that too heav'nly form, pretended[1]
To hellish falsehood, snare them. But for thee
I had persisted happy, had not thy pride
875   And wand'ring vanity, when least was safe,
Rejected my forewarning, and disdain'd
Not to be trusted, longing to be seen
Though by the Devil himself, him overweening
To over-reach, but with the Serpent meeting
880   Fool'd and beguil'd, by him thou, I by thee,
To trust thee from my side, imagin'd wise,
Constant, mature, proof against all assaults,
And understood not all was but a show
Rather than solid virtue, all but a Rib
885   Crooked by nature, bent, as now appears,
More to the part sinister[2] from me drawn,
Well if thrown out, as supernumerary
To my just number found. O why did God,
Creator wise, that peopl'd highest Heav'n
890   With Spirits Masculine, create at last
This novelty on Earth, this fair defect
Of Nature, and not fill the World at once
With Men as Angels without Feminine,
Or find some other way to generate
895   Mankind?[3] this mischief had not then befall'n,
And more that shall befall, innumerable
Disturbances on Earth through Female snares,
And strait conjunction with this Sex: for either
He never shall find out fit Mate, but such
900   As some misfortune brings him, or mistake,
Or whom he wishes most shall seldom gain
Through her perverseness, but shall see her gain'd

---

1. Stretched in front as a covering serving as a mask.
2. Left; also corrupt, evil, base. The notion that woman is formed from a bent rib, and therefore crooked, had appeared in tracts like Joseph Swetnam's *The Arraignment of*

Lewd, Idle, Froward, and Unconstant Women (page 1447).
3. Another ancient piece of antifeminism; see Euripides, *Hippolytus* 616ff. Aristotle had said in the *De generatione* that the female is a defective male.

By a far worse, or if she love, withheld
By Parents, or his happiest choice too late
905 Shall meet, already linkt and Wedlock-bound
To a fell° Adversary, his hate or shame: *bitter*
Which infinite calamity shall cause
To Human life, and household peace confound.
  He added not, and from her turn'd, but *Eve*
910 Not so repulst, with Tears that ceas'd not flowing,
And tresses all disorder'd, at his feet
Fell humble, and imbracing them, besought
His peace, and thus proceeded in her plaint.
  Forsake me not thus, *Adam*, witness Heav'n
915 What love sincere, and reverence in my heart
I bear thee, and unweeting° have offended,   *unintentionally*
Unhappily deceiv'd; thy suppliant
I beg, and clasp thy knees; bereave me not,
Whereon I live, thy gentle looks, thy aid,
920 Thy counsel in this uttermost distress,
My only strength and stay: forlorn of thee,
Whither shall I betake me, where subsist?
While yet we live, scarce one short hour perhaps,
Between us two let there be peace, both joining,
925 As join'd in injuries, one enmity
Against a Foe by doom express assign'd us,
That cruel Serpent: On me exercise not
Thy hatred for this misery befall'n,
On me already lost, mee than thyself
930 More miserable; both have sinn'd, but thou
Against God only, I against God and thee,
And to the place of judgment will return,
There with my cries importune Heaven, that all
The sentence from thy head remov'd may light
935 On me, sole cause to thee of all this woe,
Mee mee only just object of his ire.
  She ended weeping, and her lowly plight,
Immovable till peace obtain'd from fault
Acknowledg'd and deplor'd,[4] in *Adam* wrought
940 Commiseration; soon his heart relented
Towards her, his life so late and sole delight,
Now at his feet submissive in distress,
Creature so fair his reconcilement seeking,
His counsel whom she had displeas'd, his aid;
945 As one disarm'd, his anger all he lost,
And thus with peaceful words uprais'd her soon.
  Unwary, and too desirous, as before,
So now of what thou know'st not, who desir'st

4. Eve cannot be moved from Adam's feet until he forgives her.

The punishment all on thyself; alas,
950   Bear thine own first, ill able to sustain
His full wrath whose thou feel'st as yet least part,
And my displeasure bear'st so ill. If Prayers
Could alter high Decrees, I to that place
Would speed before thee, and be louder heard,
955   That on my head all might be visited,
Thy frailty and infirmer Sex forgiv'n,
To me committed and by me expos'd.
But rise, let us no more contend, nor blame
Each other, blam'd enough elsewhere,[5] but strive
960   In offices of Love, how we may light'n
Each other's burden in our share of woe;
Since this day's Death denounc't, if aught I see,
Will prove no sudden, but a slow-pac't evil,
A long day's dying to augment our pain,
965   And to our Seed (O hapless Seed!) deriv'd.
      To whom thus *Eve*, recovering heart, repli'd.
Adam, by sad experiment I know
How little weight my words with thee can find,
Found so erroneous, thence by just event°   consequence
970   Found so unfortunate; nevertheless,
Restor'd by thee, vile as I am, to place
Of new acceptance, hopeful to regain
Thy Love, the sole contentment of my heart
Living or dying, from thee I will not hide
975   What thoughts in my unquiet breast are ris'n,
Tending to some relief of our extremes,
Or end, though sharp and sad, yet tolerable,
As in our evils, and of easier choice.
If care of our descent° perplex° us most,   descendants / torment
980   Which must be born to certain woe, devour'd
By Death at last, and miserable it is
To be to other cause of misery,
Our own begott'n, and of our Loins to bring
Into this cursed World a woeful Race,
985   That after wretched Life must be at last
Food for so foul a Monster, in thy power
It lies, yet ere Conception to prevent
The Race unblest, to being yet unbegot.
Childless thou art, Childless remain: So Death
990   Shall be deceiv'd his glut, and with us two
Be forc'd to satisfy his Rav'nous Maw.
But if thou judge it hard and difficult,
Conversing, looking, loving, to abstain
From Love's due Rites, Nuptial embraces sweet,

---

5. Either "heaven" or the "place of judgment" of line 932.

995   And with desire to languish without hope,[6]
      Before the present object° languishing   *Eve*
      With like desire, which would be misery
      And torment less than none of what we dread,
      Then both ourselves and Seed at once to free
1000 From what we fear for both, let us make short,
      Let us seek Death, or he not found, supply
      With our own hands his Office on ourselves;
      Why stand we longer shivering under fears,
      That show no end but Death, and have the power,
1005 Of many ways to die the shortest choosing,
      Destruction with destruction to destroy.
          She ended here, or vehement despair
      Broke off the rest; so much of Death her thoughts
      Had entertain'd, as dy'd her Cheeks with pale.
1010 But *Adam* with such counsel nothing sway'd,
      To better hopes his more attentive mind
      Laboring had rais'd, and thus to *Eve* replied.
          Eve, thy contempt of life and pleasure seems
      To argue in thee something more sublime
1015 And excellent than what thy mind contemns;
      But self-destruction therefore sought, refutes
      That excellence thought in thee, and implies,
      Not thy contempt, but anguish and regret
      For loss of life and pleasure overlov'd.
1020 Or if thou covet death, as utmost end
      Of misery, so thinking to evade
      The penalty pronounc't, doubt not but God
      Hath wiselier arm'd his vengeful ire than so
      To be forestall'd; much more I fear lest Death
1025 So snatcht will not exempt us from the pain
      We are by doom to pay; rather such acts
      Of contumacy° will provoke the Highest   *contempt*
      To make death in us live: Then let us seek
      Some safer resolution, which methinks
1030 I have in view, calling to mind with heed
      Part of our Sentence, that thy Seed shall bruise
      The Serpent's head; piteous amends, unless
      Be meant, whom I conjecture, our grand Foe
      Satan, who in the Serpent hath contriv'd
1035 Against us this deceit: to crush his head
      Would be revenge indeed; which will be lost
      By death brought on ourselves, or childless days
      Resolv'd, as thou proposest; so our Foe
      Shall 'scape his punishment ordain'd, and wee
1040 Instead shall double ours upon our heads.

6. See Dante, *Inferno* 4.42: "without hope we live in desire."

No more be mention'd then of violence
Against ourselves, and wilful barrenness,
That cuts us off from hope, and savors only
Rancor and pride, impatience and despite,
1045 Reluctance° against God and his just yoke   resistance
Laid on our Necks. Remember with what mild
And gracious temper he both heard and judg'd
Without wrath or reviling; wee expected
Immediate dissolution, which we thought
1050 Was meant by Death that day, when lo, to thee
Pains only in Child-bearing were foretold,
And bringing forth, soon recompens't with joy,
Fruit of thy Womb: On mee the Curse aslope
Glanc'd on the ground, with labor I must earn
1055 My bread;[7] what harm? Idleness had been worse;
My labor will sustain me; and lest Cold
Or Heat should injure us, his timely care
Hath unbesought provided, and his hands
Cloth'd us unworthy, pitying while he judg'd;
1060 How much more, if we pray him, will his ear
Be open, and his heart to pity incline,[8]
And teach us further by what means to shun
Th' inclement Seasons, Rain, Ice, Hail and Snow,
Which now the Sky with various Face begins
1065 To show us in this Mountain, while the Winds
Blow moist and keen, shattering the graceful locks
Of these fair spreading Trees; which bids us seek
Some better shroud,° some better warmth to cherish   shelter
Our Limbs benumb'd, ere this diurnal Star[9]
1070 Leave cold the Night, how we his gather'd beams
Reflected, may with matter sere foment,[1]
Or by collision of two bodies grind
The Air attrite° to Fire, as late the Clouds   ground down
Justling° or pusht with Winds rude in thir shock   jostling
1075 Tine° the slant Lightning, whose thwart flame driv'n down   ignite
Kindles the gummy bark of Fir or Pine,
And sends a comfortable heat from far,
Which might supply° the Sun: such Fire to use,   take the place of
And what may else be remedy or cure
1080 To evils which our own misdeeds have wrought,
Hee will instruct us praying, and of Grace
Beseeching him, so as we need not fear
To pass commodiously this life, sustain'd
By him with many comforts, till we end

---

7. Referring to Christ's words at lines 201–5.
8. Biblical diction; see Psalms 24.4, 119.36, 112, and 1
Peter 3.12.
9. The sun.

1. Cherish; but alluding also to Latin *fomes* (tinder).
Adam envisages making fire: focusing the sun's rays onto
dry combustibles ("matter sere") with a parabolic mirror.

1085   In dust, our final rest and native home.
     What better can we do, than to the place
     Repairing where he judg'd us, prostrate fall
     Before him reverent, and there confess
     Humbly our faults, and pardon beg, with tears
1090   Watering the ground, and with our sighs the Air
     Frequenting,° sent from hearts contrite, in sign   *filling*
     Of sorrow unfeign'd, and humiliation meek.[2]
     Undoubtedly he will relent and turn
     From his displeasure; in whose look serene,
1095   When angry most he seem'd and most severe,
     What else but favor, grace, and mercy shone?
        So spake our Father penitent, nor Eve
     Felt less remorse: they forthwith to the place
     Repairing where he judg'd them prostrate fell
1100   Before him reverent, and both confess'd
     Humbly thir faults, and pardon begg'd, with tears
     Watering the ground, and with thir sighs the Air
     Frequenting, sent from hearts contrite, in sign
     Of sorrow unfeign'd, and humiliation meek.[3]
            The End of the Tenth Book.

Book 11
The Argument

The Son of God present to his Father the Prayers of our first Parents now repenting, and intercedes for them: God accepts them, but declares that they must no longer abide in Paradise; sends Michael with a Band of Cherubim to dispossess them; but first to reveal to Adam future things; Michael's coming down. Adam shows to Eve certain ominous signs; he discerns Michael's approach, goes out to meet him: the Angel denounces thir departure. Eve's Lamentation. Adam pleads, but submits: The Angel leads him up to a high Hill, sets before him in vision what shall happ'n till the Flood.

     Thus they in lowliest plight repentant stood
     Praying, for from the Mercy-seat above
     Prevenient Grace descending had remov'd
     The stony from thir hearts,[1] and made new flesh
5   Regenerate grow instead, that sighs now breath'd
     Unutterable, which the Spirit of prayer
     Inspir'd, and wing'd for Heav'n with speedier flight
     Than loudest Oratory: yet thir port°   *bearing*
     Not of mean suitors, nor important less
10   Seem'd thir Petition, than when th' ancient Pair

---

2. Having passed on from conviction of sin Adam, now "contrite" (line 1103), is ready for confession, the third stage of repentance. An allusion to the Penitential Psalm: "The sacrifices of God are a broken spirit: a broken and a contrite heart, O God, thou wilt not despise" (Psalm 51.17).

3. Repeating lines 1086–92, modulated into narrative discourse (only the last two verses remain identical).
1. In Milton's Arminian view, grace precedes human choice. People remain free to accept grace or reject grace, but in neither case does it produce repentance.

In Fables old, less ancient yet than these,
Deucalion and chaste *Pyrrha* to restore
The Race of Mankind drown'd, before the Shrine
Of *Themis* stood devout.[2] To Heav'n thir prayers
15   Flew up, nor miss'd the way, by envious winds
Blown vagabond or frustrate: in they pass'd
Dimensionless through Heav'nly doors: then clad
With incense, where the Golden Altar fum'd,
By thir great Intercessor, came in sight
20   Before the Father's Throne: Then the glad Son
Presenting, thus to intercede began.
    See Father, what first fruits on Earth are sprung
From thy implanted Grace in Man, these Sighs
And Prayers, which in this Golden Censer, mixt
25   With Incense, I thy Priest before thee bring,
Fruits of more pleasing savor from thy seed
Sown with contrition in his heart, than those
Which his own hand manuring° all the Trees   *cultivating*
Of Paradise could have produc't, ere fall'n
30   From innocence.[3] Now therefore bend thine ear
To supplication, hear his sighs though mute;
Unskilful with what words to pray, let mee
Interpret for him, mee his Advocate
And propitiation,[4] all his works on mee
35   Good or not good ingraft, my Merit those
Shall perfet, and for these my Death shall pay.
Accept me, and in mee from these receive
The smell of peace toward Mankind, let him live
Before thee reconcil'd, at least his days
40   Number'd, though sad, till Death, his doom° (which I   *judgment*
To mitigate thus plead, not to reverse)
To better life shall yield him, where with mee
All my redeem'd may dwell in joy and bliss,
Made one with me as I with thee am one.
45   To whom the Father, without Cloud, serene.
All thy request for Man, accepted° Son,   *approved*
Obtain, all thy request was my Decree:
But longer in that Paradise to dwell,
The Law I gave to Nature him forbids:
50   Those pure immortal Elements that know
No gross, no unharmonious mixture foul,
Eject him tainted now, and purge him off

---

2. A mythic version of Noah's salvation, itself a type of Christ's. Advised by his father Prometheus, Deucalion built an ark and escaped the flood. When it subsided, he and Pyrrha consulted Themis, who told them to restore the race by throwing stones behind them, which became people.
3. Varying the parable of the sower (Mark 4.14–30),
with the help of Hebrews 13.15, "Let us offer the sacrifice of praise to God continually, that is, the fruit of our lips giving thanks to his name."
4. Echoing 1 John 2.1ff, "We have an advocate with the Father, Jesus Christ the righteous: And he is the propitiation of our sins."

As a distemper, gross to air as gross,
And mortal food, as may dispose him best
55 For dissolution wrought by Sin, that first
Distemper'd all things, and of incorrupt
Corrupted.[5] I at first with two fair gifts
Created him endow'd, with Happiness
And Immortality: that fondly° lost,   *foolishly*
60 This other serv'd but to eternize woe;
Till I provided Death; so Death becomes
His final remedy, and after Life
Tri'd in sharp tribulation, and refin'd
By Faith and faithful works,[6] to second Life,
65 Wak't in the renovation of the just,
Resigns him up with Heav'n and Earth renew'd.
But let us call to Synod° all the Blest   *assembly*
Through Heav'n's wide bounds; from them I will not hide
My judgments, how with Mankind I proceed,
70 As how with peccant° Angels late they saw;   *sinning*
And in thir state, though firm, stood more confirm'd.
He ended, and the Son gave signal high
To the bright Minister that watch'd: hee blew
His Trumpet, heard in *Oreb* since perhaps
75 When God descended,[7] and perhaps once more
To sound at general Doom. Th' Angelic blast
Fill'd all the Regions; from thir blissful Bow'rs
Of *Amarantin* Shade,[8] Fountain or Spring,
By the waters of Life, where'er they sat
80 In fellowships of joy, the Sons of Light
Hasted, resorting to the Summons high,
And took thir Seats; till from his Throne supreme
Th' Almighty thus pronounc'd his sovran Will.
O Sons, like one of us Man is become
85 To know both Good and Evil, since his taste
Of that defended° Fruit; but let him boast   *forbidden*
His knowledge of Good lost, and Evil got,
Happier, had it suffic'd him to have known
Good by itself, and Evil not at all.
90 He sorrows now, repents, and prays contrite,
My motions° in him; longer than they move,   *impulses*
His heart I know, how variable and vain
Self-left.° Lest therefore his now bolder hand   *left to itself*
Reach also of the Tree of Life, and eat,
95 And live for ever, dream at least to live

5. The expulsion is not punishment but a necessary consequence of the change in human nature.
6. Milton shared the general Protestant belief in justification by faith; see *De doctrina* 1.22, "we are justified by faith without the works of the law, but not without the works of faith."

7. Horeb, where God descended to the sound of a trumpet to deliver the ten commandments on Mt Sinai (Exodus 19.16).
8. The unwithering amaranth flower was a symbol of immortality; see 3.353n.

For ever, to remove him I decree,
And send him from the Garden forth to Till
The Ground whence he was taken, fitter soil.[9]
   Michael, this my behest have thou in charge,[1]
100   Take to thee from among the Cherubim
Thy choice of flaming Warriors, lest the Fiend
Or° in behalf of Man, or to invade   *Either*
Vacant possession[2] some new trouble raise:
Haste thee, and from the Paradise of God
105   Without remorse drive out the sinful Pair,
From hallow'd ground th' unholy, and denounce°   *proclaim*
To them and to thir Progeny from thence
Perpetual banishment. Yet lest they faint
At the sad Sentence rigorously urg'd,
110   For I behold them soft'nd and with tears
Bewailing thir excess,° all terror hide.   *transgression*
If patiently thy bidding they obey,
Dismiss them not disconsolate; reveal
To *Adam* what shall come in future days,
115   As I shall thee enlighten, intermix
My Cov'nant in the woman's seed renew'd;[3]
So send them forth, though sorrowing, yet in peace:
And on the East side of the Garden place,
Where entrance up from *Eden* easiest climbs,
120   Cherubic watch, and of a Sword the flame
Wide waving, all approach far off to fright,
And guard all passage to the Tree of Life:[4]
Lest Paradise a receptacle prove
To Spirits foul, and all my Trees thir prey,
125   With whose stol'n Fruit Man once more to delude.
   He ceas'd; and th' Archangelic Power prepar'd
For swift descent, with him the Cohort bright
Of watchful Cherubim; four faces each
Had, like a double *Janus,*[5] all thir shape
130   Spangl'd with eyes more numerous than those
Of *Argus,* and more wakeful than to drowse,
Charm'd with *Arcadian* Pipe, the Pastoral Reed
Of *Hermes,* or his opiate Rod.[6] Meanwhile
To resalute the World with sacred Light

---

9. Contrast with Genesis 3.22ff, "the Lord God said, Behold, the man is become as one of us, to know good and evil: and now, lest he put forth his hand, and take also of the tree of life, and eat, and live for ever: Therefore the Lord God sent him forth from the garden of Eden."
1. Michael was the angel of the apocalypse, and the history he shows Adam is ultimately apocalyptic.
2. Legal terminology for "encroach on my property while it has no possessor."
3. The covenant was the contract between God and the Israelites, whereby they paid obedience and sacrificial worship.
4. Echoing Genesis 3.24.
5. Janus Quadrifons, the four-faced Janus, god of gates and beginnings—including the month of January. Apt for the expulsion into a world of historical change: Janus' four heads, like the four doors of his temple, symbolized the seasons of the year.
6. Argus was set to guard Io, since his 100 eyes could watch by turns; but Mercury lulled all 100 with his reed pipe. See Ovid's *Metamorphoses* 1.671ff.

135 *Leucóthea* wak'd,[7] and with fresh dews imbalm'd
The Earth, when *Adam* and first Matron *Eve*
Had ended now thir Orisons, and found
Strength added from above, new hope to spring
Out of despair, joy, but with fear yet linkt;
140 Which thus to *Eve* his welcome words renew'd.
    Eve, easily may Faith admit, that all
The good which we enjoy, from Heav'n descends;
But that from us aught° should ascend to Heav'n   *anything*
So prevalent° as to concern the mind   *efficacious*
145 Of God high-blest, or to incline his will,
Hard to belief may seem; yet this will Prayer,
Or one short sigh of human breath, up-borne
Ev'n to the Seat of God. For since I sought
By Prayer th' offended Deity to appease,
150 Kneel'd and before him humbl'd all my heart,
Methought I saw him placable and mild,
Bending his ear; persuasion in me grew
That I was heard with favor; peace return'd
Home to my Breast, and to my memory
155 His promise, that thy Seed shall bruise our Foe;
Which then not minded in dismay, yet now
Assures me that the bitterness of death
Is past, and we shall live. Whence Hail to thee,
Eve rightly call'd, Mother of all Mankind,
160 Mother of all things living, since by thee
Man is to live, and all things live for Man.
    To whom thus *Eve* with sad° demeanor meek.   *serious*
Ill worthy I such title should belong
To me transgressor, who for thee ordain'd
165 A help, became thy snare; to mee reproach
Rather belongs, distrust and all dispraise:
But infinite in pardon was my Judge,
That I who first brought Death on all, am grac't
The source of life; next favorable thou,
170 Who highly thus to entitle me voutsaf'st
Far other name deserving. But the Field
To labor calls us now with sweat impos'd,
Though after sleepless Night; for see the Morn,
All unconcern'd with our unrest, begins
175 Her rosy progress smiling,[8] let us forth,
I never from thy side henceforth to stray,
Where'er our day's work lies, though now enjoin'd
Laborious, till day droop; while here we dwell,
What can be toilsome in these pleasant Walks?
180 Here let us live, though in fall'n state, content.

7. Leucothea is Mater Matuta, Roman goddess of dawn.   8. The morning marks day 33 of the action.

     So spake, so wish'd much humbl'd *Eve*, but Fate
Subscrib'd not; Nature first gave Signs, imprest
On Bird, Beast, Air, Air suddenly eclips'd
After short blush of Morn; nigh in her sight
185   The Bird of *Jove*, stoopt° from his aery tow'r,   *swooping*
Two Birds of gayest plume before him drove:
Down from a Hill the Beast that reigns in Woods,
First hunter then, pursu'd a gentle brace,
Goodliest of all the Forest, Hart and Hind;
190   Direct to th' Eastern Gate was bent thir flight.
Adam observ'd, and with his Eye the chase
Pursuing, not unmov'd to *Eve* thus spake.
     O *Eve*, some furder change awaits us nigh,
Which Heav'n by these mute signs in Nature shows
195   Forerunners of his purpose, or to warn
Us haply too secure of our discharge
From penalty, because from death releast
Some days; how long, and what till then our life,
Who knows, or more than this, that we are dust,
200   And thither must return and be no more.
Why else this double object in our sight
Of flight pursu'd in th' Air and o'er the ground
One way the self-same hour? why in the East
Darkness ere Day's mid-course, and Morning light
205   More orient° in yon Western Cloud that draws   *bright*
O'er the blue Firmament a radiant white,
And slow descends, with something heav'nly fraught.
     He err'd not, for by this the heav'nly Bands
Down from a Sky of Jasper lighted° now   *descended*
210   In Paradise, and on a Hill made halt,°   *halted*
A glorious Apparition, had not doubt
And carnal fear that day dimm'd *Adam's* eye.
Not that more glorious, when the Angels met
Jacob in *Mahanaim*,[9] where he saw
215   The field Pavilion'd with his Guardians bright;
Nor that which on the flaming Mount appear'd
In *Dothan*, cover'd with a Camp of Fire,
Against the *Syrian* King, who to surprise
One man, Assassin-like had levied War,
220   War unproclaim'd.[1] The Princely Hierarch
In thir bright stand,° there left his Powers to seize   *station*
Possession of the Garden; hee alone,
To find where *Adam* shelter'd, took his way,
Not unperceiv'd of *Adam*, who to *Eve*,

---

9. In Genesis 32.1–2, Jacob called the place of the meeting Mahanaim.
1. Juxtaposing 2 Kings 6.13–17 and Genesis 37.16ff. The Syrian king besieged Dothan to catch one man, Elisha, who was unconcerned to hear of this. At his prayer God opened the servant's eyes "and, behold, the mountain was full of horses and chariots of fire round about Elisha."

225 While the great Visitant approach'd, thus spake.
  Eve, now expect great tidings, which perhaps
Of us will soon determine,° or impose   *decree the future*
New Laws to be observ'd; for I descry
From yonder blazing Cloud that veils the Hill

230 One of the heav'nly Host, and by his Gait
None of the meanest, some great Potentate
Or of the Thrones above, such Majesty
Invests him coming; yet not terrible,
That I should fear, nor sociably mild,

235 As *Raphaël*, that I should much confide,
But solemn and sublime, whom not to offend,
With reverence I must meet, and thou retire.
He ended; and th' Arch-Angel soon drew nigh,
Not in his shape Celestial, but as Man

240 Clad to meet Man; over his lucid° Arms   *bright*
A military Vest of purple flow'd
Livelier than *Melibæan*, or the grain°   *dye*
Of *Sarra*, worn by Kings and Heroes old
In time of Truce; *Iris* had dipt the woof;[2]

245 His starry Helm unbuckl'd show'd him prime
In Manhood where Youth ended; by his side
As in a glistering *Zodiac* hung the Sword,
Satan's dire dread, and in his hand the Spear.
Adam bow'd low, hee Kingly from his State°   *dignity*

250 Inclin'd not, but his coming thus declar'd.
  Adam, Heav'n's high behest no Preface needs:
Sufficient that thy Prayers are heard, and Death,
Then due by sentence when thou didst transgress,
Defeated of his seizure many days

255 Giv'n thee of Grace, wherein thou mayst repent,
And one bad act with many deeds well done
May'st cover: well may then thy Lord appeas'd
Redeem thee quite° from Death's rapacious claim; *completely*
But longer in this Paradise to dwell

260 Permits not; to remove thee I am come,
And send thee from the Garden forth to till
The ground whence thou wast tak'n, fitter Soil.[3]
  He added not, for *Adam* at the news
Heart-strook with chilling gripe° of sorrow stood, *spasm*

265 That all his senses bound; *Eve*, who unseen
Yet all had heard, with audible lament
Discover'd° soon the place of her retire.° *revealed / withdrawal*
  O unexpected stroke, worse than of Death!
Must I thus leave thee Paradise? thus leave

---

2. Sarra is the city Tyre, famous for its dye. Iris dyed the
woof (threads woven across a warp), because the iris
flower was "lilium purpureum," and because she was the
rainbow, sign of God's covenant or "truce."
3. Michael delivers the divine decree verbatim, as befits
his solemn mission (11.96–8).

270　Thee Native Soil, these happy Walks and Shades,
　　Fit haunt of Gods? where I had hope to spend,
　　Quiet though sad, the respite of that day
　　That must be mortal to us both. O flow'rs,
　　That never will in other Climate grow,
275　My early visitation, and my last
　　At Ev'n, which I bred up with tender hand
　　From the first op'ning bud, and gave ye Names,
　　Who now shall rear ye to the Sun, or rank
　　Your Tribes, and water from th' ambrosial Fount?[4]
280　Thee lastly nuptial Bower, by mee adorn'd
　　With what to sight or smell was sweet; from thee
　　How shall I part, and whither wander down
　　Into a lower World, to° this obscure   *compared with*
　　And wild, how shall we breathe in other Air
285　Less pure, accustom'd to immortal Fruits?
　　　　Whom thus the Angel interrupted mild.
　　Lament not *Eve*, but patiently resign
　　What justly thou hast lost; nor set thy heart,
　　Thus over-fond, on that which is not thine;
290　Thy going is not lonely, with thee goes
　　Thy Husband, him to follow thou art bound;
　　Where he abides, think there thy native soil.
　　　　Adam by this from the cold sudden damp°   *stupor*
　　Recovering, and his scatter'd spirits return'd,
295　To *Michael* thus his humble words address'd.
　　　　Celestial, whether among the Thrones, or nam'd
　　Of them the Highest, for such of shape may seem
　　Prince above Princes, gently hast thou told
　　Thy message, which might else in telling wound,
300　And in performing end us; what besides
　　Of sorrow and dejection and despair
　　Our frailty can sustain, thy tidings bring,
　　Departure from this happy place, our sweet
　　Recess, and only consolation left
305　Familiar to our eyes, all places else
　　Inhospitable appear and desolate,
　　Nor knowing us nor known: and if by prayer
　　Incessant I could hope to change the will
　　Of him who all things can,° I would not cease   *knows*
310　To weary him with my assiduous cries:[5]
　　But prayer against his absolute Decree
　　No more avails than breath against the wind,
　　Blown stifling back on him that breathes it forth:

4. Recalling 4.240, where the fountain "ran nectar," another immortal food. The fountain of Paradise was often termed a Fountain of Life (from the "living water" in John 4.10) within which was sheltered an elaborate Well of Life.

5. The first of Adam's many errors in the course of his instruction. See Luke 18.5–7 for an instance of the effectiveness of such prayers.

Therefore to his great bidding I submit.
315 This most afflicts me, that departing hence,
As from his face I shall be hid, depriv'd
His blessed count'nance;[6] here I could frequent,
With worship, place by place where he voutsaf'd
Presence Divine, and to my Sons relate;
320 On this Mount he appear'd, under this Tree
Stood visible, among these Pines his voice
I heard, here with him at this Fountain talk'd:
So many grateful Altars I would rear
Of grassy Turf, and pile up every Stone
325 Of lustre from the brook, in memory,
Or monument to Ages, and thereon
Offer sweet smelling Gums and Fruits and Flow'rs:
In yonder nether World where shall I seek
His bright appearances, or footstep trace?
330 For though I fled him angry, yet recall'd
To life prolong'd and promis'd Race, I now
Gladly behold though but his utmost skirts
Of glory, and far off his steps adore.
      To whom thus *Michael* with regard benign.
335 *Adam*, thou know'st Heav'n his, and all the Earth,
Not this Rock only; his Omnipresence fills
Land, Sea, and Air, and every kind that lives,[7]
Fomented° by his virtual° power and warm'd: *nurtured / virtuous*
All th' Earth he gave thee to possess and rule,
340 No despicable gift; surmise not then
His presence to these narrow bounds confin'd
Of Paradise or *Eden*: this had been
Perhaps thy Capital Seat, from whence had spread
All generations, and had hither come
345 From all the ends of th' Earth, to celebrate
And reverence thee thir great Progenitor.
But this preëminence thou hast lost, brought down
To dwell on even ground now with thy Sons:
Yet doubt not but in Valley and in Plain
350 God is as here, and will be found alike
Present, and of his presence many a sign
Still following thee, still compassing thee round
With goodness and paternal Love, his Face
Express,° and of his steps the track Divine.   *exactly imaging*
355 Which that thou may'st believe, and be confirm'd,
Ere thou from hence depart, know I am sent
To show thee what shall come in future days

---

6. Cain complains similarly: "Behold, thou hast driven me out this day from the face of the earth; and from thy face shall I be hid; and I shall be a fugitive and a vagabond in the earth" (Genesis 4.14).

7. Michael corrects Adam's post-Fall tendency to practice local devotions. For God's omnipresence, see 7.168ff; Jerome 23.24; Malachi 1.11; and John 4.21.

To thee and to thy Offspring; good with bad
Expect to hear, supernal° Grace contending   *heavenly*
360   With sinfulness of Men; thereby to learn
True patience, and to temper joy with fear
And pious sorrow, equally inur'd
By moderation either state to bear,
Prosperous or adverse: so shalt thou lead
365   Safest thy life, and best prepar'd endure
Thy mortal passage when it comes. Ascend
This Hill; let *Eve* (for I have drencht° her eyes)   *applied medicine to*
Here sleep below while thou to foresight° wak'st,   *prophetic vision*
As once thou slep'st, while Shee to life was form'd.
370   To whom thus *Adam* gratefully repli'd.
Ascend, I follow thee, safe Guide, the path
Thou lead'st me, and to the hand of Heav'n submit,
However chast'ning, to the evil turn
My obvious° breast, arming to overcome   *exposed*
375   By suffering, and earn rest from labor won,
If so I may attain. So both ascend
In the Visions of God: It was a Hill
Of Paradise the highest, from whose top
The Hemisphere of Earth in clearest Ken
380   Stretcht out to the amplest reach of prospect lay.
Not higher that Hill nor wider looking round,
Whereon for different cause the Tempter set
Our second *Adam* in the Wilderness,
To show him all Earth's Kingdoms and thir Glory.[8]
385   His Eye might there command wherever stood
City of old or modern Fame, the Seat
Of mightiest Empire, from the destin'd Walls
Of *Cambalu*, seat of *Cathaian Can*,[9]
And *Samarchand* by *Oxus*, *Temir's* Throne,
390   To *Paquin* of *Sinœan* Kings, and thence
To *Agra* and *Lahor* of great *Mogul*
Down to the golden *Chersonese*, or where
The *Persian* in *Ecbatan* sat, or since
In *Hispahan*, or where the *Russian Ksar*
395   In *Mosco*, or the Sultan in *Bizance*,
Turchestan-born; nor could his eye not ken

---

8. To tempt Christ, the devil "taketh him up into an exceeding high mountain, and showeth him all the kingdoms of the world, and the glory of them." (See Matthew 4.8.) Milton portrays this scene in *Paradise Regained* 3.251ff.
9. Adam first sees Asian kingdoms: Cambalu is Cambalus, capital of Cathay. Samarchand is Timur's capital, near the Oxus River. Paquin (Peking) is the capital of China, a separate kingdom from Cathay. Sinoean means Chinese. Agra is a kingdom in the north central region of India, whereas Lahor is in northwest Punjab. The wealthy Chersonese peninsula is vaguely located in India's extreme east—now Malacca in Malaysia. Ecbatan was the summer capital of Persian kings. Hispahan (or Ispahan) became a capital in the sixteenth century, when the Safavid dynasty moved their seat from Kazvin. Bizance is Byzantium, Constantinople, or Istanbul—then capital of the Turkish sultan. The sultans belonged to a tribe that haled from Turkestan, a central Asian region between Mongolia and the Caspian.

Th' Empire of *Negus* to his utmost Port[1]
Ercoco and the less Maritime Kings
Mombaza, and *Quiloa*, and *Melind*,
400 And *Sofala* thought *Ophir*, to the Realm
Of *Congo*, and *Angola* fardest South;
Or thence from *Niger* Flood to *Atlas* Mount
The Kingdoms of *Almansor*, *Fez* and *Sus*,
Marocco and *Algiers*, and *Tremisen*;
405 On *Europe* thence, and where *Rome* was to sway
The World: in Spirit perhaps he also saw
Rich *Mexico* the seat of *Montezume*,[2]
And *Cusco* in *Peru*, the richer seat
Of *Atabalipa*, and yet unspoil'd
410 *Guiana*, whose great City *Geryon's* Sons
Call *El Dorado*: but to nobler sights
Michael from *Adam's* eyes the Film remov'd[3]
Which that false Fruit that promis'd clearer sight
Had bred; then purg'd with Euphrasy and Rue[4]
415 The visual Nerve, for he had much to see;
And from the Well of Life three drops instill'd.
So deep the power of these Ingredients pierc'd,
Ev'n to the inmost seat of mental sight,
That *Adam* now enforc't to close his eyes,
420 Sunk down and all his Spirits became intranst:
But him the gentle Angel by the hand
Soon rais'd, and his attention thus recall'd.
    Adam, now ope thine eyes, and first behold
Th' effects which thy original crime hath wrought
425 In some to spring from thee, who never touch'd
Th'excepted Tree, nor with the Snake conspir'd,
Nor sinn'd thy sin, yet from that sin derive
Corruption to bring forth more violent deeds.
    His eyes he op'n'd, and beheld a field,
430 Part arable and tilth,° whereon were Sheaves   *ploughed field*
New reapt, the other part sheep-walks° and folds;   *pasture*
I' th' midst an Altar as the Land-mark stood
Rustic, of grassy sward;° thither anon°   *turf / soon*
A sweaty Reaper from his Tillage brought

---

1. As with the Asian kingdoms, Adam and Michael see nine African realms. Negus was the hereditary title of the Abyssinian empire. Ercoco or Arkiko is a port on the Red Sea. Melind or Malindi was Vasco's last port of call before his audacious voyage to India to found Portugal's short-lived empire. These are both on the coast of modern Kenya; Quiloa or Kilwa is on the coast of Tanzania. Sofala is a port in Mozambique, from its wealth sometimes supposed to be Ophir. The Niger River is in modern Guinea and Mali, and the Atlas Mountains in Morocco. Almansor (or Mansur, "Victorious") was the name of several Mohammedan princes. Fez was part of the Sultanate of Fez and Morocco. Sus is a province in southern Morocco, formerly independent. And Tremisen or Tlem-

cen is part of Algeria.
2. Even from the hill Adam could not physically see the hemisphere, so he sees it "in spirit." The empire of Montezuma was plundered by Cortez. The empire of Atahuallpa (Atabalipa), with its capital Cusco was plundered by Pizarro. But Manoa, the fabulous capital of Guiana, remained yet unspoiled by the Spanish. Hercules killed the mythical monster Geryon, which had three heads — thus the three kingdoms described here.
3. So Homer's Pallas clears Diomedes' eyes (*Iliad* 5.127); Virgil's Venus clears Aeneas' (*Aeneid* 2.604), and Tasso's Michael clears Goffredo's (*Gerusalemme Liberata* 18.92ff).
4. Euphrasy (or eyebright) and rue are herbal restoratives for the eyes.

435 First Fruits, the green Ear, and the yellow Sheaf,
Uncull'd,° as came to hand; a Shepherd next   *not select*
More meek came with the Firstlings of his Flock
Choicest and best; then sacrificing, laid
The Inwards and thir Fat, with Incense strew'd,
440 On the cleft Wood, and all due Rites perform'd.
His Off'ring soon propitious Fire from Heav'n
Consum'd with nimble glance,° and grateful steam;[5]   *swift flash*
The other's not, for his was not sincere;
Whereat hee inly rag'd, and as they talk'd,
445 Smote him into the Midriff with a stone
That beat out life; he fell, and deadly pale
Groan'd out his Soul with gushing blood effus'd.
Much at that sight was *Adam* in his heart
Dismay'd, and thus in haste to th' Angel cri'd.
450   O Teacher, some great mischief hath befall'n
To that meek man, who well had sacrific'd;
Is Piety thus and pure Devotion paid?
    T' whom *Michael* thus, hee also mov'd, repli'd.
These two are Brethren, *Adam*, and to come
455 Out of thy loins; th' unjust the just hath slain,
For envy that his Brother's Offering found
From Heav'n acceptance; but the bloody Fact°   *crime*
Will be aveng'd, and th' other's Faith approv'd
Lose no reward, though here thou see him die,
460 Rolling in dust and gore. To which our Sire.
    Alas, both for the deed and for the cause!
But have I now seen Death? Is this the way
I must return to native dust? O sight
Of terror, foul and ugly to behold,
465 Horrid to think, how horrible to feel!
    To whom thus *Michaël*.[6] Death thou hast seen
In his first shape on man; but many shapes
Of Death, and many are the ways that lead
To his grim Cave, all dismal;° yet to sense   *dreadful*
470 More terrible at th' entrance than within.
Some, as thou saw'st, by violent stroke shall die.
By Fire, Flood, Famine, by Intemperance more
In Meats and Drinks, which on the Earth shall bring
Diseases dire, of which a monstrous crew
475 Before thee shall appear; that thou may'st know
What misery th' inabstinence of *Eve*
Shall bring on men. Immediately a place
Before his eyes appear'd, sad, noisome, dark,
A Lazar-house° it seem'd, wherein were laid   *hospital*
480 Numbers of all diseas'd, all maladies

---

5. The fire and steam are common signs that a sacrifice
was acceptable. See Leviticus 9.24; Judges 6.21; 1 Kings
18.38; 1 Chronicles 21.26; 2 Chronicles 7.1.
6. Trisyllabic, as befits the passage's slow gravity.

Of ghastly Spasm, or racking torture, qualms
Of heart-sick Agony, all feverous kinds,
Convulsions, Epilepsies, fierce Catarrhs,
Intestine Stone and Ulcer, Colic pangs,
485   Dæmoniac Frenzy, moping Melancholy[7]
And Moon-struck madness, pining° Atrophy,   *emaciating*
Marasmus,° and wide-wasting Pestilence,   *wasting of the body*
Dropsies, and Asthmas, and Joint-racking Rheums.°   *rheumatic pains*
Dire was the tossing, deep the groans, despair
490   Tended the sick busiest from Couch to Couch;
And over them triumphant Death his Dart
Shook, but delay'd to strike, though oft invok't
With vows, as thir chief good, and final hope.
Sight so deform what heart of Rock could long
495   Dry-ey'd behold? *Adam* could not, but wept,
Though not of Woman born; compassion quell'd
His best of Man,[8] and gave him up to tears
A space, till firmer thoughts restrain'd excess,
And scarce recovering words his plaint renew'd.
500   O miserable Mankind, to what fall
Degraded, to what wretched state reserv'd!
Better end here unborn. Why is life giv'n
To be thus wrested from us? rather why
Obtruded on us thus? who if we knew
505   What we receive, would either not accept
Life offer'd, or soon beg to lay it down,
Glad to be so dismist in peace. Can thus
Th' Image of God in man created once
So goodly and erect, though faulty since,
510   To such unsightly sufferings be debas't
Under inhuman pains? Why should not Man,
Retaining still Divine similitude
In part, from such deformities be free,
And for his Maker's Image sake exempt?[9]
515   Thir Maker's Image, answer'd *Michael*, then
Forsook them, when themselves they vilifi'd°   *demeaned*
To serve ungovern'd appetite, and took
His Image whom they served, a brutish vice,
Inductive° mainly to the sin of *Eve*.   *giving rise*
520   Therefore so abject is thir punishment,
Disfiguring not God's likeness, but thir own,
Or if his likeness, by themselves defac't
While they pervert pure Nature's healthful rules
To loathsome sickness, worthily, since they
525   God's Image did not reverence in themselves.

---

7. Melancholy was a more comprehensive category at the time.
8. A man's tears, and softer feelings generally, were attributed to his feminine part.
9. Protestant theology emphasized disfiguring of the *imago Dei*, or image of God.

I yield it just, said *Adam*, and submit.
But is there yet no other way, besides
These painful passages,° how we may come   *deaths*
To Death, and mix with our connatural dust?

530   There is, said *Michael*, if thou well observe
The rule of not too much, by temperance taught,
In what thou eat'st and drink'st, seeking from thence
Due nourishment, not gluttonous delight,
Till many years over thy head return:

535   So may'st thou live, till like ripe Fruit thou drop
Into thy Mother's lap, or be with ease
Gather'd, not harshly pluckt, for death mature:
This is old age; but then thou must outlive
Thy youth, thy strength, thy beauty, which will change

540   To wither'd weak and gray; thy Senses then
Obtuse, all taste of pleasure must forgo,
To what thou hast, and for the Air of youth
Hopeful and cheerful, in thy blood will reign
A melancholy damp of cold and dry

545   To weigh thy Spirits down, and last consume
The Balm of Life. To whom our Ancestor.
    Henceforth I fly not Death, nor would prolong
Life much, bent rather how I may be quit
Fairest and easiest of this cumbrous charge,

550   Which I must keep till my appointed day
Of rend'ring up, and patiently attend°   *await*
My dissolution. *Michaël* repli'd.
    Nor love thy Life, nor hate; but what thou liv'st
Live well, how long or short permit to Heav'n:

555   And now prepare thee for another sight.
    He look'd and saw a spacious Plain, whereon
Were Tents of various hue; by some were herds
Of Cattle grazing: others, whence the sound
Of Instruments that made melodious chime

560   Was heard, of Harp and Organ; and who mov'd
Thir stops and chords was seen: his volant° touch   *nimble*
Instinct° through all proportions low and high   *impelled*
Fled and pursu'd transverse the resonant fugue.
In other part stood one who at the Forge

565   Laboring, two massy clods of Iron and Brass
Had melted (whether found where casual° fire   *accidental*
Had wasted woods on Mountain or in Vale,
Down to the veins of Earth, thence gliding hot
To some Cave's mouth, or whether washt by stream

570   From underground); the liquid Ore he drain'd
Into fit moulds prepar'd; from which he form'd
First his own Tools; then, what might else be wrought
Fusile° or grav'n in metal. After these,   *cast*
But on the hither side a different sort

575 From the high neighboring Hills, which was thir Seat,[1]
Down to the Plain descended: by thir guise
Just men they seem'd, and all thir study bent
To worship God aright, and know his works
Not hid, nor those things last which might preserve
580 Freedom and Peace to men: they on the Plain
Long had not walkt, when from the Tents behold
A Bevy of fair Women, richly gay
In Gems and wanton dress; to the Harp they sung
Soft amorous Ditties, and in dance came on:
585 The Men though grave, ey'd them, and let thir eyes
Rove without rein, till in the amorous Net
Fast caught, they lik'd and each his liking chose;
And now of love they treat° till th' Ev'ning Star   *talk*
Love's Harbinger appear'd; then all in heat
590 They light the Nuptial Torch, and bid invoke
Hymen, then first to marriage Rites invok't;
With Feast and Music all the Tents resound.
Such happy interview and fair event
Of love and youth not lost, Songs, Garlands, Flow'rs,
595 And charming Symphonies attach'd the heart
Of *Adam*, soon inclin'd to admit delight
The bent of Nature; which he thus express'd.
      True opener of mine eyes, prime Angel blest,
Much better seems this Vision, and more hope
600 Of peaceful days portends, than those two past;
Those were of hate and death, or pain much worse,
Here Nature seems fulfill'd in all her ends.
      To whom thus *Michael*. Judge not what is best
By pleasure, though to Nature seeming meet,
605 Created, as thou art, to nobler end
Holy and pure, conformity divine.
Those Tents thou saw'st so pleasant, were the Tents
Of wickedness, wherein shall dwell his Race
Who slew his Brother; studious they appear
610 Of Arts that polish Life, Inventors rare,
Unmindful of thir Maker, though his Spirit
Taught them, but they his gifts acknowledg'd none.
Yet they a beauteous offspring shall beget;
For that fair female Troop thou saw'st, that seem'd
615 Of Goddesses, so blithe, so smooth, so gay,
Yet empty of all good wherein consists
Woman's domestic honor and chief praise;
Bred only and completed° to the taste   *equipped*
Of lustful appetence,° to sing, to dance,   *desire*
620 To dress, and troll° the Tongue, and roll the Eye.   *wag*

---

1. In Genesis 5, these are descendants not of Cain but of Seth. They inhabited mountains neighboring Paradise and so on the hither side of the plain, whereas Cain lived "on the east of Eden" (Genesis 4.16).

To these that sober Race of Men, whose lives
Religious titl'd them the Sons of God,
Shall yield up all thir virtue, all thir fame
Ignobly, to the trains° and to the smiles   *enticements*
625 Of these fair Atheists, and now swim in joy,
(Erelong to swim at large) and laugh; for which
The world erelong a world of tears must weep.
  To whom thus *Adam* of short joy bereft.
O pity and shame, that they who to live well
630 Enter'd so fair, should turn aside to tread
Paths indirect, or in the mid way faint!²
But still I see the tenor of Man's woe
Holds on the same, from Woman to begin.
  From Man's effeminate slackness it begins,
635 Said th' Angel, who should better hold his place
By wisdom, and superior gifts receiv'd.
But now prepare thee for another Scene.
  He look'd and saw wide Territory spread
Before him, Towns, and rural works between,
640 Cities of Men with lofty Gates and Tow'rs,
Concourse° in Arms, fierce Faces threat'ning War, *hostile encounter*
Giants of mighty Bone,³ and bold emprise;°   *chivalric deeds*
Part wield thir Arms, part curb the foaming Steed,
Single or in Array of Battle rang'd
645 Both Horse and Foot, nor idly must'ring stood;
One way a Band select from forage drives
A herd of Beeves, fair Oxen and fair Kine
From a fat Meadow ground; or fleecy Flock,
Ewes and thir bleating Lambs over the Plain,
650 Thir Booty; scarce with Life the Shepherds fly,
But call in aid, which makes a bloody Fray;
With cruel Tournament the Squadrons join;
Where Cattle pastur'd late, now scatter'd lies
With Carcasses and Arms th' ensanguin'd° Field *blood-stained*
655 Deserted: Others to a City strong
Lay Siege, encampt; by Battery, Scale,° and Mine, *ladder*
Assaulting; others from the wall defend
With Dart and Jav'lin, Stones and sulphurous Fire;
On each hand slaughter and gigantic deeds.
660 In other part the scepter'd Heralds call
To Council in the City Gates: anon
Grey-headed men and grave, with Warriors mixt,
Assemble, and Harangues are heard, but soon
In factious opposition, till at last

---

2. This line marks the "midway" of the first, destroyed world. It is the midpoint between the first vision's first line (11.423) and the fifth vision's last line (11.839).

3. "Giants" is not exaggeration, in view of the tradition that giants were offspring of angels. See 1.195–200; 3.461ff; 11.621–22, 688.

665 Of middle Age one rising,[4] eminent
In wise deport, spake much of Right and Wrong,
Of Justice, of Religion, Truth and Peace,
And Judgment from above: him old and young
Exploded,° and had seiz'd with violent hands,   *shouted down*
670 Had not a Cloud descending snatch'd him thence
Unseen amid the throng: so violence
Proceeded, and Oppression, and Sword-Law
Through all the Plain, and refuge none was found.
Adam was all in tears, and to his guide
675 Lamenting turn'd full sad; O what are these,
Death's Ministers, not Men, who thus deal Death
Inhumanly to men, and multiply
Ten thousandfold the sin of him who slew
His Brother; for of whom such massacre
680 Make they but of thir Brethren, men of men?
But who was that Just Man, whom had not Heav'n
Rescu'd, had in his Righteousness been lost?
      To whom thus *Michael.* These are the product
Of those ill-mated Marriages thou saw'st;
685 Where good with bad were matcht, who of themselves
Abhor to join; and by imprudence mixt,
Produce prodigious Births of body or mind.
Such were these Giants, men of high renown;
For in those days Might only shall be admir'd,
690 And Valor and Heroic Virtue call'd;
To overcome in Battle, and subdue
Nations, and bring home spoils with infinite
Man-slaughter, shall be held the highest pitch
Of human Glory, and for Glory done
695 Of triumph, to be styl'd great Conquerors,
Patrons of Mankind, Gods, and Sons of Gods,
Destroyers rightlier call'd and Plagues of men.
Thus Fame shall be achiev'd, renown on Earth,
And what most merits fame in silence hid.
700 But hee the sev'nth from thee, whom thou beheld'st
The only righteous in a World perverse,
And therefore hated, therefore so beset
With Foes for daring single to be just,
And utter odious Truth, that God would come
705 To judge them with his Saints: Him the most High
Rapt in a balmy Cloud with winged Steeds
Did, as thou saw'st, receive, to walk with God
High in Salvation and the Climes of bliss,
Exempt from Death; to show thee what reward
710 Awaits the good, the rest what punishment;

4. Enoch, who was seven generations from Adam (11.700), and Noah's grandfather. He was taken directly into heaven by God when 365 years old. See Genesis 5.21–4; Jude 14; Hebrews 11.5. The apocryphal book of Enoch, like Michael, treats the Flood as judgment on sin.

Which now direct thine eyes and soon behold.
　　He look'd, and saw the face of things quite chang'd;
The brazen Throat of War had ceast to roar,
All now was turn'd to jollity and game,
715　To luxury° and riot, feast and dance,　　　　　　　　　*lust*
Marrying or prostituting, as befell,
Rape of Adultery, where passing° fair　　　　　　　　　*surpassing*
Allur'd them; thence from Cups to civil Broils.
At length a Reverend Sire among them came,[5]
720　And of thir doings great dislike declar'd,
And testifi'd against thir ways; hee oft
Frequented thir Assemblies, whereso met,
Triumphs or Festivals, and to them preach'd
Conversion and Repentance, as to Souls
725　In Prison under Judgments imminent:
But all in vain: which when he saw, he ceas'd
Contending, and remov'd his Tents far off;
Then from the Mountain hewing Timber tall,
Began to build a Vessel of huge bulk,
730　Measur'd by Cubit, length, and breadth, and highth,
Smear'd round with Pitch, and in the side a door
Contriv'd, and of provisions laid in large
For Man and Beast: when lo a wonder strange!
Of every Beast, and Bird, and Insect small
735　Came sevens, and pairs, and enter'd in, as taught
Thir order; last the Sire, and his three Sons
With thir four Wives; and God made fast the door.
Meanwhile the Southwind rose, and with black wings
Wide hovering, all the Clouds together drove
740　From under Heav'n; the Hills to their supply°　　　　*assistance*
Vapor, and Exhalation° dusk and moist,　　　　　　　*mist*
Sent up amain; and now the thick'n'd Sky
Like a dark Ceiling stood; down rush'd the Rain
Impetuous, and continu'd till the Earth
745　No more was seen; the floating Vessel swum
Uplifted; and secure with beaked prow
Rode tilting o'er the Waves, all dwellings else
Flood overwhelm'd, and them with all thir pomp
Deep under water roll'd; Sea cover'd Sea,
750　Sea without shore; and in thir Palaces
Where luxury late reign'd, Sea-monsters whelp'd°　　*had offspring*
And stabl'd;° of Mankind so numerous late,　　　　　*lived as in a stable*
All left, in one small bottom° swum embark't.　　　　*boat*
How didst thou grieve then, *Adam*, to behold
755　The end of all thy Offspring, end so sad,
Depopulation; thee another Flood,

5. Milton's flood account follows Genesis 6.9–9:17 with few changes.

Of tears and sorrow a Flood thee also drown'd,
And sunk thee as thy Sons; till gently rear'd
By th' Angel, on thy feet thou stood'st at last,
760   Though comfortless, as when a Father mourns
His Children, all in view destroy'd at once;
And scarce to th' Angel utter'd'st thus thy plaint.
    O Visions ill foreseen! better had I
Liv'd ignorant of future, so had borne
765   My part of evil only, each day's lot
Anough to bear; those now, that were dispens't
The burd'n of many Ages, on me light
At once, by my foreknowledge gaining Birth
Abortive, to torment me ere thir being,
770   With thought that they must be. Let no man seek
Henceforth to be foretold what shall befall
Him or his Children, evil he may be sure,
Which neither his foreknowing can prevent,
And hee the future evil shall no less
775   In apprehension than in substance feel
Grievous to bear: but that care now is past,
Man is not whom to warn:[6] those few escap't
Famine and anguish will at last consume
Wand'ring that wat'ry Desert: I had hope
780   When violence was ceas't, and War on Earth,
All would have then gone well, peace would have crown'd
With length of happy days the race of man;
But I was far deceiv'd; for now I see
Peace to corrupt no less than War to waste.
785   How comes it thus? unfold, Celestial Guide,
And whether here the Race of man will end.
    To whom thus *Michael*. Those whom last thou saw'st
In triumph and luxurious wealth, are they
First seen in acts of prowess eminent
790   And great exploits, but of true virtue void;
Who having spilt much blood, and done much waste
Subduing Nations, and achiev'd thereby
Fame in the World, high titles, and rich prey,
Shall change thir course to pleasure, ease, and sloth,
795   Surfeit, and lust, till wantonness and pride
Raise out of friendship hostile deeds in Peace.
The conquer'd also, and enslav'd by War
Shall with thir freedom lost all virtue lose
And fear of God, from whom thir piety feign'd
800   In sharp contest of Battle found no aid
Against invaders; therefore cool'd in zeal
Thenceforth shall practice how to live secure,°   *heedlessly*

6. That is, "there is no one left to warn."

Worldly or dissolute, on what thir Lords
Shall leave them to enjoy; for th' Earth shall bear
805   More than anough, that temperance may be tri'd:
So all shall turn degenerate, all deprav'd,
Justice and Temperance, Truth and Faith forgot;
One Man except, the only Son of light
In a dark Age, against example good,
810   Against allurement, custom, and a World
Offended; fearless of reproach and scorn,
Or violence, hee of thir wicked ways
Shall them admonish, and before them set
The paths of righteousness how much more safe,
815   And full of peace, denouncing° wrath to come   *proclaiming*
On thir impenitence; and shall return
Of them derided, but of God observ'd
The one just Man alive; by his command
Shall build a wondrous Ark, as thou beheld'st,
820   To save himself and household from amidst
A World devote° to universal rack.°   *doomed / destruction*
No sooner hee with them of Man and Beast
Select for life shall in the Ark be lodg'd,
And shelter'd round, but all the Cataracts°   *sluices*
825   Of Heav'n set open on the Earth shall pour
Rain day and night, all fountains of the Deep
Broke up, shall heave the Ocean to usurp
Beyond all bounds, till inundation rise
Above the highest Hills: then shall this Mount
830   Of Paradise by might of Waves be mov'd
Out of his place, push'd by the horned flood,
With all his verdure spoil'd, and Trees adrift
Down the great River⁷ to the op'ning Gulf,
And there take root an Island salt and bare
835   The haunt of Seals and Ores,° and Sea-mews'° clang.   *sea monsters / gulls'*
To teach thee that God attributes to place
No sanctity, if none be thither brought
By Men who there frequent, or therein dwell.
And now what further shall ensue, behold.
840   He look'd, and saw the Ark hull° on the flood,   *drift*
Which now abated, for the Clouds were fled,
Driv'n by a keen North-wind, that blowing dry
Wrinkl'd the face of Deluge, as decay'd;
And the clear Sun on his wide wat'ry Glass
845   Gaz'd hot, and of the fresh Wave largely drew,
As after thirst, which made thir flowing shrink
From standing lake to tripping° ebb, that stole   *dancing*
With soft foot towards the deep, who now had stopt

7. The modern Tigris or Euphrates.

His Sluices, as the Heav'n his windows shut.
850 The Ark no more now floats, but seems on ground
Fast on the top of some high mountain fixt.[8]
And now the tops of Hills as Rocks appear;
With clamor thence the rapid Currents drive
Towards the retreating Sea thir furious tide.
855 Forthwith from out the Ark a Raven flies,
And after him, the surer messenger,
A Dove sent forth once and again to spy
Green Tree or ground whereon his foot may light;
The second time returning, in his Bill
860 An Olive leaf he brings, pacific sign:
Anon dry ground appears, and from his Ark
The ancient Sire descends with all his Train;
Then with uplifted hands, and eyes devout,
Grateful to Heav'n, over his head beholds
865 A dewy Cloud, and in the Cloud a Bow
Conspicuous with three listed° colors gay,   *arranged in bands*
Betok'ning peace from God, and Cov'nant new.[9]
Whereat the heart of *Adam* erst° so sad   *previously*
Greatly rejoic'd, and thus his joy broke forth.
870   O thou who future things canst represent
As present, Heav'nly instructor, I revive
At this last sight, assur'd that Man shall live
With all the Creatures, and thir seed preserve.
Far less I now lament for one whole World
875 Of wicked Sons destroy'd, than I rejoice
For one Man found so perfet and so just,
That God voutsafes to raise another World
From him, and all his anger to forget.
But say, what mean those color'd streaks in Heav'n,
880 Distended° as the Brow of God appeas'd,   *expanded*
Or serve they as a flow'ry verge to bind
The fluid skirts of that same wat'ry Cloud,
Lest it again dissolve and show'r the Earth?
     To whom th' Arch-Angel. Dext'rously thou aim'st;
885 So willingly doth God remit his Ire,
Though late repenting him of Man deprav'd,
Griev'd at his heart, when looking down he saw
The whole Earth fill'd with violence, and all flesh
Corrupting each thir way; yet those remov'd,
890 Such grace shall one just Man find in his sight,
That he relents, not to blot out mankind,
And makes a Cov'nant never to destroy
The Earth again by flood, nor let the Sea

8. Milton rejects the locale given by Genesis 8.4, "upon the mountains of Ararat."
9. Echoing Genesis 9.13–15, "I do set my bow in the cloud, and it shall be for a token of a covenant between me and the earth . . . the waters shall no more become a flood to destroy all flesh."

Surpass his bounds, nor Rain to drown the World
895   With Man therein or Beast; but when he brings
Over the Earth a Cloud, will therein set
His triple-color'd Bow, whereon to look
And call to mind his Cov'nant: Day and Night,
Seed-time and Harvest, Heat and hoary Frost
900   Shall hold thir course, till fire purge all things new,[1]
Both Heav'n and Earth, wherein the just shall dwell.

The End of the Eleventh Book.

Book 12
The Argument

The Angel Michael *continues from the Flood to relate what shall succeed; then, in the mention of* Abraham, *comes by degrees to explain, who that Seed of the Woman shall be, which was promised* Adam *and* Eve *in the Fall; his Incarnation, Death, Resurrection, and Ascension; the state of the Church till his second Coming.* Adam *greatly satisfied and re-comforted by these Relations and Promises descends the Hill with Michael; wakens* Eve, *who all this while had slept, but with gentle dreams compos'd to quietness of mind and submission.* Michael *in either hand leads them out of Paradise, the fiery Sword waving behind them, and the Cherubim taking thir Stations to guard the Place.*

As one who in his journey bates° at Noon,   pauses
Though bent on speed, so here the Arch-Angel paus'd
Betwixt the world destroy'd and world restor'd,
If *Adam* aught perhaps might interpose;
5   Then with transition sweet new Speech resumes.
Thus thou hast seen one World begin and end;
And Man as from a second stock proceed.[1]
Much thou hast yet to see, but I perceive
Thy mortal sight to fail; objects divine
10   Must needs impair and weary human sense:
Henceforth what is to come I will relate,
Thou therefore give due audience, and attend.
This second source of Men, while yet but few,
And while the dread of judgment past remains
15   Fresh in thir minds, fearing the Deity,
With some regard to what is just and right
Shall lead thir lives, and multiply apace,
Laboring° the soil, and reaping plenteous crop,   tilling
Corn, wine and oil; and from the herd or flock,
20   Oft sacrificing Bullock, Lamb, or Kid,
With large Wine-offerings pour'd, and sacred Feast,

---

1. The three colors of the bow are blue, yellow, and red. 2 Peter 3.6ff and 3.13ff links the Flood (blue) with the final conflagration (red): "The world that then was, being overflowed with water, perished: But the heavens and the earth, which are now, by the same word are kept in store, reserved unto fire against the day of judgment and perdition of ungodly men."

1. "Stock," an ambiguity, refers not only to the literal replacement of one source of the human line of descent (Adam) by another (Noah), but also to the grafting of mankind onto the stem of Christ, according to the Pauline allegory of regeneration (Romans 11). The covenant with Noah was a type of the New Covenant.

Shall spend thir days in joy unblam'd, and dwell
Long time in peace by Families and Tribes
Under paternal rule; till one shall rise[2]

25 Of proud ambitious heart, who not content
With fair equality, fraternal state,
Will arrogate Dominion undeserv'd
Over his brethren, and quite dispossess
Concord and law of Nature from the Earth:[3]

30 Hunting (and Men not Beasts shall be his game)
With War and hostile snare such as refuse
Subjection to his Empire tyrannous:[4]
A mighty Hunter thence he shall be styl'd
Before the Lord, as in despite of Heav'n,

35 Or from Heav'n claiming second Sovranty;[5]
And from Rebellion shall derive his name,
Though of Rebellion others he accuse.
Hee with a crew, whom like Ambition joins
With him or under him to tyrannize,

40 Marching from *Eden* towards the West, shall find
The Plain, wherein a black bituminous gurge°   *whirlpool*
Boils out from under ground, the mouth of Hell;
Of Brick, and of that stuff they cast to build
A City and Tow'r, whose top may reach to Heav'n;[6]

45 And get themselves a name, lest far disperst
In foreign Lands thir memory be lost,
Regardless whether good or evil fame.[7]
But God who oft descends to visit men
Unseen, and through thir habitations walks

50 To mark thir doings, them beholding soon,
Comes down to see thir City, ere the Tower
Obstruct Heav'n Tow'rs, and in derision sets
Upon thir Tongues a various Spirit to rase
Quite out thir Native Language, and instead

55 To sow a jangling noise of words unknown:
Forthwith a hideous gabble rises loud
Among the Builders; each to other calls
Not understood, till hoarse, and all in rage,
As mockt they storm;[8] great laughter was in Heav'n

60 And looking down, to see the hubbub strange
And hear the din; thus was the building left

2. Nimrod is not connected with the builders of the Tower in Genesis 10.8. The connection is made, however, in Josephus, *Antiquities* 1.4.2ff., where we also learn that Nimrod "changed the government into tyranny."
3. In *The Tenure of Kings and Magistrates*, Milton denies the natural right of kings and insists that their power is committed to them in trust by the people.
4. See *Eikonoklastes:* "The Bishops could have told him, that 'Nimrod,' the first that hunted after Faction is reputed, by ancient Tradition, the first that founded monarchy; whence it appears that to hunt after Faction

is more properly the King's Game."
5. "Before the Lord," Genesis 10.9; Milton takes it in a constitutional sense; see *The Tenure:* "To say Kings are accountable to none but God, is the overturning of all Law."
6. The materials of the Tower—brick with bitumen as mortar—are specified in Genesis 11.3.
7. See Genesis 11.4.
8. In the 17th century it was generally believed that the separation of language into distinct individual languages had its beginning at the confusion of tongues at Babel.

Ridiculous, and the work Confusion nam'd.[9]
   Whereto thus *Adam* fatherly displeas'd.
O execrable Son so to aspire
65   Above his Brethren, to himself assuming
Authority usurpt, from God not giv'n:
He gave us only over Beast, Fish, Fowl
Dominion absolute; that right we hold
By his donation; but Man over men
70   He made not Lord; such title to himself
Reserving, human left from human free.
But this Usurper his encroachment proud
Stays not on Man; to God his Tower intends
Siege and defiance: Wretched man! what food
75   Will he convey up thither to sustain
Himself and his rash Army, where thin Air
Above the Clouds will pine his entrails gross,
And famish him of breath, if not of Bread?
   To whom thus *Michael.* Justly thou abhorr'st
80   That Son, who on the quiet state of men
Such trouble brought, affecting to subdue
Rational Liberty;[1] yet know withal,
Since thy original lapse, true Liberty
Is lost, which always with right Reason dwells
85   Twinn'd, and from her hath no dividual° being: *separate*
Reason in man obscur'd, or not obey'd,
Immediately inordinate desires
And upstart Passions catch the Government
From Reason, and to servitude reduce
90   Man till then free. Therefore since hee permits
Within himself unworthy Powers to reign
Over free Reason, God in Judgment just
Subjects him from without to violent Lords;
Who oft as undeservedly enthral
95   His outward freedom: Tyranny must be,
Though to the Tyrant thereby no excuse.
Yet sometimes Nations will decline so low
From virtue, which is reason, that no wrong,
But Justice, and some fatal curse annext
100   Deprives them of thir outward liberty,
Thir inward lost: Witness th' irreverent Son
Of him who built the Ark,[2] who for the shame
Done to his Father, heard this heavy curse,

9. See Genesis 11.9, "Therefore is the name of it called Babel"; marginal gloss: "that is, Confusion."
1. Lines 80–101 recall the regicide tracts and follow St. Augustine's *City of God* 19.15, where we read that the derivation of servitude, whose mother is sin, is the "first cause of man's subjection to man: which notwithstanding comes not to pass but by the direction of the highest, in whom is no injustice." For the connection between psychological and political enslavement, see 9.1127–31.
2. Because of Ham's perverse act committed with the drunken Noah, his own son Canaan was cursed: "a servant of servants shall he be unto his brethren" (Genesis 9.25).

Servant of Servants, on his vicious Race.°   *descendants*

105 Thus will this latter, as the former World,
     Still tend from bad to worse, till God at last
     Wearied with their iniquities, withdraw
     His presence from among them, and avert
     His holy Eyes; resolving from thenceforth

110 To leave them to thir own polluted ways;
     And one peculiar° Nation to select   *special*
     From all the rest, of whom to be invok'd,
     A Nation from one faithful man to spring:
     Him on this side *Euphrates* yet residing,[3]

115 Bred up in Idol-worship; O that men
     (Canst thou believe?) should be so stupid grown,
     While yet the Patriarch° liv'd, who scap'd the Flood,   *Noah*
     As to forsake the living God, and fall
     To worship thir own work in Wood and Stone

120 For Gods! yet him God the most High voutsafes
     To call by Vision from his Father's house,
     His kindred and false Gods, into a Land
     Which he will show him, and from him will raise
     A mighty Nation, and upon him show'r

125 His benediction so, that in his Seed
     All Nations shall be blest; he straight obeys,
     Not knowing to what Land, yet firm believes:
     I see him, but thou canst not, with what Faith
     He leaves his Gods, his Friends, and native Soil

130 *Ur of Chaldæa*,[4] passing now the Ford
     To *Haran*, after him a cumbrous Train
     Of Herds and Flocks, and numerous servitude;°   *slaves and servants*
     Not wand'ring poor, but trusting all his wealth
     With God, who call'd him, in a land unknown.

135 *Canaan* he now attains, I see his Tents
     Pitcht about *Sechem*, and the neighboring Plain
     Of *Moreh*; there by promise he receives
     Gift to his Progeny of all that Land;
     From *Hamath* Northward to the Desert South

140 (Things by thir names I call, though yet unnam'd)
     From *Hermon* East to the great Western Sea,
     Mount *Hermon*, yonder Sea, each place behold

3. On Abraham's origins, see Joshua 24.2, "Thus saith the Lord God of Israel, Your fathers dwelt on the other side of the flood in old time, even Terah, father of Abraham, and the father of Nachor: and they served other gods." 4. Nine places are named in the Holy Land — the number of heavenly things. Milton may have put Ur in Mesopotamia, on the strength of Acts 7.2. Haran was far to the northwest. Sechem (Shechem) was the scene of Joshua's covenant with Israel. Moreh, like Sechem, was near the pass between Mt Ebal and Mt Gerizim; Jacob buried his people's idols under the oak there (Genesis 35.4). Hamath marked the northern border of the Promised Land, as the great western sea marked the western border, and the wilderness of Zin marked the southern (Numbers 34.3–8). Mt Hermon is a boundary between Lebanon and Syria (Joshua 13.5ff); it is the highest mountain in Palestine. Mt Carmel's position is something to swear by (Jerome 46.18). The double-fonted stream reflects the notion that the Jor and Dan formed by confluence the Jordan. Senir was the Amorite name for Hermon (Deuteronomy 3.9).

In prospect, as I point them; on the shore
Mount *Carmel*; here the double-founted stream
145   *Jordan*, true limit Eastward; but his Sons
Shall dwell to *Senir*, that long ridge of Hills.
This ponder, that all Nations of the Earth
Shall in his Seed be blessed; by that Seed
Is meant thy great deliverer, who shall bruise
150   The Serpent's head;[5] whereof to thee anon
Plainlier shall be reveal'd. This Patriarch blest,
Whom *faithful Abraham* due time shall call,
A Son,° and of his Son a Grandchild° leaves,   *Isaac / Jacob*
Like him in faith, in wisdom, and renown;
155   The Grandchild with twelve Sons increast, departs
From *Canaan*, to a Land hereafter call'd
Egypt, divided by the River *Nile*;
See where it flows, disgorging at seven mouths
Into the Sea: to sojourn in that Land
160   He comes invited by a younger Son[6]
In time of dearth, a Son whose worthy deeds
Raise him to be the second in that Realm
Of *Pharaoh*: there he dies, and leaves his Race
Growing into a Nation, and now grown
165   Suspected to a sequent King,[7] who seeks
To stop thir overgrowth,° as inmate guests   *overpopulation*
Too numerous; whence of guests he makes them slaves
Inhospitably, and kills thir infant Males:
Till by two brethren (those two brethren call
170   *Moses* and *Aaron*) sent from God to claim
His people from enthralment, they return
With glory and spoil back to thir promis'd Land.
But first the lawless Tyrant, who denies
To know thir God, or message to regard,
175   Must be compell'd by Signs and Judgments dire;
To blood unshed the Rivers must be turn'd,
Frogs, Lice and Flies must all his Palace fill
With loath'd intrusion, and fill all the land;
His Cattle must of Rot and Murrain° die,   *plague*
180   Botches and blains° must all his flesh imboss,   *sores and blisters*
And all his people; Thunder mixt with Hail,
Hail mixt with fire must rend th' *Egyptian* Sky
And wheel on th' Earth, devouring where it rolls;
What it devours not, Herb, or Fruit, or Grain,
185   A darksome Cloud of Locusts swarming down
Must eat, and on the ground leave nothing green:

---

5. This is the promise to Abram, renewing that of the serpent's curse (see 10.180ff, and Genesis 12.1–3). "Abraham" is changed from "Abram" (Genesis 17.5), implying by etymological wordplay "father of a (great) multitude."

6. Jacob went down to Egypt at the bidding of Joseph (the "younger son"); see Genesis 45.6.
7. Named as Busiris at 1.307.

Darkness must overshadow all his bounds,
Palpable darkness, and blot out three days;
Last with one midnight stroke all the first-born
190   Of *Egypt* must lie dead. Thus with ten wounds
The River-dragon° tam'd at length submits[8]   *crocodile*
To let his sojourners depart, and oft
Humbles his stubborn heart, but still as Ice
More hard'n'd after thaw, till in his rage
195   Pursuing whom he late dismiss'd, the Sea
Swallows him with his Host, but them lets pass
As on dry land between two crystal walls,
Aw'd by the rod of *Moses* so to stand
Divided, till his rescu'd gain thir shore:
200   Such wondrous power God to his Saint will lend,
Though present in his Angel, who shall go
Before them in a Cloud, and Pillar of Fire,
By day a Cloud, by night a Pillar of Fire,[9]
To guide them in thir journey, and remove
205   Behind them, while th' obdurate King pursues:
All night he will pursue, but his approach
Darkness defends° between till morning Watch;   *wards off*
Then through the Fiery Pillar and the Cloud
God looking forth will trouble all his Host
210   And craze thir Chariot wheels: when by command
Moses once more his potent Rod extends
Over the Sea; the Sea his Rod obeys;
On thir imbattl'd ranks the Waves return,
And overwhelm thir War:° the Race elect   *army and equipment*
215   Safe towards *Canaan* from the shore advance
Through the wild Desert, not the readiest way,
Lest ent'ring on the *Canaanite* alarm'd
War terrify them inexpert, and fear
Return them back to *Egypt*, choosing rather
220   Inglorious life with servitude; for life
To noble and ignoble is more sweet
Untrain'd in Arms, where rashness leads not on.
This also shall they gain by thir delay
In the wide Wilderness, there they shall found
225   Thir government, and thir great Senate choose
Through the twelve Tribes, to rule by Laws ordain'd:[1]
God from the Mount of *Sinai*, whose gray top
Shall tremble, he descending, will himself
In Thunder, Lightning and loud Trumpet's sound

---

8. In Ezekiel 29.3, the Pharaoh is called "the great dragon that lieth in the midst of his rivers." Milton uses the Pharaoh as an example of heart-hardening in *De doctrina* 1.8.
9. In *De doctrina* 1.5, Milton says that if God himself had gone with the Israelites, it would have destroyed them; he sent "the representation of his name and glory in some angel."
1. Milton uses "senate" for the Seventy Elders, the origin of the Sanhedrin. See Numbers 11.16–25; Exodus 24; and Acts 5.21. Milton took the Sanhedrin as a model for contemporary senates.

230   Ordain them Laws; part such as appertain
      To civil Justice, part religious Rites
      Of sacrifice, informing them, by types
      And shadows, of that destin'd Seed to bruise
      The Serpent, by what means he shall achieve
235   Mankind's deliverance. But the voice of God
      To mortal ear is dreadful; they beseech
      That *Moses* might report to them his will,[2]
      And terror cease; he grants what they besought,
      Instructed that to God is no access
240   Without Mediator, whose high Office now
      Moses in figure bears, to introduce
      One greater, of whose day he shall foretell,
      And all the Prophets in thir Age the times
      Of great *Messiah* shall sing. Thus Laws and Rites
245   Establisht, such delight hath God in Men
      Obedient to his will, that he voutsafes
      Among them to set up his Tabernacle,
      The holy One with mortal Men to dwell:
      By his prescript a Sanctuary is fram'd
250   Of Cedar, overlaid with Gold, therein
      An Ark, and in the Ark his Testimony,
      The Records of his Cov'nant, over these
      A Mercy-seat of Gold between the wings
      Of two bright Cherubim, before him burn
255   Sev'n Lamps as in a Zodiac representing
      The Heav'nly fires; over the Tent a Cloud
      Shall rest by Day, a fiery gleam by Night,
      Save when they journey, and at length they come,
      Conducted by his Angel to the Land
260   Promis'd to *Abraham* and his Seed: the rest
      Were long to tell, how many Battles fought,
      How many Kings destroy'd, and Kingdoms won,
      Or how the Sun shall in mid Heav'n stand still
      A day entire, and Night's due course adjourn,
265   Man's voice commanding, Sun in *Gibeon* stand,
      And thou Moon in the vale of *Aialon*,[3]
      Till *Israel*° overcome; so call the third   Jacob
      From *Abraham*, Son of *Isaac*, and from him
      His whole descent, who thus shall *Canaan* win.
270   Here *Adam* interpos'd. O sent from Heav'n,
      Enlight'ner of my darkness, gracious things
      Thou hast reveal'd, those chiefly which concern

---

2. Frightened by the thunder and lightning and trumpeting, the Israelites said to Moses: "Speak thou with us, and we will hear: but let not God speak with us, lest we die" (Exodus 20.19).
3. Echoes Joshua 10.12ff, "Then spake Joshua to the Lord in the day when the Lord delivered up the Amorites . . . and he said in the sight of Israel, Sun, stand thou still upon Gibeon; and thou, Moon, in the valley of Ajalon. And the sun stood still, and the moon stayed, until the people had avenged themselves upon their enemies."

Just *Abraham* and his Seed: now first I find
Mine eyes true op'ning, and my heart much eas'd,
275 Erewhile perplext with thoughts what would become
Of mee and all Mankind; but now I see
His day, in whom all Nations shall be blest,
Favor unmerited by me, who sought
Forbidd'n knowledge by forbidd'n means.
280 This yet I apprehend not, why to those
Among whom God will deign to dwell on Earth
So many and so various Laws are giv'n;
So many Laws argue so many sins
Among them; how can God with such reside?
285   To whom thus *Michael*. Doubt not but that sin
Will reign among them, as of thee begot;
And therefore was Law given them to evince°   *subdue*
Thir natural pravity,° by stirring up   *depravity*
Sin against Law to fight; that when they see
290 Law can discover sin, but not remove,
Save by those shadowy expiations weak,
The blood of Bulls and Goats, they may conclude
Some blood more precious must be paid for Man,
Just for unjust, that in such righteousness
295 To them by Faith imputed, they may find
Justification towards God, and peace
Of Conscience, which the Law by Ceremonies
Cannot appease, nor Man the moral part
Perform, and not performing cannot live.
300 So Law appears imperfet; and but° giv'n   *only*
With purpose to resign them in full time
Up to a better Cov'nant, disciplin'd
From shadowy Types to Truth, from Flesh to Spirit,
From imposition of strict Laws, to free
305 Acceptance of large Grace, from servile fear
To filial, works of Law to works of Faith.[4]
And therefore shall not *Moses*, though of God
Highly belov'd, being but the Minister
Of Law, his people into *Canaan* lead;
310 But *Joshua* whom the Gentiles *Jesus* call,[5]
His Name and Office bearing, who shall quell
The adversary Serpent, and bring back
Through the world's wilderness long wander'd man
Safe to eternal Paradise of rest.

4. Outlining the central Protestant doctrine of Justification by Faith. Too concise for assignment of sources, but see Romans 3.20; 4.22–5; 5.1–21; 7.7ff; 8.15; 10.5; Hebrews 7.19; 9.13ff; 10.1–5; Galatians 3.4.
5. In *De doctrina* 1.26, Milton states that the law fails to promise what faith in God through Christ attains, eternal life: "the imperfection of the law was made apparent in the person of Moses himself. For Moses, who was the type of the law, could not lead the children of Israel into the land of Canaan, that is, into eternal rest. But an entrance was granted to them under Joshua, that is, Jesus." See also Deuteronomy 34; Joshua 1. "Jesus" is the Greek equivalent of the Hebrew "Joshua."

315   Meanwhile they in thir earthly *Canaan* plac't
        Long time shall dwell and prosper; but° when sins   *except*
        National interrupt thir public peace,
        Provoking God to raise them enemies:
        From whom as oft he saves them penitent
320   By Judges first, then under Kings; of whom
        The second, both for piety renown'd
        And puissant deeds, a promise shall receive
        Irrevocable, that his Regal Throne
        For ever shall endure;[6] the like shall sing
325   All Prophecy, That of the Royal Stock
        Of *David* (so I name this King) shall rise
        A Son, the Woman's Seed to thee foretold,[7]
        Foretold to *Abraham*, as in whom shall trust
        All Nations, and to Kings foretold, of Kings
330   The last, for of his Reign shall be no end.
        But first a long succession must ensue,
        And his next Son for Wealth and Wisdom fam'd,[8]
        The clouded Ark of God till then in Tents
        Wand'ring, shall in a glorious Temple enshrine.
335   Such follow him, as shall be register'd
        Part good, part bad, of bad the longer scroll,
        Whose foul Idolatries, and other faults
        Heapt to the popular sum,[9] will so incense
        God, as to leave them, and expose thir Land,
340   Thir City, his Temple, and his holy Ark
        With all his sacred things, a scorn and prey
        To that proud City, whose high Walls thou saw'st
        Left in confusion, *Babylon* thence call'd.
        There in captivity he lets them dwell
345   The space of seventy years, then brings them back,[1]
        Rememb'ring mercy, and his Cov'nant sworn
        To *David*, stablisht as the days of Heav'n.
        Return'd from *Babylon* by leave of Kings
        Thir Lords, whom God dispos'd,° the house of God   *put into a good mood*
350   They first re-edify, and for a while
        In mean estate live moderate, till grown
        In wealth and multitude, factious they grow;
        But first among the Priests dissension springs,[2]
        Men who attend the Altar, and should most
355   Endeavor Peace: thir strife pollution brings

---

6. The prophet Nathan promised David "thine house and thy kingdom shall be established for ever before thee: thy throne shall be established for ever" (2 Samuel 7.16).
7. The royal line of David had Messianic significance; see Psalm 89.36; Isaiah 11.10; Luke 1.32.
8. Solomon, who built the Temple to give the ark its first fixed location (1 Kings 5–8; 2 Chronicles 2–5) — the occasion of another divine covenant (1 Kings 9.1–9).

9. That is, added to people's accumulated faults.
1. For the Babylonian captivity, see Jerome 25.12; 33.20–6 relating the return from exile to the covenant with David.
2. Maccabees 4–6 relates strife between intriguing priests, and for Milton provides an exemplum of the Church's betrayal by prelates and Presbyterians.

Upon the Temple itself: at last they seize
The Sceptre, and regard not *David's* Sons,
Then lose it to a stranger,[3] that the true
Anointed King *Messiah* might be born
360   Barr'd of his right; yet at his Birth a Star
Unseen before in Heav'n proclaims him come,
And guides the Eastern Sages, who enquire
His place, to offer Incense, Myrrh, and Gold;
His place of birth, a Solemn Angel tells
365   To simple Shepherds, keeping watch by night;
They gladly thither° haste, and by a Choir   *to Bethlehem*
Of squadron'd Angels hear his Carol sung.
A Virgin is his Mother, but his Sire
The Power of the most High; he shall ascend
370   The Throne hereditary, and bound his Reign
With earth's wide bounds, his glory with the Heav'ns.[4]
       He ceas'd, discerning *Adam* with such joy
Surcharg'd,° as had like grief been dew'd in tears,   *overwhelmed*
Without the vent of words, which these he breath'd.
375   O Prophet of glad tidings, finisher
Of utmost hope! now clear I understand
What oft my steadiest thoughts have searcht in vain,
Why our great expectation should be call'd
The seed of Woman: Virgin Mother, Hail,
380   High in the love of Heav'n, yet from my Loins
Thou shalt proceed, and from thy Womb the Son
Of God most High; So God with man unites.
Needs must the Serpent now his capital° bruise   *on the head*
Expect with mortal pain: say where and when
385   Thir fight, what stroke shall bruise the Victor's heel.
       To whom thus *Michael*. Dream not of thir fight,
As of a Duel, or the local wounds
Of head or heel: not therefore joins the Son
Manhood to Godhead, with more strength to foil
390   Thy enemy; nor so is overcome
Satan, whose fall from Heav'n, a deadlier bruise,
Disabl'd not to give thee thy death's wound:
Which hee, who comes thy Saviour, shall recure.
Not by destroying *Satan*, but his works[5]
395   In thee and in thy Seed: nor can this be,
But by fulfilling that which thou didst want,
Obedience to the Law of God, impos'd
On penalty of death, and suffering death,

3. The stranger is Antipater the Idumean, father of Herod the Great and Procurator of Judaea from 47 B.C.E., under Julius Caesar.
4. Christ's terrestrial reign is prophesied, among other places, in Isaiah 9.7; Daniel 7.13–22; Revelation 2.25–7.
5. Echoing 1 John 3.8, "For this purpose the Son of God was manifested, that he might destroy the works of the devil."

The penalty to thy transgression due,
400   And due to theirs which out of thine will grow:
So only can high Justice rest appaid.°   *satisfied*
The Law of God exact he shall fulfil
Both by obedience and by love, though love
Alone fulfil the Law; thy punishment
405   He shall endure by coming in the Flesh
To a reproachful life and cursed death,
Proclaiming Life to all who shall believe
In his redemption, and that his obedience
Imputed becomes theirs by Faith, his merits
410   To save them, not thir own, though legal works.[6]
For this he shall live hated, be blasphem'd,
Seiz'd on by force, judg'd, and to death condemn'd
A shameful and accurst, nail'd to the Cross
By his own Nation, slain for bringing Life;
415   But to the Cross he nails thy Enemies,
The Law that is against thee, and the sins
Of all mankind, with him there crucifi'd,
Never to hurt them more who rightly trust
In this his satisfaction; so he dies,
420   But soon revives, Death over him no power
Shall long usurp; ere the third dawning light
Return, the Stars of Morn shall see him rise
Out of his grave, fresh as the dawning light,
Thy ransom paid, which Man from death redeems,
425   His death for Man, as many as offer'd Life
Neglect not, and the benefit embrace
By Faith not void of works: this God-like act
Annuls thy doom, the death thou shouldst have di'd,
In sin for ever lost from life; this act
430   Shall bruise the head of *Satan*, crush his strength
Defeating Sin and Death, his two main arms,
And fix far deeper in his head thir stings
Than temporal° death shall bruise the Victor's heel,   *bodily*
Or theirs whom he redeems, a death like sleep,
435   A gentle wafting to immortal Life.
Nor after resurrection shall he stay
Longer on Earth than certain times to appear
To his Disciples, Men who in his Life
Still follow'd him; to them shall leave in charge
440   To teach all nations what of him they learn'd
And his Salvation, them who shall believe
Baptizing in the profluent° stream, the sign   *flowing profusely*
Of washing them from guilt of sin to Life

6. In the Protestant doctrine of Justification by Faith, Christ's obedient righteousness was imputed to the believer. Fulfillment of the law cannot save, there being no justification by works.

Pure, and in mind prepar'd, if so befall,
445 For death, like that which the redeemer di'd.
All Nations they shall teach; for from that day
Not only to the Sons of *Abraham's* Loins
Salvation shall be Preacht, but to the Sons
Of *Abraham's* Faith wherever through the world;
450 So in his seed all Nations shall be blest.
Then to the Heav'n of Heav'ns he shall ascend
With victory, triumphing through the air
Over his foes and thine; there shall surprise
The Serpent, Prince of air, and drag in Chains
455 Through all his Realm, and there confounded leave;
Then enter into glory, and resume
His Seat at God's right hand, exalted high
Above all names in Heav'n; and thence shall come,[7]
When this world's dissolution shall be ripe,
460 With glory and power to judge both quick and dead,
To judge th' unfaithful dead, but to reward
His faithful, and receive them into bliss,
Whether in Heav'n or Earth, for then the Earth
Shall all be Paradise, far happier place
465 Than this of *Eden*, and far happier days.
      So spake th' Arch-Angel *Michaël*, then paus'd,
As at the World's great period;[8] and our Sire
Replete with joy and wonder thus repli'd.
      O goodness infinite, goodness immense![9]
470 That all this good of evil shall produce,
And evil turn to good; more wonderful
Than that which by creation first brought forth
Light out of darkness! full of doubt I stand,
Whether I should repent me now of sin
475 By mee done and occasion'd, or rejoice
Much more, that much more good thereof shall spring,
To God more glory, more good will to Men
From God, and over wrath grace shall abound.[1]
But say, if our deliverer up to Heav'n
480 Must reascend, what will betide the few
His faithful, left among th' unfaithful herd,
The enemies of truth; who then shall guide
His people, who defend? will they not deal
Worse with his followers than with him they dealt?

---

7. The Second Coming foretold at 3.321ff. For the phrase "the quick [living] and dead," see the Apostles' Creed; Acts 10.42; 2 Timothy 4.1; 1 Peter 4.5.
8. This is Michael's second pause; the first was at 12.2. The three divisions of Adam's instruction are meant to correspond to "three drops" of the well of life placed in his eyes (11.416). Here the pause is compared with the world's period the dawning of the present age, from the first to the second coming of Christ.
9. The Final Cause or end of the Fall: a greater "glory" for God and an opportunity for him to show his surpassing love through the sacrifice of Christ.
1. See Romans 5.20 ("where sin abounded, grace did much more abound") and 2 Corinthians 4.15.

485   Be sure they will, said th' Angel; but from Heav'n
   Hee to his own a Comforter will send,[2]
   The promise of the Father, who shall dwell
   His Spirit within them, and the Law of Faith
   Working through love, upon thir hearts shall write,[3]
490   To guide them in all truth, and also arm
   With spiritual Armor, able to resist
   Satan's assaults, and quench his fiery darts,[4]
   What Man can do against them, not afraid,
   Though to the death, against such cruelties
495   With inward consolations recompens't,
   And oft supported so as shall amaze
   Thir proudest persecutors: for the Spirit
   Pour'd first on his Apostles, whom he sends
   To evangelize the Nations, then on all
500   Baptiz'd, shall them with wondrous gifts endue°   *endow*
   To speak all Tongues, and do all Miracles,
   As did thir Lord before them. Thus they win
   Great numbers of each Nation to receive
   With joy the tidings brought from Heav'n: at length
505   Thir Ministry perform'd, and race well run,
   Thir doctrine and thir story written left,
   They die; but in thir room, as they forewarn,
   Wolves shall succeed for teachers, grievous Wolves,[5]
   Who all the sacred mysteries of Heav'n
510   To thir own vile advantages shall turn
   Of lucre and ambition, and the truth
   With superstitions and traditions taint,
   Left only in those written Records pure,
   Though not but by the Spirit understood.[6]
515   Then shall they seek to avail themselves of names,
   Places and titles, and with these to join
   Secular power, though feigning still to act
   By spiritual, to themselves appropriating
   The Spirit of God, promis'd alike and giv'n
520   To all Believers;[7] and from that pretense,
   Spiritual Laws by carnal° power shall force   *worldly*
   On every conscience; Laws which none shall find
   Left them inroll'd, or what the Spirit within

---

2. The Holy Spirit. See John 14.18 and 15.26.

3. See Galatians 5.6: "faith which worketh by love."

4. Alluding to the allegory in Ephesians 6.16: "Above all, taking the shield of faith, wherewith ye shall be able to quench all the fiery darts of the wicked."

5. "For I know this, that after my departing shall grievous wolves enter in among you, not sparing the flock" (Acts 20.29). See the simile comparing Satan to a wolf in the fold, at 4.183–87; see also *Lycidas* 113ff, page 1711.

6. It was an important article of Protestant belief that in doctrinal matters the ultimate arbiter is individual conscience rather than mere authority.

7. The corruption of the Church through its pursuit of "secular power" is a subject Milton had dealt with in *Of Reformation*. In *De doctrina* 1.30 he condemns the enforcement of obedience to human opinions or authority.

Shall on the heart engrave.[8] What will they then
525   But force the Spirit of Grace itself, and bind
His consort Liberty; what, but unbuild
His living Temples, built by Faith to stand,[9]
Thir own Faith not another's: for on Earth
Who against Faith and Conscience can be heard
530   Infallible?[1] yet many will presume:
Whence heavy persecution shall arise
On all who in the worship persevere
Of Spirit and Truth; the rest, far greater part,
Will deem in outward Rites and specious forms
535   Religion satisfi'd; Truth shall retire
Bestuck with sland'rous darts, and works of Faith
Rarely be found: so shall the World go on,
To good malignant, to bad men benign,
Under her own weight groaning, till the day
540   Appear of respiration[2] to the just,
And vengeance to the wicked, at return
Of him so lately promis'd to thy aid,
The Woman's seed, obscurely then foretold,
Now amplier known thy Saviour and thy Lord,
545   Last in the Clouds from Heav'n to be reveal'd
In glory of the Father, to dissolve
Satan with his perverted World, then raise
From the conflagrant° mass, purg'd and refin'd,   burning
New Heav'ns, new Earth, Ages of endless date
550   Founded in righteousness and peace and love,
To bring forth fruits Joy and eternal Bliss.
      He ended; and thus Adam last repli'd.
How soon hath thy prediction, Seer blest,
Measur'd this transient World, the Race of time,
555   Till time stand fixt: beyond is all abyss,
Eternity, whose end no eye can reach.
Greatly instructed I shall hence depart,
Greatly in peace of thought, and have my fill
Of knowledge, what this Vessel can contain;
560   Beyond which was my folly to aspire.
Henceforth I learn, that to obey is best,
And love with fear the only God, to walk
As in his presence, ever to observe
His providence, and on him sole depend,
565   Merciful over all his works, with good
Still overcoming evil, and by small
Accomplishing great things, by things deem'd weak

8. The wolves will enforce laws written neither in Scripture nor in the individual conscience.
9. See 1 Corinthians 3.17: "The temple of God is holy, which temple ye are."
1. Even though the doctrine of papal infallibility was not formally adapted until 1870, there can be no doubt that Rome is Milton's main target here. In A Treatise of Civil Power he writes that the "Pope assumes infallibility over conscience and scripture."
2. Opportunity for breathing again; rest.

Subverting worldly strong, and worldly wise
By simply meek; that suffering for Truth's sake
570   Is fortitude to highest victory,
And to the faithful Death the Gate of Life;
Taught this by his example whom I now
Acknowledge my Redeemer ever blest.
     To whom thus also th' Angel last repli'd:
575   This having learnt, thou hast attain'd the sum
Of wisdom; hope no higher, though all the Stars
Thou knew'st by name, and all th' ethereal Powers,
All secrets of the deep, all Nature's works,
Or works of God in Heav'n, Air, Earth, or Sea,
580   And all the riches of this World enjoy'dst,
And all the rule, one Empire; only add
Deeds to thy knowledge answerable, add Faith,
Add Virtue, Patience, Temperance, add Love,
By name to come call'd Charity, the soul
585   Of all the rest;[3] then wilt thou not be loath
To leave this Paradise, but shalt possess
A paradise within thee, happier far.
Let us descend now therefore from this top
Of Speculation;[4] for the hour precise
590   Exacts our parting hence; and see the Guards,
By mee encampt on yonder Hill, expect
Thir motion,[5] at whose Front a flaming Sword,
In signal of remove, waves fiercely round;
We may no longer stay: go, waken *Eve*;
595   Her also I with gentle Dreams have calm'd
Portending good, and all her spirits compos'd
To meek submission: thou at season fit
Let her with thee partake what thou hast heard,
Chiefly what may concern her Faith to know,
600   The great deliverance by her Seed to come
(For by the Woman's Seed)[6] on all Mankind,
That ye may live, which will be many days,[7]
Both in one Faith unanimous though sad,
With cause for evils past, yet much more cheer'd
605   With meditation on the happy end.
     He ended, and they both descend the Hill;
Descended, *Adam* to the Bow'r where *Eve*
Lay sleeping ran before, but found her wak't;
And thus with words not sad she him receiv'd.

---

3. Compare 2 Peter 1.5–7: "Add to your faith virtue; and to virtue knowledge; and to knowledge temperance; and to temperance patience; and to patience godliness; and to godliness brotherly kindness; and to brotherly kindness charity."

4. Vantage point but also height of theological speculation.
5. Await deployment, marching orders.
6. Alluding to the birth of Jesus.
7. Adam lived to be 930 years of age (Genesis 5.5).

610   Whence thou return'st, and whither went'st, I know;
        For God is also in sleep, and Dreams advise,
        Which he hath sent propitious, some great good
        Presaging, since with sorrow and heart's distress
        Wearied I fell asleep: but now lead on;
615   In mee is no delay; with thee to go,
        Is to stay here; without thee here to stay,
        Is to go hence unwilling; thou to mee
        Art all things under Heav'n, all places thou,
        Who for my wilful crime art banisht hence.[8]
620   This further consolation yet secure
        I carry hence; though all by mee is lost,
        Such favor I unworthy am voutsaf't,
        By mee the Promis'd Seed shall all restore.
            So spake our Mother *Eve*, and *Adam* heard
625   Well pleas'd, but answer'd not; for now too nigh
        Th' Arch-Angel stood, and from the other Hill
        To thir fixt Station, all in bright array
        The Cherubim descended; on the ground
        Gliding meteorous,° as Ev'ning Mist   *meteoric*
630   Ris'n from a River o'er the marish° glides,   *marsh*
        And gathers ground fast at the Laborer's heel
        Homeward returning. High in Front advanc't,
        The brandisht Sword of God before them blaz'd
        Fierce as a Comet; which with torrid heat,
635   And vapor as the *Libyan* Air adust,°   *scorched*
        Began to parch that temperate Clime; whereat
        In either hand the hast'ning Angel caught
        Our ling'ring Parents, and to th' Eastern Gate
        Led them direct, and down the Cliff as fast
640   To the subjected° Plain; then disappear'd.   *underlying*
        They looking back, all th' Eastern side beheld
        Of Paradise, so late thir happy seat,
        Wav'd over by that flaming Brand,[9] the Gate
        With dreadful Faces throng'd and fiery Arms:
645   Some natural tears they dropp'd, but wip'd them soon;
        The World was all before them, where to choose
        Thir place of rest, and Providence thir guide:[1]
        They hand in hand with wand'ring steps and slow,
        Through *Eden* took thir solitary way.
                        The End

---

8. Eve has assimilated Michael's exhortation at 11.292: "where [Adam] abides, think there thy native soil." There is also a resonance with Eve's song at 4.635–56 (every time of day is pleasing with Adam, none is pleasing without him).

9. See Genesis. 3.24: "a flaming sword which turned every way."

1. Note that "Providence" can be the object of "choose": decisions of faith lie ahead.

RESPONSES

Mary Wollstonecraft: from *A Vindication of the Rights of Woman*[1]
from Chapter 2. *The Prevailing Opinion of a Sexual Character Discussed*

To account for, and excuse the tyranny of man, many ingenious arguments have been brought forward to prove, that the two sexes, in the acquirement of virtue, ought to aim at attaining a very different character: or, to speak explicitly, women are not allowed to have sufficient strength of mind to acquire what really deserves the name of virtue. Yet it should seem, allowing them to have souls, that there is but one way appointed by Providence to lead *mankind* to either virtue or happiness.

If then women are not a swarm of ephemeron[2] triflers, why should they be kept in ignorance under the specious name of innocence? Men complain, and with reason, of the follies and caprices of our sex, when they do not keenly satirize our headstrong passions and groveling vices.—Behold, I should answer, the natural effect of ignorance! The mind will ever be unstable that has only prejudices to rest on, and the current will run with destructive fury when there are no barriers to break its force. Women are told from their infancy, and taught by the example of their mothers, that a little knowledge of human weakness, justly termed cunning, softness of temper, *outward* obedience, and a scrupulous attention to a puerile kind of propriety, will obtain for them the protection of man; and should they be beautiful, every thing else is needless, for, at least, twenty years of their lives.

Thus Milton describes our first frail mother; though when he tells us that women are formed for softness and sweet attractive grace,[3] I cannot comprehend his meaning, unless, in the true Mahometan strain, he meant to deprive us of souls, and insinuate that we were beings only designed by sweet attractive grace, and docile blind obedience, to gratify the senses of man when he can no longer soar on the wing of contemplation.

How grossly do they insult us who thus advise us only to render ourselves gentle, domestic brutes! For instance, the winning softness so warmly, and frequently, recommended, that governs by obeying. What childish expressions, and how insignificant is the being—can it be an immortal one? who will condescend to govern by such sinister methods! "Certainly," says Lord Bacon, "man is of kin to the beasts by his body; and if he be not of kin to God by his spirit, he is a base and ignoble creature!"[4] Men, indeed, appear to me to act in a very unphilosophical manner when they try to secure the good conduct of women by attempting to keep them always in a state of childhood. Rousseau was more consistent when he wished to stop the progress of reason in both sexes, for if men eat of the tree of knowledge, women will come in for a taste;

---

1. Written by the leading feminist of the late eighteenth century, this essay rebuts the notion that woman is naturally submissive to man. Wollstonecraft explains that this view was promoted by the Genesis story of the creation of Eve from Adam's rib and by Milton's description of Eve as created for "softness . . . and sweet attractive grace" (*Paradise Lost* 4.298). The author, however, also finds evidence of Milton's siding with her point of view when he portrays Adam's arguing with God in *Paradise Lost* 8.381–91. Where does Milton stand on the relationship between man and woman? Does he side more with the view of woman as submissive or with Adam's contestation of that view? Wollstonecraft's reading of Milton opens up *Paradise Lost* to contested readings; her reading of Genesis also bears comparison with that of Rachel Speght in terms of contrasting views of the biblical presentation of the nature of woman. (For Speght's work, see *Perspectives: Tracts on Women and Gender*, page 1445.)
2. Winged insect that lives for only a day.
3. Satan's first view of Adam and Eve in *Paradise Lost*: "Not equal, as thir sex not equal seem'd; / For contemplation hee and valor form'd, / For softness shee and sweet attractive Grace, / He for God only, shee for God in him" (4.296–99). Fordyce quotes these lines in *Sermons to Young Women*, ch. 13.
4. Francis Bacon, *Essay 16*, "Of Atheism" (1606).

but, from the imperfect cultivation which their understandings now receive, they only attain a knowledge of evil.[5]

Children, I grant, should be innocent; but when the epithet is applied to men, or women, it is but a civil term for weakness. For if it be allowed that women were destined by Providence to acquire human virtues, and by the exercise of their understandings, that stability of character which is the firmest ground to rest our future hopes upon, they must be permitted to turn to the fountain of light, and not forced to shape their course by the twinkling of a mere satellite. Milton, I grant, was of a very different opinion; for he only bends to the indefeasible right of beauty, though it would be difficult to render two passages which I now mean to contrast, consistent. But into similar inconsistencies are great men often led by their senses.

> To whom thus Eve with *perfect beauty* adorn'd.
> "My Author and Disposer, what thou bidst
> *Unargued* I obey; So God ordains;
> God is *thy law, thou mine:* to know no more
> Is Woman's *happiest* knowledge and her *praise.*"[6]

These are exactly the arguments that I have used to children; but I have added, your reason is now gaining strength, and, till it arrives at some degree of maturity, you must look up to me for advice—then you ought to *think*, and only rely on God.

Yet in the following lines Milton seems to coincide with me; when he makes Adam thus expostulate with his Maker.

> Hast thou not made me here thy substitute,
> And these inferior far beneath me set?
> Among *unequals* what society
> Can sort, what harmony or true delight?
> Which must be mutual, in proportion due
> Giv'n and receiv'd; but in *disparity*
> The one intense, the other still remiss
> Cannot well suit with either, but soon prove
> Tedious alike: of *fellowship* I speak
> Such as I seek, fit to participate
> All rational delight[7]—

In treating, therefore, of the manners of women, let us, disregarding sensual arguments, trace what we should endeavour to make them in order to co-operate, if the expression be not too bold, with the supreme Being.

By individual education, I mean, for the sense of the word is not precisely defined, such an attention to a child as will slowly sharpen the senses, form the temper, regulate the passions as they begin to ferment, and set the understanding to work before the body arrives at maturity; so that the man may only have to proceed, not to begin, the important task of learning to think and reason. ***

Probably the prevailing opinion, that woman was created for man, may have taken its rise from Moses's poetical story,[8] yet, as very few, it is presumed, who have

---

5. See Rousseau's *Émile* (1.1): "Only reason teaches us good from evil."
6. *Paradise Lost* 4.634–38; Wollstonecraft's emphases.
7. *Paradise Lost* 8.381–91; Wollstonecraft's emphases.

8. The first five books of the Old Testament are traditionally attributed to Moses; in Genesis 2.21–23, followed by Milton, God creates Eve out of Adam's rib.

bestowed any serious thought on the subject, ever supposed that Eve was, literally speaking, one of Adam's ribs, the deduction must be allowed to fall to the ground; or, only be so far admitted as it proves that man, from the remotest antiquity, found it convenient to exert his strength to subjugate his companion, and his invention to shew that she ought to have her neck bent under the yoke, because the whole creation was only created for his convenience or pleasure.

Let it not be concluded that I wish to invert the order of things; I have already granted, that, from the constitution of their bodies, men seem to be designed by Providence to attain a greater degree of virtue. I speak collectively of the whole sex; but I see not the shadow of a reason to conclude that their virtues should differ in respect to their nature. In fact, how can they, if virtue has only one eternal standard? I must therefore, if I reason consequentially, as strenuously maintain that they have the same simple direction, as that there is a God.

It follows then that cunning should not be opposed to wisdom, little cares to great exertions, or insipid softness, varnished over with the name of gentleness, to that fortitude which grand views alone can inspire.

William Blake: A Poison Tree[1]

I was angry with my friend:
I told my wrath, my wrath did end.
I was angry with my foe:
I told it not, my wrath did grow.

5 And I water'd it in fears,
Night & morning with my tears:
And I sunned it with smiles.
And with soft deceitful wiles.

And it grew both day and night.
10 Till it bore an apple bright.
And my foe beheld it shine.
And he knew that it was mine.

And into my garden stole.
When the night had veiled the pole.
15 In the morning glad I see.
My foe outstretched beneath the tree.

1. In "The Word Made Flesh: Blake's 'A Poison Tree' and the Book of Genesis" *Studies in Romanticism* 16 (1977); 237–249, the Blake scholar Philip J. Gallagher connects Blake's "A Poison Tree" from *Songs of Experience* with Milton's *Paradise Lost*. First both texts are readings of Genesis and in some sense contain parodies of the concept of "the word made flesh." If Milton's Satan out of his "malice . . . and disdain" (V.666) gives birth to Sin, the speaker of Blake's lyric conceives an anger that through being repressed gives birth to murder—palpably represented in Blake's illustration to this poem by a dead body under the "Poison Tree." Seeing the same critique of conventional morality in Blake's *The Marriage of Good and Evil* (see *The Longman Anthology of British Literature: The Romantic Period*), at work in "A Poison Tree" allows Gallagher to read the poem as "a counter-myth which exposes the biblical narrative as a fraud." To what extent can Blake's poem be seen as a critique of the biblical narrative, and of the notion that because of man's "first disobedience" all human beings are born with original sin? In what respects are the murderous and hypocritical envy of Blake's speaker like that of Milton's Satan? To what extent is the Poison Tree an alternative reading of the Tree of the Knowledge of Good and Evil, in which the poison that is born forth comes from denying knowledge rather than partaking of it? How does Blake's rewriting of the Genesis story compare with Milton's?

CREDITS

COLOR PLATE CREDITS

INDEX

Sparkling Cyanide

BOOK 1

ROSEMARY

"What can I do to drive away
remembrances from mine eyes?"

Six people were thinking of Rosemary Barton who had died nearly a year ago. . . .

One

I

Iris Marle was thinking about her sister, Rosemary.

For nearly a year she had deliberately tried to put the thought of Rosemary away from her. She hadn't wanted to remember.

It was too painful—too horrible!

The blue cyanosed face, the convulsed clutching fingers. . . .

The contrast between that and the gay lovely Rosemary of the day before . . . Well, perhaps not exactly *gay*. She had had 'flu—she had been depressed, run-down . . . All that had been brought out at the inquest. Iris herself had laid stress on it. It accounted, didn't it, for Rosemary's suicide?

Once the inquest was over, Iris had deliberately tried to put the whole thing out of her mind. Of what good was remembrance? Forget it all! Forget the whole horrible business.

But now, she realized, she had got to remember. She had got to think back into the past . . . To remember carefully every slight unimportant seeming incident. . . .

11

That extraordinary interview with George last night necessitated remembrance.

It had been so unexpected, so frightening. Wait—*had* it been so unexpected? Hadn't there been indications beforehand? George's growing absorption, his absentmindedness, his unaccountable actions—his—well, *queerness* was the only word for it! All leading up to that moment last night when he had called her into the study and taken the letters from the drawer of the desk.

So now there was no help for it. She had got to think about Rosemary—to *remember*.

Rosemary—her sister. . . .

With a shock Iris realized suddenly that it was the first time in her life she had ever thought about Rosemary. Thought about her, that is, objectively, as a *person*.

She had always accepted Rosemary without thinking about her. You didn't think about your mother or your father or your sister or your aunt. They just existed, unquestioned, in those relationships.

You didn't think about them as *people*. You didn't ask yourself, even, what they were *like*.

What had Rosemary been like?

That might be very important now. A lot might depend upon it. Iris cast her mind back into the past. Herself and Rosemary as children. . . .

Rosemary had been the elder by six years.

II

Glimpses of the past came back—brief flashes— short scenes. Herself as a small child eating bread and milk, and Rosemary, important in pigtails, "doing lessons" at a table.

The seaside one summer—Iris envying Rosemary who was a "big girl" and could swim!

Rosemary going to boarding school—coming home for the holidays. Then she herself at school, and Rosemary being "finished" in Paris. School-girl Rosemary; clumsy, all arms and legs. "Finished" Rosemary coming back from Paris with a strange new frightening elegance, soft voiced, graceful, with a swaying undulating figure, with red gold chestnut hair and big black fringed dark blue eyes. A disturbing beautiful creature—grown up—in a different world!

From then on they had seen very little of each other, the six-year gap had been at its widest.

Iris had been still at school, Rosemary in the full swing of a "season." Even when Iris came home, the gap remained. Rosemary's life was one of late mornings in bed, fork luncheons with other débutantes, dances most evenings of the week. Iris had been in the schoolroom with Mademoiselle, had gone for walks in the Park, had had supper at nine o'clock and gone to bed at ten. The intercourse between the sisters had been limited to such brief interchanges as:

"Hullo, Iris, telephone for a taxi for me, there's a lamb, I'm going to be devastatingly late," or

"I don't like that new frock, Rosemary. It doesn't suit you. It's all bunch and fuss."

Then had come Rosemary's engagement to George Barton. Excitement, shopping, streams of parcels, bridesmaids' dresses.

The wedding. Walking up the aisles behind Rosemary, hearing whispers:

"What a *beautiful* bride she makes. . . ."

Why had Rosemary married George? Even at the time Iris had been vaguely surprised. There had been so many exciting young men, ringing Rosemary up, taking her out. Why choose George Barton, fifteen years older than herself, kindly, pleasant, but definitely dull?

George was well-off, but it wasn't money. Rosemary had her own money, a great deal of it.

Uncle Paul's money. . . .

Iris searched her mind carefully, seeking to differentiate between what she knew now and what she had known then: Uncle Paul, for instance?

He wasn't really an uncle, she had always known that. Without ever having been definitely told them she knew certain facts. Paul Bennett had been in love with their mother. She had preferred another and a poorer man. Paul Bennett had taken

14

his defeat in a romantic spirit. He had remained the family friend, adopted an attitude of romantic platonic devotion. He had become Uncle Paul, had stood godfather to the firstborn child, Rosemary. When he died, it was found that he had left his entire fortune to his little goddaughter, then a child of thirteen.

Rosemary, besides her beauty, had been an heiress. And she had married nice dull George Barton.

Why? Iris had wondered then. She wondered now. Iris didn't believe that Rosemary had ever been in love with him. But she had seemed very happy with him and she had been fond of him— yes, definitely fond of him. Iris had good opportunities for knowing, for a year after the marriage, their mother, lovely delicate Viola Marle, had died, and Iris, a girl of seventeen, had gone to live with Rosemary Barton and her husband.

A girl of seventeen. Iris pondered over the picture of herself. What had she been like? What had she felt, thought, seen?

She came to the conclusion that that young Iris Marle had been slow of development— unthinking, acquiescing in things as they were. Had she resented, for instance, her mother's earlier absorption in Rosemary? On the whole she thought not. She had accepted, unhesitatingly, the fact that Rosemary was the important one.

Rosemary was "out"—naturally her mother was occupied as far as her health permitted with her elder daughter. That had been natural enough. Her own turn would come someday. Viola Marle had always been a somewhat remote mother, preoccupied mainly with her own health, relegating her children to nurses, governesses, schools, but invariably charming to them in those brief moments when she came across them. Hector Marle had died when Iris was five years old. The knowledge that he drank more than was good for him had permeated so subtly that she had not the least idea how it had actually come to her.

Seventeen-year-old Iris Marle had accepted life as it came, had duly mourned for her mother, had worn black clothes, had gone to live with her sister and her sister's husband at their house in Elvaston Square.

Sometimes it had been rather dull in that house. Iris wasn't to come out, officially, until the following year. In the meantime she took French and German lessons three times a week, and also attended domestic science classes. There were times when she had nothing much to do and nobody to talk to. George was kind, invariably affectionate and brotherly. His attitude had never varied. He was the same now.

And Rosemary? Iris had seen very little of Rosemary. Rosemary had been out a good deal. Dressmakers, cocktail parties, bridge. . . .

What did she really *know* about Rosemary when she came to think of it? Of her tastes, of her hopes, of her fears? Frightening, really, how little you might know of a person after living in the same house with them! There had been little or no intimacy between the sisters.

But she'd got to think now. She'd got to remember. It might be important.

Certainly Rosemary had *seemed* happy enough. . . .

III

Until that day—a week before it happened.

She, Iris, would never forget that day. It stood out crystal clear—each detail, each word. The shining mahogany table, the pushed back chair, the hurried characteristic writing. . . .

Iris closed her eyes and let the scene come back. . . .

Her own entry into Rosemary's sitting room, her sudden stop.

It had startled her so; what she saw! Rosemary, sitting at the writing table, her head laid down on her outstretched arms. Rosemary weeping with a deep abandoned sobbing. She'd never seen Rosemary cry before—and this bitter, violent weeping frightened her.

True, Rosemary had had a bad go of 'flu. She'd only been up a day or two. And everyone knew that 'flu *did* leave you depressed. Still—

Iris had cried out, her voice childish, startled:

"Oh, Rosemary, what is it?"

Rosemary sat up, swept the hair back from her disfigured face. She struggled to regain command of herself. She said quickly:

"It's nothing—nothing—don't stare at me like that!"

She got up and passing her sister, she ran out of the room.

Puzzled, upset, Iris went farther into the room. Her eyes, drawn wonderingly to the writing table, caught sight of her own name in her sister's handwriting. Had Rosemary been writing to her then?

She drew nearer, looked down on the sheet of blue notepaper with the big characteristic sprawling writing, even more sprawling than usual owing to the haste and agitation behind the hand that held the pen.

Darling Iris,

There isn't any point in my making a will because my money goes to you anyway, but I'd like certain of my things to be given to certain people.

To George, the jewellery he's given me, and the little enamel casket we bought together when we were engaged.

To Gloria King, my platinum cigarette case.

18

To Maisie, my Chinese Pottery horse
that she's always admired—

It stopped there, with a frantic scrawl of the pen as Rosemary had dashed it down and given way to uncontrollable weeping.

Iris stood as though turned to stone.

What did it mean? Rosemary wasn't going to *die,* was she? She'd been very ill with influenza, but she was all right now. And anyway people didn't die of 'flu—at least sometimes they did, but Rosemary hadn't. She was quite well now, only weak and run-down.

Iris's eyes went over the words again and this time a phrase stood out with startling effect:

"*. . . my money goes to you anyway. . . .*"

It was the first intimation she had had of the terms of Paul Bennett's will. She had known since she was a child that Rosemary had inherited Uncle Paul's money, that Rosemary was rich whilst she herself was comparatively poor. But until this moment she had never questioned what would happen to that money on Rosemary's death.

If she had been asked, she would have replied that she supposed it would go to George as Rosemary's husband, but would have added that it seemed absurd to think of Rosemary dying before George!

But here it was, set down in black and white, in Rosemary's own hand. At Rosemary's death the money came to her, Iris. But surely that wasn't legal? A husband or wife got any money, not a *sister*. Unless, of course, Paul Bennett had left it that way in his will. Yes, that must be it. Uncle Paul had said the money was to go to her if Rosemary died. That did make it rather less unfair—

Unfair? She was startled as the word leapt to her thoughts. Had she been thinking that it was unfair for Rosemary to get *all* Uncle Paul's money? She supposed that, deep down, she must have been feeling just that. It *was* unfair. They were sisters, she and Rosemary. They were both her mother's children. Why should Uncle Paul give it all to Rosemary?

Rosemary always had everything!

Parties and frocks and young men in love with her and an adoring husband.

The only unpleasant thing that ever happened to Rosemary was having an attack of 'flu! And even *that* hadn't lasted longer than a week!

Iris hesitated, standing by the desk. That sheet of paper—would Rosemary want it left about for the servants to see?

After a minute's hesitation she picked it up, folded it in two and slipped it into one of the drawers of the desk.

It was found there after the fatal birthday party, and provided an additional proof, if proof was necessary, that Rosemary had been in a depressed and unhappy state of mind after her illness, and had possibly been thinking of suicide even then.

Depression after influenza. That was the motive brought forward at the inquest, the motive that Iris's evidence helped to establish. An inadequate motive, perhaps, but the only one available, and consequently accepted. It had been a bad type of influenza that year.

Neither Iris nor George Barton could have suggested any other motive—*then.*

Now, thinking back over the incident in the attic, Iris wondered that she could have been so blind.

The whole thing must have been going on under her eyes! And she had seen nothing, noticed nothing!

Her mind took a quick leap over the tragedy of the birthday party. No need to think of *that!* That was over—done with. Put away the horror of that and the inquest and George's twitching face and bloodshot eyes. Go straight on to the incident of the trunk in the attic.

IV

That had been about six months after Rosemary's death.

Iris had continued to live at the house in Elvaston Square. After the funeral the Marle family solicitor, a courtly old gentleman with a shining bald head and unexpectedly shrewd eyes,

21

had had an interview with Iris. He had explained with admirable clarity that under the will of Paul Bennett, Rosemary had inherited his estate in trust to pass at her death to any children she might have. If Rosemary died childless, the estate was to go to Iris absolutely. It was, the solicitor explained, a very large fortune which would belong to her absolutely upon attaining the age of twenty-one or on her marriage.

In the meantime, the first thing to settle was her place of residence. Mr. George Barton had shown himself anxious for her to continue living with him and had suggested that her father's sister, Mrs. Drake, who was in impoverished circumstances owing to the financial claims of a son (the black sheep of the Marle family), should make her home with them and chaperon Iris in society. Did Iris approve of this plan?

Iris had been quite willing, thankful not to have to make new plans. Aunt Lucilla she remembered as an amiable friendly sheep with little will of her own.

So the matter had been settled. George Barton had been touchingly pleased to have his wife's sister still with him and treated her affectionately as a younger sister. Mrs. Drake, if not a stimulating companion, was completely subservient to Iris's wishes. The household settled down amicably.

It was nearly six months later that Iris made her discovery in the attic.

The attics of the Elvaston Square house were used as storage rooms for odds and ends of furniture, and a number of trunks and suitcases.

Iris had gone up there one day after an unsuccessful hunt for an old red pullover for which she had an affection. George had begged her not to wear mourning for Rosemary, Rosemary had always been opposed to the idea, he said. This, Iris knew, was true, so she acquiesced and continued to wear ordinary clothes, somewhat to the disapproval of Lucilla Drake, who was old-fashioned and liked what she called "the decencies" to be observed. Mrs. Drake herself was still inclined to wear crêpe for a husband deceased some twenty-odd years ago.

Various unwanted clothes, Iris knew, had been packed away in a trunk upstairs. She started hunting through it for her pullover, coming across, as she did so, various forgotten belongings, a grey coat and skirt, a pile of stockings, her skiing kit and one or two old bathing dresses.

It was then that she came across an old dressing gown that had belonged to Rosemary and which had somehow or other escaped being given away with the rest of Rosemary's things. It was a mannish affair of spotted silk with big pockets.

Iris shook it out, noting that it was in perfectly good condition. Then she folded it carefully and returned it to the trunk. As she did so, her hand felt something crackle in one of the pockets. She thrust in her hand and drew out a crumpled-up piece of paper. It was in Rosemary's handwriting and she smoothed it out and read it.

Leopard darling, you can't mean it . . . You can't—you can't . . . We love each other! We belong together! You must know that just as I know it! We can't just say good-bye and go on coolly with our own lives. You know that's impossible, darling— quite impossible. You and I belong together—forever and ever. I'm not a conventional woman—I don't mind about what people say. Love matters more to me than anything else. We'll go away together—and be happy—I'll make you happy. You said to me once that life without me was dust and ashes to you—do you remember, Leopard darling? And now you write calmly that all this had better end—that it's only fair to me. Fair to me? But I can't live without you! I'm sorry about George—he's always been sweet to me—but he'll understand. He'll want to give me my freedom. It isn't right to live together if you don't love each other anymore. God meant us for each other, darling—I know He did. We're going to be wonderfully happy—but we must be brave. I shall tell George myself—I want to be quite straight about the whole thing—but not until after my birthday.

I know I'm doing what's right, Leopard darling—and I can't live without you— can't, can't—CAN'T. How stupid it is of me to write all this. Two lines would have done. Just "I love you. I'm never going to let you go." Oh darling—

The letter broke off.

Iris stood motionless, staring down at it.

How little one knew of one's own sister!

So Rosemary had had a lover—had written him passionate love letters—had planned to go away with him?

What had happened? Rosemary had never sent the letter after all. What letter had she sent? What had been finally decided between Rosemary and this unknown man?

("Leopard!" What extraordinary fancies people had when they were in love. So silly. *Leopard* indeed!)

Who was this man? Did he love Rosemary as much as she loved him? Surely he must have done. Rosemary was so unbelievably lovely. And yet, according to Rosemary's letter, he had suggested "ending it all." That suggested—what? Caution? He had evidently said that the break was for Rosemary's sake. That it was only fair to her. Yes, but didn't men say that sort of thing to save their faces? Didn't it really mean that the man, whoever he was, was tired of it all? Perhaps it had been to him a mere passing distraction. Perhaps he had never really cared. Somehow Iris got the impression that the unknown man had been very determined to break with Rosemary finally. . . .

But Rosemary had thought differently. Rosemary wasn't going to count the cost. Rosemary had been determined, too. . . .

Iris shivered.

And she, Iris, hadn't known a thing about it! Hadn't even guessed! Had taken it for granted that Rosemary was happy and contented and that she and George were quite satisfied with one another. Blind! She must have been blind not to know a thing like that about her own sister.

But who was the man?

She cast her mind back, thinking, remembering. There had been so many men about, admiring Rosemary, taking her out, ringing her up. There had been no one special. But there must have been—the rest of the bunch were mere camouflage for the one, the only one, that mattered. Iris frowned perplexedly, sorting her remembrances carefully.

Two names stood out. It must, yes, positively it must, be one or the other. Stephen Farraday? It must be Stephen Farraday. What could Rosemary have seen in him? A stiff pompous young man— and not so very young either. Of course people did say he was brilliant. A rising politician, an undersecretaryship prophesied in the near future, and all the weight of the influential Kidderminster connection behind him. A possible future Prime Minister! Was that what had given him glamour in Rosemary's eyes? Surely she couldn't care so desperately for the man himself—such a cold self-contained creature? But they said that his own wife was passionately in love with him, that she had gone against all the wishes of her powerful family in marrying him—a mere nobody with political ambitions! If one woman felt like that about him, another woman might also. Yes, it *must* be Stephen Farraday.

Because, if it wasn't Stephen Farraday, it must be Anthony Browne.

And Iris didn't want it to be Anthony Browne.

True, he'd been very much Rosemary's slave, constantly at her beck and call, his dark good-looking face expressing a kind of humorous desperation. But surely that devotion had been too open, too freely declared to go really deep?

Odd the way he had disappeared after Rosemary's death. They had none of them seen him since.

Still not so odd really—he was a man who travelled a lot. He had talked about the Argentine and Canada and Uganda and the U.S.A. She had an idea that he was actually an American or a Canadian, though he had hardly any accent. No, it wasn't really strange that they shouldn't have seen anything of him since.

It was Rosemary who had been his friend. There was no reason why he should go on coming to see the rest of them. He had been Rosemary's friend. But not Rosemary's lover! She didn't want him to have been Rosemary's lover. That would hurt— that would hurt terribly. . . .

She looked down at the letter in her hand. She crumpled it up. She'd throw it away, burn it. . . .

It was sheer instinct that stopped her.

Someday it might be important to produce that letter. . . .

She smoothed it out, took it down with her and locked it away in her jewel case.

It might be important, someday, to show why Rosemary took her own life.

V

"And the next thing, please?"

The ridiculous phrase came unbidden into Iris's mind and twisted her lips into a wry smile. The glib shopkeeper's question seemed to represent so exactly her own carefully directed mental processes.

Was not that exactly what she was trying to do in her survey of the past? She had dealt with the surprising discovery in the attic. And now—on to "the next thing, please!" What was the next thing?

Surely the increasingly odd behaviour of George. That dated back for a long time. Little things that had puzzled her became clear now in the light of the surprising interview last night. Disconnected remarks and actions took their proper place in the course of events.

And there was the reappearance of Anthony Browne. Yes, perhaps that ought to come next in sequence, since it had followed the finding of the letter by just one week.

Iris couldn't recall her sensations exactly. . . .

Rosemary had died in November. In the following May, Iris, under the wing of Lucilla Drake, had started her social young girl's life. She had gone to luncheons and teas and dances without, however, enjoying them very much. She had felt listless and unsatisfied. It was at a somewhat dull dance towards the end of June that she heard a voice say behind her:

"It *is* Iris Marle, isn't it?"

She had turned, flushing, to look into Anthony's—Tony's—dark quizzical face.

He said:

"I don't expect you to remember me, but—"

She interrupted.

"Oh, but I do remember you. Of course I do!"

"Splendid. I was afraid you'd have forgotten me. It's such a long time since I saw you."

"I know. Not since Rosemary's birthday par—"

She stopped. The words had come gaily,

unthinkingly, to her lips. Now the colour rushed away from her cheeks, leaving them white and drained of blood. Her lips quivered. Her eyes were suddenly wide and dismayed.

Anthony Browne said quickly:

"I'm terribly sorry. I'm a brute to have reminded you."

Iris swallowed. She said:

"It's all right."

(Not since the night of Rosemary's birthday party. Not since the night of Rosemary's suicide. She wouldn't think of it. She would *not* think of it!)

Anthony Browne said again:

"I'm terribly sorry. Please forgive me. Shall we dance?"

She nodded. Although already engaged for the dance that was just beginning, she had floated on to the floor in his arms. She saw her partner, a blushing immature young man whose collar seemed too big for him, peering about for her. The sort of partner, she thought scornfully, that debs have to put up with. Not like this man— Rosemary's friend.

A sharp pang went through her. *Rosemary's friend.* That letter. Had it been written to this man she was dancing with now? Something in the easy feline grace with which he danced lent substance to the nickname "Leopard." Had he and Rosemary—

She said sharply:

"Where have you been all this time?".

He held her a little way from him, looking down into her face. He was unsmiling now, his voice held coldness.

"I've been travelling—on business."

"I see." She went on uncontrollably, "Why have you come back?"

He smiled then. He said lightly:

"Perhaps—to see you, Iris Marle."

And suddenly gathering her up a little closer, he executed a long daring glide through the dancers, a miracle of timing and steering. Iris wondered why, with a sensation that was almost wholly pleasure, she should feel afraid.

Since then Anthony had definitely become part of her life. She saw him at least once a week.

She met him in the Park, at various dances, found him put next to her at dinner.

The only place he never came to was the house in Elvaston Square. It was some time before she noticed this, so adroitly did he manage to evade or refuse invitations there. When she did realize it she began to wonder why. Was it because he and Rosemary—

Then, to her astonishment, George, easy-going, noninterfering George, spoke to her about him.

"Who's this fellow, Anthony Browne, you're going about with? What do you know about him?"

She stared at him.

31

"Know about him? Why, he was a friend of Rosemary's!"

George's face twitched. He blinked. He said in a dull heavy voice:

"Yes, of course, so he was."

Iris cried remorsefully:

"I'm sorry. I shouldn't have reminded you."

George Barton shook his head. He said gently:

"No, no, I don't want her forgotten. Never that. After all," he spoke awkwardly, his eyes averted, "that's what her name means. Rosemary—remembrance." He looked full at her. "I don't want you to forget your sister, Iris."

She caught her breath.

"I never shall."

George went on:

"But about this young fellow, Anthony Browne. Rosemary may have liked him, but I don't believe she knew much about him. You know, you've got to be careful, Iris. You're a very rich young woman."

A kind of burning anger swept over her.

"Tony—Anthony—has plenty of money himself. Why, he stays at Claridge's when he's in London."

George Barton smiled a little. He murmured:

"Eminently respectable—as well as costly. All the same, my dear, nobody seems to know much about this fellow."

"He's an American."

"Perhaps. If so, it's odd he isn't sponsored more by his own Embassy. He doesn't come much to this house, does he?"

"No. And I can see why, if you're so horrid about him!"

George shook his head.

"Seem to have put my foot in it. Oh well. Only wanted to give you a timely warning. I'll have a word with Lucilla."

"Lucilla!" said Iris scornfully.

George said anxiously:

"Is everything all right? I mean, does Lucilla see to it that you get the sort of time you ought to have? Parties—all that sort of thing?"

"Yes, indeed, she works like a beaver. . . ."

"Because, if not, you've only got to say, you know, child. We could get hold of someone else. Someone younger and more up to date. I want you to enjoy yourself."

"I do, George. Oh, George, I do."

He said rather heavily:

"Then that's all right. I'm not much hand at these shows myself—never was. But see to it you get everything you want. There's no need to stint expense."

That was George all over—kind, awkward, blundering.

True to his promise, or threat, he "had a word" with Mrs. Drake on the subject of Anthony Browne, but as Fate would have it the moment

33

was unpropitious for gaining Lucilla's full attention.

She had just had a cable from that ne'er-do-well son who was the apple of her eye and who knew, only too well, how to wring the maternal heartstrings to his own financial advantage.

"Can you send me two hundred pounds. Desperate. Life or death. Victor."

"Victor is so honourable. He knows how straitened my circumstances are and he'd never apply to me except in the last resource. He never has. I'm always so afraid he'll shoot himself."

"Not he," said George Barton unfeelingly.

"You don't know him. I'm his mother and naturally I know what my own son is like. I should never forgive myself if I didn't do what he asked. I could manage by selling out those shares."

George sighed.

"Look here, Lucilla. I'll get full information by cable from one of my correspondents out there. We'll find out just exactly what sort of a jam Victor's in. But my advice to you is to let him stew in his own juice. He'll never make good until you do."

"You're so hard, George. The poor boy has always been unlucky—"

George repressed his opinions on that point. Never any good arguing with women.

He merely said:

"I'll get Ruth on to it at once. We should hear by tomorrow."

Lucilla was partially appeased. The two hundred was eventually cut down to fifty, but that amount Lucilla firmly insisted on sending.

George, Iris knew, provided the amount himself though pretending to Lucilla that he was selling her shares. Iris admired George very much for his generosity and said so. His answer was simple.

"Way I look at it—always some black sheep in the family. Always someone who's got to be kept. Someone or other will have to fork out for Victor until he dies."

"But it needn't be you. He's not *your* family."

"Rosemary's family's *mine.*"

"You're a darling, George. But couldn't *I* do it? You're always telling me I'm rolling."

He grinned at her.

"Can't do anything of that kind until you're twenty-one, young woman. And if you're wise you won't do it then. But I'll give you one tip. When a fellow wires that he'll end everything unless he gets a couple of hundred by return, you'll usually find that twenty pounds will be ample . . . I daresay a tenner would do! You can't stop a mother coughing up, but you can reduce the amount—remember that. Of course Victor Drake would never do away with himself, not he! These people who threaten suicide never do it."

Never? Iris thought of Rosemary. Then she pushed the thought away. George wasn't thinking of Rosemary. He was thinking of an unscrupulous, plausible young man in Rio de Janeiro.

The net gain from Iris's point of view was that Lucilla's maternal preoccupations kept her from paying full attention to Iris's friendship with Anthony Browne.

So—on to the "next thing, Madam." The change in George! Iris couldn't put it off any longer. When had that begun? What was the cause of it?

Even now, thinking back, Iris could not put her finger definitely on the moment when it began. Ever since Rosemary's death George had been abstracted, had had fits of inattention and brooding. He had seemed older, heavier. That was all natural enough. But when exactly had his abstraction become something more than natural?

It was, she thought, after their clash over Anthony Browne, that she had first noticed him staring at her in a bemused, perplexed manner. Then he formed a new habit of coming home early from business and shutting himself up in his study. He didn't seem to be doing anything there. She had gone in once and found him sitting at his desk staring straight ahead of him. He looked at her when she came in with dull lacklustre eyes. He behaved like a man who has had a shock, but to her question as to what was the matter, he replied briefly, "Nothing."

As the days went on, he went about with the careworn look of a man who has some definite worry upon his mind.

Nobody had paid very much attention. Iris certainly hadn't. Worries were always conveniently "Business."

Then, at odd intervals, and with no seeming reason, he began to ask questions. It was then that she began to put his manner down as definitely "queer."

"Look here, Iris, did Rosemary ever talk to you much?"

Iris stared at him.

"Why, of course, George. At least—well, about what?"

"Oh, herself—her friends—how things were going with her. Whether she was happy or unhappy. That sort of thing."

She thought she saw what was in his mind. He must have got wind of Rosemary's unhappy love affair.

She said slowly:

"She never said much. I mean—she was always busy—doing things."

"And you were only a kid, of course. Yes, I know. All the same, I thought she might have said something."

He looked at her inquiringly—rather like a hopeful dog.

She didn't want George to be hurt. And anyway

Rosemary never *had* said anything. She shook her head.

George sighed. He said heavily:

"Oh, well, it doesn't matter."

Another day he asked her suddenly who Rosemary's best women friends had been.

Iris reflected.

"Gloria King. Mrs. Atwell—Maisie Atwell. Jean Raymond."

"How intimate was she with them?"

"Well, I don't know exactly."

"I mean, do you think she might have confided in any of them?"

"I don't really know . . . I don't think it's awfully likely . . . What sort of confidence do you mean?"

Immediately she wished she hadn't asked that last question, but George's response to it surprised her.

"Did Rosemary ever say she was afraid of anybody?"

"Afraid?" Iris stared.

"What I'm trying to get at is, did Rosemary have any enemies?"

"Amongst other women?"

"No, no, not that kind of thing. Real enemies. There wasn't anyone—that you knew of—who—who might have had it in for her?"

Iris's frank stare seemed to upset him. He reddened, muttered:

"Sounds silly, I know. Melodramatic, but I just wondered."

It was a day or two after that that he started asking about the Farradays.

How much had Rosemary seen of the Farradays? Iris was doubtful.

"I really don't know, George."

"Did she ever talk about them?"

"No, I don't think so."

"Were they intimate at all?"

"Rosemary was very interested in politics."

"Yes. After she met the Farradays in Switzerland. Never cared a button about politics before that."

"No. I think Stephen Farraday interested her in them. He used to lend her pamphlets and things."

George said:

"What did Sandra Farraday think about it?"

"About what?"

"About her husband lending Rosemary pamphlets."

Iris said uncomfortably:

"I don't know."

George said, "She's a very reserved woman. Looks cold as ice. But they say she's crazy about Farraday. Sort of woman who might resent his having a friendship with another woman."

"Perhaps."

"How did Rosemary and Farraday's wife get on?"

Iris said slowly:

"I don't think they did. Rosemary laughed at Sandra. Said she was one of those stuffed political women like a rocking horse. (She is rather like a horse, you know.) Rosemary used to say that 'if you pricked her sawdust would ooze out.' "

George grunted.

Then he said:

"Still seeing a good deal of Anthony Browne?"

"A fair amount." Iris's voice was cold, but George did not repeat his warnings. Instead he seemed interested.

"Knocked about a good deal, hasn't he? Must have had an interesting life. Does he ever talk to you about it?"

"Not much. He's travelled a lot, of course."

"Business, I suppose."

"I suppose so."

"What is his business?"

"I don't know."

"Something to do with armament firms, isn't it?"

"He's never said."

"Well, needn't mention I asked. I just wondered. He was about a lot last Autumn with Dewsbury, who's chairman of the United Arms Ltd . . . Rosemary saw rather a lot of Anthony Browne, didn't she?"

"Yes—yes, she did."

"But she hadn't known him very long—he was more or less of a casual acquaintance? Used to take her dancing, didn't he?"

"Yes."

"I was rather surprised, you know, that she wanted him at her birthday party. Didn't realize she knew him so well."

Iris said quietly:

"He dances very well. . . ."

"Yes—yes, of course. . . ."

Without wishing to, Iris unwillingly let a picture of that evening flit across her mind.

The round table at the Luxembourg, the shaded lights, the flowers. The dance band with its insistent rhythm. The seven people round the table, herself, Anthony Browne, Rosemary, Stephen Farraday, Ruth Lessing, George, and on George's right, Stephen Farraday's wife, Lady Alexandra Farraday with her pale straight hair and those slightly arched nostrils and her clear arrogant voice. Such a gay party it had been, or hadn't it?

And in the middle of it, Rosemary—*No, no, better not think about that.* Better only to remember herself sitting next to Tony—that was the first time she had really met him. Before that he had been only a name, a shadow in the hall, a back accompanying Rosemary down the steps in front of the house to a waiting taxi.

Tony—

She came back with a start. George was repeating a question.

"Funny he cleared off so soon after. Where did he go, do you know?"

She said vaguely, "Oh, Ceylon, I think, or India."

"Never mentioned it that night."

Iris said sharply:

"Why should he? And have we got to talk about—that night?"

His face crimsoned over.

"No, no, of course not. Sorry, old thing. By the way, ask Browne to dinner one night. I'd like to meet him again."

Iris was delighted. George was coming round. The invitation was duly given and accepted, but at the last minute Anthony had to go North on business and couldn't come.

One day at the end of July, George startled both Lucilla and Iris by announcing that he had bought a house in the country.

"Bought a *house?*" Iris was incredulous. "But I thought we were going to rent that house at Goring for two months?"

"Nicer to have a place of one's own—eh? Can go down for weekends all through the year."

"Where is it? On the river?"

"Not exactly. In fact, not at all. Sussex. Marlingham. Little Priors, it's called. Twelve acres—small Georgian house."

Farradays? Why this costly method of achieving an incomprehensible aim?

Did George suspect that Rosemary and Stephen Farraday had been something more than friends? Was this a strange manifestation of postmortem jealousy? Surely that was a thought too far-fetched for words!

But what *did* George want from the Farradays? What was the point of all the odd questions he was continually shooting at her, Iris? Wasn't there something very queer about George lately?

The odd fuddled look he had in the evenings! Lucilla attributed it to a glass or so too much of port. Lucilla would!

No, there was something queer about George lately. He seemed to be labouring under a mixture of excitement interlarded with great spaces of complete apathy when he sunk in a coma.

Most of that August they spent in the country at Little Priors. Horrible house! Iris shivered. She hated it. A gracious well-built house, harmoniously furnished and decorated (Ruth Lessing was never at fault!). And curiously, frighteningly *vacant*. They didn't live there. They *occupied* it. As soldiers, in a war, occupied some lookout post.

What made it horrible was the overlay of ordinary normal summer living. People down for weekends, tennis parties, informal dinners with the Farradays. Sandra Farraday had been charming to them—the perfect manner to neighbours who were already friends. She introduced them to the county, advised George and Iris about horses, was prettily deferential to Lucilla as an older woman.

And behind the mask of her pale smiling face no one could know what she was thinking. A woman like a sphinx.

Of Stephen they had seen less. He was very busy, often absent on political business. To Iris it seemed certain that he deliberately avoided meeting the Little Priors party more than he could help.

So August had passed and September, and it was decided that in October they should go back to the London house.

Iris had drawn a deep breath of relief. Perhaps, once they were back George would return to his normal self.

And then, last night, she had been roused by a low tapping on her door. She switched on the light and glanced at the time. Only one o'clock. She had gone to bed at half past ten and it had seemed to her it was much later.

She threw on a dressing gown and went to the door. Somehow that seemed more natural than just to shout "Come in."

George was standing outside. He had not been to bed and was still in his evening clothes. His breath was coming unevenly and his face was a curious blue colour.

He said:

"Come down to the study, Iris. I've got to talk to you. I've got to talk to someone."

Wondering, still dazed with sleep, she obeyed.

Inside the study, he shut the door and motioned her to sit opposite him at the desk. He pushed the cigarette box across to her, at the same time taking one and lighting it, after one or two attempts, with a shaking hand.

She said, "Is anything the matter, George?"

She was really alarmed now. He looked ghastly.

George spoke between small gasps, like a man who has been running.

"I can't go on by myself. I can't keep it any longer. You've got to tell me what you think—whether it's true—whether it's *possible*—"

"But what is it you're talking about, George?"

"You must have noticed something, seen something. There must have been something she *said*. There must have been a *reason*—"

She stared at him.

He passed his hand over his forehead.

"You don't understand what I'm talking about. I can see that. Don't look so scared, little girl. You've got to help me. You've got to remember every damned thing you can. Now, now, I know I sound a bit incoherent, but you'll understand in a minute—when I've shown you the letters."

He unlocked one of the drawers at the side of the desk and took out two single sheets of paper.

They were of a pale innocuous blue, with words printed on them in small prim letters.

"Read that," said George.

Iris stared down at the paper. What it said was quite clear and devoid of circumlocution:

"YOU THINK YOUR WIFE COMMITTED SUICIDE. SHE DIDN'T. SHE WAS KILLED."

The second ran:

"YOUR WIFE ROSEMARY DIDN'T KILL HERSELF. SHE WAS MURDERED."

As Iris stayed staring at the words, George went on:

"They came about three months ago. At first I thought it was a joke—a cruel rotten sort of joke. Then I began to think. Why *should* Rosemary have killed herself?"

Iris said in a mechanical voice:

"Depression after influenza."

"Yes, but really when you come to think of it, that's rather piffle, isn't it? I mean lots of people have influenza and feel a bit depressed afterwards—what?"

Iris said with an effort:

"She might—have been unhappy?"

"Yes, I suppose she might." George considered the point quite calmly. "But all the same I don't see Rosemary putting an end to herself because she was unhappy. She might threaten to, but I don't think she would really do it when it came to the point."

"But she *must* have done, George! What other explanation could there be? Why, they even found the stuff in her handbag."

"I know. It all hangs together. But ever since these came," he tapped the anonymous letters with his fingernail, "I've been turning things over in my mind. And the more I've thought about it the more I feel sure there's something in it. That's why I've asked you all those questions—about Rosemary ever making any enemies. About anything she'd ever said that sounded as though she were afraid of someone. Whoever killed her must have had a *reason*—"

"But, George, you're crazy—"

"Sometimes I think I am. Other times I know that I'm on the right track. But I've got to *know*. I've got to find out. You've got to help me, Iris. You've got to *think*. You've got to remember. That's it—*remember*. Go back over that night again and again. Because you do see, don't you, that if she was killed, it *must have been someone who was at the table that night?* You do see that, don't you?"

Yes, she had seen that. There was no pushing aside the remembrance of that scene any longer. She must remember it all. The music, the roll of drums, the lowered lights, the cabaret and the lights going up again and Rosemary sprawled forward on the table, her face blue and convulsed.

Iris shivered. She was frightened now—horribly frightened. . . .

She must think—go back—remember.

Rosemary, that's for remembrance.

There was to be no oblivion.

Two

RUTH LESSING

Ruth Lessing, during a momentary lull in her busy day, was remembering her employer's wife, Rosemary Barton.

She had disliked Rosemary Barton a good deal. She had never known quite how much until that November morning when she had first talked with Victor Drake.

That interview with Victor had been the beginning of it all, had set the whole train in motion. Before then, the things she had felt and thought had been so far below the stream of her consciousness that she hadn't really known about them.

She was devoted to George Barton. She always had been. When she had first come to him, a cool, competent young woman of twenty-three, she had seen that he needed taking charge of. She had taken charge of him. She had saved him time, money and worry. She had chosen his friends for him, and directed him to suitable hobbies. She had restrained him from ill-advised business adventures, and encouraged him to take judicious risks on occasions. Never once in their long association had George suspected her of being anything other than subservient, attentive and entirely directed by himself. He took a distinct pleasure in her appearance, the neat shining dark head, the smart tailor-mades and crisp shirts, the small pearls in her well-shaped ears, the pale discreetly powdered face and the faint restrained rose shade of her lipstick.

Ruth, he felt, was absolutely right.

He liked her detached impersonal manner, her complete absence of sentiment or familiarity. In consequence he talked to her a good deal about his private affairs and she listened sympathetically and always put in a useful word of advice.

She had nothing to do, however, with his marriage. She did not like it. However, she accepted it and was invaluable in helping with the wedding arrangements, relieving Mrs. Marle of a great deal of work.

For a time after the marriage, Ruth was on slightly less confidential terms with her employer. She confined herself strictly to the office affairs. George left a good deal in her hands.

Nevertheless such was her efficiency that Rosemary soon found that George's Miss Lessing was an invaluable aid in all sorts of ways. Miss Lessing was always pleasant, smiling and polite.

George, Rosemary and Iris all called her Ruth and she often came to Elvaston Square to lunch. She was now twenty-nine and looked exactly the same as she had looked at twenty-three.

Without an intimate word ever passing between

them, she was always perfectly aware of George's slightest emotional reactions. She knew when the first elation of his married life passed into an ecstatic content, she was aware when that content gave way to something else that was not so easy to define. A certain inattention to detail shown by him at this time was corrected by her own forethought.

However distrait George might be, Ruth Lessing never seemed to be aware of it. He was grateful to her for that.

It was on a November morning that he spoke to her of Victor Drake.

"I want you to do a rather unpleasant job for me, Ruth?"

She looked at him inquiringly. No need to say that certainly she would do it. That was understood.

"Every family's got a black sheep," said George. She nodded comprehendingly.

"This is a cousin of my wife's—a thorough bad hat, I'm afraid. He's half ruined his mother—a fatuous sentimental soul who has sold out most of what few shares she has on his behalf. He started by forging a cheque at Oxford—they got that hushed up and since then he's been shipped about the world—never making good anywhere."

Ruth listened without much interest. She was familiar with the type. They grew oranges, started chicken farms, went as jackaroos to Australian stations, got jobs with meat-freezing concerns in New Zealand. They never made good, never stayed anywhere long, and invariably got through any money that had been invested on their behalf. They had never interested her much. She preferred success.

"He's turned up now in London and I find he's been worrying my wife. She hadn't set eyes on him since she was a schoolgirl, but he's a plausible sort of scoundrel and he's been writing to her for money, and I'm not going to stand for that. I've made an appointment with him for twelve o'clock this morning at his hotel. I want you to deal with it for me. The fact is I don't want to get into contact with the fellow. I've never met him and I never want to and I don't want Rosemary to meet him. I think the whole thing can be kept absolutely businesslike if it's fixed up through a third party."

"Yes, that is always a good plan. What is the arrangement to be?"

"A hundred pounds cash and a ticket to Buenos Aires. The money to be given to him actually on board the boat."

Ruth smiled.

"Quite so. You want to be sure he actually sails!"

"I see you understand."

"It's not an uncommon case," she said indifferently.

"No, plenty of that type about." He hesitated. "Are you sure you don't mind doing this?"

"Of course not." She was a little amused. "I can assure you I am quite capable of dealing with the matter."

"You're capable of anything."

"What about booking his passage? What's his name, by the way?"

"Victor Drake. The ticket's here. I rang up the steamship company yesterday. It's the *San Cristobal*, sails from Tilbury tomorrow."

Ruth took the ticket, glanced over it to make sure of its correctness and put it into her handbag.

"That's settled. I'll see to it. Twelve o'clock. What address?"

"The Rupert, off Russell Square."

She made a note of it.

"Ruth, my dear, I don't know what I should do without you—" He put a hand on her shoulder affectionately; it was the first time he had ever done such a thing. "You're my right hand, my other self."

She flushed, pleased.

"I've never been able to say much—I've taken all you do for granted—but it's not really like that. You don't know how much I rely on you for everything—" he repeated: "*everything.* You're the kindest, dearest, most helpful girl in the world!"

Ruth said, laughing to hide her pleasure and

embarrassment, "You'll spoil me saying such nice things."

"Oh, but I mean them. You're part of the firm, Ruth. Life without you would be unthinkable."

She went out feeling a warm glow at his words. It was still with her when she arrived at the Rupert Hotel on her errand.

Ruth felt no embarrassment at what lay before her. She was quite confident of her powers to deal with any situation. Hard-luck stories and people never appealed to her. She was prepared to take Victor Drake as all in the day's work.

He was very much as she had pictured him, though perhaps definitely more attractive. She made no mistake in her estimate of his character. There was not much good in Victor Drake. As coldhearted and calculating a personality as could exist, well masked behind an agreeable devilry. What she had not allowed for was his power of reading other people's souls, and the practised ease with which he could play on the emotions. Perhaps, too, she had underestimated her own resistance to his charm. For he had charm.

He greeted her with an air of delighted surprise.

"George's emissary? But how wonderful. What a surprise!"

In dry even tones, she set out George's terms. Victor agreed to them in the most amiable manner.

"A hundred pounds? Not bad at all. Poor old

George. I'd have taken sixty—but don't tell him so! Conditions:—'Do not worry lovely Cousin Rosemary—do not contaminate innocent Cousin Iris—do not embarrass worthy Cousin George.' All agreed to! Who is coming to see me off on the *San Cristobal*? You are, my dear Miss Lessing? Delightful." He wrinkled up his nose, his dark eyes twinkled sympathetically. He had a lean brown face and there was a suggestion about him of a toreador—romantic conception! He was attractive to women and knew it!

"You've been with Barton some time, haven't you, Miss Lessing?"

"Six years."

"And he wouldn't know what to do without you. Oh yes, I know all about it. And I know all about you, Miss Lessing."

"How do you know?" asked Ruth sharply.

Victor grinned. "Rosemary told me."

"Rosemary? But—"

"That's all right. I don't propose to worry Rosemary any further. She's already been very nice to me—quite sympathetic. I got a hundred out of her, as a matter of fact."

"You—"

Ruth stopped and Victor laughed. His laugh was infectious. She found herself laughing too.

"That's too bad of you, Mr. Drake."

"I'm a very accomplished sponger. Highly finished technique. The mater, for instance, will always come across if I send a wire hinting at imminent suicide."

"You ought to be ashamed of yourself."

"I disapprove of myself very deeply. I'm a bad lot, Miss Lessing. I'd like *you* to know just how bad."

"Why?" She was curious.

"I don't know. You're different. I couldn't play up the usual technique to you. Those clear eyes of yours—you wouldn't fall for it. No, 'More sinned against than sinning, poor fellow,' wouldn't cut any ice with you. You've no pity in you."

Her face hardened.

"I despise pity."

"In spite of your name? Ruth *is* your name, isn't it? Piquant that. Ruth the ruthless."

She said, "I've no sympathy with weakness!"

"Who said I was weak? No, no, you're wrong there, my dear. Wicked, perhaps. But there's one thing to be said for me."

Her lip curled a little. The inevitable excuse.

"Yes?"

"I enjoy myself. Yes," he nodded, "I enjoy myself immensely. I've seen a good deal of life, Ruth. I've done almost everything. I've been an actor and a storekeeper and a waiter and an odd job man, and a luggage porter, and a property man in a circus! I've sailed before the mast in a tramp steamer. I've been in the running for President in a South American Republic. I've been in prison!

There are only two things I've never done, an honest day's work, or paid my own way."

He looked at her, laughing. She ought, she felt, to have been revolted. But the strength of Victor Drake was the strength of the devil. He could make evil seem amusing. He was looking at her now with that uncanny penetration.

"You needn't look so smug, Ruth! You haven't as many morals as you think you have! Success is your fetish. You're the kind of girl who ends up by marrying the boss. That's what you ought to have done with George. George oughtn't to have married that little ass Rosemary. He ought to have married *you*. He'd have done a damned sight better for himself if he had."

"I think you're rather insulting."

"Rosemary's a damned fool, always has been. Lovely as paradise and dumb as a rabbit. She's the kind men fall for but never stick to. Now you— you're different. My God, if a man fell in love with you—he'd never tire."

He had reached the vulnerable spot. She said with sudden raw sincerity:

"If! But he wouldn't fall in love with me!"

"You mean George didn't? Don't fool yourself, Ruth. If anything happened to Rosemary, George would marry you like a shot."

(Yes, that was it. That was the beginning of it all.)

Victor said, watching her:

"But you know that as well as I do."

(George's hand on hers, his voice affectionate, warm—Yes, surely it was true . . . He turned to her, depended on her . . .)

Victor said gently: "You ought to have more confidence in yourself, my dear girl. You could twist George round your little finger. Rosemary's only a silly little fool."

"It's true," Ruth thought. "If it weren't for Rosemary, I could make George ask me to marry him. I'd be good to him. I'd look after him well."

She felt a sudden blind anger, an uprushing of passionate resentment. Victor Drake was watching her with a good deal of amusement. He liked putting ideas into people's heads. Or, as in this case, showing them the ideas that were already there. . . .

Yes, that was how it started—that chance meeting with the man who was going to the other side of the globe on the following day. The Ruth who came back to the office was not quite the same Ruth who had left it, though no one could have noticed anything different in her manner or appearance.

Shortly after she had returned to the office Rosemary Barton rang up on the telephone.

"Mr. Barton has just gone out to lunch. Can I do anything?"

"Oh, Ruth, would you? That tiresome Colonel

Race has sent a telegram to say he won't be back in time for my party. Ask George who he'd like to ask instead. We really ought to have another man. There are four women—Iris is coming as a treat and Sandra Farraday and—who on earth's the other? I can't remember."

"I'm the fourth, I think. You very kindly asked me."

"Oh, of course. I'd forgotten all about you!"

Rosemary's laugh came light and tinkling. She could not see the sudden flush, the hard line of Ruth Lessing's jaw.

Asked to Rosemary's party as a favour—a concession to George! "Oh, yes, we'll have your Ruth Lessing. After all she'll be pleased to be asked, and she is awfully useful. She looks quite presentable too."

In that moment Ruth Lessing knew that she hated Rosemary Barton.

Hated her for being rich and beautiful and careless and brainless. No routine hard work in an office for Rosemary—everything handed to her on a golden platter. Love affairs, a doting husband—no need to work or plan—

Hateful, condescending, stuck-up, frivolous beauty. . . .

"I wish you were dead," said Ruth Lessing in a low voice to the silent telephone.

Her own words startled her. They were so unlike her. She had never been passionate, never

61

vehement, never been anything but cool and controlled and efficient.

She said to herself: "What's happening to me?"

She had hated Rosemary Barton that afternoon. She still hated Rosemary Barton on this day a year later.

Someday, perhaps, she would be able to forget Rosemary Barton. But not yet.

She deliberately sent her mind back to those November days.

Sitting looking at the telephone—feeling hatred surge up in her heart. . . .

Giving Rosemary's message to George in her pleasant controlled voice. Suggesting that she herself should not come so as to leave the number even. George had quickly overridden *that!*

Coming in to report next morning on the sailing of the *San Cristobal.* George's relief and gratitude.

"So he's sailed on her all right?"

"Yes. I handed him the money just before the gangway was taken up." She hesitated and said, "He waved his hand as the boat backed away from the quay and called out 'Love and kisses to George and tell him I'll drink his health tonight.'"

"Impudence!" said George. He asked curiously, "What did you think of him, Ruth?"

Her voice was deliberately colourless as she replied:

"Oh—much as I expected. A weak type."

And George saw nothing, noticed nothing! She felt like crying out: "Why did you send me to see him? Didn't you know what he might do to me? Don't you realize that I'm a different person since yesterday? Can't you see that I'm *dangerous?* That there's no knowing what I may do?"

Instead she said in her businesslike voice, "About that San Paulo letter—"

She was the competent efficient secretary. . . .

Five more days.

Rosemary's birthday.

A quiet day at the office—a visit to the hair-dresser—the putting on of a new black frock, a touch of makeup skilfully applied. A face looking at her in the glass that was not quite her own face. A pale, determined, bitter face.

It was true what Victor Drake had said. There was no pity in her.

Later, when she was staring across the table at Rosemary Barton's blue convulsed face, she still felt no pity.

Now, eleven months later, thinking of Rosemary Barton, she felt suddenly afraid. . . .

Three

ANTHONY BROWNE

Anthony Browne was frowning into the middle distance as he thought about Rosemary Barton.

A damned fool he had been ever to get mixed up with her. Though a man might be excused for that! Certainly she was easy upon the eyes. That evening at the Dorchester he'd been able to look at nothing else. As beautiful as a houri—and probably just about as intelligent!

Still he'd fallen for her rather badly. Used up a lot of energy trying to find someone who would introduce him. Quite unforgivable really when he ought to have been attending strictly to business. After all, he wasn't idling his days away at Claridge's for pleasure.

But Rosemary Barton was lovely enough in all conscience to excuse any momentary lapse from duty. All very well to kick himself now and wonder why he'd been such a fool. Fortunately there was nothing to regret. Almost as soon as he spoke to her the charm had faded a little. Things resumed their normal proportions. This wasn't love—nor yet infatuation. A good time was to be had by all, no more, no less.

Well, he'd enjoyed it. And Rosemary had enjoyed it too. She danced like an angel and wherever he took her men turned round to stare at her. It gave a fellow a pleasant feeling. So long as you didn't expect her to talk. He thanked his stars he wasn't married to her. Once you got used to all that perfection of face and form where would you be? She couldn't even listen intelligently. The sort of girl who would expect you to tell her every morning at the breakfast table that you loved her passionately!

Oh, all very well to think those things now.

He'd fallen for her all right, hadn't he?

Danced attendance on her. Rung her up, taken her out, danced with her, kissed her in the taxi. Been in a fair way to making rather a fool of himself over her until that startling, that incredible day.

He could remember just how she had looked, the piece of chestnut hair that had fallen loose over one ear, the lowered lashes and the gleam of her dark blue eyes through them. The pout of the soft red lips.

"Anthony Browne. It's a nice name!"

He said lightly:

"Eminently well established and respectable. There was a chamberlain to Henry the Eighth called Anthony Browne."

"An ancestor, I suppose?"

"I wouldn't swear to that."

"You'd better not!"

He raised his eyebrows.

"I'm the Colonial branch."

"Not the Italian one?"

"Oh," he laughed. "My olive complexion? I had a Spanish mother."

"That explains it."

"Explains what?"

"A great deal, Mr. Anthony Browne."

"You're very fond of my name."

"I said so. It's a nice name."

And then quickly like a bolt from the blue: "Nicer than Tony Morelli."

For a moment he could hardly believe his ears! It was incredible! Impossible!

He caught her by the arm. In the harshness of his grip she winced away.

"Oh, you're hurting me!"

"Where did you get hold of that name?"

His voice was harsh, menacing.

She laughed, delighted with the effect she had produced. The incredible little fool!

"Who told you?"

"Someone who recognized you."

"Who was it? This is serious, Rosemary. I've got to know."

She shot a sideways glance at him.

"A disreputable cousin of mine, Victor Drake."

"I've never met anyone of that name."

"I imagine he wasn't using that name at the time you knew him. Saving the family feelings."

Anthony said slowly. "I see. It was—in prison?"

"Yes. I was reading Victor the riot act—telling him he was a disgrace to us all. He didn't care, of course. Then he grinned and said, 'You aren't always so particular yourself, sweetheart. I saw you the other night dancing with an ex-gaolbird—one of your best boyfriends, in fact. Calls himself Anthony Browne, I hear, but in stir he was Tony Morelli.'"

Anthony said in a light voice:

"I must renew my acquaintance with this friend of my youth. We old prison ties must stick together."

Rosemary shook her head. "Too late. He's been shipped off to South America. He sailed yesterday."

"I see." Anthony drew a deep breath. "So you're the only person who knows my guilty secret?"

She nodded. "I won't tell on you."

"You'd better not." His voice grew stern. "Look here, Rosemary, this is dangerous. You don't want your lovely face carved up, do you? There are people who don't stick at a little thing like ruining a girl's beauty. And there's such a thing as being bumped off. It doesn't only happen in books and films. It happens in real life, too."

"Are you threatening me, Tony?"

"Warning you."

Would she take the warning? Did she realize that he was in deadly earnest? Silly little fool. No sense in that lovely empty head. You couldn't rely on her to keep her mouth shut. All the same he'd have to try and ram his meaning home.

"Forget you've ever heard the name of Tony Morelli, do you understand?"

"But I don't mind a bit, Tony. I'm quite broadminded. It's quite a thrill for me to meet a criminal. You needn't feel ashamed of it."

The absurd little idiot. He looked at her coldly. He wondered in that moment how he could ever have fancied he cared. He'd never been able to suffer fools gladly—not even fools with pretty faces.

"Forget about Tony Morelli," he said grimly. "I mean it. Never mention that name again."

He'd have to get out. That was the only thing to do. There was no relying on this girl's silence. She'd talk whenever she felt inclined.

She was smiling at him—an enchanting smile, but it left him unmoved.

"Don't be so fierce. Take me to the Jarrows' dance next week."

"I shan't be here. I'm going away."

"Not before my birthday party. You can't let me down. I'm counting on you. Now don't say no. I've been miserably ill with that horrid 'flu and I'm still feeling terribly weak. I musn't be crossed. You've got to come."

He might have stood firm. He might have chucked it all—gone right away.

Instead, through an open door, he saw Iris

coming down the stairs. Iris, very straight and slim, with her pale face and black hair and grey eyes. Iris with much less than Rosemary's beauty and with all the character that Rosemary would never have.

In that moment he hated himself for having fallen a victim, in however small a degree, to Rosemary's facile charm. He felt as Romeo felt remembering Rosaline when he had first seen Juliet.

Anthony Browne changed his mind.

In the flash of a second he committed himself to a totally different course of action.

Four

Stephen Farraday

Stephen Farraday was thinking of Rosemary—thinking of her with that incredulous amazement that her image always aroused in him. Usually he banished all thoughts of her from his mind as promptly as they arose—but there were times when, persistent in death as she had been in life, she refused to be thus arbitrarily dismissed.

His first reaction was always the same, a quick irresponsible shudder as he remembered the scene in the restaurant. At least he need not think again of *that*. His thoughts turned further back, to Rosemary alive, Rosemary smiling, breathing, gazing into his eyes. . . .

What a fool—what an incredible fool he had been!

And amazement held him, sheer bewildered amazement. How had it all come about? He simply could not understand it. It was as though his life were divided into two parts, one, the larger part, a sane well-balanced orderly progression, the other a brief uncharacteristic madness. The two parts simply did not fit.

For with all his ability and his clever, shrewd intellect, Stephen had not the inner perception to see that actually they fitted only too well.

Sometimes he looked back over his life, appraising it coldly and without undue emotion, but with a certain priggish self-congratulation. From a very early age he had been determined to succeed in life, and in spite of difficulties and certain initial disadvantages he *had* succeeded.

He had always had a certain simplicity of belief and outlook. He believed in the Will. What a man willed, that he could do!

Little Stephen Farraday had steadfastly cultivated his Will. He could look for little help in life save that which he got by his own efforts. A small pale boy of seven, with a good forehead and a determined chin, he meant to rise—and rise high. His parents, he already knew, would be of no use to him. His mother had married beneath her station in life—and regretted it. His father, a small builder, shrewd, cunning and cheeseparing, was despised by his wife and also by his son . . . For his mother, vague, aimless, and given to extraordinary variations of mood, Stephen felt only a puzzled incomprehension until the day he found her slumped down on the corner of a table with an empty eau-de-Cologne bottle fallen from her hand. He had never thought of drink as an explanation of his mother's moods. She never drank spirits or beer, and he had never realized that her passion for eau de Cologne had had any other origin than her vague explanation of headaches.

He realized in that moment that he had little affection for his parents. He suspected shrewdly that they had not much for him. He was small for his age, quiet, with a tendency to stammer. Namby-pamby his father called him. A well-behaved child, little trouble in the house. His father would have preferred a more rumbustious type. "Always getting into mischief *I* was, at his age." Sometimes, looking at Stephen, he felt uneasily his own social inferiority to his wife. Stephen took after her folk.

Quietly, with growing determination, Stephen mapped out his own life. He was going to succeed. As a first test of will, he determined to master his stammer. He practised speaking slowly, with a slight hesitation between every word. And in time his efforts were crowned with success. He no longer stammered. In school he applied himself to his lessons. He intended to have education. Education got you somewhere. Soon his teachers became interested, encouraged him. He won a scholarship. His parents were approached by the educational authorities—the boy had promise. Mr. Farraday, doing well out of a row of jerry-built houses, was persuaded to invest money in his son's education.

At twenty-two Stephen came down from Oxford with a good degree, a reputation as a good and witty speaker, and a knack of writing articles. He had also made some useful friends. Politics were what attracted him. He had learnt to overcome his natural shyness and to cultivate an admirable social manner—modest, friendly, and with that touch of brilliance that led people to say, "That young man will go far." Though by predilection a Liberal, Stephen realized that for the moment, at least, the Liberal Party was dead. He joined the ranks of the Labour Party. His name soon became known as that of a "coming" young man. But the Labour Party did not satisfy Stephen. He found it less open to new ideas, more hidebound by tradition than its great and powerful rival. The Conservatives, on the other hand, were on the lookout for promising young talent.

They approved of Stephen Farraday—he was just the type they wanted. He contested a fairly solid Labour constituency and won it by a very narrow majority. It was with a feeling of triumph that Stephen took his seat in the House of Commons. His career had begun and this was the right career he had chosen. Into this he could put all his ability, all his ambition. He felt in him the ability to govern, and to govern well. He had a talent for handling people, for knowing when to flatter and when to oppose. One day, he swore it, he would be in the Cabinet.

Nevertheless, once the excitement of actually being in the House had subsided, he experienced swift disillusionment. The hardly fought election had put him in the limelight, now he was down in the rut, a mere insignificant unit of the rank and file, subservient to the party whips, and kept in his place. It was not easy here to rise out of obscurity. Youth here was looked upon with suspicion. One needed something above ability. One needed influence.

There were certain interests. Certain families. You had to be sponsored.

He considered marriage. Up to now he had thought very little about the subject. He had a dim picture in the back of his mind of some handsome creature who would stand hand in hand with him sharing his life and his ambitions; who would give him children and to whom he could unburden his thoughts and perplexities. Some woman who felt as he did and who would be eager for his success and proud of him when he achieved it.

Then one day he went to one of the big receptions at Kidderminster House. The Kidderminster connection was the most powerful in England. They were, and always had been, a great political family. Lord Kidderminster, with his little Imperial, his tall, distinguished figure, was known by sight everywhere. Lady Kidderminster's large rocking horse face was familiar on public platforms and on committees all over England. They had five daughters, three of them beautiful, and one son still at Eton.

The Kidderminsters made a point of encouraging likely young members of the Party. Hence Farraday's invitation.

He did not know many people there and he was standing alone near a window about twenty minutes after his arrival. The crowd by the tea table was thinning out and passing into the other rooms when Stephen noticed a tall girl in black standing alone by the table looking for a moment slightly at a loss.

Stephen Farraday had a very good eye for faces. He had picked up that very morning in the Tube a "Home Gossip" discarded by a woman traveller and glanced over it with slight amusement. There had been a rather smudgy reproduction of Lady Alexandra Hayle, third daughter of the Earl of Kidderminster, and below a gossipy little extract about her—". . . always been of a shy and retiring disposition—devoted to animals—Lady Alexandra has taken a course in Domestic Science as Lady Kidderminster believes in her daughters being thoroughly grounded in all domestic subjects."

That was Lady Alexandra Hayle standing there, and with the unerring perception of a shy person, Stephen knew that she, too, was shy. The plainest of the five daughters, Alexandra had always suffered under a sense of inferiority. Given the same education and upbringing as her sisters, she had never quite attained their *savoir faire*, which annoyed her mother considerably. Sandra must make an effort—it was absurd to appear so awkward, so *gauche.*

Stephen did not know that, but he knew that the girl was ill at ease and unhappy. And suddenly a rush of conviction came to him. This was his chance! *"Take it, you fool, take it! It's now or never!"*

He crossed the room to the long buffet. Standing beside the girl he picked up a sandwich. Then, turning, and speaking nervously and with an effort (no acting, that—he *was* nervous!) he said:

"I say, do you mind if I speak to you? I don't know many people here and I can see you don't either. Don't snub me. As a matter of fact I'm awfully s-s-shy" (his stammer of years ago came back at a most opportune moment) "and—and I think you're s-s-shy too, aren't you?"

The girl flushed—her mouth opened. But as he had guessed, she could not say it. Too difficult to find words to say "I'm the daughter of the house." Instead she admitted quietly:

"As a matter of fact, I—I am shy. I always have been."

Stephen went on quickly:

"It's a horrible feeling. I don't know whether one ever gets over it. Sometimes I feel absolutely tongue-tied."

"So do I."

He went on—talking rather quickly, stammering a little—his manner was boyish, appealing. It was a manner that had been natural to him a few years ago and which was now consciously retained and cultivated. It was young, naïve, disarming.

He led the conversation soon to the subject of plays, mentioned one that was running which had attracted a good deal of interest. Sandra had seen it. They discussed it. It had dealt with some point of the social services and they were soon deep in a discussion of these measures.

Stephen did not overdo things. He saw Lady Kidderminster entering the room, her eyes in search of her daughter. It was no part of his plan to be introduced now. He murmured a good-bye.

"I have enjoyed talking to you. I was simply hating the whole show till I found you. Thank you."

He left Kidderminster House with a feeling of exhilaration. He had taken his chance. Now to consolidate what he had started.

For several days after that he haunted the neighbourhood of Kidderminster House. Once Sandra came out with one of her sisters. Once she left the house alone, but with a hurried step. He shook his head. That would not do, she was obviously en route to some particular appointment. Then, about a week after the party, his patience was rewarded. She came out one morning with a small black Scottie dog and she turned with a leisurely step in the direction of the Park.

Five minutes later, a young man walking rapidly in the opposite direction pulled up short and stopped in front of Sandra. He exclaimed blithely:

"I say, what luck! I wondered if I'd ever see you again."

His tone was so delighted that she blushed just a little.

He stooped to the dog.

"What a jolly little fellow. What's his name?"

"MacTavish."

"Oh, very Scotch."

They talked dog for some moments. Then Stephen said, with a trace of embarrassment:

"I never told you my name the other day. It's Farraday. Stephen Farraday. I'm an obscure M.P."

He looked inquiringly and saw the colour come up in her cheeks again as she said: "I'm Alexandra Hayle."

He responded to that very well. He might have been back in the O.U.D.S. Surprise, recognition, dismay, embarrassment!

"Oh, you're—you're Lady Alexandra Hayle—you—my goodness! *What* a stupid fool you must have thought me the other day!"

Her answering move was inevitable. She was bound both by her breeding and her natural kindliness to do all she could to put him at his ease, to reassure him.

"I ought to have told you at the time."

"I ought to have known. What an oaf you must think me!"

"How should you have known? What does it matter anyway? Please, Mr. Farraday, don't look so upset. Let's walk to the Serpentine. Look, MacTavish is simply pulling."

After that, he met her several times in the Park. He told her his ambitions. Together they discussed political topics. He found her intelligent, well-informed and sympathetic. She had good brains and a singularly unbiased mind. They were friends now.

The next advance came when he was asked to dinner at Kidderminster House and to go on to a dance. A man had fallen through at the last moment. When Lady Kidderminster was racking her brains Sandra said quietly:

"What about Stephen Farraday?"

"Stephen Farraday?"

"Yes, he was at your party the other day and I've met him once or twice since."

Lord Kidderminster was consulted and was all in favour of encouraging the young hopefuls of the political world.

"Brilliant young fellow—quite brilliant. Never heard of his people, but he'll make a name for himself one of these days."

Stephen came and acquitted himself well.

"A useful young man to know," said Lady Kidderminster with unconscious arrogance.

Two months later Stephen put his fortunes to the test. They were by the Serpentine and MacTavish sat with his head on Sandra's foot.

"Sandra, you know—you must know that I love you. I want you to marry me. I wouldn't ask you if I didn't believe that I shall make a name for myself one day. I do believe it. You shan't be ashamed of your choice. I swear it."

She said, "I'm not ashamed."

"Then you do care?"

"Didn't you know?"

"I hoped—but I couldn't be sure. Do you know that I've loved you since that very first moment when I saw you across the room and took my courage in both hands and came to speak to you. I was never more terrified in my life."

She said, "I think I loved you then, too. . . ."

It was not all plain sailing. Sandra's quiet announcement that she was going to marry Stephen Farraday sent her family into immediate protests. Who was he? What did they know about him?

To Lord Kidderminster Stephen was quite frank about his family and origin. He spared a fleeting thought that it was just as well for his prospects that his parents were now both dead.

To his wife, Lord Kidderminster said, "H'm, it might be worse."

He knew his daughter fairly well, knew that her quiet manner hid inflexible purpose. If she meant to have the fellow she would have him. She'd never give in!

"The fellow's got a career ahead of him. With a bit of backing he'll go far. Heaven knows we could do with some young blood. He seems a decent chap, too."

Lady Kidderminster assented grudgingly. It was not at all her idea of a good match for her daughter. Still, Sandra was certainly the most difficult of the family. Susan had been a beauty and Esther had brains. Diana, clever child, had married the young Duke of Harwich—the *parti* of the season. Sandra had certainly less charm— there was her shyness—and if this young man had a future as everyone seemed to think. . . .

She capitulated, murmuring:

"But, of course, one will have to use *influence*. . . ."

So Alexandra Catherine Hayle took Stephen Leonard Farraday for better and for worse, in white satin and Brussels lace, with six brides-maids and two minute pages and all the accessories of a fashionable wedding. They went to Italy for the honeymoon and came back to a small charming house in Westminster, and a short time afterwards Sandra's godmother died and left her a very delightful small Queen Anne Manor house in the country. Everything went well for the young married pair. Stephen plunged into Parliamentary life with renewed ardour, Sandra aided and abetted him in every way, identifying herself heart and soul with his ambitions. Sometimes, Stephen would think with an almost incredulous realization of how Fortune had favoured him! His alliance with the powerful Kidderminster faction assured him of rapid rise in his career. His own ability and brilliance would consolidate the position that opportunity made for him. He believed honestly in his own powers and was prepared to work unsparingly for the good of his country.

Often, looking across the table at his wife, he felt gladly what a perfect helpmate she was—just what he had always imagined. He liked the lovely clean lines of her head and neck, the direct hazel eyes under their level brows, the rather high white forehead and the faint arrogance of her aquiline nose. She looked, he thought, rather like a racehorse—so well groomed, so instinct with breeding, so proud. He found her an ideal companion, their minds raced alike to the same quick conclusions. Yes, he thought, Stephen Farraday, that little disconsolate boy, had done very well for himself. His life was shaping exactly as he had meant it to be. He was only a year or two over thirty and already success lay in the hollow of his hand.

And in that mood of triumphant satisfaction, he went with his wife for a fortnight to St. Moritz, and looking across the hotel lounge saw Rosemary Barton.

What happened to him at that moment he never understood. By a kind of poetic revenge the words he had spoken to another woman came true. Across a room he fell in love. Deeply, overwhelmingly, crazily in love. It was the kind of desperate, headlong, adolescent calf love that he should have experienced years ago and got over.

He had always assumed that he was not a passionate type of man. One or two ephemeral affairs, a mild flirtation—that, so far as he knew, was all that "love" meant to him. Sensual pleasures simply did not appeal to him. He told himself that he was too fastidious for that sort of thing.

If he had been asked if he loved his wife, he would have replied "Certainly"—yet he knew, well enough, that he would not have dreamed of marrying her if she had been, say, the daughter of a penniless country gentleman. He liked her, admired her and felt a deep affection for her and also a very real gratitude for what her position had brought him.

That he could fall in love with the abandon and misery of a callow boy was a revelation. He could think of nothing but Rosemary. Her lovely laughing face, the rich chestnut of her hair, her swaying voluptuous figure. He couldn't eat— he couldn't sleep. They went skiing together. He danced with her. And as he held her to him he knew that he wanted her more than anything on earth. So this, this misery, this aching longing agony—this was love!

Even in his preoccupation he blessed Fate for having given him a naturally imperturbable manner. No one must guess, no one must know, what he was feeling—except Rosemary herself.

The Bartons left a week earlier than the Farradays. Stephen said to Sandra that St. Moritz was not very amusing. Should they cut their time short and go back to London? She agreed very amiably. Two weeks after their return, he became Rosemary's lover.

A strange ecstatic hectic period—feverish, unreal. It lasted—how long? Six months at most. Six months during which Stephen went about his work as usual, visited his constituency, asked questions in the House, spoke at various meetings, discussed politics with Sandra and thought of one thing only—Rosemary.

Their secret meetings in the little flat, her beauty, the passionate endearments he showered on her, her clinging passionate embraces. A dream. A sensual infatuated dream.

And after the dream—the awakening.

It seemed to happen quite suddenly.

Like coming out of a tunnel into the daylight.

One day he was a bemused lover, the next day he was Stephen Farraday again thinking that perhaps he ought not to see Rosemary quite so often. Dash it all, they had been taking some terrific risks. If Sandra was ever to suspect—He stole a look at her down the breakfast table. Thank goodness, she didn't suspect. She hadn't an idea. Yet some of his excuses for absence lately had been pretty thin. Some women would have begun to smell a rat. Thank goodness Sandra wasn't a suspicious woman.

He took a deep breath. Really he and Rosemary had been very reckless! It was a wonder her husband hadn't got wise to things. One of those foolish unsuspecting chaps—years older than she was.

What a lovely creature she was. . . .

He thought suddenly of golf links. Fresh air blowing over sand dunes, tramping round with clubs—swinging a driver—a nice clean shot off the tee—a little chip with a mashie. Men. Men in plus fours smoking pipes. And no women allowed on the links!

He said suddenly to Sandra:

"Couldn't we go down to Fairhaven?"

She looked up, surprised.

"Do you want to? Can you get away?"

"Might take the inside of a week. I'd like to get some golf. I feel stale."

"We could go tomorrow if you like. It will mean putting off the Astleys, and I must cancel that meeting on Tuesday. But what about the Lovats?"

"Oh, let's cancel that too. We can think of some excuse. I want to get away."

It had been peaceful at Fairhaven with Sandra and the dogs on the terrace and in the old walled garden, and with golf at Sandley Heath, and pottering down to the farm in the evening with MacTavish at his heels.

He had felt rather like someone who is recovering from an illness.

He had frowned when he saw Rosemary's writing. He'd told her not to write. It was too dangerous. Not that Sandra ever asked him who his letters were from, but all the same it was unwise. Servants weren't always to be trusted.

He ripped open the envelope with some annoyance, having taken the letter into his study. Pages. Simply pages.

As he read, the old enchantment swept over him again. She adored him, she loved him more than ever, she couldn't endure not seeing him for five whole days. Was he feeling the same? Did the Leopard miss his Ethiopian?

He half-smiled, half-sighed. That ridiculous joke—born when he had bought her a man's spotted dressing gown that she had admired. The Leopard changing his spots, and he had said, "But you mustn't change your skin, darling." And after that she had called him Leopard and he had called her his Black Beauty.

Damned silly, really. Yes, damned silly. Rather sweet of her to have written such pages and pages. But still she shouldn't have done it. Dash it all, they'd got to be *careful!* Sandra wasn't the sort of woman who would stand for anything of that kind. If she once got an inkling—Writing letters was dangerous. He'd told Rosemary so. Why couldn't she wait until he got back to town? Dash it all, he'd see her in another two or three days.

There was another letter on the breakfast table the following morning. This time Stephen swore inwardly. He thought Sandra's eyes rested on it for a couple of seconds. But she didn't say anything. Thank goodness she wasn't the sort of woman who asked questions about a man's correspondence.

After breakfast he took the car over the market town eight miles away. Wouldn't do to put through a call from the village. He got Rosemary on the phone.

"Hullo—that you, Rosemary? Don't write any more letters."

"Stephen, darling, how lovely to hear your voice!"

"Be careful, can anyone overhear you?"

"Of course not. Oh, angel, I have missed you. Have you missed me?"

"Yes, of course. But don't write. It's much too risky."

"Did you like my letter? Did it make you feel I was with you? Darling, I want to be with you every minute. Do you feel that too?"

"Yes—but not on the phone, old thing."

"You're so ridiculously cautious. What does it matter?"

"I'm thinking of you, too, Rosemary. I couldn't bear any trouble to come to you through me."

"I don't care what happens to me. You know that."

"Well, I care, sweetheart."

"When are you coming back?"

"Tuesday."

"And we'll meet at the flat, Wednesday."

"Yes—er, yes."

"Darling, I can hardly bear to wait. Can't you make some excuse and come up today? Oh, Stephen, you *could!* Politics or something stupid like that?"

"I'm afraid it's out of the question."

"I don't believe you miss me half as much as I miss you."

"Nonsense, of course I do."

When he rang off he felt tired. Why should women insist on being so damned reckless? Rosemary and he must be more careful in future. They'd have to meet less often.

Things after that became difficult. He was busy—very busy. It was quite impossible to give as much time to Rosemary—and the trying thing was she didn't seem able to understand. He explained but she just wouldn't listen.

"Oh, your stupid old politics—as though *they* were important!"

"But they *are*—"

She didn't realize. She didn't care. She took no interest in his work, in his ambitions, in his career. All she wanted was to hear him reiterate again and again that he loved her. "Just as much as ever? Tell me again that you *really* love me?"

Surely, he thought, she might take that for granted by this time! She was a lovely creature, lovely—but the trouble was that you couldn't *talk* to her.

The trouble was they'd been seeing too much of each other. You couldn't keep up an affair at fever heat. They must meet less often—slacken off a bit.

But that made her resentful—very resentful. She was always reproaching him now.

"You don't love me as you used to do."

And then he'd have to reassure her, to swear that of course he did. And she *would* constantly resurrect everything he had ever said to her.

"Do you remember when you said it would be lovely if we died together? Fell asleep forever in each other's arms? Do you remember when you said we'd take a caravan and go off into the desert? Just the stars and the camels—and how we'd forget everything in the world?"

What damned silly things one said when one was in love! They hadn't seemed fatuous at the time, but to have them hashed up in cold blood! Why couldn't women let things decently alone? A man didn't want to be continually reminded what an ass he'd made of himself.

She came out with sudden unreasonable demands. Couldn't he go abroad to the South of France and she'd meet him there? Or go to Sicily or Corsica—one of those places where you never saw anyone you knew? Stephen said grimly that there was no such place in the world. At the most unlikely spots you always met some dear old school friend that you'd never seen for years.

And then she said something that frightened him.

"Well, but it wouldn't really matter, would it?"

He was alert, watchful, suddenly cold within.

"What do you mean?"

She was smiling up at him, that same enchanting smile that had once made his heart turn over and his bones ache with longing. Now it made him merely impatient.

"Leopard, darling, I've thought sometimes that we're stupid to go on trying to carry on this hole-and-corner business. It's not worthy, somehow. Let's go away together. Let's stop pretending. George will divorce me and your wife will divorce you and then we can get married."

Just like that! Disaster! Ruin! And she couldn't see it!

"I wouldn't let you do such a thing."

"But, darling, I don't care. I'm not really very conventional."

"But I am. But I am," thought Stephen.

"I do feel that love is the most important thing in the world. It doesn't matter what people think of us."

"It would matter to me, my dear. An open scandal of that kind would be the end of my career."

"But would that really matter? There are hundreds of other things that you could do."

"Don't be silly."

"Why have you got to do anything anyway? I've got lots of money, you know. Of my own, I mean, not George's. We could wander about all over the world, going to the most enchanting out-of-the-way places—places, perhaps, where nobody else has ever been. Or to some island in the Pacific—think of it, the hot sun and the blue sea and the coral reefs."

He did think of it. A South Sea Island! Of all the idiotic ideas. What sort of a man did she think he was—a beachcomber?

He looked at her with eyes from which the last traces of scales had fallen. A lovely creature with the brains of a hen! He'd been mad—utterly and completely mad. But he was sane again now. And he'd got to get out of this fix. Unless he was careful she'd ruin his whole life.

He said all the things that hundreds of men had said before him. They must end it all—so he wrote. It was only fair to her. He couldn't risk bringing unhappiness on her. She didn't understand—and so on and so on.

It was all over—he must make her understand that.

But that was just what she refused to understand. It wasn't to be as easy as that. She adored him, she loved him more than ever, she couldn't live without him! The only honest thing was for her to tell her husband, and for Stephen to tell his wife the truth! He remembered how cold he had felt as he sat holding her letter. The little fool! The silly clinging fool! She'd go and blab the whole thing to George Barton and then George would divorce her and cite him as co-respondent. And Sandra would perforce divorce him too. He hadn't any doubt of that. She had spoken once of a friend, had said with faint surprise, "But of course when she found out he was having an affair with another woman, what else could she do but divorce him?" That was what Sandra would feel. She was proud. She would never share a man.

And then he would be done, finished—the influential Kidderminster backing would be withdrawn. It would be the kind of scandal that he would not be able to live down, even though public opinion was broaderminded than it used to be. But not in a flagrant case like this! Good-bye to his dreams, his ambitions. Everything wrecked, broken—all because of a crazy infatuation for a silly woman. Calf love, that was all it had been. Calf love contracted at the wrong time of life.

He'd lose everything he'd staked. Failure! Ignominy!

He'd lose Sandra. . . .

And suddenly, with a shock of surprise he realized that it was that that he would mind most. *He'd lose Sandra.* Sandra with her square white forehead and her clear hazel eyes. Sandra, his dear friend and companion, his arrogant, proud, loyal Sandra. No, he couldn't lose Sandra—he couldn't . . . Anything but that.

The perspiration broke out on his forehead.

Somehow he *must* get out of this mess.

Somehow he must make Rosemary listen to reason . . . But would she? Rosemary and reason didn't go together. Supposing he were to tell her that, after all, he loved his wife? No. She simply wouldn't believe it. She was such a stupid woman. Empty-headed, clinging, possessive. And she loved him still—that was the mischief of it.

A kind of blind rage rose up in him. How on earth was he to keep her quiet? To shut her mouth? Nothing short of a dose of poison would do that, he thought bitterly.

A wasp was buzzing close at hand. He stared abstractedly. It had got inside a cut-glass jampot and was trying to get out.

Like me, he thought, entrapped by sweetness and now—he can't get out, poor devil.

But he, Stephen Farraday, was going to get out somehow. Time, he must play for time.

Rosemary was down with 'flu at the moment. He'd sent conventional inquiries—a big sheaf of flowers. It gave him a respite. Next week Sandra and he were dining with the Bartons—a birthday party for Rosemary. Rosemary had said, "I shan't do anything until after my birthday—it would be too cruel to George. He's making such a fuss about it. He's such a dear. After it's all over we'll come to an understanding."

Supposing he were to tell her brutally that it was all over, that he no longer cared? He shivered. No, he dare not do that. She might go to George in hysterics. She might even come to Sandra. He could hear her tearful, bewildered voice.

"He says he doesn't care anymore, but I *know* it's not true. He's trying to be loyal—to play the game with *you*—but I know you'll agree with me that when people love each other honesty is the *only* way. That's why I'm asking you to give him his freedom."

That was just the sort of nauseating stuff she would pour out. And Sandra, her face proud and disdainful, would say, "He can have his freedom!"

She wouldn't believe—how could she believe? If Rosemary were to bring out those letters—the letters he'd been asinine enough to write to her. Heaven knew what he had said in them. Enough and more than enough to convince Sandra—letters such as he had never written to *her*—

He must think of something—some way of keeping Rosemary quiet. "It's a pity," he thought grimly, "that we don't live in the days of the Borgias. . . ."

A glass of poisoned champagne was about the only thing that would keep Rosemary quiet.

Yes, he had actually thought that.

Cyanide of potassium in her champagne glass, cyanide of potassium in her evening bag. Depression after influenza.

And across the table, Sandra's eyes meeting his.

Nearly a year ago—and he couldn't forget.

Five

ALEXANDRA FARRADAY

Sandra Farraday had not forgotten Rosemary Barton.

She was thinking of her at this very minute—thinking of her slumped forward across the table in the restaurant that night.

She remembered her own sharp indrawn breath and how then, looking up, she had found Stephen watching her. . . .

Had he read the truth in her eyes? Had he seen the hate, the mingling of horror and triumph?

Nearly a year ago now—and as fresh in her mind as if it had been yesterday! *Rosemary, that's for remembrance.* How horribly true that was. It was no good a person being dead if they lived on in your mind. That was what Rosemary had done. In Sandra's mind—and in Stephen's, too? She didn't know, but she thought it probable.

The Luxembourg—that hateful place with its excellent food, its deft swift service, its luxurious *décor* and setting. An impossible place to avoid, people were always asking you there.

She would have liked to forget—but everything conspired to make her remember. Even Fairhaven was no longer exempt now that George Barton had come to live at Little Priors.

It was really rather extraordinary of him. George Barton was altogether an odd man. Not at all the kind of neighbour she liked to have. His presence at Little Priors spoiled for her the charm and peace of Fairhaven. Always, up to this summer, it had been a place of healing and rest, a place where she and Stephen had been happy—that is, if they ever had been happy?

Her lips pressed thinly together. Yes, a thousand times, yes! They could have been happy but for Rosemary. It was Rosemary who had shattered the delicate edifice of mutual trust and tenderness that she and Stephen were beginning to build. Something, some instinct, had bade her hide from Stephen her own passion, her single-hearted devotion. She had loved him from the moment he came across the room to her that day at Kidderminster House, pretending to be shy, pretending not to know who she was.

For he *had* known. She could not say when she had first accepted that fact. Sometime after their marriage, one day when he was expounding some neat piece of political manipulation necessary to the passing of some Bill.

The thought had flashed across her mind then: "This reminds me of something. What?" Later she realized that it was, in essence, the same tactics he had used that day at Kidderminster House. She accepted the knowledge without surprise, as though it were something of which she had long been aware, but which had only just risen to the surface of her mind.

From the day of their marriage she had realized that he did not love her in the same way as she loved him. But she thought it possible that he was actually incapable of such a love. That power of loving was her own unhappy heritage. To care with a desperation, an intensity that was, she knew, unusual among women! She would have died for him willingly; she was ready to lie for him, scheme for him, suffer for him! Instead she accepted with pride and reserve the place he wanted her to fill. He wanted her cooperation, her sympathy, her active and intellectual help. He wanted of her, not her heart, but her brains, and those material advantages which birth had given her.

One thing she would never do, embarrass him by the expression of a devotion to which he could make no adequate return. And she did believe honestly that he liked her, that he took pleasure in her company. She foresaw a future in which her burden would be immeasurably lightened—a future of tenderness and friendship.

In his way, she thought, he loved her.

And then Rosemary came.

She wondered sometimes, with a wry painful twist of the lips, how it was that he could imagine that she did not know. She had known from the first minute—up there at St. Moritz—when she had first seen the way he looked at the woman.

She had known the very day the woman became his mistress.

She knew the scent the creature used. . . .

She could read in Stephen's polite face, with eyes abstracted, just what his memories were, what he was thinking about—that woman—the woman he had just left!

It was difficult, she thought dispassionately, to assess the suffering she had been through. Enduring, day after day, the tortures of the damned, with nothing to carry her through but her belief in courage—her own natural pride. She would not show, she would never show, what she was feeling. She lost weight, grew thinner and paler, the bones of her head and shoulders showing more distinctly with the flesh stretched tightly over them. She forced herself to eat, but could not force herself to sleep. She lay long nights, with dry eyes, staring into darkness. She despised the taking of drugs as weakness. She would hang on. To show herself hurt, to plead, to protest—all these things were abhorrent to her.

She had one crumb of comfort, a meagre one—Stephen did not wish to leave her. Granted that that was for the sake of his career, not out of fondness for her, still the fact remained. He did not want to leave her.

Someday, perhaps, the infatuation would pass. . . .

What could he, after all, see in the girl? She was attractive, beautiful—but so were other women. What did he find in Rosemary Barton that infatuated him?

She was brainless—silly—and not—she clung to this point especially—not even particularly amusing. If she had had wit, charm and provocation of manner—those were the things that held men. Sandra clung to the belief that the thing would end—that Stephen would tire of it.

She was convinced that the main interest in his life was his work. He was marked out for great things and he knew it. He had a fine statesmanlike brain and he delighted in using it. It was his appointed task in life. Surely once the infatuation began to wane he would realize that fact?

Never for one minute did Sandra consider leaving him. The idea never even came to her. She was his, body and soul, to take or discard. He was her life, her existence. Love burned in her with a medieval force.

There was a moment when she had hope. They went down to Fairhaven. Stephen seemed more his normal self. She felt suddenly a renewal of the old sympathy between them. Hope rose in her heart. He wanted her still, he enjoyed her company, he relied on her judgement. For the moment, he had escaped from the clutches of that woman.

He looked happier, more like his own self.

Nothing was irretrievably ruined. He was getting over it. If only he could make up his mind to break with her. . . .

Then they went back to London and Stephen relapsed. He looked haggard, worried, ill. He began to be unable to fix his mind on his work.

She thought she knew the cause. Rosemary wanted him to go away with her . . . He was making up his mind to take the step—to break with everything he cared about most. Folly! Madness! He was the type of man with whom his work would always come first—a very English type. He must know that himself, deep down— Yes, but Rosemary was very lovely—and very stupid. Stephen would not be the first man who had thrown away his career for a woman and been sorry afterwards!

Sandra caught a few words—a phrase one day at a cocktail party.

". . . Telling George—got to make up our minds."

It was soon after that that Rosemary went down with 'flu.

A little hope rose in Sandra's heart. Suppose she were to get pneumonia—people did after 'flu—a young friend of hers had died that way only last winter. If Rosemary were to die—

She did not try to repress the thought—she was not horrified at herself. She was medieval enough to hate with a steady and untroubled mind.

She hated Rosemary Barton. If thoughts could kill, she would have killed her.

But thoughts do not kill—

Thoughts are not enough. . . .

How beautiful Rosemary had looked that night at the Luxembourg with her pale fox furs slipping off her shoulders in the ladies' cloak-room. Thinner, paler since her illness—an air of delicacy made her beauty more ethereal. She had stood in front of the glass touching up her face. . . .

Sandra, behind her, looked at their joint reflection in the mirror. Her own face like something sculptured, cold, lifeless. No feeling there, you would have said—a cold hard woman.

And then Rosemary said: "Oh, Sandra, am I taking all the glass? I've finished now. This horrid 'flu has pulled me down a lot. I look a sight. And I feel quite weak still and headachy."

Sandra had asked with quiet polite concern:

"Have you got a headache tonight?"

"Just a bit of one. You haven't got an aspirin, have you?"

"I've got a Cachet Faivre."

She had opened her handbag, taken out the cachet. Rosemary had accepted it. "I'll take it in my bag in case."

That competent dark-haired girl, Barton's secretary, had watched the little transaction. She came in turn to the mirror, and just put on a slight dusting of powder. A nice-looking girl, almost handsome. Sandra had the impression that she didn't like Rosemary.

Then they had gone out of the cloakroom, Sandra first, then Rosemary, then Miss Lessing— oh, and of course, the girl Iris, Rosemary's sister, she had been there. Very excited, with big grey eyes, and a schoolgirlish white dress.

They had gone out and joined the men in the hall.

And the headwaiter had come bustling forward and showed them to their table. They had passed in under the great domed arch and there had been nothing, absolutely nothing, to warn one of them that she would never come out through that door again alive. . . .

Six

GEORGE BARTON

Rosemary. . . .

George Barton lowered his glass and stared rather owlishly into the fire.

He had drunk just enough to feel maudlin with self-pity.

What a lovely girl she had been. He'd always been crazy about her. She knew it, but he'd always supposed she'd only laugh at him.

Even when he first asked her to marry him, he hadn't done it with any conviction.

Mowed and mumbled. Acted like a blithering fool.

"You know, old girl, anytime—you've only got to say. I know it's no good. You wouldn't look at me. I've always been the most awful fool. Got a bit of a corporation, too. But you do know what I feel, don't you, eh? I mean—I'm always there. Know I haven't got an earthly chance, but thought I'd just mention it."

And Rosemary had laughed and kissed the top of his head.

"You're sweet, George, and I'll remember the kind offer, but I'm not marrying anyone just at present."

And he had said seriously: "Quite right. Take

104

plenty of time to look around. You can take your pick."

He'd never had any hope—not any real hope.

That's why he had been so incredulous, so dazed when Rosemary had said she was going to marry him.

She wasn't in love with him, of course. He knew that quite well. In fact, she admitted as much.

"You do understand, don't you? I want to feel settled down and happy and safe. I shall with you. I'm so sick of being in love. It always goes wrong somehow and ends in a mess. I like you, George. You're nice and funny and sweet and you think I'm wonderful. That's what I want."

He had answered rather incoherently:

"Steady does it. We'll be as happy as kings."

Well, that hadn't been far wrong. They had been happy. He'd always felt humble in his own mind. He'd always told himself that there were bound to be snags. Rosemary wasn't going to be satisfied with a dull kind of chap like himself. There would be *incidents!* He'd schooled himself to accept— incidents! He would hold firm to the belief that they wouldn't be lasting! Rosemary would always come back to him. Once let him accept that view and all would be well.

For she was fond of him. Her affection for him was constant and unvarying. It existed quite apart from her flirtations and her love affairs.

He had schooled himself to accept those. He had told himself that they were inevitable with someone of Rosemary's susceptible temperament and unusual beauty. What he had not bargained for were his own reactions.

Flirtations with this young man and that were nothing, but when he first got an inkling of a serious affair—

He'd known quick enough, sensed the difference in her. The rising excitement, the added beauty, the whole glowing radiance. And then what his instinct told him was confirmed by ugly concrete facts.

There was that day when he'd come into her sitting room and she had instinctively covered with her hand the page of the letter she was writing. He'd known then. She was writing to her lover.

Presently, when she went out of the room, he went across to the blotter. She had taken the letter with her, but the blotting sheet was nearly fresh. He'd taken it across the room and held it up to the glass—seen the words in Rosemary's dashing script, "My own beloved darling. . . ."

His blood had sung in his ears. He understood in that moment just what Othello had felt. Wise resolutions? Pah! Only the natural man counted. He'd like to choke the life out of her! He'd like to murder the fellow in cold blood. Who was it? That fellow Browne? Or that stick Stephen Farraday? They'd both of them been making sheep's eyes at her.

He caught sight of his face in the glass. His eyes were suffused with blood. He looked as though he were going to have a fit.

As he remembered that moment, George Barton let his glass fall from his hand. Once again he felt the choking sensation, the beating blood in his ears. Even now—

With an effort he pushed remembrance away. Mustn't go over that again. It was past—done with. He wouldn't ever suffer like that again. Rosemary was dead. Dead and at peace. And he was at peace too. No more suffering. . . .

Funny to think that that was what her death had meant to him. Peace. . . .

He'd never told even Ruth that. Good girl, Ruth. A good headpiece on her. Really, he didn't know what he would do without her. The way she helped. The way she sympathized. And never a hint of sex. Not man-mad like Rosemary. . . .

Rosemary . . . Rosemary sitting at the round table in the restaurant. A little thin in the face after 'flu—a little pulled down—but lovely, so lovely. And only an hour later—

No, he wouldn't think of that. Not just now. His plan. He would think of The Plan.

He'd speak to Race first. He'd show Race the letters. What would Race make of these letters? Iris had been dumbfounded. She evidently hadn't had the slightest idea.

Well, he was in charge of the situation now. He'd got it all taped.

The Plan. All worked out. The date. The place.

November 2nd. *All Souls' Day.* That was a good touch. The Luxembourg, of course. He'd try to get the same table.

And the same guests. Anthony Browne, Stephen Farraday, Sandra Farraday. Then, of course, Ruth and Iris and himself. And as the odd, the seventh guest he'd get Race. Race who was originally to have been at the dinner.

And there would be one empty place.

It would be splendid!

Dramatic!

A repetition of the crime.

Well, not quite a repetition. . . .

His mind went back. . . .

Rosemary's birthday. . . .

Rosemary, sprawled forward on that table—dead . . . ?

BOOK 2

ALL SOULS' DAY

"There's Rosemary,
that's for remembrance."

One

Lucilla Drake was twittering. That was the term always used in the family and it was really a very apt description of the sounds that issued from Lucilla's kindly lips.

She was concerned on this particular morning with many things—so many that she found it hard to pin her attention down to one at a time. There was the imminence of the move back to town and the household problems involved in that move. Servants, housekeeping, winter storage, a thousand minor details—all these contended with a concern over Iris's looks.

"Really, dear, I feel quite anxious about you—you look so white and washed out—as though you hadn't slept—did you sleep? If not, there's that nice sleeping preparation of Dr. Wylie's or was it Dr. Gaskell's?—which reminds me—I shall have to go and speak to the grocer *myself*—either the maids have been ordering things in on their own, or else it's deliberate swindling on his part. Packets and packets of soap flakes—and I never allow more than three a week. But perhaps a tonic would be better? Eaton's syrup, they used to give when I was a girl. And spinach, of course. I'll tell cook to have spinach for lunch today."

Iris was too languid and too used to Mrs.

Drake's discursive style to inquire why the mention of Dr. Gaskell should have reminded her aunt of the local grocer, though had she done so, she would have received the immediate response: "Because the grocer's name is Cranford, my dear." Aunt Lucilla's reasoning was always crystal clear to herself.

Iris merely said with what energy she could command, "I'm perfectly well, Aunt Lucilla."

"Black under the eyes," said Mrs. Drake. "You've been doing too much."

"I've done nothing at all—for weeks."

"So you think, dear. But too much tennis is overtiring for young girls. And I think the air down here is inclined to be enervating. This place is in a hollow. If George had consulted *me* instead of that girl."

"Girl?"

"That Miss Lessing he thinks so much of. All very well in the office, I daresay—but a great mistake to take her out of her place. Encourage her to think herself one of the family. Not that she needs any encouragement, I should say."

"Oh, well, Aunt Lucilla, Ruth *is* practically one of the family."

Mrs. Drake sniffed. "She means to be—that's quite clear. Poor George—really an infant in arms where women are concerned. But it won't do, Iris. George must be protected from himself and if I were you I should make it very clear that nice as

Miss Lessing is, any idea of marriage is out of the question."

Iris was startled for a moment out of her apathy.

"I never thought of George marrying Ruth."

"You don't see what goes on under your nose, child. Of course you haven't had my experience of life." Iris smiled in spite of herself. Aunt Lucilla was really very funny sometimes. "That young woman is out for matrimony."

"Would it matter?" asked Iris.

"Matter? Of course it would matter."

"Wouldn't it really be rather nice?" Her aunt stared at her. "Nice for George, I mean. I think you're right about her, you know. I think she is fond of him. And she'd be an awfully good wife to him and look after him."

Mrs. Drake snorted and an almost indignant expression appeared on her rather sheep-like amiable face.

"George is very well looked after at present. What more can he want, I should like to know? Excellent meals and his mending seen to. Very pleasant for him to have an attractive young girl like you about the house and when you marry some day I should hope I was still capable of seeing to his comfort and looking after his health. Just as well or better than a young woman out of an office could do—what does she know about housekeeping? Figures and ledgers and shorthand and typing—what good is that in a man's home?"

Iris smiled and shook her head, but she did not argue the point. She was thinking of the smooth dark satin of Ruth's head, of the clear complexion and the figure so well set off by the severe tailor-made clothes that Ruth affected. Poor Aunt Lucilla, all her mind on comfort and house-keeping, with romance so very far behind her that she had probably forgotten what it meant—if indeed, thought Iris, remembering her uncle by marriage, it had ever meant much.

Lucilla Drake had been Hector Marle's half-sister, the child of an earlier marriage. She had played the little mother to a very much younger brother when his own mother died. Housekeeping for her father, she had stiffened into a pronounced spinsterhood. She was close on forty when she met the Rev. Caleb Drake, he himself a man of over fifty. Her married life had been short, a mere two years, then she had been left a widow with an infant son. Motherhood, coming late and unexpectedly, had been the supreme experience of Lucilla Drake's life. Her son had turned out an anxiety, a source of grief and a constant financial drain—but never a disappointment. Mrs. Drake refused to recognize anything in her son Victor except an amiable weakness of character. Victor was too trusting—too easily led astray by bad companions because of his own belief in them. Victor was unlucky. Victor was deceived. Victor was swindled. He was the cat's-paw of wicked

114

men who exploited his innocence. The pleasant, rather silly sheep's face hardened into obstinacy when criticism of Victor was to the fore. She knew her own son. He was a dear boy, full of high spirits, and his so-called friends took advantage of him. She knew, none better, how Victor hated having to ask her for money. But when the poor boy was really in such a terrible situation, what else could he do? It wasn't as though he had anyone but her to go to.

All the same, as she admitted, George's invitation to come and live in the house and look after Iris, had come as a godsend, at a moment when she really had been in desperate straits of genteel poverty. She had been very happy and comfortable this last year and it was not in human nature to look kindly on the possibility of being superseded by an upstart young woman, all modern efficiency and capability, who in any case, so she persuaded herself, would only be marrying George for his money. Of course that was what she was after! A good home and a rich indulgent husband. You couldn't tell Aunt Lucilla, at her age, that any young woman really *liked* working for her living! Girls were the same as they always had been—if they could get a man to keep them in comfort, they much preferred it. This Ruth Lessing was clever, worming her way into a position of confidence, advising George about house furnishing, making herself indispensable—

but, thank goodness, there was *one* person at least who saw what she was up to!

Lucilla Drake nodded her head several times, causing her soft double chins to quiver, raised her eyebrows with an air of superb human sapience, and abandoned the subject for one equally interesting and possibly even more pressing.

"It's the blankets I can't make up my mind about, dear. You see, I can't get it clearly laid down whether we shan't be coming down again until next spring or whether George means to run down for weekends. He won't say."

"I suppose he doesn't really know." Iris tried to give her attention to a point that seemed completely unimportant. "If it was nice weather it might be fun to come down occasionally. Though I don't think I want to particularly. Still the house will be here if we do want to come."

"Yes, dear, but one wants to *know*. Because, you see, if we aren't coming down until next year, then the blankets ought to be put away with mothballs. But if we *are* coming down, that wouldn't be necessary, because the blankets would be *used*— and the smell of mothballs is so unpleasant."

"Well, don't use them."

"Yes, but it's been such a hot summer there are a lot of moths about. Everyone says it's a bad year for moths. And for wasps, of course. Hawkins told me yesterday he's taken thirty wasps' nests this summer—thirty—just fancy—"

Iris thought of Hawkins—stalking out at dusk—cyanide in hand—*cyanide*—*Rosemary*—why did everything lead back to that—?

The thin trickle of sound that was Aunt Lucilla's voice was going on—it had reached by now a different point—

"—and whether one ought to send the silver to the bank or not? Lady Alexandra was saying so many burglaries—though of course we do have good shutters—I don't like the way she does her hair myself—it makes her face look so hard—but I should think she was a hard woman. And nervy, too. Everyone is nervy nowadays. When I was a girl people didn't know what nerves were. Which reminds me that I didn't like the look of George lately—I wonder if he could be going to have 'flu? I've wondered once or twice whether he was feverish. But perhaps it is some business worry. He looks to me, you know, as though he has got something on his mind."

Iris shivered, and Lucilla Drake exclaimed triumphantly: "There, I said you had a chill."

Two

"How I wish they had never come here."

Sandra Farraday uttered the words with such unusual bitterness that her husband turned to look at her in surprise. It was as though his own thoughts had been put into words—the thoughts that he had been trying so hard to conceal. So Sandra, too, felt as he did? She, too, had felt that Fairhaven was spoiled, its peace impaired, by these new neighbours a mile away across the Park. He said, voicing his surprise impulsively:

"I didn't know you felt like that about them, too."

Immediately, or so it seemed to him, she withdrew into herself.

"Neighbours are so important in the country. One has either to be rude or friendly; one can't, as in London, just keep people as amiable acquaintances."

"No," said Stephen, "one can't do that."

"And now we're committed to this extraordinary party."

They were both silent, running over in their minds the scene at lunch. George Barton had been friendly, even exuberant in manner, with a kind of undercurrent of excitement of which they had both been conscious. George Barton was really very odd these days. Stephen had never noticed

118

him much in the time preceding Rosemary's death. George had just been there in the background, the kindly dull husband of a young and beautiful wife. Stephen had never even felt a pang of disquiet over the betrayal of George. George had been the kind of husband who was born to be betrayed. So much older—so devoid of the attractions necessary to hold an attractive and capricious woman. Had George himself been deceived? Stephen did not think so. George, he thought, knew Rosemary very well. He loved her, and he was the kind of man who was humble about his own powers of holding a wife's interest.

All the same, George must have suffered. . . .

Stephen began to wonder just what George had felt when Rosemary died.

He and Sandra had seen little of him in the months following the tragedy. It was not until he had suddenly appeared as a near neighbour at Little Priors that he had reentered their lives and at once, so Stephen thought, he had seemed different.

More alive, more positive. And—yes, decidedly *odd*.

He had been odd today. That suddenly blurted-out invitation. A party for Iris's eighteenth birthday. He did so hope Stephen and Sandra would both come. Stephen and Sandra had been so kind to them down here.

Sandra had said quickly; of course, it would be

119

delightful. Naturally Stephen would be rather tried when they got back to London and she herself had a great many tiresome engagements, but she did hope they would be able to manage it.

"Then let's settle a day now, shall we?"

George's face—florid, smiling, insistent.

"I thought perhaps one day the week after next—Wednesday or Thursday? Thursday is November 2nd. Would that be all right? But we'll arrange any day that suits you both."

It had been the kind of invitation that pinned you down—there was a certain lack of social *savoir faire.* Stephen noticed that Iris Marle had gone red and looked embarrassed. Sandra had been perfect. She had smilingly surrendered to the inevitable and said that Thursday, November 2nd, would suit them very well.

Suddenly voicing his thoughts, Stephen said sharply, "We needn't go."

Sandra turned her face slightly towards him. It wore a thoughtful considering air.

"You think not?"

"It's easy to make some excuse."

"He'll only insist on us coming some other time—or change the day. He—he seems very set on our coming."

"I can't think why. It's Iris's party—and I can't believe she is so particularly anxious for our company."

"No—no—" Sandra sounded thoughtful.

Then she said:

"You know where this party is to be?"

"No."

"The Luxembourg."

The shock nearly deprived him of speech. He felt the colour ebbing out of his cheeks. He pulled himself together and met her eyes. Was it his fancy or was there meaning in the level gaze?

"But it's preposterous," he exclaimed, blustering a little in his attempt to conceal his own personal emotion. "The Luxembourg where—to revive all that. The man must be mad."

"I thought of that," said Sandra.

"But then we shall certainly refuse to go. The— the whole thing was terribly unpleasant. You remember all the publicity—the pictures in the papers."

"I remember the unpleasantness," said Sandra.

"Doesn't he realize how disagreeable it would be for us?"

"He has a reason, you know, Stephen. A reason that he gave me."

"What was it?"

He felt thankful that she was looking away from him when she spoke.

"He took me aside after lunch. He said he wanted to explain. He told me that the girl—Iris— had never recovered properly from the shock of her sister's death."

She paused and Stephen said unwillingly:

"Well, I daresay that may be true enough—she looks far from well. I thought at lunch how ill she was looking."

"Yes, I noticed it too—although she has seemed in good health and spirits on the whole lately. But I am telling you what George Barton said. He told me that Iris has consistently avoided the Luxembourg ever since as far as she was able."

"I don't wonder."

"But according to him that is all wrong. It seems he consulted a nerve specialist on the subject—one of these modern men—and his advice is that after a shock of any kind, the trouble must be faced, not avoided. The principle, I gather, is like that of sending up an airman again immediately after a crash."

"Does the specialist suggest another suicide?"

Sandra replied quietly, "He suggests that the associations of the restaurant must be overcome. It is, after all, just a restaurant. He proposed an ordinary pleasant party with, as far as possible, the same people present."

"Delightful for the people!"

"Do you mind so much, Stephen?"

A swift pang of alarm shot through him. He said quickly: "Of course I don't mind. I just thought it rather a gruesome idea. Personally *I* shouldn't mind in the least . . . I was really thinking of *you*. If you don't mind—"

She interrupted him.

"I do mind. Very much. But the way George Barton put it made it very difficult to refuse. After all, I have frequently been to the Luxembourg since—so have you. One is constantly being asked there."

"But not under these circumstances."

"No."

Stephen said:

"As you say, it is difficult to refuse—and if we put it off the invitation will be renewed. But there's no reason, Sandra, why *you* should have to endure it. I'll go and you can cry off at the last minute—a headache, chill—something of that kind."

He saw her chin go up.

"That would be cowardly. No, Stephen, if you go, I go. After all," she laid her hand on his arm, "however little our marriage means, it should at least mean sharing our difficulties."

But he was staring at her—rendered dumb by one poignant phrase which had escaped her so easily, as though it voiced a long familiar and not very important fact.

Recovering himself he said, "Why do you say that? *However little our marriage means?*"

She looked at him steadily, her eyes wide and honest.

"Isn't it true?"

"No, a thousand times no. Our marriage means everything to me."

She smiled.

"I suppose it does—in a way. We're a good team, Stephen. We pull together with a satisfactory result."

"I didn't mean that." He found his breath was coming unevenly. He took her hand in both of his, holding it very closely—"Sandra, don't you know that you mean all the world to me?"

And suddenly she did know it. It was incredible—unforeseen, but it was so.

She was in his arms and he was holding her close, kissing her, stammering out incoherent words.

"Sandra—Sandra—darling. I love you . . . I've been so afraid—so afraid I'd lose you."

She heard herself saying:

"Because of Rosemary?"

"Yes." He let go of her, stepped back, his face was ludicrous in its dismay.

"You knew—about Rosemary?"

"Of course—all the time."

"And you understand?"

She shook her head.

"No, I don't understand. I don't think I ever should. You loved her?"

"Not really. It was you I loved."

A surge of bitterness swept over her. She quoted: "From the first moment you saw me across the room? Don't repeat that lie—for it was a lie!"

He was not taken aback by that sudden attack. He seemed to consider her words thoughtfully.

"Yes, it was a lie—and yet in a queer way it wasn't. I'm beginning to believe that it was true. Oh, try and *understand,* Sandra. You know the people who always have a noble and good reason to mask their meaner actions? The people who 'have to be honest' when they want to be unkind, who 'thought it their duty to repeat so and so,' who are such hypocrites to themselves that they go through to their life's end convinced that every mean and beastly action was done in a spirit of unselfishness! Try and realize that the opposite of those people can exist too. People who are so cynical, so distrustful of themselves and of life that they only believe in their bad motives. You were the woman I needed. That, at least, is true. And I do honestly believe, now, looking back on it, that if it hadn't been true, I should never have gone through with it."

She said bitterly:

"You were not in love with me."

"No. I'd never been in love. I was a starved, sexless creature who prided himself—yes, I did— on the fastidious coldness of his nature! And then I did fall in love 'across a room'—a silly violent puppy love. A thing like a midsummer thunderstorm, brief, unreal, quickly over." He added bitterly: "Indeed a 'tale told by an idiot, full of sound and fury, signifying nothing.' "

He paused, and then went on:

"It was here, at Fairhaven, that I woke up and realized the truth."

"The truth?"

"The only thing in life that mattered to me was you—and keeping your love."

"If I had only known. . . ."

"What did you think?"

"I thought you were planning to go away with her."

"With Rosemary?" He gave a short laugh. "That would indeed have been penal servitude for life!"

"Didn't she want you to go away with her?"

"Yes, she did."

"What happened?"

Stephen drew a deep breath. They were back again. Facing once more that intangible menace. He said:

"The Luxembourg happened."

They were both silent, seeing, they both knew, the same thing. The blue cyanosed face of a once lovely woman.

Staring at a dead woman, and then—looking up to meet each other's eyes. . . .

Stephen said:

"Forget it, Sandra, for God's sake, let us forget it!"

"It's no use forgetting. We're not going to be allowed to forget."

There was a pause. Then Sandra said:

"What are we going to do?"

"What you said just now. Face things—together. Go to this horrible party whatever the reason for it may be."

"You don't believe what George Barton said about Iris?"

"No. Do you?"

"It could be true. But even if it is, it's not the real reason."

"What do you think the real reason is?"

"I don't know, Stephen. But I'm afraid."

"Of George Barton?"

"Yes, I think he—knows."

Stephen said sharply:

"Knows what?"

She turned her head slowly until her eyes met his.

She said in a whisper:

"We mustn't be afraid. We must have courage—all the courage in the world. You're going to be a great man, Stephen—a man the world needs—and nothing shall interfere with that. I'm your wife and I love you."

"What do you think this party is, Sandra?"

"I think it's a trap."

He said slowly, "And we walk into it?"

"We can't afford to show we know it's a trap."

"No, that's true."

Suddenly Sandra threw back her head and

laughed. She said: "Do your worst, Rosemary. You won't win."

He gripped her shoulder.

"Be quiet, Sandra. Rosemary's dead."

"Is she? Sometimes—she feels very much alive. . . ."

Three

Halfway across the Park Iris said:

"Do you mind if I don't come back with you, George? I feel like a walk. I thought I'd go up over Friar's Hill and come down through the wood. I've had an awful headache all day."

"My poor child. Do go. I won't come with you—I'm expecting a fellow along sometime this afternoon and I'm not quite sure when he'll turn up."

"Right. Good-bye till teatime."

She turned abruptly and made off at right angles to where a belt of larches showed on the hillside.

When she came out on the brow of the hill she drew a deep breath. It was one of those close humid days common in October. A dank moisture coated the leaves of the trees and the grey cloud hung low overhead promising yet more rain shortly. There was not really much more air up here on the hill than there had been in the valley, but Iris felt nevertheless as though she could breathe more freely.

She sat down on the trunk of a fallen tree and stared down into the valley to where Little Priors nestled demurely in its wooded hollow. Farther to the left, Fairhaven Manor showed a glimpse of rose red on brick.

Iris stared out sombrely over the landscape, her chin cupped in her hand.

The slight rustle behind her was hardly louder than the drip of the leaves, but she turned her head sharply as the branches parted and Anthony Browne came through them.

She cried half angrily: "Tony! Why do you always have to arrive like—like a demon in a pantomime?"

Anthony dropped to the ground beside her. He took out his cigarette case, offered her one and when she shook her head took one himself and lighted it. Then inhaling the first puff he replied:

"It's because I'm what the papers call a Mystery Man. I *like* appearing from nowhere."

"How did you know where I was?"

"An excellent pair of bird glasses. I heard you were lunching with the Farradays and spied on you from the hillside when you left."

"Why don't you come to the house like an ordinary person?"

"I'm not an ordinary person," said Anthony in a shocked tone. "I'm very extraordinary."

"I think you are."

He looked at her quickly. Then he said:

"Is anything the matter?"

"No, of course not. At least—"

She paused. Anthony said interrogatively:

"At least?"

She drew a deep breath.

"I'm tired of being down here. I hate it. I want to go back to London."

"You're going soon, aren't you?"

"Next week."

"So this was a farewell party at the Farradays?"

"It wasn't a party. Just them and one old cousin."

"Do you like the Farradays, Iris?"

"I don't know. I don't think I do very much—although I shouldn't say that because they've really been very nice to us."

"Do you think they like you?"

"No, I don't. I think they hate us."

"Interesting."

"Is it?"

"Oh, not the hatred—if true. I meant the use of the word 'us.' My question referred to you personally."

"Oh, I see . . . I think they like *me* quite well in a negative sort of way. I think it's us as a family living next door that they mind about. We weren't particular friends of theirs—they were Rosemary's friends."

"Yes," said Anthony, "as you say they were Rosemary's friends—not that I should imagine Sandra Farraday and Rosemary were ever bosom friends, eh?"

"No," said Iris. She looked faintly apprehensive but Anthony smoked peacefully. Presently he said:

"Do you know what strikes me most about the Farradays?"

"What?"

"Just that—that they are the Farradays. I always think of them like that—not as Stephen and Sandra, two individuals linked by the State and the Established Church—but as a definite dual entity—the Farradays. That is rarer than you would think. They are two people with a common aim, a common way of life, identical hopes and fears and beliefs. And the odd part of it is that they are actually very dissimilar in character. Stephen Farraday, I should say, is a man of very wide intellectual scope, extremely sensitive to outside opinion, horribly diffident about himself and somewhat lacking in moral courage. Sandra, on the other hand, has a narrow medieval mind, is capable of fanatical devotion, and is courageous to the point of recklessness."

"He always seems to me," said Iris, "rather pompous and stupid."

"He's not at all stupid. He's just one of the usual unhappy successes."

"Unhappy?"

"Most successes are unhappy. That's why they are successes—they have to reassure themselves about themselves by achieving something that the world will notice."

"What extraordinary ideas you have, Anthony."

"You'll find they're quite true if you only

examine them. The happy people are failures because they are on such good terms with themselves that they don't give a damn. Like me. They are also usually agreeable to get on with— again like me."

"You have a very good opinion of yourself."

"I am just drawing attention to my good points in case you mayn't have noticed them."

Iris laughed. Her spirits had risen. The dull depression and fear had lifted from her mind. She glanced down at her watch.

"Come home and have tea, and give a few more people the benefit of your unusually agreeable society."

Anthony shook his head.

"Not today. I must be getting back."

Iris turned sharply on him.

"Why will you never come to the house? There must be a reason."

Anthony shrugged his shoulders.

"Put it that I'm rather peculiar in my ideas of accepting hospitality. Your brother-in-law doesn't like me—he's made that quite clear."

"Oh, don't bother about George. If Aunt Lucilla and I ask you—she's an old dear—you'd like her."

"I'm sure I should—but my objection holds."

"You used to come in Rosemary's time."

"That," said Anthony, "was rather different."

A faint cold hand touched Iris's heart. She said,

"What made you come down here today? Had you business in this part of the world?"

"Very important business—with you. I came here to ask you a question, Iris."

The cold hand vanished. Instead there came a faint flutter, that throb of excitement that women have known from time immemorial. And with it Iris's face adopted that same look of blank inquiry that her great-grandmother might have worn prior to saying a few minutes later, "Oh, Mr. X, this is so sudden!"

"Yes?" She turned that impossibly innocent face towards Anthony.

He was looking at her, his eyes were grave, almost stern.

"Answer me truthfully, Iris. This is my question. Do you trust me?"

It took her aback. It was not what she had expected. He saw that.

"You didn't think that that was what I was going to say? But it is a very important question, Iris. The most important question in the world to me. I ask it again. Do you trust me?"

She hesitated, a bare second, then she answered, her eyes falling: "Yes."

"Then I'll go on and ask you something else. Will you come up to London and marry me without telling anybody about it?"

She stared.

"But I couldn't! I simply couldn't."

"You couldn't marry me?"

"Not in that way."

"And yet you love me. You do love me, don't you?"

She heard herself saying:

"Yes, I love you, Anthony."

"But you won't come and marry me at the Church of Saint Elfrida, Bloomsbury, in the parish of which I have resided for some weeks and where I can consequently get married by licence at any time?"

"How can I do a thing like that? George would be terribly hurt and Aunt Lucilla would never forgive me. And anyway I'm not of age. I'm only eighteen."

"You'd have to lie about your age. I don't know what penalties I should incur for marrying a minor without her guardian's consent. Who is your guardian, by the way?"

"George. He's my trustee as well."

"As I was saying, whatever penalties I incurred, they couldn't unmarry us and that is really all I care about."

Iris shook her head. "I couldn't do it. I couldn't be so unkind. And in any case, *why?* What's the point of it?"

Anthony said: "That's why I asked you first if you could trust me. You'd have to take my reasons on trust. Let's say that it is the simplest way. But never mind."

Iris said timidly:

"If George only got to know you a little better. Come back now with me. It will be only he and Aunt Lucilla."

"Are you sure? I thought—" he paused. "As I struck up the hill I saw a man going up your drive—and the funny thing is that I believe I recognized him as a man I"—he hesitated—"had met."

"Of course—I forgot—George said he was expecting someone."

"The man I thought I saw was a man called Race—Colonel Race."

"Very likely," Iris agreed. "George does know a Colonel Race. He was coming to dinner on that night when Rosemary—"

She stopped, her voice quivering. Anthony gripped her hand.

"Don't go on remembering it, darling. It was beastly, I know."

She shook her head.

"I can't help it. Anthony—"

"Yes?"

"Did it ever occur to you—did you ever think—" She found a difficulty in putting her meaning into words.

"Did it ever strike you that—that Rosemary might not have committed suicide? That she might have been—*killed?*"

"Good God, Iris, what put that idea into your head?"

She did not reply—merely persisted: "That idea never occured to you?"

"Certainly not. Of course Rosemary committed suicide."

Iris said nothing.

"Who's been suggesting these things to you?"

For a moment she was tempted to tell him George's incredible story, but she refrained. She said slowly:

"It was just an idea."

"Forget it, darling idiot." He pulled her to her feet and kissed her cheek lightly. "Darling morbid idiot. Forget Rosemary. Only think of me."

Four

Puffing at his pipe, Colonel Race looked speculatively at George Barton.

He had known George Barton ever since the latter's boyhood. Barton's uncle had been a country neighbour of the Races. There was a difference of over twenty years between the two men. Race was over sixty, a tall, erect, military figure, with sunburnt face, closely cropped iron-grey hair, and shrewd dark eyes.

There had never been any particular intimacy between the two men—but Barton remained to Race "young George"—one of the many vague figures associated with earlier days.

He was thinking at this moment that he had really no idea what "young George" was like. On the brief occasions when they had met in later years, they had found little in common. Race was an out-of-door man, essentially of the Empire-builder type—most of his life had been spent abroad. George was emphatically the city gentleman. Their interests were dissimilar and when they met it was to exchange rather lukewarm reminiscences of "the old days," after which an embarrassed silence was apt to occur. Colonel Race was not good at small talk and might indeed have posed as the model of a strong silent man so beloved by an earlier generation of novelists.

Silent at this moment, he was wondering just why "young George" had been so insistent on this meeting. Thinking, too, that there was some subtle change in the man since he had last seen him a year ago. George Barton had always struck him as the essence of stodginess—cautious, practical, unimaginative.

There was, he thought, something very wrong with the fellow. Jumpy as a cat. He'd already re-lit his cigar three times—and that wasn't like Barton at all.

He took his pipe out of his mouth.

"Well, young George, what's the trouble?"

"You're right, Race, it is trouble. I want your advice badly—and your help."

The colonel nodded and waited.

"Nearly a year ago you were coming to dine with us in London—at the Luxembourg. You had to go abroad at the last minute."

Again Race nodded.

"South Africa."

"At that dinner party my wife died."

Race stirred uncomfortably in his chair.

"I know. Read about it. Didn't mention it now or offer you sympathy because I didn't want to stir up things again. But I'm sorry, old man, you know that."

"Oh, yes, yes. That's not the point. My wife was supposed to have committed suicide."

Race fastened on the key word. His eyebrows rose.

139

"Supposed?"

"Read these."

He thrust the two letters into the other's hand. Race's eyebrows rose still higher.

"Anonymous letters?"

"Yes. And I believe them."

Race shook his head slowly.

"That's a dangerous thing to do. You'd be surprised how many lying spiteful letters get written after any event that's been given any sort of publicity in the Press."

"I know that. But these weren't written at the time—they weren't written until six months afterwards."

Race nodded.

"That's a point. Who do you think wrote them?"

"I don't know. I don't care. The point is that I believe what they say is true. My wife was murdered."

Race laid down his pipe. He sat up a little straighter in his chair.

"Now just why do you think that? Had you any suspicion at the time. Had the police?"

"I was dazed when it happened—completely bowled over. I just accepted the verdict at the inquest. My wife had had 'flu, was run-down. No suspicion of anything but suicide arose. The stuff was in her handbag, you see."

"What was the stuff?"

"Cyanide."

"I remember. She took it in champagne."

"Yes. It seemed, at the time, all quite straight-forward."

"Had she ever threatened to commit suicide?"

"No, never. Rosemary," said George Barton, "loved life."

Race nodded. He had only met George's wife once. He had thought her a singularly lovely nitwit—but certainly not a melancholic type.

"What about the medical evidence as to state of mind, etcetera?"

"Rosemary's own doctor—an elderly man who has attended the Marle family since they were young children—was away on a sea voyage. His partner, a young man, attended Rosemary when she had 'flu. All he said, I remember, was that the type of 'flu about was inclined to leave serious depression."

George paused and went on.

"It wasn't until after I got these letters that I talked with Rosemary's own doctor. I said nothing of the letters, of course—just discussed what had happened. He told me then that he was very surprised at what had happened. He would never have believed it, he said. Rosemary was not at all a suicidal type. It showed, he said, how even a patient one knew well might act in a thoroughly uncharacteristic manner."

Again George paused and then went on:

"It was after talking to him that I realized how

absolutely unconvincing to *me* Rosemary's suicide was. After all, I knew her very well. She was a person who was capable of violent fits of unhappiness. She could get very worked up over things, and she would on occasions take very rash and unconsidered action, but I have never known her in the frame of mind that 'wanted to get out of it all.'"

Race murmured in a slightly embarrassed manner:

"Could she have had a motive for suicide apart from mere depression? Was she, I mean, definitely unhappy about anything?"

"I—no—she was perhaps rather nervy."

Avoiding looking at his friend, Race said:

"Was she at all a melodramatic person? I only saw her once, you know. But there is a type that—well—might get a kick out of attempted suicide—usually if they've quarrelled with someone. The rather childish motive of—'I'll make them sorry!'"

"Rosemary and I hadn't quarrelled."

"No. And I must say that the fact of cyanide having been used rather rules that possibility out. It's not the kind of thing you can monkey about with safely—and everybody knows it."

"That's another point. If by any chance Rosemary *had* contemplated doing away with herself, surely she'd never do it that way? Painful and—and ugly. An overdose of some sleeping stuff would be far more likely."

"I agree. Was there any evidence as to her purchasing or getting hold of the cyanide?"

"No. But she had been staying with friends in the country and they had taken a wasps' nest one day. It was suggested that she might have taken a handful of potassium cyanide crystals then."

"Yes—it's not a difficult thing to get hold of. Most gardeners keep a stock of it."

He paused and then said:

"Let me summarize the position. There was no positive evidence as to a disposition to suicide, or to any preparation for it. The whole thing was negative. But there can also have been no positive evidence pointing to murder, or the police would have got hold of it. They're quite wide awake, you know."

"The mere idea of murder would have seemed fantastic."

"But it didn't seem fantastic to you six months later?"

George said slowly:

"I think I must have been unsatisfied all along. I think I must have been subconsciously preparing myself so that when I saw the thing written down in black and white I accepted it without doubt."

"Yes." Race nodded. "Well, then, let's have it. Who do you suspect?"

George leaned forward—his face twitching.

"That's what is so terrible. *If* Rosemary was killed, one of those people round the table, one of our friends, must have done it. No one else came near the table."

"Waiters? Who poured out the wine?"

"Charles, the headwaiter at the Luxembourg. You know Charles?"

Race assented. Everybody knew Charles. It seemed quite impossible to imagine that Charles could have deliberately poisoned a client.

"And the waiter who looked after us was Giuseppe. We know Giuseppe well. I've known him for years. He always looks after me there. He's a delightful cheery little fellow."

"So we come to the dinner party. Who was there?"

"Stephen Farraday, the M.P. His wife, Lady Alexandra Farraday. My secretary, Ruth Lessing. A fellow called Anthony Browne. Rosemary's sister, Iris, and myself. Seven in all. We should have been eight if you had come. When you dropped out we couldn't think of anybody suitable to ask at the last minute."

"I see. Well, Barton, who do you think did it?"

George cried out: "I don't know—I tell you I don't know. If I had any idea—"

"All right—all right. I just thought you might have a definite suspicion. Well, it oughtn't to be difficult. How did you sit—starting with yourself?"

"I had Sandra Farraday on my right, of course. Next to her, Anthony Browne. Then Rosemary.

Then Stephen Farraday, then Iris, then Ruth Lessing who sat on my left."

"I see. And your wife had drunk champagne earlier in the evening?"

"Yes. The glasses had been filled up several times. It—it happened while the cabaret show was on. There was a lot of noise—it was one of those negro shows and we were all watching it. She slumped forward on the table just before the lights went up. She may have cried out—or gasped—but nobody heard anything. The doctor said that death must have been practically instantaneous. Thank God for that."

"Yes, indeed. Well, Barton—on the face of it, it seems fairly obvious."

"You mean?"

"Stephen Farraday of course. He was on her right hand. Her champagne glass would be close to his left hand. Easiest thing in the world to put the stuff in as soon as the lights were lowered and general attention went to the raised stage. I can't see that anybody else had anything like as good an opportunity. I know those Luxembourg tables. There's plenty of room round them—I doubt very much if anybody could have leaned across the table, for instance, without being noticed even if the lights were down. The same thing applies to the fellow on Rosemary's left. He would have had to lean across her to put anything in her glass. There *is* one other possibility, but we'll take the obvious person first. Any reason why Stephen Farraday, M.P., should want to do away with your wife?"

George said in a stifled voice:

"They—they had been rather close friends. If—if Rosemary had turned him down, for instance, he might have wanted revenge."

"Sounds highly melodramatic. That is the only motive you can suggest?"

"Yes," said George. His face was very red. Race gave him the most fleeting of glances. Then he went on:

"We'll examine possibility No. 2. One of the women."

"Why the women?"

"My dear George, has it escaped your notice that in a party of seven, four women and three men, there will probably be one or two periods during the evening when three couples are dancing and one woman is sitting alone at the table? You did all dance?"

"Oh, yes."

"Good. Now before the cabaret, can you remember who was sitting alone at any moment?"

George thought a minute.

"I think—yes, Iris was odd man out last, and Ruth the time before."

"You don't remember when your wife drank champagne last?"

"Let me see, she had been dancing with Browne.

I remember her coming back and saying that had been pretty strenuous—he's rather a fancy dancer. She drank up the wine in her glass then. A few minutes later they played a waltz and she—she danced with me. She knew a waltz is the only dance I'm really any good at. Farraday danced with Ruth and Lady Alexandra with Browne. Iris sat out. Immediately after that, they had the cabaret."

"Then let's consider your wife's sister. Did she come into any money on your wife's death?"

George began to splutter.

"My dear Race—don't be absurd. Iris was a mere child, a schoolgirl."

"I've known two schoolgirls who committed murder."

"But Iris! She was devoted to Rosemary."

"Never mind, Barton. She had opportunity. I want to know if she had motive. Your wife, I believe, was a rich woman. Where did her money go—to you?"

"No, it went to Iris—a trust fund."

He explained the position, to which Race listened attentively.

"Rather a curious position. The rich sister and the poor sister. Some girls might have resented that."

"I'm sure Iris never did."

"Maybe not—but she had a motive all right. We'll try that tack now. Who else had a motive?"

"Nobody—nobody at all. Rosemary hadn't an enemy in the world, I'm sure. I've been looking into all that—asking questions—trying to find out. I've even taken this house near the Farradays' so as to—"

He stopped. Race took up his pipe and began to scratch at its interior.

"Hadn't you better tell me everything, young George?"

"What do you mean?"

"You're keeping something back—it sticks out a mile. You can sit there defending your wife's reputation—or you can try and find out if she was murdered or not—but if the latter matters most to you, you'll have to come clean."

There was a silence.

"All right then," said George in a stifled voice. "You win."

"You'd reason to believe your wife had a lover, is that it?"

"Yes."

"Stephen Farraday?"

"I don't know! I swear to you I don't know! It might have been him or it might have been the other fellow, Browne. I couldn't make up my mind. It was hell."

"Tell me what you know about this Anthony Browne? Funny, I seem to have heard the name."

"I don't know anything about him. Nobody does. He's a good-looking, amusing sort of

148

chap—but nobody knows the first thing about him. He's supposed to be an American but he's got no accent to speak of."

"Oh, well, perhaps the Embassy will know something about him. You've no idea—which?"

"No—no, I haven't. I'll tell you, Race. She was writing a letter—I—I examined the blotting paper afterwards. It—it was a love letter all right—but there was no name."

Race turned his eyes away carefully.

"Well, that gives us a bit more to go on. Lady Alexandra, for instance—she comes into it, if her husband was having an affair with your wife. She's the kind of woman, you know, who feels things rather intensely. The quiet, deep type. It's a type that will do murder at a pinch. We're getting on. There's Mystery Browne and Farraday and his wife, and young Iris Marle. What about this other woman, Ruth Lessing?"

"Ruth couldn't have had anything to do with it. She at least had no earthly motive."

"Your secretary, you say? What sort of a girl is she?"

"The dearest girl in the world." George spoke with enthusiasm. "She's practically one of the family. She's my right hand—I don't know anyone I think more highly of, or have more absolute faith in."

"You're fond of her," said Race, watching him thoughtfully.

"I'm devoted to her. That girl, Race, is an absolute trump. I depend upon her in every way. She's the truest, dearest creature in the world."

Race murmured something that sounded liked "Umhum" and left the subject. There was nothing in his manner to indicate to George that he had mentally chalked down a very definite motive to the unknown Ruth Lessing. He could imagine that this "dearest girl in the world" might have a very decided reason for wanting the removal of Mrs. George Barton to another world. It might be a mercenary motive—she might have envisaged herself as the second Mrs. Barton. It might be that she was genuinely in love with her employer. But the motive for Rosemary's death was there.

Instead he said gently: "I suppose it's occurred to you, George, that you had a pretty good motive yourself."

"I?" George looked flabbergasted.

"Well, remember Othello and Desdemona."

"I see what you mean. But—but it wasn't like that between me and Rosemary. I adored her, of course, but I always knew that there would be things that—that I'd have to endure. Not that she wasn't fond of me—she was. She was very fond of me and sweet to me always. But of course I'm a dull stick, no getting away from it. Not romantic, you know. Anyway, I'd made up my mind when I married her that it wasn't going to be all beer and skittles. She as good as warned me. It hurt, of course, when it happened—but to suggest that I'd have touched a hair of her head—"

He stopped, and then went on in a different tone:

"Anyway, if I'd done it, why on earth should I go raking it all up? I mean, after a verdict of suicide, and everything all settled and over. It would be madness."

"Absolutely. That's why I don't seriously suspect you, my dear fellow. If you were a successful murderer and got a couple of letters like these, you'd put them quietly in the fire and say nothing at all about it. And that brings me to what I think is the one really interesting feature of the whole thing. Who wrote those letters?"

"Eh?" George looked rather startled. "I haven't the least idea."

"The point doesn't seem to have interested you. It interests me. It's the first question I asked you. We can assume, I take it, that they weren't written by the murderer. Why should he queer his own pitch when, as you say, everything had settled down and suicide was universally accepted? Then who wrote them? Who is it who is interested in stirring the whole thing up again?"

"Servants?" hazarded George vaguely.

"Possibly. If so, what servants, and what do they know? Did Rosemary have a confidential maid?"

George shook his head.

"No. At the time we had a cook—Mrs. Pound—we've still got her, and a couple of maids. I think

151

they've both left. They weren't with us very long."

"Well, Barton, if you want my advice, which I gather you do, I should think the matter over very carefully. On one side there's the fact that Rosemary is dead. You can't bring her back to life whatever you do. If the evidence for suicide isn't particularly good, neither is the evidence for murder. Let us say, for the sake of argument, that Rosemary *was* murdered. Do you really wish to rake up the whole thing? It may mean a lot of unpleasant publicity, a lot of washing of dirty linen in public, your wife's love affairs becoming public property—"

George Barton winced. He said violently:

"Do you really advise me to let some swine get away with it? That stick Farraday, with his pompous speeches, and his precious career—and all the time, perhaps, a cowardly murderer."

"I only want you to be clear what it involves."

"I want to get at the truth."

"Very well. In that case, I should go to the police with these letters. They'll probably be able to find out fairly easily who wrote them and if the writer knows anything. Only remember that once you've started them on the trail, you won't be able to call them off."

"I'm not going to the police. That's why I wanted to see you. I'm going to set a trap for the murderer."

"What on earth do you mean?"

"Listen, Race. I'm going to have a party at the Luxembourg. I want you to come. The same people, the Farradays, Anthony Browne, Ruth, Iris, myself. I've got it all worked out."

"What are you going to do?"

George gave a faint laugh.

"That's my secret. It would spoil it if I told any-one beforehand—even you. I want you to come with an unbiased mind and—see what happens."

Race leant forward. His voice was suddenly sharp.

"I don't like it, George. These melodramatic ideas out of books don't work. Go to the police—there's no better body of men. They know how to deal with these problems. They're professionals. Amateur shows in crime aren't advisable."

"That's why I want you there. You're not an amateur."

"My dear fellow. Because I once did work for M.I.5? And anyway you propose to keep me in the dark."

"That's necessary."

Race shook his head.

"I'm sorry. I refuse. I don't like your plan and I won't be a party to it. Give it up, George, there's a good fellow."

"I'm not going to give it up. I've got it all worked out."

"Don't be so damned obstinate. I know a bit

more about these shows than you do. I don't like the idea. It won't work. It may even be dangerous. Have you thought of that?"

"It will be dangerous for somebody all right."

Race sighed.

"You don't know what you're doing. Oh, well, don't say I haven't warned you. For the last time I beg you to give up this crackbrained idea of yours."

George Barton only shook his head.

Five

The morning of November 2nd dawned wet and gloomy. It was so dark in the dining room of the house in Elvaston Square that they had to have the lights on for breakfast.

Iris, contrary to her habit, had come down instead of having her coffee and toast sent up to her and sat there white and ghostlike pushing uneaten food about her plate. George rustled his *Times* with a nervy hand and at the other end of the table Lucilla Drake wept copiously into a handkerchief.

"I know the dear boy will do something dreadful. He's so sensitive—and he wouldn't say it was a matter of life and death if it wasn't."

Rustling his paper, George said sharply:

"Please don't worry, Lucilla. I've said I'll see to it."

"I know, dear George, you are always so kind. But I do feel any delay might be fatal. All these inquiries you speak of making—they will all take *time.*"

"No, no, we'll hurry them through."

"He says: 'without fail by the 3rd' and tomorrow *is* the 3rd. I should never forgive myself if anything happened to the darling boy."

"It won't." George took a long drink of coffee.

"And there is still that Conversion Loan of mine—"

"Look here, Lucilla, you leave it all to me."

"Don't worry, Aunt Lucilla," put in Iris. "George will be able to arrange it all. After all, this has happened before."

"Not for a long time" ("Three months," said George), "not since the poor boy was deceived by those dreadful swindling friends of his on that horrid ranch."

George wiped his moustache on his napkin, got up, patted Mrs. Drake kindly on the back as he made his way out of the room.

"Now do cheer up, my dear. I'll get Ruth to cable right away."

As he went out in the hall, Iris followed him.

"George, don't you think we ought to put off the party tonight? Aunt Lucilla is so upset. Hadn't we better stay at home with her?"

"Certainly not!" George's pink face went purple. "Why should that damned swindling young crook upset our whole lives? It's blackmail— sheer blackmail, that's what it is. If I had my way, he shouldn't get a penny."

"Aunt Lucilla would never agree to that."

"Lucilla's a fool—always has been. These women who have children when they're over forty never seem to learn any sense. Spoil the brats from the cradle by giving them every damned thing they want. If young Victor had once been told to get out of this mess by himself it might have been the making of him. Now don't argue, Iris. I'll get something fixed up before tonight so that Lucilla can go to bed happy. If necessary we'll take her along with us."

"Oh, no, she hates restaurants—and gets so sleepy, poor darling. And she dislikes the heat and the smoky air gives her asthma."

"I know. I wasn't serious. Go and cheer her up, Iris. Tell her everything will be all right."

He turned away and out of the front door. Iris turned slowly back towards the dining room. The telephone rang and she went to answer it.

"Hallo—who?" Her face changed, its white hopelessness dissolved into pleasure. "Anthony!"

"Anthony himself. I rang you up yesterday but couldn't get you. Have you been putting in a spot of work with George?"

"What do you mean?"

"Well, George was so pressing over his invitation to your party tonight. Quite unlike his usual style of 'hands off my lovely ward!' Absolutely insistent that I should come. I thought perhaps it was the result of some tactful work on your part."

"No—no—it's nothing to do with me."

"A change of heart all on his own?"

"Not exactly. It's—"

"Hallo—have you gone away?"

"No, I'm here."

"You were saying something. What's the matter, darling? I can hear you sighing through the telephone. Is anything the matter?"

"No—nothing. I shall be all right tomorrow. Everything will be all right tomorrow."

"What touching faith. Don't they say 'tomorrow never comes'?"

"Don't."

"Iris—something *is* the matter?"

"No, nothing. I can't tell you. I promised, you see."

"Tell me, my sweet."

"No—I can't really. Anthony, will you tell *me* something?"

"If I can."

"Were you—ever in love with Rosemary?"

A momentary pause and then a laugh.

"So that's it. Yes, Iris, I was a bit in love with Rosemary. She was very lovely, you know. And then one day I was talking to her and I saw you coming down the staircase—and in a minute it was all over, blown away. There was nobody but you in the world. That's the cold sober truth. Don't brood over a thing like that. Even Romeo, you know, had his Rosaline before he was bowled over for good and all by Juliet."

"Thank you, Anthony. I'm glad."

"See you tonight. It's your birthday, isn't it?"

"Actually not for a week—it's my birthday party though."

"You don't sound very enthusiastic about it."

"I'm not."

"I suppose George knows what he's doing, but it

seems to me a crazy idea to have it at the same place where—"

"Oh, I've been to the Luxembourg several times since—since Rosemary—I mean, one can't avoid it."

"No, and it's just as well. I've got a birthday present for you, Iris. I hope you'll like it. *Au revoir.*"

He rang off.

Iris went back to Lucilla Drake, to argue, persuade and reassure.

George, on his arrival at his office, sent at once for Ruth Lessing.

His worried frown relaxed a little as she entered, calm and smiling, in her neat black coat and skirt.

"Good morning."

"Good morning, Ruth. Trouble again. Look at this."

She took the cable he held out.

"Victor Drake again!"

"Yes, curse him."

She was silent a minute, holding the cable. A lean, brown face wrinkling up round the nose when he laughed. A mocking voice saying, "the sort of girl who ought to marry the boss . . ." How vividly it all came back.

She thought:

"It might have been yesterday. . . ."

George's voice recalled her.

"Wasn't it about a year ago that we shipped him out there?"

She reflected.

"I think so, yes. Actually I believe it was October 27th."

"What an amazing girl you are. What a memory!"

She thought to herself that she had a better reason for remembering than he knew. It was fresh from Victor Drake's influence that she had listened to Rosemary's careless voice over the phone and decided that she hated her employer's wife.

"I suppose we're lucky," said George, "that he's lasted as long as he has out there. Even if it did cost us fifty pounds three months ago."

"Three hundred pounds now seems a lot."

"Oh, yes. He won't get as much as that. We'll have to make the usual investigations."

"I'd better communicate with Mr. Ogilvie."

Alexander Ogilvie was their agent in Buenos Aires—a sober, hard headed Scotsman.

"Yes. Cable at once. His mother is in a state, as usual. Practically hysterical. Makes it very difficult with the party tonight."

"Would you like me to stay with her?"

"No." He negatived the idea emphatically. "No, indeed. You're the one person who's got to be there. I need you, Ruth." He took her hand. "You're too unselfish."

"I'm not unselfish at all."

She smiled and suggested:

"Would it be worth trying telephonic communication with Mr. Ogilvie? We might get the whole thing cleared up by tonight."

"A good idea. Well worth the expense."

"I'll get busy at once."

Very gently she disengaged her hand from his and went out.

George dealt with various matters awaiting his attention.

At half past twelve he went out and took a taxi to the Luxembourg.

Charles, the notorious and popular headwaiter, came towards him, bending his stately head and smiling in welcome.

"Good morning, Mr. Barton."

"Good morning, Charles. Everything all right for tonight?"

"I think you will be satisfied, sir."

"The same table?"

"The middle one in the alcove, that is right, is it not?"

"Yes—and you understand about the extra place?"

"It is all arranged."

"And you've got the—the rosemary?"

"Yes, Mr. Barton. I'm afraid it won't be very decorative. You wouldn't like some red berries incorporated—or say a few chrysanthemums?"

"No, no, only the rosemary."

161

"Very good, sir. You would like to see the menu. Guiseppe."

With a flick of the thumb Charles produced a smiling little middle-aged Italian.

"The menu for Mr. Barton."

It was produced.

Oysters, Clear Soup, Sole Luxembourg, Grouse, Poires Hélène, Chicken Livers in Bacon.

George cast an indifferent eye over it.

"Yes, yes, quite all right."

He handed it back. Charles accompanied him to the door.

Sinking his voice a little, he murmured:

"May I just mention how appreciative we are, Mr. Barton, that you are—er—coming back to us?"

A smile, rather a ghastly smile, showed on George's face. He said:

"We've got to forget the past—can't dwell on the past. All that is over and done with."

"Very true, Mr. Barton. You know how shocked and grieved we were at the time. I'm sure I hope that Mademoiselle will have a very happy birthday party and that everything will be as you like it."

Gracefully bowing, Charles withdrew and darted like an angry dragonfly on some very inferior grade of waiter who was doing the wrong thing at a table near the window.

George went out with a wry smile on his lips. He

was not an imaginative enough man to feel a pang of sympathy for the Luxembourg. It was not, after all, the fault of the Luxembourg that Rosemary had decided to commit suicide there or that someone had decided to murder her there. It had been decidedly hard on the Luxembourg. But like most people with an idea, George thought only of that idea.

He lunched at his club and went afterwards to a directors' meeting.

On his way back to the office, he put through a phone call to a Maida Vale number from a public call box. He came out with a sigh of relief. Everything was set according to schedule.

He went back to the office.

Ruth came to him at once.

"About Victor Drake."

"Yes?"

"I'm afraid it's rather a bad business. A possibility of criminal prosecution. He's been helping himself to the firm's money over a considerable period."

"Did Ogilvie say so?"

"Yes. I got through to him this morning and he got a call through to us this afternoon ten minutes ago. He says Victor was quite brazen about the whole thing."

"He would be!"

"But he insists that they won't prosecute if the money is refunded. Mr. Ogilvie saw the senior partner and that seems to be correct. The actual sum in question is one hundred and sixty-five pounds."

"So that Master Victor was hoping to pocket a clear hundred and thirty-five on the transaction?"

"I'm afraid so."

"Well, we've scotched that, at any rate," said George with grim satisfaction.

"I told Mr. Ogilvie to go ahead and settle the business. Was that right?"

"Personally I should be delighted to see that young crook go to prison—but one has to think of his mother. A fool—but a dear soul. So Master Victor scores as usual."

"How good you are," said Ruth.

"Me?"

"I think you're the best man in the world."

He was touched. He felt pleased and embarrassed at the same time. On an impulse he picked up her hand and kissed it.

"Dearest Ruth. My dearest and best of friends. What would I have done without you?"

They stood very close together.

She thought: "I could have been happy with him. I could have made him happy. If only—"

He thought: "Shall I take Race's advice? Shall I give it all up? Wouldn't that really be the best thing?"

Indecision hovered over him and passed. He said:

"9:30 at the Luxembourg."

Six

They had all come.

George breathed a sigh of relief. Up to the last moment he had feared some last minute defection—but they were all here. Stephen Farraday, tall and stiff, a little pompous in manner. Sandra Farraday in a severe black velvet gown wearing emeralds around her neck. The woman had breeding, not a doubt of it. Her manner was completely natural, possibly a little more gracious than usual. Ruth also in black with no ornament save one jewelled clip. Her raven black hair smooth and lying close to her head, her neck and arms very white—whiter than those of the other women. Ruth was a working girl, she had no long leisured ease in which to acquire sun tan. His eyes met hers and, as though she saw the anxiety in his, she smiled reassurance. His heart lifted. Loyal Ruth. Beside him Iris was unusually silent. She alone showed consciousness of this being an unusual party. She was pale but in some way it suited her, gave her a grave steadfast beauty. She wore a straight simple frock of leaf green. Anthony Browne came last, and to George's mind, he came with the quick stealthy step of a wild creature—a panther, perhaps, or a leopard. The fellow wasn't really quite civilized.

165

They were all there—all safe in George's trap. Now, the play could begin. . . .

Cocktails were drained. They got up and passed through the open arch into the restaurant proper.

Dancing couples, soft negro music, deft hurrying waiters.

Charles came forward and smilingly piloted them to their table. It was at the far end of the room, a shallow arched alcove which held three tables—a big one in the middle and two small ones for two people either side of it. A middle-aged sallow foreigner and a blonde lovely were at one, a slip of a boy and a girl at the other. The middle table was reserved for the Barton party.

George genially assigned them to their places.

"Sandra, will you sit here, on my right. Browne next to her. Iris, my dear, it's your party. I must have you here next to me, and you beyond her, Farraday. Then you, Ruth—"

He paused—between Ruth and Anthony was a vacant chair—the table had been laid for seven.

"My friend Race may be a bit late. He said we weren't to wait for him. He'll be along some time. I'd like you all to know him—he's a splendid fellow, knocked about all over the world and can tell you some good yarns."

Iris was conscious of a feeling of anger as she seated herself. George had done it on purpose—separated her from Anthony. Ruth ought to have

166

been sitting where she was, next to her host. So George still disliked and mistrusted Anthony.

She stole a glance across the table. Anthony was frowning. He did not look across at her. Once he directed a sharp sideways glance at the empty chair beside him. He said:

"Glad you've got another man, Barton. There's just a chance I may have to go off early. Quite unavoidable. But I ran into a man here I know."

George said smilingly:

"Running business into pleasure hours? You're too young for that, Browne. Not that I've ever known exactly what your business is?"

By chance there was a lull in the conversation. Anthony's reply came deliberately and coolly.

"Organized crime, Barton, that's what I always say when I'm asked. Robberies arranged. Larcenies a feature. Families waited upon at their private addresses."

Sandra Farraday laughed as she said:

"You're something to do with armaments, aren't you, Mr. Browne? An armament king is always the villain of the piece nowadays."

Iris saw Anthony's eyes momentarily widen in a stare of quick surprise. He said lightly:

"You mustn't give me away, Lady Alexandra, it's all very hush-hush. The spies of a foreign power are everywhere. Careless talk."

He shook his head with mock solemnity.

The waiter took away the oyster plates. Stephen asked Iris if she would like to dance.

Soon they were all dancing. The atmosphere lightened.

Presently Iris's turn came to dance with Anthony.

She said: "Mean of George not to let us sit together."

"Kind of him. This way I can look at you all the time across the table."

"You won't really have to go early?"

"I might."

Presently he said:

"Did you know that Colonel Race was coming?"

"No, I hadn't the least idea."

"Rather odd, that."

"Do you know him? Oh, yes, you said so, the other day."

She added:

"What sort of a man is he?"

"Nobody quite knows."

They went back to the table. The evening wore on. Slowly the tension, which had relaxed, seemed to close again. There was an atmosphere of taut nerves about the table. Only the host seemed genial and unconcerned.

Iris saw him glance at his watch.

Suddenly there was a roll of drums—the lights went down. A stage rose in the room. Chairs were pushed a little back, turned sideways. Three men and three girls took the floor, dancing. They were followed by a man who could make noises. Trains, steam rollers, aeroplanes, sewing machines, cows coughing. He was a success. Lenny and Flo followed in an exhibition dance which was more of a trapeze act than a dance. More applause. Then another ensemble by the Luxembourg Six. The lights went up.

Everyone blinked.

At the same time a wave of sudden freedom from restraint seemed to pass over the party at the table. It was as though they had been subconsciously expecting something that had failed to happen. For on an earlier occasion the going up of the lights had coincided with the discovery of a dead body lying across the table. It was as though now the past was definitely past—vanished into oblivion. The shadow of a bygone tragedy had lifted.

Sandra turned to Anthony in an animated way. Stephen made an observation to Iris and Ruth leaned forward to join in. Only George sat in his chair staring—staring, his eyes fixed on the empty chair opposite him. The place in front of it was laid. There was champagne in the glass. At any moment, someone might come, might sit down there—

A nudge from Iris recalled him:

"Wake up, George. Come and dance. You haven't danced with me yet."

He roused himself. Smiling at her he lifted his glass.

"We'll drink a toast first—to the young lady whose birthday we're celebrating. Iris Marle, may her shadow never grow less!"

They drank it laughing, then they all got up to dance, George and Iris, Stephen and Ruth, Anthony and Sandra.

It was a gay jazz melody.

They all came back together, laughing and talking. They sat down.

Then suddenly George leaned forward.

"I've something I want to ask you all. A year ago, more or less, we were here before on an evening that ended tragically. I don't want to recall past sadness, but it's just that I don't want to feel that Rosemary is completely forgotten. I'll ask you to drink to her memory—for Remembrance sake."

He raised his glass. Everyone else obediently raised theirs. Their faces were polite masks.

George said:

"To Rosemary for remembrance."

The glasses were raised to their lips. They drank.

There was a pause—then George swayed forward and slumped down in his chair, his hands rising frenziedly to his neck, his face turning purple as he fought for breath.

It took him a minute and a half to die.

BOOK 3

IRIS

"For I thought that the dead had peace
But it is not so . . ."

One

Colonel Race turned into the doorway of New Scotland Yard. He filled in the form that was brought forward and a very few minutes later he was shaking hands with Chief Inspector Kemp in the latter's room.

The two men were well acquainted. Kemp was slightly reminiscent of that grand old veteran, Battle, in type. Indeed, since he had worked under Battle for many years, he had perhaps unconsciously copied a good many of the older man's mannerisms. He bore about him the same suggestion of being carved all in one piece—but whereas Battle had suggested some wood such as teak or oak, Chief Inspector Kemp suggested a somewhat more showy wood—mahogany, say, or good old-fashioned rosewood.

"It was good of you to ring us, colonel," said Kemp. "We shall want all the help we can get on this case."

"It seems to have got us into exalted hands," said Race.

Kemp did not make modest disclaimers. He accepted quite simply the indubitable fact that only cases of extreme delicacy, wide publicity or supreme importance came his way. He said seriously:

"It's the Kidderminster connection. You can imagine that means careful going."

Race nodded. He had met Lady Alexandra Farraday several times. One of those quiet women of unassailable position whom it seems fantastic to associate with sensational publicity. He had heard her speak on public platforms—without eloquence, but clearly and competently, with a good grasp of her subject, and with an excellent delivery.

The kind of woman whose public life was in all the papers, and whose private life was practically nonexistent except as a bland domestic background.

Nevertheless, he thought, such women *have* a private life. They know despair, and love, and the agonies of jealousy. They can lose control and risk life itself on a passionate gamble.

He said curiously:

"Suppose she 'done it,' Kemp?"

"Lady Alexandra? Do you think she did, sir?"

"I've no idea. But suppose she did. Or her husband—who comes under the Kidderminster mantle."

The steady sea-green eyes of Chief Inspector Kemp looked in an untroubled way into Race's dark ones.

"If either of them did murder, we'll do our level best to hang him or her. *You* know that. There's no fear and no favour for murderers in this country. But we'll have to be absolutely sure of our evidence—the public prosecutor will insist on that."

Race nodded.

Then he said, "Let's have the doings."

"George Barton died of cyanide poisoning—same thing as his wife a year ago. You said you were actually in the restaurant?"

"Yes. Barton had asked me to join his party. I refused. I didn't like what he was doing. I protested against it and urged him, if he had doubts about his wife's death, to go to the proper people—to you."

Kemp nodded.

"That's what he ought to have done."

"Instead he persisted in an idea of his own—setting a trap for the murderer. He wouldn't tell me what that trap was. I was uneasy about the whole business—so much so that I went to the Luxembourg last night so as to keep an eye on things. My table, necessarily, was some distance away—I didn't want to be spotted too obviously. Unfortunately I can tell you nothing. I saw nothing in the least suspicious. The waiters and his own party were the only people who approached the table."

"Yes," said Kemp, "it narrows it down, doesn't it? It was one of them, or it was the waiter, Giuseppe Bolsano. I've got him on the mat again this morning—thought you might like to see him—but I can't believe he had anything to do with it. Been at the Luxembourg for twelve years—good reputation, married, three children, good record behind him. Gets on well with all the clients."

"Which leaves us with the guests."

"Yes. The same party as was present when Mrs. Barton—died."

"What about that business, Kemp?"

"I've been going into it since it seems pretty obvious that the two hang together. Adams handled it. It wasn't what we call a clear case of suicide, but suicide was the most probable solution and in the absence of any direct evidence suggesting murder, one had to let it go as suicide. Couldn't do anything else. We've a good many cases like that in our records, as you know. Suicide with a query mark. The public doesn't know about the query mark—but we keep it in mind. Sometimes we go on quite a bit hunting about quietly.

"Sometimes something crops up—sometimes it doesn't. In this case it didn't."

"Until now."

"Until now. Somebody tipped Mr. Barton off to the fact that his wife had been murdered. He got busy on his own—he as good as announced that he was on the right track—whether he was or not I don't know—but the murderer must have thought so—so the murderer gets rattled and bumps off Mr. Barton. That seems the way of it as far as I can see—I hope you agree?"

"Oh, yes—that part of it seems straightforward enough. God knows what the 'trap' was—I noticed that there was an empty chair at the table. Perhaps it was waiting for some unexpected witness. Anyhow it accomplished rather more than it was meant to do. It alarmed the guilty person so much that he or she didn't wait for the trap to be sprung."

"Well," said Kemp, "we've got five suspects. And we've got the first case to go on—Mrs. Barton."

"You're definitely of the opinion now that it was *not* suicide?"

"This murder seems to prove that it wasn't. Though I don't think you can blame us at the time for accepting the suicide theory as the most probable. There was some evidence for it."

"Depression after influenza?"

Kemp's wooden face showed a ripple of a smile.

"That was for the coroner's court. Agreed with the medical evidence and saved everybody's feelings. That's done every day. And there was a half-finished letter to the sister directing how her personal belongings were to be given away— showed she'd had the idea of doing away with herself in her mind. She was depressed all right, I don't doubt, poor lady—but nine times out of ten, with women, it's a love affair. With men it's mostly money worries."

"So you knew Mrs. Barton had a love affair."

"Yes, we soon found that out. It had been discreet—but it didn't take much finding."

"Stephen Farraday?"

"Yes. They used to meet in a little flat out Earl's Court way. It had been going on for over six months. Say they'd had a quarrel—or possibly he was getting tired of her—well, she wouldn't be the first woman to take her life in a fit of desperation."

"By potassium cyanide in a public restaurant?"

"Yes—if she wanted to be dramatic about it—with him looking on and all. Some people have a feeling for the spectacular. From what I could find out she hadn't much feeling for the conventions—all the precautions were on his side."

"Any evidence as to whether his wife knew what was going on?"

"As far as we could learn she knew nothing about it."

"She may have, for all that, Kemp. Not the kind of woman to wear her heart on her sleeve."

"Oh, quite so. Count them both in as possibles. She for jealousy. He for his career. Divorce would have dished that. Not that divorce means as much as it used to, but in his case it would have meant the antagonism of the Kidderminster clan."

"What about the secretary girl?"

"She's a possible. Might have been sweet on George Barton. They were pretty thick at the office and there's an idea there that she was keen on him. Actually yesterday afternoon one of the telephone girls was giving an imitation of Barton holding Ruth Lessing's hand and saying he couldn't do without her, and Miss Lessing came out and caught them and sacked the girl there and then—gave her a month's money and told her to go. Looks as though she was sensitive about it all. Then the sister came into a peck of money—one's got to remember that. Looked a nice kid, but you can never tell. And there was Mrs. Barton's other boyfriend."

"I'm rather anxious to hear what you know about him?"

Kemp said slowly:

"Remarkably little—but what there is isn't too good. His passport's in order. He's an American citizen about whom we can't find anything, detrimental or otherwise. He came over here, stayed at Claridge's and managed to strike up an acquaintance with Lord Dewsbury."

"Confidence man?"

"Might be. Dewsbury seems to have fallen for him—asked him to stay. Rather a critical time just then."

"Armaments," said Race. "There was that trouble about the new tank trials in Dewsbury's works."

"Yes. This fellow Browne represented himself as interested in armaments. It was soon after he'd been up there that they discovered that sabotage business—just in the nick of time. Browne met a good many cronies of Dewsbury—he seemed to have cultivated all the ones who were connected with the armament firms. As a result he's been shown a lot of stuff that in my opinion he ought never to have seen—and in one or two cases there's been serious trouble in the works not long after he's been in the neighbourhood."

"An interesting person, Mr. Anthony Browne?"

"Yes. He's got a lot of charm, apparently, and plays it for all he's worth."

"And where did Mrs. Barton come in? George Barton hasn't anything to do with the armament world?"

"No. But they seem to have been fairly intimate. He may have let out something to her. *You* know, colonel, none better, what a pretty woman can get out of a man."

Race nodded, taking the chief inspector's words, as meant, to refer to the Counterespionage Department which he had once controlled and not—as some ignorant person might have thought—to some personal indiscretions of his own.

He said after a minute or two:

"Have you had a go at those letters that George Barton received?"

"Yes. Found them in his desk at his house last night. Miss Marle found them for me."

"You know I'm interested in those letters, Kemp. What's the expert opinion on them?"

"Cheap paper, ordinary ink—fingerprints show

George Barton and Iris Marle handled them—and a horde of unidentified dabs on the envelope, postal employees, etc. They were printed and the experts say by someone of good education in normal health."

"Good education. Not a servant?"

"Presumably not."

"That makes it more interesting still."

"It means that somebody else had suspicions, at least."

"Someone who didn't go to the police. Someone who was prepared to arouse George's suspicions but who didn't follow the business up. There's something odd there, Kemp. He couldn't have written them himself, could he?"

"He could have. But why?"

"As a preliminary to suicide—a suicide which he intended to look like murder."

"With Stephen Farraday booked for the hangman's rope? It's an idea—but he'd have made quite sure that everything pointed to Farraday as the murderer. As it is we've nothing against Farraday at all."

"What about cyanide? Was there any container found?"

"Yes. A small white paper packet under the table. Traces of cyanide crystals inside. No fingerprints on it. In a detective story, of course, it would be some special kind of paper or folded in some special way. I'd like to give these detective

181

story writers a course of routine work. They'd soon learn how most things are untraceable and nobody ever notices anything anywhere!"

Race smiled.

"Almost too sweeping a statement. Did anybody notice anything last night?"

"Actually that's what I'm starting on today. I took a brief statement from everyone last night and I went back to Elvaston Square with Miss Marle and had a look through Barton's desk and papers. I shall get fuller statements from them all today—also statements from the people sitting at the other two tables in the alcove—" He rustled through some papers—"Yes, here they are. Gerald Tollington, Grenadier Guards, and the Hon. Patricia Brice-Woodworth. Young engaged couple. I'll bet they didn't see anything but each other. And Mr. Pedro Morales—nasty bit of goods from Mexico—even the whites of his eyes are yellow—and Miss Christine Shannon—a gold-digging blonde lovely—I'll bet she didn't see anything—dumber than you'd believe possible except where money is concerned. It's a hundred to one chance that any of them saw anything, but I took their names and addresses on the off chance. We'll start off with the waiter chap, Giuseppe. He's here now. I'll have him sent in."

Two

Giuseppe Bolsano was a middle-aged man, slight with a rather monkey-like intelligent face. He was nervous, but not unduly so. His English was fluent since he had, he explained, been in the country since he was sixteen and had married an English wife.

Kemp treated him sympathetically.

"Now then, Giuseppe, let's hear whether anything more has occurred to you about this."

"It is for me very unpleasant. It is I who serve that table. I who pour out the wine. People will say that I am off my head, that I put poison into the wine glasses. It is not so, but that is what people will say. Already, Mr. Goldstein says it is better that I take a week away from work—so that people do not ask me questions there and point me out. He is a fair man, and just, and he knows it is not my fault, and that I have been there for many years, so he does not dismiss me as some restaurant owners would do. M. Charles, too, he has been kind, but all the same it is a great misfortune for me—and it makes me afraid. Have I an enemy, I ask myself?"

"Well," said Kemp at his most wooden, "have you?"

The sad monkeyface twitched into laughter. Giuseppe stretched out his arms.

"I? I have not an enemy in the world. Many good friends but no enemies."

Kemp grunted.

"Now about last night. Tell me about the champagne."

"It was Clicquot, 1928—very good and expensive wine. Mr. Barton was like that—he liked good food and drink—the best."

"Had he ordered the wine beforehand?"

"Yes. He had arranged everything with Charles."

"What about the vacant place at the table?"

"That, too, he had arranged for. He told Charles and he told me. A young lady would occupy it later in the evening."

"A young lady?" Race and Kemp looked at each other. "Do you know who the young lady was?"

Giuseppe shook his head.

"No, I know nothing about that. She was to come later, that is all I heard."

"Go on about the wine. How many bottles?"

"Two bottles and a third to be ready if needed. The first bottle was finished quite quickly. The second I open not long before the cabaret. I fill up the glasses and put the bottle in the ice bucket."

"When did you last notice Mr. Barton drinking from his glass?"

"Let me see, when the cabaret was over, they drink the young lady's health. It is her birthday so I understand. Then they go and dance. It is after that, when they come back, that Mr. Barton drinks and in a minute, like *that!* he is dead."

"Had you filled up the glasses during the time they were dancing?"

"No, monsieur. They were full when they drank to mademoiselle and they did not drink much, only a few mouthfuls. There was plenty left in the glasses."

"Did anyone—*anyone* at all—come near the table whilst they were dancing?"

"No one at all, sir. I am sure of that."

"Did they all go to dance at the same time?"

"Yes."

"And came back at the same time?"

Giuseppe screwed up his eyes in an effort of memory.

"Mr. Barton he came back first—with the young lady. He was stouter than the rest—he did not dance quite so long, you comprehend. Then came the fair gentleman, Mr. Farraday, and the young lady in black. Lady Alexandra Farraday and the dark gentleman came last."

"You know Mr. Farraday and Lady Alexandra?"

"Yes, sir. I have seen them in the Luxembourg often. They are very distinguished."

"Now, Giuseppe, would you have seen if one of those people had put something in Mr. Barton's glass?"

"That I cannot say, sir. I have my service, the other two tables in the alcove, and two more in the

185

main restaurant. There are dishes to serve. I do not watch at Mr. Barton's table. After the cabaret everyone nearly gets up and dances, so at that time I am standing still—and that is why I can be sure that no one approached the table then. But as soon as people sit down, I am at once very busy."

Kemp nodded.

"But I think," Giuseppe continued, "that it would be very difficult to do without being observed. It seems to me that only Mr. Barton himself could do it. But you do not think so, no?"

He looked inquiringly at the police officer.

"So that's your idea, is it?"

"Naturally I know nothing—but I wonder. Just a year ago that beautiful lady, Mrs. Barton, she kills herself. Could it not be that Mr. Barton he grieves so much that he too decides to kill himself the same way? It would be poetic. Of course it is not good for the restaurant—but a gentleman who is going to kill himself would not think of that."

He looked eagerly from one to the other of the two men.

Kemp shook his head.

"I doubt if it's as easy as that," he said.

He asked a few more questions, then Giuseppe was dismissed.

As the door closed behind Giuseppe, Race said: "I wonder if that's what we are meant to think?"

"Grieving husband kills himself on anniversary

of wife's death? Not that it was the anniversary—but near enough."

"It was All Souls' Day," said Race.

"True. Yes, it's possible that *was* the idea—but if so, whoever it was can't have known about those letters being kept and that Mr. Barton had consulted you and shown them to Iris Marle."

He glanced at his watch.

"I'm due at Kidderminster House at 12:30. We've time before that to go and see those people at the other two tables—some of them at any rate. Come with me, won't you, colonel?"

Three

Mr. Morales was staying at the Ritz. He was hardly a pretty sight at this hour in the morning, still unshaven, the whites of his eyes bloodshot and with every sign of a severe hangover.

Mr. Morales was an American subject and spoke a variant of the American language. Though professing himself willing to remember anything he could, his recollections of the previous evening were of the vaguest description.

"Went with Chrissie—that baby is sure hard-boiled! She said it was a good joint. Honey pie, I said, we'll go just where you say. It was a classy joint, that I'll admit—and do they know how to charge you! Set me back the best part of thirty dollars. But the band was punk—they just couldn't seem to swing it."

Diverted from his recollections of his own evening, Mr. Morales was pressed to remember the table in the middle of the alcove. Here he was not very helpful.

"Sure there was a table and some people at it. I don't remember what they looked like, though. Didn't take much account of them till the guy there croaked. Thought at first he couldn't hold his liquor. Say now, I remember one of the dames. Dark hair and she had what it takes, I should say."

"You mean the girl in the green velvet dress?"

"No, not that one. She was skinny. This baby was in black with some good curves."

It was Ruth Lessing who had taken Mr. Morales' roving eye.

He wrinkled up his nose appreciatively.

"I watched her dancing—and say, could that baby dance! I gave her the high sign once or twice, but she had a frozen eye—just looked through me in your British way."

Nothing more of value could be extracted from Mr. Morales and he admitted frankly that his alcoholic condition was already well advanced by the time the cabaret was on.

Kemp thanked him and prepared to take his leave.

"I'm sailing for New York tomorrow," said Morales. "You wouldn't," he asked wistfully, "care for me to stay on?"

"Thank you, but I don't think your evidence will be needed at the inquest."

"You see I'm enjoying it right here—and if it was police business the firm couldn't kick. When the police tell you to stay put, you've got to stay put. Maybe I *could* remember something if I thought hard enough?"

But Kemp declined to rise to this wistful bait, and he and Race drove to Brook Street where they were greeted by a choleric gentleman, the father of the Hon. Patricia Brice-Woodworth.

General Lord Woodworth received them with a good deal of outspoken comment.

What on earth was the idea of suggesting that his daughter—*his* daughter!—was mixed up in this sort of thing? If a girl couldn't go out with her fiancé to dine in a restaurant without being subjected to annoyance by detectives and Scotland Yard, what was England coming to? She didn't even know these people what was their name—Hubbard—Barton? Some City fellow or other! Showed you couldn't be too careful where you went—Luxembourg was always supposed to be all right—but apparently this was the second time a thing of this sort had happened there. Gerald must be a fool to have taken Pat there—these young men thought they knew everything. But in any case he wasn't going to have his daughter badgered and bullied and cross-questioned—not without a solicitor's say so. He'd ring up old Anderson in Lincoln's Inn and ask him—

Here the general paused abruptly and staring at Race said, "Seen you somewhere. Now where—?"

Race's answer was immediate and came with a smile.

"Badderpore. 1923."

"By Jove," said the general. "If it isn't Johnny Race! What are you doing mixed up in this show?"

Race smiled.

"I was with Chief Inspector Kemp when the question of interviewing your daughter came up. I suggested it would be much pleasanter for her if Inspector Kemp came round here than if she had to come down to Scotland Yard, and I thought I'd come along too."

"Oh—er—well, very decent, of you, Race."

"We naturally wanted to upset the young lady as little as possible," put in Chief Inspector Kemp.

But at this moment the door opened and Miss Patricia Brice-Woodworth walked in and took charge of the situation with the coolness and detachment of the very young.

"Hallo," she said. "You're from Scotland Yard, aren't you? About last night? I've been longing for you to come. Is father being tiresome? Now don't, daddy—you know what the doctor said about your blood pressure. Why you want to get into such states about everything, I can't think. I'll just take the inspectors or superintendents or whatever they are into my room and I'll send Walters to you with a whisky and soda."

The general had a choleric desire to express himself in several blistering ways at once, but only succeeded in saying, "Old friend of mine, Major Race," at which introduction, Patricia lost interest in Race and bent a beatific smile on Chief Inspector Kemp.

With cool generalship, she shepherded them out of the room and into her own sitting room, firmly shutting her father in his study.

"Poor daddy," she observed. "He *will* fuss. But he's quite easy to manage really."

The conversation then proceeded on most amicable lines but with very little result.

"It's maddening really," said Patricia. "Probably the only chance in my life that I shall ever have of being right on the spot when a murder was done—it is a murder, isn't it? The papers were very cautious and vague, but I said to Gerry on the telephone that it must be murder. Think of it, a murder done right close by me and I wasn't even looking!"

The regret in her voice was unmistakable.

It was evident enough that, as the chief inspector had gloomily prognosticated, the two young people who had got engaged only a week previously had had eyes only for each other.

With the best will in the world, a few personalities were all that Patricia Brice-Woodworth could muster.

"Sandra Farraday was looking very smart, but then she always does. That was a Schiaparelli model she had on."

"You know her?" Race asked.

Patricia shook her head.

"Only by sight. He looks rather a bore, I always think. So pompous, like most politicians."

"Did you know any of the others by sight?"

She shook her head.

"No, I'd never seen any of them before—at least I don't think so. In fact, I don't suppose I would have noticed Sandra Farraday if it hadn't been for the Schiaparelli."

"And you'll find," said Chief Inspector Kemp grimly as they left the house, "that Master Tollington will be exactly the same—only there won't even have been a Skipper—skipper what—sounds like a sardine—to attract his attention."

"I don't suppose," agreed Race, "that the cut of Stephen Farraday's dress suit will have caused him any heart pangs."

"Oh, well," said the inspector. "Let's try Christine Shannon. Then we'll have finished with the outside chances."

Miss Shannon was, as Chief Inspector Kemp had stated, a blonde lovely. The bleached hair, carefully arranged, swept back from a soft vacant baby-like countenance. Miss Shannon might be as Inspector Kemp had affirmed, dumb—but she was eminently easy to look at, and a certain shrewdness in the large baby-blue eyes indicated that her dumbness only extended in intellectual directions and that where horse sense and a knowledge of finance were indicated, Christine Shannon was right on the spot.

She received the two men with the utmost sweetness, pressing drinks upon them and when these were refused, urging cigarettes. Her flat was small and cheaply modernistic.

"I'd just love to be able to help you, chief inspector. Do ask me any questions you like."

Kemp led off with a few conventional questions about the bearing and demeanour of the party at the centre table.

At once Christine showed herself to be an unusually keen and shrewd observer.

"The party wasn't going well—you could see that. Stiff as stiff could be. I felt quite sorry for the old boy—the one who was giving it. Going all out he was to try and make things go—and just as nervous as a cat on wires—but all he could do didn't seem to cut any ice. The tall woman he'd got on his right was as stiff as though she'd swallowed the poker and the kid on his left was just mad, you could see, because she wasn't sitting next to the nice-looking dark boy opposite. As for the tall fair fellow next to her he looked as though his tummy was out of order, ate his food as though he thought it would choke him. The woman next to him was doing her best, she pegged away at him, but she looked rather as though she had the jumps herself."

"You seem to have been able to notice a great deal, Miss Shannon," said Colonel Race.

"I'll let you into a secret. I wasn't being so much amused myself. I'd been out with that boyfriend of mine three nights running, and was I getting

194

tired of him! He was all out for seeing London—especially what he called the classy spots—and I will say for him he wasn't mean. Champagne every time. We went to the Compradour and the Mille Fleurs and finally the Luxembourg, and I'll say he enjoyed himself. In a way it was kind of pathetic. But his conversation wasn't what you'd call interesting. Just long histories of business deals he'd put through in Mexico and most of those I heard three times—and going on to all the dames he'd known and how mad they were about him. A girl gets kind of tired listening after a while and you'll admit that Pedro is nothing much to look at—so I just concentrated on the eats and let my eyes roam round."

"Well, that's excellent from our point of view, Miss Shannon," said the chief inspector. "And I can only hope that you will have seen something that may help us solve our problem."

Christine shook her blonde head.

"I've no idea who bumped the old boy off—no idea at all. He just took a drink of champagne, went purple in the face and sort of collapsed."

"Do you remember when he had last drunk from his glass before that?"

The girl reflected.

"Why—yes—it was just after the cabaret. The lights went up and he picked up his glass and said something and the others did it too. Seemed to me it was a toast of some kind."

The chief inspector nodded.

"And then?"

"Then the music began and they all got up and went off to dance, pushing their chairs back and laughing. Seemed to get warmed up for the first time. Wonderful what champagne will do for the stickiest parties."

"They all went together—leaving the table empty?"

"Yes."

"And no one touched Mr. Barton's glass."

"No one at all." Her reply came promptly. "I'm perfectly certain of that."

"And no one—no one at all came near the table while they were away."

"No one—except the waiter, of course."

"A waiter? Which waiter?"

"One of the half-fledged ones with an apron, round about sixteen. Not the real waiter. He was an obliging little fellow rather like a monkey—Italian I guess he was."

Chief Inspector Kemp acknowledged this description of Giuseppe Bolsano with a nod of the head.

"And what did he do, this young waiter? He filled up the glasses?"

Christine shook her head.

"Oh, no. He didn't touch anything on the table. He just picked up an evening bag that one of the girls had dropped when they all got up."

"Whose bag was it?"

Christine took a minute or two to think. Then she said:

"That's right. It was the kid's bag—a green and gold thing. The other two women had black bags."

"What did the waiter do with the bag?"

Christine looked surprised.

"He just put it back on the table, that's all."

"You're quite sure he didn't touch any of the glasses?"

"Oh, no. He just dropped the bag down very quick and ran off because one of the real waiters was hissing at him to go somewhere or get something and everything was going to be his fault!"

"And that's the only time anyone went near the table?"

"That's right."

"But of course someone might have gone to the table without your noticing?"

But Christine shook her head very determinedly.

"No, I'm quite sure they didn't. You see Pedro had been called to the telephone and hadn't got back yet, so I had nothing to do but look around and feel bored. I'm pretty good at noticing things and from where I was sitting there wasn't much else to see but the empty table next to us."

Race asked:

"Who came back first to the table?"

"The girl in green and the old boy. They sat down and then the fair man and the girl in black came back and after them the haughty piece of goods and the good-looking dark boy. Some dancer, he was. When they were all back and the waiter was warming up a dish like mad on the spirit lamp, the old boy leaned forward and made a kind of speech and then they all picked up their glasses again. And then it happened." Christine paused and added brightly, "Awful, wasn't it? Of course I thought it was a stroke. My aunt had a stroke and she went down just like that. Pedro came back just then and I said, 'Look, Pedro, that man's had a stroke.' And all Pedro would say was, 'Just passing out—just passing out—that's all' which was about what *he* was doing. I had to keep my eye on him. They don't like you passing out at a place like the Luxembourg. That's why I don't like Dagoes. When they've drunk too much they're not a bit refined anymore—a girl never knows what unpleasantness she may be let in for." She brooded for a moment and then glancing at a showy looking bracelet on her right wrist, she added, "Still, I must say they're generous enough."

Gently distracting her from the trials and compensations of a girl's existence Kemp took her through her story once more.

"That's our last chance of outside help gone," he said to Race when they had left Miss Shannon's flat. "And it would have been a good chance if it had come off. That girl's the right kind of witness.

Sees things and remembers them accurately. If there had been anything to see, she'd have seen it. So the answer is that there wasn't anything to see. It's incredible. It's a conjuring trick! George Barton drinks champagne and goes and dances. He comes back, drinks from the same glass that no one has touched and Hey Presto it's full of cyanide. It's crazy—I tell you—it couldn't have happened except that it did."

He stopped a minute.

"That waiter. The little boy. Giuseppe never mentioned him. I might look into that. After all, he's the one person who was near the table whilst they were all away dancing. There *might* be something in it."

Race shook his head.

"If he'd put anything in Barton's glass, that girl would have seen him. She's a born observer of detail. Nothing to think about inside her head and so she uses her eyes. No, Kemp, there must be some quite simple explanation if only we could get it."

"Yes, there's one. He dropped it in himself."

"I'm beginning to believe that that *is* what happened—that it's the only thing that can have happened. But if so, Kemp, I'm convinced he didn't know it was cyanide."

"You mean someone gave it to him? Told him it was for indigestion or blood pressure—something like that?"

"It could be."

"Then who was the someone? Not either of the Farradays."

"That would certainly seem unlikely."

"And I'd say Mr. Anthony Browne is equally unlikely. That leaves us two people—an affectionate sister-in-law—"

"And a devoted secretary."

Kemp looked at him.

"Yes—she could have planted something of the kind on him—I'm due now to go to Kidderminster House—What about you? Going round to see Miss Marle?"

"I think I'll go and see the other one—at the office. Condolences of an old friend. I might take her out to lunch."

"So that *is* what you think."

"I don't think anything yet. I'm casting about for spoor."

"You ought to see Iris Marle, all the same."

"I'm going to see her—but I'd rather go to the house first when she isn't there. Do you know why, Kemp?"

"I'm sure I couldn't say."

"Because there's someone there who twitters—twitters like a little bird . . . A little bird told me—was a saying of my youth. It's very true, Kemp—these twitterers can tell one a lot if one just lets them—twitter!"

Four

The two men parted. Race halted a taxi and was driven to George Barton's office in the city. Chief Inspector Kemp, mindful of his expense account, took a bus to within a stone's throw of Kidderminster House.

The inspector's face was rather grim as he mounted the steps and pushed the bell. He was, he knew, on difficult ground. The Kidderminster faction had immense political influence and its ramifications spread out like a network throughout the country. Chief Inspector Kemp had full belief in the impartiality of British justice. If Stephen or Alexandra Farraday had been concerned in the death of Rosemary Barton or in that of George Barton no "pull" or "influence" would enable them to escape the consequences. But if they were guiltless, or the evidence against them was too vague to ensure conviction, then the responsible officer must be careful how he trod or he would be liable to get a rap over the knuckles from his superiors. In these circumstances it can be understood that the chief inspector did not much relish what lay before him. It seemed to him highly probable that the Kidderminsters would, as he phrased it to himself, "cut up rough."

Kemp soon found, however, that he had been somewhat naïve in his assumption. Lord

Kidderminster was far too experienced a diplomat to resort to crudities.

On stating his business, Chief Inspector Kemp was taken at once by a pontifical butler to a dim book-lined room at the back of the house where he found Lord Kidderminster and his daughter and son-in-law awaiting him.

Coming forward, Lord Kidderminster shook hands and said courteously:

"You are exactly on time, chief inspector. May I say that I much appreciate your courtesy in coming here instead of demanding that my daughter and her husband should come to Scotland Yard which, of course, they would have been quite prepared to do if necessary—that goes without saying—but they appreciate your kindness."

Sandra said in a quiet voice:

"Yes, indeed, inspector."

She was wearing a dress of some soft dark red material, and sitting as she was with the light from the long narrow window behind her, she reminded Kemp of a stained glass figure he had once seen in a cathedral abroad. The long oval of her face and the slight angularity of her shoulders helped the illusion. Saint Somebody or other, they had told him—but Lady Alexandra Farraday was no saint—not by a long way. And yet some of these old saints had been funny people from his point of view, not kindly ordinary decent Christian folk, but intolerant, fanatical, cruel to themselves and others.

Stephen Farraday stood close by his wife. His face expressed no emotion whatever. He looked correct and formal, an appointed legislator of the people. The natural man was well buried. But the natural man was there, as the chief inspector knew.

Lord Kidderminster was speaking, directing with a good deal of ability the trend of the interview.

"I won't disguise from you, chief inspector, that this is a very painful and disagreeable business for us all. This is the second time that my daughter and son-in-law have been connected with a violent death in a public place—the same restaurant and two members of the same family. Publicity of such a kind is always harmful to a man in the public eye. Publicity, of course, cannot be avoided. We all realize that, and both my daughter and Mr. Farraday are anxious to give you all the help they can in the hope that the matter may be cleared up speedily and public interest in it die down."

"Thank you, Lord Kidderminster. I much appreciate the attitude you have taken up. It certainly makes things easier for us."

Sandra Farraday said:

"Please ask us any questions you like, chief inspector."

"Thank you, Lady Alexandra."

"Just one point, chief inspector," said Lord

Kidderminster. "You have, of course, your own sources of information and I gather from my friend the Commissioner that this man Barton's death is regarded as murder rather than suicide, though on the face of it, to the outside public, suicide would seem a more likely explanation. *You* thought it was suicide, didn't you, Sandra, my dear?"

The Gothic figure bowed its head slightly. Sandra said in a thoughtful voice:

"It seemed to me so obvious last night. We were there in the same restaurant and actually at the same table where poor Rosemary Barton poisoned herself last year. We have seen something of Mr. Barton during the summer in the country and he has really been very odd—quite unlike himself—and we all thought that his wife's death was preying on his mind. He was very fond of her, you know, and I don't think he ever got over her death. So that the idea of suicide seemed, if not natural, at least possible—whereas I can't imagine why *anyone* should want to murder George Barton."

Stephen Farraday said quickly:

"No more can I. Barton was an excellent fellow. I'm sure he hadn't got an enemy in the world."

Chief Inspector Kemp looked at the three inquiring faces turned towards him and reflected a moment before speaking. "Better let 'em have it," he thought to himself.

"What you say is quite correct, I am sure, Lady

Alexandra. But you see there are a few things that you probably don't know yet."

Lord Kidderminster interposed quickly:

"We mustn't force the chief inspector's hand. It is entirely in his discretion what facts he makes public."

"Thanks, m'lord, but there's no reason I shouldn't explain things a little more clearly. I'll boil it down to this. George Barton, before his death, expressed to two people his belief that his wife had not, as was believed, committed suicide, but had instead been poisoned by some third party. He also thought that he was on the track of that third party, and the dinner and celebration last night, ostensibly in honour of Miss Marle's birthday, was really some part of a plan he had made for finding out the identity of his wife's murderer."

There was a moment's silence—and in that silence Chief Inspector Kemp, who was a sensitive man in spite of his wooden appearance, felt the presence of something that he classified as dismay. It was not apparent on any face, but he could have sworn that it was there.

Lord Kidderminster was the first to recover himself. He said:

"But surely—that belief in itself might point to the fact that poor Barton was not quite—er—himself? Brooding over his wife's death might have slightly unhinged him mentally."

"Quite so, Lord Kidderminster, but it at least shows that his frame of mind was definitely not suicidal."

"Yes—yes, I take your point."

And again there was silence. Then Stephen Farraday said sharply:

"But how did Barton get such an idea into his head? After all, Mrs. Barton *did* commit suicide."

Chief Inspector Kemp transferred a placid gaze to him.

"Mr. Barton didn't think so."

Lord Kidderminster interposed.

"But the police were satisfied? There was no suggestion of anything but suicide at the time?"

Chief Inspector Kemp said quietly:

"The facts were compatible with suicide. There was no evidence that her death was due to any other agency."

He knew that a man of Lord Kidderminster's calibre would seize on the exact meaning of that.

Becoming slightly more official, Kemp said, "I would like to ask you some questions now, if I may, Lady Alexandra?"

"Certainly." She turned her head slightly towards him.

"You had no suspicions at the time of Mr. Barton's death that it might be murder, not suicide?"

"Certainly not. I was quite sure it was suicide." She added, "I still am."

Kemp let that pass. He said:

"Have you received any anonymous letters in the past year, Lady Alexandra?"

The calm of her manner seemed broken by pure astonishment.

"Anonymous letters? Oh, no."

"You're quite sure? Such letters are very unpleasant things and people usually prefer to ignore them, but they may be particularly important in this case, and that is why I want to stress that if you did receive any such letters it is most essential that I should know about them."

"I see. But I can only assure you, chief inspector, that I have received nothing of the kind."

"Very well. Now you say Mr. Barton's manner has been odd this summer. In what way?"

She considered a minute.

"Well, he was jumpy, nervous. It seemed difficult for him to focus his attention on what was said to him." She turned her head towards her husband. "Was that how it struck you, Stephen?"

"Yes, I should say that was a very fair description. The man looked physically ill, too. He had lost weight."

"Did you notice any difference in his attitude towards you and your husband? Any less cordiality, for instance?"

"No. On the contrary. He had bought a house, you know, quite close to us, and he seemed very grateful for what we were able to do for him—in the way of local introductions, I mean, and all that. Of course we were only too pleased to do everything we could in that line, both for him and for Iris Marle who is a charming girl."

"Was the late Mrs. Barton a great friend of yours, Lady Alexandra?"

"No, we were not very intimate." She gave a light laugh. "She was really mostly Stephen's friend. She became interested in politics and he helped to—well, educate her politically—which I'm sure he enjoyed. She was a very charming and attractive woman, you know."

"And you're a very clever one," thought Chief Inspector Kemp to himself appreciatively. "I wonder how much you know about those two—a good deal, I shouldn't wonder."

He went on:

"Mr. Barton never expressed to *you* the view that his wife did not commit suicide?"

"No, indeed. That was why I was so startled just now."

"And Miss Marle? She never talked about her sister's death, either?"

"No."

"Any idea what made George Barton buy a house in the country? Did you or your husband suggest the idea to him?"

"No. It was quite a surprise."

"And his manner to you was always friendly?"

"Very friendly indeed."

"And what do you know about Mr. Anthony Browne, Lady Alexandra?"

"I really know nothing at all. I have met him occasionally and that is all."

"What about you, Mr. Farraday?"

"I think I know probably less about Browne than my wife does. She at any rate has danced with him. He seems a likeable chap—American, I believe."

"Would you say from observation at the time that he was on special terms of intimacy with Mrs. Barton?"

"I have absolutely no knowledge on that point, chief inspector."

"I am simply asking you for your impression, Mr. Farraday."

Stephen frowned.

"They were friendly—that is all I can say."

"And you, Lady Alexandra?"

"Simply my impression, chief inspector?"

"Simply your impression."

"Then, for what it is worth, I did form the impression that they knew each other well and were on intimate terms. Simply, you understand, from the way they looked at each other—I have no concrete evidence."

"Ladies have often very good judgement on these matters," said Kemp. That somewhat fatuous smile with which he delivered this remark would have amused Colonel Race if he had been present. "Now, what about Miss Lessing, Lady Alexandra?"

"Miss Lessing, I understand, was Mr. Barton's secretary. I met her for the first time on the evening that Mrs. Barton died. After that I met her once when she was staying down in the country, and last night."

"If I may ask you another informal question, did you form the impression that she was in love with George Barton?"

"I really haven't the least idea."

"Then we'll come to the events of last night."

He questioned both Stephen and his wife minutely on the course of the tragic evening. He had not hoped for much from this, and all he got was confirmation of what he had already been told. All accounts agreed on the important points—Barton had proposed a toast to Iris, had drunk it and immediately afterwards had got up to dance. They had all left the table together and George and Iris had been the first to return to it. Neither of them had any explanation to offer as to the empty chair except that George Barton had distinctly said that he was expecting a friend of his, a Colonel Race, to occupy it later in the evening—a statement which, as the inspector knew, could not possibly be the truth. Sandra Farraday said, and her husband agreed, that when the lights went up after the cabaret, George had stared at the empty chair in a peculiar manner and had for some moments seemed so absentminded as not to hear what was said to him—then he had rallied himself and proposed Iris's health.

The only item that the chief inspector could count as an addition to his knowledge, was Sandra's account of her conversation with George at Fairhaven—and his plea that she and her husband would collaborate with him over this party for Iris's sake.

It was a reasonably plausible pretext, the chief inspector thought, though not the true one. Closing his notebook in which he had jotted down one or two hieroglyphics, he rose to his feet.

"I'm very grateful to you, my lord, and to Mr. Farraday and Lady Alexandra for your help and collaboration."

"Will my daughter's presence be required at the inquest?"

"The proceedings will be purely formal on this occasion. Evidence of identification and the medical evidence will be taken and the inquest will then be adjourned for a week. By then," said the chief inspector, his tone changing slightly, "we shall, I hope, be further on."

He turned to Stephen Farraday:

"By the way, Mr. Farraday, there are one or two small points where I think you could help me. No need to trouble Lady Alexandra. If you will give me a ring at the Yard, we can settle a time that will suit you. You are, I know, a busy man."

It was pleasantly said, with an air of casualness, but on three pairs of ears the words fell with deliberate meaning.

With an air of friendly cooperation Stephen managed to say:

"Certainly, chief inspector." Then he looked at his watch and murmured: "I must go along to the House."

When Stephen had hurried off, and the chief inspector had likewise departed, Lord Kidderminster turned to his daughter and asked a question with no beating about the bush.

"Had Stephen been having an affair with that woman?"

There was a split second of a pause before his daughter answered.

"Of course not. I should have known it if he had. And anyway, Stephen's not that kind."

"Now, look here, my dear, no good laying your ears back and digging your hoofs in. These things are bound to come out. We want to know where we are in this business."

"Rosemary Barton was a friend of that man, Anthony Browne. They went about everywhere together."

"Well," said Lord Kidderminster slowly. "You should know."

He did not believe his daughter. His face, as he went slowly out of the room, was grey and perplexed. He went upstairs to his wife's sitting room. He had vetoed her presence in the library, knowing too well that her arrogant methods were apt to arouse antagonism and at this juncture he felt it vital that relations with the official police should be harmonious.

"Well?" said Lady Kidderminster. "How did it go off?"

"Quite well on the face of it," said Lord Kidderminster slowly. "Kemp is a courteous fellow—very pleasant in his manner—he handled the whole thing with tact—just a little too much tact for my fancy."

"It's serious, then?"

"Yes, it's serious. We should never have let Sandra marry that fellow, Vicky."

"That's what I said."

"Yes—yes . . ." He acknowledged her claim. "You were right—and I was wrong. But, mind you, she would have had him anyway. You can't turn Sandra when her mind is fixed on a thing. Her meeting Farraday was a disaster—a man of whose antecedents and ancestors we know nothing. When a crisis comes how does one know how a man like that will react?"

"I see," said Lady Kidderminster. "You think we've taken a murderer into the family?"

"I don't know. I don't want to condemn the fellow offhand—but it's what the police think— and they're pretty shrewd. He had an affair with this Barton woman—that's plain enough. Either she committed suicide on his account, or else he—Well, whatever happened, Barton got wise to it and was heading for an exposé and scandal. I suppose Stephen simply couldn't take it—and—"

"Poisoned him?"

"Yes."

Lady Kidderminster shook her head.

"I don't agree with you."

"I hope you're right. But somebody poisoned him."

"If you ask me," said Lady Kidderminster, "Stephen simply wouldn't have the nerve to do a thing like that."

"He's in deadly earnest about his career—he's got great gifts, you know, and the makings of a true statesman. You can't say what anyone will do when they're forced into a corner."

His wife still shook her head.

"I still say he hasn't got the nerve. You want someone who's a gambler and capable of being reckless. I'm afraid, William, I'm horribly afraid."

He stared at her. "Are you suggesting that Sandra—*Sandra*—?"

"I hate even to suggest such a thing—but it's no use being cowardly and refusing to face possibilities. She's besotted about that man—she always has been—and there's a queer streak in Sandra. I've never really understood her—but I've always been afraid for her. She'd risk anything—*anything*—for Stephen. Without counting the cost.

And if she's been mad enough and wicked enough to do this thing, she's got to be protected."

"Protected? What do you mean—protected?"

"By you. We've got to do something about our own daughter, haven't we? Mercifully you can pull any amount of strings."

Lord Kidderminster was staring at her. Though he had thought he knew his wife's character well, he was nevertheless appalled at the force and courage of her realism—at her refusal to blink at unpalatable facts—and also at her unscrupulousness.

"If my daughter's a murderess, do you suggest that I should use my official position to rescue her from the consequences of her act?"

"Of course," said Lady Kidderminster.

"My dear Vicky! You don't understand! One can't do things like that. It would be a breach of—of honour."

"Rubbish!" said Lady Kidderminster.

They looked at each other—so far divided that neither could see the other's point of view. So might Agamemnon and Clytemnestra have stared at each other with the word Iphigenia on their lips.

"You could bring government pressure to bear on the police so that the whole thing is dropped and a verdict of suicide brought in. It has been done before—don't pretend."

"That has been when it was a matter of public policy—in the interests of the State. This is a personal and private matter. I doubt very much whether I could do such a thing."

"You can if you have sufficient determination."

Lord Kidderminster flushed angrily.

"If I could, I wouldn't! It would be abusing my public position."

"If Sandra were arrested and tried, wouldn't you employ the best counsel and do everything possible to get her off however guilty she was?"

"Of course, of course. That's entirely different. You women never grasp these things."

Lady Kidderminster was silent, unperturbed by the thrust. Sandra was the least dear to her of her children—nevertheless she was at this moment a mother, and a mother only—willing to defend her young by any means, honourable or dishonourable. She would fight with tooth and claw for Sandra.

"In any case," said Lord Kidderminster, "Sandra will not be charged unless there is an absolutely convincing case against her. And I, for one, refuse to believe that a daughter of mine is a murderess. I'm astonished at you, Vicky, for entertaining such an idea for a moment."

His wife said nothing, and Lord Kidderminster went uneasily out of the room. To think that Vicky—*Vicky*—whom he had known intimately for so many years—should prove to have such unsuspected and really very disturbing depths in her!

Five

Race found Ruth Lessing busy with papers at a large desk. She was dressed in a black coat and skirt and a white blouse and he was impressed by her quiet unhurried efficiency. He noticed the dark circles under her eyes and the unhappy set line of her mouth, but her grief, if it was grief, was as well controlled as all her other emotions.

Race explained his visit and she responded at once.

"It is very good of you to come. Of course I know who you are. Mr. Barton was expecting you to join us last night, was he not? I remember his saying so."

"Did he mention that before the evening itself?"

She thought for a moment.

"No. It was when we were actually taking our seats round the table. I remember that I was a little surprised—" She paused and flushed slightly. "Not, of course, at his inviting you. You are an old friend, I know. And you were to have been at the other party a year ago. All I meant was that I was surprised, if you were coming, that Mr. Barton hadn't invited another woman to balance the numbers—but of course if you were going to be late and might perhaps not come at all—" She broke off. "How stupid I am. Why go over all

217

these petty things that don't matter? I *am* stupid this morning."

"But you have come to work as usual?"

"Of course." She looked surprised—almost shocked. "It is my job. There is so much to clear up and arrange."

"George always told me how much he relied upon you," said Race gently.

She turned away. He saw her swallow quickly and blink her eyes. Her absence of any display of emotion almost convinced him of her entire innocence. Almost, but not quite. He had met women who were good actresses before now, women whose reddened eyelids and the black circles underneath whose eyes had been due to art and not to natural causes.

Reserving judgement, he said to himself:

"At any rate she's a cool customer."

Ruth turned back to the desk and in answer to his last remark she said quietly:

"I was with him for many years—it will be eight years next April—and I knew his ways, and I think he—trusted me."

"I'm sure of that."

He went on: "It is nearly lunchtime. I hoped you would come out and lunch quietly with me somewhere? There is a good deal I would like to say to you."

"Thank you. I should like to very much."

He took her to a small restaurant that he knew

of, where the tables were set far apart and where a quiet conversation was possible.

He ordered, and when the waiter had gone, looked across the table at his companion.

She was a good-looking girl, he decided, with her sleek dark head and her firm mouth and chin.

He talked a little on desultory topics until the food was brought, and she followed his lead, showing herself intelligent and sensible.

Presently, after a pause, she said:

"You want to talk to me about last night? Please don't hesitate to do so. The whole thing is so incredible that I would like to talk about it. Except that it happened and I saw it happen, I would not have believed it."

"You've seen Chief Inspector Kemp, of course?"

"Yes, last night. He seems intelligent and experienced." She paused. "Was it really *murder,* Colonel Race?"

"Did Kemp tell you so?"

"He didn't volunteer any information, but his questions made it plain enough what he had in mind."

"*Your* opinion as to whether or not it was suicide should be as good as anyone's, Miss Lessing. You knew Barton well and you were with him most of yesterday, I imagine. How did he seem? Much as usual? Or was he disturbed—upset—excited?"

She hesitated.

"It's difficult. He was upset and disturbed—but then there was a reason for that."

She explained the situation that had arisen in regard to Victor Drake and gave a brief sketch of that young man's career.

"H'm," said Race. "The inevitable black sheep. And Barton was upset about him?"

Ruth said slowly:

"It's difficult to explain. I knew Mr. Barton so well, you see. He was annoyed and bothered about the business—and I gather Mrs. Drake had been very tearful and upset, as she always was on these occasions—so of course he wanted to straighten it all out. But I had the impression—"

"Yes, Miss Lessing? I'm sure your impressions will be accurate."

"Well, then, I fancied that his annoyance was not quite the usual annoyance, if I may put it like that. Because we had had this same business before, in one form or another. Last year Victor Drake was in this country and in trouble, and we had to ship him off to South America, and only last June he cabled home for money. So you see I was familiar with Mr. Barton's reactions. And it seemed to me this time that his annoyance was principally at the cable having arrived just at this moment when he was entirely preoccupied with the arrangements for the party he was giving. He seemed so taken up by the preparations for it that he grudged any other preoccupation arising."

"Did it strike you that there was anything odd about this party of his, Miss Lessing?"

"Yes, it did. Mr. Barton was really most peculiar about it. He was excited—like a child might have been."

"Did it occur to you that there might have been a special purpose for such a party?"

"You mean that it was a replica of the party a year ago when Mrs. Barton committed suicide?"

"Yes."

"Frankly, I thought it a most extraordinary idea."

"But George didn't volunteer any explanation— or confide in you in any way?"

She shook her head.

"Tell me, Miss Lessing, has there ever been any doubt in your mind as to Mrs. Barton's having committed suicide?"

She looked astonished. "Oh, no."

"George Barton didn't tell you that he believed his wife had been murdered?"

She stared at him.

"George believed *that?*"

"I see that is news to you. Yes, Miss Lessing. George had received anonymous letters stating that his wife had not committed suicide but had been killed."

"So that is why he became so odd this summer? I couldn't think what was the matter with him."

"You knew nothing about these anonymous letters?"

"Nothing. Were there many of them?"

"He showed me two."

"And I knew nothing about them!"

There was a note of bitter hurt in her voice.

He watched her for a moment or two, then he said:

"Well, Miss Lessing, what do you say? Is it possible, in your opinion, for George to have committed suicide?"

She shook her head.

"No—oh, no."

"But you said he was excited—upset?"

"Yes, but he had been like that for some time. I see why now. And I see why he was so excited about last night's party. He must have had some special idea in his head—he must have hoped that by reproducing the conditions, he would gain some additional knowledge—poor George, he must have been so muddled about it all."

"And what about Rosemary Barton, Miss Lessing? Do you still think her death was suicide?"

She frowned.

"I've never dreamt of it being anything else. It seemed so natural."

"Depression after influenza?"

"Well, rather more than that, perhaps. She was definitely very unhappy. One could see that."

"And guess the cause?"

"Well—yes. At least I did. Of course I may have

been wrong. But women like Mrs. Barton are very transparent—they don't trouble to hide their feelings. Mercifully I don't think Mr. Barton knew anything . . . Oh, yes, she was very unhappy. And I know she had a bad headache that night besides being run-down with 'flu."

"How did you know she had a headache?"

"I heard her telling Lady Alexandra so—in the cloakroom when we were taking off our wraps. She was wishing she had a Cachet Faivre and luckily Lady Alexandra had one with her and gave it to her."

Colonel Race's hand stopped with a glass in mid air.

"And she took it?"

"Yes."

He put his glass down untasted and looked across the table. The girl looked placid and unaware of any significance in what she had said. But it *was* significant. It meant that Sandra who, from her position at table, would have had the most difficulty in putting anything unseen in Rosemary's glass, had had another opportunity of administering the poison. She could have given it to Rosemary in a cachet. Ordinarily a cachet would take only a few minutes to dissolve, but possibly this had been a special kind of cachet, it might have had a lining of gelatine or some other substance. Or Rosemary might possibly not have swallowed it then but later.

He said abruptly:

"Did you see her take it?"

"I beg your pardon?"

He saw by her puzzled face that her mind had gone on elsewhere.

"Did you see Rosemary Barton swallow that cachet?"

Ruth looked a little startled.

"I—well, no, I didn't actually see her. She just thanked Lady Alexandra."

So Rosemary might have slipped the cachet in her bag and then, during the cabaret, with a headache increasing, she might have dropped it into her champagne glass and let it dissolve. Assumption—pure assumption—but a possibility.

Ruth said:

"Why do you ask me that?"

Her eyes were suddenly alert, full of questions. He watched, so it seemed to him, her intelligence working.

Then she said:

"Oh, I see. I see why George took that house down there near the Farradays. And I see why he didn't tell me about those letters. It seemed to me so extraordinary that he hadn't. But of course if he believed them, it meant that one of us, one of those five people round the table must have killed her. It might—it might even have been *me!*"

Race said in a very gentle voice:

"Had you any reason for killing Rosemary Barton?"

He thought at first that she hadn't heard the question. She sat so very still with her eyes cast down.

But suddenly with a sigh, she raised them and looked straight at him.

"It is not the sort of thing one cares to talk about," she said. "But I think you had better know. I was in love with George Barton. I was in love with him before he even met Rosemary. I don't think he ever knew—certainly he didn't care. He was fond of me—very fond of me—but I suppose never in that way. And yet I used to think that I would have made him a good wife—that I could have made him happy. He loved Rosemary, but he wasn't happy with her."

Race said gently:

"And you disliked Rosemary?"

"Yes, I did. Oh! she was very lovely and very attractive and could be very charming in her way. She never bothered to be charming to me! I disliked her a good deal. I was shocked when she died—and at the way she died, but I wasn't really sorry. I'm afraid I was rather glad."

She paused.

"Please, shall we talk about something else?"

Race responded quickly:

"I'd like you to tell me exactly, in detail, everything you can remember about yesterday—

from the morning onwards—especially anything George did or said."

Ruth replied promptly, going over the events of the morning—George's annoyance over Victor's importunity, her own telephone calls to South America and the arrangements made and George's pleasure when the matter was settled. She then described her arrival at the Luxembourg and George's flurried excited bearing as host. She carried her narrative up to the final moment of the tragedy. Her account tallied in every respect with those he had already heard.

With a worried frown, Ruth voiced his own perplexity.

"It wasn't suicide—I'm sure it wasn't suicide—but how can it have been murder? I mean, how can it have been done? The answer is, it couldn't, not by one of us! Then was it someone who slipped the poison into George's glass while we were away dancing? But if so, who could it have been? It doesn't seem to make sense."

"The evidence is that *no one* went near the table while you were dancing."

"Then it really doesn't make sense! Cyanide doesn't get into a glass by itself!"

"Have you absolutely no idea—no suspicion, even, who might have put the cyanide in the glass? Think back over last night. Is there nothing, no small incident, that awakens your suspicions in any degree, however small?"

He saw her face change, saw for a moment uncertainty come into her eyes. There was a tiny, almost infinitesimal pause before she answered "Nothing."

But there *had* been something. He was sure of that. Something she had seen or heard or noticed that, for some reason or other, she had decided not to tell.

He did not press her. He knew that with a girl of Ruth's type that would be no good. If, for some reason, she had made up her mind to keep silence, she would not, he felt sure, change her mind.

But there had been *something.* That knowledge cheered him and gave him fresh assurance. It was the first sign of a crevice in the blank wall that confronted him.

He took leave of Ruth after lunch and drove to Elvaston Square thinking of the woman he had just left.

Was it possible that Ruth Lessing was guilty? On the whole, he was prepossessed in her favour. She had seemed entirely frank and straight-forward.

Was she capable of murder? Most people were, if you came to it. Capable not of murder in general, but of one particular individual murder. That was what made it so difficult to weed anyone out. There was a certain quality of ruthlessness about that young woman. And she had a motive—or rather a choice of motives. By removing Rosemary she had a very good chance of becoming Mrs. George Barton. Whether it was a question of marrying a rich man, or of marrying the man she had loved, the removal of Rosemary was the first essential.

Race was inclined to think that marrying a rich man was not enough. Ruth Lessing was too coolheaded and cautious to risk her neck for mere comfortable living as a rich man's wife. Love? Perhaps. For all her cool and detached manner, he suspected her of being one of those women who can be kindled to unlikely passion by one particular man. Given love of George and hate of Rosemary, she might have coolly planned and executed Rosemary's death. The fact that it had gone off without a hitch, and that suicide had been universally accepted without demur, proved her inherent capability.

And then George had received anonymous letters (From whom? Why? That was the teasing vexing problem that never ceased to nag at him) and had grown suspicious. He had planned a trap. And Ruth had silenced him.

No, that wasn't right. That didn't ring true. That spelt panic—and Ruth Lessing was not the kind of woman who panicked. She had better brains than George and could have avoided any trap that he was likely to set with the greatest of ease.

It looked as though Ruth didn't add up after all.

Six

Lucilla Drake was delighted to see Colonel Race.

The blinds were all down and Lucilla came into the room draped in black and with a handkerchief to her eyes and explained, as she advanced a tremulous hand to meet his, how of course she couldn't have seen anyone—anyone at all—except such an old friend of dear, *dear* George's—and it was so dreadful to have no man in the house! Really without a man in the house one didn't know how to tackle *anything*. Just herself, a poor lonely widow, and Iris, just a helpless young girl, and George had always looked after everything. So kind of dear Colonel Race and really she was so grateful—no idea what they ought to do. Of course Miss Lessing would attend to all business matters—and the funeral to arrange for—but how about the inquest? And so dreadful having the police—actually in the house—plain clothes, of course, and really very considerate. But she was so bewildered and the whole thing was such an absolute tragedy and didn't Colonel Race think it must be all due to *suggestion*—that was what the psychoanalyst said, wasn't it, that everything is *suggestion?* And poor George at that horrid place, the Luxembourg, and practically the same party and remembering how poor Rosemary had died there—and it must have come

229

over him quite suddenly, only if he'd listened to what she, Lucilla, had said, and taken that excellent tonic of dear Dr. Gaskell's—run-down, all the summer—yes, thoroughly run-down.

Whereupon Lucilla herself ran down temporarily, and Race had a chance to speak.

He said how deeply he sympathized and how Mrs. Drake must count upon him in every way.

Whereupon Lucilla started off again and said it was indeed kind of him, and it was the shock that had been so terrible—here today, and gone tomorrow, as it said in the Bible, cometh up like grass and cut down in the evening—only that wasn't quite right, but Colonel Race would know what she meant, and it was so nice to feel there was someone on whom they could rely. Miss Lessing meant well, of course, and was very efficient, but rather an unsympathetic manner and sometimes took things upon herself a little too much, and in her, Lucilla's, opinion, George had always relied upon her *far too much,* and at one time she had been really afraid that he might do something foolish which would have been a great pity and probably she would have bullied him unmercifully once they were married. Of course she, Lucilla, had seen what was in the wind. Dear Iris was so unworldly, and it was nice, didn't Colonel Race think, for young girls to be unspoilt and simple? Iris had really always been very young for her age and very quiet—one didn't know half the time what she was thinking about. Rosemary being so pretty and so gay had been out a great deal, and Iris had mooned about the house which wasn't really right for a young girl—they should go to classes—cooking and perhaps dressmaking. It occupied their minds and one never knew when it might come in useful. It had really been a mercy that she, Lucilla, had been free to come and live here after poor Rosemary's death—that horrid 'flu, quite an unusual kind of 'flu, Dr. Gaskell had said. Such a clever man and such a nice, breezy manner.

She had wanted Iris to see him this summer. The girl had looked so white and pulled down. "But really, Colonel Race, I think it was the situation of the house. *Low,* you know, and *damp,* with quite a *miasma* in the evenings." Poor George had gone off and bought it all by himself without asking anyone's advice—such a pity. He had said he wanted it to be a surprise, but really it would have been better if he had taken some older woman's advice. Men knew nothing about houses. George might have realized that she, Lucilla, would have been willing to take any *amount* of trouble. For, after all, what was her life now? Her dear husband dead many years ago, and Victor, her dear boy, far away in the Argentine—she meant Brazil, or was it the Argentine? Such an affectionate, handsome boy.

Colonel Race said he had heard she had a son abroad.

For the next quarter of an hour, he was regaled with a full account of Victor's multitudinous activities. Such a spirited boy, willing to turn his hand to anything—here followed a list of Victor's varied occupations. Never unkind, or bearing malice to anyone. "He's always been unlucky, Colonel Race. He was misjudged by his house-master and I consider the authorities at Oxford behaved quite disgracefully. People don't seem to understand that a clever boy with a taste for drawing would think it an excellent joke to imitate someone's handwriting. He did it for the fun of the thing, not for money." But he'd always been a good son to his mother, and he never failed to let her know when he was in trouble which showed, didn't it, that he trusted her? Only it did seem curious, didn't it, that the jobs people found for him so often seemed to take him out of England. She couldn't help feeling that if only he could be given a nice job, in the Bank of England say, he would settle down much better. He might perhaps live a little out of London and have a little car.

It was quite twenty minutes before Colonel Race, having heard all Victor's perfections and misfortunes, was able to switch Lucilla from the subject of sons to that of servants.

Yes, it was very true what he said, the old-fashioned type of servant didn't exist any longer. Really the trouble people had nowadays! Not that she ought to complain, for really they had been very lucky. Mrs. Pound, though she had the misfortune to be slightly deaf, was an excellent woman. Her pastry sometimes a little heavy and a tendency to overpepper the soup, but really on the whole most reliable—and economical too. She had been there ever since George married and she had made no fuss about going to the country this year, though there had been trouble with the others over that and the parlour maid had left—but that really was all for the best—an impertinent girl who answered back—besides breaking six of the best wineglasses, not one by one at odd times which might happen to *anybody,* but all at once which really meant gross carelessness, didn't Colonel Race think so?

"Very careless indeed."

"That is what I told her. And I said to her that I should be obliged to say so in her reference—for I really feel one has a *duty,* Colonel Race. I mean, one should not mislead. Faults should be mentioned as well as good qualities. But the girl was—really—well, quite *insolent* and said that at any rate she hoped that in her next place she wouldn't be in the kind of house where people got bumped off—a dreadful common expression, acquired at the cinema, I believe, and ludicrously inappropriate since poor dear Rosemary took her own life—though not at the time responsible for her actions as the coroner very rightly pointed out—and that dreadful expression refers, I believe, to gangsters executing each other with tommy guns. I am so thankful that we have nothing of that kind in England. And so, as I say, I put in her reference that Betty Archdale thoroughly understood her duties as parlourmaid and was sober and honest, but that she was inclined to have too many breakages and was not always respectful in her manner. And personally, if *I* had been Mrs. Rees-Talbot, I should have read between the lines and not engaged her. But people nowadays just jump at anything they can get, and will sometimes take a girl who has only stayed her month in three places running."

Whilst Mrs. Drake paused to take breath, Colonel Race asked quickly whether that was Mrs. Richard Rees-Talbot? If so, he had known her, he said, in India.

"I really couldn't say. Cadogan Square was the address."

"Then it *is* my friends."

Lucilla said that the world was such a small place, wasn't it? And that there were no friends like old friends. Friendship was a wonderful thing. She had always thought it had been so romantic about Viola and Paul. Dear Viola, she had been a lovely girl, and so many men in love with her, but, oh dear, Colonel Race wouldn't even know who she was talking about. One did so tend to re-live the past.

Colonel Race begged her to go on and in return for this politeness received the life history of Hector Marle, of his upbringing by his sister, of his peculiarities and his weaknesses and finally, when Colonel Race had almost forgotten her, of his marriage to the beautiful Viola. "She was an orphan, you know, and a ward in Chancery." He heard how Paul Bennett, conquering his disappointment at Viola's refusal, had transformed himself from lover to family friend, and of his fondness for his godchild, Rosemary, and of his death and the terms of his will. "Which I have always felt *most* romantic—such an enormous fortune! Not of course that money is everything—no, indeed. One has only to think of poor Rosemary's tragic death. And even dear Iris I am not quite happy about!"

Race gave her an inquiring look.

"I find the responsibility most worrying. The fact that she is a great heiress is of course well known. I keep a very sharp eye on the undesirable type of young man, but what can one do, Colonel Race? One can't look after girls nowadays as one used to do. Iris has friends I know next to nothing about. 'Ask them to the house, dear,' is what I always say—but I gather that some of these young men simply will *not* be brought. Poor George was worried, too. About a young man called Browne. I myself have never seen him, but it seems that he and Iris have been seeing a good deal of each other. And one does feel that she could do better. George didn't like him—I'm quite sure of that. And I always think, Colonel Race, that men are so much better judges of other men. I remember thinking Colonel Pusey, one of our churchwardens, such a charming man, but my husband always preserved a very distant attitude towards him and enjoined on me to do the same—and sure enough one Sunday when he was handing round the offertory plate, he fell right down—completely intoxicated, it seems. And of course afterwards—one always hears these things *afterwards,* so much better if one heard them *before*—we found out that dozens of empty brandy bottles were taken out of the house every week! It was very sad really, because he was truly religious, though inclined to be Evangelical in his views. He and my husband had a terrific battle over the details of the service on All Saints' Day. Oh, dear, All Saints' Day. To think that yesterday was All Souls' Day."

A faint sound made Race look over Lucilla's head at the open doorway. He had seen Iris before—at Little Priors. Nevertheless he felt that he was seeing her now for the first time. He was struck by the extraordinary tension behind her stillness and her wide eyes met his with something in their expression that he felt he ought to recognize, yet failed to do so.

In her turn, Lucilla Drake turned her head.

"Iris, dear, I didn't hear you come in. You know Colonel Race? He is being so very kind."

Iris came and shook hands with him gravely, the black dress she wore made her look thinner and paler than he remembered her.

"I came to see if I could be of any help to you," said Race.

"Thank you. That was kind of you."

She had had a bad shock, that was evident, and was still suffering from the effects of it. But had she been so fond of George that his death could affect her so powerfully?

She turned her eyes to her aunt and Race realized that they were watchful eyes. She said:

"What were you talking about—just now, as I came in?"

Lucilla became pink and flustered. Race guessed that she was anxious to avoid any mention of the young man, Anthony Browne. She exclaimed:

"Now let me see—oh, yes, All Saints' Day—and yesterday being All Souls.' All Souls'—that seems to me such an *odd* thing—one of those coincidences one never believes in in real life."

"Do you mean," said Iris, "that Rosemary came back yesterday to fetch George?"

Lucilla gave a little scream.

"Iris, dear, don't. What a terrible thought—so un-Christian."

"Why un-Christian? It's the Day of the Dead. In Paris people used to go and put flowers on the graves."

"Oh, I know, dear, but then they are Catholics, aren't they?"

A faint smile twisted Iris's lips. Then she said directly:

"I thought, perhaps, you were talking of Anthony—Anthony Browne."

"Well," Lucilla's twitter became very high and birdlike, "as a matter of fact we did just *mention* him. I happened to say, you know, that we know *nothing about* him—"

Iris interrupted, her voice hard:

"Why should you know anything about him?"

"No, dear, of course not. At least, I mean, well, it would be rather nice, wouldn't it, if we did?"

"You'll have every chance of doing so in future," said Iris, "because I'm going to marry him."

"Oh, Iris!" It was halfway between a wail and a bleat. "You mustn't do anything rash—I mean nothing can be settled at present."

"It *is* settled, Aunt Lucilla."

"No, dear, one can't talk about things like marriage when the funeral hasn't even taken place yet. It wouldn't be decent. And this dreadful inquest and everything. And really, Iris, I don't think dear George would have approved. He didn't like this Mr. Browne."

"No," said Iris, "George wouldn't have liked it and he didn't like Anthony, but that doesn't make any difference. It's my life, not George's—and anyway George is dead. . . ."

Mrs. Drake gave another wail.

"Iris, Iris. What has come over you? Really that was a most unfeeling thing to say."

"I'm sorry, Aunt Lucilla." The girl spoke wearily. "I know it must have sounded like that but I didn't mean it that way. I only meant that George is at peace somewhere and hasn't got to worry about me and my future anymore. I must decide things for myself."

"Nonsense, dear, nothing can be decided at a time like this—it would be most unfitting. The question simply doesn't arise."

Iris gave a sudden short laugh.

"But it has arisen. Anthony asked me to marry him before we left Little Priors. He wanted me to come up to London and marry him the next day without telling anyone. I wish now that I had."

"Surely that was a very curious request," said Colonel Race gently.

She turned defiant eyes to him.

"No, it wasn't. It would have saved a lot of fuss. Why couldn't I trust him? He asked me to trust him and I didn't. Anyway, I'll marry him now as soon as he likes."

Lucilla burst out in a stream of incoherent protest. Her plump cheeks quivered and her eyes filled.

Colonel Race took rapid charge of the situation.

"Miss Marle, might I have a word with you before I go? On a strictly business matter?"

Rather startled, the girl murmured "Yes," and found herself moving to the door. As she passed through, Race took a couple of strides back to Mrs. Drake.

"Don't upset yourself, Mrs. Drake. Least said, you know, soonest mended. We'll see what we can do."

Leaving her slightly comforted he followed Iris who led him across the hall and into a small room giving out on the back of the house where a melancholy plane tree was shedding its last leaves.

Race spoke in a businesslike tone.

"All I had to say, Miss Marle, was that Chief Inspector Kemp is a personal friend of mine, and that I am sure you will find him most helpful and kindly. His duty is an unpleasant one, but I'm sure he will do it with the utmost consideration possible."

She looked at him for a moment or two without speaking, then she said abruptly:

"Why didn't you come and join us last night as George expected you to do?"

He shook his head.

"George didn't expect me."

"But he said he did."

"He may have said so, but it wasn't true. George knew perfectly well that I wasn't coming."

She said: "But that empty chair . . . Who was it for?"

"Not for me."

Her eyes half closed and her face went very white.

She whispered:

"It was for Rosemary . . . I see . . . It was for Rosemary. . . ."

He thought she was going to fall. He came quickly to her and steadied her, then forced her to sit down.

"Take it easy. . . ."

She said in a low breathless voice:

"I'm all right . . . But I don't know what to do . . . I don't know what to do."

"Can I help you?"

She raised her eyes to his face. They were wistful and sombre.

Then she said: "I must get things clear. I must get them"—she made a groping gesture with her hands—"in sequence. First of all, George believed Rosemary didn't kill herself—but was killed. He believed that because of those letters. Colonel Race, who wrote those letters?"

"I don't know. Nobody knows. Have you yourself any idea?"

"I simply can't imagine. Anyway, George believed what they said, and he arranged this party last night, and he had an empty chair and it was All Souls' Day . . . that's the Day of the Dead—and it was a day when Rosemary's spirit could have come back and—and told him the truth."

"You mustn't be too imaginative."

"But I've felt her myself—felt her quite near sometimes—I'm her sister—and I think she's trying to tell me something."

"Take it easy, Iris."

"I *must* talk about it. George drank Rosemary's health and he—died. Perhaps—she came and took him."

"The spirits of the dead don't put potassium cyanide in a champagne glass, my dear."

The words seemed to restore her balance. She said in a more normal tone:

"But it's so incredible. George was killed—yes, *killed*. That's what the police think and it must be true. Because there isn't any other alternative. But it doesn't make sense."

"Don't you think it does? If Rosemary was killed, and George was beginning to suspect by whom—"

She interrupted him.

"Yes, but Rosemary *wasn't* killed. That's why it doesn't make sense. George believed those stupid letters partly because depression after influenza isn't a very convincing reason for killing yourself.

But Rosemary *had* a reason. Look, I'll show you."

She ran out of the room and returned a few moments later with a folded letter in her hand. She thrust it on him.

"Read it. See for yourself."

He unfolded the slightly crumpled sheet.

"Leopard darling. . . ."

He read it twice before handing it back.

The girl said eagerly:

"You see? She was unhappy—brokenhearted. She didn't want to go on living."

"Do you know to whom that letter was written?"

Iris nodded.

"Stephen Farraday. It wasn't Anthony. She was in love with Stephen and he was cruel to her. So she took the stuff with her to the restaurant and drank it there where he could see her die. Perhaps she hoped he'd be sorry then."

Race nodded thoughtfully, but said nothing. After a moment or two he said:

"When did you find this?"

"About six months ago. It was in the pocket of an old dressing gown."

"You didn't show it to George?"

Iris cried passionately:

"How could I? How could I? Rosemary was my sister. How could I give her away to George? He was so sure that she loved him. How could I show him this after she was dead? He'd got it all wrong, but I couldn't tell *him* so. But what I want to know is, what am I to do *now?* I've shown it to you because you were George's friend. Has Inspector Kemp got to see it?"

"Yes. Kemp must have it. It's evidence, you see."

"But then they'll—they might read it out in court?"

"Not necessarily. That doesn't follow. It's George's death that is being investigated. Nothing will be made public that is not strictly relevant. You had better let me take this now."

"Very well."

She went with him to the front door. As he opened it she said abruptly:

"It does show, doesn't it, that Rosemary's death *was* suicide?"

Race said:

"It certainly shows that she had a motive for taking her own life."

She gave a deep sigh. He went down the steps. Glancing back once, he saw her standing framed in the open doorway, watching him walk away across the Square.

Seven

Mary Rees-Talbot greeted Colonel Race with a positive shriek of unbelief.

"My dear, I haven't seen you since you disappeared so mysteriously from Allahabad that time. And why are you here now? It isn't to see me, I'm quite sure. You never pay social calls. Come on now, own up, you needn't be diplomatic about it."

"Diplomatic methods would be a waste of time with you, Mary. I always have appreciated your X-ray mind."

"Cut the cackle and come to the horses, my pet."

Race smiled.

"Is the maid who let me in Betty Archdale?" he inquired.

"So that's it! Now don't tell me that the girl, a pure Cockney if ever there was one, is a well-known European spy because I simply don't believe it."

"No, no, nothing of the kind."

"And don't tell me she's one of our counter-espionage either, because I don't believe that."

"Quite right. The girl is simply a parlourmaid."

"And since when have you been interested in simple parlourmaids—not that Betty is simple—an artful dodger is more like it."

"I think," said Colonel Race, "that she might be able to tell me something."

"If you asked her nicely? I shouldn't be surprised if you're right. She has the close-to-the-door-when-there's-anything-interesting-going-on technique very highly developed. What does M. do?"

"M. very kindly offers me a drink and rings for Betty and orders it."

"And when Betty brings it?"

"By then M. has very kindly gone away."

"To do some listening outside the door herself?"

"If she likes."

"And after that I shall be bursting with Inside Information about the latest European crisis?"

"I'm afraid not. There is no political situation involved in this."

"What a disappointment! All right. I'll play!"

Mrs. Rees-Talbot, who was a lively near-brunette of forty-nine, rang the bell and directed her good-looking parlourmaid to bring Colonel Race a whisky and soda.

When Betty Archdale returned, with a salver and the drink upon it, Mrs. Rees-Talbot was standing by the far door into her own sitting room.

"Colonel Race has some questions to ask you," she said and went out.

Betty turned her impudent eyes on the tall grey-haired soldier with some alarm in their depths. He took the glass from the tray and smiled.

"Seen the papers today?" he asked.

"Yes, sir." Betty eyed him warily.

"Did you see that Mr. George Barton died last night at the Luxembourg Restaurant?"

"Oh, yes, sir." Betty's eyes sparkled with the pleasure of public disaster. "Wasn't it dreadful?"

"You were in service there, weren't you?"

"Yes, sir. I left last winter, soon after Mrs. Barton died."

"She died at the Luxembourg, too."

Betty nodded. "Sort of funny, that, isn't it, sir?"

Race did not think it funny, but he knew what the words were intended to convey. He said gravely:

"I see you've got brains. You can put two and two together."

Betty clasped her hands and cast discretion to the winds.

"Was he done in, too? The papers didn't say exactly."

"Why do you say 'too?' Mrs. Barton's death was brought in by the coroner's jury as suicide."

She gave him a quick look out of the corner of her eye. Ever so old, she thought, but he's nice looking. That quiet kind. A real gentleman. Sort of gentleman who'd have given you a gold sovereign when he was young. Funny, I don't even know what a sovereign looks like! What's he after, exactly?

She said demurely: "Yes, sir."

"But perhaps you never thought it *was* suicide?"

"Well, no, sir. I didn't—not really."

"That's very interesting—very interesting indeed. Why didn't you think so?"

She hesitated, her fingers began pleating her apron.

So nicely he said that, so gravely. Made you feel important and as though you wanted to help him. And anyway she *had* been smart over Rosemary Barton's death. Never been taken in, she hadn't!

"She was done in, sir, wasn't she?"

"It seems possible that it may be so. But how did you come to think so?"

"Well," Betty hesitated. "It was something I heard one day."

"Yes?"

His tone was quietly encouraging.

"The door wasn't shut or anything. I mean I'd never go and listen at a door. I don't like that sort of thing," said Betty virtuously. "But I was going through the hall to the dining room and carrying the silver on a tray and they were speaking quite loud. Saying something she was—Mrs. Barton I mean—about Anthony Browne not being his name. And then he got really nasty, Mr. Browne did. I wouldn't have thought he had it in him—so nice looking and so pleasant spoken as he was as a rule. Said something about carving up her face—ooh! and then he said if she didn't do what he told her he'd bump her off. Just like that! I didn't hear any more because Miss Iris was coming down the stairs, and of course I didn't think very much of it at the time, but after there was all the fuss about her committing suicide at that party and I heard he'd been there at the time—well, it gave me shivers all down my back—it did indeed!"

"But you didn't say anything?"

The girl shook her head.

"I didn't want to get mixed up with the police— and anyway I didn't know anything—not really. And perhaps if I had said anything I'd have been bumped off too. Or taken for a ride as they call it."

"I see." Race paused a moment and then said in his gentlest voice: "So you just wrote an anonymous letter to Mr. George Barton?"

She stared at him. He detected no uneasy guilt— nothing but pure astonishment.

"Me? Write to Mr. Barton? Never."

"Now don't be afraid to tell about it. It was really a very good idea. It warned him without your having to give yourself away. It was very clever of you."

"But I didn't, sir. I never thought of such a thing. You mean write to Mr. Barton and say that his wife had been done in? Why, the idea never came into my head!"

She was so earnest in her denial that, in spite of himself, Race was shaken. But it all fitted in so well—it could all be explained so naturally if only the girl had written the letters. But she persisted in her denials, not vehemently or uneasily, but soberly and without undue protestation. He found himself reluctantly believing her.

He shifted his ground.

"Whom did you tell about this?"

She shook her head.

"I didn't tell anyone. I'll tell you honest, sir, I was scared. I thought I'd better keep my mouth shut. I tried to forget it. I only brought it up once—that was when I gave Mrs. Drake my notice—fussing terribly she'd been, more than a girl could stand, and now wanting me to go and bury myself in the dead of the country and not even a bus route! And then she turned nasty about my reference, saying I broke things, and I said sarcastic-like that at any rate I'd find a place where people didn't get bumped off—and I felt scared when I'd said it, but she didn't pay any real attention. Perhaps I ought to have spoken out at the time, but I couldn't really tell. I mean the whole thing might have been a joke. People do say all sorts of things, and Mr. Browne was ever so nice really, and quite a one for joking, so I couldn't tell, sir, could I?"

Race agreed that she couldn't. Then he said:

"Mrs. Barton spoke of Browne not being his real name. Did she mention what his real name was?"

"Yes, she did. Because he said, 'Forget about Tony'—now what was it? Tony something . . .

Reminded me of the cherry jam cook had been making."

"Tony Cheriton? Cherable."

She shook her head.

"More of a fancy name than that. Began with an M. And sounded foreign."

"Don't worry. It will come back to you, perhaps. If so, let me know. Here is my card with my address. If you remember the name write to me at that address."

He handed her the card and a treasury note.

"I will, sir, thank you, sir."

A gentleman, she thought, as she ran downstairs. A pound note, not ten shillings. It must have been nice when there were gold sovereigns. . . .

Mary Rees-Talbot came back into the room.

"Well, successful?"

"Yes, but there's still one snag to surmount. Can your ingenuity help me? Can you think of a name that would remind you of cherry jam?"

"What an extraordinary proposition."

"Think Mary. I'm not a domestic man. Concentrate on jam making, cherry jam in particular."

"One doesn't often make cherry jam."

"Why not?"

"Well, it's inclined to go sugary—unless you use cooking cherries, Morello cherries."

Race gave an exclamation.

"That's it—I bet that's it. Good-bye, Mary, I'm endlessly grateful. Do you mind if I ring that bell so that the girl comes and shows me out?"

Mrs. Rees-Talbot called after him as he hurried out of the room:

"Of all the ungrateful wretches! Aren't you going to tell me what it's all about?"

He called back:

"I'll come and tell you the whole story later."

"Sez you," murmured Mrs. Rees-Talbot.

Downstairs, Betty waited with Race's hat and stick.

He thanked her and passed out. On the doorstep he paused.

"By the way," he said, "was the name Morelli?"

Betty's face lighted up.

"Quite right, sir. That was it. Tony Morelli that's the name he told her to forget. And he said he'd been in prison, too."

Race walked down the steps smiling.

From the nearest call box he put through a call to Kemp.

Their interchange was brief but satisfactory. Kemp said:

"I'll send off a cable at once. We ought to hear by return. I must say it will be a great relief if you're right."

"I think I'm right. The sequence is pretty clear."

Eight

Chief Inspector Kemp was not in a very good humour.

For the last half hour he had been interviewing a frightened white rabbit of sixteen who, by virtue of his uncle Charles's great position, was aspiring to be a waiter of the class required by the Luxembourg. In the meantime, he was one of six harried underlings who ran about with aprons round their waists to distinguish them from the superior article, and whose duty it was to bear the blame for everything, fetch and carry, provide rolls and pats of butter and be occasionally and unceasingly hissed at in French, Italian and occasionally English. Charles, as befitted a great man, so far from showing favour to a blood relation, hissed, cursed and swore at him even more than he did at the others. Nevertheless Pierre aspired in his heart to be no less than the headwaiter of a *chic* restaurant himself one day in the far future.

At the moment, however, his career had received a check, and he gathered that he was suspected of no less than murder.

Kemp turned the lad inside out and disgustedly convinced himself that the boy had done no less and no more than what he had said—namely, picked up a lady's bag from the floor and replaced it by her plate.

"It is as I am hurrying with sauce to M. Robert and already he is impatient, and the young lady sweeps her bag off the table as she goes to dance, so I pick it up and put it on the table, and then I hurry on, for already M. Robert he is making the signs frantically to me. That is all, monsieur."

And that *was* all. Kemp disgustedly let him go, feeling strongly tempted to add, "But don't let me catch you doing that sort of thing again."

Sergeant Pollock made a distraction by announcing that they had telephoned up to say that a young lady was asking for him or rather for the officer in charge of the Luxembourg case.

"Who is she?"

"Her name is Miss Chloe West."

"Let's have her up," said Kemp resignedly. "I can give her ten minutes. Mr. Farraday's due after that. Oh, well, won't do any harm to keep *him* waiting a few minutes. Makes them jittery, that does."

When Miss Chloe West walked into the room, Kemp was at once assailed by the impression that he recognized her. But a minute later he abandoned that impression. No, he had never seen this girl before, he was sure of that. Nevertheless the vague haunting sense of familiarity remained to plague him.

Miss West was about twenty-five, tall, brown-haired and very pretty. Her voice was rather conscious of its diction and she seemed decidedly nervous.

"Well, Miss West, what can I do for you?"

Kemp spoke briskly.

"I read in the paper about the Luxembourg—the man who died there."

"Mr. George Barton? Yes? Did you know him?"

"Well, no, not exactly. I mean I didn't really *know* him."

Kemp looked at her carefully and discarded his first deduction.

Chloe West was looking extremely refined and virtuous—severely so. He said pleasantly:

"Can I have your exact name and address first, please, so that we know where we are?"

"Chloe Elizabeth West. 15 Merryvale Court, Maida Vale. I'm an actress."

Kemp looked at her again out of the corner of his eye, and decided that that was what she really was. Repertory, he fancied—in spite of her looks she was the earnest kind.

"Yes, Miss West?"

"When I read about Mr. Barton's death and that the—the police were inquiring into it, I thought perhaps I ought to come and tell you something. I spoke to my friend about it and she seemed to think so. I don't suppose it's really anything to do with it, but—" Miss West paused.

"We'll be the judge of that," said Kemp pleasantly. "Just tell me about it."

"I'm not acting just at the moment," explained Miss West.

Inspector Kemp nearly said "Resting" to show that he knew the proper terms, but restrained himself.

"But my name is down at the agencies and my picture in *Spotlight* . . . That, I understand, is where Mr. Barton saw it. He got into touch with me and explained what he wanted me to do."

"Yes?"

"He told me he was having a dinner party at the Luxembourg and that he wanted to spring a surprise on his guests. He showed me a photograph and told me that he wanted me to make up as the original. I was very much the same colouring, he said."

Illumination flashed across Kemp's mind. The photograph of Rosemary he had seen on the desk in George's room in Elvaston Square. That was who the girl reminded him of. She *was* like Rosemary Barton—not perhaps startlingly so—but the general type and cast of features was the same.

"He also brought me a dress to wear—I've brought it with me. A greyish green silk. I was to do my hair like the photograph (it was a coloured one) and accentuate the resemblance with makeup. Then I was to come to the Luxembourg and go into the restaurant during the first cabaret show and sit down at Mr. Barton's table where there would be a vacant place. He took me to lunch there and showed me where the table would be."

"And why didn't you keep the appointment, Miss West?"

"Because about eight o'clock that night— someone—Mr. Barton—rang up and said the whole thing had been put off. He said he'd let me know next day when it was coming off. Then, the next morning, I saw his death in the papers."

"And very sensibly you came along to us," said Kemp pleasantly. "Well, thank you very much, Miss West. You've cleared up one mystery—the mystery of the vacant place. By the way, you said just now—'someone'—and then, 'Mr. Barton.' Why is that?"

"Because at first I didn't think it *was* Mr. Barton. His voice sounded different."

"It was a man's voice?"

"Oh, yes, I think so—at least—it was rather husky as though he had a cold."

"And that's all he said?"

"That's all."

Kemp questioned her a little longer, but got no further.

When she had gone, he said to the sergeant:

"So that was George Barton's famous 'plan.' I see now why they all said he stared at the empty chair after the cabaret and looked queer and absentminded. His precious plan had gone wrong."

"You don't think it was he who put her off?"

"Not on your life. And I'm not so sure it was a man's voice, either. Huskiness is a good disguise through the telephone. Oh, well, we're getting on. Send in Mr. Farraday if he's here."

Nine

I

Outwardly cool and unperturbed, Stephen
Farraday had turned into Great Scotland Yard
full of inner shrinking. An intolerable weight
burdened his spirits. It had seemed that morning
as though things were going so well. Why had
Inspector Kemp asked for his presence here with
such significance? What did he know or suspect?
It *could* be only vague suspicion. The thing to do
was to keep one's head and admit nothing.

He felt strangely bereft and lonely without
Sandra. It was as though when the two faced a
peril together it lost half its terrors. Together
they had strength, courage, power. Alone, he
was nothing, less than nothing. And Sandra, did
she feel the same? Was she sitting now in
Kidderminster House, silent, reserved, proud and
inwardly feeling horribly vulnerable?

Inspector Kemp received him pleasantly but
gravely. There was a uniformed man sitting at a
table with a pencil and a pad of paper. Having
asked Stephen to sit down, Kemp spoke in a
strongly formal manner.

"I propose, Mr. Farraday, to take a statement
from you. That statement will be written down
and you will be asked to read it over and sign it

259

before you leave. At the same time it is my duty to tell you that you are at liberty to refuse to make such a statement and that you are entitled to have your solicitor present if you so desire."

Stephen was taken aback but did not show it. He forced a wintry smile. "That sounds very formidable, chief inspector."

"We like everything to be clearly understood, Mr. Farraday."

"Anything I say may be used against me, is that it?"

"We don't use the word against. Anything you say will be liable to be used in evidence."

Stephen said quietly:

"I understand, but I cannot imagine, inspector, why you should need any further statement from me? You heard all I had to say this morning."

"That was a rather informal session—useful as a preliminary starting-off point. And also, Mr. Farraday, there are certain facts which I imagined you would prefer to discuss with me here. Anything irrelevant to the case we try to be as discreet about as is compatible with the attainment of justice. I daresay you understand what I am driving at."

"I'm afraid I don't."

Chief Inspector Kemp sighed.

"Just this. You were on very intimate terms with the late Mrs. Rosemary Barton—"

Stephen interrupted him.

"Who says so?"

Kemp leaned forward and took a typewritten document from his desk.

"This is a copy of a letter found amongst the late Mrs. Barton's belongings. The original is filed here and was handed to us by Miss Iris Marle, who recognizes the writing as that of her sister."

Stephen read:

"Leopard darling—"

A wave of sickness passed over him. Rosemary's voice . . . speaking—pleading . . . Would the past never die—never consent to be buried?

He pulled himself together and looked at Kemp.

"You may be correct in thinking Mrs. Barton wrote this letter—but there is nothing to indicate that it was written to me."

"Do you deny that you paid the rent of 21 Malland Mansions, Earl's Court?"

So they knew! He wondered if they had known all the time.

He shrugged his shoulders.

"You seem very well informed. May I ask why my private affairs should be dragged into the limelight?"

"They will not unless they prove to be relevant to the death of George Barton."

"I see. You are suggesting that I first made love to his wife, and then murdered him."

261

"Come, Mr. Farraday, I'll be frank with you. You and Mrs. Barton were very close friends—you parted by your wish, not the lady's. She was proposing, as this letter shows, to make trouble. Very conveniently, she died."

"She committed suicide. I daresay I may have been partly to blame. I may reproach myself, but it is no concern of the law's."

"It may have been suicide—it may not. George Barton thought not. He started to investigate—and he died. The sequence is rather suggestive."

"I do not see why you should—well, pitch on me."

"You admit that Mrs. Barton's death came at a very convenient moment for you? A scandal, Mr. Farraday, would have been highly prejudicial to your career."

"There would have been no scandal. Mrs. Barton would have seen reason."

"I wonder! Did your wife know about this affair, Mr. Farraday?"

"Certainly not."

"You are quite sure of that statement?"

"Yes, I am. My wife has no idea that there was anything but friendship between myself and Mrs. Barton. I hope she will never learn otherwise."

"Is your wife a jealous woman, Mr. Farraday?"

"Not at all. She has never displayed the least jealousy where I am concerned. She is far too sensible."

The inspector did not comment on that. Instead he said:

"Have you at any time in the past year had cyanide in your possession, Mr. Farraday?"

"No."

"But you keep a supply of cyanide at your country property?"

"The gardener may. I know nothing about it."

"You have never purchased any yourself at a chemist's or for photography?"

"I know nothing of photography, and I repeat that I have never purchased cyanide."

Kemp pressed him a little further before he finally let him go.

To his subordinate he said thoughtfully, "He was very quick denying that his wife knew about his affair with the Barton woman. Why was that, I wonder?"

"Daresay he's in a funk in case she should get to hear of it, sir."

"That may be, but I should have thought he'd got the brains to see that if his wife was in ignorance, and would cut up rough, that gives him an additional motive for wanting to silence Rosemary Barton. To save his skin his line ought to have been that his wife more or less knew about the affair but was content to ignore it."

"I daresay he hadn't thought of that, sir."

Kemp shook his head. Stephen Farraday was not a fool. He had a clear and astute brain. And he had been passionately keen to impress on the inspector that Sandra knew nothing.

"Well," said Kemp, "Colonel Race seems pleased with the line he's dug up and if he's right, the Farradays are out—both of them. I shall be glad if they are. I like this chap. And personally I don't think he's a murderer."

II

Opening the door of their sitting room, Stephen said, "Sandra?"

She came to him out of the darkness, suddenly holding him, her hands on his shoulders.

"Stephen?"

"Why are you all in the dark?"

"I couldn't bear the light. Tell me."

He said:

"They know."

"About Rosemary?"

"Yes."

"And what do they think?"

"They see, of course, that I had a motive. . . . Oh, my darling, see what I've dragged you into. It's all my fault. If only I'd cut loose after Rosemary's death—gone away—left you free—so that at any rate *you* shouldn't be mixed up in all this horrible business."

"No, not that . . . Never leave me . . . never leave me."

She clung to him—she was crying, the tears coursing down her cheeks. He felt her shudder.

"You're my life, Stephen, all my life—never leave me. . . ."

"Do you care so much, Sandra? I never knew. . . ."

"I didn't want you to know. But now—"

"Yes, now . . . We're in this together, Sandra . . . we'll face it together . . . whatever comes, together!"

Strength came to them as they stood there, clasped together in the darkness.

Sandra said with determination:

"This shall *not* wreck our lives! It shall not. It shall not!"

Ten

Anthony Browne looked at the card the little page was holding out to him.

He frowned, then shrugged his shoulders. He said to the boy:

"All right, show him up."

When Colonel Race came in, Anthony was standing by the window with the bright sun striking obliquely over his shoulder.

He saw a tall soldierly man with a lined bronze face and iron-grey hair—a man whom he had seen before, but not for some years, and a man whom he knew a great deal about.

Race saw a dark graceful figure and the outline of a well-shaped head. A pleasant indolent voice said:

"Colonel Race? You were a friend of George Barton's, I know. He talked about you on that last evening. Have a cigarette."

"Thank you, I will."

Anthony said as he held a match:

"You were the unexpected guest that night who did not turn up—just as well for you."

"You are wrong there. That empty place was not for me."

Anthony's eyebrows went up.

"Really? Barton said—"

Race cut in.

"George Barton may have said so. His plans were quite different. That chair, Mr. Browne, was intended to be occupied when the lights went down by an actress called Chloe West."

Anthony stared.

"Chloe West? Never heard of her. Who is she?"

"A young actress not very well known but who possesses a certain superficial resemblance to Rosemary Barton."

Anthony whistled.

"I begin to see."

"She had been given a photograph of Rosemary so that she could copy the style of hairdressing and she also had the dress which Rosemary wore the night she died."

"So that was George's plan? Up go the lights— Hey Presto, gasps of supernatural dread! *Rosemary has come back.* The guilty party gasps out: 'It's true—it's true—I dunnit.'" He paused and added: "Rotten—even for an ass like poor old George."

"I'm not sure I understand you."

Anthony grinned.

"Oh, come now, sir—a hardened criminal isn't going to behave like a hysterical schoolgirl. If somebody poisoned Rosemary Barton in cold blood, and was preparing to administer the same fatal dose of cyanide to George Barton, that person had a certain amount of nerve. It would take more than an actress dressed up as Rosemary to make him or her spill the beans."

"Macbeth, remember, a decidedly hardened criminal, went to pieces when he saw the ghost of Banquo at the feast."

"Ah, but what Macbeth saw really *was* a ghost! It wasn't a ham actor wearing Banquo's duds! I'm prepared to admit that a real ghost might bring its own atmosphere from another world. In fact I am willing to admit that I believe in ghosts—have believed in them for the last six months—one ghost in particular."

"Really—and whose ghost is that?"

"Rosemary Barton's. You can laugh if you like. I've not seen her—but I've felt her presence. For some reason or other Rosemary, poor soul, can't stay dead."

"I could suggest a reason."

"Because she was murdered?"

"To put it in another idiom, because she was bumped off. *How about that, Mr. Tony Morelli?*"

There was a silence. Anthony sat down, chucked his cigarette into the grate and lighted another one.

Then he said:

"How did you find out?"

"You admit that you are Tony Morelli?"

"I shouldn't dream of wasting time by denying it. You've obviously cabled to America and got all the dope."

"And you admit that when Rosemary Barton

discovered your identity you threatened to bump her off unless she held her tongue."

"I did everything I could think of to scare her into holding her tongue," agreed Tony pleasantly.

A strange feeling stole over Colonel Race. This interview was not going as it should. He stared at the figure in front of him lounging back in its chair—and an odd sense of familiarity came to him.

"Shall I recapitulate what I know about you, Morelli?"

"It might be amusing."

"You were convicted in the States of attempted sabotage in the Ericsen aeroplane works and were sentenced to a term of imprisonment. After serving your sentence, you came out and the authorities lost sight of you. You were next heard of in London staying at Claridge's and calling yourself Anthony Browne. There you scraped acquaintance with Lord Dewsbury and through him you met certain other prominent armaments manufacturers. You stayed in Lord Dewsbury's house and by means of your position as his guest you were shown things which you ought never to have seen! It is curious coincidence, Morelli, that a trail of unaccountable accidents and some very near escapes from disaster on a large scale followed very closely after your visits to various important works and factories."

"Coincidences," said Anthony, "are certainly extraordinary things."

"Finally, after another lapse of time, you reappeared in London and renewed your acquaintance with Iris Marle, making excuses not to visit her home, so that her family should not realize how intimate you were becoming. Finally you tried to induce her to marry you secretly."

"You know," said Anthony, "it's really extraordinary the way you have found out all these things—I don't mean the armaments business—I mean my threats to Rosemary, and the tender nothings I whispered to Iris. Surely those don't come within the province of M.I.5?"

Race looked sharply at him.

"You've got a good deal to explain, Morelli."

"Not at all. Granted your facts are all correct, what of them? I've served my prison sentence. I've made some interesting friends. I've fallen in love with a very charming girl and am naturally impatient to marry her."

"So impatient that you would prefer the wedding to take place before her family have the chance of finding out anything about your antecedents. Iris Marle is a very rich young woman."

Anthony nodded his head agreeably.

"I know. When there's money, families are inclined to be abominably nosy. And Iris, you see, doesn't know anything about my murky past. Frankly, I'd rather she didn't."

"I'm afraid she is going to know all about it."

"A pity," said Anthony.

"Possibly you don't realize—"

Anthony cut in with a laugh.

"Oh! I can dot the i's and cross the t's. Rosemary Barton knew my criminal past, so I killed her. George Barton was growing suspicious of me, so I killed him! Now I'm after Iris's money! It's all very agreeable and it hangs together nicely, but you haven't got a mite of proof."

Race looked at him attentively for some minutes. Then he got up.

"Everything I have said is true," he said. *And it's all wrong.*"

Anthony watched him narrowly.

"What's wrong?"

"You're wrong." Race walked slowly up and down the room. "It hung together all right until I saw you—but now I've seen you, *it won't do. You're not a crook.* And if you're not a crook, you're one of *our* kind. I'm right, aren't I?"

Anthony looked at him in silence while a smile slowly broadened on his face. Then he hummed softly under his breath.

" '*For the Colonel's lady and Judy O'Grady are sisters under the skin.*' Yes, funny how one knows one's own kind. That's why I've tried to avoid meeting you. I was afraid you'd spot me for what I am. It was important then that nobody should know—important up to yesterday. Now, thank goodness, the balloon's gone up! We've swept our gang of international saboteurs into the net. I've been working on this assignment for three years. Frequenting certain meetings, agitating among workmen, getting myself the right reputation. Finally it was fixed that I pulled an important job and got sentenced. The business had to be genuine if I was to establish my *bona fides*.

"When I came out, things began to move. Little by little I got further into the centre of things—a great international net run from Central Europe. It was as *their* agent I came to London and went to Claridge's. I had orders to get on friendly terms with Lord Dewsbury—that was my lay, the social butterfly! I got to know Rosemary Barton in my character of attractive young man about town. Suddenly, to my horror, I found that she knew I had been in prison in America as Tony Morelli. I was terrified for *her!* The people I was working with would have had her killed without a moment's hesitation if they had thought she knew that. I did my best to scare her into keeping her mouth shut, but I wasn't very hopeful. Rosemary was born to be indiscreet. I thought the best thing I could do was to sheer off—and then I saw Iris coming down a staircase, and I swore that after my job was done I would come back and marry her.

"When the active part of my work was over, I turned up again and got into touch with Iris, but I kept aloof from the house and her people for I knew they'd want to make inquiries about me and I had to keep under cover for a bit longer. But I got worried about her. She looked ill and afraid—and George Barton seemed to be behaving in a very odd fashion. I urged her to come away and marry me. Well, she refused. Perhaps she was right. And then I was roped in for this party. It was as we sat down to dinner that George mentioned *you* were to be there. I said rather quickly that I'd met a man I knew and might have to leave early. Actually I *had* seen a fellow I knew in America—Monkey Coleman—though he didn't remember me—but I really wanted to avoid meeting you. I was still on my job.

"You know what happened next—George died. I had nothing to do with his death or with Rosemary's. I don't know now who did kill them."

"Not even an idea?"

"It must have been either the waiter or one of the five people round the table. I don't think it was the waiter. It wasn't me and it wasn't Iris. It could have been Sandra Farraday or it could have been Stephen Farraday, or it could have been both of them together. But the best bet, in my opinion, is Ruth Lessing."

"Have you anything to support that belief?"

"No. She seems to me the most likely person— but I don't see in the least how she did it! In both tragedies she was so placed at the table that it would be practically impossible for her to tamper with the champagne glass—and the more I think over what happened the other night, the more it seems to me impossible that George could have been poisoned at all—and yet he was!" Anthony paused. "And there's another thing that gets me— have you found out who wrote those anonymous letters that started him on the track?"

Race shook his head.

"No. I thought I had—but I was wrong."

"Because the interesting thing is that it means that there is *someone, somewhere,* who knows that Rosemary was murdered, so that, unless you're careful—that person will be murdered next!"

Eleven

From information received over the telephone Anthony knew that Lucilla Drake was going out at five o'clock to drink a cup of tea with a dear old friend. Allowing for possible contingencies (returning for a purse, determination after all to take an umbrella just in case, and last-minute chats on the doorstep) Anthony timed his own arrival at Elvaston Square at precisely twenty-five minutes past five. It was Iris he wanted to see, not her aunt. And by all accounts once shown into Lucilla's presence, he would have had very little chance of uninterrupted conversation with his lady.

He was told by the parlourmaid (a girl lacking the impudent polish of Betty Archdale) that Miss Iris had just come in and was in the study.

Anthony said with a smile, "Don't bother. I'll find my way," and went past her and along to the study door.

Iris spun round at his entrance with a nervous start.

"Oh, it's you."

He came over to her swiftly.

"What's the matter, darling?"

"Nothing." She paused, then said quickly, "Nothing. Only I was nearly run over. Oh, my own fault, I expect I was thinking so hard and mooning across the road without looking, and the car came tearing round a corner and just missed me."

He gave her a gentle little shake.

"You mustn't do that sort of thing, Iris. I'm worried about you—oh! not about your miraculous escape from under the wheels of a car, but about the reason that lets you moon about in the midst of traffic. What is it, darling? There's something special, isn't there?"

She nodded. Her eyes, raised mournfully to his, were large and dark with fear. He recognized their message even before she said very low and quick:

"I'm afraid."

Anthony recovered his calm smiling poise. He sat down beside Iris on a wide settee.

"Come on," he said, "let's have it."

"I don't think I want to tell you, Anthony."

"Now then, funny, don't be like the heroines of third-rate thrillers who start in the very first chapter by having something they can't possibly tell for no real reason except to gum up the hero and make the book spin itself out for another fifty thousand words."

She gave a faint pale smile.

"I want to tell you, Anthony, but I don't know what you'd think—I don't know if you'd believe—"

Anthony raised a hand and began to check off the fingers.

"One, an illegitimate baby. Two, a blackmailing lover. Three—"

She interrupted him indignantly:

"Of course not. Nothing of *that* kind."

"You relieve my mind," said Anthony. "Come on, little idiot."

Iris's face clouded over again.

"It's nothing to laugh at. It's—it's about the other night."

"Yes?" His voice sharpened.

Iris said:

"You were at the inquest this morning—you heard—"

She paused.

"Very little," said Anthony. "The police surgeon being technical about cyanides generally and the effect of potassium cyanide on George, and the police evidence as given by that first inspector, not Kemp, the one with the smart moustache who arrived first at the Luxembourg and took charge. Identification of the body by George's chief clerk. The inquest was then adjourned for a week by a properly docile coroner."

"It's the inspector I mean," said Iris. "He described finding a small paper packet under the table containing traces of potassium cyanide."

Anthony looked interested.

"Yes. Obviously whoever slipped that stuff into George's glass just dropped the paper that had contained it under the table. Simplest thing to do. Couldn't risk having it found on him—or her."

To his surprise Iris began to tremble violently.

"Oh, no, Anthony. Oh, no, it wasn't like that."

"What do you mean, darling? What do you know about it?"

Iris said, "*I* dropped that packet under the table."

He turned astonished eyes upon her.

"Listen, Anthony. You remember how George drank off that champagne and then it happened?"

He nodded.

"It was awful—like a bad dream. Coming just when everything had seemed to be all right. I mean that, after the cabaret, when the lights went up—I felt so relieved. Because it was *then,* you know, that we found Rosemary dead—and somehow, I don't know why, I felt I'd see it all happen again . . . I felt she was there, dead, at the table. . . ."

"Darling. . . ."

"Oh, I know. It was just nerves. But anyway, there we were, and there was nothing awful and suddenly it seemed the whole thing was really done with at last and one could—I don't know how to explain it—*begin again.* And so I danced with George and really felt I was enjoying myself at last, and we came back to the table. And then George suddenly talked about Rosemary and asked us to drink to her memory and then *he* died and all the nightmare had come back.

"I just felt paralysed I think. I stood there,

shaking. You came round to look at him, and I moved back a little, and the waiters came and someone asked for a doctor. And all the time I was standing there frozen. Then suddenly a big lump came in my throat and tears began to run down my cheeks and I jerked open my bag to get my handkerchief. I just fumbled in it, not seeing properly, and got out my handkerchief, but there was something caught up inside the handkerchief—a folded stiff bit of white paper, like the kind you get powders in from the chemist. Only, you see, Anthony, *it hadn't been in my bag when I started from home.* I hadn't had anything like that! I'd put the things in myself when the bag was quite empty—a powder compact, a lipstick, my handkerchief, my evening comb in its case and a shilling and a couple of sixpences. *Somebody had put that packet in my bag*—they must have done. And I remembered how they'd found a packet like that in Rosemary's bag after she died and how it had had cyanide in it. I was frightened, Anthony, I was horribly frightened. My fingers went limp and the packet fluttered down from my handkerchief under the table. I let it go. And I didn't say anything. I was too frightened. Somebody meant it to look as though *I* had killed George, and I *didn't.*"

Anthony gave vent to a long and prolonged whistle.

"And nobody saw you?" he said.

Iris hesitated.

"I'm not sure," she said slowly. "I believe Ruth noticed. But she was looking so dazed that I don't know whether she really *noticed*—or if she was just staring at me blankly."

Anthony gave another whistle.

"This," he remarked, "is a pretty kettle of fish."

Iris said:

"It's got worse and worse. I've been so afraid they'd find out."

"Why weren't your fingerprints on it, I wonder? The first thing they'd do would be to fingerprint it."

"I suppose it was because I was holding it through the handkerchief."

Anthony nodded.

"Yes, you had luck there."

"But who could have put it in my bag? I had my bag with me all the evening."

"That's not so impossible as you think. When you went to dance after the cabaret, you left your bag on the table. Somebody may have tampered with it then. And there are the women. Could you get up and give me an imitation of just how a woman behaves in the ladies' cloakroom? It's the sort of thing I wouldn't know. Do you congregate and chat or do you drift off to different mirrors?"

Iris considered.

"We all went to the same table—a great long

glass-topped one. And we put our bags down and looked at our faces, you know."

"Actually I don't. Go on."

"Ruth powdered her nose and Sandra patted her hair and pushed a hairpin in and I took off my fox cape and gave it to the woman and then I saw I'd got some dirt on my hand—a smear of mud and I went over to the washbasins."

"Leaving your bag on the glass table?"

"Yes. And I washed my hands. Ruth was still fixing her face I think and Sandra went and gave up her cloak and then she went back to the glass and Ruth came and washed her hands and I went back to the table and just fixed my hair a little."

"So either of those two could have put something in your bag without your seeing?"

"Yes, but I can't believe either Ruth or Sandra would do such a thing."

"You think too highly of people. Sandra is the kind of Gothic creature who would have burned her enemies at the stake in the Middle Ages—and Ruth would make the most devastatingly practical poisoner that ever stepped this earth."

"If it was Ruth why didn't she say she saw me drop it?"

"You have me there. If Ruth deliberately planted cyanide on you, she'd take jolly good care you didn't get rid of it. So it looks as though it wasn't Ruth. In fact the waiter is far and away the best bet. The waiter, the waiter! If only we had a strange waiter, a peculiar waiter, a waiter hired for that evening only. But instead we have Giuseppe and Pierre and they just don't fit. . . ."

Iris sighed.

"I'm glad I've told you. No one will ever know now, will they? Only you and I?"

Anthony looked at her with a rather embarrassed expression.

"It's not going to be just like that, Iris. In fact you're coming with me now in a taxi to old man Kemp. We can't keep this under our hats."

"Oh, no, Anthony. They'll think I killed George."

They'll certainly think so if they find out later that you sat tight and said nothing about all this! Your explanation will then sound extremely thin. If you volunteer it now there's a likelihood of its being believed."

"Please, Anthony."

"Look here, Iris, you're in a tight place. But apart from anything else, there's such a thing as *truth*. You can't play safe and take care of your own skin when it's a question of justice."

"Oh, Anthony, must you be so grand?"

"That," said Anthony, "was a very shrewd blow! But all the same we're going to Kemp! Now!"

Unwillingly she came with him out into the hall. Her coat was lying tossed on a chair and he took it and held it out for her to put on.

There was both mutiny and fear in her eyes, but

Anthony showed no sign of relenting. He said:

"We'll pick up a taxi at the end of the Square."

As they went towards the hall door the bell was pressed and they heard it ringing in the basement below.

Iris gave an exclamation.

"I forgot. It's Ruth. She was coming here when she left the office to settle about the funeral arrangements. It's to be the day after tomorrow. I thought we could settle things better while Aunt Lucilla was out. She does confuse things so."

Anthony stepped forward and opened the door, forestalling the parlourmaid who came running up the stairs from below.

"It's all right, Evans," said Iris, and the girl went down again.

Ruth was looking tired and rather dishevelled. She was carrying a large-sized attaché case.

"I'm sorry I'm late, but the tube was so terribly crowded tonight and then I had to wait for three buses and not a taxi in sight."

It was, thought Anthony, unlike the efficient Ruth to apologize. Another sign that George's death had succeeded in shattering that almost inhuman efficiency.

Iris said:

"I can't come with you now, Anthony. Ruth and I must settle things."

Anthony said firmly:

"I'm afraid this is more important . . . I'm

awfully sorry, Miss Lessing, to drag Iris off like this, but it really *is* important."

Ruth said quickly:

"That's quite all right, Mr. Browne. I can arrange everything with Mrs. Drake when she comes in." She smiled faintly. "I can really manage her quite well, you know."

"I'm sure you could manage anyone, Miss Lessing," said Anthony admiringly.

"Perhaps, Iris, if you can tell me any special points?"

"There aren't any. I suggested our arranging this together simply because Aunt Lucilla changes her mind about everything every two minutes, and I thought it would be rather hard on you. You've had so much to do. But I really don't care what sort of funeral it is! Aunt Lucilla *likes* funerals, but I hate them. You've got to bury people, but I hate making a fuss about it. It can't matter to the people themselves. They've got away from it all. The dead don't come back."

Ruth did not answer, and Iris repeated with a strange defiant insistence: "The dead don't come back!"

"Come on," said Anthony, and pulled her out through the open door.

A cruising taxi was coming slowly along the Square. Anthony hailed it and helped Iris in.

"Tell me, beautiful," he said, after he had directed the driver to go to Scotland Yard. "Who exactly did you feel was there in the hall when you found it so necessary to affirm that the dead are dead? Was it George or Rosemary?"

"Nobody! Nobody at all! I just hate funerals, I tell you."

Anthony sighed.

"Definitely," he said. "I must be psychic!"

Twelve

Three men sat at a small round marble-topped table.

Colonel Race and Chief Inspector Kemp were drinking cups of dark brown tea, rich in tannin. Anthony was drinking an English café's idea of a nice cup of coffee. It was not Anthony's idea, but he endured it for the sake of being admitted on equal terms to the other two men's conference. Chief Inspector Kemp, having painstakingly verified Anthony's credentials, had consented to recognize him as a colleague.

"If you ask me," said the chief inspector, dropping several lumps of sugar into his black brew and stirring it, "this case will never be brought to trial. We'll never get the evidence."

"You think not?" asked Race.

Kemp shook his head and took an approving sip of his tea.

"The only hope was to get evidence concerning the actual purchasing or handling of cyanide by one of those five. I've drawn a blank everywhere. It'll be one of those cases where you *know* who did it, and can't ever prove it."

"So you know who did it?" Anthony regarded him with interest.

"Well, I'm pretty certain in my own mind. Lady Alexandra Farraday."

"So that's your bet," said Race. "Reasons?"

"You shall have 'em. I'd say she's the type that's madly jealous. And autocratic, too. Like that queen in history—Eleanor of Something, that followed the clue to Fair Rosamund's Bower and offered her the choice of a dagger or a cup of poison."

"Only in this case," said Anthony, "she didn't offer Fair Rosemary any choice."

Chief Inspector Kemp went on:

"Someone tips Mr. Barton off. He becomes suspicious—and I should say his suspicions were pretty definite. He wouldn't have gone so far as actually buying a house in the country unless he wanted to keep an eye on the Farradays. He must have made it pretty plain to her—harping on this party and urging them to come to it. She's not the kind to Wait and See. Autocratic again, she finished him off! That, you say so far, is all theory and based on character. But I'll say that the *only* person who could have had any chance whatever of dropping something into Mr. Barton's glass just before he drank would be the lady on his right."

"And nobody saw her do it?" said Anthony.

"Quite. They might have—but they didn't. Say, if you like, she was pretty adroit."

"A positive conjurer."

Race coughed. He took out his pipe and began stuffing the bowl.

"Just one minor point. Granted Lady Alexandra is autocratic, jealous and passionately devoted to her husband, granted that she'd not stick at murder, do you think she is the type to slip incriminating evidence into a girl's handbag? A perfectly innocent girl, mind, who has never harmed her in any way? Is that in the Kidderminster tradition?"

Inspector Kemp squirmed uneasily in his seat and peered into his teacup.

"Women don't play cricket," he said. "If that's what you mean."

"Actually, a lot of them do," said Race, smiling. "But I'm glad to see you look uncomfortable."

Kemp escaped from his dilemma by turning to Anthony with an air of gracious patronage.

"By the way, Mr. Browne (I'll still call you that, if you don't mind), I want to say that I'm very much obliged to you for the prompt way you brought Miss Marle along this evening to tell that story of hers."

"I had to do it promptly," said Anthony. "If I'd waited I should probably not have brought her along at all."

"She didn't want to come, of course," said Colonel Race.

"She's got the wind up badly, poor kid," said Anthony. "Quite natural, I think."

"Very natural," said the inspector and poured himself out another cup of tea. Anthony took a gingerly sip of coffee.

"Well," said Kemp. "I think we relieved her mind—she went off home quite happily."

"After the funeral," said Anthony, "I hope she'll get away to the country for a bit. Twenty-four hours' peace and quiet away from Auntie Lucilla's nonstop tongue will do her good, I think."

"Aunt Lucilla's tongue has its uses," said Race.

"You're welcome to it," said Kemp. "Lucky I didn't think it necessary to have a shorthand report made when I took her statement. If I had, the poor fellow would have been in hospital with writer's cramp."

"Well," said Anthony. "I daresay you're right, chief inspector, in saying that the case will never come to trial—but that's a very unsatisfactory finish—and there's one thing we still don't know—who wrote those letters to George Barton telling him his wife was murdered? We haven't the least idea who that person is."

Race said: "Your suspicions still the same, Browne?"

"Ruth Lessing? Yes, I stick to her as my candidate. You told me that she admitted to you she was in love with George. Rosemary by all accounts was pretty poisonous to her. Say she saw suddenly a good chance of getting rid of Rosemary, and was fairly convinced that with Rosemary out of the way, she could marry George out of hand."

"I grant you all that," said Race. "I'll admit that Ruth Lessing has the calm practical efficiency that

289

can contemplate and carry out murder, and that she perhaps lacks that quality of pity which is essentially a product of imagination. Yes, I give you the first murder. But I simply can't see her committing the second one. I simply cannot see her panicking and poisoning the man she loved and wanted to marry! Another point that rules her out—why did she hold her tongue when she saw Iris throw the cyanide packet under the table?"

"Perhaps she didn't see her do it," suggested Anthony, rather doubtfully.

"I'm fairly sure she did," said Race. "When I was questioning her, I had the impression that she was keeping something back. And Iris Marle herself thought Ruth Lessing saw her."

"Come now, colonel," said Kemp. "Let's have your 'spot.' You've got one, I suppose?"

Race nodded.

"Out with it. Fair's fair. You've listened to ours—*and* raised objections."

Race's eyes went thoughtfully from Kemp's face to Anthony and rested there.

Anthony's eyebrows rose.

"Don't say you still think I am the villain of the piece?"

Slowly Race shook his head.

"I can imagine no possible reason why you should kill George Barton. I think I know who did kill him—and Rosemary Barton too."

"Who is it?"

Race said musingly:

"Curious how we have all selected women as suspects. I suspect a woman, too." He paused and said quietly: "I think the guilty person is Iris Marle."

With a crash Anthony pushed his chair back. For a moment his face went dark crimson—then with an effort, he regained command of himself. His voice, when he spoke, had a slight tremor but was deliberately as light and mocking as ever.

"By all means let us discuss the possibility," he said. "Why Iris Marle? And if so, why should she, of her own accord, tell me about dropping the cyanide paper under the table?"

"Because," said Race, "she knew that Ruth Lessing had seen her do it."

Anthony considered the reply, his head on one side. Finally he nodded.

"Passed," he said. "Go on. Why did you suspect her in the first place?"

"Motive," said Race. "An enormous fortune had been left to Rosemary in which Iris was not to participate. For all we know she may have struggled for years with a sense of unfairness. She was aware that if Rosemary died childless, all that money came to her. And Rosemary was depressed, unhappy, run-down after 'flu, just the mood when a verdict of suicide would be accepted without question."

"That's right, make the girl out a monster!" said Anthony.

"Not a monster," said Race. "There is another reason why I suspected her—a far-fetched one, it may seem to you—Victor Drake."

"Victor Drake?" Anthony stared.

"Bad blood. You see, I didn't listen to Lucilla Drake for nothing. I know all about the Marle family. Victor Drake—not so much weak as positively evil. His mother, feeble in intellect and incapable of concentration. Hector Marle, weak, vicious and a drunkard. Rosemary, emotionally unstable. A family history of weakness, vice and instability. Predisposing causes."

Anthony lit a cigarette. His hands trembled.

"Don't you believe that there may be a sound blossom on a weak or even a bad stock?"

"Of course there may. But I am not sure that Iris Marle *is* a sound blossom."

"And my word doesn't count," said Anthony slowly, "because I'm in love with her. George showed her those letters, and she got in a funk and killed him? That's how it goes on, is it?"

"Yes. Panic *would* obtain in her case."

"And how did she get the stuff into George's champagne glass?"

"That, I confess, I do not know."

"I'm thankful there's something you don't know." Anthony tilted his chair back and then forward. His eyes were angry and dangerous. "You've got a nerve saying all this to me."

Race replied quietly:

"I know. But I consider it had to be said."

Kemp watched them both with interest, but he did not speak. He stirred his tea round and round absentmindedly.

"Very well." Anthony sat upright. "Things have changed. It's no longer a question of sitting round a table, drinking disgusting fluids, and airing academic theories. This case has *got* to be solved. We've *got* to resolve all the difficulties and get at the truth. That's got to be my job—and I'll do it somehow. I've got to hammer at the things we don't know—because when we do know them, the whole thing will be clear.

"I'll re-state the problem. Who knew that Rosemary had been murdered? Who wrote to George telling him so? Why did they write to him?

"And now the murders themselves. Wash out the first one. It's too long ago, and we don't know exactly what happened. But the second murder took place in front of my eyes. I *saw* it happen. Therefore I ought to know *how* it happened. The ideal time to put the cyanide in George's glass was during the cabaret—but it couldn't have been put in then because he drank from his glass immediately afterwards. I *saw* him drink. After he drank, nobody put anything in his glass. Nobody touched his glass, nevertheless next time he drank, it was full of cyanide. He *couldn't* have been poisoned—but he was! There was cyanide in his

293

glass—*but nobody could have put it there!* Are we getting on?"

"No," said Chief Inspector Kemp.

"Yes," said Anthony. "The thing has now entered into the realm of a conjuring trick. Or a spirit manifestation. I will now outline my psychic theory. Whilst we were dancing, the ghost of Rosemary hovers near George's glass and drops in some cleverly materialized cyanide—any spirit can make cyanide out of ectoplasm. George comes back and drinks her health and—oh, *Lord!*"

The other two stared curiously at him. His hands were holding his head. He rocked to and fro in apparent mental agony. He said:

"That's it . . . that's it . . . the bag . . . the waiter. . . ."

"The waiter?" Kemp was alert.

Anthony shook his head.

"No, no. I don't mean what you mean. I did think once that what we needed was a waiter who was not a waiter but a conjurer—a waiter who had been engaged the day before. Instead we had a waiter who had always been a waiter—and a little waiter who was of the royal line of waiters—a cherubic waiter—a waiter above suspicion. And he's still above suspicion—but he played his part! Oh, Lord, yes, he played a star part."

He stared at them.

"Don't you see it? *A* waiter could have

poisoned the champagne but *the* waiter didn't. Nobody touched George's glass but George was poisoned. *A,* indefinite article. *The,* definite article. George's glass! George! Two separate things. And the money—lots and lots of money! And who knows—perhaps love as well? Don't look at me as though I'm mad. Come on, I'll show you."

Thrusting his chair back he sprang to his feet and caught Kemp by the arm.

"Come with me."

Kemp cast a regretful glance at his half-full cup.

"Got to pay," he muttered.

"No, no, we'll be back in a moment. Come on. I must show you outside. Come on, Race."

Pushing the table aside, he swept them away with him to the vestibule.

"You see that telephone box there?"

"Yes?"

Anthony felt in his pockets.

"Damn, I haven't got two pence. Never mind. On second thoughts I'd rather not do it that way. Come back."

They went back into the café, Kemp first, Race following with Anthony's hand on his arm.

Kemp had a frown on his face as he sat down and picked up his pipe. He blew down it carefully and began to operate on it with a hairpin which he brought out of his waistcoat pocket.

Race was frowning at Anthony with a puzzled

face. He leaned back and picked up his cup, draining the remaining fluid in it.

"Damn," he said violently. "It's got sugar in it!"

He looked across the table to meet Anthony's slowly widening smile.

"Hallo," said Kemp, as he took a sip from his cup. "What the hell's this?"

"Coffee," said Anthony. "And I don't think you'll like it. I didn't."

Thirteen

Anthony had the pleasure of seeing instant comprehension flash into the eyes of both his companions.

His satisfaction was short-lived, for another thought struck him with the force of a physical blow.

He ejaculated out loud:

"My God—that *car!*"

He sprang up.

"Fool that I was—idiot! She told me that a car had nearly run her down—and I hardly listened. Come on, quick!"

Kemp said:

"She said she was going straight home when she left the Yard."

"Yes. Why didn't I go with her?"

"Who's at the house?" asked Race.

"Ruth Lessing was there, waiting for Mrs. Drake. It's possible that they're both discussing the funeral still!"

"Discussing everything else as well if I know Mrs. Drake," said Race. He added abruptly, "Has Iris Marle any other relations?"

"Not that I know of."

"I think I see the direction in which your thoughts, ideas, are leading you. But—is it physically possible?"

"I think so. Consider for yourself how much has been taken for granted *on one person's word.*"

Kemp was paying the check. The three men hurried out as Kemp said:

"You think the danger is acute? To Miss Marle?"

"Yes, I do."

Anthony swore under his breath and hailed a taxi. The three men got in and the driver was told to go to Elvaston Square as quickly as possible.

Kemp said slowly:

"I've only got the general idea as yet. It washes the Farradays right out."

"Yes."

"Thank goodness for that. But surely there wouldn't be another attempt—so soon?"

"The sooner the better," said Race. "Before there's any chance of our minds running on the right track. Third time lucky—that will be the idea." He added: "Iris Marle told me, in front of Mrs. Drake, that she would marry you as soon as you wanted her to."

They spoke in spasmodic jerks, for the taxi driver was taking their directions literally and was hurtling round corners and cutting through traffic with immense enthusiasm.

Turning with a final spurt into Elvaston Square, he drew up with a terrific jerk in front of the house.

Elvaston Square had never looked more peaceful.

Anthony, with an effort, regained his usual cool manner, murmured:

"Quite like the movies. Makes one feel rather a fool, somehow."

But he was on the top step ringing the bell while Race paid off the taxi and Kemp followed up the steps.

The parlourmaid opened the door.

Anthony said sharply:

"Has Miss Iris got back?"

Evans looked a little surprised.

"Oh, yes, sir. She came in half an hour ago."

Anthony breathed a sigh of relief. Everything in the house was so calm and normal that he felt ashamed of his recent melodramatic fears.

"Where is she?"

"I expect she's in the drawing room with Mrs. Drake."

Anthony nodded and took the stairs in easy strides, Race and Kemp close behind him.

In the drawing room, placid under its shaded electric lights, Lucilla Drake was hunting through the pigeon holes of the desk with the hopeful absorption of a terrier and murmuring audibly:

"Dear, dear, now where *did* I put Mrs. Marsham's letter? Now, let me see. . . ."

"Where's Iris?" demanded Anthony abruptly.

Lucilla turned and stared.

"Iris? She—I beg your pardon!" She drew herself up. "May I ask who you *are?*"

Race came forward from behind him and

299

Lucilla's face cleared. She did not yet see Chief Inspector Kemp who was the third to enter the room.

"Oh, dear, Colonel Race! How kind of you to come! But I do wish you could have been here a little earlier—I *should* have liked to consult you about the funeral arrangements—a man's advice, so valuable—and really I was feeling so upset, as I said to Miss Lessing, that really I couldn't even *think*—and I must say that Miss Lessing was really very sympathetic for once and offered to do everything she could to take the burden off my shoulders—only, as she put it very reasonably, naturally *I* should be the person most likely to know what were George's favourite hymns—not that I actually *did,* because I'm afraid George didn't very often go to church—but naturally, as a clergyman's wife—I mean widow—I do know what is *suitable*—"

Race took advantage of a momentary pause to slip in his question: "Where is Miss Marle?"

"Iris? She came in some time ago. She said she had a headache and was going straight up to her room. Young girls, you know, do not seem to me to have very much stamina nowadays—they don't eat enough spinach—and she seems positively to dislike talking about the funeral arrangements, but after all, *someone* has to do these things—and one does want to feel that everything has been done for the best, and proper respect shown to the dead—not that I have ever thought motor hearses really *reverent*—if you know what I mean—not like horses with their long black tails—but, of course, I said at once that it was quite all right, and Ruth—I called her Ruth and not Miss Lessing—and I were managing splendidly, and she could leave everything to us."

Kemp asked:

"Miss Lessing has gone?"

"Yes, we settled everything, and Miss Lessing left about ten minutes ago. She took the announcements for the papers with her. No flowers, under the circumstances—and Canon Westbury to take the service—"

As the flow went on, Anthony edged gently out of the door. He had left the room before Lucilla, suddenly interrupting her narrative, paused to say: "Who *was* that young man who came with you? I didn't realize at first that *you* had brought him. I thought possibly he might have been one of those dreadful reporters. We have had such *trouble* with them."

Anthony was running lightly up the stairs. Hearing footsteps behind him, he turned his head, and grinned at Chief Inspector Kemp.

"You deserted too? Poor old Race!"

Kemp muttered.

"He does these things so nicely. I'm not popular in that quarter."

They were on the second floor and just preparing

to start up the third when Anthony heard a light footstep descending. He pulled Kemp inside an adjacent bathroom door.

The footsteps went on down the stairs.

Anthony emerged and ran up the next flight of stairs. Iris's room, he knew, was the small one at the back. He rapped lightly on the door.

"Hi—Iris." There was no reply—and he knocked and called again. Then he tried the handle but found the door locked.

With real urgency now he beat upon it.

"Iris—Iris—"

After a second or two, he stopped and glanced down. He was standing on one of those woolly old-fashioned rugs made to fit outside doors to obviate draughts. This one was close up against the door. Anthony kicked it away. The space under the door at the bottom was quite wide—sometime, he deduced, it had been cut to clear a fitted carpet instead of stained boards.

He stooped to the keyhole but could see nothing, but suddenly he raised his head and sniffed. Then he lay down flat and pressed his nose against the crack under the door.

Springing up, he shouted: "Kemp!"

There was no sign of the chief inspector. Anthony shouted again.

It was Colonel Race, however, who came running up the stairs. Anthony gave him no chance to speak. He said:

"Gas—pouring out! We'll have to break the door down."

Race had a powerful physique. He and Anthony made short shrift of the obstacle. With a splintering, cracking noise, the lock gave.

They fell back for a moment, then Race said:

"She's there by the fireplace. I'll dash in and break the window. You get her."

Iris Marle was lying by the gas fire—her mouth and nose lying on the wide open gas jet.

A minute or two later, choking and spluttering, Anthony and Race laid the unconscious girl on the landing floor in the draught of the passage window.

Race said:

"I'll work on her. You get a doctor quickly."

Anthony swung down the stairs. Race called after him:

"Don't worry. I think she'll be all right. We got here in time."

In the hall Anthony dialled and spoke into the mouthpiece, hampered by a background of exclamations from Lucilla Drake.

He turned at last from the telephone to say with a sigh of relief:

"Caught him. He lives just across the Square. He'll be here in a couple of minutes."

"—but I must know what has *happened!* Is Iris ill?"

It was a final wail from Lucilla.

Anthony said:

"She was in her room. Door locked. Her head in the gas fire and the gas full on."

"Iris?" Mrs. Drake gave a piercing shriek. "Iris has committed *suicide?* I can't believe it. I *don't* believe it!"

A faint ghost of Anthony's grin returned to him.

"You don't need to believe it," he said. "It isn't true."

Fourteen

"And now, please, Tony, will you tell me all about it?"

Iris was lying on a sofa, and the valiant November sunshine was making a brave show outside the windows of Little Priors.

Anthony looked across at Colonel Race who was sitting on the windowsill, and grinned engagingly:

"I don't mind admitting, Iris, that I've been waiting for this moment. If I don't explain to someone soon how clever I've been, I shall burst. There will be no modesty in this recital. It will be shameless blowing of my own trumpet with suitable pauses to enable you to say 'Anthony, how clever of you' or 'Tony, how wonderful' or some phrase of a like nature. Ahem! The performance will now begin. Here we go.

"The thing as a whole *looked* simple enough. What I mean is, that it looked like a clear case of cause and effect. Rosemary's death, accepted at the time as suicide, was not suicide. George became suspicious, started investigating, was presumably getting near the truth, and before he could unmask the murderer was, in his turn, murdered. The sequence, if I may put it that way, seems perfectly clear.

"But almost at once we came across some

apparent contradictions. Such as: A. George could not be poisoned. B. George *was* poisoned. And: A. Nobody touched George's glass. B. George's glass was tampered with.

"Actually I was overlooking a very significant fact—the varied use of the possessive case. George's ear is George's ear indisputably because it is attached to his head and cannot be removed without a surgical operation! But by George's watch, I only mean the watch that George is wearing—the question might arise whether it is his or maybe one lent him by someone else. And when I come to George's glass, or George's teacup, I begin to realize that I mean something very vague indeed. All I actually mean is the glass or cup out of which George has lately been drinking—and which has nothing to distinguish it from several other cups and glasses of the same pattern.

"To illustrate this, I tried an experiment. Race was drinking tea without sugar, Kemp was drinking tea with sugar, and I was drinking coffee. In appearance the three fluids were of much the same colour. We were sitting round a small marble-topped table among several other round marble-topped tables. On the pretext of an urgent brainwave I urged the other two out of their seats and out into the vestibule, pushing the chairs aside as we went, and also managing to move Kemp's pipe which was lying by his plate to a similar position by my plate but without letting him see me do it. As soon as we were outside I made an excuse and we returned, Kemp slightly ahead. He pulled the chair to the table and sat down opposite the plate that was marked by the pipe he had left behind him. Race sat on his right as before and I on his left—*but mark what had happened*—a new A. and B. contradiction! A. Kemp's cup has sugared tea in it. B. Kemp's cup has coffee in it. Two conflicting statements that *cannot* both be true—but they *are* both true. The misleading term is *Kemp's* cup. Kemp's cup when he *left* the table and Kemp's cup when he *returned* to the table are *not the same.*

"And that, Iris, *is what happened at the Luxembourg that night.* After the cabaret, when you all went to dance, you dropped your bag. A waiter picked it up—not *the* waiter, the waiter attending on that table who knew just where you had been sitting—but *a* waiter, an anxious hurried little waiter with everybody bullying him, running along with a sauce, and who quickly stooped, picked up the bag and placed it by a plate— actually by the plate one place to the left of where you had been sitting. You and George came back first and you went without a thought straight to the place marked by your bag—just as Kemp did to the place marked by his pipe. George sat down in what he thought to be his place, on your right. And when he proposed his toast in memory of

307

Rosemary, he drank from what he thought was *his* glass but was in reality *your glass*—the glass that can quite easily have been poisoned without needing a conjuring trick to explain it, because the only person who did *not* drink after the cabaret, was necessarily the *person whose health was being drunk!*

"Now go over the whole business again and the setup is entirely different! *You* are the intended victim, not George! So it looks, doesn't it, as though George is being *used*. What, if things had not gone wrong, would have been the story as the world would see it? A repetition of the party a year ago—and a repetition of—suicide! Clearly, people would say, a suicidal streak in that family! Bit of paper which has contained cyanide found in your bag. Clear case! Poor girl has been brooding over her sister's death. Very sad—but these rich girls are sometimes very neurotic!"

Iris interrupted him. She cried out:

"But why should anyone want to kill me? Why? *Why?*"

"All that lovely money, angel. Money, money, money! Rosemary's money went to you on her death. Now suppose you were to die—unmarried. What would happen to that money? The answer was it would go to your next of kin—to your aunt, Lucilla Drake. Now from all accounts of the dear lady, I could hardly see Lucilla Drake as First Murderess. But is there anyone else who would benefit? Yes, indeed. Victor Drake. If Lucilla has money, it will be exactly the same as Victor having it—Victor will see to that! He has always been able to do what he likes with his mother. And there is nothing difficult about seeing Victor as First Murderer. All along, from the very start of the case, there have been references to Victor, mentions of Victor. He has been in the offing, a shadowy, unsubstantial, evil figure."

"But Victor's in the Argentine! He's been in South America for over a year."

"Has he? We're coming now to what has been said to be the fundamental plot of every story. 'Girl meets Boy!' When Victor met Ruth Lessing, this particular story started. He got hold of her. I think she must have fallen for him pretty badly. Those quiet, levelheaded, law-abiding women are the kind that often fall for a real bad lot.

"Think a minute and you'll realize that all the evidence for Victor's being in South America depends on Ruth's word. None of it was verified because it was never a main issue! *Ruth* said that she had seen Victor off on the S.S. *San Cristobal* before Rosemary's death! It was *Ruth* who suggested putting a call through to Buenos Aires on the day of George's death—and later sacked the telephone girl who might have inadvertantly let out that she did no such thing.

"Of course it's been easy to check up now! Victor Drake arrived in Buenos Aires by a boat leaving England the day *after* Rosemary's death a year ago. Ogilvie, in Buenos Aires, had no telephone conversation with Ruth on the subject of Victor Drake on the day of George's death. *And Victor Drake left Buenos Aires for New York some weeks ago.* Easy enough for him to arrange for a cable to be sent off in his name on a certain day—one of those well-known cables asking for money that seemed proof positive that he was many thousands of miles away. Instead of which—"

"Yes, Anthony?"

"Instead of which," said Anthony, leading up to his climax with intense pleasure, "he was sitting at the next table to ours at the Luxembourg with a not-so-dumb blonde!"

"Not that awful-looking man?"

"A yellow blotchy complexion and bloodshot eyes are easy things to assume, and they make a lot of difference to a man. Actually, of our party, *I* was the only person (apart from Ruth Lessing) who had ever seen Victor Drake—and I had never known him under *that name!* In any case I was sitting with my back to him. I did think I recognized, in the cocktail lounge outside, as we came in, a man I had known in my prison days— Monkey Coleman. But as I was now leading a highly respectable life I was not too anxious that he should recognize me. I never for one moment suspected that Monkey Coleman had had anything

310

to do with the crime—much less that he and Victor Drake were one and the same."

"But I don't see now how he did it?"

Colonel Race took up the tale.

"In the easiest way in the world. During the cabaret he went out to telephone, passing our table. Drake had been an actor and he had been something more important—a *waiter*. To assume the makeup and play the part of Pedro Morales was child's play to an actor, but to move deftly round a table, with the step and gait of a waiter, filling up the champagne glasses, needed the definite knowledge and technique of a man who had actually *been* a waiter. A clumsy action or movement would have drawn your attention to him, but as a *bona fide* waiter none of you noticed or saw him. You were looking at the cabaret, not noticing that portion of the restaurant's furnishings—the waiter!"

Iris said in a hesitating voice:

"And Ruth?"

Anthony said:

"It was Ruth, of course, who put the cyanide paper in your bag—probably in the cloakroom at the beginning of the evening. The same technique she had adopted a year ago—with Rosemary."

"I always thought it odd," said Iris, "that George hadn't told Ruth about those letters. He consulted her about everything."

Anthony gave a short laugh.

"Of course he told her—first thing. She knew he would. That's why she wrote them. Then she arranged all his 'plan' for him—having first got him well worked up. And so she had the stage set—all nicely arranged for suicide No. 2—and if George chose to believe that you had killed Rosemary and were committing suicide out of remorse or panic—well, that wouldn't make any difference to Ruth!"

"And to think I liked her—liked her very much! And actually wanted her to marry George."

"She'd probably have made him a very good wife, if she hadn't come across Victor," said Anthony. "Moral: every murderess was a nice girl once."

Iris shivered. "All that for money!"

"You innocent, money is what these things are done for! Victor certainly did it for money. Ruth partly for money, partly for Victor, and partly, I think, because she hated Rosemary. Yes, she'd travelled a long way by the time she deliberately tried to run you down in a car, and still further when she left Lucilla in the drawing room, banged the front door and then ran up to your bedroom. What did she seem like? Excited at all?"

Iris considered.

"I don't think so. She just tapped on the door, came in and said everything was fixed up and she hoped I was feeling all right. I said yes, I was just a bit tired. And then she picked up my big rubber-covered torch and said what a nice torch that was and after that I don't seem to remember anything."

"No, dear," said Anthony. "Because she hit you a nice little crack, not too hard, on the back of the neck with your nice torch. Then she arranged you artistically by the gas fire, shut the windows tight, turned on the gas, went out, locking the door and passing the key underneath it, pushed the woolly mat close up against the crack so as to shut out any draught and tripped gently down the stairs. Kemp and I just got into the bathroom in time. I raced on up to you and Kemp followed Miss Ruth Lessing unbeknownst to where she had left that car parked—you know, I felt at the time there was something fishy and uncharacteristic about the way Ruth tried to force it on our minds that she had come by bus and tube!"

Iris gave a shudder.

"It's horrible—to think anyone was as determined to kill me as all that. Did she hate me too by then?"

"Oh, I shouldn't think so. But Miss Ruth Lessing is a very efficient young woman. She'd already been an accessory in two murders and she didn't fancy having risked her neck for nothing. I've no doubt Lucilla Drake bleated out your decision to marry me at a moment's notice, and in that case there was no time to lose. Once married, I should be your next of kin and not Lucilla."

"Poor Lucilla. I'm so terribly sorry for her."

"I think we all are. She's a harmless, kindly soul."

"Is he really arrested?"

Anthony looked at Race, who nodded and said:

"This morning, when he landed in New York."

"Was he going to marry Ruth—afterwards?"

"That was Ruth's idea. I think she would have brought it off too."

"Anthony—I don't think I like my money very much."

"All right, sweet—we'll do something noble with it if you like. I've got enough money to live on—and to keep a wife in reasonable comfort. We'll give it all away if you like—endow homes for children, or provide free tobacco for old men, or—how about a campaign for serving better coffee all over England?"

"I shall keep a little," said Iris. "So that if I ever wanted to, I could be grand and walk out and leave you."

"I don't think, Iris, that is the right spirit in which to enter upon married life. And, by the way, you didn't once say 'Tony, how wonderful' or 'Anthony, how clever of you!'"

Colonel Race smiled and got up.

"Going over to the Farradays for tea," he exclaimed. There was a faint twinkle in his eye as he said to Anthony: "Don't suppose you're coming?"

Anthony shook his head and Race went out of

the room. He paused in the doorway to say, over his shoulder:

"Good show."

"That," said Anthony as the door closed behind him, "denotes supreme British approval."

Iris asked in a calm voice:

"He thought I'd done it, didn't he?"

"You mustn't hold that against him," said Anthony. "You see, he's known so many beautiful spies, all stealing secret formulas and wheedling secrets out of major-generals, that it's soured his nature and warped his judgement. He thinks it's just got to be the beautiful girl in the case!"

"Why did you know I hadn't, Tony?"

"Just love, I suppose," said Anthony lightly.

Then his face changed, grew suddenly serious. He touched a little vase by Iris's side in which was a single sprig of grey-green with a mauve flower.

"What's that doing in flower at this time of year?"

"It does sometimes—just an odd sprig—if it's a mild autumn."

Anthony took it out of the glass and held it for a moment against his cheek. He half-closed his eyes and saw rich chestnut hair, laughing blue eyes and a red passionate mouth. . . .

He said in a quiet conversational tone:

"She's not around now any longer, is she?"

"Who do you mean?"

"You know who I mean. Rosemary . . . I think she knew, Iris, that you were in danger."

He touched the sprig of fragrant green with his lips and threw it lightly out of the window.

"Good-bye, Rosemary, thank you. . . ."

Iris said softly:

"That's for remembrance. . . ."

And more softly still:

"Pray love remember. . . ."

About the Author

Agatha Christie is the most widely published author of all time and in any language, outsold only by the Bible and Shakespeare. Her books have sold more than a billion copies in English and another billion in a hundred foreign languages. She is the author of eighty crime novels and short-story collections, nineteen plays, two memoirs, and six novels written under the name Mary Westmacott.

She first tried her hand at detective fiction while working in a hospital dispensary during World War I, creating the now legendary Hercule Poirot with her debut novel *The Mysterious Affair at Styles*. With *The Murder at the Vicarage*, published in 1930, she introduced another beloved sleuth, Miss Jane Marple. Additional series characters include the husband-and-wife crime-fighting team of Tommy and Tuppence Beresford, private investigator Parker Pyne, and Scotland Yard detectives Superintendent Battle and Inspector Japp.

Many of Christie's novels and short stories were adapted into plays, films, and television series. *The Mousetrap*, her most famous play of all, opened in 1952 and is the longest-running play in history. Among her best-known film adaptations are *Murder on the Orient Express*

(1974) and *Death on the Nile* (1978), with Albert Finney and Peter Ustinov playing Hercule Poirot, respectively. On the small screen Poirot has been most memorably portrayed by David Suchet, and Miss Marple by Joan Hickson and subsequently Geraldine McEwan and Julia McKenzie.

Christie was first married to Archibald Christie and then to archaeologist Sir Max Mallowan, whom she accompanied on expeditions to countries that would also serve as the settings for many of her novels. In 1971 she achieved one of Britain's highest honors when she was made a Dame of the British Empire. She died in 1976 at the age of eighty-five. Her one hundred and twentieth anniversary was celebrated around the world in 2010.

www.AgathaChristie.com

Also by Agatha Christie and available from
Center Point Large Print:

Center Point Large Print
600 Brooks Road / PO Box 1
Thorndike ME 04986-0001 USA

(207) 568-3717

US & Canada:
1 800 929-9108
www.centerpointlargeprint.com